February 15–19, 2014
Baltimore, Maryland, USA

Association for Computing Machinery

Advancing Computing as a Science & Profession

CSCW 2014

CSCW'14

Proceedings of the 17th ACM Conference on Computer Supported Cooperative Work & Social Computing

Sponsored by:

ACM SIGCHI

Supported by:

NSF, Facebook, Microsoft Research, Grand NCE, IBM Research, Drexel University, Google and UMBC

Association for
Computing Machinery

Advancing Computing as a Science & Profession

The Association for Computing Machinery
2 Penn Plaza, Suite 701
New York, New York 10121-0701

Notice to Past Authors of ACM-Published Articles
ACM intends to create a complete electronic archive of all articles and/or other material previously published by ACM. If you have written a work that has been previously published by ACM in any journal or conference proceedings prior to 1978, or any SIG Newsletter at any time, and you do NOT want this work to appear in the ACM Digital Library, please inform permissions@acm.org, stating the title of the work, the author(s), and where and when published.

ISBN: 978-1-4503-2752-7 (Digital)

ISBN: 978-1-4503-3165-4 (Print)

Additional copies may be ordered prepaid from:

ACM Order Department
PO Box 30777
New York, NY 10087-0777, USA

Phone: 1-800-342-6626 (USA and Canada)
+1-212-626-0500 (Global)
Fax: +1-212-944-1318
E-mail: acmhelp@acm.org
Hours of Operation: 8:30 am – 4:30 pm ET

Printed in the USA

Welcome from the Conference Chairs

We warmly welcome you to Baltimore, Maryland, USA, for the 2014 ACM Conference on Computer Supported Cooperative Work and Social Computing! In keeping with previous years, CSCW 2014 presents premier research on computer-mediated collaboration, social computing, and social media, from the design of technical systems for collaboration to ethnographic studies of use in the wild. The mission of the conference is to share the novel research that will advance the state of our art. The conference program embraces a variety of perspectives, reflecting how collaboration permeates different aspects of people's work, social, and civic lives. This diversity of perspectives is mirrored by geographic diversity among contributors.

The CSCW 2014 program retains the richly articulated structure of previous conferences in this series including a robust program of workshops, papers, panels, demonstrations, videos, and interactive posters. This year, we also introduce CSCWhat's Next, a selection of forward-looking research-in-progress papers intended to foster discussion. Another innovation this year is the option for demos, videos and poster presenters to give short talks about their work immediately preceding Monday night's reception.

Special highlights this year include our opening plenary talk, "**Making a Difference In and Through Playful Design,**" by Mary Flanagan of Dartmouth University and our closing plenary, "**Next Generation Humanitarian Computing,**" by Patrick Meier of Qatar Computing Research Institute. We will also present the inaugural CSCW Lasting Impact Award to Jonathan Grudin for his groundbreaking 1988 paper "**Why CSCW applications fail: Problems in the design and evaluation of organizational interfaces.**"

Interest in CSCW'14 is as high as ever, including a record number of paper submissions. The welcome message from our technical program chairs highlights the modifications to the review process this year as we continue to optimize our new revise and resubmit system.

Putting together CSCW'14 was a team effort. We first thank the authors for providing the content that is the core of our dynamic program. We are grateful to the program committee, who worked hard in reviewing papers and providing detailed feedback for authors. We heard from many about how this process truly helped improve the final papers. We thank our entire hard-working conference committee, from the papers chairs to the treasurer to the webmasters, an incredible group of people who donated countless hours of their time. We also thank Lisa Tolles at Sheridan Communications, Yvonne Lopez at RegOnline, and Ashley Cozzi and Stephanie Sabal from ACM for all of their assistance with arrangements, registration, and publications. Special thanks go out to John and Joanne Lateulere for their invaluable help with conference planning and management. Finally, we thank our sponsors ACM and SIGCHI, and generous sponsors, Facebook, Microsoft Research, National Science Foundation, Grand NCE, IBM Research, the iSchool at Drexel University, Google, and Information Systems at UMBC.

We hope that you find this program interesting and thought provoking and that the conference provides you with a valuable opportunity to share ideas with other researchers and practitioners from institutions around the world. Take time to enjoy all that Charm City has to offer.

Susan Fussell
Conference Co-Chair
Cornell University, USA

Wayne Lutters
Conference Co-Chair
UMBC, USA

From the Program Chairs

The CSCW research community is expanding at a tremendous pace. This year, we received a record 497 submissions – an increase of 27% from last year. Authors from 38 countries on 6 continents submitted papers. We accepted 134 papers for an acceptance rate of 27%. The growth in the number of submissions speaks to the increasing interest in CSCW. The papers range from traditional topics of interest to the CSCW community such as collaboration in work settings to newer topics such as crowdsourcing and social computing. The papers presented in this year's conference highlight the intellectual diversity of research in CSCW.

This was also the third year for the revise and resubmit (R&R) process for the conference. Similar to the process last year, we did not have page limits for the submissions, nor did we have a separate submission category for "notes" (short papers); rather, research contributions of any length were considered for the papers category. Out of the 497 papers submitted to the conference, 43% were invited to be revised and resubmitted. The overall response to the R&R process has been very positive. Many of the accepted papers were greatly improved through the revision process.

We would especially like to thank the external reviewers and Program Committee (PC) members. The revise and resubmit process would not be possible without the dedicated work of the reviewers and PC members. We had one of the largest PCs for CSCW with 64 members representing both the intellectual and geographical diversity of our community. This was a particularly challenging year for reviewing because of the record number of submissions and the reduced time frame for the review process. Without the amazing efforts of the PC members and external reviewers, we would not have been able to present the outstanding set of papers in the conference. Enjoy!

Meredith Ringel Morris
Program Co-Chair
Microsoft Research, USA

Madhu Reddy
Program Co-Chair
Penn State University, USA

Table of Contents

Session Order 6: Building Communities and Relationships

Session Chair: Vanessa Evars *(University of Twente)*

Session Order 7: Filter Bubbles & News

Session Chair: Kate Starbird *(University of Washington)*

Session Order 8: Performing Crowd Work

Session Chair: Dan Cosley *(Cornell University)*

Session Order 9: Work in Hospitals

Session Chair: Aleksandra Sarcevic *(Drexel University)*

Session Order 10: Craft, Repair, and DIY

Session Chair: David Randell *(University of Siegen)*

Session Order 11: Q&A

Session Chair: David McDonald *(University of Washington)*

Session Order 12: Social Media in the Enterprise

Session Chair: Jennifer Thom *(Amazon)*

Session Order 13: Values & Social Norms

Session Chair: Ingrid Erickson *(Rutgers University)*

Session Order 14: Social Media: Online and Off

Session Chair: Andrea Forte *(Drexel University)*

Session Order 19: Social Technologies and Well-Being

Session Chair: Michael Massimi *(Microsoft Research)*

Session Order 20: Shopping and Collecting

Session Chair: Moira Burke *(Facebook)*

Session Order 21: ICT4D

Session Chair: Susan Wyche *(Michigan State University)*

Session Order 22: Leadership

Session Chair: Gilly Leshed *(Cornell University)*

Session Order 23: Technology and Information Workers

Session Order 24: Collaborative Search and Sharing

Session Order 25: Romance

Session Order 26: Crowds in Crises

Session Order 27: Supporting Communities

Session Order 29: Locations and Maps

Session Order 30: Promoting Participation and Engagement

Session Chair: Mark Handel *(The Boeing Company)*

Session Order 31: Building on Others

Session Chair: Steven Dow *(Carnegie Mellon University)*

Session Order 32: Identifying Opportunities for Collaboration

Session Chair: Jeremy Birnholtz *(Northwestern University)*

Session Order 33: The Office

Session Chair: Melissa Mazmanian *(University of California, Irvine)*

Session Order 39: Parents and Children

Session Chair: Svetlana Yarosh *(AT&T Research)*

Session Order 40: Civic Participation

Session Chair: Andrés Monroy-Hernández *(Microsoft Research)*

Session Order 41: Gaming

Session Order 42: Multiple Dimensions and Displays

CSCW 2014 Organization

General Chairs:	Susan Fussell, *Cornell University*
	Wayne Lutters, *UMBC*
Treasurer:	N. Sadat Shami, *IBM*
Papers Chairs:	Meredith Ringel Morris, *Microsoft Research*
	Madhu Reddy, *Penn State University*
Interactive Posters Chairs:	Rogerio de Paula, *IBM Research*
	Erika Poole, *Penn State University*
Workshops Chairs:	Eric Gilbert, *Georgia Tech*
	Jacki O'Neill, *Microsoft Research India*
Panels Chairs:	Hideaki Kuzuoka, *University of Tsukuba*
	Charlotte Lee, *University of Washington*
Demonstrations Chairs:	Stephan Lukosch, *Delft University of Technology*
	Hao-Chuan Wang, *National Tsing Hua University*
Videos Chairs:	Katie Derthick, *University of Washington*
	Scott McCrickard, *Virginia Tech*
Doctoral Colloquium Chairs:	Claus Bossen, *Aarhus University*
	Darren Gergle, *Northwestern University*
CSCWhat's Next Chairs:	Mark Handel, *The Boeing Company*
	Susan Wyche, *Michigan State University*
Industry Liaison Chairs:	Sean Goggins, *University of Missouri*
	Steve Poltrock
Student Volunteers Chairs:	Victoria Schwanda Sosik, *Cornell University*
	Kathy Weaver, *UMBC*
Webmasters and Graphic Design Chairs:	Serena Hillman, *Simon Fraser University*
	Pablo Quinones, *University of Michigan*
Social Media Chairs:	Irina Shklovski, *ITU Copenhagen*
	Sarita Yardi Schoenebeck, *University of Michigan*
Social Interaction Chairs:	Jofish Kaye, *Yahoo Research*
	Michael Massimi, *Microsoft Research*

Publications Chairs: Yong Ming Kow, *City University of Hong Kong*
Bryan Semaan, *University of Hawaii*

Accessibility Chairs: Jennifer Rode, *Drexel University*
Amy Hurst, *UMBC*
Shaun Kane, *UMBC*
Ravi Kuber, *UMBC*

Local Arrangements Chairs: Anita Komlodi, *UMBC*
Jessica Vitak, *University of Maryland, College Park*

PC Meeting Local Arrangements Chairs: Andrea Forte, *Drexel University*
Aleksandra Sarcevic, *Drexel University*

Program Committee Chairs: Meredith Ringel Morris, *Microsoft Research*
Madhu Reddy, *Penn State University*

Program Committee: Paul M. Aoki, *Google Inc.*
Louise Barkhuus, *Stockholm University*
Michael Bernstein, *Stanford University*
Mary Beth Rosson, *Penn State University*
Jacob Biehl, *FX Palo Alto Laboratory*
Jeffrey P. Bigham, *Carnegie Mellon University*
Jeremy Birnholtz, *Northwestern University*
Pernille Bjørn, *IT University of Copenhagen*
Marcos Borges, *UFRJ - Universidade Federal do Rio de Janeiro*
A.J. Bernheim Brush, *Microsoft Research*
Moira Burke, *Facebook*
Jack Carroll, *Penn State University*
Ed Chi, *Google Inc.*
Dan Cosley, *Cornell University*
Ed Cutrell, *Microsoft Research India*
Steven Dow, *Carnegie Mellon University*
Ingrid Erickson, *Rutgers University*
Vanessa Evers, *University of Twente*
Morten Fjeld, *Chalmers University of Technology*
Andrea Forte, *Drexel University*
Eric Gilbert, *Georgia Tech*
Carl Gutwin, *University of Saskatchewan*
Ido Guy, *IBM Research Haifa*
Mark Handel, *The Boeing Company*
James Herbsleb, *Carnegie Mellon University*
Karrie Karahalios, *University of Illinois at Urbana-Champaign*
Wendy Kellogg, *IBM Research*
Niki Kittur, *Carnegie Mellon University*
Joseph Konstan, *University of Minnesota*
Robert Kraut, *Carnegie Mellon University*
Hideaki Kuzuoka, *University of Tsukuba*
Gilly Leshed, *Cornell University*

Program Committee (Continued):

Myriam Lewkowicz, *Troyes University of Technology*
Christopher Lueg, *University of Tasmania*
Gloria Mark, *UC Irvine*
Michael Massimi, *Microsoft Research Cambridge (U.K.)*
Melissa Mazmanian, *UC Irvine*
David McDonald, *University of Washington*
Helena Mentis, *UMBC*
Andrés Monroy-Hernández, *MSR FUSE Labs*
Les Nelson, *Palo Alto Research Center, Inc.*
Jacki O'Neill, *Xerox Research Centre Europe*
Andrea Grimes Parker, *Northeastern University*
Sameer Patil, *Helsinki Institute for Information Technology*
Sharoda Paul, *GE Global Research*
Anne Marie Piper, *Northwestern University*
Daniele Quercia, *Yahoo! Labs Barcelona*
Erika Poole, *Penn State University*
Dave Randall, *University of Siegen*
Aleksandra Sarcevic, *Drexel University*
Steven B. Sawyer, *Syracuse University*
m. c. schraefel, *University of Southampton*
Kate Starbird, *University of Washington*
Gunnar Stevens, *University of Siegen*
Jennifer Thom, *IBM Research*
Max Van Kleek, *University of Southampton*
Gina Venolia, *Microsoft Research*
Daniel Wigdor, *University of Toronto*
Max L. Wilson, *University of Nottingham*
Volker Wulf, *University of Siegen*
Susan Wyche, *Michigan State University*
Naomi Yamashita, *NTT Communication Science Lab*
Svetlana Yarosh, *AT&T Research Labs*
Chen Zhao, *Microsoft*

Best Paper Award Chairs:

Joseph Konstan, *University of Minnesota*
Helena Mentis, *UMBC*

Best Papers Committee:

Pernille Bjorn, *IT University Copenhagen*
Carl Gutwin, *University of Saskatchewan*
Niki Kittur, *Carnegie Mellon University*
Hideaki Kuzuoka, *University of Tsukuba*
Jenn Thom, *IBM Research*

Ninja Review Team Chair:

Aaron Genest, *Solido Design Automation*

2014 Lasting Impact Award Committee:

Saul Greenberg, *University of Calgary* (CSCW 1998 & 2006 Papers Chair)
Irene Greif, *IBM Research* (CSCW 1986 Papers Chair)
Sara Kiesler, *Carnegie Mellon University* (CSCW 2000 Papers Chair)
Cliff Lampe, *University of Michigan* (CSCW 2013 Papers Chair)
Meredith Ringel Morris, *Microsoft Research* (CSCW 2014 Papers Chair)
Gary Olson, *UC Irvine* (CSCW 1996 Papers Chair)
Madhu Reddy, *Penn State University* (CSCW 2014 Papers Chair)
Tom Rodden, *University of Nottingham* (CSCW 2002 Papers Chair)
Loren Terveen, *University of Minnesota* (CSCW 2013 Papers Chair)
Steve Whittaker, *UC Santa Cruz* (CSCW 2010 Papers Chair)

CSCW 2014 Reviewers

Reviewers whose names appear in **bold** are being recognized by the Associate Paper Chairs for one or more excellent reviews.

Mark Aakhus
Margunn Aanestad
Joanna Abraham
Mark Ackerman
Lada Adamic
Bram Adams
Eytan Adar
Ana Afonso
Elena Agapie
Leila Alem
Florian Alt
Brian Amento
Morgan Ames
Kenneth Anderson
Paul André
Craig Anslow
Judd Antin
Ana Paula Appel
Jorge Aranda
Gabriela Avram
Leif Azzopardi
Naveen bagalkot
Brian Bailey
Saeideh Bakhshi
Eytan Bakshy
Ramnath Balasubramanyan
Rebecca Balebako
Elizabeth Bales
Stinne Ballegaard
Amartya Banerjee
Wolmet Barendregt
Scott Bateman
Benjamin Bederson
Ben Bedwell
Andrew Begel
Fabrício Benevenuto
Steve Benford
Edward Benson
Nicola Bidwell
Matthew Bietz
Christian Bird
Staffan Björk
Florian Block
Bridget Blodgett
Sara Bly
Alexander Boden
Marcela Borge
Sebastian Boring
Alan Borning
Christophe Bortolaso
Nina Boulus
Stacy Branham
Deana Brown
Barry Brown
Jed Brubaker
Amy Bruckman
Merijn Bruijnes
A.J. Brush
Michael Brzozowski
Martin Burkhard
Béatrice Cahour
Chris Callison-Burch
Maria Luiza Campos
Heloisa Candello
Jose Canos
Yiwei Cao
Xiang Cao
Robert Capra
Carlos Castillo
Marcelo Cataldo
Grevet Catherine
Daniel Cernea
Xiang ´Anthony´ Chen
Weiqin Chen
Nicholas Chen
Jilin Chen
Yunan Chen
Zhiyuan Cheng
Karen Cheng
Justin Cheng
Zhiyuan Cheng
Marshini Chetty
Lydia Chilton
Alvin Chin
Lars Rune Christensen
Hao-Hua Chu
Justin Chung
Luigina Ciolfi
Benjamin Collier
Tommaso Colombino
Rob Comber
Gregorio Convertino
Eric Cook
Dan Cosley
Lisa Cowan
David Coyle
Crabb Crabb
Henriette Cramer
Kevin Crowston
Mary Czerwinski
Laura Dabbish
Peng Dai
Elizabeth Daly
Catalina Danis
Antonella De Angeli
Munmun De Choudhury
Cleidson de Souza
Roelof de Vries
Morteza Dehghani
Katie Derthick
Prasun Dewan
Nicholas Diakopoulos
E.Ilana Diamant
Michael Dickard
Dominic DiFranzo
Tawanna Dillahunt
Xianghua Ding
Carl DiSalvo
Betsy DiSalvo
Morgan Dixon
Tao Dong
Brian Dorn
Andre Doucette
Sebastian Draxler
Honglu Du
Nicolas Ducheneaut
Andy Echenique
Dean Eckles
Hal Eden
Kate Ehrlich
Gunnar Ellingsen
Nicole Ellison
Niklas Elmqvist
Jenny Englert
Dmitry Epstein

Thomas Erickson
Chris Esposito
Jerry Fails
Shelly Farnham
Rosta Farzan
Haakon Faste
Jesus Favela
Jennifer Fernquist
Bruce Ferwerda
Megan Finn
Andrew Fiore
Scott Fleming
Fred Fonseca
Benjamim Fonseca
Laura Forlano
Marcus Foth
Mike Fraser
Chris Frisina
Wai-Tat Fu
Michael Gamon
Ge Gao
R. Kelly Garrett
Nadia Gauducheau
Rich Gazan
Aaron Genest
Elizabeth Gerber
Darren Gergle
Marco Gerosa
Werner Geyer
Elisa Giaccardi
Lorna Gibson
Sean Goggins
Jennifer Golbeck
Scott Golder
Jorge Goncalves
Victor Gonzalez
Roberto González-Ibáñez
Visda Goudarzi
Eric Graham
Raphael Grasset
Antonietta Grasso
Rebecca Gray
Mary Gray
Michael Greenberg
Beki Grinter
Miria Grisot
Diane Gromala
Jens Grossklags
Jonathan Grudin
Shion Guha
Jamie Guillory
Philip Guo
Frode Guribye
David Gurzick
Joerg Haake
Eija Haapalainen Ferreira
Eben Haber
Joshua Hailpern
Julia Haines
Maria Håkansson
Kayla Hales
Michael Haller
Kim Halskov
Christine Halverson
Martin Halvey
Keith Hampton
Kyungsik (Keith) Han
Jeff Hancock
Mark Handel
Alexander Hanna
John Hannon
Benjamin Hanrahan
Preben Hansen
Derek Hansen
Kotaro Hara
Richard Harper
Franklin Harper
Steve Harrison
Drew Harry
Mark Hartswood
Ari Hautasaari
Kirstie Hawkey
Gillian Hayes
Steven Haynes
Mike Hazas
Brent Hecht
Eric Hekler
Libby Hemphill
Morten Hertzum
Benjamin Mako Hill
Serena Hillman
Starr Roxanne Hiltz
Ken Hinckley
Jon Hindmarsh
Joanne Hinds
Christina Hochleitner
Lichan Hong
Hwajung Hong
Jason Hong
Alexis Hope
Michael Horn
Andrew Howes
James Howison
Yuheng Hu
Yun Huang
Shih-Wen Huang
Jeff Huang
David Huffaker
Amanda Hughes
Jina Huh
Christian Huitema
Jonathan Hurlock
CJ Hutto
Marleen Huysman
Ebba Thora Hvannberg
Inseok Hwang
Ioanna Iacovides
Kori Inkpen
Joshua Introne
Panos Ipeirotis
Shamsi Iqbal
Pourang Irani
Lilly Irani
Germaine Irwin
Petra Isenberg
Corey Jackson
Steven Jackson
Mohit Jain
Timo Jakobi
Jacek Jankowski
Mohammad Hossein Jarrahi
Rasmus Jensen
Carlos Jensen
Aditya Johri
Adam Joinson
Michiel Joosse
Elisabeth Joyce
Malte Jung
Sasa Junuzovic
Sanjay Kairam
Denis Kalkofen
Santosh Kalwar
Matthew Kam
Shaun Kane
Bridget Kane
David Karger
Hirokazu Kato
Andrea Kavanaugh
Joseph 'Jofish' Kaye
Brian Keegan
Caitlin Kelleher
Patrick Kelley
Ryan Kelly

Logan Kendall
Emad Khazraee
Andrea Kienle
Julie Kientz
Sara Kiesler
Taemie Kim
SeungJun Kim
Juho Kim
John King
David Kirk
Funda Kivran-Swaine
Predrag Klasnja
Mark Klein
Bart Knijnenburg
Stefan Knoll Knoll
Michael Koch
Yong Ming Kow
Adam Kramer
Jennifer Kraschnewski
Sven Kratz
Travis Kriplean
Per Ola Kristensson
Chinmay Kulkarni
Ranjitha Kumar
Andreas Kunz
Takeshi Kurata
Raja Kushalnagar
Diana Kusunoki
Lynette Kvasny
Ioanna lacovides
Richard Ladner
Mounia Lalmas
Nicolas LaLone
Shyong Lam
Cliff Lampe
Airi Lampinen
Jonas Landgren
Joel Lanir
Andreas Larsson
Walter Lasecki
Celine Latulipe
Eric Laurier
Yann Laurillau
Shaun Lawson
Robert Layton
Christopher Le Dantec
Matthew Lease
Michael Lee
Jinha Lee
Adam Lee
Ilias Leontiadis
Gilly Leshed
Na Li
Daniel Liebling
Rhema Linder
SiÃ¢n Lindley
Jessica Lingel
Yefeng Liu
Claudia López
Weiquan Lu
Stephan Lukosch
Kurt Luther
Kris Luyten
Rui Madeira
Charlotte Magnusson
Scott Mainwaring
Julie Maitland
Lena Mamykina
Clara Mancini
Regan Mandryk
Osama Mansour
Gabriela Marcu
Tiago Marino
Jennifer Marlow
Paul Marshall
David Martin
Christopher Mascaro
Afra Mashhadi
Winter Mason
Masood Masoodian
Tara Matthews
Stina Matthiesen
Michelle Mazurek
Nora McDonald
Poppy McLeod
Donald McMillan
Yevgeniy Medynskiy
Johanna Meurer
David Millen
Robert Miller
Andrew Miller
Tanushree Mitra
Karyn Moffatt
Sue Moon
Claudia Motta
Vicki Moulder
Martin Muehlpfordt
Ruth Mugge
Ingrid Mulder
Michael Muller
Heiko Müller
Sean Munson
Kyle Murray
Dave Murray-Rust
Elizabeth Mynatt
Mor Naaman
Miguel Nacenta
Hideyuki Nakanishi
Bonnie Nardi
Lisa Nathan
Carman Neustaedter
Dong Nguyen
Jeffrey Nichols
Jeffrey Nickerson
Sylvie Noël
Blair Nonnecke
Maria Normark
Oded Nov
Diarmuid Ó Séaghdha
Kieron O'Hara
Kenton O'Hara
Aisling O'Kane
Michael O'Mahony
Rosalie Ocker
Anne Oeldorf-Hirsch
Corinna Ogonowski
Alice Oh
Jonice Oliveira
Gary Olson
Tihomir Orehavacki
Myle Ott
Heather Packer
Xinru Page
Aditya Pal
Joshua Palay
Leysia Palen
Karljohan Palmerius
Katherine Panciera
Katrina Panovich
Nadia Pantidi
Katrina Paovich
Hugo Paredes
Tapan Parikh
Praveen Paritosh
Sun Young Park
Souneil Park
Sun Young Park
Shwetak Patel
Daniel Patel
Rupa Patel
Celeste Paul
James Pennebaker
Mark Perry

Daniel Perry
Anicia Peters
Helen Petrie
Tamara Peyton
Mark Pfaff
Martin Pielot
Jacqueline Pike
Fabiano Pinatti
Kathleen Pine
Niels Pinkwart
Volkmar Pipek
John Pollak
Nathan Prestopnik
Reid Priedhorsky
Michael Prilla
Kermit Purdy
Yan Qu
Alexander Quinn
Pablo-Alejandro Quinones
Emilee Rader
Rebecca Randell
Nimmi Rangaswamy
Dennis Reidsma
Katharina Reinecke
Philippe Renevier Gonin
Paul Resnick
Lindsay Reynolds
Rebecca Reynolds
Laurel Riek
Lionel Robert
Scott Robertson
Christine Robson
John Rooksby
Daniela Rosner
Chiara Rossitto
Mary Beth Rosson
Mattias Rost
Mark Rouncefield
Daniel Russell
Ian Ruthven
Jeffrey Rzeszotarski
Alan Said
Antti Salovaara
Nithya Sambasivan
Pedro Sanches
Christian Sandvig
Vagner Santana
Flavia Santoro
Stephanie Santoso
Christopher Scaffidi
Florian Schaub
Holger Schnädelbach
Oliver Schneider
Niko Schönau
Victoria Schwanda Sosik
Lauren Scissors
Stacey Scott
Kate Sellen
Bryan Semaan
Shilad Sen
Lauren Sessions Goulet
Leslie Setlock
Orit Shaer
Chirag Shah
Dafna Shahaf
N. Sadat Shami
Bin Shao
Sarika Sharma
Nikhil Sharma
Aaron Shaw
Haifeng Shen
S. Andrew Sheppard
Patrick Shih
Katie Shilton
Irina Shklovski
Garth Shoemaker
Leif Singer
Manya Sleeper
Nedim Slijepcevic
Daniel Smith
Madeline Smith
Ole Smørdal
Jaime Snyder
Emma Spiro
Ann Steele
Aaron Steinfeld
Stephanie Steinhardt
David Stillwell
Jennifer Stromer-Galley
H. Colleen Stuart
Fred Stutzman
Norman Su
Bongwon Suh
Nicole Sultanum
Chengzheng Sun
S. Shyam Sundar
Anthony Tang
Charlotte Tang
John Tang
Andrea Tapia
Yla Tausczik
Nick Taylor
Jaime Teevan
Loren Terveen
Alexander Thayer
William Thies
Elizabeth Thiry
John Thomas
Peter Tolmie
Stephanie Tong
Tammy Toscos
Zachary Toups
W. Ben Towne
Christoph Trattner
Jason Tsay
Jennifer Turns
Murray Turoff
Michael Twidale
Judith Uchidiuno
Kalle Ulvstig
Nancy Van House
Jos van Leeuwen
Sander van Splunter
Kami Vaniea
Radu-Daniel Vatavu
Sarah Vieweg
John Vines
Erik Vinkhuyzen
Thomas Visser
Jessica Vitak
Adriana Vivacqua
Juergen Vogel
Daniel Vogel
Amy Voida
Patrick Wagstrom
Jim Wallace
Yi-Chia Wang
William Yang Wang
Taowei Wang
Jing Wang
Hao-Chuan Wang
Jamie Wardman
Rick Wash
Nic Weber
Ingmar Weber
Carolyn Wei
Nadir Weibel
Astrid Weiss
Justin Weisz
Ryen White
Mark Whiting
Jason Wiese
Andrea Wiggins

Lauren Wilcox
Wesley Willett
Amanda Williams
Matt Willis
Mathew Wilson
Pamela Wisniewski
Donghee Yvette Wohn
Maria Wolters
Allison Woodruff
Shaomei Wu
Leslie Wu
Eugene Wu
Yan Xu
Kim Xu
Anbang Xu
Huahai Yang
Mika Yasuoka
Jude Yew
Daisy Yoo
Alyson Young
G. Michael Youngblood
Lixiu Yu
Nicola Yuill
Mark Zachry
Qiping Zhang
Jun Zhang
Haoqi Zhang
Dejin Zhao
Xiaomu Zhou
Mengxiao Zhu
Haiyi Zhu
Juergen Ziegler
Roshanak Zilouchian
Moghaddam
John Zimmerman
Thomas Zimmermann
Arkaitz Zubiaga

CSCW 2014 Sponsor & Supporters

Sponsors: SIGCHI

Champion: NSF

Benefactors: Facebook, Microsoft Research

Contributors: GRAND (Graphisme, animation et nouveaux médias / Graphics, Animation and New Media), IBM Research, Drexel University College of Computing & Informatics

Friends: Google, Information Systems UMBC

Teammate Inaccuracy Blindness: When Information Sharing Tools Hinder Collaborative Analysis

Ruogu Kang[1], Aimée A. Kane[2], Sara Kiesler[1]

Human Computer Interaction Institute[1]
Carnegie Mellon University
5000 Forbes Ave., Pittsburgh, PA 15213
{ruoguk,kiesler}@cs.cmu.edu

Palumbo-Donahue School of Business[2]
Duquesne University
600 Forbes Avenue, Pittsburgh, PA 15282
kanea@duq.edu

ABSTRACT

Asynchronous collaborative analysis is important in many fields, but information sharing can be a bottleneck. Tools for annotating, organizing, and summarizing information can help, but their value will likely depend on the accuracy of teammates' information. To document this claim, two experiments examined participants' performance on a complex detective task when they asynchronously received information from a teammate in a collaboration tool or received no such information. We found that receiving a progress report containing accurate information was associated with improved performance (vs. no information shared in a tool) but worse performance when the information was inaccurate. Teammates were evaluated as helpful even when they were not. Our findings point to a phenomenon of *teammate inaccuracy blindness* that arises when teammates provide inaccurate information. We propose some strategies for helping collaborators avoid or lessen this effect.

Author Keywords

Asynchronous collaboration, collaborative analysis, information sharing, teams, groups, sensemaking, problem solving

ACM Classification Keywords

H.5.3. Group and Organizational Interfaces: Asynchronous interaction, Computer-supported cooperative work.

INTRODUCTION

Remote asynchronous collaboration is increasingly common as analysts in domains ranging from science to intelligence tackle problems with large amounts of complex data [4, 11]. However, information sharing can be challenging for them. Remote asynchronous collaboration reduces the kinds of spontaneous communication that help analysts resolve discrepancies [2], and it also provides fewer opportunities for analysts to integrate one another's expertise [31]. If so, analysts may fail to effectively share information and collaborative performance may suffer.

CSCW'14, February 15–19, 2014, Baltimore, Maryland, USA.

ACM 978-1-4503-2540-0/14/02...$15.00.
http://dx.doi.org/10.1145/2531602.2531681

Researchers have developed IT-enabled tools to help analysts make sense of large amounts of complex data [29]. Increasingly, these tools support collaborative information sharing among analysts. Annotation tools, for example, enable analysts to highlight specific pieces of evidence for one another [16]. Organizing and visualizing tools enable analysts to display linkages across dispersed pieces of evidence, helping them point out patterns [2, 10, 13].

Researchers have not yet examined how the quality of the information conveyed through different tools affects collaborative analysis. Teammates' information could be highly accurate and useful, but it also could be inaccurate, erroneous, or irrelevant. In other domains, when teammates share inaccurate information, it can send them off in the wrong direction [12]. This possibility is especially critical in teams working asynchronously. Team members may assume others on the team offer help only when the help is useful. Not having continual communication with each other may hinder collaborators from spotting and ruling out misunderstandings [23]. In this paper, we tackle this issue in the context of asynchronous collaborative analysis of a complex crime problem.

This research addresses whether team members will distinguish between inaccurate and accurate information conveyed in information sharing tools. We experimentally examine how receiving information that varies in its accuracy affects the problem solving performance of a remote team member. We find evidence that the recipient may fail to recognize that teammates' information is inaccurate. In our studies, failure occurred when inaccurate information was shared in a progress report tool. We coin the term *teammate inaccuracy blindness* to highlight the influence that inaccurate information can have on problem-solving performance and on inflated evaluations of teammates.

Levels of sensemaking in collaborative analysis

Our consideration of information accuracy in asynchronous collaborative analysis builds on the concept of "sensemaking." Sensemaking refers to a process of making data intelligible by identifying evidence, schematizing and perceiving patterns and anomalies, and, at the highest level, developing insights, hypotheses, and conclusions [28]. Pirolli and Russell [29] have pointed to an emerging recognition that sensemaking is increasingly conducted by teams. They argue research is needed to understand how to facilitate the transfer of useful sensemaking information from one collaborator to another.

Analysts can use collaboration tools to share sensemaking information [16]. Generally, these tools should be more useful to collaborators if the information provider is on the right track and uses the tool to share accurate sensemaking information. But there is no guarantee that an analyst teammate is on the right track [12]. The usefulness of information sharing tools may depend on the accuracy of the sensemaking information the teammate conveys.

For purposes of our argument, we simplify the process of sensemaking by positing three key levels: (1) identifying evidence, (2) using categorization or schemas to organize evidence, and then (3) generating hypotheses and conclusions, and marshaling evidence to support them [28]. We propose that when analysts work together, annotation or tagging tools afford collaborative information sharing at the first level of sensemaking. Organizing worksheets, visualizations, and other ways of identifying categories and patterns afford collaborative information sharing at the second level of sensemaking. Summary report tools that convey hypotheses or conclusions, and give evidence in support of them, afford collaborative information sharing at the third level of sensemaking.

Because any sensemaking information added to complex data analysis potentially contributes cognitive load to an analysts' work [29], it is important to consider whether this information provides help to analysts beyond what they can glean from the underlying data. We now consider the possibly variable quality of the information collaborators may share through tools at each level of sensemaking.

Annotating, tagging, and highlighting

The sensemaking framework suggests theoretical reasons to believe that an initial analyst's annotations or tags of data may be helpful to a teammate when the information space is complex. Shared annotations may be helpful because they direct attention to different parts of a problem or evidence, thus helping analysts decide what parts of a problem are important or how to decompose the problem [24,37]. For instance, a police detective in one department who is familiar with the geography of a city might tag a crime location report with a comment that the neighborhood has experienced similar crimes.

Nonetheless, there is a risk associated with sharing inaccurately annotated information. Annotations may be irrelevant notations that only increase cognitive load and time spent in analysis. Annotations also may direct a problem solver's attention to an incorrect strategy. Sloppy or incorrect annotations could guide collaborators to erroneous conclusions [16].

Organizing, categorizing, and creating schemas

The second level of sensemaking information represents knowledge categories and schemas that can help collaborators. The organization of information is itself a shared information space that may be even more useful than the information itself [8]. Researchers have proposed strategies such as creating new categories to help solve insight problems [17, 21]. Categorizing and creating schemas highlights associations across data; distant associations can trigger innovative thinking and insights [22]. For example, when detectives group crimes according to the weapon used, their teammates may more readily detect a pattern, if one is present. Along related lines, visualization tools that display otherwise hidden linkages across dispersed information have improved complex problem solving [2, 10,13, 33].

There is a risk of sharing inaccurate organizing information. Categories and schemas are higher-level representations of information, and using them may require expertise in the domain [5]. Teammates may misunderstand or misuse the categories or schemas created by collaborators. Patterns can reveal relationships that look interesting but are innocent (false positives). If teammates highlight inaccurate categories or schemas and insufficiently link them to sources in the data, they could be misleading.

Summarizing and pointing to solutions

The highest level of representation in sensemaking is the process of creating hypotheses and drawing inferences, and connecting evidence to those ideas [28]. Analysts who communicate their hypotheses and conclusions, with evidence in their favor, provide shortcuts for their colleagues. Information sharing tools that afford sharing these developed hypotheses and conclusions should be a powerful aid to analysts and help their efficiency. The first person to close in on a demonstrably correct solution could share this knowledge and save teammates' time and effort [23].

There is a risk of sharing inaccurate hypotheses and conclusions. If the shared hypothesis or conclusion is the wrong one, is weakly supported by the evidence, or is poorly explained, then the teammate could be sent in the wrong direction. It would also magnify confirmation bias, that is, searching only for evidence in favor of a particular hypothesis [25]. Using an information-sharing tool to exchange summary hypotheses or conclusions may be worse than not sharing information at all.

In sum, we argue that the accuracy of different levels of sensemaking information shared through tools by an analyst teammate will affect the subsequent problem solving of a remote analyst. In this research, we examine the use and effects of three existing tools intended to aid each level of sensemaking. We compare the effects of an initial analyst who shares no information, other than his or her case data (no tool control), with the effects of an initial analyst's information conveyed in an annotation tool meant to help analysts identify evidence (sensemaking level 1), an organizing worksheet tool meant to help analysts share interconnections among categories of evidence (sensemaking level 2), or a summarizing report tool meant to help analysts share hypotheses and evidence in support of hypotheses (sensemaking level 3).

Taking together our reasoning about the importance of information accuracy and the levels of sensemaking conveyed in a tool, we hypothesize the following:

H1a. When an asynchronous partner uses collaboration tools to share accurate information, the receiver of this information will show better problem solving than a control partner who receives no extra information.

H1b. When an asynchronous partner uses collaboration tools to share inaccurate information, the receiver of this information will show worse problem solving than a control partner who only receives no extra information.

H2. The different effects of accurate and inaccurate information will be greater when the partner uses the summarizing report tool because that tool conveys the highest level and most efficient sensemaking information.

EXPERIMENT 1

To test the hypotheses, we used a homicide detective task in which participants needed to cull through numerous police reports, crime statistics, and bus routes, and piece together clues to identify a serial killer [2]. Two remote analysts collaborated in a sequentially interdependent manner. Each of them used three tools for information sharing, an annotation tool, a worksheet organizing tool, and a progress report. Halfway through the task, initial analysts shared their cases and, in all conditions except the no tool control, information about those cases with final analysts using one of the tools (i.e., annotation, worksheets, or reports). The final analysts ultimately prepared a final summary report and provided an evaluation of their collaborator. We coded these summary reports for evidence that the analysts had identified the serial killer, which provided an outcome measure of effective problem solving. We measured the evaluations that analysts made of one another because we wondered if their evaluations would reflect the quality of information they had received.

Method

Participants and design

Fifty-nine pairs participated in the experiment. All participants were undergraduate or graduate students. Each participant was paid $15 for participating in the experiment for 1.5 hours.

Participants were instructed to solve as many of the eight homicide cases as possible and to write a summary report on behalf of their team. The pairs were randomly assigned to one of three tool conditions or a control condition. Within each pair, one participant was randomly assigned to be the initial analyst and the other participant to be the final analyst. In subsequent discussion we refer to these participants by their roles of initial or final analyst.

The final analyst could not solve the serial killer case without case data held by the initial analyst. These data were shared midway through the task with all final analysts. In the tool conditions, the initial analyst shared additional information about these newly-shared case data. We were mainly concerned with the accuracy of the information that the initial analyst provided and the subsequent performance of the final analyst. We tested the hypotheses by comparing the problem-solving performance of final analysts who had received information from the initial analyst in information-sharing tools against the performance of final analysts who received no extra information in tools from the initial analyst. We also examined how these final analysts evaluated their asynchronous collaborator.

Task

We adapted the homicide detective task involving a serial killer used by Balakrishnan et al. [2]. Analysts needed to review multiple, complex homicide case files and other data such as bus route information and maps to piece together disparate clues across five cases that identified a serial killer responsible for four homicides. To simulate the complexity of real-world data, in addition to the four homicides perpetrated by the serial killer, analysts also had information on two unrelated homicides and two homicides that could not be solved with the evidence given. Whether or not analysts solved the serial killer crime was the problem solving success criterion.

During the first phase of the task, serial killer related cases and material were distributed unequally between teammates to create a situation in which the final analyst might benefit from receiving information from the initial analyst about the serial killer crime. Each teammate initially received four different crime case documents and relevant supplementary materials such as bus route information and an area map. The initial analyst received three serial killer cases and one unrelated case. The final analyst received one unrelated case, two unsolvable cases, and one serial killer case. They each set about their task of crime analysis, trying to identify the perpetrator of each homicide.

Halfway through the period for analysis, final analysts received access to all case data, including data from the initial analyst's four cases. In the tool conditions, final analysts also received information provided by the initial analyst in one of the tools. As noted above, by design, the final analysts could not solve the serial killer crime with the information provided at the start of the experiment because they had only one serial killer case. The other case data provided by their teammate at the mid-point was essential for solving the serial killer crime because it included three additional serial killer cases and an unrelated case in which the serial killer appeared as a witness. Our question was whether the additional sensemaking information from the initial analyst would help the final analyst in solving the serial killer crime beyond what was provided in newly shared case data.

Tools

To help analysts share their insights about cases, all participants were encouraged to use the annotation tool, the organizing worksheet tool, and the summarizing report tool.

Annotation tool. All documents were in a main folder on a website for annotating documents (http://a.nnotate.com/). Participants created annotations and highlighted text directly on their documents (as shown in Figure 1).

Figure 1. A screenshot of the annotation interface

Organizing worksheet tool. We used a "modus operandi" (MO) worksheet to help analysts organize evidence and clues in different categories. The worksheet listed all eight cases and provided categories for organizing evidence. As shown in Figure 2, participants entered data into this document and, optionally, added new rows in the worksheet to connect evidence across cases.

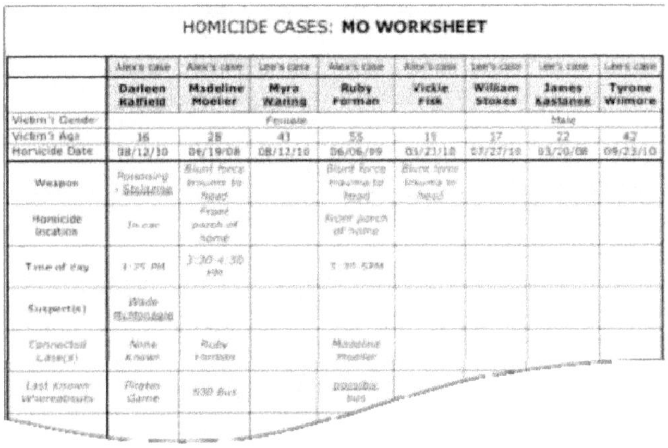

Figure 2. Organizing worksheet (italic added by a participant)

Report Tool. This tool was a simple form for conveying a progress report halfway through analysis. The progress report asked participants to provide an open-ended summary of their progress. The instructions reminded analysts their goal was to solve as many cases as possible and, in the report to "identify suspects and clues" (Figure 3).

Procedure

Each experimental session began with two practice cases as used in Balakrishnan et al. [2]. Next, the experimenter gave instructions for using the information sharing tools. Participants were instructed to use the tools to help them

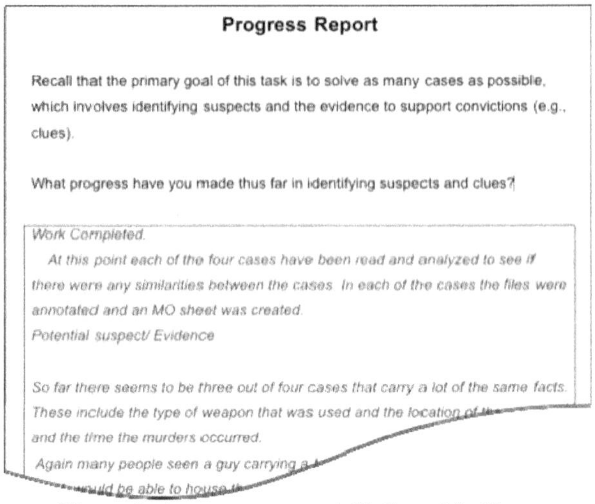

Figure 3. A progress report (italics added by a participant)

solve the cases and to communicate their ideas to their teammates, with whom they would share cases at the mid-point.

After training and instructions, participants were moved into two separate rooms. Each experimental session was split into two equal phases. During the first phase, participants worked alone on half of the total cases, and used the annotation tool and organizing worksheet tool to conduct their analysis. At the end of this phase, participants were asked to write a progress report.

At the midpoint, final analysts received the four crime case documents that initial analysts had worked on and either (1) the initial analyst's annotations, (2) the initial analyst's organizing worksheet, (3) the initial analyst's mid-point progress report, or (4) no information in any tool from the initial analyst (control condition). Crime documents and annotations were shared via annotate.com. MO worksheets and progress reports were saved as PDF documents by an experimenter and were shared with participants via Dropbox (www.dropbox.com).

The final analysts then worked on all eight cases with access to all crime documents. This period ended with final analysts writing a final report that identified suspects and evidence. Finally, the participants completed an online survey to assess analyst evaluations of their teammate.

Measures

Information accuracy was assessed with a proxy measure obtained from coding the initial analysts' midpoint progress reports. If the initial analysts identified the serial killer in their progress reports, the information they provided to the final analysts (in their annotations, worksheet, or report) was considered to be accurate. On the contrary, if they identified no suspect or an incorrect suspect as the serial killer in their progress reports, the information they provided to the receivers was considered to be inaccurate.

We observed more cases of final analysts receiving inaccurate than accurate information, particularly in annotation and the worksheet tool conditions. These results are shown in Table 1, below.

	Accurate information	Inaccurate information
Annotation tool	5	10
MO worksheet tool	5	10
Report summary tool	8	7
No tool control	14	

N = 45 in six cells of 2x3 design, 59 in all seven cells

Table 1. Experiment 1 information accuracy in each condition

Problem-solving performance was measured as a binary variable that reflected whether the final analyst solved the serial killer crime, evidenced by a final report correctly identifying by name the perpetrator of the four serial killer homicide crimes.

Collaborator evaluation was measured with a continuous variable obtained from the post-analysis survey in which final analyst teammates rated how much the initial analyst teammate had helped them solve the homicide cases they received at the midpoint. On the survey, they used a 5-point scale ranging from 1 ("not helpful at all") to 5 ("very helpful") to evaluate their teammate's helpfulness on each homicide case. We averaged these ratings across the three serial killer cases provided by the initial analyst teammates to form a composite rating of collaborator helpfulness on the serial killer problem.

Results

Our statistical analysis used a 2 (information accuracy: accurate, inaccurate) × 3 (information shared in tool: annotation, organizing worksheet, or summary report) design with an additional control group (no information shared in a tool). As noted below, we considered the control group to be a benchmark condition against which to evaluate the efficacy of information shared in a tool.

Problem-solving performance

In Hypotheses 1a and 1b we predicted that final analysts who received accurate information in tools would do better than final analysts in the no tool control condition (H1a) and that final analysts who received inaccurate information in tools would do worse than the controls (H1b). Because the dependent variable is a discrete variable (1: solved serial killer crime, 0: did not solve serial killer crime), we conducted a logistic regression analysis that estimated the effect of receiving accurate information in a tool and the effect of receiving inaccurate information in a tool. Each of these situations was compared to the benchmark no tool

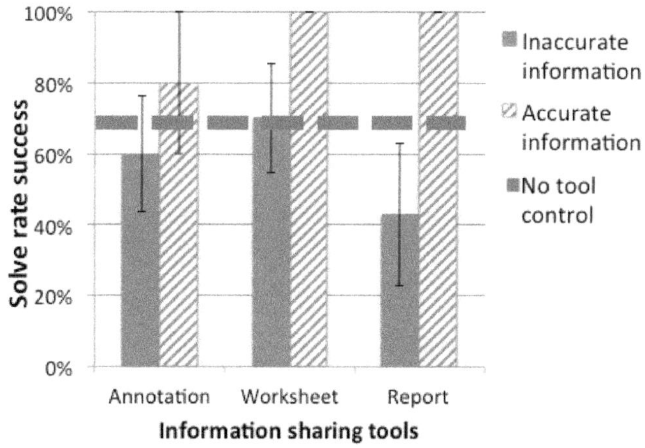

Figure 4. Experiment 1 solve rate success when teammate provides accurate or inaccurate information using one of three tools, compared with the no tool condition.

control, which served as the statistical reference group in the analysis.

As shown in Figure 4, the analysis revealed a significant main effect of information accuracy (X^2 [n=59] = 8.00, p = .02). As predicted in Hypothesis 1a, final analysts performed better when they received accurate information in a tool (i.e., annotations, worksheet, or report) from the initial analyst than when they received no information in a tool. The odds of solving the serial killer crime were 4.30 times greater for analysts receiving accurate information than for analysts in the control condition (X^2 [n=59] = 6.32, p = .01). As predicted in Hypothesis 1b, analysts performed worse when they received inaccurate information in a tool than when they received no information in a tool. The odds of solving the crime were .37 times lower for analysts receiving inaccurate information than for their counterparts in the control condition (X^2 [n=59] = 5.30, p = .02).

Hypothesis 2 posited that the effect of information accuracy would be most pronounced when the information is received in a progress report because this tool conveys the highest level of sensemaking. We used nested-by-values effects coding to estimate an additional logistic regression (see [32; 34, p. 391]). This supplementary analysis allows use of all the observations in the 2 (information quality) x 3 (information tools) cells, but alters the parameterization with one parameter for each of the three tools conditional on information accuracy. This analysis reveals that the odds of solving the case were 7.30 times greater for analysts receiving a report tool containing accurate rather than inaccurate information (X^2 [n=45] = 7.52, p = .006), but the odds of solving the case did not differ as a function of information accuracy for annotation (X^2 [n=45] = 1.68, *ns*) or worksheet tools (X^2 [n=45] = 1.68, *ns*).

Collaborator evaluation

Those in the control condition who received no information in tools rated their teammate comparatively poorly (M = 1.67, SD = 1.76) when contrasted with those who did receive information in tools ($M = 3.07$, $SD = 1.45$, t [57] = 3.02, $p = .004$). However, the 2 (information accuracy) x 3 (information sharing tool) ANOVA yielded just one significant main effect for the type of information sharing tool (F [2, 41] = 6.14, $p = .005$). Final analysts evaluated the collaborator more positively when they received information conveyed in the summary report tool (M = 4.07, SD = 1.22) than when they received information conveyed in an organizing worksheet tool ($M = 2.67$, SD = 1.43) or an annotation tool ($M = 2.49$, $SD = 1.19$). There was no overall accuracy effect.

Because significant problem solving differences due to information accuracy were found only for the report tool, we conducted an ANOVA of teammate evaluations comparing the no tool control condition with the accurate and inaccurate summary report conditions. The analysis showed an overall effect (F [2, 26] = 12.16, $p < .0002$). A planned contrast comparing the evaluations of the accurate teammate (M = 4.75, SD = .46) with the evaluations of inaccurate teammate (M = 3.29, SD = 1.38) showed a marginally more favorable evaluation of the accurate teammate (F [1, 26] = 3.92, p = .059), and the planned contrast comparing the inaccurate teammate with the control teammate (M = 1.67, SD = 1.76) showed a significantly more favorable evaluation of the inaccurate teammate (F [1, 26] = 5.98, $p = .02$).

In sum, analysts evaluated asynchronous teammates more positively when information was conveyed in a report tool, and they evaluated these teammates more positively than teammates who provided no report even when they received inaccurate information in the report and performed worse than those receiving no additional information. Consistent with this finding, we did not find a significant association between analysts' problem-solving performance and their evaluations of their teammate ($r = -.28$, *n.s.*).

Discussion of Experiment 1

Our results suggest that analysts may be misled by inaccurate sensemaking information provided in a high-level information-sharing collaboration tool. Overall, final analysts receiving accurate information in a tool (annotation, worksheet, or report) performed better than their counterparts who received no sensemaking information from analyst teammates (hypothesis 1a). This increment in performance suggests that sharing accurate information can be helpful. By contrast (hypothesis 1b), final analysts receiving inaccurate information in a tool (annotation, worksheet, or report) performed worse than their counterparts who received no sensemaking information from analyst teammates.

The decrement in performance due to inaccurate information was driven primarily by the result of information sharing in the progress report condition (hypothesis 2). We found limited support for hypothesis 2. As shown in Figure 4, analysts performed better when they received accurate rather than inaccurate information, but the increment was only statistically significant for the report tool. The lack of statistical significance for annotations and worksheets cannot be interpreted to suggest that the accuracy of the information conveyed in these tools does not affect asynchronous collaborative analysis. It is possible, for example, that the smaller sample of accurate than inaccurate information made it difficult to detect differences. Nonetheless, the results do suggest that receipt of accurate information in a summarizing report tool can help analysts, whereas receipt of inaccurate information in a report tool can harm analysts.

We also discovered that analysts receiving sensemaking information in tools (annotations, worksheets, or reports) evaluated their collaborator more positively than analysts receiving no information in tools. This positivity was the case even for analysts who not only received inaccurate information in the report tool but also performed worse than analysts receiving no information in tools. These results showing inflated evaluations of a teammate who is associated with a decrement in performance raises a question about how accurately asynchronous analysts can evaluate one another's contributions.

A major limitation of this study is that we measured rather than manipulated the quality of the information conveyed in the information sharing tools. Given the complexity of the task, fewer than half of the initial analysts had solved the case by the midpoint, which resulted in fewer observations of accurate than inaccurate information sharing. This imbalance was not an issue in the summary report tool condition, but the small sample size (8 accurate reports vs. 7 inaccurate reports) warrants replication.

EXPERIMENT 2

The main purpose of Experiment 2 was to replicate and extend Experiment 1. Because the effects were greatest in the summary report tool conditions of Experiment 1, we examined the effects of the accuracy of the information conveyed in a summary report. We addressed a key limitation of Experiment 1 by manipulating the accuracy of the information conveyed in the reports. We also increased the sample size twofold.

We extended our examination to an asynchronous collaboration with more than one other teammate and source of information because this structure is increasingly common (e.g., [12]). We increased the team size to three. Final analysts received either two reports from their teammates that conveyed inaccurate information (inaccurate-inaccurate report condition) or they received one report conveying inaccurate information and another report conveying accurate information (inaccurate-accurate report condition). This design allowed for replication of Experiment 1 in a team of three and an examination of whether an accurate report could offset the detrimental effects of an inaccurate report.

Method

Participants and design

We recruited 38 native English-speaking participants for the experiment. All participants were undergraduate or graduate students. Each participant was paid $10 for participating in the experiment for 1 hour.

All participants took on the role of final analyst. As in Experiment 1, they could not solve the case without case data from teammates. Participants were randomly assigned to either the inaccurate-inaccurate report condition or the inaccurate-accurate report condition, resulting in 19 observations per condition.

Task

We used the same experimental homicide detective task involving a serial killer as in Experiment 1 with a few modifications. The procedure was altered by simulating the first phase of the sequentially interdependent collaboration with initial analyst reports compiled from progress reports provided by participants in Experiment 1. Participants were led to believe that two teammates had been working on the cases during an initial phase and had each prepared a progress report. With access to these two initial analyst progress reports and all underlying case data, participants began their analysis. They were instructed, as in Experiment 1, to solve as many of the cases as possible and to write a summary report on behalf of their team.

Procedure

Each experimental session lasted approximately one hour and followed a procedure similar to Experiment 1 with the exception that participants did not go through an initial phase before they were provided with teammates' sensemaking information conveyed in two summary reports.

We manipulated information accuracy. Participants were randomly assigned to one of the information accuracy conditions. To create the inaccurate-inaccurate and inaccurate-accurate report conditions, we compiled three reports of equal length (214 words) from the progress reports provided by participants in Experiment 1. Each report conveyed the third level of sensemaking information (e.g., suspect hypotheses) about three of the four serial killer cases and one unrelated case. Two of these progress reports were inaccurate, mentioning different, wrong suspects and an unrelated case suspect, and one report was accurate, mentioning the serial killer and an unrelated case suspect.

Measures

The measures of problem-solving performance and collaborator evaluation were the same as in Experiment 1.

Results

Problem-solving performance

As seen in Figure 5, analysts receiving an inaccurate report and an accurate report performed better than their counterparts whose teammates provided them with two

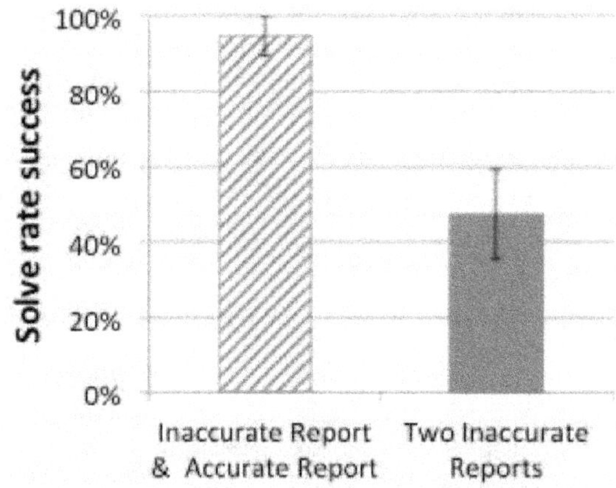

Figure 5. Experiment 2 solve rate success when teammates provide analysts with an inaccurate and an accurate report or two inaccurate reports.

different inaccurate reports ($X^2 = 10.36, p = .001$). Whereas the vast majority of the analysts receiving an inaccurate and an accurate report solved the case (94.7%), only half of the analysts receiving two inaccurate reports solved the serial killer case (47.4%). The latter result is comparable to the performance of analysts receiving one inaccurate report in Experiment 1.

Collaborator evaluation

Analysts in the inaccurate-accurate report condition evaluated their teammate who provided an accurate report ($M = 4.08$, $SD = .80$) as significantly more helpful than their other teammate who provided an inaccurate report ($M = 2.39$, $SD = 1.08$, $t\,(16) = 4.42$, $p = .0004$). Analysts in the inaccurate-inaccurate report condition whose teammates provided them with two different inaccurate reports did not evaluate one teammate as more helpful than another (*M*s= 3.08 and 3.13, SDs = 1.08 and 1.00, $t\,(15) = 0.27$, *ns*). However, analysts receiving two inaccurate reports rated their two teammates, on average, just as positively ($M = 3.10$, $SD = .99$) as did analysts receiving an inaccurate report and an accurate report ($M = 3.24$, $SD = .50$, $t\,(31) = -.48$, *ns*) even though the former were half as likely to solve the case as the latter.

Discussion of Experiment 2

Experiment 2 accomplished its primary goals of replicating and extending Experiment 1. First, it confirmed, in a larger sample, that inaccurate sensemaking information from teammates conveyed in a report tool has a detrimental effect on problem-solving performance, and that analysts erroneously evaluated these collaborations as helpful. The manipulation of information accuracy establishes that these findings are independent of other characteristics of reports or teammates. (In Experiment 1, information accuracy was measured rather than manipulated so we could not separate accuracy from other aspects of reports or teammates, such as writing style.) Second, we extended the study to a three-person team, and showed that accurate information from one teammate can cancel out inaccurate information from another. This finding suggests the value of having more than one teammate. A third teammate increases coordination costs but also increases the chances of receiving accurate sensemaking information and may counteract the tendency for asynchronous collaborative analysts to accept a teammate's information, even when it is inaccurate.

LIMITATIONS

Some limitations of our studies are worth noting before we discuss their implications. Although our participants underwent a thirty-minute training session on collaborative analysis, they were not experienced detectives or intelligence analysts. Experts in these fields may be better able to discern the quality of their collaborators' contributions than were our naïve participants. Another limitation is that we compared a small set of text-based information sharing tools. We also focused on small team collaborations rather than on larger-scale analysis situations. In future work, it would be worthwhile to expand the populations, tools, and groups tested.

IMPLICATIONS FOR COLLABORATIVE SENSEMAKING

When they function effectively, teams of collaborative analysts can be especially useful for solving analysis problems because they leverage the insights of teammates [9]. When they function poorly, collaborative performance is even worse than when analysts work alone [35].

Our research simulated information sharing in the context of remote asynchronous collaboration—a collaboration mode increasingly used by teams facing complex problems [4]. In two experiments, we examined whether participants could identify a serial killer from unsolved homicides after they received raw case data and, in all conditions except the Experiment 1 no tool control condition, additional sensemaking information from a teammate. These experiments help to identify the benefits and costs of asynchronously sharing sensemaking information in a controlled setting.

Experiment 1 measured information accuracy and compared an annotation tool meant to help analysts share evidence attached to a problem (sensemaking level 1), an organizing worksheet tool meant to help analysts share interconnections among categories of evidence (sensemaking level 2), and a summarizing report tool meant to help analysts share new associations and hypotheses (sensemaking level 3). Experiment 2 replicated and extended Experiment 1 with a manipulation of the accuracy of the information conveyed in two summarizing reports.

Taken together, results suggest that the degree to which information sharing tools help collaborative analysis depends on the level and the accuracy of the sensemaking information they convey, as follows:

1. Sensemaking information from a teammate at the third level (summarizing report containing hypotheses and/or conclusions) was associated with significant differences in problem-solving performance, either positive if the information was accurate, or negative if the information was inaccurate (Experiment 1; replicated in Experiment 2).

2. Analysts evaluated information sharing collaborators, especially those conveying the third level of sensemaking information, as helpful even when they were not (Experiment 1; replicated in Experiment 2).

3. Accurate sensemaking information at the third level from an additional teammate mitigated the negative effects of inaccurate sensemaking information at the third level from another teammate (Experiment 2).

These findings contribute to an understanding of the kind of information sharing that underlies effective asynchronous collaborative analysis. They expose a problem we call *teammate inaccuracy blindness* whereby people take a teammate's contributions at face value without looking closely at their accuracy. Although previous sensemaking literature has addressed issues that may arise from an analyst's own confirmation bias [25, 28], only recently have researchers considered the accuracy of sensemaking information contributed by others [12, 36]. Our work highlights how challenging it can be for analysts to recognize when utilizing teammates' sensemaking information at the highest level might harm, rather than aid, their problem-solving performance. These results have implications for the many situations in which collaborators share high-level sensemaking information that varies in accuracy.

Similarities exist between teammate inaccuracy blindness and other group phenomena, such as in-group favoritism [1] and groupthink [14]. Although in each case group members make poor use of information provided by others, there are some differences. Groupthink and in-group favoritism stem from group identity and conformity to the group, and predict globally positive evaluations of insiders. These phenomena harm decision quality, in large part, because group members reject accurate information from outsiders [1, 14]. By contrast, our notion of teammate inaccuracy blindness stems from misguided cognitive efficiency; it harms problem-solving performance because people, perhaps mindlessly, incorporate inaccurate sensemaking information from teammates. (A related phenomenon, called "social recognition memory," is documented in forensic analysis and false eyewitness testimony [38].) Adopting sensemaking information at the highest level is cognitively efficient. As a result, teammate inaccuracy blindness occurs most at this level, and analysts evaluate teammates providing this level of sensemaking information more positively than teammates sharing lower level or no sensemaking information at all.

It is noteworthy we uncovered teammate inaccuracy blindness in the context of teammates sharing data and information critical to solving a complex analysis task with a correct solution. Research indicates that it is rare for solutions to be so highly demonstrably that "truth wins" [19]. Demonstrability can be limited, in part, because people tend to lack sufficient information and cognitive resources to distinguish inaccurate from accurate information. These limiting factors provide insights into why teammate inaccuracy blindness occurred for participants receiving two different inaccurate reports but not for participants receiving an inaccurate and an accurate report—the accurate report would have directed attention to the serial killer and caused the participant to see the pattern revealed by his behavior. This logic suggests that teammate inaccuracy blindness is likely to be more prevalent in lower demonstrability situations characterized by greater problem complexity and information overload.

OVERCOMING TEAMMATE INACCURACY BLINDNESS

Even given the limitations of our studies, our results provide some insights for avoiding or mitigating teammate inaccuracy blindness. In the ideal case when teammates have developed accurate hypotheses or conclusions, it seems advisable to use information sharing tools, especially those that convey higher-level representations such as summary reports. However, when teammates lack expertise or the solution is not very demonstrable, high-level sensemaking tools could be harmful for subsequent analysts, especially because analysts tend to perceive their teammates as helpful even when, objectively, they are not.

Experiment 2 and research in CSCW and organizational science suggest some strategies for overcoming teammate inaccuracy blindness. Experiment 2 showed that adding an accurate report to an inaccurate report raised performance. This finding suggests the value of tools that facilitate identifying and adding competent asynchronous teammates through organizational expertise directories [7], work logs to identify structurally similar others [30], or reputation-rating systems for collaborators [9].

One study of collaborative peer production systems shows that displaying controversy or inconsistent contributions tends to increase accuracy [36]. To the extent these findings generalize to asynchronous collaborative analysis teams, software might be used to evaluate the overlap in teammates sensemaking information and display the similarity or dissimilarity of their contributions. It is possible that a simple indicator of a multiplicity of views could cause receivers to put more mindful thought into their judgments and to avoid teammate inaccuracy blindness.

CONCLUSION

Tools for summarizing information can assist analysts in their sensemaking process, but the value of these tools for sharing information will be limited by the accuracy of teammates' information. Accurate information improves performance but inaccurate information can cause performance to fall below the level obtained when no information is shared. This work uncovers teammate inaccuracy blindness and identifies a few ways to overcome it.

ACKNOWLEDGMENTS

We thank all the participants and Lisa Kim, Sarah Deluiis, and Kerry Chang for their help. The National Science Foundation supported this work (OCI-1025656 and IIS-0968583).

REFERENCES

1. Abrams, D., M. Wetherell, S. Cochrane, M.A. Hogg, J.C. Turner. 1990. Knowing what to think by knowing who you are: Self-categorization and the nature of norm formation, conformity and group polarization. *British Journal of Social Psychology* 29, (1990), 97-119.
2. Balakrishnan, A.D., Fussell, S.R., and Kiesler, S. Do visualizations improve synchronous remote collaboration? In *Proc. of CHI 2008*, (2008), 1227–1236.
3. Bier, E.A., Card, S.K., and Bodnar, J.W. Entity-based collaboration tools for intelligence analysis. *Visual Analytics Science and Technology, 2008. VAST'08. IEEE Symposium*, (2008), 99–106.
4. Bruns, H. Working alone together. Coordination in collaboration across domains of expertise. *Academy of Management Journal 56,* 1 (2013), 62-83.
5. Chase, W. G., & Simon, H. A. Perception in chess. *Cognitive Psychology*, 4 (1973), 55-81.
6. Chung, H., Yang, S., Massjouni, N., Andrews, C., Kanna, R., and North, C. VizCept: Supporting synchronous collaboration for constructing visualizations in intelligence analysis. *Visual Analytics Science and Technology (VAST), 2010 IEEE Symposium on, IEEE* (2010), 107–114.
7. Cross, R., & Baird, L. Technology is not enough: Improving performance by building organizational memory. *Sloan Management Review* (Spring), (2000), 69-78.
8. Fisher, K., Counts, S., Kittur, A., and Ave, F. Distributed sensemaking : Improving sensemaking by leveraging the efforts of previous users. *Proc. of CHI 2012*, ACM Press (2012), 247-256.
9. Furtadoa, V., Ayresa, L, de Oliveirac, M., Vasconcelosb, E., Caminhaa, C., D'Orleansa, J., and Belchiora, M. Collective intelligence in law enforcement – The WikiCrimes system. *Information Sciences 180*, 1 (2010), 4-17.
10. Goyal, N., Leshed, G., and Fussell, S. Effects of visualization and note-taking on sensemaking and analysis. In *Proc. of CHI 2013*. ACM (2013), 2721-2724.
11. Hackman, J.R. *Collaborative intelligence: Using teams to solve hard problems*. Berrett-Koehler Publishers, San Francisco, (2011).
12. Hansen, D. L., Schone, P. J., Corey, D., Reid, M., & Gehring, J. Quality control mechanisms for crowdsourcing: peer review, arbitration, & expertise at

familysearch indexing. In *Proc. CSCW 2013*, ACM Press (2013), 649-660.

13. Heer, J., Viégas, F.B., and Wattenberg, M. Voyagers and voyeurs: Supporting asynchronous collaborative visualization. *Communications of the ACM 52*, 1 (2009), 87–97.

14. Janis, I. L. *Victims of groupthink*. Boston: Houghton Mifflin, (1972).

15. Kane, A. A., Argote, L., & Levine, J. M. (2005). Knowledge transfer between groups via personnel rotation: Effects of social identity and knowledge quality. *Organizational Behavior And Human Decision Processes 96*, 1 (2005), 56-71.

16. Kang, R. and Kiesler, S. Do collaborators ' annotations help or hurt asynchronous analysis? In *Proc. CSCW 2012*, ACM Press (2012), 123–126.

17. Knoblich, G., Ohlsson, S., and Haider, H. Constraint relaxation and chunk decomposition in insight problem solving. *Journal of Experimental Psychology: Learning, Memory, and Cognition 25*, (1999), 1534-1555.

18. Laughlin, P.R., B.L. Bonner, A.G. Miner, P.J. Carnevale. Frames of reference in quantity estimations by groups and individuals. *Organanizatioal Behavior and Human Decision Processes 80*, 2 (1999), 103-117.

19. Laughlin, P.R., A.L. Ellis. Demonstrability and social combination processes on mathematical intellective tasks. *Journal of Experimental Social Psychology 22*, 3 (1986), 177-189.

20. Lojeski, K.S., Reilly, R., and Dominick, P. The role of virtual distance in innovation and success. *Proc. Conf on System Sciences (HICSS'06),* (2006), 25c–25c.

21. McCaffrey, T. Innovation relies on the obscure: A key to overcoming the classic problem of functional fixedness. *Psychological Science 23*, 3 (2012), 215-218.

22. Mednick, S. The associative basis of the creative process. Psychological Review 69, 3 (1962), 220.

23. Mesmer-Magnus, J.R. and DeChurch, L.A. Information sharing and team performance: A meta-analysis. *Journal of Applied Psychology 94*, 2 (2009), 535.

24. Munro, A.J., Höök, K., and Benyon, D.R. *Personal and social navigation of information space.* Springer-Verlag London, (1999).

25. Nickerson, R. S. Confirmation bias: A ubiquitous phenomenon in many guises. *Review of General Psychology*, *2* (1998),175-220.

26. Nobarany, S., Haraty, M., & Fisher, B. Facilitating the reuse process in distributed collaboration: a distributed cognition approach. In *Proc. of CSCW 2012*, ACM Press (2012), 1223-1232.

27. Pioch, N.J. and Everett, J.O. POLESTAR: collaborative knowledge management and sensemaking tools for intelligence analysts. *Proceedings of the 15th ACM international conference on Information and knowledge management*, ACM (2006), 513–521.

28. Pirolli, P. and Card, S. The sensemaking process and leverage points for analyst technology as identified through cognitive task analysis. *Proceedings of International Conference on Intelligence Analysis*, (2005), 2–4.

29. Pirolli, P. and Russell, D.M. Introduction to special issue on sensemaking. *Human Computer Interaction*, (2011), 1–8.

30. Reagans, R., & McEvily, B. Network structure and knowledge transfer: The effects of cohesion and range. *Administrative Science Quarterly 48*, 2 (2003), 240-267.

31. Ren, Y. and Argote, L. Transactive memory systems 1985–2010 : An integrative framework of key dimensions, antecedents, and consequences. *Academy of Management Annals 5*, 1 (2011), 189–229.

32. SAS Knowledge Base Two-Factor Logistic Model Using Dummy and Effects Coding http://support.sas.com/kb/24/447.html#ex3

33. Stasko, J., Goerg, C., and Liu, Z. Jigsaw: Supporting investigative analysis through interactive visualization. *Information Visualization 7*, 2 (2008), 118–132.

34. Stokes, M.E., David, C. S., Koch, G. G. *Categorical data analysis using the SAS system* (2nd Ed). Cary, NC: SAS.

35. Tindale, R. S., Smith, C. M., Dykema-Engblade, A., and Kluwe, K. Good and bad group performance: Same processes--different outcomes. *Group Processes & Intergroup Relations 15*, (2012), 603–618.

36. Towne, W. B., Kittur, A., Kinnaird, P., & Herbsleb, J. Your process is showing: controversy management and perceived quality in wikipedia. In *Proc. of CSCW 2013*, ACM Press (2013), 1059-1068.

37. Weng, C. and Gennari, J.H. Asynchronous collaborative writing through annotations. In *Proc. of CSCW 2004*, ACM (2004), 578–581.

38. Wright, D. B., & Mathews, S. A., & Skagerberg, E.M. Social recognition memory: The effect of other people's responses for previously seen and unseen items. *Journal of Experimental Psychology: Applied 11*, 3 (2005), 200–209.

Collaborative Web Search in Context: A Study of Tool Use in Everyday Tasks

Ryan Kelly
Department of Computer Science
University of Bath, United Kingdom
r.m.kelly@bath.ac.uk

Stephen J. Payne
Department of Computer Science
University of Bath, United Kingdom
s.j.payne@bath.ac.uk

ABSTRACT
Recent research efforts have led to the creation of a number of systems that provide specialised support for collaborative web search. However, the use of these tools has not been studied outside of the laboratory, and as collaborative search becomes increasingly commonplace in everyday life, there is a need to understand whether the support provided by collaborative search systems fits with real-world information seeking practices. In the present study, we deployed two collaborative search tools to pairs of searchers with genuine information needs. We report findings from in-depth interviews conducted after searchers had used their assigned system for an extended period of time. Our findings show how system features were used and appropriated in pursuit of collaboration, throwing light on the way in which collaborative search is conducted in quotidian settings. Theoretical and practical implications of the results are discussed.

Author Keywords
Collaborative information seeking; Collaborative search

ACM Classification Keywords
H.5.3 Information Interfaces and Presentation (e.g. HCI): Collaborative Computing

INTRODUCTION
Information seeking on the web often occurs as a collaborative act between two or more searchers with a shared information need. Research has revealed that such behaviour is fairly prevalent [3, 14] and appears to be on the increase [15]. In response to these findings, a number of prototype systems offering specialised support for collaborative search have been developed within the research community (e.g. [6, 12, 13, 16, 17, 18]) and some commercial systems (e.g. *SearchTeam, Bing*) now provide support for collaborative and other socially-oriented search behaviours [15].

Despite this progress, the actual success of collaborative search systems, in terms of mainstream takeup, has been fairly limited. To the best of our knowledge, none of the tools presented in the research literature has achieved widespread adoption. Morris [15] further notes that the majority of commercial systems are either defunct (e.g. *Aardvark, Flock*) or remain in the early stages of development (e.g. *Pinterest, So.cl*). One potential reason for this is that existing collaborative search tools may require too much effort or do not offer meaningful benefit over ad hoc practices (e.g. link sharing via email) used during everyday tasks like travel planning and online shopping [14]. However, neither of these possibilities has been investigated. A related issue is that collaborative search tools have only been studied in relatively short-term laboratory evaluations. While such studies are fine for testing specific hypotheses and evaluating initial designs, they do not provide information about how systems are used over the longer term. No work has, as yet, studied the efficacy of collaborative search tools in quotidian settings. It is, therefore, unclear as to how well existing tools fit with everyday collaborative search practices.

In the present study, we deployed two collaborative web search tools to pairs of searchers conducting everyday information seeking tasks. Our immediate aim was to understand whether the tools were useful in supporting actual collaborative search, and thus we recruited pre-established collaborators with information needs that were intrinsically collaborative—tasks were self-selected and participants used their assigned system for as long as they wished, creating high external validity. By interviewing our participants about their experiences, our study allows us to understand how the tools were used in accordance with existing routines, in turn contributing to a broader theoretical understanding of collaborative search behaviour 'in the wild'. And, by detailing how our participants used and appropriated particular system features, this research provides implications for the design of future tools to support everyday collaborative search tasks.

BACKGROUND & RELATED WORK
Within the broader area of social search, collaborative web search describes situations "in which participants work together to satisfy an information need" [15, pg.1182]. Such activity can occur either synchronously or asynchronously, and participants may be co-located or geographically distributed [9]. Collaborative search is usually scoped to consider explicit, intentional collaboration (cf. [8]), precluding consideration of filtering or recommendation tools that utilise prior searches from anonymous 'collaborators'.

Several studies have revealed that collaborative search occurs during a variety of professional and personal tasks, including medical research, travel planning, and online shopping

CSCW'14, February 15–19, 2014, Baltimore, MD, USA.

http://dx.doi.org/10.1145/2531602.2531617

[14, 15]. However, searchers report that managing such collaboration can be arduous, requiring workarounds such as link sharing via email [14, 15] or the use of 'tools-at-hand' (e.g., blogs, text documents) to keep track of search results [3]. Researchers have suggested that these behaviours can be supported at the user interface, and, to this end, a number of systems have been designed by the research community. Examples include *CoSearch* [1] *Results Space* [2], *Cerchiamo* [6], *Querium* [7], *Coagmento* [12], *ViGOR* [13], *SearchTogether* [16], *WeSearch* [17], and *CoSense* [18]. While the specific functionality offered by each tool is different, and can vary according to the anticipated scenario of use, the common goal has been to alleviate the need for workarounds by providing browser-based support for collaborative search. As an in-depth review of these systems is beyond the scope of this paper, it is instructive to focus on the general aspects of collaboration that such tools aim to support. These are *awareness, division of labour, persistence*, and *sensemaking* [5, 13, 16, 18].

Awareness refers to the ability to acquire knowledge about the current and past activities of one's interaction partners [21]. Such knowledge promotes coordination and lessens the need for explicit communication about task progress [21]. Features for supporting awareness during collaborative search include shared query, browsing, and page visitation histories [2, 12, 16]; commenting of pages [12, 16]; and increased salience of particular results based on collaborator ratings [2].

Division of Labour refers to the process of distributing a task across members of a group [5]. The aim here is to facilitate concurrent work while preventing redundancy and duplication of effort. In collaborative search tools, division of labour has been supported through text chat systems, which allow collaborators to establish division of labour through communication [12]; automated splitting of search results [16]; allocation of tasks by role [6]; and algorithms for selective filtering [5].

Persistence, referring to the storage and display of activity from prior search sessions, enables asynchronous collaboration through information re-finding and resumption of prior search sessions [2, 16]. Persistence has been supported through retention of chat logs, pageview statistics, and session histories [12, 13, 16]; automatic generation of session summaries [16]; and relevance rating tools [2].

Finally, *sensemaking* support allows collaborators to understand the search process, in terms of *what* has been found, *how* it was found, and where tasks have been handed off between collaborators [18]. Example features include: context awareness through visualisation of search strategies and trajectories [18]; functions to exchange sections of webpages [17]; and browsable timelines of pages viewed by collaborators [12, 18].

While studies have suggested that the features described above are beneficial for supporting collaborative search, no work has yet examined the success of any tool when used in natural field settings. Instead, most have been studied using artificial tasks completed under the constraints of short-term laboratory evaluations. This is problematic because real-world search may involve protracted behavioural patterns that are not well supported by current systems. Additionally, a growing body of empirical work suggests that various factors, including awareness [21], communication channel [11], time [10], and spatial proximity [20], can impact the collaborative search process. While such studies serve to advance theoretical accounts of collaborative search, they do not offer findings regarding the use of tools outside the lab.

Given the considerable research effort invested in supporting collaborative search, we believe that studying how current tools fare in everyday settings would be beneficial for directing future design activities. To this end, we designed a field study of collaborative search tool use, with the aims of gaining a better understanding of collaborative search in the wild and of identifying potential enhancements for future systems. We used two existing systems to study collaborative search behaviour. The fact that we did not develop either system means that we cannot access system logs containing quantitative data about tool use. This paper focuses on qualitative analysis of interviews conducted after our participants had used an assigned system to complete a real-world collaborative search task.

FIELD STUDY

System Choices

Our first system was *Coagmento*[1], a freely available tool that incorporates a range of features designed to support collaborative search (e.g. shared bookmarks, chat functionality) [12]. This tool can be regarded as a 'general purpose' collaborative search tool in that it is not intended to support any particular task over another. Since we did not specify in advance that our participants should engage in any particular type of search, this made Coagmento an appropriate choice for our study.

Our initial intention was to have all of our participants use Coagmento. However, a software update introduced a number of bugs (e.g. SQL database errors, malfunctioning UI elements) halfway through the study. These problems were beyond our control as we are not responsible for the creation of Coagmento. To avoid the problems affecting our remaining participants, we decided to switch to *Diigo*[2]. While this choice was partly pragmatic (very few of the systems presented in the literature are available for outside use) Diigo's overall functionality is actually very similar to Coagmento, meaning that a change of system did not require a large departure from our established methodology. And, as will be seen in our results, using a second system was beneficial in that differences between the two tools allowed us to obtain some valuable comparative insights.

System Functionalities

Both Coagmento (see Figure 1) and Diigo (Figure 2) are web-based systems. Each is comprised of two parts: a web browser plugin that provides rapid access to features intended for collecting, sharing, and saving information; and an online space to which users can save pages and view the results of prior search sessions. Both tools are also available as mobile applications, but these will not be discussed here as none of our participants opted to use them during our study.

[1] `http://www.coagmento.org`

[2] `http://www.diigo.com`

Figure 1. Coagmento for Mozilla Firefox: (A) The Coagmento toolbar. (B) The CSpace with drop down selections for filtering saved results. (C) Shared history displaying thumbnails of recorded pages. (D) A larger preview of a page, accessed by clicking on the relevant thumbnail. (E) Information about a page's time of capture, project, and username of the original viewer. (F) Sidebar providing chat functionality, history, notifications, and a notepad. Image captured April 2013. Coagmento, Copyright © Chirag Shah. Image used with permission.

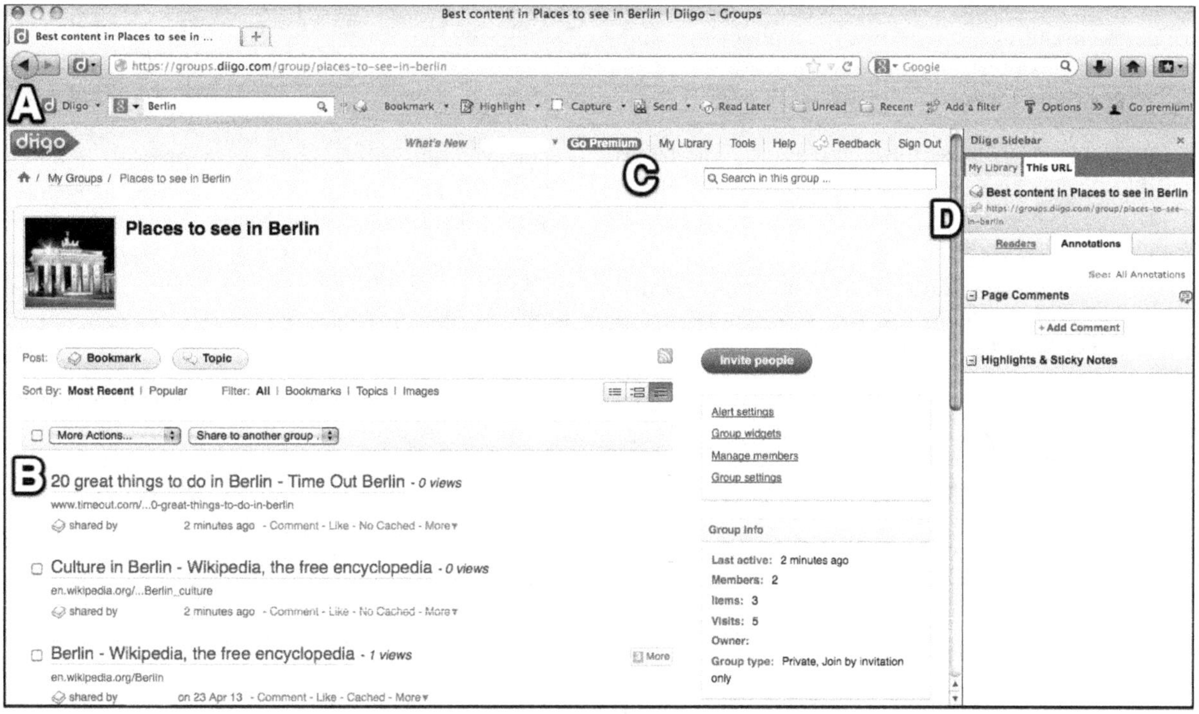

Figure 2. Diigo for Mozilla Firefox: (A) The Diigo toolbar. (B) Shared history with links to recorded pages. (C) Link to the user's personal library ('My Library'). (D) Sidebar providing a list of pages from the user's personal (but not group) library and a list of annotations on the current webpage. Image captured April 2013. Diigo, Copyright © Diigo Inc. Image used with permission.

Figure 1 shows the Coagmento system installed on a user's browser. The browser is open at the online 'CSpace' repository (B) to which pages are saved during search sessions. When the user is logged in to the system, all webpages visited are recorded to this history, appearing as thumbnails in chronological order (C). Each thumbnail can be clicked to reveal a larger preview of the relevant hyperlink (D), alongside the date and time of viewing and the username of the visitor (E). This history is then shared with all collaborators in a dedicated project folder, accessible via the CSpace.

The Coagmento plugin provides two components: a toolbar (Fig. 1, A) and a sidebar (F). The former includes buttons that allow users to bookmark whole pages, collect annotations and snippets, and recommend pages to collaborators. Pages captured using these tools are saved to the shared history and appear as an image bearing the relevant icon (the second thumbnail in area C shows the icon for a bookmarked page). Users can then selectively filter their history according to these differing types of content using the 'All Objects' dropdown (B). Of the remaining buttons, 'Resources' opens and closes the Coagmento sidebar, which contains a shared chat, a notepad, a history of recent bookmarks, and a notification submenu. 'Editor' provides access to a shared document for collaborative editing. Finally, the toolbar displays a summary of the current page in terms of views, snippets, and annotations [12].

Diigo (Fig. 2) provides a toolbar plugin (A) with functionality similar to Coagmento. Users are able to bookmark pages, leave highlights on relevant sections, or capture (screenshot) particular sections of a page. Each of these can then be saved to the Diigo webspace, either to a private library (accessed via the 'My Library' tab in area C of Fig. 2) or, in the case of bookmarks and highlights, to a shared 'group' space listing captured links in chronological order (Fig. 2, B). Of the remaining buttons, 'Send' allows users to email a page directly to a collaborator, and 'Read Later' allows for the webpage to be saved to a private library for later reading. The Diigo sidebar (D) provides quick access to the user's private library, a list of annotations for the user's current page, and a view of all prior readers of a particular webpage.

Comparison of Figures 1 and 2 reveals some differences which are worth considering due to their reference later in the paper. The first concerns the way in which each system saves and presents pages to users. In Coagmento, pages are represented using small thumbnails, each of which must be clicked to reveal further information about the represented page. In Diigo, no thumbnail is visible; instead, the title of the page is shown alongside a hyperlink and the username of the person who made the bookmark. Thus, the provision of initial descriptive information is different in each system—Coagmento relies solely on visual information, whereas Diigo uses text.

A second difference concerns the way in which each system tracks user behaviour. While active, Coagmento records *all* of the pages a user visits while logged in to the system, with individual pages represented by individual screenshots in the CSpace area (Fig. 1, C). This means that every page a user visits is captured by the system, regardless of whether or not the content is relevant to the user's primary information need. In contrast, the only pages captured by Diigo are those that the user explicitly tells the system to save, either by bookmark, highlight, or capture (area B of Fig. 2 displays some examples). As will be seen in our results, this 'all or nothing' dichotomy leads to a number of concerns related to sensemaking and privacy during the display of shared search histories.

At this point, we should stress that it is not the aim of this paper to 'evaluate' Coagmento and Diigo in terms of their usability or relative successes and failures. Rather, our use of these systems is guided by the fact that they can be regarded as exemplary tools that might be used to support collaborative search—indeed, Coagmento has been designed in accordance with the research literature on collaborative search [12]. We have no investment in either system and no desire to to demonstrate that one is better than the other. Our aim is to use these tools as probes to learn more about real-world collaborative search while identifying broader lessons for future systems.

METHOD

Study Design

Beyond our use of Coagmento and Diigo, we designed the present study to be as naturalistic as possible. Our first concern here was choice of tasks—this is a difficult yet critical issue when studying information seeking. As we were aiming for high external validity, we allowed participants to choose their own search tasks. This encourages intrinsic motivation while providing insights into real everyday search behaviour.

Second, the present study was open-ended and we did not impose any time constraints on our participants' search process. Not only did this provide ample time for our participants to explore and become familiar with system features, it allowed us to understand tool use during the broader collaborative search process, spanning tentative exploration through to results collection, refinement, and eventual selection.

Lastly, we allowed participants to use the systems according to their own preferences: at home, at work, or even on the move. We felt that learning about where, when, and how collaborative search occurs would help to understand how tools are used in the wild, and might also prove useful in terms of designing future technologies.

Participants

A total of 16 participants (eight pairs) took part in our study. Participants' ages ranged from 19–34 (M = 24.4, SD = 4.7). Pair 3 were both male; pairs 6 and 7 both female; and all other pairs were male/female. Pairs were comprised of friends or romantic partners, i.e. there were no anonymous pairings of unfamiliar participants. Participants were recruited via Facebook and our University noticeboard. Our adverts stated that we were looking for groups of people who would soon be completing a collaborative search task, offering the "opportunity to use a system designed to support collaborative information seeking behaviour". We used purposive sampling, vetting those who responded to our advert to ensure that their information needs were genuine. We did not have cause to turn away any of those who responded to our adverts. We offered each participant £20 as a goodwill gesture for completing the study.

Pair	System	Chosen task(s)	Distinct search sessions over time, by task	Pages saved, by task	Total duration of use
1	Coagmento	Travel planning	10 sessions over 14 days	27	14 days
2	Coagmento	Travel planning; House hunting	6 sessions over 16 days; 3 sessions over 8 days	10; 8	35 days
3	Coagmento	Concert venues	3 sessions over 12 days	4	12 days
4	Coagmento	Travel planning	3 sessions over 7 days	9	7 days
5	Diigo	Houses; Shopping	3 sessions over 5 days; 8 sessions over 3 days	3; 10	10 days
6	Diigo	Houses; Travel planning; Shopping	15 sessions over 14 days; 4 over 7; 3 over 3	18; 8; 14	21 days
7	Diigo	Houses; Travel planning	3 sessions over 7 days; 2 sessions over 8 days	22; 8	21 days
8	Diigo	Travel planning; Shopping	8 sessions over 6 days; 5 sessions over 8 days	10; 8	14 days

Table 1. Participants' assigned system, task choices, distinct search sessions, number of items saved, and total duration of use. The 'Pages saved, by task' column refers to the total number of items captured using bookmarks, snippets, or annotations. Note that some tasks were completed concurrently and others were distinctly separate, meaning that aggregations of task completion do not equate to total duration of participation.

All participants were made aware from the outset that their payment was fixed and that it was not related to performance or time spent using their assigned system.

Table 1 provides information about the system assigned to each pair alongside task choices. Each pair used only one system and none changed tool during the study. The tasks chosen by our participants fit well with what the literature identifies about collaborative search [14, 15], and several pairs actually chose to complete more than one task during the study. While the nature of the information required by each of the tasks is different, we consider them to be qualitatively similar in that each is open-ended and allows for considerable latitude in terms of exploratory search behaviour. Furthermore, each involves an evolving information need that calls for the search and comparison of multiple sources with the aim of arriving at an agreed outcome, i.e. a specific location, hotel, or other item of choice. We felt this stylistic similarity would permit generalisation of insights over different tasks.

Table 1 also displays statistics regarding distinct search sessions, the number of items captured during each task, and total duration of use. We requested these figures from participants after task completion (this helped prevent advance notice of scrutiny impacting behaviour during searches) and all participants consented. It is worth noting that the total duration of use refers to the elapsed time between participants' first and last search sessions during the entire study. This means that aggregations of completion time for different tasks do not always equate to total duration of participation; some tasks were completed concurrently, whereas others were distinctly separate. Although the lack of precise log data makes these somewhat coarse indicators of usage, it is clear that all participants used their assigned system for at least one week and engaged in multiple information seeking episodes during that time. This in turn increases our confidence in the meaningfulness of participants' experiences with their assigned system.

Materials & Procedure

Each pair of participants was provided with all necessary software alongside installation instructions and a briefing script introducing the study, tailored according to the system assigned to each pair. The script clarified that participants should use the software we had provided each time they were searching for information towards their chosen task. The script also stated that there were no expectations about the way in which the tool should be used. Rather, participants were encouraged to use their tool in whatever way they deemed appropriate. We also provided a detailed instruction document explaining the functionality of the relevant system. The document described each system feature in full by providing a screenshot alongside explanatory text.[3] All features were given equal descriptive treatment (roughly one page per item) so as not to suggest the importance of any feature over another. We were also careful to ensure that we only described the workings of each feature, rather than how it should be used to support search behaviour.

After installing the relevant system, participants created their own user accounts and were allowed to search at their leisure. As mentioned above, no constraints were placed on participants in terms of process. Participants were free to decide when to engage in search sessions, how long to spend on each session, and when to terminate their information seeking activities. Participants were asked to email the first author once they felt they had satisfied their information need and no longer had use for the system. A semi-structured interview was then performed with each participant. Thirteen of these interviews were conducted face-to-face in a quiet office; two were over the telephone; and one was via Skype. Interviews were one-to-one between participant and the first author; searchers did not, therefore, discuss their information seeking behaviours while their partners were present. This allowed us to cross-check statements and ensure consistency of behavioural accounts. During interviews, participants were invited to access their assigned system if they could not remember exact details or wanted to elaborate on particular functionalities.

All interviews lasted less than one hour. To avoid response bias and to dissuade participants from trying to please us with their answers [4], we began by reminding participants that we did not design the system and there were no right or wrong answers insofar as this study was concerned. We used a basic framework of 30 questions (see Appendix A), which were directed by the concerns of our study and questions used in prior work on collaborative search [3]. These questions allowed us to explore participants' search process, interactions with their tool and collaborator, and how search products were used in accordance with their chosen tasks. As our protocol was semi-structured, we were able to probe issues as and when they arose, and we invited participants to elaborate on their remarks, allowing novel topics to emerge.

[3] All documents are available on request.

Analysis

All interviews were recorded and transcribed by the first author, allowing for early familiarisation with the dataset and development of initial understanding. We used open, axial, and selective coding [22] to identify initial codes, structure codes into concepts, and then group concepts into themes relating to participants' search process and tool usage. The coding process was iterative; transcripts were read several times and initial codes were evaluated and refined during each reading, with internal consistency strengthened by scrutinising the data for counter-examples. We should acknowledge that some codes were influenced by our interview questions. For example, by asking about division of labour, it was inevitable that a related code would arise during analysis. However, many new codes also emerged, indicating to us that the results had novelty beyond current knowledge.

RESULTS

To bring clarity to our results while making sense of our participants' experiences, we cluster our themes using three categories: *search process & management*, *appropriations & afforded behaviours*, and *interface design issues*. The first encapsulates general information about our participants' collaborative search process; such insights are detailed independently of specifics concerning how system features were used. The second pertains to the emergent forms of interaction centred around the use and appropriation of particular system features in support of collaborative search. The final category allows us to drill down into specific issues linked to interface design, many of which are best understood through consideration of participants' search behaviours. As our data are primarily qualitative, we present themes alongside direct quotations from our participants. To identify speakers, we use the form [P*x*,*y*] where *x* indicates the ID number of the pair, as listed in Table 1, and *y* refers to the first or second member of that pair.

It is worth noting that participants were generally positive about the design concepts behind the two tools, and all participants believed that their assigned system had merit over ad hoc solutions. Regarding use of system features, all participants stated that they used their system's toolbar, and that they had accessed the shared online space to view search results. In Coagmento, searchers reported using bookmarks, annotations, and snippets. All participants stated that they did not use recommendations, the shared editor, or any of the resources in the sidebar. In Diigo, participants reported using highlights, bookmarks, and screenshots. All participants stated that they did not use Send, Read Later, or any of the functionality within the sidebar. While the absence of log data means that we cannot definitively state that particular features were or were not used during our study, participants' statements are revealing about preferences for some features over others. Before providing more specific details about how features were used to support collaboration, the following subsection paints a general picture of participants' search process and management strategies.

Search Process & Management

Circumstances of Search

Table 2 outlines the search scenarios reported by each pair of participants. Although we cannot specify exactly how many

	Co-located		Distributed	
Pair ID	Synchronous	Asynchronous	Synchronous	Asynchronous
1	✓	✓		✓
2		✓		✓
3		✓		✓
4	✓			✓
5			✓	✓
6	✓			✓
7	✓			✓
8	✓	✓		✓

Table 2. Participants' reported circumstances of search activity. A ✓in a cell indicates that participants engaged in the relevant type of search.

times each type of search occurred, we did ask participants which of their identified scenarios occurred most often. Responses indicated that distributed, asynchronous search was the most frequent scenario for pairs 1, 2, 3, 5, and 6. Pairs 4, 7, and 8 identified co-located, synchronous search as their most common scenario. While one might expect that such choices would be determined by living arrangements, this was not always the case. Pair 2, for example, were a cohabiting couple who reported conducting all of their searches asynchronously.

Perhaps a more valuable aspect of these results is the fact that tool use was not isolated to a single setting. Rather, all pairs reported engaging in at least two different scenarios of search, and participants described how search activities shifted according to everyday life. Pair 1, for example, reported working only asynchronously when apart, but engaged in both synchronous and asynchronous search sessions when co-located at the weekends. Our participants did not report any immediate difficulties in managing these transitions; this may be due to the fact that, as identified earlier, both tools used in our study are general purpose systems intended to support search across a range of scenarios.

Task Management Strategies

Four pairs reported using division of labour as a way of organising their task. Pairs 1 and 2 divided their travel planning by determining a set of locations and splitting them to create targeted individual searches. Pair 3 established a very distinct role assignment, where different aspects of the search process were divided using semi-formal roles: one searcher was responsible for finding a venue for their band's concert, while another sought places to promote the event. Finally, pair 7 reported dividing the web space during house hunting, with one searcher checking private rental sites and another scouring university-hosted pages. These strategies reflect variations of the *divide-and-conquer* approach described by Morris [14].

The remaining four pairs did not plan a division of labour. These pairs described a 'dive in and do it' approach, akin to the *brute force* management strategy identified by Morris [14]. However, participants did not report any negative experiences related to organising the task in this way.

Search Process

While we were not able to log behavioural data about search activity, participants did provide verbal accounts of their search process, and these are instructive in terms of understanding what searchers were actually doing during our study. All participants reported following a broadly similar process, beginning with the use of familiar search engines to learn about the information space at a high level. Participants then reported narrowing their search focus to be more specific:

"We started by simply Googling what we're looking for, and when you get leads you search for those specific things, like that specific realtor or a specific area." [P6, 2]

Participants reported that this process was directed by their existing knowledge, and by external factors such as an available shopping budget, dates of travel, or availability of particular venues in the local area:

"I already knew which websites to target, I started off with a few commercial websites and others, looking at StudentPad and the [University] noticeboard." [P6, 1]

After identifying relevant websites, behaviour shifted to the selective capture and bookmarking of results. For all our participants, search and bookmarking were fragmented over multiple sessions. Searchers stated that sessions were interspersed with communication, both during and between searches. As well as ordinary conversation, email, and message exchanges, participants reported using system features like comments and annotations to further their task-related discussions. Participants reported that their overall tasks would end with discussion of the results to reach consensus over an outcome, i.e. the 'chosen products' from their search. In broad outline, this process corresponds well with existing theoretical accounts of web search, where exploratory information seeking has been characterised as an extended, fragmented process, involving multiple search sessions, queries, and information sources [7].

We now delve into the way in which system features were adopted in support of this general pattern of collaborative search behaviour. Our later Discussion section then considers the broader implications of the results, in terms of lessons for collaborative search systems.

Appropriations & Afforded Behaviours

Page Capture for Re-Access and Suggesting Relevance

During their information seeking process, all eight pairs made use of system features intended for information capture: bookmarks, snippets, and annotations in Coagmento; and bookmarks and highlights in Diigo. At the most basic level, these features were used to overcome the ad hoc practice of sharing hyperlinks via email. Participants valued the ability to save pages to a joint repository and, correspondingly, to see pages saved by their collaborator:

"I thought it was really helpful to know exactly what he had looked at and what he wanted to go see. Instead of him having to send me a variety of different emails and links, it's all been saved visually right there for you." [P4, 1]

In providing different features for capturing information, the designers of both systems have anticipated that searchers may wish to retain different types of content. For instance, bookmarks are intended as a way of saving whole pages, whereas annotations and snippets allow capture of particular subsections or page elements. Our participants, however, tended to adopt just one of these features to achieve the same outcome: that of capturing pages to 'pull out' particular results from the web space. Pair, 1, for example, used Coagmento's 'Snippet' feature to achieve this, whereas pairs 2, 3 and 4 used 'Bookmark' for the same purpose. Furthermore, responses indicated that capture behaviour was more nuanced than simply 'saving pages for later'. First, capture was intended as a way of favouring particular results for more rapid re-access:

"It was particularly useful because I could go back quite easily and know what I'd already put up there, so I wasn't reposting it or covering the same ground." [P5, 2]

Second, capture was sometimes used as way of increasing the salience of particular results, with the aim of suggesting potential relevance to a partner. The intent was not necessarily to return to a particular page but was instead an attempt at bringing something to the partner's attention:

"Looking through Expedia, when I found some good hotels I would snippet them and then I would say to him, oh I've found these ones that look good, and I've snippeted them." [P1,1]

Forming and Discussing Shortlists

We identified that page capture was actually related to a more general strategy—that of *shortlisting*, where features like bookmarks and snippets were used to form lists of potential choices and, eventually, reach an agreed outcome. All participants engaged in this behaviour:

"We would aim towards a list of five nice hotels" [P2, 2]

"In the final decision, we had a top five possibles to choose. Which is where the bookmarking came in." [P4,2]

Participants testified that shortlisting was an existing behaviour, but espoused the benefits of the tools in terms of bringing structure to this process:

"Normally we would put links on Facebook, drop all the links into a conversation. But that is chaotic. So it was nice to have them all there without going through our conversation trying to find the link we're talking about." [P7,1]

Participants reported engaging in conversation about their shortlists, either verbally or, in the case of Diigo, by annotating shortlisted links using comments. This occurred as a back and forth process of contributing and evaluating suggestions to the list. Participants stated that using comments on Diigo was useful in supporting this behaviour, indicating the value of features that allow discussion of shortlisted items:

"We would keep commenting on each other's things, so one link had three comments, I would comment and she would comment, then I would comment back. And they weren't all mixed up." [P6,1]

While the actual content of the lists was qualitatively different between tasks (i.e. some pairs were choosing houses, others shopping items) the overall goal was the same: form a list of candidates, discuss and refine the list, and then settle on a 'good enough' outcome in line with the goal of the information seeking process. However, this process was not always linear or in sequence. Some participants reported that they would be more careful about relevance by evaluating sources on-the-go, keeping only 'definite' possibilities in the shortlist. Others would take a more carefree approach, forming a longer list of potentially relevant sources and then narrowing them down at a later stage. Participants reported that shortlists were eventually used and reviewed to reach final consensus:

"*A lot of it was down to seeing what the other person thought, and then between the two of us, we decide, oh let's go for that one. If there's no availability there, you go to the next choice on your list. So you almost rank them between the two of you, for personal preference.*" [P1,2]

Sharing versus Saving: Sensitivity to Time Constraints

In forming shortlists, participants reported that if their task was time pressured and needed to be completed in a short time frame, they would change their behaviour to ensure that their partner checked recorded links more quickly. In other words, rather than wait for their partner to check the system at some unspecified time, participants would use external communication methods to alert their partner about the information:

"*We want a house quickly because it's a little late, so we had to speed up the process. I had to call her up and tell her ok, please go and check this house, I've posted it on the group. It's possible she would go and check, but we were in a hurry, so I have to convey the message to her ASAP.*" [P6, 1]

Participants also explained that information was itself often time-critical, in that pages could be subject to expiry. For instance, holiday deals and special offers can be available for limited periods of time, and houses can disappear quickly from the rental market. The knock-on impact for collaboration was one of requiring fast action:

"*If it comes up with a great hotel price you click on more details and it would say, there's only two more rooms with this price left... if there's only two rooms left, we need to be quick otherwise we might not be able to get this room at this price.*" [P1, 2]

However, participants spoke of using out-of-band channels to notify their partner more quickly in this instance:

"*Because it gets updated quite often, London seems like quite a quick turnaround on properties. So we chatted over Facebook a bit and then I could send links to websites over Facebook and say does this look ok?*" [P2, 1]

This behaviour is interesting given that both systems have features allowing webpages to be sent directly to the email inbox of a collaborator, both of which might be used in a time-pressured search scenario. Yet none of our participants used these features; instead, ad hoc methods of communication were preferred.

Interface Design Issues

In addition to the behavioural patterns identified above, participants described a number of experiences and issues related to interface design and collaborative search.

Shared Search Histories: Information Overload

Participants described how, during search sessions, they would visit the online repository of their assigned system to review their own results and explore what had been found by their partner. Recall that our first system, Coagmento, provides a complete history of search behaviour by capturing all pages visited by the user during information seeking episodes. Previous work suggests that such 'search trajectories' can be beneficial for sensemaking and facilitating awareness [18, 19]. However, seven out of eight Coagmento users actually reported that they found the history overwhelming:

"*I'd open up the hostel search and there'd be a list of a hundred hostels... and when I'd try and go back to look at which ones were the cheapest, I'd have to look through all of them again to try and find the one in the history. I ended up just searching it again because it was too hard to find.*" [P4, 2]

This problem was partly related to the collection of landing pages, portals, and otherwise irrelevant material that held little utility for sensemaking. Participants suggested that they wanted to get rid of such pages and see only the most relevant information without having to trawl through the entire history:

"*I never looked at the history because the snippets were the core information. I just want something that jumps out and says... this is the information that she has found.*" [P1, 2]

Participants suggested that it would be helpful if Coagmento's history was searchable, or that, rather than allowing the system to indiscriminately record all pages, the process of information capture could be more selective:

"*It's almost like when you're searching you want to be able to dictate what's saved. So even if it's just a little 'plus' button, where maybe you don't want your Google search to come up, but, whatever site, even if you don't think it has anything to do with it, but you might want to look at it again, you can just hit a button and it's going to come up there.*" [P4, 2]

Some users did mention benefits of the timeline view. One member of pair 1 reported retracing their partner's search results to see what had been done earlier. Members of pair 2 reported using the timeline to direct their own work based on the results of their partner, while one member of pair 4 thought the ability to rediscover past results could be useful.

Responses from Diigo users provide an interesting contrast on this issue. Such participants did not express any dissatisfaction about not being able to view a complete search history, and none expressed any desire to have more information about their partner's search process. Some were actually skeptical about the need to understand their partner's process:

"*As long as you both know what you're looking for, it doesn't matter how you go about finding it. I didn't feel like I needed to know what he typed into Google.*" [P8, 1]

Shared Search Histories: Privacy Concerns

The fact that Coagmento captures images of all pages visited made three users hesitant about the potential consequences of having personal information recorded:

"*While I'm searching for hostels I'm using Facebook and Gmail at the same time... I think if you're working in a group that history could get a little weird, because you're going back to your bank account to figure out how much you still have left."* [P4, 2]

This highlights how, for our participants, real-world collaborative search was not an isolated endeavour; instead, it occurred as part of a broader planning activity that required access to personal and private information. Clearly a screenshot image of such content would risk a privacy violation. Participants were not specific about whether any such violations occurred during the study, but the mere threat of information leakage was enough to affect behaviour. In line with earlier statements concerning information overload, participants suggested the solution of selective tracking:

"I was always making sure that I wasn't logging in to other things while logged in to that. Maybe if it had a way of knowing it was on a page for logging in to your emails... it would know not to record those kinds of pages." [P3, 2]

In contrast, privacy did not arise as an issue during discussion with Diigo users, likely due to the fact that no pages are captured unless specifically requested by the user.

Shared Search Histories: Sensemaking and Rationale

Several issues arose related to sensemaking of the shared history, in terms of understanding *what* and *why* information had been found. Regarding the former, responses suggest that searchers need to be able to appraise page representations both quickly and easily, and do not want to spend a long time making sense of shared results. This was exemplified by participants' experiences with Coagmento, where each item in the shared history appears as a small thumbnail showing an image of the webpage (see Figure 1). However, rather than simple thumbnail images, participants wanted an up-front summary of contextual information about each page: a descriptive headline, a preview of its contents, and the time it was saved. We note that this contextual information is available within Coagmento but requires the user to click on each thumbnail to view it. Our responses imply that such information should be presented up-front, with low interaction costs, to facilitate rapid assessment of relevance and sensemaking of pages:

I would want to see the header you'd get if you bookmarked it in a browser. So, under 'hotel search', then the name of the hotel, that sort of thing. The thing is that it's either two or three links you have to click through before you even get to the page itself...And so I would've used that more if I'd had the ability to go, I know what that is... that's what I want... without having to click, click, click." [P2, 2]

Although Diigo records pages using a title and contextual information, sites are not listed with thumbnail images (see Figure 2). Somewhat ironically, all Diigo users indicated a desire for thumbnail previews of each page, as with the style used by Coagmento. This suggests providing both types of information could be beneficial for sensemaking:

"You know like on Facebook when you put a link they give you a small image and a description of what's in the website... it would be nice to have that feature because it triggers your mind about the thing you saw... a picture of the house could appear there automatically." [P7, 1]

A second issue related to sensemaking was that searchers wanted to understand *why* particular pages had been visited by their partners. This was true of both the search history and pages shortlisted using bookmarks:

Without the other person telling you what they'd gleaned from each of the links, it was difficult. You need some explanation, he could have looked at all this stuff and thought, this is a load of rubbish. Then what's the point of you looking at it? [P1, 1]

Participants wanted to annotate and append specific pages to provide rationale about why results had been selected, and to draw attention to specific aspects of webpages. Both practices are in line with the act of suggesting relevance:

"When I would bookmark a whole page, it wasn't necessarily the whole page that I wanted her to look at... I wanted her to pick out the Regent's Canal, but if I'd bookmarked the page, she wouldn't necessarily know that." [P4, 2]

Users of Diigo reported using a short description at the point of page capture to inform their partners about why particular links were relevant. This information would then appear alongside each result in the shared space. Searchers also described appending links with information gleaned from the page so that their partner did not necessarily have to re-run the search. However, users also mentioned that they wanted more ways of tagging or marking captured results. One goal was to indicate that certain pages were temporarily irrelevant. Users did not want to delete such pages in case they became useful later on:

"I added 'TAKEN' to the house because I didn't want to delete it, it's better to have it there for future reference because you never know, so I just put that tag." [P7, 2]

Segregation and Manipulation of Shared Information

Our chosen systems allowed shared results to be viewed in two forms: either as a list of one's own results, or as a combined list of with those of one's partner. However, four participants desired to see *only the results of their partner*. This action was not possible in either system, but this type of separation would clearly be advantageous when attempting to make sense of a partner's work:

"It came up with all of your stuff to start with, what you'd done when you go on it... which I really didn't care about as much, because you know what you've done. That's not the immediate reason you go on there, you go on to see what the other person has done." [P1, 1]

Participants also wanted the ability to distinguish different aspects of their work from others. For example, pages related to flights, hotels, and sightseeing were treated equally by the systems, i.e. as superficially equivalent 'pages'. But to searchers, these pages were related to different subtasks. Users wanted more ways to differentiate and classify these results by creating subcategories and folders that would allow results to be directed towards particular sections. Only one of our tools, Diigo, provided support for this. Participants were able to create specific groups to manage the overlap in concurrent completion of different search tasks:

"We made different groups, one was for house hunting, one was for holiday hunting, and the third one was on these dresses that we were shopping for online." [P5, 1]

Additionally, users reported that they wanted the ability to manipulate the results in greater depth; for example, by moving sources from project to project in accordance with changes in information need and the overall progress of task completion. Users of both systems also wanted to rank and reorder results in their shortlists, so as to allow for visual comparisons. This related to the practice of shortlisting and reaching consensus:

"if I have a preferred order for all these houses, like if I want to call this one first and that one second, I would like to have the possibility of rearranging them." [P7, 2]

Awareness and Notifications

In discussing their partner's activities, participants' responses imply that notifications of recent work (e.g. searches, bookmarks) would help to maintain a general level of awareness:

I think it would be nice to get actual notifications of things. If she'd bookmarked a page, I could get a notification of a bookmark, or a tag, something like that. [P4, 2]

Interestingly, both systems do provide notifications but in different ways. Coagmento's notifications appear in the sidebar but, as all of our participants stated they did not use this feature, likely went unnoticed. By contrast, Diigo provides daily email notifications alerting collaborators to the presence of new links in shared groups. Although one participant found the emails useful in terms of being able to check recent links with her mobile device, the remaining participants said they did not actually read the emails; instead, they were mainly used to gain awareness of the mere fact that *something* had been done. Again, this speaks to a desire for some general level of awareness about the fact that contributions are being made. When checking their assigned system, participants wanted to be able to find these contributions quickly and easily:

"It could highlight that this is the new comment, or this is the new thing, instead of me having to search constantly." [P6, 2]

Two users stated that it would be helpful to have awareness of when their saved results had been viewed by their partner, i.e. a confirmation that results had actually been seen. Responses also indicated a desire for such notifications to be more immediate and situated in the web browser, rather than the system itself. Several drew on their experiences with Facebook to suggest how these notifications might be implemented:

"It could work like Facebook, where you get the notification, you click on it and it takes you to the page." [P4, 2]

Effort Requirements

Finally, throughout our dataset, there was a general undercurrent of wanting a minimal threshold for effort. The perception was that, when search was the primary task, any additional effort above and beyond an ad hoc solution was undesirable:

"All you wanted was something easy, you didn't want something that was going to add a load of time, because the search was quite time intensive. You didn't wanna feel like you were going to have to do loads of extra work on it." [P1, 1]

Users of Coagmento made more specific remarks about effort, in that that they would prefer aspects of the tool to have lower interaction costs. In addition to the earlier statements concerning the number of operations required to access contextual information in the search history, participants remarked upon the excessive number of stages involved in other tasks. For example, when the system asks users to rate and leave comments about bookmarks at the point of page capture:

"I guess the reason the bookmark thing asks for a one to five rating is so it could do some filtering. But at the time it's too much effort. I don't want to do that, I want to automatically know what's important." [P2, 1]

DISCUSSION

The present study sought to investigate the use of collaborative search tools in everyday settings. At a broad level, the fact that searchers found merit in their assigned system suggests that the design concepts embodied by each are on the right track—it was not the case that participants considered the tools unusable or inappropriate, and many stated informally that they planned to use the tools again outside of our study. Some of the primary benefits noted by our participants included the ability to save links to a shared space, thereby negating the need for ad hoc workarounds, and the fact that the tools brought structure and persistence to the otherwise ephemeral process of collaboration over time.

General aspects of participants' search behaviour are revealing about how the tools were used in everyday circumstances. Beginning with the search process, collaboration among our participants was not isolated to a single configuration of time and space. Instead, all participants reported engaging in multiple scenarios. Although no work has argued otherwise, these findings suggest that tools should aim to support search across a range of settings rather than a single time/space configuration. The systems we used were not restrictive in this regard, but some other tools (e.g. [2, 13]) have been designed with specific circumstances in mind.

One of our most consistent behavioural findings was the generalised use of page capture features (snippets, bookmarks, and annotations). While this stresses the importance of allowing searchers to save pages to a shared space, our results suggest that capturing pages is actually more nuanced than simply 'saving pages for later'. Rather, searchers used these features to save pages for re-access; to share results with their partner with the aim of suggesting relevance; and to form *shortlists*, i.e. subsets of results that are collected as potential candidate outcomes for the group's collaboration. However, we saw that pairs tended to settle on, and persist with, a single means of page capture to achieve all three (e.g. Pair 1 used only snippets for shortlisting and suggesting relevance). Given that these are essentially distinct behaviours, which might appeal to different users in the light of different nuanced needs, we suggest that each is potentially worthy of independent support. Future tools could provide separate methods for *page saving*, *page sharing*, and *suggesting relevance*. Regarding the latter, some existing tools allow collaborators to suggest relevance by 'liking' pages [7] or through up- and down-voting of results [2], but future systems could do more to separate shortlisted pages from those that are awaiting judgements of relevance. This would avoid conflation of the two, as occurred for some of the participants in our study.

In forming shortlists, participants wanted to annotate saved results to share rationale about *why* pages had been selected; to make pertinent information salient (e.g. the rent of a saved property or the price of a hotel); and to engage in task-related discussion about the quality or relevance of results. Several systems [16, 18] allow commenting of saved items in the manner offered by Diigo; our study reiterates the value of allowing annotation of links to facilitate sensemaking and sharing of knowledge in the context of everyday tasks.

However, we found that searchers wanted to rearrange listed items to express an order of preference, or 'check off' items by deleting some while retaining others. This process of bringing structure to data is part of sensemaking [23] but our chosen systems did not allow users to repurpose results in any meaningful fashion at the end of their tasks. The implication here is that, as well as supporting aspects of the search process, future tools might also do more to support the manipulation and reuse of search *products*. Since searchers want more ways of interacting with their results, different workspaces could be provided to allow segregation of items; searchers could then be allowed to move items between these spaces in accordance with relevance judgements and task progress. Such an approach can be seen in the ViGOR system [13], which includes a workspace that allows searchers to drag and drop results into groups that can then be reorganised and restructured at will.

Some broader issues related to sensemaking and awareness concerned searchers' difficulty in understanding *what* had been found during their partner's searches. This is a foremost challenge during collaborative search [18] and indeed this was true for our participants. An initial issue concerned identifying the location of recent work when checking their assigned system—searchers often found it hard to identify recent collaborative contributions (e.g. new annotations) in the presence of a large search history. Future tools can benefit by ensuring that notifications are available and that they lead straight to recent contributions. A second lesson is that sufficient information must be given to allow searchers to appraise shared representations with relative ease. Prior laboratory studies suggest that rapid sensemaking can be promoted by displaying contextual information about search results [18, 19]. Our participants' statements align with this, and indicate that representations should combine content previews (e.g. a visual thumbnail) with contextual information (e.g. a page description) that allow comprehension while lessening the need for collaborators to click through and revisit every individual result.

An important design challenge raised by the present study concerns the vexed question of history logging and the extent to which page capture should be deliberate or automatic. Earlier work suggests that the approach of capturing all pages, which provides a persistent account of a collaborator's 'search trajectory', is beneficial for sensemaking [18, 19]. However, we found that, with this approach, the quantity of information captured was regarded as overwhelming. Rather than wade through a large history, our searchers simply wanted to identify only the most relevant information. This finding is similar to that obtained in a laboratory evaluation of CoSense [19], where searchers reported feeling overwhelmed by search histories and struggled to identify 'good' from 'bad' information. In suggesting solutions to this problem, Paul & Morris [19] recommended that designers allow filtering of search histories by content. This solution would not, however, necessarily overcome the problem of information overload as pages accumulate over time—even filtered lists could become difficult to comprehend. One interesting aspect of our results is that none of our Diigo users felt the need for a complete search history. This tentatively suggests that a complete history may not always be necessary for quotidian tasks, especially if collaborators communicate about their progress as part of their daily routines. (As in our study.) That Diigo users did not complain about the effort of saving pages also hints that page capture could be left entirely under the control of the user. This would, in turn, prevent the collection of interstitial pages that appear to offer little utility for sensemaking.

This work has also identified issues that arise only in real-world search. One example pertained to time-criticality, both of search processes and information itself, with some items available only for short windows. We are not aware of any prior work that has raised time constraint as an issue for collaborative search—perhaps future systems could elaborate on this issue and provide more pointed ways of delivering results to one's partner (e.g. through mobile devices). A second issue was the subject of privacy, which highlights the need to ensure that tools are capable of interleaving with the broader tasks in which collaborative searches are embedded. Searchers in our study were nervous about the potential capture of personal or private material. While an obvious answer to this issue would be to allow deletion of pages from the system's history, a more elegant solution would be to record only pages relevant to the user's information need. This could be achieved by allowing the user to enable or suppress tracking in specific browser tabs—this would compartmentalise search to a specific location, leaving other areas safe for private multitasking.

As many of these implications concern specific issues, it is worth considering how the present study can direct future collaborative search tools more generally. First, our results lend support to Morris' recent assertion that collaborative search solutions must be low-effort and "sufficiently lightweight compared with status quo ad hoc solutions" [15]. Our participants expressed dissatisfaction if interactional demands imposed by their tool exceeded those of their previous solution (e.g. email, Facebook). Since the implication here is that any tool with unnecessary effort requirements stands to fail, features in collaborative search systems should be benchmarked against the equivalent ad hoc solution. Additionally, the tools used in our study included many features which, according to our participants, were not necessary for their task. This suggests that future solutions could be scaled back in favour of lightweight support for core collaborative search behaviours. An example system might support the rapid sharing of pages between two linked browsers, with simple awareness mechanisms, like those desired by our participants, that notify collaborators of recent activity after their web browser is opened.

Alternatively, more specialised systems could be developed to provide targeted support for specific tasks. Some of our participants mentioned informally that they would value support beyond that for search. In travel planning, for example, searchers could be able to apply their shortlists to a map, helping them with their journey or sightseeing plans. The wider implication here is that collaborative search tools could be embedded in larger applications that support a broader range of high-level planning tasks.

Limitations & Future Work

One limitation of this study is that were only able to report on a small number of pairs from a single culture. Larger groups of three or more could differ in terms of their search and sharing practices. Since demographic, cultural, or other socio-economic factors may also impact search behaviour and system usage, future work should explore these issues.

While our study results were based on search tasks with high external validity, the patterns of behaviour reported here may not generalise to every other form of collaborative search. For example, we were not able to examine the very commonplace task of literature review, an endeavour that will no doubt be familiar to readers of this paper. Future work should examine how our findings map to other tasks.

Finally, this work is limited in ways that would be encountered in any study involving retrospective self-reports. Our results are reliant upon what our participants were able to recall about their experiences, and might also have been tempered by our choice of interview questions. We were unable to access quantitative data collected at the system level—future work might employ such an approach to reach more precise measures of tool use. Reliable data about which features are, and are not, used in field settings would help to confirm our findings and guide the design of collaborative search tools.

REFERENCES

1. Amershi, S., and Morris, M. R. Cosearch: a system for co-located collaborative web search. In *Proc. CHI* (2008), 1647–1656.
2. Capra, R., Chen, A. T., Hawthorne, K., and Arguello, J. ResultsSpace: An experimental collaborative search environment. In *Proc. ASIST*, vol. 49 (2012), 1–4.
3. Capra, R., Marchionini, G., Velasco-Martin, J., and Muller, K. Tools-at-hand and learning in multi-session, collaborative search. In *Proc. CHI* (2010), 951–960.
4. Dell, N., Vaidyanathan, V., Medhi, I., Cutrell, E., and Thies, W. "Yours is better!": Participant response bias in HCI. In *Proc.*, CHI '12 (2012), 1321–1330.
5. Foley, C., and Smeaton, A. Division of labour and sharing of knowledge for synchronous collaborative information retrieval. *Information Processing & Management 46* (2010), 762–772.
6. Golovchinsky, G., Adcock, J., Pickens, J., Pernilla, Q., and Back, M. Cerchiamo: a collaborative exploratory search tool. In *Proc. CSCW*, Demo Session (2008).
7. Golovchinsky, G., Diriye, A., and Dunnigan, T. The future is in the past: designing for exploratory search. In *Proc. IIIX* (2012), 52–61.
8. Golovchinsky, G., Diriye, A., and Pickens, J. Designing for collaboration in information seeking. In *Proc. HCIR* (2011).
9. Golovchinsky, G., Pickens, J., and Back, M. A taxonomy of collaboration in online information seeking. In *Proc. JCDL Workshop on Collaborative Exploratory Search. Pittsburgh, PA.* (2008).
10. González-Ibáñez, R., Haseki, M., and Shah, C. Time and space in collaborative information seeking. In *Proc. ASIST* (2012), 1–10.
11. González-Ibáñez, R., Haseki, M., and Shah, C. An analysis of communication and performance in collaborative information seeking. *Information Processing & Management 49* (2013), 1165–1179.
12. González-Ibáñez, R., and Shah, C. Coagmento: A system for supporting collaborative information seeking. In *Proc. ASIST* (2011), 1–4.
13. Halvey, M., Vallet, D., Hannah, D., Feng, Y., and Jose, J. M. An asynchronous collaborative search system for online video search. *Information Processing & Management 46*, 6 (2010), 733–748.
14. Morris, M. R. A survey of collaborative web search practices. In *Proc. CHI '08* (2008), 1657–1660.
15. Morris, M. R. Collaborative search revisited. In *Proc. CSCW* (2013), 1181–1192.
16. Morris, M. R., and Horvitz, E. Searchtogether: an interface for collaborative web search. In *Proc. UIST* (2007), 3–12.
17. Morris, M. R., Lombardo, J., and Wigdor, D. Wesearch: supporting collaborative search and sensemaking on a tabletop display. In *Proc. CSCW* (2010), 401–410.
18. Paul, S. A., and Morris, M. R. Cosense: enhancing sensemaking for collaborative web search. In *Proc. CHI* (2009), 1771–1780.
19. Paul, S. A., and Morris, M. R. Sensemaking in collaborative web search. *Human-Computer Interaction 26*, 1-2 (2010), 72–122.
20. Shah, C., and González-Ibáñez, R. Spatial context in collaborative information seeking. *Journal of Information Science 38*, 4 (2010), 33–349.
21. Shah, C., and Marchionini, G. Awareness in collaborative information seeking. *Journal of ASIST 61*, 10 (2010), 1970–86.
22. Strauss, A., and Corbin, J. M. *Basics of Qualitative Research*. Sage, 1998.
23. Tao, Y., and Tombros, A. An exploratory study of sensemaking in collaborative information seeking. In *AIRS*. Springer, 2013, 26–37.

APPENDIX A: INTERVIEW MATERIALS

The following script was read to each participant prior to the commencement of each interview.

Thank you for participating in our study, today I will be asking questions about your use of Coagmento/Diigo. Before beginning, I would like to tell you a few things about the interview.

- First of all, please feel free to be frank and honest when talking about your experiences with the system. We didn't build the tool and we have no reason to be offended by anything you say about it, so please feel free to speak truthfully and be honest about your experiences.
- Also, there are no right or wrong answers in this study. So please feel free to share your opinions and ideas, even if you think they might not be relevant.
- I have basic framework of 30 questions but sometimes they get answered during conversation, so I may not need to ask all of them. The interview shouldn't last more than an hour in total. We can follow up on your experiences if there is something particular that you want to talk more about.

Do you have any questions before we begin?

Interview Questions

Overview of the Project

I'd like to start by asking you some general questions about your search activity.

1. What type of information were you and your partner looking for? (*If more than one task: ask for each*).
2. What was the overall goal of the search? (*If more than one task: ask for each*).
3. Where did you do most of the searches? (*Where did they take place*).
4. Did you search at the same time as your partner or at different times? Were you together or apart?
5. How long did it take to complete the task?
6. How many search sessions were there? (*Ask then verify if necessary by inviting them to check the system*).
7. How would you normally go about looking for information when doing tasks like the one you did during the study?

Information Seeking

Let's talk about the process you followed when searching for information.

8. Can you give me a general idea of your approach towards achieving your goal?
9. How did you organise the task between the two of you?
10. What challenges, if any, did you encounter related to searching and managing results found?
11. What did you do with information once you had found it? (*Probe why they did what they did with the information*)
12. Did you encounter any problems during the execution of the task?
13. How did you resume your searches from previous sessions?

Communication

Let's talk about how and your partner communicated and exchanged information regarding your chosen task.

14. How did you share information with your partner?
15. How did they share information with you?
16. How did you and your partner communicate during the time you were working on your tasks? (*What methods did they use to discuss what they had found?*)
17. Did you ever communicate during searches?
18. What did you do to understand what your partner had searched for and looked at during their work?

Tool Use

Let's talk about the tool you were using.

19. Thinking back to your use of the toolbar, which features did you use most frequently? (*Ask them to elaborate on what they used them for. Ask them about each feature and whether or not they used them*).
20. Were there any features you chose not to use? (*If so, why didnt they use them?*)
21. Did you use any of the toolbar's communication features, for example the chat or sidebar?
22. In what ways was this tool useful during your task?
23. Were there any problems during your use of the system? (*If so, what were they?*)
24. Are there any ways in which you would improve this tool?
25. Did you use any other tools or methods to capture information? (*e.g. paper notes, spreadsheets*)
26. Can you give me an opinion of what you thought about the toolbar, overall?

Ending the Process

27. How did you decide that the quantity of information you found was enough? (*As in, at what point did they decide to terminate information seeking activities*)
28. How did you achieve consensus regarding the outcome of the work? (*As in, how did they decide which option to select*)
29. Overall, how would you describe your success in achieving what you wanted to achieve by using the tool?
30. Is there anything else you would like to add that we have not covered?

Modeling Search Processes using Hidden States in Collaborative Exploratory Web Search

Zhen Yue
University of Pittsburgh
135 North Bellefield Ave.
Pittsburgh, PA, 15260
Zhy18@pitt.edu

Shuguang Han
University of Pittsburgh
135 North Bellefield Ave.
Pittsburgh, PA, 15260
shh69@pitt.edu

Daqing He
University of Pittsburgh
135 North Bellefield Ave.
Pittsburgh, PA, 15260
dah44@pitt.edu

ABSTRACT

Investigations of search processes that involve complex interactions, such as collaborative search processes, are important research topics. Previous approaches of directly applying individual search process models into collaborative settings have proven to be problematic. In this paper, we proposed an innovative approach to model collaborative search processes using Hidden Markov Model (HMM), which is an automatic technique for analyzing temporal sequential data. Obtained through a user study, the data used in this paper consist of two different tasks in both collaborative exploratory Web search and individual exploratory Web search conditions. Our results showed that the identified hidden patterns of search process through HMM are compatible with previous well-known models. In addition, HMM generates detailed information on the transitions of hidden patterns in search processes, which demonstrated to be useful for analyzing task differences, and for determining the correlation of search process with search performance. The findings can be used for evaluating collaborative search systems as well as providing guidance for the system design.

Author Keywords

Collaborative information behavior; exploratory search; Hidden Markov Model; information seeking process.

ACM Classification Keywords

H.5.3 [Information Interfaces and Presentation]: Group and Organization Interfaces – Collaborative computing, Computer-supported cooperative work.

MOTIVATION AND BACKGROUND

A recent survey reported that the percentage of respondents engaged in collaborative Web search on a daily basis had increased from 0.9% in 2006 to 11% in 2012 [25] . As the needs of collaborative exploratory search continue to gain more and more attentions, researchers have developed many new systems and interfaces to support collaborative information seeking and retrieval [2, 9, 15, 26, 33]. Studies that seek to investigate and model search processes had played important roles in the development of Web search interfaces for individuals. For example, Bates [3] incorporated an information seeking model into a real search interface designing, and Hearst [16] emphasized the necessity to understand human information search processes in designing successful search systems. We assert that the design of a collaborative search system can benefit from a study of collaborative search processes. Previous researches [18, 32] found that it is inappropriate to directly apply individual information seeking models in collaborative search. This is because collaborative search involves more complex interactions--not only the interactions between users and the system but also the communication among users. We need new approaches that can tackle the complexity of interactions.

In individual search, researchers had employed two major approaches to investigate the information search process. One approach focuses on qualitative constructs, such as stages and context in the search process. Kuhlthau's model [20] and Marchionini's [22] model adopted such an approach. The other approach tries to derive search patterns through the analysis of logged user behaviors. These studies are based on units of search behaviors, such as actions [7, 8, 20], search tactics [42] or search strategies [4, 22], which are labeled either by human raters [22, 42] or automatic methods [7, 8, 20]. The manually labeling method is more controllable but requires huge human efforts and is difficult for scaling to large datasets. Automatic methods [7, 8, 20] need fewer human interventions, but these methods make it difficult to connect the outputs with existing theoretical models.

To investigate the collaborative search process, both [18] and [32] attempted to map the individual information search model into a collaborative Web search; both papers found this approach to be inappropriate. Although not specifically targeting a collaborative Web search, Evans and Chi's social search model [12] benefits the study of the collaborative search process. The model was built upon survey data rather than logged user data. Considering the complexity of interactions involved in the collaborative search, studying collaborative search processes through logged user behaviors remains a problem.

CSCW'14, February 15 – 19, 2014, Baltimore, MD, USA.
Copyright 2014 ACM 978-1-4503-2540-0/14/02...$15.00.
http://dx.doi.org/10.1145/2531602.2531658

In this paper, we focus on automatic methods for analyzing the collaborative information search process using logged user behavior. Previous studies on investigating the search process using logged data either focuses on the observed action level [7, 8, 20] or on the manually coded search tactics/strategies level [22, 42]. The connections between the observed actions and search tactics/strategies are missing. To capture such connections, we took a two-level view of the basic unit in the search process in this paper. The first level is observable actions, which are the manifestation of users' behavior. The second level is unobservable search tactics or strategies. We assumed that users can move between different search tactics. In each tactic, users have a list of choices (each choice is an action), and each choice has its probability of being adopted by the user. The observed actions represent the users' adopted choices. Fuhr's theoretical framework for interactive retrieval [13], which assumes that a user moves between situations in interactive information retrieval, supports this assumption.

In order to model the temporal sequential user behaviors and simultaneously leverage these two levels, we proposed using the Hidden Markov Model (HMM) [21]. Because search tactics usually represent the users' internal choices and are difficult to observe, it is reasonable to model the search tactics as the hidden variables. Moreover, unlike the Markov models that have been employed [6, 38] to analyze individual search processes, HMM assumes a Markov chain on the unobserved hidden tactics rather than the observed user actions. This approach helps to remove the over-simplistic assumption in Markov models: user's future action depends only upon the present user action, not on the other actions before the present action. One additional benefit of HMM is that instead of manually labeling user actions; HMM is an automatic method that easily applies to large datasets.

Although HMM is a well-established model, the majority of its applications focus on predicting future events, such as the weather and stock prices. To the best of our knowledge, the use of HMM in analyzing search processes is rare; we know of no previous works that applied HMM in collaborative Web search. Therefore, little available information explains how to categorize the observable user actions, how to choose appropriate parameters and how to make sense and interpret the outputs. This leads us to focus on investigating the following three research questions:

RQ1. How to apply HMM in the analysis of information search processes, especially in collaborative Web search?

RQ2: How to interpret the outputs of HMM? How to determine whether HMM is a valid method for analyzing collaborative exploratory Web search process?

RQ3: What are the potential applications of the HMM outputs? Can these outputs be used to analyze the connections between the patterns of search processes and the search task difference or the search performance?

RELATED WORK

The literature related to our study can be divided into three areas: collaborative Web search and systems, individual search processes, and collaborative search processes.

Golovchinsky et al. [14] classified the collaboration in Web search using three dimensions – location, concurrency, and intent. Morris [24] surveyed 204 information workers about when they collaboratively used Web search tools and on what tasks they usually collaborated with others. Evans and Chi [12] also investigated 150 people using Mechanical Turk on collaborative and social search strategies. Their study revealed that collaborative Web search is a surprisingly common activity. A most recent survey [25] suggested that the increased prevalence of collaborative Web search is a result of the significant change of the technology landscape, particularly the rise of social networking sites and the growing usage of smartphones. The survey also suggested that users expressed frustration regarding their lack of awareness of collaborators' activities; as a result, redundant work emerges as the primary concern in current collaborative Web search practice. Shah and Marchionini [33] presented a user study to examine the awareness in collaborative information-seeking. They showed that support for group awareness is more effective than an awareness of personal actions and history. Morris [27] conducted a study to investigate the sensemaking in collaborative Web search. Her study pointed out that sensemaking is an important component in collaborative search processes, and compared several different system features for supporting collaborative sensemaking.

In individual search, researchers explored many theoretical models to investigate the search processes of single users. There are several well-known search process models, such as Kuhlthau's [20] and Ellis' [10] model. Marchionini [22] proposed an information search process model of eight stages with possible transitions between each stage. This model highlights the likelihood of one stage transitioning into another stage in three types: most likely transitions, high-probability transitions, and low-transition probabilities. Other studies look into the search patterns through the analysis of user-system interactions. Holscher and Strube [17] compared action sequences between Internet experts and "newbies". Chen and Cooper [6] used a stochastic model to examine usage patterns in a Web-based library catalog. These studies examined search processes through the actions in the log without recognizing user intentions behind those actions. Xie and Joo [38] raised the importance of investigating transitions of search tactics as a means of examining search processes. Using a predefined scheme of search tactics, they first manually coded the transaction logs. Then, they developed a five-order Markov chain to find the common search tactics in the behavior sequence of the user. Elsweiler et al. [11] proposed using the Markov model to investigate search processes in Personal Information Management

(PIM). Most of the above-mentioned works use the Markov model on the observed action level, which made the over-simplistic Markov assumption.

One way to overcome the inappropriate assumption is to model the action sequence on the unobserved level. For example, Fuhr [13] extended the classical Probability Ranking Principle (PRP) into Interactive Information Retrieval (IIR) contexts. Fuhr's model assumes that users move between situations. In each situation, users have a list of choices, and each choice (e.g. a user action) has its cost, acceptance probability, and benefit. However, this model only provided a theoretical framework without detailing how these parameters can be estimated. Later, Tran and Fuhr [36] combined both user click logs and eye-tracking data to model the search process as a Markov chain. However, the authors did not make a clear distinction between the situations and the actions. The Markov model is built on four pre-defined Areas of Interests (AOIs).

The Hidden Markov Model (HMM) is a well-established model with mature techniques for parameter estimation. The information retrieval area has used HMM. For example, HMM has been adopted in inferring users' search contexts [5] and predicting next user behavior [37]. However, the goal of both of these papers is to improve the performance information retrieval algorithm rather than investigating and interpreting the search process.

In collaborative search, Evans and Chi [8] proposed a social search model consists of before, during and after search stages and suggested the information exchange is valuable in the whole process. The model provides a holistic view of search process while a fine-grained model is still needed to provide more details. Several studies attempted to expand Kuhlthau's model in collaborative setting. Hyldegard [18] explored Kuhlthau's model in a group educational setting based on a qualitative preliminary case study. She found that collaborative search process cannot be modeled the same way as individual search process. She suggested that the Kuhlthau's model should be extended to incorporate the impact of social and contextual factors in relation to collaborative information seeking process. Shah and Gonzalez-lbanez [32] also attempted to map Kuhlthau's model to collaborative information search process. Similar to Hyldgard, they also declared that social elements were missing when applying the Kuhlthau's model in a collaborative setting.

Based on the above literature review, we can see that the investigation on collaborative search processes is limited and problematic. Markov chain on observed actions had been used for studies in individual search settings, but the oversimplified Markov property may be inappropriate for analyzing search processes that involve complex interactions, such as collaborative search processes. While HMM had been proved to be a more powerful approach than Markov chain, there was no study investigating the application of HMM in studying search processes.

EXPERIMENT DESIGN

CollabSearch: a Collaborative Search System

CollabSearch[1] is a web search system for either a single user or a group of users. As with other collaborative search systems, CollabSearch has both search and collaboration features. As shown in Figure 1, the left side of the system's interface offers a space for chatting. Team users can communicate with each other by sending instant messages. The chat feature is turned off and the chat box is hidden in individual search mode.

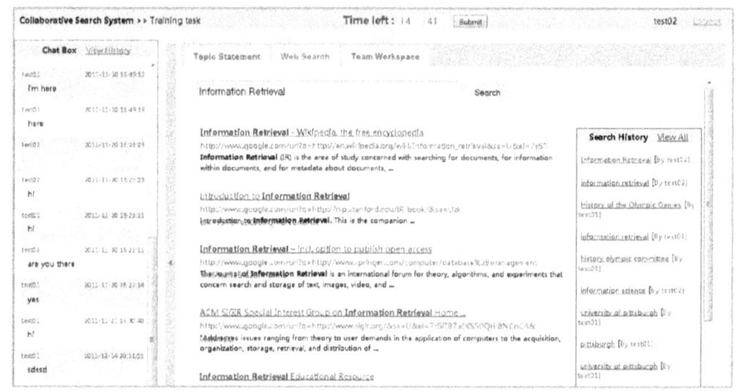

Figure 1: The web search frame

The main interface of CollabSearch contains three frames: topic statement, search and team workspace. The topic statement frame shows the current task description. In the navigation bar, they can see the time remaining for the current task. The search frame connects a user's query to the Google search engine, displaying the Google search results. This frame also reveals users' search history as well as that of their teammates. Users examine search results in the returned list for relevant information, and can save a whole web page or a snippet of the page.

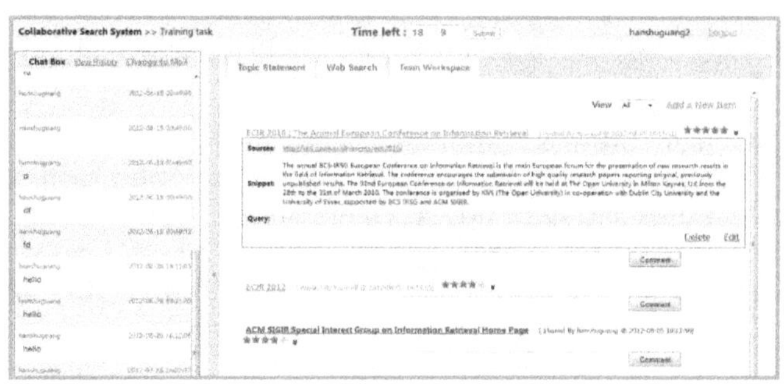

Figure 2: The workspace frame

All of the saved web pages and snippets, collected by the users in the same team, are stored in the team workspace frame. A notice is displayed at the top when new items have been saved to the team workspace. Users can click to view more details about an item in the workspace. Users can also decide whether a particular item is visible to other team members or not. The items saved by the user and the teammates are displayed in different colors and the user can choose to view a particular sets of items by using the filter.

[1] http:// crystal.exp.sis.pitt.edu:8080/CollaborativeSearch/

Experiment Conditions

We adopted a mix-method experiment with one within-subject factor: search task; and one between-subject factor: search condition, which refers to two search modes:

Collaborative search condition (COL). In this condition, two participants formed a team, and they worked on the same task simultaneously. As we were trying to simulate remotely-located collaboration, the team members could only communicate with each other by sending instant messages or reading each other's search histories. The collected results are shared in the team workspace, but no face-to-face communication was allowed.

Individual search condition (IND). This condition was devised as a baseline. In this condition, participants work on the exploratory search tasks individually.

Search Tasks

Two exploratory web search tasks were used in this study. Both of them had been used in other collaborative web search studies [23, 19]. One task is related to academic work, asking participants to collect information for a report on the effect of social networking service and software. The other one is the project-based leisure task [35], asking participants to collect information for planning a trip to Helsinki. Morris [24] noted that academic work and travel planning are the two common collaborative search tasks. Therefore, both of them are appropriate to study collaborative Web search.

The reason that we chose these two tasks is that they represent two different types of exploratory Web search tasks. First, the academic task (T1) is a recall-oriented information-gathering task, whereas the leisure task (T2) is a utility-based decision-making task. Second, the relevance criteria in these two tasks are different according to Saracevic's relevance theory [30]. Topical relevance is probably the most important criterion in T1 because the whole task is more objective in relevance judgments, whereas T2 involves users' subjective judgments and even personal preferences, so the relevance criteria contain many subjective and personal flavors.

Experiment Procedure

Each team in COL worked on both tasks. The order of the two tasks was rotated to reduce the learning and fatigue effect. During the experiment, participants were introduced to the study and the system, and completed an entry questionnaire to establish their search background. Then, participants worked on a training task for 15 minutes to become familiar with the system. They went on T1 or T2, depending on the task order assigned to each team. They had 30 minutes for each task. At the end of each task, participant completed a post-search questionnaire about their satisfaction on the performance and the cognitive load of search experiences. The experiment procedure in IND is identical to the COL condition except that only one participant undertaking the entire process.

Participants

Fifthy-four participants including 26 females and 28 males were recruited from the University of Pittsburgh. Among all of the participants, 36 signed up in pairs and thus formed 18 teams, which were assigned to the COL condition. The remaining 18 individual participants were assigned to the IND condition. All participants are students and they use computers and conduct Web searches on daily basis. Twenty-four participants are graduate students whereas the other 30 are undergraduates. According to a question asking them to rate their search experiences from 1-7 (with 1 as the least experienced and 7 as the most experienced), the response ranged from 4 to 7; thus most of our participants were experienced searchers.

Data Analysis Method

Since our study contains both within-subject and between-subject factors, and data maybe correlated, we adopted generalized estimating equation (GEE) to fit the model to the data, and analyzed the relationships between the independent variables and dependent variables, as well as the correlations. $p \leq .05$ was used to test any significant differences. GEE is a flexible statistical tool which deals with repeated measure and non-normal distributed data.

MODELING SEARCH PROCESS USING HMM

Categorizing user interactions

Before using HMM, we preprocessed user actions by classifying them into meaningful categories. Belkin et al. [4] classified user interactions using four dimensions: method of searching, mode of retrieval, goal of retrieval, and resource considered. The combination of dimensions defines multiple user interactions. In his model, each dimension was presented as binary values. Later Kim [19] expanded some dimensions with more than two values and removed some dimensions and values that do not apply to Web search environment. Xie [38] used two dimensions—methods and resources to classify user interactions, and she defined 8 values for methods and 6 values for resources.

For team users, the interactions are more complex than individual users. For example, when team users use CollabSearch for a collaborative Web search, the items saved in the workspace are both the ones saved by user him or herself and the partner. Therefore, it is useful to distinguish the interactions in which the user clicks the workspace to check on his/her own saved items from the interactions where the user checks on the partners' items.

Inspired by those ideas of classifying interactions using dimensions, we employed the following three dimensions to categorize user interactions in collaborative Web search: method, object and source, as shown in Figure 3. Some of the values of the method dimension, like search, scan, select and capture were also used in Kim's model [19]. However, we added another value communicate, which is unique in collaborative search. The values of the object dimension include all the possible objects that may exist in the collaborative Web search process, including query, topic statement, single item in search result, chat messages, list of saved items, and single saved items. The source dimension is unique in collaborative search context because it is important to distinguish the source of a particular object in collaborative process, whether it is from the user him/herself or from the partner or it is a shared/mix object.

Method	Object	Source
Search	Query	Self
Scan	Topic statement	Partner
Select	Item in search result	Shared/ mix
Capture	Chat messages	
Communicate	List of saved items	
	Single saved item	

Figure 3: Three dimensions for classifying user interactions

Using the combination of the following three dimensions, a set of observable user interactions is defined (see Table 1). Search-query-self (Q) represents the user issuing a query. In terms of using the workspace, users can scan the whole workspace without clicking on any particular item; this kind of interaction is the scan-list of saved item-mix (Wm). If the user clicks on a particular item, depending on whether the item is saved by the user or the partner, the interaction can be select-single saved-item-self (Ws) or select –single saved item- partner (Wp). All the possible combinations of the three dimensions that can be observed in the CollabSearch system are listed in Table 1.

Interactions	Description
Search – query – self (Q)	A user issues a query
Select- item-self (V)	A user clicks on a result in the returned result list
Capture-item-self (S)	A user saves a snippet or bookmarks a webpage
Scan-list of saved item – mixed (Wm)	A user checks the workspace without clicking on any particular item.
Select – single saved item –self (Ws)	A user clicks on an item in the workspace saved by him/herself
Select – single saved item – partner (Wp)	A user clicks on an item in the workspace saved by the partner
Scan-topic -shared (T)	A user clicks on the topic statement for view
Communicate-messages-self (Cs)	A user sends a message to the other user
Communicate-message-partner (Cp)	A user receives a message from the other user

Table 1: User interaction categorization

There are other possible combinations like select – item – partner, which means the user can click on an item in the partner's search result. However, this interaction is not supported in CollabSearch because team users do not share the screen and they cannot see the process when the partner issues a query and gets a returned results list. We acknowledge that clicking/viewing the topic statement is an artificial action that only exists because of the experiment setting. However, no matter whether it is because of the vagueness or the evolving nature of the exploratory information needs, users in exploratory search often have to consult their understanding of the search task to assess their progress in search. This consultation usually happens in users' mind without many external signals. Therefore, our topic statement action, though it sounds artificial, actually resembles a step that does exist in exploratory searches. We use the activities recorded in search logs to identify clicking/viewing topic statement.

Modeling Search Process

In this study, we introduced the Hidden Markov Model (HMM) method to model search tactics and search actions simultaneously. The model is described in Figure 4. We have a sequence of user actions from A_1 to A_M, and each action is one of those predefined nine actions: {Q, V, S, Wm, Ws, Wp, T, Cs, Cp}. HMM assumes that we also have a sequence of hidden states, from H_1 to H_M, and each action is generated by a corresponding hidden state, but different actions can be generated by the same hidden state with different probabilities. In this case, each action is corresponding to only one hidden state, and the hidden state sequence forms a Markov Chain.

A HMM model has several parameters: the number of hidden states N, the start probability of each states $\boldsymbol{\pi}$, the transition probabilities among any two hidden states $\boldsymbol{A_{ij}}$ and the emission probability from each state to each action $\boldsymbol{b_{ij}}$. By only defining the N and $\boldsymbol{\pi}$, a Baum-Welch algorithm [21] can be used to estimate the emission and transition probabilities.

Model Selection

It is still an open issue for determining the number of hidden states. Determining number of hidden states **N** is a model selection problem in learning the Hidden Markov Model. A complex model with large number of states will help to increase the sequence likelihood because there are more parameters that can be used to describe the model more precisely. But it has a high risk of causing over-fitting. A simple model is less likely to over-fit on the given dataset, but it may not be able to uncover the natural feature of datasets. In model selection, the information criterion such as the Akaike information criterion (AIC) or its variants [1] and Bayesian information criterion (BIC) [23] can be used to determine the optimal number of states. In this paper, we used BIC because it considers sample size.

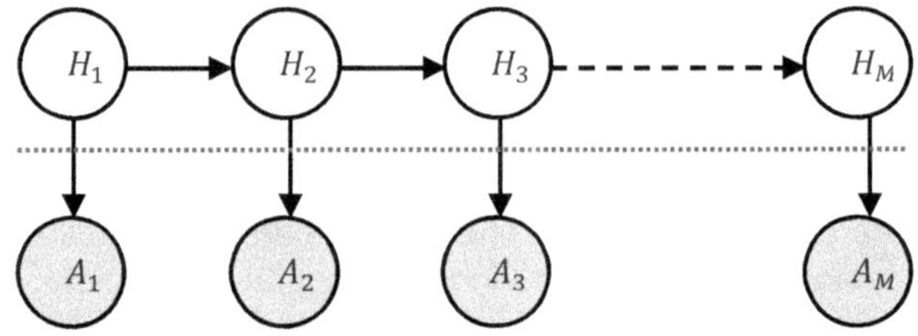

Figure 4: A Hidden Markov Model for Search Tactics

Suppose the number of parameters in HMM is p, and the number of total samples is s. The BIC is defined in

Formula (1), in which L denotes the log-likelihood of all samples. p can be computed using $(N-1)+(N-1)\times(N-1)+N\times(M-1)$, considering the summation of all probabilities is 1. M denotes the number of action types. A large log-likelihood with less parameters is preferred.

$$BIC = -2 \times \log(L) + \log(s) \times p \qquad \text{Eq. (1)}$$

VALIDATION OF HMM

Validating HMM in Individual Search

In this section, we validated the application of HMM in the individual search process. Figure 5 plots the BIC values against the number of hidden states in the IND condition. We can see that BIC has the optimal value when the number of hidden states is set to 4.

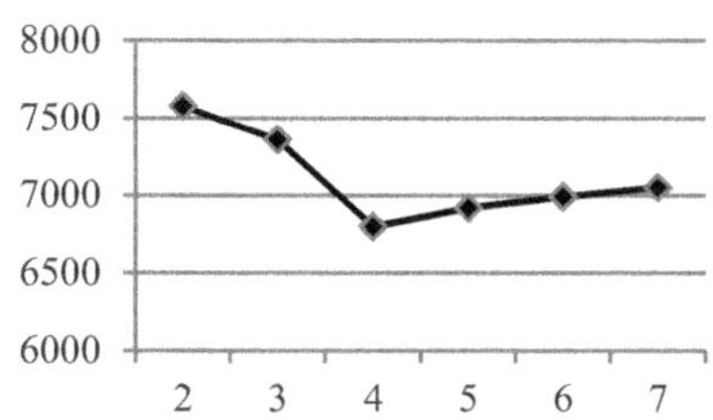

Figure 5: BIC Evaluation of HMM parameters in IND

Hidden states of HMM are represented by the emission probability distribution over observable user actions. The results of emission probability distribution in IND are shown in Table 2, in which we removed the probabilities that are smaller than 0.05 for better visualizing each hidden state. The first hidden state has a very high probability (0.99) of generating the interaction Q (defined in Table 1). Therefore, we named it HQ. Using the same naming criteria, we defined the second and third hidden states as HV and HS, respectively. It is clear that these three hidden states are directly related to search. The fourth hidden state is the most interesting one; it has a 0.57 probability of generating Ws and a 0.42 probability of generating T. We think that this hidden state is related to sensemaking, which is the process of bridging a knowledge gap that prevents the user from accomplishing the task [8]. In the exploratory search, participants may lack knowledge about the information problem, result space or the needed vocabulary for search [28]. In this hidden state, the participants were trying to evaluate the current search stage and define the current search problem in order to advance the search. Therefore, we named it the hidden state of defining search problem (HD).

	Q	V	S	Ws	T
HQ	0.99				
HV		0.91			
HS			0.96		
HD				0.57	0.42

Table 2: Hidden States and Emission Probability in IND

In HMM, each observed action corresponds to a hidden state in Table 2. To compare the differences between two tasks (this is for a later section), we computed the mean transition probabilities from each hidden state to any of the four (including itself) hidden states across all the participants. The transition probabilities are visualized in Figure 6 (probabilities lower than 0.05 are omitted). We can see a pattern of high transition probabilities on HQ→HV→HS, which represents a typical search pattern – a query is issued and results are viewed and saved if they are relevant. After saving an item, the participant may continue view another item HS→HV, issue another query HS →HQ, or transitioned to the sensemaking states before issuing another query HS→HD→HQ.

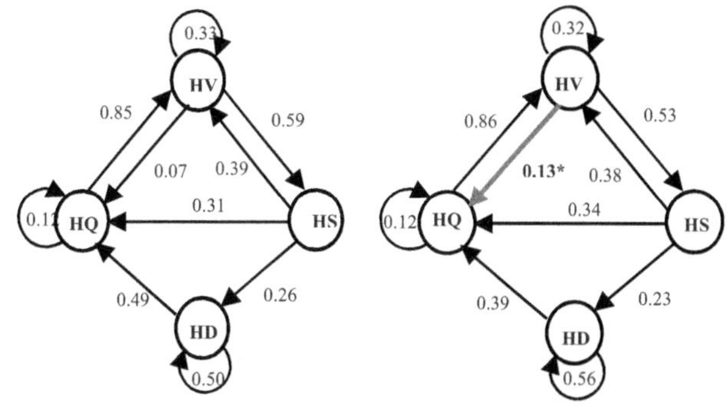

Figure 6: Comparison of transition probabilities of hidden states in IND for two tasks (left: T1, right: T2; a red arrow indicates significant difference: *p<0.05)

To validate HMM, we compared its output with Marchionini's information search process (ISP) model [22], which is a well-established model in the information seeking field. We found that the transitions among hidden states were very similar to the transitions among sub-processes in the ISP model. The default transitions in the ISP model can be mapped into HD→HQ→HV→HS→HD (Table 3), which is also the pattern of the highest transition probabilities in Figure 6. The ISP model also described the high and low transition probabilities among different sub-processes. For example, "extract information" (HS) had a high probability of transitioning to "examining results" (HV) and "formulate query" (HQ). Those transitions were also represented in the HMM output, with more details on the probabilities. Another model that can be used to validate the HMM result is the model of sensemaking loop [29]. The sensemaking loop is also reflected in the HMM output (transitions between sensemaking-related hidden states and search-related hidden states) with more details on the transition probabilities.

Sub-processes in the ISP model	HMM
Define Problem	HD
Select Source, Formulate Query, Execute Query	HQ
Examine Results	HV
Extract Information	HS
Reflect/Iterate/Stop	HD

Table 3: Mapping from sub-process in Marchionini's ISP model to the hidden states

Validating HMM in Collaborative Search

In this section, we validated the application of HMM in the collaborative search process. In Figure 7, we can see that the BIC has the optimal value when the number of hidden states in the COL condition is set to 6.

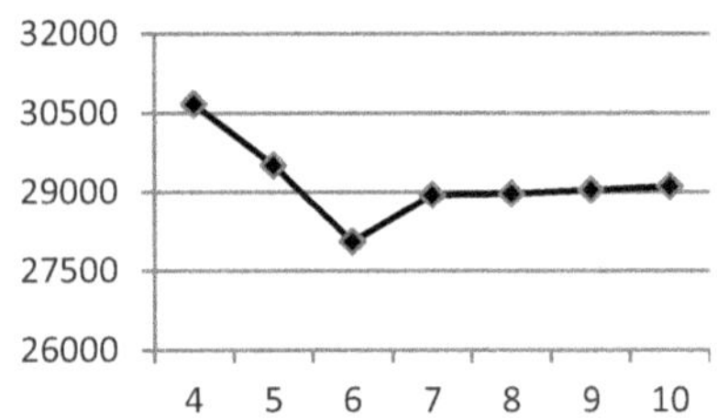

Figure 7: BIC Evaluation of HMM parameters in COL

The emission probabilities of each hidden state over observable interactions are shown in Table 4. The first three hidden states have high probabilities of generating Q, V and S respectively, which are similar to the first three hidden states in the IND condition. Therefore, we assigned them with the same names as in IND. These hidden states are directly related to the search while the rest three are related sensemaking. HD has a 0.36 probability of generating Wm, a 0.36 probability of generating T and a 0.21 probability of generating Cs. We think that this is a sensemaking hidden state in which the participants define the current search problem. Besides looking at the information in workspace and topic statement, the participants may also communicate with their partner to discuss the current search problem. The remaining two hidden states HW and HC are related to the communication between team members during the sensemaking stage. HW represents the state of checking the saved item details in the workspace whereas HC represents the continuous communication between team members.

	Q	V	S	Wm	Ws	Wp	T	Cs	Cp
HQ	0.82							0.13	
HV		0.87							0.1
HS			0.88						
HD				0.36			0.36	0.21	
HW					0.37	0.44			0.12
HC								0.44	0.47

Table 4: Hidden States and Emission Probability in COL

The transition probabilities were visualized for each search task respectively in Figure 8 (probabilities lower than 0.05 are omitted). Our results showed that sensemaking in the collaborative exploratory search (HD+HW+HC) were more important and complex than that in the individual search (HD only). We also recognized different types of sensemaking tactics, such as chat-centric sensemaking (HC) and workspace-centric sensemaking (HW). These results are consistent with the sensemaking types mentioned in [27]. In addition, our HMM outputs were consistent with Evans and Chi's model [12]. Their model consists of three phases: before search, during search and after search. In the before-search stage, users mainly focus on gathering requirements, which can be mapped to the HD in the HMM output. The during-search stage for informational tasks highlights the fact that "the foraging and sensemaking loops are tightly coupled," which is also reflected in the HMM output. The sharing of information with others in the after-search stage is also reflected in the HMM output with more details on what follows the sharing. The HMM output shows that after sharing, users could explicitly communicate about it or continue to the next round of defining a search problem.

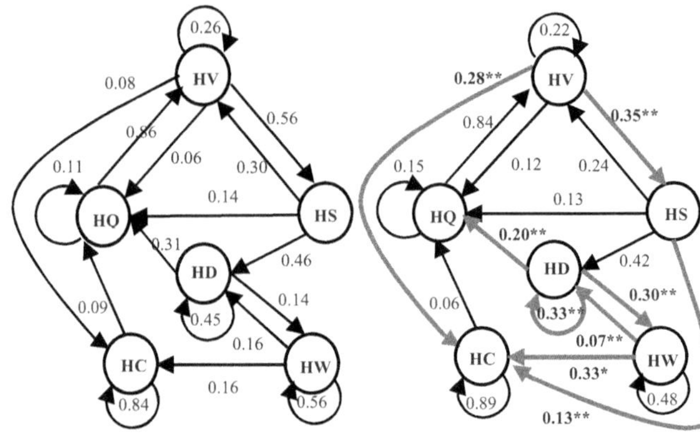

Figure 8: Comparison of Transition Probabilities of Hidden states in COL for two tasks (left: T1, right: T2; red arrows indicate significant difference: *p<0.05, **p<0.01)

The consistency of our HMM results with that of previous search process models in both individual search and collaborative search demonstrate the validity of HMM. The HMM results not only reveal the patterns found by previous models, but also provided more detailed information than previous model such as probabilities of transitions among different hidden tactics, which can be utilized to better understand users' search behavior.

APPLICATION OF HMM

The benefit of HMM is that it provides detailed information on the transition probabilities among different states in the search process. In this section, we showed the applications of such information through two cases.

Case I: Comparing Task Difference

Evans and Chi's model [12] built different search processes for three different types of user needs: informational, navigational and transactional. However, their model cannot distinguish two tasks within the same category. In this study, we showed that the HMM outputs can be used to reveal task differences.

The task comparison of individual search and collaborative search using HMM outputs are visualized in Figure 6 and Figure 8, respectively. In individual search, the patterns in the two tasks are very similar except HV→HQ, which we found it is significantly lower in T1 than in T2 (Mean diff = -.06, SE=.02, p=.012). In T2, participants were more likely to issuing another query after viewing a result, which might because the item was irrelevant. This may reflect the differences of task requirements. T2 is a decision making task, the participants are more concerned about the integration of information rather than collecting information. Therefore, they may be more selective on what information to save.

In the collaborative search, we can see that there are several significant differences between the two tasks, especially for the transitions between search related hidden states and sense-making related hidden states. HV→HC is significantly lower in T1 than in T2 (Mean diff = -.20, SE=.03, p<.001), so does HS→HC (Mean diff = -.10, SE=.03, p=.001). These differences suggest that when working on decision-making task T2, the participants were more likely to communicate with each other after they viewed or saved an item. Also, HW→HC is significantly lower in T1 than in T2 (Mean diff = -.17, SE=.07, p=.013). After viewing an item saved in the workspace, the participants were more likely to discuss what they think about the saved item in decision-making task T2. The transitions from HD are also different in the two tasks. HD→HQ is significantly higher in T1 than in T2 (Mean diff =.11, SE=.03, p<.001) whereas HD→HW is significantly lower in T1 than in T2 (Mean diff = -.16, SE=.06, p=.003). These results may indicate that in the information-gathering task such as T1, the participants preferred to have an overview of the workspace when they need to make sense of the current search problem whereas the users in decision-making task such as T2 preferred to look at the details of each saved items.

In both of the individual search and the collaborative search process, HMM recognized two types of hidden tactics, *i.e.* the search-related tactics and the sensemaking-related tactics. The search-related tactics remain similar in both search conditions, but sensemaking-related tactics are more complex in the collaborative search than that in the individual search. In terms of task difference, the collaborative search process exhibits more sensitivity on task differences. The ability of HMM on detecting task differences can be used for intelligent system design. When certain task type is detected, the system can provide support that is more suitable for the task.

Case II: Correlation between the Search Process and the Search Outcome

The ultimate goal of studying search process is to locate the core factors that influence search outcomes and provide better support for those factors. In this section, we are interested in locating those factors in collaborative web search process from real user behaviors, particularly how sense-making tactics influence the overall search performance.

Since we used the open Web as search collection, there is no ground-truth to calculate traditional precision and recall. In order to measure precision and recall, we defined the relevant Webpages (Ground-Truth data denoted by G) as those were saved by at least two teams. Then, for each participant u, the precision (P) and recall (R) were computed using Equation (2) and Equation (3), in which S(u) are a set of webpages saved by participant u.

$$P(u) = \frac{|G \cap S(u)|}{|S(u)|} \quad \text{Eq. (2)}$$

$$R(u) = \frac{|G \cap S(u)|}{|G|} \quad \text{Eq. (3)}$$

An advantage of collaborative search is that users are able to discover hard to find webpages [31]. Likelihood of discovery has been used to measure how hard a Webpage can be found [31], which is inversely proportional to the number of teams visited the Webpage. However, it doesn't consider the quality of a webpage. And we defined a weighted likelihood of discovery (WLD) for each Webpage w by multiplying the likelihood of discovery of a Webpage by the quality of the Webpage, which is measured by the number of teams saved divided by number of teams visited. WLD is calculated using Equation (4), in which $S'(w)$ is the total number of teams saved w and $V'(w)$ is the total number of teams visited w. Since WebPages saved by at least two teams are considered as relevant, $S'(w) - 1$ and $V'(w) - 1$ is used.

$$WLD(u) = \sum_{w \in S(u)} \frac{|S'(w) - 1|}{|V'(w) - 1|} \frac{1}{|V'(w) - 1|} \quad \text{Eq. (4)}$$

User satisfaction (Sat) is a subjective measurement which reflects the participants' perception of the search outcome [34]. In this study, we measure the participants' satisfaction based on their responses to a question asking them to evaluate their satisfaction on the overall performance using 7-point Likert scale. A higher score indicates a better satisfaction. Cognitive load (Cog) can measure how hard one have to work for solving a complex problem, which can be used as a subjective measurement to evaluate the participants' perception towards their search experience. We used the instrument which has been used in another collaborative Web search study [31] to measure participants' cognitive load. A high cognitive load indicates a negative user perception to the search experience.

In this study, we are particularly interested in how sense-making are related to search performance. Therefore, we examined the correlation of the following transitions with the search performance, including HS→HD, HS→HC, HV→HC, HD→HQ and HC→HQ. These transitions are chosen based on two criteria: 1) the probability in either task is higher than 0.05; 2) it represents a transition between search and sense-making. We also considered HW→HC because it represents the transition between two different types of communication: from implicit communication to explicit communication.

	HS→HD	HD→HQ	HW→HC	HC→HQ
P	-	-	-	-
R	↓(p<0.01)	↑(p<0.01)	-	-
WLD	↓(p=0.01)	↑(p<0.01)	-	↑(p=0.06)
Sat	-	↑(p<0.01)		↓(p<0.01)
Cog		↓(p<0.01)	↑(p<0.01)	

Table 6: Correlation of Search Process and Search Outcome: ↓ denoting negative and ↑ denoting positive correlation

The results are shown in Table 6. ↑ means the transition is positively related to the performance and user perception while ↓ represents a negative relationship. We didn't find any significant differences on HV→HC and HS→HC, thus they are not shown in the table. We found that the transition from sense-making to search (HD→HQ) is positively related to performance and user perception. However, the transition from search to sense-making (HS→HD) is negatively related to performance and user perception. This might be caused by the fact that when participants are facing knowledge gap during exploratory search, they need to transit to sense-making states; and when the problems were solved, they transit back to the search states. Another interest finding is about HC→HQ. It's positively related to WLD but negatively related to Sat. It might suggest that explicit communication helped the participants to improve the search performance. However, explicit communication maybe triggered by a problem in search; which makes the participants feel less satisfied with their performance. In addition, we found that HW→HC is positively related to Cog, which means that a transition from implicit communication to explicit communication increases the participants' cognitive load. This might indicate that team members had something to negotiate through explicit communication, which increases the cognitive load.

Future Applications

We believe that there are still many applications that can also make use of HMM outputs. As for our next step, we would explore the following directions: 1) through detecting patterns in search process, the system can predict which type of search tactic a user is employing and should employ in the next step. Through this way, the system can provide support intelligently; 2) it can be used to evaluate a search system works based on how well it supports the particular transition process and to identify how to make the transition smoothly and thus increase the performance.

DISCUSSION AND CONTRIBUTION

Through the analysis of search processes in exploratory search using HMM, we have several important findings. First, two types of hidden states are recognized in both individual and collaborative search processes: the search related hidden states and the sense-making related hidden states. This is compatible with previous studies that exploratory search can be viewed as an intertwine process of search and sense-making [28]. Second, using HMM in analyzing the individual search process and the collaborative search process, we obtained similar transition patterns as defined in several well-established information seeking process models, which demonstrates the validity of our model. Third, we found that the search-related states are similar in both individual and collaborative search, but sense-making related states are more complex in collaborative search. This again is consistent with previous findings. The ability to capture different types of sense-making demonstrates the generalizability of our model.

In terms of task type, collaborative search is more sensitive to the task difference. We didn't find many differences on the search process between two tasks in the individual search. However, the search processes between the two tasks in collaborative search are quite different. There are more transitions between search and explicit communications in the utility-based decision-making task. It indicates that this type of task requires users to be more active in the collaboration, which might be caused by the need for negotiation and agreement.

Based on the analysis of relationship between search process and search performance, we found that the transition from search to sense-making has a negative relationship with the performance while the transition from sense-making to search has a positive relationship with the performance. Here we refer to correlation not casual effects. We are not arguing that low performance is caused by the transition to sense-making. Instead, we think that when sense-making is needed, it means the user has to spend time on absorbing information or on resolving problems. If we can make the transition less frequent and smoother, it may improve the search performance. For example, a summary of workspace in the search frame may be able to help users to make sense of current search status without breaking the current search activity. In this case, users need less effort on sense-making so that they can keep searching without being interrupted. In future studies, we are planning to test whether the easiness of sense-making can help to improve collaborative search performance.

Our contributions include: 1) we demonstrated that HMM is a valid method for analyzing collaborative search process. The benefit of HMM is that it can model users' intent or hidden search tactics without input from a theoretical model or manual label. Collaborative Web search is an ideal case for applying HMM since collaborative search tactics have not been well-defined in literature. HMM can be useful for analyzing search processes that involve complex user interactions, such as e-discovery or multimedia retrieval; 2) we explored and identified the important procedures for applying HMM. We found that categorizing user interactions and conducting model selection are two important components in HMM. Our approach of categorizing user interactions using three dimensions: method, object and source can be applied to other studies. Future applications of HMM can follow the rules and methods we provided; 3) Comparing to the previous models, HMM provides more detailed information of transition probabilities among different states in the search process. Our study demonstrated that such information can be used for analyzing task differences and correlation with search performance. The findings can be used for evaluating collaborative Web search systems and guiding the design of the system.

We do acknowledge some limitations of this study. First, our search performance measures mainly consider topical relevance, whereas other measures might be needed for the utility-based decision-making task. This is because users' personal judgment matters for the relevance in this kind of tasks rather than the topical relevance. Second, we found that the recall is significantly lower in decision-making tasks. One reason is that the goal of this type of task is not to exhaust relevant information. Furthermore, we defined the relevant documents as those were saved by at least two teams, which might not be a good indicator of relevance in utility-based decision-making tasks. In the future, we will explore measures for more accurate reflection of search performance in collaborative Web search.

CONCLUSION

In this paper, we applied a novel approach for modeling search process automatically using hidden states. A user study was conducted to compare the search process in collaborative exploratory search and individual exploratory search. Through the analysis, we demonstrated that HMM is a valid method for automatically analyzing search processes. Different patterns of hidden states were recognized and compared in both individual and collaborative search. In addition, the patterns of hidden states between two types of tasks were quite different in collaborative search. We also discovered the relationships between search processes and search outcomes. Future works will focus on the application of these findings to facilitate collaborative exploratory Web search.

REFERENCES

[1] Akaike, H. 1974. A new look at the statistical model identification. *IEEE Transactions on Automatic Control*. 19, 6 (1974), 716–723.

[2] Amershi, S. and Morris, M.R. 2008. CoSearch: a system for colocated collaborative web search. *Proceeding of ACM SIGCHI* (Florence, Italy, 2008), 1647–1656.

[3] Bates, M.J. 1989. The design of browsing and berrypicking techniques for the online search interface. *Online Review*. 13, (1989), 407–424.

[4] Belkin, N. 1995. Cases, Scripts, and Information-Seeking Strategies: On the Design of Interactive Information Retrieval Systems. *Expert Systems with Applications*. 9, 3 (1995), 379–395.

[5] Cao, H. et al. 2009. Towards context-aware search by learning a very large variable length hidden markov model from search logs. *Proceedings of the 18th international conference on World wide web WWW 09*. 11, (2009), 191.

[6] Chen, H.-M. and Cooper, M.D. 2002. Stochastic modeling of usage patterns in a web-based information system. *Journal of the American Society for Information Science and Technology*. 53, 7 (2002), 536–548.

[7] Chen, H.-M. and Cooper, M.D. 2001. Using clustering techniques to detect usage patterns in a Web-based information system. *Journal of the American Society for Information Science and Technology*. 52, 11 (2001), 888–904.

[8] Dervin, B. et al. 2003. *Sense-Making methodology reader: Selected Writings of Brenda Dervin*. Hampton Press, Inc.

[9] Diriye, A. et al. Querium : A Session-Based Collaborative Search System. 2–3.

[10] Ellis, D. 1993. Modeling the information seeking patterns of academic researchers: a ground theory approach. *Library Quarterly*. 63, 4 (1993), 469–486.

[11] Elsweiler, D. et al. Evaluating Personal Information Management Behaviour using Markov Models. 8, 280–288.

[12] Evans, B.M. and Chi, E.H. 2008. Towards a model of understanding social search. *Proceeding of the 2008 ACM workshop on Search in social media - SSM '08*. (2008), 83.

[13] Fuhr, N. 2008. A probability ranking principle for interactive information retrieval. *Information Retrieval*. 11, 3 (Feb. 2008), 251–265.

[14] Golovchinsky, G. et al. 2009. Collaborative information seeking. *IEEE Computer*. 42, 3 (2009).

[15] Golovchinsky, G. and Adcock, J. 2008. Cerchiamo: a collaborative exploratory search tool. *Proceedings of the computer supported cooperative work*. (2008).

[16] Hearst, M. 2009. *Search User Interfaces*. Cambridge University Press.

[17] Holscher, C. and Strube, G. 2000. Web search behavior of Internet experts and newbies. 33, (2000), 337–346.

[18] Hyldegard, J. 2006. Collaborative Information Behavior - Exploring Kuhlthau's Information Search Process Model in a Group-based Educational setting. *Information Processing & Management*. 42, 1 (2006), 276–298.

[19] Kim, J. 2009. Describing and Predicting Information-Seeking Behavior on the Web. *Journal of the American Society for Information Science and Technology*. 60, 4 (2009), 679–693.

[20] Kuhlthau, C.C. 1991. Inside the search process: Information seeking from the user's perspective. *Journal of the American Society for Information Science*. 42, 5 (Jun. 1991), 361–371.

[21] L.E.Baum et al. 1970. A maximization technique occuring in the statistical analysis of probabilistic functions of Markov chains. *Ann. Math. Statist.* 41, 1 (1970).

[22] Marchionini, G. 1995. *Information seeking in electronic environments*. Cambridge University Press.

[23] McQuarrie, A. and Tsai, C. 1998. *Regression and Time Series Model Selection.*

[24] Morris, M.R. 2008. A survey of collaborative web search practices. *Proceeding of the twenty-sixth annual CHI conference on Human factors in computing systems - CHI '08.* (2008), 1657.

[25] Morris, M.R. 2013. Collaborative search revisited. *Proceedings of the 2013 conference on Computer supported cooperative work - CSCW '13* (New York, New York, USA, Feb. 2013), 1181.

[26] Morris, M.R. and Horvitz, E. 2007. *SearchTogether: An interface for collaborative web search.* ACM Press.

[27] Paul, S.A. and Morris, M.R. Sensemaking in Collaborative Web Search. *Social Cognition.* 1–66.

[28] Qu, Y. and Furnas, G. 2007. Model-driven formative evaluation of exploratory search: A study under a sensemaking framework. *Information Processing & Management.* 44, (Nov. 2007), 534–555.

[29] Russell, D.M. et al. 1993. The cost structure of sensemaking. *Proceedings of the SIGCHI conference on Human factors in computing systems CHI 93* (1993), 269–276.

[30] Saracevic, T. 2007. Relevance : A Review of the Literature and a Framework for Thinking on the Notion in Information Science . Part II : Nature and Manifestations of Relevance *. 30, October (2007), 1915–1933.

[31] Shah, C. and González-Ibáñez, R. 2011. Evaluating the synergic effect of collaboration in information seeking. *Proceedings of the 34th international ACM SIGIR conference on Research and development in Information - SIGIR '11.* (2011), 913.

[32] Shah, C. and González-ibáñez, R. 2010. Exploring Information Seeking Processes in Collaborative Search Tasks Chirag Shah. *ASIS&T* (2010).

[33] Shah, C. and Marchionini, G. 2010. Awareness in Collaborative Information Seeking. *Journal of the American Society for Information Science and Technology.* 61, 10 (2010), 1970–1986.

[34] Spink, a 2002. A user-centered approach to evaluating human interaction with Web search engines: an exploratory study. *Information Processing & Management.* 38, 3 (May. 2002), 401–426.

[35] Stebbins, R.A. 2009. Leisure and its relationship to library and information science: Bridging the gap. *Library Trends.* 57, (2009), 618–631.

[36] Tran, V.T. and Fuhr, N. 2012. Using eye-tracking with dynamic areas of interest for analyzing interactive information retrieval. *Proceedings of the 35th international ACM SIGIR conference on Research and development in information retrieval (SIGIR '12).* (2012).

[37] Wang, K. and Gloy, N. 2010. Inferring Search Behaviors Using Partially Observable Markov (POM) Model. *Web Search and Data Mining* (2010), 211–220.

[38] Xie, I. and Joo, S. 2010. Transitions in Search Tactics During the Web-Based Search Process. *Journal of the American Society for Information Science.* 61, 11 (2010), 2188–2205.

Romantic Partnerships and the Dispersion of Social Ties: A Network Analysis of Relationship Status on Facebook

Lars Backstrom
Facebook Inc.

Jon Kleinberg
Cornell University

ABSTRACT

A crucial task in the analysis of on-line social-networking systems is to identify important people — those linked by strong social ties — within an individual's network neighborhood. Here we investigate this question for a particular category of strong ties, those involving spouses or romantic partners. We organize our analysis around a basic question: given all the connections among a person's friends, can you recognize his or her romantic partner from the network structure alone? Using data from a large sample of Facebook users, we find that this task can be accomplished with high accuracy, but doing so requires the development of a new measure of tie strength that we term 'dispersion' — the extent to which two people's mutual friends are not themselves well-connected. The results offer methods for identifying types of structurally significant people in on-line applications, and suggest a potential expansion of existing theories of tie strength.

Categories and Subject Descriptors: H.2.8 [**Database Management**]: Database applications—*Data mining*
Keywords: Social Networks; Romantic Relationships.

INTRODUCTION

In a social network, an individual's network neighborhood — the set of people to whom he or she is linked — has been shown to have important consequences in a wide range of settings, including social support [12,24] and professional opportunities [5, 15]. As people use on-line social networks to manage increasingly rich aspects of their lives, the structures of their on-line network neighborhoods have come to reflect these functions, and the complexity that goes with them.

A person's network neighbors, taken as a whole, encompass a profoundly diverse set of relationships — they typically include family members, co-workers, friends of long duration, distant acquaintances, potentially a spouse or romantic partner, and a variety of other categories. An important and very broad issue for the analysis of on-line social networks is to use features in the available data to recognize this variation across types of relationships. Methods to do this effectively can play an important role for many applications at the interface between an individual and the rest of the network — managing their on-line interactions [9], prioritizing content they see from friends [1], and organizing their neighborhood into conceptually coherent groups [23, 25].

CSCW'14, February 15–19, 2014, Baltimore, Maryland, USA.

http://dx.doi.org/10.1145/2531602.2531642

Tie Strength.

Tie strength forms an important dimension along which to characterize a person's links to their network neighbors. Tie strength informally refers to the 'closeness' of a friendship; it captures a spectrum that ranges from strong ties with close friends to weak ties with more distant acquaintances. An active line of research reaching back to foundational work in sociology has studied the relationship between the strengths of ties and their structural role in the underlying social network [15]. Strong ties are typically 'embedded' in the network, surrounded by a large number of mutual friends [6,16], and often involving large amounts of shared time together [22] and extensive interaction [17]. Weak ties, in contrast, often involve few mutual friends and can serve as 'bridges' to diverse parts of the network, providing access to novel information [5, 15].

A fundamental question connected to our understanding of strong ties is to identify the most important individuals in a person's social network neighborhood using the underlying network structure. What are the defining structural signatures of a person's strongest ties, and how do we recognize them? Techniques for this problem have potential importance both for organizing a person's network neighborhood in on-line applications, and also for providing basic insights into the effect of close relationships on network structure more broadly.

Recent work has developed methods of analyzing and estimating tie strength in on-line domains, drawing on data from e-mail [19], phone calls [27], and social media [14]. The key structural feature used in these analyses is the notion of *embeddedness* — the number of mutual friends two people share [22], a quantity that typically increases with tie strength. Indeed, embeddedness has been so tightly associated with tie strength that it has remained largely an open question to determine whether there are other structural measures, distinct from embeddedness, that may be more appropriate for characterizing particular types of strong ties.

Romantic Relationships.

In this work we propose a new network-based characterization for intimate relationships, those involving spouses or romantic partners. Such relationships are important to study for several reasons.

From a substantive point of view, romantic relationships are of course singular types of social ties that play powerful roles in social processes over a person's whole life course [4], from adolescence [2] to older age [7]. They also form an important aspect of the everyday practices and uses of social media [28].

And they are an important challenge from a methodological point of view; they are evidently among the very strongest ties, but it has not been clear whether standard structural theories based on embeddedness are sufficient to characterize them, or whether they possess singular structural properties of their own [11, 18].

Our central finding is that embeddedness is in fact a comparatively weak means of characterizing romantic relationships, and that an alternate network measure that we term *dispersion* is significantly more effective. Our measure of dispersion looks not just at the number of mutual friends of two people, but also at the network structure on these mutual friends; roughly, a link between two people has high dispersion when their mutual friends are not well connected to one another.

On a large random sample of Facebook users who have declared a relationship partner in their profile, we find that our dispersion measure has roughly twice the accuracy of embeddedness in identifying this partner from among the user's full set of friends. Indeed, for married Facebook users, our measure of dispersion applied to the pure, unannotated network structure is more effective at identifying a user's spouse than a complex classifier trained using machine learning on an array of interaction measures including messaging, commenting, profile-viewing, and co-presence at events and in photos. Further, using dispersion in conjunction with these interaction features produces significantly higher accuracy.

The main contributions of our work are thus the following.

- We propose a new network measure, *dispersion*, for estimating tie strength. Given the ubiquity of embeddedness in existing analyses of tie strength, the availability of this new measure broadens the range of tools available for reasoning about tie strength, and about mechanisms for tie-strength classification in on-line domains.
- We provide a new substantive characterization of romantic relationships in terms of network structure, with potential consequences for our understanding of the effect that such relationships have on the underlying social network.
- Given this characterization, we examine its variation across different conditions and populations. We find, for example, that there are significant gender differences in the extent to which relationship partners are recognizable from network structure, and that relationships are more likely to persist when they score highly under our dispersion measure.

It is also important to delineate the scope of our results. Our approach to analyzing romantic partnerships in on-line social settings is through their effect on the network structure, and the ways in which such relationships can be recognized through their structural signatures. As such, there is potential for it to be combined with other perspectives on how these relationships are expressed on-line, and the conventions that develop around their on-line expression; a complete picture will necessarily involve a synthesis of all these perspectives.

DATA AND PROBLEM DESCRIPTION

We analyze romantic relationships in social networks using a dataset of randomly sampled Facebook users who declared a relationship partner in their profile; this includes users who listed their status as 'married,' 'engaged,' or 'in a relationship'. To evaluate different structural theories on a common footing, we begin with a simply stated prediction task designed to capture the basic issues. We take a Facebook user with a declared relationship partner, and we hide the identity of this partner. Then we ask: given the user's network neighborhood — the set of all friends and the links among them — how accurately can we identify the relationship partner using this structural information alone? Figure 1 gives an example of such a Facebook user's network neighborhood [21], drawn so that the user is depicted at the center; such diagrams are the 'input' from which we wish to identify the user's partner. By phrasing the question this starkly, we are able to assess the extent to which structural information on its own conveys information about the relationships of interest.

We note that our question has an important contingent nature: *given* that a user has declared a relationship partner, we want to understand how effectively we can find the partner. There are different questions that could be asked in a related vein — for example, inferring from a user's network neighborhood whether he or she is in a relationship. We briefly discuss the connections among these questions in a subsequent section, but the problem of identifying partners is our main focus here.

As data for our analyses, we principally use two collections of network neighborhoods from Facebook. The first consists of the network neighborhoods of approximately 1.3 million Facebook users, selected uniformly at random from among all users of age at least 20, with between 50 and 2000 friends, who list a spouse or relationship partner in their profile. These neighborhoods have an average of 291 nodes and 6652 links, for an overall dataset containing roughly 379 million nodes and 8.6 billion links.

We also employ a smaller dataset — a sample of approximately 73000 neighborhoods from this first collection, selected uniformly at random from among all neighborhoods with at most 25000 links. We refer to this sample as the *primary dataset*, and the larger dataset in the preceding paragraph as the *extended dataset*. We compute our main structural and interaction measures on both the primary and extended datasets, and these measures exhibit nearly identical performance on the two datasets. As we discuss further below, we evaluate additional network measures, as well as more complex combinations of measures based on machine learning algorithms, only on the primary dataset.

All Facebook data in these analyses was used anonymously, and all analysis was done in aggregate.

EMBEDDEDNESS AND DISPERSION

To evaluate approaches for our task of recognizing relationship partners from network structure, we start with a fundamental baseline — the standard characterization of a tie's strength in terms of its *embeddedness*, the number of mutual friends shared by its endpoints [22]. Embeddedness has also served as the key definition in structural analyses for the special case of relationship partners, since it captures how much the two partners' social circles 'overlap' [11, 18]. This sug-

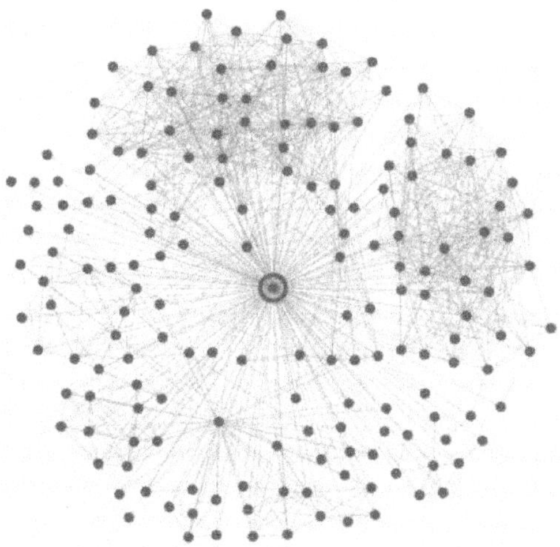

Figure 1. A network neighborhood, contributed by a Facebook employee (drawn as the circled node at the center), and displayed as an example in the work of Marlow et al [21]. Two clear clusters with highly embedded links are visible at the top and right of the diagram; in the lower left of the diagram are smaller, sparser clusters together with a node that bridges between these clusters.

gests a natural predictor for identifying a user u's partner: select the link from u of maximum embeddedness, and propose the other end v of this link as u's partner.

We will evaluate this embeddedness-based predictor, and others, according to their *performance*: the fraction of instances on which they correctly identify the partner. Under this measure, embeddedness achieves a performance of 24.7% — which both provides evidence about the power of structural information for this task, but also offers a baseline that other approaches can potentially exceed.

Next, we show that it is possible to achieve more than twice the performance of this embeddedness baseline using our new network measure, *dispersion*. In addition to this relative improvement, the performance of our dispersion measure is very high in an absolute sense — for example, on married users in our sample, the friend who scores highest under this dispersion measure is the user's spouse over 60% of the time. Since each user in our sample has at least 50 friends, this performance is more than 30 times higher than random guessing, which would produce a performance of at most 2%.

Theoretical Basis for Dispersion.

We motivate the dispersion measure by first highlighting a basic limitation of embeddedness as a predictor, drawing on the theory of *social foci* [10]. Many individuals have large clusters of friends corresponding to well-defined foci of interaction in their lives, such as their cluster of co-workers or the cluster of people with whom they attended college. Since many people within these clusters know each other, the clusters contain links of very high embeddedness, even though they do not necessarily correspond to particularly strong ties. In contrast, the links to a person's relationship partner or other closest friends may have lower embeddedness, but they will often involve mutual neighbors from several different foci, reflecting the fact that the social orbits of these close friends are

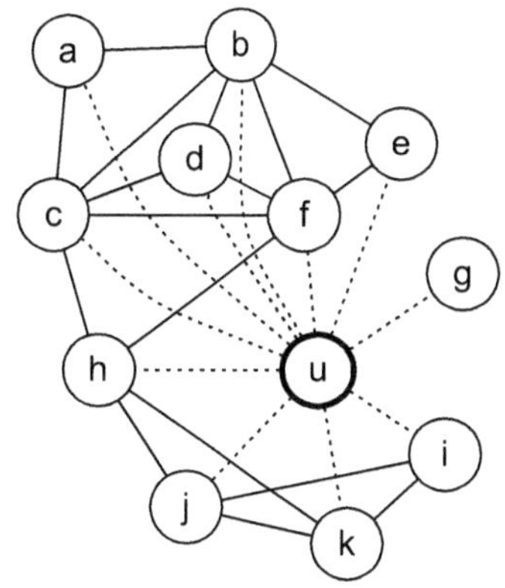

Figure 2. A synthetic example network neighborhood for a user u; the links from u to b, c, and f all have embeddedness 5 (the highest value in this neighborhood), whereas the link from u to h has an embeddedness of 4. On the other hand, nodes u and h are the unique pair of intermediaries from the nodes c and f to the nodes j and k; the u-h link has greater dispersion than the links from u to b, c, and f.

not bounded within any one focus — consider, for example, a husband who knows several of his wife's co-workers, family members, and former classmates, even though these people belong to different foci and do not know each other.

Thus, instead of embeddedness, we propose that the link between an individual u and his or her partner v should display a 'dispersed' structure: the mutual neighbors of u and v are not well-connected to one another, and hence u and v act jointly as the only intermediaries between these different parts of the network. (See Figure 2 for an illustration.)

We now formulate a sequence of definitions that captures this idea of dispersion. To begin, we take the subgraph G_u induced on u and all neighbors of u, and for a node v in G_u we define C_{uv} to be the set of common neighbors of u and v. To express the idea that pairs of nodes in C_{uv} should be far apart in G_u when we do not consider the two-step paths through u and v themselves, we define the *absolute dispersion* of the u-v link, $disp(u, v)$, to be the sum of all pairwise distances between nodes in C_{uv}, as measured in $G_u - \{u, v\}$; that is,

$$disp(u, v) = \sum_{s,t \in C_{uv}} d_v(s, t),$$

where d_v is a distance function on the nodes of C_{uv}. The function d_v need not be the standard graph-theoretic distance; different choices of d_v will give rise to different measures of absolute dispersion. As we discuss in more detail below, among a large class of possible distance functions, we ultimately find the best performance when we define $d_v(s, t)$ to be the function equal to 1 when s and t are not directly linked and also have no common neighbors in G_u other than u and v, and equal to 0 otherwise. For the present discussion, we will use this distance function as the basis for our measures of dispersion; below we consider the effect of alternative distance functions. For example, in Figure 2, $disp(u, h) = 4$ under this definition and distance function, since there are four pairs of nodes in C_{uh} that are not directly linked and also have no neighbors in common in $G_u - \{u, h\}$. In contrast, $disp(u, b) = 1$ in Figure 2, since a and e form the only pair

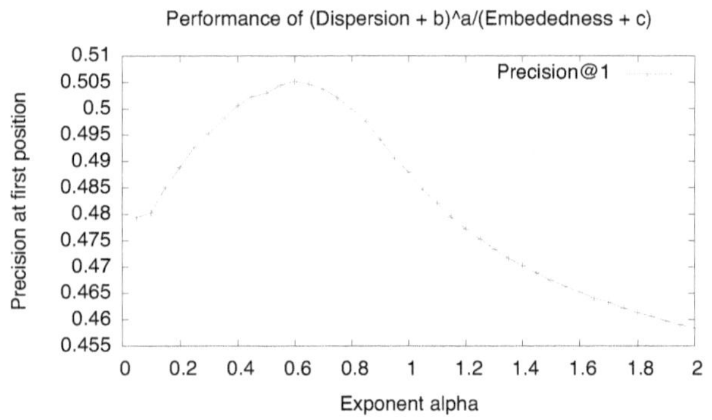

Figure 3. Performance of $(disp(u, v) + b)^{\alpha}/(emb(u, v) + c)$ as a function of α, when choosing optimal values of b and c.

type	embed	rec.disp.	photo	prof.view.
all	0.247	0.506	0.415	0.301
married	0.321	0.607	0.449	0.210
married (fem)	0.296	0.551	0.391	0.202
married (male)	0.347	0.667	0.511	0.220
engaged	0.179	0.446	0.442	0.391
engaged (fem)	0.171	0.399	0.386	0.401
engaged (male)	0.185	0.490	0.495	0.381
relationship	0.132	0.344	0.347	0.441
relationship (fem)	0.139	0.316	0.290	0.467
relationship (male)	0.125	0.369	0.399	0.418

Figure 4. The performance of different measures for identifying spouses and romantic partners: the numbers in the table give the *precision at the first position* — the fraction of instances in which the user ranked first by the measure is in fact the true partner. Averaged over all instances, recursive dispersion performs approximately twice as well as the standard notion of embeddedness, and also better overall than measures based on profile viewing and presence in the same photo.

of non-neighboring nodes in C_{ub} that have no neighbors in common in $G_u - \{u, b\}$.

Strengthenings of Dispersion.

We can learn a function that predicts whether or not v is the partner of u in terms of the two variables $disp(u, v)$ and $emb(u, v)$, where the latter denotes the embeddedness of the u-v link. We find that performance is highest for functions that are monotonically increasing in $disp(u, v)$ and monotonically decreasing in $emb(u, v)$: for a fixed value of $disp(u, v)$, increased embeddedness is in fact a negative predictor of whether v is the partner of u. A simple combination of these two quantities that comes within a few percent of more complicated functional forms can be obtained by the expression $disp(u, v)/emb(u, v)$, which we term the *normalized dispersion* $norm(u, v)$ since it normalizes the absolute dispersion by the embeddedness. Predicting u's partner to be the individual v maximizing $norm(u, v)$ gives the correct answer in 48.0% of all instances.

There are two strengthenings of the normalized dispersion that lead to increased performance. The first is to rank nodes by a function of the form $(disp(u, v) + b)^{\alpha}/(emb(u, v) + c)$. Searching over choices of α, b, and c leads to maximum performance of 50.5% at $\alpha = 0.61$, $b = 0$, and $c = 5$; see Figure 3. Alternately, one can strengthen performance by applying the idea of dispersion recursively — identifying nodes v for which the u-v link achieves a high normalized dispersion based on a set of common neighbors C_{uv} who, in turn, also have high normalized dispersion in their links with u. To carry out this recursive idea, we assign values to the nodes reflecting the dispersion of their links with u, and then update these values in terms of the dispersion values associated with other nodes. Specifically, we initially define $x_v = 1$ for all neighbors v of u, and then iteratively update each x_v to be

$$\frac{\sum_{w \in C_{uv}} x_w^2 + 2\sum_{s,t \in C_{uv}} d_v(s,t) x_s x_t}{emb(u, v)}.$$

Note that after the first iteration, x_v is $1 + 2 \cdot norm(u, v)$, and hence ranking nodes by x_v after the first iteration is equivalent to ranking nodes by $norm(u, v)$. We find the highest performance when we rank nodes by the values of x_v after the third iteration. For purposes of later discussion, we will call this value x_v in the third iteration the *recursive dispersion* $rec(u, v)$, and will focus on this as the main examplar from our family of related dispersion-based measures. (See the Appendix for further mathematical properties of the recursive dispersion.)

type	embed	rec.disp.	photo	prof.view.
all	0.391	0.688	0.528	0.389
married	0.462	0.758	0.561	0.319
married (fem)	0.488	0.764	0.538	0.350
married (male)	0.435	0.751	0.586	0.287
engaged	0.335	0.652	0.553	0.457
engaged (fem)	0.375	0.674	0.536	0.492
engaged (male)	0.296	0.630	0.568	0.424
relationship	0.277	0.572	0.460	0.498
relationship (fem)	0.318	0.600	0.440	0.545
relationship (male)	0.239	0.546	0.479	0.455

Figure 5. The performance of the four measures from Figure 4 when the goal is to identify the partner or a family member in the first position of the ranked list. The difference in performance between the genders has largely vanished, and in some cases is inverted relative to Figure 4.

PERFORMANCE OF STRUCTURAL AND INTERACTION MEASURES

We summarize the performance of our methods in Figure 4. Looking initially at just the first two columns in the top row of numbers ('all'), we have the overall performance of embeddedness and recursive dispersion — the fraction of instances on which the highest-ranked node under these measures is in fact the partner. As we will see below in the discussion around Figure 6, recursive dispersion also has higher performance than a wide range of other basic structural measures.

We can also compare these structural measures to features derived from a variety of different forms of real-time interaction between users — including the viewing of profiles, sending of messages, and co-presence at events. The use of such 'interaction features' as a comparison baseline is motivated by the way in which tie strength can be estimated from the volume of interaction between two people [8, 17]. Within this category of interaction features, the two that consistently display the best performance are to rank neighbors of u by the number of photos in which they appear with u, and to rank neighbors of u by the total number of times that u has viewed their profile page in the previous 90 days. The last two columns of Figure 4 show the performance of these two measures; on the set of instances as a whole, recursive dispersion performs better than these features.

The remaining rows of Figure 4 show the performance of these measures on different subsets of the data. Most users who report a relationship partner on Facebook list themselves as either 'married' or 'in a relationship,' with a smaller number who are 'engaged.' The performance of the structural measures is much higher for married users (60.7%) than for users in a relationship (34.4%); the opposite is true for profile viewing, which in fact achieves higher performance than recursive dispersion for users in a relationship. The performance for users who are engaged is positioned between the extremes of 'married' and 'in a relationship.'

In addition, we see important differences based on gender. The performance of structural measures is significantly higher for males than for females, suggesting some of the ways in which relationship partners produce more visible structural effects — at least according to these measures — on the network neighborhoods of men. And for certain more focused subsets of the data, the performance is even stronger; for example, on the subset corresponding to married male Facebook users in the United States, the friend with the highest recursive dispersion is the user's spouse 76.9% of the time.

We can also evaluate performance on the subset of users in same-sex relationships. Here we focus on users whose status is 'in a relationship.'[1] The relative performance of our structural measures is exactly the same for same-sex relationships as for the set of all relationships, with recursive dispersion achieving close to twice the performance of embeddedness, and slightly higher performance than absolute and normalized dispersion. For female users, the absolute level of performance is almost identical regardless of whether their listed partner is female or male; for male users, the performance is significantly higher for relationships in which the partner is male. (For a same-sex relationship listed by a male user, recursive dispersion identifies the partner with a performance of .450, in contrast with the performance of .369 for all partners of male users shown in Figure 4.)

Finally, returning to the set of all relationships, when the user v who scores highest under one of these measures is not the partner of u, what role does v play among u's network neighbors? We find that v is often a family member of u; for married users (Figure 5), the friend v that maximizes $rec(u, v)$ is the partner or a family member over 75% of the time. We also see that when we ask for the top-ranked friend to be either the partner or a family member, rather than just the partner, the performance gap between the genders essentially vanishes in the case of married users, and becomes inverted in the case of users in a relationship — in this latter case, female users are more likely to have their partner or a family member at the top of the ranking by recursive dispersion.

[1] There is significant informal evidence that the 'married' relationship status is employed by younger users of the same gender for a range of purposes even when they are not, in fact, married. While we only include users of age at least 20 in our sample, the effect is present in that age range. Listing a relationship status that does not correspond to one's off-line relationship is of course a concern across all categories of users, but from investigation of this issue, the 'married' status for users of the same gender is the only category for which we see evidence that this is a significant factor.

distance	type	all	marr.	eng.	rel.
threshold 2	absolute	0.279	0.361	0.205	0.152
	normalized	0.305	0.394	0.227	0.168
	recursive	0.210	0.279	0.141	0.105
threshold 3	absolute	0.430	0.530	0.359	0.270
	normalized	0.486	0.588	0.425	0.322
	recursive	0.506	0.607	0.446	0.344
threshold 4	absolute	0.473	0.568	0.414	0.321
	normalized	0.483	0.570	0.434	0.342
	recursive	0.455	0.539	0.405	0.319
diff component	absolute	0.380	0.461	0.317	0.253
	normalized	0.364	0.433	0.308	0.258
	recursive	0.323	0.384	0.276	0.228
diff community	absolute	0.286	0.368	0.212	0.160
	normalized	0.296	0.379	0.221	0.167
	recursive	0.216	0.283	0.156	0.115
spring length	absolute	0.379	0.474	0.307	0.229
	normalized	0.454	0.553	0.387	0.296
	recursive	0.396	0.480	0.341	0.261

Figure 6. Performance of variants of the dispersion measure using different underlying distance functions.

measure	all	married	engaged	relationship
betweenness	0.441	0.535	0.374	0.293
network constraint	0.307	0.394	0.232	0.171

Figure 7. Performance of betweenness and network constraint as alternate measures of bridging.

A Broader Set of Measures.

Since measures of dispersion are based on an underlying distance function d_v, it is interesting to investigate how the performance depends on the choice of d_v. In Figure 6, we consider dispersion measures based on a range of natural choices for d_v. as follows.

- First, we can set a distance threshold r, and declare that $d_v(s,t) = 1$ when s and t are at least r hops apart in $G_u - \{u, v\}$, and $d_v(s,t) = 0$ otherwise. The measure of dispersion we use above corresponds to the choice $r = 3$; setting the threshold $r = 2$ simply requires that s and t are not directly connected, while setting $r = 4$ imposes a stricter requirement.

- In a related vein, we could declare $d_v(s,t) = 1$ if s and t belong to different connected components of $G_u - \{u, v\}$, and $d_v(s,t) = 0$ otherwise. This in effect follows the preceding approach, but with the distance threshold r conceptually set to be infinite.

- Since the idea of dispersion at a more general level is based on the notion that the common neighbors of u and v should belong to different 'parts' of the network, it is also natural

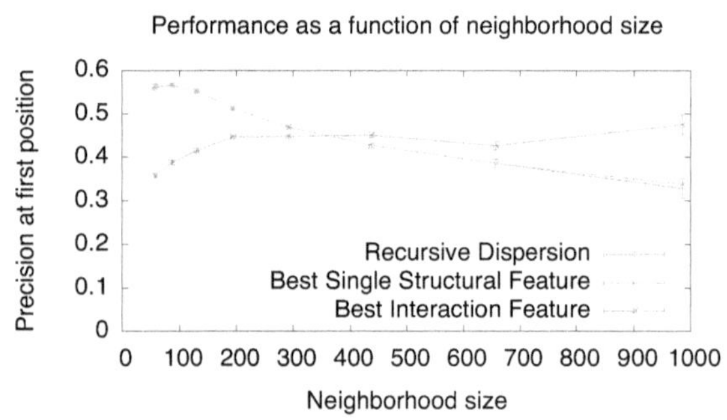

Figure 8. Performance as a function of user u's neighborhood size.

to divide $G_u - \{u\}$ into *communities* according to a network clustering heuristic, and then declare $d_v(s,t) = 1$ if and only if s and t belong to different communities. For this purpose, we use the *Louvain method* of Blondel et al for optimizing modularity [3], as implemented in the software package NetworkX. There is a wide range of methods available for inferring communities from network data [26]; we choose the Louvain method as a baseline because the graph $G - \{u\}$ for most users tends to have clearly defined *modules* of nodes, corresponding roughly to social foci, with a high density of links inside each module and a low density of links between them. Such modular structure is what the Louvain method is designed to identify.

- Related to partitions into communities, one can embed $G_u - \{u\}$ in the plane using an energy-minimization heuristic that treats each link of the graph as a spring with a fixed rest length. After computing such a spring embedding of $G_u - \{u\}$, one can then define $d_v(s,t)$ simply to be the distance between the locations of s and t in their embedding in the plane. Here too we use a heuristic implemented in NetworkX, in this case for spring embedding.

Figure 6 shows the performance of the absolute, normalized, and recursive dispersion based on all these possible distance functions d_v. (For all these distance functions, when the recursive process was carried out, the iteration other than the first producing the highest performance was always the third iteration, and so we continue to use the results in this third iteration as the definition of recursive dispersion.) As noted above, recursive dispersion using a distance function d_v based on a distance threshold of 3 produces the highest accuracy.

Finally, there are other measures of bridging that cannot be naturally expressed using the framework of dispersion. Two standard such measures are are *betweenness* and *network constraint* [5] applied to $G_u - \{u\}$. Figure 7 shows their performance; both score below the strongest dispersion measures, although betweenness has strong performance.

Performance as a Function of Neighborhood Size and Time on Site.

A further important source of variation among users is in the size of their network neighborhoods and the amount of time since they joined Facebook. These two properties are related; after a user joins the site, his or her network neighborhood will generally grow monontonically over time. This growth has two potential effects on the level of performance for our problem, acting in opposite directions: a more mature network neighborhood will have a greater level of complexity, which may hurt performance; but it will also likely reflect the user's off-line relationships in richer detail, which may help performance. It is thus natural to evaluate performance as a function of these parameters.

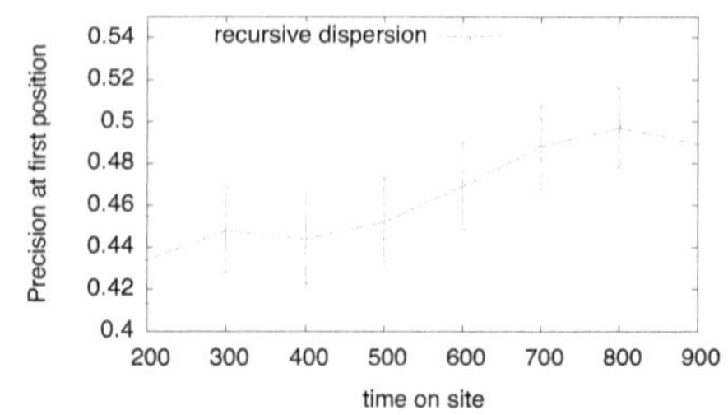

Figure 9. Performance as a function of time on site, for a subset of users where we control both the neighborhood size (between 100 and 150) and the time since the relationship was reported (between 100 and 200 days).

We begin by considering the size of the network neighborhood of the user u; recall that in our data, this size ranges from 50 to 2000. We find that recursive dispersion performs well across this full range: Figure 8 shows that, while performance is best when the neighborhood size is around 100 nodes (56%), it only drops moderately (to 33%) as the neighborhood size increases by an order of magnitude to 1000 nodes. This decline is quite small compared to the decline of the baseline that simply guesses a node uniformly at random, which would decrease in performance by a factor of 10 (from $1/100$ to $1/1000$). The modest decline of recursive dispersion may reflect the ways in which larger neighborhoods are also more informative about a user's full set of off-line relationships, which helps offset the considerably increased number of options for identifying the relationship partner. Furthermore, recursive dispersion is the highest-performing structural measure among those considered for every range of neighborhood sizes except the extremes (50 to 100, and above 1000); at the extremes, the (non-recursive) normalized dispersion is slightly better, although even here the recursive measure is within the margin of error of the best. Note that the median neighborhood size in our dataset is 205.

The benefits of large neighborhoods are reflected even more clearly when we consider the performance of interaction features — their performance tends to be approximately constant, or even increasing, as a function of neighborhood size. To elaborate on the arguments discussed above for how a larger neighborhood may help performance, we make two further observations. First, users with large neighborhoods also tend to be more active, and thus the relative variance of the interaction signals is smaller. Second, despite their large neighborhoods, previous analysis [21] has shown that the number of relationships that are actively maintained grows slowly in the total neighborhood size, and so the number of plausible candidates for the relationship partner grows more slowly than the pure neighborhood size would suggest.

We also consider a user's *time on site* — the number of days since they joined Facebook. This is strongly correlated with neighborhood size, since users continue acquiring friendship

type	max. struct.	max. inter.	all. struct.	all. inter.	comb.
all	0.506	0.415	0.531	0.560	0.705
married	0.607	0.449	0.624	0.526	0.716
engaged	0.446	0.442	0.472	0.615	0.708
relationship	0.344	0.441	0.377	0.605	0.682

Figure 10. The performance of methods based on machine learning that combine sets of features. The first two columns show the highest performing individual structural and interaction features; the third and fourth columns show the highest performance of machine learning classifiers that combine structural and interaction features respectively; and the fifth column shows the performance of a classifier that combines all structural and interaction features together.

links over their time on Facebook, and it is also correlated with the time since the relationship was first reported. (As we will see later in Figure 11, performance varies as a function of this latter quantity as well.) To understand whether there is any effect of a user's time on site beyond its relation to these other parameters, we consider a subset of users where we restrict the neighborhood size to lie between 100 and 150, and the time since the relationship was reported to lie between 100 and 200 days. Figure 9 shows that for this subset, there is a weak increase in performance as a function of time on site; while the effect is not strong, it points to a further source of enhanced performance for users with mature neighborhoods.

COMBINING FEATURES USING MACHINE LEARNING

Different features may capture different aspects of the user's neighborhood, and so it is natural to ask how well we can predict partners when combining information from many structural or interaction features via machine learning.

Machine Learning Techniques.

For our machine learning experiments, we compute 48 structural features and 72 interaction features for all of the nodes in the neighborhoods from our primary dataset. This gives us a total of approximately 18.7 million labeled instances with 120 features each — each instance consists of a node v in a neighborhood G_u, with a positive label indicating v is the partner of u, or a negative label indicating v is not.

The 48 structural features are the absolute and normalized dispersion based on six distinct distance functions defined for Figure 6, as well as the recursive versions using iterations 2 through 7 (recall that the recursive dispersion corresponds to the third iteration, and is hence included). The 72 interaction features represent a broad range of properties including the number of photos in which u and v are jointly tagged, the number of times u has viewed v's profile over the last 30, 60, and 90 days, the number of messages sent from u to v, the number of times that u has 'liked' v's content and vice versa, and measures based on a number of forms of interaction closely related to these.

To improve the performance of the learning algorithms, we transformed each of the 120 features into 4 different versions: (a) the raw feature, (b) a normalized version of the feature with mean 0 and standard deviation 1, (c) a rank version of the feature (where the individual with highest score on this feature has rank 1, and other individuals are sorted in ascending rank order from there), and (d) a rank-normalized version where we divide (c) by total number of friends a user has. Thus, the input to our machine learning algorithms has 480 features derived from 120 values per instance. In addition to the full set of features, we also compute performance using only the structural features, and only the interaction features.

We performed initial experiments with different machine learning algorithms and found that gradient tree boosting [13] out-performed logistic regression, as well as other tree-based methods. Thus, all of our in-depth analysis is conducted with this algorithm. In our experiments, we divide the data so that 50% of the users go into a training set and 50% go into a test set. We perform 12 such divisions into sets A and B; for each division we train on set A and test on B, and then train on B and test on A. For each user u, we average over the 12 runs in which u was a test user to get a final prediction.

Performance of Machine Learning Methods.

We find (Figure 10) that by using boosted decision trees to combine all of the 48 structural features we analyzed, we can increase performance from 50.8% to 53.1%. We can use the same technique to predict relationships based on interaction features. We find that, overall, interaction features perform slightly better than structural features (56.0% vs. 53.1%), though for married users, structural features do much better (62.4% vs. 52.6%). In addition, on all categories we find that the combination of interaction features and structural features significantly outperforms either on its own. When combining all features with boosted trees, the top predicted friend is the user's partner 70.5% of the time.

Machine Learning to Predict Relationship Status.

Earlier we noted that our focus is on the problem of identifying relationship partners for users where we know that they are in a relationship. It is natural to ask about the connection to a related but distinct question — estimating whether an arbitrary user is in a relationship or not.

This latter question is quite a different issue, and it seems likely to be more challenging and to require a different set of techniques. To see why, consider a user u who has a link of high dispersion to a user v. If we know that u is in a relationship, then v is a good candidate to be the partner. But our point from the outset has been that methods based on dispersion are useful more generally to identify individuals v with interesting connections to u, in the sense that they have been introduced into multiple foci that u belongs to. A user u can and generally will have such friends even when u is not in a romantic relationship. For example, Figure 5 suggests that family members often have this property, and this can apply to users who are not in romantic relationships as well as to users in such relationships. Thus, simply knowing that u has links of high dispersion should not necessarily give us much leverage in estimating whether u is in a relationship.

We now describe some basic machine-learning results that bear out this intuition. We took approximately 129,000 Facebook users, sampled uniformly over all users of age at least 20 with between 50 and 2000 friends. 40% of these users were single, while the remaining were either in a relationship, engaged, or married. We attempt two different predic-

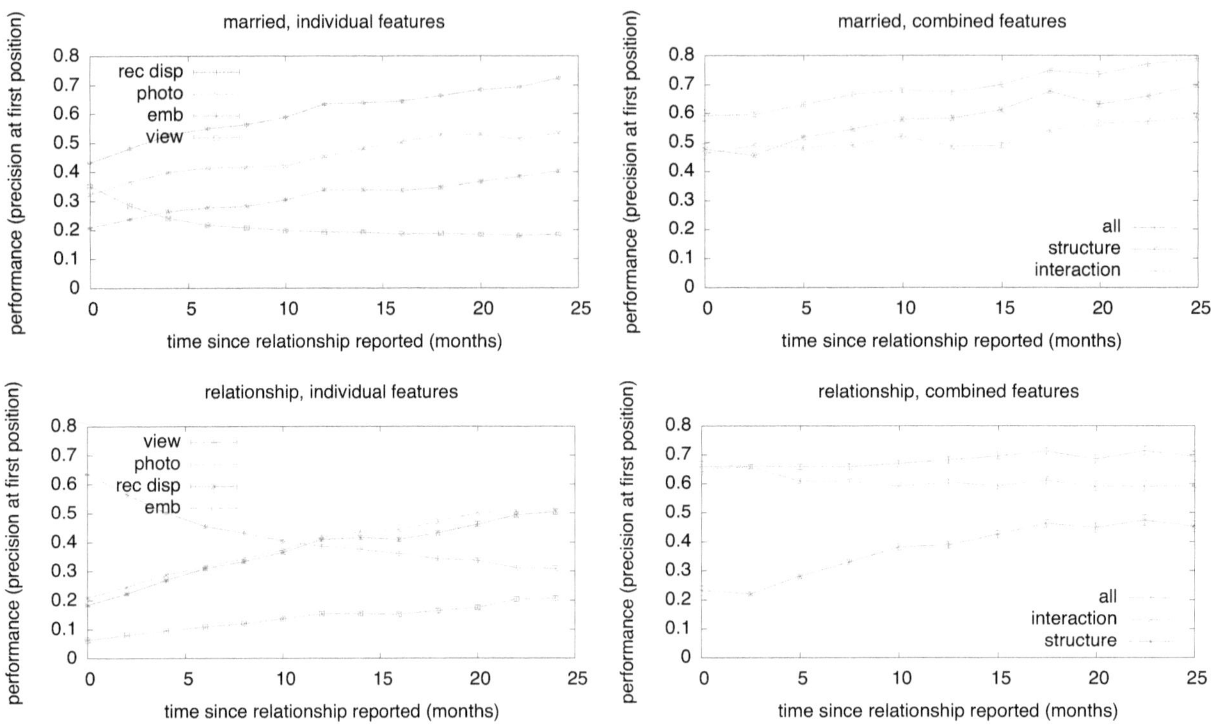

Figure 11. Performance at identifying partners for users who are (top row) married and (bottom row) in a relationship, as a function of the time since the relationship was reported on Facebook. In the two figures in the left-hand column, the four measures from Figure 4 are used individually. Here the structural measures have higher performance on older relationships, while the profile viewing feature has lower performance on older relationships; the profile viewing feature outperforms recursive dispersion for relationships reported recently, with the relative performance crossing at approximately one year. In the two figures in the right-hand column, the performance as a function of time is shown for prediction rules constructed using machine learning on a large set of features. Separate curves show the performance using only structural features, only interaction features, and when using the union of the two. Structural features peform best on older marriages, while interaction features perform best on new relationships.

Task	baseline	demo.	network	both
Single vs. Any Rel.	59.8%	67.9%	61.6%	68.3%
Single vs. Married	56.6%	78.0%	66.1%	79.0%

Figure 12. Performance on predicting relationship status. Baseline accuracy comes from predicting the more common class in each of the classification tasks. Demographic features seem more important, but network features also provide incremental improvement.

tion tasks: first, determining whether a user is in any sort of a relationship; and second, an easier task in which we look only at single and married users, and attempt to determine which category a user belongs to. We consider three different sets of features for these tasks: (i) demographic features (age, gender, country, and time on site); (ii) structural features of the network neighborhood, based on the definitions presented earlier; and (iii) the union of these two sets.

Figure 12 shows the performance on these tasks. Because age is a powerful feature for predicting relationship status, demographic features do well. Network features are not as strong, reflecting the notion discussed above that even users not in relationships have friends with similar structural properties. Despite this, network features convey non-trivial information about relationship status; they perform significantly above baseline prediction on their own, and add predictive power to demographic features. Of the network features, the maximum normalized dispersion (where the maximum is taken over all of the user's friends) has the highest feature importance.

TEMPORAL PROPERTIES

We now explore some of the ways in which these measures change over time. We first consider how performance varies based on the time since the relationship was first reported by the user — an approximate surrogate for the age of the relationship itself, although the relationship may clearly have existed for some time before it was reported (especially in the case of users who are already in a relationship when they join Facebook). We find (Fig. 11) that the structural measures are more accurate on older relationships than on newer ones, while the profile viewing feature is less accurate; in effect, the structural signature of the relationship needs time to 'burn in' to the network, while the interaction level via profile viewing is high almost immediately. For married users, recursive dispersion has the highest performance across the full time range, but for users in a relationship, an interesting crossover occurs: for relationships less than a year old, the profile viewing featured produces the highest performance, and then recursive dispersion and photo viewing surpass it at approximately one year. This illustrates a trade-off between a decreasing level of observation as a relationship goes on, contrasted with an increasing level of dispersion in the network as the link structure adapts around the two individuals.

Next, we ask how these measures change over time in the period leading up to a change in relationship status. For this purpose, we take a random sample of 29000 married users

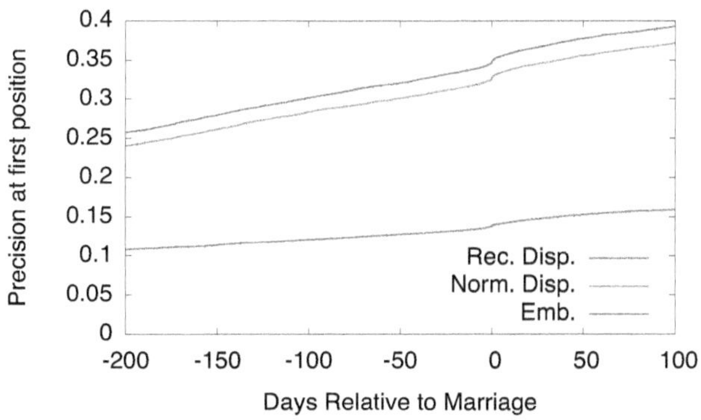

Figure 13. The performance of embeddedness and normalized and recursive dispersion increase as two people approach the point at which they announce their relationship status as 'married' (at time 0).

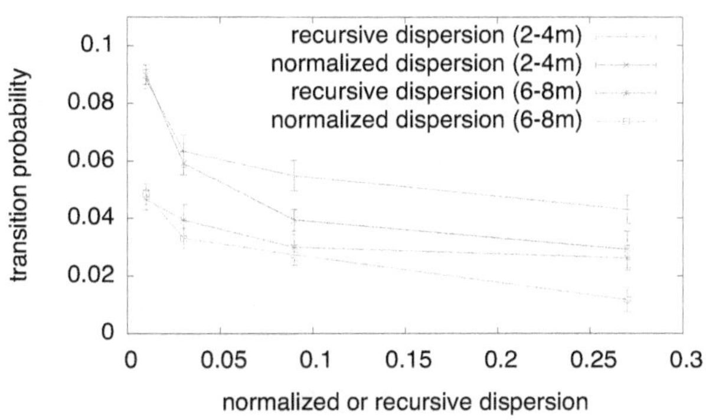

Figure 14. For different subsets of users, we can evaluate their *transition probability* from the status 'in a relationship' to the status 'single' over a 60-day period. These transition probabilities are shown as a function of both normalized and recursive dispersion, separately for relationships that are 2-4 months old and for relationships that are 6-8 months old. The transition probabilities decrease monotonically, and by significant factors, for users with high normalized or recursive dispersion to their respective partners.

whose relationship went through a succession of stages that were all reported on Facebook — first in a relationship, next engagement, and then (after a period of at least a month of engagement) marriage. For each user u in the sample, we compute embeddedness as well as normalized and recursive dispersion for all users in G_u as a function of time, declaring time 0 for u to be the moment at which u's marriage was reported. For a given network measure m, we then let $f_m(t)$ denote the fraction of instances in which u's (future or current) spouse scores highest with respect to m. We see (Fig. 13) that normalized and recursive dispersion rise quickly to the point of marriage, while embeddedness not only has lower performance but also rises more slowly. When both embeddedness and recursive dispersion eventually identify the spouse correctly, recursive dispersion does so an average of approximately 80 days sooner; in the analogous comparison between normalized and recursive dispersion, the latter identifies the spouse an average of approximately 10 days sooner.

Finally, we consider the persistence of relationships [20]. Given the effectiveness of these measures in detecting partners, is it also the case that partnerships that are more strongly identified by the measures are also more 'robust,' in the sense that they are more likely to persist over time? We address this

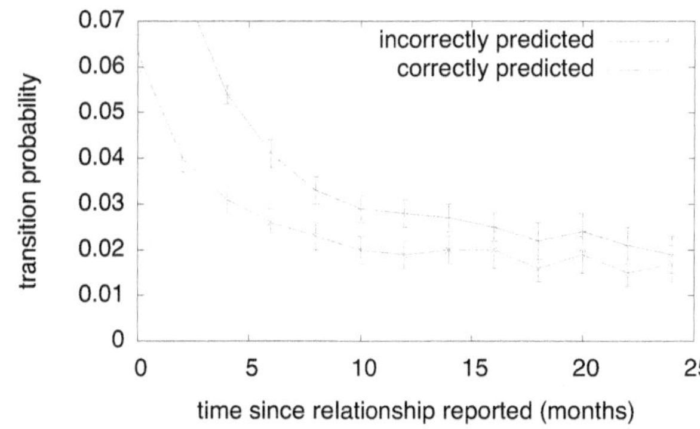

Figure 15. We plot the transition probability from 'in a relationship' to 'single' as a function of the age of the relationship, separately for relationships on which recursive dispersion correctly identifies the partner and those on which it does not. The transition probability is significantly higher when recursive dispersion fails to recognize the partner.

question by considering those users in our sample who listed themselves as being in a relationship (rather than married or some other relationship status, a set of roughly 400,000 individuals), and seeing which of them lists their relationship status as 'single' 60 days later. We perform these analyses on subsets of the data on which all relationships have roughly the same age since they were reported on Facebook, and on which all users were approximately the same age, to separate these effects from the underlying structural parameters. We find (Fig. 14) that a user whose partner has a high normalized or recursive dispersion is significantly less likely to transition to 'single' status over this time period.

We can view the persistence of relationships in a closely related way by comparing relationships on which recursive dispersion correctly identifies the partner to those on which it does not. We find (Fig. 15) that relationships on which recursive dispersion fails to correctly identify the partner are significantly more likely to transition to 'single' status over a 60-day period. This effect holds across all relationship ages and is particularly pronounced for relationships up to 12 months in age; here the transition probability is roughly 50% greater when recursive dispersion fails to recognize the partner.

BEYOND IMMEDIATE NEIGHBORHOODS

All of the network measures discussed above are based on the immediate 1-hop neighborhoods of individuals. It is interesting to consider how accurate more expansive methods might be, if they take the broader structure of the network into account. Because many individuals have 2-hop neighborhoods with hundreds of thousands of nodes, doing this is computationally challenging, and we must come up with heuristics to make it feasible.

Our approach is to take a single structural measure, recursive dispersion, and filter down to an individual's top 20 friends as ranked by this metric. We then compute the network measures discussed above in the (1-hop) neighborhoods of each of these 20 people. To evaluate a given friend v as the potential partner of u, we can then use the measures computed in u's neighborhood and also in v's. We find that the simple heuristic of taking u's top 20 friends with respect to $rec(u, v)$, and then ranking them by $\min(rec(u, v), rec(v, u))$, improves performance by about 6% to 0.534. This performs almost as well as more complex models, and confirms the intuitive result that relationship partners are best found by looking for pairs of people who have high scores in both directions.

CONCLUSION

Understanding the structural roles of significant people in online social network neighborhoods is a broad question that requires a combination of different approaches. Here we have considered this issue in the context of romantic partners, and have identified a novel network measure, dispersion, that provides a powerful method for recognizing the structural positions occupied by such partners from network data alone.

Drawing on the theory of social foci [10], we have argued that dispersion is a structural means of capturing the notion that a friend spans many contexts in one's social life — either because they were present through multiple life stages, or because they have been systematically introduced into multiple social circles. This suggests why it is not only spouses or romantic partners who exhibit high dispersion, but also family members — dispersion identifies people who span foci.

There are several applications where measures based on dispersion may play a role. For estimating which types of content from friends will be most engaging to a user [1], identifying individuals with this focus-spanning property can be useful for assessing their properties both as producers and consumers of content from different parts of a user's network neighborhood. And for organizing neighborhoods into distinct clusters or circles [23, 25], dispersion can help identify 'hard-to-categorize' individuals who may need manual annotation from a user — high dispersion arises precisely because a friend doesn't naturally fit into the obvious categories

Beyond these specific applications, our measures suggest new perspectives on basic questions in social network analysis. Overall, the notion that our mutual friends with a person may be clustered in a single context or may alternately span multiple contexts offers a novel type of trade-off in the study of tie strength. Certain important types of strong ties — including romantic and family relations — connect us to people who belong to multiple parts of our social neighborhood, producing a set of shared friends that is not simply large but also diverse, spanning disparate portions of the network and hence correspondingly sparse in their internal connections. In this way, the notion of dispersion combines concepts of network closure [6, 16] (since there must be mutual network neighbors to bridge) and brokerage between groups [5] (since the two ends of a link with large dispersion are jointly acting as brokers between disconnected mutual neighbors). The success of the measures resulting from this notion suggests some of the ways in which closure and brokerage are intertwined in the structure of strong ties.

The analysis shows how these classes of strong ties produce an extremely clear structural signature, but subtle network measures different from the standard formulations are needed to extract this signature. Crucial aspects of our everyday lives may be encoded in the network structure among our friends, provided that we look at this structure under the right lens.

Acknowledgments.
We thank Matt Brashears, Ben Cornwell, Lillian Lee, Michael Macy, Cameron Marlow, Sendhil Mullainathan, Brian Rubineau, and Johan Ugander for valuable discussions, and the Simons Foundation and NSF for support.

REFERENCES

1. Backstrom, L., Kleinberg, J. M., Lee, L., and Danescu-Niculescu-Mizil, C. Characterizing and curating conversation threads: expansion, focus, volume, re-entry. *Proc. 6th ACM WSDM*, 2013.
2. Bearman, P., Moody, J., and Stovel, K. Chains of affection: The structure of adolescent romantic and sexual networks. *American J. Sociology 110*, (2004).
3. Blondel, V. D., Guillaume, J.-L., Lambiotte, R., and Lefebvre, E. Fast unfolding of communities in large networks. *Journal of Statistical Mechanics* (2008).
4. Bott, E. *Family and Social Network: Roles, Norms, and External Relationships in Ordinary Urban Families*. Tavistock Press, 1957.
5. Burt, R. S. *Structural Holes: The Social Structure of Competition*. Harvard University Press, 1992.
6. Coleman, J. S. Social capital in the creation of human capital. *American J. Sociology 94*, (1988).
7. Cornwell, B. Spousal network overlap as a basis for spousal support. *J. Marriage and Family 74* (2012).
8. Eagle, N., Pentland, A. S., and Lazer, D. Inferring friendship network structure by using mobile phone data. *Proc. Natl. Acad. Sci. USA 106*, (2009).
9. Farnham, S., and Churchill, E. F. Faceted identity, faceted lives: social and technical issues with being yourself online. In *Proc. 14th ACM CSCW* (2011).
10. Feld, S. L. The focused organization of social ties. *American J. Sociology 86*, (1981).
11. Felmlee, D. H. No couple is an island: A social network perspective on dyadic stability. *Social Forces 79* (2001).
12. Fischer, C. *To Dwell Among Friends*. U. Chicago, 1982.
13. Friedman, J. H. Greedy function approximation: A gradient boosting machine. *Ann. Statistics 29* (2000).
14. Gilbert, E., and Karahalios, K. Predicting tie strength with social media. In *Proc. 27th ACM Conference on Human Factors in Computing Systems* (2009), 211–220.
15. Granovetter, M. The strength of weak ties. *American Journal of Sociology 78* (1973), 1360–1380.
16. Granovetter, M. Economic action and social structure: The problem of embeddedness. *Amer. J. Soc.* 91(1985).
17. Jones, J. J., Settle, J. E., Bond, R. M., Fariss, C. J., Marlow, C., and Fowler, J. H. Inferring tie strength from online directed behavior. *PLoS ONE 8* (2013)
18. Kalmijn, M. Shared friendship networks and the life course. *Social Networks 25* (2003).

19. Kossinets, G., and Watts, D. Empirical analysis of an evolving social network. *Science 311* (2006), 88–90.

20. Le, B., Dove, N. L., Agnew, C. R., Korn, M. S., and Mutso, A. A. Predicting nonmarital romantic relationship dissolution: A meta-analytic synthesis. *Personal Relationships 17*, 3 (Sept. 2010), 377–390.

21. Marlow, C., Byron, L., Lento, T., and Rosenn, I. Maintained relationships on Facebook, 2009. On-line at http://overstated.net/2009/03/09/maintained-relationships-on-facebook The cited figures and results from this work, including Figure 1, are reproduced with permission in the book *Networks, Crowds, and Markets* (D. Easley and J. Kleinberg, Cambridge University Press, 2010.).

22. Marsden, P. V., and Campbell, K. E. Measuring tie stength. *Social Forces 63*, 2 (Dec. 1984), 482–501.

23. McAuley, J. J., and Leskovec, J. Learning to discover social circles in ego networks. *Proc. NIPS* (2012).

24. McPherson, M., Smith-Lovin, L., and Brashears, M. E. Social isolation in America: Changes in core discussion networks over two decades. *Am. Soc. Rev. 71* (2006).

25. Min, J.-K., Wiese, J., Hong, J. I., and Zimmerman, J. Mining smartphone data to classify life-facets of social relationships. In *Proc. 16th ACM CSCW* (2013).

26. Newman, M. E. J. The structure and function of complex networks. *SIAM Review 45* (2003), 167–256.

27. Onnela, J.-P., Saramaki, J., Hyvonen, J., Szabo, G., Lazer, D., Kaski, K., Kertesz, J., and Barabasi, A.-L. Structure and tie strengths in mobile communication networks. *Proc. Natl. Acad. Sci. USA 104* (2007).

28. Zhao, X., Sosik, V. S., and Cosley, D. It's complicated: how romantic partners use Facebook. In *Proc. 30th ACM Conf. Human Factors in Computing Systems* (2012).

APPENDIX: MATHEMATICAL PROPERTIES OF THE RECURSIVE DISPERSION

This section provides some motivation and further mathematical detail related to the recursive dispersion, to help isolate the ingredients that make up its functional form.

First, fix a distance function d_v on the graph $G - \{u, v\}$. We first note that if we assign a value $x_s = 1$ to each node s in G_u, then $\sum_{s,t \in C_{uv}} d_v(s,t)x_s x_t$ is precisely the dispersion of v, since it is a sum over all pairwise distances in C_{uv}. Hence,

$$\frac{\sum_{s,t \in C_{uv}} d_v(s,t)x_s x_t}{emb(u,v)}$$

is the normalized dispersion.

The premise underlying the recursive dispersion is to elevate x_v when u and v act as intermediaries between many node pairs s and t that, recursively, have large values of x_s and x_t. A simple way to carry out this idea would be to define an iteration in which x_v is updated to be

$$x_v \longleftarrow \frac{\sum_{s,t \in C_{uv}} d_v(s,t)x_s x_t}{emb(u,v)}, \qquad (1)$$

directly using the functional form of the normalized dispersion. The problem with this approach on the graphs G_u that we have in the data is that the sum in the numerator is equal to 0 for many nodes v. This in turn means that even more nodes will acquire a 0 value in subsequent iterations; the end result is that very few nodes end up with a positive value x_v, and this would hurt the performance in identifying partners.

As a result, it is useful to have a mechanism that continuously introduces non-zero weight into the system. As a working guideline for how to do this, we would like the first iteration to produce values x_v whose sorted order agrees with the order of values according to normalized dispersion, so that subsequent iterations can be viewed as building from this measure. We would also like additional terms in the numerator to be quadratic, to match the quadratic degree of the existing terms in the numerator of (1). Adding $\sum_{w \in C_{uv}} x_w^2$ to the numerator achieves these two properties in a simple way — it is quadratic, and in the first iteration it is equal to $emb(u,v)$, and hence is canceled by the denominator. This gives us the functional form that we use as the recursive dispersion:

$$x_v \longleftarrow \frac{\sum_{w \in C_{uv}} x_w^2 + 2\sum_{s,t \in C_{uv}} d_v(s,t)x_s x_t}{emb(u,v)}. \qquad (2)$$

Depending on the structure of G_u, the right-hand side of (2) can simplify in several instructive ways. In what follows, we will also write $emb(u,v)$ in an equivalent form as $|C_{uv}|$.

- First, suppose G_u has the property that $d_v(s,t) = 1$ whenever s and t belong to the set C_{uv}. For example, with our distance function d_v, this would hold if the graph $G_u - \{u\}$ had no cycle of length less than 5; in this case, for any v and any $s, t \in C_{uv}$, there could be no common neighbor of s and t other than u and v, and so $d_v(s,t) = 1$. In this case, the iteration in (2) becomes

$$x_v \longleftarrow \frac{\sum_{w \in C_{uv}} x_w^2 + 2\sum_{s,t \in C_{uv}} x_s x_t}{emb(u,v)} = \frac{\left(\sum_{w \in C_{uv}} x_w\right)^2}{|C_{uv}|} \qquad (3)$$

  and so the values evolve according to an iteration that simply sums values at neighboring nodes and then squares the sum (with normalization).

- Alternately, suppose G_u has the property that $d_v(s,t) = 0$ for all pairs of nodes s and t that belong to the same set C_{uv}. For example, again using our distance function d_v, this would be true if every pair of nodes at distance 2 in G_u had at least two common neighbors other than u. In this case, if in a given iteration we have $x_s = c$ for all s, then in the next iteration

$$x_v \longleftarrow \frac{\sum_{w \in C_{uv}} x_w^2}{emb(u,v)} = \frac{c^2|C_{uv}|}{|C_{uv}|} = c^2, \qquad (4)$$

  and so all values remain equal to each other. Thus, for such a G_u, all nodes have the same recursive dispersion.

These two special cases represent different conceptual extremes, and most graphs will lie in between. It is an interesting open question to understand the convergence properties of recursive dispersion in arbitrary graphs.

Facebook Makes the Heart Grow Fonder: Relationship Maintenance Strategies Among Geographically Dispersed and Communication-Restricted Connections

Jessica Vitak
College of Information Studies
University of Maryland
4105 Hornbake Bldg, South Wing
College Park, MD 20742
jvitak@umd.edu

ABSTRACT

The increasing ubiquity of information and communication technologies has dramatically impacted interpersonal communication and relationship maintenance processes. These technologies remove temporal and spatial constraints, enabling communication at a distance for low to no physical costs. Research has established that technologies such as email supplement other forms of communication in relationship maintenance, but to what extent do newer technologies—which contain a unique set of affordances—facilitate these processes? Furthermore, do SNS users engage in different practices through the site and obtain different relational benefits based on specific characteristics of the tie? Findings from a survey of adult Facebook users (N=415) indicate that geographically distant Facebook Friends, as well as those who rely on the site as their primary form of communication, engage in relationship maintenance strategies through the site to a greater extent and perceive the site to have a more positive impact on the quality of their relationships.

Author Keywords

Facebook; relationship maintenance; social network sites; computer-mediated communication; interpersonal communication

ACM Classification Keywords

H.5.3. Group and Organization Interfaces – Web-based Interaction

INTRODUCTION

Research over the last decade has established that technologies such as email [2, 3, 23, 26, 42] and instant messaging [37, 47] play an important role in the relationship maintenance process, often supplementing other forms of communication when physical distance prohibits frequent face-to-face communication. These technologies have generally taken a back seat to "richer" communication channels such as phone calls and in-person interactions, with mediated channels often—but not always (e.g., [2])—rated as less important for maintaining relationships. That said, a major difference exists between email and IM, in which individuals communicate through a more private channel and interactions are often one-on-one, and SNSs like Facebook, which prioritize public, one-to-many communication. Facebook provides a low-cost mechanism through which to connect and interact with a wide range of people, and users appear to be embracing the site's many interaction-centric features, as seen in the high frequency of daily and weekly use of features such as "Liking" content, commenting on status updates, and commenting on photos by American adults [21].

Furthermore, communication technologies make it increasingly easy to maintain relationships at a distance through a variety of channels. While keeping in touch with friends who had moved away was once costly—both in terms of time and financial investments—these technologies have removed temporal and spatial constraints that once caused many long-distance relationships to fade away. Instead, friends are able to keep in touch through emails, text messages, and Facebook posts, all for a minimal investment. Even Robin Dunbar [15], who has generally been dismissive of SNSs as a source of meaningful interaction, conceded: "I suspect that Facebook's one great contribution has been to slow down that rate of relationship decay by allowing us to keep in touch with friends over long distances" (p. 83).

But can these technologies do more than simply "slow down" relational decay? Instead, can sites meant to connect people and facilitate communication benefit the relationship maintenance process and, for some dyads, even improve relational quality? While face-to-face communication is undoubtedly important for relationship maintenance, and especially important for one's closest ties [12, 13], Facebook may serve an important role for those

CSCW'14, February 15–19, 2014, Baltimore, Maryland, USA.
Copyright © 2014 ACM 978-1-4503-2540-0/14/02...$15.00.
http://dx.doi.org/10.1145/2531602.2531726

connections for whom one cannot see in person but can stay connected to through the site. Therefore, the present study presents results from an empirical study of adult Facebook users on their use of the site to stay connected with a randomly[1] selected Facebook Friend. The data will be analyzed to determine if there are main effects of geographic distance and communication channel on users' engagement in a set of relationship maintenance strategies, as well as the degree to which they perceive their use of the site impacts the quality of their relationship with that Friend.

Findings from this study expand research on new communication technologies' role in relationship maintenance processes, especially among more casual relationships, which are an understudied group but comprise the majority of relationships on these sites.

TECHNOLOGY'S ROLE IN RELATIONSHIP MAINTENANCE

How do people use computer-mediated communication (CMC) to maintain relationships with various types of connections? Early research focused on email and instant messaging's (IM) role in relationship maintenance, highlighting differences between email's asynchroncity and IM's more natural, "real-time" interactions. For example, Stafford, Kline, and Dimmick [42] found that email was used more frequently for interpersonal communication than for personal gain, business, or gratification opportunities, while Johnson and colleagues [26] found a number of differences in the maintenance strategies employed in emails sent to family, friends, and romantic partners, but few differences between emails sent to recipients geographically close versus those who lived much farther away. Longitudinal research by both Ramirez and Broneck [37] and Valkenburg and Peter [47] found that IM was employed as a relationship maintenance mechanism and was positively correlated with various relational outcome measures.

When considering long-distance relationships, statistics suggest that millions of Americans are involved in long-distance relationships at any given time [39], and CMC has become a mainstay for maintaining these relationships while partners are physically separated. Research has established positive correlations between use of CMC in long-distance relationships and increased levels of love and intimacy [20] and trust [8]. More recent research by Johnson and colleagues [27] found similarities in how geographically close and long-distance friends defined closeness, with a focus on "self-disclosure" and "help and support," both of which can be provided through CMC (as opposed to other resources that may require physical proximity).

[1] See Method section for details regarding how participants selected the Friend they rated in the study.

Facebook and Relationship Maintenance

The emergence of social media—and specifically social network sites—in recent years has further encouraged relationship maintenance through online communication channels. Tong and Walther [46] note four features of SNSs that aid the relationship maintenance process: asynchronous communication, which removes temporal constraints; control over dissemination of content; features to foster interaction, participation, and feedback; and the ability to share and embed multimedia messages, including photos, links, and video. These features expand on previous forms of communication in a number of ways, most notably by simplifying the process of passively consuming content produced by one's Friends (via Facebook's News Feed, Twitter's tweet stream, etc.) and by providing diverse communication methods that include both text-based and audio-visual sources. And contrary to some recent commentary (e.g., [15]) suggesting these sites' only contribution to relationship maintenance is extending their lifespan beyond what would have existed without the technology, recent empirical data suggest that SNS users have more close connections [21], more face-to-face interactions with close friends [4], more acquaintances [4], and more diverse networks [21] than non-users. Furthermore, relationship maintenance is consistently referenced as a major reason for use of SNSs across different populations [28, 29, 33].

The most popular SNS, Facebook, currently maintains a user base exceeding one billion active users worldwide. Among Internet-using U.S. adults, 72% have profiles on a SNS [5] and 92% of SNS-using adults [21] (67% of all Internet users [14]) have a Facebook profile. Relationship maintenance occurs at a number of levels through Facebook. At its most basic level, Friending another user provides access to profile information and (typically) increases the ability to interact with another user, as well as to passively consume information without formal interaction. Users can communicate with each other through public (status updates, comments, and Likes) and private (chat, closed groups, and messages) features, exchanging personal information and providing resources such as support and information. Use of Facebook to send birthday wishes is viewed by many as a form of relationship maintenance [45] and in some cases, constitutes the only directed communication between two Friends [48].

While communicating through Facebook is generally seen as a supplement to other forms of interaction, much as email was in the work of Barry Wellman more than a decade ago [23], research has yet to address whether using Facebook may function in a role beyond just "filling in the gap" when other forms of communication are unavailable or less desirable. In other words, researchers have yet to empirically address whether specific uses of Facebook improve the quality of users' relationships with some of their Facebook Friends and, if so, for whom those improvements are most likely to occur. For example,

Facebook may be the only communication channel employed by some relational dyads. In these cases, Facebook is not supplementing other forms of communication; rather, it is the sole link keeping the two people connected. These questions will be addressed in the next section.

Research Questions and Hypotheses

Even though CMC researchers have pointed to the affordances of technology in facilitating communication and relationship maintenance among more casual relationships, many researchers still focus on individuals' closest ties—who also tend to be geographically proximate. While it is likely that people use a greater quantity of communication channels [24] and use certain channels with more frequency when interacting with their closer ties, little research has examined differences in communication patterns across various types of relational dyads, with a few notable exceptions (e.g., [1]). On Facebook, this is of special interest, as users may be relying on the site as the primary form of communication to stay in touch with more geographically distant and weaker ties.

To determine how Facebook use affects individuals' relationship maintenance strategies—and how that use varies across different types of relationships—a number of analyses will be proposed. Specifically, research questions and hypotheses will examine differences between geographically proximate versus distant ties, as well as between individuals who rely on Facebook as their sole or primary communication method with a specific Friend versus those who communicate through a wider variety of channels (e.g., phone, email, face-to-face, IM).

At its most basic level, relationship maintenance is about communication and interaction between partners. As Dindia [10] notes, "To maintain a relationship, partners must communicate with one another... The end of a relationship occurs when people stop communicating" (p. 1). While various studies have established communication behaviors individuals perform on the site (e.g., [21]), only Ledbetter et al. [32] has examined differences in communication across variations in ties, finding that frequency of communication (both on Facebook and through more traditional channels) positively predicted relational closeness. In other words, as engagement in interaction through Facebook's many communication features increased, so did perceived emotional closeness ratings. The present study will first determine if differences exist in how Facebook users employ the site's communication features to interact with Friends who live both nearby (i.e., in the same town) and far away (i.e., more than a day's travel).

> RQ1: Does frequency of Facebook communication vary based on geographic proximity of the Friend?

A more rigorous evaluation of relationship maintenance on Facebook requires examining the strategies users employ to stay connected with their Friends. Once formed, relationships are maintained through a series of behaviors and routines [12]. The most commonly used measure for relationship maintenance, Stafford and Canary's Relationship Maintenance Strategies Measure (RMSM) [41], includes five subscales: positivity, openness, assurances, networks, and shared tasks. As noted in the Method section, this measure has a number of flaws when applied to a setting such as Facebook, which includes significant variance in both the relational closeness of ties [19] as well as geographic proximity. Recent research by Vitak [49] developed a four-factor relationship maintenance measure that accounts for both the specific affordances of SNSs as well as the extensive previous work on relationship maintenance in offline settings. If Facebook is serving a supplemental or relationship-enhancing role, we would expect to see geographically distant Friends more engaged in these relationship strategies. Furthermore, because of the site's many communication features, we would expect that Friends who live at a greater distance from one another would perceive Facebook as having a greater impact on the quality of the relationship than Friends who live near one another (and can presumably meet up in person more frequently).

> H1: Individuals will report greater engagement in Facebook relationship maintenance strategies with a geographically distant Facebook Friend than with a geographically proximate Friend.

> H2: Individuals will perceive their use of Facebook as having a more positive impact on the quality of their relationship with a geographically distant Facebook Friend than with a geographically proximate Friend.

In addition—and perhaps concurrent—to geographically distant connections, another type of dyad that might see relational benefits from using Facebook are those who rely on the site as their primary form of communication. Facebook users have large networks on the site, with the majority of those connections categorized as weak ties [50]. Whether living in the same town or in another country, Facebook may be the only point of connection between these connections, who may include old high school friends, coworkers from previous jobs, people met at a conference or on a vacation, friends of friends, and more. As there is no cost to staying "Friends" once the technical connection has been made, many Facebook users see little reason to remove these weaker ties from their network [51]. Furthermore, Facebook may provide the only point of contact with these people, enabling them to passively keep in touch through viewing content the other has posted, and through more interactive communication, such as commenting and sharing posts, such as birthday wishes [48]. While geographic constraints are likely to be a factor in many of these relationships, another major reason for preferring Facebook communication is the ease and convenience of using the site over more costly forms of communication.

That said, people who primarily rely on Facebook to communicate with a social tie are likely to place a higher value on the site and be more engaged in relationship maintenance than those who interact through other channels in addition to Facebook because the site is providing them with valuable relational information that would be more difficult to obtain or would likely be delayed if it were obtained through alternate channels. Therefore:

> H3: Compared with those who communicate through multiple channels, those for whom Facebook serves as a primary form of communication will report higher engagement in Facebook relationship maintenance strategies with a specific Facebook Friend.

> H4: Compared with those who communicate through multiple channels, those for whom Facebook serves as a primary form of communication will perceive Facebook to have a greater impact on the quality of their relationship with a specific Facebook Friend.

METHOD

In order to compare usage characteristics across a diverse set of relational dyads, 3000 non-faculty staff at a large U.S. university were invited, via email, to participate in an online survey regarding their use of Facebook in October 2012. The invitation email stated that having a Facebook account was a requirement for participation. The survey remained open for two weeks and garnered 415 responses. Respondents were generally female (76.2%), 44 years old (*SD*=11.12; range: 22–71), White (88.9%), and well-educated, with the majority of participants having a college degree (72.2%), and 32.5% having post-graduate training.

Procedure

Upon providing informed consent, participants were instructed to log into their Facebook account and select a Facebook Friend for whom they would then respond to a series of questions. At the time of data collection, all profiles had been converted to the Timeline layout and a rectangular Friends box appeared in the right column immediately below the main header. Participants were told to select the person in the top left position of the Friends box to provide a pseudo-random distribution of connections (see [32] for more details). This method was chosen to move beyond the common practice of having participants select a "friend" to evaluate, which skews responses heavily toward very close ties (e.g., [30, 35]). This method appeared to be successful in creating more variance in perceived tie strength, as the closeness scale employed in the study [9] was normally distributed (*M*=2.95, *SD*=1.10 on a 5-point Likert-type scale).

After selecting a Friend for the survey, participants entered the person's name (or a pseudonym if they so chose) and continued on with the survey. Whatever name they entered into this field auto-filled throughout the rest of the survey for all items to reinforce that the participant should focus only on their relationship and behaviors with that one person. Participants answered questions about the frequency with which they communicated with the person on- and offline; their relational closeness, satisfaction, and access to social provisions; the specific behaviors they engaged in with the person through Facebook; the extent to which they perceived Facebook impacted their relational quality; and demographic items. Finally, participants were invited to enter their email address to be entered into a drawing for one of 20 $25 Amazon gift cards. Email addresses were removed from the dataset prior to analysis.

Measures

Below are details for measures included in the present study's analyses.

Facebook's Impact on Relational Outcomes

From a corpus of 19 items, exploratory factor analysis (principal components analysis with Promax rotation) extracted two factors that captured various ways in which use of the site might make one feel closer to another Friend and maintain a relationship that might otherwise fade away without the technology (see Table 1 for items, means, and standard deviations). *Facebook's Impact on Relational Closeness* (α=.92, *M*=2.91, *SD*=.99) includes five items capturing positive relational outcomes associated with Facebook use, including helping one understand a friend better, feel closer to that friend, and improving the relationship (e.g., "Facebook helps me understand (person's name) better"). *Facebook's Impact on Relational Stability* (α=.83, *M*=2.76, *SD*=1.01) includes four items that focus on the users' perceptions of the role Facebook plays in keeping the relationship in existence (e.g., "Without Facebook, (person's name) and I would fall out of touch").

Relationship Maintenance Behaviors

As previously noted, researchers have used Stafford and Canary's [41] relationship maintenance measure for over two decades. While this scale has been validated [31] and applied [36, 52] in various online settings, a major limitation to this measure is that many of the individual items in the measure are predicated on geographic proximity. Furthermore, revisions to the scale (e.g., [7, 40]) have continued to stress face-to-face interactions. For example, friends who live in different cities are less likely to share tasks or engage in joint activities. A second critique of research on relationship maintenance has been its narrow focus on close, typically romantic, relationships, and the most widely used measures (e.g., [40, 41]) have focused on strategies romantically involved couples use to keep their relationship equitable. However, this becomes problematic when trying to measure relationship maintenance behaviors among a more diverse set of relationships.

A goal of the larger research project (of which this study is a part) was to evaluate existing streams of research on relationship maintenance and develop a new measure that accounted for the specific affordances of SNSs, as well as

Facebook's Impact on Relational Closeness (*M*=2.91, *SD*=.99)	**M**	**SD**
Facebook makes me feel closer to (person's name).	2.91	1.19
Facebook has positively impacted my relationship with (person's name).	3.08	1.14
Facebook helps me understand (person's name) better.	2.90	1.12
Interacting with (person's name) through Facebook makes me feel like I know him/her better.	2.91	1.16
Being Facebook Friends with (person's name) has improved our relationship.	2.78	1.06
Facebook's Impact on Relational Stability (*M*=2.76, *SD*=1.01)	**M**	**SD**
Without Facebook, (person's name) and I would fall out of touch.	2.28	1.24
Facebook is the only way I stay in touch with (person's name).	3.20	1.24
Overall, Facebook isn't very important in maintaining my relationship with (person's name).	2.80	1.17
Facebook plays an important role in maintaining my relationship with (person's name).	3.17	1.31

Table 1: Means and standard deviations for dependent variables

to more accurately account for the types of relationships represented in users' Facebook networks. Based on the results of the study (see [49] for details), a four-factor measure of Facebook Relationship Strategies was developed. These factors are used in all analyses.

Supportive Communication (*M*=3.68, *SD*=.82, α=.88) includes seven items that target specific behaviors users perform through the site to signal support for a specific Friend, such as liking a post or sending birthday wishes, and are indicative of social grooming [11], which is an important component of relationship maintenance. *Shared Interests* (*M*=2.33, *SD*=.88, α=.87) includes seven items that focus on how users engage with Facebook's features to share content and interact about commonalties they share with a Friend, whether through a Facebook Group they both belong to, through posting links on each others' Walls, or using other site features to communicate with each other. *Passive Browsing* (*M*=2.91, *SD*=.89, α=.85) includes four items that measure both the frequency and the level of agreement participants report about browsing a Friend's profile page and photo albums. As identified by Metzger et al. [34] and Burke et al. [6], passive behaviors, such as viewing a Friend's profile, are among the most common behaviors users perform on the site. *Social Information Seeking* (*M*=2.73, *SD*=.86, α=.79) includes five items tapping into two inter-related reasons for using the site: first, to keep up-to-date on individuals' more mundane activities (i.e., everyday news), which numerous relationship maintenance researchers have highlighted as a key component to maintaining a relationship in a satisfactory state (e.g., [10]); and, second, to learn new things about the other person, which may help establish common ground and strengthen the relationship.

Relational Closeness

Dibble et al.'s [9] validated 10-item unidimensional relationship closeness scale was included in the instrument. Confirmatory factor analysis suggested the full, 10-item scale was not a good fit to the data, so one item was removed and several covariance paths were added between error estimates. The final, nine-item scale included in analyses (*M*=2.69, *SD*=.61) was a good fit to the data, $\chi 2(19)=44.64$, p=.001, CFI=.994, RMSEA=.058, and was reliable (α=.85).

Geographic Distance Between Friends

Participants were asked to estimate how far away the selected Friend lived from among six options: (1) less than a 30-minute drive, (2) 30 minutes-1 hour drive, (3) 1-2 hour drive, (4) 2-4 hour drive, (5) 4-6 hour drive, (6) 6+ hour drive. The options were meant to provide a range of responses from in-town friends to those requiring a flight or multiple days worth of travel. Participants reported that their selected Friend lived, on average, slightly over two hours away (*M*=3.13, *SD*=2.05), although the item exhibited a bimodal distribution, with a significant percentage of responses in the closest geographic category (33.9%) and the farthest geographic category (27.8%). See Figure 1 for a histogram of the distribution of the variable (range=1-6).

Traditional Communication Frequency

The instrument asked participants to rate the frequency with which they interacted with their selected Friend through six communication channels that were non-Facebook-specific: in-person, phone calls, text messages, email, non-Facebook instant messages, and video calls like Skype. Items were measured on a five-point scale ranging from 1=Never to 5=Very Often.

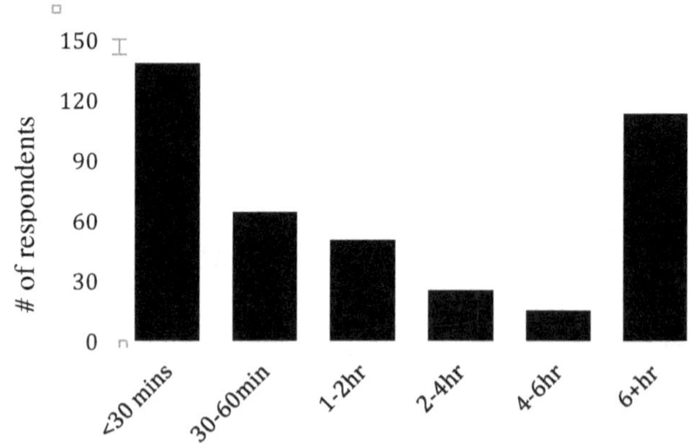

Figure 1. Histogram of responses to geographic distance question

Full Variable Name	Shorthand	Description
Facebook's Impact on Relational Closeness	FBClose	DV measuring extent to which use of Facebook affects perceived closeness
Facebook's Impact on Relational Stability	FBStability	DV measuring extent to which user perceives Facebook keeps relationship in existence
Supportive Communication	SuppComm	Maintenance strategy performed to signal support
Shared Interests	SharedInt	Maintenance strategy supporting a shared interest
Passive Consumption	PassCon	Maintenance strategy involving passive consumption of content
Social Information Seeking	SocialInfo	Maintenance strategy performed to learn new information and keep up-to-date on everyday information
Relational Closeness	RelCloseness	Emotional intensity of relationship
Geographic Closeness	GeoCloseness	Geographic proximity between two people
Traditional Communication Frequency	Identified by behavior	Frequency of engagement in face-to-face, phone calls, text messages, email, IM, and video calls with Facebook Friend (measured individually)
Facebook Communication Frequency	Identified by behavior	Frequency of engagement in private messages, Chat, private Groups, Wall posts, comments, Likes, profile browsing, photo album browsing, and viewing Friend's content in their News Feed (measured individually)
Facebook as Primary Communication	FBPrimary	Computed variable derived for H3 and H4 analysis that only includes subset of sample that scores highest on FBComm and lowest on TradComm (see Findings section).

Table 2: Summary of variables used in analyses

Facebook Communication Frequency

Participants were asked to rate the frequency with which they interacted with the specified Facebook Friend through six public and private channels (private messages, Chat, private Groups, Wall posts, comments, and Likes), as well as three passive behaviors (profile browsing, photo album browsing, and viewing the Friend's content in their News Feed)on a five-point scale ranging from 1=Never to 5=Very Often.

Analysis

See Table 2 for a summary of all variables included in analyses. As noted in the Measures section, the geographic distance measure is bimodally distributed, with 61.7% of participants describing their selected Friend as living either geographically proximate (i.e., within a 30-minute drive; 33.9%) or very far away (i.e., greater than a six-hour drive away; 27.8%). This suggests that treating it as an interval variable would likely cause misleading results. Furthermore, many of analyses in this study control for relational closeness; as seen in Scheffe post-hoc analyses of an ANOVA comparing means for geographic and relational closeness, there is no statistically significant relationship between these two variables. Therefore, because such a large percentage of respondents evaluated Friends at one of the two extremes (geographically proximate vs. geographically distant), these cases were isolated and a new variable was computed to examine differences in engagement in relationship maintenance strategies and relational outcomes between Friends who live near one another and those who live very far apart.

But isolating these two extremes leaves out over one-third of the responses and ignores a wide range of (physical) distance—Friends that might be reached in a day, but getting there requires a significant time investment. These are ties who may live in the same state but not in the same city, or in a neighboring state. If we only look at the extremes, it becomes harder to address the question of whether the findings regarding Facebook's potential effect on relational quality increases with distance or is more of an all-or-nothing phenomenon (i.e., if you live nearby, Facebook won't help; if you don't live nearby, it will). Therefore, an ANOVA was run first using a three-item geographic distance variable and including the middle group of participants (those rating a Friend who lived at least 30 minutes but less than six hours away). Scheffe post-hoc analyses revealed no differences across the three groups for the four relationship maintenance variables; however, significant differences were observed for the two relational outcomes, with Facebook's perceived impact increasing with each step except between the mid-distance and farthest distance for Facebook's impact on relational closeness. Therefore, when testing relationships between geographic distance and these two outcome variables, the three-item variable will be used.

FINDINGS

RQ1: Communication frequency

The research question addressed differences in communication patterns between geographically proximate and long-distance Friends. To answer this question, I first ran a series of independent samples t-tests using the dichotomous distance variable as the grouping variable. Results indicated no significant differences for any of the nine Facebook communication behaviors. However, when looking at engagement in non-Facebook based communication behaviors (which is not directly assessed in the RQ), significant differences did emerge, with geographically proximate Friends more likely to meet face-to-face, talk on the phone, send text messages, email, and IM. Geographically distant Friends were slightly more likely to use a video chat service like Skype.

These results may have been influenced by participants' relational closeness to the Friend they were evaluating, which was negatively correlated with the dichotomous geographic distance variable (r=-.17, p<.01). Therefore, a series of follow-up ANCOVAs were run to control for relational closeness while comparing means for each of the Facebook communication behaviors. Of the nine, only commenting on a Friend's Wall (F(6, 244)=3.21, p<.01, R^2=.05) and browsing a Friend's photo album (F(6, 244)=5.26, p<.001, R^2=.09) were statistically significant while controlling for relational closeness. In both cases, these behaviors were performed more frequently by participants responding about a Friend who lived more than six hours away.

H1 & H2: Geographic proximity and relationship maintenance strategies

The first set of hypotheses tested the relationship between geographic proximity and (H1) engagement in the four relationship maintenance strategies and (H2) the perceived role Facebook plays in their relational quality.

Looking at the four relationship maintenance strategies, independent samples t-tests revealed significantly higher engagement in Passive Consumption (M=3.06, SD=.80 vs. M=2.81, SD=.94), t(248.69)=-2.33, p<.05, and Social Information Seeking (M=2.85, SD=.85 vs. M=2.60, SD=.88), t(249)=-2.25, p<.05 amongst geographically distant Friend dyads. There were no significant differences observed in engagement in the Supportive Communication or Shared Interests strategies. This provides only partial support to H1. In order to account for the potential impact of relational closeness on engagement in these strategies, a MANCOVA was conducted with the four relationship maintenance strategies as dependent variables. Findings indicated a significant effect of geographic distance on engagement in relationship maintenance strategies while controlling for relational closeness, Wilks' Λ= .91, F(4, 244)=4.847, p<.001, η2=.090. In examining the between-subjects effects, Supportive Communication, F(1, 248)=4.58, p<.05, η2=.02; Passive Consumption, F(1, 248)=17.19, p<.001, η2=.07; Social Information Seeking, F(1, 248)=5.49, p<.05, η2=.02; and Facebook Communication Frequency, F(1, 248)=4.76, p<.05, η2=.02, were significant. Therefore, when controlling for relational closeness, support for H1 should be revised, being supported for all strategies but Shared Interests.

A similar process was used for the two relational outcomes. Results from ANOVAs show that, first, as the distance between dyads increases, participants generally perceived Facebook to have a larger impact on their relational closeness (M=2.70, SD=1.02 for the closest Friends, M=2.97, SD=1.00) for the middle group, and M=3.11, SD=.89 for the furthest Friends), F(2, 402)=5.78, p<.01. Scheffe post-hoc analyses, however, show that the only significant (p<.05) difference between groups is between the closest and farthest group. Second, when looking at relational stability, the difference is even stronger (M=2.31, SD=.91 for the closest Friends, M=2.86, SD=.88 for the middle group, and M=3.17, SD=1.04 for the furthest Friends), F(2, 402)=24.42, p<.001. Here, Scheffe post-hoc tests show significant differences between each step. Next, using MANCOVA analyses to control for the effect of relational closeness, geographic distance emerges as a significant predictor in the model, Wilks' Λ= .90, F(3, 401)=10.91, p<.001, η^2=.052. Geographic distance remains significant for both Facebook's Impact on Relational Closeness, F(1, 403)=6.94, p<.01, η^2=.017 and Facebook's Impact on Relational Stability, F(1, 403)=45.15, p<.001, η^2=.125, providing support for H2.

H3 & H4: Facebook as a primary form of communication

In order to create a measure that accurately reflects the subset of users for whom Facebook is most likely to be seen as the primary form of communication, both frequency of communication through traditional and Facebook channels must be considered. First, composite variables for Traditional Communication and Facebook Communication were created by running exploratory factor analysis on the individual behaviors (once for traditional communication behaviors and once for Facebook communication behaviors), creating two new variables: TradComm (α=.85, M=2.36, SD=1.01) measures frequency of in-person, phone calls, text messages, and email, while FBComm (α=.908, M=2.92, SD=.98) measures frequency of engagement in public interactions (Wall posts, comments, and Likes) with a Facebook Friend.

Next, the data were explored to find the optimal "cut-point" to divide the data between the group of users who would be defined as primarily Facebook communicators and everyone else. This process was complicated by the large number of cases at specific frequencies (e.g., 21.8% of participants' Facebook communication frequency score was a 3). See Table 3 for a breakdown of the two variables into deciles. Furthermore, as the computed measure needed to account for low interaction through traditional communication channels and high interaction through Facebook communication channels, this further limited the number of cases. Several variables were tested using different ranges of TradComm and FBComm scores; for analyses, a measure was constructed including cases where participants reported, on average, communicating with their selected friend at a score below 2.25 for the traditional communication measure (where 1=never, 2=rarely and

		TradComm	FBComm
Mean		2.358	2.916
Median		2.250	3.000
Standard Deviation		1.006	.9780
	10th	1.000	1.666
	20th	1.250	2.000
	30th	1.750	2.334
	40th	2.000	3.000
	50th	2.250	3.000
	60th	2.500	3.000
	70th	2.750	3.335
	80th	3.250	3.666
	90th	3.750	4.000

Table 3: Deciles for TradComm and FBComm variables

3=sometimes) and a score above 3 for the Facebook communication measure (where 4=often and 5=very often). Scores below 2.25 on traditional communication comprised the lowest 45.5% of responses, while scores above 3 on Facebook communication comprised the highest 38.6% of responses. Fifty-two participants (12.8% of the full sample) met both requirements.

Once the variable was computed, independent samples t-tests were conducted to test for differences in engagement in the four relationship maintenance strategies using "Facebook as Primary Communication" (FBPrimary) as the grouping variable. Results indicated that those who primarily interact with a Facebook Friend through public, site-based communication engage in a greater amount of Supportive Communication (M=4.02, SD=.45 vs. M=3.64, SD=.85), $t(114.11)$=-5.00, $p<.001$; Passive Consumption (M=3.14, SD=.84 vs. M=2.88, SD=.88), $t(405)$=-2.01, $p<.05$; and Social Information Seeking (M=3.24, SD=.80 vs. M=2.65, SD=.84), $t(405)$=-4.81, $p<.001$, when compared with the rest of the sample, providing partial support for H3. To test whether this finding held when taking into consideration one's level of relational closeness, which was significantly lower for those who primarily interacted through Facebook (M=2.69, SD=.61) compared with those who did not (M=2.98, SD=1.15), $t(112.74)$=2.80, $p<.01$, a MANCOVA was conducted including the four maintenance strategies as dependent variables, FBPrimary as the fixed factor, and Relational Closeness as a covariate. MANCOVA was used rather than separate ANCOVAs due to the moderate correlations between the four relationship strategies (r=.46–.57; see [46]). Results indicated that, even when controlling for relational closeness, a significant difference exists between those who primarily interact through Facebook and the rest of the sample, Wilks' Λ= .92, $F(4, 401)$=8.94, $p<.001$, η^2=.082. As with the previous analysis, significant differences were found for Supportive Communication, $F(1, 404)$=21.01, $p<.001$, η^2 = .050; Passive Consumption $F(1, 404)$=11.22 , $p<.001$, η^2=.027; and Social Information Seeking strategies, $F(1, 404)$=25.45, $p<.001$, η^2=.059.

Finally, to test whether individuals who primarily use Facebook to interact with a specific Friend perceive the site as having a greater impact on their relational closeness and relational stability, independent samples t-tests show that those primarily interacting through Facebook see the site as positively impacting how close they feel to that person (M=3.34, SD=.93 vs. M=2.85, SD=.98), $t(405)$=-3.41, $p<.001$ and that relationship's stability (M=3.52, SD=.81 vs. M=2.65, SD=.99), $t(405)$=-6.88, $p<.001$, when compared with the rest of the sample, supporting H4. A MANCOVA conducted on the two dependent variables to control for the effect of relational closeness was also significant, Wilks' Λ=.93, $F(2, 403)$=16.44, $p<.001$, η^2=.075. Both Facebook's Impact on Relational Closeness, $F(1, 404)$=13.28 , $p<.001$, η^2=.032 and Facebook's Impact on Relational Stability, $F(1, 404)$=32.95, p=.001, η^2=.075 were significantly higher for those who primarily communicated through Facebook, even when controlling for their reported level of relational closeness.

DISCUSSION

This research extends our understanding of relationship maintenance processes in the age of "social supernets" in several important ways. Notably, while engagement in these Facebook-based maintenance strategies is generally correlated with relational closeness, findings from statistical analyses suggest that one's closest relationships do not benefit the most from being connected on the site; rather, those who primarily rely on Facebook as their source of communication and those who live at a greater physical distance from each other see the site as having the greatest positive impact on the quality of their relationship. In this way, while Facebook may serve a supplemental role for closer relationships—similar to Hampton and Wellman's [23] findings about email more than a decade ago—findings suggest the site may actually serve to enhance the quality of weaker relationships and prevent those connections from fading away completely.

While face-to-face interactions are best for some kinds of relationships [12, 13], research has consistently shown over the last decade that CMC serves a supplemental role in maintaining relationships, especially when other forms of communication are unavailable (e.g., [2, 23, 47]). This study goes a step further by considering the entire spectrum of relationships individuals maintain through CMC rather than focusing solely on close-tie maintenance, as has been the focus of previous work (e.g., [25, 30, 35]). First, looking at engagement in relationship maintenance strategies, we find those who live farther away and communicate primarily through Facebook report significantly higher engagement in Supportive Communication, Passive Consumption, and Social

Information Seeking. As these strategies are not limited to collocated behaviors in the same way that Stafford and Canary's [41] measures were, there was little risk of that impacting engagement, with the exception of Shared Interests; the physical proximity required for certain types of activities related to common interests (e.g., baseball fans going to a game together) may limit its effect size, although it is important to note that the wording of the items for this strategy specifically avoided offline components.

These two categories—Facebook as Primary Communication and Geographic Distance—were also analyzed to determine whether differences emerged in the extent to which participants believed their use of the site positively affected the quality of their relationship with that Friend through two measures, one assessing relational closeness and one assessing relational stability. Again, findings indicate that, regardless of one's existing level of relational closeness, those who rely primarily on Facebook to interact with a specific Facebook Friend and those who live very far from that Friend see Facebook as playing a much more significant role in their relationship. In fact, when looking at relational stability, one does not even need to live very distant at all, but merely not be within the same town and an effect can be seen. For these Friends, Facebook may be the difference between a relationship in existence and the memory of that relationship. Because these people have chosen to rely on mediated channels to interact—whether because of a physical distance separating them, the convenience of quick updates and content browsing, or another reason—Facebook's role has transformed from mere intermediary to (oftentimes) the sole source connecting these people.

If we consider Facebook's affordances and the benefits of using the site for relationship maintenance rather than other forms of (mediated or non-mediated) communication, Facebook serves as a virtual, networked rolodex that auto-updates every time a user enters new information. Even if that user has not entered direct contact information such as an email address, as long as the technical connection between two Friends exists, communication can take place. This process is much more complicated without tools like Facebook, where the impetus is on the individual to update their files with new contact information when a friend moves, or gets married and changes her last name, or gets a new phone. Of course, if this information is needed but not available through Facebook, it can be requested—on channel or off—but the important takeaway here is that while our social contacts' personal information is constantly changing over time, Facebook has reduced the effort associated with organizing, editing, and updating that information to a single component: the Friend link. This argument has received additional support in previous empirical work by Steinfield and colleagues [43], whose qualitative interviews with college students highlighted the instrumental role of Friending as a way to keep in touch with those contacts one might wish to interact with at some point in the future, and Ellison et al. [17], who found that students' emotional connection to the site (i.e., "Facebook Intensity") positively predicted their use of the site to keep to keep in touch with high school friends (i.e., "maintained social capital").

The findings presented here also echo recent work by Keith Hampton and colleagues [22], who present a convincing argument for the *persistent* and *pervasive* nature of ICTs like Facebook, going so far as to suggest that "ICTs afford relationship maintenance in ways that reduce the likelihood that ties will ever become completely dormant" (p. 1046). When the cost to remove a social tie from one's social network is higher than simply allowing it to remain, ignored or perhaps hidden, users have little motivation to delete someone once they become Facebook Friends. Furthermore, Facebook has raised awareness about an issue that Hampton et al. [22] describe in terms of "pervasive awareness" while Vitak [51] and others have framed it in terms of "context collapse": the idea that SNS users broadcast content across numerous social contexts, and that this breakdown in the existing relational structures that is so inherent in our offline self-presentation (e.g., work, church, hometown, spouse) may raise a number of relational issues. Context collapse is facilitated by SNSs' affordances, including the visibility and persistence of content, as well as the association of people (e.g., Friends of Friends) and the association of content (e.g., tagging, retweeting).

A final consideration in light of these findings is to reflect on how they speak to Haythornthwaite's [24] work on media multiplexity, a simple construct that posits that tie strength is positively correlated with the quantity of communication channels a dyad uses. The findings here suggest that, while Facebook may be important for some close-tie dyads, it is unlikely these ties would see their relationship fall apart if they lost access to the site. For many weaker relationships—and even closer relationships separated by geographic distance—Facebook can become more than the supplement that email was a decade ago [23]. Perhaps this is because, as Tong and Walther [46] suggest, SNSs' features foster feedback, participation, and interactivity, and allow users to embed a variety of multimedia sources. Finally, as described in this paper, users can keep in contact from a distance through passive strategies, which also helps foster the maintenance of weak ties. Facebook's technical structure—and especially the News Feed—keep users on top of their network's activity. One of the most interesting questions for future research will be if this constant stream of content reduces the need for other interaction among certain types of connections and, if so, how the technology reshapes media multiplexity.

Limitations

The analyses provided in this study assess correlations between variables and cannot establish causality. While the sample in this study was generally representative of the population, the population itself is not representative of

Facebook users, especially in terms of education. Therefore, other populations' engagement in these strategies and their perceived impact on relational outcomes should be assessed to determine if similar results occur with different types of users. For example, research has identified that college students' network composition is substantively different from non-students in terms of the number of "actual friends" (see [17, 18]). Likewise, this sample was highly skewed toward White users; however, Pew Internet data show that minorities are slightly more likely to use SNSs as Whites [5] and are more likely to access SNSs through mobile devices [38], which could impact the strategies they employ. Finally, the use of an ordinal variable to measure geographic distance may have over-simplified the relationship between geographic distance and the other variables examined. A more nuanced examination is warranted in future studied.

CONCLUSION

This study has addressed questions related to relationship maintenance in the Facebook age by showing that, while relational closeness is positively correlated with engagement in relationship strategies, specific types of Friend dyads are more likely to use these strategies and, consequently, benefit from their engagement. Specifically, those who rely on Facebook as their primary communication channel and those who live farther away both engage in these strategies to a greater extent and view Facebook as having a greater impact on their relational closeness and stability than those who communicate through other channels, and those who live close to each other.

When considering these findings in light of the structure of the website, it becomes clear that Facebook should make strides to identify and encourage interaction between dyads who may benefit from communication on the site. A straightforward approach to this would be to begin showing more content from Friends after a user visits their profile page. A more difficult problem would be to predict who a Facebook user might *want* to interact with; one way this could be done would be by comparing interaction patterns with mutual Friends and then increasing prominence in the News Feed. Facebook may also consider testing features that suggest users visit a Friend's profile or interact with a Friend in some way, although these may be viewed as invasive and would need to be pre-tested. In the end, however, these types of analyses would be beneficial to Facebook's overarching goal and having users generate more content via increased interactions.

Finally, these findings provide significant evidence for the supportive role Facebook plays in maintaining the wide range of weaker connections that comprise the majority of most users' Friend networks. The site's features—most notably the straightforward nature through which a relationship is articulated, the simple presentation of content in reverse chronological order and the ease of communicating with other users through a wide range of behaviors representing various degrees of engagement and time commitment—have significantly impacted how we maintain relationships in the digital age. Returning to Dunbar's suggestion, as quoted in the introduction, that Facebook may help slow the pace of relational decay, these findings go even further by suggesting that individuals not only see the site as a repository to store contacts, but as an interactive forum that improves the quality of relationships, and specifically benefits weaker and more distant ties.

ACKNOWLEDGMENTS

This study was funded by a research grant from the College of Communication Arts and Sciences at Michigan State University. As this paper is based on data from my dissertation, I would like to thank Dr. Nicole Ellison for providing a tremendous amount of feedback throughout both the study development and data collection/analysis processes.

REFERENCES

1. Baym, N.K., Zhang Y.B., Kunkel, A., Ledbetter, A., and Lin, M. Relational quality and media use in interpersonal relationships. *New Media Society 9* (2007), 735-752.
2. Baym, N.K., Zhang, Y.B., and Lin, M.-C. Interpersonal communication on the internet, telephone and face-to-face. *New Media & Society 6* (2004), 299-318.
3. Boneva, B., Kraut, R., and Frohlich, D. Using e-mail for personal relationships: The difference gender makes. *American Behavioral Scientist, 45* (2001), 530-549.
4. Brandtzaeg, P.B. Social networking sites: Their users and social implications—a longitudinal study. *Journal of Computer-Mediated Communication 17* (2012), 467-488.
5. Brenner, J. and Smith, A. *72% of Online Adults Are Social Networking Site Users*. Pew Internet Project, 2013.
6. Burke, M. Kraut, R. and Marlow, C. Social capital on Facebook: Differentiating uses and users. In *Proc. CHI*, ACM Press (2011), 571-580.
7. Canary, D. J., and Stafford, L. Relational maintenance strategies and equity in marriage. *Communication Monographs 59* (1992), 243-267.
8. Dainton, M., and Aylor, B. Patterns of communication channel use in the maintenance of long-distance relationships. *Communication Research Reports 19* (2000), 118-129.
9. Dibble, J.L., Levine, T.R., and Park, H.S. The unidimensional relationship closeness scale (URCS): Reliability and validity evidence for a new measure of relationship closeness. *Psychological Assessment 24* (2012), 565-572.
10. Dindia, K. Definitions and perspectives on relational

maintenance communication. In D.J. Canary and M. Dainton, eds., *Maintaining Relationships Through Communication: Relational, Contextual, and Cultural Variations*. Lawrence Erlbaum, Mahwah, NJ, 2003, 51-77).

11. Donath, J.S. Signals in social supernets. *Journal of Computer-Mediated Communication 13* (2007), 231-251.

12. Duck, S. *Relating to Others*. Open University Press, Milton Keynes, UK, 1988.

13. Duck, S., and Pittman, G. Social and personal relationships. In M.L. Knapp and G.R. Miller, eds., *Handbook of Interpersonal Communication (2nd ed.)* Sage, Thousand Oaks, CA, 1994, 676-695.

14. Duggan, M., and Brenner, J. *The Demographics of Social Media Users – 2012*. Pew Internet Project, 2013.

15. Dunbar, R. I. M. (2011, June). How many "friends" can you really have? *IEEE Spectrum, 81*, 83.

16. Ellison, N., Steinfield, C., and Lampe, C. The benefits of Facebook "friends": Exploring the relationship between college students' use of online social networks and social capital. *Journal of Computer-Mediated Communication 12* (2007), 1143-1168.

17. Ellison, N.B., Steinfield, C. and Lampe, C. Connection strategies: Social capital implications of Facebook-enabled communication practices. *New Media & Society 13* (2011), 873-892.

18. Ellison, N., Vitak, J., Gray, R., and Lampe, C. Cultivating social resources: The relationship between bridging social capital and Facebook use among adults. *Journal of Computer-Mediated Communication,* (in press).

19. Gilbert, E. and Karahalios, K. Predicting tie strength with social media. In *Proc. CHI,* ACM Press (2011), 211-220.

20. Gunn, D. O., and Gunn, C. W. Electronic relationship maintenance processes. Paper presented at the annual meeting of the Association of Internet Researchers, Lawrence, KS, 2000.

21. Hampton, K., Goulet, L.S., Rainie, L., and Purcell, K. Social Networking Sites and Our Lives. Pew Internet Project, 2011.

22. Hampton, K.N., Lee, C.J., and Her, E.J. How new media affords network diversity: Direct and mediated access to social capital through participation in local social settings. *New Media & Society 13,* (2011), 1031-1049.

23. Hampton, K., and Wellman, B. Long distance community in the network society: Contact and support beyond Netville. *American Behavioral Scientist 45* (2001), 476-495.

24. Haythornthwaite, C. Social networks and Internet connectivity effects. *Information, Communication & Society 8* (2005), 125-147.

25. Johnson, A.J. Examining the maintenance of friendships: Are there differences between geographically close and long-distance friends? *Communication Quarterly 49* (2001), 424-435.

26. Johnson, A.J., Haigh, M.M., Becker, J.A.H., Craig, E.A., and Wigley, S. College students' use of relational management strategies in email in long-distance and geographically close relationships. *Journal of Computer-Mediated Communication 13* (2008), 381-404.

27. Johnson, A.J., Becker, J., Craig, E., Gilchrist, E., and Haigh, M. Changes in friendship commitment: Comparing geographically close and long-distance young-adult friendships. *Communication Quarterly 57* (2009), 395-415.

28. Joinson, A.N. (2008). "Looking at", "looking up," or "keeping up with" people? Motives and uses of Facebook. In *Proc. CHI,* ACM Press (2008), 1027-1036.

29. Lampe, C., Ellison, N., and Steinfield, C. A Face(book) in the crowd: Social searching vs. social browsing. In *Proc. CSCW*, ACM Press (2006), 167–170.

30. Ledbetter, A.M. Measuring online communication attitude: Instrument development and validation. *Communication Monographs 76* (2009), 463-486.

31. Ledbetter, A. Assessing the measurement invariance of relational maintenance behavior when face-to-face and online. *Communication Research Reports 27* (2010), 30-37.

32. Ledbetter, A.M., Mazer, J.P., DeGroot, J.M., Meyer, K.R., Mao, Y., and Swafford, B. Attitudes toward online social connection and self-disclosure as predictors of Facebook communication and relational closeness. *Communication Research 38* (2011), 27-53.

33. Lenhart, A. *Adults and Social Network Websites*. Pew Internet Project, 2009.

34. Metzger, M.J., Wilson, C., Pure, R.A., and Zhao, B.Y. Invisible interactions: What latent social interaction can tell us about social relationships in social network sites. In D. Comunello, ed., *Networked Sociability and Individualism: Technology for Personal and Professional Relationships*. IGI Global, Hershey, PA, 2012, 79-103.

35. Miczo, N., Mariani, T., and Donahue, C. The strength of strong ties: Media multiplexity, communication motives, and the maintenance of geographically close friendships. *Communication Reports 24* (2011), 12-24.

36. Rabby, M.K. Relational maintenance and the influence of commitment in online and offline relationships. *Communication Studies 58* (2007), 315 337.

37. Ramirez, A., and Broneck, K. 'IM me': Instant

messaging as relational maintenance and everyday communication. *Journal of Social and Personal Relationships 26* (2009), 291-314.

38. Smith, A. *Mobile Access 2010.* Pew Internet Project, 2010.

39. Stafford, L. *Maintaining Long-Distance and Cross-Residential Relationships*. Lawrence Erlbaum, Mahwah, NJ, 2005.

40. Stafford, L. Measuring relationship maintenance behaviors: Critique and development of the revised relationship maintenance behavior scale. *Journal of Social and Personal Relationships 28* (2010), 278-303.

41. Stafford, L., and Canary, D.J. Maintenance strategies and romantic relationship type, gender, and relational characteristics. *Journal of Social and Personal Relationships 8* (1991), 217-242.

42. Stafford, L., Kline, S.L., and Dimmick, J. Home e-mail: Relational maintenance and gratification opportunities. *Journal of Broadcasting and Electronic Media, 43* (1999), 659-669.

43. Steinfield, C., Ellison, N.B., and Lampe, C. Social capital, self-esteem, and use of online social network sites: A longitudinal analysis. *Journal of Applied Developmental Psychology 29* (2008), 434-445.

44. Tabachnick, G.G., and Fidell, L.S. *Experimental Designs Using ANOVA.* Duxbury, Belmont, CA, 2007.

45. Thelwall, M. and Wilkinson, D. Public dialogs in social network sites: What is their purpose? *Journal of the American Society for Information Science and Technology 61* (2010), 392-404.

46. Tong, S., and Walther, J.B. (2011). Relational maintenance and CMC. In K.B. Wright and L.M. Webb, eds., *Computer-Mediated Communication in Personal Relationships*. Peter Lang Publishing, New York, 98-118.

47. Valkenburg, P.M., and Peter, J. The effects of instant messaging on the quality of adolescents' existing friendships: A longitudinal study. *Journal of Communication 59* (2009), 79-97.

48. Viswanath, B., Mislove, A., Cha, M., and Gummadi, K. P. On the evolution of user interaction in Facebook. In *Proc. ACM workshop on online social networks,* ACM Press (2009) 37-42.

49. Vitak, J. Keeping connected in the Facebook age: The relationship between Facebook use, relationship maintenance strategies, and relational outcomes. PhD dissertation, Michigan State University. East Lansing, MI.

50. Vitak, J. The impact of context collapse and privacy on social network site disclosures. *Journal of Broadcasting and Electronic Media 56* (2012), 451-470.

51. Vitak, J., and Kim, J. "You can't block people offline": Examining how Facebook's affordances shape the disclosure process. In *Proc. CSCW*, ACM Press (2014).

52. Wright, K.B. Online maintenance strategies and perceptions of partners within exclusively Internet-based and primarily Internet-based relationships. *Communication Studies 55* (2004), 239-253.

"Real, but Glossy" – Technology and the Practical Pursuit of Magic in Modern Weddings

Michael Massimi, Richard Harper, Abigail Sellen
Microsoft Research
Cambridge, UK
{mmassimi, r.harper, asellen}@microsoft.com

ABSTRACT

Planning a wedding is arguably one of the most complicated collaborative tasks people ever undertake. Despite the commonplace use of technologies in "wedding work," little research has looked at this from an HCI perspective. Based on an interview study, we illustrate how technology is used to deliver the sought-after fantasy and a practical, yet entertaining, affair. We identify four ways that technology helps people do this: (a) by allowing much of the practical planning work to become "invisible;" (b) by easing navigation through the delicate rules of family configurations made manifest in the guest list; (c) by helping create a spectacle-like event that adroitly balances excess and realism; and (d) by documenting the wedding in ways that allows re-experiencing the magic after the event. The paper concludes by discussing the implications of this pursuit on social graphs, place, and photography, contributing to the literature on technology and major life events.

Author Keywords

Weddings, magic, life events, spectacle, marriage, ritual.

ACM Classification Keywords

H.5.m. Information interfaces and presentation (e.g., HCI): Miscellaneous.

INTRODUCTION

"As one of the few recently democratized portals to reenchantment in life, the wedding does not so much hold up a mirror to who we really are, but instead offers a temporary dream world for all in attendance, a celebrity-like world of elegance, elaborateness, emotion, and ease. Other rituals can promise lavishness, but none can convey a memory of once having felt like Cinderella and Prince Charming." – Otnes and Pleck [22] (pp. 15-16).

CSCW'14, February 15 - 19 2014, Baltimore, MD, USA

ACM 978-1-4503-2540-0/14/02...$15.00.
http://dx.doi.org/10.1145/2531602.2531682

A wedding is arguably the most transformative and meaningful event in a person's life. Particularly in North American and British society, brides and grooms are encouraged by the wedding industry and the media to make their wedding the "perfect day," as the above quote makes clear. This day is expected to be an elegant, dreamlike affair that celebrates the personalities, history, and future of the couple in the presence of adoring friends and family. In the United States, weddings are generally one of the largest occasions for spending money - not as much as purchasing a home, but certainly conspicuous in its scale and excess [16].

To be sure, not all weddings are lavish, expensive events. The North American and British model – if it can be treated as homogenous for the moment – is certainly not representative of weddings everywhere. Even within this context, it is certainly not uncommon to hear about people opting out of conventional wedding arrangements. However, a feature of weddings that is widely accepted is the need to create a special event that is set apart from the everyday. Making this day special is a significant effort, if not sometimes a Herculean task that requires months of dedicated effort. To begin with, planning a wedding unfolds in a unique social setting, where the needs and preferences of two or more families, as well as the friendship groups of the marrying couple, must be acknowledged. Beyond this, these diverse concerns must be weighed against financial costs and the desire to have a "once-in-a-lifetime" event that will be remembered for years to come. Of course, romance needs to be sustained throughout; the couple must not fall out before they get to the altar.

A range of technologies are mobilized in this process. General purpose websites such as Pinterest and Etsy provide inspiration and ideas for wedding themes, favors, flowers, and dresses; this is to say little of the material to be found in online bridal magazines, blogs, and portals such as The Knot [28]. Productivity software such as Microsoft Office or Google Docs are used to track invitations, balance budgets, and manage to-do lists. Mobile users can find a thousands of mobile apps dedicated to wedding planning (a search for "wedding" on the Google Play store yields over 1000 results, for example). Start-ups and established companies alike are also profoundly concerned with the event itself, launching products and services specifically for the wedding ceremony, for its recording and documenting, and much else besides; the bridal industry is a competitive multimillion dollar affair where companies try to acquire "a customer for life" [20].

Weddings are, in other words, already suffused by technology. Yet, and to date, there appears to have been relatively little in the HCI or CSCW communities that focuses on weddings as a domain for technology use in its own right. There are various papers that look at weddings indirectly, or as motivating examples for a broader category of action. For example, Zarro, Hall, and Forte note that wedding boards are common repositories in their investigation of Pinterest [35]. Other studies focused on photography [18, 24], automatic video segmentation [4], and intelligent agents for wardrobe selection [17] have used weddings as motivating examples.

There is also a growing body of literature looking at major life events and HCI, including the birth of a child [9], divorce [21, 34], moving to a new home [26], and the death of a loved one [19]. All of this literature draws into focus the changing social, psychological, and technical infrastructure of the modern world. However, weddings themselves have not yet been studied, despite their importance in economic, social, psychological, and cultural terms. There might be a range of reasons for this but as CSCW has turned away from its origins in work systems towards technology and society in the large, this absence seems all the more conspicuous: after all, weddings are fundamentally collaborative and central to the organization of relationships between people.

Following the framing of life events as crucibles for technology adoption, design and use, this study of weddings provides CSCW with a fertile arena for studying how existing technologies are appropriated in a setting with heightened stakes. Our findings provide material for future work through design exploration, and highlight some of the deficiencies in current systems that cast weddings as a form of project management. It is finally our goal to provide the CSCW community with a rich example of how technology is mobilized to make an event feel special, magical, and memorable. Weddings, like other life events, push our understanding of technology use beyond the everyday into the exceptional.

We organize the paper in the following way. First, we set the scene by providing some background on Western-style wedding culture. We then present an interview study we undertook to understand the interplay among culture, technology, and the practical action of making a wedding happen. Our approach emphasizes the agency of people, and how their practices may be thought of dialogues with the possibilities offered by Western wedding culture. To put it in terms familiar to the CSCW community, our approach is to treat people, as Garfinkel advises, as co-producers of the world known-in-common [8]. We show how technologies are used to plan, organize, augment, document and recall weddings. This suggests how technologies for weddings might unfold through sensitive, informed future design.

SETTING THE SCENE

The Modern Wedding: Elaborate and Growing

Weddings are extraordinarily variable occasions within the North American and British contexts. From a "shotgun" elopement to Las Vegas to a formal weekend-long affair with hundreds of guests at a Gothic castle, the wedding is a concept that is continually reinvented. In Martin King Whyte's book *Dating, Mating, and Marriage* from 1990, he outlines some of the demographic trends associated with weddings based on a large-scale survey held with a general population of the USA. He points out that receptions have become more common, and more people are attendance (an average of 50 guests in the 1940s, versus 150 in 1990). He goes on to point out that engaged couples are more likely to hold bachelor or bachelorette parties now than ever before, and participate in events in the lead-up to the actual ceremony [33]. When we consider that each of the approximately 2.1 million weddings held in the US each year [3] may contain multiple elaborate events, a turn towards technology to manage these affairs seems not only logical but near-essential.

Technologies for Weddings

Like weddings themselves, the landscape of available technologies specifically targeted at weddings in the North American and UK context is continually changing, and an exhaustive list is not possible here. However, blog posts and articles frequently summarize the latest options available for brides and grooms. One published on May 7, 2013 at PopSugar suggests "8 ways to completely digitize your wedding planning," and overviews software packages for coordination, design inspiration, shopping lists, registry creation, group communication, sketching, budgeting, and tracking RSVPs [23]. Applications can be found that integrate with existing platforms like Facebook (e.g., Weduary allows users to create a Facebook-integrated wedding site [32]). Other apps focus more squarely on mobile device experiences, such as Appy Couple [1] which offers pre-designed wedding websites and associated functionality for the iPhone.

Technology of course is not limited to the planning process; it is integral to the successful execution of the day. Coordinating vendors, guests, and other attendees relies on mobile phones, email, and websites to coordinate. The use of CMC on the day may even include video chat systems for broadcasting the event to those who cannot attend (as with one bride in our sample, who shared her wedding ceremony in India with her uncle in New Jersey). This bride was hardly alone; one marketing research firm found that over 50% of brides considered using Skype for their wedding [29]. iPhone apps such as Wedding Party allow guests at a wedding to upload photos automatically to shared photo albums that the bride and groom can then browse [31].

Cultural Visions of the "Perfect Day"

As this brief summary of available software tools makes clear, the weddings we are focusing on here cannot be understood without reference to mass media and modern forms of consumption. Weddings are nothing if not contemporary, even if they echo the past. Nor are they vague and underspecified affairs, even with the turn away from religious solidarity towards more "liquid forms" of connection [2]. Weddings in North America and the UK are enormously managed cultural productions (as they are elsewhere, doubtlessly, though with different nuance and form).

While a full treatment of the cultural apparatus that is weddings is not possible here (see Otnes and Pleck [22] and Ingraham [13]), what can be noted is how cultural theorists have critiqued the valence of the ideology around "magical white weddings" in the North American context particularly. This ideology is said to produce not only ephemeral consumer desires but also to instill unrealistic and potentially harmful notions of gender norms [13, 20]. As De Certeau notes, ideas about identity and social practice (such as those exemplified by weddings, though these are not something he writes about himself), provide a space for "possibilities and interdictions" [6]. Foreshadowing some of our findings from our empirical work, people have to navigate their way through their own experience and the relationship between that and the all-too-often perfect world portrayed in ideologies of various kinds:

"These websites that are supposed to give insight into how to plan your wedding but I don't think I used a lot of the websites, and it's because they're very much focused on the princess bride phenomenon." – Bride, Couple A

"People try to outdo royalty – it's not reality, you're losing the purpose of what a wedding is.... sites like ruffled.com have real weddings but even those real weddings aren't real weddings – these are wealthy Californians who have everything at their fingertips." – Bride, Couple N

These quotes, representative of the study we outline shortly, illustrate the navigation that is part of our concern, placing as it does the human as the engaged creature in the center: at once beholden to the magical wedding, but indignant towards its implications and frivolousness. The term "magic" in our sense refers to a practical pursuit – a property of the wedding that couples strive to make happen. We borrow our concept of magic from ritual scholars Ronald Grimes, and wedding researchers Cele Otnes and Elizabeth Pleck, who argue that magic is perceived transformation by ritual where specific objects and actions casually produce the sought-after transformation [10, 22]. Whatever individual choices people make about the balance between "real" and "magic," the sheer logistics of weddings – aligning the objects and actions for the ritual – is a prominent and real concern for those seeking the transition into marriage.

INTERVIEW STUDY

As outlined above, our purpose is to expose the work that goes into a wedding, and how technology is mobilized as part of this. Our data derives from semi-structured interviews in which participants to talk about how they used technology in relationship to their wedding. The interview began with demographic information and then turned to how technology was used in three time periods: before the wedding, the day of the wedding, and after the wedding. Key questions for each of these periods were: "How did you use technology to help you get ready for your wedding?", "What was your wedding day like? How did you use technology on the day?", and "How do you use technology to manage things you kept from your wedding?" Interviews took place over the course of 6 months, and each session lasted between 1 and 2 hours. All interviews were transcribed.

Data were analyzed using an affinity diagramming process where the first author identified codes in the data using open coding. Codes were reorganized, collapsed, and reread in the context of the literature. An intermediate schema was then discussed by the research team until a central theme concerning the production of magic emerged, and codes were reorganized under this heading.

Participants

Participants were recruited primarily through advertisements on a community website for southeastern England; this was supplemented with convenience sampling and snowballing. Though it would have been preferable to enroll subjects from a wider geographical locale, we treated these subjects as sufficient for at least an initial inquiry. Where possible, we asked to speak with both partners in their homes in order to allow participants the use of materials in telling their stories, but accommodated where scheduling or travel conflicts made this infeasible by speaking to only one partner or conducting interviews by telephone. In order to participate, participants simply had to be willing to talk about their wedding, and we placed few restraints on what this meant. This resulted in a diverse set of participants (Table 1).

As our goal was to gather rich accounts of participants' experiences in this domain, the heterogeneity within the sample was helpful because it allowed us to make some illustrative contrasts. For example, Couple N consisted of two divorcees who recently started their own professional wedding photography service, and were planning their own wedding as well. Couple O was a same-sex couple who invented their own style of wedding. Destination weddings, international/multicultural weddings, and non-Western weddings were also represented. However, and as should be clear, no strong claims are being made about representativeness; our set of subjects are simply diverse and the character of their experiences sufficiently rich to warrant investigation and reporting.

FINDINGS: THE PRACTICAL PURSUIT OF MAGIC

"From a photographer's perspective, there's a disconnect between what's real and what's a dream. Some people say your wedding is supposed to be a dream and your happiest day of your life. We've had clients get upset when it looks real. People want their faces blown out where they don't have wrinkles or movement – the cheesy dream filter – people have a feeling that even if it's phony – they're not real weddings...You have to be aspirational and have a nice gloss to the presentation but it's a fine line to tread – you want it to be real but glossy." – Groom, Couple N

All participants were familiar with the idea of the perfect white wedding, but recognized that it was a fantasy that was produced and reproduced by movies, magazines, and television. Participants avoided words that suggested this sense of delusion, but instead described their wedding using words that reflected its experiential aspects and importance in their lives: "amazing, very special, a day about the two of you," (Couple B); "almost perfect" (Couple M). Others emphasized the wedding as a time to reinforce social bonds: "a family affair" (Couple E), "intimate" (Couple L). Still others emphasized their reaction against the fairytale white wedding by underscoring their restraint in planning and execution: "a relaxed thing" (Couple K), "low profile" (Couple L), "a party thing, a very nonchalant, non-wedding vibe" (Couple O).

To briefly outline our findings, we start with the observation that the execution of a "magical event" requires *managing the visibility of effort.* Technology is involved in hiding some aspects of wedding work and highlighting others. One of the key ways technology is employed is to invite the *participation* of friends, family, and members of society more generally. This in turn enables the creation and execution of *spectacle* – that is, the deliberately unusual performance of an act that demands attention and entertains the assembly, and is increasingly accomplished using consumer technologies. Finally, in order for spectacle to be recognized as a measure of life made special, it must necessarily be *documented;* cameras and increasingly mobile phones make this possible. Technology not only records the event, but is applied in a way to assert the "magic" of the event thereafter.

Before the Big Day: Managing the Visibility of Effort

"The thing about the wedding is all the work happens beforehand. If you have planned everything the way it's supposed to be, it's just execution...So on the wedding day, you just go ahead and have a good time." – Bride, Couple A

Most of the guests at a wedding arrive with the expectation that a certain set of things will happen: that everyone will arrive at the right place at the right time, that the couple will go through with the ceremony, and that the reception will be festive. On the surface, the day should flow smoothly

Couple	Months since wedding	Years together (total)	Ages and genders	Interview type	Occupations
A	15	3.5	**35 (F),** 27 (M)	Face-to-face (outside home)	Researcher, contractor
B	5	8	**29 (F), 28 (M)**	Phone	Teacher, industrial designer
C	6	9	**30 (F), 35 (M)**	Home	Graphic designer, graphic/web designer
D	16	4	**26 (F), 28 (M)**	Phone	Ph.D. student (philosophy) (both)
E	180	16	**40 (F), 39 (M)**	Phone	Stay-at-home mom, project manager
F	12	6	**38 (F), 40 (M)**	Phone	Information architect, copywriter
G	42	13	**32 (F), 32 (M)**	Home	Book publisher, financial advisor
H	2	7	**29 (F), 29 (M)**	Home	Communications manager, scientist
I	Engaged 2 months	8.5	**26 (F),** 27 (M)	Phone	Medical doctor, accountant
J	36	4	**29 (F),** 29 (M)	Phone	Ph.D. student (archaeology), IT/software
K	15	7	**26 (F),** 29 (M)	Phone	Homemaker, sales advisor
L	36	6	**37 (F), 49 (M)**	Phone	Translator, project manager
M	31	5	**30 (F), 49 (M)**	Phone	Stay-at-home mom, sales assistant
N	Engaged 1 month	4	**29 (F), 31 (M)**	Home	Photographer, user experience manager
O	27	7	**33 (M), 34 (M)**	Phone	Non-profit development, TV producer

Table 1. Participants (15 couples). The 26 individuals who participated in an interview are highlighted in bold.

and appear to occur effortlessly. All those we interviewed explained that what guests experience is actually the final output of an enormous amount of effort on the part of the wedding organizers. They explained too that the appearance of success requires a great deal of work – to seem effortless is a task in itself. At the same time, and apparently opposite to this, some effort must be made visible to particular people at particular times. Some kinds of work express and convey such things as gratitude, sincerity, love, or humility. All participants talked about the challenge of managing the visibility-invisibility trade-off of these types of work. Following on from Star and Strauss, we lay out here some of the "indicators" of work participants described in order to artfully manage visibility [27]. We first remark on the invisible work that couples performed, and then turn to the ways in which couples made their efforts highly visible in other dimensions. As we shall see, these two sides go hand-in-hand: invisible work makes visible work more valuable, more demonstrative; visible work draws attention away from the pedantic and logistical, making things invisible and, in some respects, making space for the magical and artful.

Participants consistently remarked on how choosing a date, hiring vendors, organizing travel, and administrative work, had to be "hidden away" from the eyes of most guests, but demanded significant coordination, planning, and the use of technology to manage the process. As in the workplace, spreadsheets, documents, to-do lists, and other project management software was critical to its accomplishment. Each couple had a different way of achieving this goal, with some using email to manage their list of items, others using Google Docs, and others using Microsoft Office.

"I used a Word document of what to do. My friend was teasing me it's like a thesis that I've done. I probably still have it – that this has to be done, this has to be bought, and where to buy it, and making a big list in a Word document and when it was done, erasing the points." – Bride, Couple J

In selecting a technology to help manage the administrative work, participants commonly sought options that allowed them to distribute work among a small set of collaborators beyond the couple themselves. This usually involved parents, siblings, close friends, and the bridal party. For example, the delicate process of choosing a wedding dress was accomplished by identifying a subset of "collaborators" whose opinions were valued, and setting up a convenient infrastructure for soliciting and reflecting on those opinions.

"I made a private Facebook album of my wedding dress choices and only shared it with my bridesmaids who were in other places all over the country." – Bride, Couple D

Another compelling example came from Couple H, who "inherited" a spreadsheet template from the bride's sister that they then adapted to their own wedding – adding and removing columns that were missing or superfluous, inserting pivot tables to explore the guest list, and so on. Wedding planning, like many workplace projects, involved small-scale coordination before producing a final "result" that is made visible to a larger audience.

Work is not just hidden wholesale from the congregated assembly on the day, but is selectively hidden and revealed to particular "insiders" including, in some cases, the couple themselves. Couple K, for example, wanted to be insulated from the work involved in wedding planning and purchased a package at a destination resort in Cyprus where a wedding planner handled the logistics of the ceremony and reception.

"I found a wedding planner online and emailed her and we arranged it all through email. It was difficult to tell whether it was real or not. I didn't speak to them on the phone...It was worrying, it was all through the internet, I could have gotten there and they might not've been real. But at the same time, she was good and organized and made sure my paperwork was into the town hall there." – Bride, Couple K

Ultimately the bride and groom arrived to find that the ceremony was arranged, the table was decorated, and that the guests' accommodations were booked. By choosing to hire a planner, the couple shifted their workload to a local expert, but this resulted in another level of "information hiding" – this time from the bride and groom themselves – that turned into a fear that the whole affair was not actually real. In this sense, the "magic" of the wedding came partially from how effortless it was for the whole thing to be accomplished.

While effort may go into hiding the drudgery of coordinating and executing a wedding, there are times where effort must be made visible. Consider this discussion of thank-you cards.

Bride: "It's not acceptable to send thank yous by email, it doesn't seem right..."
Groom: "Because they're personal."
Bride: "Yes I guess it doesn't suggest like you've put enough effort into it."
Groom: "Yes and you could have just copy and pasted the same message."
Bride: "That would be nice wouldn't it?" – Couple H

This quote illustrates several points about making effort visible. First, effort is indicative of a relationship and of the involved parties' interests in maintaining that relationship – the thank you cards are "personal" in this way. To use technology to reduce this effort, such as by copying and pasting emails, diminishes in some way the investment in the relationship that the senders are willing to make. However, this investment in relationships comes at a cost – writing cards by hand is tedious, slow, and potentially more expensive than mass-producing cards. The bride's lamentation – "That would be nice, wouldn't it?" – captures this tension. Couples at once want to reduce the effort that goes into planning a wedding and are quick to adopt tools for that purpose, but purposefully eschew tools that may suggest they are lazy, ungrateful, or frivolous about the credibility and gravity of their wedding. As it happens, many current systems for managing the efforts around a wedding overlook this distinction by providing tools for automating all aspects of the wedding (e.g., tools for mass-inviting Facebook friends). This is something we shall come back to in the conclusion.

What makes this circumstance somewhat unique is the fact that the organizers use technologies selectively for their ability to *manage the visibility of their efforts*. This is not merely for functional purposes, but in order to generate a sense of wonderment that is sought for in weddings. Hiding effort in the right ways, while revealing it in others, contributes to making the wedding feel like "it is meant to be:" it is somehow magical.

People and Participation

Part of this is consequent on how weddings are occasions where an audience – friends, family, coworkers, and so on – congregates to witness something. Our interviews with couples highlighted the tensions associated with this process of inviting and involving people. Those who participate in the event are not any old set of people – they have to be the *right set of people*: those who it is believed "ought" to come to the marriage, those people that "must" be invited out of obligation, those it would be "nice" to have; the ambiguity of these words suggests how this is far from unproblematic.

"We both come from very large families...so we had about 100 people who were just family people, and then our friends, because both of us socialize in groups of friends. Within those groups, obviously there are some people who we don't really have that much of a relationship with other than when you see them in social situations. But it would never be people you'd call, but it would be a bit awkward if you didn't invite them to the wedding because you see them socially." – Groom A, Couple O

In other words, participants spoke of their weddings as times to take stock of their social networks. While some invitees (e.g., the biological family) are an easily identified starting point for the guest list, there are others who are more distant: casual acquaintances who, though likely encountered more frequently than most family members, are seen as less involved. Their status is unclear: should they be invited, or not? Our participants struggled with these questions, and used Facebook, email address books, and other social media to help them identify and determine who should be invited. This was especially pronounced when considering the cost associated with each additional guest (the bride from Couple A emphasized that every bride can report the cost per guest off the top of their head). The same social media that could be seen as a resource for compiling the guest list also exacerbated this problem by making the engagement and the upcoming nuptials more public.

"Now that you're engaged and your wedding is coming, it seems like more people will Like your page. Like 'Oh I want an invite to the wedding'." – Bride, Couple I

One technique some couples reported for attempting to side-step these complicated questions was to hold a destination or international wedding, where the logistics and cost of travel would serve as a forcing function for a small guest list. Still others had to be selective about who the "right set" of people for each part of the wedding was.

While some used destination weddings as a way to escape the need to involve many people, technology enabled new configurations where the people involved in making the wedding happen need not even be in the same place. Couple D lived in Los Angeles but held their ceremony in New Jersey by coordinating with the bride's mother. Couple G lived in Toronto but held their ceremony in New Orleans, and booked all of their vendors sight-unseen. The bride from Couple J lived in England, the groom lived in Saudi Arabia, and the ceremony was held in their hometown in India.

"Because I was living in England and he was in Saudi Arabia, we were always dependent on computers, Google, Skype, Windows, all those things. We had to plan for everything through the internet and we had to see the prices, do the selections, because my mom is from Calcutta and she didn't know what to buy...I went to India for my wedding 2 days before and everything was done through seeing what to buy and where to get it on the internet." – Bride, Couple J

Interesting here is the fact that the internet enabled the couples to perform the "work" of planning a wedding even if they did not necessarily have the bodily ability to see the venue, taste the food, or hear the band beforehand.

Not all people who are invited are invited to participate in the same way. Some take on more responsibilities or perform special actions, while others are expected to stay out of the process and simply appear and witness the event. Technology changed when and who could participate in the lead-up to the wedding. For example, Couple D shared a playlist on Spotify and used Facebook to ask guests to help select songs that they wanted to hear at the reception. In this sense, technology enabled participants to involve more people than they previously would have been able to, and allowed them to take on new roles as enabled by the technology.

Configuring participation – who will give speeches, who will attend which event – is also a highly variable and intricate piece of social labor. All of this occurs even before the wedding takes place and continues beyond the wedding day as well. Couple F noted that while on their honeymoon, they were delighted to discover that guests became Facebook friends and were commenting on one another's posts – *"it's created this really cool group of friends that didn't exist before."* With technology configuring participation both before and after the event, we now turn to how it enables forms of participation during the wedding day itself.

Spectacle: Giving Them Something to Talk About

Whether it is something as modest as giving a speech at a wedding with 20 guests, or something as flashy as indoor fireworks at a wedding with 800 (with Couple I), creating the right amount of spectacle was a consistent goal among participants: after the right people gather and the roles are assigned, magic demands action.

Unusual Experiences

One of the primary ways that couples achieved a sense of spectacle was to provide their guests with experiences that they would not encounter every day. Special experiences were arranged to demarcate and mirror the importance of the day, and these came in many forms: music, dancing, food and drink, elaborate costumes or formalwear, photo slideshows, giving speeches, party games, throwing the bouquet, providing small novelties at the tables, photo booths, and so on. Technology was similarly used in order to provide guests with unusual experiences. Couple K gave the children at their wedding disposable cameras in order to keep them entertained, and enjoyed reviewing the often silly photos that the children took. Couple B used an iPad in order to create a video booth at the reception where guests could record a message for the bride and groom. More prosaic, everyday forms of technology were woven into the more unusual ones: all couples described their guests using mobile phones to take and post photos throughout the day. In this way, using technology contributes to the occurrence of the event; it is made more special and noteworthy because family and friends are involving themselves through the use of these technologies in the demarcation of the day.

Personalization

As we saw at the outset, North American and British wedding culture is something that many people seek to resist – even if they cherry-pick certain acceptable and preferred aspects from it. Our couples worked to make the activities and tone of their wedding day a crafted experience, one that alloyed their disdain for the commonplace or "tacky" and yet remained somehow traditional and fashionable. Participants frequently used the term "personal" to refer to this task of making the wedding reflective of the couple's personality. The internet was a constantly-regarded source that affirmed cultural standards and norms, tacky or refined as they may be, but provided a vast set of examples of personalization:

"I was happy to find there were a lot of alternatives to that online...Rock 'n Roll Bride and Alternative Bride. Both of those were quite nice in the way that they showed you. And they had lots of forums where people talked about all of the alternative things they did or the way they did it their way." – Bride, Couple A

Personalizing aspects of the wedding helped to create a sense of spectacle – guests might reasonably attend expecting one type of experience, only to be served with a different one. As the quote above illustrates, these personal touches worked in subtle ways. The groom from Couple G explained:

"I suppose you do want it to reflect you a little bit, and you want it to be interesting for people and not just feel like the same lame idea everyone else has had...I suppose it was partly for personal satisfaction just to make it more interesting for ourselves." – Groom, Couple G

What couples struggled with is the fact that in order to have a wedding, it must seem magical, but practical; traditional, but personalized; recognizable as a wedding but unique nonetheless. No longer limited by the number and variety of materials available locally and to-hand, the web enabled participants to select from nearly endless combinations of options. This personalization was another form of work that was selectively hidden and revealed to create a sense of spectacle. Technology can present the opportunity and perceived need to make an event as unique as possible.

Limiting the Role of Technology on the Special Day

With all of the lengths that people go to in order to transform themselves and their surroundings for one day, it is not entirely surprising that technology was commonly seen as a symbol of the everyday, and accordingly an uncomfortable presence on the wedding day. Only certain people could use certain technologies and for certain purposes. Many of the brides in the sample chose to rid themselves of their mobile phones on their wedding day, seeing it as too symbolic of the frustrations of planning up until that point:

"I felt like I had spent a year organizing it, and on the wedding day I did have my phone around in the morning and then I left it at my mum's house...everyone I know was going to be there, so I didn't really need it." – Bride, Couple H

What is even more interesting here is the fact that this bride not only associated her phone with the headaches of planning and organization, but on the day, it became functionally useless to her because all of the people she could potentially contact were already physically present. Indeed, this may be one of the few times in life where one's entire social network assembles in person. Thus, a wedding prompts the utility of some everyday technologies to diminish, while the value of others increases enormously.

"I was glad there were all these photos and I didn't have to take them because I could just focus on being at the party and seeing all these people and living my wedding day, and not having to do that, be distracted by taking photos. I can see how taking photos might be distracting for someone if they're standing there watching someone do their first dance through a lens." – Bride, Couple D

As this quote shows, the bride wished to avoid using technology at her own wedding, but others were uniquely enlisted to do so on her behalf. The way they did so reminds of the problems of defining participation and attendance at a wedding. Photographers, videographers, and DJs do work at a wedding, but curiously are not attendees (c.f., Everett Hughes's "Good People and Dirty Work" [12]). These individuals are sanctioned to perform the necessary work of documentation and entertainment so that the rest of the congregation may instead focus on the pure aspects of participation.

Documenting the Magic Day

Participants brought this about in two primary ways: going to great and creative lengths to document aspects of the day itself, and to make reminders of the day easily encountered and visible in the time following the wedding. In both of these goals, technology played a central role.

Documenting the Day

All of our participants documented their weddings (or planned to) through photos, videos, websites, and documents. They did so in a highly coordinated, though common sense, way: through structuring the documenting practices around the features of the event, and ensuring that these features were there for the documenting. They knew ahead of time what was worth documenting, and made arrangements about how the documentation would take place.

The most obvious manifestation of this was in the planned presence of a photographer or videographer at the event. Participants saw both positive and negative aspects of this. Some saw the photographer/videographer as an outsider, an uninvited guest; others saw these individuals as necessary because they were able to capture elements of the day in ways different from their friends and family. Couple F represented several of the couples in the sample:

"[Our friend] captured like this whole, and he put together an amazing video. I would never have considered a videographer at the wedding, because I just think that's crazy, but in retrospect it was such an amazing gift that they gave us in putting all that together. If it was a video-for-hire then it might have changed the tone of it a bit...I can't watch it though, because I cry too much." –Bride, Couple F

In the cases where a friend or family member undertook the role of videographer, the output was treasured all the more, perhaps because of this: at least they were welcome even if they were doing work rather than participating. Participants often coordinated with their videographer or photographer to create a "shot list" – predetermining the set of shots that needed to be taken on the day. Couple N, the professional wedding photographers, noted that this list is commonly compiled through collaboration between the photographers and the couple, with the couple identifying the important people, and the photographers responsible for gathering the people on the day, arranging them in the shot, and ensuring it is actually taken. Examples of shots include ones like "couple with bridal party at church" or "groom and his father." The value of the shot list became particularly evident when speaking to the bride from Couple J:

"I regret not having a proper photo of me, my groom, and my mom and dad...I'm the only daughter so the 4 of us together. My mom was very busy then and she wasn't paying attention to have a photo done but now I so wish we had a proper photo of us together." – Bride, Couple J

The shot list illustrates again how weddings are about particular times where particular people are engaged in a particular activity that is especially meaningful or important – the (sought for) magical moments. Missing a photograph of an uncle eating at the reception is fine; missing a photograph of the first kiss is not. One is prosaic, not to be documented; the other is special, to be revisited, shown, talked about for years to come. At the same time, documenting attendance is crucial: this is hardly surprising given the time, effort and skill put into selecting those who are invited. Kirk et al.'s study of video creation and storage confirms our own findings [15].

Photos and videos were not the only types of mementos that were kept from the wedding. Participants kept a wide range of physical artifacts: the wedding dress, corks from the champagne bottles, flowers from the bouquet, copies of the invitations, the guestbook, and so on. These objects were valued due to their role in the achievement of the day, and were seen as irreplaceable but somehow still secondary in importance to the photos. For example, the bride from Couple D was representative of the sample when she talked about how it was important to place these mementos in perspective:

"I do have a sentimental attachment to this dress I wore for my wedding, but I have the photos, and I have the husband, and the sentimental attachment isn't tied to me holding onto this thing. I want to donate it to this place called Brides Against Breast Cancer." – Bride, Couple D

For technology design and use, this would outwardly suggest that capturing particular moments for the official record is more important than capturing the entire event from multiple angles. This might also have implications for ways of filtering through large sets of photos or videos, by focusing on these particular moments as "search terms." Furthermore, there is an ethos associated with holding onto materials from the day – the rule of thumb was not that "keeping more is better." These are issues well covered already in the HCI and CSCW literatures (see, for example Cosley et al. [5]). Weddings have special moments of spectacle that act as indices into the event and orient documentation efforts.

Re-Experiencing the Magic

Despite the effort put into documenting the event, our participants rarely spent a great deal of time reviewing the results. The mere fact of creating the documents was obviously more important than any planned revisiting of them [24]. Nevertheless, our participants did make some efforts to put photos in places where they would encounter them. Some of the more obvious ways were to make a wedding photo one's Facebook profile picture, or the background image on one's phone. Some couples kept the playlist of songs that they used at the wedding alongside their other playlists, and would revisit it. Participants valued photos as places to "go" when they wanted to relive aspects of their wedding. For Couple K, they substituted for visiting the actual wedding location.

"Yeah I go through the photos and the emails from the lady that organized it, they're still saved in my Hotmail. So I occasionally look through them again. It's really nice because like I said we got married abroad it's not like we can drive to where we got married and say 'Oh look that's where we got married.'" – Bride, Couple K

Participants also talked about how their lived experience of the day was so frantic that the photos made it possible for them to actually revisit the day in a way that they weren't able to experience the first time.

"I've really enjoyed watching the video and looking at the photos. It really brings it back because it does go in a bit of a blur when you're the bride and groom." – Bride, Couple H

The first few months after the wedding was regarded as a time for talking about and working with the mementos. This was a kind of timeframe or window that followed the event where revisiting it is expected and indulged, and the production of photo albums, memory books, thank you cards, and so on is done.

"For ages afterwards I intended to make one of those photo books, you make them online and have it printed but I just never got round to doing that...I suppose once the event has passed there's no deadline for getting it done so there's nothing to motivate you into thinking 'I should have that done by so and so's birthday' or something like that. I am still stuck kind of half-intending to do it." – Bride, Couple G

As this quote illustrates, the period of time following a wedding is at once an acceptable time to make a wedding album, but without a firm deadline in place, it can be delayed indefinitely. While some participants felt pressure to produce the album as a gift to their family members, and many were eager to see their photos, the level of engagement with photos tapered off over time. In fact, Facebook and other photo sharing services often surprised participants, who – long after they finished thinking about their wedding – found new photos of the event. This was seen as a welcome kind of surprise.

"I quit Facebook 'til I finished my qualifying exam... When I got back on a few weeks ago I went 'Oh wow look at all these wedding photos people have!' Otherwise I don't look at my wedding photos too often." – Bride, Couple D

This suggests that opportunities for spacing out the revealing of photos, or other forms of mementos, might be of potential benefit. Rather than showing all of the photos of the wedding at once – as with many services – it might be helpful to carefully mete out their arrival so as to "make the magic last." Further to this point, the sharing of photos in this way could potentially help to reconstitute the set of people involved in the wedding, thus serving to preserve a sense of community among the guests. All the more so when one considers these remarks about showing wedding pictures at family events:

[On father's 60th birthday] "His dad set up a massive slide show on the computer of all the official photos... they sent all their guests through the house to look at it. No one escaped! Everyone had to go through and admire our wedding." – Bride, Couple G

"I went to my grandmother's funeral...and so my aunts and my cousins there, they didn't come to the wedding. So I got that book so I could show them...so it was good to show to people who couldn't be there." – Groom A, Couple O

Outwardly we might assume that a 60th birthday party or a funeral has little to do with a recent wedding, but in fact, the wedding became a primary topic of conversation at these events. Efforts to make the magic of the wedding last were partially achieved by using technologies to create artifacts to talk about at subsequent social gatherings.

DISCUSSION

Our research has sought to capture the full lived moment of weddings: from the logistical work when it is planned, the celebration itself, and the reliving thereafter. What should be clear is that technology of all kinds is suffused through this experience. It is used to plan, to celebrate, and to recall; it is also used, as Sarvas & Frohlich note [24] to constitute the event - picture taking being as much part of doing a wedding as a technique for reminiscing thereafter.

Doubtless weddings are not unusual events in this regard; much, if not every, aspect of contemporary society is touched by technology. Even the most traditional event, like a wedding, attests to the fact that we are now living in a world of ubiquitous computing. Mark Weiser would be pleased, even if a little startled, at quite how ubiquitous it is. That this is so should not elide recognition of the subtle ways that technology gets used, however, nor equally subtle explorations of how it might be used through better design and development.

The first part of our discussions alluded to some of the aspirations that Mark Weiser outlined when he coined the term ubiquitous computing: that technology should disappear. What we found is not that the technology disappears (though it is taken for granted), but that more importantly it allows some of the work the technology enables to disappear. Various aspects of planning, scheduling and logistics, for example, amongst other paraphernalia of organization, are made easier and less "visible" with the use of spreadsheets, common email addresses and such like. A fuller, more detailed treatment of the organization of work among couples and their extended networks would be a fruitful area for future study and informative for designing planning systems.

We also saw something in relation to this which points toward the essential concerns of CSCW as outlined by Schmidt and Bannon [25]. The tools that allow invisibility also allow the humans engaged in the work to articulate themselves or, rather, to do *articulation work*. This was most conspicuous with regard to the work which is not merely practical or functional but that which entails delicate political acts: choices that, if messed up, produce emotional costs. Who gets invited is not just a question that the bride and groom can answer, for instance; sometimes the extended families on both sides have a role too. Participation in a wedding, being on the "invitee list," is then not just a matter of affection. Some people have to come to reciprocate prior invitations; others to honor aspects of family that cannot be provided in any other way. There is good reason to fear such mistakes: they can lead to recriminations, complaints, hurts. Choices about these matters articulate the auspices and nature of collaboration in the work of weddings.

This has immediate implications for some state of art technologies and related conceptions of social practice – articulation technologies especially. For if what we found is correct, then attendance at a wedding cannot be predicted to be, or modelled as, a graph-based, social network; the articulation that Schmidt and Bannon say is so fundamental to cooperative enterprises is absent [25]. The issue is not simply that those who get invited might be appalled by the use of a social graph to identify them; we are not alluding to the possibility that invitees might complain that they have been selected by dint of, say, a Facebook model. Indeed, our research suggests they would be right to complain and find that offensive. Of greater moment is that fact that their ire would derive from their knowledge – common sense, everyday knowledge - that the "configuration of participation" at weddings is a complex product of social and political negotiation. It is an emergent property derived from the patterns of power and bargaining skill manifest in those who have rights to select who can and cannot come – not just the bride and groom, but other family members, influential friends and so on. Thus those who find an invitation on their doormat and post boxes (paper invites still being preferred) will know that this is the result not of a model, but of delicate and complex affair; all the more gratified they feel when that invitation comes.

If this is so, then one important implication is that social network models cannot be used to help automate or make invisible this aspect of the work of weddings. Beyond this, it also begs the question of whether such social graph-based models have the utility that is widely claimed if an event that purports to be about robust kinship and friendships structures cannot be so modeled. If not weddings what then what of other looser affiliations? Of course, it may be that the emergent social configuration of weddings is extreme; other social connections might be easier to map and hence model because they are more stable, more "predictable." But this does suggest that the emergent nature of social relations is an important issue that might be neglected in social graph theory and practice: a contrast might be drawn between the views of society to be found in, say, Duncan Watts [30] and Schmidt and Bannon [25] already mentioned, also Tim Ingold [14]. The former privileges graph models, the latter, practice and its articulation. A system that foregrounds the practice of social configuration – that recognizes social affairs are delicately produced and difficult to pin down in models – might be more useful here. For example, a method of communicating that only allows messages to be delivered to particular people in a particular order (rather than everyone at the same time, as with email or Facebook) could be helpful.

A second important set of issues arise in relation to place. One might imagine that new technologies would reduce the need to participate in, or attend weddings. One might simply Skype in, say. Our research shows that this will only occur in the exception for two main reasons. To begin with, place is used as a determination both of who can attend and who cannot. A ceremony held far away is undertaken there so as to prohibit the need to invite all and sundry, for example (or to allow reasonable declined invitations say); a wedding nearby the reverse. Place is a tool for social selection, then.

In addition to this, place is also crucial to ensuring the right sort of event happens: that the magic sought for is attained while the adroit management of semblances also - not too extravagant with foolish expense, but tasteful, with the right ambience. Here, who attends is just as vital. To paraphrase Dourish, place is where the action is [7]. Though similar realism may motivate those who choose to accept an invitation, not many will accept simply because they think magic will be seen; many more (if not most) accept because they want to enjoy the entertainment, the ceremony, the food, the company. They are at once seeking and helping create something more than this list implies: they help foster *the spectacle*. The spectacle sought for is in some particular place: not anywhere will do. Magic – even the foolish swooning of wedding magic – is situated; its geography and its participants matter. An interesting and startling contrast can be made with Harper's study of the importance of place in the work of the IMF: though that organization seeks to undertake rational decision-making, place turns out to be important in sanctifying its decisions [11]. Here too place is bound to the sacredness sought in weddings. Technology that seeks to dissolve distance and thereby reduce the salience of place misses the point. This does not mean that technologies of communication and "digital presence" might not have a role, but it does mean that they need reimagining if they are to aid in weddings. It is unlikely that they will replace the importance of place, but it is possible they might be able to augment it.

Third, the value of technology in documenting the event cannot be underestimated. But what our research suggests is that the formal creations (e.g., the "Wedding Album") are not always visited or examined as much as one might expect, especially when one considers how much effort is put into their production. Without diminishing the importance of the official records of the day, a great deal of joy and unexpected value comes out of the unplanned and more serendipitous collections and showings of wedding traces. The sudden placing of wedding pictures on someone's Facebook account a year after the event, the sharing of hitherto unseen pictures at a subsequent but unconnected family gathering, attests to the possibility that digital traces might be gathered and made available more widely. The joy that unexpected views produces is also suggestive that these traces might take novel forms – supplements to the staged photos for example; unusual traces – sounds, say, or perhaps social media content that returns and is made strange by its appearance [5]. This points towards the absence of control over the collection of traces at the wedding: if the official album is an artful creation, the product of an imagined world of perfection, then the traces that are captured outside this envelope of editorial control might appeal precisely because they are contrastive, mocking the sought-for perfection through documenting the less-than-perfect, the foolish dress, the infelicitous speech. Just how this might be managed without offence is a difficult question, though it is one that might need to rely on the good grace of those who do the collecting.

Like other major life events, we have seen how the use of technology with respect to weddings creates opportunities and challenges for design. The problematic nature of a formal social graph emerges again throughout these events (c.f., what happens when a user of a social network dies, or seeks support following a loss [19]) – the modeling of human relationships as nodes in a graph seems to fail when life arrangements are changing drastically. We also see the importance of planning raised across life events; whether planning for a wedding, or for a new child [9], or for a residential move [26], software is used to coordinate and track progress but is often imported from the workplace and carries its moral trappings. Finally, technology changes the way we are informed of, and reflect upon, these events. Delivering news and evidence (i.e., photos) of a wedding is increasingly accomplished using social media that can inadvertently upend traditions for notification (i.e., that close family find out first, and then friends, and then looser acquaintances). Similar concerns exist for notifying people about a birth, death, new job, and so on. Major life events are often worth sharing, but the order and audience of this sharing needs to be carefully considered to enable more flexible methods of notification and documentation.

CONCLUSION

We have presented the results of the first study in HCI and CSCW exploring weddings as a domain for inquiry in their own right, revealing a set of rich and varied practices concerning technology's role in their achievement. Our findings illustrate how couples engage in a dialogue with contemporary notions of the "magical wedding day," carefully orchestrating an event that is special and memorable, but at the same time realistic and practical. We have outlined four ways in which the semblance of magic is brought about: by managing the visibility of effort, by carefully configuring who participates and how, by personalizing the event and providing spectacle, and by documenting the day so that its magic can be revisited. These findings point towards considerations for technology design and use, and suggest more nuanced notions of relationships beyond the social graph, the implications of place, and considerations for alternative forms of documentation. Like other life events, weddings surface complex, subtle, and important relationships that people create with technology, and with one another.

ACKNOWLEDGMENTS

Thanks to our participants and colleagues in the Socio-Digital Systems group.

REFERENCES

1. Appy Couple. http://www.appycouple.com.
2. Bauman, Z. *Liquid Life*. Polity Press (2005).
3. Centers for Disease Control and Prevention. http://www.cdc.gov/nchs/nvss/marriage_divorce_tables.htm.
4. Cheng, W. et al. Semantic-event based analysis and segmentation of wedding ceremony videos. *Proc. MIR 2007*, 95-104.
5. Cosley, D. Sosik, D. Schultz, J. Peesapati, S. & Lee, S. Experiences with designing tools for everyday reminiscing. *HCI* 27, 1-2 (2012), 175-198.
6. De Certeau, M. *The practice of everyday life*. Berkeley: University of California Press (1984).
7. Dourish, P. Re-space-ing place: "place" and "space" ten years on. *Proc CSCW 2006*, 299-308.
8. Garfinkel, H. *Studies in ethnomethodology*. Prentice Hall (1967).
9. Gibson, L. and Hanson, V. L. Digital motherhood: how does technology help new mothers? *Proc. CHI 2013*, 313-322.
10. Grimes, R. *Rite out of place*. Oxford (2006).
11. Harper, R. Gatherers of information: Some remarks on the mission process at the international monetary fund. *Proc. ECSCW 1997*, 361-377.
12. Hughes, E. C. Good people and dirty work. *Social Problems 10*, 1 (1962), 3-11.
13. Ingraham, C. *White weddings: Romancing heterosexuality in popular culture*. Taylor & Francis (2008).
14. Ingold, T. *Being alive: Essays on movement, knowledge, and description*. Routledge (2011).

15. Kirk, D. S., Sellen, A., Harper, R. & Wood, K. Understanding videowork. *Proc. CHI 2007,* 61-70.

16. Leeds-Hurwitz, W. *Wedding as text: Communicating cultural identities through ritual*. Routledge (2002).

17. Liu, S., et al. Hi, magic closet, tell me what to wear!. *Proc. MM* 2012, 619-628.

18. Luo, S., Shen, I., Hsu, H., and Chen, B. Attention-oriented photo slideshow. *SIGGRAPH Posters 2012*. Article 23.

19. Massimi, M. Exploring remembrance and social support behavior in an online bereavement support group. *Proc. CSCW 2013*, 1169-1180.

20. Mead, R. *One perfect day: The selling of the American wedding*. Penguin Books (2008).

21. Odom, W., Zimmerman, J., and Forlizzi, J. Designing for dynamic family structures: divorced families and interactive systems. *Proc. DIS 2010*, 151-160.

22. Otnes, C., and Pleck, E. H. *Cinderella dreams: The allure of the lavish wedding*. U. California Press (2003).

23. PopSugar. Best wedding planning apps. http://bit.ly/15NjTM9

24. Sarvas, R. & Frohlich, D. *From Snapshots to Social Media*, Springer (2011), London.

25. Schmidt, K. and Bannon, L. Taking CSCW seriously. *JCSCW* 1, 1-2 (1992), 7-40.

26. Shklovski, I., Kraut, R. and Cummings, J. Keeping in touch by technology: maintaining friendships after a residential move. *Proc. CHI 2008*, 807-816.

27. Star, S. L. and Strauss, A. Layers of silence, arenas of voice: The ecology of visible and invisible work. *JCSCW 8*, 1-2 (1999), 9-30.

28. The Knot. http://www.theknot.com

29. USA Today. http://bit.ly/1704QxM

30. Watts, D. *Six degrees: The science of a connected age.* Vintage (2004).

31. Wedding Party. https://itunes.apple.com/us/app/wedding-party-getting-married/id494214305?mt=8

32. Weduary. http://www.weduary.com.

33. Whyte, M. K. *Dating, mating, and marriage.* New York: Aldine de Gruyter (1990).

34. Yarosh, S., Tang, A., Mokashi, S., and Abowd, G. "Almost touching": Parent-child remote communication using the ShareTable system. *Proc. CSCW 2013,* 181-192.

35. Zarro, M., Hall, C., and Forte, A. Wedding dresses and wanted criminals: Pinterest.com as an infrastructure for repository building. *Proc. ICWSM 2013.*

Digital Mobilization in Disaster Response: The Work & Self-Organization of On-Line Pet Advocates in Response to Hurricane Sandy

Joanne I. White, Leysia Palen & Kenneth M. Anderson
Project EPIC
University of Colorado Boulder
joanne.white, palen, kena@colorado.edu

ABSTRACT

This ethnographic study of a Facebook Page founded on 28 October 2012 in anticipation of Hurricane Sandy's US landfall reveals how on-line pet advocates—a large but loosely organized social movement—mobilized their ad hoc discretionary activities to more cooperative, organized work to assist numerous displaced pets. The investigation shows how innovations around "crossposting" to create a more persistent form of visual data management were important. It describes how these innovations produced an improvised case management system around which members of the pet-advocacy crowd could collectively work to help displaced pets. The paper connects to the CSCW and organizational science literature to consider how this emergent community articulated work and structured the mission of the Page.

Author Keywords

Activism; Animals; Computer-Mediated Communication; Crisis Informatics; Disasters; Organizing; Pets; Self-Organizing; Social Computing; Social Media; Structuration

ACM Classification Keywords

H.5.3 Groups & Organization Interfaces—collaborative computing, computer-supported cooperative work; K.4.2 Social Issues

INTRODUCTION

Much attention has been paid to the possibilities of "crowd computing" [e.g. 20, 30], including how it might be used effectively in disaster response [3, 32, 34, 37]. This paper examines how crowd work emerged naturalistically in the 2012 Hurricane Sandy event. In the domain of pet advocacy, the latent potential for crowd interaction comes from intrinsic and extrinsic motivations—we focus on how that potential was transformed into a viable form of distributed, decentralized cooperative work. We combine practice- and structurational-based understandings of human action [29] to show how work practice and mechanisms of self-organizing interact with one another, where the features of the environment, the varying skills of the convergent crowd, and the problems that face the subjects of their interest come together to articulate a socio-technical cooperative work environment.

Pets & Disaster. Pets and their "owners" are unheralded sufferers in disasters: for example, in 2005's Hurricane Katrina, about 70,000 pets were separated from their owners because of the damage to property, rapid human evacuation, and lack of formal support for pets in evacuation procedures. Of these, only 15,000 pets were rescued and just 2,300 were reunited—3% of the total. Many were euthanized or left to die at great emotional cost to families and financial cost to the state [17, 23, 25].

Pet Advocacy. Like other "convergers" onto a disaster [6, 12, 18, 32], pet advocates are present in both the physical and digital disaster scene. They bring their existing knowledge and very strong identities as advocates to assist in the disaster cause [3]. In non-disaster situations, pet advocates have taken to on-line activities in what Golbeck calls "passion-based networks" [10]. Message boards and forums were early internet destinations that remain highly frequented locations for pet advocates. However, like other topical groups that organize on-line, how they might mobilize into action is of great interest, particularly with respect to today's social media use where the differences between activism and "slacktivism" are at issue. "Slacktivism" [9] refers to the observation that on-line advocacy in its simplest forms (such as collective profile changes and the simple passing on of information to show support for a cause—which happens frequently in pet advocacy) have unclear benefits to the causes themselves [22, 28, 30]. However, the conditions of disaster response call upon advocacy in temporally accelerated and constrained ways that allow examination of how loose coalitions reorganize to engage in coordinated work—an important element of mobilization.

We examine a central on-line site for pet activism during and after Hurricane Sandy, which made US landfall on 29 October 2012 in New Jersey, exacting its worst damage there and in New York. How people's on-line advocacy is reshaped and restructured within a digital environment [2]

CSCW'14, February 15 - 19 2014, Baltimore, MD, USA

ACM 978-1-4503-2540-0/14/02...$15.00.
http://dx.doi.org/10.1145/2531602.2531633

to support both centralized and decentralized forms of distributed, cooperative work is the topic of this paper.

The Pet Problem in Disasters

The impact of a disaster greatly increases the number of pets that enter shelters. The hazard event itself can disrupt the physical environment—fences are compromised and windows are broken. Pets might be scared by the hazard and run away. Their owners may not be able to return home, or perhaps assume temporary accommodations where pets are not allowed. Rebuilding efforts can further compromise the built environment because the usual security measures are looser. For areas in great distress, people might simply be unable to care for their pets.

The loss of a pet from a disaster may carry a higher risk for mental health issues [17, 19, 24, 27]. A study of pet-owning survivors of Hurricane Katrina found significantly higher levels of acute stress, depression, and post-traumatic stress disorder in those who lost their pets than those who did not, even when controlling for the other effects of the disaster [14]. In addition to devastating emotional loss, the logistical consequences of lost pets to the region can be high: Animals must be gathered, transported, sheltered, fed, fostered, and re-homed if possible. Following the 2005 Hurricane Katrina event, the US government passed the PETS Act [26] to help address the multi-faceted problems of pets in disasters. The Act has seen improvements in the treatment and logistical management of animals though it has not been a silver bullet for large disasters where the problems are so vast. The most reliable method of pet-family matching during non-disaster situations—microchipping—depends on proprietary software, and on owners to update phone and address details—major obstacles to seamless reunions in the aftermath of disasters.

The effects on pet welfare during Hurricane Sandy were far less than in Katrina, but still significant. One of the difficulties faced by both pet advocates and emergency managers is that so little comprehensive information is available about the pet population after disasters (see, e.g., [7]). At the time of writing, nine months after Sandy made US landfall, partial data helps explain the magnitude: The Humane Society deployed over 140 paid and volunteer staff, assisted with the rescue of more than 350 animals, and cared for over 700 total in their shelters; 400 of these animals were reclaimed by owners. In the initial days of Sandy, its 24-hour hotline received more than 900 calls [13]. The American Society for Prevention of Cruelty to Animals (ASPCA) reports that its combined response helped more than 30,000 pets in NY and NJ alone [1].

Finally, a message of distrust of established organizations pervades grassroots pet activism during times of normalcy. This distrust interacts with the disaster response in ways that influence advocates' behavior. In particular, some advocates distrust how sheltering organizations manage pets. According to ASPCA, 5-7 million pets enter animal shelters nationwide annually, and 60% of dogs and 70% of cats are euthanized. The Animal Care and Control group and the Humane Society make counter claims to pet management practices, and scholarship adds further to this conflicted space, describing the "neat and tidy" picture offered to the public as obscuring the issues that arise with the enormous number of unwanted and stray pets [15, 16]. A 72-hour stay is the minimum required time that an animal be sheltered before euthanasia, though some are euthanized earlier if they are judged to have health or behavioral problems. During disaster, however, a large number of pets—who are otherwise wanted—are newly subject to emergency shelters. Pet advocates therefore feel that it is urgent to alert rescue organizations to "pull" the pet from the shelter and help it find a "forever home" during what is perceived as a critical 72-hour window.

Objective & Theoretical Approach

With respect to the on-line response to Hurricane Sandy, the pet advocacy community participated in ways that echoed earlier events: social media accounts appeared, including Facebook Pages and Groups. However, the nature of the volunteer response to disaster is changing in often observable ways with each event, and *The Hurricane Sandy Lost and Found Pets Page* on Facebook, a central place of convergence, captured an important state change in pet advocacy response that is worth investigating from cooperative work and self-organizing points of view.

The decisions made—even when seemingly small—on this Page to organize the information about lost pets interacted powerfully with the existing but ad hoc work of on-line pet advocates ("crossposting"). The yield of this combination articulated a new form of work for pet advocates, which helped to realize the potential of organized collective behavior through volunteerism in disaster response.

Following Orlikowski [29], this analysis unites both practice-based [35] and structurational-based interpretations of coordination and social organization [8] to understand the nature of collective work in large, distributed, and emergent groups—groups that have some existing common motivation to help but have little prior precedent for how that work might be conducted [21]. By examining work practices, and tracing how those practices are reified in the social-technical organization of a group that is forming and stabilizing *as they do the work*, we learn not just what this particular group did, but also how the mechanisms by which collective action in digital environments are organized bottom-up. We also learn how those lessons are graduated into prescriptive top-down direction to sustain and direct future action.

METHODS

Data collection primarily took place in the form of ethnographic, non-participant observation of the Hurricane Sandy Lost and Found Pets Page over seven months from October 2012 to May 2013. In keeping with the ethnographic method of both collection and analysis, we digitally captured interactions and took extensive field notes about user and administrator behavior, including features of their communication, collaboration, and organization. To supplement, we collected basic statistics about the Page using Facebook's Graph API to pull available data into a relational database. The data collected are specific to Timeline Posts, Album Photos, Likes, and Comments for the same seven-month period.

To ascertain reasons for behaviors that we could not directly observe, we followed up with an "email interview" to informants who, based on their observed activity on the Page, could speak to decisions that were made by members and admins individually and collectively. These open-ended questions queried issues common across all participants, including elements about their pet advocacy as well as their disaster response backgrounds. In addition, a second section was tailored to each participant to deeply inquire about their observed role on the Page. We initially contacted Page admins and active non-admins for a total of 38 people. Twelve people (three admins and nine non-admins) followed up with first-round responses to the email interview. Most elaborated their answers extensively, which supported the ethnographic quality of the investigation. Additional questions were sent after initial responses came in to clarify and elaborate points, just as in an offline interview. In one case, follow-up came in the form of a telephone interview per the participant's choice. Finally, one of the admins made critical measures from the Page analytics available. As an ethnographic investigation, the analysis uses a grounded, immersive, data-driven, triangulated approach in the interpretivist tradition [4].

THE HURRICANE SANDY LOST & FOUND PETS PAGE

Origins

The Hurricane Sandy Lost and Found Pets Page was launched on 28 October 2012. Sandy was expected to cause a great deal of damage on the US eastern seaboard; landfall a day out was known to be imminent by the storm that had earlier made landfall in Jamaica and Cuba. By 28 October, Sandy was already the largest Atlantic storm on record. After making landfall in New Jersey on 29 October, the storm exacted the worst of its damage there and in coastal areas of New York, with total damage estimated at over $50 billon by the time it dissipated on 31 October [36].

As Hurricane Sandy approached on 28 October, the founder of the Hurricane Isaac Lost and Found Pets page appealed there for "someone to create a page similar to this one but for Sandy" with a request to "...please comment here so we don't have a million different pages...so that it can be organized and people can add each other." Within a few minutes of the first share of this post, the newly created Hurricane Sandy Lost and Found Pets Page added a comment saying, "Done."

The Sandy Page founder lives well outside the affected region, but had experienced Hurricane Katrina and the pet loss in the aftermath of that event. She is also connected to numerous animal rescue and advocacy groups on-line. The Page About section states:

> Posting photos of lost or found pets in the areas affected by Sandy, as well as posting animal shelters in need and temporary shelters that allow animals. We are animal lovers and advocates trying to help with networking to get animals reunited with their families. We do not accept donations here nor can we direct you to a specific organization to donate to . If you post to our wall, your information may be shared so please keep this in mind before posting information you do not want shared

The elements here are important. First, the Page describes itself as a place for the posting of photos. As we explain, photo posting is one of the primary tasks taken up by a segment of pet advocates outside of disasters such that the very act of posting photos is tied quite strongly to the identity of pet advocacy. Second, the Page makes clear its role as a place for connection between people helping and searching for pets. Members reinforced early and often that the Page serve as a kind of hub that authoritatively organized information on behalf of the dispersed Sandy-related pet work happening across the social web. This, we believe, was to compel not just the Page's value, but the value and meaning of pet advocacy disaster work in general. Third, implied here and then clarified in posts, the pets represented on the Page were distinct from the numerous pets already in need of help. Members had to educate some advocates that animals lost in Sandy did not happen out of negligence: some pet advocates admonished owners of lost pets without appreciating how damaging a storm like Sandy could be to both pet and human welfare.

Membership & Content Volume

Three days into the Page's launch and two days after Sandy made landfall, the Page reached 6,000 Likes on 31 October 2012. By mid-November, it had achieved and then maintained more than 25,000 Likes with continued growth through 5 May 2013 to 28,436 Likes.

The Page had 12 administrators over its life, with six core admins persisting as primary admins. More active members would be invited to be admins, and many of the decisions that shaped the direction of the Page—and therefore the work of the Page—were made by these members. Other Admins rotated out when they could not be active. All admins (former and current) are female.

In terms of magnitude of activity, 6,683 unique users commented on the Timeline posts, and 3,932 unique users commented on the Photo Albums of the Page (a separate section where a lot of the "pet matching" work was done). Most of the active members were female. Page members produced the content shown in Table 1.

Early Organizing & Activity

The site was initiated as a Facebook (FB) *Page* rather than a *Group,* which carry different affordances. FB Pages were

Number of Timeline posts	1,572
Number of Comments on Timeline posts	24,509
Number of Albums	25
Number of Photos in Albums	1,061
Number of Comments on Photos in Albums	10,639
Number of Comments Made by Admins	4,280

Table 1. Number and Types of Page Content

first designed to support official presentation of organizations or public figures. A FB Page is visible to everyone on the Internet. People simply need to "Like" the Page for posts to appear in their own timeline. FB Pages feature five different admin roles, each with different permissions. FB Groups are intended for small group communication and can be set up to be public, private, or secret. Unlike Pages, posts in Groups can be made by any member. FB states that Groups are most successful when the number of members is kept small. It is not possible to transfer a Group to the larger scope of a Page after the fact.

Elicitation of Goals & Connection to Implementation

Within the first 24 hours, people began posting suggestions about how to structure the Page, sometimes tagging others to attract them to the Page and solicit their advice. The founder demonstrated an understanding of the impact this kind of disaster had on pets, which informed decisions about how to organize the Page's operations. After a person who belonged to more than 70 pet-focused FB Groups/Pages suggested that different Pages be dedicated to each State affected by the disaster (much as other pet advocacy is organized outside of times of disaster), the founder explained that administration would be too difficult under that kind of architecture:

> Also if animals are left behind and rescued or get lost during the evacuation it is quite possible for them to be located in a different state from the owner. That was the situation with Hurricane Katrina and to a limited extent with Hurricane Isaac.

This early decision to maintain one Page also foreshadowed evidence indicating that the founder envisioned it as a destination for the information-sharing work of pet advocates rather than the usual bulletin board-like waypoints of other sites that field sometimes repetitious information posting. We discuss this point at further length in the *From Advocacy to Action* section.

Adapting Practice to Design Constraints

The admins established policies early on to direct practice: people were asked to provide as much detail as possible about lost pets. Early users tagged themselves (and sometimes each other) in photos of lost pets so that they would receive automatic notifications when someone asked a question or perhaps suggested a match. Members also asked owners of lost pets to tag themselves in photos to self-track the work being done on their pet. These were the initial steps of an improvised case management system.

Division of Labor

People started becoming admins to distribute labor and responsibilities, a critical step in the self-organization of loose coalitions [21]. Four days into the Page's life, as more people became admins, one initiated the practice of adding initials to the end of each post they made to differentiate from each other and to internally organize their work. This practice was immediately adopted by other admins. In addition, the admins set up a Facebook Secret Group that was "filled with spreadsheets" (P10) that contained personal contact and address information about foster-offer homes, as well as lists of URLs that tracked from whom and where pet information originally came. They discussed ideas and created files noting work that needed to be done. When those tasks were completed, the files were deleted. In addition, the admins communicated using email and phone.

The admins described the following tasks as part of their work over the life of the Page: Answering private messages, answering comments under photos of lost pets, creating flyers, contacting pet owners for follow-up, deleting duplicate pet entries, organizing pet photo albums, organizing pet transports, and going out "old school" to areas that did not have electricity or access to the Page with paper flyers to post on trees and telephone poles.

Establishing Relevance to Achieve a Broader Net of Support

In the first two days of the Page's life, multiple other pet-advocacy pages on FB shared the Page with their own communities. Mainstream news outlets around the world covering Hurricane Sandy also included reports about the Page, tying it to stories of reunion and rescue. Such campaigning helped to meet the objective of establishing a larger net of people who could be on the lookout for missing pets or for matching lost to found pet photos.

Organizing around Roles

In addition to the administration of the Page and the division of labor articulation [21, 31], we characterize the visible work of the Page as a set of behaviors originally based in acts of simple photo broadcasting (that many engaged in), which were then extended to more cooperative work that expressed more durable objectives. We describe the transition between these interactions and how they structured the environment (and vice versa) below.

Still, many people sat in the "long tail" of Page interaction: Of the thousands of people who "Liked" the Page, many did nothing more. However, others minimally engaged in Liking or Sharing photos of Timeline posts: By "Liking" a photo, it would show up on that person's Timeline for their FB friends to see (and was the only mode of sharing on mobile devices at the time). "Sharing" (that is, choosing the Share link) was more deliberate, but had the same effect across all devices of making the photo visible to FB friends. Some commented to say that they shared a pet's photo, and several used the convention of typing just "s" (for "shared") that had previously been adopted by on-line pet advocates in non-disaster efforts. This mild engagement served the function of distributing information about lost and found pets, a necessary condition for the more elaborate "matching" and case management work that followed.

Administrators encouraged members to work with the content of the Page beyond their normal pet advocacy activities. Some members who had breed- or species-specific interests would work on advertising and trying to match up those particular animals. However, active members made appeals that everyone work on both dogs and cats regardless of personal preference. Recall too that a few members admonished owners who lost their pets in the disaster. These characteristics signal how strong some incoming identities were—they were advocates aligned to the animals rather than the owners. Others who were more familiar with disasters made appeals to suspend individual predispositions found in everyday advocacy (e.g. [10]) and instead apply broad concern to all pets and owners.

"Crossposting" as Page Launching Point

Of critical import to the understanding of both the origins and the progression of the mission and organization of the Page are the members who identify as "crossposters." Crossposters are pet advocates who deliberately crosspost information about pet issues from one site to the next. This straightforward task—and the strong identity that happens to be associated with it—is the taken-for-granted work upon which the Page rests. Curiously, though crossposting has been discouraged since essentially the birth of the Internet—early Usenet groups dealt with the issue of repetitious posts in FAQs, and some sites today ban crossposting in their Terms of Use—pet advocates view their form of crossposting *as favorable and central to their identity*. Some crossposters have set up special personal accounts dedicated to crossposting pet information, naming themselves "Francie Downey-Crossposter" or "Mary Crossposter Smyth." Crossposters connect with each other, and a few crossposters publicly collate the names and social media accounts of other crossposters—believing that "crossposting saves lives." Interviewees write:

> "The more people share a post, the more likely the person who lost/found the pet may see the post OR the more publicity a pet that needs a home gets the more likely he is to find that home." [P12]

> "What we do is have our friends who are with rescue groups all over the United States, animal lovers, [and] shelter volunteers send us pictures of dogs and cats who are more than likely to be killed at any time….when I share the photos a rescue group in that area [it] may save that animal, or a person wanting to adopt will see the animal and adopt, or [one] of [my] 5,000 friends will share my post to their friends and it continues to be posted by others."[P8]

The strong identity of on-line pet activists as crossposters—a term that seems reserved for use within the pet activist community—is critical here. Crossposting was the basis for the genesis of the emergent group [21]. Crossposting was nothing new for pet advocates, but what *was* new for them was managing the sudden flood of lost pets in a region, and understanding how disasters affect people and pets. Also new was the realization that the likelihood of finding matches between lost and found pets was far higher than normal, because the animals were accidently and suddenly displaced—not surrendered. This difference between routine crossposting and the information-sharing that could happen on a site built for the special conditions of disaster, transforms, we propose, activists' understanding of what they can do and achieve in their on-line advocacy work.

From Advocacy to Action

The desire to assist in disaster events in some way is broad [12, 18], but the mechanisms for enabling action in the form of on-line work or commitment, as with other causes, can be unclear [22, 28, 30]. In addition to the socio-psychological methods for motivating action, we must consider what kind of socio-technical features and mechanisms create an environment that supports transition from latent potential to cooperative work.

We see the information architecture for this Page as a turning point in how simple on-line individual pet advocacy was transformed into cooperative work. Pet information is strongly visual—reports of missing pets without visual information are far less useful and far less likely to be propagated to audiences. Crossposting as a pet advocacy practice seems to have arisen after the advent of "Web 2.0" when photos could be very easily uploaded to message forums and social networking sites by most anyone. The ease with which photos of animals could then be distributed to find a willing adopter gave rise to the role of the "crossposter" in the domain of pet welfare. Curiously, "crossposters" of this positive kind seem to exist only in a persistent way in the pet welfare world.

We explain below how the admins re-organized photo information posted by others to catalog the pets they were helping and to organize the work done around each pet. These acts of organization of visual data for crowd work transformed the simple activity of crossposting—which is all about posting early, often, quickly, and widely—to include cooperative tasks that more persistently focused on each pet in an improvised case management system.

Albums

At the start, the Page founder took information posted to the Timeline and organized it into Photo Albums, a feature that FB supports for its Pages (see Fig. 1). Facebook automatically creates three albums when the founder uploads any image: Timeline Photos, Cover Photos, and Profile Pictures. Page admins can add more albums. During the first few days of the Page, admins focused on listing the pets reported as lost, found, or reunited in the different

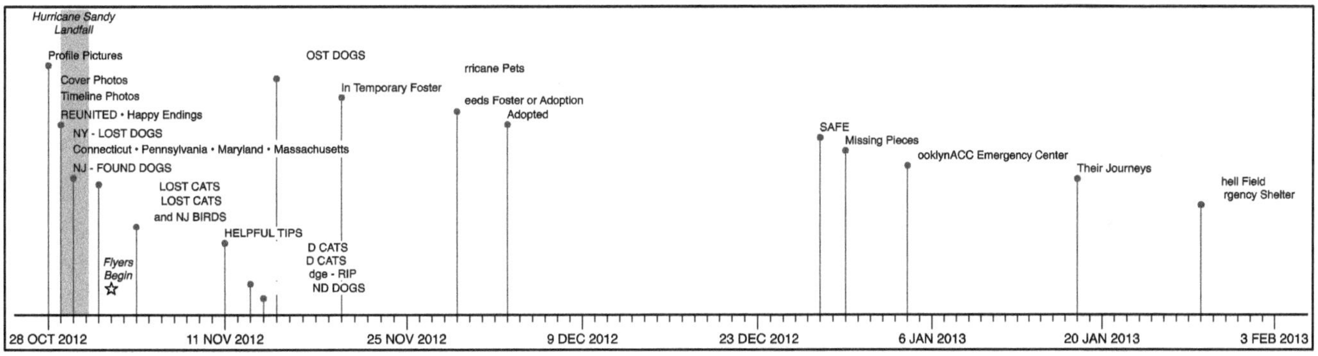

Figure 1. Timeline of Photo Album Creation & Flyer Invention

location-based albums, based on the information posted to the Page timeline by crossposters. We note that one member who was active in thinking about the information architecture of the Page was invited to be an admin because of her ideas about information management. Adapting the design constraints of FB, she customized the album faces to make the collection a clear destination for on-line work: Rather than use the FB default of the most recent photo, she created graphics for button-like navigation (Fig. 2). We note, too, that the graduation of active workers to the admin role demonstrates that the membership itself was based on a strong work-driven model.

The first album created was the "Reunited/Happy Endings" album, which shows an orientation to making sure that old information about previously lost pets was not propagated. It also shows an orientation to the goal of matching lost pet photos with found pet photos and achieving resolution. At the end of the 7-month observation, the Reunited/Happy Endings and the Adopted albums were the largest on the site with 208 and 246 photos respectively. In interviews, the more active members said that they would work until all the "hurricane kids" found homes.

Other albums created in the Page's first days reflect early suggestions by members to organize multiple Pages by State and animal type; instead that architecture was incorporated internally into albums in the single destination page: NY - Lost Cats, NJ - Found Dogs, etc. There were 10 albums of these types created by 15 November. The admins added others on topics for which people sought information for a total of 25 albums.

Figure 2. Photo Albums

The admins constantly updated the albums as a way of organizing incoming information about lost and found pets. When a case was resolved (that is, a pet was matched, reunited, adopted, or found deceased), the admins moved it to the appropriate album. This information management demonstrates a strong commitment to the arc and completion of the work. The albums as an information architecture for visual information brought the reasons for crossposting work into focus.

However, this organization also implicitly challenged the goals of some crossposters, which are to post often and widely. When people were found to be posting pet information about animals that had already been organized into an album, the admin deleted the replication posts "so as not to miss any [new] pictures or posts." The Page made this policy public with a post saying they did not want to offend anyone, which received 65 likes, but also received two comments from people who stated that they were trying to make the information "as visible as possible" to counteract that pets had been filed away "on the forgotten list." The crossposting principles that the Page was set up to foster were then challenged because the Page effectively solved a problem that crossposters usually face—that of the ephemerality of posts. The information architecture of the Page was organized in a way that enabled information to persist and for pet advocacy work to shift from individual ad hoc crossposting to the more collaborative efforts of "matching" lost/found pets.

Flyer Templates

Another critical element to support the information architecture of visual information was the introduction of "flyers" that used a template to describe each pet that was lost by an owner or found by someone looking for the pet's owner. When possible, it included a description, location, contact, information about prior crossposts, and the original source of the information. A member who graduated to admin took the lead on creating flyers that were "easy to read" and fit standard American paper sizes for printability and postability on trees, sign posts, and so on (see Fig. 3).

Figure 3. A Standardized Flyer Used to Represent Each Pet Case in the Photo Albums

This work began on 2 November. Then, critically, each flyer was put in the relevant album, effectively creating a more navigable case management system. This action kept all the relevant information about each pet within the image of the post, ensuring all the details were kept every time the images were shared on Facebook, so people seeing the image did not need to click on it to open additional information attached to the image. A participant explained in an interview the effect this had on the organizing functions of the site:

> "When you have crossposters, you might get the same image from 8 different people. By creating our own flyer, it identifies for me right away that we already have this animal. I know we already have it, it's in an album, it's being shared. I think it's a draw for the page, but it also shows us that we've already got it." [P10]

The idea that they "had" the animal indicates that they had cataloged it and formally incorporated it into their production functions. It also suggests a kind of caretaking concern in two ways: 1) that the flyers were a kind of proxy for the pets and that they were being accounted for, and 2) that the responsibility of the site was to be a useful terminus for crossposted information that otherwise pings around uncertainly in the ether. The admin posted on 3 November:

> EXHAUSTED! I will continue to make flyers and post in the am…I have not blinked, moved or eaten today because I wanted to get these stories shared. Thank you all for crossposting/sharing so we can have happy reunions. That's what it's all about right?

Matching Work & Connections to the Ground Response

The organization of the flyers in albums and a consistent effort to ensure that details from crossposters were correct set the stage for an element of work that connected the on-line advocacy with on-the-ground usefulness. The posts containing the flyers were the micro-places of work coordination; even when photos were moved between albums, the commenters could "stay" with the pet.

The Rise of "Matching" Work

On 1 November, one day after the storm dissipated and three days after the Page launched, an admin posted:

> Please help try to match pets. Look at photos of lost and found pets and try to help match them. You can do that from anywhere. I am in <a far-away State> and may have matched two within the last hour.

This is telling because the idea of "matching" pets between the lost photos and the found photos (that is, pets found by someone other than their owners) was not common practice. Some crossposters seem to do this, but it was not an explicit or well-articulated task. Crossposting seems largely focused on rescue activities and amplifying messages of help (because during non-disaster times, most pets are voluntarily surrendered and then need to be rescued by someone else). The idea that their work could lead to reunions was new enough that it got a response: 169 likes and 41 shares. Ten members wrote in support, indicating that it was not something they had thought of, saying: "OMG...that's awesome" and "Great idea!"

Some needed additional information about how to go about matching. Someone replied:

> you need to look real close at markings but just making someone aware that there is a similar match around is good. Never know it could be the same one.

Another member suggested that the scope of the matching work could be broad, and that people could look on findtoto.com and Craigslist for matches. Such comments reinforced the idea that the Page could serve as a matching hub for the much larger world of the 'net. The admins would move pets to one of the end-story albums no matter how or where the match happened on-line.

After this initial period, it became standard for people to work within the albums on individual pets to identify matches. People made suggestions for matches, and conversations ensued over their likelihood. The suggested matches were given to the contact for each pet listing for follow up. Often the owner of a lost pet would give feedback by commenting on their pet's post. Before a pet's flyer was moved to the Reunited Album, members sought proof of the resolution (similar to other verification tasks in disaster-related problem solving [37]).

An example was the case of "Butterscotch," a male orange and white tabby cat missing since 29 October from one of the hardest hit areas of the hurricane: Breezy Point, New York. Butterscotch was posted in the "NY - Lost Cats" album on 9 November. The post received 254 shares, 92 likes, and 32 comments. Many comments pertain to matching work, with suggested matches to pets elsewhere on the Page as well as on other on-line sites. The comment stream ran until 11 April, with members and admins giving feedback about the match suggestions. The updates showed the Page was invested in sustaining the community that had mobilized around pet matching.

Connections to On-the-Ground Response

Some of the work went to physical search for lost animals. Analysis of posted data and interviews reveal that non-admin members who were geographically local to the disaster went to the neighborhoods of lost pets to distribute flyers. One Page member explained in an interview how she corrected information and translated the work of remote volunteers into meaningful work on the ground:

> "As I was sharing posts from the page, I would often notice incorrect information. Things like flyers with "Neptune, NY" on them, when I knew Neptune was here in NJ. So I would comment on those posts to have them make corrections... At the time, I didn't realize the people volunteering behind the scenes on the page weren't locals! So they had no sense of which town was where, or what areas were close to others. They started asking me questions about specific missing animals - "Could this found cat in ANYTOWN be the same one that is missing from OTHERTOWN?"" [P3]

"Napolean," a Rottweiler, was found in the Cliffwood Beach Area of New Jersey. Before he was captured, he was added to the Page's Albums with a picture of just the dog's paw print and "search and rescue needed" (Fig. 4). Eventually, Napolean was captured and housed by someone who knew to report about his case on the Page. People then shared a new photo of Napolean so that he could be matched. He was suggested as a match for other missing Rottweilers, but these were never correct. However, because of the public work on this case, a family came forward to adopt him when his owner could not be found.

The matching work still rested strongly on the idea that crossposting spread news of the plight of animals far and wide, as the person who helped find a missing dog posted:

> I just want to thank everyone again for all the cross posting. Without it, this dog might never have found his parents. The final sharing total was over 11,000 posts. Thank you everyone!

Figure 4. Napolean's Flyer

Disaster management designates the post-rescue stage as "recovery," which extends over a long period. Long-term recovery efforts can be hard to sustain for digital volunteers [34], even though their subjects of interest are still affected. The Page was involved in long-term on-the-ground recovery work: Three months after the hurricane, temporary shelters to house pets whose owners were most in need began announcing closure. Only about half the owners returned. One of the Page admins who was volunteering on the ground offered to create a Page album to help the pets find homes. With the assistance of Page members, many were adopted. The interviewee said that this experience helped "to grow our network even bigger" (P10).

Offering Resolution

The Page community's commitment to the successful homing of the pets is seen in the steady growth of the Reunited and Adopted albums. The Reunited album, created on 29 October, had over 200 posts and is matched in size only by the Adopted album. News of reunions was encouraging to workers, as a poster wrote: "that's just wonderful!...several of us have been scanning the pics looking to match the lost/found pictures!!"

Curiously, many people appeared to believe the Page was critical in the reunion of pets with owners, even though matching work included links from other on-line sources, and even though very few of the culminating narratives written about the pet directly identified a match made on

Figure 5. An End-Story Narrative Flyer

the Page itself. In interviews, admins and members alike were unsure of the number of successful matches made on the Page. Though all felt matches happened, none had a readily available record. Nevertheless, people believed that the reunions of pets with their owners happened as a result of the Page, which likely encouraged people to persist in the face of a difficult, uncertain task:

> Out of all the FB posts, this site is my favorite. You can see results. This is amazing how people have taken the time out to help. Truly amazing and I cry every time I see it work.

The admins created more albums and updated flyers to provide a conclusion to the pets' "journeys," which we believe had the strong effect of showing an arc of collective work toward some completion. The SAFE album collected information about animals successfully "pulled" by rescue organizations from shelters. The Rainbow Bridge RIP album memorialized pets that died either directly because of the hurricane or because they were euthanized. The pets' completed stories often were told in a narrative compiled from the comments made by members, another instance of reinforcing the importance of collective action (Fig. 5).

PROPAGATION OF THE ORGANIZATION

During the final writing of this paper, an EF5 tornado devastated the town of Moore, Oklahoma on 20 May 2013, killing 24 people. People from the Sandy Page are part of a similar effort for the pets of Moore, and their stated mission represents an evolution with a new claim to be "trained 'online' first responders":

> …a group of volunteers who utilize social media and other offline resources to help reunite lost pets with their owners in the aftermath of disasters.
>
> We combine our talents and knowledge, gained from reuniting families and animals after other disasters, such as Katrina, Joplin, Sandy, the Bastrop Wildfires, and the North TX tornadoes and most recently the West TX Fertilizer Plant Explosion. You might say we are trained "online" first responders.

The Moore Oklahoma Tornado Lost & Found Animals Page was launched employing similar practices that developed over the course of the Sandy Page. An admin said she ensured that it began with separate albums and a consistent look to the flyers, just as the Sandy one evolved to. A few members of the Sandy Page began to suggest possible matches on the Moore Page. We see early evidence in this of an attempt at sustained self-organization with repeating patterns of coordination [5, 21, 34].

POST-EVENT ACCOUNTING: HOW MANY HANDS?

With thousands of commenters and Likes on the Page, and a great deal of organization happening to make the Page viable, it would be easy to believe this volume of work was widely distributed. It is hard to know how much attention the Sharing and Liking of pets drew to the Page. From the Page analytics, we see that 60% of those who commented

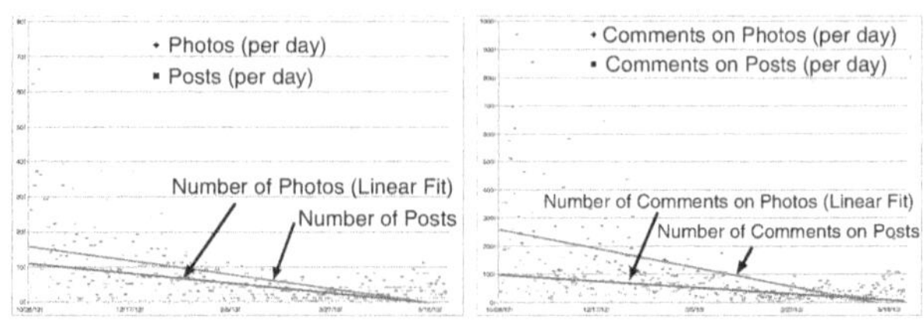

Figure 6. Daily activity for creation of posts and photos (left) and comments on photos/posts (right).

on the Timeline and 68% of those who commented within the albums left just a single comment, suggesting transient engagement. However, it could be that even one comment was valuable: the person who found Napolean commented just once upon Napolean's capture to notify others (with others verifying the claim). Across the seven months, data show that the number of posts, photos, and comments remained high in the first couple of months, which is a indication of ongoing engagement into the recovery period after Sandy was no longer in the news (Fig. 6). There is drop-off as the pet issue becomes less salient, but the photo activity shows less of a drop-off than the commenting and other non-photo posting, suggesting that a core group were committed to the work of pet matching.

Not everything was rosy: The tedious matching work was described by a participant as the necessary "dirty work" of the Page that not everyone wanted to do (P10). Other respondents said that they lost FB friendships because of crossposting, which some found to be overbearing. The lesson here might not be to aim for everyone mobilizing for a cause, but rather to create environments that make tedious work more attractive while still making functional use of a larger but only mildly engaged crowd.

DISCUSSION

Mobilizing advocacy is a central question in today's networked world [9, 28, 33]. This paper considers how work practice and a digital environment as a site of interaction for a highly distributed group of volunteers were co-adapted so that it might achieve the goals of accomplishing tasks as a group. Advocacy organizations may see social media as effective, but it is often difficult to integrate it with existing practices of connecting with audiences [28], and to engage long-term committed volunteers [38]. One could tackle the issue of mobilization as a matter of attaining critical mass, or understanding the social psychology of advocacy, or other theoretical frames. Here, we see that design decisions—even those for which there are many imposed constraints by the service provider—are important in igniting mobilization.

In recent years, disaster events have given rise to the influx of on-line digital convergers who want to help [6, 12, 18, 32]. Among these digital convergers are those who were already performing advocacy work on-line, though often in an ad hoc fashion. In the site we examine here, which we believe to be "the state of the art" in on-line pet welfare disaster response volunteer work at the point in time that it was instituted, came to be built upon implicit knowledge of the crossposting that pervades on-line pet advocacy. A few of the lead people had prior disaster experience, but most other members and admins had little experience with respect to the particular matters of pet welfare in disasters.

In on-line crowd work, the matter of structure of the work is central. This is because much of the work that can be done includes manipulation of data, or the consumption or generation of information resources. In their study of the digital volunteers who instituted the "disaster desk" in response to the 2011 Peru earthquake, Starbird and Palen [34] reveal how work was restructured in response to the restructuring of the information environment volunteers were working in—which itself was an exasperated response to a confused division of labor and in the end enabled the group to sustain itself relative to its production functions.

In this case of matching lost pets, the information architecture was highly organizing to the group and graduated the information dissemination activity into a more structured case management system. Both the work and the mission came into focus, connected to efforts on the ground, and brought this special interest group to a workable state of mobilization. The information structuring here had to make use of the highly visual information that pet advocates needed to work—photos of pets. The visual nature of the information was already the reason crossposting in pet advocacy was as it was: so that people could be repeatedly appealed to about the plight of particular animals that crossposters believe needed rapid help. The admins made use of existing crossposting behaviors but organized the information generated so that it could be housed, standardized, and made persistent. This in turn had the effect of making clear what the production functions of the Page should be to a newly banded group of inexperienced disaster volunteers: that of rapid matching to quickly reunite suddenly displaced pets with people.

Such attention to the information architecture transformed the work of advocacy from an impulsive and transient "clicktivism" [28] into action that had a chance to be sustained for longer engagement—if not for very long volunteering commitments [38] then at least for longer task commitments. This observation maps to that of earlier work by Kreps and Bosworth [21] on the nature of self-organizing among (often volunteer) groups responding to disaster. In their terms, the Page would be described as arising out of loosely defined "activities" (crossposting) for most of the active members, which were then shaped by the "resources" in the form of the affordances of Facebook's Page features. This then gave rise to the articulation of the "task" of matching, which surprisingly had not previously been an explicit notion in crossposting work—the focus had been on pet rescue in non-disaster situations. In this case, people reoriented to the understanding that matching between lost and found pets—rather than the rescue of abandoned pets—is the solution for the setting of disaster and is a natural off-shoot of the visual information-sharing they were already engaging in. It also set the stage so that "site seers" [12] who had not previously been a part of the crossposting movement could become a part of the mobilization. Imposing structure on previously unarchitected, highly visual work brought the idea of advocacy work—mobilization—within this community clearly to the fore.

The admins also communicated resolution of the pet cases, which was a critical part of mobilization—and they did so in keeping with the information architecture they developed for the problem-solving work. These practices created the sense of completion of work—which communicated that there was work being done in the first place. Even when the actual matching work happened on another site or privately, the Page assumed the responsibility of calling the work completed for the entire large and amorphous pet advocacy world. This, we believe, appeals to the value of mobilized pet activism writ large.

Summary

The Hurricane Sandy Lost and Found Pets Page on Facebook sprung from a special interest group that represented an existing large segment of on-line society—pet lovers and advocates—that needed a structured information environment to spur further self-organization to assist in the aftermath of Hurricane Sandy. Innovations around the organization of visual information as well as other social practices articulated the cooperative work they could conduct—an improvised case management system—and in turn that work clarified the mission and larger social ordering of pet advocacy.

ACKNOWLEDGMENTS

We are grateful to members of the Facebook Sandy Pets page for their participation. We thank Amrutha Rajiv for data collection assistance. This research is funded through the US National Science Foundation grant IIS-0910586.

REFERENCES

1. ASPCA. (2013). ASPCA Urges NYC Pet Owners to Reclaim Pets at Emergency Boarding Facility in Brooklyn. <http://www.aspca.org/Pressroom/pressre-leases/010213>.
2. Atkinson, S. and Ayers, A. (2010). The potential of the Internet for alternative caring practices for health. *Anthropology Medicine*, 17(1): 75-86.
3. Barrenechea, M., Barron, J., and White, J. (2012). No Place Like Home: Pet-to-Family Reunification after Disaster. In *Ext. Abs. of CHI 2012*, 1237-1242.
4. Denzin, N.K. and Lincoln. Y. (2011). *The Sage Handbook of Qualitative Research, 4th edition.* Sage Publications.
5. Dynes, RR. (1970). *Organized Behavior in Disaster.* Heath.
6. Fritz, C. and Mathewson, J. (1957). Convergence Behavior in Disasters: A Problem in Social Control, *Committee on Disaster Studies, National Academy of Sciences, National Research Council*, Washington DC.

7. Gibbs, L. and Holloway, C. (2013). *NYC Hurricane Sandy After Action Report and Recommendations to Mayor Michael R. Bloomberg.* <http://www.nyc.gov/-html/recovery/downloads/pdf/sandy_aar_5.2.13.pdf>.
8. Giddens, A. (1984). *The Constitution of Society: Introduction of the Theory of Structuration.* UC Press.
9. Gladwell, M. (2010). Why the Revolution will not be Tweeted. *The New Yorker.* <http://www.newyorker-.com/reporting/2010/10/04/101004fa_fact_gladwell>.
10. Golbeck, J. (2011). The More People I Meet, the More I Like my Dog: A Study of Pet-Oriented Social Networks on the Web. *First Monday* 16(2-7).
11. Harper, R. (2000). The Organisation in Ethnography: A Discussion of Ethnographic Fieldwork Programs in CSCW. *CSCW Journal*, 9(2): 239-264.
12. Hughes, A., Palen, L., Sutton, J., Liu, S., and Vieweg, S. (2008). "Site-Seeing" in Disaster: An Examination of On-Line Social Convergence. In *Proc. of ISCRAM*, 324-333.
13. Humane Society of the US. (2013). *Hurricane Sandy Relief.* <http://www.humanesociety.org/issues/animal-_rescue/hurricane-sandy/>.
14. Hunt, M., Al-Awadi, H., and Johnson, M. (2008). Psychological Sequelae of Pet Loss Following Hurricane Katrina. *Anthrozoos*, 21(2): 109-121.
15. Irvine, L. (2003). The Problem of Unwanted Pets: A Case Study in How Institutions "Think" about Clients' Needs. *Social Problems*, 50(4): 550-566.
16. Irvine, L. (2004). Pampered or Enslaved? The Moral Dilemmas of Pets. *International Journal of Sociology and Social Policy*, 24(9): 5-17.
17. Irvine, L. (2007). Ready or Not: Evacuating an Animal Shelter during a Mock Emergency. *Anthrozoos*, 20(4): 355-364.
18. Kendra, J. and Wachtendorf, T. (2003). Reconsidering Convergence and Converger: Legitimacy in Response to the World Trade Center Disaster. *Terrorism and Disaster: New Threats, New Ideas: Research in Social Problems and Public Policy*, 11: 97-122.
19. Kilijanek, T. and Drabek, T. (1979). Assessing Long-Term Impacts of a Natural Disaster: A Focus on the Elderly. *The Gerontologist*, 19: 555-556.
20. Kittur, A., Nickerson, J., Bernstein, M., Gerber, E., Shaw, A., Zimmerman, J., Lease, M., and Horton, J. (2013). The Future of Crowd Work. In *Proc. of CSCW 2013*, 1301-1318.
21. Kreps, G. and Bosworth, S. (1994). *Organizing, Role Enactment,and Disaster: A Structural Theory.* University of Delaware Press.
22. Lee, Y-H and Hsieh, G. (2013). Does Slacktivism Hurt Activism?: The Effects of Moral Balancing and Consistency in Online Activism. In *Proc. of CHI 2013*, 811-820.
23. Lewis, T. (2006). ASPCA takes lead in relief effort. *PR Week*, 32.
24. Lowe, S., Rhodes, J., Zwiebach, L., and Chan, C. (2009). The Impact of Pet Loss on the Perceived Social Support and Psychological Distress of Hurricane Survivors. *Journal of Traumatic Stress*, 22(3):244-247.
25. McCully, R. (2007). Saving Pets from Another Katrina. *Time Magazine*, <http://www.time.com/time/nation/-article/0,8599,1629962,00.html>.
26. Mike, M., Mike, R., Lee, C. (2011). Katrina's Animal Legacy: The PETS Act. *Journal of Animal Law and Ethics*, 4(1): 133-160.
27. Mileti, D. (1999). *Disasters by Design: A Reassessment of Natural Hazards in the United States.* Joseph Henry Press,
28. Obar, J., Zube, P., and Lampe, C. (2012). Advocacy 2.0: An Analysis of How Advocacy Groups in the United States Perceive and Use Social Media as Tools for Facilitating Civic Engagement and Collective Action. *Journal of Information Policy*, 2: 1-25.
29. Orlikowski, W. (2000). Using Technology and Constituting Structures: A Practice Lens for Studying Technology in Organizations. *Organization Science* 11(4): 404-428.
30. Rotman, D., Vieweg, S., Yardi, S., Chi, E., Preece, J., Shneiderman, B., and Glaisyer, T. (2011). From Slacktivism to Activism: Participatory Culture in the Age of Social Media. In *Proc. of CHI 2011*, 819-822.
31. Schmidt, K. and Bannon, L. (1992). Taking CSCW Seriously: Supporting Articulation Work. *CSCW Journal*, 1(1): 7-40.
32. Starbird, K. and Palen, L. (2011). "Voluntweeters:" Self-Organizing by Digital Volunteers in Times of Crisis. In *Proc. of CHI 2011*, 1071-1080.
33. Starbird, K. and Palen, L. (2012). (How) Will the Revolution be Retweeted? Information Propagation in the 2011 Egyptian Uprising. In *Proc. of CSCW 2012*, 7-16.
34. Starbird, K. and Palen, L. (2013). Working and Sustaining the Virtual "Disaster Desk." In *Proc. of CSCW 2013*, 491-502.
35. Suchman, L. (1987). *Plans and Situated Actions.* Cambridge University Press.
36. Sullivan, K. and Uccellini, L. (2013). *Hurricane/Post-Tropical Cyclone Sandy. NOAA Service Assessment.* <http://www.nws.noaa.gov/os/assessments/pdfs/Sandy13.pdf>.
37. Vieweg, S., Palen, L., Liu, S., Hughes, A., and Sutton, J. (2008). Collective Intelligence in Disaster: Examination of the Phenomenon in the Aftermath of the 2007 Virginia Tech Shootings, In *Proc. of ISCRAM*, 44-54.
38. Voida, A., Harmon, E., & Al-Ani, B. (2012). Bridging between Organizations and the Public: Volunteer Coordinators' Uneasy Relationship with Social Computing. In *Proc. of CHI 2012*, pp. 1967-1976.

Collaboration Surrounding Beacon Use During Companion Avalanche Rescue

Audrey Desjardins[1], Carman Neustaedter[1], Saul Greenberg[2], and Ron Wakkary[1]
[1] School of Interactive Arts + Technology, Simon Fraser University, Surrey, British Columbia, Canada
[2] Department of Computer Science, University of Calgary, Calgary, Alberta, Canada
{adesjard, carman_neustaedter, rwakkary}@sfu.ca, saul.greenberg@ucalgary.ca

ABSTRACT
When facing an avalanche, backcountry skiers need to work effectively both individually and as a group to rescue buried victims. If they don't, death is likely. One of the tools used by each person is a digital beacon that transmits an electromagnetic signal. If buried, others use their beacons to locate victims by searching for their signals, and then dig them out. This study focuses on the collaborative practices of avalanche rescue and the interactions with beacons while backcountry skiing. We conducted interviews with backcountry recreationists and experts, and we observed avalanche rescue practice scenarios. Our results highlight aspects and challenges of mental representation, trust, distributed cognition, and practice. Implications include three considerations for the redesign of beacons: simplicity, visibility and practice.

Author Keywords
Avalanche, backcountry, snowboard, transceiver, beacon, ski, collaboration, communication, distributed cognition.

ACM Classification Keywords
H.5.3 **[Group and Organization Interfaces]:** Computer-supported cooperative work; H.1.2 **[User/Machine Systems]:** Human factors.

INTRODUCTION
Backcountry skiing is becoming more popular every year with an increasing number of skiers and snowboarders seeking untouched snow, new lines, and challenging but rewarding adventures [17]. When traveling in the backcountry – areas where there is no avalanche control – skiers and snowboarders assume the risk of being caught in an avalanche that can lead to injuries or fatalities. An avalanche is loose snow that rapidly slides down a slope [16]. If buried in the avalanche, victims rely on rescue teams for their survival – usually their backcountry skiing companions through a process called *companion rescue*.

Rescue is far from easy. Avalanche accidents are extreme, stressful and challenging situations demanding efficiency, speed and team effort. Time is of the essence, as the chance of survival decreases significantly after 15 minutes in a complete burial [8]. Collaboration and coordination is vital: the group – typically comprising friends, acquaintances and even strangers of various skill levels – must quickly choose a leader to direct and distribute roles amongst them, and each person must perform their part of the rescue in concert with others if they are to successfully rescue the victim.

As victims can be completely buried under avalanche debris, specialized equipment – almost always carried by the prepared backcountry recreationist – is required to search for and dig out the victim to achieve any chance of survival. *Beacons* are electronic transmitters/receivers that rescuers use to search for the victim, where rescuers try to identify the snowpack surface directly above or nearby the victim [5]. Collapsible *probes* (long poles) are used to pinpoint that search, where a rescuer probes that area at intervals to physically strike – and thus find – the victim. *Avalanche shovels* are used to dig out the victim. See [3, p.27-33] for an account of a real accident.

While there is much research concerning avalanche causes, medical implications, and technological advancement in beacon technology (e.g., [1,6,8,17]), little research investigates avalanche rescues from computer-supported cooperative work (CSCW) or interaction design perspectives. Currently, much of the focus in equipment design is oriented towards a single user, in particular his use of the beacon. The problem is that the overall success of the rescue relies heavily on the ability of the group to collaborate. Thus the specific goal of our research is to investigate collaboration in avalanche rescue as facilitated by the use of beacons.

In this paper, we explore how groups train with beacons, how beacons fit into daily routines, and how groups use beacons during rescues. We are particularly interested in how existing beacon designs serve well or poorly as a collaborative artifact. Our results show the complexity of this distributed effort and provide insights on the challenges of creating and sharing mental representations of the rescue scene and the quality of trust within the team and with the beacon. We also reveal the importance of the scene itself and how we see distributed aspects of cognition through the acts of the rescuers, the tools they use and the environment they act in. Finally, we discuss the challenges of performing meaningful practice and training. These results lead us to a discussion of visibility, simplicity and practice that can

CSCW'14, February 15–19, 2014, Baltimore, Maryland, USA.

http://dx.doi.org/10.1145/2531602.2531684.

influence and re-orient the design of tools for avalanche rescue.

BACKGROUND INFORMATION

Backcountry skiing and avalanche rescue are activities that need training and basic knowledge to perform successfully. In this section, we briefly present background information regarding accepted backcountry skiing protocols, avalanche rescue coordination, and avalanche survival technologies. Additional detail can be found in books such as [5].

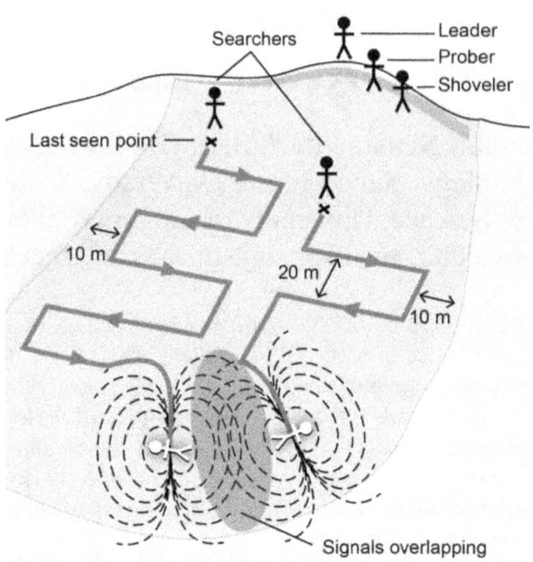

Figure 1. S-shaped search pattern (red) taken by searchers to find the signal. Flux lines of the victims' beacons signal are shown in black.

Backcountry skiing protocol

Backcountry skiing involving avalanche accidents, while relatively rare, have life and death consequences. Thus, route planning includes analyzing the avalanche and weather forecast, and using that information to select an area within the group's risk tolerance. Equipment is prepared accordingly; typically including the rescue tools mentioned earlier, food and water, a first aid kit, compass and map, and clothing.

On the day of the trip, mountaineers put on their beacon as they are putting on their outdoor clothing. At the trailhead, groups do a *beacon check* in order to make sure that everyone's beacon is working, i.e. it is emitting a signal and that it can be picked up at a certain distance. To perform the check, one person is elected to be the "searcher" and puts their beacon in search mode. Each person from the group skis by this person, who verifies that he can pick up their signal. Once everyone has passed, the searcher switches his beacon to transmit and (ideally) someone else checks his signal.

Route-finding through the terrain is heavily influenced by the perceived risk of avalanches on particular terrain features. When one has to ski through an area with avalanche risk (e.g., when descending a steep ski slope), the protocol is to send one skier at a time with others acting as spotters. This reduces the risk of the entire group being buried, while allowing other skiers to be well positioned to rescue a skier caught in an avalanche.

Companion rescue

Almost all avalanche rescues rely on *companion rescue,* where rescuers are the victim's companions[1]. Companion rescues are framed around a prescribed protocol of action, which implies that every recreationist is prepared to learn and practice that protocol. This is why professional bodies strongly advocate that skiers take avalanche courses (although these range considerably in their length and depth of treatment). Prepared skiers will train with their equipment several times a year, either individually (e.g., practicing beacon searches) or as a group (e.g., running through avalanche scenarios). In reality, practice and experience levels within and between groups vary considerably.

Leadership and collaboration in avalanche rescue

Collaboration is an important aspect of companion rescue. The first step taught in classes and emphasized in training sessions is to choose a leader who will overview the scene and assign roles to other rescuers (e.g., searchers, shovelers, probers, lookouts). The leader assigns each searcher a search path to ensure that: (a) every area of the avalanche scene is being searched and (b) no victim is left buried on higher terrain.

Rescue protocol for burials

Once the leader has assigned roles, the next step is the *coarse search*. Those chosen as searchers start at the victim's last seen point (Fig. 1). They move downhill searching for physical signs of the victim (e.g., a body part above the snow) and for a signal with their beacon. Because beacons have limited range, searchers must coordinate their search into a pattern. The idea is that their collective patterns of search will cover the entire avalanche path. For example, a single rescuer on a wide path may follow a wide S pattern to ensure the whole avalanche area is covered. As more people search, each person's S-pattern can be narrower (Fig. 1), until all are descending in a straight line.

The beacon signals when it first acquires another beacon's signal (which should be the victim's beacon) and provides cues to guide the searcher towards it (described in the next section). When the searcher is close to the victim, she starts a *fine search* to find the closest point on the surface to the victim. The searcher moves the beacon across the snow surface to discover the area covered by the beacon's highest reading, and marks those as boundaries. This area may range from .2 to 2 m or more in width, depending on the depth of the burial. Within this bounded area, the rescuer(s) then systematically probe into the snow pack until they 'touch' the victim, after which they start shoveling to create an airway to the victim. During this process, rescuers shout about their activity and needs, e.g. "I got a signal" or "I need a prober" or "I need some shovelers".

[1] Professionally organized rescues are normally reserved to areas where ski patrollers and professionals can arrive on-scene very quickly, such as within or immediately around ski areas, or by helicopter-assisted skiing. In recreational backcountry skiing, delays mean that organized rescues are typically targeted towards body recovery.

With multiple burials, the leader must monitor the scene to ensure that searchers do not congregate on a single victim at the expense of others that are still buried. Even with this guidance, communication amongst teammates is the weakest link in many rescues and it is often what makes the difference between survival and fatality [6].

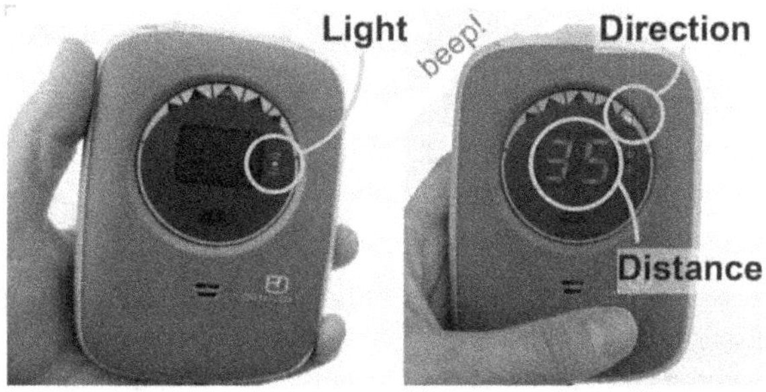

a) Transmit *b) Receive (search)*

Figure 2. Beacon modes.

The Beacon

Various tools are available to backcountry skiers to increase their chance of survival in the case of an avalanche [2]. We focus on the beacon, because it is the most common tool used by backcountry recreationists [5], and because it is the only tool that realistically shortens burial duration.

While beacons vary considerably, all have two primary modes of operation, illustrated by the sample beacon in Figure 2. In *transmit mode,* it broadcasts an electromagnetic signal of 457 kHz along a radial flux line pattern[2] (Fig. 1, dashed black lines): a blinking light provides feedback that it is active (Fig. 2a). In *receive mode*, it displays auditory and visual information to help a person search for this signal [9]: a digital numeric display estimates the buried victim's distance (here ~35 meters), the approximate direction to the victim (the small arrows), and audio feedback as an intermittent beep that increases in speed, pitch and/or volume as the rescuer approaches the victim's beacon (Fig. 2b). Distances and direction are approximate, as they follow the curved flux lines of the signal (Fig. 1) rather than a linear path. If multiple burials occur, the light below the number turns on to signal multiple victims and the beacon will display alternating signals for each victim. Some beacons allow the searcher to mark (hide) certain signals, allowing one to concentrate on other signals.[3]

RELATED WORK

While seemingly very specific, avalanche rescue relates to CSCW theories relevant to emergency and high stress situations. There is also a smattering of HCI work on the human factors of avalanche rescue beacons.

CSCW theories relevant to stressful and emergency situations

Within CSCW, various theories of social behaviors have focused on small teams of people who must coordinate their activities. These theories contribute to our ability to define, structure, analyze and interpret studies of collaborative teams and the development of interactive tools in stressful and emergency situations.

Hutchins' framework of *distributed cognition* [10,11] is most relevant to our study of collaborative avalanche rescue [3, p.27-33]. Distributed cognition argues that in many situations 'cognition' involves social aspects: the coordination between individuals (e.g., their social interactions and their social relationships), and how people coordinate their interactions between themselves and the artifacts within their collective environment. Thus distributed cognition is fundamentally embodied, where the body and the world are central to cognition aspects. It is also part of a cultural context where people accumulate partial solutions to situations over time and are able to use these in new situations [10]. Hutchins originally used distributed cognition to study ship navigation and to highlight the importance of the interactions between multiple navigators and their various tools on the ship [11]. We believe distributed cognition is highly relevant to the study of emergency situations like companion rescue: overall coordination of the situation relies on how individuals monitor and interact with other team members, the use of the beacon as an artifact, and how all are situated in the surrounding environment.

Implicit collaboration is a construct within distributed cognition that "describes the ability of team members to act in concert without the need for overt communication" [13, p.2]. Implicit collaboration is necessarily a part of efficient emergency teamwork (including companion rescue) since it allows teammates to concentrate on tasks to achieve and reduce the amount of explicit communication they have to do. For example, studies of firefighters highlight the importance of tacit communication [12] and implicit coordination [19]. Toups and Kerne [19] state that clear shared mental models are crucial to good collaboration in stressful and extreme situations because they eliminate the need for explicit communication and allow the process to be "streamlined" [p.714].

Situation awareness (SA) is "the perception of the elements in the environment within a volume of time and space, the comprehension of their meaning, and the projection of their status in the near future" [7, p.36]. SA highlights the importance of how a person understands 'what is going on' in order to help the decision-making process in dynamic domains such as aircraft piloting [7], ship navigation [11], air traffic control, and tactical situations like those involving firefighters [19], police, or military command personnel. The SA theoretical framework includes three

---

[2] Beacon signals emanate in space as a *flux field*: a curved 3D aura centered around the beacon. Figure 1 illustrates a cross section of this 3D field as curved *flux lines*. Thus, a searcher following a signal's flux line first moves in a slight curve *away* from the victim, and then back towards him. 'Dead spots' are also present along the antenna axis, affecting fine-search accuracy. Modern transceivers mitigate this through multiple antennas.

[3] Beacons vary considerably in how they track, manage and display multiple signals. Algorithms distinguishing such signals are quite complex where, for example, rapid movements can confuse this tracking.

levels: *perception*, *comprehension*, and *projection*. In brief, SA is necessary in emergency situations like companion rescue: it allows people to understand the situation, the context they are in, to predict what might happen next, and to take decisions accordingly as they conduct an efficient rescue.

The context of avalanche rescue is somewhat similar to how others have investigated stressful and emergency situations. Companion rescue, like some other dynamic domains mentioned above, require potentially life or death decisions. As we will see, distributed cognition, situational awareness and implicit coordination manifest themselves in successful avalanche rescues, similarly to how firefighters, pilots, and ship crews rely on the same constructs. Companion rescue, however, has its own unique circumstances. Recreationists – who may not have worked together in a rescue situation before – become *ad hoc* rescuers. Individuals are mostly non-experts, and thus their familiarity with technology can considerably influence the team effort. The situation is highly unpredictable due to weather and terrain features, the location of people (who, for example, may be scattered around the slope), the abilities of the rescuers, the risk of further avalanches, fatigue, cold, and so on.

The professional avalanche community is not blind to the collaborative nature of companion rescue, although they rarely use the above theoretical constructs to frame their work. The new generation of both research [1,14] and avalanche safety classes [18] focus on group dynamics and decision making surrounding backcountry skiing, such as "tools for planning, communication and group management" [1,6]. Classes teach students to be familiar with beacon use through simple exercises such as finding a buried beacon under snow (an individual activity to gain device proficiency), to more elaborate settings such as avalanche scenarios with multiple burials (a group activity).

Beacons and HCI research

Beacon design has evolved over the years, in part by advances made by manufacturers and in part by feedback from avalanche rescue professionals. However, most have centered on increasing an individual's performance rather than considering the beacon as a collaborative artifact. For example, Hereford and Edgerly propose that future avalanche beacons include an additional signal that uniquely IDs each mountaineer [9]. This would help rescuers separate multiple signals in multiple burial situations, particularly in scenarios where two victims are situated very close together.

One noteworthy exception is the work by Michahelles et al. [15]. At issue is how significant time may be lost uncovering dead victims or victims who may be deeply buried at the expense of other live victims. Their focus was to redesign beacons to support *triage*, where the team decides which victim to rescue first, and thus where their efforts should be concentrated. They added sensors that collected and transmitted data about the victim to support triage: heart rate, oxygen blood level, victim orientation under the snow, and depth of the burial.

The aforementioned theories as used in CSCW help us frame our study of avalanche rescues in order to focus on the collaborative aspects of the rescue as well as the interactions with the beacons themselves. By using this perspective, we contribute research on beacon technological advancement and human factors in avalanche rescues.

METHODOLOGY

In order to gain an overview of the collaborative rescue practices and the use of beacons, we used two methods for collecting data: semi-structured interviews with experienced backcountry recreationists, and observation of practice avalanche rescue scenarios. We chose these two qualitative inquiry methods because of our study's explorative nature, where they would help (a) uncover the broad and holistic collaborative practice of avalanche rescue and the use of beacons [4], (b) triangulate findings, and (c) provide more diverse and in-depth exploration than a single method [20].

Interviews with recreationists and experts

We met with ten participants (one female), where individual backcountry expertise ranged from 2 to 30 years of experience. Four were recreationist backcountry skiers. The other six were considered experts in the field of avalanche control or education: one ski patroller, one backcountry skiing guide, three avalanche safety instructors and one researcher in avalanche snow and weather conditions in Washington, USA, and in Alberta and British Columbia, Canada. Participants were chosen through snowball sampling. They were not remunerated.

For each participant, we conducted a semi-structured interview in person, or via phone or Skype: interviews lasted from 30 to 90 minutes. Hand written notes were collected and used to create a report for each interview. Interviews included questions related to three topics: backcountry traveling history, avalanche rescue situations, and the use of beacons and tools in avalanche rescues. We started with ice-breaking questions to learn about the participant, his goals, and his experience and motivations for doing backcountry skiing. We then focused on the two aspects that are closely related to CSCW and interaction design and that are missing from the literature: the aspects of collaboration and the use of tools (i.e. beacons) by the participants. Lastly, we opened the conversation to discuss challenges and potential improvements in the future development of beacons.

Observations of avalanche rescue scenario

In order to gain more insight on how beacons are really used in avalanche settings, one of the authors observed avalanche scenario sessions at the Mount Baker Ski Area in Washington, USA (another author is also a domain expert). Since it is very problematic to observe real avalanche rescues, these scenarios were the next best opportunity to see how people use beacons in a time-constrained and real environmental setting. We observed two types of groups doing avalanche rescue scenarios: three groups of five students of a MEC 2 class (with varied levels of experience typical of companion rescue teams) and two groups of seven patrollers from the Mount Baker Ski Area (with high level of experience). The MEC 2 class allowed each group of five to practice three different rescue scenarios on the mountain (total observation time: 3 hours). The pro patroller groups performed one rescue each on the mountain (total observation time: 5 hours). In both cases, we collected hand written data about the team organization and process, and how the beacons were used. In the both patroller groups, we videotaped the scenarios. Since things happen quickly in these situations, video proved valuable for documenting otherwise hard to observe information.

Analysis method

All data was analyzed with a thematic analysis. We extracted themes that could be clustered in three areas:

- team collaboration during an avalanche scene (including search steps, multiple burials situations, general protocol on scene, and the beacon in the environment),
- the beacon itself (including physical aspects, technical aspects, use issues, potential additional functions, and the simplicity of the tool), and
- training and practice aspects of using beacons (including education, practice, skills and beacon checks).

We now present the results and analysis based on our data. Data from interview participants is labeled with P# for participant number, while observational data is labeled with O# for observational participant.

CREATING MENTAL REPRESENTATIONS

On the avalanche scene, rescuers work to construct a representation of where the victims might be buried based on the information provided by the beacon and by other physical hints in the environment. To work as a team, rescuers must try to share this mental idea with others. However our data show the various challenges in doing so. Some of these come from challenges in how people share information, while others come from an individual's difficulty in obtaining and interpreting beacon readings.

Sharing mental representations

In scenarios with multiple burials and multiple rescuers, rescuers collaborated to find the buried victims by partitioning the search zone. That is, one person may search one area while another person may search an area lower down the hill. The goal is to not repeat search areas. This can be challenging since the second searcher does not have the same mental representation as the first searcher who was able to pick up the signal from further up the hill.

"It is hard to pick up on someone else's signal. The person who found the first victim has already an idea of how the signals are present in the scene and should be the one continuing to the second victim. He already has this mental model. More intuitiveness for where to go." – P4

Figure 3. The beacon is worn on the torso in a harness. Some functions and buttons are challenging to use with gloves.

Thus shared mental representations between rescuers in the group are extremely important, especially in the case of multiple burials. Yet we observed that the information gathered from one beacon by one rescuer is not often communicated to others on scene. Instead, each individual rescuer is working hard to understand his beacon and create one's own accurate mental representation (see below). There is little time to discuss another person's mental representation, let alone understand it.

Single burial challenges

Even before sharing a mental representation with others, rescuers need to first create a representation for themselves of the possible location of victims. We observed multiple challenges in the design of beacons that constrain the collaborative process. First, P2 and P10, two instructors, said that many backcountry skiers do not understand that the beacon functions by tracking the non-linear radial 3D electromagnetic signals (Fig. 1, dashed black flux lines). Because the signal follows the curved flux lines, the orientation will change as the rescuer moves on the site. This means that distance and orientation readings are at best approximations; while knowledgeable searchers can make assumptions and conclusions based on how this information changes, this is hard for those with fewer skills. In order to assess potential places for burial and create a mental image of where the victim might be, rescuers need to understand and apply this knowledge of the beacon's operation. Another problem is that rapid movements of the beacon, including beacon rotation, will affect how the beacon discriminates between signals and how it estimates direction and distance. Thus, success hinges in part on a rescuer's ability to correctly hold and move the beacon, and to correctly understand, interpret and make decisions based on its information in an efficient manner while under stress.

The second problem in creating an accurate mental representation arises from issues with device ergonomics. One example is difficulties in correctly reading beacon information. We observed participants of the MEC 2 class having difficulty reading the beacons' distance numbers.

For example, one participant was not able to differentiate "2.0" from "20" or "1.0" from "10". Similarly, P10 mentioned that older mountaineers can have difficulty reading the display without reading glasses, which are rarely handy. Obviously, such misreads could dramatically slow the search. Another example is that most beacons are physically difficult or awkward to handle (Fig. 3). When worn under the clothes, beacons must be extracted. Because they are usually tethered to the body in an elastic harness, they are sometimes difficult to move to particular positions. Because people wear gloves, their controls are at times difficult to use.

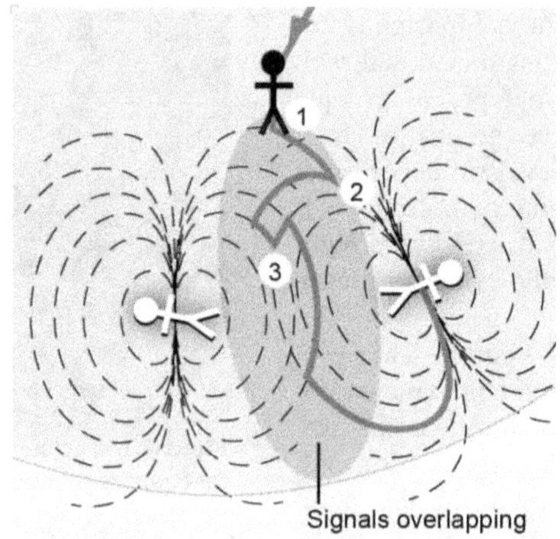

Figure 4. A situation where distance readings flip between victims. The rescuer would read the alternating signals at the following points: (1) 30 – 25; (2) 30 – 15; (3) 12 – 15.

Multiple burial challenges

All experts in our interviews told us that multiple burial accidents were the most challenging rescues to perform. P4, P7 and P9 said that separating two signals was the hardest thing to do with a beacon, e.g., "*it needs practice since it is not intuitive*" (P7). To explain: as the searcher moves, the beacon indicates smaller or bigger numbers on the display. While modern beacons try to 'lock onto' the strongest signal, the process is imperfect. Thus they may flip between the data readings for each buried victim (Fig. 4). This often results in what appears to be contradictory or random readings, or signals that change unpredictably. P2, P4 and P9 further explain that in order to perform a multiple burial search successfully, the rescuer needs to use the readings on the beacon to track the beacons worn by all victims within range. This is difficult: the rescuer must retain several mental images or construct a more complex representation. For many first-time users, this was the most challenging aspect of understanding the beacon's readings. We observed in the MEC 2 class that most participants were not certain if they were still picking up the first signal they found or if they were on the right path to look for a second victim. For example, one participant said: "*I keep getting a soft second reading but I can't pinpoint it*" (O1).

Most advanced digital beacons remedy this somewhat by allowing the searcher to 'mark' a signal during multiple burials, which removes it from the display. However, we did not observe the MEC 2 participants using this function on their beacons: they indicated that they simply did not know how to use it. Even so, marking has its own associated issues that require expert interpretation, e.g., marked signals may 'come alive' due to the difficulty the device has in differentiating between competing signals.

BUILDING TRUST

Sharing information (e.g. mental representations) and coordinating tasks on scene are crucial for the team to perform successful rescues. These activities, however, also rely heavily on social dynamics. A theme that appeared recurrently in our data analysis is trust: trust in the other rescuers on site, and trust in the beacon.

Trust between team members

Our interviews and observations revealed that team members must work together in both tightly-coupled and loosely-coupled situations, where trust is vital to both.

Loosely-Coupled Collaboration

Loosely-coupled collaboration occurs when rescuers work together but each has one's own specific task and goal. As mentioned, each rescue group appoints a leader and the leader assigns different search roles to people in the group. This is challenging in companion rescue due to the lack of information about team member abilities, especially in situations when skiing groups are created *ad hoc* at the trailhead or in the ski area. For example, when choosing who will be doing the beacon search, a leader often does not know who has the best search skills. Trust in the leader's decisions as well as the abilities of the other group members to perform their assigned roles within the group may be easily questioned.

When groups know each other very well, the distribution of the roles and the collaboration between rescuers can be fluid and efficient. We observed a close collaboration effort in the scenarios with the pro patrollers who worked together as a team on a daily or weekly basis.

"*We were all really fluid in our roles. We all know each other and can switch between roles. But this would not work with a different group and customers.*" - *O2*

We observed that clear communication between rescuers allowed for faster searches. Rescuers that were not beacon searchers were aware of the scene and ready to come help with the tools for the next steps. We observed implicit coordination in the pro patrollers teams where roles were established and understood without explicit communication.

In contrast, in the MEC 2 class, groups comprised people that did not know each other; hence, the teammates did not find a leader as fluidly as the pro patrollers. However, since each group performed three rescues, we observed a clear evolution in the leadership roles and team sense from the first rescue to the last rescue. This led to improved collaboration and trust, which ultimately can help achieve more efficient rescues.

Tightly-Coupled Collaboration

Rescuers also work in tightly-coupled situations, where two or three rescuers typically work together to rescue the same victim. For example, as one person fine-tunes the victim's location, another may start probing or shoveling. In these cases, precise coordination is necessary to know when the beacon search is advanced enough so that the other tasks can efficiently be started. Hence, team members must trust the efforts of each other and also relay information while searching. Team members must trust that the information shared with them by other team members is accurate.

To illustrate, one rescuer in the pro patrollers group did a fine search with the beacon and set the area for the second rescuer to probe the snow. The second rescuer started to probe and did not get a strike even after probing multiple times. The instructor asked him to redo the beacon fine search, however, the rescuer trusted his partner and decided to continue to probe. A few seconds later, he probed and found the victim. This is in an interesting example since it shows the trust and confidence a rescuer has in his teammate's abilities. We also saw the sharing of mental representations about the scene: the rescuers shared the information they had through signals with their hands by pointing at the area and the center of the fine search results, and the searcher with the beacon used lines he made in the snow to show to the prober where to start probing. In brief, team members trusted each other's abilities to perform their tasks, but also used visual clues to indicate the mental representation they had about the victim's position. In contrast, ad hoc companion rescue groups rarely have the opportunity to form this tight-knit expertise relationship.

Trust in the tool

In some cases, a lack of understanding of the flux lines and the shape of these lines brought multiple questions, confusion, and frustration to less experienced beacon users.

For example, one participant of the MEC 2 class was walking in circles on the scene and she said three times within a few minutes interval: "*I don't trust it. I just don't trust it*" (O1). As she was getting various readings, she did not know where to direct herself and how to manage this information. She started to doubt her tool and was not able to find a victim without the help of her teammates. Other participants said "*the readings were lying to us*", "*the beacon is confused*", and "*the beacon locked on one victim*" (O1). In all cases, the beacons were functioning normally and it was the interpretation of the signals that participants were struggling with. In situation awareness terms, the first step of situational awareness – perception – is lacking. P2 argued that these questions and lack of trust come from a misunderstanding of how a beacon follows a flux line. These situations were also used by the instructors to remind participants that although the theory of using a beacon is rather simple, the execution can be more challenging.

Beacon precision was also a challenge for rescuers and limited how fast they could do the fine search. Confusing and unreliable readings can occur if the beacon is moved too fast since it does not have time to interpret the buried beacon signal. In order to counter this, some instructors, like P9, encouraged students to physically place the beacon on the snow, read the signal, then pick up the beacon and move it 20 cm away and repeat. Here, trust between the rescuer and the beacon is built by consciously creating the best context for the beacon to show reliable data.

Perceived simplicity of beacons

All participants told us that beacons have improved dramatically in the past few years. Participants with less experience explained that they saw the beacon as a very "*straight forward*" (P5), "*easy to use*" (P6), and "*not confusing*" (P1, P6) tool. These participants perceived beacons as simple and passive technologies: "*beacons are a very passive technology, invisible technology. You put it in the morning and then you forget about it*" (P5).

Interestingly, the more experienced participants generally presented a different perspective. Through their work and experience, they had seen many cases were beacon use broke down and users were not able to use them properly, particularly when there was a lack of practice and training. Thus, we observed a tension between how participants perceived the ease of use of beacons, how challenging they can be in practice to use and how the lack of trust in the beacon can bring doubts and hinder rescue efficiency.

DISTRIBUTED COGNITION ON THE RESCUE SCENE

Our data showed that distributed cognition and an understanding of the broader scene and environment are important aspects of avalanche rescues. As presented in the related works section, we know that distributed cognition allows people to share what they understand through the acts they are doing with their artifacts and in the environment. This way of externalizing and embodying cognition should be central to the teamwork happening between avalanche rescuers on an avalanche scene. However, we observed that different aspects of the team strategies and of the beacon itself hinder fluid distributed cognition.

Ephemeral and invisible data

First, we found that there was no way to record beacon data on what had been searched and what had not. Thus it was impossible to see and visualize this data on the scene. Moreover, as soon as a rescuer moved, the data she had in one position was lost and replaced by new data. During the observations of both the pro patrollers and the students in the MEC 2 class, we saw rescuers asking others (and sometimes the leader) if certain areas were explored yet. For this reason, rescue leaders in both groups often stayed at the top of the avalanche scene in order to keep track of what has been explored and to communicate that to the team. Yet this was also challenging as leaders would need to survey and understand what had been searched from afar. In addition, the leader is in charge of depicting a clear and dynamic picture of what is going on: mostly knowing how many victims have been retrieved, how many are still unfound. The leader must also be aware of the role of each person, the problems they encounter, and reassign them as needed. All this is difficult to achieve since rescuers might be far away from the leader. Sharing information between the rescue team becomes challenging: verbal or gestural communication might not be possible due to distance, or because searchers are so engrossed in their local activity as to effectively ignore those communications. All this leads to a breakdown in explicit and implicit communications.

During beacon search in multiple burials scenarios, we observed some rescuers who were closer together than was necessary on the terrain. This was because rescuers do not often evaluate and visualize how far their beacon can search. For this specific reason, during training P7 said he had groups start a beacon check close together but then walk as far away as they can from a transmitting person until that signal could not be received. The group's spread provides a visual image of their beacons' range. However, on scene, rescuers cannot 'see' how far their search tool can pick up a signal and align properly with others on site. Another problem arises when two searchers target the same victim without realizing it and thereby reduce the number of searchers looking for victims buried elsewhere. This can easily arise because search zones overlap (e.g. Fig. 1).

Being aware of others and the environment

Rescuers also need to be aware of the other rescuers on scene and to understand if everyone in the group has switched their beacons to search mode from transmit. This is the first thing rescuers must do when they are on an avalanche scene so the searchers do not accidentally pick up their signal instead of the victims'. Yet this first step is often missed in scenarios and brings much confusion to the scene: searchers end up 'chasing' the moving signal of another searcher. A similar situation arises if the beacon turns back to transmit by error (e.g., many beacons auto-revert to transmit mode after a timeout period). Such errors can be detected by practiced rescuers who detect unusual signal changes as part of their situational awareness, but this comes at the cost of time.

Distributed cognition also states that a part of cognition happens through the environment. Rescuers observe the terrain and use this information to support and orient the interpretation of the beacon's reading. However rescuers tend to rely on the beacon to create a mental representation of where the victim could be despite instructors constant refrain that students should also focus on the site to find additional clues from such features as the terrain shape (which suggests where victims may come to rest after the slide) to pieces of personal equipment on the snow surface (e.g., a ski pole). P7 and P9, both experienced avalanche safety instructors, explain that "*your brain is your best tool*" (P9) meaning that additional thought is needed to take the information provided by the beacon and mentally map it to real world geography. Yet switching one's attention between the beacon and the environment is challenging, since once a rescuer finds a signal, most of his attention is focused on getting as fast as he can to the victim's location.

We observed that both new users and pro patrollers tried to "*beat the myopia of the device*" (P8).

PRACTICE AND PREPAREDNESS

Challenges presented earlier – misunderstanding of how the beacon sends and receives signals, sharing mental representations, identifying searched *vs.* unexplored territory, dividing the avalanche scene between rescuers, and how to trust a beacon – could, in theory, be mitigated by good training and practice. P8, an instructor and head of the mountain safety education department, argued "*beacons [are] just outside the intuitive realm that they need practice.*" However, our interviews revealed that a variety of challenges occur in practice.

Lack of seriousness and attention

The first challenge is that, naturally, practicing is not the preferred activity. The main goal of recreationists is to go skiing. Hence, any time used to practice as a group can be seen as a waste of precious time that could be used on the mountain to ski. Practice time is also often seen as "*lame, dry and boring*" (P6). Weather also affects this: practice in cold or wet conditions is far from pleasant. In consequence, there is a chance that skiers will not practice, or will not take practice seriously, or will not be fully focused on the practice and what they need to do. P2, P5, P8 and P9 all mentioned that, from their own observations as instructors or guides, recreationists need to practice more. Some participants talked about trying to make practice time fun. For example, when P6 practices with his group, they try to make it more fun by placing rewards with the hidden beacons or by timing everyone in the group to bring more competition and excitement. While beneficial, this can easily present a mismatch in the goal of a practice scenario and associate rescue attempts with the wrong frame of mind. This opportunity could also be used to build team trust and observe each other's skills in preparation for distributing roles on a real avalanche scene. However, this was rarely reported in our interviews.

Beacon check

We mentioned that beacon checks should be done by the ski group before entering the backcountry area [16]. However, our interviews revealed that beacon checks are not done systematically and that the group of people and the chosen area of skiing influenced this decision. For example, P2 explained that for shorter runs close to the ski area, it felt less important to complete all the safety steps. He also explained that if he travels with people he knows better, he sometimes skips this step. This finding points to human factor considerations, where P2 argues that we need to find a way to encourage beacon checks.

Although there are multiple ways of doing a beacon check, in most situations the group concludes the beacon check with one person not being checked. Since one person turns his beacon to search, he can check everyone else; however, when he is done, others may not check him as they have already skied by.

The generalizability of mock practice scenarios

Beyond the need to simply practice more, we also found that the way recreationists practice is not always ideal and does not represent the reality of an avalanche rescue. Because of the time required to set up practice scenarios that were similar in nature to a real avalanche, some participants talked about overly simplistic forms of practice. For example, P3 hides a beacon in the parking lot before leaving for a day of backcountry skiing. The beacon is not under snow and is not on a slope. Similarly, P1 reported that he hides a beacon in a backpack and buries it under snow on flat terrain. In this case, the challenges brought by an angled slope cannot be tested and practiced. These unrealistic scenes also mean that one does not learn how to interpret the avalanche area for additional cues of where the victim may lie. Yet due to their 'success' in these simplistic scenarios, recreationists may feel overly comfortable and confident with using beacons in a search.

As we described earlier, avalanche rescues are rare and companion rescuers themselves may not be experienced or up-to-date on their practice. This reveals the challenge of designing tools that can easily be picked up and used correctly in a stressful situation by such rescuers. As we observed in the MEC 2 course, even a practice scenario can bring a high level of stress and a range of emotions to the participants. One of the students said that "*I know this is just practice, but I can't stop thinking I could be searching for my husband or for my daughter*" (O1). In a real avalanche accident, these emotions are even stronger. Yet there is no way of truly simulating a practice scenario with the extreme emotional conditions that rescuers would face in a real avalanche.

DISCUSSION

Our results reveal that many challenges in collaborative practices of avalanche rescue and use of beacons come from: a lack of regular practice; a lack of understanding of the beacon itself; or from deficiencies in the human factors of beacon design. In order to help recreationists coordinate better on a scene and understand and use their tools better, we propose three considerations in beacon redesign: visibility, simplicity and practice.

However, these considerations are provided with a large caveat: they are not guidelines, nor should they be even considered correct. Rather, they are best viewed as broad suggestions for those exploring the future design of safety tools in avalanche conditions, especially for designs that depart considerably from the current status quo. We recognize that much work would be required to produce 'good' designs from these implications, not only because of human factors issues but because of limitations in beacon technology. Even if reasonable designs are found, much work needs to be done to see if they are provable better than existing beacons, and if the improvement is worth disrupting current technology standards and avalanche protocol practices.

Visibility

We found that working with 'invisible' signals was an issue in several situations: a) coordinating how much space to leave between rescuers on the hill to do the coarse search, b) understanding the flux line between the searcher's beacon and the victim's beacon and sharing this with others, and c) differentiating multiple signals in a multiple burial scene. We believe that these three challenges are related to the lack of information rescuers have about the flux line and how it would be represented on the terrain. Moreover, rescuers have trouble sharing or knowing what has been searched on the terrain and what has not. Challenges were also present for rescuers trying to keep track of what signals were being followed and which ones were yet to take care of. In both cases, the lack of visual feedback made it difficult to share or track this useful information.

In order to increase distributed cognition and better teamwork, we believe that the first step is to allow the translation between the distance and direction on the beacon and the physical space to be clear (this could only work if beacon algorithms were able to estimate this information accurately from the data it collects). Only the more experienced backcountry skiers were able to explain how they can construct a representation of the scene that allows them to perform the search faster. This mental image is not only based on the beacon's feedback but is also informed by keeping situational awareness. However, even within their description, they were not able to pinpoint where the victims were, let alone share that with others. Instead, they were only able to approximate the victim's area.

In this case, tools that support the 'seeing' of beacon data within the terrain could be extremely valuable. For example, one interviewee suggested that future beacons could have a larger LCD screen showing the position of the victims in relation to the terrain and landscape features. This would allow users to gain even more information from the beacon and reduce the amount of assumptions they have to make to reach the victim. This strategy, although potentially efficient for orienting oneself on the scene, would require the rescuers to constantly keep their eyes on the device. In addition, creating a way to combine and show information collected by networked beacons held by multiple rescuers could help keep a connection and awareness between rescuers in multiple burial situations. This would also support a structured way of keeping track of the process towards different victims.

There are certainly technical issues as to whether beacons can individually or collectively create an accurate view of the scene based on the limited data they can gather. Even if they could, there is a fine balance between having a tool that shows 'everything on the screen' and a tool that allows the user to take his eyes off the screen to be more aware of the environment. We mentioned that expert users emphasize the importance of maintaining an awareness of the physical environment. One possible – albeit quite futuristic – way to mitigate this problem is an augmented reality approach that integrates the virtual view of beacon data with the physical scene.

Simplicity

Our results also point to the importance of simplicity in the design of beacons used by backcountry recreationists. Questions and confusion can arise because of the lack of simplicity. Practice and training are necessary because beacons are not simple enough to be picked up and used immediately. Since avalanches are rare events, even if recreationists wear a beacon every time they travel in the backcountry, they can use them inefficiently in a stressful and urgent situation like a companion rescue. For this reason, we believe it is useful to design with casual users in mind, and assume that users have only modest training and minimal practice. While our findings revealed a perceived simplicity of the beacon by inexperienced users, experienced users understood the subtlety and complexity of beacon search. This shows that beacons are precise instruments that require practice to lead to proficiency and adding more functionality would only delay this.

Simplicity also relates to proposed additional functionalities for beacons. We previously mentioned that unique IDs can better identify beacons in multiple burials [15] or that sensors could afford display of vital signs [9]. Yet unless great care is taken, this can make the interface and beacon visuals more complex, thus negating possible benefits. With simplicity, we advocate only those functions that keep people directly on task; to the extent that extra information would be helpful, they must be seamlessly integrated into the beacon's visual representation so that the scene can be understood at a glance. Removing less-critical functions implies less decision-making, less unnecessary team coordination, and less analysis of the beacon's interface while on the avalanche scene[4]. Interviewees also argued that all additional functions will require more practice: while potentially useful for guides and patrollers, they would not be appropriate for recreationists. There is clearly a tradeoff here: while beacons should be enhanced to increase their accuracy, interface and representation complexity and the need for interpretation needs to be kept to a minimum.

The unique ID and sensor enhancements proposed by Hereford and Edgerly [9] and Michahelles et al. [15] include tools for a faster triage of victims in a multiple burial setting. While these make sense for professional searchers who may not know the victims, they do raise significant issues for casual teams with differing interpersonal relationships. Both P8 and P10 felt that these additional functions would 'get in the way' and create conflict on the avalanche scene. In our interviews, participants expressed concern around the ethical issues of such a function. "*It makes you ask the question – who do I dig out first? I would want to know where my wife is. Would that be fair?*" (P5). Indeed, one of the authors of this paper was involved in an avalanche burial with multiple victims (all survived) – an account is found in the opening chapter of [3]. During the search, it was likely no coincidence that the first person to arrive at each victim's site was that person's mate. Thus we argue for safety tools that are not only simple in their interface, but also in the ways they shape the very real human emotions and choices surrounding the search process. Additional triage information can create ethical questions: this can potentially hamper decision-making happening on scene that can cost precious rescue time and lead to bad choices.

Practice

Finally, we reflect on the importance of practice with safety tools and as a group. One of the interviewees, a ski guide with 30 years of experience, compared beacon search with wood working: "*Because I have been making furniture for 40 years, my hands know how to do it. It is automatic*" (P9). He argues that beacon search has to become as automatic as practicing a craft at length. In order to help rescuers gain a better understanding of their beacons, we advocate different training tools and environments that would highlight (and maybe make visible) different aspects of the beacon and how it is used over time by a person. These training aids should also consider group aspects and allow recreationists to better structure their practice time to strengthen and reflect on both the tool and the group activities. For example, practice beacon parks – a series of beacons permanently buried under snow that are placed for practice – now allow recreationists to practice beacon searches. We foresee that such parks could track a team's movements, and allow them to 'play back' their search efforts for review and reflection. By practicing together, teams could reach more powerful implicit coordination in the event of an accident. Certain tools could also support the development of routines for critical aspects of the tightly-coupled collaboration, such as when to start to probe while another rescuer is still completing the fine search.

In summary, we believe that avalanche rescue performance can be partially improved by redesigning beacons – if possible – to support distributed cognition. However, this must be supplemented by training tools and practice strategies oriented to increase situational awareness and distributed cognition.

CONCLUSION AND FUTURE WORK

We contributed a description of avalanche rescue practice and the use of beacons. More generally, our results also

[4] Indeed, some beacons are already designed for simplicity, with the casual user in mind. Without getting into detail, some beacons provide a wide range of settings in how signals are presented on the audio and visual channel as the search progresses, which is useful for those experts who understand signal nuances. Other beacons are designed for casual users: there are few or no options, and only a single way to look at the signal. While less confusing for casual use, information is lost for those who know how to exploit it.

point to the added need to support distributed cognition in emergency situations managed by non-professionals.

Unlike other emergency situations studied in CSCW, companion rescues are usually performed by non-expert casual users, which reveals unique issues. Our results present multiple challenges in using the beacon that are barriers to accomplishing better teamwork through distributed cognition or situation awareness. Challenges emerge in creating and sharing mental representations of the scene, trusting the rescue team and the tool itself, being aware of what is on scene and what other rescuers are doing, and finally in practice and training contexts. These challenges can in part be addressed by gaining a better understanding of the tool. We believe that the three approaches of visibility, simplicity and practice are worth considering in future designs. Some point to radical redesign and require new technologies that go far beyond what today's beacons supply. Yet by deeply rethinking the way beacons shape interactions between rescuers on scene, we argue that better rescue and training tools could be created. Our future work will focus on furthering our understanding of collaborative avalanche rescue with beacons and on the development of concepts and prototypes for future beacons and training tools.

ACKNOWLEDGMENTS

We thank all the backcountry recreationists and the pro patrollers at Mount Baker who participated in the study.

REFERENCES

1. Adams, L. A systems approach to human factors and expert decision-making within Canadian avalanche phenomena. 2005.
2. Brugger, H. and Falk, M. Analysis of avalanche safety equipment for backcountry skiers. *Avalanche News (66)*, (2004), 34–38.
3. Buxton, B. *Sketching User Experiences: Getting the Design Right and the Right Design*. Morgan Kaufmann, 2007.
4. Creswell, J.W. *Qualitative Inquiry and Research Design: Choosing Among Five Approaches*. SAGE, 2012.
5. Daffern, T. *Backcountry Avalanche Safety: Skiers, Climbers, Boarders, Snowshoers*. Rocky Mountain Books Ltd, 2009.
6. Edgerly, B. and Baugher, P. Talking the Talk: Human Factors, Group Communication, and the Next Frontier in Snow Safety. *Proc, ISSW 2012,*
7. Endsley, M.R. Toward a Theory of Situation Awareness in Dynamic Systems. *Human Factors: The Journal of the Human Factors and Ergonomics Society 37*, 1 (1995), 32–64.
8. Falk, M., Brugger, H., and Adler-Kastner, L. Avalanche survival chances. *368*, 6466 (1994), 21–21.
9. Hereford, J. and Edgerly, B. 457 khz electromagnetism and the future of avalanche transceivers. *Proc. ISSW*, (2000).
10. Hollan, J., Hutchins, E., and Kirsh, D. Distributed cognition: toward a new foundation for human-computer interaction research. *ACM Trans. Comput.-Hum. Interact. 7*, 2 (2000), 174–196.
11. Hutchins, E. *Cognition in the Wild*. Mit Press, 1995.
12. Jiang, X., Chen, N., Hong, J.I., Wang, K., Takayama, L., and Landay, J. Siren: Context-aware Computing for Firefighting. In A. Ferscha & F. Mattern, eds., *Pervasive Computing*. Springer, 2004, 87–105.
13. MacMillan, J., Entin, E.E., and Serfaty, D. Communication overhead: The hidden cost of team cognition. *Team cognition: Process and performance at the interand intra-individual level. American Psychological Association, Washington, DC*, (2004).
14. McCammon, I. Heuristic Traps in Recreational Avalanche Accidents: Evidence and Implications. *Avalanche News (68)*, (2004), 1–10.
15. Michahelles, F., Matter, P., Schmidt, A., and Schiele, B. Applying wearable sensors to avalanche rescue. *Computers & Graphics 27*, 6 (2003), 839–847.
16. O'Bannon, A. *Allen and Mike's Really Cool Backcountry Ski Book, Revised and Even Better!: Traveling and Camping Skills for a Winter Environment*. Globe Pequot, 2007.
17. Radwin, M.I. and Grissom, C.K. Technological Advances in Avalanche Survival. *Wilderness & Environmental Medicine 13*, 2 (2002), 143–152.
18. The American Institute for Avalanche Research and Education. *The American Institute for Avalanche Research and Education*. http://avtraining.org/.
19. Toups, Z. and Kerne, A. Implicit coordination in firefighting practice: design implications for teaching fire emergency responders. *Proc. CHI'07*, ACM, 707.
20. Yin, R.K. *Case Study Research: Design and Methods*. SAGE, 2009.

Designing for the Deluge: Understanding & Supporting the Distributed, Collaborative Work of Crisis Volunteers

Camille Cobb
Computer Science & Engineering
University of Washington
cobbc12@cs.washington.edu

Ted McCarthy
Biomedical & Health Informatics
University of Washington
epmccart@uw.edu

Annuska Perkins, Ankitha Bharadwaj, Jared Comis, Brian Do, Kate Starbird
Human Centered Design & Engineering
University of Washington
{annuska, abharadw, jcomis, bdo6, kstarbi}@uw.edu

ABSTRACT
Social media are a potentially valuable source of situational awareness information during crisis events. Consistently, "digital volunteers" and others are coming together to filter and process this data into usable resources, often coordinating their work within distributed online groups. However, current tools and practices are frequently unable to keep up with the speed and volume of incoming data during large events. Through contextual interviews with emergency response professionals and digital volunteers, this research examines the ad hoc, collaborative practices that have emerged to help process this data and outlines strategies for supporting and leveraging these efforts in future designs. We argue for solutions that align with current group values, work practices, volunteer motivations, and organizational structures, but also allow these groups to increase the scale and efficiency of their operations.

Author Keywords
Civic participation; crisis informatics; crowdsourcing; digital volunteers; disaster response; machine learning; natural language processing; social computing.

ACM Classification Keywords
H.5.3 Groups & Organization Interfaces—collaborative Computing, computer-supported cooperative work

INTRODUCTION
The converging trends of mobile computing, social media use, and citizen reporting have precipitated a rich and potentially valuable new stream of information during crises [24]. During natural disasters and other mass emergency events, social media data have—among other uses—become a source of real-time, first-hand information.

Research suggests that this information could help improve situational awareness for affected people, aiding them in making better decisions [37]. For example, after a hurricane, knowledge about the locations of downed power lines could help individuals avoid hazardous areas. Individuals stranded by high water could use social media to connect with nearby neighbors who have extra supplies or a safe means of transportation.

CSCW'14, February 15 – 19, 2014, Baltimore, MD, USA.
Copyright 2014 ACM 978-1-4503-2540-0/14/02$15.00.
http://dx.doi.org/10.1145/2531602.2531712

This information has potential value for formal response efforts as well. Emergency managers (EMs) and first responders are increasingly considering strategies for leveraging it for their own situational awareness [12;15;31]. However, there are several difficulties in utilizing these new information streams, including the massive volume of available information after events and the fact that much of the data can be considered noise [33].

In recent years, some research and development efforts have focused on building tools to help people process this information, e.g. TweetTracker [14], Geofeedia, and Crisis Tracker. Related research seeks computational solutions for automatically processing social media data, using algorithms to classify and filter the streams [2;13]. The ongoing research program outlined by Meier [20] examines the potential for automatically processing tweets using machine learning classifiers.

Another approach to addressing the information-processing problem can be seen within the emerging phenomenon of *digital volunteerism*. Digital volunteers are unaffected individuals who use social media and other online tools to assist in disaster response efforts, often taking on information-processing tasks, e.g. filtering and mapping crisis-related social media data [34]. After disaster events, digital volunteer efforts often *emerge* [3]—i.e. groups of remote volunteers (and often locals as well) come together and self-organize response efforts [34]. This work has sometimes been referred to as *crowdsourcing* [6]. However, it is worth noting that these collaborative efforts are less like the microwork variety of crowdsourcing (i.e. that enabled by Amazon's Mechanical Turk) and more like the Open Source roots of that term [10].

Recently, ongoing communities of digital volunteers have taken shape (e.g. CrisisMappers, the Standby Task Force, CrisisCommons) and a few groups have established non-profit organizations for their work, (e.g. Humanity Road). In the realm of formal emergency response, another organizational form, the Virtual Operations Support Team (VOST), was created to address challenges related to information overload [38]. VOSTs are distributed teams of volunteers who assist emergency managers in information processing and communicating during disasters [32;38].

Digital volunteers often work collaboratively, initially improvising and later formalizing and sharing work practices within and across groups [34;35]. A core task of many of these efforts is *media monitoring*— monitoring incoming feeds, including social media posts, to find new, relevant, actionable information. Volunteers often work to assemble—or *curate*— this data into usable resources.

Through this research, we seek to gain insight into how emergency managers and experienced digital volunteers currently curate social media data during crisis events. We conducted contextual interviews with emergency managers and experienced digital volunteers to (1) assess commonly used tools for monitoring a disaster and finding relevant social media posts; (2) assess commonly used tools for collaborating during a disaster; (3) understand processes for collaborating in this space; and (4) gain insight into participants' motivations for doing this type of work. We report on common themes, concerns, and insights from our interviews and suggest implications for design motivated by these findings.

Our research outlines a complementary approach to the computational solutions recently put forward by Meier and his colleagues [1;13]. Evidence suggests that machine learning classifiers will need training and re-training across event types and event stages [36]. We also argue that the output of these algorithms will need human validation and interpretation to be usable for decision-making in safety-critical situations. This research points to a strategy that integrates these computational tools into the existing and evolving work practices of digital volunteers and distributed teams of emergency managers.

BACKGROUND AND PREVIOUS WORK

Social Media and Crisis Response

Research studies show people turn to social media sites after disasters to look for and share information [e.g. 25;27;30], to help coordinate response efforts [29;34], and to collectively make sense of the event [9].

Twitter as a Crisis-Reporting Platform

Several affordances of the Twitter platform, including the short message format and the public searchability of tweets, make it particularly useful in the crisis context. Vieweg et al. [37] report that a significant percentage of tweets sent during disasters contain information that could contribute to situational awareness, and evidence suggests that some emergency responders are turning to this platform as a potential information source, as well as an outgoing communication channel, during events [12].

Photo-sharing Sites

Eyewitness photographs taken on mobile phones and shared through photo-sharing sites like Flickr and Instagram are another potentially valuable information source [18], providing near real-time evidence of damage and emerging hazards.

Making Social Media Data Useful

Though social media are enabling new information-sharing behaviors and providing a potentially valuable information source during disaster events, significant challenges remain in converting the tremendous stream of social media data into usable bits of information [2]. Affected citizens and emergency managers have limited capacity for analyzing this data during events. Considering these new information streams, responders complain of having to "drink from the fire hose" [6].

Disaster events often spark online convergence events, where people—locals as well as remote "participants" from all over the world—come together to make sense of the event [11], generating a large amount of data, much of which can be considered noise. Even for the subsection of the data that is on-topic and relevant to response, only a small fraction is new information coming into the space for the first time [33]. Misinformation is another significant problem with this data, and was cited as such after Hurricane Sandy [4].

A final aspect of the information-processing problem relates to the unstructured nature of social media data. Though many posts have some metadata (e.g. timestamps, author details, and geo-coordinates for tweets), the primary content of status updates and photos is "unstructured" and requires significant processing to get it into standard formats for analysis on a large scale [6].

Computational Solutions for Automated Processing

Researchers have proposed a number of computational solutions to filter, classify, or process incoming tweets. As the amount of social media data generated during disasters increases, automated means of processing this data become increasingly desirable. Solutions that leverage natural language processing (NLP) or machine learning (ML) could help cull, verify, and categorize Twitter posts.

Meier and others have proposed a "Twitter Dashboard" to support automatic tagging and filtering of incoming tweets [21]. Automated techniques can identify tweets posted by an eyewitness, including photos or video, communicating caution or advice, contributing to situational awareness, or otherwise containing informative content [2;13;23;36]; however, these classifiers only achieve high accuracy when trained on posts from the same or a similar event [36].

Most of these techniques identify tweets with around 80% accuracy and precision compared to manual work; the maximum precision was 90% for a classifier trained on data from the same event [13]. While these accuracies and precisions seem high, they may privilege certain types of information—possibly information that is already known—over others. For example, an ML tool may find that tweets containing URL links are more likely to be relevant, which could mean that citizen-reported "nuggets" will be missed. Additionally, all of these are post-hoc analyses; there are currently few tools for real-time processing.

Digital Volunteerism

Catalyzed by the challenge of making citizen-reported information usable, and enabled by online tools that allow them to access this information and coordinate their work with others, digital volunteerism has quickly become an established feature of crisis events [35]. Palen and colleagues have connected this new phenomenon to well-established patterns of "convergence" and "spontaneous volunteerism" that are known to occur after disaster events [11;26;34]. Digital volunteer work currently takes place within a handful of different organizational forms.

Emergent Organizations of Digital Volunteers

Empirical research on historical disaster events shows response efforts taking four different organizational forms: established, extending, expanding, and emerging [3]. Emerging organizations are ones that have no pre-existing structure and come together as individuals who begin to connect and coordinate their work [3]. Starbird & Palen characterized a group of digital volunteers who came together on Twitter and attempted to provide remote assistance after the Haiti earthquake as an emergent organization [34]. Similar groups of Twitter volunteers formed after the Alabama and Joplin tornados in 2011 to help in relief efforts. Following Hurricane Sandy, communities in New Jersey turned to Twitter to help locate open gas stations, and digital volunteers played a role in connecting those seeking information with those who had it [19]. These examples suggest that emergent organizations of remote actors connected through social media are now a feature of the disaster response milieu.

Ongoing Virtual Volunteer Organizations

Though many emergent groups dissipate as relief efforts wind down, some virtual volunteer groups have established an ongoing presence with a more formalized organizational structure. CrisisCommons, CrisisMappers, the Standby Task Force, and Humanity Road are all examples of virtual organizations that attempt to use online tools to provide remote assistance during disaster events. Most of these groups can be considered *expanding* organizations—ones that have an established structure between events, but increase capacity for response during events by activating part time volunteers and bringing in new ones [35].

Ziemke provides a high level description of "crisis mapping" and outlines the structure, role and mission of groups like CrisisMappers and the Standby Task Force who have developed an ongoing presence in virtual disaster response [39]. Starbird & Palen [35] offer a detailed account of the organizational structure and evolving work practices within the Humanity Road organization.

Virtual Operations Support Teams

The concept for Virtual Operations Support Teams (VOSTs) originated in 2011, developed by emergency manager Jeff Phillips [38]. VOSTs seek to integrate distributed teams of "trusted agents" (often other emergency response professionals) into emergency monitoring and response by establishing volunteer teams to monitor social media, manage communication with the public, and handle other matters than can be dealt with remotely; notably, VOSTs conduct both information processing and outgoing communication. VOSTs utilize remote volunteers, some of whom are professional EMs, and serve to connect emergency management and digital volunteerism.

> *Beth (emergency manager & VOST leader): "A VOST is different from a digital volunteer because it has a pinpoint, an internal connection to an emergency operation."*

VOSTs arose from a need to address information overload, as emergency managers struggled to deal with an increasingly tech savvy public communicating via social media. The cooperative, distributed work of VOSTs melds together professionals and volunteers, as well as disaster response veterans and relative novices. Early leaders within the VOST community shaped the idea around existing volunteer-based disaster response structures, including Voluntary Organizations Active in Disaster (VOADs) and Community Emergency Response Teams (CERTs). A VOAD is a group of individuals and organizations who work to share knowledge and resources during crisis events. CERTs work to bring together and train individuals to be active in emergency response within their community.

Existing Tools that Support Crisis Curation

Those monitoring crises online often use client applications designed for general use, but a few tools have been developed specifically for crisis monitoring, including *TweetTracker*[1], *Crisis Tracker*[2], *Geofeedia*[3], *Ushahidi*[4], *and SwiftRiver*[5]. These tools support manual monitoring of Twitter data through filtering and labeling tweets, mapping and data visualization. A few provide some computational analysis. Though many of these tools have overlapping functionality, no tool fulfills the needs of every crisis monitoring group, and many are in limited use or remain at various stages of development.

[1] http://tweettracker.fulton.asu.edu/

[2] http://ufn.virtues.fi/crisistracker/about.php

[3] http://corp.geofeedia.com/

[4] http://www.ushahidi.com/

[5] https://swiftapp.com

METHODS

We designed our research study to assess the work practices of people who have worked to remotely process social media streams during crisis events either as digital volunteers or as emergency response professionals. Our methodology reflects dual goals of understanding the work practices of these individuals and the groups within which they work and of designing to support this activity.

Contextual Interviews

We recruited participants for this study using Twitter posts with the hashtag "#SMEM" (Social Media in Emergency Management). This hashtag is used to organize conversations within a growing community of Twitterers interested in the use of social media for emergency response, including emergency managers, humanitarian response professionals, and digital volunteers. Nine individuals participated in this study—six emergency response professionals (i.e., individuals connected with official response in a particular geographic area) and three digital volunteers. Most of the emergency managers interviewed also act as digital volunteers for events outside their jurisdiction.

The two-hour interviews were conducted in our lab (two interviews), on-site at the participant's workspace (one interview), and virtually (six interviews). Virtual interviews were conducted via WebEx. Interviews were either audio recorded or a combination of audio recorded and screen captured, depending on the participants' preferences. In all interviews, participants used their own devices—laptops, iPads, and mobile phones.

These were contextual interviews because participants used their own hardware and software tools. Interviews conducted at our lab simulated their mobility and flexibility of working in multiple environments (ex. home, coffee shops, office). To avoid hindering crisis response efforts, we interviewed participants at a time when they were not actively contributing to a response effort.

Interview Structure and Questions

We conducted semi-structured interviews to establish consistency across interviews, plus allow opportunity to drill into emerging topics. Participants were generally enthusiastic and often spoke freely, answering many of our prepared questions without prompting. Thus, each participant fielded questions in a different order and/or context. Participants were asked about their:

- Responsibilities, goals, and motivations in their role as either a digital volunteer or an Emergency Manager
- Workspace and technology devices
- Workflow in a crisis situation, from initial assessment to the end of involvement for an event
- Formal and informal collaborations with others online and on the ground
- Use and perceptions of social media
- Reflections on impact and workload

Throughout the interviews, participants were encouraged to demonstrate and articulate their processes using the think aloud protocol. Researchers were aware of current disaster events and in some cases prompted participants to simulate their processes for an unfolding event.

Monitoring Exercise by Research Team Members

To gain better insight into the experience of conducting social media monitoring, members of the research team also performed a social media monitoring exercise and self-reflection during Hurricane Sandy and during the Pemex explosion and building collapse in Mexico.

Persona	Description
Newcomer	New to group. New to crisis monitoring in general. May struggle with use of social media monitoring tools. May struggle with emotional difficulties of this work.
Local expertise	Gets involved in a specific event because of a connection to the geographic area. Has specific skills related to local expertise (knowledge of language, culture, contacts on the ground etc.) that can help the group. Likely to work on different tasks than other newcomers (i.e. ones that use their special skill set).
Experienced team member	Has already worked remotely on multiple crisis events. Identifies as a part of the team. Often helps mentor newcomers.
Free Agent	Has worked several events, but not always with the same group. Moves from team to team. Shares knowledge and experience across teams.
Team Leader	Determines crisis monitoring tasks. Coordinates shifts of team members. Looks out for team member wellbeing. May delegate tasks (or members might self-select tasks). Corresponds with EMs, humanitarian responders, and other digital volunteer groups.

Table 1. Abstractions of Personas

Human-Centered Design Process

To generate insights from our contextual interviews, we created affinity diagrams. Themes emerged around managing information, collaboration models, and factors influencing workload and gratification. We created detailed personas based on the study participants and collaborators they described in the interviews. Table 1 provides short abstractions of those personas for reference here. These personas are representative of the roles an individual may have within a distributed crisis monitoring group; however, many of interviewees take on more than one role or change roles depending on the event. For example, some participants act as VOST leaders for events in certain geographical locations and volunteer for events in other locales. The participants in our study are not evenly distributed amongst these roles. Most are experienced team members, free agents, and/or team leaders. Newcomers and individuals who participate because they have local expertise for a specific event were not represented in our sample, likely because our recruiting method reached only individuals who already identified either as emergency managers or digital volunteers. However, there is substantial evidence of these other two personas in the interviewees' descriptions of their co-workers and in existing research [34;35].

Grounded Qualitative Analysis

Finally, we conducted a second round of qualitative analysis. Taking the themes identified through our affinity building activity along with questions we wanted to explore in greater depth, we returned to the interview notes and transcripts with the goal of substantiating and expanding our initial findings. Through this process, we categorized parts of each interview according to the pre-identified themes and design implications that we missed in the initial affinity building exercise.

FINDINGS

Characteristics and Work Practices of Distributed Crisis Monitoring Groups

We interviewed individuals from different virtual volunteer organizations and communities, though almost all had experience working in multiple groups and group boundaries were often porous. Because they were all participants in the #SMEM Twitter community, most of the participants were connected online and had worked with each other (virtually) previously.

Although the groups with which participants affiliated have developed distinct work practices, they have some common characteristics. Interviewees described their activities as occurring in small groups of three to 15 active members. In all of them, members work collaboratively but are geographically distributed. Some, especially VOSTs, have a hierarchical leadership structure, while others try to maintain a more lateral structure. During an event, there is often some kind of "backchannel" conversation among group members—where they coordinate their efforts and collaboratively make judgments about the relevance, importance, or truth of certain pieces of information. Five participants mentioned having a "trusted group" of team members who help process information.

Beyond these shared characteristics, there is a significant amount of variation in work practices due to group leaders' preferences; the nature, size, or location of the crisis; organizational values or structures; or the availability and specific expertise of volunteers.

The Work of Crisis Monitoring

The interviewees' responses, along with our observations of them at work, revealed the process of monitoring social media to be fast-paced and somewhat frantic. Members use a variety of tools and employ sophisticated work processes to accomplish varied goals for monitoring and collaboration. While monitoring, they often have to deal with a tremendous amount of incoming information and manage a large cognitive load to keep track of all the information at any one time.

Individuals monitoring crises use a variety of general-purpose tools, including TweetDeck, TweetGrid, TwitterFall, HootSuite, Bottlenose, and Monitter, with participants in our study indicating different preferences depending on task, familiarity, and expertise. Four of our interviewees explicitly reported that tools must be free (or inexpensive) if they are to be adopted by EMs and disaster response organizations. Two participants mentioned that although Radian6[6] could be a powerful tool, it did not fit in their small budgets.

In explaining their preferences for different tools, interviewees cited features that enabled them to display multiple searches in columns across a page, filter tweets based on location or retweet, create lists of twitterers, save and share searches, color-code search terms, view analytics such as related hashtags or "influential" users, and search for geolocated tweets within a given radius. Some interviewees expressed a desire for a tool that allows users to tag both social media posts and authors, and to share that tagging information with collaborators.

Participants used a number of tools to accomplish a variety of goals. We found that individuals often use various tools for different functions successively, taking the output from one tool and moving it over manually (copying/pasting) to use as the input to another. John, an experienced digital volunteer who works officially as an emergency responder, laid out a sophisticated strategy: first, he identifies the terms that he is "supposed to be looking for" (often using Bottlenose), then he inputs the terms into Twitter, Hootsuite or Tweetgrid for ongoing monitoring. Similarly, Rachel, a technically savvy social media user who is new to online crisis response, initially discovers hashtags on Twitterfall, uses them in Twitter to verify that they are "relevant", and then adds them to her Twitterfall page for continued monitoring. Throughout our interviews, it was clear that individuals monitoring crises use a wide array of tools concurrently to perform different tasks. Beth (emergency manager and VOST leader) commented on the positive effects of this, suggesting information might be missed if all team members are using the same tool.

[6] http://www.salesforcemarketingcloud.com/products/ social-media-listening/

Some tools are preferred for their ability to enable the monitoring of a large number of streams of tweets, as many interviewees often need to do. John, for instance, uses a 2x3 grid of six different hashtags he follows in Tweetgrid, but will use Tweetdeck or Hootsuite if he is only following one or two hashtags. The work of these individuals often involves monitoring many sources of tweets covering different topics. Beth described how she usually has eight to ten columns open for monitoring in Tweetdeck, and has had as many as 26 open at one time. She also operates at least three different crisis-related Twitter accounts. Another interviewee, Abe, uses nine different Twitter handles for monitoring and communicating during disasters.

Through the research members' experiences monitoring social media during crises during this study, we were able to experience first-hand the stressful environment of social media monitoring. An important factor we noted was the speed with which new tweets came in during a disaster. By the time a tweet had been noted, saved, or otherwise processed, too many more had accumulated at the top of the page to be able to read. Interviewees mentioned that the speed at which tweets pass by while using one application is too fast for them to handle, and that managing information is easier in some applications than in others.

> *Rachel (technically savvy newcomer): "Twitterfall is too much information. It's good for seeing trends and commonality but it's too fast for specific things."*

Working Collaboratively

Emergency monitoring professionals and volunteers do not work in isolation—they often connect with others as they collectively monitor events. Skype and shared Google documents are used extensively for coordination and backchannel communication. Seven interviewees explicitly mentioned using Skype, and six said they use Google Drive documents. Group members discuss the relevance or credibility of certain posts in Skype chat rooms, and have conversations to coordinate tasks and provide emotional support to one another. Google Drive documents are used to schedule shifts, coordinate work, and collaboratively collect and curate relevant data by copying and pasting social media posts and their metadata into spreadsheets.

Verifying Information

All of the interview participants mentioned verifying information as an important part of their work. Rick, whose job involves monitoring social media for information about hyperlocal events, verifies claims made on social media by physically going to the location of the incident (e.g. fallen tree, downed power line). Other interviewees discussed techniques for virtually verifying information, including considering something verified if they could find multiple distinct reports, glancing at the public profile of the person who posted the information to determine their reliability, and searching for other information about the poster's reliability (e.g. a LinkedIn profile).

Division of Labor and Assigning Tasks

Groups have a variety of techniques for determining, assigning, and managing tasks. Some of the interviewees described group practices where leaders define what the tasks are and assign them to specific individuals. Others described work practices that allowed team members to self-select tasks based on their availability and expertise.

A common tactic for dividing work is to split up search terms so that every individual monitors different terms and therefore sees a different set of tweets. Other methods include giving volunteers distinct geographic regions to monitor and having volunteers look for different types of data—e.g. injury reports vs. damage reports.

The work of assigning tasks becomes its own task and leads to more division of labor. Experienced volunteers and leaders determine which searches to do, which regions to cover, and what kinds of reports to monitor, while less experienced volunteers execute those searches.

Working within VOSTs

Within the SMEM community, the VOST concept is growing in popularity. Five study participants act as VOST team members. Three of those work as team leaders, and two of these three are EMs who coordinate VOSTs as part of their official job.

VOST groups have a more hierarchical structure than emergent virtual volunteer organizations and other ongoing digital volunteer communities. This hierarchical structure, along with a related desire for standardization across groups, aligns well with traditional practices in official response. Within VOSTs, EMs serve as the connection between the team and official response. This is an important distinction, as other digital volunteer groups do not always have a formal connection with an emergency response team during an event. Study participants explained that EMs rarely act as leaders for their "own events."

Many VOSTs are established outside of any specific event, often for response within a certain geographic region. When a crisis event occurs or events such as extreme weather are predicted, EMs in those areas can deploy the VOST by contacting their trusted group of team members.

Though some elements of workflow vary across VOSTs, two participants in our study who were affiliated with them discussed a push for interoperability and standardization among teams. In response to this perceived need, VOST teams use "workbooks"—Google Drive spreadsheet templates that leaders can quickly adapt for a specific event. Within these workbooks, leaders specify "missions" for team members based on the EM's requests. The EM also determines how and when the team leader should report back with the group's findings, which might affect how the leader structures or describes missions.

Though their structure is more top-down than other digital volunteer organizations, VOSTs maintain a collaborative, team-oriented approach, reflected in their use of the term "mission" instead of "task." Leaders attempt to foster a sense of work ownership among team members. Compared with other volunteer groups, VOSTs have more people who overlap between different teams, and are growing similar in some of their practices.

Becoming a Digital Volunteer

Volunteers become involved in digital response teams for a variety of reasons. High among the motivators, regardless of background, is the evident belief that social media and non-local responders can have an impact during crises.

> *Sara (leader of a digital volunteer organization): "So the volunteers, why they engage varies. It may be for their career, it may be to give back to society because they want to pay it forward and they were impacted, or it may be because they have some extra time on their hands... Sometimes it's because they have a personal connection to that area."*

Eight of the participants in our study were either currently employed as emergency response professionals or had previous experience in the emergency and/or humanitarian response domain. However, about half of these entered the digital response space first as a volunteer. Among participants' whose first forays into social media were in an official capacity, three reported that they started using these tools as a means of gauging community opinions and misunderstandings so that outgoing messages could be tailored to specific needs. They then connected with other people in this space already doing digital volunteer work, and two of these individuals became active digital volunteers themselves. All but one participant mentioned having become connected to the community via Twitter through the #SMEM hashtag.

Some volunteers described how they first responded as a digital volunteer for a specific event that they felt impacted them, and then continued on to volunteer with other events. For these participants, their volunteerism was catalyzed by a disaster situation that hit especially close to home—e.g., a crisis in an area where they formerly lived or where they had loved ones.

> *Rick (emergency responder & PIO): "I was active in the week after the hurricane [Sandy], putting out info to my own friends & followers, because it was so close to me."*

Continuing as a Digital Volunteer

The motivations for becoming a digital volunteer are not always the same as the motivations for continuing on as a volunteer. Many of the interviewees described how responding to event after event could produce a kind of disaster fatigue, indicating that continued participation had a significant cost and suggesting that these volunteers must have reasons to keep going.

Altruism is certainly a factor for sustained membership. Making an impact is a related driver. Many interviewees offered anecdotes connecting their work to outcomes on the ground or expressed the frustration of wondering if their work was helpful, suggesting that knowledge of definitive impact is an important motivating factor in continued participation as a digital volunteer.

A related motivation is tied to the formation of an identity as a digital volunteer. Starbird & Palen [34] reported that some volunteer Twitterers after the 2010 Haiti earthquake changed their online profiles to include "crisis tweeter," a reflection of this same effect. Seven interviewees tie their work in the crisis space into their self-identity. For example, Phil, now an experienced digital volunteer and free agent, traces his interest in disaster response back to his previous work ensuring that museums were safe from damage due to disasters and to his involvement in the Ham radio community.

Another motivator for continued involvement may be the personal relationships that volunteers forge with each other. The following quote alluded to the bonds that volunteers form while working together:

> *Sara: "I get a sense for the fact that they [the other volunteers] feel like a family."*

Finally, one community leader suggested volunteers may seek to gain new skills through this work, skills that may benefit them in other areas of their lives or in future disaster (and non-disaster) scenarios.

Some volunteers only participate in digital volunteerism for a short time. Although former volunteers were not included among the participants, we were able to learn about these individuals through the observations of the interviewees. Sara suggested that some volunteers may stop working because the work of social media monitoring is intimidating, or because they had a connection to a specific event that did not carry over to subsequent disasters.

Membership in the Virtual Volunteer Team

Through our interviews with volunteers and personal reflections on monitoring during a major event, we gained insights into the processes, stressors, and challenges of working as a digital volunteer or VOST team member.

What it's Like to be a Team Member

Being a team member in a distributed crisis-monitoring group often involves a great deal of stress. Volunteers try to do the right thing—to complete assigned tasks for their teams or to respond directly to affected people. But to do this often requires filtering through a massive amount of information that is literally moving too fast to process. The information deluge can be stressful in and of itself, a fact that Beth made clear in her remark about a VOST training exercise in 2012: "The Superbowl gave us all PTSD."

In the context of an actual crisis, the stakes and the stress get higher. Volunteers worry that they might be missing things, or that the information they find is incorrect. Additionally, the content of many of these posts can be traumatizing, as social media contain messages about people trapped in collapsed building after earthquakes, images of homes burnt in wildfires, and names of people missing in floods. Beth, an emergency responder and VOST team leader, discussed fears that inexperienced volunteers are unprepared to deal with some of these impacts:

> *"With digital volunteering, we have to switch leaders every four hours. It's more emotionally intense... I see paralysis [among volunteers] when things happen online. People are getting to the emotional brink during the event, and we need to evaluate volunteers who aren't emergency responders."*

In addition, distributed crisis monitoring can be a lonely experience. Volunteers are rarely collocated, and new volunteers may not yet feel that they are part of the surrounding community. Whereas offline emergency responders have access to a concrete, physical network of individuals around them when they experience something traumatic, digital volunteers are not often afforded this.

> *Beth: "Partly it's being alone when you're activated virtually ... and not really sure how the info's being used. Sometimes they [EMs] get so wrapped up in response that they don't touch back as often as you'd like them to."*

Team leaders employ several strategies to ease the stress. For example, Beth maintains a steady schedule of work and break, which she feels discourages individuals from over-exerting themselves. Additionally, virtual volunteer groups organize trainings for new volunteers to help them become more familiar with crisis response and to forestall severe adverse reactions to trauma on the job.

Integrating New Volunteers

An important part of sustaining the virtual volunteer organization is integrating new volunteers into the group [35]. Sara (leader of a digital volunteer organization) reported assigning new members different amounts and different kinds of work—easier tasks that do not require the technical or contextual expertise that experienced volunteers bring to their work. Other interviewees share similar strategies:

> *Rachel (technically savvy newcomer): "People flagging things don't need to think too much, they're just flagging things... you might be able to pull people in... who aren't being needed right now but don't have a lot of experience in the area."*

Since many new volunteers are "spontaneous"—i.e. they only show up after an event occurs—training volunteers before their first deployment is difficult. The interviewees described different methods for utilizing inexperienced volunteers so that they have opportunities to become more included into the group over time. Sara described how this structure helps integrate new volunteers and discussed how the group with which she works has online training "modules" to, in theory, address this problem, but she mentioned these are difficult to keep up-to-date, indicating a low priority and possibly a perceived low utility for this method. Carey and Beth described similar aims to develop structured training materials that can be shared across the entire VOST community:

> *Carey (EM and VOST leader): "I would like to see us develop something to help train people to do this kind of [social media monitoring] work."*

Almost all of the digital volunteer groups and VOST teams described by the participants had an outgoing, broadcast component to their work that accompanied their information gathering and processing tasks. Interviewees, however, pointed out that new volunteers are often not given access to transmit outgoing information, and are instead encouraged to gain a better understanding of the crisis response context before going on to perform this task.

> *Sara: "When it comes to new volunteers, we don't just put them right behind the seat and let them start driving the car. They're going to be working with the more seasoned volunteers for a while."*

Research shows that new volunteers sometimes develop unofficial mentoring relationships with more experienced volunteers [34], a relationship that both provides them a means of learning and helps them become integrated into the social structure of the group.

Continued Learning and Sharing Knowledge

Individuals performing social media crisis monitoring have devised a number of techniques for transmitting work practices and supporting continued learning. One way this is done is through the explicit sharing of search and monitoring strategies. Phil (experienced volunteer and free agent) stated that he creates a series of searches on Tweetgrid and then posts a link to the search page to a shared Skype window during an event so other volunteers can bring up a window with the search terms he defined. Phil also demonstrated how he creates templates for executing different levels of a geographical search—setting up one search within a region with a radius of one mile from a given GPS location, another search with a radius of ten miles, etc. When a disaster strikes, he can quickly access his templates, change the center point for each search, and start monitoring posts from the affected regions. These templates are designed for his future use, but he also suggested that they could be shared with other volunteers. This method of sharing search strategies facilitates work in the moment for less experienced volunteers and also provides them a learning opportunity, but is currently employed by only a few volunteers.

Other sharing of community and "professional" know-how occurs through groups such as the "leadership coalition," a network of VOST leaders from various locations who meet monthly by phone to share tools and skills. Beth (emergency manager and VOST leader) mentioned that she sends out messages to the coalition looking for specific expertise when needed, and described how she and others from her organization engage in local "tweetups," stressing the value of these as places where individuals could participate in a "collaborative learning environment."

Sharing work practices within and across groups can also aid in interoperability between teams. Beth noted that despite her experience with digital volunteerism and VOSTs, it takes her at least 45 minutes to become adjusted and begin working when she joins a new VOST group. This may not sound like much time, but during a crisis, when information is accumulating quickly, it can be incredibly important. Interoperability is seen as a method for easing this transition between groups.

DISCUSSION

This research investigates the work practices of crisis monitoring teams with the aim of informing the design of tools and platforms to support this work.

Current Work Practices

Currently, digital volunteers and VOST members primarily use freely available, online tools to cobble together ad hoc infrastructures that are extremely flexible and often in flux. Their work is both collaborative and distributed—i.e. they work with others, but they rarely see each other in person. Along with the manual work of monitoring, they currently do considerable work "by-hand" to stitch together the separate pieces of information, such as copying and pasting information into Skype conversations or shared Google documents, which become their work products. Previous research examining how a digital volunteer community works during active events reveals heavy articulation work to coordinate action within textual chatrooms [35], something to which interviewees in this study also alluded.

Distributed Crisis Curation within Communities of Practice

This research supports a view of digital volunteer groups as communities of practice [16, 35] organized around a core group of "trusted" volunteers but with others at the periphery, including occasional and spontaneous volunteers who elect to help in various capacities during an event. By participating in relatively simple tasks, those on the periphery are able to contribute while learning skills used within the group, enabling them to gradually become more involved and move toward the center of the community.

New digital volunteers are often assigned different yet meaningful tasks from more experienced group members. Sara said, "Volunteers are motivated by self-actualization. They want to be masters, they want mastery of their skill sets." Because communities of practice cannot be sustained or grown without new members moving from the periphery to the center, it is vital that systems for collaborative crisis curation are designed to allow inexperienced volunteers to legitimately participate and learn relevant skills.

Motivations for Participating

An important aspect of digital volunteer and VOST work is *why* they do it. This is significant for understanding the capacity of this work, and speaks to the sustainability of these efforts over time [35]. This research reveals, through interviewees' descriptions of themselves and of other volunteers, a variety of motivations for participation. Significantly, it suggests that individuals with previous emergency management experience may enter the space for different reasons—and with different skillsets and expectations—than those who spontaneously volunteer in response to a specific event. However, volunteers from both of these persona types appear to be partially driven by a sense of identity drawn from their activities in the space—a finding that supports Starbird & Palen's account of crisis-volunteering Twitter users [34]. Social interactions with other team members and a growing sense of community are also important factors in ongoing participation.

Designing to Support Distributed Crisis Curation

Repeated evidence of emergent volunteer groups and the establishment of ongoing virtual volunteer communities suggests that people continue to make themselves available to help remotely and participate in information processing tasks during disaster events. During crisis events, there will be workers available to monitor social media and other sources. However, to increase their effectiveness and to accommodate the ever-increasing flood of data, individuals and teams who do this work need flexible tools that allow them to collaborate, coordinate, and sync their work with other people and other platforms in real time.

Our research reveals several design opportunities in this space. Importantly, informed by the empirical findings presented here, we argue for situating solutions within current work practices and infrastructures.

Situating Solutions with Current Work Practices

Digital volunteer work often takes place within communities. Even when volunteers begin alone, many soon connect and coordinate their work [34].

Value Sensitive Design (VSD) emphasizes consideration of stakeholder values when making design decisions [5]. Applying this rationale to the goal of leveraging the capacity of digital workers during crisis events, we identify design solutions that fit the underlying community dynamics, including current work practices, organizational structures, and motivations of digital volunteer work.

In introducing new tools and processes into this work, we risk inadvertently designing out the creative appropriation work that has heretofore characterized these groups. This could have the undesired effect of making them less flexible and less adaptable to emerging needs—a consistent feature of crisis events—and new technologies. In a related vein, one interviewee emphasized the need to use a variety of tools and strategies to get diverse input, saying, "I think that if we prescribe one way of doing things, [the volunteers] will miss things." Additionally, prescribing a top-down work process may have detrimental effects on volunteer motivations. This is particularly true for a process that supports the institutional context of the VOSTs, as equality and lateral organization are valued within digital volunteer communities. Therefore, our design seeks to support current work practices without disrupting the ecosystems within individual or collective communities.

Our research suggests that current communication practices have dual effects: to coordinate action *and* to support the social (and therefore motivational) structure of participation. We therefore situate solutions within an existing, multi-channel communication infrastructure that includes Skype, Twitter, and other tools.

Figure 1 illustrates a potential new system for supporting the work of distributed crisis monitoring teams, highlighting several design implications that emerged from this research. This design represents part of an ongoing research effort, and we are working to develop a usable platform based on it.

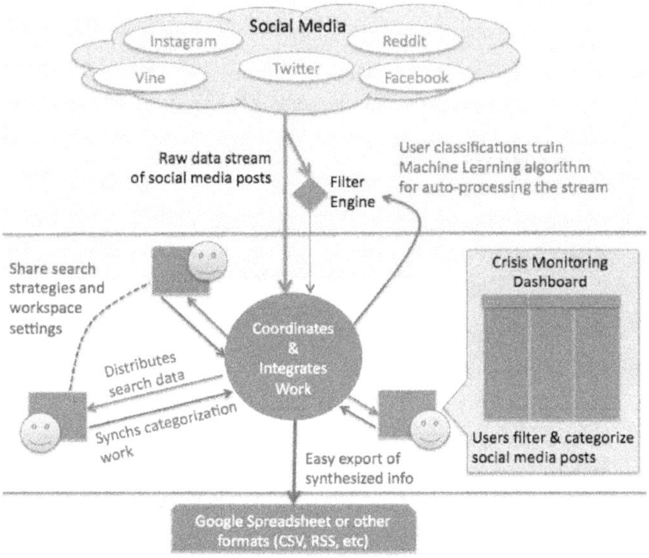

Figure 1. Design to Support Current Work Practices

Crisis Monitoring Dashboard

At the primary point of user-interaction within this design is a Crisis Monitoring Dashboard that enables collaborative monitoring of social media data (see Figure 1). It consists of multi-column streams of tweets defined by search terms, geographic regions, user lists, and more—aligning with similar features in existing platforms that interviewees indicated are popular in crisis monitoring groups. Our design aims to help volunteers collaborate and coordinate by integrating their work within a common data store—i.e. when one user categorizes a social media post, other users will be able to see and work off of that categorization. By making the work of individual volunteers visible to the whole group, this could increase situational awareness within the group, and help less experienced volunteers learn new skills. A central data store also allows for the data stream to be divided into different subsets—e.g. randomly, by search term, by geolocation, etc.—and distributed across the volunteers, which could reduce redundancy and help volunteers deal with information overload.

Shared Search Strategies and Work Space Configurations

Related to the idea of learning within a community of practice, another design idea that emerged from our interviews is a feature that enables easy sharing of search strategies and workspace configurations. Currently, this process involves considerable meta-work, including moving between different tools, and is very time consuming. A collaborative system that enables team members to seamlessly share dashboard configurations (Fig. 1, dotted line on the left) could extend the impact of this technique, allowing members to share new search strategies as event conditions change, and, perhaps more importantly, to help train less experienced workers during events.

Exporting Curated Data in Structured Formats

To facilitate connections between the various applications used by digital volunteer groups, and to help eliminate the time-consuming work of copying, pasting, and toggling between windows, our findings also suggest features for easily exporting "found information" in structured formats. For example, our proposed design includes one-click functionality for exporting social media posts and associated meta-data, including user tags, into shared Google Spreadsheets that groups are already using to coordinate and synthesize (see Fig. 1, at bottom).

Using "Natural" Actions to Train Automatic Classifiers

One promising area of research explores the use of computational solutions, such as automatic filtering and classification tools, to process crisis data during disaster events [2;13;23;36]. Importantly, current solutions require large amounts of "training" data that has been manually classified by humans. Meier, a leader in the online crisis response community, outlines a research program for creating real-time tools for computational processing and advocates using a microwork approach both for increasing the scale of manual classification efforts and to help train automatic classifiers [20]. Microwork is a form of crowdsourcing that distributes small "micro" tasks to an (often anonymous) crowd using small financial or other incentives.

Our research findings support a slightly different approach, one that situates these computational solutions within digital volunteer communities and other distributed crisis monitoring teams. Following Quinn & Bederson's vision of tightly integrating human and machine work in hybrid systems [28], and instead of a microwork approach that attempts to recruit a new crowd using micropayments or other incentives, we advocate designing workflows that take advantage of digital volunteers' current work practices—i.e. algorithms that learn from manual work to filter and categorize social media posts (e.g. the Filter Engine in Fig. 1), perhaps nudging volunteers to do specific categorization tasks as needed. The actions within the system would provide the training data for the machine learning algorithms. We suggest a classifier "fuel gauge" in the shared monitoring dashboard that declines over time and can be "filled" by dedicating a few minutes to a training task—e.g. classifying unmarked tweets as relevant or not relevant, or verifying that a set of automatically classified photos have accurate labels. Importantly, within our proposed design, this classification work is integrated with the "real" work of identifying important posts. Since classification can be seen as an entry-level task that allows new volunteers to productively—and *legitimately* [16]—participate in the team's work while they learn skills, integrating computational solutions in this way may provide opportunities for incorporating inexperienced volunteers.

Additionally, the products of these machine learning algorithms (the filtered and pre-processed data streams) become input streams for the digital volunteer communities. By providing volunteers with data that has already been automatically filtered and classified, these algorithms could increase their ability to sift through massive amounts of data. In other words, the products of their work have utility to the groups themselves.

Importantly, the work discussed here would be visible and integrated into the community, rather than separated off on another platform or site, and could access the full range of motivations for digital volunteers—moving beyond mere altruism to the sense of community, social connections, identity, and reputation motivations currently driving the more experienced volunteers.

Informed by the findings of this research, we advocate designing a workflow that integrates automatic classifiers and other machine-computational strategies with the rich work practices of digital volunteers. Instead of designing volunteers out, we suggest creating computational solutions that learn from their work, producing an invaluable resource for volunteers and external clients of the data.

CONCLUSION

From interviews with digital volunteers and emergency response professionals, this research examines the current work practices of distributed teams who work to curate social media data during crisis events. We describe the tools and processes currently used by digital volunteer teams to collaborate and work together, as well as their inherent motivations for continued participation in crisis response. From our findings, we identify design implications for supporting this work, including coordinating and integrating the activities of distributed volunteers; facilitating connections between different tools and tasks; enabling team members to share their actions (i.e., making them visible to others) to scaffold learning for less experienced and spontaneous volunteers; and using the current work of volunteers to train machine learning algorithms to increase the scale of their impact.

ACKNOWLEDGMENTS

We would like to thank all participants and participating organizations who allowed access to their time and knowledge for this research. In particular, we thank the members of the #SMEM and VOST communities for their time. Additionally, we thank Apurva Dawale, Mania Orand, Daniel Shank, Archana Suresh, and Thomas Stanton for their work on this project. This work was supported in part by the NIH National Library of Medicine (NLM) Training Grant Nr. 2T15LM007442 at the University of Washington.

REFERENCES

1. Castillo, C., Mendoza, M. & Poblete, B. Predicting information credibility in time-sensitive social media. To appear in *Internet Research* (2013).
2. Cameron, M. A., Power, R., Robinson, B. & Yin, J. Emergency situation awareness from Twitter for crisis management. *Proc. of WWW* (2012), 695-698.
3. Dynes, R. R. Organized behavior in disaster. *Heath*, (1970).
4. FEMA. Hurricane Sandy: Rumor Control. (Dec. 2012) http://www.fema.gov/hurricane-sandy-rumor-control.
5. Friedman, B., Kahn Jr, P. H., & Borning, A. Value sensitive design and information systems. *Human-computer interaction in management information systems: Foundations*, *5*, (2006), 348-372.
6. Harvard Humanitarian Initiative. Disaster relief 2.0: The future of information sharing in humanitarian emergencies. *Washington, D.C. and Berkshire, UK: UN Foundation & Vodafone Foundation Technology Partnership* (2011).
7. Hecht, B., Hong, L., Suh, B. & Chi, E. H. Tweets from Justin Bieber's heart: The dynamics of the location field in user profiles, *Proc. of CHI* (2011), 237-246.
8. Heinzelman, J. & Waters, C. Crowdsourcing crisis information in disaster-affected Haiti. *United States Institute of Peace, Special Report* (2010), 252.
9. Heverin, T. & Zach, L. Use of microblogging for collective sense-making during violent crises: A study of three campus shootings. *J. Am. Soc. Inf. Sci. 63, 1* (2011), 34-47.
10. Howe, J. Crowdsourcing: Why the power of the crowd is driving the future of business. *New York: Crown Business* (2008).
11. Hughes, A. L. & Palen, L. Twitter adoption and use in mass convergence and emergency events. *Proc.of ISCRAM* (2009).
12. Hughes, A. L. & Palen, L. The evolving role of the public information officer: An examination of social media in emergency management. *Journal of Homeland Security and Emergency Management*, *9, 1* (June 2012).
13. Imran, M., Elbassuoni, S., Castillo, C., Diaz, F. & Meier, P. Practical extraction of disaster-relevant information from social media. *Proc. of WWW* (2013).
14. Kumar, S., Barbier, G., Abbasi, M. A., & Liu, H. TweetTracker: An analysis tool for humanitarian and disaster relief. *Proc. of ICWSM* (2011).
15. Latonero, M. & Shklovski, I. Emergency management, Twitter, & social media evangelism. *International Journal of Information Systems for Crisis Response and Management 3, 4,* (2011), 67-86.
16. Lave, J. & Wenger, E. Situated learning: Legitimate peripheral participation. *Cambridge university press* (1991).
17. Leetaru, K., Wang, S., Cao, G., Padmanabhan, A. & Shook, E. Mapping the global Twitter heartbeat: The geography of Twitter," *First Monday*, *18, 5,* (April 2013).

18. Liu, S., Palen, L., Sutton, J., Hughes, A. & Vieweg, S. In search of the bigger picture: The emergent role of on-line photo sharing in times of disaster, *Proc. of ISCRAM* (2008).

19. Medley, E. Hurricane Sandy: Use Twitter to find open gas stations and business, *nj.com* (Oct 31, 2012). http://www.nj.com/news/index.ssf/2012/10/hurrican_sandy_use_twitter_to.html.

20. Meier, P. *iRevolution.* http://irevolution.net/.

21. Meier, P. Towards a Twitter dashboard for the humanitarian cluster system. *iRevolution.* (July 30, 2012). http://irevolution.net/2012/07/30/twitter-for-humanitarian-cluster/.

22. Meier, P. Verily: Crowdsourced verification for disaster response. *iRevolution.* (Feb 19, 2013). http://irevolution.net/2013/02/19/verily-crowdsourcing-evidence/.

23. Mendoza, M., Poblete, B. & Castillo, C. Twitter under crisis: Can we trust what we RT?, *Proc. of the 1st Workshop on Social Media Analytics* (2010), 71-79.

24. Palen, L., Anderson, K. M., Mark, G., Martin, J., Sicker, D., Palmer, M., & Grunwald, D. A vision for technology-mediated support for public participation and assistance in mass emergencies and disasters. *Proc. of ACM-BCS Visions of Computer Science* (2012), 1-12.

25. Palen, L & Liu, S. B. Citizen communications in crisis: Anticipating a future of ICT-supported participation, *Proc. of CHI* (2007), 727-736.

26. Palen, L., Vieweg, S., Liu, S. & Hughes, A. Crisis in a networked world: Features of computer-mediated communication in the April 16, 2007 Virginia Tech Event. *Social Science Computing Review, Sage* (2009), 467-480.

27. Qu, Y., Huang, C., Zhang, P. & Zhang, J. Microblogging after a major disaster in China: A case study of the 2010 Yushu Earthquake, *Proc of CSCW* (2011), 25-34.

28. Quinn, A. & Bederson, B. Hybrid human-machine hybrid computation. Position Paper for the *CHI 2011 Workshop on Crowdsourcing and Human Computation.*

29. Sarcevic, A. Palen, L., White, J., Starbird, K., Bagdouri, M. & Anderson, K. "Beacons of Hope" in decentralized coordination: Learning from on-the-ground medical Twitterers during the 2010 Haiti earthquake. *Proc. of CSCW* (2012), 47-56.

30. Shklovski, I., Palen, L. & Sutton, J. Finding community through information and communication technology in disaster response. *Proc. of CSCW* (2008), 127-136.

31. Shih, G. Over 20 Million Tweets Sent as Sandy Struck. *Reuters* (Nov. 2, 2012). http://www.reuters.com/article/2012/11/02/us-storm-sandy-twitter-idUSBRE8A116020121102.

32. St. Denis, L. A., Hughes, A. L., & Palen, L. Trial by fire: The deployment of trusted digital volunteers in the 2011 Shadow Lake Fire. *Proc. of ISCRAM* (2012).

33. Starbird, K., Palen, L., Hughes, A. & Vieweg, S. Chatter on the red: What hazards threat reveals about the social life of microblogged information. *Proc. of CSCW* (2010), 241-250.

34. Starbird, K. & Palen, L. "Voluntweeters:" Self-organizing by digital volunteers in times of crisis. *Proc. of CHI* (2011), 1071-1080.

35. Starbird, K. & Palen, L. Working & sustaining the virtual disaster desk. *Proc. of CSCW* (2013), 491-502.

36. Verma, S., Vieweg, S., Corvey, W. J., Palen, L., Martin, J. H., Palmer, M., Schram, A. & Anderson, K. M. Natural language processing to the rescue?: Extracting 'situational awareness' Tweets during mass emergency, *Proc. of ICWSM* (2011).

37. Vieweg, S., Hughes, A., Starbird, K., & Palen, L. Micro-Blogging during two natural hazards events: What Twitter may contribute to situational awareness. *Proc. of CHI* (2010), 1079-1088.

38. Virtual Operations Support Group (VOSG), History. http://vosg.us/history/.

39. Ziemke, J. Crisis mapping: The construction of a new intrdisciplinary field? *Journal of Map & Geography Libraries*, *8*, 2, (2012).

Beyond End User Content to Collaborative Knowledge Mapping: Interrelations Among Community Social Tools

Tara Matthews[1], Steve Whittaker[2], Hernan Badenes[3], Barton A. Smith[1]
[1]IBM Research - Almaden, San Jose, CA, USA, {tlmatthe, barton.smith}@us.ibm.com
[2]UC Santa Cruz, Santa Cruz, CA, USA, swhittak@ucsc.edu
[3]IBM, Buenos Aires, Argentina, hbadenes@ar.ibm.com

ABSTRACT
Most studies of social tools examine usage of each tool in isolation. Instead, we explore how online communities (a) *combine* multiple social tools, and (b) use social tools together with *external* tools. Based on interviews with community leaders and quantitative analysis of 128 online community spaces, we explored the combined use of *six social software tools*—wikis, blogs, forums, social bookmarks, social file repositories, and task-management tools. We contribute a detailed characterization of how enterprise online communities combine multiple social tools, adding to our understanding of community behaviors: Communities combine social tools to curate and organize complex information spaces. When combined, each tool is used for limited "core" functions; thus "social" features are not always leveraged for every tool. Leaders and members divide labor by tool boundaries. Our results suggest that an important overlooked aspect of social media concerns how different tools can be effectively combined. While most prior work on communities emphasizes end user content, we identify additional important design activities where community participants curate and organize pre-existing content from multiple tools to serve their community needs.

Author Keywords
Online communities; social software; interrelationships; user study; workplace; office.

ACM Classification Keywords
H5.m. Information interfaces and presentation (e.g., HCI): Miscellaneous.

INTRODUCTION
Online communities have long used online forums and email to interact [8]. With the explosion of social software and Web 2.0 applications, there is a host of new tools available, including wikis, social file repositories, forums, blogs and microblogs. This rapid emergence of new social tools and new tool features, means that online communities often do not know *which* tools to deploy or *how to use them effectively* [2,17,21,27]. If communities were limited to a single social tool for all their needs, choices might be easier, but communities can now combine multiple tools for interaction, archiving, and other needs. The problem is exacerbated in mature communities, who may have multiple older tools to manage as well [17]. In this new context, how are enterprise online communities composing multi-tool technology environments, and can we provide guidance to leaders about effective tool combination practices? Our study focuses on enterprise online communities, but the same questions are relevant for internet communities who have the same complex portfolio of tools to choose from.

Researchers have documented how individuals and groups in organizations appropriate social tools [23]. However, such studies generally explore use in a *single tool situation*, where appropriation is really common. For example, wikis afford publishing information, collaborative editing, and team coordination [21]. Blogs enable workers to access and share information, solve problems, give and get feedback, build their network and collaborate [7]. Social file sharing supports discovery of, and discussions about content [20]. Social bookmarks enable people to organize, share, and find resources [18]. Across these studies, "social" features—such as tags, comments, "like" options, identification of authors and commenters, and the ability for multiple people to edit—enhance these tools, enabling content sharing and discovery, collaboration, and contributor visibility. However, it is unclear if these benefits will accrue when communities combine multiple tools. Also, the results of single-tool studies may have unknowingly been influenced by users' use of other tools.

In this paper, we study how enterprise online communities combine social tools in a multi-tool environment. In theory, a multi-tool context should enable communities to evaluate the strengths of each tool and avoid sub-optimal tool appropriations. Multi-tool environments can be incredibly complex, involving many tools and resources. We therefore selected a sub-set of multi-tool use cases we could study for a broad set of communities, triangulating both qualitative and quantitative methods. In particular, we examined cases where *multiple social tools are combined* to support a single activity. We call these tool *interrelations*. We address the following questions about *interrelations* between social tools used by enterprise online communities:

CSCW'14, February 15–19, 2014, Baltimore, Maryland, USA.

http://dx.doi.org/10.1145/2531602.2531694

- When a community has access to *multiple social software tools*, do they combine tools to exploit their different functions?
- If tool combination does occur, what *interrelations* do we see between different social tools? *How* are the tools used together and in support of *what activities*?
- *Why* do certain types of interrelations occur? What social and technology design features encourage these interrelations?

To tackle these questions we studied how *six different social tools*—wikis, blogs, forums, social file repositories, social bookmarks, and task-oriented spaces (called "Activities" [2])—were used *together* by communities in an enterprise. We examine long-term communities, managing complex, diverse sets of information. Such communities also often exploited *external overlapping tools*, i.e., tools outside their community space that duplicate internal tools, such as basic file repositories. Thus we wanted to know:

- How do communities combine *external overlapping tools* with social tools inside their community space?

The six social tools we studied are integrated in a web application, Connections Communities (www.ibm.com/software/lotus/products/connections/communities.html). A "Community" is a single shared space that gives members options to activate any of the six tools, providing one UI to access them. The Communities application provides a unique opportunity to evaluate how communities combine the six generic social tools. We can therefore determine: (a) how frequently communities combine tools, and (b) how different tools are combined. These questions are important because several tools support overlapping functions, e.g. both wikis and activities can coordinate tasks [2,21]; blogs and forums can be used to share group news and gather feedback [7,27]; wikis, activities, and shared repositories can be used to attach files [2,20,21]; and so on. And certain external tools' capabilities directly overlap with social tool functions (e.g., basic vs. social file tools [20]).

Combination supported three major tasks: *organization,* i.e., making internal resources findable; *curation,* i.e., drawing in external resources; and *notification,* i.e., alerting others to new content, to provide feedback or simply for awareness. Communities had a tool-delineated division of labor between leaders and members for these tasks. We describe how tools were combined and labor divided to accomplish these tasks. We offer implications for community and technology design. Our data also quantifies the huge efforts dedicated to organization and curation, revealing a new understanding of community dynamics.

RELATED WORK

Prior research provides guidelines for how communities can collaborate using multiple tools [10,22,26,27]. Wenger et al. motivate our study, highlighting critical challenges communities have in selecting, setting up, and managing technology [27]. They provide guidelines for *community technology stewards* to handle these tasks, describing how different communities emphasize different "orientations." Orientations affect the tools groups select, but there are still many possible multi-tool configurations per orientation.

Applying Wenger et al.'s framework, most studies of *actual technology deployment* focus on communities with a single orientation using a single configuration of tools, e.g. technology use by communities within Wikipedia [11], Encyclopedia of Life [24], MovieLens [11], Facebook [25], QuitNet [14], Slashdot [12], and Stack Overflow [15]. Early studies of technology use by communities described similar case studies [8]. There is little empirical work presenting *quantitative and qualitative* data, describing multi-tool use by a *range* of enterprise communities who can *select from and configure* a generic set of social tools.

We are aware of one study by Muller et al. of multi-social-tool appropriation by a range of communities [19]. Muller et al. described how the types of enterprise communities included in our study—Communities of Practice (CoP), Teams, and Technical Support Communities (Tech)—used different tools. They found some differences in how different community types initiated and used different social tools. However, their study was purely quantitative, and did not describe rationale or practices for using the different tools, as we do in this paper. Nor did they study combination of tools, which is our focus.

We examined technology use by both community leaders and members, who enact different activity types [3,4,9]. To foster successful communities, prior work advocates that leaders should: encourage contributions and discussion [9,10,22], contribute and read content [4], organize and curate content [22,27], deal with disruptive behavior [4,9,10], create a positive environment [4,9], foster connections [10,26], manage new members [10], advertise [4,9], and maintain infrastructure [4,9,22,27]. Members' should: contribute and read content, and interact with other members (asking/answering questions, providing/receiving social support, etc.) [4,8,9,10]. However, prior work does not directly observe patterns of how leaders and members *combine* a variety of tools to accomplish these activities.

STUDY CONTEXT

We examine communities in a global enterprise offering technology products and services to businesses. The commercial tool, Connections Communities ("Communities") was available to all employees, and the company encouraged employee leadership of, and participation in, internal online communities. As a result, there were 166,000+ communities and 580,000+ distinct members. Communities was used by a variety of community types: including CoPs, organizational teams, and technical support communities [19]. These groups used Communities primarily to *connect and build relationships among employees* who could *share information and resources* with each other, and sometimes *collaborate* on a shared deliverable. CoPs did these activities in the context of a shared interest or practice; teams in the context of producing a shared deliverable; and technical support communities in the context of a mutually used technology. Relating these community types to the "orientations" described by Wenger et al., there was a strong emphasis on *content*, *projects*, and *access to expertise* [27].

The default Community homepage includes three columns (see **Figure 1**): *left column*, top to bottom, includes the community's logo, links to tools, and a tag cloud; *middle column* starts with an community description, then one box per tool (Blog, Forum, Files, etc.) listing latest updates (**Figure 1** only shows the first tool for this community, Blog); *right column* includes "Important Bookmarks" (communities choose these), Members, and an optional list of Related Communities (manually configured by leaders).

Communities is an example of highly configurable end-user software [23], meaning that it includes a set of general-purpose tools that can be appropriated in multiple ways. The Blog, Wiki, Forum, Files, and Bookmarks tools have the standard functionality of similar tools widely available on the internet, plus typical "social" features: author profiles, comments, tagging, sorting, and "liking." The Activities tool provides task-oriented spaces with structured fields for to-dos, text content, file uploads, and the ability to organize content into "sections" [2].

STUDY METHOD

We wanted to understand *which* tools were combined and *how* they were used together. Thus we collected detailed qualitative data by interviewing expert community leaders about how and why they combined tools, and by directly examining community spaces. We also gathered broad quantitative data characterizing communities' multi-tool environments and tool inter-linking. We describe interviews with 8 leaders, observations of 67 community spaces, and a quantitative linkage analysis of 128 community spaces.

Interviews With Community Leaders

To collect descriptions of *how* and reasons *why* communities combined tools, we interviewed 8 community architects. Architects were *expert community leaders* who worked with multiple communities in their business division (e.g., Software, Hardware, Services, Sales, HR, etc.). Their jobs were to determine best practices for community tool usage, set up technology, and train and consult with community managers [5]. Generally they were responsible for the success of all the communities in a particular division or sub-division within the company. Because they worked with multiple communities, this enabled us to collect data about a range of practices across the company. The other leader role at the company was *community managers*, who were responsible for the day-to-day activities of a single community through its life cycle. All our participants were community managers for at least one community, in addition to their architect roles.

Our participants represented a broad set of divisions, including Hardware, Sales, and multiple sub-divisions of Software, Services, and Corporate Development. Each led

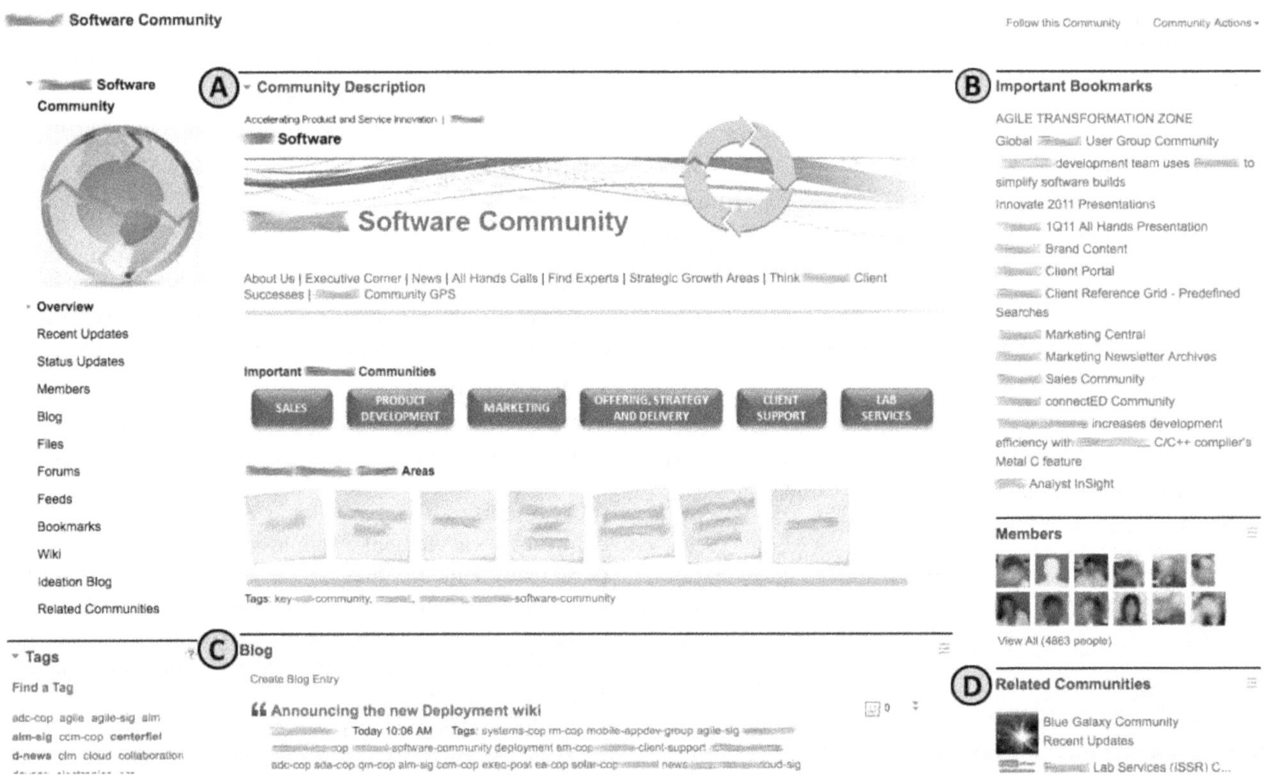

Figure 1. Communities default landing page for an example community (only top third of page is shown). (A) Community description, configured to link to top community content. (B) Important bookmarks, configured to link to more top community content. (C) Preview of each tool's contents, configured to start with the Blog. (D) Related Communities list.

both CoPs and Teams with experience leading and consulting with many communities. To recruit such a diverse set of people, we identified an initial 4 community architects representing different divisions through our working relationships with them, developed from our work designing tools for community leaders [16]. We identified an additional 3 architects who worked in different business divisions. We identified 1 participant in a new division based on a recommendation from another participant.

In 30-60 min phone interviews, we asked architects about the *types* of communities they led, *how these communities used each of the six social tools* in Communities, and what *other tools* (like external file repositories, wikis, forums, or communication tools like email) they used and how. We made it clear to participants that we wanted to understand how their communities *actually* used the tools, rather than how architects *intended* people to use the tools. Indeed we will provide multiple instances of where members did not do what architects wanted or expected. Interviews were audio recorded and detailed notes were taken to create a list of usage goals and practices for each individual tool and interrelation between tools mentioned by participants. We used this list to determine common interrelations between social tools. We did multiple passes through interview notes to identify themes related to these interrelations.

Exploratory Examination of Community Spaces

Our interviews did not allow us to observe *actual tool* usage by community participants. Thus to supplement our qualitative data, we conducted a small-scale, exploratory examination of community spaces, observing and interpreting how communities used the six social tools. We sampled 67 public communities with the highest overall posting in and viewing of their community space (54 CoPs and 13 Teams). Our goal was to understand if the themes from our interviews occurred in communities other than those led by our interviewees, and to observe concrete examples of how leaders and members enacted the themes, but not to quantitatively assess how frequently they occurred in a large population of communities. Thus we did not conduct a content analysis with a formal coding scheme, but instead examined community spaces, observing the ways tools were used and interpreting the purposes of posts in those tools.

For each of the 67 communities, we viewed the pages that summarized every post. The summary pages for all the tools except the Wiki included, for each post, the title, author, date updated, and number of comments. The summary page for Blogs also included the entire article. For the Wiki, we viewed the top-level parent page and a tree-structure listing the titles of all the Wiki pages. On each of these summary pages, we used the available information to assess the purpose of each post. The post titles were informative because members also used these pages to determine when to click on a post, so authors made the titles descriptive of the purpose and contents. We clicked on posts when their purpose was not apparent, to view all of their content. We took notes about the variety of purposes the posts in each tool served. We also noted the practices used to accomplish these goals, such as linking to other tools. This analysis, importantly, confirmed that *linking* was the primary way in which people enacted the interrelations described in our results.

Quantitative Linkage Analysis

The exploratory examination of community spaces showed that communities combined tools by linking from one to another. We performed a *linkage analysis* to quantitatively characterize *how* inter-linked the tools were, as well as the *patterns* of different links, i.e., which tools commonly linked to each other, and whether links were formed within the community or across communities. Tools that interview participants said were important to the community had many links to them in the linkage analysis, even non-social tools (e.g., email linked by "mailto" links, meetings indicated by links to web-conferencing and scheduling tools). Also during our interviews, the *community description* on the homepage emerged as an important place for the activities observed in our study. Even though the homepage description is not a "tool," we added it to our linkage analysis and present it in the results.

To analyze interrelationships, we crawled all leader- or member-posted text in 128 Communities (excluding text inside Files) to identify links (URLs). For each link, we captured the source Community (where it was posted), the source tool (Wiki, Blog, Forum, Bookmark, Activity, Community description), whether its target was internal (inside the Community) or external (outside the Community), and the target tool (see Table 2 for a list of external target tools and **Table 1** for a list of internal target tools). When an Activity was the *target* tool, we could not determine if it was part of the same or some other community, so we exclude Activities from internal target tool analyses (**Table 1** columns). We analyzed the data to understand: How many tools does each community typically use? How inter-connected are tools in the community space both internally and externally? What tools do communities commonly combine? Our criteria for inclusion in the linkage analysis were:

- *Active management*: Leaders had to sign up for Community Insights [16], a tool to help leaders enhance their community. A research goal is to make community design recommendations, so we wanted active leaders.
- *Mature*: Greater than one year old, allowing time to develop norms for using the tools, and materials describing these norms to new members.
- *Active*: Updated in the last month. We wanted relatively successful communities since our aim was to describe effective tool usage practices.
- *Type*: We chose 3 of the 5 community types described in [19]: CoPs, Teams, and Tech. (IdeaLabs and Recreational communities were excluded because there were not enough of them that met the other criteria.)

Table 1. Internal Tool Linkages: For each source tool inside a community, the number of its links that point internally to each target tool within the community, aggregated across the 128 communities in our dataset. The "total" column and row include the total number and percent. Results: As a center of curation and organization, wikis are the source and target of most links. As common "attachments," files are a target of many links.

Internal Source Tool (linked from) \ Internal Target Tool (linked to)	Wiki	File	Blog	Cmty Home	Forum	Total
Wiki	9885	4015	289	912	370	15471 (77%)
Blog	436	194	2303	270	84	3287 (16%)
Forum	313	120	77	161	171	842 (4%)
Cmty description	251	6	25	21	9	312 (2%)
Bookmark	107	13	18	11	12	161 (1%)
Activities	25	4	0	6	14	49 (0.2%)
Total	11017 (55%)	4352 (22%)	2712 (13%)	1381 (7%)	660 (3%)	20122

508 communities met these criteria. We selected all 17 Tech communities and randomly sampled 57 each of CoPs and Teams, totaling 131 communities. We were unable to collect full-text data from 3 communities, leaving us with a dataset of 103,900 links from 128 communities.

Use of Multiple Methods

Our use of multiple methods enabled us to *compare the results* of each method to ensure they were *consistent.* Below, we describe only those results that aligned across all three methods. This approach is known as methodological triangulation [5]. Characterizing tool interrelationships based on results that were consistent across multiple, complementary methods, adds credibility to our findings (e.g., interviews elucidated in depth perspectives of a limited set of people, but linkage data quantified practices for a broad set of communities and people). Note that the data from our three methods were not analyzed together, but rather the final results were compared for consistency.

The methods were designed to complement each other. Together the qualitative methods provided an understanding of the phenomenon of tool interrelationships: the interviews provided rich descriptions and rationale for the interrelations. The examination of community spaces showed whether the interrelations occurred in the spaces and provided concrete instances of what interviewees described. The quantitative linkage analysis design was informed by the qualitative findings that communities purposefully used tools together and that links were used to mark interrelationships. This suggested we explore links between specific tools inside and outside the community.

RESULTS

Our results show that combining social tools is common and the reasons and ways communities did so. The results demonstrate new use cases introduced by tool combination, e.g., *layering* social functionality of one tool onto another and *dividing work* for a single activity into multiple tools. The practice of linking tools and resources together also reveals a new emphasis on content curation (in contrast to end user content creation) in enterprise communities.

Combining Tools is Common

Our quantitative analysis showed that communities commonly use multiple tools: 88% of communities used (i.e., posted at least once to) 4 or more social tools in their Community. Tools were used with the following overall frequency per community: Wiki (89%), Files (88%), Forum (88%), Bookmarks (88%), Blog (71%), and Activities (19%). However, communities did not use tools independently; rather, we found considerable linkage between tools. Each type of tool had links, with the vast majority pointing to tools other than themselves, inside and outside the community. As shown in Table 2, Wikis contained the most links (average of 588 for 114 communities with Wikis), then Blogs, Forums, Bookmarks, and Activities.

For *internal* links, Communities had an average of 154 links pointing to their own community (out of an average total of 812 links). As shown in **Table 1**, the most referenced internal tools were Wikis (55% of internal links), Files (22%), and Blog (13%). Surprisingly very few links pointed to the community's homepage (7%) or Forum (3%). While each tool contained within-tool references (especially the Wiki and Blogs), many links were to other tools (see **Table 1**). Some frequently linked tools included Wiki to Files (4015 links, 26% of internal Wiki links), Blog to Wiki (436 links, 13% of internal Blog links), Forum to Wiki (313 links, 37% of internal Forum links), and Bookmark to Wiki (107, 66% of internal Bookmark links).

Our linkage analysis also showed which tools were used *in isolation.* Activities had very few links: 400 total (0.38% of all links), and only 49 pointed to other tools in the same community (see in **Table 1**). Activities seemed to be used in a fairly isolated way, even within a multi-tool environment.

Our link analysis showed that communities also relied on *external tools:* i.e. resources outside the community space. Communities signaled which external tools were relevant by linking to them. Table 2 lists the categories of tools linked to by our dataset of 128 communities. For external links, the biggest category was links to *other communities*

(22.5%), indicating significant interrelationships between communities (also noted in [17]). The next biggest category was internal links to the *same community* (19.4%). A large number of links were to *external overlapping tools* (13.7%) (i.e., external tools with similar functions to an internal tool, such as external file repositories or wikis). People are key to communities, so many links pointed to *individuals'* intranet profiles or email addresses (10.6%). These links referenced experts, people in particular roles, and so on.

Which community space tools were linked to primarily internal vs. external targets? Virtually all Bookmarks (98%) and Forum links (93%) pointed *outside* the community space. Though the majority of Wiki and Blog links also pointed outside the community, a substantial proportion pointed inside (23% and 19% respectively). See Table 2.

These data show that tool combination is common, but do not tell us *how and why* different tools are combined. Why do communities link different tools so often? What activities do the interrelations serve? Why are some tools more externally focused than others? Why are different communities so interlinked? How do communities use content in external overlapping tools as compared to internal tools? What social and technology design features encourage these interrelations? We address these questions by presenting results from our leader interviews. We identified three main categories of interrelationships among the six tools in Communities and overlapping external tools. These interrelationships do not cover *all* use cases for the six social tools, but rather uses where tools were combined.

(1) Leaders Organize and Curate Content

The first three interrelationships involved *activities performed by community leaders*. For all the communities led by our participants, the Wiki, homepage, and links to other communities were owned and edited by leaders.

Wiki as knowledge map to internal and external tool content

Our linkage analysis showed communities used multiple tools, inside and outside Communities. Interviews revealed that before adopting new social media tools, long-term communities had already built up considerable resources in external tools. Such established communities thus had to manage this pre-existing external content, along with new social tools after adopting Communities. To organize their complex information landscape, a very common practice was to use social tools within Communities, particularly the Wiki, to create a *knowledge map* for the complex resources the community managed. Wiki maps helped members locate content distributed across many tools.

Such Wikis acted as static reference pages enabling new members to *get acquainted* with community resources. It also *highlighted* key content and helped members *navigate to* specific content spread across other tools. The Wiki therefore included many links to individual items in other tools (e.g., "more information about product release in the Blog post") and/or the tools themselves (e.g., "post product questions in this Forum"). See Figure 2 for an example.

> *"We tend to use Wikis more as index pages, or content curation pages... So we'll have a page in the Wiki that has the details about [product] client references, so it'll have some information about what the client references are... and it'll link to the place in the Community Files where you can actually download the presentations." –M1*

Wiki knowledge maps were not usually community-wide collaborative efforts. Leaders stated that in all their communities, a small set of people on the leadership team created and maintained the Wiki. This is consistent with prior research [4] indicating that leaders take responsibility for organizing community content. For example, notice how at the bottom of Figure 2, two Wiki owners ask "Do you have a suggestion for new content or an update? Please send your suggestions to [name] and [name]."

Our linkage analysis supports this interrelation: Wikis held the majority of community links. Table 2 shows 65% of all links posted were in Wiki pages. This is especially striking given the small number of Wiki pages per community (an average of 15 pages), adding support to leaders' claim that the knowledge map was the primary use of Wikis. Also, aside from community descriptions, Wikis were the main

Table 3. Most link targets are *external* to the community. For each target category of tool, the average number of links and the percentage of links pointing to it in the community spaces of the 128 communities in our dataset.

Target Tool (linked to)	avg. # links (N=128)	% links
Other community	183.0	22.5
Same community	157.2	19.4
Internet	120.9	14.9
Other intranet	114.0	14.0
External overlapping tools	111.6	13.7
People (profile, mailto)	86.1	10.6
Meeting tool	6.0	0.7
Unknown	33.0	4.1
Total	811.7	100

Table 2. In our dataset of 128 communities, for each source tool (column 1), # communities using the tool (column 2), the average # of posts in the tool per community that uses the tool (forums includes topics + replies, the rest only include top-level posts) (column 3), the average # of links in the tool per community that uses the tool (column 4), and the percentage of links pointing inside and outside the community space (columns 5-6).

Source Tool	#cmty use	avg #post	avg #link	%link inside	%link outside
Cmty descr	128	1	5	49.9%	50.1%
Wiki	114	15	588	23.1%	76.9%
Blog	93	61	186	19.0%	81.0%
Activities	27	188	15	12.3%	87.8%
Forum	113	341	102	7.3%	92.7%
Bookmark	113	63	63	2.3%	97.7%

way to index *internal* content: 23% of Wiki links were to internal tools, the source tool with the second-highest proportion of internal links (see Table 2). The Wiki identified key internal resources that were otherwise hard to find, in particular, other Wiki pages (64% of internal Wiki links) and Files (26% of internal Wiki links) (**Table 1**).

Homepage links to organize critical content

Communities helped members navigate to critical community content, internal and external, with the "Community Description" and "Important Bookmarks" areas, which we refer to collectively as *homepage links*. These always appeared in the top portion of the Community homepage (**Figure 1** A and B). Homepage links were salient on the homepage, making them one of the first things people saw upon visiting the community. They included a very small number of links (average of 5 in the community description), but leaders considered them important navigation aids, so selected them carefully. The links pointed to critical *internal and external* content—50% of community description links were internal, 50% external, as shown in Table 2. Among all community tools, they were the *most internally focused* (see Table 2), and usually linked to the Wiki knowledge map when present (80% of internal community description links pointed to the Wiki).

> *What we'll do is on our front page... here are the top five things that you probably want to see... I think that's helped a lot versus saying, 'just come to our community and figure out where you want to go, you know, navigate the Wiki on your own.' It gives people a high level entry point." –D1*

While Community Descriptions could only be edited by Community leaders, any member could classify a bookmark

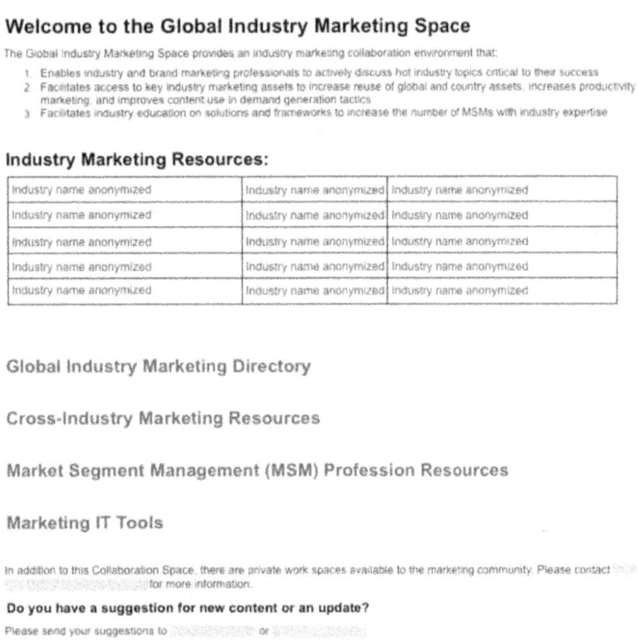

Figure 2. Wiki as a knowledge map. This wiki links to various parts of the Community, including files and other wiki pages, as well as an external overlapping file repository. Notice at the bottom that two leaders ask for feedback on new wiki content rather than encouraging members to change the wiki themselves.

they added to the Bookmark tool as "important," moving it to this prominent area. This posed a problem for leaders, who wanted to control homepage links, since these were key navigation guides to the content owners managed and where they believed they were the experts.

> *"We specifically tell [members] not to post Important Bookmarks, because it does mess up our right sidebar, and I actually go in and delete them as I see someone has done something, even if they read the warning or they just ignored it... [The Important Bookmarks] are just the ones we put in there. I have to clean it out like every week." –M2*

Other Communities generate relevant content

Other related communities were major sources of relevant content. Communities drew in that content by linking to it, leading to significant interlinking between communities. On average 23% of links in a community were to other communities (Table 2). Relationships usually resulted from a collaboration or shared topic of interest. Several communities embedded feeds in their Wiki pages to automatically collect and display related content posted in any other community. One leader described this:

> *"We have something like 40 of these communities that we call 'smart communities.' All of these... rely on the same tagging taxonomy... What we use the Wikis for, is to embed these feed windows so that instead of having your community manager go out and find all the assets that they want to put links to on the Wiki... we set up feeds to look for specific tags based on that community and the interest... You can post it anywhere... and we'll populate those Wiki pages." –D1*

In addition to the Wiki, communities frequently linked to a small set of related communities in their *homepage links* (described next) and in a widget called "Related Communities" (**Figure 1**D). The sole function of the Related Communities widget was to link to other communities. All of these tools—the Wiki, homepage links, and related communities widget—were primarily maintained by community leaders.

(2) Members Curate Content

All leaders reported explicitly encouraging members to contribute to Bookmarks and Forums. One of the activities members did in these tools was to curate external content.

Bookmarks to curate external content

The vast majority of bookmarks (97.7%, see Table 2) catalogued a wide variety of *external* content. Unlike the Important Bookmarks, leaders actively encouraged members to add to the collection of general bookmarks, soliciting members' knowledge of external resources. For example, one community of practice leader wrote in their community charter (published in the Wiki):

> *"We aim to become the "home base" or "one stop shop" for all of your [Community Name] collaboration needs. In order to do so, it's important that we provide links to the other valuable communities in [our company], as well as any other content relevant to the [Community Name] Community. Please feel free to add to our collection of Bookmarks..."*

Forum and Blog engage people who curate external content

Forums pointed primarily to resources *outside* the community (92.7% of Forum links, Table 2). Leaders noted that members congregated in the Forums to share their knowledge in support of other members. By answering questions, discussing topics, or brainstorming, members drew external resources into the community space via links. A few leaders told us the Blog was also used by members to draw in external resources (81% of Blog links pointed externally). Whereas leaders pre-planned and mapped relevant external content in the Wiki, members dynamically created a map of relevant external content in ad hoc Forum and Blog posts. A leader discussed layering these social software "conversations" over external content:

> *"It used to be 'content is king,' you know everybody used to say that. To me, content without a conversation around it, nobody's ever going to find the asset. And I think that's been hard for a lot of people, because I think most of us grew up when there was a manageable number of assets, even though we thought it was a lot. But today, there's just tons more. And we've got [employees] who go, 'well I posted it out on iRAM, why didn't everybody find it?' And you're like, 'cuz there's about a billion places.'" – D1*

(3) Notifications of New Content: Blog announces new content in Files or Wiki; Forum used to discuss Files

In addition to organization and curation, another function of linking social tools was to *draw attention* to new content and to *solicit* and *organize feedback* to that content. Leaders and members used the Forum and Blog for notifications.

Blog posts often *announced* new Files or Wiki content in the Community or externally (e.g., see Figure 1C). A similar interrelation involved using the Forum to *discuss* files posted to the Community or externally. The Files tool supported commenting on files, so feedback *could* be gathered and organized in that tool. However, these interrelationships existed because people expected others to check the Blog and Forum for new information. Conversely, they did *not* expect people to check the File or Wiki tools themselves for new content.

Our linkage analysis shows that the Blog points to the internal Wiki, and internal and external Files fairly commonly, an average of 3.4 times and 18 times per community, respectively. Forums point to internal and external Files an average of 13.7 times per community. Of course, not all of these references were notifications and content analysis would be needed to determine exactly how many of these links to Files and Wikis were notifications.

While leaders advocated using Blogs for announcements, we observed other instances where members instead used Forums. When asked about this, leaders saw it as a misuse of tools caused by member confusion between the two tools because of their similar functionality and affordances.

> *"We try to make it so that you use the Blog for... a one-to-many announcement... And then try to use Forums for when it truly is a many-to-many conversation. But we still have people get them confused." –D1*

For notification activities, the Forum and Blog competed with email. When we asked leaders about other tools they used besides those in the community space and external file repositories, the only other tool discussed by all of them was email. Most leaders said their communities were trying to *replace email* use by the community, with the Forum and Blog. However, email continued to be used since adoption of newer social tools was an ongoing change in most communities' interaction practices.

(4) Organizing Files

Both leaders and members helped organize community Files, which were often spread across multiple repositories.

Blogs, Forums, and Wiki index information stored in Files

Leaders and members organized Files, linking to them in the Wiki, Blogs, and Forums. After the Wiki, Files were the most commonly linked to internal tool (see **Table 1**). We extended this analysis to examine how often different tools linked to any internal or external file repository. File repositories got many pointers from the Wiki (10659 links across 128 communities, an average 83 links/community, or *10% of all links*), the Blog (2366, or an average 18 links), and the Forum (1757 links, or an average 14 links).

Leaders noted how members would describe a file in another social tool and include a link to the file. The link served to supplement information being shared in a Blog post, help answer a Forum question, and so on. In all cases, the source tool provided the mechanism to help members discover the target file to determine if they wanted to download it. Thus, people were *not* relying on Files' intrinsic "social" features—such as tags, recommendations and notifications—to help others become aware of, describe, and find them. Instead the primary interrelation in which Files participated was as a reference "attachment" to another type of post in the Community.

> *"What we've done is a very simple practice of, when you find an asset, wherever it is, it could be in Files, Cattail [an external file repository], Twitter, you just post a note with the URL in the content of that Blog." – D1*

External overlapping vs. Community file repositories

Many communities used multiple file repositories. Communities had an average of 68 links to files in external overlapping file repositories (8.5% of all links in our dataset). Mature communities needed to incorporate legacy file repositories. File repository technologies have changed over time, sometimes leaving mature communities with multiple instances. One leader showed us a diagram with ten file repositories used by her communities, saying,

> *"The community leaders are curating content... [Members] still come to the Community as their first stop. The whole point is, don't sent them out to the 10 repositories. Send them to the community and then they can access that content... 'Business Value Accelerators' go in the BVA repository. That's where they should go. Practitioner Portal is used for 'work product,' and it has to be harvested and scrubbed and tagged, but that's where it should go... And we'll help you*

build Wikis and links and stuff to that content, but that's easy to find for people in your community." –R1

The quote above also illustrates how communities sometimes had very specific repositories for certain file types (e.g., assets, work products, etc.). We saw a clear partitioning between external overlapping and social tools. The external overlapping file tools tended to be for storing "assets" or "work products", which was a specific designation given to high-value, reusable materials that usually went through a review process. The Community Files tool was for anything else.

Despite these programmatic efforts, the abundance of file repositories led to liberal attitudes about where files were stored. Leaders described encouraging members to post files anywhere and link to them in the Community, e.g.:

"I personally think we ought to keep [the Community] separated from the file repositories, and you just use links, you know just URLs… So more of a people-centric approach than telling people which file repository to use… Let's all blog about it and tag it, so we don't all have to know where and how people are storing stuff" –D1

Technology Features, Social Norms Affect Interrelations

These interrelations occurred because of a combination of technology features and community social norms. For example, knowledge maps and homepage links were carefully crafted by community leaders. Not only did leaders *want to control* these critical navigation resources (social), they also felt members were *unable to contribute* (technology design). Leaders described the Wiki as too flexible to lay out and simultaneously difficult to format. One leader described how enabling community members to use it was virtually impossible:

"In terms of posting content, I find myself explaining what a Wiki is… When people explain to me what they are trying to do… I say to do that in an Activity because you have features designed specifically for that. Whereas a Wiki page… is more complicated." –S1

Similarly members linked to external resources in Forums partly because they tended to do most of their posting there. Forum design encouraged this by focusing on conversations that resembled Internet Forums with which workers were already familiar. Similarly, members frequently posted to Bookmarks because they were easy to use. These interrelationships was enforced by norms fostered by community leaders, who posted guidelines encouraging members to post in the Forums and Bookmarks.

Files were frequently referenced in other tools because it was difficult to find files. Despite Files including tags, sorting features and folders, leaders still described Files as "one big bucket" where individual files were "hard to find." The summary page listing a community's Files showed only meta-data, without the textual descriptions, making it hard for people to evaluate a file. Leaders favored the Wiki to organize file navigation and the Blog to announce them, since these tools allowed customizable ways of describing the relevance of a file to members.

DISCUSSION

Our major result is a characterization of how the six social tools in Communities are combined with each other and with external tools. We now discuss high-level themes and implications for social and collaboration software design.

Combining Social Tools is a Common Practice to Support Organization, Curation, and Notification

Combination of tools was a common and important practice that is not well documented in prior work. Communities combined tools to support three major uses: *organization,* or making the community's internal resources findable (done with the Wiki, homepage); *curation,* or drawing in external resources (Wiki, homepage, Bookmarks, Forum); and *notification,* or asking others to look at new content, for awareness or to provide feedback (Forum, Blog). These activities as performed by leaders and members, were clearly partitioned into different tools—partly as a social practice to make it clear where and how members should participate, and partly because of tool affordances. The sheer quantity of links between tools, plus confirmation from interviews, shows that much effort was put into these activities. Our results point to the importance of understanding how communities combine multiple tools.

Limited Use of Individual Tools in a Multi-Tool Context

One important unexpected implication of tool combination was that individual social tools were not themselves used for multiple purposes. Thus a community tended to use an individual tool for a single function (e.g., storing Files), but combined it with other tools if multiple functions were required (e.g., Forums or Blogs for discussing Files). Some tools might be appropriated for a couple of functions, but leaders noted communities were careful to limit this to avoid confusing members.

Limited appropriation is clearly demonstrated for Files. The primary function of Files was to serve as a reference "attachment" to other types of posts in the Community. Thus, people did not rely on Files' "social" features—such as tags, recommendations, and notifications—to help others become aware of them, describe them, and find them later. Instead, other tools such as Forums and Blogs were used for these purposes. Our findings are contrary to previous studies that looked at social file tools [20], which found that social features within Files were used to announce, rate, and solicit feedback. However this discrepancy between our results and prior studies may arise because prior work explored tool use in isolation rather than in relation to other tools used by the same community.

In the same way we saw Wikis being used for a limited set of purposes when combined with other tools. The Wiki's primary use for communities was as a knowledge map or static reference document. However, leaders did not commonly talk about Wikis as a collaboration or coordination tool, as is often cited in literature studying

Wiki use in isolation [21], because collaboration usually happened in Activities [2]. Again this difference may arise from the multi-tool context of our study

Social Tools Are Not Always Used Socially

The uses of Files and Wikis imply that social tools are not always used "socially" when combined with other social tools. For example, announcing files in the Blog reduces the number of places a community has to look for new information. But this suggests that people do not expect others to discover their file using just the Files tool, despite its social features such as tags, feeds, recommendations, and listing the author along with the file. The usage of Files in combination with the Blog is practical: communities do not want too many places to check for new information, so they consolidate announcements in the Blog. This finding emphasizes the need for communities to develop common practices for where to discuss, monitor, curate, and so on, an issue discussed next.

Managing Complex Info Spaces with Tool Usage Rules

Overlapping functionality among a community's tools can cause confusion. For example, leaders reported that members were confused about when to use the Blog versus Forum. Similarly, we observed different communities appropriating the same use cases differently across the two tools; e.g., some groups allocated announcements to the Forum, others to the Blog. To mitigate confusion, community leaders defined practices for using each tool for a specific purpose that did not overlap with the other tools. The fact that we were able to find so many communities with thriving online spaces indicates that such efforts can lead to effective utilization of complex resources.

Prominence of Content Curation and Organization

Our data also quantifies the huge efforts put into organization and curation activities, representing a new understanding of enterprise community behaviors. Communities strongly emphasized *content curation and organization* as key activities, i.e., architecting information spaces. This is markedly different from the emphasis in prior literature on *member content creation* as the main community activity [6,9,10,13]. That literature emphasizes the leader's role as a *facilitator of peer interaction*, not as an information source or curator [8]. Community design guidebooks have chapters dedicated to helping leaders encourage contributions among members [9,10]. Researchers offer study after study that look for ways to increase participation [10,13] or use contributions as a primary community success metric [6]. However, the community leaders in our study described a shift in their own focus *from content creation to curation*: "*It used to be content is king. Now you're never going to find it without people.*" Several expressed the opinion: 'the information is already out there somewhere so why duplicate it.' Curation seemed to be a coping mechanism for information overload, enabling communities to create a place to collect and find relevant information. Leaders described members as providing access to external information via the Forum and Bookmarks. They described their own role as information architects creating Wiki knowledge maps and carefully selecting community homepage links. They wanted their members to post information in predictable ways that would allow others to access it. Our quantitative data supports these qualitative findings, showing considerable linking between community tools and to resources inside and outside the community.

This study contributes to an emerging literature describing curation processes in communities [11,24]. As the amount of information on the intranet and internet increases to levels no one person could consume, it may become less important for communities to create content, and more important for them to curate content. On the web, bloggers [1], content strategists for aggregator sites (like The Daily Beast and Huffington Post), and users who rate on Slashdot [12], curate content of interest to their audience. In a similar way, we contribute a detailed view of how enterprise communities divide labor and appropriate social tools in their curation and organization processes.

An emphasis on curation and organization has implications for community design, technology design, and success metrics. The prevalence of Wiki knowledge maps indicates that an index of the community's information space offers an important way to orient members. Technology might automatically create these maps to ease the burden on community leaders and ensure up-to-date information. This might be achieved by analyzing frequently accessed links and resources. Also, technology might surface resources buried in a Forum discussion, making them easier to find and browse. We also observed that labor was divided along tool boundaries, indicating that technology should support the different curation roles of leaders and members, and provide restricted access to centrally curated content. Regarding success metrics, number of *views* may be more important than *contributions* in communities that emphasize information curation. This is supported by recent work studying metrics needs among enterprise community leaders [16]. Our work also suggests new success metrics: the *diversity* of links posted might be considered important indicators of the community's progress in curating content.

Communities Divided Labor by Tool

While both leaders and members curated content, they did so in different tools. Leaders curated in the Wiki and homepage, while members curated in Bookmarks and Forums. This division of labor by tool is a useful way for communities to help members learn how to contribute. Leaders described selecting the tools where members could participate based on which were easiest to use and most likely familiar. For example, Bookmarks were easier to use than Wikis, so leaders encouraged members to curate via Bookmarks and maintained the Wiki themselves.

Implication for Design: Goal-based Abstractions

Both the existence of interrelationships between tools and member's confusion over when to use certain tools argues for a new way of designing complex community collaboration spaces. These need to be organized around *activity- or goal-based abstractions* rather than tool-based distinctions. For example, tool designers should enable leaders to organize the Community into areas for key community needs—like knowledge map, announcements and discussion, and contributing new assets. Communities should then use the appropriate tool—or tools, in the case of an interrelationship—to support these. Our study indicates that the above needs would be useful abstractions for enterprise communities. The interrelationships we observed show how social tools might be combined to support these abstractions, providing concrete implications for system integration. For example, announcements could be supported by a tool people monitor (Forum, Blog) that could easily link to reference materials (Files, Wiki pages).

Generalizing to Internet Communities

While this is an investigation of intranet communities, some lessons are also relevant to internet communities. First, our study points to the importance of understanding how communities combine social tools. Internet communities commonly use multiple tools and our results suggest that social tool use may be different in multi-tool versus single-tool environments. Second, our study emphasizes the importance of curation in online communities, as a coping mechanism for information overload. Curation is directly relevant to internet communities, and it deserves more study as emerging research have also indicated [11,23]. Third, some of the specific interrelationships identified in this paper may hold in an internet environment, serving to guide future research. The tools studied here were generic and widely available to internet communities (wikis, forums, blogs, etc.). Fourth, our observation that curation duties were different for leaders and members and relied on different tools may also be general. Finally, our study showed that links and curated content provide a way to identify related communities.

CONCLUSION

This paper represents a first step toward an understanding of how communities combine multiple social tools. This points to avenues for future research. We studied inter-relationships from the perspective of community leaders and more could be understood about this topic by studying the perspective of community members, though the linkage analysis documents behaviors of members. Different types of communities have different collaboration needs and might combine tools differently, something future studies could elucidate. We studied a particular set of six tools, but a different set of tools might yield different interrelationships. Because there are so many possible combinations used by many types of communities, studying interrelationships is complex. This complexity encourages researchers to study tools in isolation, because it is simpler. However, we have demonstrated that interrelationships are a real phenomenon, one that seems to be increasingly common. We call for future work to study other combinations of tools and types of communities.

REFERENCES

1. Ammann, R. Reciprocity, Social Curation and the Emergence of Blogging: A Study in Community Formation. *Procedia - Social and Behavioral Sciences 22*, (2011), 26-36.
2. Balakrishnan, A.D., Matthews, T., Moran, T.P. Fitting an activity-centric system into an ecology of workplace tools. *Proc. of CHI* (2010), 787-790.
3. Bourhis, A., Dubé, L., Jacob, R. The Success of Virtual Communities of Practice: The Leadership Factor. *Electronic J. of Knowl. Mgt. 3*, 1 (2005), 23-34.
4. Butler, B., Sproull, L., Kiesler, S., Kraut, R. Community effort in online groups: Who does the work and why? In *Leadership at a distance*. Erlbaum, 2002.
5. Denzin, N.K. *Sociological Methods: A Sourcebook*. Aldine, '06.
6. Iriberri, A., Leroy, G. A life-cycle perspective on online community success. *ACM Comput. Surv. 41*, 2 (2009), 1-29.
7. Jackson, A., Yates, J., Orlikowski, W. Corporate blogging: Building community through persistent digital talk. *HICSS '07*.
8. Johnson, C.M. A survey of current research on online communities of practice. *The Internet & Higher Ed. 4*, 1, '01.
9. Kim, A.J. *Community building on the web : Secret strategies for successful online communities*. Peachpit Press, 2000.
10. Kraut, R.E. Resnick, P. *Building successful online communities: Evidence-based social design*. MIT, 2012.
11. Lam, S.K. *Collaborative curation in social production communities*. University of Minnesota, 2012.
12. Lampe, C. Resnick, P. Slash(dot) and burn: distributed moder-ation in a large online conversation space. *Proc. of CHI '04, 543*.
13. Ludford, P., Cosley, D., Frankowski, D., Terveen, L. Think different: increasing online community participation using uniqueness and group dissimilarity. *Proc. of CHI*, (2004).
14. Ma, M., Agarwal, R. Through a glass darkly: Information technology design, identity verification, and knowledge contribution in online communities. *Info. Sys. Res. 18*, 1, '07.
15. Mamykina, L., Manoim, B., Mittal, M., et al. Design lessons from the fastest Q&A site in the west. *Proc. of CHI* (2011).
16. Matthews, T., Whittaker, S., Badenes, H., et al. Community Insights: Helping community leaders enhance the value of enterprise online communities. *Proc. of CHI* (2013), 513.
17. Matthews, T., Whittaker, S., Moran, T.P., et al. Productive Interrelationships between Collaborative Groups Ease the Challenges of Dynamic and Multi-Teaming. *CSCW 21*, 4-5, '12.
18. Millen, D.R., Feinberg, J., Kerr, B. Dogear: Social bookmarking in the enterprise. *Proc. of CHI*, (2006), 111.
19. Muller, M., Ehrlich, K., Matthews, T., et al. Diversity among enterprise online communities: collaborating, teaming, and innovating through social media. *Proc. of CHI*, (2012).
20. Muller, M., Millen, D.R., Feinberg, J. Patterns of usage in an enterprise file-sharing service: publicizing, discovering, and telling the news. *Proc. of CHI* (2010), 763–766.
21. Poole, E.S., Grudin, J. A taxonomy of Wiki genres in enterprise settings. *Proc. of WikiSym* (2010), 14:1–14:4.
22. Preece, J. *Online communities: Designing usability and supporting sociability*. Wiley, 2000.
23. Richter, A. and Riemer, K. Malleable End-User Software. *Business & Info. Systems Eng. 5*, 3 (2013), 195-197.
24. Rotman, D., Procita, K., Hansen, D., et al. Supporting content curation communities: The case of the Encyclopedia of Life. *JASIST 63*, 6 (2012), 1092–1107.
25. Wang, Q., Woo, H.L., Quek, C.L., et al. Using the Facebook group as a learning management system: An exploratory study. *BJET 43*, 3 (2012), 428–438.
26. Wenger, E., McDermott, R.A., Snyder, W. *Cultivating communities of practice: A guide to managing knowledge*. Harvard Bus., 2002.
27. Wenger, E., Smith, J.D., White, N. *Digital habitats: Stewarding technology for communities*. CPsquare, 2012.

Think Globally, Act Locally: A Case Study of a Free Food Sharing Community and Social Networking

Eva Ganglbauer, Geraldine Fitzpatrick, Özge Subasi, Florian Güldenpfennig
HCI group, Vienna University of Technology
Argentinierstrasse 8, 1040 Vienna, Austria
{eva.ganglbauer, geraldine.fitzpatrick, oezge.subasi, florian.gueldenpfennig} @tuwien.ac.at

ABSTRACT

Social networking has a long history of supporting communities online. In this paper we are concerned with a specific community that has formed around free food sharing to save food from being wasted. Specifically, Foodsharing.de is a platform that enables consumers, farmers, organizations and retailers to offer and collect food. Associated with this is the Foodsharing Facebook group where broader community discussions take place. We report on a qualitative analysis of the Foodsharing Facebook group to understand its role in emerging and sustaining the community. The Facebook group is a place where the individual values and motives, socio-political discussions and mass media interrelate and create new social patterns through narratives and local community building. We present our findings as interplay between a number of factors: individual, community, and organisational levels; public relations and media, the operational platform Foodsharing.de that enables local communities and the Facebook group where global ideological framing of the community takes place.

Author Keywords

Social networking sites; communities; Facebook; food waste; empowerment; free share economy; activism;

ACM Classification Keywords

H.5.m. Information interfaces and presentation (e.g., HCI): Miscellaneous.

INTRODUCTION

Sharing food has been a cultural and social practice in communities since ancient times and is re-gaining popularity now. This is because societal developments of overproduction of food in industrialized countries results in half of the food being produced thrown away along the food chain [10]. The advance of web and social technologies offer new possibilities to connect people who want to offer or receive food for free to save it from being wasted. This gives rise to interesting online and offline sharing interactions, as people who meet online have to meet offline to actually hand over the food articles. However little has been researched about the values and ideals of such free share economy [27] communities and how technologies facilitate these online-offline practices.

The focus of the study here is a German community that shares food supported by the platform Foodsharing.de. This platform enables activities such as offering food, accepting the offer, and negotiating a time and place to meet and hand over the food. Complementing this, active discussions around Foodsharing and its community happen at the Foodsharing Facebook page, where the Foodsharing Association posts messages to invite community interactions and discussions. Community members are also allowed to post to the Facebook group. 3242 posts and comments from December 2012 until March 2013 on this Facebook group served as the material for our qualitative thematic analysis. The focus of our analysis was on individual values and the overall picture that makes such a community work. We identified individual values and needs of social, ecological and economic nature as motivations to engage in sharing food. Here public relations and mass media not only played a significant role in promoting the community but also in creating through narratives a new social pattern of sharing food. Public relations also played a role in building local communities, as sharing food requires a critical mass of active participants in a geographically bounded area. We also analyzed interactions between community members and found pro-active appeals and critical awareness of community members. The key contribution of this paper for the CSCW community is how participants use the social media and web platforms to facilitate fluid transitions between online-offline and local-global interactions. We draw out the interplay between individual, community, organisational levels, public relations and media, the operational platform Foodsharing.de that enables local

CSCW'14, February 15 - 19 2014, Baltimore, MD, USA
Copyright is held by the owner/author(s). Publication rights licensed to ACM. ACM 978-1-4503-2540-0/14/02...$15.00.
http://dx.doi.org/10.1145/2531602.2531664

communities and the Facebook group where global ideological framing of the community takes place.

RELATED LITERATURE

This paper builds on prior research on food as a social and cultural phenomenon, the phenomenon of food waste, communication and social networking sites, and food communities.

Food and its passage to waste

The main motivation behind the Foodsharing community is to save food from being wasted by giving it to other individuals and institutions for free. In this section we first want to engage with food itself, as food is an inherent part of our lives. Everybody has to eat to survive. Beyond this primary need there is a social and cultural dimension, where food is inherent in the enactment of cultural and social practices. Food is graspable, tangible, visible, and related to living organisms. Evans points to this materiality of food as "susceptible to spoilage, decay, and rapid transformation" that "suggests a vitalism that animates foodstuffs" [7].

If food is wasted somewhere along the food supply chain, it is not just the food itself that is wasted but also the energy that has been invested in growing, nurturing, harvesting, producing, packaging and transporting. According to Gustavvson et al. [9] medium and high income countries are mainly responsible for food waste, with 95-115 kg a year per person, whereas in developing countries it is 6-11 kg a year per person. The majority of food waste happens at the household consumer and retailer level for industrialized countries like Germany, which cause up to 40 percent of all food waste. The remaining 60 percent of waste happens during food production, agriculture, post-harvesting and processing [9]. Besides the ecological effects it is also the ethical implications that accompany food. It is important to emphasize that for individuals, food waste usually occurs unintentionally. For example, the participants in studies of Evans [7] and Ganglbauer et al. [8], in most instances, did not want to waste food. Food was wasted inadvertently, accompanied by ethical as well as economic concerns and because somewhere else in the world 'people suffer from hunger' or 'it just feels wrong to throw food away'.

Food communities

Given the importance and social nature of food in people's everyday lives, it is not surprising that communities around food are formed. Communities serve as a foundation where experiences and knowledge are discussed and reflected upon. There are various communities with food as a common theme and these include alternative food cultures that might be supported by technology [2]. Odom [19] looked at the agricultural aspect of urban food production and how this might be supported by technology, as technology can potentially play a role in tracking food to 'grower management software' or 'garden sensors'. Communities are often built on the idea of sharing, such as the one studied by Parker et al. who looked at the reflective aspects when people share healthy eating ideas through audio-recordings on health [21]. Participants in this study discussed and shared more than healthy eating ideas and also had debates about wider systemic implications of healthy food and 'become advocates of change apart from the tool' [22]. Gross et al [11] talk about Foodmunity, a social networking site that facilitates people meeting together around shared experiences with food. Our Foodsharing community is extended by the notion of actually sharing food articles, which in turn results in discussions and engagement around broader issues we want to present in this paper.

Communities and social networking sites

Individuals are often part of a broader community, where there are different dynamics at work. An integral part of communities is communication, as it is only through communication that the interior values and motives can be exteriorized [9]. It is also communication that enables cooperation and collaboration [14] between members, which is central to a community. Social networking is an umbrella term for the infrastructures where people with similar interests can meet, interact, create, share and exchange information online. Platforms like Facebook provide the possibilities to connect, investigate and network socially to share identities, content and statuses [12]. For people with common interests there are Facebook pages that enable an online space for people who like and follow a certain theme. Facebook users 'liking' the page and participating in it can benefit from being able to socialize, entertain, seek self-status and information [20], contribute and discover [13]. The members of such online communities are often geographically distributed and independent as a common interest acts as social lubricant for the community. Such social networking sites can also be used in local geographical areas to build social relationships, negotiate ways to take collective action and social norms [17], negotiate local events and services, and share information and advice [15]. In this case interactions happen online as well as offline [18].

ABOUT FOODSHARING

Foodsharing.de[1] is a community platform in Germany that enables consumers, farmers, organizations and retailers to offer and collect food articles to save them from being wasted. Sharing food in this community involves no transactions of money and attracts all sorts of participants. Foodsharing therefore is theoretically open to all levels of the food supply chain.

The Foodsharing initiative originated in Cologne when several committed people came together to form an Association. It mainly started around Valentin Thurn, a documentary film-maker. Thurn had created a documentary called "Taste the Waste"[2] that presented the problem of

[1] http://foodsharing.de/

[2] http://www.tastethewaste.com/

food being wasted from different perspectives including farmers, wholesalers, food retailers and consumers. Besides many other vey active members he was key in actually starting the Association and is still part of it. Following the documentary the newly formed Foodsharing Association started a crowdfunding campaign and raised enough money in Germany to get funding for an online platform, giving evidence that there were already many people who believed enough in the idea to invest money for its development. Foodsharing.de was subsequently released on Dec 12th 2012. While it was started in Cologne, the site now can be accessed by anyone anywhere in Germany and actual food sharing could take place wherever people could physically access each other.

Figure 1: Screenshot from Foodsharing.de webpage

As at March 2013[3] the Foodsharing.de community had 17000 active members distributed over Germany and 1788 food baskets had been handed over. On the date we downloaded our data for analysis, there were 271 food baskets on offer to be collected. A food basket is created by someone who has food to offer and can contain one or more food articles. The food basket page of Foodsharing.de displays all currently available food baskets across a map of Germany and also provides the same information (available baskets) in a list view (see Figure 1). Community members can filter on different parameters such as location and adjacency on a map, timeliness of food baskets, content, or ending time for collecting them. If somebody wants to take up the offer of a food basket, s/he can then send a request to the person, organization or institution offering the basket. The offering side in turn can accept or decline a request. If both sides agree, they then negotiate where and when to hand over the food basket in the offline world.

The Foodsharing Facebook community

The Foodsharing webpage also links to a Facebook group called Foodsharing[4], which will be referred to as the Foodsharing Facebook page or just Facebook page in this paper. The Facebook page was started on September 13th 2012, before the platform itself started, as a forum for interested people. Whereas the Foodsharing.de platform is mainly functional, enabling the practical sharing of food, the Facebook page is the place where we can see the emergence of the community itself: where broader community discussions take place, and where members are invited to post, comment or 'like'. This paper will therefore focus on the community interactions on the Foodsharing Facebook page.

METHODS

To understand the mechanisms of this community and the role of the platform the posts of the Facebook community were qualitatively analyzed using inductive thematic analysis [3]. As at March 2013, there were 22405 'likes' (Facebook's mechanism for showing support for a page), and 1012 contributing members. The data set comprised 3242 contributions, made up by 243 posts contributed from the Foodsharing Association, 401 posts by members and 2598 comments to posts. Everybody who 'likes' and is subscribed to the page has access to all the posts and comments.

To create the dataset for analysis, we expanded all posts, starting from the beginning of September 2012 until beginning of March 2013, to make all comments visible, and printed out 208 pages of material. As a first pass in the thematic analysis, two coders made notes on two separate prints-outs, from which they identified and agreed 14 broad types of contributions, such as users requesting help or the Foodsharing Association celebrating a milestone. We then started to look for the deeper themes underlying the posts and repeatedly reviewed the material together to draw out important issues. The themes and codes were further reviewed in a collaborative analysis session with other group members. In this paper we focus on two themes, 'individual values and needs' and the 'emergence of the community'.

From the first analysis we could see that public relations and mass media played important roles in promoting the community and engaging new members. Hence, we analyzed 11 videos that were still available from the 17

[3] As at October 2013 the Foodsharing.de community had 27600 members and 4800 food baskets have been handed over.

[4] https://www.facebook.com/foodsharing.de

video links that were posted to the site. We observed these 11 videos and made notes of the main content topics. We were also looking for themes in these videos to analyse how they contribute to the emergence of the community. One illustrative video that was highly influential (surpassing all others by number of comments, likes and shares) was transcribed and thematically coded to uncover the possible new relations of sub-themes to the emergence of the community.

At our request, the Foodsharing Association also made us 'insight analysts' for this group, which granted us access to aggregated Facebook data and descriptive statistics behind the group. This provided us with information about basic demographic data of the members and to identify posts that were most 'viral', meaning we could see how many people commented, liked or shared a post.

FINDINGS

As background to understanding the Foodsharing Facebook community, we first provide a picture of the age group and gender of people engaging in this group, drawn from an analysis of the aggregated data of the Foodsharing Facebook page.

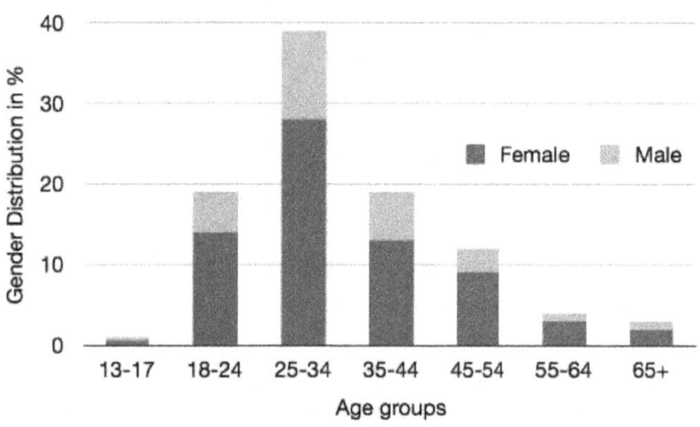

Figure 2: Gender and age distribution within the Foodsharing Facebook community.

More users 'like' the page who identify themselves to be female (69.6 percent) than male (27.4 percent). This resonates with other reports that women often play "central roles in shaping and furthering alternative agrifood movements and institutions" [1, p.12]. Allen and Sachs discuss the ways in which food practices such as cooking are often still a predominantly female domain, with women being mainly responsible for food-related work at the home as well as at the labour market [1]. This could be one aspect why more women (at least on the Facebook page) than men are present.

The most common age group for Foodsharing Facebook 'likers' is between 25 and 34 (39 percent of total). Almost a third (28 percent) of the users in the Foodsharing Facebook group are female and between 25 and 34 years old. See Figure 2 for more details.

We go on here to characterise the posts and comments in terms of topics. There were a plethora of issues discussed by the community, ranging from dumpster diving (freeganism)[5], agriculture, gardening, and everyday practices of food and waste, to sharing experiences offline and online, food waste cooking events and other initiatives.

To determine the nature of the information provided and how users engaged with Foodsharing, we categorised different types of contributions from Foodsharing users:

- *Foodsharing experiences*: Experiences, both positive and negative, from online and offline interactions with other members with whom food was shared.
- *Finding a local community*: Requests to connect to/ find others in a specific local area.
- *Calls for internationalization*: Remarks about wanting to have such a community in their country. (Foodsharing.de is provided for Germany only at the time of analysis).
- *Offering help:* Offers not only to share food but also to engage in voluntary work.
- *Plaudit to the Foodsharing initiative:* Appreciation for the initiative and how useful it is.
- *Wider systemic implications:* Discussions of the systemic effects of Foodsharing and if individual actions might have consequences if Foodsharing gains a critical mass.
- *Links to other initiatives:* The dynamics of Foodsharing seemed to attract users to link to other initiatives with a similar mindset.
- *Everyday practices and food waste:* Discussions about how food waste in private households, food retailers, restaurants or agri-industry emerges or not.
- *Feedback on the design of the Foodsharing.de platform:* Remarks about what could be improved and which features would be desirable.

The Foodsharing Association also made particular types of contributions:

- *Requesting help*: Asking for help on a range of issues, from asking for legal expertise (e.g., lawyers to consult about food legislation and Foodsharing activities) to asking for volunteers to be interviewed and report about Foodsharing experiences on TV.
- *Providing feedback to members:* Giving answers to questions, contributing to discussions.
- *Showcasing Foodsharing:* Sharing links to media where Foodsharing was presented, ranging from reports on TV to newspaper magazines.
- *Promoting networking:* Providing links to other initiatives with a similar mindset or political intention, such as for petitions, events, etc.

[5] The practice of foraging dumpsters for edible food (freeganism) or other goods.

- *Celebrating collective community milestones* such as the thousandth food basket that has been handed over.

Within these contributions, we identified emerging themes following the thematic analysis procedure described in the methods section. Here we start with unpacking the underlying motivations and values of individuals to participate in such a community. Posts may also entail a number of other themes than the one we primarily identify, as topics were often discussed in a non-linear way, where personal experiences are mixed with arguments for political perspectives or general expressions of praise or dispraise for the community. Statements of the members have been translated from colloquial German into English to make it understandable for an international audience. Pseudonyms are used to refer to members.

INDIVIDUAL VALUES AND NEEDS

This community included a highly diverse set of active Foodsharing Facebook members. To enact practices of sharing food requires additional effort in people's everyday lives – to create and/or respond to posts, to negotiate meeting places and times, and to physically meet to exchange the food. This implies that there are motivations and added values beyond the food that is provided to members. We were looking for the motivations that are inherent in the practice of sharing food in such a community. Two underlying and interdependent aspects as incentives to take action in this food sharing community were identified, namely *social and ecological* values and *economical* needs.

Social and ecological values

When people described their experiences on sharing food on Facebook, we often came across statements such as "*gives me a good feeling*" or "*doing a good thing*" in sharing food to save it from being wasted. So there seems to be something in not throwing food away that feels inherently right for these members and gives people an intrinsic reward from being 'socially responsible'.

There were also social side effects and some specific instances where people reported that they built new social relationships through Foodsharing activities. This is because the online interaction on Foodsharing.de leads to people actually meeting up, i.e., while the initial contact is made online via the platform, actually meeting and handing over the food has to happen offline at a place users can decide themselves.

> Isabel: "Even if it [food] was only a small amount I gave away, it gave me a good feeling. I get rid of my food baskets so quickly and you get to know so many brilliant and interesting people. Next week I have an arrangement with one for dinner … it is fun doing good and at the same time making new friends."

For others, the social motivation was more about wishing to "*do good*", to help and support people "*who don't have it so easy*" (Sophie). This social motivation in some cases went even further. Michael solely wanted to offer to people who are in need and not those who are economically well off:

> Michael: "Foodsharing is a great idea, I can finally give left over food to people in need of help. […] I just don't see a point in helping people who are NOT in need of it."

This statement was then discussed with other Foodsharing members, questioning who is in need and how one might be sure that only people in need are receiving food. The discussion, along the dimension of who has or has not economic and social need, points to wider systemic discussions we often encountered in the data when members discussed Foodsharing, an aspect which we will discuss later on.

Given the effort involved in sharing food, it is not surprising to see that people also expressed frustration when members of the community made an appointment to hand over the food but those collecting were not reliable. The Facebook group then acted as a forum for those who had been disappointed by a member who did not show up. It was suggested by members that these happenings should be translated into technological changes insofar that not only members offering food baskets should be rated but also those who collect them.

Besides intrinsic social values that mattered for sharing food, active members also demonstrated ecological motivations. These played out not just in terms of local practices, but connected to broader concerns for societal change.

> Karoline: "I hope even more people become enthusiastic about Foodsharing, at least this would be great for humanity and the environment."

This statement implies the humanistic nature of sharing food and how the social and environmental impacts go together in an idealized account of striving for a better world. This statement also reveals that users think about Foodsharing having systemic effects in a social (humanity) and ecological (environment) way. It is not only about the practice of sharing food on a local micro-level, but, given that more people participate, it will have macro-effects and systemic changes along the food chain. Doris similarly expresses this:

> Doris: "Our resources are limited and we should ALL catch on to this finally".

Such discussions pointed to the importance of getting a critical mass in order to achieve a notable effect on scarce limited resources of the environment. However, these environmentally optimistic posts were often counter-argued by people who pointed out that more than just a critical mass is needed, that it needs interventions from the state to reduce food waste on the agri-industrial side. There were a vast number of posts, particularly during discussions about more systemic and political aspects, that condemned the food industry for resource and food depletion, the state who does nothing against it, and retailers who deliberately prefer to throw away instead of giving to people in need. Those in need refer to our next motivation, which is an economical as well as social one.

Economic need

It is clear from other posts the economic need played a big part in food sharing, given how often people in the 'giving' position commented about people in need. However there was only a minority of posts to the Facebook group from users who were in need of food support to make or improve their living. Of all the 3242 posts there were only five instances where people explicitly articulated their own economic need. This points potentially to feelings of shame that might go with social and economical needs of sharing food and discussing this publicly.

> Tory: "If I go to the food bank twice a week already und cannot give a lot [of food] myself...can I still get any?"

> Anna: "Just register online and have a look if somebody has to give something away. I don't think that it is about "who collects also has to give" but rather those who have, give, and those who need, just take."

Though we could not find many posts from users who collect food baskets, the free-rider phenomenon that is criticized in many other communities is actually welcome for the Foodsharing community. Tory is seeking help and asking for the conditions under which she can get food, and is encouraged and supported through Anna, telling her it is endorsed if "*those who need, just take*". Michael's social motivation to share food (noted previously) was even to give only to people who are socially disadvantaged. We could not find at any point a member complaining (at least on Facebook) about people who only seek and not give food.

In summary, in this section we were looking for the motivations that are inherent in the practice of sharing food in such a community. Social, ecological as well as economic values and needs are incentives to take action. The motivations between and within participants are manifold, some emphasizing a general '*doing good*', some writing more about their social, ecological and/or economic motives. Help-seekers, help-givers, social, ethical ecological and economic values and engagements are all able to co-exist and in some cases mutually re-enforce each other. These values are reflected and made visible by the various discussions at the Facebook community. What is interesting to note too is that while the different roles of giving and receiving make this sharing community work, since both roles are needed for any food exchange, the discussions on the Facebook community are largely presented from the activists and giver perspective.

EMERGENCE OF THE COMMUNITY

We can see the emergence of Foodsharing at both local and global levels, with the public media also playing a key role. We define the term 'global' in this paper to have a non-local, geography-independent and issue-based connotation. This section is started with the initial role of the media.

Creating visibility and narrative through media

Public relations and mass media played an important role in the emergence and sustainability of the Foodsharing community. Specifically we focus on the emergence of the Facebook community through the inter-relation between Facebook and public relations and mass media, and how members support local community building through advertising and pro-active appeals. We also focus on the development of critical awareness through community interactions and the emergent narratives that are used to communicate the values and practices of the Foodsharing Association.

As noted previously, Foodsharing started off with a crowdsource campaign to attract funding for the development of Foodsharing.de, at a point where the Facebook group already existed to promote and discuss Foddsharing.de's development. The platform was released on December 12th 2012 with a press conference, accompanied by local strategies such as posters, flyers and billboards close to food retailers. Foodsharing has since had significant media interest, with a very frequent presence on prominent TV news, newspapers and online news. The Foodsharing Facebook page links to: 17 reports about the community on TV channels, 3 of those channels being the biggest in Germany who broadcast about Foodsharing in their main evening news; 44 newspaper articles, with 6 of those being amongst the biggest national newspapers or magazines in Germany; and 3 links to radio entries and 2 mentions on blogs. This mass media coverage served as a starting point for motivating people to get active themselves in Foodsharing and posting this to the Facebook page. The activating potential was visible on the Facebook page with 31 posts where members got to know Foodsharing through a TV report in the main news on a prominent German TV channel and were encouraging about the initiative.

> Pam: "We just watched it on TV, tried it out and classify it as PERFECT! Great idea :D".

Media coverage not only prompted people becoming actively engaged in food sharing, but also to actively talk to other people who had more power and control over the distribution of food and so try to change their instant environment.

> Cora: "Just watched it on TV ... it's a great thing ... I am working in a big supermarket chain and will talk about it with my boss".

The various responses showed how media coverage could have important effects on awareness with follow-up actions, moving from watching TV reports to actively engaging in the community or their specific local environment. In fact so many people tried to visit the Foodsharing website after one broadcast report about it on one of the major German TV news shows, that the Foodsharing.de page was accessed unexpectedly often and was not reachable for days. This also resulted in numerous posts on the Facebook page remarking on the unattainability of Foodsharing.de.

To understand the nature of these reports with their activating potential, we observed reccuring issues across these reports: Stories started with presenting the problem space of food waste to raise awareness, presented Foodsharing.de as an alternative, and showed role-playing and exemplifying how the platform can be used. To understand the way these TV reports encouraged interested members, we analysed the narrative content of an illustrative example of the TV report that Facebook users 'shared' the most (most viral) on Facebook; 29.3 percent of all users who saw the post with the TV report also reacted (liked, shared or commented) to it.

The TV report starts off with the overall story of wasted food and introduces Foodsharing.de as a platform that enables individuals to waste less through the new evolving practice of meeting online to share offline. The main narrative behind the report told an individual story to "*show how it works*" (speaker announcing the report). The report then depicted a woman to show online interactions with the platform Foodsharing.de as well as offline interactions when another woman comes by with her children to collect the offered food. She says:

> "One has to bring the right attitude to this, others would throw it away, and that you can accept Foodsharing confidently and don't have to feel weird doing this."

The content of this TV report serves to attract people who want to engage in food sharing and directly addresses stigmas that could potentially be attached to it. This is illustrated in the remarks "*don't have to feel weird about doing this*" and "*accept Foodsharing confidently*" about collecting food baskets. That such social stigmas might otherwise exist is suggested by the fact that only five people posting to the Facebook page identify themselves as being in economic need (see section economic needs). The TV report also serves to practically demonstrate sharing food and how this constructs and narrates a new social pattern, potentially aiming to achieve cultural change ("*bringing the right attitude to this*") for TV audiences. The moderator's words to announce the report, "*show how it works*", point to the demonstration and play-acting of the new social pattern.

In sum, the values of Foodsharing and its social patterns are narrated and exteriorized through broadcasting and at the same time promote acceptance of it. The Facebook page played a critical role in a) keeping the report alive by linking to it and b) keeping the issue alive and being able to mobilise the energy, concerns and debates arising from the report by providing a focal point for people to gather, discuss and learn.

Building local communities

While the media played a role in making Foodsharing an accepted social pattern globally in a cultural, societal, and political way, local communities are still needed to make Foodsharing productive and sustainable. Active agents enabled through the global Facebook page promoted local community building and Foodsharing members engaged in broadcasting, advertising strategies and local interactions.

> Dora: "Is there a possibility to advertise for Foodsharing in your own town? Ideas anybody? It just works if enough people participate..."
>
> Carla: "It depends how you imagine advertising, you can have advertising material sent to you, I have done that too and was sent posters, stickers and flyers in different sizes. There is an email address I forgot that you can write to"
>
> Foodsharing: "info@foodsharing.de"

This conversation shows that to make Foodsharing reach enough people it is inherently dependent on local communities and pro-actively engaged members such as Dora. Therefore public relations and the organisational means of a community play a crucial role on a local level to advertise offline with flyers and posters, both of which can be ordered from and sent out by the Association. This conversation also points to online-offline interactions in advertising online and offline, similar to the practice of sharing food itself. Building and instantiating local communities are necessary to make the community as a whole work, to reach a critical mass, as Dora remarked. Such interactions on the global Foodsharing Facebook page resulted in 17 new local Foodsharing Facebook groups being founded to enable local interactions and food sharing.

Online support in the community did not necessarily come from the Foodsharing Association itself and often happened between members. Support often takes the form of encouraging statements or pro-active appeals.

> Sandra: "I really love the idea, unfortunately there are no food articles provided in my city."
>
> Kathy: "Sandra, offer food articles yourself, mine have been requested and collected within minutes! If everybody just waits until others are offering food articles, it will not work."

There were many other instances where community members supported each other. Examples include: advice on how to use the platform; how to initiate a local community; and discussing relevant food topics such as how to start dumpster diving.

Pro-active appeals were not only exchanged between members of the community to form bottom-up local Foodsharing communities, but also from the active agents behind the Foodsharing Association in a top-down manner. Hence it is also the pro-active involvement of the Foodsharing Association that matters, such as in Dora's and Carla's case where the exchange of information is accompanied by someone from the Association actively providing information.

The Association also repeatedly posted pro-active top-down appeals for engagement to the Facebook community members to offer foodstuffs which members not need any more.

> Foodsharing: "Dear Friends, holidays are coming soon and everybody still has foodstuffs at home that could be offered on Foodsharing.de before they spoil. Take part and comb through your pantry, fridge and kitchen. Now is the right time! Over 15.000 Foodsharing members are waiting for your food basket."

The role of the remark "*over 15.000 Foodsharing members are waiting for you*" is to communicate to interested members that they are part of a bigger movement and story, that another 15000 active people have already adopted the practice of sharing food. This pro-active call also provides direct instructions ("*comb through your pantry*") to engage potential or existing members in sharing food.

Creating critical 'global' awareness

Accompanying the emergence of the community was also the development of critical awareness at a more general level, through which people developed a critical understanding of the socio-political sphere their community moves in. Members regularly engaged with topics on the Facebook page that were actively discussed, questioned and negotiated, such as hunger in the world and the context of wasted food, genetically modified organisms, the role of marketing at food retailers, product packaging or practices of the agri-industry, etc. The vast numbers of topics, though not directly associated with Foodsharing, were actively discussed and provide evidence that food practices are inherently cultural and political.

Discussions also allowed members to develop critical awareness towards potential systemic impacts of Foodsharing and often took place within the context of discussed topics. An illustrative instance for the ongoing development of critical awareness was Tom and Hannah discussing the wider systemic impacts of Foodsharing:

> Tom: "Foodsharing cannot change the throw-away practices of agriculture and industry. Foodsharing can also not contribute to reduce hunger in the world. Foodsharing should then only communicate what it can do: Saving food at the consumer level. Not more, not less."

> Hannah: "But Foodsharing connects people with each other – and this is the basis for all other changes, because enterprises will not change their strategies voluntarily, together we are strong. Foodsharing raises awareness, and awareness is the key."

Here Tom and Hannah discuss their individual belief of what Foodsharing can achieve, where Tom questions and negates wider systemic implications, and Hannah argues that people together can achieve change though raising awareness and collective action ("*together we are strong*"). It is this interaction between members - where they provide different critical perspectives, the debate between them - which potentially contributes to raising critical awareness of individual members. The Facebook page offered the medium through which people could engage critically with the community, its purpose, its aims, its attitude, its technologies and systemic consequences. Through this critical process people acquire a greater understanding of the cultural and social circumstances that shape their lives.

DISCUSSION

In this paper we have been concerned with understanding an activist community around the issue of food sharing and its use of social networking, drawing particularly on contributions from the first 19 months of its Facebook page. Overall, what is impressive across the data is how quickly this community grew over a short period of time and, by definition, how engaged so many people needed to be. The very emergence of Foodsharing as a grassroots initiative and the growing levels of activity both on Foodsharing.de in the food baskets exchanged, and on the Facebook page in the number of 'likes' and the active contributions and discussions, give evidence of people feeling and being empowered to act. Empowerment links to levels of individual, community and organisational empowerment [23]. The Facebook group has been a key focal point and enabler at the levels of the individual, community and organisation (here, the Association) as well, along with key roles of Foodsharing.de and public media, in enabling the emergence of a community that engaged in intertwined 'global' thinking and local acting.

Think globally, act locally

As for many communities the principle of '*think globally, act locally*' is a valid description of the interactions between individuals, the community, the Association and across the data there were strong patterns of *global-local* as well as *online-offline* interactions.

The Facebook page, representing the online world, provided the basis to form global identities and ideas that guide and frame this community. Various discussions, links to similar interventions, the links to mass media where Foodsharing is portrayed, all act as *ideological framing* processes for the community. The Facebook page also has a global-local dimension as people there connect with each other to build new local communities, which resulted in 17 new local Facebook groups. The platform Foodsharing.de acted on a national level and is provided for all Germany as a functional and operational tool. But there is also a strong local element that is the lifeblood of Foodsharing. First users search, request, accept and meet online to negotiate where and when to meet. It is then at the offline local place where the act of handing over of food takes place.

Apart from the overarching patterns of global–local, and offline–online, we could observe interactions to be *top-down* as well *as bottom-up*. This was most visible for e.g. local community building which was a bottom-up approach by engaged community members, at instances supported top-down by Foodsharing through providing advertising material. Pro-active appeals were used as encouragement between members as well as top-down by the Foodsharing Association as posts to all members of the Facebook community. This was, for example, the case at the instances where they pro-actively promoted Foodsharing with mass media. Mass media presented narratives of *new social patterns* how the community works and direct instructions and encouragements to engage in sharing food. Thus actions happen at multiple levels, by local agents as well as the Association.

Individuals of the community enact through social, ecological and economic motives, to save food from being wasted. Through the social networking platforms, they are enabled to translate needs, values, and 'good intentions' (around eco-beliefs, concern for environment, social good, etc.) into practical offers or collection of food. They are also able to connect with others to exchange food in local geographical areas. It was also the belief in a wider systemic change and being part in a bigger intervention that encouraged people to participate. The relationship for individuals to the narratives told via various (mass) media was, according to our data, very influential. Not only the guiding values of the Foodsharing community were shown, but also how the new social pattern of meeting online to share food offline is played out in very explicit and explanatory ways. This had impact on individual encouragement to pro-actively engage in the community. It is the Facebook page that makes this engagement visible and notions of *empowerment*, the process of being motivated to act [23] were visible - such as for Michael who reported to "*finally give left over food to people in need of help*" or Cora who watched a report about Foodsharing on TV and felt encouraged to talk to her boss in the supermarket to actively change her environment. Individuals saw stories where they could identify themselves as part of a bigger movement able to change their circumstances that empower them to act. This was also discussed by Dimond et al. [4] who described the positive impact of collaborative storytelling online. Overall it is the individuals that can realize an emerging and sustained community only, individuals that need to feel agency to change their respective environments according to their values, needs and beliefs.

The **community** itself lives and is enlivened by the various interactions between individuals that fulfil different roles. Mutual understanding, helping behaviours between and within community members, engaged voluntary action, and receiving help add up to collective problem solving. The Facebook group of the community acts as a forum for direct encouragement (pro-active appeals) to act, to post questions, find answers, get support, connect to others and being pointed to most relevant resources in a just-in-time way by other people in the community responding to questions and comments. This is accompanied by tensions and hot debates about political and cultural implications of food and waste practices that characterise this community. Interactions between community members can shape the nature of debates and support the development of critical awareness. Members discuss wider possible or non-possible systemic change through the community or question the systemic impacts of Foodsharing, as illustrated in the conversation between Tom and Hannah. Moreover the Facebook page provided a platform for people to form a community of interest, passion and activism around the issue of food waste and sharing food. It enabled people to mobilise and to act as a 'global-issue-based' community, to seed new local communities, while Foodsharing.de enabled people to form a local community of practical action to hand over food between the members.

The Foodsharing Association provided **organisational** means and technological resources to enable the emergence of this community. They provided the development and maintenance of the operational platform Foodsharing.de that made this free food sharing community possible. Through the Facebook group they were able to provide the information, materials, resources and respond directly to people, to point them to these resources, contribute to conversations, discussions through their posts, and make more powerful use of public media by linking stories through to Facebook. They could effect change, both by empowering individuals to act locally and form local food exchange groups, and empowering people more generally, even if they didn't have a local group, to change thinking, to be more aware and to act politically through giving information, stimulating discussions, pro-active appeals and establishing public discourses.

From a design perspective, there were two key characteristics that made this particular type of local-global, online-offline community work. Firstly, the platform Foodsharing.de enabled practical and operational local community exchanges. Secondly, the Facebook page facilitated broader discussions and framing processes for the community. These sites of inter-dependent global interactions then also facilitated the development of local interactions and communities, which is a crucial aspect for distributing power to local agents of change, such as the instances where local communities were built and advertised by local agents to initiate their own local Foodsharing Facebook page.

It is crucial to acknowledge for CSCW and HCI researchers who aim to design for communities that the foodsharing Association itself was the main actor who intervened and was visible as a change actor beyond the provided platforms Foodsharing.de and Facebook. The community would not have worked without their guiding initiative, help, support and intervention. However the community is still growing because different roles are offered to individuals that they can fulfil and act out. The effect of media also adds to a holistic perspective on how this community could emerge. Community policy and framing also includes rather than excludes political issues and values that are [22] or should be addressed [5, 6, 16].

Moreover the Foodsharing community is a very specific one as the nature of food and food waste is a tangible, graspable and visible one, as opposed to the invisibility of electricity or water [26], resources that are implicitly, naturally, and invisibly delivered to the household. For these reasons, some of the dimensions of local-global, online-offline [18] might be inherently part of this type of free share economy [27] community.

Limitations of our study

While this study had access to a large number of posts starting from the beginning of the Facebook group of the Foodsharing community, the findings might not reflect all members. This is because we only had material about those members who post to Facebook. We could not include the voices of members who are using Foodsharing.de but do not engage with the Facebook group. Conversely, we might also have heard voices that engage with the Facebook group but do not actually engage in food sharing.

CONCLUSION

Foodsharing is a vibrant active community of members engaging in very practical ways at local levels to exchange food, mediated by Foodsharing.de, and in more political and mutually supportive ways at a global level, using the Foodsharing Facebook group. Here we have focused on the role of the Facebook group and explored how the discussions and links provide a means for the values, motivations and growth of the Foodsharing community to play out and evolve. The key contributions are showing how participants use the social media and web platforms to facilitate fluid transitions between online-offline and local-global interactions and the empowering impact of these interactions. We draw out the interplay between individual, community, organisational levels; public relations and media, the operational platform Foodsharing.de that enables local communities and the Facebook group where global ideological framing of the community takes place. The study also points to the relationship between mass media coverage and the follow up public communication on the Facebook page, which proved to be of central importance for establishing cultural change and new institutional practices and social patterns that are oriented towards sustainability and social values.

For future work we plan to interview members of the Foodsharing community who are actively using the operational platform Foodsharing.de to gain more understanding how and why such new social patterns evolve within a community.

ACKNOWLEDGMENTS

Thanks to the Foodsharing Association for providing the aggregated Facebook page data and all the members of Foodsharing who make this community happen.

REFERENCES

1. Allen, P. and Sachs, C. 2007. Women and food chains: The gendered politics of food, *International Journal of Sociology of Food and Agriculture*, 15(1), pp. 1–23.
2. Blevis, E. and Morse, S. 2009. SUSTAINABLY OURS: Food, dude. *interactions* 16, 2 (March 2009), 58-62.
3. Braun, V. and Clarke, V. 2006. Using thematic Analysis in Psychology, *Qualitative Research in Psychology*, 3(2). p. 77-101.
4. Dimond, J. P., Dye, M., Larose, D., and Bruckman, A. S. 2013. Hollaback!: the role of storytelling online in a social movement organization. In Proc. of CSCW '13. ACM, New York, NY, USA, 477-490.
5. DiSalvo, C., Light, A., Hirsch, T., Le Dantec, C. A., Goodman, E., and Hill, K. 2010. HCI, communities and politics. In CHI EA '10. ACM, NY, USA, 3151-3154.
6. Dourish, P. 2010. HCI and environmental sustainability: the politics of design and the design of politics. In Proc. of DIS '10. ACM, NY, USA, 1-10.
7. Evans, D. 2012. Binning, gifting and recovery: the conduits of disposal in household food consumption. *Environment and Planning D: Society and Space*. 30(6) pp. 1123 – 1137.
8. Ganglbauer, E., Fitzpatrick, G., Comber, R. 2013. Negotiating food waste: Using a practice lens to inform design. ACM Trans. Comput.-Hum. Interact. 20, 2, Article 11 (May 2013), 25 pages.
9. Godemann, J., & Michelsen, G. (2011). Sustainability communication: interdisciplinary perspectives and theoretical foundations. Springer Science+ Business Media.
10. Gustavsson, J., Cederberg, C. and Sonesson, U. 2011. Cutting food waste to feed the world global food losses and food waste, Interpack2011.
11. Gross, S., Toombs, A., Wain, J., and Walorski, K. 2011. Foodmunity: designing community interactions over food. In Proc. of CHI EA '11, New York, NY, USA, 2011, ACM, pp. 1019–1024.
12. Joinson, A. N. 2008. Looking at, looking up or keeping up with people?: motives and use of facebook. In Proc. of CHI '08. ACM, New York, NY, USA, 1027-1036.
13. Karnik, M., Ian Oakley, Jayant Venkatanathan, Tasos Spiliotopoulos, and Valentina Nisi. 2013. Uses & gratifications of a facebook media sharing group. In Proc. of CSCW '13. ACM, New York, NY, USA, 821-826.
14. Lozano, R. (2007). Collaboration as a pathway for sustainability. *Sustainable Development*, 15(6), 370-381.
15. López, C. A. and Butler, B. S. 2013. Consequences of content diversity for online public spaces for local communities. In Proc. of CSCW '13. ACM, New York, NY, USA, 673-682.
16. Le Dantec, C. 2012. Participation and publics: supporting community engagement. In Proc. of CHI '12. ACM, New York, NY, USA, 1351-1360.

17. Lewis, S. and Lewis, D. A. 2012. Examining technology that supports community policing. In Proc. of CHI '12. ACM, New York, NY, USA, 1371-1380.

18. McCully, W., Lampe, C., Sarkar, C., Velasquez, A., and Sreevinasan, A. 2011. Online and offline interactions in online communities. In Proc. of WikiSym '11. ACM, NY, USA, 39-48.

19. Odom, W. 2010. "Mate, we don't need a chip to tell us the soil's dry": opportunities for designing interactive systems to support urban food production. In Proc. of DIS '10. ACM, New York, NY, USA, 232-235.

20. Park, N., Kee, K. F., and Valenzuela, S. (2009). Being immersed in social networking environment: Facebook groups, uses and gratifications, and social outcomes. *CyberPsychology & Behavior*, 12(6), 729-733.

21. Parker, A., Landry, B. M. and Grinter, R. E. 2010. Characteristics of shared health reflections in a local community. In Proc. of CSCW '10. ACM, New York, NY, USA, 435-444.

22. Parker, A. Kantroo, V., Lee, H. R., Osornio, M., Sharma, M. and Grinter, R. 2012. Health promotion as activism: building community capacity to effect social change, in Proc. of CHI '12, New York, NY, USA, 2012, ACM, pp. 99– 108.

23. Rappaport, J. (1987). Terms of empowerment/exemplars of prevention: Toward a theory for community psychology. *American journal of community* psychology, 15(2), 121-148.

24. Robson, C., Hearst, M., Kau, C and Pierce, J. 2013. Comparing the use of social networking and traditional media channels for promoting citizen science. In Proc. of CSCW '13. ACM, New York, NY, USA, 1463-1468.

25. Shirky, C. Here comes everybody: the power of organizing without organizations, Penguin Group USA, 2008.

26. Strengers, Y. A. A. 2011. Designing eco-feedback systems for everyday life. In Proc. of CHI '11. ACM, New York, NY, USA, 2135-2144.

27. Weitzman, M. L. (1984). *The share economy: Conquering stagflation*. Harvard University Press.

From Rookie to All-Star: Professional Development in a Graphic Design Community of Practice

Jennifer Marlow
Human-Computer Interaction Institute
Carnegie Mellon University
5000 Forbes Avenue, Pittsburgh, PA
jmarlow@cs.cmu.edu

Laura Dabbish
Human-Computer Interaction Institute and
Center for the Future of Work, Heinz College
Carnegie Mellon University
dabbish@cmu.edu

ABSTRACT
Communities of practice have traditionally supported learning and knowledge exchange within a professional field. However, little work to date has examined how individuals use social network functionality for professional development in these types of communities. We present a qualitative investigation into how the social transparency provided by SNS functionality influences two important components of professional activity: social learning and professional identity development. We focus on activity within Dribbble, a social media enabled community of practice for graphic designers. Through a series of interviews with novice and experienced Dribbble users who work within and outside of traditional organizations, we identified ways they leverage social media features for learning and skill development. We find that benefits of the site are dependent on extensive social capital development activities in order to garner attention for posted work. Our results inform the design of online social settings for professional development.

Author Keywords
Social network software; Professional development; Online communities; Communities of practice

ACM Classification Keywords
H.5.2 [Information Interfaces and Presentation]: User Interfaces - Interaction styles.

General Terms
Human Factors; Design; Measurement

INTRODUCTION
With the rise in popularity of social networking sites (SNS), communities oriented around particular professional domains are beginning to incorporate social networking functionalities into their site design. On these sites, which we refer to as social media-enabled communities of practice [1], individuals can improve their skills and manage a professional identity independent from traditional institutions like universities or corporations. In many fields such as software development, these sites are becoming the means by which potential employees are identified and evaluated for employment [6]. In creative professions such as the design field, the profiles built on these social networks can serve as portfolios to attract freelancing or contract-based work.

Despite the popularity of these sites, it remains unclear whether and how individuals are actually using social networking functionality for professional development. Previous research in CSCW touches on limited aspects of this issue. A majority of the research on SNS use has examined relationship and well-being impacts of different types of social interaction on Facebook (e.g. [5]). Research on professional SNS use has focused predominantly within organizational boundaries (e.g. [26, 34]) and found that members use SNS for non-work activities such as photo-sharing or to build connections outside of their own team or department.

Instrumenting communities of practice with SNS features increases the degree of social transparency within the community by providing increased visibility of an individual's identity, the content (or artifacts) they have created, and interactions with others around these artifacts [33]. Early work on social translucence highlighted its potential for supporting different types of communication and collaboration, letting people learn through observation and imitation, and enabling people to notice and follow social conventions [11]. Research in socially transparent collaborative settings such as GitHub suggests that social transparency can radically improve collaboration and learning in complex, knowledge based activities like software development [9].

However, it is unclear whether these benefits translate from a peer production setting to professional communities of practice that do not involve interdependent work or where members may have other motivations for participation besides learning. The professional nature of communities of practice may lead to different dynamics when social networking functionalities (such as publicly-visible personal profiles, displays of connection, and directed interactions) make one's activity viewable to a variety of potential audiences.

ACM 978-1-4503-2540-0/14/02...$15.00.
http://dx.doi.org/10.1145/2531602.2531651

On one hand, this increased transparency of who does what could support social learning by making it easier to navigate relevant content, observe the design process of experts and learn community norms by seeing how others react to content. On the other hand, when the community is large, access to all members' connections and creations could make seeking and allocating attention more difficult. People may need to learn and develop strategies for getting the attention they need to achieve their goals. Finally, when a community of practice is public and work linked to an individual's real identity can be viewed by both site members and outside observers, the way in which professional identity management occurs may happen differently depending on one's targeted audience.

In this paper, we examine how the transparency provided by SNS features in a social media-enabled community of practice influences professional activity outside the boundaries of an organization. We focus on the following research question:

> ***How do social networking functionalities support learning and professional identity development in a design-oriented community of practice?***

In particular, we were interested in the influence of site functionalities on social learning and on how perceived attention and audience shaped member behaviors with regards to building a professional identity through sharing their work and interacting with others. We conducted a series of semi-structured interviews with members of the SNS site Dribbble. We selected Dribbble because it is an example of a social media-enabled community of practice, is growing in popularity, and is increasingly used for hiring and employment opportunities [40]. We examined how and why people used the various social networking functionalities within the site for social learning and professional identity management. We also include some quantitative analysis on general site use as background for our descriptions of user behavior.

We found that the combination of a community of practice with artifact sharing and social networking functionalities enabled people to navigate design examples within a connected community of creators and to use this to develop their own skills. Our results suggest the importance of community level signals of attention to shared work artifacts in social media-enabled communities of practice. Visible cues about aggregate patterns of member attention supported professional development opportunities provided by the site (e.g. feedback on work shared, promotion by other users, enhanced reputation). Reputation building in this context, given the meritocratic nature of the design field, often involved strategic work-sharing and interaction behaviors to gain more attention from other designers and potential clients. Members were strategic about using the visible social network to maximize attention to their shared work examples. Our findings highlight social and design related challenges in supporting the site's dual use as a community of practice and a place to show off. We conclude with recommendations for the design of social media-enabled communities of practice in other professional domains.

RELATED WORK

In our research, we examine how a professionally focused, social media-enabled community of practice for designers supports community of practice activities associated with learning and information sharing as well as identity management. Our work builds upon previous literature on communities of practice, social networking, and artifact sharing in hobbyist domains, which suggest that online tools are important for transferring certain types of knowledge among community members.

Participation in online communities of practice/ communities of interest

Professionals often participate in online special-interest groups in order to gain professional status and reputation, as well as to improve work-relevant skills [36]. To achieve these aims, people have traditionally turned to communities of practice (CoPs). These groups share several defining characteristics, where members: (1) Focus on a domain of shared interest, (2) interact and learn together by engaging in joint activities and discussions, helping each other, and sharing information, and (3) develop a shared collection of experiences, stories, best practices and ways of solving problems [37]. Social networking functionality, such as the ability to communicate around shared artifacts, should support these types of activities, particularly the ability to interact, learn, and share information through viewing and navigating networks of people and content.

Perhaps unsurprisingly, activities undertaken in professional communities of practice differ from non-professional ones. According to Amin & Roberts [3], professional communities of practice share defining characteristics that imply the importance of social interaction for learning. The type of knowledge that circulates in professional CoPs focuses on how to perform activities associated with the profession (e.g. for doctors how to manage patients but also how much pressure to use during a particular surgical procedure). This knowledge includes conventions, rules of thumb, intuitions and shared world views that can typically only be transferred through face-to-face social interaction, the use of artifacts and in-person observation of and imitation of experts [3].

However, there is at least one study suggesting that after members have achieved mastery in the professional activity, they can better transfer this knowledge in virtual communities [30]. This albeit limited work on online interaction and learning in professional CoPs suggests that the value of different types of social interactions or social information may depend on a member's expertise in the particular field.

The way a professional CoP works and the degree to which it is successful also depend on the dynamics of the professional domain (while non-professional CoPs are less affected by these issues). For example, while teachers freely share practices aided by tools like Twitter [13], architects or scientists have difficulty forming communities of practice partly due to the competitive nature of these fields [12]. Therefore, the area of practice (i.e. the broader professional domain) could influence the ways in which individuals interact within communities of practice in that field. Norms about collaborative activity, the nature of work in the domain, the value of interactivity, and how learning takes place could affect what work people share and why they share it.

Social networking functionality may support knowledge transfer and exchange of best practices among members of CoPs in new and potentially unanticipated ways. In the next section we consider the features a social networking site provides and potential implications for professional communities.

Social networking site functionalities

Whether they are intended for a general audience or a more specific community of practice, many online sites aimed at encouraging interaction share a common set of social networking features and functionalities. These include visible *individual profile spaces* for each member, facilities for uploading *content, public displays of connection* with other members, and the ability to message other members [4,17] or engage in *directed interaction* via comments or "likes" [5]. These features have been used in social and friendship contexts for impression management, building social capital and learning about people in one's social circle [21].

The majority of the previous research on online work sharing has focused on settings involving amateurs or people engaged in "serious leisure" for fun or entertainment. Several studies have examined how people use photo sharing sites like Flickr. This work has revealed that photo enthusiasts often used artifact-sharing sites both to improve their practice and develop a social network around the activity. On Flickr, photographers browse photos uploaded by others to find inspiration or models of good technique. They post photos to receive feedback on their work. Amateur photographers use photo-sharing sites to connect with others in the field, build relationships with other photographers, generate interest in their work, and establish reputation [5, 19, 27].

Other research looking at work sharing in DIY craft communities found that skill development was also a motivation for participation [13, 23]. Similar to photographers, DIYers and crafters participated in work-sharing sites to learn new things and get feedback on their projects. The previous work on social networks of hobbyists also suggests the unique potential for the social aspects of these sites. These studies noted that work-sharing sites allowed individuals working alone to connect with a larger community of individuals also building a similar skill. The work on hobbyist work sharing also showed that connecting with a broader social network is an important motivation for participation. DIYers had a similar desire to improve their reputation within the community [35].

Social media-enabled communities of practice differ from other types of social networking sites (or SNS) in a few ways. First, they are dedicated to professional activity rather than friendship or leisure pursuits (e.g. Facebook or Ravelry.) Second, they are typically very narrowly focused around one professional activity or field (e.g. Thingiverse.com for 3D prototyping, Dribbble.com for graphic design) versus professional activity more generally (e.g. LinkedIn). Third, the central activity of the site is sharing and interacting around digital artifacts connected to the professional practice (e.g. posting images of graphic designs) rather than text-based communications or non-work related artifacts. Shared artifacts are tied to individual social network site user's profiles and represent or embody elements of work practice associated with the skilled activity or field. For example, Thingiverse.com supports posting CAD diagrams for 3D prototype projects users have created and allows users to comment on those projects.

Professional identity development, attention, and audience

The previous work suggests that work-sharing sites can support skill development through exposure to others' work and interaction around created artifacts. The site design also shapes the ways in which users appropriate the technology available to them to create a professional identity [2]. In artifact sharing sites, users first make a creation and then decide whether or not to share it on the site, and work artifacts are not interdependent or part of a larger collective activity. When work sharing is directly connected to a professional activity, patterns of behavior may be quite different. People may be more reluctant to share and post work they typically create for pay. The goals for participation in this kind of site may therefore vary considerably from a hobbyist work-sharing site.

People using professionally-oriented communities of practice may also use them to develop a professional identity, both by observing role models and imitating what they see [16]. The kind of professional identity people seek to build may depend on who they want to see their work and who they think is looking at what they do. In addition to fellow community members, the audience for professional work (as opposed to hobbyist work) could include potential employers. The presence of dual audiences with access to publicly visible behavior has the potential to influence what kind of work people share and how they share it. Related work in open source software development suggests that developers motivated by career concerns may wish to signal their talent to a different audience than developers seeking peer recognition [22].

In the next section we describe the setting for our study, Dribbble, a social media-enabled community of practice for graphic designers. We discuss the professional context of graphic design, how designers develop skill in the domain and the social norms of the professional community. This informs our qualitative investigation of how members of the Dribbble community use the social networking functionality to support professional goals.

DRIBBBLE: A SOCIAL GRAPHIC DESIGN COMMUNITY

Our research focuses on a social media-enabled community of practice for graphic designers called Dribbble. We chose the graphic design domain because of the existing body of research describing the role of social interaction in design activities (e.g. [6, 18, 25]). This research highlights the importance of in-person critiques of created designs for learning and improving the quality of work output [28] and suggests social interaction is important both for skill development and reputation building, meaning participants should be likely to leverage social networking functionality for professional goals.

In addition, there are several studies describing the ways graphic designers leverage the Internet for their work prior to SNS development (e.g. [28]). These studies found that designers used the web to seek out examples created by others. Designers used the examples they found online to get ideas and learn how to create specific examples [8, 11]. This existing body of research provides a baseline that lets us examine what social features may influence a known set of design activities.

The Dribbble site was founded in 2009, and as of March 2013, had over 270,000 registered users. The site describes itself as "Show and tell for designers," where "web designers, graphic designers, illustrators, icon artists, typographers, logo designers, and other creative types share small screenshots (shots) that show their work, process, and current projects" [41].

In order to be a full member of Dribbble (known on the site as a "player,") a person must be invited to the site, or "drafted," by an existing member or by the site admins. Full members can post shots, follow other members, view the work of others in the community and "like" or comment on their work. Non-members (known on the site as "scouts,") can also follow players, view their work, and like (but not comment on) individual posts.

Dribbble provides a good setting for understanding how SNS functionality supports professionals because it incorporates the following key aspects of SNS [4,5]:

1. **Profiles**: Players on the site each have a personal profile where work items they have chosen to share (called "shots") are displayed (see Figure 1). Profiles contain information about a person including:

a) Biographical details (including name, location, website, Twitter handle);

b) Shots: Images of a person's work (limited to a 300x400 pixel view.) Details below each shot include the number of views (how many times someone has clicked on the thumbnail to view the larger version of the shot,) number of comments, and number of likes (see Figure 2.) Clicking on an individual shot takes a user to a more detailed view of the work, where one can see it in a larger view along with further details such as a short description and any likes or comments that other people have given it, and

c) Number of people the user follows and is following.

2. **Public displays of connection**: Network information including details and links to profiles of a user's followers and people the user is following.

3. **Directed interactions**: Dribbble supports the ability to directly (publicly) communicate with other site members through commenting on their work. It is also possible to "like" their shots as a more lightweight means of communicating approval or admiration.

4. **Activity feeds**: Activities are featured in a profile's "activity feed" (see Figure 3,) where an individual's most recent actions are displayed and it is possible to see what shots they have uploaded, who they have followed, and what work they have commented on and liked.

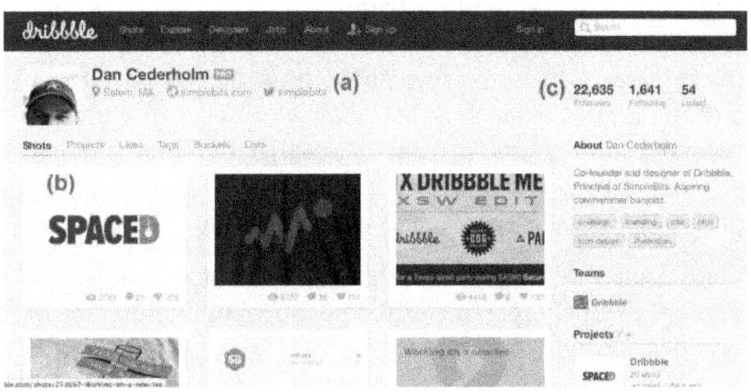

Figure 1. Dribbble profile of site co-founder Dan Cederholm

Figure 2. Shot overview with number of views, comments, and likes

Figure 3. Activity feed on member's profile

INTERVIEW STUDY

In order to understand how graphic designers used Dribbble for professional development, we conducted interviews with 23 Dribbble users. In the next sections we describe participant recruitment and our interview technique.

Participants

Participants were recruited from a subset of recent site users. Using the Dribbble site API, we first identified a list of 332 people who had posted something the most recently (within the last two months.) We used the approach of Torrey et al. [35], focusing on users with recent activity, because this meant interviewees would more accurately recall specific details about their activities on the site. We next contacted a random sample of 139 people selected from the list of recent posters via e-mail, inviting them to participate in an interview about how they used Dribbble and other sites to accomplish their work as a designer. We received 23 responses from the active Dribbble members we contacted. This 16% response rate is consistent with participation rates reported in other studies of this type [29].

Our 23 interviewees (4 females and 19 males) represented a diverse segment of the Dribbble site population and the broader design community. Fourteen were primarily graphic designers, eight were UI/UX/web designers, and four also did illustration. Four participants were students (referred to here as S1-S4), thirteen worked for companies but also engaged in part-time freelance work (PT1-PT13), and six were full time, independent freelance designers (FT1-FT6).

They varied in terms of the length of time they had been members of Dribbble, and level of activity/followers on the site itself. They were also geographically dispersed: 19 were based in various cities throughout the United States (ten in large metropolitan areas and nine in smaller towns,) three were located in Europe and one was in Asia. Table 1 summarizes basic characteristics of the interviewees' relative standing in the community, broken down by employment category. These are displayed alongside general site statistics for all "active" players on the site based on data obtained through the site's API in March 2013.

	Studnt	PT freel.	FT freel.	All interviews	All active members
	Mean			Mean (median)	
# shots on profile	25	27.3	43.5	31 (22)	19.48 (10)
Followers	47.5	141.92	351.16	181 (35)	174 (34)
Following	32.5	114.76	88.3	93 (54)	110 (50)
Length of time on site (yrs.)	.93	1.08	1.06	1.11 (1.08)	1.59 (1.58)

Table 2. Characteristics of interview sample (student, part-time/full-time freelancer), and all active site members

While all of our interviewees had been members of the site for roughly one year, there were some disparities in their statistics. In particular, members who were full time freelancers and using Dribbble as a tool for their livelihood were on average more active in uploading shots and had more followers than the rest of the interviewees.

Method

We conducted semi-structured interviews focusing on the participant's most recent activity on the Dribbble site. Interviews lasted between 30 and 45 minutes and were conducted over Skype, with screen sharing enabled so that interviewees could share their Dribbble accounts and refer to specific examples of items on the screen.

First, participants explained how they originally got involved in Dribbble and why they had last visited the site. We then followed up with additional questions about a work creation they had recently shared, someone else's work they had recently looked at and comments made on other people's work. For each activity on the site, we probed about what happened and their motivations for engaging in the activity.

In our analysis we wanted to identify how SNS features of Dribbble supported skill development and reputation building. All interviews were transcribed and then analyzed using an iterative process. First, we identified all examples of recent items people had looked at and shared and their reasons for doing so. Using qualitative analysis software we first categorized these examples based on the rationale provided by the participant for looking at or sharing something. Behaviors were coded as either motivated by skill development or relating to giving or seeking attention. Within these two categories we used focused coding [7] based on the behavior undertaken, the rationale provided by the participant for the behavior, and the role of SNS features in supporting this behavior. This second level of coding revealed sets of skill development and reputation building behaviors. We then compared answers across expertise level and job role to look for similarities and differences. Our analysis also identified cross-cutting themes associated with using the site for professional activities.

RESULTS

Our interviews suggested that Dribbble users relied heavily on visible indicators of community level attention to derive professional benefit from the site and navigate the large volume of posted work. Visible cues of member attention supported community level agreement on best practices and norms for the field. They allowed members to find solutions to problems in their work and locate examples that demonstrated particular skills. In addition, members used these cues to gauge the quality of their work in terms of its 'fit' with member expectations. Members used their own mental models of site usage to structure their own actions in terms of seeking out work and making personal connections.

An individual's status in the community was based on the attention to them (followers) and their shared work. Attention conferred status and raised an individual's professional profile and reputation. Thus a great deal of effort was put into leveraging the social features of the site to increase the likelihood posted work would get attention. Designers who were serious about advancing in status within the community observed and learned models of behavior from high status users and then strategically used the site to garner more attention. In the next sections we present examples of how these behaviors occurred.

SOCIAL LEARNING

The first area of professional development we focused on was social learning, both in terms of learning skills through observing others' behavior [27] and in learning how to make use of the site technology [32]. We were interested in how members leveraged the site to improve their own graphic design abilities and learn over time. Skill development took two unique forms that lined up with behavior found in the previous work: 1) observation-based social learning of skills (through looking at examples of others' work) and 2) interactive learning through engaging with feedback provided by others.

Learning through looking at others' work

The social functionality on the site, particularly being able to find and follow other members, supported learning through access to others' work. Specific examples from particularly skilled users supported inspiration and learning a specific skill, while trend-spotting let users understand community norms. Being able to follow other designers in order to have access to their latest work in one place was an important functionality that supported inspiration and trend-spotting. Navigating the social connections on individual profiles and by seeing who interacted with who helped newcomers to the site figure out who was most influential as a source of learning and inspiration.

Inspiration

Inspiration, as mentioned by many interviewees (S1, S2, S3, PT1, PT2, PT3, PT13, FT1, FT2, FT3, FT4, FT5), consisted of searching for specific examples of a particular style or object in order to inform a personal approach to designing something specific. Social functionalities allowed people to find and follow respected others and to easily keep up with what they were doing. For example, one person mentioned how as a result of following some of his favorite developers on Dribbble, he could easily access their work and get inspiration from it:

> *"it's really nice to be able to go around my [Dribbble] feed and see how other people...are able to mimic Apple's aesthetic... this one's one of my favorites because the way it uses-- what do you call it?-- the perspective. The way the perspective works, it's a square icon, but it looks 3-D, and I really like the creativeness of that. It's nice to see what other people are doing. It gives you ideas." (FT4)*

Reverse-engineering skills through observing examples

Another type of learning behavior facilitated by the site was looking at examples of a skill or technique and then trying to replicate that independently. One person described how he was able to teach himself how to do hand-drawn typography through looking at examples of work on the site. He used the visible social connections on the site to deduce who were the big players in the area of hand-lettering by seeing who interacted with who:

> *FT2: There was a lot of trial and error and a lot of looking at people who are already doing it extremely well and seeing what they're doing-- just studying everything that they did and trying to redo it. So.*
>
> *Q: Okay, how did you find people who were doing it really well?*
>
> *FT2: Dribbble. Dribbble is huge. I mean, I was able to, through people that I found early on-- seeing who they were following and who they were interacting with and seeing who were friends and who worked together and who did this and that.*

This participant, who started out on Dribbble with no formal design training and knew no one in the design community, was able to gradually improve his skills through observing and imitating work done by well-known members. By seeing who well-known people were connected to via their social network and directed interactions, he expanded his set of quality examples.

Trend-spotting (continuing development by keeping up)

A third type of learning and skill development that occurred on Dribbble was the ability to understand general trends and popular styles in the industry at the moment by looking at the body of work as a whole that was displayed on the "popular" page. It is possible to filter the work on Dribbble by the members one follows ("Following"), most recent ("Everyone"), most popular ("Popular"), and the first shots from new members ("Debuts"). Work featured on the popular page generally had received a large number of likes and comments from other members in the community, and this caused many people to use these social signals to infer the types of styles that were most appreciated by the community at large. One person described using this as part of his general inspiration search process:

> *I'll also usually browse what the popular shots on Dribbble are just to see what is some of the best work right now. (FT1)*

Access to the most popular work allowed people to see what styles and types of work were trendy and current. However, frequent visitors to the site noticed that the popular content was often repetitive and homogeneous:

> *you'll clearly see some very, very, very visible trends. Like icon design-- very popular, and in very specific 3-D styles. You can see trends in logo design. There's kind of a retro-minimalist style going on. (S2)*

Through learning what was gaining attention in the community at large, new designers could decide to what extent they should try to emulate current trends in developing their own style:

> *Like say if I wanted to go into advertising, I mean, if I can do what we're seeing now in these kind of emerging trends, it'll make it easier for me to get a job and come off as avant-garde or very groundbreaking, and that sort of thing. So I think it makes it easier to keep up with what's trending, what's cool, what's appealing, but it also sacrifices a little bit of that individuality as well. (S2)*

As a result, several interviewees who were starting out in the design field used the popular work to give them a sense of how they could create new and different styled work in order to stand out from the crowd.

Getting feedback on work in progress

The social functionalities of likes and comments also supported skill development by supporting feedback on posted work from others in the community (S1, S2, S3, PT4, PT5, PT6, PT7, PT8, FT2.) In describing what they shared and why, there were two main types of feedback that people reported seeking. The first of these was to get help improving specific aspects of a piece of work that was not yet finalized.

> *I specifically asked if the ampersand looked too much like an E and asked if anybody had any particular things that they saw that looked really weird or anything that maybe me having looked at it for several hours and not having fresh eyes on-- something they might see that I missed or something. And a lot of them said the ampersand looked fine, but this looks like an F. This is crowded, and because I prompted for that feedback, they all gave me excellent feedback. So that was cool. (FT2)*

In this case, the participant received useful feedback through comments that other site members gave him.

People also used site feedback about attention to their work to get an overall sense of the community's relative like or dislike of a given creation. Designers would post work without asking explicitly for feedback, but would use likes and views as a proxy to infer community interest in or acceptance of their work compared to other designers and to other shots they had previously posted.

For example, one interviewee posted a logo he had designed in order to see if it would get the same amount of views and likes as other high-quality creations he had seen on the site.

> *It did not, so I guess I missed the mark...I have 135 views which is more than most of my others. So that means from the small thumbnail view on the homepage of Dribbble, it probably looked really good, and then when they got more into it-- I don't know, maybe it started to look less great. (S1)*

He interpreted the different social signals, in this case, the ratio of views to likes, as an indication that his work missed the mark. Whether or not the feedback desired or received came in the form of useful written comments or number of "likes," the interaction transparency helped people assess the quality of their posted work in a way that would not have been possible on a personal portfolio website.

Novices vs. experts

While inspiration was used almost universally, the main difference between novices and experts came with regards to the desire for and type of feedback received. Moving from a novice to an expert involved determining who one's desired audience was and then both needing to learn to improve one's skills, but also on learning what strategies or site norms were needed to achieve success. Experts rarely sought substantive feedback on specific things. In some cases, they felt that their skills were developed enough that they knew what they were doing.

> *I'm happy, personally about what I'm doing at the moment with it, so-- yeah, as I said, I wasn't looking for, like, anybody to kind of solve problems for me. (PT3)*

In other cases, getting detailed feedback from other fellow designers could not impact work that had already been completed for a client, but was useful for general reactions:

> *definitely I don't use Dribbble as a feedback-- I mean, after my client approves something, I upload it here. Then, depending on if they like it or not, it doesn't matter, because I got paid, but definitely for next project it gives me a sort of insight what people think. (PT9)*

In contrast, novices were most likely to want feedback on work in progress. They were also the least likely to get it. When they did, it came most often from people they knew already and who were at a similar level of expertise as themselves.

> *I was working on these buttons and my initial idea was to have it kind of animate a little bit like you can see happening in this preview here. And so I thought I'd toss this up and see what people thought. Nobody actually commented on it but I did get some comments from other friends I shared it with. (PT4)*

In terms of interviewees' willingness to offer feedback to others, the number of followers a person had was often a cue that factored into deciding whether or not to comment on others' work. People were often less likely to give feedback to prominent designers, either because they felt intimidated by their celebrity, or because they felt their voice would be lost among the crowd. Fewer followers was a signal that a person might be more receptive to comments:

> *If that person especially has less followers and they're looking for feedback, I'm much more willing to put my time in and say, "Hey, you really want feedback and no one's giving it to you. I'll help you out. Whereas the other people who are posting stuff who might not even be looking for feedback, and they're getting a ton of feedback. (FT1)*

This highlighted the importance of building up one's social capital on the site. An important prerequisite for getting feedback on work was gaining followers who would be more likely to see the work an individual member posted. Members worked to build interpersonal relationships with other designers who would then be more likely to respond when a new piece of work was shared. We address ways people pursued some of these community aims in the next section.

PROFESSIONAL IDENTITY DEVELOPMENT

The second major activity we were interested in investigating on Dribbble was how people appropriated the site and its features to develop a professional identity. We found that members on the site attempted to gain attention to enhance their professional identity and improve their standing in the community. Compared to other online sites focused around making and sharing creative artifacts, such as Scratch or Newgrounds [15, 23], professional identity was often a concern for people deciding how to position themselves either within their professional community, to outside observers or to both audiences simultaneously.

Attention from whom?: Membership and status

The fact that membership in Dribbble was invite-only seemed to increase the value of attention from site members (versus the internet at large). The first step to becoming a Dribbble member was to receive an invitation to become a "player" and fully participate in the community by sharing work and commenting on others' work. This invitation-only requirement was, for many people, a motivation to join the site because an invitation signaled some level of skill in and of itself. Many Dribbble site members (S1, S2, PT1, PT5, PT9, PT10, FT1,FT4, FT6) mentioned how being invited to the site helped to build their reputation both with other designers and with clients or employers. The signal of site membership helped members gain employment or other work opportunities.

> *my manager directly said, "Oh, the presentation of your website and the added fact that you had a Dribbble account really appealed to us." Because the people I work with were familiar with Dribbble; they don't use it very frequently, but I think that having an account and being able to upload your work is almost a bit of-- it seems a bit of a status symbol at this point, especially for students, because it's a heavily vetted process. (S2)*

The impact of the invite-only system not only had implications for the reputations of the designers who were accepted, but also was seen as beneficial for the creation of a repository of high quality work as a source of examples.

> *You can upload almost anything on Deviantart be it beautiful or crap but I can only find an essence of great works on Dribbble. The preliminary evaluation guarantees that only good designers get into the community so being a member gives you kinda proof that you reached a level of quality. (PT7)*

However, although site members had all demonstrated a certain baseline of quality to be invited, hierarchies still emerged with some people becoming more popular than others (as determined by the number of followers they had and the number of likes their work typically received.)

> *but there's definitely a sense of hierarchy...It's all about-- it's also about seniority, like who's been on Dribbble the longest, and who has the most followers. I think who has the most followers is probably the strongest way to tell. (S2)*

With so many members and so much content, the number of followers a person had and the likes their work received was often a quick and easy way to assess quality. Work with little audience response would reflect badly on the individual, because audience response to work was a signal of quality. By comparing the response various works received, people would remove an individual piece if it didn't achieve a certain level of success (as determined by likes and views.)

> *there are things that I like-- I put on the site because I want to put on the site because I think it's going to get a lot of attention. And then there are things that I think I'm going to put on the site, and then I'll get to that point where I put it on and I realize, "You know what? This isn't actually that great, so I'm going to pull it down." (PT2)*

One problem with this was that the audience's response was not always predictable, especially for non-established designers. Interviewees mentioned encountering discrepancies between what they felt was their best work and what received the best response on Dribbble.

Sharing work to show off

Once they had "made it," members were strategic about how and what they shared and who they sought out to advance their status in the community and with outside clients. In describing why they had shared recent examples of their work, members talked about "showing off" or sharing examples that indicated a particular level of skill or effort invested that only other designers on the site, or peers could appreciate (PT2, PT7, PT9, PT10, PT11, FT2, FT4, FT5). For example, one person uploaded a 3D phone icon he had created in order to showcase his approach:

> *it was showing off how you could have-- like it's showing the 3-D and a really subtle line-- like just really subtle accenting around edges and stuff.... Well, normal people-- like they'll see, but they won't look in depth and think about the amount of work that has to go into make a-- to do detailing like that.*

> *Whereas designers will-- they don't really need to read this to see that a lot of work went into it. (FT4)*

Another person wanted to "show off" to other designers in the community some work he had put a lot of time into for a prestigious client:

> *Because some people know who my clients are or you can guess it from the colors. I don't know if that's relevant for you but I think if you're a designer and you know me and you know my company then you can see the colors, where they came from, so yes, I post it to show off. (PT12)*

These kinds of examples were shared to impress other members of the community and to earn credibility as a very skilled member of the profession. Showing off to other designers was seen as useful in terms of not only forming new friendships and mutually giving feedback to each other, but also for the possibility of collaborations or getting referrals for clients.

On the other hand, some members, particularly full-time freelancers, were interested in increasing their reputation with the goal of being viewed by potential clients.

> *I post stuff so it's current with what I'm working on, as current as I can be. And just a way to demonstrate to potential clients that this is what I do and this is kind of the best of what I'm working on. Because I actually don't have a dedicated portfolio. (FT1)*

It was not necessarily always clear who was actually viewing the work that was posted. Different site members had different hypotheses about who was looking at their work. For example, one person thought it was fellow designers:

> *I really don't think that people are really looking at it beyond kind of like an exclusive group of design people. (PT6)*

Another thought it was external observers:

> *I think there's a lot of designers who post to it and use it. There are more people who watch it who are not creative people. You know like they're in the marketing field or they're in communications but they don't know how to design a logo. (FT5)*

Lack of audience awareness meant that for people who sought attention, it was not always easy to tell if they were getting the right amount of attention from the audience that they were targeting or how to interpret the amount of attention they got. For example, it was possible to see the number of views a work received but not the details of who had looked at it. There was also the issue in which signaling quality to outsiders vs. insiders may have taken different forms. While some people mentioned that other designers would "get" what they were showing off by appreciating the inherent skill being demonstrated, they also felt that outsiders would be more likely to rely on things like popular work as signals of quality.

Novices vs. experts: Strategies for gaining attention

Gaining reputation through getting more followers and likes involved getting more attention to oneself and one's work. We found that interviewees who were more concerned with these objectives were likely to adopt strategies in order to increase the attention they received from site members, often leveraging the work size constraints of the site and utilizing the visible network connections to their advantage.

Users who were concerned about rising in the community were careful about how they displayed their work within the size limits imposed by Dribbble. Two people mentioned participating in an unspoken norm amongst serious users to create what they called "Dribbble bait," or specially-formatted versions of their work designed to look good in the particular setting.

> *I particularly made a 300 by 400 layout with a focus on this. I designed a Dribbble shot rather than just posting a screen shot of something I'm working on... So by Dribbble bait, I mean it was specifically customized to be on Dribbble and to get feedback or likes on Dribbble. (FT1)*

Using the visible activity traces of directed interactions between other members served as another strategy for gaining attention and reputation by increasing one's following from other members. Members interested in advancing within the site's hierarchy used the activity traces of people they already followed to discern social networks featuring the top members and then decided to follow these people as well in order to start learning about who was who.

> *I was able to, through people that I found early on-- seeing who they were following and who they were interacting with and seeing who were friends and who worked together and who did this and that. And clicking through to their portfolios and things from their Dribbble profiles and following them on Twitter and listening to what they were saying and viewing all the new work that they were putting out there. (FT2)*

In addition to discovering new people who were important to know in the community, an additional step in gaining their attention was to reach out to them via commenting on their work.

> *I feel like-- I kind of comment strategically. When I comment on people's stuff, I either am looking for them to look at my profile back, so kind of showing my face on their shot so that they can kind of see what I'm doing, like, "Oh, I want to check out this guy's stuff"...And that's kind of how I got the attention of the more popular Dribbble users is continually commenting on their shots. (PT2)*

The outcome of networking with other site members in this way was frequently the formation of friendships or feedback relationships. In some cases, people were invited to collaborate or contribute to projects based on people they networked with through Dribbble.

> *So by commenting on stuff for other people, you can get involved with things that could-- you can get involved with*

people that could potentially turn into people that you could collaborate with later down the road. (PT2)

DESIGN IMPLICATIONS

Augmenting a community of practice with social networking features may enhance a community's ability to develop shared understanding of best practices and standards. Transparent signals of community attention helped members of Dribbble easily find work artifacts and other professionals to serve as sources of inspiration and learning. The site's design at the time of our interviews may have been responsible for these social dynamics, making popular work most readily accessible and explicitly highlighting followers, likes, and comments. These design choices emphasize the importance of attention and popularity for people seeking to advance within the site. Although the design focus on community-level attention supported professional development in some ways, it also led to tensions between groups of users with different levels of status and with different objectives (e.g. getting feedback vs. showing off.) In addition, the fact that work on Dribbble can simultaneously be viewed both by other designers and by external clients leads to the "context collapse" seen in other social sites such as Facebook or Twitter [25], where people may often wish to target their posts to different audiences, some of whom leave no trace.

To some extent, the behaviors seen on Dribbble may be unique to the design profession. For example, the type of work being shared is visual and easy to quickly and rapidly view and assess. For the most part, people were able to freely share their work (either after it had been launched for a client or because it was their own creation.) In addition, the intrinsic role of critique and feedback inherent in design as a profession makes it easy to carry out this type of behavior online, although there are still challenges in enticing people to give helpful feedback, both on Dribbble and elsewhere [39].

Changing elements of the site design could influence the social dynamic and social importance of attention. For example, currently the site showcases "popular" work on its landing page for non-members, and showcases "Following" work as the default landing page for members who are signed in to the site. This creates incentives for those who wish to make it onto the Popular page by copying popular styles, reformatting their work to look as good as possible in a small format, or seeking to expand their network so that more people will see their work in their "following" feed. Removing signals about how much attention a particular shared artifact has received may reduce its importance in evaluating quality.

We also found evidence that skill development on the site was limited by the focus of attention. In order to receive feedback in the form of detailed critique on posted work, it was necessary to attract the attention of an audience. Novices who could most benefit from this type of feedback were least likely to have this type of audience. Domain focused SNSs need to think about how to support novice members who may want to develop their skills while simultaneously supporting established professionals who want to "show off." It is not clear whether the same site can support both of these goals. On Dribbble there is currently no dedicated section of content for people seeking in depth feedback on works in progress. It is not always easy to understand who wants critical comments in response to a piece of posted work, especially given that many of our interviewees did not. Therefore, creating a special section of the site where people can explicitly call for feedback could facilitate that behavior.

Supporting professional development elsewhere

Some aspects of Dribbble's site design (invite only, sharing small parts of work rather than the whole, and incorporating social media functionalities) could be used in other types of professional sites in related fields where people produce and share digital work (e.g. journalism, translation, academia.) Professionals in other fields beyond design also have the ability to share their work and interact in sites focused around their field. Most sites devoted to professional skill development and practice are currently either focused on learning or primarily dedicated to self-promotion. In the former case, MOOCs provide a rising context in which encouraging peer feedback is a challenge. In the latter case, sites like oDesk or specialized sites for freelance translation like Proz.com act as digital matchmakers to help translators get work, with crowdsourced "kudos" serving as signals of their expertise [19]. Work-sharing and invite-only sites are also taking hold in the field of journalism (e.g. Svbtle.com), a professional field which is evolving towards more independent work. However, challenges seem to exist when an individual's activities on a single professional site receive attention for both hiring and non-hiring related purposes.

Another example of a site which is starting to be used for hybrid purposes is GitHub, a software development site where people collaborate on open source projects. While the main use of the site is to create an artifact (software code,) each individual on the site also has a profile that shows a history of their work and interactions. Employers are increasingly paying attention to these profiles to recruit and hire software developers, viewing GitHub membership as a signal of certain positive characteristics such as passion for coding [24, 31]. This has implications for the types of behaviors people will engage in on the site if and when they think another unrelated audience may see what they have done, such as removing old projects that could help others but may not be an accurate signal of their current abilities.

CONCLUSION

Social media-enabled communities of practice have the potential to provide great professional benefits to members. By increasing social transparency regarding who created what, how they created it, and who paid attention to it, a site like Dribbble allows users to engage in skill development through learning from and interacting with others in a wider community and to build a professional identity to an intended audience. Dribbble provides a unique case of a site that has evolved from a feedback-oriented community to a site that, once it was opened up to view from a wider audience, enabled dual uses (some of which involved conflicting goals between learning for novices and self-promotion for full-time freelancers.) Our findings illustrate the challenges of designing increased transparency through social networking features into a site for users with different levels of experience and diverse professional objectives. Nonetheless, they show promise for the ability of professional social networking sites to enable various types of professional development and success of individuals engaging in independent creative production.

ACKNOWLEDGMENTS

This work was supported by National Science Foundation grants IIS-1111750, CNS-1040801, OCI-0943168, STC-1221006, and grants from the Center for the Future of Work, Heinz College, Carnegie Mellon University.

REFERENCES

1. Allen, W. Rewarding Participation in Social Media Enabled Communities of Practice. *Proc. ICWSM,*, (2013), n.p.
2. Allen, W. Exploring Hybrid-Economic Communities and the Technology-Mediated Identities Performed There. *Proc. iConference,* 576-582.
3. Amin, A. and Roberts, J. Knowing in action: Beyond communities of practice. *Research Policy 37*, 2 (2008), 353–369.
4. boyd, d. and Ellison, N. Social network sites: Definition, history, and scholarship. *Journal of Computer-Mediated Communication 13*, 1 (2007), 210–230.
5. Burke, M., Kraut, R., and Marlow, C. Social capital on Facebook: Differentiating uses and users. *Proc. CHI,* (2011), 571–580.
6. Capiluppi, A., Serebrenik, A., and Singer, L. Assessing technical candidates on the social web. *IEEE Software 30*, 1 (2013), 45–51.
7. Charmaz, K. Grounded theory as an emergent method. *Handbook of emergent methods*, (2008), 155–170.
8. Cox, A.M., Clough, P.D., and Marlow, J. Flickr: a first look at user behaviour in the context of photography as serious leisure. *Information Research 13*, 1 (2008), 5.
9. Dabbish, L., Stuart, C., Tsay, J., and Herbsleb, J. Social coding in GitHub: transparency and collaboration in an open software repository. *Proc. CSCW,* (2012), 1277–1286.
10. Dow, S., Fortuna, J., Schwartz, D., Altringer, B., Schwartz, D., and Klemmer, S. Prototyping dynamics: sharing multiple designs improves exploration, group rapport, and results. *Proc. CHI*, (2011), 2807–2816.
11. Erickson, T. and Kellogg, W.A. Social translucence: an approach to designing systems that support social processes. *ACM Transactions on Computer-Human Interaction (TOCHI) 7*, 1 (2000), 59–83.
12. Faulconbridge, J. Global Architects: Learning and Innovation Through Communities and Constellations of Practice. *SSRN eLibrary*, (2010).
13. Forte, A., Humphreys, M., and Park, T.H. Grassroots Professional Development: How Teachers Use Twitter. *ICWSM*, (2012), 106–113.
14. Herring, S.R., Chang, C.C., Krantzler, J., and Bailey, B.P. Getting inspired!: understanding how and why examples are used in creative design practice. *Proc. CHI*, (2009), 87–96.
15. Hill, B.M., Monroy-Hernández, A., and Olson, K. Responses to Remixing on a Social Media Sharing Website. *Proc. ICWSM*, (2010), 74–81.
16. Ibarra, H. Provisional selves: Experimenting with image and identity in professional adaptation. *Administrative Science Quarterly 44*, 4 (1999), 764–791.
17. Joinson, A.N. Looking at, looking up or keeping up with people?: motives and use of facebook. *Proc. CHI*, (2008), 1027–1036.
18. Kumar, R., Talton, J.O., Ahmad, S., and Klemmer, S.R. Bricolage: Example-based retargeting for web design. *Proc. CHI*, (2011), 2197–2206.
19. Kushner, S. The freelance translation machine: Algorithmic culture and the invisible industry. *New Media & Society*, (2013), 1-18.
20. Kuznetsov, S. and Paulos, E. Rise of the expert amateur: DIY projects, communities, and cultures. *Proc. NordiCHI*, (2010), 295–304.
21. Lampe, C., Ellison, N.B., and Steinfield, C. Changes in use and perception of facebook. *Proc. CSCW,* (2008), 721–730.
22. Lerner, J. and Tirole, J. Some simple economics of open source. *The Journal of Industrial Economics 50*, 2 (2002), 197–234.
23. Luther, K., Caine, K., Ziegler, K., and Bruckman, A. Why it works (when it works): success factors in online creative collaboration. *Proc. GROUP,* (2010), 1–10.
24. Marlow, J. and Dabbish, L. Activity traces and signals in software developer recruitment and hiring. *Proc. CSCW,* (2013), 145–156.
25. Marwick, A.E. I tweet honestly, I tweet passionately: Twitter users, context collapse, and the imagined audience. *New Media & Society 13*, 1 (2011), 114–133.
26. Muller, M., Ehrlich, K., Matthews, T., Perer, A., Ronen, I., and Guy, I. Diversity among enterprise online communities: Collaborating, teaming, and

innovating through social media. *Proc. CHI,* (2012), 2815–2824.

27. Muller, M. Lurking as personal trait or situational disposition: lurking and contributing in enterprise social media. *Proc. CSCW*, (2012), 253–256.
28. Muller, M.J. and Carey, K. Design as a minority discipline in a software company: toward requirements for a community of practice. *Proc. CHI*, (2002), 383–390.
29. Nov, O., Naaman, M., and Ye, C. Motivational, structural and tenure factors that impact online community photo sharing. *Proc. ICWSM*, (2009), 138–145.
30. Russell, J., Greenhalgh, T., Boynton, P., and Rigby, M. Soft networks for bridging the gap between research and practice: illuminative evaluation of CHAIN. *BMJ 328*, 7449 (2004), 1174.
31. Singer, L., Figueira Filho, F., Cleary, B., Treude, C., Storey, M.-A., and Schneider, K. Mutual assessment in the social programmer ecosystem: An empirical investigation of developer profile aggregators. *Proc. CSCW,* (2013), 103–116.
32. Stewart, J. and Williams, R. The wrong trousers? Beyond the design fallacy: social learning and the user. *Beyond the Design Fallacy: Social Learning and the User*, (2005), 195-221.
33. Stuart, H.C., Dabbish, L., Kiesler, S., Kinnaird, P., and Kang, R. Social transparency in networked information exchange: a theoretical framework. *Proc. CSCW,* (2012), 451–460.
34. Thom-Santelli, J. and Millen, D.R. Learning by seeing: photo viewing in the workplace. *Proc. CHI,* (2009), 2081–2090.
35. Torrey, C., McDonald, D., Schilit, B., and Bly, S. How-To pages: Informal systems of expertise sharing. *Proc. ECSCW*, (2007), 391–410.
36. Wasko, M.M. and Faraj, S. Why Should I Share? Examining Social Capital and Knowledge Contribution in Electronic Networks of Practice. *MIS Quarterly 29*, 1 (2005), 35–57.
37. Wenger, E. Supporting communities of practice. *A survey of community-oriented technologies*, (2001).
38. Xu, A. and Bailey, B. What do you think?: a case study of benefit, expectation, and interaction in a large online critique community. *Proc. CSCW*, (2012), 295–304.
39. Xu, A. and Bailey, B.P. A crowdsourcing model for receiving design critique. *Proc. CHI Extended Abstracts* (2011), 1183–1188.
40. http://www.dribbble.com/site/testimonials
41. http://www.dribbble.com

Mind the Map: The Impact of Culture and Economic Affluence on Crowd-Mapping Behaviours

Giovanni Quattrone
Dept. of Computer Science
University College London
Gower Street
London WC1E 6BT, UK
g.quattrone@cs.ucl.ac.uk

Afra Mashhadi
Bell Labs
Alcatel Lucent
Dublin, Ireland
afra.mashhadi@alcatel-lucent.com

Licia Capra
Dept. of Computer Science
University College London
Gower Street
London WC1E 6BT, UK
l.capra@cs.ucl.ac.uk

ABSTRACT

Crowd-mapping is a form of collaborative work that empowers citizens to collect and share geographic knowledge. OpenStreetMap (OSM) is a successful example of such paradigm, where the goal of building and maintaining an accurate *global* map of the changing world is being accomplished by means of *local* contributions made by over 1.2M citizens. While OSM has been subject to many country-specific studies, the relationship between national culture and economic affluence *and* users' participation has been so far unexplored. In this work, we systematically study the link between them: we characterise OSM users in terms of who they are, how they contribute, during what period of time, and across what geographic areas. We find strong correlations between these characteristics and national culture factors (e.g., power distance, individualism, pace of life, self expression), and well as Gross Domestic Product per capita. Based on these findings, we discuss design issues that developers of crowd-mapping services should consider to account for cross-cultural differences.

Author Keywords

OSM; crowd-sourcing; volunteered geographic information; cross-cultural

ACM Classification Keywords

H.2.8 Database Management: Database Applications—*Spatial Databases and GIS*; H.5.3 Group and Organization Interfaces: Computer-Supported Cooperative Work

INTRODUCTION

Crowd-sourcing has become a popular paradigm to harvest user-generated content into meaningful and informative collections. A specific domain where this paradigm has been widely applied to is that of volunteered geographic information: citizens have become surveyors, with council-monitoring applications like FixMyStreet;[1] local reporters, as powered by Ushaidi's Crowdmap;[2] and cartographers, with geo-wikis like Cyclopath[3] and OpenStreetMap.[4] We refer to this instantiation of the crowd-sourcing paradigm as crowd-mapping.

OpenStreetMap (OSM) is perhaps one of the most successful examples of crowd-mapping, with currently over 1M users, collectively building a free, openly accessible, editable map of the world. Various country-specific studies of OSM have been conducted, mainly to quantify the accuracy (e.g., in the UK [8], France [7], and Germany[21]) and coverage (e.g., in London, UK [23]) of its information, with respect to centrally-maintained geographic datasets. However, an important aspect that has so far been neglected is the relationship between national culture and economic affluence *and* this form of collaborative work.

Previous research has shown that cultural values shape our thinking, behaviours and social procedures [17]. Such cultural differences have visible manifestations not only in the actions people undertake in the physical world, but also in the behaviour they manifest in the online world (e.g., [28, 6]). We thus hypothesize that users' participation in computer-mediated crowd-mapping activities like OSM varies significantly between countries. As such initiatives heavily rely on local volunteers to accomplish their goals, quantifying users' engagement in countries around the world, through the lens of national culture and economic affluence, should highlight important design considerations that engineers of crowd-mapping systems might ponder, to better account for national diversities.

In this paper, we study the behaviour of nearly 165,000 OSM users spread across 35 countries, who have collectively made over 13M contributions to OSM to date. We describe OSM crowd-mapping characteristics, on a per country basis, in terms of: *who* the contributors are (power vs. normal users); *how many* contributions they make, and over *how long* a period of time; *how detailed* contributions are; *when* edits are

[1] `http://www.fixmystreet.com`
[2] `http://www.ushahidi.com/products/crowdmap`
[3] `http://cyclopath.org/`
[4] `http://www.openstreetmap.org/`

CSCW'14, February 15–19, 2014, Baltimore, Maryland, USA.
Copyright 2014 ACM 978-1-4503-2540-0/14/02...$15.00.
http://dx.doi.org/10.1145/2531602.2531713

made (both to capture speed of OSM adoption, and burstiness of activity); and, finally, *where* in the country edits are done (how geographically spread they are). We then correlate these OSM factors with cultural and economic factors that anthropologists have found to be most accountable for cross-country differences: *power distance*, that is, the extent to which people (especially those less powerful) accept power to be unequally distributed [13]; *individualism vs. collectivism*, that is, the extent to which social relationships are loose (e.g., people look after themselves), as opposed to relationships integrated in strong and cohesive groups [13]; *pace of life*, that is, the speed at which we move, the high-pressure at which we work, and the density of experiences and activities we undertake daily [18]; *self-expression vs. survival*, that is, the extent to which subjective well-being and quality of life take precedence over economic and physical security, as captured by the World Value Survey [15]; and, finally, *Gross Domestic Product*, to capture a country's standard of living. We find that GDP per capita and power distance are strongly correlated with users' engagement (how many OSM users exist in a country, to what extent they contribute, and over what period of time); self-expression and pace of life are strongly correlated with the quality of the edits (how detailed they are, and how geographically spread); finally, GDP per capita is strongly correlated with the speed of technology adoption and burstiness of contributions. We discuss the implications of these findings in assessing the long-term sustainability of OSM across cultures, and suggest design questions that engineers of crowd-mapping initiatives should consider, to account for cross-cultural differences. We finally conclude the paper with a discussion of known limitations and future work.

RELATED WORK

The relationship between cultural values and users' social behaviours has been the subject of extensive research in the domain of online communities, following seminal work of social psychologist Geert Hofstede [13]. Hofstede administered opinion surveys to IBM employees in over 70 countries. After analysing over 100,000 questionnaires, he discovered significant differences between cultures; he was then able to attribute most of the variance in the data to five cultural factors: individualism vs. collectivism (i.e., the extent to which individual goals take precedence over collective ones), power distance (i.e., the extent to which social hierarchies are accepted), masculinity vs. femininity (i.e., the importance of values such as competitiveness, ambition and power as opposed to relationships and quality of life), uncertainty avoidance (i.e., a society's propensity to accept unusual changes and the resulting uncertainty), and long-term orientation (i.e., a disposition to favour long-term rewards vs. short-term ones). Various cultural anthropologists and psychologists have subsequently proposed other (related) cultural factors, that help understand people's differing behaviours when faced with the same situation in the real world. For example, Hall [9] proposes the concept of polychronic versus monochronic time orientation, to differentiate between cultures that give higher importance to human interactions rather than strict time management and punctuality; Levine and Norenzayan [18] suggest the concept of pace of life, measured as a combination of people's walking speed, the work speed of postal clerks, and the accuracy of bank clocks, to analyse behavioural difference across cultures; and Inglehart and Baker [15] refer to self-expression vs. survival values, that is, the extent to which subjective well-being and quality of life take precedence over economic and physical security (which tend to be taken for granted in more industrialised countries), as captured by the World Value Survey.

These theories have been used as a framework to analyse people's differing behaviour not only in the physical world, but also in their manifested actions in online communities. A very thorough and recent survey of such studies has been compiled by Gallagher and Savage [5]. A common aim behind these works is to help improve our understanding of how cultural variations impact online community dynamics, so to more effectively manage them. Studies span a variety of aspects: from understanding the impact of cultural differences on people's motivation to use an online community [22], to the impact of culture on behavioural dynamics, both in social networking websites [4, 16, 6] and more recently within online group decision-making tools [28].

Hofstede's cultural attributes (power distance and individualism vs. collectivism in particular) have been used to understand online crowd-sourcing behaviours too, more specifically in the context of Wikipedia (e.g., [26, 10]). In this case, language has often been chosen as unit of analysis. For example, Pfeil et al. [26] have analysed Wikipedians' editorial actions in light of cultural factors, and found strong negative correlation between power distance and 'delete' actions, strong positive correlation between collectivism and 'expand' actions, and strong positive correlation between individualism and 'modify' actions. They went on to explain these findings as follow: Wikipedians from countries where subordinate relationships are well accepted (high power distance), are more reluctant to adopt subversive (i.e., delete) actions, as they accept they do not have the right or privilege to do so. Wikipedians from collectivist countries are more likely to add information to expand already existing Wikipedia pages, while those from countries with high individualism tend to have their own opinions prevail over group consensus, as exhibited by the higher number of modifications (i.e., corrections) to existing articles. Findings about editing behaviours in Wikipedia cannot be directly transferred to the crowd-mapping domain, as the unit of cultural analysis they used (i.e., the language edition of Wikipedia) is too coarse grained. More precisely, in the crowd-mapping domain exemplified by OSM, where the task to be accomplished (i.e., mapping geographic information) requires contributors to have detailed local knowledge, a finer (country) level of granularity is required.

Studies conducted to date in the domain of crowd-mapping can be broadly grouped in two streams: on one hand, analyses of the quality of the volunteered geographic information; on the other hand, investigations into the motivation behind users' engagement with the mapping tasks. Quality of information has been measured in OpenStreetMap in terms of accuracy (e.g., in the UK [8], France [7], and Germany[21]), and more recently coverage (e.g., in Germany [30] and in London, UK [23]). While the former has been found to be consistently high, coverage is presently low, especially as one moves away from urban areas to more rural ones. This finding raises concerns in terms of the long-term sustainability of crowd-mapping: is coverage going to spontaneously grow, or are there going to be areas that will continue to be neglected? Studies so far have been limited in that they quantify coverage at one specific point in time, and in so doing they cannot disclose the factors that contribute to crowd-mapping participation over time; furthermore, comparative studies between different countries are lacking.

A second stream of research has looked into users' motivation behind the mapping task. OpenStreetMap contributors' motivation has been studied by means of an online questionnaire [3]: 444 contributors of differing age, education, and past OSM experience took part. Among them, ideology (i.e., the willingness to contribute to the community that is behind the OSM project) emerged as the single highest motivational factor; they also found geography to be a community-wide motivator, with both casual and serious mappers concerned with building a complete map of their local territory. These motivational factors emerged also in studies of Cyclopath, another successful geo-wiki that is being used to digitally map route information for cyclists in Minneapolis. Indeed, researchers found that, after being attracted to volunteer information in response to a call to fix a problem, contributors remain engaged to aid the local cycling community [25, 27]. However, findings from these studies cannot be generalised to differing countries, as even in [3] over 90% of respondents where from either the UK or North America.

A challenging question that has so far been left unexplored is thus the extent to which people's engagement with a crowd-mapping initiative varies with respect to national characteristics: are there countries where a crowd-mapping task will succeed more than in others? Can we identify them, both to raise awareness (of importance, for example, to those building location-based services on top of such maps), as well as to intervene with purpose-planned corrective actions? As a first step to provide answer to these questions, we present in this paper a large-scale, quantitative analysis of the extent that national *cultural factors* and *economic affluence* correlate with users' crowd-mapping behaviour in OpenStreetMap.

DATA DESCRIPTION

OpenStreetMap

We begin our study with a detailed description of the crowd-sourcing dataset at hand, that is, OpenStreetMap. The dataset is freely available to download[5] and contains the history (since 2006) of all edits (over 2 billions) performed by all users (over 1M) on all spatial objects. In OSM jargon, spatial objects can be one of three types: *nodes*, *ways*, and *relations*. Nodes are single geospatial points and typically represent Points-of-Interest (POIs) (e.g., cafes, restaurants, hospitals, schools); ways mostly represent roads (as well as streams, railway lines, and the like); finally, relations are used for grouping other objects together, based on logical (and usually local) relationships (e.g., administrative boundaries, bus routes).

[5] `http://www.geofabrik.de/data/download.html`

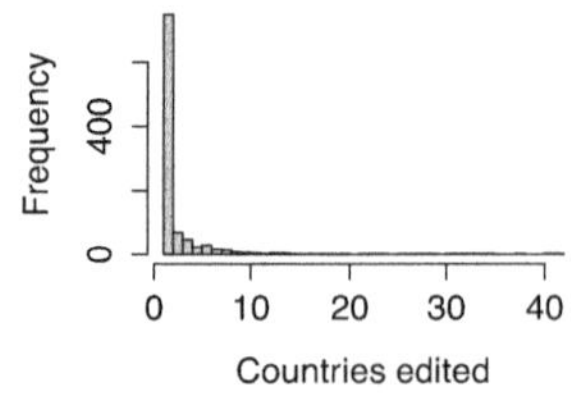

Figure 1. Distribution of number of edited countries per user

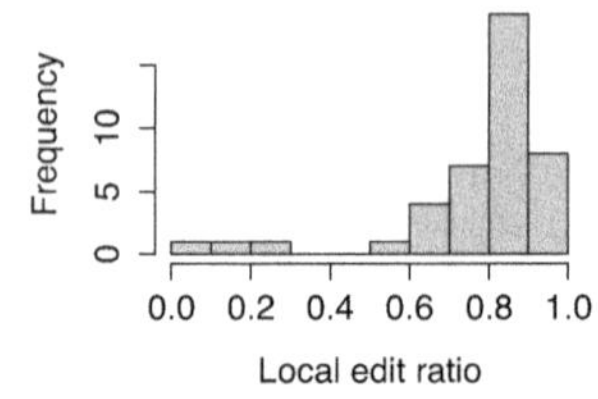

Figure 2. Distribution of local edits per country

In order to reduce the OSM dataset to a more manageable size, we restricted our attention to nodes only. A node consists of three main attributes: a geographical position (latitude and longitude), a name, and an optional amenity type (e.g., hospital, cafe). Furthermore, we used stratified sampling and selected 43 countries, out of the 133 presently mapped in OSM, so to have representatives across the whole range of cultural and economic values we focus on in this study (further details about these values in the next section). From this sample, we removed all contributions that appeared to be 'bulk imports' (i.e., over 1K edits, performed by a single user, within a single session, and spread over a large geographic area). We chose to discard these edits as not representatives of 'human' crowd-sourcing activity, but rather of 'data donations' given to the wider OSM community by external organisations. These imports represent less than 30% of the total edits considered.

Last but not least, if we are to examine crowd-mapping behaviour in relation to national cultural factors, we need to grow confidence in the fact that OSM edits in a given country are indeed performed by users who are representative of the country's culture. We cannot know if OSM users were 'born and bred' in any given country or if, for instance, they were migrants who only recently moved there; however, we can grow confidence in our analysis by performing the following processing: first, we infer a 'home country' for each OSM user with more than 5 edits (while marking 'homeless' those with less than that); there was no ambiguity in this inference, as all users had over 90% of their edits (and the vast majority exactly 100%) done in a single country, as shown in Figure 1. We then compute, for each of the 43 pre-selected countries, the ratio of edits done by home users, over all edits done in that country; Figure 2 illustrates the resulting distribution. Finally, we remove from our analysis countries with less than 70% of contributions made by (inferred) locals. Eight countries were removed during this processing, including four (Canada, Libya, Nigeria and Peru) where the majority of edits are indeed 'foreign'. In the end, we are left with a dataset comprising nearly 165,000 users, who have collectively made over 13M contributions to OSM to date, across the 35 countries coloured in Figure 3. We next describe the cultural and economic factors we chose to investigate in our analysis of cross-country crowd-mapping behaviours.

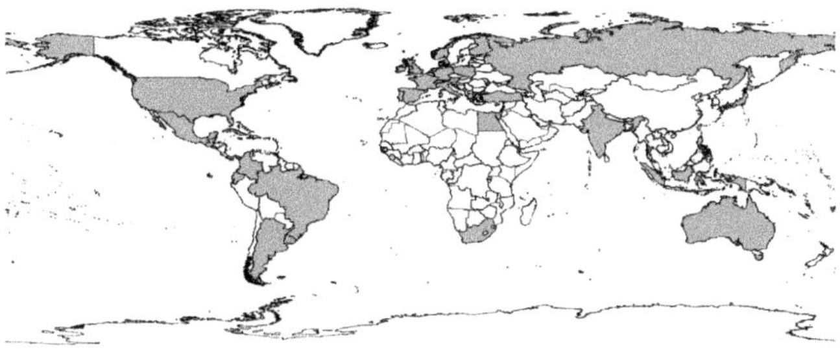

Figure 3. Map of final 35 countries under analysis.

Cultural and Economic Factors

Based on previous cross-cultural studies of users' behaviours in online communities [5], we have selected the following five cultural and economic factors to analyse manifested crowd-mapping behaviours in OSM.

Power Distance Index (PDI). The first cultural feature we consider is Hofstede's Power Distance Index [13]. This feature represents the extent to which a nation expects power to be unequally distributed. For example, in countries where PDI is higher, decision making is accepted to be in the hands of a few powerful people, rather than a broader citizen base. Pfeil et al. [26] have studied the relationship between this feature and editing activity in different language editions of Wikipedia, and found that the higher the PDI, the lower the number of 'delete' actions on each other's work (as if people did not feel they had the power or the right to make the decision of deleting somebody-else's work). In the context of OSM, we expect PDI to be strongly correlated with *who* OSM editors are (power vs. normal users), and *how* they map (using what actions).

Individualism vs Collectivism (IDV). The second cultural feature we consider is Hofstede's Individualism index [13]. This feature measures the extent to which individuals are integrated into groups: the higher the individualistic score, the higher the importance given to personal achievements and individual rights (or of those within very close circles), as opposed to wider community interest. Western cultures tend to have high IDV, as opposed to Eastern ones, that are more collectivist instead. This feature has also been studied in the context of Wikipedia, where it has been observed that: the lower the IDV (the higher the collectivism), the higher the number of 'addition' to Wikipedia articles; while the higher the IDV (the higher the individualism), the higher the number of 'modification' to Wikipedia articles [26]. In other words, 'modifications' are signals of individual opinions prevailing over group consensus, while 'additions' are signals of cross-group collaborations towards the growth and development of Wikipedia. As for the power distance index, we expect IDV to correlate both with *who* OSM editors are (power vs. normal users), and with *how* they map (using what actions).

Gross Domestic Product Per Capita (GDP-pc). The third metric we use is Gross Domestic Product per capita, as obtained from the CIA World Factbook.[6] This index is often considered a good indicator of a country's standard of living. To participate in crowd-mapping, citizens must be able to afford the technology (i.e., a desktop computer and an Internet connection) in the first place, so we expect GDP-pc to manifest itself in relation to *who* the OSM contributors of a country are (how many of them, with respect to the country population), and *where* (how spread) edits are across the whole territory (the poorer the country, the more geographically clustered the edits are likely to be, around a few centers of relative wealthier status).

Self-Expression Index (SEI). As our fourth factor, we use the Self-Expression Index measured by Inglehart and Baker [15] using data collected by the World Value Survey [1]. This survey provides a comprehensive country-level measurement of major areas of human concern, from religion to politics, from economics to social life. After analysing the data, Inglehart and Baker found that most of the cross-national variance in the survey data could be explained using the Self-Expression Index. Intuitively, the higher the score, the greater the extent to which subjective well-being and quality of life take precedence over basic survival values, such as economic and physical security (which tend to be taken for granted in most post-industrial societies). We expect our analysis to highlight a significant correlation between SEI and *how much* OSM users contribute.

Pace of Life Index (PLI). The fifth and final cultural factor we consider is Pace of Life Index, originally defined by Levine et. al [19] as a combination of walking speed, work speed, and accuracy of public clocks. The index was computed for 31 countries, so that the higher the pace, the lower the PLI value (to be interpreted as number of seconds). Many Western Europe countries (e.g., Switzerland, Germany, Sweden) as well as Japan exhibit very fast pace of life (very low PLI), while Latin American ones have a much slower paced lifestyle (high PLI). Reinecke et. al. have analysed the relationship between pace of life and users' participation in group decision making [28], and indeed found that, in countries with faster pace, the number of Doodle polls completed per Internet user is higher. PLI has been widely analysed in cross-cultural studies of users behaviours in online communities [5]; we have thus chosen to include it in our analysis, despite the fact we have this value for only 16 of the selected 35 countries. Even in this restricted sample, we expect PLI to manifest itself in a variety of ways: from *how much* OSM users edit, to *when/where* edits enter the map.

Figure 4 illustrates how the five cultural/economic factors above vary among the countries under exam – the darker the shade, the higher the corresponding factor. As it emerges from these maps, these factors are not independent of each other: for example, countries with higher GDP per capita also exhibit higher individualism index, while countries with lower GDP per capita tend to have a slower pace of life (higher PLI). Table 1 details the dependency (measured as Pearson Correlation coefficients) between these five factors. We note that, as often the case when performing cross-cultural analysis, we risk stereotyping the people within a country based on the country's dominant cultural values [5];

[6]`https://www.cia.gov/library/publications/the-world-factbook`, last access: 27/05/2013.

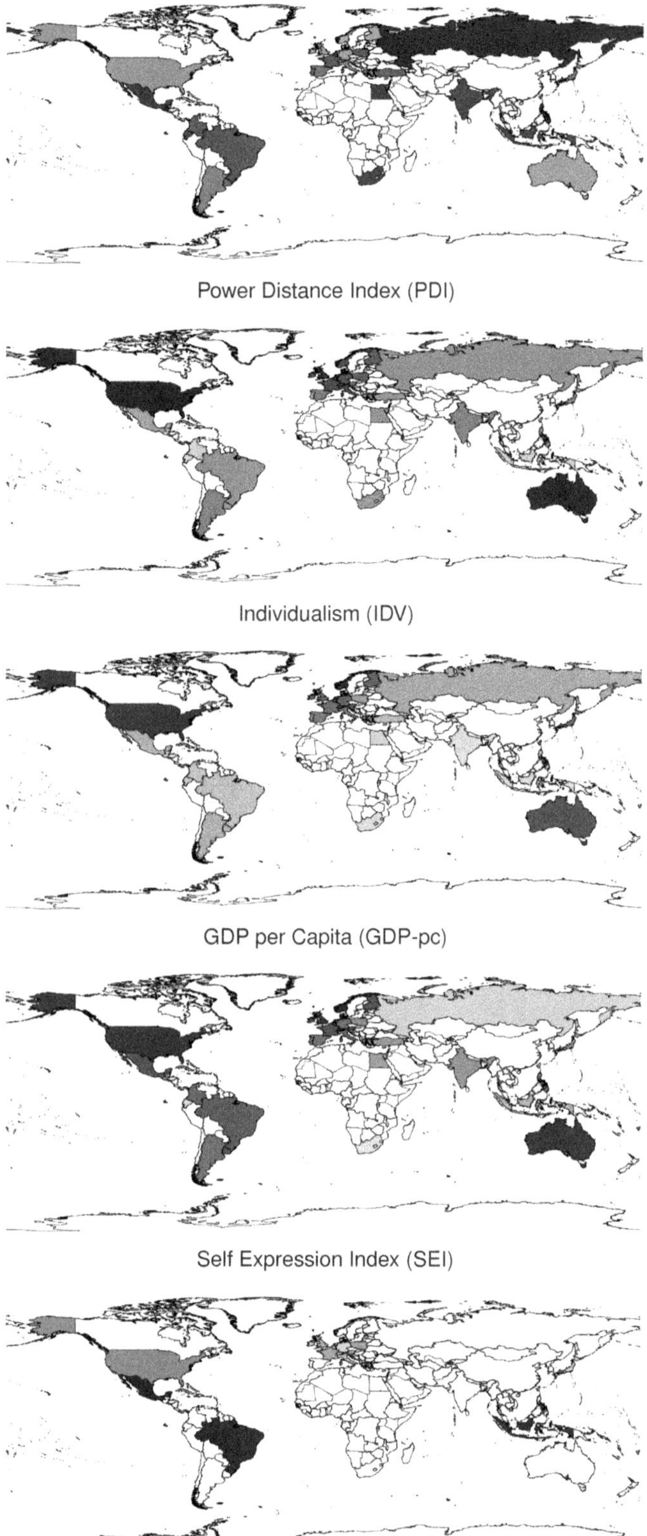

Figure 4. Choropleth Maps of Countries' Cultural/Economic factors – the darker the shade, the higher the corresponding index. White areas mark countries that have not been included in the study.

however, the purpose of the study is not to capture within-country cultural differences, but rather to analyse contrasting behavioural tendencies. As OSM users have been observed to be a rather homogeneous group of people (i.e., young, male, educated, in full-time employment and with Internet access) [3], we may actually assume they have a comparable sub-culture, so that potential differences in crowd-mapping behaviour between countries are indeed most likely due to the influence of cultural and economic factors.

	PDI	IDV	GDP-pc	SEI	PLI
PDI	—	-0.69 ***	-0.72 ***	-0.71 ***	0.72 ***
IDV	-0.69 ***	—	0.69 ***	0.67 ***	-0.71 ***
GDP-pc	-0.72 ***	0.69 ***	—	0.65 ***	-0.87 ***
SEI	-0.71 ***	0.67 ***	0.65 ***	—	-0.29
PLI	0.72 ***	-0.71 ***	-0.87 ***	-0.29	—

Table 1. Correlations among the cultural/economic factors with p-values codes: 0 '*' 0.001 '**' 0.01 '*' 0.05 ' ' 1**

METHODOLOGY

In order to understand to what extent crowd-mapping behaviour in OSM correlates with the cultural and economic factors described in the previous section, we adopt the following methodology. First, we describe the manifested OSM behaviour *for each country* under exam along the following dimensions.

Who the OSM Users are. We compute both the number of OSM contributors per country population, as well as the ratio of OSM users over a country Internet population. We expect the former to be strongly correlated to GDP-pc, while with the second we are partly controlling for individual economic wealth. A consistent finding in the study of collaborative-work platforms has been that a small fraction of users is responsible for the vast majority of contributions (e.g., [2, 14]). In these cases, the 80-20 rule-of-thumb is frequently found to hold: that is, less than 20% of users (often called 'power users'), are responsible for more than 80% of the content. A substantial body of research has indeed studied motivation and commitment of such participants in user-generated content systems, acknowledging the central role they play in the sustainability of such systems. In this study, we thus also compute the ratio of OSM power users over a country's population/Internet population/OSM users population. To do so, we first need to define what a OSM power user is. We proceeded in steps: first, we computed the frequency distribution of OSM user edits on a per country basis, and found them to be very similar among each other (Figure 5 shows the frequency distribution plots – in log scale – for two sample countries, France and United Kingdom). We then ordered OSM contributors per country (from the most to the least active), computed their cumulative ratio of contributions, and finally considered 'power users' the minimum number of contributors required to cover 80% of the country's OSM content. If we look at Figure 6, where the cumulative contribution plots are illustrated for the case of France and United Kingdom, we find that power users are those that make more than 100 edits. We used this threshold across all 35 countries; in all countries, the OSM power user population was less than 10% of the OSM population.

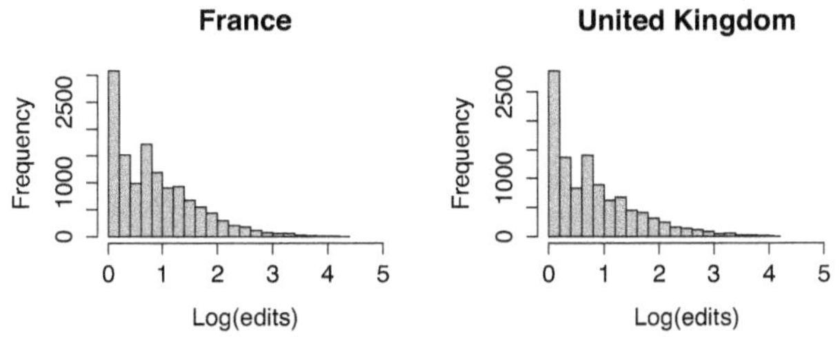

Figure 5. Frequency distribution of OSM user edits

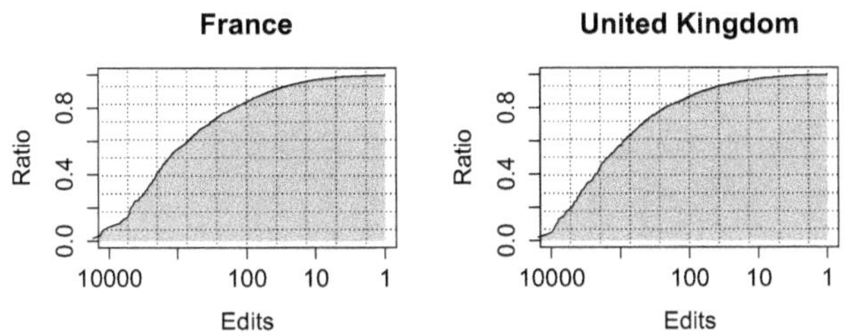

Figure 6. Cumulative ratio of contributions of OSM users

How long/how much OSM users edit. We describe the 'average OSM contributors' in each country in terms of: longevity, that is, the time passed between their first and last edit; and the average number of edits their perform during their OSM lifetime. We also consider the 'average OSM power contributors' separately, and compute how long/how much they edit on average. As these values follow a power law distribution, we compute their geometric mean.

How the edits themselves are performed. In studies of Wikipedia, cultural factors have been linked to the proportion of add/modify/delete actions performed on articles. In OSM, the objects being edited are of a much simpler nature than Wikipedia articles, so we look at the following two editorial characteristics instead: first, the (in)completeness of the information provided. In OSM, nodes only require to have a name and spatial (latitude/longitude) information, while the amenity type (e.g., cafe, school, etc) is optional. Previous studies have shown that the less 'complete' the information being provided about a POI, the lower its spatial positional accuracy [24]. We thus compute the proportion of OSM POI edits within a country where the amenity type field is left blank. Second, we compute the number of edits that modify information previously entered.

When the edits are performed. We capture two different aspects: first, we look at how quickly the OSM user base grows in the first year of OSM adoption in that country; second, we capture how consistent the influx of contributions is over time. To quantify the former, we compute the average monthly contributors that OSM attracted during its first year of usage across each country. To quantify the latter, we count how many edits are performed in each month, then compute the ratio of the Simpson diversity index[7] on such vector of values over the number of considered months (the higher the *normalised temporal* diversity, the lower the burstiness of contributions over time).

Where the edits are performed. Finally, we compute how spatially clustered edits are in a country. To do so, we divided each country into 5Km by 5Km grid cells, computed how many edits fall within each cell, then calculated the Simpson diversity index on such vector of values (the higher the *spatial* diversity, the more geographically distributed edits are over the whole country territory). Note that, depending on the country's territory, there might be areas that have no urbanisation at all (e.g., deserts), and would thus require no edits. To account for this, we normalise the computed value by the size of the country's urbanised areas.

Table 2 summarises all the above mentioned parameters, together with a plot of their frequency distribution. We also list three countries following the top/bottom values.

Once parameters were determined, we computed the Pearson Correlation between the above OSM characteristics and the previously selected cultural/economic factors (for parameters that were moderately/strongly skewed, we first computed the square root/log value); a complete set of results is shown in Table 3. As Table 1 previously highlighted, cultural/economic factors are correlated with each other. To better understand what cultural/economic factors are most strongly linked to what OSM characteristics, we proceeded as follow: for each OSM characteristic, we built a series of regressions, starting from the simplest (using as single dependent variable the cultural/economic factor with the highest correlation value as per Table 3), then adding one by one the other factors. Each time, we checked the adjusted R^2 value of the more complex models, to see if the newly added cultural/economic factors where indeed improving the model, or whether they were not adding any information w.r.t. the OSM characteristic under exam. We elaborate on these results in the next section.

RESULTS

Who are OSM users?

To begin with, we look at the penetration of OSM in a country, in terms of the number of OSM users, both relative to the country population, and relative to the number of Internet users in that country. We expect the former ratio to have strong correlation with GDP-pc: citizens must be able to afford the technology in the first place, so that richer countries are more likely to have a larger user base. However, with the second ratio we partly control for wealth, so that we should be able to observe what other cultural values are correlated with OSM engagement. The first two rows of Table 3 show the result of these correlations. As expected, GDP-pc has a very strong correlation (0.78) with the former, but less so with the latter (0.56). It is interesting to observe that at the top of the scale, countries such as Austria, Germany and Switzerland (characterised by a high GDP-pc), exhibit the highest penetration of OSM users, both relative to the country population and relative to the number of Internet users in that country. This is however not the case when looking at countries scoring lowest on this OSM factor. To understand if other cultural

[7]The Simpson diversity index is a measure that reflects how many different entries there are in a data set and the value is maximized when all entries are equally high [29].

	Parameter	Min	Distribution	Max	Bottom 3 countries	Top 3 countries
Who	OSM users per population	2.0e-06		8.2e-04	India, Egypt, Indonesia	Austria, Germany, Switzerland
	OSM users per million internet users	22		1097	Japan, Egypt, Brazil	Austria, Switzerland, Germany
	OSM power users per population	1.1e-07		6.1e-05	India, Egypt, Sierra Leone	Austria, Germany, Switzerland
	OSM power users per million internet users	0.80		82	Egypt, Sierra Leone, Taiwan	Austria, Germany, Switzerland
	OSM power users per OSM users	0.023		0.11	Uruguay, Egypt, Sierra Leone	Japan, Germany, Finland
How much	Geometric mean edits per user	2.4		7.9	Sierra Leone, Uruguay, Egypt	Germany, Portugal, Finland
	Geometric mean edits per power user	204		571	Portugal, Indonesia, Taiwan	Sierra Leone, Russia, UK
How long	Geometric mean user lifetime (days)	2.1		7.8	India, Mexico, Sierra Leone	Germany, Switzerland, Austria
	Geometric mean power user lifetime (days)	7.0		316	India, Guatemala, Colombia	Sierra Leone, UK, Germany
How	Null amenity ratio	0.43		0.77	UK, Guatemala, Philippines	Sierra Leone, Turkey, Egypt
	Overwrite ratio	0.19		0.50	Sierra Leone, US, Turkey	Finland, Austria, Germany
When	Speed of adoption (active users per month)	0.25		16	Guatemala, Ecuador, Sierra Leone	Finland, UK, Spain
	Normalised temporal diversity	0.054		0.89	Egypt, Sierra Leone, Guatemala	UK, Germany, Switzerland
Where	Normalised spatial diversity	2.5e-05		5.5e-03	Australia, Brazil, Russia	Belgium, Switzerland, Netherlands

Table 2. Description of our parameters

		PDI		IDV		GDP-pc		SEI		PLI	
Who	OSM users per population	-0.71	***	0.60	***	0.78	***	0.64	***	-0.77	***
	OSM users per Internet users	-0.53	***	0.46	**	0.56	***	0.52	**	-0.57	*
	OSM power users per population	-0.74	***	0.63	***	0.78	***	0.62	***	-0.75	***
	OSM power users per Internet users	-0.59	***	0.51	***	0.61	***	0.50	**	-0.63	**
	OSM power users per OSM users	-0.37	*	0.46	**	0.48	**	0.19		-0.57	*
How much	Geometric mean edits per user	-0.23		0.45	**	0.34	*	0.04		-0.67	*
	Geometric mean edits per power user	-0.04		0.13		-0.04		-0.09		-0.63	**
How long	Geometric mean user lifetime	-0.62	***	0.69	***	0.66	***	0.44	*	-0.68	**
	Geometric mean power user lifetime	-0.29		0.39	*	0.21		0.26		-0.53	*
How	Null amenity ratio	0.37	*	-0.41	*	-0.38	*	-0.42	*	0.12	
	Overwrite ratio	-0.44	**	0.40	*	0.40	*	0.29		-0.67	**
When	Speed of adoption	-0.40	*	0.21		0.46	**	0.40	*	-0.40	
	Normalised temporal diversity	-0.59	***	0.68	***	0.69	***	0.62	***	-0.62	*
Where	Normalised spatial diversity	-0.38	*	0.33		0.57	***	0.30		-0.85	***

Table 3. Pearson Correlation with p-values codes (0 '*' 0.001 '**' 0.01 '*' 0.05 ' ' 1)**

factors are correlated with OSM adoption, we computed a series of multiple linear regressions: we first added Pace of Life Index (second highest correlation in Table 3) to GDP-pc, but found the model not improving over the basic one with GDP-pc only; we then discovered that by adding Power Distance Index we improved the model the most (adjusted R^2 growing from 0.29 to 0.36). Indeed, PDI has a strong negative correlation (-0.53) with OSM users per Internet population. Although there might well be hidden factors that this correlation analysis does not capture, we might speculate that countries where people do not perceive a strong hierarchical structure and division of power (low PDI) are more likely to take part in collaborative work, as represented by OSM.

To illustrate this further, we plot in Figure 7 the number of OSM contributors per full population (left) and the number of OSM contributors per Internet population (right) as they vary with GDP per capita (x axis) and Power Distance Index (size of the circle). As shown, when we consider the correlation between GDP per capita and the number of OSM contributors per country population (left), there are very few outliers, reflecting the strong correlation between the two parameters. However, when considering the correlation between GDP per capita and the number of OSM contributors per Internet population (right), the number of outliers increases significantly, signalling that GDP per capita alone is no longer able to capture OSM user engagement. If we look at the outlier countries, we observe that many countries with low Power Distance Index cluster above the fitted line (and viceversa).

We then repeated the same analysis as above, but focusing on OSM *power* users (rows 3 and 4 of Table 3): results are very similar to those obtained when looking at the broader OSM population, confirming the above observations.

Finally, we looked at the number of OSM power users over the OSM population itself, to see if the emerging contributors' roles in OSM vary between countries. We observe a strong negative correlation with PLI (-0.57): that is, the more 'relaxed' the pace of the country (high PLI), the lower the number of power users within the OSM user base, as if people would not add 'OSM mapping' to their schedules as a frequent activity to engage in. Rather, most OSM contributors engage equally in these countries. For countries where we do not have PLI values (recall we have PLI for only 16 out of 35), the other factor that counts the most is GDP-pc instead: in this case, wealthier countries also have a higher number of power users.

We have so far analysed the composition of the OSM user base, but have not yet looked into how much they contribute when they do engage. We address this next.

How much do they edit?

We have computed the average number of OSM contributions made every month. The higher the average, the higher the continuous engagement with the system, the higher the OSM long-term sustainability overall (a recent study conducted for the city London, UK, has found that OSM users who do not edit for 3 to 6 months tend to leave the system entirely [14]). We first consider the whole OSM user base, and computed the geometric mean of monthly edits. As shown in Table 3, PLI is again negatively correlated with this OSM characteristic (-0.67): not only countries with a slower pace have fewer power users, they also overall make much fewer contributions

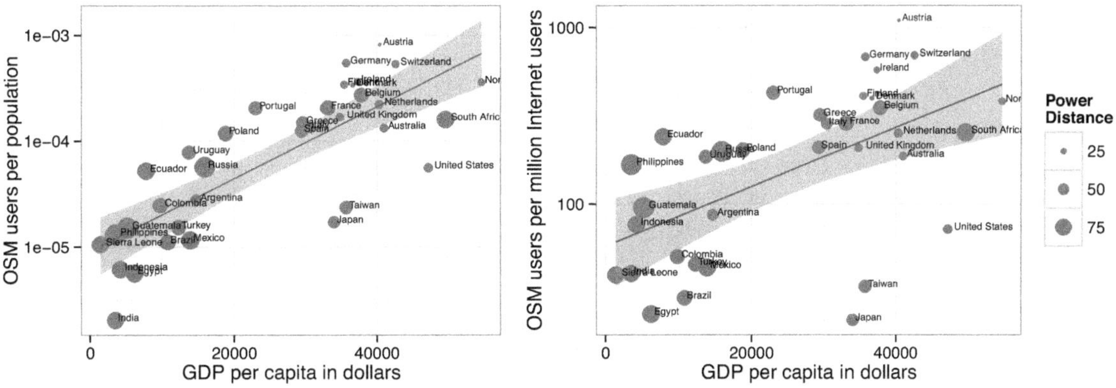

Figure 7. Engagement of OSM user around the world

than countries where people tend to fit many different activities in their daily life. Using linear regressions, we found that power distance was also useful to further understand this OSM characteristic: that is, the higher the power distance in the country, the fewer the average number of contributions per OSM user. Editors from countries such as Uruguay, Egypt and Sierra Leone, characterised by a slow pace of life and high power distance, tend to edit significantly less than contributors from Germany, Portugal and Finland (i.e., countries with faster pace of life and lower power distance). Based on this finding, we might speculate that in countries where citizens expect the few in power to 'do something', they are less apt to take the initiative to contribute to crowd-sourcing platforms like OSM, where users are all equally expected to contribute.

We repeated this analysis focusing on power users only. As observed when looking at the whole OSM user base, we found PLI to be negative correlated with this OSM characteristic (-0.63): both normal and power users from countries with a slower pace make much fewer contributions than those from countries with more active lifestyles. Using linear regression, we then tried to see if other cultural factors (e.g., power distance) were related to how much power users edit: in contrast to what observed with the whole OSM user base, we found no other cultural factors to be significant.

How long do they remain engaged?

We next analyse OSM user engagement in terms of how long users keep contributing to the map (that is, the time passed between the first and last edit of each user). We first consider all OSM users, and compute the geometric mean of their lifespan. As shown in Table 3, this factor has the strongest correlation with Individualism (0.69): we might speculate that editors from countries where one's goals and desires are highly valued, tend to remain engaged for longer. For example, OSM users from countries such as Germany, Switzerland and Austria, which are characterised by high individualism, are those who are engaged for the longest time; this is in contrast to users from countries such as India, Mexico, and Sierra Leone, where individualism is low instead, and so is OSM users' longevity. The only other factor that significantly contributes to this OSM characteristic, when performing multiple linear regression, is power distance (correlation -0.62): OSM users tend to disengage with collaborative-work platforms quicker, if they come from countries where the norm is to have the few in power to take charge of common-good tasks.

When we look at power users' longevity, Individualism is confirmed as an important cultural factor; however, pace of life bears even stronger relevance (-0.53): power users remain engaged longer in countries with active and full lifestyles (low PLI).

How are the edits performed?

Having characterised OSM users, we now look at their edits. The first aspect we are interested in is the 'null amenity ratio': previous studies have shown that OSM objects with a non-null amenity field also have higher spatial accuracy [24]. Are there cultural/economic factors that would enable us to expect lower null amenity ratio (thus higher accuracy) for the countries under exam? As Table 3 shows, Self-Expression Index has the highest (negative) correlation (-0.42): we might speculate that in countries that particularly care about quality of life and subjective well-being, OSM edits tend to be conscientiously done (lower null amenity ratio). Adding other factors(e.g., PDI, GDP-pc, IDV) to a regression model does not improve the model further.

The second characteristic we look at is the overwrite ratio, or simply the number of 'modify/delete' actions over the total number of edits. When performing a mapping task, we need to be aware of the saturation effect: if the digital map is near complete, modify actions are likely to be more frequent than add actions, relative to a country whose digital map is still very sparse. We do not know the level of saturation of OSM in the countries under exam; according to a recent study [23], the OSM map in London, UK, is still rather sparse in terms of Points-of-Interest, and the UK is the country where OSM was born and where it has been edited the most. We could then speculate that OSM is not yet at a stage where saturation emerges. In this case, two cultural factors are most strongly (negatively) correlated with the overwrite ratio: first, the Pace of Life Index; that is, the more 'relaxed' the pace of the country (high PLI), the less engaged OSM users are in overwrites. Second, the Power Distance Index: in line with findings from Pfeil et al. [26] for Wikipedia, people from countries with high power distance are less likely to modify/delete others' work, as if they do not feel to have the power or right to do so.

When are contributions made?

We are next interested in looking at the speed of adoption of OSM. To do so, we look at the first year of use of OSM in each selected country, and compute the monthly average number of unique users that contribute to the map. As Table 3 shows, the factor that most strongly correlates with this metric is GDP per capita; that is, OSM penetration is faster in richer countries. There are a number of factors we cannot control for and that might bias results (e.g., local events organised by OSM to recruit more participants). We re-computed the correlation, after discarding countries where we knew the OSM organisation to be particularly active in terms of recruitment campaigns (i.e., UK, US, Germany, France); even in this case, results were confirmed, with GDP-pc being the single most relevant factor in explaining OSM speed of adoption.

We also correlated cultural/economic factors with a metric aimed at capturing the 'burstiness' of contributions; we do so as we expect burstiness to be low (i.e., Simpson temporal diversity to be high), in countries where OSM has become a mature and stably-adopted technology, with a solid and loyal user base whose contributions keep coming in over time (and predictably so). Viceversa, burstiness may be high in countries where the OSM user base is very volatile, with large contributions sometimes coming in, followed by periods with near no activity, so that the long-term sustainability of the map is much more difficult to predict. Regression analysis shows that two factors are most accountable for high diversity (low burstiness): GDP-pc and Self-Expression, that is, the higher the wealth and well-being of the country, the more organic the growth of the map. Countries such as United Kingdom, Germany and Switzerland, that are characterised by high GDP-pc and high Self-Expression, are in the top three position for low 'burstiness' of contributions.

Where are contributions made?

The last OSM factor we measure is the geographic spread of the edits made on a per country basis. The lower the spatial diversity, the higher the geographic clustering of OSM user edits in a few urbanised areas; this might be problematic, as it signals that some areas are being mapped, while many others are being severely neglected. As shown in the last row of Table 3, we observe a very strong negative correlation with PLI (-0.85): that is, the faster the pace of life and work in the country (low PLI), the higher the spatial diversity; at the same time, the higher the economic affluence of a country (GDP-pc), the higher the spatial diversity. This may suggest that countries with low PLI and high GDP-pc, such as Belgium, Switzerland and Netherlands, are more uniformly developed and better connected internally, so that OSM edits cover a much wider area (relative to the country's urbanised areas).

DISCUSSION

Implications

The previous results have highlighted strong correlations between the culture and economic affluence of a country, and the way OpenStreetMap is being used within it. Although cultural and economic characteristics of a country do not capture all factors that may contribute to the observed OSM users' behaviours, they help highlighting important national differences that engineers of crowd-mapping initiatives should consider to account for cross-cultural differences. We elaborate on them below.

On User Engagement. Our analysis has revealed that GDP per capita is negatively correlated with the size of the OSM user base severely. Once we control for that (by computing the ratio of OSM users over Internet users), power distance is negatively correlated with the size of the participating crowd. A design question we may then ask is how to enlarge the user base in this context. Word-of-mouth dissemination is unlikely to attract new contributors, as the task at hand (i.e., building a map of the world) is possibly perceived as one to be undertaken by 'those in power', rather than by all citizens. Public recruitment campaigns, backed up by people or institutions that are highly regarded within countries with high PDI, may have a better chance of succeed in this goal. Having the financial means to acquire the technology needed remains a hindrance, but mapping does not necessarily have to be done with personal devices. Indeed, schools could make use of OSM to teach subjects such as geography, while engaging new users in the mapping task.

Power distance has a strong negative correlation not only with the size of the user base, but also with how much they contribute. As mentioned above, being asked to contribute by those in power may act as good motivator to start engaging users more. Further research is needed to evaluate to what extent we can rely on intrinsic motivation to contribute (as OSM does now), and to what extent reward systems should be brought in instead, to stimulate and to improve the user engagement within the collaborative work platform. In countries with high power distance index, rank in a society is usually highly regarded, so that leveraging a (virtual) social status within the OSM community could be used as reward system to foster user engagement: for example, from new user, to mayor of an area, to curator of content (as in Wikipedia). This may also help address another issue for which Power Distance seemed 'culpable', that is, the short lifetime of OSM users.

Apart from PDI, Pace of Life is correlated with the amount of contributions people make: countries with a slow pace do not seem to add crowd-mapping to the range of activities they wish to allocate their time to. If this is indeed the case, a possible venue for exploration in this case is implicit crowd-sourcing, that is, embedding the crowd-mapping task within (or disguised as) another task they would normally do anyway (e.g., by children in schools, as part of teaching a geography class).

On Task Quality. A common concern in crowd-sourcing activities is related to the quality of the task, once performed by skilled employees, and now done by any volunteer. Quality in OSM can be measured in a variety of ways, including accuracy and coverage. We did not explicitly measure these two metrics as part of this work, but we can consider 'null amenity ratio' as proxy for the former, and spatial diversity ratio as proxy for the latter. Null amenity ratio is lowest (expected highest accuracy) when Self-Expression Index is highest. What interventions can we plan in countries where survival needs dominate over subjective well-being instead? We may speculate that OSM users in such countries do not have the time to carefully edit OSM objects, pressed by other more basic needs. This is a case where a different design may easily help: for example, using a voting mechanism so that a new edit is not immediately added to the map, but first needs to be checked and approved by others for correctness. Voting may also be seen as a less strong action than a delete or modify, and might thus help in those countries where high power distance results in a very low overwrite ratio.

As for spatial diversity, we found that countries with lower economic affluence, as well as countries with slower pace of life, tend to have their edits clustered around few areas, with many other urban areas being largely neglected. To remedy this, a form of more 'directed' crowd-sourcing could be designed, similar to what Cyclopath first tried [25, 27]: rather than letting the OSM task be completely self-driven, attention of the OSM community could be explicitly driven towards more neglected areas. This could be subtle (e.g., highlighting neglected areas on the map), or be explicitly linked to the reward system mentioned above.

On Technology Adoption. Finally, we look at the speed of penetration of OSM and the level of burstiness of its use. In both cases, the factor that mostly correlates with these OSM characteristics is GDP per capita: the richer the country, the faster the technology adoption and the stabilisation of its use. When similar crowd-mapping initiatives are launched in countries of low GDP-pc, it may be worth planning low-cost recruitment campaigns coupled with shared access to mapping technologies, so to speed up the penetration of the crowd-mapping initiatives. Where there is a simple way of linking the collaborative task to educational institutions and their practices, this may represent a happy combination.

Limitations

The results presented in this study suffer from three main limitations: first, we acknowledge that the results presented in this paper do not imply any causality between a country's cultural and economic factors *and* its OSM user characteristics. There might indeed exist other underlying factors that contribute to the above correlations and that our analysis does not fully capture. For example, it might be that OSM is better known in Western countries than in the Eastern ones, and these Western countries also happen to have higher GDP-pc and individualism. Despite this limitation, we believe this study offers valuable insights on the differing crowd-mapping behaviours that emerge around the world; cultural and economic characteristics of the analysed countries represent a useful lens through which to present and quantify results.

Second, one may argue that a user could live in a country while editing mostly another, so that the inference scheme we use to associate a user to its home country (with related cultural and economic factors) would fail as an effect of the globalisation of online communities. However, there have been quite a few studies now, especially on Wikipedia, showing that most contributors to this online collaborative platform actually exhibit strong geographic locality in the articles they edit [11, 20, 12]. When the task undertaken has an even stronger geographic component than Wikipedia (i.e., mapping POIs), we may assume geographic distance to matter even more.

Third, assuming that the geographic boundaries of a country act as a sort of containment for it cultural and economic values (that we then equally apply to all its citizens), may attract criticism. This issue has indeed been acknowledged to be a limitation in any cross-cultural studies [13]; however, despite the fact that geographical countries may not be the best way to study culture, these are often the only kind of units available for comparison.

Future Work

The study presented in this paper has looked at users' engagement with OSM, while remaining agnostic of *what* people edit in different countries. A preliminary investigation on the types of OSM objects that people map around the world revealed that the range is indeed huge: from topographic information (e.g., roads, rivers), to basic services (e.g., schools, hospitals), from leisure offerings (e.g, restaurants, cafes), to possibly 'unusual' and very 'personal value' information (e.g., trees, benches, etc.). A future direction of research is to analyse what (combination of) categories of OSM objects are being edited around the world, possibly revealing interesting correlations between national characteristics of the examined countries and the type of information maps being created. A second direction of research we intend to pursue is to understand the within-country characteristics of crowd-mapping: in particular, we wish to quantify how spatially concentrated the contributions of OSM users are, whether this concentration depends on countries' characteristics (e.g., GDP-pc), and/or whether it varies with the type of information being mapped (i.e., some categories having very localised value only).

Acknowledgment

This work was partly supported by the Knowledge and Innovation Community EIT ICT Labs, and by the Intel Collaborative Research Institute on Sustainable Connected Cities.

REFERENCES

1. W. V. S. Association et al. World values survey 1981-2008 official aggregate v. 20090901. *Madrid: ASEP/JDS*, 2009.
2. S. L. Bryant, A. Forte, and A. Bruckman. Becoming Wikipedian: transformation of participation in a collaborative online encyclopedia. In *Proceedings of the 2005 international ACM SIGGROUP conference on Supporting group work*, GROUP '05, pages 1–10, 2005.
3. N. Budhathoki and C. Haythornthwaite. Motivation for open collaboration: Crowd and community models and the case of OpenStreetMap. *American Behavioral Scientist*, 2012.

4. C. N. Chapman and M. Lahav. International ethnographic observation of social networking sites. In *CHI'08 Extended Abstracts on Human Factors in Computing Systems*, pages 3123–3128. ACM, 2008.
5. S. E. Gallagher and T. Savage. Cross-cultural analysis in online community research: A literature review. *Computers in Human Behavior*, 2012.
6. R. Garcia-Gavilanes, D. Quercia, and A. Jaimes. Cultural Dimensions in Twitter: Time, Individualism, and Power. In *AAAI ICWSM*, July 2013.
7. J. Girres and G. Touya. Quality assessment of the French OpenStreetMap dataset. *Transactions in GIS*, 14(4):435–459, 2010.
8. M. Haklay. How good is volunteered geographical information? A comparative study of OpenStreetMap and Ordnance Survey datasets. *Environment and Planning B: Planning and Design*, 37(4):682–703, 2010.
9. E. Hall. *The Dance of Life: The Other Dimension of Time*. Anchor Books. Knopf Doubleday Publishing Group, 1984.
10. N. Hara, P. Shachaf, and K. F. Hew. Cross-cultural analysis of the wikipedia community. *Journal of the American Society for Information Science and Technology*, 61(10):2097–2108, 2010.
11. D. Hardy, J. Frew, and M. F. Goodchild. Volunteered geographic information production as a spatial process. *International Journal of Geographical Information Science*, 26(7):1191–1212, 2012.
12. B. J. Hecht and D. Gergle. On the localness of user-generated content. In *Proceedings of the 2010 ACM conference on Computer supported cooperative work*, pages 229–232. ACM, 2010.
13. G. H. Hofstede and G. Hofstede. *Culture's consequences*. SAGE Publications, Incorporated, 2001.
14. D. Hristova, G. Quattrone, A. Mashhadi, and L. Capra. The Life of the Party: Impact of Social Mapping in OpenStreetMap. In *AAAI ICWSM*, July 2013.
15. R. Inglehart and W. E. Baker. Modernization, Cultural Change, and the Persistence of Traditional Values. *American Sociological Review*, 65(1):19–51, 2000.
16. K. Karl, J. Peluchette, and C. Schlaegel. Who's posting facebook faux pas? a cross-cultural examination of personality differences. *International Journal of Selection and Assessment*, 18(2):174–186, 2010.
17. D. E. Leidner and T. Kayworth. A Review of Culture in Information Systems Research: Toward a Theory of Information Technology Culture Conflict. *Management Information Systems Quarterly*, 3(2):357–399, 2006.
18. R. Levine. *A Geography of Time: The Temporal Misadventures of a Social Psychologist, Or how Every Culture Keeps Time Just a Little Bit Differently*. BasicBooks, 1997.
19. R. V. Levine and A. Norenzayan. The pace of life in 31 countries. *Journal of cross-cultural psychology*, 30(2):178–205, 1999.
20. M. D. Lieberman and J. Lin. You are where you edit: Locating wikipedia contributors through edit histories. In *3rd International AAAI Conference on Weblogs and Social Media*, 2009.
21. I. Ludwig, A. Voss, and M. Krause-Traudes. A Comparison of the Street Networks of Navteq and OSM in Germany. *Advancing Geoinformation Science for a Changing World*, 1(2):65–84, 2011.
22. V. Madupu and D. O. Cooley. Cross-cultural differences in online brand communities: an exploratory study of indian and american online brand communities. *Journal of International Consumer Marketing*, 22(4):363–375, 2010.
23. A. Mashhadi, G. Quattrone, and L. Capra. Putting Ubiquitous Crowd-sourcing into Context. In *Proceedings of the 2013 Conference on Computer Supported Cooperative Work*, pages 611–622, 2013.
24. A. Mashhadi, G. Quattrone, L. Capra, and P. Mooney. On the accuracy of urban crowd-sourcing for maintaining large-scale geospatial databases. In *Proceedings of the 8th International Symposium on Wikis and Open Collaboration*, WikiSym '12, pages 15:1–15:10, 2012.
25. K. Panciera, M. Masli, and L. Terveen. "How should i go from ___ to ___ without getting killed?:" motivation and benefits in open collaboration. In *Proceedings of the 7th International Symposium on Wikis and Open Collaboration*, WikiSym '11, pages 183–192, 2011.
26. U. Pfeil, P. Zaphiris, and C. S. Ang. Cultural differences in collaborative authoring of wikipedia. *Journal of Computer-Mediated Communication*, 12(1):88–113, 2006.
27. R. Priedhorsky, M. Masli, and L. Terveen. Eliciting and focusing geographic volunteer work. In *Proceedings of the International Conference on Supporting Group Work*. ACM, 2010.
28. K. Reinecke, M. K. Nguyen, A. Bernstein, M. Näf, and K. Z. Gajos. Doodle around the world: online scheduling behavior reflects cultural differences in time perception and group decision-making. In *Proceedings of the 2013 Conference on Computer Supported Cooperative Work*, pages 45–54, 2013.
29. E. H. Simpson. Measurement of diversity. *Nature*, 163:688–688, 1949.
30. D. Zielstra and A. Zipf. A comparative study of proprietary geodata and volunteered geographic information for germany. In *Proceedings of the 13th International Conference on Geographic Information Science*, 2010.

Aesthetic Capital: What Makes London Look Beautiful, Quiet, and Happy?

Daniele Quercia
Yahoo Labs, Barcelona, Spain
dquercia@acm.org

Neil O'Hare
Yahoo Labs, Barcelona, Spain
nohare@yahoo-inc.com

Henriette Cramer
Yahoo Labs, Sunnyvale, USA
henriette@yahoo-inc.com

ABSTRACT
In the 1960s, Lynch's "The Image of the City" explored what impression US city neighborhoods left on its inhabitants. The scale of urban perception studies until recently was considerably constrained by the limited number of study participants. We here present a crowdsourcing project that aims to investigate, at scale, which visual aspects of London neighborhoods make them appear beautiful, quiet, and/or happy. We collect votes from over 3.3K individuals and translate them into quantitative measures of urban perception. In so doing, we quantify each neighborhood's aesthetic capital. By then using state-of-the-art image processing techniques, we determine visual cues that may cause a street to be perceived as being beautiful, quiet, or happy. We identify effects of color, texture and visual words. For example, the amount of greenery is the most positively associated visual cue with each of three qualities; by contrast, broad streets, fortress-like buildings, and council houses tend to be associated with the opposite qualities (ugly, noisy, and unhappy).

Author Keywords
urban informatics; crowdsourcing; aesthetics; visual, urban aesthetics; cities; streets.

ACM Classification Keywords
H.5.m. Information Interfaces and Presentation (e.g. HCI): Miscellaneous

General Terms
Human Factors; Design; Measurement.

INTRODUCTION
Appearances matter in people's perceptions and affective experience of their urban environments. Visual features can distinguish one locale from another, and help people perceive a city as unique and recognizable. Doersch *et al.* [4], for example, identify visual elements such as windows, balconies, and street signs that distinguish Paris or London from other cities (e.g., street signs in Paris, Victorian houses in London). The visual qualities of urban facades not only affect aesthetic responses and people's judgments of urban locale [34], but also have stark social and psychological effects on their inhabitants [14].

CSCW'14, February 15–19, 2014, Baltimore, MD, USA.
Copyright 2014 ACM 978-1-4503-2540-0/14/02. . .$15.00.
http://dx.doi.org/10.1145/2531602.2531613

One famous theory of urban appearance and social effects was articulated by Kelling & Coles [12]. Their theory of 'broken windows' posits that cues of disorder in public are highly visible and constitute a salient marker of urban spaces. The idea behind the theory is that neighborhood *appearances* drive the reality of neighborhood *safety*: one broken window leads to another broken window and, in turn, to future crime. This theory was not confined to academic circles but made its way into public policy, starting from the city of New York. However, basing public policy on stark notions of aesthetics and cracking down on minor transgressions has notable social and cultural downsides [27]. Nevertheless, since the importance of visual features in perceptions of the built environment has been given a major role in public policy, understanding their effects is key.

To explore visual assessments at scale, we make a number of contributions. We have built a crowdsourcing website under `UrbanGems.org` to collect ratings about how beautiful, quiet, and happy London's streets are. It picks up two random locations from Google Street View and Geograph[1], and ask users which one is more beautiful, quiet, or happy: we choose those three qualities as proxies for urban aspects that have been consistently discussed in 1960s urban studies. We have collected subjective aesthetic judgments of different parts of the city from more than 3.3K users. The goal of this paper is to focus on a specific aspect of this crowdsourcing effort; that is, whether it is possible to *automatically* extract aesthetically-informative features of annotated city scenes. To this end, we apply three state-of-the-art computer vision techniques on each urban scene, and identified effects of color, texture and a number of 'visual words'. We find, for example, that nature-made elements (generally characterized by diagonal and smooth lines) tend to be associated with happy scenes. By contrast, man-made elements (generally characterized by horizontal and vertical lines) tend to be associated with ugly scenes. We also extract visual patches (called 'visual words') from our urban scenes and find that visual words in happy scenes are associated with Victorian houses, public gardens, red bricks, and residential trees, while those in unhappy scenes are associated with council housing and highway road signs. After this visual analysis, three architects are interviewed and asked to reflect on the findings

[1]`http://www.geograph.org.uk`: geographically representative photographs of the whole Great Britain and Ireland.

presented here to gain a perspective from practicing domain experts on the applicability and (dis)advantages of our approach.

Our analysis is an exploration of how various techniques could assist the design of urban environments by, for example, identifying features with positive or negative effects. It might also result in practical applications in the city context such as affective route recommendation [24, 23], and automatic aesthetic profiling of streets and neighborhoods - while also considering the limitations of such automatic approaches.

RELATED WORK

Beyond Lynch's [15] classic notion of legibility and the ease with which a city can be 'read' in terms of layout, aesthetics are of crucial importance in people's evaluation of their surroundings [19, 32, 34]. Various urban planning and urban design researchers have established criteria that affect people's preferences for certain environments, and their aesthetic responses [34, 18].

The perception of 'urban disorder' from trash, abandoned property, and decay, for example, has been taken as a signal of a breakdown of the local social order [30]. Visual qualities can also affect people's mental states in a physical environment. Lindal and Hartig [14] investigated the effects of architectural variation and physical building attributes (e.g., height) on judgments of the (imagined) psychologically restorative quality of a street scene. Even when considering the inherent social and cultural biases in what is considered to be aesthetically pleasing, researchers have found a persistent correlation of perceived disorder with individual-level affective outcomes, with psychological distress [25], and with perceived powerlessness [6].

Authors such as Weber [34] identified factors such as vegetation, uniformity in style, scale, and symmetry as primary factors in aesthetic judgments. Nasar [19] proposed aesthetic programming could help develop guidelines for visual qualities to gain specific factions from different populations in particular contexts. They find that, to optimize for 'pleasantness', moderate complexity, references to historical elements, removing artificial nuisances, and ordering elements would all be beneficial. To increase interestingness and excitement, more natural materials, higher complexity and atypicality, as well as ordering and familiar elements would help.

So far the most detailed studies of perceptions of urban environments and their visual appearance have, however, relied on personal interviews and observation of city streets: for example, some researchers relied on annotations of video recordings by experts [28], while others have used participant ratings of simulated (rather than existing) street scenes [14].

Using the web to survey a large number of individuals has been recently done. Place Pulse is a website that asks binary perception questions (e.g., "Which place looks safer?") across a large number of geo-tagged images [26]. The goal is to create quantitative measures of urban perception, and results for the city of Boston and New York have been made available[2]. The authors do not focus on visual features but rather on relating socio-demographic factors to user ratings. Quercia *et al.* proposed a web game, called `UrbanOpticon.org`, that puts the recognizability of London's streets to the test. It picks up random locations from Google Street View and tests users ability to judge the location (e.g., closest subway station) [22]. By analyzing the data from the site, the authors found that areas with low recognizability significantly suffer from social problems of housing deprivation, poor living conditions, and crime.

CROWDSOURCING URBAN AESTHETICS

The main idea behind `UrbanGems.org` is that players compare a series of urban scenes and vote on which one is more beautiful, quiet or happy. Users compare two side-by-side street views from various neighborhoods around London. They must decide which scene best represents one of three qualities: happy, beauty and quiet. They can also opt for "Can't Tell", if undecided on which picture to click on.

Choosing Rating Qualities

One might well wonder why we chose to study the three qualities of beauty, quiet, and happy. For this exploration, a choice was made to return to classic urban studies, as well as more popular discussions on 'city life'.

Quiet. In the noise of a city, it might be hard to find quiet places. That is why a variety of mobile applications has been built to discover such places in big cities. The Economist 'Thinking Spaces' application allows the global community of Economist readers to create, share and explore the spaces where they think and get new ideas[3]. This has resulted in interactive maps of major cities around the world features readers' beloved thinking spaces. More recently, sound artist Jason Sweeney proposed a platform where people crowdsource and geo-locate quiet spaces, share them with their social networks, and take audio and visual snapshots. It is called Stereopublic[4] and is "an attempt to both promote 'sonic health' in our cities and offer a public guide for those who crave a retreat from crowds" - both for those in need of quietness and for people with disabilities, like autism and schizophrenia.

Beauty. In *The Death and Life of Great American Cities*, Jane Jacobs [10] offered a critique of 1950s urban planning policy and of modernism. She argued against authoritarian top-down urban planning and separation of uses (i.e., residential, industrial, commercial), while instead emphasizing the importance of mixed functions and human activity. She dedicated an entire chapter on 'Visual Order', in which, amongst other topics, she discusses how streets provide the principal visual scenes in cities, and how 'visual interruptions' can used to create visual order without sacrificing the intensity and diversity that a city's functional order demand. Visual order and harmony are linked to 'beauty', which forms the basis of our second question as it is easy for people to grasp (as opposed to concepts such as 'visual order' or 'aesthetically pleasing') and is thus amenable to an open crowd-sourcing setting. Note

[2] http://pulse.media.mit.edu/results/

[3] `http://thinkingspace.economist.com/`

[4] `http://www.stereopublic.net/`

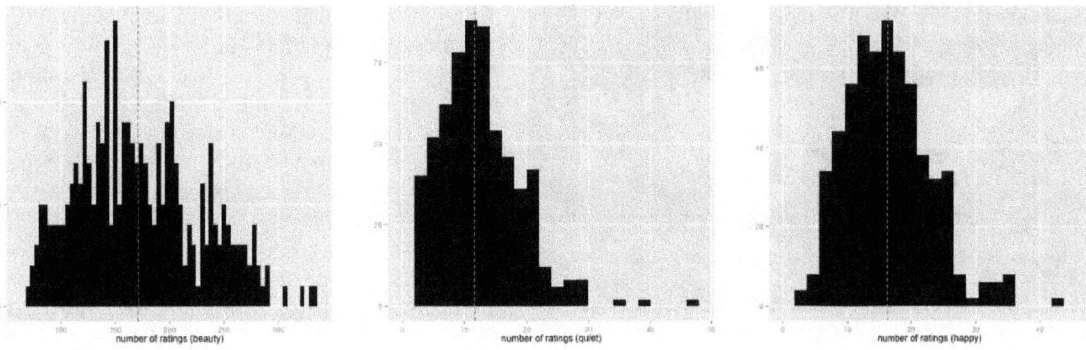

(a) Beauty (b) Quiet (c) Happy

Figure 1. Number of Answers for Each Urban Scene. The number of answers each scene has received are centered around means thanks to randomization: 171 answers per scene for beauty (default question), 12 for quiet, and 16 for happy.

that we are certainly not the first to measure perceptions of beauty. In 1967, Peterson proposed a quantitative analysis of public perceptions of neighborhood visual appearance [21]. He did so by choosing ten variables that reflected visual appearance (e.g., preference for the scene, greenery, open space, safety, beauty) and having 140 individuals rate 23 pictures of urban scenes in the Chicago metropolitan area for each of those ten variables. He found that beauty and safety are approximately collinear with preference for a scene, suggesting that "beauty of visual appearance is in fact synonymous with perception of visual pleasure and, hence, desirability of visual appearance" [21].

Happiness. Additional urban studies from the 1960s tried to systematically relate well-being in the urban environment (including happiness) to the desire for visual order, beauty, and aesthetics. In *The Image of the City* [15], Kevin Lynch illustrated what elements appeared to make cities more vivid and memorable to city dwellers. More recently, in *The Architecture of Happiness* [3], Alain de Botton dwells on how different architectural styles talk about cultural values. He analyzed how people's needs and desires manifest their ideals of *beauty* and *happiness* in architecture, considering that there is an intimate relationship between our visual taste (e.g., what we consider quiet and beautiful) and our values (e.g., search for happiness).

While we most certainly do not claim to address the full gamut of observations and proposals of the classic authors above, we here aim to explore whether some prior observations related to visual characteristics of city streets can be reproduced using crowd ratings and visual analysis.

Selecting Scenes

To avoid sparsity problems (too few answers per picture), a random scene is selected within a 300-meter radius from a subway station and within the bounding boxes of census areas. This results in 258 Google Street views and 310 Geograph images whose ratings are not sparse (the number of images is different in the two sets as individual census areas contain more than one Geograph image). To see why we choose those two sources of pictures, consider that, in general, photos might not necessarily show what they are supposed to show (representative urban scenes in each neighborhood), and some pictures might be of better quality than others. For this reason, we did not opt for Flickr images, as people often upload pictures of extremely different levels of quality and character. We instead use two kinds of pictures for which quality is comparable: Google Street View pictures captured by camera-mounted cars, and Geograph pictures provided by volunteers with the goal of mapping the whole Great Britain and Ireland in a crowdsourcing fashion. We use multiple images of the two types at the *same* locations. We find that the visual features associated with our three qualities are almost the same for the two sets of pictures, and that ratings are not correlated with objective measures of image quality - there is no correlation between images' ratings and their sharpness and contrast levels, both of which have been used as proxies for quality [36].

Setting up the site

To increase the likelihood that people will adopt the platform, we added some simple engagement strategies. Those strategies include giving points, creating a sense of freshness and of purpose. In our platform, with each selection, the user is asked to guess the percentage of other people who shared their view. The player then scores points for correct guesses. After being presented with 10 pairs of scenes, the player has completed one round and can share the resulting score on Facebook or Twitter with a single click. The purpose of the score is to facilitate the player's assessment of their performance against previous game rounds or against other players [33]. After the first round, each player is also asked to complete a small questionnaire (e.g., age, gender, location). Participants engaging in multiple rounds are identified through browser cookies, which uniquely identify users[5]. Pictures are chosen randomly to create a sense of freshness and increase replay value. In addition, for experimental sake, randomization reduces biases and leads to reliable results, producing a distribution of answers for each picture that is

[5]Unless multiple individuals use the same computer with exactly the same username. This situation, however, represents an unlikely exception.

Figure 2. Screenshot of the Crowdsourcing Task. The question "Which place do you find more beautiful?" is displayed on top of the two urban scenes. By clicking on that question, the other two questions, about quietness and happiness, are made available.

Race (%)			
White 92.1	Asian 3.1	Black 0.6	Indian 0.6
Country (%)			
UK 65.1	France 4.5	USA 4.3	Netherlands 3.2
City (%)			
London 40.3	Cambridge 6.5	Manchester 1.6	Amsterdam 1.4
Profession (%)			
Student 15.5	IT Prof 12.3	Scientist 7.5	Architect 6.6

Table 1. Statistics of Participants about Race (census terminology used), Country of Origin, City of Origin, and Profession. This data is available for those 515 participants (at most) who have been willing to provide their personal information.

centered around a typical number of answers. In our analysis, the median is of 171 answers per scene for beauty, 12 for quiet, and 16 for happy (Figure 1). These mean values are different as the default question is that on beauty, and it thus preferentially attracts more votes, while the other two are accessible from a drop-down menu. Interestingly, despite the fact that the ordering has the happiness question last, that question has still attracted more votes than the question on quietness.

To increase the sense of belonging to a community, users could post their scores on Facebook and Twitter after each round. These posts are expected to not only foster a preliminary sense of community but also increase awareness among other social media users. Additionally, users' votes are used to rank the urban scenes, and top-ranked images are shown under three different pages on the site, each of which corresponds to beautiful, quiet, and happy scenes.

Statistics after Launch

After two beta tests, we have made the final version of the platform publicly available and issued a press release in September 2012. Shortly after that, the site was featured in major newspapers and news sites, including BBC News. After 4 months, we collected data from as many as 3,301 participants: 36% connecting from London (IP addresses), 35% from the rest of UK, and 29% outside UK. A fraction of those participants (515) answered a surveyed in which they specified their personal details. The percentage of male-female for those participants is 66%-34%. Their average age was 38 years old (range: 18 - 77 years old). Compared to the 2001 UK census, our sample was fairly representative (Table 1), in that, (as per census terminology[6]) White participants were slightly overrepresented by +6.4%, and participants of Asian descent, Black, Indian, Mixed and Irish were represented in a balanced way. The top country of origin was United Kingdom (65.1%) and the top city of origin was London (40.3%). Professions were quite diverse, the most common being Student, IT Professional, Academic/Scientist, and Architect/Urbanist.

After processing 17,261 rounds of annotation (each of which annotates at most ten pairs of pictures), we rank pictures by their score for beauty, quiet, and happiness based on the fraction of votes they received. Based on those rankings, we are now able to quantify perceptions.

Quantifying urban perceptions has already been done for the concept of imaginability: in 1969, Milgram quantified recognizability (proxy for imaginability) for New York City by running a variety of small-scale experiments that resulted in collective mental maps of the city. More recently, web crowdsourcing has been used to take such an experimentation to a larger scale [22]. Since the data from this crowd-sourcing effort in London is publicly available, we are also able to correlate recognizability scores for 98 of our locations with their scores of beauty, quiet, and happiness. We find that recognizability is correlated with beauty ($r = 0.28$), quiet ($r = -0.35$), and happiness ($r = 0.14$), and those correlations are statistically significant with p-value < 10^{-3}. We are also able to compute the correlations between each pairwise combinations of the three qualities. All correlations are statistically significant (i.e., all p-values are 10^{-4}): happy-quiet has $r = 0.29$, quiet-beauty $r = 0.33$, and beauty-happy is $r = 0.64$. We find that the strongest affiliation happens to be between beauty and happiness. The intimate relationship between the two has been aptly crystallized by Stendhal in his book "On Love": "Beauty is the promise of happiness" [31].

VISUAL ANALYSIS OF SCENES

Stendhal also knew that there is not only one acceptable visual style: "There are as many styles of beauty as there are visions of happiness". In this vein, we should think about our urban environments as visual representation of our values (e.g., pursuit of happiness), that is, as the transubstantiation of our ideals into a material form. Next, we will explore this rendition of values for the city of London by studying what it is about certain neighborhoods that makes them appear to speak of beauty, quiet and, ultimately, happiness. To this end, we will start our analysis by focusing on colors and answering the following question: Which *colors* correlate the most/least with pictures of happy/quiet/beautiful scenes? After this, we analyze the texture of images to see which types of texture correlate with the same qualities. Finally, we do the same for visual words, which represent local, salient, patches in an image.

[6] `http://en.wikipedia.org/wiki/Ethnic_groups_in_the_United_Kingdom`

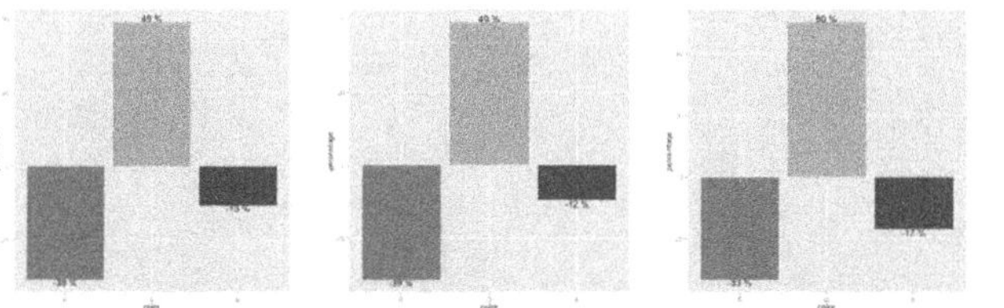

(a) Beauty (b) Quiet (c) Happy

Figure 3. The Relative (percentage) Importance of the Three Color Components. Red, green, and blue for scenes considered to be: a) beautiful; b) quiet; and c) happy. While the bars visually suggest the relative importance of the three color components, the actual values are reported in Section "Presence of Colors".

Presence of Colors

We use two methods to analyze the color distribution of images. The first method represents the color of each pixel as an RGB triplet (r, g, b), each component of which can vary from 0% (absent completely) to 100% (maximum value). If all the components are at 0% the result is black; if all are at 100%, the result is the brightest representable white. We then average each of these components separately, giving the average *redness*, *greenness* and *blueness* of the pixels in the image. Although other color spaces (e.g., HSV) are known to better approximate the human visual system, we chose the RGB here since it allows for an intuitive analysis of the amount of red, green and blue in the image.

To test each color component's contribution to the three qualities of beauty, quiet and happiness while controlling for interaction effects between colors, we build a simple linear model in which we represent a scene's rating for any given quality (e.g., beauty) as a linear combination of the ith scene's RGB triplet (r_i, g_i, b_i). That is, the regression is of the form $beauty_i = \alpha + \beta_1 r_i + \beta_2 g_i + \beta_3 b_i + \epsilon_i$, where, say, β_1 reflects the importance of red, and the corresponding relative importance is β_1 normalized by the sum of the absolute values of the three beta coefficients.

We build three linear models, one for each of the three qualities, and we report the relative importance of the triplet (r, g, b) in Figure 3 (all the beta coefficients are statistically significant at least at level 0.001). The relative importance for the triplet (r, g, b) is (-38%, 49%, -13%) for beauty, (-39%, 49%, -12%) for quiet, and (-33%, 50%, -17%) for happiness. Green (second element) is the strongest positively associated color for all the three qualities, while red and, to a lesser extent, blue are slightly negatively associated (i.e., associated with the opposite qualities of ugly, noisy, and unhappy).

The strong association of green with the three qualities is no surprise. In our urban scenes, green is associated with trees, and, more generally with nature [13]. As one cited by Komar and Melamid puts it: "Green's my favorite color - and I'm wearing green. It reminds me of forests, trees, nature, nice things like that - everything opposite of New York City." More generally, the importance of green has been widely discussed in urban studies (see [1] as an example).

To then go beyond the three primary colors, we create a 64-bin color histogram in the RGB color space by quantizing each of the color components into 4 bins. The histograms count the number of pixels that belong in each of these 64 color bins; we can consider each bin as representing a unique color in a reduced palette. Given the ratings for all pictures for beauty, quiet, and happiness, we calculate the Pearson correlation coefficient between each of the 64 colors and these ratings. To remove spurious correlations, we retain the colors that have correlation coefficient $r > 0.15$, leaving 14 colors associated with beauty, 18 with quiet, and 12 with happiness. We then build a simple linear model in which a scene's rating for any given quality (e.g., beauty) is the linear combination of those remaining colors. Figure 4 reports the β coefficients (and corresponding colors) that are statistically significant in the linear regression. Different greens (reflecting nature) are positively associated with beauty, while gray (reflecting roads) and dark red are negatively associated with it (i.e., associated with the opposite quality - ugliness). For the quality of quiet, green becomes the only color that matters (gray's importance is as low as 1%). For happiness, green is again positively associated, and grey and dark red are negatively associated (are associated with unhappy scenes). These results match the previous ones, in that green and its shades are positively associated with our three qualities.

The main drawback of color histograms is that its representation is dependent on the color of the object being studied, ignoring shape and texture. Color histograms can potentially be identical for two images depicting different objects that happen to share similar color information. In the next section, we look at image texture and answer this question: Which types of *texture* (e.g., smooth vs. sharp lines) correlates the most/least with pictures of happy/quiet/beautiful scenes?

Texture

To represent the texture of images, we follow the approach of Park *et al.* [20] and extract a global edge histogram from the region-based MPEG-7 Edge Histogram descriptor [17]. The image is divided into a number of small blocks, and blocks corresponding to edges (i.e., local areas of high contrast) are detected. These edge blocks are then further classified into four types: vertical, horizontal, 45°and 135°diagonals, and non-directional. We also count the total number of blocks that are classified as edges as a percentage of all blocks. Images with a high number of these 'classified' blocks tend to contain fine-grained details and, as such, tend to be visually rich. We will see to which extent the level of detail in a scene contributes to its beauty, happiness and quietness.

As we have done for color in the previous section, we build a linear regression model in which the dependent variable is beauty (or quiet or happiness) and the predictors are the four types of edges (i.e., horizontal, vertical, diagonal, non-directional) plus the fraction of *classified* blocks as edges. The corresponding (normalized) beta coefficients, shown in Figure 4(d), will measure the relative contribution of a certain edge type to, say, beauty. Beautiful pictures tend to not contain horizontal edges but do contain vertical, diagonal and non-directional edges. Since images depicting buildings and

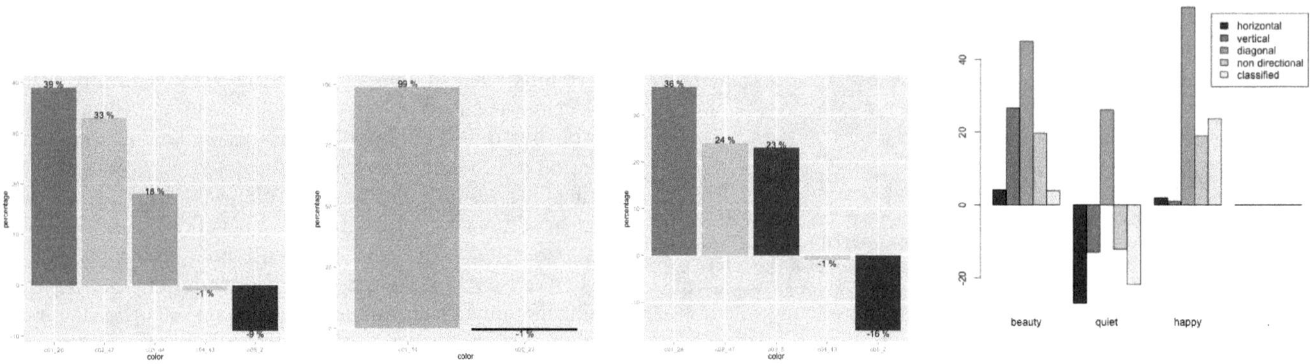

(a) Beauty (b) Quiet (c) Happy (d) Edge Types

Figure 4. The Relative (percentage) Importance of Colors. The urban scenes considered are: a) beautiful; b) quiet; and c) happy. Out of the 64 colors (our color space), we report only the colors that are correlated with the ratings for the three qualities. (d) Relative importance of different edge types.

man-made structures tend to contain many horizontal and vertical edges [16], it is quite likely that these horizontals corresponds to buildings. The fact that vertical edges contribute more than horizontal ones is somewhat puzzling: perhaps people are less likely to find vertical lines in buildings ugly than they are to find horizontal lines ugly. The positive contributions of diagonal and non-directional edges to beauty and happiness are likely explained by the presence of 'natural' scenes and shapes in those images [16]. Based on the number of classified blocks (as edges), we see that high level of detail does not contribute to beauty as much as it does to happiness. By contrast, for quiet scenes, the 'classified' bar is negative, suggesting that the more detailed a scene, the less quiet it is perceived to be. Again, we find that, as one expects, quiet scenes tend to also be "visually quiet" (i.e., they are smooth and flat).

Visual Words

The color and edge histograms discussed in the previous sections ignore spatial information in an image: they do not give us any hint as to the specific regions within images that correspond to beauty, happiness and quietness. To address this, we now set out to answer this last question: Which *visual elements* (e.g., building styles) correlate the most/least with pictures of happy/quiet/beautiful scenes? To answer this question, we use a popular approach for exploiting local information in images that creates *visual words* [11, 29]. These are *interest points* of an image and typically correspond to a change in intensity (i.e., an edge). These local interest points are represented by a feature vector, which describes "a small patch on the image (array of pixels) which can carry any kind of interesting information in any feature space (color changes, texture changes)" [35]. We use a codebook of visual words from these interest points by applying a clustering algorithm to the set of interest points. After that, an image can be considered as a bag of visual words, similar to bag of words in text retrieval, allowing text retrieval techniques to be applied to image collections.

In this work, we use Speeded Up Robust Features (SURF), a texture based descriptor based on Haar wavelets [2], to detect and describe interest points. We quantize the interest points into a set of 500 visual words using the K-Means algorithm. We represent each urban scene as a histogram of 500 visual words, and we calculate correlations between each visual word and the three qualities.

Since the individual visual words do not have an intuitive interpretation, we highlight them (filtering away those with correlations $r < 0.1$) on example images that rank highly for beauty, happiness and quietness (we do the converse for bottom-ranked images). One should consider that visual words are based not on colors but on texture. Hence, if associated with trees, visual words reflect the trees' texture and do not reflect the presence of green. Despite this, we still find that greenery is positively associated with our three qualities in the analysis of visual words.

For beauty, Figure 5 shows the top-ranked scenes (top row) and bottom-ranked scenes (bottom row). Each scene contains red dots next to the visual words that positively (top row) correlate with beauty or negatively (bottom row) correlate with beauty (i.e., they correlated with the opposite quality - ugly). Visual words affiliated with beauty include those around: Figure 5*(a)* Victorian houses; *(b)* public gardens; *(c)* red bricks; *(d)* residential trees. Those affiliated with low value of beauty include those present on *(e)* council housing; *(f)* bridges; *(g)*, again, council housing; and *(h)* highway road signs and guardrails. The red dots on top-ranked pictures and those on bottom-ranked ones mean two different things - the former reflect positive (e.g., happy) visual words, while the latter reflect negative (e.g., ugly) ones. This is best exemplified by the bottom-ranked picture in Figure 5(e), in which no red dot is present on trees, as opposed to what happens in top-ranked pictures, where trees and, more generally, greenery, receive many red dots.

For quiet, Figure 6 shows the top-ranked scenes (top row) and bottom-ranked scenes (bottom row). Visual words affiliated with quiet include those on *(a,c,d)* trees and hedgerows; and *(b)* residential windows. Those affiliated with low values of quiet include those on *(e)* construction sites and public buses;

(a) (b) (c) (d)

(e) (f) (g) (h)

Figure 5. Visual Words for Beauty (top row) and Ugly (bottom row).

(f) council housing; *(g)* typical architecture of central London buildings; and *(f)* guardrails. Scenes considered to be quiet are characterized not only by fewer salient edges (as we have seen in the previous section, e.g., in Figure 4(d)) but also by fewer salient visual words. We might say that quiet scenes are also quiet (smooth) in the visual sense. Beauty and quiet do not go always hand in hand, however. Buildings with texture similar to that of the building in Figure 6(g) are generally associated with noisy scenes (because they are in central London) yet are also considered beautiful.

Finally, Figure 7 shows the top-ranked scenes (top row) and bottom-ranked scenes (bottom row) for happiness. Visual words affiliated with happiness include those on *(a)* trees and buses; *(b)* trees; *(c)* trees and London letterbox; and *(d)* people. Less happy visual words include those on *(e)* street billboard; *(f)* construction site; *(g)* chain link fence; and *(h)* bridge.

PRACTITIONER REACTIONS

To gain a perspective from practitioners in the realm of the built environment as a starting point for discussion, we asked three architects (2 males, 1 female, NY and Barcelona-based) to reflect on the work presented here, and the role of 'visual words'. They were interviewed in person or over Skype. First, they were given a basic overview of the project and were asked to, according to their own preference, either draw or describe a 'happy scene in London'. Then, they were primed with 10 red-dotted street views indicating visual words (such as those in Figure 5) that were highly ranked on happiness. They then were asked to either redraw their scene or explain how they would change it. They were asked to which extent relationships between visual features and people's reactions currently play a role in their work, and how visual words such as those identified here could help, or perhaps hinder.

All three indicated that such visual words could be useful in providing insight in features affecting people's reactions. Asked which features stood out, they specifically noted the markings related to the importance of green spaces (well-known in their field); the positive effect of pedestrians and cyclists (one architect remarked that the presence of people humanized London and reminded him of Jane Jacobs' work, noting her emphasis on the presence and activity of people, without referencing a specific scholarly work); suggestions of the variety of color, type of materials and features (e.g., traditional middle-class housing material) associated with happiness & beauty; the appearance of mostly private buildings, buildings leaving more space for walkway, and buildings whose facades included windows and ornaments; and features that influence familiarity and comfort (such as common 'artisanal' lamp posts) or create the 'London identity' with typical red letterboxes, red buses, and red telephone cabins.

They also remarked on potential business or investment opportunities. Knowing what makes people - customers - happy, and then designing for such 'happiness' could increase profits. It could guide investment in urban landscaping by business and property owners. Ratings would indicate appeal to a greater population, and could steer the adding of value to space in a certain way, potentially having consequences for real estate development.

Limitations were also noted. The composition of features, for example, plays a role in how urban facades are rated. One noted that visual features would be useful to know, but that she would not rely on them as they might not necessarily reflect the experience of 'being there'. Additional drawbacks of visual words from crowdsourced ratings include that they tend to reflect traditional styles of architecture and, as such, reflect a 'democratic' view of English beauty, which may not necessarily match with modernist or more forward-looking architecture. Similarly to critique on 'democratization of art' [13], it was noted that democratizing architecture may have considerable drawbacks. When asked for a reaction, the third practitioner noted that algorithms might start to pigeonhole certain types of buildings, yet algorithms might also be an interesting reference, opening the floor for discourse.

(a) (b) (c) (d)

(e) (f) (g) (h)

Figure 6. Visual Words for Quiet (top row) and Noisy (bottom row).

(a) (b) (c) (d)

(e) (f) (g) (h)

Figure 7. Visual Words for Happy (top row) and Sad (bottom row).

(a) (b)

Figure 8. Visual Words for Tall Buildings in Happy Scenes.

PUTTING RESULTS INTO CONTEXT

To rephrase our findings in the broader context of the literature, we consider three simple elements that have been found to be universally present in most urban environments: tall buildings, cars, and trees.

Tall Buildings

One architectural element that has been widely discussed in the literature is tall buildings:

Four-story Limit (`Pattern 21` in A Pattern Language [1]) "There is abundant evidence to show that high buildings make people crazy". Therefore, the authors of A Pattern Language suggested that: "In any urban area, no matter how dense, keep the majority of buildings four stories high or less. It is possible that certain buildings should exceed this limit, but they should never be buildings for human habitation."

Connected Buildings (`Pattern 108`) "Isolated buildings are symptoms of a disconnected sick society. "

In Chapter *Salvaging Projects* [10], Jane Jacobs wrote: "All housing projects with tall buildings are especially handicapped in supervision of children . . . The corridors of the usual high-rise, low-income housing building are like corridors in a bad dream: creepy lit, narrow, smelly, blind."

We have indeed found that tall *residential* buildings are negatively associated with beauty and happiness. For example, the visual words in Figure 5(e) and Figure 5(h) are associated with the opposite qualities, that is, they are associated with ugly and unhappy scenes. Two specific types of tall buildings are exceptions to this general rule: tall *office* buildings (e.g., Figure 8(a)) and landmarks (e.g., Figure 8(b)). The former type is generally represented by glass buildings of the " international skyscraper style": in London, it is common to see ancient bricks contrasting thrillingly with soaring verticals of glass and steel. These buildings are considered to be beautiful by our participants, and the corresponding visual words tend to occur on windows and, more generally, on glass materials. The latter type of tall buildings (i.e., landmarks) and their importance have been discussed at length in the literature. A case in point is the paragraph in Chapter *Visual Order* [10] in which Jacobs noted: "Landmarks, as their name says, are prime orientation clues. But good landmarks in cities also perform two other services in clarifying the order of cities. First, they emphasize (and also dignify) the diversity of cities; they do this by calling attention to the fact that they are different from their neighbors, and important because they are different. This explicit statement about themselves carries an implicit statement about the composition and order of cities. Second, in certain instances landmarks can make functional fact but need to have that fact visually acknowledged and dignified. "

Cars

The second element frequently discussed in the literature is that of cars; more generally, that of transportation systems.

Local Transport Areas (`Pattern 11`) "Cars give people wonderful freedom and increase their opportunities. But they also destroy the environment, to an extent so drastic that they kill all social life."

Ring Roads (`Pattern 17`) "It is not possible to avoid the need for high speed roads in modern society; but it is essential to place them and build them in such a way they they do not destroy communities or countryside"

In Chapter *Lost areas* [15], Kevin Lynch added: "Many [Los Angeles] subjects had difficulty in making a mental connection between the fast highway and the remainder of the city structure ... A high-speed artery may not necessarily be the best way of visually delimiting a central district"

The presence of moving cars and buses is indeed *negatively* associated not only with quiet scenes (as one would expect and, for example, sees in the pictures at the bottom of Figure 6) but also with beauty (e.g., Figure 5(h)). By contrast, despite the presence of cars, some scenes are still considered to be quiet (pictures at the top of Figure 6).

Trees

Among all colors, green enjoyed the strongest associations with all the three qualities. Green emerged not only in the color histogram analysis but also in the visual word analysis, which has nothing to do with colors but is based on image texture. Visual words in happy scenes tend to occur on trees (e.g., pictures at the top of Figure 7), and that, again, relates to what the literature would suggest:

Tree Places (`Pattern 171`) " ... shape the nearby buildings in response to trees, so that trees themselves, and the trees and buildings together, form places which people can use."

Again, in the chapter *Visual Order* [10], Jacobs observed that: "There are some city streets which need unifying devices, to suggest that the street, with all its diversity, is also an entity. ... One of the simplest such devices is trees along the stretch to be unified ... "

The presence of those three elements in our findings speaks to their external validity and potential generalizability.

DISCUSSION

Beyond the visual and 'pleasant'. Cities are not just collections of buildings and views. Recreating a visual 'identical copy' of a city would not 'feel' like the original. Even with all the visually pleasant elements in place, it it not the same. Aesthetics extend beyond the visual; experiencing a city is not about seeing singular viewpoints, or looking at buildings, it is about moving through the city, experiencing it with all of the senses. This entails moving through a city [8] and developing judgments over time through familiarity and social changes [19]. The potential of cities lies in the 'life between buildings' [5] and their role as meeting places of people [7]. Perceptions about whether this potential is being met are not just about in-the moment sights, sounds and smells; memories, culture, history and all human activity could not be captured by simply analyzing visual properties. Platforms such as ours should be enriched to investigate additional factors at play such as stylistic references, personality, affective state, cultural background and to ultimately further refine existing models [19] of aesthetic responses to the built environment. Our work is simply a first step, and analyzes one element: the effects of visual characteristics on people's perceptions of the streets they encounter. We have here started with three specific qualities, but our approach could be used to assess other aspects and perceptions of urban surroundings as well; for example safety, excitement, expectations of the availability of certain services and businesses, expectations of demographics, or prices. An intended contribution of this work is the investigation of the merits - and limitations - of the presented crowdsourcing and visual analysis approach, and the comparison with other work addressing perceptions of the urban environment. Input from architecture, urban design, and social geography is crucial in going further than just these first steps. As pointed out by Hillier, "buildings are not just objects, but transformations of space through object" [9], and they need to be considered as systems of spatial relations and not as just physical objects. Jacobs [10] points out the essential interplay of the 'bits and pieces' of a city, warns against bland consensus, and points out that unifying design elements should not be so ubiquitous that they be rendered ineffective.

Variety matters, and opposing qualities such as diverse excitement and calm order are both necessary to support pleasant experiences. In addition, contemporary urban designers such as Jan Gehl [5] offer a wealth of criteria for designing 'good public spaces', and these are not just about visual qualities alone. While visual aesthetics are a definite influential feature, the visual words in this work still have to be translated for use by non-computational-oriented audiences. We need to further develop the ways to get at these essential characteristics, to determine how their interplay affect perceptions, and to combine larger-scale quantitative and in-depth qualitative projects that reflect diversity.

Tool, not a directive. There are a number of potential applications of crowdsourced scores such as those generated by this platform. From the perspective of mobile applications, these scores can be used as input for generating local recommendations that go beyond recommending local venues and that consider the aesthetic value of the trajectory. We are currently working on techniques that automatically generate routes that are not only short but also emotionally pleasant [24, 23]. To quantify the extent to which urban locations are pleasant, we combine the data generated by our crowdsourcing project with Flickr metadata. This can lead to practical applications in the city context such as affective route recommendation, aesthetic profiling of streets and neighborhoods, and affective-aesthetic extensions of local 'walk-scores' (see, e.g., `walkscore.com`). On the scale of the built environment itself, perception scores could be mapped and used to identify areas that are most in need of improvement. With an increased understanding of social perception of urban environments, it may be possible for targeted changes. This could benefit local authorities, city planners, real estate agents, architects and homeowners, and members of urban participatory platforms deciding on which interventions to adopt that would make a place appealing. However, this raises the question of whether striving for the visually pleasant 'mean' is truly the way to go. The identification of elements correlated to perceptions of beauty may appear to pose a risk of striving for 'cultural continuity and reduplication', rather than 'architectural design' as defined by Hillier [9]. Revolutionary designs, as well as preservation of urban history, may well be considered 'ugly' to the algorithm. Just blindly applying a computational judgment would not suffice, and more work is thus needed to understand when using these algorithms is appropriate and when it is not. At the same time, these types of platforms allow for much wider audiences to run, and contribute to, studies of perceptions of the urban environment. They can help identify features that affect people's perceptions and affective effects, and add to existing small-scale studies using qualitative ratings of desirable features for specific contexts. Human interpretation is still necessary to apply the outcomes of the process presented here. In this regard, it is interesting to note that the architects' interpretation of what was marked as important, for example, may not necessarily match the exact feature identified by the algorithm. All this goes to suggest that the work presented here should not be taken as a directive for urban design. Rather, it should be taken as a contribution to the discussion on computational approaches in profiling streets, neighborhoods and cities; and as an addition to the toolkit available to those disciplines engaged with people's perceptions of outdoor settings.

TECHNICAL LIMITATIONS

Limitations of Visual Analysis. A limitation of this study is that 'what is perceived' is not necessarily 'what is there', nor 'what would be perceived in-place and in-the-moment'. Users' votes might be influenced by picture quality, cultural and socio-economic factors, and shared priors (e.g., reputation of a neighborhood built over the years). Urban experiences are highly socially constructed, and do not depend on visual characteristics alone. Different kinds of people may engage with cities in different ways and (visual) characteristics may convey different meanings to various demographic groups. Visual characteristics do not necessarily reflect human activity and history, and social or political meanings that require in-depth local knowledge and experience to be understood. Future studies should extend the analysis presented here and further tease out such differences and the effects of a multitude of factors.

Limitations of Image Processing Algorithms. Although our results show that it is possible to use automatic image analysis to gain real insights into why people find certain urban scenes to be happy, quiet or beautiful, there are limitations to this analysis. While the color analysis show interesting associations between certain colors and beauty, quietness and happiness, average color and histograms give a very coarse representation of the content of an image, and the color distribution is very dependent on factors like the time of day. The edge histogram results suggest that people prefer scenes containing more 'natural' shapes. This feature can be affected by the distortion in the Google Street View images caused by the fish-eye lens, however, and correcting the images for this distortion would improve the reliability of this feature. Finally, while the visual words help us to localize the most beautiful, happy and quiet areas in a scene, the result of this are perhaps *too* local, in that, they represent points in the scene, whereas a single object can be made up of the interplay of many such points. An intermediate representation of areas, such as that used by Doersch *et al.* [4], might offer further insights into the types of objects within a scene corresponding to each of the features. Also, given that these local correspondences were calculated based on a relatively small dataset, based on annotations of entire scenes, a more reliable identification of the happy, quiet or beautiful areas within a scene could be achieved by soliciting sub-scene annotations from users, and from obtaining a larger dataset.

CONCLUSION

Our aim has been to identify the visual cues that are generally associated with concepts that are difficult to define, such as beauty, happiness, and quietness. The difficult task of deciding what makes a building beautiful, or what is sought after in a quiet location, is outsourced to the users of our site using comparisons of pictures. Using three existing image processing techniques that extracted colors, edges, and visual words, we were able to find interesting visual associations with the three qualities of beauty, quietness, and happiness.

More generally, we have offered a tool to better understand people's visual perceptions of the urban environment, starting with visual ratings of urban sceneries. Rather than aiming for a 'consensus' in what 'is averagely pleasing', we here aimed to explore the usage of crowdsourcing tools and visual analytics in identifying visual urban features that people appear to react to. Those initial steps call for new research and a critical debate across a variety of disciplines, including urban informatics, planning and architecture. Ultimately, the vision behind this project is that, with a comprehensive list of aesthetic features at hand, we would be more likely to systematically understand people's reactions to their surroundings, without striving for a lovable but bland mean.

Acknowledgments. We thank Adam Barwell for his role in building the site; Jon Crowcroft of Cambridge and the whole NetOS for continuous support; Fred Lewsey for contributing to the launch of the site; the anonymous reviewers for shepherding the submission; and Michael Batty and Licia Capra of UCL for their feedback.

REFERENCES

1. Alexander, C., Ishikawa, S., and Silverstein, M. *A Pattern Language: Towns, Buildings, Constructions*. Oxford University Press, 1977.
2. Bay, H., Ess, A., Tuytelaars, T., and Van Gool, L. Speeded-up robust features (surf). *Computer Vision and Image Understanding 110*, 3 (June 2008), 346–359.
3. De Botton, A. *The Architecture of Happiness*. Knopf Doubleday, 2008.
4. Doersch, C., Singh, S., Gupta, A., Sivic, J., and Efros, A. A. What makes Paris look like Paris? *ACM Transaction Graphics* (2012).
5. Gehl, J. *Cities for People*. Island Press, 2010.
6. Geis, K., and Ross, C. A new look at urban alienation: The effect of neighborhood disorder on perceived powerlessness. *Social Psychology Quarterly* (1998).
7. Glaeser, E. *Triumph of the City*. Penguin Press, 2011.
8. Heft, H., and , J. L. Evaluating environmental scenes using dynamic versus static displays. *Environment and Behavior 32*, 3 (2000), 301–322.
9. Hillier, B. *Space is the machine, e-version*. Cambridge University Press, 2006.
10. Jacobs, J. *The Death and Life of Great American Cities*. Random House, 1961.
11. Jurie, F., and Triggs, B. Creating Efficient Codebooks for Visual Recognition. In *Proceedings of the* 10th *IEEE International Conference on Computer Vision (ICCV)*, IEEE Computer Society (2005).
12. Kelling, G., and Coles, C. *Fixing Broken Windows: Restoring Order And Reducing Crime In Our Communities*. Free Press, 1998.
13. Komar, V., Wypijewski, J., and Melamid, A. *Painting by Numbers: Komar and Melamid's Scientific Guide to Art*. University of California Press, 1997.
14. Lindal, P. J., and Hartig, T. Architectural variation, building height, and the restorative quality of urban residential streetscapes. *Journal of Environmental Psychology* (2012).
15. Lynch, K. *The Image of the City*. Urban Studies. MIT Press, 1960.
16. Malobabic, J., le Borgne, H., Murphy, N., and O'Connor., N. Detecting the presence of large buildings in natural images. In *CBMI 2005 - 4th International Workshop on Content-Based Multimedia Indexing* (2005).
17. Manjunath, B. S., Ohm, J. R., Vasudevan, V. V., and Yamada, A. Color and Texture Tescriptors. *IEEE Transactions on Circuits and Systems for Video Technology 11*, 6 (2001), 703–715.
18. Nasar, J. L. Perception, cognition, and evaluation of urban places. *Human Behavior and Environment* (1989), 31–56.
19. Nasar, J. L. Urban design aesthetics: The evaluative qualities of building exteriors. *Environment and Behavior 26*, 3 (1994), 377.
20. Park, D. K., Jeon, Y. S., and Won, C. S. Efficient use of local edge histogram descriptor. In *Proceedings of the ACM Workshops on Multimedia* (2000).
21. Peterson, G. L. A Model of Preference: Quantitative Analysis of the Perception of the Visual Appearance of Residential Neighborhoods. *Journal of Regional Science 7*, 1 (1967), 19–31.
22. Quercia, D., Pesce, J. P., Almeida, V., and Crowcroft, J. Psychological Maps 2.0: A web gamification enterprise starting in London. In *Proceedings of ACM International Conference on World Wide Web (WWW)* (2013).
23. Quercia, D., Schifanella, R., and Aiello, L. M. Shortest Urban Paths or Shortcuts to Happiness? *IEEE Computer Society Special Technical Community on Social Networking E-Letter* (2013).
24. Quercia, D., Schifanella, R., and Aiello, L. M. The shortest path to happiness: Recommending beautiful, quiet, and happy routes in the city. *To Appear* (2014).
25. Robert J. Sampson and Jeffrey D. Morenoff and Thomas Gannon-Rowley. Assessing 'Neighborhood Effects': Social Processes and New Directions in Research. *Annual Review of Sociology* (2002).
26. Salesses, P., Schechtner, K., and Hidalgo, C. The Collaborative Image of The City: Mapping the Inequality of Urban Perception. *PLoS ONE* (July 2013).
27. Sampson, R. J. When Things Aren't What They Seem: Context and Cognition in Appearance-Based Regulation. *Harvard Law Review Forum 125* (May 2012).
28. Sampson, R. J., and Raudenbush, S. W. Seeing Disorder: Neighborhood Stigma and the Social Construction of Broken Windows. *Social Psychology Quarterly 67*, 4 (2004).
29. Sivic, J., Russell, B. C., Efros, A. A., Zisserman, A., and Freeman, W. T. Discovering objects and their location in images. In *In IEEE International Conference on Computer Vision* (2005).
30. Skogan, W. *Disorder and Decline: Crime and the Spiral of Decay in American Neighborhoods*. University of California Press, 1990.
31. Stendhal. *De L'Amour (On Love)*. Penguin Classics, 1822.
32. Taylor, N. Legibility and aesthetics in urban design. *Journal of Urban Design 14*, 2 (2009), 189–202.
33. Von Ahn, L., and Dabbish, L. Designing games with a purpose. *Communications of ACM* (2008).
34. Weber, R., Schnier, J., and Jacobsen, T. Aesthetics of streetscapes: Influence of fundamental properties on aesthetic judgments of urban space 1, 2. *Perceptual and motor skills 106*, 1 (2008), 128–146.
35. Yang, J., Jiang, Y.-G., Hauptmann, A. G., and Ngo, C.-W. Evaluating bag-of-visual-words representations in scene classification. In *Proceedings of the* 9th *ACM SIGMM International Workshop on Multimedia Information Retrieval* (2007).
36. Yeh, C.-H., Ho, Y.-C., Barsky, B. A., and Ouhyoung, M. Personalized photograph ranking and selection system. In *Proceedings of the International Conference on Multimedia (MM)* (2010).

Leveraging the Contributory Potential of User Feedback

Mikhil Masli
IBM
1 New Orchard Road, Armonk, NY, USA
mnmasli@us.ibm.com

Loren Terveen
GroupLens Research
University of Minnesota, Minneapolis, MN, USA
terveen@cs.umn.edu

ABSTRACT

Under contribution is an important problem in online social production communities: important tasks don't get done, and only a small minority of participants are active contributors. How can we remedy this situation? We explore the feasibility of using the act of *consuming* information as a gateway to *contributing* information; specifically, we investigate semi-automated means to extract useful information from standard types of *user feedback*. We explore this approach in the context of a geographic wiki and route-planning system for bicyclists. We analyzed naturally occurring textual route feedback, finding that the feedback was rich in information such as bikeability ratings, tags and notes that are useful to improve the system's route finding and navigational assistance capabilities. We also present a technique to extract such information by engaging users in dialogue immediately after they obtain a route. We believe that our results and ideas are applicable to a broad class of social production systems.

Author Keywords

User feedback; under-contribution; increasing participation; social production; online communities

ACM Classification Keywords

H.5.m. Information Interfaces and Presentation (e.g. HCI): Miscellaneous

General Terms

Human Factors, Design

INTRODUCTION

In social production communities, large numbers of people freely collaborate to produce common goods [2]. In recent times, online social production communities have become a part and parcel of our daily lives. For example, breaking news now appears on Twitter and Wikipedia, household items are sold and exchanged on Craigslist and eBay, and available parking spaces, cycling and running routes are shared via Google Maps-based mash-ups.

However, *under contribution* is a major problem for such communities. For example, 1,661 Wikipedia articles were marked as needing expansion in April 2013 alone[1], and 87.4% of collaboratively-made Flash games and animations on the site Newgrounds[2] are incomplete [14].

CSCW'14, February 15–19, 2014, Baltimore, MD, USA.
Copyright 2014 ACM 978-1-4503-2540-0/14/02...$15.00.
http://dx.doi.org/10.1145/2531602.2531686

Consumers of socially produced knowledge resources greatly outnumber contributors to these resources: for example, readers of Wikipedia are estimated to outnumber Wikipedia editors by a ratio of 10,000:1 [10]. Research on other online groups reports that about 90% of the total membership of the online group never makes a contribution [12, 18].

Our fundamental hypothesis is that we can harness information consumption activities as a gateway to elicit contributions and perhaps develop new contributors. We explore this hypothesis in the context of Cyclopath (`cyclopath.org`), a bicycle route-planner and geographic wiki for the Minneapolis/St. Paul metropolitan area of the United States.

In the remainder of this paper: we survey relevant related work and provide a brief introduction to Cyclopath; we then report on a study that shows that naturally occuring user feedback on routes contains potentially useful information; in a second study, we introduce a semi-automated technique for obtaining useful information from another common type of user feedback, visual route modification; we conclude by discussing the generality, benefits, and limitations of our work, and directions for future work.

RELATED WORK

Nature of Online Social Production

A majority of contribution in online social production communities is done by a few contributors [25]. Most participants are information consumers. Many will never contribute, while others may be learning about the community [21] and may transition into contribution and organization-related activities as they gain more experience [24].

An important motivation to contribute is to fill gaps or fix problems; in other words, to improve information consumption. For example, Bryant et al. found that new users primarily use Wikipedia for information gathering, and identify problems and mistakes in passing and fix them [3]. In the context of open source software development, Hertel et al. discovered that one reason people contributed code was to make the software meet their own needs [11]. Prior research on Cyclopath revealed that a major reason for users to edit the map and rate road segments is to get Cyclopath to compute the route they desire [23]. However, there are barriers to contributing information, including: (a) a perception that one has

[1] `en.wikipedia.org/wiki/Category:Articles_to_be_expanded_from_April_2013`
[2] `www.newgrounds.com`

no information to contribute, and (b) the combination that contribution is not required and that it is perceived to be a high-cost activity [22].

A related body of research has studied ways to motivate users to contribute information to public resources. Intelligent Task Routing systems match users with tasks they are likely to be willing and able to perform; these systems have been shown to boost contributions [5, 26]. However, matching tasks to users accurately is challenging. *Gamification* is a popular technique that attempts to make activities fun and game-like; the ESP Game is the seminal example [33]. Finally, techniques that manipulate users into participating and contributing information may succeed in the short-term but might cause longer-term harm, because users tend to recognize the manipulations and may consider them unfair [6, 17].

Nature of User Feedback

Several instances of prior research and experience have highlighted the utility of user feedback. First, user feedback can contain useful content. It is well known in the field of user interface design, that users are better able to communicate interface requirements when presented with prototypes, even if they are low-fidelity. Various research studies and practical use cases have demonstrated the utility of employing the *recognition-over-recall* principle for effectively capturing user requirements and reactions to interfaces [20].

Second, user feedback on the output of a system can be used to improve the system itself. Chen and Pu [4] suggest that a combination of system-generated and user-driven critiquing is the best way for a recommender system to incorporate user feedback and improve its recommendations. An evaluation of a simple tool on Wikipedia demonstrated that consumers can be persuaded to make small contributions in a low-cost, low-risk way [10] through the medium of providing feedback on the article they are reading. Several artificial intelligence and machine learning techniques rely on user feedback to improve their internal models and performance, including the well-known Winston Learning Algorithm which does so through examples and counter-examples [34].

Third, the cognitive processes behind generation of feedback are often automatic and hence, low-cost for people. When presented with a stimulus, natural human tendency is to develop an evaluation about it. To some extent, this construction of evaluation is automatic and happens without one's knowledge. This is due to the use of associative/heuristic-based cognitive information processing [7, 29]—one of the two channels described by dual-processing models of cognition. Evaluations that are more "intuitive" or affective, involving how one subjectively feels about the stimulus, appear to be more associatively driven, compared to more analytic, rational judgments such as those about causation [8]. Further, it seems likely that more richly detailed, specific stimuli are better cues for responses from the associative system [7].

Prior work suggests our opportunity: a pathway from naturally-occurring evaluation and feedback processes to contributions of information has the potential to overcome barriers to contribution and shortcomings of previous work elicication techniques.

THIS RESEARCH: CONTEXT AND OUTLINE

Cyclopath is a route-planning system for bicyclists that generates personalized, bicycle-friendly routes. As of May 25, 2013, Cyclopath had 5,128 registered users, visits from 196,263 different IP addresses and 128,330 routes requested. However, unlike traditional route-planning systems, Cyclopath is also a geographic wiki—a map that anyone can edit—and relies on community knowledge to compute these routes. Cyclopath went live in the summer of 2008.

Like any wiki, users contribute information to Cyclopath in sets of edits called revisions[3]. Each revision may contain edits to points, roads, regions, notes and tags. Roads and trails (e.g. *Kennilworth Trail*) are useful for route-finding, points help define route endpoints (e.g., from *CS Building* to *Lagoon Theater*), ratings enable smart and personalized routes, tags enable more customized route requests (e.g., a route that is more *scenic*, but less *bumpy*) [31], and notes supplement road segments included in a route with subjective information useful for evaluating the route (e.g., "icy during the winter"). In order to maintain quality, all revisions are publicly visible and revertible (via the Recent Changes list). As of May 25, 2013, the Cyclopath map has seen 17,559 revisions (13,892 by 999 registered users and 3,667 anonymously). Prior research has demonstrated that user-contributed information has helped improve route-finding [26] as well as transportation planning tasks [15].

We instantiate our idea of a pathway from naturally occurring feedback to contribution in Cyclopath as follows. After obtaining a route, user can submit feedback about the route—including specific segments—while their evaluation of the route is fresh in their minds. We present two studies as evidence for this method.

Study 1. We analyzed naturally occurring textual route feedback, finding that it contains contributory potential—information that, through appropriate techniques, may be assimilated into Cyclopath's database.

Study 2. We studied one such technique, user modification of a computed route by "dragging" the route. We showed that machine learning algorithms can identify automatically part of the contributory potential; this in turn makes it easier for users to translate their route evaluation into concrete contributions such as ratings, tags and notes.

STUDY 1: ANALYZING TEXTUAL FEEDBACK

Aim: To determine whether naturally occurring route feedback contains contributory potential

Data

From May 2009 to January 2012, Cyclopath included a simple route feedback tool. When a user obtained a route from

[3]See [27] for a more in-depth description.

Question (Does this feedback...)	% Yes	N
...include positive evaluations about any roads/areas?	24%	394
...include negative evaluations about any roads/areas?	48%	392
...include any objective facts about any roads, their surroundings and/or vehicles on them?	51%	399
...suggest any alternative roads or areas to take?	39%	440

Table 1. Findings from our textual route feedback analysis: the majority of naturally occuring route feedback contains contributory potential. Combining the first two rows, 57% of comments contained either a positive or negative evaluation. The N varies across questions and is less than 488 because we ignored responses that did not meet our 67% agreement threshold for that question.

Cyclopath, a button was displayed next to the route details, inviting feedback about the route. When the user clicked this button, a simple form popped up that asked them to tell us how satisfied they were with route on a 5-point Likert scale (very dissatisfied to very satisfied) and optionally, express in text, what they thought of the route.

While this feature was active, 688 instances of route feedback were submitted, 488 of which had textual comments. The median comment length was 137 characters ($mean = 169.020$, $sd = 132.256$). 120 comments were submitted by 90 registered users, and 368 comments were submitted by anonymous users.

Method

We developed a coding scheme to evaluate the contributory potential contained in the route feedback comments. For each comment we asked: *Does this feedback...*

1. ...include positive evaluations about any roads/areas?
2. ...include negative evaluations about any roads/areas?
3. ...include any objective facts about any roads, their surroundings and/or vehicles on them?
4. ...suggest any alternative roads or areas to take?

These questions let us identify specific types of information useful for Cyclopath: positive/negative evaluations correspond to bikeability ratings of road and trail segments, and objective information corresponds translate to tags and notes. We also looked for the occurrence of alternative route suggestions since this is an intuitive way of expressing route feedback used on popular mapping sites like Google Maps.

We coded the route feedback via crowdsourcing, using CrowdFlower[4] to deploy the coding task on Amazon Mechnical Turk. CrowdFlower provides a service that augments Mechanical Turk's platform with survey-building interfaces, quality-control mechanisms and reporting tools. As a quality-control measure, we created 32 artifical route route feedback comments with known answers ("gold standard items") and added them to the set of 488 actual comments to be coded, resulting in a dataset of 520 total items[5]. We omitted responses submitted by workers whose accuracy on the gold standard items (their "trust score") was less than 70%.

Our goal was 3 responses per question per item, but due to the way Crowdflower manages the process, we received an average of 3.14 responses per item. We only considered responses where there was at least 67% agreement between workers, where responses were weighted by the workers' trust scores. For example, if three workers had the same trust scores, then 67% agreement would mean a simple 2-out-of-3 majority. See the CrowdFlower documentation[6] for more detail on their quality control mechanisms.

[4] `crowdflower.com`

[5] The recommended amount of quality control items is about 5% of the data set size.

Findings

Naturally occurring route feedback contains evaluations of roads/areas. 24% of comments contained positive evaluations about roads/areas, 48% contained negative evaluations, and 57% contained one or the other or both.

> "Totally smooth, pleasant route, not much interaction with cars, felt very safe." (positive evaluation)

> "Biking straight down Ramsey Hill from Summit Ave to Grand Ave is an awful idea and I would never bike that way. It is a very steep hill with a stop light at the bottom. No way." (negative evaluation)

Naturally occurring route feedback contains objective facts about roads, etc. 51% of comments contained such information.

> "The part of the route from 3.65 to 5.29 is wretched. The bicycle path (in the directions, it's called "unnamed bicycle path") is downright dangerous, too. The path crosses two sets of railroad tracks and the seams are dangerously deep and wide. In addition, the path sweeps down onto a driveway to an industrial site, and that driveway is filled with grit and rubble. I take my chances on Country Road C, which is not great, either, but at least I avoid the wheel-swallowing railroad tracks."

Naturally occurring route feedback contains descriptions of alternative routes. 39% of comments contained such information.

> "A better route is getting on E River Road to Franklin Ave Bridge, cross the River, get on West River Road, tkae that to Greenway Trail and follow all the way to The Depot. Too much traffic on Cedar Ave."

Non-contributors offer feedback. We wondered whether most route feedback came from people who already contributed to Cyclopath; this would be disappointing, as it would decrease the chance of attracting new contributors through a route-feedback-based mechanism. However, this was not the case. First, as already noted, 368 of 488 route feedback comments came from anonymous users. And

[6] `crowdflower.com/solutions/self-service/faqs`

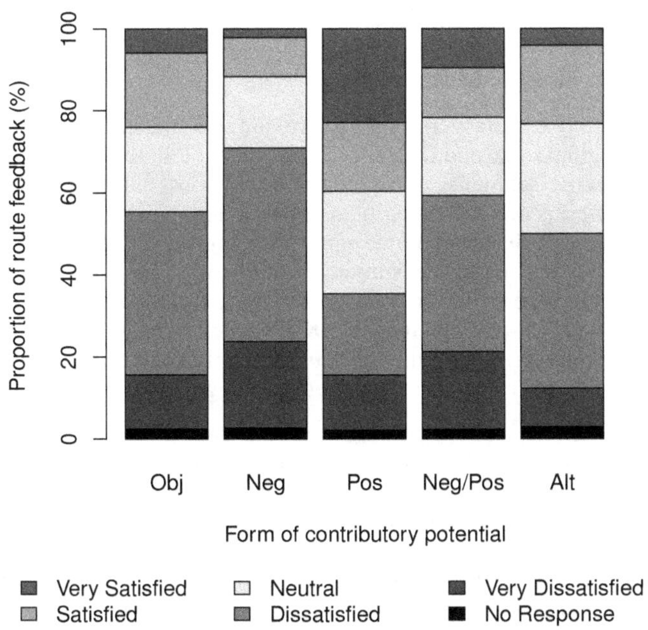

Figure 1. Relationship between users' satisfaction with routes and the contributory potential of their route feedback. Obj = Objective Information, Neg = Negative Evaluation, Pos = Positive Evaluation, Alt = Alternative Route Suggestion. It is not only the dissatisfied who submit useful feedback.

anonymous users account for a small proportion of contribution to Cyclopath (3,667 out of 17,559 revisions, or 21%). Therefore, we can infer that most of the anonymous route feedback came from non-contributors. Second, route feedback comments from anonymous users were more likely to include contributory potential than comments from registered users: negative evaluations (52% vs 37%, $p = .012$), objective information (55% vs 39%, $p = .007$), alternative routes (43% vs 28%, $p = .010$)[7]. Third, only half of the 90 registered users who submitted comments had contributed to Cyclopath. Therefore, route feedback offers a significant opportunity to obtain contributions from new sources.

Not only dissatisfied users provide useful feedback. Most useful content came from users who said they were dissatisfied with their routes. However, users who were satisfied or very satisfied with their routes accounted for 22% of comments with positive or negative evaluations of roads, 23% of comments with alternative route suggestions, and 24% of comments with objective information (see Figure 1).

Discussion and Implications

We found that naturally occurring route feedback is rich in several kinds of useful information. How can that information be mapped on to Cyclopath constructs?

Evaluations → Ratings. Evaluations of roads can be expressed as bikeability ratings. A simple ratings widget could be displayed along with a route, enabling users to quickly identify segments they want to rate higher or lower.

[7]To compute statistical significance, we used the 2-sample test for equality of proportions with continuity correction.

Objective Facts → Tags, Notes. Cyclopath represents factual information as tags (short phrases) and notes (longer, freeform text). As with ratings, an appropriate widget could be displayed to enable easy annotation of road segments. Further, techniques like Tag Expression [32] have been shown to be effective in eliciting tags and tag preferences.

Alternative Routes → *???*. When a user specifies an alternative route, there is no direct correspondence to specific Cyclopath constructs. Indeed, various things could be changed in order for Cyclopath to produce a different route: bikeability ratings, tags, or the details of the routing algorithm (e.g., how various parameters are weighted). Instead, an alternative route suggestion—along with the rejection of the original route—constitutes an opportunity for Cyclopath to learn. *How* that learning might be done is the topic of the next study.

STUDY 2: ANALYZING VISUAL FEEDBACK

Aim: To investigate a semi-automated technique for learning from visual route feedback

We have shown that naturally occurring route feedback often includes a suggestion of an alternative route. Further, an intuitive means for users to specify an alternative route is by "dragging" the route, as on Google Maps and Cyclopath. There are two ways a system could respond to this learning opportunity: (1) Automatically modify the route planner's internal models and/or algorithms, thus producing better routes in the future [36, 37, 19]; (2) Engage the user in a dialogue to elicit reasons for preferring the new route over the old route [28]; these reasons then can be analyzed to produce new system knowledge.

We explored the second approach for the following reasons: (1) Richer types of information can be gathered, e.g., notes and tags in addition to ratings. Indeed, in the context of recommender systems, researchers have recommended a hybrid system-and-user-generated critiquing approach to improving system performance [4]. (2) The consumer is introduced to and nudged towards contribution through simple, easy steps. This is consistent with theories such as Legitimate Peripheral Participation [13] and the Reader-to-Leader framework [24] that model the transition from consumption to contribution. These approaches have been demonstrated to have value in the context of Wikipedia [10]. Thus, the result of a semi-automated, dialogue approach may be not just a *contribution*, but also a new *contributor*.

The following use case illustrates the type of dialogue we have in mind.

1. A user requests a route.

2. Cyclopath computes the best path based on available information.

3. The user is not satisfied with the route, and corrects it by dragging the route line to follow their preferred path.

4. Cyclopath automatically identifies segments along the original and new routes that it thinks caused the user to modify the route, highlights the segments, and offers the

user the opportunity to provide ratings, tags, and notes for the segments. The user responds as he/she desires.

This use case is plausible under three conditions: (1) The user's route preference is based on preferences for individual segments of the route. (2) The system can identify the approriate route segments with sufficient accuracy. (3) The user will provide information about these segments. We consider each of these in turn.

Users might prefer one route over another because of properties of individual segments of the routes: for example, they might want to avoid hilly or high traffic segments and instead ride on quiet, scenic off-road facilities. Alternatively, users might prefer one route over another for more holistic reasons, for example, to ride near certain resources (say, places to stop for a drink). Given the way our route-finder works, the former preference is more directly useful. We use the A* graph search algorithm, and at each step in the search process, the system considers only the properties of the possible next segments that could be added to the route (and not global properties like "make sure some part of the route passes within a kilometer of a place to get a drink"). Thus, we conducted a study to explore the reasons why users prefer one route over another, specifically, the extent to which they do so because of properties of specific segments (Study 2A).

If users do tend to prefer one route over another because of the properties of specific segments, then the next challenge is for the system to identify these segments. We therefore developed a machine learning classifier to predict such segments and evaluated its accuracy (Study 2B).

But even if the system can identify these segments—segments in an old route that a user is apt to dislike, segments in the user's suggested route that the user is apt to like—why would a user go to the trouble of providing knowledge (ratings, tags, notes) about them? Besides the likelihood that the user will have this information fresh in their mind, prior work offers compelling answers. As we noted above, fixing problems and improving one's own experience are common reasons people begin contributing to a social production system; Panciera et al. found that fixing problems was the most common reason for Cyclopath users to begin editing [23]. Moreover, prior work on Cyclopath has shown that focusing users' attention on specific geographic areas makes them more likely to contribute information [26]. Given this prior work, we did not study user motivation further in this research.

Data and Method

We modified the Cyclopath interface to elicit visual route feedback. When a user generated a route using Cyclopath's route planner, a button was displayed in the route details panel labeled "Suggest Different Route". Clicking this button led to the user being guided through a two-step procedure.

In step 1, users were asked to drag the route to meet their preferences. (Route dragging was an existing feature of Cyclopath, which works similarly to other mapping applications such as Google Maps: clicking on the route line introduces an intermediate waypoint at the location of the click and dragging it changes the route line in such a way that it is forced to pass through the waypoint.)

In step 2, users were asked to provide specific feedback on the original route and their suggested route, including identifying specific segments of either route that most influenced their preference. These segments constituted a data set that we used to train and evaluate a machine-learning classifier. Users also were asked to estimate how much of an improvement their suggested route was over the route Cyclopath computed. Note that we implemented step 2 solely for the purpose of data gathering—in the wild, users would only be required to drag their routes for Cyclopath to suggest road segments to annotate.

We received 85 instances of route feedback between October 25, 2012 and April 16, 2013. Each feedback instance consisted of the original route, the suggested route, one or more waypoints, zero or more marked segments, optional reasons for changing the original route and suggesting the alternative and an evaluation of how much of an improvement the suggested route was over the original.

In 38 of these 85 cases, users had marked specific segment(s) as reasons for modifying the route. In most cases (36 of 38) where users marked segments, they also provided an explanation for modifying the route. An additional 17 feedback instances carried explanations (for changing the original or for suggesting the alternative) but no marked segments, making a total of 53 feedback instances with explanations.

As in Study 1, most of the feedback was submitted anonymously: 23 instances were submitted by 20 registered users and the remaining 62 anonymously. Anonymous users also provided more feedback than registered ones, accounting for 24 of 36 instances where liked/disliked segments, and 33 of 53 instances where comments were submitted. However, 18 of the 20 registered users had made at least 1 contribution.

Study 2A: Why did the user modify the route?

Aim: To identify why users modified their routes, and specifically, to what extent did they do so because of the segments they marked

Method

We manually coded the comments users specified along with their visual route feedback to to understand why users chose to modify their routes. For the first question, coders assigned one or more of the following sets of codes to the reasons users gave for rejecting the original route and for suggesting the alternative:

- Longer vs. Shorter
- Unsafe vs. Safe
- No dedicated bike facilities vs. Dedicated bike facilities
- Hills vs. No hills
- Bad surface vs. Good surface
- High traffic vs. Low traffic

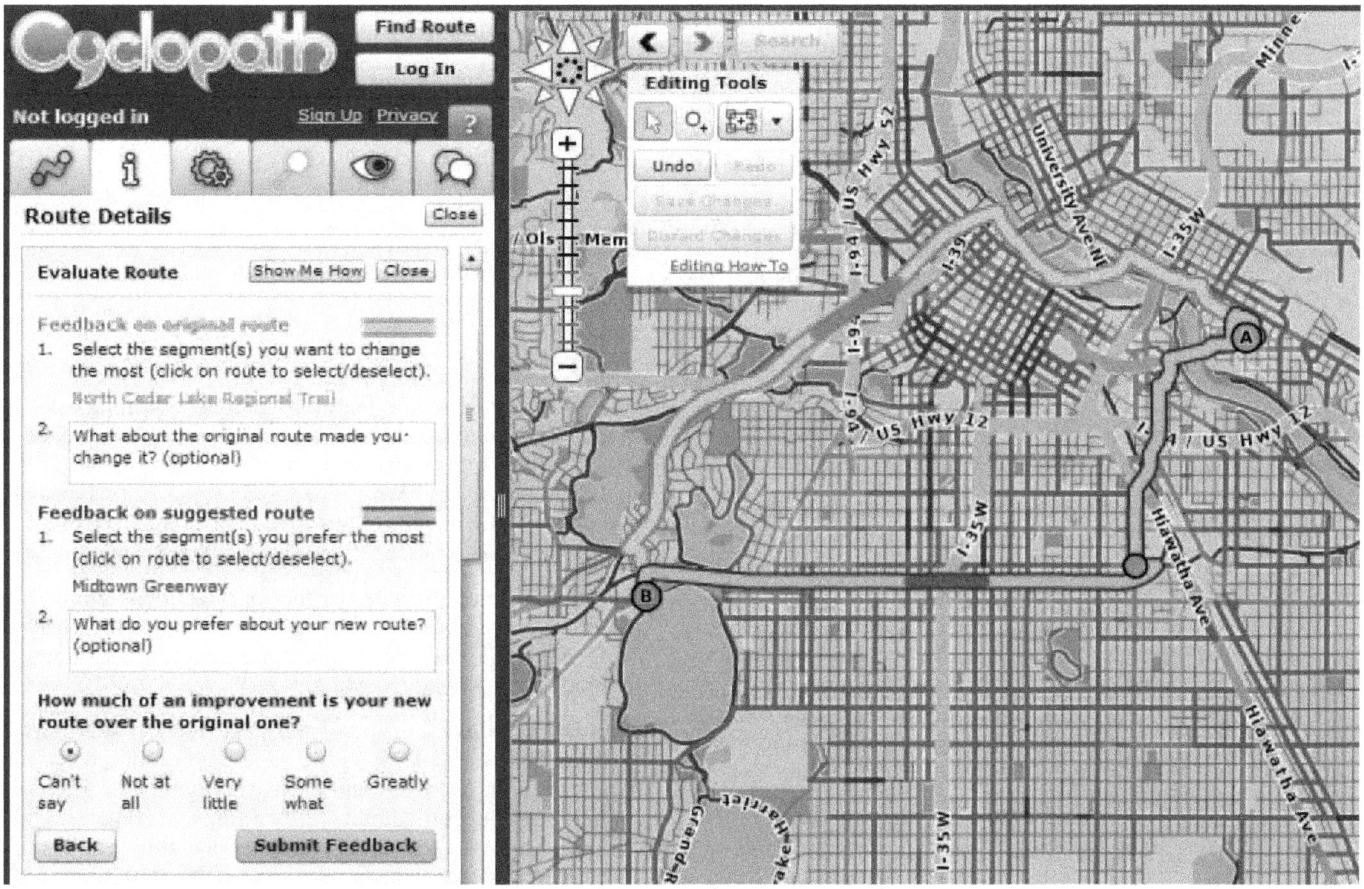

Figure 2. The Cyclopath interface to collect visual route feedback through dragging. This images is showing step 2 of the 2-step process where the user is being asked to mark road segment(s) that caused them to modify their route. The "Show Me How" button led users to a tutorial video describing the process.

- Noisy vs. Quiet
- Many stoppages vs. Few stoppages
- Bad intersection vs. Good intersection

One of the authors developed these codes by identifying prominent patterns within the feedback comments. These patterns are consistent with those used by prior research on bicycling route choice [30].

For the second question, we used the following ordered set of rules to code the comments. That is, if Rule 1 let us conclude that the user modified route because of the segment(s) they marked, then rules 2 and 3 were not considered. *We conclude that the user modified the route because of the segments they marked if...*

Rule 1. ...the user mentions a road segment by name in the feedback and has also marked a road segment with the same name. For example, one comment said *"Big hill on North St, too much traffic on University, freeway on/off traffic on 12th St"* and the user marked segments of North St. or 12th St.

Rule 2. ...the feedback content is highly synonymous with the road type and the contents of the tags and notes attached to the marked segments. To help make this determination, we augmented each feedback instance with road types, tags and notes attached to the corresponding marked segments. For example, a comment said *"This is a long, steep hill."* and the "hill" tag was applied to one of the marked segments.

Rule 3. ...we find factual, objective information with the feedback that we can verify applies to the marked segments using aerial imagery or by browsing around the area. For example, a comment said *"I don't wanrt [sic] to ride through the U [University of Minnesota]. Don't like the traffic and vibe."* and browsing the map around the marked segment reveals that the segments were within the University of Minnesota neighborhood.

Thus, for this coding task, coders assigned one of two codes to user comments: "Yes" (by Rules 1, 2 or 3) or "No evidence". Three independent coders coded the feedback instances for the both the coding tasks.

Findings

Why did users modify the route? We found evidence for several important reasons. The most common reasons for rejecting the original route were *high traffic* (17/53; inter-rater

Attribute	Entire Section				Marked Segments Only			
	Original	Suggested	p	sig	Original	Suggested	p	sig
Avg. annual daily automotive traffic	6240	5250	< .001	$***$	8030	4300	< .001	$***$
Shoulder width (m)	0.831	1.16	< .001	$***$	0.856	1.12	.309	
Outer lane width (ft)	9.91	12.1	< .001	$***$	12.0	13.5	.0502	$\diamond$
Speed limit (mph)	31.6	31.6	.79		32.0	31.0	.011	$*$
Avg. user bikeability rating	4.09	4.73	< .001	$***$	2.97	2.96	.943	

Table 2. Differences between the original and suggested route sections. All values are means. Suggested sections had lower automotive traffic, wider shoulders and outer lanes, and higher user-submitted bikeability ratings. All road attributes were loaded into Cyclopath when map data was initially imported from the Minnesota Department of Transportation in 2008 and except average annual daily traffic, the others can be modified and kept up to date by users. P-values and statistical significance codes (sig) are computed using the Welch 2-sample t-test ($\diamond :< .1, * :< .05, ** :< .01, *** :< .001$).

agreement for this category using Fleiss' Kappa, $\kappa = 0.85$) and *hilliness* (10/53; $\kappa = 0.91$), whereas those for suggesting the alternative route were *presence of dedicated bicycle facilities* (12/53; $\kappa = 0.79$) and *low traffic* (11/53; $\kappa = 0.79$).

These findings are consistent with prior research on commuter bicyclists: The most important factors in choosing a route are: travel time, the presence of a bicycle facility (bike lane or separate path on a bridge), the level of automobile traffic, quality of the pavement or riding surface [30]. This is also consistent with the data we collected. Table 2 shows quantitative differences between the original and suggested sections of routes. We see that on an average, the suggested section had much lower automotive traffic, wider shoulders and outer lanes, and a higher average user-submitted bikeability rating.

Did users modify the route because of the segment(s) they marked? Yes, in many cases. Marking segments was an optional step of the data collection process—users could successfully submit route feedback by simply dragging the route and doing nothing else. Despite this, in 29 out of 85 cases, users marked segment(s) as a response to the prompt "Select the segment(s) you want to change the most" and in 26 out of 85 cases, users marked segment(s) as a response to the prompt "Select the segment(s) you prefer the most". In sum, in 38 out of 85 cases (45%), users indicated at least one segment as a reason why they modified their route.

Further, combining "Yes (by Rule 1)", "Yes (by Rule 2)" and "Yes (by Rule 3)" into a single code "Yes", we found evidence that the marked segments were a part of the reason why users modified the route in 23 of the 36 instances (64%) where users had marked segments ($\kappa = 0.50$). Note that this is a lower-bound: in the remaining 34% cases, we could not reliably conclude from our manual coding whether the feedback was about the segments marked.

Finally, as a response to the question, "How much of an improvement is your new route over the original one?", we obtained the following results: *can't say* (34 cases), *very little* (3 cases), *somewhat* (26 cases) and *greatly* (22 cases). This suggests that obtaining information about why users preferred one route over another, and then mapping it into a form usable by the route finder will result in demonstrably better routes.

Study 2B: Predicting liked/disliked segments

Aim: Given the original and suggested sections, to predict the segments that the users marked

Method

We adopted a machine learning approach for this task. For our choice of classifier to use, we chose the Random Forest classifier due to its sensitivity towards handling data sets with imbalanced classes. We trained and evaluated this classifier using the Weka data mining software package [35]. We evaluated the classifier using 10-fold cross-validation.

We used several attributes of the road segments in question, the routes (original and suggested versions) to which they belonged, and the user that requested the routes (and submitted the feedback, whenever available):

- **Road attributes:** Type of the road (local road, highway, bike trail, etc.), lane width, lane count, shoulder width, speed limit, average annual daily automotive traffic, number of user-recorded bikeability ratings, average user bikeability rating, Cyclopath-estimated bikeability rating (calculated based on road properties), presence of bike lane (or similar tags such as bike trail), presence of hills, presence of roughness (or similar tags such as unpaved), presence of traffic (or similar tags such as busy).
- **Route attributes:** Length (in metres), number of road segments, average bikeability rating.
- **User properties:** Number of revisions made, number of routes requested, number of map views done, number of days since registering for Cyclopath.

We used three primary metrics in reporting the performance of our machine learning classifiers: sensitivity, specificity, and area under the Receiver-Operator-Characteristic (ROC) curve (also called area-under-curve or AUC) [9]. Our metrics may be interpreted as:

- **Sensitivity:** proportion of marked road segments that are correctly classified
- **Specificity:** proportion of unmarked road segments that are correctly classified
- **AUC:** a single scalar value representing the overall performance of the classifier.

We used the 0-R classifier to provide a baseline model as a frame of reference for interpreting our results. A 0-R algorithm always predicts the most commonly occurring class. Due to the design of our data gathering procedure (the instructions we gave to the users), there will be many fewer marked than unmarked road segments in any given old/new

(a) Given the original section, predict the road segment(s) the user marked.

Attributes Used	Sensitivity	Specificity	AUC
Road	0.346	0.978	0.814
Road + User	0.365	0.987	0.857
Road + Route	0.738	0.984	0.951
Road + User + Route	0.757	0.985	0.962

(b) Given the suggested section, predict the road segment(s) the user marked.

Attributes Used	Sensitivity	Specificity	AUC
Road	0.339	0.983	0.870
Road + User	0.347	0.984	0.883
Road + Route	0.771	0.989	0.964
Road + User + Route	0.792	0.989	0.974

Table 3. Classifier performance. Using all three sets of attributes (road, user and route), we can detect about 76% of marked segment(s) for the original section of the route, and about 79% for the suggested section. The values are average of 10-fold cross-validation. User attributes had a small effect on sensitivity because a majority of the feedback was submitted anonymously.

route pair. So, given an old (or new) route section, the 0-R algorithm will always predict that none of its road segments were marked: sensitivity = 0, specificity = 1, AUC = 0.5. Note that our baseline outperforms random guessing, which would converge to an overall performance of sensitivity = 0.5 and specificity = 0.5.

Findings

Our classifier outperformed the baseline 0-R in all our cross-validation tests. On an average, given the original section of the route, the marked road segments within it were correctly identified in about 76% (sensitivity = 0.757) of the cases when road, route and user attributes were all utilized for prediction (see Table 3(a)).

Similarly, given the suggested section of the route, the marked segments were correctly identified in about 79% (sensitivity = 0.792) of the cases on an average by using all three sets of attributes (see Table 3(b)).

Discussion, Implications and Limitations

In this study, we have presented a technique to leverage the intuitive action of correcting a route when dissatisfied with it to capture the content of the underlying route evaluation. We now address the generality, utility and limitations of this study.

Generality of Results and Ideas

Social production communities such as Wikipedia and Cyclopath offer contributors tasks across a wide spectrum of expertise and difficulty: some tasks are quite easy and do not require topic or work-type expertise (e.g. slightly modifying a route in Cyclopath, correcting a typo in Wikipedia) whereas other tasks can require both (e.g. fixing road segment connectivity around a complex intersection, or composing and editing an entire article in Wikipedia). Prior research suggests that consumers take their first steps into becoming a contributor by performing the simpler tasks [13, 24], a pattern that is observed in both Wikipedia [3] and Cyclopath [16]. Fixing or tweaking the output that the system computes and presents is one such simple task that consumers have a propensity to do: after all, it brings them direct benefit. Consequently, in Study 2, we explored how route dragging can be used to engage the consumer in a dialogue that may help translate some naturally-occurring route evaluations into concrete contributions such as ratings, tags and notes.

This basic idea is applicable in a wide spectrum of social production systems. For example, when a recommender system presents the consumer with a list of recommended items, the consumer could correct it by rating the items listed or specifying different items. To some extent, Amazon already does this with the "Fix this recommendation" feature. Similarly, another domain where this idea is applicable is the collaborative construction of the semantic web. It may be easier to identify the inaccuracy and correct the output of a information query on a structured knowledge graph, than to identify the holes by browsing through the graph itself.

Estimation of Utility

How useful might the contributions resulting from the system-user dialogue explored in Study 2 be? Study 2A highlighted several reasons users mentioned for modifying their routes. Many of the reasons can be expressed as tags: e.g., hilliness can be represented by the *hill* tag and dedicated bicycle facilities can be recorded using the *bikelane* tag. By automatically predicting a part of users' feedback in the form of especially liked/disliked segments, we can reduce the cost of contribution to just that involved in submitting ratings, tags, and notes.

A more interesting approach is to estimate the potential "conversion rate", i.e., the proportion of route-modification actions that might be leveraged to obtain a contribution. It is precisely those times when users modify computed routes (by dragging) when they are dissatisfied with the route; thus, these consitute opportunities for Cyclopath to learn. Our results let us estimate the conversion rate. To do so, must enumerate and analyze the various steps involved in the process. See Figure 3 for a back-of-the-envelope version of this analysis. Recall that for a route-modification action to be "converted" to a contribution, two things must happen:

1. *The modification must be due to the user liking/disliking specific segments.* Study 2A showed that in 45% of cases when users described an alternative route, they marked segments they liked/disliked; further, we have evidence that at least 64% of the time, segments were marked because of issues with the segments themselves, as opposed to issues with their surroundings. Thus, we that when a user modifies a computed route, the probability that specific road or trail segments caused the modification is 45% $\times$ 64% = 29%.

2. *Cyclopath should be able to successfully predict these segments.* In Study 2B, we built a predictor that could identify these segments with a sensitivity of about 76%. In other words, when users modified a route because of specific segments, the classifier had a 76% probability of predicting the segments correctly.

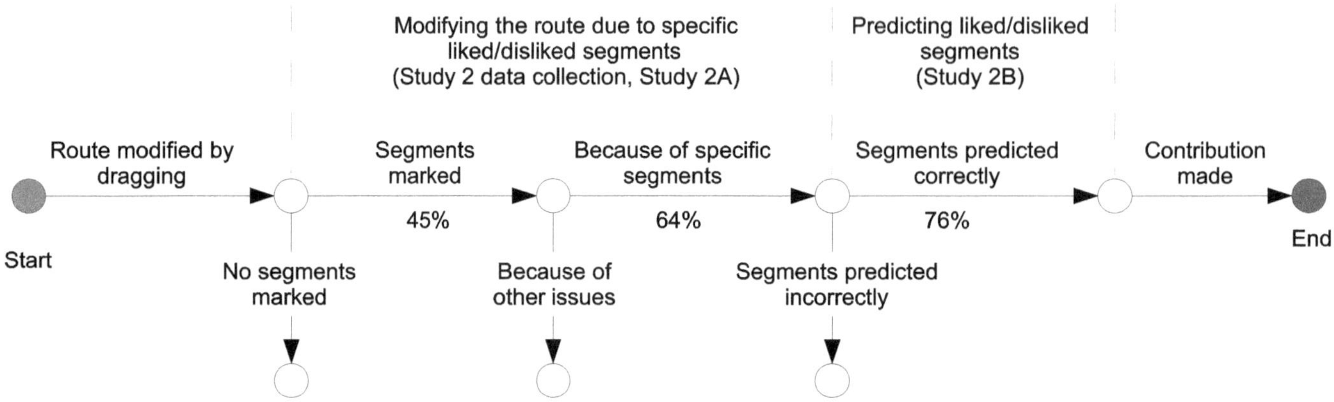

Figure 3. Flowchart illustrating the back-of-the-envelope calculation used to estimate the probability that a user would make a contribution after dragging a route through the technique explored in Study 2. Note that in a real-life use-case, the user would drag their route and then directly contribute information about the predicted segments—the intermediate steps would happen internally (either within the user's mind or within the system).

Thus, if each route-modification action with correctly-predicted segments yielded one contribution, we would get a route-modification-to-contribution conversion rate of about 29% × 76% = 22% (22 contributions per 100 route-modification actions). This may be an underestimate, as prior research has shown that users may contribute beyond what they are asked directly [26]. A controlled field study is required to provide more concrete evidence in this regard.

How sustainable is this process for eliciting contributions? Since users modify routes for self-benefit, we think the first part of the process will continue to be "triggered" until the route finder is perfect for all users... which likely never will happen. And we already have presented an argument why users are likely to provide simple explanations (in the form of ratings, tags, and notes) for why they modified a route.

Moreover, the utility extends beyond getting more *contributions*: we may be able to get more *contributors* too. Indeed, research has shown that having consumers do simple contribution tasks, such as providing feedback, may convert them into regular contributors [10]. This is valuable in and of itself, because an increased inflow of contributors into the community is an important force to combat attrition and increase the diversity and quality of the community resource [1].

Limitations

An important limitation of the process we have outlined for eliciting contributions from a route modification is that it captures only one possible type of preference, i.e., preference for (or against) individual route segments. However, as we noted, it is possible that users may have more holistic preferences. For example, one user gave the following reason for modifying their route: "It brings me by Freewheel Cycle."

Another limitation of this process is that dragging-based feedback depends on the road network being connected correctly. For example, intersection faults (road segments that visually cross but are not connected in the database) can cause routing to work incorrectly. While collecting visual route feedback, we observed several cases where users who had the motivation and skills to make geographic edits, made the required connections in the road network in order to enable them to drag their route. On the other hand, some users who had the motivation but not the skills wrote to us complaining that they were not able to drag the route on paths they wanted. After investigating why, we found out that some roads were not connected appropriately. We connected these roads and the users were then able to record their feedback correctly.

Some users mentioned this limitation as a part of their feedback comments.

> "Shorter distance, wide shoulders, and new path on east side of Flying Cloud between ValleyView and Technology. Couldn't make the route follow Flying Cloud there..."

> "System doesn't seem to know that both Sibley and Jackson connect to Shepard Rd"

With a modification to the route-dragging mechanism, we believe we can convert this limitation to an advantage. For example, if we made the route-dragging permissive enough to allow the route to treat intersection faults like regular connections, we may be able to either automatically create connections and fix the faults, or at least flag them for user attention.

SUMMARY AND FUTURE WORK

In this research, we have explored the possibility of harnesssing a commonly-found information consumption behavior to drive contribution into a social production system. We have done so in the context of Cyclopath, a route-planner and geographic wiki, shown that route feedback contains contributory potential, and outlined a process for focusing it on specific road segments.

Important future work is to investigate further how users choose to express their feedback in the context of a modified route. We might do this by inviting the user to modify their route (like our Study 2) and if the user accepts the invitation, employ our new classifier to automatically predict and highlight road segments that might be the reason the user modified the route. Then, for each highlighted segment, we could ask the user to express feedback in one or more of three different ways: ratings, tags and notes. We may then be able to study any association between the route modification and the existence and nature of the information elicited.

ACKNOWLEDGEMENTS

We thank the members of GroupLens Research, the Cyclopath team, the Cyclopath user community, and our reviewers. We also thank Jacob Thebault-Spieker for proof-reading an earlier draft. This work was supported in part by the National Science Foundation grant IIS 08-08692 and a University of Minnesota Doctoral Dissertation Fellowship.

REFERENCES

1. Arazy, O., Morgan, W., and Patterson, R. Wisdom of the crowds: Decentralized knowledge construction in wikipedia. In *16th Annual Workshop on Information Technologies & Systems (WITS) Paper* (2006).
2. Benkler, Y. *The wealth of networks: How social production transforms markets and freedom.* Yale University Press, 2006.
3. Bryant, S. L., Forte, A., and Bruckman, A. Becoming wikipedian: transformation of participation in a collaborative online encyclopedia. In *Proceedings of the 2005 international ACM SIGGROUP conference on Supporting group work*, ACM (2005), 1–10.
4. Chen, L., and Pu, P. Critiquing-based recommenders: survey and emerging trends. *User Modeling and User-Adapted Interaction 22*, 1-2 (2012), 125–150.
5. Cosley, D., Frankowski, D., Terveen, L., and Riedl, J. Suggestbot: using intelligent task routing to help people find work in wikipedia. In *Proceedings of the 12th international conference on Intelligent user interfaces*, ACM (2007), 32–41.
6. Cosley, D., Lam, S. K., Albert, I., Konstan, J. A., and Riedl, J. Is seeing believing?: how recommender system interfaces affect users' opinions. In *Proceedings of the SIGCHI conference on Human factors in computing systems*, ACM (2003), 585–592.
7. Epstein, S. Cognitive-experiential self-theory of personality. *Handbook of psychology* (2003).
8. Epstein, S., Lipson, A., Holstein, C., and Huh, E. Irrational reactions to negative outcomes: Evidence for two conceptual systems. *Journal of Personality and Social Psychology 62*, 2 (1992), 328.
9. Fawcett, T. ROC graphs: Notes and practical considerations for researchers. *Machine Learning 31* (2004), 1–38.
10. Halfaker, A., Keyes, O., and Taraborelli, D. Making peripheral participation legitimate: reader engagement experiments in wikipedia. In *Proceedings of the 2013 conference on Computer supported cooperative work*, ACM (2013), 849–860.
11. Hertel, G., Niedner, S., and Herrmann, S. Motivation of software developers in open source projects: an internet-based survey of contributors to the linux kernel. *Research policy 32*, 7 (2003), 1159–1177.
12. Katz, J. Luring the lurkers, slashdot, 1998.
13. Lave, J., and Wenger, E. *Situated learning: Legitimate peripheral participation.* Cambridge university press, 1991.
14. Luther, K., Caine, K., Ziegler, K., and Bruckman, A. Why it works (when it works): success factors in online creative collaboration. In *Proceedings of the 16th ACM international conference on Supporting group work*, ACM (2010), 1–10.
15. Masli, M., Bouma, L., Owen, A., and Terveen, L. Geowiki + route analysis = improved transportation planning. In *Proceedings of the 2013 conference on Computer supported cooperative work companion*, ACM (2013), 213–218.
16. Masli, M., Priedhorsky, R., and Terveen, L. Task specialization in social production communities: The case of geographic volunteer work. *Proc. ICWSM* (2011).
17. Masli, M., and Terveen, L. Evaluating compliance-without-pressure techniques for increasing participation in online communities. In *Proceedings of the 2012 ACM annual conference on Human Factors in Computing Systems*, ACM (2012), 2915–2924.
18. Mason, B. Issues in virtual ethnography. *Ethnographic studies in real and virtual environments: Inhabited information spaces and connected communities* (1999), 61–69.
19. McGinty, L., and Smyth, B. Personalised route planning: A case-based approach. In *Advances in Case-Based Reasoning*. Springer, 2000, 431–443.
20. Nielsen, J., and Hackos, J. T. *Usability engineering*, vol. 125184069. Academic press Boston, 1993.
21. Nonnecke, B., and Preece, J. Why lurkers lurk. In *Americas Conference on Information Systems* (2001), 1–10.
22. Nonnecke, B., Preece, J., and Andrews, D. What lurkers and posters think of each other [online community]. In *System Sciences, 2004. Proceedings of the 37th Annual Hawaii International Conference on*, IEEE (2004), 9–pp.
23. Panciera, K., Masli, M., and Terveen, L. How should I go from _ to _ without getting killed?: motivation and benefits in open collaboration. In *Proceedings of the 7th International Symposium on Wikis and Open Collaboration*, ACM (2011), 183–192.
24. Preece, J., and Shneiderman, B. The reader-to-leader framework: Motivating technology-mediated social participation. *AIS Transactions on Human-Computer Interaction 1*, 1 (2009), 13–32.

25. Priedhorsky, R., Chen, J., Lam, S. T. K., Panciera, K., Terveen, L., and Riedl, J. Creating, destroying, and restoring value in wikipedia. In *Proceedings of the 2007 international ACM conference on Supporting group work*, ACM (2007), 259–268.

26. Priedhorsky, R., Masli, M., and Terveen, L. Eliciting and focusing geographic volunteer work. In *Proceedings of the 2010 ACM conference on Computer supported cooperative work*, ACM (2010), 61–70.

27. Priedhorsky, R., and Terveen, L. Wiki grows up: arbitrary data models, access control, and beyond. In *Proceedings of the 7th International Symposium on Wikis and Open Collaboration*, ACM (2011), 63–71.

28. Rogers, S., Fiechter, C.-N., and Langley, P. An adaptive interactive agent for route advice. In *Proceedings of the third annual conference on Autonomous Agents*, ACM (1999), 198–205.

29. Smith, E. R., and DeCoster, J. Dual-process models in social and cognitive psychology: Conceptual integration and links to underlying memory systems. *Personality and social psychology review 4*, 2 (2000), 108–131.

30. Stinson, M. A., and Bhat, C. R. Commuter bicyclist route choice: analysis using a stated preference survey. *Transportation Research Record: Journal of the Transportation Research Board 1828*, 1 (2003), 107–115.

31. Torre, F., Sheppard, S. A., Priedhorsky, R., and Terveen, L. bumpy, caution with merging: An exploration of tagging in a geowiki. In *Proceedings of the 16th ACM international conference on Supporting group work*, ACM (2010), 155–164.

32. Vig, J., Soukup, M., Sen, S., and Riedl, J. Tag expression: tagging with feeling. In *Proceedings of the 23nd annual ACM symposium on User interface software and technology*, ACM (2010), 323–332.

33. Von Ahn, L., and Dabbish, L. Designing games with a purpose. *Communications of the ACM 51*, 8 (2008), 58–67.

34. Winston, P. H. Learning structural descriptions from examples. Tech. rep., DTIC Document, 1970.

35. Witten, I. H., and Frank, E. *Data Mining: Practical machine learning tools and techniques*. Morgan Kaufmann, 2005.

36. Ziebart, B. D., Maas, A. L., Dey, A. K., and Bagnell, J. A. Navigate like a cabbie: Probabilistic reasoning from observed context-aware behavior. In *Proceedings of the 10th international conference on Ubiquitous computing*, ACM (2008), 322–331.

37. Zita, K., Jonathan, H., Shewchuk, R., and Veloso, M. M. Exploiting domain geometry in analogical route planning. *Journal of Experimental & Theoretical Artificial Intelligence 9*, 4 (1997), 509–541.

A Comparison of Social, Learning, and Financial Strategies on Crowd Engagement and Output Quality

Lixiu Yu, Paul André, Aniket Kittur, Robert Kraut
Carnegie Mellon University
5000 Forbes Avenue, Pittsburgh, PA 15213
{lixiuyu, pandre, nkittur, robert.kraut}@cs.cmu.edu

ABSTRACT

A significant challenge for crowdsourcing has been increasing worker engagement and output quality. We explore the effects of social, learning, and financial strategies, and their combinations, on increasing worker retention across tasks and change in the quality of worker output. Through three experiments, we show that 1) using these strategies together increased workers' engagement and the quality of their work; 2) a social strategy was most effective for increasing engagement; 3) a learning strategy was most effective in improving quality. The findings of this paper provide strategies for harnessing the crowd to perform complex tasks, as well as insight into crowd workers' motivation.

Author Keywords

Crowds; incentives; strategies; motivations

ACM Classification Keywords

H.5.3 [Information Interfaces and Presentation]: Group and Organization Interfaces – Collaborative computing, Computer-supported cooperative work, Web-based interaction

INTRODUCTION

A major research challenge in crowdsourcing has been increasing crowd worker engagement and output quality [4,8,16,19,20,21,26,33,37]. One significant issue has been that crowd platform features aimed at lowering market transaction costs – such as simplified work histories, de-identification of worker names, and lack of long-term contracts – can, on the one hand, enable employers to hire workers without the significant vetting and handshake costs prevalent in other markets, leading to high-speed, scalable transactions. On the other hand, they do not promote a particularly fulfilling or engaging environment for workers, who can feel like "just another cog in the machine" [12], with corresponding negative implications for motivation, effort, and output quality [4,17,20,34].

CSCW'14, February 15 - 19 2014, Baltimore, MD, USA.
Copyright 2014 ACM 978-1-4503-2540-0/14/02...$15.00.
http://dx.doi.org/10.1145/2531602.2531729

As a result, large crowd employers (such as CrowdFlower or MobileWorks) have begun to build up and train their own trusted workforces of crowd workers, and researchers have investigated "retainer" models to keep workers around [22]. However, such approaches may not work for many crowd employers, who do not have the volume of work to continuously feed a dedicated workforce. In this paper we compare combinations of three task design strategies – social, learning, and financial – to determine what kinds of features can be incorporated into marketplaces to create rewarding or fulfilling experiences for crowd workers, and thereby increase crowd worker engagement and output quality. Specifically, we examine the effects of these strategies on attracting workers to come back to take additional tasks from the employer (engagement) as well as changes in the quality of their work (output quality). Furthermore, we go beyond investigating individual strategies to look at interactions between strategies.

Job Design Strategies

In traditional organizations, a variety of strategies are designed to encourage employees' engagement and productivity. Theories on job design and motivation theory in conventional work organizations indicate that job design should focus on human needs and workers' motivations [24]. Job design researchers stress the importance of performance feedback, learning, and interaction with other people in determining the attitudes and behavior of employees in organizations [35]. Literature on human resource management suggests that individual performance appraisal (and the rewards associated with the appraisal), training, and team building are the main activities that motivate workers [3]. In brief, the strategies that are effective for improving engagement and output quality mainly include a social, learning or training, and financial component, and these strategies are very often implemented together.

While the effects of job design are well established in conventional work organizations, the features of crowdsourcing markets, including their reliance on one-off impersonal transactions, crowd workers' demographics, and lack of effective punishment mechanisms [20, 34], make it unclear how crowd workers will respond to these strategies. In traditional organizations, employees are situated in a hierarchical and long-term situation, and their behaviors are influenced by such an environment. For example, employees are motivated by a social strategy because maintaining a good relationship with coworkers is important to gain resources, mentorship, or promotion [e.g., 30,31]. In contrast, crowdsourcing markets have little concept of such resources, mentorship or hierarchy. Therefore crowd workers might not be interested in putting in the effort to maintain certain relationships, and a social strategy might not be effective. As for a learning strategy, most crowd workers treat the work in crowdsourcing markets as complementary to their main jobs [34]. Therefore, they may only want to earn quick money by working on simple tasks instead of learning skills. Lastly, micro- and low-pay tasks are prevalent in crowdsourcing markets, and the hourly-rate is a few dollars [34]. A financial strategy within the current payment range is unlikely to make big changes to crowd workers' income and thereby might not affect their behavior. To summarize, due to the fundamental differences between crowdsourcing markets and traditional organizations, it is not clear whether strategies that work in traditional organizations would be effective in improving crowd workers' engagement and performance.

We therefore try to apply such strategies and test their effects on crowd workers. The goal for this strategy design is two-fold: 1) increase a worker's predisposition to return to work for a particular employer without requiring a longer-term employment contract; 2) increase a worker's motivation and ability (expertise) to perform high quality work for that employer. Specifically we extend the piece rate pay model typical of crowdsourcing markets with a *financial strategy* based on long-term rewards contingent upon quality work. We augment these financial strategies with a novel *social strategy*, that involves building teams and allowing interaction between workers as well as between workers and employer, and a *learning strategy* that involves providing detailed performance feedback to workers. These three strategies aim to redesign crowd worker/employer interactions to support greater opportunities for relationships to develop between workers and employers (and potentially between workers as well). In addition to these individual strategies, we create different mechanisms by combining the strategies in order to find optimal ways of increasing both engagement and quality.

Our results suggest that the social strategy has positive effects on worker engagement and the learning strategy improves output quality, while the financial strategy has neither effect. Additionally, the social, learning, and financial strategies seem to undermine each other's positive effects when used together.

The contributions of this work are two-fold. First, this work provides empirical test to the effects of incentive strategies on crowd workers' engagement and performance. Second, our findings can be used to guide the design of crowdsourcing platforms, including incorporating interaction and training features.

RELATED WORK

Financial strategies have been studied to improve the quality of crowd work. However, researchers showed that while increasing payment attracts more workers faster, it does not consistently improve the quality of their work [26, 33, 37]. These studies applied simple financial incentives, such as paying more on single tasks. Among simple tasks with similar levels of difficulty, ones offering higher payment can stand out and attract more workers. Increasing complex tasks' payment might not produce the same effect, because these tasks compete for workers with simple tasks in the same market. It is difficult for workers to determine whether the extra effort required by the difficult tasks is worth the extra payment. Thus, we can't predict workers will behave in the same way as they did in performing simple tasks. In addition, there are many types of financial incentives, such as base salaries, bonus contingent on performance, long-term accumulated reward, and their combinations, which can be used to increase employees' commitment and performance [18]. Their effects on crowd workers remain to be tested.

Increasing the intrinsic motivation of a task has also been tried. In this view, researchers framed tasks in a meaningful context, such as labeling tumor cells in order to assist medical researchers, but found that while the framing motivated individuals to do more work, again work quality (i.e., accuracy) did not improve [4]. A later study appealed to altruism by contrasting work for a non-profit versus a profit-making corporation, and found that appeals to altruism increased the quality of work [33]. These studies were based on the assumption that if workers find the task more engaging, interesting, or worth doing in its own right, they may produce higher quality results. Unfortunately, most tasks don't seem engaging to workers and can't be framed as altruistic work.

Other techniques, such as providing instant feedback and establishing connection with workers' peers, have also been tried. For example, Dow and colleagues found that providing crowd workers with instant feedback increased the quality of work [8], and Salganik and colleagues showed that asking subjects to consider the answers of their peers increased accuracy on a content analysis task [37]. In addition, a recent study found that revealing demographic information of workers' teammates could motivate workers to put more effort into the task and thereby improve quality [16]. While valuable, these studies focused on simple tasks where low quality is not likely due to inherent difficulty of the task, but through worker carelessness or lack of effort. Although complex tasks can suffer from similar issues, they also suffer from workers' limited expertise. That is, even if workers are motivated enough to pay attention, they still can't improve their output quality because they lack the required skills.

STRATEGY DEVELOPMENT

Social Strategy

Social factors such as the desire to feel a sense of involvement and 'belong' to a social group, and the forming and maintaining of interpersonal bounds, are a fundamental human need [2, 14]. Traditional organizations have tried many ways of building up social relations between employees to facilitate collective actions [e.g., 25]. Empirical studies also show that social motivation is an important driver for people taking part in online activities, ranging from knowledge contribution to providing emotional support [e.g., 32, 40].

Crowdsourcing markets are centered on work and pay. There is limited direct social interaction in current crowdsourcing markets. Whether social motivation is important to crowd workers, and whether a social strategy can keep workers around, is unclear. Crowd workers might have self-selected into a system of financial reward, and therefore would not be interested in social motivation. Additionally, most crowd workers have their own formal jobs and working in crowdsourcing markets is just a way of earning quick money [34]. Thus they might think of social factors as unnecessary or even a burden. However, in slightly different online environments researchers who study the relation between socialization tactics and newcomers' commitment to peer-production projects found that social interaction increases participation [5]. Although crowdsourcing markets are different from peer production communities, they share two important features in common: participants are self-selected and this activity is not their main job. Researchers argue that people can become committed to a group or community through identity or bound-based commitment [29]. Self-disclosure plays a central role in the development and maintenance of relationships [6]. Therefore, we designed a social strategy to build bounds between workers, as well as between workers and employers. Specifically, we will invite workers to be part of a team, encourage them to introduce themselves, and allow workers to talk to each other. We predict,

H-S1: A social strategy will improve workers' engagement.

The effect of social factors on the quality of work is complex due to many possible dynamics. On one hand, high commitment resulting from social factors might increase work performance [27]. On the other hand, different social dynamics can affect work performance in different directions [e.g., 10]. For example, positive interaction with team members might benefit performance and conflicts might reduce performance.

In crowdsourcing markets, recent work has shown visual presentation of co-workers changed workers' perceptions of co-workers, and that the more co-workers participants saw, the lower their work quality [19]. But another recent study found that revealing demographic information of co-workers could increase social transparency, motivating workers to put more effort into the task when interacting with their teammates [16]. Although such studies and some practices tried indirect collaboration and coordination among crowd workers, there isn't yet any study focused on allowing workers to interact with each other socially in the way we propose in crowdsourcing markets. In our proposed social strategy, there will be awareness, interaction and self-disclosure. These social factors are intended not only to increase social transparency, but also build workers' trust and bond with their co-workers and the requester, which might improve the quality of their output. Therefore, we predict that,

H-S2: A social strategy will improve the quality of crowd work.

Learning Strategy

There are many studies in traditional organizations showing feedback can improve quality. Feedback can be provided by either superiors or peers. For example, on-going feedback from instructors can improve students' learning [41], employer feedback can foster employee development [23], and providing or receiving peer feedback for students reinforces their learning and enables them to achieve higher understanding [9].

Related work shows several ways of improving the quality of crowd work in crowdsourcing markets [e.g., 8, 19]. However, we argue that these motivators largely improve quality by reducing lazy or careless work. For example, Dow et al. showed that instant feedback improved crowd workers' output quality [8]. It is unclear whether the improved work resulted from learning or from a supervision effect: workers feeling monitored and therefore paying more attention. In addition, the task was writing a product review, and the finding may not apply to more difficult tasks. As argued before, crowd workers might not be willing to spend time on gaining knowledge or learning skills considering that most of them have formal jobs. Workers may also not trust the feedback provided either by their peers or the requester. However, workers might like to learn skills while making money. Feedback tailored to their previous performance can help them be aware of the issues they had, and they might try to correct these issues next time when they work on similar task. We designed a learning strategy by means of providing feedback asynchronously, on more difficult tasks, given either by experimenters or co-workers. We posit feedback can improve quality by improving workers' expertise. We predict,

H-L1: A learning strategy in the form of providing feedback will improve the quality of crowd work.

Although we created a learning strategy to improve quality, we are also interested in seeing how it influences engagement. Hackman and Lawler describe feedback as one of four task dimensions that are important in the generation of intrinsic rewards, and thereby increase employees' engagement [12]. However, in many situations, feedback's effect on engagement is mediated through motivations. Positive or negative feedback can provoke different motivations and therefore lead to different effects on engagement. For example, researchers found that positive feedback led to higher levels of intrinsic motivation [38], but studies in peer production show that providing negative feedback can reduce newcomers' general motivation [43].

The effect of feedback on engagement has not been studied in a crowdsourcing context. On one hand, workers might like to learn skills while making money and therefore be more likely to participate. On the other hand, learning might demotivate workers because feedback often involves negative assessments about the workers' output quality. Such assessments might discourage workers and therefore decrease their engagement rate [42]. Therefore, we predict,

H-L2: A learning strategy will not improve workers' engagement.

Financial Strategy

The effects of financial strategies on the quantity and quality of an employee's work have been controversial in traditional organizations (reviewed by [17]). As discussed previously, crowdsourcing markets have a new model of employer-employee relationship. The effect of financial incentives in such markets deserves investigation.

Previous studies used one-off short-term financial incentives. These studies showed an effect on quantity of crowd work but no effect on the quality of work [e.g., 26]. Researchers explain this finding as an "anchoring" effect: workers who are paid more also perceive the value of their work to be greater, and thus are no more motivated than workers paid less.

These studies focused on one-time fixed payments or a bonus. Many types of financial incentives in traditional organizations, such as base salaries, bonus contingent on performance, long-term accumulated reward, and their combinations are used to increase employees' commitment and performance [18]. There are few studies of systematic financial incentives in crowdsourcing markets. To design a long-term systematic financial strategy, we enhance the standard payment rate by paying an extra bonus to returning workers, provide performance-contingent incentives such as building credits in our system over time, and promise to solve disputes fairly. Workers were told they would receive such special financial treatment if they kept taking our tasks and individually or as a team performed well in a task. This financial strategy is designed for long-term and contingent on engagement and performance. Therefore, we predict,

H-F1: The financial strategy will improve workers' engagement.

H-F2: The financial strategy will improve the quality of crowd work.

Combining Strategies

This paper aims to explore optimal ways of increasing crowd workers' engagement and output quality for complex tasks. As discussed above, we are interested in the effects of both individual strategies and their combination. If these individual strategies produce positive effects, can we create an even more effective strategy by combining them?

There has been little research on the interactive effects of multiple strategies except on the interaction between extrinsic and intrinsic incentives. In the motivation literature, "crowding out" effects were found with external incentives such that students paid to play with a puzzle later played with it less, and reported less interest than those who were not paid to do so [7]. However, researchers also found that one can combine extrinsic and intrinsic motivators in a synergistic way and thereby gain a higher level of employee satisfaction and performance [1]. In addition, researchers in the crowdsourcing literature found a synergistic interaction between intrinsic and extrinsic motivators: workers provided highest quality results when intrinsic motivation was stronger than extrinsic motivation. Once extrinsic motivation took over, accuracy converged to equal (and lower) levels regardless of the level of extrinsic motivation provided [33]. These findings indicate the complexity of interaction among incentives. Many factors, including the phrasing of the treatments, and the way of integrating different types of strategies, could affect workers' behavior. Therefore, we take an exploratory approach to experiment with different ways of combining strategies in order to find an optimal way of designing strategies for crowd workers.

We conducted three experiments. In each we presented multiple tasks in different steps across several months to test the effects of strategies. The participants were all recruited from Amazon Mechanical Turk. To avoid sampling bias, we first recruited a pool of subjects to perform an initial task and then sent them messages to invite them to complete more tasks. Depending on the experimental conditions, different strategies were used in invitations–a social strategy, learning strategy, financial strategy, or interactive (combined) strategies.

We first conducted an omnibus experiment in which we compared the effects of an invitation with all three strategies to the control condition with only the notification of the new task, looking at workers' engagement and output quality. We then tested the individual strategies and the interactive strategies in two subsequent experiments. Workers were asked to summarize portions of scientific articles (for example, the first two paragraphs from an academic paper [15]). We selected this task because writing tasks are complex tasks that call for particular skills, effort, and potential collaboration.

EXPERIMENT 1: AN OMNIBUS WAY OF TESTING STRATEGIES

In Experiment 1, we aim to test the overall effect on engagement and quality from all strategies. To do so, we used a multiple-tasks procedure. We posted a first task recruiting a pool of workers and then divided them into two groups receiving different treatments. We then invited them back to take more tasks. Our experimental condition invited workers back with a combination of social, learning and financial strategies, and a control condition only notified workers about new tasks with simple messages.

Subjects

Overall 236 workers participated in the experiment. Thirty-eight percent of participants were women, 69% were native English speakers, and 64% received college or higher education. Their average age was 32, and ranged from 18 to 75.

Design and Procedure

Step 1. We posted a summarization task requiring workers to summarize two paragraphs taken from a scientific article into a few sentences [15]. Workers self-selected to take the task.

Step 2. We posted a second summarization task (four paragraphs taken from [39]). We divided participants from Step 1 into two groups: a control group and a strategy group. The control group received a simple notification about the task, as shown below.

Looking for HITs? We are going to offer HITs on reading and writing. The goal of these HITs is the production of news articles. The tasks include reading articles, summarizing articles, writing sentences and judging writing.

The strategy group received an invitation about joining a news-article writing team with rewards (bonus and credits) as well as learning promises (learn the skills to be a journalist). The main part of the message is shown below.

We are building a news article writing team. The goal of the team is the production of news articles through a series of tasks. The tasks include reading articles, summarizing articles, writing sentences and judging writing.

We are seeking good and responsible workers as partners. We are only inviting participants who did well on the initial writing assignment. You took our previous task "News article writing!" We would like to invite you to be on our writing team.

The reasons you might be interested in doing this: 1) You will get an extra five cents bonus for every task you complete. 2) By working on our tasks, you will be building up your credits in our system. You will get a final reward depending on your credits: we will select the team member with the most credits every other month and reward him/her 10 dollars. 3) You will know about the task as soon as we post it. 4) You are going to learn the skills of a journalist. 5) You will belong to a news article writing team.

What we need from you is simple: please take all the tasks you accept seriously and do your best on every task. Please introduce yourself by replying to this invitation (e.g. What do you do for a living? What is your expertise? What kind of tasks do you like to do on Mechanical Turk? Why are you working on Mechanical Turk?)

Workers in the strategy team then sent their self-introductions to employers. Below is an example of the self-introduction from one worker:

*Let me start by saying how very glad I am that you invited me to your writing team. I am currently in the process of studying law at the **University. Writing articles and/or reviews for numerous sites, including Mechanical Turk, is my source of extra income and a way to fill my free time. I mostly write and summarize news articles, movie and music reviews, and basically all kinds of articles on general topics, or the ones I'm particularly interested in. I would also be interested in editing/judging others' writing. Concerning my personal information, I have no problem sharing it with other workers, but please inform me if your intentions were to create some kind of work groups.*

Step 3. We posted a third summarization task (two paragraphs from [36]), and sent different messages to the two groups notifying them of this task. The control group received a simple notification message about the task. The strategy group received messages that confirmed workers' membership in the news-article writing team and the bonus and credits they received from doing the previous task.

Step 4. At the end of Task 3, the strategy group received bonus and credits.

Rating

A good summary needs to cover the key ideas in the original text accurately but concisely. Two judges rated the summaries on 7-point Likert scales of *coverage*, *accuracy* and *conciseness*. We averaged these assessments using the geometric mean to normalize differences among the variance in the judgments [11]. The geometric mean of three assessments is the cube root of their product. The inter-rater agreement scores on the quality measures for the summaries were adequate: Intraclass Correlation Coefficient (ICC) was .76. The final analysis was based on the averaged scores of the two judges.

Analysis and Results

Engagement was measured by return rate, which is the proportion of the participants who returned in the final task, given they received a message in the first task. The quality of the summaries was calculated as the geometric mean of accuracy, conciseness and coverage. Thus, the dependent variables were return rate and quality. The independent variables were conditions: the control condition and the strategy condition. We included two control variables in the analyses: education and language. Education was a binary variable, measured by whether the participants received college or higher education. Language was also a binary variable, measured by whether the participant's native language is English or not. Both the variables were coded as 1 and 0 using dummy coding. They were selected as control variables because workers with higher education and higher English skills might be more likely to come back, which may result in sample bias.

The first goal was to examine how strategies resulted in changes in return rate. We constructed a logistic regression model with return rate as the dependent variable, conditions as independent variables, and education and language as control variables.

The second goal was to examine the changes in the quality of the summaries. To do so, we used a multiple regression analysis with quality as a dependent variable, and conditions as independent variables. Only a subset of participants had been invited to perform Task 2 and Task 3. (This is because we wished to observe changes in behavior of participants who received the complete treatment. Since some participants dropped out at each step, we focused on the subset of

Conditions	Probability of Return	SE	Mean of Quality	SE
Control group	.24(27/117)	.04	4.87	1.27
Strategy group	.36(40/119)*	.04	5.74*	1.28

p < .001 = ***, p < .01 = **, p < .05 = *

Note: The first numbers in the parentheses were the numbers of participants in the final task and the second numbers were the numbers of participants in the first task.

Table 1. Experiment 1: Effects of strategies on return rate and quality

participants who stayed throughout the process.) The characteristics of the workers, such as their education level and native language, can influence both whether they would stay through the tasks and their quality, so it was necessary to control the selection biases when modeling changes in quality. To do so, we used the Heckman two-step selection model [13], which performs multiple regressions to generate a derived variable predicting whether a participant would complete a new summary. This propensity score was then used as a control variable in the second stage of the analysis predicting changes in quality. When modeling the worker's propensity to persist, we included in the first stage of the Heckman analysis the education and the language variables.

Table 1 summarizes the results: compared to being in the control condition, being in the strategy condition increased the return rate by .12 ($p<.05$), and the quality by .87 on average ($p<.05$), holding all other variables constant. These results suggest that an invitation with all strategies motivated crowd workers to return, and the workers produced better work when they returned.

Discussion

The strategy condition included social, learning and financial elements. As a whole, these strategies improved workers' engagement and their output quality. However, it was unclear which strategy led to the effects, and we couldn't determine interaction effects between strategies. In addition, in this instance the learning strategy was a promise of learning about news article writing, but this was not operationalized. To improve Experiment 1 and test the effects of every individual and pairs of strategies, we designed Experiment 2.

EXPERIMENT 2: INVITATION WITH SINGLE AND INTERACTIVE STRATEGIES

Similar to Experiment 1, we used a summarization task to recruit workers and then divide them into groups receiving different treatments for the following tasks. Different from Experiment 1, we are interested in the effect of individual strategies and their interaction. Thus we break the overall invitation with all strategies into three separate conditions: *Social*, *Learning,* and *Financial* conditions. We also created three conditions with interactive strategies: *Social & Learning, Social & Financial,* and *Learning & Financial.*

Subjects

Overall 1,171 workers participated in the experiment. Forty-four percent of participants were women, 73% were native English speakers, and 63% received college or higher education. Their average age was 30, and ranged from 18 to 74.

Design and Procedure

Step 1. We posted a summarization task and workers self-selected to take the task (same as used in Experiment 1).

Step 2. We posted a second summarization task (same as Experiment 1). We divided participants who completed Task 1 into seven groups and then sent them invitations with different messages.

Control group. Workers received a notification about the new task that was similar to the one used in Experiment 1.

Social group. Workers received an invitation to join a news article writing team. Part of the message is shown below.

We are building a team of dedicated workers to produce news articles. The tasks will include reading articles, summarizing articles, writing content, proofing, copy-editing, and judging others' writing. We are seeking good and responsible workers as members of this team. We would like to invite you to be part of the team.

To build a strong team, we would like to get to know you better and encourage team members to know each other. Please introduce yourself by filling out the following information.

What do you do for a living? What is your expertise? What kind of tasks do you like to do on Mechanical Turk? Why are you working on Mechanical Turk? Would you like to share your information with other team members?

Learning group. Workers received an invitation with promises of providing knowledge about scientific discoveries and providing feedback on their summaries. Part of the message is shown below.

You will learn about cutting-edge scientific discoveries when you take our tasks. The topics of the tasks range from social science to natural science. Articles you are writing about are from top researchers around the world. We will also provide you feedback on your tasks, including the quality of your writing and ways of improving it. You will also learn some skills that are important for writing news articles professionally.

Financial group. Workers received an invitation with promises of providing extrinsic strategies such as paying bonuses, giving credits and solving disputes appropriately. Part of the message is shown below.

By taking our tasks, you will enjoy the following benefits:

1) You will get an extra five cents bonus for every task you complete.

2) By working on our tasks, you will be building up your credits in our system. You will get a final reward depending on your credits: we will select the team member with the most credits every other month and reward him/her 10 dollars.

3) You will know about a task as soon as we post it, notified by e-mail.

4) We will pay you promptly and if any problems arise will contact you for dispute resolution rather than rejecting your work.

There were three interactive strategy groups: *Social &*

Learning group, Social & Financial group and *Learning & Financial group*. The messages these groups received were pairs of the messages shown above and the appearance orderings of the messages were randomized.

Step 3. We posted a third task (same as the one used in Experiment 1), and only participants who took Task 2 were allowed to take the new task. Before taking Task 3, groups received different messages.

The control group received a simple notification saying that a new task was available.

Groups involving the social strategy (*Social group, Social & Learning group* and *Social & Financial group*) sent their self-introductions to employers and received confirmations of their group membership.

Groups involving the learning strategy (*Learning group, Social & Learning group* and *Learning & Financial group*), received feedback tailored to their summaries for Task 2. Below is an example of feedback from the experimenters,

You did a good job in summarizing the DARPA text! Our main suggestion for you is to try to cover all important information in the text and leave out the unimportant information. Here are a few places that can be improved: 1. About MIT's incentive strategy: the amount of money for people involved is detailed information which can be removed from the summary. 2. An important piece of information was missing in your summarization: GTRI team's financial strategy was to donate all money to charity.

Groups involving the financial strategy (*Financial group, Learning & Financial group* and *Social & Financial group*) received bonuses and credits.

Step 4. At the end of Task 3, groups with the financial strategy received bonus and credits, and groups with the learning strategy received feedback.

Rating

We rated the summaries in a similar process as in Experiment 1. Due to the large number of summaries, only a sample of summaries (50 summaries) were selected and rated by two judges. The inter-rater agreement score on the overall quality was good (ICC=.81). One judge rated the remainder of summaries.

Analysis and Results

The analysis was similar to Experiment 1, the main difference being the independent variables. We were interested in the effects of every single strategy and the interactive strategies. So rather than using conditions as independent variables, we used strategies as independent variables: conditions were coded into three dummy variables: social, learning and financial. If a variable existed in a condition, it was coded as 1. Otherwise it was coded as 0.

We conducted a logistic regression model with return rate as dependent variable, strategies and the interaction between strategies as independent variables, education and language as control variables.

	Probability of Return	SE	Mean of Quality	SE
Control	.13 (22/176)	.27	3.81	.61
Social	.21 (35/169) *	.30	4.69 *	.62
Learning	.12 (19/160)	.33	4.76 *	.63
Financial	.15 (25/165)	.32	4.62 *	.63
Social&Learning	.13 (23/172)	.45	4.35	.65
Social&Financial	.20 (34/167)	.42	4.35	.61
Learning&Financial	.09 (14/163)	.49	3.98	.72

$p < .001$ = ***, $p < .01$ = **, $p < .05$ = *

Table 2. Experiment 2: Effects of strategies on return rate and quality

Regarding quality, we conducted a Heckman two-step selection model with quality as dependent variable, strategies and the interaction between strategies as independent variables, and education and language included in the first stage.

The results are shown in Table 2. The second and the third column show the return rates and standard errors. The logistic regression analysis shows that compared to receiving the control invitation, receiving an invitation with just the social strategy increased the odds of participants' return by .61 (p<.05), holding all other variables constant. The rest of the strategies, including the single strategy and the interactive strategies, didn't predict return rate.

The fourth and fifth column of the table show the means and standard errors of quality for the final task. Heckman regression analysis shows that the presence of one unit of social, learning or financial strategy increased the quality by .89 (p<.01), .95 (p<.05), and .82 (p<.05) on average, holding all other variables constant. This means all single strategies improved the quality.

We observed a negative interaction between every pair of strategies. Examining the improvement in quality as compared to control, the social strategy improved quality by .89 (3.81 to 4.69), the learning strategy by .95 (3.81 to 4.76), and the financial strategy by .82 (3.81 to 4.62). Therefore, one might expect that combining social and learning strategies should lead to a 1.84 increase in quality, but we saw a .55 (3.81 to 4.35) increase. Similarly, combining social and financial should lead to 1.70, but we again saw a .55 (3.81 to 4.35) increase. Combining learning and financial should lead to 1.77, but we saw a .17 (3.81 to 3.98) increase. This means adding strategies together did not produce additive effects. Particularly, adding the learning strategy to the financial strategy even reduced each positive effect.

Discussion

Experiment 2 results show that a social strategy improved both workers' engagement and output quality. These results support H-S1 and H-S2. As we discussed in the previous section, this manipulation might increase a worker's sense of belonging and build bonds between workers, as well as between workers and experimenters. Therefore the workers were more likely to return and do better. However, in Experiment 2, there was no direct interaction between team members of social groups.

As predicted by H-L1 and H-L2, the learning strategy only improved the workers' output quality. This suggests that workers could learn skills by reading feedback. However, negative feedback such as "you missed one of key ideas in the original article" might discourage them to return.

The financial strategy improved quality, not the return rate, which supports H-F2 but not H-F1. This finding contradicts findings in previous studies that financial rewards led to higher engagement but had no effect on quality. It might be because participants were told that they were only invited back when they did well in the tasks, so unlike prior work the reward was contingent on quality. This demotivated workers who did not want to work hard to come back.

Another finding was the negative interaction between strategies: when we added a second strategy to the existing one, it either did not provide an additional effect, or even reduced the existing positive effect of the single strategy on quality and return rate. This negative interaction was especially strong for the interaction between learning and financial strategies: the mean quality was as low as that of the control condition. This finding can be explained by the "crowding out" effect in previous literature [7]. Without theoretical support for the negative interaction between other strategies (social and learning, and social and financial), we have two conjectures. First, the negative interaction might be caused by the design of the conditions: we simply put together the two independent messages. Without appropriate integration of the strategies, workers might be confused by the large amount of information and therefore only paid attention to one of the strategies. Second, there might be a ceiling effect: given that summarization tasks are not easy, there is only a limited amount of space for workers to improve and the improvement resulting from the single strategy already reached the limit. We conducted Experiment 3 to better understand the interaction between strategies.

EXPERIMENT 3: IMPROVED INTERACTIVE STRATEGIES

To improve interactive strategies, we created mechanisms to better integrate the strategies rather than just put strategies together. For example, in Experiment 2 the social and learning message was simply the individual messages concatenated. In Experiment 3, we ask team members to provide feedback for each other, so the social element and the learning element are dependent on each other.

In addition to improving the interactive strategies, Experiment 3 is also designed to improve several other aspects of Experiment 2. We found a positive effect on engagement and quality from the social strategy. But there was only an imaginary team and no real interaction between team members in Experiment 2. To strengthen the effect of the social strategy, we here add interaction between team members by allowing them to chat to each other. Moreover, Experiment 2 did not test the interaction between all three strategies. This is added in Experiment 3. Lastly, messages with treatments were sent to the participants in emails in Experiment 2, and we were not sure whether these messages were read by participants. To ensure that participants are actually exposed to the treatments, in Experiment 3 we ask participants to read the treatment messages by taking tasks like surveys.

Subjects

Overall 2,018 workers participated in the experiment. Forty-three percent of participants were women, 80% were native English speakers, and 50% received college or higher education. Their average age was 32, and ranged from 18 to 70.

Design and Procedure

Step 1. We posted Task 1 and workers self-selected to take the task (the article was the same used in the previous experiments).

Step 2. We divided workers from Task 1 into eight groups and sent them messages inviting them to take a survey containing different treatments.

The treatments in control, social, learning, and financial groups were similar to the ones used in Experiment 2. The main changes were in the interactive strategy groups.

Social & Learning group. Participants were invited to join a team. They would provide and read feedback for and from their team members. This design intended to create a group-learning environment. Part of the message is shown below.

...The team members will evaluate each other's answers and provide feedback, including the quality of the writing and ways of improving it...

Social & Financial group. Participants were invited to join a team. As a team they would compete with other teams and would receive rewards based on their performance. This design intended to create a group competitive environment. Part of the message is shown below.

...Your team will compete with another team. If your team wins, all your members will enjoy the following benefits:

1) You will get an extra five cents bonus. 2) By working on our tasks, you will be building up your credits in our system. You will get a final reward depending on your credits: we will select the team member with the most credits every other month and reward this team member 10 dollars. 3) You will know about a task as soon as we post it, notified by e-mail. 4) We will pay you promptly and if any problems arise we will contact you to resolve the problem instead of rejecting your work...

Learning & Financial group. Participants were informed that they would receive feedback and they would receive a reward if they improved. This design intended to motivate the participants to learn by using rewarded learning. Part of the message is shown below.

...We hope you will learn the skills of writing news articles by taking our tasks. We will provide you feedback on your quality, including the quality of your writing and the way of improving it. If your skills improve, which is measured by the number of errors you make, you will enjoy the following benefits...

Social & Learning & Financial group. Workers were invited to join a team. They would provide and read feedback for and from their team members. In addition, as a team if they win, they would get a reward. This design intended to encourage teams to improve together. Part of the message is shown below.

... As a member of the team, you will be asked to evaluate each other's summaries. That is, you will provide feedback on one of your team members' summary and will also read the feedback on your summary given by your team members. We hope as a team you can help with each other and do your best. In the meantime, your team will compete with another team. If you win, all members will enjoy the following benefits...

Step 3. Groups with social and learning strategies (*Social & Learning* and *Social & Learning & Financial group*) were asked to read and give feedback on their team members' summaries. They were told that their team members took the same tasks and they were asked to evaluate their summaries for coverage, accuracy and conciseness. They also needed to provide feedback including the merits and the flaws of the summaries. At the same time, experimenters produced feedback for the non-social learning group (*Learning group* and *Learning/Financial group*). After all the feedback was generated, groups with the learning strategy (*Learning group, Social & Learning group, Learning & Financial group* and *Social & Learning & Financial*) received feedback.

The financial group received rewards. Groups with a social strategy (*Social group, Social & Financial group, Social & Learning group* and *Social & Learning & Financial group*) sent us their self-introductions and then received welcome messages with a short introduction to their team members.

Step 4. We posted Task 2 and sent different messages to groups (two different articles were used in the task: [36] and [39]. Participants were presented with one of them randomly). For groups with social strategies, there were chat boxes (we customized chat boxes from cbox.ws) embedded in the task interface to increase the interaction between team members. For the *Financial group*, there was a reminder of reward at the top of task. For the groups with learning strategies, feedback was reminded at the top of the task.

Step 5. After Task 2, participants in the groups involving financial reward received rewards. Participants in the groups involving learning received feedback.

Rating

Different from the previous experiments, we used crowd workers (who were independent of the experiment) to evaluate the summaries. Each summary was rated by three workers on its accuracy, conciseness and coverage on 7-point scales. To control the quality of the rating, verification questions were embedded in the task: two questions were about the content of the original text and the raters were also asked to provide feedback for the summaries. After the rating was finished, experimenters examined the ratings and removed the ratings from turkers who did not pass the verification questions. Only the ratings from the judges who gave reasonable answers to the verification questions and summary feedback were used. The ratings were averaged across raters: each summary received average scores on its accuracy, conciseness and coverage. These scores were converted into a final quality score by using the geometric mean. To check the reliability of the crowd's ratings, one experimenter rated a sample of 34 summaries independently. The inter-rater agreement on the sample was adequate (ICC=.63).

	Probability of Return	SE	Mean of Quality	SE
Control	.06 (18/290)	.33	4.82	.70
Social	.13 (31/244) *	.31	5.20	.67
Learning	.05 (13/281)	.38	5.81 **	.73
Financial	.10 (24/243)	.33	5.27	.67
Social&Learning	.10 (22/218)	.48	5.28	.73
Social&Financial	.10 (24/245)	.44	5.07	.72
Learning&Financial	.09 (24/259)	.48	5.11	.70
Social&Learning& Financial	.13 (32/238)	.64	5.28	.67

p < .001 = ***, p < .01 = **, p < .05 = *

Table 3. Experiment 3: Effects of strategies on return rate and quality

Analysis and Results

The analysis for Experiment 3 was similar to the analysis in Experiment 2. The results are shown in Table 3. The second and third column show return rates and standard errors. Logistic regression analysis showed that one unit presence of social strategy increased the odds of participants' return by .78 (p<.01). The rest of the single strategies and interactive strategies did not predict the return rate.

The fourth and fifth column show the means and standard errors of quality. We can see that one unit presence of learning strategy increased the quality by 1.00 (p<.01) on average. The other two individual strategies did not predict the quality.

We also observe a negative interaction between two pairs of strategies. The learning strategy alone increased quality by 0.99 (4.82 to 5.81). Therefore, one would expect that combining social and learning strategy should lead to at least a 0.99 increase, but instead we observed a .46 (4.82 to 5.28) increase. Similarly, combining financial with learning, we saw a .29 (4.82 to 5.11) increase. This means adding either a social or financial strategy reduced the learning strategy's positive effect. However, when we added both social and financial strategies to the learning strategy, this negative interaction was mitigated: given that both strategies reduced learning strategy's effect, we would expect an even lower quality in three-strategy condition. However, we found that every presence of social & learning & financial strategy increased the quality by .46 (4.82 to 5.28) (p<.05).

Discussion

Experiment 3 produced some consistent and inconsistent results with that of Experiment 2. First, the learning strategy's effect was consistent: a positive effect on quality but not return rate. This result suggests that it is possible to create a process allowing workers to provide feedback for each other and improve their skills.

Second, the social strategy continued to have a positive effect on return rate but not on quality. In Experiment 3, we added chatboxes to increase the interaction between workers, (in Experiment 2, there was no direct interaction between participants), which might distract them from focusing on the tasks. This may indicate that social interaction between workers should be controlled at the appropriate level, and designed in a task-centered way. We examined the content of the chatting between team members. Some were task-related and some were not. We did not keep track of an individual's chat messages, so we are unable to undertake further analysis to confirm our conjecture.

Third, the financial strategy no longer had an effect on either quality or return rate. As we can see from the design of the new interactive strategies, participants need to learn or compete with each other or other teams to receive reward. This might demotivate them. In addition, in some conditions, the reward was not delivered until the end of the final task. Participants might not be motivated until they received a reward.

Fourth, even after we designed new ways of integrating the strategies, the paired interactive strategies still had a negative effect on quality: both social and financial strategies reduced the learning strategy's positive effects. Even adding a third strategy reduced such negative interaction, the average quality for *Social & Learning & Financial* (M=5.28) was still lower than that of using the learning strategy alone (M=5.81). This means the negative interaction among strategies might not be caused by the method of integrating them, but something else. We further discuss this issue in the discussion section.

SUMMARY AND DISCUSSION

In this paper, we explored strategies to increase crowd workers' engagement and performance. We used social, learning, and financial strategies, as well as their combinations. We conducted three experiments to test the effects of every single strategy and the interaction of strategies.

The Social Strategy

Social strategies were shown to be most effective in improving crowd engagement. In our study, even though we either only promised a team, or added simple chatboxes, we still found powerful positive effects on workers' engagement across tasks. This finding is interesting for two reasons. First, considering that complex tasks benefit from a sustained workforce and might require collaboration between workers, this finding suggests that using social job design mechanisms may be effective for building teams of workers who could work together across multiple tasks. Second, a social strategy might improve crowd workers' wellbeing by satisfying their social motivation rather than treating them as independent workers. Regarding the social strategy's effect on *quality*, it had a positive effect when there was only an imaginary team and self-disclosure of workers' information, and the effect disappeared when real interaction between workers was provided. This indicates that task irrelevant interaction might distract workers from focusing on the tasks. However, this needs to be further tested in the future.

The Learning Strategy

A learning strategy was shown to be most effective in improving quality. This finding is consistent with previous research from Dow et al. [8]. However, we provide new insights: 1) Workers are able to provide feedback to each other's work and learn through feedback on complex tasks. 2) Unlike the previous study where feedback was presented synchronously, our feedback was provided asynchronously and workers made progress in a different new task. This shows the promise of training crowd workers over time, and building a skilled workforce for complex tasks.

The Combined Strategy

The social and learning strategies seem to make an ideal strategy to incentivize workers: using a social strategy to attract workers and a learning strategy to improve their skills. One might assume combining multiple strategies can improve both engagement and quality. However, when we tried to combine strategies, we found that the effects were not additive on either engagement or task quality. Indeed, some combinations, especially the learning and financial combinations even undercut the positive effect from the single strategy. Except for the negative interaction between the financial and learning strategy, we are not aware of theories to explain such complex interaction among the other strategies.

As discussed in the beginning of the paper, interaction among different factors could be complex, especially considering that in online experiments it is not clear which part of the treatments the participants were exposed to and focused on. The integrated mechanisms might change the initial intention of each single strategy and induce a different mindset in crowd workers and lead to worse results. That the effects of social and learning strategies were not additive might be because workers who concentrated on learning either did not care about social interactions, or were distracted by them. For example, in Experiment 2, workers not only need to read feedback but also introduce themselves, which might result in higher cognitive load and therefore a lower level of performance. Regarding the interaction between social and financial strategies, the financial strategy involves competition between workers (being rewarded if accumulating most credits among all workers) and this relation might undercut the bonding effect we tried to build with the social strategy.

However, the interaction between the three strategies in Experiment 1 and Experiment 3 resulted in a more positive effect. This may be because even though in Experiment 1 we combined all the strategies, each one of them was not fully operationalized and therefore didn't lead to strong conflicts. In Experiment 3, the three-strategy-interaction was constructed differently with a common goal: group members help each other to compete with another group. This design conveyed a clear and non-conflicting goal.

Therefore, we conjecture that when using multiple strategies, they should be designed in a way that signals a clear and coherent goal and involves minimum cognitive load for workers. However, these conjectures need further investigation and evidence. It is also likely that there is a ceiling effect on participants' behavior: even if participants are motivated by multiple strategies, there is only a limited space to improve for both return rate and quality.

Limitations

This work is limited in several ways. Even though we tried to operationalize the three strategies, such as adding chat boxes to allow interaction, asking workers to provide feedback to each other, and providing rewards, these strategies still functioned more as recruitment strategies than systematic strategies, because they were only implemented for three tasks. For example, we didn't successfully build real teams to compete with each other or work together synchronously. Regarding the learning strategy, we didn't differentiate between learning about general science versus learning job skills. It may be interesting in future work to test these types of learning apart. For example, crowd workers who are intrinsically motivated might like to learn about general science, while those who are extrinsically motivated might be more interested in learning job skills. Learning strategies could be tailored to these differences.

In addition, we only tested the strategies in Amazon Mechanical Turk. We varied the base payment from 40 cents to 150 cents in the three experiments, and the bonus included 5 cents and 10 dollars (conditional to the credits they accumulated), with consistent findings across experiments. Because these payments roughly cover the price range of many micro-task (and even some macro-task) crowdsourcing markets, we think the findings, especially findings about the learning and social strategies, may be generalizable among crowdsourcing markets such as Amazon Mechanical Turk, CrowdFlower, MobileWorks, and others. Other crowd communities such as Wikipedia involve many different motivations other than pay, including reputation, altruism, and fun [28]. Therefore, while our financial strategy findings are likely less relevant, some of our findings on social and learning strategies might apply to such communities.

Through experiments involving thousands of workers, we found that the final return rate was about 15%. This low final return rate was partially caused by the experiment itself. We needed to focus on participants who accepted the complete treatments. Participants who were not able to take a task within the given time slot were excluded in the following tasks. Ignoring that constraint, after the first task 50% participants were willing to come back. This suggests the opportunity and possibility of building stable long-term strategies with ad-hoc collections of crowd workers.

CONCLUSION

This paper attempts to improve our understanding of applying job design mechanisms – including social, learning, and financial strategies – to increasing engagement and output quality in crowdsourcing markets. Through three experiments we showed that a social strategy is most effective in building the crowd's loyalty, and a learning strategy is most effective in improving their skills. The complex findings about interactions between strategies suggest that multiple strategies should be carefully designed. Strategies applied in parallel can cancel out each other's positive effects.

This work provides ways of increasing crowd engagement and output quality. Techniques we described provide opportunities for improving the interaction between employers and workers, and the interactions between workers themselves, as well as training and learning possibilities. In this way, mechanisms can be built to improve crowdsourcing markets that will enable better crowds and more complex and high quality crowd work.

ACKNOWLEDGEMENT

This work was supported by NSF grants IIS-1149797, IIS-1217559, OCI-0943148, IIS-0968484, IIS-1111124, Bosch, Google, and Microsoft, and Carnegie Mellon's Center for the Future of Work.

REFERENCES

1. Amabile, T. M. Motivational synergy: Toward new conceptualizations of intrinsic and extrinsic motivation in the workplace. *Human Resource Management Review*, 3(3), (1993), 185-201.
2. Baumeister, R.F. and Leary, M.R. The need to belong: desire for interpersonal attachments as a fundamental human motivation. *Psychological bulletin 117*, 3 (1995), 497.
3. Bowen, D.E. and Lawler, E.E. Total quality-oriented human resources management. *Organizational Dynamics 20*, 4 (1992), 29–41.
4. Chandler, D. and Kapelner, A. Breaking monotony with meaning: Motivation in crowdsourcing markets. *University of Chicago mimeo*, 2010.
5. Choi, B., Alexander, K., Kraut, R. E. and Levine J. M., Socialization tactics in Wikipedia and their effects. In Proc. *CSCW* 2010.
6. Collins, N. L. and Miller, L. C., Self-disclourse and Liking: a meta-analytic review. *Psychological bulletin 116*, 3 (1994), 457-475.
7. Deci, E.L., Koestner, R., and Ryan, R.M. A meta-analytic review of experiments examining the effects of extrinsic rewards on intrinsic motivation. *Psychological bulletin 125*, 6 (1999), 627.
8. Dow, S., Kulkarni, A., Bunge, B., Nguyen, T., Klemmer, S., and Hartmann, B. Shepherding the crowd: managing and providing feedback to crowd workers. In *Proc. CHI EA 2011*.
9. Ertmer, P. A., Richardson, J. C., Belland, B., Camin, D., Connolly, P., Coulthard, G., Lei, K., and Mong, C., Using peer

feedback to enhance the quality of student online postings: an exploratory study. *JCMC*, 12(2), (2007).

10. Jehn, K. A. The dynamic nature of conflict: a longitudinal study of intragroup conflict and group performance. *Academy of Management Journal* 44, 2(2001), 238-251.
11. Galton, F. The geometric mean, in vital and social statistics. *Proceedings of the Royal Society of London 29*, 196-199 (1879), 365–367.
12. Hackman, J.R. and Oldham, G.R. Motivation through the design of work: Test of a theory. *Organizational behavior and human quality 16*, 2 (1976), 250–279.
13. Heckman, J.J. Sample selection bias as a specification error. *Econometrica: Journal of the econometric society*, (1979), 153–161.
14. Hill, C.A. Affiliation motivation: People who need people... but in different ways. *Journal of personality and social psychology 52*, 5 (1987), 1008.
15. Hsieh, G., Hudson, S.E., and Kraut, R.E. Donate for credibility: how contribution strategies can improve credibility. In *Proc. CHI 2011,* 3435–3438.
16. Huang, S.-W. and Fu, W.-T. Don't Hide in the Crowd! Increasing Social Transparency Between Peer Workers Improves Crowdsourcing Outcomes. In *Proc. CHI 2013.*
17. Jenkins, G. D., Mitra, A., Gupta, N. and Shaw, J. D., Are financial incentives related to performance? A meta-analytic review of empirical research. *Journal of Applied Psychology* 83, 5(1998), 777-787.
18. Jensen, M. and Murphy, K., Competition and Incentives: Practice vs Theory. *Journal of Finance* 43 (1988), 593-616.
19. Kinnaird, P., Dabbish, L., Kiesler, S., and Faste, H. Coworker transparency in a microtask marketplace. In *Proc. CSCW 2013,* 1285–1290.
20. Kittur, A., Nickerson, J. V., Bernstein, M. S., Gerber, E. M., Shaw, A., Zimmerman, J., Lease, M., and Horton, J. J. The future of crowd work. In *Proc. CSCW 2013.*
21. Kittur, A., Smus, B., Khamkar, S., and Kraut, R.E. Crowdforge: Crowdsourcing complex work. In *Proc. UIST 2011.*
22. Lasecki, W., Murray, K., White, S., Miller, R. C., and Bigham,J. P. Real-time crowd control of existing interfaces. In *Proc. UIST 2011,* 23–32.
23. Lave, J. and Wenger, E. *Situated Learning: Legitimate Peripheral Participation.* Cambridge University Press, 1991.
24. Lawler III, E.E. 3. Job design and employee motivation. *Personnel Psychology* 22, 4 (1969), 426–435.
25. Leana, C. R., & Van Buren, H. J. Organizational social capital and employment practices. *Academy of Management Review* 24, (1999). , 538-555.
26. Mason, W. and Watts, D.J. Financial strategies and the quality of crowds. *ACM SigKDD Explorations Newsletter* 11, 2 (2010), 100–108.
27. Meyer, J. P., Paunonen, S. V., Gellatly, I. R., Goffin, R. D. and Jackson, D. N. Organizational commitment and job performance: It's the nature of the commitment that counts. *Journal of Applied Psychology* 74(1), 1989, 152-156.
28. Nov, O. What motivates Wikipedians? *Communications of the ACM* 50, 11(2007), 60-64.
29. Prentice, D. A., Miller, D. T., and Lightdalel,J. R. Asymmetries in attachments to groups and to their members: Distinguishing between common-identity and common-bond groups. *Personality and Social Psychology Bulletin* 20, 5 (1994), 484–49.
30. Podolny, J. M., & Baron, J. N. Relationships and resources: Social networks and mobility in the workplace. *American Sociological Review*, 62, (1997), 673-693.
31. Randel, A.E. and Ranft, A. L. Motivations to maintain social ties with coworkers. *Group and Organization Management* 32, 2(2007), 208-232.
32. Ren, Y., Kraut, R. E., Kiesler, S., & Resnick, P. (2012). *Encouraging commitment in online communities*. In R. E. Kraut & P. Resnick (Eds.), Building successful online communities: Evidence-based social design (pp. 77-124). Cambridge MA: MIT Press.
33. Rogstadius, J., Kostakos, V., Kittur, A., Smus, B., Laredo, J., and Vukovic, M. An assessment of intrinsic and extrinsic motivation on task quality in crowdsourcing markets. In *Proc. ICWSM 2011.*
34. Ross, J., Irani, L., Silberman, M. S., Zaldivar, A., and Tomlinson, B. (2010). Who are the crowdworkers?: shifting demographics in mechanical turk. *In CHI EA'10: Proceedings of the 28th of the international conference extended abstracts on Human factors in computing systems*, pp. 2863–2872, New York, NY, USA. ACM.
35. Rousseau, D.M. Technological differences in job characteristics, employee satisfaction, and motivation: A synthesis of job design research and sociotechnical systems theory. *Organizational Behavior and Human Performance 19*, 1 (1977), 18–42.
36. Salganik, M.J., Dodds, P.S., and Watts, D.J. Experimental study of inequality and unpredictability in an artificial cultural market. *Science* 311, 5762 (2006), 854–856.
37. Shaw, A.D., Horton, J.J., and Chen, D.L. Designing strategies for inexpert human raters. In *Proc. CSCW 2011.*
38. Tang, T. L. and Sarsfield-Baldwin, L. The effects of self-esteem, task label, and performance feedback on task liking and intrinsic motivation. *The Journal of Social Psychology* 131, 4 (1991), 567-572.
39. Tang, J.C., Cebrian, M., Giacobe, N.A., Kim, H.W., Kim, T., and Wickert, D.B. Reflecting on the Darpa red balloon challenge. *Comm. of the ACM* 54, 4 (2011), 78–85.
40. Wang, Y., Kraut, R., and Levine, J. To stay or leave? The incentive of emotional and informational support to commitment in online health support groups. In *Proc. CSCW* 2011.
41. Wiggins, G., Educative assessment. *Designing assessments to inform and improve student quality*. Jossey-Bass Publishers, CA, 1998.
42. Zhu, H., Kraut, R., and Kittur, A. Effectiveness of shared leadership in online communities. In *Proc. CSCW* 2012.
43. Zhu, H., Kraut, R.E., & Kittur, A. Effects of Peer Feedback on Contribution: A Field Experiment in Wikipedia. In *Proc. CHI 2013.*

Motivating Contribution in a Participatory Sensing System via Quid-Pro-Quo

Anthony Tomasic **John Zimmerman** **Aaron Steinfeld** **Yun Huang**
{tomasic,johnz,astein,yunhuang}@cs.cmu.edu
Carnegie Mellon University

ABSTRACT
Participatory sensing systems (PSS) require frequent injection of information that has a short shelf-life. The use of crowds to gather information for PSS is therefore particularly challenging. In this study, we explore the impact of two policies on user contributions. A quid-pro-quo policy exchanges contributions from users for access to critical information in the system. A request policy simply reminds the user that information is needed to make the system function well. Prior research has shown that request for help in crowdsourced system is an effective mechanism to increase contributions. During a large-scale experimental study within a publicly deployed, crowdsourced, transit information system, we analyzed metrics associated with frequency of contribution and commitment to long-term use over a 10-month period. Our results confirmed that quid-pro-quo led to more contribution, but at a cost of faster departure from the study. When a participant was simply requested to contribute, but could still access community-generated data if they ignored a request, was largely ineffective and was statistically similar to the control condition where no request for contribution occurred. Thus crowdsource system designers should consider imposing quid-pro-quo type policies for PSS that concentrate on fewer users, but makes them more productive.

Author Keywords
Crowdsourced transit information systems; quid-pro-quo; participatory sensing

ACM Classification Keywords
H.5.3.

INTRODUCTION

The recent emergence of social computing along with the meteoric adoption of smartphones has given rise to the concept of participatory sensing [3]. This is a new embodiment for socio-technical systems that blends crowdsourcing and the ubiquity of mobile phones, positioning this as a sensing platform that can generate valuable information about the world. Examples of participatory sensing systems (PSS) include the commercial service Waze [22], a mobile app that motivates car drivers to report traffic conditions that benefit others. On the research side, a great example can be found in Tiramisu [26], a smartphone service that allows transit riders to generate their own real-time arrival information system by sharing location traces as they commute across a city. One critical challenge PSS like Waze and Tiramisu face is how to motivate users to continually observe and contribute information. Part of the challenge comes from the fact that in the case of many PSS, such as Waze and Tiramisu, the contributed information does not directly benefit the person who makes the contribution. For example, by the time a user can report a traffic breakdown, it is generally too late for them to avoid the problem spot. Additionally, observations such as emergent traffic conditions and transit vehicle locations are time and place sensitive. They have a very short shelf life, and they only benefit a small segment of a larger user community who need the information in the next few minutes.

Understanding why people contribute to online communities has been an ongoing topic of interest in CSCW. A recently book [15] details many strategies for motivating contributions, including asking people as well as intrinsic and extrinsic approaches. In addition, research on free-riding — people who use a service but do not contribute — in peer-to-peer systems [8] and with recommenders [7] have investigated the idea reciprocity, of requiring users to make a contribution in order to gain access to the service or information they desire. A question we chose to investigate is if this "quid pro quo" approach could be successful in the context of participatory sensing.

To investigate this question and to better understand the unrealized potential of PSS, we conducted a ten-month long field study. We deployed a PSS version of the Tiramisu app with three conditions. One condition followed a *quid pro quo* approach, requiring participants to share location traces in order to access arrival time information; one condition simply made a *request* for contributions to participants who engaged in free-riding; and the final condition functioned as a *control*, allowing participants to access arrival information regardless of whether they shared location traces when commuting. Users were randomly assigned to one of the three conditions upon download of the app.

CSCW'14, February 15–19, 2014, Baltimore, Maryland, USA.
Copyright © 2014 ACM 978-1-4503-2540-0/14/02...$15.00.
HTTP://DX.DOI.ORG/10.1145/2531602.2531705

Participants in the *quid pro quo* condition made significantly more contributions than the other participants. However, they also abandoned their use of the app at a higher rate than participants in the other conditions. On average, they used the app for fewer days. In addition, a few even publically complained about the quid-pro-quo design in reviews they made in the app stores. We observed no differences in contributions between the control and request conditions. Interestingly, we did observe that participants who shared location traces, regardless of condition, were more likely to share reports about their transit experience. This observation indicates a possible relationship between contribution and engagement with the service.

In this paper, we first summarize related research that motivated and informed the design of our study. Next, we describe the Tiramisu, the context for our study, and the three experimental conditions. We then report our findings and discuss what they mean and how they might aid in the design of a participatory sensing system.

RELATED WORK

Related work falls into two distinct categories: previous research on participatory sensing and crowdsourcing systems, and previous work on motivating contributions in online communities.

PPS and crowdsourcing Systems

Many smart city concepts have been developed based on the idea of urban infrastructures that are instrumented with robust sensors. While many of these concepts have yet to be realized due to challenges of costs and machine-learning, recently *participatory sensing* has emerged as an alternative way to developing these kinds of systems. Participatory sensing recognizes the many people out in the world with mobile phones as a new type of sensing infrastructure [3]. It combines human observers and their phones' sensing and communication abilities to create new services.

Waze [22], a system that crowdsources traffic information provides a great commercial example. This service encourages users to contribute observations of traffic as they drive. Users can attach clarifying details to specific geographic points so fellow users have insight on sources of congestion (e.g., "Construction in right lane"). Like many PSS, Waze employs a gamification approach. They motivate people to share reports by making the interaction feel like a game. Users earn points for each observation. The potential success of this participatory approach can partially be seen in Google's $966 million purchase of Waze.

Researchers and developers have both recognized motivating participation as a key challenge to developing participatory sensing systems. One of the main challenges with PSS in an urban sensing context is that it requires very time-sensitive and place-sensitive contributions. Often an observation has a short shelf life and benefits only a tiny segment of other users. Consider Tiramisu, the crowdsourced transit information system, as an example. A Tiramisu user shares a location trace when commuting. This live information is only good for the remainder of the trip this user is on. In addition, it only benefits other users who are considering riding this specific bus in the next few minutes. Most other crowdsourced information systems do not face this challenge. For example, if a user adds or updates a Wikipedia entry, the benefits of their effort can persist for days, weeks, months, or even years.

Researchers have suggested that one approach to addressing this problem might be to transition from a participatory sensing to opportunistic sensing framing [16]. The difference is that, with participatory sensing, the human explicitly makes an observation. With opportunistic sensing, the mobile phone acts without requiring user input. Researchers have developed systems that employ this approach to generate transit arrival information similar to Tiramisu [20, 25]. This approach, however, raises two issues. One is privacy when a phone shares potentially personal information like location without explicit consent. Another is in the robustness of the information. For example, a phone can report its location on the bus, but it cannot easily report the route number when multiple routes share the same roadways. In this case the human observers ability to add information beyond what a phone can sense helps to demonstrate the potential of PSS.

Recent work in time-sensitive crowdsourcing has focused on the use of multiple, remote contributors (workers) who work together in support of an individual user (requestor). For example, Soylent utilized Mechanical Turk to provide on-demand, real-time document editing [2]. Another example, SCRIBE, also uses Mechanical Turk as a labor force and brings four Turkers together to transcribe live events in place of a traditional transcriptionist [17]. While these systems are successful and work well for their target applications, it is difficult to tell if they can scale to support millions of requestors. It is difficult to tell if there are enough workers to do all of the work people might request. Another key difference in the embodiment of these other time-sensitive crowdsourcing services is that they make a clear distinction between requestors and workers. In PSS systems the users that want the sensed information are often the same users who are in a position to make and share the observations.

Motivating contribution

Encouraging users to contribute to online systems has been an ongoing research topic within CSCW going back to early investigations of why workers failed to enter data into shared calendars [11]. Over the years, many studies have built up a rich set of theories designers can draw on in order to envision more effective, collaborative systems. A recent book by Kraut and Resnick does a wonderful job of digesting this research and putting it into language that is actionable by designers [15]. Kraut and Resnick note that people are more likely to contribute when they are asked, and when they are asked personally, based on their individual knowledge and abilities. In addition, they detail a number of approaches that use intrinsic and extrinsic motivations to drive contribution. On the intrinsic side, systems can be designed to be fun or social, both of which has been found to increase contribution. On the extrinsic side, systems can offer rewards such as money, game points, or rewards such as reputation or status. They connect the results of many different studies around a model of how a user perceives the individual value they receive and the effort being asked of them. When the benefit (individual value) outweighs the effort, the user will contribute.

One ongoing challenge with social systems that require user contribution is free-riding, people that use a system but who never make a contribution. Adar and Huberman conducted one of the first studies on free-riding. They investigated usages patterns in the peer-to-peer (P2P) file sharing system Gnutella and found that 70% of users free-ride. They also reported that 25% of users provided 99% of the shared content and the top 1% provided almost 40% of the shared content [1]. More recent work looking at Gnutella reported even higher levels of free-riding, with more 85% of users exhibiting this behavior over different durations [12].

Some P2P systems have attempted to address the problem of free-riding by employing a reciprocity based incentive model where users are required to contribute in order to access the information they desire [14]. Many researchers have investigated BitTorrent's use of this incentive model [6, 14]. BitTorrent employs a "tit for tat" approach where the speed with which a user can download a file is controlled by their willingness to contribute, to allow others to download information from their own machine. When users do not share, they are choked out. This research generally describes BitTorrent's approach as effective, though a number of papers detail how users can cheat the system and engage in free-riding and propose variations to refine the incentive design, i.e. [13]. While "tit for tat" is an abstractly similar policy to quid-pro-quo, the BitTorrent user experience is completely different from a PSS. The quid-pro-quo policy of a PSS requires human effort to generate contributions with every use of the system. BitTorrent simply requires a user to agree (by default) to expend some computational resources.

Researchers working on recommender systems have also investigated reciprocity as a way to motivate contribution. It is important to note that the usage model of recommenders is a different than for PSS and P2P. With most recommenders, users need to enter information (make a contribution) before the recommender can make a recommendation. Many other social systems, such as online dating services, follow this same usage model. With PSS and P2P, the data any user might want is often already available, so it is possible to gain the benefit of the system prior to making any contribution. While recommenders are different from PSS, they have a shared challenge of time-sensitive information. They need to generate ratings for new content in order to be able to recommend this content to others. Some of the recommender users must rate a new thing before any other ratings have been made. However, the shelf-life of these contributions made to recommenders are generally much longer than for PSS.

The need to make an initial contribution for receiving a service has been viewed as a barrier to adoption. Researchers looking at recommenders have investigated this issue. One very relevant study of the movie recommender MovieLens made a great advance on understanding the use of reciprocity during the initial use [7]. In this study, researchers created several versions of MovieLens: one required participants to enter in 25 tags in addition to an initial set of ratings; one required them to enter 5 additional tags; and one required no tagging, but allowed participants to tag if they desired. Participants who were required to enter more tags generated more tag information than participants in the other conditions. However, they also had a higher rate of abandoning the system during their initial use than participants in the other conditions. Nevertheless, even with the higher rate of abandonment, the high contribution requirement generated the most contributions even taking abandonment into account. Most interesting was that fact that participants who were required to enter the most information during their initial use of the system on average continued to enter more information during extended use of the system.

Our study advances understanding on contribution by applying current theories around motivating online contribution to a new domain: participatory sensing systems. We wanted to understand if these theories generated in experiments with systems like recommenders and wikis could work on this different kind of social computing system. In particular, because of the requirements of PSS, quid-pro-quo continuously monitors user behavior, unlike previous approaches that only set an initial barrier. In addition, we wanted to push of the ecological validity of these theories. While many of them had been developed and refined of lab studies and short-term field deployments, we intended to test them with a long-term (10-month) field study with a relatively large number of participants (8000+). A long-term field study exposes the research to additional effects, such as the impact of media announcements and product reviews.

STUDY

We wanted to investigate if a quid-pro-quo approach, which has been successful for driving contribution in P2P services and for recommenders, could be effective at motivating high and sustained levels of contribution in the context of a PSS.

Study Context

For the context of our study, we selected the Tiramisu system, which allows transit riders to crowdsource arrival information by sharing location traces on a smart phone. In the current implementation, users begin by selecting a bus stop from a map. The service then displays a list of arrival times for all buses within a 90-minute window (those that should have passed 30 minutes ago to those that should arrive within 60 minutes) (Figure 1a). When another user is on a bus and contributing a location trace, the system provides a "real-time" arrival estimate to other users. When there is no real-time, but enough traces for this specific trip have been contributed in the past, the system provides a "historical" estimate of the arrival time. When there is neither real-time nor historical data of sufficient quality, the system provides "scheduled" arrival information from the transit agency's static schedule.

To contribute a trace, users select the route number of the vehicle they board (Figure 1a) and identify their destination stop. This transitions them to the "Record" screen (Figure 1b). Here they indicate how full the bus is and then select the green "Start Recording" button to begin contributing a location trace (Figure 1b). When they are near their destination, the trace is automatically stopped, and the user is provided with a summary of their current and cumulative contributions. For more details on the design and rationale, please see [26].

While real-time arrival information systems are quite common in most European and many Asian cities, they are less available in the US. In the US only 5% percent of commuters use public transit to get to work [21]. Access

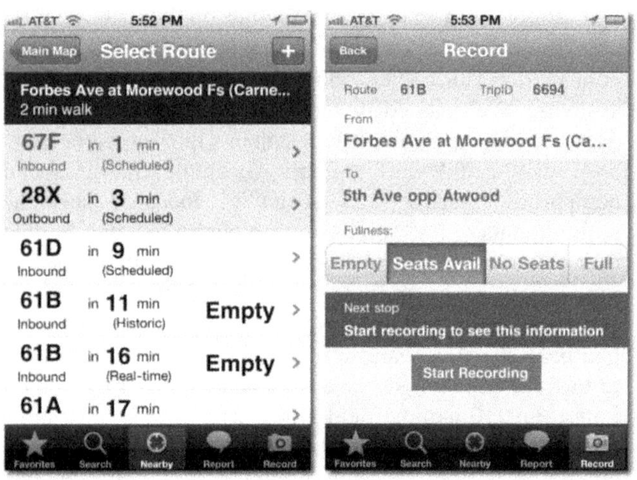

Figure 1. (a) Select Route Screen: users see three kinds of arrival information and select the vehicle they board. (b) Record Screen: users to report fullness and start sharing a location trace.

to arrival time estimates can increase ridership [5], particularly when delivered to mobile devices [9]. However, an embedded arrival information system including networked GPS units installed on all transit vehicles and electronic signage for display of the arrival information at the stops is expensive to purchase, install, and maintain. We suspect that the relatively small number of citizens who use public transit systems in the US make installation of an embedded real-time information system a challenging prospect for the taxpayers to accept. Given this situation, a PSS, where transit users co-produce the arrival information they desire, seems a possible solution.

In addition to being able to crowdsource arrival information, the Tiramisu app allows users to submit notes: questions, compliments, or complaints about the transit service. During a field trial of Tiramisu [26], researchers observed that usage of the app seemed to drive use of the notes feature. Most participants in the field trial reported that they had never contacted the transit service to share a compliment or complaint, yet when given this mobile service, more than half of the participants submitted a note about the transit service within the three-week trial. The research team did not know if this behavior was driven by simply having the phone in hand, with a transit app in focus, when experiencing a problem worthy of reporting, or if the act of sharing location traces (co-producing this new service) actually increased participants' engagement with the transit service.

Conditions and Hypotheses

To run our study, we configured Tiramisu to run three experimental conditions parallel to its normal interaction design. Below we describe the conditions:

Request Condition (Req): When participants are observed to be free-riding, they are prompted via a popup message to contribute a location trace (Figure 2a).

Quid-pro-quo Condition (QPQ): When participants are observed to be free-riding, they are informed by a popup message that access to arrival information has been blocked (Figure 2b), and when they close the popup, they see only a list of upcoming buses and the word "Blocked" in place of the arrival time information (Figure 2c).

Control Condition: Follows the normal interaction design previously described where the system makes no attempt to detect free-riding behavior.

Our system detected free-riding by observing the number of sessions where participants accessed arrival information and the number of sessions where they shared a location trace. We used a point system. For each day a participant accessed the arrival information, they were awarded one *usage-point*. Regardless on how many times they accessed the arrival information, the most they could earn was one usage-point for a day. For each day where they shared a location trace, they were awarded one *contribution-point*. Again, it did not matter how long they shared a location trace or how many times they shared location traces in a day. The maximum they could earn was one *contribution-point* per day. We used the ratio *contribution-point/usage-point* to infer free-riding behavior. When a new participant joined the study by downloading the app, they began with a default score of 1 *contribution-point* and 2 *usage-points*; a starting ratio of ½.

For the QPQ and Req conditions, we added a high and low threshold for the free-riding detector. Participants in the high-level (QPQ-High and Req-High) were considered to be free-riding if they earned three usage-points and no contribution-points (three days of accessing information without contributing a location trace). Participants in the low-level (QPQ-Low and Req-Low) were considered to be free-riding if they earned six usage-points and no contribution-points (six days of accessing information without contributing a location trace).

After the system detected free-riding, it continued to accrue usage-points for each day participants accessed the system and did not share a location trace. When free-riding, if they shared a location trace, the points reset. This reset turned off the popups for both QPQ and Req participants and turned on the arrival information to participants in the QPQ condition. For participants in QPQ-High and Req-High, a reset changed *contribution-point* to 1 and *usage-point* to 3. For participants in QPQ-Low and Req-Low, a reset changed the contribution-point to 1 and usage-point to 6. These reset values meant that if the following day, the participant accessed the arrival information without sharing a location trace, the system would once again consider them to be free-riding. With this reset behavior, participants needed to only contribute once to be seen as not free-riding, regardless of the number of days they had exhibited free-riding behavior. The actual total number of contributions and usage sessions for a device were recorded separately from this scoring system to aid in our analysis.

We had several hypotheses drawn from the literature:

H1: Participants in QPQ will contribute more location traces than participants in the other two conditions. The success of BitTorrent [6] and the work on recommenders [7] made QPQ appear to be a more successful strategy that simply asking participants to make a contribution.

H1.1: Participants in QPQ-High will submit more location traces than participants in QPQ-Low. The Drenner study [7] indicated that requiring more contribution should result in more total contributions, even after people quit using the service.

H2: Participants in Req will share more location traces than participants in Control. Requesting contribution has been shown to be more effective than not requesting [15].

H2.1: Participants in Req-High will share more location traces than participants in Req-Low. It seems logical that simply asking more frequently should generate more action from participants.

H3: Participants in QPQ will stop using the app after fewer days than participants in Control and Req. The Drenner et al. study [7] observed that for their recommenders, the requirement to contribute caused people to abandon the service a higher rate during initial use than without the requirement.

H3.1: Participants in QPQ-High will quit using the app at a higher rate than participants in QPQ-Low. Again,

Figure 2a. Popup message participant sees in the request condition.

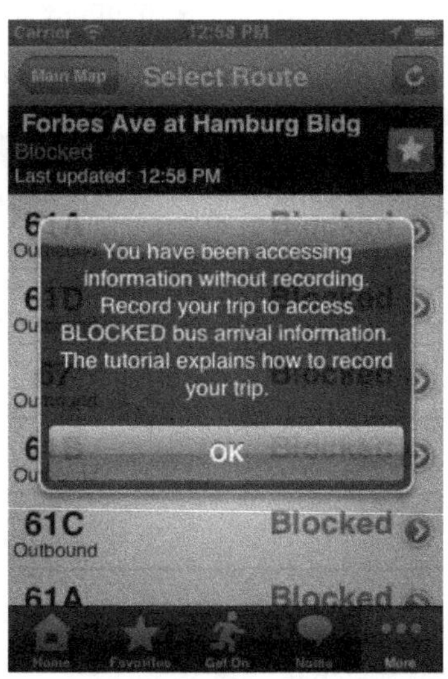

Figure 2b. Popup message participant sees in the quid-pro-quo condition.

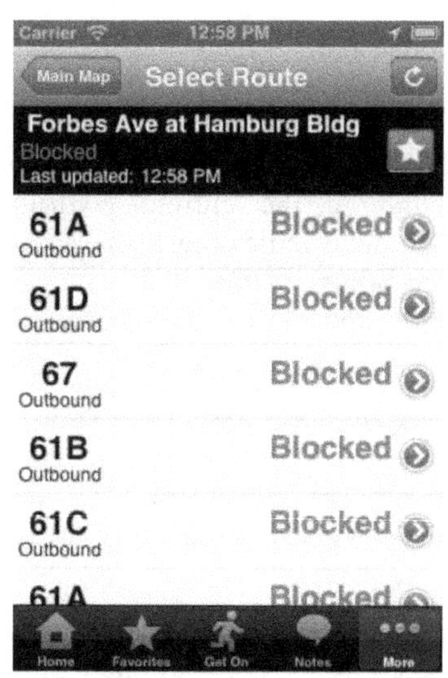

Figure 2c. Arrival information the seen in the quid-pro-quo condition.

the Drenner et al. study [7] noted that requiring more contribution cause more people to quit using their recommender during initial use.

H4: Participants that share location traces will contribute more notes than participants that submit fewer location traces. We have two rationales for this. First, the Drenner et al. recommender study [7] showed that people who were required to contribute more during their initial sessions continued to contribute more. Second, results from the field trail of Tiramisu hinted that there might be a connection between sharing location traces and generation of notes.

Measures

Our study had 3 conditions and five possible configurations (Control, Req-High, Req-Low, QPQ-High, QPQ-Low). In the Control condition, there was no level as the system never attempted to detect free-riding and change its behavior.

For all configurations, we logged a series of device interaction measures. We used Device ID as a proxy for participant. When participants installed the app, the app would assign them to one of the conditions based on the Device ID. If they deleted and reinstalled the app, they were reenrolled in the same condition and recognized as the same participant. If they upgraded to a new phone during the course of this study, they appeared to be a new participant using the service for the first time. They could be assigned to any of the configurations.

Each device log record contained a GPS location and counts for the following: *Usage:* the number of days where the participant accessed information at least once. *Contribution:* the number of days where the participant shared at least on location trace. *Impressions:* the total count of schedule, historical and real-time *impressions* delivered. An impression is generated when a particular bus arrival time prediction, i.e. trip row, is displayed on the device (horizontal panels in Figure 1a). *Notes:* the total number of notes submitted from a device.

The log record also contained data about each device's configuration, the current contribution count, and a boolean value indicating if the device was considered to be free-riding. Additional data on other interactions within the app were also collected.

This data was used to compute a variety of summary statistics of each participant's use of the system. For example, the contribution percentage is the fraction of days that the participant shared a location traced out of all days the participant used the system.

Study Timeline

A deliberate effort was made to manage the mass media influence on this study so that external factors associated with public awareness would be somewhat controlled. While never a problem in lab studies, these real-world factors can influence how people use a system in the wild. We deployed our system via Apple's App Store as a free app and held a press event on July 27, 2011 for the local papers, television news channels, and radio stations. The event was successful and resulted in very high saturation throughout the Pittsburgh media market. All major, local news outlets mentioned the application service. As desired, this saturation led to a dramatic surge in participant enrollment. We intentionally did not run a marketing campaign to increase participation and contribution rates. One exception to this was a press release we issued when an Android version became available (October 19, 2011).

External events occurred during the deployment that we assume could impact usage of the app. As with most agencies, Port Authority of Allegheny County (PAAC) changes their schedule periodically to adjust route timings, route offerings, and provide drivers a chance to change routes (i.e., a new "bid"). During the ten months of this deployment (August through May), the transit service released three new schedules. These occurred three months apart and are important in the system. The representation of the transit schedule complicates efforts to link data across bid changes. Each time a new schedule was released, the system discarded the historical estimates and used new location traces to generate new estimates.

In addition, during the initial release we encountered complaints that sharing a location trace led to unwanted battery drain. The software was update to reduce the location sampling rate, making use of the app much less battery draining. This change occurred during the second month of the deployment.

The study ended on May 15, 2012 when a new version of the software that removed the two experimental conditions, Req and QPQ. However, the system continued to operate, thus permitting tracking of the devices that continued to use the system (either under the old or new release). We continued to track devices after the study. This additional data permits a precise designation of the participants that continued to use the system after the new version of the software was deployed. This designation (called "right-censoring") allows us to properly account for participants who continued to use the service beyond the end of our data sample in survivability analyses.

RESULTS

8447 participants (smartphone device IDs) took part in our study over the 10-month duration. Results are organized below around the four hypotheses. Table 1 shows a summary of the results including the number of participants in each condition and level. Condition and level nested within condition were tested for significance. Participants in the QPQ condition had a contribution rate of 19.1%. This rate is the number of days they shared at

Table 1. Measurement of participant behavior by condition.

Condition	Level+	Total devices (n)	Total device days	Total trace days	Contribution %	Total trace duration (min)	Average trace duration (min)
Condition main effect results:			$F(2, 8444) = 7.1$ $p = 0.0008$	$F(2, 8444) = 8.5$ $p = 0.0002$	$F(2, 8444) = 10.7$ $p < 0.0001$	$F(2, 8444) = 4.7$ $p = 0.009$	$F(2, 8444) = 2.6$ $p = 0.075$ n.s.
Control			A++	A	A	A	
	Subtotal	2825	25124	6,017	15.5%	67,614	2.67
Request			AB	A	A	AB	
	High	1352	10,744	3,231	17.2%	40,654	3.78
	Low	1467	12,044	3,514	17.0%	42,721	3.55
	Subtotal	2819	22,788	6,745	17.1%	83,375	3.66
Quid-pro-quo			B	B	B	B	
	High	1379	9,858	4,938	19.9%	54,979	5.58
	Low	1424	11,076	4,101	18.2%	46,806	4.23
	Subtotal	2803	20,934	9,039	19.1%	101,785	4.86
Total		8447	68,846	21,801	17.2%	252,774	

\+ There were no significant main effects for Level nested within Condition on the measures in this table.

++ Conditions not connected by letters (A, B, etc) are significantly different from each other for Tukey HSD post hoc test. For example, Control has significantly more Device Days than QPQ, but Req is not significantly different from either Control or QPQ.

least one location trace over the total number of days they used the app.

Participants in the Req condition had a contribution rate of 17.1% and Control had contribution of 15.5%. Tukey HSD post hoc analyses show that the QPQ mode was significantly different from the Control and from Req for contribution percentage and also for the total number of days where at least one location trace was shared. H1 was confirmed.

Participants in QPQ-High had a contribution rate of 19.9% while participants in QPQ-Low had a contribution rate of 18.2%. However, there was no significant effect for Level. Therefore, H1.1 was not confirmed. Requiring more contribution for participants in the QPQ-High configuration at twice the rate of contribution for participants in the QPQ-Low configuration did not result in significantly more contributions. H1.1 was not confirmed.

Participants in the Req condition had a higher rate of contribution than participants in Control; however, the effect was not significant. Asking participants to contribute did not result in significantly more contributions than not asking. H2 was not confirmed.

Table 2. Summary statistics for days in study.

Condition	Level	Days In Study		
		Mean	**Median**	**St Dev**
Control		50.3	23	62.1
Req	High	47.1	21	59.5
	Low	46.6	23	57.6
	Subtotal	46.9	22	58.5
QPQ	High	38.3	14	52.0
	Low	44.3	22	55.5
	Subtotal	41.4	18	53.9
Total		46.2	21	58.4

Participants in Req-High had a 17.2% contribution rate and those in Req-Low had a 17.0% contribution rate. This effect was not significant. Prompting participants more frequently to contribute did not result in significantly more contributions. Therefore H2.1 was not confirmed.

Participants in QPQ used the app for an average duration 41.4 days (Table 2). Participants in Req had an average duration of 46.9 days and those in Control a duration of 50.3. To better tease out the details of duration we performed a parametric survival analysis using a Weibull distribution (Figure 3). This test showed significance for condition ($X^2 = 31.5$, $DF = 2$, $p < 0.0001$) and condition*Level ($X^2 = 2.69$, $DF = 1$, $p < 0.05$), but not Level ($X^2 = 7.8$, $DF = 2$, $p = 0.101$). Participants in QPQ dropped out 18% faster than participants in Control and 12% faster than Req. Therefore, QPQ participants left the study faster than those in the other conditions. This trend can also be seen in the number of participants who continued to use the system after the new release ("right-censored"), with QPQ retaining 176 censored devices while Req and Control retaining 233 and 259, respectively. H3 was confirmed.

Participants in QPQ-High stopped using the app after an average of 38.3 days while those in QPQ-Low stopped after an average of 44.3 days. Due to the mixed results for the parametric survival analyses and difficulty in running post hocs for this analysis method, we performed a regular survival analysis on Level for only the QPQ data. There was no difference between QPQ-Low and QPQ-High for a Log-Rank test ($X^2 = 2.4$, $DF = 1$, $p = 0.12$) but there was for a Wilcoxon test ($X^2 = 3.8$, $DF = 1$, $p < 0.05$). Given these mixed results and the large sample size in this study, H3.1 was not confirmed.

We conducted analysis of note submission and contribution of location traces. We wanted to understand if submission of notes was more related to simply having the phone in hand, such as accessing the arrival information, or if it was related to contribution and the co-producing of a service with a service provider. We discovered that the quantity of notes submitted was significantly correlated with contribution rate (0.150, $p < 0.0001$) and total number of share location traces (0.353, $p < 0.0001$). Participants who shared more location traces also submitted more notes about their transit experience. H4 was supported.

The mobile client application is available on iTunes and Google Play. These systems provide an opportunity for users to rate and comment on the application. We evaluated all 60 reviews for some mention of the fact that providing traces helps the crowd. For example, a 5-star review on July 28, 2011 begins "*Using the app seems straightforward. It gets me everything my usual approach does- with the promise of real time info when there are enough users. So c'mon everybody! ...*". Of all the reviews, 24 contained some reference to the crowdsourced nature of the application. Some reviews however viewed the crowdsourced nature of the application as a negative feature, for example, a 3-star review on August 7, 2012 beings "*Because this app relies on riders using it to track the busses, it only works well when lots of people use it. On the lines that I ride here in Pittsburgh, it appears that no one else is using this app ..*"

Reviewers also commented on the quid-pro-quo policy. Two reviews explicitly reference this policy and complain about it, giving a very low rating to the mobile application. For example, a 1-star review dated April 7, 2012, "*... if I don't record my trip, times are blocked. Thanks for ruining my night out (and ride home). Guess what? I don't need ... App deleted.*"

The quantity of popup messages received by participants in the request and QPQ conditions varied. Analysis of the number of popup messages received by participants showed significant differences for Condition ($F(5620,1) = 142.3$, $p < 0.0001$) and Level ($F(5620,1) = 35.3$, $p < 0.0001$). Participants in Req received three times as many popup messages as participants in QPQ (means of 1.1 and 3.1, respectively). Participants in the High level received 1.6x more popup messages than those in the Low level (2.6 and 1.6, respectively).

DISCUSSION

The main question of our research was to investigate if reciprocity, which has to encourage contribution for recommenders and for P2P systems, could be used to effectively motivate contribution for a participatory sensing system. Contribution in a PSS is different than in these other social systems because of the time-place sensitive. PSS need near constant sense input from all points along the network because the shelf-life of any

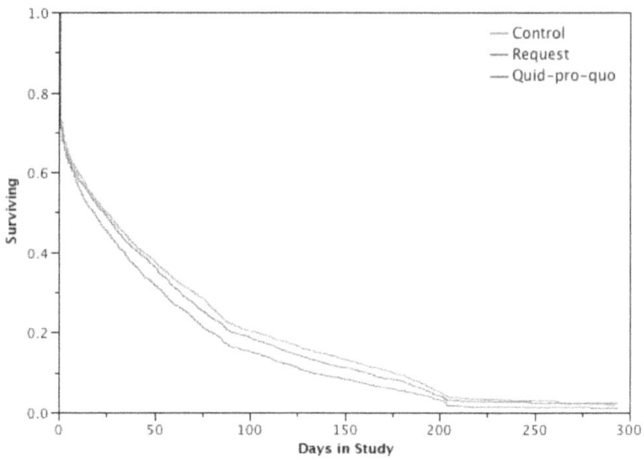

Figure 3. Survival by Condition.

contribution is often very, very short. Our first hypothesis, that participants in the QPQ condition would contribute more was confirmed. However, H3, our hypothesis that participants in the QPQ condition would abandon the app faster than participants in the other conditions also proved true. Together these make the choice to use a quid-pro-quo approach for a PSS more complicated.

If the goal of the system is simply to produce as much sense data as possible, then reciprocity seems like a good choice. Note that H1 automatically accounts for abandonment by participants, so QPQ produces more data despite the fact that participants quit using the system after fewer days. If a good user experience is also a critical goal, then reciprocity might not be the answer. This might particularly be the case where a PSS is simply one of many apps within a single product brand. The reviews participants submitted to the app stores also cloud this issue. The poor reviews clearly related to the reciprocity design might drive future users away, especially in cases where there are competing apps that follow a different motivational approach.

We caution PSS designers to carefully consider the specific goals of their system before committing to a specific motivational approach. Reciprocity seems a viable choice for generating more contribution, and in the case of Tiramisu, more data from more users produces more real-time arrival information, making the overall system more valuable to all users. At the same time, blocking negatively impacted user experience and might drive future users away.

Level had no effect in terms of contribution. Our hypothesis that requiring more contributions would increase contributions was not confirmed. One possible reason we observed no effect while [7] saw an effect could be a result of the different demands between QPQ-High and Low. In [7], participants had to contribute five-times as much information during their initial use, while in our study, participants in QPQ-High were only required to provide twice as much as those in QPQ-Low. This issue deserves more investigation. We suggest a study with several different levels in order to better understand where the impact thresholds reside.

Req had no effect when compared to control. This result is counter-intuitive since previous research has shown that asking people to contribute will make a difference. We suspect this behavior depends on the specific embodiment of the request in our design. Participants in our study experienced this condition as a popup pushed to their phone. Participants may have been or became quite savvy at dismissing the popup without actually reading the text or without experiencing the popup as an actual request. This unexpected outcome also deserves more investigation. It would be helpful for designers to know if specific designs are more appropriate to specific motivational approaches. Other automated request forms, such as email, SMS, robocall, etc. may have had a very different effect than our design. This open research issue is part of the challenge designers face when attempting to move from theory to practice. They often have many different options within a design and no way to estimating the impact of a choice. There currently is no literature they can turn to that describes the best design patterns for working with the different motivational approaches.

In our study, participants in the Req condition received a lot of popups — three times as many as those in QPQ — yet they did not contribute more traces. This fact raises the issue that a Req approach used for a PSS could potentially have a negative impact on the user experience, but without the positive impact of producing more data. The lack of of negative evidence experience in terms of higher abandonment between Req and Control does not mean that the experience of the two was equal.

The findings supporting H4 show a link between contribution of location traces and submission of notes about the transit service. The finding hints that there may indeed be a connection between the co-production of a service, in this case the co-production of the real-time information system, and increased engagement that drives people to submit more notes and to take more care and concern for their transit agency. From this study, it is impossible to tell if people who already have more engagement simply share traces and notes more frequently than other users or if the action of sharing traces or the action of submitting notes works to increase engagement. The issue requires a more carefully crafted study to tease out the underlying mechanism. The results should be of particular interest to the service research and service design communities who claim that co-production of service can be linked to customer engagement.

The reviews Tiramisu proved to be an unanticipated source of information on user experience. We had not considered these at the time we were designing the experiment. While an interesting source of qualitative information, the reviews raise some concerns for conducting behavioral experiments in the wild. In our case, the reviews could easily reveal that the app had several conditions. For example, two of the reviews clearly talked about the quid-pro-quo design, and participants assigned to other conditions might realize that they are using a different version of the app. It is hard to tell what specific impact this might have, but it simply indicates another challenge of running studies in the wild that focus on ecological validity.

CONCLUSION

Changes in technology raise the possibility of creating participatory sensing systems as an alternative to fully embedded sensing systems. With participatory sensing, a community of people use their mobile phones to report conditions, thus producing a sensor network made up of people and phones. One key challenge in designing a PSS is motivating people to make contributions. A second challenge is the high rate of contribution that is needed. PSS are time and place sensitive. Generally each contribution only impacts a tiny section of the network for a very short amount of time. To build an effective PSSS, designers need to figure out how to motivate users across the network to continually make contributions.

Reciprocity, where systems require users to make contributions in order to access the information they desire, has been shown to be effective for recommenders and for peer-to-peer file sharing systems. An open research question is if reciprocity might work for PSS. We conducted a 10-month field study to investigate this approach, by instrumenting Tiramisu, a participatory sensing transit information system. Our results show that reciprocity can help to increase contribution. However, the choice to use it is complicated by the fact that reciprocity also negatively impacts the user experience. Designers need to carefully consider the harmony they seek between collecting data and user experience when designing their systems.

This study also raised issues with the challenge of moving from theory to practice. Previous research has shown that asking people to contribute can increase contributions; however, in our study we observed no effect when we attempted to operationalize this previous finding. Additional research is clearly needed to better match specific interaction design patterns to behavioral theory so that designers can more effectively apply these theories and get the results they expect. Finally, the study showed an interesting interaction between the co-production of the real-time arrival service and participants' engagement with the transit service as evidenced through the increased submission of notes about the service. Again, more work is needed to better explicate this relationship.

ACKNOWLEDGEMENTS

This research and development are activities of the Rehabilitation Engineering Research Center on

Accessible Public Transportation (RERC-APT). The RERC-APT is funded by grant number H133E080019 from the United States Department of Education through the National Institute on Disability and Rehabilitation Research. Additional support was provided by Traffic21 at Carnegie Mellon University, a program developed with the support of the Hillman Foundation; a University Transportation Center grant (DTRT12-G-UTC11) from the US Department of Transportation.

REFERENCES

1. Adar, E. and Huberman, B. A. Free Riding on Gnutella. *First Monday*, *5*, 10 (2000).
2. Bernstein, M., Little, G., Miller, R. C., Hartmann, B., Ackerman, M. S., Karger, D. R., Crowell, D., & Panovich, K. Soylent: a word processor with a crowd inside. In *Proceedings of UIST,* (2010) ACM Press, 313-322.
3. Burke, J. A., Estrin, D., Hansen, M., Parker, A., Ramanathan, N., Reddy, S. & Srivastava, M. B. Participatory Sensing. In *Workshop on World-Sensor-Web*, 2006
4. Burton, M. A., Brady, E., Brewer, R., Neylan, C., Bigham, J. P., & Hurst, A. Crowdsourcing subjective fashion advice using VizWiz: challenges and opportunities. In *Proceedings of ASSETS,* (2012) ACM Press, 135-142.
5. Casey, C. April 2003. Real-Time Information: Now Arriving. *Metro Magazine.*
6. Cohen, B. Incentives Build Robustness in Bittorrent. In *Proceedings of Workshop on Economics of Peer-to-Peer systems*, (2003), 68-72.
7. Drenner, S., Sen, S., & Terveen, L. Crafting the initial user experience to achieve community goals. In *Proceedings RecSys*, (2008) ACM Press.
8. Feldman, M. and Chuang, J. Overcoming Free-Riding Behavior in Peer-to-Peer Systems. *ACM SIGecom Exchanges, 5*, 4 (2005), 41-50.
9. Ferris, B., Watkins, K. & Borning, A. One bus away: results from providing real-time arrival information for public transit. In *Proceedings of CHI*, (2010) ACM Press, 1807-1816
10. Fuglestad, P., Dwyer, P., Filson Moses, J., Kim, J. Anna Mannino, C., Terveen, L., & Snyder, M. What makes users rate (share, tag, edit...)? Predicting patterns of participation in online communities, In *Proceedings of CSCW*, (2012) ACM Press.
11. Grudin, J. Why Groupware Applications Fail: Problems in Design and Evaluation. *Information Technology & People*, *4*, 3 (1989).
12. Hughes, D., Coulson, G. and Walkerdine, J. Free Riding on Gnutella Revisited: The Bell Tolls? *IEEE Distributed Systems Online*, *6*, 6 (2005).
13. Jun, S. and Ahamad, M. Incentives in BitTorrent Induce Free Riding. In *Proceedings of ACM SIGCOMM Workshop on Economics of Peer-to-Peer Systems*, (2005) ACM Press, 116-121.
14. Karakaya, M., Korpeoglu, I. and Ulusoy, O. Free Riding in Peer-to-Peer Networks. *IEEE Internet Computing*, *13*, 2 (2009), 92-98.
15. Kraut, R. E. & Resnick, P. 2012. *Building successful online communities: Evidence-based social design*. Cambridge, MA: MIT Press.
16. Lane, N. D., Eisenman, S. B., Musolesi, M., Miluzzo, E. and Campbell, A. T. Urban Sensing Systems: Opportunistic or Participatory? In *Proceedings of HotMobile*, (2008) 11-16.
17. Lasecki, W., Miller, C., Sadilek, A., Abumoussa, A., Borrello, D., Kushalnagar, R., & Bigham, J. 2012. Real-time captioning by groups of non-experts. In *Proceedings of UIST,* (2012) ACM Press, 23-34.
18. Lasecki, W. S., Song, Y. C., Kautz, H., & Bigham, J. P. Real-time crowd labeling for deployable activity recognition. In *Proceedings of CSCW*, (2013) ACM Press, 1203-1212.
19. Steinfeld, A., Zimmerman, J, Tomasic, A., Yoo, D., Aziz, R.D. Mobile transit rider information via universal design and crowdsourcing, *Transportation Research Record - Journal of the Transportation Research Board 2217*, (2012) 95-102.
20. Thiagarajan, A., Biagioni, J., Gerlich, T. and Eriksson, J. Cooperative transit tracking using smart-phones. In *Proceedings of SenSys,* (2010) ACM Press.
21. US Census Bureau (2010) http://www.census.gov/prod/2010pubs/acsbr09-5.pdf Accessed: September 1, 2012.
22. Waze (2013) http://www.waze.com Accessed: May 30, 2013.
23. Wilson, J. Volunteering. *Annual Review of Sociology*, *26* (2000) 215-240.
24. Yoo, D., Zimmerman, J., Steinfeld, A., Tomasic, A. Understanding the space for co-design in riders' interactions with a transit service. In *Proceedings of CHI* (2010), ACM Press.
25. Zhou, P., Zheng, Y., Li, M. How long to wait? Predicting bus arrival time with mobile phone based participatory sensing. In *Proceedings of MobiSys,* (2012) ACM Press.
26. Zimmerman, J., Tomasic, A., Garrod, C., Yoo, D., Hiruncharoenvate, C., Aziz, R., Thiruvengadam, N.R., Huang, Y., Steinfeld, A. Field trial of Tiramisu: Crowdsourcing bus arrival times to spur co-design. In *Proceedings of CHI,* (2011) ACM Press.

Crowd Synthesis: Extracting Categories and Clusters from Complex Data

Paul André, Aniket Kittur, Steven P. Dow
Human-Computer Interaction Institute, Carnegie Mellon University
{pandre,nkittur,spdow}@cs.cmu.edu

ABSTRACT

Analysts synthesize complex, qualitative data to uncover themes and concepts, but the process is time-consuming, cognitively taxing, and automated techniques show mixed success. Crowdsourcing could help this process through on-demand harnessing of flexible and powerful human cognition, but incurs other challenges including limited attention and expertise. Further, text data can be complex, high-dimensional, and ill-structured. We address two major challenges unsolved in prior crowd clustering work: scaffolding expertise for novice crowd workers, and creating consistent and accurate categories when each worker only sees a small portion of the data. To address these challenges we present an empirical study of a two-stage approach to enable crowds to create an accurate and useful overview of a dataset: A) we draw on cognitive theory to assess how re-representing data can shorten and focus the data on salient dimensions; and B) introduce an iterative clustering approach that provides workers a global overview of data. We demonstrate a classification-plus-context approach elicits the most accurate categories at the most useful level of abstraction.

Author Keywords

synthesis; clustering; crowd; categorization; classification

ACM Classification Keywords

H.5.m. Information Interfaces and Presentation (e.g. HCI)

INTRODUCTION

Analysts and researchers commonly cluster and analyze data to uncover themes and comprehend disparate pieces of information as a whole. Whether for insight into interview data or getting an overview of product reviews or a news event, the underlying process of synthesis requires complex cognition. Multiple stages of sensemaking, such as moving from specific to higher-level concepts, clustering, and classification of data [28], draw on aspects of concept learning, abstraction, and schema induction [16, 25]. The synthesis process typically requires significant amounts of time and effort, and expertise in both the domain and process. Qualitative researchers have discussed problems or even bias that might arise when analysis is from a single point of view and open to debate [18].

CSCW'14, February 15–19, 2014, Baltimore, Maryland, USA.

ACM 978-1-4503-2540-0/14/02...$15.00.
http://dx.doi.org/10.1145/2531602.2531653

Tools to support the synthesis process can assist in an analyst's understanding of a dataset. Ongoing work in automatic text clustering and visualization generates automatically grouped words or topics and ways to navigate them [4, 10, 7, 13], but analysts must still perform the "arduous task of inferring meaningful concepts" [11] from the unlabeled groupings. An alternative approach is to try to leverage the human cognition necessary for deeper analysis of qualitative data. Crowdsourcing provides the opportunity to quickly access a large pool of people, but introduces the question of *how* to harness crowd members for this cognitively complex task. Such a process removes key assumptions in traditional analysis, providing several challenges.

- *Transient.* While analysts often immerse themselves in the full dataset to gain a rich understanding of themes, crowd members may only interact for a short period of time with a small portion of the data, meaning high-level similarities or categories might be missed.
- *Inexpert.* Workers may not have domain expertise, resulting in superficial or shallow categories rather than deeper concepts at higher levels of abstraction.
- *Conflicting.* Many workers, looking at complex data, mean potentially multiple (accurate and inaccurate) interpretations and disagreements over validity.

Recent work has begun to examine the use of crowds to cluster and discover partitions in data [17, 34, 41]. Most of this work has focused on creating clusters from image datasets, and has not attempted to elicit labels for newly discovered clusters. Exceptions that consider text are Cascade [9], a workflow for online crowds to generate taxonomies of datasets, and experiments in communitysourcing clusters of conference papers [2]. However, across all prior work, two major challenges for using the crowd to help with synthesis tasks remain unsolved.

One open challenge is how to enforce global constraints when each worker only sees a small sample of the data. Without a global overview of the data, workers could create incorrect or redundant categories. For example, Chilton et al.'s [9] report of running Cascade on a sample of 100 random colors resulted in a taxonomy with top level categories of "green" and "blue", but also "seafoam green" and "aqua"; another top-level category of "pastels" further included shades of blues and greens that could plausibly belong in these other categories as well. We introduce an *iterative clustering* approach in which workers can see all of the current categories when categorizing items in order to provide global context for their judgment. While workers can still create a new category if none of the current ones fit, the goal of the approach is to minimize redundancy across items and promote a consistent and useful level of abstraction for category labels.

Another major challenge we address in this paper is how to extend crowd synthesis to more complex qualitative data in potentially unfamiliar domains. While previous work has focused on datasets such as images or travel tips that most people are already familiar with, supporting expert analysis often involves textual data which can be highly domain-specific and of which the average worker may have little knowledge. This is especially problematic because novices have different mental models than experts and may categorize problems using surface features rather than deep structure [8], may use terms at a different level of abstraction [35], or may even ignore features that would be apparent to experts [27]. Here we compare a variety of methods aimed at *scaffolding expertise for novice crowd workers* so that they can function effectively despite limits on the time and experience they bring. Specifically, we draw from cognitive theory to examine tradeoffs in how items are represented; having the context of multiple items; and whether items are categorized one-by-one or categories are induced by comparing multiple items.

- *Re-representation.* Raw text is long and unfocused on salient dimensions. Re-representing the data will shorten and simplify, reducing distraction or burden of unnecessary information. On one hand, keeping the raw form will preserve all information that may be needed [23], but on the other, summaries help to abstract data and may aid in categorization [16].
- *Context.* Providing context (by showing multiple text items at once) may aid in producing rerepresentations using a standardized common language, and an understanding of what the most salient dimensions are [25]. On the other hand, multiple items at a time may prove more burdensome (in time or effort) than just one.
- *Classification vs. Comparison.* One approach to eliciting information is to predict a category label for each individual text item–a *classification* approach [25]. While context may help, crowd workers do not necessarily know the space they are classifying into. An alternative cognitive approach is to infer a single label for a group of items. While context in classification implicitly asks the worker to draw connections between the presented items, creating a single label for a group of items explicitly enforces mapping and *comparison*, techniques which have been shown to facilitate schema induction [16]. Additionally, making inter-property relationships more salient may result in more nuanced categories [20]. However, such grouping may mean losing less frequent relationships if two similar items are never shown together, or producing overly generic labels if very different items are shown together.

To address challenges in providing a crowd-generated overview of qualitative text datasets, we make the following unique contributions:

1. While prior work used datasets that build on workers' everyday knowledge, we focus on rich text datasets where a worker has no prior knowledge, asking: How can we get a crowd to generate meaningful categories in an unfamiliar domain?
2. We generate clusters as well as semantic labels and reasons for clustered data, distinct from automated approaches and the majority of prior crowd clustering work.
3. We conduct a formal evaluation of techniques within a two-stage workflow where we: (A) re-represent data in a short, salient form more conducive to clustering; (B) introduce a simple iterative clustering mechanism that enforces global constraints.

We demonstrate that a classification plus context approach is the most effective at creating useful categories at the right level of abstraction.

RELATED WORK

Topic Modeling and Visualization

Many linguistic and statistical methods to automate text clustering and classification have been proposed. In particular, LDA (Latent Dirichlet Allocation) [4] is a statistical generative model to uncover hidden (latent) topics in a corpus, by learning distributions of words that co-occur. A list of k topics (described by n most common words) is produced, along with distributions of topics for each document. However, such methods still require extensive work by the researcher to infer concepts from the list of words, fine-tune parameters, or manually add and remove words or topics [11].

Visualization of topic models [10, 7], or other forms of visual analytics [13] also offer insight into datasets. An analyst may find these valuable to support understanding and exploration of data (though again, many require knowledge or parameter tuning [13]). Though future work might incorporate such visualizations, our immediate focus is on generating clusters of data using human crowds, and providing descriptive rationale for the clusters.

Crowd-Based Labeling with Existing Categories

Dataset labeling can be used for direct analysis or as training data before model fitting. Researchers have used crowdsourcing services to perform data labeling against pre-existing categories, e.g., for use in natural language processing [30], computer vision [31], or social media analysis [1]. Willet et al. [40] used crowds to generate hypotheses for features of visual charts. Their work suggests strategies such as prompts and examples that may aid workers in generating useful output, though unlike synthesis, their goal was not to learn a global schema of a dataset.

Semantic attributes have also been elicited through 'games with a purpose' – metadata elicitation of image [38] or music [22] datasets through gameplay. The 'output-agreement' mechanism (rewarding a player for agreeing with their partner) can produce common and uninformative tags, even with restrictions such as taboo words [26]. To address this, researchers have proposed 'complementary-agreement' [21], which asks players to provide positive or negative examples of a given attribute.

Crowd-Based Clustering without Existing Categories

Recently there has been a movement to cluster datasets using crowd labeling without providing predefined categories. Tamuz et al. [34] use adaptive triadic comparisons (e.g., "is object A more similar to B or C") to create a similarity matrix for supervised learning. Gomes et al. [17] use an algorithm for aggregating worker annotations from partial clusterings of an entire dataset (i.e., multiple overlapping samples of items). Extending this approach, Yi et al. [41] use a matrix completion technique to reduce the number of comparisons needed for partitioning of the entire dataset. Each process was successfully able to uncover meaningful categories within the image data, such as types of indoor/outdoor scene, or features of neckties. Most recently, researchers have experimented with text datasets. Chilton et al. [9] introduced Cascade, a workflow for crowd-generated taxonomies of text datasets such as Quora questions, and André et al. [2] experiment with communitysourced partial clustering and Cascade techniques for clustering conference papers.

We focus on more complex datasets than prior work, extending to data where a worker lacks firsthand knowledge. We also conduct a formal evaluation of cognitively-grounded approaches for re-representing data to shorten and focus on salient dimensions, before utilizing a novel iterative clustering approach that enforces global constraints (helping to eliminate redundant top-level categories or misclusterings). In the experiment below we first discuss challenges of text data, before describing techniques to address those challenges in a crowd synthesis process.

CLUSTERING HIGH-DIMENSIONAL TEXT DATA

Prior crowd clustering approaches have been successful with image datasets [34, 17, 41], or with text datasets containing mostly everyday knowledge, e.g., travel tips from Quora [9]. However, analysts often work with datasets that use domain-specific, rich text data, posing a number of challenges:

- There are many (even infinite) potential dimensions of text [5], though only higher-level conceptual dimensions are likely to be of value, e.g., "number of vowels" is likely unhelpful, while "emotion" may be an important distinction.
- These dimensions are rarely as salient and obvious as visual features such as shape and color, which we can quickly or pre-attentively assess [37].
- Each data point may be long, complex, and outside the expertise or attention span of a crowd worker.

To address these challenges, we consider the cognitive factors involved in synthesis to inform our workflow. Synthesis involves categorization, concept learning, and schema induction (learning a global pattern or template to determine where

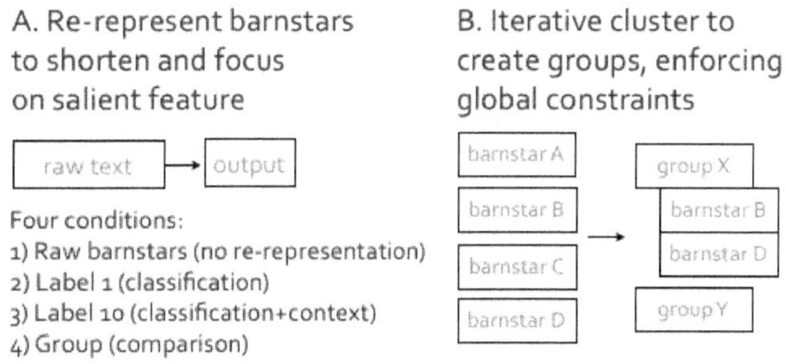

Figure 1. Two-stage process to cluster and elicit categories from text data. Stage A: four conditions to transform raw data to shortened salient form. Stage B: an iterative clustering technique to group outputs from stage A and extract themes from data.

to place individual items) [12, 16, 25]. We propose a two-stage process to scaffold aspects of these concepts towards producing an overview of a dataset; we elaborate below but first introduce the overall process (see Figure 1). *Stage A*: we propose to test three key concepts for how to re-represent text to shorten and simplify prior to clustering. *Stage B*: we utilize the Stage A outputs in an iterative clustering process that enforces global constraints by providing workers an overview of existing categories.

First, we describe an experiment empirically examining the effect of re-representation on text items, as input to an iterative clustering technique. Then, in the Discussion, we report the mostly unsuccessful results of two existing techniques (LDA and partial clustering) on our text dataset.

METHOD

Text Dataset

To investigate clustering performance, we chose a text dataset with two properties in particular:

1. Sufficiently complex, such that a crowd would not necessarily have prior knowledge or domain expertise. This allows us to test our approach with the type of unfamiliar data an analyst may use.
2. A dataset that had already been analyzed by researchers in order to provide a 'ground truth' for comparison. (Note that while we do not expect to fully recreate an expert analysis, our aim is to evaluate how and where crowd synthesis succeeds and fails.)

We utilized a dataset consisting of Wikipedia 'barnstar' awards, previously analyzed by Kriplean et al. [19]. A barnstar is a token or message of appreciation given to a participant. For example:

> *...Mani, you have contributed a great deal of Estonian articles and done major and useful copyedits in a short time. You are a very productive user and deserve recognition.*

Kriplean's analysis focused on understanding what work was valued in Wikipedia, essentially asking, "What type of work does this barnstar recognize?" Their analysis revealed 7 high-level categories, with 42 total sub-categories (see Table 1).

Editing Work		**89**	**31.1%**
minor	copy-editing	13	14.6%
media	images, audio	10	11.2%
initiative	starting articles, stubs	9	10.1%
major	substantial textual addition to an article	5	5.6%
achievement	shepherding article to a higher quality level	3	3.4%
classification	categorizing articles, adding templates	4	4.5%
redesign	large-scale refactoring, merging pages	-	-
translation	to or from another language	-	-
attribution	citing sources, removing unsourceable	1	1.1%
general		44	49.4%
Social and Community Support Actions		**87**	**30.4%**
commitment	to an article, a wiki-project	34	39.1%
teaching	mentorship, question-answering	11	12.6%
leadership	of wikiprojects & other initiatives	7	8.0%
humor & cheer	being funny, cheering others up	3	3.4%
user page design	helping to design another's user page	2	2.3%
rewarding	recognizing achievements of others	1	1.1%
welcoming	welcoming newcomers	2	2.3%
general		27	31.0%
Border Patrol		**35**	**9.1%**
vandal fighting	reverting damage to unspecified namespace	13	37.1%
deletion	article notability, spam removal	8	22.9%
vandal fighting	reverting damage to user pages	3	8.6%
vandal fighting	reverting damage to articles	6	17.1%
sockpuppets	finding users operating multiple accounts	2	5.7%
legal	copyright violations, fair use rationale	-	-
general		3	8.6%
Administrative		**9**	**3.1%**
privilege granting	helping vet potential administrators	1	1.1%
intervention	formal mediation of user conflicts	-	-
quality designation	determining article status (e.g. Featured)	4	4.4%
technical action	exercise of privileged power	3	3.3%
general		1	1.1%
Collaborative Actions and Disposition		**27**	**9.4%**
disposition	civility, accepting of criticism, keeping cool	17	26.0%
adherence	policy interpretation, integrity	12	44.4%
diplomatic action	conflict mediation, consensus-seeking	2	7.4%
explanation	rationale for an edit, decision, or standard	1	3.7%
general		5	18.5%
Meta-Content Work		**7**	**2.4%**
template	design of applicable templates	2	28.5%
tool programming	design & support of tools (e.g. bots)	3	42.9%
forums/portals	creation & support of help desks	2	28.5%
classification	category creation & organization	-	-
process & policy	policy authoring & process design	-	-
archiving	storing old discussions	-	-
general		-	-
Undifferentiated Work		**32**	**11.1%**
	Total work codes applied	**286**	**100.0%**

Table 1. Distribution of work codes for the sample of 200 coded barnstars from Kriplean et al.'s analysis. Top-level work categories are bolded. Work dimensions within each category are given. Global and within-category percentages are given. The general coding represents barnstars that clearly fall into a category, but were not specific enough to be able to identify a specific dimension.

The full dataset consists of 2,272 barnstars, coded with potentially multiple of the categories. We randomly sampled the dataset for 200 barnstars. Table 1 details the description of the categories, and associated counts in our sample. From now on, we refer to this analysis as the 'expert hierarchy'.

Study Design

We evaluate a two-stage workflow to re-represent and cluster barnstars. In the first stage, we compare techniques for re-representing barnstars. Drawing on the discussion of re-representation, context, and classification vs grouping in the Introduction, we operationalize these concepts into three tasks, along with a fourth condition that uses raw barnstars. We briefly discuss the motivation, pros and cons, and operationalization of each condition, summarized in Table 2. Images of the the tasks can be seen in Figure 2. Each task asks a similar question to Kriplean's [19] original analysis: "What type of action or work is being rewarded?"

Stage A: Re-Representation. We test the three re-representation conditions below, against a fourth: Raw data.

Label 1. Shortening and simplifying the text may help to abstract data and aid in categorization [16], but on the other hand, keeping the raw form preserves all information that may be needed [23]. We test simple re-representation by displaying one barnstar and asking the worker to answer the above question. This is a *classification* technique, predicting the category label for one item.

Label 10. Showing multiple items at once may aid in understanding what the most salient dimensions are, as well as providing a standardized common language [25]. On the other hand, multiple items at a time may prove more burdensome (in time or effort) than just one. We test the additional context by extending the Label 1 technique, but rather than seeing just one barnstar, ten are shown, each with corresponding textboxes to answer the above question.

Group. Rather than classifying each individual barnstar, an alternative approach is to generate a single label for a group of items. This process explicitly asks the worker to consider multiple barnstars, highlighting common aspects of items and promote mapping and *comparison*, processes that have been shown to facilitate schema induction [16]. However, such grouping may mean losing less frequent relationships if two similar items are never presented together. We test this concept by displaying ten items. Workers are asked to create groups of barnstars, and label the groups as appropriate.

Stage B: Iterative Clustering. We then apply a second stage to elicit categories from the data. Techniques like partial clustering [17] and Cascade [9] do not explicitly enforce global constraints, potentially leading to incoherent top-level categories or misclusterings (i.e., two redundant high-level groups could be created). We propose a simple iterative clustering technique to test the effect of the re-represented barnstars, while enforcing global constraints. Using the output from the four techniques in Stage A, items are grouped. This is a similar mechanism to the 'Group' task, in that a worker is asked to group similar barnstars (or, re-representations of barnstars). The difference is that after an initial worker performs a task, subsequent workers see existing group names and can either group into them, or create new groups. In this way, the technique enforces global constraints by providing workers an overview of the categories, and the workers perform a complete clustering themselves (without need for a machine clustering step). To reduce any ordering effects of workers or data, and to yield potentially different results, we created five separate threads for each condition. See Figure 2 for examples of Label 1, Group, and iterative clustering tasks.

Hypotheses

We posit that extra context in Label 10 as compared to Label 1 will result in better precision and recall. While classification

Study Condition	Concept	Benefits	Drawbacks
Raw	—	Retain all information	Long, salient dimension unclear
Label 1: Summarize individual item	Classification	Shorten, simplify, focus on salient feature	Lose some detail, little context, requires n workers
Label 10: Summarize individual items in groups of ten	Classification plus Context	As above, standardized language, requires n/10 workers	As above, and possible boredom or exhaustion after multiple items
Group: infer m groups from n items	Comparison	As above, but different type of context: infer groups rather than classify	Lose detail, bias against less frequent or rare themes

Table 2. Summary of Stage A re-representation techniques to transform original raw barnstars. Concepts of context, classification, and inference are operationalized within three mechanisms: Label 1, Label 10, and Group.

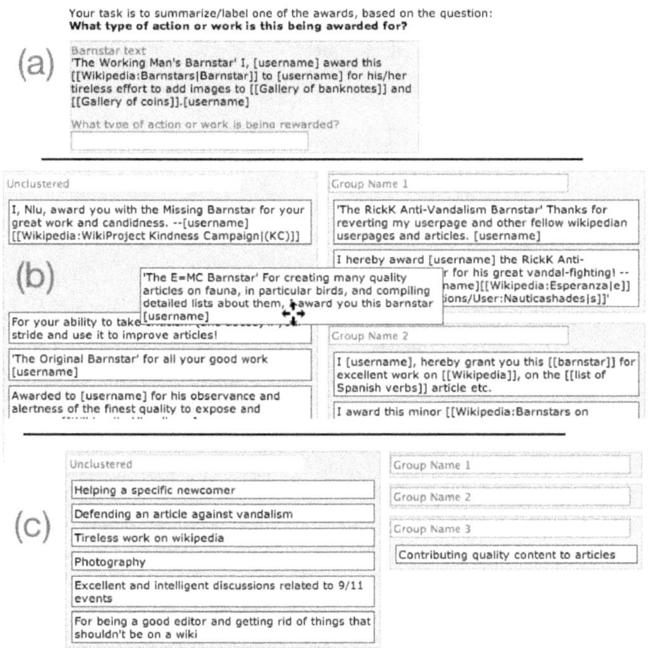

Figure 2. Examples of tasks in Stage A and B. (a) Stage A, Label 1: A worker sees one barnstar and is provided a textbox to identify the salient work done. (Label 10 task is similar but with 10 instances on the same page.) (b) Stage A, Group: A list of ten items are shown, workers are asked to create groups and label the group. (c) Stage B, Iterative Cluster: input is from one of 4 outputs in Stage A. Here showing summarized forms from 'Label 10' output. Workers see prior group names, and are asked to group into them or create new groups.

(Label 1 and Label 10) and comparison (Group) both have pros and cons, we believe that the extra context in Label 10, combined with the iterative clustering in Stage B, will result in superior performance for the classification methods. As for re-representation in general, we posit that all methods will outperform Raw, though Label 10 will perform the best.

Participants

Amazon's Mechanical Turk was used as a source of relatively novice crowd worker. We restricted to US-only workers, with 95% HIT acceptance rate. Each worker could only complete one HIT to ensure no 'domain expertise' was learnt.

Procedure

After a worker accepted the task entitled 'Label groups of Wikipedia messages (barnstar awards)' or a close variant, they were shown instructions, a brief description of Wikipedia barnstars, and workers were asked to perform a labeling or grouping to answer a similar question to Kriplean et al.'s original paper: "What type of action or work is being rewarded?" In Stage A, one of three re-representation conditions was shown (Label 1, Label 10, Group), and workers had to label, or group and label, raw barnstars. In Stage B, iterative clustering, output from one of the three conditions was shown (or a fourth condition: raw barnstars), and workers were asked to group and label, see Figure 2. After initial workers in Stage B, subsequent workers were able to see existing group names and group into them or create their own.

Measures

Stage A: Re-Representation. We measure the *time* taken to complete the task; *conciseness*: length of the resulting label; *precision*: whether the label captured the most salient code of the original barnstar; and *recall*: how many of the potentially multiple codes of the original barnstar were retained.

Stage B: Iterative Clustering. We again measure time and other descriptive statistics such as *number of groups* in a thread, and *number of barnstars* in a group. We calculate *internal consistency*: how many barnstars in the group match the group name and theme; *precision*: whether the group matches an expert code; *recall*: how many concepts from the hierarchy were named in the groups. These are distinct from the Stage A precision and recall measures in that we assess at group-level against the expert hierarchy. We also present sample final outputs from each technique.

RESULTS

Two raters assessed the outputs. The raters were familiar with Wikipedia having edited numerous articles in the past, one with over 10,000 edits. After an initial period of training, the two raters independently assessed all outputs. Stage A outputs (barnstar labels) were assessed to determine if they matched the most salient code of an original barnstar (as judged by the raters), as well as how many of the potentially multiple codes from the original barnstar. Stage B outputs (groups of barnstars and the group name) were assessed as matching a category from the expert hierarchy or not. There was substantial agreement between raters (Cohen's kappa: 0.74).

Since we are motivated by cognitive differences in conditions, and have specific comparisons of interest, we use a planned comparisons approach to test our hypotheses [36]. This also enables us to combine conditions to test hypotheses; we test the effect of *context* (Label 1 vs Label 10), of *classification*

Raw Barnstar	Label 1	Label 10	Group
Thanks for your comments and inspiration on [[Wikipedia talk:Esperanza]]. I think you've given a very succinct explanation of what Esperanza should be about, even during this difficult time. It might even help me change my mind and come back, despite recent turmoil.	Comments and inspiration	Community interaction	Exceptional work on a topic
Thanks for all you help on my user page! May this lead you to more and even greater contributions to Wikipedia. :) Thanks [username]	For making contributions to the user's wikipedia page	Helpfulness	Contributions
'The Working Man's Barnstar' Your tireless work on improving the [[2006 FIFA World Cup controversies]] article is more than worthy of this barnstar - the level head you have shown in dealing with an issue which could have easily got out-of-hand was a lesson for us all. Well done.	Dealing with an issue that could have gotten out of hand	Delicate wording	Hard Work

Table 3. Examples of outputs from re-representing barnstars in Stage A. Label 1 outputs are often more specific. Label 10 tends to capture more context to put into a more standardized and abstract language. Group tends to produce very abstract or even generic labels.

		Label 1	Label 10	Group	Raw
Stage A	Time (sum total, min)	283	108	67	—
	Conciseness (chars)	41.02	34.42	19.57	167
	Precision	73%	82%	62%	—
	Recall	63%	69%	61%	—
Stage B	Time (sum total, min)	312	337	64	392
	# Groups per Thread	6.6	6.8	4.2	6
	Barnstars per Group (sd)	30.3 (24.9)	29.3 (17.5)	36.7 (24.6)	34.2 (26.3)
	Precision	45% (15 / 33)	65% (22 / 34)	40% (6 / 15)	53% (16 / 30)
	Recall	59% (20 / 34)	82% (28 / 34)	35% (12 / 34)	68% (23 / 34)
	Cost ($)	90	72	72	60

Table 4. Results of Stage A: Re-Representation (top), and Stage B: Iterative Clustering (bottom).

vs comparison (Label 1 & Label 10 vs Group), and of *re-representation* in general (Raw vs Label 10). We introduce the results in terms of these comparisons.

Stage A Results: Re-Representation

Label 1 and Label 10 have a 1-to-1 correspondence, i.e., 200 barnstars result in 200 labels. Since Group does not force all barnstars to be in groups, some do not get grouped; this resulted in 50 groups that contained a total of 155 barnstars.

To illustrate the differences in output, Table 3 presents examples of raw barnstar text and the outputs from the three processing methods. As hypothesized, there is a general trend for Label 1 to more directly capture the barnstar, but without a broader context, the output tends to be specific and potentially not abstract enough to capture the higher-level concepts at work. Label 10, with more context, is able to capture these abstractions (see, for example, the difference between specifics of "comments and inspiration" vs "community interaction", or "contributions to user's wikipedia page" vs "helpfulness".) The Group technique results in labels more abstract and with a slightly different focus, "exceptional work" vs "community interaction", or "hard work" vs "delicate wording". All of these concepts appear in the expert hierarchy, but the clustering may focus on the more prevalent concepts, removing the more subtle ones. It remains to be seen whether these abstractions are helpful in clustering, or whether the loss of detail is harmful to creating groupings. Details for the following measures are summarized in Table 4.

Conciseness. Label 1 and Label 10 differed significantly in length of label, Wald test: $\chi^2(1, N = 400) = 8.95$, $p<.01$, with Label 1 labels an average of 41 characters in length, compared to 34 for Label 10. Comparison (Group) and classification (Label 1, Label 10) techniques also differed significantly, Wald test: $\chi^2(1, N = 555) = 75.13$, $p<.01$, with Group outputs an average of 20 characters. The raw barnstars, by comparison, were an average of 167 characters.

Precision. Raters assessed the most salient code of the original barnstar (given the coding from the expert hierarchy), and categorized the label as either capturing that most salient code or not. Label 1 outputs captured the salient aspect of the original barnstar 73% of the time, compared to 82% for Label 10, and 46% for Group. Planned contrasts reveal that Label 1 and Label 10 differed, $\chi^2(1, N = 400) = 4.65$, $p<.05$, as did classification (Label 1 and 10) and comparison (Group), $\chi^2(1, N = 555) = 52.14$, $p<.01$.

Recall. Raters assessed how many of the potentially multiple codes of the original barnstar were retained in the label. Label 1 outputs retained on average 63% of all codes from the original barnstar, compared to 69% in Label 10, and 61% in Group. Planned contrasts indicate there was marginal difference between Label 1 and Label 10, $\chi^2(1, N = 400) = 3.38$, $p=.07$, while Group differed significantly from the classification conditions (Label 1 and Label 10), $\chi^2(1, N = 555) = 34.37$, $p<.01$.

Summary of Stage A

Lengths of output from each condition varied, suggesting that the technical and cognitive mechanisms did have an effect on the labels, as seen in the examples. The context of multiple barnstars allowed a higher level of abstraction and shorter la-

	Label 1	Label 10	Group	Raw
Match Expert	Adding Images Community / Helping Others Hard Work / Diligence Other / Unknown Editing / Content	Editing / Fixing Helpfulness / Friendliness Community Improvement Fighting Vandalism Hardworking Administrative Details	Hard Work Editing Community Behind the Scenes Vandalism	Generating / Improving an Article Dealing with Vandals Being a Good Person Art and Media Administrative Work Longterm Accomplishment
Not Match	How-to's for articles Unneeded changes to articles Jibberish Continuity	Driving Content Contributing to a Charity Suspicious Category Heroic Behavior	Work Contributions Negative Specialization	Make Wikipedia Better! Excellent Contributions Politics Video Games

Table 5. Examples of group names from each condition: matching an expert (top), and not matching (bottom).

bels in Label 10, while the Group technique resulted in labels of just 20 characters, suggesting a higher level of abstraction due to inferring groups that fit multiple barnstars as opposed to classifying individual items. The extra context of Label 10 over Label 1 seemed to enable better precision (more likely to create a label matching the salient feature of the original), with marginal difference in recall. Group performed surprisingly poorly. This is partially inherent in the process—inferring a group name for multiple barnstars is likely to incur some loss of precision, but we had hypothesized better performance. It is possible that workers were overeager to group items, or that with complex, unfamiliar items, classification is a more promising technique than the induction by comparison. We next discuss how these re-representation techniques affected clustering.

Stage B Results: Iterative Clustering

We used a crowd-based iterative clustering technique to cluster the raw or processed barnstars into mutually exclusive groups. Five separate threads of iterative clustering were performed for each condition, to attempt to control for worker quality or ordering effects. We collapse these threads (since each may result in slightly different information), to report a single measure for each condition. Details, including descriptive statistics, are presented in Table 4.

Internal Consistency. Raters assessed whether individual barnstars matched the crowd-generated group name and apparent theme of the group. There was no difference between condition, one-way ANOVA, $F(3,114)=1.23$, $p=.30$.

Precision. We investigate the proportion of groups matching an expert concept to get a precision measure. There was marginal difference between Label 1 and 10, $\chi^2(1, N = 67) = 3.36$, $p=.07$. There was a significant difference between Group and the Label 1, Label 10 conditions, $\chi^2(1, N = 88) = 4.55$, $p<.05$, with 40% of Group groups, compared to an average of 55% of classification groups, matching an expert concept. There was no significant difference between Label 10 and Raw, $\chi^2(1, N = 64) = 1.37$, $p=.24$.

Recall. We measured two versions of recall. First, whether a concept from the expert hierarchy was at all present in the groupings (a fine-grained but overly generous measure), and second, whether a concept from the hierarchy was explicitly named in a group name (a coarse but overly conservative measure). We believe both are valuable—an analyst looking at output is likely to consider the group name as well as the contained barnstars in order to get a feel for the dataset. There was a difference in fine-grained recall between Label 1 and Label 10, $\chi^2(1, N=68) = 4.53$, $p<.05$; Label 1 groups covered 59% of the expert hierarchy, compared to 82% of Label 10 groups. The difference between Group and the Label conditions was also significant, $\chi^2(1, N=102) = 11.66$, $p<.01$, with Group covering 35% of the expert hierarchy. There was no difference between Raw and Label 10, $\chi^2(1, N=68) = 1.96$, $p=.16$. There was no difference in coarse-grained recall.

Abstraction and Usefulness of Output

Table 5 presents a sample of the group names that did or did not match categories in the concept hierarchy. When a group did match an expert concept, it was for the same reasons across conditions: obviously matching either a high-level or specific concept. There were varying reasons for a group not matching an expert concept. Group is the simplest to characterize, the group names were often too generic or abstract to be of use, due to clustering already abstract names. Within Label 1 we see examples of workers misinterpreting the barnstars or the focus of the group being unclear. It is possible we are seeing a curvilinear effect of conciseness or specificity. Raw barnstars contain a lot of information but are unfocused, while Label 10 output has a lot less information but is more focused. Both conditions performed well. Label 1 falls in-between, and it is feasible there is not enough focused information to be of use in determining categories (part of the motivation for providing more context with a Label 10 option).

While Label 10 and Raw were statistically similar in precision and recall, there were differences in the types of group name generated. Based on our hypotheses around classification and context, we investigated instances where a group name was overly specific or focused on irrelevant surface features as opposed to a more abstract category, or more focused on content rather than the activity being rewarded. We see a difference between Label 10 and Raw, $p<.05$, (Fisher's Exact Test). While both conditions had instances of overly generic or unclear names, Raw groupings were more likely to not be at a useful level of abstraction, for example, 'National Award' (specific countries mentioned), 'Video Games' (specific to video games as opposed to editing), and 'Emotion' (focused on words or feelings in the barnstars, not the reason for awarding the barnstars). Label 10 largely avoided these issues because of the re-representation and context to focus the label on the salient features of the barnstar.

Summary of Stage B

In summary, Label 10 and Raw performed similarly in terms of precision and recall, though Label 10 was more likely to produce categories at a correct or useful level of abstraction, not focused on specifics or surface features. We found more nuanced differences for context (Label 1 vs Label 10), and classification vs comparison (Label vs Group). The higher precision of Label 10 over Label 1 in Stage A resulted in a marginal difference in precision in Stage B, though did result in higher recall (coverage of expert categories). Group again performed poorly, outperformed by Label conditions in both precision and recall.

DISCUSSION

We drew on cognitive theory in categorization and concept learning to motivate three approaches in re-representation of text, hypothesizing advantages compared to raw data, and an iterative clustering step that enforced global constraints. A classification plus context approach (Label 10) performed the best in terms of precision, recall, and eliciting category names at a useful level of abstraction. The Raw barnstars condition also performed surprisingly well on precision and recall measures, but upon closer inspection the category names were less useful in terms of level of abstraction. We begin by expanding on the results according to our planned contrasts, before discussing other issues and future work.

Effect of Re-Representation on Clusters

Context: Label 1 vs Label 10

We posited that the added context of Label 10 in Stage A would produce labels more focused on salient dimensions and in a more standardized common language, aiding in clustering similar items in Stage B. This appears to be partially supported. Label 10 re-representations were more accurate, and resulted in higher coverage of concepts in resulting groups, with marginally more groups matching an expert concept.

Comparison (Group) vs Classification (Label 1 & Label 10)

Label 1 and 10 are a classification style of concept learning, albeit with the added advantage of context, compared to Group's comparison style [25, 27]. The classification re-representations matched and retained more concepts in Stage A, and produced more groups matching an expert concept in Stage B, though there was no difference in recall (number of unique concepts matched). Though we had posited superior performance for Label 10 in particular, the generally poor performance of Group was a surprise. The Group output went through two stages of grouping/clustering, and output may have been harmed as a result; relatively rare items were lost in initial re-representation and thus could not be present in Stage B, and the highly concise and perhaps overly generic labels from re-representation meant that subsequent cluster names were even more generic. Since workers could not see the underlying barnstars within those group names, it seems that there was not enough context or detail to create useful and meaningful clusters.

Raw vs Re-Representation (Label 10)

We had hypothesized that the length and complexity of the raw barnstars would result in an overload of information for crowd workers, making it harder to judge what was salient or similar, and thus resulting in clusters not as likely to be coherent or match the expert hierarchy. Based on precision and recall measures, this does not appear to have been the case; there were similar numbers of high-quality groupings and coverage of the expert hierarchy compared to Label 10. However, a comparison of the level of abstraction of group names revealed that some Raw groups were more specialized, more focused on surface features, or more focused on content rather than activity. For example, categories such as 'National Award' (specific to a country), or 'Video Games' were present in the Raw but not Label 10 groups. It seems that Label 10 was able to produce group names at a more consistently useful level of abstraction through the contextual re-representation process.

Utility of Barnstar Synthesis

Although our focus was on the effect of technical and cognitive aspects of re-representation, a question still remains as to whether the overall output would be useful to a Wikipedia analyst. We recruited two Wikipedia-related researchers in our lab, though not experts in barnstars specifically, to provide their informal thoughts on the output. The general consensus was that the groupings, along with an ability to drill down into constituent barnstars, was a useful overview of the data. Their comments highlighted the importance of ensuring an appropriate level of abstraction, with group names such as 'Contribution' eliciting comments such as *"doesn't really tell me much... a context miss,"* while 'Computer Knowledge' was *"too close to the barnstar, doesn't provide much value."* A question of abstraction was brought up: *"some seem to be directly sampling from barnstar text, not adding value to it.'* Some slightly unclear group names elicited more positive reactions: *"really intriguing that this is encoded, what does it mean?"* (before looking to the raw barnstars). Asked to provide an informal ranking, Group output was clearly last, *"on one hand, these are interesting categories that I can imagine would split types of work. But doesn't give me much information about what is helpful in Wikipedia."* Label 1 next, *"most are valid, in that I'd like to see them in this list, but not well formulated."* Label 10 was ranked highest, though Raw was *"almost similar, both provide value."*

Comparing to Existing Approaches

As a point of comparison, we also elicited clusters of barnstars using two existing techniques: topic modeling using LDA, and partial clustering (a technique to create a global clustering of items by grouping subsets of the dataset). We used the full 2,272 barnstar dataset for LDA, pre-processed to clean the data [39] before constructing 30 topics using GibbsLDA++. For partial clustering we created Mechanical Turk HITs using an object distribution algorithm used in recent crowd clustering work [17, 32], clustered using an agglomerative clustering tool [14].

While both methods were able to extract some meaningful categories, both had large numbers (around two-thirds) of unhelpful or uninterpretable groupings. LDA produced topics with linguistically similar terms, but the majority were not able to be mapped onto the conceptual groupings of the expert hierarchy. Some concepts such as vandalism defense were separated into three or four separate groups because of the different terms used to describe the actions. Partial clustering produced 49 second-level clusters, with an average of 4.00 barnstars. There was a lot of redundancy in groupings, and the groups that did not match were not useful, either too specific (e.g., South American related articles), or completely spurious. However, the clustering did have an advantage of producing small groups, some perfectly matched, or at least easily able to be assessed as matching or not matching.

Although future developments may make machine learning approaches more powerful, our experience indicated a number of issues that motivated the approaches tested here.

Crowd, Novice, and Expert Distinctions

This work focuses on novice crowds, as distinct from merely novices. This meant an explicit focus on crowd challenges such as interchangeable transient workers, leading to the need to coordinate via global constraints, and the iterative clustering mechanism. One or two novices looking at the same data would be able to spend more time and get a better sense of the structure of the data, and mechanisms to aid in that process would likely be different.

In our text dataset of Wikipedia barnstars, some data required specific knowledge of Wikipedia terms, but workers likely had little prior knowledge of the domain. However, most could reasonably be interpreted. We also used a similar prompt to Kriplean [19] in assessing the barnstars – "What type of work is being rewarded?" – thereby focusing the task.

Other datasets may not have the same structure, or analysts might wish to ask a more open-ended question initially to understand different metrics for similarity that people may use, in which case techniques such as confusion matrices to highlight different ways of categorizing may be useful [17]. There is a rich history of novice vs expert categorization and learning, and, e.g., Shafto and Coley [29] discuss how novice generalizations are explained by notions of similarity, while experts tend to use prior knowledge about causal, taxonomic, or conceptual issues to guide them in reasoning. In other words, novices' reasoning is decontextualized. As with our Wikipedia dataset, this may not be an issue, but for biological or medical datasets it may be harder to create categories that match an expert's understanding; though for some areas novice categorization may be useful to understand how a layperson reasons about features.

Qualitative researchers have noted how analysis can be open to debate [18]. One in-depth example comes from a 2010 workshop to discuss software design.[1] Three videos of professionals working on a software design exercise were analyzed by teams drawn from 54 participants, "*resulting in many different perspectives including cognition, representation, ... interaction design, coordination, tools, and design theory*" [3]. The variety of perspectives likely reflects the different backgrounds of the participants, but the analyses were not mutually exclusive: "*sometimes, findings were contradicted, sometimes wholeheartedly affirmed, and sometimes clarifying interpretations resulted in new insight*" [3].

[1] `http://www.ics.uci.edu/design-workshop/`

Implications of Utilizing Novices

In a broader sense, classification systems can be viewed as "*artifacts embodying moral and aesthetic choices that in turn craft people's identities, aspirations, and identity*" [6]. Bowker and Star [6] cite examples of categories linked with social movements, such as homosexuality or postpartum depression included in the *Diagnostic and Statistical Manual* (DSM), or racial categories in the U.S. census. As Suchman notes, "*categories have politics*" [33]. As above, a novice may be able to reason based on perceptual similarity, but they do not have the domain knowledge to make other conceptual judgments, nor the political knowledge to understand the broader impact of the categorization.

Limitations and Future Work

We restricted workers to one task only to emphasize novice crowds and a lack of domain expertise. However, throwing away workers who gain knowledge is not optimal, and future work should consider how best to utilize workers who wish to do more than one task, as well as workers who have been trained through performing the tasks. A further limitation of our approach was little or no error checking or redundancy, though these mechanisms would increase number of tasks and cost, adaptive sampling [34] or training workers may offset these costs as well as improve output.

Data items presented to workers should be carefully considered, both in terms of scalability and information gain, but also in terms of the order and similarity of items. The order of new features affects learning and generalizations about categories. For example similar items in a sequence might correctly be considered part of the same category, but when separate, the categorizations are often missed [24]. Variability of examples may also affect concept learning: diverse examples can lead to superior categorization (though these findings are based on training data being available), but perceptual categories are learned more slowly when examples are highly variable [15]. These findings suggest that automated methods such as TF-IDF or LDA may be beneficial to explore pre-grouping similar items.

We have discussed results from one text dataset, and next steps are to see if these findings replicate. Particularly interesting might be a different form of data such as longer form product reviews, or interview data, where partitioning of data, temporal dependencies, and tradeoffs of verbatim words vs re-representation may be important. We used Amazon Mechanical Turk as a participant pool, and future work might further investigate the potential of multiple perspectives from a diverse crowd, or look to other crowds with different properties: size of crowd, expertise, incentives, and availability.

Finally, the crowd synthesis process could be more interactive, particularly focused on crowd-requester interaction. For example, an analyst might have an open-ended initial question of the data, or multiple questions, and decide to focus on particular subsets of the data, or throw away particular questions or areas of data, as real-time results are explored.

CONCLUSION

There are many complex datasets and not enough time or expert effort to uncover the potentially valuable categories and insights contained within them. Motivated by recent work in crowd clustering of simple image and text datasets, we explored issues and approaches for utilizing novice crowds to create simple overviews of more complex data than in prior work. In a two-stage process for synthesis of qualitative text data, we provide a theory-grounded approach to re-representation and clustering of data. A classification-plus-context approach (Label 10) performed best in terms of precision and recall of expert categories. Raw data also performed surprisingly well, although the Label 10 approach resulted in group names at a more useful level of abstraction. Further, we utilize a simple iterative clustering approach that differs from prior work by enforcing global constraints, providing workers an overview of data and reducing potential for global misalignments or misclustering.

ACKNOWLEDGMENTS

We thank Travis Kriplean for the barnstar dataset, and Bob Kraut and Kurt Luther for helpful discussions. This work was supported by NSF grants IIS-1149797, IIS-1217559, OCI-0943148, IIS-0968484, IIS-1111124, IIS-1208382, IIS-1217096, Bosch, Google, and Microsoft.

REFERENCES

1. André, P., Bernstein, M., and Luther, K. Who gives a tweet?: evaluating microblog content value. In *Proc. CSCW 2012*, 471–474.
2. André, P., Zhang, H., Kim, J., Chilton, L. B., Dow, S., and Miller, R. Community clustering: Leveraging an academic crowd to form coherent sessions. In *Proc. HCOMP 2013*.
3. Baker, A., van der Hoek, A., Ossher, H., and Petre, M. Guest editors' introduction: Studying professional software design. *Software, IEEE 29*, 1 (2012), 28–33.
4. Blei, D., Ng, A., and Jordan, M. Latent dirichlet allocation. *Journal of Machine Learning Research 3* (2003), 993–1022.
5. Blum, A. L., and Langley, P. Selection of relevant features and examples in machine learning. *Artificial intelligence 97*, 1 (1997).
6. Bowker, G. C., and Star, S. L. *Sorting things out: Classification and its consequences*. The MIT Press, 2000.
7. Chaney, A. J., and Blei, D. M. Visualizing topic models. In *Proc. ICWSM 2012*.
8. Chi, M. T., Feltovich, P. J., and Glaser, R. Categorization and representation of physics problems by experts and novices. *Cognitive science 5*, 2 (1981), 121–152.
9. Chilton, L. B., Little, G., Edge, D., Weld, D., and Landay, J. Cascade: Crowdsourcing taxonomy creation. In *Proc. CHI 2013*.
10. Chuang, J., Manning, C. D., and Heer, J. Termite: Visualization techniques for assessing textual topic models. In *Proc. AVI 2012*.
11. Chuang, J., Ramage, D., Manning, C., and Heer, J. Interpretation and trust: Designing model-driven visualizations for text analysis. In *Proc. CHI 2012*, 443–452.
12. Clapper, J. P., and Bower, G. H. Learning and applying category knowledge in unsupervised domains. *Psychology of Learning and Motivation 27* (1991), 65–108.
13. Endert, A., Fiaux, P., and North, C. Semantic interaction for visual text analytics. In *Proc. CHI 2012*, 473–482.
14. Fernández, A., and Gómez, S. Solving non-uniqueness in agglomerative hierarchical clustering using multidendrograms. *Journal of Classification 25*, 1 (2008), 43–65.
15. Fried, L., and Holyoak, K. Induction of category distributions: A framework for classification learning. *J Exp Psychol Learn Mem Cogn. 10*, 2 (1984), 234.
16. Gick, M., and Holyoak, K. Schema induction and analogical transfer. *Cognitive psychology 15*, 1 (1983), 1–38.
17. Gomes, R., Welinder, P., Krause, A., and Perona, P. Crowdclustering. In *Advances in Neural Information Processing Systems (NIPS 2011)*.
18. Kolbe, R., and Burnett, M. Content-analysis research: An examination of applications with directives for improving research reliability and objectivity. *Journal of consumer research* (1991), 243–250.
19. Kriplean, T., Beschastnikh, I., and McDonald, D. Articulations of wikiwork: uncovering valued work in wikipedia through barnstars. In *Proc. CSCW 2008*, 47–56.
20. Lassaline, M., and Murphy, G. Induction and category coherence. *Psychonomic Bulletin & Review 3*, 1 (1996), 95–99.
21. Law, E., Settles, B., Snook, A., Surana, H., von Ahn, L., and Mitchell, T. Human computation for attribute and attribute value acquisition. In *Proc. FGVC 2011*.
22. Law, E., Von Ahn, L., Dannenberg, R., and Crawford, M. Tagatune: A game for music and sound annotation. In *Proc. ISMIR 2007*.
23. Marr, D. *Vision*. W. H. Freeman and Company, San Francisco, 1982.
24. Medin, D., and Bettger, J. Presentation order and recognition of categorically related examples. *Psychonomic Bulletin & Review 1*, 2 (1994), 250–254.
25. Medin, D. L., and Schaffer, M. M. Context theory of classification learning. *Psychological review 85*, 3 (1978), 207.
26. Robertson, S., Vojnovic, M., and Weber, I. Rethinking the esp game. In *Proc. CHI'09 EA*, ACM, 3937–3942.
27. Rosch, E., Mervis, C. B., Gray, W. D., Johnson, D. M., and Boyes-Braem, P. Basic objects in natural categories. *Cognitive psychology 8*, 3 (1976), 382–439.
28. Russell, D., Stefik, M., Pirolli, P., and Card, S. The cost structure of sensemaking. In *Proc. InterCHI 1993*, 269–276.
29. Shafto, P., and Coley, J. D. Development of categorization and reasoning in the natural world: Novices to experts, naive similarity to ecological knowledge. *J Exp Psychol Learn Mem Cogn. 29*, 4 (2003).
30. Snow, R., O'Connor, B., Jurafsky, D., and Ng, A. Cheap and fast—but is it good?: evaluating non-expert annotations for natural language tasks. In *Proc. EMNLP 2008*, 254–263.
31. Sorokin, A., and Forsyth, D. Utility data annotation with amazon mechanical turk. In *Proc. CVPR Workshops 2008*, 1–8.
32. Strehl, A., and Ghosh, J. Cluster ensembles—a knowledge reuse framework for combining multiple partitions. *J. Mach. Learn. Res. 3* (2003), 583–617.
33. Suchman, L. Do categories have politics? the language/action perspective reconsidered. In *Proc. ECSCW 1993*, 1–14.
34. Tamuz, O., Liu, C., Belongie, S., Shamir, O., and Kalai, A. Adaptively learning the crowd kernel. In *Proc. ICML 2011*.
35. Tanaka, J. W., and Taylor, M. Object categories and expertise: Is the basic level in the eye of the beholder? *Cognitive psychology 23*, 3 (1991), 457–482.
36. Thompson, B. Planned versus unplanned and orthogonal versus nonorthogonal contrasts: The neo-classical perspective. In *Advances in Social Science Methodology*, B. Thompson, Ed. JAI Press, 1994.
37. Treisman, A., and Gelade, G. A feature-integration theory of attention. *Cognitive psychology 12*, 1 (1980), 97–136.
38. Von Ahn, L., and Dabbish, L. Labeling images with a computer game. In *Proc. CHI 2004*, 319–326.
39. Wang, Y.-C., Burke, M., and Kraut, R. E. Gender, topic, and audience response: an analysis of user-generated content on facebook. In *Proc. CHI 2013*, 31–34.
40. Willett, W., Heer, J., and Agrawala, M. Strategies for crowdsourcing social data analysis. In *Proc. CHI 2012*, 227–236.
41. Yi, J., Jin, R., Jain, A., and Jain, S. Crowdclustering with sparse pairwise labels: A matrix completion approach. In *Proc. HCOMP 2012*.

Standing on the Schemas of Giants: Socially Augmented Information Foraging

Aniket Kittur, Andrew M. Peters, Abdigani Diriye, and Michael R. Bove
Carnegie Mellon University
5000 Forbes Ave, Pittsburgh, PA 15213
{akittur, andrewpe, adiriye}@cs.cmu.edu, mbove@andrew.cmu.edu

ABSTRACT

People spend an enormous amount of time searching for complex information online; for example, consumers researching new purchases or patients learning about their conditions. As they search, people build up rich mental schemas about their target domains; which, if effectively shared, could accelerate learning for others with similar interests. In this paper we introduce a novel approach for integrating the schemas individuals develop as they gather information online and surfacing them for others with similar interests. Through a controlled experiment we show that having access to others' schemas while foraging for information helps new users to induce more useful, prototypical, and better-structured schemas than gathering information alone.

Author Keywords

Schema; social search; foraging; search; structure.

ACM Classification Keywords

H.5.2 [Information Interfaces and Presentation]

General Terms

Human Factors; Design; Measurement.

INTRODUCTION

People spend an enormous amount of time online searching for information about unfamiliar domains, whether they are patients trying to make sense of their symptoms; consumers deciding which digital camera to buy; scientists learning the literature of an unfamiliar field; or voters trying to understand which issues they should support. The amount of time spent online globally is estimated at 35 billion hours per month (comscoredatamine.com), of which approximately ⅓ is estimated to be spent on such complex information foraging activities [23]. Thus accelerating online knowledge acquisition could have significant and widespread benefits.

As people engage with an unfamiliar domain they learn not only about the *content* of a domain but also its *structure*. Specifically, users build up mental models and rich knowledge representations that capture the structure of a domain in ways that serve their goals [45, 21, 25]. Such schemas change over time as a user moves from being a novice to an expert, with greater expertise enabling schemas that focus on deeper and more meaningful features [6, 25]. For example, a novice photographer may begin their search for a new digital camera focusing on how many megapixels a camera has, but upon learning more about the domain might come to the conclusion that the size of the sensor and low-light sensitivity are more important dimensions.

How can schema acquisition for novices be augmented? One approach is to leverage the schemas that other novices have already induced as they learn about a new domain [12, 47]. Enabling people to build on each others' learning could increase the speed and depth of their sensemaking across a variety of fields [11, 17]. However, such an approach also raises potential challenges. Capturing structured information can be time consuming for users, who may be focused on their own interests rather than on helping others. Even if users were motivated to capture structured information, mismatches with the goals and expertise of those consuming their information could make it too costly to consume and with little benefit. In the limit, if each persons' schema were idiosyncratic, there would be no easy way to aggregate across schemas.

In this paper we begin to explore these challenges by augmenting an online sensemaking tool [25] with features that enable the integration and surfacing of schemas from multiple users during information foraging. Our key contributions include:

- A scalable approach for capturing and aggregating schemas across individuals
- Methods for surfacing the schemas of others during sensemaking
- Empirical evidence of the value of others' schemas during information foraging

APPROACH

How can we capture the schemas that people build up as they make sense of an unfamiliar domain, integrate the schemas of multiple people, and usefully surface those schemas to others? One promising line of work highlights the utility of capturing and iterating on schemas across us-

CSCW'14, February 15–19, 2014, Baltimore, Maryland, USA.

http://dx.doi.org/10.1145/2531602.2531644

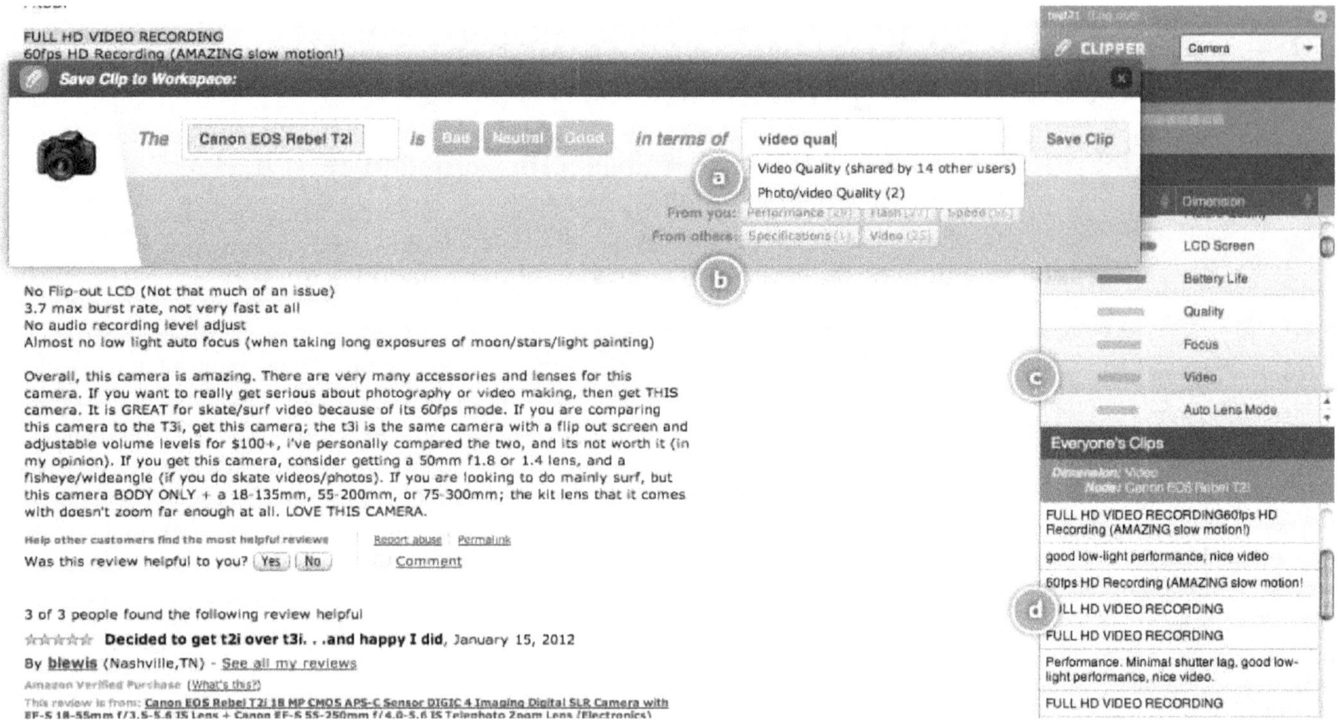

Figure 1. A novel interface to support social sensemaking. Social autocompletion (a) and dimension hints (b) assist users while they create clips. At right, the workspace panel shows information about the domain's dimensions (c) and their corresponding clips (d).

ers. Fisher, Counts & Kittur [12] engaged users in the open-ended creation of "knowledge maps", and found that users often created two-dimensional structured schemas involving options (e.g., *Canon T2i*, *Sony A55*) and dimensions (e.g., *lens, picture quality*) of the information space. Furthermore, they found that having users iteratively build on the maps of others led to improved maps that new users found useful. However, new users preferred to start from scratch rather than use maps created by only one individual. This raises the challenge of getting over the "hump" that raw, individual maps are not found useful, yet generating useful iterated maps requires someone to start from a raw, non-iterated map. Another challenge for this approach is how to aggregate maps across users, as each map in their study had an idiosyncratic spatial layout.

Instead of trying to combine entire maps across users, here we introduce the approach of breaking down schemas into their constituent elements and aggregating those elements. Given that users consistently structured their maps according to options (e.g., Canon Rebel T2i) and dimensions (e.g., picture quality) [12], here we use *dimension* as the element on which to aggregate across users' information spaces. To capture options and dimensions in a lightweight way we build on the sensemaking system described in [25], which elicited structure using an {*item*, *valence*, *dimension*} paradigm framed as a sentence (e.g., "The *Canon T2i* was *good* on *picture quality*"). This approach was shown to be useful and robust in eliciting people's structure of an information space. However, the system in [25] was designed for individual sensemaking, and users foraged for information completely independently from others. In this paper we add *asynchronous social aggregation*: aggregating the dimensions of previous users as potentially useful ways for a new user to structure their information workspace.

On the one hand, such an approach could expose users to more useful and expert dimensions that could augment their schema acquisition. Conversely, it is possible that the dimensions of others might not be valuable and just add to the burden of information to consume. Indeed, [25] found that eliciting dimensions from users during the information foraging process was likely to produce dimensions that are obsolete, irrelevant, novice, or idiosyncratic. For example, the previously mentioned novice photographer might start off creating dimensions such as *megapixels*, but upon learning more about the domain realize that *sensor size* or *lens selection* were more important factors. Aggregating and surfacing obsolete dimensions could be worse than showing none at all. However, if more useful or expert dimensions are more commonly input by users than obsolete or idiosyncratic dimensions, then aggregating dimensions across users could be a way to find valuable dimensions to surface.

We hypothesize that augmenting the approach introduced by [25] so that the captured dimensions could be integrated across individuals and then surfaced to new users might simultaneously address a number of fundamental challenges: 1) the foraging interface could capture and aggregate schemas across individuals without requiring them to interact with raw schemas, 2) aggregating by dimensions provides a scalable and segmentable method for combining multiple users' data; and 3) aggregating schemas across individuals could filter out noisy, obsolete, or idiosyncratic schemas. Below we introduce novel asynchronous social aggregation features to the Clipper interface [25] that enable capturing, aggregating, and surfacing schemas across individuals. We then describe a controlled experiment aimed at understanding the conditions under which socially augmented information foraging is effective.

RELATED WORK

Information Seeking

Users engage in a variety of information exploration tasks online ranging from finding the price of a camera they have in mind to deciding on the model of a carseat to purchase [7, 23, 33]; there is a large body of work that has looked at understanding and supporting how users navigate the web to find information (e.g., [5, 32, 42, 44, 50]). During online information seeking people engage in a process of information foraging and integration [45, 24]. To support these behaviors, a number of tools exist – for example, WebBook and WebForager by Card et al. [4], which use a book metaphor to find, collect, and manage web pages; Elastic Windows, which provided information overview and location context [22]; Webcutter, which collects and presents URL collections in tree, star, and fisheye views [31]; SenseMaker [2] for evolving collections of information; and Scatter/Gather [8] a text-clustering interface for iteratively navigating through document collections. Some of the more recent tools include Hunter Gatherer [46] which supports fine-grain clipping of information from web pages; and Dontcheva et al.'s suite of tools to assist users' browsing, collecting and sharing information found on web pages [10]. Our approach is similar in spirit to Dontcheva's in organizing collected information in a structured way, but instead of having predefined templates and extraction patterns, in our system structure continually emerges from and is refined by the aggregate behavior of many individuals. Furthermore our structure aims to reflect the schemas that underlie the structure of the conceptual information space rather than the elements of the web page.

Social Data

Data created by people using one of the above tools has started to be repurposed for other means. Social annotation and data is used by most systems to either augment the content surfaced to the user or to enrich the content presented. Social annotation and data is derived from user behavior (e.g. selecting a specific search result) or generated content (e.g. tags assigned to a given web page). Social data can benefit users to make sense of information and search and browse more effectively. Social data is becoming more visible; we see social footprints and annotations in the forms of "likes", "shares", +1's and reviews on sites like Facebook, Yelp, and Google+. Several different approaches have been proposed on how to use social data to personalize and re-rank search results, and enrich information sharing [17, 18, 34, 3, 54, 53].

Systems developed by Golder et al. looked at the structure of systems leveraging user annotations and tags [17]; Wu et al. leveraged social data and annotations to build statistical models in search and browsing [52]; Dmitriey et al. used social data to enrich anchor text and improve intranet search [9], and Muralidharan et al. studied the content and presentation that make social annotations useful [39]. Research into social data during information seeking can inform us of what type of information is useful during users' sensemaking.

Social and Collaborative Sensemaking

Other aspects of sensemaking such as the social and collaborative dimensions are seeing more attention. Collaborative sensemaking involves people interacting, sharing, searching and understanding information with each other while collaborating [42], and according to Morris and Horvitz [37], the support provided by existing tools for collaborative sensemaking falls under two categories: awareness features, that is features intended to support the group's status and work product, and division of labour, features intended to support how work is divided up. One notable piece of work is by Sharma et al. [47], who studied how artifacts handed-off and available online affect subsequent sensemaking. They found that resources that were accessed online resulted in more structured sensemaking whereas information that was handed-off to people resulted in less structure added.

We are also seeing work that looks at how people turn to others for recommendations [11, 36] or actively work together to search and filter information for each other [28, 36, 51]. Some work has looked at saving information from the search process so that others can re-use it in the future [1, 37, 41]. Research in personalized web search often uses the implicit traces of others' opinions of behaviors to train collaborative filtering systems to recommend items matching individuals' information seeking needs [15, 16, 19, 27, 49]. Similarly, social navigation uses the traces of others' behaviors to point people to useful places that others have found [38, 13]. An increasing number of social web sites are collecting and aggregating information from many users, including social bookmarking systems such as del.icio.us [29], DogEar [35], and Spartag.us [20]; social news aggregators such as Digg [30]; and many other commercial systems (e.g., diigo, CiteULike, Connotea, ConnectBeam). Our work builds on these approaches but instead of focusing on navigation and suggesting items to look at, we aim to make use of the deeper cognitive processing and myriad judgments that individuals engage in while sensemaking and using them to help others build up rich relational schemas of the information space.

PLATFORM – DESIGN RATIONALE

Overview

We started with the design of the existing Clipper web tool [25], which assists individuals in the gathering and structuring of information in a given domain. Clipper allows the user to save textual information ("clips") from a web page, along with a structured summary of the text. This summary is captured in a well-defined schema, where each contains an *item* (the topic of the clip), a *valence* (whether the sentiment is positive, negative, or neutral) and a *dimension* (the attribute of the item in question). This approach leads to summaries that can be surfaced in sentence form, such that "The *[item]* is *[valence]* in terms of *[dimension]*." We follow the approach of [25] in operationalizing schemas as the *dimensions* that structure the information space, due to the simplicity, tractability, and grounding in empirical evidence of the approach, though we recognize that real mental schemas can be richer and deeper. Thus, for a given domain, a collection of its clips' dimensions begins to define the important and differentiable criteria between items in the space.

We used two distinct versions of the interface that elicit this schema at different points of the information foraging process. The "full" clipper prompts the user to supply node, valence, and dimension when the Clipper is activated and text on the page is highlighted (see Figure 1); the "mini" clipper prompts only for node during clip creation and defers valence and dimension selection until a later review phase. Although we were interested in whether different versions of the interface would lead to differences in how social schema information was used, our results did not show any significant differences in our primary outcome measures; hence, going forward we collapse our data across the two interface conditions.

We then created a social version of the Clipper tool, which integrates and surfaces the schemas of multiple users. In order to provide users with assistance with creating dimensions, we leveraged schemas that had been collected using the Clipper interface from a previous study [25]. These data were comprised of 55 users, 2388 clips, and 560 distinct dimensions. We surface this information in a number of ways in the socially augmented interface:

Autocomplete

Dimensions are suggested to users as they begin to type in the dimension selection field while saving clips. In the social condition, users see autocomplete suggestions from other users' workspaces in addition to their own, along with a measure of dimension overlap (see Figure 2).

Dimension hints

We surface dimension hints to users whenever they are prompted to select dimensions while creating clips (see Figure 3). For each clip, we suggest up to five dimensions, including: the user's last used dimension; the user's most popular dimension; a random dimension from the user's workspace; a random dimension from all social workspaces; and the most overlapping dimension from other users, given the words comprising the clip. Specifically, the latter *social overlap* method involved summing the distribution of dimensions for each word in the clip across all social workspaces, and selecting the dimension with the highest total weight. Ties were broken by the heuristic of selecting the dimension with the higher average clip length. Dimension hints were generated independently, with one "slot" for each of the five methods. When the same dimension was generated for two or more slots it was randomly assigned to one of the slots so that no dimension was shown more than once. In the non-social condition, only the user's random, most popular, and last dimension were shown as hints.

Workspace Pane

The workspace pane is overlaid on the web pages where the user browses to gather information (see Figure 5). It contains a list of all dimensions the user has specified for the domain (marked with a head in the *You* column in Figure 5), and, in the social condition, the most popular dimensions specified by all users with their corresponding clips. The blue bar in the *Others* column (specific to the social condition) corresponds to the number of other users who have saved the dimension. It serves as a running summary of the most popular dimensions; users may refer to it while foraging for clips or hide it if desired.

Review Table

The review table, the final view of clips the user is shown after finishing their foraging (see Figure 4), contains a table of a user's nodes vs. dimensions, with corresponding clips in each cell organized by valence (e.g., good/neutral/bad). In the social condition, this table additionally contains nodes, dimensions, and clips from all users who have previously completed the task, which are shown in a less saturated hue than the users' own. Hovering over a node shows the actual text of the clip.

CORE HYPOTHESES

A core idea behind the interface features described above is that integrating and surfacing dimensions across individuals

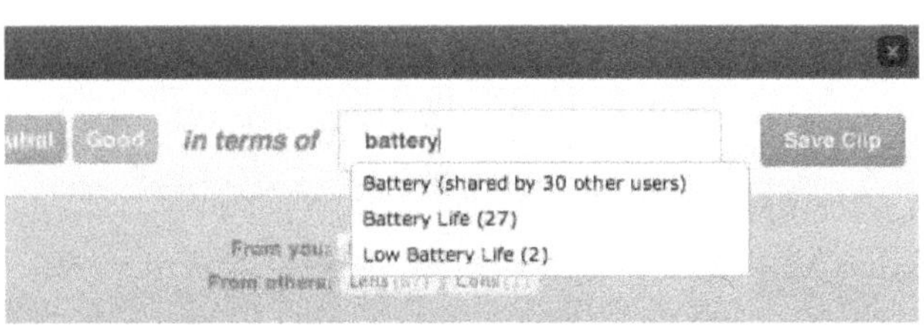

Figure 2. The social autocomplete feature suggests socially relevant dimensions to users as they type in the input field.

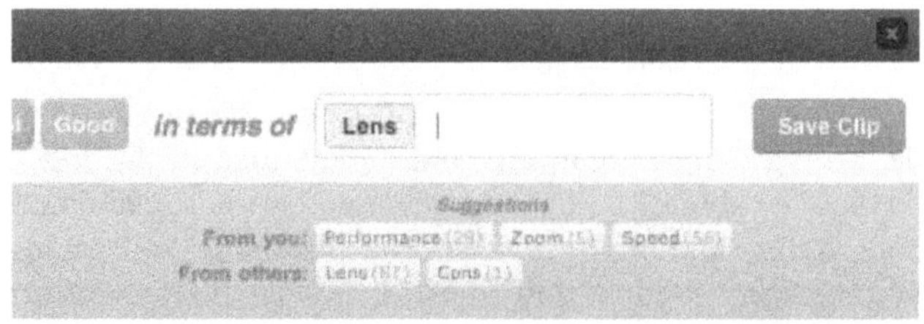

Figure 3. Dimension hinting provides users with suggestions derived from a variety of social and individual contexts.

will accelerate learning the important structure of a new knowledge domain. However, there are many reasons that this might not occur. Below we discuss three core challenges we examine through a controlled experiment.

Overlapping Dimensions

First, simply aggregating dimensions from multiple individuals might not be a useful approach for identifying useful dimensions. One challenge is that users may use dimension names that are too diverse to aggregate. For example, Furnas et al. [14] showed that the probability of two people generating the exact same name for an object was below 20% for a variety of tasks; even expanding to the three most popular names led to less than 50% overlap on most tasks. Furthermore, it is not clear whether dimensions that are more prototypical are more useful for learning about the structure of a domain. Thus the impact of social dimension aggregation depends on whether 1) there is sufficient overlap density of dimensions across individuals, and 2) more prototypical dimensions are found more useful.

Hyp 1.1: *Aggregating dimensions across users will result in overlapping dimensions.*

Hyp 1.2: *Dimensions that are shared across more people will be more useful.*

Noticing and Using Social Data

Second, users might not want to see or interact with the social data from other users. Information foraging is already a cognitively demanding task, and adding even more information from other users might prove overwhelming. We tried to address these issues by providing social data in an unobtrusive way, enabling (but not forcing) the user to drill down for further information (e.g., showing the clips associated with a dimension). However, this approach raises the risk that users would not even notice or look at social data. Conversely, if social data is found sufficiently useful then users might interact with the interface even more than they would if such data was not present.

Hyp 2.1: *People will notice and use social data in the interface.*

Hyp 2.2: *When social data is present people will interact with the interface more than when it is not present.*

Impact of Social Schemas

Finally, even if social schema information is present and noticed that does not mean that it will actually change users' mental representations of an information space. Users might not trust data from others, especially if those others are anonymous, with unknown expertise, motivations, or goals [26, 47]. Schemas from other users might be difficult to understand, especially if the schema provider is already familiar with the domain and the schema consumer is not -- exactly the situation we are trying to support. Relatedly, just seeing the abstracted dimension name may not be sufficient information to help users develop a better mental model of the information space.

However, if the social schema information conveys useful information it could help users to understand the structure of the domain, and do so faster than if such information was not available. We expect such understanding to manifest in more prototypical and useful dimensions generated, espe-

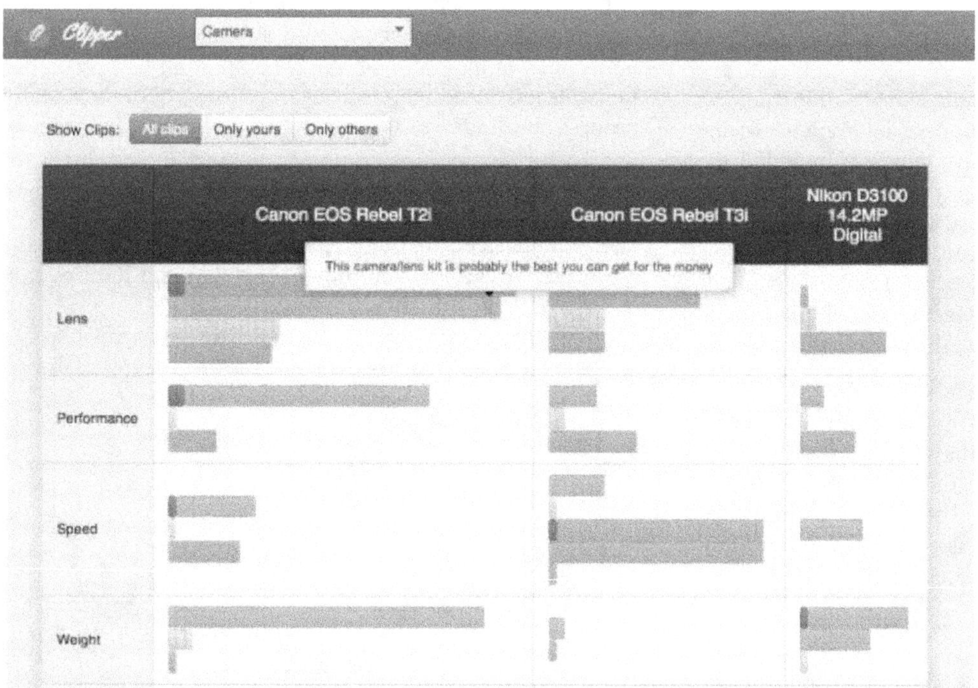

Figure 4. The review table shows a final, graphical summary of a user's workspace.

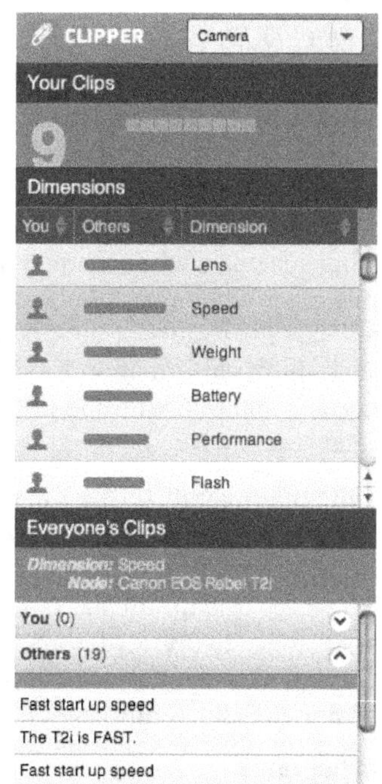

Figure 5. The workspace pane shows dimensions and clips.

cially early on in the process where people are still unfamiliar with a domain. It could also result in better structured workspaces involving fewer "throwaway" or singleton dimensions, which are often created when a person is unfamiliar with the structure of a domain and uses a dimension that later becomes obsolete or irrelevant [25].

Hyp 3.1: *The social condition will generate more prototypical and more useful dimensions than the non-social condition.*

Hyp 3.2: *The social condition will generate more prototypical and more useful dimensions* ***earlier*** *than the non-social condition.*

Hyp 3.3: *Workspaces in the social condition will be better structured than the non-social condition.*

In addition to improving the explicit structure of their workspace, we are also interested in how participants' mental models changed over the period of the task. If social schemas are useful and impactful we would expect participants' mental models to change more when in the social condition, for example in terms of the dimensions that they find important at the end of the task versus what they thought important going into the task. We might also expect them to converge faster on a common vocabulary, as they are exposed to an already-common vocabulary from others' schemas.

Hyp 3.4: *The social condition will lead to greater changes in participants' mental models from before the information foraging task to afterwards.*

Hyp 3.5: *The social condition will converge to a common vocabulary faster than the non-social condition.*

EXPERIMENTAL APPROACH

To test these hypotheses we conducted a within-subjects experiment comparing social vs. non-social versions of the interface. The social version of the interface included the various social features for capturing, integrating, and surfacing schemas, while the non-social version maintained the same basic functionality but was limited so that individuals only saw the results of their own work. Each participant engaged in two information foraging tasks, one with the social interface and one with the non-social interface (counterbalanced across participants).

Evaluating overall schema quality is challenging and unreliable: any single approach will have its weaknesses. Instead, we opted to operationalize multiple metrics in tandem (e.g. structure of the overall workspace, usefulness of dimensions, overlap of dimensions, etc.) to provide converging evidence for overall schema quality in the social and non-social conditions.

Participants

We recruited 64 participants from a university subject pool. Our participants were 28 females and 36 males, and their ages ranged from 18 – 63 years old with an average age of 24.8 years old (SD = 8.1 years). Our participants identified having a variety of backgrounds from undergraduate and graduate students to graphic designers and retired military staff. Almost all of our participants identified spending at least 5 hours online engaged in information foraging activities (61/64 participants). Our participants spent 90 minutes conducting our experiment and were paid $15 for their time.

Procedure

The experiment was a within-subjects design in which each participant interacted with both the social and non-social versions of the interface (counterbalanced for order). Participants were asked to perform information foraging tasks in two domains – cameras and carseats (fixed order, respectively). Half of the participants used the "full" interface (which captures node, valence and dimension during clipping) and the other half used a "mini" interface that captured only node during clipping, then valence and dimension in subsequent steps.

In each condition, participants were seated at computers and presented with a browser window with many open tabs comprising the experiment. The tabs contained a survey, two clipping tasks, and instructions and videos throughout to help assist participants during the experiment.

Participants were asked to proceed through the tabs in order. They began by entering demographic information in the survey, then proceeded to perform clipping tasks for both the camera and carseat domains. Each clipping task consisted of saving information from a group of three Amazon product pages using the tool, reviewing the resulting clips in spreadsheet form, and finally seeing a review table of the results. Participants could switch between the products pages as they wished. After completing each task, participants answered more survey questions about their search process and findings.

RESULTS

Overlapping Dimensions

We hypothesized that aggregating dimensions from multiple users would result in dimensions that had high overlap

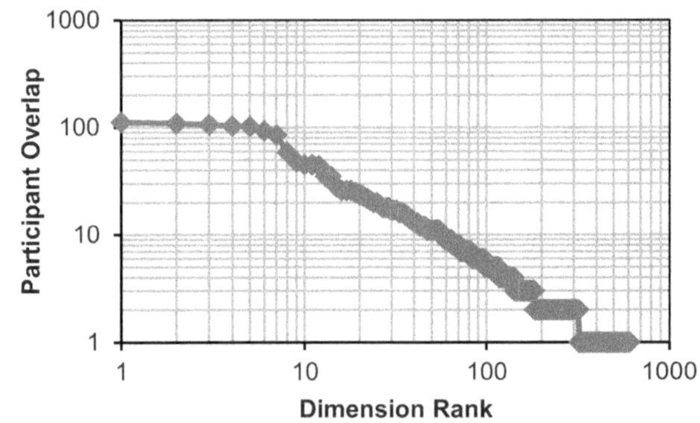

Figure 6. Distribution of dimensions by how many participants' workspaces they overlapped.

across users, and that those dimensions would be found more useful than low overlap dimensions.

Hyp 1.1: *Aggregating dimensions across users will result in overlapping dimensions.*

As shown in Figure 6, we found a highly skewed distribution in which a small number of dimensions were shared across many participants and many dimensions shared by only a few or unshared, similar to the long-tail distributions found in studies of unstructured tagging [17, 40].

Hyp 1.2: *Dimensions that are shared across more people will be more useful.*

Two domain experts independently labeled all 510 unique dimensions generated by our participants according to how useful they would be to new users engaging in the task on a scale of 1 – 5 (1 = low; 5 = high). We defined usefulness as how well the dimension described the domain to a novice. For example, dimensions such as "safety" or "affordability" would score highly on usefulness, while dimensions such as "operate" or "pro & cons" would score lower on usefulness. We compared our domain experts' ratings for the 510 dimensions, and found a weighted Cohen's kappa (κ) of 0.69 indicating a significant level of agreement between our raters on how useful the dimensions were.

Using this data, we performed a regression analysis which showed that increased dimension overlap was significantly positively associated with greater usefulness ($b = 0.21$, $p < .001$), indicating that dimensions that are shared across more people are also more useful. These results provide empirical evidence that surfacing high overlap dimensions may be indeed be a useful strategy for supporting social schema induction.

Noticing and Using Social Data

Hyp 2.1: *People will notice and use social data in the interface.*

We recorded the mouse hovering interactions of all users, and found that people did notice and interact with social data elements. This included both dimensions and clips in the workspace pane (M=10.3; M=2.8), and clips in the review table (M=10.4). These results suggest that many users did notice and interact with social elements of the interface.

We were particularly interested in how people would interact with the dimension hints, as we tested five different methods for surfacing potentially useful dimensions, either from the participants' own workspace (their last used, most popular, or random) or from others' workspaces (highest social overlap or random). The social overlap method (i.e., selecting from others' dimensions given the text of the clip) was selected most frequently, although an ANOVA controlling for within-subject effects with post-hoc Tukey HSD comparisons showed that only the difference between the social overlap method and random was significant ($p < .05$), with the difference between social overlap and user-last of marginal significance ($p = .079$).

	Hover counts	
	Social	**Non-social**
Dimension	545	116
Clip	169	11
Review	4757	1896

Table 1. Total interactions (as measured by hover counts) for interface elements in the social and non-social conditions.

Hyp 2.2: *When social data is present people will interact with the interface more than when it is not present.*

Although ***Hyp 2.1*** indicates that people interacted with social data, many of the elements they interacted with exist for both the social and non-social conditions. To test whether participants interacted with the interface more in the social condition we aggregated counts of all of the instances when a participant hovered over an element in the dimension pane or in the review view, regardless of whether it was their own or another's clip or dimension (see Table 1). The social condition had significantly more hover counts than the non-social condition ($F_{1,63}=17.4$, $p < .001$). This effect was significant for hover counts for the review page, pane dimensions, and pane dimension clips – in other words, all of the elements that existed in both conditions and had social data embedded in them in the social condition. Interestingly, there was no difference between the social and non-social conditions as to how much they interacted with their own clips ($F_{1,63}=.20$, $p > .6$). This is a somewhat surprising and promising result: increasing their interaction with social data did not reduce participants' interaction with their own data. This suggests that social data was beneficial on top of participants' own data, rather than competing with it for attention.

Impact of Social Schemas

So far two of our prerequisite challenges have been addressed: aggregating dimensions across participants led to more useful dimensions; and participants noticed and interacted with social data. However, the most important question is whether interacting with useful social data actually changes participants' mental schemas. As it can be difficult to identify exactly when and how a mental schema has been changed and improved, below we address this question through converging evidence involving a number of variants operationalizing the question.

Hyp 3.1: *The social condition will generate more prototypical and more useful dimensions than the non-social condition.*

One question we looked was how the structure of a participant's workspace changed as a function of being in the social condition. In this hypothesis we look specifically at effects on prototypicality (i.e., participant overlap) and usefulness of the dimensions generated. We conducted nested

	Overlap		
	Coeff.	SE	P
Intercept	24.6	1.85	***
Social	5.55	2.31	*
Dimension order	-.849	.27	**
Social X Dimension order	-.278	.38	

Table 2. Regression model predicting dimension overlap.

linear regressions with participant as a random factor to determine whether being in the social condition would lead to more prototypical and more useful dimensions. Our results (see Table 2) show that participants' workspaces when in the social condition had dimensions with greater overlap with other participants' dimensions than when in the non-social condition ($b = 3.14$, $SE = .78$, $p < .001$). Dimensions generated in the social condition were also rated as more useful than in the non-social condition ($b = .12$, $SE = .035$, $p < .001$).

Hyp 3.2: *The social condition will generate more prototypical and more useful dimensions* ***earlier*** *than the non-social condition.*

We hypothesized that the social condition would lead to more prototypical and useful dimensions earlier in participants' information foraging process than the non-social condition. While participants did tend to produce higher overlapping dimensions earlier in the process, this effect did not differ between the social and non-social conditions Furthermore, there were no temporal effects associated with rated usefulness of dimensions. These results disconfirm our hypothesis, and suggest that the beneficial effects of surfacing social schemas continue even beyond the early period of information foraging.

Hyp 3.3: *Workspaces in the social condition will be better structured than the non-social condition.*

We operationalized workspaces as being better structured if they had fewer singleton dimensions, which often reflect dimensions that users created but later found irrelevant or obsolete [25]. To determine if workspaces in the social condition were better structured we conducted a nested logistic regression with participant as a random factor, predicting whether a dimension will be a singleton or not. We found that the social condition was a significant negative predictor of generating a singleton dimension ($b = -0.80$, $p < .001$). This effect was quite substantial: seeing others' schemas was associated with a .45 factor reduction in the likelihood of a dimension being a singleton.

Hyp 3.4: *The social condition will lead to greater changes in participants' mental models from before the information foraging task to afterwards.*

Previous research [25] has shown that people's mental models change depending on the support facilitated by a

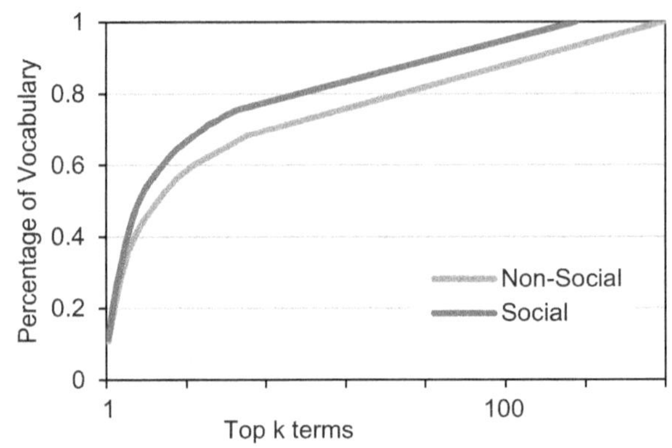

Figure 8. Vocabulary convergence over time in the social and non-social conditions. Users in the social condition achieved greater convergence in less time.

tool. We sought to extend this finding by studying the effects of social data. We hypothesized that the participants' mental models will change the most in the social condition. We used data pertaining to which dimensions our participants thought were important before and after the task to address this question. We find that on average participants in the social condition changed 0.98 dimensions compared to 0.77 for the non-social condition, and the participants in the social condition identified more dimensions (5.41 dimensions) than the non-social condition (5.14 dimensions). However, these findings were only marginally significant (change in dimensions: $t_{63} = 1.284$, $p = 0.103$; dimension sizes: $t_{63} = 1.619$, $p = 0.055$).

To shed some light on the rationale behind our participants change in mental models, we examined the qualitative data gathered from our surveys. Using our participants' responses to how their choice of dimensions changed over the task, we performed content analysis and categorized their responses into groups depending on the theme. We find that our participants' mental models changed during the task in four key ways: by certain dimensions becoming more important and visible in their mental models (27.3%) resulting in participants prioritizing them over others; by expanding through learning and encountering more information (28.9%); becoming more confident of their decision-making (2.3%); no change due to existing knowledge (28.9%); and other (12.5% participants). These findings support similar results published by [25].

Hyp 3.5: *The social condition will converge to a common vocabulary faster than the non-social condition.*

We hypothesize that the presence of social data will influence people to use a common vocabulary. Once again, using the dimensions identified by our participants as important, we compared the data from the social and non-social condition to understand the characteristics and differences of the vocabularies used in the two conditions. After stemming and cleaning the data (i.e. removing stopwords, e.g. 'the', 'a', 'were', etc.), we computed the frequency of each term within the social and non-social vocabularies.

	Social Condition	Non-Social Condition
Vocab. Size	346	329
# Unique Dimensions	118	140
# Non-Unique Dimensions	228	118

Table 3. Vocabulary size and dimension sharing, for social and non-social conditions. Users in the social condition built a larger vocabulary with more shared dimensions.

Table 3 shows that the characteristics of the social and non-social vocabularies differ: the social condition has a larger number of dimensions, but fewer unique ones used, and there is a large number of repeat dimensions found in the social condition vocabulary (228 vs. 118) compared to the non-social condition. What we can understand from this is that participants in the social condition are identifying more dimensions but are re-using ones used by other participants.

We tabulated this data, and in Figure 8 we see that fewer number of terms comprise the majority of the vocabulary in the social condition compared to the non-social condition. What is also of interest is that the social condition has a much smaller tail compared to the non-social conditions and fewer singleton dimensions suggesting that a smaller vocabulary with a high re-use of terms was found for the social condition.

Subjective Data

After performing both tasks, our participants provided feedback on the usability of the social Clipper tool via our survey. The feedback comprised the overall utility of the tool as well as the helpfulness and use of specific social features. Feedback took the form of evaluations on a 7-point Likert scale as well as open-ended responses. Overall results show that participants rated the system highly (5+) across all features and dimensions, including whether they felt effective and confident using it, whether it was helpful, enjoyable, and easy to use, and whether they would like to continue using it for their own use (Figure 9). Ratings for specific social features showed that participants found all features easy to use and useful, with ratings above 5 for the review table, dimension suggestions, autocomplete, and the dimension pane sidebar (Figure 10).

From our survey we also collected open-ended responses about what aspects of the tool our participants liked and what aspects they would improve. When asked what aspects of the tool our participants liked, a number of responses were given such as its ability to provide social awareness of others' information seeking and having this information at hand (15.6% participants):

"*The community aspect with others' clips was very helpful overall.*" – Participant 48

Most participants liked the features provided by Clipper and identified specific features like the review table and the dimensions (18.7% participants):

"*Review Table was very helpful. Interface for saving clips was intuitive.*" – Participant 8

"*Dimensions, seems to me like a time saver, very easy to use*" – Participant 29

More generally, a number of participants mentioned the positive aspects of how the tool organizes and structures information (17.2%) and the general functionality (18.7%), though this feedback was not specific to the social features we implemented. However, it is encouraging that despite the increased amount of information involved in using social data, participants still mentioned the tool's ease of use (15.6%):

"*It was so simple and intuitive – and I am thrilled to use it for my shopping purposes in the future*" – Participant 41

To assist in future iterations, we asked our participants what improvements they would make. Our participants identified a number of suggestions including additional features (23.4% participants) such as chat and Q&A features, previews of the product, snippets of content and summarizing the main content and dimension. A significant number of participants (23.4%) identified improvements being needed with the performance and responsiveness; these were primarily due to bugs that led to dimension suggestions taking

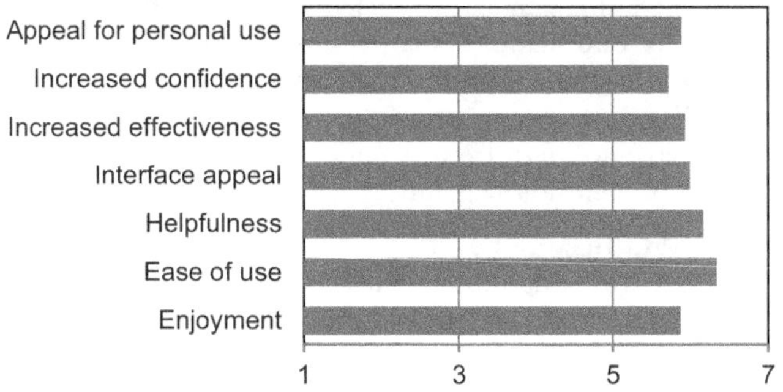

Figure 9. Participants gave the Clipper high marks for measures of usability.

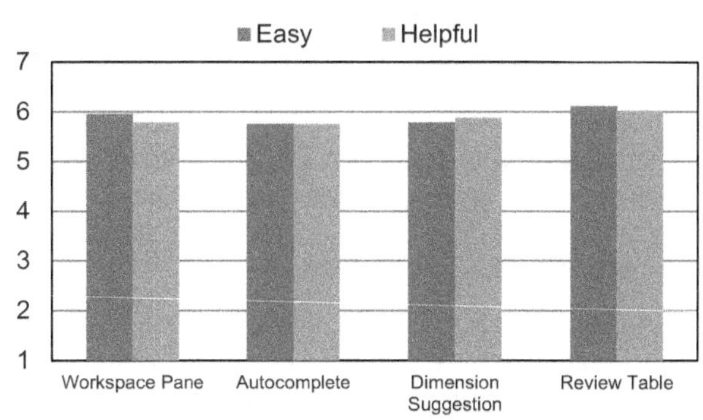

Figure 10. Participants found the interface's social features both easy to use and helpful.

2-3 seconds to generate. Other issues arose from constraints of the study in which we surfaced random suggestions as a baseline, which may have undermined perceived performance.

DISCUSSION

In this paper we examined how capturing, integrating, and surfacing the schemas of users as they engage in information foraging could help others to learn about the structure of a new domain. We designed and implemented novel social features into an information foraging interface which addresses the dual challenges of algorithmically integrating the schemas generated by multiple individuals while simultaneously filtering out less useful dimensions. Users found this interface and its various social elements useful and helpful for information foraging. We conducted an experiment to explore a number of potential challenges for socially augmented information foraging including: whether users would generate useful, overlapping dimensions; whether users would notice and use the dimensions of others; and whether others' dimensions would impact users' workspace structure, mental models, and vocabulary.

Our results indicated that the dimensions generated by users showed significant overlap, and that dimensions with more overlap across users were rated as more useful. This link between dimension overlap and usefulness is an interesting result that may have implications for interfaces aimed at supporting information foraging, and more generally for social tagging. We also showed that users noticed and used the social elements we introduced, with preliminary support for the usefulness of our social dimension suggestion method. These results are promising given our design rationale of making such elements unobtrusive and not forcing users to interact with them. Furthermore, users did not reduce their interaction with non-social elements of the interface, suggesting that the social elements were useful but not competing with the non-social elements.

Finally, we presented results indicating that being exposed to others' schemas changed users' behavior in a number of ways. In the social condition, users generated more prototypical and more useful dimensions than when they were in the non-social condition. They also had better structured workspaces with fewer singleton dimensions and converged on a common vocabulary faster than when in the non-social condition. Interestingly, these results were consistent whether participants added structure to their clips during (full version) or after (mini version) clip creation, suggesting that the workspace pane was effective in influencing their mental models even if they were not explicitly adding dimensions at the time of clipping.

Our approach demonstrates a scalable and effective way for users to learn from each others' schemas while learning about a new domain online. In many cases when users search they are not looking for a single piece of content but instead trying to understand the structure of a new information space and how multiple pieces of content fit into that structure. Framing search as a process of learning and schema induction [12, 25, 33] highlights this as a critical need that we begin to address here.

Our results provide an important step towards a future of distributed sensemaking [12], in which the effort that individuals put forth in learning about a new domain is not lost but instead accelerates the learning process for individuals coming after them. A key challenge for that future is determining how to capture, aggregate, and surface schemas so that they are useful to others. By algorithmically aggregating schemas and showing that more overlapping schemas are also rated as more useful, we identify a method of overcoming the "hump" paradox introduced by [12] -- that individual schemas are less valuable than starting from scratch, but iterated schemas are more valuable. Our approach also naturally deals with the challenge raised in [25], that early dimensions generated before a user is familiar with a domain become obsolete and irrelevant: by aggregating dimensions across users, these idiosyncratic and less relevant dimensions drop to the bottom of the pile.

At the same time, our study suggests a number of areas that would profit from further research. While we aim to minimize user effort through features such as dimension hinting, computational approaches to automatically infer important dimensions could further streamline the process. Aggregating and summarizing similar clips is another area that computational approaches could help. However, any such approaches would need to provide clear orientation, provenance, and the ability for the user to override the machine in order to support and privilege the process of learning and schema induction in information foraging.

There may also be drawbacks to using the social Clipper system for users with differing viewpoints than the common view. For example, people may use different dimensions for the same information if they have different goals, background, experience, or cultures, and valuable minority views could be lost through aggregation. However, there may be ways of addressing this, such showing dimensions from people like themselves, where similarity could be determined by browsing or clipping characteristics.

In summary, we have demonstrated an approach for capturing, aggregating, and surfacing schemas from others and its benefits for information foraging. Further reducing the costs and increasing the benefits for schema acquisition by novices will help us move to a future where new learners no longer have to start from scratch, and can stand on the schemas of their fellow giants.

ACKNOWLEDGMENTS

This work was supported by NSF grants IIS-1149797, IIS-1217559, OCI-0943148, IIS-0968484, IIS-1111124, Bosch, Google, and Microsoft.

REFERENCES

1. Amershi and Morris, M.R. CoSearch: A system for colocated collaborative web search. In *Proc. CHI 2008.*
2. Baldonado, M.W. and Winograd, F. SenseMaker: an information-exploration interface supporting the contextual evolution of a user's interests. In *Proc. CHI 1997.*
3. Bao, S., Wu, X. Fei, B., Xue, G., Su, Z. and Yu, Y. Optimizing web search using social annotations. In *Proc. WWW 2007.*
4. Card, S.K., Robertson, G.G. and York, W. The WebBook and the Web Forager: Video use scenarios for a World-Wide Web information workspace. In *Proc. CHI 1996.*
5. Catledge, L.D. and Pitkow, J.E. Characterizing browsing strategies in the World Wide Web. In *Proc. WWW 1995.*
6. Chi, M.T.H., Feltovich, P.J. and Glaser, R. Categorization and representation of physics problems by experts and novices. *Cognitive Science 5,* 2, (1981), 121-152.
7. Choo, C.W., Detlor, B. and Turnbull, D. Information seeking on the Web: An integrated model of browsing and searching. *First Monday* 5, 2, (2000).
8. Cutting, D.R., Karger, D.R. and Pedersen, J.O. Constant interaction-time scatter/gather browsing of very large document collections. In *Proc. SIGIR 1993.*
9. Dmitriev, P.A., Eiron, N., Fontoura, M. and Shekita, E. Using Annotations in Enterprise Search. In *Proc. WWW 2006,* 811-817.
10. Dontcheva, M., Drucker, S., Wade, G., Salesin, D. and Cohen, M. Collecting and Organizing Web Content. In *Proc. SIGIR 2006.*
11. Evans, B.M. and Chi, E.H. Towards a Model of Understanding Social Search. In *Proc. CSCW 2008.*
12. Fisher, K., Counts, S. and Kittur, A. Distributed sensemaking: improving sensemaking by leveraging the efforts of previous users. In *Proc. CHI 2012,* 247-256
13. Freyne, J., Farzan, R., Brusilovsky, P., Smyth, B. and Coyle, M. Collecting community wisdom: integrating social search & social navigation. In *Proc. UIST 2007,*
14. Furnas, G.W., Landauer, T.K., Gomez, L.M. and Dumais, S.T. The vocabulary problem in human-system communication. *CACM 30,* 11, ACM Press (1987), 964-971.
15. Glance, N. S. Community search assistant. In *Proc. IUI 2001.*
16. Goldberg, D., Nichols, D., Oki, B.M. and Terry, D. Using collaborative filtering to weave an information tapestry. *CACM 35*, 12, (1992), 61–70.
17. Golder, S.A. and Huberman, B.A. Usage Patterns of Collaborative Tagging Systems. *Journal of Information Science 32,* 2, (2006), 198-208.
18. Hammond, T., Hannay, T., Lund, B. and Scott, J. Social book marking tools (i) - a general review. *D-Lib Magazine 11,* 4, (2005).
19. Hofgesang, P.I. Web personalisation through incremental individual profiling and support-based user segmentation. In *Proc. IEEE 2007.*
20. Hong, L, Chi, E.H., Budiu, R., Pirolli, P. and Nelson, L. SparTag.us: Low Cost Tagging System for Foraging of Web Content. In *Proc AVI 2008.*
21. Hummel, J.E. and Holyoak, K.J. Distributed representations of structure: A theory of analogical access and mapping. *Psychological Review 104*, (1997), 427-466.
22. Kandogan, E. and Shneiderman, B. Elastic Windows: evaluation of multi-window operations. I*n Proc CHI 1997.*
23. Kellar, M., Watters, C. and Shepherd, M. A Field Study Characterizing Web-Based Information-Seeking Tasks. *Journal of the American Society for Information Science 58,* 7, (2007), 999-1018.
24. Klein, G., Moon, B. and Hoffman, R.R. Making Sense of Sensemaking 2: A Macrocognitive Model. In *Proc. IEEE 2006.*
25. Kittur, A., Peters, A.M., Diriye, A., Telang, T. and Bove, M.R. Costs and benefits of structured information foraging. In *Proc. CHI 2013*, 2989-2998.
26. Kittur, A., Suh, B. and Chi, E.H. Can you ever trust a wiki?: impacting perceived trustworthiness in Wikipedia. In *Proc. CSCW 2008*, 477-480.
27. Konstan, J.A., Miller, B.N., Maltz, D., Herlocker, J.L., Gordon, L.R. and Riedl. J. GroupLens: Applying collaborative filtering to Usenet news. *CACM 40,* 3, (2007), 77–87.
28. Large, A., Beheshti, J. and Rahman, T. Gender Differences in Collaborative Web Searching Behavior: An Elementary School Study. *Information Processing and Management 38*, (2002), 427-433.
29. Lee, K.J. What Goes Around Comes Around: An Analysis of del.icio.us as Social Space. In *Proc. CSCW 2006.*
30. Lerman, K. Social Information Processing in News Aggregation. In *Proc. IEEE 2007.*
31. Maarek, Y.S., Jacovi, M., Shtalhaim, M., Ur, S., Zernik, D. and Ben-Shaul, I.Z. WebCutter: a system for dynamic and tailorable site mapping. In *Proc. WWW 1997,* 1269-1279.
32. MacKay, B., Kellar, M. and Watters, C. An evaluation of landmarks for re-finding information on the Web. *Ext. Abstracts CHI 2005.*
33. Marchionini, G. Information seeking in electronic environments. Cambridge, UK: Cambridge University Press, (2000).
34. Mathes, A. Folksonomies – Cooperative Classification and Communication through Shared Metadata. http://www.adammathes.com/academic /computer-mediatedcommunication/folksonomies.html. (December 2004).
35. Millen, D.R., Feinberg, J. and Kerr, B. Dogear: Social bookmarking in the enterprise. In *Proc. CHI 2006.*
36. Morris, M.R. A Survey of Collaborative Web Search Practices. In *Proc. CHI 2008.*

37. Morris, M.R. and Horvitz, E. SearchTogether: An Interface for Collaborative Web Search. In *Proc. UIST 2007.*
38. Munro, A.J., Hook, K., and Benyon, D.R. Eds. *Personal and Social Navigation of Information Space.* Springer-Verlag (1999).
39. Muralidharan, A, Gyongyi, Z. and Chi, E. Social annotations in web search. In *Proc. CHI 2012*, ACM Press (2012), 1085-1094.
40. Marlow, C., Naaman, M., boyd, d. and Davis, M. HT06, Tagging Paper, Taxonomy, Flickr, Academic Article, To Read. In *Proc. HT06,* 31-40.
41. Paul, S.A. and Morris, M.W. CoSense: Enhancing Sensemaking for Collaborative Web Search. In *Proc. CHI 2009.*
42. Paul, S.A., Reddy, M.C. Sensemaking in collaborative web search. Human Computer Interaction 26, 72–122 (2011).
43. Pirolli, P. and Card, S.K. Information foraging in information access environments. In *Proc. CHI 1995.*
44. Pirolli, P. and Card, S.K. Information foraging. *Psychological Review 106*, (1999), 643-675.
45. Russell, D.M., Stefik, M.J., Pirolli, P. and Card, S.K. The cost structure of sensemaking. In *Proc. CHI 1993*, 269-276.
46. Schraefel, M., Zhu, Y., Modjeska, D., Wigdor, D. and Zhao, S. Hunter gatherer: interaction support for the creation and management of within-web-page collections. In *Proc. WWW 2002.*
47. Sharma, N. Role of available and provided resources in sensemaking. In *Proc. CHI 2011.*
48. Shneiderman, B. Designing trust into online experiences. *CACM 43*, 12, (2000), 57-59.
49. Smyth, B., Balfe, E., Boydell, O., Bradley, K., Briggs, P., Coyle, M. and Freyne, J. A liveuser evaluation of collaborative web search. In *Proc. International Joint Conference on Artificial Intelligence 2005.*
50. Tauscher, L. and Greenberg, S. How people revisit Web pages: Empirical findings and implications for the design of history systems. *International Journal of Human–Computer Studies 47*, (1997), 97–137.
51. Twidale, M., Nichols, D. and Paice, C. Browsing is a Collaborative Process. *Information Processing and Management 33*, 6, (1997), 761-783.
52. Wu, X., Zhang, L. and Yu, Y. Exploring Social Annotations for the Semantic Web. In *Proc. WWW 2006*, 417-426.
53. Yanbe, Y., Jatowt, A., Nakamura, S. and Tanaka, K. Can social bookmarking enhance search in the web? In *Proc. ACM/IEEE-CS joint conf. on Digital libraries 2007,* 107.
54. Zanardi, V. and Capra, L. Social ranking: uncovering relevant content using tag-based recommender systems. In *Proc. ACM RecSys 2008*, 51.

The Antecedents of Remix

Giorgos Cheliotis
National University of Singapore
Blk AS6, #03-41
11 Computing Drive
Singapore 117416
gheliotis@nus.edu.sg

Hu Nan
University of Wisconsin
1908 Lasalle St
Eau Claire, WI 54702
hun@uwec.edu

Jude Yew
National University of Singapore
Blk AS6, #03-41
11 Computing Drive
Singapore 117416
jude.yew@nus.edu.sg

Huang Jianhui
Singapore Management University
80 Stamford Road
Singapore 178902
jhhuang.2009@phdis.smu.edu.sg

ABSTRACT

Reuse of the works of others has become common practice on the Internet and has formed the basis for collaboration in some online communities. However, some works are reused much more frequently than others. In this article we build a quantitative model that explains which factors are most salient in determining the likelihood that an author's work will be reused. Controlling for common factors, such as the work's popularity, we show that the probability of reuse depends on (a) the degree of derivativity of the work in question, (b) the specific ways in which it derives meaning from other works (intertextuality), (c) the audience's preferential attachment to authors of high fecundity, and (d) the author's social embeddedness in networks of reuse. We use trace data from an online community that was built for the purpose of demonstrating the ability of open sharing and reuse to spur collaboration and innovation in music. Although our model is designed for broad applicability, we explain that the size and direction of the effects reported in this paper may vary, when reuse is performed with other media or for different purposes.

Author Keywords
Remix; reuse; derivativity; intertextuality; fecundity; social embeddedness; social network analysis.

ACM Classification Keywords
H.5.3. **[Information Interfaces and Presentation]**: Group and Organizational Interfaces – collaborative computing, computer-supported cooperative work, theory and models, web based interaction. J.0 **[Computer Applications]** General.

General Terms
Measurement, Human Factors, Theory, Legal Aspects

CSCW'14, February 15–19, 2014, Baltimore, Maryland, USA.

ACM 978-1-4503-2540-0/14/02...$15.00.
http://dx.doi.org/10.1145/2531602.2531730

INTRODUCTION

Digital content is increasingly produced by amateurs, hobbyists and professionals, working alone, in small teams, or collaborating with others in online communities of practice, using the Internet for communication and as resource pool for samples, designs, textures, and other elements they can incorporate in their work [1, 3, 21, 31]. Some of these communities promote collaboration through the reuse of member contributions [13, 14, 23]. The ability to reuse each other's work has been essential to the success of free/open source software, Wikipedia, open education, open data, and many collaborative music-making, storytelling, and film-making initiatives [13]. In software, reuse has long been a design goal, and thus designing for reuse is taught in every computer programming class. Similar examples of designing for reuse can be found in engineering, education, graphic design, music, video games, etc.

Often the term 'remix' is used instead of 'reuse', especially in the context of music, whence the term originated [37]. In more recent years the word has gained currency outside of music, largely thanks to the rise of social media, improvements in the capacity of the Web to support user-generated content, and the growth of what is commonly termed a 'remix culture', in reference to the increasing popularity of the practice and the ways in which it permeates contemporary culture [29, 31, 34]. In this paper we will attempt to produce a general understanding of reuse, but with a focus on creative works and drawing inspiration from remix in music primarily. To this end we will build an explanatory model of remix that will include some of the social and cultural factors that drive remixing activity and will help us investigate their relative salience in predicting the likelihood that a given work will be taken up by others and reused.

BACKGROUND

Remix is defined by Navas [37] as "a reinterpretation of a pre-existing song, meaning that the 'spectacular aura' of the original will be dominant in the remixed version". He identifies three types of remix in the history of music: (i) the *extended* remix, which is a longer reinterpretation of the original music track, suitable for performance in clubs, (ii) the *selective* remix, which selectively adds or removes material from the original recording, but keeping the 'essence' of the original intact, and (iii) the *reflexive* remix, in which the original work is left largely intact, but with the remix claiming autonomy as an alternative version of the recording rather than a derivative work, thus challenging the 'spectacular aura' of the source by attempting to be its equal. Yet even in the latter case, Navas claims that the remix is still "completely dependent" on the source for validation.

Intertextuality

The definitions of remix in music offered in [37] present a tension between the authority of the 'parent' source work and the remix 'child'. This is a familiar theme in critical literary theory, where the tension is often considered unresolvable: any work that recontextualizes source material is as much an homage to the source (the work and by extension possibly also its author), as it is a departure from it (see for example the translator's preface in [19]). More generally, any work of the intellect can be said to derive meaning from its relationships to other works that have preceded it, and even to those that have followed it. This is the premise of intertextuality [18], an approach towards understanding texts through their relationships to other texts, and by extension, works in other mediums as well. For example, an academic article becomes meaningful to the reader not only by what it claims as a contribution, but also by means of its reference to academic literature and thus its relationship to the works of other authors that the reader may be familiar with. Similarly, works of creative expression, such as musical works, are always implicated in networks of meaning-making (e.g. with respect to genre) that are defined largely by their relationships to other works [36]. The appreciation of remix then is intimately related to the works it is reusing and the audience's familiarity with them. Indeed, experiencing familiarity in something new (through repetition with variation) is one of the greatest pleasures of adaptation [24].

Derivativity

The definitions of remix discussed earlier, as well as the notion of adaptation theorized in [24], pertain to works that reuse recognizable elements from usually just one source work. In such cases, as already stated, the adaptation, or remix in other words, depends on the source for validation, i.e. even when it may try to escape the 'aura' of the original and stand on its own, it will be largely perceived in relation to the original work (a comparison which may work in its favor, or not [24, 26]). However, more recently, the word 'remix' has become almost synonymous with the more general term 'reuse' and has come to encapsulate, as an umbrella term, many more forms of reuse of prior work [30, 34]. Mash-ups for example combine two sources into a new creation and thus derive their meaning from the juxtaposition of two sources rather than the reinterpretation of one [22]. With increasing access, ease of reproduction, and growing availability of free and affordable audiovisual editing tools, it is becoming easier for authors to reuse an ever larger number of sources in their works. In other words, it is becoming easier to produce works that are *more derivative*, in the sense that authors rely on many different sources for their production. In musical tradition, this would be sometimes referred to as 'sampling' rather than 'remix' [37], but given the transformation in public discourse of the once more specific term 'remix' into a more general term that is also not anymore medium-specific, we will use it here in this broader sense.

This tension between an original work and its derivatives has been explored by [35, 38] who criticize that widespread remixing produces low quality works that lack originality. More recently, [30] empirically explored this tension in a specific online community, Scratch. The authors found that remixes involving reuse of computer code tended to be rated higher than remixes of non-interactive media. Here we will look in greater detail at the issue of derivativity for creative works, while remaining cognizant of the fact that derivativity and other variables may operate differently across various types of media.

Social embeddedness

As already noted in the introduction, in a contemporary remix culture, remix refers not only to a creative process, but also to the ability to collaborate with others online through the reuse of each other's works. Yochai Benkler has described the production model that underpins this process as "commons-based peer production" [6], because the works produced by such communities of practice are typically licensed in a manner that allows for their open sharing and reuse, thus forming a digital *commons*, while community members are assumed to regard each other as equal *peers*, eschewing hierarchy and task division for organizational flexibility and ad-hoc, interest-based contribution. Participants can reap a number of rewards through their active engagement: laboring on a contribution might be a fun and fulfilling activity in and of itself [4, 27, 38], not the least because of the personal learning that the practice may involve [38, 44, 45]. Additionally, the publication of a contribution to the community may bring with it a number of additional and important social rewards, such as enhancing the status of the participant in the community [42, 46] and possibly providing opportunities for interpersonal or group communication with other members. A factor that is known to influence commitment to the group, is a person's degree of embeddedness in the network of group interactions, which is also a predictor of one's propensity to be an active contributor [46]. Likewise, recent work on social media has examined how contextual factors such as network topology or position within a network can impact the popularity and reuse of user contributions. For example, there exists an interesting parallel between the practice of reposting (or 'retweeting') in micro-blogging and remixing in music, as both practices, though clearly distinct, involve the propagation and recontextualization of personal expressions. Recent work has found that retweeting is the result of both contextual factors (such as network position) and the content of the tweet (such as the type of tweet that is being posted) [12, 33, 54]. Likewise in this paper we examine the role that an author's position in the network (in terms of embeddedness in reposting/remixing activity) and the characteristics of a contribution by the author (in terms of its derivativity and intertextuality) determine whether the contribution will be remixed or not.

Online communities rely critically on a small core of committed contributors *but also* on the maintenance of an extended circle of more ephemeral participants [28], so the extent to which the network structure is such that it engenders high and sustained levels of contribution by a critical mass of participants [35] while also accommodating newcomers is essential, especially in light of frequent changes in member motivation and activity level [5, 10]. Through remix, relationships are formed not only between works, but also by extension between their respective authors [14], and so reuse becomes a conversation between works, their authors, and their audience. It is in the context of such relationships that we will examine how an author's embeddedness in networks of reuse influences their creative output and relations to other authors, as well as the reception and reuse of their work by others.

Fecundity

Preferential attachment theory predicts that core members will not only be more committed to the community and more productive, but also more attractive as 'hubs' to connect to for newcomers [2, 12]. More generally, an individual's historical record of linking to others will be a predictor of the probability of new link formation, in what is also known as the 'rich get richer' or 'Matthew effect'. In the context of remix, this means that works produced by authors with a high historical rate of reuse are more likely to be reused in the future. Preferential attachment to core members of a community should further increase their embeddedness in the network of community interactions, thus also their motivation to contribute more, leading to a virtuous circle. However, the potential downside is that core members (usually also those with longer tenure in the community, as the theory of preferential attachment predicts [2]), while perhaps respected for their contributions to the community, may also, intentionally or not, create an exclusionary social structure by promoting their own interests and developing own norms that may redefine group boundaries [39, 40], and make them more differentiating in their treatment of other members [32], possibly at the expense of contributions from the periphery and from newcomers.

We refer to the ability of some authors to produce works that are highly reused by others, as *fecundity*, although in [23] it is conceptualized as 'generativity', in reference to Jonathan Zittrain's development of the concept in [47]. We avoid using the term generativity in relation to authors or works, because it can be misleading. The term was used in [47] to develop a theory of 'generative systems' and explain how the Internet has been effective in accommodating for unanticipated innovation by being moderately specified and thus also moderately complex (based on 'rough consensus and running code' rather than being fully specified in advance). But it is not clear that this extends to individual works or to people, i.e. whether an author or say a piece of music can be said to be inherently generative in the sense that the Internet is generative as a system.

Complexity and modularity

However, it is conceivable that the complexity of a source work may indeed influence its attractiveness for reuse, at least in the sense that it may, in some cases, where complexity is pertinent and objectively measurable, increase the cognitive load on those potential remixers who will consider engaging with the material. Using data that is akin to procedural software from an online community that produces interactive works, the authors in [23] demonstrate that the probability of reuse of a work produced in this community is indeed maximized for moderate complexity, where complexity is measured in terms of the number of blocks of computer code in a work. Although an interesting finding, we do not attempt to measure complexity in our study, where the focus is on non-procedural creative works, and also express some reservations as to whether generativity theory would be applicable to such works, as already explained.

Related to complexity is the concept of modularity. Media theorist Lev Manovich has postulated in an essay [34] that the modularity of a work should be positively associated with its 'remixability', i.e. the ease with which it can be remixed, thus presumably making the work more likely to be reused by others. This is also the foundational logic behind the dominant paradigm of object-oriented programming in software, and in music too, we observe that when authors wish to encourage remixing of their works (for example, when organizing remix contests), they make the 'stems' available individually, i.e. they offer the work up for remix divided into modules that are more malleable and easier to recombine in new creations.

Incentives

In an attempt to maintain a constant flow of new content and participants, as well as engage successful professionals with their fans and with new talent, online communities often resort to the organization of contests offering additional, extrinsic incentives for contributing a remix. These usually take the form of non-monetary incentives, such as promises of social recognition and exclusive promotion of the most popular remixes, but sometimes also include monetary awards.

Remix contests have proven particularly popular and able to generate large amounts of remixing activity [14]. However, they come with their own sets of issues. One is the risk that frequent use of contests to motivate remix will alter the incentive structure of the community [25, 41, 46], possibly undermining intrinsic motivations for participation. Another is that contests reinforce a culture of fandom rather than supporting commons-based peer production, by diverting attention away from engaging with peers, towards honoring the works of famed individuals, and moreover, in a mode of competition with other community members, rather than cooperation [43]. When considering the factors that lead to remixing activity we must thus also take into account the presence of any additional incentives for production.

CCMIXTER

We will test our model using a large dataset of remixing activity from the ccMixter online community. ccMixter was first formed to serve as an online submissions platform for a music remix contest organized by Wired magazine, using Creative Commons licenses, to encourage legal reuse. It is unique in that it was built from the bottom up to support and importantly, *track* reuse by its members.

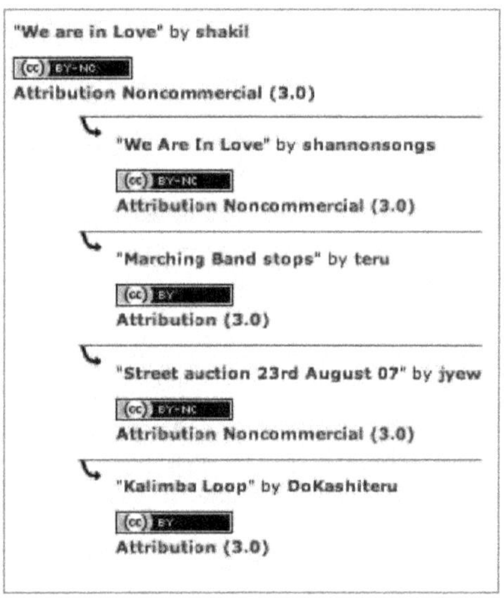

Figure 1: Screenshot of ccMixter user interface – song information page displaying reuse of material from other songs and licensing information

Whenever a work is uploaded, the author of the work is requested to declare whether it is a de novo contribution, or a remix of other works in the community, and in the latter case, declare also the sources that were used in the remix (see). Then the authors of the source works are notified and can track the number of remixes that their works receive. The submitter must also select a license for the work, among a set of Creative Commons licenses that allow for remix, but in some cases only under the condition that the remix will not be exploited commercially. Licensing options for remixes are generated automatically, based on the restrictions in the licenses of the source works used in the remix. Thus licensing restrictions are propagated from one work the next through remix.

ccMixter outlived the purposes of that first contest and continued to organize more remix contests, while also increasingly encouraging organic growth of remix activity outside of the confines and special incentives of contests [43]. Table 1 presents a summary of all works posted to the community at the time of data collection. We notice that the community produced a sizeable amount of works (9,300), with more than half of them reusing elements of other works posted by the community. Contests were particularly effective in contributing to remix activity, although the majority of remixes were not contest-related.

Table 1: Summary of works posted on ccmixter

Works	Sources	Remixes	Total
Total	4253	5047	9300
(% of total works)	*46%*	*54%*	*100%*
Contest-related	57	1699	1756
(% of column total)	*1%*	*34%*	*19%*
Contest entries	57	1193	1250
Byproducts	n/a	506	506
Non-contest	4196	3348	7544
(% of column total)	*99%*	*66%*	*81%*

MODEL

Based on our literature review regarding the pertinence of various factors, we will now proceed with the development of an explanatory model for the probability of remix. Then we will test the model using the ccMixter dataset.

Author-related variables

Considering that some of the factors we have discussed thus far concern the work itself, and some the track record and position of the author in the community, our model will focus on two factors that are author-related (embeddedness and fecundity), and two factors that are content-related (derivativity and intertextuality). Figure 2 lists the main factors at these two levels of analysis.

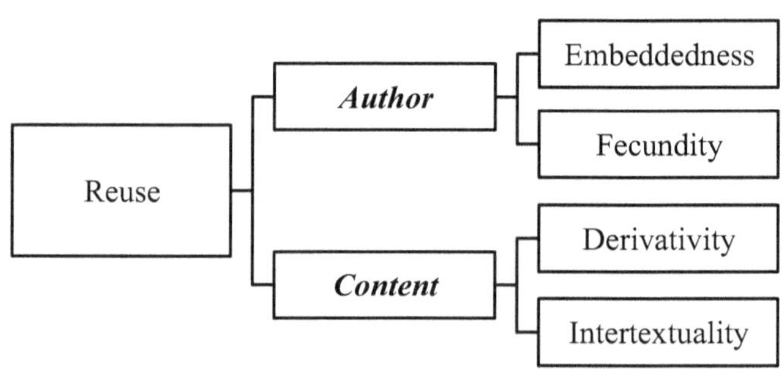

Figure 2: Main hypothesized factors affecting the reuse of a creative work (*simplified*)

Social embeddedness

As discussed, the social embeddedness of an author in community interactions is expected to be positively associated with the author's level of commitment and contributions to the community. However, there exists no unique way of operationalizing embeddedness. The network of relations under consideration here consists of relations of remix (where a link from author A to author B suggests that B has remixed at least one work of A), and an author contributes not only by making a submission, but also by making it available and attractive for reuse. In a remix network, embeddedness should be naturally associated with higher remix activity (by definition, since the network consists of remix relations), but to investigate the directionality of this activity and consequently who remixes whom, we need to go further than this.

Given that, as noted in the literature review, communities typically consist of a small core and a more expansive periphery, and understanding that remix defines a flow of cultural influence and information from one author to the next, we decided to operationalize embeddedness as membership in the three primary network components of a bow-tie structure. Bow-tie analysis was famously used in analyzing the structure of the Web in [11]. It is premised on the observation that networks of directional information flow (such as hyperlinks between web pages, or, in our case, a network of remix relationships) can be characterized as consisting of three critical components: a strongly-connected CORE, an IN component which flows into the CORE, and an OUT component which flows out of the CORE. The three components can be visualized as having the shape of a bowtie, with the knot representing the CORE in the middle. Table 2 shows the main results of the bow-tie analysis we applied to the network of authors connected through the remix of each other's works in ccMixter. Every author in the IN component has been remixed by an author in the CORE, without having remixed an author in the CORE. Authors in the OUT component have remixed authors in the CORE, but *have not* been remixed by authors in the CORE. Authors in the CORE remix authors in the IN component, and other authors in the CORE. Remix thus can be said to flow mainly in the direction IN->CORE->OUT (although this is an oversimplification of information flow dynamics in the community and it does not prescribe which authors are most likely to be remixed in the community as a whole).

All authors classified under 'Other' in Table 2 are connected to the rest of the network either through the IN or OUT components. These are community members who form the periphery of the remix network by virtue of forming small disconnected components (islands) or being connected by the act of remix to one or more authors in either the IN or OUT components (thus forming what Broder et al. call 'tendrils' [11]). In this analysis we focus on the three more central components CORE, IN and OUT, without which large numbers of authors would become disconnected from the rest of the remix network.

Table 2: Summary of bow-tie analysis

Components	CORE	IN	OUT	Other
Authors	12% (205)	17% (290)	20% (338)	51% (865)

After examining the authors classified in the CORE (see Table 3), we find that they exhibit a much higher level of sustained contributions (uploads) to the community, as predicted by social embeddedness theory. They also, as expected, remix and are remixed (average degree) more than twice as often as the average author, while they also tend to reciprocate another author's remix of their work.

Table 3: Comparison of core to network

Group	Core		Entire network	
	Value	Rel. SD	Value	Rel. SD
Reciprocal ties	114	n/a	115	n/a
Avg. tie strength	2.15	1.44	1.95	1.20
Avg. degree (in,out)	6.8	1.5, 1.3	2.9	2.8, 4.7
Average uploads	21.4	1.3	5.0	2.4

Authors in the IN component do not belong to the prolific CORE group, but their works are nevertheless deemed valuable and reused by authors in the CORE, who otherwise exhibit a preference for remixing each other. Assuming that imitation (and thus also reuse) is the sincerest form of flattery and drawing on our literature review regarding the intellectual debt of the remix to the source material, we will assume that authors in the IN component will enjoy at least as high, if not higher reuse than authors in the CORE. In a sense, they may come to be viewed as innovators by the rest of the community by means of the CORE's acceptance and adaptation of their works. We expect that the works of authors in the OUT component will on the other hand have an at least slightly lower probability of reuse, because these authors remix the CORE, but are not remixed by it (nor by anyone in the IN component). In other words, the favor is not returned, and the intellectual debt remains with the authors in the OUT component. In summary, although this is a reduction that would not do justice to each individual author in these components, it is conceptually useful to think of the IN, CORE, and OUT components as the 'mavericks', the 'incumbents', and the 'followers' respectively This leads us to formulate the following hypothesis:

Hypothesis 1: Works by authors classified in the IN component are more likely to be reused, followed by the CORE, and OUT component.

Fecundity

We also mentioned how works by authors with a record of having been frequently remixed by others are more likely to be remixed, as predicted by preferential attachment theory. This leads us directly to the second hypothesis:

Hypothesis 2: Works by authors with a higher historical rate of reuse are more likely to be reused.

Content-related variables

Intertextuality

We mentioned that familiarity is one of the main pleasures experienced in the appreciation of adaptations. Therefore, reusing popular works should improve the reception of the remix by the community. However, it should have a negative effect on the likelihood that the remix will be further reused by others, because it will be harder for the remix to escape the aura of the works it incorporates, the more popular these works are. In other words, audience familiarity may improve likability, but it should affect negatively remixability. If anything, fans of the remix are more likely to produce another remix of the popular and thus presumably instantly recognizable source work, rather than consider remixing further the remix.

Hypothesis 3: Reuse of popular works will decrease a work's attractiveness for further reuse

This hypothesis, and the related hypothesis on derivativity that follows, are in the opposite direction from the hypothesis in [23] regarding the probability of remix for a work that is itself a remix. The authors of that paper base their hypothesis on a rather incorrect interpretation of preferential attachment theory, but find their hypothesis validated by empirical findings, possibly because the data used concerned procedural works that may be more amenable to iterative remixing practices, compared to the works that we consider here. See also [13] for a discussion of the differences in the organization of production for different media types and purposes.

Derivativity

We explained that a remix of a single creative work cannot escape the 'aura' of the source, in that it inevitably derives validation from its relationship to the recognizable source material. Even if the source material may not be instantly familiar to the audience, it will be identified in the metadata accompanying the remix, and as the remix will be structured around that single source work whose influence will likely permeate every aspect of the remix, we expect that if the audience is going to reuse a work, then it is more likely that this will be the parent work, and not the remix itself. Therefore the probability of remix should be negatively associated with the derivativity of the work. Remixes that appeal to the audience, will, if anything, encourage further remix of the sources they used. However, since this intellectual debt of the remix to the source is premised on the existence of a unique, recognizable parent work casting its shadow over the remix, we assume that, as the number of sources in a work increases, the association with any individual source work or parent author is weakened by diffusion in the number of sources. Source material will likely also become less recognizable and in any case will be less critical in defining the character of the remix, the more sources are included in the work. We therefore also hypothesize a positive second-order effect of including many sources in a remix.

Hypothesis 4: There exists a U-shaped relationship between the derivativity of a work and its attractiveness for further reuse.

Control variables

Popularity (content-level)

We explained in the literature review section that remix of popular works is more likely, as familiarity with the source material is one of the greatest pleasures in adaptation, and moreover remixing is always also an homage to the source. Therefore we hold it for almost self-evident that popularity will affect the probability of remixing and do not wish to highlight it as an important factor and contribution of our model. We nevertheless need to control for it. We expect that both exposure and quality assessments (user ratings) will be relevant as indicators of a work's popularity, as there is evidence to suggest that while perceptions of quality matter, exposure is in itself positive (as in the popular saying 'any publicity is good publicity').

For example, there is an interesting corollary in the finance literature, where analyst visibility is measured in two ways: analyst reputation [8] and analyst exposure [9]. There is another corollary in product reviews in e-commerce sites: while some studies show that the mean of online product reviews has a significant effect on sales [16, 17], other studies in the context of online book sales present evidence to the contrary [15, 20, 33], because book reviews largely serve the purpose of informing consumers about the books' contents, and not their intrinsic quality. For books it seems any publicity is good publicity, since even negative reviews can lead to increases in sales [7].

Assessment (content-level)

As the results of prior studies on the impact of reviews are not entirely conclusive and peer assessments may after all affect perceptions of posted content to some extent, we will also control for the average user rating of a work.

Contest participation (author-level)

We noted that contests generate a great amount of non-organic growth in the community, under additional incentives for participation and in conditions of competition among members. We must therefore also control for the effect of contests on remix. One way we can do this, is by controlling for author participation in contests (authors of contest source material would only ever participate in contests, because they were not otherwise active members of the community). Also, contests were successful in attracting many new members to the community, but several new members never participated beyond a single contest, which contributed to the community's ultimately skeptical view of contest participation [43].

Contest submission (content-level)

We also control for the effect of contests on remixing by controlling for works that were submitted as contest entries.

License restrictiveness (content-level)

As noted, all content posted to ccMixter is licensed under Creative Commons, but some licenses used by the community forbid commercial use. As this may deter some prospective remixers from investing time and effort into producing a remix that cannot be exploited commercially in the future without the consent of the copyright owner, we also include license choice as a control variable.

MODEL SPECIFICATION

To investigate which factors influence the probability that an item will be remixed after it is posted online, we use logistic regression. This allows us to interpret the dependent variable as the probability of remix, which is helpful in building intuition regarding the size of the observed effects and consistent with the tradition of random graph modeling and the development of preferential attachment theory in network science. The use of logistic regression requires that we define the dependent variable as a dichotomous or ternary variable (see next subsection for detailed variable definitions). Several variables had to be log-transformed to obtain normal distributions.

Equation 1: Logistic regression of the probability of reuse

$$\begin{aligned}\text{logit}(remix_{dummy}) &= \alpha + \beta_1 * cont_{src}^2 + \beta_2 * cont_{src} + \beta_3 * cont_{play} \\ &+ \beta_4 * cont_{rate} + \beta_5 * cont_{score} + \beta_6 * cont_{ncl} + \beta_7 * cont_{contest} \\ &+ \beta_8 * cont_{top\_played\_p} + \beta_9 * cont_{top\_remixed\_p} + \beta_{10} * usr_{remix} \\ &+ \beta_{11} * usr_{contest\_tracer} + \beta_{12} * usr_{in} + \beta_{13} * usr_{core} + \beta_{14} * usr_{out}\end{aligned}$$

Based on Lack of Fit test and global F test, our model fits the data very well. To check the robustness of the results we have also tried using the number of remixes as the dependent variable (i.e. sans the logit transformation) and estimating the model with ordinary least squares (OLS). Qualitatively the results do not change. Because both dependent and independent variables can be driven by the age (i.e. tenure in the community) of an author or work, for both logistic regression and OLS we tried weighted logistic regression and weighted least squares respectively and quantitatively and qualitatively the results do not change. We also tested for multicollinearity in the independent variables with the VIF statistic and found no issues. Finally, we also ran the regression with clusters at the author level, to account for the possibility that observations clustered into authors may not be independent, which could lead to residuals that are not independent within authors.

VARIABLE DEFINITIONS

We will now present in more detail the specific operationalization of the constructs in the regression.

Dependent Variable

$remix_{dummy}$: ternary variable, 0 for items which have never been remixed, and 1 or 2 for those that have been remixed at least once. Among the items which have been remixed at least once, we first rank them according to the number of times they have been remixed. Then we assign the value 2 to items that fall within the top 20%; and 1 for the rest. This will provide us with some more insight into the salience of the effects of independent variables on the dependent variable.

Independent variables – author level

Social embeddedness

usr_{in}: binary variable, 1 for authors (or, equivalently, 'users') classified in the IN component and 0 otherwise.

usr_{core}: binary variable, 1 for authors classified in the CORE component and 0 otherwise.

usr_{out}: binary variable, 1 for authors classified in the OUT component and 0 otherwise.

Fecundity

usr_{remix}: on average, how many times a work created by a specific author is remixed. For a specific author i who uploaded n works, we compute $usr_{remix,i}$ thus:

$$usr_{remix,i} = \frac{1}{n} \times \sum_{j=1}^{n} n\_remix_{i,j}$$

where $n\_remix_{i,j}$ is the number of times the jth work created by author i was remixed.

Contest participation (control)

$usr_{contest\_tracer}$: binary variable, 1 for authors who only upload works in contests and 0 for all other authors.

Independent variables – content level

Derivativity

$cont_{src}$: number of source works used to generate a remix

Intertextuality (operationalized as familiarity)

$cont_{top\_played\_p}$: Out of all the sources used in a remix, the percentage that belongs to the most played works in the community. It is calculated thus:

$$cont_{top\_played\_p} = \frac{n_{top\_played\_p}}{n_{src\_items}}$$

where $n_{top\_played\_p}$ is the number of sources which belong to the most-played group and n_{src_items} is the total number of sources used in the remix. We define the most-played group like this: first we rank all posted works in the community according to the number of times they have been played; then we mark the top 2% as the most-played works, taking into account the typically long-tailed distribution of attention in online communities.

Similarly,

$$cont_{top\_remixed\_p} = \frac{n_{top\_remixed\_p}}{n_{src\_items}}$$

is defined as above, but with works ranked according to the number of times they have been remixed instead of the number of plays.

Popularity (control)

$cont_{play}$: number of times a work has been played.

$cont_{rate}$: number of times a work has been reviewed.

Assessment (control)

$cont_{score}$: average rating (score) for a work.

License restrictiveness (control)

$cont_{ncl}$: binary variable, 1 for works with a 'non-commercial' license (i.e. forbidding commercial use) and 0 otherwise.

Contest submission (control)

$cont_{contest}$: binary variable, 1 for works submitted as contest entries and 0 otherwise.

RESULTS

Table 4 summarizes the results of the regression. The findings support our hypothesis regarding network embeddedness (Hypothesis 1). Authors classified in the OUT component are the least likely to have their submissions remixed by others (b=-0.5176), followed by the CORE group (b=2.9078), and the IN group (b=3.2884). The coefficient for the OUT component is not significant, however F-tests on the differences between the coefficients show that these are significant, leading us to accept the hypothesis. Figure 3 shows the mean probability of reuse for each author group, after applying inverse logit on the dependent variable to obtain probability values. Even after having controlled for many other factors in the regression, authors in the IN group enjoy an impressive 50% chance of having their works remixed, and a 6.2% chance of their works reaching the top 2% in the community, in terms of the number of remixes they receive (see also earlier introduction to the bow-tie analysis for an explanation of the salience of these results regarding CORE, IN and OUT groups). Total probability of receiving at least one remix per work for the group is obtained by adding the two values, i.e. for the IN group it is 56%. Authors in the CORE also enjoy a high probability of having their works remixed. This is in stark contrast to the OUT group, whose works will be remixed with a very low probability on average. The distinction between IN, CORE, and OUT group has thus proven to be very salient in the context of remix. However, the much lower levels of the dotted line in Figure 3 suggest that having one's work remixed by CORE authors will only go so far. Becoming a highly remixed author will depend on many other factors.

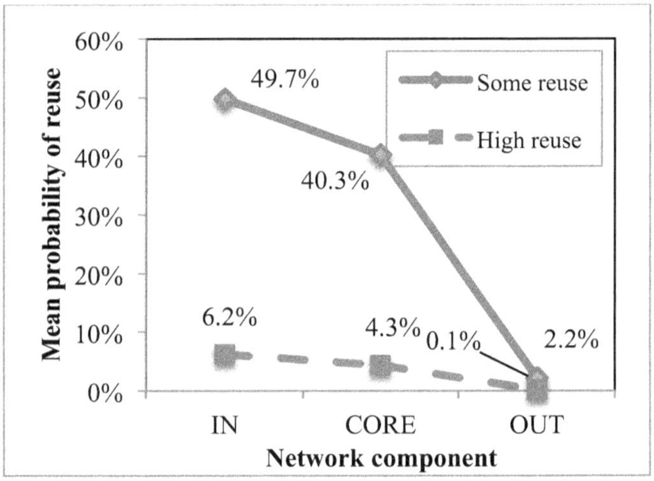

Figure 3: Mean probability of some reuse (solid line), and high reuse (dotted line), i.e. chances that a work will be remixed and that the number of remixes will rank in the bottom 80% or top 20% respectively compared to all other remixed works

With respect to the impact of the author's fecundity on the probability of remix for a work by that author, we find that our hypothesis is supported (b=0.9724, $p<0.0001$, supporting Hypothesis 2). This suggests that preferential attachment to authors of high fecundity is indeed a factor that determines remixing activity, and should lead to concentration of remixing activity on the works of a small number of authors, unless authors of higher inherent 'fitness' appear, because, after all, the quality of a work does matter, as also indicated by the significant positive effect of the average rating of a work on its remixing probability. As expected, popularity (exposure), as measured by the number of plays (b=0.1168, p=0.0003), or the number of ratings (b=0.2228, p=0.0071), is also a predictor of remixing activity.

We also find that the reuse of popular works, in terms of plays or remixes, will indeed have an adverse effect on the attractiveness of the content as material for further reuse (b=-0.9951, p=0.0024 when reusing from the 'most-played group' and b=-1.2195, $p<0.0001$ for reusing from the 'most-remixed group'). Thus the hypothesis on intertextual familiarity benefitting the source rather than the remix is also supported (Hypothesis 3).

Table 4: Results of ordered logistic regression of the probability of reuse

Regression variables	Beta (logit)
Intercept 2	-5.958***
Intercept 1	-3.3427***
Derivativity	
Number of sources (squared)	0.2993*
Number of sources	-1.3182***
Intertextuality *(operationalized as familiarity)*	
Reuse of most-played items	-0.9951**
Reuse of most-remixed items	-1.2195***
Fecundity	
Avg. reuse per author's work	0.9724***
Social embeddedness	
Author in IN group	3.2884***
Author in CORE group	2.9078***
Author in OUT group	-0.5176
F-test for IN and CORE group	p=0.0016
F-test for OUT and CORE group	p<.0001
Controls	
Number of plays	0.1168***
Number of reviews	0.2228**
Score (average rating)	0.1196*
License restrictiveness	-0.2156*
Contest submission	0.0773
Contest participation	0.5171
Testing Global Null Hypothesis: Beta = 0	
Test	$\chi 2$
Likelihood Ratio	1379.21***
Score	1115.312***
Wald	733.606***

* *p*<.05 ** *p*<.01 *** *p*<.001

We mentioned earlier that we suspected the existence of a nonlinear relationship between the degree of derivativity of a work and its reception by the community. The coefficient of the linear term for the number of sources is significantly negative (b= -1.3182, p<0.0001), while the coefficient of the squared term is significantly positive (b=0.2993, p<0.0001). This suggests that the relationship between the number of sources that a work is reusing, and the chances that it will be remixed is indeed non-linear. Specifically, the data points to a convex relationship, lending support to Hypothesis 4. We present this relationship graphically in Figure 4, after applying an inverse logit on the dependent variable and converting the log-transformed independent variable back to its original form. We notice how the probability of reuse drops steeply as derivativity increases, but then slowly increases again as the number of sources grows beyond a threshold value of 5-10 sources. It therefore appears that works that incorporate many different sources are indeed better able to stand alone, independently of their borrowing from source material, thus becoming more attractive for remix, though the effect size is small. Also, the dotted line in Figure 4 shows that derivativity has virtually no influence on making a work really popular for remix. The popularity of the work itself, preferential attachment, and perhaps other factors that we couldn't control for here (such as complexity, modularity, and perhaps also the perceived originality of the work) will likely play a more important role in propelling a work from having just a couple of remixes, to becoming a source of inspiration for many remixers.

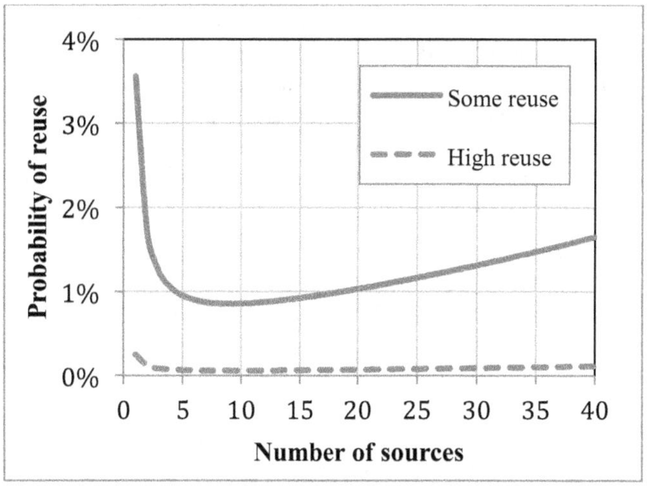

Figure 4: Influence of derivativity (number of sources) on the probability of reuse, shown separately for the bottom 80% of reused works (solid line) and for the top 20% of works that exhibit the highest levels of reuse (dotted line)

Finally, it is interesting to note from Table 4 that license restrictiveness does seem to matter: content made available under more restrictive licenses, specifically licenses forbidding commercial use without the consent of the copyright owner, was found to be significantly less likely to be reused in new productions (beta=-0.2156, p=0.0419).

DISCUSSION

In this paper we started by explaining how remixing practice has become a central component of commons-based peer production in online communities, while some communities in particular are built around the practice and thus critically depend on it. The chances then that a work will be remixed by others, whether conceptualized as 'remixability' in [34], or 'generativity' in [23], is then a central question for collaboration through remix. Focusing our attention on creative works, and using elements of network theory and literary/media theory, as well as earlier findings on cooperation and attention in online communities, we developed and tested a quantitative model that explains how the probability of reuse depends on a work's intertextuality and derivativity, as well as the author's fecundity and social embeddedness in networks of reuse. Not surprisingly, we found that it also depends on the work's popularity and on the restrictiveness of the licensing conditions under which remix is taking place.

Specifically, we found that the works of authors who have enjoyed an overall higher rate of reuse, are more likely to be reused in the future, which is in agreement with the theory of preferential attachment. It follows that it may be hard for newcomers to a community who may want to have their works reused by others to divert attention from already established sources of inspiration and existing remix projects. However, that is not necessarily an issue, as newcomers are likely to also engage in remixing the works of popular authors in the community at first, and thus practice their skill, while learning more about the community and how it appraises the works of others. We can also speculate that the primary concern of newcomers will be to produce remixes that are validated by the community as remixes, rather than expecting that any original creations they produce will become instantly popular for remix by others. At least our findings suggest that any such expectation would be misplaced.

We also found that the more derivative a work, the less likely it is to be further reused (except for works that incorporate so many different elements, that they ultimately attain a life and character of their own). This seems perhaps obvious in retrospect, but we have found at least one example of a study where the authors claim the opposite effect [23]. Although we already mentioned that there exists some confusion with respect to theorizing remix and associated concepts such as preferential attachment (see footnote 1), we also believe that results with respect to the direction and size of some of the effects we report will be medium- and purpose-specific, as also suggested in [13]. In other words, one must ask: what medium is being remixed and for what purpose? Although the results we report here seem sensible in light of related theory and in the context of musical remix, it is conceivable that in other communities and with other media, a work that is already a remix, will be more likely to be further remixed. For instance, the authors in [23] focus on the remixing of programming code in Scratch and conceptualized 'originality' as the "edit distance", or amount of change in the text/code between two works. In this case, we speculate that the medium of programming code helps to promote the remixing of derivative works, where blocks of code can be easily reused from one program to another, unlike music remixing where it may be harder to create remixes from derivative works because of the lack of "modularity" in the medium. This speculation deserves greater investigation of the differences in the dynamics of remixing as a result of different mediums.

Perhaps the most striking result was with respect to the influence of an author's embeddedness in networks of reuse on the probability that a work by the author will be remixed. We showed that community members seeking to have their works remixed by others will have a much higher chance of achieving their goal if at least one member of the core group of community contributors remixes a work by the member in question. Core members frequently remix each other, and so remixing one of their works will probably not be reciprocated, unless one is already in the core. On the contrary, if a community member remixes the work of a core author without being remixed back by the same (reciprocity) or another member in the core (generalized reciprocity), the chances of this author's works being remixed appear very slim indeed. Since the reciprocation is unlikely, we conclude that preemptively remixing the works of core members, though perhaps beneficial for other purposes, will be a poor choice for community members who want to become recognized as authors of original works that are an inspiration for others. There appears to be a tradeoff between seeking the recognition of other community members by engaging in remixing popular works and authors on the one hand, and being valued for one's own original contributions on the other.

IMPLICATIONS FOR DESIGN

We thus far focused our attention on the theoretical import of our findings. This begs the question: what of the design of user interfaces, algorithms, and systems that will optimally support remix in an online community? Although we are somewhat reluctant to speculate based on the findings of a cross-sectional study, our findings do point in some interesting directions. Firstly, building on the findings regarding network embeddedness, we would recommend that an online community based on remix, features not only most-remixed and most-liked content, but also contributions by newcomers to the community. A popularity-based algorithm determining which works will be featured in the front page of the community could for example weigh popularity according to a member's tenure in the community, such that works by new members will have a higher chance of being featured compared to works of similar popularity by incumbent members.

Another means of promoting a culture of collaboration as opposed to reproducing a culture of fandom would be to create incentives for members to remix the works of specific other members who are either new to the community or otherwise deserving of greater attention based on their track record in the community. In fact, the ccMixter community has already taken measures in this regard, whereby the leadership of the community has more recently decided to supplant the practice of remix contests with remix collaborations, whereby members are paired and asked to remix each other's works, thus also encouraging the development of reciprocity as a community norm.

Finally, if a community's shared objective is to promote the practice of remix (as is the case with ccMixter), it would be advisable to encourage members to use as liberal a copyright license as they can be comfortable with, seeing as license restrictiveness can affect the probability of remix negatively.

LIMITATIONS

A methodological limitation of this study is that we have not included a survey of the community or interviews with community members that might shed more light into their personal motivations and thought processes. An advantage on the other hand is that we avoid the pitfalls of sampling online populations and generalizing from a usually small and statistically non-representative sample. Also, as discussed, although our model is designed to have more general applicability, we have focused on music, which seems appropriate seeing as it is the birthplace of remix, but our findings regarding the size, significance, and direction of effects may vary for other media types and purposes. Finally, our model is based on cross-sectional data and as such is limited in its applicability as a causal model. In future work we would like to build a hierarchical (HLM) model to better account for the structure inherent in the data (works nested into authors) or a p^* model, as well as explore how to better incorporate time with lag/sequential models.

ACKNOWLEDGMENTS

We wish to thank Mike Linksvayer, Victor Stone, and ccMixter community members for their generous help with data collection and for the many insights they shared regarding the workings and history of the ccMixter community. We also thank the reviewers for the many valuable suggestions.

REFERENCES

1. Anderson, C. *The long tail: Why the future of business is selling less of more.* Hyperion, London, UK, 2006.
2. Barabási, A.-L. An introduction and keynote to a networked self. In Z. Papacharissi (ed.) *A networked self: identity, community and culture on social network sites*, (2011), 1-14.
3. Bauwens, M. The Political Economy of Peer Production. *CTheory e-Publication* (2005).
4. Benkler, Y. Coase's Penguin, or, Linux and the Nature of the Firm. *Yale Law Journal*, *112*, 3 (2002), 367-445.
5. Benkler, Y. Peer Production and Sharing. In *The Wealth of Networks*, (2006), 59-90.
6. Benkler, Y. *The Wealth of Networks: How Social Production Transforms Markets and Freedom.* Yale University Press, New Haven, 2006.
7. Berger, J., Sorensen, A. T. and Rasmussen, S. J. Positive Effects of Negative Publicity: When Negative Reviews Increase Sales. *Marketing Science*, *29*, 5 (September/October 2010), 815-827.
8. Bonner, S., Walther, B. and Young, S. Sophistication-related differences in investors' models of the relative accuracy of analysts' forecast revisions. *The Accounting Review*, *78* (2003), 679-706.
9. Bonner , S. E., Hugon, J. A. and Walther, B. R. Investor reaction to celebrity analysts: The case of earnings forecast revisions. *Journal of Accounting Research*, *45*, 3 (2007), 481-513.
10. Bouas, K. and Arrow, H. The development of group identity in computer and face-to-face groups with membership change. *Computer Supported Cooperative Work (CSCW)*, *4*, 2 (1995), 153-178.
11. Broder, A., Kumar, R., Maghoul, F., Raghavan, P., Rajagopalan, S., Stata, R., Tomkins, A. and Wiener, J. Graph Structure In The Web. *Computer Networks*, *33*, 1-6 (2000), 309-320.
12. Capocci, A., Servedio, V., Colaiori, F., Buriol, L., Donato, D., Leonardi, S. and Caldarelli, G. Preferential attachment in the growth of social networks: The internet encyclopedia Wikipedia. *Physical Review E*, *74*, 3 (Sep 1 2006), 6.
13. Cheliotis, G. From open source to open content: Organization, licensing and decision processes in open cultural production. *Decision Support Systems*, *47*, 3 (2009), 229-244.
14. Cheliotis, G. and Yew, J. An analysis of the social structure of remix culture. In *Proc. Fourth international conference on Communities and Technologies (C&T 2009)*, ACM (2009), 165-174.
15. Chen, P. Y., Wu, S. Y. and Yoon, J. The impact of online recommendations and consumer feedback on sales. In *Proc. of the International Conference on Information Systems* (2004), 711-724.
16. Chevalier, J. and Goolsbee, A. Measuring prices and price competition online: Amazon and Barnes and Noble. *Quantitative Marketing and Economics*, *1*, 2 (2003), 203-222.
17. Clemons, E. K., Gao, G. and Hitt, L. M. When online reviews meet hyperdifferentiation: A study of craft beer industry. *Journal of Management Information Systems*, *23*, 2 (2006), 149-171.
18. Culler, J. Presupposition and Intertextuality. *MLN*, *91*, 6 (1976), 1380-1396.
19. Derrida, J. *Of Grammatology*. Johns Hopkins University Press, Baltimore, MD, 1997.
20. Duan, W., Gu, B. and Whinston, A. B. Do online reviews matter? — An empirical investigation of panel data. *Decision Support Systems*, *45*, 4 (2008), 1007-1016.
21. Grossman, L. Time's Person of the Year: You. *Time Magazine* (2006). http://www.time.com/time/magazine/article/0,9171,1569514,00.html.

22. Gunderson, P. A. Danger Mouse's Grey Album, Mash-Ups, and the Age of Composition. *Postmodern Culture*, *15*, 1 (2004).
23. Hill, B. M. and Monroy-Hernández, A. The Remixing Dilemma: The Trade-Off Between Generativity and Originality. *American Behavioral Scientist* (December 21, 2012).
24. Hutcheon, L. *A Theory of Adaptation*. Routledge, New York, 2006.
25. Johnson, B. K. Incentives to Contribute in Online Collaboration: Wikipedia as Collective Action. In *Proc. International Communication Association* (2008).
26. Keen, A. *The Cult of the Amateur: How Today's Internet is Killing Our Culture*. Doubleday, New York, NY, 2007.
27. Kim, M. *An Analysis of the Creative Commons as a Solution for Copyright Protection in the Digital Era*. University of North Carolina at Chapel Hill, Chapel Hill, NC, 2005.
28. Kittur, A., Chi, E. H., Pendleton, B. A., Suh, B. and Mytkowicz, T. Power of the few vs. wisdom of the crowd: Wikipedia and the rise of the bourgeoisie. In *Proc. Alt.CHI at CHI 2007* (2007).
29. Lessig, L. *Free Culture: The Nature and Future of Creativity*. The Penguin Press, New York, NY, 2004.
30. Lessig, L. Free(ing) Culture for Remix. *Utah Law Review*, *961* (2004), 961-975.
31. Lessig, L. *Remix: Making Art and Commerce Thrive in the Hybrid Economy*. Penguin Press HC, New York, NY, 2008.
32. Linville, P. W., Fischer, G. W. and Salovey, P. Perceived Distributions of the Characteristics of In-Group and Out-Group Members: Empirical Evidence and a Computer Simulation. *Journal of Personality and Social Psychology*, *57*, 2 (1989), 165-188.
33. Liu, Y. Word of mouth for movies: Its dynamics and impact on box office revenue. *Journal of Marketing Research*, *70*, 3 (2006), 74-89.
34. Manovich, L. *Remixing and Remixability*, 2005. http://manovich.net/DOCS/Remix_modular.doc.
35. Marwell, G. and Oliver, P. *The critical mass in collective action: a micro-social theory*. Cambridge University Press, New York, 1993.
36. Miller, P. D. *Rhythm science*. MIT Press, Cambridge MA, 2004.
37. Navas, E. *Remix Theory: The Aesthetics of Sampling*. SpringerWien, 2012.
38. Nov, O. What motivates Wikipedians? *Communications of the ACM*, *50*, 11 (2007).
39. Postmes, T., Spears, R. and Lea, M. Breaching or Building Social Boundaries? *Communication Research*, *25*, 6 (December 1, 1998), 689-715.
40. Postmes, T., Spears, R. and Lea, M. The formation of group norms in computer-mediated communication. *Human Communication Research*, *26*, 3 (2000), 341-371.
41. Roberts, J. A., Hann, I.-H. and Slaughter, S. A. Understanding the Motivations, Participation and Performance of Open Source Software Developers: A Longitudinal Study of the Apache Projects. *Management Science*, *52*, 7 (2006), 984-999.
42. Spears, R. and Lea, M. Panacea or Panopticon? *Communication Research*, *21*, 4 (August 1, 1994), 427-459.
43. Stone, V. ccMixter: A Memoir (2009). http://fourstones.net/ccmixter-a-memoir.
44. von Hippel, E. Horizontal innovation networks - by and for users. *Industrial and Corporate Change*, *16*, 2 (May 16 2007), 293-315.
45. von Hippel, E. and von Krogh, G. Open Source Software and the "Private-Collective" Innovation Model: Issues for Organization Science. *Organization Science*, *14*, 2 (Mar-Apr 2003), 209-223.
46. Wasko, M. M. and Faraj, S. Why Should I Share? Examining Social Capital and Knowledge Contribution in Electronic Networks of Practice. *MIS Quarterly*, *29*, 1 (2005), 35-57.
47. Zittrain, J. The Generative Pattern. In *The Future of the Internet - And How to Stop It* (2010).

Remixers' Understandings of Fair Use Online

Casey Fiesler, Amy Bruckman
GVU Center
Georgia Institute of Technology
85 5th St. NW, Atlanta, GA 30332 USA
casey.fiesler@gatech.edu, asb@cc.gatech.edu

ABSTRACT
How do online content creators make decisions about copyright law? In the course of day-to-day online activities, Internet users are forced to make subtle judgments about one of the most confusing and nuanced areas of law, copyright and fair use. In this study, we conducted semi-structured interviews with eleven content creators who participate in remix and fan creation activities online, to try to probe their legal understandings and attitudes. We found that social norms that emerge among these content creators do not always track to what the law actually says, but are often guided more by ethical concerns. Our participants showed surprisingly similar patterns of understandings and confusions, impacting technology use and interaction online.

Author Keywords
copyright; creativity; fair use; fandom; intellectual property; internet; law; remix; social norms; user-generated content

ACM Classification Keywords
K.4.1 **[Computers and Society]:** Public Policy Issues --- *Intellectual property rights*

INTRODUCTION
In online spaces, a number of aspects such as technical limitations or cultural norms influence what users can and cannot do. In understanding group dynamics, CSCW research often focuses on the entire socio-technical system. However, a part of this system infrequently examined is the role of law. One striking example of the law (or perceptions of the law) impacting online behavior is in the realm of copyright and content creation. From the massive popularity of peer-to-peer networks to the rise of remix culture and user-generated content sites like YouTube, the notion of what sorts of uses someone can make of copyrighted work is touching amateur content creators in a way that it simply didn't a decade ago. As a result, the answer to "Can I do this?" in an online creative space may have a legal rather than a technical answer.

CSCW'14, February 15–19, 2014, Baltimore, Maryland, USA.

ACM 978-1-4503-2540-0/14/02...$15.00.
http://dx.doi.org/10.1145/2531602.2531695

In the United States, *fair use* is the legal mechanism that allows for uses of copyrighted content under certain conditions. Without it, we would not be able to quote from books in book reviews, or parody film and music on comedy television shows like *Saturday Night Live*. However, since determinations of what constitutes fair use are made on a case-by-case basis, the concept is deliberately vague and notoriously ambiguous [2,13]. Content re-use has long been considered one of the most complex areas of copyright law. In 1841, Justice Story referred to the problem as the "metaphysics" of law (*Folsom v. Marsh*), and in 1992 the United States Supreme Court agreed that fair use remains the "most troublesome" aspect of all of copyright law (*Campbell v. Acuff Rose*). This is a problem that has only grown along with technology, and if lawmakers, judges, and legal scholars can have reasonable debates about what may or may not be a fair use, then it is not surprising that ordinary Internet users have trouble drawing these lines as well. Yet, "Can I do this?" is a question that many online content creators have to ask themselves in the context of using pieces of copyrighted works.

Traditionally, copyright was not an area of the law that held much relevance for the majority of people. However, the amount of agency that people have with technology has changed drastically, and so has the way that consumers interact with copyrighted material. We have seen a significant cultural shift toward using previously existing content in new ways [24]. Consumers are not only producers but remixers—that is, not just creating from scratch but also making use of existing content—thanks to the digitization of nearly all media which makes manipulating it possible for anyone with common computer software, and to the wide dissemination of amateur content made possible by the Internet. However, just because the law is more relevant to more people does not mean it is more easily understandable. Technological advances have only exacerbated the same confusions that have always existed in applications of copyright law.

Understanding and knowledge of applicable legal doctrines can change in this environment as well. In situations in which the law is unclear or largely unenforced, it is not uncommon for community constructions to become social norms that can carry more weight than written law [10].

Though the term "remix" originally applied to music, the concept has become much broader in recent years. As

Lawrence Lessig describes in his book on the subject, remix is an act of read-write creativity—not just consuming content but using it to make something new [24]. By "remixer" we mean anyone who makes use of content created by someone else in new, creative ways. We wanted to better understand how remixers might think about copyright law and its relationship to their online creative activities. In the absence of bright line legal rules, how do they make decisions about what they can or can't do when it comes to creative appropriation?

Though we wanted to study "remixers," we did not want to focus on a specific online site or media type. Our subjects responded to an ad asking for "online content creators," and specifically those who create "remixes" and "fanworks" in a variety of media (see Methods section below). Because all of our participants self-identified as being creators of fanworks, we consider this our population, a subset of remix.

Therefore, we conducted interviews with online content creators who specialize in fanworks—art, writing, music, video, or other media based on media properties such as television shows, books, or videogames. The "fandom" community forms a set of subcultures focused on shared significant interests in these media. These practices date back to the days of Sherlock Holmes and Jane Austen, but have flourished since the 1970s when fans congregated around science fiction television shows such as *Star Trek* [8]. The first author has experience as a fan writer.

Like the issue of fair use itself, copyright complications with fanworks do not begin and end with the Internet. Fan creators have been remixing works since long before digital technology was prevalent [8,20]. However, as in many other contexts, changing technology has exacerbated already-existing tensions [11,33]. Fan creators provide us with an example of social norms that derive from the creative community itself rather than being dependent on a specific online site or technology. The current study therefore does not focus on a specific online site but rather on the shared activity of creating fanworks.

RELATED WORK

Research in the field of creativity and technology emphasizes that creativity does not exist in a vacuum, and indeed, it is inevitably influenced by context, including the connection between artist and broader cultural and technological factors [6]. We see these common themes appearing again and again in studies of amateur content creators—such as the importance of attribution, and tension over commercialization. This is true both for creators of original content, such as digital musicians [6,30] or knitters [18], and for remixers, such as fan fiction authors [11,16] or video mash-up artists [9]. Sometimes the online spaces they frequent might have technical support for these kinds of norms, though very often not [29], which suggests that online community designers may not always be aware of them.

One example is the Scratch online community, made up of young people sharing user-generated content they create through programming, in which norms about reuse and attribution have evolved within their remix practices [27]. Researchers found that whereas there are both positive and negative reactions to work being remixed within the community, the idea of attribution and credit was of near-universal importance. Even with (presumably) little knowledge of copyright law, norms emerged in the community about when remixing was okay based on whether appropriate credit was given to the creator. Remixing in this context will only become more important—Lange and Ito note that many of the activities in which youth are developing creative identities and competencies involve appropriation, such as music remixing and anime video creation [22]. Hill and Monroy-Hernandez have also discussed ways to promote remixing and originality among their young Scratch users, [17] a goal that has been posited by other researchers as well [5,20,22].

In the interest of advocating remix within the combative copyright environment, Aufderheide and Jaszi studied different communities of creators to reveal practices and attitudes about using copyrighted material, and then published a book as a guide to fair use for online content creators [2]. In one of their studies, of college students who upload online video, nearly half of the participants said that they never incorporated copyrighted material in their work [1]. Some were simply confused about what is copyrighted, but for others, they purposefully did not incorporate material for fear of getting into trouble—possibly a chilling effect of the law. Though traditionally referring to when free expression is "chilled," this effect comes into play when any conduct is suppressed for fear of penalty.

Another major finding of Aufderheide's study was that participants did not understand even elementary facts about copyright; with respect to fair use, three fourths of participants believed that it permitted them use of copyrighted materials but none were able to describe the doctrine accurately. Other studies have revealed similar misunderstandings of copyright law, such as among documentary filmmakers [23] and librarians [14]. Legal scholarship on the subject of social norms and content production has suggested that people may have intricate intuitions about the law without actual knowledge to back it up—and that this phenomenon is particularly pronounced in communities of online content creation such as fan creators [11,16,33].

Fan culture is particularly interesting with respect to issues of copyright and appropriation. The community of fan creators does not fit within the bounds of a particular online site. Instead migrating to some degree with changing technologies [8], the group has established highly ingrained social norms that are not tied to a particular technology [11]. Researchers have examined how fandom communities make use of different technologies, such as Livejournal [31] or Twitter [26], as well as the norms that form. Communities of fan creators are notoriously tight-knit [20], and Ito notes from her interviews with members of the anime music video community that standards for behavior and creativity derive from this closeness [22]. They have specialized practices that rely on deep knowledge of the subject matter and the community, an environment that makes it easy for norms to proliferate. Fans have also been struggling with legal issues for decades, much longer than most remix communities, but chilling effects have become more common in recent years [7].

METHODS

In the current study, we interviewed eleven online content creators—two in-person interviews for local participants, and nine conducted by phone. Our criteria for inclusion was that each participant dealt with issues of appropriation in their creative work, and identified fanworks as a major part of their online creative activities. Participants were recruited through postings in online remix communities. We also attempted to use fliers on a college campus, but were unsuccessful in gaining any participants this way. Though we posted to websites that catered to fiction and music as well, the participants that contacted us came from communities that focused on art (DeviantArt) and video (a Livejournal fan video community), though also participated in a wider range of activities (see Table 1) and a large number of different online content creation websites.

Recruitment materials sought "online content creators," specifying a particular interest in those who created remix works or fanworks. Because we asked our participants to recommend others who might be interested in participating, word of mouth was also a recruitment tool; therefore, we had in part a "snowball sample" of participants [3]. Five of our participants came to us directly from seeing our recruitment materials, and six heard about the study from other participants. Though this technique does produce a more homogeneous sample, it also has the benefit of allowing the interviewer to explore shared meanings among the community being studied [30]. Additionally, though our sample size is only eleven participants, research has shown that data saturation can occur quickly in thematic analysis of qualitative interview data, and that most codes/themes can be present in as few as six interviews [15].

Participants were 10 women and 1 man, ranging in age from 19 to 36. This gender breakdown is not unusual for the community of fan creators, which is traditionally predominantly female [7,19]; though the Internet has shifted demographics of fan communities, this is largely with respect to age (younger) and nationality (more global) while maintaining the gender gap [21]. All participants lived in the U.S. and participated in primarily U.S.-based online communities. As detailed in Table 1, our participants covered a range of different media types in their remixing activities, including fan art, fan video, and fan fiction and roleplaying (both types of writing), as well as music and graphics remix. We also captured non-remix content creation that might be relevant to the discussion (blogging, and original art and fiction); for example, some of the participants with blogs brought up copyright issues with respect to using images in their blog posts.

Interviews were semi-structured, and included questions about online activities, including types of content creation and sharing, as well as online communities participated in; scenarios related to copyright and content creation, asking for their judgments about how the law applied and how they thought it should apply; and knowledge about U.S. copyright law. The purpose of these questions was to tease out their attitudes about different aspects of the law, how they felt it applied to their work, and the ways in which different technologies as well as their knowledge of the law affect their online creative activities. The semi-structured interview protocol gave us the flexibility to dynamically adjust questioning based on the participants' responses. The idea behind this technique is to consider not just a behavior itself as stated, but the meaning behind it [28].

After transcribing the interviews, we conducted a thematic analysis of the data. This method of identifying, analyzing, and reporting emergent patterns (or themes) within a set of data is a type of open qualitative coding that maintains some theoretical freedom [4]. Our analysis relied in part on the first author's expertise in copyright as a law school graduate. Though a number of themes emerged from our interviews, one concept that came up consistently was that of fair use. After having coded all of the data, we considered just the data that had been coded for fair use concepts, and examined it more closely.

RESULTS

After coding our data, we focused our analysis on one emergent theme: fair use. Of our eleven participants, nine were familiar with the fair use doctrine by name even if they could not articulate it correctly, and the remaining two still had intuitions about an exception to copyright law—for example, one participant stated when asked about one activity, "No, I think it's okay, but I think you have to follow certain rules."

Judging from previous research, including studies of documentary filmmakers and remix video creators, we expected to see misunderstandings of the law; however, a more surprising finding was just how similar the misconceptions were among our participants. Even across different types of creators—writers, visual artists, filmmakers—intuitions about what makes a use "fair" were by and large the same. What follows is a discussion of these common understandings (and misunderstandings) of fair use, as well as patterns of heuristics and judgments used in thinking about the law. In order to emphasize the relationship between these understandings and the actual law, we organize our findings based on the four fair use factors. Though a judge determines whether something is fair use on a case-by-case basis, the Copyright Act of 1976

	Fan Fiction	Fan Art	Fan Video	Fan Roleplaying	Music Remix	Graphics Remix	Original Fiction	Original Art	Blogging
1	■			■					■
2		■				■		■	
3	■			■					■
4				■	■		■		■
5			■		■	■			■
6			■						■
7	■			■					■
8	■								■
9	■		■			■			■
10		■				■			■
11	■	■						■	■

Table 1: Types of Content Creation by Participant

codified these four factors that must be weighed in making this determination:

> 1. the purpose and character of the use, including whether such use is of a commercial nature or is for nonprofit educational purposes;
>
> 2. the nature of the copyrighted work;
>
> 3. the amount and substantiality of the portion used in relation to the copyrighted work as a whole; and
>
> 4. the effect of the use upon the potential market for or value of the copyrighted work (17 U.S.C. § 107).

The Purpose and Character of the Use

1. the purpose and character of the use, including whether such use is of a commercial nature or is for nonprofit educational purposes (17 U.S.C. § 107)

Noncommercial Use

Whether a use is commercial or noncommercial is only one part of the first factor weighed in fair use determinations. Generally, noncommercial use weighs more toward a finding of fair use. This factor is usually a point in favor of remixers who typically do not profit from their work. However, the definition of "noncommercial" is not clearly defined in case law [33].

Most participants (eight out of eleven) implied that this was the single most important factor in determining whether a use is fair. This backs up previous legal scholarship that has pointed out the deeply ingrained norm of noncommercial use within fan communities [11,16].

Some participants (P4, P5, P7, P8) also expressed frustration that, like the doctrine itself, a judgment of commerciality is in a gray area. When pushed to define the boundaries of noncommercial use, they disagreed over where this line should be. Some thought that having ads on a website that displays remixed work was a deal breaker, whereas others stated that the remixer has to be explicitly selling something.

On my website, it has Amazon ads that help pay for the bandwidth or whatever for it. But I don't know that I would consider that as a profit-making enterprise that would be a big deal since I think I've made like 13 dollars in two years, which isn't enough to cover even the space. – P5

I don't think they should be making money from it. It's like a hobby, right? I mean, if you were making money, like if you were selling a DVD of your vids that had such and such song and clips from such and such show then the owners of that stuff should get some of the proceeds. If you profit from ads, same thing. – P8

In fact, many participants (five out of eleven) when discussing commercial use spoke in terms of "profiting." The issue was not whether any money exchanged hands at all, but whether the person making use of the copyrighted work was personally benefiting from the use. For example, charity auctions in fan communities are not uncommon. One participant (P11) spoke of the "Help Haiti" initiative on Livejournal (a blogging community) in which fan fiction writers and artists offered their services (to write or draw to specifications) to the highest bidder, with the proceeds going to the Red Cross. She noted that the noncommercial norm within the community doesn't seem to apply to this situation because the artists are not personally profiting from the original works.

Another community norm that several participants articulated but had difficulty explaining is the significance of media with respect to noncommercial norms—specifically, the fact that within fan communities there is more tolerance for selling fan art than fan fiction. With the exception of charity auctions, there have been documented instances of fan fiction writers being ostracized for attempting to sell their work [11,16]; however, the same does not seem to be true for art. One fan fiction writer (P9) expressed envy that artists can sell their work at conventions, noting that "you could never get away with that" as a writer. Another participant (P11) was an artist who regularly takes commissions to draw characters from books or movies such as *Harry Potter* or *Pirates of the Caribbean,* for as much as $50 a piece. She stated that she "sometimes feel[s] guilty" that she can make money from her art when writers can't.

Neither this artist, nor the others who brought up this inconsistency, could explain exactly why it exists. However, there seems to be a related norm of more tolerance for selling art from books over art from television shows, though some participants had a vague idea of publicity rights of actors factoring into this as well. Some (P4, P11) did note that for books, it is more difficult to "prove" that the image is of a particular character—is that Harry Potter or just a boy with glasses? This could explain both why the noncommerciality norm within fandom seems to be less enforced for art, and why legal scrutiny (cease-and-desist letters, etc.) have more often been seen with fiction than with art.

Despite the ambiguity regarding boundaries and differences in media, commercial use does play an important role within understandings of fair use: it is consistently judged as being more legally important than it likely is. Since the landmark case *Campbell v. Acuff-Rose*, courts have recognized that commercial uses can still be fair. However, it is also true that noncommercial uses are less frequently litigated, and since fair use is determined on a case-by-case basis, there is no bright line rule as to the weight of the factor [16]. Though our participants made statements like "I think that... would be okay, like legal, though because they're not making money" (P3), a more technically correct interpretation would be to pragmatically say that it (a noncommercial use of a copyrighted work) would be "okay" because it would be much less likely to be challenged in court.

In sum, the noncommercial part of the first prong of fair use is seen as an important factor. This in itself is not a misconception, but there is a misconception when it is seen as the sole deciding factor. However, perhaps more interestingly, this norm seems to be largely a moral judgment rather than a legal or market-based one. Judgments extend to the fairness of profiting from someone else's work. As one creator of fan videos (P5) stated, "It's just tacky. Completely aside from fair use issues of commercial/non-commercial, you just don't do it because fandom's a gift economy."

Educational Use

Like commerciality, the potential educational purpose is considered part of the first "nature of the use" fair use prong. If a use is for nonprofit educational purposes, it is more likely to be judged a fair use.

The misconception concerning this part of the test is a simple and consistent one. When specifically asked about an educational use of content, nearly all of the participants (nine out of eleven) thought that there was a blanket exception for educational use of copyrighted material. The recognition of the concept does show some understanding of copyright exceptions; however, educational use is simply one part of the entire fair use test rather than a different exception altogether as most participants thought.

Transformativeness

Transformativeness—part of the "purpose and character of the use" stated in the first prong of the fair use test—covers how much a new work is "transformed" from the original, extending to the purpose and function of the new work. Two significant examples of this from case law are the 2 Live Crew "Pretty Woman" rap as defended in *Campbell v. Acuff Rose* and Google's use of thumbnail images in their search engine in *Perfect 10 v. Google.*[1] The more transformative a use is, the more likely it is to be judged fair use. Though currently considered to be a very important aspect of fair use analysis [2], like fair use itself, the definition of what constitutes transformativeness has been ambiguous.

With the exception of often pulling out parody as an important copyright exception, participants by and large conflated transformativeness with the third fair use factor, amount and substantiality of the original work used—discussed more below.

The Nature of the Work

2. the nature of the copyrighted work (17 U.S.C. § 107)

The second fair use factor concerns the nature of the original copyrighted work—specifically whether it is fiction or nonfiction, or published or unpublished. If the original

[1] The Supreme Court stated in *Campbell v. Acuff-Rose* that what "lies at the heart of fair use doctrine" is whether the work "merely supersede[s] the objects of the original creation, or instead adds something new, with further purpose or different character, altering the first with new expression, meaning, or message"; the transformative use in that case was parody. In *Perfect 10 v. Amazon*, the Ninth Circuit Court of Appeals found that a search engine providing "social benefit" as an "electronic reference tool" could actually be *more* transformative than a parody because it provides an entirely new function for the work.

work is fiction or unpublished, this weighs slightly in favor of the new work being a fair use.

None of our participants had any concept of this factor, with the exception of the common misconception that some process is required to receive a copyright in something (such as registering). When pushed on this issue, several participants (P2, P6, P10) reconsidered or expressed confusion—for example, stating that their work isn't copyrighted unless they have applied for it like a patent, but then also saying that their work posted online cannot be used without permission.

However, note that for our participants, this factor would be largely irrelevant. Fictional works are much more often the subject of fanworks than non-fiction. Non-publication is even more rare, since putting something on the Internet would constitute publication.

Amount and Substantiality

3. the amount and substantiality of the portion used in relation to the copyrighted work as a whole 17 U.S.C. § 107).

The third factor of the test—amount and substantiality used—relates to how much of the original work is in the new work. The less of the original used, the more likely the new work is a fair use. Again, participants by and large conflated transformativeness with this factor. One might consider the underlying difference between the two to be quantitative versus qualitative—amount and substantiality is a largely objective measure of how much of the original remains, where as transformativeness looks more to the *spirit* of the original in purpose or character.

The general heuristic we saw from participants was that the more different from the original the new work is, the better—whether with respect to purpose or more tangible changes. One participant articulated this idea with respect to graphics, and the amount of transformation that can occur in creating user icons for blogs:

There really is an art to making a good icon, to choosing the right shot, to cropping it right, to tweaking the color in whatever way it has to happen, and obviously not everyone does that; there are icons that are less transformative just like there are vids that are less transformative. – P5

As with the gray area in determining whether a use is commercial, the majority of participants (seven out of eleven) were able to articulate vaguely that a remixed work needs to be different than the original in order to qualify for fair use. However, they differed on where this line should be (and many were not able to even guess where it might be). Of the fair use factors, this was the one for which participants had the most legally accurate idea of the balance that courts must find. Even without an idea of clear boundaries, they had consistent intuitions about the third fair use factor, particularly by virtue of believing that remixes are far more likely to be fair use than wholesale copying.

Market Harm

4. the effect of the use upon the potential market for or value of the copyrighted work (17 U.S.C. § 107)

The final fair use factor concerns the effect of the use upon the potential market for the original work. If a new work is interfering with a potential source of revenue for the original copyright owner, then it is less likely to be considered a fair use.

A number of themes involving market harm emerged from our interviews, reflecting in large part a utilitarian stance from our participants. For example, though they conceded that this concept likely does not have legal weight, some participants (P1, P3, P5, P7) expressed that some people should be more entitled to copyright protection than others—i.e., the "little guy." They were less likely to obtain illegally and more likely to correctly attribute a source when that source is a smaller artist as opposed to a large corporation. When pressed, they admitted that this was a moral judgment rather than a legal one.

Another theme that emerged is that of the potential for remix to do a market *good* rather than harm. The basic idea is that if a work is included in a remix (such as a song, or clips from a television show), then that work reaches a larger audience, thus increasing exposure rather than discouraging sales. One participant put it thus:

What's better advertisement for a TV show than a [fan video]? Oh and I can't tell you the number of times I've bought a song because I heard it on a vid. I'm pretty sure that Regina Spektor owes a ton of sales to Lim [a popular creator of fan videos]. I mean not only are the fans not making money from this but they're putting money in the pockets of the owners. At least I think so. I don't think the law should mess with creative works that aren't hurting anybody. – P7

Piracy

Though for the most part we limited the discussion to remix and appropriation, when discussing issues of market harm, participants often went off on tangents related to piracy and illegal downloading, with the related heuristic being "it's okay if it doesn't hurt anyone." The main idea that came up was the "fairness" of being able to copy when the material is unavailable through legitimate means.

I don't download music from the Internet, I use iTunes or I'll get it from Amazon. Unless I can't. I am so annoyed that neither iTunes or Amazon has [recording artist] ACDC. There's no mp3s, you can't buy it. And I want Thunderstuck and I want it now! – P4

With Doctor Who, I'm not going to wait a whole year to watch it just because I'm in the wrong country and with the Internet it's like a forced pop culture divide. My

[Livejournal] friends list doesn't care who's in the UK and who's in the US and if I read it the day after [UK television show] Doctor Who airs I'm going to get spoiled at worst or at least not be able to participate in the conversation. –P10

The participants that discussed this did, however, acknowledge that this was an ethical judgment and not a legal one. Additionally, those who do not pirate noted that they choose not to do so because of fear of viruses or legal ramifications rather than believing that it is wrong to do so in all cases (P5, P7, P10). Those who do pirate also do not always abide by their own ethical heuristics—the same participant who spoke of her unwillingness to download music unless absolutely necessary (P4) has no qualms about pirating software "if it's too expensive." In fact, all participants who mentioned software seem to have fewer reservations about pirating it than other types of media, suggesting further utilitarian calculations relating to cost.

Attribution

Another issue that came up repeatedly with respect to the idea of "good" and "harm" is that of attribution. Attribution is the idea that if a work is used, its source should be properly credited. Though courts might consider this as part of an overarching sense of good faith, and it factors into moral rights in some cases, attribution is generally irrelevant to the fair use test.

However, the idea of "credit where credit is due" is an important norm within communities of fan creators in particular. Fandom has even been described as an "attribution economy" [32]. This idea extends beyond reuse and into sharing and copying as well. To a large degree, this is a "good faith" norm. Some participants said that though they don't necessarily credit every image they use in a blog post, for example, they would remove something without question if they were asked to do so.

We also saw some degree of *implicit* attribution at work in our participants' values and judgments about copyright law—the idea that attribution isn't necessary when the content source is obvious.

If you're writing a post about Sherlock Holmes, like a movie review, then yeah, put up a picture of the movie poster. No need to say where it's from, it's obvious. But if you have some picture you got from Flickr then you should give the photographer credit. – P8

Another participant (P3) noted that for some types of content (such as music by indie recording artists), she will include links to purchase CDs or ask people to buy them, but that this isn't necessary for well-known works—that everyone knows she "didn't make up" Harry Potter, as well as where to buy the product if they want to do so.

Along with how well-known the source is, with respect to value judgments (as opposed to a consideration for what the law actually says), the importance of attribution seems to be related to how public the forum is—i.e., the bigger an audience the remixer has, the more important it is to correctly attribute sources. Again, to some of our participants this was a show of good faith, and is true of fan works also. Though most of the participants (seven out of eleven) cited a preference for disclaimers ("I don't own this"), they also thought that though they were not necessary, they were polite. In fact, disclaimers typically carry no legal weight when it comes to copyright infringement [33].

Though attribution is not a factor in fair use determinations, except perhaps relating to good faith, our participants consistently brought up the issue with respect to fair use or broader judgments of what is fair. This "hidden factor" represents a common misconception that correct attribution carries more legal weight than it actually does. However, it also represents a clear norm among original content creators to be properly credited; in early studies of the use of Creative Commons licenses, it was found that 97-98% of users were selecting attribution as a characteristic for their licenses, to the point where the organization made it a requirement of *all* licenses [25].

DISCUSSION

Of the themes that emerged from the analysis of our interview data, the commonality of ideas related to fair use among our participants was the most striking. The common thread among our participants is that they all create and share fanworks online. Many of the heuristics described therefore likely stem from the social norms of that larger community. What is also interesting, however, is that our participants also represent a number of different media types: fiction, art, video, graphics, and music. Though their understandings of fair use were similar across these different types of creators, we also saw that treatment of different media types are not always the same when it comes to accepted norms—for example, the different standards for noncommerciality for art.

More generally, we saw these common legal misconceptions about fair use:

1. Perception of noncommerciality as a sole deciding factor of fair use

2. Blanket exception for educational use

3. Addition of attribution as an explicit fair use factor

In addition, though participants recognized that these did not translate to legal doctrine, we saw these ethical judgments related to fair use, sometimes tracking to norms within the fan community:

1. Distinction between "profiting" from someone else's work and commerciality

2. More consideration for the "little guy" with respect to market harm

3. Potential for "market good"

4. Implicit attribution

Moreover, participants' reported behavior did not always track to either legal understandings or ethical judgments, such as the decision to pirate software; or in some cases, reported behavior represented a failure to consider the implications at all.

With respect to fair use, or even more granular down to individual factors, we see that the following five dimensions of copyright decisions can be completely different: (1) what the law says; (2) what people think the law says; (3) what is ethical; (4) what people think is ethical; and (5) what people actually do. The following table illustrates one example of this from our results:

Dimension	Participant Scenario
What the law says	One part of a fair use judgment is whether a new use is noncommercial.
What they think the law says	It is always illegal to make money from fan fiction.
What they think is ethical	It is not right to profit from someone else's work.
Community norm	Fan fiction writers are heavily sanctioned by the community for selling their work.
What they actually do	There are fan fiction auctions where the proceeds go to charity are common.

Table 2: Five Dimensions of Copyright Decision-Making

Additionally, though we did not discuss with participants at length specific online community policies, it is sometimes the case that those policies may not track exactly to the law or to ethical judgments. Some participants did express that they have more comfort in distributing their work via some online communities than others. YouTube in particular seems to have a poor reputation when it comes to protecting creators' rights; several of our participants (P4, P5, P9) reported not using the site due to the fear of being served DMCA takedown notices (though none had a clear understanding of the Digital Millennium Copyright Act). For example:

For vidding [creating fan videos], I [post to] my personal journal just because of the hassles of the copyright violations associated with vidding... because YouTube and sites like that have all those things where they can take down your video. Once YouTube took down one of my vids because of copyright violations. Just because I know that I'm not violating the law doesn't mean that they know that... I really wish I could share with more people. – P5

Interestingly, those participants who said that they know more about the law were more confident about their online activities; some of our participants did seem to be the victims of chilling effects of the law, particularly the DMCA, and those who were generally had the least knowledge.

However, we found generally that participants had more nuanced understandings of the law than we expected based on previous research—though they could not articulate fair use as written in law, they had some correct intuitions, and those that were not correct were often based on sound ethical judgments. Additionally, it was these ethical judgments that often inspired calls for change in the law. As one participant noted:

I wish they would just come out and say that fan fiction is legal and be done with it. It's not hurting anyone, and we shouldn't have to be scared of doing our art. –P1

CONCLUSION

The socio-technical system of the Internet is shaped by both the law as written and the law as understood by software designers and end users. The professionals who contribute to shaping this space are strangely disconnected in their knowledge and methods. Legal scholars rarely use an empirical approach to understanding human behavior. Designers of social computing systems rarely have legal training. Policy makers often know little about software design. Where does this leave users? In this study, we have taken an empirical approach to gain insight into how online content creators understand ethical and legal questions that impact their daily practice. One goal of this research was to begin to help bridge these professional gaps, and foster more dialog about the role of law within the field of CSCW.

Though some of the patterns of knowledge and intuition that we saw among our participants did track correctly to the law, there was a general sense of confusion over the current state of legal doctrine when it came to their online activities. For some, it is simply something that they do not think about; for others, this uncertainty has some chilling effect on the ways that they choose to share their creative works online.

There are more questions to ask in this space, for a more detailed picture. The patterns we saw from this small sample of fan creators suggest further threads of inquiry, particularly in terms of looking at different types of content creation communities. It is unclear how much of these findings might be generalizable to other types of content creation or other groups of creators. For example, might we see different norms or ethical intuitions in a community of creators that does not skew so heavily female, such as music remix? In our ongoing work, we are studying how intellectual property rules and norms differ across Internet sites, and are using both qualitative and quantitative methods to understand to what extent users understand those differences.

With respect to a legal doctrine that is infamously ambiguous, a better understanding of those who are forced to engage with fair use could benefit both policy makers and online community designers. Legal problems might be bad business for user-generated content sites, but so are chilling effects that might drive users away. One legal scholar has suggested that the risk inherent in the ambiguity of fair use has led to unnecessary licensing—better to pay for use of something than take the risk of being sued [13]. However, for amateur content creators who would not know how to go through traditional media licensing channels, this same risk aversion might simply chill creative expression instead.

YouTube's "copyright school," a video that copyright violators are required to watch, tells them how to file a counter-notice if they think their video was wrongfully flagged as a copyright violation. However, it also notes that taking action could be risky: "You could get in a lot of trouble. That's how the law works." A more positive example might be Wikipedia, which scaffolds fair use knowledge with their image upload wizard [12], asking uploaders for the appropriate information that would signal fair use of an image. This not only helps with the legal ambiguity, but it shifts some of the balance of power to the content creator since they are able to explain their decision-making pre-emptively to copyright holders.

As user-generated content continues to be a huge part of online communities, designers should be thoughtful about how their users deal with these ubiquitous and ambiguous copyright issues. Aufderheide and Jaszi argue in *Reclaiming Fair Use* that because judges often consult patterns of use in surrounding communities of practice when making fair use determinations, it would be in the best interest of communities to articulate their own understandings of fair use in order to strengthen these norms as well as the ability of judges to make reasonable decisions [2]. This is a strategy that has worked well within the documentary filmmaking community, for example. What the community typically believes and does can actually affect what is judged legal. However, what about creative communities that do not have the cohesion or motivation to craft codes of best practice?

Community designers are able to observe, and indeed help mold, patterns of use in an online community. In this role, designers can help develop an understanding of social norms and practices that could be used as a model for policymaking and legal interpretation. Ideally there should be a congruence between what people believe is legal, what is legal, and what fairly balances the interests of diverse stakeholders. More dialog about legal issues and evidence of user understandings of the law can help the CSCW community to create systems that help protect the rights of both copyright holders and content creators.

ACKNOWLEDGMENTS

We would like to thank our participants in this study, as well as reviewers who provided valuable feedback. This work is supported by NSF IIS-1216347.

REFERENCES

1. Aufderheide, P., Jaszi, P., and Brown, E.N. *The Good, The Bad, and The Confusing: User-Generated Video Creators on Copyright*. 2007.
2. Aufderheide, P. and Jaszi, P. *Reclaiming Fair Use: How to Put Balance Back Into Copyright*. University of Chicago Press, Chicago, IL, 2011.
3. Babbie, E.R. *The Basics of Social Research*. Wadsworth, Belmont, CA, 2009.
4. Braun, V. and Clarke, V. Using thematic analysis in psychology. *Qualitative Research in Psychology 3*, 2 (2006), 77–101.
5. Cheliotis, G. and Yew, J. An analysis of the social structure of remix culture. *Proceedings of the fourth international conference on Communities and technologies - C&T '09*, (2009).
6. Cook, E., Teasley, S.D., and Ackerman, M.S. Contribution, commercialization & audience: understanding participation in an online creative community. *Proceedings of the ACM 2009 International Conference on Supporting Group Work*, (2009), 41–50.
7. Coppa, F. and Tushnet, R. How to Suppress Women' s Remix. *Camera Obscura 26*, 2 (2011), 131–139.
8. Coppa, F. A Brief History of Media Fandom. In K. Hellekson and K. Busse, eds., *Fan Fiction and Fan Communities in the Age of the Internet*. McFarland Press, 2006, 41–59.
9. Diakopoulos, N., Luther, K., Medynskiy, Y. (Eugene), and Essa, I. The evolution of authorship in a remix society. *Proceedings of the 18th conference on Hypertext and hypermedia - HT '07*, (2007), 133.
10. Ellickson, R.C. Of Coase and Cattle: Dispute Resolution Among Neighbors in Shasta County. *Stanford Law Review 38*, (1986), 623–687.
11. Fiesler, C. Everything I Need To Know I Learned from Fandom: How Existing Social Norms Can Help Shape the Next Generation of User-Generated Content. *Vanderbilt Journal of Entertainment and Technology Law 10*, 3 (2008), 729–762.
12. Fiesler, C. The Chilling Tale of Copyright in Online Creative Communities. *XRDS: Crossroads, The ACM Magazine for Students 19*, 4 (2013).

13. Gibson, J. Risk Aversion and Rights Accretion in Intellectual Property Law. *The Yale Law Journal 116*, (2007), 882–951.

14. Graveline, J. Debunking Common Misconceptions and Myths. *College & Undergraduate Libraries 17*, 1 (2010), 100–105.

15. Guest, G., Bunce, A., and Johnson, L. How Many Interviews Are Enough?: An Experiment with Data Saturation and Variability. *Field Methods 18*, 1 (2006), 59–82.

16. Hetcher, S.A. Using Social Norms to Regulate Fan Fiction and Remix Culture. *University of Pennsylvania Law Review 157*, (2009), 1869–1935.

17. Hill, B.M. and Monroy-hernández, A. The Remixing Dilemma : The Trade-off Between Generativity and Originality. *American Behavioral Scientist 57*, 5 (2013), 643-663.

18. Humphreys, S. The Challenges of Intellectual Property for Users of Social Networking Sites : A Case Study of Ravelry. *Mind Trek*, (2008).

19. Jenkins, H. *Textual Poachers: Television Fans and Participatory Culture*. Routledge, 1992.

20. Jenkins, H. *Convergence Culture*. NYU Press, 2006.

21. Karpovich, A.I. The Audience as Editor: The Role of Beta Readers in Online Fan Fiction Communities. In K. Hellekson and K. Bussee, eds., *Fan Fiction and Fan Communities in the Age of the Internet*. McFarland & Company, North Carolina, 2006, 171–188.

22. Lange, P.G. and Ito, M. Creative Production. In M. Ito, ed., *Hanging Out, Messing Around, and Geeking Out: Kids Living and Learning with New Media*. MIT Press, Boston, MA, 2010.

23. Larsen, L.O. and Nærland, T.U. Documentary in a Culture of Clearance: A Study of Knowledge of and Attitudes Toward Copyright and Fair Use Among Norwegian Documentary Makers. *Popular Communication 8*, 1 (2010), 46–60.

24. Lessig, L. *Remix: Making Art and Commerce Thrive in the Hybrid Economy*. Penguin Group, New York, 2008.

25. Loren, L.P. Building a Reliable Semicommons of Creative Works: Enforcement of Creative Commons Licenses and Limited Abandonment of Copyright. *George Mason Law Review 14*, 1 (2007), 271–328.

26. Magee, R.M., Sebastian, M., Novak, A., Mascaro, C.M., Black, A., and Goggins, S.P. #TwitterPlay: A Case Study of Fan Roleplaying Online. *CSCW '13*, (2013), 199–202.

27. Monroy-hernández, A., Hill, B.M., Gonzalez-Rivero, J., and boyd, danah. Computers can't give credit: how automatic attribution falls short in an online remixing community. *CHI 2011*, (2011), 3421–3430.

28. Seidman, I. *Interviewing as Qualitative Research*. Teachers College Press, 1998.

29. Seneviratne, O. and Monroy-hernández, A. Remix Culture on the Web: A Survey of Content Reuse on Different User-Generated Content Websites. *Proceedings of Web Science Conference 2010*, (2010).

30. Sinnreich, A. *Mashed Up: Music, Technology, and the Rise of Configurable Culture*. University of Massachusetts Press, Amherst, MA, 2010.

31. Stein, L.E. "This Dratted Thing": Fannish Storytelling Through New Media. In K. Hellekson and K. Busse, eds., *Fan Fiction and Fan Communities in the Age of the Internet*. McFarland Press, 2006, 245–260.

32. Tushnet, R. Payment in Credit: Copyright Law and Subcultural Creativity. *Law & Contemporary Problems*, (2007).

33. Tushnet, R. User-Generated Discontent: Transformation in Practice. *Columbia Journal of Law and the Arts 10*, 2007 (2008), 101–120.

Unsupervised Classification and Visualization of Unstructured Text for the Support of Interdisciplinary Collaboration

Lisa J. Miller
ljmiller@hawaii.edu

Rich Gazan
gazan@hawaii.edu

Susanne Still
sstill@hawaii.edu

Department of Information and Computer Sciences
University of Hawaii at Mānoa
Honolulu, HI 96822-2327

ABSTRACT

We present a computer supported tool for cooperative work in interdisciplinary fields, which we tested within the area of astrobiology. Our document classification and visualization system is fully automated and data driven, based on unsupervised learning algorithms and network visualization tools. A new feature selection algorithm was created to aid this process that indicates which words should be used for mutual information-based clustering. Our system can extract information about collaborations from unstructured databases with no meta-data and reveals structure that can aid the planning of collaborative research. We analyzed publications produced by researchers from NASA's Astrobiology Institute. We presented this analysis as a cultural probe and recorded reactions from researchers that indicated that our method can help scientists from different disciplines to work together. We have made an interactive version of our visualization and analysis available as a website for long-term use.

Author Keywords

interdisciplinary science; document analysis; unsupervised learning; feature selection

ACM Classification Keywords

H.5.3 Group and Organization Interfaces:

General Terms

Algorithms; Measurement

INTRODUCTION

The field of Computer Supported Cooperative Work (CSCW) can contribute useful tools to interdisciplinary scientific collaborations. In practice, however, the use of CSCW as a bridge to more productive collaborations has been modest and situational. Challenges involved in making CSCW applicable to aiding interdisciplinary cooperation have been identified in the CSCW literature, which we discuss below.

CSCW'14, February 15–19, 2014, Baltimore, Maryland, USA.

ACM 978-1-4503-2540-0/14/02...$15.00.
http://dx.doi.org/10.1145/2531602.2531666

We present here a computer supported tool, designed for scientists funded by the NASA Astrobiology Institute (NAI), to facilitate cooperative work in this highly interdisciplinary field. We have analyzed a corpus of documents published under the current NAI funding period, looking for commonalities by means of automated cluster analysis. This allowed us to identify clusters of related documents, to extract topics that characterize these clusters, and to evaluate how these relate to the Science Objectives listed in the NAI planning guidelines [13].

The cluster analysis furthermore reveals a meta-structure, which we visualized using a force-directed graph. This visualization provides an opportunity for scientists to look at the large body of unstructured document data in a structured way, and thereby identify how their work fits into the entire body of work produced under NAI funding. One explicit goal of the funding agency is to "carry out, support and catalyze collaborative, interdisciplinary research". Our data analysis and visualization tool allows for a time efficient way of assessing where cooperation between teams and/or interdisciplinary research occurs within the funded work. Thus, it may be useful in helping to plan in which areas new collaborations could be pursued. Furthermore, the visualization aids both scientists and the funding agency in identifying potentially relevant areas that are not yet being actively addressed within the funded body of work.

CSCW and Interdisciplinarity

There is a long history of CSCW research in the domain of interdisciplinary science collaborations [27, 28, 31]. Distributed interdisciplinary collaborations have been studied from a CSCW perspective at several levels of analysis, including organizational forms [17], interfaces [42], and human infrastructure [33].

One study conducted retrospective interviews of principal investigators (PIs) and Co-PIs of distributed interdisciplinary teams [3]. Those teams explicitly stated dissemination and integration across fields as their goals. Integration was defined as "the extent to which a research team combines its distinct expertise and work into a unified whole" [3]. Integrated teams required both administrative support and internal commitment, and the authors call for CSCW tools that create opportunities for cross-team discussion and feedback [3].

Within an interdisciplinary collaboration, individual researchers will use tools that work for them, and are less likely to use groupware or similar common tools [12]. However, scientific research at the boundary between disciplines can result in the negotiation of new roles [24] and lead to the creation of boundary objects [46], artifacts across which diverse collaborators can communicate and negotiate shared meaning.

Cultural probes [19], defined as "designed objects, physical packets containing open-ended, provocative, and oblique tasks to support early participant engagement with the design process" [8], are artifacts designed to engage a group or community and elicit interactions. Introducing cultural probes can generate both boundary objects [25] and more lightweight, transient, boundary-negotiating objects [32], which in turn, can elicit cross-boundary communication [25].

The results of our analysis were presented to scientists as a cultural probe and they remain available to them as an interactive tool on our website. This work is part of the ongoing development of the Astrobiology Integrative Research Framework (AIRFrame) [1], a system [20, 35, 21, 23] funded by the NASA Astrobiology Institute (NAI) that uses document analysis techniques to allow astrobiology researchers from diverse fields to identify the subset of publications relevant to their work, but which may have appeared in journals specialized for a different audience, as well as relevant concepts and researchers from outside their discipline. The goal of AIRFrame is to foster understanding across areas, and thereby catalyze interdisciplinary collaboration.

Astrobiology and the NAI

The field of astrobiology is concerned with questions of life in the universe. Researchers in areas as diverse as astronomy, geology, biology, chemistry, and oceanography address questions about habitable environments, prebiotic chemistry, water in the universe, extremophiles, and the physical limits of life, to name a few examples. Understanding more about the evolution and distribution of life may also help to understand more about the future of life on Earth.

NASA is the main funding agency for astrobiology. The NASA Astrobiology Institute (NAI) is a virtual, distributed research organization consisting of 14 teams across the US and approximately 840 researchers, hospitable for CSCW. Researchers work both in their areas of expertise and on interdisciplinary research projects. NAI teams share science results internally and with other teams in weekly meetings; principal investigators at each site have monthly meetings to share results; and each team is responsible for producing an annual report of its publications, presentations, outreach, and other activities. Critically, both publications and annual reports are the primary means by which researchers and teams are evaluated.

The NAI requires researchers to articulate in what way their work is interdisciplinary. However, little or no support structure is in place for researchers to find potential interdisciplinary collaborations or to assess how their work fits into the body of research being conducted. The AIRFrame system addresses these issues. AIRFrame analysis results are shared with researchers in team meetings and seminars to elicit feedback as input to iterative development [18].

CSCW for the NAI

A crucial challenge in providing CSCW tools to scientists is that they naturally have a preference for more traditional means of communication. However, established methods of transmitting scientific information such as journal publications can be used to create tangible tools and assessment instruments [29, 34, 11]. Scientists can employ these tools to identify areas of potentially productive crossover in large distributed collaborations, and to provide evidence of their interdisciplinary impact.

We chose to analyze the articles produced by the NAI teams without causing disruption to ongoing research. Instead of using expert help to construct a structured database that fit into a given set of criteria, we use unsupervised machine learning algorithms to extract interpretable structure directly from document texts by means of cluster analysis. We visualize the results of the cluster analysis to further aid ease of interpretation. This automatization is useful as it saves valuable expert time. Not imposing pre-conceived criteria may also be useful, as that allows for the possibility of discovering, for example, which Science Objectives appear together in document clusters, revealing the extent to which the clusters correspond to stated NAI funding guidelines.

The collected documents are publications reported by the 14 NAI-funded research teams in three years of annual reports. Some of these were available to us as full text, for others we only had access to abstracts. NAI does not have a structured citation database, hence no bibliographic metadata was used in the automated analysis. We used unsupervised learning (cluster analysis) based on the distributions of words over documents, as estimated from the data. In the Methods Section, we detail data collection, discuss the challenges that have to be overcome to perform meaningful cluster analysis of document data, and discuss how we addressed them using existing algorithms. We saw fit to develop a new preprocessing method which provides an automated indication of how many words should be used in the analysis. This method has not been published elsewhere and is also described in the Methods Section.

Results of the cluster analysis are discussed in the Results Section, together with their visualization and the resulting meta-structure that was observed. These were presented to the University of Hawaii NAI team. Both the automated document analysis and the visualization of the results met with great success, and were deemed useful by the team. We have created a website to allow continued and more detailed access to these results. We report on the presentation of our work and reactions of our audience in the Presentation and User Reaction Section.

METHODS

Astrobiology Document Dataset

Often, only the abstract text is used in cluster analysis, but prior research with the Textpresso semantic search engine [36] suggests that abstracts of scientific journal articles are not enough to discover important connections among documents. Abstracts are rich with keywords, but they traditionally do not include more subtle evidence of linkage such as common research methods, equipment, and shared references.

We manually collected 1,346 publications, compiled from the 2009, 2010, and 2011 NAI annual reports. We attempted to retrieve the full text of all articles but if it was unavailable the article abstract was used. This resulted in a corpus of 724 long multi-page articles including references, 106 long abstracts or short articles with references, 484 short abstracts, and 32 very short database posting records or citations. Of these, 832 were in pdf format, the rest were retrieved as plain text. Pdf documents were converted to plain text using the Unix utility *pdftotext.*

The *NASA Astrobiology Roadmap* document [13] is the planning guide for the NAI research represented in the dataset. It outlines 18 high-priority Science Objectives ranging from strict astronomy topics (e.g., *Indirect and direct astronomical observations of extrasolar planets*) to interdisciplinary topics (e.g., *Biosignatures to be sought in Solar System materials*) to strongly biological themes (e.g., *Co-evolution of microbial communities*). This document was included in the document data set and was used to analyze and evaluate the output of cluster analysis (detailed in the Results Section).

Cluster Analysis

By grouping the documents into a number of different clusters we wish to extract useful structure from this diverse and unstructured collection for which manual analysis by an expert is too time consuming. We are particularly interested in the topics that emerge within clusters when as few assumptions as possible are made about the data.

Clustering can be viewed as a form of summarizing data in a meaningful way and a large number of different clustering methods have been developed, e.g., [5, 30, 22, 15]. There are a few serious challenges involved in cluster analysis [22]. Determining what level of detail should be used in the summary, or equivalently choosing the appropriate number of clusters, is considered the hardest problem in clustering [22]. Choosing an appropriate clustering criterion such that similar objects end up in one cluster is another fundamental issue, involving both selection of a measure of similarity and identification of relevant features in the data [22, 15].

Many popular text clustering methods are based on text modeling algorithms developed within the area of Information Retrieval for querying large databases [5, 10, 16, 7]. These methods, such as Latent Dirichlet Allocation (LDA) [7] and Latent Semantic Analysis (LSA) [16], use statistical modeling methods to reduce document representation from a vector of word counts to a more compact vector of model features. A simple similarity measure, such as the cosine distance or average linking, is then used to group the reduced vectors into clusters [5, 10, 16]. LSA identifies a linear subspace in a matrix of document-word vectors which captures variance between the documents [16, 7]. LDA is a probabilistic expansion of LSA where latent multinomial variables (referred to as topics in this literature) are modeled as discrete distributions over words, while documents are modeled as discrete distributions over "topics".

Statistical document models require assumptions be made about the structure of the data and what part of it is relevant for clustering. For example, with LDA one must use *ad hoc* methods to estimate the parameters which fix the shape of the assumed prior distributions of words over topics and topics over documents. Additionally, the number of topics must be estimated. Model-based, parametric clustering methods have the drawback that incorrect assumptions or poor selection of parameters can lead to poor performance or skew results toward finding certain types of clusters [52, 34, 22].

Alternatively, one can define a notion of relevance directly, using information theory [48]. This results in a framework, the Information Bottleneck (IB) method, within which a clustering algorithm and a notion of similarity can be derived mathematically [48], rather than needing *ad hoc* specification.

Applied to document clustering, the IB method can be interpreted as lossy compression of documents into clusters in such a way that the information about the words is maximally retained. Thus, the words are defined as the relevant variable, W. The mutual information between clusters, C, and documents, D, $I[C;D]$ is minimized, while the mutual information between clusters and words, $I[C;W]$, is maximized. The parameter β controls a trade-off between the amount of compression and keeping relevant information, that is, information about words.

$$\min_{p(c|d)} \left(I[C;D] - \beta I[C;W]\right) \tag{1}$$

Minimizing this equation yields the optimal cluster assignments, $p(c|d)$, the probability of cluster c given document d.

Even prior to the development of the Information Bottleneck framework, information theoretic methods were shown to be preferrable to parametric methods in data analysis for science studies [34]. For more than ten years, the IB framework and related methods, have been viewed as the state of the art for clustering highly multidimensional data, such as text [5]. It is difficult to compare outcomes of different clustering methods because of diverse definitions of relevance and similarity, and the relatively ambiguous meaning of correctness in grouping unlabeled data. However, tests using labeled benchmark document datasets have shown that IB-based methods produce as good or better clustering precision with regard to the labeling than parametric models such as LDA [6, 43]. Additionally, with the IB framework, perturbation theory allows one to work out the difficult problem of how many clusters can be used maximally without over-fitting the data [47].

Document Preprocessing

Before documents can be clustered, preprocessing must be done to extract valid text and format it for input into the clustering algorithm. Most commonly, each document is initially represented as a single *feature vector* whose dimensions or *features* are normalized word counts [5, 7, 15, 22]. Removing or combining words to reduce the dimensionality of the feature space while maintaining the most important elements is known as *feature selection*. Important elements are those features which define subsets in the data relevant to the intended goal of a particular clustering project [22, 15, 45].

In different clustering methods, feature selection may be an integral part of the clustering process or it can be just another step in the preprocessing before clustering occurs. With text modeling, such as LDA, most of the processing to differentiate between clusters is done within the feature selection step itself and it is considered part of the clustering process. With other methods, such as the IB, a complex clustering algorithm performs most of the work to fit the data into clusters and feature selection is part of preprocessing, used only to eliminate extraneous elements.

The System for the Mechanical Analysis and Retrieval of Text (SMART) project worked to evaluate and develop feature selection methods for more than 30 years [26]. We employ two of those methods which remain standard practice [41]: *stop word* removal which removes a list of extremely common function words; and *stemming* which removes the endings of words, transforming related words into identical word stems.

For all of the documents, a standard list of stop words were removed and all remaining words were stemmed using the Porter Stemming Algorithm [40]. We then applied our new feature selection method to determine which and how many of those words to keep for clustering.

New Feature Selection Method

A feature selection method particularly popular and methodologically consistent in IB-based clustering is to build a list of words, w, ranked by $I[w]$, their individual contribution to the mutual information between all words and documents in the data, $I[W;D]$, as in Equations 2 and 3 [44, 45, 14].

$$I[w] = \sum_{d \in D} p(w|d)p(d) \log_2 \left(\frac{p(w|d)}{p(w)} \right) \quad (2)$$

$$I[W;D] = \sum_{w \in W} I[w]. \quad (3)$$

Where $p(w|d)$ is the probability of word w given document d, $p(w)$ is the probability of w over the whole dataset, and $p(d) = \frac{1}{N_D}$ is the probability of a particular document, with N_D being the number of documents .

However, with this method, the number of words to keep is not indicated, a cutoff threshold must be decided upon. We developed a new method, introduced here, to address this issue.

Algorithm 1 Greedy Corrected $I[W;D]$ Word Ranker

for all words w in the data **do**
  Calculate and save $I[w]$, Equation 2.
end for
while all words not ranked **do**
  for all not yet ranked words, w **do**
    Calculate $C[w]$ from Equation 4.
    Calculate corrected information contribution: $I_{corr}[w] = I[w] - C[w]$.
    Keep track of the maximum $I_{corr}[w]$.
  end for
  Add word with largest $I_{corr}[w]$ to ranked list
  Add N_{Dw} for that word to N_{Dr}
  Add N_w of that word to N_r
  Add $I_{corr}[w]$ to I_{sum}
end while
return The ranked word list.

Based on ideas taken from [47, 49, 38, 37], our new method for choosing words attempts to correct the error made when estimating information from finite samples. The idea is to retain only those words that give an increase to the corrected mutual information between words and documents. Words that do not increase this value are seen as adding noise to the data due to finite sampling effects.

A greedy algorithm is used due to the combinatorial nature of the problem. Complete pseudo-code is given in Algorithm 1 and Equation 4, where N_{Wr} is the number of ranked words, N_{Dr} is the number of documents containing any ranked word (a document is only counted once, the first time any word it contains is ranked), N_r is the total number of occurrences of all ranked words in the data, N_w is the number of occurrences of a single word w in the data, and N_{Dw} is number of documents a word w occurs in not already counted in N_{Dr}.

$$C[w] = \frac{(N_{Dr} + N_{Dw} - 1) * N_{Wr}}{2 \log(2) (N_r + N_w)} \quad (4)$$

The correction term changes as each word is added to the ranked list. Therefore, it must be recomputed for each as-yet unranked word in each round of ranking. In each round, the word with the largest corrected contribution, $I_{corr}[w]$, is added to the ranked list. After all are ranked, all words that increase I_{sum}, the cumulative $I_{corr}[w]$, are retained for clustering.

For this dataset, the cumulative per-word contributions of the top-ranking 10,000 words out of a total of 48,421 are shown in Figure 1. Our method indicated 1,943 words to be kept as can be seen by the red square at the maximum of the inset in the figure. Those words were then used for all clustering procedures.

Visualization of Cluster Analysis Results

The use of node-link plots in association with text clustering to visualize structure in scientific research has a long history [50, 9, 34, 11]. Commonly, metadata or modeled text are

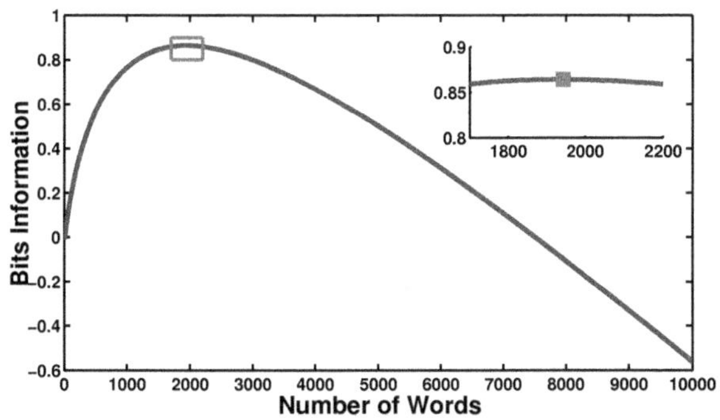

Figure 1. Cumulative corrected per-word contribution to mutual information between documents and words. 10,000 highest contributing words. Words ranked by largest to smallest contribution. Inset shows the section within the red box of the larger plot, highlighting the point at 1,943 words after which contributions become negative. All words giving a positive contribution were kept for clustering.

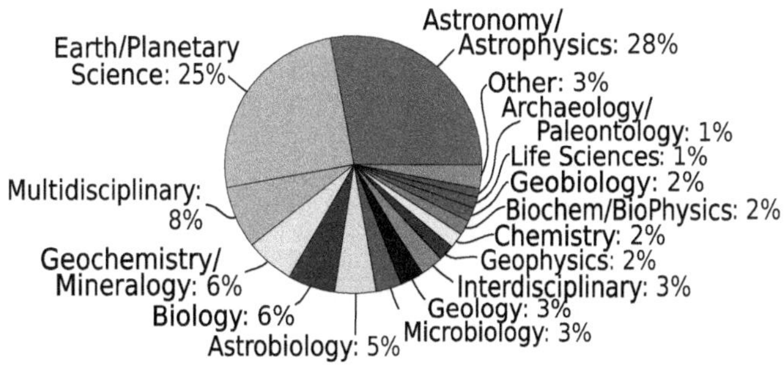

Figure 2. Breakdown of astrobiology document dataset by discipline. The multidisciplinary category includes articles in journals such as *Science, Nature* and *PNAS*. The interdisciplinary category contains articles in journals which specifically state that they publish interdisciplinary studies, such as *The Journal of Cosmology.*

represented on a network graph framework, graph clustering algorithms are used to simplify and group the representation, and layout algorithms are employed to spatially manipulate the graph for easier visual comprehension [51, 50, 9, 34].

In our method, we use the IB to cluster mixed-length documents into several different numbers of clusters. Then, we use the Gephi graph visualization program [4] to visualize the combined multiple clustering results on one force-directed node-link plot. The graph layout was done using Gephi's Force Atlas algorithm and Gephi's partition functionality was used to color the document nodes. All other data analysis and processing was done outside of Gephi.

An exponentially large number of edges would have resulted if we had represented each cluster as a fully connected subplot, where all document nodes in a cluster are connected to each other by an edge, as is common. Inspired by network topology for large-scale networks, we reduced the number of edges by representing the clusters as star networks with each document represented by a small node connected to a central cluster node, often referred to as a hub [39]. Each cluster node is sized by the number of documents assigned to that cluster, and each document node has an edge connecting it to the cluster it was assigned to. This is visualized simultaneously for several clustering results with different numbers of clusters.

Our method of reducing edges is related to graph reduction techniques such as node and edge aggregation into metanodes or aggregating edges into a single meta-edge [51, 2], but different in that we aggregate edges into the hub. The original document nodes are retained and are connected to each other through the hub. This allows us to preserve both the overall structure of the entire dataset and the ability to visualize properties of individual document nodes, such as coloring by discipline.

RESULTS OF CLUSTER ANALYSIS

For a given number of clusters, k, the IB clustering algorithm returns a representation of each cluster, which is a list of words sorted by their probability of occurring in that cluster. The algorithm also returns a list of assignments of documents to each cluster.

We looked at the 50 most probable words in each cluster and inspected the documents assigned to each. The documents are listed by projects in the annual reports to the NAI, those projects include a subset of Science Objectives from the Astrobiology Roadmap. From this, we obtained both projects and related Science Objectives for each document. We identified the most prominent Science Objectives in each cluster. This evaluation allowed us to identify topics that appeared in each cluster.

We hand-labeled the documents with 22 disciplines listed on their publishers' websites, the distribution of these is shown in Figure 2. Over half of the documents appeared in Astronomy/Astrophysics (AAP) or Earth and Planetary Sciences (EPS) journals and conferences. Approximately 8% were published in multidisciplinary journals such as *Science* and *Nature*, while the rest come from 19 disciplines that each make up 6% or less of the total. The "Other" category in contains the least represented disciplines: Marine Science, Chemical Physics, Aerospace/Astronautics, Physics, Meteorology/Climate, and Information Science. Discipline labels were used only in our evaluation and visualization, not as input to the clustering algorithm.

We examined the best cluster analysis results and chose to evaluate $k = 8$, 12, and 16 clusters in detail to show a progression in relationships amongst the documents at different levels of compression. Less than 8 clusters compressed the data too much. Clusters were very large and detailed topics were not present. More than 16 clusters resulted in very small clusters with few documents in them. These were no longer a useful summary of the data. Within the chosen range of 8, 12, and 16 clusters, the differences between clustering results were enough to discern obvious changes in the cluster memberships without adding too much complexity for evaluation.

In our results, most clusters are a mix of long full-text documents and shorter abstracts all related to the same topic.

However, some small clusters containing only abstracts were made. These indicate a limitation of clustering short documents. Despite having similiar topics, the sparsity of words in some shorter abstracts make their representations very different from longer documents with much richer word content, so much so, that they can be forced into separate clusters.

In the following sections, clusters are identified with a number-letter combination, such as 8a, where the number indicates k, the number of clusters made, and the letter is an arbitrary name for the cluster. Cluster topics are listed in italics following the cluster identifier.

Eight Clusters

Classifying the dataset into 8 clusters results in 6 with topics directly related to combinations of Science Objectives. Three clusters contain documents from very mixed disciplines, with no single discipline making up more than 30% of the total: 8a - *beginning of life and biosignatures*; 8c - *prebiotic materials in ice and water*; and 8d - *genetics and biomolecules*. Two clusters contain a mix of primarily AAP and EPS documents: 8f - *detecting planetary habitability* and 8h - *planet formation and planetary qualities*. Cluster 8b - *observations and properties of stars and planetary systems* contains only AAP documents.

Cluster 8g - *methods of research, equipment and instruments, field expeditions, and planning for future missions* is about methods and planning, rather than NAI Science Objectives. This cluster contains mixed disciplines with 46% of them from EPS. Predictably, it includes the Astrobiology Roadmap document. The smallest cluster, 8e - *observations of extrasolar planets* is a collection of AAP abstracts from a single NAI team.

Twelve Clusters

Seven of the 12 clusters contain topics closely related to Science Objectives, quite similar to clusters 8a-c, 8f, and 8h, but split slightly more along disciplinary lines. Out of those 7 only 2 contain very mixed disciplines (no individual discipline makes up more than 30% of the total): 12j - *origins of organic matter, early Earth ecosystems, microbes, and biosignatures* and 12l - *microbes, RNA, and biomolecules*. EPS documents make up more than 30% of clusters 12g - *habitable planet environments, early Earth and Mars*; 12h - *planet, asteroid, and meteorite surface features*; and 12k - *microbial fossils and evolution of minerals*. AAP makes up slightly more than 30% of cluster 12a - *ice chemistry, icy worlds, prebiotic materials, and chemical complexity* and more than 90% of cluster 12c - *stars, planetary systems and exoplanet detection*.

Both 12b - *general discussions of astrobiology, exploration missions, and planning* and 12i - *environment and instrument testing* are directly related to cluster 8g. 12b is a cluster of general topics including the Astrobiology Roadmap, while 12i contains only 32 EPS abstracts.

Additionally, there are 2 small clusters of under 40 abstracts each which have the same topic: *extrasolar and habitable planets*, 12d, which is all AAP articles, and 12f with mixed disciplines. Finally, there is a large cluster containing mostly EPS documents, 12e - *MESSENGER mission to Mercury*. Interestingly, the MESSENGER mission to Mercury is not listed in the Astrobiology Roadmap.

Sixteen Clusters

When 16 clusters are used, the topics of 6 do not change significantly from 12 clusters. Listing their identities: 12a - 16f; 12e - 16e; 12h - 16i; 12j - 16g; 12k - 16c; 12g - 16o. We now discuss the remaining 10.

There is more than one biology-based cluster: 16d - *evolution, genetics and RNA* which contains the Roadmap document and 16p - *microbes, bacteria and extremophiles*. The previously discussed AAP clusters, 8a and 12c, split into 16n - *stars, planetary systems and observations of extrasolar planets* and 16h - *planet formation and planet qualities*. Documents contained in clusters 12b and 12i recombine and split into 3 mixed-discipline clusters: 16l - *instruments, analysis methods, analog environments, and field studies*; 16m - *Earth as model for habitable extrasolar planets*; and an all abstract cluster, 16k - *bio-signatures in meteorite materials and asteroids*.

Three small clusters of abstracts each contain less than 30 documents: 16j - *extrasolar planet detection*; and 16a and 16b which are too small, containing only very short documents, such that we could not identify meaningful topics. This is an indication that using more than 16 clusters would result in a summary that contains meaningless detail.

Visualization

To visualize the meta-structure resulting from cluster evaluation over different numbers of clusters, we plotted all clustering results in one graph, with node size based on degree and document nodes colored by discipline (Figure 3).

The layout was made using the Force Atlas algorithm provided with Gephi [4]. This algorithm causes all nodes to repel each other with a force based on size while edges draw connected nodes together. Therefore, document nodes were drawn toward the hubs representing their assigned clusters. The plot expanded along directions where there are less connecting edges (documents and cluster topics are less closely related) and contracted towards areas with similar topics where many connections occur. The resulting structure reveals cluster topic relatedness; how different disciplines are spread over the result space; and how documents are reassigned when the number of clusters is changed.

The graph shows that there is no clear hierarchical structure. Clusters do not split up evenly when going from 8 to 16 clusters. Instead, re-assignments are complex as indicated by the large number of isolated documents in the graph. Some documents, however, do stay together and we discuss this behavior in detail later in this section. We now discuss the highlighted areas in Figure 3.

The area inside the dashed line marked with I in Figure 3, contains clusters with star and exoplanet detection topics

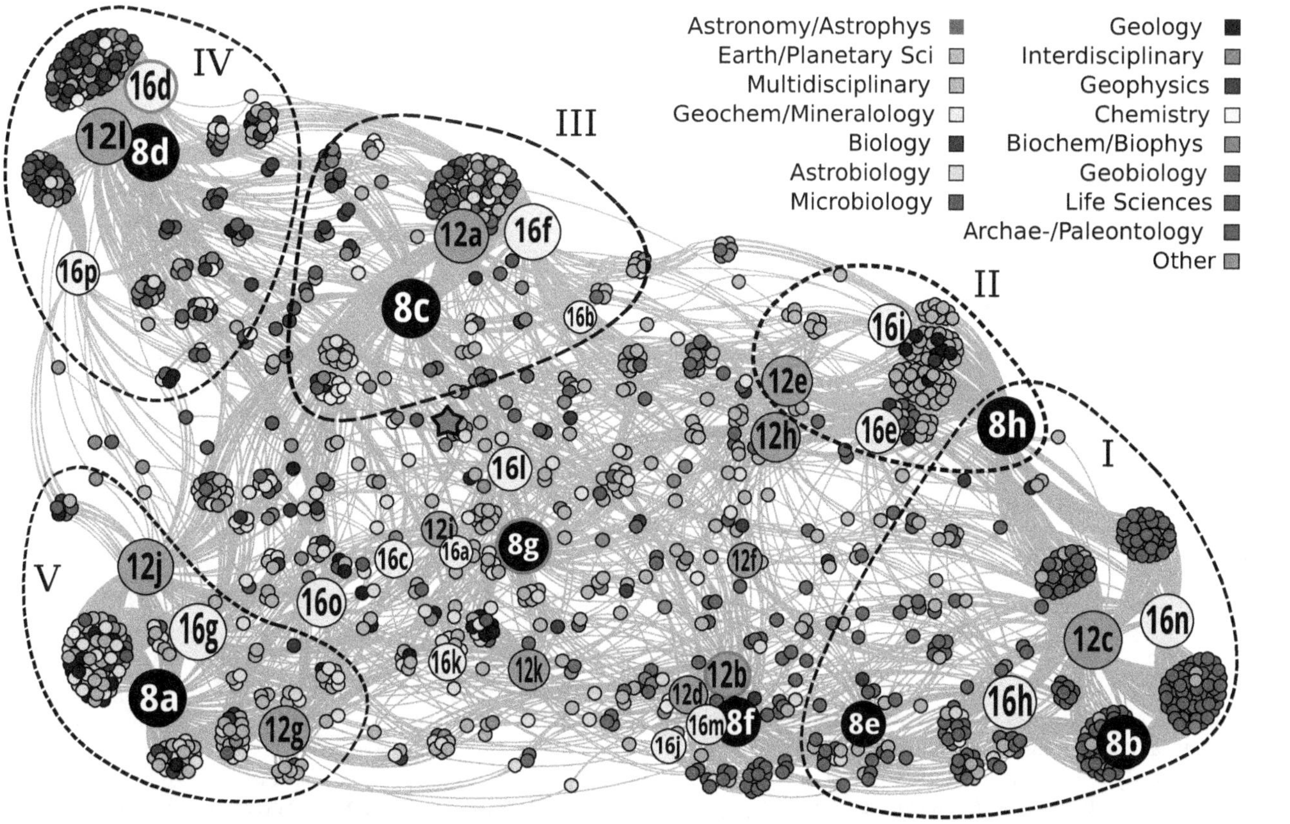

Figure 3. Force directed plot of clusters and documents for k = 8, 12, and 16 clusters, showing clumping behavior and distribution of disciplines. Cluster hubs, colored gray or black, are labeled with k plus a letter to aid evaluation. Document nodes are colored by discipline as indicated. Areas within dashed lines are approximate locations of topics discussed in the text. The dark pink star node is the NASA Astrobiology Roadmap document, its assigned clusters are outlined in the same pink.

and their associated documents. These are almost exclusively AAP publications as indicated by the majority of purple nodes. When assigned to different numbers of clusters, documents either stay together, such as in cluster 12c, or they split up into subtopics, such as in 16h and 16n. This is the most prominent place in the graph where an almost hierarchical structure can be found. Many documents in area I never cluster with other documents outside of this area. They remain very close together because there are few edges to pull them away. This causes the area to be somewhat segregated from the rest of the graph.

Within area II we find a predominantly green group of document nodes, which are the EPS documents related to the MESSENGER Mercury mission that make up cluster 12e. A large portion of those documents is also assigned to cluster 8h, together with large groups of AAP documents found in area I. Therefore, there are short paths connecting documents in these two groups pulling the document nodes and their related clusters closer together, giving a visual clue about the bi-disciplinary content of cluster 8h.

Area III contains an heterogeneous selection of disciplines (indicated by document node colors), but most of the documents share similar topics, namely the study of prebiotic materials (particularly ice and water) in lab experiments, on Earth, in the Solar System, and outside the Solar System.

Inside area IV are many dark purple biology, magenta microbiology, and brown geology document nodes. These are the documents clustered into genetics, microbes, and biomolecule-related topics. The large group of documents near the cluster 16d node stay together when different numbers of clusters are used. They are also assigned to clusters 12l and 8d.

Clusters with topics related to biosignatures and the beginning of life are located in area V with cluster nodes 8a, 12g, 12j, and 16g. These are multidisciplinary, indicated by the amount of differently colored document nodes. They are also not as separated from the bulk of the data as the biology-based clusters (in area IV) due to the fairly large amount of connections they share with the ice-related work contained in area III, and the more loosely connected documents related to mission planning, analog environments, and instrument testing located near the center of the plot and cluster 8g.

The *NASA Astrobiology Roadmap* document contains descriptions of all of the 18 Science Objectives. It is by definition a summary of the intended outcomes of research produced by the NAI Teams. In Figure 3, the *Roadmap's* location is marked by a node shaped as a pink star with a thick black border. The clusters it was assigned to, 8g, 12b, and 16d, are highlighted by pink borders. This document is located close to the center of the plot, as should be expected, and the clus-

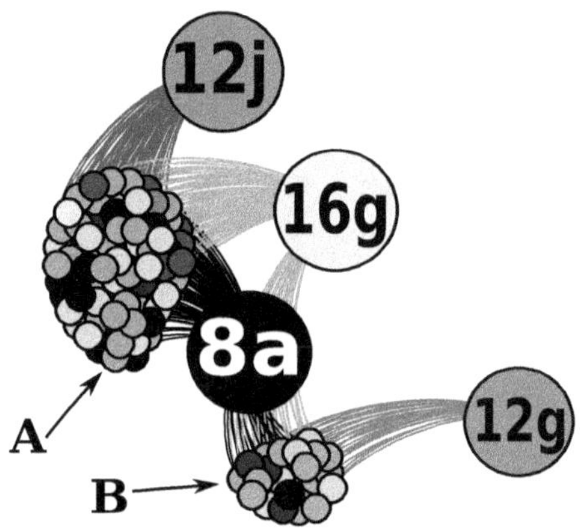

Figure 4. Detail from area V from Figure 3 showing how documents always assigned together to the same clusters form clumps of nodes. As explained in the text, the documents contained in clumps marked "A" and "B" are all assigned to clusters 8a and 16g, but are split at k=12 into 12g and 12j. Document nodes colored by discipline as in previous figures.

ters it was assigned to do not consistently represent the same topic or the same disciplines. This illustrates an advantage of looking at more than one clustering solution on the plot. Examining only one solution would make it appear that a single cluster topic (where the *Roadmap* is assigned) represents the research guidelines much more strongly than any of the others.

Plotting multiple clustering solutions also reveals how some document nodes are always assigned together to the same cluster, for all values of k considered. These documents form clumps in the force directed plot. However, one clump of document nodes rarely makes up an entire cluster itself and examination of these clumps reveals further insights into the data.

As an example, we focus on area V from Figure 3. A detail is provided in Figure 4, with two clumps of documents labeled **A** and **B**. In-depth examination of all documents within **A** and **B**, respectively, including texts, authors, and citations, reveals a high degree of relatedness within each clump.

The 84 documents in **A** are predominantly geochemistry (light blue), multidisciplinary (orange), and geology (dark brown). Most of these articles originate from projects tagged with Science Objectives pertaining to the early Earth and the search for biosignatures in materials of extraterrestrial origin (such as meteorite samples.) All clusters that the documents in **A** were assigned to have topics related to the beginning of life and biosignatures.

The 26 documents in **B** contain a larger percentage of EPS articles (green). The majority of these articles come from projects tagged with Mars exploration and general planetary habitability-related Science Objectives.

Interestingly, the documents in **B** cluster together with those in **A** in both 8a and 16g, but they separate into clusters 12g and 12j at the intermediate compression level of 12 clusters.

The authorship and citations within both clumps are very tightly coupled. We find that active collaborations between many authors and connections via direct citation are present. Some authors are represented in both **A** and **B**. These authors have done work on the formation of both the Earth and Mars. Their papers about Earth are in **A**, and their papers about Mars are in **B**. Several of the Mars papers by these authors are cross-institutional collaborations with other authors also represented in **B**.

From this examination it can be seen that our method extracts a large amount of relevant detail from the unstructured database we had at hand. Documents that cluster together share similar topics and some share authorship and citations. Documents that clump together over a range of k, are indicative of active collaboration and citation amongst the authors, thus providing, for example, an excellent starting point for CSCW researchers looking for existing collaborations in an unstructured database.

PRESENTATION AND USER REACTION

Our analysis results were presented to 17 NAI researchers from the University of Hawaii (roughly $\frac{2}{3}$ of the entire University of Hawaii Team), during a planning session. The primary goals of the session were to examine (i) the team's collaborative efforts and research output, and (ii) how both could be compared with other NAI teams. The visualizations generated in the present study served as cultural probes during the session, providing researchers in diverse areas a data-driven representation of the larger context of their work and a basis to explore potential connections across disciplines. We noted 4 main reactions:

1. The scientists thought that the model-free nature of the clustering process, which included no preconceptions about the disciplinary membership of any paper, was appropriate to the nature of astrobiology research. It contributed to the perceived objectivity and trustworthiness of the results.

2. The Hawaii team thought that their primary distinguishing strengths were in the areas of astronomy and earth and planetary sciences. However, the visualization suggested that those strengths are relatively common across NAI. One of the strongest interdisciplinary clusters, and one of the rarest across NAI, is in ice chemistry and related areas (seen in area III of Figure 3). The researchers had not been aware of this and realized this was an area of strength unique to Hawaii that should be emphasized in forthcoming reports to NASA. This led to a discussion about whether a physical chemist specializing in ice chemistry might have a productive collaboration with an astronomer specializing in comets. Those researchers and several others used the visualization to form themselves into breakout groups, map out the next steps of their research, and discuss areas of potential crossover.

3. The researchers were not surprised to see documents in the biological sciences cluster together, somewhat removed from those in astrobiology's other constituent fields. They

discussed the relative benefit of having some teams specialize in biological aspects of astrobiology as opposed to trying to force interdisciplinary connections in every area. They argued that the Hawaii team's focus on water, a precursor and substrate for life, might help bridge biological and physical sciences.

4. The scientists expressed interest in examining documents from outside their home discipline that consistently clustered within their own areas, suggesting that this clustering process might also be used as an interdisciplinary document discovery and recommendation system.

As a result of the feedback from the NAI scientists, we have built a website with a fully interactive version of our analysis visualization. This is located at: **http://airframe.ics.hawaii.edu/visualizations/**. The site allows a much richer experience with our data and analysis than is possible to represent here. The entire graph, similar to Figure 3, can be zoomed and panned. Mousing-over nodes pops up document bibliographic information or cluster topic. Clicking a node highlights related clusters and documents, hiding all others. Users can choose to see different numbers of clusters, from 2 - 16, or combinations of those. They may also choose to color the document nodes by discipline or by NAI team. We anticipate that the site will be useful not only for astrobiology researchers, but for NASA administrators and interested members of the public as well.

CONCLUSION AND OUTLOOK

Interdisciplinary research is, by definition, open to contributions from diverse fields, and it is useful to have a mechanism for information to migrate across domains. In this paper we used computer supported methods, powered by unsupervised learning (clustering) and network visualization, to aid cooperative work by helping interdisciplinary scientists work together.

We have created a document classification and analysis tool to aid interdisciplinary research in the field of astrobiology. To that end we created a new algorithm for document preprocessing, resulting in an indication of how many words to use for the mutual-information based clustering method we applied. We have presented the resulting document analysis to scientists at a planning session, as a cultural probe, and have recorded their reactions. We have created a website providing a web-based version of our analysis to allow for its continued use.

Our classification and visualization method is automated and uses unsupervised machine learning (clustering) methods that make minimal assumptions about the structure of the data. It thus saves valuable expert time.

Analysis of the astrobiology documents shows that our method reveals useful structure in an unstructured database without bibiographic meta-data. We were able to identify: (i) which documents are topically related, (ii) how a given document fits into the entire body of work, and (iii) where collaborations take place. This is useful as it provides a time efficient visual guidance that can help researchers to identify both publications and other researchers that are relevant to their own interests. It can thus aid in strengthening existing collaborations and the formation of new ones. It can also aid in guiding searches and in building reading lists.

Most importantly, our method met with success when it was presented to a subset of astrobiology researchers. Our document analysis contained some expected results, but also contributed new insights. It elicited interest and discussions. This demonstrates that our document clustering and visualization method can be a valuable collaborative tool.

The utility of our method should become even more obvious in application areas in which the number of publications is much larger than what we analyzed here. The size of our database ($< 10^3$ documents) implies that probably most PI's are aware of a large fraction of most of the published articles. However, in areas where there are one or even two orders of magnitude more documents, our automated and systematic approach may provide a valuable starting point to guide search and discovery of connections between documents, thereby saving time and making an otherwise infeasible task more tractable. Computing speed limitations are being addressed in active research by others [5] and should be less of an issue in the future.

ACKNOWLEDGMENTS

This material is based upon work supported by the National Aeronautics and Space Administration through the NASA Astrobiology Institute under Cooperative Agreement No. NNA08DA77A issued through the Office of Space Science.

REFERENCES

1. AIRFrame. Astrobiology Integrative Research Framework Project. **http://airframe.ics.hawaii.edu/**.

2. Archambault, D., Munzner, T., and Auber, D. Grouseflocks: Steerable exploration of graph hierarchy space. *Visualization and Computer Graphics, IEEE Transactions on 14*, 4 (2008), 900–913.

3. Balakrishnan, A. D., Kiesler, S., Cummings, J. N., and Zadeh, R. Research team integration: what it is and why it matters. In *Proc. CSCW 2011*, ACM Press (2011), 523–532.

4. Bastian, M., Heymann, S., and Jacomy, M. Gephi: An open source software for exploring and manipulating networks. In *ICWSM 2009*, vol. 2, AAAI Press (2009).

5. Bekkerman, R., Bilenko, M., and Langford, J. *Scaling up machine learning: Parallel and distributed approaches*. Cambridge University Press, 2011.

6. Bekkerman, R., and Scholz, M. Data weaving: scaling up the state-of-the-art in data clustering. In *Proc. CIKM 2008*, ACM Press (2008), 1083–1092.

7. Blei, D. M., Ng, A. Y., and Jordan, M. I. Latent dirichlet allocation. *The Journal of Machine Learning Research 3* (2003), 993–1022.

8. Boehner, K., Vertesi, J., Sengers, P., and Dourish, P. How HCI interprets the probes. In *Proc. CHI 2007*, ACM Press (2007), 1077–1086.

9. Börner, K., Chen, C., and Boyack, K. W. Visualizing knowledge domains. *Annual review of information science and technology 37*, 1 (2003), 179–255.

10. Boyack, K. W., Newman, D., Duhon, R. J., Klavans, R., Patek, M., Biberstine, J. R., Schijvenaars, B., Skupin, A., Ma, N., and Börner, K. Clustering more than two million biomedical publications: Comparing the accuracies of nine text-based similarity approaches. *PLoS One 6*, 3 (2011), e18029.

11. Callon, M., Law, J., and Rip, A. *Mapping the dynamics of science and technology*. Springer, 1986.
12. Cummings, J. N., and Kiesler, S. Who collaborates successfully?: prior experience reduces collaboration barriers in distributed interdisciplinary research. In *Proc. CSCW 2008*, ACM Press (2008), 437–446.
13. Des Marais, D. J., Nuth III, J. A., Allamandola, L. J., Boss, A. P., Farmer, J. D., Hoehler, T. M., Jakosky, B. M., Meadows, V. S., Pohorille, A., Runnegar, B., et al. The NASA astrobiology roadmap. *Astrobiology 8*, 4 (2008), 715–730.
14. Dhillon, I. S., Mallela, S., and Modha, D. S. Information-theoretic co-clustering. In *Proc. KDD 2003*, ACM Press (2003), 89–98.
15. Duda, R. O., Hart, P. E., and Stork, D. G. *Pattern classification*. Wiley-interscience, 2012.
16. Dumais, S. T. Latent semantic analysis. *Annual review of information science and technology 38*, 1 (2004), 188–230.
17. Finholt, T. A., and Olson, G. M. From laboratories to collaboratories: A new organizational form for scientific collaboration. *Psychological Science 8*, 1 (1997), 28–36.
18. Fiore, S. M. Interdisciplinarity as teamwork: How the science of teams can inform team science. *Small Group Research 39*, 3 (2008), 251–277.
19. Gaver, B., Dunne, T., and Pacenti, E. Design: Cultural probes. *interactions 6*, 1 (Jan. 1999), 21–29.
20. Gazan, R. AIRFrame: integrating diverse digital collections in astrobiology. In *Proc. JCDL 2010*, ACM Press (2010), 375–376.
21. Gazan, R. Identifying crossover documents in an interdisciplinary research environment. In *Proc. iConference 2013*, iSchools (2013), 457–460.
22. Gordon, A. D. *Classification*. CRC Press, June 1999.
23. Gowanlock, M., and Gazan, R. Assessing researcher interdisciplinarity: a case study of the University of Hawaii NASA Astrobiology Institute. *Scientometrics 94*, 1 (2013), 133–161.
24. Halpern, M. K. Across the great divide: Boundaries and boundary objects in art and science. *Public Understanding of Science 21*, 8 (2012), 922–937.
25. Halpern, M. K., Erickson, I., Forlano, L., and Gay, G. K. Designing collaboration: comparing cases exploring cultural probes as boundary-negotiating objects. In *Proc. CSCW 2013*, ACM Press (2013), 1093–1102.
26. Harmon, D. K. *Overview of the Third Text Retrieval Conference (Trec-3)*. DIANE Publishing, Oct. 1995.
27. Howison, J., and Herbsleb, J. D. Incentives and integration in scientific software production. In *Proc. CSCW 2013*, ACM Press (2013), 459–470.
28. Jackson, S. J., Ribes, D., Buyuktur, A., and Bowker, G. C. Collaborative rhythm: temporal dissonance and alignment in collaborative scientific work. In *Proc. CSCW 2011*, ACM Press (2011), 245–254.
29. Jackson, S. J., Steinhardt, S. B., and Buyuktur, A. Why CSCW needs science policy (and vice versa). In *Proc. CSCW 2013*, ACM Press (2013), 1113–1124.
30. Jain, A. K. Data clustering: 50 years beyond k-means. *Pattern Recognition Letters 31*, 8 (June 2010), 651–666.
31. Kraut, R., Galegher, J., and Egido, C. Relationships and tasks in scientific research collaborations. In *Proc. CSCW 1986*, ACM Press (1986), 229–245.
32. Lee, C. P. Between chaos and routine: Boundary negotiating artifacts in collaboration. In *ECSCW 2005*, H. Gellersen, K. Schmidt, M. Beaudouin-Lafon, and W. Mackay, Eds., Springer Netherlands (2005), 387–406.
33. Lee, C. P., Dourish, P., and Mark, G. The human infrastructure of cyberinfrastructure. In *Proc. CSCW 2006*, ACM Press (2006), 483–492.
34. Leydesdorff, L. *The challenge of scientometrics: The development, measurement, and self-organization of scientific communications*. Universal-Publishers. com, 2001.
35. Miller, L., and Gazan, R. Adaptation of an open source semantic and conceptual retrieval framework to the astrobiological domain. In *AbSciCon 2010*, vol. 1538 (2010), 5154.
36. Müller, H., Kenny, E. E., and Sternberg, P. W. Textpresso: An Ontology-Based information retrieval and extraction system for biological literature. *PLoS Biol 2*, 11 (2004), e309.
37. Panzeri, S., Senatore, R., Montemurro, M. A., and Petersen, R. S. Correcting for the sampling bias problem in spike train information measures. *Journal of Neurophysiology 98*, 3 (2007), 1064 –1072.
38. Panzeri, S., and Treves, A. Analytical estimates of limited sampling biases in different information measures. *Network-Computation in Neural Systems 7*, 1 (1996), 87–108.
39. Peterson, L. L., and Davie, B. S. *Computer networks: a systems approach*. Elsevier, 2007.
40. Porter, M. F. An algorithm for suffix stripping. *Program: electronic library and information systems 14*, 3 (1980), 130–137.
41. Salton, G. *Automatic text processing: the transformation, analysis, and retrieval of information by computer*. Addison-Wesley, 1989.
42. Shneiderman, B. Creating creativity: user interfaces for supporting innovation. *ACM Trans. Comput.-Hum. Interact. 7*, 1 (Mar. 2000), 114–138.
43. Slonim, N., Friedman, N., and Tishby, N. Unsupervised document classification using sequential information maximization. In *Proc. SIGIR 2002*, ACM Press (2002), 129–136.
44. Slonim, N., and Tishby, N. Document clustering using word clusters via the information bottleneck method. In *Proc. SIGIR 2000*, ACM Press (2000), 208–215.
45. Slonim, N., and Tishby, N. The power of word clusters for text classification. In *ECIR 2001*, vol. 1 (2001).
46. Star, S. L., and Griesemer, J. R. Institutional ecology, translations, and boundary objects: Amateurs and professionals in Berkeley's Museum of Vertebrate Zoology, 1907-39. *Social studies of science 19*, 3 (1989), 387–420.
47. Still, S., and Bialek, W. How many clusters? an Information-Theoretic perspective. *Neural Computation 16*, 12 (Mar. 2004), 2483–2506.
48. Tishby, N., Pereira, F. C., and Bialek, W. The information bottleneck method. In *Proc. Allerton Conf. 1999*, Univ. of Illinois (1999), 368–377.
49. Treves, A., and Panzeri, S. The upward bias in measures of information derived from limited data samples. *Neural Computation 7*, 2 (1995), 399–407.
50. Vargas-Quesada, B., and de Moya Anegón, F. *Visualizing the structure of science*. Springer, 2007.
51. von Landesberger, T., Kuijper, A., Schreck, T., Kohlhammer, J., van Wijk, J., Fekete, J.-D., and Fellner, D. Visual analysis of large graphs: State-of-the-art and future research challenges. *Computer Graphics Forum 30*, 6 (2011), 1719–1749.
52. Wallach, H. M., Mimno, D. M., and McCallum, A. Rethinking lda: Why priors matter. In *NIPS 2009*, vol. 22 (2009), 1973–1981.

Pair Research: Matching People for Collaboration, Learning, and Productivity

Robert C. Miller[1], Haoqi Zhang[2], Eric Gilbert[3], Elizabeth Gerber[2]

[1]MIT CSAIL
Cambridge, MA
rcm@mit.edu

[2]Northwestern University
Evanston, IL
{hq,egerber}@northwestern.edu

[3]Georgia Tech College of Computing
Atlanta, GA
gilbert@cc.gatech.edu

ABSTRACT

To increase productivity, informal learning, and collaborations within and across research groups, we have been experimenting with a new kind of interaction that we call *pair research*, in which members are paired up weekly to work together on each other's projects. In this paper, we present a system for making pairings and present results from two deployments. Results show that members used pair research in a wide variety of ways including pair programming, user testing, brainstorming, and data collection and analysis. Pair research helped members get things done and share their expertise with others.

INTRODUCTION

Academic research is a hard endeavor. The path to discovery has many hurdles that can dampen enthusiasm for making progress. While collaboration and help-seeking can boost productivity and produce better research, few mechanisms in academic research directly promote and facilitate it. This is particularly troubling for young researchers, who may only receive feedback on their work in group meetings, work with only a few collaborators (one of whom is their advisor), and be more easily frustrated by setbacks, real or imagined.

We have been experimenting with a new kind of interaction within a research group that we call *pair research*, as a generalization of pair programming. Each week, group members pair up, guided by a matching algorithm. Each pair meets for a one- or two-hour session, of which half the time is spent working together on one person's project, and the other half working on the other person's project. The work might be any activity involved in computer science research, including pair programming, user testing and design critique, data collection and analysis, brainstorming and research discussion, and mentoring and advising. The following week, different pairs are formed, and the process repeats.

Inspired by pair programming, pair research seeks to increase collaboration, promote informal learning, and boost productivity within and across research groups. For collaboration,

CSCW'14, February 15 - 19 2014, Baltimore, MD, USA

ACM 978-1-4503-2540-0/14/02$15.00.
http://dx.doi.org/10.1145/2531602.2531703

Figure 1. Pair research in action: two group members working together on each other's projects.

it offers people the chance to interact with many partners with diverse perspectives and expertise, and to get to know them better by working closely with them. Reciprocation [5, 12] is built into the process, so neither partner needs to feel in debt to the other afterwards. For learning, it may spread knowledge and skills within a group, and between groups if multiple groups participate in the same pairing system. For productivity, it helps people make concrete progress on their own projects, by drawing on other people's expertise, effort, and social pressure. We chose research groups as our context because—while convenient—they exemplify a kind of creative work where the benefits of pair programming have not been explored.

Pair research is a new socio-technical system consisting of both a social process, meeting to work as a pair, and a technical system that supports the process, collecting people's preferences and automatically matching them to help each other do work. We developed a spreadsheet prototype to manage pair research. Each week, the system automatically reminds group members to submit what they want help on and what they can help with, makes an optimal pairing given that information, and notifies members of their partners.

This paper makes the following contributions: (1) the design space for pair research, drawing from literature, existing systems, and early prototyping experience; (2) a pair research system which collects needs and preferences and matches members automatically; and (3) the results of two deployments, one with roughly 10 people over 2 months, the other with almost 30 people over 6 months, still ongoing. The deployments show that members used pair research in a wide variety of ways, and that it helped them start and complete tasks, share expertise, and learn about other group members.

RELATED WORK

Pair research is inspired in part by pair programming [2], in which two programmers work at the same workstation, with one writing code while the other watches and reviews the code as it is typed. Pair programming has been shown in some studies to be more efficient than solo programming, producing higher-quality code. The effect of pair programming on learning is less clear. One controlled study of introductory computer science showed no benefit for exam scores, but an improvement in attitude toward the course [20]. The two partners in pair programming are typically working on the same development project, sharing a common overall goal. Pair research differs in that its two partners are usually working on different projects.

In pair programming, pairs typically spend a full iteration of the software project working together, which may last for weeks. Belshee has argued for *promiscuous pair programming* instead [3]. Experimenting with pair-switching at various intervals from every 30 minutes to every 3 days, he found the highest task completion rate for 90-minute switching intervals. At this rate, pairs typically consisted of one person already familiar with the task, and one person who was still learning. Frequent switching seemed to propagate knowledge quickly around the development team. By switching partners every week, pair research similarly seeks to spread knowledge and skills quickly within a group.

Pair research is intended to increase informal workplace learning, or *over-the shoulder learning (OTSL)* [18]. One of the benefits of OTSL over more formal learning approaches is shared context. The helper understands the task the learner is trying to do and the learner's goals for doing it. Twidale also argues that encouraging OTSL may require not only tool support but also organizational changes that assign positive value to giving help to colleagues. Pair research as a practice may help to induce these changes.

Also related is apprentice learning [4]. Berlin and Jeffries followed several graduate student interns and their mentors in a computer science research laboratory for several months, a similar setting and duration as the results reported in this paper. One finding was that incidental learning, triggered by specific incidents in problem-solving, was a major benefit of interactions between apprentices and mentors. But apprentices also had to use strategies to minimize their use of the mentor's time. By matching people who can best help one another and rotating pairs frequently, pair research seeks to provide some of the benefits of apprenticeship learning without reliance on a particular mentor.

DESIGN SPACE

In designing the pair research process, we faced a number of design decisions. This section discusses these decisions and some alternatives. Some decisions were based on prior work, and others learned from experience of early design iterations.

How many people should work together? We use pairs by extension of pair programming, and for simplicity. We briefly experimented with 3-person teams as a way to resolve the problem of an odd-numbered pool. The small teams were harder to schedule, took longer to work together, and could not always manage a fair three-way exchange of effort. This finding is consistent with decades of small group research [9]. The current process simply leaves an odd person unpaired for the week. Larger groups have occasionally been suggested. For example, one week a member noticed several people asking for help with learning Node.js, so a study group formed independently of the pair research process.

How should people be matched? Initial experiments used randomized matching, which often led to people tailoring the pair research session to their partner's expertise rather than their needs. To support people receiving help from those who are most able to help, our current prototype solicits preferences from members and computes an optimal pairing given those preferences.

Should preferences be expressed about activities or people? An *activity* is the particular work to be done or kind of help needed. The people are *consumers* who need help and *providers* who give help. Considering other systems in the people-matching design space, online dating sites typically focus on people, but some (e.g. HowAboutWe.com) allow members to propose dating activities and have other members rate that activity. In contrast, marketplaces typically focus on the products or services for sale, but some (e.g. AngiesList) rate the service providers. Our system focuses on activities rather than people, in order to make pair research primarily about work progress rather than social interaction. Members nevertheless used preferences in complex ways, to specify interest in both the activity and the other person.

Who should specify the activities? An activity might be proposed by the consumer, e.g. "I need help with R", or by the provider, like "I can help anybody with design sketching." We chose to focus on consumer-specified activities in order to make productivity a primary goal. A project to-do item then becomes a natural activity. If we had wanted to prioritize learning instead, we might use provider-specified activities, as does Skillshare.com, or for that matter, traditional classroom education. Although consumer-specified help requests were the norm, we also saw provider-specified activities, mainly by one group member who preferred not to ask for help but offered it instead.

How public should the matching process be? Labor markets and dating sites usually keep preferences and matchings private. We chose instead to make them visible to all members of the system, in order to make it easier to learn about the skills and interests of others.

How long should a pair work? We want each person to walk away from pair research with the feeling that they have accomplished something in the time they worked together. But we also want to keep the time commitment low to encourage participation and to avoid fatigue. Based on the Pomodoro technique [6], our normal minimum is 30 minutes for each

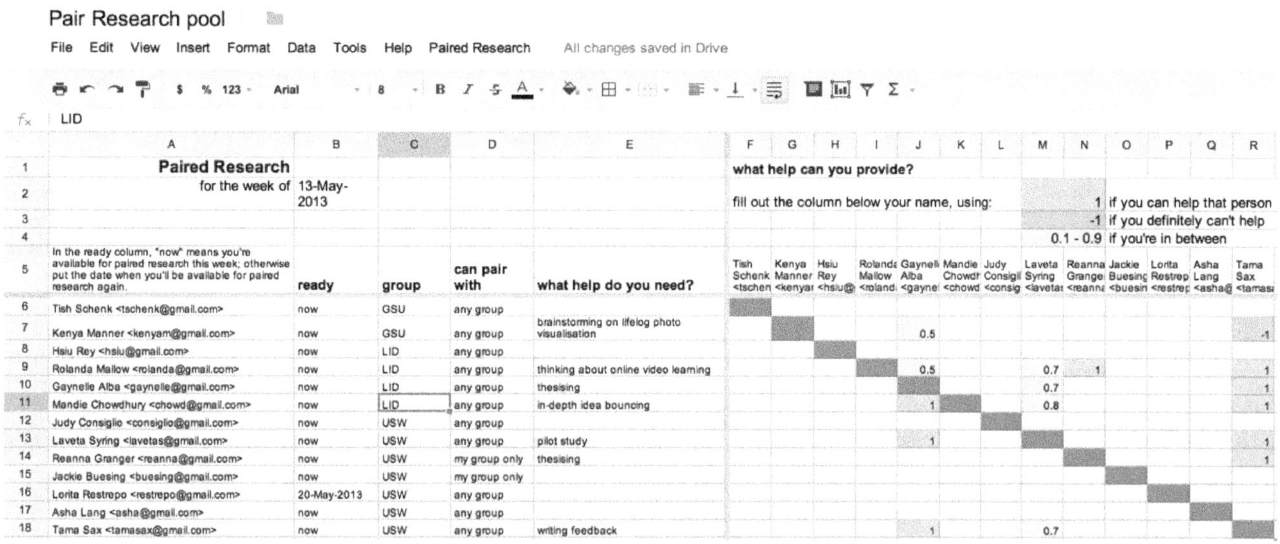

Figure 2. Prototype interface for managing the pair research pool. Each week, members describe what they need help with, and enter preference scores on how well they can help others. Members can also remove themselves from the pool temporarily.

partner. This includes a few minutes to talk informally and off-topic, which helps establish the trust and personal connection critical for learning. With each partner taking a turn, the normal result is a one-hour session. In practice, the duration is negotiated by each pair based on the goals they set for themselves, so some pairs meet for longer than an hour.

How often should pairs change? A secondary objective to matching people with those who are best able to help is to spread knowledge and skills. To promote this objective, we bias the matching to encourage new collaborations and discourage repeating recent pairings.

Should pair meetings be fixed-time or independently-scheduled? We initially prototyped the process at a regularly-scheduled group meeting time, but members requested more flexibility, so pairs now decide on their own when to meet. This flexibility also allowed people from other time zones to join the pool without having to negotiate a common meeting time for the whole pool. In practice, however, flexibility can lead to scheduling failures, discussed more later in this paper.

What pool of people should be involved? A large number of members in the pool provides a more diverse set of expertise, but may be uneven in quality. Our two deployments were centered on existing work groups, and varied in size between 10 and 30 members. Both deployments also included members with a range of seniority, from undergraduates to faculty.

USER INTERFACE

We developed a prototype user interface to manage the process, implemented as a collaborative spreadsheet (Figure 2). The heart of the user interface is a preference matrix for person matching. Each week, group members specify the help they need that week (e.g. "debugging Django," "feedback on my writing," "need a pilot user for my prototype"). Other members then fill out the preference matrix according to how able and interested they are to provide that help, where 1 is maximum interest, -1 is maximum disinterest, and 0 or blank is neutral. The preference matrix may be sparse, because

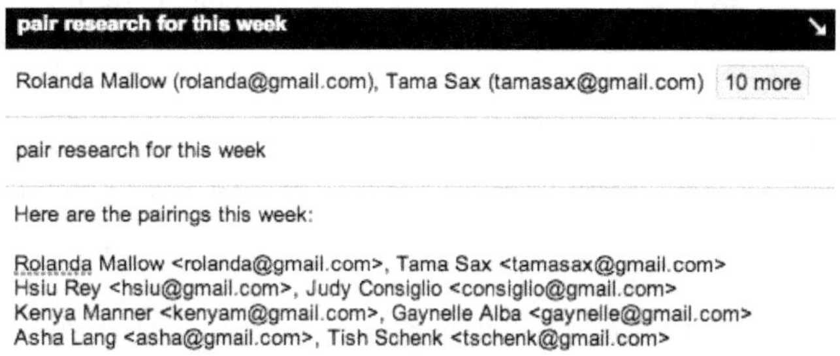

Figure 3. The pairing is computed and emailed automatically.

some members may not fill it out. Members are matched with others even if they do not fill out the matrix.

The preference ratings are used to bias the pair assignment for the week, so that people with high mutual preference are very likely to be paired, people with negative mutual preference are never paired, and people with neutral preference receive a random partner. To generate pairings, the system uses collected preferences to construct a weighted graph. Nodes in the graph represent members in the pool, and the graph contains an edge between two members if and only if both members have nonnegative preferences. The weight of an edge between two members is the average of their mutual preferences, plus a bonus if the pair has not been matched recently. A small random perturbation is added to break ties, and to cause random assignment for members who did not provide any preferences. The system then finds a *maximum weighted matching* on the constructed graph. Matching problems like this one are well-studied in the literature [14], and have applications in matching students to school [1], residents to hospitals [15], and donors to patients [16].

The system sends weekly email notifications to remind members to submit their needs and preferences. Members enter their needs in the spreadsheet on Saturday, then return to the spreadsheet again on Sunday to look at what others need and fill out the preference matrix. The pairs are assigned on Sunday night and emailed automatically. Figure 3 shows an example of a typical matching.

	Group A	Group B
N	29	10
gender	18M, 11W	7M, 3W
age	20–40	20–33
role	6U, 16G, 5P, 2F	9G, 1F
time period	26 weeks (Nov '12 – May '13)	7 weeks (Jan-Feb '13)
pairings	244	31
help requests	207 (100%)	46 (100%)
programming	83 (40%)	4 (9%)
user study	41 (20%)	7 (15%)
writing	36 (17%)	15 (33%)
brainstorming	18 (9%)	8 (17%)
data analysis	7 (3%)	8 (17%)
offering help	18 (9%)	2 (4%)
other	4 (2%)	2 (4%)

Figure 4. Results of two deployments of pair research. Roles are (U)ndergraduate, (G)rad student, (P)ostdoc, and (F)aculty.

New columns were added to the spreadsheet as the process evolved. The *ready* column allows a member to temporarily drop out of the pool, for example while traveling or going away for holidays, but requires a date on which they will return, so that the reminder emails can automatically resume. The *group* and *can pair with* columns were added when the pool broadened to multiple research groups, so that a member can keep their pairing local if they choose. Undergraduates, in particular, expressed a reluctance to engage with members of remote research groups, perhaps because they do not (yet) feel ready to make a long-term investment in getting to know people in the wider research field.

The pair research spreadsheet is a low-fidelity prototype [19] of what may become a full-fledged web application. In general, we have found that collaborative spreadsheets and documents are excellent for this purpose, similar to paper prototyping [13] but for collaborative sociotechnical systems that might otherwise require programming to experiment with. Even though our spreadsheet now has a programmed backend that matches people and sends emails automatically, we could have run these parts by hand using a simple but nonoptimal greedy matching algorithm executed by a human wizard. Low-fidelity spreadsheets and docs permit early experimentation with potentially-risky social parts of a sociotechnical system, without investing development effort in the technical parts before it can be justified.

DEPLOYMENT STUDY

Pair research has been deployed in two university research groups, A and B, each run by one of the authors. Group A initially had 15 members at a single school, and the pool grew to include 29 people, including collaborators from five other schools. Group B had 10 members at a single school. Figure 4 shows statistics about the two deployments, including demographics of group members.

Method

We collected and analyzed three kinds of data about the deployments. First, to learn about the pair assignment process, we collected the spreadsheets containing help requests, preference ratings, and the resulting pairs for each week. The help requests were coded by one researcher using the categories shown in Figure 4.

Second, in order to learn about how pairs actually worked together, we sent a short weekly survey to group A for the last 9 weeks of its deployment. Group B did not receive the survey, because its deployment had already ended. The survey asked for how long pairs spent working together, what they actually worked on, the usefulness of the pairing session on a scale from 1 to 5, and open-ended comments on positive and negative aspects of the week's experience. The survey produced responses for 55 of the 244 group A pairings, from 18 distinct members.

Third, to gather some experience from group B in the absence of survey data, we conducted in-person or video interviews with two members of group B and a remote member of group A, covering the same questions as the survey and also asking about collaboration outside of pair research and about opportunities for informal learning.

Results

Members requested specific help in the spreadsheet only some of the time. In group A, the median person asked for specific help only 20% of the time (5 weeks out of 26), and the most frequent asked for help 70% of the time (18 weeks out of 26). The system assigns partners even without a specific help request, so group A members regarded it as optional. Group B had far more specific help requests, because the spreadsheet was filled out synchronously in meetings to encourage participation. The median group B member made a specific help request 70% of the time (5 weeks out of 7).

Figure 4 shows the kinds of help requested, which varied between the groups. The most common Group A request was programming and debugging help (40%), while the most common request in B was for writing (33%). Both groups showed significant requests for user study design and testing (20% for A, 15% for B). We also saw instances where the specific-help field of the spreadsheet was used to make an offer of help instead of a request. One group A member was responsible for all 18 of these offers, suggesting that he preferred to give help than get it.

Pairing was promiscuous. Group A members had a mean 16.8 pairings over 26 weeks, with a mean 12.0 different partners, so 71% of the time they were working with a partner they had never had before. For contrast, most of group A's members would normally work closely with only 1-2 other group members, counting the adviser. Pair research increased their number of close contacts by an order of magnitude.

Turning to the survey data, which collected the outcomes of a sample of pairings in group A, the mean time spent on pair work was 1.3 hours per week. But pair work failed to happen 16% of the time (9 instances out of 55 pairings in the survey) because of scheduling difficulties between the partners, suggesting that the practice might benefit from a regular scheduled time, at least for co-located groups. When pairs succeeded in meeting, group A members rated the usefulness of the experience as a mean 4.5 on a scale of 1 to 5, though these ratings may be biased by awareness that other group members might see them.

Comments in both the survey and interviews expressed the value of having a fresh perspective, different from the person's usual set of collaborators: *"It brings together people who are interested in each others' work but wouldn't otherwise act on that interest."*

Many members said the process helped spur them to action. *"It helped me do something that I was ambivalent about." "It is a 'forcing function' ... to work on things I have been putting off." "I [said] 'this week I need help with this and committed to do it."*

Others suggested that more preparation would have been useful before the pair work session. *"This could have been improved had we specifically written down our goals prior to the start."* The time gap between filling out the spreadsheet and meeting to work together also came up as a problem: *"I often find it restricting to 'commit' to working on a certain subject ...up to a week before I actually work on it." "Lately I have not known [what I want to do] far enough in advance."*

Pair research was frequently cited as a way to learn about other group members and their work. A new member of group A expressed this very strongly: *'Our group's paired research is the best thing that happened to me since I came – [getting] to know individual's work one by one, face-to-face."* Members of group B found this value in the spreadsheet alone, perhaps because they filled it out more than group A: *"Even though we're in the same lab, I don't know what specific tasks they're working on." "It's a good way to know who's doing what."*

Some members learned new tools or practices from working closely with their partners. *"I switched to Sublime because of pair research." "When I worked with [my partner] she decided to drop what she was planning to do for paired research and learn about bootstrap (we had talked about it when I showed her my experiment during paired research)."*

The fair exchange of the process was important to several participants. *"[I like] that we both got something out of it." "She helped me, but I feel a little bit guilty because I couldn't help (but it was her fault because she wasn't ready)." "I wish we had not spent as much time on my stuff and had spent more equal time on his."*

Finally, a number of comments showed that the process provided emotional and social support. *"I was able to help [him] on his thesis when he was stressed." "I felt energized and excited about my work after every pair research."*

DISCUSSION

The goals of the pair research system were to improve productivity, informal learning, and collaboration. For productivity, the results suggest that members feel motivated by the process, and do succeed in making progress on their work. For collaboration, members interact with far more people than they normally would, which increases opportunities for further collaboration. For learning, we saw some mentions of specific tools, skills, and work practices, and also learning about other group members and their work and their abilities, which again may lay the groundwork for future collaboration.

It is instructive to look at the differences between the group A and group B deployments, because each had different successes and failures that shed light on how the system could be improved. Group B used the spreadsheet far more effectively than group A because they didn't just rely on email reminders over Saturday and Sunday, but filled out the spreadsheet together at a Friday group meeting. Another contrast was the length of deployment. Group A continued using pair research throughout the spring semester, but group B stopped partly because the group leader is a bottleneck in the current system, having to approve the pairing before emailing it out to the group. On one occasion, the pairing wasn't announced until Thursday, leaving only two days left in the week to actually work. We have since changed the system to send the final pairing automatically.

Even the pair work session may need to happen more automatically. Both group A and group B struggled with fitting pair research into already-busy schedules. Group A experienced 16% failures due to scheduling, and group B stopped after 7 weeks in part because the entire group got busy, not just the group leader. One way to address this would make the entire process happen in one synchronous session, in which members fill out the spreadsheet, immediately determine the pairing, and then immediately break up to work in pairs.

Prior to deployment, it may be important to understand how pair research integrates in the organizational context. Group B may have stopped after 7 weeks in part because the team's reward structure may have recognized and reinforced individual excellence as opposed to team collaboration and learning [8]. Group B's membership may have been unclear [11] or not stable enough to learn and adopt a new collaborative practice [7]. Moreover, Group B's members could have relied on outside resources or support or felt that they were too similar to each other to support each other. Member personality types, such as openness and extraversion [10], and ability to communicate may have also influenced adoption. Assessing the organizational context prior is one way to address this concern.

One co-author's research group, inspired by pair research but not using the spreadsheet matching system, combined group meetings and one-on-one meetings into a single synchronous time block. The group meeting starts with brief updates and requests for ad-hoc meetings with other group members (which are recorded on a whiteboard), and then breaks up into those ad-hoc meetings, which continue until everybody's meeting needs are satisfied. Conducting pair research synchronously may be the right solution for a co-located group, though as groups grow and become geographically distributed, like group A, it becomes more challenging to bring the entire group together at the same time.

Limitations

To design and develop pair research, we deployed the system in two technical labs within universities characterized by high research activity. While the diversity and size of the sample was limited, like other systems designers [21] we found that small deployments are useful for developing a proof of concept and identifying social and technical factors to consider in future designs. Further, we conducted observations throughout the deployment. The advantage to this research approach is the ability to collect in situ data, not just reflective data; the disadvantage is that bias is introduced through participant observation [17].

Future Work

Based on the initial outcomes, we will continue to deploy the system to better understand the social (i.e. size, gender) and technical (i.e. matching algorithm, capturing shared content) factors in academic research as well other domains such as public policy research in government and curriculum development in education. In addition, we understand that pair research likely does not come without costs. We will investigate whether confusion about the ownership of ideas occurs after meetings, whether the method prevents self-directed learning or novices from gaining sufficient expertise to advise others, or whether the method encourages social comparison.

CONCLUSION

This paper presented pair research, a new socio-technical system that pairs members of a work group to work together on each other's projects each week. In two deployments, we found that the system motivates participants, helps them learn about their colleagues, and makes opportunities for further collaboration.

While we have been motivated by the academic research setting, the pairing system may find application to groups in other domains, particularly other kinds of hard knowledge work that involves diverse expertise. In particular, we find pair research to be effective as a form of transient, low-commitment collaboration, especially to overcome hurdles and promote progress on hard tasks by drawing on other people's expertise, effort, and social pressure. We look forward to expanding pair research to other research groups and experimenting in other work settings in future work.

ACKNOWLEDGMENTS

We gratefully acknowledge valuable help and suggestions from Katrina Panovich, Greg Vargas, Geza Kovacs, Hubert Pham, Elena Agapie, the anonymous reviewers, and all the wonderful people in the MIT UID group, the Georgia Tech comp.social lab, and the Northwestern Delta Lab. This work was supported in part by the National Science Foundation under SOCS-1111124 and IIS-1217225. Any opinions, findings, conclusions, or recommendations in this paper are the authors' and do not necessarily reflect the views of the sponsors.

REFERENCES

1. Abdulkadirolu, A., Pathak, P. A., and Roth, A. E. The New York City high school match. *American Economic Review 95*, 2 (May 2005), 364–367.
2. Beck, K. *Extreme programming explained: embrace change*. Addison-Wesley Longman Publishing Co., Inc., Boston, MA, USA, 2000.
3. Belshee, A. Promiscuous pairing and beginner's mind: Embrace inexperience. In *Proc. Agile Development Conference*, ADC '05 (2005), 125–131.
4. Berlin, L., and Jeffries, R. Consultants and apprentices: observations about learning and collaborative problem solving. In *Proc CSCW* (1992), 130–137.
5. Cialdini, R. B. *Influence : the psychology of persuasion*. HarperCollins, 2009.
6. Cirillo, F. *The pomodoro technique*. Lulu.com, 2009.
7. Cohen, W. M., and Levinthal, D. A. Absorptive capacity: a new perspective on learning and innovation. *Administrative Science Quarterly* (1990), 128–152.
8. Edmonson, A. Psychological safety and learning behavior in work teams. *Administrative Science Quarterly 44*, 2 (1999), 350–383.
9. Levine, J. M., and Moreland, R. L. Progress in small group research. *Annual Review of Psychology 41*, 1 (1990), 585–634.
10. McCrae, R. R., and John, O. P. An introduction to the five-factor model and its applications. *Journal of Personality 60*, 2 (1992), 175–215.
11. Mortensen, M., and Hinds, P. Fuzzy teams: Boundary disagreement in distributed and collocated teams. *Distributed Work* (2002), 284–308.
12. Regan, D. T. Effects of a favor and liking on compliance. *Journal of Experimental Social Psychology 7*, 6 (1971), 627–639.
13. Rettig, M. Prototyping for tiny fingers. *Commun. ACM 37*, 4 (Apr. 1994), 21–27.
14. Roth, A., and Sotomayor, M. *Two-Sided Matching: A Study in Game-Theoretic Modeling and Analysis*. Econometric Society Monographs. Cambridge University Press, 1992.
15. Roth, A. E. The evolution of the labor market for medical interns and residents: A case study in game theory. *Journal of Political Economy 92*, 6 (1984), 991–1016.
16. Roth, A. E., et al. Kidney exchange. *Quarterly Journal of Economics 119*, 2 (May 2004), 457–488.
17. Spradley, J. P. *Participant Observation*. Holt, Rinehart and Winston, 1980.
18. Twidale, M. B. Over the shoulder learning: Supporting brief informal learning. *Comput. Supported Coop. Work 14*, 6 (Dec. 2005), 505–547.
19. Virzi, R. A., Sokolov, J. L., and Karis, D. Usability problem identification using both low- and high-fidelity prototypes. In *Proc. CHI* (1996), 236–243.
20. Williams, L., et al. In support of pair programming in the introductory computer science course. In *OOPSLA* (2002), 197–212.
21. Zimmerman, J., Forlizzi, J., and Evenson, S. Research through design as a method for interaction design research in HCI. In *Proc. CHI*, ACM (New York, NY, USA, 2007), 493–502.

Supporting Group Interaction in Museum Visiting

Peter Tolmie, Steve Benford, Chris Greenhalgh, Tom Rodden and Stuart Reeves
Mixed Reality Lab, School of Computer Science, University of Nottingham
Nottingham, United Kingdom
firstname.secondname@nottingham.ac.uk

ABSTRACT

Ethnographic study in two contrasting museums highlights a widespread but rarely documented challenge for CSCW design. Visitors' engagement with exhibits often ends prematurely due to the need to keep up with or attend to fellow group members. We unpack the mechanics of these kinds of phenomena revealing how the behaviours of summoning, pressurizing, herding, sidelining, and rounding up, lead to the responses of following, skimming and digging in. We show how the problem is especially challenging where young children are involved. As an initial prompt we explore two ways in which CSCW could help address this challenge: enabling a more fluid association between information and exhibits; and helping reconfigure the social nature of visiting.

Author Keywords
Museums; collaboration; visiting practices; ethnography.

ACM Classification Keywords
H5.m. Information interfaces and presentation (e.g., HCI)

INTRODUCTION

The appropriate provision of information to support people in activities such as visiting is a significant topic in the design of CSCW systems. It touches numerous fields of work and expertise. It might therefore seem that most of the core requirements associated with group visiting would have been uncovered by now. However, in this paper we want to introduce a feature of information support that has, to date, been left largely undiscussed in the literature, despite its pervasive character.

The issue we want to look at was first uncovered during intensive ethnographic studies at two major museums. At the heart of the problem is the work groups of people, or even couples engage in, in order to preserve the coherence of the group. It reveals some potential issues with existing approaches to physical displays of information that might be open to technological intervention and design.

CSCW'14, February 15 - 19 2014, Baltimore, MD, USA
Copyright 2014 ACM 978-1-4503-2540-0/14/02...$15.00.
http://dx.doi.org/10.1145/2531602.2531619

Discussion in this paper is going to revolve around the ways people manage their engagement with exhibits and with one another in order to keep together as they go around museums. In particular we note that, to accomplish this, members of groups regularly interrupt themselves and one another in their engagements with information regarding the exhibits. As a result members of groups often have to abandon interactions with specific exhibits before those interactions are properly concluded. The fact that they have not yet finished their interactions is made manifest through the way they sometimes try to resist these interruptions or to hasten their mode of consumption. This means that aspects they would have liked to have read about and seen are recurrently being lost to them over the course of a visit.

At heart there is a tension that has to be managed when visiting museums as part of a group. This tension resides between wanting, as an individual, to attend to exhibits and associated information (such as labels, noticeboards and guides), whilst also wanting to preserve the coherence of the group. The tension is exacerbated by the ways in which exhibits and their associated information are routinely physically co-located. This means that leaving the exhibit also requires breaking off from any consumption of that information. In order to delineate the nature of the issue here and the challenge it presents to design we look at certain aspects of how people work to maintain group coherence in museum environments. We also look at some of the ways in which people resist simply complying with that work. We then conclude with some reflections upon different kinds of strategies that might serve to improve the character of support. First of all we consider the implications of this for existing ideas regarding enabling a more fluid association between exhibits and information. Then we move on to exploring ways in which the social nature of visiting might be reconfigured so as to offset some of the tension we have identified.

PREVIOUS WORK

The nature of people's with exhibits and with one another in museums and galleries has been an abiding interest in both CSCW and in the broader HCI community. This interest has spread across a variety of technological agendas. One body of work, for instance, looks at the use of mobile technologies in museums [e.g. 5 &17]. Others focus more broadly upon the support of collaboration [e.g. 14], with some extending this to the ways in which exhibits can be assembled to encourage different kinds of interactions [e.g. 21]. Others again consider the use of different kinds of media to accomplish different ends [e.g. 25], with one especially notable concern being the use of technology to support learning [e.g. 35]. Inevitably the focus of actual studies of such environments has therefore been somewhat varied, according to the interests of the parties involved. Sometimes that interest is centred upon how people move around museums [e.g. 32 & 38]. Sometimes the discussion is more concerned with how people engage with exhibits [1]. Sometimes there is an effort to do both [7]. Yet few studies explicitly attend to how people go around museums together and interact with one another as *groups*. This is the case even though the cooperative work involved in actually managing to keep together as a group is often quite significant. The nature of that work is one of the principal topics of this paper. In cases where group interactions *are* discussed a strong emphasis is put upon the collaborative character of people's engagement with exhibits [e.g. 8]. Some previous (and rather old) studies have documented certain ways in which children can impact on how families progress through museums [e.g. 20 & 36]. However, only one study seems to concretely allude to the kinds of issues we will be focusing on in this paper:

> "younger children pull the adults away from one exhibit toward any other exhibit before they have had a chance to digest the science behind the first exhibit" [24].

Related to all of this a wide variety of different works focus upon the actual provision of technology to support users visiting museums in various ways. This includes: ways of personalizing visits [e.g. 2 & 17]; mechanisms for accessing information [e.g. 4, 9 & 23]; the provision of guidance [e.g. 12 & 39]; and new ways of encouraging interaction [e.g. 18, 27 & 33]. More foundational literature can be seen to examine the constitution of various kinds of *information ecologies* and the situated support of information consumption and use [e.g. 28]. However, the need to support *simultaneously* the management of group interaction, physical movement through space, and engagement with exhibits, largely stands beyond this literature to date. Brown et al [6] and Szymanski et al [35] are amongst the few who have even begun to move in this direction, though without specific explication of the mechanics of managing group coherence. We therefore wish to highlight here what might be seen to constitute an important new challenge for design.

RESOURCES

The materials we shall be drawing upon here relate to a series of studies conducted at two very different but popular and well-known European museums. One of these was the Acropolis Museum in Athens. This is a new, purpose-built museum that presents a significant and valuable collection of artefacts gathered from various chronological periods on the Acropolis. It also includes the much discussed marble friezes from the Parthenon. The museum is a major tourist destination and is visited by people from all over the world as well as various local parties of school children and university students. The other site studied was the Cite de l'Espace in Toulouse. This museum hosts a wide range of exhibits concerned with space exploration. It includes full-scale replicas of rockets and space-stations, together with a large number of highly interactive exhibits designed to enhance visitors' understanding of mankind's relationship with space. The whole complex includes a park, an IMAX cinema and a planetarium and is a popular destination for days out with families, as well as educational visits from all over France. In the year prior to our study a total of 274,680 visitors went to the Cite de l'Espace and over 1.3 million to the Acropolis Museum. Whilst the two sites are, in a variety of ways, very different from one another, it is important to note that at both sites the vast majority of visitors come in groups. For instance, a tiny 3.4% of visitors to the Cite de l'Espace came to the site on their own in 2010. Equivalent figures for the Acropolis Museum are not available but a third of its visitors are made up of organized groups such as tours and school visits. This preponderance of group visits to cultural sites and the importance of its impact upon visiting behaviours has been previously documented by a number of researchers [11, 22, 29].

Two weeks of intensive ethnographic observation were conducted at each of the sites in Spring and Summer 2011. In the initial week at each site a series of sensitizing studies were undertaken, This involved systematic observations of visitor comportment being conducted across all of the principal locations within each site so as to get a gross sense of the kinds of interactions taking place. In the second week at each site visitors entering the museums were recruited at entry and followed systematically around the museum throughout the course of their visit, capturing video recordings of their interactions where appropriate. In these cases the ethnographer acted as an adjunct member of the group so as to get first-hand access to how the visit was organized and reasoned about it as it actually unfolded. Six different groups were followed in this fashion at the Cite de l'Espace and ten at the Acropolis Museum. The resultant data includes just under 50 hours of video recordings of natural action and interaction across the two sites as well as several volumes of fieldnotes. Subsequent analysis of the data adopted an ethnomethodological approach [15]. This involves transcription and extensive fine-grained analysis of situated practices and interactions in order to explicate people's 'ethno-methods'. 'Ethno-methods' refers to the practical, situated exercise of commonsense such that people's activities can be seen to be accountable, organized and recognisable local instantiations of social order. This analysis in turn provided a means of unpacking how the experience and reasoning of specific visitors was being made manifest through their actual situated interactions. As such this work can be seen as part of a growing trajectory of ethnomethodological studies of cultural sites [6, 19].

PRESERVING GROUP COHERENCE – EXAMPLES

In this part of the paper we will first of all present a range of examples illustrative of the kinds of phenomena we are discussing. After that we will explore aspects of these phenomena in greater depth to tease out their workings and the orientations in human interaction they exhibit.

The basic character of the interactions we are looking at here is as follows: A group of people are moving through a public setting where various physical objects are present and are accompanied by information relating to them. One or more of the group stops to look at an object and/or read the information about it. Other members of the group continue to follow a trajectory away from the object. At some point the member(s) of the group who paused to look and read is/are obliged to stop looking and reading in order to follow the other members of the group.

The specific examples from each of the sites we are going to be looking at here have been chosen to illustrate the complex nature of the problem. However, the kind of phenomena we are talking about abound and endless examples of people being dragged away from both information and exhibits were visible in the fieldwork data. Despite the two sites being radically different in a number of respects, the same issues of managing both engagement and group coherence at the same time were recurrently visible in both sites to equal degrees. In fact these issues arose repeatedly amongst all of the different groups followed, regardless of age or group complexion, and were witnessed on numerous occasions during static observations as well. This gives us considerable confidence in proposing that these are issues that visitors continually have to manage when they visit museums in groups.

Example 1: The Acropolis Museum

[In this example an older couple who were approaching retirement age were going round the museum together]

Figure 1: Keeping up with the wife

Both of them are looking at an object on the glass ramp [the first set of displays one encounters in the museum] – They try to peer at it more closely but are asked to step back by a security man – The woman notices an information panel over to one side on the wall relating to the exhibit and points it out to her husband, then she goes over to read it - After a few moments of continuing to look at the exhibit her husband goes over to join her – They stand there reading together for a short while but then the wife finishes and heads off along the display cabinets – The husband glances at his wife then follows her, abandoning reading the panel.

Example 2: The Cite de l'Espace

[In this example the observations were of a family with 3 children: a boy of 12, a girl of 10 and a younger girl of 5 years old]

Figure 2: Keeping up with the youngest child

The family are walking together down l'Allee de l'Infini [a pathway in the park presenting multiple panels demonstrating shifts in scale towards infinity] – The father and the two older children regularly stop to look at the panels showing increasing scale views – The mother and younger daughter are continually ahead, with the little girl pointing to and eager to get to the Ariane rocket [a full size replica visible at the end of the path] – The father and two older children constantly have to move on from panel to panel to keep pace with the mother and the youngest child.

Example 3: The Acropolis Museum:

[Here an older woman in her 50s and her daughter in her 20s are going round the museum together]

Figure 3: a) Reading an information panel; b) Being called over; c) Accounting for the summons

The daughter is stood looking at a part of a frieze in the Roman gallery - Her mother is further down the gallery, reading an information panel (Figure 3a) - The daughter calls out to her mother sotto voce (Figure 3b) - The mother looks round then walks over to her daughter - As she heads over her daughter points to the frieze (Figure 3c) and they both go to look at it together more closely.

Example 4: The Cite de l'Espace

Figure 4: a) Getting left behind & b) Being tacitly summoned by being visibly waited for

The whole family [see Example 2] are looking at an information panel about the Ariane 5 - The two girls stay looking at the panel as the others move on towards the Astralia building [where they are headed to see a film at the IMAX cinema] (Figure 4a) - The mother waits and looks back towards them as the father and son head on (Figure 4b) - The two girls leave the panel and run to catch up with the mother, who falls in behind them once they have arrived.

Example 5: The Acropolis Museum

[Here a Canadian family with two adults in their 40s and their 3 children, a boy and a girl in their teens and a 7 year old girl, are spending the morning in the museum as part of a visit to Athens]

Figure 5: a) & b) Making sure Mum doesn't get left behind

All of the family are grouped around an object on the glass ramp – The mother turns and starts to read an information panel to one side – The rest of the group head off – The youngest daughter looks back and her mother hurries on to catch up with them - They stop and look at an object and the father comments on it briefly – The mother is stood at the back trying to see - As the rest move off the mother looks at the object more closely then starts to read about it - Both of the daughters go back and she looks up and joins them and follows along behind the father and son towards the stairs leading up to the next level.

Example 6: The Cite de l'Espace
[Same family as in examples 2 and 4]

Figure 6: Sacrificing your own interests to the kids

The youngest girl and her sister are in an interactive display where they can look at a screen and see themselves as an astronaut at take off – Their mother is reading an adjacent information panel but is called over by the girls - She tries to help the youngest to make the display work but the girl insists on managing it for herself - The father and son come over as well to join them from a jet-pack display and lean in to watch for a while - Everyone tries to move on but the little girl remains, still trying to push various buttons, so the mother returns to stay with her

Apart from Example 2 each of the above examples shows various members of the group being dragged away from information panels adjacent to the objects they relate to. In Example 2 the display conveys information in its own right. Example 6 is subtly different again. Here the mother does not only allow herself to be called away but then also works to support a 'safe' bifurcation of the group. This ensures that the youngest child continues to be accompanied by at least one parent. Indeed, in this one instance we might say that it is the child, not the adult, who has successfully resisted being moved on. We shall return to this particular matter of handling children later on.

SO WHAT'S GOING ON?

Having introduced the kinds of interactions we are interested in, we shall now proceed to unpack them in more detail. This shall involve teasing out the key interactional features that provide for the ongoing work members of groups engage in to maintain their coherence as a group. As we noted above you can find these sorts of interactions happening, not just in museums, but in pretty well any public setting where groups of people are attempting to navigate through space together. Key to the associated issue we want to unpack is the way in which the work of coherence can result in a necessary truncation of the consumption of information. This truncation is exacerbated by the physical tying of information to related physical objects. To keep the coherence of the group you are obliged to move on from the object and its physical position in space and to thereby move on from the information as well.

Some grossly observable features:

The interactions we are describing here have several important grossly observable characteristics. First of all, they are all about group dynamics and visible attention to one another's rights, responsibilities and mutual accountability. This reflects the following social concerns:

People are accountable for their actions not only to the group and their understanding of what the group is doing and where it is going, but also to various individuals within the group. In all of the above examples it is specific members of the group who make visible to those who are not keeping up that they are in danger of breaching the group's coherence. This may be done explicitly or in the course of their own ordinary progression

Members of groups moving through space together do not routinely have the right to ignore everyone else's movements. However, they do have limited rights to pursue activities on their own, as long as they display due attention to what the others in the group are doing. These rights go hand-in-hand with the matter of accountability. In all of the above examples some presumption of being able to at least look at the exhibits for yourself is manifest. Otherwise the problem of keeping up would not arise and everyone would follow one another around like sheep. In examples 1 and 2 it is the individuals who might fall behind who recognize the danger of extending beyond their rights of separation and who move to rectify the situation for themselves. In examples 4 and 5 other members of the group, in one case the mother, in another the children, actively remind the straying individuals to keep up. In neither case is the right to issue such a summons brought into question. This makes it clear that what is going on is not just about parental rights over children. Instead it's about expectations on the part of all competent members of a group regarding what work everyone in the group should be doing to keep the group together. Examples 3 and 6 are different again. This time it is one member of the group actively summoning another member of the group away from what they are doing to attend to something different instead. Here the unchallenged rights lay with the summoning party. This adds to the complexity of the issue we are describing here because interruption of the consumption of information is about more than just keeping up. What is going on is also about different members of the group exercising a right to interrupt and call away.

Some members of a group may consider themselves responsible for the continuing engagement and group orientation of others in the group, e.g. parents/grandparents of younger children. In example 2 the mother keeps up with the youngest child instead of pausing to look at the panels like her husband and her other children. In example 4 the same mother actively takes it upon herself to shepherd her two daughters. And in example 6 she makes even clearer her willingness to defer her own interests to that of keeping the youngest child happy. She does this by abandoning her own reading to accompany the child in the activity she is pursuing. It is in these kinds of doings that a sense of responsibility is made manifest (to just about anyone caring to take notice, in fact). The summons issued by the youngest child in example 6 trades upon this.

Secondly, it is important to note that the need to preserve group coherence is attended to by orientation as well as by being expressly dragged away. In other words, it is frequently the case that members of a group will notice one another's movements and break engagement with whatever they are doing for themselves so as to maintain suitable proximity. This is made visible in the first two examples, as noted above. What it demonstrates is a careful monitoring of the other members of the group on the part of individual group members. This monitoring is also demonstrated on the occasions where some kind of breach occurs. What happens quite often is that this oriented to expectation of monitoring is disrupted in some way. This can be for a variety of different reasons such as: a) the environment is too dark or cluttered to see what other members of the party are up to; b) because someone gets engrossed in what they are looking at and fails to notice the others have moved away; c) because some other visitor interrupts them to ask them a question; and so on. A to-the-point anecdote was recently provided to the authors where a visitor to the site of Pompeii was following a guided tour wearing a headset through which the guide addressed the members of the party. The visitor in question got involved in looking at some information panels. However, because she could still hear the guide at the same volume within her headset, she did not notice that the rest of the party had moved on. In all of these cases the recognition of the orientation to preserving group coherence is made immediately visible when the breach is recognized. Firstly the individuals concerned look up and then visibly look around with rapid head and body movements in ways that can become increasingly describable as 'frantic'.

Thirdly, these issues can impact anyone in the group. It should not be considered solely a matter of concern to those leading a group or those with children, etc. All members work to keep with the group in various ways. The above examples show variously spouses, parents, siblings and children attending to the same considerations. In other examples not presented here we also saw grandparents and even friends and couples engaging in the same kinds of monitoring and group preservation activities.

Exploring some specific aspects of the work of group coherence:

In the following material we shall look in closer detail at particular ways in which attention to group coherence can become manifest, and how it can result in interrupted consumption of information. Our primary concern in this section is to provide an outline of the kinds reasoning upon which the work of group coherence in museum visiting might be seen to turn. It is important to understand, therefore, that this explication of certain aspects of commonsense reasoning about group coherence is just that: a set of commonsense, member-recognisable categories. It is not being provided as a formal taxonomy of the interactions in play. Nor is it exhaustive. Rather it is provided as a means of making visible various ways in which people may reason about the work of group coherence, even when it is apparently similar phenomena they are reasoning about. Thus it will be found that different descriptions will sometimes overlap simply because members can reason about what is going on in different ways according to circumstance.

Summoning: This aspect involves the physical drawing of one person's attention away from what they are doing by another person. This can be done by means of tapping, gesturing, calling, etc. It is clearly oriented to as a summons and it is visibly difficult for people to ignore a direct summons of this kind. Some members of the group may have special rights of summoning and demand. Parents, for instance, can expressly demand that children 'come along'. An overt summons, where someone is called by name, is particularly hard to ignore. In example 3, for instance, a daughter looking at one exhibit, calls to her mother, who is some way off and looking at an information panel. Even though the mother is currently occupied and the daughter does not make explicit what she wants, the mother's orientation to her name being called as a summons is quite clear. Instead of continuing to read she stops what she is doing and goes to join her daughter. From the point of view of the summoner this is also highly economical, requiring a simple utterance and no displacement at all on their part. In this case the mother does not get to finish reading the panel, which may or may not be of concern to her. At the same time there is potential recompense in terms of the proposed interest of the feature her daughter has called her over to see. This, however, is not the only kind of verbal summons one can see, with others being merely callings by name to remind someone to keep up with the group. This is closer to what we see in examples 4 and 5, even if the reminder is accomplished in those examples by other means.

Pressurizing: A related but more overt form of the above that can be seen in family groups and amongst school parties is sibling and/or peer pressure. Older children often drag younger siblings away by actual tapping, pushing, calling, gesturing, etc. In school parties children can be seen to also act in a similar fashion. This kind of interruption is mostly visible amongst younger interactants, but accomplishes the same result of taking potentially interested consumers of information away from its point of consumption. Between interactants of different ages the pressure to move on is accomplished in more subtle ways, such as the rounding-up visible in example 5.

Herding: In example 4 above, as the rest of their family move on two girls remain behind continuing to look at an information display. Their mother then stops and looks directly back at them, waiting. As the two girls notice her they stop reading and hurry off to join the rest of the group, the mother following along behind them. Several features in particular are worth noting about this. First of all as soon as the girls see their mother waiting they become accountable for any continued delay. Not only have they seen their mother waiting but they have seen their mother seeing that they have seen her waiting and it is this mutual witnessability of the situation that plies pressure so effectively. Having seen their mother waiting there and that she has seen that they have noticed her, just ignoring her is no longer an option. Indeed, ignoring people in these situations can produce more direct interventions e.g. utterances such as 'we've still got loads to see'; 'the film starts in 10 minutes' etc., or coughing, tutting, sighing, and so on. In addition, the waiting ensures that they do not ever become truly split off from the group, which would be a risk if she simply continued with the others and assumed they would follow. Finally, the way the mother waits until they have physically passed her enables her to keep them in view from now on. This also ensures that they know that she is behind them, attending to their progress such that further delay can be directly noted and commented upon. Altogether this sequence of interaction, which involves no spoken words at all, accomplishes neatly a restored group coherence and a form of supervised continuation or, what one might call a form of 'herding'. We also observed instances where members of a group went physically back to loiter next to people in order to achieve the same ends. The use of gaze and spatial position here can equally be seen as a tacit form of summoning. The visible waiting and looking act as the first part of the summons, with movement to re-join counting as the second, compliant part. Of course, what it also ensures is that an ongoing consumption of information is abandoned.

Sidelining: An aspect of group interactions that is related to both pressurizing and herding is the problem of being sidelined. This can lead to the same kinds of tensions between honouring the coherence of the group and trying to get enough time to engage properly with an exhibit. What happens here is that others in the group may block your access to the information/exhibit. We can see this happening in example 5 above. Here a mother who has already been obliged to abandon one exhibit is stuck behind the rest of her family as they look at another one. When they finish and move on she tries to take a look herself, but her daughters come back to ensure she keeps up with them again. This happened at a number of exhibits with this particular family. The mother repeatedly got stuck in a pattern of being pressurized to keep up but then being the last to arrive at the next exhibit. This resulted in her often being sidelined and unable to look at the exhibit more closely because the rest of the family were in the way. Each time they finished she would try to look herself. However, she would then be forced to cut her perusal short as the trajectory adopted by the rest of the group obliged her to abandon looking or rush the engagement. If she did pause she again became accountable for falling behind and therefore subject to further summoning, pressurizing or herding to ensure she kept up. The husband trailing behind his wife in example 1 and the girls trying to read an information panel the rest of the family have been looking at in example 4 also exhibit similar issues. Here the need to abandon interaction with information about an exhibit is itself a result of not being able to get access to it at the same time as the rest of the group.

Rounding up: Note that our previous discussion of example 5 with regard to pressurizing is not the whole story. The ways in which maintaining group coherence can be reasoned about can prove to be quite distinct according to who is looking to keep the group together and who is understood to be lagging behind. For the mother who was being collected by her daughters in example 5, the work being done by her daughters is accountable as a form of pressure being put upon her to keep up. However, for others in the party the work they are doing is equally describable as the work of 'rounding up', because they have noticed a potential breach in the overall coherence of the group. Rounding up, for the rest of the group, looks like some of the group specifically going to locate the laggardly or missing person. This may involve directly pointing out the risk they are posing to keeping the group together. Indeed, it is a blatant exercise of the licence to remind others in the group of their obligation to keep up. This licence extends to all members of the group but is usually tacit in the ways it gets recognized. Thus a part of its exercise may often include some kind of direct summons, with the person in question being called by name. A further feature we can see in example 5 is that the parties doing the rounding up do not necessarily have to be the whole of the group. This being the case, there is a concomitant expectation that those who are not dispatched will hold their position until the other party has joined them rather than moving on. It can, of course, happen that when some members of a group are sent back to get someone else, the rest of the group then carry on moving in the opposite direction. However, this immediately exacerbates the problem of preserving group coherence and becomes accountable in its own right.

The ways in which various people were seen to *respond* to the above aspects of the work of maintaining group coherence are detailed below, ranging from simple compliance with the interruption to wholesale resistance. Once again the aim is to provide some aspects of member reasoning rather than a formal or comprehensive taxonomy.

In particular note here how, as we observed above, accounts for what is going on are not only subject to circumstance but also relate to just who is doing the reasoning:

Following: In examples 1 and 2 the parties who interrupt their own consumption of information in various ways are largely oriented to simply following other members of their party. Should the 'leading individual' move on, that stands as sufficient reason for them to abandon what they are doing in order to keep up. In example 1 it was mostly the wife who was directing the visit and her husband simply made a point of keeping up with her. In example 2 the visit was almost entirely organised around keeping the youngest member of the family happy. In many cases the others therefore allowed her to set the pace and lead the way. Her parents did, however, sometimes intervene to structure this in certain ways, depending upon a broader schedule and the overall direction chosen. We shall discuss the particular character of maintaining group coherence where small children are present in due course. However, a strong corollary of this compliance with the lead of some other party (or parties) in the group is a fairly careful monitoring of their movements. In this way those following can, indeed, be actively seen to be following rather than requiring one of the more active forms of management outlined above. There is another aspect of this willingness to subserve one's interests to someone else when visiting a cultural site such as a museum, however. By abbreviating their own engagement the following parties are potentially seeable as being somehow less interested than the principal party. This is not to ascribe definite preferences to these individuals. Rather it is to say that at least one way of making manifest a lack of interest is to simply follow other members of your party around. The most extreme realization of this is to follow others without showing any manifest engagement with the surrounding exhibits at all.

Skimming: It is, of course, the case that compliance with the lead of other parties can be accomplished without simply abandoning everything the moment you see them moving on. Often the strategies we've outlined for keeping the group together are met with more subtle responses. One such response is to not just stop outright but rather to speed up one's looking at exhibits or consumption of information. This can be accomplished, variously, by rapidly glancing through the rest of the text, rushing through interactions with displays, and so on. Whilst the three others in the family group in example 2 are oriented to keeping up with the mother and youngest child, they do not simply stop looking at the various displays along l'allee d'infini. Instead they manage the situation by 'skimming' through the contents, stopping and starting, as they endeavour to keep pace. There is manifest engagement with the displays but also manifest attention being paid to 'keeping up with the youngest child' such that no-one could call them to account for falling behind. So skimming is an effective strategy for respecting the coherence of the group without abandoning all semblance of interest in the contents of the site.

Digging-in: Usually there is a strong orientation amongst most groups towards an overall compliance with maintaining the coherence of the group. However, on occasion one does witness people trying to resist the pressure to keep up with the rest of the group as it moves on. Summoning, pressurizing, herding, and rounding-up are all manifestations of efforts to maintain group coherence in the face of someone resisting the interruptions to their engagement with information or exhibits to some degree. In example 4, for instance, the two girls, having been sidelined, exhibit reluctance to move on before having a look at the information panel themselves. This results in the mother's intervention so as to ensure they do not get left behind. In example 5 the mother is continually being put under pressure to keep up in all sorts of ways, pressure she is also constantly exhibiting resistance to. What is important to note about digging-in behaviour is that it almost invariably leads to more direct callings to account and/or summonses. It also results in increasing escalation of the kinds of 'bringing to heel' behaviours adopted, with increasingly evident annoyance on the part of those being obliged to stop. The youngest daughter in the family presented in example 4 ultimately resorted to taking her mother by the hand and occasionally trying to pull her along with the rest of them. Similarly the mother in the family presented in various examples at the cite de l'espace frequently took her youngest daughter by the hand in an effort to keep her with them.

The presence in the group of young children can make the work of preserving group coherence particularly troublesome. This makes both breaches and efforts to manage group coherence more overtly visible. It is therefore a particularly useful scenario for being able to elucidate the orderly practices group coherence turns upon. In the following discussion we elaborate further upon some of the observations we have already made:

Managing young children: Something notable in our observations of family groups with young children is the extent to which certain shared orientations to their management are visible across the whole of the family group. Thus and for instance, very young children can be understood by the whole party to have a low 'attention threshold'. In this case members of the group will continually cut short their reading of information / looking at exhibits in order to match their flow to the flow of the child. Example 2 reveals three members of a family doing just this so that they can keep pace with the youngest child and her mother.

Directing the family: Young children can demand a break-off in engagement through things like pointing gestures indicating where they want to go next. Trouble rapidly ensues if these demands are not met so families learn to bow down to the pressure and 'avoid a scene'. They can also insist on staying in one location and resist all of the strategies we were discussing above for moving them on.

Thus they can, in a disproportionate sense, come to direct the trajectory of the whole family through spaces like museums. In example 6 the youngest child gets involved in repeating over and over the same engagement with a simple rocket launch interactive. She not only summons over her mother to watch but then also resists everyone's efforts to move on. Thus, and without any overt discussion, the mother elects to stay with her as she continues to play with the exhibit. The very way in which this election is treated as wholly unremarkable and the group is allowed to bifurcate without discussion speaks volumes. It illustrates just how much this management strategy has become an ordinary aspect of the way this family organizes its days out. And it economically provides for the giving of parental attention when out visiting such that the youngest one will not cause trouble, without simultaneously obliging the whole group to remain by her side.

Preferential rights: What the preceding point makes visible is the question of rights we have already discussed in our grosser observations above. Young children in many family visiting situations have ongoing preferential rights to summon parents. They will get increasingly difficult if parents do not respond, even resorting to trying to physically drag the parent where they want them to go. Parents, by contrast, rarely directly insist or drag in this way. Resistance to this from young children can become quite 'vocal'. Thus what we see unfolding in these situations is not just a capacity to direct the family trajectory. Instead it is an unspoken acceptance that they do, for the present at least, have a right to direct the trajectory in this way, rather than have it become a continuing source of trouble. As we shall be discussing further below, this ceding of rights comes with a definite expiry date, though the exact point at which the right expires is something specific to individual family cohorts.

Keeping Up: Young children's consumption of exhibits can be at high speed, dragging parents / siblings along in their wake. Others in the party may try to look at the information and exhibits as they pass, but, as we have already discussed, they have a primary orientation to accompanying the child. People in this position are accountable also for stopping and looking for themselves and allowing the child to carry on and possibly 'go missing'. Young children going missing is understood by the whole party as a 'serious matter'. It takes precedence over all other activities and everyone is accountable for showing due attention to finding them again. This was seen during our observations on a number of occasions. This amounts to another implicit pressure to avoiding letting the child become lost in the first place. Thus, with regard to the issue of interrupted engagement with information and exhibits, this means that, for members of families with young children, you have to grab what opportunities you can to look and read. There is, however, a constant expectation that you may be obliged to move on.

Acquiring a sense of coherence: Something we noted above is the fact that, whilst rights for directing the trajectory of the group are at least partially ceded to young children whilst they *are* young, this is usually a temporary arrangement. Understandings of how to attend to group coherence are matters children are inducted into as much as anything else. So, we saw in example 4 how the youngest child in that family, albeit in the company of her sister, was effectively called to account for not keeping up. This is at least one way in which young children can begin to acquire a sense of accountability for attending to the coherence of the group. When they themselves breach it they too can be called to account, jollied along, nagged, and a range of other parental herding activities, that stop short of physical dragging along (as observed above). All of these things do, of course, happen, as well as the ceding of certain disproportionate rights for governing the trajectory of the group through space. An upshot of this is that even young children are subject to a certain amount of disruption in their engagement with information and exhibits. Thus the management of such interruptions and the adoption of strategies to minimize their impact is something else into which they are inducted over time.

Beyond the various matters of management and breaching discussed above, the importance of preservation of group coherence is recurrently visible through a range of other phenomena. This includes things such as waiting behaviors, running to catch up, watching where the others go, calling one another together, and so on. It should be noted that separation *is* allowed within groups but with clear and accountable limits such that your engagement with exhibits and information is continually open to being interrupted by others in the group. This can be in order to bring to your attention things they've noticed (as in example 3). It can also be about keeping you in line for preservation of the group coherence (as was the case in examples 4 and 5). Of particular importance is that separation is rarely tolerated once line of sight is broken. This is made manifest by the way that, if people do fall out of the line of sight, someone will actively say 'where is X?'. Meanwhile, if someone in a group realizes they have fallen behind they will rapidly move to disregarding any potential objects of interest in the environment. At this point they will instead focus their efforts upon trying to locate the rest of their group.

REVISITING GROUP VISITING

The data discussed above, gathered in two major museums, highlights a tension that may serve to present an interesting challenge for design. The tension in question is that the work undertaken to solve one problem – *the management of group coherence* – can give rise to a different kind of problem – *the interruption of engagement with information and exhibits*. We now consider the implications of this finding for the design of future visiting experiences and the collaborative technologies to support them.

The first implication is quite simply to recognize the widespread nature of the challenge: that groups of visitors frequently struggle to interleave their engagement with exhibits and accompanying information with their social interactions with peers. At the very least, it is important to avoid designing experiences that exacerbate this tension. For instance, assuming long dwell times at exhibits or arranging exhibits in a way that requires members of a group to be out of line-of-sight for significant periods may cause trouble. However, such principles are by and large already well known to museum experience designers. What is perhaps more interesting, and certainly more relevant to CSCW, is to consider the implications for new collaboration technologies. We explore various possibilities under two broad approaches: 1) how a more fluid association between information and exhibits might enable visitors to better interleave the informational and social aspects of visiting; and 2) how we might reshape the social nature of the visit.

A fluid association between exhibits and information

Part of the problem here lies in the tight coupling of exhibits to associated information. Placing labels, placards and other informative signs at an exhibit obviously requires visitors to remain there so as to read them. This may even require them to prolong their stay in order to fully engage with both the exhibit and the information. Recently interest has grown in location-based technologies in museums, from QR codes and RFID tags that trigger information when near an exhibit, to full-blown augmented reality with digital images directly overlaid on exhibits. Whilst intended to deliver information when most relevant, our analysis suggests that this may exacerbate the tension we have identified. At the other extreme, visitors can carry both traditional and digital guidebooks with them as they move between exhibits, affording flexibility as to when they access information. However, looking up information while on the move can be challenging and it becomes more difficult to associate detailed information with fine-grained features of an exhibit.

We suggest an alternative approach that involves a more fluid association between information and exhibits, combining elements of delivery in context with access on the move. Recent explorations of designing 'trajectories' through a sculpture garden enabled pairs of visitors to receive a multisensory experience of each sculpture before accessing official guide information as they walked away from it [12]. Drawing inspiration from this, we propose that designers should explicitly differentiate (and that mobile technologies should directly support) a fluid approach that distinguishes between four classes of information:

- Information that is delivered in advance of first encountering an exhibit, for example that advertises it, summarises its relevance, or guides the visitor to it;
- Information delivered while at an exhibit, for example augmented reality interactions that guide or amplify the immediate viewing experience;
- Information to be carried away from the exhibit and consumed on the move, especially when visitors are called away by peers. For example, an augmented reality presentation may morph into a virtual reality presentation as the visitor steps away from an exhibit.
- Information to be accessed later on, possibly in a quite different context such as at home or in a classroom. This might include souvenirs, virtual reconstructions, or access to supplementary sources of information.

This *temporally* structured approach is firmly grounded in research on the sequential order of visiting [10]. It also reflects existing strands of research in ubiquitous computing that explore ways in which to break the traditional use of proximity to relate exhibits and associated information whilst supporting access over time [31]. We believe it can increase the flexibility with which visitors access information regarding exhibits and enable them to more gracefully interleave information consumption with their engagement with fellow visitors. For examplethey may complete their reading while walking away or resume it some time later on. In short, it may be possible to bridge the physical and digital worlds by *associating* information with an object rather than it being *bound* to the object by co-location. This offers the possibility of maintaining a fluid association between the physical and digital worlds. In that way the fixity of an object in space no longer has to equate to fixity of consumption of the information about the object that is first encountered in that space.

Reconfiguring the social nature of visiting

Our second, complementary approach is expressly focused upon the social relationships between the visitors themselves. The importance of supporting collaboration in museums and galleries has been widely recognized in CSCW. The focus of much of this work has been on designing collaboration with and immediately around exhibits. This includes extensive interest in tabletop and tangible interfaces as natural enablers of collaboration [9, 16]. It also includes recognition of the challenges of deploying headphones in group visits. Attempts to overcome such challenges have included techniques like eavesdropping [13 & 35] where awareness of what others are doing can actually serve to ameliorate some of the pressures to maintain proximity. In response to ethnographic studies in museums and galleries [21] there is also a general recognition of the need to design interaction with spectators in mind [30].

While supporting collaboration through and around exhibits should remain an important focus, we wish to draw attention to wider possibilities concerned with enabling groups to coordinate their activities across exhibits. One possibility lies in promoting awareness of others' activities.

This might include things like signaling people are currently busy but will be available in a short while. This may in turn encourage some visitors to delay interruptions until a more opportune moment, although we suspect that this may prove challenging for parent-child interactions.

Another possibility that we wish to emphasise is to restructure to the group experience. The professional tour guide is an established feature of many museums and provides a range of services to visiting groups from directly delivering interpretative material, to answering questions, to coordinating the progress of the group. Our studies have revealed examples in which some group members already assume aspects of being a tour guide. Parents, in particular, may take responsibility for coordinating a visit, ensuring that members of the party do not get lost, while also furnishing information about exhibits and answering questions. This raises the prospect as to how we might better support and also reward visitors in this role. Might we provide them with additional information to convey to others or use to help them engage with exhibits, for example, giving parents additional nuggets of information to pass on to children. This, of course, needs to be flexible enough to support a range of different family dynamics with different ages of children also impacting on interaction in various ways [34].

We conclude our discussion of this approach with a further intriguing possibility for future work – that of 'gifting' experiences to others. Previous studies have shown the extent to which group visits can be occasioned by special events such as people's birthdays or anniversaries [10]. This opens up the possibility of visitors customizing aspects of the experience such as information delivered through mobile devices for others in the party. This might include things like choosing their favourite exhibits, highlighting new ones not seen before, or adding personal references. While the idea of personalizing visiting experiences may be familiar, the approach of getting one group member to personalize for another has not been widely discussed. This approach may be particularly appropriate as it could serve to strengthen people's sense of accountability to one another. Those giving the experience would have a vested interest in seeing it completed, while those receiving would see a need to demonstrate engagement. Thus approaches such as supporting informal guides or gift experiences may mitigate problems with interruption by demanding a greater 'buy in' to the experience.

CONCLUSION

An ethnographic study of visitor interactions in two contrasting museums has revealed what would appear to be a widespread, important, and relatively undiscussed tension in group visits to public spaces such as museums. This tension resides in the way that the management of group coherence in public spaces may result in visitors prematurely disengaging from exhibits and/or related information. Through a series of examples, we have unpacked the various ways in which the maintenance of group coherence becomes manifest. This includes the various ways in which group members attempt to summon, pressurize, herd, sideline, and round up other members of their party. We have also noted, in turn, how those other members are variously seen to respond, by simply following, skimming or sometimes by digging in. We have taken particular note of how this tension between the orientation to group coherence and the interest in engagement with exhibits can be further aggravated by the presence of young children.

Interruptions of engagement are not, of course, inevitably a problem in their own right. Previous research has pointed out the ways in which interruptions can have a range of situated understandings and consequences that preclude from seeing them as necessarily undesirable [37]. Furthermore, as pointed out by [26] short dwell times in front of exhibits does not necessarily mean that information has not been absorbed. However, so much as they do limit the scope for engaging with information about exhibits that might otherwise be considered desirable, we have briefly outlined some strategies that might be pursued in designing future support. These have been grouped under the two complementary and general approaches of creating a more fluid association between information and exhibits while also potentially reconfiguring the social nature of visiting. At this stage these suggestions are necessarily nascent. However, the primary concern to emphasise here is the way in which visitors have to manage multiple matters as they go around museums. For members of groups, group coherence is one of the principal things that have to be managed. Engagement with exhibits is another. In view of the fact that one can regularly witness manifest resistance to being moved on by the group one can see that there clearly is a potential tension here. This alone indicates that there is still plenty of room here for improved support of group visiting in order to enhance the visiting experience. These findings are therefore intended to sensitise designers to the complex challenges of social visiting while also identifying some initial avenues for research into CSCW technologies that may offer some promise.

ACKNOWLEDGMENTS

This research was supported by the EC FP7-IST collaborative project CHESS, No. 270198. Our thanks also to the staff and visitors at the Cite de l'Espace in Toulouse, France and The Acropolis Museum in Athens, Greece.

REFERENCES

1. Bannon, L J, et al (2005) Hybrid design creates innovative museum experiences. *Communications of the ACM* 48(3): 62-65
2. Basile, P, et al (2009) SpIteR: A Module for Recommending Dynamic Personalized Museum Tours, in *Proc* WI-IAT '09, IEEE, Washington, DC, 584-587
3. Bell, G, (2002) *Making Sense of Museums*, Intel Labs

4. Blöckner, et al (2009) Please touch the exhibits!: using NFC-based interaction for exploring a museum, *MobileHCI '09*, ACM
5. Brown, B & Chalmers, M (2003) Tourism and mobile technology, *ECSCW'03*, 335-354, Kluwer
6. Brown, B, et al (2003) Lessons from the Lighthouse: collaboration in a shared mixed reality system. *CHI 2003,* pp.577-584
7. Callaway, C, et al (2005) Personal Reporting of a Museum Visit as an Entrypoint to Future Cultural Experience, *IUI 05,* pp. 275-277
8. Ciolfi, L, & Bannon, L (2002) Designing interactive museum exhibits: Enhancing visitor curiosity through augmented artifacts, in *Proc European Conference on Cognitive Ergonomics.* (Catania, Italy), 311–317.
9. Correia, N, et al (2010) A multi-touch tabletop for robust multimedia interaction in museums, in *Proc ITS '10*, ACM, New York, 117-120
10. Crabtree et al (2013) "How many bloody examples do you want?!" – Fieldwork and Generalisation, *ECSCW '13*, Springer
11. Falk, H J, & Dierking, L D (1992) *The Museum Experience,* Whalesback Books, Washington
12. Fockler, P, et al (2005) PhoneGuide: museum guidance supported by on-device object recognition on mobile phones, *Proc MUM '05*, ACM, New York, 3-10
13. Fosh, L., Benford, S., Reeves, S., Koleva, B., & Brundell, P. (2013) "See Me, Feel Me, Touch Me, Hear Me": Trajectories and Interpretation in a Sculpture Garden, *CHI '13*, Paris, France, ACM.
14. Fuks, H, et al (2012) Collaborative museums: an approach to co-design, *CSCW '12*, 681-684, ACM
15. Garfinkel, H, (1967) *Studies in Ethnomethodology*, Prentice-Hall
16. Geller, T, (2006) Interactive Tabletop Exhibits in Museums and Galleries, *IEEE Computer Graphics and Applications* (vol. 26 no. 5), pp. 6-11, IEEE Press
17. Grinter, R E, et al (2002) Revisiting the visit: understanding how technology can shape the museum visit, *CSCW '02*, ACM, New York, 146-155
18. Hall, T & Bannon, L (2005) Designing ubiquitous computing to enhance children's interaction in museums, *Proc* IDC '05, ACM, New York, 62-69
19. Hemmings, T, et al (2000) Task, Talk and Closure: Situated learning and the use of an 'interactive' museum artifact, *Local Educational order; ethnomethodological studies of knowledge and action*, Benjamins
20. Hensel, K A (1987) Families in a museum: Interactions and conversations at displays, Unpublished Doctoral Dissertation, Columbia University
21. Hindmarsh, J, et al (2005) Creating Assemblies in Public Environments: Social Interaction, Interactive Exhibits and CSCW. *CSCW Journal, 14 (1)*, Kluwer
22. Hope, T, et al (2009) Familial collaborations in a museum,. *CHI 2009*, Boston, MA, USA
23. Hornecker E, & Stifter, M (2006) Digital backpacking in the museum with a SmartCard, in *Proc CHINZ '06*, ACM, New York, 99-107
24. Hsi, S & Fait, H (2005) RFID Enhances Visitors' Museum Experience at the Exploratorium, *Communications of the ACM*, Sept 2005/ 48 (9), 60-65
25. Luff, P, et al (2004) Only touching the surface: creating affinities between digital content and paper, *CSCW '04*, 523-532, ACM
26. McManus, P M (1989) Oh, yes, they do: How museum visitors read labels and interact with exhibit texts, *Curator: The Museum Journal*, *32*(3), 174-189
27. Naemura, T, et al (2010) Mixed reality technologies for museum experience, *Proc* VRCAI '10. ACM, New York, 17-20
28. Nardi, B & O'Day, V (1999) *Information Ecologies: Using Technology with Heart*, MIT Press
29. Petrelli, D, & Not, E (2005) User-centred Design of Flexible Hypermedia for a Mobile Guide: Reflections on the HyperAudio Experience. *User Modelling and User Adapted Interaction.* 15 (2005), 303-338
30. Reeves, S., Benford, S., O'Malley, C., (2005) Designing the Spectator Experience, *CHI 2005*, ACM
31. Semper, R, Exploratorium, & Spasojevic, M (2002) The electronic guidebook: Using portable devices and a wireless web-based network to extend the museum experience, http://www.museumsandtheweb.com/mw2002/papers/semper/semper.html
32. Serrell, B (1994) The Question of Visitor Styles. In: S. Bitgood (Ed.). *Visitor Studies: Theory, Research, and Practice*, *6*(1), 48-53. Jacksonville AL
33. Sparacino, F (2004) Scenographies of the past and museums of the future: from the wunderkammer to body-driven interactive narrative spaces, in *Proc MULTIMEDIA '04*, ACM, New York, 72-79
34. Sterry, P & Beaumont, E (2006) Methods for studying family visitors in art museums: A cross-disciplinary review of current research, *Museum Management and Curatorship*, *21*(3), 222-239
35. Szymanski, M, et al (2008) Sotto Voce: Facilitating Social Learning in a Historic House. *Comput. Supported Coop. Work* 17, 1 (February 2008), 5-34
36. Taylor, S M (1986) Understanding processes of informal education: a naturalistic study of visitors to a public aquarium, Unpublished Doctoral Dissertation, UC Berkeley
37. Tolmie, P et al (2008) '"Are you watching this film or what?": interruption and the juggling of cohorts'. In *Proc. CSCW 2008,* ACM, 257-266
38. Véron, E, & Levasseur, M (1983) Ethnographie de l'exposition: l'espace, le corps et le sens, BPI, Centre Georges Pompidou, Paris
39. Wakkary, R, & Hatala, M (2007) Situated play in a tangible interface and adaptive audio museum guide, *Personal and Ubiquitous Computing*, v.11 n.3, p.171-191, February 2007

Trustworthy By Design

Bran Knowles[1], Mike Harding[1], Lynne Blair[1], Nigel Davies[1], James Hannon[2], Mark Rouncefield[1], John Walden[2]
[1] Lancaster University, Lancaster, UK, and [2] InTouch Ltd, Morecambe, UK
bran@highwire-dtc.com, hardingm@comp.lancs.ac.uk, lb@comp.lancs.ac.uk, nigel@comp.lancs.ac.uk, james@intouch-ltd.com, m.rouncefield@lancaster.ac.uk, john@intouch-ltd.com

ABSTRACT
Driven by changes in working practices and technology trends, organizations are increasingly reliant on mobile workers and the data they capture. However, while significant work has been carried out on increasing the usability of mobile devices and applications, little attention has been paid to the quality of data captured by mobile workers. If this data is inaccurate or untrustworthy, serious consequences can ensue. In this paper we study a system targeted at mobile workers in the highways sector that is deliberately designed to increase the accuracy and trustworthiness of the data collected. The resulting Inspections application has been very positively received by workers and we present lessons that we believe can be applied to other applications of this type.

Author Keywords
Trust, data collection, mobile computing, mobile work, highways maintenance, ethnography

ACM Classification Keywords
H.5.m. Information Interfaces and Presentation (e.g. HCI): Miscellaneous

General Terms
Human Factors; Design; Measurement.

INTRODUCTION
While the average citizen rarely considers such issues, the drains (or gullies) that keep our streets from flooding accumulate silt and debris over time, requiring regular cleaning to maintain safe conditions. Collecting accurate information on these gullies is important to improve maintenance operations and to meet legislative requirements (e.g. [21]), but it is also a difficult data management problem for the highways contractors involved. Firstly, these contractors must locate the gullies they are responsible for, which requires collection of these assets over a large area. Secondly, contractors have to keep track of which are cleaned, when, and when they might need to be cleaned again.

CSCW'14, February 15–19, 2014, Baltimore, Maryland, USA.
Copyright © 2014 ACM 978-1-4503-2540-0/14/02...$15.00.
http://dx.doi.org/10.1145/2531602.2531699

Traditionally, paper records were used to record this information, but increasingly mobile tools have been introduced to help with data capture. First generation solutions recorded instances of gully cleaning through linking of GPS and sensors that detected when a maintenance truck was actively cleaning. Second generation solutions added extra buttons that allowed operators to input additional relevant information, e.g. 'Gully is blocked'. More recently, third generation mobile management tools have emerged for the collection of asset data histories and integration with multiple forms of asset data.

Our interest for this paper is not so much to explore the ins and outs of gully collection — as fascinating as we have grown to think it is — but rather to explore the elements of design that enable accurate, and above this, *trusted* data collection in this domain, with a view toward applying these more generally to other mobile data capture domains. The issue of trust in data collected in the field is of critical importance to many organizations. For example, in the context of gullies, accurate data can significantly improve the efficiency and effectiveness of maintenance — potentially helping to avert serious flooding in extreme cases. Additionally, if more mundanely, accurate data can reduce the need for, and therefore the cost of, maintenance by some 80 percent according to recent estimates. Trusted data is also critical in a wide range of domains such as health, policing, environmental monitoring, surveying and disaster management where inaccurate or untrustworthy data from the field can have serious consequences.

However, verifying data collected in such domains, is challenging — how do you check the accuracy of the data collected without incurring significant extra cost? Indeed, in many cases post-hoc verification of data collected in the field is simply not possible. For example, in health scenarios there is almost certainly no way to go back and check that the initial data captured on a patient at the scene was accurate. Similarly, for gullies, knowing when they became blocked relative to an inspection is a difficult task. As a result, a key challenge is to collect, at the outset, accurate data in which organizations can place significant trust. This trusted data, as we will show, links with a range of other important qualities to do with successful completion and management of work, and can change for the better the way business process is organized.

In this paper, we describe the development of a third generation mobile data collection system (Inspections), which has been built and deployed since May, 2011, in a total of five

Figure 1. Using the iPad app on site.

locations. We begin by describing the extensive ethnographic fieldwork that inspired our focus on trust and informed the requirements of our system design. Next, we describe the system features in terms of how they respond to the particularities of gully maintenance work, and how these features are intended to contribute toward accurate data. Finally, we use trust as an analytical lens for reflecting on lessons learned from our experience in creating a successful mobile asset collection system, and from this, develop several principles of successful system design that can be applied to a range of domains. We hope to show that trust is not easily retrofitted into systems, but that when trust is a clear design aim throughout the development process, it can be successfully engineered by carefully attending to requirements of the application domain whilst exploring the unique affordances of mobile technology.

RELATED WORK AND NOVELTY

Trust is a familiar if not well-developed concept in the CSCW literature, particularly as it relates to the difficulties of trust surrounding remote work activities. Although precedents for such inquiry exist (e.g. [18, 19, 34, 35]), recent mobile technologies innovation presents new opportunities for investigation.

We adopt a definition of trust fitting with [13], i.e. trust is a subjective assessment of reliability, and we explore trust specifically as it relates to 'trusted data' in the context of developing quality systems. Our research engages with a multidisciplinary body of trust literature that has resulted in a range of competing understandings and theoretical frameworks (e.g. [3, 4, 14, 19, 25, 43, 46]). In contrast to these theoretical angles on trust, we approach the subject from a practical perspective, exploring the concept as an explicit design goal of technological systems that can produce tangible benefits to organizations.

The principle novelty of our work is exploring trust as a complex and emergent phenomenon resulting from design decisions related, but not limited to, the goal of producing *accurate data*. Furthermore, as there is very little research in the way of broadly applicable principles for developing systems that work, whether or not they pertain to the role of trust in doing so, this paper offers a unique contribution to the vast community of researchers who develop such systems.

Given our chosen focus on mobile solutions for producing accurate data as a prerequisite for trusted data, it is worth contextualizing our contribution within not only trust literature, but also within literature related to the challenge of accurate mobile data capture. Many previous studies related to accurate data capture report on the use of cheap and relatively basic mobile phones, such as can be deployed in resource-poor scenarios (e.g. healthcare [26, 28] and business [36] in the developing world). In recent years there has been an increased interest in smartphones for data capture, though many of these studies focus on data capture for purposes of crowd-sourcing and participatory sensing [6, 20], experience capture [41], feedback [12], etc., in which accuracy and trust play a less critical role. Most data collection of governmental and/or business importance (such as in our chosen highways maintenance domain) has historically been done using Windows Mobile data collection devices (DCDs), such as those we are familiar signing when receiving a package delivery. Our system, however, leverages the affordances of commodity consumer hardware, i.e. smartphones, for generating accurate data collection.

While we have made clear that our interest is primarily but not always in highways maintenance work itself, there is little existing CSCW work in this area to draw from in terms of design insights for a data collection system in this domain. Liu et al's [22] study of public service workers in Seattle examines a number of different public service workers with only a marginal interest in road maintenance. And whilst [16] does concern itself with roads, the emphasis is entirely on safety and document work rather than standard, manual maintenance work. Our understanding of design issues related to this domain, therefore, result directly from our own ethnographic research, detailed below.

FIELDWORK

In this section we document some of the empirical issues about trust — how trust is manifested in various observed interactions in the workplace — by presenting some of the ethnographic findings from our fieldwork on aspects of highway maintenance and repair. The fieldwork was not only helpful for generating insight into lack of trust, but also how this lack of trust was remedied in order to accomplish work as a practical everyday matter. In the process, is it possible to identify the important role of trust in such organizational work, how people 'perform' trust, how it is instantiated in various paper and electronic documents and how it enters into everyday work through aspects of planning, coordination and awareness (cf. [14]). We include findings from the wider context of highways maintenance and repair, within which sit gully maintenance activities, to provide necessary context for what has ultimately informed the design of our gully intervention. After all, this context is the basis of our inspiration for focusing on trust. Having drawn out some insights from general highways maintenance work, we focus specifically on the nature of gully maintenance work and elicit further specific insights.

Methods

Our fieldwork involved informal, semi-structured interviewing (asking about work and trust incidents) and periods of observation (shadowing highways inspectors or highways maintenance gangs as they went about their everyday work). The (ongoing) fieldwork reported here was carried out by two ethnographers at seven different sites in the UK over the course of a year and amounted to approximately 70 interviews (of differing durations) and approximately three months worth of observation. Interviews were transcribed and fieldnotes typed up and examined for broad, recurring themes which acted not as precursors to the development of theory but as broad requirements for design. Of particular interest was the detailed explication of the work of the highways inspectors (employed by the council) and road maintenance and gully clearance gangs (employed by the contractor).

We look to our fieldwork to reveal instances of how trust is woven into the fabric of everyday organizational life — or not; instances of how trust is achieved in everyday work — or not; and what sort of things produce trust and trustability — or distrust and suspicion. In our fieldwork studies we paid attention to the social process of trust production, to specify the social mechanisms which generate trust and to examine and document the various ways in which trust is woven into the fabric of everyday organizational life as part of the taken for granted moral order [15].

Behind this work is the idea that electronic devices of various kinds might be used to improve the work process, so our interest in understanding the details of everyday work and how trust is manifested is as a precursor to design — to move from a current paper based system to an electronic system of some kind. Our exploration of issues of trust in road maintenance began by identifying several different stakeholders or parties (or 'users') between whom and for whom issues of trust arise. One major stakeholder is the public who obviously use the roads. The 'council' whose staff initiate and inspect (and sometimes carry out) the work and who are most likely to face complaints from the public is another stakeholder. Our final stakeholder is the contractor who carries out the road maintenance work. In the section to follow, we describe these roles in the context of how they contribute toward an overall organizational workflow, and how this workflow reveals potential trust issues relevant to the design of a technological intervention.

Trust issues within highways maintenance work

Defects needing repair or maintenance are identified via two mechanisms: council highways inspectors locate them during the course of their inspections routines, or members of the public call in with complaints. When reported by the public, an inspector will have to go out and examine it to determine that it is, in fact, a defect and decide what action is needed to remedy it. At the moment, this is necessary because reports are made over the phone and are not accompanied by photographic evidence and a time/location stamp, which might serve to verify these claims.

Defects are then logged on the local council's asset management system and allocated a due date according to the level of danger it poses to the public. Once receiving a list of defects, contractors are expected to complete them by their due date. Schedulers, who are responsible for allocating jobs to their team of gangs, reported suspecting the council of "artificially escalating" jobs to force the contractors to work faster. What councils fail to realize, they argue, is that escalating jobs reduces overall efficiency, requiring gangs to run around like "headless chickens". There is a perception that public pressure, and a greater role for the public, is a driver of inefficient scheduling: *"You're then empowering people that don't really know a lot about the job. And then everyone wants everything done outside their own house... People that are actually paid to make decisions don't make decisions"* (Scheduler).

The contractor's highway maintenance gangs are given a list of jobs to complete (either for the week or for the day). While onsite, gangs will typically be visited every day by their own supervisor — who checks for compliance with safety regulations and ensures work is being carried out according to plan — as well as by a council inspector, who they will have to phone to get permission for deviations from the schedule. Throughout the day, gangs' locations may be monitored via tracking devices: a feature that allows monitoring in the absence of trust.

What seems especially notable in highway maintenance work, an observably physically demanding job, is the sheer amount of paperwork involved. When a gang arrives onsite, they go up and down the street looking for the markings left by the inspector. They find the job, and begin filling out paperwork:

- Two Minute Risk Assessment (mandatory, all): These need to be done for each job (each street).
- Site Briefing (mandatory, per day): These need to be signed by all gangers (i.e. each member of the gang), one per day. They have to list the kind of Traffic Management™ they will use, referring to the diagram numbers in the TM book.
- Traffic Management Audit (mandatory, per judgment): Usually traffic management audits are completed by Inspectors. But sometimes the gang will arrive onsite and feel they cannot proceed without contacting the Supervisor to get him to come to site to complete a traffic management audit.
- Permit to dig (mandatory, if digging): This is completed by the Supervisor. If a crew finds unexpectedly that they need to dig, they will have to contact the Supervisor, who will then have to deliver it to site.

- Ordering materials (as needed): If for some reason they have run out of materials, the gang will have to contact the Supervisor to get an order number for new materials.

Then they complete the work and fill out more paperwork:

- Record sheet (mandatory, all): Gangs need to record who the operatives were, weather conditions, the actual works carried out (and how they may have differed from the job description), time on and off site, plant used, material used, and whether it was a temporary or permanent fix.

Completed work is reported back to the council, along with all of this documentation. In some cases, the council will then send an inspector out to verify the completion of these jobs before removing them from the system. The public is perceived as aggressively litigious, and management ensures the gangs spend time documenting their work: *"I'd rather have them not do as much work in the day than have a 15 grand's worth insurance claim."* Contractors understand that the public is not always aware of all the repairs that have been made, and were keen to get a system to enable them to *"actually go to a member of the public if they like and say, 'Look, this is what we've done.'"*

This lack of trust and the apparent need to continually inspect work has major implications for the efficiency of highways maintenance. As a result, it has major cost implications, resulting in an estimated overspend of tens of millions of pounds per year, or approximately 30% of total expenditure (by our calculations). As schedulers and gangers themselves have noted, efficiency is not easily increased through top down measures (e.g. escalating jobs), and often result in a cycle of distrust. By not trusting the contractor to get work done efficiently, the council ends up decreasing the contractors' efficiency; this then decreases the council's trust in the contractor's ability to deliver jobs on time. It has also apparently decreased contractors' trust in the council. Like 'the boy who cried wolf', contractors may over time be less inclined to take seriously the deadlines set by the council, potentially increasing the chance of instances of unreliability with more damaging consequences to accrued trust. In contrast, were the council to trust contractors, efficiency would result as a natural consequence of empowering people who are best able to make decisions, thereby catalyzing a virtuous circle of trust. The design challenge, it would seem, is providing those with managerial control (e.g. the council over schedulers, supervisors over gangers) a *reason* to place this trust in workers.

The emphasis on continuing and continual audit [30, 31, 40], the importance of recording activity, and the importance of paperwork as a permanent record of that activity, points to further interesting issues regarding trust (and distrust). Our analysis reveals that 'trust' resides in these different paper documents in various ways. On a basic level, documents handle information; information about defects, various assets, or activity occurring around these assets (e.g. when a road was last checked). Trust, here, relies on data being accurate or checkable in various ways. Documents seem to enable trust in part by creating a 'stratified trace' of the orderliness of activities. A document provides history, in this case of a stretch of road; but that historical record is only trustworthy as a result of lower level instantiations of trust: trust in location, trust in the represented order of events, and so on. A document further acts as a coordinating device, and trust placed in that document can be translated into an appropriate organizational formulation — what needs to be done, by whom and when it needs to be done by.

These insights reveal several important trust considerations, which served to guide our initial thoughts about development of a mobile data capture system intended to increase trust between various parties:

- *Supporting the identification and persistent storage of evidence.* This evidence is the kind of evidence that people use to make reliability assessments — a key metacognition in the formulation of trust.
- *Understanding and graphing the complexity of interdependent processes and relationships to deliver on organizational assertions.* Understanding processes provides the context that is necessary for individuals to evaluate the equitability of the process, identify worker expertise and competencies in which trust might be placed, and share relevant information for successful completion of work.
- *Providing trust warnings in the form of data visualizations and inline user interfaces to involved stakeholders.* Realtime evidence capture will be used to prepare people for possible failures to deliver on expectations, mitigating the erosion of trust between parties.
- *Visualizing the impact of individuals' actions throughout the system and process.* This will invoke social scripts, which will make people more accountable to themselves and to one another. In turn, this accountability will likely lead to greater integrity of individuals. Furthermore, this visual feedback is necessary to continually reinforce this integrity. Ultimately, this may provide one mechanism for generating a *reason* to trust.

Development of our mobile data capture system for gully maintenance was inspired and guided by this understanding of trust in the context of the highways maintenance sector, which we formulated over the course of approximately two years of ethnographic research as part of the development of a separate but related works orders management system. Further fieldwork was undertaken over the course of several months (by two ethnographers) to explore the particularities of gully cleaning.

Unique aspects of gully maintenance

The core responsibility of gully gangs is to ensure that water is able to drain into and flow through gullies. In addition to cleaning gullies, gangers must also repair damaged lids. In instances when they cannot repair a lid with the materials they have on their trucks (e.g. if they run out of a particular type of lid), they must generate a work order for another crew to complete at a later date. The overall workflow of the process is as follows. A gang is given a list of streets requiring gully maintenance. They go up and down each of these streets, stopping at each accessible gully. A ganger lifts a lid off of the gully, blasts water down the gully to break up any sediment, sucks up the liquid to remove the silt, and runs water through to check whether it is flowing properly. This process is repeated as needed until it is flowing properly. Then the gangers get back in the truck and drive up to the next gully and clean/repair it. They do as many gullies as they can do in a given day. If they are not on track to complete all of the gullies within a given timeframe as agreed by the council and contractor, additional gangs may be brought on to complete the work.

In addition to the trust issues endemic to highways maintenance work generally, we were able to derive additional trust issues worth considering in the context of gully maintenance. The most noticeable feature of this particular work is the way in which decision making opportunities are effectively designed out of the process. Gangers work to a cyclical cleaning regimen, which they follow blindly. While this approach does enable thorough, systematic cleaning of the council's gullies, it is highly inefficient, since many gullies do not actually require cleaning. Furthermore, and in terms of trust, while it is easy to fall short of expectations, it is not particularly easy to exceed expectations. Whereas a pothole repair gang might increase productivity by attending to jobs in an order which reduces travel time, a gully gang cannot devise any intelligent solution for increasing productivity. This creates a scenario in which trust is far more easily lost than gained.

Secondly, in contrast to reactive repair work like pothole filling, gangers do not record each gully as they clean it. Rather, they record the completion of a portion of road, which may contain many gullies. This means that the council does not have a history of maintenance activity for each gully (in many cases, they do not even know the number of gullies in their district). While it may seem unnecessary to trace activity for individual gullies, this information could be leveraged toward the development of more efficient maintenance routines. Furthermore, it would allow contractors to attend to problem gullies, such as the ones filled to the lid and sprouting plant life, whether or not they had met their legal obligation to clean it every six months. This would cut down on the number of complaints from the public, and help generate confidence that gangers can be trusted to do a good job.

The ethnographic fieldwork we conducted for gullies was intended not only to reveal further insight into trust, but also, more fundamentally, to capture requirements for our system design. The two ethnographers produced write-ups for the software development team that included minute details of carrying out gully maintenance work that must be designed for to ensure system success. These requirements, along with the understanding of trust we had developed up to this point, informed the design of our mobile data capture system, Inspections, which we describe in the next section.

THE SYSTEM

Overview

The mobile management tool, Inspections, that we have designed and studied allows mobile workers in the field to collect and manipulate a wide range of assets and to send this data back to a central office for processing and review. A demonstration of the system can be found at `http://www.intouch-ltd.com/gully_cleaning.asp`. The requirements for the system were derived from an extensive capture process involving several ethnographic visits, interviews, evaluation of several prototypes and analysis of past experiences with prior systems.

Figure 2. Locating gullies on the iPad.

The system is structured as a web application for office workers and an iOS based mobile client for the workers in the field. While the system allows the collection of different types of highways asset, in this study we have focused exclusively on the mobile component and its use as a tool for collecting gully data. While many systems designed for mobile workers rely on ruggedized hardware designed for niche markets, we have found that commodity consumer hardware (specifically iPhones) are able to function effectively in this environment with suitable cases.

The mobile application can be used for two purposes: conducting an initial survey of the state of gullies and supporting subsequent cleaning and maintenance of gullies.

Gully Collection

The mobile application initially allows users to accurately map assets. We have found that GPS provides adequate coarse grained positioning but in many cases users need to be able to reposition assets (e.g. in instances when they cannot position the device directly over the asset due to an obstruction, such as a parked vehicle), and this is supported by the application. In addition to position, users capture a range of data about the state of the gully including reports of any damage and a photograph of the current state of the gully. Once assets have been plotted on the map, users are able to see the data that they have just entered on their device — helping them place assets relative to each other providing visual conformation that asset data has been accurately recorded. As many assets occur in groups (e.g. several traffic lights might be sited at the same junction) the system enables users to enter data on multiple assets as a group.

Figure 3. iPhone use in the field.

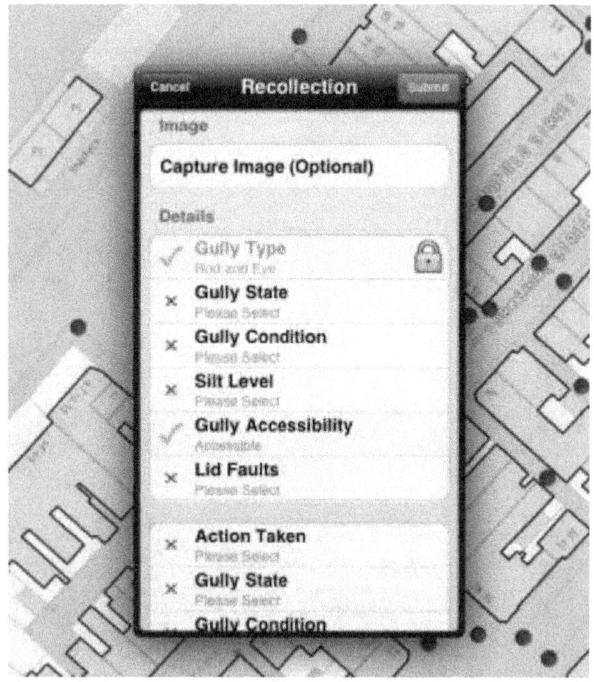

Figure 4. Recollection using the iPhone app (detail).

Gully Re-Inspection and Maintenance

Once an initial data set has been collected, the application can be used on a daily basis by maintenance workers to update information on individual assets. This support for re-inspections, which is the principle advance from second to third generation asset collection, enables users to recollect that same asset again and again, building a history of data against that asset. Users can also change any data that is incorrect by doing a recollection. They do not have to create a new inspection every time; data is pulled forward — some of which is immutable, some mutable, some blank, as appropriate (see Figure 4). In particular, the system allows users to reposition assets. This is important as assets may have been located in the wrong position during an initial inspection.

While inspection and re-inspection of assets is important, the true value of the system comes from its ability to provide maintenance operatives in the field with tools to view collected data in order to inform their maintenance decisions. Given the very large number of gullies that need to be collected (in excess of 200,000 is not uncommon) the system provides a sophisticated set of filters to enable viewers to hide irrelevant data from view. This combination of filtering and access to all the past data on local assets can transform the way highways maintenance operations are performed. In particular, it provides empowerment to the users, allowing them to be in control of their work and to choose how to carry it out, e.g. inspectors can choose to see all the gullies that they did not have time to check last time.

Visibility of past cleaning information can also be used to support a business process switch from a cyclic cleaning regime to an *intelligent* cleaning regime, whereby decisions about which gullies need cleaning can be predicted based on historical patterns. Crucially, proactive management is not done by managers in the office, but can be done by the workers themselves in the field. This is supported both by enabling mobile workers to access asset history on their devices and by allowing workers to add 'frequency prediction' information to an asset. More specifically, when a gully is collected/cleaned the user can select from a drop down menu how soon they think it will need to be cleaned again.

ANALYSIS

User feedback indicates that Inspections is a system that works, and works well. Both the gully crews and management had quickly learned to use and appreciate the various features of the system and, importantly, indicated that they both trusted and liked it. Some of this success can be put down to the extensive ethnographic research done up front and careful planning to attend to the needs highlighted by this research through iterative ethnographic/development cycles throughout. For example, users appreciated the way the system closely followed existing procedures for gully cleaning, the way in which it speeded up the work process, and the use of photographs to document, to provide a trustable record of, their work. Much of this success, however, we put down to serendipity, in the sense that we recognize the dynamic complexity of introducing a system into any organization; yet in hindsight we can glean a fair understanding of the design elements (planned or not) that contribute to the system's success.

There are particularities of the highways maintenance sector, and gully cleaning within that, that entail specific design constraints and UI solutions to match these constraints. In addition, there are design considerations that pertain to our chosen device and platform (Apple/iOS). While we could extract lessons from our experience with Inspections that apply to these particularities, we suggest that it would be of greater benefit to the community to distill more generalizable lessons

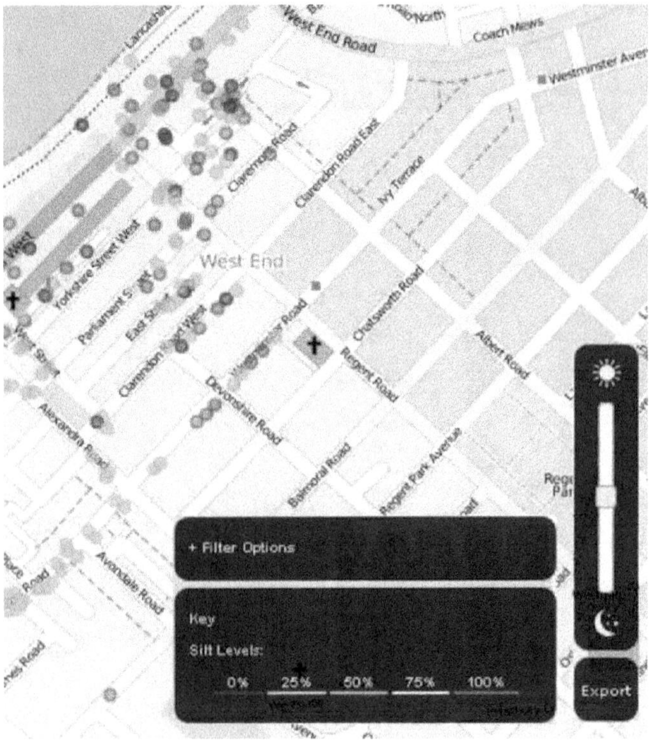

Figure 5. Filtering collected assets on the web portal (detail).

with broad applicability to other problem spaces. To do so, we begin with a brief discussion of the affordances of our mobile data capture system and explore how these affect *empowerment*. Next we explore additional characteristics that contribute to system success. Finally, we conclude by discussing how all of these factors contribute toward trusted data.

Organizational affordances

When designing mobile solutions, one issue affecting uptake relates to the desirability of the mobile devices themselves, and the 'sexiness' of the UI. Understanding the characteristics that engender this desirability has been explored by others (e.g. [27]), and while we are convinced that this desirability played an important role in getting users to want to use the system and to take good care of their devices, we cannot claim a great deal of credit for these successes. We can, however, claim credit for having designed a system that allows the easy and reliable capture of all necessary information — and all otherwise *useful* data — which can then be utilized in developing process improvements within highways maintenance.

At a minimum, mobile solutions must allow the collection of the same data as the paper-based systems they replace. However, they can offer so much more, in terms of generating what we would call a 'quality system'. Some of the affordances Inspections capitalizes on include the following:

- *'Wizarding':* Collection and recollection both force the user to enter all mandatory data before they are able to move on.
- *Pinpointing location:* The device's inbuilt GPS is used to generate initial locations (accurate to within 2m), but these can be further refined by allowing the user to adjust that location to give pinpoint accuracy (to within 50cm).
- *Filtering data:* Users can not only view relevant data, but also hide irrelevant data.
- *Gathering asset histories:* The system ties data collection to a specific asset, and users can continue to add information to this same asset over time.

These examples serve to highlight the distinct 'functional affordances' [17] of the technology we employed in comparison to traditional paper-based management systems.

But just as a quality system does not result inevitably from developing on quality devices, it also does not arise from these added affordances alone (though this should in no way undermine the UI work that went into making these elements function as well as they do). As [44] notes, introducing a system into an organization entails a complex emergent dynamic between the system and what that system enables users within the organization to do. "These factors," the authors write, "go beyond basic functionality, dialogue and representations of a technology and encompass organization culture, changes in organizations, users' identity and power differences and their emotional, symbolic and functional values related to the technology". We argue below that Inspections makes possible several further organizational-level affordances: 1) it empowers crews to engage their creative intelligence; 2) it empowers the organization as a whole to shift to an intelligent management model; and 3) this empowerment is enabled by — and in turn perpetuates — the fostering of *trust* throughout the different levels of the organization.

Empowerment

The term 'empowerment' has been defined in various ways and applied to various 'levels'. At the individual level, there are two commonalities across competing definitions which are particularly relevant to our experience with Inspections: 1) people have natural strengths that they can use and build upon [45]; 2) people understand their own needs better than anyone else does, and should have the power to act on them [8] (cf. [23]). At the organizational level, researchers differentiate between 'empowering organizations' and 'empowered organizations': the former serves to foster psychological empowerment for individuals within that organization or otherwise influenced by that organization [47]; whereas the latter ('empowered') are those that "influence the larger systems of which they are a part" [29], increasing their own effectiveness in achieving goals. Below we describe how Inspections empowers at both of these levels.

Crew empowerment

In previous gully collection (both paper based and first/second generation gully systems), workers were expected to stick to a cleaning routine that ensured compliance with governmental requirements. This did not accommodate the fact that gullies need more or less frequent cleaning depending on a range of environmental factors, resulting in some gullies being cleaned unnecessarily, or more problematically, some gullies not being cleaned as often as needed. Meanwhile, the cleaners themselves had relevant, local knowledge about these gullies that was not being utilized.

Our goal with Inspections was to design a system to enable individual workers to engage their creative capabilities in exercising greater control over their daily work. To this end, Inspections makes use of crews' previously untapped knowledge by asking them to predict the frequency of cleaning required for each gully. But further, it enables them to act on this creatively and independently, giving them the power to craft their maintenance schedules in accordance with their expertise, and being able to make these decisions by utilizing relevant data from their devices in the field (i.e. without needing scheduling input from supervisors). As a result, workers tell us they like using the system, which we think reflects the psychological benefits typically associated with empowerment, including increased job satisfaction [10, 37, 42]. And this makes intuitive sense: rather than feeling like robots or slaves to inflexible routines, workers can feel competent and engaged, and contribute toward making their cleaning efforts more successful.

Organizational empowerment

A key goal of the target organization (the highways contractors and the maintenance crews) is to maintain safe road conditions. In the absence of tools such as Inspections, local councils' solution to this rather complex management problem was to commit contractors to a related though somewhat different goal: to clean each gully within a given timeframe (whether or not it actually needed cleaning). As a result, organizational efficiency was bounded by the number of gullies in their area and the number of gullies their workforce was physically capable of cleaning per day. Within these constraints, the most obvious way to increase efficiency was to ask the crews to work harder, resulting in inevitable tensions.

Inspections, on the other hand, enables the organization to increase efficiency through strategic means while enabling the workforce to operate at a safe, healthy, *realistic* pace — with the added benefit that this is conducive to data accuracy. Ultimately, this has revolutionized these organizations, freeing them from a blind, cyclical cleaning regimen and enabling them to proactively target the gullies that are likely to cause unsafe road conditions. Efficiency and quality improvements both result from the fact that the system allows inspectors, crews, and management to work together in deciding which work they do *not* need to do, so that they can devote resources where they are most needed.

Successful characteristics

With empowerment we have isolated a fairly high-level contributor to success. It is important to recognize that this empowerment is itself enabled by lower-level successes; and that certain characteristics of the design contribute in other ways toward producing a successful system. We highlight three such characteristics that have played a particularly important role in Inspections' success.

Performance

In situations where the data entry is an onerous process, users may be unwilling to correct errors by re-entering data. We have witnessed, in contrast, the benefits that come with using high-performing devices. Inspections forces users to fill in all mandatory data fields, but because the device (and the UI decisions we have made) make doing so a very quick process, users are able to complete a collection or recollection quickly, knowing that they can recollect again just as quickly if they need to make corrections. Workers are more likely, as a result, to correct mistakes that they may have made in data collection.

Provenance

Many organizations now exhibit a highly visible and ubiquitous 'audit culture' [30, 40], and must demonstrate competence and compliance to a variety of audiences. For example, councils require appropriate data in order to defend, in court, claims of negligence or claims of failing in the council's 'duty of care'. So, for Inspections, complete factual 'audit' information regarding gully-emptying data, including any supplementary photographs, must be electronically signed (authentication enables the stamping of data with the users' identifier) and must be easily and immediately available. When compared to a current paper-based process[1] that Inspections will replace, it is easy to see why the system offers such an attractive and efficient alternative process.

We are cautious to adopt the term 'auditability' as a descriptor of our system design, as this has connotations related to 'people management' issues (e.g. catching and disciplining unwanted behavior). But beyond this, the benefit of these metadata traces is that they enable those that manage the data (whether or not they actively manage personnel) to determine the data's *validity*. We are also aware of the closer association between provenance and trust (e.g. [1, 2, 24]), which indicates that 'provenance' is in greater alignment with our intended design ambitions.

Translucency

The information that is relevant to doing work differs for different users of the system. Web users frequently manage and report on the organization's productivity over a given time period (e.g. annually), and therefore have access to all of the data in the system. Field workers actually need *less* information to work effectively: they need to know which gullies need to be collected or recollected. Inspections enables visibility of relevant peer activities, i.e. only the most recent collections and recollections captured by themselves and their co-workers. This optimizes usability in three ways: 1) it makes for an uncluttered interface on a small screen; 2) it avoids performance reductions that would be caused by pulling down the entire database; and 3) it makes that much

[1] An inspector makes manual notes in a notebook while on an inspection route. When back at the office, s/he fills in appropriate fields on paper forms. Key fields are then transcribed into an electronic system that manages any necessary works orders (tickets), and the paper forms are filed. Following any request for information, e.g. regarding a legal claim, the paper forms are retrieved, electronically scanned and sent to the legal team to form part of a portfolio of evidence.

more accessible what [11] describe as 'socially relevant' information.

Summary: how this all relates to trust

Trust is widely recognized as bringing about a wide range of benefits, including individual, community and organizational well-being, and economic growth [39]. It is cumulative and self-perpetuating in nature [9, 32], and a necessary precondition for successful collaboration. We contend there is an important distinction between accurate data and trusted data. While accuracy is a prerequisite of trusted data, it does not guarantee it; data can be accurate and still not be trusted. So what can design do to foster confidence both in the accuracy of that data and in the workers generating that data, and build trust within the organization?

In empowering crews, Inspections gives them certain responsibilities, and it is therefore important to ensure that they are going to succeed (particularly when failing to record activity can have legal consequences). The 'wizarding' functionality does just that, making sure they remember to fill out all necessary information. Additionally, the system is designed to be forgiving of mistakes — e.g. allowing users to recollect an asset if they have entered it wrong. These features contribute to the generation of 'accurate' data, and go some way toward indicating that workers can be trusted; but more is needed to foster genuine trust.

We suggest that an important element in bridging accurate and trusted data pertains to an understanding of the incentives that motivate workers to collect accurate data. In previous models of gully collection, crew were paid according to the number of gullies they cleaned. In this model, the workers needs (payment) were not aligned with the organizational need to get good quality data and cleaning. To some extent, this problem was addressed by first and second generation GPS tracking solutions, which ensured that cleaning activity could not be forged (i.e. gullies were collected at the point of active cleaning, so workers could not claim to have cleaned additional gullies). At the same time, however, these previous generation solutions did nothing to resolve the rift between worker and organizational needs, so trust in the accuracy of that data was not a designed outcome of these systems; instead the burden was on management to implement top-down organizational (often disciplinary) practices that contributed toward trustworthy data.

Inspections, on the other hand, attends to this problem from the bottom-up by giving users a reason to capture accurate data. As was shown in the discussion of crew and organizational empowerment, there are benefits to all involved for workers to collect accurate data: the system makes everyone's jobs easier, and everyone can be *trusted* to be working toward this mutual incentive. On top of this, the translucency that enables peer visibility contributes further to a sense of collective effort toward a shared goal, which not only breeds trust, but also may contribute to increased job performance (cf. [7]), which in itself would contribute to greater trust in the workers and in the organizational strategy.

Our feedback supports the conclusion that the features that have been designed into Inspections — conscious of its ultimate impact on trust at the early stages of development — combine dynamically to ensure that the data collected is *trusted* as well as accurate.

TRUSTWORTHY BY DESIGN

In 'The Mechanics of Trust: A Framework for Research and Design,' Rieselsberger et al [33] argue that: "If we are to realize the potential of new technologies for enabling new forms of interactions without these undesirable consequences, trust and the conditions that affect it must become a core concern of systems development. The role of systems designers and researchers is thus not one of solely increasing the functionality and usability of the systems that are used to transact or communicate, but to design them in such a way that they support trustworthy action and — based on that — well-placed trust." Our fieldwork and early design thinking identified a series of important and relevant trust considerations for the development of the design.

The examples provided above suggest that many aspects of trust require support to be built very deeply into the application. For example, deciding to ensure that data flows back to mobile users as part of their regular work cycle needs to be addressed at the point at which the overall business process is designed and specified.

More generally, our experience suggests that *trust cannot be easily retrofitted to an application once it is complete*. In this regard we draw a parallel with recent research in the area of privacy support. Like trust, privacy is a fairly abstract concept without clear definitions or boundaries. Engineering support for privacy is known to be extremely challenging at many levels. For example, anonymizing data sets is difficult without complete knowledge of how they might be combined with other data sources while the correct design of user interfaces for describing and managing user privacy needs has proved elusive. The result is that the privacy community have focused on the notion of "Privacy by Design", i.e. the incorporation of privacy principles already at design time, rather than as an afterthought [5].

A good example of privacy by design is the 'Whereabouts clock' [38] that illustrates how privacy can become an active design ingredient. In this work the designers created a wall clock that could only be seen by people in the home — supporting implicit and intuitive 'access control'; was coarse grained (home, work, and school) in line with the information needs of people; and, their wall clock design made the system a shared source of information rather than feeling like a surveillance tool.

We believe that a similar approach, i.e. *trustworthy by design*, is required for building trusted data-gathering systems. While developing a comprehensive toolkit to support trustworthy by design is out of the scope of this paper, we have have drawn on lessons learned from our experiences (above) to suggest eight key principles that should be embedded into the system and its interface at design time:

- *Security:* Trusted data capture must necessarily be underpinned by a secure infrastructure, e.g. it must include measures that ensure tamper resistance.
- *Performance:* Systems — both devices and web portals — must be quick and easy to use in order to encourage users to amend data as necessary.
- *Provenance:* The system must enable users to trace the source of any data capture and amendment activity in a way that aids verification of the validity of that activity.
- *Translucency:* Users must be able to see all relevant data that would help them undertake their work, but no more.
- *Flexibility:* The system must allow users to adjust data when the device is unable to deliver accuracy, e.g. if an obstruction prevents the user from positioning the device over the asset.
- *Value to users:* The system must be designed to deliver value to the user — as opposed to a model that treats users as 'dumb sensors' — to ensure they benefit from producing accurate data.
- *Empowerment:* The system must bring people 'into the loop' and engage their knowledge and intelligence toward a shared goal, such as increasing the quality and ease of work.
- *Competence:* In empowering people and giving them responsibility, the system must build in assurances that users will succeed, e.g. facilitating the submission of all necessary data.

CLOSING REMARKS

We have reported on a data collection system that appears to work toward delivering not only accurate data, but highly trusted data. Much of what we have offered here is post-hoc rationalization of why we have come to believe Inspections works, informed in part by the conversations we have had with users. Having said that, our ambitions at the start had always explicitly pertained to delivering trust, and we are confident that having this goal in mind throughout the development process is a key ingredient in our eventual success. Additional goals, such as providing value to and empowering users, were also explicit in our development process, though we did not understand at the start how integrally it would relate to trust. And finally, while we are confident that design in accordance with our 'trustworthy by design' principles will contribute toward the development of successful systems, successful design further requires open and frequent communication with the users of that system to understand, respond to, and indeed capitalize on emergent organizational affordances. In the future we plan to refine and enrich these 'trustworthy by design' principles, illustrating them in action with further ethnographic accounts and user feedback gathered as the development of Inspections moves from controlled trials to full deployment.

ACKNOWLEDGEMENTS

The research leading to these results has been conducted as part of the FAITH: Building Trust Between Citizens, Local Authorities and Contractors project funded by the EPSRC/TSB under grant TS/I002537/1.

REFERENCES

1. B. T. Adler, K. Chatterjee, L. de Alfaro, M. Faella, I. Pye, and V. Raman. Assigning trust to wikipedia content. In *Proc. WikiSym'08*, pages 26:1–26:12. ACM, 2008.
2. P. Buneman and W.-C. Tan. Provenance in databases. In *Proc. SIGMOD'07*, pages 1171–1173. ACM, 2007.
3. L. Capra. Engineering human trust in mobile system collaborations. *SIGSOFT Softw. Eng. Notes*, 29(6):107–116, Oct. 2004.
4. J. Cassell and T. Bickmore. External manifestations of trustworthiness in the interface. *Commun. ACM*, 43(12):50–56, Dec. 2000.
5. A. Cavoukian. Privacy by design: The 7 foundational principles. White paper, Information and Privacy Commissioner of Ontario, Canada, 2009.
6. X. Chen, E. Santos-Neto, and M. Ripeanu. Crowdsourcing for on-street smart parking. In *Proc. DIVANet'12*, pages 1–8. ACM, 2012.
7. C.-F. Chiang and T.-S. Hsieh. The impacts of perceived organizational support and psychological empowerment on job performance: The mediating effects of organizational citizenship behavior. *International Journal of Hospitality Management*, 31(1):180 – 190, 2012.
8. M. Cochran. The parental empowerment process: Building on family strengths. In J. Harris, editor, *Child psychology in action: Linking research and practice*, pages 12–33. Croon Helm Publishers, Brookline, MA, 1986.
9. D. Cohen and L. Prusak. *In Good Company: How social capital makes organizations work.* Harvard Business School Press, Boston, MA, 2001.
10. M. Engström, B. Wadensten, and E. Häggström. Caregivers' job satisfaction and empowerment before and after an intervention focused on caregiver empowerment. *Journal of Nursing Management*, 18(1):14–23, 2010.
11. T. Erickson and W. A. Kellogg. Social translucence: an approach to designing systems that support social processes. *ACM Trans. Comput.-Hum. Interact.*, 7(1):59–83, Mar. 2000.
12. J. Froehlich, M. Y. Chen, S. Consolvo, B. Harrison, and J. A. Landay. MyExperience: a system for in situ tracing and capturing of user feedback on mobile phones. In *Proc. MobiSys'07*, pages 57–70. ACM, 2007.
13. D. Gambetta. Can we trust trust. *Trust: Making and breaking cooperative relations*, pages 213–237, 2000.

14. H. Garfinkel. A conception of and experiments with "trust" as a condition of concerted stable actions. *The production of reality: Essays and readings on social interaction*, pages 381–392, 1963.
15. H. Garfinkel. Studies of the routine grounds of everyday activities. *Social problems*, 11(3):225–250, 1964.
16. R. Harper, R. Procter, D. Randall, and M. Rouncefield. 'Safety in numbers': calculation and document re-use in knowledge work. In *GROUP'01*, pages 242–251. ACM, 2001.
17. R. Hartson. Cognitive, physical, sensory, and functional affordances in interaction design. *Behaviour & Information Technology*, 22(5):315–338, 2003.
18. P. Hinds and C. McGrath. Structures that work: social structure, work structure and coordination ease in geographically distributed teams. In *CSCW'06*, pages 343–352. ACM, 2006.
19. A. Jøsang, R. Ismail, and C. Boyd. A survey of trust and reputation systems for online service provision. *Decis. Support Syst.*, 43(2):618–644, Mar. 2007.
20. S. S. Kanhere. Participatory sensing: Crowdsourcing data from mobile smartphones in urban spaces. In *Proc. MDM'11*, pages 3–6, Washington, DC, USA, 2011. IEEE Computer Society.
21. Legislation.gov.uk. Flood and water management act 2010. `http://www.legislation.gov.uk/ukpga/2010/29/contents`.
22. S. M. Liu, K. Unsworth, R. Fidel, and H. J. J. Scholl. Fully mobile wirelessly connected technology applications: Organizational communication, social, and information challenges. *Proc. ASIS&T*, 44(1):1–20, 2007.
23. J. Lord and P. Hutchison. The Process of Empowerment: Implications for Theory and Practice. *Canadian Journal of Community Mental Health*, 12(1):5–22, 1993.
24. C. A. Lynch. When documents deceive: Trust and provenance as new factors for information retrieval in a tangled web. *Journal of the American Society for Information Science and Technology*, 52(1):12–17, 2001.
25. S. Marsh and J. Meech. Trust in design. In *CHI EA '00*, pages 45–46, New York, NY, USA, 2000. ACM.
26. I. Medhi, M. Jain, A. Tewari, M. Bhavsar, M. Matheke-Fischer, and E. Cutrell. Combating rural child malnutrition through inexpensive mobile phones. In *Proc. NordiCHI'12*, pages 635–644. ACM, 2012.
27. D. A. Norman. *The Design of Everyday Things*. Basic Books, Inc., New York, NY, USA, 2002.
28. S. Patnaik, E. Brunskill, and W. Thies. Evaluating the accuracy of data collection on mobile phones: a study of forms, SMS, and voice. In *Proc. ICTD'09*, pages 74–84. IEEE Press, 2009.
29. N. A. Peterson and M. A. Zimmerman. Beyond the individual: Toward a nomological network of organizational empowerment. *American Journal of Community Psychology*, 34(1–2):129–145, September 2004.
30. M. Power. *The Audit Explosion*. Demos, London, 1994.
31. M. Power. The audit society: Rituals of verification. *OUP Catalogue*, 1999.
32. R. Putnam. *Bowling Alone: The Collapse and Revival of American Community*. Simon and Schuster, New York, 2000.
33. J. Riegelsberger, M. A. Sasse, and J. D. McCarthy. The mechanics of trust: a framework for research and design. *International Journal of Human-Computer Studies*, 62(3):381–422, 2005.
34. E. Rocco. Trust breaks down in electronic contexts but can be repaired by some initial face-to-face contact. In *CHI'98*, pages 496–502. ACM Press/Addison-Wesley Publishing Co., 1998.
35. E. Rocco, T. Finholt, E. C. Hofer, and J. Herbsleb. Designing as if trust mattered. *Collaboratory for Research on Electronic Work (CREW) Technical Report*, 2000.
36. Y. Schwartzman and T. S. Parikh. Establishing relationships for designing rural information systems. In *CHI EA'07*, pages 1845–1850. ACM, 2007.
37. S. E. Seibert, G. Wang, and S. H. Courtright. Antecedents and consequences of psychological and team empowerment in organizations: A meta-analytic review. *Journal of Applied Psychology*, 96(5):981–1003, September 2011.
38. A. Sellen, R. Eardley, S. Izadi, and R. Harper. The whereabouts clock: early testing of a situated awareness device. In *CHI EA'06*, pages 1307–1312. ACM, 2006.
39. B. Shneiderman. Designing trust into online experiences. *Commun. ACM*, 43(12):57–59, Dec. 2000.
40. M. Strathern. *Audit Cultures*. Routledge, London, 2000.
41. D. Tjondronegoro and T.-S. Chua. Transforming mobile personal life log into autobiographical multimedia echronicles. In *Proc. MoMM'12*, pages 57–63. ACM, 2012.
42. I. O. Ugboro and K. Obeng. Top management leadership, employee empowerment, job satisfaction, and customer satisfaction in TQM organizations: an empirical study. *Journal of Quality Management*, 5(2):247 – 272, 2000.
43. L. Viljanen. Towards an ontology of trust. In *Proc. TrustBus'05*, pages 175–184, Berlin, Heidelberg, 2005. Springer-Verlag.
44. D. M. Vyas, C. M. Chisalita, and A. J. Dix. Dynamics of affordances and implications for design. Technical Report TR-CTIT-08-36, Centre for Telematics and Information Technology University of Twente, Enschede, May 2008.

45. E. Whitmore. Participation, empowerment and welfare. *Canadian Review of Social Policy*, 22:51–60, 1988.

46. X. Zhang and Q. Zhang. Online trust forming mechanism: approaches and an integrated model. In *Proc. ICEC'05*, pages 201–209. ACM, 2005.

47. M. A. Zimmerman. Empowerment theory: Psychological, organizational, and community levels of analysis. In J. Rappaport and E. Seidman, editors, *Handbook of Community Psychology*, pages 43–63. Plenum, New York, 2000.

Tracking Serendipitous Interactions: How Individual Cultures Shape the Office

Chloë Brown
Computer Laboratory
University of Cambridge
chloe.brown@cl.cam.ac.uk

Christos Efstratiou
Computer Laboratory
University of Cambridge
christos.efstratiou@cl.cam.ac.uk

Ilias Leontiadis*
Telefonica Research
Barcelona
ilias@tid.es

Daniele Quercia*
Yahoo Labs
Barcelona
dquercia@yahoo-inc.com

Cecilia Mascolo
Computer Laboratory
University of Cambridge
cecilia.mascolo@cl.cam.ac.uk

ABSTRACT
In many work environments, serendipitous interactions between members of different groups may lead to enhanced productivity, collaboration and knowledge dissemination. Two factors that may have an influence on such interactions are cultural differences between individuals in highly multicultural workplaces, and the layout and physical spaces of the workplace itself. In this work, we investigate how these two factors may facilitate or hinder inter-group interactions in the workplace. We analyze traces collected using wearable electronic badges to capture face-to-face interactions and mobility patterns of employees in a research laboratory in the UK. We observe that those who interact with people of different roles tend to come from collectivist cultures that value relationships and where people tend to be comfortable with social hierarchies, and that some locations in particular are more likely to host serendipitous interactions, knowledge that could be used by organizations to enhance communication and productivity.

Author Keywords
Cultural dimensions; interaction sensing; serendipitous spaces

ACM Classification Keywords
H.5.3 [**Information Interfaces and Presentation**]: Group and Organization Interfaces— *Organizational design*

*Data collection was undertaken while the authors were at the Computer Laboratory of the University of Cambridge.

CSCW'14, February 15–19, 2014, Baltimore, Maryland, USA.
Copyright © 2014 ACM 978-1-4503-2540-0/14/02...$15.00.
http://dx.doi.org/10.1145/2531602.2531641

INTRODUCTION
In many knowledge-based work environments, where creativity and innovation are key, it is intuitive that serendipitous interactions between members of different teams, with complementary expertise or skill sets, can be highly beneficial as a source of fresh perspectives, information, and ideas. Chance conversations between individuals who are not necessarily part of the same group have long been judged to be essential for team coordination, cohesiveness and productivity [2, 10, 11, 25]. This idea was recently further confirmed by Pentland *et al.*, in a study of workplace communication patterns at a Prague bank [16]. They discovered a key characteristic of successful teams: members periodically interact with others outside of their team, and bring back new information. They dubbed this critical dimension of communication 'exploration', the tendency for a team to seek inter-group connections, and found that teams with high exploration tended to be more successful, demonstrating the power of serendipitous interactions in the office.

One factor that could clearly affect the ease of such interactions is the physical spaces of the workplace itself; for example, high-traffic areas such as coffee machines and photocopiers may be particularly likely places for inter-group meetings [6, 10]. In general, if spaces encourage the mixing and meeting of a diverse range of people, serendipitous meetings between individuals from different teams or social groups will occur more readily, which could be crucial; face-to-face communication has been shown to be more important than electronic means such as email or SMS [16, 20].

Indeed, designing the layout of workspaces in accordance with office social dynamics resulting from the background of employees can help them work more effectively, as was shown by a recent study of offices across 11 different countries [4]. While this approach takes into account the national culture of the country where an office is situated, it does not consider what happens in very culturally diverse environments that accommodate workers from many different backgrounds.

The effects of cultural variations between countries on organisations have been studied by Geert Hofstede, by means of administering opinion surveys to IBM employees in over 70 countries. He derived five main factors, or cultural dimensions, that can account for most of the variance he observed [9], and found that workers' cultural backgrounds can shape the way they think, feel, and act. Besides the workplace environment itself, cultural differences between its occupants could affect office social dynamics and, therefore, the propensity of workers to engage in beneficial serendipitous inter-group interactions.

Since interactions between people with different areas of expertise or social circles are so beneficial for the exchange of information and ideas, it is important to understand what facilitates or hinders them. Studies of workplace communication have traditionally used pen-and-paper methods from the social sciences, with data being gathered through direct manual observations and participant surveys. These approaches have various disadvantages and limitations: the presence of an observer may cause people to reflect upon and change their natural behavior [26], and surveys can suffer from participants giving answers they feel are socially desirable, or misremembering [1, 22]. Recently, technological methods such as wearable badges and sensors have enabled social interaction patterns to be studied in a less obtrusive way [13, 27]. In this work, we make use of this technology to investigate the impact of cultural differences on serendipitous interactions in the workplace in a way that was not available to Hofstede doing his original work in the 1970s.

In addition, we can make use of localization available from the sensing technology to study the characteristics of different spaces within the workplace, and their potential to host encounters between people from different groups, knowledge that could be used by organizations to stimulate inter-group meetings and perhaps enhance productivity.

We present a study of serendipitous interactions in an office environment, making the following contributions:

- We analyze a dataset captured using the SocioPatterns proximity-sensing platform[1]. For a period of 2 weeks, 61 people at a research laboratory in the UK wore lightweight electronic badges that can capture face-to-face interactions (as opposed to Bluetooth devices, which simply capture colocation information) [3]. The use of these badges allows us to study face-to-face interactions and mobility in the office environment in a less obtrusive way than older sensing technologies.

- We investigate the relationship between Hofstede's cultural dimensions and detected interactions. We analyze Power Distance (how comfortable people are with hierarchy), Individualism (how individualist or collectivist a culture is), and Masculinity (task-orientation vs. person-orientation), finding that those who interact with people of different roles tend to come from collectivist and person-oriented cultures comfortable with social hierarchies. This suggests that cultural effects depend not only on the location of the office itself, but on the cultural diversity of the people working there.

- We assess the potential for particular rooms to host serendipitous interactions between people from different groups, by counting visitors to the room from groups defined according to a variety of dimensions: research group, role, nationality, age, and gender. We determine the extent to which different kinds of spaces allow for serendipitous interactions between visitors, and find that while social spaces such as kitchens and common rooms score highly for all dimensions, others such as shared offices score more highly in some dimensions than others. This means that different locations may be more important for the promotion of interactions between individuals from different groups in the workplace, depending on the kind of diversity it is wished to achieve.

Our work demonstrates the feasibility of detecting serendipitous interactions in the workplace using unobtrusive sensing technology. Given the importance of interactions between people from different teams and groups for productivity, information flow, and idea exchange, being able to sense and quantify such effects could potentially be highly beneficial to organizations.

RELATED WORK

Electronic sensing of office social interactions

From as early as 1992, the design of the Active Badge [24] system was motivated by the need for location-based services in business environments. Most of these early attempts were focused on the design of context-aware systems, placing less emphasis on the potential of using location technologies to understand and analyze social interactions.

Olguín-Olguín *et al.* [13] demonstrated the feasibility of using wearable computing devices to measure, among a variety of factors, face-to-face interactions in the workplace. They showed that the data collected by the devices could be used in combination with email communication data to predict employees' perceptions of group interaction. Their work differs from the study we present here in that that the sensing devices used were bigger, and thus potentially more obtrusive, than the tiny badges we use. Moreover, they were not looking explicitly to study encounters between individuals from different cultural backgrounds.

The same technology has been used in a variety of studies of social interactions in the workplace, for example by Waber et. al. [23], who studied the effect of social

[1] `http://www.sociopatterns.org`

group strength on productivity, and by Wu *et al.* [27], who compared face-to-face network structure with the network formed by electronic communication.

Recently, research projects have shown that social interactions in the workplace can be detected using mobile phones [5]. Although mobile phones are demonstrably less accurate in detecting face-to-face interactions than specialised wearable devices, these attempts signify an interest in the design of mobile applications that can track social interactions, and deliver tailored services to the end user.

Effects of physical spaces on social interactions

Those who plan and design buildings have long been interested in the 'social logic of space' [8], that is, how the nature and layout of spaces can affect patterns of usage and group behavior. One set of methods to aid such study is those of *space syntax*, used by Penn *et al.* [15] in a 1999 study finding that the spatial configuration of a work environment can directly affect the frequency of face-to-face communication between office workers. Furthermore, the frequency of such contact affected how useful employees found work-related interactions to be. The same importance of the role of space in the frequency of communication between workers was also found in a later study by Sailer and Penn [18].

In the same vein, Toker and Gray [21] studied the effect of workspace layout specifically in the context of research offices and laboratories, such as that that we study here, and found that spatial configuration affected the frequency and location of unplanned face-to-face interaction between workers.

Cultural dimensions

Beginning in 1971, Geert Hofstede conducted an extensive study of the way that cultural differences shape the way that people think, feel, and act, and can therefore influence workplace environments and office social dynamics. He administered over 100,000 opinion surveys to IBM employees in 70 countries, and through his analysis derived five *cultural dimensions* that could explain most of the variation between cultures in his observations [9].

These factors were recently shown, in a study by Reinecke *et al.* [17], to correlate with differences in behavior of office workers in different countries scheduling meetings, which demonstrates that cultural differences continue to have an effect on workplace behavior especially in today's highly international business world.

The idea of Hofstede's cultural dimensions was also recently applied in the context of office space layout by researchers from the office furniture company Steelcase [4]. Over a period of 5 years, they studied offices in 11 different countries including China, India, Italy, Germany, and Britain, and showed how differences in national culture could mean that difference office layouts would be more effective in different countries. For example, in countries where competition tends to be valued over collaboration, private offices are important and collaboration spaces may be very basic, while in countries placing higher value on cooperation, workers may be helped by more open, fluid spaces.

In this study, we show that besides cultural differences between countries where offices are situated, in a highly international work environment there may also be such effects at work in a single office.

MEASURING SERENDIPITOUS INTERACTIONS

We study a culturally diverse environment, populated by workers from many different backgrounds. We have two aims: firstly, to examine how cultural differences, as measured by Hofstede's cultural dimensions, may affect the serendipitous interactions of individuals. Secondly, we wish to identify the spaces within the workplace that are most likely to host such interactions. Our approach is based on the collection of real-world traces of social interactions in a culturally diverse research institution, then exploring how cultural dimensions are related to serendipitous interactions, through quantitative analysis.

Cultural dimensions and interactions of individuals

As a result of his study of cultural variations across countries in the 1970s, Hofstede defined five *cultural dimensions* that could explain most of the variance in his data [9]. In this work, we study three of these[2]:

- **Power Distance** describes how comfortable people tend to be with unequally distributed power and a clear social hierarchy. In a typical office environment the distribution of power is reflected by the different roles that are defined in the workplace, and the explicit or implicit hierarchy across them. Given Hofstede's definition of Power Distance, we consider that people less comfortable with differences in power may be less likely to interact with those with colleagues with a different role from their own, and propose the hypothesis:
HP1: Individuals from cultures with lower Power Distance tend to have a lower proportion of their interactions with those outside their own roles.
- **Individualism** concerns the extent to which self-sufficiency is valued and people largely look after only themselves (high Individualism), or whether group well-being is important and people have more responsibility for others. Collaborations in many office environments are commonly carried out by clearly defined

[2]The remaining two, Uncertainty Avoidance and Long-Term Orientation, are less directly associated with short-term interactions between people as considered by our study. For example, uncertainty avoidance is often reflected in whether company managers are focused on day-to-day operations, which demand less tolerance of uncertainty, or on strategic problems, which are by nature more uncertain. Long-term orientation is relevant in situations such as businesses deciding whether to focus on short-term profits or future growth [9].

groups consisting of people in a variety of roles, where all members work together to achieve a common goal. We consider that people from more collectivist cultures (lower Individualism) may perceive interactions with others in different roles important to maintaining group well-being, and form the hypothesis:
HP2: Individuals from cultures with lower Individualism tend to have more of their interactions with those outside their own roles.

- **Masculinity** quantifies how task-oriented (as opposed to person-oriented) a culture tends to be. Cultures with high Masculinity place higher value on achievement and competition, while cultures with lower Masculinity regard relationships and co-operation as more important. We consider that people from more person-oriented and less task-oriented cultures may regard a person's work role as less relevant to their willingness to interact, and test the hypothesis:
HP3: Individuals from cultures with lower Masculinity tend to have more of their interactions with others outside their own roles.

In this work we attempt to answer these research questions experimentally, through the collection of real-world traces of social interactions in a culturally diverse office environment.

DATA COLLECTION

We conducted a study over 2 weeks in 2012 within a research laboratory in the UK. We collected traces of face-to-face interactions, using the SocioPatterns proximity-sensing platform, which was made available to us in order to carry out the measurements. The measurements were captured by active RFID badges [3], worn on the body as shown in Figure 2. The badges are lightweight radio transceivers, programmed to transmit a low signal strength beacon periodically, and to listen continuously for beacons from other badges nearby. The badges are configured to transmit low signal strength beacons that were experimentally evaluated to have a range of 1.5m - 2m with clear line-of-sight. When worn by the participants, the beacons are shielded by the body, meaning that successful communication can occur only when another badge is facing that of the participant. This way the tags can assess continued face-to-face proximity between users. We assume continued face-to-face proximity to be a good proxy for a social interaction between users. Defining the threshold for such matching to be 2m (the maximum range of the radio transmission) makes the likelihood of false positives in the dataset negligible. Reducing the number of false negatives (face-to-face proximity not detected by the tags) can be controlled by using time windows within which detected beacons can be considered as indicators of proximity for that duration. In the study by Panisson *et al.* [14] the authors established that the use of a 20-second window offers a 99% probability for a face-to-face proximity detection.

Figure 2. The SocioPatterns tag worn on the chest is able to track face-to-face interactions.

We also augmented the office environment with a number of active RFID tags placed on the walls of rooms. The 26 rooms with static tags on the walls were: 4 kitchens, the common room, the cafeteria, reception, 13 offices, 4 printers, and 2 meeting rooms (Figure 1). The room tags were programmed to beacon a unique location ID at a higher signal strength than the participants' badges, achieving a range of 5m - 6m.

Traces from both badge-to-badge interactions, and from contacts between badges and location tags, were collected by RFID readers installed throughout the building. This instrumentation allowed us to capture two sets of data: the first consisting of timestamped face-to-face contacts between participants, and the second involving proximity of participants to particular locations within the building.

Study participants were recruited based on the physical locations of their offices, with the aim of including the majority of people working within a specific geographic space (the north wing of the main laboratory building). After briefing all employees working within the target area, we recruited 61 participants, which represents more than 80% of the total number of employees in the participating areas.

At the start of the 2-week data collection period, the participants completed a survey indicating their job role (e.g., PhD student, postdoc, lecturer), their working group (team), their age, and their gender. They also identified among the other participants people with whom they collaborate on work projects, and people they consider to be their friends. The demographics of the participants reflect the overall demographics of the particular research institution. The participant group was 78.6% male and 21.3% female, with age distributed as 34.4% 20–30, 22.9% 30–40, 14.7% 40–50, 21.0% over 50, and 4.9% not specified. The participants were spread across different roles as shown in Figure 3. With respect to different nationalities, as expected, the group was dominated by UK nationals (Figure 4). However,

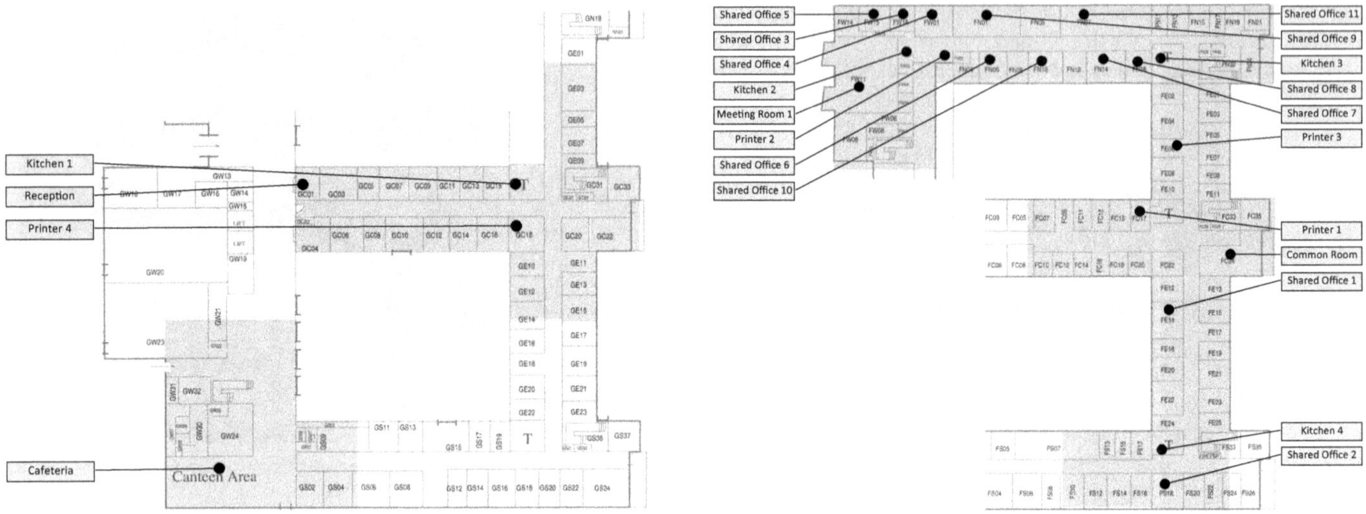

Figure 1. Data was collected on the shadowed areas of the ground floor (left) and the first floor (right) in a UK research laboratory.

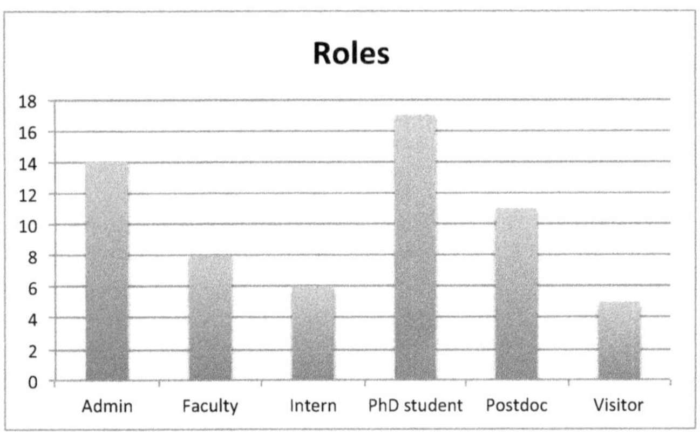

Figure 3. Distribution of roles across the study participants.

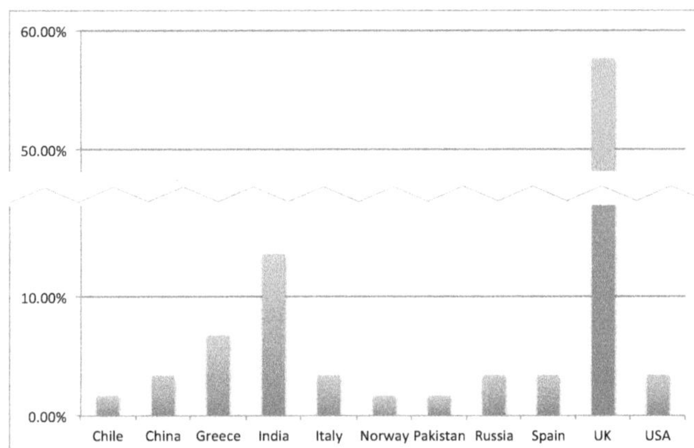

Figure 4. Distribution of nationalities across the study participants.

UK nationals made up only 57% of the total population, making this a diverse working environment where people from different cultural backgrounds interact on a daily basis.

Over the 2 weeks of the deployment, the badges and tags generated over 270,000 face-to-face contact reports, and over 730,000 location proximity traces.

Individual interactions

Hofstede assigned each of the countries he studied a score from 1 to 120 for each dimension (Table 1). To test our hypotheses, we therefore assign to each study participant the score for their self-reported country of origin, for each dimension[3]. We then compute for each individual their *Interaction Diversity*, ID, defined for each participant p to be:

$$ID(p) = \frac{\#\text{people } p \text{ interacted with in different role to } p}{\#\text{people } p \text{ interacted with}} \quad (1)$$

We then test our hypotheses by examining the relationship between individuals' Interaction Diversity and their scores for each of the three cultural dimensions.

Serendipitous spaces

We also study the nature of different kinds of space within the building, aiming to characterize their potential to host encounters between people from different teams or groups. Static tags were placed on the walls of shared offices, individual offices, kitchens, printer rooms, and a common room and cafeteria, allowing the occupants of the room to be detected by means of the signals from their badges.

Specifically, for each room, we compute the diversity of the visitors to that room by using the Shannon index H',

[3]Note that we did not administer Hofstede's original questionnaire, as this would have risked biased results due to participants altering the way they interacted, being overly aware of their behavior in relation to the cultural dimensions.

Country	Power Dist.	Individualism	Masculinity
Chile	63	23	28
China	80	20	66
Germany	35	67	66
Greece	60	35	57
India	77	48	56
Italy	50	76	70
Norway	31	69	8
Pakistan	55	14	50
Russia	93	39	36
Spain	57	51	42
UK	35	89	66
USA	40	91	62

Table 1. Hofstede's cultural dimensions of the participants' nationalities. Each dimension can have a value from 1 to 120.

Power Distance	How comfortable people tend to be with unequally distributed power and a clear social hierarchy
Individualism	How much self-sufficiency is valued and people largely look after only themselves, or group well-being is important and people have more responsibility for others
Masculinity	How much achievement and competition are valued, as opposed to relationships and co-operation

Table 2. Descriptions of cultural dimensions

a measure often used in ecology to measure the diversity of populations, and originally proposed by Claude Shannon to quantify the entropy in strings of text [19].

The index is defined as:

$$H' = -\sum_{i=1}^{R} p_i \ln p_i \qquad (2)$$

where p_i is the proportion of visitors to the room belonging to group i out of R. The higher the Shannon index, the more diverse the population of visitors to a room and, as such, the more potential the room has for hosting serendipitous interactions between members of different groups. If all the visitors to the room are from the same group, H' has a value of 0.

We measure H' based on several different definitions of 'group', these being: job role, research group (team), gender, age, and nationality. We aim to answer two questions:

1. *Which places are visited by people from many different groups, and therefore likely places for serendipitous meetings?* This question is motivated by the statement in [10] that cafeterias and photocopiers are particularly likely places for such encounters.

2. *Are the same places the most diverse across all definitions of 'group', or are some more diverse in some terms than in others?* Serendipitous meetings between those from different groups may be beneficial for the exchange of ideas and information whether those encountering one another are from different social circles, different teams, or have different job roles and therefore different perspectives and expertise. The answer to this question could provide insight into which kinds of places are the best for fostering serendipitous interactions between people from different groups depending on the type of group being considered.

Pre-processing

We pre-processed the data collected by the RFID badges in order to extract locations of participants in rooms, and face-to-face contacts between participants.

To record a person as visiting a room, for the purpose of computing diversity in that room as described above, we required that there be a contact between that person's badge and the static badge in the room. We further required that more than 90% of the contacts between the person's badge and static badges in rooms be from the room in question, over a 30-second time window. The reason for this window was to remove noise from events where, for example, people were walking around and were 'seen' by multiple room badges over a short period of time.

To record a face-to-face contact between two people, we aggregated all contacts between the same two badges with an interval less than 30 seconds in between into the same interaction, resulting in a total of 4646 interactions being recorded. In the analysis that produced the following results, we considered these aggregated interactions.

RESULTS

Cultural dimensions and interactions of individuals

We now present the results of testing the hypotheses stated earlier. For each cultural dimension we compute Pearson's correlation coefficient r and the corresponding p-value. The descriptions of the cultural dimensions are given again in Table 2 for easy reference.

HP1: Individuals from cultures with lower Power Distance tend to have a lower proportion of their interactions with those with different roles. Table 3 shows a positive correlation between Power Distance and Interaction Diversity, as defined earlier. When all contacts are considered, $r = 0.31$, confirming that individuals from cultures with lower power distance do indeed have a lower proportion of their interactions with those having roles different from their own. Considering only contacts with those the study participants identified as collaborators, the correlation is stronger ($r = 0.36$), and weaker considering only contacts with those identified as friends ($r = 0.25$). If only interactions with those in a different team are considered, the result is much the same as that where all contacts are considered ($r = 0.32$, as opposed to $r = 0.31$), so the relationship appears to be

	Power distance	Individualism	Masculinity
All contacts	**0.31** (0.02)	**-0.27** (0.04)	**-0.27** (0.04)
Collaborators	**0.36** (0.01)	**-0.32** (0.03)	**-0.36** (0.01)
Friends	0.25 (0.13)	-0.23 (0.17)	**-0.35** (0.03)
Inter-team only	**0.32** (0.04)	**-0.31** (0.04)	-0.27 (0.08)

Table 3. Pearson's correlation coefficient r (and p-value) for the three cultural dimensions under study vs. Interaction Diversity.

unaffected by whether workers are on the same team or not. These results effectively mean that individuals from cultures where there is lower acceptance of inequality of power are less likely to interact with those above or below them in the workplace hierarchy, and that this effect is strongest for working relationships.

HP2: Individuals from cultures with lower Individualism tend to have more of their interactions with those with different roles. Table 3 shows a negative correlation between Individualism and Interaction Diversity, which confirms that those from cultures with lower Individualism, where the group is considered to be important (rather than the self alone), tend to interact more with those in different roles from themselves. Again, the correlation considering interactions with collaborators ($r = -0.32$) is slightly stronger than that obtained from considering all interactions ($r = -0.27$), which suggests that this effect may be particularly important in the context of working relationships and less relevant for purely social relationships. If only interactions with those in a different team are considered, the result is much the same ($r = -0.31$) as that where all contacts are considered, so the relationship appears to be unaffected by whether workers are on the same team or not. Individuals from cultures with low Individualism may perceive that interacting with their colleagues having different roles is important for the wellbeing of the group as a whole, to a greater degree than those from backgrounds where self-sufficiency is valued more highly.

HP3: Individuals from cultures with lower Masculinity tend to have more of their interactions with others outside their own roles. Table 3 shows a negative correlation between Masculinity and Interaction Diversity, in agreement with the hypothesis: those from more task-oriented cultures, where achievement and competition are more valued, interact less with those in different roles than those from more person-oriented cultures, where co-operation and relationships are more valued. As for the other two cultural dimensions, the correlation is stronger for working relationships ($r = -0.36$) than when considering any relationship ($r = -0.27$). For Masculinity in particular, there is also a stronger correlation ($r = -0.35$) when considering only interactions with those the participant in question identified as friends. If only interactions with those in a different team are considered, the result is much the same as that where all contacts are considered ($r = -0.27$), although the p-value in that case is 0.08, rather than 0.04. People from cultures with low Masculinity are more likely to engage in interaction with those in different roles from themselves, but the effect is equally strong for working relationships and social relationships – those with a less task-oriented and more person-oriented background may be more open to social interaction with those in different roles from themselves.

Serendipity of rooms

The results of computing the diversity of visitors to rooms according to five different ways of defining groups (role, research group, gender, age, and nationality) are given in Table 4. To facilitate understanding of these results, we should remember that the two floors under study consisted of a variety of places where diverse people could potentially meet, as shown by Figure 1. The ground floor included reception, administrative offices, a printer, a kitchen, and one big cafeteria, and the first floor included three printers and three kitchens shared by different research groups, offices shared by PhD students and postdocs, and one common room. The table shows the top 10 locations with the most diverse range of visitors, according to the Shannon index H' computed over the various kinds of group.

With regard to our first question posed earlier:
1. Which places are visited by people from many different groups, and therefore likely places for serendipitous meetings? We can see that all 4 printers feature in at least one of the lists, and all the lists except that for Nationality feature at least two printers. This would support the idea that printers are likely places for serendipitous, inter-group encounters. Similarly, at least one of the social spaces including the kitchens, cafeteria, and common room appears among the top 3 places on each of the lists, and all of the lists except that for Nationality include two kitchens. This would also suggest that kitchens are indeed likely places for serendipitous meetings between people from different groups.

We can also consider the second question:
2. Are the same places the most diverse across all definitions of 'group', or are some more diverse in some terms than in others? The bolded entries in the table show that there are indeed some rooms that are highly-ranked only in one list, and all but 2 of these places are shared offices. It seems likely that this is because while kitchens and printers are, by nature of the usage of the space, ideal for mixing between people from different groups, shared offices are often occupied by people from the same research group and having the same role. These results meet what one would expect, and

	Role		Research group		Gender		Age		Nationality	
1	Printer 2	1.79	Shared office 1	1.72	Kitchen 1	0.63	Reception	1.61	Shared office 3	2.04
2	Common room	1.79	**Printer 1**	**1.71**	Printer 4	0.57	Cafeteria	1.58	Kitchen 2	2.02
3	Shared office 3	1.77	**Shared office 2**	1.67	Reception	0.56	Common room	1.57	Meeting room 1	2.02
4	Shared office 1	1.77	Common room	1.64	**Shared office 4**	**0.54**	Printer 4	1.57	**Shared office 5**	**1.94**
5	Printer 3	1.77	Kitchen 1	1.63	Cafeteria	0.52	Printer 3	1.56	Shared office 6	1.93
6	Cafeteria	1.76	Reception	1.63	Common room	0.51	Kitchen 1	1.54	**Shared office 11**	**1.92**
7	Kitchen 2	1.76	Printer 4	1.63	Shared office 6	0.50	Kitchen 3	1.53	**Shared office 8**	**1.92**
8	Kitchen 3	1.75	Cafeteria	1.63	Printer 2	0.45	Printer 2	1.47	**Shared office 9**	**1.92**
9	Meeting room 1	1.72	**Kitchen 4**	**1.63**	Kitchen 2	0.41	Shared office 7	1.41	Shared office 7	1.90
10	Reception	1.71	Printer 3	1.63	Shared office 3	0.41	Meeting room 1	1.36	**Shared office 10**	**1.86**

Table 4. Top 10 most diverse rooms and the corresponding values of H', for each way of defining groups. Bolded entries indicate rooms that do not appear in the top 10 for any other definition of groups.

that speaks to their external validity and to the quality of our experimental design.

The Nationality list is noticeably different in that most of the entries in the list are offices. This can be regarded as a reflection of the highly culturally diverse environment of the research lab as a workplace. Offices are populated by many different people from many different cultural backgrounds, and this highlights the relevance of the relationships between Hofstede's cultural dimensions and social interaction patterns in the workplace that we presented above.

DISCUSSION

From a theoretical standpoint, this study provides a modern perspective on an established set of metrics that are commonly used to explain inter-culture interaction. Our work shows how new technology, such as the sensing badges that we have deployed here, can be used alongside well-established theory, and our results provide evidence in support of the validity of these metrics and theories.

In practical terms, we have demonstrated that the way that space in the workplace is used can indeed result in more or less diversity, according to a variety of definitions, in certain locations. Our work paves the way for new application opportunities, such as better tools to understand and visualize the cultural interactions within an organization.

Theoretical implications. Past experimental work has suggested that ideas for productive collaboration will most likely come from 'idea brokers', those who maintain broad networks across many company divisions [7, 12]. Furthermore, that the best-performing groups seek fresh perspectives by frequently interacting with other groups [13]. Informal interactions can foster serendipitous mixing of ideas, which fuels innovation, but these interactions evolve so rapidly that they are not easy to track. Using the active RFID tags, we have been able to track them and validated the corresponding serendipity metric: it is highest in spaces in which it is expected to be so, which suggests that the badges are good for performing this type of study. In contrast to previous technological solutions like collar devices, the badges are much less obtrusive (they are small, barely noticeable, and lightweight) and can capture data at scale (they allow for tracking a large number of participants). They are able to observe, quantify, and measure interaction dynamics that are often associated with productive teams. Previous work has found that the most valuable form of communication is face-to-face ("35% of the variation in a team's performance can be accounted for simply by the number of face-to-face exchanges among team members" [16]), while the least valuable forms are e-mail and mobile text messages.

The significance of these results extends beyond merely tracking interactions: they provide evidence that not only the culture of an office, but also the cultures of individuals within an office, could shape interactions. To appreciate the importance of this insight, consider that past research has focused on offices as self-contained entities in the countries where they are situated [4, 9], but not on how cultural differences between individuals in highly international work environments can shape office social dynamics. In addition, our research makes key informal dynamics measurable to an unprecedented degree, producing findings based upon highly reliable observations.

Practical implications. Our results show that the way that space in the workplace is used can indeed result in more or less diversity in certain locations, depending on the kind of diversity that it is desirable to achieve. From the location results, we can see that some shared offices are ranked highly for diversity along certain dimensions (e.g., gender or nationality) and appear in no other list. This is because in the lab in question, shared offices are often occupied by people from the same research group and having the same role (e.g., offices occupied entirely by PhD students with the same supervisor). Therefore, these offices will not promote interactions between people from different roles or research groups, but will have a diverse population along dimensions not closely related to role or research group. It is true that the assignment of people to offices does not completely preclude diverse interactions, since others may visit the office. However, these interactions may more commonly take place in other spaces, to avoid disturbing the other occupants of the office.

On the other hand, other areas such as kitchens and printers are located more centrally, such as between corridors used by different research groups, and may therefore be visited by people from both groups. Similarly, common areas such as these are not used exclusively by people of one or two roles, e.g., a single printer or coffee machine will be used by faculty and students alike, so there is more diversity in these areas along dimensions such as role.

To the best of our knowledge, this is the first investigation into workplace spaces, culture, and types of interaction conducted using purely automatic mechanisms. This has implications for future such studies, in showing how workplace interactions could be studied in conjunction with new physical workplace configurations.

Our findings might translate into a number of practical applications. To give one example, we are currently planning to create maps of the lab's floor plans reflecting the extent to which each area hosts serendipitous conversations, and graphs showing how a research group is doing in terms of serendipitous interactions. If these maps were to be made accessible, they would provide instant visual feedback to anyone, and their impact on group interactions could be measured. In the future, one could imagine a lab's entire staff wearing our name badges, creating what Pentland calls a 'God's-eye view' of the organization [16].

Limitations. This study has three limitations that call for further investigation in the future. The first is that our results do not speak to causality. While we have found that Hofstede's cultural dimensions of Power Distance, Individualism, and Masculinity are correlated with interactions with others across different roles, the root cause of this is not clear from this study, and there would therefore be benefit to be gained from more studies of a similar nature.

Secondly, we did not compare serendipitous interactions to any performance metric. In the research lab, it is difficult to find a well-defined performance metric apart from publications and research impact, which do not change frequently enough to warrant real-time tracking of informal interactions. However, this does not mean that such interactions do not have an important effect, just that it is difficult to measure formally using existing metrics. As a next step, we are planning to collect subjective daily measures (e.g., frustration, satisfaction) from our participants using experience sampling, and to investigate any relationship between these measures and sensed serendipitous interactions.

A third limitation is that we have not studied exactly how the sensing of employees' inter-group interactions, and meetings in serendipitous spaces, could be used in practice by an organization, for example, to foster more such interactions. One could envisage that making workers aware of the sensed information could prompt them to consider their own interactions and might have a positive effect on productivity by increasing the exchange of information and ideas.

CONCLUSIONS

In this work, we have used state-of-the-art active RFID tags to track serendipitous interactions in the workplace between individuals from different groups, in a less obtrusive and therefore potentially more accurate way than was possible using previous sensing technology.

Our results suggest that cultural differences between individuals in a highly international office environment can affect the likelihood that people engage in serendipitous interactions with others from different groups. We have also been able to characterize certain spaces in the workplace, such as kitchens and printers, as being particularly likely to host serendipitous interactions, and shown that different kinds of spaces may be more likely to host intergroup interactions, depending on the kind of group considered. Knowledge of these effects could be important for organizations, given that such interactions have been shown by previous work to be beneficial for group productivity, by enabling the exchange of information and ideas.

ACKNOWLEDGEMENTS

We thank the ISI Foundation and Bitmanufaktur for their support. We acknowledge the SocioPatterns collaboration (`http://www.sociopatterns.org`). We also thank Jon Crowcroft, and Kerstin Sailer for valuable discussions and feedback. Chloë Brown is a recipient of the Google Europe Fellowship in Mobile Computing, and this research is supported in part by this Google Fellowship.

REFERENCES

1. Bradburn, N. M., Sudman, S., Blair, E., and Stocking, C. Question threat and response bias. *Public Opinion Quarterly 42*, 2 (1978).
2. Burt, R. S. Structural holes and good ideas. *American Journal of Sociology 110*, 2 (2004).
3. Cattuto, C., Van den Broeck, W., Barrat, A., Colizza, V., Pinton, J.-F., and Vespignani, A. Dynamics of person-to-person interactions from distributed RFID sensor networks. *PLoS ONE 5*, 7 (2010).
4. Congdon, C., and Gall, C. How culture shapes the office. *Harvard Business Review 91*, 3 (2013).
5. Efstratiou, C., Leontiadis, I., Picone, M., Rachuri, K., Mascolo, C., and Crowcroft, J. Sense and sensibility in a pervasive world. In *Pervasive Computing* (2012).
6. Fayard, A.-L., and Weeks, J. Photocopiers and water-coolers: The affordances of informal interaction. *Organization studies 28*, 5 (2007).
7. Fishman, M., Cross, R., and Tadmor, B. Better connected. *Nature 493* (2013).
8. Hillier, B., and Hanson, J. *The social logic of space*, vol. 1. Cambridge University Press Cambridge, 1984.

9. Hofstede, G. H., Hofstede, G. J., and Minkov, M. *Cultures And Organizations: Software For The Mind.* McGraw-Hill USA, 2010.
10. Isaacs, E. A., Tang, J. C., and Morris, T. Piazza: a desktop environment supporting impromptu and planned interactions. In *CSCW*, ACM (1996).
11. Jeffrey, P., and McGrath, A. Sharing serendipity in the workplace. In *CVE*, ACM (2000).
12. Krackhardt, D., and Hanson, J. R. Informal networks: the company behind the chart. *Harvard business review 71*, 4 (1993).
13. Olguín-Olguín, D., Waber, B. N., Kim, T., Mohan, A., Ara, K., and Pentland, A. Sensible organizations: Technology and methodology for automatically measuring organizational behavior. *IEEE Transactions on Systems, Man, and Cybernetics, Part B: Cybernetics 39*, 1 (2009).
14. Panisson, A., Barrat, A., Cattuto, C., Van Den Broeck, W., Ruffo, G., and Schifanella, R. On the dynamics of human proximity for data diffusion in ad-hoc networks. *Ad Hoc Networks* (2011).
15. Penn, A., Desyllas, J., and Vaughan, L. The space of innovation: interaction and communication in the work environment. *Environment and Planning B 26* (1999).
16. Pentland, A. The new science of building great teams. *Harvard Business Review 90*, 4 (2012).
17. Reinecke, K., Nguyen, M. K., Bernstein, A., Näf, M., and Gajos, K. Z. Doodle around the world: online scheduling behavior reflects cultural differences in time perception and group decision-making. In *CSCW*, ACM (2013).
18. Sailer, K., and Penn, A. Spatiality and transpatiality in workplace environments. In *7th International Space Syntax Symposium* (2009).
19. Shannon, C. E., and Weaver, W. A mathematical theory of communication, 1948.
20. Stryker, J. B., and Santoro, M. D. Facilitating face-to-face communication in high-tech teams. *Research-Technology Management 55*, 1 (2012).
21. Toker, U., and Gray, D. O. Innovation spaces: Workspace planning and innovation in US university research centers. *Research Policy 37*, 2 (2008).
22. van de Mortel, T. F. Faking it: social desirability response bias in self-report research. *Australian Journal of Advanced Nursing 25*, 4 (2008).
23. Waber, B., Olguin Olguin, D., Kim, T., and Pentland, A. Productivity through coffee breaks: changing social networks by changing break structure. *Available at SSRN 1586375* (2010).
24. Want, R., Hopper, A., Falcao, V., and Gibbons, J. The active badge location system. *ACM Transactions on Information Systems 10*, 1 (1992).
25. Whittaker, S., Frohlich, D., and Daly-Jones, O. Informal workplace communication: What is it like and how might we support it? In *CHI*, ACM (1994).
26. Whyte, W. F. *Street corner society: The social structure of an Italian slum.* University of Chicago Press, 1943.
27. Wu, L., Waber, B., Aral, S., Brynjolfsson, E., and Pentland, A. Mining face-to-face interaction networks using sociometric badges: Predicting productivity in an IT configuration task. *Available at SSRN 1130251* (2008).

Capturing the Mood: Facebook and Face-to-Face Encounters in the Workplace

Gloria Mark[1], Shamsi Iqbal[2], Mary Czerwinski[2], Paul Johns[2]

[1]Department of Informatics
University of California, Irvine
Irvine, CA 92697 USA
gmark@uci.edu

[2]Microsoft Research
One Microsoft Way
Redmond, WA 98052 USA
{shamsi,marycz,Paul.Johns}@microsoft.com

ABSTRACT

What makes people feel happy, engaged and challenged at work? We conducted an *in situ* study of Facebook and face-to-face interactions examining how they influence people's mood in the workplace. Thirty-two participants in an organization were each observed for five days in their natural work environment using automated data capture and experience sampling. Our results show that online and offline social interactions are associated with different moods, suggesting that they serve different purposes at work. Face-to-face interactions are associated with a positive mood throughout the day whereas Facebook use and engagement in work contribute to a positive feeling at the end of the day. Email use is associated with negative affect and along with multitasking, is associated with a feeling of engagement and challenge throughout the day. Our findings provide initial evidence of how online and offline interactions affect workplace mood, and could inform practices to improve employee morale.

Author Keywords

Mood; affect; Facebook; face-to-face interaction; multitasking; email

ACM Classification Keywords

H.5.3 [Information Interfaces and Presentation (e.g., HCI)]: Group and Organization Interfaces; K.4.m [Computers and Society]: Miscellaneous.

INTRODUCTION

Mood in the workplace has long been a subject of interest in fields ranging from organizational science to psychology. In the field of CSCW, although some attention has been given to how interactions in general influence mood (e.g., [44]), and how affect is conveyed through computer-mediated interaction (e.g., [20]) and social media [4], little attention has been given to how workplace interactions affect mood. This is important, as mood has been shown to impact performance in the workplace [3].

Understanding how such interaction affects mood in the workplace is important for organizations as both online and offline interactions continue to be integral parts of the daily routine of workers. Social networking sites (as well as other social media) are being deployed increasingly more in organizations and they amplify opportunities for online interactions.

In a work environment, it is an open question how face-to-face and online interactions compare in affecting mood. To our knowledge, this has never been investigated before. On the one hand, we might expect online interactions to positively affect mood, as has been found with face-to-face interaction in field experiments [43, 44]. On the other hand, interactions could be associated with work interruptions and task demands which have been shown to increase stress [37, 38], which in turn could negatively impact mood. In this paper we investigate how face-to-face and online social network interactions influence mood in the workplace. These interactions typically occur in an environment where task switching and interruptions are prevalent [10, 17]; we also investigate how this multitasking context affects mood.

To gain a deeper understanding of how online and offline social interactions affect people's mood at work, we conducted an *in situ* study at a large U.S. corporation. Our focus was to examine the influence of both face-to-face interaction and Facebook use on a breadth of workplace affective states. We chose Facebook because of its reported versatility and fairly high adoption in the workplace [50]. This research is part of a larger project: WorkSense, which has the goal of understanding people's workplace behavior via automated data capture and other methods. We found that online and offline social interactions are associated with different mood experiences suggesting that they serve different purposes at work. Face-to-face interactions are associated with people being happy throughout the day whereas Facebook use and being engaged in work contribute to an overall positive feeling at the end of the day. Our results showing the effects of online and offline

CSCW'14, February 15 - 19, 2014, Baltimore, MD, USA.
Copyright 2014 ACM 978-1-4503-2540-0/14/02...$15.00.
http://dx.doi.org/10.1145/2531602.2531673

social interactions on mood may have implications for workplace practices to improve employee morale.

EFFECTS OF SOCIAL MEDIA USAGE ON MOOD

Pew reports show that in 2012, 67% of internet users said that they used at least one social network site (SNS) [14]. This is over double the percentage from a similar study in 2008 (as reported in Hampton et al, [18]). Over half of these SNS users (71%) were female, and while the largest demographic continues to be 18-29 years of age, 52% of 50-64 year olds were using SNS sites and 32% were over 65. Of these sites, Facebook has been the dominant site used, with 92% of SNS users reporting they were on Facebook. The Pew report also documents that between 10-26% of users update their status, comment, "like" or send private messages at least once a day. But more specific to our study, how does the use of Facebook influence users' emotional states? The Pew report finds that Facebook users are more trusting than others, have more close relationships, get more social support and are more politically engaged than most people [18]. Does this mean that they are happier or turn to Facebook when they need this kind of support?

Pea et al. [43] used a large, online survey of girls from North America aged 8-12 and examined the relationships between social well-being and young girls' media use—including video, games, music, reading/homework, e-mailing/posting on social media sites, texting/instant messaging, and talking on phones/video chatting and face-to-face communication. These researchers found a strong negative association between personal communication in media and social well-being. For example, using the phone, chatting, listening to music, reading and especially watching video were highly correlated with negative social well-being. Media multi-tasking was also correlated with negative social well-being. On the other hand, face-to-face communication was strongly associated with positive social well-being. While these findings have direct implications for pre-teens' social well-being, do they translate into mood effects in the workplace?

Kramer (2012) did a large-scale study of emotional contagion by studying Facebook status updates [30]. His research suggested that if someone from your social network made a status update with emotional content, the friends of the poster are more likely to post in a similar emotional vein. His original group of participants included one million random Facebook users. He found that this effect was long-lasting (lasting up to 3 days after the original post) and held when controlling for emotional expressions by posters and their friends in the past. This study was important because it may have demonstrated the contagion of emotion through indirect textual posts in social networks (though of course it could not control for face-to-face interactions with close friends that might also be your friend in Facebook). The speculation proffered by the author is that these public expression strategies might help users maintain psychological health, by inviting friends to share in each other's joy or by gaining social support when needed. It was also conjectured that sharing negative emotions on Facebook might be important for garnering feelings of closeness.

There may also be gender differences to consider. For instance, Kivran-Swaine et al. [29] analyzed the language used on Twitter exchanges in addition to aspects of users' networks, to analyze the influence of gender on emotion, while controlling for the strength of connection between the users. Their findings showed that women expressed positive emotions more than men, especially when exchanging tweets with other women.

According to reasoning by Hampton and Wellman [19], Facebook might enhance current, place-based community and help generate social capital, which may help explain why so many people use it on a frequent basis. Another study has shown that using Facebook may actually boost your self-esteem, largely due to users and their social networks portraying their best possible selves [16]. Yet it is unclear whether these factors could also positively impact mood in the workplace.

Research questions

In this study we ask the following two research questions.

1) How are Facebook (FB) use and face-to-face (F2F) encounters related to mood as it fluctuates throughout the day? Mood varies throughout the day depending on workload changes, task engagement, interactions, and breaks that one may take. Measuring mood at a single point in time fails to capture the dynamic nature of interactions at work and how they affect mood. Continually tapping into mood as the environment and context change can provide us with insight into how specific phenomena (interactions, computer use) affect mood. It also enables us to capture mood while the experience is still recent in memory [21]. Therefore, in this research question we examine how online and offline interactions may impact mood changes throughout the day. As interactions may occur in a context of dynamic task-switching [17] we also examine how multitasking influences mood throughout the day.

2) How are the amount of FB use and F2F encounters over the course of the day related to one's mood state at the end of the day? In this research question, we are interested to examine whether FB or F2F encounters have a longer temporal effect such that at the end of the day, one's mood might be affected. Mood at the end of the day is important to consider as mood in work and home life can have carryover effects [56]. In particular, we are interested in whether the amount of FB or F2F encounters could influence a *change* in mood over the course of the day. Again, as interactions occur in a context of multi-tasking, we also examine factors related to task-switching.

VARIABLES TO ASSESS MOOD IN THE WORKPLACE

An assumption in studying mood or "feeling" is that it can be broken down into different dimensions that are consciously accessible [46]. A range of variables have been used to assess mood [46]. As our focus was on interaction and mood in the workplace, we considered the following dimensions to be the most relevant: valence, engagement, and challenge. Since personality's effects have been well studied on mood, we felt it was important to consider personality traits in our exploration. Finally, given the potential of disruption to ongoing work caused by interactions, we incorporate prior knowledge on how task-switching behavior may impact a user's affective state.

Dimensions of mood

We selected *Valence* as a measure to capture the positive (e.g., happy, upbeat) and negative (e.g., sad, gloomy) affective dimensions of an emotion [5]. Informed by the study of Pea et al [43], who examined media and face-to-face interactions, we deemed it important to understand the type of valence associated with offline and online interactions. The valence measure has been validated in assessing positive and negative affect. Steptoe et al. [51] measured affect using a self-report sampling method (as in the current study) and validated it with physiological measures of cortisol samples and heart rate monitoring. Positive and negative affect have been examined in a range of different contexts in the workplace. See [3, 21] for reviews.

We selected *Engagement* as a measure to capture the degree to which people felt involved in or distracted from their work, particularly relevant in information work where people are constantly interrupted and switch tasks [10, 17]. We follow the definition of Schaufeli et al. [48] who defines engagement as "*a positive, fulfilling, work-related state of mind that is characterized by vigor, dedication, and absorption*". Experience-sampling studies typically query subjects with either 'engagement', 'concentration', or 'involvement' in an activity to capture the degree of engagement [21]. Others have studied and visualized self-reports of engagement to help users reflect upon their work activities and mood using various sensors [40]. We were motivated to build upon and extend this work. For a review of how engagement has been used in self-reports, see [21].

We also focus on *Challenge*, as we felt that when someone in the workplace is faced with juggling interactions and work demands, then this could at times create a feeling of being challenged, e.g., due to time pressure [37]. This may especially be the case if online or offline interactions are viewed as distractions as opposed to benefits [41]. One's perception of 'challenge' can be dynamic, depending on the activity; interacting with someone face-to-face during a coffee break might yield a different feeling of challenge compared to dealing with an interruption amidst other task activities. We define challenge as the amount of mental effort involved in performing an activity. The construct of challenge in the workplace has long been emphasized for its significant contribution to job satisfaction (e.g., [22]). The feeling of challenge has been studied extensively and has been validated as part of the experience of "flow", or optimal experience [21].

Effects of personality on mood

Personality, as related to interactions and mood, has long been a topic of interest, with recent studies beginning to address online interactions. The Big Five dimensions of personality have been widely employed as a measure [39], as they are well-validated, and consistent and comprehensive in scope [13]. The Big Five characterizes personality using five different traits [39]. *Agreeableness* refers to cooperative behavior, as well as deferring to others during a conflict. *Conscientiousness* refers to the propensity for planning and to seek high achievement. *Extraversion* is the tendency to want to be with others, to have strong social skills, and to seek social stimulation. *Openness to Experience* refers to being open to change and variety and seeking diversity. *Neuroticism* is the tendency to feel guilty, depressed or anxious.

In terms of mood, Neuroticism is generally associated with negative affective states while Extraversion is associated with positive affective states (cf [54]). Some research has addressed the relationship of personality with face-to-face and online communication. Extraversion was shown to be positively correlated with using the Internet to maintain both face-to-face and remote friendships [53]. Facebook users were found to score high on Extraversion [47], and social network site use [6]. Conscientiousness has been shown to be negatively correlated with time spent on Facebook [47] while Neuroticism was found to be positively correlated with time spent on Facebook [47]. Openness to Experience was positively correlated with social network site use [6].

Thus, though positive and negative affect are generally related to specific personality traits, the results relating personality to communication, especially online social network use, is mixed. As prior studies show correlations with Extraversion, Conscientiousness and Openness, we examined these personality traits in our study.

Effects of interruptions, email and task switching on mood

Broadly speaking, both Facebook and face-to-face interactions typically interrupt the flow of ongoing work at the workplace, which can in turn affect mood. A large body of prior work has explored the effects of interruption on a user's affective state, mostly focusing on negative affect such as frustration, anxiety and annoyance caused by inopportune interruptions [1, 2, 24, 57]. McFarlane and Latorella demonstrated that interruptions that are unpredictable and cannot be controlled result in more stress and affect task performance [41]. Mark et al. [37] also showed that interruptions can lead to increased stress and higher frustration.

On the other hand, external interruptions to ongoing work caused by emails and instant messages have been shown to have positive benefits including supporting near instant communication [9, 11, 32], maintaining awareness of peripheral information [34], reminding upcoming activities [12] or helping users perform complex tasks [33, 45]. Such benefits can lead to positive affect. Self-interruptions can also have positive or negative impact on an individual [27].

Other studies have looked at how interruptions from digital media such as email or IM notifications, or physical interruptions such as phone calls or face-to-face interactions, cause people to continue to be distracted by switching tasks with effects on task performance [10, 25, 26]. Notifications also are associated with emotional experiences and are correlated with types of notifications people would like to receive in the future [42]. Email use in particular has been found to be associated with an increase in stress [37, 38].

Thus, it is unclear how FB and F2F interactions, and digital media use in general, might influence mood in the workplace. To the best of our knowledge, no study has looked at the effects of social interactions on mood in the context of the workplace. As it is an open question, based on this prior body of work, we examine FB and F2F interaction, as well as task switching of applications and documents, along with email usage. Our broader goal is to understand factors that impact mood at work.

RESEARCH STUDY

To understand effects of FB and F2F interactions on mood in the workplace, we conducted an *in situ* study. The research was conducted in the fall of 2012 at a large U.S. corporation.

Participants

Participants were recruited primarily from volunteers who responded to email advertising done throughout a research division in the company. The rest of the participants were recruited through convenience sampling or snowball sampling, (i.e., recommendations of names from people who participated.). Our criteria for recruitment were that people should be FB users and that they use the Windows 7 operating system (which was compatible with our logging software). Thirty-two people (17 females, 15 males), volunteered to participate. This sample is over double that of samples used in similar *in situ* work tracking studies [10, 17, 38]. We feel that the data collected from 32 people over five full work days was sufficient for enabling us to gain a representative sample of their mood in their daily work environment.

All participants were knowledge workers. Most participants were involved in research (15), but there were also managers, admins, engineers, a department director, a designer, and consultant.

Methodology

Following a paradigm of precision workplace shadowing [17, 38], our goal was to capture as complete a picture as possible about online workplace behaviors and mood. Each participant was observed for a period of five days. For most participants, this was Monday through Friday, i.e., a regular work week. Some participants traveled during the week or missed a day for other reasons; in these cases, they made up the missed day (in most cases) the following week.

We used mixed methods for our data collection: computer logging was used to capture online actions, a wearable SenseCam camera [23] was utilized to capture face-to-face interactions, experience sampling probes were used to capture self-reported moods throughout the day, and a series of surveys were collected for other subjective and demographic measures. On the day before the participant began the study (usually a Friday), the computer logging software and experience sampling software were installed on their computer. The study and tracking approaches were explained to the participant. Participants were assured that their data would be private and aggregated, that no content would be retraced to their information, and that they would remain anonymous. They were also assured that their data would be deleted in a timely manner.

Participants were instructed to work as they normally would throughout the workday. They were instructed to answer the (experience sampling) probes when the probe windows popped up on their computer screens, but they also could cancel the probe window when they chose. We emphasized that it was important to answer the probe questions as accurately as possible. Participants were told that at any time they could turn off the SenseCam camera. In the post-study interviews, 11 participants reported that they turned the camera off when they left the office for brief periods (e.g., for meetings, a demo, and a doctor's office). In these cases, we did not collect probe or logging data either. For two people we lack SenseCam data for ½ day each.

Measures

Below we explain the details of the measures taken. Table 1 provides a summary of the measures and their explanations, along with abbreviations used to refer to them in the paper.

Data collection: sensors and experience sampling

In collecting data we had to decide between using highly precise sensor-based data and human observation data which is more effective in capturing the context of the participant's work. Previous ethnographic studies that track workplace behavior, e.g. [17], while capturing rich data, are very labor intensive for capturing precision data, i.e., users' actions tracked to the second. Automatic data collection by sensors, though lacking contextual information and intentional data that ethnography provides, enables the collection of a wider array of data, with more participants simultaneously, and at a higher precision level than human ethnographic observation.

Measure	Explanation	Abbrev.
Computer Logging		
FB use (seconds)	The amount of time spent in a web browser where a Facebook page is in the foreground tab.	**FB**
Email use (seconds)	The amount of time an email is open and in the foreground, whether one is reading a received mail, composing a new mail, or replying or forwarding.	**Email/Use**
Email/Calendar (seconds)	The amount of time any part of the Email/Calendar Application is open and in the foreground, including email, calendar, contacts, tasks, etc. Email usage in Email/Cal is distinct from usage in Email/Use. Email/Use refers to operations of reading and writing, whereas Email/Cal refers to simply viewing the inbox.	**Email/cal**
Document switches (counts, per unit of time)	The number of document switches *within* an application, e.g. within Word or Excel or Internet Explorer. In web browsing, each new page is a document switch.	**Doc**
Application switches (counts, per unit of time)	The number of switches *between* applications, e.g., from Internet Explorer to Word.	**App**
SenseCam		
F2F interactions (counts)	The SenseCam captured images on average once every 15 seconds.	**F2F**
Experience Sampling Probe		
Valence (-200 to +200. Neutral = 0)	Ranging from negative to positive affect.	**Valence**
How Engaged (0=not at all to 5=high)	The extent to which people feel involved with or distracted from work	**Engaged**
How Challenged (0=not at all to 5=high)	The amount of mental effort involved in performing an activity	**Challenged**
Surveys		
PANAS	Rating scale of mood of positive (PA) and negative (NA) affect dimensions [55]; deployed at beginning (BEG) and end (END) of each day	**PA-BEG, NA-BEG PA-END, NA-END**
Big 5 traits	Personality inventory [39]	**Extroversion Neuroticism Conscientiousness**
Demographic info	Age, gender, job role, education	

Table 1. Summary table of measures, explanations and their abbreviations.

Thus, the choice of using sensors to capture human behavior as opposed to ethnographic approaches involves a tradeoff between precision and contextual richness. Since for this study the precision of data was central to understanding mood changes we chose for our methodology the use of sensors. To compensate for the lack of context that human observation could have provided, we collected participant self-reports to supplement our automated data with the participant's perspective. We collected the following data:

Mood throughout the day: Experience sampling

To collect mood data throughout the day we used the experience sampling method. Experience sampling is designed to capture people's perception of daily life as it changes throughout the day. This method has been proven to have internal validity [8] as well as external validity [21]. Experience sampling works well paired with computer logging as it provides information on how the participant is experiencing the events and context. Experience sampling has been used in a large number of studies and particularly has been used for measuring mood in the workplace: some example studies examined work and home life balance [56] and time pressure [52]. For a review see [21].

Experience sampling was done with custom built software that presented a probe, a small pop-up window on the computer screen, to participants using predetermined sampling rules. We used a hybrid interval-contingent and event-contingent sampling approach [21]. The sampling occurred whenever a user left email after being active in that application for at least three consecutive minutes, or in FB after a full minute of uninterrupted use. Sampling also was triggered whenever a user logged into Windows or unlocked the screen saver (event-contingent). If fifteen minutes passed without a sampling, then a probe was triggered (interval-contingent).

The probe presented the instructions “Please rate how you feel right now”. We used rating scales as is commonly used in experience sampling approaches [21]. To measure Valence, participants saw a sliding scale which corresponded to a range of -200 (negative affect) to +200 (positive affect) and were asked to click with their cursor on that point that best expresses their feeling "right now". To measure Engagement, participants were asked 'How Engaged Were You?' using a 6-point Likert scale (0=Not at All; 5=Extremely). To measure Challenge, participants were asked 'How Challenged Were You?' using the same Likert scale. Participants were asked if they just had any face-to-face interactions, and if so, a second screen was shown, asking whether the participant had a scheduled meeting. The timestamp when participants submitted the probe was recorded.

Beginning and end of day mood: PANAS

To answer the second research question, we needed to collect overall mood data at the beginning of the day and at the end of the day so that we could quantify any changes. We deployed surveys at the beginning and end of each day to measure mood using the PANAS scale [55], a well-validated 20-item inventory of mood which is comprised of two scales to measure positive and negative affect. Items included feelings such as interested, excited, distressed, upset, and irritable. Participants were asked to rate to what extent they felt that way at the present moment on a scale ranging from *very slightly/not at all* to *extremely*.

Facebook interactions: Computer logging

Online interactions were logged with a custom-built application that captured all activity in the Windows Operating System. Captured activity includes beginning and end times for the lifespan of every window, and the beginning and end times for every instance of every foreground window. Computer sleep mode, mouse and keyboard activity were also logged, so that periods of time in which an application was in the foreground window, but the user was not actively using the computer, could be ignored.

Note that we were unable to capture activities that occurred within a window itself, e.g., capturing what a person was looking at while on FB or any other application due to privacy and technical limitations. While there are APIs that can collect data on what one posts – statuses, comments, photos, etc., there is no public API that allows one to track actions to the second on Facebook. Even such APIs would provide access to only a small fraction of what one does on Facebook and would miss interactions that involve scanning for awareness which can be only detected via over-the-shoulder shadowing. We therefore focused on measuring the total time one spends on FB as a holistic measure of FB interaction, though we hope to be able to capture more fine-grained interaction data in future research.

Face-to-face interactions: SenseCam

F2F interactions were measured through SenseCam [23], a lightweight wearable camera that participants wore around their necks. The camera automatically takes a picture and stores it locally, and as soon as the image is processed and saved the next picture is taken. The average length of time between photos is 15 seconds. SenseCam images were processed by a face detection module, a publicly available application produced by Microsoft Research (http://research.microsoft.com/en-us/projects/facesdk/). It is important to note that with this software, we cannot distinguish whether the faces were the same person or not. Therefore, the counts in our F2F variable should be considered as a proxy for amount of F2F interaction over the course of the day, and not necessarily *distinct* interactions. It is thus a measure of how much interaction a person experienced, and not precisely how many different interactions one engaged in.

RESULTS

We first present an overview of results of the data collected, the probe responses measuring mood, and then an overview of FB and F2F interactions.

Data overview

Our 32 participants were observed for 5 days each, for a total of 160 person-days, or a total of 1,509 hours of data collection. Our computer logging software collected a total of 91,409 computer window switches. We collected 2,809 experience sampling probes and analyzed 204,922 SenseCam photos.

Mood: probe responses

Our 32 participants averaged 17.56 probe responses per day, for an average of 87.8 probe responses per participant. The average Valence rating over participants was 38.83 (on a scale of -200 to +200), showing a net positive affect. Females (M=44.78, sd=74.98) reported significantly higher Valence than males (M=32.75, sd=62.30), $t(2807)=4.62$, $p<.0001$. The average Engaged rating over participants was 3.01 (sd=1.37), on a scale of 0-5 (high). Females (M=3.09, sd=1.37) reported being significantly more Engaged than males (M=2.93, sd=1.38), $t(2808)=9.25$, $p<.004$. The average Challenged rating over participants was 1.82 (sd=1.42) on a scale of 0-5 (high). There was no significant difference between females (M=1.78, sd=1.36) and males (M=1.86, sd=1.47), $t(2807)=1.43$, $p<.15$, in feeling Challenged. Thus, in our sample females reported higher positive Valence, and reported to be more engaged in their tasks than males, throughout their workday.

FB and F2F interactions

We next present an overview comparison of FB and F2F interactions over the course of the day. Table 2 shows average daily FB use in seconds and F2F interactions, broken down by age and gender.

	N	FaceBook (sec.)	F2F (SenseCam counts)
Females	17	715.14 (1662.65)*	78.51 (81.16)
Males	15	320.33 (827.64)*	74.62 (90.04)
Age			
< 30	6	941.83 (2536.02)	37.33 (56.13)**
30-40	16	425.16 (830.71)	93.83 (95.62)**
> 40	10	454.58 (830.71)	72.18 (73.55)**
Overall mean	32	529.92 (1348.19)	162 (76.69)

Table 2. Means (S.D.) of daily FB use and F2F interaction, as measured by SenseCam counts, N=32 subjects, each measured over five days, **=p<.001, *=p<.05.

A 2 (Gender) x 3 (Age) ANOVA conducted on the dependent variable of FB shows a significant Gender difference (F(1, 161)=5.39, p<.02), and a trend showing Age x Gender interaction (F (2, 161)=2.64, p<.08). Age is not significant. Females use FB over twice as long on an average day as males.

A 2 (Gender) x 3 (Age) ANOVA conducted on the dependent variable of F2F interactions shows a significant effect of Age (F(2, 162)=5.19, p<.007, but no Gender, or Age x Gender interactions. In sum, people in the age range of 30-40 had the most F2F encounters during the day on average, with people under 30 having the least. In contrast, people under 30 had the most FB usage, with ages 30-40 the least. Work roles could somewhat explain the difference. Participants under 30 were all researchers (researcher, intern, postdoc) whereas participants 30-40 had more of a range of positions (researcher, intern, manager, admin, designer, and consultant). Younger participants may use social media more than their older counterparts, and this might have an effect on their number of F2F interactions.

Comparing activities in 5-minute time units, time spent in FB is weakly correlated with both App switching (r=.09, p<.0001) and Doc switching (r=.11, p<.0001), N=37,788. F2F is very weakly correlated with both App switching (r=.05, p<.0001) and Doc switching (r=.08, p<.0001), N=37,788.

Mood throughout the day: Valence, Engagement, and Challenge

Our first research question addressed how FB use and F2F interactions influence mood throughout the day. We report the results of three mood states: Valence (positive and negative affect), and feelings of Engagement and Challenge in the current activity.

We collected data on the same participant for five days. To account for the nested interdependence in our data, we ran linear mixed models in SPSS using random and fixed effects, and did this for all three mood measures. As we had no a priori notion of what variables might be associated with mood change, the ideal procedure would be an automatic model fitting based on selecting those variables that would result on the best fitting model. As SPSS does not have an automatic model building procedure for linear mixed models, we built the models by hand. We emulated a backward elimination procedure as in stepwise regression, where we started with all variables in the model and then by hand gradually eliminated different combinations of variables until we found the best fitting model based on the BIC criterion[1]. We tested variable measures in different time units (1, 5 and 10 minutes) prior to each probe response and included the results that showed the strongest correlation in the model.

An R^2 statistic for linear mixed models must account for the variance explained by both the fixed and random effects; however, there is no standard method for specifying an R^2 in these models [15]. To provide a sense of how much variance the model explains, we ran a linear model including only fixed effects to get an R^2 value. By not including random effects (participants), this of course will underestimate the amount of variance explained but we feel it is a reasonable estimate since the random effects are small.

We tested models that included all the variables shown in Table 1. As some variables were not normally distributed, we did a log transformation on these variables: F2F, FB, Email/Use, Email/Cal, App and Doc.

Valence model	β	t	p
Intercept	*-32.37*	-1.06	.30
F2F prior 5 min. (counts)	*4.90*	2.44	.03
Email/Use prior 5 min. (sec.)	*-3.41*	-2.85	.005
Big 5 Extroversion	*2.69*	2.32	.03

Table 3: Beta coefficients of variables for best fitting model for Valence throughout the day. N=2809 cases.

Influencing Valence throughout the day

We first report the results of the model for Valence change over the course of the day. Table 3 shows the independent variables in the model that best fit Valence as a dependent variable. The model shows that the more F2F interaction in the 5 minutes prior to the probe (i.e., F2F counts as measured in the SenseCam photos), the higher (i.e., more positive) the Valence measure. Email/Use, on the other hand, shows an inverse relationship with Valence: the *lower* the seconds of

[1] In linear mixed models, Schwarz's Bayesian Criterian (BIC) is the criterion used to find the best fitting model [49.]. The lower the score, the better the fit of the model. The absolute number itself is not meaningful—the BIC is used to compare between models and is a well-established metric of model selection.

email use in the 5 minutes prior to the probe (i.e. reading or writing emails), the more positive the Valence measure. There is also a significant positive relationship with the Big 5 Extroversion personality score and Valence: the more extroverted participants are, the more positive is the Valence measure. There were no significant interactions. FB was not found to impact Valence. There was no significant difference in Valence if one had a scheduled meeting or not before the probe. The R^2 of a linear model of the fixed effects alone is 14.4% (see explanation above).

Influencing Engagement throughout the Day

We next focus on variables that might influence Engagement over the course of the day. Our dependent variable was Engagement, as measured by participants' responses to the probe, "How Engaged Were You?" on a 6-point scale ranging from 0='not at all' to 5='extremely'. Table 4 shows the best fitting model.

Here, the model shows that the *fewer* seconds of FB use prior to the probe, the more Engaged one reports. In contrast, the *more* F2F interaction prior to the probe, the more Engaged one reports to be. Contrary to Valence, the more time spent in Email/Use, the higher the reported engagement. The more task switching (as measured by App), the more engaged one reports to be. Email/Cal use is inversely related to Engagement. Interestingly, Conscientiousness, from the Big 5 personality inventory, is positively associated with Engagement. No interactions were significant. Though linear mixed models in SPSS do not report multi-collinearity, a regression analysis of these factors shows all variance inflation factors (VIF) to be <1.1, indicating that multi-collinearity is not a problem. The R^2 of a linear model of the fixed effects alone is 30.6%.

Engagement model	*β*	t	p
Intercept	1.97	3.32	.002
FB use prior 10 min. (sec.)	-.10	-3.29	.004
F2F prior 5 min. (counts)	.08	1.93	.05
Email/Use prior 5 min. (sec.)	.16	5.63	.0001
App prior 10 min. (counts)	.10	3.03	.002
Email/Cal prior 10 min. (sec.)	-.08	-3.60	.0001
Big 5 Conscientiousness	.04	2.05	.05

Table 4: Beta coefficients of variables for best fitting model for Engagement throughout the day. N=2809 cases.

Influencing Challenge throughout the Day

What leads people to feel challenged throughout the day? Our dependent variable was Challenge, as measured by the probe question: 'How Challenged were you?' using the 6-point Likert scale. Table 5 shows the independent variables that produce the best fitting model.

The model shows that FB use is inversely related to Challenge: the more one uses FB, the *less* challenged one feels. Email/Use is positively related to Challenge: the more time spent email reading/writing, the more challenged one self-reports. Task switching (as measured by App switches) is positively related to feeling challenged. However, Email/Cal use is inversely related to feeling challenged. One's negative mood at the beginning of the day (as measured by the PANAS NA BEG), is positively associated with feeling challenged throughout the day.

Challenge model	β	t	p
Intercept	1.07	2.70	.007
FB use prior 10 min. (sec.)	-.18	-3.99	.001
Email/Use prior 5 min. (sec.)	.11	2.98	.005
App prior 10 min. (counts)	.08	2.48	.013
Email/Cal prior 10 min. (sec.)	-.06	-2.89	.004
PANAS NA BEG	.86	2.88	.004
Age X Gender	<30, F: -.71 <30, M: -.18 30-40, F: .07 30-40, M: -.68 >40, F: -.80 >40, M: 0*	1.65	.04

Table 5: Beta coefficients for best fitting model for Challenge throughout the day. N=2809 cases. *=This parameter is set to 0 because it is redundant.

Age	Gender	Mean (SE)
<30	F	1.38 (.27)
	M	1.91 (.40)
30-40	F	2.16 (.16)
	M	1.41 (.24)
>40	F	1.29 (.37)
	M	2.09 (.21)

Table 6: Mean (SE) of Age x Gender levels that influence How Challenged one is throughout the day.

We also find a significant Age x Gender interaction but no other interactions. In Table 5, the beta coefficients show that females 30-40 feel positively challenged; all other Age x Gender levels show that participants feel negatively challenged. As Table 6 shows, for those under 30, males report being more challenged than females; for those 30-40, females are more challenged than males; and for those over 40, males are more challenged than females. The variance inflation factor is < 1.8 for all variables indicating that multi-collinearity is not a problem. The R^2 of a linear model of the fixed effects alone is 39.6%.

We summarize the results of our first research question. The more F2F interaction one has, the more positive is one's Valence rating and the more one feels Engaged. The longer one spends in FB, the less Engaged and Challenged one feels. Length of time of Email/Use is consistently a strong influence on all three types of mood: negatively related to Valence, and positively related to Engagement and Challenge. Task switching is positively related to both Engagement and Challenge. If one starts out the day with a negative affect, then this shows a spillover effect in making people feel more challenged throughout the day. Personality traits are also associated with mood: the higher the Extroversion score, the more positive the Valence, and the higher the Conscientiousness score, the higher the Engagement rating.

Changes in mood at the end of day

Our second research question asked what factors would be associated with a person's mood at the end of the day. Would cumulative time in FB and amount of F2F interactions have an effect on one's mood at the end of the day? What other types of user actions throughout the workday make one feel more positive or negative by the end of the day?

Positive mood at the end of the day

To investigate positive mood at the end of the day, we looked at the *change* in positive affect over the course of the day, computing a dependent variable based on [PANAS PA-END score – PANAS PA-BEG score]. We were particularly interested to see if FB use or F2F interactions were associated with a more positive mood at the end of the day compared to the beginning of the day. We examined a dataset consisting of each participant's measures totaled for each day. We ran a stepwise regression in SPSS entering the following variables, controlling for individual differences: FB, F2F, Email, Email/Cal App, Doc, App, Age, Gender, Sociability, FB Import, Engaged, and Challenged. Individual differences were not found to be significant. The following model best fit the data, as shown in Table 7: $F(2,99)=9.99$, $p<.0001$, $R^2=16.8$. There is no significant Engaged x FB interaction.

Positive End of Day Mood	β	t	p
Constant	-13.13	-4.31	.0001
How Engaged	3.76	3.89	.0001
FB Use (seconds)	.778	2.50	.01

Table 7: Beta coefficients to model the change in positive affect at the end of the day.

This model shows that the more one feels engaged in their activity during the day, the more positive one feels at the end of the day (compared to the beginning of the day). FB also plays a role in influencing affect over the course of the entire day: the longer one spends in FB over the course of the day, the greater the increase in positive affect. Time in FB contributed 5.3% of the R^2, i.e. the variance explained, of the change in affect.

Negative mood at the end of the day

To investigate what might be associated with negative affect at the end of the day, we computed a dependent variable based on [PANAS NA END score – PANAS NA BEG score]. Using the same dataset as positive mood at the end of the day (see above), and entering the same variables into a stepwise regression analysis, we found none of our measures to significantly influence negative mood at the end of the day.

DISCUSSION

In this study we examined the open question of how FB use and F2F interaction influence workplace mood. We studied influences on mood from two perspectives: how mood fluctuates throughout the day and how mood is experienced at the end of the workday. Our study provides initial evidence that FB and F2F both influence positive affect, albeit in different ways. Moreover, workplace interactions, as discussed, generally occur within a broader context of other task activity and we found that email and task-switching influence workplace mood as well. Demographic and personality variables also contribute to explaining workplace mood.

Our results suggest that online and offline interactions serve different purposes in the workplace in terms of influencing mood. F2F interactions are associated with positive affect throughout the day whereas amount of FB use contributes to an overall positive feeling at the end of the day. Our results further show that throughout the day, F2F interactions were positively associated with Engagement whereas FB use was inversely associated with Engagement and Challenge. F2F showed no relation to Challenge.

Our findings show that when people are engaged in F2F interactions, it makes them feel more positive. F2F interaction involves different stages: an opening phase (e.g., greeting, adjusting proximity), the interaction, and a closing phase (parting rituals), which contributes to creating a social commitment to some degree [28]. FB, on the other hand is negatively associated with engagement and challenge. FB is an online interaction that can be done quickly, in a "grazing" fashion, without a greeting, involvement, or closing stage. This can explain why FB is not associated with high engagement or challenge, though of course our users could have chosen to go to FB precisely because they were in a state of low engagement in the first place!

To understand the FB results more holistically (i.e., that it influences positive affect at the end of the day, and involves low engagement and low challenge), we can be informed by the results of the Engagement variable, also associated with positive affect at the end of the day. Engagement was a fairly strong influence of end of day positive affect, explaining most of the variance. In our post study interviews, nearly all participants reported that being productive puts them in a good mood. Engagement in work could be equated with feeling productive.

How are FB use and Engagement then tied together to influence positive affect? FB use is weakly correlated with both App switching and Doc switching which suggests it may be used in a context of high task switching. Consistent with the idea of grazing, people can quickly move in and out of FB. As FB was not associated with high engagement or challenge, together with its use during task switching, it suggests that FB may be a "light" interaction experience. If people are also highly engaged in their work for that day, then FB could serve the purpose of offering a “break” from other work. High engagement in work, along with light breaks as FB affords, contribute then to people being in a positive mood at the end of the day.

Negative affect at the beginning of the day, as measured by the PANAS survey, also influenced feeling challenged throughout the day. This spillover effect that we found extends the work of Marco et al. [35] who, using an experience sampling study, found that a person's negative personality disposition leads to a feeling of distress in handling events throughout the day.

What makes people feel happy at work? Our results thus suggest that having F2F interactions and being engaged in work influences positive affect. However, "light" interactions of FB (as measured by negative challenge and engagement) are also important in contributing to a positive affect at work. Our result showing that F2F influences positive affect extends the findings of Pea et al. [43] who focused on moods of adolescent girls. Our results in an *in situ* workplace environment also show that F2F encounters impact positive affect.

Email, task-switching and mood

While our main focus was on examining FB and F2F interaction and mood, it is important to consider that these activities are done within a context of digital media use in the workplace. Email was a factor that surfaced as significantly influencing all three mood measures throughout the day. We found that the more time spent reading and answering emails (Email/Use) throughout the day, the lower was one’s positive affect. Studies of email use have uncovered that it leads to stress [37, 38]. Our study additionally shows that reading and responding to emails is associated with feeling engaged and challenged. Responding to email may disrupt ongoing work, making resumption of tasks more challenging [26]. Email also influences negative affect. Put simply: reading a lot of email at work puts people into a "bad mood".

If we consider email as a communication tool we can examine how it compares with F2F and FB as communication mediums. F2F interaction and Email/Use both elicit similar results of feeling engaged in the workplace. F2F requires a degree of engagement to attend to verbal and nonverbal information and also to respond to the conversation partner [28]. Reading and responding to emails also requires a certain degree of engagement as it involves communicating with another.

On the other hand, FB and Email/Cal both showed similar results of being inversely related to feeling engaged or challenged. Checking one's Inbox and calendar (Email/Cal) are aspects of task and time management which involves gaining quick awareness. FB actions of reading status updates can also be used to gain a quick awareness of friends' status. Future research could distinguish FB activities in a more fine-grained manner to examine whether distinct activities are associated with different aspects of mood.

Task switching, as measured by App switching, was positively related to both Engagement and Challenge. We might expect that when one is task switching one would be engaged in this activity, as this involves constantly shifting focus and it can be challenging to reorient back to an interrupted task [17]. This result extends previous work on multitasking which shows it is related to stress [37].

Personality and mood

We found that personality traits influence mood throughout the day. Extraversion has been previously found to be associated with positive affect in single self-reports [31, 54] Our study demonstrates that Extraversion influenced Valence using continual measurements in the context of a dynamic workplace. We also found that Conscientiousness was positively related to Engagement as it was measured throughout the day. Though no personality study has ever directly addressed Engagement, we would expect these results. According to the Big 5 Inventory, self-discipline and achievement-striving are facets of Conscientiousness [7] which we expect are related to feelings of Engagement. Therefore, our results contribute to studies of personality by showing it influences mood as a person's context changes.

Gender and mood

Females use FB over twice as long on average per day as males. Females report over the course of the day as having significantly more positive Valence and they are significantly more engaged in work than males. Our results extend the findings of Kivran-Swaine et al. [29] who found that females express more positive emotions than males with Twitter use. Our results together suggest that females in the workplace use FB more and are happier (though these two results do not imply causality).

We found an Age x Gender interaction with the Challenge measure: in both the younger and older age groups, males report being more challenged than females; in our mid-range age group, females report being more challenged than males. We find this result important as it reveals that gender and mood effects in the workplace are related to age. We hope that this result can lead to more detailed examination of gender differences and work.

Alternative explanations to mood rating

We consider alternative explanations to our mood results. Demand characteristics are always a potential explanation of the results, i.e., that participants rated their mood according to how they believed the researcher wanted them to behave. However, we do not believe that demand characteristics played a major role. First, it was not clear to participants what kind of mood they should expect to report. Second, there was variability in mood assessments. If people presumably believed that the researcher was looking, for example, for positive (or negative) affect, we would expect that mood would be rated consistently throughout the day, and it was not.

Another possible explanation of our result showing no end of day mood effect for F2F is that F2F interaction creates positive feelings that dissipate very quickly or are not remembered at the end of the day. FB, on the other hand, could create feelings that are longer lasting throughout the day. A mechanism that could lead to long lasting feelings is that FB use constantly reminds people of close friends who are remote. More research is needed to test the notion of the temporal span of feelings with F2F interaction and FB use.

Sensors and human observation

A contribution of our study was to show that sensors are a viable means for capturing *in situ* workplace behavior. Sensors enable the continual capture of behavior with minimal disruption for the participant. Another advantage of automated capture of behavioral data is that it can be scaled up enabling the investigation of more complex phenomena such as workgroup or even organizational behavior. Though our technology did not enable us to capture fine-grained details of FB use or types of F2F interaction, we hope that our study can spark research in this direction.

Limitations

Our participants were all highly educated (at least having a Bachelor's degree) and about half were researchers. They thus represent highly skilled knowledge workers. We therefore can only generalize our results to similar types of workers. The use of researchers as participants has been used in other activity tracking studies, e.g. [10, 38]. However, we believe that task characteristics of our participants are very similar to what is found in many kinds of information work: dealing with multiple tasks, deadlines, and heavy reliance on information technology at work.

A known issue with the Experience Sampling method is that the probe can be a source of interruption [21]. However, in the post-study interviews, participants did not report this as a problem. We believe that the reason is because the probe was able to be answered in seconds. Another potential limitation is that raised by Columbetti [5] who argues that a positive-negative valence scale misses complexity as a measure of affect. However, studies such as Steptoe et al. [51] have carefully validated this dichotomous valence measure and we feel that the level of discrimination was adequate for the goal of our study.

Another limitation was our use of the SenseCam to measure face-to-face interaction. As explained, the SenseCam can only be considered a proxy for amount of F2F interaction; the face detection software that we used cannot distinguish unique faces. Therefore, the F2F interaction measure should be regarded as "amount" of interaction rather than distinct interactions. This is similar to measuring FB use, as we could not distinguish whether people were reading one post, or scanning over many posts. The SenseCam also would have failed to photograph faces if people were standing sideways when they spoke to someone. It also does not capture interactions that occurred within the 15 second window of time between SenseCam photo shots. Therefore, our measure of F2F interaction could have underestimated interaction counts.

CONCLUSION

Our results showed that both F2F interactions and FB use do influence positive affect in the workplace though differently. F2F involves more engagement in interactions, whereas the low engagement and challenge associated with FB use is consistent with a lightweight interaction that contributes, together with engagement in work, to making people feel good by the end of the day.

Our findings provide initial evidence of how social interactions affect mood at the workplace, suggesting the usefulness of incorporating social media platforms in the workplace as well as in promoting informal workplace interactions. This has important implications for decision-makers in the workplace who wish to balance interactions and task engagement with positive affect of employees.

ACKNOWLEDGMENTS

This material is based upon work supported by the National Science Foundation under Grant Number 1218705. We thank Munmun de Choudhury and Scott Counts for their valuable comments.

REFERENCES

1. Adamczyk, P.D. and Bailey, B.P., If Not Now When? The Effects of Interruptions at Different Moments Within Task Execution. in *Proceedings of the ACM Conference on Human Factors in Computing Systems*, (2004), 271-278.

2. Bailey, B.P. and Konstan, J.A. On the Need for Attention Aware Systems: Measuring Effects of Interruption on Task Performance, Error Rate, and Affective State. *Journal of Computers in Human Behavior*, 2006, *22* (4). 709-732.

3. Brief, A. and Weiss, H. Organizational behavior: Affect in the workplace. *Annual Review of Psychology*, 2002, *53*. 279-307.

4. Choudhury, M.D. and Counts, S. Understanding Affect in the Workplace via Social Media *Proceedings of Computer Supported Cooperative Work*, 2013, 303-315.

5. Columbetti, G. Appraising valence. *Journal of Consciousness Studies*, 2005, *12* ((8-10)). 103-126.

6. Correa, T., Hinsley, A. and Zúñiga, H.G.d. Who interacts on the Web?: The intersection of users' personality and social media use. *Computers in Human Behavior*, 2010, *26*. 247-253.

7. Costa, P.T. and McCrae, R.R. Revised Personality Inventory (NEO-PI-R) and NEO Five-Factor Inventory (NEO-FFI) manual. *Psychological Assessment Resources*, 1992.

8. Csikszentmihalyi, M. and Larson, R. Validity and reliability of the experience sampling method. . *Journal of Nervous and Mental Disease*, 1987, *175*. 526-536.

9. Czerwinski, M., Cutrell, E. and Horvitz, E., Instant Messaging: Effects of Relevance and Timing. in *People and Computers XIV: Proceedings of HCI*, (2000), British Computer Society, 71-76.

10. Czerwinski, M., Horvitz, E. and Wilhite, S., A diary study of task switching and interruptions. in *Proceedings of the ACM Conference on Human Factors in Computing Systems*, (2004), 175-182.

11. Dabbish, L. and Kraut, R.E., Controlling interruptions: awareness displays and social motivation for coordination. in *Proceedings of the ACM Conference on Computer Supported Cooperative Work*, (2004), 182-191.

12. Dey, A.K. and Abowd, G.D., CybreMinder: A Context-Aware System for Supporting Reminders. in *Proceedings of 2nd International Symposium on Handheld and Ubiquitous Computing*, (2000), 172-186.

13. Digman, J.M. Personality structure: Emergence of the five-factor model. *Annual Review of Psychology*, 1990, *41*. 417-440.

14. Duggan, M. and Brenner, J. The demographics of social media users - 2012. *Pew Internet and American Life Project*, 2012, http://www.pewinternet.org/Reports/2013/Social-media-users/The-State-of-Social-Media-Users.aspx.

15. Edwards, L., Muller, K., Wolfinger, R., Qaqish, B. and Schabennerger, O. An R^2 statistic for Fixed Effects in the Linear Mixed Model. *Stat Med.* , 2008 (27(29)). 6137.

16. Gonzales, A.L. and Hancock, J.T. Mirror, mirror on my facebook wall: Effects of facebook exposure on self-esteem. *Cyberpsychology, Behavior and Social networking*, 2011, *14*. 79-83.

17. Gonzalez, V.M. and Mark, G., "Constant, Constant, Multi-tasking Craziness": Managing Multiple Working Spheres. in *Proceedings of the ACM Conference on Human Factors in Computing Systems*, (Vienna, Austria, 2004), 113-120.

18. Hampton, K., Goulet, L.S., Rainie, L. and Purcell, K. Social networking sites and our lives. *Pew Internet and American Life Project*, 2011, http://pewinternet.org/Reports/2011/Technology-and-social-networks.aspx.

19. Hampton, K. and Wellman, B. Neighboring in Netville: How the internet supports community and social capital in a wired suburb. *City and Community*, 2003, *2* (4). 277-311.

20. Hancock, J., Gee, K., Ciaccio, K. and Lin, J.M.-H. I'm sad you're sad: emotinoal contagion in CMC. *Proceedings of Computer Supported Cooperative Work*, 2008, 295-298.

21. Hektner, J., Schmidt, J. and Csikszentmihalyi, M. *Experience Sampling Method: Measuring the quality of everyday life*. Sage, Thousand Oaks, CA, 2007.

22. Herzberg, F. *The Motivation to Work*. Transaction Publishers, 1993.

23. Hodges, S., Williams, L., Berry, E., Izadi, S., Srinivasan, J., Butler, A., Smyth, G., Kapur, N. and Wood, K. SenseCam: A Retrospective Memory Aid *Ubicomp*, 2006, 177-193.

24. Iqbal, S.T. and Bailey, B.P., Investigating the Effectiveness of Mental Workload as a Predictor of Opportune Moments for Interruption. in *Proceedings of the ACM Conference on Human Factors in Computing Systems*, (Portland, Oregon, USA, 2005), 1489-1492.

25. Iqbal, S.T. and Horvitz, E., Conversation Amidst Computing: A Study of Interruptions and Recovery of Task Activity. in *The 11th International Conference on User Modeling*, (Corfu, Greece, 2007), Berlin: Springer.

26. Iqbal, S.T. and Horvitz, E., Disruption and Recovery of Computing Tasks: Field Study, Analysis and Directions. in *Proceedings of the ACM Conference on Human Factors in Computing Systems*, (San Jose, California, USA, 2007), 677-686.

27. Jin, J. and Dabbish, L.A. Self-interruption on the computer: a typology of discretionary task interleaving *Proceedings of the SIGCHI Conference on Human Factors in Computing Systems*, ACM, Boston, MA, USA, 2009, 1799-1808.

28. Kendon, A., Harris, R.M. and Key, M.R. *Organization of Behavior in Face-To-Face Interaction*. Walter de Gruyter, 1975.

29. Kivran-Swaine, F., Brody, S., Kiakopoulos, N. and Naaman, M. Of joy and gender: emotional expression in online social networks *ACM 2012 Conference on Computer Supported Cooperative Work*, 2012, 139-142.

30. Kramer, A.D. The spread of emotion via facebook *Conference on Human Factors in Computing Systems (CHI)*, 2012, 767-770.

31. Larsen, R. and Ketelaar, T. Personality and susceptibility to positive and negative emotional states. *Journal of*

Personality and Social Psychology, 1991, *61* (1). 132-140.

32. Latorella, K.A. Investigating Interruptions: Implications for Flightdeck Performance. 1999, http://www.interruptions.net/literature/Latorella-NASA-99-tm209707.pdf.
33. Maes, P. Agents that Reduce Work and Information Overload. *Communications of the ACM*, 1994, *37* (7). 30-40.
34. Maglio, P. and Campbell, C.S., Tradeoffs in Displaying Peripheral Information. in *Proceedings of the ACM Conference on Human Factors in Computing Systems*, (2000), 241-248.
35. Marco, C.A. and Suls, J. Daily Stress and the Trajectory of Mood: Spillover, Response Assimilation,Contrast, and Chronic Negative Affectivity. *Journal of Personality and Social Psychology*, 1993, *64* (6). 1053-1063.
36. Marder, B., Joinson, A. and Shankar, A., Every Post You Make, Every Pic You Take, I'll Be Watching You: Behind Social SPheres on Facebook. in *45th Hawaii International Conference on System Sciences (HICSS)*, (2012), 859-868.
37. Mark, G., Gudith, D. and Klocke, U. The cost of interrupted work: more speed and stress *Proceedings of CHI'08,* ACM Press, Florence, Italy, 2008, 107-110.
38. Mark, G., Voida, S. and Cardello, A. "A Pace Not Dictated by Electrons": An Empirical Study of Work Without Email. *Proceedings of CHI'12.* ACM Press, 555-564.
39. McCrae, R. and Costa, P. The five factor theory of personality. in *Handbook of Personality: Theory and Research*, L.A. Pervin, O.P. Johns, NY: Guilford, 1999, 139-153.
40. McDuff, D., Karlson, A.K., Kapoor, A., Roseway, A. and Czerwinski, M. AffectAura: an intelligent system for emotional memory *Proceedings of CHI'12*, 849-858.
41. McFarlane, D.C. and Latorella, K.A. The Scope and Importance of Human Interruption in HCI Design. *Human-Computer Interaction*, 2002, *17* (1). 1-61.
42. Paul, C. and Komlodi, A. Emotion as an indicator for future interruptive notification experiences *Proceedings of CHI '12 Extended Abstracts,* ACM Press, 2012, 2003-2008.
43. Pea, R., Nass, C., Meheulla, L., Rance, M., Kumar, A., Bamford, H., Nass, M., Simha, A., Stillerman, B., Yang, S. and Zhou, M. Media use, face-to-face communication, media multitasking, and social well-being among 8- to 12-year-old girls. *Developmental Psych*, 2012, *48* (2). 327-336.
44. Rhoades, J. and O'Connor, K. Affect in computer-mediated and face-to-face work groups: The construction and testing of a general model. *Computer Supported Cooperative Work*, 1996, *4*. 203-228.
45. Rich, C. and Sidner, C.L. COLLAGEN: A Collaboration Manager for Software Interface Agents. *User Modeling and User-Adapted Interaction*, 1998, *8* (3/4). 315-350.
46. Russell, J. Core affect and the psychological construction of emotion. *Psychological Review*, 2003, *110* (1). 145-172.
47. Ryan, T. and Xenos, S. Who uses Facebook? An investigation into the relationship between the Big Five, shyness, narcissism, loneliness, and Facebook usage. *Computers in Human Behavior*, 2011, *27*. 1658-1664.
48. Schaufeli, W., Salanova, M., Gonzalez-Rom, V. and Bakker, A. The measurement of engagement and burnout: A two sample confirmatory factor analytic approach. *Journal of Happiness studies*, 2002, *3*. 71-92.
49. Schwartz, G. Estimating the dimension of a model. *Annals of Statistics*, 1978, *6* (2). 461-464.
50. Skeels, M. and Grudin, J. When social networks cross boundaries: A case study of workplace use of facebook and linkedin *ACM Group '09*, 2009. 95-104.
51. Steptoe, A., Wardle, J. and Marmot, M. Positive affect and health-related neuroendocrine cardiovascular and inflammatory processes. *Proceedings of the National Academy of Sciences*, 2008, *102* (18). 6508-6512.
52. Teuchmann, K., Totterdell, P. and Parker, S.K. Rushed, unhappy, and drained: an experience sampling study of relations between time pressure, perceived control, mood, and emotional exhaustion in a group of accountants. *Journal of Occup Health Psychology*, 1999, *4* (1). 37-54.
53. Tosun, L.P. and Lajunen, T. Does Internet use reflect your personality? Relationship between Eysenck's personality dimensions and Internet use. *Computers in Human Behavior*, 2010, *26* (2). 162-167.
54. Watson, D. and Clark, A.L. On traits and temperament: General and specific factors of emotional experience and their relation to the five-factor model. *Journal of Personality*, 1992, *60* (2). 441-476.
55. Watson, D., Clark, A.L. and Tellegen, A. Development and validation of brief measures of positive and negative affect: The PANAS scales. *Journal of Personality and Social Psychology*, 1988, *56* (6). 1063-1070.
56. Williams, K. and Alliger, G. Role stressors, mood spillovers and perceptions of work-family conflict in employed parents. . *The Acad of Mgt J*, 1994, *37* (4).
57. Zijlstra, F.R.H., Roe, R.A., Leonora, A.B. and Krediet, I. Temporal Factors in Mental Work: Effects of Interrupted Activities. *Journal of Occupational and Organizational Psychology*, 1999, *72*. 163-185.

Social Influences on Secure Development Tool Adoption: Why Security Tools Spread

Shundan Xiao, Jim Witschey, and Emerson Murphy-Hill
North Carolina State University
890 Oval Drive, Raleigh, NC 27695
{sxiao,jwshephe}@ncsu.edu, emerson@csc.ncsu.edu

ABSTRACT
Security tools can help developers build more secure software systems by helping developers detect or fix security vulnerabilities in source code. However, developers do not always use these tools. In this paper, we investigate a number of social factors that impact developers' adoption decisions, based on a multidisciplinary field of research called diffusion of innovations. We conducted 42 one-on-one interviews with professional software developers, and our results suggest a number of ways in which security tool adoption depends on developers' social environments and on the channels through which information about tools is communicated. For example, some participants trusted developers with strong reputations on the Internet as much as they trust their colleagues for information about security tools.

Author Keywords
adoption; security tools; social factors

ACM Classification Keywords
D.2.0 SOFTWARE ENGINEERING: Tools

General Terms
Human Factors; Security

INTRODUCTION
Software security is a non-functional requirement of software that ensures that software functions correctly even under malicious attack [18]. Many types of software vulnerabilities can compromise security, including memory safety violations, input validation errors, and race conditions. According to the National Institute of Standards and Technology, the number of new software vulnerabilities discovered each year has more than doubled in the last decade; in 2012, more than 5,000 new vulnerabilities were reported[1].

[1]http://web.nvd.nist.gov/view/vuln/statistics

ACM 978-1-4503-2540-0/14/02...$15.00.
http://dx.doi.org/10.1145/2531602.2531722

The cost of fixing defects in software, including vulnerabilities, increases over time [4]. Vulnerabilities can be particularly expensive, taking into account the costs of losing customer trust, handling bad publicity, and, potentially, facing litigation. For instance, a single vulnerability in Microsoft's Internet Information Server cost an estimated $2 billion in repair, lost productivity, and support [7]. In comparison, previous work indicates that fixing vulnerabilities can take as little as three minutes of a developer's time if found early enough [6]. However, finding these vulnerabilities in order to fix them can require significant skill and resources.

Because the cost of changing software to fix vulnerabilities increases over time [4], we focus on tools that help developers find and fix vulnerabilities in source code during the implementation phase of the software development lifecycle. We call these tools secure-software development tools, or *security tools* for short. We consider two types of security tools: static analysis tools and dynamic analysis tools. Static analysis tools, such as Fortify SCA[2], Armorize CodeSecure[3], and FindBugs[4], scan application source code for vulnerabilities. Dynamic analysis tools, such as HP WebInspect[5] and IBM AppScan[6], scan running applications for such vulnerabilities as memory leaks and SQL injections. Such tools can augment the security practices, if any, that a development team already uses.

When developers do not use security tools, they may deploy software containing vulnerabilities they could have prevented by using these tools during implementation. We previously explored the problem of software development tool underuse for tools available in integrated development environments (IDEs) [22]. However, the consequences of security tool underuse — such as the release of needlessly vulnerable software — are more severe than those of, for example, refactoring tool underuse. In addition, understanding the existing culture surrounding security tool use is critical if we are to create a culture of secure development. Thus, security tool underuse deserves special attention. We will refer to it as the *security tool adoption problem*.

[2]http://www.hpenterprisesecurity.com/products/hp-fortify-software-security-center/hp-fortify-static-code-analyzer

[3]http://www.armorize.com/codesecure/

[4]http://findbugs.sourceforge.net/

[5]http://www.hpenterprisesecurity.com/products/hp-fortify-software-security-center/hp-webinspect

[6]http://www-01.ibm.com/software/awdtools/appscan/

In this paper, we investigate the security tool adoption problem by studying the factors that influence the adoption of security tools, based on a multidisciplinary field of research called *diffusion of innovations* [34]. This paper's primary contribution is a qualitative account of social factors influencing security tool adoption. We consider software development companies as the social systems in which security tools are spread. Thus, many of these social factors are manifested in and shaped by the organizational structure and policies of these companies. We also address social factors by investigating how developers communicate about security tools and how their attitudes toward different communication channels affect adoption. Our findings, based on an interview study with 42 software developers, can help organizations predict return on investment for new security tools, toolsmiths to understand the needs of their users, and educators decide how to teach and present security tools to their students.

We feel that an account of adoption focusing on such social factors is overdue. Previous work in software engineering has focused on developing better tools, but such work does not account for tool adoption behavior. Previous work in human aspects of software engineering has described social factors on the adoption of software process [37] and programming languages [19], but such work has not, until now, been extended to programming tools in general or security tools in particular. Future security tools would be better positioned to improve the state of the practice if they were designed and presented to developers in ways that make adoption more likely. This foundational work will help us develop an understanding of adoption that we hope will help increase the impact of future research into security tool development.

RELATED WORK

In this section, we discuss existing theories of technology diffusion, as well as related studies of developers' adoption of tools and technologies.

Adoption Theory

To make our investigation of as the security tool adoption problem as comprehensive and principled as possible, we used an existing theory of *diffusion*, or the spread of new ideas and technologies. This theory, Rogers' diffusion of innovations (DOI) theory, is one of the most widely used diffusion theories across disciplines. Rogers defines DOI as "the process by which an innovation is communicated through certain channels over time among the members of a social system" [34]. DOI explains the process by which a technology or idea spreads through a population. It describes how a group of people learn of a new technology, try it for themselves, then decide whether or not to adopt it for long-term use. DOI also names social and technological factors that speed or hinder this process. For instance, highly influential early adopters and organizational mandates can increase both the probability and speed of adoption. Technological factors, like the complexity of a technology and its compatibility with existing technologies, also influence adoption patterns. The present paper focuses on social aspects as they are manifested in software development companies.

Other theories describe what influences individuals' intentions to use information technology. These include the Technology Acceptance Model [8, 40], Perceived Characteristics of Innovating [20], Theory of Planned Behavior [1], and Model of Personal Computer Utilization [39]. Though DOI shares many traits with these theories, DOI accounts for communication in ways other theories do not. Our previous findings indicate that the way developers learn about tools affects their adoption behavior [23], and DOI's focus on communication about new technologies allows us to study this phenomenon further.

Software Technology Transfer

An area of research related to DOI is software technology transfer (STT), in which software engineering innovations are transferred from an idea to common practice [5]. Researchers have studied STT in different contexts. Nahar and colleagues studied transfer of software development tools and methods from a multinational Finnish company to its Indian subsidiary, and described how well-trained internal consultants helped this process succeed [24]. Gorschek and colleagues developed a model of STT based on their experiences collaborating with industry [10]. They found that training adopters in using the technology and long-term commitment from management, among other factors, increase the probability of successful STT. Our paper extends such results to security tools.

Adoption of Software Engineering Technologies

We also expand other research on the adoption of some kinds of software tools, methodologies, and programming languages. One of the most widely studied classes of tools is that of Computer-Aided Software/Systems Engineering (CASE) tools. For example, Premkumar and Potter surveyed developers to evaluate a model of factors that influence CASE adoption found five important factors, such as presence of a product champion and support from management [28]. Iivari conducted a similar study evaluating ten factors; his results suggest the importance of management factors, voluntariness, and the perceived advantages of CASE tools [15]. Kemerer demonstrated how learning curves can affect CASE adoption and the challenges in applying traditional learning curve models to CASE tools [16]. Other studies of CASE adoption identified factors that were part of or extended factors from DOI theory [30, 31, 14].

Researchers have also studied diffusion of software development methodologies. For example, Raghavan and Chand used DOI in an informal case study to investigate why the adoption of structured design methodologies was slow [29]. They recommend that researchers produce more evidence for the benefits of such methodologies and find ways to effectively communicate these benefits. Riemenschneider and colleagues showed that developers' intention to adopt is determined by the presence of an organizational mandate, the compatibility of the methodology, and peer influence [32]. Hardgrave and colleagues investigated the determinants of developers' intention to follow methodologies, showing that an organizational mandate cannot guarantee the sufficient use of the software methodology [12]. Singer and Schneider studied how to improve the adoption rate of software engineering methodologies using social software [36].

Recent work has also investigated the diffusion of programming languages and language features. We previously empirically investigated the adoption of Java generics by mining the history of 40 popular open-source Java programs, and found that adoption of generics there is typically incomplete and championed by one or two individual developers [26]. In their work, Meyerovich and Rabkin posed several open-ended questions and hypotheses about the adoption of programming languages and features [19].

One particularly relevant set of methodologies are Secure Development Lifecycles (SDLs), which prescribe practices that integrate security into the software development process. McGraw suggests the use of tools to help build more secure software [18], making policies relevant to our work. The Microsoft SDL suggests a list of static analysis tools to use in the implementation phase and a list of dynamic analysis tools to be used in the verification phase [13]. Because using security tools is part of SDLs, the adoption of an SDL entails the adoption of security tools, which is the main concern of the present work. However, according to Geer's survey, few software development companies formally adopt SDLs [9]. The main self-reported reasons for non-adoption are that formal SDLs are too time consuming, developers are not aware of the existence of SDLs, and formal SDLs require too many resources. In "A Few Billion Lines of Code Later" [3], Bessey and colleagues discuss challenges faced when trying to deploy the security tool Coverity in industry. Our work empirically investigates some of the social and technical issues described anecdotally there.

Finally, though it does not specifically concern tool adoption, Xie and colleagues' study on the reasons developers make security errors [41] is similar to ours methodologically and in spirit. We also use an interview study and are concerned with developers' attitudes toward secure development. One of their central findings is that many developers feel that security is not their responsibility. While Xie and colleagues' interview study focused on developers' reasons for not considering security when they write software, ours also focuses on tools and developers' reasons for using or not using security tools.

METHODOLOGY

We conducted one-on-one interviews with 42 software professionals to collect data with which to study the security tool adoption problem. More specifically, our research objective was to qualitatively describe the factors that influence adoption or rejection decisions, as well as to describe how those factors interact. In this section, we describe how we recruited participants, some characteristics of the participants we interviewed, how we conducted the interviews, and the how we analyzed the data we collected.

Recruitment and Incentives

We sought to interview professional software developers from diverse backgrounds. We planned to recruit approximately the same numbers of developers working in large, medium-sized, and small companies. To that end, we recruited study participants in four ways: we emailed invitations to 50 software development companies listed on Guru[7], a recruitment website that connects freelance software developers with those who want to hire them. We also emailed personal and professional contacts working in software development. We posted flyers in break rooms at a large software development company. Finally, we asked developers who had already participated in our study to help recruit friends and colleagues who might be interested in participating. We incentivized participation by offering $50 gift cards for completing the interview.

When developers expressed interest in participating, we asked them to sign a consent form and complete a screening survey online. We used the results of this survey to select developers who were at least 18 years old, held a job related to software development, and actively wrote code as part of their professional activities in the past six months. We emailed developers who reported meeting these criteria to schedule the interview.

Participants

Forty-four developers signed the consent form and completed the screening survey. However, we later learned that one of these people did not meet our selection criteria; another could not complete the interview due to significant communication difficulties. We excluded these interviews from our analysis. Participants worked in various countries and developed software in many application areas, including banking, military, financial, and clinical software, as well as web browsers, and software as a service. They used popular programming languages such as Java, JavaScript, C, C++, C#, Python, Ruby, and Perl. Their work experience ranged from 1 to 28 years, with a mean of 11.0 years and a median of 7.3 years.

We sought to interview developers who program as part of their jobs, but also those who may be involved in the tool adoption decision-making processes: managers, security experts, and software consultants. Table 1 shows the numbers of participants who reported working in each development role. Table 1 also shows how many developers worked in small, medium-sized, or large companies. We classified companies thus: small companies employ 50 or fewer developers, medium-sized companies employ more than fifty but fewer than 500 developers, and large companies employ 500 or more developers. As shown, we interviewed 31 programmers, 5 software development managers, 4 software security experts (some of whom developed security tools themselves), and 2 software development consultants. The majority of our participants are programmers, because we were interested in programmers' experience, or lack thereof, with security tools. We also asked managers, security experts, and consultants questions about their activities outside programming if time allowed after asking the more general tool adoption questions. Specifically, we asked managers what factors they considered in deciding whether to adopt a security tool for their team; we asked security experts what factors contributed

[7]http://www.guru.com/

to the adoption of a security tool, how best to advertise security tools, and how to increase awareness of the importance of secure coding practices among ordinary programmers; and we asked consultants questions about differences between domains with respect to secure coding.

Interview Methodology

We interviewed each participant for 45 minutes to an hour over Skype or phone. The interviewer used a script to guide the interview[8]; this script contained open-ended questions about participants' security tool adoption choices, and more directed questions about the importance of social and technological factors from DOI theory.

As in other exploratory studies [41], we used a semi-structured interview methodology [35]: if the interviewer found a participant's answer particularly interesting, she asked questions not in the script to collect more detailed data. If one of these impromptu questions yielded useful information, we added it to the script for the next interview. If a question stopped yielding new information, we stopped asking participants that question. Thus, we did not ask every participant every question.

Because the interview was retrospective in nature, participants might have forgotten about tools that they no longer use. To mitigate the risk of formerly-used tools being unreported, we tried to prompt responses about such tools by giving examples of security tools they may have used and security problems they may have solved in the past. This gave participants an opportunity to recall security tools that they had forgotten about or not have previously thought of as security tools.

Before we started each interview, we confirmed with each participant that we could record his or her voice. After the participant consented, we explained the purpose of our study and our definition of security tools. At the end of the interview, we thanked the participant and arranged for delivery of the gift card offered as incentive.

Data Analysis

We recorded each interview we conducted, then transcribed each recording. We used a qualitative data analysis program called Atlas.ti[9] to analyze the interviews using open coding [35]. We started with an initial set of codes based on findings in Rogers' discussion of diffusion of innovations [34]. We created new codes when we found interesting patterns that were previously unaccounted for. For example, our "evaluation process" code, which accounts for companies and managers having a formal process in place to evaluate new security tools, was not part of our initial set of possible relevant factors. When evaluating whether a participant actually adopted a tool, we considered an instance of adoption to occur when a developer used a tool on a regular basis for at least one week.

[8]The interview script is available at **http://www4.ncsu.edu/~sxiao/adoption/interview_script.pdf**

[9]http://www.atlasti.com/

In our results sections, we will refer to each participant by an alias of the form Pi, from P1 to P42, to allow the reader to track individual participants. When discussing responses to questions that we only asked a subset of participants, we will use expressions such as "x out of y participants said A" to indicate that of the y developers who we asked a particular question, x answered A. Note that this work is exploratory and qualitative, and considers a relatively small number of participants. While we will present some statistical information about our participants and their behavior, such information serves only to summarize our results — the reader should not infer any generalizations about developers' behavior from our data.

PARTICIPANTS' SECURITY TOOL USE RATES

In this section, we discuss general patterns we discovered in participants' use of security tools. We divided the participants into 3 categories based on their statements in our interviews: regular users, who used security tools regularly in their daily programming work; occasional users, who used security tools only when they considered it necessary to search for vulnerabilities; and non-users, who never used security tools.

When we initially asked participants if they had used any security tools, many participants said that they had not. However, when we gave these participants examples of what we considered security tools, some participants reported using them. We attribute this to our deliberately liberal definition of security tools. Some tools that participants used, like Coverity, are marketed as security tools, with finding vulnerabilities given as a primary use case. However, we also consider a tool a security tool if it can be used to find vulnerabilities, even if that is not its exclusive purpose. For instance, memory profilers like Valgrind[10] help developers find buffer overruns and other memory errors that can, in some cases, allow an attacker to gain control of the instruction pointer and execute arbitrary code on a compromised machine. As another example, FindBugs can analyze code for API misuse that leaves a server open to cross-site scripting and SQL injection attacks. Thus, we considered the participants who regularly used Valgrind or FindBugs to be regular users, even though finding vulnerabilities is not these tools' primary use case. We have chosen this broad definition because, at this exploratory stage, we would rather overgeneralize than miss a factor we had not previously accounted for.

The nineteen occasional users reported many reasons for not using security tools regularly. Nine of the nineteen reported using a tool to fix a security problem, then discontinuing use of the tool after fixing it. For example, P33 once used a memory profiler to find memory leaks in his code, then stopped using it once he had repaired the leaks. Seven of the nineteen said that they stopped using a security tool because they moved to a development team in a different application area in which they felt security tools were not needed. Two of the nineteen reported that they stopped using a security tool out of "laziness", and the other three said they were not sure why they discontinued use of a tool.

[10]http://valgrind.org/

Company Size	*Programmer*	*Manager*	*Security Expert*	*Consultant*	**Total**
Large (500+ Developers)	14	3	3	2	22
Medium (51-499 Developers)	8	1	0	0	9
Small (1-50 Developers)	9	1	1	0	11
Total	31	5	4	2	42

Table 1. Participants' Backgrounds

Among the ten non-users, six participants worked at small companies and reported that these companies did not require that they use secure coding practices. Participants who worked for these small companies appeared to know less about secure development and secure coding than other participants. Some thought of security as a narrow concern mainly focused on operational security, software access control, and user authentication.

In general, most of the regular users came from large companies where security tools have been integrated into the standard development process, while many of the non-users came from small companies that do not require developers to use secure coding practices.

ORGANIZATIONAL FACTORS

One of the strengths of DOI theory is that it accounts for how characteristics of the social systems in which innovations diffuse affect their adoption. Since all our participants were software developers working in industry, we consider the companies in which they work as the main social systems in which they use and learn about security tools. The social norms and standards of these companies manifest themselves as the company's policies, structure, culture, and practices. In this section, we will discuss the impact these social environments have had on participants' adoption decisions concerning security tools. Specifically, developers work in different companies with different cultures, practices, standards, and structures that could influence adoption in many ways. Our results show that these characteristics of the company for which a developer works can greatly influence her decisions in adopting security tools.

Policies and Standards

A company's policies and standards refers specifically to the policies or standards a company holds that relate to secure coding and the use of security tools. Several participants reported that the standards of their company directly influence the perceived necessity of security tools and their actual use of security tools.

Only two participants reported that their companies have formal secure development lifecycles that require them to use security tools. Fewer than half of the participants reported that their companies have and enforce formal secure coding standards at all. Of the thirteen regular users, seven reported that their companies require them to use some specific security tools as part of the development process, while none of the nineteen occasional users and ten non-users reported their companies have these policies or standards. In other words, all participants who were required to use security tools used them; this is notable, as other research shows that people will circumvent security policies if they are inconvenient, even in hospitals, where the consequences of circumvention can be harmful to patients [17]. However, this conforms to Straus and colleagues' finding [38] that mandates effectively encourage adoption of new technologies in organizations.

In most cases, however, security standards are informal, verbal "best practices". Participants reported following these practices and expecting their coworkers to follow them, though no policies or guidelines were written or enforced by their employers. P11 said that the standards in his department were "informal" and not "well-promoted". P21 said that there was no formal requirement that passwords be stored encrypted, but that doing so was an "unwritten standard". These decisions might be enforced by informal communication between colleagues, such as pointing out vulnerabilities on mailing lists.

Two participants reported that in their companies, using a tool that is new to the company requires written authorization; obtaining this authorization sometimes takes weeks. Thus, these participants rarely, if ever, investigated new tools on their own to avoid this long wait. For example, P36 reported that at his company, if he wanted to start using a new security tool, he would "have to get approval from [his] manager" or through a more complex process, "depending on the tool". Tools to be "only [used] internally", that were not involved in any client-facing services, might be approved or rejected by management in "in a week or... a couple of weeks", which P36 considered a "very short time". Tools used in customer-facing services and products would "take a lot longer" to approve. P19 said that at his company, tools were evaluated to ensure that the were cost-effective and fit into the organization's existing workflow.

The managers we spoke to shed some light on this evaluation process. For instance, P5 and P7 indicated they evaluated tools based on their cost. Both considered developer time part of that cost. P5 who, he managed development of a system with components written in many languages, said that the initial cost in time to set up security tools for these varied components was disproportionate to the benefits it could have. P7 said he prefers tools that "can be scripted to run automatically".

Among the thirteen regular users, seven worked in large companies where security tools were integrated into the development process. Three of these seven were required to use a security tool on their local workstation. The other four reported that security tools were integrated into their companies' build server; the security tools automatically check for vulnerabilities as part of a nightly build or before participants check in their changes. These participants were able to circumvent the costs of installing, configuring, learning, and running these security tools — they needed only to read and understand the reports generated by the tools.

Four participants reported feeling they did not need to use security tools because they felt mandatory manual code reviews already ensured security. Two participants mentioned they had used security tools in conjunction with manual code review; this practice gave them more confidence in their code's security. Overall, seven of the thirteen non-users reported feeling no need to use security tools because they could depend on code reviews or testing by others in the company ensure security. P9 trusted security experts to "catch the problems" in his code. This corroborates Xie and colleagues' finding that developers tend to place trust in process when it comes to software security [41].

Culture

By culture, we mean the beliefs and social norms surrounding security and security tools in a company. Different company cultures can influence developers' security tool use: for example, P28 worked in a company where installing new tools on his workstation is free and encouraged. He and his coworkers consider such exploration "cool".

However, other companies seem to have a culture that discourages using new tools. For instance, as mentioned previously, P36 worked in a company where the approval process for the use of a new tool might take weeks. He reported that management would "encourage" developers to see if there was a tool that was already approved for use in order to avoid this process. Between this encouragement from management and the length of the approval process, P36 said that he would need a particularly "compelling reason" to use a tool that had to be approved. Thus, policies that necessitated a long evaluation period helped create a culture of avoiding new security tools.

Our interviews with managers confirmed that managerial involvement affected company culture around security. P5, a manager, said it was "very clear" that security is "everybody's responsibility" in his company, and that is was "a culture thing" in his company. He and other managers actively fostered that culture by encouraging collaboration between security experts and other developers and offering security classes to developers.

Domain and Security Concerns

By a company's domain and security concerns, we mean the importance of security in the domain in which the company develops software. Of thirty-four participants, twenty-six considered their companies' domains security-sensitive. Despite this high awareness of security issues, only ten participants were regular users, as mentioned previously. There is a dissonance, then, between developers' knowledge and behaviors: Sixteen participants think the security of their code is important, but do not use tools to help increase that security. Most developers may not have a concrete understanding of the consequences of deploying insecure software: five participants reported that they only started using security tools after vulnerabilities in their companies' code were exploited. Three participants said they do not use security tools because they never had been "hacked". This is predicted by DOI theory, as it is a common problem for other *preventive innovations* [34]; we will discuss this issue further in the Discussion section.

The perceived user base of the applications developed by software developers had an influence on participants' security tool adoption decisions as well. Four participants said they did not use security tools primarily because the applications they developed were only used internally by authenticated users, so they felt they did not need to worry about the security of these applications. Their conception of software security mainly concerned data access control and user authentication, as opposed to other kinds of security, like memory safety and input sanitization. Six participants mentioned that they care about security because their applications have a large number of users. For instance, P28 said that developers "need to make sure that [their software wasn't] opening up security holes" for the software's 400 or 500 million users. P19 said that security was less important than other requirements of his software because he developed "internal applications". Both considered user-facing applications more likely to be attacked and were more concerned about security if many users might suffer from an exploit.

Seven participants said that in their companies, functionality is the first concern because of tight deadlines for delivering products. Like participants in Xie and colleagues' study [41], they reported not having time to worry about security, as security is a non-functional requirement. P19, for instance, said that, partly because of limited development time, his team felt that for the software he developed, "achieving the task [was] more important than having a fully secure solution".

Structure

A company's structure, with respect to security tool adoption, refers to whether the company has dedicated security and testing teams. Of 31 participants, 17 reported that the companies they work in have dedicated security teams. Security teams perform different functions in different companies. P13 reported that the security team at his company held regular meetings with developers to suggest the use of new tools. In P6's company, developers could request security audits from the security teams. These security teams would use security tools to find vulnerabilities.

Security teams design security guidelines, offer security trainings and look for security tools for ordinary programmers to use. However, only six of the security teams interacted often with ordinary developers to consult and to review developers' code. The other security teams, which did not often interact with developers, tended to focus on operational security — they prioritized access control and authentication concerns, penetration testing, and auditing open-source software used in the company but developed outside it. For instance, P25 reported that the security team at his company would scan his software for vulnerabilities just before a release, not through the entire development lifecycle.

P32's statements illustrate the attitude of one developer who rarely interacts with his company's security team. He reported that the security team was "less than helpful" and "never checked any code" that he or his coworkers wrote. Rather, they looked for vulnerabilities in open-source code used by the company's products. P32 considered this a "waste of time" and thought that "they should have [spent] their time analyzing [the company's] code base".

While Xie and colleagues [41] found that developers hold a relaxed attitude towards security when they have security teams or testing teams to back them up, we found that not all of our participants held this attitude. Only two out of twenty-six participants thought ordinary developers were less responsible for security than security and testing teams. The other participants believed they had a, to quote P35, "shared responsibility" for writing secure software. They said that while security experts and testers helped ensure software security, writing secure code is ultimately the developers' responsibility. Especially in cases where ordinary developers interacted often with the security team, participants reported that they felt social pressure from the security team by having them audit the code and review the new features from a security perspective. This ultimately made developers feel personally responsible for their code's security. Nov and Arazy found that personality traits also influence peoples' decisions to help others in computer-supported cooperative work contexts when they know that they could defer responsibility to others [25]. This notion of personal responsibility for security is complex, and warrants further study.

Education and Training

Education and training refers to the training a company provides for general security problems and for specific security tools. Overall, no participants reported adopting a security tool through education and training. Though three of thirty-two participants mentioned that they learned about some security vulnerabilities in a software engineering course, none of the participants had had any security-specific courses in college. Twelve of thirty-one participants said that their companies provided training that touched upon security. However, only three of them have training for specific security tools. Rather, most of the training consisted of education on specific vulnerabilities and security best practices. Most trainings are optional, some are held only once a year, and some are just for newly hired developers. P6 indicated that questions about security were part of his employer's interview process. Thus, he assumed that developers who joined the company already understand security vulnerabilities, so he felt security training was unnecessary in his company.

P36 explained why security tool training may be uncommon in his company. To avoid the time costs of training all of its developers to use security tools, his company "want[ed] to let certain individuals be more specialized about security" and not "[have] the whole team understand security". This shows another way that the presence of security teams can negatively affect developers' security tool adoption behavior: while security teams can make developers feel social pressure to code securely, as discussed previously, they also can make developers feel that security is not their responsibility.

COMMUNICATION CHANNEL FACTORS

Rogers [34] makes a number of claims about the characteristics of communication channels that make people more or less likely to adopt the use of a tool that they hear about through those channels. Through our interviews, we have found two high-level characteristics of these channels that influenced participants' adoption behavior: the amount of *exposure* that the channel gives the innovation to individuals, and the extent to which the individuals *trust* that communication channel.

DOI theory accounts for three types of communication channels: mass media, interpersonal channels, and interactive communication on the Internet. Examples of mass media channels include webpages, television, radio, newspaper and magazines. Interpersonal channels involve face-to-face communication between two or more people, such as in peer recommendation. Interactive communication on the Internet happens on online forums and discussion websites, where people can discuss common interests, and social networks, such as Twitter and Facebook.

Exposure

To learn what communication channels expose developers to security tools, we asked participants what security tools that they had heard about and how they heard about them. Specifically, we asked them to list the security tools they had used, then asked how they first learned about each. We also asked participants if they had ever learned of any security tools through each of the channels listed in Table 2. We did so to prompt them to discuss tools that they had heard of but never used.

In Table 2, we list the channels that participants mentioned and the number of participants who mentioned each. In the following subsections, we indicate what participants said about each type of channel with respect to how and how much they exposed participants to security tools.

Interpersonal Communication

Our previous work [23] indicates that developers sometimes learn about tools through interpersonal channels — specifically, from their peers. The results of our interviews corroborate this finding: participants mentioned a total of 34 instances of learning about a tool through an interpersonal channel, 18 of which were through coworkers' suggestions.

P37 recalled a time when he discovered a security tool when a coworker who sat next to him shared a new tool with him in person. However, P3 mentioned that such peer recommendation happens rarely because developers do not often drop by other developers' offices; this corroborates our previous findings [23].

Twenty-two of thirty participants reported that they had recommended security tools to other developers. All eight of the other participants indicated that they did not recommend security tools to their friends because of the tools' cost. P5, for instance, reported that one tool his company evaluated cost 50,000 dollars per license. They felt that these tools are prohibitively expensive for individual users, and that adopting a

Communication Channel Type	Channel	Participants Mentioned	Total
Interpersonal Channels	Coworker Recommendation	18	34
	Required by Management	6	
	Conference	6	
	Security Team Recommendation	4	
	Security Tool Vendor	4	
	Required by Customer	2	
Mass media	Technical Blogs and Websites	4	7
	Security Tool's Official Website	3	
	Web Advertisements	–	
	Television	–	
	Radio	–	
	Newspapers and Magazines	–	
Interactive Communication on the Internet	Online Forums and Discussion Boards	4	4
	Social Networks	–	

Table 2. Security Tool Discovery Channels

tool is a managerial, not individual, decision. Eighteen of another thirty participants reported actually using a security tool or tools recommended to them by peers. We were surprised that participants reported six instances of first hearing of tools at security conferences and trade shows; we did not expect so many participants to learn about tools through interpersonal channels outside their companies.

Mass Media Communication

Participants reported seven instances of discovering a tool through mass media channels. However, no participants discovered tools through traditional mass media channels like television, magazines, or radio. They only mentioned mass media channels that presented information to them on the Internet.

Participants reported four instances of discovering a security tool by reading a technical blog or website. Participants also said that they sometimes searched for security tools online when they felt the need to use them; for example, when participants suspected their code had memory leaks, they might search for the terms "security tools for memory leaks". These searches sometimes brought them to security tools' official websites. Participants reported three instances of learning about a security tool through a tool's official website discovered through web search.

Though two participants recalled seeing security tools advertised online, neither recalled what tool they saw advertised. Moreover, participants reported that they had never seen security tool advertisements through traditional mass media channels, such as television and radio. Three participants reported they had seen security tool advertisements in software magazines, but none remembered the names of the security tools advertised. Overall, the Internet played a more important role than traditional mass media channels in participants' awareness of security tools.

We find it interesting that only five out of thirty-four participants recalled noticing security tool advertisements in Google search, forums, and software magazines. Participants reported that they generally ignored security tool advertisements because they did not trust such advertisements; we discuss the issue of trust further in the following section.

Interactive Communication on the Internet

Participants reported four times that they saw a security tool in online forums and discussion threads in their research about security tools. However, participants reported that they had never learned of security tools through social networks, which is consistent with our previous finding that developers rarely discover tools on Twitter [23].

Trust

Trust refers to the reliance of a developer on a communication channel to deliver relevant and useful information about security tools. We asked participants to tell us how much they trust different communication channels, both individually and relative to other channels.

Interpersonal Communication

Participants generally trusted "word of mouth" more than other sources — for instance, P3 said that he would be likely to try a tool recommended by someone he knew, more so than one he read about. Three participants reported trusting tool recommendations most from people with similar professional duties. P33 indicated that he trusted tool recommendations from technical managers, but not those from managers without a technical background. This also conforms with DOI research [34] and our previous computer supported cooperative work research [23], both of which suggest that people are more likely to trust information from individuals who share similar socioeconomic and educational status.

Mass Media Communication

Participants reported that they do not trust advertisements in mass media, such as those on webpages and magazines, because they considered mass media advertisements "biased". P37 indicated that he "did not trust [advertisements] to be unbiased" and would rather seek information from an expert he trusted. Only five of twenty-seven participants recalled noticing security tool advertisements on webpages or in magazines; most said they did not trust advertisements and ignored them.

Two participants also mentioned that they trust security tools and advertisements for them more if the tool is made by a well-known company. For example, participants mentioned they trust security tool advertisements from Microsoft and Hewlett-Packard more than from other companies that they had never heard of.

Interactive Communication on the Internet

We found it particularly interesting that some participants showed nearly equal trust toward recommendations received in person from peers and recommendations on the Internet given by people with good reputations or demonstrated credibility. P28 claimed that he trusted people he interacted with on the Internet, such as Stack Overflow users, more than he trusted some people he interacted with physically, such as his coworkers. Another participant reported that he would trust a well-moderated, high-scoring answer to a question on Stack Overflow over a recommendation from a colleague, particularly if the answer was from a highly-ranked Stack Overflow user. However, he also reported that he would trust a colleague's recommendation over a less thorough answer from a Stack Overflow user without a high rank.

DISCUSSION

We find it remarkable that so many participants believed that security is important and that they were personally responsible for the security of the software they develop, and yet did not use security tools. We believe that this is partly because security tools are what Rogers calls a *preventive innovation*. Preventive innovations are technologies that lower the probability of some unwanted future event. Condoms and vaccines, for instance, are preventive innovations. Preventive innovations diffuse slowly because of the temporal distance between the use of the technology and its effects, and because it's easier to see the negative effects of not using them than the positive effects of using them [34]. We believe that the challenges to creating cultures around thorough testing, as detailed by Pham and colleagues [27], may be due to the preventive nature of writing good tests.

We consider security tools a preventive innovation because security tools are used to lower the probability of security problems before deploying the software, but security problems generally occur after software is deployed. We found that a developer's code being "hacked" works as a *cue-to-action* for that developer to adopt a tool. A cue-to-action, in DOI theory, is an event that crystallizes a favorable attitude towards an innovation into a behavioral change [34]. In security tool adoption, being "hacked" can push developers who are considering using security tools to start using them. This indicates that one way to prevent losses that occur when vulnerabilities are exploited and must be repaired is to find more effective ways to warn developers about such losses.

The results of our study suggest a number of strategies for educators, software development companies, toolsmiths, and developers to increase adoption of security tools. These are preliminary recommendations that we hope to expand in more detail and to further justify in our future work.

Educators

We found some developers believe most security problems concern user authentication and access control. We think educators are in a unique position to present the broad spectrum of security problems to computer science students. Educators can also introduce students to tools that help solve those problems and encourage them to learn and explore new tools throughout their careers. Thus, educators are in a unique position to instill their students with inquisitive and enthusiastic attitudes toward security and security tools. Classroom studies such as Singer's [37] demonstrate that educators can effectively teach testing in the classroom, and we hold that they can also effectively promote other good software engineering practices, like the use of security tools.

Software Development Organizations

Companies can design policies regarding security tools to increase adoption among developers. We found, perhaps surprisingly, that policies requiring developers to use security tools seem quite effective. While secure development processes help developers code more securely, trust in process can make developers complacent and less likely to code securely, as reflected in our findings and those of Xie and colleagues [41]. Our findings also suggest that if companies structure their security processes so that security teams and other developers often interact, developers are more likely to feel personally responsible for security.

Companies might also encourage and support security tool use training developers to use tools that support it; this does not seem to be a common practice. Companies seeking to use the best and newest security tools to find vulnerabilities in their code might encourage developers to attend security conferences and make it easy to start using new tools in their organizations.

Finally, developers might be more security-conscious if their employers emphasize the potential costs to users of exploits on their code; developers who are conscious of these costs may be more likely to use security tools.

Toolsmiths

We found a number of ways that toolsmiths might focus their efforts to increase awareness of their tools. Toolsmiths might increase adoption of their tools by focusing their efforts on trusted channels like word-of-mouth, blogs, and Stack Overflow, and not using their resources promoting their tools with advertisements.

Toolsmiths designing tools to support code review and security auditing might also keep our results in mind. We found that developers who interact with security teams as part of the auditing process are more likely to adopt security tools, so future code review tools might be designed to support social as well as technical aspects of the code review process. Previous work has found that code review already serves social as well as code-improving purposes [2], and that code review tools already provide social benefits, like traceability, that other means of review do not [33]. Future code review tools might be designed to support the social interaction of developers and security teams.

Developers

We find it unlikely that this paper's audience includes developers unconcerned with software security. However, we remind those who are concerned that their peers are likely to take their security tool recommendations seriously. Our findings, here and elsewhere [23], indicate that developers are more likely to adopt tools they learn about from their peers than ones they learn about elsewhere. These findings show that individuals who tell others about the tools they use can be forces for change in their organizations. In addition, developers with good reputations on the Internet can act as forces for change within communities of developers in the software development community at large.

LIMITATIONS

One limitation for our retrospective interview study is the *recall problem*. Some participants noted that it was difficult to remember the tools they have tried out. Thus, our data on instances of adoption may be incomplete. For example, participants might remember the functionality of a security tool, but forget how complete its documentation was. We asked pointed questions to try to obtain this data. If a participant did not remember, we assumed the missing data was not important in his decision-making. Also, participants tended to forget the names of security tools they rejected more than those they adopted. In order to remind participants of the tools they might have tried, we created a list of well-known security tools, grouped by the programming languages they work with. After participants mentioned all the security tools they remember, we asked them to read this list based on the language they used most to find if they missed any tools.

This retrospective interview study also could not adequately capture the temporal aspects of DOI theory. An observational study might be better suited for evaluating how well the DOI adoption process describes security tool adoption.

Another limitation of our interview study is that, given the nature of semi-structured interviews, we did not ask all participants the same questions. Thus, we cannot guarantee that our data is complete since we cannot know how participants would respond to questions we did not ask them. However, we think that the breadth of our results justifies this possible incompleteness.

Because we designed our interview questions based on DOI theory and our initial ideas of how it would apply to security tool adoption, we may have biased our results with our preconceptions. To reduce this risk, we asked participants many open-ended questions to describe their adoption and rejection experiences before we started asking any pointed questions based on our interpretation of DOI. We tried to record all factors that we had not initially predicted and integrate these factors into our questions for subsequent interviewees.

The participants we recruited may not be representative of all software developers for a number of reasons. Though we did not specifically choose participants based on location, more than half of our participants reported working in the United States. All participants we recruited speak English, while many potential security tool adopters do not speak English. Also, developers who were willing to participate our study might hold more positive attitudes than average toward the software engineering research community, and perhaps are more likely to be aware of and adopt new security tools. We did not speak with any developers outside of industry, such as those who contribute to open-source software. This limits the kinds of social systems to which our work generalizes to those in industry. Most of our subjects' primary responsibility was writing code. While we did interview security experts and managers, our implications apply more reliably to those whose primary activity is writing code. Finally, we did not collect detailed demographic information from participants. Such qualities of individuals, such as age [21] and gender [11], can affect various aspects of software development, and may also affect social processes such as adoption.

FUTURE WORK

As mentioned in the Limitations section, we did not interview developers about open-source development. An interview study of developers who write open-source software would help determine if our findings generalize to developers outside of industry.

We believe that a qualitative and comprehensive model of influences on developer adoption of security tools would be more actionable than the current descriptions of participants' responses. Such a model would incorporate developers' perception of technological qualities of security tools as well as the factors concerning interpersonal communication presented here. For instance, several participants mentioned that automatabilty and interoperability with technologies they already used were important factors when deciding whether or not to adopt a tool. Our analysis currently does not account for these more technical factors, but could with further investigation.

A survey study would also be helpful in evaluating and quantifying our findings. We hope that this will result in validated recommendations we can make to managers seeking to increase security tool adoption in their organizations and a quantified predictive model that can predict whether or not developers in a given organization will adopt a given tool.

Our results have also shown that some developers attribute their tool use to having seen exploits on their companies' code; others attribute their disuse to having never been "hacked". This indicates that one way to persuade developers to use security tools may be to frame the results of such tools in terms of specific attacks that would successfully exploit vulnerabilities in developers' code. Future study could explore this.

CONCLUSION

There are many security tools that can help software developers write more secure code, but not all developers use these tools. In this paper, we have presented a number of social and organizational factors that we found influenced developers' security tool adoption decisions. We found these factors by conducting interviews, based on an established framework for understanding adoption called diffusion of innovations, with 42 professional software developers about their past experience about security tools. Our results suggest several ways for people in different roles in the software development community to improve the adoption rate of security tools, and thus to foster a culture that produces more robust and secure software.

Acknowledgment
Thanks to all participants for their time, to Michael Bazik for his comments and feedback, and to the National Security Agency for funding this research.

REFERENCES

1. Ajzen, I. The theory of planned behavior. *Organizational Behavior and Human Decision Processes 50*, 2 (Dec. 1991), 179–211.
2. Bacchelli, A., and Bird, C. Expectations, outcomes, and challenges of modern code review. In *Proceedings of the 35th International Conference on Software Engineering* (2013).
3. Bessey, A., Block, K., Chelf, B., Chou, A., Fulton, B., Hallem, S., Henri-Gros, C., Kamsky, A., McPeak, S., and Engler, D. A few billion lines of code later: using static analysis to find bugs in the real world. *Communications of the ACM 53*, 2 (Feb. 2010), 66–75.
4. Boehm, B. W. *Software Engineering Economics*, 1st ed. Prentice Hall PTR, Upper Saddle River, NJ, USA, 1981.
5. Buxton, J., and Malcolm, R. Software technology transfer. *Software Engineering Journal 6*, 1 (Jan. 1991), 17 –23.
6. Cornell, D. Remediation statistics: What does fixing application vulnerabilities cost? RSA Conference, 2012.
7. Cowley, S. Code red costs could top $2 billion. PCWorld, August 2001. `http://www.pcworld.com/article/57744/article.html`.
8. Davis, F. D. Perceived usefulness, perceived ease of use, and user acceptance of information technology. *MIS Quarterly 13*, 3 (Sept. 1989), 319–340.
9. Geer, D. Are companies actually using secure development life cycles? *IEEE Computer 43*, 6 (June 2010), 12–16.
10. Gorschek, T., Wohlin, C., Carre, P., and Larsson, S. A model for technology transfer in practice. *IEEE Software 23*, 6 (Nov.-Dec. 2006), 88–95.
11. Grigoreanu, V., Burnett, M., Wiedenbeck, S., Cao, J., Rector, K., and Kwan, I. End-user debugging strategies: A sensemaking perspective. *ACM Transactions on Computer-Human Interaction 19* (2012), 5:1–5:28.
12. Hardgrave, B. C., Davis, F. D., and Riemenschneider, C. K. Investigating determinants of software developers' intentions to follow methodologies. *Journal of Management Information Systems 20*, 1 (July 2003), 123–151.
13. Howard, M., and Lipner, S. *The Security Development Lifecycle*. Microsoft Press, Redmond, WA, USA, 2006.
14. Iivari, J. From a macro innovation theory of IS diffusion to a micro innovation theory of IS adoption: An application to CASE adoption. In *Proc. of the IFIP WG8.2 Working Group on Information Systems Development* (1993), 295–320.
15. Iivari, J. Why are CASE tools not used? *Communications of the ACM 39*, 10 (Oct. 1996), 94–103.
16. Kemerer, C. F. How the learning curve affects CASE tool adoption. *IEEE Software 9*, 3 (May 1992), 23–28.
17. Koppel, R., Wetterneck, T., Telles, J. L., and Karsh, B.-T. Workarounds to barcode medication administration systems: Their occurrences, causes, and threats to patient safety. *Journal of the American Medical Informatics Association 15*, 4 (2008), 408 – 423.
18. McGraw, G. Software security. *IEEE Security and Privacy 2*, 2 (Mar.-Apr. 2004), 80–83.
19. Meyerovich, L. A., and Rabkin, A. S. Socio-plt: principles for programming language adoption. In *Proc. of Onward!*, ACM (2012), 39–54.
20. Moore, G. C., and Benbasat, I. Development of an Instrument to Measure the Perceptions of Adopting an Information Technology Innovation. *Information Systems Research 2*, 3 (Sept. 1991), 192–222.
21. Morrison, P., and Murphy-Hill, E. Is programming knowledge related to age? *Mining Software Repositories* (2013), 3–6.
22. Murphy-Hill, E., Jiresal, R., and Murphy, G. C. Improving software developers' fluency by recommending development environment commands. In *Proc. of FSE*, ACM (2012), 42:1–42:11.
23. Murphy-Hill, E., and Murphy, G. C. Peer interaction effectively, yet infrequently, enables programmers to discover new tools. In *Proc. of CSCW* (2011), 405–414.
24. Nahar, N., Kakola, T., and Huda, N. Diffusion of software technology innovations in the global context. In *Proc. of the Hawaii International Conference on System Sciences* (Jan. 2002), 2749–2757.
25. Nov, O., and Arazy, O. Personality-targeted design: theory, experimental procedure, and preliminary results. In *Proc. of CSCW*, ACM (New York, NY, USA, 2013), 977–984.
26. Parnin, C., Bird, C., and Murphy-Hill, E. Java generics adoption: how new features are introduced, championed, or ignored. In *Proc. of MSR*, ACM (2011), 3–12.
27. Pham, R., Singer, L., Liskin, O., Figueira Filho, F., and Schneider, K. Creating a shared understanding of testing culture on a social coding site. In *Proc. of ICSE*, IEEE Press (Piscataway, NJ, USA, 2013), 112–121.
28. Premkumar, G., and Potter, M. Adoption of computer aided software engineering (CASE) technology: an innovation adoption perspective. *SIGMIS Database 26*, 2–3 (May 1995), 105–124.

29. Raghavan, S., and Chand, D. Diffusing software-engineering methods. *IEEE Software 6*, 4 (July 1989), 81–90.

30. Rai, A., and Howard, G. Propagating case usage for software development: An empirical investigation of key organizational correlates. *Omega 22*, 2 (Mar. 1994), 133–147.

31. Rai, A., and Patnayakuni, R. A structural model for CASE adoption behavior. *Journal of Management Information Systems 13*, 2 (Sept. 1996), 205–234.

32. Riemenschneider, C., Hardgrave, B., and Davis, F. Explaining software developer acceptance of methodologies: a comparison of five theoretical models. *IEEE TSE 28*, 12 (Dec. 2002), 1135–1145.

33. Rigby, P. C., and Bird, C. Convergent Software Peer Review Practices. In *Proceedings of the the joint meeting of the European Software Engineering Conference and the ACM SIGSOFT Symposium on The Foundations of Software Engineering (ESEC/FSE)*, ACM (2013).

34. Rogers, E. M. *Diffusion of Innovations*. Free Press, 1995.

35. Seaman, C. Qualitative methods in empirical studies of software engineering. *IEEE TSE 25*, 4 (1999), 557–572.

36. Singer, L., and Schneider, K. Influencing the adoption of software engineering methods using social software. In *Proc. of ICSE* (2012), 1325–1328.

37. Singer, L.-G. *Improving the Adoption of Software Engineering Practices Through Persuasive Interventions*. PhD thesis, Gottfried Wilhelm Leibniz Universitt Hannover, 2013.

38. Straus, S. G., Bikson, T. K., Balkovich, E., and Pane, J. F. Mobile technology and action teams: Assessing blackberry use in law enforcement units. *Proc. of CSCW 19*, 1 (2010), 45–71.

39. Thompson, R. L., Higgins, C. A., and Howell, J. M. Personal Computing: Toward a Conceptual Model of Utilization. *MIS Quarterly 15*, 1 (Mar. 1991), 125.

40. Venkatesh, V., and Davis, F. D. A theoretical extension of the technology acceptance model: Four longitudinal field studies. *Management Science 46*, 2 (Feb. 2000), 186–204.

41. Xie, J., Lipford, H., and Chu, B. Why do programmers make security errors? In *Proc. of Visual Languages and Human-Centric Computing* (Sept. 2011), 161–164.

"Figure Out How to Code with the Hands of Others": Recognizing Cultural Blind Spots in Global Software Development

Stina Matthiesen[1] **Pernille Bjørn**[1,2] **Lise Møller Petersen**[1]

[1]The IT University of Copenhagen
Rued Langgaards Vej 7, 2300 Copenhagen,
Denmark

[2]University of California, Irvine
Irvine, CA 92697
USA

{matthiesen, pbra, lmp}@itu.dk

ABSTRACT

We report on an ethnographic study of an outsourcing global software development (GSD) setup between an Indian IT vendor and an IT development division of a Danish bank. We investigate how the local IT development work is shaped by the global setup in GSD and argue that the bank had cultural blind spots toward the changes in Denmark. Three critical issues were neglected due to the cultural blind spots: 1) increased number of interruptions, 2) lack of translucence of remote colleagues' work, and 3) the re-definition of boundaries between work and articulation work. The implications of these findings include considerations for how to organize GSD practices and prepare the organizational changes that occur when moving from a co-located software development organization to an inter-organizational geographically distributed organization. Also, our findings open up discussions about the professional identity of IT developers within GSD, including extending the qualifications for IT developers.

Author Keywords

Global software development (GSD); ethnographic study; cultural blind spots; articulation work; local work practices

ACM Classification Keywords

K.4.3 [Organizational Impacts]: Computer-supported collaborative work; H.5.3 [Group and Organization Interfaces]: Computer-supported cooperative work

INTRODUCTION

The CSCW community has an increased interest in global work practices within software development. Working remotely across time zones and geography impact the local work practices of IT developers, and issues such as trust [e.g. 1], coordination [e.g. 12], and awareness [e.g. 14] are crucial enablers for global software development (GSD). For companies determined to reap the benefits of global software development, methods for assuring the quality of software engineering processes and end product have tended to steal the focus, while the actual concrete practices have attracted less attention. Echoing the call for further understanding of actual concrete practices in software development through "*empirical studies of software development teams using extensive field study methods*" [3, p. 480], we present a study that focuses on local practices in a global collaborative setup.

In this paper we ask: *How is the local work shaped by the global setup in GSD?* Answering this question, we provide empirical data from an outsourcing setup between a large Indian IT vendor and a Danish financial enterprise that have been collaborating for the last 7 years. Interestingly, in this case the local Danish developers still articulate and experience many problems and challenges. At first glance, the obvious explanation for this observation might entail linking the complexities of working cross-culturally to "*Hofstede-type studies*" that understand cultures as nationally determined characteristics. However, this understanding poorly links to detailed work-related attitudes and actions when used as a basis for analyzing cross-cultural working [32]. Thus, if we are to move away from this "stereotypical" understanding and instead dive into the empirical complexities, a totally different set of reasons emerges.

We use the notion of "cultural blind spots" to encompass an unidentified knowledge that exists in parallel within organizations [9]. Cultural blind spots can be understood as unnoticed tacit knowledge we have about ourselves in relation to our culture, mind, action, or motivation that are typically overlooked when paying attention elsewhere. Cultural blind spots may encumber the collaboration, as people and organizations may have blind spots toward their cultural self-awareness. In relation to knowledge sharing in organizations and the processes through which people manage to act appropriately within a certain context, the cultural blind spots then represent unattended knowledge that, if attended to, may be a resource in the organizational context.

CSCW'14, February 15 - 19 2014, Baltimore, MD, USA
Copyright 2014 ACM 978-1-4503-2540-0/14/02...$15.00.
http://dx.doi.org/10.1145/2531602.2531612

We propose that one of the major reasons for the challenges in our case concerns the cultural blind spots of the Danish IT division toward the Danish local site. Although the Danish IT division has focused its attention toward the Indian IT vendor, ensuring alignment of processes and practices toward the Danish bank, it has paid less attention to the changes at the local Danish site. In this paper, we point to how this unbalanced attention from Danish IT division has brought about issues and concerns from the Danish site. Moreover, we point to how three crucial cultural blind spots in particular have been neglected by the Danish IT division: 1) how the global setup brings with it an increased number of interruptions that forces the coordinating and prioritizing of tasks to be reviewed differently at the local Danish site, 2) how the local work related to coordination within projects needs realignment to include translucence of the global collaboration and the work of the remote colleagues, and 3) how boundaries between work and articulation work at the local Danish site are re-defined when engaging in GSD.

The paper begins with a presentation of related work followed by a description of the research method. Then, approaching an answer to our research question, the case is described and the empirical results are presented. Finally, findings are discussed before the paper concludes.

RELATED WORK

Global software development is characterized by collaboration between IT developers with different national and organizational cultures in different geographic locations and across time zones using various traditional and IT-enabled means to collaborate [15, p. 88]. GSD is widely studied within CSCW, both in terms of open-source development [14, 22] and in corporate settings [6, 8, 17, 30]; our focus is on the latter.

Working across organizational boundaries entails malleable structures around the collaborative setup [21], providing opportunities to continuously align and readjust the global work arrangement. It is important to remember that people work locally and are part of the local organizational setup even when working globally, since the global organizational context is a conglomeration of the local organizational setup people bring to the table [5]. Thus, the local organizational setup impacts the global setup. In addition, the global setup impacts local work of the IT developers, since the developers also have to readjust and align to the new ways of working.

The question then becomes, which practices in the local organizational context are impacted by the global setup? Looking into the literature, the key collaborative practices in GSD are coordination [12, 14], knowledge management [2, 6, 17], organizational culture [6, 32], and trust/commitment [1, 30]. Examining how the local collaborative practices become impacted by the global setup, it is essential to realize that GSD is not the opposite of local software development [3] but rather software development with additional complexities in handling the extra effort of articulation work, which must be present to reach the global objective. Our interest is to "localize the global" [19, p.173 ff] in GSD, which means that we will study the global engagement through the local practices.

Articulation work is the extra work required to handle the mutual dependencies when more than one person is involved in solving a task [31]. Articulation work as a theoretical concept aims to help us understand the interdependence of activities where more than one individual is needed to solve a task. Articulation work has been studied in the practical setting of global software development, where it was found to be essential for handling the large number of interdependencies between the developers [7]. The complexity of articulation work in the context of GSD tends to be overlooked by the IT developers, even though it plays an important role in the management of distributed projects [7]. It is important to note that work for some professions might be articulation work for others. For example, a secretary might have it as her work task to organize meetings, whereas for a system developer organizing meetings would be articulation work. Therefore, what counts as work for a particular profession influences what counts as articulation work for the same profession. In this way, activities might be identified as articulation work, depending on the role of the employee.

Articulation work in GSD is closely related to coordination. Working remotely while being mutually dependent on each other for completion of interdependent work requires a lot of communication to mediate and control the cooperative relationship. Distribution of tasks across organizational, spatial, and temporal boundaries has been referred to as increased reach [12]. Increased reach has consequences for the organization of work and "*implies that the problem of coordinating tasks and people (never easy) becomes markedly more complex*" [12, p. 195].

Agile methods, originally assumed for collocation, are increasingly applied in GSD in an effort to mitigate the challenges of coordination stipulated by temporal, geographical, and socio-cultural distance [15]. Still, issues of increased coordination costs and inconsistent work practices impact coordination, and several papers [e.g. 6, 14] report reduced cooperation arising from misunderstandings. When we investigate how the local work is shaped by the global setup, we will include studying the local coordination practices as an approach to comprehend the global coordination practices.

Misunderstandings are closely related to how knowledge is managed between geographically dispersed participants [2]. Being able to communicate as well as to interpret the requirements of an IT system [8] to achieve a shared understanding of the work [14] poses great challenges. When operating in geographically distributed and intercultural collaborative work settings, distinct interpretations of concepts and meanings were found to challenge the communication of shared tasks [17]. Based on the experiences that we collect as individuals and as part of groups, we are each left with an unarticulated frame of reference that we act on and live in [5]. When people's frames of reference are distinctly different, a shared meaning may be difficult to reach. Acknowledging the necessity of knowledge and skill in a team, it is not sufficient if team members cannot coordinate their expertise [11]. Technologies such as instant messaging offer synchronous communication. However, when answers are not needed instantly, an asynchronous use has been reported: sending off a question and continuing to work until the answer arrives later [7]. Instant messaging has been found useful in supporting knowledge work in GSD [2]. But, interestingly, the tools only played a secondary role; instead, the human factors such as communication and social skills were critical for success. The exchange of knowledge is a challenge further increased in situations where domain and task experts are distributed [13]. For example, if the majority of the domain experts are located at the headquarters in Germany, less motivation for knowledge exchange was found at the headquarters in comparison to the subsidiaries in, for example, Italy and India [13]. Here the sub-grouping of experts is overlapping with the sub-grouping of locations, thus increasing the impact of the sub-groups on the collaboration [10], making the us/them division more pertinent. The distribution and strict division of labor has also been reported to cause problems when dealing with exceptional cases in work processes where workers are lacking understanding and knowledge of the work of other division [25]. Examining the empirical data in our case, we will study sub-group dynamics as well as knowledge practices to understand how the global setup impacts the local work of the IT developers.

The socio-emotional relations between colleagues at the local sites are critical for the collaboration and are based on the trust and expectations toward remote colleagues [1, 30]. Social relationships are related to cultural aspects of the local contexts. Interestingly, asymmetry in cultural training in inter-organizational GSD setups has been reported [18]. In these cases it was perceived as necessary for the staff from the IT vendor to learn about the culture of their client organization's country and not the other way around. In these cases culture is perceived as a stable national entity that can be "translated" for others to understand. Studying cultural complexities, we join others by examining culture not as a stable entity based on nationality, but rather as a dynamic entity which gets re-negotiated and which we can only study through its manifestation in artifacts, practices, and routines [6, 17]. Understanding culture in GSD thus requires us to study the local practices and the negotiated processes of language, practices, and artifacts. Often cultural differences emerge in situations of conflict or communication breakdown [5], since these are the situations where differences become pertinent in practice. However, culture also manifests in local practice, even though these practices often appear as blind spots locally. The term *blind spot* comes from human biology and refers to a small region of the eye where there are no cells to detect light, and thus a part of the visual field is obscured. The brain typically compensates for the blind spot based on the surrounding details and information from the other eye. Which visual information falls into the blind spot differs depending on where the eye is directing attention. When attention is moved, the blind spot moves as well; however, the human eye can never access the visual information that falls in the blind spot directly. Cultural blind spots comprise the knowledge that exists in parallel within organizations without being identified [9]. For example, organizations might focus on creating a "global mindset" while completely ignoring the many international experiences that already exist at the organization's headquarters. So, by focusing on "something," other important knowledge might become opaque and out of sight. In many cases information that falls into the organizational cultural blind spot is about our own cultural behaviors and practices, since we simply take these for granted. Not just organizations have cultural blind spots; groups and individuals also have cultural blind spots. Each cultural blind spot is different depending on the direction of attention; thus, cultural blind spots across groups will to some extent be incongruent. Different directions of attention may therefore provide the opportunity for other group members to compensate in the same way that the other eye also compensates for the blind spot in the first eye. However, compensating for cultural blind spots is not automatic. Organizations need to direct attention toward such processes to be able to utilize the opportunity.

When we investigate our empirical case, we will study, in particular, the aspects of the local practices that become neglected or overlooked as cultural blind spots when attention is directed toward the global work. In this process, we will include examinations at the different locations to determine how coordination, knowledge management, and cultural practices are shaped by the global setup.

METHOD

To determine how the global setup impacts the local practices, we conducted a workplace study [20] applying ethnographical approaches [27]. Investigating GSD work practices, we took seriously the many challenges that research in distributed software development poses [26], and we conducted extensive fieldwork at the two sites involved. We studied the IT division in a Danish financial enterprise that employs more than 20,000 people in northern Europe. For confidentiality reasons, we have anonymized the company, to be referred to as *ScandiaBank*, as well as the IT division, which we here call *BankIT*. Since 2006, BankIT has been engaged in GSD by outsourcing development tasks to an IT vendor in India, *ITS* (name also anonymized). ITS is a well-reputed company working out of Bangalore, India, with 102 years of history. It provides IT services, among other things, and ITS was originally chosen by ScandiaBank among many other IT services companies in India due to its standards in human resource management. The IT division, BankIT, comprises more than 2,000 people responsible for handling, maintaining, and developing the IT services within ScandiaBank. In India, around 750 ITS developers are associated with the BankIT, but ITS also serves other clients and customers.

The Empirical Case

The empirical case concerns the outsourcing relationship between ScandiaBank and ITS. ScandiaBank first established the outsourcing arrangement with ITS to ensure scalability of skilled labor, which was difficult to obtain onshore in Denmark in 2006. Nonetheless, a large presence in Denmark was still required to maintain business and domain-specific knowledge. However, over time the official reason for the outsourcing setup has changed to concern cost reductions. Although it is referred to as an outsourcing relationship, many of the structures resemble those of an offshore relationship where closely coupled work is required due to the distribution of knowledge and staffing across the two sites. While ScandiaBank decides which tasks and projects are dedicated to the ITS employees, and domain knowledge and business logic required for accomplishing the development work reside in Denmark, ITS is responsible for providing the needed complement of Indian employees to be associated with the bank. Because ITS possesses the required reputation in India to attract and recruit skilled labor, ITS is critical for ScandiaBank, which is not a well-known company within India and thus not prestigious enough to attract competent workers in India. Moreover, an expatriated Danish resource manager is posted in India. This individual is responsible for ScandiaBank's activities in Bangalore, together with four Danish liaison officers responsible for coordinating the different IT development projects in BankIT, sitting at the table when new employees are hired, and bridging the communication between ScandiaBank and ITS if needed.

ScandiaBank has a visual identity in terms of logo, posters, website, coffee cups, and other merchandise, all bearing the mark of a range of ScandiaBank's brand colors that are unavoidably noticeable when moving inside the walls of the BankIT building in Denmark.

In Bangalore, India, ITS is servicing different customers around the globe, one being ScandiaBank. The ITS precinct is surrounded by fences and walls demarcating ITS and the outside pulsating life of Bangalore. Clients of ITS reside in different office buildings among flourishing clean and quiet gardens. ScandiaBank has its own building where only ITS employees working for ScandiaBank are allowed access. Flags of both ITS and ScandiaBank are flying outside the entrance of the building as well as inside. The workstations are formed into cubicles and distributed into 4 large, open office environments. The walls are decorated with ScandiaBank posters in English or Danish language, and throughout the offices time zone wall clocks are hanging displaying the time in India and in Denmark. Recently the ITS employees moved into a new building, concurrent with the increase in staffing over the last seven years. The new building went through a renovation in order to meet the standards required by ScandiaBank. For example, the bank made requirements for the working environment: the colors of the office interiors needed to match the ScandiaBank brand's colors, and the ceiling height needed to be lifted.

Data Sources and Analysis

From October 2012 to March 2013, two of the authors conducted fieldwork in Denmark at a department within BankIT with a total of 80 employees and in India at their counterpart team in ITS with a total of 30 employees. More specifically, we focused on 9 BankIT employees of different occupation: system managers, IT developers, and business developers all located at one location in Denmark. From the counterpart team in India, we studied 12 ITS employees: task managers and IT developer. Furthermore, we interviewed 2 ScandiaBank expats at ITS.

Our data sources collected in Denmark and India cover 12 interviews and 80 hours of observations, as well as 12 pages of field diary, 41 pages of reflections, and 98 minutes of video-recorded accounts of our confessional statements (cf. Table 1). In total, over 300 pages of rich descriptions and interviews were created. Furthermore, internal department documents were analyzed, including outsourcing strategy documents, meeting agendas, an overview of human resources in the department, organizational diagrams, and task descriptions.

Gathering Technique \ Field Site	DK	IN
Interviews (no./hours)	5/10.0	7/16.2
Observation (no./hours)	32/29.2	40/51.1
Confessional statements (no.)	8	20
Field diary entry (no.)	5	24
Reflections (no.)	60	79

Table 1. Data sources of the ethnographic fieldwork conducted in Denmark (DK) and India (IN).

In an effort to convert the data source comprising rich detailed empirical insight into concepts and premises that underlie the practices we studied, we investigated the patterns of thought and practice by combining various data-gathering techniques with a self-reflective method from action research by conducting confessional statements [4]. During the study this helped us keep track of, reflect upon, and improve the direction and inquiry of the research while being in the field. After data collection, we did several iterative write-ups, coding, and identified the critical incidents concerning the cultural blind spots. In this work we were also guided by the theoretical framing.

RESULTS

In the following we provide background information on how the global collaboration between ITS and ScandiaBank was initiated. This includes a description of how the goals of inter-organizational collaboration were first laid out to the BankIT department. Then we present the increased extra work that emerged in the global setup. Following this, we have two main sections focusing on the local work in India and in Denmark. In each of those sections, including subsections, we present empirical data on how the local work at each site was affected by the global setup.

Initiating the Inter-Organizational Collaboration

Initially, the global collaboration was operationalized in the form of quantitative goals, which were difficult for employees to translate into concrete work arrangements and therefore failed to make the Danish employees fully committed to the collaboration with their Indian counterparts:

"When we were assigned the development organization in Bangalore there was this quantitative goal: "now everyone should have 10% of the staff in Bangalore, here you go!" [...] And it did not go very well, and we were not whole-hearted about it." (Interview, system manager, Denmark, 10/01/2012)

According to the system managers, the engagement in GSD with ITS was challenging for the people who had to collaborate on a daily basis because the IT developers themselves had to figure out suitable ways to collaborate globally without any particular guidelines from the management in BankIT.

Since 2006, though, BankIT has made efforts to provide some global collaboration guidelines; however, it is still a challenge to make the collaboration work well, and serious issues remain.

Increased Extra Work

One of the major changes when engaging in global software development work is the increased "extra work" required to handle the dependencies across time and space. For the BankIT department the increase in extra work gave rise to doubts about whether their effort in the global collaboration was a worthy investment.

Several of our informants announced that the mentality and the general assumption about the global collaboration was that it entails a lot of effort without knowing if it is actually paying off. An IT developer expressed a need for information that could help him convince people to invest time and effort in the global collaboration:

"But we have no idea what the accounts say, we have no idea whether they are paid back in two years, or 5 years. And then again take all those opinions and prejudices and skepticism that are in... amongst all, or almost all of the employees here. Concerning, well, they do not believe fully in that it can pay off." (Interview, IT developer, Denmark, 10/05/2012)

Interestingly, this *investment* is understood in two ways: 1) in terms of the extra work and time required to make it work and 2) by the business' accounts – the investment of setting up and maintaining the apparatus of outsourcing IT development to India.

Even the BankIT system manager, who is responsible for leading and motivating his staff to engage in the global collaboration, is having a hard time believing in the actual financial output of the work required:

"There's actually something that goes into production [...] I do not believe that they are efficient enough yet, that we must honestly say. There is still an imbalance relative to the effort and output." (Interview, system manager, Denmark, 10/01/2012)

One reason for his misgivings is embedded in the way tasks are managed and solved in BankIT. The overhead of specifying the development tasks is, according to the system manager, a big investment, and it poses different and extra work than what they are used to in the department:

"If you pay someone to do some tasks that are incredibly well-described, i.e., down to a detail that just needs to be developed, then you have a big investment up front in describing all this. It is something we have never been very good at, and I do not think that this is the right way to do it." (Interview, IT developer, Denmark, 10/05/2012)

While documentation is a part of software development practices, the criteria for quality documentation increase in a global work setting, since remote collaborators should be able to continue work based on this documentation. The demand for quality documentation very much impacts the local IT development work of the Danish IT developers as well as the need for describing methods and processes:

"This is something I have been doing for a long time now... describing processes and so. So this has also been started up because they [the Indian IT developers] are extremely focused on following processes and templates, and doing things right. So we have to pull ourselves together and produce these things for them, right. Thing is, we know how we do things; these are simply not written down." (Interview, IT developer, Denmark, 10/05/2012)

Moving from knowing how to do things within the walls of BankIT to actually creating high-quality documentation and specifications requires different types of competences than simply expertise in programming and concomitant tacit knowledge. As such, the type of work required locally is changing and is experienced as "extra work" that emerges due to the global setup. As one developer states, the code was not structured enough as it had been gemmating for many years:

"Just to be able to set up the apparatus to give to the Indians – it has been quite necessary. [...] It has both required an effort from a business developer aspect because there must be documents, but it has required the code to be structured, and that it has not been previously. It has been, it has sprouted in ten years." (Interview, IT and business developer, Denmark, 10/02/2012)

Extra work is emerging for BankIT employees due to the global work – work that BankIT employees do not perceive as part of the work fitting their professional identity. No doubt the work is essential for global work, but there continues to be a "feeling" that this kind of work does not add directly to the production and earning of ScandiaBank and that therefore it is only a matter of time before the global setup might be closed. A system manager explains:

"We may risk that from tomorrow on someone decides that we should not use the ITS anymore, and then we cannot afford that they are the ones sitting with the knowledge, and it is obviously another parameter relative to the cooperation we can have and how much responsibility we can lay down with them when we have the little protective attitude toward our source code" (Interview, System manager, Denmark, 10/02/2012)

The changed requirements for the work by BankIT employees and the persistent doubt in the global setup, despite seven years of engagement, is a complication which makes the global work difficult to accomplish with all benefits. The lack of attention toward the complexities experienced at the Danish site has been experienced as problematic. According to the liaison officer, the Danish perspective has been de-prioritized in the past:

"One of the things we have not worked much with is the Danish employees throughout this sourcing setup. As it is no secret – it's come out to people that, yes, if in 5 years from now you're not adept at using sourcing, then you might not be here [in ScandiaBank]." (Interview, Liaison officer, India, 11/08/2012)

Clearly, the outsourcing strategy impacts the Danish employees. It changes their work assignments and creates new criteria for relevant competences and continued learning. The BankIT employees have to take on the responsibility of continuously improving their own market value through persistent education and qualification. According to the liaison officer, the employees in BankIT must be willing and ready to adapt in the future, and the work practiced in BankIT might also adapt accordingly:

"I thought about a role description... I call it 'Integration Manager' [...] An integration manager is a person who can figure out how to code with the hands of others, send off some tasks, with everything it entails, which is not simple, send off some tasks, get them fixed, get them back, put them together so they can go into production. [...] If you can do that, then you're still here [employed in BankIT]. However, if you want to sit and build your own LEGO castle with your own bricks then you're not." (Interview, liaison officer, India, 11/08/2012)

The message coming from the liaison officer in Bangalore is clear: the IT developer in BankIT must adapt to work in a global setting. Also, s/he must accept that the distribution of work will change in the future, moving from actual coding and programming to orchestrating and supporting the programming executed in a global collaborative setting. The global setup thus shapes the work in BankIT.

Local Work in India

In the next section we bring forward two examples: one concerning how the accomplishment of work at the Indian site is challenged by the global setup, and a second exemplifying how new management styles are introduced – shaping the local work.

Blocking or Prolonging the Work

A vital part of the work executed at the Indian site entails understanding the contextual information about the actual task that the IT developers are to solve. As we have earlier explained, the domain knowledge and the business logic reside mainly in Denmark. This arrangement means ITS employees are often waiting for BankIT employees to get back to them concerning documentation or answers to questions. In a task clarification meeting we observed from the Danish site, a Danish business developer (James) attempted to provide additional necessary information on a task to an Indian IT developer (Nikhil). Unfortunately, they both find the decisions in the task description incomprehensible:

James says he will then ask his system manager who initially made the design decision [...] "I understand, there is no reason for us to go through it!" James says. It seems like he is explaining to Nikhil that he fully understands the issue; however, he is not able to give more relevant information before he has discussed this matter with the system manager. (Observation notes, Denmark, 10/04/2012)

In the above observation, the Indian IT developers are highly dependent on receiving the correct information to accomplish the tasks. Unfortunately, the originator of the proposed task and its description is the system manager, who rarely, if ever, attends these kinds of meetings due to his many other obligations as a system manager and a leader with daily HR responsibility. Thus, when sufficient information is not obtainable, the goal of clarifying a particular task is not met, and unwanted breaks then emerge. As an attempt to overcome similar situations, the Indian developers must then act proactively by continuously asking for the information whenever they are in contact with the Danish employees. At another audio meeting between a Danish business developer and two Indian IT developers, we observed how one of the Indian IT developers seized the chance to procure some extra information about another task:

As Shashi gets to speak, it's really mostly about some other tasks than what the meeting would be about, and it is welcomed by James [...] Shashi sees a chance just to get some updates on some other issues, a kind of briefing, as well as to get some advice from James. (Observation notes, India, 10/03/2012)

The Indian IT developers are facing a lot of waiting for the Danish team to get back to them, and typically a few key actors become the bottlenecks blocking the provision of needed information. This makes it difficult to continue work, and in some situations the Indian IT developers might be lacking work, which was expressed explicitly at an internal team meeting in ITS:

Muthu says that he does not have much to do and he informs [the ITS task manager and team] that he has started looking at a new task. To that, the task manager says that he should not spend time on that [particular task] as it has not been given the go-ahead by James yet, but they are still waiting to hear what is going to happen with this task. [...] Muthu, Shan, and Nikhil would soon have nothing to do. (Observation notes, India, 11/20/2012)

Evidently, what is blocking or prolonging the work among Indian IT developers is mostly related to the work of the Danish team, for example, having the Danes spending time on preparing new tasks for the Indians to solve. Here, the "extra work" required to make the global work function is missing due to key actors like "James," who was mentioned several times at the meeting and who appears to have quite a lot of work in his hands, or at least it is not a priority that several ITS employees cannot move forward because they are awaiting information.

New Management Styles

To create an environment at ITS where people in general may be more inclined to challenge leaders as well as colleagues, a mailbox has been set up for the ITS employees to be able to anonymously submit feedback or ideas. The resource manager then reads the submissions, and according to him, it is one step toward adapting an Indian top-down management hierarchy to *"our [Danish] form of management."* Additionally, an increase in employee involvement has been enacted, and the ITS employees are now involved in new initiatives such as the introduction of ScandiaBank's new strategy in Denmark. This initiative was announced through a two-hour event with stage performances by ITS employees, a red carpet, and popcorn machines, to which the resource manager commented:

"Yesterday's strategy event was an approach that hopefully will help building a sense of ownership here. In the past, this kind of information would not reach all the way down to India." (Interview, resource manager, India, 10/31/2012)

At the event, we also witnessed the resource manager trying to act more informal by wearing a tuxedo and 3D glasses, to which he told us he wanted to show that he was not so different from them. Likewise, he prefers to pick up his own coffee instead of having it served, and he makes an effort to greet people in the morning when he comes into the office.

While most changes since 2006 have concerned the Indian site, one major change influencing the Danish employees is a recent re-definition of the travel policy. Historically, only directors travelled to ITS. However, recently IT developers from BankIT started visiting Bangalore for education or/and for building collaborative relationships with their ITS colleagues. This change was also initiated to overcome some of the major resistance from the BankIT employees, as the employees visiting ITS will act as ambassadors when they return home. One of the arguments for this approach is to address the problem of making the Danish employees work globally. A liaison officer agrees that by visiting ITS in Bangalore, ambassadors for pro-global collaboration are formed:

"But it is evident that when you come down here you get something completely different, a completely different impression of what is going on. [...] and there will also be some of those skeptics, as there have been many down here, and they see what the conditions are down here and how and so. And when they come home, they actually act as ambassadors to the rest of the business at home and say, 'That global collaboration could damn well make sense.'" (Interview, liaison officer, India, 11/08/2012)

Not only does this liaison officer advocate for sending employees to Bangalore to have ambassadors returning back home to Denmark, he advocates for sending the skeptics of the global collaboration. A ScandiaBank IT developer who recently visited ITS in Bangalore for 14 days also shared the understanding of what impact an onsite visit may have:

"I think it was really good, professionally speaking, to be over there, and when you come back, you can say that the cooperation continues also when you return home [...] When I got home, I did not give it a thought when four Indians were writing me in one morning. Before I was like this: "Oh.. is it them again!" [laughs]" (Interview, IT developer, Denmark, 10/03/2012)

Getting to know one's global collaborators, in this case, was shown to impact the work afterward. However, what made this trip favorable was the changed perspective on the global collaboration for the Danish IT developer, namely the renewed focus of work, changing from thinking of instant messaging chat inquiries as interrupting work to becoming part of work.

Over the last seven years the collaboration between ITS and BankIT has developed and improved. However, most changes have been directed at ITS, while BankIT employees have been less of a focus. We found that the solo focus on the new remote site created problems because it neglected the important changes that also occur at the local site when a company engages in global work. This neglect, we argue, complicates the global work, and the possible benefits of global collaboration are less than what could be because successful collaboration requires engagement and participation from all partners. We will provide examples.

Local Work in Denmark

Interestingly, the local work in Denmark received much less attention than the local work in India after the global collaboration was implemented. This meant that formally local work practices in Denmark continued unchanged. However, in practice the local work in Denmark was indeed affected by the global setup. In this section we will provide empirical data illustrating this point.

Staff in the BankIT department are used to working really closely with their co-located colleagues, discussing news, urgent deadlines, or roadblocks in progressing a task by having a quick chat at the coffee machine, or by stepping into each other's offices or discussing things over lunch. Here we bring forward two examples of how work practices in the local work are challenged by the global work.

Coordinating Work with Kanban Meetings

This particular department in BankIT does not use agile development methods such as Scrum; however, they use a certain Kanban meeting mechanism as a strategy to improve translucence of the progress of tasks that people are working on in the department, as the system manager described:

"We meet every morning, just to talk about who's up to what, like, 'what kind of challenges am I facing, and is there someone who can help me?' And it has definitely given us something ... it has at least given us some visibility on what each other is doing." (Interview, System manager, Denmark, 10/01/2012)

In the field we observed a couple of these Kanban meetings executed within a local team in the BankIT department consisting of 16 employees, a combination of business developers and IT developers. At the meeting, the IT developers gathered around a large whiteboard they call a Kanban board, which shows a big chart with all their names written downward in rows and the different states of the development process presented in columns. The tasks are written down and represented by post-it notes sticking to the board. Typically, a system manager or the like would then function as moderator and each employee goes through the status of their tasks and updates the board by moving the post-its with tasks around, for example, moving a task from the state of analysis to construction.

People take turns going to the Kanban board and informing the team about the status of their tasks [...] The system manager is uttering small sounds of consent, expressing that he is in on what they are talking about: "well," "yes," "yeah," "yeah well," "yes, it just sounds so," "yes, definitely," and when he is not completely following, he asks kindly, "what is it that you stand with there?" (Observation note, Denmark, 10/03/2012)

This mechanism of interaction functions as a way of communicating, coordinating, and creating translucence around what is going on. However, this mechanism does not include the global collaboration and their colleagues in ITS to the same extent as the local BankIT employees. While observing one of the Kanban meetings we noticed the limited presence of ITS, and we were told by the system manager that ITS was only represented by a single entity/row on the boards.

The system manager asked Jim about ITS because it is Jim who is the main contact [...] the information from Jim was only directed to Andy [the system manager] (Observation note, Denmark, 10/03/2012)

The work executed by the ITS team and the work executed in collaboration with ITS is not visible to the same extent as the work that is performed by the employees situated in BankIT. The information from India is, in this case, mostly mediated through a single IT developer, and therefore the work of and with the Indian counterpart is not perceptible at the meetings. Acknowledging the need to create translucence around the progress of tasks being solved in India, a Danish system manager explains the rationale for now introducing a virtual Kanban board and meetings to their Indian colleagues:

"But there has just been very little managing of the tasks. And of course it is quite unfortunate because it sends out ... it may send some signals to both the business but also to other developers that they are not producing anything when they've said something will be done tomorrow, and tomorrow it is still not done... and these are some of the things we have to work with; it simply needs to be more visible, possibly through Kanban [...] And it is both for the business but also internally, among other developers, so they can see that there actually is progress. Something is happening." (Interview, system manager, Denmark, 10/02/2012)

By creating translucence around task progression and deliverables, the increased visibility of work of the global collaboration may lead to a better understanding of what is going on and what kind of support the global collaborative work requires. However, participation in the newly established Kanban meetings appeared to include only employees already engaged in the global collaborative work, and the board was not being merged with the Kanban board already used by the Danish team. Unfortunately, the argument of enhancing the visibility of the otherwise imperceptible work for the customer and the IT developers not directly involved in the global collaboration is not followed up on.

Inquiry or Interruption

While in the field at the Danish site, a frustrated IT developer came to see us after we had observed an audio conference meeting with IT developers from both sites. The language barrier, he explains, is an obstacle in the collaboration, and he finds it to be easier to manage for the people who have been working with the Indian colleagues much longer than he has.

Martin says several times that it is "difficult" and that he normally tends to evade these kinds of meetings. "It is different for Allan [the Danish colleague also present at the meeting]; he talks to them every day and has done so for a year or more." (Informal talk, Denmark, 10/04/2012)

When discussing alternative communication tools he tells us that he prefers to use e-mail, whereas the Indian IT developers "are crazy about" using the internal instant messaging (IM) system provided by ScandiaBank. This obviously disparate view on the use of communication tools in the collaboration triggers a certain behavior when the Indian colleagues contact him using IM:

He explains that they do sometimes write "Hi Martin," and then they will wait for his response on the chat. The Danish IT developer finds it silly, and he would prefer if they first wrote what it was about so he did not have to respond with only a "Hi." The Danish IT developer says that he actually started to ignore these requests if they only contact him by writing him a "Hi" on the chat and without anything concrete in the message. (Informal talk, Denmark, 10/04/2012)

Interestingly, we found that chatting through IM in ITS was highly preferred, as it conforms to the physical environment of the open office cubicles by being nearly noiseless and thus less disturbing to colleagues nearby. A common work practice of using IM seems to have been adopted inside the cubicles of ITS both when communicating with co-located colleagues and when inquiring with BankIT colleagues. Unfortunately, the use of IM in BankIT is less preferred as a practice of work. Instead, we were told and observed how the employees in BankIT exchange information informally at lunch, by knocking on a co-worker's door, or by having a quick discussion in the corridor on the way to the coffee machine. Whereas IM inquiries may be perceived as interruptions, knocks on the door are regarded as part of the work and are beneficial for co-located colleagues, though disadvantageous for remote colleagues.

Summarizing our empirical results, we have pointed to how the global setup provided extra work effort in making the collaboration function well. Also, we have pointed to how the local work (both formal an informal) in India was very much shaped and re-organized based on the global setup. On the contrary, the formal work practices in Denmark were kept without aligning to the global practices. Still, we found examples where the local work in Denmark was clearly affected by the global setup, despite this being neglected by the BankIT management in their formal organization of the work.

DISCUSSION

How is the local work shaped by the global collaborative setup? First, it becomes evident that local work practices continuously transform over time as a result of the global setup. For example, the Indian local work situation is being directed toward the Danish company, both in terms of the physical surroundings (as in the logo and branding), but also in terms of mindset. An example of how the mindset of the Indian site is being directed toward the Danish company is that the Danish resource manager in India insists on picking up his own coffee or playing along during social events, which demonstrate the Danish management style. The attention toward BankIT at the Indian location was very evident by the clocks on the walls and the Indian employees' attitudes and engagement toward the Danish remote colleagues. But the changes from the global work setup were not only at the Indian location. Working in a global setup shapes all geographical sites, which includes the Danish location. The changes at the Danish site were, for example, in terms of renewed focus on methods and processes, and even more pertinent, the changing nature of what counted as "work" and "articulation work" for the IT developers in Denmark. Prior research has pointed to the malleable structures of inter-organizational and remotely distributed teams [21]. Here the argument is that over time, guided by disrupted events, reflections on the work help support the creation of new collaborative structures. We also found that working remotely created some new opportunities for reconfiguring the local practices, and as such the collaborative structures could be said to be more malleable. However, we also identified uneven attention from BankIT toward these changes. While much attention was given to the Indian location and their changes, little to no attention was given to the transformation of the Danish location. Only a few prominent changes have been made at the Danish site, for example, the travel policy that enables the Danish employees to go to India and establish a broader familiarity with their Indian colleagues. Neglecting to notice and acknowledge the changes at the Danish site related to the increase in disruptions, for example, could be interpreted either as a strategic choice by the Danish management to ignore local changes to avoid resistance to the outsourcing model, or simply lack of reflection on the matter. Studying the data in our case, we found that neglecting the changes at the Danish site was *not* a result of bad intention or a planned management strategy to avoid resistance. Instead, we will argue that the Danish location fell in the cultural blind spot [9] of BankIT. The local Danish site did not feel prepared for global collaboration and felt they were standing alone in figuring out how to collaborate with remote colleagues. The management in BankIT had its attention on making the Indian location directed toward the business and organizational culture of the ScandiaBank [18]. This included changing the physical surroundings and management style at the Indian site. However, in this process, the local Danish site ended up in the cultural blind spot of the organization.

The global collaborative setup shapes the local work at all involved locations, both in India and in Denmark. What is interesting is that despite the many years of engagement and the continued expansion of the collaboration, the local Danish developers still articulate and experience many problems and challenges. We propose that one of the major reasons for this diverse perspective on the collaboration concerns the asymmetry in attention from BankIT toward the collaborative setup, where the Danish site is in the cultural blind spot. However, important changes occurred at the Danish site as a result of the global setup.

One of the major changes concerned the nature of the work for the IT developers at the Danish site. Collaboration consists of work and articulation work, which are seamlessly integrated in practice [28]. Still, the distinction between what counts as work and what counts as articulation work is important for the professional identity of different organizational members. Prior to the global setup, the Danish IT developers had their professional identity as technical experts focusing on system architecture, programming, and highly sophisticated technical knowledge; however, the global setup changed this, and they started to do all the "extra work." The IT developers in our empirical case clearly referred to a distinction between their work and the extra work required to work in a global setup. This "extra work" was the articulation work for global collaboration. Danish IT developers found themselves spending much time on tasks related to methods and formal processes, which to some extent were perceived as an external demand that constrained the actual work. We are aware that methods and formal processes for some might be viewed as "the work" of IT developers [16]. However, in our empirical case, the IT developers in Denmark did not. Prior to the global setup the Danish IT developers perceived the close, friendly relationship they had with local colleagues and which was accomplished through the daily face-to-face encounters to be directly beneficial for supporting collaboration, and all additional time spent on methods and processes was a waste of time. In the global setup, this balance changed and the Danish IT developers now had to submit to methods and formal processes due to the global engagement, where their strategy previously had been to ignore such external requirements. In addition, it was clear that all business as well as system integration knowledge was located at the Danish site, which meant that extra time was required by the Danish IT developers to communicate frequently with their remote counterparts, reducing the time to be spent on programming. The global setup thus impacted the local work for the Danish IT developers by increasing their efforts invested in articulation work while reducing the time for actually developing code. You might argue that the extra work required for communication and coordination simply became part of the Danish IT developers' work – their formal job description; however, as long as their professional identity perceived communication, processes, and methods as outside their core work, this change created tensions. What counts as work or articulation work, and for whom, is dependent upon the professional role of the collaborators. In a group of globally distributed IT developers, who share a professional context, what counts as the *real* work is often related to the activities of writing code, working with business and system requirements, conducting tests, etc. In these cases, articulation work concerns, for example, the coordination of activities and dependencies. When working globally, the increased reach of the activity [12] requires extra effort in handling articulation work. Therefore, the effort involved in handling articulation work is more time and resource demanding on the participants. This increased time spent on communication in global software development has also been reported elsewhere [6, 17]. However, our argument here is that this shift in the balance between work and articulation work is a more fundamental debate about the kind of competences and qualifications that make up the job descriptions for IT developers working in global settings. It is no longer enough to have high technical qualifications; instead, qualifications now include global work competences such as communication and coordination, and this is part of the work required to succeed in collaborating globally. The boundaries between what counts as work and what counts as articulation work are re-defined for the IT developer. For the IT developer, articulation work now becomes part of the formal work required when participating in global work; it is no longer *extra* work.

Coordination is a strategy to handle the extra effort of articulation work [12]. Coordination has typically been organized through standards, protocols, and coordination mechanisms [29], or in terms of timely coordination [23, 24]. The increased effort spent on articulation work also requires increased focus on coordination practice. Part of the extra effort concerns applying formal processes and methods to create standards for work across sites. However, we also found that a critical change of the global setup concerned the prioritizing of tasks. Prior to the global setup, the IT developers did the prioritizing of tasks and activities autonomously through face-to-face discussions or simply by making decisions and conducting the task. If colleagues experienced issues or problems and need help, they would simply go to other colleagues who then would prioritize to spend time supporting each other. Interruptions were not seen as disruptive but as a part of the normal, natural trouble [27]. In the global setup, the number of colleagues increases, as does the number of colleagues who need to interrupt to solve issues or questions. In our case, this situation was further increased by business knowledge only being present at the local Danish site. People do not physically knock on the door in a global setting; moreover, awareness of whether remote colleagues are working toward a tight deadline or are busy is also not automatically available in the global setting [14]. Instead, "knocking on the door" will manifest as digital interruptions through instant messaging or similar tools. However, whether interruptions are perceived as disruptions or normal, natural trouble is very dependent upon the relationships between colleagues, as well as the type of inquiry. If inquiries are perceived as questions that a colleague could get answered by other means (e.g., reading documentation) and are thus not important enough to warrant interruption, then the interaction will be problematic. In our case, it was evident that employees at the Danish site experienced increasing interruptions from their remote colleagues. However, there were clear differences in how these interruptions were perceived. When the Danish IT developers knew and had a relationship with the remote colleagues, they would engage in knowledge work [2], seeing such interruptions as though local colleagues were knocking on their door, and would provide the answer in a timely manner, also taking into account the time zones. In addition, they knew more about each other's work [25] and would be aware of situations where remote colleagues could not move forward before getting an answer, thus prioritizing such inquiries. In contrast, Danish IT developers without close relationships with the remote colleagues would view each interruption as a disruption that required an instant response and, as a strategy, choose to ignore remote colleagues "knocking on the door." In other words, the asynchronous use of instant messaging [7] was not considered as an option for some developers. Further complicating the matter in our case was that the Danish system manager took great interest in technical details of the solutions yet was very busy and difficult to get a hold of, which in several situations disrupted the project with unwanted breaks. Moreover, these unwanted breaks were also a product of the challenges of equal motivation for knowledge exchange across sites [13] and the dynamics of sub-groups [10]. All domain experts were at the same location, and the IT developers solving the actual programming tasks were at another. This division of expertise in concurrence with the geographical location increased the us/them dichotomy, forming apparent sub-groups between domain experts at one location and IT developers who were solving the actual programming tasks at another location. The competences of coding "with the hands of others" includes timely coordination and frequent interaction based on relationships among remote colleagues, taking into account time zones and ensuring that unwanted breaks do not occur. While previous research has pointed to the importance of frequent and timely interaction [e.g. 23, 24], our argument here is that the global setup impacts the local setting by increasing the number of colleagues who need to interrupt the work of others in order to do their own work, and as such the increase in interruptions and acting upon these must be part of the employees' work and professional identity. We found that this change due to the global setup impacted the work at the local Danish site but was outside the attention of BankIT.

Translucence in communication structures is critical for global work [5]. Remote colleagues need to make their work visibly available for others to monitor to create accountability. When the work becomes increasingly dispersed between participants as well as across geography and time, bringing translucence into the work practices becomes essential. In our case, it was very evident that the remote work of the Indian colleagues was absent in the everyday work of most of the Danish IT developers. Only the few Danish employees who had daily contact with their remote colleagues knew and were aware of what was going on remotely; however, the majority of the Danish IT developers had no relationship with their remote colleagues. This was evident, for example, in the Kanban board, where the work of the entire Indian counterpart team was reported briefly by one of the Danish IT developers. The remote colleagues were visualized in a single row on the board, whereas each Danish colleague had his or her own row. The invisibility of the remote colleagues created extra work for the few who worked closely with the developers in India because all interactions became mediated by them and translated to others; however, all the work required to continuously make visible in the Danish setting the huge amount of work that was conducted in a global setup was an add-on work task. The invisibility also made the Danish employees (not working closely with their counterparts in India) even more alienated from the global setup. The lack of translucence of the global work among the larger group of IT developers in Denmark had further impact by reducing chances for them to create relationships with their remote colleagues, which were essential for perceiving the necessary interruptions as part of the everyday work rather than as disruptions.

By directing all attention toward the Indian local site, the management of BankIT neglected to notice the changes in the local work at the Danish site. The Danish location fell into the cultural blind spot of management. By neglecting attention toward the changes at the Danish site, it created obstructions for the global work in general, particularly related to the Danish IT developers' perception of interruptions, as well as to the nature of work. The cultural blind spot of the Danish organization thus affected the ability to take a critical stance toward its own practices, and thus hindered the development into a global organization.

CONCLUSION

In this paper, we presented empirical observations from our ethnographic study of global software development between Denmark and India, demonstrating how a global setup impacts the local work practices of both sites. We found that the Danish outsourcing company in our case focused only on the Indian site of the collaboration, while lacking attention toward the changes in their own organization and the local work conducted by Danish IT developers. We refer to this lack of attention as a cultural blind spot. Due to the cultural blind spot, tensions were created in the global setup, influencing the collaborative work practices between remote colleagues.

Cultural blind spot serves as a helpful concept when seeking to open up critical issues of global cooperative work in CSCW research. The cultural blind spot is the information and practices embedded within our own cultural behavior and practices that we take for granted and thus risk neglecting. By introducing the notion of cultural blind spots to CSCW, we argue that there is a need for organizations to compensate for their blind spots by making visible the critical issues in the local work that otherwise go unnoticed. In our empirical case, we identified three local issues that fell into the cultural blind spot of the Danish organization: 1) the increased number of interruptions, 2) the lack of translucence of remote colleagues' work, and 3) the re-definition of the boundaries between what counts as professional work and what counts as articulation work for the Danish IT developers.

The increased interruptions that the IT developers experienced based on the increased number of colleagues to collaborate with (locally and remotely) were overlooked and thus disregarded as an important issue to engage with by management because it fell into the cultural blind spot of the Danish company. Still, the increasing interruptions were an enormous change that the outsourcing relationship brought to the home ground of the Danish company. The impact of transitioning from working with software development locally to globally showed when the Danish company failed to notice the extra work required to integrate the coordination of remote work into the local coordinative artifacts like the Kanban board at the Danish site. Here it was clear that the global setup was lacking translucence because of the Danish participants' cultural blind spot that caused them to overlook the necessity of representing the day-to-day work and coordination with their remote colleagues on the board. This oversight had a significant negative impact on the global collaboration because the articulation work required to handle the global collaboration became opaque and the people handling it were not given credit for their efforts.

It is evident from our study, also supported by previous studies [e.g. 12], that the effort required to handle articulation work increases in the global setting. As it is, the participants involved in GSD do articulation work to make the work work. However, in this paper we showed how the increase in effort involved in handling articulation work required to make GSD function better tends to be neglected. We argue that the increase in effort required to handle articulation work for global collaborative work is inevitable. It also changes the balance between the efforts and resources that an IT developer involved in software development spends on programming and testing, for example, and the efforts that same individual spends on articulation work to make the collaboration function well. In this way, our study suggests it is important to re-define what counts as work and what counts as articulation work in the formal descriptions of IT developers' work when they become involved in global software development. Thus, we argue that global software development practices change the qualifications and competences involved in being an expert IT developer in global collaborative work. Working in a global setting changes the conditions for IT development, and we need to figure out how we can support the expert IT developers, who have the critical business knowledge to better work in global setups, to *"figure out how to code with the hands of others"* while developing their own skills and continuously improving their own professional profile. Actions must be taken to address organizations' cultural blind spots, to solve the inability to take a critical stance toward one's own practices, and to continuously make changes that go along with becoming a global organization.

ACKNOWLEDGEMENT

This study is conducted within the context of the interdisciplinary and inter-organizational research project "Next Generation Technologies and Processes for Global Software Development," #10-092313 a research project that is financially supported by the National Council for Strategic Research, Ministry of Science, Innovation and Higher Education in Denmark. For further information, see www.nexgsd.org. We would like to thank all the anonymous volunteers from the global team in ScandiaBank and ITS who generously offered their time and energy for this research. Finally, we would like to thank Morten Esbensen, Steven Jeuris, Anne-Marie Søderberg, and Rasmus Eskild Jensen for valuable discussions about the study, and the anonymous reviewers for insightful comments and suggestions.

REFERENCES

1. Al-Ani, B., et al. (2013). Globally distributed system developers: their trust expectations and processes. Proceedings of the 2013 conference on Computer supported cooperative work. ACM: 563-574.
2. Avram, G. (2007). Knowledge Work Practices in Global Software Development. *The Electronic Journal of Knowledge Management*. 5(4): 347-356.
3. Avram, G., et al. (2009). Bridging, Patching and Keeping the Work Flowing: Defect Resolution in Distributed Software Development. *Computer Supported Cooperative Work (CSCW)*. 18(5-6): 477-507.
4. Bjørn, P. and N. Boulus (2011). Dissenting in reflective conversations: Critical components of doing action research. *Action Research*. 9(3): 282-302.

5. Bjørn, P. and O. Ngwenyama (2009). Virtual team collaboration: building shared meaning, resolving breakdowns and creating translucence. *Information Systems Journal*. 19(3): 227-253.

6. Boden, A., et al. (2009). Knowledge Management in Distributed Software Development Teams - Does Culture Matter? In *Proc. Conference*, IEEE Computer Society: 18-27.

7. Boden, A., et al. (2007). Coordination Practices in Distributed Software Development of Small Enterprises. Proceedings of the International Conference on Global Software Engineering. IEEE Computer Society: 235-246.

8. Boden, A., et al. (2009). Trust and Social Capital: Revisiting an Offshoring Failure Story of a Small German Software Company. ECSCW 2009. I. Wagner, H. Tellioğlu, E. Balka, C. Simone and L. Ciolfi. Published, Springer London: 123-142.

9. Clausen, L. and M. Zølner (2010). Cultural Awareness Processes in Corporate Knowledge Sharing: Turning "Cultural Blind Spots" into Resources. Paper presented at The Academy of Management Annual Meeting 2010, Montréal, Canada.

10. Durnell Cramton, C. and P. J. Hinds (2005). Subgroup Dynamics in Internationally Distributed Teams: Ethnocentrism or Cross-National Learning? . *Research in Organizational Behavior*. 26(0): 231- 263.

11. Faraj, S. and L. Sproull (2000). Coordinating Expertise in Software Development Teams. *Manage. Sci*. 46(12): 1554-1568.

12. Gerson, E. M. (2008). Reach, Bracket, and the Limits of Rationalized Coordination: Some Challenges for CSCW. Resources, Co-Evolution and Artifacts. Published, Springer London: 193-220.

13. Gumienny, R., et al. (2013). Supporting creative collaboration in globally distributed companies. In *Proc. Conference*, ACM: 995-1007.

14. Herbsleb, J. D. (2007). Global Software Engineering: The Future of Socio-technical Coordination. 2007 Future of Software Engineering. IEEE Computer Society: 188-198.

15. Hossain, E., et al. (2011). Scrum practices in global software development: a research framework. In *Proc. Conference*, Springer-Verlag: 88-102.

16. Iversen, J. H., et al. (2004). Managing risk in software process improvement: an action research approach. *MIS Q*. 28(3): 395-433.

17. Jensen, R. E. and P. Bjørn (2012). Divergence and Convergence in Global Software Development: Cultural Complexities as Social Worlds. From Research to Practice in the Design of Cooperative Systems: Results and Open Challenges. J. Dugdale, C. Masclet, M. A. Grasso, J.-F. Boujut and P. Hassanaly. Published, Springer London: 123-136.

18. Krishna, S., et al. (2004). Managing cross-cultural issues in global software outsourcing. *Commun. ACM*. 47(4): 62-66.

19. Latour, B. (2005). Reassembling the Social: An Introduction to Actor-Network-Theory, OUP Oxford.

20. Luff, P., et al. (2000). Workplace Studies: Recovering Work Practice and Informing System Design, Cambridge University Press.

21. Majchrzak, A., et al. (2000). Technology adaption: the case of a computer-supported inter-organizational virtual team. *MIS Q*. 24(4): 569-600.

22. Marlow, J., et al. (2013). Impression formation in online peer production: activity traces and personal profiles in github. Proceedings of the 2013 conference on Computer supported cooperative work. ACM: 117-128.

23. Massey, A. P., et al. (2003). Because Time Matters: Temporal Coordination in Global Virtual Project Teams *Journal of Management Information Systems*. 19(4): 129-155.

24. Maznevski, M. L. and K. M. Chudoba (2000). Bridging Space Over Time: Global Virtual Team Dynamics and Effectiveness *Organization Science*. 11(5): 473-492.

25. O'Neill, J., et al. (2011). When a little knowledge isn't a dangerous thing. Proceedings of the SIGCHI Conference on Human Factors in Computing Systems. ACM: 1667-1676.

26. Prikladnicki, R., et al. (2013). Data collection in global software engineering research: learning from past experience. *Empirical Software Engineering*: 1-35.

27. Randall, D., et al. (2010). Fieldwork for Design: Theory and Practice, Springer.

28. Schmidt, K. and L. Bannon (1992). Taking CSCW seriously. *Computer Supported Cooperative Work (CSCW)*. 1(1-2): 7-40.

29. Schmidt, K. and C. Simone (1996). Coordination mechanisms: Towards a conceptual foundation of CSCW systems design. *Computer Supported Cooperative Work (CSCW)*. 5(2-3): 155-200.

30. Søderberg, A.-M., et al. (2013). Global Software Development: Commitment, Trust and Cultural Sensitivity in Strategic Partnerships. *Journal of International Management*. (in press).

31. Strauss, A. (1988). The articulation of project work: An organizational process. *The Sociological Quarterly*. 29(2): 163-178.

32. Walsham, G. (2002). Cross-cultural software production and use: a structurational analysis. *MIS Q*. 26(4): 359-380.

Articulation Spaces: Bridging the Gap between Formal and Informal Coordination

Alexander Boden
Fraunhofer FIT
Schloss Birlinghoven
D-53754 St. Augustin
alexander.boden@fit.fraunhofer.de

Frank Rosswog
University of Siegen
Hölderlinstr. 3
D-57076 Siegen
frank.rosswog@uni-siegen.de

Gunnar Stevens
University of Siegen
Hölderlinstr. 3
D-57076 Siegen
gunnar.stevens@uni-siegen.de

Volker Wulf
University of Siegen
Hölderlinstr. 3
D-57076 Siegen
volker.wulf@uni-siegen.de

ABSTRACT
The high complexity of knowledge-intensive work such as software development makes it beneficial to have spaces for formal and informal articulation work. Existing information systems (IS) tend to treat these different aspects of coordination separately, resulting in problems of awareness and coordination. To bridge this gap, we present the concept of Articulation Spaces which combines aspects of Coordination Mechanisms and Common Information Spaces (CIS) in order to provide a room for mediating between the formal and informal aspects of coordination. Based on a design study in the form of a lightweight public display that has been tested in a medium-sized German software company, we show how Articulation Spaces provide information for meta-coordination, encourage ad-hoc coordination and support decision-making processes. Our findings provide insights into the design of support systems for flexible and coordination-intensive contexts such as software development work.

Author Keywords
Lightweight Displays; Software Development; Small Companies; Coordination; Formal and Informal Communication; Articulation Work; Common Information Spaces; Coordination Mechanism.

ACM Classification Keywords
H.5.3 [Group and Organization Interfaces]: Computer Supported Cooperative Work.

INTRODUCTION
Workgroups in knowledge-intensive areas such as software development demand efficient team coordination and knowledge exchange [2]. Small and medium-sized enterprises (SMEs) have particular needs in this regard, as they often follow business models that depend on close cooperation with the customer and on high flexibility [10].

CSCW'14, February 15–19, 2014, Baltimore, Maryland, USA.

http://dx.doi.org/10.1145/2531602.2531621

Arguably, this means that responsiveness, both to customers and to each other, is a more pressing problem. Certainly, there is some evidence that SMEs typically embed more flexibility and informality, for instance, in their customer relations (see e.g. [18]). In practice, such demands can be problematic and call for adequate organizational and technological solutions. This is especially important with regard to managing in-situ coordination and learning, which have turned out to be important success factors of such forms of work [34].

We have investigated coordination and the related use of information systems (IS) in software teams in previous studies in two small German software companies. Both studies have already been published [8, 9]. In summary, our studies revealed a complex interrelationship between the formal protocols of using systems like source-code repositories and the informal practices to contextualize them. The information systems used did not support these problems very well, as they tended to focus on formal aspects, while neglecting the informal parts of coordination. As a result, awareness about changes of plans was often less than adequate, and further informal communication was needed to raise awareness and announce the changes in the team—a difficult and time intensive task, which often led to problems, for example when changes went unnoticed or details were overlooked. Common problems concerning the use of IS in software development recognized in previous work reference the fact that the information in these systems is often not up to date and not self-explanatory, requiring informal communication and coordination in order to make sense of and contextualize it against the background of the specific work context [8, 9].

The CSCW community has developed numerous analytic concepts for understanding and supporting coordination in complex work contexts, such as Coordination Mechanisms [39] and Common Information Spaces [19, 20]. Based on this prior work, we have developed the concept of *Articulation Spaces*. It aims at bridging the gap we found in our empirical studies by integrating diverse information sources and communication channels that have become separated in current IS applications and providing a space for mediation between them. In this paper, we present findings from a design study in which we tested an implementation of our concept over a period of seven weeks in a medium-sized German software company. We chose software development as an example due to its high reliance on heterogeneous IS systems, but we think that the concept can be easily adapted to other application areas. The design intervention allowed us to get a better understanding of our concept, as well as of how it can be implemented in knowledge-intensive areas of work such as software development.

RELATED WORK

Tools for supporting coordination of software development work can be roughly divided into two different areas [2, 8]: the first includes tools for information management such as bug-trackers or version control systems. They provide the basic infrastructure for working on source-code and managing tasks for software developers. The second includes tools for personal communication such as Instant Messaging, micro-blogs or Email. Both fields differ not only with regard to their focus on informal versus formal forms of coordination, but also with regard to the social protocols that guide their usage. While the information stored in bug-trackers or in project planning tools is usually considered to be rather formal, standardized and obligatory, information shared in personal communication is usually rather more informal, unofficial and often subject to changes in the course of projects [27]. However, there can be a crossover of both forms: informal information can be formalized if its context is changed, for example, by posting private chat-logs into an official and public bug-tracking ticket—a process that can change the character of the information substantially. Equally, formal information can be discussed in informal contexts, and actors can decide ad-hoc to re-interpret or ignore formal information without necessarily updating the status of information systems. In our own studies, we found that while formal systems played a very important role for the coordination of the development work, their use was highly embedded in informal discussions that took place before, during and after the tasks mandated in the formal systems were accomplished. The informal discussions were crucial for the actors in order to make sense of the information stored in the formal systems, which was often rather abstract and needed to be interpreted against the context of the current situation of the projects [9].

Frameworks such as "Continuous Coordination" combine the benefits of formal and informal coordination to stimulate communication, provide context, and raise awareness [14]. The authors of this framework developed different tools like Palantír, an artifact centered workplace awareness tool, or Ariadne, which visualizes the socio-technical relations between software artifacts [34]. Similar solutions for practitioners focus on organizational practices that are closer to agile methodologies [43], and on the use of specialized tools that attempt to support group awareness by analyzing socio-technical congruency between actors and artifacts [37]. Hence, coordination is meant to be supported by making predictions about possible breakdowns and notifying developers thereof, ideally preventing the breakdown from occurring in the first place. Problems with such approaches include that they rely on up-to-date information in the IS (thus often focusing on the formal side), and that they can be annoying in the case of inaccurate predictions because notifications can be intrusive and cause interruption [36]. Hence, the problem of visualizing the information is one of the main challenges of implementing such systems in practice.

Several tools try to address the problems of visualizing coordination-related information in software projects by embedding collaboration and communication features directly into the development environments, namely IBM's Jazz or Microsoft's CollabVS [17]. Such approaches are promising, but have the disadvantage of focusing on the individual workplace tools of software developers, which can lead to problems of acceptance, and are subject to space limitations on the screen. At the same time, they often tend to provide all-in-one solutions at the cost of excluding other established development tools (cf. [10]). Other approaches provide information on (semi-)public displays placed at central places in companies. For instance, approaches such as CommunityMirrors support peripheral awareness and serendipity [32] and provide a shared working context for cooperating actors [17]. In software development, a special approach of using public displays has been tried in the form of "dashboards" that represent project related information [7, 45]. Usually, such approaches are rather focused on formal aspects of the project, which can be easily obtained from the deployed Information Systems. Despite the apparent advantages of using public displays for supporting group awareness in companies, they are hardly established in practice [35].

The concepts described above provide interesting approaches for fostering awareness and supporting coordination in software development. They will play an important role for the implementation of our concept that we will present in the next chapter. The studies of Redmiles et al., in which design aims to support "Continuous Coordination" [34], and also approaches for providing dynamic forms of awareness in software teams with public displays are particularly valuable. We want to contribute to this stream of research by paying closer attention to the interconnections between formal and informal aspects of coordination, and by presenting a concept for a support tool that provides a space for mediating between the two forms.

THE CONCEPT OF ARTICULATION SPACES

Analytically, we can distinguish between formal and informal practices of coordination in the sense that the formal is often institutionally sanctioned and mediated by mandated IS systems, while the informal involves any practical means of getting the work done [4]. However, while there is a clear analytical distinction between formal and informal forms of coordination, in practice both are interwoven in quite complex ways [34]. Our Articulation Spaces concept explicitly integrates two existing CSCW concepts, in order to address these complex interrelations between formal and informal forms of coordination: Coordination Mechanisms, and Common Information Spaces.

A Coordination Mechanism can be defined as "specific organizational construct, consisting of a coordinative protocol imprinted upon a distinct artifact, which, in the context of a certain cooperative work arrangement, stipulates and mediates the articulation of cooperative work so as to reduce the complexity of articulation work of that arrangement" [39]. The concept is based on the theoretical framework of articulation work, introduced originally by the sociologist Anselm Strauss, and based on his studies of medical work in hospitals [42]. Articulation work describes a kind of meta-work that is needed to coordinate different tasks and responsibilities of cooperating actors. The practical application of Coordination Mechanisms itself requires articulation work, as these mechanisms are often constructed in a way that allows them to be interlinked with each other [39].

Common Information Spaces (CIS), on the other hand, promote the meaning and interpretation of artifacts as a core aspect of supporting teamwork [38]. In early studies, CIS were mainly understood as relevant to local control rooms and similar settings. Studies in this field increasingly concentrate on distributed contexts and teamwork where the collaboration takes place asynchronously or infrequently [6]. The emphasis on these studies is the distinction between the common access to information and the interpretation of this information, and the way it needs to be communicated (or, in Strauss' terms, articulated) to make team coordination successful. From this perspective, providing rich information channels is not enough [22], as different perspectives and interpretations of information need to be taken into account—a thought which has also been discussed in the context of "second generation" knowledge management studies [1]. Instead of just providing a shared access, group awareness systems should support different perspectives.

Articulation Spaces refer to these two concepts with the aim of improving the visibility of articulation work by identifying and filtering individual articulation work events in the existing communication media and development IS and presenting them on a shared display or a similar device (such as a Media Space). There are already some research projects in the field of practical support of cooperative work through Common Information Spaces that rely on public displays. One example using public displays as the output medium is the concept of tickets-to-talk, which was developed for academic conferences [30]. The concept of awareness cues also fits into this category [33]. It has been shown that these approaches can support social interaction and animate the knowledge exchange of actors by providing relevant contextual information. Our concept extends these ideas to solving the problem that articulation work is often invisible for the team [41]. At the same time, it aims to improve the traceability of articulation work, which often is hard to reconstruct by referring to the formal coordination tools and artifacts, like bug-trackers or project plans [10]. While most components of Articulation Spaces have been discussed in the literature before, we think that the combination of the different concepts can be seen as a new paradigm of supporting flexible and knowledge intensive work, such as software development.

At its basis, the concept of Articulation Spaces relies on an "articulation pipeline" which, similar to an awareness pipeline [23, 25], aggregates and filters information about articulation work events from the various tools, media and artifacts. It provides interfaces for in- and outputs and a back channel to the deployed artifacts, IS and communication media (see Figure 1). Due to its flexible nature, an Articulation Space allows for individual appropriation, for example with regard to which sources of information are connected. Relevant design considerations concern similar issues as the discussion on providing awareness, including filtering at the input-side (to ensure privacy), but also the appropriate visualization at the output-side and the avoidance of information overload [23, 24, 28].

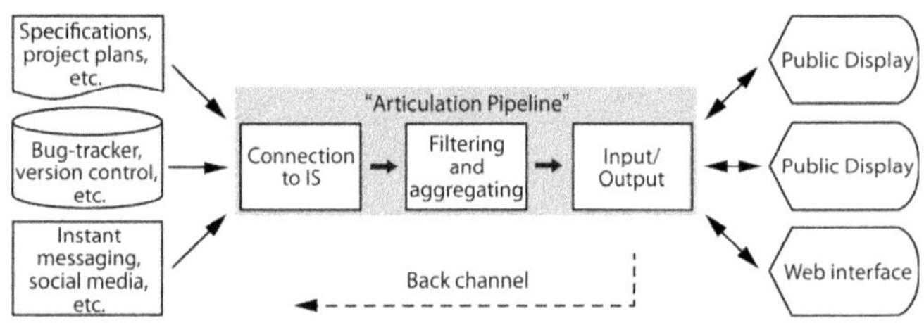

Figure 1. The concept of Articulation Spaces.

The gathered information is presented on an output device such as a wall mounted display, which might, for instance, be placed in a public or semi-public space in the company, such as a coffee kitchen. Design decisions in this regard are related to the debate on Media Spaces, which has a long tradition in the fields of HCI and CSCW, following the early studies at Xerox PARC at the end of the 1980s [26]. Media Spaces usually use large wall displays to support synchronous collaboration of small and distributed teams by means of video and audio links. The underlying concept holistically supports distributed cooperation by a virtual enhancement of the room, by means of different communication channels [31] and the support of group awareness through concepts such as peripheral visualization (like colored lights, which represent the status of a project [5, 44]). Articulation Spaces visualize information by means of technology that has been developed in the context of Media Spaces, but rather aim at sharing small chunks of information that provide hints towards what is going on in the company and who could be asked for which problems, than to provide fully self-sufficient and codified knowledge in form of a public repository. At the same time, Articulation Spaces do not focus on providing as much information as possible, but on putting the available information into context [22]. Hence, like CIS they should not be designed as central knowledge repositories [21], but should allow practitioners to order the information as it fits their work contexts.

In the next section, we will present a specific implementation of the Articulation Space that we have developed in order to study how practitioners appropriate the concept in practice.

DESIGN & IMPLEMENTATION

Based on the conceptual considerations outlined above, we have implemented an Articulation Space that consists of a small public display, which presents information from the development IS, as well as other sources such as blogs and news forums in the form of “sticky notes”. The system is designed to be used by software developers in small teams, and aims to raise awareness about formal and informal aspects of their cooperative work, provide a space for mediating between the two aspects of coordination, and facilitate the flexibility we have argued is necessary.

Overview

The system was implemented as client-server architecture. A middleware acts as an articulation pipeline that aggregates RSS and Atom feeds from different sources, such as bug-trackers or version control systems. It combines these formal items with information of tools used for informal communication and external sources, such as newsfeeds of blogs and websites. The items are managed via a micro-blogging server, using account names that correspond to the information sources (for example, news items from a bug-tracking tool are posted on an account that is called “bug-tracker”).

A (semi-public) display serves as client for the micro-blogging server and regularly requests the server for updates. If available, new entries are presented as sticky notes on the display. In addition, the server also can be accessed by a web interface or off-the-shelf micro-blogging clients, allowing users to read the messages individually. If needed, multiple displays can be connected to the server, for example to support distributed work groups. Micro-blogging is an interesting metaphor to implement an Articulation Space related solution, as this technology seems to combine several advantages of Instant Messengers (informal character, not intrusive, etc.) with a better traceability and visibility [13, 47].

In the next sections, we give a more detailed description of the different parts of the system.

Client

According to the concept of Articulation Spaces, we have used a public display for visualizing data and providing awareness in teams. (Semi-)Public displays have considerable advantages in this regard compared to desktop applications, as they allow information to be presented in an unobtrusive way, hence providing for peripheral awareness [29]. At the same time, they can be used cooperatively and thus provide a shared context for cooperative work [46]. In order to address the flexible nature of the software development work that we aim to support, we used a standard tablet PC as display device (in our case an iPad 1, see Figure 2a) that was attached to the wall by a Velcro fastener (see Figure 2b). The display software was developed using Adobe Flash CS 5.5 and packaged as an App by including the Packager for iOS and the runtime environment Adobe Air 3. All functions of the software can be used by standard touch gestures. The lightweight form factor makes it easy to install the device in different rooms or to simply carry it around (for example taking it to a meeting). If the battery is charged overnight, the display can remain turned on for a whole working day, thus making the display very flexible.

In accordance with the conceptual argument above, we wanted to create a design that reflects the users’ different perspectives on their shared work context, is open to everyone and invites people to interact with the device. Based on our concept of sharing small chunks of information in a non-linear way and on the results of an internal design workshop, we decided to implement our prototype in the form of a bulletin board [15], presenting all messages as sticky notes on the display (see Figure 2). A bulletin board allows for other types of interaction (compared to the usual timeline view of micro-blogs), as messages can be rearranged, can overlap each other, and can show new (or important) items at the top or next to each other. Users can browse through the messages and arrange notes on the display by dragging them around, overlapping them with each other, or by scaling or deleting them via a context menu (triggered by a long touch on a note). The context menu also provides links and corresponding QR codes to the source of the messages, e.g. an entry in the bug-tracking system, or a blog post (see Figure 2c).

These simple interaction mechanisms provide users with the possibility of highlighting messages they find important, and covering (or deleting) unimportant ones. Users can also create new messages directly on the display by touching a button, which opens the standard iPad keyboard. If users want to post messages from their own accounts, they have to use a client or the web-interface, as we wanted to make the use of the display as easy (without needing to log-in) as possible and to stress the status of the frontend as a device that is free to use for all team members.

New notes appear on a pile in the upper left corner of the display, and have to be rearranged by users. This stimulates interaction with the display, and increases the peripheral awareness for new project related news. There is also the possibility of answering notes on the display; in this case, the corresponding note appears just next to the first one, in order to show the relation between the two. Also, there is an auto-sorting feature in case the pile of new messages gets too big in order to be useful, which can be called by touching a button on the side of the display.

In order to visualize the different sources to which the notes are related, we use different account names as well as different colors for the notes (e.g. the different IS systems). The color codes make it very easy to recognize important messages even from a distance (for example, new bugs are displayed in red). After a certain time, the notes begin to disappear by becoming transparent, providing hints towards the immediacy of the message. Users can also make transparent messages visible again by simply touching them. As there is a (configurable) limit to the number of notes that can be displayed at the same time, older notes disappear automatically from the display after a while, depending on the amount of messages that are created.

Server

The server of our prototype is based on the micro-blogging server StatusNet (www.status.net) and a middleware that acts as an articulation pipeline. We decided to use micro-blogging to manage and store events because of the many similarities to the Instant Messengers that users demonstrably preferred for in-situ coordination and knowledge exchange [11]: micro-blogging is informal, easy to use, not intrusive, and makes it easy to share links to web resources or the IS. At the same time, micro-blogging has some advantages with regard to Instant Messaging, as it allows for fine-grained control of what is displayed (filtering by users, groups, hash-tags), and offers a shared timeline for all users—besides the also possible direct messages, which remain private.

Hence, micro-blogging seems to be an interesting technology for supporting informal coordination within work groups, without introducing high overheads to use [13]—thus making it the ideal base for design with regard to the problems we have identified in our previous studies [10, 11]. Due to its Twitter-compatible API, StatusNet also can be easily integrated with other systems such as our own middleware, but also with Instant Messaging solutions. As the server can also be accessed via several freely available standalone clients, as well as a usable web interface, it enables a very high integration into the work of the software developers, even apart of the display.

The aggregation of different sources of information is handled by a middleware that we have developed to serve as an articulation pipeline. It parses XML feed sources (e.g. RSS or ATOM feeds) on a regular basis and searches for new items. RSS feeds are provided by most recent Information Systems (such as bug-trackers or version control systems), but also by a number of websites, making it easy to connect formal systems for team coordination and relevant news (such as from the company website) with more informal sources such as interesting blogs and news forums.

The middleware also filters and publishes items to the micro-blogging server which serves as a repository that is accessible via the client. Before they are published, postings are reformatted, supplied with corresponding hash-tags and afterwards sent via special user accounts that resemble the sources of the information. Users can enter new feeds into the system (or delete unwanted ones) by using a simple web interface. For sources with many new items each day (such as highly active news blogs) there is also a special "digest" mode that only posts messages from these feeds to the server when no new message has been posted in the last couple of hours, in order to prevent a spamming of the display (and the timeline) and to keep the display active even during times with hardly any user interaction.

DESIGN INTERVENTION

Methodology

For our design intervention, the system was tested for seven weeks in a web and software development company that employs about 110 people. We provided practitioners with our implementation of Articulation Spaces, consisting of an iPad running the client software. The server was hosted on a virtual machine at the authors' University, giving full access to server logs and to all sent messages. The team consisted of five employees who used our system in a small project that aimed at the concept development of an E-learning platform for a local public institution. For doing so, the display was positioned at an open space in the office, close to a water dispenser (see Figure 2b). The project manager took responsibility for taking care of the display in terms of charging it overnight.

We used empirical qualitative methods, notably participant observation and interviews to investigate the usage of our prototype during the study. The main focus of our investigation was how the design was used for formal and informal forms of coordination in the project. Further foci were the appropriation of the lightweight form factor, its influence to the team communication and coordination, as well as the usability of the display in everyday work situations of the project members.

The investigation started with a small workshop during which two members of our research team presented the prototype to practitioners, explaining its features and the main vision of our concept. The aim was to give practitioners a basic idea about the aims and possibilities of our system, and to stimulate a discussion about how the company could integrate the prototype into their daily work routines, where the display could be placed, and how it could be integrated into the technical infrastructure of the project. During the workshop, the team members expressed

Figure 2: (a) The display, attached to a wall with Velcro fastener, (b) The display in the field, (c) Close-up of the Application.

their need for improved and up-to-date communication by collecting different kinds of information on the display, and also their interest in discovering relations between different tasks by presenting them on the screen. Through the semi-public character of the design intervention, the actors were also hoping for serendipitous participation on the part of colleagues who were not part of the project team by allowing them to make suggestions or post critical comments. After the workshop, the system was rolled out in the company, and one of the researchers visited the company regularly one day per week in order to observe usage of the platform. Furthermore, we checked the timeline and log data of the micro-blogging server on a daily basis to see how the system was used. At the end of the design intervention, we conducted qualitative interviews with all project participants in order to understand their view of the design (30 minutes each). We also performed 90 minutes design workshops with two of the participants in order to collaboratively scribble and discuss ideas about possible improvements of our prototype. All interviews were transcribed and analyzed together with field notes and other materials, such as server log files. For doing so, we followed a grounded theory-oriented approach, which consisted of sessions of iterative coding and concept-building based on the material until a theoretical saturation was reached.

Results

During our design intervention, the practitioners mainly used the system as a digital task board for their agile SCRUM software development practices, for informal communication within the team and (as a mobile display) in meetings. For doing so, the project manager created a new StatusNet account with the name "Sprints" for posting tasks as notes on the public display. During their regular meetings, the practitioners discussed these tasks and arranged them on the display according to their priorities, or grouped tasks that belonged together. The notes then served as means for coordinating the development work in a similar fashion to conventional SCRUM task boards used in the company. These, we should note, were regarded as rather inflexible, and so the company often used Excel sheets for managing SCRUM tasks prior to our intervention.

In that regard, the practitioners liked the fact that that the virtual sticky notes did not crumple, fall down or get lost. At the same time, despite its small size, the display allowed the display of all tasks at once. The possibility of automatically creating notes by adding RSS feeds from formal development systems or websites that we had included was not substantially used by the practitioners during the field trial, as they preferred to focus on the SCRUM-related tasks: *"For me as a project manager this was a possibility to communicate the tasks and their statuses—done, not done. I could have done that with Excel too, but this way it was more comprehensible in a graphical sense"*. In this context, we learned from our observations that messages from tools for formal coordination can be recognized as unfriendly: *"Sometimes you get several bugs, but it's always the same problem. For example an image for a button that appears at several places and only needs to be replaced once"*. This also hints at the importance of informal communication, or a different visualization of formal incidents: *"People are annoyed by getting a lot of Jira-bugs and sometimes they get angry about it. This needs to be friendlier"*. The display was also used to coordinate the work tasks that were shown via the "Sprints" account: *"How far did we get with sprint 3?"* Feedback to the work tasks could be found in statements like the following: *"Today we continue with the visualization of the use cases within our #prototype"* and informal, sprint related comments: *"First thoughts to the activity streams [sprint 3]. Who sees what, how, where, and why?"*

The users also used the display to communicate with their colleagues in different ways. For example, one user sent a request for suggestions to the colleagues over the display: *"To all spontaneous - creative people, answer this question: How shall we name the online-community for studying, teaching & learning at the (local public institution)?"* Other messages were notifications about current tasks in the project, such as: *"Today we will work on the #prototype. On the agenda are the starting pages of the learning rooms."* For posting such messages, the web-interface played a more important role during the field trial than the input interface of the display itself. Users expressed the view that they could well imagine posting messages to the display via the web client from the home office, in order to stay in touch with their colleagues and thus coordinating their work in a more informal way. The possibility of integrating the prototype into an Instant Messenger was also deemed interesting for sharing extracts of chat protocols in an easy and informal way with the team.

With regard to the general usability of the display interface, the practitioners expressed a wish for further filtering and grouping options as well as more fine-grained color-coding of the notices. Our design study distinguished between different sources of notifications, but not between different user accounts. As much of the communication took place using the "Sprints" account, the practitioners also wanted to choose the color of the sticky note before sending it to the display. In this way it would be possible for them to build their own color-coding scheme for the messages. The possibility of grouping messages was perceived in different ways. On one hand peopled liked the easy and intuitive way of grouping and making stacks by dragging messages on the screen, but on the other hand the stacks were sometime recognized as annoying because it was difficult to find a note within a stack. Another issue was the number of messages displayed on the screen: users complained the display became chaotic when too many messages were displayed. The possibility of enlarging messages on the display to highlight their importance was used by the team members to overcome this problem when the screen was crowded. Nevertheless, users expressed the wish to mark messages with different levels of priority. The users would also have liked the possibility of archiving the content of the display (i.e. the state of how the messages were arranged). The functionality of deleting messages or using QR codes to save links was not used during the design intervention.

Regarding the form factor of the display, our study also showed that the lightweight character of the iPad allowed for a very flexible usage of our system. The position of the display near the water dispenser turned out to be less serendipitous than expected, as the time taken for perusal was far lower than expected at this place in the office. However, the possibility of taking the display from the wall and using it in a different location alleviated this disadvantage. As the strong battery made the display more or less independent from electrical outlets during a workday, the display could be used in different contexts such as the aforementioned SCRUM meetings. This strongly suggests that the use of our device was seldom casual and almost always associated with specific purposes. On one occasion the practitioners even took the display with them to a meeting at the customer's site to show the progress of the project and coordinate the next steps of the development work—an interesting practice that would not have been possible with a heavier wall-mounted display.

DISCUSSION

The results of our design intervention are creating new challenges for the (re-)design of the implementation and raise new questions regarding the concept of Articulation Spaces. During our study, we were able to observe both formal and informal use of the provided system, which combined both aspects on a common surface for the team members.

With regard to the former, the actors used the display for coordinating their development tasks according to the formal suggestions of the SCRUM development approach. Even though this manual kind of usage had not been anticipated by us, the role of the messages for the ongoing (re-)articulation of the project work was quite similar to that of bug-trackers and project planning tools in our previous studies. In this way the team used the system to implement their own formalized Coordination Mechanism by the adaptation of an already used process model (SCRUM), but without connecting external sources. They used the display to assign tasks and visualize the work process in an official and—according to our conceptual understanding—formalized way. With regard to informal coordination of the work, the practitioners used the display for sending messages that were meant to provide a general awareness or related to specific tasks of the project organization apart of the actual development work (such as choosing a name for the software solution). By referencing more official, SCRUM related messages with questions or statements posted from a personal account, we have also seen aspects of mediation between the different kinds of coordination.

With regard to the underlying concept, this usage of the system can be interpreted in the sense of a CIS. Actors used the possibility to promote the meaning of coordination-relevant information by posting them as sticky notes on the display. Their colleagues again interpreted these artifacts against the context of their work and reacted to this information. In this respect, it became apparent that the formal and informal aspects of coordination are not independent from each other. For example, the possibility to annotate formal messages with informal notes was used by the actors to provide more detailed information or pose questions regarding the project progress as well as open tasks. It became apparent that the nature of the information could be changed by posting on the display, depending on the context or person posting. Due to the semi-public status of the display, it was not clear who would be able to see the message, implying a different context than for example directly talking to a colleague in the coffee kitchen. Even though this effect is similar to what we have observed with regard to the use of IS in our previous studies [8, 9], it was interesting to observe how the different form factor of our solution as well as the semi-public and playful context of our design intervention affected the negotiation of SCRUM tasks and the communication within the team.

Besides the SCRUM-related display postings, the use of the display and micro-blogging system was generally rather playful and non-mandatory. At the beginning of the design intervention, an anonymous user of the display (posts send by the display) wrote mainly jokey messages with regard to the display itself but after a while the usage changed to a more organizationally relevant one: They used it to express their project related thoughts, asked coordination related questions, made appointments, asked project-specific questions to the team or the whole company, gave task related status updates, shared folder structures or announced meetings and visitors.

In this regard, we could find suggestions as to how far corporate culture and individual usage strategies are an important part of appropriation, as the system needed to address overall company requirements as well as the interests of the individual developers. As an open tool, the practitioners were able to use the system according to their individual needs. At the same time, due to the small team size, informal communication often took place directly, but with the indirect involvement of the display. For example, we observed that a question posted on the display addressing the whole company wasn't answered on the display, but the practitioner got plenty of feedback at a meeting scheduled later that day. Hence, the awareness that was raised by the message on the display can have positive impact on teamwork, even if not all communication is mediated by the artifact. Overall, the specific use practices that emerged were strongly related to the small number of team members in the given project, the immediate proximity of their workstations in the same office, and the clear arrangement of the project that only lasted a couple of months. The conceptual intention to provide a flexible system that is usable in dynamic software projects was certainly fulfilled, as the actors were able to adapt the system to their needs and use the display in the context of their work.

Our analysis of the appropriation of the system also showed some interesting insights with regard to the role of the lightweight form factor in the context of appropriating the Articulation Space. First of all, we found that the visualization of the content was of essential importance for a successful usage of a tablet computer as a "public display". Readability of content is a challenge given that public displays need to be seen from medium as well as close-range. For this specific operational scenario, smartphone and tablet Apps are generally not well suited and call for different design and presentation metaphors. The lightweight form factor also influenced the awareness for the display and the platform: while use of the display was strongly recognized by the entire staff of the office at the beginning of the experiment, the interest of colleagues that were not part of the immediate study faded over time. However, practitioners reported that absence or change of location raised awareness and brought the system back to peoples' minds. At the same time, the flexibility of the lightweight display helped to leverage the disadvantages of the chosen place for the display beside the water dispenser. Furthermore, the practitioners found it interesting that they were able to take the display with them to meetings in the company or at a customer, to show the progress of their work and coordinate the next steps.

The bulletin board metaphor of our system was accepted and understood in this regard, but participants requested that the visualization be even more "bulletin board"-like. In the design workshops, we also discussed different approaches to visualizing streams of messages on a tablet computer and providing the possibility of annotating formal messages with informal comments. While classic "timeline" approaches would be more orderly and scalable, the bulletin board had the advantage of allowing the visualization of connections between messages in a more tangible way (for example by overlapping them, or placing them next to each other) and being more flexible with regard to sorting and piling messages, as the participants did in the context of their SCRUM development. Non-linearity seemed to better support awareness of small chunks of information in regard of the Articulation Spaces concept. As a consequence, a hybrid system that combines the advantages of both approaches (for example by showing a bulletin board next to a timeline and offer possibilities for dragging messages from one into the other) might be a good idea.

The requests for grouping and sorting features were strongly based on the specific practices that emerged in the context of using the system as a SCRUM notice board. For example, practitioners also suggested adding functions for muting specific accounts during meetings to avoid interruption by informal messages, but still allowing new (for example) "Sprints" to appear on the display. Some requested possibilities, for instance for archiving messages and conversation or exporting functions into other software (e.g. Outlook Calendar), would probably change the character of the messages and the usage of the board to a more formal project management tool—an aspect that we want to explore in further studies.

CONCLUSION

There is a need for supporting formal and informal coordination in software development projects and, as importantly, mediating between the two. As we have suggested above, this is particularly important for small project teams, or small companies where there are additional demands for flexibility, and where "informality" of communication amongst members of the team and in "customer facing" aspects of the work, is more common. As both forms are not independent from each other, approaches are needed that take the complex interrelations between these aspects into account [10, 34, 40]. In this paper, we have outlined "Articulation Spaces" as a concept that borrows ideas from other fields like awareness tools [16], public displays [32], Common Information Spaces [19] and Coordination Mechanisms [39] and combines them in a specific way to provide a new space for formal, mandated coordination and more informal modes of communication. Our concept provides a level of integration and ease-of-use in both formal and informal channels, serving as a central medium for negotiating coordinative practices deployed by members of software teams. During our design intervention in a small software company, the practitioners used the display for both formal and informal coordination, allowing us to learn more about the practical implications of our concept. The implementation of the Articulation Space allowed the sharing of information of varying content and from different sources, but with the same goal: the coordination of the software project. This involved formal aspects such as the organization of meetings, reports about the work progress, but also informal ones such as questions to team members, the announcement of visitors/customers, just to name the most important ones. In that regard, it is important to stress that it was not our aim to combine all formal and informal coordination in a single artifact, but to provide a new space for mediation in order to better understand the complex relationship between the two aspects of articulation work, and to test of novel ways of visualizing and interacting with coordination-related information in small, dynamic teams.

Interestingly, we observed that the use of the display changed over time, as the actors appropriated our provided system in the context of their work. In this context, we could observe how the system improved visibility of articulation work and raised awareness about current issues in the company, which guided of coordination and facilitated knowledge exchange between the team members in the sense of a tickets-to-talk approach. The related processes were triggered and supported by the display, which allowed for informal questions as well as formal announcements. At the same time, we observed that connections between the formal and informal messages remained often implicit, hinting towards the need for better forms of visualizing cross-connections as compared to the lightweight implementation of our design study. In this regard, our field study provided insights into combining public displays [7] with aspects of ubiquitous computing [14] for enabling new forms of team coordination with such devices by showing how our study also showed that actors dealt with the issue of filtering and sorting mechanisms by the re-arrangement notes or enlarging them for others to see. At the same time, the design metaphor of a bulletin board that we chose for our design study provided an equitable visualization of formal and informal information. For the design of CIS systems, the bulletin board metaphor seems to have some potential, as it allows for playful interaction and exploration, supporting the informal character of the prototype as well as serendipity and team communication [32], as we have seen in our design study. We are currently experimenting with different approaches to visualization that combine the advantages of a bulletin board with the classic timeline visualization, which we want to explore in further studies.

At a conceptual level, it became apparent, that our system could be used as classic Coordination Mechanism in the sense of a SCRUM-Board [39], but that it also served as a mediator for existing Coordination Mechanisms. Based on our findings, we conclude that the concept of Articulation Spaces can be characterized as an information space that aggregates information about Coordination Mechanisms commonly used by a software team (such as bug-trackers and source-code repositories) and allows actors to make sense of this information in the context of their work [3, 12]. Similar to Schmidt's and Simone's suggestion to use arrays of specialized Coordination Mechanisms for regulating articulation work [39], we see Articulation Spaces as a means to devise a Coordination Mechanism for this purpose. In other words, Articulation Spaces can serve as a "Meta Coordination Mechanism" that helps to understand the coordination steps that are made, encourages ad-hoc coordination and supports decision-making processes. In this regard, the mobility of the deployed display allowed the actors to enlarge the information space into different contexts. Taking the device to different rooms or to the customers' site allowed for a nuanced use and had interesting implications for the range of "awarenesses" that our concept might support, with clear implications for the design of CIS applications in other contexts with similar demands for flexibility.

ACKNOWLEDGMENTS

The study presented in this paper was partially supported by the German Research Foundation (DFG) within the research project ARTOS.

REFERENCES

1. Ackerman, M.S., Dachtera J., Pipek V. and Wulf, V. (2013): 'Sharing knowledge and expertise: The CSCW view of knowledge management'. In *Computer Supported Cooperative Work,* vol. 22, no. 4-6, pp. 531-573.
2. Aranda, G.N., Vizcaino, A., Cechich, A. and Piattini, M. (2006): 'Technology selection to improve global collaboration'. In *Proc. of the international Conference on Global Software Engineering,* IEEE Computer Society Press, pp. 223-232.
3. Bannon, L. and Bødker, S. (1997): 'Constructing common information spaces'. In *Proc. of the European Conference on Computer Supported Cooperative Work,* Kluwer, pp. 81-96.
4. Bardram, J.E. (1997): 'Plans as situated action: an activity theory approach to workflow systems.' In *Proc. of European Conference on Computer Supported Cooperative Work*, Kluwer, pp. 17-32.
5. Bardram, J.E., Gueddana, S., Houben, S. and Nielsen, S. (2012): 'ReticularSpaces: activity-based computing support for physically distributed and collaborative smart spaces.' In *Proc. of the Conference on Human Factors in Computing Systems,* ACM Press, pp. 2845-2854.

6. Bertelsen, O.W. and Bødker, S. (2001): 'Cooperation in massively distributed information spaces.' In *Proc. of the European Conference on Computer Supported Cooperative Work*, Kluwer, pp. 1-17.
7. Biehl, J. T., Czerwinski, M., Smith, G. and Robertson, G.G. (2007): 'FASTDash: A visual dashboard for fostering awareness in software teams'. In *Proc. of the International Conference on Human Factors in Computing Systems*, ACM Press, pp. 1313-1322.
8. Boden, A., Nett, B. and Wulf, W. (2009): 'Trust and social capital: Revisiting an offshoring failure story of a small german software company'. In *Proc. of the European Conference on Computer Supported Cooperative Wor*k, London, pp. 123-142.
9. Boden, A., Nett, B. and Wulf, W. (2010): 'Operational and strategic learning in global software development - Implications from two offshoring case studies in small enterprises'. In *IEEE Software,* vol. 27, no. 6, IEEE Computer Society Press, pp. 58-65.
10. Boden, A. (2011): '*Coordination and learning in global software development. articulation work in distributed cooperation of small companies'*. Univ. Diss., Siegen. http://dokumentix.ub.uni-siegen.de/opus/volltexte/2012/598/.
11. Boden, A., Avram, G., Bannon, L. and Wulf, V. (2012): 'Knowledge sharing practices and the impact of cultural factors: Lessons from two case studies of offshoring in SME'. In *Software Maintenance and Evolution: Research, and Practice*, vol. 24, no. 2, pp. 139-152.
12. Bossen, C. (2002): 'The parameters of common information spaces:: the heterogeneity of cooperative work at a hospital ward'. In *Proc. of the Conference on Computer Supported Cooperative Work,* ACM Press, pp. 176-185.
13. Bougie, G., Starke J., Storey, M.-A. and German, D. M. (2011): 'Towards understanding Twitter use in Software Engineering'. In *Proc. of the International Workshop on Web 2.0 for Software Engineering,* ACM Press, pp. 31-36.
14. Chen, C. and Zhang K. (2012): 'Continuous awareness: a visual mobile approach'. In *Proc. of the International Symposium on Visual Information Communication and Interaction,* ACM Press, pp. 69-76.
15. Churchill, E.F., Nelson, L. and Denoue, L. (2003): 'Multimedia fliers: Information sharing with digital community bulletin boards'. In *Proc. of the International Conference on Communities and Technologies,* Springer Press, 97-117.
16. Desouza, K.C., Awazu, Y. and Baloh, P. Managing (2006): 'Knowledge in global software development efforts'. In *IEEE Software,* vol. 23, no. 5, IEEE Computer Society Press, pp. 30-37.
17. Dewan, P., Agarwal P., Shroff, G. and Hegde, R. (2009): 'Distributed side-by-side programming'. In *ICSE Workshop on Cooperative and Human Aspects on Software Engineering,* IEEE Computer Society Press, pp. 48-55.
18. Dittrich, Y., Eriksén, S. and Hansson, C. (2002): PD in the Wild; Evolving practices of design in use. In *Proc. of the 7th Biennial Participatory Design Conference*, pp. 124-134.
19. Dullemond, K., van Gameren, B. and van Solingen R. (2010): 'Virtual open conversation spaces: Towards improved awareness in a GSE setting'. In *Proc. of the Conference on Global Software Engineering*, IEEE Computer Society Press, pp. 247-256.
20. Dourish, P. and Bly, S. (1992): 'Portholes: supporting awareness in a distributed work group'. In *Proc. of the SIGCHI Conference on Human factors in computing systems*, ACM Press, pp. 541-547.
21. Fields, B., Amaldi, P. and Tassi, A. (2005): 'Representing collaborative work: the airport as common information space'. In *Cognition, Technology & Work,* vol. 7, no. 2, Springer Press, pp. 119-133.
22. Fuchs, L., Pankoke-Babatz, U. and Prinz, W. (1995): 'Supporting cooperative awareness with local event mechanisms: the groupdesk system'. In *Proc. of the European Conference on Computer-Supported Cooperative Work,* Springer Press, pp. 247-262.
23. Fuchs, L., Sohlenkamp, M., Genau, A., Kahler, H., Pfeifer, A. and Wulf, V. (1996): 'Transparenz in kooperativen Prozessen: Der Ereignisdienst in POLITeam'. In *Deutsche Computer Supported Cooperative Work,* Springer Press, pp. 3-16.
24. Fuchs, L. (1998): '*Situationsorientierte Unterstützung von Gruppenwahrnehmung in CSCW-Systemen*'. Univ. Diss., Essen. http://publica.fraunhofer.de/documents/B-73127.html.
25. Fuchs, L. (1999): 'AREA: a cross-application notification service for groupware'. In *Proc. of the European Conference on Computer Supported Cooperative Work,* ACM Press, pp. 61-80.
26. Harrison, S. (2009). *Media Space 20+ Years of Mediated Life.* Springer Press, Heidelberg, Germany.
27. Herbsleb, J.D., Atkins, D. L., Boyer, D. G., Handel, M. and Finholt, T. A. (2002): 'Introducing instant messaging and chat in the workplace'. In *Proc. of the Conference on Human factors in computing systems,* ACM Press, pp. 171–178.
28. Kraut, R.E., Fussell, S. R., Brennan, S. E. and Siegel, J. (2002): 'Understanding effects of proximity on collaboration: Implications for technologies to support remote collaborative work'. In P. Hinds & S. Kiesler (Eds.) *Distributed Work,* MIT Press, pp. 137-162.

29. Koch, M. and Richter, A. (2007): '*Enterprise 2.0: Planung, Einführung und erfolgreicher Einsatz von Social Software in Unternehmen*'. Oldenbourg Verlag, München, Germany.

30. McCarthy, J.F., McDonald, D.W., Soroczak, S., Nguyen, D.H. and Rashid, A.M. (2004): 'Augmenting the social space of an academic conference'. In *Proc. of the Conference on Computer Supported Cooperative Work,* ACM Press, pp. 39-48.

31. Olson, G. and Olson, J. (2000): 'Distance Matters'. *Human-Computer Interaction,* vol. 15, no. 2, pp. 139-178.

32. Ott, F. and Koch, M. (2010): 'CommunityMirrors – Large interactive screens as natural user interfaces for cooperation systems'. In *Workshop-Proc. of the International Conference on Human Factors in Computing Systems,* ACM Press, pp. 1-5.

33. Oulasvirta, A., Petit, R., Raento, M. and Tiitta, S. (2007): 'Interpreting and acting on mobile awareness cues'. *Human-Computer Interaction*, vol. *22*, no. 1, pp. 97-135.

34. Redmiles, D., van der Hoek, A., Al-Ani, B., Quirk, S., Sarma, A., Silva Filho, R.S., de Souza, C. and Trainer, E. (2007): 'Continuous coordination: A new paradigm to support globally distributed software development projects'. *Wirtschaftsinformatik,* vol. 49, no. 3, pp. 28-38.

35. Reeves, S. (2011): *'Designing Interfaces in Public Settings: Understanding the Role of the Spectator in Human-Computer Interaction'.* Springer Press, Heidelberg, Germany.

36. Rittenbruch, M. (1999): 'Atmosphere: towards context-selective awareness mechanisms'. In *Proc. of HCI International Conference on Human-Computer Interaction,* ACM Press, pp. 328-332.

37. Sarma, A., Maccherone, L., Wagstrom, P. and Herbsleb, J. (2009): 'Tesseract: Interactive visual exploration of socio-technical relationships in software development'. In *IEEE 31st International Conference on Software Engineering,* IEEE Computer Society Press, pp. 23-33.

38. Schmidt, K. and Bannon, L. (1992): 'Taking CSCW Seriously: Supporting Articulation Work'. In *CSCW: An international Journal,* vol. 1, no. 1, pp. 7-40.

39. Schmidt, K. and Simone, C. (1996): 'Coordinaton mechanisms: Towards a conceptual foundation of CSCW systems design'. *CSCW: An international Journal,* vol. 5, no. 2-3, pp. 155-200.

40. Schmidt, K. (1997): 'Of maps and scripts – The status of formal constructs in cooperative work'. In *Proc. of the International Conference on Supporting Group Work,* ACM Press, pp. 138-147.

41. Star, S.L. and Strauss, A.L. (1999): 'Layers of silence, areas of voice: The ecology of visible and invisible work'. *In Proc. of the Conference on Computer Supported Cooperative Work*, ACM Press, pp. 9-30.

42. Strauss, A.L. (1988): 'The articulation of project work: An organizational process'. In *The Sociological Quarterly*, vol. 29, no. 2, pp. 163-178.

43. Sutherland, J., Viktorov, A., Blount J. and Puntikov, N. (2007): 'Distributed scrum: Agile project management with outsourced development teams'. In *System Sciences HICSS*, IEEE Computer Society Press, pp. 274a.

44. Tang, J.C., Marlow, J., Hoff, A., Roseway, A., Inkpen, K., Zhao, C. and Cao, X. (2012): 'Time travel proxy: Using lightweight video recordings to create asynchronous, interactive meetings'. In *Proc. of the Conference on Human Factors in Computing Systems*, ACM Press, pp. 3111-3120.

45. Treude, C. and Storey M.A. (2010): 'Awareness 2.0: Staying aware of projects, developers and tasks using dashboards and feeds'. In *Proc. of the International Conference on Software Engineering*. ACM Press, pp. 365-374.

46. Wilson, S., Galliers, J., and Fone, J. (2006): 'Not all sharing is equal: the impact of a large display on small group collaborative work.' In *Proc. of the Conference on Computer Supported Cooperative Work*, ACM Press, pp. 25-28.

47. Zhao, D. and Rosson, M.B. (2009) 'How and why people Twitter: The role that micro-blogging plays in informal communication at work'. In *Proc. of the International Conference on Supporting Group Work*, ACM Press, pp. 243-252.

Everyday Dwelling with WhatsApp

Kenton O'Hara[1], Michael Massimi[1], Richard Harper[1], Simon Rubens[2], Jessica Morris[2]

[1]Microsoft Research Cambridge
Cambridge, UK
{keohar, mmassimi, r.harper}@microsoft.com

[2]New Experience
London, UK
{simon.rubens, jessica.morris@new-experience.com}

ABSTRACT

In this paper, we present a study of WhatsApp, an instant messaging smartphone application. Through our interviews with participants, we develop anthopologist Tim Ingold's notion of dwelling, and discuss how use of WhatsApp is constitutive of a felt-life of being together with those close by. We focus on the relationship "doings" in WhatsApp and how this togetherness and intimacy are enacted through small, continuous traces of narrative, of tellings and tidbits, noticings and thoughts, shared images and lingering pauses; this is constitutive of dwelling. Further, we discuss how an intimate knowing of others in these relationships, through past encounters and knowledge of coming together in the future, pertain to the particular forms of relationship engagements manifest through the possibilities presented in WhatsApp. We suggest that this form of sociality is likely to be manifest in other smartphone IM-like applications.

Author Keywords

Dwelling; WhatsApp; mobile phones; communication; texting; SMS; Instant Messaging.

ACM Classification Keywords

H.5.m. Information interfaces and presentation (e.g., HCI): Miscellaneous.

PREAMBLE

The development of information and communication technologies continues unabated. An ever-richer array of channels confront the user - email, SMS, social networking sites, audio calling, video calling, instant messaging and so on. Accompanying new channels are an increasing number of devices - laptops, tablets and mobile phones - and it is through these that people engage with each other in ever more diverse and nuanced ways. In this regard, the high levels of smartphone adoption have been particularly noticeable, since they provide perhaps one of the most powerful platforms for accessing combinations of communication modalities. This use is, some argue, transformative of the ways in which communications patterns are assembled to particular social effect [10]. Such assemblies are not simply a reflection of the novel aspects of this hardware and the channels it supports; they also relate to how familiar forms of communication are coming to be deployed in delicately new ways – one speaks face to face because of a prior text; one writes an email because of a picture sent via an IM client; one 'Facetimes' because of the SMS one received moments before; one's smartphone allows one to do all this even as one sits down to watch TV [16].

Of particular note here has been the massive adoption of a raft of mobile instant messenger applications and services on smartphones, such as WhatsApp [26], Line [22], WeChat [25], iMessage [19], Viber [24], Skype [23], Facebook Messenger [20], and KaKao Talk [21]. These are often called Over The Top applications (OTT) since they are independent of the network being used at any time just as they are of the smartphone itself, the device. Such applications are free or inexpensive to download and use, and offer various capabilities for sharing media - images, video, audio clips, and even location data. What is curious about these applictions is that, *prima facie*, they seem to offer little in the way of conceptual novelty; their cheapness eliding the fact that much of this functionality has been present on communication tools provided on PCs and Laptops for some time – in Gmail, Outlook, Skype. Yet many of these OTT applications now have an active user base numbering in the hundreds of millions; some providers deal with billions of messages daily. Questions as to why these OTT applications are benefiting from such high rates of adoption and usage then emerge; the success of WhatsApp and similar seems to fly in the face of what seems obvious – that these apps aren't really offering anything new, not at first glance anyway.

Explanations of this success in the mass media often highlight economic factors: the relative low cost of using these apps, especially when compared to historically more prevalent channels such as SMS, is indisputable. These new applications deliver content across the Internet (either via Wi-Fi or mobile data networks) and hence any messaging costs seem quite negligible or are perceived to be free by the user since they get 'lost' within a 'data plan'. While there will be undoubtedly economic considerations, in particular in regard to initial motivations for adoption,

CSCW'14, February 15 - 19 2014, Baltimore, MD, USA
Copyright 2014 ACM 978-1-4503-2540-0/14/02...$15.00.
http://dx.doi.org/10.1145/2531602.2531679

'cheapness' it seems to us is too simple an account. Such an explanation lends very little to understanding the everyday meanings given to messaging practices with these applications. For one thing, the ubiquity of multiple channels – the deployment of one OTT app alongside others on the smartphone – can't be explained by cost alone. After all, the scale of use seems to beg the question not of whether people can afford to pay for their messaging practices, as how they can pay for the time and manage so many. Even the boldest of economists would baulk at these questions, even the likes Becker who famously claimed all cultural practices can be explained economically [7].

The other explanation to be found in the media - albeit less often articulated - points towards the rich feature set of these applications as being the driver for succss. In this view, it is the application's capacity to combine photos, video and messages that is the trick. But this too must be overly simplistic. As we have noted, this functionality has been available for a while. People certainly use these capacities, but it is not clear that one can understand the scale of their actions as merely determined by them. What is required, we believe, is a much fuller, richer explanation of what is at play; attempts to reduce practices to cost or functionality serve to obscure what needs to be understood rather than make it available. There is a requirement, in other words, to capture the quiddity of the experiences sought for and enabled by these applications in ways that reaches beyond economic or technological determinism and which accounts both for scale and the purpose of this use in ways that colours how that use is experienced and oriented to; how it is lived, if you like.

OUR PURPOSE

In this paper we want to reveal this quiddity – or at least begin its uncovering. To do so we adopt a particular perspective that draws on a set of themes from anthropology [e.g. 17, 27], communication and media studies [e.g. 10, 33], sociology [e.g. 29, 30, 40] and HCI [e.g. 1, 12, 18]. These themes pertain to Simmel's notion of *faithfulness* [40] (see also [9]) which labels the motivations that bind people despite the separating tides of modernity; Licoppe and Smoreda's notion of *sociability* [30, see also 29] – alluding the manner in which people 'do' friendship' in the age of the smartphone (as background to this concept see also [4]); Farman's observation that contemporary friendships are articulated through heterogeneous *mobile enabled tellings* [10]; and the concept of *dwelling*, from Ingold [27], which he devised in an attempt to transcend crude models of social action as being 'situated' into an alternative view in which human affairs consist of an intersection of trajectories that produce a felt-life of embodied forms.

Key to bringing these ideas together is our assumption that they can be treated as resources for our exploration of the evidence rather than being merely outcomes asserted by that evidence. This will make some readers uneasy, as it highlights important differences in the approaches of CSCW, some being of the sociology and anthropology kind and others being more psychological. The former is more explorative and philosophical, the latter more committed to the idea of a discovering kind of science.

Be that as it may, the concept of faithfulness here concerns the ways in which people are disposed to experience and sustain commitment to our various human relationships. Simmel came to this notion through his interest in how modern urban society affected social relations. He observed that faithfulness in friendship would would appear to be under strain – the bonds of friendship were likely be made weak by the way society was evolving. He noted that in mass urban settings, for example, the *geographic proximity* of people is not matched by their *moral proximity*. In a modern city, strangers might find themselves sat side by side on a bus or train but this close physical proximity does not reflect any moral closeness between these persons – they remain strange despite touching. Simmel noted that whilst this happens, those whom these same persons are morally close to, their friends, partners, family for example, might be some distance away, at different workplaces, say, or living in districts well removed from their own homes. Who people are close with, those they are *morally proximate* with, are then not mirrored in whom they are physically beside at any moment in time – their geography. Does this mean that society is breaking up? Simmel observes that this is evidently not so; he proposes that it is faith that keeps those physically separate morally close, that is to say, despite the physical separations created by modern living, people put effort into keeping connections alive. They trust in the continuity of friendship despite the hardship of separation; they rely on the friendship of others just as they invest in that friendship themselves. They do so through faith and *faithfulness*. We see this argument in recent work on social capital [e.g. 7, 35].

The point is that to understand why communications technologies are used one needs to understand first and foremost why people turn to them: it has to do with the desire to make and sustain bonds [5, 15, 16]. A version of this argument can be seen to preoccupy the intellectual landscape of HCI and CSCW today, even if Simmel's insights are not mentioned. Here we see the contours of this argument being altered to emphasise how it is digital technologies that create a new inflection on geographical and moral proximity; it is not 'mass society' that threatens connection. These arguments derive from contemporary sociologists, such as Rainie & Wellman [36] and Castells [7] who argue that geography, crudely speaking, no longer matters in social connection, with space dissolving in the weave of digital connection: the moral only exists in the digital, in this view.

Such a perspective, when put in extreme, is easily criticised in its exaggeration of the uniformity of access to and control of digital connection and in its oversimplification of the willingness of people from different social groups to take up the digital and thus create moral bonds [16]. But it can also be criticised for oversimplifying the relationship between the nature of moral proximity and geography and the interplay of these in the ways we live together: the digital binds and transcends these in ways that is much more subtle and contradictory than Rainee & Wellman or Castell's allow.

As Licoppe and Smoreda put it [30, see also 29], ways of living together in the current world are made up of various flowings, of interactions and interconnection, of exchanges and encounters both face and face and mediated. These are ordered and patterned through time and space in delicately achieved rhythms of presence and absence. Different technologies of communication create and organise a set of "possibilities and interdictions" [8] that are leveraged and appropriated in the ongoing production of *sociability* in ways that is rich, artful, managed. In this sense, Licoppe and Smoreda's notion of sociabilty highlights how different sites of social encounters, whether in the real or digital world, are intimately interrelated and bound in a weave of mutually interdependent meaningful acts.

Online encounters, then, are not so much discrete, bounded entities and connections to remote others in the digital; they are instead constitutive of an ensemble of encounters that comprise our various relationships in and through the real and the virtual. Farman [10], meanwhile, draws attention to the substance in these relational exchanges; central to this is how these exchanges occur within and are experienced across a wide range of media and practical circumstances in which the fitting and appropriating of modes of communication entails elaborating narratives across time and space and in reference to the channels and devices used. In Farman's view, people do sociability through using messaging applications as not only the the technical means of communication, but as a resource to make content. A smartphone allows people to tell stories anytime and place, but it allows those stories to include images from where the storyteller is. Messaging technology becomes part of the palette of meaning and content production; smartphones and the apps they support make discourse as well as enable it to be couried.

What this points to, then, is the wrapping of the geographic, the technological and the moral into a spatio-temporal patterning through narrative actions. Simmel's original formulation of the problem of the moral and geographic thus seems at once archaic and crude. Today one can see that geographic and moral proximity are mixed and managed through the digital and the real. The articulation of absence and presence is not so much a problem as it is a resource for justifying and giving content to acts of faith.

Instead of focusing on distance, then, one should approach questions like why new OTT smartphone apps get used so extensively through thinking about how contemporary connection and forms of sociability transcend the real and the virtual, and how faithfulness - if it is still exists – must therefore have new inflections and forms. Instead of thinking of how faithfulness heals the separaton created by 'place', one might think of how faithful doings occur both in and through place and yet also through newly created digital spaces; where going to Facebook is as much a geographic locale for shared experience as being side-by-side on a couch.

The kind of lifeworld being produced in these circustamces is only now beginning to be characterized – Harper's *Texture* [16] comes to mind, though it doesn't offer any nomenclature for these circumstances. A term from current anthropology might cut it. Ingold [27] proposes that a good definition of and label for 'being' is to be found in his notion of *dwelling* [cf. 10, 16, 33]. In his view, human affairs entail a movement through and between sites of engagement, where trajectories of individuals intersect and create a texture of joint being together, a felt-life of sociality. In our view, this can be extended to include trajectories in the digital and the physical and the interweaving of the two into narratively produced dwellings that consist of a digital and real hybrid state of praxiological experience, of 'being in' and 'through' time and space [17, 33]. The argument holds that people are not simply responding to what is presented to them in any given situation; rather all situations consist of an intersection of trajectories through space and time making situatedness merely momentary co-ordinates in movement.

Our proposal then is to draw on these arguments, and use them to show how new forms of mobile instant messenging, the OTT applications like WhatsApp, are constitutive of a kind of dwelling – a dwelling in the digital age [27]. In doing this, we need to explicate how these applications enable articulations of Simmel's faithfulness but where these articulations are evidently contemporary, bound to and governed by the possibilities and interdictions of technologies, yet leveraged in everyday encounters of narrative exchange and chitchat. We need to ask if and show how they are bound to the geographies, temporalities and engagements of ongoing relationships told in and through moment by moment acts of messaging and pausing; of silences followed by fleeting 'instant' conversation.

OUR CASE STUDY

In order to do this we present a study of the application WhatsApp as a representative example of contemporary technologies of digital dwelling. WhatsApp, as the dominant player in the European market, represents a choice from our methodological point of view that is pragmatic. While it does have certain unique features in its design, it essentially shares many characteristics with other OTT applications of this genre but it also happens to be the most popular. If we were to chose any, then WhatsApp seems appropriate.

WhatsApp presents IM chats as a series of threaded messages on a wall, using spatial position and colour to differentiate sender and receiver messages (see Figure 1). These chats can be performed either between 2 individuals (as in the left image of Figure 1) or as a group (as in the right image of Figure 1). As well as text, messages can also include URLs, images, video or audio clips. All messages are timestamped and include one or two ticks next to the time to indicate the massage has been sent and delivered respectively. Various status messages are also included such as when the recipient was "last seen online". In the UK, where our study was based, data packages for smart phones, combined with unlimited use of Wi-Fi where available, mean that in practical terms there is not a constraining upper bound on the number of messages that can be sent through WhatsApp. With SMS, while certain expensive packages offer unlimited texting, other packages set upper bounds on the number of messages that can be sent - of the order of several hundred per month[1].

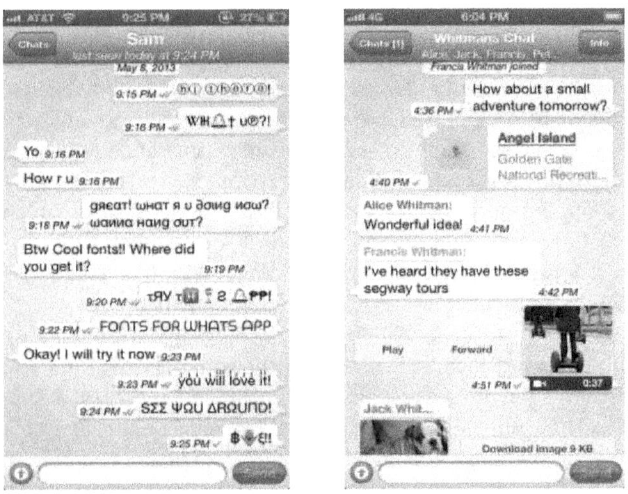

Figure 1. WhatsApp screenshot (iOS version)

RELATED WORK

Over the years, computer-mediated communication (CMC) in its various forms has been a central concern within CSCW and extensively studied both within the community and beyond. While a full treatment of all CMC issues echoed in our work is not possible here, there are a number of studies that we wish to briefly review here. Of particular relevance are those concerned with understanding the practices of instant messaging and SMS [e.g. 3, 11, 12, 13, 14, 15, 31, 32, 34, 37, 41]. Overwhelmingly, what these studies point to is the use of such messaging systems, in particular by teenagers and young adults, to maintain social relations and contact among friends and family outside of their face-to-face interactions. More specifically, such interpersonal connection is found within "close ties" rather than "weak ties", reflecting real space relationships - something that we draw on in our own work later. As well as characterising certain practices, a number of these studies aim to highlight how particular characteristics of the technologies (and related infrastructures) "shape" such practices - for example, the fact that they are lightweight, quick, cheap, and offer certain abilities to time-shift and place-shift their communications in ways relating to their particular social and physical circumstances.

While we get a sense of the similarities between IM and texting in terms of the relationships for which they are used, there is less emphasis on highlighting points of contrast. This is raised by Grinter et al. [12] in their more explicit attempts to explore the two forms side by side. While these highlight certain differences such as the use of media sharing and group chat in IM, much of the differences are bound up in how and when these different communications can be performed in relation to mobilities of SMS vs. the fixity of IM (their study, as they acknowledge, coming before large scale adoption of IM on phones) – rather than with whom. More recent work though, would indicate that there are potential relational differences in terms of the use of the different forms on the mobile. Reynolds et al. [38], for example, found that "*BBM social contacts are relationally closer and include more friends but fewer family and acquaintances than SMS.*" This would suggest that these are being oriented to in different ways.

What this also begins to point to is the shifting communications landscape that has taken place over the last few years. The adoption of current mobile devices running platforms such as iOS, Windows Phone 8, Blackberry, and Android now offers people a much richer variety communication possibilities beyond what was available in the earlier studies. In this respect we are starting to see greater concern with these communication dealings as a whole and how people manage across this multiplicity of possibilities [e.g. 2, 18, 28]. In their study of smartphone users, Barkhuus and Polichar [2] note that while this complexity of choice would outwardly appear problematic, users are actually quite resourceful and capable customizers of their devices. They found that communication "flexibility was paramount," and that users exploited the "seams" created by the technical properties of different modes of communication in order to manage their various relationships [ibid]. Others have pointed to the process of integrating and combining these apps in what is described as "channel blending" [e.g. 18, 39]. In this respect users expertly move among the different channels in order to

[1] It is worth noting here that smartphone based SMS clients are evolving more resemblances to the kinds of mobile IM applications exemplified by WhatsApp. Most notable here is in the representation of texts as threaded conversations. In addition, for some carriers in some countries there are also options for group SMS chat of the form discussed here whereby a message can both be sent to a group as well a replies being returned to all members of the group. This is carrier/country specific and was not available in the UK at the time of writing.

continue recurring, episodic conversations and draw in content from various sources, or to manage particular features of a social situation. Here, then we start to get a sense of the multi-layered nature and weave of communication possibilities where considerations of a narrative across time and channels are of concern. As Isaacs et al. [18] articulate, *"rather than thinking in terms of technology-based sessions, we might think about coherent social acts that may take place over time and across channels (including F2F), and allow people to build on the context created during the ongoing interaction"* [18].

More recent work has described additional styles of communication that young adults associate with particular applications or platforms. Barkhuus and Tashiro [1], for example, point out that Facebook is the "glue" that holds together the nomadic social existences of university students [1]. In their work, students leveraged different parts of Facebook to organize different kinds of face-to-face meetings and events; for example, they find that structured events are organized through the Facebook event feature, but more semi-structured meetings occur by posting a status update and awaiting responses in several channels, including SMS, Facebook, and voice calls.

While these studies present some important characterisations of the multi-channeled nature of communications, and indeed some reasons related to the choices being made, it is also apparent that something more is afoot. The issue here pertains more to the relationship "doings" of these communications. More than conceiving them just in terms of "relationship maintenance" or a social "glue", it becomes important to think of these as constitutive of the particular ways people experience and enact their relationships across time. It is here where attention is drawn back to the likes of Licoppe & Smoreda, Simmel, Farman, and Ingold [30,40,10,27] and their orientation to these encounters, their various constraints and possibilities, in terms of what is enacted in ongoing sociability and dwelling together.

To state again, then, our intentions are as follows: first, despite the range of work investigating diverse communication platforms and uses of smartphones, there has been relatively little investigation into OTT apps like WhatsApp. Second, in taking the perspective of dwelling, we want to contribute to the ways in which we might approach an understanding of WhatsApp as illustrative of how this and other kinds of communication technology more broadly are to be understood analytically.

THE STUDY

For the purposes of our study, we recruited a total of 20 participants from the UK (10 male and 10 female) who owned a smartphone and were regular users of WhatsApp. The participants were aged between 17 and 49 years (median 28yrs). The participants were drawn from a range of occupational backgrounds and domestic circumstances. These included a teacher, air steward, health manager, events manager, border agency controller, civil servant, executive manager, music producer, customer services manager, full time mother, sales person, and a number of school and university students. These were variously living alone, with partners, flat sharing, living with family or away from home. Of the 20 participants, 8 were recruited as individuals. The other 12 comprised various relationship pairs, including partners, siblings, cousins and friends.

For each of the 8 participants recruited as individuals we conducted a semi-structured interview lasting approximately 1 hour. The other 12 participants were interviewed in two groups of six, each comprising 3 relationship pairs. We used relationship pairs to provide an additional resource for considering the use and experience of WhatsApp in the context of a specific relationship and from the perspective of both parties. Further, by conducting these particular interviews in groups, there was opportunity for the participants to compare and contrast their experiences with others, yielding points of agreement, tension and distinction and facilitating critical reflection on their own experiences. To help initial scaffolding of the discussion, we also employed a number of exercises to surface communication patterns across different relationships defined by the participants. For example, we employed a network elicitation task where the participant identified different groups and relationships of significance to them and drew lines of different colors to indicate which types of communication channels were used most frequently with each one. Participants were also asked to show us examples of actual exchanges in WhatsApp that they had recently experienced with a variety of their contacts. The participants would talk us through the context and circumstances of these exchanges and why they had been enacted in particular ways. These provided a more concrete grounding with which to explore the themes emerging from the interviews.

To complement our note-taking during the interviews, all of the interviews were video recorded, allowing us to revisit the details of what the participants articulated and reflect more closely on these in the context of emerging themes. An initial pass through the interviews by the research team was used to assemble together a collection of behaviours, episodes, participant explanations and evocative quotes that related to particular orientations to WhatsApp encounters. The items in the collection were clustered together by the research team to yield a set of high-level themes, which were then refined and iterated with reference to confirmatory and non-confirmatory evidence in the data.

FINDINGS

Enacting friendships

We begin with some high level articulations by participants about their doings in WhatsApp that help render salient particular social orientations to it. Consider the following:

"I don't really know what I say on WhatsApp. It's rubbish really...It's a bit embarrassing -you know what I mean."

"Mine is really trivial. It doesn't have to have a point like it does with a text message."

"Just doing tosh."(nonsense)

While such articulations are painted with a broad brush they provide a useful start to how we might grasp the essence of WhatsApp. They point to a particular kind of exchange and encounter in WhatsApp that are often without a clearly articulable functional purpose. Participants at times were almost embarrassed to explain this but in this very lack of [functional] "*reason*" and its "*triviality*" we begin to glimpse its very quiddity. Underpinning these experiences, then, would appear to be a broader set of phatic concerns. Of significance here is not simply that these exchanges *are* performed without functional reason, but that they *can be* performed without reason. This is bound up in both the specific interdictions and possibilities of the technology and the particular type of relationships being enacted through it. Overwhelmingly, such relationships were with those who were emotionally and geographically close - with people who lived close by and seen on a regular basis.

"The majority of people I use WhatsApp with are based in the UK and most of them are based in London – they are actually quite close to me – so I think its to arrange to do things with people nearby."

"With WhatsApp I use it with friends that I see more regularly so you can kind of just ditch the conversation – there's no fuss – it comes back to being stuck in a conversation."

"It's for people I am living with day to day."

What is key in these relationships is an existing intimate understanding of each other's day-to-day lives built up through their frequent encounters. WhatsApp in this sense is not concerned with the finding out about these friends because they are already known to each other.

"You can't really catch up with WhatsApp."

"You don't really learn about your friends with WhatsApp 'cause you know them already."

So, while the technology makes no distinction between different geographical distances, the geographies of these relationships are often central to people's experiences with it. With some exception, geographically distant friends were not typically communicating through WhatsApp. The nature of such relationships and their rhythms entail a different form of engaged encounter – a "catch-up" – that is not easily performed in WhatsApp. That the geographies of these relationships matter is highlighted in particular by one of the university students who uses WhatsApp with her particular set of friends in London only when she is back home in London; when away at university, her WhatsApp use shifts to her friendship group based there.

Our arguments here are that participants' experiences in WhatsApp, appear bound up in the enactment of their day-to-day relationships. They talk of planning their doings together with and through WhatsApp, of how they giggle with these friends in those events and through WhatsApp, of how they recollect and inquest about those events afterwards. What is apparent is an ongoing weave of text and media-based tittle-tattle and "tosh" with an emphasis on the phatic rather than the functional. WhatsApp here is a site of encounter with these friends; a means by which, we would argue, they can exhibit small but frequent acts of commitment and faithfulness. It is part of the way these relationships are experienced and constructed as an ongoing matter; in essence, part of the way they live and dwell together even when apart.

What lends additional substance to these arguments is participants' orientation to these relational encounters in WhatsApp as an ongoing concern. Participants described it as being without end – "*it's for on-going conversation*". This is not to suggest that these participants are locked in a perpetual round of continuous second-by-second exchanges that they cannot get out of. While participants do engage in some episodes of back and forth message exchange, these were not typically of the sustained kind possible when using IM with a keyboard at a PC or laptop. Within the context of these close relationships, participants in WhatsApp described being less concerned with the normal delicacies of ending a conversation gracefully. With such closeness of relationships and intimate knowledge of friends, any disinterest or lack of response was not taken as an immediate threat to the friendship. The threads were viewed by participants as something that would be picked up again whenever and wherever. Just as the friendship is never ending, so the thread of encounters is in WhatsApp.

What we would want to argue is that never-endingness of WhatsApp is critical to how we understand its quiddity and use. In part this relates to how it is constitutive of the ongoing performance of the friendship and indicative of a certain commitment to that relationship. But it is also in the *potential* for this ongoing thread that it comes to be used in the context of particular relationships and not others. We can see this illustrated in the following episode where one of the participants discussed an uncomfortable and inappropriate relationship being played out in WhatsApp.

"I've got in situations – it's a very free way of communicating – it's not on phone bills and I've got into situations where it is so chatty and soon you are in a situation where the person is saying very rude things and I have had that and it goes into – it's casual to the point of flirting – people approach you who have already got your phone number – I have had a text from a guy today saying how has your year gone so far – and he's like just trying to instigate a chat."

Apparent in this example is how she does not want this relationship played out in a particular way. She does not want the ongoing casualness of exchange but rather wants to maintain a certain relational distance. Indeed as we see here, the possibilities of an ongoing exchange with this particular person led to a misinterpretation of the relationship - an intimacy that is not reflected in any substantial friendship in the real world. What this points to is a concern with particular relationship boundaries. It is here that we see interesting points of departure from more traditional SMS. Consider some of the following remarks:

"Friends I don't know so well I would much rather send a text to because it just keeps a little barrier up – I wouldn't want them to come back and then – so with a text it just needs one answer."

"With work colleagues? – I wouldn't WhatsApp. WhatsApp is much more to be in contact with people I want to be in contact with – my work friends are not anywhere near close to me so it's few and far between that I would need to contact them – so I would just get on and text them – because I know it's not going to be a running conversation its just going to be text messages."

On first inspection, this all seems rather curious for channels that, on the face of it, bear some strong resemblances with each other. Yet what is revealed here are nuanced ways to which these different channels are oriented. SMS messages here are seen as enabling a delicate way of providing a barrier and a distance as particular relationships dictate, be that work colleagues or more distant friends. They were viewed as something that, where necessary, could be treated as discrete and bounded entities. With the particular character limit, SMS messages had potential to be designed to be more complete. They could be used in a less open-ended way, inviting a single response in contrast to any ongoing commitment. WhatsApp was seen not just in terms of discrete messages but as an ongoing conversation.

We glean more insights here in some related sentiments contrasting SMS with WhatsApp and how these may pertain to particular kinds of relationship doings.

"Texting is more formal whereas WhatsApp is more informal and social."

Again, the idea that text messaging is regarded as a more formal channel would appear to be a somewhat surprising pronouncement. Yet it is clear from this that people are orienting to the respective quiddities of SMS and WhatsApp in subtle but important ways. In part we can attribute some of these qualities to the different economies of these channels.

"It [WhatsApp] tends to be shorter messages – not like with text where you are aware of paying for a text so you send one long text."

"[WhatsApp] is more conversational – whereas if I get a text its more of a long response so I wont reply to it whereas with WhatsApp it can just be one word."

With SMS, one participant discussed his effort to design a message within the constraints of the message character limit – as we see, this can then be oriented to with particular social effect. In WhatsApp, by contrast, there is less of a concern with doing this. A single "conversational" turn in a WhatsApp exchange can be spread across multiple messages without recourse to conscious concerns about message economics. With this comes the possibility for a greater looseness and casualness of the exchange: a greater informality. It is these possibilities, it would seem, that people orient to in the context of their dwelling with certain types of people but not within the context of enacting other types of relationships.

Enacting groups

Our everyday relationships are not just comprised of a collection of one-to-one relationships but are played out too in a variety of collective concerns. Of significance in our arguments about dwelling is a concern with groups not just as a bounded and defined collection of people but with the ongoing encounters and enactments of relations that comprise the experience of the collective. Within WhatsApp, multiple participants can be added to a dedicated thread of conversation. Again, these groupings are bound to particular kinds of collective encounters and relationships in the real world whether these are housemates, groups of friends or specific familial relationships. Their significance lies not in their initial formation but in the ways they enable the ongoing performance of group relations. One of the participants in a shared household told of various behaviours around household organisation that are enacted through a group thread in WhatsApp with her housemates. She recounts examples of when passing the supermarket she will send a WhatsApp message to her housemates to see if any household items are needed. Similarly she will WhatsApp them to say she will be late home or to see if they will be in so as to inform the organisation of any cooking. For her, while such exchanges serve particular practical concerns of coordination, they also hold additional phatic value, being expressions of courtesy, consideration and generosity. Simply enquiring is often enough; simply informing is often enough. Such exchanges, we would argue, become part of the fabric through which being a good member of that shared household is performed and experienced.

We see other examples of WhatsApp group threads for friendship groups who live in the same area and see each other on a regular basis. Again, the enactment of these relationships combines both the practical and the phatic possibilities of WhatsApp relating to the geographies and rhythms of the real. From a pragmatic perspective, WhatsApp group exchanges were used by our participants as a way of planning and organising a night out or place to meet. The group messages were seen as providing efficiencies over individual messages for quickly ascertaining availabilities or negotiating locations and schedules. But again in such exchanges there are other ways that the group is enacted and experienced. Inviting, negotiating, agreeing, disagreeing of these coordination activities, through the group WhatsApp exchanges are also ways in which faithfulness and commitment to the other members of the group can be demonstrated.

What we also see from our interviews is that such planning and coordination encounters are not just discrete and bound communication events but rather are constitutive of the ongoing trajectories of a group's encounters. Perhaps most salient here is the continuation into what one participant referred to as the *"morning after nights out debriefs"*. In these, he describes how WhatsApp exchanges turn to group commentary and reflection about how the night's events went. Photos are exchanged, social interactions are played over, critiqued and analysed, and playful teasing carried out - all ways of participating in the group's ongoing narrative construction. This then flows into the ongoing exchange of tosh and gibberish in a never-ending thread. These threads then are not a matter of minutes, hours or days. Many of the WhatsApp groups we heard about had taken place for several years as part of the ongoing weave of other encounters among its members. In highlighting these timescales here our concerns are not with some longitudinal demonstration of repeated utility or social value of WhatsApp group messaging; i.e., that people find it useful so they keep using it. Rather, what is apparent from the interviews is how the social significance of these groups is experienced (and, we would argue, needs to be understood) in the context of these timescales – their historical narrative and prospective commitment to group relations.

The significance of this ongoing social construction of group relations through WhatsApp is further highlighted in an episode drawing on a participant's contrast with a Facebook group. In question here was a WhatsApp group comprising ten of her close university friends that had been established for several years. The participant recounted how the group exchanges messages of "absolute gibberish" all day every day – it is an ongoing concern. When planning a gathering, the participant discussed how they used a Facebook group rather than WhatsApp:

"If there was a party or something then we would use Facebook for that – messaging and groups – Facebook group messages have partners in it."

Key here was that such a gathering was also to include romantic partners of the group members. By using Facebook to organise this, the participant discussed orienting to a particular set of social concerns. In the first instance she described how she was able to confer a welcoming gesture to the partners of the group. But in the second instance she wanted to do so without conferring any ongoing commitment. So she articulated how adding partners to the WhatsApp group in this instance would not have been appropriate. So, while it may have served a similar practical function, it would also have entailed a deeper and ongoing commitment to the partners which would be at odds with their enactment and status in the real world. What this highlights is her orientation to different levels of *faithfulness* across the different relationships and how these become bound up in the organisation of online group enactment.

Awareness and Notification

We turn our attention now to consider ways that people come to acquire lightweight information about others through WhatsApp and how this becomes inscribed with particular social meaning. As we described earlier, WhatsApp has a number of notification and awareness mechanisms. These include, for example, the automatically updated "*last seen online at [date/time]*" status attached to each contact, and the tick marks attached to each message, one tick appearing to indicate a message has been sent and a second tick when that the message has been delivered (see figure 1). These features can be seen as offering some pragmatic functions (e.g. ensuring the phones and network are working properly). However, what is revealed is an additional set of concerns relating to accountabilities, moral implicatives and temporal meanings bound up in what can be perceived, interpreted and revealed through these mechanisms.

Let us consider for example the "last seen online" statement. What is critical here is that such a statement is not some immediate representation of the here-and-now. While it provides some information about contacts' temporal behaviours, there remain certain ambiguities about their current state – which, in essence, is more open to interpretation. It is worth making a point of contrast, here, with related mechanisms found in some other systems where the online status is used to represent the here-and-now of a contact's activity.

"With WhatsApp if I am online that isn't telling people that I am available for a chat – I am there with a purpose to message someone reading a message – it's just that. It's not an invitation to talk. With Skype if I am online – it's an invitation."

"With WhatsApp you have to look to see who's online – whereas with Skype it shows you everyone that is online – that's the difference. It discourages you from being online all the time with Skype."

What this suggests is that while more accurate real-time online status might on the face of it offer better information to make these judgements, it also opens up a wider set of moral implicatives and accountabilities. For example, such real time visibility is sometimes perceived by participants as representing an invitation to talk. When viewed in these terms, there would appear to be a confounding of notions of presence and notions of social availability. We can see here that such a confounding creates a certain burden that is dealt with by altering any indications of visible presence to obfuscate the "true" state of affairs.

By contrast, the "last seen online" status of WhatsApp can be seen to be oriented to in a different way. Here, such information is not regarded as an invitation to talk but rather appears bound up in the notions of knowing about. The information comes to be given meaning in the context of what we know about the other in the context of our dwelling together. While it may be suggestive of certain activity, there is a particular latitude in terms of exactly what this means. This leads us to understood notions of plausible deniability [32, 12] in which such interpretive latitude lends itself to socially graceful ways of accounting for one's presence and rhythms of response. These are argued to be important concerns in the ways we dwell together and the ways we choose to save face and express continued faithfulness to those with whom we dwell.

What we want to argue further, though, is that such latitude is important in the scope of interpretive possibilities available to the person viewing the status update. In this respect, it is not simply an issue of *plausible deniability* on the part of one party but a *plausible accounting* on the part of the other. This points to a different way in which such awareness information is being oriented to – that is, not necessarily as a precursor to interaction and communication *per se* but something that might arguably be conceived of as a social encounter in and of itself. To illustrate this let us consider a couple of notable examples from the interviews. The first example here is drawn from discussions with a mother of a 15-year-old son and highlights something particular about what it means for her to be absent from her son. She articulates an ever-present concern on her part for his safety and well-being and how this, at times, can sit uncomfortably alongside her needs to respect his evolving independence and freedom. For her, negotiating these concerns is a delicate balance in their relationship and we see this being played out in the orientation to WhatsApp.

"On the way home he switches his phone off – to save the battery. I want to see that he is safely home... When he gets home he charges his phone to switch it on – I can see that he is online and home safe."

Here, she invokes her intimate knowledge of his everyday habitual behaviours in the real world to enable particular forms of interpretation in WhatsApp. The "last seen online" time update that takes place when he switches his phone on at home is interpreted by her in a way that renders his geography (and safety) visible. She discussed how this was important for her because it avoids any explicit need to check up on him allowing her to maintain the delicate balance of expressing trust in him and her motherly concern for his safety. What is illustrated here, we would argue, is an *encounter of knowing* as opposed to an encounter of communication.

In a related example, our discussions revealed accounts of people simply going into the application to see when certain people were last online. Significantly, such checks were not motivated by specific needs to understand particular response patterns, nor were they motivated by specific intention to communicate. Rather, their motivations resided simply in the evidence of activity.

"Seeing when they are last on line. It's a weird way of keeping track on your friends"

At first glance, these behaviours might appear somewhat curious, in particular when viewed through a lens of awareness-as-coordination device or a precursor to communication. It highlights, though, how awareness information is being viewed as an encounter in itself, motivated by phatic rather than pragmatic appeal.

Moving on from this, let us consider now participants' orientations to the message notification ticks. Generally speaking, participants regarded these as useful indications that a message had been read – in particular for time-dependent messages, such as those involved in planning, meeting up and coordination activities. But, again, a more interesting picture emerged in relation to accountabilities and moral implicatives bound up in these notifications and the ways these played out in the context of particular relationships. There were times for our participants where temporal properties of response (or not) to a message that has been visibly read came to acquire significance. Here again the issue of dwelling comes into play. For many of the close relationships enacted in WhatsApp, there was a sufficient knowing of the other to interpret these temporal properties without threat to the friendship. Certain temporal patterns were interpreted in particular ways in relation to the habits of others, for example, whether a particular contact always responded quickly when they read something or whether a contact typically respond slowly. Anything unusual or out of the ordinary in this sense is what would become significant and it is the unusual that would become a prompt for further enquiry by participants.

"I had something recently where both my best friend and boyfriend couldn't get in touch with me and I hadn't been using WhatsApp so they were getting worried I wasn't OK - so they called."

But typically, there was sufficient depth and trust in the ongoing friendship that such temporal qualities would be easily explained away in response to other knowings about their lives – they are at work, they are out playing sport and so on and so forth. But participants also talked about particular relationships or circumstances in a relationship when these accountabilities and moral implicatives did create certain social pressures to respond.

"In a way it [the ticks] is good and in a way it isn't. I wouldn't always want people to know that I have read it so seeing that people read it rather than assuming it but again it's up to a point. It's give and take. Most people aren't but a few of my friends are like 'you read this two minutes ago why haven't you replied?', even if I'm driving. I've stopped at the traffic lights I see that I have got it swipe it open – 'oh it's from Emily, big deal – will reply to it later.'"

In orienting to these accountabilities we see how people learn to deal with them in particular ways that are revealing of the tensions that can be at play in these mechanisms.

"They know that you have read it to so you have to respond. Sometimes I will get it where it pops up on my screen. I will read it on screen but not go into the app to show that I have read it. If I am avoiding them or I am at work or I can't get into it now, I won't respond at that point."

Here, the participant seeks to read the message in a way that he thinks doesn't reveal anything to the sender – by not explicitly entering the application to *read* the message, his assumption is that the double ticks will not be revealed to the sender thereby bypassing any source of these tensions[2].

That people were orienting to different relationship concerns in their WhatsApp encounters is further illustrated by a participant discussing the use of WhatsApp in boyfriend/girlfriend relations.

"A lot of my friends have boyfriends and they won't WhatsApp each other – even if it's been going for a while. If they are having a conversation, especially if they are at different universities because they know that if they send a WhatsApp and he has read it and if he doesn't reply she can see that he has been online for the next few hours on and off has not replied for the next few hours – and it's not cause he doesn't want to talk to her it's just because he is busy... When you go into the conversation – it will say if they are typing. The girl will sit there for 10 minutes trying to word and reword things and you can see then it stops and then typing again."

What the participant is pointing to here are a specific set of insecurities and vulnerabilities at play in such newly formed romantic relationships. For her girlfriends, the minutiae of these encounters are subject to detailed scrutiny, interpretation and reflection. In this respect, the temporal properties of response (or lack thereof) in relation to a notification that a message has been read acquire particular significance. While she suggests there may be rational and reasonable explanations for these response properties, and while these may even be understood by her friends, the implication is that ambiguities and alternative explanatory possibilities sow seeds of doubt. Likewise, the visibility of typing activity is seen to hint at levels of investment in the crafting of the response. Implied here is how this temporal investment is subject to social scrutiny both in terms of what the sender thinks it may reveal and what the recipient thinks it reveals. This leads to experienced or anticipated anxieties that are dealt with through a deliberate avoidance of WhatsApp in these scenarios.

[2] Note though that the user has misunderstood the meaning of the double tick marks; technically, because the message has reached his phone, his conversation partner would have seen the double ticks.

Enacting Friendship in Media Exchange

What is further notable about these encounters is how they are constructed not simply through a textual exchange but also through the exchange of various media objects. Such objects include photos, short video clips, audio clips and URLs for web pages of noteworthiness. What we argue here is that more than simply getting these media object from one person to another, their significance lies in how they are invoked for particular forms of social enactment. To illustrate this, let us consider the common practice among our participants of sending photos as part of the "*debriefing*" following a night out. Here the real world encounters between friends are extended and continued through subsequent encounters in WhatsApp. The posting of photos and their particular juxtaposition with textual comments become part of the resources through which an ongoing narrative is produced, being constructed to sit alongside other sites of narrative production on which relationships are built and through which they are experienced and encountered. Participants describe how photos are chosen to render particular features of the events salient. The photos are used to provide contextual cues and points of orientation to augment or be supplemented by comments in the text. The significance lies not just in the retelling of events in particular ways, say for the purposes of reminiscing. Rather, through the sharing, participants constructed opportunities for the co-participation in these narrative assemblies. Key here is not so much the collective assembly of narrative details but in the selective forms of participation enabled. They are used to invite additional comment and humourous banter or simple expressions of evaluation and approval in relation to the referents being invoked. Through this, we would argue, there is the enactment of solidarity and the performance of bonding among the participants. It is a means through which they can build a shared identity and history.

We see this too in other forms of shared cultural reference by participants: *"[We] send pictures, news – have you seen this on BBC website."* Here URLs are embedded and sent, again inviting comment and evaluation and other forms of co-participation in the narrative around these. Likewise, photos are sent of other recent happenings and doings: *"I sent a photo [her hand with new nails] 2 hours ago to my Mum – I just had my nails done."* One couple spoke of how they send images to each other of things they would like to buy. In doing this, a number of things are being enacted in their relationship. First of all, the photo serves as an expression of her taste and the kind of things that she likes. In sending these images, she informed us, she is soliciting the opinion of her partner. This was not simply about the pragmatics of informing a buying decision but was also seen as showing that her partner's opinion was important and valued to her. What this suggest is that in such acts, there is a construction of a sense of we-ness: they are things she thinks they both like or need; they are things they both need to contribute to; they are things that will become constituted in their home and in the way they live together; things that can be part of their evolving identity together and so on.

Of further interest to our arguments in the interviews were some intriguing episodes of media exchange concerning the exchange of snippets of other WhatsApp threads. One of our participants, a final year student, described:

"You can copy the whole chat and get it to another person like one of the other girls – like if I want to show my friends the conversation."

In these episodes, the participant takes a copy of a WhatsApp conversation and then forwards it on to another friend. The particular details of one encounter are made the subject of another encounter in which the first is scrutinised and discussed, re-examined. By sending these snippets, the participant opens up for analysis the minutiae and social nuances bound up in the particular conversation in question; its way of wording, its sequence of response, the back stories of those involved which give those nuances colour and meaning. Again, what we see apparent in these episodes are various forms relationship 'doings'. First of all, we argue, the sharing entails the enactment of a certain contract of trust between the communicating parties. They enable particular readings to be inspected and their validity tested so that this trust can be invoked and tested collaboratively, through friendship. So, for example, 'Is this person being weird by what they have written or have I misinterpreted it?', or 'Do you think this means he likes me or am I reading too much into it?' and so on. Through these various interpretations and reinterpretations, these turns at chat on and around WhatsApp conversations, insights can be revealed into a whole variety of feelings, insecurities, hopes, and expectations on the part not only of the sender and the receiver, but all those who are somehow involved in these conversations. These are ways, we would argue, that the friends in question open up to each other and come to know each other - the ways of doing their friendship.

DISCUSSION

Before offering a discussion we should remark on some of the limits of this kind of investigation. In this work, our concerns are not simply with a straightforward documentation of practices, nor with any claims of universality of practices across cultures. Furthermore it is not our intent to argue that any such practices and our discussions of them, are, in their entirety, exclusive to WhatsApp. Indeed, it is to be expected that there will be certain similarities with SMS, in particular as it evolves from its more traditional form toward some of the capabilities found in WhatsApp. Rather, and what emerged from out interviews, was a more particular concern with relationship "doings" in WhatsApp use; the ways in which such doings are constitutive of these relationships and the ways that these relationships are secured and continued.

The kinds of relationships and friendships that are apparent and articulated in our analysis are about being together or having a sense of being together through the ebb and flow of lives lived as a piece. Key here is that such a sense of being together does not equate to the people in question sharing the same physical space; the shared domain is at once real and virtual but tied together into a delicate world of felt-life. The kind of relationship and friendship that we saw in our analysis was typically geographically-bound in the sense it entailed being together in a district, but this real geography is given valence through digital connection that transforms and transcends that space.

This is not the being together of, let us say, marriage where togetherness is more emphatically about a close physical proximity. It is togetherness and intimacy enacted through small, continuous traces of narrative, of tellings and tidbits, noticings and thoughts, shared images and lingering pauses. This friendship has a history and an ongoing trajectory into the future. It has a rhythm whereby people are coming together and then parting knowing they will come back not to the same space but through the next act of communication, the next expression of 'what's happening'. Some of this is in and through WhatsApp, but more of it is through a sharing of lives, a being together. Each of these facets of being together, one aspect of which is enabled by WhatsApp, is only partial; the friendship in question is woven through time and space and trajectory. There is a tying together of the real and virtual, interconnecting with other webs of connection in the production of moral proximity and felt-life with others with whom we dwell: whose trajectories bind with our own.

What is important to note here is that the term dwelling not only labels the locales of embodied spaces we inhabit but draws attention to how the life in question, the practices in question, need to be understood praxiologically. Dwelling is not simply a place but a "doing" and needs to be seen as constituted by things done and felt endlessly in the moment-by-moment of togetherness and directionality.

A particular quality of felt-life of the relationships highlighted in our evidence is that it would seem more secure and less requiring of the functional maintenance and deeper "catch-ups" we might associate with those outside of this space of dwelling such as with more distant friends. Connections there also need acts of sorts, ones that do the work necessary to keep connection alive. But the doings and showing of faithfulness in these relationships are arguably of a different order. The casual remarkings and postings of WhatsApp would seem to make less sense outside of those with whom we dwell. They seem too ephemeral and, we would argue, less likely to be meaningful to those far away. What is key here is a knowing enough about the everyday life circumstances and happenings - their details and rhythms - to engage in these ways with WhatsApp. Further, it is in the knowing that you will be with these people a few hours or a few days later that there opens up the opportunity for these kinds of engagements to make sense; they can be made in relation to these knowings. Given these particular ways of being together, of knowing and of dwelling, the enactments of faithfulness and the communication in WhatsApp can assume a form that is casual and never-ending.

The apparent absence of purpose would seem to suggest that it lacks fertility; that it affords no oxygen for friendship. But as we have tried to highlight, these acts of communication are grounded in phatic concerns. That they often seem to lack immediate function is precisely how they offer the oxygen required. It is in the pointless chit-chat, the garbling of asides, the jokes, and the non-sequitors in WhatsApp that friendship is at once made and displayed. At the same time, the intimacy that ensures these acts of communication have meaning is made partly through these acts. It is in these ways that friendship is kept fresh, vibrant, close.

We can see too how certain kinds of relationship doings sometimes sit less comfortably within these communication forms and how other forms, such as SMS or Facebook may be used to enact certain forms of moral distance. This is illustrated for example in instances where the more bounded form of SMS messages were deliberately constructed to accountably close off the communication – to communicate without any ongoing commitment to the relationship. This is not to argue that SMS is always used like this. On the contrary, it is clear that there remains some significant overlap with what we see in WhatsApp. Rather, it is to argue that there are certain nuances of form in these technologies, in the character limit of SMS, for example, that present subtly different opportunities for producing moral distance. We saw further evidence for this in a particular use of a Facebook Group rather than amend an existing WhatsApp Group to communicate with peripheral members of a social group. Here again, the communication was performed without enacting any form of long-term commitment. The relationships we see played in WhatsApp are ongoing and committed, not requiring of such closure.

The various forms of presence and notification mechanisms available in WhatsApp need to be understood from a praxiological perspective: in the things done and felt through people's engagement with these features. Through dwelling together, significant knowledge of the circumstances of others is brought to bear on the interpretation and meaning of these particular signals. We saw for example, how the appearance of a "last seen online" status message at a particular time in the afternoon was sufficient indication for a mother to know her son was home safely. In light of her knowledge of his routine and phone habits on returning home from school, she uses the status update as reassurance of his safety. That is, these features are not simply a means by which we might know when to contact someone, or whether they have received a message. Rather they enable us to know something about others in light of our existing knowing of them. Our knowing of others also comes to bear on the accountabilities and moral implicatives associated with particular notifications and presence indicators. Lack of response to a message that had been visibly read by the other was not necessarily viewed as a threat to faithfulness in the context of these close friendships. In the context of other relationships, where there is less assumed faithfulness, the same lack of response to a visibly read message comes to mean something different. Faithfulness needs to be worked at differently in these relationships and cannot be assumed in the same ways. This is what we saw in the case of courting couples who avoided the use of WhatsApp early on in their dating because of uncertain interpretations of behaviours and faithfulness made visible through these awareness and notification mechanisms.

In conclusion, our investigation demonstrates how WhatsApp is used by our participants as a key component their way of dwelling with others. By positioning it in this way, we situate it within the ebb and flow of lives lived together, within the web of other connections, both real and virtual. Along with these other connections, we argue that it is constitutive of the felt-life with those with whom we dwell. This helps draw our attention not just to practices with WhatsApp but to the forms of commitment, faithfulness and knowledge manifest through the possibilities presented in this form of communication.

REFERENCES

1. Barkhuus, L. and Tashiro, J. Student socialization in the age of Facebook. In *Proc. of CHI '10,* 133-142.
2. Barkhuus, L. and Polichar, V. (2010) Empowerment through seamfulness: Smart phones in everyday life. *Personal and Ubiquitous Computing, 15(6),* 629-639.
3. Barkhuus, L. (2006) Mobile Networked Text Communication: The case of SMS and its Influence on Social Interaction. In Heilesen and Jensen (eds.): *Designing for Networked Communication: Strategies and Development.* Idea Group Publishing.
4. Barthes, R., (2002). *Comment vivre ensemble: Cours et seminaires au College de France (1976–1977).* Paris, Seuil (Eng. Trans. Briggs, K. (2012) How to Live Together. Columbia University Press).
5. Baym, N. (2010) *Personal Connections in the Digital Age*, Cambridge, Polity Press.
6. Becker, H. (1996) Accounting for Tastes Harvard, Harvard University Press.
7. Castells, M. (2009) *Communication Power.* Oxford: Oxford University Press.
8. De Certeau, M. (1984) *The Practice of Everyday Life*, Berkeley: University of California Press.
9. Durkheim, É. (1984) *The Division of Labour in Society (De la Division Du Travail Social)*, Translated by W. D. Halls, Second Edition, Free Press, New York.

10. Farman, J. (2012). *Mobile interface theory: Embodied space and locative media*. Routledge: New York.

11. Faulkner, X., & Culwin, F. (2005). When fingers do the talking: A study of text messaging. In *Interacting with Computers, 17,* 167-185.

12. Grinter, R.E., Palen, L. and Eldridge, M. (2006) Chatting with teenagers: Considering the place of chat technologies in teen life. In *ACM Transactions on. Computer-Human Interaction*, *13(4),* 423-447.

13. Grinter, R.E. and Eldridge, M.A. (2001) y do tngrs luv 2 txt msg? In *Proceedings of CSCW 2001*, 219-239.

14. Grinter, R.E. and M. A. Eldridge. (2003) Wan2tlk? Everyday text messaging. In *Proc. of CHI '03*. 441-448.

15. Hall, J., & Baym, N. (2011). Calling & texting (too much): Mobile maintenance expectations, (over)dependence, entrapment, and friendship satisfaction. *New Media & Society*, 1-16.

16. Harper. R (2011) *Texture: Human expression in the age of communications overload*, Boston: MIT Press.

17. Harper. R. Bird, C., Zimmerman, T. and Murphy, B. (2013) Dwelling in Software: Aspects of the felt-life of engineers in large software projects. In *Proc. of ECSCW 2013*, Paphos, Cyprus.

18. Isaacs, E. Szymanski, M., Yamauchi, Y., Glasnapp, J. and Iwamoto, K. (2012) Integrating local and remote worlds through channel blending. In *Proc. of CSCW '12,* 617-626.

19. http://www.apple.com/uk/ios/messages/

20. https://www.facebook.com/mobile/messenger

21. http://www.kakao.com

22. http://line.naver.jp/en/

23. http://www.skype.com/en/features/instant-messaging/

24. http://www.viber.com/

25. http://www.wechat.com/en/

26. http://www.whatsapp.com

27. Ingold, T. (2011). *Being alive: Essays on movement, knowledge and description*. Abingdon, UK: Routledge.

28. Kim, H., Kim, G., Park, H. and Rice, R. (2007) Configurations of Relationships in Different Media: FtF, Email, Instant Messenger, Mobile Phone, and SMS. In *J. of Computer-Mediated Communication, 12,* 1183–1207.

29. Licoppe, C. (2004) Connected presence: The emergence of a new repertoire for managing social relationships in a changing communication technoscape. In *Environment and Planning Part D*, *22*, 135-156.

30. Licoppe, C. and Smoreda, Z. (2005) Are social networks technologically embedded? How networks are changing today with changes in communication technology. In *Social Networks, 27(4)*, 317–335.

31. Ling, R. and Yttri, B. (2002) Hyper-Coordination via mobile phones in Norway. In Katz, J. and Aakhus, M. (Eds) *Perpetual Contact: Mobile Communication, Private Talk, Public Performance*. Cambridge: Cambridge University Press, 139–169.

32. Nardi, B., Whittaker, S. and Bradner, E. (2000) Interaction and outeraction: instant messaging in action. In *Proceedings of CSCW '00*, 79-88.

33. Page, R., Harper, R. and Frobenius, M. (in press) From small stories to networked narrative: The evolution of personal narratives in Facebook status updates. In *Narrative Enquiry*.

34. Pettigrew, J. (2009) Text messaging and connectedness within close interpersonal relationships. *Marriage & Family Review 45*, 6-8, (2009), 697-716.

35. Putnam, Robert D. (2000). *Bowling Alone: The Collapse and Revival of American Community*. New York: Simon & Schuster.

36. Rainie, L. & Wellman, B. (2012) *Networked: the new social operating system.* Boston: MIT Press.

37. Ramirez, A., & Broneck, K. (2009) "IM me": Instant messaging as relational maintenance and everyday communication. *Journal of Social and Personal Relationships, 26,* 291-314.

38. Reynolds, L., Gillette, S., Marder, J., Miles, Z., Vodenski, P., Weintraub, A., Birnholtz, J. and Hancock, J. (2011) Contact stratification and deception: blackberry messenger versus SMS use among students. In *Proc. of CSCW '11,* 221-224.

39. Scissors, L. E., Gergle, D. (2013) Back and forth, back and forth": Channel switching in romantic couple conflict. In *Proc. of CSCW 2013*, 237-248.

40. Simmel, G. (1908) *Sociology: Investigations on the Forms of Sociation*. Berlin: Duncker & Humblot.

41. Taylor, A. S., & Harper, R. (2003). The gift of the gab: a design oriented sociology of young people's use of mobiles. In *J. of Computer Supported Cooperative Work, 12(3),* 267-296.

Enhancing Community Awareness of and Participation in Local Heritage with a Mobile Application

Kyungsik Han, Patrick C. Shih, Mary Beth Rosson, John M. Carroll
College of Information Sciences and Technology
The Pennsylvania State University
{kuh178, patshih, mrosson, jcarroll}@ist.psu.edu

ABSTRACT
One goal of local communities is to create and reinforce community identity by connecting residents to their local heritage. Technologies have enabled and facilitated the creation and consumption of digitized history content provided by official history institutions as well as individuals. Although much research has been conducted to understand technical and social aspects of digital cultural heritage, little empirical research has investigated how people perceive, experience, and interact with community content that is socially generated and tied to locations, particularly with respect to building community heritage. To address this, we developed a mobile application called Lost State College (LSC) and conducted a user study with 34 local residents. The study results indicate that meaningful historic places evoked special attention from the participants, and that those who have lived in the community longer tended to contribute more to the community heritage effort. Participants utilized *social features* as a way of learning local history, reflecting personal experiences and stories, and co-creating rich layers of local history information from their perspectives.

Author Keywords
Community awareness, participation, digital cultural heritage, mobile application.

ACM Classification Keywords
H.5.m. Information interfaces and presentation (e.g., HCI): Miscellaneous.

INTRODUCTION
The history of a community is a part of its identity and is the essence of the communal roots that local residents inherit or share by cohabiting or visiting a physical region [7]. Prior to the widespread dissemination of information and communications technology (ICT), the act of archiving and provisioning historical content was limited to cultural heritage institutions, and individuals simply accessed the resulting official history information as information consumers. However, the introduction of ICT has enabled and eased the digitization, management, and provision of archived content of all kinds, including community-related content. With the emergence of Web 2.0 and social network platforms, it is now possible for individuals to create and share their personal experiences with others in the form of user-generated content [25]. These newly evolved ICT platforms have the ability to augment interactions among people and their local history, and *digital cultural heritage* has emerged as an opportunity for engaging civic participation in creating and preserving community heritage. In particular, the mobility afforded by smart mobile devices (e.g., smartphones and tablet PCs) allows people to access either static or more context-specific locational information more instantaneously and opportunistically than any other technologies (e.g., web) and to create new or broader forms of documenting, collecting and sharing diverse types of history information, such as texts, photos, or videos on the go. These new opportunities and affordances have been well appreciated and embraced in mobile tourism [5].

CSCW'14, February 15 - 19 2014, Baltimore, MD, USA

http://dx.doi.org/10.1145/2531602.2531640.

Although much research has been conducted to understand technical and social aspects of digital cultural heritage, little empirical research has investigated how people perceive, experience, and interact with socially generated locational content to build community heritage. In this paper, we present a mobile application called Lost State College (LSC) that provides official historical information about local landmarks in a downtown area in the northeastern U.S.

Research in mobile tourism has stressed the importance of sociability on enhancing tourism experience [5,21]. We build on this notion as well as adding four specific social features (visits, likes, comments, and photo sharing) to the LSC application. These features were designed to allow people to access local historical contents generated by other LSC users and to encourage them to contribute their own perspectives and experiences to historic buildings. Our goal in this project is not to propose a specific novel feature or interface, but rather to explore user interactions and experiences with such an application in the context of community heritage. In particular, our research objective is to explore how people use LSC as a *civic application* that aims to turn local landmarks into interactive places that are more historically meaningful, to promote historical awareness of various places in the local community, and to understand how digitized historical content combined with public storytelling could create or reinforce community identity and engagement [7].

To pursue these research objectives, we conducted a field study with 34 participants. Our study results show that: (1) participants utilize *social features* as a way of learning local history and interacting with others, co-creating digital traces and rich layers of local history information; (2) participants who have lived in a community longer tend to contribute more to the community heritage effort by adding more comments and photos; and (3) some particularly meaningful historic places evoke special attention from the participants. Overall, participants shared information using social features, which created novel affordances and allowed different types of connection to the local history. We present and discuss these findings using a combination of user interaction data, qualitative observations, and post-study interviews in the context of community heritage.

RELATED WORK

Mobile-based social interactions

Several research efforts have investigated how mobile technology transforms social connectivity and interactions, pointing to positive effects from connecting people more closely through increased mobility and high availability. For example, Humpherys described how people create and maintain their social relationship with others through use of Dodgeball, a mobile application that enables users to meet up by distributing location-based information of user whereabouts [17]. Dodgeball users found that the mobile social network facilitated social connection and also transformed the traditional notion of public space into a socially interpreted space. Similarly, Hampton *et al.* presented new insights to an ongoing debate about the extent of social isolation in America [16]. By analyzing data collected from people's mobile phone usage, they found that Americans are not as isolated as has been previously reported by many other researchers. This was in part due to mobile technology allowing users to participate within a larger and more diverse social network.

Along with these conceptual analyses of how mobile technologies may facilitate social interactions, researchers have explored applications that incorporate specific social mechanisms. For example, Lindtner *et al.* introduced a mobile photo sharing system named *mopix*. They analyzed how these sharing technologies mediated collective social relations. Their focus was not on the technical advances of media sharing, but on the practice of social and cultural production and social interaction and connection [22]. Carter *et al.* described digital *e-graffiti,* an application through which people shared their annotations of content displayed on publicly situated digital community poster boards. They found that the mobile device facilitated the practice of adding different media types of annotations [8].

In a tourism context, Brown and Chalmers studied tourists' practices in the wild, noting that the ability to share social interactions (e.g., commenting) was an essential feature that could enhance users' tourism experiences [5]. They also stressed the importance of having interactive maps and guides in mobile platforms. Aoki *et al.* developed a mobile tour application called *Sotto Voce* that incorporated an audio sharing mechanism. Participants were able to share audio clips through an "eavesdropping" mechanism, which created a strong interaction between companions [2]. Tintarev *et al.* described a system that offered personalized mobile recommendations as opposed to general, popular Points-Of-Interests (POIs) recommendations. The study showed a higher level of participants' satisfaction from more rare and serendipitous recommendations over general ones [27]. *Explore!* is a mobile game application that is used in archaeological parks. A number of groups, consisting of three to four participants, perform a game to explore and enjoy heritage by interacting with each other and using mobile devices [4]. *ArtLinks* is a visualization tool that allows museum visitors to leave text-based impressions about artifacts and presents these to others. The study emphasizes the importance of considering social connections and interactions as part of museum experiences [10].

While these studies have explored the effects of specific social aspects of user experiences (e.g., eavesdropping, recommendation, gamification, text-based visualization), we are interested in investigating the impact of social features (i.e., visits, likes, comments, photos) that are common in commercial social networking systems like Yelp, where users share experiences associated to physical places among strangers.

Heritage connection

Storytelling of community history is as an effective way to increase civic engagement and participation in preserving and developing community heritage [13]. Gaver et al. developed *Cultural Probes* as a storytelling technique where participants are given a set of physical artifacts (e.g., postcards, maps, diary, etc.) to inspire self-reflections and engender personal experience to local community heritage [13]. In LSC, we provide a list of historical photos of famous local landmarks as a trigger to personal reflection, storytelling, and co-creating local heritage.

Digital storytelling has a synergy with the evolution of mobile devices and the introduction of Web 2.0 applications, and research has experimented with enabling digital storytelling by allowing users to easily upload digital photos and share personal experience narrations [18]. In the local community context, digital storytelling encourages people's interests in their community and is effective in creating feelings of engagement and attachment among community members [6,7,19]. Shared stories of community history could also strengthen sense of community [12]. For local residents, the history of a community contributes to feelings of a sense of belonging or emotional connection, often regarded as an essential component of community identity [7].

Many efforts have studied the discovery of heritage connections through digital storytelling, for example exploring the use of ICTs in helping people express their experiences and expectations about heritage. For example, *Mukurtu* is a mobile platform designed for managing and sharing digital cultural heritage [1]. *Urban Tapestries* is a mobile platform that supports authoring as well as sharing content created by its users, highlighting the actions of cooperative co-creation and accretion of community knowledge [20]. Giaccardi and Palen emphasize cross-media interaction created by multiple media and technologies with respect to producing social experience to physical places [14]. Similarly, Ciolfi argues for the importance of enhancing people's social experience while visiting museums and other heritage sites, so as to enrich their experiences and personal connection to heritage [9]. These studies investigate the concept of *placemaking*, which refers to "the active process of connecting and relating to locations that become meaningful in our lives" [9] and "a living and sustainable relationship with heritage" [14] by allowing users to share personal and community memories through annotated photos and notes or capturing of sonic experiences of the natural heritage.

By leveraging mobile technology, LSC seeks to integrate storytelling and placemaking in the context of digital cultural heritage. Its design rationale and motivation are similar to the aforementioned research with respect to addressing how the mobile system could provide and support a notion of *agency* in community residents, allowing them to co-create personalized content and make meaningful associations to physical places. As part of this, LSC incorporates social features from popular social network platforms for facilitating creation and sharing of social activities; we expect that it reinforce an individual's identity within a community. In our study, we carefully examine the relationship between user-generated content and storytelling and its impacts on how people perceive, experience, and interact with socially generated locational content to build community heritage.

MOBILE TOUR APPLICATION

Aligning with the placemaking perspective of constructing local heritage, the meaning of LSC underscores the preservation goals of local history – or else it might be "[L]ost" in the future. Our intention in developing LSC is to make local heritage more visible and available to community members and visitors, aiming to capture and share the collective memories of a town's history; user interfaces supporting socially generated content could allow local participants to contribute their own perspectives and experiences about local landmarks as well as appreciating meaningful contributions shared by others.

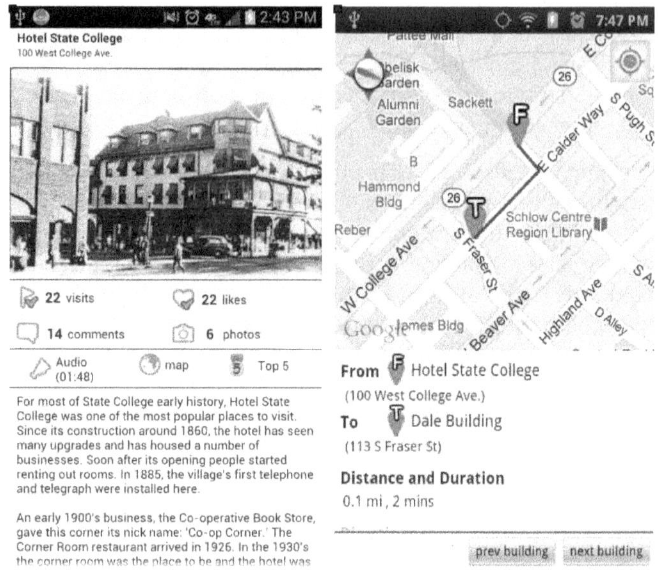

Figure 1. Information displayed on a landmark page (left) and a walking route between two landmarks (right).

Official features	Explanation
Official photo	View historical & current photos provided by city officials
Official text	Text description of landmark
Audio	Listen to pre-recorded audio description
Social features	**Explanation**
Add visit	Indicate the user has been to this place
Add like	Indicate the user likes this place
Add comment	Add a comment about this place
Add user photo	Take a photo of a landmark
View visit	See who else checked-in at this place
View like	See who else liked this place
View comment	See others' comments about this place
View user photo	View photos taken by others

Table 1. Eleven application features.

LSC was developed for the Android mobile phone platform, to provide information about historical landmarks that are part of a traditional college town in the Northeastern U.S. With help from city officials, we gathered photos (dated from over a century ago to more recently) and text descriptions of 14 historical downtown landmarks including houses, churches, diners, and shops. While walking through the downtown with LSC, users can thus access the history of nearby landmarks and leverage community efforts to archive the history of the downtown area using an interactive map and other features. Like other tour applications, LSC provides a name, address, official historical or current photos (each landmark has at least three official photos), text description, and a pre-recorded audio description for each landmark. Importantly, LSC also supports creating and accessing user-generated social data such as visits, likes, comments, and uploaded photos.

USER STUDY

The research goals of this study were as follows: (1) to characterize the general usage of the mobile application; (2) to investigate how user-generated content is utilized as a storytelling and placemaking mechanism; and (3) to understand the creation and perception of user-generated content and how it differs from official historical content. We conducted a user study with 34 participants. We discuss these findings based on the analyses of a combination of the user interaction data, qualitative observations, and post-study interviews in the context of community heritage.

Participants

We recruited 34 participants via mailing lists, local news websites, and word of mouth. We designed the study as a history tour so that the participants could visit all historical landmarks in the downtown area. Each participant took the history tour on their own. Among the participants, 21 were male and 13 were female, with ages between 20 and 50 (Mean = 30.2, SD = 9.6). Participants had differing familiarity with the town and downtown location of the tour, ranging from having resided in the community for less than one year (11 participants), 1-2 years (4), 2-4 years (7), and more than 4 years (12). All of the participants owned at least one Android, iPhone, iPad or iPod device and were generally familiar with the use of mobile applications; 24 of 34 participants had their own smartphones. In a survey administered prior to taking the tour, 17 of this subset of 24 told us that they would look for a mobile tour application when they visit indoor or outdoor attractions, indicating that a smartphone-based tour was a common expectation among such users. 90% of the participants were not aware of the history of the downtown area, but expressed high interest in learning more through the study.

Procedure

The study consisted of three steps. Prior to taking the tour, participants completed a brief online survey that asked for demographic information (e.g., age, gender, length of residency, technology use); they were introduced to the LSC app in the controlled conditions of a research lab. Then, they embarked on a tour using LSC. They were asked to follow a predefined walking route to ensure some comparability across users' experiences. Participants who owned an Android smartphone downloaded the application and used their own phones for the tour, while others used an Android smartphone that we provided (we first demonstrated its use). All walking tour took place when the weather was warm and sunny. Researchers walked behind the participants and took notes on their behaviors; they also answered questions regarding use of the application throughout the tour. Afterwards, participants returned to the lab to participate in a semi-structured interview. The tour included 14 landmarks covering a total distance of about 2 miles. The average tour duration was approximately 56 minutes.

Interaction Data

The interaction data we collected and analyzed comprise any application input that came in the form of touchscreen actions. For example, participants touched the Visit icon to indicate that they had visited a landmark; they touched the Visit text to see a list of people who had visited previously. They touched Official photo to access the 3-5 historical photos we had uploaded for each landmark; they scrolled up and down the text area to read Official text.

When analyzing the data, if there were repeated actions in a row (e.g., a series of touches on the same feature), we considered them to be a single interaction. For example, a set of user actions such as (Official text, Official text, Official text, Official photo, Official photo, Official text, Official text, Add comment) recorded in the system log was converted into (Official text, Official photo, Official text, Add comment) prior to conducting any analysis.

It is important to note that our intention to use interaction data as a data analysis is not to suggest a generalized usage of LSC but to elicit the meanings of its usage with respect to the connection to local community heritage.

RESULTS

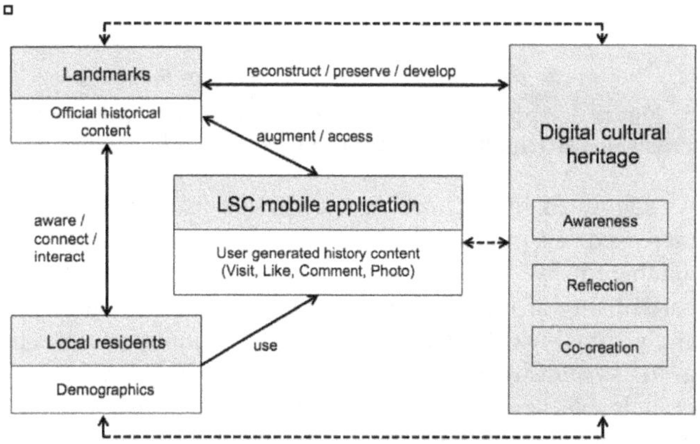

Figure 2. Digital cultural heritage through a lens of the usage of user-generated content, local residents, and landmarks (Note: dashed lines: analysis points).

Local residents and landmarks are core entities in a community; however, there might be no connection or relation between them. By placing LSC between people and places, it creates a channel for people to be aware of and become closer to the landmarks, not only by providing official historical content but also by allowing people to augment their own reflections and experiences regarding the landmarks. This can be viewed as a process of co-creating cultural heritage mediated by mobile technology. These continuous actions and activities will reconstruct the landmarks into interactive historical places, which not only serves to preserve but also to *develop* socially constructed local heritage.

We now discuss how our study participants, who are local residents, used LSC to co-create digital cultural heritage around existing landmarks and describe how people, landmark, and user-generated content can be understood through a lens of awareness, reflection, and co-creation (see Figure 2).

Overall application usage

From the user study, we collected a total of 2909 interactions generated by 34 participants.

To obtain a sense of overall application usage, we calculated the usage percentage for Social and Official features. "Social" refers to the usage percentage for all eight Social features (i.e., whether viewing or adding), and "Official" refers to the percentage of usage of Official photo and Official text. Audio was excluded in the data analysis because we found that most participants tended not to listen to the audio and rather relied on the official photos and text for seeking information of the landmarks.

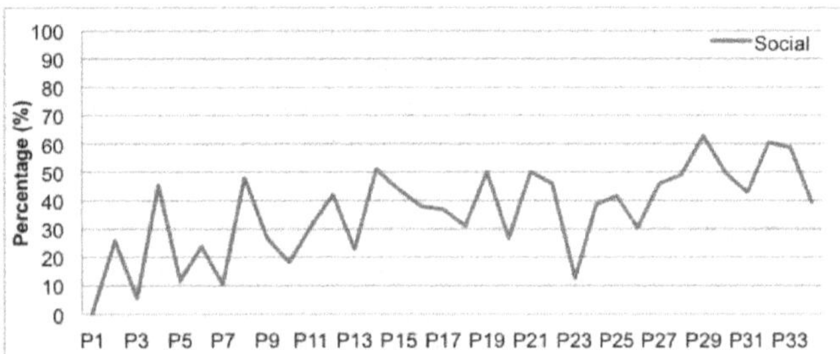

Figure 3. Application usage of Social features. The x-axis refers to participant number, i.e., in sequence of participation.

As suggested by Figure 3, use of Social features generally increased as more tours took place (participants are numbered by their temporal sequence). The first few participants of the study relied primarily on Official photo and Official text because there were no primary social data in the system for participants to interact with. However, as participants began to use the Social features to contribute new content to the landmark pages, the overall use of Social features gradually increased. Although we could not identify the saturation point in this study, and the use of Social features varies across the individuals, the key aspect of this result is the attractiveness of content created through social mechanisms. We did not intentionally insert social data for this study because we were interested in how participants created and used social data in a naturalistic setting; all content provided through Social features came from participants. This led to the situation where there was no social data presented in LSC for the first two participants. As a result in the following data analysis, we excluded them and used the data from the remaining 32 participants.

Digital history placemaking and storytelling

We were interested in the use of specific social features (Visit, Like, Comment, and Photo), so that we could explore how their use might impact placemaking and storytelling. Thus we focused on Social feature usage with respect to (1) *awareness* (2) *personal reflection* and (3) *co-creation*, to understand collective activities and social production of local heritage. Table 2 shows the summary of interactions in Social features.

Social features	Interaction counts
Visits	363 (35%)
Likes	200 (19%)
Comments	225 (22%)
Photos	248 (24%)

Table 2. Summary of interactions in Social feature.

First, Visit was the most used Social feature. The first action taken by many participants on accessing a landmark's page was to note their Visit, which was easy to do. Several participants mentioned that they liked to mark their visit because they wanted to leave a digital trace and expected that others (e.g. their friends) might see this in the future. This activity promotes creating an additional layer of one's *presence* to the landmarks. It is also pertinent to a personal reflection to the landmarks because people will be able to trace their visits back later.

Like is similar to Visit, but it implies a different relation to the landmarks, suggesting more of a personal preference. More specifically, it seemed that participants simply touched the "like" button to express personal enjoyment, whenever they thought the landmark looked interesting or found unique or meaningful information in the official or user-generated content (*"It's simple. I just clicked it when I liked the landmark."* (P16)). It also engenders co-creation of overall positive appreciations to the landmarks.

Types	#	Examples
T1. Personal appreciation	37	*"nice hotel", "quite a big pig", "classic structure"*
T2. Sharing a personal experience or story	21	*"There's an orthodontist office up there and it has an awesome fish tank in the waiting room"*
T3. Landmark features	18	*"Had no idea that it was originally a dump", "Love the fallout shelter"*
T4. Current state of the landmark	17	*"The nittany quill is here and a close store dragon chaser"*
T5. Asking a question	5	*"Why would they want to ruin the natural architecture with that front?"*
T6. Adding information	4	*"The delta program is housed here I think"*

Table 3. Question types, counts and exemplary comments (a total of 102; ordered by counts).

Regarding checking others' visiting or liking activities, we found some participants tended not to do this because they would see a list of people they did not know. As Visit and Like are only binary interactions, it might be useful to add features that could aid discovery of social connections among people who have or are currently experiencing the landmarks. For example, several participants indicated that seeing a list of people who are somehow connected to him/herself would be more interesting; this might be done using friend lists from other social network sites.

We collected a total of 102 comments contributed via the Comment button. We inductively coded the comments and grouped them into six types. Table 3 lists the types, counts, and examples. We noted that 36% of the comments (T1) simply expressed appreciation toward a landmark in a few words, 34% (T3, T4) consisted of physical observations about the landmarks, and 25% (T2, T6) provided additional information or stories to the landmarks. We observed that participants did read the comments left by others, using diverse forms of text-based information to experience the places and then contributing their own reflections.

Participants also used the Photo feature frequently; 109 photos were shared during the study. Photo sharing with smartphones is already identified as popular and interactive social practice [24], and our study confirms such findings. We observed similar interaction patterns from Comment in which many participants checked photos posted from other participants first, aiding awareness or appreciation, before deciding whether or not to add one of their own. If they found any interesting aspects of the landmark or its surroundings, which is pertinent to either personal reflection or interest, they tended to take and post a photo unless they determined that there were already many existing photos or photos that captured their reflections.

Figure 4. Examples of official photos and user-generated photos. Participants took various types of photos related to the landmarks.

As with the diversity of comments left at each landmark, participants added a variety of photos for landmarks; for example, ones that captured different angles, interesting architectural or decorative features, close-ups, insides, surroundings and so on as depicted in Figure 4. We found these user-generated digital photos tended not to be a set of redundant images, but rather ones that expanded landmark coverage, co-creating a rich body of visual information about the landmarks. A few participants mentioned they did not want to add similar photos to the landmarks (*"I did not want to add redundant photos if there were already a number of existing ones shared by other participants."* (P19)). Each photo was also given a short caption, typically consisting of 5 to 10 words, briefly describing the content of the photo. As a design suggestion, a few participants mentioned that they wished to leave further comments or Likes on photos posted by others. They also suggested a filtering mechanism such as sorting photos by popularity. This reinforces that many participants wanted to interact with other users more broadly, and that the application should offer features that support these desires. From these results, we can reasonably say that participants seemed to use Visit to log their activities and Like to express their preference for a given landmark; in contrast, they used Comment and Photo to augment the system with additional information about a landmark. Contents from Visit and Like consist of numbers and a list of users, thus they might not be as informative as the information portrayed by Comment and Photo.

This led us to examine the interplay between different Social behaviors. We ran a Pearson's correlation test between the actions of adding Visits or Likes and those of viewing Visits or Likes. We found no significant relation between adding and viewing these data ($r = .35$, $p = .21$). We speculate that participants were attracted to Visit and Like because they require only a one-click interaction, but they did not find as much benefit in seeing who else had Visited or Liked the landmark.

However, we also examined the correlation of adding versus viewing Comments or Photos. Here, we found a strong correlation; people who added comments or photos were much more likely also view these content types ($r = .75$, $p < .01$). We speculate that there was adding and viewing Comments and Photos were mutually reinforcing. This result also emphasizes the importance of providing a simple but interactive interface to support adding and viewing comments and photos as a way to increase user experience and participation.

Application usage by length of residence

Features (N)	High (11)	Mid (11)	Low (10)	F(2,31)
Add Visit	9.8 (1.7)	5.2 (1.7)	10.2 (4.8)	2.4
Add Like	4.7 (3.9)	3.3 (3.0)	4.6 (3.8)	0.4
Add Comment	4.7(3.6)[a]	2.0(1.8)[b]	2.3(2.8)	2.9*
Add Photo	5.1(4.9)[a]	3.0 (2.9)	1.4(2.0)[b]	2.9*
View Visit	2.4 (3.3)	1.9 (2.3)	4.5 (4.3)	1.6
View Like	1.8 (1.8)	1.4 (1.8)	1.8 (1.7)	0.1
View Comment	4.0 (1.8)	4.0 (2.8)	3.9 (2.8)	0.1
View Photo	4.3 (3.8)	4.0 (4.2)	4.7 (3.8)	0.1

Note: Reporting format: Mean (SD); a > b, $p < .05$; * $p < .05$

Table 4. Social feature usages by three groups of the length of residence.

People who have lived in a community for a long time might know more about its history than relative newcomers. For instance, with respect to LSC use, those people might have had personal experiences at the landmarks or already know interesting information about them. For these reasons, we were interested in the relationship between length of residence and application usage. Because most of the participants were undergraduate students, and assuming that students live in our town 2 to 4 years before graduation, we used the demographic survey to segment time of residence into three groups of approximately the same size: high – more than 4 years; mid – between 1 and 4 years; low – less than a year.

We ran a between-subjects ANOVA with Tukey-Kramer post-hoc analyses to assess possible differences according to residence length, as well as to explore how such patterns might relate to cultural heritage activities. As seen in Table 4, the behaviors that varied across residence length were adding Comments and Photos. Participants with the longest residence times added more content of these two types. More specifically, participants in the high group left more comments for local historical landmarks than those from the mid group ($t = 3.1$, $p < .05$); they also added more photos than those from the low group ($t = 3.4$, $p < .05$).

One possible interpretation of these findings is that residents who have lived in a town have more comments and ideas for photos when experiencing its past history; in this sense the effect may be evidence of participants' experiences with a historical site. The use of LSC would thus make such community information and activities more visible to oneself and other local residents, already identified as a strong motivations for participation [7]. Another possibility is that these participants already feel more identity with the community and as a result are more motivated to participate in this active fashion.

It is important to note that the viewing Comments and Photo were quite similar across the groups varying in residence time. Participants who had lived here for a short time still seem interested in checking comments and photos created by others. They may simply have less to add, or perhaps less motivation to contribute. Independent of these groupings, many participants indicated that they found Comment and Photo helpful and checked them as many times as they did Official photo or Official text. This suggests that user-generated content can enrich all users' experiences, and we will discuss more detailed analyses on this later. We also tested for age and gender effects on application usage, but found no significant differences.

In the previous section, we discussed the types of comments added by the participants (Table 2). Working from these data, we further investigated if the local information from knowledgeable local citizens might be as insightful or interesting as the official history. This inference could be echoed by the fact that the content of comments might vary among people with differing residence histories. Thus, our exploratory hypothesis was that participants with a longer residence history would share more informative content and story related to the landmark (which refers to those in T3 and T6, accounting for a total of 25 comments from 102; 25%) because they might have more knowledge or experiences.

To test this, we combined the comments of the mid and low residency groups and compared them to those from the high group using a Pearson's chi-square method (*2 (two groups of comments) X 2 (high vs mid/low residency)*). We found a significant difference between the two groups of comments with respect to length of residence (X^2 (1, N=102) = 3.4, $p < .05$). This result indicates that the comments from the high-residence-time group (68%) had more shared personal experiences and stories or provided additional information about the landmarks than the mid- and low-residence-time group (32%). In contrast, participants from the mid- and low-residence-time group (54%) tended to add more comments describing interesting features, current state, or their personal feelings of appreciation toward the landmarks than those from the high-residence-time group (46%). It clearly reflects different actions toward digital storytelling among local residents and suggests design directions to support different levels of motivations.

Constructing heritage at meaningful landmarks

In parallel with characterizing participants' interactions, we investigated the relationship between individual *landmarks* and people's heritage connection. In this analysis we assume that landmarks that tend to evoke more use of social features are experienced as more meaningful.

Features (N)	High (4)	Low (10)
Add Visit	19.5 (1.0)	19.1 (1.4)
Add Like*	14.8 (1.5)	8.1 (0.9)
Add Comment*	9.3 (0.9)	6.0 (0.6)
Add User photo	9.3 (1.8)	7.2 (1.1)
View Visit	6.3 (0.7)	6.9 (0.4)
View Like	6.0 (2.0)	3.6 (2.1)
View Comment*	12.0 (1.1)	8.0 (0.7)
View User photo	11.3 (1.4)	9.4 (0.9)

Note: Reporting format: Mean (SD); * $p < .05$

Table 5. Social feature usage at high-interaction and low-interaction landmarks.

To explore this possibility, we used k-means clustering to search for contrasting clusters of landmarks based on usage frequency of all social features. To decide a starting point of *k*, we performed the centroid hierarchical clustering on the total interactions recorded for each landmark. This led us to cluster the landmarks into two groups; the k-means output showed that the clustering variables' means differ significantly ($p < .001$). Table 5 summarizes the feature usage across these two clusters of landmarks. It points to several differences among them; for example, more adding of Likes ($t(12) = 3.6$, $p < .05$), as well as adding ($t(12) = 2.8$, $p < .05$) and viewing Comments ($t(12) = 2.9$, $p < .05$).

We found no patterns related to *who* contributed the Likes. Many participants told us that they were aware of which landmarks were high in Likes; however, that did not necessarily warrant the extra step of viewing who liked the landmark, mainly because they did not expect to know most of other participants (*"I did not check other users, because*

I do not know them." (P25)). However, as previously described, this aspect could possibly create another motivation to use Like because a few participants indicated they would be more engaging in using Like if they could see activities and content from their friends (*"I will use this feature more if my friends use this app."* (P29)). This also implies that participants wanted to create and maintain social interactions with others if the opportunity exists.

Regarding the Comment feature, both the adding and viewing of comments varied across the two clusters. We speculate that if a landmark is meaningful to participants, they will leave and check more comments. Perhaps they know more stories and information about those landmarks, or perhaps they want learn more about them because they seem particularly interesting.

Lastly, we had expected to see more use of adding and viewing of Photos for landmarks clustering in the high-interaction group. Although the means of adding and viewing photos were tended to be higher for this group, the differences were not reliable enough to lead to a significant difference between the two groups.

Figure 5. Example landmarks in the high-interaction cluster. On the top is a historical building that has housed a hotel and restaurant for almost 100 years and is still a popular place; below is a public park that many local residents visit.

These results raise the question of *why* participants used LSC more for the four landmarks in the high-interaction group and *whether* those landmarks should really be regarded as being more "meaningful." By making a qualitative comparison of those four landmarks with the other ten, we noted characteristics that make these places uniquely interesting: These are all places that people know well but not well enough to know their history. More specifically, two of the landmarks are buildings that have housed a similar business for nearly 100 years. One has been operated as a hotel and restaurant since 1926 (Figure 5), and the other is a barber shop that is the oldest such establishment in this community; it has been in business since 1919. Many residents visit these locations on a regular basis, going to eat or getting a haircut. A number of participants mentioned they were surprised to learn that these places have historic stories and value, and are still operating as the same business (*"I love the long history and also food"* (hotel; P13); *"wow this is cool that they keep it original!"* (barbershop; P9)).

A third landmark is a statue of a pig family. It was built to commemorate the town's agrarian roots; most of the town's avenues were dirt roads in 1896 when the statue was installed, and farm animals freely roamed the village. Because it is the only statue in the downtown area, our participants paid considerable attention to it during the tour and showed interest when finding new information about its history. For example, as depicted in Figure 6 (right), participants mentioned, *"I didn't know animals were prohibited from running around State College so early in its history."* (P31) and *"I always wondered what the story was behind here."* (P27)

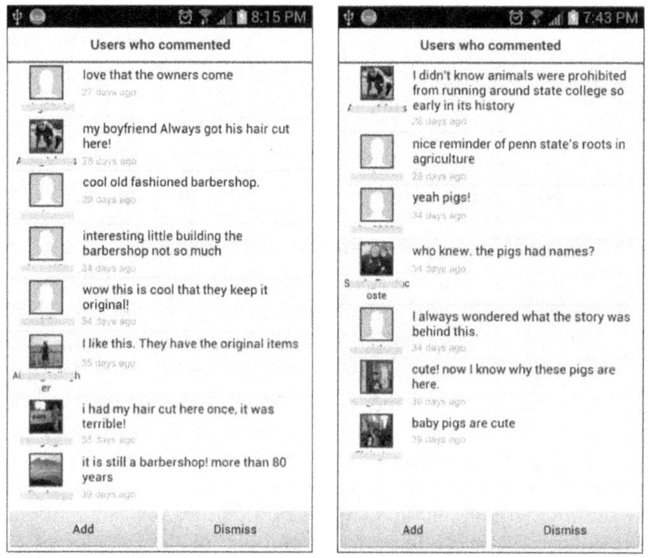

Figure 6. User comments (names anonymized) added to the two popular landmarks: barbershop (left) and a statue of a pig family (right). Participants appreciated historical values at the landmarks.

The fourth landmark is a public playground or park. The interesting fact is that this location is a naturally occurring sinkhole, and for many years it served as the town dump. Some participants indeed were surprised of this fact. *"(I) never knew it was originally a dump, (it is) quite interesting to know about this."* (P16) Similarly to the hotel and the barbershop, participants shared close connections to this landmark because a lot of local residents spend time together with family and friends there (*"My daughter loves this park."* (P26)), and a number of annual local events, such as musical concerts and festivals, are held in this place attracting more people to come (*"some good concerts at the parklet in the summer."* (P17)).

We could see that the other ten landmarks did not have a similarly clear uniqueness, because most of them are now offices, residential buildings, or a school. In contrast to comments made about the four landmarks in the first group, some participants mentioned they did not know the other ten locations at all or failed to find a historical value from them. Although this cannot be generalized to perspectives from all participants – in fact some participants said they learned new information about these other landmarks – it seems that the four high-interaction locations were indeed experienced as more *meaningful landmarks* by most participants in our study.

Overall, these findings indicate that locations with unique back stories may attract more interaction from participants, including user-generated historical commentary. Many participants seemed to be more interested to know others' reactions toward those landmarks and wanted to explore them to find interesting stories or facts, increasing their awareness through different perspectives. They also shared their personal reflections on those landmarks, augmenting and co-creating the history information not only with respect to the landmarks themselves, but also to the community as a whole. This perspective well accounts for the notion of placemaking, because socially generated content has reconstructed the spatial environment into more meaningful interactive historical landmarks. Evidently, they have become more aware of local community history.

Official and user-generated historical contents

While the contributions made through use of Social features can be interesting and reflect personal stories, these data are not official in their historical content and in fact may be inaccurate due to lack of knowledge or personal subjectivity [11]. Therefore, it is necessary to examine the impacts or validity of Social features with respect to learning experience or enjoyment.

A number of participants expressed positive reactions about the Social features. They found the use of these features to be fun and interactive, saying, *"It's easier and more interactive, more fun. I would definitely use the app for a tour with my friends, using features like visits, photos, etc."* (P25) They also found that Social features provided a unique and intriguing viewpoint that the official content could not. For example, participants said, *"I think comments are quite informative. There were some good photos that I liked a lot."* (P17) and *"I think so. I made some observations from them since they are all related to landmarks."* (P26)

Although most participants were actively involved in using Social features or appreciated social content with respect to learning and being more aware of a history of their community, a small number of participants perceived Social features quite differently, preferring official content as a means of learning about history of this community. This seemed be a pronounced personal preference with respect to learning. For example, some participants mentioned, *"Not really, I wanted to learn something more about the landmarks from official photos and description because those were from historians or someone in Borough, and I think social data is more for do I like it or this place is popular or not."* (P19) and *"Like appreciating arts in museum, I read text descriptions more while looking at the buildings."* (P31)

Regardless of the method or preference when using LSC, most participants acknowledged that user-generated content was a valuable part of the historical information that could not be added or managed by the city officials. This came from active and voluntary participation as content created by participants became part of each landmark's "story," along with official content. As depicted in Figure 6, LSC was utilized as creating a *digital guestbook* in a sense that (1) participants provided their different types of inputs to the landmarks with different motivations or purposes and (2) making their content more visible and accessible to other local community members.

LSC also enabled participants to realize that the place where they live has its own long and rich history as well as giving them heartfelt appreciation for the people and families who built up the town over many generations. Some participants mentioned, *"I really didn't know buildings have some stories and history. Giving more different perspectives to my community."* (P20) and *"I have learned a lot about this community, like it used to be a bank, theatre, and it got burned, etc. I think it is a learning experience."* (P28) They also mentioned that they felt more identity and belonging to a community after completing the tour. *"I love to know about the story of each building. Knowing a little bit more makes me feel even more like 'townie'."* (P30)

Overall, our study is an excellent example of how mobile technology can be used for placemaking and storytelling as a way to make community historical landmarks more meaningful, interactive, and visible to community members, as well as increasing community awareness. The mobile application certainly offers new ways of learning about a community's history, both through official content and socially generated content among local residents. As smartphones become more affordable and pervasive, we expect to see more interactive online social activities that lead to interesting and rich community historical stories. This expectation is also echoed by participants' comments: *"It gives you online social interaction, and I can see how technology can be applied to learning about community history"* (P22) and *"It is easier and more interactive, more fun. I would definitely use the app with my friends, using features like visits, comments, photos, etc."* (P25)

DISCUSSION AND CONCLUSION

We have investigated how participants used LSC by conducting a small study that yielded a variety of user interaction data and participants' comments. Through a mix of statistical and qualitative analyses, we specifically investigated how application usage and user experience (grouped both by participant activity level and landmark interest) could turn landmarks into more active and interactive places and connect to community history storytelling and feelings of community heritage.

First, the study results show that participants not only appreciated and became aware of existing official and newly added social content, they also shared their digital traces, demonstrating an important role for user-generated content in user experience. Participants interacted with Visit and Like, showing their presence and preference, and shared personal reflections or stories by leaving Comment and Photo. Participants also took both adding and viewing actions together when interacting with Comment and Photo, presenting interdependence of the usage of those features. These results show that LSC supports an action of co-creating additional layers of local history information to the landmarks and the community as a whole. Second, we also found that participants who have lived in a local community longer were more likely to leave comments and add photos. Third, regarding landmarks, there were a small number of meaningful places that drew more attention from participants, producing higher volume in adding and viewing user-generated content. We also identified the significant differences in the content from the comments, clearly indicating a role that local residents can play with respect to information provision.

All of these findings demonstrate how digital cultural heritage transforms the way of experiencing or learning community heritage [15], making a local community as a living history and heritage site [9,14]. It is a result of the integration of people, places, and history information that contributes to co-creating meaning to a local community. It is done by combining both static and official information provided by history institutes and dynamic and social information, including people's reflection, presence, and activities.

Our study has a number of implications. With respect to theoretical implications, we showed how a digital tool makes local community history information more visible and supports social interactions, creating and sharing additional content to local history. LSC leverages the effort to identify the history of places in communities and shows how storytelling can be used to create and reinforce community identity. Our comprehensive analyses that incorporated both interaction and interview data provide a unique lens for understanding the connection between people and their local and cultural heritage.

Our study also revealed the relationship between local residents and the spatial features of their community. Landmarks that participants visited and appreciated are the historical places that were originally designated and geometrically defined by a local historic institution. Following the Lynch's theory of spatial cognition and the physical environment [23], these landmarks are what constitute the mental map of the city. However, social connections and interactions created by user-generated content within places are more consistent with Appleyard's study [3], because they have become reformed and transformed into more personal, historical, and cultural places. Our exploration of the characteristics of each social feature (visits, likes, comments, photos) based on awareness and appreciation, reflection and interest, and co-creation of the landmark clearly show different motivations and intentions in creating distinctive historical information to the landmark.

Utilizing mobile technology in digital cultural heritage also creates the opportunities where people can appreciate the landmarks and create and access official and social content while they are physically located at the landmarks. It creates more vivid and interactive cultural experiences that are similar to those encountered in mobile tourism. It also supports some situations in which people can access and create information on their mobile devices without physically visiting the sites. Providing the fact that more people are adopting smartphones, delivering local history information to their devices would make them more aware of local history and encourage them to be involved in activities of preserving and contributing to local heritage.

One obvious practical implication of our study includes the need for interfaces to support creating and accessing user-generated content in various ways because people perceived existing four social features as useful channels to learn more about community history and interact with others. Perhaps providing other types of interfaces, for example, supporting audio or video inputs might create another set of history content creation or social interaction by people. Our findings about participants' different motivations and involvements of reconstructing landmarks also suggest a need for systematic mechanisms to make meaningful landmarks more visible and salient to residents, to make other landmarks more interactive, and to increase participation and engagement from more diverse community members from senior citizens to the younger generation.

We identified several limitations in this study. First, we only studied individual user's interactions and experiences to the local landmarks and community. As a result, participants only had the option to pass on ideas or knowledge to future tourists. As described in [5] participating in a group setting can be a very sociable activity. There is an opportunity to design a mobile application that allows members who belong to the same group (i.e., by proximity to the landmark or by closeness of members' social ties) to share and reflect on their experiences. Second, 32 participants do not necessarily represent the general population, and our findings might not generalize to other broader contexts. Scalability is also another issue as we realized that properly managing the increased number of social data would be additional challenges if the application is used by more people. Some participants have also suggested that having an interface for sorting user-generated content and displaying them based on popularity might be helpful. Third, although we found the length of residency to be a factor that affected application use, there might be other factors such as the degree of a sense of community, personal interests to history in general, and more. While it is hard for us to present a broad understanding of local heritage connection given that this study focuses on the individual use of the LSC app, we believe that our approach reflects experiences and connection to community heritage from an individual's perspective and presents novel contribution to the literature.

Our findings hinge on the analysis of interaction data and user-generated content from a single usage scenario. We might have different patterns of application use or different experiences or perceptions to local heritage from local residents or potential visitors who will take a tour or visit a landmark multiple times. The idea of utilizing LSC as a guestbook and storytelling mechanism to local history could generate additional insights. Future work that explores different usage scenarios and local heritage connections in different contexts and conditions could unveil more interesting results of local heritage.

As part of its technological implications, LSC supports a notion of agency in construction, in that people can create and in a sense "authorize" their own content regarding local shared landmarks. We did observe evidence of social construction of local heritage as participants wanted to be connected with other local residents and interact with them with respect to preserving and developing cultural heritage. If we were to enable even more persistent communications among local residents, the system might take the socially constructed co-creation experience to another level, which may or may not be desirable and could have interesting additional implications for community engagement (i.e., might residents use such a system to debate current plans for renovation or removal of sites). Such broader implications are not visible in the one-time usage scenario we studied, again pointing to the importance of investigating naturalistic heritage and community identity creation and formation in a long-term deployment study.

Finally, this paper sheds light on how we might broaden the design applications that support interactions among people and local heritage. We believe these insights will help local history institutions, local heritage researchers, and designers who are particularly interested in cultural heritage enrich their perspectives on the design processes and create more effective and user-friendly applications that can be easily and widely used to provide connection to cultural heritage.

ACKNOWLEDGEMENTS

We thank Harry Robinson for helping us design and conduct the user study. We also thank the reviewers for their valuable comments which helped to considerably improve the quality of the paper.

REFERENCES

1. Mukurtu, http://www.mukurtu.org/
2. Aoki, P., Grinter, R., Hurst, A., Szymanski, M., Thornton, J., Woodruff, A. (2002). Sotto Voice: Exploring the interplay of conversation and mobile audio spaces, In *Proc. of CHI 2002*, pages 431-438.
3. Appleyard, D. (1969). Why buildings are known. *Environment and Behavior*, 1(2), pages 131-156.
4. Ardito, C., Buono, P., Costabile, M., Lanzilotti, R., Pederson, T., Piccinno, A. (2008). Experiencing the past through the senses: An m-learning game at archaeological parks, *IEEE Multimedia*, 15(4), pages 76-81.
5. Brown, B., Chalmers, M. (2003). Tourism and mobile technology, In *Proc. ECSCW 2003*, pages 335-354.
6. Carroll, J.M., Rosson, M.B. (1996). Developing the blacksburg electronic village, *Communication of the ACM*, 39(12), pages 69-74.
7. Carroll, J.M., Rosson, M.B. (2008). Theorizing mobility in community contexts, *International Journal of Human Computer Studies*, 66(12), pages 944-962.
8. Carter, S., Churchill, E., Denoue, L., Helfman, J., Nelson, L. (2004). Digital graffiti: public annotation of multimedia content, In *Proc. of CHI 2004*, pages 1207-1210.
9. Ciolfi, L. (2012). Place-centred interaction design: situated participation and co-creation in places of heritage. *Museum and design principles, Proceedings of the conference*, Venezia, Fondazione di Venezia, pages 57-68.
10. Cosley, D., Lewenstein, J., Herman, A., Holloway, J., Baxter, J., Nomua, S., Boehner, K., Gay, G. (2008). ArtLinks: Fostering Social Awareness ad Reflection in Museums, *In Proc. CHI 2008*, pages 403-412.
11. Dellarocas, C. (2003). The digitization of word-of-mouth: promise and challenges of online reputation mechanisms, *Management Science*, 49(10), pages 1407-1424.
12. Freidus, N., Hlubinka, M. (2002). Digital storytelling for reflective practice in communities of learners, *ACM SIGGROUP Bulletin*, 23(2), pages 24-26.
13. Gaver, B., Dunne, T., & Pacenti, E. (1999). Cultural Probes, *Interactions*, 6(1), pages 21-29.
14. Giaccardi, E., Palen, L. (2008) The Social Production of Heritage through Cross-media Interaction: Making Place for Place-making, *Journal of Heritage Studies*, 14(3), pages. 281-297.
15. Giaccardi, E. (2012). *Heritage and social media: Understanding heritage in a participatory culture*, Routledge, Taylor & Francis Group.
16. Hampton, K., Goulet, L.S., Her, Eun Ja., Rainie L. (2009). Social isolation and new technology: How the internet and mobile phones impact american's social

networks. *Pew Internet & American Life Project*.

17. Humphreys, L. (2010). Mobile social networks and urban public space, *New Media Society*, 12(5), pages 763-778.
18. Jokela, T., Lehikoinen, J., Korhonen, H. (2008). Mobile multimedia presentation editor: enabling creation of audio-visual stories on mobile devices, In *Proc. of CHI 2008*, pages 63-72.
19. Klaebe, H., Foth, M., Burgress, J., Bliandzic, M. (2007). Digital storytelling and history lines: Community engagement in a master-planned development, In *Proc. of VSMM 2007*, pages 108-120.
20. Lane, G. (2003). Urban Tapestries: Wireless networking, public authoring and social knowledge, *Journal of Personal and Ubiquitous Computing*, 7(3,4), pages 169-175.
21. Larsen, J., Urry, J., Axhausen, K. W. (2007). Networks and tourism: Mobile social life. *Annals of Tourism Research,* 34(1), pages 244-262.
22. Lindtner, S., Chen, J., Hayes, G., Dourish, P. (2011). Towards a framework of publics: Re-encountering media sharing and its user, *Journal ACM Transaction on Computer-Human Interaction*, 18(2), pages 1-23.
23. Lynch, (1960). *The Image of the City*, MIT Press, Cambridge, MA.
24. Miller, A.D., Edwards, W.K. (2007). Give and take: A study of consumer photo-sharing culture and practice, *In Proc. CHI 2007*, pages 347-356.
25. O'Connor, P. (2008). User-generated content and travel: A case study on TripAdvisor.com, *Information and Communication Technologies in Tourism*, pages 47-58.
26. Stuedahl, D. (2009). Digital Cultural Heritage Engagement – A New Research Field for Ethnology. *Ethnologia Scandinavica*, 39, pages 67-81.
27. Tintarev, N., Amatriain, X., Flores, A. (2010). Off the beaten track – a mobile field study exploring the long tail of tourist recommendations, In *Proc. of MobileHCI 2010*, pages 209-218.

GEMS: The Design and Evaluation of a Location-Based Storytelling Game

Jason Procyk and Carman Neustaedter
School of Interactive Arts & Technology, Simon Fraser University
250 – 13450 102nd Avenue, Surrey, BC, Canada, V3T 0A3
jep4@sfu.ca, carman_neustaedter@sfu.ca

ABSTRACT
It is now possible to capture geotagged photos and videos and share them with family and friends. Yet the reality is that applications for capturing and viewing this information are not particularly rich offering little more than maps and simple textual information about a location. Given this, we wanted to explore this design space to find new and exciting ways for people to document and share their experiences. We designed a location-based game called GEMS to support storytelling amongst family members and close friends. The game narrative and mechanics prompt players to reflect on meaningful places from their past and create geolocated digital memory. Other players can then visit the locations to collect and view the records. A user study revealed that location can provide a rich foundation for storytelling activities. We learned that location-based storytelling strategies often elicit a sense of discovery through exploration, sharing, and conscious reflection.

Author Keywords
Location-based games, pervasive games, family storytelling

ACM Classification Keywords
H.5.3. Group and Organization Interfaces: Computer-supported cooperative work.

INTRODUCTION
Presently we are seeing a proliferation of digital technologies that easily permit families to capture and share their experiences [28]. For example, the integration of high-resolution image and video capture within mobile phones makes it easy to capture one's experiences anytime, anywhere [18,27,28]. Online tools such as social media and social networking sites make it easy for people to share their thoughts and experiences with their contacts, along with a broader community of individuals [17]. We are also increasingly seeing new commercial and research technologies permit the recording of place-based information along with people's accounts of their experiences. For example, it is now possible for people to record their geographic location along with captured photos or videos. This creates new opportunities for people to tie records of their experiences to the places that they inhabit.

CSCW'14, February 15–19, 2014, Baltimore, Maryland, USA.

http://dx.doi.org/10.1145/2531602.2531701

The challenge is that existing methods for sharing and viewing locative media (e.g., geotagging photos on Facebook, 'checking in' on Foursquare) are limited and the sense of place is not very compelling. Location may be simply shown as a specific point on a map or conveyed through a single line of text, such as "Near Seattle." The goal of our research was to explore new ways for people to capture, preserve, and share location-based experiences. We wanted to understand how to design a flexible system that would enable people to use location as a context for reflecting on and documenting meaningful personal experiences. We imagined that such a system could be used in two primary ways. First, people could reflect on their experiences and leave place-based memories for close contacts to view over time. For example, a parent may create records for a child to see once the child grows older. Second, people could create records for present-day friends or family to view. This would extend current practices of place-based record keeping (e.g., Foursquare usage).

To this end, we designed a location-based storytelling game called the Geolocated Embedded Memory System (GEMS). In the game, players are asked to contribute to a location-based chronicle of human life by reflecting on and documenting meaningful personal experiences. Players record their experiences through photos, videos, and textual descriptions and digitally store them in real-world places. GEMS explores how game systems can not only support the act of storytelling but can also engage the motivations that surround it by structuring the activity with a series of goals and framing it as part of a larger narrative that challenges the player to imagine how much of their personal history could be passed on to future generations or present contacts and how it might be communicated.

To evaluate GEMS, we conducted a user study in which participants played the game for a period of three weeks. Our evaluation focused on personal reflection in two scenarios. First, we evaluated the game's ability for players to create place-based records for future users to view across time. This explored intergenerational play from the perspective of the person creating the content for future players. Second, we evaluated the game's ability for present-day groups of close contacts to record and share place-based experiences. Here we explored play by close friends. Our findings show that location-based games offer a compelling way to support place-based storytelling. Yet to be successful, they must support both extrinsic and intrinsic motivation, create an audience or the sense of one in the future (e.g., a grown-up child), and provide both remote and location-based content creation and collection.

RELATED WORK

Documenting and Sharing Experiences

There has been a wealth of research that documents how people capture and share experiences using photos and video. We know that people capture a large amount of photos and (more recently) videos and this has increased dramatically since the arrival of digital cameras [11,28]. Photo and video management can be challenging and many people have large archives of media [28]. People also view and review photos in group settings [1,14] where they routinely tell stories about their photos and associated experiences [1,14]. People prefer the tangibility of printed photos [14,28] because it can be cumbersome to view photos on laptops or computers in a group setting [14,23,31,36]. People most often look at recent photos rather than older ones [33]. Viewing also happens while people are 'mobile' where they view photos immediately after capture [18] or during meet-ups with others [2,18,28].

Online sharing of photos and videos has rapidly proliferated over the last decade [27,28,36] despite concerns about privacy [1]. Studies have shown that online photo sharing allows people to choose when and how to view photos shared by others, if at all [28]. Online pictures are thought of as being transitory and ephemeral [37]. Despite the success of online photo sharing, storytelling is often lost when photos are shared this way [27] because the 'storyteller' (photo taker) is not around to discuss or present the photos to others. We focus on this aspect to make it easy and fun to create stories and share them with others.

Storytelling can be a challenging process where it is often difficult to come up with ideas for a story and know what to focus on out of daily life [22]. Digital storytelling is a workshop practice where computer and media experts help amateurs tell stories with digital media [16,22]. Freidus and Hlubinka identify digital storytelling as a reflective practice that can strengthen communities [12]. History Lines is a tool that allows people to map out places they have lived and share comments and multimedia for each location [20]. Balabanović, Chu, and Wolff report on the use of physical photographs to support storytelling, and developed technology to improve the use of digital photographs for the same purpose [3].

Location-Based Games

Location-Based games (LBGs) are games that extend the gameplay experience into the real world by incorporating aspects of the player's environment into the game system. Over the past decade, researchers and designers have created and studied a variety of LBGs. This includes games focused on technological issues in present society [5,7], social issues such as trust, security, and privacy [8,24], and aspects of community and culture [4]. We detail the LBGs that are most similar to our explorations.

First, Geocaching is a location-based treasure hunt game where players routinely create places of importance by physically embedding content (i.e., a container with a log book) in outdoor locations [29,30,32]. See It is a location-based treasure hunt game designed to investigate scalability and player-generated content in LBGs [30]. See It expands the treasure-hunt model seen in Geocaching to explore how locative media can enrich one's sense of place. GEMS iterates on this idea and makes the media the prize rather than the clue: the memory records players create double as content for other players (e.g., friends and family) to view.

Eyespy is a LBG in which players earn points by tagging real-life places with geolocated text and photos and by verifying tags created by other players [6]. While Eyespy uses this create-and-collect pattern to generate a reliable catalogue of visible geographic details for route navigation [6], our design uses it to encourage the sharing of personal stories through the context of place. Feeding Yoshi is a location-based game where teams of players try to collect the most points by moving around the city to gather and deliver digital fruit to digital animals called Yoshis [5]. The authors suggest that mobile games must be compatible with all of "home life, commuting, and work" so that players can find a way to interweave the game with everyday life [5]. We designed GEMS with this requirement in mind.

Serendipitous Family Stories (SFS) is a system that enables family members to create and collect geolocated video messages [9]. Elderly parents record a video message and then link it to a location using a computer interface. Their adult children can then use a mobile interface to track down and view the video in the location it is associated with. GEMS is similar to this yet we explore the idea of traveling to the locations of interest to *record* stories. Moreover, SFS focuses on videos that are conversational in nature; in GEMS, the format is very flexible and users can choose video, audio, photos, and text.

There also exists a set of more casual games that one could argue are location-based. For example, Foursquare allows users to tag locations that they are currently at and record textual descriptions. Yet research has shown that the game attributes found in Foursquare are less motivating over time for players [25]. Moreover, we argue that the manner in which people are able to document experiences in Foursquare is not very rich.

DESIGN OF GEMS

We created a LBG called the Geolocated Embedded Memory System (GEMS). The design of GEMS was drawn from an interaction scenario for supporting intergenerational communication amongst family members.

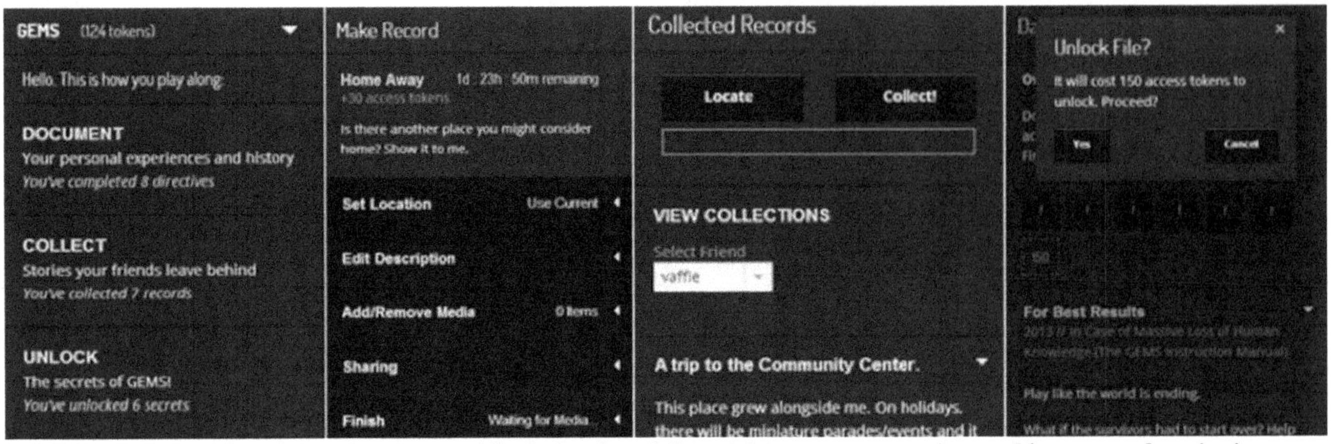

Figure 1. The GEMS interface as seen on a mobile device, from left to right: progress overview, making a record, reviewing a collected record from a friend, and unlocking databank information.

We imagined what it would be like for a person to visit places where her parents or grandparents spent time and to be able to find traces of their past experiences in those places. We also recognized that people may want to share their place-based experiences with close contacts in the present in a richer way than is currently afforded by present day technologies. Thus, we wanted to build a flexible system that would allow users to document and share memories for both types of scenarios.

With GEMS, players can document location-based stories for personal reflection and, in concept, for future generations to find. Players can also play together to share their stories with close friends or family. GEMS encourages them to reflect on their experiences, to consider which places are worth revisiting, and to consider which experiences are worth sharing. It is designed to situate location at the heart of a set of interactions for recording personal experiences and to implement game mechanics to structure and motivate this storytelling process. The main components of the interface are shown in Figure 1. We describe them in subsequent sections.

The game is set in an alternate reality fiction where the player learns of an impending natural disaster. We selected this kind of scenario to establish a narrative frame that might compel a person to reflect on her personal legacy in the face of instability and tumultuous change. In the game, players are asked to contribute to a location-based chronicle of human life by reflecting on and documenting meaningful personal experiences. We iteratively designed and implemented GEMS over several months, drawing on our past experiences studying [29,30] and playing LBGs as well as our understanding of the LBG literature. We also piloted the game throughout its design.

GEMS was implemented as a cross-platform web site accessible on smartphone and computer web browsers. We developed the site as a Node.js web application with HTML5 and Javascript for the user interface. The system stores persistent data using MongoDB, an open source document-oriented database system, and it interfaces with a private Amazon S3 bucket to store media files.

Gameplay Scenarios

This scenario illustrates typical gameplay in GEMS:

Larry has decided to play GEMS. He learns that by recording a history of his own place-based experiences, he will learn about an upcoming (fictional) natural disaster. It's Saturday afternoon, and Larry is riding a bus on his way to meet friends for lunch at a restaurant. He uses his smartphone to check his directives in GEMS. His current directive reads, "show me a place where you experienced triumph." He takes a few minutes to think, and he realizes that the restaurant he's going to is near Citadel Park—the park where he hit his first and only homerun in little league baseball. He goes to the park and uses his phone to take a picture of home plate and to record a video in which he admits the steep downward slope in right field could turn a well-struck ground ball into a homerun. He calls the record "Homer", and GEMS embeds it at his current position for his family to find later. He also earns access tokens that enable him to reveal part of the game storyline.

The next scenario illustrates how Larry's story might find its way to another player in his family.

It's five years after Larry created his "Homer" record in GEMS and his daughter, Lucy, is now playing the game. She is 24 and has a 5-year-old son, Tommy. It's Monday afternoon and Lucy is at Citadel Park for Tommy's first little league game. Between innings she uses her smart phone to see if there's anything stored nearby on GEMS. She checks the map and notices a pin from her dad, Larry. Lucy opens up the record to see what her dad had to say about this park and learns about his first homerun – she is emotionally touched as she sees the present day connection to the park as well. Once Tommy's game is done, Lucy shows him the GEMS record and tells him the story of how his grandfather used to play at the same baseball diamond and hit his first home run there.

The above scenario illustrates the desired intergenerational play that we imagined for GEMS over time. The scenario shows a time separation of only five years, but one could imagine longer periods of time (given technology and data storage persistence). Similar scenarios could be imagined for sharing with close contacts in present day where groups of friends or family play together at the same point in time.

Gameplay Components

Play in GEMS is designed to unfold like a conversation. An artificial intelligence (AI) character named "MALColm" periodically asks players about their past, and they respond by recording and sharing a relevant story or memory. We felt that this conversational format would create a sense of an audience for players who are thinking of future generations and encourage players to create content as if it might be read by someone else in the future.

Directives

Throughout the game, players receive directives from the AI character. Directives are brief questions or prompts that provide players with short-term goals and help structure the content they must create. For example, Figure 1, Column 2, shows a directive, 'Home Away,' received by a player that asks for information about the player's home. GEMS includes directives we created based on four main themes:

a. Specific Locations, e.g., Where are you from?

b. Emotions/Abstract Concepts, e.g., Show me a place where you experienced fear; Take me to a beautiful place.

c. Social Reflection, e.g., Where are your parents? Is there a place you go with your friends? What draws you there?

d. Daily Life, e.g., Where do you find your favourite meal?

We selected themes iteratively by testing them out amongst the designers during the design process. We chose these themes because we felt they would challenge players to create content that would be meaningful and interesting both in personal reflection and in sharing with close contacts. We wanted the directives to be open-ended enough to allow room for interpretation and reflection so that the content created could vary from player to player. The set of directives is pre-defined, and players cannot create their own; they can, however, create free-form records not tied to a directive.

Directives are a crucial part of the design because they catalyze the storytelling process with both a push and a pull. As a question, a directive prompts the player to reflect and to begin formulating a story. As a game objective, a directive gives the player a short-term goal to work toward in the storytelling process. There is a two-day time limit for each directive. After the time expires, the player loses the directive and receives a new one. This mechanic was included to establish a sense of urgency in gameplay.

Memory Records

In order to complete a directive, players must create a memory record. A memory record uses a combination of GPS coordinates, text, audio, photographs, or video clips to capture a particular experience and the place it originates. There are two ways to create a record. Primarily, players can travel to the location in question and use a mobile device (Android phone or iPhone) to capture media and make a record on the spot. In this case, the game determines the player's location using the device's GPS unit. We believe this method of record creation offers the player a unique way to reflect on a personal experience and a novel way to document it. By revisiting a location for the specific purpose of telling the story of what happened there, players can become investigators of their own histories. They can experience the place again in a new context and, using their mobile device, they can produce media that helps to communicate the significance of the place. Alternatively, players may create a record when not at the location by using a map in a computer web browser. In this case, players are expected to upload existing media rather than capture new media at the scene. This method was intended to enable players to document places that they cannot visit due to time constraints, distance, or other obstacles. Figure 1, Column 2, shows the 'Make Record' user interface as seen on a mobile device.

The Databank

In the context of game fiction, the databank is a pool of secret information relating to the role of the AI character and to the impending disaster. As players make records and complete directives, they earn access tokens that can be used to unlock narrative content in the databank. Recording memories at an actual location, as opposed to doing it remotely from a computer, earns additional bonus points to encourage place-based activities. Figure 1, Column 4, shows the databank interface for selecting and unlocking game information. Each fictitious fragment is presented as a blog post, report, or file pertaining to the storyline.

This fragmented style was intended to give players a sense of a puzzle with missing pieces. In order to gather all of the pieces, they need to indulge the AI character and complete more directives. We believe this kind of narrative can act as a hook to sustain players' interest and motivation over multiple gameplay sessions. Each directive players complete brings them closer to a clear understanding of the fictional threat and, ultimately, to the resolution of the story. Thus, as can be seen, GEMS includes game elements to increase players' extrinsic motivation. Our goal was to use this as a way to entice players to play, especially at the onset, in case they did not initially see the intrinsic value in recording place-based information. We hoped that players would gradually become more intrinsically motivated over time to play because they felt the experience was valuable, wanted to leave place-based memories behind for others, or wanted to see what other family or friends recorded.

Group Play through Record Collection

Players may 'follow' each other in order to locate, collect, and view each other's records. Figure 1, Column 3, shows the user interface for record collection. Players search for another player's username and request permission to follow her. If a player agrees, the follower gains access to her content. When created, players can set records to be viewable from anywhere, or only when another player is at the record's location. The former creates an overlap of experiences across distance and time, while the latter creates an overlap of experiences across time. Together, record collection allows players to leave content for one another. Thus, as a flexible tool, it supports personal reflection and intergenerational communication across time as well as sharing of place-based information amongst present-day groups of close contacts.

USER STUDY

We carried out a user study with fifteen participants over three weeks to understand how people used GEMS as a way to document and share personal memories and as a way to connect these memories to concrete locations. Our evaluation focuses on two scenarios: players creating content for future generations to view and players creating and viewing content amongst present day close contacts.

Participants

We recruited fifteen participants (five female) via email advertisements within our university and a local elementary school, and snowball sampling through family and friends. Thirteen participants were between the age of 20 and 29, and two were between 37 and 50. Participants' occupations varied and all were experienced with using email, social media, and software for sharing photos and videos.

Participants were comprised of two sets of players: seven participants who knew each other and were all close friends (labeled as Group Players) and eight who were playing individually (labeled as Individual Players). This allowed us to learn from two different perspectives: the experience of those with a present day 'audience,' and the experience of those with the potential for a future audience (e.g., parents leaving content behind for their children or grandchildren). Naturally, in the Individual Players' case, we could only study the perspective of the player creating records and not the future generation finding them. The perspective of the future player would be extremely interesting to learn about, yet largely impractical to study.

Our participant set was comprised of only 15 people because we wanted to observe participants closely over the three-week period. It would not have been possible to attend to the participants with the level of detail that we did (described next) if we had recruited as many participants as studies of shorter duration sometimes include (e.g., 20-30).

Method and Data Collection

At the beginning of study, we met with each participant individually to conduct a semi-structured interview regarding their current practices relating to documentation of personal experiences, storytelling, and family communication. We also used this initial meeting to explain GEMS and introduce the player to the game interface. We explained that the game would try to help them document their experiences in two ways: 1) for sharing with future generations, or 2) for sharing amongst present-day close contacts. This pre-play session typically took between 30 and 60 minutes.

Next, players played GEMS over a period of three weeks. Players used their own devices—typically an Android phone or iPhone in combination with a desktop computer—to play the game. We felt this would better allow them to incorporate GEMS into their existing daily routine, as opposed to providing them with a new device that they were unaccustomed to using. During gameplay, players received diary questions from the investigators through the game's mail system. Questions asked them to document their experience playing the game. We also actively monitored participants throughout the three-week period by reviewing server data and checking in through email and in-person visits.

At the end of the three-week period, we conducted a semi-structured interview that focused on enjoyable, problematic, or otherwise memorable gameplay moments. We also asked players to provide step-by-step descriptions of the process of creating a memory record. This kind of information helped us investigate why players chose particular memories or locations and how they put the 'story' together. This post-play interview usually took between 30 and 60 minutes. At the end of the study, all participants were entered into a draw for a new tablet (~$200). Thus, it did not matter to what extent they played GEMS, and participants were explicitly told so.

Data Analysis

We gathered the transcripts of both the pre-play and follow-up interviews together with the diary entries into a single collection of qualitative responses. We used open, axial, and selective coding [35] to analyze our data at the individual player level. We present a number of specific quotations that are representative of the trends we discovered.

Our results first explore the ways in which players created and collected records while playing and the processes they used to reflect on locations and create content. Next we outline the ways in which players were motivated to play and how this affected engagement in the game.

RECORD CREATION AND COLLECTION

In our study, we examined the practices of both Individual and Group Players for creating records and, for Group Players, how they collected and viewed shared records.

Types of Content

Participants created a total of 54 records (3 median records per person, with a range of 0-11). We had hypothesized that the completion of a directive would take place over a period of hours; however, we were surprised to learn that players often took multiple days to contemplate directives. We learned that they needed time to think of a meaningful place and an appropriate story. Thus, engaging with a directive and creating a record required a significant amount of thought. For this reason, even though the number of records players created seems low, it is actually reflective of the challenging nature of creating personal records with meaningful content. We discuss this in detail later.

We categorized player records on a number of different axes. First, 67% of records were responses to directives while 33% were free form and not responses to directives. We found the writing style of records included: accounts of specific events (39%), general descriptions of a location's significance (54%), and messages directed at the potential audience (6%). Most records related to public places (e.g., stores, parks) (52%), while others referred to a country or city (11%), private places (e.g., a home) (20%), vehicles (6%), or no real location (11%). For example, P14 documented a run-down neighbourhood. He attached a photo of a city street, and the text he included said:

"The place near my house is a sight which I pass by everyday, and quite frankly it's less than pleasant. The houses are out-dated, the walls are less than clean, and some of the houses feel like they came out of a ghetto area. A renovation of this hood would be an ideal thing to have, and it has somewhat began as the building which I live in is very modern" (city; general description; concerted effort).

P9 created a record at a local candy shop that included a photograph of the storefront. The text she added said:

"This is hands down the best sweet shop in town, and the girls love it." (public place; general description; brief yet complete).

P1 made a record of a hiking trail where he had encountered a bear. He attached a photo of the bear, and he used text to describe what happened:

"I was quite intrigued to run into a black bear during hiking and was delighted to see it. I was excited to take a close up look and take some photos until it hit me that this was quite dangerous. The gravity of the situation got even heavier when I realized it was a black bear cub, the threat of a mother bear was a serious possibility and it was a quick decision to move away and be wary of running into the mother bear on the way back to the car" (public place; specific event; concerted effort).

None of the participants chose to attach audio or video to their records; 78% of records included at least one photo. We did not find any substantial differences between Group and Individual Players in terms of content creation.

Planned Play vs. Opportunistic Play

Both Individual and Group Players had similar practices for creating records and completing directives. These practices can be situated on a spectrum from planful to opportunistic behavior. A *planned approach* to completing a directive used conscious reflection to identify a relevant place and to recall a story to tell. For example, upon receiving a directive, some players would actively think about the question to formulate an idea and a course of action. Part of this reflection involved interpreting the directive in order to narrow down the range of possible locations to select from.

"I stopped and thought about [the directive] and came up with an answer. I asked myself, what is the most meaningful place for places where I feel most at peace, most comfortable?" –P9 (on "show me a place for thought")

Alternatively, an *opportunistic approach* relied on inspiration, convenience, and a chance to create records. Some players created records when they found themselves in a particularly interesting place. In some cases, this meant stumbling across a place that could be used to respond to a directive. In others, it meant making free-form records (records with no directive) for the sake of sharing an experience that did not relate to the current directive. Either way, these players did not build a record around a pre-formed mental picture. Instead, they waited for a location and a memory to emerge before they created a record.

"When I was taking pictures one day, I was like, 'That question is asking me where I eat, so I might as well take pictures of that kind of place'. One was really close to my house. I ended up there, took pictures...then later I accepted the directive and put the record together."-P14 (on "show me a place where you find your favourite meal")

"I actually liked the free form records... I could take a picture any time and then build something around it and upload and that would be it. The one I made about the library, It happened at the moment. I was there, and then it happened."-P10

Players' behavior was not always strictly planful or opportunistic. Some participants exhibited a hybrid approach that involved both planning and opportunism.

"I had accepted [the directive] and left it for a few days. I was thinking of what type of triumph [to document], and I couldn't think of anything. Then when I was walking by my old school, I remembered how I had played a basketball tournament there, so I took a picture and made the entry on my phone."-P1 (on "show me a place where you experienced triumph")

Discovery

We found that the acts of creating and collecting memory records could enhance the meaning of familiar places and create new meaning in unfamiliar places. On a personal level, players discovered forgotten or overlooked aspects of familiar places as they reflected on the game directives. This occurred for both Individual and Group Players when creating records and for Group Players when collecting them from other players. As mentioned above, P1 rediscovered a forgotten childhood memory as he struggled to identify a place where he had felt triumph. In this way, he developed a richer personal understanding of that place by documenting his experience of it. Other players had new experiences in the process of documenting familiar places. For example, P14 decided to spend some more time at his favourite restaurant as he was documenting it in GEMS:

"My favourite directive was the one about where I like to eat....one spot was Cactus Cafe. I passed by, and I was like, 'Might as well go for a drink!' –P14 (on "show me a place where you find your favourite meal")

These cases highlight one aspect of the value of using location as a medium for storytelling. By revisiting a place as part of the storytelling process, players created a new experience that added to their history with the place. Similarly, players also seemed to connect with new places by consuming the stories created by their friends.

"One record I collected showed a place I didn't know about that was in Richmond, so that was interesting. He pinpointed a restaurant at Bridgeport, and I didn't know it even though it was in my neighbourhood. So in my mind I thought, 'Oh, maybe next time I can check that out.'" – P10

Effect of a Present-Day Audience

We noticed for Group Players that the players' sense of a present-day audience influenced the content they created. A player's rationale for documenting a particular place or experience often related to their understanding of who would be collecting the record later. This kind of behavior could be considered "impressed management"; according to Goffman [15], an actor performs for a target audience in such a way as to give them an impression that suits the actor's goals. In this way, players explained how they sometimes chose a certain location or took a certain photo in order to elicit a specific reaction from the other players.

"The game asked me to show a place for thought. There are a lot of places I thought would be helpful for me to think. I ended up doing the washroom which was funny. But it did make me think about, 'Which one do I want to show my friends?' I chose the washroom because I thought it would be funny for them." –P10 (on "show me a place for thought")

"[The record] was a different perspective I wanted to share with other people. Something they don't usually see. I felt like I had a responsibility to make that post." –P2

Conversely, Individual Players typically did not think about their audience when creating records. They found it harder to 'imagine' this audience, and, instead, play was about personal reflection only. When we asked them about whether they would continue to play after the study was over, they expressed an interest in having a stronger sense of audience and playing with a group of 'the right people':

"I'm not sure it's something I would play for years unless I had the right network of people to play it with... I think people I know would relate to those memories are people I would definitely want to include. Either family or friends I think would enjoy learning about these things." –P12

"I would be interested in playing over a longer period of time if it was more social. I would want to see what [other players] are doing." –P4

This finding suggests that the design of GEMS failed to evoke a strong sense of a 'future audience' in the act of recording place-based experiences and raises the question of how to represent this kind of audience effectively in storytelling interactions. We return to this in our discussion section. Overall, these results also show that a player's motivation and goals may change between individual and group play. Factors such as introspection, reflection, and posterity may be important for an individual player, but in a group setting, they may be superseded by the social goals that drive impression management.

MOTIVATION AND ENGAGEMENT

GEMS was designed to leverage personal, player-generated content as the core attraction: we wanted players to *want* to play because they were intrinsically motivated [34]. Yet we also had components to encourage play via extrinsic motivation (e.g., game narrative, directives) [34]. We discuss each next and identify how group play and travel acted as additional factors that influenced engagement.

Extrinsic Motivation

Our interviews revealed that participants were first motivated to play GEMS extrinsically. The design of GEMS included mechanics intended to help draw players into the game and prompt them to start creating stories: directives, time limits, and access tokens and narrative.

Directives

In general, directives seemed to be effective in supporting the storytelling process. First, they gave players an entry point for the game itself. All but two players completed the first directive which asks the player to document the place that feels most like home. Afterwards, players went on to complete further directives and some began to experiment with free-form records. The directives also gave players a point of departure for individual storytelling activities. As mentioned, interpretation of the directive was the first step in the storytelling process for many players.

"When I was trying to complete a specific objective, I thought about how certain places have more meaning than others." –P1

"[The directives] tried to invoke me to learn more about myself. It helped having someone ask me questions." –P4

Time Limit

When a player accepts a directive, they have two days to complete it and earn points before it expires and they receive a different directive. As mentioned, players were mindful of this limit, but they were not mindful of it in the way we intended. In the design process, we introduced a time limit in order to set a pace for the game that encouraged players to engage on a somewhat regular basis. In practice, however, we found many players would circumvent this mechanic by 'putting off' accepting the directive until they had selected a location to talk about and had prepared media or travelled to the location. They described this tactic as a deliberate, strategic choice. This highlights the fact that participants saw record keeping as a reflective act where they preferred to have time to perform it rather than be 'rushed' and do it 'in the moment'.

Access Tokens and Narrative

Outside of content created by other players, the primary rewards in GEMS were access tokens and game narrative, which could be purchased with the tokens. Most players acknowledged access tokens as a light but encouraging reward. They expressed a feeling of delight in accumulating access tokens even though they were not a top priority.

"[Earning tokens] felt good. It was good. It was nice to get a reward for certain things. I probably would've done it without them, but at the same time, it was nice." –P6

Moreover, we found that the application of access tokens toward unlocking fragments of information in the databank served as a more substantial reward for some players who were interested in pursuing the narrative. Part of this interest stemmed from a general curiosity for storylines while part stemmed from a desire to complete the game. They understood the narrative as a measure of their progress in the game and wanted to unlock databank items for the sake of reaching the end.

"I guess it would be the motivation to the game for me. If you didn't have the narrative, it would be more like a twitter feed and the narrative was the motivation for me to continue on." –P10

"[Databank items] are kind of the story behind it. I really love stories, so I think it's kind of a fun way and an interesting way to think about what you're doing. It's kind of like reading a book while you're playing a game which is kind of an interesting concept" –P12

Conversely, some players felt indifferent towards the databank. They did not feel that it was an important or necessary part of the game, or they were not particularly interested in the style and content of the narrative. Consequently, they simply ignored it. Similarly, some players seemed to forget it existed.

"I didn't know how or why [unlocking databank items] would benefit me. I was indifferent." –P13

While the narrative was not completely effective, we believe the more positive responses indicate that it can function as a source of extrinsic motivation for some people. Other people may simply not need narrative to be compelled to create records, which we describe next.

Intrinsic Motivation

Our interviews revealed that the motivation for participants to play GEMS was not initially intrinsic. Yet, over time, once players 'got into the game,' personal content engaged players on an intrinsic level. For many players, the moments that stood out from their experience with the game were the ones that involved a novel discovery through personal reflection. They expressed a sense of delight in working through a thought-provoking directive and discovering some new aspect of their own identity or history. One participant said that the directive that stood out for him was one that asked him to show a place of triumph:

"I expanded my concept and had to think of a triumph that was a little farther back in time when I was a lot younger. I had to think about it more than usual" –P1

This player was aware of how many points he earned and how many directives he had completed, but the internal discovery was his favorite part of the game. Other players expressed a similar delight in moments that challenged them to produce something personal or think in a new way.

"I found I became more aware of potential areas that I could document. For example, I would do ritual visits to the library. And I had already done one log of the library, so I was looking to find somewhere besides the library. I wanted to find somewhere new." –P10

"Those are definitely places I wouldn't think about when I'm present there. But when it's prompting me to think about these places...where are they? Why are they? It's a more reflective process." –P12

This kind of engagement occurred for those who were playing with other people they knew. Group play seemed to enhance the level of engagement with the game. Collecting or creating a record with an audience in mind resulted in novel or meaningful moments.

"For me, I have the disconnect of not being at home anymore. I have friends here who don't know about where I'm from, so I could tell them if you go here, here's an extra reason why it would be kind of fun to check out." –P12

In these cases, players were interested in creating stories in GEMS as a way to fulfill some interpersonal goal. They considered location as a reflection of a person's personality and history, and described a level of engagement that reached beyond points or progress in the game.

All but one of the Group Players claimed to be interested in the activities of the others. Moreover, they suggested that a high level of activity among friends generated interest playing the game. Conversely, they admitted to losing interest during periods where their friends were not creating many records.

"As I got busier with school, it became the last thing on my mind...But the least I could do was collect other people's records." –P2

"I tried to see who was uploading new things. My ritual of checking on them started to taper off when they didn't make any records for a while." –P10

For most players, this group of players needed to include people they were comfortable sharing with and people who had some similar interests and experiences with a social tie to them. They described this as close friends or family.

Travel

We learned that players were much less willing to travel for the sake of creating and collecting records than we anticipated. In the design process, we assumed players would enjoy the opportunity to experience the past and present 'simultaneously' by physically visiting locations. In practice, the cost of time and distance outweighed the novelty or nostalgia of authoring or consuming a story in its location of origin. Most participants felt it was too difficult to travel to each location to embed stories.

"Some of the places were not as easy to get to. When they were too hard to get to, I didn't feel like I was really playing properly. But it was awesome to get the bonus points for making the record in place. That made me want to go make the entries in the actual location more." –P1

Similarly, many players felt that it was too difficult to collect distant records because they did not have the time to travel to far-away locations. We allowed players to decide if their own records had to be physically visited in order to be collected or if they could be collected remotely. Most Group Players commented that it was too difficult to collect the ones that required them to travel.

"I wish I could venture out and collect the far away ones, but I don't know when that's going to happen. It makes it more interesting, but it's also too hard." –P2

"[Collecting records] seemed like a really interesting idea. I did do that. I did the general pickup. I didn't go looking for records....I'm confined to transit, and most participants were out of my range. It was like, 'You are here. Everyone else is over here. Darn.'" –P6

DISCUSSION

We now summarize and discuss our findings and outline the lessons we learned for the design of new experiences to capture and share location-based experiences.

The Role of Location for Storytelling

First, our design work and study revealed that location can function as an entry point for storytelling. When we asked players to think about location first, they were able to generate meaningful content. This happened both opportunistically and in a planned manner with additional reflection. Location also provided opportunities for rediscovery. Together, this illustrates the value in designing richer interactions for collecting and sharing location-based experiences that go beyond simple 'check-ins' and geo-tagged pictures and video. It also shows a different pattern of usage than studies of people who play Foursquare [25]. Systems like Foursquare allow individuals to visit a place and say, "I was here". GEMS shows that there is room beyond this basic 'check in' to enrich a place with detailed personal stories: people can not only indicate the places they have been to but also the reasons they had for going, the things they did, and the feelings that had.

Presence vs. Convenience

We did not expect players to perceive distance as a discouraging obstacle for location-based storytelling. Originally, and perhaps naively, we imagined that players would be excited to visit unfamiliar or forgotten places and that distance would be understood as more of a measurement of challenge or a sign of potential adventure. Instead, players often considered physically travelling to a location (for both creation and collection) an obstacle and used the remote creation features more often than expected. This suggests that games or systems designed for users to create location-based stories should consider alternative, remote methods of creating and collecting records.

Comparing this to commercially-available systems (e.g., Foursquare, geotagged photos), we see this is not the norm where content must be created at the location of interest [25,28]. We also see that this contrasts play in other LBGs like Geocaching where players *must* go to locations to create content [29,32]. When consuming content, players of games like Foursquare can view content anywhere. This reflects the way participants in our study wanted to view records created by others. Conversely, for Geocaching, many people report on the enjoyment in visiting new locations to consume content [29,32]. We believe this difference stems from the volume of players in Geocaching when compared to our study of GEMS. In Geocaching, players can consume content placed by anyone and because of this, there are large amounts of it around. Yet in GEMS, content is much more limited and widespread across large distances, depending on where other players reside. Thus, players are likely to have to travel further to view content.

The Role of the Audience

We also learned that the 'audience' is important for player-created content. Participants purposely thought about who would view their content when they created it. This was especially the case for Group Players who had an easier time since they were playing with others they knew. On the other hand, Individual Players had a more difficult time with this and talked about the need for some kind of more explicit audience or group when they imagined leaving content for future generations to collect. In related systems, like Foursquare or Geocaching, an audience is implicitly provided because of the large volume of players [29,32]. Yet with games like GEMS, the audience will be much smaller and more targeted, and harder to 'imagine' when creating content for future players.

This suggests that presentations of a future social circle, albeit fabricated by the game, may be compelling to try to explore for the case of intergenerational play. For example, games could create representations of what a future child may look like and include this person in the game's narrative or structure. Of course, this is a preliminary idea that needs to be tried and tested. There are also likely many other ways to create the sense of an audience for intergenerational play. Designers should think carefully about how future players are presented to support the wide range of individuals and relationships that players may wish to create records for.

The Value of Motivation

GEMS included elements to support extrinsic motivation and we also hoped the activity of recording location-based experiences would encourage intrinsic motivation. Open-ended objectives (our directives) worked well for structuring the storytelling process and inspiring reflection. People also wanted to have the time to think about a directive and reflect on it without feeling pressure to complete a record in a short time period. This contrasts the way people quickly check-in to systems like Foursquare [25] or take multitudes of digital photos on cameras [18,28], often based on fleeting thoughts and moments. It was obvious from our interviews that recording stories of one's experiences in GEMS was emotionally-involved and sometimes felt like work. Thus, participants required additional intrinsic motivation to fully engage with the game and create records. This is more similar to the ways in which people carefully plan and construct content in Geocaching [29]. Overall, these findings suggest that both extrinsic and intrinsic motivation are important for games designed to support the act of location-based reflection and storytelling. Without extrinsic motivation, it is unlikely that players will actively engage with the game, at least initially. Similarly, without intrinsic motivation, players will not have a deep enough investment in the game to create and leave behind compelling content.

Generalizing to Other Applications and Scenarios

Beyond the scope of personal record keeping and intergenerational communication, we believe GEMS could provide a model for designing similar systems in other areas. It could, for example, be adapted for tourism to help tourists connect with locals or with other tourists. One could imagine that a digital network of geolocated personal stories would be compelling for travellers in search of 'authentic' or novel places in popular destinations. This kind of application suggests a system like Bedwell et al.'s Anywhere game [4] but with a focus on personal stories. Similarly, we believe a system like GEMS holds potential to enhance genealogy and family history activities. If the game directives were adjusted to refer to the player's family members instead of to the player, the game could help family historians match different branches of their family trees to specific places. Of course, these are initial design ideas, and they would need to be further refined and evaluated as part of future work.

CONCLUSION

In this paper we have contributed the design and implementation of a fully-playable location-based game called GEMS that provides people with a new way to document and share place-based experiences. GEMS explores how designs can give location a prominent role in the process of documenting and sharing experiences. Our goal was to leverage location both as inspiration for telling stories and as a strong context for listening to them. We also contributed a study of GEMS where players participated in the game over the course of three weeks. Our study findings show that narrative and game mechanics can encourage storytelling, yet intrinsic motivation is also needed to support longer term play and full engagement with the creation of meaningful content. Audiences are also important and designs that attempt to capture user content over time and share it with others must ensure appropriate audiences exist, even if they are future users.

ACKNOWLEDGMENTS

This research was funded by a SSHRC Insight Development grant and the GRAND Network of Centres of Excellence. We thank members of the Connections Lab for their help and support.

REFERENCES

1. Ahren, S. Eckles, D., Good, N., King, S., Naaman, M., and Nair, R. Over-Exposed? Privacy Patterns and Considerations in Online and Mobile Photo Sharing, *Proc. CHI,* ACM Press (2007).
2. Ames, M., Eckles, D., Naaman, M., Spasojevic, M., and House, N. Requirements for Mobile Photoware, *Personal & Ubiquitous Computing,* 14(2), (2010).
3. Balabanović, M., Chu L. L., and Wolff, G.J., Storytelling with Digital Photographs, *Proc CHI 2000,* ACM Press (2000).
4. Bedwell, B., Schnadelbach, H., Benford, S., Rodden, T., and Koleva, B., (2009) In Support of City Exploration, *Proceedings of the Conference on Computer Human Interaction,* ACM Press.
5. Bell M., Chalmers, M., Barkhuus, L., Hall, M., Sherwood, S., Tennent, P., Brown, B., Rowland, D., Benford S., Capra, M., Hampshire, A., Interweaving Games With Everyday Life, *Proc Chi 2006*, ACM Press (2006).
6. Bell, M., Reeves, S., Brown, B., Sherwood, S., McMillan, D., Ferguson, J., and Chalmers, M., Eyespy: Supporting Navigation Through Play, *Proc CHI 2009*, ACM Press (2009).
7. Benford, S., Crabtree, A., Flintham, M., Drozd, A., Anastasi, R., and Paxton, M. Can You See Me Now? (2006) In *ACM Transactions on Computer Human Interaction*, Vol. 13, No. 1, March, ACM Press, pp. 100–133.
8. Benford, S., Crabtree, A., Reeves, S., Flintham, M., Drozd, A., Sheridan, J., and Dix, A. (2006) The Frame of the Game: Blurring the Boundary between Fiction and Reality, *Proceedings of the Conference on Computer Human Interaction,* ACM Press.
9. Bentley, F., Basapur, S., and Chowdhury, S., Promoting Intergenerational Communication Through Location-Based Asynchronous Video Communication, *Proc. UbiComp '11*, ACM Press (2008).
10. Capra, M., Radenkovic, M., Benford, S., Oppermann, L., Drozd, A., and Flintham, M., The Multimedia Challenges Raised by Pervasive Games, *Proc MM '05,* ACM Press (2005).
11. Chalfen, R. *Snapshot Versions of Life*, Popular Press (1987).
12. Crabtree, A., Rodden, T., and Mariani, J. Collaborating around Collections: Informing the Development of Photoware, *Proc. CHI,* ACM Press (2004).
13. Freidus, N., and Hlubinka, M. Digital Storytelling for Reflective Practice in Communities of Learners. ACM SIGGROUP Bulletin, 23(2), 24-26.
14. Frohlich, D., Kuchinsky, A., Pering, C., Don, A., and Ariss, S. Requirements for photoware, *Proc. CSCW*, ACM Press (2002).
15. Goffman, E., The Presentation of Self, Doubleday (1959).
16. Hartley, J., McWilliam, K. Computational power Meets Human Contact. in Hartley J., and McWilliam T. ed. *Story Circle: Digital Storytelling Around the World.* Chichester, UK: Wiley-Blackwell.
17. Joinson, A.N., 'Looking at', 'Looking up' or 'keeping up with' People? Motives and Uses of Facebook. Proc. CHI, ACM Press (2008).
18. Kindberg, T., Spasojevic, M., Fleck, R., and Sellen, A. The Ubiquitous Camera: An In-Depth Study of Camera Phone Use, IEEE Pervasive Computing, 4(2), IEEE Computer Society (2005).
19. Kirk, D., Sellen, A., Rother, C., and Wood, K. Understanding Photowork, *Proc. CHI,* ACM Press (2006).
20. Klaebe, H., Foth, M., Burgess, J., and Bilandzic, M. Digital Storytelling and History Lines: Community Engagement in a Master-Planned Development, *Proc.* VSMM 2007, Springer (2007).
21. Kun, L. and Marsden, G. Co-Present Photo Sharing on Mobile Devices, *Proc. MobileHCI,* ACM Press (2007).
22. Lambert, J. Digital Storytelling: Capturing Lives,

Creating Community. Berkeley, CA: Digital Diner Press (2006).

23. Lindley, S. and Monk, A. Designing Appropriate Affordances for Electronic Photo Sharing Media, *Proc. CHI,* ACM Press (2006).

24. Linehan, C., Kirman, B., Lawson, S., and Doughty, M. Blowtooth: Pervasive Gaming in Unique and Challenging Environments, *Proc. CHI*, ACM Press (2010).

25. Lindqvist, J., Cranshaw, J., Wiese, J., Hong, J., and Zimmerman, J. I'm the Mayor of My House: Why People Use foursquare, *Proc. CHI,* ACM Press (2011).

26. McAuley, E., Duncan, T., and Tammen, V. V. Psychometric properties of the Intrinsic Motivation Inventory in a competitive sport setting: A confirmatory factor analysis. *Research Quarterly for Exercise and Sport*, 60 (1989), 48-58.

27. Miller, A., and Edwards, K. Give and Take: A Study of Consumer Photo-Sharing Culture and Practice, *Proc. CHI,* ACM Press (2007).

28. Neustaedter, C., and Fedorovskaya, E. Understanding and Improving Flow in Digital Photo Ecosystems, *Proc. Graphics Interface,* ACM Press (2009).

29. Neustaedter, C., Tang, A., and Judge. T, The Role of Community and Groupware in Geocache Creation and Maintenance, Proc. CHI 2010, ACM Press (2010).

30. Neustaedter, C. and Judge. T, See It: A Scalable Location-Based Game for Promoting Physical Activity, *Extended Proc. CSCW*, ACM Press (2012).

31. Nunes, M., Greenberg, S., and Neustaedter, C. Sharing Digital Photos in the Home through Mementos, *Proc. DIS 2008,* ACM (2008).

32. O'Hara, K. Understanding Geocaching Practices and Motivations, *Proc. CHI 2008*, ACM Press (2008).

33. Rodden, T. and Wood, K. How do people manage their digital photographs?, *Proc CHI,* ACM Press (2003).

34. Ryan, R.M., and Deci, E.L., Intrinsic and Extrinsic Motivations: Classic Definitions and New Directions, *Contemporary Educational Psychology,* 25 (2000), 54-67. doi:10.1006/cep.1999.1020.

35. Strauss, A. and Corbin, J., *Basics of Qualitative Research*, 2nd Edition, Sage Publications (1998).

36. Van House, N. Collocated photo sharing, story-telling, and the performance of self, *Int. J. Human-Computer Studies,* 67, Elsevier (2009).

37. Van House, N. Flickr and Public Image-Sharing: Distant Closeness and Photo Exhibition, *Proc. CHI,* ACM Press (2007).

VidWiki: Enabling the Crowd to Improve the Legibility of Online Educational Videos

Andrew Cross, Mydhili Bayyapunedi[1], Dilip Ravindran[1], Edward Cutrell, and William Thies

Microsoft Research India
{t-across, cutrell, thies}@microsoft.com

ABSTRACT

Videos are becoming an increasingly popular medium for communicating information, especially for online education. Recent efforts by organizations like Coursera, edX, Udacity and Khan Academy have produced thousands of educational videos with hundreds of millions of views in their attempt to make high quality teaching available to the masses. As a medium, videos are time-consuming to produce and cannot be easily modified after release. As a result, errors or problems with legibility are common. While text-based information platforms like Wikipedia have benefitted enormously from crowdsourced contributions for the creation and improvement of content, the various limitations of video hinder the collaborative editing and improvement of educational videos. To address this issue, we present VidWiki, an online platform that enables students to iteratively improve the presentation quality and content of educational videos. Through the platform, users can improve the legibility of handwriting, correct errors, or translate text in videos by overlaying typeset content such as text, shapes, equations, or images. We conducted a small user study in which 13 novice users annotated and revised Khan Academy videos. Our results suggest that with only a small investment of time on the part of viewers, it may be possible to make meaningful improvements in online educational videos.

Author Keywords

Online education; massive open online course; crowdsourcing; wiki; video annotation

ACM Classification Keywords

H.5.2 [**Information Interfaces and Presentation**]: User interfaces; K.3.0 [**Computers and Education**]: General

[1] Mydhili Bayyapunedi and Dilip Ravindran were interns at Microsoft Research India during this work. They can be reached at mydhilib@gmail.com and diliprr@berkeley.edu.

CSCW'14, February 15 - 19 2014, Baltimore, MD, USA

ACM 978-1-4503-2540-0/14/02...$15.00.
http://dx.doi.org/10.1145/2531602.2531670

INTRODUCTION

Today we are seeing a paradigm shift in online education. In the last 5 years, organizations such as Coursera, edX, Khan Academy, and Udacity have released thousands of hours of video that have been viewed millions of times by learners. Proponents of Massive Open Online Courses (MOOCs) envision a world where videos serve as the primary delivery vehicle for educational content distributed to learners across the planet via the Web. Further, the concepts of "flipped classrooms" and blended learning are gaining traction in K-12 and university classrooms worldwide. These teaching techniques replace primary in-person instruction with video tutorials, reserving class time for more in-depth interaction. In short, online educational videos have the potential to revolutionize education in both living rooms and traditional classrooms throughout the world. As a result, high-quality, legible, up-to-date content that is also customized for local languages and idioms is of utmost importance for educational videos.

Despite the appeal of educational video content, it remains very time-consuming to create, update, and localize videos. Professors spend enormous quantities of time creating content for their classes; this time and expense is one of the main bottlenecks to the growth of MOOCs. This situation is not unlike prior production of encyclopedias – Britannica, Encarta, etc. – where a huge compendium of information was slow and expensive to create. However, time has shown that the crowd can greatly reduce these costs while also improving quality and timeliness. While not an absolute authority, Wikipedia has been shown to be accurate [10], covering a wide range of topics [12], and is available in numerous languages worldwide. With that in mind, we ask: Can the crowd play a similar role in improving educational videos? In particular, can we leverage the vast number of students who are closely viewing educational videos, enabling them to "give back" a small amount of effort that benefits current and future classmates?

In this work, we take a small step towards this vision by creating a "wiki" for educational videos. While such a platform could evolve to allow editing many aspects of video, in this paper we restrict our attention to two things: legibility of text and graphics, and language localization.

Legibility of text and graphics remains an unrecognized challenge in many educational videos. Prior research has shown that viewers of videos enjoy seeing handwriting in real-time as a form of engagement, drawing users into the

Figure 1. TypeRighting example. Typeface fades in to replace each handwritten phrase soon after it is drawn.

lesson despite being physically separate from the speaker [5]. However, for reviewing or skimming a video for specific content, typeface presentation is preferred for its legibility and visual appeal [5]. A recently-proposed style of presentation called TypeRighting, illustrated in Figure 1, combines the benefits of handwriting and typeface by morphing each handwritten phrase into a typewritten version shortly after it appears [5]. While TypeRighting has shown strong potential – about 80% of viewers prefer to watch Khan Academy videos in this style, compared to the original – until now it has been difficult to produce videos in this format.

Language localization for the content of videos has also received little attention to date. While there are subtitling platforms to convey audio in different languages, the text in the video itself remains untranslated. Until now, the main remedy for this was to record a new video (or just leave the handwriting in the original language).

To address these problems, this paper describes the design, implementation, and usability evaluation of VidWiki: a tool that enables the crowd of students viewing educational videos to easily improve and localize those videos. While VidWiki bears some similarity to other tools for video annotation, none of these tools offer the features necessary for collaborative improvement of educational content. Using VidWiki, users can overlay text, shapes, images, equations, and hand-drawn content on top of a video to improve legibility and enable translation to multiple languages. Additionally, the annotations could be used to index textual content in the video, to convert the video to presentation slides (such as PowerPoint or similar), and potentially to save network bandwidth by loading only the audio and annotations, instead of the full video. Figure 2 illustrates an example video frame with overlain type in English and Hindi produced using VidWiki.

To explore the VidWiki user experience, we conducted a small user study asking 13 participants to annotate segments of Khan Academy videos. We measured their performance annotating videos from scratch, as well as incrementally improving on others' annotations. An expert administrator fine-tuned the annotations further to arrive at a final version of each video. On average, the annotating process required about 9.5 minutes of human effort for every 1 minute of video. When considering the size of the crowd viewing educational videos, the amount of work for a single user could be reduced drastically at scale. With just modest usage on the part of students, we believe that VidWiki could offer significant improvements to the overall viewing experience.

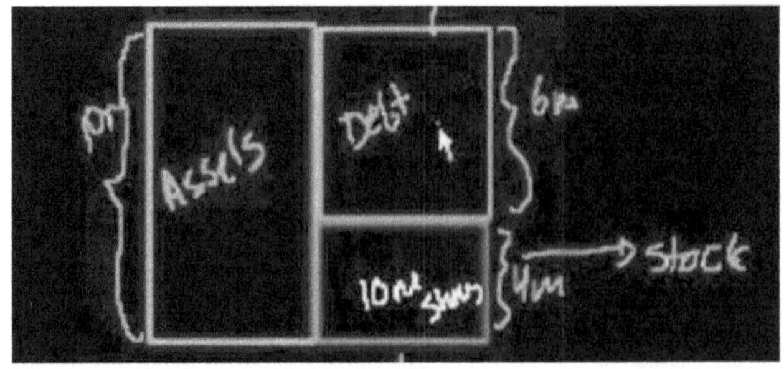

Figure 2a. Frame from original video

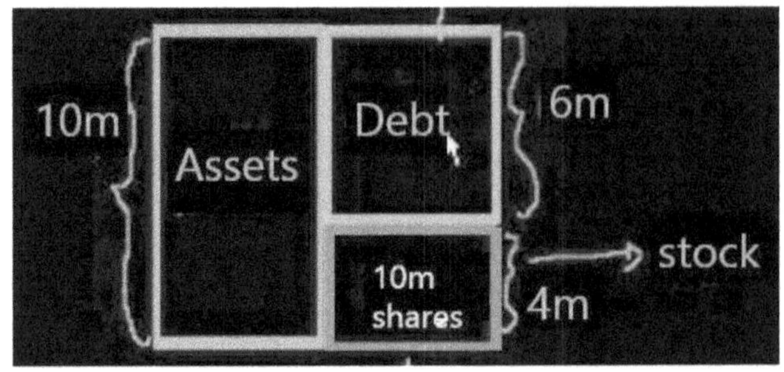

Figure 2b. Frame with annotations in English

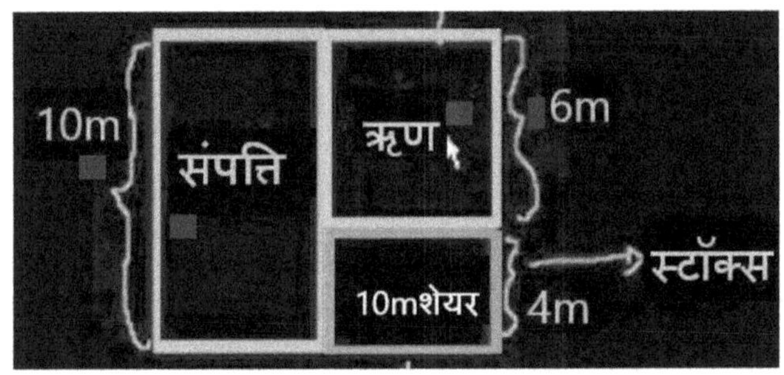

Figure 2c. Frame with annotations in Hindi

RELATED WORK

Prior tools for video annotation fall in three categories: annotating videos for indexing or object identification; adding captions; and altering videos by overlaying new content as a lens to highlight or obscure features in the video.

Several tools allow a user to create video annotations as a means to indexing videos or identifying objects in the video [16, 21, 25, 26]. These tools are all designed for marking up videos with metadata and do not have the capability to overlay text or other objects to obscure background content as part of seamless video playback. Annotations are used as additional content to build an index of objects or timings, rather than as a method to improve a video's visual quality.

Other captioning tools, such as YouTube Annotations [24] and Ambulant Captioner [18], allow users to add interactive features to videos with captions or links to other videos. However, these annotations do not fully obscure the text below, and do not allow custom shapes, equations, or images, making them inadequate to convert content to TypeRighting style.

A final group of annotation tools are designed to augment the video viewing experience by overlaying different kinds of content [11, 20, 22]. These tools are mostly domain-specific and are intended as supplemental content to draw attention to points in the video, rather than improve visual quality.

A recent release by Mozilla called PopcornMaker[1] combines several annotation concepts, allowing users to remix videos by adding additional content such as Wikipedia articles, online maps, or simple plain text. Although a powerful tool, remixes made using this platform are produced by a single user and not designed for collaborative editing. Produced videos are meant to be remixes, or collages of data, rather than an improved version of the original. The tool also lacks certain features necessary for annotating educational content such as panning events to shift annotations when an author scrolls the screen, or the ability to add equations for math or science videos.

Extensive research has examined the properties of collaborative crowdsourcing platforms, including volunteer incentives and editing behavior [1, 7], how most work is done by a minority of users [23], quantifying time spent editing or moderating an article [8], and optimizing the final quality while dealing with vandalism [2, 9, 13, 14]. This literature heavily influenced our design of VidWiki as a crowdsourcing platform.

GUIDING DESIGN PRINCIPLES

The purpose of VidWiki is fundamentally different from prior video annotation tools. While prior tools sought to *augment* videos with useful annotations, we seek to *replace* handwritten text with a typed overlay that exactly mirrors the content, style, and layout of the original video. Specifically, we aim to facilitate users' creation of TypeRighting annotations for handwritten content in videos. In the case of language translation, translated text entirely replaces the content underneath.

Design Goals

The most commonly-used tools influencing our initial design were PowerPoint animations and YouTube Annotations. However, there are several unique aspects of online educational videos that these tools are not well-equipped to address.

First, traditional caption annotations either persist throughout an entire video or frequently come and go (e.g., subtitles or YouTube Annotations). In contrast, in the majority of handwritten videos, objects such as text and drawings only disappear at two times: when the author clears the entire screen, or when they scroll the screen to reveal more blank space.

Second, because the added TypeRighting annotations aim to replace the original handwritten content, it is important for annotations to be opaque. That is, they should be filled with a background color that fully obscures the original content of the video. While this might seem like a simple feature, several existing tools support only transparent annotations. This makes them unfit for our purposes.

Third, given the vast audience of potential collaborators educational videos attract, the ability to crowdsource video annotations means that any annotation tool should support collaborative creation of content.

VidWiki is therefore a browser-based tool designed so that someone unfamiliar with video editing software can contribute. Annotations are modular, such that a video can be annotated all at once or revised in pieces at different times.

Constraints

There are several constraints that limit the capabilities of VidWiki. For example, one limitation is that it is difficult to programmatically access the pixel data of a video hosted in an outside domain, or frames within the video through a browser, and difficult for the server to process files without hosting or mirroring the videos ourselves. Because of this limitation, tools like an eyedropper tool to select color, or automatic recognition of on-screen text is difficult. Therefore, in its current incarnation, all annotations must be added manually. Future research will work toward automating steps that currently require human effort, for example, automatically generating some annotations that can later be checked, corrected or tweaked by annotators.

Since VidWiki is not a video editor, annotations are simply layers on top of the video that alter the appearance of the video without manipulating the actual pixel data. These layers are well-suited to our goals in this work, though they also have some limitations, such as at times obscuring recorded cursor or pointer movements in the video.

Other limitations affect the type of video that can be seamlessly annotated. When viewed as a tool to clean up legibility of text, VidWiki works particularly well with videos that maintain a stable background that primarily features text, like most Khan Academy videos and many other MOOC videos. However, videos that follow a speaker around or do not have a fixed background can be hard to annotate since the text location is unstable.

VIDWIKI

VidWiki allows users to draw annotations over a video canvas, altering the visual appearance of the video without modifying the video itself. A screenshot of the tool is shown in Figure 3, with various features highlighted. A video demonstration is also available online[2].

A user watching the video in a browser can toggle into the editing mode at any time. This mode reveals the extended toolset and properties shown in Figure 3. The various features are as follows:

[1] https://popcorn.webmaker.org/

[2] http://youtu.be/qtkymHwsRzo

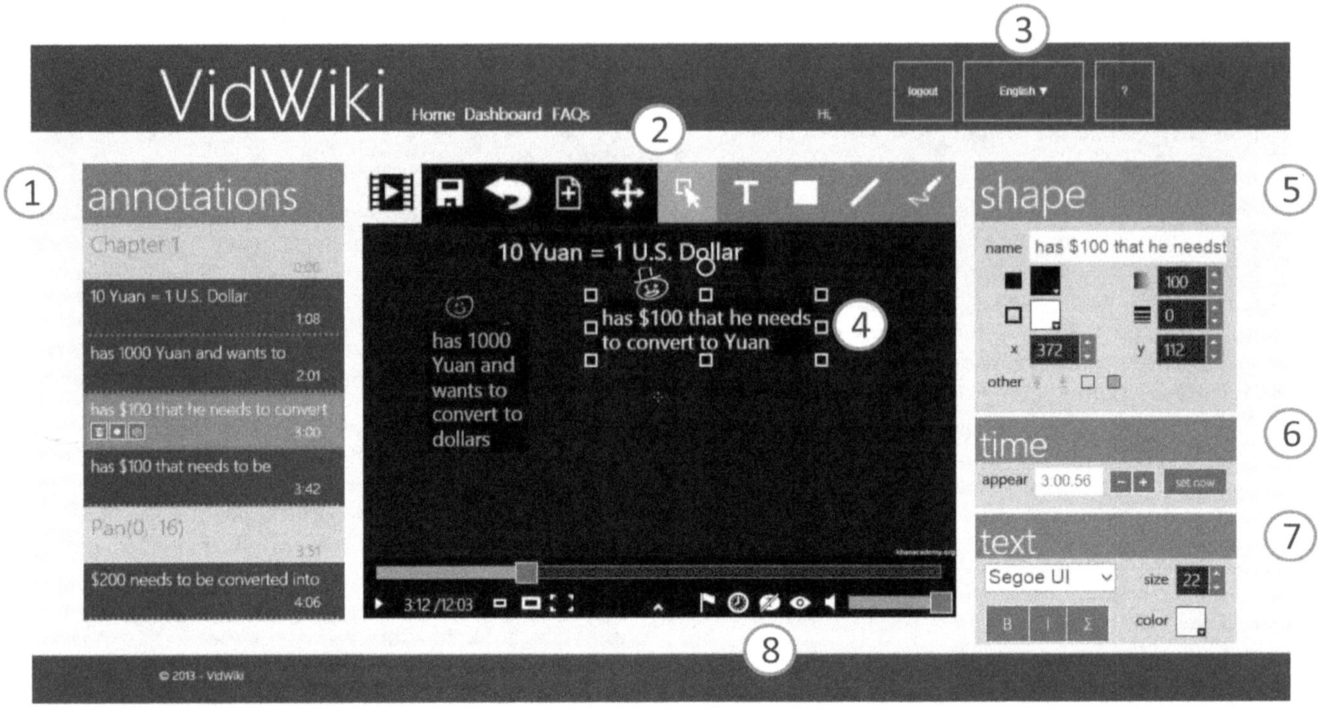

Figure 3. VidWiki and several salient features (see text for discussion).

1. An annotation list shows the current annotations and the time at which they appear.
2. The toolbar above the video allows a user to add annotations. The most commonly used tools are: a text tool, allowing entry of plaintext or LaTeX equations which are rendered over the video; a shape tool, which draws common shapes and also allows users to add images by their URL; a pen tool, which allows users to draw custom content; a chapter tool, which mimics a 'slide change' and clears all visible annotations; and a pan tool, which scrolls all visible annotations by a given pixel count.
3. A language selection menu. One usage for VidWiki is to create annotations in languages other than the original text language.
4. The annotations are drawn over the video, and are selectable to adjust sizing or position.
5. Shape properties including fill and stroke color, opacity, stroke width, and position.
6. Timing properties for when the annotation should appear. Annotations can only disappear with a chapter or pan event.
7. Text properties for color, font, size, decoration, and for rendering text as a LaTeX equation.
8. Video properties to show or hide annotations or subtitles. Users can also flag inappropriate content, or adjust the timing of all annotations relative to what the annotator specified. For example, one could introduce a delay in all the annotations, causing handwritten content to remain visible for a longer time before being obscured by typeface.

ADDING AN ANNOTATION

To add an annotation at a given time, a user follows the steps outlined in Figure 4. While in edit mode, the user selects the desired tool and draws the annotation directly over the video canvas. For text content, the user types the text, adjusts the font and color, and finally moves it into position over the original handwriting. The timing of the annotation can be tweaked in the timing panel, or set to the current video time.

Other annotations such as equations, images, shapes, or free-drawn content can be added in a similar way. Chapter and pan events, which clear and scroll the screen, respectively, are added by clicking on corresponding tool icons. Each annotation is a distinct unit, and any user can move, resize, delete, or adjust the timing.

Getting Annotations from the Crowd

While there is high potential to automate many of the features described above (e.g., using OCR), in the current incarnation, annotations are created manually by members of the crowd. They can be added piecemeal, or all at once; they can be edited, tweaked, or changed by other users of the platform.

Any platform that draws participation from the crowd faces challenges of merging conflicting annotations or vandalism. Many of these issues have been sorted out by projects such as Wikipedia. For now, VidWiki allows users to flag inappropriate content for a moderator to consider and take action. The history of revisions is available to system administrators, but is not yet exposed to users.

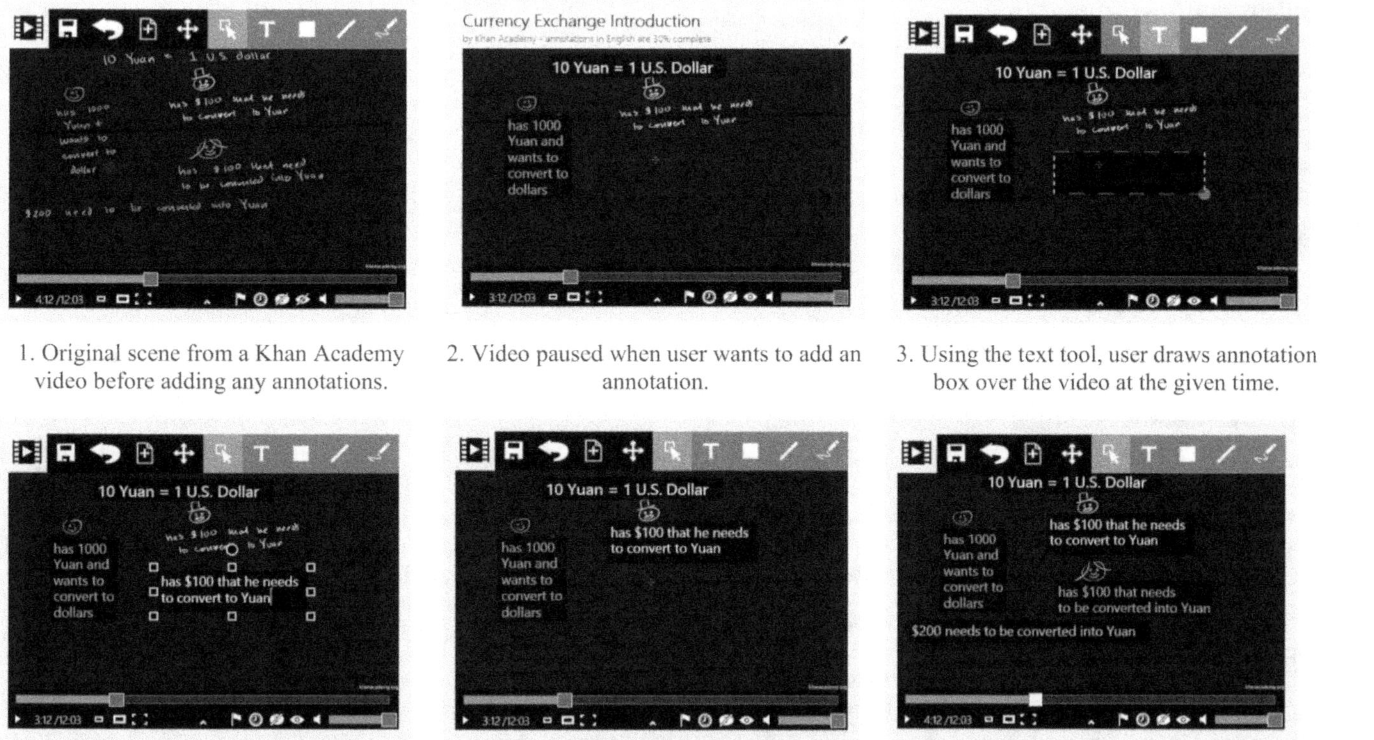

1. Original scene from a Khan Academy video before adding any annotations.
2. Video paused when user wants to add an annotation.
3. Using the text tool, user draws annotation box over the video at the given time.
4. User types the text for the annotation.
5. User adjusts font to match the video and moves annotation into place over the text.
6. Scene after user has added multiple annotations over the text.

Figure 4. Adding an annotation in VidWiki.

Translation of On-screen Text

Many MOOCs aspire to reach a global audience, including viewers who do not speak English as their primary language. Given the amount of time and effort required to create high-quality videos, it would be highly desirable to translate content from one language to another without having to re-record it from scratch. While tools such as Amara[3] enable subtitling of videos, they focus only on the audio track and do not translate the text content in the video itself.

VidWiki extends the capabilities of video translators by using annotations to display translations of on-screen text. The tool currently supports user-generated translations, where the author indicates the language in which text is typed, and the viewer can select among all of the available languages. In the future, machine translation can be used to produce the first pass of translated annotations, and a human can later make adjustments where needed. This model has previously been explored in the context of Wikipedia [17] but has not been applied to video content until now.

USER STUDY

Study Goals

There were two primary goals to our user study. The first was to evaluate the usability of VidWiki by novice users. As VidWiki introduces several novel concepts in video annotation, we sought to understand users' first time experiences with the tool.

The second goal was to explore the dynamics of annotating a video as a member of the crowd, including review and improvement of other users' annotations. In short, we wanted to explore the quality of annotations produced by novice users, how much time it took to annotate a set of videos, and how users managed this process in a collaborative setting.

The user study did not explore the translation aspect of VidWiki because we believe the authoring experience would be similar, provided the correct keyboard tools are available to type in a given language. Also, this study is not a substitute for a large-scale field trial of VidWiki, which (as discussed later) will be an important focus for future work.

[3] http://www.amara.org/

Participants

We conducted a usability evaluation of VidWiki with 13 students. All students were pursuing undergraduate or graduate studies in India, and 12 of the 13 specialized in computer science or a related technical field. None of them had ever used the VidWiki tool before. These students are typical of many viewers of online educational videos.

Methodology

Before initiating the task, each participant was given a 5-minute tutorial on using VidWiki. This in-person tutorial introduced the notion of annotating a video in the TypeRighting style, and demonstrated the various tools available for annotation in VidWiki. This demonstration used a previously annotated video different from those participants would work with later. We suggested that participants use large text when possible, keep the color scheme as similar to the video as possible, and have the annotations appear roughly three seconds after the author had finished handwriting a word, phrase, or number.

Each participant was given two separate Khan Academy videos to convert from handwritten style to TypeRighting style. The videos came from two economics playlists, and one statistics playlist from the Khan Academy website; they covered the topics of financial and capital markets, currency exchange, and an introduction to probability and statistics. The first video given to each participant was unannotated, and the participant's task was to annotate the first four minutes of the video from scratch. After completing the first task, each participant filled out a short survey on their experience using the tool and was directed to the second video.

The second video had been previously annotated by another participant, and the participant's task was to review the existing annotations and to fix or adjust where the annotations were inadequate with regards to content, color, position, or timing. If the current annotations were perfect, users could re-submit them without any changes. To bootstrap this process, the first participant revised a video prepared by the researchers. Following this, participants filled out a second survey on their experience to complete the trial.

We asked participants to annotate only the first four minutes of each video to keep the experiment short and because the videos varied in total duration. Therefore, 13 study participants annotated 52 minutes of video content, and revised another 52 minutes of video content. VidWiki was instrumented to track user actions and timing throughout the study. Though the trials were unassisted, a researcher was available nearby if a participant had any questions. Early questions were due to bugs in the initial system, or were about how to handle certain situations in videos such as when graphics and text were very close, requiring the text annotation to obscure the graphics as well. We extended our tutorial to cover these common issues and the amount of assistance towards the end of the experiment was minimal.

All timing data and survey results were anonymous and analyzed in aggregate. Both surveys used 5-point Likert-scale questions to assess the usability of VidWiki, the perceived quality of annotations, and the participants' willingness to annotate videos based on the final output and potential audience benefitting from their work. Participants were also given two free-response questions asking about the positive and negative aspects of the tool.

Results

To estimate the feasibility of using VidWiki to crowdsource video annotations, we wanted to understand both the usability of the system as well as how long it takes users to annotate videos. The participants annotated 52 minutes of video in a cumulative 321 minutes of work (M = 24.7, SD = 7.14 per four-minute video); participants revised 52 minutes of video in 121 minutes of work (M = 9.28, SD = 3.39 per video). Therefore, in total, it took a combined 8.5 minutes of novice work to annotate and revise each minute of the original video. Variability in annotation time was a product of both the participant's speed and the complexity of the video, as some videos had more text to annotate than others.

While our study aimed to examine usage by novices, there is obvious potential for users to become more efficient as they gain experience with the tool. As an example measure of how much efficiency could improve, a person familiar with the tool annotated each of the 13 videos from scratch, annotating 52 minutes of video in 101 minutes (M = 8.38, SD = 3.68 per video) corresponding to 1.93 minutes of annotation work for every minute of video.

Post-task surveys suggest that participants felt that 1) the video quality improved after each round of annotation and revision; 2) the tool was usable (also including many suggestions for further improvements); and 3) that participants felt the amount of time spent was reasonable if a large audience would benefit from their work. However, as participants were answering questions about the experimenter's technology, we acknowledge that the results may be biased by demand characteristics [6]. Summaries of survey responses on a 5-point Likert-scale (1 – Strongly Disagree, 5 – Strongly Agree) are shown in Figures 5 and 6.

Quality of Annotations

To assess the quality of participants' annotations, the first author served as a moderator, taking the revised annotations and fixing or improving them if necessary. Like moderators in online forums, this individual was familiar with the tool as well as the expected style and quality of the final annotations. It took the moderator 54.4 minutes to revise the existing 52 minutes of annotations (M = 4.18, SD = 1.46 per video). This amounts to only slightly more time than watching the videos to ensure correctness, a reasonable expectation of moderators on this and related platforms.

Adding this moderation time to the annotation and revision phases, it took a total of 496 minutes for novice workers to annotate, and a more experienced user to moderate the 52

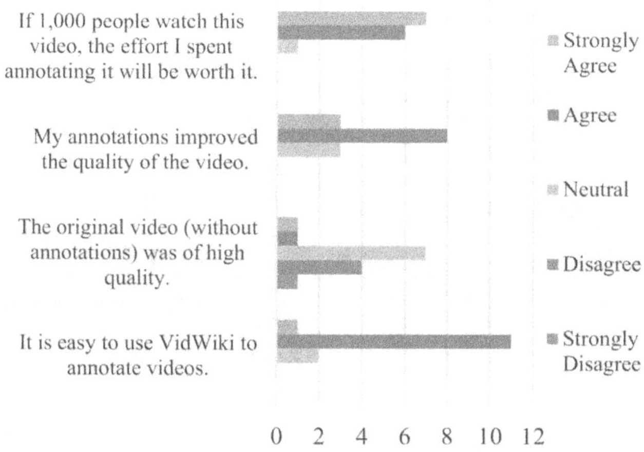

Figure 5. Results of survey after annotating a video.

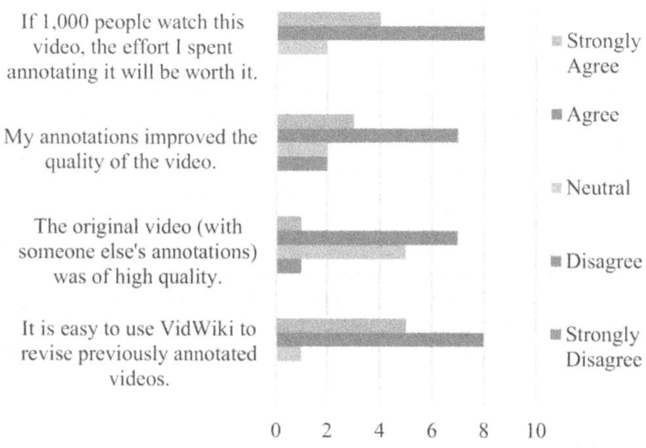

Figure 6. Results of survey after revising a video.

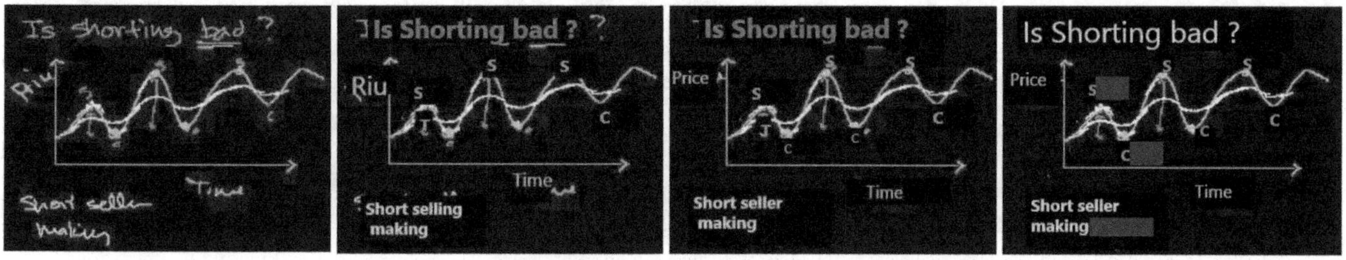

Scene from original video First user's annotations Second user's revisions of first user's annotations Final version after moderator's revisions

Figure 7. Iterative improvement of annotations during user study.

minutes of video; this corresponds to 9.5 minutes of combined novice and moderator work to annotate each minute of the original video.

Figure 7 shows a sample progression of a frame from the original video to the annotated final product. Figure 8 shows three additional videos before and after annotation, demonstrating the improvement in visual quality.

Common struggles, or situations that took the most time for users, involved perfecting the timing, location, or color of an annotation. Many of the tweaks in revisions were slight adjustments to these three annotation properties. Two videos included panning in the first four minutes which required more effort than adding text annotations, but participants were able to correctly add pan events.

After the annotations were revised, the videos had an average of 17 total annotations per video. Revisers changed the text content in 7% of annotations. Most changes were minor such as altering the text spacing by adding new lines or capitalizing words. Annotation timing was changed in 19% of annotations, where the average time adjustment was 6.9 seconds. Annotation text or shape color was changed in 9% of annotations. Some original annotators had not bothered to match color schemes at all, in which case the revisions added color. In other cases, revisers adjusted the colors to better match the background video.

DISCUSSION

In this study, novice users were able to use the VidWiki tool to successfully annotate and revise 52 minutes of content. Though it may seem expensive to invest 9.5 minutes of work for every minute of video and to involve three different users in the process, dividing the annotation tasks across thousands of students in a common MOOC context may be quite reasonable.

As an example, consider edX's inaugural course (MIT 6.002x), that enrolled almost 155,000 students. Even with the high attrition rates typical to MOOCs, over 7,000 people passed the course [19]. These students are highly motivated and invested, and, similar to contributors to Wikipedia, they represent the top percentage and those most likely to contribute video annotations. The 14-week course contained roughly 28 hours of lecture material, requiring 15,960 minutes of work to completely annotate given our experience in the user study. If each of those motivated 7,000 students invested about 2.3 minutes – either as volunteer work, an assignment, or even paid work – they could annotate the entire course. Since most MOOC video lectures are intended to be reused year after year, the cumulative effort of several consecutive classes of students could author the annotations and continuously revise them as needed. Khan Academy videos, while targeted at a younger, less-experienced audience, attract equally high numbers of viewers and potential annotators.

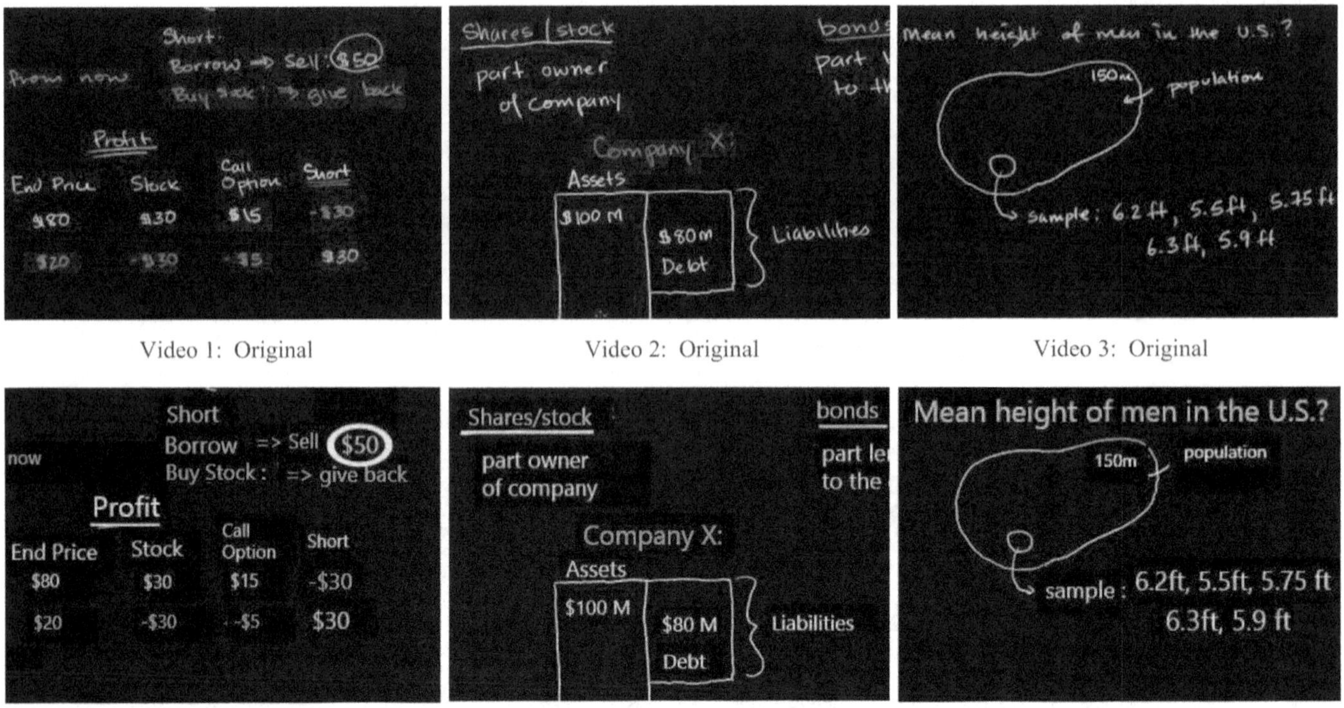

Video 1: Final with annotations   Video 2: Final with annotations   Video 3: Final with annotations

Figure 8. Frames from original and final versions of videos during user study.

A study on Wikipedia contributors estimates that the average session length, the time a user spends editing an article, is 10 minutes with some more expert users spending hours or entire days editing articles [8]. While annotating Wikipedia articles is predominately text editing, and annotating videos introduces other facets such as visual quality and timing, such findings suggest that it is feasible to ask each viewer to contribute 2.3 minutes of time to enhance an entire course.

As another point of comparison, a wiki on Coursera discusses the time required for contributors to add subtitles for the audio track and sync them with the video [5]. It suggests that it is not unreasonable to expect non-professionals to spend 15 minutes subtitling a single minute of video, which is about 50% longer than the time required for VidWiki annotations.

As an initial study into the usability of VidWiki, this paper does not observe patterns of real-world use, which will only be evident upon releasing the tool to a larger audience. A future deployment at scale may reveal interesting new facets of collaborative annotating that could promote or hinder VidWiki's success.

Motivation to Contribute

There are open questions regarding students' motivation and willingness to contribute annotations, either voluntarily or in response to incentives. The survey responses show that while annotating videos takes time, students are willing to contribute knowing that their work can benefit a large number of peers. Augmenting this intrinsic motivation with the right incentive structure could be key for the future success of the platform.

There are several models that might prove fruitful, such as assigning annotation work as homework, leveraging a teaching assistant (or similar role) to help contribute, or paying workers to annotate. Any of these schemes could tap into the large audience already watching educational videos; this is the population most familiar with the content and, arguably, most motivated to want to improve it. In contrast to more complicated video editing tasks that require experts, VidWiki allows the annotation process to be broken up into smaller tasks appropriate for volunteers with little training. Khan Academy has an integrated "points" system whereby learners earn credit for watching videos or answering questions; annotating could be another way to earn points. More formal MOOC classes have certificates based on credit, so annotating could even become a requirement for receiving credit.

Subsets of users do contribute to forums and Wikipedia articles without any direct benefits such as course credit or financial incentives. Prior research has explored how to maximize the likelihood that a reader or viewer of crowdsourced content might contribute [15]; a similar exploration for VidWiki could evaluate related incentives.

CONCLUSIONS AND FUTURE WORK

We present VidWiki, an online browser-based tool to facilitate on-screen annotation of educational videos to improve their visual quality and localize their language. The tool allows novice users to add layers on top of a video, overlaying handwritten content with more legible typeface, or extending a video by adding other annotations like equations, shapes, images, or free-drawn custom content.

We tested the tool with 13 users unfamiliar with the system who annotated several Khan Academy videos, requiring 9.5 minutes of work for each minute of the video to be annotated. Extending this to the online scenario where Khan Academy videos have over 200,000 viewers, and MOOC courses have anywhere from 10,000 to 160,000 students on each iteration of the course, such a tool could enable large crowds of students to collaboratively annotate and improve lecture videos through various incentive schemes.

In the future, one could extend VidWiki to include audio recording and real-time capture of typed or penned annotations, so that an author could record entire lectures through the browser. This would further lower the expertise required to author an instructional video. Once a video or course is authored in the tool, the annotations are already inserted as modular objects, ready for translation, resizing, rearrangement, recoloring, etc., by authors or collaborators who seek to modify, update, or extend the video.

ACKNOWLEDGMENTS

We are grateful to Jessica Herron for her contributions to the design and user experience of VidWiki, and to Steven Drucker for his support for the project. We thank Nakull Gupta for preparing VidWiki for a broader release, and Vidya Natampally and the Microsoft Research Connections team for their ongoing support. We also thank the participants and the anonymous reviewers for their thoughtful feedback.

REFERENCES

1. Antin, J., Cheshire, C., & Nov, O. Technology-mediated contributions: editing behaviors among new Wikipedians. *CSCW,* (2012).
2. Arazy, O., & Nov, O. (2010). Determinants of wikipedia quality: the roles of global and local contribution inequality. *CSCW,* (2010).
3. Ayache, S., Quénot, G., & Tseng, A. The ligvid system for video retrieval and concept annotation. *CBMI,* (2010).
4. Coursera: Video Subtitles, https://share.coursera.org/wiki/index.php/Video_Subtitles
5. Cross, A., Bayyapunedi, M., Cutrell, E., Agarwal, A., & Thies, W. TypeRighting : Combining the Benefits of Handwriting and Typeface in Online Educational Videos. *CHI,* (2013).
6. Dell, N., Vaidyanathan, V., Medhi, I., Cutrell, E., and Thies, W., "Yours is Better!" Participant response bias in HCI. *CHI*, (2012).
7. Dow, S., Kulkarni, A., Klemmer, S., & Hartmann, B. Shepherding the crowd yields better work. *CSCW,* (2012).
8. Geiger, R., & Halfaker, A. Using edit sessions to measure participation in Wikipedia. *CSCW,* (2013).
9. Geiger, R., & Ribes, D. The work of sustaining order in Wikipedia: the banning of a vandal. *CSCW,* (2010).
10. Giles, G. Internet encyclopaedias go head to head. Nature, 438 (2005), 900-901.
11. Goldman, D., & Gonterman, C. Video object annotation, navigation, and composition. *UIST,* (2008).
12. Halavais, A., & Lackaff, D. An analysis of topical coverage of Wikipedia. *Journal of Computer-Mediated Communication*, (2008).
13. Halfaker, A., Keyes, O., & Taraborelli, D. Making peripheral participation legitimate: reader engagement experiments in Wikipedia. *CSCW,* (2013).
14. Hansen, D., Schone, P., & Corey, D. (2013). Quality control mechanisms for crowdsourcing: peer review, arbitration, & expertise at family search indexing. *CSCW,* (2013).
15. Hoffmann, R., Amershi, S., Patel, K., Wu, F., Fogarty, J., & Weld, D. S. (2009). Amplifying community content creation with mixed initiative information extraction. *CHI,* (2009).
16. Kipp, M. (2008). Spatiotemporal coding in anvil. *LREC,* (2008).
17. Kumaran, A., Saravanan, K., & Maurice, S. (2008). wikiBABEL: community creation of multilingual data. *WikiSym,* (2008).
18. Laiola Guimarães, R., Cesar, P., & Bulterman, D. Creating and sharing personalized time-based annotations of videos on the web. *DocEng,* (2010).
19. Lessons Learned from MITx's prototype course, (2012). http://web.mit.edu/press/2012/mitx-edx-first-course-recap.html.
20. Lux, M., & Riegler, M. (2013). Annotation of endoscopic videos on mobile devices: a bottom-up approach. *MMSys,* (2013).
21. Müller, S., Miller, G., & Fels, S. Using temporal video annotation as a navigational aid for video browsing. *UIST,* (2010).
22. Singh, V., Latulipe, C., Carroll, E., & Lottridge, D. The choreographer's notebook: a video annotation system for dancers and choreographers. *ACM C&C,* (2011).
23. Stuckman, J., & Purtilo, J. (2009). Measuring the wikisphere. *WikiSym,* (2009).
24. Yuen, J., & Russell, B. Labelme video: Building a video database with human annotations. *IEEE Conference on Computer Vision*, (2009).
25. YouTube Annotations, http://www.youtube.com/t/annotations_about
26. Zimmermann, T., & Weber, M. CoVidA: pen-based collaborative video annotation. *VIGTA,* (2012).

Should Your MOOC Forum Use a Reputation System?*

Derrick Coetzee dcoetzee@eecs.berkeley.edu **Armando Fox** fox@cs.berkeley.edu **Marti A. Hearst** hearst@ischool.berkeley.edu **Björn Hartmann** bjoern@eecs.berkeley.edu
Computer Science Division and School of Information
University of California, Berkeley, CA 94720, USA

ABSTRACT
Massive open online courses (MOOCs) rely primarily on discussion forums for interaction among students. We investigate how forum design affects student activity and learning outcomes through a field experiment with 1101 participants on the edX platform. We introduce a reputation system, which gives students points for making useful posts. We show that, as in other settings, use of forums in MOOCs is correlated with better grades and higher retention. Reputation systems additionally produce faster response times and larger numbers of responses per post, as well as differences in how students ask questions. However, reputation systems have no significant impact on grades, retention, or the students' subjective sense of community. This suggests that forums are essential for MOOCs, and reputation systems can improve the forum experience, but other techniques are needed to improve student outcomes and community formation. We also give a set of guidelines for running field experiments on MOOCs.

Author Keywords
Massive open online course; MOOC; forum; reputation system.

ACM Classification Keywords
H.5.3. Information Interfaces and Presentation (e.g. HCI): Group and Organization Interfaces; K.3.1. Computers and Education: Computer Uses in Education

INTRODUCTION
Massive open online courses (MOOCs), such as those currently operated by Coursera, edX, and Udacity, typically include hundreds to thousands of students in each course. Traditional social structures of on-campus courses, such as direct interaction of teachers with each student, become infeasibly expensive at this scale. As Chamberlin and Parish lamented, "The number of people in a course can be overwhelming! How does someone connect with 2000-plus people?" [4].

CSCW'14, February 15–19, 2014, Baltimore, Maryland, USA.
ACM 978-1-4503-2540-0/14/02.
http://dx.doi.org/10.1145/2531602.2531657

A scalable alternative is interaction among students in an online discussion forum, in which students can assist one another. This model has been pervasive and successful in learning communities on the open web [36]. However, some forums are effective in creating learning communities while others are not, and a poor sense of community has been linked to high student attrition [39], which has been observed in practice in MOOCs [8].

Large, popular question answering forums on the web, such as Yahoo! Answers and Stack Overflow, have been successful in generating communities with high participation, quick responses, and quality content [1, 24]. These forums generally rely on *reputation systems* [29], which provide extrinsic rewards such as "reputation points" for timely, high-quality contributions. We investigate whether forums in general — and reputation systems in particular — can help to promote learning and a successful student community in the MOOC context. We target five main research questions:

1. *Is forum participation correlated with student learning outcomes*, such as student retention and final grades? Online forums benefit students in traditional courses [5] — do they have similar effects in a MOOC?
2. *Do reputation systems improve forum participation metrics* like number of unanswered questions and response time? Prior work showed that Stack Overflow's reputation system helps to keep response times close to the minimum possible [24]. Can a reputation system achieve similar benefits in a MOOC forum?
3. *Do reputation systems affect the type of content posted on class forums?* Different incentive systems change the kinds of questions that are asked [19]. Will the reputation system alter how students ask questions?
4. *Do reputation systems affect student learning outcomes?* If reputation systems increase forum participation, students may have access to alternative explanations of concepts and spend more time explaining material to others (as in reciprocal teaching [28]), which could lead to improved learning as measured by course assessments.
5. *Do reputation systems affect the student's subjective sense of community*, their sense that they belong to a community of learners who they can rely upon? The incentives provided by reputation systems may have a positive effect if they lead to increased engagement, or a negative effect, if they interfere with students' intrinsic motivations and promote competition over cooperation [19, 12].

We investigate these questions in a between-subjects field experiment on a single course on the edX platform. $N = 1101$ participants were assigned to forums with and without reputation features. In line with previous work on traditional courses [5], we find that forum participation is correlated with higher grades and higher retention. Presence of forum reputation features significantly affects forum participation, increasing the number of responses and decreasing the time to first response. Reputation features also curtail certain language usage patterns like appeals for help. However, reputation features did not have a significant impact on students' assessment outcomes or their sense of community. Overall, these results suggest that reputation systems can improve the forum experience, but do not contribute substantially to assessment outcomes or community formation in the current MOOC context.

RELATED WORK

Relevant prior work includes research on forums in traditional classes; answering sites for informal learning communities; language use in online forums; and the current generations of MOOCs. We discuss each area in turn.

Students and Forums

Online discussion forums have been used to support on-campus courses since the early 1990s, when they were based on mailing lists and Usenet [7]. Effective forums contribute to learning through community building and collaborative dialogues. The cognitive apprenticeship model in learning theory, wherein more experienced peers and experts provide the minimal assistance needed to complete tasks until autonomy is achieved, helps to explain the benefits of forums for problem solving [20].

Students who voluntarily participate in forums have been found to achieve better exam grades and perform better overall, even when only viewing content and with minimal instructor interaction [5]. We expect that forum use will also improve student outcomes in MOOCs. Intent to participate in forums has been linked to two motivational factors: the perceived importance of learning, and peer pressure, the sense that peers are putting effort into the forum [41]. The importance of peer pressure suggests that even interventions that generate small changes to participation can have a larger indirect effect.

Q&A Sites and Reputation Systems

Question and answer (Q&A) sites provide responses to specific questions and often discourage discussion not related to a question. Nevertheless, they are used both for informational purposes (as intended) as well as for conversational purposes [18]. Popular examples include Yahoo! Answers, for general topics, and Stack Overflow, for software development. Investigations of existing sites typically focus on characterizing usage patterns through large scale data analysis, without comparing design alternatives, as researchers are unable to modify the system. For example, Adamic et al. characterize activity on Yahoo! Answers by clustering categories of questions based on text and user features [1]; Mamykina et al. measure response times on Stack Overflow and categorize users based on quantitative behavior metrics [24].

Q&A sites rely on reputation systems, in which participants receive extrinsic rewards such as "reputation points" when their contributions are rated as useful by others. Reputation systems are thought to encourage participation, increase contribution quality, and identify reliable information. They originate on electronic marketplaces where they help identify trustworthy participants [29], and have been used to support both student discussion forums [6] and social collaborative learning systems [32]. In Tausczik's investigation of Math Overflow [34], a Q&A site for mathematics research, "[u]ser behavior suggests that building reputation is an important incentive, even though users do not report this in the survey."

Reputation systems as extrinsic motivators may also have negative consequences. Dearman found that Yahoo! Answers users employed reputation as a cue to withhold answers – if the questioner was known for assigning low scores to increase their own points, then others would be reluctant to respond [11]. Tangible extrinsic motivators such as money or candy can also diminish feelings of community and bonding [12]. On the other hand, in a comparison of a for-fee market-based answer forum to a system with a top-10 leader board [19], the reputation-based system had more socially-conducive community building questions, suggesting that the discouraging effects of reputation points are not as severe as those of tangible extrinsic motivators.

Despite their ubiquity, there has been little systematic investigation into whether and how reputation systems benefit sites which use them. Researchers have however systematically studied the impact of other design features on online communities. Harper [16, 17] and Ludford [21] report on online field experiments motivated by social design to increase participation at the MovieLens film recommender site. Our work similarly is a field experiment designed to study the impact of specific design features (reputation systems) on course participation and assessment outcomes.

Communication in Forums

Our work investigates language differences between the two experimental forums. In particular, in the absence of the extrinsic incentives of a reputation system, students may have to take extra steps to encourage responses. Studies from social psychology have shown that demonstrations of gratitude can increase efforts to assist someone even when those efforts are costly, and that gratitude can increase assistance provided to strangers [2, 14]. Other language usage such as ending an information need with a question mark, explicitly scoping the audience, and being succinct, can also increase the likelihood of quickly receiving many high-quality answers on social networks [35]. As described in the results, we focus on appeals for help such as "thanks for any help," which can be interpreted as pre-emptive expressions of gratitude.

MOOCs

Massive open online courses (MOOCs) are online courses with open enrollment that typically have thousands of active students. They originated with the University of Manitoba's Connectivism and Connective Knowledge MOOC in 2008 [22], and have precursors in instructional video sites like Khan Academy [37]. Forums are pervasive in MOOCs and have been characterized as "an essential ingredient of an effective online course" [23], but early investigations of MOOC forums show struggles to retain forum users over time. In one example, half of forum users ceased participation due to factors such as lack of forum facilitation, an overwhelming number of messages, and rude behavior of other students [23]. Published research on MOOCs has thus far focused on reflections on the MOOC experience and the great number and diversity of students who participate [25, 9]. In contrast, we provide a systematic, comparative study of design alternatives and their impact on MOOC students.

Recently, researchers have begun to develop and evaluate new technology to facilitate learning in MOOCs. ARTful [33] uses EEG technology to track student attention and later uses this information to suggest material for review, while Pex4Fun [38] uses automated test generation techniques to assist in automated grading in programming courses. Although these techniques are valuable, they are presently limited by special hardware requirements and a restricted topic domain, respectively. We aim instead to evaluate enhancements to existing forum systems that are easy to deploy in current MOOC settings.

METHOD

We conducted a between-subjects field experiment on a seven-week, open-enrollment software engineering course offered on the edX platform ("CS169.1x: Software as a Service" from University of California, Berkeley).

Course Testbed

The course features 11 video lectures recorded during a corresponding on-campus course, 4 homeworks and 4 quizzes. Lectures incorporate short assessments that test the material just presented. The course has been offered three times on the Coursera platform and three times on the edX platform, each time with similar content.

All edX courses include a simple forum designed for answering specific factual questions with limited thread depth (at most three). Posts can be upvoted or reported for misuse, but not downvoted. Posts are listed in the order they were posted. Each post shows the author's name, when it was posted, and the number of upvotes. Users can be manually marked as moderators. Each user has a user page listing all their contributions; there are no reputation scores or badges. Threads are searched using full-text search, rather than tags, and can be ordered either by date or number of votes. Other MOOC providers such as Coursera have similar forum designs.

In the particular course under study, the forum is self-moderated by students and a set of community teaching assistants (community TAs), volunteers who took the previous offerings of the course. Instructors generate content but do not participate in the forum.

We modified the course software to replace the standard edX forum with two variants of an experimental forum. When students and community TAs first visit the forum, they are randomly assigned to one of the two experimental forum websites based on a hash of their username, and are unable to access the other. The assignment of participants to forums remains stable throughout the course, and the two forums share no content. Although using separate content databases leads to less available content for each forum, and divides the efforts of the community TAs, it avoids complex interactions between students using different features, and allows differences in passive participation to be examined.

Both sites were based on the open-source OSQA software [27], which is similar to Stack Overflow (see Figure 1). Like the edX forum, OSQA is designed for answering specific factual questions with thread depth at most three, rather than for extended complex discussions. This model encourages asking concrete questions on individual assignments over general class-related discussions. On one of the experimental forums, the *basic forum*, students can post questions, answers, and comments, search content using tags and full-text search, and follow or send private messages to other users. The *full-featured forum* additionally provides a reputation system with the following features:

- Users can upvote and downvote questions, answers, and comments to indicate the most useful ones. Answers with more upvotes are listed first.
- Users receive a reputation score based primarily on how many upvotes their posts receive. Reputation points reward users and highlight which users are reliable to others. As users gain reputation points, they gradually acquire access to moderation features on the forum.
- Users who ask questions can select a best answer among the answers.

An *anchor* is a piece of course material that naturally stimulates discussion, such as a homework or lecture. [15] We follow the best practice of making relevant discussion easily accessible from anchors by inserting forum links into anchor pages which show posts with related tags.

After the course completed, we sent all participating students an optional survey gathering qualitative information about the usefulness of the forum, usefulness of the reputation system features, their motivation for contributing to the forum, and their sense of community.

Participants

MOOCs are characterized by varying participation over the duration of the course, with considerable attrition between milestones [3]. The March 2013 course we examined exhibited this pattern, starting with 5985 enrolled students and ending with 532 passing students; students who use the forum depart somewhat more slowly, with 1572 students starting the course and 442 passing (see Table 1). First-Class-to-Course-Completion-Rate (FCCR), a metric devised by Russell measuring the ratio of the number of students who received a passing grade to the number who viewed the first video lecture, was 11%, lower than the 19% and 36% reported by Google for their Power Searching course, [13] suggesting higher attrition.

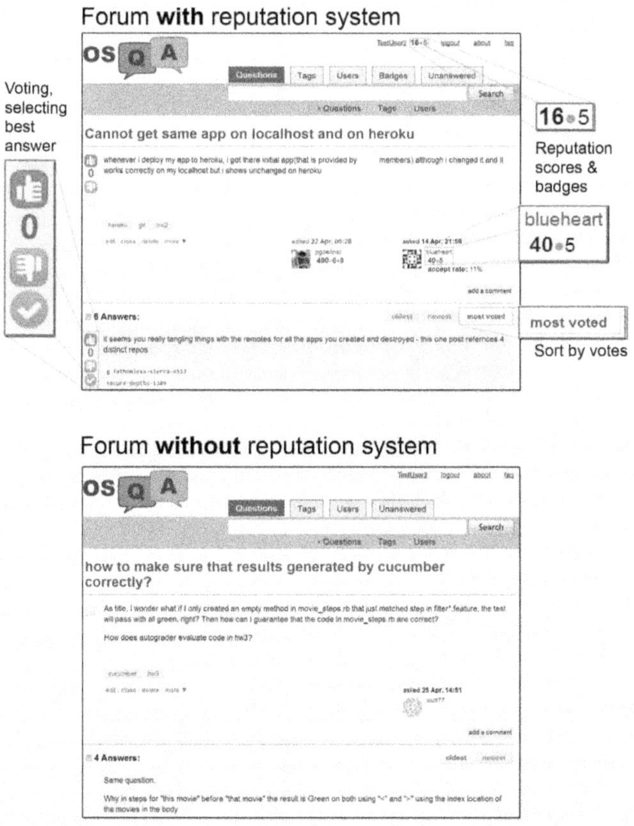

Figure 1. The full-featured forum has several voting and reputation features; the basic forum does not.

Milestone	Total students	Forum users	Non-forum users
Enrolled	5985	1572	4413
Viewed any lecture/HW/quiz	4963	1305	3658
Viewed first video lecture	3266	791	2475
Completed first quiz	2594	1127	1467
Started first homework	1874	985	889
Watched final lecture	1078	638	440
Started final homework	996	625	371
Completed final quiz	925	594	331
Received passing grade	532	442	90

Table 1. Number of students reaching various milestones during the course. Attrition occurs rapidly at the beginning and continues over time. Forum users (using either the experimental or edX forums at any point in the course) abandon the course more slowly, starting at 25% of students and ending at 64%. Most passing students (83%) used the forum.

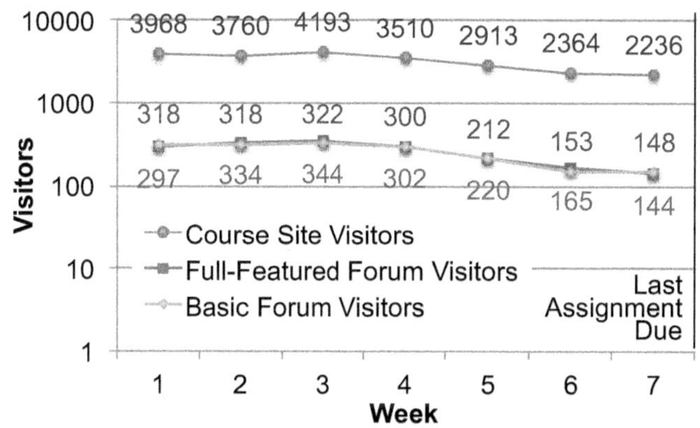

Figure 2. Forum and class visitors by week.

1101 students opted in to participate in the experiment, with 548 in the full-featured forum and 553 in the basic forum; 471 students who opted out instead used the standard edX forum. 3391 students (68%) viewed at least one lecture or assessment, but never visited any forum. Students opt in when they first visit the forum, and all subjects retained access to the standard edX forum to enable them to opt out of the experiment at any time. All students, regardless of whether they participated in the forum experiment, agreed to the edX terms of service which allow researchers to study their edX data. In any given week, 13%–17% of students who accessed the course website also accessed the experimental forum website, as shown in Figure 2.

Different information was available for different course participants. Aggregate grade and participation information was available for all students. For the 1101 students who consented to the experiment, detailed information about their forum usage is available. Additionally, 216 students opted in to a more permissive consent form that allowed us to correlate their detailed forum activity with their edX grades.

Hypotheses

Prior work indicates that students who use forums achieve better grades. Our first goal is to establish whether in the MOOC setting there is a connection between mere use of the forum and course outcomes. Because forum use was self-selected by students and not manipulated in our experiment, we can only show correlation, but such a correlation would support the potential usefulness of performing forum interventions and provide context for our other results. This gives two hypotheses:

H1. Forum participants will have higher course grades than non-participants.
H2. Forum participants will have higher retention than non-participants (they drop out later).

Next, we exploit our controlled forum intervention to seek strong connections between forum reputation features and important student outcomes: course grades and course retention. In addition, we also study factors directly linked to forum participation such as time to first response and number of responses. Such factors can help explain changes in outcomes (or the lack thereof). We also investigate the students' subjective *sense of community*. Reputation features could promote sense of community by encouraging more participation and by providing more information about which users are experienced in the context of a forum discussion.

H3. Reputation features will improve forum participation metrics, such as time to first response.
H4. Reputation features will improve grades.
H5. Reputation features will improve student retention.
H6. Reputation features will affect the student's subjective *sense of community*.

Although useful, simple quantitative forum metrics are unable to distinguish forum threads that have similar structures. Subjective metrics like sense of community are subject to bias as they are based on self-reported and incomplete data. For this reason we also sought to investigate differences in the *content* of the forums using text analysis techniques. Although many questions can be investigated with text analysis, for the purposes of this work we focus on one example that is straightforward to analyze, namely, whether students in the basic forum use more linguistic cues such as "can anyone help me" to persuade others to assist them. As noted in related work, we expect this because reputation systems offer extrinsic rewards to users posting answers, reducing the need for social rewards.

H7. Users of the basic forum will use more appeals for help in their questions.

Dependent Measures

Course Outcomes: Final grades and retention

We operationalize *retention* as days from the beginning of the course until the last student activity, defined as any access to any webpage associated with the course. We extract student activity from clickstream data provided by edX and forum activity, recorded by our own forum server.

Similarly to on-campus courses, a student's *final grade* is a summative assessment of their work throughout the course on a 0-100 scale, and students with a score of 50 pass. However, due to low completion rates, final grades in a MOOC have a different interpretation: they are a combined measure of the portion of the course that the student completed and the student's performance in that portion. For example, a student who scored 100% on the first assignment and then dropped out, and a student who scored 25% on all four assignments would receive the same final grade.

Although final grades remain useful as a combined metric, we also wish to effectively separate performance on completed work from attrition. One straightforward and flexible way to do this is to compare results on individual assessments, including only students who completed the assessment.

Forum Participation

We operationalize forum participation by following the model of prior analyses, e.g. [24]. In particular, we investigate *number of responses to questions*. A high number of questions without any responses indicates an inactive forum and has been linked to a low sense of community [10], while questions that receive many answers are indicative of multiple solutions or discussions. We also investigate *time to first response* – the interval between the time a new question is posted, and the time the first answer to that question is posted.

Sense of Community

We use Rovai's Classroom Community Scale [30] to measure subjective sense of community by users of each forum. In this self-report survey instrument, participants answer 20 questions on a five-point Likert scale about their perceptions of community, e.g. *"I feel that students in this course care about each other."* The results are aggregated into a numerical rating from 0 to 80. Rovai's Scale has been used, for example, to connect certain quantitative forum metrics to sense of community [10]. We assessed sense of community as part of the end-of-course survey.

	Full-featured forum	Basic forum
Total posts	819	587
Questions (threads)	115	144
Answers	358	286
Comments	346	157
Total users	546	555
Posters or upvoters	152	—
Post authors	119	152
Question authors	70	88
Answer authors	81	108
Comment authors	59	58

Table 2. Basic descriptive statistics for each forum. Deleted content is included.

RESULTS

The two experimental forums had roughly equal number of students (562 vs. 578), with more posts on the full-featured forum (819 vs. 587). Additional overall statistics are shown in Table 2. Each thread has one question (original post) and zero or more answers (responses to questions giving solutions) and comments (other posts).

Fisher's exact test shows that users on the full-featured forum are less likely to post ($p \approx 0.036$)—it has more posts overall but less users posting questions and answers. The basic forum also has more questions, and a post on the basic forum is more likely to be a question than a post on the full-featured forum ($p \approx 10^{-6}$). Although fewer users answered questions on the full-featured forum, it also has less users posting overall—as a result we found no evidence that posters on either forum are more likely to answer questions (Fisher's exact test, $p > 0.5$).

The top 10 posters in each forum contribute a substantial portion of overall posts: 54% and 32% in the full-featured and basic forums, respectively. The behavior of these authors can have substantial influence on the forum as a whole, particularly in the full-featured forum where the top two posters are responsible for 23% and 9% of all posts. Posts not by the top 10 posters (46% and 68% respectively) are contributed by a long tail of authors; see Figure 3. Because of the holistic nature of the forum, where all posts are available to all users and affect behavior of others, there is no simple way to account for or exclude top posters during analysis. For example, examining the average number of answers per question after removing top posters would produce a misleading underestimate, because the software is designed to discourage answering questions that already have a good answer.

Users applied an average of two tags to each question (at least one is required), with 43% of tag uses related to homeworks or quizzes, 31% related to the course topic (software engineering terms), and the remainder largely related to course administrative issues.

In analyzing our results, since the distributions being compared usually cannot be shown to be normal, we rely on the

	Hypothesis and Result	Data	Test	Significance
H1	**Forum Use → Higher Grades.** Supported.	88% of students who don't visit forum receive zeros as final grades, compared with 26% of those who visit at least once.	Mann-Whitney U = 701305.5, n_1 = 1321, n_2 = 2622	$p < 0.001$
H2	**Forum Use → Higher Retention.** Supported.	Students who visit the forum participate in the course for a median of 39 out of 42 days, versus 19 out of 42 for those who don't visit.	Mann-Whitney U = 1722209 n_1 = 1528, n_2 = 4634	$p < 0.001$
H3	**Reputation Features → Number of Responses.** Supported.	Questions in the full-featured forum received a mean of 3.5 responses, versus 2.3 in the basic forums.	Mann-Whitney U = 5609 n_1 = 115, n_2 = 144	$p < 0.001$
	Reputation Features → Time to First Response. Supported.	Median time to first response for an answered question in the full-featured forum was 59 min, versus 2 hr 21 min for the basic forum.	Mann-Whitney U = 4626 n_1 = 110, n_2 = 120	$p < 0.001$
H4	**Reputation Features → Higher Grades.** Not Supported.	Median final grades in the full-featured forum and basic forum respectively were 73 and 71.	Mann-Whitney U = 4235.5 n_1 = 89, n_2 = 97	$p > 0.4$
H5	**Reputation Features → Higher Retention.** Not Supported.	The median forum retention in the full-featured and basic forums respectively was 24.5 and 26.1 days.	Mann-Whitney U = 147315 n_1 = 546, n_2 = 555	$p > 0.2$
H6	**Reputation Features → Sense of Community.** Not Supported.	The full-featured and basic forums had mean community scores of 48.5 and 49.8 out of 80, respectively.	$t(81) = -0.35$	$p > 0.7$
H7	**Reputation Features → Less Appeals for Help.** Supported.	The full-featured forum had 24 of 819 posts with appeals for help; the basic forum contained 43 of 587 such posts.	Fisher's exact test	$p \approx 0.0002$

Table 3. Summary of the quantitative support for each hypothesis.

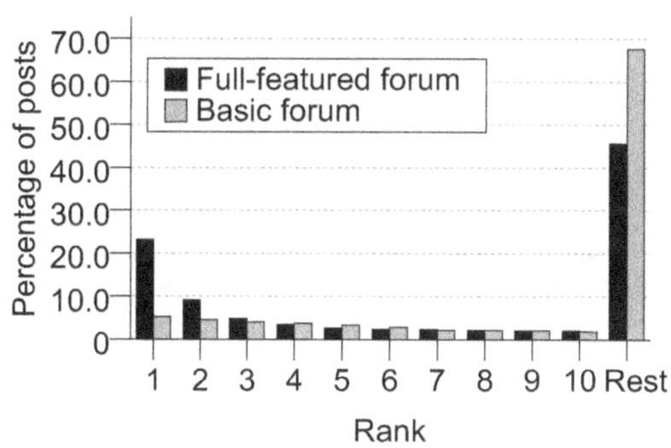

Figure 3. Number of posts contributed by top posters. The top two posters in the full-featured forum stand out with 23% and 9% of all posts. Both distributions are long-tailed.

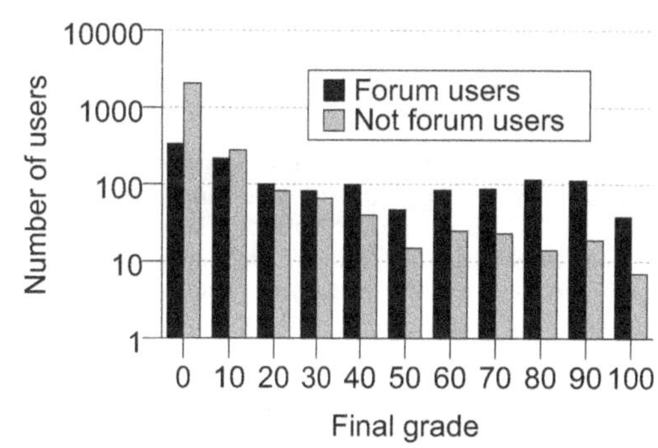

Figure 4. Comparison between final grades of users who visited forum at least once and users who did not. Note that vertical axis is logarithmic. Grades for students who visited the forum are significantly higher.

nonparametric Mann-Whitney U rank-sum test to determine whether one tends to have larger values than the other.

Forum Use Correlated With Higher Grades and Retention

Cheng et al. [5] have shown that students who voluntarily participate in forums perform better and receive higher exam grades. In our setting, we define a *forum user* as a user who visited the experimental forum or the edX forum (1572 users), and a *non-forum user* as a user who is not a forum user but viewed at least one lecture, homework, or quiz (3221 users); this excludes the 1192 users who enrolled in the course but never participated. With these definitions, students who participate in the forum, even by just visiting it once, have considerably higher grades than those who don't: 78% of those who don't visit the forum receive zeros as final grades, as compared to only 26% of those who visit the forum, and the median score is 22% as opposed to 0%, as shown in Figure 4. This difference is significant (Mann-Whitney U = 701305.5, n_1 = 1321, n_2 = 2622, $p < 0.001$), and hypothesis H1 is supported. The difference remains significant even if the non-forum users are restricted to the 1321 highest grades in the set (Mann-Whitney U = 480786.0, $p < 0.001$).

Moreover, students who visit the forum participate in the course longer before dropping out, lasting for a median of 39 out of 42 days as opposed to 19 of 42 days for students who don't visit the forum, as shown in Figure 5. This difference is significant (Mann-Whitney U = 5609, n_1 = 115, n_2 = 144, $p < 0.001$), supporting H2. Note that because forum users were self-selected, both these results are solely correlational.

Forum Use Correlated With Higher Assessment Scores

As noted above, retention is poor for non-forum users, and this severely skews their final grade distribution, with 78% receiving zeroes. To separate the effects of retention from student understanding of the material, we also investigate whether non-forum users also received lower scores on assessments that they completed.

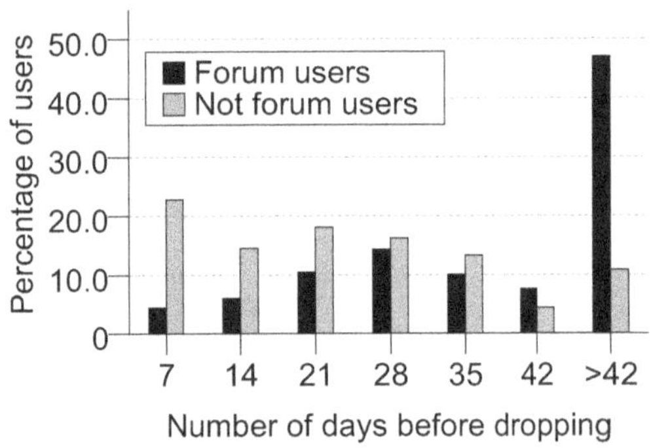

Figure 5. Percentage of forum users and non-forum users, respectively, who drop each week of the course, with the last bar showing those who are still participating at the end of the course after six weeks. Forum users are defined as users who visit the forum at least once. Forum users participate significantly longer. In particular, over 20% of non-forum users quit the first week, and nearly 50% of forum users participate until the end.

Assessment	# forum users, median		# non-forum users, median		U	Significance
HW1	737	700	216	610	60099	$p < 0.001$
HW2	471	300	85	300	17308	$p < 0.02$
HW3	350	500	56	500	9110	$p > 0.1$
HW4	259	500	47	500	5658	$p > 0.2$
Quiz 1	703	8	290	7	84436	$p < 0.001$
Quiz 2	476	11	164	10	31025	$p < 0.001$
Quiz 3	401	8	290	8	19839	$p < 0.008$

Table 4. Comparison of forum users and non-forum users on particular assessments, examining only students who completed those assessments. Mann-Whitney U tests show that forum users receive better assessment scores on most assessments, but are inconclusive on the last two homeworks. More forum users than non-forum users attempted every assessment.

By examining particular assessments and the students who completed them, we found that forum participation was associated with significantly better scores on all assessments except for the last two homeworks, where no difference could be shown. For example, the median score of both forum and non-forum users on Homework 3 was 500, the maximum, and no significant difference was found (Mann-Whitney U=9109.5, n_1 = 350, n_2 = 56, $p > 0.1$). Table 4 summarizes results for all assessments. Again, because forum users were self-selected, this result is correlational.

Reputation Features Improve Forum Response Metrics

Passive participation in the forum is similar in the two groups: most students view only a few discussion threads during the course (over 70% viewed 10 or fewer threads), and we could show no significant difference in the number of threads users of each forum viewed (Mann-Whitney U = 150996, n_1 = 546, n_2 = 555, $p > 0.4$). The histogram in Figure 6 shows strikingly similar distributions.

Active participation shows clear differences across forums. Questions in the full-featured forum received more responses and received their first response more quickly. Questions received a mean of 3.5 responses as opposed to 2.4 in the basic forum, and this difference was significant. To measure the time to first response we exclude questions that received no

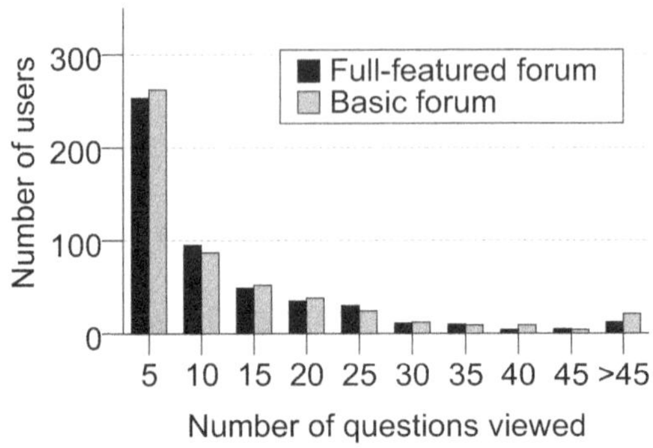

Figure 6. Histogram of number of thread views per user in each forum, showing similar distributions for both forums. Neither forum's users were found to view significantly more threads.

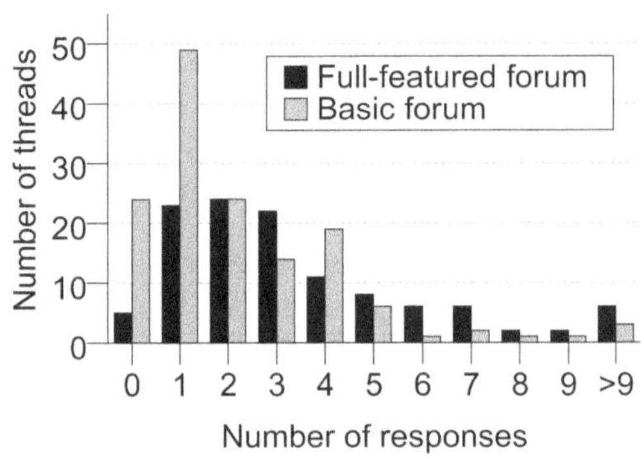

Figure 7. Number of responses questions received in each forum. Questions in the full-featured forum received significantly more responses. In particular, unanswered questions were much more common in the basic forum (21 or 15% as opposed to just 1 in the full-featured forum).

response, which is conservative since these were rare in the full-featured forum. Median time to first response was 59 minutes as opposed to 2 hours and 20 minutes in the basic forum, and this was also significant (Mann-Whitney U = 4626, n_1 = 110, n_2 = 120, $p < 0.001$), supporting H3. See Figures 7 and 8.

No Significant Effect of Reputation System on Student Outcomes

The median final grade in the full-featured forum and basic forum respectively were 73 and 71 (see Figure 9). No significant difference was found (Mann-Whitney U = 4235.5, n_1 = 89, n_2 = 97, $p > 0.4$), and H4 was not supported. Since the grade of a student incorporates both their progress in the course and assessment outcomes, it falls into a bimodal distribution where both forums include students who quit the course with zero grades and students who completed the course with more typical grades.

The comparison above used only the subset of users who opted in to have their forum activity correlated with their course outcomes. This subset of users had very high retention (more than 85% in both forums participated until the end of the course), providing insufficient data to confirm or reject H5. A more meaningful comparison can be made without correlating forum activity and course outcomes if we instead

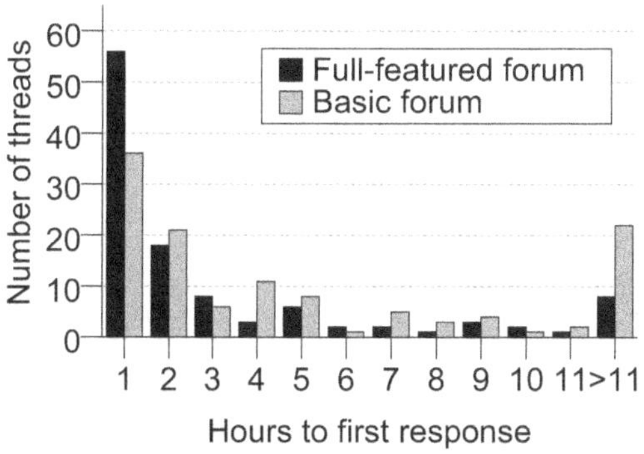

Figure 8. Number of hours for a question to receive its first response in each forum, among questions receiving at least one response. The full-featured forum has a significantly faster time to first response, as evidenced by the much larger number and proportion of questions answered in under one hour (49 or 50% of all answered questions as opposed to 35 or 30%), as well as having less than half as many posts requiring 12 or more hours.

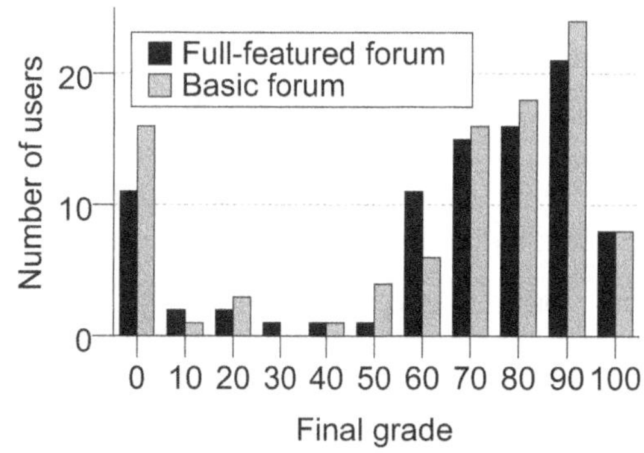

Figure 9. Histogram of final course grades for users of each forum. Neither group was found to have higher scores.

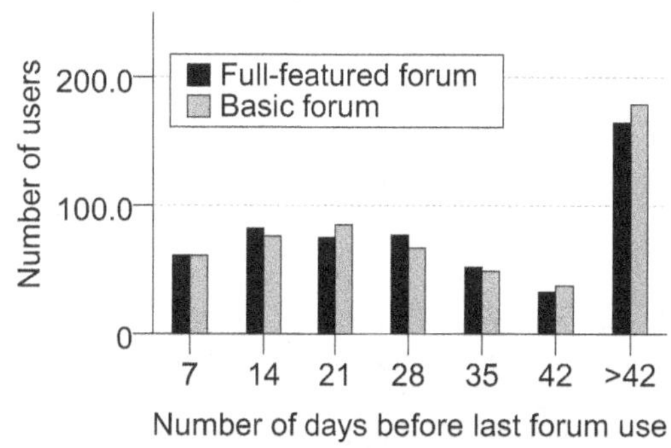

Figure 10. Number of forum users who cease to visit the forum each week, with the last bar showing those who are still participating at the end of the course. No significant difference was shown.

compare only *forum retention* of all users on the two forums; that is, the number of days from the beginning of the course to their last forum access, shown in Figure 10. The median forum retention was 24.5 and 26.1 days in the full-featured and basic forums respectively, and no significant difference was shown (Mann-Whitney U = 147315, $n_1 = 546$, $n_2 = 555$, $p > 0.2$), providing no evidence for H5.

No Significant Effect of Reputation System on Sense of Community

Participants' self-report score to Rovai's Classroom Community Scale [30] follow a normal distribution (SciPy omnibus normaltest, [31] $k_2 = 0.25, 2.8, p > 0.2$), so a parametric test can be used. The Rovai Scale questions were included with the qualitative survey, and the full-featured and basic forum groups had 43 and 40 responses respectively. Mean scores were similar: the full-featured and basic forums had mean scores of 48.5 and 49.8 out of 80, respectively, suggesting a moderate sense of community. See Figure 11. No significant difference between forums was found ($t(81) = -0.35$, $p > 0.7$), and H6 is not supported.

Reputation Features Decrease Appeals for Help

We used the exploratory text analysis tool WordSeer [26] to explore a number of plausible hypotheses regarding differences in language between the forums. Among the examined phrases were expressions of community and discussions of reputation features, but these had insufficient data to analyze.

We isolated one feature suitable for analysis: appeals for help. Our hypothesis is that, in the absence of a reputation system, users will rely on linguistic cues such as "any help is appreciated" to persuade others to answer them. The following words, with stemming, were used to search for sentences in the questions containing appeals for help: "appreciate," "help," "anyone," "anybody," "somebody," "someone," "thank." Posts containing these words were identified and then the posts were rated blindly (without knowledge of the forum it came from) by three independent raters as either representing or not representing an appeal for help, and the final classification was determined by majority. Fleiss' kappa gives a strong inter-rater reliability of $\kappa = 0.80$. An example sentence that all raters agreed was an appeal for help: "Any and all help is greatly appreciated." An example that all raters agreed was not: "It helps me in the homework 1."

In the full-featured forum, 24 of 819 posts (2.9%) by 19 of 546 unique users (3.5%) contained language appealing for help. The basic forum contained 43 of 587 such posts (7.3%) by 31 of 555 unique users (5.6%). This is a significant difference (Fisher's exact test, $p \approx 0.0002$), and H7 is supported. Note however that there is some subjectivity in the rating process, and we cannot necessarily infer that users intended to persuade others to help them; for example, these comments might have been expressions of frustration.

Qualitative Results

Students using the full-featured and basic forums provided 43 and 45 responses, respectively, to the optional end-of-course survey, a response rate of 8%. All questions were optional. 83% of students gave their pseudonym; this lack of anonymity may introduce bias.

No Significant Difference in Usefulness

On a scale of 0 to 4, the median rating of usefulness of both forums was 2.0, and we found no significant difference (Mann-Whitney U = 629.0, $n_1 = 37$, $n_2 = 39$, $p > 0.1$). Similarly, when asked how often they find the answers they were

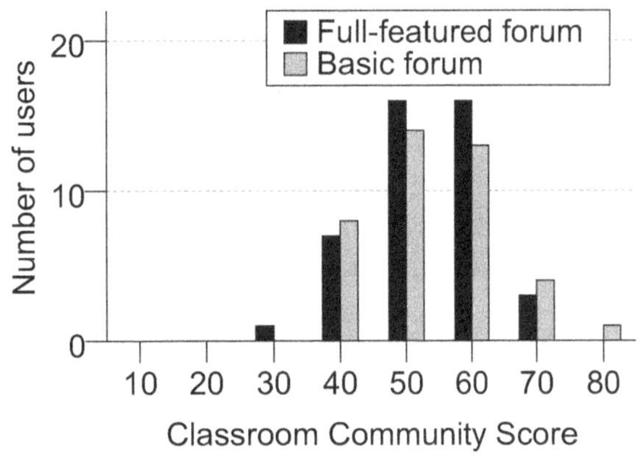

Figure 11. Histogram of Rovai's Classroom Community Scale scores for users of each forum. Neither group was found to have higher scores.

looking for on a 0-4 scale, median ratings were 2.5 and 3.0, and again there was no significant difference (Mann-Whitney U = 665.5, $n_1 = 36$, $n_2 = 39$, $p > 0.3$).

Reputation Features Moderately Useful

Full-featured forum users were asked some questions about their experience with the reputation system. When asked how often features were useful, both upvotes and the "select best answer" feature were given a median rating of 2.0 on a 0 to 3 scale, with 60% of students rating them "always" or "usually" useful. 62% of students said "Yes" or "Usually" when asked whether the reputation system was "fair."

Motivating Students to Care About Reputation Score

One limitation of our study is that students have limited incentive to increase their reputation score when it has no impact beyond the forum of a single short course. 40% of students said they would be more motivated to increase their reputation score if it carried over into other edX courses, and 23% said they would be more motivated if it carried over into future iterations of the same course. This suggests that the use of a sitewide reputation system that preserves scores over time could be more effective. 23% of students also said they would be more motivated to increase their score if it affected their final grade in the course.

Motivated By Altruism, Not Self-Interest

As shown in Figure 12, students self-reported that their main reason for responding to forum posts was in order to be helpful to others, rather than to increase their reputation score or benefit their own learning. Similarly, 89% of students reported it was "unimportant" or only "a little important" to increase their reputation score. On the other hand, [34] found that users of the Math Overflow forum tended to understate their desire to increase their reputation score on surveys, when compared with their behavior. Particularly since surveys were not fully anonymous, students may have avoided answers that make them appear selfish. Some motivators may be underrepresented due to being excluded from the survey, for example having the answer with the most upvotes or getting an answer selected as the best answer.

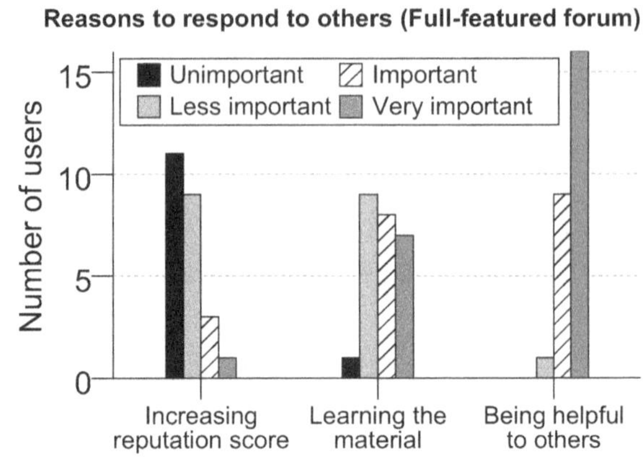

Figure 12. Though presence of reputation features did impact behavior, students self-reported that increasing reputation was not a major goal.

DISCUSSION

We review our results in context, list important limitations, and give advice for running field experiments on MOOCs.

Interpretation of Results

Reputation systems provide concrete, yet limited benefits for MOOC forums. They can result in faster response times and larger numbers of responses per post, improving the students' objective forum experience; and surveys suggest that students found the reputation features useful, improving their subjective forum experience. But we could not show a significant difference in the students' final grades or their subjective sense of community, suggesting that reputation systems do not contribute substantially to assessment outcomes or student community formation.

Users are more likely to post on the basic forum, but posts are more likely to be questions, and a larger proportion of questions are not answered, so these posts might not be productive. The number of users who posted or upvoted on the full-featured forum is also the same as the number who posted on the basic forum (see Table 2), suggesting that upvotes may be displacing some types of posts on the full-featured forum.

The strong correlation between forum usage and student outcomes like retention and grades is difficult to interpret due to a range of possible confounding factors, which we explore below, but to the extent that a causal link exists, it may be attributed to the use of the forum to get "unstuck" when a student is unable to make progress in the course on their own. In learning theory terms, the student is operating in their zone of proximal development [40], which is considered important for advancing individual learning. In the absence of a forum, students frustrated by an obstacle are, intuitively, more likely to cease participation. It is therefore unsurprising that forum software is widely deployed in MOOCs today.

The finding that forum users receive better scores on most individual assessments but not the last two homeworks can be explained in several ways. Steadily increasing p-values from one homework to the next suggest that as students depart, sample size shrinks and statistical tests can no longer detect differences, but they still exist. Additionally, assessments that are too easy can fail to distinguish two groups even if their competency is very different; perfect median scores like we observed suggest low difficulty. The overall disadvantage of non-forum users on individual assessments suggests that poor retention is not the sole cause of their lower grades.

Limitations and Biases

Our study has a number of important issues that limit validity and generalizability.

Single Course Offering

We studied a single offering of a single course. It is not clear to what extent our results would generalize to other settings; e.g., student demographics may be different in other course subjects. Because software engineers are tech savvy, they may be more familiar with discussion forums than other types of students (18% of participants use them "frequently" and 21% "on a daily basis"). In addition, class size may lead to different forum behavior. The most popular MOOCs have an order of magnitude more students than the class we studied.

Small Number of Very Active Users

As in many other systems, participation resembles a power law distribution: the top contributors author a substantial proportion of posts. In the full-featured forum, 43% of posts were by the top 5 users, and in the basic forum 21% of posts were by the top 5 users. The behavior of these particular users may have had a strong effect on metrics like average number of responses, and it is difficult to determine to what extent their behavior is based on the presence or absence of the reputation system. There is no simple way to analyze the forum without the effects of top contributors because the forum is a holistic system in which every post affects all users.

Self-Selection Bias

The study required subjects to consent to participation, and only 67% of forum visitors did so. Students who opted out were directed to the traditional edX forum. This self-selection may have resulted in a biased sample, for example because students who opted out preferred the traditional edX forum experience, or because they had experience with reputation systems and disliked them. Of these participants, only 20% also consented to have their grades correlated with forum activity, and only 8% responded to the survey at the end of the course. Because these interventions were conducted late in the course, they are more likely to have excluded students who had already abandoned it. In particular, this suggests that sense of community scores may be biased upwards.

No Claims of Causation

Although participation in forums was correlated with increased retention and higher grades, there is no evidence of a causal relationship that forum participation leads to improved outcomes. Several alternative explanations are possible. First, students who are more seriously committed to completing the course and the assignments may be more likely to encounter difficulties which require forum support to resolve. Second, students who drop out very early in the course, and so exhibit very low retention and grades, may not ever have encountered a situation in which the forum would have been useful. Finally, students who are unable to use the forum due to limited English-language proficiency or technical literacy may also struggle with the rest of the course.

External Validity and Contamination

Although our experimental forum was used in a real class setting, it does not provide the fully-integrated forum experience that students would normally receive. When they first join the forum, users must visit another website at another domain, log in again using their edX credentials, and complete a consent form before accessing it. These extra steps may deter some users. Additionally, students may have interactions outside of the experimental forum, such as in the edX forum or in private study groups on Facebook or Skype. This could result in the spread of information between users of the two experimental forums, affecting both course outcomes and subsequent forum activity.

Lessons for MOOC studies

MOOCs are attractive for controlled experiments because of their large number of participants and the ability to deploy designs rapidly. However, such experiments face unique challenges that are not encountered in traditional classroom studies. In this section we outline some advice for MOOC researchers and for operators of MOOC platforms.

Advice for MOOC researchers

1. **Study retention and performance separately**: In a MOOC, high attrition is the norm. Metrics like grades, although still valuable, conflate student progress in the course and understanding of material. To separate these factors, it is useful to examine retention directly, to compare performance on individual assignments, and to break subjects into cohorts for analysis based on retention.
2. **Use clickstreams to infer retention**: By logging every page load, clickstreams simplify computing student retention, since a large variety of interactions could potentially indicate continued interest in a course.
3. **Don't rely on late surveys**: Because of attrition, late surveys tend to capture a small, biased set of "survivors" who participated until the end. Early surveys can capture information about other students and their intent for taking the course, and also function as a pretest, enabling measurement of individual improvement over the course.
4. **Use established platforms, but work around limitations**: Reaching large subject pools means leveraging existing platforms with large market share and limited extensibility. In our study, we inserted external links that directed students to another site hosted by the experimenters, sacrificing an integrated experience for more control. We authenticated with edX's OpenID interface and reused edX usernames, simplifying signup and data integration.

Advice for MOOC platforms

To enable continual innovation, MOOC platforms need to empower individual instructors and researchers to deploy new designs and technologies in classes with as few barriers as possible. Our field study ran up against several limitations that a more research-friendly platform could have avoided:

1. **Enable extensibility**: Instructors and researchers should have the opportunity to build and deploy sophisticated extensions and client-side scripts on the MOOC platform, without resorting to the use of an external site. These should be able to transparently replace or extend existing functionality in courses, and be easy to share with others.
2. **Enable interoperability**: When new technology can't be integrated directly with the platform, it still has to interact with it. Support federated identity, and make it easy for external sites to request information about a user or take action on their behalf (with their permission). All functionality available on the web should also be exposed through a service API.
3. **Make data easy to access**: To the extent it is possible, MOOC platforms should secure explicit and broad prior permission from all students to disseminate their data for research purposes, and should make less sensitive data freely available to the general public. When researchers need to go beyond this blanket permission, the platform should make it easy to direct students to a consent form before they can participate in a course.

CONCLUSION AND FUTURE WORK

We presented results from a field experiment on the impact of forums and forum reputation systems on MOOC students. Our work focused on a single offering of a single course, and an important question is the extent to which our results generalize to other courses. Replicating the results would provide evidence that they are not due to the influence of individual prolific users or the topic being studied. Another open question is whether reputation systems would be useful in student forums that center around long, complex discussions of course concepts, rather than the simple question-answer format explored here. Noticeable differences between our forum and success stories like Stack Overflow include the community size and duration of forum use, suggesting that a forum used with a larger course or set of courses over a longer period of time may be more successful.

Our analysis focused primarily on significant relationships between factors; an interesting question is whether metrics of participation such as number of posts and number of threads viewed can be related by regression to course outcomes. Another important question is how to develop analyses of holistic systems like forums that are robust against undue influence from the most prolific users.

The forum used in this work represents a single forum design, and the possibility remains that other forum designs, including novel designs, may produce different results. In particular, due to the short timespan of this experiment, we used OSQA's "bootstrap mode" which allows users to earn privileges with less points. Both bootstrap mode and standard mode in OSQA have different point rewards from other sites like Stack Overflow, and another choice of point rewards may be more effective in encouraging participation. A more ambitious direction that may better improve course outcomes like grades is to create a new forum design based on sound pedagogical principles such as conceptual change, metacognition, and project-based learning.

Beyond forums, there is a wide array of MOOC interventions that could be studied using a similar setup to ours, ranging from simple web design changes, to changes in course materials and assessments, to novel interaction technologies. The strong correlation between forum usage and student outcomes suggests that making an overall improvement in student outcomes requires new interventions that will effectively target the 66% of students who never set foot in the forum. We hope that our work can provide a blueprint for future field experiments in live MOOCs.

ACKNOWLEDGMENTS

We thank Sam Joseph and the World TAs of CS169.1x for coordinating support of students on the forums. This work was funded by the National Science Foundation under award IIS-1149799 and partially funded by the National Endowment for the Humanities under grant HK-50011.

REFERENCES

1. Adamic, L. A., Zhang, J., Bakshy, E., and Ackerman, M. S. Knowledge sharing and Yahoo Answers: everyone knows something. In *Proceedings of WWW 2008*, ACM (New York, NY, USA, 2008), 665–674.
2. Bartlett, M. Y., and DeSteno, D. Gratitude and prosocial behavior helping when it costs you. *Psychological science 17*, 4 (2006), 319–325.
3. Belanger, Y., and Thornton, J. Bioelectricity: A Quantitative Approach — Duke Universitys First MOOC. *Duke University Report* (2013).
4. Chamberlin, L., and Parish, T. MOOCs: Massive open online courses or massive and often obtuse courses? *eLearn 2011*, 8 (Aug. 2011).
5. Cheng, C. K., Par, D. E., Collimore, L.-M., and Joordens, S. Assessing the effectiveness of a voluntary online discussion forum on improving students course performance. *Computers & Education 56*, 1 (2011), 253 – 261.
6. Cheng, R., and Vassileva, J. Adaptive reward mechanism for sustainable online learning community. *Artificial Intelligence in Education* (2005), 152–159.
7. Chizmar, J. F., and Williams, D. B. Altering time and space through network technologies to enhance learning. *CAUSE EFFECT 19* (1996), 14–21.
8. Clow, D. MOOCs and the funnel of participation. In *LAK '13: 3rd International Conference on Learning Analytics & Knowledge* (2013).
9. Cooper, S., and Sahami, M. Reflections on Stanford's MOOCs. *Commun. ACM 56*, 2 (Feb. 2013), 28–30.
10. Dawson, S. P. Online forum discussion interactions as an indicator of student community. *Australasian Journal of Educational Technology 22*, 4 (2006), 495–510.
11. Dearman, D., and Truong, K. N. Why users of Yahoo! Answers do not answer questions. In *Proceedings of CHI 2010*, ACM (2010), 329–332.

12. Deci, E. L., Koestner, R., and Ryan, R. M. A meta-analytic review of experiments examining the effects of extrinsic rewards on intrinsic motivation. *Psychological bulletin 125*, 6 (1999), 627.

13. Google. Power searching with Google: second course FCCR. `https://plus.google.com/+ResearchatGoogle/posts/cSTrtKHyQh6`, Oct. 2012. [Online; accessed 28-May-2013].

14. Grant, A. M., Gino, F., et al. A little thanks goes a long way: Explaining why gratitude expressions motivate prosocial behavior. *Journal of personality and social psychology 98*, 6 (2010), 946–955.

15. Guzdial, M., and Turns, J. Effective discussion through a computer-mediated anchored forum. *Journal of the Learning Sciences 9*, 4 (2000), 437–469.

16. Harper, F. M. *The impact of social design on user contributions to online communities*. PhD thesis, University of Minnesota, 2009. AAI3358616.

17. Harper, F. M., Frankowski, D., Drenner, S., Ren, Y., Kiesler, S., Terveen, L., Kraut, R., and Riedl, J. Talk amongst yourselves: inviting users to participate in online conversations. In *IUI 2007*, ACM (2007), 62–71.

18. Harper, F. M., Moy, D., and Konstan, J. A. Facts or friends? Distinguishing informational and conversational questions in social Q&A sites. In *CHI 2009*, ACM (2009), 759–768.

19. Hsieh, G., and Counts, S. mimir: A market-based real-time question and answer service. In *Proceedings of CHI 2009*, ACM (2009), 769–778.

20. Luca, J., and Mcloughlin, C. Using online forums to support a community of learning. In *ED-MEDIA 2004*, AACE (2004), 1468–1474.

21. Ludford, P. J., Cosley, D., Frankowski, D., and Terveen, L. Think different: increasing online community participation using uniqueness and group dissimilarity. In *CHI 2004*, ACM (2004), 631–638.

22. Mackness, J., Mak, S., and Williams, R. The ideals and reality of participating in a MOOC. In *International Conference on Networked Learning 2010*. 266–275.

23. Mak, S., Williams, R., and Mackness, J. Blogs and forums as communication and learning tools in a MOOC. In *International Conference on Networked Learning 2010*. 275–285.

24. Mamykina, L., Manoim, B., Mittal, M., Hripcsak, G., and Hartmann, B. Design lessons from the fastest Q&A site in the west. In *Proceedings of CHI 2011*, ACM (2011), 2857–2866.

25. Martin, F. G. Will massive open online courses change how we teach? *Commun. ACM 55*, 8 (Aug. 2012), 26–28.

26. Muralidharan, A., and Hearst, M. A. Supporting exploratory text analysis in literature study. *Literary and Linguistic Computing* (2012).

27. OSQA: The open source Q&A system. `http://www.osqa.net/`, 2013. [Online; accessed 28-May-2013].

28. Palinscar, A. S., and Brown, A. L. Reciprocal teaching of comprehension-fostering and comprehension-monitoring activities. *Cognition and instruction 1*, 2 (1984), 117–175.

29. Resnick, P., Kuwabara, K., Zeckhauser, R., and Friedman, E. Reputation systems. *Commun. ACM 43*, 12 (Dec. 2000), 45–48.

30. Rovai, A. Development of an instrument to measure classroom community. *The Internet and Higher Education 5*, 3 (FebMar 2002), 197–211.

31. SciPy v0.12 Reference Guide: scipy.stats.normaltest. `http://docs.scipy.org/doc/scipy/reference/generated/scipy.stats.normaltest.html`, May 2013. [Online; accessed 28-May-2013].

32. Sterbini, A., and Temperini, M. Socialx: Reputation based support to social collaborative learning through exercise sharing and project teamwork. *Int. J. Inf. Syst. Soc. Chang. 2*, 1 (Jan. 2011), 64–79.

33. Szafir, D., and Mutlu, B. ARTFul: adaptive review technology for flipped learning. In *Proceedings of CHI 2013*, ACM (2013), 1001–1010.

34. Tausczik, Y. R., and Pennebaker, J. W. Participation in an online mathematics community: differentiating motivations to add. In *CSCW 2012* (2012), 207–216.

35. Teevan, J., Morris, M. R., and Panovich, K. Factors affecting response quantity, quality, and speed for questions asked via social network status messages. In *ICWSM 2011* (2011).

36. Thomas, D., and Brown, J. *A New Culture of Learning: Cultivating the Imagination for a World of Constant Change*. CreateSpace, 2011.

37. Thompson, C. How Khan Academy is changing the rules of education. *Wired Magazine 126* (2011).

38. Tillmann, N., De Halleux, J., Xie, T., Gulwani, S., and Bishop, J. Teaching and learning programming and software engineering via interactive gaming. In *ICSE 2013* (2013), 1117–1126.

39. Tinto, V. *Leaving College: Rethinking the Causes and Cures of Student Attrition*. University of Chicago Press, 1993.

40. Vygotsky, L. L. S., et al. *Mind in society: The development of higher psychological processes*. Harvard University Press, 1978.

41. Yang, X., Li, Y., Tan, C.-H., and Teo, H.-H. Students' participation intention in an online discussion forum: Why is computer-mediated interaction attractive? *Information and Management 44*, 5 (July 2007), 456–466.

Integrating On-demand Fact-checking with Public Dialogue

Travis Kriplean[1,4], Caitlin Bonnar[1], Alan Borning[1], Bo Kinney[2], Brian Gill[3]
Dept. of Computer Science & Engineering and DUB Group, University of Washington[1],
Seattle Public Library[2], Dept. of Mathematics, Seattle Pacific University[3], Invisible College LLC[4]

ABSTRACT

Public dialogue plays a key role in democratic society. Such dialogue often contains factual claims, but participants and readers are left wondering what to believe, particularly when contributions to such dialogue come from a broad spectrum of the public. We explore the design space for introducing authoritative information into public dialogue, with the goal of supporting constructive rather than confrontational discourse. We also present a specific design and realization of an archetypal sociotechnical system of this kind, namely an on-demand fact-checking service integrated into a crowdsourced voters guide powered by deliberating citizens. The fact-checking service was co-designed with and staffed by professional librarians. Our evaluation examines the service from the perspectives of both users and librarians.

Author Keywords

Deliberation; fact-checking; civic engagement; libraries; Value Sensitive Design

ACM Classification Keywords

H.5.3. Information Interfaces and Presentation (e.g. HCI): Group and Organization Interfaces

INTRODUCTION

Public deliberation can help uncover solutions to public policy questions and help establish the political will to act [14, 20, 22]. But public deliberation is challenging, requiring communicators to consider tradeoffs, listen to others, seek common ground, and be open to change given evidence [47]. Unfortunately, many people do not even want to talk with people holding different views [36]. In addition, current communication interfaces do not generally support the people who are interested. A few interfaces such as OpinionSpace [13] and ConsiderIt [29] have demonstrated that it is possible to create lightweight communication interfaces that encourage constructive interactions when discussing difficult issues. However, such systems also have a significant problem: the contributions often include factual claims, but participants have difficulty identifying which ones are trustworthy.

We describe a new approach for helping discussants decide which factual claims to trust. Specifically, we designed and deployed a fact-checking service staffed by professional librarians and integrated into a crowdsourced voters guide. Overall, this research approach continues that used in our earlier work [29]: a field deployment of a real system, in a real election, with discretionary users who decide to participate to help with their electoral deliberations. It thus complements other research involving rigorously controlled experiments that, for example, use tasks presented in a laboratory experiment or paid participants. It also serves as an archetype of a more general class of systems that integrate the contributions of professionals and established institutions into what Benkler [4] calls "commons-based peer production."

Much of our design effort went into crafting an interaction design that let the fact-checking enhance public deliberation rather than diminishing it. For example, one key design element is that the fact-checks are performed at the behest of discussion participants, rather than being imposed from outside. Our results indicate that participants welcomed the librarians as authoritative sources of information. We also found that librarians were willing and qualified to carry out the fact-checking. However, the fact-checking frame, emerging from journalistic practice, did not map smoothly into librarian reference practice. These findings inspire our design implications, where we discuss a shift to *interactive fact-seeking*.

BACKGROUND: FOSTERING PUBLIC DELIBERATION

To help explore design alternatives and evaluate this work, we turn to Value Sensitive Design (VSD), a methodology that accounts for human values in a principled and systematic way throughout the design process [6, 18]. As with prior work involving VSD in the civic realm [5], we distinguish between stakeholder values and explicitly supported values. Stakeholder values are important to some but not necessarily all of the stakeholders, and may even conflict with each other. For example, discussion participants may differently value environmental sustainability and property rights. While we do not build in support for stakeholder values, we provide a venue in which users can act on their stakeholder values.

Explicitly supported values, on the other hand, guide designers' choices in the creation of the system: here, the values are democratic deliberation, respect, listening, fairness, and civility. Our explicitly supported values are only a small subset of the values at play in public dialogue. Deliberation in particular is just one normative ideal of political communication [3, 8, 16, 48]. Freelon [16] maps out two other prominent communicative ideals: liberal individualism [11] which values self-expression over listening, manifesting in monologues and flaming, while communitarianism [15, 45] emphasizes group identification with like-minded people for mutual support and to better organize against groups with whom they

CCSW'14, February 15 - 19 2014, Baltimore, MD, USA.
Copyright 2014 ACM 978-1-4503-2540-0/14/02$15.00.
http://dx.doi.org/10.1145/2531602.2531677

disagree. With respect to our explicitly supported values, unfortunately most commonly used communication interfaces, especially online comment boards, *implicitly* support liberal individualist and communitarian values through the particular interface mechanisms they provide. Kriplean et al. found that these interfaces make it far easier to speak into than to actively listen through creating an imbalanced communication model [30]. Because communicative behaviors are context sensitive and can be altered by interface design [35, 38, 44], we believe we can design lightweight interfaces that gently nudge people toward finding common ground and avoiding flame wars, thus supporting a deliberative environment while still accommodating some stakeholder values aligned with these other communicative paradigms (such as advocating for a belief).[1]

We implemented ConsiderIt as an approach to this challenge [29]. In ConsiderIt, participants are first invited to create a pro/con list that captures their most important considerations about the issue. This encourages users to think through tradeoffs — a list with only pros or cons is a structural nudge to consider both sides. Second, ConsiderIt encourages listening to other users by enabling users to adopt into their own pro/con lists the pros and cons contributed by others. Third, ConsiderIt aggregates users' expressions of their primary considerations to help everyone better understand and explore facets of the issue being deliberated; they can even view the most important pros and cons for different voter segments (e.g. supporters), enabling users to find common ground. Finally, a per-point discussion facility was added in the 2011 deployment to help participants drill down into a particular pro/con point and have a focused conversation about it. We call special attention to this functionality because one component of our evaluation is an examination of how the focused discussion progressed before and after fact-checks.

Our primary deployment of ConsiderIt is the Living Voters Guide (LVG). The LVG is an ongoing collaboration started in Spring 2010 between our research team and the non-partisan Seattle CityClub, with the goal of inventing and piloting a new method for facilitating civic engagement [17, 28]. We identified deliberation on Washington State ballot measures as a high need area. In 24 states, these ballot measures can be added to the ballot directly by citizens (with the sufficient number of registered voters' signatures), while a legislative referendum process is allowed in all states. These measures are frequently hotly contested, such as Proposition 8 on same-sex marriage in California's 2008 election. They are also often opaquely worded and confusing. For example, in Washington's 2010 election, there were two irreconcilable measures for privatizing the sale of liquor. Unfortunately, there are few avenues, online or offline, for citizens to work through the various arguments and claims being made by campaigns and pundits, or hear the considerations of "everyday" people.

[1]There have been many efforts at to create deliberation systems, most prominently argumentation visualization techniques (see [41, 42] for an overview). But these systems tend to require a high level of learning and investment from users and administrators [24, 40], which limits their scope and sustainability. We focus on interfaces that can be easily learned and used widely, even if they lack the semantic richness of these other approaches.

We have run the LVG for the past three elections in Washington State, with 30,000 unique visitors from over 200 Washington cities using LVG for nearly ten minutes on average. Our analysis of behavioral data has revealed a high degree of deliberative activity; for example, 41.4% of all submitted pro/con lists included both pros and cons [17, 28, 30]. Moreover, the tone of the community discussion has been civil: although CityClub actively monitored the site for hate speech and personal attacks, less than ten out of a total of 424 comments have been removed over the three deployments. We encourage readers to visit `http://livingvotersguide.org` to better understand the design of ConsiderIt and the LVG application.

Our summative user studies also revealed the paramount limitation of the original LVG platform (and the motivation for the work reported here): in a crowdsourced voters' guide, participants have difficulty understanding what information to trust. Content analysis of the pro/con points in 2010 found that around 60% contained a verifiable statement of fact, such as a claim about what the ballot measure would implement, or included a reference to numerical data from an external source. Anyone can state a claim, but how do others know whether that claim is accurate?

GROUNDING DIALOGUE WITH AUTHORITATIVE INFO

Before delving into the design of our embedded, on-demand fact-checking service, we sketch the broader design space and touch on design-oriented related work.

What: Framing Authoritative Information

A basic design question for introducing authoritative information is its provenance and the format in which it is delivered.

Primary sources. Authoritative information can be provided directly using primary sources. However, suitable primary sources are often unavailable, and most deliberating bodies do not have the ability to commission a report from a dedicated organization like the Congressional Budget Office. Another option is to find experts in the relevant field, or advocates on either side of a public policy question, who are willing to discuss the subject. For example, face-to-face deliberation methodologies like Consensus Conferences and Citizen Juries incorporate expert Q/A as part of the process by which citizens come together to learn about, discuss, and jointly craft a policy recommendation [14]. Unfortunately, scalability is challenging because it is difficult to secure and coordinate time commitments of experts.

Fact-checking. Fact-checkers produce an evaluation of verifiable claims made in public statements through investigation of primary and secondary sources. A fact-check usually includes a restatement of the claim being investigated, some context to the statement, a report detailing the results of the report, and a summative evaluation of the veracity of the claim (e.g., Politifact's "Truth-O-Meter" ranging from "True" to "Pants-on-Fire"). Fact-checks provide a wealth of information and explicit guidance to the reader about whether to believe the claim or not. Unfortunately, establishing the legitimacy of fact-checks can be challenging because the format of a fact-check juxtaposes the claim and the fact-check, creating an environment of competing claims [19]. This is problematic because those whose prior beliefs are threatened by the result of the fact-check are psychologically prone to dismiss counter-attitudinal information and delegitimate the source of the challenging information [31, 33, 34, 46], sometimes even strengthening belief in the misinformation [37].

Secondary source synthesis. Another approach is to synthesize information available in reliable secondary sources. This differs from fact-checking in that (1) the investigation does not create new interpretations of original sources and (2) the report does not explicitly rate the veracity of the claims. This approach may help reduce the confrontational nature of fact-checking, while still making information ready-at-hand (though less easily assessable by participants).

Who: Creating and Introducing Authoritative Information

To help ground dialogue, someone needs to identify, synthesize, and introduce the information. Design considerations regarding who does this work and how the process is organized impact the resulting trust in the information and the sustainability of the service.

Professional. A number of professions have developed practices for identifying, synthesizing, and introducing authoritative information. For example, modern political fact-checking emerged from the journalism profession [10], and many current fact-checking enterprises are housed in news organizations (e.g., *Tampa Bay Times* runs Politifact). The journalistic roots of fact-checking are apparent in the emphasis on investigating original sources and publishing an evaluation as a breaking report. Other professionals with relevant skills are reference librarians. One of the main roles of librarians is to help patrons find the information they seek amidst a sometimes overwhelming amount of source material. Librarians assess the content of resources for accuracy and relevance, determine the authority of these resources, and identify any bias or point of view in the resource [2]. As we explore in this paper, librarians can help introduce authoritative information into public dialogue, even though they typically do not provide their services outside of libraries.

Crowdsourcing. Crowdsourcing can also help identify, synthesize, and introduce authoritative information. Both of the aforementioned techniques (fact-checking and secondary source synthesis) have been crowdsourced. Reddit has crowdsourced political fact-checking, where members post claims, the community researches their accuracy, and forum moderators read through the discussion and evaluate the accuracy based on community consensus. Secondary source synthesis is crowdsourced by Wikipedia. While traditional encyclopedias rely on subject-matter experts, Wikipedia relies on many contributors' synthesis of secondary sources, encoded by Wikipedian policies like "No Original Research" [43]. Establishing trust in the results of these crowdsourced efforts is often a challenge [7, 9], but can be accomplished to some extent by transparency of process [27].

Where: Connecting Authoritative Info with Dialogue

Authoritative information can be tailored and introduced into a discussion in a number of ways.

Via participant link to dedicated entity. Authoritative information is usually published and promoted by dedicated entities. For example, fact-checking is often provided as a stand-alone service, as with Snopes, Politifact, and factcheck.org. The authoritative information is thus not explicitly tied to any particular ongoing discussion about the wider issue; only if discussants link to the resource does it potentially help ground a discussion. Even if participants are motivated to do so, other participants may call into question the motives of the individual who provided the link, the reliability of the source, the comprehensiveness of the given resource, and its applicability to the discussion.

Via embedded response. Professionals facilitating a discussion can shepherd authoritative information directly into a discussion. The authoritative information might be researched and introduced at the request of participants, or at the discretion of the professionals. We are unaware of any socio-technical system that embeds a fact-checking service into an ongoing dialogue. However, the aforementioned resource-intensive face-to-face deliberative methodologies often employ experts to help inform participants during a dialogue.

Via personal overlay. Systems like Dispute Finder [12] and Hypothes.is annotate claims at a sentence-by-sentence granularity at the point of consumption as users browse the web. This line of system building focuses on helping individuals be more responsible consumers of information they encounter, rather than grounding an ongoing discussion.

A FACT-CHECKING SERVICE FOR PUBLIC DIALOGUE

In this section, we present our primary socio-technical contribution: a design for introducing authoritative information by a trusted institution into ongoing public dialogue.

As discussed in the previous section, there are a number of potential institutional resources for a fact-checking service. We suggest that libraries and librarians have qualities that make them compelling for this activity (and more generally, as an institutional home for voter education and dialogue forums). The professional practice of librarianship, as embodied in the ALA's Code of Ethics [1], emphasizes the role of libraries in a democracy: "In a political system grounded in an informed citizenry, we are members of a profession explicitly committed to intellectual freedom and the freedom of access to information. We have a special obligation to ensure the free flow of information and ideas to present and future generations." The Code explicitly calls out such values as equitable access; accurate, unbiased, and courteous responses to all requests; and a clear distinction between personal convictions and professional duties. Further, in an era characterized by declining trust in most of our society's established institutions, public libraries continue to enjoy a high level of trust and respect by the public [25, 49]. Reference librarians in particular have well-developed techniques for finding, assessing, and communicating about reliable and useful sources of information [2]. For example, standard practice in addressing a request from a patron for information is the reference interview — as stated in the Reference & User Services Association guidelines, "A librarian treats the user as a collaborator and partner in the information seeking process." However, libraries and reference librarian practice have limitations, such as a prohibition on doing legal research. This is significant because the ballot measures being fact-checked in LVG have legal status and implications.

After the 2011 election we established a partnership with the Seattle Public Library (SPL) to provide on-demand fact-checking for the LVG. Any LVG user could request that a librarian fact-check any pro or con point contributed by another user on the site. Librarians reviewed these requests, identified verifiable claims, researched the accuracy of those claims, and posted a public evaluation and report about each claim. SPL sees its participation in the LVG as an opportunity to reimagine and expand its role in serving the public.

The LVG fact-checking service was co-designed by our team and the participating SPL librarians. Librarians made recommendations regarding the functionality of the system, provided feedback on iterations of the design, and wrote web copy explaining the service to LVG users. As part of this preparation, they studied the pro/con points submitted in 2011, created criteria for the kinds of claims they would be able to fact-check, and wrote sample responses to a set of hypothetical fact-check requests based on the 2011 points. The specific guidelines that the librarians settled on were: (1) We will not conduct in-depth legal or financial analysis, but we will point users to research that has already been conducted; (2) We will not evaluate the merits of value or opinion statements, but we will evaluate their factual components; (3) We will not evaluate the likelihood of hypothetical statements, but we will evaluate their factual components.

Following a VSD approach, we consider both direct and indirect stakeholders in our analysis of the fact-checking service. Direct stakeholders are the users of the technology or its outputs. For this work, we call out the following direct stakeholders: (1) users of the Living Voters Guide, (2) authors of points that are fact-checked and (3) the reference librarians. We separate out the authors of points that are fact-checked because one can imagine a range of reactions on the part of someone whose contribution was fact-checked. While there are other possible categories of direct stakeholders (such as users who request the fact-checks), we suggest that the above list includes the most significant cases.

Indirect stakeholders are people or organizations that are significantly affected by the technology even though they do not use it directly. We call out the Seattle Public Library as an institution as an important indirect stakeholder because of our focus on the librarians' role as fact-checkers, and since this activity represents a significant extension of its traditional role. There are numerous other indirect stakeholders, including voters in general, campaigns with interests in the measures being discussed, and government officials in charge of running the elections.

We now describe the fact-checking service's sociotechnical design from the perspective of the direct stakeholders, and identify value tensions implicated by this design.

From the Perspective of Living Voters Guide Users

The primary design tension we faced was enabling LVG users to easily get a sense of which factual claims in the pro/con points were accurate (in support of deliberative values), while not making the fact-checking a confrontational, negative experience that would discourage contributors from participating again (or at all). This is a delicate design task because having one's political beliefs challenged can actually reinforce the original belief. For example, Garrett [19] shows that even introducing a small delay between showing a false claim and a correction of the claim to someone whose prior beliefs are bolstered by the false claim significantly improves the participants' receptivity to updating their prior belief and reduces their likelihood of rejecting the legitimacy of the fact-check. We now step through a few of the difficult design choices arising from this tension.

When: Origination of the Request

The service was on-demand: any registered user could request a fact-check, submitted with a brief description of what he or she wanted to have checked. The primary design alternative, as implemented by sites like Politifact, would have been to have librarians select which pro/con points to fact-check. By relying on LVG participants themselves to initiate a fact-check, we hypothesized that the degree of confrontation with an authority would be diffused. Further, we hoped that requests would come from supporters of the point to be checked, not just opponents — for example, a supporter (or even the author) might request a check as a way of bolstering the point's credibility. This design decision is consistent with the values of librarians, as they provide information in response to requests rather than imposing it into discussion. It also enabled librarians to focus on questions that citizens actually cared about, potentially reducing their load and improving the sustainability of the service.

What: Substance of the Fact-Check

Each fact-check comprised (1) a restatement of each factual claim in the pro or con, (2) a brief research report for each claim, and (3) an evaluation of the accuracy of each claim. Dividing points into multiple claims provided an opportunity to address questions directly and reduce confrontation if some of the claims could be marked as accurate. Selecting the categories and labels for accuracy was difficult. We settled on a simple scheme of "accurate," "unverifiable," and "questionable." Each of the evaluation categories was accompanied by a symbol representing the result: a checkmark for accurate, an ellipsis for unverifiable, and a question mark for questionable. The wording "questionable" was chosen to lessen the potential confrontational nature of the evaluation (e.g. in contrast to "wrong" with a red X symbol).

Where: Presentation of Results

There are two primary levels for communicating the result of the fact-checks: (1) when users are browsing multiple points at once and see only the summary of the point, choosing which ones to include in their list, and (2) when viewing the details of a pro/con point and discussing it.

The evaluations of claim accuracy primarily helped users quickly assess general trustworthiness as they browsed the

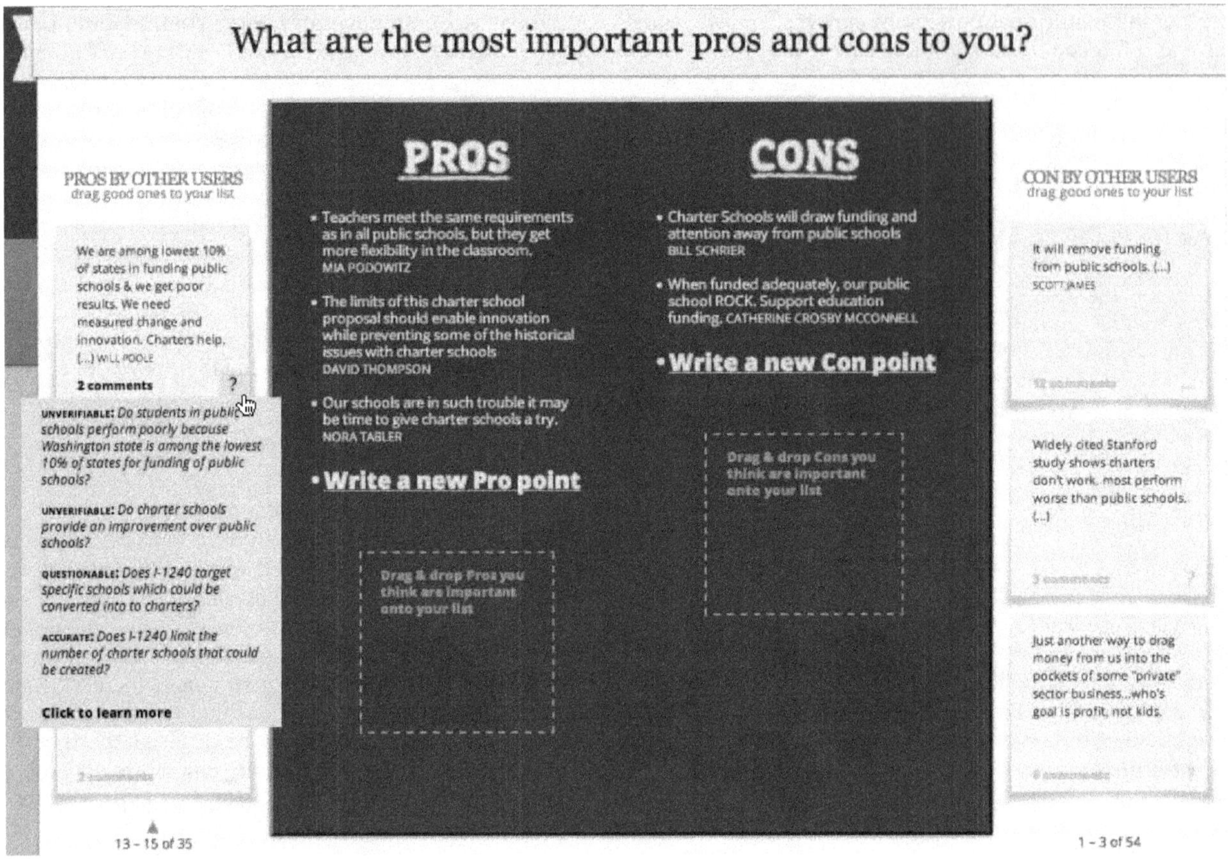

Figure 1. Users can browse the pros and cons contributed by other users while crafting their own pro/con lists. A summary verdict of each fact-checked point is shown in the lower-right corner. A question mark denotes that the point contains at least one inaccurate claim; an ellipsis means that the lowest rating is unverified; a checkmark indicates that all claims are accurate. Upon hovering on the icon, all the claims and their ratings are shown.

points. For each fact-checked pro or con, an icon representing the *most negative* evaluation was shown at the bottom. When a user hovered over the icon, a fact-check summary was shown (Figure 1). We hoped that putting a question mark for points that contained inaccurate claims would not be perceived as exceptionally confrontational to point authors, while being intriguing enough for general users that they would probe into what the question mark meant.

The full fact-check was presented immediately below the text of the point when users drilled into the point details and discussion page (Figure 2). This made the fact-check easily accessible, at the expense of not integrating well into the ongoing dialogue about that point.

From the Perspective of SPL Librarians

While high-level SPL management participated in planning the fact-checking service, the service was implemented by eight reference librarians and managed by a single librarian who also helped perform fact-checks. Librarians took shifts to cover each day during the three weeks leading up to election that the service was deployed. We initially suggested a prioritization scheme for the fact-check requests, but in keeping with the professional values of equitable service policies and access [1] the librarians chose instead to deal with all the requests, in the order received, and committed to responding within a 48-hour period (which they did).

Every fact-check request generated a notification e-mail to the librarians. Librarians then logged into a custom fact-checking dashboard. The dashboard listed each point where a user had requested a fact-check, showing the fact-check status (e.g. completed), which librarian was taking responsibility for it, and the result of the fact-check (if applicable). Librarians could claim responsibility for new requests, and then conduct the fact-check.

The fact-checking page enabled librarians to restate each factual claim made in a pro or con as a researchable and verifiable question, and then answer the research question. The librarians would spend up to two hours researching each of these claims and writing a brief report on their findings (preferably including references to the information sources drawn upon). Finally the librarians would evaluate whether each claim was "accurate," "unverifiable," or "questionable." The fact-checking team decided that the librarians should always identify as many researchable, verifiable questions as a pro or con point contained, even if the request was only for a very specific claim to be checked. This helped scale the service because each point then only had to be checked once.

Every fact-check was a collaboration between at least two librarians. One librarian would write the initial fact-check, which was then reviewed by a second librarian before being published. Additionally, since they worked in close proxim-

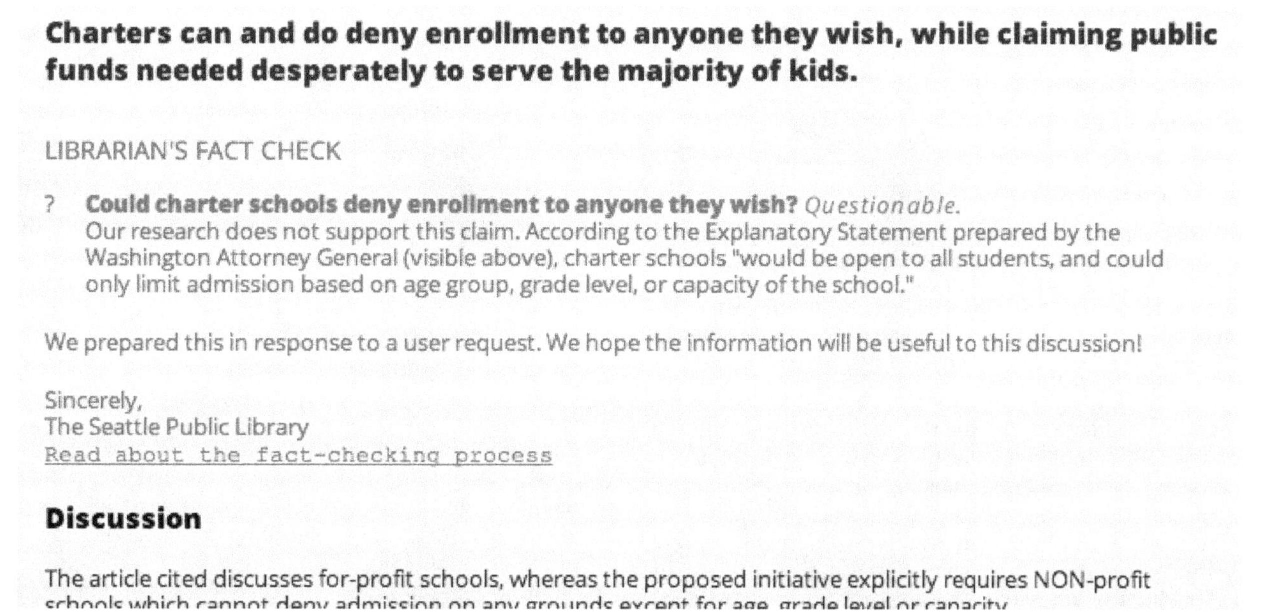

Figure 2. If users open a pro or con point summary, they access a page with additional point details and a discussion space for that point. If that point has been fact-checked, the librarians' report is displayed immediately below the point author's description. In this case, the librarians only identified a single claim and marked it as questionable.

ity, librarians often discussed the fact-checks. This communication facilitated learning and coherence for the service, and also drove functionality changes during the early stage of the pilot.

After each fact-check was published, a notification e-mail was sent out to the requester of the fact-check, the author of the pro/con point, and any other interested party (such as people who were participating in a discussion on that point). Each fact-check was signed collectively as "The Seattle Public Library," not as the individual librarian, in order to protect the librarian from possible harassment. As many of the librarians pointed out in interviews, this was also a way to distinguish personal opinion from a professional response.

METHODS

Following the Value Sensitive Design approach, we used a variety of methods to help us evaluate the fact-checking service from the point of view of each of the main stakeholder groups identified in our conceptual investigations. For users, we relied on three sources. The first was the log files from the LVG deployment. In the 2012 implementation of LVG, this data captures activity by 549 registered users who wrote 332 pro/con points and 424 comments on these points. Seven out of eight of the ballot measures had at least one point that was fact-checked; we therefore constrain our analysis to the 294 pro/con points written for these seven ballot measures. The second was a survey sent out by our collaborator CityClub. The survey asked users about the general usefulness of the LVG and also included a section of six questions specifically about the fact-checking facility. Respondents were asked five questions about the impact and importance of the fact-checking facility. They were scored using a 5-point Likert scale ranging from "strongly disagree" to "strongly agree." The other question asked if they had read at least one of the librarians' fact-checks. The survey overall received 55 responses (10.7% response rate); out of these, 33 (60%) indicated that they read at least one of the librarians' fact-checks and 14 provided additional comments on the fact-checking facility. The third was another survey, sent to the 40 authors of points that were fact-checked. This survey included both fixed and open-ended questions. We received 16 responses (40% response rate). For the librarians, the second author interviewed seven of the eight reference librarians who did the fact-checking, using a value-oriented semi-structured interview [26]. The interviews ranged from 25 to 60 minutes (μ = 36 minutes). Questions were divided into two categories: individual (e.g., whether the librarians felt qualified to perform this service, and how they felt they represented the SPL's values and roles in the community), and organizational (e.g., how they felt this project affected SPL's reputation, and ways in which this project differed from traditional reference practice). Finally, for the Seattle Public Library as an institution, we interviewed two SPL managers, using the above organizational questions as well as a final question regarding the library's future involvement with the LVG.

Each of these data sources is partial, but together, we believe they help enrich our understanding of the strengths and weaknesses of the fact-checking service, even if the limitations of the data preclude us from making strong generalized claims. The next section weaves this data together to communicate about fruitful next directions.

RESULTS

Our goal is to enhance public dialogue by providing authoritative information from a trusted third party. We first answer a fundamental question: whether or not there was demand for this service. Before we launched, we did not know whether users would be interested in requesting fact-checks, and if

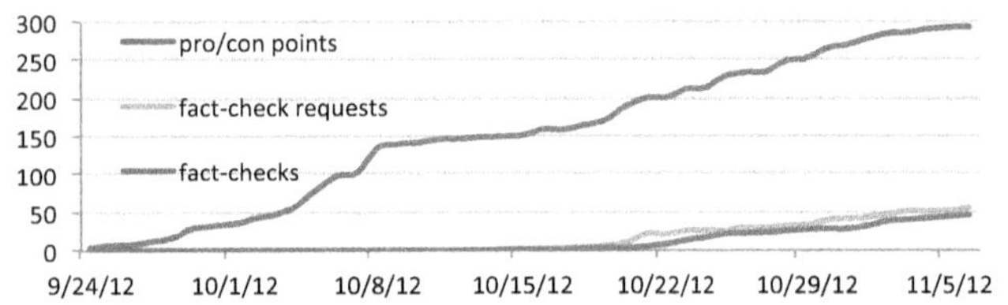

Figure 3. Cumulative time series showing total pro/con points, fact-check requests and completed fact-checks aggregated across all ballot measures that received at least one fact-check. The fact-checking service launched midway on 10/17/2012. Total requests are slightly greater than the completed fact-checks because sometimes several people requested the check before the librarians could publish the fact-check.

they were, would act on that interest. After establishing that there was significant demand for the service, we then analyze three aspects of the goal of enhancing dialogue with authoritative information: first, whether the library was perceived as a legitimate, welcomed, authoritative participant; second, whether the particular way in which authoritative data was introduced helped invite wider, deeper participation; and third, whether the service did in fact inform public dialogue. We undertake this analysis first from the viewpoint of LVG users, and then from the viewpoint of the librarians and the library.

Broad Trends

Demand

When we launched the fact-checking pilot, we did not know whether users would request fact-checks at all, or conversely, whether they would request fact-checks about nearly every point and overburden the librarians.

In this deployment, users demonstrated demand for fact-checks and the willingness to submit requests for them. Through the course of the 3 weeks the fact-checking service was live, SPL librarians responded to 55 requests by 30 distinct users to fact-check 47 distinct pro/con points related to 7 of the 8 statewide ballot measures (Figure 3).

Users thus requested fact-checks of 14.2% of the pros and cons submitted. We consider this a respectable, even high, level of participation, for a number of reasons. First, many pros and cons do not contain checkable claims because they are statements of principle, such as the vast majority of pros and cons submitted to discussion around 2012's ballot measure for legalizing gay marriage. In an informal analysis, librarians found that approximately half of all submitted pros and cons in 2011 contained claims checkable by their criteria. Second, not all pros and cons are examined with the same degree of scrutiny by other users. For example, some are poorly worded or even incoherent. Because of ConsiderIt's PointRank algorithm [29], these points rapidly fall to the bottom and are only seen by the most persistent users. Finally, because of an inopportune illness, the fact-checking interface was launched midway through the deployment, necessarily limiting participation. We were pleased therefore that many of the prominent points with factual claims on popular measures had fact-checks requested, suggesting that users were overall parsimonious with their requests.

Though the librarians were challenged at times to respond to the requests, the demand matched capacity. Librarians were able to respond to each fact-check request within the 48-hour time frame that they promised. In 2012, we were pleased to have hit a sweet spot between capacity and demand. However, in the future, the service could be overwhelmed. One factor mitigating this possibility is a structural resiliency in ConsiderIt that disincentivizes political gaming of the fact-checking service: if a strong advocate decides to request fact-checks of all the points he or she disagrees with, the claims could be evaluated as accurate and end up bolstering the opposing side's case. The more likely risk in overloading the librarians stems from pranksters operating without a political agenda. This could be handled by triaging requests based on the user requesting the fact-check.

Requesting Fact-Checks

Fact-check requests demonstrated a variety of information needs. According to a post-mortem report by the librarian who managed the fact-checking project, requests usually took one of five forms: (1) a simple paraphrase or copy and paste of the original claim, (2) a request for a specific aspect of the claim to fact-check, (3) a request based on implicit assumptions made within a point, (4) a request on the reliability of a source cited by the author of the pro or con point, or (5) a question that was related to the pro or con point.

We expected that users would request fact-checks of points that opposed their own positions (e.g. a proponent of a ballot measure requesting a fact-check of a con point). This was borne out, with 28 (75.7%) of the requests targeted to position-opposing points, eight requests (21.6%) targeting position-supporting points and one request submitted by a neutral user. (Thirteen requests were made by users who did not register their positions, which were excluded from this analysis.) The 21.6% of requests that targeted position-supporting points is notable because it is potentially evidence of normatively desirable deliberative behavior, with users questioning and probing considerations posted in favor of their own positions. (An alternative explanation is that these requests reflected a desire to bolster the point's legitimacy in order to better persuade other users, which still seems normatively desirable, in that it is seeking to ground deliberation in fact.)

Librarian Responses

Overall, the librarians demonstrated that they were able to evaluate complex requests and find specific information to help evaluate the accuracy of claims made on the LVG.

Librarians divided the fact-check requests of 47 points into 65 claims. The librarians' investigations of those claims resulted in 19 claims marked as "accurate," 34 marked as "unverifiable," and 12 marked as "questionable." One reason for the large number of "unverifiable" claims is that, for the political domain, what one might think are straightforward factual questions turn out to be more nuanced on closer examination. Another reason was SPL's policy about not doing legal research; this meant that claims asking whether the ballot measure actually stipulated some specific change had to be marked "unverifiable," even though the librarian was often able to find and report specific relevant quotes in the text of the measure. Additionally, about half of the "unverifiable" claims were hypothetical statements. Regardless of whether the accuracy of the claim could be established, librarians were always able to write an informative response to each fact-check request.

From the Living Voters Guide Users' Perspective

Legitimacy and Welcome

We hypothesized that librarians would be perceived as a qualified, credible source of information and be welcomed by users. To assess these hypotheses, we draw upon our survey results. Users generally agreed with the librarian's analysis and found value in it (8.6% strongly agreed, 65.7% agreed, 25.7% neutral, 0% disagreed, 0% strongly disagreed). People who were fact-checked felt that librarians generally assessed their points in a fair manner (62.5% "fair," 0% "unfair," 37.5% "neither").

Users who were fact-checked were divided on how accurate they found the resulting fact-check to be (53.3% answered "accurate," 6.7% "inaccurate," 40.0% "partly"). All respondents who answered that the resulting fact-check was either "partly accurate" or "inaccurate" received ratings of either "unverifiable" or "questionable," while all who received "accurate" ratings responded that the fact-check on their point was "accurate." Four respondents whose points had been labeled "questionable" responded that they felt the fact-check was "accurate" — an encouraging result.

Users did express a desire for better communication with the librarians. One user, for example, stated:

> But you could never ask a second question or counter the fact checking. ... I'd say it was a good service to have, we just didn't seem to know how to properly communicate with it.

Perhaps most importantly, the fact-checking service improved users' perception of the overall credibility of the LVG (65.7% strongly agreed, 25.7% agreed, 8.6% neutral, 0% disagreed, 0% strongly disagreed). Even those who were fact-checked stated they were either more likely to return (56.3%) or neutral (37.5%), suggesting that the fact-checking at least did not harm the group most likely to perceive the service as illegitimate or unwelcome. The extensive positive press coverage that the service received also suggests that the legitimacy of LVG increased. For example, a *Seattle Times* column [21] praised the librarian's contribution to the LVG, stating that "there's something refreshing in such a scientific, humble approach to information."

Inviting of wider, deeper participation

It is difficult to assess the impact of the fact-checks on users' overall propensity to participate. Since the LVG received more pros and cons than in the previous two elections, it did not appear to significantly deter users from contributing new pros and cons; furthermore, the favorable press coverage of the fact-checking service likely attracted additional users. However, we can begin to evaluate the impact fact-checking had on the discussions rooted to each pro/con point, though we cannot make authoritative causal claims.

We examined the data to determine if pro or con points that were fact-checked tended to receive fewer comments after the fact-check compared to points that did not receive a fact-check. Our dataset contains timestamped comments, as well as timestamped views of each pro/con point, by registered users. We can therefore operationalize the commenting rate as the number of comments per view over a given period of time. We expected the commenting rate to drop slightly after the point was fact-checked because a fact-check should eliminate the need for many of the comments people might make, such as asking a question of the point author or challenging the claims. However, we expected this effect to be partially offset by the fact-check spurring further discussion about the result of the fact-check.

To properly analyze the impact of fact-checks generally on the commenting rate, the statistical analysis needs to control for a major temporal factor: *users in general, even for non-fact-checked points, were less likely to comment on points as the election drew closer.* In other words, LVG users as a whole become more passive consumers of the voters guide as the election neared. This temporal effect also holds for point inclusions, as discussed later.

We therefore conducted a permutation test to assess whether the decrease in the commenting rate from before the fact-check to after was significantly larger than the change that would be expected due to temporal effects alone. If the fact-check had no effect on the commenting rate, then we would expect to see similar before/after differences if we simply randomly reassign the fact-checks and their timestamps to a different set of points. To conduct the permutation test, Monte Carlo simulation was used to repeatedly randomly reassign the 47 fact-checks and their original timestamps to 47 of the 294 points. In the randomization process, each fact-check was assigned at random to a point which had at least one view prior to the timestamp at which the original request for the fact-check was submitted. For each of these new simulated groups of 47 "fact-checked" points, we then computed the before-after difference in comment rates. We repeated this permutation process 10,000 times, recording these differences for each permutation. We then obtained a Monte Carlo estimated p-value for the test by determining the proportion of the permutations that produced differences as extreme or more extreme than the difference observed in our actual data.

In our data, 3.1% of users who viewed a fact-checked point prior to the actual fact check commented on the point; after the fact-check this comment rate decreased to only 0.5%. The permutation test revealed that this before-after decrease in the comment rate for fact-check points was significantly larger ($p=.024$) than would be expected based purely on the temporal effect. The observed decrease in commenting rates before-after fact-checking was an estimated 1.57 times as large as would be expected from temporal effects alone.

One possible explanation is that the fact-check resolved the questions which subsequent commenters might have had. This user's quote conveys this perspective:

> I accepted the fact checking as the end of the discussion. Can't fight the facts ... it definitely felt like once something had been fact checked, any speculations about something were put to rest.

However, we need more data to know how common was this view and whether we can attribute causality. At this point there are other possible explanations, based on factors that our statistical test could not control for, such as the particular persuasive style these points employed. Interestingly, the points that were eventually fact-checked generated significantly more comments before the fact-checking service launched than points that were not fact-checked (p=.0098).[2] By the last week before the election, there was virtually no commenting on any of the points. It is possible that the commenting had largely run its course and would have died out by late October on all points even if there were no fact-checking, and that the sorts of points that had fact-checks had a shorter "commenting half life" — that is, they attracted a stronger initial burst of discussion that then died off more quickly.

Informing Public Dialogue

Though our high-level goal is to foster a deliberative environment in which slow, long-term opinion change might take place, we still want to know whether the librarian's fact-check made an impact on a person's decision about which pro or con points were important to their decision, and also whether the fact-check resulted in a more informed decision (even if the stance remained the same). Our first hypothesis was that the fact-checking service would help people make their decisions about whether to vote for a ballot measure or not. Secondly, we expected that points labeled "accurate" would be included in people's pro/con lists at a higher frequency after the fact-check and that points given a label of "questionable" would be included less frequently.

According to our survey data, general users overwhelmingly self-reported that they thought library fact-checks increased their understanding of the pro/con points as well as helped them become more generally informed about the ballot measure itself (31.4% strongly agreed, 48.6% agreed, 11.4% neutral, 8.6% disagreed, 0% strongly disagreed). The same held true for the users who were fact-checked (68.8% said fact-checks were "informative," 18.8% "confusing," 6.3% "neither," 6.3% gave no response). As one fact-checked user shared, *"I learned things about several issues that I did not know. In one case, my vote was changed."* One author whose point was fact-checked stated that the fact-check caused him to think more critically about validity of his source:

> I found the most interesting part to be that the Librarian fact checker not only checked the fact I submitted, but also the source from whence it came. I had accepted and regurgitated this think-tank's fact and when the library cautioned that the think-tank source was "unverifiable" in its trustworthiness, this really forced me to think critically about the source of the fact that I had thoughtlessly used.

However, in practice, we found no evidence that the fact-checks changed participants' likelihood of including a pro or con point, regardless of whether the point contained accurate or inaccurate claims.

[2]There were 248 points with at least one view prior to the launch of the fact-check system, 44 of which would later be fact-checked. Under a null hypothesis that there is no difference in comment rates for points that would later be fact-checked and points that would not later be fact-checked, we conducted a permutation test in which we randomly assigned 44 of the 248 points as the "fact-checked" points, repeating this process 10,000 times. For each permutation, we computed the difference between the comment rate for the points randomly assigned as "fact-checked" points and the comment rate for the points not assigned to be "fact-checked." This permutation test showed that there is a significant difference in comment rate for points that would eventually be fact-checked with a Monte Carlo p-value of .0098.

As with the analysis of commenting rates, we employed a Monte Carlo permutation test with 10,000 repetitions of the simulation to answer the question of whether the change in the rate of inclusions before/after fact-checking is different from what would be expected based on temporal effects alone. The Monte Carlo estimated p-value of .160 suggests that the change in inclusion rates is consistent with what would be expected based on temporal effects alone. Moreover, we find no evidence that the evaluation of the factual accuracy affected inclusion rates. Thus, we found no support for our hypotheses regarding the impact of fact-checks on users' decisions about which points are important.

There are several possible reasons why fact-checks may not have broadly influenced inclusion rates. First, people's values and self-perception may not be aligned with their actual behavior. And second, opinions may have changed, but only for those whose prior beliefs were not threatened by the fact-check [19]. On the whole, it appears that there was little evident short-term opinion change, at least as exhibited through the adoption of other users' pro/con points.

From the Librarian's Perspective

We now analyze the fact-checking service from the perspective of the librarians, and their experience in acting as authorities in the service of public dialogue.

Legitimacy and Welcome

There are three aspects that contributed to the librarians' view of whether their contributions were perceived as legitimate: (1) if the provision of this service fit within the library's core mission and goals, (2) if the librarians felt qualified to fact-check, and (3) if the librarians felt welcomed. To answer these questions, we draw on our one-on-one interviews with the participating librarians and managers, and an internal report compiled by the librarian who acted as project manager.

We first address whether the design of the fact-checking facility aligns with the library's core mission and values, traditional reference practice, and SPL's goals to innovate. On the innovation side, both librarians and managers alike saw this project as a way to reach out to the community on a larger scale, as well as highlight one of the core services that the library can provide. As one manager put it,

> I think we get lots of advantage from putting our answers to people's questions in a public setting. Foremost of which is that other people can see those answers too. The information is not limited to this one-on-one exchange that we have with a person ... it starts from that, but you know, we know that we had fifty-some requests that we responded to, but we don't have any idea of how many other people read those responses and also learned something from that exchange. So that's something that we don't get from the traditional experience which I think is really valuable.

Some librarians liked the ability to provide information that might aid voter decisions and felt that they could contribute balanced (if not neutral) information while maintaining their non-partisan stance. However, some librarians raised concerns about the ability of the library to maintain their reputation as a neutral institution. These two viewpoints are epitomized by the following quotes from two different librarians:

> I think ultimately what we are doing is helping people find information, and I don't think ... we want to strive for absolute neutrality at

> the expense of informing people. ... it's hard, it's a difficult thing to do well, but I do think that it is something that is possible to do.

> We're a neutral territory. Anyone could come in here, regardless of your political persuasion and so forth and we try to give you equitable service and so on. I think when we get into the realm of political discourse around campaigns and initiatives and so forth, we can get pulled one way or another, and then become labeled as an advocate for this position or an advocate for that position.

However, despite the concerns about the library maintaining a non-partisan stance, the librarians felt that they were able to keep their own political positions separated from their responses. Some mentioned the fact that they already handle this in their day-to-day question answering, and that they are professionally trained to separate their opinion from their work. Others also described that by reading and discussing each others' fact-checks they were able to further mitigate the risk of injecting their own viewpoints.

Five of the librarians reported that they felt qualified, claiming that providing fact-checks was similar to their everyday reference work. One librarian felt his lack of legal background prevented him from properly evaluating some claims. Other librarians who gave an affirmative response brought this up as well, stating that they had to be more cautious because of the legal implications of many points, but felt that they were overall able to uphold the guidelines. This mix of feelings is well captured here:

> In a sense, I did feel qualified but then in [another] sense, I didn't because I didn't have the expertise in government or the types of things that they were looking for in those types of questions. But after reading on the different things that they were trying to pass, all the initiatives, all the measures, and after answering a few of them over time, I felt more and more comfortable and more qualified to be able to answer or point them to different resources that they could look at.

All seven librarians felt qualified to check whether a source was consistent with a claim; however, many cited the fact that in traditional reference practice they leave the final analysis to the patron. Comfort with this varied. Some felt they had the skills and the experience to perform it even if the analysis was not normal. One felt that the "unverifiable" category gave him the opportunity to leave the analysis up to the reader if he did not feel they could provide a definitive answer. Another felt that she should not be conducting any analysis at all.

Lastly, we consider how the librarians regarded their participation and whether they felt welcomed. As previously discussed, users were receptive but wished there were better ways to communicate with the librarians. Librarians shared this desire. Librarians often felt that they needed to make assumptions about what the requester of the fact-check was asking or what the original poster intended. Six of the seven librarians, as well as both managers, mentioned that this was at odds with their day-to-day reference practice where they converse with patrons in order to get at the heart of the question and make sure they are providing the correct information.

> ... sometimes it would have helped to get a little more clarification or to have some of that back and forth. When you have a face-to-face interaction with someone, that is a big part of what we do, sort of a conversation before we start looking for sources is figuring out what is this person really looking for, what is going to be most useful to them.

The lack of a communication mechanism also prevented librarians from knowing how their fact-checks were received by the author of the point, the requester(s) of the fact-check, and anyone reading the fact-check, leading to a general disconnect between librarian and user.

Inviting of Wider, Deeper Participation

All librarians and managers interviewed felt that they provided fact-checks in a responsive, non-discriminatory manner that was inviting to the public. The project manager decided on a 48-hour timeframe for answering a fact-check request. Librarians felt this was reasonable, and were able to complete all fact-checks within that time period. Only a few felt they could have used more time on a particular fact-check. And while the lack of communication mechanisms as discussed above was problematic, librarians sometimes still found ways to respond to concerns. In one instance, a user posted on the LVG's Facebook page a concern with the evaluation that the librarians had made on a fact-check relating to same-sex parenting. The librarian in charge of the fact-check went back and reworded the claim to provide more clarity, as well as adding additional explanation of the assessment. This suggests that librarians were not only willing to listen to user's concerns, but that they also took their suggestions seriously.

Informing Public Dialogue

Both managers and librarians felt that their specific skill sets were conducive to providing reliable and helpful information. As mentioned previously, many librarians see themselves as navigators of the vast amount of information found not only within the library, but also on the Web.

> Our job is helping people become informed in whatever realm that means, so certainly we can contribute information to political discussion. ... I think LVG showed actually several different ways that we can participate in that, you know, just by inserting ourselves into a conversation and saying, 'here is some information that might help,' or ... just by letting people know that we are available to help them find information is making a contribution to the discussion.

However, some felt that the labels associated with the fact-checks — "accurate," "questionable," and "unverifiable" — could sometimes be misleading. For example, since points sometimes contained multiple claims, librarians broke fact-checks into separate claims, rephrased them as a question and provided a label for each. The interface then displayed the lowest rating associated with the point.

> Yeah, I mean, one thing that might have been confusing for the people using it was the fact that you have an original post, which then somebody flags, and then we restate it, and then we reflag it with one of the [labels]. And so when we flag it as one of the three, what we were doing was flagging that in response to the way we restated the question, which worked I think because we were able to very carefully do that. I think if the person wasn't very carefully figuring that out, they could see our flag and read it as back to the original point.

In summary, librarians felt able to provide authoritative, relevant information to the public. They felt that this project was not only a good way to showcase the skills that they possess in terms of providing answers to complex questions, but also a way to reach a wider audience. Their concerns centered primarily around the way the service was manifested on the LVG, which we believe can be mitigated by redesign.

DISCUSSION AND DESIGN IMPLICATIONS

We suggest three takeaways from this work. First, crowdsourcing systems can benefit from reintroducing professionals and institutions that have been up to now omitted. They can provide their professional skills and the authority of their institutions as design assets, for example in support groups for ongoing health conditions in which health care professionals may occasionally participate [23]. Conversely, some of these organizations see engagement in public dialogue and other crowdsourcing systems as a way to help cultivate a new or evolved identity. As socio-technical architects, we should be combining old and new to create entirely new possibilities.

Second, users welcomed the librarians' contributions, even those whose statements were challenged. Our perspective is that correcting widely held, deep misperceptions is something that cannot be quickly fixed (e.g., with a link to a Snopes article), but is rather a long process of engagement that requires a constructive environment [32]. Our initial data indicates that participants were willing to consider the library as an authoritative source of information, even if our data does not suggest that the fact-checks influenced participants' short-term opinions. This willingness to welcome SPL lays the groundwork for long-term opinion change and cultural shifts within an environment for constructive public dialogue.

Third, we found that the journalistic fact-checking frame did not map smoothly to librarian reference practice. Librarianship is rooted in guiding people to sources rather than evaluating claims. Discomfort stepping outside these bounds was magnified by the lack of opportunities for librarians to communicate with users to clarify request and the original point. This points to an evolution of our approach to introducing authoritative information into public dialogue that we call *interactive fact-seeking*. In the remainder of this section, we outline ideas for this new approach.

Interactive Creation. In our implementation, there was a glaring lack of communication among the librarians, the user whose point was being fact-checked, and the fact-check requester. Librarians were hamstrung in knowing with confidence whether they were addressing requesters' needs; they also did not have a way to ask clarifying questions of the author of the point. Participants, on the other hand, could not readily ask followup questions. Straightforward solutions are possible, such as providing mechanisms for private communication between librarians and users, and the ability for users to thank librarians for fact-checks they found useful. A more comprehensive solution might enable the interactive creation of fact-checks. Each fact-check request could open a new forum to which the author of the point, the requester of the fact-check, and anyone else following the point are invited. Librarians can use the forum to ask clarifying questions, post sources they are consulting, and seek feedback. After the fact-check is completed, the forum would serve as a transparent log of the fact-check, helping to establish the legitimacy and participatory nature of the process. The principal challenge with this approach is likely the management of conflicts between the point author and the requester of the fact-check.

Integrate Fact-Checks with Other Comments. Fact-checks are displayed immediately below the pro/con point (Figure 2). While this maximizes visibility, it also highlights competing claims [19], overshadows the discussion section, and obfuscates when the fact-check happened with respect to the discussion. In fact, this could have been a factor in the drop in commenting rates after a fact-check occurred. An interactive fact-seeking approach might situate the fact-check in the flow of the comments as just one part of a larger effort by discussants to ground the discussion and build from it. This design gives librarians the opportunity to frame the fact-checks in a conversational (though professional) manner that maximizes receptivity (e.g. by framing the fact-check in an affirming manner that heightens the chance that people will respect the authoritative information and update their prior beliefs [19, 32]).

Separate Research from Evaluation. Some librarians felt they were overstepping their professional practice when evaluating the veracity of many claims. This problem could be mitigated by creating categories better suited to librarianship, such as evaluating a claim's consistency with reputable sources, or enabling librarians to signal their confidence in the evaluation. However, the problem might be eliminated if the librarians do not evaluate the claims, and instead only seek out and synthesize reliable information on the claim. The evaluation of the claim could be carried out by some other process, such as by an independent panel of trusted community members formed ahead of the election, or crowdsourced by community vote. This latter option is intriguing from an interactive fact-seeking perspective because it invites users to participate in assessing truth, which in turn may encourage opinion change grounded in accurate information because opinion change is most likely to occur if users synthesize and re-articulate information themselves [39].

Encourage Self Fact-Check Requests. Ideally, participants would experience being fact-checked as a learning opportunity and not be embarrassed or offended. While not always possible, the design can do more to foster this fact-seeking attitude. One design direction might encourage participants who are writing a pro or con to actually request a fact-check of themselves, such as by making a "double-check this please" option salient in the authoring process. If it becomes routine to request a fact-check of one's own contribution, the potential confrontational aspect of fact-checks could be lessened.

As of this writing (October 2013), we are in the midst of our second election with the fact-checking service. We implemented many of the above changes in collaboration with SPL librarians, including (1) a facility for the reference librarians to email the fact-check requester or the author of the original point; (2) revised evaluation categories that state whether the claim is consistent with authoritative sources, rather than accurate or inaccurate; and (3) incorporated the results of the fact check chronologically in the comment thread, with a short note at the top that links to the main fact check.

ACKNOWLEDGMENTS

Many thanks to our other collaborators at the University of Washington, Seattle CityClub, and the Seattle Public Library; and in particular to the reference librarians at SPL who took part in the experiment, and to all the Washington voters who participated by using LVG. This research was supported in part by the National Science Foundation under Grant No. IIS 0966929 and in part by a Google Research Award.

REFERENCES

1. American Library Association. Code of ethics of the American Library Association, 2008. Available at **http://www.ala.org/advocacy/proethics/codeofethics/codeethics**.
2. American Library Association. Reference and user services association guidelines, 2013. Available at **http://www.ala.org/rusa/resources/guidelines**.
3. Anderson, C. Deliberative, agonistic, and algorithmic audiences. *Int. J. of Communication 5* (2011).
4. Benkler, Y. *The Wealth of Networks*. Yale University Press, 2006.
5. Borning, A., Friedman, B., Davis, J., and Lin, P. Informing public deliberation: Value sensitive design of indicators for a large-scale urban simulation. In *Proc. 9th European Conference on Computer-Supported Cooperative Work* (Paris, Sept. 2005).
6. Borning, A., and Muller, M. Next steps for value sensitive design. In *CHI* (2012).
7. Castillo, C., Mendoza, M., and Poblete, B. Information credibility on twitter. In *Proceedings of the 20th international conference on World wide web*, WWW '11, ACM (New York, NY, USA, 2011), 675–684.
8. Dahlberg, L. Democracy via cyberspace. *New Media & Society 3*, 2 (2001).
9. Denning, P. J., Horning, J., Parnas, D. L., and Weinstein, L. Wikipedia risks. *Communications of the ACM 48*, 12 (2005), 152.
10. Dobbs, M. The rise of political fact-checking: How Reagan inspired a journalistic movement: A reporter's eye view. New America Foundation, Feb. 2012. Available at **http://newamerica.net/sites/newamerica.net/files/policydocs/The_Rise_of_Political_Fact-checking.pdf.pdf**.
11. Dryzek, J. *Liberals, Critics, Contestations*. Oxford Press, 2002.
12. Ennals, R., Trushkowsky, B., and Agosta, J. M. Highlighting disputed claims on the web. In *Proceedings of the 19th International Conference on World Wide Web*, WWW '10, ACM (New York, NY, USA, 2010), 341–350.
13. Faridani, S., Bitton, E., Ryokai, K., and Goldberg, K. OpinionSpace: A scalable tool for browsing online comments. In *CHI* (2010).
14. Fishkin, J. Strategies of public consultation. *Integrated Assessment 6*, 2 (2006).
15. Fraser, N. A contribution to the critique of actually existing democracy. *Social Text*, 25/26 (1990).
16. Freelon, D. Analyzing online political discussion using three models of democratic communication. *New Media & Society 12*, 7 (2010).
17. Freelon, D., Kriplean, T., Morgan, J., Bennett, W. L., and Borning, A. Facilitating diverse political engagement with the living voters guide. *Journal of Information Technology & Politics 9*, 3 (2012), 279–297.
18. Friedman, B., Kahn Jr., P. H., and Borning, A. Value Sensitive Design and information systems: Three case studies. In *Human-Computer Interaction and Management Information Systems: Foundations*. M.E. Sharpe, Armonk, NY, 2006.
19. Garrett, R. K., and Weeks, B. The promise and peril of real-time corrections to political misperceptions. In *CSCW* (2013).
20. Gastil, J. *Political Communication and Deliberation*. Sage, 2008.
21. Guzmán, M. Seattle library fact check experiment risky, but valuable. *Seattle Times* (Oct. 2012). See **https://wash.livingvotersguide.org/home/media** for this and other links to press coverage.
22. Habermas, J. *The Structural Transformation of the Public Sphere: An Inquiry into a Category of Bourgeois Society*. MIT Press, 1991.
23. Huh, J., Patel, R., and Pratt, W. Tackling dilemmas in supporting "the whole person" in online patient communities. In *CHI* (2012).
24. Isenmann, S., et al. IBIS: a convincing concept . . . but a lousy instrument? In *DIS* (1997).
25. Jaeger, P. T., and Fleischmann, K. Public libraries, values, trust, and e-government. *Information Technology and Libraries 26*, 4 (2007), 34–43.
26. Kahn Jr., P. H. *The Human Relationship with Nature: Development and culture*. MIT Press, 1999, ch. 5: Structural-developmental methods, 77–93.
27. Kittur, A., Suh, B., and Chi, E. H. Can you ever trust a wiki?: Impacting perceived trustworthiness in Wikipedia. In *CSCW* (2008).
28. Kriplean, T. *Encouraging Reflective Discussion on the Web*. PhD thesis, Dept. of Computer Science & Engineering, University of Washington, Dec. 2011.
29. Kriplean, T., Morgan, J., Freelon, D., Borning, A., and Bennett, W. L. Supporting reflective public thought with ConsiderIt. In *CSCW* (2012).
30. Kriplean, T., Toomim, M., Morgan, J., Borning, A., and Ko, A. Is this what you meant? promoting listening on the web with reflect. In *CHI* (2012).
31. Kuklinski, J. H., Quirk, P. J., Jerit, J., Schwieder, D., and Rich, R. F. Misinformation and the currency of democratic citizenship. *Journal of Politics 62*, 3 (2000), 790–816.
32. Lewandowsky, S., Ecker, U., Seifert, C., Schwarz, N., and Cook, J. Misinformation and its correction: Continued influence and successful debiasing. *Psychological Science in the Public Interest 13* (2012), 106–131.
33. Lord, C. G., Ross, L., and Lepper, M. R. Biased assimilation and attitude polarization: The effects of prior theories on subsequently considered evidence. *Journal of Personality and Social Psychology 37*, 11 (1979), 2098–2109.
34. MacCoun, R. J., and Paletz, S. Citizens' perceptions of ideological bias in research on public policy controversies. *Political Psychology 30*, 1 (2009), 43–65.
35. MacKuen, M., et al. Resolute partisanship or reflective deliberation. *Am. J. of Pol. Sci. 54*, 2 (2010).
36. Mutz, D. *Hearing the Other Side: Deliberative versus Participatory Democracy*. Cambridge, 2006.
37. Nyhan, B., and Reifler, J. When corrections fail: The persistence of political misperceptions. *Political Behavior 32*, 2 (June 2010), 303–330.
38. Park, S., et al. Newscube: Delivering multiple aspects of news to mitigate media bias. In *CHI* (2009).
39. Price, V., Nir, L., and Cappella, J. N. Normative and informational influences in online political discussions. *Communication Theory 16*, 1 (Feb. 2006), 47–74.
40. Shipman, F., et al. Formality considered harmful. *JCSCW 8*, 4 (1999).
41. Shum, S. *Visualizing Argumentation*. Springer, 2003.
42. Shum, S. Cohere: Towards web 2.0 argumentation. In *COMMA* (2008).
43. Stvilia, B., Twidale, M. B., Smith, L. C., and Gasser, L. Information quality work organization in Wikipedia. *Journal of the American Society for Information Science and Technology 59*, 6 (2008), 983–1001.
44. Sukumaran, A., et al. Normative influences on thoughtful online participation. In *CHI* (2011).
45. Sunstein, C. *Republic.com 2.0*. Princeton Univ. Press, 2009.
46. Taber, C. S., and Lodge, M. Motivated skepticism in the evaluation of political beliefs. *American Journal of Political Science 50*, 3 (July 2006), 755–769.
47. Thompson, D. Deliberative democratic theory and empirical political science. *Annual Review of Political Science 11* (2008).
48. Wahl-Jorgensen, K. Letters to the editor as a forum for public deliberation. *Crit. Stud. in Media Comm. 18*, 3 (2001).
49. Zickuhr, K., Rainie, L., and Purcell, K. *Library Services in the Digital Age*. Pew Internet & American Life Project, 2013. Available at **http://libraries.pewinternet.org/2013/01/22/library-services/**.

Tweet Acts: How Constituents Lobby Congress via Twitter

Libby Hemphill and Andrew Roback
Illinois Institute of Technology
3301 S. Dearborn St., Chicago, IL 60616
{libby.hemphill, aroback}@iit.edu

ABSTRACT

Twitter is increasingly becoming a medium through which constituents can lobby their elected representatives in Congress about issues that matter to them. Past research has focused on how citizens communicate with each other or how members of Congress (MOCs) use social media in general; our research examines how citizens communicate with MOCs. We contribute to existing literature through the careful examination of hundreds of citizen-authored tweets and the development of a categorization scheme to describe common strategies of lobbying on Twitter. Our findings show that contrary to past research that assumed citizens used Twitter to merely shout out their opinions on issues, citizens utilize a variety of sophisticated techniques to impact political outcomes.

Author Keywords

Politics; Twitter; lobbying; linguistics; speech acts; political communication

ACM Classification Keywords

K.4.1 [**Computers and Society**]: Public policy issues

INTRODUCTION

For nearly two decades, we have been debating the potential of computer-mediated communication (CMC) to impact democracy and political engagement. Grossman [6] proposed that the internet could allow citizens to engage directly in political decision-making processes. Then the late 1990's saw a proliferation of online political groups [2] and people continued to discuss politics online, even in seemingly apolitical spaces [15]. Today, the popular press, especially, attributes the success of campaigns to their effective use of CMC. Twitter itself has invested in politics and elections; their "Government and Politics team" maintains an account (@gov), developed a sentiment monitor for the 2012 presidential election, and "verifies" accounts maintained by members of Congress and other elected officials.

CSCW'14, February 15 - 19 2014, Baltimore, MD, USA

ACM 978-1-4503-2540-0/14/02..$15.00.
http://dx.doi.org/10.1145/2531602.2531735

Much of the existing research about political discussion online has focused on how citizens talk to one another [12,14,15]. Recent research asks how they use CMC in general [5,8] and whether they exploit the interactive capabilities of the medium [8]. Here, we turn our attention to the other side of that interactivity and examine how citizens use CMC to talk to their representatives. Specifically, we analyze whether and how people use Twitter to lobby members of the U.S. Congress (MOCs) about particular issues. We see lobbying as something distinct from soapboxing (merely shouting out personal opinions on issues).

The primary purpose of this paper is to provide a classification of linguistic approaches constituents use to lobby their representatives through social media. We provide a "social realist" [10] account of how people are actually employing technology to influence political outcomes. Twitter's public-ness provides a way for us to investigate how citizens lobby that traditional mail, phone calls, and email can't. We illustrate the myriad ways in which citizens use Twitter to try to participate in the political process. We contribute to the literatures on online political activity and political engagement generally by identifying and providing examples of various categories of issue-oriented interactions between citizens and their elected officials. We also analyze the linguistic distinctions between those interactions and discuss the different approaches citizens use when lobbying for an issue.

RELATED LITERATURE

Talking About Politics Online

Much of the existing literature about political conversations online focuses either on citizen-citizen interactions [12] or official-official interactions [5,8]. Few studies of interactions between governments or officials and their constituents focus on specific moments such as disasters [23] or on e-government services.

While Twitter is a (relatively) new forum for political interaction, all of the newly elected members of the 113th Congress had Twitter accounts maintained by their staff, or sometimes by the MOC him/herself. Some recent research suggests elected officials are starting to use Twitter to interact directly with citizens [8]. While prior work has claimed that citizens use social media as a soapbox from which they shout their own opinions at elected officials

[17], recent research provided evidence that users act in much more varied and sophisticated ways on Twitter [18]. We expand on this earlier literature by examining whether Twitter serves only as a soapbox where users can express their views or whether users actually use Twitter to engage in discussions and produce political change.

Doing Things with Words

Austin [1] first documented ways in which communication is more than just a series of utterances that provide information; most often speakers are attempting to accomplish something with their speech, such as trying to get someone to do something or describing a state of affairs to someone. Austin called these *speech acts*. Each speech act consists of two separate actions: the locutionary act and the illocutionary force. The locutionary act is the physical act of making an utterance (e.g. a child speaking the words "I want a balloon"), whereas the action that the speaker performs with that utterance is referred to as the illocutionary force (e.g. the above child expressing his desire for a balloon to his parent) [16].

Searle later refined Austin's taxonomy of illocutionary acts into five categories that more or less capture the range of possible speech acts a speaker can perform [21]:

- *directives*, which attempt to get the listener to do something;
- *commissives*, which commit the speaker to a course of action;
- *representatives*, which serve to report on the state of the world;
- *expressives*, which express a speaker's emotional state; and
- *declarations*, which change the state of a person or object (e.g. saying "I resign" actually changes your status as an employee).

Similar to Parker & Riley [16], we observe the distinction between directives and *questions*, which attempt to solicit information from the hearer, as they occupy a special place in our discussion of lobbying strategies.

Speech acts are a useful place to begin categorizing lobbying strategies because they differentiate approaches the speakers (constituents) take to motivate the listener (MOC) to take some sort of action or recognize a point of view on an issue. They also provide a theoretical framework for examining semi-public speech (tweets) by letting us focus on the impact speech acts have on their audiences. Here, we focus on the impact tweets have on only one audience: members of Congress. Each tweet in our dataset is directed at one or more MOCs using Twitter's "@" reply convention. Because these utterances are on Twitter, they are visible to the public, but they are aimed specifically at MOCs. We do not discuss the illocutionary force tweets have toward the public.

DATA

Data Collection

SOPA/PIPA was an issue that elicited a large amount of public feedback, but most of that feedback was directed in very narrow rhetorical channels, and nearly all of it was in opposition to the legislation [18]. To analyze lobbying strategies in a wider range of issues, we chose four political issues with well-established hashtags: immigration reform, the federal budget and sequestration, gun control, and internet freedom. We deliberately focused on hashtags in order to limit our analysis to issue lobbying instead of examining all kinds of political speech.

The Collaboration and Social Media Lab at Illinois Institute of Technology provides lists of all members of both the House and Senate for the 112th and 113th Congresses. We used Twitter's streaming and search APIs to collect tweets that mentioned members of Congress and that contained any of our hashtags of interest between 12/22/11 and 10/29/12, 1/25/13 and 1/29/13, and again between 4/30/13 and 5/16/13. In all, we collected 76,454 tweets from 43,079 users directed at a total of 566 Twitter accounts owned by members of the 112th and/or 113th Congress. Of those tweets, 42,398 were traditional retweets (shared content preceded by "RT") and were not included when coding. We excluded RTs because they are linguistic duplicates of the original tweet. RTs redistribute the original message without using a new rhetorical strategy. Retweeting certainly represents a lobbying strategy but not a linguistic one and is therefore beyond the scope of our current analysis. From the remaining original tweets, we randomly selected a subsample for coding. Table 1 breaks down our sample by issue and hashtag (note that hashtag categories

Issue	Hashtags	Tweets	Users
Immigration reform	#immigration	4845	3083
	#dreamact	2591	1838
	#dreamers	3175	2495
Federal budget and sequester	#budget	13249	8767
	#fiscalcliff	978	674
	#sequestration	914	647
Gun control	#guncontrol	1743	733
	#2ndamendment	1443	1014
	#nra	1819	747
Internet freedom	#sopa	36985	21265
	#pipa	25009	15633
	#cispa	5498	3712
Total		76,454*	43,079*
* Some tweets contained multiple hashtags, and some users posted more than one tweet. These numbers represent unique tweets and unique users.			

Table 1. Frequency of tweets containing hashtags associated with our selected issues.

are not mutually exclusive, meaning the sum of all categories is greater than the totals listed above).

Data Analysis

For our purposes, hashtags serve as metadata for identifying potentially relevant tweets. For us, relevant tweets are those that make lobbying efforts. We searched Twitter for hashtags that were clearly related to popular political issues during 2011-2013 expecting to retrieve some lobbying tweets and some tweets that accomplished other ends. We coded mainly for lobbying strategies, but constituents used hashtags for more reasons than lobbying for or against specific legislation or issues. For instance, constituents may have included hashtags to ensure that their tweets appeared in search results even if the content of the tweet doesn't clearly match the hashtag. @FreeRepublicUSA provides a good example: "@BachusAL06 We need #Benghazi answers BEFORE the election! #tcot #tlot #bcot #ccot #gop #nra #ocra #sgp #teaparty #twisters #breitbart" (10/28/2012). The tweet appears in our collection because it contains the "#nra" hashtag, but the tweet is actually about the Libyan embassy tragedy. We chose hashtags based on their issue relationships, but some are more general than others (e.g., #budget vs. #cispa) and therefore appear in tweets that are more or less identifiable as lobbying efforts.

In order to categorize this subset of lobbying tweets, we used an iterative approach to developing a list of categories. We extended the list of seven lobbying strategies (including "other") that was presented in [18] to include seven additional strategies, bringing our total to fourteen lobbying strategies (including "other"). After coding 300 tweets, we calculated interrater reliability using Stata's kappa command and reached a substantial [11] level of agreement (k=0.73). In the next iteration of coding, we identified two additional lobbying strategies, bringing the total number of lobbying strategies in our list to sixteen (including "other"). Both authors coded a 300 tweet training set plus a combined 625 additional tweets individually[1], and we discussed all edge cases until we reached agreement. We also negotiated all changes to the number and nature of categories until we agreed on new or amended categories.

LOBBYING EFFORTS

We identified sixteen distinct categories of tweets about our four selected issues. Table 9 (after References) lists all the categories and gives examples of tweets from each. In this section, we define those categories and organize our discussion by the type of speech act they perform. Table 2 lists the types of speech acts and the number of tweets in our sample that fell in each speech act category.

As Table 9 shows, *Directly oppose/support* was the most common lobbying strategy employed in 17% (N = 108) of tweets, but three other categories appeared more than 10% of the time as well. Tweets that point the audience to additional information accounted for nearly a quarter of all

Speech Act Type	N (%)
Directive	228 (37%)
Commissive	14 (2%)
Representative	145 (23%)
Expressive	100 (16%)
Questions	90 (14%)
N/A	48 (8%)

Table 2. Frequency of tweets by speech act type

tweets (*Promotional* [N = 85, 14%] and *FYI* [N = 75, 12%]). Expressives, where constituents express their emotional state, were more positive (*Thank you for opposing/supporting* [N = 66, 11%]) than negative (*I want a response from you* [N = 14, 2%] and *Disappointed* [N = 20, 3%]). "Polite" tweets (*Thank you for opposing/supporting* and *Please oppose/support*) combined with more neutral, informational tweets (*Promotional* and *FYI*) make up 41% of all tweets in our sample, demonstrating that civil and fact-based political discourse does occur on Twitter. More complex figures of speech (*Rhetorical Question* [N = 33, 5%], *Loaded Policy Question* [N = 39, 6%], and *Analogy* [N = 5, 1%]) were infrequent individually. Those kinds of comments are more linguistically complex than others, so it's not surprising to see fewer of them in such an informal, character-limited outlet. Their combined proportion (12%) demonstrates that sophisticated framing of issues is still a substantial part of citizen lobbying efforts on Twitter.

Directives

We identified four kinds of lobbying efforts that used directive speech acts: *please oppose/support, directly oppose/support, general directive,* and *FYI*. To distinguish between them, we look for markers of politeness (e.g., "please", "I would appreciate"), and specific legislation. When those markers are present, we categorized the tweet as *please oppose/support*. When specific legislation is mentioned but no markers of politeness were present, we categorized the tweet as *directly oppose/support*. When no specific legislation is mentioned, we categorized the tweet as *general directive* whether or not politeness markers appeared. Finally, *FYI* tweets are indirect speech acts where the illocutionary force is a directive (e.g. "Read this"), but the syntactic structure is representative (e.g. "Here is an article that discusses this issue") and includes a link to information that the user wants the MOC to read. We provide further detail on *FYI* tweets below. See Table 3 for examples of tweets in each category and our rationale.

The *Please oppose/support* tweets (N = 27, 4%) resemble the more popular *Directly oppose/support* tweets but include explicit politeness words such as "please" and "thank you". Given Twitter's 140 character limit, it's somewhat surprising that more than one-third of the tweets directly opposing or supporting an issue used some of those limited characters to advocate politely. The differences between these two types of tweets doesn't end at word

[1] Our codebook and dataset are available at http://repository.iit.edu/handle/10560/3057.

Tweet Text	Category	Rationale
@farenthold Please don't trade our Liberty for Poker. #CISPA can't improve #Cybersecurity and has huge potential for abuse. #CongressTMI (Noah_Vail, 04/20/2012)	Please support/ oppose	Implies opposition to CISPA and uses "please"
@FPizarro_DC @marcorubio @SenatorReid @UnivisionNews We need to pass the Dream Act. Pass #CIR Pass #DreamAct (SilvestreReyes, 03/27/2012)	Directly support/ oppose	Tweeter directly requests that MOCs pass a specific piece of legislation
@RepLankford #Sequestration would mean a $68.9 million cut & 69,000 fewer students served! Find a balanced solution! #saveTRiO #NDDUnited (simpson_kris, 10/12/2012)	General Directive	Clearly this tweet is about the budget, but it doesn't express support or opposition for any particular budget bill.
@marcorubio @MarshaBlackburn We can reform our system without the amnesty path to citizenship.#immigration http://t.co/9m0eVucTns (VictoriaSells1, 0505/2013)	FYI	Indirect directive that includes information intended for the MOC to read (the link is to an editorial on immigration reform).

Table 3. Examples and rationale for directives

choice, though. We used separate categories for tweets that included these etiquette markers because the tone, punctuation, and presentation of polite tweets were so different from those without politeness markers.

The examples for each category in Table 9 illustrate these differences. In the *Directly oppose/support* tweet, @HartKnight employs all caps in both the text and hashtag, essentially shouting at three MOCs; this tweet closely resembles the more threatening *I'd have to vote against you tweet* in punctuation and style. In the *Please oppose/support* tweet, @valentin_tintin provides context for his comment using the "#Aurorashootings" hashtag, employs traditional punctuation and capitalization, and directs his/her tweet at a single senator. Similarly polite tweets appear in the *Thank you for opposing/supporting* category. These *Thank you* tweets express appreciation for a position or action the MOC has already taken rather than one the user would like to see. This kind of polite tweet accounts for 11% of the tweets we saw (N = 66). Together, these polite tweets account for about 15% of the sample and illustrate the remarkable linguistic differences between appeals that are polite and those that are not. The conscious decisions users make to spend limited characters on politeness markers and punctuation set them apart from other tweets.

Directly oppose/support included implied positions. Sometimes people indicated their support or opposition explicitly (e.g., "@BillOwensNY VOTE NO! AGAINST #SOPA #PIPA i hope you are aware how these could affect the internet" [@mesaStreet, 01/18/2012]) and sometimes implicitly (e.g., "@ChuckSchumer @SenGillibrand @cbrangel #SOPA and #PIPA will destroy the free and open internet," [QiSites, 01/18/2012]).

Categories for issue tweets were less clear than for legislation-specific tweets. Without a specific piece of legislation to reference, it could be difficult for citizens to concisely tell a representative what kind of action to take. Some of these tweets fell into "general directive" because they did clearly ask representatives to do *something* but the something wasn't vote for or against a particular bill. For instance, @simpson_kris asks Rep. James Lankford (R-OK) to find a balanced solution and implies that he should avoid sequestration, but doesn't ask Rep. Lankford to vote on any particular resolution: "@RepLankford #Sequestration would mean a $68.9 million cut & 69,000 fewer students served! Find a balanced solution! #saveTRiO #NDDUnited" (simpson_kris, 10/12/2012).

In the case of immigration, the Dream Act was a specific piece of legislation that citizens could lobby for or against. Such *directly oppose/support* lobbying attempts were much more focused: "@FPizarro_DC @marcorubio @SenatorReid @UnivisionNews We need to pass the Dream Act. Pass #CIR Pass #DreamAct" (SilvestreReyes, 03/27/2012).

Commissives

The only commissive type of lobby that we identified is the *I'd have to vote against you...* category. In this lobby type, users state their position and then indicate explicitly or implicitly that they will vote for an opposing candidate in the next election if the MOC does not adopt their position. We witnessed this strategy most often in the internet freedom debate which preceded the 2012 elections and less often on more recent issues. Obviously our sample is too small to definitively link this strategy to a particular point in time in the congressional election cycle, but that is one possible explanation for our observations. Users may also have been trying to show how strongly they felt about specific legislation, i.e. they cared so much about stopping SOPA, PIPA, or CISPA that they were willing to change their voting behavior. This kind of issue voting has been well-studied in political science (see [9] for a thorough review). We often assume that issue voters are more sophisticated than average voters because they base voting behavior on policy concerns rather than party loyalty or individual candidates [3]. While all users who include issue hashtags are likely paying attention to issues, those who use

Tweet Text	Explicit/ Implicit	Rationale
@JerryMoran #SOPA and #PIPA are bad bills. Please withdraw your support for them or you will lose my vote in the next election. (donaldrossberg, 01/06/2012)	Explicit	User explicitly states that failure to support his/her position will result in a loss of his/her vote in the next election.
@RepJohnYarmuth @SenRandPaul, I will not ever support any candidate who actively supports/votes for censorship. #SOPA #PIPA #STOPSOPA (TehLamonTeh, 01/04/2012)	Implicit	A promise to act regarding issue voting is present, though no request for a position is explicitly stated.

Table 5. Examples and rationale for commissives

commissives are more clearly marking themselves as issue voters. It wasn't possible for us to analyze initial user sentiment in juxtaposition with probable MOC position on issues, so we relied wholly on the linguistic structure when identifying tweets in this category, fully recognizing that constituents who did not support an MOC to begin with still employed this strategy. Likewise, we have no way to measure whether these voters actually follow through with their threats, but a commissive is a reasonable strategy for anyone wanting to sway a representative while indicating their own sophistication. Table 5 provides examples of both the explicit and implicit use of this strategy.

Representatives

Most representatives attempt to convey information about a particular state of affairs concerning an MOC. In the case of *Promotional* tweets, the user typically composes a short blurb about an event an MOC is speaking at or a quotation from a news piece and then links to that document. Negative promotion occurs when sentiment expressed by user is negative, but structure (content association and promotion) is the same. Later in this paper we go into more detail about the difference between *Promotional* tweets and *FYI* tweets. We found that not all promotional messages reflected the MOC in a positive light (e.g. @ItsShoBoy writes "@LuisGutierrez supports @marcorubio even if hurting #Latinos families http://t.co/UWn7ejlU --- #DREAMAct #immigration #p2 #tcot #latism" [05/31/2012]). Since this was an issue of negative versus positive sentiment (as opposed to an issue of a fundamentally different strategy) we include these tweets with other *Promotional* tweets.

Tweet Text	Category	Rationale
@RepReneeEllmers introduces bill to reverse #sequestration cancer cuts #stopcancercuts http://t.co/VLYBK59UbS (communitycts, 04/10/2013)	Promotional	The user composes a short headline for an article about an MOC and links to that document.
@DWStweets Wrong. It's up to Obama and the Dems to come up with $1.2T in cuts to avoid #Sequestration. @GOP has done their job. (Jmonwater, 02/19/2013)	Campaign ad accusation	Accuses the MOC of a position but does not provide additional information or evidence.
@LuisGutierrez @jsethanderson #Justice4AZ #SB1070 Sadly, we *CAN* have 50 different #immigration laws. We do it with marriage. #NoH8 (communitycts, 04/10/2013)	Analogy	Responding to the assertion that we need a comprehensive immigration law by equating that issue to the fragmentary and conflicting state-level marriage laws.
@DarrellIssa As your constituent, please make sure to vote 'NO' on #CISPA. It violates Internet freedom on the pretense of #cybersecurity. (AvrilPrakash, 04/18/2013)	I'm your constituent and I oppose	The user is representing a state of affairs about him/herself, and pairs a constituency reminder with a lobbying statement.

Table 4. Examples and rationale for representatives

A *Campaign ad accusation* is a special type of representative, in that the tone of the user is accusatory and the veracity of the statements is questionable or taken for granted by the author in lieu of providing evidence or support. The category name stems from the type of accusatory voiceover that traditionally adorns television campaign attack advertisements.

An *Analogy* tweet equates the issue being lobbied with another current political issue. These tweets have complex linguistic structures and usually apply a consequential or substantial relationship between the two issues.

Tweet Text	Category	Rationale
Thank you @SenatorBoxer 4 your leadership on #immigration, women & families today! #womentogether #4immigrantwomen (WomenBelong, 03/19/2013)	Thank you for opposing/ supporting	The user thanks the MOC for existing support on an issue.
@RepDennisRoss we're here outside your luncheon and we would love if you came out and show support for #CIR #immigration #11MilliomDreams (veronikaperz, 05/01/2013)	I want a response from you	The user expresses a feeling, implying a request for action but not a vote on a particular issue.
@robportman Even though you aren't my senator, I need to tell you how disappointed I am in you. We need #guncontrol NOW. (Magpiemusing, 04/18/2013)	Disappointed	Especially because the user can't vote for or against the MOC, the primary purpose of the tweet is to state how the user feels.

Table 7. Examples and rationale for expressives

The final type of representative, *I'm your constituent and I oppose*, represents the user as a member of the MOC's constituency. The persuasive power of this type of statement seems self-evident, in that a user probably assumes that this lobbying strategy will garner more attention from the MOC or that their message will carry additional weight. Table 4 shows examples of each type of representative category.

Expressives

The illocutionary point of tweets in this category is to "express the psychological state [of the speaker]" [21, p.12], i.e. not to bring about a state or to assert the truth of something, but to say how one feels about the state of things. Pure expressives are rare in political speech because most political speech does aim to bring about change or assert a claim even if it does so implicitly. In our scheme, expressives fall under *Thank you for opposing/supporting*, *I want a response from you*, and *Disappointed*. Table 7 shows examples of tweets from these categories.

Questions

Above we discussed the special place questions occupy in our classification scheme. Questions are typically asked to illicit information from a listener [16]. Tweets classified as *What is your position?* do just that, asking the MOC to declare support or opposition on a particular issue.

Questions can also be transformed as indirect illocutionary acts to both signal a position/express frustration (*Rhetorical question*) and presuppose the position of the listener, creating a condition where no answer can allow the listener to save face (*Loaded policy question*); in the former, a reply is not expected, while in the later, no reply would likely be offered. Table 6 offers examples of each type of question.

Whereas we elected to categorize certain speech acts by their illocutionary force rather than their syntactic form (e.g. *FYI*), we elected to group *Rhetorical* and *Loaded policy questions* with actual interrogatives because we feel they rely heavily on the syntactic form to deliver the intended illocutionary force. For instance, we could change any indirect *FYI* tweet to a directive and the utterance would retain its illocutionary force ("I want you to read this"), but converting a rhetorical question to a statement would compromise the intended rhetorical effect evoked by phrasing the directive, accusation, etc. as a question. Posing these challenges as questions is a sophisticated rhetorical strategy that deserves further inquiry, and we plan to return to them in future work.

Tweet Text	Category	Rationale
@SenJohnMcCain What is your view of President Obama's Announcement today #DreamAct (aaronazbartlett, 06/15/2012)	What is your position?	User directly asks MOC for a statement responding to someone else's position. Many users fail to punctuate syntactic interrogatives with question marks.
@LuisGutierrez: so what happen, I thought obama was going to reform #immigration, Obama throw you under the bus, huh!! how it feel? (CowboySpurs12, 05/08/2012)	Rhetorical question	This is actually a string of rhetorical questions. The user likely does not expect a response to any of them; the comment is more to express dissatisfaction and/or to preen.
@jasoninthehouse Do you not care that married couples cannot be together because of #Immigration laws? #UAFA #RFMA #CIR (Song1964, 04/23/2012)	Loaded policy question	The question presupposes the opposition of the MOC on the issue and creates a situation where no response allows the MOC to save face.

Table 6. Examples and rationale for questions

DISTINGUISHING ILLOCUTIONARY FORCES

We chose to assign tweets to a single category based on their primary lobbying strategy as determined by the coder, though some tweets made clear efforts at more than one strategy; however, the character limit of Twitter also serves to limit the number of approaches a user can take in one individual tweet, so most of the tweets we coded utilized a single approach. Early in the coding process, we recognized the difficulty in distinguishing between the sixteen categories we articulated. To address this, we constructed a decision tree to guide our classification of tweets. Still, some categories are similar in their content or speech act type, and so we justify our distinctions by providing additional information about how we assigned those tweets to a single category.

FYI vs Promotion

Some tweets' content suggested it could be either *FYI* or *Promotion*, but it was difficult to tell which one from the content of the tweet alone. Most tweets in these two categories contained links to other content, so we used information from the link (specifically whether the content was intended for the MOC to read or whether it contained information about the MOC) to determine which strategy the tweet employed.

Searle [21] describes a fundamental distinction between directives (*FYI*) and representatives (*Promotional*): direction of fit between words and the world. Searle's example describes a man at a grocery store with a shopping list given to him by his spouse and a detective following the man and writing down everything he puts in his basket. At the end of the shopping trip, both lists will contain the same information (a list of items), but the fundamental speech acts behind them are different because of how the words fit with the world. The shopping list is intended to fit actions in the world to the words on the list (i.e. a directive, "buy these items"), whereas the detective's list is intended to fit the words on the page to actions taken in the world (i.e. a representative, "that man bought these items").

Tweets in the *FYI* category provide information about a topic or issue with the intention of having the world fit their words through directing MOCs to read or understand that information. The users sometimes provide information in the text of the tweet, but most often link to the information that they want MOCs to read or understand by providing a short description or directive paired with a URL. Ultimately, there is a want or need [21] expressed by the user to direct the linked to information at the MOC, making this category an indirect directive (i.e. the implied force of the indirect utterance "here is something to read that is related to this issue" when transformed to a direct utterance would look something like "I want you to read this").

On the other hand, *Promotional* tweets attempt to make their words fit the world by describing actions taken by MOCs or rebroadcasting quotations from MOCs on particular policy issues. These tweets are meant to transmit the opinions and positions of MOCs on an issue rather than direct information at the MOC. We categorized tweets as *FYI* when they contained information the tweeter wanted the MOC to access and as *Promotional* when the link contained information about the MOC (see Table 8).

"I'd have to vote against you" vs "I'm your constituent and I oppose"

While these categories appear quite similar, *I'd have to vote against you* explicitly commits the user to a course of action while *I'm your constituent and I oppose* only implies consequences. One could argue that the constituency reminder, if read as an implication of consequences, is akin to an indirect speech act (where the syntactic form differs from the illocutionary force), e.g. a speaker saying "it's pretty cold in here" when the speaker wants the listener to close a window. We read the constituency reminder as a signifier to the MOC to pay greater attention to the message, and thus it serves as more of an amplification of the message's persuasive power rather than as an indirect threat or commissive. The sheer number of lobbying websites that ask for a zip code or address in order to direct a message to the user's members of Congress testifies to the importance of constituency in citizen lobbying. This is, of course, a fine distinction that requires further exploration, but our experience with a large volume of tweets leads us to believe that these are distinct strategies.

Notable "others"

Some tweets eluded classification based only on their linguistic features or the content of the URLs they contained. One set of tweets that fell into this "Other" category came from a tool for tweeting and emailing Congress provided by Fight for the Future (FFTF), an online freedom lobbying group. FFTF was aiming to defeat CISPA and encouraged users to share "inappropriate, awkward, often embarrassing personal details — the kind that the FBI, NSA, CIA, IRS, and local police will soon have access to if CISPA passes." The tweets generated by

Tweet Text	Link Info	Category
@ChrisCoons #Immigration reform is critical to US economic competitiveness. Watch our videos on the issue: http://t.co/BpzYlWYQ (imovement, 02/13/2013)	YouTube video from The Innovation Movement, a immigration reform lobbying group	FYI
@BuckMcKeon: "#sequestration would do what no other external enemy could -- cripple our economy and defenses" http://t.co/AbCBLYjS (AIAspeaks, 06/25/2012)	An opinion piece about sequestration authored by Rep. Buck McKeon (R-CA) at Politico	Promotional

Table 8. Examples distinguishing *FYI* from *Promotional* tweets

their site (http://www.congresstmi.org) contain the #CISPA hashtag, so they appear in our dataset, but the content of tweets is arcane by design. For instance, @bnowbh said, "@Call_Me_Dutch #EndingOurPrivacy with #CISPA? OK: I'm off to the shower now. #CongressTMI. http://t.co/wKCrSAN1" (04/20/2012). The canonical link for that short URL is FFTF's CongressTMI website. The #CongressTMI tweets employ a more social lobbying strategy than a linguistic one. They rely on shared knowledge and not on language to do their lobbying and therefore fell into our "Other" category.

Another type of "Other" contained tweets in which the content and hashtags either didn't match or the relationship was unclear. As mentioned earlier, tweets about the Libyan embassy tragedy often included the #nra hashtag. Often these tweets contained many hashtags that are commonly associated with Republicans [7] but are otherwise unrelated. It's not clear from the content of the tweet what the tweeter hopes to accomplish legislatively, or at least the author makes no clear lobbying effort.

Finally, some tweets in this category contained no clear message and were just amalgamations of usernames and hashtags (e.g. "@ChuckSchumer @DeptEducation #DISCLOSE #DreamAct #EBTCards #ACA. @federalreserve #AUDITFED #ENDtheFED...@DeptTransportation #Gasoline taxes" [Joseywalesful, 07/16/2012]) or were in a language other than English (e.g. "@LuisGutierrez y De que sirvio. El fue el primero en sugerir no tocar el problema migratorio, me equivoco? #DreamAct" [jchc24141, 05/03/2012]).

DISCUSSION AND FUTURE WORK

Social Media Lobbying May be Unlike Other Lobbying

Social media lobbying may differ in significant ways from email/letter writing lobbying and/or off-line lobbying. The 140 character limit of tweets does not allow the user to provide a great deal of context or lead in to their message, hence they may write more concisely than they do in emails or letters. This may also limit the amount of personalization or the telling of anecdotes, which literature on traditional lobbying suggests is important (for a discussion of web interfaces and personalization see [22] and [24]). Our example of the Fight for the Future campaign demonstrates that tweets can often appear bizarre out of the context of their larger organizational movement.

MOC websites typically require an in-district address to direct messages at MOCs, but Twitter enables any user to direct any stock message at any MOC on Twitter, whether that MOC represents them in Congress or not. Individuals may use different tactics when lobbying their own representatives (e.g., our *I'm your constituent* category) than they do when lobbying others' representatives. We were unable to identify how often users directed messages at people who don't represent them, in part because of the low usage of Twitter's geotagging feature, but future research may shed light on this issue.

Some Twitter accounts that address MOCs are lobbying groups (e.g., AIASpeaks, imovement) rather than individuals. Future work could also examine how professional lobbyist use social media in messaging campaigns.

Sarcasm

Like any qualitative coding scheme, ours has edge cases and produced disagreements between coders. We made efforts to resolve disputes by more explicitly defining categories and including example tweets for each, but some rhetorical strategies, such as sarcasm, limit the comprehensiveness of our scheme.

Tweets that contain sarcasm are difficult to categorize based solely on their content, but sarcasm is a popular tool in political speech. We categorized some sarcastic tweets as directives and sometimes as expressives. For instance, "@benquayle That's right, go after innocent kids! Way to pick your battles! #Congress #DreamAct" (droskosz, 06/18/2012) fell into *directly support/oppose* because the tweeter implies support for the DreamAct. However, that reading of the tweet requires that one know what the Dream Act entails and to recognize "go after innocent kids" is sarcastic in this context. The content alone doesn't provide that information.

Effectiveness

Our analysis does not allow us to make claims about the effectiveness or impact of these lobbying efforts. We cannot know the effectiveness of these tweets without knowing both what it means to be effective and what happens after the tweet is sent. Effectiveness is an important avenue for future work, but first we will have to define what effectiveness means in this context. Here are just a few examples of possible definitions: whether an MOC responds (on Twitter or elsewhere), whether an MOC changes his/her position, whether a user thinks the tweet is effective. We recognize that our analysis does not provide insight about effectiveness, but we consider that beyond the scope of our current study. In terms of speech acts, we would normally judge the effectiveness of a speech act on its ability to bring about the outcome the speaker wanted. The content alone doesn't allow us to claim intent though. The content and frequency of tweets allow us only to infer that people find some benefit in tweeting at their MOCs (or they wouldn't do it), not to judge whether these tweets were effective. Also, it's unlikely that any individual tweet actually influences how an MOC will vote. Before we begin discussing effectiveness of action, we need to know whether and how that action occurs. Our paper provides a taxonomy of constituent lobbying efforts, helps us understand those efforts, and enables future work on the effectiveness of constituent lobbying.

Future work could examine whether some lobbying efforts receive more responses from MOCs, for instance. Our "Other" category reveals that some of the tweets directed at MOCs are actually part of longer conversations. A larger statistical analysis of the tweets and their eventual replies may reveal which lobbying strategies produce the highest response rates from MOCs. For instance, it may be that tweets with a clear, directive approach may be more effective than tweets that link to other documents and, through their linguistic structure, transfer persuasive power to the author of the referred to document as opposed to the author of the referring tweet.

Similarly, it would be interesting to disentangle how issue type, party affiliation of the user/MOC, or timeframe (i.e. when an issue is in the public discourse versus when it actually goes up for a vote in Congress) impact the type of lobbying strategies that citizens employ. Likewise, a study of how often tweets directed at MOCs come from users in that MOC's legislative district may reveal patterns of communication that differ with traditional, geographic conceptions of citizen lobbying.

We don't yet know what citizens' goals are when they engage in lobbying efforts. Earlier work provides some ideas including soapboxing and grassroots organizing [17]. Evidence of lobbying efforts on Twitter implies that users think *something* will happen, but without knowing what citizens know about issues and what they expect to accomplish, it's hard to say *what* they think will happen. Users may just want to feel like they're making a difference. These questions relate to the ongoing discussion of "slacktivism" in social media [4,13,20]. Our results indicate users are trying to influence political outcomes and not just expressing opinions.

Finally, we are conducting work on using machine learning algorithms to automatically classify tweets into the lobbying categories we described above. Past work with machine learning algorithms employed an automated text classification algorithm, but we identified necessary and interesting categories beyond those earlier research identified [18]. Reliable automated classification would allow researchers to examine this approach on a macro level to better understand how citizens communicate with their elected officials on social media. This paper provides a comprehensive codebook for use in automated classification efforts. For a longer discussion of our use of this codebook for automated efforts, see [19].

LIMITATIONS

Our study has a few limitations worth noting - some related to what data is included and others related to what our analysis allows us to claim. We included tweets only when they were are directed at the Twitter accounts of members of Congress and included hashtags. In order to appear in our dataset, users needed to be Twitter- and politically-savvy enough to know how to use hashtags, how to find an MOC's Twitter account, and how to direct their tweets at an individual user. Our findings, then, are limited to issue campaigning where users explicitly labeled both the conversation and the audience. Users who discussed the issues we analyzed but without using a hashtag or directing the tweet at Congress may use different rhetorical strategies than those we identified. We did not capture tweets that complained to the public about an MOC's position on an issue, for instance. Such tweets are certainly implicit lobbying efforts, but they are not aimed directly or explicitly at individual representatives and therefore fall outside our analysis.

CONCLUSION

By allowing people to communicate with their representatives and to do so publicly, Twitter provides space for broader conversations about political issues. We cannot yet measure the impact of that conversation, but we can clearly see that people try to influence politics directly through their social media use. We have described several ways constituents use Twitter to lobby their representatives about political issues and specific legislation. We applied speech acts theory to constituent-authored tweets to explain the ways in which constituents attempt to lobby MOCs. We developed a robust, sixteen-category classification scheme that captures the various strategies citizens adopt when lobbying MOCs and made this codebook and our complete dataset publicly and freely available so that other researchers may build on our work. We also demonstrated that users employ diverse and sophisticated lobbying techniques and don't only "soapbox." Finally, we elaborated on different approaches for future research, specifically how social media relates to other forms of lobbying, the challenges of dealing with classifying sarcastic speech acts, and various metrics of effectiveness that could be applied to citizen lobbying on Twitter.

ACKNOWLEDGEMENTS

Thanks to the Amazon Web Services Education Grants Program for supporting this work.

REFERENCES

1. Austin, J.L. *How to do things with words.* Oxford University Press, Oxford, 1962.
2. Browning, G. *Electronic Democracy: Using the Internet to Influence American Politics*. Pemberton Press, Wilton, CT, 1996.
3. Carmines, E.G. and Stimson, J.A. The Two Faces of Issue Voting. *The American Political Science Review 74*, 1 (1980), 78–91.
4. Christensen, H.S. Political activities on the Internet: Slacktivism or political participation by other means? *First Monday 16*, 2 (2011).
5. Golbeck, J., Grimes, J.M., and Rogers, A. Twitter use by the U.S. Congress. *Journal of the American Society for Information Science and Technology 61*, 8 (2010), 1612–1621.
6. Grossman, L.K. *The Electronic Republic*. Viking, New York, 1995.
7. Hemphill, L., Culotta, A., and Heston, M. *Framing in Social Media: How the U.S. Congress uses Twitter hashtags to frame political issues* (2013). Available at: http://papers.ssrn.com/sol3/papers.cfm?abstract_id=2317335.

8. Hemphill, L., Otterbacher, J., and Shapiro, M. What's Congress doing on Twitter? *Proceedings of CSCW 2013*, ACM (2013), 877–886.
9. Kessel, J. Comment: The Issues in Issue Voting. *The American Political Science Review 66*, 2 (1972), 459–465.
10. Kling, R. Hopes and Horrors: Technological Utopianism and Anti-Utopianism in Narratives of Computerization. In R. Kling, ed., *Computerization and Controversy, Second Edition: Value Conflicts and Social Choices*. Academic Press, San Diego, CA, 1996, 40–58.
11. Landis, J. and Koch, G. The Measurement of Observer Agreement for Categorical Data. *Biometrics 33*, 1 (1977), 159–174.
12. Mascaro, C., Black, A., and Goggins, S. Tweet recall: examining real-time civic discourse on Twitter. *Proceedings of GROUP 2012*, ACM Press (2012), 307.
13. McCafferty, D. Activism vs. slacktivism. *Communications of the ACM 54*, 12 (2011), 17–19.
14. Morgan, J.S., Lampe, C., and Shafiq, M.Z. Is news sharing on Twitter ideologically biased? *Proceedings of CSCW 2013*, ACM (2013), 887–896.
15. Munson, S.A. and Resnick, P. The prevalence of political discourse in non-political blogs. *Proceedings of ICWSM 2011*, (2011).
16. Parker, F. and Riley, K. *Linguistics for non-linguists*. Pearson, Boston, MA, 2010.
17. Parmelee, J.H. and Bichard, S.L. *Politics and the Twitter Revolution: How Tweets Influence the Relationship Between Political Leaders and the Public (Google eBook)*. Lexington Books, 2011.
18. Roback, A. and Hemphill, L. "I'd have to vote against you": issue campaigning via twitter. *Proceedings of CSCW 2013*, ACM (2013), 259–262.
19. Roback, A., and Hemphill, L. *How Constituents Lobby Members of Congress on Twitter*. APSA 2013 Annual Meeting Paper (2013). Available at SSRN: http://ssrn.com/abstract=2301133.
20. Rotman, D., Vieweg, S., Yardi, S., et al. From slacktivism to activism: participatory culture in the age of social media. *CHI '11 Extended Abstracts,* ACM (2011), 819–822.
21. Searle, J.R. A classification of illocutionary acts. *Language in Society 5*, 1 (1976), 1–23.
22. Sidler, M. and Jones, N. Genetics Interfaces: Representing Science and Enacting Public Discourse in Online Spaces. *Technical Communication Quarterly 18*, 1 (2009), 28–48.
23. Starbird, K. and Palen, L. Pass It On?: Retweeting in Mass Emergency. *Proceedings of the 7th International ISCRAM Conference*, (2010), 1–10.
24. Yang, H. and Callan, J. Near-duplicate detection by instance-level constrained clustering. *Proceedings of SIGIR '06*, ACM (2006), 421–428.

Code	Description	Example	Speech Act Type	N (%)
Directly oppose/ support	User expresses his/her opinion on issue to MOC without a polite request.	@jim_jordan @sensherrodbrown @robportman DO NOT SUPPORT #PIPA! http://t.co/i8no0A3z (HartKnight, 01/13/2012)	Directive	108 (17%)
Promotional	Link to promotional media *or* simply promoting the MOC without explicitly requesting action.	@LuisGutierrez I told Piers Morgan to contact you. I think he would be a great media if he listens. #DreamAct and immigration reform** (MarkChristianPr, 01/13/2012)	Representative	85 (14%)
FYI	Directing MOC to a page on the internet via a hyperlink	@ChrisCoons #Immigration reform is critical to US economic competitiveness. Watch our videos on the issue: http://t.co/BpzYlWYQ (imovement, 02/13/2013)	Directive	75 (12%)
Thank you for opposing/ supporting	Thanking MOC for opposing/supporting an issue	@RosLehtinen heard you on 1020 AM. Gotta get GOP on board for #DreamAct. Thanks for supporting the bright minds who were raised here! (josephedison, 02/27/2012)	Expressive	66 (11%)
Other	Does not fall in any of the other categories or doesn't contain enough content to classify	@gopwhip @wsj #BoycottMSM #Propaganda wing of #BarackObama #DNC2012 #coverup #treason #unemployment #DreamAct #ExecutiveOrder #tyranny (USAFBro1964, 09/08/2012)	N/A	48 (8%)

Campaign ad accusation	An allegation or accusation posited as fact that one would expect to encounter in a campaign advertisement.	@OrrinHatch, just like you, the original Repiblican #DREAMAct Sponsor, decided to turn your back on it for political points w/ REP voters. (deftbeta, 01/09/2012)	Representative	46 (7%)
Loaded policy question	Question with a presupposition about the MOC's issue position, an answer to which would force a positioning statement.	@SenatorLeahy You sure you want #PIPA to pass!?!? Forgive me for this, but do you realize the magnitude of such an error!?!? PIPA kills jobs (mySCRIPPSDTW, 12/29/2011)	Question	39 (6%)
Rhetorical question	Figure of speech question with no expectation of reply.	@SenatorReid Harry Reid is paid by our tax dollars to take away our internet. #sopa #pipa since when [d]o we pay the enemy ? (peplepowerusa, 12/27/2011)	Question	33 (5%)
Please oppose/ support	Polite request to MOC to oppose/support an issue	@SenJohnMcCain Please, put #GunControl in your agenda. No more weak NRA laws. We can stop future massacres. #Aurorashootings #Colorado (valentin_tintin, 07/20/2012)	Directive	27 (4%)
Disappointed	Expressing disappointment or dissatisfaction with something the MOC has already done or voted on	@SenatorBegich Ashamed of you and your vote for the background check bill! When will you stop being a pawn of the #NRA (mitamuk, 04/08/2013)	Expressive	20 (3%)
General directive	Asking MOCs to "do something" that is less specific than a particular bill but more specific than a rhetorical question.	@RepLankford #Sequestration would mean a $68.9 million cut & 69,000 fewer students served! Find a balanced solution! #saveTRiO #NDDUnited (simpson_kris, 10/12/2012)	Directive	18 (3%)
What is your position?	Request for clarification or positioning statement from MOC on an issue	@SenatorBarb When the UN asks if you'll support their global gun ban on the 27th what will you say? #tcot #guncontrol #lnyhbt (kwall76, 07/23/2012)	Question	18 (3%)
I want a response from you	Author is requesting a response from the MOC.	@repaaronschock and you still haven't responded to any of my emails about #SOPA and #PIPA ruining the internet and free speech (frozensolidone, 01/05/2012)	Expressive	14 (2%)
I'd have to vote against you...	Some indication that user will withdraw support for MOC. Does not take into account initial sentiment, position or constituency, only linguistic construction.	@SenatorBarb IF YOU DARE TREAD ON OUR 2nd AMENDMENT,KISS YOUR CAREER GOODBYE!@BarackObama #GunControl #tcot #lnyhbt #ATT #teaparty (GirlMonson, 07/26/2012)	Commissive	14 (2%)
I'm your constituent and I oppose	User positioning statement that explicitly or implicitly implies constituency	@repjohncampbell wanted to voice my opposition to #SOPA #PIPA and as a tax paying citizen, #dreamact please vote for your constituents (Common__Cents, 01/18/2012)	Representative	9 (1%)
Analogy	Equates or transfers support/opposition of an issue to another issue or state of affairs	@RepDianaDeGette Supporting the #DREAMact HR.1751 is supporting the economy that put #USA in front! Thanks for listening. (Emanuel5280, 02/13/2012)	Representative	5 (1%)

Table 9. Definitions of the 16 categories of lobbying tweets, examples of each, their speech act types, and frequency.

Catalyst: Triggering Collective Action with Thresholds

Justin Cheng, Michael S. Bernstein
Stanford HCI Group, Computer Science Department
Stanford University
{jcccf,msb}@cs.stanford.edu

ABSTRACT
The web is a catalyst for drawing people together around shared goals, but many groups never reach critical mass. It can thus be risky to commit time or effort to a goal: participants show up only to discover that nobody else did, and organizers devote significant effort to causes that never get off the ground. Crowdfunding has lessened some of this risk by only calling in donations when an effort reaches a collective monetary goal. However, it leaves unsolved the harder problem of mobilizing effort, time and participation. We generalize the concept into *activation thresholds*, commitments that are conditioned on others' participation. With activation thresholds, supporters only need to show up for an event if enough other people commit as well. *Catalyst* is a platform that introduces activation thresholds for on-demand events. For more complex coordination needs, Catalyst also provides thresholds based on time or role (e.g., a bake sale requiring commitments for bakers, decorators, and sellers). In a multi-month field deployment, Catalyst helped users organize events including food bank volunteering, on-demand study groups, and mass participation events like a human chess game. Our results suggest that activation thresholds can indeed catalyze a large class of new collective efforts.

Author Keywords
Collective action, activation thresholds, critical mass.

INTRODUCTION
By lowering barriers to participation, the web has transformed how people work together [12]. Successful collective efforts include the compilation of encyclopedic knowledge on Wikipedia [26], disaster relief for major earthquakes [48], and planning and organizational support for the Arab Spring uprisings [25]. However, for every successful cause, there are many that never reach critical mass. For example, Wikipedia was the only large-scale success out of eight independent, simultaneous attempts at creating a collaborative online encyclopedia [23]. Moreover, successful causes are typically limited to online tasks. Causes that try to mobilize offline participation, effort, and hours have far less design support.

CSCW'14, February 15–19, 2014, Baltimore, Maryland, USA.

ACM 978-1-4503-2540-0/14/02...$15.00.
http://dx.doi.org/10.1145/2531602.2531635

Many efforts struggle because participation incurs significant costs and risks, regardless of the eventual outcome [27]. Supporters run the risk of committing time to a cause that never captures enough interest to achieve its goals. Similarly, organizers risk putting time and emotional investment into a cause that never catches on. Many collective efforts need critical mass to be successful, for example study groups, flash mobs, or musical ensembles. Further, the significant upfront cost of organizing a cause, and discouragement that results from past failure [10], may prevent organizers from trying again.

Catalyst is a platform designed for crowds to take action predicated on the concept of *activation thresholds*. Activation thresholds condition commitment on the participation of others: a cause gets activated only if enough participants commit. Organizers can pitch ideas, only putting effort into those that reach success thresholds, and participants need only participate if enough others also commit to doing so. For instance, a benefit concert might get put on only if at least 100 people commit to attending. Activation thresholds are an explicit manifestation of the *threshold point* described in models of collective behavior, where the benefits of participation begin to outweigh its drawbacks [21, 38]. As each participant's utility is dependent on the number of fellow participants, they typically want to join efforts that reach this threshold and are guaranteed to succeed. As the commitment to organize or participate in an event is conditioned on the activation threshold being reached, one's time is only spent on coordinating or attending successful events. Thus, these thresholds can significantly reduce the upfront risks of organizing causes.

The funding model used in crowdfunding systems such as Kickstarter [1] is essentially a type of activation threshold: a project is funded only if supporters commit a sufficient amount of money. Motivated by the success of using activation thresholds in crowdfunding, we hypothesize that these thresholds can generalize to new classes of efforts that raise person-hours, and not just money. In doing so, we broaden the design space of such systems to include commitments that require later action (such as attendance), instead of an automatic transfer of funds.

Many collective action efforts also involve more complex forms of coordination than a threshold number of participants. In many volunteer organizations, for example, significant effort is spent in coordination and communication [51, 48]. Beyond simple participation thresholds, Catalyst minimizes back-and-forth coordination by enabling more highly-structured activation thresholds, for example by requiring that

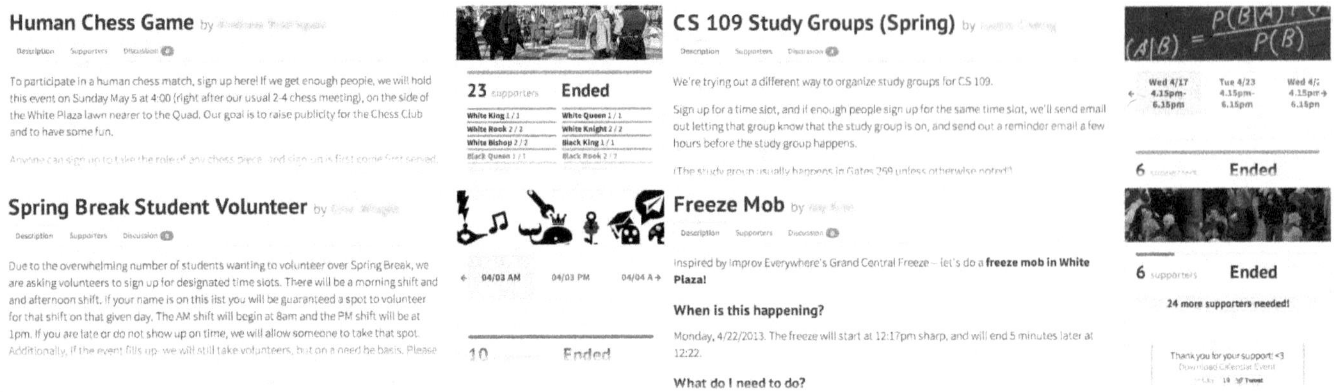

Figure 1. A variety of causes were organized on Catalyst, each using different activation thresholds, and succeeding to different degrees.

different roles or time slots all be filled. Roles end up being critical in many types of events: bake sales require both bakers and sellers, and office hours require both teaching assistants and students. This approach can also help overcome the free rider effect and promote peer commitment [15].

In this paper, we first review theories of collective behavior and existing online systems for collective action. We then describe the design of Catalyst, its support for activation thresholds and other mechanisms for coordination. Next, we detail Catalyst's evaluation through a field deployment where it was used to organize real-world causes including volunteering at a large food bank, on-demand study groups and flash mobs. We find that activation thresholds help both in group coordination and deferring commitment, with most participants following through on their initial commitments.

RELATED WORK

Activation thresholds are inspired by the threshold theories (e.g. critical mass theory) of collective action advanced by Granovetter and Oliver [21, 38], and generalize the use of similar thresholding mechanisms found in many crowdfunding platforms. Drawing on the literature on specialization and small group sizes and their impact on collective action, we extend these thresholds beyond simple minimum participation to support roles and time slots.

Collective action

The term *collective action* is used differently in fields such as sociology, political science, economics, and social computing. In particular, we refer to collective action broadly as a group of people coming together to achieve a shared goal. This definition has been applied to social computing efforts such as Wikipedia [23]. However, some literature focuses on social movements such as revolutions [25] or environmentalism, which is largely outside the scope of this work.

Triggers

There is a tipping point beyond which the benefit of participating in a cause exceeds its cost [40]. Threshold models suggest that individuals have unique tipping points, with each adopting the cause only if the proportion of people in the network who also support it exceeds this threshold [21, 38]. With the right conditions, initial support can precipitate a chain reaction that ultimately spreads to all members of a community.

These theories aim to explain several characteristics of collective action, including numeric thresholds and their tendency to either fail completely or succeed wildly [38]. A common framing is that the value of participating as a function of other number of participants may be "S"-shaped. In particular, collective action begins with a period of startup costs and low but increasing marginal returns from each additional participant, which accounts for the high failure rate of many potential causes. This then leads to a period of higher marginal returns (i.e. the tipping point), and finally satiation where returns are high, but the marginal returns diminishing. In other words, there is "some threshold of participation that is crossed before a social movement 'explodes' into being" [38]. Catalyst makes explicit this notion of a numeric threshold. Users who commit to Catalyst events are, in a sense, agreeing that its activation threshold is at or above their own personal threshold.

Efforts that fail to reach this tipping point, or critical mass, including online encyclopedias and WikiProjects, may never achieve their goals [49, 19]. Critical mass is also key to groupware acceptance [22]. Solving critical mass problems can thus benefit a large class of social computing platforms.

Collective action platforms

Where many systems exist to support specific types of group action including crowdfunding [1], crisis organization [37], creative projects [32], and public deliberation [28], Catalyst represents the first attempt at supporting the organization of arbitrary threshold-based collective activities. Motivation schemes can also be layered on top of such platforms; for example, the MIT DARPA Red Balloon Challenge team offered financial incentives to encourage effective organization [41]. In an organizational setting, crowdfunding was shown to encourage diverse proposals and promote collaboration [36].

"All or nothing"

Thresholding is ubiquitous in online crowdfunding web sites such as Kickstarter. On these sites, the funding model is predicated on the concept of *critical mass*, or that a project succeeds only if it reaches a specific funding goal. Crucially, they use the concept of "all or nothing" in canvassing support from its users. When supporters back a project, their money is first held in escrow; depending on whether the project's funding goal is met, this money is either released to the project creators, or returned to the supporter. This "all or nothing" approach ensures supporters risk-free commitment: either the project succeeds and they obtain what the project promised, or it fails and they get their money back. Groupon also uses thresholding to activate deals: a deal is only active when enough users have claimed it. This thresholding positively correlates with the number of deals sold [14]. Sites such as Zokos [5] also require a minimum number of attendees. Still, the primary goal and commitment mechanism in many of these systems is the monetary pledge, which is optional in Catalyst. Our work generalizes these mechanisms for financial critical mass to commitments involving time and effort. Rather than raising money, Catalyst raises person-hours.

Motivating commitment

Social signaling can help people estimate an event's probability of success. A project's funding status acts as social proof, with the amount of funding and number of backers signaling the quality of the project. "People are persuaded more by the actions of others than by any proof we can offer," [15]. For example, peers' listening patterns have large effects on an individual's preferences [47].

Social signaling helps later participants make inferences based on previous participants' decisions, and can create social pressure to conform. When faced with a lack of information, people tend to mirror the decisions that others made previously [8], with the strength of this effect correlated with the size of the conforming group [34]. This signaling also affects a participant's perception of whether an event will achieve a critical mass of users. This perceived critical mass was shown to significantly influence a user's intention to use groupware technology [30]. Thus, Catalyst provides information about the current state of an event such as how close an event is to its threshold.

Many types of collective action also involve specialized roles. Wikipedia is organized hierarchically into administrators, editors, trusted users, and untrusted users, with resource and interest heterogeneity shown to be key factors contributing to its sustainability [43]. In creative systems like Pipeline, leaders delegate the creation of specific art to different individuals [32]. Further, individuals are more likely to contribute to online communities when given specific tasks, or reminded of the uniqueness of their contributions [11].

In contrast to crowdfunding, where contribution is purely monetary, in collective action, "time is the ultimate resource" [39]. This introduces several complications, most importantly the free-rider problem, as well ensuring follow-up commitment. Collective efforts also suffer from social loafing: the larger a group, the larger the loss of individual motivation and coordination [45]. Smaller groups can mitigate this effect as individuals are more likely to take action when they stand to gain a substantial proportion of the total benefit [40]. While Catalyst can support events of arbitrary size, roles and time slots help break up larger events into smaller, more manageable ones.

In contrast to crowdfunding, the commitment contracts on Catalyst are primarily social, implicitly with both the organizer and other participants. Thus, it is significantly harder to enforce followthrough on Catalyst than on many crowdfunding web sites, where money is immediately taken into escrow, or when the commitment contract is material or financial. In such cases, commitment devices can serve to discourage people from reneging on their promises to participate [20], and act to filter out the less committed.

CATALYST

Motivated by the challenges of organizing group action, our work translates threshold models into a general design mechanism of *activation thresholds*. In activation thresholds, users' commitments are only called in if the event gathers a minimum number of participants. In this section, we introduce Catalyst, a platform that demonstrates the opportunities for activation thresholds, including variants such as minimum thresholding, maximum thresholding, and role-based thresholding. We motivate Catalyst's design with an example, then the system and its use.

Alfred is trying to organize a neighborhood bake sale in support of a local charity. He creates an event on Catalyst, specifying the date and time of the sale, as well as a minimum number of people that need to participate to ensure its success (the *activation threshold*). As he needs volunteers to donate baked goods, decorate the booth for the bake sale, and sell the baked goods, he creates specific roles for these (*role-based thresholding*, Figure 2a); only when enough people fill these roles will the sale take place. Alfred links to the event on Facebook and posts flyers to recruit potential volunteers. Later, Beth sees that 3 of her neighbors have already signed up for the event in various roles. Confident in her oatmeal cookies, she signs up as a baker by entering her name and email address (*coordinating action*, Figure 2b). Several signups later, Cole, who can neither bake nor decorate, decides to help out as a seller instead (*differing levels of commitment*). Cole's support brings the number sign-ups to the requisite 10, including committed individuals for each role (*the threshold point*, Figure 2c). Having reached its threshold, the bake sale is on! Catalyst emails everyone who signed up with an email Alfred had prepared to confirm the event.

Activation thresholds

In Catalyst, activation thresholds are the minimum number of people who need to commit to an event for it to occur. To create a sense of urgency, and drawing from crowdfunding techniques, the organizer must attract the minimum number of commitments within a specific time span. Catalyst reinforces this urgency by reminding committed participants roughly 72 hours before a deadline.

Catalyst primarily focuses on lower bounds for a number of participants (minimum thresholding). However, early field studies of the system made clear that there was more complexity to collective action than Catalyst captured. Thus, organizers may also limit the number of participants (maximum thresholds) to create additional urgency, or specify multiple roles or repetitions of an event.

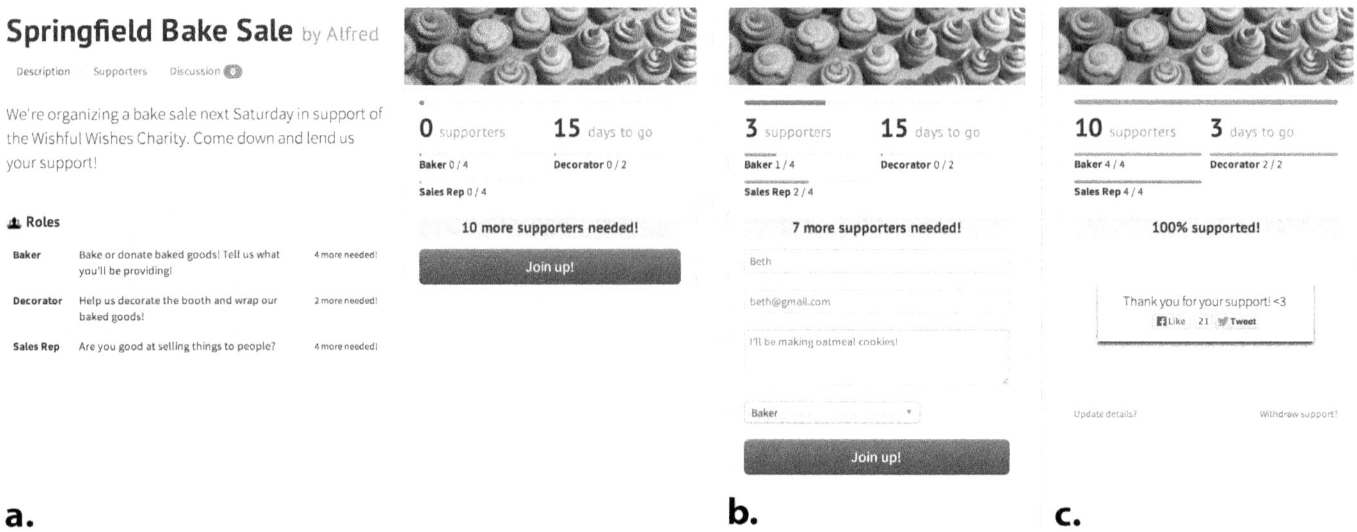

Figure 2. (a) A Catalyst event page shows the event description, the roles that participants can take on, as well as the current status of the cause. (b) A user supports a cause by typing in her name and email address, along with an optional message, picking a role if necessary. (c) A successful cause where the requisite number of supporters was achieved, with every role filled.

Minimum thresholding

In Catalyst, minimum thresholding is based on the assumption that many events require at least some number of people to be successful, and is grounded in critical mass theory [21, 38]. Additionally, minimum thresholding implicitly sets a participation goal to meet, which has been effective in persuading people to donate to charitable causes [17].

Maximum thresholding

While minimum thresholds show how "close" one is to success, maximum thresholds create artificial limits on the number of signups, thus making them appear more desirable. The time limit imposed on every cause also acts as a type of maximum threshold. Artificial scarcity causes participation to be perceived as more valuable, and can motivate participants to support and subsequently participate in an event [15]. In particular, the effect of limited supply on perceived value is strongest together with popularity, suggesting that maximum thresholds are most effective with popular events [50].

Role-based thresholding

While simple activation thresholds are intuitively appealing, many events require complex coordination — a potluck dinner might require different attendees to bring different dishes; study groups may occur at different times in a day, with each requiring one tutor and five students. It may also be necessary to condition spots on the roles that other participants pick. For example, supporters may only be able to sign up as students if there is at least one peer tutor in a study group session.

Also, many events are temporal and repetitive in nature: study groups might meet several times a week, and beach cleanups might occur over several different weekends. Thus, Catalyst supports multiple time slots for a single event, allowing participants to choose a slot that fits best in their schedule. All time slots that reach their threshold will be activated.

By introducing roles or specialization, participants can concentrate on a narrower set of tasks, improving their effectiveness [9]. In collective action systems like Wikipedia, participation begins at the periphery, with users assuming roles of increasing importance as they get more familiar with the system [13]. Similarly, roles in Catalyst allow for supporters of differing expertise, and differing commitment levels.

In many volunteer organizations, volunteer coordination, which includes scheduling and role assignment, presents an even larger issue than recruitment [51]. Role-based thresholds partially alleviate the cost of coordination by requiring participants to commit to specific roles or time slots.

Monetary commitment

Unlike crowdfunding or fundraising, where the commitment is automatically executed through a donation held in escrow, it is always possible that a Catalyst volunteer may fail to follow through on a commitment. As commitment devices can serve to discourage people from reneging [20], Catalyst also allows organizers to require a higher-friction commitment, for example donating $1 using Paypal to sign up.

Coordinating action via email

Catalyst allows organizers to contact supporters to remind them about their commitments. For instance, activation goal emails let supporters know if a cause they supported has been activated, while failure emails let supporters know a cause failed to get off the ground. Reminder emails sent a few days before can act to increase the tension and urgency in supporting the cause, and can be effective when used with negative frames ("we're not going to succeed without enough supporters!") and statistical support ("we're only 10 supporters away from our goal!") [50].

Designing for Collective Action

The organization of an event involves different costs: those of supporters *committing* or *participating*, and those of organizers *preparing* for, and *coordinating* the event. Each factor represents different tradeoffs which affect an event's scale, impact or success. The design of collective action systems such as Catalyst can encourage events with particular cost levels, and they may even aim to raise or lower these costs.

Here, we characterize the design of Catalyst and other systems along these axes. Considering different points in this design space may lead to platforms that support very different purposes — for example, an online system for reporting sensed data require initially high commitment (e.g. setting up one's phone to sense the environment), but subsequently less effort to participate (walking around with a phone). One focused on localized, realtime events (low commitment and preparation, but high coordination cost) may focus more on short-term dynamics and recruitment strategies.

Commitment cost relates to the initial effort required to participate in a cause. Events may require high commitment costs to guarantee participation, while those hoping to gather as many people as possible may seek lower costs. Systems for volunteer organizations like VolunteerMatch err on the side of high friction signups, requiring potential volunteers to fill out several forms and pass in-person interviews. While this filters for highly committed volunteers, potential participants may be discouraged by the up-front effort [46]. On the other hand, if the initial commitment is low-cost, participants are less committed to the cause [6]. Crowdfunding, while having a low participation cost in requiring only a monetary pledge, has high commitment cost because this pledge is up-front. Catalyst aims for a balance: just enough friction to provide an honest signal about the intent to participate [18]. Since commitment devices like an initial monetary commitment can potentially improve follow-through, in Catalyst, organizers can require a monetary donation to support a cause, and can offer to return the donation when participants show up to the event.

Participation cost describes the amount of time or energy desired from participants. For instance, volunteering a morning for a beach cleanup may be a substantial commitment, but supporting a petition requires significantly less effort. Differing motivations also influence a participant's desired commitment level — activities with clear personal benefits (e.g., office hours) may be more motivating than those without (e.g., a flash mob). As Catalyst is designed primarily for offline events where participants needed to show up at a specific location and time, events tended to require greater effort. Nevertheless, roles allow for variable participation cost, where not all participants are involved to the same extent.

Preparation cost describes the up-front cost to organizers in preparing an event. For instance, large concerts may require venue reservation months in advance (high cost), and tend to use event management platforms that support ticket sales, as the event's occurrence is usually guaranteed regardless. On the other hand, social media platforms like Twitter favor low-cost, ad-hoc event organization [48]. Planned events are generally well-organized and coordinated, but lack the flexibility of ad-hoc systems which can respond quickly to crises. Catalyst requires organizers to create events, but supports low-cost event creation, so preparation can be deferred until an event's success is guaranteed.

Coordination cost describes the effort required in coordinating and organizing participants. Petitions and fundraisers require little coordination between organizers and participants, as participants need only donate or sign a petition. Thus, platforms like Kickstarter and We The People [4] are designed to primarily support this single transaction, but not more complex coordination. For instance, platforms like ConsiderIt require the crowd to collectively decide on public issues [28]; Doodle requires all participants to report availability and then agree on a specific time. Through activation thresholds (or the lack thereof) and roles, Catalyst supports events which have low to medium coordination costs, such as minimum participation, or a division of labor. In particular, Catalyst can reduce this coordination cost for smaller-scale, local causes that lack resources to develop specialized platforms. As the centralization of ties has a positive effect on collective action [33], a single organizer is responsible for a cause on Catalyst.

DEPLOYMENT AND EVALUATION

Catalyst instantiates our design hypothesis that activation thresholds support collective action. To test this hypothesis, as well as understand the types of events that are well or poorly supported by activation thresholds, we launched Catalyst and studied its use from February through May 2013. We did not pursue a controlled field experiment as early pilots suggested that events exhibited large variance in participation. We instead aimed to attract a large amount of naturalistic usage so we could probe the strengths and weaknesses of the system.

Catalyst attracted interested organizers from a local volunteer food bank, lecturers and faculty at a large American university, student interest organizations, organizers of a massive online open course, and others. The authors mined contact information for these organizations from the web, and then reached out to the organizers via email to explain how Catalyst might support their goals. As each organizer was responsible for organizing their own event, we did not perform any additional participant recruitment. Organizers used their organization's web site or email to direct participants to the Catalyst web site. Table 1 presents a sample of these events, the types of activation thresholds they used, and whether they succeeded. In the case of the volunteer food bank, a computer running Catalyst was also set up on-site.

For events that occurred locally, at least one author was present to verify the number of people that showed up to events that succeeded. To understand subjective perceptions of commitment on Catalyst versus in-person or social-network based invitations, we sent an email survey at the end of the deployment to all organizers and participants who had registered for events on Catalyst. The questions asked can be found in Appendix A.

Results

Catalyst was successful in coordinating hundreds of supporters across tens of events. From February to May 2013, Catalyst saw 2,300 visitors, 15,000 page views, and 368 supporters across all events. 16 leaders created 30 events, with 24

Event (Type)	Activation threshold	Supporters (Sparkline)	Slots	Conv. %	Description
Human chess game (Mass participation)	Min 18 2 Players, 16 Pieces	23	—	8	Act as a chess piece in an outdoor human chess game.
Peer office hours (Self-improvement)	Min 4, Max 6 1 Leader, 3-5 Learners	55	13	23	Tutor students on demand, or be tutored.
Massive online course discussion sessions (Self-improvement)	Min 10, Max 20 1 Mod, 9 Learners	177	28	28	Moderate or attend optional weekly small-group discussion sections on Google Hangouts.
Peer study groups (Self-improvement)	Min 4, Max 6	35	12	12	Attend peer-led, on-demand study groups.
On-demand labs (Self-improvement)	Min 20	61	4	N/A	Lab topics that attracted enough interest were added to the course schedule.
Spring Break volunteering (Volunteer)	Max 8-10	79	10	80	Volunteer at a food bank: there was a maximum number of volunteers each day.
Teatime meetup (Meeting)	Min 4	29	5	20	Weekly teatime meetings occurred if there was sufficient interest.
Food Bank volunteering (Volunteer)	Min 1	62	20	N/A	Volunteer at a local food bank on a given day.
Reading group (Self-improvement)	1 Discussion Leader	6 —	6	N/A	Reading group occurred each week if a discussion leader committed.
Finals study session (failed) (Self-improvement)	Min 20	4	—	0.2	Committed $1 to attend a finals week study session providing candy.
Freeze mob (failed) (Mass participation)	Min 30	6	—	3	Join a flash mob.
Document translation (failed) (Volunteer)	Min 2	1 —	3	2	Volunteer to translate documents for a food bank.

Table 1. The events organized on Catalyst ranged from meetings to study groups to volunteer opportunities to flash mobs. The sparklines show the number of supporters over the lifetime of the event.

obtaining at least 1 supporter (4 of the 16 leaders were personal contacts of the authors). Analyzing participant names using data from the U.S. Census Bureau [3], we estimate that overall, 42% of participants were female; 40% were White, 44% were Asian or Pacific Islander, 10% were Black, and the remainder Hispanic. Nonetheless, the demographic makeup of participants varied depending on the event — office hours involved undergraduate students, while food bank volunteering saw a more diverse range of ages and professions.

Eleven (46%) of the causes eventually succeeded, or reached their activation thresholds, comparable to Kickstarter's 42% success rate as of May 2013 [2]. Catalyst had a mean conversion rate of 16%, meaning that on average, 16% of an event's visitors signed up for it.

Events organized on Catalyst tended to fall into three main categories—volunteer efforts, fun mass-participation events, and self-improvement (Table 1). For a volunteer event, participants committed to packing or distributing food during a particular time slot. As an example of a mass-participation event, participants signed up to act as different chess pieces in a large outdoor human chess game (Figure 3). In the self-improvement category, study groups and office hours for computer science classes were organized on-demand if enough students expressed interest. In particular, additional office hours were only organized if there was also at least one experienced peer facilitator to lead the discussion. Organizers also used Catalyst to organize meetings and social events, including informal tea gatherings and reading groups.

Figure 3. A local chess club used Catalyst to organize a game of human chess, where participants wearing black or white represented chess pieces on a life-size game board.

As predicted by prior work, the sparklines in Table 1 demonstrate empirical evidence of the hypothesized "S"-shaped production function, especially in events with substantial activity (e.g. the human chess game).

A total of 35 participants (labelled P#) and 5 organizers completed the post-deployment survey. Participants are labelled P# and organizers O#.

Figure 4. A computer running Catalyst at a local food bank allowed volunteers to sign up for events.

Activation thresholds supported coordination
The visibility of peer commitment served as a valuable signal of future success: participants clustered around topics or slots that others were also beginning to support. Many appreciated that "you could see who else [was] going" (P12, P13). For instance, the online class discussion sections were divided into seven different sections focusing on different topics, each studio having four different meeting times. In almost all cases, only one or two of these four time slots exceeded the minimum number of attendees. Similarly, when a class was polled to figure out which topics should be covered in labs, only two of the four suggested topics exceeded the minimum threshold of 20 supporters (obtaining 22 each), with the other two receiving far less support (6 and 11).

Through maximum thresholds, Catalyst helped generate demand and manage volunteer flow at a local food bank (Figure 4). The food bank expressed that they had previously struggled with large variance in volunteer numbers day-to-day [51]. While students would typically show up on Monday or Tuesday, with little to none on Thursday or Friday, using Catalyst, an average of 7.9 ($\sigma = 1.85$, Gini $G = 0.125$) students signed up for each of 10 slots spread out over the week.

Activation thresholds supported deferred commitment
Activation thresholds helped organizers push back preparation for an event until they had an better idea of how many people were interested. On Catalyst, mass-participation events like flash mobs had the highest failure rates out of all event types. Deferred commitment helped organizers gauge interest before committing time and resources to coordinating participants: "Using Catalyst allowed me to make the event page without committing to it happening, which was good because I was unsure if enough people would be interested" (O4). Similarly, O5 mentioned that during busier weeks, he would "not...[hold office hours] for [only] 2 people."

In other cases, Catalyst also helps organizers better estimate the number of people who participate, as was the case for volunteer food bank signups. For example, the local food bank coordinator used Catalyst to better forecast the number of volunteers to expect each day, then prepare an appropriate number of tasks for those volunteers.

Committed supporters followed through on commitments

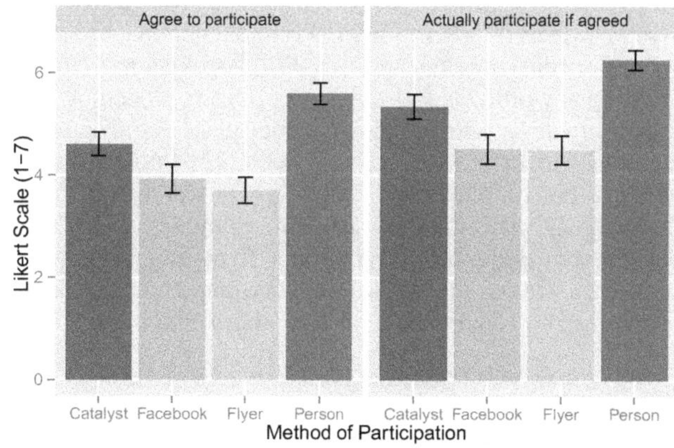

Figure 5. Participants were more likely to both agree to attending an event on Catalyst, and participate if they previously agreed to, compared to an event on Facebook or one advertised through a flyer or email.

While Catalyst successfully gathers commitments, events that might appear successful can still fail to actually mobilize supporters if they do not honor these commitments. Followthrough was thus a major concern while developing Catalyst. However, across the hundreds of committed supporters for Catalyst events, we observed that the vast majority of commitments for triggered events were truthful. For instance, almost all students who signed up for peer office hours attended them. Similarly, more than 90% of participants who signed up for volunteer food bank events followed through on their commitments.

While motivation strongly influences commitment, we observed that group size also affected the follow-through rate—fewer participants showed up when there was a larger committed group. This result corroborates previous research relating larger group sizes with decreased motivation [45]. Because each peer office hour or study group session only involved 4 to 6 students, each student was highly likely to show up. On the other hand, for the human chess game, only 70% of committed participants showed up (16/23). In this case, the event's minimum threshold was just eighteen people, and the initial gathering of sixteen attracted a few interested onlookers, so the event had a sufficient buffer to still succeed; even a small group of people engaging in some action is sufficient to induce a large proportion of passers-by to also do so [34]. In the future, Catalyst might predict the number of follow-throughs for a given minimum threshold to help event organizers ensure a sufficient buffer.

Our post-deployment survey suggests that Catalyst was also effective in motivating participants to sign up or commit, as well as follow through on their commitment. We compared participants' self-reported likelihood of commitment and followthrough between common recruiting methods such as Facebook events, flyers, an in-person request (our gold standard), and Catalyst (Figure 5). A Friedman test on the Likert-scale responses revealed a significant effect of the recruiting method on both the likelihood of committing to an event ($\chi^2(4) = 90.9$, $p < 10^{-16}$) and the likelihood of following through on that commitment ($\chi^2(4) = 82.5$, $p < 10^{-16}$). Post-hoc Wilcoxon tests demonstrated that participants were more likely to sign up for, and participate in events on Catalyst, compared to being invited on Facebook or after seeing a flyer or mass mailing ($p < 0.05$). As expected, in-person invitations would be still the most effective at getting people to participate ($p < 0.01$), possibly because "personal requests take top priority" (P3), and "in person...[one doesn't] want to hurt that person's feelings" (P20). Thus, Catalyst is more effective than other popular means of organizing events online, but less so than personal invitations. To overcome possible response bias in our results, future work could compare signups for the same event on Catalyst, Facebook and in-person.

Roles supported complex coordination

Organizers used role-based participation for the more complex event setups. For example, in peer office hours, the organizer used multiple time slots and a role-based threshold such that students could only join a specific time if at least there was at least one peer facilitator who had already signed up for that slot. Similarly, in the online class discussion sections, students could sign up as moderators to lead a Google Hangout, or to sign up as a participant to attend one.

Role-based thresholds were especially applicable to the human chess game, which required 16 different people to play 16 different chess pieces, and to peer office hours, which required a peer facilitator and 4 students — "I couldn't see it any other way" (O5).

While every event that employed roles succeeded, some organizers had reservations about using roles: while "it makes planning automation easier...there's no way to know if...role[s] encouraged or discouraged people" (O1). Future work could study the effect roles have on commitment levels and on creating artificial scarcity.

Long-running events initially succeeded, then struggled

On Catalyst, recurring events tended to stop recurring: events like study groups and class studios were designed around weekly, repeating events, where participants had to commit to attending each. However, sustaining causes is difficult unless such they demonstrate very tangible benefits to participants [7]. While the initial instantiations of such events were successful, subsequent instances saw significantly less commitment: "we had attendance for the first [discussion session], but then it just fell apart." (P8)

Nonetheless, several individual sessions in a massive online course saw sustained participation through the end of the deployment. Though there was a drop-off in attendance, users that stuck around continued to do so for several weeks. In one session, though there were 7 participants in the first week, 4 continued to participate through the next three weeks. This suggests that utilizing small-group commitment may be useful for long-running events.

Reminders played a significant role in ensuring the success of some long-running events: "A reminder 1 hour before the event would definitely help me not forget it" (P16). For the weekly social teatime meet-ups, not only was the activation threshold low, but weekly emails were sent out to remind participants to join in. Where reminders were infrequent or not used, participant attendance decreased week after week.

Motivation is the primary factor driving participation

While activation thresholds are useful in signaling quality and deferring commitment, the actual acts of committing and attending an event are still largely dependent on a participant's motivation. Many participants echoed the sentiment that "regardless of [how] I was invited," (P15, P16), "I will go only if I want to" (P15) or "when I am interested" (P9).

Nevertheless, feedback suggested that activation thresholds may be the most persuasive when participants are on the fence, unsure whether or not to participate. In these situations, their decision could be strongly influenced by peer and social signals like the number of other people going [8].

Similarly, events that conferred larger and more specific benefits to participants (e.g., study groups, office hours and class studios) saw higher success rates and conversion rates than those where the benefit of participation was less clear (e.g., flash mobs). While participants joined class studios "to get feedback on my project from like-minded people" (P6) and peer office hours because of the "good, focused attention from the professor" (P9), flash mobs "were kind of stupid" (P17).

Deployment limitations

Participant feedback was primarily positive, and our deployment allowed us to understand how Catalyst was able to support several types of causes using different activation thresholds, Nonetheless, it was not a field experiment. Experiments that control for whether the activation threshold is shown, or compare participation in similar events across different web sites such as Facebook or Meetup.com, would help quantify the effectiveness of activation thresholds. Though our deployment lasted several months, we also cannot extrapolate to how the system would be used if it gained further popularity.

DISCUSSION

In our three-month initial field deployment, participants adopted Catalyst to mobilize hundreds of people for causes ranging from education to social gatherings and fun. Here, we reflect on open challenges and opportunities for activation thresholds and for Catalyst in particular.

Enforcing followthrough

Activation thresholds generalize two components of crowdfunding: 1) the *form* of the commitment (from a monetary pledge to participation), and 2) the *execution* of that commitment (from financial escrow to a social contract for followthrough). The challenge is that a social contract may be more difficult to enforce. Some of crowdfunding's success can be attributed to the hardness of a financial commitment, which discourages participants from reneging on their promises to fund projects. Catalyst makes an explicit design decision *not* to use hard commitments such as money, and instead to focus on social commitments to encourage followthrough. In this sense, Catalyst has a strictly harder problem to solve: it not only needs to raise interest, it also needs to encourage follow-through on that commitment.

We experimented with allowing organizers to require monetary commitment similar to Kickstarter. However, the conversion rates for events with monetary commitments was significantly lower, with few to no people signing up for them. Such commitment devices may instead be appropriate for larger events, where demand far outstrips availability. Alternatively, reputation systems like on eBay or Stack Overflow could help build trust among organizers and participants in the long term[44].

Slacktivism or activism?

While many of the flash mobs organized never succeeded, they gained a substantial number of Facebook likes (19, 12 and 7). Many people supported the idea on Facebook, but most of them did not commit to attending the event. The result is an intermediate, "slacktivist" level of commitment on Catalyst. This suggests that when faced with a decision about how much to support a cause, most people will pick the path of least resistance. Rather than joining in a demonstration, most people would rather support the demonstrators [29].

Allowing for weaker, more tentative commitment with the ability to later escalate such commitment to actual participation may thus be more effective in encouraging slacktivists to participate: "I wish Catalyst had a way to indicate that people were 'maybe' attending...people would be more comfortable responding...see who else was coming, then change their mind" (O3). We hypothesize that this approach might decrease follow-through, but the concomitant increase in participation might be enough to offset it. Another approach might allow the less committed individuals on Facebook — who may even be remote and unable to participate — to leave messages for and motivate the committed users. Participation could also be motivated with appropriate task or role recommendations (e.g. SuggestBot on Wikipedia [16]).

Controlling for participant quality

Many volunteer organizations face the challenge of retaining volunteers in the long-term, as well as ensuring that participants who signed up are committed to carrying out the tasks they were assigned [51]. Several volunteer organizations expressed interest in Catalyst but were concerned that its framing around single events could not yet support the kind of long-term commitment they require.

Nevertheless, we believe Catalyst embodies an interesting middle ground between online signups and offline volunteerism. While organization online is highly ad-hoc, and more about accomplishing a task than about forming social bonds [52], Catalyst seems to support a combination of both ad-hoc gatherings and bond-building. While intrinsic motivation plays a large factor in participation, especially in the case of recurring events, participants reported they were more likely to commit via Catalyst than through most other mechanisms. Participants who signed up to volunteer at the local food bank generally followed through, and animated, long-lived discussions sprang up in the online discussion sessions.

Limitations

While Catalyst is useful for predetermined events, it lacks the "flexibility afforded by email" (O1) or a Doodle poll, where there is more room for negotiation and the balance of power between all stakeholders more equitable. Further, though requiring separate commitments for each event in a recurring series potentially strengthens one's resolve to attending each, it can also discourage the initial commitment and hence the success of the event. And like Kickstarter, the organizer is solely responsible for the specifics of an event including the setting of appropriate thresholds and roles. This also means a large amount of a cause's success is dependent on the organizer, like in other collective action systems. Kickstarter projects which lacked video introductions or had spelling errors were significantly less likely to be funded [35]. Despite the low barrier to entry, creators reported that organizing and marketing successful, large-scale Kickstarter campaigns was significantly harder than they believed [24]. Still, such "front loading", where the goals and details of a project are specified upfront, has been shown to be more effective at gathering contributors than projects which are more spontaneous [31].

"Let a hundred flowers bloom"

While many Catalyst events reached their activation threshold, many others did not. The organizers may have been disappointed, but the fact that Catalyst encouraged failed events is a kind of success. Likewise, YouTube is valuable not just for its popular videos, but also for its publish-then-filter model that encourages failures as well as out-of-the-box successes. In this way, Catalyst leads to many failures as a side effect of generating more collective action successes. Akin to design prototyping, the low cost of failure suggests that Catalyst potentially supports *event prototyping*, where organizers create and iterate on several potential events.

Most research has focused on models for collective action and case studies of successful causes, rather than the identification and analysis of failed efforts [42]. However, many of Grudin's exhortations for groupware developers are relevant here [22]; often, the organizer's view of an event's latent interest did not match those of the potential participants. But even then, some events that did not reach their activation thresholds still succeeded — some online discussion sessions that had only six participants instead of ten still ended up being organized, subsequently generating lively discussion.

We believe that it will be important to explore how systems can help organizers predict, understand and learn from failure. For example, often organizers were left wondering whether an event failed because it received insufficient exposure, or if it succeeded in reaching people but failed because no one was interested. Analytics like page views or historical event data could help organizers design events that appeal to larger audiences and create realistic thresholds to improve the chances of future events succeeding.

CONCLUSION AND FUTURE WORK

In this paper, we introduce *activation thresholds* for collective action. Catalyst embodies this idea by allowing participants to condition their commitment on others' participation. A three-month field deployment demonstrated that Catalyst could organize hundreds of individuals to gather for small-scale events ranging from on-demand tutoring, volunteerism and social events. Future work lies in three main areas. First, many events require more thorough consideration of activation thresholds, including events with multiple stages and long-term commitments. Second is further analysis of how to encourage participants to commit to new events and follow through once they do commit. Third, it will be important to quantify the effect of activation thresholds in comparison to other commitment mechanisms.

Our work suggests that social computing design can help support many new classes of events. Could Catalyst have helped organize Wikipedia or Tahrir Square? In its current form, probably not. However, its vision of low-risk collective efforts will lower barriers. Online classes could be kickstarted based on the interests of students; local citizens could gather to more actively improve their communities; major movements may even take root. The web has already lowered the threshold for connecting like-minded people — we envision its potential for likewise catalyzing real-world action.

ACKNOWLEDGMENTS

This work is supported by NSF Grants XXX and a Stanford Graduate Fellowship.

REFERENCES

1. Kickstarter. `http://www.kickstarter.com`.
2. Kickstarter stats. `http://www.kickstarter.com/help/stats`.
3. U.S. census bureau genealogy data. `http://www.census.gov/genealogy/www/data/index.html`.
4. We the people. `http://petitions.whitehouse.gov`.
5. Zokos. `http://www.zokos.com`.
6. Arkes, H. R., and Blumer, C. The psychology of sunk cost. *Organizational behavior and human decision processes* (1985).
7. Backman, E. V., and Smith, S. R. Healthy organizations, unhealthy communities? *Nonprofit Management and Leadership* (2000).
8. Banerjee, A. V. A simple model of herd behavior. *The Quarterly Journal of Economics* (1992).
9. Becker, G. S., and Murphy, K. M. The division of labor, coordination costs, and knowledge. *The Quarterly Journal of Economics* (1992).
10. Bédoyan, I., Aelst, P. V., and Walgrave, S. Limitations and possibilities of transnational mobilization: the case of eu summit protesters in brussels, 2001. *Mobilization: An International Quarterly* (2004).
11. Beenen, G., Ling, K., et al. Using social psychology to motivate contributions to online communities. In *Proc. CSCW* (2004).
12. Benkler, Y. Coase's penguin, or, linux and" the nature of the firm". *Yale Law Journal* (2002), 369–446.
13. Bryant, S. L., Forte, A., and Bruckman, A. Becoming wikipedian: transformation of participation in a collaborative online encyclopedia. In *Proc. GROUP* (2005).
14. Byers, J. W., Mitzenmacher, M., Potamias, M., and Zervas, G. A month in the life of groupon. *CoRR* (2011).
15. Cialdini, R. B. *Influence: Science and practice*. 2001.
16. Cosley, D., Frankowski, D., Terveen, L., and Riedl, J. Suggestbot: using intelligent task routing to help people find work in wikipedia. In *Proc. IUI* (2007).
17. Das, E., Kerkhof, P., and Kuiper, J. Improving the effectiveness of fundraising messages: The impact of charity goal attainment, message framing, and evidence on persuasion. *Applied Communication Research* (2008).
18. Donath, J. S. Identity and deception in the virtual community. *Communities in cyberspace* (1999).
19. Forte, A., Kittur, N., et al. Coordination and beyond: social functions of groups in open content production. In *Proc. CSCW* (2012).
20. Giné, X., Karlan, D., and Zinman, J. Put your money where your butt is: a commitment contract for smoking cessation. *American Economic Journal: Applied Economics* (2010).
21. Granovetter, M. Threshold models of collective behavior. *American Journal of Sociology* (1978).
22. Grudin, J. Groupware and social dynamics: eight challenges for developers. *Communications of the ACM* (1994).
23. Hill, B. M. Almost wikipedia: What eight collaborative encyclopedia projects reveal about mechanisms of collective action. 2011.
24. Hui, J., Greenberg, M., and Gerber, E. Understanding crowdfunding work: implications for support tools. In *Proc. CHI Extended Abstracts* (2013).
25. Khondker, H. H. Role of the new media in the arab spring. *Globalizations* (2011).
26. Kittur, A., and Kraut, R. E. Harnessing the wisdom of crowds in wikipedia: quality through coordination. In *Proc. CSCW* (2008).
27. Klandermans, B. Mobilization and participation: Social-psychological expansisons of resource mobilization theory. *American Sociological Review* (1984).
28. Kriplean, T., Morgan, J., et al. Supporting reflective public thought with considerit. In *Proc. CSCW* (2012).
29. Lee, Y.-H., and Hsieh, G. Does slacktivism hurt activism?: the effects of moral balancing and consistency in online activism. In *Proc. CHI* (2013).
30. Lou, H., Luo, W., and Strong, D. Perceived critical mass effect on groupware acceptance. *European Journal of Information Systems* (2000).
31. Luther, K., and Bruckman, A. Leadership in online creative collaboration. In *Proc. CSCW* (2008).

32. Luther, K., Fiesler, C., and Bruckman, A. Redistributing leadership in online creative collaboration. In *Proc. CSCW* (2013).

33. Marwell, G., Oliver, P. E., and Prahl, R. Social networks and collective action: A theory of the critical mass. iii. *American Journal of Sociology* (1988).

34. Milgram, S., Bickman, L., and Berkowitz, L. Note on the drawing power of crowds of different size. *Journal of Personality and Social Psychology* (1969).

35. Mollick, E. The dynamics of crowdfunding: Determinants of success and failure. *Journal of Business Venturing* (2013).

36. Muller, M., Geyer, W., et al. Crowdfunding inside the enterprise: employee-initiatives for innovation and collaboration. In *Proc. CSCW* (2013).

37. Okolloh, O. Ushahidi, or'testimony': Web 2.0 tools for crowdsourcing crisis information. *Participatory learning and action* (2009).

38. Oliver, P., Marwell, G., and Teixeira, R. A theory of the critical mass. i. interdependence, group heterogeneity, and the production of collective action. *American Journal of Sociology* (1985).

39. Oliver, P. E., and Marwell, G. Mobilizing technologies for collective action. *Frontiers in social movement theory* (1992).

40. Olson, M. *The logic of collective action: public goods and the theory of groups*. 1965.

41. Pickard, G., Rahwan, I., et al. Time critical social mobilization: The darpa network challenge winning strategy. *CoRR* (2010).

42. Poteete, A. R., Janssen, M., and Ostrom, E. *Working together: collective action, the commons, and multiple methods in practice*. Princeton University Press, 2010.

43. Prasarnphanich, P., and Wagner, C. Creating critical mass in collaboration systems: Insights from wikipedia. In *DEST* (2008).

44. Resnick, P., and Zeckhauser, R. Trust among strangers in internet transactions: Empirical analysis of ebay's reputation system. *Advances in applied microeconomics* (2002).

45. Ringlemann, M. Recherches sur les moteurs animés: Travail de lhomme. In *Annales de lInstitut national Agronomique* (1913).

46. Ross, L., and Nisbett, R. *The Person and the Situation: Perspectives of Social Psychology*. 1991.

47. Salganik, M. J., Dodds, P. S., and Watts, D. J. Experimental study of inequality and unpredictability in an artificial cultural market. *Science* (2006).

48. Starbird, K., and Palen, L. "voluntweeters": self-organizing by digital volunteers in times of crisis. In *Proc. CHI* (2011).

49. Suh, B., Convertino, G., Chi, E. H., and Pirolli, P. The singularity is not near: slowing growth of wikipedia. In *Proc. WikiSym* (2009).

50. Verhallen, T. M., and Robben, H. S. Scarcity and preference: An experiment on unavailability and product evaluation. *Journal of Economic Psychology* (1994).

51. Voida, A., Harmon, E., and Al-Ani, B. Bridging between organizations and the public: volunteer coordinators' uneasy relationship with social computing. In *Proc. CHI* (2012).

52. Wang, L. S., Chen, J., Ren, Y., and Riedl, J. Searching for the goldilocks zone: trade-offs in managing online volunteer groups. In *Proc. CSCW* (2012).

APPENDIX A — POST-DEPLOYMENT SURVEY

The post-deployment survey was emailed to all event organizers, and participants who had provided their email address when signing up for an event on Catalyst. Demographic information was not collected. Questions that appeared in the survey sent to organizers are prefixed with an "O", and those sent to participants with a "P".

- General questions (open-ended)
  - (O) About how many people showed up to the events you organized? How many were you expecting?
  - (O) How did you publicize the event you organized?
  - (P) There are many kinds of events that people want you to participate in: some aren't that interesting to you, some are moderately interesting, and some are extremely interesting. Would you respond differently via Facebook (where you RSVP), via Catalyst (where you are only committed if many other people also commit), or in person (where you're telling a friend if you'll go)?
  - (O, P) What did you like about Catalyst? What didn't you like?
- (O) Understanding thresholds and roles (open-ended)
  - How did creating an event on Catalyst compare to simply announcing it (via email, Facebook, flyers)? Were there differences in how and when you made preparations for the event?
  - Catalyst also allowed you to specify minimum or maximum thresholds (i.e. this event would only happen if 5 people join, or this event can have at most 10 people). Were those useful?
  - Catalyst allowed the use of roles in your event. For example, one for a bake sale may have roles for bakers and sellers. Did you use roles in your event? Were they useful? Why or why not?
- (O, P) Comparing Catalyst to other platforms for organizing events (7-point Likert scale)
  - How likely would you be to agree to attending an event you were somewhat interested in, if you were invited to it using Facebook?
  - How likely would you be to agree to attending an event you were somewhat interested in, on Catalyst?
  - How likely would you be to agree to attending an event you were somewhat interested in, if a friend invited you in person?
  - How likely would you be to agree to attending an event you were somewhat interested in, and found out about through an email list/flyer/the local paper?
  - Supposing that you've agreed to attend an event on Facebook, how likely would you be to actually show up to it?
  - Supposing that you've agreed to attend an event on Catalyst, how likely would you be to actually show up to it?
  - Supposing that you've agreed to attend an event a friend invited you to in person, how likely would you be to actually show up to it?
  - Supposing that you've agreed to attend an event you found out about through an email list/flyer/the local paper, how likely would you be to actually show up to it?

Competing or Aiming to be Average? Normification as a Means of Engaging Digital Volunteers

Chris Preist, Elaine Massung, David Coyle
University of Bristol
Merchant Venturers Building
Woodland Road, Bristol, BS8 1UB
{chris.preist, elaine.massung, david.coyle}@bristol.ac.uk

ABSTRACT

Engagement, motivation and active contribution by digital volunteers are key requirements for crowdsourcing and citizen science projects. Many systems use competitive elements, for example point scoring and leaderboards, to achieve these ends. However, while competition may motivate some people, it can have a neutral or demotivating effect on others. In this paper we explore theories of personal and social norms and investigate normification as an alternative approach to engagement, to be used alongside or instead of competitive strategies. We provide a systematic review of existing crowdsourcing and citizen science literature and categorise the ways that theories of norms have been incorporated to date. We then present qualitative interview data from a pro-environmental crowdsourcing study, Close the Door, which reveals normalising attitudes in certain participants. We assess how this links with competitive behaviour and participant performance. Based on our findings and analysis of norm theories, we consider the implications for designers wishing to use normification as an engagement strategy in crowdsourcing and citizen science systems.

Author Keywords

Citizen science; crowdsourcing; gamification; competition; social norms; personal norms; normification

ACM Classification Keywords

H.5.m. Information interfaces and presentation (e.g., HCI): Miscellaneous.

INTRODUCTION

Crowdsourcing and citizen science projects face key challenges in engaging contributors – namely how to recruit them, and how to get them to make an active ongoing contribution. In a review of crowdsourcing literature, Doan et al. [9] categorise common approaches, including (amongst others) coercion, payment, intrinsic enjoyment and competition. In citizen science literature, Kim et al. [23] report the use of incentives, competition, entertainment and education to support ongoing engagement. Also within the realm of citizen science, Rotman et al. [40] report a complex network of factors at play, with initial scientific interest and curiosity moving towards a desire for attribution and acknowledgment over time. Within HCI and CSCW research more generally, gamification is an approach that has rapidly gained prominence as a motivational and engagement technique [8, 26, 52]. Deterding et al. define it as "using game design elements in non-gaming contexts" [8]. Elements can include point scoring, leaderboards, goal setting, questing, and artefact collecting. These gaming techniques have been applied in diverse domains including eco-feedback [13, 28], health and exercise [4, 7], image labelling [50], and service industries [20]. Gamification aims to increase the motivation of participants partly by engaging with competitive urges and partly by increasing intrinsic enjoyment in an activity. It has also been used to encourage paid crowdsourcing participants to perform tasks more rapidly and with greater accuracy, leading to higher quality data [11]. In this paper, we particularly consider those aspects of gamification focused around competition and achievement, which we refer to as *competitive gamification.*

Though competitive gamification may motivate some people, there is evidence to suggest that it can have a neutral or demotivating effect on others. Nicholson [30] has argued that competitive gamification can reduce peoples' intrinsic motivation to contribute to a given activity. More generally, Duffy and Kornienko [10] have found that encouraging competitive behaviour has the potential to reduce altruism. Our paper explores the possible negative effects of competitive gamification in greater detail, and considers an alternative approach, which we term *normification*. Normification focuses on ideas of collective engagement by a community, with individuals within the community each "playing their part". Rather than encouraging competition, it encourages normalising behaviour where community members aim to emulate others in the community and behave similarly to them.

Normification applies theories from psychological literature on social and personal norms [6, 39, 46]. Within CSCW research to date, norm theory has been applied to

CSCW'14, February 15-19, 2014, Baltimore, MD, USA.
ACM 978-1-4503-2540-0/14/02.
http://dx.doi.org/10.1145/2531602.2531615

understand and influence the development of online communities. It has also received some attention in the context of persuasive technologies. In this paper we focus on the potential of normification to support engagement amongst participants in crowdsourcing and citizen science systems. Normification is not seen as a direct replacement for competitive gamification. Instead the paper considers a range of situations in which gamification and normification strategies may prove more or less effective, and how the two approaches may interact with, and complement, each other.

Our discussion is grounded in a qualitative analysis of interview data from a pro-environmental crowdsourcing study called Close the Door (CTD) [28]. In CTD participants used mobile phone apps to collect data about whether shops in a city kept their doors open or closed in cold weather. The study was designed to explore the effects of competition on participants through the use of leaderboards, badges and pay-for-results financial incentives. Whereas high performing participants were clearly motivated by competition, analysis of semi-structured interviews with participants shows that may low performing participants were demotivated by competition. However, it also became clear that some participants, in particular those performing at a mid-level, were using the leaderboard in an unexpected way. For example, one participant stated the leaderboard *"was an indication obviously on how much other people were using it and I wanted to make sure I was sort of in the middle or top half rather than the bottom end."* The CTD study did not make explicit use of normification strategies, however attitudes such as this indicate the potential for motivational approaches based on normification to encourage those who are not motivated, or indeed demotivated, by competition.

This paper makes several contributions to CSCW research. It provides a review of three major psychological theories on the behavioural influences of norms. Following this we review the impact of normative theories on prior research in crowdsourcing and citizen science, and categorise the ways in which these theories have been used. We then provide a qualitative analysis of attitudes of participants in the CTD study. Three broad motivational/demotivational factors are identified: self-competition, other-competition and normalising attitudes. We consider relationships between performance, motivation and attitude and also assess our findings in terms of the theories of norms. Finally, based on findings from the study and our analysis of norm theories, we consider the implications and make recommendations for designers wishing to use normification in crowdsourcing and citizen science systems.

PROBLEMS ADDRESSED BY CROWDSOURCING

Depending on the key aims of a crowdsourcing or citizen science system, it may desirable to identify and maximise the contribution of key individuals. For example, Foldit [21] uses point scoring and leaderboards to motivate solving problems of protein structure prediction. The scientists and designers behind Foldit are interested in identifying a small number of high quality solutions, which warrant further exploration. Given the nature of the problem addressed (protein folding), the system benefits most from regular participants with some basic skills, which participants may have inherently, or which may be developed through ongoing interaction with the system. Competition and high-ranking status may be an effective means of promoting excellence in such a community.

In many cases, however, the objective of crowdsourcing is to maximise the overall output of the crowd. Many such systems require less skill and involve rapid or widespread data collection and/or assessment. For example, GalaxyZoo [25] involves the rapid assessment and categorisation of photos of galaxies, while WhatsInvasive [15] involves the spotting and logging of invasive plant species. Competitive, highly engaged, high performing volunteers can provide a substantial contribution to such systems. However there is also significant benefit from engaging larger numbers of more casual or occasional volunteers. In such cases, if gains among high performers, induced by competition, are offset by a loss in performance or participation by the wider community, then competition may reduce the overall output of the system. As we will see in the CTD study, which aimed to maximise the overall contribution of unskilled volunteers, there is evidence that competition did demotivate lower-level contributors. The question therefore arises: what techniques can we apply to maximise the effectiveness of both high and low level contributors? The norm theories discussed in the next section have the potential to help in addressing this challenge.

THEORIES OF BEHAVIOURAL INFLUENCES OF NORMS

Theories of norms and norm activation have developed primarily within research on the psychology of behaviour change, often in the context of pro-environmental and pro-health behaviours. Three major theoretical models exist for the role that different norms play in influencing the action of an individual: the Focus Theory of Normative Conduct, the Theory of Normative Social Behavior, and the Norm Activation Model.

The Focus Theory of Normative Conduct

The Focus Theory of Normative Conduct [6] distinguishes between two kinds of normative beliefs that can affect behaviour. *Descriptive normative beliefs* are beliefs regarding what others tend to do in a particular situation. These can be used to guide behaviour as a heuristic and can affect the decision to adopt pro-social behaviour. For example, Nolan et al. [31] found a strong correlation between an individual's descriptive normative beliefs regarding the energy conservation behaviour of others and that individual's decision to conserve energy in their home. *Injunctive normative beliefs* are beliefs regarding what actions others approve or disapprove of, and again can influence choice as to whether to engage in pro-social behaviour. For example, a householder may believe that their friends or neighbours approve of energy efficiency and disapprove of wasteful behaviour, and may thus be influenced to be more energy efficient in their own home.

A person's actions are affected by both descriptive and injunctive norms to varying extents, and research has been conducted to explore their relative strengths and interactions. Schultz and Khazian et al. [42] found that a message that linked both descriptive and injunctive norms was more effective in encouraging towel reuse at hotels than a purely information-based message. Schultz and Nolan et al. [41] found that descriptive information about average energy use in similar households encouraged a move towards the mean by both high and low energy users. However, when combined with an injunctive indicator – a smiley face for low energy use and a frowning face for high use – the increase in energy consumption by low energy users was reduced.

Descriptive and injunctive norms can operate in opposition to each other. For example, Cialdini et al. [6] demonstrated that people are more likely to litter in an area that already contains rubbish than in an area that is clear. Hence the descriptive norm that 'people tend to litter here' reduces the effect of the injunctive societal norm against littering. Interestingly, Reno et al. [38] compared the effect on littering in a litter-free environment of the observation of a single person discarding something, and found the reverse: viewing someone littering in a litter-free environment reduces the probability of an individual littering themselves. The Focus Theory argues that the norms that affect our behaviour at any given time depend on which norms are *salient* in any given situation. There is also evidence that norms operate subconsciously. Nolan et al. [31] found that, despite the strong correlation between descriptive normative belief regarding energy efficiency and an individual's decision, the behaviour of others was rated as the least important reason for their actions.

The Theory of Normative Social Behavior

With the Theory of Normative Social Behaviour Rimal and Real [39] built on concepts within Focus Theory. In particular they focused on injunctive norms and developed a model of how they operate. They argue that injunctive normative beliefs gain their weight either from threat of sanctions or from social approval – "because people important to them expect them to do so". They also argue that the effect of such norms on an individual's actions is influenced by two other categories of factors. Firstly, the individual's perceived *outcome expectations* of engaging or not in an action – namely what subjective benefits or disbenefits they believe they will experience. Secondly, the individual's *group identity* and the descriptive norms of that particular group: individuals aspire to a varying degree to behave like others within a given social group, and experience positive emotions when conforming to in-group norms. Hence an individual's course of action is influenced by a combination of injunctive norms operating on them, their subjective perception of 'outcome expectations' of different courses of action, and a desire to conform to the descriptive norms of a certain social group.

The Norm Activation Model

The Norm Activation Model of Harland et al. [17] further extended norm theory by introducing the concept of *personal norms* – namely the individual's feelings of moral obligation to engage in or avoid particular behaviours. They argue that injunctive norms and other factors affecting the actions of an individual are significantly influenced by these personal norms. In a study of self-reported reasons for choosing to use unbleached paper or not, they found that personal norms were a stronger predictor than attitudes towards the product (a form of outcome expectation). They also found that personal norms were a stronger predictor of use than beliefs that others approved of such use (i.e. injunctive norms).

The Norm Activation Model aims to explain the way in which personal norms come into being over the longer term [46]. The model states that personal norms are activated by a combination of (1) Awareness of Consequences – namely an awareness of the benefits of success or cost of failure of the collective action; (2) Ascription of Responsibility – a sense that the individual is partly responsible for bringing about the collective action, and; (3) Outcome Efficiency – whether they believe that the actions individually and collectively taken will have some positive impact. The model was primarily developed and presented as a model for the development of pro-environmental personal norms. However, in a more general form it can be applied to arbitrary collective action problems – namely those problems where a set of individual choices can result in a collective benefit to the community, though each choice may have an immediate cost on the individual.

As with our two other theories, the Norm Activation Model has been the subject of experimental investigation. For example, the interplay between personal norms and descriptive normative beliefs has been explored by Göckeritz et al. [14]. They observe that the impact of descriptive normative beliefs on the uptake of energy conservation behaviour is reduced when an individual is highly "involved" – namely they are consciously engaged with the issue and so have knowledge and strong personal norms around energy conservation. They propose that descriptive norms influence behaviour without conscious processing, while strong personal norms are associated with greater conscious engagement, which in turn weakens the influence of descriptive norms.

Overview

The theories described above, and the associated experimental work, explore the relative influence of different norm types in varying situations. Each theory prioritises different norm types and motivational triggers. The Focus Theory of Normative Conduct distinguishes between descriptive and injunctive norms, and emphasises how environmental factors can make certain norms more "salient" at a given time. The Theory of Normative Social Behavior provides a more detailed model of the factors underlying the operation of injunctive norms in a given social situation. Finally, the Norm Activation Model adds the concept of personal norms, which when strong enough can override both descriptive and injunctive norms. It also provides a model for how personal norms become active.

Later in the paper we will return to these theories to see how they can be used to explain the results of the CTD study. Prior to this, we consider the extent to which norm theories have impacted on HCI and CSCW research to date, and the ways in which have been used to guide the design of crowdsourcing systems.

PRIOR USE OF NORMS IN CSCW AND HCI RESEARCH

Within CSCW literature, norm theories have featured in research aimed at understanding, influencing and developing online communities. Postmes et al. [36] explore how norms regarding the use of email are socially constructed over time by groups of collaborating students. In addition, Postmes et al. [35] have found that online communities with a strong social identity can reinforce the effect of pre-existing norms, despite participant anonymity. In a lab-based study, Sukumaran et al. [48] demonstrated that pre-existing contributions in an online news discussion site affect the thoughtfulness of contributions made by new arrivals. With regard to the use of social norms in influencing the behaviour of online communities, Chen et al. [5] explore how they can be used to increase contribution to MovieLens. They explored the effect of sending social comparison information regarding the performance of an individual and the mean performance of similar individuals. They found it resulted in an increase in contribution by those below the mean, and a decrease by those above – a similar phenomenon to that observed by Schultz and Nolan et al. [41]. However, the increase by those below the mean was significantly greater than the decrease by those above. Furthermore, they found that those who expressed a competitive preference in a questionnaire (defined as valuing achievement over social popularity) were more likely to increase their contribution if below the mean, and less likely to decrease it if above. This insight is of particular relevance to the focus of our paper on the interaction between competition and normification.

The design of an online environment can also influence the norms that develop or express themselves within it. Lea et al. [24] present a collaborative learning environment for use by students, which is designed in such a way to promote 'team player' behaviour – mutually supportive coordinated contributions. It does this through the use of "collectivised" activities, which encourage a common group identity. Sukumaran et al. [48] demonstrate the effect visual design has on a news discussion website, with a more serious and formal style promoting more thoughtfulness of contribution.

Research in persuasive technology, particularly in environmental contexts, has also begun to consider theories of norms. He et al. [18] include the use of norms in their set of recommendations for environmental persuasion, and several trials have incorporated consideration of norms into their design. Thieme et al. [49] consider how social monitoring can encourage injunctive norms around recycling, whilst Mankoff et al. [27] consider how social networking can develop community norms around environmental behaviour, e.g. greenhouse gas emissions reduction. Several projects [12, 34, 47] explore how social feedback can influence domestic electricity use. Finally [43] suggests that comparative social feedback can be used, not only as a means to influence behaviour directly, but also as 'an inquiry instrument to discover opportunities to save energy'.

In this paper we are specifically focused on the implications of norm theories for the design of crowdsourcing and citizen science systems. To determine the extent to which psychological theories of norms have been applied in this context we conducted a survey of prior literature. We extracted all papers from the ACM Guide to Computing Literature[1] that include either "crowdsourcing" or "citizen science" as an author keyword. This yielded a corpus of 538 papers. Within this, we identified all mentions of the substring "norm", and categorised the way in which different papers used it. We filtered out those papers which only used the substring in the word "normal" etc., and those which used it in a statistical sense, to leave only those which referred to social or personal norms. Of the original corpus, we found that 12 (2.2%) discussed norms in some way. The ways in which they discussed norms can be categorised as follows:

Emergence of social norms in crowdsourcing environments. Three of the papers [16, 33, 45] discuss how crowdsourcing environments result in the emergence of new social norms. For example, Starbird and Palen [45] observe the emergence of norms around retweeting behaviour of digital volunteers in the aftermath of the 2010 earthquake in Haiti.

The incorporation of social norms in design of crowdsourcing environments. Two of the papers touch on the relationship between the social norms of a community and the design of a crowdsourcing environment they use. Wiggins [51] discusses how existing community norms within the birding community were reflected subtly in the design of leaderboards as part of the eBird system. Reeves and Sherwood [37] observe that design choices when developing a crowdsourcing application can affect the norms that emerge in a user community – either unintentionally or intentionally.

[1] Though this corpus contains over 2M publications both within and outside of the ACM, we recognize that this cannot be considered a complete literature survey due to the interdisciplinary nature of crowdsourcing research.

The influence of social norms on reporting of motivation in crowdsourcing. Antin and Shaw [1] report on how social norms in different cultures can affect self-reporting of motivational factors in crowdsourcing.

Social Norms as a motivational factor for participants in crowdsourcing and citizen science. Kim et al. [22] refers to social norms as one of several motivational factors for data collectors in citizen science, but does not explore it further. Nov et al. [32] conducted a survey on self-reported motivations of volunteers with stardust@home, and analysed the results to determine which factors were most salient. They found that collective and intrinsic factors were the most salient, with social identification and norm-related factors being secondary. Rotman et al. [40] explored the motivation of volunteers in projects making a scientific contribution and found a complex network of factors at play, with initial scientific interest and curiosity moving towards a desire for attribution and acknowledgment over time, but did not explore the role of social norms in this process. The only example in our corpus of work that attempts to actively use norm theory (along with other interventions) to affect behaviour is [44]. Shaw et al. explored the effect of a number of messages and questions on motivating qualitative coders in an online labour market. Among the messages, two were connected to social norm theory. For example, they attempted to activate an injunctive social norm encouraging good behaviour through the message "It is your job to provide accurate answers to these questions. It is important that you do your job well." This was found to have no significant effect on job performance. This is an interesting finding, and one that we return to in our Discussion and Analysis section when considering the results presented in the current paper.

Influencing of Social Norms through Crowdsourcing. Prior research with the CTD environmental campaign has considered two distinctive, but complementary perspectives on social norms and crowdsourcing. As previously stated, Massung et al. [28] investigated the use of different gamification strategies in supporting crowdsourcing of pro-environmental data. The current paper extends that work by considering normification as an additional engagement strategy for volunteers in crowdsourcing projects. They [28] also considered, but did not investigate, a longer-term possibility. Namely, if crowdsourcing can support large-scale environmental data collection, this data could then be brought to bear in influencing ingrained, negative social behaviour. The possibility of using crowdsourced data to influence third party social norms was discussed further in Massung and Preist. [29]. This is an interesting longer-term research goal, but beyond the scope of the current paper.

This literature review has shown that whilst norms have received attention in the CSCW community more generally, they have received only limited attention as an active design strategy in prior crowdsourcing research. We now consider the CTD study in more detail.

THE CLOSE THE DOORS STUDY

Close the Door (CTD) is a UK-based pro-environmental campaign that encourages shops to reduce energy waste by keeping their doors shut when running heating during the winter. A detailed study of typical 150m^2 UK high street shops found that keeping doors closed can reduce carbon emissions and the amount of heating energy used by 30-50% [3]. The campaign operates across several UK cities and is lead by a core group of dedicated and highly motivated members. The aim of the CTD study was to investigate how mobile crowdsourcing could be used to increase the scalability of campaign groups like CTD by engaging and enabling casual, digital volunteers to collect relevant data. This approach has the potential to allow small campaign groups to collect data on a much larger scale than previously possible and also free core members to focus on advocacy activities. In line with Massung and Preist. [29] we believe large-scale data collection, and focused advocacy, will ultimately support third party change.

Overall we developed three apps for the iPhone. As users went about their daily routines, the app allowed them to collect information about whether shop doors were opened or closed, with each app using a different strategy to try to engage and motivate the digital volunteers. The Virtual app used competitive gamification to encourage engagement through game mechanics including points, badges, and a leaderboard. The Financial app was similar to the Virtual app, incorporating the same competitive gamification techniques, but with the addition of financial incentives to encourage participants to carry out data collection tasks. The Control app did not use any explicit motivational strategies and so acted as a control. Control participants did not receive points or badges for rating shop doors, nor did they see the activity of other participants. Further details of the app design are available in [28].

Experimental procedure

The CTD study lasted two weeks. 48 participants were randomly assigned to three groups, each using one app – Control, Virtual or Financial – with 16 participants per group. In all cases, participants were asked to record data on as many shop doors as possible while going about their normal routine. Control and Virtual participants received a flat fee for taking part. Financial participants received a share of a fixed pot based on the number of badges and points they earned. The pot size was chosen to ensure that the average earned by the Financial group would be the same as the flat fee in the two other groups. Quantitative data on the number of shops rated was collected for all participants over the two weeks. Qualitative data was gathered through semi-structured interviews with 18 participants. These interviews explored participants' reactions on the different motivational strategies used in the CTD apps, e.g. leaderboards and badges. Six interviewees were selected from each app group: the two highest, two mid-range and two lowest performers in the data collection exercise.

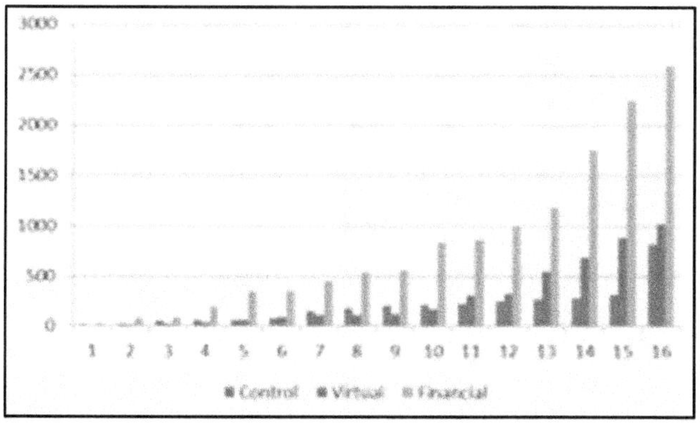

Figure 1: Points scored by the 16 participants in each group in the CTD study [28].

Competitive and normative attitudes in Close the Door

The initial purpose of the CTD study was to explore the effect of competition on participants, and the "leaderboard" was framed in this way. The quantitative results of the study are reported in [28]. Here we summarise those relevant to this paper. Figure 1 shows the points scored by the 16 participants in each group[2]. We found that virtual rewards (points and badges) increased performance over the control group, though not to a statistically significant level. Combining financial rewards with leaderboards led to a statistically significant increase in the amount of data collected. Z-score analysis of performance showed that in both the virtual and financial groups, those at the top of the leaderboard were relatively stronger while those in mid and low positions were relatively weaker than the control group. In the case of the virtual group, this difference could also be observed in absolute terms: though the top 4 participants notably outperformed the control group, this was offset by comparative underperformance by those at mid and low positions resulting in no statistically significant difference in performance between the two groups.

During our preliminary analysis of the qualitative interview data we also noted that some participants in the CTD study related to the leaderboard in an unexpected way. They used it more as a means to see how their performance compared with the community in general – i.e. a way more in line with theories of social norms rather than theories of competition. This observation raised interesting questions regarding the role of competition versus normification for our participants.

Building on this observation we now return to this qualitative data to assess/determine what attitudes people express towards the leaderboard, and present further analysis and results. Having presented our results we will begin our discussion and analysis by considering several inter-related research questions:

[2] The Control app maintained a log of the shops ranked by participants and through this their effective points total; however, this information was not revealed to control participants.

	Financial	Virtual
Low scorers	Other-competitive (-ive)	Normalising
	Other-competitive (-ive)	Other-competitive (+ive)
Medium scorers	Other-competitive (+ive)	Normalising
	Self-competitive & Normalising	Self-competitive & Normalising
High scorers	Other-competitive (+ive)	Other-competitive (+ive)
	Self-competitive & Other-competitive (+ive)	Other-competitive (+ive)

Table 1: The attitudes expressed by 12 interviewees, with respect to the leaderboard. Tags in brackets indicate the motivational impact (+ive or –ive) expressed in other-competitive statements. All self-competitive and normalising statements were associated with positive motivational impacts.

- How do participants describe the attitudes they hold as motivating or demotivating? How do the expressed attitudes and motivations link to actual performance on the leaderboard? How do these different attitudes interact with each other?

Following this we will step back and consider the broader question:

- What explanations do the three psychological theories of norms offer for the expressed attitudes?

Method

Of the 18 interviews conducted with participants of CTD, 6 were with the control group who had no access to the leaderboard. We analysed the transcripts of the remaining 12, tagging examples of language that reflected different attitudes to the leaderboard. We then sorted these statements into different categories of attitude, and used these to categorise attitudes expressed by the different interviewees. Next, we tabulated the results against participant group (virtual and financial) and score (low, medium, high). Then, based on this tabulation, we carried out a second pass of the qualitative data to identify other factors, which may explain 'anomalies' in the table. Finally, we returned to the six interviews with the control group and tagged any examples of statements that corresponded to the attitudes identified in other groups, to explore to what extent these attitudes emerged, even in the absence of a leaderboard.

Results

The analysis of language used by the 12 participants in the financial and virtual groups identified three broad categories of attitude towards the leaderboard: other-competitive, self-competitive, and normalising. Table 1 charts the attitudes observed in interviewee statements against participant group and scoring band. As can be seen some interviewees made statements expressing more than one attitude. In the case of other-competitive statements, we also record whether the participant described being motivated (+ive) or demotivated (-ive) by competition. All self-competitive and normalising statements were associated with positive motivational expressions.

Other-competitive: We define an other-competitive statement as one in which the interviewee compares their behaviour with that of others on the leaderboard, with an expressed wish to beat others and/or not be beaten by others. In some cases, particularly for high scoring participants, an other-competitive attitude was linked to engagement and positive motivation. For example, one interviewee [Virtual Group, High Scorer] stated: *"I would check [the leaderboard] ... to see if people were coming up near me and if they were then I'd be like, 'Right, I've got to get on with it.'"* However, in other cases, it was demotivating and had a negative impact. One participant [Financial Group, Low Scorer] observed *"I think the score board put me off a little bit. ... after a few days I think people were on hundreds and I was trailing behind."* Interestingly, both of the low scoring participants in the financial group described how the competitive aspect was initially motivating prior to becoming demotivating. For example, one stating that "*to begin with* [the leaderboard] *spurred me on and then after getting so far behind it felt a bit oppressive really*". This suggests that it may not have been competition per se, but rather poor performance in a competitive environment that was demotivating.

There is an anomaly in our data that that can be explained at this point. At first sight the low scorer in the virtual group who described other-competition as positively motivating appears inconsistent. However at interview this person stated that they found competition motivating, but also revealed that they had left Bristol for much of the trial period, thus limiting their ability to accumulate points.

Self-competitive: We define a self-competitive statement as one in which the interviewee used their score to monitor their own progress, but not in comparison with others or with regard to improving or maintaining a position on the leaderboard. For example, one participant [Financial Group, Mid Scorer] stated that they used the leaderboard *"kind of competitive with myself like today I'll do a few more than I did yesterday"* and that the leaderboard was motivating through *"seeing the numbers go up just for me more than seeing who was above or below me."* Another interviewee [Virtual Group, Mid Scorer] stated that they were motivated by getting badges and that scoring points *"helped me do more because I was like I want to get more."* Interestingly, unlike other-competitive statements, all self-competitive statements were associated with increased motivation.

Normalising: We define a normalising statement as one in which the interviewee used activity on the scoreboard as a guide to what other people were doing, with a view to following them or making a representative contribution. For example, one interviewee [Financial Group, Mid Scorer] stated that observing activity on the leaderboard *"did make me go oh okay [...] I should probably make sure that I make an effort to do it when I go out."* Another [Virtual Group, Mid Scorer] stated that they viewed the leaderboard as *"an indication obviously of how much other people were using it and I wanted to make sure I was sort of in the middle or top half rather than the bottom end."*

Other normalising statements were more complex. One interviewee [Virtual Group, Low Scorer] stated that the sight of activity on the leaderboard before she had actually begun using the app meant *"I felt guilty that I hadn't started using it so then I used it."* This low performer is an interesting case. She expressed normalising attitudes not towards the score, but towards the use of the app. Overall it appears that she was spurred on by the activity of others to do something, but felt no need to compare her score with others, or to make an average or high level of contribution.

Our analysis of six interviews with the control group found, unsurprisingly, that these participants expressed no competitive or normalising attitudes. One of them did highlight the lack of feedback, in what appears to be a request for feedback to allow self-competition as a motivator: *"There should have been a guideline to how many shops we recorded [...] there was no incentive!"*

Discussion and Analysis

18 interviews, including 6 with control participants, is not sufficient to warrant strong conclusions. However, based on our results we can make a number of observations and give initial answers to our research questions. We will begin by considering our research questions around participants' stated attitudes. Following this we consider the insights on this provided by psychological theories of norms. We then consider our findings in light of prior CSCW research incorporating norm theories.

- *How do participants describe the attitudes they hold as motivating or demotivating? How do the expressed attitudes and motivations link to actual performance on the leaderboard? How do these different attitudes interact with each other?*

The results presented in Table 1 broadly show a pattern of low scorers having an other-competitive attitude linked to demotivation and high performers having an other-competitive attitude linked to motivation. Many people with an other-competitive attitude were initially motivated, but ultimately became demotivated by competition. Hence it appears that demotivation occurs when a participant is other-competitive but falls behind and feels they cannot catch up with others. Taken together other-competitive statements by our participants, and their contrasting performance, highlight both the benefits and possible negative effects of other-competitive gamification.

Mid performers in our study expressed a normalising and/or self-competitive attitude to the leaderboard, with three of the four mid-performing interviewees expressing a normalising attitude. Self-competitive and normalising attitudes were always associated in our dataset with positive motivation – though not always high performance or positive emotion, as the quote referring to guilt above shows. We found no evidence that demotivation occurs in those adopting only self-competitive or normalising attitudes. Statements indicate that they remained motivated to act despite the emergence of significant high scorers.

While two interviewees expressed both self-competitive and normalising attitudes, and one expressed both self- and other-competitive attitudes, no interviewees expressed both other-competitive and normalising attitudes. This indicates an inconsistency between other-competitiveness and normalising attitudes, suggesting they are unlikely to be simultaneously held by the same person. The fact that all four high scorers expressed an other-competitive attitude, suggests that a competitive attitude is a necessary (but not sufficient) condition for high scoring, while a normalising attitude tends to encourage mid-range performance (corroborating the findings of Chen et al. [5]).

More broadly, it is interesting to consider how the behaviour of those holding one set of attitudes affects those holding another set. As Figure 1 shows, mid range performers in the virtual group (who typically expressed normalising attitudes in interviews) actually perform less well than the mid range performers in the control group. This is likely to be because of interaction, through the leaderboard, with low performers who were demotivated by other-competition. Consider again the words of a mid-performing virtual app user: *"I wanted to make sure I was sort of in the middle or top half rather than the bottom end."* This statement emphasises a leaderboard position rather than outright scores. Interestingly, the leaderboard in the CTD app was presented as a list. It therefore highlighted positions, and it is the low scorers on a leaderboard that determine the score needed to achieve a mid-level position. Hence if those low on the scoreboard are demotivated by other-competition, and therefore score less, the required score to achieve a mid-level position is also reduced. Hence, even though normalising attitudes acted as a positive motivator, they may have actually resulted in reduced performance of mid-range participants. This is analogous to the findings of Schultz and Nolan et al. [41] with regard to energy usage and Chen et al. [5] with regard to online community contribution. It is possible that a different feedback approach, which emphasised the size of individual contributions or the mean contribution, might have had a different effect on normalising participants.

- *What explanations do the three psychological theories offer for the expressed attitudes?*

The theory of Normative Social Behaviour [39] suggests that injunctive norms act through desire for social approval from specific individuals or groups. Participants in the CTD study did not know each other and the leaderboard used pseudonyms, which enforced anonymity. It is therefore unlikely that this theory provides a strong explanation for results in our study.

The Focus Theory and Norm Activation Model offer greater insight. One possible explanation for the expressed attitudes is as follows. Recall that *personal norms* [17] operate to encourage a behaviour that the individual believes is the "right" thing to do, based on their own self image rather than what they believe others will think of them. We hypothesise that two kinds of personal norms were at work in CTD. Some participants have a personal norm that encourages competition – "I must be one of the best in what I do" – while others have a personal norm around contribution – "I must contribute sufficiently and appropriately to this collective effort in line with what others do". In other words, a personal norm that follows a *descriptive norm* of what others contribute. Some, perhaps most, people have both contributory and competitive personal norms to a greater or lesser extent, yet which one is activated will depend on which is given salience in the specific environment [6].

Our leaderboard and badges environment provided primarily competitive cues, and thus likely reduced activation of normalising motivations in users. However, it was (unintentionally) structured in such a way that those with strong personal norms towards contribution could use it in a normalising manner. In such cases, the leaderboard provided a representation of what others were doing, allowing individuals to form a descriptive norm of what a typical contribution was and therefore what they should aim for. So, for those with significantly stronger personal norm of contribution over competition, this descriptive norm of collective activity would activate their personal norm, resulting in the observed behaviour.

This finding is consistent with the observations of Sukurman et al. [48] that the environmental cues provided by an online system affect which behavioural norms are made salient to its users. Our findings are less consistent with Shaw et al.'s findings about the use of incentives with inexpert human raters [44]. They found that an injunctive norm statement, "It is your job to provide accurate answers to these questions. It is important that you do your job well." had no significant effect on job performance when sent to paid contributors in a crowdsourcing system, suggesting it did not motivate them. This approach is very different from ours – where individuals are able to discern norms from the leaderboard rather than being explicitly ordered to obey them – which may explain the difference in reported motivation.

As noted earlier, Nolan et al. [31] found that social norms were not explicitly stated as a motivator in interviews with householders, even though they were found to be a strong predictor of energy efficiency behaviour. Why our approach to interviewing did identify the role of normalising behaviour where theirs did not is a subject for further exploration. One possible explanation is the structure of our interview: the role of social norms emerged when participants were questioned about their feelings about the leaderboard, not about their motivation for participation. Those expressing normalising attitudes when talking about the leaderboard would give other explanations of their motivations to use the app – for example *"I enjoyed doing it. When I went places I suddenly went 'Hey, I could use the open and closed app"* [Virtual, Mid] and *"It was just out of interest to see what you were up to really because I'd never done anything like that before so it was quite fun to have a go with it."* [Financial, Mid]. This may also explain why Rotman et al. [40] do not report social normalising behaviour as a motivator of participants in citizen science experiments.

DESIGN IMPLICATIONS

Building on our findings regarding norms and competition in the CTD study, we are now in a position to discuss implications for the design of crowdsourcing and citizen science systems. In presenting these implications we also draw on our review of norm theories and prior CSCW research. These implications should be viewed as tentative recommendations as this point. They can provide useful guidance for designers and are a worthwhile subject for further experimental validation.

1. *Designers should consider whether a crowdsourcing system requires cultivation of a set of exceptional performers to produce a small number of high quality results, or a broad community of "average" contributors. In the first case, competitive-gamification should be considered. In the latter case, normification may also provide an effective strategy for engagement.*

Some crowdsourcing systems (e.g. Foldit) aim to generate of a small number of high quality results, and require skill on the part of the participants, which may require time to develop. In this case it may be desirable to identify and maximise the contribution of key individuals. Here an explicitly competitive, indeed other-competitive, approach may be most appropriate, helping to filter out those who are less motivated or less able to contribute to the task, whilst motivating high performers to contribute further. Other crowdsourcing systems (e.g. CTD) involve relatively simple tasks, but require a large coverage. Here the objective of crowdsourcing is to maximise the overall output of the crowd, so a broad community, including a large number of average contributors, may be preferable. In such cases normification strategies should also be considered, as environments that emphasise competition may demotivate large parts of the overall crowd.

2. *Designers should consider the development of systems that combine gamification and normification to get the "best of both worlds" – but be aware that interactions between the two approaches can be negative.*

Building on our first point, there are many systems in which designers may want to combine gamification and normification. The aims in such a system may include:

- Allow high performers to compete with each other in such a way that other participants are not demotivated.
- Provide a mechanism that allows self-competition and normalising behaviour, without enforcing either.
- Encourage a sense of engagement in a collective, meaningful endeavour, and reduce environmental cues that specifically emphasise competition.

When combining competition and normification designers need to carefully consider how these strategies interact. Our results suggest that it may be fairly safe to mix self-competitive elements (badges, goal setting, personal scores) with normifying information. Chen et al. [5] have also provided evidence that achievement oriented individuals will largely ignore normalising cues, so normalising information should not overly demotivate high performing, self-competitive people. Combining normification and other-competition is more risky, for several reasons. Firstly, our results suggest this combination will demotivate those who are not performing well. If feedback mechanisms in the system are poorly designed, this in turn can have the effect of dragging down the performance of those with strong normalising tendencies. Finally, over emphasis on other-competition may make contributory norms less salient, and so reduce the impact of normification strategies. Finally, evidence from Sukumaran [48] (in line with the Focus Theory of Normative Conduct) indicates that the design of a virtual environment can affect the expression of norms, suggesting that over emphasis on other-competition may make contributory norms less salient, thus reducing the impact of normification strategies.

Overall, in a system combining competition and normification, competition should not be upfront in the system, should be easy to opt in and out of, and should be focused primarily on those who are already achieving strong results. Future version of the CTD system will reflect this advice. For example, by default the initial screen will display the total number of shops rated by the community, the average number of shops rated by each member over a given period, e.g. the last 7 days, and the number rated by the user in this time. A "contribution" screen will also be included. This will displays target numbers of ratings to be awarded a "bronze", "silver" or "gold" contributor award for a given 7 day period, together with the user's current score. To emphasise this is in recognition of contribution, not an achievement, the message accompanying successful completion would be phrased as a "Thank you" message, rather than "Congratulations!". This will cater for those motivated by personal achievement, but will do so in a way that promotes a sense of contribution to a collective endeavour rather than winning over others. Finally, the app will include a "star contributors" screen that lists the scores of the top 10% of contributors. This will be accessible through an "opt-in" function. Once selected, the user can then set it as their default view. This will allow other-competition between those at the top who "opt-in", while reducing the potential to demotivate others. We hypothesise that this combination of competitive and normalising strategies will result in an overall improvement in the performance of the community. However, we acknowledge that further research is necessary to investigate this hypothesis.

3. *Designers should carefully consider which of the norm types are most likely to encourage engagement in their user population and application context.*

The psychological theories of norm offer three different norm types – descriptive, injunctive, and personal – each of which has the potential to influence users positively or negatively. For example, Schultz and Nolan et al. [41] and Chen et al. [5] have found that *descriptive norms* can encourage low performing users to move towards the "typical" contribution level of a community. A potential disadvantage of descriptive norms, particularly in the early days of community development, is that the norm of contribution may not be high enough to sustain the community. If participants observe low levels of activity by other community members, it may have a demotivating effect.

Depending on the social characteristics of a system, *injunctive norms* may also be an option. Normative Social Behaviour suggests that individuals are influenced both by seeking social approval of people important to them, and by the expected behaviour of the groups they identify with. By sharing identities of participants in a community rather than remaining anonymous, individuals may experience a stronger motivation to contribute, particularly if they know others in the community. However this decision will involve trade-offs against other concerns, e.g. how important is privacy in a given system. If participants come to consider the community owners as people from whom they want social approval, then the theory would suggest that highlighting the visibility of performance to the owners, together with gentle encouragement and messages of thanks, would enhance motivation.

Finally, when *personal norms* are strongly held they can override the influence of other norms types, according to the Norm Activation Model. Those whose personal norms are aligned with the objectives of a crowdsourcing project are likely to be motivated to contribute beyond levels suggested by descriptive norm feedback. An environment can potentially be designed to appeal to those with a specific set of personal norms – perhaps leading to a reduced "pool" of recruits, but with higher levels of contributional commitment.

4. *Designers should consider alternate mechanisms to provide normifying feedback, both in terms of content and delivery modality.*

Research on the relative effectiveness of different approaches to providing norm feedback is at an early stage. Chen et al. [5] have used an email message stating an individual's contribution and comparing it with the average contribution of others who are similar. Our leaderboard allowed individuals to view the ranked performance of all participants, which some used in a normifying way. (This was not our original intention.) These two approaches involved different degrees of subtlety and had differing effects on the users. A wide range of other approaches could be applied, for example:

- Push messages of the form *"Together we can <do the task>. Most participants contribute at least X ratings a week"*. This wording draws on the findings of Schultz and Khazian et al. [42].
- Visualisations featuring contribution "bands" for a given period, including information on how many participants are in each band at a given time, and the participant's current band.
- Rather than focusing on individual comparison, a real-time visualisation of collective progress towards a group target, together with some form of notification whenever others have made a contribution.

Where injunctive norm feedback is used, important design decisions also are required regarding how explicitly this feedback is provided. For example, a participant's contribution could be displayed in red when well below average, and shading to green as it reaches the average. A more explicit message such as "We would like you to contribute at least X ratings a week" could also be used.

CONCLUSIONS AND FUTURE WORK

In many crowdsourcing and citizen science applications, the aim is to maximise the overall effectiveness of the crowd. In such situations, the motivating effect of competition on some may be outweighed by the demotivating effect it has on others. To that end, we have considered "normification" as an alternative design philosophy, aiming to encourage a sense of playing ones part in a collective effort. Whilst norm theories have influenced other areas of CSCW research, our review of crowdsourcing literature found little evidence of the use of norms as a design strategy.

Our analysis of qualitative data from the CTD study provides initial evidence that some participants in crowdsourcing systems relate to comparative performance data in a normalising way, even when it is framed competitively as a "leaderboard". These participants tend to be mid-range contributors. Such contributors can play a valuable role in increasing the overall effectiveness, and output, of crowdsourcing systems. In the case of the CTD study, we hypothesise that such people have a personal norm of sufficient contribution (as opposed to achieving more than others) and that the leaderboard allowed them to quantify what a sufficient contribution is, based on descriptive norms of others behaviour. However, with the leaderboard used in our system, we found evidence that normalising behaviour, interacting with the depressed scores from those demotivated by other-competition, lead to a reduction in the contribution of normalising participants. We believe more explicit norm strategies will increase the performance of normalising crowdsourcing participants.

In preparing this paper we are keenly aware of the ongoing debate within the HCI and CSCW communities regarding the role, and the gap between, theory and design-driven approaches [2, 19]. For example, Hekler et al. [19] have highlighted the role of differing experimental design strategies and the need for experimental validation of both theoretical predictions and new designs. We welcome this call. In the CTD study normification behaviour emerged somewhat accidentally. Research is now required to design and evaluate crowdsourcing systems that make more deliberate use of normification strategies. Two broad arguments presented in this paper are ripe for experimental examination: (1) that normification can improve the overall effectiveness of crowdsourcing systems, and (2) a combination of normification and competition will be most effective for systems requiring broad coverage, but not requiring high skill levels. These broad predictions, and the tentative design implications we have outlined, can also be examined at a more detailed level. For example, what are the most effective ways of combining normification and competition? Do opt-in strategies for competitive elements motivate people with strong competitive tendencies, whilst not demotivating others? Experiments can also be undertaken to investigate different types of norm feedback (e.g. text messages vs. visualisations, mean vs. individual scores), the effectiveness of subtle versus explicit injunctive feedback, and the impact of anonymity versus participant identification.

Subject to this ongoing research, we believe normalisation will provide a powerful additional strategy for designers of crowdsourcing and citizen science systems. This paper provides initial answers and a starting point for new research in this area.

ACKNOWLEDGEMENTS

We would like to thank Marc Jay and Kirsten Cater of University of Bristol, Sue Pollard and Phil Holtam from the Bristol branch of the Close the Door campaign, and the participants of the study. This work was in part funded by UK Research Council Digital Economy grant number EP/K012509/1.

REFERENCES

1. Antin, J. & Shaw, A. *Social desirability bias and self-reports of motivation: a study of amazon mechanical turk in the US and India.* ACM CHI 2012, 2925-2934.
2. Arriaga, R.I., Miller, A.D., Mynatt, E.D., Pagliari, C., & Poole, E.S. *Theory vs. design-driven approaches for behavior change research.* CHI EA 2013, 2455-2458.
3. Basarir, M. & Overend, M. Interim Report on the Energy Appraisal of Retail Units: Assessing the effect of open doors on energy consumption and thermal comfort. 2010, University of Cambridge. CUED/D-STRUCT/TR232.
4. Campbell, T., Ngo, B., & Fogarty, J. *Game design principles in everyday fitness applications.* ACM CSCW 2008, 249-252.
5. Chen, Y., Harper, F.M., Konstan, J., & Xin Li, S. *Social comparisons and contributions to online communities: A field experiment on MovieLens.* The American Economic Review, 2010. **100**(4), 1358-1398.
6. Cialdini, R.B., Reno, R.R., & Kallgren, C.A. *A focus theory of normative conduct: Recycling the concept of norms to reduce littering in public places.* J of Personality and Social Psychology, 1990. **58**(6), 1015-1026.
7. Consolvo, S., McDonald, D., Toscos, T., Chen, M., Froehlich, J., Harrison, B., Klasnja, P., LaMarca, A., LeGrand, L., Libby, R., Smith, I., & Landay, J. *Activity sensing in the wild: a field trial of ubifit garden.* ACM CHI 2008, 1797-1806.
8. Deterding, S., Sicart, M., Nacke, L., O'Hara, K., & Dixon, D. *Gamification. using game-design elements in non-gaming contexts.* ACM CHI EA 2011, 2425-2428.
9. Doan, A., Ramakrishnan, R., & Halevy, A.Y. *Crowdsourcing systems on the World-Wide Web.* Communications of the ACM, 2011. **54**(4), 86-96.
10. Duffy, J., & Kornienko, T. *Does competition affect giving?* . J. Economic Behavior & Organization, 2010. **74**(1-2), 82-103.
11. Eickhoff, C., Harris, C.G., Vries, A.P.d., & Srinivasan, P. *Quality through flow and immersion: gamifying crowdsourced relevance assessments.* ACM SIGIR 2012, 871-880.
12. Foster, D., Lawson, S., Blythe, M., & Cairns, P. *Wattsup? motivating reductions in domestic energy consumption using social networks.* NordiCHI 2010, 178-187.
13. Froehlich, J., Findlater, L., & Landay, J. *The design of eco-feedback technology.* ACM CHI 2010, 1999-2008.
14. Göckeritz, S., Schultz, P.W., Rendón, T., Cialdini, R.B., Goldstein, N.J., & Griskevicius, V. *Descriptive normative beliefs and conservation behavior: The moderating roles of personal involvement and injunctive normative beliefs.* European J of Social Psychology, 2010. **40**(3), 514-523.
15. Graham, E., Henderson, S., & Schloss, A. *Using mobile phones to engage citizen scientists in research.* Eos Trans. AGU, 2011. **92**(38), 313-15.
16. Hansen, D.L., Schone, P.J., Corey, D., Reid, M., & Gehring, J. *Quality control mechanisms for crowdsourcing: peer review, arbitration, & expertise at familysearch indexing.* ACM CSCW 2013, 649-660.
17. Harland, P., Staats, H., & Wilke, H.A.M. *Explaining proenvironmental intention and behavior by personal norms and the Theory of Planned Behavior 1.* Journal of Applied Social Psychology, 1999. **29**(12), 2505-2528.
18. He, H.A., Greenberg, S., & Huang, E.M. *One size does not fit all: applying the transtheoretical model to energy feedback technology design.* ACM CHI 2010, 927-936.
19. Hekler, E., Klasnja, P., Froehlich, J., & Buman, M. *Mind the theoretical gap: interpreting, using, and developing behavioral theory in HCI research.* ACM CHI 2013, 3307-16.
20. Huotari, K. & Hamari, J. *Defining gamification: a service marketing perspective.* MindTrek 2012, 17-22.
21. Khatib, F., Cooper, S., Tyka, M.D., Xu, K., Makedon, I., Popovifá, Z., & Baker, D. *Algorithm discovery by protein folding game players.* Nat Acad of Sciences, 2011. **108**, 18949-53.
22. Kim, S., Mankoff, J., & Paulos, E. *Sensr: evaluating a flexible framework for authoring mobile data-collection tools for citizen science.* ACM CSCW 2013, 1453-1462.

23. Kim, S., Robson, C., Zimmerman, T., Pierce, J., & Haber, E.M. *Creek watch: pairing usefulness and usability for successful citizen science.* ACM CHI 2011, 2125-2134.
24. Lea, M., Rogers, P., & Postmes, T. *SIDE-VIEW: Evaluation of a system to develop team players and improve productivity in Internet collaborative learning groups.* British Journal of Educational Technology, 2002. **33**, 53-63.
25. Lintott, C., Schawinski, K., Slosar, A., Land, K., Bamford, S., Thomas, D., Raddick, J., Nichol, R.C., Szalay, A., Andreescu, D., Murray, P., & Vandenberg, J. *Galaxy Zoo: morphologies derived from visual inspection of galaxies from the Sloan Digital Sky Survey.* Monthly Notices of the Royal Astronomical Society, 2008. **389**(3), 1179-1189.
26. Malone, T. *Heuristics for designing enjoyable user interfaces: Lessons from computer games.* ACM CHI 1982, 63-68.
27. Mankoff, J., Matthews, D., Fussell, R., & Johnson, M. *Leveraging social networks to motivate individuals to reduce their ecological footprints.* HICSS 2007, 87-96.
28. Massung, E., Coyle, D., Cater, K.F., Jay, M., & Preist, C. *Using crowdsourcing to support pro-environmental community activism.* ACM CHI 2013, 371-380.
29. Massung, E. & Preist, C. *Normification: using crowdsourced technology to affect third-party change.* ACM CHI EA 2013, 1449-54.
30. Nicholson, S. *A user-centered theoretical framework for meaningful gamification.* Games, Learning & Society 8.0 2012, 223–230.
31. Nolan, J., Schultz, P., Cialdini, R., Goldstein, N., & Griskevicius, V. *Normative social influence is underdetected.* Personality and Social Psych Bulletin, 2008. **34**, 913-23.
32. Nov, O., Arazy, O., & Anderson, D. *Dusting for science: motivation and participation of digital citizen science volunteers.* iConference 2011, 68-74.
33. Oomen, J. & Aroyo, L. *Crowdsourcing in the cultural heritage domain: opportunities and challenges.* Communities and Technologies 2011, 138-149.
34. Petkov, P., Kobler, F., Foth, M., & Krcmar, H. *Motivating domestic energy conservation through comparative, community-based feedback in mobile and social media.* Communities and Technologies 2011, 21-30.
35. Postmes, T., Spears, R., & Lea, M. *Breaching or building social boundaries? SIDE-effects of computer-mediated communication.* Comms Research, 1998. **25**(6), 689-715.
36. Postmes, T., Spears, R., & Lea, M. *The formation of group norms in computer-mediated communication.* Human Communication Research, 2000. **26**(341-371).
37. Reeves, S. & Sherwood, S. *Five design challenges for human computation.* NordiCHI 2010, 383-392.
38. Reno, R., Cialdini, R., & Kallgren, C. *The transsituational influence of social norms.* J of Personality and Social Psychology, 1993. **64**(1), 104-112.
39. Rimal, R.N. & Real, K. *How behaviors are influenced by perceived norms: A test of the theory of normative social behavior.* Communication Research, 2005. **32**(3), 389-414.
40. Rotman, D., Preece, J., Hammock, J., Procita, K., Hansen, D., Parr, C., Lewis, D., & Jacobs, D. *Dynamic changes in motivation in collaborative citizen-science projects.* ACM CSCW 2012, 217-226.
41. Schultz, P.W., Nolan, J.M., Cialdini, R.B., Goldstein, N.J., & Griskevicius, V. *The Constructive, Destructive, and Reconstructive Power of Social Norms.* Psychological Science, 2007. **18**(5), 429-434.
42. Schultz, W.P., Khazian, A.M., & Zaleski, A.C. *Using normative social influence to promote conservation among hotel guests.* Social Influence, 2008. **3**(1), 4-23.
43. Schwartz, T., Stevens, G., Ramirez, L., & Wulf, V. *Uncovering practices of making energy consumption accountable: A phenomenological inquiry.* ACM Trans. Comput.-Hum. Interaction, 2013. **20**(2).
44. Shaw, A.D., Horton, J.J., & Chen, D.L. *Designing incentives for inexpert human raters.* ACM CSCW 2011, 275-284.
45. Starbird, K. & Palen, L. *"Voluntweeters": self-organizing by digital volunteers in times of crisis.* ACM CHI 2011, 1071-80.
46. Steg, L. & de Groot, J. *Explaining prosocial intentions: Testing causal relationships in the norm activation model.* British J of Social Psychology, 2010. **49**(4), 725-743.
47. Studley, M., Chambers, S., Rettie, R., & Burchell, K. *Gathering and presenting social feedback to change domestic electricity consumption.* Workshop on Persuasion, Influence, Nudge & Coercion Through Mobile Devices 2011.
48. Sukumaran, A., Vezich, S., McHugh, M., & Nass, C. *Normative influences on thoughtful online participation.* ACM CHI 2011, 3401-3410.
49. Thieme, A., Comber, R., Miebach, J., Weeden, J., Kraemer, N., Lawson, S., & Olivier, P. *"We've bin watching you": designing for reflection and social persuasion to promote sustainable lifestyles.* ACM CHI 2012, 2337-2346.
50. von Ahn, L. & Dabbish, L. *Labeling images with a computer game.* ACM CHI 2004, 319-326.
51. Wiggins, A. *Free as in puppies: compensating for ICT constraints in citizen science.* ACM CSCW 2013, 1469-1480.
52. Zichermann, G. & Cunningham, C. *Gamification by design: Implementing game mechanics in web and mobile Apps* 2011. Sebastopol, CA. O'Reilly Media.

Capturing Quality: Retaining Provenance for Curated Volunteer Monitoring Data

S. Andrew Sheppard
University of Minnesota &
Houston Engineering, Inc.
Minneapolis, MN, USA
sheppard@umn.edu

Andrea Wiggins
University of New Mexico &
Cornell University
Ithaca, NY, USA
andrea.wiggins@cornell.edu

Loren Terveen
GroupLens Research
University of Minnesota
Minneapolis, MN, USA
terveen@cs.umn.edu

ABSTRACT
The "real world" nature of field-based citizen science involves unique data management challenges that distinguish it from projects that involve only Internet-mediated activities. In particular, many data contribution and review practices are often accomplished "offline" via paper or general-purpose software like Excel. This can lead to integration challenges when attempting to implement project-specific ICT with full revision and provenance tracking. In this work, we explore some of the current challenges and opportunities in implementing ICT for managing volunteer monitoring data. Our two main contributions are: a general outline of the workflow tasks common to field-based data collection, and a novel data model for preserving provenance metadata that allows for ongoing data exchange between disparate technical systems and participant skill levels. We conclude with applications for other domains, such as hydrologic forecasting and crisis informatics, as well as directions for future research.

Author Keywords
volunteer monitoring; citizen science; VGI; provenance; data models; EAV; spreadsheets; mobile applications; data exchange; ICT

INTRODUCTION
Citizen science, a form of scientific collaboration that engages non-professionals in research, is an increasingly valuable means for collecting robust scientific data sets. The benefits of including volunteers in scientific research include local ownership of environmental concerns, an increased "sense of place", and improved understanding of scientific matters, as well as enabling new research that was previously impossible. Recent high-profile citizen science projects like Galaxy Zoo [18] are largely *virtual* [32], taking advantage of the the web as infrastructure to facilitate data processing via human computation.

CSCW'14, February 15–19, 2014, Baltimore, Maryland, USA.

http://dx.doi.org/10.1145/2531602.2531689

However, the majority of citizen science projects still focus on collecting *observational data* of such phenomena as weather and precipitation, air and water quality, and species abundance and distribution. This form of citizen science, also known as *volunteer monitoring*, has actively contributed to science and decision-making for over 100 years [4]. While most such projects now also take advantage of the web, field-based data collection tasks will always involve a physical component, leading to interesting tensions in the use of Information and Communication Technologies (ICT) for citizen science.

Virtual projects share features with the crowdsourcing style of distributed work [8], in which large contributor bases are usually required for success. In contrast, the geographic and human scale of field-based citizen science can vary widely. On one end of the spectrum are *large-scale projects* like eBird, which collects global bird abundance and distribution data [26], and the Community Collaboratorive Rain, Hail & Snow Network (CoCoRaHS) [1], a network of precipitation observers across North America. Approximately 150,000 active participants generate around 5 million observations of birds per month for eBird, with a total data set size of around 140 million records in mid-2013. The data are used for scientific research as well as policy and land management decisions. CoCoRaHS data are requested nearly 3,000 times a day; the largest of several data sets includes 22 million data points, each representing daily precipitation for a specific location. Notable data users for CoCoRaHS include the U.S. National Weather Service, National Climatic Data Center, and other climate and weather organizations.

On the other end are *local scale projects*, sometimes referred to as community-based monitoring [34]. These projects are often organized by local community leaders who are generally experts in the topic area, but may or may not have prior professional experience. Projects like River Watch [23] and Mountain Watch [30] usually have specific conservation or social justice goals. These projects benefit from working with support from, and exchanging data with, government entities and other related organizations. For example, River Watch data is shared with the Minnesota Pollution Control Agency and becomes a part of the official state record for the rivers monitored by the program. Mountain Watch data were used in testimony to lawmakers to demonstrate the value of maintaining Clean Air Act protections.

Like other aspects of citizen science, the *quality of data* collected by volunteers is an ongoing area of research. Data quality is often critical to achieving project goals, and while it is generally defined as "fitness for its intended purpose" by most field research disciplines [9], its precise formulation is inherently context-dependent [23].

There are a number of mechanisms for handling data quality in citizen science [33]. Online projects can often verify results by having multiple volunteers complete the same task. However, in field-based monitoring, the data are much more individualized, containing time and location-sensitive information[1]. These data are often unique observations of changing natural phenomena; as such, they may not be directly verifiable. An eBird project leader described the act of observation as "the intersection of a person, a bird, a time, and a place," emphasizing that for these data, the observation is never repeatable.

The distributed nature of participation means that supervision is often minimal and organizers must trust volunteers to follow instructions accurately. Thus, there is a strong emphasis on precise *task definition* and training to reduce error and maintain the comparability of data points [23], and expert review to validate the data. *Expert review* remains the most popular and broadly used mechanism for data validation in citizen science projects collecting observational data [33]; therefore, it is the primary focus of our discussion.

The experts conducting data quality review may be volunteers, staff, or affiliated scientists who evaluate incoming data. Among other approaches, data review may take the form of a project leader reviewing data summaries for outliers (e.g., The Great Sunflower Project), an intern entering hard copy data sheets into a database (e.g., Mountain Watch), or a global network of expert volunteer data reviewers using an integrated, customized, distributed data review tool (e.g., eBird).

One might assume that observational data remain unchanged as long as they are recorded as intended by the original observer. In practice, however, *some data do change*, usually through the review process. A common procedure is checking for and flagging or removing outliers. This is not as simple as just marking a record as "invalid", because the initial data review may not be the final word. For example, in some data sets that include species for whom range shifts are observed, outliers might be judged invalid upon initial review. If additional evidence of a range shift accrues over time, however, the original records would be re-reviewed and marked as valid. Where supported, data may also be changed by the individuals who submit it, e.g., due to post hoc development of further expertise, or after communication with a reviewer clarifies an uncertainty.

[1]The location-dependent nature of field observations can also lead to complex privacy issues, which fall outside of the scope of this paper.

Finally, the task definition (protocol) itself can change, or multiple protocols may be supported; knowing which protocol and which "version" of the task was in place is necessary for accurate data interpretation. This is particularly important during the early stages of project development, as establishing workable procedures and quality control mechanisms can take several iterations, each of which may require a full field season.

With this in mind, it is clear that projects should ideally track changes to data for a number of reasons:

- for accurate provenance;
- in case future reversal is needed;
- to facilitate process improvement;
- to support participant skill development; and
- to demonstrate scientific rigor through appropriate data documentation.

A number of recent developments in ICT for citizen science have led to promising approaches for managing data. However, the complexity of the data management task means that familiar general-purpose tools like Excel may still be preferred by participants. Even if a project has the resources to build or contract custom ICT for data management, important revisions to the data can and do continue to occur externally.

In this paper, we explore a *general workflow* common to many field-based monitoring projects. We discuss five citizen science projects as examples and identify aspects of data management important to each step of the workflow process. We then present a *new data model* for field monitoring workflows that handles some of the complexities inherent in managing these kinds of data.

RELATED WORK

Technologies supporting public participation in scientific research are swiftly advancing, but with little consideration for the complexities of data management processes. To date, general-purpose ICT rarely support quality control processes such as data review outside of simple moderator approval. Metadata standards focus on documenting data rather than facilitating retention of provenance, and while wikis might seem a suitable solution to some key concerns, most citizen science projects violate the assumptions upon which wikis are built.

General-purpose ICT for citizen science

Despite the centrality of data in these projects, scientific data management is not a skill that project coordinators necessarily bring to the table, nor do partnering scientists or participants. Therefore, guidelines for data management plans, policies, and practices for these projects have only recently begun emerging [31, 13]. Persistent challenges in storing project data and metadata include suboptimal ICT for smaller projects [30]. Cumulative data sets, such as those produced by ongoing, long-term projects, also defy some of the usual practices in data management because there is no "finished" data product to archive as a standalone object.

Table 1. Example Citizen Science Projects

Project	Focus	Data Type	Geographic Range	Organizational Sector
CoCoRaHS	Precipitation	Measurement	U.S.A. & Canada	NGO
eBird	Birds	Observation	Global	NGO partnership
Great Sunflower Project	Bees	Observation	North America	Academic
Mountain Watch	Alpine plants	Observation	New Hampshire	NGO
RRB River Watch	Water quality	Measurement	Red River Basin	NGO & state agency partnership

Given these challenges, several tools have been developed to make it easier for new projects to get started. Online systems like CitSci.org [14], Sensr [11], and CrowdMap by Ushahidi [15] provide platforms to launch new projects with little or no programming knowledge. However, these systems are also harder to customize for more complex workflows; project leaders must either adapt their workflow to fit the software, pay someone to make modifications to meet their needs, or both.

Other projects like Open Data Kit [7] and wq [22] offer customizable, open source software platforms for field data collection. These platforms provide an alternative to both "from scratch" development and hosted solutions. wq's modular codebase is designed to support project-specific customization, and the framework did not previously support the complex data management workflow common to many field-based projects. We have provided an implementation of the ERAV data model proposed in this work as an extension to wq[2].

Provenance Models

There have been a number of efforts to create and standardize models for describing the provenance of citizen science and other types of monitoring data. Some prominent examples include Ecological Metadata Language (EML) [3], the Federal Geographic Data Committee's Content Standard for Digital Geospatial Metadata [2], and the Darwin Core [29] - as well as a number of other field-specific metadata standards. More general provenance models for the semantic web include the PROV standard by the W3C [5], and the conceptual W7 model [19], designed to address the "7 W's" of provenance: what, how, when, where, who, which, and why.

These models can be useful for describing the provenance of monitoring data sets, but they do not fully address the data management challenges we explore in this work. At a superficial level, the goals are slightly different: these models standardize ways to *document* provenance, while the model proposed in this work is intended to facilitate *recording and retaining* provenance data throughout the project workflow. In this respect, the model proposed in this work has more in common with FilteredPush [28], as a platform for tracking and incorporating revisions from third parties into scientific datasets.

[2]See `http://wq.io/vera` for more details.

However, there is a more serious underlying concern. We have observed that in practice, not every party involved in a data exchange can be expected to utilize the recommended metadata standards and software tools. Thus, the model proposed in this work is intended to facilitate the incorporation of revisions to data received from multiple parties, *whether or not* those parties are actively tracking and reporting those revisions internally.

Wikis

Wikis are a well studied method for maintaining online repositories of community knowledge, with built-in mechanisms for versioning and some provenance tracking. Wikis generally incorporate a timeline or revision history, tracking changes to data with timestamps and usernames. Importantly, old values are preserved and changes can be reverted, supplemented by log messages to explain why data were changed. Previous research has explored the usefulness of revision logs for provenance [12, 16], and as a way to evaluate the quality control process [6, 25]. Other efforts work to extend wikis with additional provenance tracking features, for example the Shortipedia project [27]. The geowiki model [17] extends wikis with concepts useful for some citizen science use cases, including the ability to track changes to interdependent objects and fine-tune permissions on a per-user basis.

With these affordances, it may appear that wikis would be ideal for maintaining repositories of citizen science data. However, there are a number of assumptions that limit the usefulness of the wiki model for this case. First, most wiki models assume that once data are in the system, all further editing will happen within the system, so there is generally limited support for offline editing and reintegration. As we will demonstrate, many important review tasks for field monitoring data are accomplished using external systems.

Second, the basic wiki model generally assumes the artifacts being described are relatively stable, and can be objectively described in increasingly better detail through iteration by additional contributors. As noted above, field data collection results in individualized, first-hand observations of changing natural phenomena.[3].

[3]This observation has been explored in previous work as a distinction between *descriptive* versus *experiential* volunteered geographic information [22]

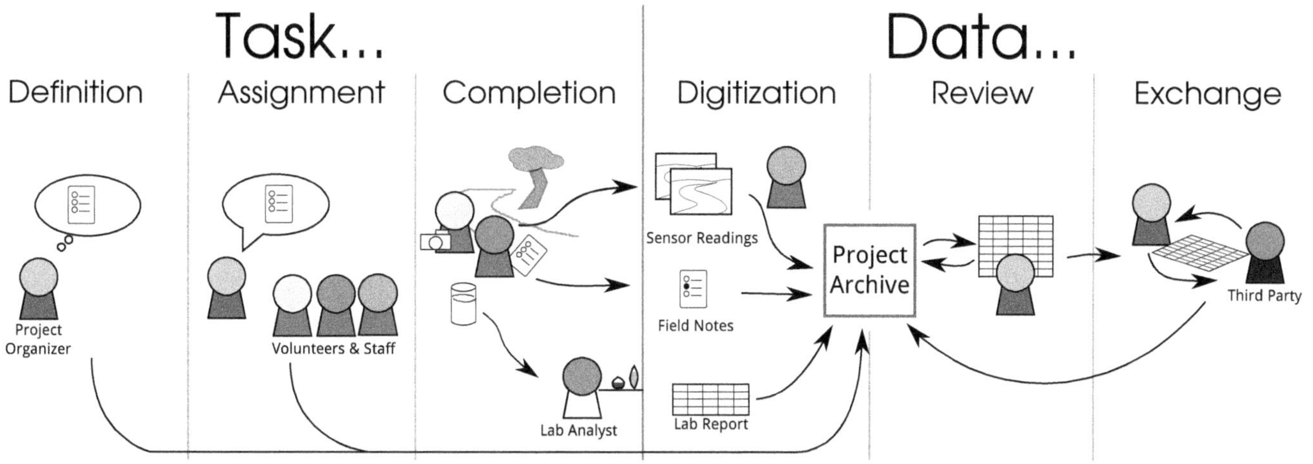

Figure 1. The field monitoring workflow. Arrows represent the flow of data and metadata between and during subtasks. (Lab analysis is relatively infrequent in citizen science projects.)

Wikis generally have poor support for time series data because the main timeline most wikis track is their own revision history. Handling time-sensitive data effectively is a general challenge given the multiple potential interpretations of time and history [21].

Wiki rules and norms are interactively worked out within the wiki and versioned like other wiki objects. Citizen science protocols, by contrast, are well-defined in order to support scientific rigor, with the primary data collection tasks usually occurring offline. These procedures change only when necessary, and with careful consideration. The quality of an individual observation must be evaluated according to the task definition in place at the time of observation, as opposed to the task definition currently in place (which may differ). Data entry is typically a secondary task, separate from data collection, sampling, and other field-based tasks, which can reduce the rates of data submission. Finally, wikis frequently are not adequately usable for project participants, many of whom struggle with fairly simple UI-driven sites [30].

THE FIELD-BASED MONITORING WORKFLOW

In this section, we explore aspects of the data management workflow common to many field-based monitoring projects. We give examples of each step in the process and draw general conclusions about ICT requirements for these projects.

Methods

The empirical data informing the inductive model development presented here were collected for two prior studies of citizen science projects [23, 30] and preliminary data from a third unpublished study. These independently conducted studies employed qualitative field research methods and shared a primary focus on *data management processes* and *ICT infrastructures* in citizen science projects. Data sources included interviews with project organizers, internal documents such as database schemata, and longitudinal participation and observation documented via field notes. Each study included standard procedures for ensuring research quality; for example, project leaders were invited to review and correct the penultimate drafts of analyses.

As such, the data sources and thematic focus of these studies were highly compatible. Further, the combined cases are reasonably representative of the known population of North American citizen science projects that focus on field-based data collection [30]. From a theoretical sampling standpoint, they also maximize diversity across several key project characteristics, while remaining comparable due to similar participation structures and levels of project maturity. As shown in Table 1, the projects discussed in the current work originated from diverse scientific domains in a variety of organizational structures. They operated at geographic scales ranging from local to global, with average contribution rates ranging from well under 7,000 data points per year to over 7,000 data points per hour.

The Workflow

The process of collecting and processing field data in a citizen science project is summarized in Figure 1. We describe a general workflow, noting that each citizen science project has its own specific variations to accommodate.

Task Definition

The monitoring task is usually defined by a project coordinator/domain expert, sometimes with participant input. Precise task design is critical for data quality and meaningful evaluation metrics [23]. Task definitions generally include step-by-step protocols for collecting data and explanations of targeted parameters.

For example, the CoCoRaHS task includes reading a rain gauge and (in winter months) melting snow samples to measure snow water equivalent. The River Watch task follows a more complex protocol based on professional monitoring processes, including readings with a chemical probe (sonde). Ideally, the task definition is digitized and stored in the project archive. In practice, it is documented primarily in the form of instructions to participants.

Task Assignment

Once volunteers agree to participate and have completed any necessary training, task assignment usually includes selecting the location(s) for collecting data. Participants typically make observations in areas near their home or school due to the practical constraint that volunteers must be able to readily access observation sites.

Participants may be assigned specific individual sites to monitor (River Watch); or they may report on data for established shared observation sites, such as permanent plots for plant species (Mountain Watch); or they may select a location in their yard (CoCoRaHS, The Great Sunflower Project); or they may make observations anywhere the phenomenon of interest is present (eBird and numerous others). In most cases, observation locations chosen by participants are resolved to a latitude and longitude based on a street address or a pin dropped on an online map.

The assignment step may also include training and/or distribution of equipment, where appropriate. In some projects, training is self-paced using online materials; in others, in-person workshops provide opportunities to learn more complex participation processes. For a few projects, training is limited to instructions for data entry: through self-selection, eBird participants are typically already "trained" in key skills for bird detection and identification, and need only learn the conventions of the eBird system.

Task Completion

Once protocols are defined and locations assigned, it is up to the volunteers to head out into the field to collect data. This step is referred to as the *event* in our proposed data model. As noted above, this is "the intersection of a person, a bird, a time, and a place" for eBird. Similarly, a River Watch sampling event is the combination of a sampling team, a time, and a predetermined site along a stream.

While CoCoRaHS and River Watch incorporate measurements from specialized sensors into their workflow, eBird, the Great Sunflower Project, and Mountain Watch each require nothing more than field observations written down on paper. Very simple task definitions are increasingly common among citizen science projects, because most organizers report a direct tradeoff between task complexity and volume of data contributions.

Data Digitization

Ideally, all information for each observation would be uploaded into a centralized system immediately as a single report for instant validation and change tracking. In practice, the conversion of data from field notes into digital form often does not happen instantly. Data entry is sometimes substantially delayed because participants consider it an unpleasant or undesirable task; this is a universal challenge for projects that require a separate data entry step. In some cases, participants intentionally delay data submission due to concerns over data visibility for sensitive species and breeding animals.

It might seem that replacing paper-based data entry with a mobile app would streamline the process and facilitate instant validation and provenance tracking, but there are some notable barriers to consider. Some contributors will always be more comfortable manually recording data in the field, or hard copy record retention may be required for quality assurance or legal purposes, making mobile entry an unwanted extra step. Not all contributors own smartphones or other technologies such as GPS devices. In some projects, the primary contributor group is older adults, the demographic with lowest smartphone adoption [24]. Under a variety of circumstances, bulk upload can be the most feasible way to entice volunteers to contribute larger volumes of data.

Collecting data in the field is subject to the conditions of the field. Technical constraints can limit the usefulness of smartphones (e.g., off-grid usage must be accommodated), but sometimes using electronics is simply impractical due to screen glare, inclement weather, or incompatibility with the flow of activities. In addition, most projects are poorly positioned to manage an additional platform (or three) for mobile data entry. Although the use of HTML5 can facilitate cross-platform deployment [22], the mobile workflow adds complexities that can be challenging to address. Further, external partners may not be able to adapt to new technologies.

Even when new technologies can be incorporated, integrating the collected data into a single submitted record is still challenging. Unannotated digital photos may require later manual matching to field data. For measurement projects like River Watch, chemical sensor readings must be transcribed manually (though newer sensors will support direct data transfer). When lab samples are involved, the original field report must be associated with a lab report created after the fact.

Data Review

In order to ensure the quality of the project results, incoming data is often reviewed to the extent feasible. Large projects like eBird may use algorithmic flagging of outliers – as defined by the data themselves, where possible [10] – to automatically identify data points that require expert review. Review is conducted by domain experts; for example, eBird's network of approximately 650 volunteer reviewers use both online and offline tools and resources for data review. Most reviews are readily completed within the custom review interface, but during spring migration, when an especially high number of records are flagged each year due to early movement of some species, bulk review is more feasible. Reviewers sift through data in Excel to manage these large batches or identify more nuanced data problems, and then update records via eBird's online review interface (re-upload of edited records is not supported.)

In smaller projects without resources for such systems, data filtering algorithms are enacted by hand, often with Excel. These manual procedures are rarely adequately documented to make the data processing itself repeatable.

For example, River Watch data is reviewed by a core team of 3-4 staff. While the project's custom ICT does support some simple range validation checking, making corrections to bulk data while importing it has been a cumbersome task. Thus, most of the review to identify and remove outliers still happens in Excel, and reviewers generally prefer to wait to import anything until after they have fully reviewed the data they receive. As a result, potentially valuable information about the review process is lost, as is the ability to easily reverse a decision to discard an outlier when reversal is warranted.

Data Exchange

An important part of enabling data use is facilitating exchange with third parties. Data are often exchanged using a standard or agreed-upon format. For example, River Watch monitoring data is sent annually for incorporation in the Minnesota Pollution Control Agency's master database, using an Excel spreadsheet with a layout based on the STORET standard. In addition to less formally structured download files, eBird data packages are made available in Bird Monitoring Data Exchange (BMDE) format, an extension of Darwin Core metadata standards, which was collaboratively developed with the Avian Knowledge Network to permit data exchange among partners.

In some cases, third parties may comment on or even modify data within their systems as part of an ongoing review process. This is certainly true for River Watch, and it has traditionally been difficult to ensure that these changes are replicated across databases. This challenge is addressed in the new data model proposed in this work.

Task Refinement

Finally, as the project evolves, the core tasks will often be refined. A new measuring tool may become available, for example, or a task is simplified to make it accessible to a larger audience. Data users and contributors often request modifications to protocols to better fit their needs. For example, in 2012 River Watch (and other similar programs in Minnesota) switched from measuring water clarity with T-Tubes to using Secchi tubes. The protocol and data structure is nearly the same, but Secchi data is treated as a different parameter for provenance purposes. Although eBird's three primary protocols remain unchanged since the project launched, 20 additional protocols appear in the data set, most of which address specific needs for projects coordinated by partner organizations.

Coordinators may also find that the way volunteers execute tasks differs from their expectations, leading to a retooling of procedural details to support more consistent task completion. For example, The Great Sunflower Project switched from 30-minute sampling on Lemon Queen (*Helianthus annus*) sunflowers exclusively (2008), to 15-minute sampling (2009), to 15-minute sampling on Lemon Queens plus a selection of common garden species (2010), to 5+ minute sampling for any flowering garden

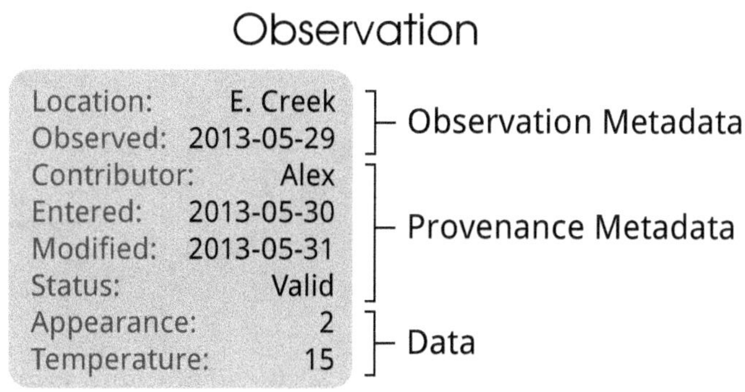

Figure 2. Example *single-table* model for representing an observation. Note that "single-table" here refers only to the structure of the observation data, as there would typically be separate Contributor and Location entities, which are represented here as text values for simplicity.

species (2013). This is neither atypical nor slow development for a new participation protocol in field-based citizen science.

Supporting changing task definitions is a common challenge for ICT in citizen science. Without careful planning, project development can be stymied by static platforms that cannot adapt to changing project needs without additional (often unavailable) programming effort. Even more flexible data models typically fail to retain the information necessary to evaluate historical data properly. This can lead to erroneous assumptions about data and misinterpretations that can have serious consequences, e.g., inappropriate land use recommendations for managing endangered species habitat. Managing changes to task definitions is another challenge addressed by our proposed data model.

Key observations

Field monitoring data often starts its life "offline" and may also be reviewed and edited offline. Despite evolving ICT capabilities, it is not reasonable to expect that all contributors will use a custom system for all editing and review practices. Especially when third parties are involved, there is simply no way to ensure that every important revision to the data will happen inside of a project's ICT system.

With this in mind, we suggest that rather than building a custom platform that supports every conceivable data review operation, it may be more valuable to build a system that is robust against *multiple imports and exports* to and from external formats. That is to say, data import is more than just a bootstrapping feature until developers can implement a full-featured data management platform, then train contributors to perform all data modification within it, where changes can be directly monitored. Instead, the ability to import new *and modified* data from external formats is, and will remain, a core part of the workflow. This can be due to contributor preferences, and to parts of the workflow not fully under project control, like data exchange with third parties.

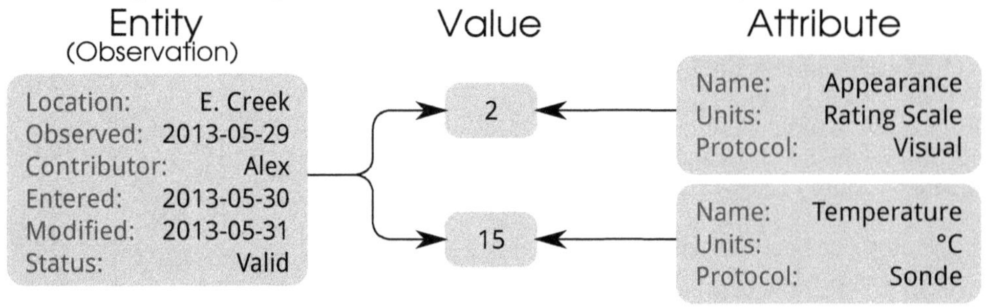

Figure 3. Simplified *Entity-Attribute-Value* model for field observations. Each rectangle represents a row in a table. Arrows represent parent-child relationships; some primary and foreign key columns are not shown.

In particular, the good old spreadsheet is how many scientific project contributors prefer to work with data [20]. Normalized data models and sophisticated apps are not necessarily seen as useful, even if there is a demonstrable overall benefit. Volunteers are rarely eager to learn new software, and data management tasks are a hurdle to participation for many individuals. Generally, our internal data model should account for the needs of contributors who are unconcerned about internal data models and just want to participate in science.

Certainly, there is great potential for mobile devices to be harnessed as a way to improve data quality and submission rates[4]. However, mobile technology is not a panacea, and in many projects, mobile entry should not be the only contribution option. A more holistic approach should incorporate new technologies where appropriate (and possible), but also allow for more traditional ways of handling data, with the understanding that technology is just one part of the larger process [30]. Toward that end, we propose a new data model that flexibly integrates data from both bulk import and mobile field entry workflows.

PROPOSED DATA MODEL

As we have discussed, data management for field-based observation is a nontrivial task. Most existing general-purpose platforms do not track changes to data, and wikis are not particularly well suited for field observation data. Even tailor-made platforms struggle with adequately maintaining history. An ideal data model would track changes to data and task definitions, allowing accurate analysis of historical data. Importantly, *the model must handle the data import task robustly and repeatedly*, by matching incoming records to data already in the database.

We propose a novel data model that has these characteristics, and hope that it will be useful to implementers of ICT for citizen science projects. We demonstrate the derivation of the new model by way of example. As a starting point, Figure 2 shows a simple "single-table" model for storing incoming observations.

The model contains a number of metadata attributes that are important for provenance, as well as the actual recorded values for the observation. Note that there are three different types of data being stored: Observation metadata, describing when and where the observation took place (Location, Observed); Provenance metadata, tracking the process of entering and maintaining the record within the ICT (Contributor, Entered, Modified, Status); and Data, or the actual values being reported per the task definition.

The single-table model conceptually matches an intuitive understanding of the task definition, and could easily be implemented in web and paper forms for entering the data. This database model is used by a number of projects, including CoCoRaHS, but can be inflexible to evolving project needs.

For example, a subset of River Watch participants now collect both precipitation and frost depth information during the winter months when streams are frozen [22]. The precipitation data is a natural fit for CoCoRaHS and so is shared with the program. However, there is currently no place in the CoCoRaHS database to record frost depth, which falls outside of the original scope of the project. Asking CoCoRaHS staff to add additional database columns and interface elements for the sake of one subcommunity is not reasonable, so as a workaround, these additional data were submitted to CoCoRaHS in the "comments" field, limiting its usefulness. Work is currently underway to explore the potential of applying the more flexible database model proposed in this work to CoCoRaHS.

In general, whenever a project task definition expands to include additional data fields, the project will need to have a developer add additional columns to the database and update hard-coded application logic. If an existing parameter definition changes in a way that will affect the meaning of the associated values, old data is either "upgraded" via computational means, or a subtle break in the data between the "old" and the "new" data is created.

EAV: Tracking Changes to the Task Definition

The entity-attribute-value model (shown in Figure 3) is a common way to address these flexibility issues. The EAV model is necessarily used by general-purpose platforms like Ushahidi to support custom task definitions. However, it is also useful for project-specific ICT systems.

[4]For example, the eBird team have noted that the BirdLog mobile app has dramatically increased submissions by core contributors.

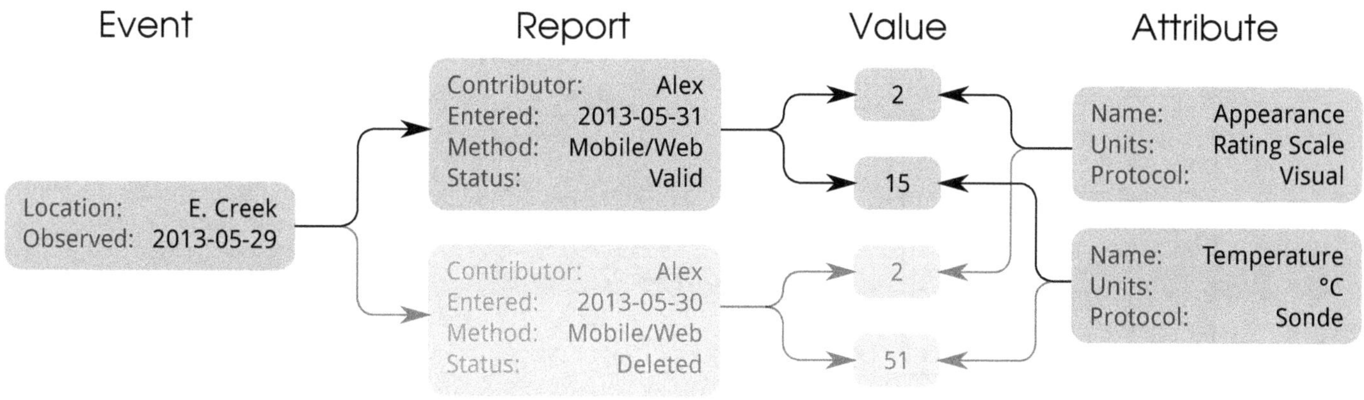

Figure 4. *Entity-Report-Attribute-Value* example showing two versions of a report. In this case, all editing happened within a web interface, making it possible to automatically deprecate the old report.

For example, eBird's internal database model includes a *Checklist* (Entity), *Species name* (Attribute), and *Observation* (Value)[5], the latter being the number of birds seen for a given species at the date and place represented by the checklist. Similarly, River Watch and other water quality projects' data are typically structured as a series of *Sampling Events* (Entities), each containing *Results* (Values) for a number of predetermined (but flexible) *Parameters* (Attributes).

By managing attribute definitions in their own table, systems designers can allow more flexibility to customize and maintain the task definition as needed. This table can also store useful metadata about each parameter (e.g., units and sampling methods) rather than hard-coding it in the application. When implementing EAV generally, it can sometimes be a challenge to determine which items to implement as attribute-values and which to leave as "normal" fields on the entity. In this case the distinction is relatively simple: metadata should generally be defined as part of the entity, while the observation or measurement data should be implemented as attribute-value pairs.

The EAV approach can also be applied as a simple but effective way to "version" task definitions, simply by creating additional attributes, though this capability is rarely exploited. New incoming observations could be associated with new attribute definitions, while leaving the existing data as-is. Where possible, it may be useful to define a mapping from the old values to the new values, but this can be done without actually changing prior data.

For example, when River Watch switched from T-Tubes to Secchi Tubes, one of the project coordinators was able to create a "Secchi Tube" parameter definition without developer intervention. While there was general agreement that the parameters should be kept separate in the database, River Watch organizers and participants wanted to evaluate their Secchi and T-Tube data on the same chart, as if they were the same parameter. This was facilitated by defining a relationship between the old and new parameters, indicating that they were numerically equivalent and could be graphed on the same scale.

[5]Note that "observation" as used elsewhere in this work refers to the entity (or checklist in eBird's case).

ERAV: Tracking Changes to Observation Data

The EAV model is useful for supporting and tracking changes to the task definition. However, as we noted, individual observation records can also be changed during the review process, and these changes should ideally be tracked as well. With the model in Figure 3, if data is modified, the only indication that anything has changed is the *modified* column; the replaced data is lost entirely.

In a wiki or similar versioning system, a *version* field on the observation could be incremented whenever data change, automatically marking the previous version as *deleted* on each new save.[6] However, this assumes that revisions are done sequentially, within the system, and that there is always only one active (non-deleted) version of the observation. As noted earlier, there can be two or more records created for the same observation, especially if there is lab work involved. We need a way to group these into a single entity for analysis, while maintaining the separate provenance information for each record.

To accomplish this, we propose a new model, ERAV, which separates the *event* (the actual observation) from its provenance record. The *event* entity retains metadata about the observation (e.g., site, date observed), while the metadata about provenance (e.g., observer id, date/time entered, review status) is moved to a separate *report* entity. *This approach enables maintaining multifaceted provenance data for the same event.*

As Figure 4 shows, whenever a report is changed within the system, a new version is created and the prior one is marked as deleted, much like in a typical wiki. Note that an explicit *last modified* column is no longer needed, as it can be derived from the *entered* date of the most recent report. As with EAV, the actual observations/measurements are recorded as attribute-value pairs. Importantly, these attribute-values are internally associated with each report, rather than the event.

To the casual data user and for most data analysis purposes, the event/report distinction is unimportant. For

[6]Note that "deleted" is really just a value for the *status* field; an actual SQL DELETE would cause historical data to be lost, contrary to the goals of the versioning system.

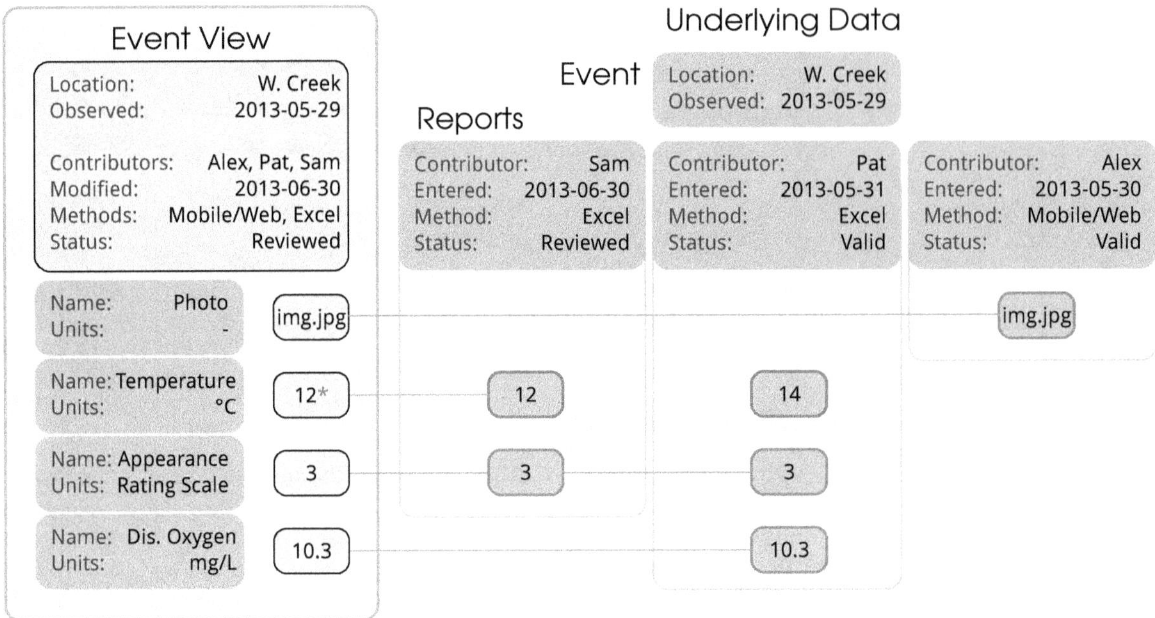

Figure 5. Resolving report information into a single "event" view. Some of the event data was imported from Excel more than once, leading to ambiguity. (For clarity, only currently active reports are shown.)

many common use cases, the attribute-values can be displayed as if they were directly associated with the event. This trick allows provenance metadata for various attribute values to be maintained internally as part of each report, while presenting a single conceptual *event* entity for analysis purposes.

"Merging" Reports & Handling Conflicts

When information about an event is created or modified outside of the system and then imported again, we cannot necessarily assume that any existing reports for the event should be deleted. For example, the incoming report may contain only supplemental data or a single additional attribute that was previously missed by mistake. Reports can also contain lab data associated with corresponding field reports, which would previously have been manually merged, obfuscating provenance metadata in the process. In the new model, the contributor can simply upload the new file; if the observation metadata matches, new reports are generated with the additional attribute-values, which are displayed together with the previously entered values as though all were directly associated with the event. This feature can be thought of as "merging" reports, though the actual data is not combined internally.

Even when the new data contains complete observation records, automatically deprecating older reports may not be desirable. Certainly, when reviewers have already validated a bulk dataset offline, they prefer to avoid manually confirming each change, and instead want the system to re-import and accept their new values without question. On the other hand, if a third party conducted the review, the person responsible for re-importing the data may want to "re-review" each change separately.

The main point here is that the appropriate time to resolve differences between versions is context, task, and contributor-dependent, so *the model must allow for ambiguities.*

This allowance can lead to discrepancies between attribute values for active reports, particularly if the incoming data set is an update to existing events incorporating data that was reviewed offline. The terminology of the conceptual model provides a convenient way to describe this situation: *conflicting reports.* This term can be used to alert contributors of the situation, where appropriate, but forcing contributors to deal with conflicts as soon as they are discovered is not always practical. Instead, the system may need to allow for ambiguities remaining in the dataset indefinitely. *This is the key difference between this model and traditional wiki models.*

Figure 5 demonstrates a number of possible outcomes when multiple imported reports describe the same event. If two active reports for an event contain values for different attributes, the data is merged without issue. Even if the reports contain values for the same attributes, the data can be merged as long as the values are also the same. However, conflicting reports must be handled differently according to the use case and skill level of each contributor.

For those only interested in using the data for analysis, conflicts can be smoothed over with a simple heuristic, as demonstrated by the Temperature value in Figure 5. By assigning a relative *authoritativeness* value to each report (e.g., the most recently *entered* report can often be treated as most authoritative), we can defer to the value from the most authoritative active report containing that attribute whenever there is a conflict. More complex workflows might assign priorities to different report status values (e.g. Provisional, Verified), allowing for more fine-tuned ordering and conflict resolution. This would also permit greater transparency for data use by third parties.

Identifying the Relevant Event for an Incoming Report

So far, we have not dealt with the issue of matching incoming reports to their associated events. The ideal approach would be to include each event's unique ID in exported files, and require that only appropriately annotated files be used for offline editing. Then, when a batch of reports was (re-)imported, the embedded event IDs could be used to match those reports to the existing events.

However, we cannot always control the format of batch files for upload, nor can we always ensure that updated files will contain the events' unique identifiers used within our system. This is especially true for file formats controlled by third parties and standard exchange formats. Fortunately, there is usually a workable *natural key* for each event we can use to match incoming reports to events. For example, assuming only one individual is monitoring a given site once a day, we can assume that any reports for the same site and date should be associated with the same event. The actual natural key used would project-specific, but the concept can be applied generally. It is important to be able to identify a usable natural key: if the key is too general, unrelated reports will be inappropriately merged as if they were the same event, but an overly specific key will prevent merging.

Obviously, this strategy works only as long as none of the fields in the natural key need to be updated. If an event is entered with e.g. the wrong date, uploading a spreadsheet with the correct date would simply create another event unassociated with the old data. One possible workaround might be to step back and compare the entire date range of the contributors' existing data against the date range of the uploaded file and point out any obvious discrepancies. Similarly, there is no explicit support for deletion: if a reviewer deletes a row or column from an exported spreadsheet, they might reasonably expect the same data to be deleted from the associated events upon re-import. As Figure 5 shows, this action would be instead interpreted as a partial update by the model.

DISCUSSION

As we have demonstrated, the proposed ERAV model facilitates useful data integration tasks that are difficult or impossible to accomplish in previous data models. The model is conceptually straightforward, with intuitive underlying concepts. ERAV builds off of the existing EAV model to implement very flexible systems that can adapt to changing project needs while preserving data provenance.

Like EAV, ERAV is much more complex than a single-table approach. ERAV has the additional complexity of allowing multiple active versions of the same data, as well as historical versions, to be present in the database at the same time. This has negative implications for system performance[7] that can be mitigated through various technical means such as indexing, caching, and denormalization to a warehouse table for analysis. However, it may also make it more difficult for new developers to quickly understand and adapt an existing project's software. In particular, the multi-table database structure is somewhat less self-documenting, and effectively requires the application software to properly maintain it. Similarly, the software itself is dependent on the database to dictate the interface layout - a useful but occasionally befuddling feature familiar to designers of EAV systems.

Nevertheless, we argue that the flexibility and provenance capabilities ERAV provides are valuable enough to merit the additional complexity for many, if not most, volunteer monitoring projects. In addition, we have released the source code for a generic implementation of ERAV[8] in an effort to mitigate this complexity and provide a bootstrapping platform for new projects interested in getting started with this approach.

Other Uses for ERAV

While this model was developed in the context of field-based citizen science, it has potential applications in a wide variety of domains. It may be useful in nearly any process that involves the exchange and revision of structured data between parties using incompatible software platforms or metadata practices. For example, citizen science data can be seen as a midpoint on a continuum between official or government-maintained datasets, and the more fluid crowdsourced data sets used in areas like crisis informatics.

Government agencies regularly exchange official datasets as part of their workflow. For example, the U.S. Bureau of Reclamation relies on streamflow data downloaded from the U.S. Geological Service to make water supply forecasts. In an ideal world, the data would only be used after it is fully validated and corrected. In practice, however, time constraints mean that the USBR must rely on provisional data sets that may be updated periodically without explicit information about when and why data was changed. This can make it a challenge to explain why a forecast result is coming out differently. With a model like ERAV, it will be possible to incorporate third party data and track changes to it, even if the third party is not explicitly reporting those changes.

FilteredPush [28] provides another approach to solving the problem of integrating updates from third parties into authoritative scientific datasets. However, FilteredPush requires that all involved parties use compatible software for sharing and receiving annotations to data. In contrast, ERAV can be used integrate changes from third parties not using ERAV, as long as the exchanged data has a minimally consistent structure.

[7] Concerns about performance were among the primary reasons CoCoRaHS initially chose not to utilize an EAV schema.
[8] `http://wq.io/vera`

Crisis informatics is another area where ERAV may prove useful. In responding to a crisis event, agencies and partners need to retrieve, organize, and evaluate data from multiple external sources (such as social networks) under rapidly changing conditions. This data must then be validated and compared against other available information. ERAV may be useful for tracking crisis reports as they move between databases and review processes. It may also prove useful in tracking revisions to public posts on social media sites that would otherwise be lost. However, the relatively unstructured nature of crisis data means that it may prove challenging to identify a usable natural key in some cases.

In summary, ERAV is most likely to be useful in cases where:

1. Structured data is being exchanged and revised between multiple parties or data management platforms,
2. The selected (or de facto) exchange format does not include complete provenance information, and
3. The entities being described (i.e. events) can be uniquely identified with a stable natural key that does not need to be centrally assigned.

Next Steps

We plan to implement and evaluate this model with River Watch and potentially with CoCoRaHS. While we believe the model itself is sound, its success will hinge on effectively facilitating the review and integration tasks. Thus, there is a need for more empirical evaluation to better understand the appropriate interfaces for representing "conflicting reports" to contributors of varying skill levels and expertise. We intend to explore this further in a future study. We also note the potential of leveraging other common uses of Excel for review that are missed when only reading cell values for import. For example, River Watch reviewers often use various highlight colors to flag questionable values, but this information is lost after the spreadsheet is ingested. Finally, more technical work is needed to address cases like deletion that the existing model does not handle well.

In closing, recent advances in ICT can help improve tracking of revisions and retention of provenance metadata for citizen science projects. However, it is important to keep in mind that participants' expectations, skill levels, and preferred software tools may not match those idealized by computer scientists. For many projects, building complex data review tools within custom ICT would be over-engineering with minimal benefit. It is often more appropriate to enable bulk import processes, not only to facilitate ingestion of historical records, but as part of the ongoing development and improvement of the quality of the project. Retaining provenance metadata can be a challenge, and our proposed model is an important step toward enabling that capability.

Acknowledgments

We would like to thank the participants and coordinators of the projects we studied, for their input into our understanding of the processes of citizen science. We especially thank Julian Turner for his help in relating CoCoRaHS to the concepts discussed in this paper. We also appreciate the feedback of anonymous reviewers that helped improve this paper. This work is supported in part by NSF Grant OCI-083094.

REFERENCES

1. Cifelli, R., Doesken, N., Kennedy, P., Carey, L. D., Rutledge, S. A., Gimmestad, C., and Depue, T. The community collaborative rain, hail, and snow network: Informal education for scientists and citizens. *Bulletin of the American Meteorological Society 86*, 8 (2005), 1069–1077.
2. Federal Geographic Data Committee and others. FGDC-STD-001-1998. *Content standard for digital geospatial metadata* (1998).
3. Fegraus, E. H., Andelman, S., Jones, M. B., and Schildhauer, M. Maximizing the value of ecological data with structured metadata: An introduction to ecological metadata language (EML) and principles for metadata creation. *Bulletin of the Ecological Society of America 86*, 3 (2005), 158–168.
4. Firehock, K., and West, J. A brief history of volunteer biological water monitoring using macroinvertebrates. *Journal of the North American Benthological Society 14*, 1 (1995), 197–202.
5. Gil, Y., Miles, S., Belhajjame, K., Deus, H., Garijo, D., Klyne, G., Missier, P., Soiland-Reyes, S., and Zednik, S. *A Primer for the PROV Provenance Model.* W3C, 2012. http://www.w3.org/TR/prov-primer/.
6. Halfaker, A., Geiger, R. S., Morgan, J. T., and Riedl, J. The rise and decline of an open collaboration system: How Wikipedia's reaction to popularity is causing its decline. *American Behavioral Scientist 57*, 5 (2013), 664–688.
7. Hartung, C., Lerer, A., Anokwa, Y., Tseng, C., Brunette, W., and Borriello, G. Open Data Kit: Tools to build information services for developing regions. In *Proceedings of the 4th ACM/IEEE International Conference on Information and Communication Technologies and Development*, ACM (2010), 18.
8. Howe, J. The Rise of Crowdsourcing. *Wired Magazine 14*, 6 (2006), 1–4.
9. Juran, J. M. *Quality control handbook.* McGraw-Hill, 1962.
10. Kelling, S., Yu, J., Gerbracht, J., and Wong, W.-K. Emergent filters: Automated data verification in a large-scale citizen science project. In *Proceedings of Workshops at the Seventh International Conference on eScience*, IEEE (2011), 20–27.

11. Kim, S., Mankoff, J., and Paulos, E. Sensr: Evaluating a flexible framework for authoring mobile data-collection tools for citizen science. In *Proceedings of the 2013 conference on Computer supported cooperative work*, ACM (2013), 1453–1462.

12. Liu, J., and Ram, S. Who does what: Collaboration patterns in the Wikipedia and their impact on article quality. *ACM Transactions on Management Information Systems (TMIS) 2*, 2 (2011), 11.

13. Lukyanenko, R., Parsons, J., and Wiersma, Y. Citizen science 2.0: Data management principles to harness the power of the crowd. In *Service-Oriented Perspectives in Design Science Research*. Springer, 2011, 465–473.

14. Newman, G., Graham, J., Crall, A., and Laituri, M. The art and science of multi-scale citizen science support. *Ecological Informatics 6*, 3 (2011), 217–227.

15. Okolloh, O. Ushahidi, or 'testimony': Web 2.0 tools for crowdsourcing crisis information. *Participatory Learning and Action 59*, 1 (2009), 65–70.

16. Orlandi, F., and Passant, A. Modelling provenance of DBpedia resources using Wikipedia contributions. *Web Semantics: Science, Services and Agents on the World Wide Web 9*, 2 (2011), 149–164.

17. Priedhorsky, R., and Terveen, L. Wiki grows up: Arbitrary data models, access control, and beyond. In *Proceedings of the Seventh International Symposium on Wikis and Open Collaboration*, ACM (2011), 63–71.

18. Raddick, J., Lintott, C., Schawinski, K., Thomas, D., Nichol, R., Andreescu, D., Bamford, S., Land, K., Murray, P., Slosar, A., et al. Galaxy Zoo: An experiment in public science participation. In *Bulletin of the American Astronomical Society*, vol. 39 (2007), 892.

19. Ram, S., and Liu, J. Understanding the semantics of data provenance to support active conceptual modeling. In *Active conceptual modeling of learning*. Springer, 2007, 17–29.

20. Ribes, D., and Finholt, T. A. Representing community: Knowing users in the face of changing constituencies. In *Proceedings of the 2008 ACM conference on Computer supported cooperative work*, ACM (2008), 107–116.

21. Roth, M., and Tan, W.-C. Data integration and data exchange: It's really about time. In *Proceedings of the 6th Biennial Conference on Innovative Data Systems Research*, CIDR (2013).

22. Sheppard, S. A. wq: A modular framework for collecting, storing, and utilizing experiential VGI. In *Proceedings of the 1st ACM SIGSPATIAL International Workshop on Crowdsourced and Volunteered Geographic Information*, ACM (2012), 62–69.

23. Sheppard, S. A., and Terveen, L. Quality is a verb: The operationalization of data quality in a citizen science community. In *Proceedings of the Seventh International Symposium on Wikis and Open Collaboration*, ACM (2011), 29–38.

24. Smith, A. Smartphone adoption and usage. Tech. rep., Pew Internet & American Life Project, Washington, DC, 2011.

25. Stvilia, B., Twidale, M. B., Smith, L. C., and Gasser, L. Information quality work organization in Wikipedia. *Journal of the American society for information science and technology 59*, 6 (2008), 983–1001.

26. Sullivan, B. L., Wood, C. L., Iliff, M. J., Bonney, R. E., Fink, D., and Kelling, S. eBird: a citizen-based bird observation network in the biological sciences. *Biological Conservation 142*, 10 (Oct. 2009), 2282–2292.

27. Vrandečić, D., Ratnakar, V., Krötzsch, M., and Gil, Y. Shortipedia: Aggregating and curating Semantic Web data. *Web Semantics: Science, Services and Agents on the World Wide Web 9*, 3 (2011), 334–338.

28. Wang, Z., Dong, H., Kelly, M., Macklin, J. A., Morris, P. J., and Morris, R. A. Filtered-Push: A Map-Reduce platform for collaborative taxonomic data management. In *Computer Science and Information Engineering, 2009 WRI World Congress on*, vol. 3, IEEE (2009), 731–735.

29. Wieczorek, J., Bloom, D., Guralnick, R., Blum, S., Döring, M., Giovanni, R., Robertson, T., and Vieglais, D. Darwin Core: An evolving community-developed biodiversity data standard. *PLoS One 7*, 1 (2012), e29715.

30. Wiggins, A. Free as in puppies: Compensating for ICT constraints in citizen science. In *Proceedings of the 2013 conference on Computer supported cooperative work*, ACM (2013), 1469–1480.

31. Wiggins, A., Bonney, R., Graham, E., Henderson, S., Kelling, S., Littauer, R., LeBuhn, G., Lotts, K., Michener, W., Newman, G., Russell, E., Stevenson, R., and Weltzin, J. *Data Management Guide for Public Participation in Scientific Research*. DataONE, 2013.

32. Wiggins, A., and Crowston, K. From conservation to crowdsourcing: A typology of citizen science. In *HICSS '11*, IEEE Computer Society (2011), 1–10.

33. Wiggins, A., Newman, G., Stevenson, R. D., and Crowston, K. Mechanisms for data quality and validation in citizen science. In *Proceedings of Workshops at the Seventh International Conference on eScience*, IEEE (2011), 14–19.

34. Wilderman, C. C. Models of community science: Design lessons from the field. In *Citizen Science Toolkit Conference* (Cornell Laboratory of Ornithology, Ithaca, NY, 2007).

Understanding Factors of Successful Engagement around Energy Consumption Between and Among Households

Tawanna Dillahunt
School of Information, University of Michigan
105 S. State Street, Ann Arbor, MI 48109
tdillahu@umich.edu

Jennifer Mankoff
HCI Institute, Carnegie Mellon University
5000 Forbes Avenue, Pittsburgh, PA 15221
jmankoff@cs.cmu.edu

ABSTRACT
An increasing number of researchers are using social engagement techniques such as neighborhood comparison and competition to encourage energy conservation, yet community reception and experience with such systems have not been well studied. We also find that researchers have not thoroughly investigated how different households use these systems and how their uses differ from one another. We explore these questions in a 4-10 month field deployment of a social-energy monitoring application across 15 households, in two distinct locations. We contribute results that describe conditions under which these techniques were effective and ineffective. Our results imply that understanding factors such as a building, or community's layout, context knowledge of community members, accountability and adherence to social norms, trust, and length of residence are key for future design of social-energy applications.

Author Keywords
Home energy, social comparison, community, renters

ACM Classification Keywords
H5.m. Information interfaces and presentation: Misc.

INTRODUCTION
Residential energy use accounts for 23% of the total energy consumption in the U.S [13], and usage highly depends on the behaviors of occupants living or working in these settings [27][31]. Other factors such as who is responsible for paying electricity, who controls the dwelling (*i.e.*, is the building leased or owned), and external groups such as community members affect energy consumption [8]. Yet the designs of energy monitors have typically been limited to the individual [5], and the deployments of these devices limited to single households.

To encourage the reduction of home energy use, researchers are moving toward understanding consumption beyond the individual and among the collective. In doing so, researchers have leveraged social techniques [15,28,36] such as historical and neighborhood comparisons [1, 15, 36], competition [15, 36], and features such as message boards [15]. One commonality among these studies is that they do not provide a rich picture of the deployment communities, the structure of these communities, and details about the participating households. It is unclear which group dynamics impact the level of responsiveness to social engagement techniques that encourage energy conservation.

To better understand these dynamics, we explored the similarities and differences in reception and experiences between two communities using a social-energy application. We deployed a community-focused, energy feedback application to 15 rental households across two distinct communities in a city known for its tapestry of neighborhoods (*e.g.,* culture, ethnicities). We staggered our recruitment and deployment over a period of 4-10 months. Households in the same community could monitor each other's average daily consumption. Households could also view their own real-time information about their energy use and use features to share home-energy reduction strategies. Though this study only represents a small sample, our results suggest that crucial factors affecting successful social engagement around energy consumption include: 1) the built environment, 2) context knowledge of community members, 3) accountability and adherence to social norms, 4) trust, and 5) length of residence.

In this paper, we contribute detailed results based on the deployment of a social-energy application across two distinct communities. Our study sheds light on social and physical factors that contribute to the success and failure of each community's engagement around energy conservation. We raise new research questions around detecting and leveraging social network structures and conclude with design implications for future social-energy applications.

RELATED WORK
We review deployments of home energy monitors (HEMs) to explore consumption beyond the individual level and within group settings. In past field deployments of HEMs that incorporate social strategies to encourage energy reduction, we find mixed results [15,26,28,35,36]. These studies also lack household and community details that make it difficult to tease apart which communities and households are more receptive to social techniques designed to curb home energy

CSCW'14, February 15 – 19, 2014, Baltimore, MD, USA.

ACM 978-1-4503-2540-0/14/02…$15.00.
http://dx.doi.org/10.1145/2531602.2531626.

consumption. To help us understand factors that facilitate community engagement, we also look outside the domain of home-energy consumption to field deployments of information and communication technologies (ICTs) across neighborhoods and communities.

Factors affecting successful social-energy applications

In some social-energy applications, comparison and competition have helped to reduce energy consumption. However, factors that contribute to their success are unclear. We review related work to identify factors and conditions that may play a role in the effectiveness of some social-energy applications.

Comparison with others is a way to establish standards of behavior and can lead to reduction of uncertainty [16]. Successful uses of energy comparison have occurred in office settings [35] and campus dormitories [4], yet the effectiveness of social comparison has been mixed in military and residential households [1, 26, 28, 36] and in settings that leverage competition as an incentive to conserve energy [4,15,36]. Unfortunately, information regarding community characteristics or individual household characteristics is not always available to help identify success and failure cases.

In a qualitative study of an energy-monitoring device in 16 households, Schwartz *et al.*, provided the social context of comparative data as a complement. As a result, people were allowed to draw practical conclusions about their household consumption, and their feedback was perceived as useful [31]. The researchers suggest that social comparison motivates behavior as it can increase the motivation to contribute by way of knowing that others are contributing [31]. It can also indicate a failure to conform [31].

In an energy-related workplace study [35], employees that received consumption comparisons with others saved more energy than employees that received feedback on their own conservation behavior. Perhaps understanding the context of the workplace setting influenced how well social comparison worked in this environment. Another factor that may have played a role in this setting is the hierarchical network structure (*e.g.*, managers and employees).

Military housing is another homogenous (*e.g.*, housing sizes, politics, fighting the same cause), hierarchical setting; the environment appears to be well suited for techniques such as social comparison and could lead to subsequent improved performance [26]. However, in a study using multiple interventions to encourage energy conservation across two military bases, the effect of social comparison did not lead to successful results. It was concluded that since up to half of the respondents were on post and moving within a year, there was less motivation to make one's neighborhood outperform everyone else's and little chance to build a group identity [26].

In essence, factors found in past work that affected the success of social-energy applications have included knowledge of the social context of social comparisons [31] and the length of time spent in an area, both of which may have contributed to group identity [26] and perhaps to the hierarchical network structure.

Factors affecting social interaction in communities

We discuss how the integration of ICTs in communities can affect community interaction and under what circumstances. We also discuss other factors that influence social interaction in communities.

In a longitudinal survey of 100 households in the Blacksburg Electronic Village, researchers found that Internet use can increase: community attachment and engagement; social contacts for those with high social use of the Internet; a sense of belonging, and community activism [23]. In a study of 109 homes provided with free Internet access, researchers found that a community mailing list increased social engagement and aided in collective action against homeowners and the housing developer [21]. This study also found that factors such as the length of residence and prior computer knowledge helped to promote community-based interactions [21]. Additional factors such as norms of reciprocity and trust, or social capital [30], have been found to promote social engagement.

On the other hand, Kavanaugh, *et al.,* note that factors such as life-cycle stage (*i.e.,* 35-64 years of age) and low levels of extroversion and education may lead to lower contributions of social capital and collective action [23]. Similarly, Hampton and Wellman raise concern for the increasing digital divide [21]. In terms of social capital they also express concern about the lack of interaction by underprivileged individuals [21]. These works suggest the need for further investigation of ways to encourage these populations to contribute to the general pool of social capital and collective action [21, 23].

Studies to understand social interaction without ICTs find that physical structure, or a building's layout, can affect social interaction and can help create new social networks. For example, Ginsberg and Churchman found that elevators in Israeli middle-class neighborhoods were a form of public commons [20]. This allowed for social interaction, which could help strengthen network ties. This study also found that other semi-public spaces (*e.g.,* hallways, outside of the building) allowed for social interaction.

Regardless of how frequently neighbors interact [2], those communities with a large proportion of residents who know and interact with each other are more likely to engage in surveillance, intervene in local disturbances, and develop movement-governing rules [2, 14]. Though social-energy applications leveraging social comparisons inherently rely on social interaction, researchers studying these applications have not explored the effect of these factors in their deployment communities. Our goal was to understand which factors contributed to the success or failure of our application in each community.

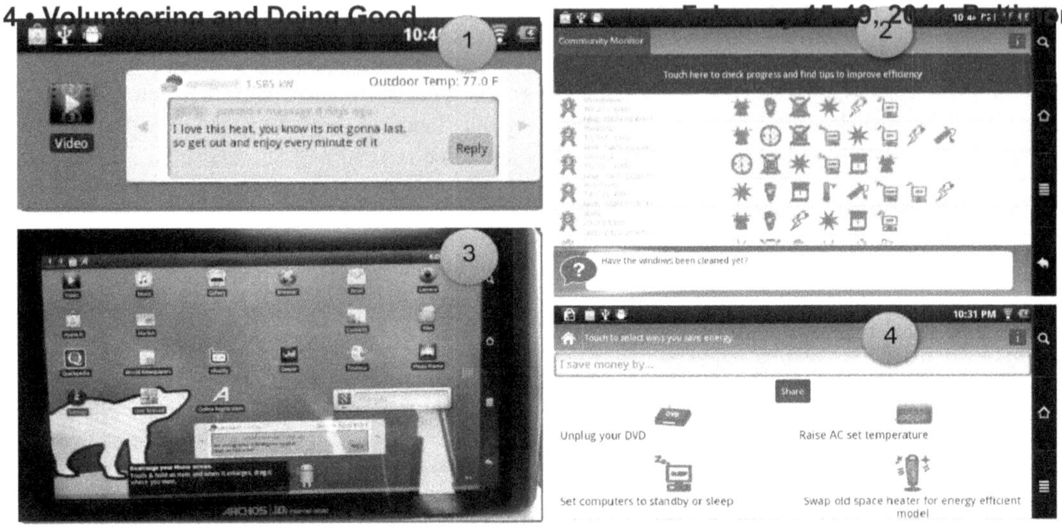

Figure 1 – Community Monitor: (1) Application widget – shows real-time energy consumption, outdoor temperature, and latest message post (2) Application main page – shows household rankings, latest community message, and ways each household saves energy; participants can send messages to the message board from this page (3) Tablet and application wallpaper (4) "Ways to Save" page

THE COMMUNITY MONITOR APPLICATION

Before providing application details, we provide an illustration to describe how we intended participants to use the Community Monitor. Imagine Daryl, a 35-year-old father of two, takes a look at his tablet because his children are upset that only one of the four polar bears appears on the tablet wallpaper. The family knows that they are currently consuming a lot of electricity (see Figure 1-3). Daryl asks the kids to turn off unused devices, he turns off the AC, and they see two more polar bears appear in the background. The kids are happy. Daryl, however, wants to see how he is doing in comparison to the other participants. He selects the Community Monitor application widget to take him to the main application, which shows him the leaderboard (see Figure 1-2). Daryl sees that he is ranked #5 out of 6, and consumed on average, 16.73 kWh in the past 24 hours. He sees that the Jones family is ranked #2 at 10.5 kWh. At the bottom of the leaderboard screen, Daryl sees that Jennifer posted a new comment on today's weather (see bottom of Figure 1-2). He then selects the message and posts, "Yes, it is a nice day outside! I'm going to take the kids outside to play around 6." Daryl selects the "tips" button at the top of the leaderboard for additional ways to save (see Figure 1-4). He selects the tip to save energy by using the sunlight and sees that a sun icon appears next to his average daily consumption on the leaderboard (see icons in Figure 1-2).

We designed the Community Monitor to include feedback and to encourage social engagement (through regular presence in households). Our goal was to integrate the application into an Internet tablet to build energy awareness into daily routines and habits, and to create a social experience with our application. Our implementation was iterative and informed by past concept validation results of social-energy applications [7, 10], past research (*e.g.,*[8,9,18,19, 24,28]), and a multi-month pilot deployment. We present the *final* version of our application, which we released on January 5, 2012.

Platform Selection: Many of our participants did not have smartphones or Internet access; therefore, we selected a platform that was relatively inexpensive as well as useful for a new Internet user. Since we wanted individuals within a household to share the device, and because tablets are low cost in comparison to laptops, we chose them as the most appropriate technology medium for our demographic. In addition to Internet access, tablets provide individuals with games, email, and other appealing applications. Additionally, because tablet devices are portable, they can be placed in common areas. The versatility of tablets also encouraged frequent use. Toward that end, we modified the tablet's wallpaper background to represent the household's real-time consumption, as this strategy was successful on mobile phones [19].

Wallpaper Design: Recent studies indicate that people understand the relationship between their actions and the environment better with the use of iconic images [23]. Studies also suggest connecting individual actions to their consequences [29]. Therefore, to demonstrate real-time consumption, we displayed a single polar bear on a block of ice to indicate high consumption (bad) and a family of polar bears to indicate low consumption (good). The images are noticeable from a distance and could be seen before household members interacted with other applications (*i.e.*, games, email, *etc.*)(see Figure 1-3).

Main Application: The main application was designed to support communication, sharing, and social comparison. Our goal was to allow households to see what was good or bad in terms of consumption, to whittle down issues, and to be able to have informed discussions with landlords or each other.

We used the Android™ platform to develop the tablet application and The Energy Detective (TED®, http://www.theenergydetective.com/) to collect home energy use data. We used the StepGreen API to manage data [25]. The application could be accessed *via* an Android widget.

Android Widget: We used an Android application widget (a small application view that can be embedded on the device home screen and can receive recurring updates) to provide additional information. The widget provides participants at-a-glance feedback about their current electricity usage, the outside temperature, and the latest posting to the community message board (Figure 1-1). The use of an Android widget was also suggested in [28]. Selecting the widget sent users to the main application and main application feature—the leaderboard.

Leaderboard: The Leaderboard provides a ranking of household members based on their average daily consumption (Figure 1-2).

Message Board: The Community Message Board allows participants to communicate with the rest of their community (*e.g.,* information sharing, event planning, and questions). This social aspect of the application provides an opportunity for knowledge transfer between individuals.

Shared Actions: The "Ways to Save" (Figure 1-4) feature allows participants to learn about possible actions and share information about how they save (Figure 1-2).

FIELD STUDY METHOD

We deployed our application across 15 households within two communities between 4-10 months (6-7 months on average across both locations Table 1). Prior to that, we piloted the first two versions of our application for one to four months across five participant households to get design feedback and to work out kinks in the study design and technology. Our official deployment began January 5, 2012, and our quantitative analysis for this study ended June 30, 2012. We continued recruiting participants during our pilot and main study.

In total, we recruited 15 households consisting of 31 household members, and at least 18 guests, including visiting friends and family (see Table 1 for details). In all, our qualitative data consists of approximately 176 interviews across our 15 primary participants. We conducted 1-3 interviews per month per household on average. Initial setup, survey and interviews lasted between 2-3 hours per household, but our ongoing monthly interviews lasted approximately 30-60 minutes each. One site observation occurred during a site tour provided to the main author by each site manager. However, we also made observations while interviewing participants, which were based on participant interview responses.

We selected our locations for several reasons. The primary reason for our selection was that these buildings were some of the few all-electric (*i.e.*, heating and cooling), individually metered buildings in the area. Though this limited us to rental households, these households are understudied in this domain, and provided us with the opportunity to explore landlord/tenant conflict around energy consumption.

Past work exploring energy consumption in low-income households [7] reveal conflict between landlords and tenants and identified factors such as social engagement and social sharing as possible solutions to this conflict [8]. Further, a deployment of households within the same community, or building, implied shared characteristics of each unit such as built-in appliances, building age, *etc.*

Community Descriptions: We deployed our application to two disparate communities, both maintained and managed by the same company. The development company recommended the most suitable locations based on our study and the factors listed above. Though rental units were not the same size, and the two sites were different ages, both sites used similar appliances and represented distinct community characteristics. Though the two locations varied significantly in the number of occupants per household, we saw the disparity as an efficient way to better study intra-communal communication and interaction with our application.

Community 1-Hamlet: Hamlet is a 60-tenant, mixed-income, 12-story building. The building was built in 1907 and renovated in 2008 into a set of affordable residential lofts. The building was equipped with a clubroom, which is a common area for residents to watch TV and/or hold meetings, a fitness center, and a rooftop deck and green space. Some residents paid market value rent plus a separate electricity bill. Others paid a reduced rate for their rent that included electricity (*i.e.,* these residents did not receive an electricity bill). Except for gas-heated hot water, paid for by the building, this was an all-electric, individually metered building. It is a Leadership in Energy and Environmental Design (LEED) Green Building. We recruited six households from Hamlet that includes two households that paid for their own electricity.

Community 2-Main Street: Main St. consists of 23 all-electric metered units that were newly constructed at the time of deployment; they consist of rehabilitated brownstones and newly constructed apartments and townhouses. Previously, the area consisted of a strip of abandoned buildings and vacant lots. A small community center was built six months after our study deployment and was used primarily as a place to deliver monthly rental payments. All homes are rented to low-income households and no participants paid an electricity bill. We recruited nine households from Main St.

Both sites shared the same type and brand of appliances (*e.g.*, refrigerator, dishwasher, and washer/dryer in most households). Table 1 represents households and household members from each community. Key variations affecting energy consumption among Hamlet households included which floors individuals lived on (*i.e.*, higher floors tend to be warmer) and, at Main St., whether or not the household was a 3-bedroom, three-story townhome (TH) or one or two-bedroom apartment (Apt).

Site	ID	Age (Young Adult < 25; Adult 25-59; Elderly >=60); Employment	Household Size (including frequent visitors)	Type of Household	Study Devices	Other Devices; Home Internet Access?	Change in Consumption	Key influencer?	Approx. Time in study (months)
1: Hamlet	**H1**	Elderly; Employed	1 Adult	Apt	1	Y; Y	Decrease	Yes	10
	H2	Elderly; Retired	2 Adults	Apt	2	Y; Y	Decrease	Yes	8
	H3	Adult; Employed	2 Adults	Apt	2	Y; Y	Increase	No	4
	H4	Elderly; Retired	1 Adult	Apt	1	N; N	Decrease	Yes	6
	H5	Adult; Employed	1 Adult	Apt	1	Y; Y	Decrease	No	6
	H6	Adult; Not Employed	3 Adults, 1 Child	Apt	1	Y; Y	Decrease	No	6
2: Main Street	**M1**	Adult; Employed	4 Adults	TH	2	Y; Y	Increase	Yes	9
	M2	Adult; Not Employed	4 Adults, 2 Children	Apt	2	N; N	Increase	No	6
	M3	Adult; Not Employed	4 Adults	Apt	2	Y; N	Increase	No	7
	M4	Adult; Not Employed	3 Adults	Apt	2	Y; N	Decrease	No	6
	M5	Young Adult; Employed	2 Adults, 1 Child	TH	2	Y; N	Decrease	No	5
	M6	Adult; Retired	1 Adult, 2 Children	TH	2	Y; N	Decrease	Yes	6
	M7	Elderly; Not Employed	4 Adults, 2 Children	Apt	2	Y; N	Increase	No	6
	M8	Adult, Not Employed	4 Adults	TH	2	Y; N	Increase	No	5
	M9	Adult; Employed R	1 Adult; 2 Children	TH	2	Y; Y	Decrease	No	4

Table 1– Household Profiles: Details are provided about the main participant's age and employment (our interviewees). Other devices include mobile devices, PCs, iPads, *etc.*; consumption change based on differences between average monthly consumption prior the intervention and average monthly consumption with the intervention.

Recruitment Strategy: To recruit participants, we posted flyers around the building and asked management to email flyers and to slide flyers under each resident's door. We also used "snowball sampling", in which existing participants recruit others from among their acquaintances. We offered referral payments as incentives.

Our recruitment was open to all residents. We did not prohibit participation by residents who were also on staff at the development company. Realistically, inclusion of staff members reflected what was expected in a real world deployment; it also gave us some insight into landlord/tenant issues that might arise. As a result, the Main St. site manager and a Hamlet resident who helps with building upkeep participated.

Household annual income ranged from less than \$10k to more than \$70k; higher-income households lived in Hamlet. The first member in each row of Table 1 represents our primary participant, and interviewee. Primary participant mean age was 52 (SD=13.56). Seven were either retired or unable to work; six worked full-time or part-time; and two were looking for work. Employed participants worked in a variety of fields including administration, human resources, maintenance, banking, environmental services, and property management. Main St. (M=3, SD=.87) had significantly more household members than Hamlet (M=1.3, SD=.52) ($F[1,15]=17.73$, $p=.001$).

Data: We conducted 1-3 interviews per month with each household. In our initial interviews, we collected data about each primary participant's social ties with other community members, what they liked most about their communities, and any issues that they needed to report to the landlords in the past month. We also logged application use data, collected monthly electricity bills, and conducted site observations.

To understand participant's social ties with other community members, we collected the names of each primary householder in the community from the site managers prior to the first interviews. Using a 5-point Likert scale, we then asked participants to indicate their levels of agreement or disagreement with the statement, "*I know this person.*" Participants engaging in offline communication were instructed to choose "*agree somewhat*" or "*agree strongly*"; if they did not know the person at all, they were instructed to choose "*disagree strongly.*" Otherwise, they selected "*disagree somewhat,*" *or* "*neither,*" to indicate that they knew the person by sight but did not engage in meaningful conversations.

The goal of our ongoing interviews was to understand each household's interaction with our application and tablet. We asked, for example, "Did you engage with others, and/or share the application and tablet? Did you discuss application data or information with others in your household and/or with neighbors?"

Application data allowed us to gather how many times a feature was accessed. Logs, in addition to interviews, also helped us determine how often participants used various features of our application and gave us insight into other applications installed on each tablet.

Site observations consisted of a guided tour of the facilities by a development company representative. We captured this information in our site descriptions but provide additional context based on data from our monthly site visits and resident interaction.

Deployment Details: Our application relied on use of TED data and Internet access. In addition to the TED installation, we provided all households with free Internet and Wi-Fi access, 10" Android Internet tablets, and technical support for the system by phone and in person as-needed. To prevent sharing-related conflicts in multiple-member households, especially those with children, we offered an additional 7" tablet.

To encourage community building, household engagement, and to increase knowledge, researchers posted messages to the board using the alias *CMBot* an average of two times per week, part way through the main study. Messages included energy-saving tips and questions about how residents save

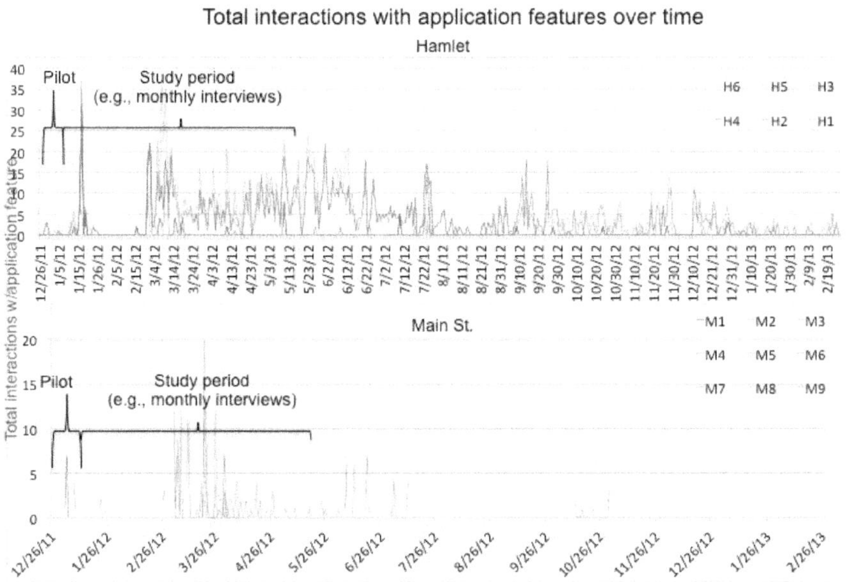

Figure 2 – Application feature interaction over time. Note that some Hamlet participants continued using the application even after the end of our formal study (top: Hamlet, bottom: Main St.)

energy. The first author also organized a casual pizza party event for both communities.

Next, we present our deployment results. We refer to our participants by anonymous IDs and location (*e.g. H1* is *household 1* from *Hamlet*, and *M2 is household 2* from *Main St.).* For clarity, a primary participant, or simply *participant*, represented each household. We present data about *households* as a whole, which includes *other household members*. Where possible, we provide IDs for participant quotes. However, because some comments deal with activities or opinions that might be frowned upon by landlords or other community members, we sometimes attribute a quote only to a "participant."

FIELD STUDY RESULTS

In this section, we discuss our deployment results. Due to several factors such as the variability across sites and households (*e.g.*, building and household size); the relatively small number of households involved in the study; the short study length; and indoor/outdoor temperature fluctuation, our consumption data did not show any significant change. Therefore, we largely present detailed qualitative results and show household change in consumption in Table 1. Our qualitative results show how differences between the two communities and interactions within each household may have affected the use of our application. However, we first present tablet and application usage results between each community and a cursory analysis of participant interaction.

Application and tablet usage

We used our application log data to gather both application and tablet usage. Generally speaking, all participants interacted with the tablet in some way. While Main St. participants used the tablet device more frequently, Hamlet participants were higher users of all application features. Hamlet's number of community message ($F[1,15]=7.59$, $p=.02$, $M=1.5$) and leaderboard views ($F[1,15]=5.14$, $p=.04$, $M=4.1$) were significantly higher than Main St.'s on an ANOVA.

The leader and message board features were the most used features across both locations. Many participants read, though very few posted messages. Participants rarely used the "Ways to Save" feature. Most Main St. participants used the polar bear display to explore their consumption. Because we were not able to track how often households viewed the main screen, these actions are not accounted for in Figure 2.

To facilitate sharing, more than half (8/15) of the households kept the tablet in a common area (*i.e.*, the kitchen, the living area, and dining room). Households also used their tablets to surf the Internet (15/15), to play games (14/15), to check email (8/15), to search for jobs (3/15), and to read the Bible (4/15). Ten of the fifteen households used their tablets on a daily basis. The remaining five households had access to devices such as iPads, smartphones, and home laptops and as a result, did not use our tablets as frequently. Next, we provide a high-level social network analysis to help us understand interactions among our participants and how the two communities differed.

Cursory analysis of participant interaction

Though our deployment only spanned two communities, we wanted to understand the nature of interaction between participants before introducing our application. We conducted a cursory social network analysis to help us understand the characteristics of each community's network structure (see Figure 3). We find that Hamlet had stronger ties and that Main Street's low centrality signaled opportunities for key influencers to promote our application. These findings were also supported by our interview data.

The analysis reveals that the Hamlet households had stronger ties, which we conclude from its transitivity score, an indication of network closure and close bonds [22]. Also, Hamlet had a lower closeness centrality, which means that information could spread more quickly within Hamlet than Main Street [22]. H5, Hamlet's outlier, became a part of the network within weeks after joining the study, and as an outlier did not affect Hamlet's results significantly. Main St. had a higher degree centrality, which is an indicator that there were key households in positions of influence [22]. Main St. also had a higher "betweenness" centrality, which relates to a network's ability to link together individuals that have few other ties between them [22]. This enables individuals to broker relationships between those with few connections. We

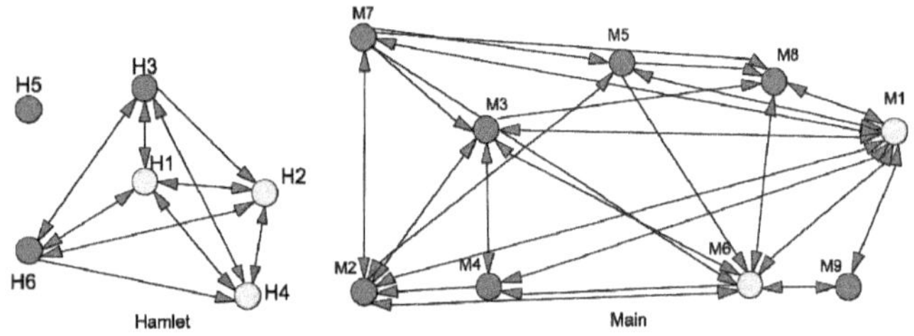

Figure 3 - Social Network Diagram (H=Hamlet, M=Main; key influencers are yellow) Degree centrality: H=.30, M=.54, Betweenness centrality: H=.02, M=.66 Closeness centrality: H=0, M=.66, Density: H=.60, M=.58, Transitivity: H=.88, M=.66, Size: H=6, M=9. Netvis analysis factors in weights of each relationship.

add context to these findings by discussing our site observations and interviews next.

Site observations and interviews

Our site observations and interviews help us to understand community characteristics and how participants used our application within and among households. Site observations suggest reasons for household bond strength, but no insight into information flow within and among householders. Our interview results help to fill this gap.

Site observations suggest a relationship between the stronger ties in Hamlet and the use of common areas that support congregation. Similarly, our site observations suggest a relationship between weaker ties in Main St. and fewer social interactions across the full community. According to Hampton and Wellman, the physical layout does not solely determine the forms of interaction [21], but it makes certain interactions easier and others more challenging.

Hamlet had three common areas: a TV/entertainment and/or meeting room, a fitness center, and a rooftop deck and green space. Per our interviews, half of our participants regularly used one or more of these spaces and residents could watch baseball games and see fireworks from the rooftop. Hamlet was a 12-story building with two main elevators. There was also a strong dog community within the building, and many people knew owners by recognizing their dogs. The common areas, presence of an elevator, and strong dog community could increase opportunities for household interaction.

Main St. consisted of townhouses and apartments spread across one side of a single street. Toward the end of our study, the development company built a small common area; surprisingly, participants rarely used this space. On sunny days, residents sat on their front porch and interacted with passers-by as well as neighbors across the street. The site manager stated, "*Hamlet is an apartment building, it is a complex. They have facilities on site. They have things right there for them. ...this area [Main St.] [is] not a recreational place.*"

Finally, the Main St. apartments and townhomes were larger and had significantly more household members than Hamlet. This factor could also lead to less engagement with neighbors. It is likely that these physical characteristics have played a role in how residents within the community interacted and formed ties outside of the household.

We were able to identify sources of conflict at Main St. from our interviews. We used a bottom-up approach to analyze our interview data, and used saturateapp to manage our data (http://www.saturateapp.com). Due to privacy concerns, the vast majority of our participants did not wish to be recorded. As a result, the primary author captured detailed notes during each interview, and created memos after each interview. We assigned low-level codes to the data and grouped them into 19 categories. Our two most emergent categories were related to community engagement and disengagement, which shed light on application use and community interaction. Other prominent categories included "barriers to saving energy" (*e.g.,* health, safety, property restrictions), "landlord/tenant issues" (*e.g.,* maintenance issues, landlord distrust), which we discuss later. "Unwillingness to compromise comfort," which we do not discuss, appeared as a category and is similar to prior findings in this area [33].

These categories help us understand how information flowed in each community and identify obstacles to information flow. We also saw interaction patterns within households, particularly among Main St. households that did not engage with the application. We explain our key categories, starting with those related to community engagement next.

Getting to know your neighbors: Though the Hamlet participant network was not fully connected at the beginning of the study, only Hamlet households were able to identify everyone using Community Monitor. H5 was initially isolated but joined the network *via* H6 once the study started. All Hamlet participants identified and spoke with other participant households outside of the application. Two of the Hamlet participants used a non-anonymous pseudonym. H1, who worked onsite, used his real name, and another used the name of the household pet—a name known in the community.

Four of nine Main St. households used non-anonymous pseudonyms such as an apartment number or pet's name. Despite this, only four Main St. participants were able to identify household participants, and only those participating in adjacent apartments (*e.g.,* next door). Knowing participating households provides additional context and could aid in information and communication flow around energy consumption.

Holding your neighbors accountable: The leaderboard enabled social comparison, which allowed households to hold each other accountable. This occurred despite the fact that the majority of our participants (13/15) did not pay their electricity bills. Though not mentioned as frequently among Main St. residents, many Hamlet participants described holding others accountable; the first author witnessed the behavior at the community pizza party.

At a researcher-sponsored pizza party, two Hamlet households mentioned that H2 was ranked much lower than normal. In a discussion about community averages, the two households (H4 and H6) brought this to H2's attention. H2 was somewhat surprised and explained that they had already put in a work order for a broken air conditioner (AC). The H2 household asked the first author to speak to the landlord because the issue was *"messing up [their] stats."*

H6 noticed that another household's data was anomalous due to an issue with the installed TED device. During an interview, she asked what was going on with the household—she felt the daily average was impossible for the building. H5 mentioned that H6 and H4 would check up on her regarding her average daily consumption. She mocked H4 as he would always say, *"What [are] you doing up there girl? Your number is always the same."* Verifying the system also forced participants to reflect about household energy consumption.

Hamlet participants knew detailed information about their neighbors (*e.g.,* when neighbors were home, their floor numbers, and the set temperatures of their thermostats). One Hamlet participant deduced detailed information about the other participants and determined that neighbors consuming less energy had to have set their thermostat to a lower temperature [in the winter] than she did: *"I know that [my neighbor] keeps his [thermostat] around 71 and [another neighbor] is below him [on the leaderboard] so I know the people who sit around in 68 degrees or lower!"*

Main St. participant M8 mentioned that, though home much more, she was ranked higher than a neighbor who had been away all summer (M6): *"If she has air on when she's not home, I'm going to kick her *ss [scold her] – she should be number one. How am I before her and she's never there?"* These two residents (M6 and M8) shared information after receiving the application.

In essence, Hamlet households got to know their neighbors while Main St. households did not engage with each other at the same level. This is likely a side effect of another theme we saw in our Main St. data, which we discuss next.

Internal isolation: We learned from our site manager and our interviews that five of the nine Main St. households were from a recently displaced neighborhood. The site manager described the former area as *"isolated...like New Jack City.*[1]*"* As a result, Main St. households referred to each other as "us" and "them" and to an extent, held themselves to different standards. This may be a form of internal separation leading to weaker Main St. ties.

Community contention with the site manager and intergenerational differences may also explain the internally isolated community. Insight from the site manager and other participants led us to believe that there may have been some conflict between the site manager and the rest of the community. For example, when asked if she (site manager) discussed the application with the rest of the community, she stated, *"At first when I started, it was cool but when I became, 'the manager,' that put a wall between us... They may not feel comfortable given [my] position."* Though not well reflected in our participant interviews, the Main St. community as a whole was also a mixed-aged community, which may imply generational differences. Two participants described this difference suggesting it to be the cause for the lack of engagement. One commented, *"I attribute it to the way our society is today...a generational thing. [A] sense of community is almost gone with regards to some of the younger folk out here. You know, it's just a different atmosphere—it's different, it's just different."* M2, another influential household at Main St., stated, *"I don't know, I don't know what's wrong with the generation today. I stay to myself [on] my own porch."* This participant did report visiting her immediate neighbors but did not discuss their status on Community Monitor.

Another key household, M6, was well known in the community but was away most of the time according to her neighbor, M8. This may have taken away from her ability to leverage her position in the network regarding the use of the application. When home, M8 said she used the polar bear screen to manage her consumption; she did not interact with the leaderboard feature.

Weaker ties, internal isolation between certain households (*i.e.,* "us" vs. "them" mentality), and the isolation of the site manager—who was key to effective communication—were signs that social interaction was needed in this community. Providing our application alone, with little encouragement for interaction, was insufficient.

Privacy concerns and community distrust around the message board: The message board feature was a source of privacy concern in our application and very rarely used. In one case, a Hamlet participant was upset about a message posted about him, while others were concerned about posts shared with the landlords. For example, one participant was troubled about a message posted about him because of underlying implications that he was consuming energy late at night. H2 posted *"It looks like <alias> is burning the midnight oil."* The participant unknowingly took the message out of context. Because the system was not designed to provide households with real-time consumption data about other households, the participant was upset and felt his privacy had been violated. The participant learned after confronting H2 that H2 saw him outside of the building late one evening. Though the participant resolved the issue, he stopped posting messages.

Concerns of privacy and distrust of landlords prevented participants from engaging with each other online *via* the message board. One Hamlet participant said, *"[A participant] could take this [tablet] and show him [building owner]."* Another Hamlet participant stated, *"They're people that go into the office a lot and talk a lot; if you say something to them, they'll take it to the office and you didn't want it there. I keep my [message board] conversations [to] general questions."* Indeed, a maintenance employee was a Hamlet

[1] (*e.g.,* Reference to a film about a drug infested American neighborhood).

participant. Though Main St. did not report issues of distrust, they were still fairly absent from the message board; it was disheartening to see the lack of posts to the message board considering institutional constraints placed upon Main St. The most active Main St. participant, M8 posted, "*Come on Community!!!! Lets try and be a community!!!!*"

Lack of collective action around institutional constraints: We wanted our application to provoke a deeper understanding of complex energy-related issues, which often appear as external factors, such as institutional constraints. We found that external factors were related to building constraints and/or infrastructural issues at Main St.

Due to concerns related to excess electricity consumption, the development company enforced a policy preventing Main St. participants from raising their thermostats above 71°F. At least three residents mentioned this to be a problem in interviews because the temperature was too cold. Even at the highest temperature, residents felt cool air coming from the system. Participants blamed the geothermal heating system, and some of those reporting discomfort in the winter admitted to using the oven to heat households. Tenants who wanted a temperature increase from 71 to 74 had to sign a lease addendum and agree to not use electric heaters. After signing the agreement, some residents continued to use their oven for additional warmth, as it was still too cold. In this case, we need to understand how the social network structure contributes to a lack of collective action. Though participants had access to Community Monitor, they did not use it as a way to negotiate household restrictions.

Variation in households and application usage: Figure 2 clearly shows differences in how the two communities interacted with our application. In analyzing our interview data, we identified three distinct groups: most active users, households with prior computer knowledge, and shared device households. We discuss the characteristics of our most active users next.

Our most active users represented our "best-case" usage model. Three of our Hamlet users (H1, H4, and H6), and only one of our Main St. users (M8) fell into this group. H4 and H6 reported checking Community Monitor's leaderboard as a part of their daily routine. For example, H4 says he checks his tablet every morning to see *"who's in first place."* He does this along with his morning devotional period: *"I [eat] my daily bread, and then I pray, and then I read the Bible...It takes about 45 minutes."* Similarly, H6 says, *"I wake up and grab the tablet, I check the Community Monitor first to see if anyone responds [to prior posts] and then I read the Bible."* She sees where people are in terms of their energy consumption. Although H1 did not check the application on a daily basis, he would use the application to confirm that there were no issues: "*I look at it every other day or so. I'm usually 2nd or 3rd. If my numbers are similar it's okay. If they were different, then I'd wonder why."* M8 was the most active Main St. household and she engaged all household members with the application. For example, M8's daughter stated, "*I can say that I used to fall asleep with my light on but now I turn my light off when I go to bed. My mom unplugs the microwave. We try to keep things unplugged when they are not in use.*" M8 was also the only family in this category, and the fact that all members were over the age of 18, may have contributed to higher levels of engagement. Three out of four routine users lived alone and three of the four were either unemployed or retired. H1 held multiple jobs.

A second group of users included those with prior access to and knowledge of technology. Six households (H1, H2, H3, H5, M1, M9) had their own computers, iPads, and/or smart phones, which they preferred using. This does not mean that they did not use our application; in interviews, members from this group reported looking at the polar bear screen and using the main application features. However, their personal devices were already a part of their daily routines, and managing one more device was perceived as impractical. For example, when asked about his thoughts on the application and tablet, H2 stated, *"It seems like H4 really likes it. It's great for people that don't have computers. We're [H2 household] oversaturated with computers."* H2, however, did like glancing at the tablet wallpaper to see how much he was consuming.

M2-M7, M9 represent our last set of users and are probably the most challenging to engage. We characterize shared device households, as those with a primary participant that managed and/or competed with multiple tablet users such as kids, loved ones, and guests. As a result of emphasizing social engagement across households within a community, we failed to successfully engage individuals within a household. Further, our application failed to compete with popular applications such as YouTube and Angry Birds. Moreover, for low-income, unemployed households, job hunting took precedence over use of our application. As M9, who was looking for work reported, "*I don't have to go to a job center or library.*"

Finally, four of our participants (M2, M4, M5, M6) used the tablet as a form of entertainment for young children (*e.g.*, their own children, grandchildren, and friends' children). At least three (M2, M3, M7) of our participants were seen sharing their tablets with their friends. M4's son used our tablet application to see how turning on devices changed the polar bear background; however, he only did this activity a few times. Many times, the tablet became a source of entertainment. When asked for application suggestions, M2 stated, "*more kids' stuff.*" M2's grandchildren used the tablet and often taught her how to play games. On one occasion, she discussed how they (1st and 2nd graders) downloaded games that she had no idea were available. According to M3, "*All they [the kids] know is videos, videos, videos—They don't want to go outside, they want to see this...*" Though the tablet as a platform worked as expected, *i.e.,* it was shared within households, our core application features (*e.g.*, leaderboard) were ignored.

Finally, the first author observed visitors during regularly scheduled interviews on several occasions (households M2, M3, and M7). Visitors used the tablet for job hunting and checking email; none were aware of Community Monitor.

DISCUSSION AND DESIGN IMPLICATIONS

Based on the application usage and qualitative data, our results suggest that factors such as the built environment, context knowledge of community members, and accountability and adherence to social norms as seen in Hamlet, attributed to social engagement around our application.

On the other hand, issues of trust and length of residence may have contributed to a lack of social engagement around our application. We also found that access to prior technology may have played a role. In addition, the sharing of devices among multiple household members and guests may have played a role in the failure of some households to engage socially around our application.

Discussion

We found from our site observations that common spaces (*e.g.,* TV room, rooftop deck space, fitness center, elevator) allowed more opportunities for social interaction among Hamlet than Main St. residents. Without opportunities for community members to get acquainted, development of trusting relationships is less likely [3]. A small common space became available at Main St. late in our study; however, no participants reported using it. Information from the site manager and certain residents suggest isolation among some residents and little social interaction.

Sernhed, *et al.,* report that users are less interested in comparisons with other households without context knowledge about the households to which they are being compared [32]. Comparably, Schwartz found that comparative feedback is perceived as useful when social context is provided as a complement [31]. We draw similar conclusions from our results. For example, M8 was able to contextualize and find issues with M6's results because she knew M6 had been away all summer. Similarly, a Hamlet participant was able to estimate thermostat settings in other households based on her knowledge of her neighbor's settings.

We saw that our social comparison feature (the leaderboard), led to Hamlet households holding each other accountable for their consumption (as reflected in their rank). Schwartz notes that social comparison can motivate behavior because it signals failure to comply with accepted social norms [31]. The leaderboard influenced two out of the three most active Hamlet users to become watchdogs who held other households accountable for their leaderboard positions, which in their eyes, became the community norm. In our pizza party, for example, H4 and H6 held H2 accountable for his increased consumption, which led H2 to report the issue. We posit that our application's leaderboard combined with Hamlet participants' social connections and context knowledge influenced social norms, which increased participant accountability.

Neither community expressed privacy concerns around sharing their average electricity consumption. Nevertheless, we saw decreased message board activity in both communities. M8's post to the community to *"Let's try and be a community,"* suggests that there was no attempt to be a community. We suspect that the presence of the site manager at Main, and maintenance at Hamlet, led to community distrust that resulted in decreased message board activity in both communities. Siegel's findings support the suspicion—privileged individuals have negative impacts within a network only when they are powerful (as the case of our site manager) [34]. However, leaders that do not have control over their networks have diminished power; therefore, leadership presence does not always dictate a lack of motivation, or action. Further, without opportunities for community members to get acquainted, there is less chance for households to build trusting relationships [3].

Kavanaugh *et al.,* suggest a lack of group or self-efficacy may cause a lack of collective action [23]; they also express concern about inaction for younger or older adults with less education and less group interaction. Similarly, Yin suggests that heterogeneity in interests can have a significant effect on the expected participation level in collective action [38]. It is likely that generational differences, or lack of self and/or group efficacy in the Main St. community were associated with the lack of action.

Past research also proposes that the length of residence [21, 26] may also play a factor into household engagement. As stated earlier, Main St. homes were newly constructed at the time of deployment. Perhaps there was not sufficient time to build group identity among residents. This, in addition to its larger households, may have led to more intra-household interaction and decreased inter-household interaction at Main St. One could also reasonably speculate that since Hamlet participants had a significantly lower number of household members, loneliness, or even boredom could have contributed to increased interaction in the community.

Next, those with prior access to technology did not engage as much with our application as our most active users. Perhaps a cross-platform application would have been more successful with this group (*e.g.,* Android and iOS).

Finally, we observed external guests and families interacting with the tablet device, but not the application. Among shared device households, the wallpaper was effective at capturing people's attention, but it failed to engage external stakeholders such as visitors and guests.

Future social-energy applications must consider factors such as the built environment, context knowledge of community members, accountability and adherence to social norms, trust and length of residence for successful reception of social engagement around energy consumption. Our results lead us to conjecture that perhaps more connected communities might be more influenced by social-energy applications.

Limitations

Though our study lasted longer than similar studies [5], we suggest a period of two years or more for collecting electricity consumption data across multiple communities. Further, our study was not randomized, and the number of household participants was low. Finally, the number of our participants was too small to conduct a more proper and more representative social-network analysis; tracking the changes among interactions may have been more intuitive. Despite this, our rich qualitative data provide us with insightful results.

Design Implications

Ensure knowledge of social context from social networks and the built environment. Existing research [6,12] demonstrates the ability to detect network structure using sensors such as Wi-Fi and to detect location using GPS or GSM. Further, existing location services, such as Google Maps Floor Plans (http://maps.google.com/help/maps/floorplans/) could help researchers analyze the built environment. With the rise of social-energy applications and mobile Internet tablets, are there ways to identify social network structures using these capabilities? If so, can we identify which populations are likely to have context knowledge of each other that would lead to effective social comparisons? Can we adjust our applications accordingly when deployed in areas that may not be as conducive to social-energy applications? The built environment may have played a role in how households interacted with each other, which may have influenced their interaction with our application. Can we use the latest location services to detect physical building infrastructure? Leveraging information such as user check-ins could provide additional context.

Future applications should encourage accountability through social comparison and social roles. Social comparison was effective in our application because of context knowledge and also as a result of our routine households holding others accountable for their leaderboard rank. Perhaps using social comparison across other aspects of the application, such as message board posts, would have been effective (given knowledge of other community members' settings, characters, and schedules).

In a way, households, especially Hamlet households played roles similar to investigators and neighborhood watch. As mentioned in [14], those communities with high resident interaction are more likely to engage in surveillance behavior and intervene in local disturbances. This type of behavior is desirable in applications leveraging social comparison to help identify excess consumption. Social comparison enables these social roles, which allows for accountability for behaviors. Roles portray how people in certain positions are expected to behave [16], and these roles come with normative beliefs (perceived social pressures to engage or not to engage in a behavior). Taking on these roles may have influenced how our participants dealt with external factors, such as broken air conditioners. Applications can infer and report potential issues to the community to enable members to take on roles (*e.g.*, investigative) to identify problems. To encourage and support these social roles, applications could leverage characteristics from social network structures to identify key influencers and focus interventions on targeted households.

Future social-energy applications should support shared device households: We saw how multiple person households played a role in the use of our application. The introduction of our technology enabled outsiders to search for jobs, and served as entertainment for household members. It is plausible that the introduction of a new technology and Internet capability increased our householders' overall consumption. In hindsight, bringing householders and guests together in one place to share resources may help to reduce consumption. Future social-energy applications could support these dynamics.

CONCLUSION

As Dourish argues, HCI must consider the political, cultural, social, economic, and historical contexts of the technology it produces to effectively address complex issues such as environmental sustainability [11]. Our paper details our longitudinal deployment of Community Monitor, a social energy application, across two distinct communities. Our results confirm prior findings that factors such as context knowledge of community members, accountability and adherence to social norms, are key for successful reception of social engagement around energy consumption. At the same time, we consider new factors that affect social engagement around energy. These include the built environment, trust, and length of residence. Our findings lead us to speculate that more connected communities might be more likely to engage in social-energy applications.

ACKNOWLEDGMENTS

We thank our participants, Google for their generous donation of the Energy Detectives, NSF IIS-0803733 and IBM for their financial support, Action Housing, and Trek Development. Thanks to Rob Thompson and the Stepgreen team for their development support and Beth Corry for her polar bear designs. We thank the students and faculty at UMSI and CMU, Candace G. Ragin and the reviewers for their insightful and thoughtful feedback.

REFERENCES

1. Allcott, H. Social norms and energy conservation. MIT Center for Energy and Environmental Policy Working Paper 09-14, 2010.
2. Bellair, P. 1997. "Social interaction and community crime: examining the importance of neighborhood networks," *Criminology,* vol. 35, no.4, pp.677-703.
3. Berger, C.R. & Calabrese, R. J. (1975). Some explorations in initial interaction and beyond: Toward a development theory of interpersonal communication. *Human Communication Research*, 1:99-112.

4. Brewer, R.S., Lee, G.E. and Johnson, P.M. The Kukui Cup: a dorm energy competition focused on sustainable behavior change and energy literacy. *HICSS 44, 2011*, 1-10, 4-7.

5. Brynjarsdóttir, H., Håkansson, M., Pierce, J., Baumer, E.P.S., DiSalvo, C., Sengers, P. Sustainability Unpersuaded: How Persuasion Narrows our Vision of Sustainability. *CHI 2012,* 947-955.

6. Cranshaw, J., Toch, E., Hong, J., Kittur, A. and Sadeh, N. Bridging the gap between physical location and online social networks. *UbiComp 2010*, 119–128, 2010.

7. Dillahunt, T., Mankoff, J. Design implications for social-energy applications. CMU-HCII-12-100, SCS, Carnegie Mellon University, Human-Computer Interaction Institute Collection.

8. Dillahunt, T., Mankoff, J., Paulos, E. Understanding Conflict Between Landlords and Tenants: Implications for Energy Sensing and Feedback. *UbiComp 2010*, 149-158.

9. Dillahunt, T., Mankoff, J., Paulos, E., Fussell, S. It's not all about green: energy use in low-income communities. *Ubicomp 2009*, 255–264.

10. Dillahunt, T., Mankoff, J. 2011. In the dark, out in the cold *XRDS* 17, 4 (June 2011), 39-41.

11. Dourish, P. Print this paper, kill a tree: Environmental sustainability research topic of HCI. LUCI-2009-004.

12. Eagle, N., Pentland, A., Lazer, D. (2009). Inferring social network structure using mobile phone data. *Proc. Natl. Acad. Sci.* USA 106:15274–15278.

13. Energy Information Administration USA. Annual energy review, 2012. Retrieved 8/23/12 from http://www.eia.doe.gov/aer.

14. Erete, S.L. Protecting the home: Exploring the roles of technology and citizen activism from a burglar's perspective. *CHI '13* (to appear).

15. Erickson, T., Podlaseck, M., Sahu, S., Dai, J.D., Chao, T., Naphade, M. The Dubuque water portal: evaluation of the uptake, use and impact of residential water consumption feedback. *CHI '10,* 675-684.

16. Festinger, L. (1954). A theory of social comparison processes. *Human Relations,* 7(2) 117-140.

17. Forsyth, D.R. (2010). *Group Dynamics* (5th edition).

18. Froehlich, J., Findlater, L. & Landay, J. The design of eco-feedback technology. *In Proceedings of CHI '10.* ACM Press, 1999-2008.

19. Froehlich, J., Dillahunt, T., Klasnja, P., Mankoff, J., Consolvo, S., Harrison, B., & Landay, J. A. UbiGreen: Investigating a mobile tool for tracking and supporting green transportation habits. *CHI '09,* 1043-1052.

20. Ginsberg, Y. & Churchman, A. The Pattern and Meaning of Neighbor Relations in High-Rise Housing in Israel. *Human Ecology*. Vol. 13 (4) 1985: 467 – 484.

21. Hampton, K. & Wellman, B., Neighboring in Netville: How the Internet supports community and social capital in a wired suburb. *City & Community,* vol.2, no.3, 2003, 277-311

22. Hansen, D. L., Schneiderman, B. (2010). *Analyzing social media networks with NodeXL: insights from a connected world.* Amsterdam: M. Kaufmann.

23. Kavanaugh, A., Carroll, J., Rosson, M., Zin, T., Reese, D., Community Networks: Where offline communities meet online. *Journal of Computer-Mediated Communication,* 10(4), art. 3.

24. Kim, T., Hong, H., & Magerko, B. Design requirements for ambient display that supports sustainable lifestyles. *DIS 2010,*103-112.

25. Mankoff, J., Fussell, S., Dillahunt, Glaves, R., Grevet, G., Johnson, M., Matthews, D., Matthews, H.S., McGuire, R., Thompson, R. (2010). Stepgreen.org: Increasing energy saving behaviors via social networks. *ICWSM 2010*, 106-113.

26. McMakin, A.H., Malone, E.L. & Lundgren, R.E. Motivating residents to conserve energy without financial incentives. *Environment and Behavior Journal*, 2002.

27. Parker, D.S., Hoak, D., Cummings, J. Pilot evaluation of energy savings from residential energy demand feedback devices (FSER-CR-1742-08), 2008.

28. Petkov, P., Köbler, F., Foth, M., Medland, R., Krcmar, H. Engaging energy saving through motivation-specific social comparison. In *CHI Extended Abstracts '11*. ACM Press, 1945-1950.

29. Pierce, J., Odom, W., and Blevis, E. (2008). Energy aware dwelling: A critical survey of interaction design for eco-visualizations. *OZCHI 2008*, 1-8.

30. Putnam, R.(2000). Bowling alone: The collapse and revival of American community. Simon & Schuster: New York.

31. Schwartz, T., Stevens, G., Ramirez, L., Wulf, V. (2013). Uncovering practices of making energy consumption accountable: A phenomenological inquiry. *TOCHI 2013,*20(2), article 9.

32. Sernhed, K., Pyrko, J., & Abaravicius, J. (2003). Bill me this way!—customer preferences regarding electricity bills in Sweden. *In Proceedings of the 2003 summer study of the European Council for an energy efficient economy,* pp. 1147–1150. Stockholm: ECEEE.

33. Shove, E. (2003). Converging conventions of comfort, cleanliness and convenience. *Journal of Consumer Policy, 26*, pp.395-418.

34. Siegel, A. David. 2009. "Social Network and Collective Action." American Journal of Political Science 53 (1): 122–38.

35. Siero, F.W., Bakker, A.B., Dekker, G.B., van den Burg, T.C. Changing organizational energy consumption behavior through comparative feedback. *Journal of Environmental Psychology 16,* 1996. 235-246.

36. Vande Moere, A., Tomitsch, M., Hoinkis, M., Trefz, E., Johansen, S. & Jones, A. Comparative Feedback in the Street: Exposing Residential Energy Consumption on House Façades. *INTERACT 2011*, 470-488.

37. Wiese, J., Kelley, P., Cranor, L., Dabbish, L., Hong, J., Zimmerman, J. Are you close with me? Are you nearby?: investigating social groups, closeness, and willingness to share. *Ubicomp '11*, 197-206.

38. Yin, C. (1998). "Equilibria of collective action in different distributions of protest thresholds." *Public Choice* 97(4):535-67.

Adolescent Online Safety: The "Moral" of the Story

Pamela Wisniewski
The Pennsylvania State University
University Park, PA
pam@pamspam.com

Heng Xu
The Pennsylvania State University
University Park, PA
hxu@ist.psu.edu

Mary Beth Rosson
The Pennsylvania State University
University Park, PA
mrosson@ist.psu.edu

John M. Carroll
The Pennsylvania State University
University Park, PA
jcarroll@ist.psu.edu

ABSTRACT
Adolescence is characterized by heightened risk-taking and independence from parents; these tendencies seem to be magnified by the opportunities afforded through online interactions. Drawing on Kohlberg's Cognitive Moral Development (CMD) theory, we conduct a qualitative study of 12 parent-adolescent dyads that examines the interplay between parenting behaviors and adolescent moral development. We show an association between adolescent moral judgment and online behavior, and we illustrate how parenting style and mediation strategies influence teens' moral growth and decision making about online behaviors. We also note that parental mediation strategies are moderated by parents' digital literacy: reduced digital literacy is associated with more restrictive or indulgent strategies; while more digitally competent parents are more likely to monitor and mediate their teen's behaviors as they engage online. We also found that experience, not restriction, facilitates the teen's moral growth.

Author Keywords
Adolescent online safety; parenting; moral development

ACM Classification Keywords
K.4.1 [Public Policy Issues]: Ethics, Human safety, Privacy

General Terms
Human Factors; Theory; Design.

INTRODUCTION
Adolescence is characterized by heightened risk-taking and independence from parents, even though many teens are not well-equipped to make these decisions on their own [12]. Teens are by nature sensation-seeking and more likely to take greater risks than children and adults [12]. Teens are also intensely focused on social life, and consequently have been eager and early adopters of the Internet and social networking applications that help them engage with their peers [8]. Because of this, adolescent online safety has become a mounting contemporary concern. For example, teens have committed suicide due to cyberbullying [19], received (and accepted) sexual solicitations online [24], viewed inappropriate pornographic or violent websites [14], and served jail time for digital piracy [6].

Many studies have examined the role of parenting as a means for positively influencing adolescent online safety [5, 7, 14-15, 20, 22, 25]. However, parents cannot shield their teens from all negative online experiences without also limiting the potential for positive online experiences that promote developmental growth. As adults, assuring that adolescents are "safe" means not only giving them tools to cope with risks that they encounter, but also teaching them not to make unethical decisions that may have severe consequences. In this sense, online parenting is a balancing act between protecting teens from excessive harm and teaching them how to cope with the sometimes ugly realities of engaging online with others. Our end goal is to protect adolescents from themselves and others while still allowing them to engage in beneficial online activities.

We frame adolescent online safety as a ***developmental process*** of adolescent growth. Through this lens, adolescent online safety should be viewed as not only a function of parents but also as independent action by adolescents enabled by their growing autonomy and pseudo-maturity [12]. Teens mature at different rates, are exposed to vastly different experiences, and respond differently to parenting strategies. Yet, few if any, studies consider the combination of parenting strategies and teen characteristics when studying or promoting positive adolescent online safety outcomes. To fill in this gap, we investigate both parenting and adolescent moral development as factors in adolescent online behavior. Ethical decision making cannot protect adolescents from all online threats, but we propose that sound moral judgment is an important contributor to appropriate online behaviors and decisions that promote adolescent online safety. Through an in-depth qualitative study of 12 parent-adolescent dyads, we illustrate how moral judgment, parenting style, and mediation techniques vary across participants and by age.

THEORETICAL BACKGROUND
Our work draws from the developmental psychology literature, with a dual focus on parents and adolescents.

Adolescent Moral Development
Psychologist Lawrence Kohlberg's Cognitive Moral Development (CMD) theory was that moral reasoning is the

CSCW'14, February 15–19, 2014, Baltimore, Maryland, USA.

http://dx.doi.org/10.1145/2531602.2531696.

foundation of ethical decision-making and that children progress through six distinct stages of moral development as they mature [9]. We apply these six stages in our qualitative analysis:

Stage 1. Punishment and obedience orientation: Characterized by compliance in order to avoid punishment and conformity to authority.

Stage 2. Naïve instrumental hedonism: Characterized by "individualistic morality" where "it's the person's life, not the law's life" [9]. Moral judgments are based on perceptions of relative value and cost, pleasure or pain.

Stage 3. "Good-boy" morality of maintaining good relations, approving of others: Decisions motivated by anticipated praise or disapproval of others, sympathy for others, and identification with authority and its goals.

Stage 4. Authority maintaining morality: Internalizes respect for authority and exhibits a sense of justice, moral indignation, and duty.

Stage 5. Authority of contract and of democratically accepted law: Identifies right and wrong based on laws or institutional rules that are assumed to have a rational basis. Recognizes conflict between the individual and society but ultimately conforms to a "moral society."

Stage 6. Morality of individual principles of conscience: Reliance on the individual's moral principles over rules, incorporating a sense of the "greater good."

Our work applies these six stages of moral development as a lens on adolescents' comments about their own online behavior. We are interested in the interplay between parenting and adolescent moral development as factors influencing teens' online behaviors; our guiding perspective is that a key element in teens' online safety is learning not to make unethical decisions, such as committing digital piracy, cyberbullying, and other online crimes.

Parenting

Two streams of research on parenting are relevant to adolescent online safety and moral development – parenting styles and parental mediation. Baumrind's seminal work on parenting styles [1-2] identified two dimensions along which parents vary: ***Demandingness*** and ***Responsiveness***. Parents are demanding to the extent that they regulate and supervise their child's activities [1-2]. Responsiveness refers to the extent in which a parent is warm, communicative, and supportive toward the child's needs of individuality and autonomy [1-2]. As parents vary along these two dimensions, they can be classified into four main parenting styles: ***Authoritative*** (high demanding, high responsive), ***Authoritarian*** (high demanding, low responsive), ***Indulgent*** (low demanding, high responsive), and ***Neglectful*** (low demanding, low responsive) [3, 11, 21]. Research suggests that authoritative parents tend to have adolescents who are more competent and well adjusted [3, 11].

Valkenburg et al. [23] created a scale to capture parental television mediation strategies; this construct was later adapted and merged with Baumrind's parenting styles for use in the Internet context [7, 13-14, 22]. Parental mediation strategies include instructive (active) mediation, restrictive mediation, and social co-viewing (monitoring). With respect to online behavior, ***active mediation*** involves interaction and discussion between parent and teen regarding online activities. ***Restrictive mediation*** occurs through rules and limits placed on a teen's online activities. ***Monitoring*** is non-interactive surveillance of a teen's online activities, such as checking text messages or web browser history [14]. Some studies have also included ***technical mediation***, such as the use of software applications [7, 14]. Active mediation has more characteristics of responsiveness while restrictive mediation is more reminiscent of demandingness. However, a study comparing parenting styles and parent mediation strategies on the Internet found that authoritative parents tend to use more active mediation, restrictive mediation, monitoring, and technical mediation strategies than authoritarian, indulgent, and neglectful parents [7]. Therefore, the relationship between parenting style and mediation strategies is not one-to-one.

Our work is unique in that it draws on Kohlberg's CMD theory to examine adolescent moral development as it relates to online behavior, and it takes into account how parenting style and mediation techniques impact adolescent moral judgment and online behavior. Few studies have explored adolescent online behavior using a dyadic parent-child level of analysis. Furthermore, research that has examined the role of parenting in adolescent online safety has focused on shielding teens from negative online experiences. Thus, our research is one of the first to frame adolescent online safety as a developmental process of adolescent growth where teens are taught through parental guidance and personal experience how to behave appropriately online and handle negative online experiences.

RESEARCH METHODOLOGY

Participants and Procedure

We conducted audio-recorded, semi-structured interviews of 12 parent-adolescent dyads. The 12 adolescents included seven females (aged 13, 13, 13, 15, 16, and 16) and five males (aged 14, 15, 15, 15, and 17). Although we only specified "parent" in our advertisement, mothers were more likely to self-select as the parent to accompany their adolescents than fathers. Thus, the parents included eleven mothers and one father. Eleven dyads were Caucasian and one (a mother-daughter pair) was Asian. All adolescents except for one came from a two-parent home. Ten dyads reported having broadband Internet access and two dyads (all from the same family) reported having dial-up access. On average, families reported having three computers (either laptop or desktop) and all adolescents had access to cell phones with texting capabilities. All participants lived in Central Pennsylvania.

Adolescents and parents arrived together but were interviewed separately; interviews lasted approximately one hour. We asked parents about their techniques for regulating their teen's online behavior as well as any associated challenges. We asked teens about their online experiences, and more specifically about how they interpreted the moral implications of online activities like illegal downloading of music, cyberbullying, identity theft, and so on.

Coding and Data Analysis

Using the parent-adolescent dyad as our level of analysis, we qualitatively coded the transcribed interview responses, using Atlas.ti and Excel®. We applied Kohlberg's six stages of moral development to the adolescents' comments and the classifications of both parenting styles and mediation strategies to the parent data. The coding was blind to each teen's age or parent; we simply coded the moral statements in the context of the interview. Two coders worked collaboratively to obtain agreement on the final codes.

We coded 270 moral statements across the 12 adolescent participants, averaging 23 statements per teen with a standard deviation of 6 statements. We also coded a total of 555 parental statements that were indicative of parenting styles and/or mediation strategies, averaging 46 statements per parent with a standard deviation of 12 statements. Parental interviews were coded independently of the adolescent interviews. We assign pseudonyms for each teen to protect their identities.

Profiles of Parent-Adolescent Dyads

Consistent with Kohlberg's CMD theory [10], we found that moral development progresses with adolescent age. As shown in **Figure 1**, 13- to 14-year-olds in our study tend to have a "Punishment and obedience orientation" (Stage 1) more often than older teens. "Authority maintaining morality" (Stage 4) and other more advanced stages of moral development increase in 15- to 17-year-olds.Since age plays such a pivotal role in moral development, we chose to present our results through adolescent profiles grouped by age in the following section.

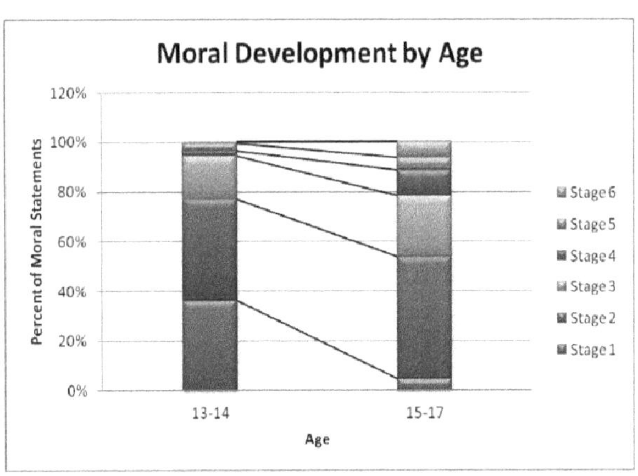

Figure 1: Moral Development by Age

RESULTS

To explore the relationships of moral development to age, we created a *"**moral compass**"* for each adolescent and grouped them by age. Each compass visualizes the six stages of moral development as a web graph, starting with Stage 1 at the top of the compass and progressing clockwise through Stage 6. Each line represents the unique moral profile of a teen participant. The lines fluctuate based on the percent of the teen's total moral statements that were classified within each Kohlberg stage.

13- & 14-Year-Olds: Monica, Emily, Paige, and Joshua

Figure 2 summarizes the moral profiles of participants aged 13 to 14. Monica, Emily, and Paige are 13-year-old females, while Joshua is a 14-year-old male.

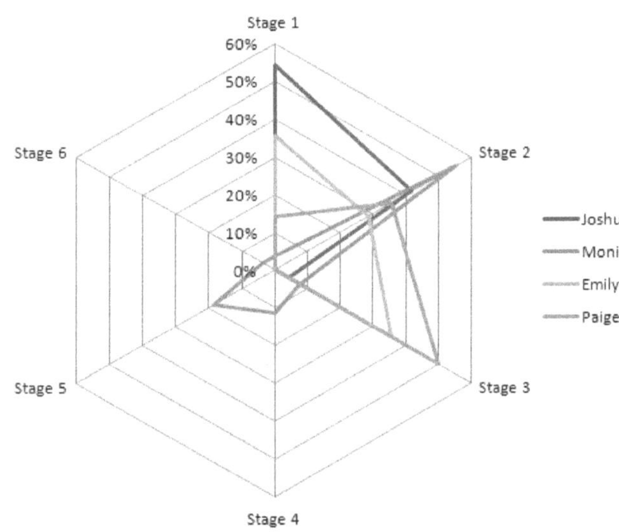

Figure 2: Moral Compass, 13- & 14-year olds

Emily and **Paige** have similar moral profiles, spreading across Stages 1 (obedience) and 3 (approval). However, Emily expressed more compliance with her parents (Stage 1), and Paige was more individualistic (Stage 2). Both girls admitted that they did not know the meaning of the word "ethical" during their interviews and often said, "I don't know" when asked about the moral implications of specific online behaviors. Both girls said that they pirated music online, though Emily's mother made her stop when she learned this was happening. When Emily and Paige were asked if they would mind their parents using a program like Net Nanny to monitor their computer usage, they said:

"I would be fine with it." –Emily, 13-year-old female

"Well... I think that they should trust their kids unless their kids give them a reason not to." –Paige, 13-year-old female

Emily and Paige also share similarities in parent profiles; both have mothers who were predominantly ***authoritative*** and described ***active mediation*** strategies for regulating the teens' online behavior. However, Paige's mom was slightly more ***authoritarian***. At home, both girls use shared computers in a common area. They are both on Facebook, but their moms have friended them to keep an eye on their activities. Both girls have cell phones and text messaging, but only Paige has Internet access on her phone .

A key difference was the level of digital literacy displayed by their mothers: Emily's mom is a programmer analyst who uses software to implement technical monitoring of her daughter's computer use. Her grasp of the technology allows her to "probe" her daughter's online behaviors and intervene when necessary. For example, she made Emily stop downloading music illegally and now only permits her to buy music from iTunes. In contrast, Paige's mom said that her husband is more "computer savvy" than she is, and that he would be the one to prevent Paige from illegal music downloads. However, according to Paige, this was not the case; she admitted to downloading pirated music. It is possible that Emily was slightly more compliant than Paige because Emily's mother was both actively engaged in her daughter's online behavior and technically competent in enforcing reasonable guidelines. However, we can only speculate because we did not interview Paige's dad.

Monica was another 13-year-old female in our sample, but she tended to be more hedonistic (Stage 2) than Emily and Paige. Monica often disregarded her mother's advice and disobeyed her orders. When asked about monitoring programs such as Net Nanny, she said:

"Oh geeze, I hope that lady over there didn't tell my mom about that ha ha." –Monica 13-year-old female

She then added that she would be okay with it because she would circumvent her parents if they tried to use it. Unlike the other girls, Monica's mom was predominantly ***authoritarian*** and ***restrictive***. She was very strict and protective with Monica and Craig (who are siblings), perhaps in part because her oldest daughter had once been abducted. Monica's mom primarily restricts her online usage through the use of parental controls on the computer that disallow downloads, some websites, and many games:

I don't even know what they are, just everything that was like 13 and up, I locked. ha ha." – Monica's Mom

Monica does not have Internet access on her phone; the family only has dial-up Internet access at home, which their mother chooses intentionally to limit usage. A condition of Monica being allowed to have a Facebook account was that she shared her password with her mom. However, Monica does have her own laptop, which she is allowed to bring into her room. It is possibly due to this limited freedom and her mom's strictness that Monica takes advantage of opportunities to exert independence from her parents.

One apparent contradiction to Monica's parents' restrictive parenting is that both mother and father condone digital piracy. When we asked Monica's mom if she had a problem with Monica downloading music illegally, Monica's mom expressed her own hedonistic (Stage 2) viewpoint:

"Downloading illegal music, oh heck no, as long as it's free." –Monica's Mom

It seems likely this type of parenting contributed to Monica's highly hedonistic moral profile.

Joshua is unique. Even though he is 14, it seems that he has not reached similar levels of moral growth as the 13-year-old females in **Figure 2**. Joshua's comments are primarily in Stages 1 (obedience) and 2 (hedonism). Many of his statements suggest a strong reliance on authority (Stage 1). When we asked him about implications of different types of online behavior, such as piracy, information sharing, and his personal digital rights, he focused on what he was allowed and not allowed to do:

"I wish I understood it more though. How it works, like, so if I get in trouble, if something happens. Yeah, the legal aspect." –Joshua, 14-year-old male

"So what am I not allowed to do? What am I allowed to do? Basically." –Joshua, 14-year-old male

In general, he complied with his mom, as if her word was law, relinquishing psychological control. Our interview with Joshua's mom confirmed that her primary parenting style was ***restrictive*** and ***authoritarian***. Joshua is not allowed to have a smart phone, Facebook account, or even a personal email address because his mom does not think he is mature enough to handle the responsibility:

"He doesn't do Facebook, yet. He wants to but, kids are dumb on Facebook." –Joshua's Mom

Joshua's only online access was from a shared computer in a common area at home or at school. His mother did not implement any parental controls on the computer, but it was due to lack of knowledge, not desire to do so. It is possible that Joshua's predominantly compliant (Stage 1) moral development may be explained by his young age and his mother's restrictive parenting style.

15-Year-Olds: Craig, Martin, Leslie, and Aaron

We interviewed four 15-year-olds, one female and three males (**Figure 3**). Two of the boys, Craig and Martin, had similar moral profiles. Aaron was unique, and Leslie's moral profile was similar to the 16-year-old girls discussed in the subsequent section.

Craig and **Martin** were skewed toward hedonism (Stage 2), with individualistic and autonomous views of actions and consequences. Neither showed remorse about pirating digital content; they framed right and wrong as what they could get away with without getting caught or punished. Martin and Craig expressed somewhat Machiavellian views on how parents should monitor their kids' online behavior:

"If they don't trust their kids, they should get a nanny program or somehow, don't tell them about history or how to check it. If they trust them, they can do what they want." –Martin, 15-year-old male

Craig responded, *"Yeah, they bought the computer,"* when we asked him if his parents should be allowed to use monitoring software, such as Net Nanny.

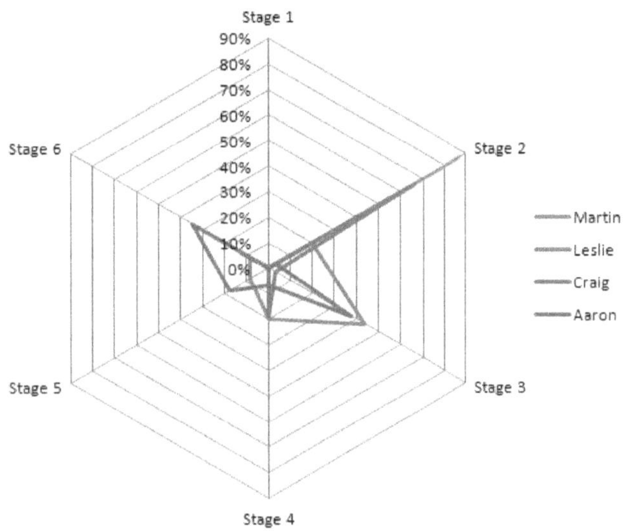

Figure 3: Moral Compass, 15-year-olds

These two teens differed in the parenting styles they experienced. Craig (Monica's brother) has ***authoritarian*** and ***restrictive*** parents. Craig's dad confirmed that his wife is highly restrictive of their teens' Internet usage and keeps a strict watch on what they do:

"My wife monitors everything. She checks their Facebook and she checks... If there was something she couldn't control, we probably wouldn't have them [computers]." – Craig's Dad

Similar to what we heard from Craig's Mom, his Dad saw no problem with Craig downloading music illegally. The parents' low level of responsiveness to their teens' need for autonomy and their own individualistic sense of cost-benefit for digital piracy may have added to Monica and Craig's tendency for hedonistic moral judgment (Stage 2).

The interview with Martin's mom suggests that parents who are ***indulgent*** and do little to mediate their teen's online behavior (***no mediation***) may also contribute to a hedonistic moral view. Martin accesses the Internet through a shared computer in a private room at home and through his iPod touch. His mom does not feel comfortable mediating his online behavior in any way (low demandingness):

"I don't want to be breathing down his neck all the time because I don't want to alienate him. At this point in his life, I feel like it's important that I'm there for him if he needs me, but yet to respect some of the privacy that he has." –Martin's Mom

She repeatedly confirmed that she had no idea what Martin did online. However, she also had very little confidence that her son would act appropriately (low responsiveness).

"I worry about that with him because he's blinded. He's not as savvy as other people so he's blinded by 'oh, I'll do it and won't get caught.' Whereas if he does it, he'll get caught." –Martin's Mom

Martin's mom is well aware of her son's moral views regarding reward versus consequences. She mimicked Martin to show us his mentality. At the same time she did nothing to address Martin's hedonistic viewpoint:

"'The police, the Facebook police aren't going to get me. I'm not going to have to be held to any consequences ...I can do whatever I want to do. [Mimicking her son]' ...And I say, well if the police haven't shown up I guess that's a good thing." –Martin's Mom

In some ways, Martin seemed interested in having more engagement from his mom. For example, he friended her on Facebook, told her that he was downloading movies illegally, and shared inappropriate pictures on his phone sent between friends. It seems he was being confronted with ethical dilemmas and was not receiving guidance. Instead, Martin's mom continued to enable Martin by indulging his hedonistic behavior and ensuring that he would not suffer negative consequences from them:

"I think I would be the fall guy. I would be the person he goes to after he did it. I would be the person that he went to and said hey, I did this, how do I get out of it? Yeah, mom to the rescue." –Martin's Mom

Aaron seemed quite different than the two other 15-year-old boys, expressing moral values that fell in Stages 3, 5, and 6. He exhibited characteristics of being a "good boy" (Stage 3) who wanted to win the approval of others. He also had a strong sense of right and wrong, institutionalized (Stage 5) by Christian beliefs that he has internalized (Stage 6) as his own personal moral beliefs. For example, when we asked Aaron if he knew what ethics meant, he asked:

"Could you define ethics, because it's different for everyone ...Yeah, I have a strong ethic. I'm a Christian, so I know what's right and wrong." –Aaron, 15-year-old male

Overall, Aaron seemed to struggle most with moral issues that may cause disapproval by others. Sometimes, when it came to upholding his personal moral beliefs (Stage 6) versus doing what he thought would please others (Stage 3), he chose to take the path of most approval. For example, Aaron has strong moral values regarding digital piracy, but he makes exceptions when it comes to sharing his legally downloaded music with his friends:

"Like my friend said 'I hate my songs on my iPod,' and I don't want them to feel all bad and stuff. And I don't want to be just that friend and say 'oh I have like 300 songs. I'm sorry I can't give you any.' I don't want to be that guy

either because then I'm a total jerk all of a sudden. So..." – Aaron, 15-year-old male

In general, Aaron had a high level of moral awareness that was expressed as personal moral integrity (Stage 6). He seemed to understand the difference between having the right to behave in a certain way but also the maturity to act how one should:

"I have rights. Freedom of speech. And I could say anything I want. It's just I don't want to be a jerk. Which is another thing ...Well, there's a difference between the right to and what you can and cannot do. I mean I can jump off a building but it's not like I'm going to so..."–Aaron, 15-year-old male

He also seeks advice regarding ethical dilemmas and incorporates the advice into his own moral deliberations:

"[I] get advice from multiples of people, write down their advice, and then clump them together, and make the best decision out of it ...and I look at each individual piece of advice, and see how it fits together and chose the best out of [the advice]." –Aaron, 15-year-old male

Our interview with Aaron's mom offered some insights as to why his moral profile was so different from the other two same-aged boys. Because of a severely negative experience concerning a family member who was involved in a serious cybercrime, Aaron and his mom are acutely aware of the dangers of engaging online. Aaron's mom was ***authoritarian***, perhaps due to this negative experience. However, she tends to mediate Aaron's online activities through ***monitoring*** rather than restriction. She monitors Aaron's Facebook posts, reviews his games, and uses monitoring software. She also often uses ***active mediation*** in a more ***authoritative*** way to learn from past experiences and teach her son right from wrong:

Well, I just try to talk to him, you know, about what's right on there and what's wrong on there and he knows. And he knows from personal experience what can happen to him ...we're brought up, and we're Christian, and we believe that it's morally wrong to do this stuff too." –Aaron's Mom

Strong Christian family beliefs and negative consequences of online behavior help to explain Aaron's advanced moral character. He witnessed drastic consequences from inappropriate Internet use; this may have promoted a deeper understanding of online risks than most boys at his age.

Leslie is a 15-year-old female with a moral profile that is more similar to the 16-year-old girls we interviewed than the same-aged boys. For the most part, Leslie identified with Stage 3, evincing a "good girl" mentality that values relationships and approval of others. For example, when she was asked if she would act differently on a school computer as opposed to her own, she answered:

"Well the schools can, like, watch everything you do, and you wouldn't want to make a bad impression on yourself." –Leslie, 15-year-old female

Leslie also expressed a respect for parental authority (Stage 4); she understands that parents monitor kids for a reason:

"I guess it kind of is [a violation of privacy] but they're your parents, and they're also doing that for a moral reason." –Leslie, 15-year-old female

At the same time, she explained that her parents do not have to monitor her online behavior because she takes the responsibility to do so herself, unlike her brother:

"I kind of limit myself with most things, like with the amount of information I put on, the amount of time I spend, those kinds of things. My brother is on Xbox, internet, all the time so he's limited. I'm not." –Leslie, 15-year-old female

Leslie's mom mirrored her daughter's sentiments; she does not feel the need to use parental controls to monitor her daughter's online behavior. Leslie has earned her Mom's trust by meeting high expectations that have been placed on her. Leslie does not exceed the limit on her monthly text messages; she does not download music illegally; and according to both Leslie and her mom, she respects parental authority. Leslie's mom explained that Leslie is an honor student and does not spend as much time on Facebook as her friends. Therefore, she gives Leslie more freedom:

"I don't feel with her that I necessarily need to [use parental controls]. But maybe with my son I will, although right now he's 13 and he's only interested in games. That might change ha ha." –Leslie's Mom

Leslie's mom practices ***active mediation*** with an ***authoritative*** parenting style. She seems well-informed about her daughter's online behaviors and encourages her to engage with others online. Leslie has Internet access on her phone and a tablet that she is allowed to bring into her bedroom. Leslie's mom helped her set up her Facebook account; all of Leslie's Facebook messages go to her mom's email address as well, so that her mom can monitor them. However, she sees this as a way to be engaged in her daughter's social life, not to restrict her online activities:

"When I get home, or if it's a weekend and I'm home, I'll just say, well even [your friend] is on Facebook right now, do you want to get on and talk with her?' Or 'So and so wants to be your friend.'" –Leslie's Mom

Leslie's mom often finds teaching moments to educate her daughter on appropriate online behaviors, even cases when she thinks Leslie's friends are behaving inappropriately:

"I have even called one of her friends a very not-nice name. And it was just 2 days ago ...I said she's advertising, you know, that's what she's doing...I quickly came off with 'you know not to post...' I forget how I exactly worded it but either 'you have to watch what you put up online or you

know not to put bad photos up online.' She gives me the eyes. The evil eyes. She looks at me and she says 'mom, you know that I wouldn't.'" –Leslie's Mom

16- & 17-Year-Olds: Kim, Erica, Mary, and Jaden

Figure 4 displays the moral profiles of our oldest group of participants, three 16-year-old females and one 17- year-old male. In this age group, **Kim** and **Erica** are most similar. Both are centered on Stage 3 (approval of others), but also exhibit Stages 2 (hedonism) and 4 (respect for authority). Being more socially focused, both girls shared their observations of acceptable social norms when explaining what they believed was right or wrong. For example, Kim and Erica both acknowledged that illegal downloading of music harms the artists, but they had an "everyone does it" mentality regarding whether it was right or wrong to do so:

"Well, I'm sure everyone does that [pirates music] sometimes." –Kim, 16-year-old female

"I mean, a lot of people do it, I guess it's wrong, but I don't know. I wouldn't really tell them not to, I guess." – Erica, 16-year-old female

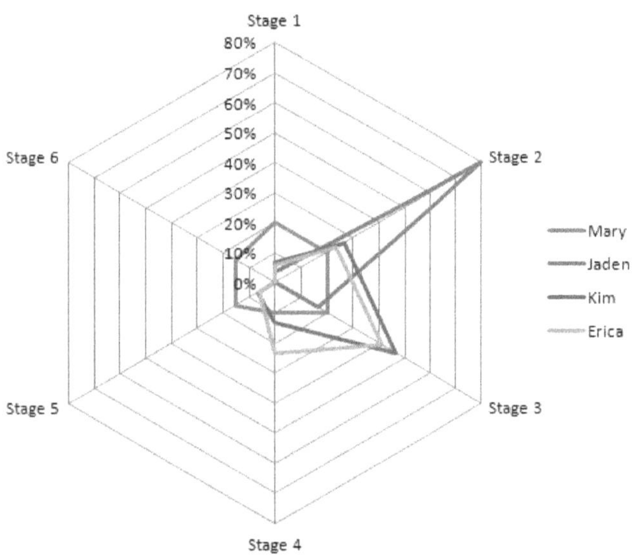

Figure 4: Moral Compass, 16 & 17-year-olds

Erica seemed to have greater respect for parental authority (Stage 4) than Kim. While both girls wanted their parents to trust them online, Kim wanted to have more autonomy:

"Um, not really. [I] just feel like it's just kind of a trust thing. Like, why do you not trust me with the things on my computer?" –Kim, 16-year-old female

Erica respected that it was the parents' role to protect their children from online threats. Therefore, Erica said she would be okay if they used a program like Net Nanny:

"Maybe but I mean it'd be alright. I want them to trust me, but if they didn't then I guess it would be okay." – Erica, 16-year-old female

Comparatively, Kim was slightly more hedonistic (Stage 2) and had less respect for parental authority (Stage 4) than Erica. This may partially be explained by the different parenting styles they experienced at home. Kim's mom was difficult to categorize, perhaps because of cultural and language differences. However, her comments suggest that her parenting style is predominantly ***neglectful*** with ***no mediation*** in regard to Kim's online behavior. However, this was coupled with a ***restrictive authoritarian*** parenting style regarding academic scholarship. Kim's mom had very high expectations about school performance; therefore, she was adamant that Kim not waste time socializing online, and expressed a fairly negative view of technology overall:

"I think whole world, I wish people would spend less time with computers and do something else.... I try to tell her you know, I cannot monitor every minute. I just say, you know it's a waste of time. Try to limit as much as you can." – Kim's Mom

Kim has Internet access through her laptop that she can use privately in her room with the expectation that she is productively doing her school-work. Kim has a Facebook account that her mom does not monitor. In fact, even though her mom currently does not have a Facebook account, Kim told her mom that she would not friend anyway. Kim's mom is aware that she downloads music illegally; however, she does not concern herself with it:

"Sometime she told me some of the music is illegal to download but everybody else download, and they share with her. I basically, I'm not interested in that music, so I say okay as long as nobody trouble you." –Kim's Mom

In contrast, Erica's mom has an ***active mediation***, ***authoritative*** parenting style and is highly involved with Erica's online behavior. Similar to the other moms in this category, she often interacts with her daughter regarding her online behavior; however, she also gives Erica freedom to engage online. Erica has her own laptop and iPod touch. Her mom is her Facebook friend but does not closely monitor Erica's Facebook account. Erica's mom trusts her to behave appropriately online and does not feel that she needs to monitor her very closely. However, she often talks to Erica about the negative consequences experienced by Erica's peers, and she also intervenes when she feels that Erica's friends are not acting appropriately:

"We've had conversations about different posts that people would post on her wall. Her friend, which is a very good friend, for a little while was putting some song lyrics on her daily whatever. Swearing. Suggestive.... [Erica told her friend that] she probably shouldn't be doing that ...because I am good friends with her mother, and that I'd tell her mother.'" – Erica's Mom

Mary is a 16-year-old with a distinctive moral profile compared to the other same-aged girls we interviewed. Mary was very articulate during her interview, generating almost twice as many moral statements than Kim or Erica.

Her moral statements ranged from Stage 1 to Stage 6, showing heightened levels of moral development. One possible explanation is that Mary is very studious. Her mother characterized her as an "honor student," and Mary herself admits that she predominantly uses her computer for school, though she does have Facebook and email accounts. Another explanation is that Mary views her online behavior as an extension of how she should behave in real life:

"I mean, to the point of what I should and shouldn't be doing, it's kind of understood I guess. Like, I wouldn't do it normally, why would I do it online?" –Mary, 16-year-old female

Mary mentioned the value of "common sense" and discussed moral dilemmas in terms of "repercussions" and "guilty conscience." Furthermore, she extended her moral convictions beyond herself (Stage 6), to what she felt was right or wrong for everyone:

"Yeah, I mean, I think people should respect others ideas. They can disagree but just disagree respectfully, and you know, if you have an opinion just back it up with facts." – Mary 16-year-old female

With her own strong moral compass, Mary would be very upset if her parents chose to use a program like Net Nanny to monitor her online behavior. She feels she has earned trust and autonomy, and it would be a betrayal of that trust:

"I don't think I would be upset as to 'oh, I'm gonna have to stop doing something.' It would be more like, 'oh you're not exactly trusting me as much.' I think that would be a major issue. It would be more like the principle rather than what it actually does." –Mary 16-year-old female

Mary's mom is ***authoritative*** and uses ***active mediation*** and ***monitoring*** to encourage appropriate online behavior. She does little to restrict Mary's online interactions. She is not Mary's Facebook friend and has no parental controls on her computer. Mary has her own laptop that she uses in a common area, but her mom offered Mary her own office, if she wanted it. Mary's mom has high expectations that Mary will take personal responsibility for her actions:

"Well I think she has, well you're talking about personal rights [online], but to me she should have the responsibility not to go there. But that's something that you're taught." – Mary's Mom

Finally, **Jaden** is male and the only 17-year-old that we interviewed. As shown in Figure 4, Jaden expressed many hedonistic views (Stage 2), similar to 15-year-olds Craig and Martin. Jaden explained that his parents were restrictive when he was younger, but no longer do much monitoring of his online behavior. As a result of the earlier restrictions, Jaden does not have a Facebook account:

"At this point, I don't really care as much, but growing up that's the reason I didn't get a Facebook. There was a point where at 10 pm each night they would turn off the internet, whereas my friends didn't." –Jaden 17-year-old male

Apparently, Jaden's parents used to be very strict, and Jaden learned then how to take subversive measures, such as deleting his browser history. At 17, Jaden feels that he is grown up and should not have any parental restrictions; those should be reserved for younger teens. In fact, when we mentioned Net Nanny, Jaden's response was simply, "*Sounds illegal*." According to Jaden, his parents no longer care about what he does online:

"I mean they don't really care that much anymore. They don't want me, well, they're really big on me not handing out personal information but they don't check. So if I wanted to..." –Jaden 17-year-old male

Unfortunately, Jaden expresses an under-developed sense of moral judgment and partakes in many negative online behaviors, such as pirating music and movies and trolling:

"I think a lot of the time it's [trolling] pretty funny." –Jaden 17-year-old male

Similar to Martin's mom, Jaden's mom is fairly ***indulgent*** regarding Jaden's online activities. For the most part, she feels that she has no control of what Jaden does online and does little to mediate this (***no mediation***). However, her secondary style is ***active mediation***, ***authoritarian***, and she has been much more restrictive of her children in the past. She did not let Jaden play T-rated video games until he was 13, and she was strongly against him having a Facebook account. Jaden's mom talked about how she had many fights with Jaden's older sister regarding these restrictions:

"We had pretty significant fights with his older sister about it, and they were not subtle. They were pretty firm, pretty unpleasant... And you know, computers getting taken, it was bad ...Like when we found out she had a, I don't think it was Facebook, it was Myspace, when she was young. That was not allowed. That had to have permission. We found out that she had done that without permission. That was a very bad, not good thing." –Jaden's Mom

Jaden's mom wants to control her son's online behaviors. She said that part of her strategy is to "torment" in hopes that Jaden has internalized some of what she has said:

"Ha ha. I used to say I shampoo their brain. That's terrible." –Jaden's Mom

However, now, Jaden's mom seems to have mostly given up trying to restrict her son, lets him do what he wants, and hopes for the best. This may be partially because she felt sorry for her son when he suffered a long-term injury:

"So 6 months he couldn't really do a whole lot. At that point, I kind of felt sorry for him and he did a lot of gaming then. And it happened kind of contemporaneously with me saying you got to start cutting back. But I think even if he hadn't [hurt himself] it would have been a bit of a struggle." –Jaden's Mom

Jaden has a Macbook Pro, iPhone, and multiple other computers. His mom cites her lack of technology savviness an important factor for why she feels she has lost control:

"Yeah, I think he sees me as technologically a nincompoop. His opinion of me is that I'm just beyond bad, and I'm full of concern. I think that would be his opinion." –Jaden's Mom

We speculate that Jaden's transition from highly demanding and restrictive parents to parents who are indulgent and give him complete autonomy over his online behavior, may have negatively impacted Jaden's moral development.

DISCUSSION OF EMERGENT THEMES

Several themes emerged from the detailed qualitative analysis of the parent-adolescent interviews. We now discuss these themes and their implications.

Age and Autonomy

By organizing adolescent-parent profiles by age, we uncovered interesting trends across cohorts of adolescents. For example, the youngest group of teens (ages 13 & 14) tended to exhibit the early stages of moral development (Stages 1 – 3) and required a fairly high level of parental supervision. Most young teens only shared computer access in a common area at home. Facebook usage was monitored or restricted. Technical monitoring was common. To some extent, however, we noted that parents who acknowledge the importance of allowing their children to engage online had teens that are more morally advanced than younger teens that were prevented from having these experiences.

In comparison, 15-year-olds exhibited less compliance toward parental authority (Stage 1) than younger teens. They also had fewer restrictions, for instance, the online devices shifted from common areas to private bedrooms. However, levels of parental mediation varied drastically. Martin's mom was reticent to interfere with her son's online activity, while Craig's mom restricted his online usage as much as possible. Perhaps age 15 is a transition period for parents who struggle to know when to parent and when to let go.

Parents afford their older teens (ages 16 & 17) greater autonomy by allowing them to have computers in their rooms and choosing not to heavily monitor their online usage. Parents of these older adolescents are less likely to use parental controls to technically monitor their teens. In fact, doing so would likely violate an older teen's sense of privacy and damage the trust relationship between parent and teen. In general, parents of older teens understand that restricting online usage is no longer an option. Some parents of older teens leveraged the high demands from school work as a means to influence older teens to self-regulate their social engagement online. Instead, they must actively engage with their teen if they want to remain part of their teens' online lives.

Predisposition toward Hedonism

Overall, we were surprised to find a pervasive moral predisposition toward hedonism (Stage 2) in our sample, particularly for the male adolescents. In **Figure 5**, we have averaged and aggregated our coding results by gender. Adolescent males tend to center around hedonism, while adolescent females tend to have a more external focus, caring more about the approval of others (Stage 3). We believe that this phenomenon can be explained by the different moral expectations placed on boys and girls. Research suggests that parents and society have lower moral expectations of boys than they do for girls. As such, girls are expected to exhibit higher levels of moral judgment and empathy than boys [18]. Our research suggests that this expectation may also carry over to the context of online behavior.

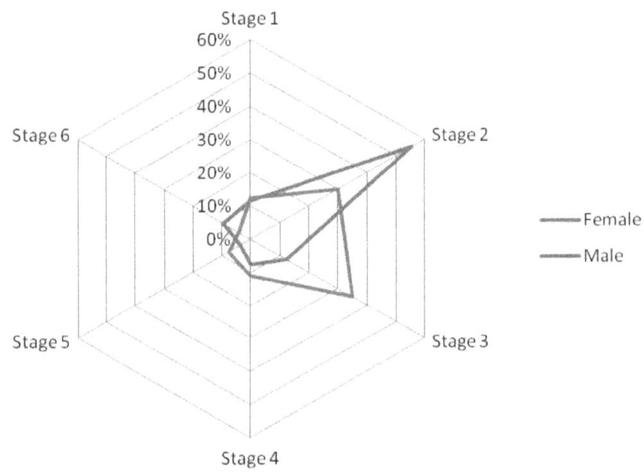

Figure 5: Moral Development by Gender

We also compared these results to Kohlberg's original findings [9]. **Figure 6** compares the moral profiles from our sample to males who were of age 13 and 16 in Kohlberg's data. While we cannot make a one-to-one comparison due to the differences in the studies, we can make one broad observation: Compared to Kohlberg's 1963 study [9], our study of today's adolescent online behaviors seems to be much more skewed toward a ***hedonistic world view***. Even the girls in our sample presented with more hedonistic characteristics than the boys in Kohlberg's studies.

For example, the teens in our sample often justified right and wrong in terms of punishment versus reward. They felt that they should be able to do whatever they want to do online as long as they don't get caught:

"If you feel comfortable doing what you're doing, then you should be able to do it." –Craig, 15-year-old male

They also had little respect for parental guidelines.

"My mom said I wasn't allowed to put my last name up on my Facebook until I just finally did it and she kind of got mad, but I didn't care. Ha ha." –Monica, 13-year-old female

And, they believed that if they did get caught for doing something illegal, such as digital piracy, the repercussions would not be very harsh:

"Well the thing is, when you're my age, they [authorities] can't exactly do a whole lot." –Martin, 15-year-old male

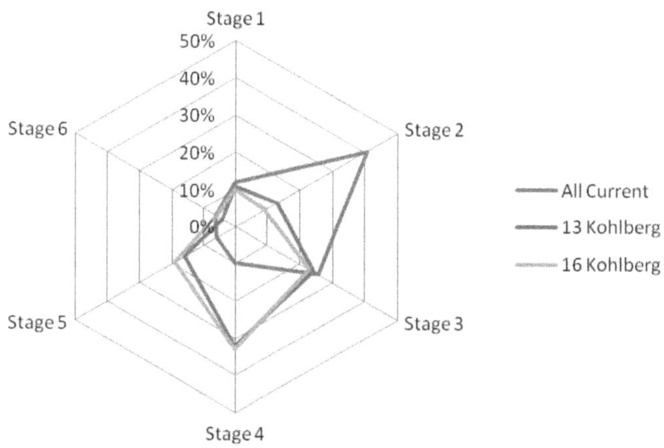

Figure 6: Moral Profiles Compared to Kohlberg[1]

Another aspect of hedonism is reciprocity or quid-pro-quo. But in our sample, reciprocity often came up as justification for retaliation. For example, Craig justified punishing his friend when he felt he had been wronged online:

"A friend found out my stuff, and he thought it'd be funny to get on there and say like, post as me, and say I'm admitting I'm gay. I kind of lost it, and the next day at school I punched him in the mouth for it. And, well we're still friends but he realized that I'm not gay, or I'm not joking around about that stuff." –Craig, 15-year-old male

Past research offers a possible explanation for a hedonistic paradigm shift: "The online world has its own etiquette, its own system of rules, and its own morality" [4]. The Internet is a completely different world, unconstrained by physical boundaries, giving teens more autonomy than ever before [4]. Online, teens consume information and have experiences that are unmediated by adults [4]. It is possible that heightened levels of individual autonomy online may predispose teens to a sense of "individualistic morality" [9] or hedonism. If this is the case, an implication of this shift would be that parenting teens online may be even more challenging than in the "real world." Online parenting may require even more active and authoritative engagement in the teen's online world. In addition, parents may want to emphasize to their adolescents that their behaviors online should be consistent with who they are offline. This strategy seemed very successful in Mary's case.

[1] Note that values for Kohlberg's stages are an approximation based on a chart in his original findings.

Experience Fosters Moral Growth

We also noticed that more advanced moral views often seemed tied to a direct or indirect negative experience. In concert with extreme negative experiences within his family, Aaron's profile was distinct from same-aged boys. Other teens made moral judgments that included examples of how they or people they knew had been victims of identity theft or cyberbullying. For example, both Craig and Emily said that their moms had her identity stolen in the past. Craig (predominantly hedonistic with 66% of his moral statements at Stage 2), may have reached a higher level of moral development (Stage 6) after internalizing this experience:

"I mean you were born a person. You were born who you were. Why are you trying to be someone else?" –Craig, 15-year-old male

Martin is consistently hedonistic (87% of his moral statements at Stage 2). When he was asked about digital rights and what he felt teens should and should not do online, he made it clear that he should be able to do what he pleases, as long as he does not get caught:

"Like my right is to download anything I want to and take the repercussions that would come afterward if I get caught ...Yeah, it's just like action-reaction. I don't remember what that is, it's one of the laws." –Martin, 15-year-old male

However, Martin exhibited some level of moral growth when he was posed with a moral dilemma:

"The hardest thing that I ever had to decide was fixing a computer from when my mom or my dad downloaded a virus . . ." –Martin, 15-year-old male

Martin had discovered pornography on his dad's computer, and was unsure about what to do. He thought *"maybe it'll be a wakeup call"* for his dad, implying that he did not approve of his dad looking at pornography. Martin's mom has not discussed pornography with Martin; she is predominantly indulgent and uninvolved with his online activities:

"Obviously he's going to be curious [about porn], I know that. But I can only hope that he only goes so far ...But I said, honestly I'd rather not know." –Martin's Mom

Meanwhile, Martin reiterated his moral disdain (Stage 4) for pornography on two separate occasions, when his advice to other teens was, *"not to get onto porn sites unless they are 18 or older,"* and, *"don't go on porn sites. Don't give away information. That's it ha ha."*

These examples illustrate that some level of direct or indirect experience can work as a positive influence on a teen's moral development. Conversely, our interviews with Joshua, Craig, and Monica suggested that lack of online social experiences can serve to stunt overall moral growth in the context of online behavior. A key implication of this finding is that restricting online experiences is not an optimal means for achieving adolescent online safety. Therefore, researchers and parents need to find more effective ways to allow teens to engage socially online while keeping them safe.

Parenting Style Influences Moral Development

A consistent theme across our analysis is that parenting style has a direct relationship to adolescent moral development. Compare **Figure 7** and **Figure 8**:

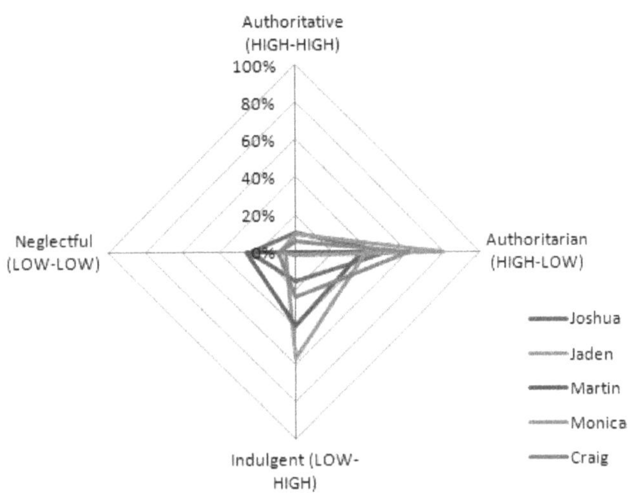

Figure 7: Adolescent Parenting Styles, Hedonistic Teens

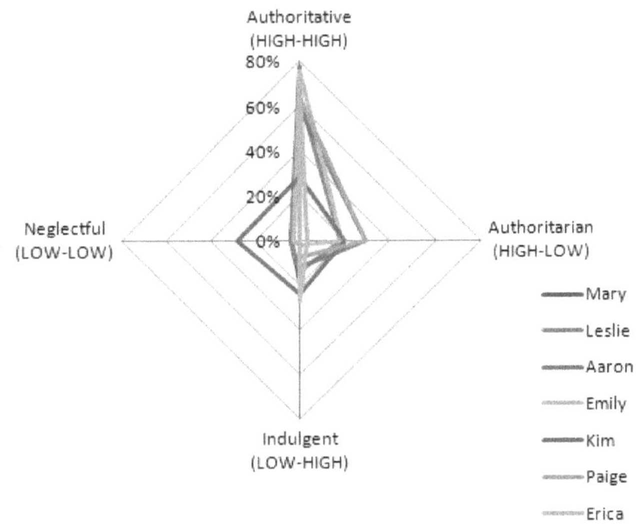

Figure 8: Adolescent Parenting Styles, Non-Hedonistic Teens

Figure 7, we have graphed the teens who displayed higher levels of hedonism (Stage 2). The figure shows a clear pattern of authoritarian and indulgent parenting styles among the more hedonistic teens. For more hedonistic teens, online parental mediation strategies tended to be more restrictive or non-existent. For example, Martin and Craig were both extremely hedonistic (Stage 2). Martin's mom gave him complete autonomy (high responsiveness) but had little trust that he was behaving appropriately online (low demandingness). Craig's mom gave him very little autonomy (low responsiveness) and carefully supervised his online activities (high demandingness). It may be that the "Goldilocks principle" applies here, where both extremes – indulgent and authoritarian parenting –lead to sub-optimal outcomes. Autonomy without any responsibility and high levels of parental control that limit overall online engagement can both hinder adolescent developmental growth.

However, teens who expressed fewer hedonistic views tended to have parents who were more authoritative (**Figure 8**). These parents often opted to actively mediate their teen's online activities or to monitor instead of restrict. For instance, Leslie experienced both high levels of demandingness coupled with high levels of responsiveness, which translated into the ability to self-regulate her online activities. Authoritative parenting that allows teens to engage online, coupled with high expectations from parents regarding appropriate behavior, seems to be linked to higher levels of moral judgment in teens. These findings are consistent with adolescent developmental psychology literature, which suggests that authoritative parenting is associated with positive adolescent outcomes, such as competence and school performance [2, 21]. However, ours is the first study to confirm the relationship between authoritative parenting styles and adolescent moral judgment in the context of online engagement.

One related question concerns parenting styles for girls versus boys. Only one female teen presented as predominantly hedonistic (Monica). We observed that mothers tended to be authoritarian and restrictive with their sons but more authoritative and using active mediation with their daughters. One interpretation is that a gender-based difference in parenting style may be confounded with the more general processes of adolescent moral development [18]. This finding deserves more scrutiny in future research.

Digital Literacy Influences Mediation Strategies

Our analysis also suggests that parents' level of digital literacy moderates their mediation strategies. Parents who knew more about technology tended to be more actively engaged in their teens' online behaviors while parents who were less technically inclined tended to be more in favor of restricting how their teens engaged with others online. Some parents, such as Aaron's mom, were successful in strictly monitoring their teens' online activities while still allowing them opportunities to engage online with others. However, other parents, such as Monica and Craig's, were restrictive to the point that they limited online risks, but also opportunities for their teens to engage with others online. This finding relates to our earlier conclusion that adolescent experience is needed for moral growth. Parents who actively engaged and monitored their teens tended to have more morally developed adolescents than the parents who focused on restriction of online social activities. This may mean that parents should increase their digital literacy in order to effectively mediate adolescent online behavior.

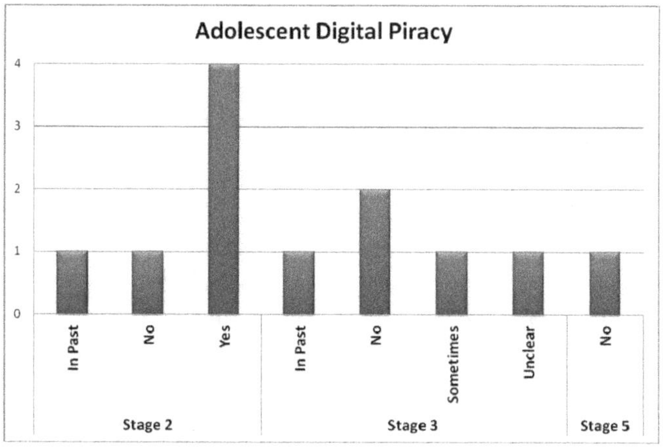

Figure 9: Digital Piracy by Moral Stage

Moral Judgment Influences Online Behavior

Our data suggests that moral judgment plays a role in ethical decision making online. In a more focused analysis, we classified teens by moral views regarding digital piracy and their decision about whether or not to pirate digital content. While consistent with previous research that found a general acceptance towards piracy among high school students [16], our data additionally suggests that moral judgment influences whether teens choose to pirate digital content or not. **Figure 9** shows that hedonism (Stage 2) is most often associated with the decision to illegally download digital content. Unlike prior research that posited piracy occurred because teens are unaware of legal consequences [17], our teens who pirate digital content seem to be aware that they are doing something illegal. Teens who pirated digital content realized that doing so was not "right," but they felt that the benefits outweighed the costs. For the teens classified in Stage 2 who chose not to download digital content illegally, the decision was made because they felt that the costs outweighed the benefits. Viruses, followed by legal consequences, were the main reason hedonistic teens chose not to pirate digital content:

"Um, not from an ethics standpoint. From a security standpoint, I don't like to torrent just because other computers connect to you that way. But from an ethics stand point, I mean I don't illegally download a lot of things, but I wouldn't feel guilty if I were to download like a movie or a bunch of songs." –Jaden, 17-year-old male

Teens who made moral justifications that were more socially based (Stage 3) than individualistic (Stage 2), chose not to pirate music due to sympathy toward the artist:

"Immoral I guess. Because you're stealing other people's stuff when they could be making a profit off of it. And that's kind of like ruining, if like a whole bunch of people do it then it's kind of like ruining them." –Leslie, 15-year-old female

Stage 3 teens who had pirated digital content in the past or in certain circumstances were influenced by peer pressure. As we mentioned earlier, Aaron thought that pirating music was wrong, but he felt compelled to share his legally downloaded music with his friends. Emily had downloaded music illegally in the past, but her mom made her stop. However, she justified her behavior because it was accepted among her friends.

Only one participant gave moral justification for not illegally downloading digital content that extended beyond a Stage 3. Mary recognized the conflict between society and the individual (Stage 5), expressing a deeper understanding of the importance to conforming to a moral society:

"No, I don't think they should because that would just kind of cause chaos. An artist makes music and the company sells it, and they make a profit off of it, and that's part of their business. It's like stealing from a regular company. Just because it's a larger organization doesn't mean you should steal from it." –Mary, 16-year-old female

In addition to seeing an association between adolescent moral character and online behavior, we saw a direct relationship between parenting and digital piracy. Parents who explicitly condoned digital piracy ***all*** had teens who pirated digital content. Parents who preferred their teens download music legally, usually through iTunes, tended to have teens who obeyed those wishes. We did not find that teens went against their parent's wishes when it came to digital piracy. An implication of this finding is that parents can directly influence specific online behaviors that could have negative, even legal, consequences for their teens.

Limitations

Before concluding, we would like to note some of the limitations of our study. First, due to the small sample size, we do not assume that our findings are generalizable to all teens. Our sample was fairly homogeneous as most participants were Caucasian and from a small proximate area. However, we believe the strength of our research is that the small sample size allowed us to do an in-depth dyadic analysis of parents and adolescents. We believe that our qualitative results can be used as a foundation for future research that can further substantiate and refine our qualitative findings through quantitative research methods (e.g., survey) with a large sample size. Second, we used subjective, quantitative coding of qualitative data in order to characterize adolescent moral growth, parenting styles, and parental mediation strategies. Our intention was not to negatively label or stereotype individuals or sub-groups of teens as "hedonists" or parents as "neglectful" or "indulgent." We used these categorizations and labels only to gain summative insights. The categorizations were drawn from previously validated theoretical models, but we want to emphasize that the resulting classifications are approximate, based only on statements that were uttered during the interviews. Our analysis assumes that statements made by participants are truthful and reflective of participant attitudes.

CONCLUSION

Today's adolescents are growing up in a world where online social interactions occur every day. Therefore, teens need to learn how to positively engage online and effectively cope with the negative aspects of online social interactions. Our paper contributes to the theoretical understanding of adolescent moral development and parental mediation as they relate to adolescent online behavior. While we confirmed that Kohlberg's CMD and Baumrind's parenting style theories can extend to the context of adolescent online social interactions and parenting, we also developed new understandings. For example, compared to Kohlberg's 1963 study [9], our study of today's adolescent online behaviors seem to be much more skewed toward online moral hedonism. Unfortunately, our evidence suggests that hedonism is associated with inappropriate online behaviors, such as digital piracy. Some parents may be contributing to this problem because they do not possess the technical expertise to authoritatively engage their teens through active mediation and monitoring. Instead, they take authoritarian approaches to restrict all online experiences or let their teens indulge without any kind of parental mediation. Yet, overly authoritarian or indulgent parents tended to have more hedonistic teens. We also found that adolescent experience facilitates moral growth; therefore, restricting does little to teach teens how to engage appropriately online.

We have already discussed some of the implications of our research for parents; however, these findings present many design opportunities for our research community. For example, we can leverage what we have learned to redesign existing technical monitoring software. New, customizable features could promote active and collaborative engagement between parents and adolescents to reinforce appropriate online behavior while being responsive to adolescents' needs for more autonomy as they mature. Furthermore, we are challenged with designing interfaces that help bridge the digital gap between parents who are often technologically disadvantaged compared to their tech savvy teens. Finally, we can move beyond technical monitoring solutions to develop new tools that encourage adolescents to engage in meaningful social interactions online while learning to be responsible digital citizens.

ACKNOWLEDGEMENTS

The authors are very grateful to the anonymous reviewers for their constructive comments, and to Lee B. Erickson and Bradley C. Dellinger for their input and assistance on data collection. The authors also thank Daniel F. Perkins for his valuable comments on an earlier version of this paper. This research was supported by the U.S. National Science Foundation under grant CNS-1018302. Any opinions, findings, and conclusions or recommendations expressed herein are those of the researchers and do not necessarily reflect the views of the National Science Foundation.

REFERENCES

1. Baumrind, D. A developmental perspective on adolescent risk taking in contemporary America. *New directions for child development*, 37 (1987), 93-125.
2. Baumrind, D. The Influence of Parenting Style on Adolescent Competence and Substance Use. *The Journal of Early Adolescence*, *11*, 1 (1991), 56-95.
3. Baumrind, D. Patterns of parental authority and adolescent autonomy. *New Directions for Child and Adolescent Development*, *2005*, 108 (2005), 61-69.
4. Bradley, K. Internet lives: Social context and moral domain in adolescent development. *New Directions for Youth Development*, *2005*, 108 (2005), 57-76.
5. Crossler, R. E., Bélanger, F., Hiller, J. S., Park, J.-M., Hsiao, M., Channakeshava, K., Bian, K. and Korbich, E. Determinants of Protection Behaviors for Online Privacy of Children. In *Proc. 39th Annual Meeting of The Decision Sciences Institute* (2008), 1641-1647.
6. Defalco, B. *Teen convicted under Internet piracy law*. 2005, http://usatoday30.usatoday.com/tech/news/techpolicy/2005-03-07-az-teen-downloader-convicted_x.htm?csp=34.
7. Eastin, M. S., Greenberg, B. S. and Hofschire, L. Parenting the Internet. *Journal of Communication*, *56*, 3 (2006), 486-504.
8. ISTTF. *Enhancing Child Safety and Online Technologies*. Harvard University's Berkman Center for Internet and Society, 2008, http://cyber.law.harvard.edu/sites/cyber.law.harvard.edu/files/ISTTF_Final_Report.pdf.
9. Kohlberg, L. The Development of Children's Orientations Toward a Moral Order. *Human Development*, *6*, 1-2 (1963), 11-33.
10. Kohlberg, L. Stage and Sequence: The Cognitive Developmental Approach to Socialisation. In D. A. Goslin (ed.) *Handbook of Socialisation Theory and Research*, (1969), 347-480.
11. Lamborn, S. D., Mounts, N. S., Steinberg, L. and Dornbusch, S. M. Patterns of Competence and Adjustment among Adolescents from Authoritative, Authoritarian, Indulgent, and Neglectful Families. *Child Development*, *62*, 5 (1991), 1049-1065.
12. Lerner, R. M. *Adolescence: Development, diversity, context, and application*. Prentice-Hall, Upper Saddle River, NJ, 2002.

13. Leung, L. and Lee, P. S. N. The influences of information literacy, internet addiction and parenting styles on internet risks. *New Media & Society*, *14*, 1 (2012), 117-136.
14. Livingstone, S., Haddon, L., Görzig, A. and Ólafsson, K. *Risks and safety on the internet: The perspective of European children*. EU Kids Online, 2011, http://eprints.lse.ac.uk/33731/.
15. Lwin, M. O., Stanaland, A. J. S. and Miyazaki, A. D. Protecting children's privacy online: How parental mediation strategies affect website safeguard effectiveness. *Journal of Retailing*, *84*, 2 (2008), 205-217.
16. Malin, J. and Fowers, B. Adolescent self-control and music and movie piracy. *Computers in Human Behavior*, *25*, 3 (2009), 718-722.
17. Malin, J. and Fowers, B. Adolescent self-control and music and movie piracy. *Computers in Human Behavior*, *25*, 2009 (2009), 718-722.
18. Nunner-Winkler, G., Meyer-Nikele, M. and Wohlrab, D. Gender Differences in Moral Motivation *Merrill-Palmer Quarterly*, *53*, 1 (2007), 26-52.
19. Press, A. *Father of gay teen who committed suicide plans nationwide walk against bullying*. 2013, http://www.lgbtqnation.com/2013/04/father-of-bullied-gay-teen-who-committed-suicide-plans-nationwide-walk/.
20. Sorbring, E. and Lundin, L. Mothers' and fathers' insights into teenagers' use of the internet. *New Media & Society*, *14*, 7 (2012), 1181-1197.
21. Steinberg, L., Lamborn, S. D., Dornbusch, S. M. and Darling, N. Impact of Parenting Practices on Adolescent Achievement: Authoritative Parenting, School Involvement, and Encouragement to Succeed. *Child Development*, *63*, 5 (1992), 1266-1281.
22. Valcke, M., Bonte, S., De Wever, B. and Rots, I. Internet parenting styles and the impact on Internet use of primary school children. *Computers & Education*, *55*, 2 (2010), 454-464.
23. Valkenburg, P. M., Krcmar, M., Peeters, A. L. and Marseille, N. M. Developing A Scale to Assess Three Styles of Television Mediation: "Instructive Mediation," "Restrictive Mediation," and "Social Coviewing". *Journal of Broadcasting & Electronic Media*, *43*, 1 (1999), 52-66.
24. Walsh, J. *Man Admits Meeting Teen Online and Keeping Her as Sex Slave*. 2006, http://www.wktv.com/news/new-york-state/2813571.html.
25. Yardi, S. A. *Social Media at the Boundaries: Supporting Parents in Managing Youth's Social Media Use*. Dissertation, Georgia Institute of Technology, Atlanta, GA, 2012.

Social Networking Site Use by Mothers of Young Children

Meredith Ringel Morris
Microsoft Research
Redmond, WA, USA
merrie@microsoft.com

ABSTRACT

In this paper, we present the first formal study of how mothers of young children (aged three and under) use social networking sites, particularly Facebook and Twitter, including mothers' perceptions of which SNSes are appropriate for sharing information about their children, changes in post style and frequency after birth, and the volume and nature of child-related content shared in these venues. Our findings have implications for improving the utility and usability of SNS tools for mothers of young children, as well as for creating and improving sociotechnical systems related to maternal and child health.

Author Keywords

Social media; social networking sites; Facebook; Twitter; mothers; motherhood.

ACM Classification Keywords

H.5.m [Information Interfaces and Presentation (e.g., HCI)]: Miscellaneous.

INTRODUCTION

Social networking sites (SNSes) have become an increasingly common aspect of daily life. As of August 2012, 69% of online American adults used SNSes; Facebook was the most popular, used by 66%, followed by LinkedIn (a professionally-focused network) at 20% penetration, and then Twitter at 16% [5].

Older adults are one of the fastest-growing SNS user segments; SNS adoption among more youthful segments (e.g., 18 – 29 year-olds) appears to be plateauing after achieving nearly ubiquitous penetration [25]. These changing demographics were notably parodied in a popular *Saturday Night Live* skit, "Mom's On Facebook" [30], which satirizes concerns of teens and young adults whose privacy or "cool" reputation may be compromised by their mother's presence in their online social network.

Although most media discussion of mothers and SNSes focuses on the aforementioned concerns resulting from an older generation's increased social media presence, the maturation of the original "Facebook generation," college students and young adults who joined the network near its inception, has resulted in the growth of a different kind of mom on Facebook, i.e., women who have recently become mothers.

This growing demographic has led to new software features, such as Facebook's addition of the ability to add an "Expecting a Baby" Life Event to one's profile [37], and the third-party Facebook application unbaby.me, which allows aggrieved users to remove what they perceive as an unwelcome deluge of baby photos from their Newsfeed [11].

In this paper, we present the first formal study of how mothers of young children (aged three and under) use social networking sites, particularly Facebook and Twitter, including mothers' perceptions of which SNSes are appropriate for sharing information about their children, changes in post style and frequency after birth, and the volume and nature of child-related content shared in these venues. We then discuss the implications of these findings, both with respect to how they inform our understanding of evolving societal norms and how they can inform the design of enhanced sociotechnical systems.

The following research questions motivated the analyses presented here:

- Does becoming a mother change the ways in which women appropriate social networking technologies?
- Are mothers using social networking sites to share and seek information about parenting young children? What categories of child-related information are shared and sought? What proportion of SNS use do parenting-related posts comprise?
- Do mothers in special circumstances (such as mothers experiencing postpartum depression or mothers whose children have special needs) have different SNS footprints than other mothers? If so, can this information offer insight into how to improve technologies or social services to better address the unique needs of these subpopulations?
- How can social networking sites be designed to better support the needs of mothers of young children?

The primary contributions of this work are twofold. From a computational social science perspective, this work contributes insight into the experience of mothering young

CSCW'14, February 15 – 19, 2014, Baltimore, MD, USA.

ACM 978-1-4503-2540-0/14/02...$15.00.
http://dx.doi.org/10.1145/2531602.2531603

children through the lens of technology use (for example, differential status update patterns distinguish mothers with postpartum depression and those whose children have developmental delays), as well as insight into the evolving role of social networks for sharing information about one's children. From an HCI perspective, this work contributes design guidelines for tailoring social networking sites (or apps within SNS ecosystems) to better support the needs of mothers of young children, including supporting information-seeking, milestone tracking, and privacy (not only privacy for a child's information, but potentially for masking signals that our analysis shows may implicitly reveal one's motherhood status).

RELATED WORK

The intersection of technology and motherhood is a small but growing field of study [1]. Foucault studied the technological needs of expectant and new parents, finding a desire for better communications tools for keeping in touch with friends and family after a child's birth, more nuanced baby monitoring technologies, and easier access to pregnancy and childcare related information [15]. Gulotta et al. [17] learned that many parents desire to leave "digital legacies" to their children upon their death, such as allowing offspring to inherit digital photo collections. Kientz et al. [21] developed BabySteps, digital journaling software that prompted mothers to archive key moments in their child's development; BabySteps provided the personal incentive of creating a digital baby book to motivate faithful collection of developmental data for sharing with a child's pediatrician. LeDantec et al. [24] studied the use of mobile phones and other ubiquitous computing technologies by homeless mothers residing in shelters, finding that such technologies could be a transformative and empowering force. Hui et al. [19] created MammiBelli, a wearable sensor band that allowed pregnant mothers to share details of fetal activity with close friends and relatives. Rather than introduce a novel technology into mothers' lives as in the aforementioned efforts, in this paper we study mothers' use of existing technologies, specifically Facebook and Twitter.

The use of online social technologies by mothers has been most prominently characterized by "Mommy Blogging," wherein mothers write public blogs that document and reflect on their children's lives, dispense advice to fellow moms, and/or endorse parenting-related products [26]. A recent study by Scarborough Research found that 14% of U.S. moms consider themselves Mommy Bloggers [23]. McDaniel et al. [27] found that new mothers' frequency of blogging correlated with feelings of social connection and support. Motherhood forums, including traditional forums hosted on parenting sites such as babycenter.com and anonymous forums such as YouBeMom [35], are also a popular online outlet for new mothers to seek and share advice. In this paper, we focus on the use of the social networking sites Facebook and Twitter by the mothers of infants and toddlers, rather than on traditional blogs and forums.

Several researchers have studied the use of social networking sites by specific sub-populations. For example, Brady et al. [4] reported results of a survey on the use of Facebook and Twitter by blind adults, Burke et al. studied Facebook use by adults on the autism spectrum [7], and Chang et al. [10] analyzed the differential use of Facebook by members of several ethnic groups. Rather than focusing on demographic traits, Brubaker et al. [6] studied how a specific life event (death of a loved one) played out in user actions on the social networking site MySpace. Our work can be considered an effort in this genre, with a particular focus on women who are the mothers of very young children (aged 0 – 3 years).

There are a small number of recent studies that are beginning to shed light on mothers' social networking use. NielsenWire [31] reported poll results indicating that 3 out of 4 American moms visited Facebook in March 2012, and that mothers are more likely than other women to access social media via mobile devices. Gibson and Hanson [16] conducted ethnographic sessions in the U.K. studying the general use of technology by new mothers, and noted that this demographic particularly valued Facebook as a way to remain socially connected during the perinatal period. Burke et al. [8] analyzed the prominence of intra-family connections on Facebook, including those between parents and children old enough to have Facebook accounts (above age 13), as well as the types of communications occurring between family members on Facebook; they found that 37% of English-speaking Facebook users have explicitly connected with either a parent or child, with mother-daughter connections being most common. De Choudhury, Counts, and Horvitz [12, 13] studied public tweets from new mothers as a method of identifying signals of postpartum depression (PPD), a mood disorder that affects about 11% – 18% of new mothers [9]. This paper studies broader patterns of new mothers' social networking use, such as the frequency and types of child-related content shared on different networks; we also discuss some findings on how such communications are influenced by PPD, which complement those of De Choudhury et al., and which enable us to quantify some of the qualitative findings suggested in Gibson and Hanson's results.

Ethical and privacy issues relating to the use of social networking technologies by children, while not the focus of this paper, inform the cultural backdrop that may influence mothers' decisions about appropriate sharing of child-related content. Most such studies focus on SNS use by teens, since 13 is the minimum registration age for most sites due to the U.S. COPPA act (www.coppa.org). boyd et al. [3] have explored the issue of SNS use by younger "tweens," and found that many use Facebook before they are officially of age, noting that about a third of parents have helped their children create Facebook accounts before the officially permitted age of 13 years. Although Facebook tries to promote a "real name" policy, as of June 2012, Facebook estimated that approximately 2.4% of accounts are "user-misclassified," such as accounts for babies, pets, duplicate identities, etc. [34]; Facebook tries to discourage parents from creating separate accounts for their babies by allowing them to add babies and even fetuses to a "Friends & Family" profile field [37]. Our study adds to the body of work concerning children and online privacy by giving insight into the types of child-related content mothers of infants and toddlers are willing to share on social networking sites.

DATA COLLECTION

Participants completed a brief online survey, which included an optional SNS data dump. Our survey instrument was available online for two months, from mid-July through mid-September, 2012. Mothers of children aged three years or younger and who had either a Facebook or Twitter account were eligible to take the survey; a drawing for a $500 gift card was offered as an incentive for participation.

The survey was advertised via several online venues (all targeted to a U.S. audience), including posts to e-mail lists for new mothers (both within our organization and within the broader community in our metropolitan area), tweets from our organization's social media accounts, paid advertisements on Facebook targeted to U.S.-based women in their twenties and thirties, and sponsored posts on BabyCenter (babycenter.com), a popular website aimed at mothers that hosts discussion forums and parenting articles.

The survey collected demographic data and data related to the child/childbirth experience (child's birthdate, whether the child is the first-born, whether the child had been diagnosed with a developmental delay, whether the mother had been diagnosed with PPD, etc.). The survey also asked whether the respondent used Facebook and/or Twitter to share several types of information about the child (status updates, photos, videos, etc.).

Respondents were then optionally asked to provide their Twitter username and/or to install a Facebook application that collected a one-time snapshot of their Wall/Timeline posts. The Twitter username allowed us to capture all of the user's public Twitter posts and account details (via our institution's access to the complete public Twitter Firehose). The Facebook data dump included status updates and captions associated with photos, videos, and links that the user shared on their Facebook Wall/Timeline. Multimedia such as photos and videos were not collected for privacy reasons.

RESULTS

After discarding invalid surveys (e.g., incomplete surveys or surveys from participants not meeting the eligibility criteria), we had 412 valid surveys. After discussing the demographics of our respondents, we then present results regarding Twitter use and Facebook use; for the latter, we further explore trends in post frequency and content, as well as trends associated with particular maternal sub-groups, such as those with PPD or with developmentally-delayed children.

Manual labeling of whether individual posts were or were not about the child would be infeasible due to the size of the data set (e.g., 59,316 postnatal Facebook posts). Instead, we used posts containing the child's name or nickname(s) as a proxy for identifying child-related posts. Note that this heuristic underestimates the total number of child-related posts – manual coding of a random sample of 144 status messages not containing the child's name identified an additional 28.5% of these as being parenting-related, e.g. "Peed on twice in one day! Lordy how life changes…"; "my oldest told me tonight that she's glad that I'm her mommy…aawwwww thanks!"; "Nothing like sitting and waiting to find out if your daycare is closing."

Note that throughout the results section we report medians rather than means and conduct non-parametric statistical tests in the situations where data is not normally distributed (e.g., number of social media posts made by participants).

Demographics

348 of the 412 participants indicated how they learned of the survey; of these, 34.2% indicated that they learned of the study through the promoted posts on BabyCenter, 23.0% were recruited via posts on e-mail lists for new mothers, 12.4% were recruited via Facebook advertisements, and 10.6% via our organization's social media posts, and the remainder indicated learning of the survey through other routes (e.g., word of mouth from a friend). Most (91.3%) were external to our own organization. This broad recruitment strategy resulted in a diverse group of participating mothers along dimensions such as age, ethnicity, occupation, and socioeconomic status.

410 of the 412 participants provided their age. The average age was 31.2 years (median = 31), and ranged from 19 to 46. 0.5% were in their teens, 34.9% in their twenties, 59.8% in their thirties, and 4.9% in their forties.

As per the study call, the children whom the mothers referred to in their surveys ranged in age from newborn to three years old. On average, the child's age was 12.3 months (median 8 months). 42.5% of the children were infants, 29.6% were one-year-olds, 17.7% were two-year-olds, and 10.2% were three-year-olds. 63.8% of the mothers were completing the survey about a first-born child, while the remainder were describing experiences with respect to non-first-born children.

408 participants reported their race/ethnicity. The majority of these (75.5%) identified as Caucasian, followed by 15.0% identifying as Asian, 3.7% as Latina, 2.7% as African-American, 0.7% as Native American, and 2.5% as "Other."

407 participants gave information about their occupation, selecting from a provided set of occupational categories. Of these, the most common occupation was "Stay at Home Mom," which described 27.8%. The other 72.2% pursued a variety of careers outside the home, including work in sectors such as law, education, healthcare, science, engineering, food preparation, personal care, the arts, sales, administrative support, and the military.

359 participants provided their annual household income. Incomes ranged from $10,400 per year to $1,100,100 per year, with an average annual household income of $111,322 (median = $90,000); 22.3% had incomes below $50K/year, 30.6% between $50K and $100K, 19.2% between $100K and $150K, and 27.9% reported household incomes exceeding $150K annually.

Note that while this group of participants is diverse in many respects, it is not a representative sample of U.S. society overall. For instance, white mothers and mothers from high-income households are overrepresented. This may be a consequence of the demographics of the venues where we advertised and/or the demographics of users who possess Facebook or Twitter accounts [10, 27]. Understanding how mothers from underrepresented groups use social media and understanding the perspectives of mothers who do not use social media at all are both valuable areas for future inquiry, but are beyond the scope of this paper.

Twitter Use

77 of the respondents (18.7%) indicated that they used Twitter; this proportion is similar to that of a recent a Pew study finding that 16% of online U.S. adults had Twitter accounts in August 2012 [5]. Of the 77 who indicated that they used Twitter, the Twitter usernames of 71 were valid. Of these accounts, 9.9% were protected (with non-public status updates).

Respondents universally did not view Twitter as a medium for sharing information about their child. Not a single respondent indicated using Twitter to share tweets, photos, or videos about their child. In the survey's comments field, two mothers explained that they do use Twitter to discuss their child indirectly, by "posting [links to news] stories relevant to my child" and by "link[ing] to blog posts about my child"; another indicated that she only posted about child-related issues to the extent that she tweeted "abstract motherhood/feminist theories."

Because no mothers reported sharing specific content about their child in their tweets, we focus the remainder of our analysis on Facebook. However, although respondents all claimed not to share details about their children in their tweets, it is interesting to note that manual inspection of the 71 valid Twitter account homepages provided found that 17 of the mothers (23.9%) used a photo containing their child's face as their Twitter profile photo, and 3 (4.2%) mention the first name(s) of their child(ren) in the public bio associated with their Twitter account.

Behaviors	Examples
Questioning	• "ask other mothers questions about concerns I have" • "inquiry of appropriate behaviors, stores, products, or illnesses" • "information seeking about care"
Curation	• "linking to blog posts about baby" • "making a memory archive"
Mommy Networking	• "Facebook messaging/email with people in online forum for my baby group" • "interacting on [Facebook] pages of mom-groups"

Table 1. Example survey comments by mothers describing parenting-related appropriations of Facebook.

Facebook Use

259 (62.9%) of the mothers indicated that they used Facebook (though only 233 provided access to a dump of their Facebook timeline data). This is comparable to the 66% of online U.S. adults found to use Facebook in a recent Pew survey [5]. Of the 259 mothers who were Facebook users, 89.2% indicated that they posted Facebook status updates about their child, 96.5% said they posted photos of their child to Facebook, and 45.6% said they posted videos of their child to Facebook.

Additionally, a few respondents (4.6%) used the comments area to describe other ways in which they used Facebook for parenting-related purposes. These other uses fell into three main categories (established using open coding): *questioning*, *curation*, and *mommy networking*. Table 1 shows examples of mothers' descriptions of appropriating Facebook for each of these three activity types. Only one mother used the comment field to raise privacy issues: "I used to post about my kid, including pics (sic) and videos, but I stopped because of privacy concerns."

For the 233 mothers who provided access to a dump of their Facebook Timeline, our analysis focused only on posts authored by the mother. These posts consisted of the text associated with status updates, and captions of photos, videos, and/or links shared on the mother's Timeline/Wall.

Post Frequency

Mothers' status updates generally taper off after birth, from a median of 0.12 statuses/day in the 100 days before the birth to a median of 0.05 statuses/day after the birth. A Wilcoxon test found this to be a significant difference, $z = -6.89$, $p < .001$. Photo posting rates remain steady, however, at a median of .02 photos/day both before and after the birth; indeed, photos make up a median of only 9.8% of mothers' posts in the 100 days before the child's birth, but comprise 26.8% of posts afterward, a significant difference according to a Wilcoxon test ($z = -10.32$, $p < .001$).

Posts containing the child's name are most common in the first month after birth, during which they represent a

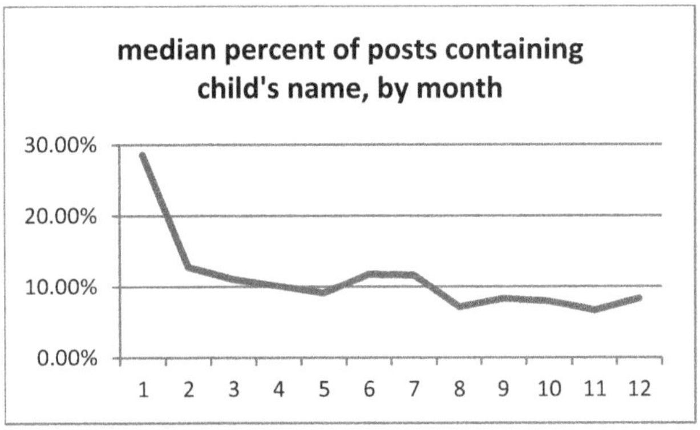

Figure 1. The proportion of a mother's Facebook posts that mention her child by name drops sharply after the first month post-birth.

median of 28.6% of all posts authored by the mother. After the first month, the proportion of posts mentioning the child's name quickly tapers off; by the second month, these comprise only 12.8% of the mother's posts, and by the end of the first year, only 8.3%; a Friedman test confirms there is a significant change in the proportion of posts mentioning the child over time, $\chi^2(2, N = 81) = 30.0, p < .001$. Figure 1 illustrates this trend over the course of the baby's first year.

Posting rate, regardless of whether the post is baby-centric, remains relatively constant after the sharp drop-off from the pre-birth median of 0.2 posts per day, holding steady at a median of 0.1 posts per day for each of the 12 months after the birth.

Post Content

A median of 13.5% of all posts written by mothers after their child's birthdate contain the child's name. For status messages, the median is 14.0%, for photos it is 14.0%, and for videos and links the median is 0%, as these latter two types of posts were relatively uncommon.

First-time mothers tend to post more about their child (median 15.3% of all posts) than non-first-time mothers (median 10.8%); a Mann-Whitney U test indicates that this is a statistically significant difference, $z = -2.98, p = .003$.

Since several mothers indicated in their survey comments that they use Facebook for questioning activities, a finding also mentioned by participants in Gibson and Hanson's (2013) ethnographic study, we examined question-asking behavior by looking at status message posts containing a question mark, a heuristic found to be reasonably satisfactory at identifying SNS questions in prior studies [18, 32]. Overall, questioning appears to be a common activity by expectant mothers and mothers of young children. For status messages posted by the mother in the 100 days before the birth of the child, the median proportion of questions is 9.4%. In contrast, after the birth of the child, question asking increases to represent 12.5% of the status updates; however, this difference is not statistically significant by a Wilcoxon test ($z = -0.79$, $p = .4$).

Category	Examples
Social Support	• "Any other moms out there have trouble falling asleep… around the 3 month postpartum mark?" • "How does one tiny person generate SO much laundry???"
Advice	• "So [anon] is going to be 6 months on the 6th and he cries everytime i try to give him solids with a spoon… any advice?" • "So dumb question...when do babies start sitting in their car seats facing forward?"
Parenting Purchases	• "Is Sophie the Giraffe really worth the price or is it just a really hyped up squeaky toy?" • "Anyone know of someone selling a crib in good condition with the new safety standards?"
Social Interaction	• "Heading to the [anonymized] Children's Center mid-day, anyone want to join us?" • "Any [anonymized location] peeps doing fun stuff for kiddos today? We need to get out some energy and would love company!"
Favor	• "Anyone have a kiddie pool I can borrow?" • "I am in need of a loving friend to watch my sweet baby for the day on Wed Jan 25. Any takers?"

Table 2. Categories of parenting-related questions asked in mothers' Facebook status messages.

A single coder iteratively developed a labeling scheme after reading samples of mothers' questions, and then two coders applied this scheme to another random sample of 100 questions. Questions were first labeled as being parenting-related or not (41% were parenting-related, Cohen's Kappa of .90). Parenting-related questions were further categorized by type (Cohen's Kappa of .81): 63.4% were seeking social support over the joys and travails of parenting, 19.5% were seeking parenting advice, 7.3% were seeking opinions or recommendations for child-related purchases, 4.9% were seeking social interaction with other parents/children, and 4.9% were seeking parenting-related favors. Table 2 shows examples of questions from each category.

We also analyzed the emotional content of mothers' Facebook posts, using the LIWC lexicon's positive emotion and negative emotion term lists. LIWC's lexicon has been validated on Internet language [33], and has been used to compute affect in several computational social science projects (e.g., [12, 13]). Each post was assigned an *emotion score* using the following process: a post's component words were compared against LIWC's positive and negative emotion lists – for each positive word, one point was added to the score, and for each negative word, one point was subtracted.

Figure 2. Word cloud depicting the most common terms appearing in the first Facebook post mothers made containing their child's name. Terms that appeared in posts from at least 10 mothers are included; word size increases proportionally to frequency of use. [wordle.net]

We call posts that have an emotion score greater than zero *positive posts* (as they had more positive than negative terms), and those with scores below zero *negative posts* (note that a *neutral post* having an emotion score of 0 is also possible, either due to a lack of use of emotionally charged terminology or due to equal use of positive and negative terms cancelling each other out). "[name] **loves** his new toy cell phone... I think it's **adorable** he **likes** to hear my voice over and over 'I **love** you [name]'!" is an example of a post identified as being positive by this method (emotion score = 4, relevant terms bolded), whereas "[name] **screamed** all **freaking** night. we finally got him to sleep and the second we put him down all **hell broke** loose." is an example of a post identified as negative (emotion score = -4, relevant terms bolded).

Overall, mothers' posts trend toward being more positive after their child's birth (mean emotion score = 0.82) than in the 30 preceding days (mean emotion score = 0.74) (t(174) = -1.81, p = .07). This is probably explained by mothers' propensity to use positive terms in posts about their child – examining only post-birth posts, those containing the child's name had significantly higher emotion scores (mean = 0.99) than those not mentioning the child's name (mean = .77) (t(225) = 5.57, p < .001). 54.3% of posts with the child's name were positive posts, compared to only 49.1% of those without the child's name (t(225) = 4.10, p < .001).

Announcing the Birth

Since we knew the date of the child's birth, but not the time, it was not possible to precisely identify the first post made after the birth (since many posts were often made on the birth date but before the birth itself, i.e., describing labor, hospitalization, or non-birth-related events). As a surrogate, we analyzed the first post on or after the birthdate that mentioned the child's name.

For the first post mentioning the child's name, 61.5% of mothers shared a traditional text-based status update, 33.6% shared a photo, 3.5% shared a link, and 1.3% shared a video. These initial posts were not necessarily made on the birth date itself (though 29.2% were); rather, the announcements came a median of two days after the birth.

Category	% of Firsts	Examples
Event	29.9%	trip; bath; swim; flight
Temporal	16.0%	night; today; tonight
Holiday	14.5%	birthday; Christmas; Easter; Halloween
Descriptive	12.7%	big; last; long; official
Developmental	12.4%	word; food; step; laugh
Health	4.1%	cold; fever; shots
Miscellaneous	10.4%	thing; duck; life

Table 3. Most prevalent categories of milestones of the form "first <X>" shared in mothers' Facebook posts containing their young child's name.

An aggregate examination of terms appearing in the first post mentioning the child confirms that these generally constitute birth announcements, with the most common co-occurring unigrams being "born" (57 posts), "baby" (45), "lbs" (44), "oz" (43),"long" (33) and "inches" (32). Figure 2 depicts the terms mentioned in first posts by at least 10 mothers.

Sharing Milestones

To understand, at an aggregate level, the ways in which mothers use Facebook to discuss child-related issues, we extracted words (unigrams) occurring in post-birth posts that mention the child's name after removing stop words, punctuation, and the child's name itself, and tally their frequencies for all 233 mothers who provided Facebook data. The five most common terms occurring in posts with a child's name were temporal: "just" (in 828 posts), "today" (755), "time" (708), "first" (695), and "day" (631).

We further explored the term "first" to understand what milestones of a child's life mothers were sharing via Facebook. We extracted the first non-stop-word unigram following the word "first" or the common phrases "first time," "first day," "first ever," or "first real" in posts containing a child's name.

We categorized these milestones using open coding with a two-pass process – a first pass to develop a set of categories based on common themes in the terms, and a second to apply a category to each term (an additional coder also applied the labeling scheme, with good inter-rater reliability of Cohen's Kappa = 0.65). All terms appearing in at least two posts were included in the categorization (93 unique terms comprising 338 "firsts"). Table 3 shows these categories and their prevalence, with examples of each; sharing milestones relating to novel events (e.g., travel, educational experiences, etc.) was most common ("[anon]'s first time sledding was a success!" "[anon]'s first Patriot's game!!"), followed by holidays ("Taking [anon] to her first Easter Egg hunt..." "[anon] went to her first Christmas party today (at dad's work)."), then by more traditional developmental milestones (e.g., walking, speaking) ("[anon] took her first steps last night! We're in for it now." "[anon]'s first words include: shoes ('szehz') and dog ('dah')..."), and lastly by health milestones (e.g., vaccinations, doctors' visits) ("Little [anon] had a day of firsts: first PB reaction, first ambulance ride and first ER visit but praise the Lord he is now doing just fine!" "First pediatrician's appointment: at 8 days old, [anon] is 3 oz above his birth weight.").

Post Reception

For each of the mother's posts, we calculated an *attention score* that equals the sum of the number of "Likes" and the number of comments the post received. While calculating the actual audience of a post is infeasible from observable post traits [2], our attention score serves as a proxy for the level of interest a user's friends had in her post (similar to the heuristics users themselves use to reflect on a post's success [2]). For example, a post receiving 2 "Likes" and 2 comments would have an attention score of 4.

On a per-mother basis, we calculated the average attention score for all post-birth posts containing their child's name, and all post-birth posts not mentioning the name. Posts mentioning the child had significantly higher mean attention scores (18.1) than those not mentioning them (9.7), according to a paired samples t-test, $t(224) = 8.35$, $p < .001$. Only 12.5% of mothers had a named/unnamed attention score ratio below 1 (indicating that this minority typically received more likes and comments for posts not mentioning their child's name).

We also identified the post receiving the highest attention score for each mother, from the date of the baby's birth onward. For these "most popular" posts, the median attention score was 55 (comprising a median of 32 "Likes" and 23 comments per post). 50.2% of these "most popular" posts mention the child's name, a much higher proportion than one would expect given that 13.5% of all post-birth posts mention the child's name ($\chi^2(1, N=233) = 269.0$, $p < .001$).

Birth announcements are highly likely to be the most attention-receiving post a mother makes. 36.5% of the "most popular" posts corresponded to those that we had automatically identified as birth announcements (the first post on or after the child's birthdate that mentioned their name). This likely underestimates the proportion of birth announcements comprising "most popular" posts – 49.4% of the posts in this set are posted within one week of the child's birth date, with most on the first 3 days (Figure 3).

Postpartum Depression

Our survey asked mothers, "Have you ever been clinically diagnosed with postpartum depression?" 92 of the mothers taking our survey (22.3%) reported having been diagnosed with Postpartum Depression (PPD), a type of depression generally commencing shortly after giving birth that the U.S. CDC estimates affects between 11% - 18% of new mothers [9].

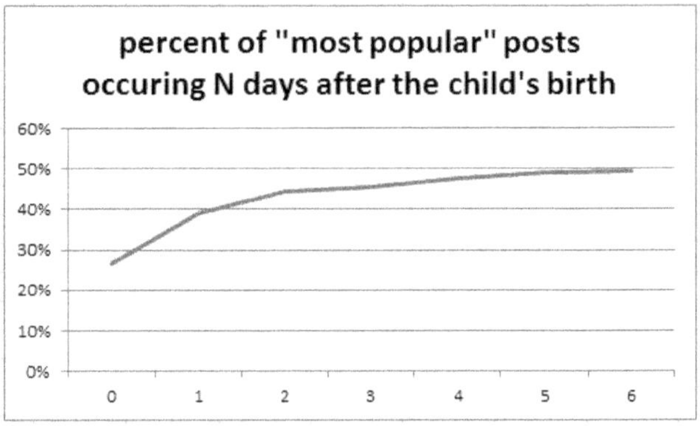

Figure 3. Of the "most popular" post for each mother (the one receiving the highest number of "Likes" and comments), almost half are likely birth announcements (49.4% occur within one week of the child's birth, and most of those occur within the first few days after birth).

Of these, 29.3% used Twitter and 79.3% used Facebook, higher rates of social networking site use than respondents without a PPD diagnosis, of whom 15.6% used Twitter and 58.1% used Facebook. These SNS usage rates of mothers with and without PPD are significantly different: Twitter: $\chi^2(1, N=92) = 13.2$, $p < .001$; Facebook: $\chi^2(1, N=92) = 17.1$, $p < .001$.

69 of the mothers who had been diagnosed with PPD provided Facebook data. Mothers with PPD were as likely to post about their child (median of 12.0% of posts, as measured by the proportion of posts containing the child's name) as those who did not report having a PPD diagnosis (median of 13.6% of posts) (no significant difference according to a Mann-Whitney U test, $z = -1.37$, $p = .17$). While there is a slight trend toward mothers with PPD posting content to Facebook more frequently, it is not statistically significant – in the 100 days before the child's birth, mothers who later received a diagnosis of PPD authored a median of 0.23 posts per day, while those without authored 0.18; after the birth, mothers with PPD authored a median of 0.12 posts per day, compared to 0.09 for those not reporting a PPD diagnosis.

Prior work [12, 13] has analyzed the relative mix of positive and negative affect of terms used in Twitter posts by mothers with and without PPD. We find that lexical analyses of emotion words also discriminates between mothers with and without PPD on Facebook. In particular, the use of negative emotional words between these two groups was significantly different post-birth (8.0% of non-depressed mothers' posts were negative compared with 9.8% for mothers with PPD, $t(231) = -2.29$, $p = .02$), though these two groups did not have significantly different proportions of negative posts in the 30 days pre-delivery ($t(173) = -1.54$, $p = .13$).

Developmental Delays

Our survey asked mothers, "Has your child been diagnosed with any of the following types of developmental delay?" Answer options were: "Language or Speech"; "Gross or Fine Motor"; "Social or Emotional"; "Cognitive"; and "Other (please specify)." 32 of the 412 mothers in our study (7.8%) reported that their child had been diagnosed with a developmental delay. Of these, 15.6% had Twitter accounts, and 53.1% had Facebook accounts (neither of which is significantly different from the proportion of mothers of children not reporting delays who have such accounts, 18.9% on Twitter, $\chi^2(1,N=32) = .22$, $p = .6$, and 63.7% on Facebook, $\chi^2(1,N=32) = 1.55$, $p = .2$).

Of those with Facebook accounts, only 58.8% reported posting status updates about their child (a much lower percentage than the 91.3% of mothers of children not diagnosed with delays who reported posting such updates, $\chi^2(1, N=32) = 49.5$, $p < .001$). However, the proportion reporting sharing photos (94.1% vs. 96.7%) and videos (47.1% vs. 45.5%) were similar to the larger pool of mothers.

15 of the mothers who reported that their child had been diagnosed with a developmental delay provided their Facebook timeline data for analysis. Mothers of children diagnosed with developmental delays tended to write fewer posts including their child's name (13.0% of posts compared to 18.1% of posts for mothers of children without a delay) – however, this is not a significant difference according to a Mann-Whitney U test, $z = -1.28$, $p = .2$; a larger sample size may be necessary to identify whether this trend reflects a true difference. The mothers of children with developmental delays used a smaller percentage of positive words in posts containing their child's name than mothers not reporting developmental delays (4.2% vs. 5.5%, $t(15) = 2.35$, $p = .03$).

DISCUSSION

Our findings provide insights into evolving sociotechnical trends regarding the media mothers find appropriate and useful for sharing information about their young children, and the ways in which they use these media. These findings have implications for the design of future technologies that meet the needs of mothers of young children.

SNS Choice

Although our participants overall had Facebook and Twitter profiles in similar proportions to the general U.S. population, our findings reveal that these networks are viewed very differently through the lens of motherhood, particularly with respect to their suitability as an outlet for sharing child-related content.

Twitter, specifically, was not viewed as an outlet suitable for posting tweets or imagery of one's child, even among the subset of users whose accounts were restricted to be private. If privacy concerns were indeed at the root of mothers' reluctance to embrace Twitter for child-related content, then the discrepancy we found in mothers' claimed avoidance of child-related posts on Twitter and the prevalence of revealing information about their child in their profile may represent a form of privacy leakage. Alternatively, the discrepancy may be due to factors such as our survey asking about what they shared in the content of tweets rather than in the account profile, inaccurate self-reporting by respondents, and/or cognitive dissonance surrounding actual versus desired behavior (i.e., embarrassment at violating social norms dictating that it may not be prudent to share a child's info on a public site).

The prevalence of photo-sharing on Facebook after a child's birth suggests another possible reason for the negative view of Twitter as an information-sharing venue – though it supports sharing imagery, Twitter's reputation and roots as a simple, text-based interaction experience may bias mothers toward using other services. Network composition might also play a role, as other studies (e.g., [4]) indicate that Twitter networks may contain lower proportions of friends and family than Facebook.

Post-Natal Changes in SNS Use

De Choudhury et al. [12] found that machine learning systems could classify major life events based on signals present in tweets, focusing largely on the positive/negative affect of terms used. Our findings indicate that similar systems could be built on Facebook, and suggest features beyond emotional valence of post terms that might be important, such as posting rate and post type. In the case of mothers of young children, a sharp and prolonged drop in posting frequency follows the birth of their child, and the use of Facebook shifts away from a text-based status update style toward a multi-media photo-sharing style. We also found that emotional terms in post-natal Facebook posts differ for specific sub-populations of mothers, with those diagnosed with PPD having higher rates of negative posts, and those whose children have developmental delays using fewer positive terms in conjunction with their child's name.

Although pop-culture sensibilities, exemplified by the Facebook app unbaby.me [11], suggest that new mothers post incessantly and exclusively about their offspring, our findings indicate that this is a greatly exaggerated perception. Indeed, mothers of young children post far less often than they did before their child's birth (at only half of their prior rate), and posts mentioning the child comprise only a small portion of their total posts. Furthermore, the proportion of posts mentioning the child drops off sharply following the first month after birth, and continues to drop as the child ages. However, the amount of attention ("Likes" and comments) given to a mother's child-related posts is much higher on average than for non-child-related posts; this may influence which of a mother's posts are given prominence in Facebook's Newsfeed algorithm (which incorporates likes and comments as a factor [14]), thus contributing to misperceptions of the proportion of parenting content in mothers' posts.

Our finding that mothers' posts are not primarily about their children substantiate the findings of an ethnographic interview study by Gibson and Hanson [16], in which new mothers indicated using social technologies, such as Facebook, to connect with others socially (in order to avoid the isolation that often comes with new motherhood) and as a channel for identity preservation, in order to maintain connections to non-mothering hobbies and interests.

Gibson and Hanson's interviewees also reported using social technologies as methods of seeking parenting advice, an increasingly common phenomenon among general SNS users, as well [29]. Our analysis shows that question posts are indeed quite common among mothers of young children, comprising 12.5% of posts, suggesting that SNSes represent an important medium not only for *sharing* information about one's child, but also for *seeking* parenting-related advice, product recommendations, favors, social interactions, and social support.

Implications and Future Directions

These insights into mothers' SNS use patterns suggest design and usability changes that such platforms might consider to optimally serve this demographic. For example, mothers of young childrens' tendency to share more photos and fewer traditional updates, their tendency to share birth announcements of a relatively uniform format, their interest in social information seeking, and their desire to curate and share key milestones in their child's life are all functionalities that could be explicitly supported by Facebook, emergent competitors, and/or app developers.

The large digital footprints created by mothers of young children have potential implications for both maternal and child health, as well. As De Choudhury et al. [12, 13] have observed, social media traces can be used to detect warning signs of serious conditions like postpartum depression. Our findings complement theirs by suggesting other related features that such algorithms might consider, such as the presence or absence of accounts on certain services, posting frequency, and the proportion of negative posts; our findings also indicate elements that do not appear to be valuable features for such distinctions, such as the proportion of posts about the child.

Although we only had a small number of mothers of children with developmental delays in our participant pool, our findings suggest that examining how technology could serve this group is an important area for further research. The decreased likelihood of sharing information about their child on Facebook that this group reported, despite being on Facebook at rates similar to other mothers, might place this group at increased risk of social isolation. Further, it might be advantageous for this group to record more detailed digital traces of their children's developmental progress – Kientz et al.'s [21] work on Baby Steps prompted mothers to record key milestones for sharing with a pediatrician in order to identify developmental delays in time for early interventions. Our findings indicate that attempting to automatically glean such milestones from mothers' Facebook posts is unlikely to be fruitful, as developmental milestones accounted for only a small percentage of the "firsts" mothers typically shared with their online social networks. However, perhaps a Baby-Steps-inspired approach could be successful if prompting for milestone entry were incorporated into Facebook, a venue where mothers are already sharing such information, rather than in the form of a standalone piece of software as originally proposed by Kientz et al.

Common patterns in mothers' Facebook use (e.g., changes in post type and frequency, similar linguistic patterns used in birth announcements, etc.) may represent privacy risks. SNS companies, app developers, advertisers, or other parties with access to users' posts may be able to automatically infer motherhood status (as well as indicators of conditions affecting a mother or her children like PPD or developmental delays) with high probability, even if users have not explicitly identified their motherhood status in their SNS profile. This information could potentially be used for ethically or legally questionable purposes, such as an employer choosing not to display "help wanted" ads to mothers of young children. The growing body of examples of implicit privacy leakages enabled by "big data" (e.g., [22]) suggest that developing social, technical, and legal protocols for handling such issues is an increasingly timely issue.

Limitations

While our study offers the first systematic insights into use of social networking sites by mothers of young children, its findings and limitations suggest valuable avenues for future work. Interviews, observations, and other ethnographic approaches (such as efforts by Foucault [15], Gibson and Hanson [16], Gulotta et al. [17], and Jomhari et al. [20]) are important complements to the types of survey- and log-based analyses we presented here. Such approaches may be particularly valuable for gaining insight into issues surrounding privacy concerns of this demographic, an issue not explicitly addressed by our study. Qualitative coding of posts might also yield more nuanced insights than the "big data" approaches used in this paper; for example, as mentioned at the beginning of the "Results" section, our heuristic of using mentions of the child's name as a proxy for identifying child-related posts underestimates the total number of such posts, but facilitated analysis of large post volumes. Manual coding of posts might yield more nuanced insights about the extent and manner of child-related social media posts.

Further log-based work may also yield new insights – for example, automated or qualitative analyses of the photos shared by mothers may shed additional light on the feasibility of using SNS traces for a "Baby Steps"-style digital diagnostic record. Understanding the richer ecosystem of SNS use by mothers of young children, including the use of within-network apps, the network structure itself, and/or the ways in which they access such sites (by phone, tablet, PC, etc.) would also be a valuable avenue for further inquiry.

Our study did not examine the intersection of fatherhood and SNS use. Understanding differences in how mothers and fathers utilize social media may be a valuable area of inquiry – for example, perhaps combining data streams from several caregivers (be they mothers, fathers, grandparents, nannies, etc.) would provide a more complete dataset for applications like automatic milestone tracking.

The use of SNSes by mothers as their children grow beyond baby- and toddler-hood is also a rich area for further study not addressed in this paper. For example, Burke et al.'s recent analysis of families on Facebook [8] indicates that SNSes provide important venues for connection and communication for parents and their teenaged and adult children.

As noted earlier, another limitation of this study is the oversampling of affluent, white women. Additionally, our sample was limited to women who currently have accounts on social networking sites. Understanding the perceptions and behaviors of mothers who choose not to use social technologies, or of those from more diverse cultural and socioeconomic backgrounds (as well as from beyond the U.S.), are open areas for further work.

CONCLUSION

In this paper, we presented the first study of how mothers of young children (aged 0 – 3 years) use the popular social networking sites Facebook and Twitter. By analyzing surveys from 412 U.S. based mothers (and associated Facebook data from 233 of them), we identified the types of content mothers share about their children, where they prefer to share it, and how their SNS use patterns change after birth. Our findings have implications for improving the utility and usability of SNS tools for mothers of young children, as well as for creating and improving sociotechnical systems related to maternal and child health.

ACKNOWLEDGEMENTS

We would particularly like to thank all of our participants, as well as Scott Counts, Munmun DeChoudhury, and Aaron Hoff (whose efforts made it possible to collect the data in this paper), and Madeline Balaam (who provided helpful pointers to related work).

REFERENCES

1. Balaam, M., Robertson, J., Say, R., Fitzpatrick, G., Hayes, G., Mazmanian, M., and Parmar, B. CHI 2013 Workshop on Motherhood & HCI.
2. Bernstein, M., Bakshy, E., Burke, M., and Karrer, B. Quantifying the Invisible Audience in Social Networks. *Proceedings of CHI 2013.*
3. boyd, d., Hargittai, E., Schultz, J., and Palfrey, J. Why parents help their children lie to Facebook about age: Unintended consequences of the 'Children's Online Privacy Protection Act.' *First Monday*, 16(11), Nov. 7, 2011.
4. Brady, E., Zhong, Y., Morris, M.R., and Bigham, J. Investigating the Appropriateness of Social Network Question Asking as a Resource for Blind Users. *Proceedings of CSCW 2013.*
5. Brenner, J. Pew Internet: Social Networking. *Pew Internet & American Life Project.* November 13, 2012.
6. Brubaker, J.R., Kivran-Swaine, F., Taber, L., and Hayes, G.R. Grief-Stricken in a Crowd: The Language of Bereavement and Distress in Social Media. *Proceedings of ICWSM 2012.*
7. Burke, M., Kraut, R., and Williams, D. Social use of computer-mediated communication by adults on the autism spectrum. *Proceedings of CSCW 2010.*
8. Burke, M., Adamic, L.A., and Marciniak, K. Families on Facebook. *Proceedings of ICWSM 2013.*
9. Centers for Disease Control and Prevention (CDC). Depression Among Women of Reproductive Age and Postpartum Depression. July 20, 2012.
10. Chang, J., Rosenn, I., Backstrom, L, and Marlow, C. ePluribus: Ethnicity on Social Networks. *Proceedings of ICWSM 2010.*
11. Considine, A. Making Facebook Less Infantile. *The New York Times.* August 8, 2012.
12. De Choudhury, M., Counts, S., and Horvitz, E. (2013a) Major Life Changes and Behavioral Markers in Social Media: Case of Childbirth. *Proceedings of CSCW 2013.*
13. De Choudhury, M., Counts, S., and Horvitz, E. (2013b) Predicting Postpartum Changes in Emotion and Behavior via Social Media. *Proceedings of CHI 2013.*
14. Facebook, Inc. "How News Feed Works." https://www.facebook.com/help/327131014036297/ Retrieved March 27, 2013.
15. Foucault, B.E. Designing Technology for Growing Families. *Technology@ Intel Magazine.* August 2005.
16. Gibson, L. and Hanson, V.L. "Digital Motherhood": How Does Technology Support New Mothers? *Proceedings of CHI 2013.*
17. Gulotta, R., Odom, W., Forlizzi, J., and Faste, H. Digital Artifacts as Legacy: Exploring the Lifespan and Value of Digital Data. *Proceedings of CHI 2013.*

18. Hecht, B., Teevan, J., Morris, M.R., and Liebling, D. SearchBuddies: Bringing Search Engines into the Conversation. *Proceedings of ICWSM 2012.*

19. Hui, M., Ly, C., and Neustaedter, C. MammiBelli: Sharing Baby Activity Levels between Expectant Mothers and their Intimate Social Groups. *CHI 2012 Extended Abstracts.*

20. Jomhari, N., Gonzalez, V.M., and Kurniawan, S.H. See the Apple of My Eye: Baby Storytelling in the Social Space. *British Computer Society HCI People & Computers*, 2009.

21. Kientz, J.A., Arriaga, R.I., and Abowd, G.D. Baby Steps: Evaluation of a System to Support Record-Keeping for Parents of Young Children. *Proceedings of CHI 2009.*

22. Kosinski, M., Stillwell, D., and Graepel, T. Private traits and attributes are predictable from digital records of human behavior. *Proceedings of the National Academy of Sciences*, Vol. 110 No. 15, Feb. 12, 2013, pp. 5802-5805.

23. Laird, S. The Rise of the Mommy Blogger. *Mashable.* May 8, 2012.

24. Le Dantec, C.A., Farrell, R.G., Christensen, J.E., Bailey, M., Ellis, J.B., Kellog, W.A., and Edwards, W.K. Publics in Practice: Ubiquitous Computing at a Shelter for Homeless Mothers. *Proceedings of CHI 2011.*

25. Madden, M. Older Adults and Social Media. *Pew Internet & American Life Project.* August 27, 2010.

26. Mendelsohn, J. Honey, Don't Bother Mommy. I'm Too Busy Building My Brand. *The New York Times*, March 12, 2010.

27. McDaniel, B.T., Coyne, S.M., and Holmes, E.K. (2012) New Mothers and Media Use: Associations between Blogging, Social Networking, and Maternal Well-Being. *Maternal and Child Health Journal*, 16(7), 1509-17.

28. Mislove, A., Lehmann, S., Ahn, Y-Y., Onella, J-P., and Rosenquist, J.N. Understanding the Demographics of Twitter Users. *Proceedings of ICWSM 2011.*

29. Morris, M.R., Teevan, J., and Panovich, K. What Do People Ask Their Social Networks, and Why? A Survey Study of Status Message Q&A Behavior. *Proceedings of CHI 2010.*

30. NBC (National Broadcasting Corporation). "Mom's on Facebook." October, 2010. http://www.nbc.com/saturday-night-live/video/moms-on-facebook/n12879/

31. NielsenWire. Infographic: The Digital Lives of American Moms. May 11, 2012.

32. Paul, S., Hong, L., and Chi, E. Is Twitter a Good Place for Asking Questions? A Characterization Study. *Proceedings of ICWSM 2011.*

33. Pennebaker, J.W., Mehl, M.R., and Niederhoffer, K.G. Psychological aspects of natural language use: Our words, ourselves. *Annual Review of Psychology*, 2002.

34. Protalinski, E. Facebook: 8.7 percent are fake users. *CNET*, August 1, 2012.

35. Schoenebeck, S.Y. The Secret Life of Online Moms: Anonymity and Disinhibition on YouBeMom.com. *Proceedings of ICWSM 2013*

36. Toma, C.L., Hancock, J.T., & Ellison, N.B. (2008) Separating fact from fiction: An examination of deceptive self-presentation in online dating profiles. *Personality and Social Psychology Bulletin*, 34, 1023-1036.

37. Van Grove, J. Facebook Lets Expectant Parents Add Unborn Children to Friends & Family. *Mashable*, August 1, 2011.

TalkBetter: Family-driven Mobile Intervention Care for Children with Language Delay

Inseok Hwang[1,2], Chungkuk Yoo[2], Chanyou Hwang[2], Dongsun Yim[3], Youngki Lee[4], Chulhong Min[2], John Kim[2], Junehwa Song[2]

[1]Center for Mobile Software Platform
KAIST
Daejeon, 305-701, Republic of Korea

[2]Dept. of Computer Science
KAIST
Daejeon, 305-701, Republic of Korea

[3]Dept. of Language Pathology
Ewha Womans University
Seoul, 120-750, Republic of Korea

[4]School of Information Systems
Singapore Management University
Singapore, 188065, Singapore

{inseok, ckyoo, chanyou, chulhong, junesong}@nclab.kaist.ac.kr
[3]sunyim@ewha.ac.kr, [4]youngkilee@smu.edu.sg, jjk12@kaist.edu

ABSTRACT

Language delay is a developmental problem of children who do not acquire language as expected for their chronological ages. Without timely intervention, language delay can act as a lifelong risk factor. Speech-language pathologists highlight that effective parent participation in everyday parent-child conversation is important to treat children's language delay. For effective roles, however, parents need to alter their own lifelong-established conversation habits, requiring extensive period of conscious effort and staying alert. In this paper, we present new opportunities for mobile and social computing to reinforce everyday parent-child conversation with therapeutic implications for children with language delays. Specifically, we propose *TalkBetter*, a mobile in-situ intervention service to help parents in daily parent-child conversation through real-time meta-linguistic analysis of ongoing conversations. Through extensive field studies with speech-language pathologists and parents, we report the multilateral motivations and implications of TalkBetter. We present our development of TalkBetter prototype and report its performance evaluation.

Author Keywords

Language delay; speech-language pathology; mobile; children; parent; smartphone; conversation; turn-taking; in-situ intervention; everyday life

CSCW'14, February 15 - 19 2014, Baltimore, MD, USA
Copyright 2014 ACM 978-1-4503-2540-0/14/02…$15.00.
http://dx.doi.org/10.1145/2531602.2531668

ACM Classification Keywords

J.3 [**Life and Medical Sciences**]: Health; C.3 [**Special-Purpose and Application-based Systems**]: Real-time and embedded systems; H.5.3 [**Group and Organization Interfaces**]: Computer-supported cooperative work

INTRODUCTION

The human ability to communicate through language is a unique blessing which is vital to develop our social relations, cognitive functions, and academic achievement [12]. The process of speech-language development is prominent in one's early childhood; young children undergo a sequence of developmental stages during which they respond to others, express themselves, and combine words to communicate with other people [28]. *Language delay* refers to a failure or difficulty in childhood to achieve these stages on the typical developmental timetable even if the child has normal nonverbal intelligence. Language delay acts as a critical risk factor during one's life; it is associated with subsequent reading/learning disorders in childhood and adolescence [12], psychiatric disorders in adulthood [2], and even serious socioeconomic outcomes such as prolonged unemployment and a paucity of social relations [5]. Language delay is also often a sign of high risk of Autism Spectrum Disorders (ASD) or Attention Deficit Hyperactivity Disorder (ADHD) [31]. An epidemiological study reports the prevalence of language impairment of 7.4% in U.S. kindergarten children [39].

Throughout decades of studies, speech-language pathologists (SLPs) have established that effective parent participation in everyday life is a crucial element for the prevention or remediation of language delay in children [9, 28, 29, 34, 36]. Toward bridging the chasm between formative clinical sessions, *parent training* emphasizes a number of guidelines and strategies for parents to keep in mind and practice in their daily interactions with their child [28]. It includes specific practices for parents to learn and become accustomed to, such as "*waiting long enough for the child to respond*," "*letting the child lead the dialogue*," "*promoting turn-taking to continue the dialogue*," etc. However, as non-experts, altering the parents' own lifelong-established interaction style is quite challenging and requires significant period of time and conscious efforts.

In this paper, we introduce new opportunities for mobile and social computing to reinforce everyday parent-child conversation, with therapeutic implications for children with language delay. As an initial effort, we aim to overlay the parent training program directly onto daily conversations, beyond a-priori prescriptions as it has been done thus far. To this end, we present the design and prototyping of *TalkBetter*, a mobile in-situ intervention service to facilitate parents' habitualization of parent training guidelines in their everyday lives. TalkBetter runs in the background on a parent's smartphone, monitoring the ongoing parent-child conversation. When the parent strays from the guidelines, TalkBetter identifies this moment and provides an in-situ reminder to the parent.

The key inspiration behind TalkBetter began with an intersection of two distinct domains: speech-language pathology and mobile social computing. Through extensive field studies with eight SLPs, we identified important implications within the parent training guidelines. We found that a meaningful number of training guidelines are not related to the linguistic contents but to a meta-linguistic perspective that abstracts a parent-child conversation as a sequence of speaking turns held by one with turn-taking from one to another. We then noted that such meta-linguistic information can be detected on-the-fly by mobile face-to-face interaction monitoring [20, 25], enabling to determine if the parent is departing from guidelines during an ongoing conversation. We carefully designed the basic service flow and key functionalities of TalkBetter. Through extensive studies with eight SLPs and 13 parents of children with language delay, we explore the parents' acceptance and the implications pertaining to the design of TalkBetter. Encouraged by their responses, we developed a working prototype and evaluated the performance of TalkBetter on real parent-child conversation data.

We propose two major CSCW contributions, extending the consistent effort in the community on computationally augmenting human conversation [20, 21]. First, we propose a vision of mobile and social computing support for out-of-clinic, life-immersive, socio-interactive care for children with language delay. Second, we propose the specific design of a mobile service for everyday reinforcement of parent training. Notably, we present inter-domain meta-linguistic intuitions which together establish the pathological foundation and the technical feasibility.

Figure 1. The treatment room for children with language delay. (Photographed at the developmental support center where we conducted our study)

BACKGROUND AND RELATED WORK

Language Delay: Etiologies, Outcomes, and Therapies

In speech-language pathology, language delay [1] broadly describes developmental problems in young children who are not acquiring language as would be expected for their chronological age [33]. The causes of language delay vary widely. For example, biological factors include anomalies in the motor cortex controlling human vocal organs, while cognitive factors include inefficient auditory processing and procedural learning. Interestingly, family environmental factors exhibit high correlations with their child's language delay. These factors include language input from parents, family socioeconomic status, and maternal education [33].

The outcomes of language delay which remain without timely intervention also largely vary in their severity levels. The child with a mild degree delay may be what is termed a *late bloomer*, who eventually catches up, learning to talk without further pathological implication. An empirical study reports that 40% of a group of two-year-old children with language delay developed into those with persistent language difficulties by the age of four [6]. Children with phonological and spelling difficulties are more likely to display difficulties in peer social interactions and problem solving [12]. A cohort with severe childhood language disorders was followed in their thirties, exhibiting severe literacy impairment, significant deficits in terms of the theory-of-mind concept, and low socioeconomic status due to prolonged unemployment [5].

For decades, SLPs have established diverse, well-structured therapeutic procedures for children with language delay. Overall, a typical clinical session for children with language delay is designed as a pair-wise playing and talking session between an SLP and the child with language delay. Figure 1 shows a treatment room with toys for language stimuli and a video camera for record keeping. While the application of specific procedures largely varies based on the preceded

[1] A delay refers to either comprehending others or producing his/her thoughts. Note that the term 'language delay' by itself includes the notion of developmental age. More specific terms such as *developmental language disorder*, or terms with notions of clinical assessments such as *specific language impairment* are also commonly used.

standardized tests and assessment strategies used, many procedures include scaffolding to promote the child's comprehension, verbalization, and sentence combining ability. For example, the SLP may present visual stimuli, syllabic or imitative clues to help the child verbalize the appropriate word. Given a word verbalized from the child, the SLP may give a two- or three-word combined phrase back to the child, such as "*mommy's shoe*" when the child has verbalized "*mommy*" while gazing at the shoe.

Our particular interest lies in the clinical implication of parents' roles and participation in the family, also known as parent training. For example, OWL "*Observe, Wait and Listen (when interacting with your child).*" is one of the guidelines for parents [28]. The basic motivation of parent training is to help the children's language development not only in clinical sessions but also in daily routines. Parent training has recently come again to the fore in speech-language pathology. While the strategy of parent training was originally proposed in the 1970s [29], its contribution has been mostly considered to be minor. However, recent empirical studies report positive changes in children's speech-language output after a parent attended parent training, such as children's increased production of initiations, requests, and information provisions in parent-child conversation [34]. Parent training also positively influences parents' perceptions of success, improving the morale of families undergoing a long struggle against their child's language delays [36]. In the section Preliminary Studies, we report example guidelines frequently given by SLPs to parents as well as the parents' difficulties of getting accustomed to parent training in daily conversations.

Computational Support for Children with Language Difficulties

A number of computer-supported systems have been proposed for SLPs to facilitate phonetics therapies in clinical sessions. Hailpern et al. presented a phonetic visualization system for SLPs, to facilitate multisyllabic speech with children with autism and language delays [10]. It provides 2-D visualization of the pitches and timings of the syllables spoken by the SLP and the child, helping the child closely to imitate the desirable pronunciation. Spoken Impact Project develops an augmented clinical environment with audiovisual cues to encourage vocalizations from children with ASD [11]. Hoque et al. reported a concept called gamification to train clinically those whose speaking rates are excessively fast [14]. By playing a teacher-controlled turtle-racing game, the subject is trained to regulate their speaking rates for better intelligibility.

LENA is a commercial speech acquisition and assessment tool for children with language delay that can be used in clinical and/or daily settings at a cost of USD 700 for a home kit [26]. The child wears on her chest a recording device which is comparable in size with a cigarette pack. Upon uploading a daily recording, the signal processing software conducts a posterior analysis to separate the recorded sound into the child's vocalizations, adult vocalizations, and other noises. LENA provides statistics over time to be examined later by SLPs, such as their vocalizing durations and the number of speaking turn exchanges between them (also known as turn-taking).

While the prior works above provide SLPs with effective computational support and clinical information, we focus on the potential of everyday contributions from the child's primary caregiver and interaction counterparts: the parents. We introduce a mobile in-situ reminder service for parents, enabling everyday conversation that momentarily reinforces the parent training. In addition, the use of commodity smartphones would encourage many parents to participate.

Life-immersive Care for Children by Mobile Sensing

Mobile sensing on children in everyday situations has been studied mostly in behavioral aspects, enabling rich contextual understanding and in-situ help. For children with autism spectrum disorder, wearable sensing technologies to detect characteristic motor behaviors were proposed to extend and enrich their clinical assessment [1, 35]. In public education programs, the children group's microscopic behaviors are monitored to find their behavioral similarities as well as individual differences under the common educational stimuli [16, 17]. Monitoring the fine-grained behavioral similarities among the classmates has been applied to keep both the children's safety and freedom in field activities [18] and to improve the children's scholastic performances [40]. These works have inspired the design goal of TalkBetter in terms of monitoring in everyday life. We believe that TalkBetter would extrapolate the efforts in life-immersive sensing for children toward the aspects of conversational interaction.

Meta-linguistic Face-to-Face Conversation Monitoring

A session of human conversation consists of a sequence of speaking turns continuously taken and given from one to another participant. In group discussion settings, Hung et al. analyzed the durations of each speaking turn and the turn-taking patterns to infer who dominated at meetings, e.g., who led the agenda or asserted themselves most often [15]. In ongoing group brainstorming settings, Meeting Mediator continuously updates the visualization of turn-related information, e.g., the durations of per-participant turns, expecting stimulatory effects such as balanced participation and active idea generation [20]. SpeakerSense is a smartphone-based system for the online identification of conversation participants based on their vocal signatures [27]. Notably, SocioPhone proposed a smartphone-based platform and meta-linguistic APIs for multi-personal face-to-face interaction monitoring in everyday natural conversations [25]. These works inspired us by suggesting that the specific ongoing mood or status of a conversation session may be intelligible by analyzing the turn-taking patterns among the participants, without inferring the linguistic meanings inside the speaking turns.

For convenience, we hereinafter use the term meta-linguistic information to refer to the turn-related attributes; i.e., for each turn, these refer to speaker's identity, the timestamps when the turn started and ended, and its prosodic effects such as pitch, tone, and speech rate.

MOTIVATION AND STUDY PROCEDURE

Initial Motivation and Intuition

It is generally known that, when the patients themselves' everyday efforts are added to existing formative treatments or medication, better clinical outcomes can be expected. The idea of parent training for children with language delay stems from such notion. Aside from a few hours a week when the child is visiting the SLP, the parents should be the primary helper for the child. To assist the parents, the SLP provides guidelines to the parents to be effective helpers. (See Table 3 for examples.) Many guidelines require the parents to alter their lifelong conversational habits, i.e., how patiently they listen and respond to their child, how fast they speak, etc. As one may expect, adhering to such guidelines during every interaction with their child requires a persistent effort and conscious attention at all times. In addition, much of the interactions can occur at any time, regardless of whether the parents themselves are tired, depressed, or preoccupied with something else.

We propose that a mobile computing opportunity exists to help parents to expedite establishing new conversational habits according to the guidelines. In particular, we identify that a meaningful subset of these guidelines are based on meta-linguistic aspects of the conversation, which implies their service feasibility based on current mobile technologies. We focus on smartphones as a platform to provide service parents with appropriate reminders at the right times to improve.

Study Procedure and Methods

Figure 2 illustrates the overall study procedure and methods. To explore our vision, our research employed a two-phase design process (Phases 1 and 2) followed by core system prototyping and performance evaluation (Phase 3).

Participants: Table 1 and Table 2 summarize the SLPs and the parents who participated in this study, respectively. We invited eight SLPs with clinical experience. For Phases 1 and 2, we recruited 13 parents who regularly visit a developmental support center (DSC) affiliated with a university in South Korea. Their children have been under treatment for only language delay or with comorbidity. For Phase 3, we recruited three parent-child pairs who visited a municipal welfare center (MWC). The children in Phase 3 were suspected of language delay based on their previous assessment but were not yet conclusively diagnosed. All the parents except one were mothers as the children are mostly accompanied by their mother when visiting the clinical facilities. We believe that this is a reasonable participant group for the purpose of our study since, particularly in the

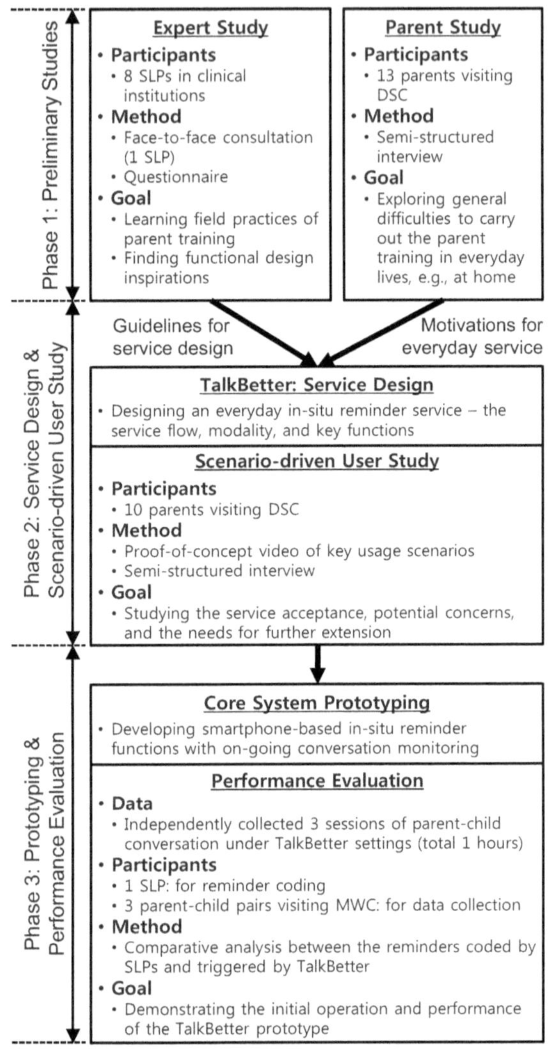

Figure 2. Overall study procedure and the phase-specific participants, methods, goals, etc. (DSC: Developmental Support Center; MWC: Municipal Welfare Center)

Korean culture, since the mother is most likely to spend significant amount of time with her child at home. As a result, the mother is often the primary caregiver and interaction counterpart of the child while having dominant influence on the child's language development. We still expected a certain extent of diverse response from the inclusion of one father (F1), but later we did not found any conflicting responses between those from F1 and his wife (M1).

Phase 1 consists of preliminary studies designed to learn the SLPs' field practices and the parents' difficulties in parent training. We first consulted one SLP via two times of face-to-face meetings (2 hours each) and a number of phone meetings. We outlined the overall clinical procedure for children with language delay and the field practices of parent training. To learn the detailed practices and extended clinical experiences from a larger group of SLPs, we conducted questionnaires with eight SLPs. Along with questions to collect their own clinical practices, the key

SLP ID	Clinical career (year)	Doctor-in-training history (year)	Approx. # of patients treated	Min. age of patients treated	Max. age of patients treated
S1	7	5	150	2	19
S2	20	7	200	0	70
S3	12.5	5	100	2	21
S4	9	6	150	2	50
S5	4	4	100	2	75
S6	5	5	70	2	31
S7	22	9	100	1	78
S8	3	3	200	0	81

Table 1. List of SLPs who participated in the study

Phases	Parent ID	Child's gender	Child's age	# of siblings (older, younger)	Child's age at beginning of treatment	Total treatment period so far (months)	Child's diagnosis
1, 2	M1, F1	F	7	0,0	5	24	LD, PDD
1	M2	F	3	1,0	3	1	LD
1	M3	F	3	0,1	2	15	LD
1	M4	M	7	0,0	7	1	LD
1, 2	M5	M	3	1,0	2	20	LD
1, 2	M6	M	3	0,0	2	8	LD, ASD, PDD
1, 2	M7	M	4	0,1	2	25	LD, ASD, PDD
1, 2	M8	M	5	0,0	3	30	LD, ASD, PDD
1, 2	M9	M	5	0,1	2	43	LD
1, 2	M10	M	5	1,0	3	24	LD
1, 2	M11	M	5	0,1	1	47	LD
1, 2	M12	M	3	0,0	3	6	LD, MR, PDD
3	M13	F	4	2,0	N/A	N/A	N/A
3	M14	M	3	0,1	N/A	N/A	N/A
3	M15	M	4	0,0	N/A	N/A	N/A

Table 2. List of parents who participated in the study (M1~M15: mothers; F1: father; LD: Language Delay; ASD: Autism Spectrum Disorder; MR: Mental Retardation; PDD: Pervasive Developmental Disorder)

questions were: "*Please list the guidelines for parent training which you frequently give to parents.*" and "*Have you received parents' feedback on the parent training guideline? If yes, please state your experiences.*"

In parallel with the study with SLPs, we conducted semi-structured interview with 13 parents individually at DSC. Each interview lasted one hour on average. (30 min~1 hour 20 min) We focused on collecting the parents' experiences in applying the parent training guidelines in their everyday conversations with their children. By coding and iteratively clustering the interview data, we found a number of difficulty factors the parents have undergone in terms of human errors, circumstantial causes, mental fatigue, etc.

Phase 2 consists of the service design of *TalkBetter* and its scenario-driven user study. Based on our findings in Phase 1, we set the major design goals of TalkBetter and designed its service flow and key functions: a background service which runs on the parent's smartphone and provides in-situ reminders based on a real-time meta-linguistic analysis of the parent-child conversation. To design the reminders, we adopted a subset of parent training guidelines which are frequently given by SLPs and would be technologically feasible with meta-linguistic information in conversations.

To study the implications of TalkBetter carefully with the clinically delicate population, we created a proof-of-concept video [18]. The video shows usage cases of TalkBetter in typical daily parent-child conversation in which five different reminders are triggered at appropriate situations. We conducted face-to-face interviews with ten parents out of those listed in Table 2. The interviews focused on finding their service acceptance levels, the prevalence of such situations in their everyday lives based on their personal episodes, and the needs for further extension.

All the interviews in Phase 1 and 2 were recorded and transcribed. Two researchers initially coded the data line by line, and iteratively clustered the codes into high-level categories until arriving at broad themes. The quotes presented in this paper are representative of the broad themes grounded in our data [37]. The interview questions are designed and organized to be nonjudgmental, open-ended, and to trigger further ideas from the participants following their responses [23]. For in-depth exploration of the participants' personal experiences in their daily lives, we adopted intensive interviewing as well [4]. All quotes in the paper are directly translated from Korean language.

Phase 3 is to study the operation and evaluate the performance of TalkBetter. Phase 3 consists of the prototyping of the core system functions and evaluating its operation with one hour of real parent-child conversation data. To avoid potential bias of the subjects influenced by the previous studies, we collected the data from parent-child pairs who did not have prior knowledge of TalkBetter (i.e., parents who were not involved in Phases 1 and 2.) We recruited three mother-child pairs who visited MWC for suspected language delay in their children. The parent-child conversation was a part of the clinical assessment process. The same conversation data were analyzed by an SLP and TalkBetter independently. The SLP listened to the conversation recording and annotated it with appropriate parent guidelines where necessary. We then conducted comparative analysis between the guidelines coded by the SLP and those triggered by TalkBetter.

PHASE 1: PRELIMINARY STUDIES

In this section, we report our major findings derived from the preliminary studies with the SLPs and the parents through the aforementioned methods.

SLPs' Field Practices in Delivery of Parent Training

The SLPs stated that the average period of language treatment for a child is roughly 12~24 months, but it largely varies depending on the child's intellectual development, the severity of language disorder, and the presence of comorbidity. Typically, a child meets her SLP two times a week, and a single clinical session takes 30~60 minutes. A session typically consists of 5~10 minutes of relaxation for the child, 20~40 minutes of clinical conversation with the child, and 5~10 minutes of a parent interview.

	Guidelines to the parents	S1	S2	S3	S4	S5	S6	S7	S8
Meta-linguistic	*"Talk more slowly."*		X	X	X	X	X	X	X
	"Wait for the child to talk back."	X			X	X	X	X	X
	"Do not interrupt the child before she completes what she says."		X			X		X	X
	"Talk in short (and simple) sentences."	X	X	X	X	X		X	X
	"Respond immediately when the child talks first."	X	X	X				X	X
	"Make more turn-takings with the child."			X			X	X	X
	"Spend more time talking with the child."					X			
	"Articulate what you speak."		X					X	X
Semantic-aware	*"Praise the child."*				X		X	X	
	"Set a topic that the child is interested in."		X			X			
	"Use positive words."				X		X	X	
	"Refrain from making one-sided instructions."			X	X		X		
	"Repeat the important keyword."	X	X						X
Facial	*"Make eye-contact with the child."*				X	X	X	X	

Table 3. Frequent parent training guidelines: the categorization and the respondents

For a parent-child pair who begins the treatment for the first time, an initial observation session is often done where the SLP observes how the parent and the child play together and interact with each other. Based on the observation, the SLP provides specific parent training guidelines to the parent. We asked the SLPs to respond with up to seven guidelines frequently given to parents. Table 3 lists the guideline responses from each SLP. These were essay questions; the original wording varied slightly, and we reworded a few responses which included multiple guidelines simultaneously, e.g., "*Praise the child and use positive words.*" SLPs sometimes give guidelines during the parent interviews in the regular sessions upon questions by a parent on how to deal with a specific situation at home.

The SLPs stated that the parents often complained about difficulties to follow the guidelines. S7 quoted a parent: "*Actually I don't talk much. I feel I became an actress. It's really weird.*" Becoming tired of the parents' own work was a common excuse. S5 quoted a parent: "*When I get back home from work, I am really tired. I'd rather turn on the TV for my kids.*" Similarly, S7 quoted a parent: "*I am too busy doing household chores, so I tend to say something first. I even yell at my kid without looking at his eyes.*"

The SLPs also noted a number of theories explaining parents' difficulties: (S1) "*Parents are often unaware of their own faults. I recorded what they said, and they were really surprised when hearing how fast they spoke.*" Sometimes the parents have an incorrect belief: (S1) "*They might believe that, if they ask again and again, then their children will eventually talk back.*", and (S3) "*They often don't understand their children's true developmental status, believing that their children are not doing what they actually can.*" The parents' former experiences of bringing up a normal child may also increase the difficulty: (S2) "*Giving totally different types of language stimuli should be hard for them.*" S2 and S4 recalled a few worse cases of parents with little effort who believed that just paying the bill for the therapy would cure their children. S6 and S7 noted that giving one guideline per week may alleviate the parents' difficulties in becoming accustomed to them.

Parents' Experiences in Reception of Parent Training

Not surprisingly, the parents we interviewed were commonly aware of many parent training guidelines. Struggling for years with their child's difficulties, some parents have studied on their own, obtaining knowledge on parent training from books or the Internet. We found there was a general consensus on positive experiences of applying the guidelines in parent training at home.

Momentary negligence: Nearly all parents confess they had (or are having) very difficult time following the guidelines all the time. A common response was, when they are busy doing household chores or preoccupied with something such as watching TV, they often do not notice that their children are talking nearby. Losing temper is a frequent reason, because the child's performance does not meet the parent's expectation: (M1) "*When I teach my daughter at home over and over, she doesn't understand what I teach her. (...) I get upset in spite of myself. (...) I start to talk faster and push her. (...) She just shuts up.*"

Extensive period of time to alter their habits: We asked how long it took until the guidelines became a part of their natural conversation habits. They responded it took almost one year on average. Notably, M1's effort was quite surprising: "*It took almost two years, but still I often make mistakes. (...) I wrote the guidelines on post-its, and put them everywhere in our home, to remind myself every moment.*" M9 was the fastest, reaching that point within three months, but she strongly emphasized: "*I was really desperate.*" We found that taking a considerable amount of time aggravated the parents' mental status, leading to, for instance, depression and feelings of failure. (M5) "*I have gone through a really long, hard time trying to get used to the [guidelines], and feel like I am a stupid mother.*"

Delayed realization of straying from the guidelines: It is also noteworthy that it often takes some significant amount of time until the parents realize themselves that they have strayed from the parent-training guidelines. (M12) "*I found myself just talking alone to explain a bird flying by, not responding to my son's responses. (...) I later realized that*

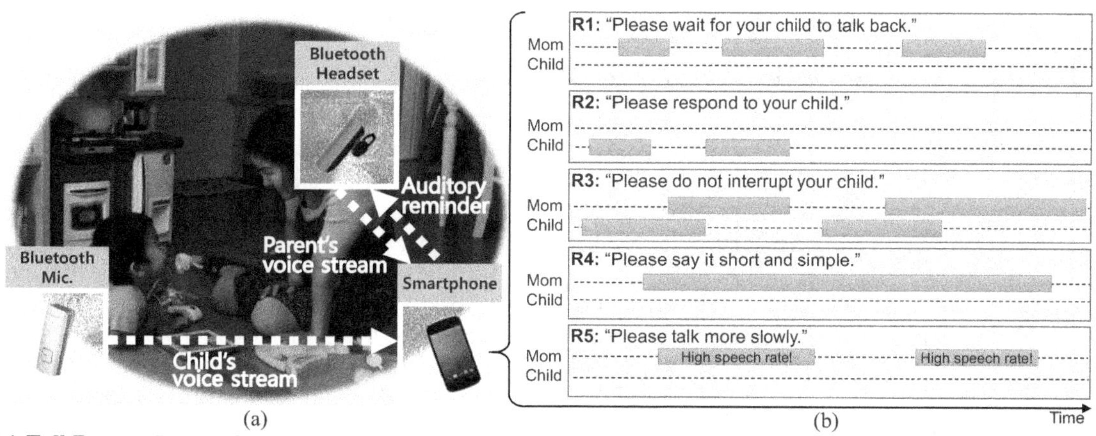

Figure 3(a) TalkBetter: data and service flow, (b) reminder IDs and triggering situations based on meta-linguistic conversation lineation (The child in the photograph does not have language delay or a developmental disorder.)

he didn't understand what I was saying, and talked to him again with just a couple of words." M6 stated a similar experience, "*I often don't realize that I am upset until somebody else asks 'what's wrong with you?'*"

Extra burden to train family members: M5 pointed out an excessive burden of herself, trying to change not only her own conversation habits but also those of other family members. "*I am usually the only one in our family who finds and learns [parent training guidelines]. You know, my husband has to make money. (...) Then, I have to teach my husband and [the older son] what I've learned.*"

Too slow start: We conjecture that the parents' perceptions of success also greatly impact upon their will whether to keep trying to practice the guidelines or not. M6 stated, "*At first, I was really enthusiastic to try anything that might help. You can find from the Internet tons of things that claim to be effective. [After several months], however, my son's change was too subtle. I could hardly see any. (...) Later on, I learned about [parent training], but I got tired of pushing myself so hard to try something new.*"

PHASE 2: SERVICE DESIGN OF TALKBETTER AND SCENARIO-DRIVEN USER STUDY

The preliminary studies delivered a number of cornerstones with which we began designing the overall system and its key functionalities. First, expediting becoming habituated to the parent training guidelines is highly beneficial to the parents to bring forward their perception of success, retain a high level of motivation, and prevent prolonged mental suffering. The parents are motivated to learn and become accustomed to the guidelines, especially early in the treatment process. However, they have undergone year-long struggles, which gradually consumed their motivation and patience. Second, opportunities to cover instances of momentary negligence in everyday life are quite prevalent. In particular, becoming aware of one's own straying from a guideline may not be immediate. A prompt reminder would be helpful to identify one's own frequent habits and to correct them as early as possible. Third, as shown in Table 3, a meaningful number of parent training guidelines frequently given by SLPs are based on meta-linguistic aspects of ongoing conversations. This observation sheds light on the technical feasibility of these guidelines in which recent advances in mobile computing and meta-linguistic conversation monitoring can be utilized.

Service Design and Key Functions

Figure 3(a) illustrates the data and service flow of TalkBetter, a mobile in-situ intervention service to reinforce parent training in daily parent-child conversation. For unobtrusive access to many of the daily conversations, TalkBetter runs on the parent's smartphone in the background. The key functions of TalkBetter are three-fold: continuous capturing of voice activities from the parent and the child, meta-linguistic conversation lineation to monitor the ongoing turn-taking patterns, and in-situ triggered gentle auditory reminders through the parent's earphone.

To reliably detect voice from the parent, the child, or both, TalkBetter employs two wearable 5-cm-long Bluetooth microphones: a clip-type microphone for the child and an ear-worn headset for the parent. In the process of meta-linguistic conversation lineation, the ongoing conversation is graphed into a turn-taking sequence, as shown in Figure 3(b). To identify moments when the parent is likely straying from a predefined guideline, the following basic attributes are monitored: the length of ongoing individual turns, the length of ongoing pauses between adjacent turns, the temporal overlap of a parent's turn over a child's turn, and the switches of turns from the parent to the child, and vice versa. In addition, TalkBetter estimates the speech rate for each turn based on the rates of syllable production [7, 41].

Figure 3(b) lists the five reminders and their IDs (R1-R5) for the initial service design, which we carefully chose out of those in Table 3. On average, 5.8 SLPs out of the eight included these guidelines within their list of guidelines frequently given to parents. Note that a few meta-linguistic guidelines in Table 3 are not included in our initial design. The guidelines "Make more turn-takings." and "Spend more time talking with your child." focus on changing the parents' overall conversation style in a comprehensive

Parent ID	Service acceptance	Personal episodes similar to the demonstrated cases					Reminder-specific extension	Concerns	
		Case 1	Case 2	Case 3	Case 4	Case 5		Wearability problem	Privacy problem
M1,F1*	Y	2	2	1	1	-	R4	N(c)	N(c)
M5	Y	1	1	3	3	1	-	N(c)	N
M6	Y(c)	2	-	1	2	-	R4	N(c)	N
M7	N	-	-	1	1	1	-	Y	N
M8	Y	1	1	-	2	2	-	N	N
M9	Y	1	1	-	1	1	-	N(c)	N
M10	Y	3	1	1	1	2	R3	N(c)	N
M11	Y	1	1	2	2	1	R3	N(c)	N
M12	Y(c)	-	-	-	2	1	R1, R5	N(c)	N

Table 4. High-level summary of the parents' responses. Y: yes | N: no | (c): with a conditional remark. (*M1 and F1 are considered as a single respondent because most responses from one were followed by the other's agreement, and also they referred to episodes they commonly experienced in their family)

manner, while we initially focus on spotting momentary opportunities for a specific reminder to be applied at once. To develop the guideline of articulation, we believe a highly sensitive speech dictation would be required for everyday application. We leave this as a future work.

A reminder of a specific guideline is triggered upon a match between the ongoing turn-taking patterns and the predefined conditions. For example, R1 in Figure 3(b) is triggered if the parent's turns appear repetitively without sufficiently long pauses between them and no child's turn appears along the parent's turns. S8 noted that the parameters – the number of repetitions and the upper limit defining an insufficient pause – are subject to the SLP's prescription followed by an assessment of each parent-child pair. Whether to activate a specific reminder or not is also subject to the prescription. The prescription depends on factors such as the developmental age of a child, her responsiveness to external stimuli, and the parent's conversational habits. However, an in-depth study of child-specific prescription is beyond the scope of this paper.

Scenario-driven User Study

When a service is used for a clinically delicate population, the premature deployment of the service on the population is unacceptable. To be cautious, we instead conducted scenario-driven user study to find the implications of service acceptance, potential concerns, and the needs for further extension. To facilitate the user studies, we created a proof-of-concept video which included multiple usage scenarios [18]. With proper consent, we filmed a half-day routine of a mother and her three-year-old son, including typical daily conversations both at home and while taking a walk. We included the following use cases in the three-minute video at which the appropriate reminders are triggered in-situ by TalkBetter.

- **Case 1:** Their activity involves cutting colored paper. The mother shows her son what she has cut out and repeatedly asks "*What does it look like?*" while the son is neither responding nor showing interest. (R1 is triggered)
- **Case 2:** The mother is focusing on her smartphone, and does not respond to her son nearby who has initiated short verbalization twice. (R2 is triggered)
- **Case 3:** In the paper cutting situation, the son babbles but the mother interrupts him, asking what she wants to ask, "*Shall we go out? When?*" (R3 is triggered)
- **Case 4:** They are playing at a local playground; the mother explains to her son playing seesaw is dangerous to him but her explanation is very long. The son remains quiet and hardly makes eye contact. (R4 is triggered)
- **Case 5:** They are walking; the mother tells her son that they should stop by a place, but she speaks so fast that her son just says "*No*" repeatedly. (R5 is triggered)

With the video, we conducted semi-structured interviews with 10 parents individually, each interview lasting approximately one hour. Table 4 summarizes their responses in major categories obtained through the methods described previously. Our questioning sequences varied depending on the parent's responses for effective exploration within the given time, but to list the key leading questions: "*Did you have personal experiences similar to [the cases in the video] this week (or month)?*", "*If TalkBetter is available now, would you like to use it with your child?*", "*What are the reasons for you to use (or not to use) TalkBetter?*", "*If you can modify or add something to the current TalkBetter service, what would you like to do?*", "*If you use TalkBetter with your child at your home, do you expect problems or concerns?*", etc. To report the detail, we present the representative quotes below.

Prevalence of personal episodes similar to the cases demonstrated: Within each individual interview, we could elicit on average five personal episodes per parent similar to the cases shown in the video. There was a consensus among the parents that such situations are very frequent in their everyday routines. Situations similar to Case 1, 3 and 5 commonly occur when they are doing what they should do, e.g., having the child eat meals, getting the child dressed, and preparing to go out, as the parents get hasty and expect their child to cooperate in doing such imminent tasks. Situations similar to Case 2 commonly occur when the parents are preoccupied with things like web surfing or texting with their mobile devices. Situations similar to Case 4 often occur when the parents keep talking and explaining, believing that doing so may elicit the children's response. Getting upset is a frequent cause for Case 3, 4, and 5.

Service acceptance of TalkBetter: Nine parents showed strong interest in using TalkBetter. (M5) "*I would not have spent a year to get used to [the guidelines] if I had [TalkBetter]. (...) I am very curious if [her son] can extend his language much faster (with TalkBetter).*" Even M1 and F1 asked: "*Can we buy this now? How much is this?*" M6 liked that TalkBetter is simple and easy: "*Once your child is diagnosed with language delay, you will find tons of* *things that claim clinical effects. It's simply impossible to learn and try everything. (...) I love that this is ready-made, doesn't ask me to learn.*" M11 liked its language-independent characteristics: "*My son is bilingual in Korean and English. I buy this, and it will work on both, right?*" A clinical implication regarding M11's comment is that parent-mediated intervention is important to facilitate the development of bilingual children's home language, which SLPs do not speak [22]. Notably, F1 liked the phone-driven reminders for an interesting reason: "*When I make a mistake (against the guidelines), [M1] points out that I was wrong. Over and over, I feel like I am insulted by my wife. (...) I like [the reminders] are coming from the machine, not my wife. (...) It would not be a matter of affection between us.*"

M6 and M12 appended minor concerns while agreeing to the effectiveness of TalkBetter. (M6) "*(Referring to her experiences that she tried many things without much effect) I might lose interest if I don't perceive improvement within several months.*" M12 pointed out that TalkBetter would be appropriate to children who attained at least a minimum level of making responses and turn-takings. "*My son could hardly do turn-takings until a few months ago. I might not have been interested if I saw [TalkBetter] at that time.*"

M7 declined to use TalkBetter because she had an urgent priority in her son over his language delay, which is the recently aggravated hyperactivity disorder accompanied by his autism. Her immediate demand was a tool to prevent her son's sudden violent behaviors such as hitting other people or taking other people's belongings.

Further needs for functional extension: The parents were enthusiastic to suggest extended features based on their own experiences. Regarding the reminder R4, M1 wanted different presets of triggering conditions or selective turn-on/off instances: "*When I read a book for her, I am supposed to keep talking.*" M6 suggested a different extension regarding R4: "*(Upon a reminder to say it short) What if I don't know how to rephrase it to be shorter? I would like a handy interface to make instant search.*"

M10 and M12 pointed out that, in urgent situations, they cannot help but ignore the reminders such as R1, R3, or R5. For example, M12 stated, "*When he is touching the electrical outlet, I must rush and say 'Don't! Don't! Don't!'*", where she is forced to say fast and repeatedly, no matter what her child says. The urgent and unpredictable nature may render the aforementioned multi-preset strategy inapplicable. A quick and simple workaround would be an one-touch reminder suspension feature that works by overriding one of the buttons embedded in the Bluetooth headset. Likewise, M11 stated that sometimes she purposely interrupted her son while he was talking in order to clarify what he meant. We believe the instant override strategy may be applicable in this case.

Besides the initial five reminder functions, M1, F1, M6, M9, and M10 wanted a reminder when they were about to lose (or have lost) their tempers. Interestingly, F1, who is a software developer, suggested technical clues such as capturing the steep rise of the vocal tone and fluctuations in the pitch. M11 asked for an additional function to determine if an utterance is either a question or a declarative sentence: "*Our SLP advises me to speak in sentences, rather than in questions, (...) such as 'Don't say 'Do you like that flower?' but instead say 'Oh, you are watching the flower.''*" A notable suggestion was given by M1, which gives verbal rewards to herself when she is conforming well to the guidelines: "*It's exhausting to care for [a child with prolonged disorder]. Sometimes I need to be cheered up.*"

Wearability of the microphone: Nine parents expected that the 5-cm-long microphone would be acceptable to their children. They expected that at first, their children might show excessive interest in the new item. M5 and M9 expected a few days for their children to get used to the microphone. M1, F1, M6, and M11 suggested redesigning the microphone to look more natural, like a button or a name-tag. M10 and M12 suggested making a small pocket on the child's shirt to hide the microphone. However, M7 was not optimistic in microphone usage because of her son's hyperactivity disorder.

Privacy concerns: Not surprisingly, the clinical concerns for the parents by far exceeded any privacy concerns. No parents raised privacy concerns as long as only the meta-linguistic features are extracted. M5 did not care whether the raw conversation would be saved or not. M8 even insisted that the raw conversation should be kept for potential future use. However, M1 and F1 were cautious in terms of third-party privacy in case of TalkBetter usage is extended beyond the family: "*We are perfectly fine, but we should respect the privacy of kindergarten teachers or other children. We may need to be careful when [TalkBetter] goes beyond family conversations.*"

PHASE 3: PROTOTYPING AND EVALUATION

Encouraged by the promising user responses in Phase 2, we proceeded toward building a working prototype. The implementation was inspired by previously proposed context sensing platforms in terms of peer detection, cross-device cooperative sensing, and conversational interaction monitoring [24, 25]. We describe the key architecture of TalkBetter prototype, and provide its performance evaluation results on parent-child conversation datasets.

Core System Prototyping

Figure 4 shows an overview of the architecture on a Google Galaxy Nexus running Android OS 4.1+. To work around the limitations of the default Bluetooth headset profiles allowing only one Bluetooth microphone to be connected, the prototype runs on two smartphones: Phone A paired

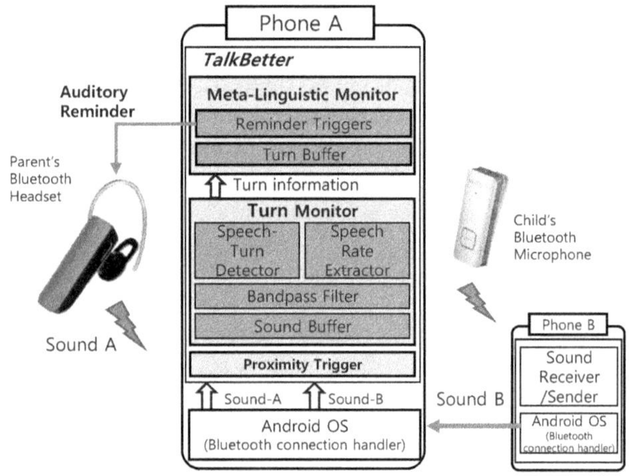

Figure 4. Architecture overview of TalkBetter prototype

with the parent's headset and Phone B with the child's microphone. [2] Each phone continuously receives sound signals from its microphone through a band-pass filter focused on the human voice spectrum. Phone B forwards the filtered signals to Phone A in real time. Phone A is responsible for combining and processing the sound signals, performing the meta-linguistic lineation as shown in Figure 3, and determining when and which reminder should be triggered. As a result, Phone A has two major processing components: a *Turn Monitor* and a *Meta-Linguistic Monitor*.

Turn Monitor extracts conversational *turns* by abstracting raw sound signals collected from both phones. As a conversation progresses, it identifies turns continually and annotates each turn with a quadruple consisting of the following information, (*speaker*, *start time*, *duration*, *speech rate*). We devised a simple but effective turn-detection method assuming reasonably calm home situations. Intuitively, a turn is detected when the volume of an input sound signal exceeds a certain threshold. Since the microphone is in close proximity to the speaker's mouth, the volume of the speaker's voice is prominent to the microphone. Accordingly, our method first segments the continuously incoming sound signal into unit of frames, e.g., 0.3 seconds, and calculates the average volume for each frame. A frame whose volume exceeds a threshold is considered as a part of a turn. This process repeats over continuous signals, growing the duration of the turn until it ends if the succeeding frame is determined as silence.

The parent and the child may talk at the same time, which we call an overlapped turn. However, we observed that a static threshold sometimes outputs falsely overlapped turns; one's utterance undesirably increases the volume captured by the other's microphone but by a far reduced scale. To filter out false overlaps, we employ a second-stage threshold determining the overlapped turns only if the ratio between two concurrent frames' volumes does not exceed it. Along with the turn information, *Speech Rate Extractor* detects the speed of a parent's speech by estimating the number of syllables pronounced during the turn [7, 41].

[2] Single-phone-based implementation is possible in many ways, for example by connecting two custom-designed sound sensors via Bluetooth serial port profile.

Session (parent's ID)	Person	# of turns	Precision	Recall
M13	Parent	301	0.83	0.93
	Child	205	0.73	0.78
M14	Parent	293	0.83	0.87
	Child	139	0.69	0.77
M15	Parent	263	0.81	0.89
	Child	239	0.73	0.83

Table 5. Summary of turn monitoring evaluation

Meta-Linguistic Monitor continuously matches the ongoing turns with the triggering conditions for the reminders in Figure 3. Upon the detection of each turn, it evaluates if any triggering conditions for reminders are newly satisfied based on the previous turn histories stored in its buffer. The conditions to trigger each reminder are as follows.

R1: triggered if a parent's turns repeat $N_{dominance}$ times in which pauses between adjacent turns are shorter than T_{wait} AND no child's turn appears during these parent turns.
R2: triggered if the following condition repeats N_{grace2} times: Given a child's turn, neither a parent's nor a child's turn follows within time duration $T_{neglect}$.
R3: triggered if a parent's turn begins before the child's turn ends for N_{grace3} times.
R4: triggered if the duration of a parent's turn is longer than T_{long} AND no child turn follows within $T_{response4}$ after the parent's turn ends.
R5: triggered if the estimated syllable rate of a parent's turn is higher than R_{fast} AND no child turn follows within $T_{response5}$ after the parent's turn ends.

Performance Evaluation

We evaluated the performance of the TalkBetter prototype in terms of turn-monitoring and reminder-triggering with real parent-child conversations. For the evaluation, we recruited three parents who visited MWC, i.e., M13, M14, and M15 in Table 2, who did not have prior knowledge of TalkBetter. For assessment purposes, each parent-child pair had a 20-minute free conversation session under an SLP's observation. We recorded the conversation from each session by deploying the TalkBetter prototype, obtaining 1 hour of conversation data consisting of 857 parent turns and 583 child turns. Note that we disabled the in-situ reminder triggers for clinical precaution so as not to affect the original assessment.

Turn-monitoring evaluation: We first report the accuracy of turn monitoring performed by TalkBetter. For each 0.3-sec frame, we compare the output from Turn Monitor with the ground truth coded manually. If a frame is classified as a part of a turn from both TalkBetter and ground truth, we consider it as a true-positive. If a frame is classified as a part of a turn from TalkBetter but not from the ground truth, we consider it as a false-positive, and so on. Table 5 summarizes the evaluation results for each session and each person of the turns (either the parent or the child).

The major factor degrading the precisions was the noises from the parent-child pairs' playing activities during the assessment. They played with various toys many of which often generate nontrivial sound such as speaking dolls. The choices of toys varied for each child, so that frequent use of sound-generating toys resulted in a lower precision such as that of M14's child. On the other hand, the recalls are degraded mainly due to mumbling or quiet utterances below the conservatively set threshold against activity noises.

Overall, we observe lower precision and recall for the children's turns than the parents'. This is mainly because the children often touched the microphone clipped on their shirts. Note that the parents in Phase 2 expected a few days to get used to or minor design modifications for the children.

Reminder-triggering evaluation: We also evaluate the validity of the reminder triggering. For the purpose, we compare the reminders generated by TalkBetter with those hand-coded by an SLP. The SLP listened to the recordings from the conversations and examined the transcriptions as well. The SLP then coded the conversations with the reminders R1 ~ R5 where she determined appropriate.

We first demonstrate a case of TalkBetter operation where it triggered an appropriate reminder. Figure 5 shows a 7-sec snapshot from the M14's session in which the parent turns repeated without a child turn in the middle, where R1 was triggered by TalkBetter. We can observe the raw sound signals of the parent-child pair, the detected turns, and the triggered reminder.

Table 6 summarizes the results: the reminders coded by the SLP, triggered by TalkBetter, and the matches between those two, for each session and each reminder type. In total, we observed 22 correctly matched reminders, 9 falsely triggered ones by TalkBetter, and 11 missed ones. We analyzed every mismatch, and discuss the findings below.

Nonverbal responses: In two cases, TalkBetter falsely triggered R1. Although there was no apparent turn from the child while the parent was making repeated turns, the SLP did not suggest reminders on these cases. Based on the recorded conversation, she presumed that the child likely made proper responses in a nonverbal, behavioral way. Similarly, in one case, TalkBetter falsely triggered R2. No parent turn followed the child's turn, but the SLP thought that the parent likely made a nonverbal response.

Speech rate changes in mid-turn: In one case, the SLP suggested R5 for a 3-sec parent turn since she determined that the parent spoke too fast, but TalkBetter did not. We found that the speech rate was fast indeed for the first one second. But it dropped and remained at a typical rate for the rest of the turn, resulting in an average rate not exceeding R_{fast}. The SLP later explained that the speech rate was fast

Session	Reminder by	The Number of Reminders					
		R1	R2	R3	R4	R5	Total
M13	SLP	0	0	4	2	5	11
	TalkBetter	1	1	3	2	4	11
	Match	0	0	3	2	3	8
M14	SLP	7	1	0	1	0	9
	TalkBetter	5	2	0	1	0	8
	Match	3	1	N/A	1	N/A	5
M15	SLP	2	8	3	0	0	13
	TalkBetter	3	7	2	0	0	12
	Match	2	6	1	N/A	N/A	9

Table 6. Summary of reminder triggering evaluation

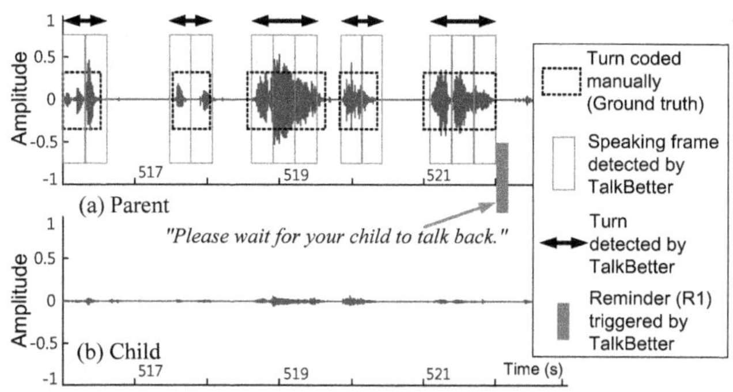

Figure 5. A snapshot of turn-detection and reminder-triggering

particularly around the keywords in the turn, thereby perceived the overall speech rate to be higher.

Linguistic factors affecting reminder suggestions: In one case, the parent repetitively made her turns more than $N_{dominance}$ times, and TalkBetter triggered R1. But the SLP thought that the parent's turns were not that many because the parent changed the topic of question after a couple of turns. In another case, the repetition of parent's turns was less than $N_{dominance}$ times but the SLP suggested R1 because those turns were exactly the same questions.

Misidentified turns: The majority of mismatched reminders were caused by the misidentified turns from the underlying Turn Monitor. We discuss potential technical approaches to improve turn-monitoring in the Discussion section.

Interestingly, we observed distinctively higher frequencies of specific reminders for each parent, which were consistent with the SLP's assessment of their individual conversation styles. In Table 6, M13 has relatively higher reminders of R3 and R5. The SLP assessed that M13 tends to speak fast, resulting in frequent interruptions and fast utterances. The SLP assessed that M14 tends to make many questions, which is consistent with the higher frequency of R1 for M14. The SLP stated that M15 tends to pay less attention to the conversation with her child, which explains the notably high frequency of R2. This observation demonstrates that each parent has certain conversation habits for which they may require focused help. We believe that the specific set of reminders fit to each parent could be determined by SLPs. By selectively enabling only the reminders prescribed, we may be able to further reduce little necessary or falsely triggered reminders and improve the usability of TalkBetter.

DISCUSSION

Limitations

Participant recruitment in Phases 1 and 2: As discussed earlier, we believe that the dominance of mothers in our participants is reasonable as an initial study group because of the Korean cultural factors. Nonetheless, including various opinions from other family members such as more fathers and siblings would make our system more concrete. It would be worth exploring to extend TalkBetter to encompass the social peers in the trusted network [13] who are willing to support the child with language delay.

Most of the recruited parents had prior knowledge of parent training at home, despite their difficulties in applying it on everyday conversations. Although we invited such experienced parents during our design process, we expect the TalkBetter service would be useful and helpful for the parents who have just started language care for their children, i.e., who lack knowledge and experience in parent training. In near future, we plan to derive the effectiveness of TalkBetter from inexperienced parents.

Social burden of the primary conversation partner: To use TalkBetter, parents need to pay attention to the auditory reminders during conversations, which might act as additional burden. However, according to our interview, the parents are willing to accept it for the treatment purposes. They state that they are able to keep their motivation high if they see the progress of their child's language. One may be concerned that the parents might feel nagged as they hear the same auditory reminders again and again for months. We expect that simplified reminders, such as short chimes, would suffice for long-term users. To be optimistic, we believe that such experienced parents may receive less and less reminders, mitigating the issue of getting bored as well.

Technical limitations: From the evaluation, we observed falsely detected turns mainly caused by unexpected noises. For example, the speaking doll's speech was misclassified as human voice. Another case occurred when a child touched the attached microphone. There are other scenarios at home that may introduce noise problems such as the TV or radio. The child's microphone may shake when the child runs around. TalkBetter may also falsely detect overlapped turns at home when the parent and the child are talking very close to each other, e.g., the mother reads a book while holding her child in her arm. In this case, one's speech may be captured by the both microphones at a similar volume.

Although these limitations have not resulted in severe concerns in our evaluation, we need to improve TalkBetter for further deployment in more diverse environments. For example, to suppress background noise and separate the speaker's voice, we can apply noise cancellation techniques [3] or employ highly selective microphones [8, 32, 38]. We internally conducted a pilot test with a throat microphone [38] that was very effective in preventing falsely overlapped turns. The throat microphone was designed to be in contact with the skin around the vocal cord, thereby sensing only the speaker's own voice. However, we are cautious about potential discomfort of the child with commercially available throat microphones. Employing a statistical model for speaker identification would be also practical, as we need only a few speaker models for home use [27]. Overall, we believe that these strategies would further help overcome the technical limitations.

Extensibility in Various Settings

We believe the key feature of TalkBetter monitoring and intervening in ongoing conversations can be extended for a broad range of applications beyond the setting of this paper.

Beyond parent-training: To assist the social lives of children with language delay, it is important to guide not only the parents but also other people in the children's daily social circles. The SLPs consider the peer friends such as kindergartens as one of the most concerning groups. They are too young to understand the language delay of their friend and the needs for attentive care. They often consider the child idiotic and make him isolated. The SLPs and we discussed a social game designed to elicit the children's responses in a well-balanced manner. It shows an interesting avatar, which gradually grows when the game detects evenly distributed utterances from the children. Not necessarily to be two-way interactive, TalkBetter can also create a log of conversational patterns for diverse daily conversations. These logs can be leveraged afterwards by SLPs to evaluate the progress of language ability in more natural settings, compensating the SLP's highly limited interaction with the child in terms of duration and place.

Other clinical training program: S8 suggested that TalkBetter can be also useful when used with the Lee Silverman Voice Treatment (LSVT) – a speech training for patients with Parkinson's disease to increase vocal loudness. These patients have difficulties in sending neural signals to voice-producing muscles, resulting in a much quieter voice even when they believe it is sufficiently loud. TalkBetter may extend LSVT toward the patients' daily lives without necessarily visiting a therapist at a clinic.

Daily face-to-face conversations: We believe there would be opportunities in normal people's daily conversations where useful in-situ assistance can be provided. We address mitigating the awkward silences [30], i.e., uncomfortable pauses in the middle of conversation. The people in the conversation feel anxieties and pressure to speak something but have no idea what to talk next. With help from social networking services, TalkBetter can be extended to suggest a topic of common interest once it detects characteristic patterns of pauses indicating a possible awkward silence [30]. Another extension of TalkBetter would be to facilitate balanced participations in group brainstorming such as in Meeting Mediator [20] with commodity smartphones.

Implications in Parents of Normal Children

The SLPs commented that they believe a large number of undiscovered children with language delay exist. Especially in Korean culture, parents are often reluctant to consult SLPs despite their suspect of slower language development in their children; they may blindly believe it will disappear, deliberately not accept the presence of it, or be afraid that people will learn that their child has a disorder. The SLPs expect that commodity services like TalkBetter may narrow the chasm between consulting an SLP and doing nothing.

Inspired by these comments, we conducted interviews with seven parents of normal children after showing our video. Two of them have pressing concerns about their children's language but mostly related to learning slang from the local community. Nevertheless, they agree the problematic situations in our video apply to their daily routines. One was shocked at her own habits and the outcomes: "*[Ignoring what my kid says] happens every day, when I am watching my smartphone. [In the video], I clearly see in [the child's] face that he is disappointed [as soon as he is ignored by his mom]. (...) Perhaps the same thing happens to my kid and I feel really sorry [to my child].*"

CONCLUSION

In this paper, we present new opportunities for mobile and social computing to facilitate everyday parent-child conversation with therapeutic implications for children with language delay. As a first step, we developed TalkBetter, an in-situ intervention service for parents to reinforce parent-training. We conducted extensive domain-specific studies with speech-language pathologists and parents whose child has language delay. We found the clinical and habitual motivations, reinforced our design, and derived further implications. We explored the inter-domain intersection from the meta-linguistic aspect of speech-language pathology and mobile computing. We envision that TalkBetter is the first step toward life-immersive socially-driven care for those with speech-language difficulties.

ACKNOWLEDGEMENTS

We thank all the anonymous reviewers for their insightful reviews which improved this paper. We thank all the SLPs and the parents who participated in this study. Especially we thank the SLPs Seokjeong Yeon, Minkyoung Kang, and Ji Young Na for their considerable effort and constructive comments. Special thanks to Cheon-Hee Park, Jeeyae Koo, and Taiwoo Park for their generous opening of their half-day family life. We also thank our colleagues and friends, Aram Choi, Miri Moon, Jaeung Lee, Jaemyung Shin, and Soonyoung Kwon for their assistance. This work was partly supported by National Research Foundation of Korea (NRF) grant (No. 2011-0018120) and by Next-Generation Information Computing Development Program through NRF (No. 2010-0020729), both funded by the Korea government (MSIP). This work was also partly supported by the IT R&D Program of MOTIE/KEIT [2012, 10041313, UX-oriented Mobile SW Platform].

REFERENCES

1. Albinali, F., Goodwin, M. S., Intille, S. S. Recognizing Stereotypical Motor Movements in the Laboratory and Classroom: A Case Study with Children on the Autism Spectrum. Proc. *UbiComp 2010*.
2. Beitchman, J. H., Wilson B., Johnson, C. J., Atkinson, L., Young, A., Adlaf, E., Escobar, M., Douglas, L. Fourteen-year Follow-up of Speech/Language-impaired and Control Children: Psychiatric Outcome. *American Academy of Child and Adolescent Psychiatry*, 40, 1 (2001), 75-82.
3. Boli, S. Suppression of acoustic noise in speech using spectral subtraction. *IEEE Trans. Acoustics, Speech and Signal Processing*, 27, 1 (1979), 113-120.
4. Charmaz, K. *Constructing Grounded Theory: A Practical Guide through Qualitative Analysis*. Sage Publications, 2006.
5. Clegg, J., Hollis, C., Mawhood, L., Rutter, M. Developmental Language Disorders: a Follow-up in Later Adult Life. Cognitive, Language, and Psychosocial Outcomes. *Child Psychology and Psychiatry*, 46, 2 (2005), 128-149.
6. Dale, P. S., Price, T. S., Bishop, D. V. M., Plomin, R. Outcomes of Early Language Delay: I. Predicting Persistent and Transient Language Difficulties at 3 and 4 Years. *J. Speech, Language, and Hearing Research*, 46 (2003), 544-560.
7. De Jong, N. H., Wempe, T. Praat Script to Detect Syllable Nuclei and Measure Speech Rate Automatically. *Behavior Research Methods*, 41, 2 (2009), pp. 385-390.
8. Electret condenser lavalier microphones. http://pro.sony.com/bbsc/ssr/product-ECM66B/
9. Girolametto, L. E., Greenberg, J., Manolson, H. A. Developing Dialogue Skills: The Hanen Early Language Parent Program. *Seminars in Speech and Language*, 7, 4 (1986), 367-382.
10. Hailpern, J., Harris, A., LA Botz, R., Birman, B., Karahalios, K. Designing Visualizations to Facilitate Multisyllabic Speech with Children with Autism and Speech Delays. *Proc. DIS 2012*.
11. Hailpern, J., Karahalios, K., Halle, J. Creating a Spoken Impact: Encouraging Vocalization through Audio Visual Feedback in Children with ASD. *Proc. CHI 2009*.
12. Hay, I., Elias, G., Fielding-Barnsley, R., Homel, R., Freiberg, K. Language Delays, Reading Delays, and Learning Difficulties: Interactive Elements Requiring Multidimensional Programming. *Learning Disabilities*, 40, 5 (2007), 400-409.
13. Hong, H., Kim, J. G., Abowd, G. D., Arriaga, R. I. Designing a Social Network to Support the Independence of Young Adults with Autism. *Proc. CSCW 2012*.

14. Hoque, M. E., Lane, J. K., El Kaliouby, R., Goodwin, M., Picard, R. W. Exploring Speech Therapy Games with Children on the Autism Spectrum. *Proc. InterSpeech 2009*.
15. Hung, H., Huang, Y., Freidland, G., Gatica-Perez, D. Estimating Dominance in Multi-Party Meetings Using Speaker Diarization. *IEEE Trans. Audio, Speech, and Language Processing*, 19, 4 (2011), 847-860.
16. Hwang, I., Jang, H., Nachman, N., Song, J. Exploring Inter-child Behavioral Relativity in a Shared Social Environment: A Field Study in a Kindergarten. *Proc. UbiComp 2010*.
17. Hwang, I., Jang, H., Park, T., Choi, A., Lee, Y., Hwang, C., Choi, Y., Nachman, N., Song, J. Leveraging Children's Behavioral Distribution and Singularities in New Interactive Environments: Study in Kindergarten Field Trips. *Proc. Pervasive 2012*.
18. Hwang, I., Yoo, C., Hwang, C., Yim, D., Lee, Y., Min, C., Kim, J., Song, J. TalkBetter: Smartphone-supported Intervention in Family Conversation for Children with Language Delay. *Proc. CSCW 2014 Videos*.
19. Jang, H., Choe, S. P., Hwang, I., Hwang, C., Nachman, L., Song, J. RubberBand: Augmenting Teacher's Awareness of Spatially Isolated Children on Kindergarten Field Trips. *Proc. UbiComp 2012*.
20. Kalnikaitė, V. Ehlen, P., Whittalker, S. Markup as You Talk: Establishing Effective Memory Cues While Still Contributing to a Meeting. *Proc. CSCW 2012*.
21. Kim, T., Chang, A., Holland, L., Pentland, A. Meeting Mediator: Enhancing Group Collaboration using Sociometric Feedback. *Proc. CSCW 2008*.
22. Kohnert, K., Yim, D., Nett, K., Kan, P. F. Intervention with Linguistically Diverse Preschool Children: A Focus on Developing Home Language(s). *Language, Speech, and Hearing Services in Schools*, 36, 3 (2005), 251-263.
23. Kuniavsky, M., *Observing the User Experience: A Practitioner's Guide to User Research*. Morgan Kaufmann, 2003.
24. Lee, Y., Ju, Y., Min, C., Kang, S., Hwang, I., Song, J. CoMon: Cooperative Ambience Monitoring Platform with Continuity and Benefit Awareness. *Proc. MobiSys 2012*.
25. Lee, Y., Min, C., Hwang, C., Lee, J., Hwang, I., Ju, Y., Yoo, C., Moon, M., Lee, U., Song, J. SocioPhone: Everyday Face-to-Face Interaction Monitoring Platform Using Multi-Phone Sensor Fusion. *Proc. MobiSys 2013*.
26. LENA. http://www.lenafoundation.org
27. Lu, H., Brush, A. J., Priyantha, B., Karson, A. K., Liu, J. SpeakerSense: Energy Efficient Unobtrusive Speaker Identification on Mobile Phones. *Proc. Pervasive 2011*.
28. Manolson, H. A. It Takes Two to Talk: A Parent's Guide to Helping Children Communicate. *Hanen Centre Publication*, 1992.
29. Manolson, H. A. Parent Training: A Means of Implementing Pragmatics in Early Language Remediation. *Human Communication* (Summer 1979), 275-281.
30. McLaughlin, M. L., Cody, M. J. Awkward Silences: Behavioral Antecedents and Consequences of the Conversational Lapse. *Human Communication Research*, 8, 4 (1982), 299-316.
31. Miniscalco, C., Nygren, G., Hagberg, B., Kadesjo, B., Gillberg, C. Neuropsychiatric and neurodevelopmental outcome of children at age 6 and 7 years who screened positive for language problems at 30 months. *Developmental Medicine and Child Neurology*, 48 (2006), 361-366.
32. Noise canceling microphone array. http://www.andreaelectronics.com/da250.html
33. Paul, R., Norbury, C. F. *Language Disorders from Infancy through Adolescence: Listening, Speaking, Reading, Writing, and Communicating*. Mosby (2011).
34. Pennington, L., Thomson, K., James, P., Martin, L., McNally, R. Effects of It Takes Two to Talk – The Hanen Program for Parents of Preschool Children with Cerebral Palsy. *J. Speech, Language, and Hearing Research*, 52, 5 (2009), 1121-1138.
35. Ploetz, T., Hammerla, N. Y., Rozga, A., Reavis, A., Call, N., Abowd, G. D. Automatic Assessment of Problem Behavior in Individuals with Developmental Disabilities. *Proc. UbiComp 2012*.
36. Romski, M., Sevcik, R. A., Adamson, L. B., Smith, A., Cheslock, M., Bakemana, R. Parent Perceptions of the Language Development of Toddlers with Developmental Delays Before and After Participation in Parent-coached Language Intervention. *American J. Speech-Language Pathology*, 20, 2 (2011), 111-118.
37. Strauss, A., Corbin, J. *Basics of Qualitative Research Techniques and Procedures for Developing Grounded Theory*. Sage Publications, 2007.
38. Throat microphones. http://www.jeancouk.com/?post_type=product&p=434
39. Tomblin, J. B., Records, N. L., Buckwalter, P., Zhang, X., Smith, E., O'Brien, M. Prevalence of Specific Language Impairment in Kindergarten Children. *J. Speech, Language, and Hearing Research*, 40, 6 (1997), 1245-1260.
40. Watanabe, J., Matsuda, S., Yano, K. Using Wearable Sensor Badges to Improve Scholastic Performance. *Proc. UbiComp 2013 Adjunct*.
41. Wyatt, D., Choudhury, T., Bilmes, J., Kitts, J. A. Inferring Colocation and Conversation Networks from Privacy-sensitive Audio with Implications for Computational Social Science. *ACM Trans. Intelligent Systems and Technology*, 2, 1 (2011), 7:1-41.

Giving is Caring: Understanding Donation Behavior through Email

Yelena Mejova
Yahoo Labs
Av. Diagonal 177
E-08018 Barcelona, Spain
ymejova@yahoo-inc.com

Ingmar Weber and Venkata Rama Kiran Garimella
Qatar Computing Research Institute
Doha, Qatar
{iweber,vgarimella}@qf.org.qa

Michael C Dougal
University of California, Berkeley
210 Barrows Hall
Berkeley, California 94720
mdougal@berkeley.edu

ABSTRACT
Every day, thousands of people make donations to humanitarian, political, environmental, and other causes, a large amount of which occur on the Internet. The solicitations for support, the acknowledgment of a donation and the discussion of corresponding issues are often conducted via email, leaving a record of these social phenomena. In this paper, we describe a comprehensive large-scale data-driven study of donation behavior. We analyze a two-month anonymized email log from several perspectives motivated by past studies on charitable giving: (i) demographics, (ii) user interest, (iii) external time-related factors and (iv) social network influence. We show that email captures the demographic peculiarities of different interest groups, for instance, predicting demographic distributions found in US 2012 Presidential Election exit polls. Furthermore, we find that people respond to major national events, as well as to solicitations with special promotions, and that social connections are the most important factor in predicting donation behavior. Specifically, we identify trends not only for individual charities and campaigns, but also for high-level categories such as political campaigns, medical illnesses, and humanitarian relief. Thus, we show the extent to which large-scale email datasets reveal human donation behavior, and explore the limitations of such analysis.

Author Keywords
donations; email; charities; social factors

ACM Classification Keywords
K.4 Computers and Society: Miscellaneous; J.4 Social and Behavioral Sciences: Sociology

General Terms
Human Factors

INTRODUCTION
The development of the Internet as a marketplace has brought about an era of online giving. The largest source of charitable giving are individuals, donating $211.77 billion in 2010[1]. The 2008 US presidential campaign saw a new wave of online mobilization, with websites like *moveon.org* collecting millions of dollars for political campaigns[2]. Campaigns used "money bombs" to set single day fundraising records. On December 16, 2007 a fundraising effort raised $6 million for the presidential candidate Ron Paul, largely by having a strong online presence[3]. Charities are increasingly fundraising online, and understanding this market may mean thousands of additional donations.

While past literature has cited the potential of the Internet for fundraising and other charitable activities [18, 21], relatively few studies look at a web-based dataset on actual donor behavior. Commonly, such studies perform user surveys focusing on a single website [9]. However, the number and diversity of potential donors on the web, as well as organizations seeking their support, provides an unprecedented opportunity for a data-driven study of the factors contributing to an individual's donating behavior online.

We take inspiration for this study from the copious sociology and psychology literature on individuals' motivations for charitable giving. Social pressure and reward have been found to be powerful motivators [8], as well as social identity in the form of social norms such as gender and income [2]. However, in a recent study of online charitable behavior on GiveIndia, Shier & Handy [41] find an inverse relationship between perceived social pressure to donate (both explicit like solicitations and implicit like other members of social group donating) and likelihood of donating to a cause. This finding puts in question the role of social propensity in an individual's motivations. Guided by these findings, we model individuals' charitable motivations using both internal and external factors – all extracted from a large set of web data.

[1] `http://www.nps.gov/partnerships/fundraising_individuals_statistics.htm`
[2] `http://www.factcheck.org/2010/08/moveonorg/`
[3] `http://www.npr.org/templates/story/story.php?storyId=17332414`

Specifically, this paper contributes a unique multi-faceted analysis of donors' behaviors and interaction with the world as captured by four respects: (1) demographics, (2) topical interest, (3) social influence, and (4) external influence. We examine the communication of hundreds of thousands of anonymous Yahoo! users with a wide range of organizations, including political campaigns, humanitarian efforts, and special-interest groups. Interactions with organizations are mined from a collection of anonymized emails spanning a two-month period of July 19 - September 19, 2012, including interactions with 480 organizations. This analysis is further enriched by demographic information about the users, their interactions with the emails, and an induced social network. Thus, we were able to explore a variety of factors contributing to donations. Finally, throughout this analysis we discuss the benefits and shortcomings of using email for human behavior research. We conclude this study with a set of guidelines to organizations aiming to solicit contributions online, and especially via email.

RELATED WORK

The literature identifies several main factors that influence whether or not an individual will donate to a particular charity: individual capacity and general inclination to donate, individual's interest in the charitable group, social influence and pressure, and the institutional ability of the charity to solicit donations. We briefly discuss these here.

Individual capacity and inclination. Individual capacity generally refers to "a person's human and financial resources (level of education and income, respectively)" [41]. To the extent that charities provide collective goods, they face a collective action problem wherein the rational self-interested individual prefers to free-ride on other people's donations rather than make a donation herself [32]. Individual inclination "typically refers to the social and psychological propensity that a person has towards giving" [41]. The degree to which an individual is altruistic, the extent to which a donation (or lack of thereof) will influence his personal reputation, the psychological benefits that accrue from making a donation, and his values are all important forces that drive charitable giving [8]. More generally, donating can provide a psychological benefit by reinforcing an individual's positive self-image [8] and providing them with an "empathetic joy" [5] or "warm glow" [3]. Related to the notion of self-image, Beckers observes that the Name-Letter Effect [31], where people have a general preference for things sharing their first name initial, can be used to increase donations [6]. For example, a Janette receiving a phone call from a Jane would have a higher donation probability. In this study, we model internal and behavioral user attributes using demographics and emailing behavior.

Interest. Individuals give to organizations because they care about their charitable work. Bekkers [7] finds that people are more willing to contribute to charities that are "more needy and deserving beneficiaries", even if these beneficiaries are geographically far away. Also, people tend to donate more to organizations when they perceive them to have a higher measure of performance and accountability [37]. Unlike in previous survey-based studies which rely on self-reporting, in our data-driven study we measure the interests of users using their daily interactions with friends and the outside world.

Social influence. Donors can also be thought of as "impure altruists" to the extent that their behavior is driven by the social and psychological benefits of donating [4, 8]. In the context of a tightly knit group, such as a small church congregation, donation behavior can be monitored to socially reward donors and punish non-donors [8]. In contrast, online donations and solicitations for charitable donations made via email are made in relative anonymity. Nevertheless, social identity can still play a large role in anonymous online donations. Social identity theory tells us that positive in-group identity is important to individual self-esteem [43] and that making a donation can reinforce that identity in response to out-group threat [13]. Choosing donations made in one's name over being paid has also been shown to increase one's credibility in the context of user-generated content [24]. In comparison to in-person solicitation, email solicitation can "increase the salience of social identity" related to a charitable group while reducing "cognitive perceptions of interpersonal differences" within a group [11]. Such social interactions can be glimpsed in the email use of the users in our dataset.

External influence. Finally, the ability of an organization to solicit donations is an important institutional factor in charitable giving. Charities can provide selective incentives to help overcome collective action problems [32], such as giving donors access to exclusive events. Donors are also responsive to decreases in the cost of donating, such as tax incentives [33] and offers to match contributions [25]. We explore both the nature of successful solicitations, as well as the effect of major events on donation behavior.

While there is a vast social science literature on charitable donations, there are relatively few studies that examine either online charitable donations or email-based charitable donation solicitations. Recently, studies of large donation websites such as *www.give-india.com* [41] and *www.kiva.org* [27] have allowed for a large population of study. Specifically, [27] build a text classifier that identifies reasons for why people donate to charities from their free-text elaborations on the topic. In contrast, our study provides a more involved analysis of the donors' interactions with the charitable organizations, as well as their social network and the rest of the world.

A number of researchers have looked at the role that new technology plays concerning fundraising. Goecks et al. [17] study 150 instances of technology for nonprofit fundraising, including Facebook Causes and Network for Good. They claim that technology like email helps in making visible an immediate need and framing a contribution as helping individuals rather than groups. Technology can also provide information about what other people have donated and legitimize small contributions. Hayes et al. [22] present several studies related to "modern" donation. They stipulate that "philanthropic organizations wishing to connect to donors strive to become part of their everyday 'small world' ". Using the American Red Cross website as an example, they illustrate how interactivity and social networking tools have drastically increased the number and depth of connections that can exist between donors and causes. Popups asking for immediate contributions are found to be ineffective in [47]. The same authors find evidence though that they can help to remind users to contribute, leading to a 23% increase in contributions. However, this effect wanes as users habituate to the popups. After the 2010 earthquake, special SMS donation numbers were setup leading to over $7M in micro donations. The technology-enabled ease of the system - just sending and SMS to a dedicated number - is widely regarded as crucial in this success [34]. Going beyond donations, Rotman et al. [35] present a discussion of open research questions related to social media and their use for engaging people in activism for certain causes.

Recently, researchers have looked at *crowdfunding* platforms to understand the arguably altruistic motivation of the contributors. Muller et al. [29] studied an intra-organization crowdfunding system where participants were each given USD 100 by the organization to "use or lose". Considered a successful pilot, it showed the importance of the social context and of achieving real change in their workplace. Though interesting, their findings might not be transferable to donations to "external" charities. Greenberg et al. [19] go beyond the focus on financial committments and apply Resource Exchange Theory to model crowdsourcing. They find that platforms support the implicit exchange of all six resources (money, love, information, status, goods, and services). The "tragedy of the commons" is a classic problem in game theory where each player's individually optimal move is not to contribute to a common good. Sakamoto et al. [36] try to tackle this problem through crowdfunding. In their envisioned system, people contribute "ageing money" to projects in their direct environment to keep them sustainable. Projects range from public toilets to office areas. They built a first prototype system for mobile devices but have not yet provided any evaluation of real results. Knowing that your crowdfunding application will or will not be successful could help you to improve your submission. Greenberg et al. [20] study the corresponding binary classification problem by applying machine learning classifiers to learn the concept of a successful online crowdfunding project at the time of project launch. The features used include the set monetary goal in USD, the topic category, how popular the person in chare is on Twitter and other features. Ultimately, crowdfunding can be viewed as a "creativity support tool" and Kuoger et al. [26] apply the "Genex (Generator of Excellence) Framework" to model platforms. They link the four phases from Genex, namely, Collect, Relate, Create and Donate to features in crowdfinancing platforms.

OBSERVING DONATIONS IN EMAIL

Data Gathering

We begin by describing our anonymized email dataset, which spans a two-month period of July 19 – September 19, 2012.[4] In the following, a "user" refers to a Yahoo! email user. For our analysis, all user identifiers (= email addresses) were replaced by random numbers ("hashes"). For simplicity, we will call any entity that may seek a donation a *charity*, regardless of its actual charitable status, thus generalizing the word to refer to political campaigns, food drives, human rights groups, etc.

Table 1. Top 10 charity domains by donation volume

barackobama.com	US President Barack Obama's Campaign
mittromney.com	Mitt Romney for President Campaign
cancer.org	American Cancer Society
lls.org	Leukemia & Lymphoma Society
alz.org	Alzheimer's Association
nmss.org	Multiple Sclerosis Society
worldvision.org	World Vision (humanitarian)
redcross.org	American Red Cross
irusa.org	Islamic Relief USA
stjude.org	St. Jude Children's Research Hospital

An initial set of charities was gathered by scraping the lists of top charities posted on reputable websites like Forbes[5] and USNews[6]. The top 100 US political campaign organizations by money raised to date in the 2012 election cycle were also added to the dataset[7]. Finally, we compiled a list of prominent news stories in that time span, using Wikipedia Current Events portal[8] and compiled lists of charities which may be affected by them. This resulted in 480 internet domains each belonging to a charity.

In order to identify an email from a charity, we matched the domain (or subdomain) of the URL in the *from* field of the email to the list of our charities. Furthermore, we identified emails thanking the user for a donation using a manually compiled set of regular expression rules. We manually checked the accuracy of these rules (having an average 86% accuracy). Table 1 shows the top 10 domains which received the most donations in our dataset. They include political campaigns, humanitarian organizations, and medical illness associations.

We then identified three groups of users who may be of interest. The *donors* are the users who have received an email from any of our 480 charities that thanks them for a donation. This set contains on the order of 100,000 users. The *interested* users are those who have received an email from one of the charities, but who have not donated, or rather received a "thank you" email. We down-sample these users to get a set of roughly the same size as the previous. Finally, we compare these groups to a *general* random subset of 10,000 users who have received at least one email in that time period and who are not in the above samples. Incoming and outgoing emails were gathered for all of these users, and the data anonymized. In total, around a billion incoming and several million outgoing emails were collected. These included metadata, such as (anonymized) *from* and *to* fields, the date

[4]Data originated from users who voluntarily opted in for their mail to be analyzed for research purposes. `http://info.yahoo.com/privacy/us/yahoo/`

[5]`http://www.forbes.com/lists/2011/14/200-largest-us-charities-11_rank.html`

[6]`http://www.usnews.com/usnews/biztech/charities/lists/intl_deve-lopment.htm`

[7]`http://www.fec.gov/data/CommitteeSummary.do?format=html&election_yr=2012`

[8]`http://en.wikipedia.org/wiki/Portal:Current_events`

email was sent/received, and the subject. The body of the emails was not collected.

In order to aggregate over the various charities, we selected the charities that received at least 100 donations within these two months and annotated them for topical category. The 49 charities in this list accounted for 99.3% of all donations in our dataset. The ten categories are (in the descending order of prominence) *Medical*, *Humanitarian*, *Politics*, *Environmental*, *Religious*, *US Military*, *Children*, *Public Broadcasting*, *Animals*, and *Internet*. Additionally, a set of distinguishing keywords were manually compiled such that if one is found in a subject of an email, it is most likely about the given topic.

Spam Filtering

As the incoming mail comes with a *spam* flag, we investigate the distribution of this flag in the emails sent by the charities. According to this flag, the email may be directed to the inbox, or to bulk or spam folders. We find that there is a significant number of emails from these charities that do not end up in the users' inbox. Although most organizations, such as *cancer.org*, *lls.org*, and *redcross.org* have less than 10% of their emails flagged as spam, more than half of the emails from *stjude.org* (St. Jude Children's Hospital) and *dscc.org* (Democratic Senatorial Campaign Committee) are labeled as bulk and do not reach the user's inbox.

We further investigate this by gathering user action statistics. These include instances of users reading, deleting, and forwarding emails, as well as tagging them as *spam*. We find that the proportion of emails tagged as spam to those read is the greatest for *wikimedia.org* – an organization responsible for Wikipedia and other projects – at 0.55. Indeed, upon examination we find the domain may have been "hijacked" by spammers. Thus, the server-side spam-filtering algorithms which are out of the user's control may affect the user's perception of the charity, and we discuss the possible effects the spam filter may have on donation behavior in the Discussion section. Also, when considering the user's interaction with the charity, we exclude those emails tagged as spam.

DONATION BEHAVIOR ANALYSIS

Demographics

Sociological studies on motivation often link motivation to group membership and identity definition. Demographics such as gender, age, and income, play an important role in an individual's formation of their self-image [39]. In order to determine if users' demographic characteristics play a role in their donation behavior, we collect the self-reported demographic information from the user profiles. This information includes age, gender, and zip code. In the case the user's zip code is in US, we use census data to obtain localized statistics such as the percentage of bachelors degrees and median household income[9]. We aggregate these for the users donating to charities within the ten topics. The age, gender (male = 1), percentage of bachelor degrees and median household income are shown in Figure 1 (note, the 95% confidence intervals are too small to plot).

[9]`http://www.census.gov`

Table 2. US Presidential Election exit polls

Age	Obama	Romney	% total
18-29	60	37	19
30-44	52	45	27
45-64	47	51	38
65 or over	44	56	16
Gender	Obama	Romney	% total
Male	45	52	47
Female	55	44	53
Bach Degree	Obama	Romney	% total
College graduate	50	48	47
No college degree	51	47	53
Family Income	Obama	Romney	% total
Under $50,000	60	38	41
$50,000 - $99,999	46	52	31
$100,000 or more	44	54	28

Several interesting trends become evident. First, note the average age is usually between 40 and 55 (even after removing the small number of instances where users claim age of > 100), showing that donors in our dataset tend to be of an older generation. Donors to political and military causes, as well as donors to public broadcasting, tend to be older. Environmental and internet (including sites like *wikipeda.org*) causes tend to attract slightly more male donors, whereas donors to animal-related causes tend to overwhelmingly be female. Public broadcasting, which is mostly operated by non-profits in US, attracts donors from neighborhoods with higher household income and a higher percentage of bachelor degrees.

Figure 2 shows the same distributions for two major political campaigns: *barackobama.com* and *mittromney.com*. On average, Romney donors are older and live in more affluent areas[10], while Barack Obama attracts significantly more women. When we compare online donation behavior to the US Presidential Election exit polls[11], we find that donors exhibit a similar gender gap as voters, but that Barack Obama's voters are much younger than his donors. This is consistent with the finding of [40] that political donors are generally older and more affluent than the electorate as a whole. Note that we show the original statistics instead of computing an "average voter" due to vagueness in classes like "65 or over".

Donor Interest

Next, we attempt to measure the effect of the user's interest on donation behavior. Intuitively, people interested in a cause are more likely to donate. First, we note that for most part donors are more likely to receive emails from the charity than those who do not donate but still receive some emails (the "interested" group). For example, Figure 3 shows the distribution of emails received from *cancer.org* and *redcross.org* by users in the two groups. We see that even though both charities deal with health issues, the difference between the

[10]Remember that we do not have data on individual income and education, only zip code level information. The average donor to any campaign is likely to be better educated and have a higher household income than their neighbors [40].

[11]`http://elections.msnbc.msn.com/ns/politics/2012/all/president/#exitPoll`

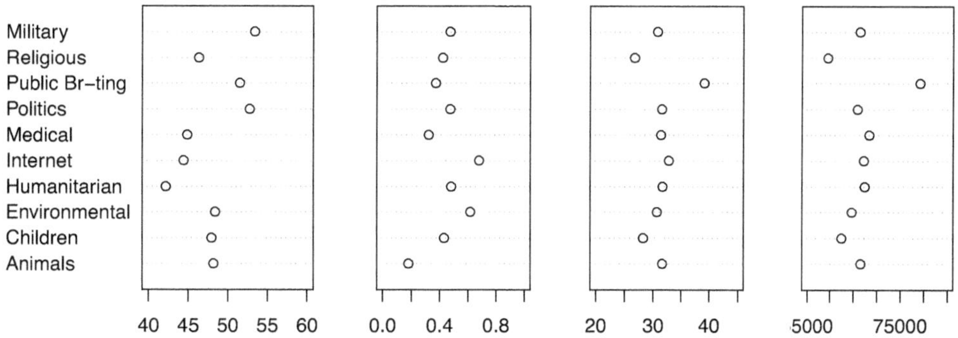

(a) Age (b) Gender (m=1) (c) % Bachelors (d) Median HHI

Figure 1. Demographics of donors to causes in 10 topical categories

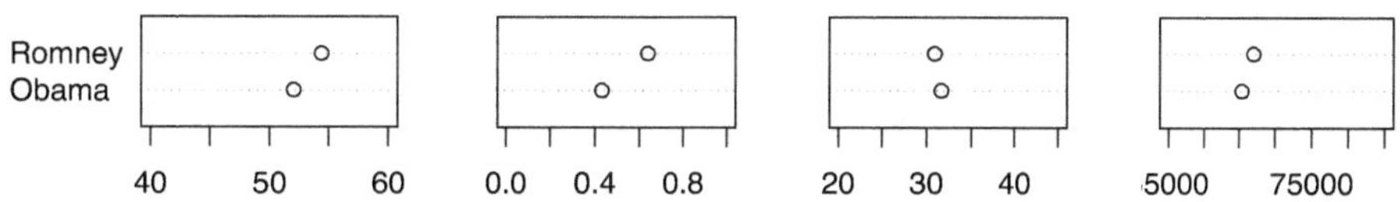

(a) Age (b) Gender (m=1) (c) % Bachelors (d) Median HHI

Figure 2. Demographics of donors to two political campaigns

number of received emails between the two groups of users is more pronounced for the former than the latter.

However, just receiving emails from a charity is not a sure sign of interest. Instead, we estimate interest by classifying the subjects of the incoming and outgoing emails according to the ten topical categories. Specifically, we use regular expressions with manually-compiled keywords such as one below for *Politics*:

$$(politic\backslash w* \mid republican\backslash w* \mid democrat\backslash w* \mid election\backslash w* \mid elect\backslash w* \mid tax\backslash w* \mid obama\backslash w* \mid romney\backslash w* \mid white\ house \mid senat\backslash w*)$$

Upon manual evaluation of a selection of 50 email titles for each topic, we find the average accuracy of these regular expressions to be 86.2% (although coverage would be more difficult to check). Figure 4 shows the topical shares of incoming and outgoing emails for the *donors*, users who have received an email from a charity but have not donated (*interested*), and a general subset of users (*general*) with 95% confidence intervals. Note here that donors and interested are not all of the people in our *donors* or *interested* groups, but people who have donated to (in case of donors) or received an email from (interested) at least once to the cause in the category.

Considering the incoming emails, we can see that in most cases (8 out of 10), the donors are more likely to receive emails about such topics than other groups. Similarly, users whose (outgoing) emails mention *animals*, *politics*, or *religion* are drastically more likely to donate to these causes.

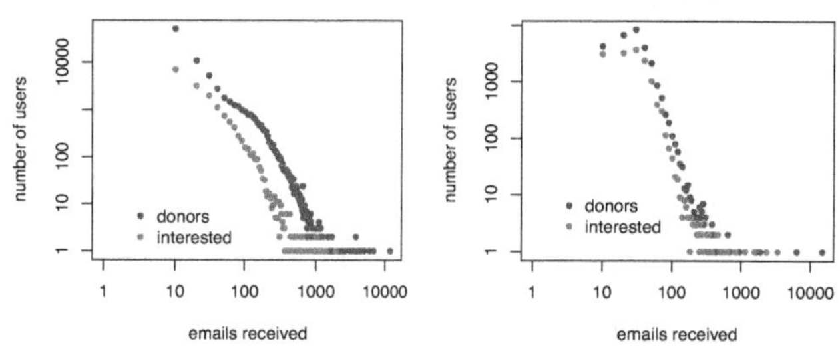

(a) cancer.org (b) redcross.org

Figure 3. Number of users receiving an email from a charity in donor and interested groups

Most other topics do not show much difference between the behavior of the three groups. Note that we saw very few incoming and no outgoing emails about public broadcasting for all three groups. This is consistent with organizations like WGBH (Boston Public Broadcasting) and PBS (Public Broadcasting Service) raising money primarily through other means, such as on-air fundraising telethons. Similar observations can be drawn about *medical* charities and *humanitarian* charities, both of which have well-established organizations that promote donations offline. An alternative explanation is that animals, politics, and religion are more natural topics of conversation for animal lovers, political junkies, and the religiously devout than, say, public radio is for NPR listeners, such that our classifier is better able to pick up an interest in election outcomes than an interest in quality public radio. Nevertheless, the relationship between the content of incoming emails and donation may be indicative of the effectiveness of solicitation campaigns. We examine this next.

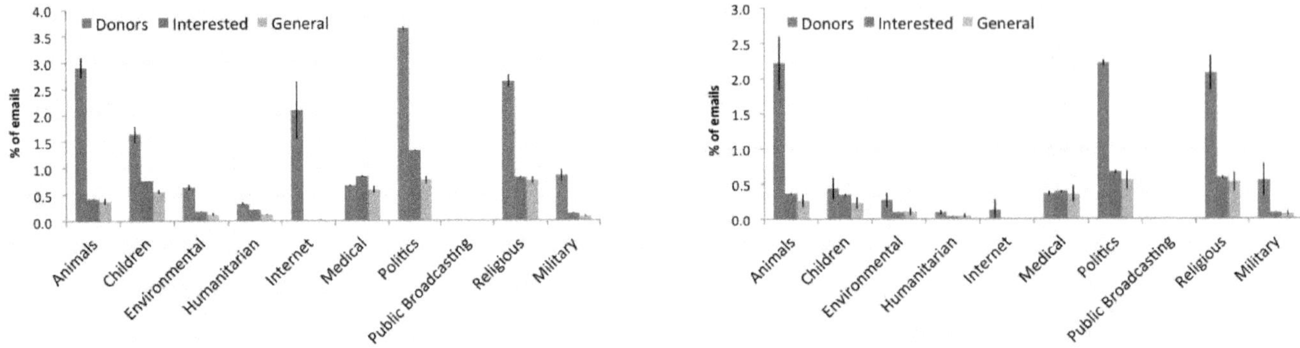

(a) Incoming emails (non-spam)

(b) Outgoing emails

Figure 4. Topical share of incoming and outgoing emails for the donors, interested, and general sets of users

Solicitation

Regardless of the user's interest in the charity, from the point of view of the charitable organization it would be useful to gauge whether donations can be encouraged by solicitation. We address this by looking at overall solicitation and donation volumes, as well as donation on a per-user basis.

Table 3. Cohen's kappa between donation volume and charity solicitations, top and bottom 10 charities

Domain	Category	kappa
toysfortots.org	Children	0.9379
firstfoodbank.org	Humanitarian	0.8070
tbn.org	Christian	0.7377
dav.org	US Military	0.7304
nationalmssociety.org	Medical	0.6873
earthisland.org	Environmental	0.6796
wikimedia.org	Internet	0.6659
smiletrain.org	Medical	0.6625
feedthechildren.org	Humanitarian	0.6423
stjude.org	Medical	0.6186
hsus.org	Animals	0.0223
cff.org	Medical	0.0216
arthritis.org	Medical	0.0205
pbs.org	Public Broadcasting	0.0046
diabetes.org	Medical	-0.0008
ucsusa.org	Environmental	-0.0379
autismspeaks.org	Medical	-0.0496
jdrf.org	Medical	-0.0670
barackobama.com	Politics	-0.0722
wgbh.org	Public Broadcasting	-0.0973

First, to understand the "burstiness" of the donation volume over time, we characterize the donations as happening in a "low", "medium", or "high" period. To do this, we compute the number of donations per day for each charity. We then order these days from least active days to most active, where activity is the number of donations, and then split these into the three terciles, each having a third of all of the days in the dataset.

Table 3 shows the Cohen's kappa between the (discretized) donation volume and incoming mail from that charity. We exclude from this analysis charities for which the donation activity was too sparse. Organizations high on this list rely more on fundraising emails or have a high precision: when they send an email, they tend to get donations. For organizations towards the bottom the relationship is reversed: people donate on any day, regardless of whether a solicitation was sent on that day. In the full list of these organizations, 43% have Cohen's kappa greater than 0.3, suggesting a positive relationship between email solicitation and donations.

In order to determine whether solicitations are effective on personal level, we compute the probability that, given the user will donate to an organization, that he or she donates within some number of days of receiving a solicitation. We compare this probability to a baseline, that uses the total number of donations the user has made to this charity over the dataset. The results are shown in Figure 5. The probabilities were first aggregated over all users donating to a charity, and then over charities (resulting in a macro-average). The cumulative probability of a user donating after a solicitation is higher by approximately 8% than the baseline probability. The organizations which have the best response (donation) rate to their solicitations are largely concerning medical illness, children's charities, and humanitarian relief. The only political campaign among the top ten most successful solicitors list is dscc.com (Democratic Senatorial Campaign Committee), with a 15.4% difference between observed and simulated donation rates.

We note that both of these measures can only capture correlation rather than causation. If charities send out solicitations only in periods where a user would have donated anyway, then our measure will overestimate the effectiveness of solicitations. If, on the other hand, charities send out emails every single day then our measure would not detect any correlation, even though donations could still be caused by these constant solicitations. One of the challenges is determining the intent of a charity's email. For instance, a Granger Causality test informs us that it is the donations which predict other emails, since we find that the policy of following up on a donation on the next day is common in our dataset. To determine the causal effect of any given email or email campaign, charities should run randomized, controlled experiments that randomly assign prospective donors to treatment (an email or email campaign) and control (no emails) and measure the difference in donation behavior.

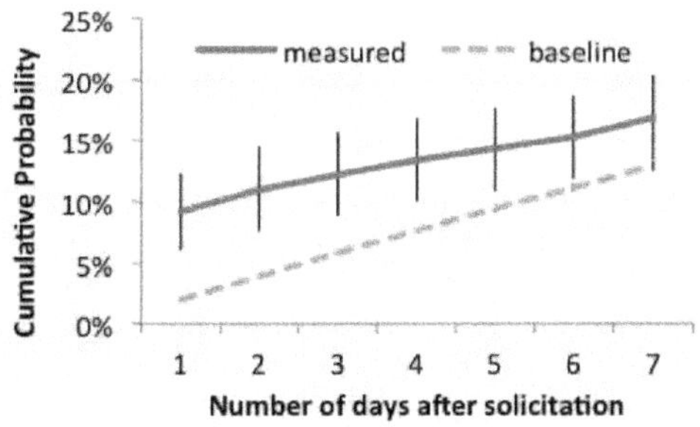

Figure 5. Cumulative probability (in %) of donation within n days of solicitation (with 95% confidence intervals)

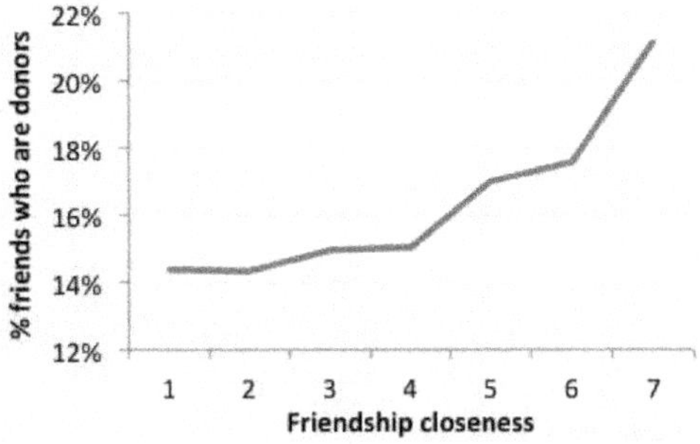

Figure 6. Percentage of donors' friends who are also donors (close friends = 7)

Social Network

Direct interaction between individuals has been shown to be important in information diffusion and has been used in marketing [23] and epidemiology [15]. Also, individuals tend to become friends with similar others, a phenomenon called *homophily* [28]. In order to examine the relationships between social ties and donation behavior, we extract a social network from the emails.

First, for each donor, we found all users they exchanged emails with, constraining these to users within the Yahoo! network. The average number of friends within this network was 47. Because our lists of donors and user who have received an email from a charity are complete, we can look up whether any of these friends are themselves in a *donors* or *interested* groups. In order to normalize the contribution of each user to our aggregate measures, we sample each user's contacts with replacement to get 100 friends. We measure the strength of the relationship between two users by the minimum of emails sent or received (that way one-sided relationships such as spam would not be considered a strong relationship). We then bucket the users by relationship strength from distant acquaintances to close friends (with each bucket containing the same number of users). Within these buckets, we calculate the percentage of donors (Figure 6). The spike in the seventh bucket, which contains the closest friends, is significant at a $p = 0.01$ level (compared to both buckets 1 and 6). When we compute these statistics on per-charity basis, we find similar results. Furthermore, we find that not only are friends of donors more likely to donate to that cause, but they are also more likely to receive solicitations from the same domain.

Not only do interests unite users, they also divide them. For instance, the two major opposing sides of the US political scene – one supporting Barack Obama, another Mitt Romney – are more connected within the party than across. In Figure 7 we show the percentage of users we found to have a connection (who have both sent and received emails to/from each other) over all users in the group. This divide has been previously observed both for the interlinkage network of political blogs [1] and for the social network of Twitter users [14]. While roughly 1 in 4 Americans have reported having regular contact with someone of the opposite political persuasion, almost none of our online donors have such a connection [30]. This extreme homophily is consistent with [30]'s finding that homophily increases political participation.

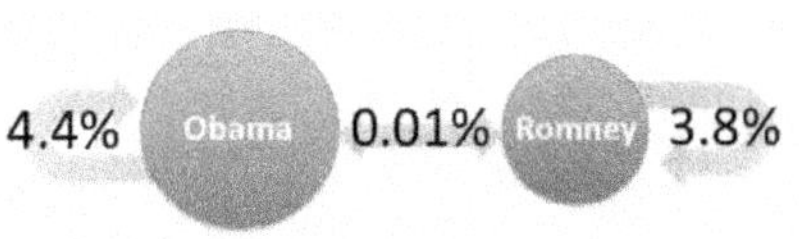

Figure 7. Percentage of donors having social ties with other donors within their own or opposing political groups

As we show in the Regression Analysis section, this relationship between friends is the most predictive factor of donation behavior when we consider interest, demographic, behavioral, and social variables.

External Influence

Next, we examine the role of external influences on donation behavior. A driving factor of charitable donations is awareness of need. In particular, donors' subjective perceptions of need is crucial [8][46]. Increased perception of need has been found to be positively related to university alumni support [48], volunteering in the community [44], and donations to international relief organizations [12]. The media can play an important role in facilitating this awareness. Increased media coverage of a particular earthquake, for example, tends to increase donations to that earthquake's relief efforts [42].

In order to capture the effect of current events on donation behavior, we manually examine the donation levels for select charities. Figure 8 shows the daily donation (in blue) and solicitation (in red) volumes. The first organization, *barackobama.com* is the official US Presidential campaign of Barack Obama, a Democrat and the second, *mittromney.com*, is that of his Republican opponent Mitt Romney. Here are several dates of interest:

July 31: "Photo going around on Facebook" (Obama)
Aug 11: Paul Ryan is Republican VP candidate
Aug 18: T-shirt promotion "I built this" (Romney)
Aug 27-30: Republican National Convention
Sep 4-6: Democratic National Convention

We see major spurs in donations following promotional emails like "Photo going around on Facebook" where a potential voter shows their support for Obama. These solicitations are not as effective on Romney's side, for example, when a promotion on August 18 did not result in a similar

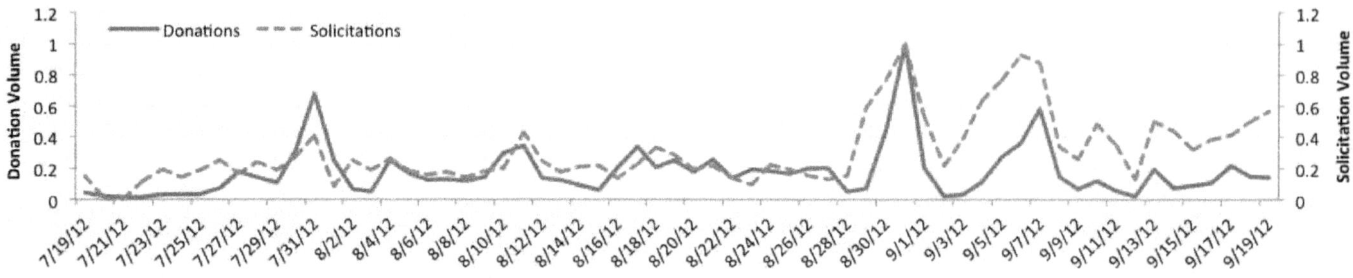

(a) barackobama.com

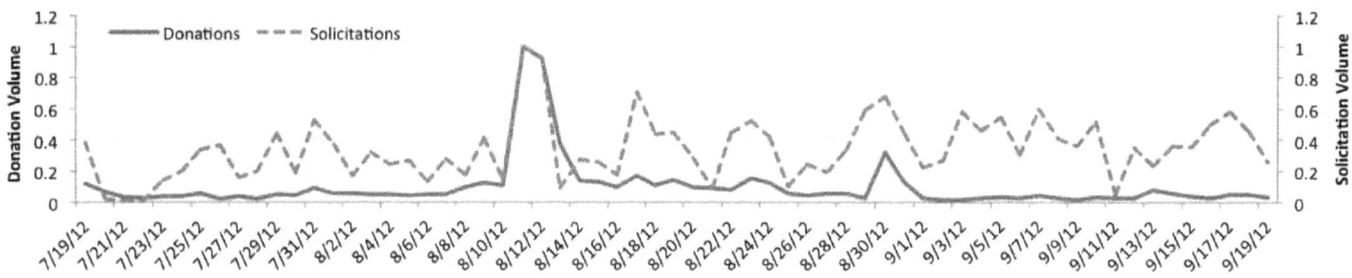

(b) mittromney.com

Figure 8. Daily donation and solicitation levels for select organizations (1 is maximum volume)

bump. However, the announcement of Paul Ryan's nomination for Vice President on Republican ticket has especially spurred solicitation and donation activity for *mittromney.com*. The national conventions in late August and early September encouraged comparatively few donations on Republican side, whereas spurring donations to *barackobama.com*.

Additionally, we have made the following observations from our manual analysis of select charities:

- Major donations spikes seem to coincide with major events, especially in the political arena.
- Explicit solicitations for donations spur more donation activity than newsletters or updates.
- Solicitations connected to real-world events are more effective than general-purpose ones.

However, a more comprehensive study linking world events, media coverage, and donation behavior is needed to qualify the effect of new information on donors behavior. We leave such a study for future work.

REGRESSION ANALYSIS

Finally, we use a regression model to examine the contributions each of the dimensions we discussed make to the likelihood of a donation. For each user/charity pair we compute the independent variables described in Table 4. These include simple behavior measures (emails sent and received), demographics, interest, and information about the friends of the user. Note that it was impossible to include the external influences such as world events as a factor. To address multicollinearity issue, we compute variance inflation factors for each variable. These range between 1.01 and 1.72, all within acceptable range for inclusion in analysis. The most related variables, as shown by Pearson correlation of 0.65, are % bachelors degrees (D3) and median household income (D4). Finally, the dependent variable is whether the user donates to a charity – one if the user has donated to a charity, and zero otherwise.

Because of the prohibitive data size, we devise a sampling strategy that is designed to mitigate the influence of the charities which have more representation (such as those on political and medical issues). Within each charity type we collect 1000 positive examples (those who have donated) and 1000 negative examples (from both interested and general groups). Table 5 shows the logistic regression coefficients, odds-ratios associated with them (exponentiated coefficients), and the mean and standard deviation statistics for each variable. All coefficients, except for I4 and S4 are significant at $p < 0.01$. For that reason it is most informative to consider the odds-ratios listed in the third column.

The effect of S1 (number of friends who are donors to the charity) is by far the greatest: for each friend who donates to a charity, the likelihood for the user to also donate to that charity goes up by 24%. These results strongly attest to homophily – a tendency of individuals to associate with similar others. Simply, you are likely to have similar interests and values as your friends, and thus donate more to the same causes. To gauge how well the model fits the data, we calculate McFadden's pseudo R^2 to be 0.319. Since this measure tends to be smaller than R^2, values of 0.2 to 0.4 are considered highly satisfactory [45].

However, the importance of these factors varies across charity groups. S1 remains to be the most powerful predictor in most cases, being strongest for Religious (87.6%), Humanitarian (49.7%), and Animals (32%). The number of emails received

Table 4. Regression variables

	Behavior
B1	# emails received
B2	# emails sent
	Demographic
D1	age (in years)
D2	gender (male = 1)
D3	% bachelors degrees
D4	median household income (in thousands of dollars)
	Interest
I1	# emails received from charity
I2	# emails received from any charity within a topic
I3	# emails received on topic judging from subject
I4	# emails sent on topic judging from subject
	Social
S1	# friends who are donors to the charity
S2	# friends who are donors to any charity on this topic
S3	# friends who got emails from the charity
S4	# friends who got emails from any charity on this topic

Table 5. Logistic regression of Behavior, Demographic, Interest, and Social factors on Donation (all coefficients are statistically significant at $p < 0.01$ except for I4 and S4)

	Coefficient	Odds-ratios	Mean	SD
intercept	7.83e-02	-	-	-
B1	2.23e-06	1.0000	1079	1351
B2	2.04e-06	1.0000	179.6	725.9
D1	1.95e-04	1.0002	46.35	14.96
D2	-1.04e-02	0.9897	0.419	0.493
D3	3.74e-04	1.0004	29.92	12.87
D4	5.38e-04	1.0005	67.07	24.39
I1	7.70e-03	1.0077	3.847	16.973
I2	-4.83e-04	0.9995	16.24	47.27
I3	5.25e-05	1.0001	15.26	50.64
I4	-3.14e-04	0.9997	0.053	1.822
S1	2.15e-01	1.2403	0.074	0.370
S2	-1.74e-02	0.9827	0.210	0.643
S3	1.48e-04	1.0001	0.841	17.57
S4	1.66e-05	1.0000	9.881	64.04

from charity (I1) is a strong predictor for Children at 8.9%, Military (5.8%), Humanitarian (4.5%), and Animals (4.4%). Gender (D2) is also important, with being male increasing the likelihood of donation by 8.2% to political causes, but decreasing by 5.1% for medical ones. Also, the number of donors to any charity on the topic (S2) is important to Children at 8.0% and Broadcasting at 7.6%. These findings illustrate the difference in behavior of the potential donors to these varying causes, and the need to adjust one's campaign to its audience.

DISCUSSION

Our findings are two-fold. First, the donation behavior we uncovered is consistent with several theories about motivation and giving. Close social connections play an important role in whether an individual donates to a cause, supporting findings of earlier studies [8]. Solicitations, as far as they make individuals aware of issues and charitable opportunities, indeed seem to have some effect on the donation behavior, and considering the low price of sending emails, may be a great way to promote one's cause. This confirms the popularity of email as a form of communication with organizations by donors found in [10]. Second, we illustrate the power of email communication to reveal human behavior as it records the daily interactions of individuals with the outside world. In this particular domain, the behavioral and social signal is strong enough to effectively predict online donation.

In light of the results above, we offer a set of general recommendations for an effective solicitation campaign. First and foremost, our findings show that such campaigns can be effective, and that users read and respond to the solicitations received via email (confirming general positive reaction to emails found in [10]). Similar to the conclusions in [38], these solicitations are even more effective if the individual is already interested in the topic, as in the case of political or religious issues. Our findings suggest that campaigns should try to make appeals more salient to prospective donors by capitalizing on relevant current events.

Furthermore, demographic targeting may benefit individual campaigns. However, in general, we find that who your friends are is a far better indicator of your propensity to donate than who you are as measured by demographic characteristics. Whether appeals from friends to friends are particularly effective we cannot say, but we have demonstrated a great degree of homophily such that appealing to a donor's friends by any means available (most likely through the donor herself) is likely to be more effective than an appeal to particular demographics (in contrary to the findings in [41]).

Finally, we caution that one size does not fit all. While we make a set of general recommendations, to determine the causal effect of any given email or email campaign, charities must run randomized, controlled experiments in which prospective donors on an email list are randomly assigned to a treatment group (an email or email campaign) or a control group (no emails), thereby allowing them to measure the difference in donation behavior between the two groups and estimate a causal effect of a particular solicitation on opening an email, click-through rates, and ultimately donation (see [16] for more details on running this kind of field experiment).

Although the size and diversity of our dataset provides a unique view of the interactions between donors and charitable organizations, there are several notable limitations to our study. As illustrated by the case of public broadcasting organizations, there are ways other than email in which the information about a cause may travel, such as via radio, television, or other forms of advertisement. Also the link between social ties and donation behavior suggests a communication of this information within the social network, possibly outside email. However, more research should be done on the effect of charity's email on a potential donor. As we mention earlier, the actions of the donor (such as making a donation) may affect the future behavior of the charity (prompting more frequent requests). Finally, our study encompasses donation behavior as witnessed in an email exchange of select users. The interactions between donors and charities outside email were not captured here. Self-selection dictates that the users in our study are more comfortable with internet and email than those who donate "offline", and may have other peculiarities we have not accounted for. However, the demographic similarity of the donors to the US Presidential campaigns to the election exit poll statistics shows the efficacy of email mining for monitoring social phenomena.

Particular to email collections is the importance of the role the email service plays in users' interactions with the email. As discussed in Spam Filtering section, the spam tagging and the routing of emails into various folders affects the final user experience with the charitable campaign. Furthermore, user-defined filters introduce variables which are difficult to incorporate into data aggregation and analysis. Thus, the policies and spam classifiers of email providers may have an unintended effect on the success of a solicitation campaign. It is obvious, then, that charities are to make sure not to spam their potential donors, as is the case for *wikimedia.org* – the questionable messages were obviously about unrelated content (with subjects like "Wonder pills for thrills" and "Check out this hot babe"), and probably come from a malicious source other than the charity. In fact, the actual donations come from *donatewikimedia.org*, whereas the others from nonsensical accounts, indicating a faked "from" field.

CONCLUSIONS

Our paper provides a unique exploration of the donation behavior of hundreds of thousands of users. Unlike most previous studies on motivation and charitable giving, we take a data-driven approach in which we examine the incoming and outgoing emails for these users over the span of two months. These two months encompass several notable world events, numerous donation drives, and hundreds of organizations. We attempt to quantify the effects of four major factors on donation behavior: demographic, interest, social network, and other external influences. By examining each factor separately and all together we show the contribution of each to the individuals' motivation to donate to various causes.

Most notably, we find a strong relationship between social ties and donations, with the odds of user donating increasing dramatically with every friend who has donated to the same cause.

However, this study provokes more questions for future research. What messages and solicitations are the most convincing to donors? What strategies can charities employ to find new potential donors? And, expanding the data sources, what other technologies support the communication between organizations and the public that leads to further donations? In an increasingly online world, the answers to these questions will determine which charities succeed and which fail at soliciting donations to help their cause.

REFERENCES

1. Adamic, L. A., and Glance, N. The political blogosphere and the 2004 U.S. election: divided they blog. In *LinkKDD* (2005), 36–43.
2. Akerlof, G., and Kranton, R. *Identity economics: how our identities shape our work, wages, and well-being.* Princeton Univ Pr, 2010.
3. Andreoni, J. Giving with impure altruism: Applications to charity and ricardian equivalence. *The Journal of Political Economy* (1989), 1447–1458.
4. Andreoni, J. Impure altruism and donations to public goods: a theory of warm-glow giving. *The Economic Journal 100*, 401 (1990), 464–477.
5. Batson, C., and Shaw, L. Evidence for altruism: Toward a pluralism of prosocial motives. *Psychological Inquiry 2*, 2 (1991), 107–122.
6. Bekkers, R. George gives to geology jane: The name letter effect and incidental similarity cues in fundraising. *International Journal of Nonprofit and Voluntary Sector Marketing 15*, 2 (2010), 172–180.
7. Bekkers, R. Who gives what and when? a scenario study of intentions to give time and money. *Social Science Research 39*, 3 (2010), 369–381.
8. Bekkers, R., and Wiepking, P. A literature review of empirical studies of philanthropy. *Nonprofit and Voluntary Sector Quarterly 40*, 5 (2011), 924–973.
9. Bennett, R. Impulsive donation decisions during online browsing of charity websites. *Journal of Consumer Behaviour 8*, 2-3 (2009), 116–134.
10. Bhagat, V., Loeb, P., and Rovner, M. The next generation of american giving. *White paper* (2010).
11. Chan, M. The impact of email on collective action: a field application of the side model. *New Media & Society 12*, 8 (2010), 1313–1330.
12. Cheung, C., and Chan, C. Social-cognitive factors of donating money to charity, with special attention to an international relief organization. *Evaluation and Program Planning 23*, 2 (2000), 241–253.
13. Collins, K. Who gives? political messages, activist motivations, and campaign contribution behavior. *Working paper* (2012).
14. Conover, M., Ratkiewicz, J., Francisco, M., Gonçalves, B., Menczer, F., and Flammini, A. Political polarization on twitter. In *ICWSM* (2011), 89–96.
15. Eubank, S., Guclu, H., Kumar, V., Marathe, M., Srinivasan, A., Toroczkai, Z., and Wang, N. Modelling disease outbreaks in realistic urban social networks. *Nature 429*, 6988 (2004), 180–184.
16. Gerber, A., and Green, D. *Field experiments: Design, analysis, and interpretation.* WW Norton, 2012.
17. Goecks, J., Voida, A., Voida, S., and Mynatt, E. D. Charitable technologies: Opportunities for collaborative computing in nonprofit fundraising. In *Proceedings of the 2008 ACM conference on Computer supported cooperative work*, ACM (2008), 689–698.
18. Gomes, R., and Knowles, P. Strategic internet and e-commerce applications for local nonprofit organizations. *Journal of Nonprofit & Public Sector Marketing 9*, 1-2 (2001), 215–245.

19. Greenberg, M. D., Hui, J., and Gerber, E. Crowdfunding: a resource exchange perspective. In *CHI* (2013), 883–888.

20. Greenberg, M. D., Pardo, B., Hariharan, K., and Gerber, E. Crowdfunding support tools: predicting success & failure. In *CHI* (2013), 1815–1820.

21. Hart, T. ephilanthropy: Using the internet to build support. *International Journal of Nonprofit and Voluntary Sector Marketing 7*, 4 (2002), 353–360.

22. Hayes, B. M. Everyday information in american philanthropy: informed giving. In *Proceedings of the 2011 iConference*, ACM (2011), 680–681.

23. Hill, S., Provost, F., and Volinsky, C. Network-based marketing: Identifying likely adopters via consumer networks. *Statistical Science 21*, 2 (2006), 256–276.

24. Hsieh, G., Hudson, S. E., and Kraut, R. E. Donate for credibility: how contribution incentives can improve credibility. In *Proceedings of the 2011 annual conference on Human factors in computing systems*, ACM (2011), 3435–3438.

25. Karlan, D., and List, J. Does price matter in charitable giving? evidence from a large-scale natural field experiment. *The American Economic Review* (2007), 1774–1793.

26. Kuo, P.-Y., and Gerber, E. Design principles: crowdfunding as a creativity support tool. In *CHI* (2012), 1601–1606.

27. Liu, Y., Chen, R., Chen, Y., Mei, Q., and Salib, S. "i loan because...": understanding motivations for pro-social lending. In *WSDM* (2012), 503–512.

28. McPherson, M., Smith-Lovin, L., and Cook, J. Birds of a feather: Homophily in social networks. *Annual review of sociology* (2001), 415–444.

29. Muller, M., Geyer, W., Soule, T., Daniels, S., and Cheng, L.-T. Crowdfunding inside the enterprise: employee-initiatives for innovation and collaboration. In *CHI* (2013), 503–512.

30. Mutz, D. *Hearing the other side: Deliberative versus participatory democracy*. Cambridge University Press, 2006.

31. Nuttin, J. Narcissism beyond gestalt and awareness: The nameletter effect. *European Journal of Social Psychology 15*, 3 (1985), 353–361.

32. Olson, M. *The logic of collective action: Public goods and the theory of groups*, vol. 124. Harvard Univ Pr, 1965.

33. Peloza, J., and Steel, P. The price elasticities of charitable contributions: a meta-analysis. *Journal of Public Policy & Marketing* (2005), 260–272.

34. Pepitone, J. Text donations raise $7m for red cross haiti effort. *CNN Money* (2010). `http://money.cnn.com/2010/01/14/technology/haiti_text_donation/`.

35. Rotman, D., Vieweg, S., Yardi, S., Chi, E., Preece, J., Shneiderman, B., Pirolli, P., and Glaisyer, T. From slacktivism to activism: participatory culture in the age of social media. In *CHI'11 Extended Abstracts on Human Factors in Computing Systems*, ACM (2011), 819–822.

36. Sakamoto, M., Nakajima, T., Liu, Y., and Alexandrova, T. Achieving sustainable society through micro-level crowdfunding. In *CHI* (2013), 1443–1448.

37. Sargeant, A., and Hudson, J. Donor retention: an exploratory study of door-to-door recruits. *International Journal of Nonprofit and Voluntary Sector Marketing 13*, 1 (2008), 89–101.

38. Sargeant, A., and Lee, S. Donor trust and relationship commitment in the uk charity sector: The impact on behavior. *Nonprofit and Voluntary Sector Quarterly 33*, 2 (2004), 185–202.

39. Shaw, K. Defining the self: Constructions of identity in community college students. *Community colleges as cultural texts* (1999), 153–172.

40. Shields, T., and Goidel, R. Who contributes? checkbook participation, class biases, and the impact of legal reforms, 1952-1994. *American Politics Research 28*, 2 (2000), 216–233.

41. Shier, M., and Handy, F. Understanding online donor behavior: the role of donor characteristics, perceptions of the internet, website and program, and influence from social networks. *International Journal of Nonprofit and Voluntary Sector Marketing* (2012).

42. Simon, A. Television news and international earthquake relief. *Journal of Communication 47*, 3 (1997), 82–93.

43. Tajfel, H., and Turner, J. An integrative theory of intergroup conflict. *The social psychology of intergroup relations 33* (1979), 47.

44. Unger, L. Altruism as a motivation to volunteer. *Journal of Economic Psychology 12*, 1 (1991), 71–100.

45. Veall, M. R., and Zimmermann, K. F. Pseudo-r2 measures for some common limited dependent variable models. *Journal of Economic Surveys 10*, 3 (1996), 241–259.

46. Wagner, C., and Wheeler, L. Model, need, and cost effects in helping behavior. *Journal of Personality and Social Psychology 12*, 2 (1969), 111.

47. Wash, R., and Lampe, C. The power of the ask in social media. In *Proceedings of the ACM 2012 conference on Computer Supported Cooperative Work*, ACM (2012), 1187–1190.

48. Weerts, D., and Ronca, J. Profiles of supportive alumni: Donors, volunteers, and those who "do it all". *International Journal of Educational Advancement 7*, 1 (2007), 20–34.

Civic Action Brokering Platforms: Facilitating Local Engagement with ACTion Alexandria

Derek L. Hansen[1], Jes A. Koepfler[2,3], Paul T. Jaeger[2], John C. Bertot[2], Tracy Viselli[4]

[1]Brigham Young University
Provo, UT, USA
dlhansen@byu.edu

[2]University of Maryland
College Park, MD, USA
{koepfler}, {pjaeger}, {jbertot} @umd.edu

[3]Intuitive Company
Philadelphia, PA, USA
jkoepfler@intuitivecompany.com

[4]BROOKINGS
Washington, DC, USA
tviselli@brookings.edu

ABSTRACT

Local communities are turning to new online systems to help motivate and coordinate local volunteerism and problem solving. Inspired by the American barn raising tradition, ACTion Alexandria is designed to help local residents and service-oriented organizations collectively take action to address pressing local needs. This paper introduces "civic action brokering" as a new theoretical concept and frames it within a year-long evaluation of ACTion Alexandria. A mixed-method, case study approach was used to understand how social practices, roles, and technologies helped or hindered successful action brokering. Successes were attributed to a competent community manager, institutional support from an existing nonprofit brokering agency, effective use of social media, a synergistic partnership with nonprofits that helped grow each group's donor network, and emphasis on promoting immediate actions and soliciting ideas for Community Challenges among residents and nonprofit organizations.

Author Keywords

Civic engagement; civic action brokering; community; case study, citizen engagement

ACM Classification Keywords

H.5.m. Information interfaces and presentation (e.g., HCI): Miscellaneous.

INTRODUCTION

In early rural American life, the barn raising tradition arose out of necessity; small efforts and contributions from large numbers of people in the surrounding area were required to construct a building that would benefit the larger community. Brought together by the harsh realities of frontier living, settlers responded to the needs of their community and peers. Whether motivated by altruism, an expectation of a returned favor, or devotion to a shared value system, the resulting local collective action helped build strong social ties and community structures.

Today's communities still face challenges as monumental as barn raising that require as many hands to construct, such as ensuring community food pantries are stocked to feed the hungry and rebuilding homes after a natural disaster strikes. Existing social media sites like Twitter and Facebook are widely used to help promote collective action, and increasingly systems are specifically designed to meet the unique needs of collective civic participation. These systems often include technical features and functions that enable crowdsourcing through social networks, but action does not occur simply because a system enables it. Though crowds do form on their own to solve social problems, there are civic challenges that go unnoticed by local residents.

One major challenge of enabling civic participation is the pairing of those who are willing to take action with those who have legitimate needs. When community problems are known, it is not always clear how one can contribute or collaborate in an unstructured, volunteer-based environment. These challenges emphasize the role of social and technical intermediaries that help match potential actors (i.e. volunteers) with those in need and the nonprofits and government agencies that serve them. We call this intermediation between those performing and those organizing civic activities *civic action brokering*.

Civic action brokering through websites and social media is part of a broader set of public engagement goals to promote what has been called "collaborative governance" or "participatory governance" – the inclusion of public agencies, non-profit civic organizations, and individuals in addressing community issues (e.g., [4,29]). Such initiatives "blur traditional boundaries between organizations, sectors, and policy design and implementation" and their success depends on meaningful involvement from all stakeholder groups in a community [29, p. 246].

This paper discusses ACTion Alexandria, a socio-technical platform designed to promote civic action brokering within the Alexandria, Virginia community. We use a case study approach to identify the social practices and technical features used by ACTion Alexandria to implement civic action brokering and assess their impact. Our analysis

CSCW '14, February 15–19, 2014, Baltimore, Maryland, USA.

http://dx.doi.org/10.1145/2531602.2531714

highlights the key factors contributing to successful collective action, as well as the challenges the community still faces for implementing effective and sustainable civic action brokering. We end by discussing key design challenges of platforms that promote civic action brokering and recapping best practices learned from the case study.

CIVIC ACTION BROKERING

This section defines the novel concept of civic action brokering, describes how it relates to other forms of online collective action, and introduces the ACTion Alexandria civic action brokering platform.

Defining Civic Action Brokering

Civic action brokering is best defined by describing its core elements:

Civic Action: The word *action* connotes "something that is done or performed, a deed, an act" [1]. In the context of civic participation, actions include acts of service (e.g., labor), provision of resources (e.g., items, money, access), sharing of expertise, and the active promotion of a cause. Actions are the primary goal of civic participation initiatives that aim to promote prosocial behaviors for the public good. The qualifier *civic* highlights that the action is "concerned with the welfare of the community as a whole, public-spirited" [10].

Brokering: The word *brokering* connotes an intermediary who negotiates an exchange between two parties [9]. The primary responsibility of a broker in a traditional, financial sense is to bring together buyers and sellers. In the context of civic action, action brokers help address social issues by matching up individuals interested in performing civic actions, called *action seekers* (e.g., potential community volunteers), with those who help organize and offer civic actions, called *action providers* (e.g., nonprofits or government agencies who work on behalf of individuals in need). Brokering may also occur between organizations who share a common mission, but who would not otherwise know about one another or work together effectively without the intermediary.

Thus, civic action brokering is the work performed by an intermediary to match action seekers with action providers so they can accomplish civic deeds. There are several potential benefits of civic action brokering. As in the financial world, the advantage of using a broker is that the broker has a comprehensive view of the market and has established relationships with the different parties. Maintaining a comprehensive network of connections takes considerable time and effort. By delegating social network maintenance to a broker, individuals and organizations can devote their scarce resources (e.g., time) to their own domain, yet remain connected via the broker to potential partnerships. In addition, brokers can help organize collective efforts that are hard for disconnected groups to perform on their own.

Civic action brokering takes place informally across many types of action seekers and action providers in local communities. It occurs, for example, when a mother invites her friend to contribute baked goods to a local PTA bake sale, when a religious congregation encourages its members to serve at the local soup kitchen, and when the local county volunteer center distributes a calendar of service events to email subscribers. In all of these cases an individual or organization plays the role of a third party broker helping to match up those seeking out or capable of volunteering with those organizing such activities. As the examples illustrate, many different individuals and organizations play the role of an action broker either intentionally or unintentionally. In this paper, we focus primarily on intentional civic action brokering via online tools, a community manager, and organizational support.

Civic Action Brokering and Online Collective Action

Civic action brokering occurs within the growing research areas of collective action, crowdsourcing, participatory challenge platforms, and technology mediated social participation. Collective action is a concept used in sociology to help explain how individuals form in a grassroots manner around an idea to create action (e.g., [18,37]). With the increase in social media tools that enable distributed collective action through online contexts, groups can form around any number of social issues to achieve goals quickly and effectively ranging from organizing protests against local regimes [34] to coordinating disaster response via online coordination networks [17].

Recently there has been increased emphasis on understanding novel platforms designed to support active participation at all levels of civic and philanthropic life [3,12,20,23,26,32]. A need to focus on both the social and technical aspects of participatory platforms has emerged in the area of technology-mediated social participation [30]. Civic action brokering advances our understanding of that broad literature by taking into account the facilitated nature of the collective actions that occur on participatory sites. Though technology is a mediating factor and we discuss its implications, this case study sheds light on the behind-the-scenes social practices of community managers, policy makers, and local citizens who use technology to mediate social participation and increase collective action.

Finally, there are some similarities between the idea of civic action brokering and crowdfunding sites, particularly philanthropic crowdfunding sites such as GiveForward and Kiva. They both leverage online resources to support micro-contributions and act as brokers to match funders with those needing funds. However, whereas crowdfunding sites are predominantly focused on fundraising, civic action brokering sites are also interested in facilitating actions (e.g., providing services, finding volunteers, collecting specific items) and ideas (e.g. community problem solving efforts). As a result, civic action brokering requires significant investments in relationship building (e.g., with local government; between nonprofits) and significant involvement by the broker who often serves as a matchmaker and helps train and support non-technically savvy organizations.

Civic Action Brokering Environment

The civic action brokering environment is presented in Figure 1. As shown, brokering occurs between Action Seekers and Action Providers. Brokering is typically mediated by a combination of technologies (e.g., web-based platform and/or social media), people (e.g., a community manager or sponsoring organization), social practices, and policies. We call this entire socio-technical system the civic action brokering platform.

A single individual or organization may serve as an Action Seeker at one time and an Action Provider at another time depending on the situation. For example, a resident may seek volunteer work at a homeless shelter and later provide service opportunities to others when organizing a neighborhood cleanup.

An implicit group of individuals within this model are the recipients or beneficiaries of the completed actions; those for whom the Action Providers and Action Seekers dedicate their work in a given action. Depending on the type of project, beneficiaries (who are also residents of the community) may themselves be Action Seekers and may come from vulnerable populations, such as those in need of housing, individuals who have been incarcerated, victims of abuse, the elderly, or the young.

Indeed, some of the better ideas for meeting the needs of vulnerable populations come from those who understand the issues best due to their own experiences. Although most civic action brokering platforms do not prevent beneficiaries of civic actions to participate as Action Seekers, the majority of interaction with beneficiaries is often mediated through Action Providers (i.e., nonprofit and government organizations in a community). This model leaves the responsibility of identifying and meeting the unique needs of various vulnerable populations in the hands of the nonprofit and government organizations most familiar with them.

A different approach would be to design a civic action brokering platform explicitly for interactions with vulnerable populations. For example, there is a small, but growing body of research considering how homeless individuals are already engaging on social media, which may be overlooked by society and other stakeholders in the social services sector (e.g., [24]). There is also some design research focused on bringing together multiple-stakeholders in specific organizations through participatory design efforts, though this has not been done in the context of designing civic action brokering platforms [19, 27, 38]. We cover this gap/opportunity further in the Discussion section.

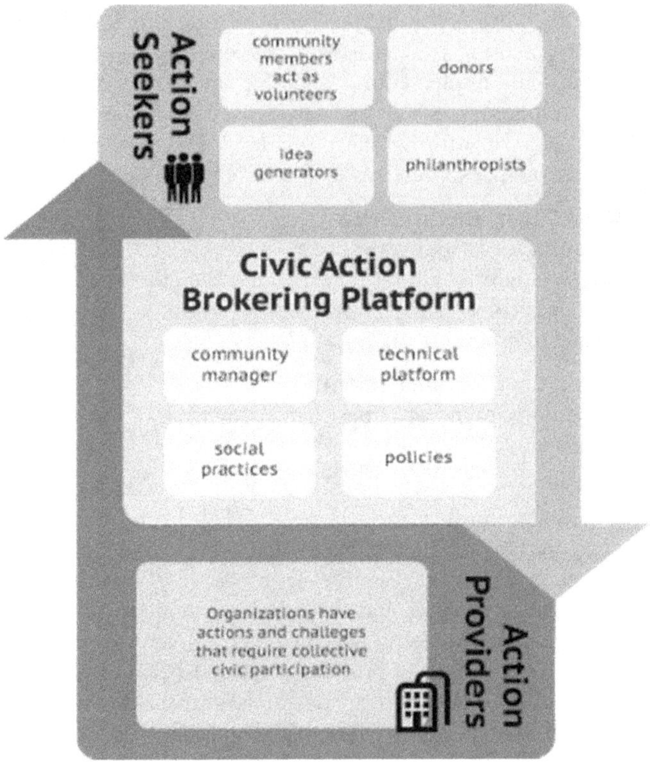

Figure 1: Civic Action Brokering Environment

Platforms that Broker Civic Action

Several large-scale platforms that broker civic action have emerged in recent years, fueled largely by advances in social media. For example, ChangeMakers by Ashoka brokers between "innovators" (civic action providers who share novel solutions to community problems) and "advocates" (action seekers who volunteer their skills and time to help innovators meet their goals). TakingITGlobal uses a similar approach, though it focuses on young adults (aged 13-30) and their schools and teachers. The "Action Tools" section of their website helps broker various types of civic actions including "commitments" in the form of pledges, "petitions" which individuals can sign and share, and "Featured Actions" (e.g., a challenge to eat a "Low Carbon Lunch"). Other platforms such as Give a Minute, Changeby.us, and BeNeighbors.org broker ideas for civic action at local levels. Puget Sound Off focuses on brokering ideas and civic actions among youth blogger journalists in a local community [13]. Despite the growing number of civic action brokering platforms, few studies have evaluated their effectiveness, or the specific technical and social aspects that lead to success or failure. The following case study of ACTion Alexandria, a city-level civic action brokering platform, illustrates the potential that such platforms have for solving community problems and sheds light on the importance of human face-to-face interactions that localized civic action brokering requires.

ACTion Alexandria Platform

ACTion Alexandria is a platform designed to broker civic actions in the form of ideas and specific activities in Alexandria, VA. As others have done, we use the term 'platform' in its broadest socio-technical sense to encompass not only the technical aspects of the system (its features and affordances), but also the core social or human elements of the system (its human mediators, participants, policies, and social context) [15,23]. The platform includes a website (Figure 2), Twitter account (@ACTionAlexVA), Facebook page (www.facebook.com/ACTionAlexandria), a full-time paid Community Manager responsible for the day-to-day operations and outreach efforts, a steering committee, and policies and procedures that underlie its use. In the sections that follow, we report on the first year of its implementation and the months leading up to its launch, which occurred on February 7, 2011.

A key component of the platform's social context is an initiative of the City's community foundation called ACT for Alexandria, which serves as a catalyst for increasing charitable efforts in the community. ACT and the City of Alexandria helped raise funding for the development of the ACTion Alexandria platform from local nonprofit organizations and a Community Information Challenge grant from the John S. and James L. Knight foundation.

ACTion Alexandria seeks to "empower citizens to take collective action on behalf of themselves and local organizations" [2]. Its three stated goals are to:

1. Create a vibrant online platform that inspires offline action, where challenges are posted, solutions are debated, successes and failures are archived, data is both disseminated and captured, stories are shared, and essential civic relationships are developed.
2. Improve the quality of life for its most vulnerable residents in a cost-efficient manner through a platform that provides everyone a voice and the opportunity to identify problems and offer solutions.
3. Engage residents and business people in problem solving to strengthen community ties and increase each individual's stake in creating positive outcomes for specific community problems.

ACTion Alexandria attempts to achieve these goals through a variety of mechanisms that help residents connect with local nonprofit organizations and government agencies. First, community members can seek out and complete *actions* – small donations of items, funds, or volunteer efforts that are posted by a local nonprofit or government agency. The "ACT Now" page (linked to from the homepage shown in Figure 2) allows people to browse and search through current and prior actions (see Figure 3). All actions can be listed and filtered by category (Arts &Culture; Education; Environment; Food & Shelter; Health; Neighborhoods), by neighborhood (of which there are 8), or keyword. By default, active actions are shown in a

Figure 2: ACTion Alexandria homepage, a civic action brokering website in Alexandria, VA.

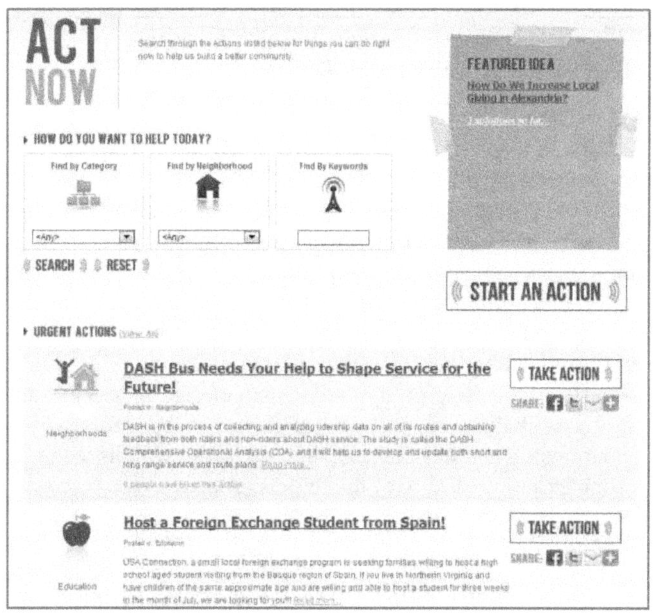

Figure 3: ACT Now page showing search functionality and 2 active actions.

list on the page. If selected, a page associated with the action is presented with a description of the action and a "Take Action" button that can be clicked to initiate the next steps in the action (e.g., take the user to a donation website or an Amazon wishlist). Additionally, certain actions are chosen by ACTion Alexandria to be Featured Actions, which show up on the main page (in the spotlight panel on the left-hand side of Figure 2 and in the list at the bottom-left column) and at the top of the ACT Now page, as well as in the email list and social media postings.

Second, residents and organizations can help brainstorm and vote on *ideas* to Community Challenges identified by ACTion Alexandria and the greater Alexandria philanthropic community. When users click on the "Share your ideas" link on the main page (see Figure 2) they are taken to a page listing all active *challenges*, along with the number of ideas already submitted to each one. Visitors can click on a specific challenge to see its description, deadlines for voting, and ideas posted by registered users. Registered users are given 3 votes per challenge to use on their preferred ideas. Users can also post comments associated with each idea. Ideas are sorted so that those with the highest number of votes are at the top.

Actions and *ideas*, as well as local events, such as in-person training for nonprofits, are promoted via the ACTion Alexandria website, Facebook page, and Twitter account, as well as emailed to a list of registered users who have opted in. Finally, residents and organizations can communicate in less structured ways by blogging (and commenting) on the ACTion Alexandria website, posting on the Facebook wall, mentioning the Twitter account, or talking in person at local meetings and events. The majority of these activities are managed on a day-to-day basis by the Community Manager with input from the ACTion Alexandria steering committee and other volunteers (e.g., bloggers).

METHODS

We chose to perform a case study of ACTion Alexandria for several reasons: 1) case studies are ideal for understanding phenomena that occur within a larger socio-technical system [14] such as a civic action brokering platform; 2) a case study approach bounds the research inquiry around the system of action that community managers and designers can influence; 3) case studies are also ideal for describing new and emerging phenomena, like civic action brokering, where little empirical investigation has been conducted to date [39]; and 4) case studies support an in-depth investigation of a phenomenon within an existing context, which leads to strong external validity of the findings.

ACTion Alexandria is an ideal case to examine for several reasons. First, the ACTion Alexandria platform brokers local civic actions in the form of what the site calls "actions" (e.g., donations of goods) as well as "ideas" (e.g., proposed solutions to known problems) allowing for a range of social practices and technical features to be examined. Second, in its first year, the platform successfully recruited over 2,000 registered users and 130 local organizations, helped raise over $100,000, and collected thousands of donated items for local nonprofit organizations allowing us to identify some of the most effective components of the system and identify areas for further inquiry. Furthermore, ACTion Alexandria allowed the authors to collect qualitative and quantitative data beginning before the platform's official launch. This unique longitudinal dataset allowed us to focus on the critical first year of civic action brokering, which is when most online communities face their greatest challenges related to increasing participation [7].

Data for this project were collected as part of a multi-year evaluation of ACTion Alexandria conducted by a team of researchers at Brigham Young University and the University of Maryland. The data collection effort for the full research and evaluation of the project includes mixed methods approaches to collect data from a variety of stakeholders (organizations, local citizens, project management team members, local government officials) and sources (digital trace data, social media data, interview and survey-based data, meeting notes) during the life of the evaluation project funding (August 2010-August 2013). In this paper we have focused on a subset of the data most relevant to illuminating the key social and technical aspects of the action brokering platform in its first year, namely interviews with organizations and key stakeholders, surveys of organizations provided as an alternative to participating in an interview, and web and social media analytics.

Prior to the launch of the site (between December 2010-February 2011) we conducted: a) a phone interview with the Community Manager, b) face-to-face interviews with four organizations identified by the Community Manager as groups who covered a range of health and human services in the community, would likely be around for the duration of the project, and were candidates to be early Featured Actions once the platform launched, and c) phone interviews with three members of the city government from Health and Human Services and Communications.

After ACTion Alexandria was active for six months, it became clear that Featured Actions (discussed more later) were a critical socio-technical feature of the early implementation phase of the platform. We reached out to organizations who were Featured Actions early on and gave them the opportunity to participate in a phone interview or to complete a questionnaire with several of our interview questions in it. In Fall 2010, we invited the 10 organizations who had been Featured Actions to that date to participate. Five elected to participate via web questionnaire, and three participated via phone interview (these individuals were also part of our early case study organizations). Three chose not to participate. Six to eight months following this period, we then conducted follow-up phone interviews with a) the Community Manager, b) three of the four original case study organizations, c) seven additional organizations who covered a broader range of services in the City including a local PTA, a historic society, a seaport foundation and others, and d) a key stakeholder from the Community Challenge that had been launched during this time period.

Interview questions (used in both the interviews and the optional questionnaire) focused on assessing the impact of the platform on organizations' actions and outcomes, effort, and time, as well as experiences of using the website, social media, and interacting with the Community Manager. For example, those who had completed Featured Actions were asked to report on how their effort to promote the action differed from other methods they had used in the past; how the results compared to their expectations and prior experiences with similar actions. Organizations were also asked what features of the ACTion Alexandria website they considered most and least useful, what role the website and social media outreach play in the community, and what could be improved.

We used a concurrent triangulation strategy to analyze the data, collecting both quantitative and qualitative data simultaneously, collecting multiple iterations of qualitative data, and then analyzing all of the data as a set [11]. In this way the weaknesses of one method can be supported by the strengths of another and a more holistic picture of the system emerges. We analyzed, summarized, and visualized website and social media analytics data using Excel 2010, Google Analytics, Facebook Insights, Bitly, and Thrive (for Twitter analytics). We analyzed qualitative data (e.g., notes and transcripts from interviews, open-ended questionnaire responses, website content) using thematic analysis [8]. Two of the authors read through all of the transcripts and iteratively identified the themes to minimize biases. Once the major themes were identified and analyzed, we were then able to relate them to existing theories and literature in the findings and discussion sections that follow. We focused on the socio-technical aspects of the platform that were most strongly emphasized in the early implementation phase of the project and identified themes that highlighted successes and challenges for the platform moving forward.

Our findings were presented to key leaders of the ACTion Alexandria initiative who provided insiders' perspectives on the data and elaborated on issues that needed further elucidation. Tracy Viselli, one of the co-authors on this paper was a member of the ACTion Alexandria leadership team. At no point in the process did ACTion Alexandria leaders discourage the evaluation team from reporting on any of their findings or being candid with limitations related to current approaches.

FINDINGS

This section reports on the first year of civic action brokering via the ACTion Alexandria platform. First, we present summary data on ACTion Alexandria from web analytics tools. Second, we present major themes related to the social practices and technical features of Featured Actions, the primary mechanism used to broker direct *actions* through the platform. Then we present the major themes for Community Challenges, the primary mechanism used to broker *ideas* for actions. We provide evidence for the impact that these two key socio-technical features had on the success of the platform as a whole, and discuss lessons learned along the way.

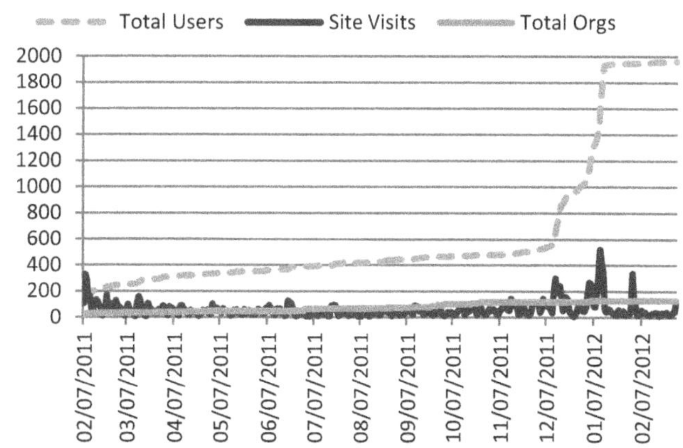

Figure 5: ACTion Alexandria registered users, organizations, and site visits over time.

ACTion Alexandria Summary Data

From February 7, 2011, to February 29, 2012, ACTion Alexandria accumulated a total of 1,963 registered members and 130 registered nonprofit organizations or government agencies. As shown in Figure 5, there was slow but steady growth from its beginning (with nearly 200 registered users in the first week) to mid-December 2011. This was followed by a month of rapid growth initiated by the Project Play Community Challenge (see Community Challenge section below), which ended in January of 2012, after which point growth continued to be incremental.

As is typical of voluntary contribution sites, users engaged with the site to varying degrees [31]. The website itself was visited 24,023 times by more than 14,621 unique visitors during this time (as reported by Google Analytics, which may overstate the number of unique visitors due to the use of different browsers and devices by a single individual). Over 9,402 of the visits (39%) were from visitors who had been to the site before. As is typical, there is a skewed distribution where 2,493 return visitors have visited 2 times, 1,173 have visited 3 times, 741 have visited 4 times. This pattern has a long tail with hundreds of people who have visited over a hundred times, indicating a core group of people who visit the site regularly.

The percent of the 1,963 registered users who logged in each month ranged from 3% to 34% depending on the actions brokered in a given month. Table 1 shows the frequency of key activities that registered users performed on the ACTion Alexandria website. Figure 6 shows a Venn diagram indicating the number of people that participated in the 3 main sections of the website: blogs (they either posted a blog or commented on one), actions (they either created or responded to an action), and challenges (they either posted an idea or voted on an idea). As shown, most people only participate in a single section, though a handful of core members participate in multiple sections. The high number of unique actors (e.g., 282 action takers) versus total actions completed (e.g., 374 actions completed) shown in Table 1

Metrics	Total Actions	Unique Actors
Website Visits	24,023	14,784
Actions Taken	374	282
Blog Posts	242	50
Blog Comments	73	64
Ideas Posted	187	36
Votes Cast	5,440	1,120

Table 1: User ACTIVITY and number of unique ACTORS on ACTion Alexandria website (02/07/2011-02/07/2012)

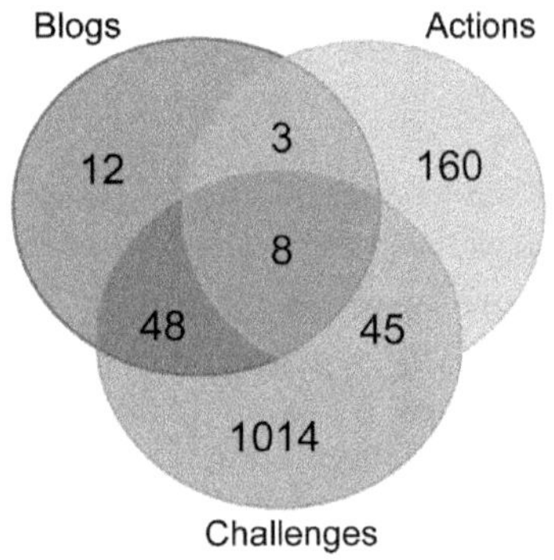

Figure 6: Venn diagram showing registered users' participation in 3 main areas of the website.

suggests that many people take only 1 action via the website (median=1 action taken). In contrast, a relatively small group of bloggers make many posts on average. Similarly, a small group of people post many ideas. Overall, there are around 100 active users who participate in multiple ways, with many others who rarely participate.

Of the 130 organizations registered on the site, only 71 (55%) have completed any actions (e.g., posted an action or blog post). This is due to the fact that many were registered by the Community Manager after getting permission from the organization, which will allow them to use the site more easily in the future.

Many people interacted with ACTion Alexandria via their Facebook and Twitter accounts. The Facebook page had an initial spike of fans, followed by steady monthly growth at an average of 20 new fans a month culminating in 464 fans as of February 29, 2012. According to Facebook Insights data collected since October 2011, the Facebook page averaged 176 contributions by engaged users (e.g., mentions, likes, shares) and 76 discussions (i.e. people talking about ACTion Alexandria) per month. ACTion Alexandria's Twitter account had 1,159 Followers as of February 29, 2012. It spurred 2,222 retweets, mentions, and replies during the first year with an average of 156 per month for the period after its initial announcement. These led to a total of 5,085 clicks on links embedded in the Tweets (according to Bit.ly), with an average of 222 per month for the period after its initial announcement. Taken together, it is clear that much of the brokering occurred via social media channels, though the website and email list also played important roles.

Actions and Featured Actions

Actions, a designated term for small acts of service such as donating goods and money or volunteering one's time, are one of the core elements brokered by the ACTion Alexandria platform. Local nonprofits or government agencies (i.e. action providers) sponsor actions, and community residents (i.e. action seekers) complete them. Actions typically require small contributions from a large number of Action Seekers over a short period of time (usually one week) to meet an immediate need. Actions are often in the form of small monetary donations, specific items such as diapers or Pedialyte, or one-time service opportunities. Any organization using the ACTion Alexandria system can post actions, which can be searched for by topic on the website. During the first year, a total of 61 actions were submitted. Most of the actions were not particularly successful, averaging only 6 action takers (median=2) as recorded on the website. This is likely due to the small number of active participants on the website itself, as opposed to other components of the platform (like social media). The word-of-mouth and viral marketing efforts were considerably lower for actions as opposed to Featured Actions, which were facilitated and promoted by the Community Manager in the project's first year.

Featured Actions are week-long campaigns that seek to meet an urgent community need identified by a local nonprofit in conjunction with the Community Manager. Often the Community Manager helped identify a corporate sponsor who matched funds for items raised by the community. Featured Actions were promoted via the ACTion Alexandria homepage, email list, Facebook page, and Twitter account, as well as by the organization sponsoring the specific Featured Action.

An example Featured Action campaign was a diaper drive for Community Lodgings, a local nonprofit dedicated to helping families exit homelessness through transitional and affordable housing and through youth and adult education programs. Community lodgings sought to raise 640 disposable diapers (a one-month supply) in one week to provide to the families they work with. By the end of the week, community members had donated 2,500 diapers to Community Lodgings, nearly 4 times the requested amount.

A total of 14 Featured Actions (including an annual Spring2Action online fundraising drive) were promoted during the first year of the project (23% of the total actions). These were far more successful than non-featured actions. They averaged 19 responses (median=21) and in total community members contributed \$115,680 in online donations and 3,720 items (valued at \$4,338) to City of Alexandria nonprofits, making the overall donation total \$120,018. Donated items included medicine, food, diapers, children's books, and toys.

Based on the number of items collected, money raised, and services provided, there is no question that the Featured Actions were successful and a critical component of the platform in its early implementation phase. All but one of the Featured Actions promoted in the platform's first year met or exceeded their goal. Featured Actions through ACTion Alexandria enabled some nonprofits to accomplish more than they would have on their own (e.g., one questionnaire respondent stated that "[we] generated more donations than a typical email blast or other drive that we would have put together ourselves."). Several of the Featured Action nonprofits mentioned that they would not have launched a campaign like the one they launched for the Featured Action had it not been for ACTion Alexandria. This was particularly the case because many nonprofits did not have the technological sophistication and experience to perform online action-based initiatives (e.g., one interviewee stated that "[ACTion Alexandria] provided something that we really couldn't bring to the table.").

Community Manager Time and Expertise

The role of the Community Manager was critical to the success of Featured Actions. Because this form of crowdsourced charity mediated by a web-based system was new to most organizations, it was not always clear to them how to craft a Featured Action that would appeal to residents. The Community Manager was able to use her experience to help organizations scope out and frame strong campaigns in this new online context:

> "[The Community Manager] was extremely helpful in helping us create an action that would be well received by the public. She also helped us choose a goal that was attainable and was supportive during the length of the campaign." (Featured Action questionnaire respondent, Fall 2011)

> "I was talking with the city about a need that we have in terms of providing resources to some of the vulnerable families that we serve and I was like wow, we should talk to [the Community Manager] and see if we can get an action [featured]..." (Non-case study interview, June 2012)

In addition, resource-poor organizations benefited from the Community Manager's help in developing promotional materials, getting matching funds from corporations, which were highly valued by the organizations, and coordinating the launch of the action. This all made the cost of participation low for organizations, despite the "extra work" needed to coordinate with the Community Manager, which was not part of their regular workflow. It was clear from the interviews and comments that without the Community Manager's heavy involvement many of the Featured Actions would not have occurred and would otherwise probably not have been as successful as they were.

Quantitative results tied to the actions support the importance of the Community Manager's ability to help craft and promote actions and Featured Actions. The Community Manager posted 23 actions (14 of which were featured). These averaged 13 responses (median=10); far greater than the average of 2 responses (median=1) for actions posted by others. Even the 9 non-featured actions posted by the Community Manager outperformed actions posted by others (average of 5 responses; median=3 compared to average of 2 responses; median=1). Table 2 summarizes best practices used by the Community Manager. While other techniques may also work, these were sufficient to have a high success rate.

Last for a short duration (e.g., one week)
Focus on a single, well-defined and measurable goal (e.g., X number of diapers, Y dollar amount to go towards Z)
Allow contributors to make micro- and macro-contributions (i.e. no contribution is too small)
Clearly demonstrate how it will benefit the organization and the individuals it serves
Relate to a popular need that resonates with the public (e.g., oriented around children)
Be a joint effort between the organization sponsoring the action and the action broker (i.e. ACTion Alexandria)
Have matching funds from a corporate sponsor to increase incentives for organizations to participate.

Table 2: Featured Action Best Practices

Leveraging ACTion Alexandria's Social Network

ACTion Alexandria helped organizations extend their reach to a larger network of residents via the Featured Action emails and promotion on Facebook and Twitter. This helped the organizations reach their goals quicker while also making more people aware of the organization. Thus, the messages from ACTion Alexandria complemented the work the organizations were already performing via their own outreach methods, which ranged from email lists to social media to on-the-ground outreach via church congregations and events.

Organizations that were smaller or less well known for other reasons (e.g., they were new) had the most to gain from being featured, since their existing network was limited. The following comments from two different nonprofits we interviewed illustrate this point:

> "We wouldn't have had the capacity to do it on our own. We don't have the network of people to put it out to. [...]Our listserv is not nearly as pervasive as the one that ACTion Alexandria has." (Case study follow-up interview, June 2012)

> "The biggest impact was [the Community Manager] being able to get the word out. We just have a sense that more people are aware of us now." (Case study follow-up interview, June 2012)

Growing ACTion Alexandria's Social Network

ACTion Alexandria also extended its own network as a result of the Featured Action mechanism, because the sponsoring organizations helped provide a continual source of new members to the site. Nonprofit organizations promoted their own actions through whatever existing channels they had including email lists, newsletters, social media accounts, contacts at religious organizations, etc. Inevitably, this reached many people not yet part of ACTion Alexandria. Those who learned about the action were taken to ACTion Alexandria's website where there was a detailed description of the action and a plea to register and click "Take Action", directing the resident to an Amazon wishlist, donation button, or other appropriate link. Website analytics and registration dates make it clear that Featured Actions accounted for the majority of the steady, if small, growth in membership throughout the first year. Unfortunately, this model was difficult to completely enforce, as nonprofit organizations could post a different link to their donation page and the nature of the action could make tracking it online difficult (e.g., delivering books in person). There is a balance that must be made between the desire to make actions as simple as possible to complete and the desire to extend the resident network associated with ACTion Alexandria.

Competition in the Nonprofit Sector

When pressed to identify concerns about the platform, nonprofits mentioned competition as a potential issue when interviewed before the launch. For example, some organizations expressed reservations about the idea of Featured Actions because they feared that it might unfairly privilege some organizations over others. Nonprofits often compete for the same scarce resources and, as a broker, ACTion Alexandria has the potential to drive attention and resources to one organization over another. A case study interviewee expressed concerns of "donor burnout" and wondered if all the nonprofits could get what they needed out of "a diminishing or exhausted pot [of funding and resources]."

Though several organizations mentioned concerns about this before the site was launched, they still felt like the opportunities would outweigh the risks, particularly if ACTion Alexandria was fair in the way they chose who to feature. In follow-up interviews, nonprofits indicated that competition had not arisen due to the use of Featured Actions, though we primarily interviewed organizations who had been featured, so it is possible other non-featured organizations felt otherwise.

Members of the ACTion Alexandria steering committee did not see the competition concern explicitly expressed by nonprofits, but noted that some organizations were hesitant to drive their constituents to the ACTion Alexandria website because of the extra work involved or due to fear of losing their own website traffic. Because the initiative was so new in this first year, the demand from nonprofits was not significant, as indicated by the need of the Community Manager to actively solicit nonprofits to partner with on Featured Actions. However, as ACTion Alexandria becomes more prominent, this issue will likely need to be revisited.

Technical Capabilities of Donor Tracking

A second concern about the platform was the difficulty that organizations had using it to track donors or to synchronize their other tracking tools with the information coming in as a result of being a Featured Action. One government official mentioned the ability to track and evaluate community impact as a key feature she hoped for in the platform:

> "...if we could track where we are now in terms of numbers and citizens who interact with the government versus where we are a year after we've fully launched with ACTion Alexandria, because once again that one notion is key – when we've reached the 'non-usual' suspects and get new ideas." (Government, pre-launch interview)

Unfortunately, tracking donors and volunteer time among the variety of organizations and features of the system remains a challenge for the platform. Organizations commented on the challenges that they had trying to combine their current systems (like Amazon.com wishlists) with the ACTion Alexandria platform:

> "[We were] not able to track the actual donors. Donors made a donation using Amazon's wishlist and we did not receive their contact information. When [we] logged in as the administrator [in ACTion Alexandria] we saw names of anyone who clicked on the action, but they did not necessarily purchase a book [for the book drive]." (Featured Action questionnaire respondent)

Civic action brokering platforms should carefully consider the importance of developing tracking technologies that might integrate with common web-based donation tools that organizations and governmental agencies are already using, as this is a key part of a nonprofit's overall workflow and efforts and may lead to increased adoption of the system over time.

Sustainability of Featured Actions Moving Forward

One downside of using the Featured Action mechanism was that it drew so much attention toward the actions that were featured that other actions posted on the site by organizations went largely unnoticed. As mentioned earlier, non-featured actions had very few if any respondents. Also, some organizations that were used to receiving assistance from the Community Manager in crafting and promoting their Featured Action were not interested in creating their own non-featured actions on the site. Indeed, several organizations did not know that actions and Featured Actions were different.

While additional training and familiarity may alleviate this issue, the prominent use of Featured Actions may obscure the use of regular actions or set up the expectation that the Community Manager needs to be heavily involved with all actions leading to sustainability issues down the road. The limited time of the Community Manager created a bottleneck that restricted the number of Featured Actions that could be promoted in a given month (e.g., Action Alexandria averaged 2 per month). Additionally, people have a limited amount of attention, which also limits the number of actions that could be featured even independent of the Community Manager's time. Training organizations to develop their own successful actions and take on more of the responsibility of running Featured Actions will be essential for the future sustainability and growth of ACTion Alexandria and is something for all civic action brokering platforms to be concerned with. Additionally, providing organizations with mechanisms to target non-featured actions to registered users who have interests in their organization may help as well. ACTion Alexandria has a notification system that allows people to "follow" an organization and get updates such as new actions tied to the organization, but was not widely promoted or used during the time of this study as it required extra effort from the user to set up.

Community Challenges and Ideas

Another core activity of ACTion Alexandria is brokering *ideas* that address community-wide concerns or opportunities. A space for citizens to generate and respond to ideas was of great importance to the local government and organizations before the launch of the platform. In particular the web-based platform was seen as a tool that might encourage voices that were otherwise missing from city meetings to participate in the local civic discourse:

> "That's always, I think, something that we work really hard to do and I think sometimes puzzles us and confounds us is getting those unheard voices to the table. For years, you try to get kids to the table, to get youth and the parents of the youth in the city to speak up and to become part of the solution and that's, you know, it's always how do you get there? How do you get to them?" (Government interview, pre-launch 2010)

The Community Manager, in conjunction with the local nonprofits and government agencies, identified a problem or issue that could benefit from community input. The Community Challenge was posted to the website, outreach (online and offline) was conducted, and residents shared their *ideas* for solutions on the website. Next, a voting round occured, which helped identify the best (i.e. most popular) submitted ideas. The Community Manager followed up and appropriate steps were taken based on the top ideas. During the first year, ACTion ran 13 challenges, which solicited 187 ideas from 36 different people (average of 14 ideas per challenge) and 5,440 votes on those ideas by 1,120 people (see Table 1). Initial challenges were seeded with ideas from the Community Manager, while later challenges solicited ideas from residents.

Community Challenge topics varied dramatically from having residents propose ideas to make Alexandria a more sustainable community to provide feedback on a new set of community quality of life indicators. The Challenge with the highest level of participation had residents nominate a playground that would receive a $15,000 Spruce Up grant from Project Play, an initiative put together by the Community Manager and several local organizations, with the goal of ensuring that "every child in Alexandria has a quality space to play." A total of 22 ideas were submitted by residents who posted detailed descriptions of why a particular playground warranted the grant and included photos to help tell the story. The leading ideas received over 1,000 votes, helping identify potential playgrounds with wide community support.

Initial Challenges did not solicit as much input as later ones, likely because awareness was greater later in the year and because of the nature of the challenges. The Project Play challenge, which was run in December of 2011 showed the potential of Challenges and was directly responsible for the site's highest increase in registered users by far (see Figure 3). It led to over 4,000 votes from 1,000 participants in under a month. All the voting was conducted through the ACTion Alexandria website. At the time of this study, it was not clear if the new members who joined in order to vote would translate into a larger number of people taking other actions or submitting other ideas. However, the Community Challenges increased the total community investment in 2011 to over $210,000 through the addition of $92,500 in grant money that was brought to the table through collaboration fostered by Community Challenges, particularly via Project Play.

Role of the Civic Action Brokering Management Team

The successes of the Community Challenges were largely a result of the ACTion Alexandria management team's connections, insights, and efforts. Since 2004, ACT for Alexandria, the primary sponsor of ACTion Alexandria, has promoted philanthropic activity through training and organizing the nonprofit and government sector in Alexandria. For example, they sponsor an annual Spring2ACTion event where they bring together nonprofit and local government organizations to network, share best practices, and teach new skills such as how to effectively use social media. Those skills are then put into action during a competitive, community-wide fundraising drive.

ACT steering committee members and the Community Manager sit on many community councils, participate in town hall meetings, and interface with the local government. Because of these endeavors, ACT for Alexandria, and by extension ACTion Alexandria, enjoyed a great deal of social capital among the philanthropic community as evidenced by the very positive comments from interviewees. Indeed, most interviewees did not differentiate between ACT for Alexandria (the parent organization) and ACTion Alexandria (the initiative centered on the website, social media initiatives, and community manager) as they discussed the merits and challenges of the platform.

ACT for Alexandria's pre-existing position as a network hub among the Alexandria nonprofit community placed its steering committee, including the ACTion Alexandria Community Manager, in an ideal position to help broker and aggregate actions among residents and organizations. Their panoramic view of the entire community-giving and volunteering network in Alexandria allowed them to see problems that nonprofits shared as well as opportunities for collaboration. ACTion Alexandria Community Challenges acted as a podium for nonprofits to draw attention to some larger social issues in the community, while at the same time getting fresh ideas from residents who could directly contribute their feedback.

The Project Play Community Challenge discussed earlier is an example where ACTion Alexandria's Community Manager helped broker a partnership between three local nonprofits that had not worked closely together before. The initial success of the challenge led to a continued partnership among these and additional nonprofit organizations and the city government officials via the Project Play Task Force. This group met regularly to improve playground policies, seek foundation funding, and coordinate joint activities. One interviewee who served on the Project Play Task Force described the benefits of having ACTion Alexandria serve as a broker in these words:

> "An interesting outcome with ACTion [Alexandria] is that we've learned a lot about additional community collaborations that we didn't know of before, particularly with several PTAs." (Community Challenge interviewee, March 2012)

A Competent Community Manager

As with Featured Actions, the Community Manager was critical in framing Community Challenges so they would resonate with residents and generate enthusiasm and ideas.

Popular challenges tend to be ones where there is a "winner" associated with the ideas that are generated through a process of community voting.
Community Challenges work well when they are sponsored by a project that spans multiple organizations and focuses on a social issue rather than a specific organization (e.g., childhood obesity, teen pregnancy, or affordable housing).
The topic should be something that affects many people in the community or be something that many people in the community care about.
Challenges last longer on the site (one to two months) and culminate in a week-long voting period by community members.

Table 3: Community Challenge Best Practices

Table 3 outlines some best practices for Community Challenges derived from interviews with the Community Manager and the researchers' comparison of the various challenges run in the first year. The importance of having a competent Community Manager that nonprofits trusted cannot be overstated. A large part of the success of the ACTion Alexandria project resulted from crafting a meaningful Community Manager role (Table 4) and hiring an experienced, enthusiastic, full-time person to fill it.

Creates and posts actions, community challenges, blog posts, Tweets, Facebook wall posts, events, and other community information.
Identifies actions that fulfill an urgent human service need in the community and works with a nonprofit partner to run a week-long Featured Action campaign to meet a specific goal (100 books, 640 diapers, $500 for a room renovation at a shelter, etc.).
Identifies community problems ripe for citizen-sourced solutions and posts them as challenges to the community on an ideation platform.
Continually conducts community outreach through a variety of methods both online and offline.
Manages most aspects of the website and public relations (website administration, community organizing, email marketing, editorial content, sponsorships, organization partners, marketing, etc.).

Table 4: Community Manager Role at ACTion Alexandria

Interviewees described the Community Manager as "amazing", "delightful to work with", "helpful and accommodating", "knowledgeable about social media and "willing to share." The following quote describes how the Community Manager helped make one Community Challenge a success:

> "I've been working pretty collaboratively with [the Community Manager]. We talk about it ahead of time; about the kinds of information she thinks will be useful, the kinds of information I think will be useful, the timing, and then I try to send her information and then she sort of translates it to the website." (Community Challenge interviewee, March 2012)

One challenge with having a Community Manager that is so central to the successful operation of civic action brokering is that it introduces a single point of failure. If a Community Manager without the right skillset is hired, the credibility of the entire civic action brokering system can be jeopardized. Additionally, relying on a single Community Manager to take on too many responsibilities may lead to burnout or a lack of scalability.

Increasing Capacity through Social Media

Another key factor leading to the success of the Community Challenges, similar to Featured Actions, was the effective use of social media. Indeed, social media is the kind of tool that several interviewees said they wished they used more effectively, but did not have the time or capacity to do well. Because Community Challenges required large amounts of participation in order to be successful, strategic campaigning through social media greatly increases the word-of-mouth communication about the challenge and drives people to the website. In this way, ACTion Alexandria filled a critical gap for its community of nonprofit and government agencies.

Raising Awareness

The benefit of a Community Challenge in particular was that it allowed organizations to get input from residents early in a project and build an audience around an issue that might not otherwise have existed. Not only were Community Challenges useful for getting the word out about ACTion Alexandria and increasing its membership, but they were useful for raising awareness about social issues in the community. The following comment from an interviewee involved in the Project Play challenge highlights this finding:

> "The awareness piece is raised and we have at least some audience to spread information out about our play equipment and sort of the next steps… It will be interesting to see whether and how we can mobilize that to a greater degree… It's another forum for spreading information to the public." (Case study follow-up interview, June 2013)

DISCUSSION

Nonprofits and government agencies at all levels in many nations are increasing their use of social technologies as a way to reach members of the public in new locations, extend government services, promote democratic participation and engagement, crowdsource solutions and innovations, and co-produce valuable community resources [5,21,30]. Despite the well-articulated potential benefits of civically-oriented social technologies, few studies have empirically demonstrated success. Some even argue that the Internet has had an overall negative effect on civic engagement so far [6].

This paper characterizes a promising approach of civic engagement as *civic action brokering*, calling for socio-technical platforms that are explicitly designed to broker between Action Seekers (i.e., volunteers) and Action Providers (i.e., organizations and individuals with ideas for improving the human condition). It is in line with earlier calls for technology that better supports connectedness within civic networks [35,36], though our focus on civic action brokering platforms is unique. Having said that, many prior studies can be viewed through the lens of civic action brokering.

Prior work on information exchange systems such as Barter [33], or public deliberation sites tied to civic action (e.g., public ballot initiatives) such as ConsiderIt [25], fit well within the construct of civic action brokering, though ACTion Alexandria's experience suggests new strategies to broker more than just ideas. The benefits that ACTion Alexandria received as a result of being a civic action brokering hub are consistent with earlier work that suggests that online spaces that support local communities are most viable when they cover a range of topics [28]. Work on technologies that support fundraising (including matching up potential donors with nonprofits, teaching to use online tools, and enabling individual and community advocacy [16]) and crowdfunding also fits well within the civic action brokering construct, though they address just part of the potential scope of action brokering as discussed earlier. Indeed, the success of ACTion Alexandria's Spring2Action event suggests that civic action brokering platforms are particularly well suited to help with community-wide fundraising efforts and may want to partner with crowdfunding sites.

There is still opportunity to expand and engage a broader conceptualization of what a civic action brokering platform could be by considering the role that *all* citizens of a community can play in the distribution of goods, services, and ideas. This includes considering the role of the beneficiaries of actions; often groups who identified as vulnerable or who may be marginalized. We raised this question to our case study organizations in pre-launch interviews and the following quote highlights a number of obstacles that stand in the way from a social norms perspective that should continue to be addressed by the CSCW community:

> Researcher: The last question I have is do you imagine any direct involvement of your constituents here, of the families that are staying here [at the shelter], with some kind of system like ACTion Alexandria?
>
> Interviewee: I don't know if they would post their needs. I don't know. That's a good question. Because most of the protocol is that you have to go through an agency to get anything, because there's a safeguard in that to some extent, because nobody's abusing it. I don't know. That's interesting. I guess we could certainly send our clients over to our computer lab and say go to ACTion Alexandria, pick out what you want and then tell them what you need. It's almost empowering, which is really what we want to do with our clients because they're supposed to be self sufficient. …but you know then that might be a mistake, I don't know. …To open it up to everybody. Whatever they want they could come get it from ACTion Alexandria… there might be a level of entitlement there. (Case study interview, pre-launch)

While overall, we believe the first year of ACTion Alexandria was a success, the experience raised several socio-technical design challenges that will need to be addressed by civic action brokering platforms more generally. First, as discussed, a heavy reliance on a Community Manager and the limits of human attention make scaling up the number of actions and challenges difficult. This may become even more of an issue for civic action brokering platforms that work with larger groups than a single city. Second, once civic action brokering platforms are well recognized and sought after by nonprofits that want to partner, the competitive nature of philanthropy must be dealt with in a reasonable or even mutually beneficial way. Mechanisms will need to be designed to address fairness (e.g., which nonprofit is featured) and create win-win opportunities for nonprofits who collaborate (as the Project Play example demonstrated are possible). Third, strategies and tools that foster continued engagement among initial participants are needed (as discussed in [31] more generally). As mentioned earlier, most participants only visited the ACTion Alexandria site once and participated in a single aspect of the site. Strategies such as transitioning winning ideas into Featured Actions may help users learn about and become more active in different aspects of the site. Finally, civic action brokering technologies must integrate with tracking tools already used by nonprofits. Otherwise, they risk being perceived as "extra work" to implement, as well as fail to demonstrate the value of the brokering relationship.

Any approach to addressing these challenges must consider the entire socio-technical system. Indeed, throughout this paper we have talked about "design" in the broad sense of the term, focusing on social relationships, technologies, and ways of structuring activities, all of which are intertwined. The novelty of ACTion Alexandria derives not so much from the specific technologies employed, as from the unique way of organizing activity into a civic action brokering platform, both in person and via online tools. Having said that, ACTion Alexandria has only slowly come to recognize their unique role as a civic action broker, and there are ample opportunities to design tools and activities and social structures that will explicitly support this function.

This paper presents a first step in understanding how to effectively support civic action brokering, particularly during the first year. Some of the practical takeaway messages derived from the case study include:

- Define the role of Community Manager and hire someone experienced with the requisite skill-set including the ability to act as a social network hub and community organizer, perform effective online (e.g., social media) and offline outreach and fundraising, and identify and frame opportunities for collective action and idea generation.
- Leverage organizations with existing social capital when launching new web-based initiatives for civic action brokering.
- Provide initial support for nonprofits that need help in crafting compelling and achievable campaigns for *actions* and *ideas* that will work in an online environment.
- Create win-win network-building opportunities where organizations and civic action brokering networks promote actions and ideas, and in so doing drive their own networks toward the other in a virtuous cycle. Starting with popular actions and ideas with well-known sponsoring organizations may be especially important in the early implementation stage.
- Broker actions and ideas between different nonprofits, as well as between nonprofits and residents.

ACTion Alexandria succeeded in part due to the fertile conditions it was planted in: the willingness of the local government to help fund the project, the leadership of an existing non-profit brokering organization, and the exceeding generosity of the people of Alexandria. Local communities without such support may prove too barren an environment for civic action brokering through web-based systems to thrive, even if such communities are the ones with the greatest need for it.

It should be noted that this paper only reviews the first year of the initiative, so these results, no matter how promising, are still early results. Subsequent years may reveal a new set of strategies necessary to successfully broker civic actions in a way that is scalable and sustainable over time. Future research will need to elucidate the changes in approach made by ACTion Alexandria, as well as other models of success from different platforms. Though our current understanding of civic action brokering is in its infancy, we hope the experience of ACTion Alexandria and the new theoretical focus will help inspire additional platforms designed to meet the needs of residents and service providers alike.

ACKNOWLEDGEMENTS

Many thanks to the members of the ACT for Alexandria team for their insights and support of this project along with funding by the Bruhn Morris Family Foundation. We would like to acknowledge Frank Bonnevier and Kaitlin Peterson of iPAC at the University of Maryland and Cheng Wan of Drexel University for their assistance with this project. Finally, a very special thank you goes to the research participants for this project who took time out of their busy schedules to participate in interviews and surveys.

REFERENCES

1. action, v. *Oxford English dictionary, 3rd Ed* (N.D.).
2. ACTion Alexandria. About ACTion Alexandria. (2011) http://www.actionalexandria.org/about
3. Ansell, C., & Gash, A. Collaborative governance in theory and practice. *Journal of Public Administration Research and Theory 18*, (2007), 543-571.
4. Bertot, J. C., Jaeger, P. T., & Grimes, J. M. Promoting transparency and accountably through ICTs, social media, and collaborative e-government. *Transforming Government: People, Process and Policy 6*, (2012), 78-91.
5. Bertot, J. C., Jaeger, P. T., Munson, S., & Glaisyer, T. Engaging the public in open government: The policy and government application of social media technology for government transparency. *IEEE Computer 43*, 11 (2010), 53-59.
6. Besser, T. L. Changes in small town social capital and social engagement. *Journal of Rural Studies 25*, (2009), 185-193.
7. Bishop, J. Increasing participation in online communities: A framework for human-computer interaction. *Computers in Human Behavior 23,* 4, (2007), 1881-1893.
8. Braun, V. & Clarke, V. Using thematic analysis in psychology. *Qualitative Research in Psychology 3,* 2, (2006), 77-101.
9. broker, v. *Oxford English Dictionary, 3rd Ed* (N.D.)
10. civic-minded, adj. *Oxford English Dictionary, 3rd Ed.* (N.D.).

11. Creswell, J. W. *Research design: Qualitative, quantitative, and mixed methods approaches*. Thousand Oaks, CA: Sage Publications (2009), pp. 213-214.

12. Desouza, K. C. Leveraging the wisdom of crowds through participatory platforms: Designing and planning smart cities. *Planetizen: Planning, Design & Development*, (2012), www.planetizen.com/node/55051

13. Farnham, S., Keyes, D., Yuki, V., and Tugwell, C. Puget sound off: Fostering youth civic engagement through citizen journalism. *Proc. of CSCW 2012*, ACM Press, (2012), 285-294.

14. Feagin, J. R., Orum, A. M., & Sjoberg, G. (Eds.). *A Case for the Case Study*. Chapel Hill, NC: The University of North Carolina. (1991).

15. Gillespie, T. The politics of 'platforms'. *New Media & Society 12*(3), (2010), 347-364.

16. Goecks, J., Voida, A., Voida, S., Mynatt, E.D. Charitable technologies: Opportunities for collaborative computing in nonprofit fundraising. *Proc. of CSCW 2008*, ACM Press, (2008), 689-698.

17. Goggins, S., Mascaro, C., Mascaro, S. Relief work after the 2010 Haiti earthquake: leadership in an online resource coordination network. *Proc. of CSCW 2012*, ACM Press, (2012), 57-66.

18. Hardin, R. *Collective Action*. Baltimore: Johns Hopkins University Press, (1982).

19. Hendry, D. G., Woelfer, J. P., Harper, R., Bauer, T., Fitzer, B., & Champagne, M. How to integrate digital media into a drop-in for homeless young people for deepening relationships between youth and adults. *Children and Youth Services Rev. 33*, 5 (2011), 774-782.

20. Jaeger, P. T., & Bertot, J. C. Designing, implementing, and evaluating user-centered and citizen-centered e-government. *International Journal of Electronic Government Research 6,* 2, (2010), 1-17.

21. Jaeger, P. T., Bertot, J. C., & Shilton, K. Information policy and social media: Framing government-citizen Web 2.0 interactions. In C. G. Reddick & S. K. Aikins (Eds.), *Web 2.0 Technologies and Democratic Governance: Political, Policy and Management Implications*, London: Springer, (2012), 11-25.

22. Janssen, M., & Estevez, E. Lean government and platform-based government – Doing more with less. *Government Information Quarterly 25*, 3, (2008), 400-428.

23. Johnston, E. & Hansen, D. L. Design lessons for smart governance infrastructures. In A. P. Balutis, T. F. Buss, & D. Ink (Eds.) *Transforming American Governance: Rebooting the Public Square. National Academy of Public Administration*, (2011).

24. Koepfler, J.A., Shilton, K., & Fleischmann, K.R. A stake in the issue of homelessness: Identifying values of interest for design in online communities. *Proc.of C&T 2013*, ACM Press (2013), 1-10.

25. Kriplean, T., Morgan, J., Freelon, D., Borning, A., and Bennett. L. Supporting reflective public thought with considerit. *Proc. of CSCW 2012*, ACM Press, (2012), 265-274.

26. Lathrop, D. & Ruma, L. (Eds.) *Open Government: Collaboration, Transparency, and Participation in Action*. Sebastopol, CA: O'Reilly Media, Inc. (2010).

27. Le Dantec, C. A., Farrell, R. G., Christensen, J. E., Bailey, M., Ellis, J. B., W. A. Kellogg, W. A., and Edwards, W. K. Publics in practice: Ubiquitous computing at a shelter for homeless mothers. *Proc. of CHI*, ACM Press (2010), 1687–1696.

28. López, C.A. and Butler, B.S. Consequences of content diversity for online public spaces for local communities. *Proc. of CSCW 2013*, ACM Press, (2013), 673-682.

29. Page, S. Integrative leadership for collaborative governance: Civic engagement in Seattle. *Leadership Quarterly 21*, (2012), 246-263.

30. Pirolli, P., Preece, J., & Shneiderman, B. Cyberinfrastructure for social action on national priorities. *Computer, 43*, 11, (2010), 20-21.

31. Preece, J. & Shneiderman, B. The reader-to-leader framework: Motivating technology-mediated social participation. *Transactions on Human-Computer Interaction 1*, 1, (2009). 13-32.

32. Schroeter, R. Engaging new digital locals with interactive urban screens to collaboratively improve the city. *Proc. of CSCW 2012*, ACM Press, (2012), 227-236.

33. Shen, D., Van Alstyne, M., Lippman, A., and Benbya, H. Barter – Mechanism Design for a Market Incented Wisdom Exchange. *Proc. of CSCW 2012*, ACM Press, (2012), 275-284.

34. Starbird, K. and Palen, L. (How) will the revolution be retweeted?: Information diffusion and the 2011 Egyptian uprising. *Proc. of CSCW 2012*, ACM Press, (2012), 7-16.

35. Stoll, J., Edwards, W.K., Foot, K.A. Between us and them: building connectedness within civic networks. *Proc. of CSCW 2012*, ACM Press, (2012), 237-240.

36. Stoll, J., Edwards, W.K., Foot, K.A. Interorganizational coordination and awareness in a nonprofit ecosystem. *Proc. of CSCW 2010*, ACM Press, (2010), 51-60.

37. Tarrow, S. *Power in Movement: Social Movements, Collective Action and Politics*. New York: Cambridge University Press, (1994).

38. Woelfer, J. P., Iverson, A., Hendry, D. G., Friedman, B., and Gill, B. Improving the safety of homeless young people with mobile phones: Values, form, and function. *Proc. of CHI*, ACM Press (2011), 1707-1716.

39. Yin, R. K. *Case study research: Design and methods, 4th ed.* Thousand Oaks, CA: Sage Publications, Inc. (2008).

MyPosition: Sparking Civic Discourse by a Public Interactive Poll Visualization

Nina Valkanova[1,2], Robert Walter[1], Andrew Vande Moere[3], Jörg Müller[4,1]

[1] Quality and Usability Lab
Telekom Innovation Laboratories, TU Berlin
firstname.lastname@tu-berlin.de

[2] Music Technology Group, Universitat Pompeu Fabra
nina.valkanova@upf.edu

[3] Research[x]Design - Department of Architecture
KU Leuven
andrew.vandemoere@asro.kuleuven.be

[4] Alexander von Humboldt Institute for Internet and Society
joerg.mueller@hiig.de

ABSTRACT
We present the design and evaluation of *MyPosition*, a public display in the form of a large projection, featuring an interactive poll visualization. *MyPosition* aims at facilitating the deliberation and comparison of individual opinions on locally relevant topics in an opportunistic and engaging way. We evaluated *MyPosition* in an in-the-wild study and demonstrated that the engaging nature of the installation was effective in enticing public discussion. We found that (i) the increased identifiability of users positively impacted the engagement with and the social debate around the installation, however lowered the actual voting rate; (ii) people submitted their personal opinion instead of playing around with the interactive features; and (iii) the display led to considerable discussion as well as nudging among people, in particular in zones beyond the interaction area in front of the screen.

Author Keywords
Public display; urban screen; urban visualization; in-the-wild study; awareness, reflection; gestural interaction.

ACM Classification Keywords
H5.m. Information interfaces and presentation (e.g., HCI): Miscellaneous.

INTRODUCTION
Interactive electronic displays are becoming increasingly ubiquitous in public space, showing up in bus stops, community centers, or museums. As situated media technology is rapidly maturing, it is likely that the trend will accelerate, so that people will become more accustomed to it [15]. Although the majority of currently existing urban displays serve mainly commercial, artistic or entertainment purposes, they might offer a promising communication platform for citizens [5, 9, 34], such as for increasing public discussion on socially and locally relevant topics [1, 31].

CSCW '14, February 15–19, 2014, Baltimore, Maryland, USA.
Copyright 2014 ACM 978-1-4503-2540-0/14/02

The identification and recognition of local concerns and views forms an essential aspect of encouraging civic engagement, allowing the deliberation of public opinion and the discussion of alternative perspectives [35]. Several initiatives have already addressed the idea of creating new, agile platforms of communication by embracing the potential of online technology [26]. For instance, it has been shown that community networks [32] are able to support local engagement and collaboration on civic topics [24, 29]. However, these platforms are often not easily accessible (i.e. people need to remember ways of accessing these tools, provided they have ways to access the Internet) or opportunistic (i.e. people need to dedicate time and effort). Furthermore, they tend not to be well situated, as they present a 'local' concern in a medium that is unrelated to the underlying social-cultural context [37]. Besides, these tools have limited ways of synchronous situated social interactivity, such as face-to-face encounters and discussion.

We propose to address issues of polling local opinions by combining the opportunistic and situated accessibility of interactive public displays with the qualities of a *social visualization*. By its original definition, social visualization describes the enriching of social (electronic) communication by making its salient qualities visible in easily accessible and understandable ways [8]. Research in this field has indicated that people seem to become encouraged to use social visualization for participative purposes, and potentially organize social activities alongside [7, 12]. While social visualization has mainly focused on graphical depictions of online and social media activities, little is known on whether it can be successfully deployed in other contexts or presentation media.

For instance, there are early indications that the public visualization of private data may incite physically situated discussions and debate by viewers, as the public externalization of private data can trigger feelings of friendly competition, social comparison, or social pressure [36]. Inspired by previous findings on situated polling for increased opinion deliberation on a given local topic [35], we thus focus on enticing situated discussions and reflections by way of moving online-style, non-scientific polls to the public realm, and explicitly visualizing the resulting statistics.

We contribute by (1) introducing the design of an interactive poll visualization of opinions originating from passers-by, and based on gesture-based interaction; (2) proposing different degrees of identifiability of the visualized opinions; (3) evaluating *MyPosition* in-the-wild; and (4) discussing the implications for design and use of public interactive visualizations as tools for increasing civic discourse. Our study demonstrated that the engaging nature of the installation was effective in enticing public deliberation and discussion. The main findings that emerged from the study are: (i) increased identifiability of the visualized votes increased the motivation to engage with the installation and forged open social discussion in the social space around the display, however less people actually submitted a vote; (ii) visitors expressed and submitted their personal opinion instead of playing around with the interactive features of the installation; (iii) the display led to significant discussion as well as nudging, in particular outside the direct interaction area.

RELATED WORK

Several in-the-wild studies of public displays have been presented, ranging from museums [17] to urban settings [23]. Such public displays are generally designed to communicate information of relevance to a specific group of people [13], support opportunistic conversations [19], provide playful information experience [17], or enrich casual interactions of people sharing a physical environment [21]. Few public displays have been specifically designed for a civic purpose, such as to increase awareness, discussion and reflection on local topics. We compare *MyPosition* to existing work regarding SMS-based civic communication displays, playful interfaces for civic discussion, and public voting systems.

SMS-based Civic Communication Displays

Some public displays create an open forum for public expression by providing a communication channel to citizens via SMS messaging, for instance *TexTales* [1] or *Discussions in Space* [31]. *TexTales* presents civic topics, such as "smoking in public places", whereas *Discussions in Space* is specifically focused on enticing civic interaction within the context of urban planning proposals. Results from these projects indicated that conversations might be sustained not only within the system, but also carried on in the physical and social space around it. We were inspired by this observation and aim to provide a more detailed analysis of the actual in-situ engagement of individuals and groups with the installation and its underlying topic. We also explore more immediate and playful interaction based on computer vision, thereby avoiding the moderation requirement of the SMS input modality and the associated feedback delay.

Playful Interfaces for Civic Engagement

Some digital urban installations aim to encourage more playful or reflective civic engagement on socially relevant topics, exploring the experiential and reflective potential of the interactive system [2]. For instance, *CO_2nfession* constitutes of a video-booth-like installation, where citizens are invited to enter and 'confess their sins' related to their CO_2 usage, which are then broadcasted on urban displays distributed across the city [20]. The system capitalized on the increased potential for reflexivity with regards to personal and civic values. In *MyPosition*, we explore a more in-situ communication between citizens, hoping to encourage active engagement with others' opinions and stimulate public discussion. Similar to *MyPosition*, *Climate on the Wall* was conceptualized to encourage passers-by to communicate their opinion (on climate change), by forming statements with their bodily movements along a projection wall [11]. A field trial showed that the playful nature of interaction was actually a hindrance for a meaningful participation, as many participants rather played with the interaction and few meaningful sentences were formed [11]. With *MyPosition*, we aimed at finding a good balance between playful interaction and meaningful participation.

Public Voting Systems

Several research projects already used voting mechanisms in a social context such as bars [25] and classrooms [3] in order to encourage public opinion deliberation. *MyPosition* extends this work towards a more civic focus and a systematic in-the-wild evaluation with a larger group of people. Recently, Taylor et al. [35] presented results of a long-term deployment of a voting device within three highly frequented public locations, allowing residents to express in-situ a *yes/no* opinion on a locally relevant topic [35]. *Viewpoint* aimed to increase community members' individual perception of their own efficacy. *MyPosition* builds on this work, while trying to promote awareness and on-site social debate among participants. *MyPosition* is also designed for rapid, opportunistic responses, yet allows for a wider range of sentiments to be submitted. Furthermore, *MyPosition* is a social visualization, in that individual opinions are still readily recognizable and identifiable, and utilizes more playful and engaging interaction.

DESIGN PROCESS

MyPosition was developed through an iterative design process involving the production of successive designs, the evaluation of low-fidelity sketches, mockups, working prototypes, and preliminary in-the-wild tests.

Design Goals

We set out to develop an urban poll visualization that would entail several design goals: a) provide awareness on individual contributions submitted by passer-by; b) motivate participation through engaging and playful design; c) provide a low-barrier entry for participation while minimizing misuse or accidental submissions of votes; d) explore anonymity in participation by exploring different degrees of identifiability of the individual contributions; and e) encourage opportunistic and spontaneous conversations.

THE PUBLIC POLL VISUALIZATION "MYPOSITION"

We used the Design Space Explorer Framework for Media Façades [6] to structure its design goals in regards to its location and situation, form and material, participation and visualization design.

Location and Situation

A public situation determines the shared understanding and social interpretation of cues present in the physical environment [16]. Therefore, we specifically aimed at locating *MyPosition* within an environmental context that naturally hosts informal, opportunistic social activities and encourages different forms of informal gathering, dwelling and transition (*design goal e)*), such as spaces in front of local cafés or shops, or entrance halls of cultural or community centers.

Physical Form and Material

MyPosition was implemented using a large rear projection canvas measuring 5x2 meters, two short-throw projectors and two Kinect cameras. All technical devices can be placed behind the screen to provide a compact setup that could be seamlessly and securely integrated in the physical environment. The interaction zone, i.e. the floor area in front of the screen in which users can be detected, measures about 5x3 meters.

Participation

MyPosition allows any passer-by to express her opinion on a given topic (*design goal a)*) by way of a full-body interaction method. We specifically chose this type of interacting in order to: i) create a more enjoyable experience when participating (*design goal b)*) in an otherwise relatively serious context [11], ii) support a more lightweight, inadvertent way of interaction [23] (*design goal c)*, and iii) allow multiple participants to simultaneously interact with our system (*design goal c)*).

A person is able to vote by consciously positioning herself along the display in front of a desired opinion section along a 4-point scale: *'strongly disagree'- 'disagree'-' agree'-'strongly agree'*. In order to place a vote, the participant has to raise her hand. This gesture was preferred as it is commonly used to visibly express opinions in public spaces such as town halls, podium discussions, or classrooms. To avoid accidental submissions, we introduced a dwell-time, for which the gesture has to be performed. By 'forcing' the potential voter to perform an explicit gesture, this 'submission' mechanism also aims to minimize possible misuse such as flippant [35] or merely playful interaction [11]. (*e.g. design goal c)*) This act of public 'submitting a personal opinion' was also meant to enhance public engagement by providing an opportunistic moment at which other passes-by could observe and discuss the action taking place (*design goal e))*.

Visualization Design

We chose a visualization style that combined the "seriousness" of the topic with a more accessible and enjoyable way of representing the voting statistics. The visualization consists of a set of square tiles, of which each corresponds to an individual opinion submitted by a passer-by (Fig. 1.D). Each of the preference options is represented by a different color and a textual label, and occupies an equally large horizontal section of the screen (Fig. 1.B). The voting topic is shown on the top (Fig. 1.A).

Animations

We implemented several dynamic visual features, to make the visualization richer, vivid, and more understandable. For instance, tiles that are in the direct proximity of a visitor who is passing through the interaction zone enlarge in a smoothly animated way to attract her attention. Once this person moves closer to the projection, her relative position – and thus her implied opinion (see subsection *Participation*) – becomes previewed as an animated 'polaroid'-like visual form, rendered over the existing visualization (Fig. 1.C and Fig. 2). An animated textual hint explains how to place a submission: "*Raise your hand to agree!*" (Fig. 2.A), as an efficient, integrated visual 'hint' to inform users on how to perform a gesture in a public display setting [38] (*design goal c)*). Once a participant starts to correctly perform the voting gesture, a clock-wise animation gradually colors her preview, thus providing real-time progress feedback on the dwell-time (Fig. 2.B). Upon registering a vote, the screen shortly flashes to visually acknowledge the submission. The newly created tile then gets added to the collection of tiles that were already submitted.

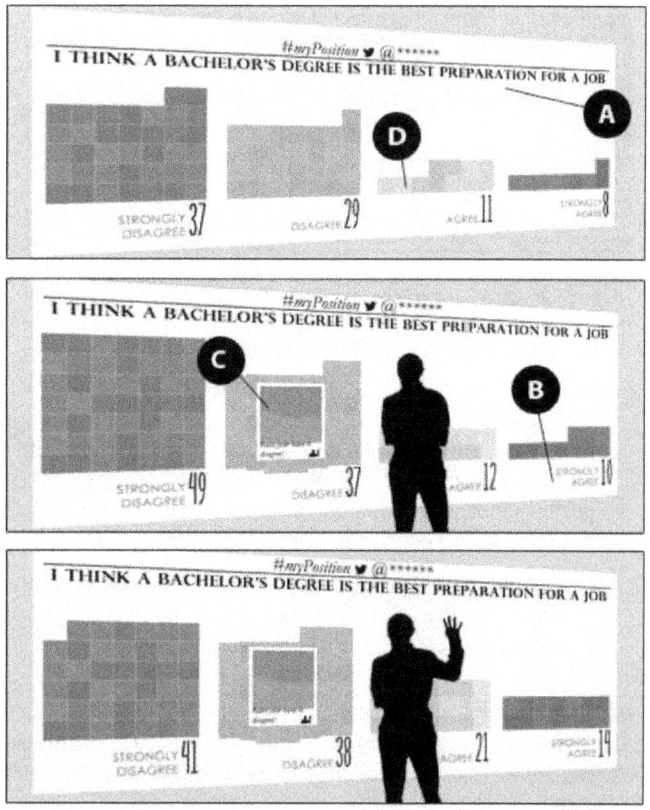

Figure 1: *MyPosition*: the poll visualization (top), a participant positioning herself (middle) and placing a vote (bottom): (A) The voting topic; (B) One of the four voting options; (C) A preview of a currently interacting participant (see Fig. 2 for details); (D) A tile corresponding to a vote.

Representation of Opinions

In order to explore the relationship between (pseudo-) anonymity and participation in the poll (*design goal d)*), we created three different representations of an individual opinion, each representing a different degree of identifiability: *color*, *contour*, and *image*.

- In ***color*** mode (low identifiability) all tiles look identical, making it impossible to identify which vote was submitted by whom (see Fig. 1-Top).

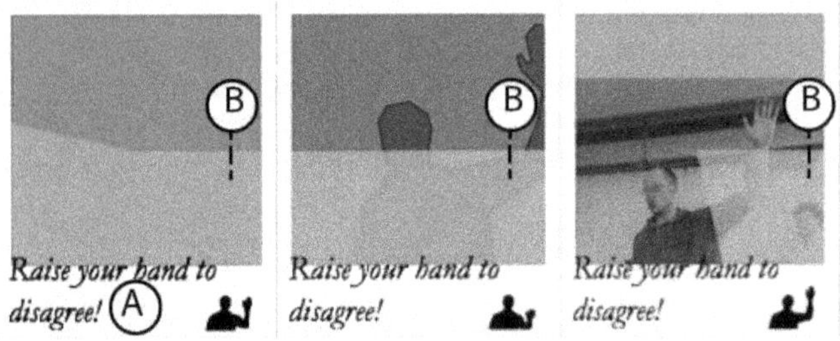

Figure 2: Close-up of the preview of a currently interacting participant in the three representation modes (color, contour, image); (A) The integrated hint for performing the gesture; (B) the clock-wise visualization of the gesture dwell-time.

- In ***contour*** mode each tile contain a graphical contour of the person who placed the vote, as captured by the camera. While it is difficult to identify other participants, a participant might be able to recognize her own submission (see Fig. 1-Middle).
- In ***image*** mode (high identifiability) each tile contains a photo of the corresponding participant, making it possible to identify who submitted what preference in the visualization (Fig. 1-Bottom).

PRELIMINARY FEEDBACK

In order to identify potential usability flaws, we evaluated *MyPosition* in an expert study consisting of three HCI researchers. The two most significant results included extending the dwell-time of the voting gesture (2s) and adding an explicit representation of the dwell-time progress (Fig. 2.B). We also collected informal feedback from five non-experts, in particular on the social aspects of the voting gesture. We did not discover any concerns about performing it in a public setting.

PILOT FIELD STUDY

MyPosition was installed for five consecutive days in the district of Wedding (Berlin, Germany), where it was accessible to passers-by and visitors via a large rear projection on the glass pane of a window of a local cultural event center (Fig. 3). We took notes on people's behavior towards the installation (e.g. attention and reactions) for 3 to 4 hours every afternoon (from 4pm to 10pm). Additionally we conducted interviews with random participants during an international freelance event hosted in a semi-public indoor lounge of the same center. After discussion with the organizers, we chose *"I think that freelancing is a good way to make a living"* as a voting topic. The interview questions dealt with the general attitude towards the installation and the submission and visualization of votes in a public setting. In total, we talked to 6 people (4 male, 35-50 years), all self-employed professionals.

Findings

While approximately a majority (70%) of all outdoor passers-by were attracted by the inadvertent visual feedback produced by their movements, only few stopped and had a closer look. The unpleasant weather conditions (i.e. below-freezing temperature and snowy conditions) hampered the overall motivation to stay, as well as the establishment of idling, exploration and discussion zones in the vicinity of the installation. In contrast, the indoor placement of *MyPosition* did not facilitate any inadvertent interactions, as events took place in an area spatially detached from the installation's vicinity, so people's paths upon entering the space did not pass by. However, the setting and in particular the social laid-back nature of the event provided situations of idling and contemplation around *MyPosition* after the end of the event. Participants who approached, considered the installation generally quite understandable and appealing. Interviewees suggested various possible venues and application areas for further integration, such as for education, general referenda, or local community issues. Several participants criticized the visualized topic as being too general for the people at the setting to engage. While people seemed comfortable with the public way of voting, we noted several concerns about the public collection and possible uncontrolled publication of private opinions, with several participants mentioning Facebook or other online platforms characterized by exposed social data.

FIELD STUDY

We deployed *MyPosition* over the course of one working week in the foyer of a large university cafeteria. As a topic, we chose *"I think a bachelor's degree is the best preparation for a job"*. This choice was motivated by a recent and highly debatable change in the university degree system in Germany. The goal of the study was to gain insight into the following questions:

(i) What is the impact of identifiability on voting behavior and participation?

(ii) Does playfulness of the display, including the public gesturing, interfere with meaningful participation?

(iii) What are the social interactions caused by the display?

Location Description

The deployment location was mainly visited around noon by students or staff of the TU Berlin and University of the Arts, as well as locals living nearby. The contextual setting of the space was characterized by several distinct zones: two *transit areas* situated between the main entries/exits and the dining-hall of the cafeteria; a *waiting* area in front of a coffee shop, as well as several *sitting* areas (Fig. 7). Based on previous research [21] and our experience from the pilot studies, we situated the projection in a transit area in front of the large sitting area, to maximize potential overlapping situations for both inadvertent interactions with the installation as well as idling, contemplation and gathering in a more broader space (Fig. 7).

Observations

Two researchers observed passers-by for 4 to 6 hours throughout the evaluation period. We kept field notes such as simple sketches annotating the relative locations and movements of passers-by. We observed and listened in to visitors, capturing their initial behaviors (e.g. direction of movement, attention, and reaction) as well as their opinions during their interactions or while discussing among themselves. To facilitate the process, we devised observational categories that were subsequently refined. In

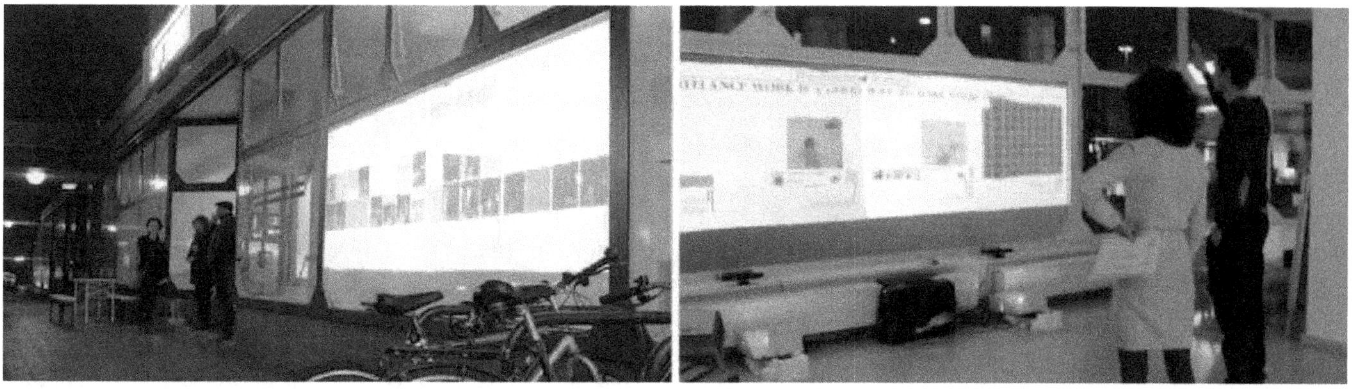

Figure 3: Pilot field study: outdoor (left) and indoor (right) settings. A participant (right) is placing a vote by raising his hand.

an overall period of 5 days (approx. 30 observation hours), we took notes of about 445 random persons who noticed the projection, 356 of which (80%) were in groups.

Semi-structured Interviews

We approached individuals and groups of people who had interacted with *MyPosition* and/or spent at least 2 minutes in front of it. The interviews lasted from 5 to 20 minutes and were typically performed after visitors placed a vote. At the beginning of each interview, we inquired about the purpose and habits of visiting the location and their initial motivation for approaching the projection. We further asked about general voting habits, civic discussion behavior, and attitudes towards engaging in issues related to the location. We also noted age and gender of participants, and their social context (e.g. whether they came alone, in group, etc.). The interviews included questions regarding *MyPosition* in terms of its understandability, its potential usefulness, its interactivity, the representation of votes, as well as any other suggestion or thought in relation to the project. Overall, we conducted 17 interviews with 26 visitors (3 female). We attribute the unbalanced gender to the higher ratio of male students at the nearby technical university. We interviewed 9 individuals, 7 couples and one group of 3 people. The majority of interviewees were between 20 to 30 years old (except of 5 who were between 55 and 65 years).

System Logs and Captures

Our system continuously recorded anonymous data of passers-by and participants, such as log files, screen video captures and depth image streams. Besides the three-dimensional position data of each individual that entered the interaction zone (captured at 30 Hz), the log files contained timestamps of all relevant user events, such as: visitors entering or leaving the interaction zone; positioning themselves in front of a specific voting option; or performing the voting gesture. The screen content was captured in full resolution at 15 frames per second (fps), while the depth image streams of the sensors was captured at 30 fps. Over the course of the deployment, we collected data of about 4980 passers-by. As 80% of passers-by occurred within the core hours (12pm-3pm), our quantitative analysis is based on that time period.

Experiment

To quantitatively assess how the different vote representation modes affected participation, the system automatically switched between *contour*, *image,* and *color* every 30 minutes (see Figure 1). Only votes that were placed during the current mode were presented on the screen. In order to minimize any effect of the order of options on voting, after half of the deployment time we reversed the order of the options.

Data Analysis

We analyzed our collection of field notes and visitor opinions using grounded theory [33] to draw bottom-up findings based on the direct quotations and to establish hierarchies and connections among remarkable findings. Apart of the the descriptive statistics of visitors' participation, we used the system logs together with the interview data to evaluate the impact of identifiability. We further used this data to triangulate participants' comments and reactions upon participation.

RESULTS

General Overview of Participation

Our quantitative data analysis is based on an average of 880 (min=760, max=960, std=75) daily passers-by between 12pm-3pm. People stayed in front of the projection on average for 4.6s (std=16.1s). Those, who placed a vote stayed for 27.9s (std=41.9s) and those who did not for 3.9s (std=14.2s).

Self-Reported Perception of Community Engagement. All interviewees turned out to be regular (daily- or weekly-basis) visitors of the university restaurant. The majority of them (77%, 21/26) were students or alumni of the university (aged 20-35 years), the rest were adults of varying backgrounds and professions ranging from 45 to 65 years, living close by. While 62% (16/26) claimed to usually participate in municipal or state elections, the majority (69%) reported to actually not engage in community or university issues. Some of them explicitly stated the reasons, which ranged from a lack of time, to the fact that they could not longer participate as they were no longer university students. In summary, the engagement reported by visitors at the deployment location was relatively low.

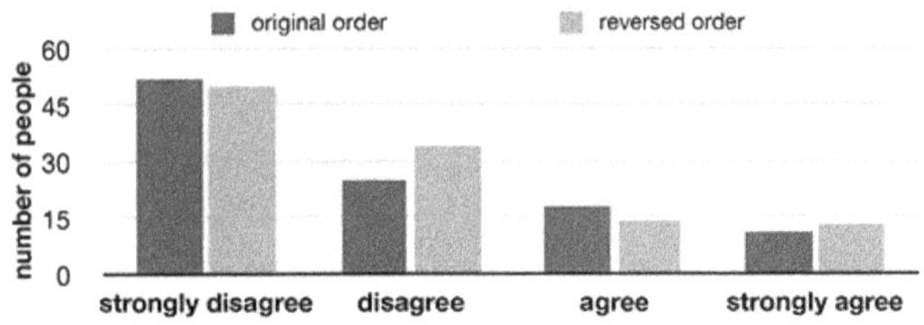

Figure 4: The change of order of the visualized options did not change the distribution of visitors' votes.

Impact of Identifiability

Did People Vote?

From the log files, we extracted the conversion rates (votes per passers-by), which we considered as a measure for the willingness of visitors to submit a vote to the system. Out of the 880 passers-by, recorded in the core hours, 217 submitted an opinion, with a conversion rate of about 5%. We observed the lowest conversion for *image* (3.9%), and higher conversions for *contour* (5.7%) and *color* (6.1%). While we could not detect significant differences between *contour* and *color*, significantly less people voted in the *image* mode compared to *color* (χ^2=6.5, p<0.02) and *contour* (χ^2=4.6, p<0.04). These results thus indicate that people are more reluctant to participate directly if their vote is more recognizable.

How Did People Perceive Their Increased Identifiability?

Interestingly, when asked whether they have any concerns with the vote representation, 79% (11/14) of the interviewees in *image* mode claimed it did not bother them at all, e.g. *"[...] It does not bother me, I think it is good like that, more interesting and evocative for the people."* (P10), or *"No, totally fine with me, people should see what I think!"* (P21). Some even stated that their participation already implied their firm position: *"Of course not, if it bothers me, I would simply not participate in the first place!"* (P3). Others explained that the image representation did not affect their privacy: *"Definitely I think image is a good option, actually it is relatively anonymous."* (P13).

On the contrary, around 78% (7/9) of the interviewees in the *contour* mode were rather skeptical towards a more recognizable vote representation in case of a *"more critical"* context, with a majority (67%) referring to poll domains with traditionally higher demand of security, e.g. *"If it's about elections of the parliament, I would rather stay more anonymous.*" (P8), or *"Hmm, if its something serious I would find it difficult to see my image displayed. It depends on the question."* (P5).

How Did People Perceive Others' Identifiability?

Our interviewees expressed differing views regarding their opinion about being able to see the votes of others. The majority of them (62%, 16/26) found that this visualization sparks curiosity in so far they felt incentivized to participate, e.g. *"Seeing others' votes makes it more interesting for you to participate."* (P7). In particular, some seemed to find the 'personalized' character of the visualization appealing. For instance, P3 (*image* mode) explained: *"[...] It's extremely cool to see the pictures of all*

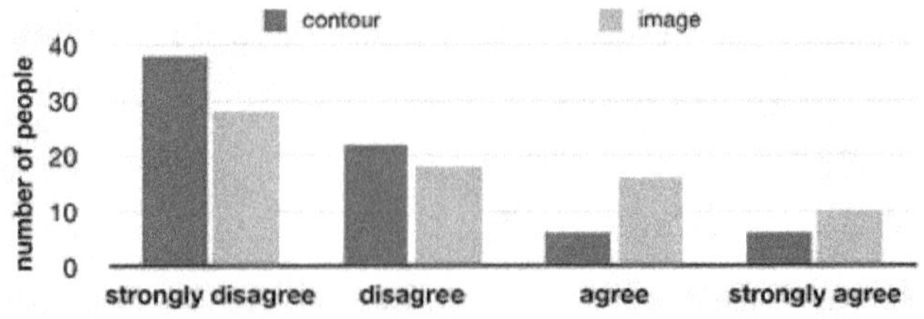

Figure 5: Visitors' votes were more evenly distributed in the *image* mode, Significantly more people chose 'in favor' in the *image* mode (χ^2=7.0, p<0.01).

others. It is not just an impersonal color chart as we know from newspapers," or (P10 – saw all modes): *"The contour is playful, it shows movement and personality, it motivates people"*. However, several participants expressed their doubts about the bias of one's opinion when all others' votes are visible, e.g. *"[...] Surely the fact that you see others influences somehow."* (P5).

How Did People Vote?

Our log files revealed that 47% of the people chose *'strongly disagree'*, 27% for *'disagree'*, 14% for *'agree'* and 12% for *'strongly agree'* (out of a total of 217). Reversing the order of the four visualized options did not influence the distribution of the submitted votes (Fig. 4). This indicates that the vast majority of people intentionally chose 'against', regardless of the order.

Further, we extracted the distributions of participant votes across the options in the three representation modes. Interestingly, significantly more users in the *image* mode were 'in favor' of the statement (*'agree'* or 'strongly agree') compared to the *contour* mode (χ^2=7.0, p<0.01). In addition, in the *image* mode, the submissions across options appeared to be more evenly distributed than in the *contour* mode (see Fig. 5).

Playful vs Meaningful Submission of Votes

Did People Vote for Their Personal Opinion?

Overall, people's voting behavior represented their actual opinion, rather than merely trying out the interactive features of the system, an problem reported in [11] and [35]. Most of the interviewed visitors (81%, 21/26) had placed a vote immediately before the interview: 91% of them were *'against'*, and 9% *'in favor'* of the topic (similar to the logged general voting results). When asking them directly about their opinion, these participants confirmed the preference position we had noted beforehand. Seven of them even went on and specifically showed us their submissions in the visualization, e.g. *"Look, that is my vote, I definitely disagree"* (P6). We observed only one case, where two guys were making funny poses while interacting and one of them accidentally chose 'agree'.However, shortly afterwards he complained, *"Oh, damn it, now I voted here, and it stays!"*. He then noticed a man nearby the installation, assuming that he was related to it, and asked *"Could I delete my vote, or move it to 'strongly disagree'?"*.

Public Character of Voting

The act of positioning oneself along the projection in order to choose the preferred option together with the explicit voting gesture imposed a publicly recognizable aspect to

Figure 6: In-the-wild deployment at a university cafeteria lounge. A man positioning himself along the visualized options and a group of friends discussing his participation.

participating, which evoked curiosity and taught other passers-by how to participate. All interviewees who had placed a vote (81%, 21/26) perceived the gesture-based voting as *"entertaining"*, *"cool"*, *"much funnier [as traditional voting mechanisms]"* and *"easy to use."* Although some visitors perceived the voting gesture as intriguing, others thought it was quite *'exposed'*. Interviewee P23 (*image* mode) was even more specific: *"People see me all the time, if everybody is against, I would think twice about what to vote for."* One interviewee claimed this was due to the 'openness' of the spatial layout around the screen: *"[...] Of course, the fact that you can be seen ... creates a sort of stage. [...] If it were in sort of a corridor, that people won't feel that observed."* (P9). Others related this 'exposure' to the time it took to place a vote: *"[the visibility] is not a problem for me because it's only for a short time and does not stay" (P10), and "[...]. If [voting] were quicker, it would be more anonymous." (P6).*

Spatial and Social Interaction Patterns

We observed that *MyPosition* also created several zones of engagement within a larger area of the deployment (see Fig. 7). Outside of the active interaction zone, passers-by engaged with *MyPosition* in a number of other zones, such as the sitting and waiting areas in the vicinity of the projection. We also noticed that visitors congregated outside of the camera field of view, such as around the two columns located on both sides of the sitting area. These observed zones relate to the "comfort spaces" discussed in [10], which tend to give "physical and psychological comfort [...] by providing a line of sight, but giving people the feeling of being 'out of the way'". However, we observed that this engagement often became more active than passive contemplation, such as reading aloud, or debating and commenting in group.

Social Learning and Social Teaching

We noted that visitors tried out the interactive features or attempted to vote as a consequence of observing others interacting, similar to the *social learning* effects perceived in other public screens [27, 38]. We noticed this behavior in approximately 8% of the observed cases (35/445), which mostly unfolded around some of the comfort zones and the zone in front of the projection (see Fig. 7. A).

A more frequently observed social configuration (approximately 31% of the observed group cases, 110/356) was *'social teaching'*, where one person teaches the other (s) about the features of the installation. This situation occurred mostly among couples or groups of acquainted people. In fewer instances, mostly around the comfort zones, we observed 'passive' social teaching, where people explained specific features to their companions. While previous work has reported 'teacher-apprentice' social configurations along an interactive multi-touch wall [27], we observed social teaching happening in a larger number of engagement zones (see Fig. 7.B), often leading to participative behaviors.

Social Discussion

The most spatially fragmented yet most frequently observed social behavior (approximately 52% of the observed group cases, 185/356) consisted of deeper discussions about *MyPosition.* The majority of discussions occurred in the waiting area in front of the coffee shop (Fig. 7. C), as well as other spots within the upper transit area, where passers-by had the most optimal overview of the installation. People engaged less frequently in debate in the interaction zone in front of the projection itself, in the comfort zones, and in lower transit area close to the exit. Discussion topics included: a) the visualized voting topic and their personal preferences; b) the visualized patterns and voting results; and c) data privacy issues.

a) Voting Topic. Often discussions about the topic were triggered by more 'implicit' interactions by one or more members of a group. Visitors would pass through the space, notice the screen and stop for a bit observing it. They would ask each other "*What do you say?*" and receive response such as, "*Well, obviously not [agreeing]!".* They would frequently start debating university degrees or graduations afterwards.

b) Visualization and Results. Over time, passers-by seemed to 'follow' the development of the visualization, as we noted several instances of people observing that *"something has changed"* [i.e. the vote representation mode, or the order of options], and discussing the possible causes of these changes, such as *"privacy reasons"*, or to *"make it statistically correct"*. The collective visualization of all submitted votes (see Fig. 1) seemed to encourage discussion about the result distribution, e.g. *"Look, only five say that they totally agree,"* or *"There is a big contrast between the votes"*.

c) Data Privacy Issues. Similar to our observations from the pilot study (see section *Pilot Field Study*), the *image* representation mode often prompted debates about the perceived privacy of the submitted votes. For instance, a girl left her group of friends, standing in the upper transit zone, to vote. Upon her coming back to the group, one of her companions said jokingly: *"Now they know everything about you!"*. Often privacy concerns also related to potential future publications of the data. One girl participated with her back to the projection, explaining to her friend: *"I don't want to be seen on Facebook!"*. We are aware such privacy issues would be even more outspoken

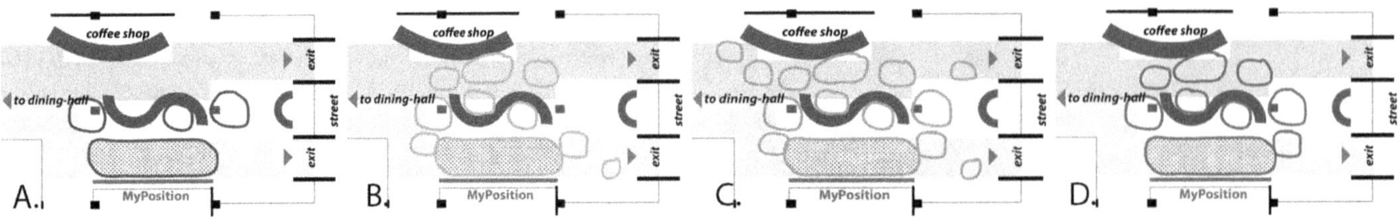

Figure 7: The engagement areas created by *MyPosition* (denoted by blobs): A. Learning; B. Teaching; C. Discussion; D. Nudging. These participative behaviors were observed in a much larger area than the interaction zone in front of *MyPosition* (dotted area).

and hazardous if opinion questions are more provocative, contested or politically sensitive.

Social Nudging and Critique

Visitors often explicitly prompted their companions to vote or criticized the intentions and opinions of others. These social behaviors were noted in approximately 16% of the observed group cases (57/356). The majority of the people who nudged other visitors had already participated. These actions were often accompanied by humorous or ironic encouragements. For example, we observed two friends passing-by, one of them knew the installation already. He drew attention to *MyPosition*, by prompting the other one: "*Look over there, that's something for you! You are so democratic, right; you always like to go voting...*". Moreover, the public visibility of submitting an opinion triggered open critical attitudes towards others, which often occurred within the social context of groups. A young male prompted his friend to participate. Upon his friend saying: "*I strongly agree.*", the first man responds, seemingly surprised: "*Are you serious!? You agree on* this?". The second one did not submit a vote. Critical attitudes were also openly expressed towards non-present participants' preferences, reflected in the visualization: "*Look over there! Somebody has agreed*!"

DISCUSSION

Whereas the most valuable effect of *MyPosition* consisted of its ability to cause cooperative discussion, reflection and contemplation of a civic concern in a public setting, several issues should be considered when designing an interactive poll visualization placed in a physical environment.

The Identifiable Self

The identifiability of the person and her vote in the *image* mode did not seem to cause concerns among interviewees. However, the biggest impact was observed in the voting conversion rate dropping by 36%, which means that some people simply did not vote in this representation mode. Furthermore, votes were more evenly distributed and significantly more positive for the *image* mode, compared to the *contour* mode.

Design Implications: There may be concerns related to individual data privacy, or social factors which influence these different behaviors, especially in settings aimed at the general public, rather than a small co-located group such as in [14, 18]. Some of those people who were against the visualized statement, would not participate due to the higher identifiability of their vote in the *image* mode. Conversely, the situation of expressing opinion on an issue, implicitly related to the institution hosting the display (in this bachelor degree/university), would lead to a more conformist behavior, when it comes to an open criticism. Future studies could explore how the explicit choice of identifiability may influence one's participation behavior.

The Identifiable Others

Generally, people seemed to consider the identifiability of votes on the screen stronger than the immediate publicness of the voting itself, as illustrated in the case of the girl voting with the face away from the screen (and towards the audience). In contrast, the ability to identify *others* was described as more "*intriguing*" and showing more "*personality*". While we did not observe any particular attitudinal differences across the different representation modes, the public and collective depiction of people's votes sparked considerable discussions. People compared and contrasted the visualized results, and often loudly reflected on the underlying implications, especially in cases of those votes, which were in line with the represented majority. Conversely, people would publicly criticize the opinion 'outliers' - e.g. the ones who have submitted a positive vote towards a statement, which is predominantly disagreed with - both the ones already depicted the visualization, as well as potential participants in the social space, they were part of.

Design Implications: This calls for attention towards the social challenges involved with the visibility of individual contributions in public visualization settings: how would people's own contribution be effectively influenced when others' are readily visible, is still an open question. Furthermore, while the open critical debate is a desired result, those who are less inclined to publicly submitting their personal data, might be even inhibited to express their views, when social pressure towards the 'correct' contribution is induced.

Naturally, our findings regarding identifiably and privacy are limited to more innocent or playful voting questions, and further studies are required to be able to extrapolate them to more sensitive, contested or controversial polls.

Playfulness vs. Meaningful Discussion

Previous research has pointed out that designing urban interactive platforms, which can both communicate meaningful information and engage, is a challenge [11]. Our field study demonstrated that *MyPosition* has achieved a relatively good balance between engaging,playful design and enticing meaningful discussion regarding the topic at hand. Compared to other public interventions with a civic purpose (e.g., [31] and [35]), we opted for a playful, bodily interaction in order to increase the engaging capabilities of the system. In spite of the expressive playfulness, our interview and log data demonstrated, that the vast majority actually did express their true opinion, instead of only engaging with the interactive features of the installation [11] and/or voting randomly [35]. Furthermore, while previous work reflected on the problem of predominantly off-topic or random communication via a participative system [31], our observational findings showed that *MyPosition* was able to communicate a socially-motivated topic and spark vivid discussions among the people on-site.

Design Implications: There could be several strategies to support a good balance between playfulness and meaningful participation. On one hand, it should be fairly easy and fast to contribute *meaningfully* (in our case, submit a vote, which is than reflected in the visualization), while at the same time misuse was relatively restricted. Indeed, there were very few instances, we observed visitors to engage in publicly 'challenging' the vote distribution by submitting twice for opposed options in order to e.g. *"do a two-fold manipulation of the results"*. While we tried to restrict that by only allowing a tracked user to participate once, we could not provide for a more sophisticated solution (such as face detection) due to ethical reasons. Yet, even initially random behavior with *MyPosition* (observed in only one case) was quickly followed by a loud reflection in terms of the visibility of the opinion, which suggest that the visible persistency of one's contribution, might also lead to a more 'considered' behavior.

Public Character of Voting

Participating was public in two regards. First, the voting mechanism implied an *'immediate publicness'*: the participants were very visible to a large audience in the deployment space. Second, participants' images (in the *image* mode) could be associated with their votes for the time of the deployment (see *"The Identifiable Self"*). Despite this 'immediate publicness', a large percentage of all passers-by (6.1% in *color* mode) did vote. However, participants often stated that they would prefer a less public setting in the case of more controversial questions, suggesting a less exposed hallway, or a shorter interaction time.

Design Implications: One possible concern is that when publicly expressing one's opinion, people could participate in a more 'socially appropriate' way. While we did not observe people stating a different opinion than what they actually submitted (agreeably, we cannot know their true opinion), people with a more controversial opinion may not have voted in the first place.

Socio-spatial Patterns of Participation

Previous work has discussed individual and social group engagement in front of, along, and in close vicinity of interactive public screens [23, 27]. We observed participative behavior in a much wider area than the interaction zone of *MyPosition* (Fig. 7). While direct participation was possible in a relatively narrow area in front of the projection, various individual and group behavior patterns emerged in relation to the installation, such as social learning, teaching, discussion and nudging. While we observed social learning mostly relatively close to the screen, discussions and nudging happened up to very large distances away from it. Those were mostly the spots, where people obtained a good view of the screen, but were relatively far away from the interaction area. While these spatial specifics relate to the "activation spaces" proposed by [10], we observed that for spaces to be advantageous for *active* participative behaviors, they ought to provide the adequate social setting for a longer encounter with installation. The queue in front of the coffee shop, for instance, implied a waiting and a gathering situation, where several people were able to contemplate and debate around *MyPosition* together, without feeling awkward or exposed. Similarly, some people seemed to avoid the interaction area, and rather congregated around columns and other "comfort spaces" [10] out of the camera view.

Design Implications: Our findings demonstrate that an interactive public display, featuring a collective depiction of individual participative efforts can influence a much larger area than the interaction zone itself. However, it is important to provide spaces for active engagement with the installation, such as social discussion, that possess both proper visibility and social affordances, yet don't intersect with the interaction area.

Limitations

Obtaining the 'true' opinion of citizens in a public context is characterized by many pitfalls, and we did not aim at collecting a representative voting result. Rather, we focused on how *MyPosition* was able to entice civic discussions and reflections on a locally relevant topic. In this sense, our conversion rate of 5% is comparable or better than conversion rates reported by other public display studies [38]. This emphasizes its usefulness for polls that are more playful and situated, however less 'representative' in nature. Furthermore, the objective of our field study was high ecological validity, so naturally, using this method we cannot generalize the results to other settings and questions. The university context might have provided a more friendly audience (e.g., more 'tech-savvy' people, 'safer' environment etc.), than for instance the grocery store investigated in [35].

CONCLUSION

Through the design and evaluation of *MyPosition,* we learned that an interactive public visualization of a local concern can be a means for civic participation and discussion. Apparently the inherent issues of voting in public (e.g. peer pressure, reluctant acceptance of intermediate results) cannot be avoided. In spite of this, increasing the visual identifiability of participants positively impacted the overall enticement of onlookers to engage with the installation and the underlying topic, however lowered the actual turnout. At the same time, the playful nature of the interaction did not seem to deter people from submitting their stated opinion. We observed considerable discussion and nudging among people, in particular beyond the interaction area in front of the screen. In future studies, it would be worthwhile to further investigate the impact of the context, such as the socio-demographic characteristics of the audience, and to study if such systems can be augmented with more societally grounded questions and more elaborate, qualitative ways of answering.

ACKNOWLEDGMENTS

This research has been supported by the European Institute of Innovation and Technology and the German Federal Ministry of Education and Research. Special thanks to SUPERMARKT and TU Mensa Berlin for facilitating our field study locations and to Tanya Valkanova, Ines Ben Said, Denitza Toteva, Martin Tomitsch, Gilles Bailly, Moritz Behrens and Christina Dicke for their valuable support.

REFERENCES

1. Ananny, M., & Strohecker, C. (2009). TexTales: Creating Interactive Forums with Urban Publics. In Foth, M. ed. *Handbook of Research on Urban Informatics: The Practice and Promise of the Real-Time City, IGI Global, Hershey, PA, 2009.*
2. Bødker, S. When Second Wave HCI Meets Third Wave Challenges. In *Proc. NordiCHI 2006*, 1-8.
3. Cheok, A.D., Fernando, O.N.N., Wijesena, J.P. Mustafa, A., Shankar, R., Barthoff, A.K., Tosa, N., Choi, Y., and Agarwal, M. BlogWall: Social and Cultural Interaction for Children. In Advances in Human–Computer Interaction (2008).
4. Coleman, S. and Gotze, J. Bowling Together: Online Public Engagement in Policy Deliberation, Hansard Society, London, UK, 2001
5. Dalsgaard, P., & Halskov, K. Designing Urban Media Façades : Cases and Challenges. In Proc. CHI 2010, 2277-2286.
6. Dalsgaard, P., Nielsen, R. and Halskov, K.: Towards a Design Space Explorer for Media Facades. In *Proc. OZCHI 2008*, 219-226.
7. Danis, C., Viegas, F., Wattenberg, M. and Kriss, J. Your Place or Mine?: Visualization as a Community Component. In Proc. CHI 2008, 275-284.
8. Donath, J., Karahalios, K. and Viegas, F. Visualizing Conversations. *Computer-Mediated Communication 4, 4* (1998).
9. Fatah Gen. Schieck, A., Briones, C. and Mottram, C. The Urban Screen as a Socializing Platform: Exploring the Role of Place within the Urban Space. In F. Eckardt, J. Geelhaar, L. Colini, K.S. Willis, K. Chorianopoulos and R. Hennig (Eds.) MediaCity: Situations, Practices and Encounters (2008), Frank & Timme GmbH, 285-305.
10. Fischer, P. T., & Hornecker, E. Urban HCI : Spatial Aspects in the Design of Shared Encounters for Media Façades, In Proc. CHI 2012, 307–316.
11. Fritsch, J. & Brynskov, M. Between Engagement, Affect and Information - Experimental Urban Media in the Climate Change Debate. In Foth, M., Forlano, L., Gibbs, M., & Satchell, C. (Eds.). From Social Butterfly to Engaged Citizen: Urban Informatics, Social Media, Ubiquitous Computing, and Mobile Technology to Support Citizen Engagement (2011), MIT Press, 115-135.
12. Gilbert, E. & Karahalios, K. Using Social Visualization to Motivate Social Production. In IEEE Transactions on Multimedia - Special Section on Communities and Media Computing 11, 3 (2009), 413-421.
13. Grasso, A., Muehlenbrock, M., Roulland, F., and Snowdon, D. Public and Situated Displays: Social and Interactional Aspects of Shared Display Technologies, Chapter 11: Supporting Communities of Practice with Large Screen Displays (2003), Springer, 261–282.
14. Greenberg, S., & Rounding, M. The Notification Collage: Posting Information to Public and Personal displays. In Proc. CHI 2001.
15. Greenfield, A., Shepard, M.: Urban Computing and Its Discontents. The Architectural League of New York, New York (2007).
16. Harrison, S. & Dourish, P. Re-place-ing Space: the Roles of Place and Space in Collaborative Systems. In Proc. CSCW 1996, 67-76.
17. Hinrichs, U., Schmidt, H., & Carpendale, S. EMDialog: Bringing Information Visualization into the Museum. IEEE Transactions on Visualization and Computer Graphics 14, 6 (2008), 1181–1189.
18. Huang, E. M., & Mynatt, E. D. Semi-public Displays for Small, Co-located groups. In Proc. CHI 2003, 49-56).
19. Jancke, G. Venolia, G., Grudin, J., Cadiz, J. and Gupta. J. Linking Public Spaces: Technical and Social Issues. In Proc. CHI 2001, 530-537.
20. Leong, T. W., & Brynskov, M. CO_2nfession: Engaging with Values through Urban Conversations. In *Proc. OZCHI* 2009, 209–216.
21. McCarthy, F.. Public and Situated Displays: Social and Interactional Aspects of Shared Display Technologies, Chapter 12: Promoting a Sense of Community with Ubiquitous Peripheral displays (2003), Springer, 283–308.
22. McCullough, M. On Typologies of Situated Interaction. Human-Computer Interaction 16, 2-4 (2001), 336-349.
23. Müller, J., Walter, R., Bailly, G., Nischt, M., & Alt, F. Looking Glass: A Field Study on Noticing Interactivity of a Shop Window, In Proc. CHI 2012, 297–306.
24. Networked Neighbourhoods Study. http:// networkedneighbourhoods.com/?page_id=409.
25. O'Hara, K., Lipson, M., Jansen, M., Unger, A., Jeffries, H. and Macer, P. Jukola: Democratic Music Choice in a Public Space. In Proc. DIS 2010, ACM (2010), 145–154.
26. Oates, B.J. The Potential Contribution of ICTs to the Political Process. Electronic Journal of e-Government 1, 1 (2003), 32–42.
27. Peltonen, P., Kurvinen, E., Salovaara, A., Jacucci, G., Ilmonen, T. Evans, J., Oulasvirta, A. and Saarikko, P. It's mine, Don't Touch!: Interactions at a Large Multi-touch Display in a City Centre. *In Proc of CHI, 2008,* 1285-1294.
28. Putnam, R.D. Bowling Alone: The Collapse and Revival of American Community. Simon & Schuster, New York, NY, USA, 2000.
29. Rogers, E.M., Collins-Jarvis, L. and Schmitz, J. The PEN Project in Santa Monica: Interactive Communication, Equality, and Political Action. Journal of the America Society for Information Science 45, 6 (1994), 401–410.
30. Satchell, C., Hearn, G., Foth, M., & Schroeter, R. Suburban Nostalgia : The Community Building Potential of Urban Screens. *In Proc. OZCHI 2008, 243-246.*
31. Schroeter, R. Engaging New Digital Locals with Interactive Urban Screens to Collaboratively Improve the City. *Proc. CSCW 2012*, 227-236.
32. Schuler, D. Community Networks: Building a New Participatory Medium. Communications of the ACM 37, 1 (1994), 38–51.
33. Strauss, A. L. and Corbin, J. Basics of Qualitative Research. Sage Publications, 1990.
34. Struppek, M. The Social Potential of Urban Screens. In Journal for Visual Communication 5, 2 (2007), 173-188.
35. Taylor, N., Marshall, J., & Blum-Ross, A. Viewpoint: Empowering Communities with Situated Voting Devices. In *Proc. CHI 2012,* 1361–1370.
36. Valkanova, N., Jorda, S., Tomitsch, M., & Vande Moere, A. Reveal-it!: The Impact of a Social Visualization Projection on Public Awareness and Discourse. In Proc. CHI 2013, 3461-3470.
37. Vande Moere A. and Hill D. Designing for the Situated and Public Visualization of Urban Data, Journal of Urban Technology 19, 2 (2012), 25-46.
38. Walter, R., Bailly, G., Müller, J. StrikeAPose: Revealing Mid-Air Gestures on Public Displays. In Proc. CHI 2013, 841-850.

How Players Value their Characters in World of Warcraft

Ian J. Livingston[1], **Carl Gutwin**[2], **Regan L. Mandryk**[2], **and Max Birk**[2]

[1]Playtest Lab
Ubisoft Divertissements Inc.
5505, St-Laurent Blvd, Montréal, H2T 1S6
ian.livingston@ubisoft.com

[2]Department of Computer Science
University of Saskatchewan
110 Science Place, Saskatoon, S7N 5C9
[first.last]@usask.ca

ABSTRACT
Characters in games such as World of Warcraft allow players to act in the game world and to interact with others. Game characters and avatars are a mediated form of self-representation for the player, but some research suggests that players also view characters in other ways that have to do with the kinds of value that the characters provide. To better understand the ways that players value their characters in an online environment, we carried out a semi-structured interview study of twenty World of Warcraft players. From our data we identify ten kinds of value that characters can provide – including utility, investment, communication, memory, enjoyment, and representations of relationships, as well as value as an opportunity for experience, creativity, sociability, and self-expression. The analytical lens of value provides a new understanding of the ways that players appreciate characters in online multi-user worlds. Our results can help developers understand and enhance an element of multi-player games that contributes greatly to player experience and satisfaction.

Author Keywords
Avatars; characters; World of Warcraft; character value.

ACM Classification Keywords
H.5.3. Group and Organization Interfaces: CSCW

INTRODUCTION
Game characters in massively multiplayer online (MMO) games provide many things to human players. In addition to being the agent through which the player acts in the game world, a character (also called an avatar) allows people to interact with other characters and players. The agency and immersion of these characters make a strong connection to the player: as Castronova states, "the avatar mediates our self in the virtual world, we inhabit it, we drive it, and we receive all of our sensory information about the world from its standpoint" ([5], p. 3).

As a result, characters and other forms of online embodiment have long been studied in terms of identity and representations of self. Researchers have looked at a many topics within this area, including the representation of different aspects of a player's identity [3], identity exploration [37], deception [10], gender roles and 'gender-bending' [44], ethnicity and race in avatar construction [40], role-play [25], community identity formation [12], and the presentation of ideal selves through characters [1].

In addition to observations that are strongly related to identity, several studies of MMOs have shown that players view their characters in other ways as well. For example, researchers have noted that characters can be created primarily for utility reasons [23], and that customizations are often strongly based on the needs of the character's game role [36]. Players can also use characters as an opportunity for aesthetic creativity, even without a strong identity connection (i.e., "doll play" [16]). Studies have also noted that characters can be created expressly as a means to explore game content [18] or to play with other people [23]. In some cases, players talk about their characters in terms that suggest a greater distance – for example, as if they were possessions [43], or chess pieces [15].

These results suggest that there are several ways that players view their characters, and several ways that characters can provide value, even in situations where identity or self-representation are also involved. This may be particularly true in games such as World of Warcraft (WoW), which allows people to create several characters on one account (i.e., 'Mains' and 'Alts'). Despite the number of these observations, however, researchers have not focused on, or thoroughly explicated, the kinds of value that characters can provide to players.

Character value can be an important factor in a player's gameplay experience, and therefore in the overall success of a game. To better understand the range of these value relationships, we carried out a field study in which we conducted observations and in-depth interviews with ten WoW players, and follow-up interviews with an additional ten players.

From our data and from a review of existing observational studies, we identified ten common types of value that WoW characters can provide to players:

- *Utility*: some characters are valuable because of what they can do – that is, what tasks they can accomplish and what goals they can achieve for the player;
- *Investment*: some characters are valuable because they represent a player's time, effort, and achievements;

CSCW'14, February 15–19, 2014, Baltimore, Maryland, USA.

ACM 978-1-4503-2540-0/14/02...$15.00.
http://dx.doi.org/10.1145/2531602.2531661

- *Communication*: some characters have value because of what their appearance communicates to a social group;
- *Memory*: some character are collections of the player's memories, recording a player's activities in the game;
- *Enjoyment*: some characters are valuable because they are simply fun to play;
- *Representation of relationships*: some characters are meaningful because they represent relationships with other players or groups;
- *New experience*: some characters are valuable because of the new experiences that they enable;
- *Creativity*: some characters are platforms on which the player can create aesthetically-pleasing forms;
- *Sociability*: some characters are valuable because they allow the player to engage in activities with friends;
- *Self-expression*: some characters are valuable because they allow a player to express a wide variety of personal attributes or beliefs.

Our work brings together a wide range of ways that players can value characters in WoW, and shows how considerations of value can enrich existing understanding of player-character relationships. Our work provides a complementary view to ongoing considerations of identity, and shows how some notions of value are strongly related to self-representation. The value categories that we identify can help game developers understand what makes characters worth having – an important element of player experience that contributes greatly to the value and success of online game environments.

BACKGROUND AND RELATED WORK

World of Warcraft and Characters in WoW

WoW is a massively multiplayer online role-playing game (MMORPG) introduced in 2004; it is the world's leading MMORPG, with more than 8 million subscribers in 2013 [42]. In WoW, human players create one or more *characters* and play the game through these avatars, exploring the game world, completing quests, or fighting monsters. Characters can be one of several races (e.g., Human, Night Elf, Orc, or Tauren) from two warring factions (Alliance or Horde). Many other aspects of a character's appearance can be customized, including sex, hairstyle, and clothing. Players also choose a character's class (e.g., Paladin, Priest, or Rogue), which determines the character's role (damage dealer, tank, or healer) [42].

Part of the gameplay in WoW involves developing the abilities, attributes, and powers of a character, represented by the character's 'level.' Progressing through the many character levels (90 as of 2013) requires considerable time and many different in-game activities (e.g., carrying out quests, killing monsters, or practicing crafting skills). Whereas some online environments severely limit the number of characters that a player can create, WoW allows ten characters per server, with a total of 50 characters per user account. Most players do create multiple characters, dividing these into one 'Main', which is the character that the players focuses on (or plays most often), and several 'Alts', which are usually played less frequently.

WoW has been the subject of significant research from an ethnographic perspective (e.g., [25,18]). In addition, several investigations have explored WoW practices within the context of HCI. Researchers have explored topics such as player demographics [46], motivations for playing [47], player behaviors [48], the integration of real-world currency [8], gaming culture [21], creative expression through machinima [29], and learning [24].

Because of the social interaction that is inherent within WoW, there has also been significant research from a CSCW perspective on collaborative practices within WoW [23, 39], including social dynamics in the game [11,12] how players enact intimate experiences within WoW [28], how real-life friends and family play together [33], and how collaboration changes when players are co-located [21].

Identity and Self-Representation in Online Games

The concept of identity in virtual worlds has been studied extensively since Turkle's work in the early 1990s [37]. Despite this breadth, however, identity is not a well-agreed-upon concept; a definition from Pavlenko and Blackledge [30] that is useful for our work suggests that identities are a kind of opportunity: they are "social, discursive, and narrative options offered by a particular society in a specific time and place to which individuals and groups appeal in an attempt to self-name, to self-characterize, and to claim social spaces and social prerogatives" (p.19, in [27]).

In addition, several theorists state that identity is not a single construct. For example, Tajfal and Turner argue that there are two broad classes of identity: social identity, which defines self in terms of groups; and personal identity, which defines self in terms of idiosyncratic traits and characteristics [34]. Even within these classes, however, there can be many identities. Omoniyi [27] proposes a hierarchy of identities, in which a person's social identity is constructed within a particular context, and may change from context to context; furthermore, multiple identities may be articulated in a given context (27, p. 2).

Theorists also propose that people actively construct representations of their self and identity for themselves and for other people, and since the self that we project has consequences for how others react, we try to control the self that we present. Many researchers build on the notions of self-representation proposed by Goffman [19], who likens this process of impression management to theatre, where people play different roles for different audiences.

Avatars and characters in online games are obvious mechanisms for self-representation because of the close connection between the player and the character. Concepts of agency (i.e., that the character enacts the player's actions in the game) and immersion (i.e., that the player receives sensory information about the game world through the character) allow both a projection of self and an emotional attachment to the character [31].

Numerous studies have explored the ways in which online representations interact with identity (e.g., [2,3,10,12,37]). Researchers have recognized that the relationships between players and characters are complex: people can have multiple accounts, and accounts can be shared, so the relationship between people and their online identities can be many to many [10]. In addition, some people expose a real-world identity, while others hide their information, provide fake information, or even impersonate others [10,37]. Bessière et al. showed that players who experience a wide gap between "who they are" and "who they want to be" build avatars to represent an ideal version of themselves [2]. Similarly, most players in Second Life create avatars that reflect aspects of themselves, although different players represent different aspects [26]. Blinka et al. [3] found that adolescents identified more with their avatars than adults, although age was not a factor in the strong interconnection between the player and the avatar.

Within these explorations of identity, and also in other studies of MMOs, researchers have also observed several other aspects of the ways that players view their characters (e.g., [15,16,22,35]). These observations indicate that players can think of characters in several ways simultaneously (e.g., using different conceptual 'frames' as discussed by Fine [15]), and that players can think about characters in value terms as well as in identity terms, based on factors such as the character's utility or aesthetics. In our categorization of value types below, we review these previous studies in more detail; but first, we consider the theoretical basis for an exploration of the idea of value.

Theories of Value

Many fields of research have considered the underpinnings of the concept of value, and the question of why objects and actions have value. Adler [1] wrote that "concepts of value can be reduced to about four basic types": value as an absolute (arising from 'eternal ideas'), value as a property of an object, value as a social construction originating in needs or desires, and value as equated with action (p. 272). Adler states that many theorists align with one of these types, although there are many examples where more than one type is relevant to a situation or object [1]. Theories of value are also often tied to ideas of evaluation and comparison, in that people need ways of judging worth in different contexts. For example, Boltanski and Thévenot [4] describe six 'economies of worth' (civic, market, inspired, fame, industrial, and domestic), which provide "systematic and coherent principles of evaluation" that operate in different social contexts. In these spheres, the principles allow arguments and behaviour to be evaluated and compared (although problems arise when people appeal to different spheres).

Many theorists allow differentiation between philosophical value (i.e., 'values'), which relate to importance or 'goodness' in terms of a belief or ethical system, and which guide how people should act and behave; and economic value, in which worth is dependent on relative factors such as context, rarity, or the goals of the individual [41]. We are concerned primarily with this latter kind of value, although it is also clear that philosophic conceptions of value often influence economic ones (i.e., 'values' often affect 'value').

Economic theories use the concept of exchange to define value – that is, the value of an object is equivalent to the price that a person is willing to pay for it (leading also to the idea of value as a relationship between the quality received and the particular price paid for an object [32]). Economists classify value as either intrinsic (i.e., the value of an object is contained only within the object itself, such as in the labour theory of value [6]), or subjective (i.e., value is determined by the consumer rather than the object's properties or production processes).

One basis of intrinsic value is the difficulty of creating or obtaining an object – for example, as reflected in the low probability of discovering a gemstone in the wild, the labour involved in extracting the gem from a mine, and the effort required to turn a rough specimen into a cut stone.

For subjective value theories, monetary value typically reflects other aspects of the object's worth, such as its utility in saving labour (e.g., a bicycle can reduce transportation time), or the enjoyment or satisfaction that a person can obtain from it. Enjoyment value can be either direct (e.g., sensory appreciation of a painting or a gourmet meal) or indirect, in which the object enables participation in enjoyable activities rather than being enjoyable itself (e.g., a bicycle might allow the owner to engage in the excitement of bike racing with friends) [41]. We note that 'subjective value' here is not entirely internal to the person, since part of the value that a person may place on something is at least partly based on the person's relationships to other people and on community notions of value (in addition, any exchange-based idea of value requires that that there be multiple people involved).

The idea of subjective value begins to decouple the idea of value from a monetary structure – a divide widened by concepts such as 'sentimental value' where monetary value is no longer important at all. As Richins suggests, in many cases "economic value cannot fully capture the actual value of many of the objects owned by consumers" [32, p. 504]. This division has been discussed as the difference between 'value in use' versus 'value in exchange' [41], and in our work we focus primarily on the idea of value in use.

Richins and other theorists suggest that the subjective value of an object is derived from its *meaning* to the object's owner [32], and meaning can be either public or private. *Public* meaning acts as communication within a social system, in which the publically-accepted value associated with an object communicates something about the owner of the object. For example, certain brands of clothing or cars can 'make statements' about a person's status, role, or interests. The meaning of these statements is highly specific to a social group. *Private* meaning involves memories and representations of other relationships or events, and builds over time – "meaning, and hence value, derives from repeated interactions with a possession" [32, p. 506].

Public and private meaning can take several forms, often in a representational sense:

- Objects can be representations of interpersonal ties (e.g., diamond earrings given on a wedding anniversary);
- Objects may be a representation of a person's past or their personal history (e.g., 'sentimental value');
- Objects can be an expression of personal values or religious beliefs, or of ethnic or national identity;
- Objects can be a representation of a person's competence, mastery, or achievement;
- Objects can differentiate oneself from others.

Although it can be difficult to separate the communicative aspects of meaning from personal aspects, it is clear that each form adds value in certain contexts. We used these ideas of value from economics and consumer research to guide our study of WoW character value. It is also important to note that public and private meaning in an object or possession can clearly involve identity as well – for example, in the idea of 'somatic displacement' discussed by Holopainen and Meyers, in which people can project themselves into objects (e.g., a car or a doll) [20].

Previous research has also considered the role of value in motivation. Expectancy-value theory [38], for example, states that people make choices about actions and behaviours based on their beliefs about the likelihood of success and the expected value to be gained. This theory can be used in a gaming context to understand why people play in different ways (see discussion section below).

Finally, we note that considering characters as valuable objects does not mean that players do not also maintain other views (e.g., based on identity). Players can maintain multiple views of characters, and different characters can be seen differently as contexts and times change.

CHARACTER VALUE STUDY: METHODOLOGY

We examined the idea of character value with twenty WoW players. We carried out data collection in two separate sessions. The first session (10 players, three female) involved direct observation of play sessions followed by an in-depth interview. The second session (10 players, two female) involved interviews only, and was used to follow up on concepts and issues identified in the first session. All twenty participants were experienced WoW players (usually playing daily). Each player had a main character but also maintained a number of 'alts', with the amount of time spent on non-main characters varying widely.

In session one, observation sessions took 2.5 hours on average and involved the player showing us each of their characters, and then engaging in one or more normal activities in the game such as raiding, trading, PVPing (competing against other human players), or socializing. After watching the gameplay, we conducted a semi-structured interview, covering planned questions about character value, and follow-up questions to explore interesting events that occurred during the game session. Each interview lasted about 1.5 hours. We audio-recorded and transcribed each session for later analysis (over 40 hours of data). We analyzed the data iteratively using a grounded theory approach [17] with open and selective coding. We used data from each session to contextualize data from the others, allowing us to refine our categories. Each new set of interview and observation data yielded new codes and modifications of old ones; the process was repeated with new data until the categories stabilized.

In session two, semi-structured interviews were carried out by e-mail. Initial questions started a discussion about the players' characters, and asked about character value and relationship. Further questions followed up on earlier answers, and the discussion moved in different directions for different players. Interviews were carried out asynchronously over a period of one month. After interviews were complete, responses were analyzed using the categories and concepts identified in session one. Finally, after the interviews were completed, we reviewed previous MMO literature for examples where researchers had observed value elements that fit into our categories. These analyses revealed that players value their WoW characters in many different ways. We identified ten types of reported value, as introduced below.

RESULTS

We first look generally at how participants viewed their characters, and then address the question of what kinds of value a character can provide to the player.

How players viewed their characters

Our interviews show a wide variety of ways that participants think about their characters. First, identity-based relationships were one of the main ways that players described their characters (particularly their main), much as has been reported in previous research (e.g., [10,15,37]). People made statements such as: "[the character] is me in the game world"; "I suppose [PH][1] is a cartoon/fantasy representation of what I try to be/hope that I am;" or "The name [HF] is my personal pseudo-identity online. It makes sense to make my main character the representation of me."

However, participants also described a number of other ways that they viewed their characters. For example, some players clearly saw their characters as a means rather than an identity – as one player said, "[I don't] refer to it almost as if it were a sentient being, really it's not. It's me playing it; it's my puppet as if I had a marionette." Another person

[1] Anonymized initials are used in place of character names.

said "It's the model I use to play the game. I don't go out there pretending that I'm this character in this realm."

Players also mentioned the possession-based and object-based relationships that were suggested by Wong and colleagues [43]. Main characters were sometimes described in these terms, even if there was also a strong identity relationship. Participants had no difficulty talking about their characters in different ways at different times – sometimes with identity language, and sometimes in value terms. The theories reviewed above, however, suggest that it is not surprising that players can view characters in multiple ways simultaneously [19].

Alt characters were more often talked about in value terms, and all participants had at least one of these characters. The language used to describe them varied widely, but often used metaphors of tools, actors, or independent entities: e.g., one person said "It's like I'm playing this chess piece to beat up this [other] chess piece, or how will a piece deal with this situation given its limited movement."

Mains can become Alts (and vice versa), and even strong identity relationships can change over time. One participant discussed a shift in their thinking about a character who used to be her Main until her guild dispersed. This character changed from being strongly associated with the player's identity to being almost entirely a utility:

"Since the guild disappearance I don't use [RG] for really much of anything anymore. The only time I hop on her is when I need to utilize her professions or need a level 90 toon to help with a raid. Unfortunately she has reverted to simply being a tool for me. When I play her I don't feel the same way as I do with my current toons or that I used to feel when I was actively playing her."

It was clear that players do attribute several kinds of value to their characters, and these values are not mutually exclusive. In the next sections, we identify and describe ten different types of value arising from the study.

Utility Value

Utility is a classic form of value in many different theories, and utility is a strong element of many WoW characters. The useful things that a character can do or accomplish are clearly a valuable aspect for many participants in the study. Almost all players described at least one character (or an attribute of a character in a situation) that was primarily about utility. In many cases, the better the utility provided by a character to the player (e.g., the better the character is at playing a particular role), the greater the perceived value: e.g., one person described a character by saying "my warrior is a good tank," but had little else to say about him.

It was also clear that players often had utility in mind when creating some characters. One person stated "I would always choose the tactical advantage over the aesthetic look;" another said "I chose Shaman because I heard they had really high DPS and heals;" and a third stated:

"To be honest, I only spent 30 seconds to create my paladin. [...] I did not spend too much time on appearance, because you can change her hair style in game. And I don't really care about it. So it can be regarded as an 'all business' style."

In many cases utility characters were created in order to fill a particular need in a guild: e.g., one player stated "The reason that I created him is my raid needed a holy paladin as their main tank healer since the previous paladin AFKed." This player was strongly utility-oriented: almost all of his characters were created because of what they could do, and he did not name any of the characters (his guild uses player's real names online).

Other characters had particular skills that were valuable for the player, and when they were performing these skills, the relationship was primarily a utilitarian one. For example, one player said "I played him only for taming a variety of wild beasts"; another said, "This makes her a very valuable tool for earning gold and crafting powerful items." Another player made it clear that when playing a character for utilitarian needs, there is no real identity relationship:

"When I am using her purely as a tool (like when I log in to her now to get materials and am not interacting with anyone or anything) I do not impart any sort of personality on her at all. If someone interacts with me while I am in this situation, 'I' am the one to respond and if people were to ask me about [RG] while I am in this situation I respond purely as if she is a game object and nothing more."

The mechanics of WoW also lead to certain types of utility characters, particularly 'bank Alts' who exist only to store items and gold for the player's other characters. Several of our participants had at least one of these characters, and one person had several characters whose role was purely to make (in-game) money:

"I used [EN] as my mule, my cash cow. This character made all the gold for all my other characters. I used him to rule the auction house which was for the longest time in WoW the best way to make money using a buyout low sell very high approach."

This player also stated that the utility-based nature of this character conflicted with another identity-based character: "Unfortunately this made [EN] a known name on the server and therefore I tried to never associate [HF] with [EN]."

WoW also has specific PVP areas that can lead players to create specialized fighting characters (similar perhaps to gladiators). As one participants described:

"I then made a few more characters [who] all shared one purpose. They were level'd up and then level locked [...] Once level locked I acquired them significantly over-powered gear for their level. These characters would then fight in player versus player (PvP) and dominate. These characters were for competition and I associated very little with them."

Finally, several participants mentioned that at a higher level, all characters are just mechanisms: as one stated, "to a certain extent, all of the characters are a tool to play the game; actually, to the most extent [they are]."

Prior work on utility value. Several researchers have also noted that players are very concerned with character utility. For example, studies of why players create certain characters show that many characters are made for specific game purposes (e.g., to serve a guild) [36,10,12,18], and as

DiGiuseppe and Nardi stated, "the single most common class choice across all classes was to be valuable to a team" ([9], p. 10). Equipment choice often has similar motivation: as Taylor states, "there is a significant focus on choosing particular clothing and weapons for very utilitarian reasons (better statistics being predominant)" ([35] p. 27). In addition, Ducheneaut and colleagues observed the practice of creating Alts that are only for storage or trading [12].

Personal Investment Value

Unlike many other objects, characters are entities that can be improved or enhanced, and these improvements take time and effort. As indicated by Richins [32], meaning and value derive from repeated interactions with something, and character development in WoW requires a great deal of work with the character. For example, becoming better at a skill requires many hours in the game world, and leveling a character to the maximum can take hundreds of hours.

Most of our participants indicated that their characters had value because of their investment: for example, one player said "It's not something that you can put a price on but it has value because I've put time and effort into it;" another said "I don't feel like protective of them, but I do feel they have value from all the time and effort I've put into them." Another simply said "Time, lots of time." Several participants explicitly used language that suggested investment, as well as comparisons to other kinds of objects in which one could invest – for example, one player said:

> "I guess it's like a car or truck, you buy it and pay it in payments – more than likely it cost a lot, you put a big investment into paying [for] your car, [so] you want to take care of it, same with your toons that you make – grinding from level 1-90 is rough."

Once the player has spent time developing a character, there is a clear attachment to that specific character (even though the character is just a digital record). Richins and other theorists state that as objects gain meaning through prolonged interaction, they become less and less fungible (i.e., they cannot be replaced with an equivalent item because the replacement does not contain the same meanings); and this was clearly true in our participants' comments. For example, one person said:

> "I could grind another character up to 85 and equip her with the same stuff and give her the abilities and she would be carbon copy, but she wouldn't feel right. She's not the original character."

The achievements and progress that players see in their characters can also be an important part of the play experience – this is of course part of the game design, in order to keep people involved, but it also provides value to the player. As one person said:

> "I put in the time and chip away at it, I'm able to work on developing her and actually see the results. They're predictable for the most part - I just have to be patient. Even when things in my life weren't working the way I wanted, I could get 'actual' things done with [PH]. I actually think that I enjoyed playing her in a few particularly stressful times simply because it was something that I could control and see the results for."

A character's level is one external and quasi-economic assessment of its worth (e.g., a high-level character would be worth more than a low-level character on the open market) that is widely understood in the WoW community. Thus, characters also have value as a representation of achievement in WoW (i.e., the degree of investment) – this is apparent in that players often include the level when talking about their characters (e.g., "She is a level 90 Blood Elf Hunter;" or "This character is still not lv90 yet. I spend about 1 hour per week to level him up").

Character level is also a game restriction (some zones are limited to certain levels), which increases awareness of this achievement. For example, one player said:

> "Since [PS] is only at level 68 she has no value in terms of her utility in regards to the latest expansion content since she does not reach the minimum level requirement for the Mists of Pandaria zone."

However, players in our study differed widely in the way that they valued both particular character enhancements and the effort needed to achieve them. While one player might see ten hours as a significant investment of time, another might consider this to be inconsequential (or, depending on what attribute was being improved, might consider the effort to be a waste of time). Some players were very interested in developing many different aspects of the character (e.g., one player said in regards to her Main, "I invested an enormous amount of time in rounding her as a character – leveling, questing, gathering, leveling my abilities, doing achievements, getting better equipment") but others were much more focused on particular attributes (e.g., the overpowered PVP characters mentioned above).

In addition to the object-based comparisons, several players described characters with considerable pride, as if they were independent people, or even one's own child. One player said "I have in my own way been creator and breathed life into him, so he would be like (in some weird crazy roundabout sense) my child;" another said:

> "Look at my character! She's grown up so much. I almost feel like I'm sharing photos of children. Like I have a daughter or something and she's grown up so much."

We also asked participants about another kind of investment – the potential real-world monetary value of their characters (characters can be bought and sold at external websites and can be worth hundreds of dollars). Players said that this was not a major concern for them. Only one of our 20 participants had ever done this – the player said that they had previously sold an old account in this fashion. Some participants even indicated that the disparity between the personal investment value and the potential real-world value made the idea somewhat ridiculous: e.g., "It's like asking for $20,000 for a pinkie. It's just something I wouldn't put a dollar value on."

Prior work on investment value. Previous studies have also identified aspects of the investments that players make, including the time that players spend in the game [45], the effort that goes into (and satisfaction that derives from) leveling a character [47, 14], and the emotional investment that players have in their characters [49].

Identity and Self-Expression Value

As discussed earlier, players and characters often have strong identity relationships. Here we consider not the nature of these relationships, but the characters' value as a means for self-expression – as noted by Richins [32], objects can allow people to express aspects of their self, such as their personality, their ethnicity, their beliefs, or their competence and mastery of a skill.

Participants stated several ways in which these personal attributes came out in their characters – we previously described how a character's level is a representation of achievement, but often the character's class or visual appearance were also seen as valuable. For example, one player who created a shaman class character stated:

> "I've always been interested in real life shamanism and how they view the world... I identify with [my character] because he is the shaman, and that is something I know; that kind of spirituality I find attractive. I mean even though it's a game, he's a shaman so he's representing this classic iconic real life station. People for thousands of years have followed these traditions and passed on to their children's children's children."

Characters were also often described as the player's "representative" – that is, an agent who can be relied on to maintain the player's reputation. As one person said, "She's my ambassador;" another stated "I suppose she is a bit of a representative of me in the gaming world, though she is a shinier version of me!". Players also mentioned choices of visual appearance in this way: for example,

> "She isn't particularly striking, particularly in comparison to other female characters like Elves, but I kind of like that about her - she is unassuming :-)"

In addition, players described aspects of their character's behaviour or imagined attributes: one person said "Like me, [PH] is good natured, she enjoys helping people, [and] she loves to gather things (items, achievements)."

Prior work on self-expression value. As described above, much research has investigated identity in MMO games. Some of this work identifies the value of avatars for self-expression, particularly in the visual appearance of the character [26,14,49]. For example, Fron and colleagues observe that "costumes, garb, attire, gear, fashion – in short, dress-up – provide players with a means to 'put on' these identities and explore the avenues they open" ([16], p.15).

Enjoyment Value

Many objects are valuable to their owners because of the enjoyable activities that they enable (i.e., intrinsic indirect value in theoretical terms), and some WoW characters are primarily created to allow players to enjoy the game. The game, after all, is intended to be fun – but because of the investment needed to develop and level a character, several participants talked about Alts that they created purely for enjoyment. As stated by one player:

> "When I had to make a character for me to just level and enjoy I made a Blood Elf Hunter [...] This was a 'just for fun on the side' character. Not much investment."

In addition, many Mains were also seen as having at least some enjoyment value (alongside other value), even given the work they required – for example, as said by one player:

> "I enjoyed being a druid - lots of magic and healing, less hand-to-hand combat [...] I enjoyed creating a character that was of great use to others [...] and I really enjoyed socializing with other characters - helping people randomly, and hooking up for quests, especially for special occasions like Children's Week or Brewfest."

Prior work on enjoyment value. Although it is very clear in previous work that people enjoy playing MMOs, we have found only a few instances where players talk about the enjoyment of their characters over and above the rewards and achievements of the game itself (e.g., [36,35]).

New-Experience Value

Some characters are valuable in the new and different experiences that they make possible for the player (of course, all game content must be experienced through an avatar, but in some cases this is the character's primary purpose). There may be elements of pure enjoyment in these new experiences, but our participants also mentioned other reasons for creating these characters. For example, several participants stated that they made characters to see what gameplay was like with a different class or role – e.g., "I created [the Disc Priest] because I was curious about what is the gameplay style of a healer in WoW." Another person reported creating a character as a kind of 'scouting report' to learn about an enemy class:

> "I created him because Mage is a big threat to my healers in PVP arenas. I have to know more about this class so that I can react better when meeting them in arena or RBG."

Prior work on experience value. Researchers have observed that some players create characters purely to explore the game world. For example, Taylor states "One woman I spoke with recounted her experiences trekking her necromancer around the world ('from one end of Norrath to the other') and the peril and excitement such a journey brought. Another told me she specifically created a druid because they 'were the ultimate explorers and at that stage of the game I just really wanted to explore'" ([35], p. 32).

Memory and Sentimental Value

Many objects have value in their ability to remind the owner of a person, a relationship, or an event. Several participants mentioned that their characters contained memories in this way; one person, who had previously characterized himself as being very focused on achievements and goals, said:

> "These characters store a lot of memories for me. Although the original reason for me to create them has some specific target, what they have left for me is not only who they are, but also what the teams have done. Teams cannot always be stable, but what my characters have done with that team [shows] the timeline of how our team has changed and progressed."

Another player described one of their characters as a tribute to another person from a former guild:

> "The only value I really have in [FX] is the sentimental value of her being made in the image of a friend's old toon [...] When he said

that he was going to retire the character and that he didn't plan on playing him ever again, I made [FX] as an homage to the Undead Priest to which I had become so close."

Characters can also represent other memories and experiences for a player – similar to the way that a scrapbook can store mementos of the past. One person made this clear using the metaphor of photographs: "My character is as valuable as a photo album, it's a collection of memories." Even if a character is not particularly useful or attractive, they may still be valuable to the player if they 'have been through a lot together' – using the character may remind the player of memorable experiences (e.g., skirmishes or particular interaction with other players).

Prior work on memory value. Wong and colleagues suggest that when characters are shared, they could record or collect information about their 'adventures' while on loan [43]. Similarly, Manninen and Kujanpää [22] discuss the idea of players journeying through a game world with their character, and building up shared memories. They state "the investment of time and the empathic approach to the character may also result in players wanting to think back on the events shared with, and the qualities built for, the character. In this way the character gains sentimental value" ([22], p. 28).

Aesthetic and Creative Value

Some possessions provide intrinsic value through sensory pleasure, and this is true of WoW characters as well. Aesthetic value involves attraction to a character's attributes (e.g., appearance or movement). Participants primarily valued the visual aesthetics of their characters, and much of the discussion involved topics related to making characters visually appealing. Players are able to express themselves creatively through the design of a character, and are able to appreciate the results of these efforts. Aesthetic value may be associated with self-expression, accomplishment, and social recognition.

Several participants stated that they made conscious choices about their characters to achieve aesthetic goals. For example, in contrast to the player above who stated that he always chose utility over looks, one player stated:

"When I play games like this I always make my choices out of flavour and never utility - this is why I am never usually among the top OP (over-powered) players. [...] I chose her race because it was my favourite at the time and I chose her appearance because it was the look that I liked best."

Another player who had originally chosen the Undead race for his Main said that the character was "the ugliest you can get in WoW. Not at all pleasing to me. I considered paying $20 to race change to Blood Elf; however [the character] had spent so much time Undead it felt wrong to change."

Other participants stated that they went further than simply making appearance-based decisions, and actively created entire 'looks' for their characters that were aesthetically pleasing. There are many ways to customize the visual appearance of a WoW avatar – e.g., through different armour, items, mounts, or pets (as one player said, "you are able to have them follow you around so they can become part of your toon's physical appearance"). These add-on items can help to create a desired visual effect, and participants stated that they could get very involved in this creative process – as one person said, "you spend 20 hours making this beautiful art piece."

The aesthetic and creative work could be for either public or private consumption. For some participants, personal goals were most important: "I like how my characters look, I like having pets that match. It matters to me, I don't care if it matters to you." Another player stated that the look they were trying to achieve matched other aspects of how they created the character:

"I wanted him to be all very black with golden eyes, which just pleased me... I thought the golden eyes were more a shaman color, you know? Somebody who'd see visions, and would be able to see the spirits, you know? His eyes had been touched in that way."

Public displays of characters were also common – in these cases, a character is a creative outlet to be shared and appreciated by the world. There is a mixture of aesthetic and public communication value in this activity – as one person said, "I see others as looking at the items she's wearing." One participant related the way in which these creative acts can be shown to the public at specific times:

"I have a black cat pet and my [Main] is black and I have a [black] Bombay cat [...] At Halloween every character that has a sinister squashling brings out a sinister squashling."

Prior work on aesthetic value. Several researchers have noted players' interests in customizing character appearance [14] and in creating particular visual appearances [16]. For example, Fron [16] describes several creative aspects of clothing and fashion practices in role playing, including crafting items of clothing and the design communities that build up within the game. Creativity and visual aesthetics have even become out-of-game interests for some sub-communities – as evidenced by 'WoW fashion' websites (e.g., the *Kirina's Closet* or *World of Dresscraft* blogs).

Sociability Value

Although WoW can be played as an individual, many players prefer to play with friends ("I don't think I would play as much if I didn't have real life friends to play with"), with family, or even with strangers [23]. Characters thus have value in that they enable social interaction with others. Many participants stated that they created Alts specifically to play with friends who were on other WoW realms (it is difficult to move characters across realms).

One person stated that one of her Alts "was primarily created to quest with a character that my husband had on the server. [Another character] was also created to play with my husband's alt." Other players related stories of being recruited by a group of friends, which required the creation of a new character. One person said "My friends were trying to get a gladiator title for season 10. So they recruited me and I decided to make a Shaman"; another stated "I only made [MN] to help my group and now that they're gone he will sit there till I see fit."

several studies [23,7,13]. A few authors have noted that characters can be created primarily to enable social relationships – for example, Nardi and Harris [23] suggest that Alts are used to allow friends to play together when their main characters are at different levels.

Social Communication Value

Public meaning gives objects value, and having certain objects communicates status, achievement, and identity to a social group [32]. Several participants stated that the publicly-visible nature of characters was important, and particularly when the player had achieved something rare or difficult. This kind of value is different from the creative act of making a character for aesthetic reasons; in WoW it often has elements of being proud of one's accomplishments and wanting to receive public acclaim for something that has been difficult to achieve. Players clearly derive value from a personal sense of accomplishment and the social recognition they receive. For example, one player related the story of acquiring new mounts with two friends:

"Our Jewelled Panther mounts that took us a few months of hard work to get. [...] the mounts required over 60k gold to make. [...] Once all three of us finally had our panthers, we spent probably about an hour just flying around together [...] and walking through town in a line and many other things to show them off (if not to other people than even just for ourselves). I played ['Swagger Like Us'] through Vent when we had finally accomplished this and were sitting around town =)."

A similar experience was reported by another player who completed a difficult game task that rewarded him with a proto-drake flying mount:

"I've gone so far as to do it in such a way as being ostentatious... I took one of those elixirs that makes you bigger, and planted my big [black proto-drake] on the landing pad, so you had to run up to the foot if you were going to fly out, and see this huge gigantic thing and me sitting there. I did that for an hour easy."

Prior work on communication value. Previous work has discussed ways that a character's visual appearance can reflect achievements or status. For example, Taylor [35] found that certain items of clothing or gear indicate a player's level of advancement or mastery: "Obtaining epic weapons or more generally owning impressive equipment [...] all become artifacts of mastery and signal to both the user and the server community their skill at the game" [35] (p. 28). Fron also states that specific items can even convey where a character has been in the game world (because certain items are only obtainable in certain places) [16].

DISCUSSION

Our analysis reveals a range of player-character relationships and ways in which players value a character in a game like WoW. We saw and described ten types of value that a player can ascribe to a character, suggesting that this is an important part of a player's enjoyment of the game.

For researchers, our focus on the value of a character helps to explicate some of the complexities in the ways that players relate to characters. Our value categories highlight the fact that players can value their characters in many ways (e.g., as one facet of an identity, as a theatrical role, as a canvas, or a memory repository). Our interviews showed us that conversations about characters are often full of different perspectives – even within a single statement. There can potentially be several ways of interpreting the ways that players talk about their characters, but value is a lens that helps us understand a quality that clearly adds importance and meaning to MMO games. Considering the value of characters in games can help user experience researchers and game developers understand players and their actions more completely. Additionally, the ten values that we listed here provide a structure that can be used to design interviews or survey instruments. While some of the values we have identified here support and reaffirm existing value research in games, we have also explicated new sources of value such as the character as a representation of a relationship, or as a repository of memory.

Prior work on sociability value. Researchers have explored the importance of sociability and collaborative play in

For developers, thinking about character value can provide new insights into player retention, and can provide a better understanding of how players interact with a game. As discussed earlier, expectancy-value theory [38] suggests that players who value different aspects of their character will react differently to game content. For example, a player who values social communication through showing off a character's rare or good-looking gear, and who knows the probability of an item drop, might spend more time in raids to get the item and will view their character as having a higher value for it. This could lead to increased activity in the game world over a longer period. Game developers can make use of our categories to encourage their players to return to the game because their characters have value to them. The long-term retention of players is an ongoing concern for developers, especially for MMOGs, and an understanding of the player-character value relationship can help designers improve retention rates. In the following paragraphs we discuss some of these opportunities.

Supporting aesthetic value. Game developers already know that aesthetics are a critical element of games – graphics, art, and soundtrack are all cited explicitly by players as a important aspects of a game. However, as a dimension of value to the player, aesthetic components have only recently begun to be explored. Over the last few years we have seen the rise of the free-to-play and 'freemium' business models in the game industry. For example, games such as WoW, Lord of the Rings Online, Dota 2, Team Fortress 2 and social environments (e.g., Second Life) have implemented additional capabilities for designing or purchasing clothing, apparel, and style items. The real monetary value of these digital items demonstrates a clear understanding of the aesthetic value players place in their characters – value that players are willing to pay for. A second possibility involves enhancing creative expression – such as the integration of player-side creation and sharing tools. These tools would allow players to create their own aesthetically-valuable objects (e.g., faces, hair, or clothing) for characters. Some games are already exploring this possibility – Valve has introduced a community market system into the Steam delivery system that allows players to buy and sell items for real money. Taking the idea further, sensing tools like the Kinect could also capture players' motion data and allow them to create customized character movements, which could then be captured, sold or traded with other players.

Supporting social value. For characters whose primary purpose is communicating and interacting with other players, game developers could add features that are commonly seen in social-network platforms like Facebook or Twitter. For example, status messages and updates could be shown as in-game artifacts similar to the 'comic blurbs' already seen in WoW. Enhanced communication and social value could encourage players to use the game system as a primary communication channel, keeping them in the game. Well-supported social value could also encourage player retention if players use the game system for other kinds of communication. WoW has seen the inclusion of some of these features such as cross-game communication with their 'RealID' system. Popular casual games such as Farmville or Settlers Online have also successfully built on the value found in social networks. Furthermore, games could make more use of the fact that players are part of different social groups (e.g., friends, family, and guild), by allowing players to customize a character depending on the social context (either in terms of information that can be queried from the character or even the in-game visual representation).

Supporting investment value. Players value both their own understanding of investment in a character, and also the public display of achievements and progress. Giving players the opportunity to improve a wider range of character attributes can enhance this kind of value. Game developers understand the need for player investment as a means for motivation and progression, but investment value could be further enhanced by making many extendable attributes that can be improved through in-game tasks, and by making progression through these improvements clearly visible. Some games (although not currently WoW) could also make use of ideas such as character sharing [43] as a way to enhance investment value (e.g., a guild could all pool their resources to improve the utility of a character, and link it with a guild rather than a single player account).

Supporting memory value. Games could do much more to enhance the value of characters as a record of experiences and adventures. Games could give players the ability to revisit these previous experiences: for example, games could provide tools for recording images or videos of a character's current appearance and capabilities, and these visual records could be stored in photo albums, scrapbooks, or 'highlight reels.' One possible configuration of such a system might be a timeline (similar to Facebook's version), where a player could quickly and easily explore their history and the history of their friends within the game. Such a system would also provide investment value since the timeline could also illustrate the player's investment as well as past experiences. Games could also make it possible to replay scenes from a character's history, so that players could relive interesting or memorable episodes that they experienced through the character, or walk through the progression of the character to its present form.

Last, we note that maximizing character value may not always be the most important consideration. Different play strategies in MMOGs lead to different player-character relationships, and some players may not want to have characters of high value, or may never see a character as having any type of high value. Nevertheless, character value is a factor in a some players' decisions about which games to pick up and which games to return to – a player's gaming activity is often split among multiple games and multiple characters, and so the higher the character value that can be generated by an individual game, the more likely it is that a player will become attached to that game.

CONCLUSION AND FUTURE WORK

Research into MMOGs suggests that there is considerable diversity in the range of player-character relationships, and in the ways that players think about character value. To investigate the concept of character value in more detail, we carried out in-depth interviews with twenty WoW players; we identified ten different types of value categories that can help in understanding the complex ways in which players think about their characters. This work can inform game developers who wish to enhance players' experiences through increased character value.

There are a number of directions for future research in this area. First, we plan to continue our observational fieldwork, to see whether our categories hold in other MMOGs. Second, we will continue our exploration of the connections between different relationships, different value dimensions, and the ways that players shift between these views based on context. Third, we will develop prototypes that provide examples of the kinds of support described above, to investigate how best to make use of the diversity of player-character relationships in game design.

ACKNOWLEDGMENTS

This work was supported by the Natural Sciences and Engineering Research Council of Canada, and by the GRAND Network of Centres of Excellence.

REFERENCES

1. Adler, F., The value concept in sociology. American Journal of Sociology, 1956, 272-279.
2. Bessière, K., Seay, A. & Kiesler, S. The ideal elf: Identity exploration in World of Warcraft, *CyberPsychology & Behavior*, 10(4), 2007, 530–535.

3. Blinka, L., The relationship of players to their avatars in MMORPGs: differences between adolescents, emerging adults and adults. *Cyberpsychology*, 2(1), 2008, 1–9.
4. Boltanski, L., & Thévenot, L. *On justification: Economies of worth*. Princeton University Press, 2006.
5. Castronova, E., *Theory of the Avatar*. Cesifo, 2003.
6. Cohen, G., The Labor Theory of Value and the Concept of Exploitation, *J. Phil. & Public Affairs*, 8, 4, 1979, 338-360.
7. Cole, H., & Griffiths, M., Social interactions in massively multiplayer online role-playing gamers. *CyberPsychology & Behavior*, 2007, *10*(4), 575-583.
8. Debeauvais, T., Nardi, B., Lopes, C., Yee, N., & Ducheneaut, N., 10,000 Gold for 20 Dollars: An exploratory study of World of Warcraft gold buyers. *Proc. FDG*, 2012, 105-112.
9. DiGiuseppe, N., & Nardi, B., Real genders choose fantasy characters: Class choice in world of warcraft. *First Monday*, 2007, 12(5).
10. Donath, J., Identity and deception in the virtual community. *Communities in cyberspace*, 1999, 29–59.
11. Ducheneaut, N., Yee, N., Nickell, E., Moore, R., Alone Together? Exploring the Social Dynamics of Massively Multiplayer Games. *Proc. CHI 2006*, 407-416.
12. Ducheneaut, N, The life and death of online gaming communities: a look at guilds in World of Warcraft. *Proc. CHI 2007*, 839-848.
13. Ducheneaut, N., Moore, R., and Nickell, E. Virtual third places: A case study of sociability in Massively Multiplayer Games. *CSCW*, 2007, 16(1-2), 129-166.
14. Ducheneaut, N., Wen, M., Yee, N., and Wadley, G., Body and mind: A study of avatar personalization in three virtual worlds. *Proc. CHI* 2009, 1151-1160
15. Fine, G., *Shared fantasy: role-playing games as social worlds*, University of Chicago Press, 2002.
16. Fron, J., Fullerton, T., Morie, J. F., & Pearce, C. Playing dress-up: Costumes, roleplay and imagination. *Proc. Philosophy of Computer Games*, 2007, 25-27.
17. Glaser, B. & Strauss, A., *The discovery of grounded theory: strategies for qualitative research*, Transaction, 1967.
18. Golub, A., Being in the world (of warcraft): raiding, realism, and knowledge production in a massively multiplayer online game. *Anthropological Quarterly*, 2010, 83(1), 17-45.
19. Goffman, E., *Frame analysis: an essay on the organization of experience*, Northeastern University Press, 1986.
20. Holopainen, J., & Meyers, S. Neuropsychology and game design. *Consciousness Reframed III*, 2000.
21. Lindtner, S., Nardi, B., Wang, Y., Mainwaring, S., and Jing, H., A hybrid cultural ecology: World of Warcraft in China. *Proc. CSCW 2008*, 371-382.
22. Manninen, T., & Kujanpää, T, The value of virtual assets–the role of game characters in MMOGs. *I.J. Business Science and Applied Management*, 2007, *2*(1), 21-33.
23. Nardi, B. and Harris, J., Strangers and Friends: Collaborative Play in World of Warcraft, *Proc. CSCW 2006*, 149-158.
24. Nardi, B., Ly, S., and Harris, J., Learning Conversations in World of Warcraft. *Proc. HICSS 2007*, 79.
25. Nardi, B., *My life as a night elf priest: An anthropological account of World of Warcraft*. Univ. of Michigan Press, 2010.
26. Neustaedter, C., & Fedorovskaya, E. Presenting identity in a virtual world through avatar appearances. *GI 2009*, 183-190.
27. Omoniyi, T., Hierarchy of identities. In T. Omoniyi & G. White (Eds.), *The sociolinguistics of identity*, 2006, 11-33.
28. Pace, T., Bardzell, S., and Bardzell, J., The rogue in the lovely black dress: intimacy in world of warcraft. *Proc. CHI'10*, 233-242.
29. Pace, T., Toombs, A., Gross, S., Pattin, T., Bardzell, J., & Bardzell, S., A tribute to Mad skill: expert amateur visuality and world of Warcraft Machinima. *Proc. CHI'13*, 2019-2028.
30. Pavlenko, A. and Blackledge, A., (eds) *Negotiation of Identities in Multilingual Contexts*, 2004.
31. Pearce, C., Towards a game theory of game. *First person: New media as story, performance, and game*, 2004, 143–153.
32. Richins, M.L., Valuing Things: The Public and Private Meanings of Possessions. *Journal of Consumer Research*, 21(3), 1994, 504-521.
33. Schiano, D. J., Nardi, B., Debeauvais, T., Ducheneaut, N., & Yee, N., A new look at World of Warcraft's social landscape. *Proc. CHI* 2011,174-179.
34. Tajfel, H., & Turner, J., An integrative theory of intergroup conflict. *Social psych. of intergroup relations*, 1979, 33-47.
35. Taylor, T., Multiple Pleasures: Women and Online Gaming. *Convergence*, 2003, 9, 1, 21-46.
36. Trepte, S., & Reinecke, L. Avatar creation and video game enjoyment: Effects of life-satisfaction, game competitiveness, and identification with the avatar. *J. Media Psychology: Theories, Methods, and Applications*, 2010, 22(4), 171.
37. Turkle, S., *Life on the screen: identity in the age of the Internet*, Simon & Schuster, 1997.
38. Wigfield, A., Tonks, S., & Klauda, S.. Expectancy-value theory. *Handbook of motivation at school*, 2009, 55-75.
39. Williams, D., Ducheneaut, N., Xiong, L., Zhang, Y., Yee, N., & Nickell, E. From Tree House to Barracks: Social Life of Guilds in World of Warcraft. *Games and culture*, 2006, 1(4), 338-361.
40. Williams, D., Martins, N., Consalvo, M., & Ivory, J. The virtual census: Representations of gender, race and age in video games. *New Media & Society*, 2009, 11(5), 815-834.
41. Wikipedia, *Subjective Theory of Value*. wikipedia.org/ /wiki/Subjective_Theory_of_Value (May 31, 2013).
42. Wikipedia, *World of Warcraft*. wikipedia.org/wiki/ /World_of_warcraft (May 31, 2013).
43. Wong, N., Tang, A., Livingston, I., Mandryk, R., Gutwin, C., Character Sharing in World of Warcraft. *Proc. ECSCW 2009*, 343-362.
44. Yee, N., Ducheneaut, N., Yao, M. and Nelson, L. Do men heal more when in drag?: conflicting identity cues between user and avatar. *Proc. CHI 2011*, 773-776.
45. Yee, N. The psychology of massively multi-user online role-playing games: Motivations, emotional investment, relationships and problematic usage. In *Avatars at work and play*, 2006, 187-207.
46. Yee, N., The Demographics, Motivations and Derived Experiences of Users of Massively-Multiuser Online Graphical Environments. *PRESENCE: Teleoperators and Virtual Environments, 15*, 2006, 309-329.
47. Yee, N., Motivations of Play in Online Games. *Journal of CyberPsychology and Behavior*, 9, 2007, 772-775.
48. Yee, N. & Bailenson, J., The Proteus Effect: The Effect of Transformed Self-Representation on Behavior. *Hum. Comm. Research*, 33(3), 2007,271-290.
49. Yee, N., Ducheneaut, N., Nelson, L., & Likarish, P., Introverted elves & conscientious gnomes: the expression of personality in world of warcraft. *Proc. CHI 2011*, 753-762.

The Effects of Consistency Maintenance Methods on Player Experience and Performance in Networked Games

Cheryl Savery[1], T. C. Nicholas Graham[1], Carl Gutwin[2] and Michelle Brown[3]

[1]School of Computing
Queen's University
Kingston, ON, Canada
{savery | graham}@cs.queensu.ca

[2]Dept. of Computer Science
University of Saskatchewan
Saskatoon, SK, Canada
gutwin@cs.usask.ca

[3]Dept. of Computer Science
York University
Toronto, ON, Canada
brown@cse.yorku.ca

ABSTRACT

Network lag is a fact of life for networked games. Lag can cause game states to diverge at different nodes in the network, making it difficult to maintain the illusion of a single shared space. Traditional lag compensation techniques help reduce inconsistency in networked games; however, these techniques do not address what to do when states actually have diverged. Traditional consistency maintenance (CM) does not specify how to make game-critical decisions when players' views of the shared state are different, nor does it indicate how to repair inconsistencies. These two issues – decision-making and error repair – can have substantial effects on players' gaming experience. To address this shortcoming, we have characterized a range of algorithmic choices for decision-making and error repair. We report on a study confirming that these algorithms can have significant effects on player experience and performance, and showing that they are often more important than degree of consistency itself.

Author Keywords
Consistency maintenance; game development; usability

ACM Classification Keywords
H.5.3Information Interfaces and Presentation: CSCW.

General Terms
Human Factors; Algorithms

INTRODUCTION

Real-time networked systems, such as multi-player games or shared-workspace groupware, often follow the principle of *distribution transparency* [26] - they attempt to provide an experience that is the same over distance as it is when people are in the same location. The illusion of transparency often breaks down, however, due to problems in the network, such as latency, jitter, or packet loss - often collectively referred to by gamers as 'lag.' In these situations, those parts of the shared environment (e.g., the game world of a multi-player game) that are stored at each node in the network diverge, leading to strange phenomena such as bullets not hitting their targets, objects jumping across space, or avatars moving in a halting and jerky fashion.

Most networked games (and other kinds of distributed systems) combat these problems with lag compensation techniques that try to ensure that information at different nodes in the network (e.g., the locations and status of players in the game world) is in the same state. There are several types of techniques that operate on different principles: for example, some use prediction to try to overcome latency, some use 'local lag' to slow down input to match the latency in the network, and some use time offsets to reduce the variance in remote update times. These techniques work well in many situations - shown both by research studies (e.g., [1,20,25]) and by their adoption by virtually all commercial networked games.

However, the focus of these techniques on 'simple consistency' does not address all of the issues caused by lag and diverging state. In the case of networked games, we have identified two additional factors that are important to player experience and performance, but that are not adequately considered by most consistency maintenance schemes. First, lag compensation techniques are never perfect, and so games need to make decisions in the presence of inconsistency. Second, when the techniques recognize a state divergence and attempt to correct it, the error must be repaired at one (or more) of the nodes.

The first issue is called the *decision-making* problem. When the game must make a fast decision about a game-critical event (e.g., whether a bullet hits a target), it must often do so with the assumption that states at different nodes have diverged. Therefore, the game must choose one of the different states to use as the basis for the decision. This choice could mean substantially different outcomes for game events, which could have a large effect on understandability and player experience.

The second issue is called the *error repair* problem. When a state divergence is identified (e.g., when a prediction algorithm has moved an avatar to the wrong location), the error must be repaired – and since errors often involve a

CSCW'14, February 15–19, 2014, Baltimore, Maryland, USA.

http://dx.doi.org/10.1145/2531602.2531616

visible object in the game, the repair must be visually understandable. Some techniques provide smoother corrections (e.g., interpolating between the incorrect and correct locations over a time period) but at the cost of reduced consistency, in that it takes longer for the two nodes to reach the same state.

Understanding the effects of the decision-making problem and the error repair problem are important in the design of a game's overall approach to consistency maintenance, but there is little information available about how important these issues are, and how they affect player performance and experience. To address this shortfall, we carried out an experiment to address three questions:

- Is simple consistency the most important issue for player experience in networked games?
- What are the effects of different choices about what state is used to make game-critical decisions?
- What are the effects of different choices about how errors are corrected?

Our study tested 26 people (13 experts and 13 novices) in three different custom games that implemented several different techniques for lag compensation, decision-making, and error repair. We recorded both player performance and subjective assessments of play experience. Our study confirms that decision-making and error repair are important design considerations for networked games. Players preferred conditions where game-critical decisions were made such that outcomes were more understandable to the local player. Players also preferred smooth animation over jerky movements caused by instantaneous 'warps' when the corrections were small. However, when larger corrections were required, players only marginally preferred smooth corrections compared to warping. These results show that simple consistency is not the most important element in player experience, since both smooth corrections and local-player understandability actually reduce the overall state consistency of the game.

Our study also provides several additional results that add to our knowledge of player experience in conditions of lag. For example, we found that there were large differences in the degree to which experts and novices noticed the effects of the consistency techniques; we also found that some players enjoyed the challenge of having to adjust for the lag, particularly when playing against a weaker opponent.

Our work makes three important contributions to the understanding and design of CM schemes for networked games. First, we demonstrate that state consistency alone does not address all of the issues that arise from lag. Second, we present an integrated CM design space that brings lag compensation together with the additional techniques of decision-making and error repair. Third, we provide the first empirical evidence of how these factors affect player experience and performance in three different game genres, and identify trade-offs in the techniques' use.

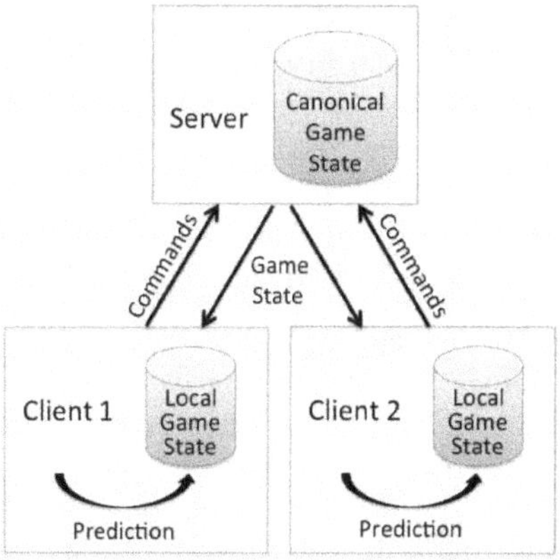

Figure 1. Typical client-server architecture: server maintains canonical game state; local clients use prediction and server updates to determine local game state.

BACKGROUND AND RELATED WORK

In this section, we describe the consistency maintenance problem and briefly review existing research related to consistency maintenance in networked games.

The Consistency Maintenance Problem

In multiplayer games, inconsistencies arise due to a combination of network latency and the use of prediction by the client to determine the local game state. Because of the real-time performance requirements of many forms of networked games, some inconsistency must typically be tolerated in exchange for faster feedback to the player and quicker resolution of game events.

Most networked games are based on an authoritative central server (Figure 1). To combat cheating, game clients are generally not allowed to make any decisions that affect player performance in the game [15]. Player inputs are passed to the server, which determines the new game state and propagates it back to the clients. Due to network latency, the client cannot wait for the next game state to arrive from the server before providing feedback to the player. Thus, the client must use prediction to calculate the local game state. Problems occur when the client's predicted state differs from the server state. For example, consider a racing game where two players attempt to move their car to the same position at the same time. Each player sees that the position is open, and locally the client predicts that the move can occur. However, when the server receives the commands, it determines that a collision has occurred. The server sends the corrected game state to the clients, which are then forced to repair this inconsistency. The use of multiple servers can reduce the latency between the server and client, but introduces the complexity of maintaining a consistent state among the servers [7].

Inconsistencies can have a negative impact on player performance and experience [4,19], such as the confusion caused by sudden warps in position, the frustration of shooting directly at another player and missing [5], or the perplexity of suffering damage from a grenade while protected by an invincibility shield [2].

Lag and Consistency in Games

Research on consistency in games can be divided into two categories: studies that look at the general effects of latency on player performance and experience [4,10,11,19], and research into specific CM techniques such as dead reckoning [1,21] and local lag [9,25]. These techniques are described in detail in the Reducing Inconsistency section.

Claypool [11] generalizes the effects of latency in networked games by categorizing game actions along two dimensions: precision (the accuracy required in performing an action) and deadline (the time period within which an action must be performed). This provides us with an understanding of the types of game actions that are most affected by network latency, but provides no guidance on techniques that can mitigate the effects of latency.

The Human Factors framework [22] discusses three aspects of multiplayer games that must be considered when determining CM requirements. First, there are the types of entities found in the shared environment. E.g., objects such as avatars typically have tighter consistency requirements than other objects in the game world. Second are the types of interactions players can have with those entities, particularly whether interaction with multiple players is possible and whether the interaction affects game critical variables. The framework then considers how player states may diverge in time and space and in rate of change. This work provides a good foundation for making CM choices, but focuses primarily on the single dimension of the CM problem of reducing inconsistency.

AN EXPANDED CONSISTENCY DESIGN SPACE

Unlike the work described above, we believe that there are three factors to be considered in the design of a CM scheme: in addition to the traditional factor of reducing inconsistency, we highlight the importance of decision-making and error repair. These factors are related and it is important to deal with them as a whole rather than looking at each factor individually. We introduce three axes (Figure 2), describing a range of approaches that help with each problem, and concluding with a discussion of how decisions in each axis influence the behavior of the others.

Reducing Inconsistency

The first line of defense in the CM problem is to deploy an algorithm that prevents or reduces inconsistency in the first place. While a core set of algorithms has been proposed, it is not yet fully understood in what situations different algorithms should be applied. In general, these algorithms trade off game responsiveness, the frequency with which the algorithm causes jarring corrections to the player's view, and the degree to which the views of different players diverge [22]. These algorithms follow three broad strategies, all of which have been used in commercial games: using *prediction* to anticipate remote updates; *delaying input* to allow simultaneous execution on all players' computers, and *offsetting time* to allow state to diverge in a controlled fashion.

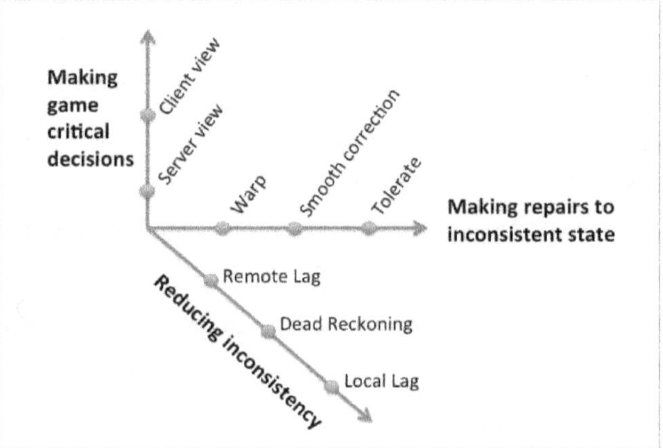

Figure 2. The design space consists of three axes capturing the issues that must be addressed in deciding on a consistency maintenance scheme

More specifically:

- *Predictive techniques,* such as dead reckoning [16,20], predict changes to remote state before those changes are propagated over the network. The predicted state can be used locally, compensating for the time to transmit the state over a network. However, if the prediction is incorrect, the local state must be updated, possibly in a jarring or confusing manner. Dead reckoning is commonly found in role-playing games such as EverQuest and World of Warcraft. Here, game clients predict the position of remote entities based on their last known position and velocity.
- *Delayed input techniques,* such as bucket synchronization [6] and local lag [17], delay local actions to allow simultaneous execution by all clients. For example, if a player presses the "W" key to move forward, he will not see his avatar move until after the delay period, providing time for the input to be sent over the network to remote game clients. Delayed input algorithms improve consistency, at the cost of slower response to player actions.
- *Time-offsetting techniques,* such as remote lag [5], apply a constant delay to updates from remote clients. For example, in the Half-Life first person shooter game, remote players' avatars are lagged by a constant 100ms. Time-offsetting increases inconsistency (since remote state updates are not applied immediately), but makes the degree of consistency predictable, something to which players may be able to adapt.

Each of these strategies embodies trade-offs. Prediction can increase consistency when the prediction is correct, at the cost of potentially jarring corrections when the prediction is wrong. Delayed input increases consistency at the cost of reduced responsiveness. Time-offsetting lends predictability to inconsistency, but increases inconsistency overall. Because time-offsetting displays an exact replica of the remote state which has been simply offset in time, its use can reduce or even eliminate the need for error repairs.

A growing body of research attempts to determine the conditions under which the various techniques are applicable [9,21,25]. For example, local lag is effective up to about 100ms of lag [25,9]; bucket synchronization is most effective in real-time strategy games where users can tolerate small delays [11]. However, little work has been done on the criteria for selecting one algorithm over another.

Decision-Making

Game-critical events are highly visible occurrences with significant impact on the game's progression. Examples include picking up a piece of treasure, crashing into an opponent's car and blowing up, or defeating a "boss" enemy to complete a level. Game-critical events are different from, for example, moving an avatar, which can generally be easily undone or corrected, and where small differences in positions may be unnoticeable.

The resolution of game-critical events in the presence of inconsistency can have an enormous impact on player experience and performance. In a shooter game, one player might be frustrated to miss an enemy who was clearly in his cross-hairs, while another might be upset at being hit while hiding behind a rock. When inconsistency causes players to see the world differently, the outcome of such game critical events can have unintuitive and negative consequences.

An important question in resolving game-critical events is the choice of perspective to use. If game clients all have a different state, which state should be used to resolve the outcome? One important case involves actions which have a source and a target: e.g., one player shoots another, or throws a pass to another. The game-critical questions to be resolved are whether the target player was shot, or whether the target player caught the ball. Three choices of perspective are available:

- *Server perspective.* The game server maintains a canonical state. The event is resolved relative to this state, even if it disagrees with what the players see.
- *Source client perspective:* The decision is based on what the initiator of the action sees. For example, Counter Strike uses this approach for shooting, in the belief that it is more noticeable to the shooter if he erroneously misses, than to the target if he is erroneously hit [5].
- *Target client perspective* resolves events based on what the target of the action sees. This is used, for example, in Halo: Reach for determining damage when a player has activated Armor Lock [2], an ability providing the player with a few seconds of invincibility. During this period, a player would be frustrated if a grenade thrown toward her inflicted damage.

Note that the choice of perspective does not necessarily imply the node within a distributed system where choices are made. For example, Counter Strike uses the shooter perspective, but the hit decision is actually made on the server (and therefore requires the server to be able to reconstruct what the shooter saw when firing) [5].

The perspective used for resolving hit decisions can have an enormous impact on player experience. Dick et al. have shown that in Unreal Tournament 2004, network latency above 100ms has a significant impact on game score, while in Counter Strike, player skill was the primary determinant of game score [12]. A primary difference between these games is that Unreal Tournament 2004 uses server-perspective for resolving hit decisions, while Counter Strike uses the perspective of the shooter.

When choosing a strategy for decision-making, game developers should consider which player is more likely to notice an unintuitive result, and which player is more negatively impacted by an erroneous determination.

Error Repair

The final axis of the design space deals with how to repair inconsistencies when they are discovered. Three basic approaches are used to resolve inconsistencies:

- *Correct immediately:* The simplest solution is to immediately update the local state to the newly arrived correct state. This may result in jarring visual artifacts, such as remote players "warping" to a new location. This warping can be confusing, and can distract the player's attention to the location of the abrupt change.
- *Correct smoothly:* Here, the incorrect local state is progressively updated to the correct state. For example, a remote avatar might quickly run to the correct location rather than simply warping. This removes the effect of jarring corrections at the cost of prolonging the period of inconsistency.
- *Tolerate:* If the inconsistency doesn't matter, it may be preferable to leave it as-is. For example, the positions of players in Blizzard's World of Warcraft are often inconsistent, with little effect on gameplay.

There are significant tradeoffs between these solutions, and to-date, these have received little attention. Correcting immediately may affect players' immersion in the game world since a player's attention will be drawn toward any sudden discontinuities in the position or motion of objects in the game [18]. A player may also lose context, for example, if an avatar that was in front of him is suddenly behind him and now out of his field of view.

Smooth corrections may reduce the jarring effect of corrections [24]; however, they prolong the inconsistency, which may be unacceptable in some game situations. Fiedler suggests the rule of thumb of moving 10% toward the true position during each frame, but if the correction is large, simply warping to the new position [13]. More sophisticated forms of smooth correction are possible; e.g. varying priorities may be given to different objects in the game to ensure the objects of higher importance deviate the least from their true position [8]. To date, there has been little effort to characterize when smooth corrections are effective, and how they should be applied.

Design Consequences

Designers need to be aware of how decisions made in one axis can affect the range of choices in other axes. We now list some examples of possible interactions. Our study, presented in the next section, explicitly tests the effects of these interactions on players' experience and performance.

- The use of local lag has positive effects on the decision-making and error repair axes. Local lag reduces inconsistency, therefore reducing the magnitude of corrections and increasing the likelihood that client and server perspectives are the same when decisions are made. Local lag may be a good choice in situations where corrections are particularly bad, e.g., to avoid race conditions when two players are concurrently picking up the same item.
- Prediction can lead to large state divergences. This can increase the importance of the choice of perspective used for decision-making, and can lead to an increasing frequency and magnitude of corrections. Prediction may be most appropriate in situations where an accurate prediction algorithm is available and where corrections do not negatively impact gameplay.
- The suitability of the remote lag algorithm depends upon the nature of game-critical decisions. If one player is more impacted by the outcome of a game decision, as in our shooter example, remote lag can allow the decision to be made from that client's perspective. However, if all players care equally about a decision, having divergent views of the game world can be confusing. For example, in a two-person racing game, if each player saw a delayed version of the other player, both players might believe that they were the first over the finish line.
- Smooth corrections may reduce the jarring effect of warps, but increase state divergence versus immediate correction of inconsistencies when they are discovered. Smooth corrections may therefore be a poor choice when state consistency is very important.

USER STUDY: TYING THE DESIGN SPACE TO USER EXPERIENCE AND PERFORMANCE

We carried out a study to provide a better understanding of how the dimensions of the design space affect player experience and performance. In particular, we designed the study to answer four questions:

Q1. Does better overall consistency in a distributed game always lead to better experience?

Q2. How does the decision perspective (client or server) affect player perception of critical game events?

Q3. How do different error repair strategies (warping or smooth correction) change experience?

Q4. Does the player's level of experience affect the results of Q1-Q3?

We answered these questions with three custom networked games designed specifically for this study. The games replicated critical aspects of real multiplayer game situations (but were otherwise kept simple to avoid the effects of strategy). The three games were *Paddle Blasters*, a cooperative canoeing game, *Eliminate*, a first-person shooter, and *Speed Daemons*, a racing game.

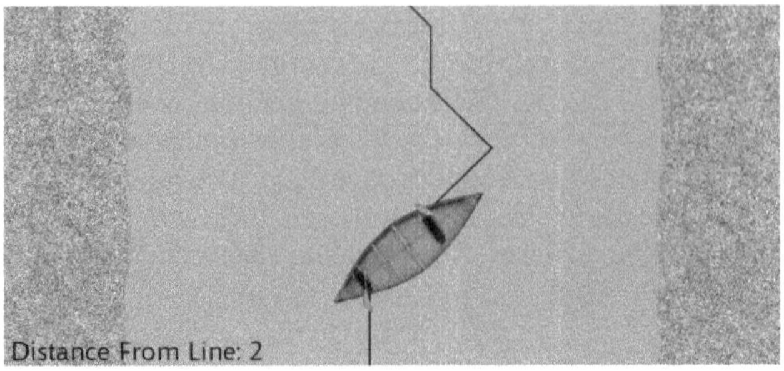

Figure 3. Paddle Blasters: Players cooperate to paddle a canoe and follow a path indicated by a black line.

Figure 4. Eliminate: FPS in which players attempt to hit their opponent while avoiding being hit themselves.

Paddle Blasters is a cooperative two-player game that was used to investigate whether overall consistency led to better player experience (Q1). In Paddle Blasters, players attempt to paddle a canoe down a river; the goal is to keep the canoe as close as possible to the black line that zigzags down the river (Figure 3). Each player paddles on one side of the canoe. If one player is paddling, the canoe turns; when both players paddle, the canoe moves ahead in its current direction.

Eliminate is a first-person shooter game used to investigate the effect of using different perspectives for game-critical decisions (Q2). In the game, players attempt to shoot their opponent while avoiding incoming shots. Simple block avatars are located on a platform separated from the other player by an open area that cannot be crossed (Figure 4). This restricts the movement of each player and forces the player to focus on the shooting task. To discourage firing without aiming, players must wait three seconds between shots.

Speed Daemons is a 2-D side scrolling game used to study two techniques for repairing location errors: immediate warping and smooth correction (Q3). Each player controls a racecar and attempts to pick up coins while avoiding mud puddles (Figure 5). Players earn one point for each coin they collect; colliding with puddles causes a loss of two points. The game scrolls from right to left at a constant rate with new coins and mud puddles appearing from the right.

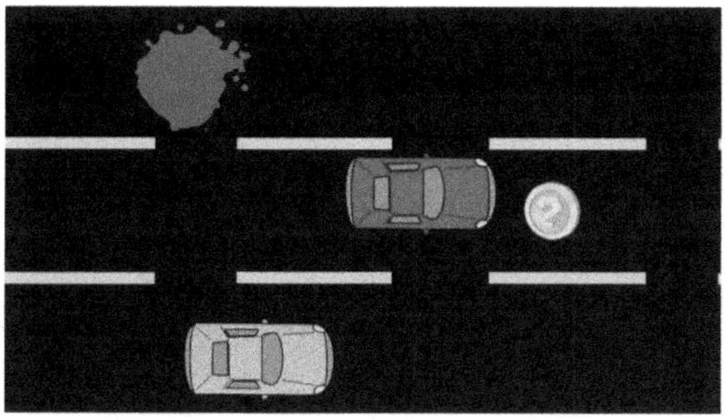

Figure 5. Speed Daemons: Racing game in which players attempt to collect coins while avoiding mud puddles.

Study Methods

Participants

26 participants were recruited from a local university. 13 of the participants were frequent and experienced gamers, and 13 were non-gamers. We classed participants as gamers if they played fast-paced games at least once per week. We did not require expertise in any given game. Although expertise might be specific to an individual game or game genre, we hypothesized that there is significant commonality between games in, for example, the ability to rapidly manipulate game controls, or to visually process game events. In addition, because our games are designed to focus on common game elements (moving, targeting, avoiding), there is a reasonable expectation that expertise will apply across all of our scenarios. We use gaming experience as a factor in the study, as described below.

Procedure

Participants played in pairs, seated at separate computers and able to communicate through a headset. For each game scenario, the players were shown the game and allowed to practice for up to five minutes. During this learning period no latency was added to the game. Typical network latency during the practice sessions, as measured by ping time, was 1ms or lower.

Following the training period, in order to simulate typical wide area network conditions, synthetic latency was introduced on the network. Based on work by Armitage [3] showing that players of games such as Quake 3 actively select servers where the latency is less than 150 to 180ms, we chose to limit the synthetic latency to 200ms. The latency was randomly distributed between 50 and 200ms according to a Poisson distribution. Because the games used synthetically created latency over a local area network, there were no large latency spikes during the trials. The participants played several trials. Each trial used a different CM technique, corresponding to the conditions from questions 1-3 above. The order of the trials was randomized and the conditions were balanced for order. Specifics of the trial conditions for each game scenario are described below.

Paddle Blasters (Q1). Participants played three different conditions. Each condition was repeated three times for one minute each. In condition A, 200ms of remote lag was used (*Lowest Consistency* between the two players' views); in condition B, 100ms of local lag was used in addition to dead-reckoning-based prediction (*Medium Consistency*); and in condition C, 200ms of local lag was used (*Highest Consistency*). In condition B, warping was applied to repair any incorrect states that occurred when latency exceeded 100ms. No information regarding the specific differences between conditions was provided to the participants.

Eliminate (Q2). There were two five-minute trials, both of which used 200ms of remote lag for displaying the position of the remote avatar. In trial A, hits were determined based on the shooter's perspective (*Shooter*), while in trial B, hits were determined based on the canonical game state as determined by an authoritative central server (*Server*). Expert gamers typically play their game of choice for many hours each week, and over weeks, they become intimately familiar with the algorithms being used in the game. As each condition was played for only five minutes, we told the participants what scheme was being used in order to simulate the experience they would have in extended play in real life.

Speed Daemons (Q3). Participants played three one-minute trials. In both trials A and B, dead reckoning was used to predict the position of the remote car. However, in trial A, immediate position warping (*Warping*) was used to fix incorrect positions, and in trial B, smooth interpolation-based correction techniques were applied (*Smooth*). In trial C, remote lag of 200ms was applied to the remote car position, meaning that no corrections were required for the position of the remote car. Smooth corrections were used to repair any incorrect states for the local car caused by collisions between the two cars (*Local Only*). No information regarding the specific differences between conditions was provided to the participants.

After each of the trials in each of the games, participants answered several Likert-style questions about their experience in that particular trial condition (Tables 1, 2, and 3). After all the trials for each game, participants were also asked to indicate which of the conditions they preferred.

Setup and Apparatus

The study used custom software written in C#, XNA, and the Janus toolkit [23], and ran on two computers connected via a dedicated network. The system maintained a frame rate of approximately 60 FPS. Each game used two clients and a server. The server arbitrated conflicts between the two clients (e.g., if both players picked up a coin at the same time in Speed Daemons).

Study Design

We analysed each game separately, using mixed-factorial ANOVAs to test for effects on performance measures. One within-participants factor was determined for each question (i.e., *Degree of Consistency* for Q1, *Decision Perspective* for Q2, and *Correction Method* for Q3, and *Expertise* (Gamer or Non-Gamer) was used as a between-participants

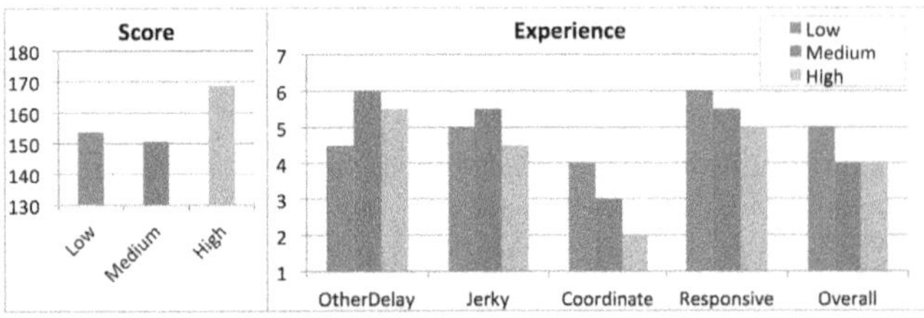

Figure 6. Paddle Blasters: Overall performance (means) (low score is best) and questionnaire measures (medians), by degree of consistency.

OtherDelay: The other player's paddling seemed delayed.
Jerky: The canoe moved in an unexpected jerky manner.
Coordinate: It was easy to coordinate my paddling with the other player.
Responsive: The canoe movement was responsive when I pressed the space bar.
Overall: Overall this version was as good as the practice version.

Table 1. Player Experience questions for Paddle Blasters

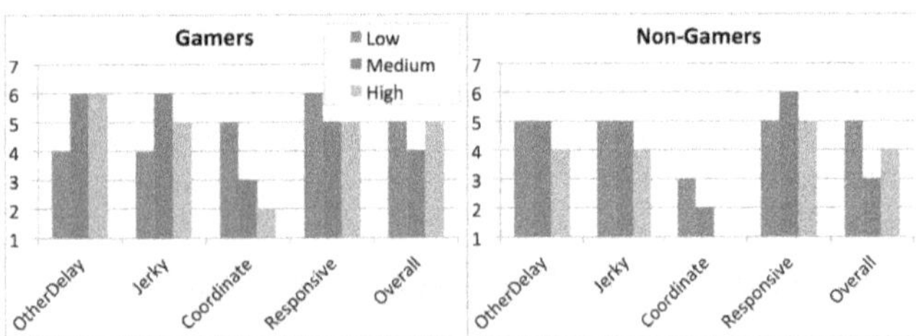

Figure 7. Paddle Blasters: Questionnaire median responses by expertise (Gamer / Non-Gamer) and degree of consistency

factor. Player experience (the questions of Tables 1, 2, and 3) was analysed with Wilcoxon tests on medians.

In the following sections, we present our results. For each question, we first consider the performance measures, and then the player experience questions.

Results

Q1: Does better consistency lead to better ***performance****?*

The Paddle Blasters game compared three different consistency maintenance schemes, providing different amounts of overall consistency between the two clients' views. Remote Lag produces the least overall consistency because the remote player's actions are delayed by 200ms. Local Lag produces the highest consistency because both players' actions are delayed by the same amount, so both players have an identical view of the game. The hybrid approach provides consistency between these two extremes.

We analysed the effects of *Degree of Consistency* on the pair's shared score (we used the mean of the pair's best two scores for each technique; note that lower scores are better in this game). One-way within-subjects ANOVA showed a significant effect of *Degree of Consistency* ($F_{(2,49)}$=3.81, p=0.038) (see Figure 6). Follow-up pairwise t-tests indicated that scores were significantly worse in the *High Consistency* condition (200ms Local Lag) compared to the *Medium* and *Low Consistency* conditions ($p<0.05$).

Q1: Does better consistency lead to better ***experience****?*

For the experience questions (Figure 6), Friedman tests showed a main effect of *Degree of Consistency* for the 'overall' question (χ^2=6.72, p=0.035) and near-significant effects for the 'jerkiness' question (χ^2=5.51, p=0.063) and the 'responsiveness' question (χ^2=5.51, p=0.063) (Fig. 6).

In addition, we divided the data by *Expertise* into Gamer and Non-Gamer groups (Figure 7). For Non-Gamers, Friedman tests show no effect of *Degree of Consistency* on any question. For Gamers, Friedman tests showed a main effect of *Degree of Consistency* for the 'jerkiness' question (χ^2=6.78, p=0.034) and a near-significant effect for the 'overall' question (χ^2=5.90, p=0.052). Follow up Wilcoxon tests showed that for the jerkiness question, the *Medium Consistency* condition was significantly worse than either *Low* or *High Consistency* ($p<0.05$). For the 'overall' question, Wilcoxon tests showed no differences.

Following the trials, the participants indicated their overall preference among the three techniques. For Non-Gamers, five chose the *Low Consistency* condition (Remote Lag), two chose *Medium Consistency* (Local Lag plus prediction), and six chose *High Consistency* (Local Lag). For Gamers, seven chose *Low Consistency*, two chose *Medium Consistency*, and four chose *High Consistency*.

Q1 – Interpretation of Results

In Paddle Blasters, the *High Consistency* condition (Local Lag) resulted in the worst overall score. This indicates that overall consistency does not necessarily result in the best performance. Interestingly, however, the results were not as clear-cut for player experience, with 10 players selecting the *High Consistency* condition as the best overall and 12 selecting the *Low Consistency* condition.

Contrary to previous evidence that 100ms is the limit for local lag for direct interaction [25], we found that fewer than half of the participants noticed 200ms of local lag. Answers to the 'responsiveness' question (Table 1) showed that 15 of the 26 participants found the *High Consistency* (Local Lag) condition to be as or more responsive than the *Low Consistency* (RemoteLag) condition. We believe that the game type has an effect on the noticeability of local lag. The fact that the local player was not the only one controlling the canoe meant that most players (even the gamers) did not notice the 200ms of local delay. However, even though the participants did not always notice the lag, it affected their score in the game.

The *Medium Consistency* condition resulted in the best overall score. However, only four of the 26 participants selected this as their preferred version of the game. This counter-intuitive result is best explained by one participant's comment: "The jerkiness of [this condition] was off-putting, but it played the best."

Our results show that players have definite opinions about the play experience of different CM techniques, but that these are not strongly related to degree of consistency (players preferred either the least or the most consistent version). In addition, it is clear that the visual jerkiness of the game is an important factor (an issue we consider in more detail below).

Q2: Effects of decision perspective on ***performance***

The Eliminate game was used to explore the importance of the perspective from which game-critical decisions were made. The two conditions were *Server*, where decisions are made based on the server view of the game, and *Shooter*, in which decisions are made based on what the shooter saw. The *Server* condition requires players to lead or predict the position of a moving enemy in order to score a hit. We analysed the effects of factor *Decision Perspective* on game performance (individual accuracy and score).

A 2x2 ANOVA showed a main effect of *Decision Perspective* on score ($F_{1,24}$=4.39, p=0.042) and on accuracy ($F_{1,24}$=8.00, p=0.007). As shown in Figure 8, both score and accuracy were lower when decisions were made based on the *Server* viewpoint.

ANOVA did not show a main effect of *Expertise* on either score ($F_{1,24}$=2.83, p=0.10) or accuracy ($F_{1,24}$=.282, p=0.60). Differences between Gamers and Non-Gamers are shown in Figure 8. There was no interaction between *Decision Perspective* and *Expertise* on score ($F_{1,24}$=0.68, p=0.41) or accuracy ($F_{1,24}$=0.165, p=0.69).

Q2: Effects of decision perspective on ***experience***

For the experience questions (Figure 9), Wilcoxon tests showed a main effect of *Decision Perspective* (Z=-2.42, p=0.015) only for the question "Aiming at the other player was easy." Since Wilcoxon tests do not determine interactions, we divided the data by *Expertise*, and carried out secondary analyses with the Gamer and Non-Gamer data (Figure 10).

For Non-Gamers, Wilcoxon tests did not show a main effect of *Decision Perspective* for any of the questions. However, for the Gamers, Wilcoxon tests showed a main effect of *Decision Perspective* for three questions: "Aiming at the other player was easy." (Z=-2.62, p=0.009), "The game felt delayed or laggy." (Z=-2.02, p=0.044) and "There were no issues with delay in this game" (Z=-2.26, p=0.024). In all three cases, participant responses favoured the *Shooter* condition.

Following the game trials, participants were asked which condition they preferred. Among Non-Gamers, 8 preferred the *Shooter* condition and 5 preferred the *Server* condition; for Gamers, 10 preferred *Shooter* and 3 preferred *Server*.

Interview comments show that for some players, the added challenge of leading when aiming (in the *Server* condition) increased enjoyment as opposed to causing frustration. For example, player 13 commented, "I preferred Game A [*Shooter*] but compensating for the lag in Game B was actually kind of fun"; player 1 stated, "Game B is better because of the increased potential for improvement of skills and increased challenge."

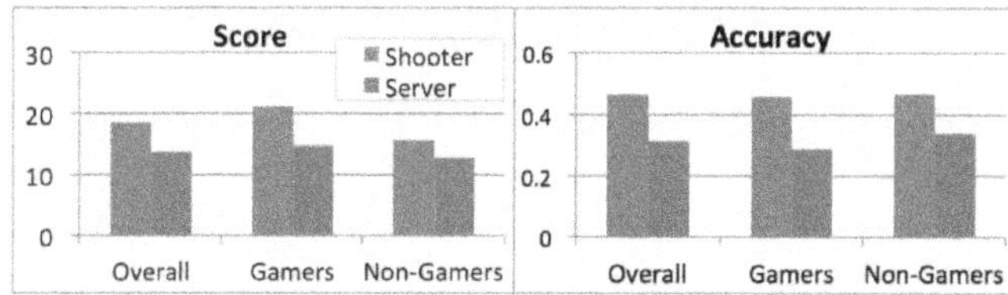

Figure 8. Eliminate: Mean performance by expertise and decision perspective (Server / Shooter).

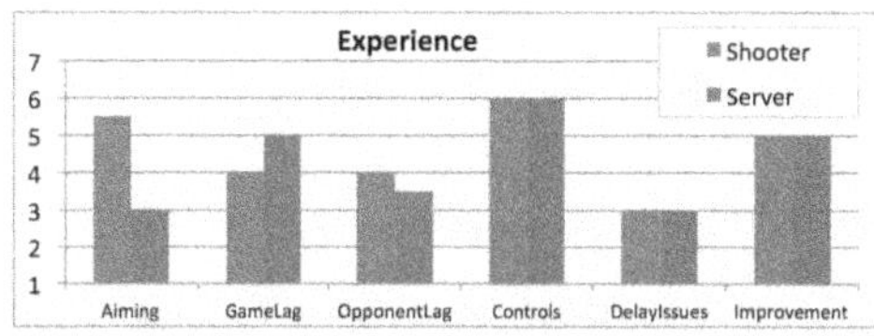

Figure 9. Eliminate: Questionnaire median responses by decision perspective (Server/Shooter)

Aiming: Aiming at the other player was easy
GameLag: The game felt delayed or laggy.
OpponentLag: The other player seemed delayed
Controls: The mouse and keyboard controls worked well.
DelayIssues: There were no issues with delay in this game.
Improvement: I was getting better at shooting/aiming throughout the game.

Table 2. Player Experience questions for Eliminate

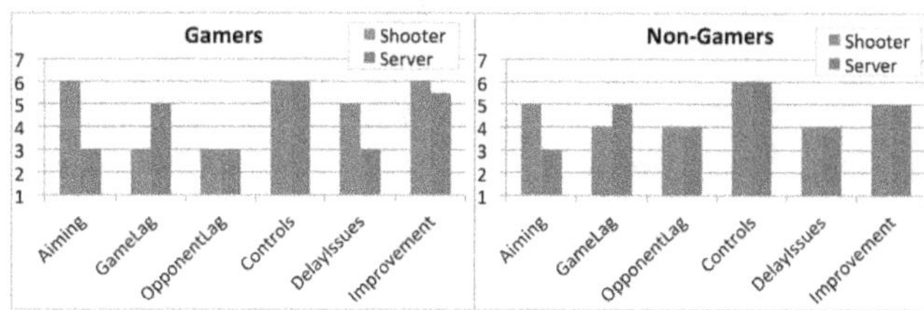

Figure 10. Questionnaire median responses by expertise (Gamer / Non-Gamer) and by decision perspective

Q2 *– Interpretation of Results*

The choice of decision perspective had a significant impact on player performance, with score and accuracy being significantly better in the *Shooter* condition. This is not surprising, as in this condition, the player scores a hit whenever he shoots with his cross-hairs over the enemy's avatar.

This performance difference was seen in both Gamers and Non-Gamers. Surprisingly, score and accuracy measures for the Gamers were not significantly better than for the Non-Gamers. We attribute this to the fact that the Gamers were frequently paired with other Gamers who were also better at avoiding being hit. When we analyzed separately the five trials in which Gamers were paired with Non-Gamers, we did find a significant effect of *Expertise* on both score ($F_{1,8}$ =13.98, p=0.002) and accuracy ($F_{1,8}$ =14.77, p=0.001) with Gamers performing significantly better than the Non-Gamers.

Gamers were more aware of the effects of latency. For the 'game lag' question, they reported that the *Server* condition felt significantly more laggy and for the 'delay issues' question they reported that the *Shooter* condition had fewer

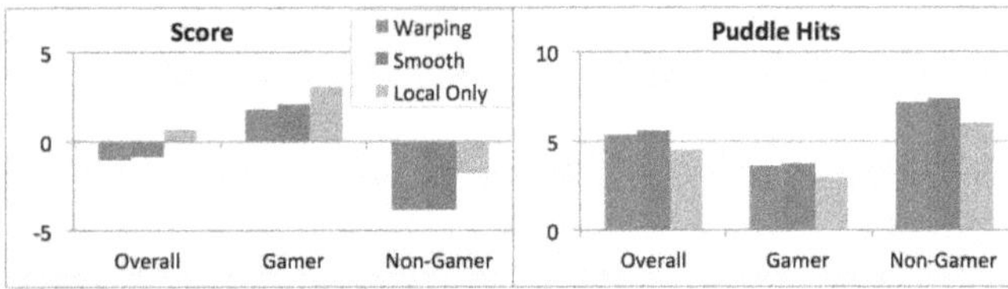

Figure 11. Speed Daemons: Performance (means) by expertise (Gamer / Non-Gamer) and by correction method

OtherJump: It was annoying when the other car jumped or moved unexpectedly.
MyJump: It was annoying when my car jumped or moved unexpectedly.
DelayIssues: There were no issues with delay in this game
Overall: Overall this version was as good as the practice version.

Table 3. Player Experience questions for Speed Daemons

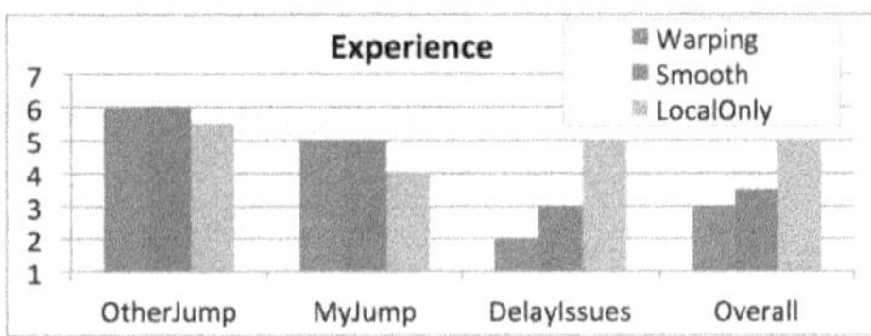

Figure 12. Speed Daemons: Questionnaire median responses by correction method

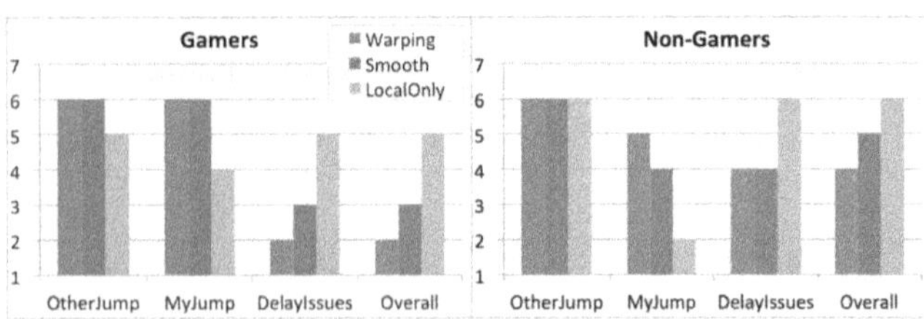

Figure 13. Speed Daemons: Questionnaire median responses by expertise (Gamer / Non-Gamer) and by correction method

issues with delay. Non-Gamers responses for these questions showed no significant difference between the conditions. However, despite not subjectively seeing a difference, Non-Gamers' performance was affected by the choice of technique. This suggests that Non-Gamers may not notice subtle differences in CM techniques because they are too busy with general gameplay, but that these differences may nevertheless impact their performance.

A main lesson is that consistency between players' views may be less important than perceived local correctness (i.e., intuitive resolution of game-critical events).

Q3: Effects of error repair strategies on ***performance***

The Speed Daemons game was used to examine the difference between three error repair techniques: instantaneous correction (*Warping*), interpolated correction (*Smooth*), and a technique that avoided all corrections of the remote car (*Local Only*). We analysed the effects of *Correction Method* on individual performance (game score and puddle hits).

ANOVA did not show a main effect of *Correction Method* on either player score ($F_{2,72}$=0.20, p=0.82) or puddle hits ($F_{2,72}$=0.29, p=0.75) and there was no interaction between *Correction Method* and *Expertise* on either measure (score: $F_{2,72}$=0.02, p=0.98; puddle hits: $F_{2,72}$=0.02, p=0.98).

ANOVA did show a main effect of *Expertise* on both score ($F_{1,72}$=5.12,p=0.027) and puddle hits ($F_{1,72}$=7.62, p=0.007). As shown in Figure 11, the score was higher for Gamers and the number of puddle hits was lower.

Q3: Effects of error repair strategies on ***experience***

For the experience questions (Figure 12), Friedman tests showed a main effect of *Correction Method* for the last three of the four questions (see Table 3). Since Friedman tests do not determine interactions, we divided the data by *Expertise*, and carried out secondary analyses with the Gamer and Non-Gamer data (Figure 13).

For the Gamers, Friedman tests showed a main effect of *Correction Method* for all of the last three questions: for the 'other jump' question, (χ^2=7.37, p=0.025); for the 'delay issues' question, (χ^2=10.3, p=0.006); and for the 'overall' question, (χ^2=13.0, p=0.002). Follow-up Wilcoxon tests showed that for the 'delay issues' question, *Warping* was significantly worse than both *Smooth* and *Local Only* and that *Smooth* was significantly worse than *Local Only* (p<0.05). For the 'overall' question, both *Warping* and *Smooth* were significantly worse than *Local Only* (p<0.05).

For Non-Gamers, Friedman tests only showed a main effect of *Correction Method* (χ^2=8.19, p=0.017), for the third question "There were no issues with delay in this game". Follow up Wilcoxon tests showed that both *Warping* and *Smooth* were worse than *Local Only* (p<0.05).

Following the trials, the participants indicated their overall preferences. Among Non-Gamers, participants were evenly split (each technique was chosen by four people, with one participant stating no preference). Among Gamers, three people preferred *Warping*, two preferred *Smooth*, seven preferred *Local Only*, and one did not state a preference.

Q3 – Interpretation of Results

In Speed Daemons, we saw that player performance was not affected by the choice of technique. We attribute this to two aspects of the game. First, collecting the coins was a very simple task and during each trial all the coins were always collected. Second, the mud puddles were large and players could find themselves cornered into a position where the puddle was unavoidable. Getting into such a position was affected more by player skill than by the choice of technique.

Surprisingly, smooth corrections provided only a marginally better player experience than warping. (Gamers found there to be more issues with delay in warping than smooth corrections, but otherwise there were no significant differences between the two.) We attribute this to the large magnitude of corrections in Speed Daemons and to the very visible nature of the corrections. Corrections occurred when the cars collided with each other and the local client predicted that they did not, or vice versa. When a correction occurred, it was possible for the cars to be on the wrong sides of each other. To do the correction smoothly, the cars quickly drove around each other. Participants' lukewarm response to smooth corrections suggests that these large, rapid movements may be as problematic as instant warping.

In the *Local Only* condition (which used Remote Lag), the position of the remote car was always correct, just delayed in time. The local client can still make incorrect predictions about whether the local car collided with the remote car, and thus there may still be corrections to the local car when the true remote position arrives over the network. However, these corrections were smaller and less frequent than with dead reckoning, and had less impact on player experience.

As with Eliminate, gamers and non-gamers had similar experiences with the different techniques, although gamers continued to be more sensitive to the differences.

The clear winner for player experience is Remote Lag, which reduced the number and magnitude of corrections. Remote Lag leads to greater divergence in state among the participants, but generally leads to smoother animation. This is another indication that factors other than overall consistency can be critical to player experience.

SUMMARY OF RESULTS

To summarize, the following are the important lessons from the study:

- The algorithm that leads to the best player performance does not always lead to the best player experience. In both Paddle Blasters and Eliminate, we saw a decoupling of player performance and experience. In Paddle Blasters, medium consistency was chosen by only 4 of 26 players as their preferred algorithm, yet delivered the best score (in a statistical tie with low consistency). While most players in Eliminate preferred the direct aiming that allowed them to score more hits, some preferred the leading version that provided more challenge.
- Similarly, the algorithm providing the best consistency does not always lead to the best player performance or the best player experience. In Paddle Blaster, the high consistency condition led to lowest scores and worst experience.
- In all three games, we saw that expert gamers are more likely to perceive anomalous behavior due to latency than are novice players. Surprisingly, novice players can fail to distinguish negative behavior even when their performance suffers from it. This was most evident in Eliminate where the novice players had significantly worse accuracy in aiming in the *Server* condition, but reported no significant difference when responding to the experience questions.
- Smooth corrections are not always better than warping, particularly for large corrections that may be required after collisions between entities. In Paddle Blasters, the participants reacted negatively to the small warps in position that caused jerky motion. However, in Speed Daemons, smooth corrections were found to be only marginally better than warping. The large corrections where a car moved quickly around the other car were disconcerting, even when they were done smoothly.

We next discuss the conclusions we can draw from these findings.

DISCUSSION

Our study shows that the CM problem is multi-dimensional, as captured in the three dimensions of our design space. The three example games show that focusing on consistency alone is insufficient, and that the factors of decision-making and error repair are important in designing a complete CM scheme. The study indicates that designers must consider questions such as the following:

- How important is consistency to decision-making? For example, in a scenario where two players attempt to pick up the same object at the same time, it is critical that all clients make the same decision, and a high-consistency CM scheme should be adopted, such as local lag.
- To what degree can decision-making be viewed as asymmetric, in the sense that the results of the decision are more critical to one player than another? If this is the case, then the remote lag CM scheme can be used.
- To what degree can corrections be tolerated? For example, in games where player movement is highly predictable, dead reckoning schemes may be appropriate as they will result in few corrections, and these can be easily and (often) imperceptibly repaired. However, if the corrections are highly noticeable, remote lag and local lag, both of which reduce the number and size of corrections, may be more suitable.

The multi-dimensional nature of the CM problem highlights the importance of user testing to determine the true effects of algorithmic choices on player experience. As we have seen, the best player experience is not always provided by the algorithm that leads to the highest consistency, or even the best player scores. We saw two reasons why the participants actually preferred games where they scored worse. First, part of the fun of playing a game is the challenge of trying to accomplish a goal. If the game is too easy, players may find it boring and not as fun as a more challenging version. For this reason, we believe some of the gamers enjoyed the version of Eliminate where they could not aim directly at their opponent, but instead had to determine how much to lead them. Second, in one condition of Paddle Blasters, warps were used to correct the canoe position as quickly as possible which allowed the players to score better than in the other two conditions. However, the warps lead to jerky animation that many players found to be visually annoying.

Play testing also showed the fallacy of assuming that smooth corrections would always provide a superior experience over warping. Testing showed that remote lag was a surprisingly good option in many situations, as it negated the need for most of the corrections.

The study shows that the type of game and the target player group are important considerations in developing a CM strategy. Games designed for casual players may be able to use a simpler strategy, as many of the subtle effects may go unnoticed by the players. However, fast paced games designed for expert gamers must carefully consider the impact of CM choices on each interaction.

We have seen that there are interesting interactions between the three axes. The use of remote lag can reduce the number of corrections making it easier to provide a smooth animation. However, remote lag also leads to the greatest state divergence and can make it more difficult to make game critical decisions that appear intuitive to all players.

Dead reckoning has the potential to help with this and works well when the movements of the game entities are highly predictable. However, when an entity moves erratically, a large number of jarring corrections can result. Smooth correction techniques can mask the negative effects of the error repairs, but when the game uses physics and entities collide with each other, the corrections may be too large to mask with smooth corrections.

In a perfect world, game developers would prefer complete consistency among all players' views of the game world. However, as a consequence of the tight performance requirements of most networked games, we must accept a degree of inconsistency and sometimes even make incorrect decisions. Ultimately, the key to a good consistency maintenance strategy is providing players with an intuitive local view of the game world. Similar to the findings of Greenberg and Marwood [14] for some classes of real time groupware, it is not necessary that each player have an identical view of the state, merely that the views are consistent enough and that the outcomes of game critical decisions can be rationalized by the players.

CONCLUSIONS AND FUTURE WORK

Our research has provided an expanded view of CM in networked games, focusing on two factors – decision-making and error repair – that can help designers improve player experience. We have performed a user study confirming that it is not sufficient to focus on consistency alone. While it is difficult to generalize the results of game performance studies because changing even small parameters in a game can possibly result in quite different results, we claim that it is productive to analyze individual games in terms of the three axes of the design space, and that surprising results can be obtained from these analyses. From our study, we saw that consistency algorithms providing the best consistency do not necessarily lead to the best user experience. We found that players preferred smooth animation and preferred the results of game-critical decisions to be consistent with their view of the game, even when this resulted in lower overall consistency. Other surprising results included that smooth corrections were not always successful in masking error corrections, and that novice players often failed to noticed the effects of lag even when it caused their performance to suffer.

In future work, we will carry out additional studies using the framework, exploring these axes in real-world gaming situations, and investigating techniques that can better manage the tradeoffs identified in our study. We plan to further investigate interaction effects among the axes such as the relationship between remote lag and corrections and whether the perspective for game critical decisions affects the choice of correction technique.

ACKNOWLEDGEMENTS

We gratefully acknowledge the funding of the GRAND Network of Centres of Excellence.

REFERENCES

1. Aggarwal, S., Banavar, H., and Khandelwal, A. Accuracy in dead-reckoning based distributed multi-player games. *SIGCOMM Workshops*, (2004), 161–165.
2. Aldridge, D. I shot you first! Gameplay networking in Halo: Reach. *Game Developers Conference*, (2011).
3. Armitage, G., An experimental estimation of latency sensitivity in multiplayer Quake 3. Networks, (2003), 137–141
4. Beigbeder, T., Coughlan, R., Lusher, C., Plunkett, J., Agu, E., and Claypool, M. The Effects of Loss and Latency on User Performance in Unreal Tournament 2003. *SIGCOMM'04 Workshops*, (2003), 144–151.
5. Bernier, Y.W. Latency compensation methods in client/server in-game protocol design and optimization. *Game Developers Conference*, (2001).
6. Bettner, P. and Terrano, M. 1500 archers on a 28.8 network: Programming in the Age of Empires and beyond. *Game Developers Conference*, (2001).
7. Brun, J., Safaei, F., and Boustead, P., Managing latency and fairness in networked games. Commun. ACM 49, 11 (2006), 46-51.
8. Chandler, A. and Finney, J. On the effects of loose causal consistency in mobile multiplayer games. *NetGames '05*, (2005), 1–11.
9. Chen, H., Chen, L., and Chen, G. Effects of local-lag mechanism on task performance in a desktop CVE system. *JCST, Vol. 20*, 3 (2005), 396–401.
10. Claypool, M. The effect of latency on user performance in real-time strategy games. Elsevier Computer Networks, Vol 49, (2005) 52–70.
11. Claypool, M. and Claypool, K. Latency and player actions in online games. *CACM 49*, 11 (2006), 40–45.
12. Dick, M., Wellnitz, O., and Wolf, L. Analysis of factors affecting players' performance and perception in multiplayer games. *NetGames'05*, (2005), 1–7.
13. Fiedler, G. Networked Physics. 2006. gafferongames.com/game-physics/networked-physics/.
14. Greenberg, S. and Marwood, D. Real time groupware as a distributed system: Concurrency control and its effect on the interface. *CSCW*, (1994), 207–217.
15. Hogland, G. and McGraw, G. *Exploiting online games: Cheating massively distributed systems*. Addison-Wesley, 2007.

16. IEEE. IEEE Standard for Distributed Interactive Simulation - Application Protocols. *IEEE Standard 1278.1-1995 (revision of IEEE Std 1278-1993)*, 1995.
17. Mauve, M., Vogel, J., Hilt, V., and Effelsberg, W. Local-lag and timewarp : Providing consistency for replicated continuous applications. *Transactions on Multimedia 6*, 1 (2004), 47–57.
18. Murphy, C. Believable dead reckoning for networked games. In E. Lengyel, ed., *Game Engine Gems, Volume 2*. CRC Press, 2011, 307–328.
19. Nichols, J. and Claypool, M. The effects of latency on online Madden NFL football. *NOSSDAV '04*, 146–151.
20. Pantel, L. and Wolf, L.C. On the suitability of dead reckoning schemes for games. *NetGames'02*, (2002), 79–84.
21. Pantel, L. and Wolf, L.C. On the impact of delay on real-time multiplayer games. *Proc NOSSDAV* (2002), 23–29.
22. Savery, C., Graham, T.C.N., and Gutwin, C. The human factors of consistency maintenance in multiplayer computer games. *GROUP'10*, (2010), 187–196.
23. Savery, C. and Graham, T.C.N. Timelines: Simplifying the programming of lag compensation for the next generation of networked games. *Multimedia Systems*, (2012).
24. Smed, J. and Hakonen, H. *Algorithms and networking for computer games*. Wiley, 2006.
25. Stuckel, D. and Gutwin, C. The effects of local lag on tightly-coupled interaction in distributed groupware. *CSCW'08*, (2008), 447–456.
26. Zhao, S., Li, D., Lu, T., and Gu, N. Back to the future: A hybrid approach to transparent sharing of video games over the internet in real time. *CSCW'11*, (2011), 187–196.

The Identification of Deviance and its Impact on Retention in a Multiplayer Game

Kenneth Shores
GroupLens Research
University of Minnesota,
Minneapolis, MN 55455
shores@cs.umn.edu

Yilin He
GroupLens Research
University of Minnesota,
Minneapolis, MN 55455
hexxx305@umn.edu

Kristina L. Swanenburg
Department of Psychology
University of Pittsburgh,
Pittsburgh, PA 15213
kls94@pitt.edu

Robert Kraut
Human-Computer Interaction Institute
Carnegie Mellon University,
Pittsburgh, PA 15213
robert.kraut@cs.cmu.edu

John Riedl
GroupLens Research
University of Minnesota,
Minneapolis, MN 55455
riedl@cs.umn.edu

ABSTRACT
Deviant behavior in online social systems is a difficult problem to address. Consequences of deviance include driving off users and tarnishing the system's public image. We present an examination of these concepts in a popular online game, League of Legends. Using a large collection of game records and player-given feedback, we develop a metric, *toxicity index*, to identify deviant players. We then look at the effects of interacting with deviant players, including effects on retention. We find that toxic players have several significant predictive patterns, such as playing in more competitive game modes and playing with friends. We also show that toxic players drive away new players, but that experienced players are more resilient to deviant behavior. Based on our findings, we suggest methods to better identify and counteract the negative effects of deviance.

Author Keywords
deviance; cooperation; retention; online games; norms; League of Legends;

ACM Classification Keywords
H.5.3. Collaborative Computing

INTRODUCTION
In this paper, we examine the impact of deviance on retention in the online multiplayer game League of Legends. Deviance can be defined as an aberration from normative behavior. Norms are shared ways of feeling, thinking and behaving [15]. Deviation from norms can lead to rejection of the deviant [27] and to decreases in a group's cohesion [31] and performance [11].

CSCW'14, February 15–19, 2014, Baltimore, Maryland, USA.

http://dx.doi.org/10.1145/2531602.2531724

The phenomenon of deviance has been explored in the past in both offline (see [14] for a review) and online settings. Research suggests that deviance is quite common in virtual groups [7][9]. Greater anonymity in a virtual environment has been linked to increased deviance [8][24], and at the same time may lead to an enhanced awareness of group-specific norms [17]. If group-specific norms encourage disruption, then an individual could adhere to their group's norms by deviating from community norms. Designers of online systems are motivated to decrease deviance because deviance is assumed to have a negative impact on user retention[2][20][7]. User retention is important online because virtual groups, from guilds in online games to Wikipedia editors, suffer from high turnover [10][23].

Since retention is so important online, and deviance poses a threat to that retention, system designers have attempted to decrease deviance in a variety of ways. Many forums utilize surveillance techniques to decrease deviance. Moderators review posts to their forums and may alter or delete inappropriate posts or even remove members who repeatedly violate the forum's rules. Some designers have developed more creative solutions to deal with a deviant user, including "hellbanning" the user by making all of that user's actions invisible to others [2]. As a result, the user is seemingly ignored by the entire community. Other techniques to dissuade deviance include allowing other users to rate specific artifacts created by their peers and to report violations when they occur. A popular extension of user-rated comments is to automatically hide comments receiving mostly negative votes. In many online games, including League of Legends, players can send reports about disruptive players to moderators who review the report and dole out punishments if necessary.

Another technique that is commonly used to decrease deviance is reputation systems. Reputation systems decrease the ephemeral consequences of poor online interaction by creating a reputation that follows a user or player. This is in contrast to applying ratings to individual comments, inventories or other system-specific artifacts. These reputations are based on ratings by other users. Reputation systems have proven effective online; positive reputations on Ebay have been linked to improved performance [26]. The threat of the "shadow of the future" is used by reputation systems. Ratings persist from one interaction to the next, threatening to harm future interactions [25]. These systems simultaneously punish deviant users and allow other users to avoid them.

Riot, the developer of League of Legends, has put substantial effort into studying player deviance, and has focused on a type of deviant behavior it labels as "toxic". Riot defines "toxicity" as any behavior that negatively impacts other players' experiences [30]. Toxic behavior is a subset of deviant behavior and is often considered "un-sportsmanlike". It includes a large range of behaviors, such as sending offensive messages or intentionally helping the opposing team. However, specific definitions of toxic behavior may be situational to subsections of the community.

In an effort to reduce toxic behavior, Riot has implemented a system called the Tribunal, which allows players to judge player behavioral reports of suspected toxic players [29]. Riot has also experimented with exposing players to a variety of messages while a match is loading. By varying message text and color, Riot has found that certain combinations decreased reports of deviance by up to 10% [20]. This demonstrates that subtle design decisions and interventions can be effective in influencing deviant behaviors.

Deviant behavior in League of Legends is complex and embedded in community norms. Some segments of the user population may have different expectations around use of profanity or giving commands. It is important to note that the reporting system used by Riot indicates behavior that is considered deviant - if cursing is acceptable, a player will not report their teammate for it. Because the Tribunal has players review the behavior of other players, a reported player is being flagged to be evaluated by peers according to community norms. Riot provides suggested guidelines for evaluating behavior [28], but determining acceptable behavior is ultimately situational.

Present Study

In order to address problems related to deviance, we first need to detect and identify deviant behavior. We can then explore the effects of this behavior on users. One specific concern to social system designers is user retention, and measuring the effect of deviance on retention is an important part of assessing it as a threat.

The present study examines deviance and retention in League of Legends. First, we develop a metric based on indications of deviant behavior in our dataset. We look specifically at indications of toxic behavior, as it is the most concerning type of deviance in League of Legends. We examine our metric in several situations, looking for situations where toxic behavior differs. We then perform a regression with this metric and several in-game behavior measures to look for predictors of players leaving the game. We explore the findings of this regression with regard to social and structural factors in the game, and use this to draw conclusions for the design of other games and social systems.

BACKGROUND: LEAGUE OF LEGENDS

League of Legends is a game which is played in many independant matches. In each match, two teams of five players compete on a symmetric map to destroy the opposing team's objectives while defending their own[1]. League of Legends has a large global player base, with about 12 million active players daily [21]. Teams are often made up of strangers who will never play together again. Effective communication and teamwork are important factors in winning a match, and a lack of cooperation often leads to losing a match [28]. This need for cooperation and communication with teammates makes a player's experience highly dependent on social interactions with other players.

League of Legends has several different game modes. Teams are composed of players who choose one of over one hundred characters, and characters can be classified into roles.[2]

In each match, players control a single character. With their character, they must destroy the enemy structures while defending their team's structures. During a match, players unlock abilities and purchase items which make their character and their teammate's characters stronger. Players must use reflexes, knowledge of the game, and cooperation to defeat the enemy team. An average match lasts 31 minutes, but can range from 20 to 60 minutes or more. League of Legends tracks many statistics through each match, including number of kills of enemy characters, number of deaths of each player's character, and number of assists (helping a nearby teammate score a kill). Kills reward gold, and assists reward gold in addition to the gold given for a kill, increasing the team's total reward and encouraging cooperation.

The primary game mode is called "normal" (or "unranked") mode. Normal is the most popular game mode, and in it a player's skill rating is hidden. A second game type is "ranked" mode, where players are given a public skill rating. Winning or losing a match in this mode will alter this rating, which is visible to other players and friends. This mode is often considered more competitive, and fewer players participate. It is also restricted to only allow maximum level players. The final game mode is "co-op vs. AI" - a mode where players fight computer-controlled enemies. Each game mode has different expectations and social norms around it, and many players play primarily a single mode. Co-op vs. AI mode will not be discussed further. It represents a qualitatively different game experience because there are not two teams of human players.

[1]The limited popularity of other game modes excluded them from our analyses. They are not discussed in this work.

[2]Each character in League of Legends has a distinct set of abilities, but differences at the level of individual characters do not affect this work and will not be discussed.

Matchmaking

In League of Legends, players are matched with teammates and enemies based on three factors: experience, player skill, and grouping. The matchmaking system attempts to make "fair" matches for each game, so both teams have an equal probability of winning when the match begins.

Experience: Players who have a similar amount of experience with the game are matched together. Players earn experience points for each match they play and these points advance a player's level until they reach the maximum level of 30. Players gain levels at a relatively consistent rate per match, so below level 30, player level is a reasonable proxy to "number of matches played." League of Legends has a steep learning curve, and giving players a level to indicate experience helps reduce frustration for newer players.

Player Skill: The matchmaking system also tries to match players with similar skill levels. This matchmaking system is based on Elo, a rating system initially designed for chess and commonly used in online competitive games [12]. Thus players who have won more matches, or matches against harder opponents, will be matched against more skilled opponents in the future.

Grouping: Finally, the matchmaking algorithm attempts to match groups of players who have queued (joined a match) together against other groups who have queued together [32]. While the impact of this is smaller than other factors, the matchmaking algorithm is designed with the assumption that players who queue together will play more effectively than strangers who are grouped together.

Character Roles

Characters are classified into roles based on a character's ability set - each character has four abilities, and these abilities can emphasize damage-dealing, defense or utility. Character roles can be defined as carry, defender and support. We further divide these roles based on community norms, as follows:

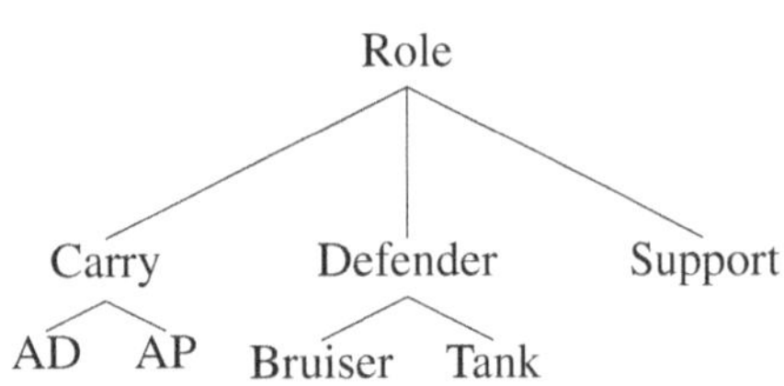

Carry is split between 'AP' and 'AD', named for their in-game damage type. Both roles deal lots of damage but have low survivability. 'Tank' and 'Bruiser' are both high-survivability roles. Tanks tend to have abilities that stun or control other characters, while bruisers are durable but also do substantial damage. The 'Support' role specializes in utility and control abilities, such as a 'stun' ability which causes an enemy to be unable to act for a few seconds. Supports often rely on cooperation with teammates playing other roles to best make use of their abilities.

Team composition in League of Legends is quite flexible. Each player's roles are chosen at the start of each match through team discussion. One group may have five carries, while another has four defenders and a support. Game knowledge and tactical decisions both contribute to group composition, and team cooperation is an important factor in winning a match.

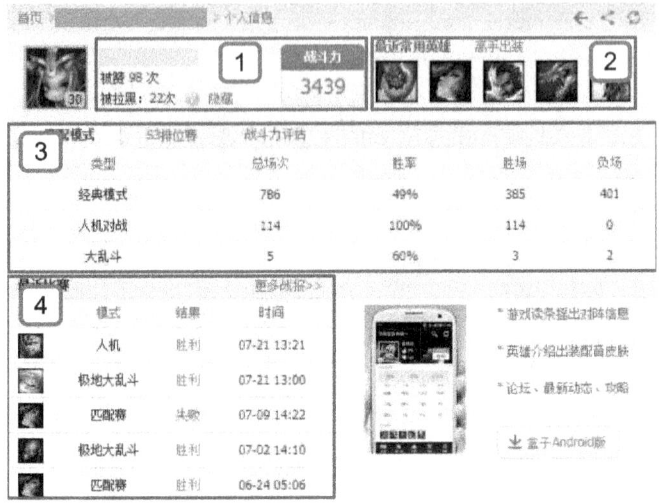

Figure 1. A screenshot of Duowan's add-on software. 1) Thumbs-up and thumbs-down scores. 2) Player's favorite characters. 3) Game modes and win statistics. 4) Recent match history.

METHODS

Dataset

Data was collected through a software add-on made by Duowan[3]. The add-on creates a reputation system for League of Legends players on a game server in China. Whenever a player using the add-on played a match, statistics for all players in that match were recorded by the add-on. The dataset contains 2.5 million players playing 18.25 million matches across three months. Players in the data set have played an average of 67.26 matches during the data collection period. The data collected by Duowan and used in this study is public data, and our analysis was performed without intervention, and without handling any private data.

In addition to game statistics, the dataset also contains feedback for each player, given by other players using the add-on. This feedback is either positive ("*Player* is a good player, have a thumbs up.") or negative ("I don't want to play a match with *Player* in the future."), and is displayed in chat for all the players at the end of the match. The message is clearly labeled as coming from the add-on, and the feedback given is stored by the add-on and displayed on a player profile on Duowan's site.

Because the data was only collected from games where at least one user is using the addon, the method of data collection risks missing some matches played. We were able to compute an estimate of the percentage of collected matches, and found that 91.6% of matches played between the first and last sighting of a player were tracked by the add-on. Because newer players are less likely to use the add-on, we suspect that

[3] `www.duowan.com`

most players missed in our dataset were very low level. This is the primary reason we do not look at the retention patterns of very new players in this work.

Toxic Behavior Detection

A survey on the Duowan's forums asked players to choose the reason that best fit why they have given players a thumbs-down [1]. Posted in July of 2012, the survey presented nine responses. However, because the survey was in Mandarin Chinese and used game-specific terminology, responses were translated and clustered by the authors into a smaller set of categories. The majority of the 138 participants (78.23%) stated that they would give a thumbs-down for various deviant behaviors, including verbal abuse (outside of socially acceptable cursing or yelling), refusing to continue to play a match and helping the enemy team win. A minority (16.98%) stated that thumbs-down was given to players who did not perform well in the match. The remaining responses indicated that some users never give thumbs-downs. The categories we consider to be deviance-related are the same as the types of reports that Riot collects regarding player behavior that indicate a violation of either community or group norms. This means that thumbs-downs are mostly given for deviant behavior. Thus we believe that thumbs-downs are a reasonable proxy for measuring deviance.

To identify players in our dataset that exhibited deviant behavior, we developed a metric using the thumbs-up and thumbs-down ratings that a player received. These counts were given on a weekly basis, so we looked at the changes in a player's scores for each week as an indication of deviant behavior. A metric was developed that combined the two scores as a way to compare between players. Called *toxicity index*, the metric was based on the ratio of thumbs-down to thumbs-up during a given week. Because players participated in a varying number of matches, we added a normalization factor (1 for thumbs-down and 4 for thumbs-ups) to the resulting ratio to reduce the likelihood of having extreme scores from a small number of matches. The constants for the normalization factor were tuned by hand, by examining the distribution of resulting toxicity indexes in our sample. We also excluded players who participated in fewer than ten matches during a given week, because a player with a small number of matches would have few thumbs-up and thumbs-downs given, which we felt gave us low confidence for making inferences about their general behavior.

The final formula for player toxicity index was defined as follows:

$$toxicity\ index = \frac{thumbs\text{-}down + 1}{thumbs\text{-}up + 4}$$

We expected that players exhibiting more deviant behavior would have a high ratio of thumbs-down to thumbs-up scores, based on the reasons for giving a thumbs-down in the survey above.

Our dataset had several factors and limitations that influenced the toxicity index. For many of our questions, we sampled players from matches during a particular week. For these players, we calculated their toxicity index in the previous week and used it as a predictor of behavior during the studied week. Because we could not determine specific matches where thumbs-ups or thumbs-downs were given, scores from the previous week were used to prevent a conflation of predictors and outcomes.

Another limitation was that a player's teammates could only give a thumbs-up to the player when they had won a match, and a thumbs-down when they lost. A concern might be "What if deviant players are just *good* at the game?". An Elo-based matchmaking system is unlikely to allow players to maintain a win-ratio that is far from .5, and to address this concern, an analysis was performed assessing player win-ratios. The analysis found an average win:loss ratio of .4961, with a standard deviation of .0633. Given that active players in our dataset have a mean of 30 and a median of 20 matches per week, this is an imbalance of only a few wins or losses for most players.

HYPOTHESES

Broadly, we have several hypotheses that can be split into two research questions:

1. *What factors predict a high toxicity index?*
2. *What factors predict quitting or continuing to play the game?*

Toxicity Index

We had several hypotheses to test with this metric. We hypothesized that the type of game modes played, a player's role in a match, attributes of a player's teammates and overall experience with the game will affect a player's toxicity index. Since competitiveness and aggression are highly correlated [6] and aggression can be considered a type of deviance, we predicted that players in more competitive game modes would act more deviantly. Ranked matches are considered more competitive because by playing them, a player's ranked Elo is prominently displayed and publicly available. Additionally, high-Elo players can earn rewards for their account.

> **Hypothesis 1.1:** Players who primarily play more competitive game modes will have a higher toxicity index than players who play primarily less competitive game modes.

To test this, we generated toxicity indexes for 139,855 ranked players and 201,145 unranked players from matches in our dataset. All players were level 30. We then compared toxicity indexes based on the game mode sampled from.

Similarly, we believed that the role a player chooses in a match is related to the player's level of deviance. The high-damage "carry" role can be viewed as the most competitive role because both "AD" and "AP" characters focus on doing lots of damage to enemy players. The primary goal of all roles is competition with the opposing team, but carries often compete within their own team to be the best damage-dealer. Scoring a high number of kills or dealing a lot of damage is a clear indicator of a successful carry, and a predictor of winning. Support roles can be viewed as the least competitive in this regard. A successful support contributes to winning by assisting and protecting their teammates, and by adapting to team needs. The focus of supports is to cooperate with their teammates and help them take objectives, and there is little competition within teams to be the "best cooperator". Defenders (including both Tank and Bruiser roles) must split focus between damage-dealing and protecting other members of their team, and thus we predict an intermediate level of competitiveness.

> **Hypothesis 1.2:** Playing characters with mostly damage-dealing abilities will predict the highest toxicity index, and playing characters with cooperative or supportive abilities will predict the lowest toxicity index.

This analysis was applied to the same samples of players selected for Hypothesis 1.1. For each sampled game, the player's toxicity index was added to the appropriate measure based on the role of their selected character, split by game mode. From this, the mean toxicity index was calculated for each role.

Playing with friends should also impact the player's perceived deviance. Deviant behavior is more likely to be reinforced when playing with a friend than with strangers, in turn increasing its frequency. Additionally, friends are likely to imitate each other's deviant behavior through social learning, which would also increase the frequency of deviance [3].

> **Hypothesis 1.3:** Playing with friends will increase the number of thumbs-downs given by non-friends.

We classified players as *friends* whenever they played two or more matches together, on the same team, in the week we measured their toxicity index. Because of the size of the game's player pool, the likelihood of two strangers being incorrectly classified as friends in this system is extremely low. A player's friends could give them a thumbs-up after winning a match, and arguably would do so for different reasons than a stranger, so we were not able to use our toxicity index here. Instead, we looked at the raw number of thumbs-up and thumbs-down votes per match played in a given week, and categorized players by the number of friends they played with in that week. We assumed that friends would not give thumbs-downs to each other, and divided the number of thumbs-downs received by the number of strangers played with during the week. Frequency of thumbs-ups received was calculated to include friends. 10,000 players were sampled for this analysis.

We also expected that a player's long-term experience with the game would impact the player's rate of deviance. Players who have played longer will have been socialized to the community norms [19]. In League of Legends, a player might assume that some behavior is normative because deviant behavior is more memorable than non-deviant behavior [4]. A player may exhibit this behavior in a later group where the behavior is considered deviant. Therefore, variations in group norms and conflict between group and community norms may lead to behavior being regarded as deviant. There are other reasons to suspect that experienced players may act in deviant ways. As players become more comfortable with the game, they may become more easily frustrated by players who do not know effective playing strategies, or with players who use strategies that disagree with their expectations. This increased frustration could lead to more deviant behavior [5]. We expect toxicity index to be a proxy to deviant behavior, therefore:

> **Hypothesis 1.4** Players who have been playing longer will have a higher toxicity index.

Retention

We were also interested in the relationship between deviance and player retention. We considered two types of retention: short-term and long-term. Being retained in the short-term means continuing to play the current game session. Players can play matches successively for as long as they wish, and a continuous block of matches is considered a session. Long-term retention refers to either permanently quitting the game, or leaving for an extended period. To better quantify these cutoffs, we performed an analysis of time between the end of one match and the beginning of the next. Referring to work by Geiger & Halfaker [13] we plotted time between matches on the bucketed log-scaled plot in Figure 2. For short-term retention we chose a threshold of one hour: any time a player has at least one hour between the end of a match and the beginning of the next, we assume they had ended their session. This cut-off was chosen for several reasons. It is the same session duration used by Geiger and Halfaker in their Wikipedia session analysis, and anecdotally, we as players feel it is a reasonable and safely-inclusive cutoff; Someone might spend fourty-five minutes waiting for friends to finish a concurrant match, but taking more than an hour between matches indicates the player is doing something else. For long term retention we chose a threshold of one week. Any time a player plays no matches for at least one week, we assume they have either left the game permanently or are taking an extended break.

> **Hypothesis 2.1:** Playing with teammates with a high toxicity index will decrease retention.

Though we consider several factors related to retention in our regressions, we predict that playing with players who frequently exhibit deviant behavior will have a negative impact on player retention. As mentioned earlier, deviance is assumed to have a negative impact on retention, and this is a central question for our work. We expect this prediction to apply to both short and long-term retention.

To discover factors that impacted retention, 341,295 players were sampled from our dataset. The toxicity index was calculated for the selected players, as well as for every player they encountered during a chosen week. For each match played, we labeled players for whether it was their last match for both short- and long-term retention; did the player quit the session or did they leave the game for an extended period after that match? A binomial logistic regression was performed for each type of retention on each player-match combination. In addition to in-game performance statistics such as "number of kills" and "did the player win the match?", the player's toxicity index and the average toxicity index of their teammates (excluding themselves) were included in the regression. We

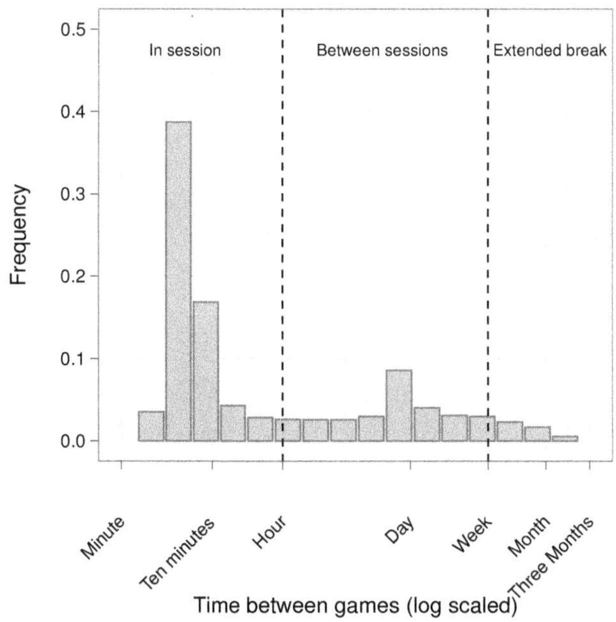

Figure 2. Distribution of time spent between matches.

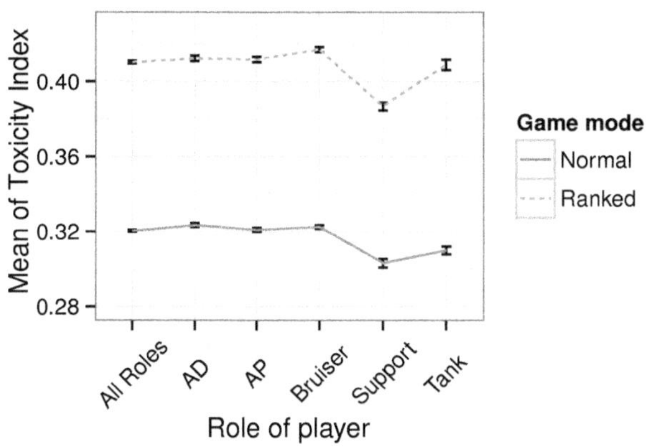

Figure 3. Toxicity index and player role. AP and AD are versions of the "carry" role. Tanks and Bruisers are types "defenders".

also partitioned our regressions by player level. Since level is a proxy to number of matches played, we consider players who are not maximum level to be at a different stage of learning the game and learning community norms. This is supported by several game design decisions, including increased character customization options for high-level players and by limiting ranked mode to only be played by maximum level players.

RESULTS AND DISCUSSION

RQ1: *What factors predict a high toxicity index?*

Hypothesis 1.1:

Players who primarily play more competitive game modes will have a higher toxicity index than players who play primarily less competitive game modes

Players were sampled and divided into into ranked (n=139,855) and unranked (n=201,145) categories. All players were level 30. A plot of the mean toxicity index of the players with standard error bars is shown in Figure 3. Ranked players had an mean toxicity index of 0.41 with a standard deviation of 0.27. Unranked players had an mean toxicity index of 0.32 with a standard deviation of 0.25. These groups are statistically significantly different (t-test $p < 0.001$).

Discussion

As predicted, players in the more competitive ranked matches were associated with higher toxicity indexes than players in normal matches. Thus, even though a more competitive attitude is the norm for players playing the ranked game mode, players were exhibiting more deviant behavior than players in normal mode matches.

Hypothesis 1.2:

Playing characters with mostly damage-dealing abilities will predict the highest toxicity index, and playing characters with cooperative or supportive abilities will predict the lowest toxicity index.

We classified 341,295 level 30 players according to role and game mode. Figure 3 plots the mean and standard error of toxicity index of different roles on the X axis. Both carry roles in Figure 3 were found to have a relatively high toxicity index. Bruisers (one type of defender) also had a high toxicity index for unranked, and the highest mean toxicity index for ranked. This disagreed with our hypothesis that both bruisers and tanks would have lower toxicity than the carry roles. For both ranked and unranked, supports had a low toxicity index. Tanks also had a lower toxicity index, relative to AP, AD and bruisers.

We performed an ANOVA for both the ranked and unranked samples and found significant differences between them: *Ranked* ($F(4, 139850) = 39.31, p < .001$)) *Unranked* ($F(4, 201160) = 23.83, p < .001$)). A Tukey's HSD test was performed between roles for each mode. For ranked, support was statistically significantly different than all other roles ($p < .05$). No other roles had significant differences in ranked mode. For unranked, support was significantly different from AP, AD and bruisers ($p < .05$). The tank role was also significantly different from AP, AD and bruiser ($p < .05$). Tanks and supports were not significantly different from one another in unranked play.

Discussion

Roles were found to vary in average toxicity index. Hypothesis 1.2 predicted that the roles with the most damage-dealing abilities would have the highest toxicity index. The least competitive role, support, was associated with lower toxicity levels than other roles in both ranked and unranked matches. Tanks were found to have significantly lower toxicity indexes than both carry roles in unranked matches, but were not significantly different in ranked matches. Bruiser mean toxicity index was not significantly different from the more damage-dealing roles in either game mode, and in ranked matches bruiser had the highest toxicity index of all roles. Differences between bruisers and tanks went against our classification, which expected them to be similar. We suspect that this difference stems from the way they are designed. The roles have different specializations: Bruisers often have abilities oriented towards dealing damage, while tanks generally have abilities that are best used to protect teammates or survive incoming damage. While the grouping of bruisers and tanks led to an incorrect prediction about bruisers, the idea that a character's ability set relates to the player's toxicity index is still reasonable. Importantly, these findings do not support or discourage a causal relationship, where players who would exhibit behavior leading to thumbs-downs are attracted to the more damage-oriented characters and roles.

Hypothesis 1.3:

Playing with friends will increase the number of thumbs-downs given by non-friends.

Players were bucketed according to the average number of friends they played with across all matches for a given week. We expected bias in the number of thumbs-ups for players who frequently played with friends, because we expect friends to be inclined to give each other thumbs-ups. Thus, the rate of thumbs-up is the number of thumbs-ups received, divided by the total number of players encounterd in the sampled time period. The thumbs-down rate is the number of thumbs-downs received divided by the total number of non-friends played with. A large number of players did not play with any friends during the sampled week - these players were put in bucket 0. Otherwise, players were bucketed by the ceiling of the mean number of friends played with across matches.

Figure 4 shows the mean and standard error plots for the rate of thumbs-ups and thumbs-downs by number of friends. We performed an ANOVA and found significant differences ($F(1, 9998) = 33.36, p < .001$), and a Tukey's HSD test was performed to assess differences between buckets. For thumbs-down, playing with 0 friends was significantly different from playing with either 1 or 2 friends ($p < .05$ for both). For thumbs-up, playing with 0 friends was significantly different from all other buckets, and playing with 1 friend was significantly different from playing with 2 or 3 friends ($p < .05$ for all).

Discussion

Our analysis shows that playing with friends increases the number of thumbs-downs a player recieves, especially for players who on average play with 1 or 2 friends. A corollary to this is that playing with friends is associated with higher levels of deviance. Players may become socialized to display deviant behaviors through positive reinforcement from friends. A player may experience a conflict between community norms and the norms of their group of friends - behavior that deviates from community norms may be encouraged by friends.

Hypothesis 1.4:

Players who have been playing longer will have a higher toxicity index.

We also examined toxicity indexes based on the total number of matches played. We computed the mean toxicity index for

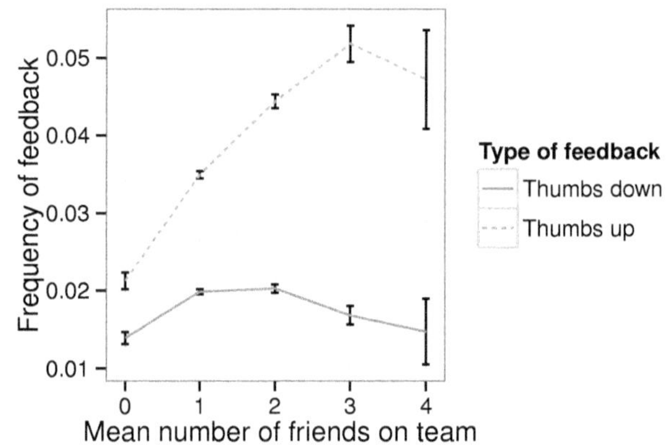

Figure 4. Average number of friends on a team vs frequency of feedback signals. Frequency is the rate of given thumbs-up or thumbs-down per encountered teammate.

players, bucketed by total number of games played. However, we found counfounds for addressing this hypothesis with our data. Further analysis indicates that a lack of data about low level players causes our normalization ratio to bias the mean toxicity index. Because total thumbs-up and thumbs-down measures will increase over time, mean toxicity index will tend to move from a mean dictated by our base toxicity index ratio to a mean that represents the community at max level. This reaffirms the notion that the dataset's collection methods discourage analysis involving low-level players. In other explorations we control for this by selecting currently active players, rather than assessing measures of whole user histories.

Discussion

While our dataset is not sufficient to explore this question, we believe that the factors suggeting the hypothesis are still reasonable. There are several potential game-situations where confidence in game-understanding may encourage deviant behavior.

One common situation is when a player believes their team can no longer win the match, leading them to quit by exiting the game. This leaves their four teammates at a severe disadvantage. While their teammates may or may not agree with this prediction, community norms dictate they should play it out or end the game by team-vote. This is a scenario where a player's experience influences their confidence about a situation, and is used as a justification for their deviant behavior. We would encourage future work to explore this concept.

Retention

Hypothesis 2.1:

Playing with teammates with a high toxicity index will decrease retention.

A binomial logistic regression was performed to look at factors that predict short-term and long-term retention. This regression was split into four categories in two dimensions: short-term vs long-term, and level<30 vs level=30.

	Short Term Retention						Long Term Retention					
	Level < 30			Level = 30			Level < 30			Level = 30		
	β	SE	P	β	SE	P	β	SE	P	β	SE	P
(Intercept)	.873	.010	< .001	.960	.006	< .001	5.502	.081	< .001	6.900	.088	< .001
Match Length	-.231	.010	< .001	-.194	.006	< .001	-.150	.059	.011	-.074	.071	.298
Win Current Match?	.082	.010	< .001	-.016	.006	.004	.113	.062	.067	.005	.073	.944
Average Teammate Toxicity Index	.011	.042	0.790	.032	.010	< .001	-.351	.178	.049	-.206	.112	.066
Player Toxicity Index	.028	.046	0.545	.086	.016	< .001	.640	.269	.017	.370	.261	.156
Player Level	.078	.025	.002				.394	.127	.002			
Friends in Match	.117	.010	< .001	.120	.006	< .001	.069	.069	.003	.398	.101	< .001
Player Level : Teammate Toxicity Index	-.005	.050	0.923				.618	.258	.016			
Player Level : Players Toxicity Index	.032	.048	0.498				-.276	.320	.388			
Player Toxicity Index : Teammate Toxicity Index	-.009	.028	0.738	-0.039	.018	.029	-.189	.217	.385	.263	.296	.374

Table 1. Four logistic regressions corresponding to short term retention and long term retention. Positive β indicates a prediction of increased likelihood of retention. Inputs are scaled. Variables omitted from certain regressions are left blank.

Short Term, Level < 30

Match length was a significant negative predictor of short term retention ($\beta = -0.231, p < .001$) meaning that longer matches predicted a reduced likelihood of continuing the session. Winning the current match was a significant positive predictor of continuing the session ($\beta = .082, p < .001$). Level was a significant predictor as well - higher level players were more likely to continue a session ($\beta = 0.078, p < .002$). Number of friends in the current match was the final significant predictor ($\beta = 0.117, p < .001$). Playing with friends increased the likelihood of continuing a session. The toxicity index of the player or the player's teammates was not a significant predictor of short-term retention behavior for players below level 30.

Short Term, Level = 30

Match length was also a significant predictor of discontinuing the session for level 30 players ($\beta = -0.194, p < .001$). Unlike players under level 30, winning the match predicted a decreased likelihood of continuing the session ($\beta = -0.016, p < .004$). A high average toxicity index of teammates was a strong predictor of continuing the session ($\beta = .032, p < .001$). Players with higher toxicity indexes were also more likely to continue a session ($\beta = .086, p < .001$). Similar to players under level 30, playing with friends was a strong predictor of continuing a session ($\beta = 0.120, p < .001$). The positive prediction of player-toxicity index and teammate-toxicity index is moderated when both factors are high ($\beta = -0.039, p < .029$), showing that an all-around high toxicity index tends to predict that a player will end their session.

Long Term, Level < 30

Match length was a significant predictor of players below level 30 taking an extended break from (or quitting) the game ($\beta = -.150, p < .011$). A high toxicity index of teammates was also a stronger predictor for driving these players to quit ($\beta = -.351, p < .049$). However, a player with a higher toxicity index was more likely to continue playing ($\beta = .640, p < .017$), and players with a higher level (who had played more matches over-all) were also less likely to leave ($\beta = .394, p < .002$). Playing with friends had a smaller impact, but increased long-term retention ($\beta = .069, p < .003$). A player's level and their teammate's toxicity had an interaction effect which suggests that higher level players were more resilient to toxic teammates ($\beta = .618, p < .016$).

Long Term, Level = 30

Number of friends was the only significant predictor of long-term retention at level 30. ($\beta = 0.397, p < .001$). Playing with friends increases the likelihood of continuing to play over long periods, and playing with more friends increases it further. Surprisingly, toxicity index had no significant impact on retention once a player reached level 30.

Discussion

Hypothesis 2.1 predicted that playing with teammates with a high toxicity index will decrease both short term and long term retention. We found that toxicity index had a variety of effects on retention.

For players who had reached level 30, a higher average toxicity index of their teammates increased the likelihood of continuing their session. And a player with a higher toxicity also has an increased likelihood of continuing their session. However, when both a player's toxicity index and their teammate's average index is high, players tend to end their session. There are several possible interpretations for this finding, and it warrants further study. We suspect that deviant players may enjoy deviant behavior, or at least are not deterred by any immediate consequences, but that a clash between a high toxicity index player and teammates with a high toxicity index may be frustrating enough to motivate taking a break.

For long term retention, the story is a bit different. Players who are below level 30 and have a high toxicity index are more likely to continue to play League of Legends. Also, playing with higher-than-average toxicity index teammates predicts long-term departure: frustrating teammates can drive off players who are learning the game. However, at level 30 players are more resistant to teammates with a high toxicity index, and are not driven away from the game for long periods by them.

Why are players below level 30 likely to be driven off when players at max level are not? One possibility is a selection effect against players with low tolerance for toxic behavior. In this situation, players must either develop tolerance for toxic behavior or be driven off. While the regression indicates that players with low toxicity indexes are more vulnerable to being driven off (supporting the notion of a selection effect), it is unclear that toxicity is learned by the surviving players. Future work could explore this dynamic.

Beyond toxicity index, the regression considers several other factors which show predictive power. Playing with friends is a consistent predictor of continuing to play the game, in both the short-term and the long-term for players at all levels of experience. Even though playing with friends also corresponds to a higher toxicity index, having friends to play with has a clear impact on retaining players. Furthermore, for players at maximum level, playing with friends was the only significant predictor of long-term retention - having friends to play with is more likely to keep an experienced player from leaving the game.

Another factor effecting both short-term and long-term retention was match length. Not surprisingly, longer matches led players to end their sessions. But longer matches were also associated with a greater chance of players under level 30 quitting the game for good. Less experienced players may have qualitatively different game experiences as they are not just playing but also learning basics of gameplay and norms around gameplay, and designers should consider this when they design to acclimate new users. In League of Legends, leaving in the middle of a match is discouraged both by community norms and by in-game warning messages, and players who are unexpectedly kept in a long match may be upset if staying causes (for example) schedule conflicts outside of the game.

CONCLUSIONS AND DESIGN IMPLICATIONS

In this paper we examined the nature and effects of a concerning type of deviant "toxic" behavior in League of Legends, a multiplayer online game. We developed a metric called the *toxicity index* for measuring this type of deviant behavior based on peer evaluations of other players, and we use it to examine several predictors of toxic behavior. We also used this metric to explore the commonly held assumption that players who exhibit this deviant behavior reduce the retention rates of other players in the community.

Our findings support the notion that interactions with toxic players decrease the retention rates of new players. Many games have similar social design elements to League of Legends. Competitive first-person shooters often highlight team-based gameplay [16], and player-versus-player options in MMORPGs are frequently team-based [22]. As such, our findings regarding player retention have many implications for designers of other systems.

Designers should take an active role in teaching and encouraging positive community norms, especially when interacting with newer players. For example, designers can propose a set of community norms in order to actively discourage common behaviors that make the game less enjoyable for others. The League of Legends "Summoner's Code" [28] is on implementation of this approach.

Our study examined the effects of a signal for deviant behavior in an online game which encourages both competitive and cooperative behavior. Our findings suggest that emphasizing the cooperative aspects of the system instead of the competitive aspects may be one technique for decreasing deviant behavior. However, some users may be attracted to the system because of its competitive aspects. It is important that interventions are designed to address deviant behavior directly, rather than by simply decreasing competitiveness. This is a problematic balance for designers because actions that are perceived to be deviant by users can influence their retention.

We also saw a consistent link between playing with friends and retention. Playing with friends was the most significant predictor of improved long term retention for players who had reached the maximum level in game. Designers should take note of referral programs like League of Legend's refer-a-friend system, and should incentivise and facilitate in-game activities with friends. This is consistent with findings of social motivation in other domains, such as the finding that relationships in blogging networks predicted better retention rates when those relationships were actively maintained [18]. Though League of Legends has a "friends list", our classification of friendships only consisted of users who played games with one another. Future work should investigate more closely the effects of different kinds of relationships on retention in a competitive space.

Limitations

In this work, variables were not experimentally manipulated and thus causal inferences are limited. Future studies should attempt to experimentally manipulate the factors found to be significantly related to deviance and retention in order to clarify causative directions.

ACKNOWLEDGMENTS

The authors would like to thank Duowan for generously providing us with data.

Additionally, we would thank Riot for making a game that is fascinating to study and fun to play.

Finally, John Riedl passed away between the writing and the publication of this paper. We would like to dedicate this work in his memory. An avid player, insightful mentor and beloved friend, he helped make this work possible.

REFERENCES

1. In what kind of situation would you thumbs-down your teammate? http://bbs.duowan.com/thread-27997215-1-1.html.
2. Atwood, J. Suspension, ban or hellban? http://www.codinghorror.com/blog/2011/06/suspension-ban-or-hellban.html.
3. Bandura, A., and McClelland, D. C. *Social learning theory*. General Learning Press, New York, 1977.
4. Baumeister, R. F., Bratslavsky, E., Finkenauer, C., and Vohs, K. D. Bad is stronger than good. *Review of general psychology 5*, 4 (2001), 323.
5. Berkowitz, L. Frustration-aggression hypothesis: Examination and reformulation. *Psychological bulletin 106*, 1 (1989), 5973.
6. Buss, A. H., and Perry, M. The aggression questionnaire. *Journal of personality and social psychology 63*, 3 (1992), 452459.

7. Davis, J. P. The experience of bad behavior in online social spaces: A survey of online users. *Social Computing Group, Microsoft Research* (2002).

8. Douglas, K. M., and McGarty, C. Identifiability and self-presentation: Computer-mediated communication and intergroup interaction. *British journal of social psychology 40*, 3 (2001), 399416.

9. Dubrovsky, V. J., Kiesler, S., and Sethna, B. N. The equalization phenomenon: Status effects in computer-mediated and face-to-face decision-making groups. *Human-Computer Interaction 6*, 2 (1991), 119146.

10. Ducheneaut, N., Yee, N., Nickell, E., and Moore, R. J. The life and death of online gaming communities: a look at guilds in world of warcraft. In *Proceedings of the SIGCHI conference on Human factors in computing systems* (2007), 839848.

11. Dunlop, P. D., and Lee, K. Workplace deviance, organizational citizenship behavior, and business unit performance: The bad apples do spoil the whole barrel. *Journal of Organizational Behavior 25*, 1 (2004), 6780.

12. Elo, A. E. *The rating of chessplayers, past and present*, vol. 3. Batsford London, 1978.

13. Geiger, R. S., and Halfaker, A. Using edit sessions to measure participation in wikipedia. In *Proceedings of the 2013 conference on Computer supported cooperative work* (2013), 861870.

14. Hogg, M. A., Fielding, K. S., and Darley, J. Fringe dwellers: Processes of deviance and marginalization in groups. *The social psychology of inclusion and exclusion* (2005), 191210.

15. Hogg, M. A., and Reid, S. A. Social identity, self-categorization, and the communication of group norms. *Communication Theory 16*, 1 (2006), 730.

16. Jansz, J., and Tanis, M. Appeal of playing online first person shooter games. *CyberPsychology & Behavior 10*, 1 (2007), 133–6.

17. Lea, M., and Spears, R. Computer-mediated communication, de-individuation and group decision-making. *International Journal of Man-Machine Studies 34*, 2 (1991), 283301.

18. Lento, T., Welser, H. T., Gu, L., and Smith, M. The ties that blog: Examining the relationship between social ties and continued participation in the wallop weblogging system. In *3rd Annual Workshop on the Weblogging Ecosystem* (2006), 12.

19. Levine, J. M., and Moreland, R. L. Group socialization: Theory and research. *European review of social psychology 5*, 1 (1994), 305336.

20. Lin, J. The science behind shaping behavior in online games. http://gdcvault.com/play/1017940/The-Science-Behind-Shaping-Player.

21. MacManus, C. League of legends the world's 'most played video game'. http://news.cnet.com/8301-17938_105-57531578-1/league-of-legends-the-worlds-most-played-video-game/.

22. Nardi, B., and Harris, J. Strangers and friends: collaborative play in world of warcraft. In *Proceedings of the 2006 20th anniversary conference on Computer supported cooperative work*, CSCW '06, ACM (New York, NY, USA, 2006), 149–158.

23. Panciera, K., Halfaker, A., and Terveen, L. Wikipedians are born, not made: a study of power editors on wikipedia. In *Proceedings of the ACM 2009 international conference on Supporting group work* (2009), 5160.

24. Resnick, P. The social cost of cheap pseudonyms. *Journal of Economics & Management Strategy 10*, 2 (2001), 173199.

25. Resnick, P., Kuwabara, K., Zeckhauser, R., and Friedman, E. Reputation systems. *Communications of the ACM 43*, 12 (2000), 4548.

26. Resnick, P., and Zeckhauser, R. Trust among strangers in internet transactions: Empirical analysis of eBay's reputation system. *Advances in applied microeconomics 11* (2002), 127157.

27. Richard, F. D., Bond, C. F., and Stokes-Zoota, J. J. One hundred years of social psychology quantitatively described. *Review of General Psychology 7*, 4 (2003), 331363.

28. Riot Games. The summoner's code. http://na.leagueoflegends.com/articles/The_Summoners_Code .

29. Riot Games. The tribunal. http://na.leagueoflegends.com/tribunal/en/faq/.

30. Skleres, G., K. T. C., and Pavlas, D., L. J. Improving player behavior in league of legends. http://east.paxsite.com/schedule/panel/improving-player-behavior-in-league-of-legends.

31. Wellen, J. M., and Neale, M. Deviance, self-typicality, and group cohesion the corrosive effects of the bad apples on the barrel. *Small Group Research 37*, 2 (2006), 165186.

32. Zileas. LOL matchmaking explained. http://na.leagueoflegends.com/board/showthread.php?p=122813 .

Quick and Dirty: Streamlined 3D Scanning in Archaeology

Jarrod Knibbe[1], Kenton P. O'Hara[1,3], Angeliki Chrysanthi[2], Mark T. Marshall[1], Peter D. Bennett[1], Graeme Earl[2], Shahram Izadi[3], Mike Fraser[1]

[1]Interaction & Graphics Group, Department of Computer Science, University of Bristol, UK
{ jarrod.knibbe, mark.marshall, peter.bennett, mike.fraser}@bristol.ac.uk

[2]Archaeological Computing Research Group, University of Southampton, UK
{ac14g09, graeme.earl}@soton.ac.uk

[3]Microsoft Research, Cambridge, UK
{v-keohar, shahrami}@microsoft.com

ABSTRACT
Capturing data is a key part of archaeological practice, whether for preserving records or to aid interpretation. But the technologies used are complex and expensive, resulting in time-consuming processes associated with their use. These processes force a separation between ongoing interpretive work and capture. Through two field studies we elicit more detail as to what is important about this interpretive work and what might be gained through a closer integration of capture technology with these practices. Drawing on these insights, we go on to present a novel, portable, wireless 3D modeling system that emphasizes 'quick and dirty' capture. We discuss its design rational in relation to our field observations and evaluate this rationale further by giving the system to archaeological experts to explore in a variety of settings. While our device compromises on the resolution of traditional 3D scanners, its support of interpretation through emphasis on real-time capture, review and manipulability suggests it could be a valuable tool for the future of archaeology.

Author Keywords
Archaeology; Interpretation; 3D scanning

ACM Classification Keywords
H.5.m. Information interfaces and presentation (e.g., HCI): Miscellaneous.

INTRODUCTION
Data capture has long been an integral part of archeological practice. Along with other disciplines, archaeology has embraced new technologies on site digs that enable an ever richer set of data to be assembled for the documentation and interpretation of archaeological discovery. A traditional separation exists in archaeology between the practices of excavation in themselves and the post excavation construction of narrative for dissemination [1]. For those working within the constructs of this division, data gathering and capture has been conceived as something that is simply done prior to stages of post-excavation interpretation [21]. That is, the act of archaeological interpretation is seen as something that is separable from processes occurring on site. This in turn has led to particular ways in which capture technologies are viewed both in their design and in their manifestations in the context of practice.

More recently, however, the separation of excavation and interpretation has come under scrutiny from the academic community and it is becoming more widely accepted that interpretation is 'insidiously ubiquitous' [17]. Within this perspective, the very act of excavation is to transform physical deposits into interpreted archaeological features [7]. This has created a drive towards 'reflexive archaeology' with the intention of recombining excavation and interpretation [6]. A primary feature of the organization of archaeology is that it is a physically irreversible process; that once a process is decided upon, based on interpretation, other lines of enquiry cannot be pursued. Those in favor of reflexivity argue that destroying the relationship between artefacts and their setting means that the moment of excavation is always the best opportunity to explore alternative interpretations [6]. In the context of these arguments, the traditional methods of trying to capture data "objectively" for later interpretation inherently constrain future generations, since they can neither participate in ongoing interpretive practices on-site nor support the subsequent reconstruction of the thinking behind an excavation in order to reconsider processes or conclusions [1].

In considering the support of on-site interpretation, our attentions are shifted to a variety of different factors. Archaeological expertise plays a significant role; for example in differentiating between different types of soil, recognizing plant matter and determining the age of pottery. In his seminal work on archaeological practice, Goodwin [11] argues that *professional vision* – the articulation of skillful seeing that demonstrates and reifies expertise – plays a key role in the production of archaeological interpretation, crucially even in situations where knowledge is objectively codified in processes or artefacts. Physical tacit knowledge also plays a large role and helps inform

CSCW'14, February 15 - 19 2014, Baltimore, MD, USA
Copyright 2014 ACM 978-1-4503-2540-0/14/02 $15.00.
http://dx.doi.org/10.1145/2531602.2531669

interpretation such as feeling changes in the texture of the floor, the cold touch of metal or the sharp edge of a cutting stone [6]. The sharing of this interpretation with other members of the excavation team through talk and body draws on a wider range of previous experience and background knowledge, helping the shared development of interpretation [10]. As a result, there is an increasing focus on collaborative process as well as resulting product, on 'documenting the documenting' [6], so that the patina of the interpretation can be retraced and the unfolding tacit site knowledge is not lost.

The interpretive work being performed and the practices surrounding this work are intimately bound up with the broad range of capture technologies available to the archeologists [14]. These include the more traditional paper-based artefacts such as finds recording forms, and excavator diaries as well a variety of digital capture technologies. For example, digital cameras are now an important method of capture within archaeology providing good two-dimensional records of finds and their surroundings, as well as depicting things such as soil color changes [32]. Likewise, video recording is used on some sites as a means of documenting key features of the excavation either through ad hoc recording or performed by a dedicated site videographer [5]. Increasingly too, more sophisticated 3D scanning and capture technologies are being adopted on archeological dig sites. These methods include geophysics [9], photogrammetry [32], spectrophotometry [31] and laser scanning [25] that all produce highly detailed 3D representations of on-site scenes and artefacts.

What is important about these capture technologies is that they have come to be appropriated in particular ways in the context of archeological practice that subsequently shape and constrain their relationship with the different locales of interpretation on- and off-site. The concerns go beyond what the different representational outputs of these capture technologies enable the archeologists to record, see and analyse. Rather there are a broad set of factors and practical considerations arising in the preparation work and production work involved in different forms of capture that come to bear on the relationship these technologies have to the locales of archeological interpretation. Indeed, even those capture technologies that on the face of it might be regarded as lightweight can often have heavyweight methodologies associated with their use on site. Consider for example the onsite use of digital cameras for capture. In producing the "right" kind of image there are a variety of issues with lighting, resolution and so on that affect how things such as color will be manifest in the captured image. This in turn will affect the extent to which an image may or not be amenable to particular forms of expert inspection and differentiations from surrounding materials. As such there is a significant amount of time consuming work done to "set-up" the captured scene to best highlight the observed and agreed phenomenon [11]. The time spent cleaning, lighting, shading, and measuring prior to this photographic capture then serves to situate such capture in the context of particular forms of post dig interpretive work that is separate from the ongoing interpretive work at the point of excavation.

Similar arguments are at play with the use of more intensive capture equipment, in particular, the various 3D scanning technologies adopted on dig sites. Such equipment is typically very expensive, of the order of tens of thousands of pounds which places financial restrictions on their use and availability on site. Their complexity also requires considerable training and skill to operate, requiring the presence of specialist individuals on site, which again leads to certain restrictions on when and how they can be deployed during excavation. Such techniques, even when they have an automated processing pipeline (e.g. [1]) typically take a significant amount of time to process and produce the actual 3D reconstructions [30, 3], which often occurs after the dig. As such they are not necessarily available for instantaneous feedback on site, making it difficult to integrate results with the on-site interpretation work. The equipment is also cumbersome and time consuming to set up which imposes limitations on the ease with which it can be moved around the site. Finally, the use of such techniques requires significant preparation of the site of scanning. Significantly, in the context of our concerns with on-site interpretation, the scanning area needs to be cleared of the people involved in the excavation so to avoid interference with signals and technologies. So while these techniques serve to produce high quality representations, the factors surrounding their production situate their use in the locale of post-dig interpretation work and inhibit opportunities to juxtapose the scans with on-site archaeological interpretation.

What we see then, as Hodder argues [14], is that despite the value of these capture technologies, the pragmatics of their use still renders them at odds with the broader changes within the discipline that are seeking to erode the division between excavation, analysis and interpretation. As Dellepiane et al argue [8], an erosion of these divisions requires a greater exploration of lightweight technologies combined with lightweight processes for capture. These arguments are not intended to be dismissive of the current capture approaches and their value but rather serve to highlight these unfulfilled niches of interpretation work which appropriately designed capture technologies could facilitate. With these arguments in mind, Dellepiane et al set out a set of key principles that capture technologies would need to adhere to in order to fulfill niches of on-site interpretation: repeatability, comparability, low-cost (in terms of money, time and skill), workflow compatibility and presentability. Based on these principles, they go on to explore a lightweight approach to 3D capture using digital cameras. While their approach addresses a number of the factors that contribute to heavyweight capture processes, they were unable to avoid the multiple hours of post-processing before the material becomes available. As such there remained key aspects of use that preserved some of the separation between excavation and capture.

The arguments and intentions of Hodder [14] and Dellepiane et al [8] provide an important launch point for the work we present in this paper. Here our concerns are with the exploration and development of a lightweight 3D scanning technology and process for archeological settings that can be situated within the locale of on-site collaborative interpretation work. Such explorations of the "lightweight" remain non-trivial in the sense that all sorts of potential trade-offs in the design space are at play that will come to bear on how such a technology can be situated in on-site interpretive practice. For example issues such as cost, portability, speed of processing, what can be captured and the quality of what is captured are all factors that can potentially be manipulated and traded off against each other in different ways; where one factor is emphasized, another may be compromised.

While there may be no singular right answer here regarding the quiddity of "lightweight-ness" of 3D scanning, what is important is that the design decisions and trade-offs embodying this essence are understood and made in the context of on-site interpretive practice. To this end, then, we begin our explorations with a more detailed inquiry in the form of two field studies carried out at two different archeological dig sites. The aim of these studies is to elicit key features of on-site interpretative practices and how they come to be collaboratively organized in particular ways. In particular, we concern ourselves with some of the temporal and spatial features of these practices and the factors that impact on the pace and scope of activities. Furthermore, our aim is to elicit more detail as to what is important about this interpretive work, what is being lost with existing capture practices and what might be gained through a closer integration of capture technology with these practices.

Drawing on the insights derived from the fieldwork, we go on to present a novel portable, battery-powered and wireless 3D modeling system and discuss its design rationale in relation to these insights. In particular, how by changing parameters such as the temporal and spatial possibilities for capture, the system might enable capture to be situated in new ways in the context of collaborative interpretation. We evaluate this rationale further by giving the system to archaeological experts to explore and critique, with a view to informing directions for future development. Our approach to this work fits within the long CSCW tradition of using ethnography to inform systems design, but we are also mindful of the longer term potential of 3D capture as a technology to enhance collaboration across a range of domains beyond archaeology.

OBSERVATIONS FROM THE EXCAVATION SITES

In order to further understand on site archaeological practices, the work of interpretation and relationship to potential opportunities for capture, we carried out a series of field studies at two archeological dig sites: Clatford in the UK and Çatalhöyük in Turkey.

Clatford

Clatford is a Neolithic site in Wiltshire UK, near to the Stonehenge World Heritage Site. 2 years previously, geophysical data had shown evidence of another 'sarsen stone' henge monument, including further stones that may have been destined for the incomplete outer ring at Stonehenge. The site had also been identified as the possible location of a prehistoric river crossing and is situated within close proximity of a number of important burial sites. Around 15 archaeologists were participating in the excavation, including site supervisors, experienced excavators, geophysical and location mapping specialists and a number of archaeology students. As well as observing on-going work practices of the excavation, we conducted informal interviews with the various participants throughout the dig to provide additional context and explanations for particular organizational features of the work.

Temporal pressures on the organization of work

An overriding feature of the excavation at Clatford was the adverse weather conditions. Given that the archeological team will be on site for a bounded period of time (2 weeks in this case), the weather comes to play a key role in determining the organization and sequencing of particular activities. While we were on site, rain halted digging at various stages, but in doing so it also served to expedite the work conducted during clear moments and highlighted some of the features and pressures of archaeological practice. Key here in the context of the weather was an uncertainty surrounding the availability of time periods where particular tasks would or wouldn't be possible. The consequence is that the site leader and the rest of the team reactively organize the work to make use of current and prospective clear periods. The uncertainty, then, led to many different work streams being conducted simultaneously over different parts of the site: photographic capture, feature excavation and location measurement.

Figure 1: Various parallel activities at the Clatford dig site.

Implications for capture and interpretation

The temporal pressures and resulting distribution of tasks across the site, then had some important consequences for the organization of certain capture activities which in turn impacted on opportunities for interpretation during excavation. To illustrate, let us consider an episode in which the site supervisor was keen to capture photographs and laser scan measurements of an uncovered feature of the site prior to the next rainfall-caused interruption. In preparing the capture area, the excavators were asked to shift their excavation activities to a different part of the site. Even throughout the increased pressure of the dig, the supervisor proceeded to spend considerable time (half a day) cleaning, framing and measuring his target area prior to capture. This also involved moving a vehicle to the edge of the trench, such that he could achieve a higher vantage point for capture.

Two further experts spent the day making detailed measurements of the site using laser range finding. This heavy, specialist equipment required interruption free, line-of-sight recording, at times leading to further disruption of the excavation work. Significantly, the scanning base stations were frequently subject to marginal movements – for example, to allow for better alignment or to simplify subsequent measurements. This leads to potential issues with the standardization of measurement accuracy across the different scans taken, but the temporal pressures of the dig mean it is not always possible to repeat all the measures from scratch. The complex nature of these capture activities and processes again demanded that the supervisor was there to oversee and direct what was happening, and thereby was away from the activities of the rest of the excavation team who focused on a small ditch running across the site.

Highlighted in this episode are a number of issues relating to our concerns. First of all, the capture process is hugely time consuming in its setup and execution. The equipment is cumbersome to assemble and demands significant expert resources to operate. Of further significance is how this complexity and time to operate can inhibit efforts to repeat or redo measures in an accurately standardized way when trying to account for various pragmatic constraints imposed by the site. Importantly too, the process removes the excavators from the point of capture. The demands of the technology and the process mean that the capture is thus conducted only as an aid to post-excavation interpretation. The temporal pressures imposed by the weather mean that excavation work continues elsewhere in parallel with these capture activities. Significantly, this excavation work continues in the absence of the site supervisor who is overseeing the capture process. Again the time demands of the heavyweight capture process means that he is removed from the point of excavation for long periods of time therefore acting to distance himself from the developing interpretation during excavation work. While it was possible for him to be 'brought up to speed' later, the heavyweight procedure associated with photographic capture prevents this work from being conducted by a less experienced member of the team, in turn freeing the supervisor to continue overseeing the wider work. Finally, as a consequence considerable work was conducted on the excavation, based on interpretation of the materials being unearthed but without any capture being conducted – both the supervisor's absence and the complexity of the capture equipment being potential factors at play here. As such much of the textural and wider contextual details surrounding the excavation work and in situ finds are left unrecorded and consumed into interpretation without availability for later re-inspection.

What this begins to point to are the variety of ways in which key points of separation between capture and excavation based interpretation are introduced that relate to the incompatibility of capture time demands with the temporal demands of excavation work. This then suggests that significant benefits in the organisation of these practices could be achieved with capture techniques that significantly reduce: time to capture, complexity of capture and required expertise to capture. In order to develop these insights and elicit more detailed understanding of interpretive capture requirements and settings we undertook further fieldwork at a second site: Çatalhöyük in Turkey.

Çatalhöyük

The Neolithic site of Çatalhöyük, Turkey is one of the first urban centres of the world (7400BC) and now a World Heritage Site. The research project at Çatalhöyük has played an important role in both revealing new information about the people who lived in the settlement and developing some of the most influential theoretical, methodological and technological changes in the field of archaeology.

Our study took place over six days of the dig and again we were able to observe and informally interview key members of the archaeological team. We also wanted to capture key episodes of interpretive practice during excavations. The aim here was to understand in more detail how the episodes come about, what kinds of things are oriented to in conversation, how they are collaboratively organised, the relationship of the interpretive work to the artefacts and setting, and how such interpretive work relates to opportunities for capture. In order to capture the events in close detail we employed a lightweight 'Looxcie' ear-mounted digital video camera to be worn by a member of the archeological team. Over the course of the study, seven members of the archeological team wore the camera during their excavation work providing us with a broad coverage of different archaeological processes and conversations as they unfolded. At the end of each day participants would review the captured footage and discuss with us their perspectives on the captured footage. The archaeological work at Çatalhöyük is conducted in English so no translation was required.

Following the deployment, the captured videos were catalogued, and watched to highlight moments of interest in understanding the working and capturing. We followed a methodology based on interaction analysis employed in workplace studies in CSCW [13, 25] that emphasizes the ways that the archaeologists themselves responded to one another's actions. Selected moments were transcribed (using Jeffersonian notation) and subjected to repeated viewing to gauge the ways in which the participants worked to create interpretation in the trenches. Of these sequences, an illustrative subset is presented that aids the further exploration of the key requirements for streamlined capture.

Pre interpretation and the capture of special finds

The majority of uncovered finds are commonplace and homogeneous, illustrative of known issues and therefore less of a concern for capture. Of greater interest are "special finds" that have greater significance to the archeological narrative of the site. Here it is important that detailed information about 'good' finds is accurately recorded; their condition, context in-situ, exact location and the surrounding area. However, this is not as straightforward as it may at first appear. Indeed the demarcation as a special find and consequently what is important for capture is an emergent product of close collaboration interpretation on site, with an emphasis on how reconstruction for later interpretation is possible. Let us consider the following sequence in which the bone handle of a tool, presumed to be an axe, is found by Earl. The field director Beth looks at the find while Amos, another excavator, focuses on finding any extra missing pieces.

```
Amos (Excavator): Did you find the rest of the rock that fits in here
Beth (Field Director): (.hhh) (hhh.) (what) a fresh err break of the umm of the stone. And it is cut marked too (.) this is really cool you should walk around the trench and show everybody (.) OK we have the find of the day slash season slash year slash century slash millennium
Amos: you need the (.) you [need]
Beth: [you will see:::]
Amos: You need the
Dave (Excavator): [(inaudible)]
Amos: (inaudible) [(whistle)] Oi whats that
Earl: Let me see a second°
Beth: [Err:::]
Amos: [You] need (.) (Eugen) you need to find the rest that was sticking in [here]
Beth: [yeah:::]
Amos: [It's a long] shaped stone
Beth: [Is it?]
Earl: [(inaudible) something else inside of it?]
Beth: Is it already in the sieve?
Earl: we ok (.) hold up one [second ((raises finger))]
Charlie: [Looks like an axe] wow::: ma:::n
Beth: But its got a
Charlie: mm::: (.) find of the day
Amos: its got a cut up the [(incisional bulb)]
Beth: [um:::]
Earl: this was next to it but this is not it
Amos: you need a stone that fits into here
Beth: did you xfind that one and you xfind that one too right? umm::: did you already send the soil to sieve that might contain the rest of that?
Earl: [yeah]
Amos: [just scratch that thing] on a bit of wood and its like an axe or an axe head
```

This fragment illustrates what we come to label as the pre-interpretive practices bound up in the capture and recording of finds. Interpretation of these finds is emergent and dependent upon the assembly of other material evidence. These pre-interpretive practices then are expressions of expertise required to anticipate how a record will support later interpretation, and therefore the necessary scope and context of that record. Here, the scope of recording a find is interwoven with the collaborative interpretation necessary to create a sufficient record for later. The object as a find is worked up into the subject of its importance, and the two are inextricably linked on site. In shaping our thinking about capture technologies, this leads us to consider the importance of how they can be situated within the context of these collaborative pre-interpretive practices with particular attention to their spatial and temporal demands (for example by exploiting faster and more mobile capture possibilities).

Revealing features: colour, texture and context

The excavation at the West Mound area of Çatalhöyük is principally concerned with the mapping and understanding the structural elements of an urban conurbation, much of which involves the delineation of walls and floors. One of the key tasks around the site is to determine where such features were located, and the order in which they were constructed. Observing the excavators at work makes it immediately apparent that differentiation of colour, texture and consistency plays an important role in guiding the direction of excavations.

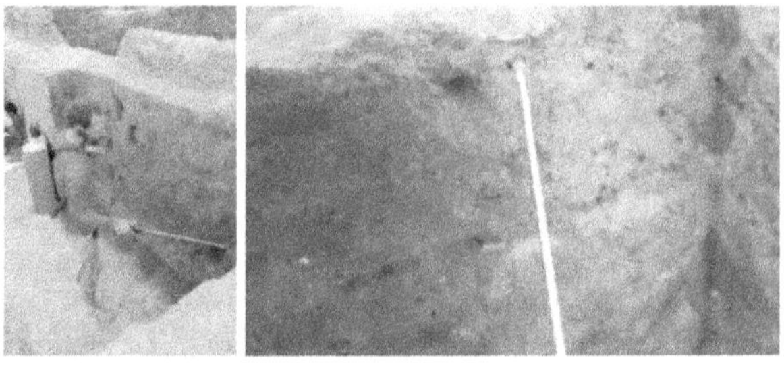

Figure 2: Images showing an excavator using a water sprayer to exaggerate color details. The excavator can be seen wearing a Looxcie on his ear (left) which captures images such as those on the right.

The most popular method for determining wall layout and building order is to trace a mortar line, a visibly darker line between lighter bricks. If it can be shown that the mortar line continues between sections of walls, then this can be interpreted as a continued wall. An excavator suggests "*When we were digging earlier I saw definite lines, but I am not seeing them now... sometimes they don't come out as well if you don't have the sprayer... with the sprayer they really pop out... See there is the line coming out more. Its proof, we got it.*" The water sprayer is one tool which can be used to exaggerate details of color, both for guiding the direction of excavation and for enhancing color differences for photographic capture (see figure 2 above). Texture proves equally important in differentiation providing the clearest definition between mortar, brick and plaster. On occasion, for example, when attempting to locate the floor, texture plays a very important role in guiding understanding of construction and use.

```
Anne: get everything out that is (0.5) related to the floor and it probably will ha- ((stutter)) will have a very bumpy base
Bella: mmhmm
```

Anne: because they might just have had umm room fill that (.hhh) altogether seems to make a little bump in the room (.) [in the centre]
Bella: [and then they flattened it] by doing a floor
Anne: yeah and then they didn't flatten the room fill [before]
Bella: [yeah]
Anne: they just filled all the bumps in the room fill with [floor]
Bella: [yeah] so maybe that is why it is thick in some areas and [thin in others (.) ok]
Anne: [yeah (0.5) yeah]
Bella: yeah
Anne: and we want to expose exactly that so
Bella: yeah ok

Here the discussion centres around exactly what constitutes the floor, and whether the rather loose fill in the bumps actually constitutes the floor, or whether the floor will be exposed upon removing the loose fill to discover a (rather counter-intuitively) bumpy floor. Thus the textural 'thinness' of the filling is found critical to the judgement of the floor's definition. Alongside the need to capture specific colour and textural detail, the excavators were also concerned with capturing this with sufficient surrounding detail to later enable wider understanding.

Losing opportunities for capture

Of particular note in our fieldwork enquiries was how particular aspects of archaeological practice were resulting in key opportunities for capture being missed through disruption, re-arrangement and destruction of material and speed pressures of work. We begin here with a look at how preparations for a particular capture narrative remove and rearrange things of relevance to a different narrative. In the following episode, the site leader interrupts the excavation to prepare it for capture but thereby disrupts the ongoing excavation and interpretive narrative being assembled.

Alan: There is no mortar here (.) there was mortar above this area but none here (.) this is like one big compacted block (.5) goes all the way down a lot thicker
Anne: what you were showing in the photo (.) is the information which (.) yeah
Alan: ((points)) well this needs to go because it just looks bad
Anne: So we will never know that it was up to here ((points))
Alan: we could sorta just clean it a bit and leave it like that (.) I don't know
...
Alan: So we sorta need to think
Anne: Water?
Alan: Water?
Anne: Take one dry photo (.) then we'll wet it then we'll have colour (2.5) we really have to take that out ((points)) because even if we leave it in nobody is gonna know what the hell it is

This process then involves precise trowelling, dusting, tidying and further cleaning before summoning the photographer to capture the scene. On the one hand the fragment highlights the constructed nature of particular capture practices; the need for framing the scene, actively removing or emphasising detail such that specific understanding can be clearly interpreted post-excavation. But at the same time in these constructed practices, the preparation and cleaning processes remove features of interest to the other narrative leading to Anne's disappointment. Had Anne had more personal control over her own capture, and been able to do it quickly, this narrative evidence might have been recorded.

In a related example we see further evidence of missed or avoided opportunities for capture. Again temporal issues are at play here in which there are discrepancies between speed of capture and speed of excavation. What is of particular significance in this example is the temporal ordering of archeology whereby particular features available at any one moment may need to be destroyed or removed in order to reveal other aspects of relevance to the interpretation. In the example, a senior excavator is describing the process of excavating features in a wall through the differentiation of texture.

Alan: this mud brick just slices (hhh) (.hhh) (hhh) maybe ((pointing gesture)) (.) maybe ((pointing gesture)) (0.5) I don't know (1.0) not terribly convincing
Bob: no
Alan: and that's one of the problems is that it's really (.) difficult to see it until you actually like cut into it
Bob: yeah
Alan: at which point you kind of lose the (.) edge a bit

In this case the edge is so poorly defined that gauging the texture requires destructive actions on the surface necessary for guiding and studying the surface itself.

In a final example, we highlight other work and time pressures precluding accurate capture. In this episode an archaeologist has been tasked with lowering an entire section of floor. In the process of this primary task, he excavates a lot of 'find' material (e.g. pottery and bone), but has to delay processing it until later. He create piles of material on an opposite surface, where additional material is then placed. This placement of material, combined with his pick-axe based excavation, leads to a significant amount of contamination and breakage. After considerable work, as the piles of finds become structurally unstable, he breaks to record data surrounding this material. He also makes it known to the capture expert that he requires a 'point' (an accurate, standardized position measurement) '*at some point (.) but no hurry*'. At this time all accurate contextual information surrounding each find and information surrounding its precise location has been lost as considerable excavation has been conducted subsequently.

RECONSIDERING OPPORTUNITIES FOR CAPTURE

With these issues in mind we wanted to consider how new forms of capture technology might offer new ways to recombine with the practices and processes of excavation. Our intention here was not to look to replace other capture practices and technologies but rather, consider niches not currently supported in this broader ecology of capture practice. In particular, we wanted to explore how new technologies could sit within the collaborative practices of interpretation in terms of their spatial and temporal organization and specific features to which they orient. More specifically we wanted to consider ways of putting capture capabilities into the hands of the excavators in ways that might support and document their excavation and interpretive work. In this regard, we were looking to avoid the need for time consuming clean up and preparation practices in the context of capture; the way this disrupts the excavation, the way this removes the excavators from the point of excavation, the way this demands the dedicated attention of site leader, the ways in which this demands dedicated technical capture expertise, and the ways that this disrupts the material assemblies of the site relating to the interpretive narratives of the excavators. Further our aim was to orient to the inherent time pressures of archeological excavation through which useful capture and review opportunities are lost – in particular where states of artefacts and assemblies at any moment may be permanently lost through the destructive requirements of interpretation.

To this end, we looked at how we could alter particular parameters and characteristics of a scanning technology (and the balance of trade-offs) to fit within the niche outlined above. First of all, then, our emphasis was first on speeding up capture activity to avoid lost opportunities and enable the review of the material in situ in support of ongoing interpretation. Second, we looked to emphasise greater mobility – to have something that could be personal to an excavator and that could be more easily positioned around the site and particular artefacts in the context of excavation based interpretation. Such shifts will entail certain compromises elsewhere, such as, for example, resolution. In making these shifts we wanted to ensure that the resolution of capture still revealed the *sufficient* detail of artifact form and texture oriented to in the development of these interpretive narratives. We move on to consider these shifts in the context of a personal 3D scanner.

A PERSONAL MOBILE 3D SCANNER

Given these requirements we turned to recent developments in real-time, small form factor scanning exemplified by recent advances in Simultaneous Localisation and Mapping (SLAM). With their Kinect Fusion algorithm [20, 28], Izadi et al present a system capable of real time dense model acquisition using a Microsoft Kinect camera. Their approach allows the near real time capture of 3D models of objects, scenes and body movement that can be integrated together or differentiated from one another - providing a bridge between the requirement of personal capture in reflexive archaeology, and the demand for 3D modeling in archaeological capture and interpretation: both capturing for interpretation and capturing interpretation. A related approach is presented in [29], where a depth camera is replaced with a traditional monocular webcam. Such an approach, though, relies heavily on movement to capture a scene, leading to an unnatural capture technique, and textural data is more heavily affected by color variation. Thus we decided to use Kinect Fusion with our device.

Hardware

To develop our mobile scanner (see figure 3), we extracted the cameras, infra-red laser and main camera board from a Kinect and combined this with a wifi dongle, a low-power Gumstix embedded linux computer, a 7.5V camera battery and a custom-made circuit board to route the resulting camera data and to provide the required voltages to power all of the components (which require a mixture of 1.8V, 3.3V or 5V). A fan, heatsinks, on/off LEDs and a charger adaptor were also added. The design reduces the physical size and power requirements of the existing Kinect, facilitating its mobility. Finally, we designed a case to enable one-handed use of the device, supporting interaction with the environment during capture. We have published our open source hardware design [27] for reuse in other applications.

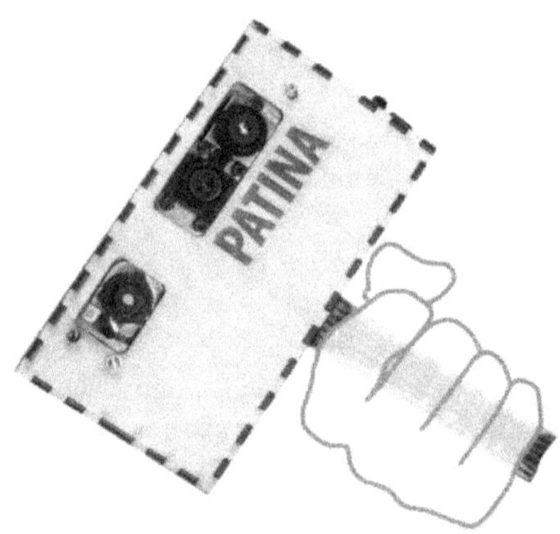

Figure 3: Our prototype personal 3D scanning device

Software

The software for the device is in two parts. Firstly, using open source drivers recompiled for the Gumstix, we built network code that would enable the Kinect to connect to a WiFi network and transmit depth images at roughly 24 frames-per-second. Given this frame rate is sufficient for our purposes, we have not optimized depth data streaming, although there are novel algorithms in this area [22]. Secondly, Microsoft's Kinect Fusion algorithm [see 20 for full description], running on a nearby server is used to construct full 3D models from the data. The algorithm determines the six degrees of freedom transformation of the Kinect between subsequent frames and uses this to integrate all captured points into a 3D voxel volume. This volume can be ray-cast in real time, producing a model of the scene. This process is carried out on the GPU in order to achieve a real-time and interactive frame-rate. The algorithm treats moving pixels in the scene as outliers, discarding them from the model. If these pixels are maintained separately, however, it can be determined when they overlap with the captured model in 3D space. This means that, should a hand enter the scene, any interaction it has with objects in the scene can be recorded.

To facilitate the use of the scanning device on large outdoor sites, we developed an application for an Android Tablet to enable remote control of the device and the software. The app allows the user to start and stop the capture process as well as control both the volume ($2m^3$ to $20cm^3$) and resolution of the area being captured (to support shifting perspectives of the archaeologists from wide areas, such as an entire wall, to specific points, for example where a piece of pottery lies). The excavators may also be capturing models for a variety of different purposes, for example as a quick reminder or for more detailed examination later. By controlling the temporal properties of the Kinect Fusion algorithm, the archaeologists can control the time taken to capture frames for the model and, thereby, the resolution of the output. This adheres to our design considerations, allowing the user to determine the trade-offs between detail and efficiency for each scan.

INITIAL EVALUATION WORK

To understand our device further within the context of archeological practice we conducted some initial evaluation studies with archaeologists. First of all we gave the system to a team of archaeologists working in the Crypt of Winchester Cathedral. This provided an interesting point of contrast for our evaluation discussion as the team had previously deployed more precise archaeological laser scanning techniques as part of their work there. We also gave our system to a number of different archeological specialists working in Lithics, Maritime, and Osteo-archaeology laboratories. The archeologists had the opportunity to use the system and review the captured outputs in the context of their work. We observed them using the system and discussed their experiences in relation to how particular system characteristics pertained to their interpretive practices.

Granularity of detail

We begin our discussion here with a look at the central issue of granularity of detail captured in the scans. What was apparent here was that the required granularity of detail in the scans was dependent on the area of expertise and, more specifically, the materials of interest. For both the osteo-archaeologists and maritime archaeologists, the concerns of their work are with less durable materials subject to erosion within their natural environment. As such, their focus is often on coarser features of their finds.

Figure 4: Maritime archaeologist explaining a ship segment (left) and the captured models (right).

For example, while scanning a hull segment of a ship with our device, a maritime archaeologist remarked that the detail captured was of sufficient quality to examine the important features, such as location of the securing bolts, the timber construction techniques used and the location of the mast (figure 4). Working in heavily constrained environments, these details are the typical focus of maritime archaeologists, as they allude to the manufacturing location and period, and overall size of the vessel. He remarked that the ability to *quickly* revisit and explore this information upon completion of his work would be useful to him. Communication within his work setting is limited, and so interpretation is typically shared immediately upon surfacing. He suggested a model of this resolution would facilitate this process.

For those working with these softer materials then, the resolutions of the scans were suitable for key aspects of their work. For the archaeologists working with stone and other similar materials there were some requirements for the finer detail of their objects. For the lithics specialists (focusing on the fine details of smaller hand axes and blades), they suggested that the capture resolution of Kinect Fusion was not sufficient for some of their analytic requirements. Of further significance in their comments was that while they invest a large amount of time in drawing and capturing data around their finds, it is not just the output of this process that is of interest. Rather, the aim is the interpretation gained by spending time focusing on the minutiae of their research materials. Much of their work is also dependent upon cleaning the finds post-excavation for use with specialist equipment in a controlled environment. As such, it was not felt that our scanner would deal well with the specific site and details that are central to the interpretive work of these specialists.

However, what we found was that the demands of resolution detail can also be dynamic and that models of the same things at different resolutions can play different roles in the interpretations they enable. We see this illustrated by the team working in the Crypt of Winchester Cathedral. During renovation works over the last few centuries, various stones have been moved from their original setting to other parts of the cathedral. Located within the crypt is an example of constructor graffiti, where one of the masons had engraved a message into the stone. The team had previously scanned this using more precise archaeological laser scanning techniques. A comparison of the output of our model against the output of a photogrammetric model can be seen below (figure 5). While it can be seen that the model produced by our device contains significantly less detail, it does show the textural detail of the surrounding wall, including brick outlines and mortar thickness. The scanning expert at the Crypt remarked that *'you managed to capture this bit a little more clearly than here [the higher resolution model],'* showing that, by removing some of the finer details of tool marks and chips, the structure of the material can be more clearly defined.

However, where these concerns really come into play is that interpretive work is not just bound up in static scans but in their additional dynamic transformations and manipulations. Resolution detail here then was not simply about what could be viewed in the static but what it meant for the way the model could be manipulated. The team articulated that high-resolution models demand a significant computational resource to render and explore. For these reasons, they deliberately invest time to reduce the resolution of their 3D models (or treat them as texturally rich 2D photographs) to support their faster manipulation and explorability, referring to this as *"throwing information away"*. Such a trade-off between resolution detail and manipulability is embodied in our scanner. This was highlighted rather nicely by one of the experts there who felt able to explore the model from our lower resolution scanner more freely than some of the other scanned material. During his manipulations, he turned the model upside down and repositioned the virtual lighting, something he had been previously unable to do. In doing this he realised that the text could in fact be read (as can be seen in figure 5, where the models have been rotated from their original capture orientation).

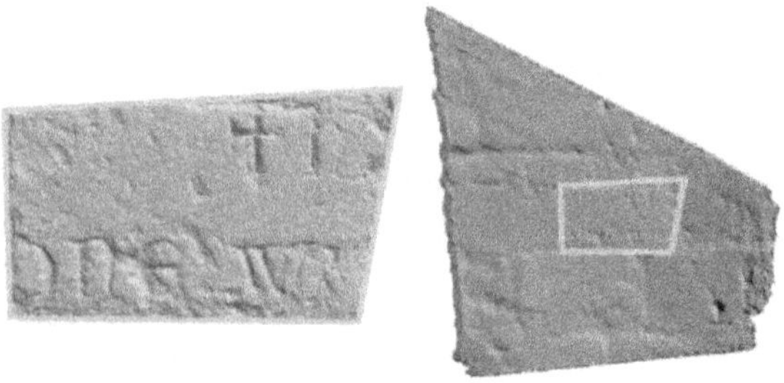

Figure 5: A comparison between a photogrammetric model (left) and our captured model (right) of masonry graffiti at Winchester Cathedral.

Speed of Capture and review

Of further significance in our discussions with the archaeologists was the ability to capture and review the scanned models in a matter of seconds. Where this becomes important is in the constructed nature of the narratives that are bound up in the process of capture – that is how they are designed to render certain features visible. For these reasons, it is important to review the outputs from capture to ascertain whether it appropriately reveals things as intended by the narrative. Such review of the capture materials can actually be problematic with the current high end scanning technologies. As the scanning expert on the team at Winchester Cathedral explained, creating a photogrammetry model takes 1 hour of on-site capture (during which time the capture process cannot be interrupted and no work can be conducted within the capture vicinity) and 6 hours to render on a powerful GPU cluster. During this time there is minimal feedback, resulting in uncertainty surrounding the final output. The total time for model acquisition makes it impractical for small changes to be made and models to be repeated. For this reason, he expressed that a significant benefit of our system lay in the instantaneous nature of our capture. This would allow outputs to be reviewed in near real time to ascertain how they were working in the context of the constructed narrative being produced.

The speed of our device would also make it possible to capture a more varied set of outputs. An example he gave here was that he would be able to capture detail surrounding the engraving, such as how the particular stone fits within the makeup of the wider wall. The ability to quickly capture multiple scans of the surrounding contexts as well as the details of particular features would add significant evidence to the kinds of interpretations they would be able to make.

We saw some related issues here with the Osteo-archaeologists. One of the problems they experience is that logs completed during excavation are often of varying quality and precision with much of the situational information surrounding the find lost. Commenting on a scanned model of a skull using the system she suggested *"if you can get some kind of 3D model in the grave to actually get an idea of bones spatially in relation to one another, and depths [that] would be useful"*. Of particular concern to her though was the degrading of artefacts of interest over time and she pointed to the opportunities opened up for repeated captures over time: *"An issue we have with skeletal remains rather than maybe hand axe stuff, is the fact that it does disintegrate a lot more... it will completely change, the bones will move, the coloration will change and you end up having a different interpretation of what you are looking at, so it is useful to be able to capture things at different stages."* Here being able to capture models quickly would greatly facilitate repeated capture over time preventing the loss of artifact states important for her interpretive work. The speed of capture of our device would allow her scanning to be conducted in a manner that results in 3D 'time-lapse' style scans, in turn affording her the ability to determine between the effects of excavation and the effects of time. This is one aspect of her archaeology that is currently not possible for her to capture. She also raised the possibility of printing 3D models from the scans that would greatly assist in these aspects of her work.

Pragmatics of use

In observing the archaeologists using the device, it was evident how they referred constantly to the monitor which depicts both what the camera can see in real time and the resultant effect on the created model. In doing this they were constantly verifying that they were focused on the area of relevance and capturing it appropriately for their concerns. Given the particular setup we employed, there were times when people were looking in the opposite direction from which they were capturing and, therefore, having to mentally translate the movements required to better frame their target object or fill holes in the model. In addition, the Kinect requires a distance of roughly 60cm between the camera and the object for depth readings to be made. While this was explained to every participant, there was a natural tendency to move towards the target object, as though 'zooming in' to enhance resolution. This behavior decreased in occurrence with continued use, but reliance on the monitor for feedback continued. This suggests that there may be some usability benefits to be gleaned from adding a small output screen on the back of the scanner – making it easier shift focus between the actual objects and corresponding capture output. We will look to explore this in future iterations. Another aspect affecting ease of use was the portable form factor of our device. Participants happily carried the device with them and continuing to converse and gesture whilst holding the device. Here we see an indication of its ability to support the interleaving of capture with the interpretive discussions surrounding it.

DISCUSSION

In this paper, we have begun to explore some of the interpretive practices in archeology and the particular ways that they are bound up with certain practices of capture. More specifically, a central concern in our work, has been with understanding some of the separations that happen between excavation, analysis and interpretation and how these relate to the ways that on site work of archeology has come to be organised. Much of this is in response to particular temporal pressures of the work and the contextual constraints at the sites of practice. Furthermore, we have highlighted some key features of current capture technologies and practices within these archaeological settings that do not sit neatly with the ongoing collaborative practices of interpretation during excavation. As a consequence, much of this interpretive practice remains unsupported by existing capture techniques – neither supporting it as it occurs, nor documenting it in aid of post excavation practices. Much of the temporal unfolding of the archaeology, and what is destroyed in the process of revealing remain lost.

In orienting to these separations, our approach is not to be critical of current capture techniques and practices per se. Indeed, these practices remain hugely important to current archaeological methods. Rather than replace these then, our aim has been to understand how new capture technologies might be positioned differently within the broader ecology of these capture practices. In particular, our concern has been with how we can develop new capture technologies that can interleave more closely with the collaborative practices of interpretation during excavation. Here we sought explicitly to investigate how we could alter key parameters of the capture process through technologies that emphasised certain performance attributes at the expense of others. With our 3D scanning system then, the emphasis here was on the portability of a device that could be personally controlled by an excavator during their work and ongoing interpretive practice. Furthermore, the device focused on the *'quick and dirty'*, placing particular emphasis on real time capture, review and manipulability of captured data in the context of interpretation, while compromising to an extent on the kinds of image resolution possible with the higher end scanning techniques. This streamlining of capture and excavation aims to be less disruptive to work practices and supports the continued development of interpretation.

In our initial evaluations of the technology, we were able to get some early indications of the ways that such a shift in the relative balance of performance trade-offs might play out – where they might offer some important benefits and where, on the other hand, they would not. Here, for example, we start to see the dependent nature of resolution requirements in a captured scan. For some concerns and some areas of archaeology, the lower resolutions work well - softer objects subject to deformation as a result of their immediate environment and handling are typically considered through their larger features, as exhibited by the examination of bones and ships. By contrast more durable materials such as stone are often examined for the minutiae of their form. But even here, in certain cases, lower resolutions were sometimes used to exaggerate features that remain hidden in more highly detailed scans. Perhaps of greater significance though is that lower resolution can bring certain benefits in terms of the dynamic manipulation of capture models. And it is in these manipulation possibilities that key features of interpretation can take place. Benefits too were to be found in the real time capture and review pointing to enhanced possibilities to monitor and review capture activity in the construction of particular interpretation narratives. This provides opportunity for frequent or repeated scans to re-capture in case of error or reframe to embody a different interpretation. Furthermore, there was a suggestion that by emphasising speed of capture, there would be greater freedom to capture more models. This would enable the documenting of degrading objects and the interpretive significance of these temporal concerns. It would also provide greater freedom to capture a greater selection of models each with different perspectives, foci and surrounding context.

In conclusion, through examination and observation of different aspects of archaeological practice we have identified key features of current capture technologies that do not sit neatly with ongoing interpretation and, more specifically, the drive towards 'reflexive archaeology.' As a result of this, we have investigated the key parameters of the capture process that could be altered to streamline the process with ongoing interpretation during excavation. We have presented a novel 3D capture device that emphasizes 'quick and dirty' capture and examined its use in a variety of settings. By working in the long tradition of ethnographic CSCW, we have shown that devices such as these, designed to support ongoing collaborative interpretation, could play an important role in archaeology in the future, providing a greater freedom to capture a wider range of data. We also believe that our work serves to highlight the longer term potential of 3D capture as a medium for digital collaboration across a range of domains.

REFERENCES

1. Allen, P., Feiner, S. Troccoli, A., Benko, H., Ishak, E., Smith, B., Seeing into the Past: Creating a 3D Modeling Pipeline for Archaeological Visualization., in *Proc. 3DPVT'04*, pp. 751-758, 2004.
2. Andrews, G., Barrett, J. C and Lewis, J. S. C., Interpretation not record: the Practice of Archaeology. *Antiquity*, 74 (285), pp. 525-530, 2000.

3. Balzani, M., Santopuoli, N., Grieco, A., Zaltron, N., Laser Scanner 3D Survey in Archaeological Field: the Forum of Pompeii, *International Conference on Remote Sensing Archaeology*, Beijing, October 2004.
4. Besl, P. and McKay, N., A Method for Registration of 3D Shapes, in *IEEE Transactions on Pattern Analysis and Machine Intelligence*, 14, pp. 239-256, 1992.
5. Brill, D., Video Recording as Part of The Critical Archaeological Process, in Hodder, I (ed), *Towards Reflexive Method in Archaeology: The Example at Çatalhöyük*, Cambridge: MacDonald Institute for Archaeological Research, 2000.
6. Carver, M., On Archaeological Value, in *Antiquity*, 70 (267), pp. 45-56, 1996.
7. Chadwick, A., Post-Processualism, prefessionalisation and archaeological methodologies. Towards reflective and radical practice, in *Archaeological Dialogues* 10 (1): 97-117, 2003.
8. Dellepiane, M., et al, Archaeological excavation monitoring using dense stereo matching techniques, in *Journal of Cultural Heritage*, 2012.
9. Gaffney, C., Detecting trends in the prediction of the buried past: a review of geophysical techniques in archaeology, in *Archaeometry*, 50 (2), pp. 313-336.
10. Goodwin, C., The semiotic body in its environment, in *Discourses of the body*, pp. 19-42, Macmillan.
11. Goodwin, C., Professional Vision, in *American Anthropologist*, 96, pp. 606-633, 1994.
12. Healey, J. and Picard, R.W., StartleCam: A Cybernetic Wearable Camera, in *Proc. Second International Symposium on Wearable Computing (ISWC'98)*.
13. Heath, C., Hindmarsh, J. and Luff, P., Video in Qualitative Research: Analysing social interaction in everyday life, Sage, 2010.
14. Hodder, I. The Archaeological Process: An Introduction, Blackwell Publishers, 1999.
15. Hodder, I. Archaeological Reflexivity and the 'Local' Voice, in *Anthropological Quarterly*, 76 (1), pp. 55-69.
16. Hodder, I. (ed), *Towards Reflexive Method in Archaeology: The Example at Çatalhöyük*, McDonald Institute for Archaeological Research / British Institute of Archaeology at Ankara Monograph, 28, 2000.
17. Hodder, I., Shanks, M., Alexandri, A., Buchli, V., Carman, J., Last, J., Lucas, G. *Interpreting Archaeology*, Routledge, London, 1995.
18. Hodges, S., Williams, L., Berry, E., Izadi, S., Srinivasan, J., Butler, A., Smyth, G., Kapur, N. and Wood, K., SenseCam: a Retrospective Memory Aid, in *Proc. Ubicomp 2006*, pp. 177-193, 2006.
19. Hori, T. and Aizawa, K., Context-based video retrieval system for the life-log applications, in *Proc. 5th ACM SIGMM international workshop on Multimedia information retrieval*, November 2003.
20. Izadi, S., Kim, D., Hilliges, O., Molyneaux, D., Newcombe, R., Kohli, P., Shotton, J., Hodges, S., Freeman, D., Davison, A. and Fitzgibbon, A., KinectFusion: Real-time 3D Reconstruction and Interaction Using a Moving Depth Camera, in *Proc. UIST 2011*, ACM.
21. Joukowsky, M. *A Complete Manual of Field Archaeology*. Prentice Hall, Englewood Cliffs, NJ, 1980.
22. Pece, F., Kautz, J. and Weyrich, T., Adapting Standard Video Codecs for Depth Streaming, in *Proc. of Joint Virtual Reality Conference of EuroVR (JVRC)*, pp. 1-8, Nottingham, UK, September 2011.
23. Lamming, M. and Flynn, M. Forget-me-not: Intimate Computing in Support of Human Memory, in *Proc. Friend 21*, 1994.
24. Levy, T. E., et al, On-site digital archaeology - new developments, delivery and the creation of a data avalanche, in M. Forte (ed.) *Introduction to cyber-archaeology*, pp. 135-153, Archaeopress, 2010.
25. Luff, P., Hindmarsh, J. and Heath, C., Workplace Studies: Recovering work practice and informing system design, Cambridge University Press, 2000.
26. Mann, S., Fung, J., Aimone, C., Sehgal, A. and Chen, D., Designing EyeTap Digital Eyeglasses for Continuous Lifelong Capture and Sharing of Personal Experiences, in *Adjunct Proc. alt.chi 2005*, ACM.
27. http://big.cs.bris.ac.uk/projects/mobile-kinect
28. Newcombe, R, Izadi, S., Kim, D., Hilliges, O., Molyneaux, D., Kohli, P., Shotton, J., Hodges, S., Freeman, D., Davison, A. and Fitzgibbon, A., KinectFusion: Real-Time Dense Surface Mapping and Tracking, in *Proc. ISMAR 2011*.
29. Newcombe, R., Lovegrove, S., Davison, A., DTAM: Dense Tracking and Mapping in Real-Time, *IEEE International Conference on Computer Vision*, 2011.
30. Novo, A., Grasmueck, M., Viggiano, D., Lorenzo, H., 3D GPR in Archaeology: What can be gained from dense Data Acquisition and Processing, in *International Conference on Ground Penetrating Radar*, Birmingham, UK, 2008.
31. Shackley, MS., An Introduction to X-Ray Fluorescence (XRF) Analysis in Archaeology, in *Geoarchaeology*, 2011.
32. Wheatley, D., *High-Dynamic Range Imaging for Archaeology*, 1996.
33. Wood, K., Fleck, R. and Williams, L., Playing with SenseCam, in *Proc. Playing with Sensors: Exploring the boundaries of sensing for playful ubiquitous computing (W3)*, UbiComp 2004, Nottingham, UK

Support for Deictic Pointing in CVEs: Still Fragmented after All These Years?

Nelson Wong and Carl Gutwin
Computer Science Department, University of Saskatchewan
110 Science Place, Saskatoon, SK, S7N 5C9, Canada
nelson.wong, carl.gutwin @usask.ca

Figure 1. A custom CVE set on a balcony with a downtown view, and avatars able to point freely.

ABSTRACT

Pointing gestures – particularly deictic references – are ubiquitous in face-to-face communication. However, deictic pointing can be much more difficult in collaborative virtual environments (CVEs) than in everyday life – early studies found that the 'fragmentation' caused by the environment greatly complicated object-based communication. In the fifteen years since these studies appeared, the technologies used in CVEs have improved substantially, and several techniques for improving pointing have been proposed or implemented. What these advances mean for the problems of fragmentation and deictic gesture, however, is not clear. To find out, we conducted a new observational study of deictic pointing in a CVE with several techniques that may reduce fragmentation: extra-wide and third-person views, precise control over an avatar's pointing arm, and visual enhancements such as object highlighting and laser pointing. Our study shows that although pointing has come a long way, problems of fragmentation still occur, and that visual and view enhancements can cause new problems for collaboration, even as they solve others. In addition, the visibility of a gesture's preparatory actions remained important to study participants, even when pointing was augmented. These results provide a richer understanding of the subtlety in avatar-based deictic communication, and of the ways that this critical communication mechanism can be better supported in CVEs.

CSCW'14, February 15 - 19 2014, Baltimore, MD, USA
Copyright 2014 ACM 978-1-4503-2540-0/14/02$15.00.
http://dx.doi.org/10.1145/2531602.2531691

Author Keywords

Pointing; gestures; avatars; CVEs.

ACM Classification Keywords

H.5.3 [**Group and Organization Interfaces**]: *CSCW*

INTRODUCTION

Indicating referents with pointing gestures during an utterance is called *deictic pointing*, or *deixis*. Deictic pointing is ubiquitous in face-to-face communication, because it lets people use spatial information about locations, directions, paths, and areas to simplify referential utterances and reduce conversational effort. Deixis is one of the most important kinds of non-verbal communication, and numerous studies have shown its ubiquity and its usefulness in face-to-face interaction [1,9,22].

The value of deictic pointing has long been recognized by designers of 2D groupware, and has been widely supported through telepointers (e.g., [10]) which allow simple and unambiguous referential gestures. However, support for deictic pointing in 3D collaborative virtual environments (CVEs) is much less developed. There are several reasons for this difference. For example, avatar-based embodiments and perspective views means that people must interpret the pointing direction of the avatar's arm in the 3D environment, rather than simply observing a telepointer in a 2D workspace. Although avatar-based pointing is closer to real-world deixis, limitations of the virtual environment often mean that interpreting (or even noticing) a pointing gesture becomes problematic.

These difficulties have been recognized by previous researchers, particularly in the 'Furniture World' studies carried out with the MASSIVE environment [13,14]. These studies identified the *problem of fragmentation* – the display cannot show all the relevant information (e.g., the pointing gesture, referent, and environment) needed for communication, forcing collaborators to change their views to see such information. This problem occurs due to narrow fields of view (FOV), poor resolution, and difficulty in seeing others' pointing actions. The fragmentation caused by these technological limitations caused serious problems in the collaborative interaction, and led to "the disruption of [what] is one of the critical and foundational elements of collaborative work—i.e., the reference to, and discussion of, objects and artefacts" [14], p.487. Hindmarsh and colleagues also proposed several techniques that could be used to combat the problems of fragmentation. For example, they suggested that FOV could be widened using compressed 'peripheral lenses' (leading to better visibility of others' pointing gestures), that pointing interpretation could be improved through visual enhancements such as object highlighting or 'extendable arms,' and that view awareness could be achieved by visualizing each avatar's view frustum.

In the fifteen years since the Furniture World studies were carried out, CVEs have become commonplace – there are currently hundreds of environments used for diverse purposes such as multi-player gaming (e.g., World of Warcraft, Call of Duty) and social interaction (e.g., Second Life, There). CVE technology has advanced considerably compared to the MASSIVE system, with high-resolution graphics, detailed models and textures, fast networking, high frame rates, and wide-screen displays. These commercial CVEs have not, in general, implemented the pointing improvements suggested by Hindmarsh and colleagues, but they have introduced other features that could be beneficial to the problem of fragmentation. In particular, recent CVEs have included techniques such as third-person views and multi-monitor support (which give a more expansive view of the scene), 'laser' pointing and object highlighting (e.g., in Second Life), and detailed control over the avatar's pointing arm [25].

What are the effects of these technical improvements and enhancements on the fragmentation that Hindmarsh and colleagues observed – and have the problems of deictic reference been solved in current CVEs? To answer this question, we carried out a new observational study in a CVE that implemented several of the techniques mentioned above – three-monitor-wide views, third-person views, object highlighting, laser pointing, and full control over the avatar's pointing arm. We recorded and analysed the communicative behaviour of twelve pairs of participants as they carried out a variety of tasks in our CVE. Our analysis focused on three main questions that derive from the concept of fragmentation and its intimate relationship to the simultaneous visibility of the target and the producer of the pointing gesture:

- Do wide-field-of-view techniques provide solutions to the visibility and context problems seen in earlier work – that is, do wide views improve the noticeability and understandability of pointing gestures?
- Do visual enhancements like object highlighting and laser pointing improve the accuracy of interpreting a deictic reference, and is increased precision desirable for all referential tasks (even those that do not require precision)?
- Does the increased visibility and precision of enhanced pointing reduce the need for people to see the preparatory stages of a pointing gesture (i.e., mutual orientation, preparation, and production)?

Our observations show that deictic pointing has greatly improved since the days of Furniture World – techniques such as wide views and laser pointing work well to make gestures visible and to simplify the process of indicating objects. However, our study shows that even with augmented techniques, there are still problems of fragmentation in object-based communication: we saw problems of gesture visibility, inappropriate precision, and the need for verbal communication to overcome limitations of the environment. We also saw that participants regularly made use of the preparatory stages of a pointing gesture, even when they had a high-visibility enhancement like laser pointing. Our results show that it is still important to set deictic pointing gestures – even augmented ones – into a context that includes the rich awareness of gestural interaction and communication in the real world.

BACKGROUND

Pointing in Co-located Settings

People primarily use pointing to indicate objects referred to in speech, which is called deictic reference or deixis [20]. Deixis allows people to simplify communication when it is difficult to rely on verbal descriptions (e.g., indicating objects with hard-to-describe shapes) [17], as long as the observer can see and interpret the pointing gesture.

A deictic pointing gesture can be divided into four stages. First, the producer of the gesture wants to ensure *mutual orientation* with the observer, such that both parties can see the gesture and the target. Since mutual orientation can be difficult to establish, this stage may overlap with later stages and finish after a pointing gesture is produced. Second, the producer may engage in *preparation* actions that indicate to the observer that a pointing gesture is going to be made. *Production* of the gesture occurs next, and the fact that this production is gradual allows people to predict the general direction of the gesture before it is completed (e.g., [21]). Finally, the producer must continue *holding* the gesture until they are sure that the observer has seen it and that mutual understanding has been reached (e.g., [15]).

While the gesture itself is crucial to the success of pointing, the immediate environment, orientation, and view are also important [7,8,12]. How people coordinate with each other depends on the objects and artifacts around them. People construct pointing gestures based on their knowledge of the environment, such as drawings on a whiteboard and text on a monitor [9,12,15,22]. The locations of artifacts, and the orientations and viewing angles of the people involved also change how pointing gestures are constructed and perceived [9,12,22] – e.g., the process of pointing at referents in front of someone is vastly different from pointing at referents behind them. The process of communicating with pointing gestures is intricate in co-located settings; the act of referencing in distributed settings is even more complex.

Pointing in Distributed Settings

The usefulness and ubiquity of pointing gestures in everyday human interaction has led to a large body of research into pointing in distributed settings. Showing referents in distributed environments is often done via embodiments (representations of people in groupware systems), which can be 2D telepointers [10,11], video images [16,18,19,23] or 3D avatars [2,3,4].

In traditional 2D groupware, the embodiment can be a simple telepointer [10,11]. A telepointer is often sufficient to indicate referents because collaborators normally share the same view – that is, when a telepointer is over an object, all collaborators can see the same pointer pointing at the same referent. Referencing is more difficult when distributed environments go beyond 2D groupware.

In video-mediated mixed realities, videos of hand gestures [16,18,23] and full bodies [19] can be projected into collaborators' workstations. While much more information can be shown with videos of hands and people, there are other challenges – for example, understanding the conduct of collaborators can be problematic due to different viewing angles, camera locations, and transmission delays.

In CVEs, collaborators interact with each other via avatars (3D representations that are usually humanoid figures). Researchers have noted several problems that make pointing gestures challenging in CVEs. Mutual orientation is difficult to achieve because of the narrow FOV in CVEs, and pointing at objects that are not close by often leads to misunderstandings [5,13,14]. 'Fragmentation' hinders fluent collaboration in CVEs – for example, collaborators need to frequently change their views to see all the relevant information for communication [5,13,14]. In addition, pointing actions in CVEs are often produced immediately (e.g., as the result of a command such as '/point'), and therefore do not provide the gradual information available from gestures in the real world [21]. Pointing in CVEs is also often restricted to targeting a set of predefined objects in the world, greatly reducing the expressiveness of people's pointing actions. Object-based pointing has been shown to cause severe communication problems in collaborative work [6].

Various techniques for improving interaction in CVEs have been suggested – such as those in the Furniture World studies [5,13,14]. Some of these techniques are intended to improve the problem of limited FOV and mutual orientation, such as wide-angle peripheral lenses to increase a user's FOV and a visible view frustum to better indicate what others can see [5,13,14]. Other techniques are aimed at improving object referencing: for example, elongated arms that can be extended to reach referents, and object highlighting that enhances awareness of what others are looking at [5,13,14]. In addition, several other techniques have been introduced in commercial CVEs, such as third-person views, flexible arm movement, and 'laser' pointing. Despite this variety of techniques, however, we do not know what impact improvements to CVE pointing have had on the overall problem of fragmentation and the success of referential communication.

OBSERVATIONAL STUDY: POINTING IN A CVE

We carried out a study to investigate how techniques for deictic pointing and for increasing FOV help reduce fragmented interaction. We developed a custom CVE and set the scene on a virtual balcony that overlooked a city's downtown area. The study asked people to carry out open-ended collaborative tasks that involved making reference to objects, paths, areas, and directions. We explored three issues in the study:

- Whether a wider FOV (using either additional monitors or third-person views) reduces the problems of fragmented interaction;
- Whether high-accuracy and high-visibility techniques like a virtual laser solve problems of referential accuracy that were identified in earlier work;
- Whether the high visibility of augmented pointing techniques (such as a laser beam or spotlight) reduce the need for people to participate in the staging actions of pointing (e.g., mutual orientation and gesture production).

Collaborative Virtual Environment Used in the Study

We built a custom CVE in XNA and C#, running on Windows 7. Participants' avatars were located on a balcony overlooking a virtual cityscape (Figure 1). Participants could move their avatars around the balcony, point at objects with the avatar's arm, and look in any direction by turning the avatar's head.

Avatar control. Participants moved their avatars using the W-A-S-D keyboard keys. All of the pointing techniques were controlled by manipulating the direction of the avatar's arm (there was no selection of objects with a mouse cursor as in CVEs like Second Life). We implemented two methods for avatar arm control (all participants used both in the study) that were previously identified as being effective and simple [25]. First, *mouse control* allowed people to move the arm when the left mouse button was pressed; the arm pointed in the direction indicated by the left-right and up-down motion of the mouse. Second, *Wiimote control* allowed people to move the arm using real-world pointing movements (pointing left, right, up, or down in the real world provided relative input to change the pointing direction of the avatar's arm). 'Natural' arm-based pointing (with no visual enhancement) was the default behavior of the avatar; when an augmented technique was available, the participant turned it on and off by pressing number keys on the keyboard.

View control. When using the mouse control technique, participants changed the avatar's view direction by moving the mouse with no buttons pressed (this meant that participants could only control either view direction or arm direction at one time). When using the Wiimote, participants controlled view direction using the thumbstick on a Nunchuk controller. In addition, participants could switch between first-person and third-person views by pressing the Tab key.

CVE view width. One of the workstations used in the study had a single 24" monitor with a 1440x900-pixel resolution. The other one had three 24" monitors with a total resolution of 4320x900 pixels, tripling the width of the CVE's view (Figure 4-9). In both cases, the CVE view width increases when changing to 3rd-person perspective where the camera is located behind and above the avatar.

Pointing Techniques Used in the Study

We implemented five pointing techniques: natural pointing (the default), natural pointing with a long arm, a virtual laser beam, a spotlight technique, and an object highlight (see Figure 2).

- *Natural pointing*. The avatar's arm and extended finger pointed as controlled by the participant.
- *Long arm*. Similar to natural pointing, but with a double-length avatar arm, making it easier to see.
- *Laser beam*. A red line (the 'laser') was drawn from the avatar's finger.
- *Spotlight*. A small red dot was drawn on the first intersecting object in the arm's pointing direction.
- *Highlight*. If a selectable object intersects the arm's pointing direction, it is highlighted in red.

We used the long arm and object highlighting because similar approaches were used in the original Furniture World studies [5,13,14]; and the laser beam and spotlight because they can be commonly found in commercial CVEs such as first-person shooter games. Our augmented techniques were focused on pointing (i.e., the locations and directions of the visual effects were based on pointing directions); therefore, we did not use a visible view frustum [5,13,14] as it was a visualization that was based on the avatar's view direction instead of the pointing direction.

There are several possible configurations of these techniques (e.g., the thickness and colour of the laser, size and colour of the spotlight, colour of highlighting, and granularity of highlightable objects). The configurations used in the study were based on observations in pilot studies. For example, we decided to use large highlightable objects to provide a wider range of specificity among the techniques (and we note that any granularity choice will be either too large or too small for some referential tasks).

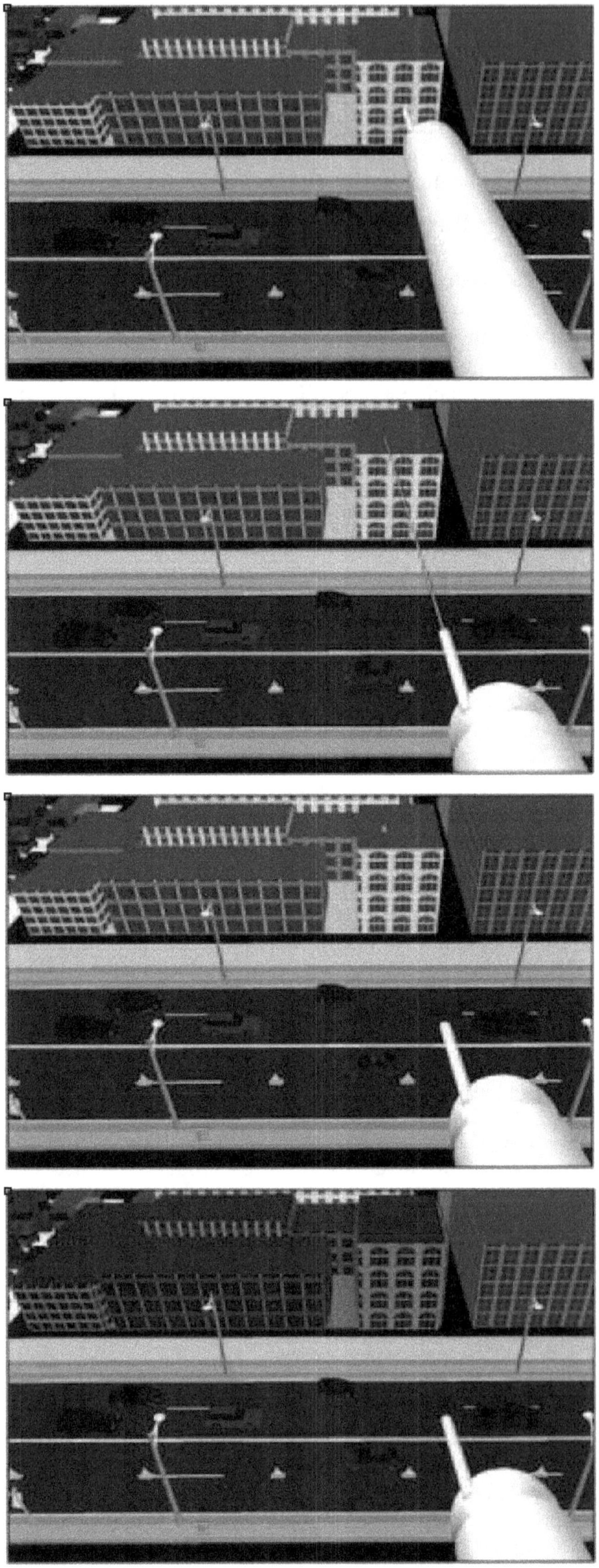

Figure 2. From top: long arm, laser beam, spotlight, highlight, all first-person view. (See color versions and video).

Participants, Procedure, and Tasks

We recruited 12 pairs (17 men and 7 women, ages 19-35) from nine different university departments. Participants sat at two computers (3m apart) at opposite ends of a room, facing outwards so they could only see their own displays, but close enough to talk to each other normally.

At the onset of each session, pairs were given time to learn all techniques and input methods until they felt comfortable using them. The pairs were then asked to work on a set of referencing tasks. In the tasks, one participant (the *gesturer*) was asked to indicate different referents in the scene to their partner (the *observer*). The gesturer chose a referent from each of five categories: large objects (e.g., buildings), small objects (e.g., cars), paths (e.g., the path from the building to the car), areas (e.g., a city block), and general directions (e.g., where the downtown area should expand next). The participants could talk to each other and use their avatars to communicate. There were 40 tasks in total: 5 categories x 2 input methods (mouse and Wiimote) x 2 displays (single and multiple monitors) x 2 roles (gesturer and observer). The participants were given the freedom to decide the order of categories, the referents within each category, and the pointing techniques to use. They were allowed to choose the technique that they thought would be the most suitable for the task and to change techniques at any time. The pairs switched roles for half of the tasks. Referencing tasks took approximately one minute each to complete.

Participants were then asked to work on three creative tasks. During the tasks, pairs collaboratively constructed stories and made decisions based on scenarios given to them. For example, participants were asked to pretend to be roommates and to look for an apartment together, taking into consideration issues such as type of neighborhood, distance to work sites, and traffic. These tasks involved referencing and pointing from both participants, and were open-ended with no defined solution. The participants decided who would use which display (one-monitor or three-monitor), and were allowed to use the input methods of their choice. Throughout all three tasks, participants could use any pointing techniques they wanted at any time, and could also switch between first- and third-person views at any time. Although tasks times varied widely, most pairs finished each creative task in less than five minutes.

At the end of the study, participants completed a questionnaire asking about their preferences for the different pointing techniques and view settings. An informal interview was then conducted asking participants both for general comments about the techniques, and for further details about specific episodes seen in the session. Overall, the session took approximately 90 minutes.

RESULTS AND OBSERVATIONS

Technique Preferences (Referencing Tasks)

In the first part of the study, participants used and saw each of the five pointing techniques for five different referencing tasks (large objects, small objects, paths, areas, and directions). At the end of each task type, participants were asked to rank preferences of techniques for that task. A summary of the mean ranks is shown in Figure 3. Note that because participants could choose the techniques to use, the techniques were not used with equal number of times.

The results showed some consistent trends, but with specific differences for particular tasks. In general, the laser was ranked first or second for all tasks, and first overall. The normal arm and the long arm were least preferred for all of the tasks that involved precise targets; for the Directions task, however, the long arm was seen as being second only to the laser beam. This task involved pointing 'in the air' rather than at a visible target, and so the techniques that need a tangible object to be seen (object highlighting and spotlight) were ranked worse; the arm-based techniques and the laser could effectively point even without a target object. Participant preferences also reflect the different specificity that is possible with each technique. The laser was the most precise, so worked well for small objects and paths, but could also be used for less-specific tasks such as areas or directions. In contrast, the object-highlight technique worked well for large objects, but poorly for small objects and paths, since these targets did not correspond well to the objects that could be highlighted. We discuss these issues further below.

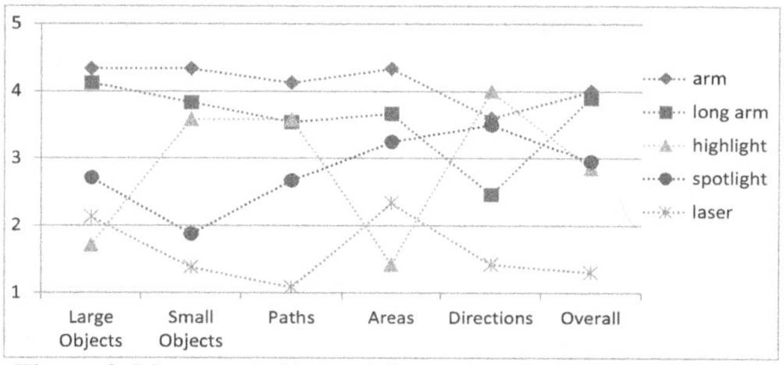

Figure 3. Mean rank (1=best) for each pointing technique, by type of target. (Note that lines are used for visual continuity).

Use of the Pointing Techniques (Creative Tasks)

In the second part of each session, participants were given an open-ended task and allowed to use whatever pointing techniques they wanted during their work. We recorded these tasks and later counted the uses of the different techniques. Table 1 summarizes these results.

Technique	Uses
Normal arm	20 uses (all objects)
Long arm	3 uses (2 objects, 1 direction)
Spotlight	11 uses (9 objects, 1 path, 1 no clear target)
Object highlight	17 uses (16 objects, 1 no clear target)
Laser	101 uses (85 objects, 7 paths, 1 area, 2 directions, 6 no clear target)

Table 1. Usage of pointing techniques in the free tasks.

The laser was by far the most popular technique in the free tasks, with almost twice as many uses as the other techniques combined; this result mirrors the preference data reported above. The primary use of all of the techniques was to indicate object referents, although there were a few instances of referring to paths and directions (and again, the laser was used more often for these). In the following sections, we present results related to our three main questions about wide views, augmented pointing techniques, and preparatory stages of pointing. The results were based on interaction analysis of study data that were collected via video analysis (over 15 hours total), notes taken during the study, questionnaires, and informal interviews. Overall, participants were consistently able to complete their tasks with relative ease.

Q1: View Preferences and Effects on Fragmentation

Our first fragmentation-based issue involves the ways that the CVE's view changes behavior and communication. Our CVE included two views that have not been studied before for collaborative referencing: a three-monitor display, and a third-person perspective. Both provided a wider view of pointing actions, and both appeared to be valuable as people carried out deictic pointing.

Twenty-three of the 24 participants reported on the survey that they preferred the three-monitor display. Many participants commented that it gave them a much better ability to see the actions of their partners as well as the referents – for example, one participant said "It was easier to see everything and determine where [the other person] was looking." The three-monitor display also changed the way that people used the CVE. People could look around without changing their view controls – this reduced the amount of view manipulation, but (as discussed below), the larger display and the increased number of visible objects also made attentional focus more of a problem.

Participants also regularly used both the first-person and the third-person views. In the interviews, people stated two main reasons for using the third-person view: it showed more of the scene, particularly in the one-monitor display, and it showed more of the avatar's arm, which gave better pointing feedback. Some participants used the first-person view for a 'zoom-in' effect; this was sometimes necessary because in the third-person view, the avatar occasionally occluded some objects (see below).

We observed several situations where the wider views allowed people to overcome view fragmentation (i.e., by being able see the pointing action and the referent without changing the view). The following example involving the third-person view is representative of these observations.

Fragment 1
M: I just wanna be sure that we're pointing to the same building.
K: yeah yeah understand.
M: ar (.) did you use Tab?
K: I'm I'm on the first person right now.
M: first person, so
K: Let me check where you're pointing at. (1.5) [switches to third person] Can you point at it?
M: Yeah of course (.) I'm (.) pointing to that building.

Mark wanted to confirm that he and Ken were both pointing at the same referent. However, at the beginning of the fragment, the pair did not have mutual orientation – Ken was using the first-person view and facing the buildings, and so he could not see Mark's avatar (Figure 4 top). Mark tried to understand what Ken was able to see, and said "did you use Tab?" to ask which perspective Ken was using (participants changed view perspective with the Tab key). Ken replied that he was in the first-person view, but switched to the third person (Figure 4 bottom) to better see Mark's pointing gesture ("Let me check where you're pointing at.")

Ken was focusing on the buildings, but he also wanted to look at where Mark was pointing, to better understand what the referent was. Instead of changing his view back and forth between Mark's avatar and the referent, Ken simply switched to the third-person view and was able to see all the relevant information. This shows that seeing the pointing activity from a third-person perspective can provide some of the information that is available when people have mutual orientation, alleviating some of the fragmentation problems seen in earlier studies [13].

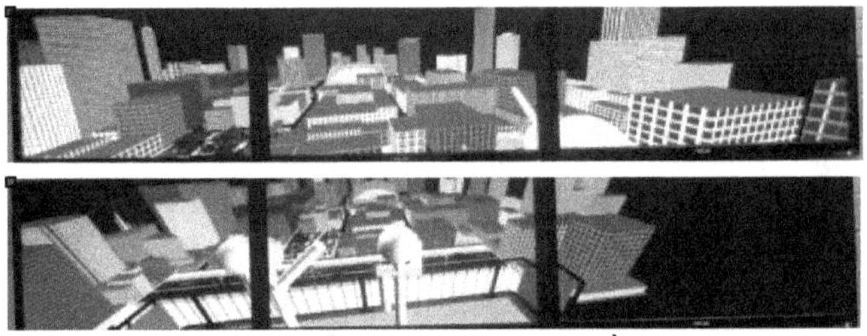

Figure 4. Ken's view: 1st-person (top) and 3rd-person (bottom).

Switching Between First-Person and Third-Person Views

While the third-person view was useful in reducing fragmented interaction, there were situations where the first-person view was more suitable. Participants used different viewing perspectives in different settings and situations. The first-person view was used more often with the three-monitor setup and the third-person view was the primary choice with the one-monitor setup. Also, participants tended to use the first-person view when they were producing gestures (rather than viewing them). The following fragment shows a typical example.

Fragment 2
D: That car::: (4) That car there (3.5) next to the pylon.
I: Okay.

Dora was using the one-monitor setup and the third-person view. She wanted to show Ivan a car on the freeway. After saying "That car:::", Dora tried to point at the car that was partially occluded by her avatar, but she had difficulty doing so (Figure 5A). She then changed the perspective to the first-person view and told Ivan "That car there." She then adjusted her view so that the car was in the center of the screen, pointed at it with the laser, and said "next to the pylon" (see Figure 5B).

Dora used the third-person view as her default viewing perspective allowing her to see more of the scene to compensate for the narrow FOV. However, in third-person view, her avatar blocked the middle of the scene. She spent a few seconds trying to point at a car that was partially occluded by her avatar, and then realized that the first-person view was the best perspective for the task. She switched to the first-person view so that she could clearly see and point to the car.

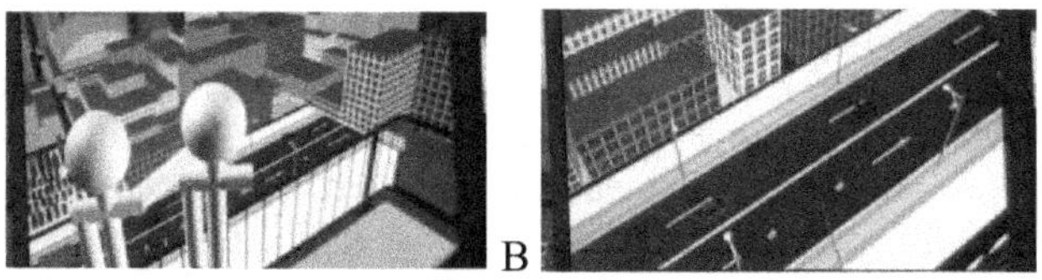

A B

Figure 5. Dora's view: 3rd-person (A) and 1st-person (B).

Awareness of Others' Viewing Perspectives

While being able to switch between first- and third-person views was useful in reducing fragmented interaction as shown above, there were also drawbacks introduced by this flexibility. Participants' actions were highly dependent on what their partners could see. Participants often made assumptions about the viewing perspectives their partners were using, but wrong assumptions could lead to confusion:

Fragment 3

T: Can you mo::ve to my position? And face yourself to the road. (5.5) If you face yourself to the road and (0.8) lower your camera view, you'll see two black cars on the road.
J: Two black cars?
T: The two black cars (0.6) on the left, on the opposite direction, there's a dark blue car
J: um::::::
T: Can you see that?
J: I can only see a black car.

Thomas wanted to show Joyce some cars. He pointed at the cars and helped Joyce finding the cars by giving her instructions ("mo::ve to my position", "face yourself to the road", and "lower your camera view"). Joyce followed his instructions, but still could not see the black cars he mentioned. Thomas then gave a further description, but without success. However, Thomas gave the instructions based on the assumption that Joyce was using the same view (first-person view) as he was, when in fact she was using the third-person view. In third-person view, Joyce's avatar was blocking her view of the objects being discussed (the black cars). Figure 6 shows what Joyce saw.

Figure 6. Joyce's avatar was blocking her own view.

Noticeability of Pointing on a Three-Monitor-Wide Display

We observed several situations where observers failed to notice an augmented pointing action – even with high-visibility techniques like the laser, and even with they were visible on the three-monitor display. For example:

Fragment 4

J: There's (0.5) a little yellow building (0.8) right in between (.) and behind these two buildings right across the street from us↑. Next in the little lot next to the parking lot. Have a yellow one (.) in the middle. You see it?
K: Yeah, I can see that.
J: Okay, and::: I guess the (.) one visible, the ground level room on the right that's actually (1.2). ( ) You can actually see more from your angle. Okay, we'll go ar:: ( ) top right. This little room right (.) he::re↑. This one on top floor. My laser pointing at it.
K: Which one? I actually can't.
J: hey, come over here and have a look.
K: Oh yeah there. I can see it.

Jason wanted to point out a room on the top floor of a yellow building. At the beginning of the fragment, after he said "There's (0.5)", he started to point at the building (on the right monitor of Kate's station; see Figure 7) with a laser beam, which was kept on for the whole fragment.

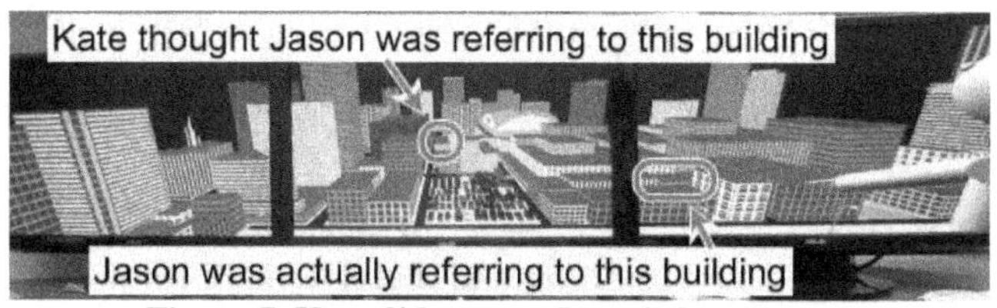

Figure 7. Kate did not see Jason's laser beam.

When Jason uttered "a little yellow building (0.8) right in between (.) and behind these two buildings right across the street from us↑", "in the little lot next to the parking lot", and "Have a yellow one (.) in the middle", Kate thought Jason was referring to another building with similar visual features (as shown in Figure 7, both buildings were in line with Jason's arm direction). Kate positioned her avatar and adjusted her view to center the mistaken building. She thought she knew the correct building until Jason said "My laser pointing at it." Kate then realized that she misunderstood ("Which one? I actually can't").

Although Jason was pointing at the building with a laser beam the whole time, Kate did not pay attention to it until he mentioned that his laser was pointing at the building. Kate commented at the end of the study that she was focusing on Jason's verbal descriptions and the mistaken referent; therefore, she did not see the laser beam and misunderstood the referent as a result. This episode shows that in a busy visual environment, it is not always easy to notice even a substantial augmentation such as the virtual laser. It is also notable that although the laser was only about 25cm from Kate's focus of attention, it was on a different monitor – it is possible that the 4cm visual gap of the monitor bezels made it more difficult to notice activity that was occurring on a different monitor.

Summary: Wider Field of View Reduces Fragmentation

Previous research has indicated the problems that occur when people's FOV is too narrow [5,13,14], and we saw several episodes that add to these findings. Our study is the first to explore the value of a wide display for referential communication in CVEs, and it was clear that wider views improved people's ability to coordinate activities in pointing-based communication. Furthermore, participants made frequent use of the third-person view, especially with the one-monitor setup, to compensate for the narrower display. Participant comments and our observations (e.g., Fragment 1) both indicate that wider FOVs help overcome some of the fragmentation problems seen in earlier work.

It is important to note, however, that while a wider FOV reduces the need to change the view between the gesture and the referent, this setup may actually provide less information about the observer's behavior. How pointing gestures are produced is largely based on the conduct of observers [5,13,14], and lack of such awareness can hinder communication. Information such as whether the observer is looking at the pointing gesture, the referent, or both (glancing between them) may not be shown (since there is no need to change the avatar's view). Similar issues could be seen in Fragment 3 where there was no visual feedback to indicate whether the observer was using a first-person or a third-person view.

While third-person views have the advantage of showing wider scenes on the screen, and multiple monitors provide extra screen real estate, these setups were not a complete solution. As seen in Fragment 2 and Figure 5A, although collaborators could see more objects, those objects were smaller and harder to see. Also, collaborators' own avatars occluded the middle of the screen, which was often the location of the referent. Although the three-monitor view was strongly preferred and provided a much wider FOV, we noted a few problems arising from the large number of objects shown on the screen, which may have made it harder to attend to important information (Fragment 4). Even a laser can be difficult to notice in a visually busy environment.

Q2: The Value of Augmented Pointing Techniques

The second fragmentation-based issue is about pointing techniques. We tested four augmented techniques (long arm, spotlight, laser, and object highlight; see Figure 2). Each technique had different characteristics that affected a deictic gesture's visibility, accuracy, and interpretation.

Feedback and Visibility

The different pointing techniques provided different types and amounts of feedback to the gesturer, changing the way that the technique was used. First, the default arms were difficult to see in the first-person view, and most participants switched to the third-person view when using this technique. Second, the spotlight did not provide strong visual feedback – the spot was small, could be hard to see when pointing at an oblique surface, and did not appear at all when pointing at the sky – and this caused some problems for participants (particularly in first-person view where the arm direction was not as visible).

The object highlight and the laser beam provided the most obvious feedback. The highlight was easy to see, although it could be difficult to determine whether objects were selectable or not (see below); in contrast, the laser beam was always visible and was seen as the easiest technique to position (as reflected from user preferences and the count of uses discussed earlier). However, as shown in Fragment 4, even the laser could be unnoticeable if the observer was not attending to the right area of the screen.

Perceived Accuracy and Specificity

There were substantial differences between the techniques in terms of accuracy and specificity. Participant preferences and comments indicated that they felt that the laser beam and the spotlight were the most specific, followed by the highlight, and then by the two arm-based techniques. Although the laser beam was considered the most specific based on participants' comments, it was not the most desirable technique in all situations. From our observations, it was clear that there was a strong relationship between the perceived accuracy of the different techniques and the size of the referent in the scene. For example, multiple participants commented that when referring to a small object or a precise location, they felt that the task was considerably easier with the laser or spotlight, and required less verbal description. For larger targets, however, participants also perceived other techniques as being accurate – for example, if the referent was a building, then the object-highlight technique was at exactly the right level of granularity. For indicating general directions, even the arm-based pointing techniques were seen as being sufficiently accurate.

Our observations also showed how people used techniques of different specificity for different-sized targets. In some cases, the participants operated the techniques much like they would in the real world. For example, when participants used a more-specific technique (like the laser beam) with a less-specific referent (e.g., an entire building or a general direction), they used verbal communication to broaden the scope of the referent (e.g., saying "this entire building") and moved the laser around the referent to avoid appearing to point to a more specific location. When people used a less-specific technique with a more-specific referent (e.g., the arm or the highlight to point to a single window in a building), they also used speech, but now to provide information that would allow the hearer to identify the specific referent. For example, when referring to a particular room, people would highlight the building and say "the leftmost room on the third floor of that building."

Issues with Augmented Techniques

Overall, participants preferred the augmented techniques to the two arm-based techniques (as seen in the technique ranking above), because of the increased specificity provided by the visual effects. These techniques, however, had issues regarding controls, visual clutter, and ownership. First, object highlighting was seen as more difficult to control than all other augmented techniques because it only worked with pre-defined objects. In a few cases, when participants did not see the highlight effect, they did not know whether they had missed with their pointing action, or whether the object was not selectable. Other participants found that this technique was hard to use because of its discrete movement (i.e., jumping from object to object).

The spotlight, laser, and highlighting provoked some discussion about the degree of visual clutter that would be produced if there were several people in the CVE. Several participants mentioned that it would be more difficult to identify referents if there were several lasers visible in the scene – and that the clutter would be worse with the larger-scale highlighting technique.

A problem related to that of visual clutter is determining who owns the visual effect of an augmented technique. This caused problems in several tasks, particularly when participants used the spotlight and highlight techniques simultaneously (which occurred frequently during the open-ended tasks). One way to help identify ownership is to use different colours. However, this may introduce mapping problem (i.e., which colour belongs to whom) that can be severe when there are several users in the CVE. Determining ownership was seen by participants as a main strength of the laser, because it always visually connected the gesturer and the referent.

Summary: Preference for Techniques with Varying Specificity
Referencing in CVEs has been shown to be an important and challenging problem [6,14,21,24,25], and augmented pointing techniques have been developed to address these problems [5,14]. In our study, where we tested different kinds of augmentation, people generally preferred the laser beam, primarily because of the added specificity and connection between the gesturer and the referent. However, while the laser was the most specific, could connect the referents to the gesturer, and was highly visible, it was not desirable for all referential tasks because the laser could be over-specific in some situations.

Different referents had different specificity requirements. Typically, participants preferred to point at less-specific referents with less-specific techniques (e.g., point at a general direction with a arm-based technique), and vice versa. As seen in the study, when there was a mismatch of specificity between techniques and referents, more verbal communication was needed to guide collaborators to the object of interest. Indicating referents with techniques of matching specificity could reduce the effort of providing complex verbal descriptions. Overall, participants stated that they preferred to have multiple techniques available, so that they could match the technique to the specificity requirements of the task.

Q3: Use of the Preparatory Stages of Pointing
Augmented pointing techniques are much more visible, and in some cases, much more specific than pointing with just the avatar's arm. These changes suggest the possibility that the communication problems identified in earlier work (e.g., related to mutual orientation or fragmentation) will be fully addressed through the additional visual information, and that users of a CVE will be freed from careful attention to the preparatory actions that are important elements of real-world referential communication.

Our observations, however, indicate that although augmented pointing techniques can improve certain elements of communication, they do not remove the need to support other aspects of the pointing process. In particular, our study showed that even when augmentations were present, people still failed to notice or see some pointing gestures (as discussed above); furthermore, it was clear that people still used the avatar's body and arm as a way to orient themselves to upcoming augmented pointing actions.

We observed several episodes where participants appeared to gather information from the other person's avatar as a way to orient themselves to an upcoming pointing action, even when the gesturer was using augmented pointing. After seeing these episodes in the first five pairs, we added a questionnaire question for the final seven pairs asking whether people looked at the other person's avatar during pointing. All of the participants replied that they did use the other person's avatar location and orientation, even when augmented pointing techniques were being used. For example, the next fragment shows one participant using the gesturer's viewing direction and arm direction to help determine where to look in the scene (see Figure 8 and 9).

Fragment 5
M: That's the room.
K: Okay.
M: Ah:::: the car:: (19) ah::: in the parking lot.
K: Okay let me come over there.

Figure 8. Ken's view showing Mark (left monitor) and cars.

Figure 9. Ken focused on Mark's laser beam (left monitor).

In this fragment, Mark had just finished showing Ken a room in an apartment building with the laser beam. Ken confirmed that he knew which room Mark was pointing at ("okay"). Right after this confirmation, Mark turned off the laser and moved to the left of the balcony. As he was moving, he started to consider which car he wanted to show Ken next ("Ah:::: the car::"). Mark took several seconds to decide, and during that time, Ken turned his avatar towards Mark's, adjusting his viewing angle so that he could see both Mark's avatar and the cars (Figure 8). Once Mark made his decision, he turned the laser beam on and said "ah::: in the parking lot." Ken immediately moved his avatar beside Mark's, such that he only saw the laser beam on his screen, not Mark's avatar (Figure 9).Knowing that Mark would use the laser beam to indicate a car, Ken could have oriented his avatar towards only the cars and waited for the laser beam to appear. However, Ken instead began by paying close attention to Mark's avatar: Ken changed his view to keep track of Mark's avatar orientation and arm direction. Before Mark turned the laser beam on and said "ah::: in the parking lot," Ken already knew roughly where the referent would be (because he could see Mark's arm) and was able to quickly respond to the pointing gesture.

Once the area of the referent was established and the laser was switched on, however, it is notable that Ken moved to a location where he could no longer see Mark's avatar or arm. Once the general orientation is determined, the laser beam provides accurate information about the referent; the observer no longer needs the avatar orientation information, and can focus their view on the target region.

Summary: the Importance of Staging Actions

While augmented pointing techniques helped referencing in many situations, it was clear that these techniques do not solve the entire problem – they are not a replacement for the context provided by staging actions (such as avatar position, direction, and arm movement), or for the disambiguation capabilities of speech. All these communication channels remained critical to the success of collaboration. Collaborators relied on different resources at different stages of referencing conduct. Before the onset of pointing actions, observers paid close attention to the locations and orientations of gesturers. When the gesturer started to point, the arm direction gave additional information about the direction of the referent, and observers often adjusted their views so that they could see both the arm and the potential referent. Once the gesturer activated a technique, observers would often change their view to focus more closely on the visual effects.

Augmented pointing definitely improved the referencing process by providing additional information. Gesturers used the techniques to precisely indicate referents, and the visual effects helped observers locate what gesturers wanted to show. However, most of the benefit of using augmented pointing came at the later stages of referencing. Observers still needed to pay attention to the avatar's body orientation and arm direction at the earlier stages of pointing, suggesting that augmented pointing will not entirely replace the need to support these other aspects of pointing behaviour. Furthermore, collaborators still needed to talk to each other even when they were using augmented pointing: the techniques helped simplify verbal descriptions, but collaborators still relied heavily on speech.

DESIGN IMPLICATIONS

There are five main lessons that designers of CVEs can make use of as they develop support for deictic pointing:

- *Free arm movement.* People paid a surprising amount of attention to avatar arm movements, even when augmented pointing techniques were used. Being able to move the arm provided a staging action that helped collaborators predict the general direction of a referent. Having the arm indicate direction as well as the augmentation simplified verbal descriptions of referents. Free arm movement would be beneficial in commercial CVEs, such as World of Warcraft, that currently only support predefined arm movements (with activation commands like '/point').
- *Large field of view.* All but one participant preferred using the three-monitor to the one-monitor setup, and all made frequent use of the third-person view. A larger FOV and more screen real estate greatly helped collaborators stay aware of each other's actions, knowledge that was crucial to smooth communication. Multiple-monitor support has been increasingly common in commercial CVEs (e.g., Far Cry 3) in recent years, underscoring the value of a large FOV.
- *Augmented techniques with varying specificity.* Augmented techniques that add visual aids were shown to be useful, especially when their specificity matches with the referents. Providing techniques with a wide range of specificity helps reduce complex verbal references. For example, asking someone in a CVE to put a book back to a bookshelf, one can simply say "put that [highlight the book] there [point at a specific location on the bookshelf with a laser beam]" instead of "put the book back to the second shelf from the top and put it in between the seventh and the eighth books from the left".
- *Clear connection between the gesturer and the referent.* A main reason for the laser's success was that it linked the gesturer and referent. The explicit connection made referents easier to identify, and reduced the problem of determining which beam belonged to which participant. This is particularly important in CVEs with many users, such as massively multiplayer online games.
- *View awareness.* There were several episodes where confusion occurred because collaborators did not know what the other person could see. Many commercial CVEs (e.g., Second Life) support both 1st- and 3rd-person view but without appropriate indications to other users. Providing an indication of the other person's view (1st- or 3rd-person) could avoid some communication errors.

Overall, our study suggests that if designers want to support deictic pointing in CVEs, the best set of techniques will be a combination of free-arm pointing for context and staging, and different visual aids with varying specificity. In addition, wide displays and third-person views should be provided to increase the visibility and interpretability of staging actions.

CONCLUSION

Deictic referencing in CVEs is far more difficult than in the real world. One main reason is that interactions in CVEs are often fragmented, causing severe communication problems.

Numerous techniques have been proposed to alleviate this problem, and CVE technology has much advanced since problems of fragmentation were first reported. In order to determine whether pointing-support techniques and the technical advances of the past fifteen years have solved these problems, we conducted an observational study looking at how pairs of participants carried out referencing tasks with a variety of view types and augmented pointing techniques. We found that a wide FOV and precise pointing techniques help reduce fragmented interaction. However, these highly-precise pointing techniques may not be suitable for all referential tasks and do not remove the need for visible staging actions such as avatar orientation and arm movement.

Our observations provide a new level of detail for designers who wish to support deictic communication in CVEs. Although we are able to make recommendations that designers can take up immediately, there are also several ways in which our work can be broadened and generalized in future studies. First, we will explore the problem of visual clutter and effect ownership in CVEs with more users. Second, we will explore visualizations that may be able to improve view awareness and reduce errors that are based on incorrect assumptions about what others can see. Third, we will explore issues related to highlight granularity, and investigate how users can adjust granularity to suit the referent without compromising other controls.

ACKNOWLEDGMENTS

This work was supported by the Natural Sciences and Engineering Research Council of Canada, and by the GRAND Network of Centres of Excellence.

REFERENCES

1. Bekker, M., Olson, J., Olson, G. Analysis of gestures in face-to-face design teams provides guidance for how to use groupware in design. *Proc. DIS,* 1995, 157–166.
2. Benford, S., Bowers, J., Fahlén, L.E., Greenhalgh, C., Snowdon, D. User embodiment in collaborative virtual environments. *Proc. CHI*, 1995, 242-249.
3. Bowers, J., Pycock, J., O'Brien, J. Talk and embodiment in CVEs. *Proc. CHI*, 1996, 58-65.
4. Ducheneaut, N., Wen, M.-H., Yee, N., Wadley, G. Body and mind: a study of avatar personalization in three virtual worlds. *Proc. CHI*, 2009, 1151-1160.
5. Fraser, M., Benford, S., Hindmarsh, J., Heath, C. Supporting awareness and interaction through collaborative virtual interfaces. *Proc. UIST* 1999, 27-36.
6. Fraser, M., Benford, S. Interaction effects of virtual structures. *Proc. CVE*, 2002, 128-134.
7. Goodwin, C., Goodwin, M. Seeing as a situated activity: Formulating planes. In Y. Engeström and D. Middleton, eds., *Cognition and Communication at Work.* Cambridge University Press, 1996, 61-95.
8. Goodwin, C. Action and embodiment within situated human interaction. *J. Prag.* 32, 10, 2000, 1489-1522.
9. Goodwin, C. Pointing as situated practice. In S. Kita, ed., *Pointing: Where language, culture and cognition meet.* Psychology Press, 2003, 217-241.
10. Greenberg, S., Gutwin, C., Roseman, M. Semantic telepointers for groupware. *Proc. OzCHI*, 1996, 54-61.
11. Gutwin, C., Penner, R. Improving interpretation of remote gestures with telepointer traces. *Proc. CSCW*, 2002, 49-57.
12. Heath, C., Hindmarsh, J. Configuring Action in Objects: From Mutual Space to Media Space. *Mind, Culture, and Activity 7*, 1, 2000, 81-104.
13. Hindmarsh, J., Fraser, M., Heath, C., Benford, S., and Greenhalgh, C. Fragmented interaction: establishing mutual orientation in virtual environments. *Proc. CSCW*, 1998, 217–226.
14. Hindmarsh, J., Fraser, M., Heath, C., Benford, S., Object-focused interaction in collaborative virtual environments. *ToCHI 7*, 4, 2000, 477-509.
15. Hindmarsh, J., Heath, C. Embodied reference: A study of deixis in workplace interaction. *Journal of Pragmatics 32*, 12, 2000, 1855-1878.
16. Kirk, D., Rodden, T., Fraser, D.S. Turn it <u>this</u> way: grounding collaborative action with remote gestures. *Proc. CHI*, 2007, 1039-1048.
17. Krauss, R.M., Fussell, S.R. Mutual knowledge and communicative effectiveness. In *Intellectual teamwork: social and technological foundations of cooperative work.* L. Erlbaum Associates Inc., 1990, 111–145.
18. Luff, P., Heath, C., Kuzuoka, H., Yamazaki, K., Yamashita, J. Handling documents and discriminating objects in hybrid spaces. *Proc. CHI*, 2006, 561-570.
19. Luff, P., Yamashita, N., Kuzuoka, H., Heath, C. Hands on hitchcock: embodied reference to a moving scene. *Proc. CHI*, 2011, 43–52.
20. McNeill, D. *Hand and mind.* Univ. Chicago. 1992.
21. Moore, R.J., Ducheneaut, N., Nickell, E. Doing Virtually Nothing: Awareness and Accountability in Massively Multiplayer Online Worlds. *Proc. CSCW*, 2007, 265-305.
22. Tang, J.C. Findings from observational studies of collaborative work. In *International Journal of Man Machine Studies.* Academic Press Ltd., 1991, 11–28.
23. Tang, J.C., Minneman, S. VideoWhiteboard: video shadows to support remote collaboration. *Proc. CHI*, 1991, 315-322.
24. Wong, N., Gutwin, C. Where are you pointing? the accuracy of deictic pointing in CVEs. *Proc. CHI*, 2010, 1029-1038.
25. Wong, N. and Gutwin, C. Controlling an Avatar's Pointing Gestures in Desktop Collaborative Virtual Environments. *Proc. Group*, 2012, 21–30.

Photoportals: Shared References in Space and Time

André Kunert Alexander Kulik Stephan Beck Bernd Froehlich

Bauhaus-Universität Weimar
Bauhausstrasse 11, 99423 Weimar, Germany
<first name>.<last name>@uni-weimar.de

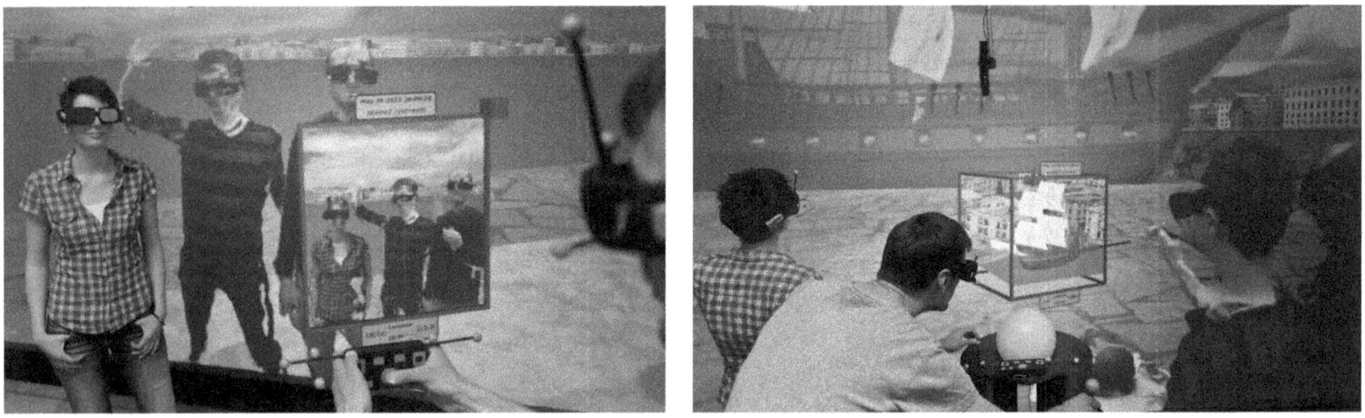

Figure 1. Collaborative interaction with Photoportals. Left: A user takes a virtual photo of a local and two remote collaborators in a virtual city model. Note that the local user (standing on the left) also appears in the virtual photo. Right: Two local users (on the left side) share a box-shaped Photoportal with two remote collaborators (on the right side). A remote user operates a virtual pointer inside the portal to manipulate the ship model in the background at a convenient scale and distance while the other users provide guidance from their individual viewpoints.

ABSTRACT

Photoportals build on digital photography as a unifying metaphor for reference-based interaction in 3D virtual environments. Virtual photos and videos serve as three-dimensional references to objects, places, moments in time and activities of users. Our Photoportals also provide access to intermediate or alternative versions of a scenario and allow the review of recorded task sequences that include life-size representations of the captured users.

We propose to exploit such references to structure collaborative activities of collocated and remote users. Photoportals offer additional access points for multiple users and encourage mutual support through the preparation and provision of references for manipulation and navigation tasks. They support the pattern of territoriality with configurable space representations that can be used for private interaction, as well as be shared and exchanged with others.

Author Keywords

Interactive Systems; Multi-User Interaction; Collaborative Virtual Environments; 3D Interaction; 3D User Interfaces

CSCW'14, February 15–19, 2014, Baltimore, Maryland, USA.

ACM 978-1-4503-2540-0/14/02...$15.00.
http://dx.doi.org/10.1145/2531602.2531727

ACM Classification Keywords

H.5.2 Information interfaces and presentation: User Interfaces

INTRODUCTION

Virtual reality allows the exploration of simulated places and objects as if they exist in real space and real time. Many 3D interaction techniques are correspondingly based on the experiences and skills we have acquired in the real world – with the restriction that the displayed objects cannot be touched and felt with bare hands. Instead, mediating tools and references are used to manipulate the virtual matter.

We suggest photography as a unifying metaphor for reference-based interaction techniques. We have learned to use photos as visual representations of places, objects and moments in time and to exchange these with others. In this sense, photography allows the appropriation of inaccessible objects and locations for review and presentations. Photos also capture viewpoints and serve as mnemonics for relations and past experiences. Scaling is an implicit parameter of the recording process. Scenes captured with contemporary digital cameras can be instantly reviewed on the built-in screen.

Our virtual photos capture scenes and actions not just as images, but in 3D and, therefore, they become portals to remote locations or alternate realities which can be entered or manipulated at any time. Our virtual camera also supports the recording and playback of 3D videos that involves animated objects, as well as actions and body representations of local and remote users (Figure 1 left). We show how this metaphor of virtual photography supports a multitude of reference-based 3D interaction techniques while maintaining the direct manipulation paradigm on the basis of a congruent input-output space.

The work presented in this paper is a first approach to provide groups of collocated and remote users acting in a truly shared 3D space with advanced collaborative tools and techniques. The main contributions of our work are:

- A novel interface concept that builds on the metaphor of digital photography for the immediate creation and the management of sharable references in space and time.
- A coherent set of interaction techniques that exploit scene references for efficient collaboration in shared virtual environments.
- A user study demonstrating the usability of Photoportals.

We designed a powerful mixed-reality system to explore the future of local and remote 3D collaboration in immersive virtual environments. We argue that reference-based interaction techniques are an important tool in such systems since they support territoriality, exchange of information and complementary activities of users. Our Photoportals demonstrate the applicability of this interface concept to address the challenges of interaction in 3D collaborative systems.

DESIGN CHALLENGES OF COLLABORATIVE SYSTEMS

Mutual awareness of participating users and their actions is a primary requirement of collaborative user interfaces. Gutwin and Greenberg defined workspace awareness as the "up-to-the moment understanding of another person's interaction with the shared workspace" and emphasized its three main elements: 1. the presence, identity and authorship of participants (who), 2. the involved artifacts, actions and intentions (what) and 3. the location, gaze, view and reach of users (where) [18]. The framework also considers the history of artifacts and events (how and when). They noted that the ease of people maintaining workspace awareness in real-world collaborative settings is based on the continuous gathering of this information through consequential communication (the observation of each other's activity), feedthrough (the sensory perception of involved artifacts) and intentional communication (verbal and gesturing).

In collocated settings, real-world workspace awareness can directly be exploited for computer-supported collaborative work. Multi-touch tabletops, for example, provide such a shared space for joint interaction with 2D data. More elaborated technologies are required for multi-user 3D applications, as the appearance of 3D geometries depends on the users' individual viewing perspectives. In 1997 Agrawala et al. presented the two-user responsive workbench [1], the first 3D display system that supported more than one user. Since then, various alternative approaches and improvements have been proposed (e.g. [3, 37, 23, 16, 26]).

In the realm of distributed collaborative systems, workspace awareness is often limited by low bandwidth and several explicit notification options have been proposed [11, 10]. Novel sensor technology and increasing network bandwidth, however, promote the introduction of high-fidelity telepresence systems that support whole-body 3D capturing and reconstruction of remote participants in real time [15, 28, 5]. The quality of remote user representations is not yet perfect and factors such as noise, missing data and latency clearly affect usability but, like in collocated settings, the systems already offer similar levels of workspace awareness. They create a seamlessly shared 3D interaction space for users at different physical locations.

The high level of workspace awareness provided in collocated and tightly coupled distributed settings supports the coordinated interaction of multiple users. However, conflicts still occur, specifically if users try to manipulate the same virtual objects simultaneously [30, 35, 22, 33]. Grossman and Balakrishnan [16] suggested the locking of manipulated objects while highlighting which user is operating on it. Riege et al. instead proposed merging the input of multiple users and visualizing the simultaneously-induced forces [35]. In both cases, only a mapping for the conflicting input is suggested. The actual conflict is not prevented.

The design space of combining the input from multiple users received particular interest. Distributing degrees of freedom among participants, for example, can enforce the users' cooperation [8, 34]. However, Pinho et al. also found that this approach negatively affected the comprehensibility of the interface [34]. Ruddle showed that merging the input from different users is likely to increase the cooperation overhead [36].

Instead of enforcing joint efforts, Benford et al. suggested encouraging collaboration with complementary tools that can be combined for additional functionalities [6]. We followed this example of complementary interfaces. Photoportals can be used to prepare location references for the manipulation input of other participants or as targets for group navigation.

Scott et al. observed the pattern of territoriality in collocated collaboration. It refers to the common behavior of individuals in a group to establish three distinct interaction areas: personal, group and storage territories [38]. Supporting this user behavior can reduce input interferences [43]. Several implementations of the concept have later been reported in the context of collaborative tabletop applications. They generally divide the screen space into individual areas (e.g. [24]). Grossman and Balakrishnan applied this approach to multi-user interaction with a volumetric display [16]. Alternatively, additional displays have been proposed for private views of details or independent content manipulation [42, 29, 39].

We adopted the pattern of territoriality. Our Photoportals support the ad-hoc creation of configurable spacelets that can be used as private or storage spaces. Users can instantly create secondary scene representation and use them for the individual examination of objects and locations from various perspectives. Manipulation conflicts are effectively prevented, as this does not affect the shared scene. If users actually want to change the configuration of the shared scene, they can apply their manipulations in individual Photoportal versions, compare their proposals and enter the one they agree on.

Avoid Input Interference	Exploit Simultaneous Input	Avoid Fragmented Visibility	Exploit Multiple Views	Avoid Unexpected Motion	Exploit Collaborative Planning
Known Techniques					
• Object locking [16] • Explicit notifications [10, 16]	• Input merging [8, 35, 36, 34] • Territoriality [16, 38, 43, 24, 42, 29, 39] • Complementary input [6]	• Extended field of view [20] • Show Through [2]	• Specialized views [1]	• Shared control [26] • Augmented group navigation [26]	• Shared WIM [5]
Novel Strategies for Collaboration Support as Provided by Reference-Based Interaction with Photoportals					
Secondary scene representations reduce demand for object manipulation.	Mutual interaction support with location references.	Perspective sharing reveals invisible fragments of the shared environment.	Individual manipulation of viewing parameters in privately used Photoportals.	Group transit through portals reduces demand for steering-based navigation.	Rapid creation and management of shared WIMs and previews of target locations.

Table 1. Several major challenges of collaborative 3D environments (in columns) have been addressed in prior work. Our Photoportals add a range of alternative strategies that exploit the concept of shareable references for collaborative interaction.

The design of collaborative 3D user interfaces involves further challenges that relate to 3D viewing perspectives and group navigation. A surrounding 3D environment cannot be overseen completely and the appearance of 3D objects depends on the viewing perspective. As a result, each user only sees fragments of a shared 3D scene at a time. Hindmarsh et al. addressed this fragmented visibility problem for the case of individually navigating users in a distributed virtual reality system. They suggested extended peripheral vision and exaggerated representations of other users' actions to improve the perception of remote participants [20]. Another type of fragmented visibility is interpersonal occlusion. Geometric features may be hidden behind other geometry from several perspectives. Argelaguet et al. suggested tackling this problem with cut-away visualizations that let indicated features show through occluding parts of the shared scene [2]. Note that both techniques imply a distorted perception of the scene which can be highly detrimental, e.g. if the evaluation of geometric properties is purposed.

We suggest an alternative approach to resolve fragmented visibility that preserves the appearance of the scene. Objects and locations that cannot directly be seen by everybody can be captured in a Photoportal and shown to everybody else. Geometry clipping at the surface of the virtual photos implicitly enables cut-away views towards occluded geometry.

Exploring a 3D virtual world requires navigation during which the visual and the vestibular perceptual systems perceive contrary motion signals: visual motion flow without physical acceleration. This perceptual conflict may induce cybersickness, even more so if the virtual motion is not expected. Input for group navigation should thus be observable by all involved users and they should be allowed to interfere easily if they do not agree. Kulik et al. suggested a large stationary device to increase mutual awareness of group-related input. They also developed a set of augmented group navigation techniques that avoid collisions of individual users with the virtual environment – at the price of temporarily giving up the notion of a shared 3D space [26].

By using Photoportals, the demand for group locomotion can be drastically reduced. Individual users can prepare a location reference to a new travel target and then invite the whole group to enter this place directly, using the photo as a portal.

Our design process was inspired by the tangible interaction framework of Hornecker and Buur [21]. Following their guidelines, our interaction techniques build on direct haptic manipulation with isomorphic mappings and enable lightweight interaction in experimental steps (Tangible Manipulation). As demanded by their concept of Spatial Manipulation, we ensure a consistent space among users and interactive objects in which the movement of objects and the users' bodies has a comprehensible meaning. While the effects of individual perspectives in 3D environments imply the problem of fragmented visibility, our Photoportals provide simple ways to solve it. The operation of our interface elements generally involves the whole body in action. With a set of complementary interfaces that include one or many Photoportals, we provide multiple access points to engage users in the collaboration (Embodied Facilitation). In the sense of preparing and exchanging scene references for further interaction, Photoportals also support the externalization of ideas and provide unambiguous references for the communication and collaboration (Expressive Representation).

Reference-based interaction techniques have rarely been applied to solve design challenges of collaborative systems. Beck et al. suggested a shared World in Miniature for collaborative tour planning, but did not consider further usage scenarios [5]. Spindler et al. suggested Tangible Windows as private views towards a shared 3D scene [39]. Their design builds on the concept of handheld magic lenses [7] and extends it with techniques for object manipulation and navigation. They also mentioned the advantage of private views for parallel interaction of multiple users, but no particular workflow of collaborative interaction was outlined in their paper. We show how the concept of secondary scene representations can minimize common collaboration obstacles including fragmented visibility and the coordination of manipulation and navigation.

REFERENCE-BASED 3D USER INTERFACES

Photoportals are visual references to captured objects and locations in a shared 3D environment. While this concept is new in the realm of collaboration support, similar reference-based interaction techniques are successfully used for manipulating virtual objects that are out of reach: A reference to a distant part of the scene held in one hand provides a reference for input from the other hand.

Such bi-manual interaction also leverages the benefits of proprioceptive cues [17]. Voodoo Dolls, for example, provide the user with an additional miniature representation of selected objects [32]; a World in Miniature (WIM) can represent the whole virtual environment on a smaller scale [40]. WIMs are often used to visually support wayfinding. Several extensions have been proposed to the technique, including scaling and scrolling [44] and a navigation technique that flies the user into selected locations of the handheld miniature [31].

Hinckley et al. suggested physically graspable props as reference objects [19]. If the prop's physical shape fits into the human hand, users can take advantage of their manual dexterity. The necessary dislocation of visual space and motor space, however, may be detrimental. We aimed for a novel interaction technique that combines the advantages of physical grasping and a congruent input-output space.

Stoev and Schmalstieg suggested building on the paradigm of magic lenses for reference-based interaction [41]. They proposed virtual lenses that show parts of the scene from a different viewpoint and defined a set of corresponding "through-the-lens" interaction techniques. Several of them, including pick ray manipulation at the remote location and virtual travel "through the lens," were similar to corresponding techniques of our Photoportals. Our work builds on this example and extends it with additional viewing modes and a refined user interface for collaborative settings.

The concept of interconnecting different virtual locations is also known as "locales" that can be assembled to virtual environments of potentially unlimited size [4]. Greenhalgh et al. extended this concept with temporal links that capture sequences of user activity [13, 12]. They explored various application scenarios for this functionality, including the intuitive authoring of dynamic 3D content and the post-hoc evaluation of user interaction. They also proposed several manifestations of temporal links mostly corresponding to the requirements of digital storytelling. Most comparable to our sequence recordings with Photoportals is Holovid, a WIM-like scene representation that includes captured motion sequences. Other than temporal links in the distributed system MASSIVE-3 [14], our Photoportals support the recording of temporal sequences that include life-sized 3D video avatars of local and remote participants. Our tangible camera interface furthermore enables inexperienced users to operate the recording and manage several of them in a virtual gallery.

Technically, our Photoportals are most closely related to the pioneering work of Stoev and Schmalstieg [41], but our implementation in the context of collaborative virtual reality goes beyond their original proposal. We created a novel tangible interface for the immediate creation and management of scene references that corresponds to the familiar functionality of digital cameras. The resulting ease of use enables the application of Photoportals in collaborative settings with naive users. Furthermore, our Photoportals incorporate other successful concepts from prior research into a unifying interface. This includes all of the above mentioned extensions to WIM-like scene representations.

The immediate creation of secondary scene representations can be compared to that of Voodoo Dolls, but instead of a grasping gesture in screen space, our interface exploits the metaphor of digital photography. This novel approach directly supports adaptations of the capturing process to create specialized representations for different use cases, as well as the management of multiple scene representations in a virtual gallery. Our tangible camera interface facilitates the handling and the exchange of Photoportals.

MULTI-USER INTERACTION IN VIRTUAL ENVIRONMENTS

We developed and tested our interaction techniques with a state-of-the-art immersive telecollaboration system that connects two multi-user 3D power walls. The participants in front of each display are captured using color-and-depth cameras. The resulting color- and depth-image streams are transferred to the other location where real-time 3D video representations of remote users are shown [5]. For a group of colocated users, each user can independently walk in front of the screen, but navigation through the environment is always performed for the entire group [26]. Otherwise, the consistency of the shared virtual environment cannot be preserved. We coupled virtual locomotion for the whole group and limited its control to input from a single group navigation device (Spheron) that is purposefully large in order to increase awareness and its accessibility for everybody in the group (Figure 1 right). The six degree-of-freedom device consists of a large 3D trackball and a separate joystick-type handle for 3D translational input. Its operation requires comparably large movements that are visible to all group members.

Both groups use a multi-user 3D power wall display with a resolution of 1920 by 1200 pixels. The larger display measures 4.3 by 2.7 meters screen size and provides stereoscopic image pairs for up to six users [26]. The smaller one supports only two users with a screen size of 3 by 2 meters.

The setup generally provides high workspace awareness – at least as long as the remote group is visible within the boundaries of the screen and the participants' actions correspond to the real-world, as in direct walking and bare-handed gesturing. As soon as augmented, non-isomorphic interaction techniques are involved, it becomes much more difficult to maintain awareness of each other's actions. However, interaction with virtual objects requires a certain level of abstraction, as the data cannot be grasped directly. Therefore, we focused our efforts on the design of interfaces and interaction techniques that support the mutual understanding of "magic" techniques like teleporting, remote manipulation or scaling.

The pick ray is a common solution for interaction with virtual objects. We also provide this basic technique, but not to everybody simultaneously. We experienced conflicts of users that try to operate on the same object. In a first attempt to increase the group's coordination, we limited direct manipulation to the selection of a virtual reference point on a geometry. The whole scene could then be rotated around this point using the 3D trackball of the Spheron device as a physical reference. The manipulation of individual objects required indirect input that was operated with motion input relative to the 3D trackball. The technique prevented input conflicts, but only at the price of inhibiting simultaneous input. Moreover, the dislocation of physical input and visual output was confusing for many users.

One of the main motivations for object manipulation is the desire for their examination from various perspectives. An unintentional side effect often is the change of the object placement relative to the surrounding scene. The demand for object manipulation can thus be reduced if users can easily view objects from every angle without actually moving them. The scene rotation around a selected reference point, as described above, provides such functionality, but only for the whole group. If someone wants to explore a particular detail, not everybody else will share this interest. Collaborating users often prefer to divide their focus temporarily in order to explore various aspects of a shared context and then exchange their findings. Consequently, we aimed to create an interaction technique that allows individual examination of different scene details and promotes immediate sharing of gathered perspectives without disturbing anybody or compromising the coherence of the shared virtual environment.

Secondary scene representations such as a WIM or Voodoo Dolls allow users to virtually get hold of some part of the virtual environment and observe it from all sides while the original scene remains unchanged. Providing users with such references can thus be very useful – if their creation and handling can be done without hassle. Successful collaboration support with a shared WIM has been shown earlier [5]; the rapid creation of a WIM with dedicated parameters, has not been considered so far. Voodoo Dolls can be created rapidly with a grasping gesture in screen space but, as a result of this gesture-based creation, the doll is attached to the user's pinched fingers and vanishes if the fingers are released. This complicates their handling; in particular, rotation beyond the range of the wrist and sharing between multiple people.

We propose the metaphor of digital photography for the immediate creation of secondary scene representations to which we refer as virtual photos or Photoportals. In correspondence to actual photography, snapshots can be made instantly and the capturing device provides a physical handle to the resulting virtual photo. Moreover, as known from photographic cameras, various controls enable the parameterization of the capturing process for different use cases and facilitate the management of multiple virtual photos in a gallery.

PHOTOPORTALS

Photoportals combine the capabilities of reference-based interaction techniques in a consistent user interface that builds on the metaphor of photography. It consists of a tracked tangible camera prop with a set of physical buttons and a virtual display through which the captured scene can be perceived. Users can take virtual photos or record a video of anything they find interesting in the scene. These virtual photos or videos are not just images like their real-world counterparts, but they can be augmented with powerful features and functionalities. We exploit the following four elements of photos for the interaction with virtual environments: 1. a frame that contains the captured scene, 2. a focused object or location of interest, 3. the camera viewpoint, and 4. recording time.

Once a view has been recorded, the respective scene features can be individually examined without necessarily involving the whole group. If interesting aspects shall be discussed, they can easily be shown to others. A collection of successively taken photos shows parts of the virtual environment that are currently not visible. During an architectural walkthrough, for example, users can take photos of details and perspectives they want to discuss with others – now or later. This approach corresponds to groups exploring real environments and it helps with structuring the collaborative review process. It is even more attractive in virtual environments. Our virtual photos are essentially portals and thus provide shortcuts to the captured locations. Consequently, we dubbed our mixed-reality interface Photoportals.

The most fundamental implementation of Photoportals is a monoscopic projection of the scene on the virtual screen of our device. This 2D viewing mode is most effective if a particular vista towards the scene shall be shown to others. It corresponds exactly to real-world photography with the liveview function of digital cameras. Alternatively, our 3D viewing mode shows the captured scene in stereo and continuously adapts the view according to the users' head positions in relation to the camera's virtual screen. In this case, the Photoportal can be considered a window to a remote place. This mode is most appropriate for accessing remote locations.

Furthermore, the visual appearance of our Photoportals can be switched from a single window to a box shape, which is a composite of six individual portal windows that are used in conjunction to show the same scene location from six orthogonal directions. The portal box is well-suited for the examination and manipulation of remote objects. In combination with the 3D viewing mode, it resembles a fish tank containing objects of interest. Protruding parts of the objects are automatically clipped. In combination with the 2D viewing mode, the display box shows six aligned orthographic projections of the captured part of the 3D scene. This mode is particularly useful for the accurate examination of geometric relations, as well as for constrained object manipulation.

We also experimented with other combinations of viewing and display parameters, but we found that the combination of two viewing modes (2D and 3D) with two display setups (Window and Box) provides the most sensible manifestation of Photoportals. The four resulting Photoportal modes are:

- 2D-Window (Figure 2 green Photoportal to the right)
- 3D-Window (Figure 2 blue Photoportal to the left)
- 2D-Box (Figure 3 green Photoportal to the right)
- 3D-Box (Figure 3 blue Photoportal to the left)

Figure 2. Capturing scene references in both window display setups. The blue Photoportal to the left illustrates the 3D-Window mode. The live preview in the blue frame integrates seamlessly with the scene behind. The green Photoportal to the right illustrates the 2D-Window mode. The captured 2D image corresponds to a real photo. It appears identical from all perspectives.

Figure 3. Captured scene references in both box display setups. The blue Photoportal to the left illustrates the 3D-Box mode. The captured scene is shown within the blue box as a miniature. The green Photoportal to the right illustrates the 2D-Box mode. The captured car model appears aligned within the green box with orthographic projections shown on all of its sides. The blue and green intersection points on the surface of the car model in the background define the selected geometry.

REFERENCE-BASED INTERACTION WITH PHOTOPORTALS

Photoportals offer a unifying interface for reference-based interaction techniques, some of which are novel, others building on prior work. The following subsections, organized by interaction goals, explain these techniques in detail. At the end of each subsection, we summarize the implemented functionalities with references to related work where applicable.

Taking Photos and Videos

Taking a virtual photo or video is an almost equivalent operation to its real-world counterpart. The user orients the camera towards the target object or location and then triggers the capturing with a button on the device (see Figures 2 and 4). We use a two-state button as known from autofocus cameras. In our case, the intermediate state enables a live preview of the Photoportal which helps to optimize the captured perspective. Fully depressing the trigger button captures the current perspective as a photo or video.

The Photoportals in our system do not only capture virtual content. The photos and videos also record the users as 3D video avatar representations (Figure 1 left). This feature can be used to capture user postures and movement sequences, e.g. for studies of ergonomics. During virtual videotaping, the current color- and depth-image streams of the captured local and remote users are stored for later playback.

In both box modes (2D-Box, 3D-Box), the capturing process is optimized for the creation of an object representation that may later serve as a reference for remote manipulation (Figure 3). If the user encloses 3D objects with the portal box, these objects become captured as they are, but with all protruding parts cut away. If, instead, the box is empty during the capturing process, the camera tries to fetch distant objects along its capturing direction. We search for candidate objects by means of an intersection ray that extends from the Photoportal camera into the scene along the capturing direction. The first intersected object will be represented in the box. The original object placement in the scene remains unaffected, but equivalent to the creation of a Voodoo Doll, [32] the view is parameterized such that the geometry will appear as a miniature inside the handheld Photoportal Box (with its size remaining equal in 2D image space). In 2D-Box mode, the algorithm sets the viewing parameters such that the bounding box of the selected object fits inside the Photoportal box and is aligned to the coordinate system of the parent node in the scene graph. The live preview in the box modes shows only the intersection point of the capturing ray with the scene.

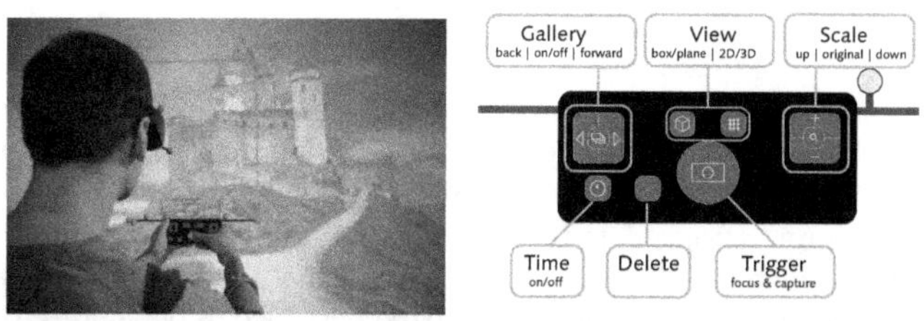

Figure 4. Left: The Photoportal in 3D-Window mode. The live-preview integrates seamlessly with the surrounding scene. Right: The assignment of buttons on the tangible camera device.

All virtual photos are automatically saved in a gallery that is associated with each Photoportal camera device. They can be reviewed, adapted and deleted at any time. After the initial capturing, the viewpoint can still be adjusted by moving the camera device while pressing the trigger button. The viewing and display modes of a virtual photo can be modified at any moment, as well. In analogy to the zoom control of real-world cameras, our Photoportal input device offers a two-way button scaling of the displayed scene representation.

Photoportals do not capture static images, but a certain viewpoint towards a 3D scene. If changes to that same scene are applied after a photo has been taken, they affect the situation that is visible on the photo. Some users expected that a scene that had been captured on a photo could not be changed anymore. Correspondingly, we extended the capturing functionality of Photoportals to record versions of the scene if the recording of temporal aspects is enabled via the *time* button on the camera device (see Figure 4 right). This allows users to go back to earlier versions of the scene if they are unsatisfied with their manipulations. In collaborative work, it also enables users to apply manipulations to a separate version and show their results to everybody else. Then the group can accept the suggested changes by entering this version of the scene. We currently record the full scene graph for a version and only support a full exchange of scenes, but we aim to include a versioning system that supports branching and merging of content.

Recording temporal aspects naturally supports the capturing of action sequences similar to the creation of temporal links in the work of Greenhalgh et al. [13]. Our virtual video sequences also include the captured performances of the life-sized 3D video avatars of local and remote users.

In summary, our capturing techniques offer the following features:

- Immediate creation of scene references
- Two display setups:
  - *Photoportal Window* for location references
  - *Photoportal Box* for object references and WIM
- Two viewing modes:
  - *2D View* for aligned perspectives
  - *3D View* for portal functionalities
- Recording of versions and animations [13]
- Capturing of local and remote users as 3D video avatars
- Storage and management of scene references in a gallery

Sharing Perspectives

Our 3D display system enables the perception of a shared 3D environment among multiple users. However, sharing the same 3D environment does not guarantee that everybody sees the same (fragmented visibility). Our Photoportals provide three techniques to increase the visibility of relevant scene details for all involved users: perspectives can be shared, occluding objects can be cut away and additional object representations can be acquired within arm's reach.

If users want to share a particular perspective of the scene, e.g., to show the alignment of several objects, they can take a photo of this view and immediately show it to others on the virtual display of the camera device (Figure 5). The 2D-Window mode is often preferable in this case. It ensures that all users can see exactly the same perspective on the Photoportal display. However, the lack of stereo and motion parallax also hampers depth perception. In cluttered environments, such as a car's engine compartment, it can become impossible to distinguish between objects that are located at different depth levels along the perspective. In these occasions, the 3D-Window mode can be the better choice.

Each group of users typically has a single camera device, but multiple devices per group are also supported. Each device maintains its own gallery but their content can be shared too. Taking a photo of the virtual screen of another camera device copies the shown photo (Figure 5 right).

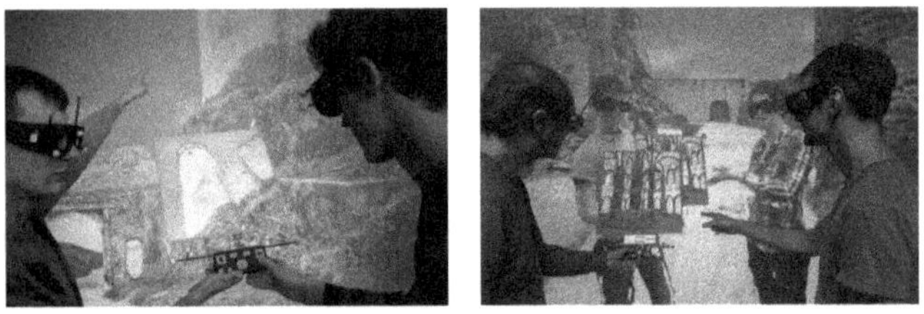

Figure 5. Left: A user shares an interesting perspective with a local collaborator. Right: The exchange of captured photos is supported with a copy functionality between Photoportal cameras.

If the groups' attention shall be drawn to a particular object that cannot easily be seen behind surrounding geometry, they can make use of the Photoportal as a cutting plane. The near clipping plane of our Photoportals is aligned to the virtual display; hence the tool facilitates the exposure of hidden objects through clipping of occluding geometry. Such cutaway views can be captured, readjusted and scaled as any other virtual photo in our system. This facilitates the group discussion of zones that cannot be reached comfortably (Figure 6). Using the display box for cutaway views provides additional information on adjacent geometry. The box's shape can even be adjusted to the object of interest.

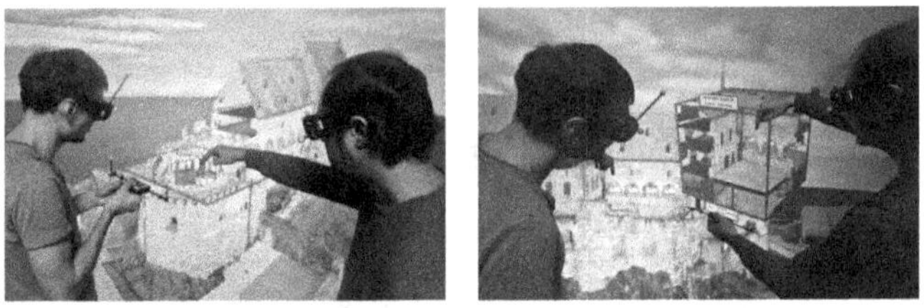

Figure 6. Two users examining interior parts of a building model with a Photoportal used as a cutting plane (left) or a 3D cutout (right).

In summary, our interface supports communication and mutual exchange with the following features:

- Rapid capturing of individual perspectives
- Shareable handheld view representations
- Cut-away views to reveal hidden geometry

Navigation Techniques

Photoportals provide references to remote locations and it seems natural to use these for navigation too. Earlier frameworks for reference-based interaction suggested navigation support in terms of camera-manipulations in a WIM [40, 41], but the resulting viewpoint motion can be uncomfortable from an egocentric perspective. Our Photoportals provide the means for the ad-hoc creation of a WIM. We simply need to scale down the scene representation in the 3D-Box mode (Figure 7). Miniaturized 3D avatar representations of local and remote users are also visible inside the WIM.

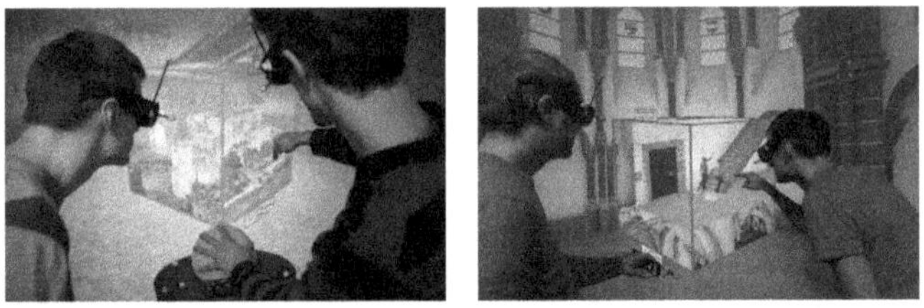

Figure 7. Using Photoportals as a WIM. The image on the right side illustrates the benefits of implicit geometry clipping for wayfinding inside a virtual building. Note the 3D video avatars of remote users in the miniature view.

For viewpoint navigation, however, we do not manipulate the position of these avatars in the WIM. Instead we switch to 3D-Window mode, adjust the scaling and enter the visible locations through the Photoportal. Each user can individually enter a remote scene directly by putting his head into a handheld Photoportal in 3D viewing mode. The user who does this experiences a seamless transition from the main scene that is shared with everybody else to the place displayed by the Photoportal. If the distance between the portal window and the user's head is less than 15 cm, the main scene becomes fully replaced by the portal scene - but only for that user. The others remain completely unaffected by this individual transition. They only see the respective user putting the head into the portal (Figure 8 left).

Group transit to another location requires more steps to ensure everybody's awareness and agreement. Our group interaction policy requires that all group-related input must be operated via a highly-visible central control station, which is generally the aforementioned Spheron in our setup. Placing the Photoportal device on the board around the 3D trackball triggers a coupling between the two input devices. In 2D- or 3D-Window mode, this coupling activates a public gallery with the device's collection of virtual photos on our large physical screen (Figure 8 right). The near clipping planes of all user views become aligned with the gallery in order to avoid occluding scene geometry in front of it. With the buttons of the camera device, the users can browse through the Photoportal collection and select a location they want to enter. Pressing the capturing button grows the selected Photoportal to full screen coverage without affecting the scale of the displayed scene. This entering process deactivates the public gallery and resets the near clipping planes of all user views to the default distance of 15 cm in front of the eyes.

The scene shown in a Photoportal can be scaled up or down before entering. Therefore, navigation in terms of entering Photoportals implicitly supports multi-scale navigation similar to that suggested by [25].

Figure 8. Two ways of entering a Photoportal. Individually, users can put their head into the portal (left). Group transitions require the selection of the target view from a public gallery (right).

In summary, Photoportals support navigation tasks with the following features:

- Shared scene overview for collaborative tour planning [5]
- Preparation of 3D location references
- Multi-scale navigation [25]
- Individual viewpoint transition to remote locations [41]
- Group transit to remote locations

Manipulation Techniques

Similar to other reference-based interaction techniques, our Photoportals enable the remote manipulation of distant objects. The basic principle for all these techniques is the transformation of pick ray input towards the Photoportal display into the shown scene. This has been described previously by Stoev and Schmalstieg [41]. Our implementation of pick ray manipulation in the 3D-Window mode corresponds to their implementation, including the suggested drag-and-drop operation to extract objects from the Photoportal into the main scene. We extended the concept with different manipulation techniques that correspond to the characteristics of our Photoportal modes and added further functionality.

We found that the single-display Photoportal does not support the manipulation of distant objects very well. Without laborious viewpoint adaptations, the distance to the captured object remains the same and it can only be accessed from one direction. The drag-and-drop operation for object extraction, instead, works well (Figure 9 left). We extended the technique with functionalities for object scaling, duplication and animation. When dragging an object from a scaled portal scene into the main scene, the object retains the scaling of the scene from which it is extracted. Inserting objects into a Photoportal works vice versa. A duplicate of an object is created if the user holds the trigger button of the camera device during the object extraction. Extracting a moving object from a video sequence retains its motion path and automatically loops this motion at the new location in the main scene. This feature facilitates the creation of simple animation sequences.

Remote manipulation with the Photoportals in 3D-Box mode corresponds largely to the Voodoo Dolls technique [32]. The corresponding capturing process fits the focused object or location into the box; hence it provides a secondary representation within arm's reach. In our implementation, the remote scene reference appears more like a WIM and is attached to the physical camera device which facilitates its handling among multiple users.

The 3D-Box mode does not support object extraction. Instead, we increased the manipulation range. Once an object inside the Photoportal has been selected with the pick ray, it can be moved beyond the borders of the box. The object does not get lost when passing the border and it is generally still visible in the main scene. The viewport of the Photoportal can be moved thereafter such that the object of interest becomes enclosed by the box again for further manipulation.

The 2D-Box mode additionally offers constrained manipulation for the precise manual alignment of remote objects. Pick ray interaction on one of the six orthogonal projection views is limited to 2D translations along the respective display plane and 1D rotation about its normal (Figure 9 right).

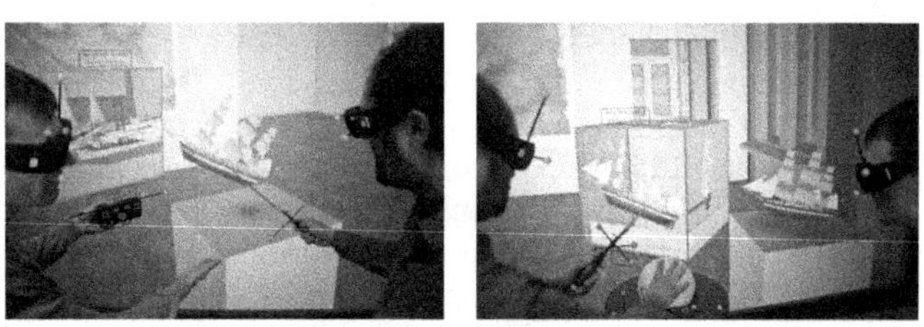

Figure 9. Left: A 3D object is extracted from a Photoportal in 3D-Window mode. Right: The Photoportal in 2D-Box mode supports constrained manipulation. For more relaxed operation, the Photoportal box can be coupled with the Spheron device.

Depending on the task, object manipulations may take time. Continuously holding the Photoportal device to provide a reference for manipulation input can become exhausting. For these situations, we couple the Photoportal interface in box display mode with the Spheron device. The Photoportal box becomes detached from the camera device and is then displayed hovering above the Spheron (Figure 9 right). Rotation input to the trackball is now directly applied to the orientation of the Photoportal box.

In summary, Photoportals support manipulation tasks with the following features:

- Manipulation of remote objects [41, 32, 40]
- Mutual provision of manipulation references
- Drag-and-drop transitions between 3D locations [41]
- Drag-and-drop copy operations with implicit scaling
- Constrained object manipulation

USER EXPERIENCE WORKSHOP

Photoportals offer novel functionalities that can improve collaborative interaction in 3D virtual environments – but only if they can be operated without hassle. Therefore, the general usability of the interface was a primary concern during development. For the evaluation of our novel interface, we invited design students from a partner university to realize their own ideas of interactive virtual environments. In preparation for this workshop, we visited the students at their university and introduced them to the interactive possibilities of our system using photos and videos to illustrate various functionalities. Groups of two to four students were then asked to develop application scenarios.

The six resulting scenarios ranged from 3D design reviews over a futuristic 3D file browser to more gaming-oriented applications. Most fascinating was the possibility of creating experiences that would not be possible in the real world, e.g. traveling through hyperlinks, walking upside-down or meeting oneself in recorded scenarios. After five weeks of preparation, eight of the students came to our lab to realize their ideas. We focused on four scenarios which had to be managed by groups of two students.

Procedure

Before we started to work on the students' scenarios, we familiarized them with the multi-user 3D displays and the 3D capturing and reconstruction technology for telepresence applications. The participants were also thoroughly introduced to the operation of the Photoportals in groups of two. In an existing virtual environment, they were shown each functionality and then asked to operate it themselves. By following a predefined script, we made sure that each user operated every function alone, but also in collaboration with the other. This took between 60 to 90 minutes per group. Then each user was asked to complete a questionnaire on the usability of the overall system and the Photoportal interface. It consisted of a system usability scale (SUS) [9] and more specific items on 7-point Likert scales. In particular, we were interested in ratings of the different Photoportal functionalities and the usefulness of the system to promote collaboration. We worked on the realization of the students' ideas during the following two days. This gave us the opportunity to observe users during the unsupervised use of the interface and to discuss their opinions in brainstorming sessions.

Results

The overall feedback was very positive. The students were excited about the system and also rated the general usability of the Photoportals positively. On a scale between 1 (worst) and 7 (best) a mean score of 5.25 (SD=1,04) was given. The mean score on the system usability scale was 71.65 (SD=10.43), which is above average [27]. One of the students added the comment that using the Photoportals primarily required learning the button mappings of modes and functions, which he considered to be normal for any new electronic device. During their independent work with the system, we observed that it took everybody a while to remember the mapping.

The ease of using the individual functionalities was also rated on the same scale (1-7). Capturing, deleting and exchanging photos, as well as entering the portals individually or as a group, were rated to be most easy with an average score of 6.17 (SD=0.86). The later adjustment of perspectives, including the scaling of the scene, was rated slightly lower (M=5.31, SD=1.10). This corresponds to our observations that users had difficulties estimating the scale of distant objects and that relocating a Photoportal capturing position in a scene can be cumbersome if the scene is shown at a large scale. The ease of using the Photoportals to create cutaway views was rated on a similar level with an average score of 5.43 (SD=1.28). In practice, it requires the same operations to create a cutaway view as any other adjustment of the perspective. When asked to decide between cutaway views in plane or box mode, all but one voted for the box view. The ease of creating object copies was rated with an average score of 5.25 (SD=1.39). We observed some users having difficulties remembering that the trigger button had to be pressed in order to create a copy rather than removing the object from the portal.

The two remote manipulation techniques were rated differently. The average score for remote manipulation of objects in the 3D box mode was 5.5 (SD=0.93). The constrained remote manipulation in 2D box mode was still rated positively, but worst among all of our functionalities (M=4.63, SD=0.92). During the discussions, one participant mentioned that, for accurate placement, the input should be further constrained (e.g. only 2D translation) and that the orthogonal viewing in 2D box mode can be hard to understand in complex scenes. We observed that our participants tended to use the portals to navigate to the optimal position for manipulation rather than using it for remote manipulation.

All but one participant agreed that using Photoportals in a multi-user environment like ours can improve the collaboration of participants. One participant was neutral on that question; the average score was 6.13 (SD=1.36). Some participants argued that the overall system clearly promotes collaboration, but that it takes more than a few days' experience to evaluate the impact of individual aspects like the Photoportals on the collaborative use of the system.

We observed that two aspects of Photoportals for collaboration were immediately used: perspective sharing and territoriality. Our test users frequently assumed Photoportals as temporary private spaces (territoriality) and used them to prepare perspectives towards interesting parts, sometimes while somebody else was steering the rest of the group through the environment. These scene references were then shown to others (perspective sharing) – in most cases they referred to detailed scene features or suggested a new target location. More closely-coupled collaboration, like preparing a reference view for another user, occurred only rarely. Instead of asking each other for such support, most users wanted to operate the device themselves – despite being otherwise busy.

DISCUSSION

Our collaborative virtual reality system supports collocated interaction in a shared 3D environment and the inclusion of remote participants through 3D video avatars. We experienced that these characteristics provide an overall high level of workspace awareness, but that it can still be hard to understand and follow each other's actions in the virtual world if these go beyond real-world behavior.

This deficit and the desire to better support parallel activities led us to the design of a novel interface metaphor: Photoportals provide powerful reference-based interaction techniques for collaborative settings. Primarily, they support the communication about details of a shared virtual environment. Users can immediately capture objects, locations and views they want to discuss. Motion sequences can also be recorded. The resulting virtual photos and videos can then be shown to others directly or stored for later use. The physical camera device further promotes exchange between users. The interface also supports post-hoc adjustment of the view towards the captured scenes, including scaling, which helps to emphasize relevant aspects.

The novel interface metaphor also supports the navigation requirements of groups in virtual environments. It only takes several seconds to create an appropriately scaled and oriented WIM that can be used for wayfinding. The possibility of entering locations of interest directly through the virtual photo reduces the need for traveling long distances, which can be particularly cumbersome for groups. Furthermore, users can enter saved versions of the scene which can also include the captured movements of objects, themselves and other users. This allows them to travel into the past of a design process, create alternative versions or observe an interaction sequence including all the movements of the users. A further important aspect in that regard is the possibility of using the interface as a private display or territory. If a user wants to inspect a particular location within the scene that might not be relevant for everybody else, a Photoportal can be used to provide an individual view of this place.

Photoportals can also be used for object manipulation. In this context, they can be considered as an amalgamation of Voodoo Dolls and tangible props. Like Voodoo Dolls, our Photoportals clearly show what they are referring to, while grasping the physical capturing device facilitates the handling of these references. Our technique contributes further advantages for collaborative scene editing. The capturing of a remote object or location for manipulation does not yet change anything in the shared scene. It only manifests the intention and provides a reference to the relevant part of the scene. The collection of photos thereby provides a storage space for planned activities. The actual editing can be postponed to a moment that fits into the collaborative workflow and allows participants to discuss the intended changes. Moreover, if the group ultimately does not agree on the applied changes, they can use Photoportals to return to an earlier captured version.

Our interfaces and interaction techniques have been designed to encourage the engagement of each individual through multiple access points and different levels of involvement. At the lowest level, each user can explore the shared scene from various angles by walking around. The consistency of the shared environment facilitates gestural communication about the application content. As a next step, one can take a camera device for capturing photos of interesting features and show them to the others. Alternatively, the pick ray can be used to select and manipulate objects in the scene. The group can also be navigated through the virtual environment. Such group-related operations are controlled through the centrally located Spheron device to increase awareness and minimize conflicts.

This selection of tools provides the users with complementary functionalities and thus invites cooperation. For example, the Photoportals provide references for manipulation with the pick ray and the Spheron can be coupled with the Photoportals. We observed that users easily distribute fully orthogonal tasks like navigation and manipulation amongst each other, but that more closely intertwined collaboration only occurs among users that are proficient with the involved technologies and know each other well.

CONCLUSION AND FUTURE WORK

We presented Photoportals as a consistent interface for reference-based 3D interaction techniques in distributed multi-user virtual reality systems. Photoportals allow the quick creation of references and provide easy access to stored ones. Our user experience workshop revealed their usability and showed indications of their benefits for collocated and remote group interaction. The development of our collaborative interaction techniques followed well-established guidelines from the field of computer-supported collaborative work. In particular, the tangible interaction framework of Hornecker and Burr guided our developments [21]. The consistency of the shared 3D space inhabited by locally and remotely collaborating users leverages workspace awareness and promotes full-body interaction.

Our Photoportals allow users to take photos and videos of the surrounding scenery while they are collaboratively exploring a virtual environment. Recordings can be shared among collocated and remote users and serve as portals into the captured 3D scenes. Photoportals provide additional access points for interaction, minimize the issue of fragmented visibility and provide unambiguous references for communication, manipulation and navigation. They also provide users with a private interaction space where they can prepare views that refer to individual areas of interest. Photoportals can also refer to alternate versions of the scene in which users can explore their ideas for modifications. In that sense, Photoportals support the externalization of ideas that can be collaboratively discussed before they are applied to the shared virtual environment.

Given the development in 3D scanning, light field acquisition and display technology, we envision that, in the future, static real-world photos will only be placeholders for interactive portals to the captured scenes in a simulated mirror world and suggest virtual reality as a development platform for appropriate user interfaces.

ACKNOWLEDGMENTS

The research leading to these results has received funding from the EC FP7 projects 3D-PITOTI (ICT-2011-600545) and VR-HYPERSPACE (AAT-2011-RTD-1-285681). Our work was also supported by the German Federal Ministry of Education and Research (BMBF) under grant 03IP704 (project Intelligentes Lernen). The 3D model of Castle Vianden (Luxembourg) that can be seen in Figures 4-8 is courtesy of ArcTron 3D GmbH (`http://www.arctron.com`). We thank the participants of our studies and the members and students of the Virtual Reality Systems group at Bauhaus-Universität Weimar (`http://www.uni-weimar.de/medien/vr`) for their support. Special thanks to Stefanie Wetzel, who realized the first software prototype of Photoportals.

REFERENCES

1. Agrawala, M., Beers, A. C., McDowall, I., Fröhlich, B., Bolas, M., and Hanrahan, P. The two-user responsive workbench: support for collaboration through individual views of a shared space. In *Proc. of Siggraph 1997*, SIGGRAPH '97, ACM Press/Addison-Wesley Publishing Co. (1997), 327–332.
2. Argelaguet, F., Kulik, A., Kunert, A., Andujar, C., and Froehlich, B. See-through techniques for referential awareness in collaborative virtual reality. *Int. J. Hum.-Comput. Stud. 69*, 6 (June 2011), 387–400.
3. Arthur, K., Preston, T., Taylor, R., Brooks, F., Whitton, M., and Wright, W. Designing and building the pit: a head-tracked stereo workspace for two users. In *Proceedings of IPT '98, Workshop CD-ROM* (1998).
4. Barrus, J. W., Waters, R. C., and Anderson, D. B. Locales: Supporting large multiuser virtual environments. *IEEE Comput. Graph. Appl. 16*, 6 (Nov. 1996), 50–57.
5. Beck, S., Kunert, A., Kulik, A., and Froehlich, B. Immersive group-to-group telepresence. *IEEE Transactions on Visualization and Computer Graphics 19*, 4 (Apr. 2013), 616–625.
6. Benford, S., Bederson, B. B., Åkesson, K.-P., Bayon, V., Druin, A., Hansson, P., Hourcade, J. P., Ingram, R., Neale, H., O'Malley, C., Simsarian, K. T., Stanton, D., Sundblad, Y., and Taxén, G. Designing storytelling technologies to encouraging collaboration between young children. In *Proc. of CHI 2000*, ACM Press (2000), 556–563.
7. Bier, E. A., Stone, M. C., Pier, K., Buxton, W., and DeRose, T. D. Toolglass and magic lenses: the see-through interface. In *Proc. of SIGGRAPH 1993*, ACM Press (1993), 73–80.
8. Bricker, L. J., Baker, M. J., and Tanimoto, S. L. Support for cooperatively controlled objects in multimedia applications. In *CHI '97 Extended Abstracts on Human Factors in Computing Systems*, CHI EA '97, ACM Press (1997), 313–314.
9. Brooke, J. SUS: A quick and dirty usability scale. In *Usability evaluation in industry*, P. W. Jordan, B. Weerdmeester, A. Thomas, and I. L. Mclelland, Eds., Taylor and Francis (London, 1996).
10. García, A. S., Molina, J. P., González, P., Martínez, D., and Martínez, J. An experimental study of collaborative interaction tasks supported by awareness and multimodal feedback. In *Proc. of VRCAI 2009*, ACM Press (2009), 77–82.
11. Greenberg, S., and Marwood, D. Real time groupware as a distributed system: concurrency control and its effect on the interface. In *Proc. of CSCW 1994*, CSCW '94, ACM Press (1994), 207–217.
12. Greenhalgh, C., Flintham, M., Purbrick, J., and Benford, S. Applications of temporal links: Recording and replaying virtual environments. In *Proc. of IEEE VR 2002*, VR '02, IEEE Computer Society (Washington, DC, USA, 2002), 101–.
13. Greenhalgh, C., Purbrick, J., Benford, S., Craven, M., Drozd, A., and Taylor, I. Temporal links: recording and replaying virtual environments. In *Proc. of ACM Multimedia 2000*, MULTIMEDIA '00, ACM Press (New York, NY, USA, 2000), 67–74.
14. Greenhalgh, C., Purbrick, J., and Snowdon, D. Inside massive-3: flexible support for data consistency and world structuring. In *Proc. of CVE 2000*, CVE '00, ACM Press (New York, NY, USA, 2000), 119–127.
15. Gross, M., Würmlin, S., Naef, M., Lamboray, E., Spagno, C., Kunz, A., Koller-Meier, E., Svoboda, T., Van Gool, L., Lang, S., Strehlke, K., Moere, A. V., and Staadt, O. blue-c: a spatially immersive display and 3d video portal for telepresence. *ACM Trans. Graph. 22*, 3 (July 2003), 819–827.
16. Grossman, T., and Balakrishnan, R. Collaborative interaction with volumetric displays. In *Proc. of CHI 2008*, CHI '08, ACM (2008), 383–392.
17. Guiard, Y. Asymmetric Division of Labor in Human Skilled Bimanual Action: The Kinematic Chain as a Model. In *Journal of Motor Behavior 19* (1987), 486–517.
18. Gutwin, C., and Greenberg, S. A descriptive framework of workspace awareness for real-time groupware. *Comput. Supported Coop. Work 11*, 3 (Nov. 2002), 411–446.

19. Hinckley, K., Pausch, R., Goble, J. C., and Kassell, N. F. Passive real-world interface props for neurosurgical visualization. In *CHI '94: Proceedings of the SIGCHI conference on Human factors in computing systems*, ACM (1994), 452–458.

20. Hindmarsh, J., Fraser, M., Heath, C., Benford, S., and Greenhalgh, C. Object-focused interaction in collaborative virtual environments. *ACM Trans. Comput.-Hum. Interact. 7*, 4 (Dec. 2000), 477–509.

21. Hornecker, E., and Buur, J. Getting a grip on tangible interaction: a framework on physical space and social interaction. In *Proc. of CHI 2006*, ACM Press (2006), 437–446.

22. Hornecker, E., Marshall, P., Dalton, N. S., and Rogers, Y. Collaboration and interference: awareness with mice or touch input. In *Proc of CSCW 2008*, ACM Press (2008), 167–176.

23. Jones, A., McDowall, I., Yamada, H., Bolas, M., and Debevec, P. Rendering for an interactive 360 degree light field display. *ACM Trans. Graph. 26* (July 2007).

24. Klinkhammer, D., Nitsche, M., Specht, M., and Reiterer, H. Adaptive personal territories for co-located tabletop interaction in a museum setting. In *Proc. of ITS 2011*, ITS '11, ACM Press (2011), 107–110.

25. Kopper, R., Ni, T., Bowman, D. A., and Pinho, M. Design and evaluation of navigation techniques for multiscale virtual environments. In *VR '06: Proceedings of the IEEE conference on Virtual Reality*, IEEE Computer Society (2006), 175–182.

26. Kulik, A., Kunert, A., Beck, S., Reichel, R., Blach, R., Zink, A., and Froehlich, B. C1x6: a stereoscopic six-user display for co-located collaboration in shared virtual environments. *ACM Trans. Graph. 30*, 6 (Dec. 2011), 188:1–188:12.

27. Lewis, J. R., and Sauro, J. The factor structure of the system usability scale. In *Proc. of HCI International 2009*, HCD 09, Springer-Verlag (2009), 94–103.

28. Maimone, A., and Fuchs, H. Encumbrance-free telepresence system with real-time 3d capture and display using commodity depth cameras. In *Proc. of ISMAR 2011*, IEEE Computer Society (2011), 137–146.

29. McGrath, W., Bowman, B., McCallum, D., Hincapié-Ramos, J. D., Elmqvist, N., and Irani, P. Branch-explore-merge: facilitating real-time revision control in collaborative visual exploration. In *Proc. of ITS 2012*, ITS '12, ACM (2012), 235–244.

30. Morris, M. R., Ryall, K., Shen, C., Forlines, C., and Vernier, F. Beyond "social protocols": multi-user coordination policies for co-located groupware. In *Proc. of CSCW 2004*, ACM Press (2004), 262–265.

31. Pausch, R., Burnette, T., Brockway, D., and Weiblen, M. E. Navigation and locomotion in virtual worlds via flight into hand-held miniatures. In *Proc. of SIGGRAPH 1995*, SIGGRAPH '95, ACM Press (1995), 399–400.

32. Pierce, J. S., Stearns, B. C., and Pausch, R. Voodoo dolls: seamless interaction at multiple scales in virtual environments. In *Proc of I3D 1999*, ACM Press (1999), 141–145.

33. Pinelle, D., Barjawi, M., Nacenta, M., and Mandryk, R. An evaluation of coordination techniques for protecting objects and territories in tabletop groupware. In *Proc. of CHI 2009*, CHI '09, ACM (2009), 2129–2138.

34. Pinho, M. S., Bowman, D. A., and Freitas, C. M. Cooperative object manipulation in immersive virtual environments: framework and techniques. In *Proc. of VRST 2002*, VRST '02, ACM Press (2002), 171–178.

35. Riege, K., Holtkamper, T., Wesche, G., and Frohlich, B. The bent pick ray: An extended pointing technique for multi-user interaction. In *Proc. of 3D UI 2006*, 3DUI '06, IEEE Computer Society (2006), 62–65.

36. Ruddle, R. A., Savage, J. C. D., and Jones, D. M. Symmetric and asymmetric action integration during cooperative object manipulation in virtual environments. *ACM Trans. Comput.-Hum. Interact. 9*, 4 (Dec. 2002), 285–308.

37. Schmalstieg, D., Fuhrmann, A., Hesina, G., Szalavári, Z., Encarnação, L. M., Gervautz, M., and Purgathofer, W. The studierstube augmented reality project. *Presence: Teleoper. Virtual Environ. 11* (February 2002), 33–54.

38. Scott, S. D., Sheelagh, M., Carpendale, T., and Inkpen, K. M. Territoriality in collaborative tabletop workspaces. In *Proc. of CSCW 2004*, CSCW '04, ACM Press (2004), 294–303.

39. Spindler, M., Büschel, W., and Dachselt, R. Use your head: tangible windows for 3d information spaces in a tabletop environment. In *Proc. of ITS 2012*, ACM Press (2012), 245–254.

40. Stoakley, R., Conway, M. J., and Pausch, R. Virtual reality on a wim: interactive worlds in miniature. In *Proc. of CHI 1995*, ACM Press/Addison-Wesley Publishing Co. (1995), 265–272.

41. Stoev, S. L., and Schmalstieg, D. Application and taxonomy of through-the-lens techniques. In *Proc. of VRST 2002*, ACM Press (2002), 57–64.

42. Tani, M., Horita, M., Yamaashi, K., Tanikoshi, K., and Futakawa, M. Courtyard: integrating shared overview on a large screen and per-user detail on individual screens. In *Proc. of Chi 1994*, CHI '94, ACM Press (1994), 202–.

43. Tse, E., Histon, J., Scott, S. D., and Greenberg, S. Avoiding interference: how people use spatial separation and partitioning in sdg workspaces. In *Proc. of CSCW 2004*, ACM Press (2004), 252–261.

44. Wingrave, C. A., Haciahmetoglu, Y., and Bowman, D. A. Overcoming world in miniature limitations by a scaled and scrolling wim. In *Proc. of 3D UI 2006*, 3DUI '06, IEEE Computer Society (Washington, DC, USA, 2006), 11–16.

Managing Political Differences in Social Media

Catherine Grevet[1], Loren Terveen[2], Eric Gilbert[1]

[1]School of Interactive Computing
and GVU Center
Georgia Institute of Technology
{cgrevet, gilbert}@cc.gatech.edu

[2]Department of Computer Science
and Engineering
University of Minnesota
terveen@cs.umn.edu

ABSTRACT

Most people associate with people like themselves, a process called *homophily*. Exposure to diversity, however, makes us more informed as individuals and as a society. In this paper, we investigate political disagreements on Facebook to explore the conditions under which diverse opinions can coexist online. Via a mixed methods approach comprising 103 survey responses and 13 interviews with politically engaged American social media users, we found that participants who perceived more differences with their friends engaged less on Facebook than those who perceived more homogeneity. Weak ties were particularly brittle to political disagreements, despite being the ties most likely to offer diversity. Finally, based on our findings we suggest potential design opportunities to bridge across ideological difference: 1) support exposure to weak ties; and 2) make common ground visible while friends converse.

Author Keywords

Social media; homophily; politics; Facebook; self-censorship; tie strength; relationship management

ACM Classification Keywords

H5.3. Group and Organization Interfaces; Asynchronous interaction; Web-based interaction.

INTRODUCTION

People tend to befriend and stay connected to others who have similar interests and values [25, 26]. This phenomenon, called *homophily,* is a widely studied social process [21]. While congregating with like-minded others can confer strong emotional support [21], inwardly focused groups also risk tunnel vision and an inability to challenge their own views [24, 32]. Exposure to diverse opinions often makes people more informed and engages society in healthy deliberation [19, 32].

CSCW'14, February 15 - 19 2014, Baltimore, MD, USA

ACM 978-1-4503-2540-0/14/02···$15.00.
http://dx.doi.org/10.1145/2531602.2531676

CSCW and HCI work has explored ways to increase exposure to diverse views. Novel algorithms and interaction design can present a mix of political perspectives in news aggregators [22], or can introduce people to others with different views [10]. This growing line of social computing work recognizes that design has the potential to nudge people towards more diverse viewpoints. Yet, systems in widespread production often reinforce homophily (e.g., Amazon's product recommendations, Facebook friend suggestions). Systems like these make suggestions based on similar interests, often creating an "echo chamber" [10]. This has also been shown in many large-scale network analyses (e.g., [1, 21]). To date, our online social life mimics our offline inclination to associate with people like us.

However, social networks are not entirely homogeneous. Three quarters (73%) of social media users have disagreed with a friend's post [25]. People already cohabitate in online communities with friends who hold different opinions. How do they make it work? Sometimes, of course, it ends with the nuclear option: unfriending. Other times, social media strengthens friendships [8, 17]. Social media enables these relationships to be expressed and maintained, despite inevitable disagreements.

We are interested in the intricacies of relationships in the context of political discussions on social media because—when they work out—they suggest the conditions under which diverse opinions can coexist online. In this paper, we present a systematic investigation of heated political discussions via social media. In 2013, three contentious federal events rattled the political landscape in the United States: budget cuts, gay marriage debates, and gun control regulations. It is in this political climate that we studied how Facebook users manage relationships with people who hold different opinions. Our mixed methods study comprises 103 survey responses and 13 phone interviews about Facebook usage and friendships during these events with social media users who have strong political opinions.

We find that our participants who perceive more friends as holding viewpoints different to their own *engage less on Facebook* than those with more similarity in their network. Echoing earlier social science work [20], we also find that weak ties *talk about politics less often*, and are brittle when those conversations happen. In other words, weak ties can easily break under pressure from contentious discussions.

Turning to design interventions, we suggest that *making common ground visible* (i.e., highlighting past interactions and shared interests) during contentious discussions could alleviate in-the-moment tension. Namely, our data suggest that this intervention could keep an argument from overshadowing a history of friendship. We also suggest opportunities to *increase exposure and engagement between weak ties* to make them more resilient in the face of political disagreement. The primary contribution of this work is an exposition of opportunities and pitfalls for social media to bridge differences.

RELATED WORK

Our inquiry was informed by two broad topics: the prevalence of homophily in social networks and the pressing need for more political deliberation. Social computing research at the intersection of these areas can provide insights into user behavior and design innovations.

Homophily and exposure to differences

Most social networks are clustered in groups of like-minded individuals [21, 25, 26]. These groups form through deliberate actions such as associating with similar others, also known as homophily. Other more indirect processes also contribute to these congregations, such as triadic closure, via which befriending a friend of a friend is highly probable [33]. These homogeneous groups are prevalent offline due to geographical, cultural, professional, and interest-based associations [21]. Cloistering with similar others may be reassuring, but this tendency can magnify already extreme views and exacerbate polarization [22, 31]. Some exposure to more diverse views can bring about new sources of information and lead to more educated decisions.

Despite the lack of physical constraints, homophily is also a widespread phenomenon online [15, 21]. Much work has shown the prevalence of the *"echo chamber"* or *"filter bubble"* effects in social network sites [10, 13]. Many widespread systems recommend people or content based on similar interests, intensifying these effects [10]. This results in our online social life mimicking our offline tendency of associating with similar others, a finding validated by many large-scale network analyses (e.g. [1, 21]).

Political discussions and public deliberation—a healthy part of democratic societies [19, 25]—face challenges online. The Internet has many communities designed for political expression, such as political blogs [13, 23], comments on political articles, or through channels administered by U.S. government officials [18, 27]. Yet, the echo chamber effect largely hinders access to dissenting views [1, 13]. Exposing people to more diverse political opinions is a growing line of work in interaction design.

Bridging across differences

Work in CSCW and HCI has looked into bridging across these political differences [2, 10, 15, 19, 21, 22, 30]. Novel algorithms and interaction design can present a mix of political perspectives in news aggregators [22], or can introduce people to others of different views [10]. Some of these interactive systems have demonstrated the potential to support political deliberation [19, 30]. For example, systems can support weighing multiple sides of issues [19].

The design of these systems rests on conflicting and complex findings. First of all, displaying opposing views can polarize people even more strongly towards their original position [22, 31]. Second, some people explicitly seek out different opinions, while others are "challenge adverse", seeking content that matches their own views [12, 22]. Finally, people of different views might use different terminology to explain political concepts [2]. Systems design has made great progress, yet results remain mottled. We contribute to this scholarship by simply asking, how do people currently manage political differences?

Managing differences

Online social networks are not entirely homogeneous. Disagreeing with a friend is not uncommon. 73% of social media users report disagreeing with a friend's post [25]. In fact, people tend to overestimate similarities with their friends [15]. Discovering this discrepancy can lead to social tension. While this has only led 18% of social media users to unfriend[1], block or hide someone [25], it does not mean that the relationship remained intact. What happens to the other 82%?

Politics are extensively discussed in online communities that are not political [2, 13, 23]. In fact, 40% of the U.S. adult population reports that their friends post political content on social network sites [25], and 15% of content that users share on Facebook is political [28]. When political tensions arise in these non-political places, people tend to employ ad-hoc mechanisms to minimize animosity [13, 23]. For example, political posts on non-political blogs often contain warnings such as "please excuse my rant" [23].

In social media, people employ a variety of mechanisms to manage tensions [11]. One relevant mechanism is self-censorship, or refraining from posting [9, 28, 34]. Politics is a topic that is often self-censored [28]. A Pew study found that 72% of survey respondents did not post political links, and 66% do not post their own political thoughts on Facebook [26]. Because people tend to overestimate similarities with their friends [15], self-censorship and engagement with social media might depend on the degree of similarity that users perceive in their network.

This prior work motivates our investigation around political disagreements in social media. Homophily suggests that most people connect to others similar to them on Facebook. However, friends do not always agree. These disagreements

[1] The term unfriend here is referenced from the cited article. Unfriending is removing a connection on a social media platform. Other websites use different terms (e.g. unfollowing on Twitter).

are particularly salient during times of contention, such as during current news debates. Expectations of backlash may impact engagement with Facebook during these times. Furthermore, designing systems to bridge across differences merits asking how this is currently done. This leads us to our two main research questions:

R1: How do perceptions of differences affect engagement on Facebook during political events?

R2: How do people manage relationships on Facebook with friends of different political opinions?

METHODS

We conducted a mixed methods study comprising a survey and follow-up interviews. The questions were about Facebook usage and interactions with friends during political events. First, we briefly contextualize our study in the socio-technical and socio-political landscapes that frame our findings. We briefly attend to these contexts to inform future researchers of the environment that shaped our results.

Research context

The U.S. political landscape and Facebook are evolving systems. Our survey and interview questions were dependent on the specifics of these systems at the time of our study in order to elicit grounded responses from our participants. In the discussion section, we generalize from these contexts to highlight what can be learned for future designs of social media for political discourse.

We conducted the study with U.S. participants around U.S political events between March and April 2013. Prior to this, in December 14th 2012, a mass murder shooting at the Sandy Hook Elementary School in Newtown, CT spawned gun law debates. In May 2013, three states—Rhode Island, Delaware, and Minnesota—legalized gay marriage. Our study spans three controversial political events in the beginning of 2013: the federal budget cuts on March 1st, the same-sex marriage debates on March 26th and 27th, and the Senate gun control vote on April 17th. Debates started before and continued after these dates, but we used them to launch our survey.

Facebook is the most widely used online social network [11]. At the time of our study, Facebook consisted of a newsfeed, personal pages, groups, business pages, inbox for directed messages, chat system, and other add-on applications. The newsfeed was the homepage and displayed the posts from a user's network as a stream. An unknown algorithm sorted the posts in the newsfeed, possibly prioritized by posts of high potential interest and posts from close ties [7]. Personal pages could be customized with a picture and information such as birthday, religion, political affiliation, and interests. Facebook included a number of privacy controls to allow users to specify audiences for posts and pictures. At the time of this study, Facebook was rolling out new features such as Graph Search, which provided more flexibility in social searching on the site, and a new newsfeed layout with more control over filtering.

Data collection and analysis

Our study consisted of a survey administered in waves between March 1, 2013 and April 30, 2013. Each survey phase was followed by a series of semi-structured interviews with a subset of the survey respondents. In total, we obtained 103 survey responses and conducted 13 interviews. Using different events was an advantage because we could see how different types of debates affected engagement and relationship management.

Recruitment

Understanding relationship management around political differences necessitated that both parties actually had opinions. As a proxy for users with opinions about U.S. politics, we used the following recruitment criteria: *"users who posted a link to a WhiteHouse.gov petition online."* The WhiteHouse.gov website prompts signatories to share the petition link to social media. A user who broadcasts such a link broadens the petition's exposure and essentially takes a political action.

For each event, we collected tweets containing a link to a WhiteHouse.gov petition, through the Twitter search API, and selected a random sample. We then replied to tweets that were written in English. We excluded retweets to focus on personal political viewpoints, and excluded verified accounts on the off chance that a celebrity mentioning our survey would induce a snowball sample. Our reply stated that we were conducting a study about Facebook usage during a specific event. This ensured that those answering our survey were Facebook users.

Instead of using Facebook directly, we used Twitter to recruit participants. While somewhat roundabout, tweets are easily searchable, and replying to a tweet is free, which allowed us to reach a large sample. By contrast, messaging non-friends on Facebook typically costs $1—somewhat prohibitive considering normal survey response rates. We also worried that Facebook users would not consider it normative for us to message them in response to a post, especially when many might not realize they made the post publicly searchable. This also allowed us to obtain a range of behaviors on Facebook: those who post about politics on Facebook and those who withhold.

Survey instrument

Our questionnaire[2] was constructed around our two research questions and included a total of 34 questions. Some questions were optional and some were conditional. To answer our question about how perceived differences affected Facebook usage, we asked participants about how many of their friends they thought had different opinions from them about the event. To answer this question, participants selected a range of percentage (e.g. 0-9%, 10-19% etc). We asked about their frequency of usage of Facebook, the amount of posts and comments they made, and whether

[2] Link to survey: http://comp.social.gatech.edu/hsurvey.pdf

Perceived difference	Interpretation	N
0%-29%	High perceived homogeneity	51
30%-59%	Mixed perceived homogeneity	43
60%-100%	Low perceived homogeneity	9

Table 1. Grouping by how much difference our participants perceived in their Facebook friend network.

	Budget cuts Mar. 1st	Same-sex marriage Mar. 26th	Gun laws debates Apr. 17th	Total
Sample	500	700	700	1,900
Responses	19	42	42	103
Response rate	3.8%	5.8%	5.8%	5.4%
Female	9 (47%)	21 (51%)	26 (62%)	54%
Age 18-40	13 (68%)	29 (69%)	24 (57%)	64%
Age >40	6 (32%)	13 (31%)	18 (43%)	36%

Table 3. Demographics of survey responders. We sent the survey to 1,900 Twitter users and obtained 103 responses (5.4% response rate).

they joined a group or liked a politician's page. If they had made a post, we asked whether they set privacy settings on that post. Then, we asked questions about a specific relationship by prompting: *Think about one friend in particular who has a different opinion from you about the event to answer the following questions.* Here, we asked participants about how close they felt to this person on a 5-point likert scale, following previous work [7, 14]. Other questions in this section pertained to the frequency of communication with this friend, and whether their relationship changed after the event. Finally, our questionnaire also included demographic questions, such as the number of Facebook friends and general political orientation. The questionnaire was customized for the specific political event under consideration by simply replacing the name of the event; the questions were the same for each event.

Our survey responses were self-report data: no data was collected directly from Facebook. We aimed to address this limitation [3] by providing a link to participants' Facebook account and Facebook activity logs, and explicitly asking them to open their account while answering our questions. In the interview we also encouraged participants to open Facebook and to browse their friends' pages. Moreover, the survey and interview were conducted within a two-week timeframe, which aimed to be as close to the debate as possible to address recall issues. By encouraging the use of Facebook during the survey and interview, we believe the responses we obtained corresponded to existing relationships and actual experiences, which is the crux of our findings. It is possible that participants misreported some of their usage of Facebook.

Tie strength	Interpretation	N
1-2	Weak ties	45
3-5	Strong ties	57

Table 2. Grouping by tie strength.

	Liberal	Moderate	Conserv.	None	Total
Social	67 (65%)	14 (14%)	19 (18%)	3 (3%)	103
Econ.	48 (47%)	22 (21%)	30 (29%)	3 (3%)	103

Table 4. Political orientation of survey responders. We grouped responses from Very Liberal and Liberal together; and responses from Very Conservative and Conservative together. Our participants leaned more liberally overall. This was more pronounced for social issues than economic issues.

Data analysis

We grouped survey responses for Facebook usage based on perceived differences, and for relationships, we grouped on tie strength:

For perceived difference (Table 1), we clustered responses into three groups: few friends perceived different (0%–29% of friends with different opinions) that included 49% of our participants; many friends perceived different (30%–59% of friends with different opinions) that included 42% of our participants; and most friends perceived different (60%–100% of friends with different opinions) that included 9% our the participants.

For tie strength (Table 2), we clustered responses into two groups: weak ties (reported tie strength as 1 or 2) that included 44% of participants; and strong ties (reported tie strength as 3, 4 or 5) that included 56% of participants. One participant could not think of a friend with different opinions, thus this section contains 102 survey responses.

Survey respondent demographics

Via our recruitment process described above, we sent our survey to 1,900 unique Twitter users. We received 103 responses, corresponding to a response rate of 5.4% (see Table 3). About half (54%) of our respondents were female, and two thirds of our participants (64%) were under 40. This is representative of Facebook users [11]. In addition, our participants tended skew liberal (65% on social issues and 47% on economic issues), also consistent with the demographics of social network sites [25] (see Table 4). However, social media users tend to be biased towards being educated, more liberal, younger, and more politically engaged than the general population [26]. Our study is based on political events happening in the United States, so cultural characteristics of American politics might affect our results. Our recruitment methods did not reach individuals who were not willing to discuss politics online; we leave this for future work in the *Limitations* section. By targeting politically engaged users, we might have also biased our sample towards diversity seekers [22].

A preliminary overview of our participant data shows that most of them perceive their friends to be similar to them. This parallels homophily research: people tend to associate with people similar to them. In addition, our data suggest that interacting with people of different political opinions was a common experience. The fact that our participants could relate to the experience of dealing with a friend of different opinion could be biased by our population sample of politically active users. This could be due to homophily (they would be most likely to be friends with others of strong political opinion) or because they were more attuned to noticing posts about politics. Most participants (71%) did not frequently talk about politics with their friends of differing opinion. Though many (60%) did see something they did not agree with, and did not comment on it. Facebook was a place to talk about politics: 79% of the survey respondents posted at least one thing during the political events. Privacy controls to limit posts to a small audience were rarely used [29]. Participants preferred to not post anything rather than set a privacy setting.

Follow-up interviews and analysis

Survey participants could choose to provide us with their contact information for a follow-up interview. From this, we interviewed 13 participants. The interview was scheduled for 1 hour and participants received $30 for their time. We conducted all the interviews over the phone, and participants were encouraged to open Facebook to support recall during the interview.

The interviews were semi-structured. The script was followed rather consistently. Questions asked during the interview centered around similar issues as those asked in the survey, but with more depth. In the interview, participants were asked about multiple relationships. We conducted an inductive thematic analysis of individual interview questions [5]. To do this, we familiarized ourselves with the interviews through transcribing and contrasting the interviews with the survey data.

IMPACT OF DISAGREEMENTS ON FACEBOOK USAGE

Our first research question was: *How do perceptions of differences affect engagement on Facebook during political events?* We obtained one to three relationships per interviewee, amounting to 33 dyads total. From our analysis of these interactions, we found that perceptions of similarities shaped behaviors during political events that left few opportunities to be exposed to differing opinions.

Logging on

Those who perceived more friends as different logged on to Facebook less than those who perceived high homogeneity, $\chi^2(4, N = 103) = 10.05$, $p = 0.04$. With a large number of dissenting friends, Facebook was less welcoming during political events:

> *I mean it can be overwhelming just being on Facebook [...]. Just like the number of people participating [...], and it was just like there's no room to voice an opinion from either side when I guess your newsfeed, your friends are just going crazy like that. (P8)*

This could be one reason that political discussions online happened in an echo chamber: those with an overwhelming number of friends with different opinions are not as present. This is not to say that these friends are never present. Rather, they are not present when it is most critical, during a debate, both as an active participant and as a viewer. One participant who logged on to Facebook more frequently than usual indicated that this was due to confounding factors like other news happening at the same time. Thus, perceptions of being in the minority directly decreased the desire to log on to Facebook while perceiving high homogeneity didn't have a noticeable effect.

Joining conversations

Those who had more friends of perceived different opinions posted fewer comments on their friends' Facebook posts during the political events than those who perceived higher homogeneity, $\chi^2(2, N = 103) = 5.61$, $p = 0.06$. In addition, users who perceived a large number of their friends to have different opinions self-censored more than those who perceived their friends to be more similar to them, $\chi^2(2, N = 103) = 8.37$, $p = 0.01$. Participating in conversations around political debates often amounted to avoiding confrontation and siding with like-minded friends.

Confrontation resulting in agreeing to disagree

Facebook arguments were described as long, emotional, and confrontational. Often, they resulted in friends "agreeing to disagree." The following quote illustrates an example of this occurrence:

> *We'll have conversations that reach 80 comments. Um... and like most political debates on Facebook it doesn't just stick to gun control, you go all over the map and then end up back on the same spot where you were and then we just agree to disagree. (P12)*

Many of the survey respondents noted that there was "no point" in engaging with friends of different opinion on Facebook because they couldn't "change their mind." These dead-end conversations were described as unproductive and unappealing, meaning that most chose to avoid engaging in them.

Lightweight cues to show support

Rather than joining heated debates, some participants wanted to show support without inviting confrontation. A simple comment or "liking" a post could provide an opportunity to show support in a semi-private setting:

> *I think like one friend wrote [how she felt] I might have commented like I do too, or like word or something like that so more so like I did those things so that friends [...] know that they're supported by me. But um.. people*

who are against it I didn't comment back or debate you know with them. (P6)

One participant mentioned "liking" a friend's posts as a "thumbs up" indicator that does not invite dissenting opinions. The appropriation of these lightweight cues to show support could increase polarization in two ways: 1) explicitly taking an action to side with a party (likely strengthening their own position), and 2) limiting the possibility for someone on the other side to confront them.

Too much agreement is uninteresting

In some cases, participants limited their postings to things that brought new insights, or just stayed away all together when there was a noticeable echo chamber effect:

I honestly didn't see a whole lot of point in posting anything else related to it because pretty much everyone was in agreement that it was an idiotic thing. (P2)

I like to keep [my friends] on top of what's going on and so I usually what they post I've maybe seen somewhere already so I consider them just an echo chamber. (P12)

This illustrates that overwhelming agreement can also cause people to hold back from posting on Facebook during political events. Munson et al. [22] found that providing some dissenting opinions in a news aggregator could be engaging for diversity seekers. Having a balance of pro and con posts could help engagement on Facebook during political events. Rather than showing extremes, all supporting or all dissenting posts, people could see a subset of each side of the argument to present a more nuanced display of opinions – this would especially help with weak ties as we will see next.

Changing someone's mind on Facebook

Our findings show that Facebook is a difficult place to maintain a friendship with someone who has different opinions during times of heated political debates. During those times, Facebook can feel like a hostile environment, conversations can quickly get stale, and the opportunities to show support with like-minded others overshadow the opportunities to engage with people of different opinion. One participant mentioned that changing a fundamental belief would happen in the context of a strong relationship, such as one between father and son rather than through weak ties – the types of relationships fostered by Facebook:

I feel like when people change their opinion about stuff like that it happens within the context of a relationship that can't be cultivated through an online connection. [...] Like when you hear about politicians who have changed their minds because their son came out. (P6)

Prior work has shown that friendships influenced behavior on a voting website [6]. We see here that stronger offline ties might have more impact on political attitudes. However, Facebook was the only way that some of our participants communicated with their friends of different opinion. Relationships that are maintained solely through Facebook are particularly vulnerable.

IMPACT OF DISAGREEMENTS ON RELATIONSHIPS

Our second research question was: *How do people manage relationships on Facebook with friends of different political opinions?* Hearing dissenting voices on Facebook created challenges, especially for weak ties. From our participants, we found that weak ties of different opinion communicated less often about politics in general than strong ties of different opinion, $\chi^2(3, N = 102) = 10.27$, $p = 0.02$. This matches Granovetter's theories about tie strength [16]. However, when they did communicate there were challenges. These experiences sometimes made our participants change their opinion about the friends. Other times, it resulted in questioning the relationship and ultimately disassociating from the friend. This was confirmed by our survey results in which we found that more people felt that their relationship had changed with weak ties than with strong ties.

Withdrawing from friends online

Our participants reported a number of negotiations employed to manage relationships with friends of different opinions. Rather than engaging with their friends, our participants discussed ways in which they actively avoided confrontation.

Unfriending, blocking, hiding

Most drastically, ending a friendship can be the result of a heated political argument. Among the 33 dyads mentioned during the interview, three were no longer friends. These relationships were all weak ties based on past common background, such as high school friends and they had not seen each other in many years. This confirms findings from [25] that people unfriend more weak ties than strong ties.

Unfriending was not an option with close family. Instead of unfriending her brother, P1 hid his posts from her newsfeed meaning that his posts no longer appeared in her social stream:

I feel like unfriending my brother on Facebook would cause a lot of strife. Whereas staying friends with him causes frustration but just for me. (P1)

They saw each other in person on a frequent to occasional basis and removing them from Facebook could cause friction in the relationship. Simply hiding him was a better alternative because he wouldn't be aware of the fact that she altered the state of their connection.

Avoiding the topic

In some cases, participants knew not to talk about politics based on previous experiences. This meant that they were more careful when talking to their friend, perhaps making explicit choices about topics that should not be discussed:

I don't really talk about anything with her other than like small talk and work things that are you know are required. (P9)

On Facebook, selectively hearing from the other person is difficult to control. As we saw from our participants, these are not people who they never want to hear from. In the case of hiding someone from the newsfeed, it might be beneficial to provide timed hiding so that the hiding can only take effect during a particularly tense time.

Lack of communication as a form of communication

In some cases, unfriending is not an option and hiding someone from the newsfeed is not necessary. Rather, the way to manage the relationship is to stop talking:

> *Just because I stopped arguing with you does not mean that I agree with you. And I find that that's very very true online. People take ... you know when you stop arguing that must mean that they won, it's like no, [laughs] it's because I'm not arguing anymore. (P13)*

One aspect of social media is that it is easy to withdraw from friends, and that the in-person nuances of withdrawing are less easily interpreted online.

Changing perceptions

In our interviews, about 30% of the dyads changed their perception of their friend after the event. From the survey responses, more people felt that their relationship had changed with weak ties than with strong ties $\chi 2(1, N = 102) = 7.68$, $p = 0.0056$. These changes happened after realizing that their friend had a position they did not know, or that their friend was not being as rational as usual:

> *We all grew up in the same general neighborhood in the same general background. You know nobody was particularly wealthy or over privileged but [...] these two women had married into a lot of money and it changed them. And that was very evident in the types of things they wrote on Facebook [...] those are the kinds of things that shocked me. (P9)*

In contrast, friends who were closer knew where the other stood and these conversations were minor compared to the overall friendship:

> *I guess you look at it like a bank account right. And over the years he's made so many donations [...]And we build a good friendship. And so when he does once in awhile gets, you know, ugly it's a small withdrawal and so he's not been corrupting the bank. [...] we'll get heated but the thing is afterwards we, you know, hug it out and that's about it (P12)*

It may be more helpful, during times of contentious discussions, to pull out common ground aspects of each person's profile. Relating on shared experiences or common values to keep perspective on differences. One of our participants experienced this during our interview. She was navigating Facebook as she was answering our questions. When we asked her to talk about a friend, she pulled up the friendship page that aggregates Facebook information about her and her friend's profile highlighting similarities, pictures tagged in together, and wall posts:

> *This Facebook [friendship page feature] is really interesting. We both like "To Kill a Mockingbird" and the Bible and music. (P6)*

This brought forward the reasons they were friends in the first place. Through reminiscing on these aspects of her friendship that were documented on Facebook, she remembered character strengths that she might consider to be "deposits in the friendship bank account." Elements that are displayed on the friendship page could be highlighted while friends communicate. This could mean leveraging the Friendship page, as a more readily available resource.

For many weak ties Facebook was the only means of communication: 42% of survey respondents who mentioned weak ties communicated with them on Facebook at least once a month, while 4% communicated by email, 4% saw each other in person, and none talked over the phone. This means that our participants gathered impressions of their weak ties almost solely based on Facebook behavior. As this participant suggests, the ability to relate and sympathize may be different in person than online:

> *"You're not able to see the look in someone's eye or um... hear their tone. I feel like some of the Christians that I know who are against marriage equality [...] they genuinely do love people. And I hear that in their voice, and I hear that tension in their voice because they know how they sound and they don't want to sound that way. Like I hear it. And you can't express that online. Like you can hear it face to face, but you can't express it online. There's just something missing that can't be captured through a screen" (P6)*

By studying these relationships in specific events of contention, we highlighted some of the tensions around managing relationships with dissenting friends. Recalling past history was a way to settle the shock of unexpected behavior, or putting the relationship into perspective by rationalizing the reasons that caused the difference. Showing common ground and allowing more opportunities to engage with weak ties could strengthen these bonds.

DISCUSSION

The behaviors of our participants around contentious events revealed effects of increased polarization and congregating with like-minded others. Those with the minority opinion in their group of friends disappeared from the conversation, and weak ties, those most likely to present different views, were more brittle to these arguments. Together, they create politically like-minded cloisters in social media.

We found that all our participants could relate to an experience of political contention on Facebook. These experiences caused significant struggles, from trying to rationalize the behavior of a friend to deciding whether to terminate the friendship. As we saw in our results, when politics appear on Facebook there is currently more opportunity for politically engaged users to become more polarized rather than to converse with the other side.

Our first design implication is *making common ground visible* (i.e., highlighting past interactions and shared interests). Past research has shown that weak ties are important for getting access to information and being exposed to other ideas [16]. Yet, supporting communication between weak ties is delicate. Our finding that weak ties primarily communicate through Facebook echoes previous work [14]. Thus as the medium through which these relationships are expressed and maintained, Facebook has the potential of helping people stay in contact with weak ties. Through bringing common ground to light, such as displaying a past history of the friendship next to an argument could help alleviate some tensions.

Second, *increasing exposure and engagement between weak ties* could make them more resilient in the face of political disagreement. Not only are people mainly friends with like-minded others, but their few friends of different opinions will not expose them to other views. Bursting the filter bubble could happen in existing social networks, simply by hearing the voices of those with different opinions. The absence of dissenting friends from the debate means missed potential for discussion and deliberation; this reinforces the echo chamber. On Facebook's newsfeed, where the algorithm for displaying posts is unknown, this effect might be redoubled: people who do not communicate with each other do not appear in each other's newsfeed. Rather than showing extremes, all supporting or all dissenting posts, the newsfeed could select a subset of each side of the argument to present a more nuanced display of opinions [22]. We speculate that these changes could bring more weak ties to light since they are the ones who are less emphasized in the newsfeed currently.

Social media might be able to create bridges across ideologies. Insofar as this cross-communication currently occurs, our findings suggest that users may remove themselves from the conversation or from the website. Currently, muffling political discussions, or at least discouraging them, might create a more welcoming environment. This has the consequence of further digging trenches between friends of differing opinions. Designing social media towards nudging users to strengthen relationships with weak ties of different opinions could have beneficial consequences for the platform, for users, and for society.

LIMITATIONS AND FUTURE WORK

Our participants present the biases of heavy social media users and a politically engaged population. They might have been more sensitive to political posts, and held stronger reactions to political disagreements than less politically inclined users. Future work could focus on two other populations: people who aren't heavy social media users (how do they stay in contact with friends of dissenting views?), and people who don't have strong political opinions. Studying the conditions under which friends of different opinion can coexist in social media suggests implications for designing bridges between homogeneous clusters.

We measured perceptions of similarity in our participant's network. A follow-up study could focus on how actual homophily affects behavior around political events. This would require data from actual user profiles. Prior work has found that people perceive greater homogeneity than what is actually present, meaning that people perceive their friends to be more similar to them than they actually are [15]. Designing systems that rectify this gap could bring to light the hidden diversity in one's social network.

Lastly, our study was culturally specific. The dual-party system and binary polarization that ensues is possibly unique to the U.S. Moreover, cultural aspects of the U.S. might exacerbate differences across party lines such as the ease of mobility and choice of lifestyle [4] that makes political issues have deep ramifications in personal choices and social associations.

CONCLUSION

By talking directly to users about their experiences with politics on Facebook, we were able to see what network analysis studies cannot: co-existing online with people of different opinions is a constant negotiation. Homophily is the process by which people tend to congregate with others similar to them. However, friends do not always see eye to eye. We found that our participants *engaged less on Facebook* when they felt overwhelmed by politics, and that weak ties *were fragile when they did talk* about politics. Our work contributes to prior scholarship through highlighting opportunities for social media to bridge across differences.

These opportunities posit that social media could better facilitate discussions across ideologies. We suggest opportunities to make weak ties more resilient. Calling attention to past interactions and shared interests could make common ground visible during arguments. These strategies, such as knowing when to step away, point to constant negotiations evolving around disagreements.

ACKNOWLEDGMENTS

Thank you to our participants for their time and insights; Gary Hsieh, Saedieh Bakhshi, Tanushree Mitra, Chaya Hiruncharoenvate, Casey Fiesler and Maia Jacobs for their comments on early versions; and the anonymous reviewers for their feedback. This work is supported by NSF grant IIS-1212338.

REFERENCES

1. Adamic, L. and N. Glance, The Political Blogosphere and the 2004 U.S. Election: Divided They Blog. *Proc. LinkKDD,* 2005.
2. Baumer, E., Sinclair, J., and Tomlinson, B. "America Is Like Metamucil": Fostering Critical and Creative Thinking about Metaphor in Political Blogs. *Proc. CHI,* 2010. 1437-1446.
3. Bernard, H.R., Killworth, P., et al. The Problem of Informant Accuracy The Validity of Retrospective Data. Annual Review of Anthropology, 1984. 495-517.

4. Bishop, B., *The Big Sort: Why the Clustering of Like-Minded America is Tearing Us Apart*. 2009. Mariner Books.
5. Braun, V. and Clarke, V. Using thematic analysis in psychology. *Qualitative Research in Psychology,* 2006. 3(2): p. 77-101.
6. Brzozowski, M., Hogg, T., and Szabo G. Friends and foes: Ideological social networking. *Proc. CHI,* 2008. 817-820.
7. Burke, M. and Kraut, R. Using Facebook After Losing a Job: Differential Benefits of Strong and Weak Ties. *Proc. CSCW*, 2013. 1419-1430.
8. Burke, M., Kraut, R., and Marlow, C. Social Capital on Facebook: Differentiating Uses and Users. *Proc. CHI,* 2011. 571-580.
9. Das, S., and Kramer, A. Self-Censorship on Facebook. *Proc. ICWSM.* 2013.
10. Doris-Down, A., Versee, H., and Gilbert, E. Political Blend: An Application Designed to Bring People Together Based on Political Differences. *Proc. C&T,* 2013.
11. Duggan, M. and Brenner, J. The Demographics of Social Media Users — 2012. P*ew Internet and American Life Project*, 2013.
12. Garrett, R.K., Echo chambers online?: Politically motivated selective exposure among Internet news users. *Journal of Computer-Mediated Communication*, 2009. 14(2): p. 265-285.
13. Gilbert, E., Blogs Are Echo Chambers: Blogs Are Echo Chambers. *Proc. HICSS.* 2008.
14. Gilbert, E. and Karahalios, K. Predicting tie strength with social media. *Proc. CHI,* 2009. 211-220.
15. Goel, S., Mason, W., and Watts, D.J. Real and perceived attitude agreement in social networks. *Journal of Personality and Social Psychology,* 2010. 99(4) 611-621.
16. Granovetter, M.S., The Strength of Weak Ties. *The American Journal of Sociology*, 1973. 78(6) 1360-1380.
17. Hampton, K., Sessions Goulet, L., et al. Social networking sites and our lives. *Pew Internet and American Life Project,* 2011.
18. Hemphill, L., Otterbacher, J., and Shapiro, M. What's Congress Doing on Twitter? *Proc. CSCW*, 2013. 877-886.
19. Kriplean, T., Morgan, J., et al. Supporting Reflective Public Thought with considerate. *Proc. CSCW*, 2012. 265-274.
20. Marsden, P.V., Core Discussion Networks of Americans. *American Sociological Review*, 1987. 52(1) 122-131.
21. McPherson, M., Smith-Lovin, L. and Cook, J.M. Birds of a feather: Homophily in social networks. *Annual review of sociology,* 2001. 415-444.
22. Munson, S. and Resnick, P. Presenting Diverse Political Opinions: How and How Much. *Proc. CHI.* 2010. 1457- 1466.
23. Munson, S. and Resnick, P. The Prevalence of Political Discourse in Non-Political Blogs. *Proc. ICWSM*, 2011.
24. Putnam, R.D. Bowling alone: the collapse and revival of American community. Simon & Schuster, New York. 2000.
25. Rainie, L. and Smith, A. Social networking sites and politics. *Pew Internet and the American Life Project,* 2012.
26. Rainie, L., Smith, A., et al., Social Media and Political Engagement. *Pew Internet and the American Life Project,* 2012.
27. Roback, A. and Hemphill, L. "I'd have to vote against you": Issue Campaigning via Twitter. *CSCW Extended Abstracts,* 2013. 259-262.
28. Sleeper, M., Balebako, R., et al. The Post that Wasn't: Exploring Self-Censorship on Facebook. *Proc. CSCW,* 2013. 793-802.
29. Stutzman, F., Gross, R. and Acquisti, A. Silent Listeners: The Evolution of Privacy and Disclosure on Facebook. *Journal of Privacy and Confidentiality*, 2013.
30. Sukumaran, A., Vezich, S., et al. Normative Influences on Thoughtful Online Participation. *Proc. CHI*, 2011. 3401-3410.
31. Sunstein, C. The Law of Group Polarization. *Journal of Political Philosophy,* 2002.
32. Sunstein, C. Republic.com 2.0. Princeton University Press, 2009.
33. Wimmer, A. and Lewis, K. Beyond and below racial homophily: ERG models of a friendship network documented on Facebook. *American Journal of Sociology*, 2010. (116) 583-642.
34. Zhao, C., Hinds, P. and Gao, G. How and To Whom People Share: The Role of Culture in Self-Disclosure in Online Communities. *Proc. CSCW,* 2012. 67-76.

Social Media Supporting Political Deliberation Across Multiple Public Spheres: Towards Depolarization

Bryan Semaan[1], Scott P. Robertson[1], Sara Douglas[2], Misa Maruyama[2]
[1]Information and Computer Sciences Department,[2]Communication and Information Sciences Program
University of Hawai'i at Mānoa
Honolulu, HI 96822 USA
{bsemaan, scott.robertson, sarad, misattm}@hawaii.edu

ABSTRACT
This paper reports on a qualitative study of social media use for political deliberation by 21 U.S. citizens. In observing people's interactions in the "sprawling public sphere" across multiple social media tools in both political and non-political spaces, we found that social media supported the interactional dimensions of deliberative democracy—the interaction with media and the interaction between people. People used multiple tools through which they: were serendipitously exposed to diverse political information, constructed diverse information feeds, disseminated diverse information, and engaged in respectful and reasoned political discussions with diverse audiences. When people's civic agency was inhibited when using a tool, they often adopted, or switched to, alternative media that could afford what they were trying to achieve. Contrary to the polarization perspective, we find that people were purposefully seeking diverse information and discussants. Some individuals altered their views as a result of the interactions they were having in the online public sphere.

Author Keywords
Social media; public sphere; depolarization; multi-mediation

ACM Classification Keywords
K.4.3 [Computers and Society]: Organizational Impacts – Computer-Supported cooperative work.

INTRODUCTION
Social media, like Social Networking Sites (SNSs), blogs and YouTube, have become popular online destinations in recent years. Researchers have studied the use of social media, with recent emphasis on SNSs such as Facebook and Twitter, from a variety of perspectives, e.g. "social searching" [22] and social capital [12].

The study of the use of social media, with respect to the political deliberation process, has become an active research topic in the CSCW and CHI communities [e.g. 17, 28, 34, 42]. The major activities that constitute deliberative democracy—information sharing, discussion, and public participation—may now be facilitated by online media as citizens can gather together virtually, irrespective of geographic location, and engage in information exchange and discussion as long as they have an Internet connection.

CSCW '14, February 15–19, 2014, Baltimore, Maryland, USA.

http://dx.doi.org/10.1145/2531602.2531605

Recent work has found that the political deliberation emerging online is complex [27, 29, 30]. Some researchers have found that people seek diverse information and discussion [38], whereas other scholars fear that Internet will lead to "polarization" as users will connect exclusively with like-minded others [16]. The latter behavior can lead to the reaffirmation and strengthening of previously held views [40].

We believe that the affordances of social media provide a space through which citizens can engage in meaningful political interactions. In this paper, we describe how people use various social media to interact in the public sphere by seeking and disseminating diverse information and opinions, as well as engaging in rational discussions with diverse audiences—only we turn our analytic attention to how people participate in deliberative activities across multiple public spheres (both political and non-political) available through several social media. We show how, contrary to the polarization perspective, people were seeking diversity in information, opinions and discussants. We report how the interactions people were having even led some individuals to alter their perspectives on political issues like civic matters, politicians and public policy.

DELIBERATIVE DEMOCRACY AND THE PUBLIC SPHERE
Deliberative democracy—also known as political deliberation—is a process where citizens voluntarily and freely participate in discussions on public issues [8]. The notion of deliberative democracy finds its roots in the utopian ideal of democracy where citizens engage and talk with one another in a civil manner. In this respect, political deliberation is a discursive system where people share information about public affairs, talk politics, form opinions, and participate in political processes [8, 19].

Deliberative democracy can only exist in the public sphere—"a domain of our social life in which such a thing as public opinion can be formed" [18, 19, 20]. As theorized by Habermas [18], the public sphere is a democratic space that facilitates open, reasoned and reflexive interaction and communication among different kinds of publics. A public sphere only functions properly when people with different views and backgrounds are able to freely express themselves, engage in rational discussion, and disseminate information.

Recent work has built on Habermas' definition by conceptualizing the public sphere as consisting of three dimensions: structures, representations and interactions [10]. Structures consist of formal institutional features, e.g. how media organizations are structured. Representations refer to the output of the media, like campaign materials. Interactions consist of two aspects, which will be the focus of this paper.

The first aspect of interaction deals with how materials made available by the media are communicated from the media to citizens and between citizens. The interaction between media and citizens focuses on how people acquire and encounter information (i.e. through the media or through other citizens), and the ways in which individuals share information and opinions with others. The second feature of interaction deals with the "deliberative" aspect of democracy that focuses on the rational discussions that emerge between citizens. Thus, three forms of interaction emerge in the public sphere: the acquisition of information and opinion, the dissemination of information and opinion, and the discussions that take place between people.

In further building on Habermas' vision, Dahlgren [11], in defining what he refers to as civic culture, contends that there exist six pre-conditions of mutual reciprocity for interaction in the public sphere, including: knowledge, values, trust, spaces, practices, and identities.

Knowledge refers to the idea that a citizens' ability to participate in the public sphere is predicated upon their ability to acquire knowledge or disseminate knowledge. *Values* refer to a citizens' ability to engage in the public sphere as dictated by the values of openness, reciprocity, discussion and accountability. *Trust* deals with how individuals must be able to adequately engage with people they may or may not know personally, but feel that they can have a satisfactory exchange. There must exist *spaces* (offline and online) through which people can meet and discuss political candidates and issues. *Practices* refer to the set of stable, individual and collective practices in which participation can be embodied, e.g. voting. Finally, *identities* involve the concept that people have an awareness of the characteristics that comprise their political beliefs and attitudes, and that they have the right to those attitudes and beliefs.

When any of these preconditions are compromised, civic agency—people's ability to interact and participate in the public sphere—can be inhibited. For example, if a conflict exists in the value systems of participants in the public sphere, agency can be constrained as people may be unwilling to discuss political issues with people who are not respectful of differing opinions.

SOCIAL MEDIA AND POLITICAL PUBLIC SPHERES

Social media can be viewed as a new type of online public sphere [6, 10, 14]. The Pew Internet and American Life project has shown increasing use of the Internet and social media for political activity [23, 32]. Raine and Smith [32] found that 25% of their interview respondents used social media to discuss or debate political issues with others. Thirty percent of respondents said that their friends post occasionally about politics and 25% said that they have become more involved politically as the result of information in their social networking feeds. Other recent work has explored the emergence of the public sphere in online spaces devoted to political discussion like political blogs [1, 13, 41], political discussion forums [31], political videos posted on YouTube [24, 25], and political and media accounts on SNSs [17, 33, 42, 44].

Amongst public sphere scholars, there is a widely shared view that the Internet serves as an "echo chamber" in which people tend to seek political information that is aligned with their beliefs, or discuss political issues and candidates with citizens who are also in support of those issues and candidates [e.g. 2, 16, 40, 43]. For example, in their study of political blogs, Adamic and Glance [1] reported that the majority of blogs in their sample only linked to blogs that shared the same political ideology. Similarly, Gilbert Bergstrom, and Karahalios [16], in analyzing blog comments, found that blogs were echo chambers: comments were more likely to be in agreement with the original blog post.

Other researchers, however, have argued that online discussion and debate is more complex and diverse [21, 27, 38, 39]. For example, in-depth interview data of online discussion group members suggests that Internet users do seek diverse information [38]. In a large-scale survey conducted during the 2004 election season, Horrigan, Garrett, and Resnick [21] found that Internet users did not filter out viewpoints contradictory to their own, and, as a result, were more aware of diverse political arguments than non-Internet users. Others have reported mixed results. Munson and Resnick [27] found that online reading behavior was user dependent—some people seek diverse information ("challenge-seeking") while others only seek information that reinforces their individual beliefs ("challenge averse"). Papacharissi [30] argues that online media are both an augmented public sphere that broadens the types of information available to participants and also a potentially polarizing public sphere. Similarly, Gentzkow and Shapiro [15] found ideological segregation online to be worse than print media, but not as polarized as Sunstein feared.

INTERACTIONS IN THE SPRAWLING PUBLIC SPHERE

Whereas the majority of scholarship has focused on the political deliberation that emerges in online spaces dedicated to politics, few studies have examined the political discussions and information exchange that emerges in non-political spaces [e.g. 3, 7, 28]. Chadwick [7] asserts that researchers should focus on the deliberation that emerges in non-political spaces, or "third spaces," as the online political interactions may more closely resemble what naturally unfolds in the physical world.

Research has shown that users of social media are exposed to diverse political information [3] and discussions [28] in non-political spaces. For example, in their study of blogging activity, Munson and Resnick [28] reported that 25% of the discussions taking place in non-political blogs were political in nature. Since they usually cater to specific ideological groups, online public spheres devoted to political discussion may be more prone to polarization. Conversely, political discussion in non-political arenas might be less polarized and possibly more conducive to reasoned consideration of alternative viewpoints.

It is important to understand the ways in which people exchange political information and opinion, and discuss politics, in online public spheres not specifically devoted to politics (in addition to political ones), as people may have access to a more diverse audience with more varying opinions. Some non-political online spaces are highly personal in that they contain friends and close acquaintances (e.g. Facebook) whereas others are less personal in that they many connect people with weak ties (e.g. Twitter).

Papacharissi [29] introduces a new way of thinking about the public sphere within the context of social media, as various tools are hybrid environments that are private with public features. She defines the "private sphere" as an online media space that provides people with the autonomy that is most associated with physical private spaces, but with the potential audience of a public act. For example, though blogging is often done as a "narcissistic" act of self-expression, it may still contribute to public discourse. The unique "hybridity" of digital media allows for different types of expression in different spaces. The proliferation of social media has thus enabled people to interact with multiple audiences in multiple expressive manners [29]—in a more private and personal manner as well as in a more public and impersonal manner. Both types of expressive manners can influence public discourse. Thus, people's interactions across media might have a democratizing value [29].

The hybridity of social media might influence the degree to which people are exposed to diverse ideas or the degree to which they engage in discussion with people holding alternative viewpoints. For example, in relationship-based networks like Facebook, people may be more inclined to listen to and engage with their audience, or to acknowledge different perspectives. Conversely, Facebook users may wish not to share their political opinions in what they consider to be a private space to keep people in their network from "unfriending" them or hiding their newsfeed activity [e.g. 32].

Recent work has attempted to characterize the political discussions that emerge in third spaces—and preliminary results have found the interactions to be diverse. Conover Ratkiewicz, Fancisco, Goncalves, Flammini, and Menczer [9], in analyzing over 250,000 tweets from the six weeks leading to the 2010 U.S. congressional midterm election, found that the network of political retweets exhibited a highly segregated partisan structure with limited connectivity between right- and left-leaning users. However, with respect to user mentions, users were targeting people with differing opinions for purposes of discussion. Similarly, Morgan, Lampe and Shafiq [26] found that Twitterers disseminate cross-ideological information.

To our knowledge, few studies have looked at how users appropriate multiple social media for purposes of political deliberation. In evaluating the public sphere by taking into account online media, Dahlgren [10] re-characterized the public sphere as having a "sprawling" characteristic—it is spread out across various online tools. Considerable cross-pollenization may occur across the various public spheres (political and non-political) as users engage with others using multiple technologies. For example, people may discuss politics with a diverse audience in one medium and disseminate links and opinions in another. Rather than study one public sphere at a time, we turn our analytic attention to the ways in which any given user appropriates one or many social media for political deliberation.

We hypothesize that the affordances of social media can support the interactional dimensions of the public sphere—access to information from media and other citizens, the dissemination of information and opinions, and discussion between citizens. We further propose that each medium may support interaction in varying ways which are relative to the affordances of each tool. Whereas social media can support interaction, although it was not a part of our hypothesis, we believe that the ongoing interactions that emerge in these networked publics between people and the media, and between people, can have a depolarizing effect on the public sphere, for several reasons. Firstly, people can interact with media from diverse perspectives outside of their own political ideology. Secondly, people can interact with other citizens who may or may not share the same views. Lastly, people may be introduced to political issues through media and other citizens that they may have otherwise never come across.

In this study, we utilize qualitative techniques to build on previous work by exploring how individuals use one or more social media tools to engage in the political deliberation process in both political and non-political spaces. We adopt the view that people's deliberative activities are multi-mediated [5] as people can use multiple media to engage in any given activity. Depending on how a tool is instantiated in practice (by a user), if an individual feels that they lack agency (when a pre-condition of civic culture is not met) within one public sphere, they may adopt, or switch to, alternative social media through which they can seek information, disseminate information, and engage in rational discussions.

METHODOLOGY

This study is part of a larger research program to understand how people use social media as part of the political deliberation process [e.g. 33]. Our data is based on a longitudinal interview study with United States citizens who already used social media to learn about and discuss politics.

The goal of the study was to understand how politically involved social media users engaged in online deliberation, and to that end we recruited social media users interested in politics. We found informants through multiple seeds with the intention of limiting sampling biases. Firstly, the study team recruited subjects through personal contacts consisting of friends and family (1 subject). Secondly, we posted recruitment fliers on and around the college campus to seek additional interview subjects (5 subjects). Thirdly, we enlisted informants through a newsletter distributed by a local news agency (9 subjects). Lastly, we recruited participants through online postings on Twitter, Facebook, and Craig's List (5 subjects). We then used a snowball sampling technique [4] to recruit additional informants (1 subject). All subjects were given a $20 dollar Amazon gift card as remuneration for their participation in the study. The study team maintained a shared list of the volunteers who responded to our inquiries, which we used to contact people to schedule interviews.

We conducted twenty-one semi-structured interviews (interviews are ongoing) with unique informants before the November 2012 US election (beginning in May), and six follow-up interviews after the election (beginning in February 2013). Interview questions were open-ended. We allowed our informants to guide the inquiry while probing them for additional information. We purposefully designed the protocol to be general because we did not want to influence informants' responses.

We first asked our informants to identify, from the social media platforms they had integrated into their daily lives, which technologies they used to engage in the political deliberation process. In order to better understand the different uses of each respective technology and the underlying personal motivations for the use of each tool, we asked the same set of questions for each medium that they said they used while asking people to provide us with relevant examples. We asked people to identify the activities they engaged in, how they engaged in those activities (i.e. which features they used to engage in the activities they previously described), who (if anyone) they deliberated with (and for what reason they did or did not engage with others), what their level of participation was in the activities they described (and for what reason(s) they did or did not participate), how often and for how long they used a given tool, and the motivation(s) for using a respective technology. We then asked our informants to describe the reason(s), if any, which motivated their use of multiple social media for political deliberation.

Interviews were conducted with individuals living in the continental United States and its territories. We conducted both face-to-face and long-distance interviews. In person interviews took place on the University of Hawaiʻi at Mānoa campus. For people who were either unable to travel to the university or lived in the continental U.S., we used the telephone or Skype™. Interviews lasted anywhere from forty minutes to two and a half hours in length. With participant permission, following the interviews the first author added participants' usernames to his social media accounts to make general observations about participants' online activity and verify the validity of their personal recollections and, in turn, our findings. All interviews were recorded and transcribed for analysis.

The lead author coded interview transcripts using Atlas.ti—a qualitative data analysis workbench. Utilizing an approach from grounded theory [37], we first used open coding to identify general themes made explicit during interviews, which went through numerous iterations as we developed new codes, evaluated existing codes, and collapsed/expanded codes following each subsequent interview. We then reduced our codes under axial coding to generate the themes presented in this paper.

Participants and Social Media

Our informants were diverse with respect to their age, gender and education levels, as well as their educational backgrounds and work roles. Our eleven male and ten female participants ranged from eighteen to sixty-seven years of age. We interviewed people who had never attended or graduated from college, as well as undergraduate and graduate students in various disciplines like Computer Science and English. Our informants were also diverse with respect to their political orientations—11 reported being Democrat, 7 reported being Independent, and 3 reported being Republican. We also interviewed people who were working in various professions, e.g. as professors and entrepreneurs. All of our informants integrated at least one social media tool into their lives.

Table 2 provides a breakdown of the primary social media platforms that emerged from our interviews, the number of participants that used each social media tool, and which participants used (or did not use) each social media tool.

Facebook is a SNS through which people maintain a semi-public profile. Facebook users can construct a network of friends, whereby the act of adding a friend is mutual. More recently, Facebook implemented the ability for people to categorize their connections into groups. Users can post "status" updates to their profiles, and these updates appear in the Facebook "newsfeed"—the main page consisting of a stream of posts from friends. Users can peruse this stream to obtain information and opinions from their connections, or to engage in lively discussions with friends and friends-of-friends. Users can also visit a friends' personal page and initiate a discussion. Facebook users can join public and private groups that can be interest based, e.g. video games, or person-based, e.g. Barack Obama, where people can discuss a wide array of issues and topics (including politics). Users can also "like" public profiles to receive updates in their respective newsfeed.

Twitter is a communication platform that allows users to broadcast 140-character messages (tweets) to other users who subscribe to their accounts (followers). Twitter does not employ a mutual relationship-based dynamic. For example, user A can *follow* user B, but it is not required that user B *follow* user A. Twitter users (twitterers) receive tweets from the set of users they elect to follow. Thus, twitterers can follow politicians and other political groups to receive timely updates. Furthermore, promoted to enhance the searchability of tweets, the #hashtag convention is now used by twitterers to mark up tweets with thematic keywords of their choice. For twitterers whose accounts are not explicitly set as private, every tweet is also posted to a public, searchable timeline. The retweet emerged as a forwarding technique whereby twitterers pass on tweets with attribution to the original author. Twitterers began to use the @ sign preceding another user's account name as a way of mentioning or addressing tweets to a specific user. This convention allows users to engage in one-on-one, yet still public, conversation.

Google+ is a social media platform that allows people to follow others and place them in "circles" based on self-created categories. Users can share information and posts of unlimited length, and target their posts to all of their connections or to a specific circle (or circles). People have access to a "stream" (similar to the Facebook newsfeed) where they can view what their connections are saying and engage in discussions, and users have the ability to filter their streams based on circles. Users can also "follow" other users without placing them in circles. Like with Facebook, Google+ users can join and create groups where people can engage in discourse.

Blogs (or weblogs) allow users to create a profile (anonymous or not) through which they can write posts of an unspecified length. People can peruse the blogosphere to obtain information and opinions from other citizens as well as politicians and media sources. Through blogs, people can engage in discussions with other people through a comments section on a post-to-post basis. People from anywhere in the world can comment on a blog post (barring privacy settings), providing their perspective on issues, sharing similar experiences, and so on.

YouTube is an account-based platform that enables people to create videos that they can, in turn, share with a global audience. People also have the ability to search for and watch videos, as well as engage in lively discussions with others. Users must be logged into their account (which is now linked to people's Google profile) to post videos or engage in discussions, though they do not need to log in to watch videos and view comments.

Online forums like Reddit are social media that allow people to create posts (typically anonymous or via an alias) based on various topics. People are free to peruse the political postings of others, as well as interact with one another, and discuss a wide array of topics with a global audience. In order to make contributions, however, users must have an account.

Social Media	Number of Users [Informants (p)]
Facebook	21 [p1 – p21]
Twitter	17 [excluding: p4, p8, p12, p17]
Google+	5 [p5, p9, p19, p20, p21]
Blogs	7 [p3, p9, p11, p15, p16, p19, p21]
YouTube	11 [excluding: p4, p5, p8, p9, p10, p11, p12, p13, p17, p20]
Online Forums (e.g. Reddit)	4 [p9, p15, p19, p21]

Table 2: Social Media used by Informants

From our sample, three informants used a single medium for political deliberation, whereas the remaining adopted two or more (see Table 2). Our informants described using social media multiple times a day, from half an hour to several hours in total. They were using these online technologies on their personal and work computers, as well as on their mobile phones when commuting.

DELIBERATION IN THE ONLINE PUBLIC SPHERE

We found many cases where our informants adopted new media, or switched to media that they already used, in order to seek and consume information, disseminate information and opinions, and engage in political discourse. Thirteen of our informants reported adopting new media and constructing networks specifically to engage in the necessary interactions that constitute a Habermasean public sphere, like open and rational discourse (whereas others switched to other media they had already adopted for political contexts).

Through informants' accounts we show how people interacted in the "sprawling public sphere" [10] available through multiple social media. We learned that informants were (1) being exposed to a wide variety of political topics from diverse perspectives and populations through social media, (2) using social media to disseminate diverse information and opinions, and (3) seeking out reasoned and respectful discussions. When people found that their ability to interact was limited in one medium, they often adopted, or switched to, different tools to maintain civic agency. Furthermore, contrary to the view that social media is associated with polarization [e.g. 40], our results show that people were acquiring and disseminating diverse information and opinions, as well as interacting with diverse audiences (as opposed to only interacting with like-minded others). The interactions that people were having in the public sphere led some individuals to change their political attitudes and beliefs.

From Serendipity to Organized Information Acquisition

Our informants reported using either one medium, or a combination of media like Facebook, Twitter, Google+, online news sites and YouTube, through which they could obtain political news and information. When people's civic agency was constrained in any given tool for information acquisition, they often adopted or switched to other media through which they could seek information more effectively.

With respect to obtaining information, many of our informants reported starting with Facebook and then evolving to use of alternative tools after determining that Facebook was lacking in some way (i.e. affordances or perception of the tool itself). In fact, the majority of our informants reported not actively seeking political information through Facebook initially. Whereas some individuals were receiving campaign updates from politicians' pages, they often commented on how the information that was made public did not help them with respect to the deliberation process as they could only receive "trivial updates". People also felt that politicians' pages were homogenous [33].

Similar to the way in which bloggers can be exposed to political information in blogs not devoted to politics [28], all of our informants reported being exposed to political information when scanning through their newsfeeds. They described how people often posted opinions about political issues and topics, as well as links to political materials outside of Facebook, e.g. news sites. In other words, people were being exposed to political information in a serendipitous fashion—through the status updates posted by members of their Facebook network. As explained by p3:

"Right now, I encounter [political information] just by accident, or just by scanning through my newsfeed..."

Our informants described how they often first learned of current events when scanning through their Facebook newsfeeds well before information was made available through traditional media sources like the television. Furthermore, they were being introduced to new and familiar views and perspectives on common topics, to problems and events with which they were unfamiliar, and to global perspectives on issues that were happening worldwide. Not all of our participants were receptive to the information being posted by people in their networks. Three informants reported "unfriending", "unfollowing", or hiding a friend's feed to avoid "listening to recurring polarizing political posts" [32].

After this serendipitous exposure to political information persisted, the majority of our informants claimed to have, at some point, shifted their use of Facebook to actively peruse their newsfeeds and seek out political news and opinions. Three of our informants reported using Facebook as their only source for political information.

For example, as described by a male journalist (p12), Facebook was an all-encompassing deliberative tool. He described how although he was unable to structure his information feed and filter out non-political topics, he did not mind spending the necessary time in order to "stay up to date with [his] newsfeed".

However, with respect to purposefully seeking political information, eight participants reported that the mixture of political and non-political topics that comprised their newsfeeds, and/or the inadequate search functionality built into the tool, limited their ability to effectively seek political information. As described by p1:

"...although I still use Facebook daily to seek political news, it is no longer the only media I use... it's so hard to filter out the political information... from all the... 'cute cat photos'..."

Furthermore, nine informants described how the way in which Facebook was tied to their real world identity further restricted its function as a tool for obtaining political news and information from multiple perspectives, thus limiting their civic agency. Before the functionality to "follow" was added, in order to receive newsfeed updates from political candidates and news media agencies, Facebook users had to "Like" a respective political candidate or news agency's Facebook profile. Our informants explained how they were unable to "Like" candidates or news agencies that did not align with their personal views as this practice was tied to their personal identities. As described by p3:

"Facebook to me is way more personal. I can't go and 'Like' a candidate's site on Facebook that I don't align with politically. I have a pretty large network on Facebook... I don't want them to see that I'm following the 'other' side... it really restricts me because I can't follow those other views so easily [and receive their updates]..."

In order to receive timely and diverse political information, fifteen of our informants adopted or switched to alternative media like Twitter and Google+ to self-organize and create more structured political newsfeeds to counter the lack of civic agency in Facebook. Importantly, our informants were structuring their networks to include information and opinions from people and media that did not align with their personal political views—a major component of depolarization.

One informant (p15), a male graduate student in Computer Science, described how his Facebook network was homogenous by design. He felt it was difficult using Facebook to actively seek political information as the majority of his newsfeed was personal in nature; though when his friends shared their political opinions he most always found himself to be in agreement as they were all "left leaning." He was also uncomfortable following more conservative media and politicians through Facebook because of the misalignment with his personal views. In order to expose himself to diverse opinions and a wider spectrum of information, he re-oriented his Twitter use (which he had initially adopted to follow the "local food truck" scene) to include media networks, politicians, and radio personalities across the political spectrum.

Similarly, a female informant (p19) who was employed as a service administrator, described how "horrible Facebook's search interface is". She had a difficult time filtering through her feed, especially when she was looking for political information. In seeking a better political information environment she first adopted Twitter to create an organized newsfeed. In finding the way in which Twitter presents information to be "too overwhelming", she began using Google+. Using the circles feature of Google+, she crafted a robust information environment. She created several circles for unique groups based on political ideology, e.g. conservative and liberal media, and would traverse her circles to peruse political information from multiple perspectives.

Through serendipity and the organization of diverse networks for political information and opinions, people were establishing common ground with others who held opposing views, reinforcing their existing views after better understanding "the other side" and, in some cases, formulating new opinions on issues that were counter to their former beliefs.

One informant who only used Facebook (p4) described how, as a conservative, she could not "wrap her head around President Obama's foreign policy." As a Republican living in Hawaii, which is a left-leaning state, the majority of her Facebook friends were liberal. She began to notice that many of her friends were often posting articles and opinions on foreign policy issues, and over time she began to better understand why people supported Obama's policies. Similarly, as she was exposed to other issues through Facebook, she even better understood the American president as she could see how his policies were affecting her friends who were not as financially stable.

Another informant (p6), who claimed to have changed his stance on issues like the Affordable Care Act ("Obamacare") as a result of his exposure to alternative perspectives, described how his interactions often helped him develop new political views on various issues:

"On Twitter I purposefully follow people and news sources with different viewpoints. For example, one user I try to [follow] is True Conservative... although I'm liberal. Then I'll go through the links they provide and look for stuff. I get a sense of what people are saying from a perspective that's not my own. Occasionally it'll even help me change my opinions."

Our informants were being exposed to diverse information, firstly, through serendipity, and secondly, by purposefully constructing diverse information networks. Contrary to the polarization perspective, people were actively seeking information from different perspectives. Some of our informants altered their beliefs as a result of this exposure to alternative viewpoints from multiple political angles.

Multiple Networks for Information and Opinion Dissemination

Our informants reported using either one medium, or a combination of media through which they disseminate political information and opinions. When people felt that their agency to post was restricted, they adopted and/or switched to alternative media.

Eighteen informants reported using one or more social media to engage in online posting behavior. They were posting information about political candidates, civic issues, or political events that were taking place locally, nationally and globally. We found that people were posting information they obtained from other individuals or news agencies within the same media, e.g. sharing a friend's Facebook status, or posting information they had come across in one medium, such as Twitter, to other media like Google+ and Twitter. As such, people had access to various networks through which they could obtain and, in turn, disseminate information and opinions. Importantly, people were disseminating cross-ideological information.

For six of our informants, Facebook served as the primary vehicle for sharing information. Using the status functionality within the medium, people posted opinions, factual links, and factual links combined with self-interpretations about political issues and candidates. They explained that the personal nature of Facebook made them feel more comfortable posting information and opinions from all sides of the political spectrum because the presence of family and friends provided them with what they felt was a "safe environment." Furthermore, they wished to expose their closest connections to more diverse opinions and information that they may not otherwise see.

For twelve informants, however, the presence of family and friends on Facebook limited their ability to share information and opinions. The factors dissuading them from posting on Facebook were mostly consistent with what has been reported in other studies [36]. Specifically, people wanted to avoid upsetting others or getting into arguments.

The way in which Facebook was tied to their real world identity limited their civic agency with respect to disseminating information and opinions. People described a reverse form of identity management—one associated with conflicting value systems. Whereas most studies have reported that individuals limit what they share when a misalignment exists between what they wanted to post and how they want to portray themselves [e.g. 36], our informants reported not posting because of a misalignment between what they were posting and other people's expectations of what they should and should not post. As described by one informant (p10):

"With Facebook there's a stamp of personal convention on what you post. I'm extremely liberal and if I would post something from the conservative slant because I felt people should be aware of that side... I would receive a TON of negative feedback... I was going against their expectations of me... so I stopped posting things like that there."

In order to freely share political information and opinions irrespective of ideology, twelve informants began using one or more media tools like Twitter, Blogs, and Google+. Our informants reported that the impersonal nature of other media made them feel like they could freely disseminate information across the political spectrum. As described by one informant:

"People understand that Twitter is a broadcast medium... even when my family and friends who are following me see what I'm tweeting and retweeting, they don't take issue... they know Twitter is just about getting the word out... what you say isn't tied to who you are as a person."

People were not restricting what they were posting to any one medium. Rather, our informants wanted to reach as broad of an audience as possible while being cognizant of the personal or impersonal nature of the networks they were reaching. One informant (p21) used several media, including Facebook, Twitter, Google+, blogs and Reddit, and targeted his posts based on where he believed he would make the most profound impact. He described this activity as "where to post calculus":

"Well... with Facebook, I had a lot of negative responses in the past. I'd post political stuff that... people thought I shouldn't be posting... So now, whenever I am going to post something political I play 'where to post calculus.' I have to carefully think about what I'm posting. Does it align with people's expectations of me? Where can I potentially make the largest impact and reach the most people? So without fail I post to Twitter because I can post anything [there], then to Google+ because I can choose which circles to target, and maybe my blog... in the end when I get to Facebook... not much ever makes it..."

Another informant (p16), a female entrepreneur and social media advocate living in Hawaii, described how although she felt limited when posting on Facebook because her friends and family always seemed to "get upset with [her] posts," she had adopted other tools through which she could disseminate information. She often targeted specific groups of people with her posts based on potential impact. For example, she used Twitter to disseminate political information and opinions that were of interest to a national audience, whereas she used Google+ to post information and opinions to various circles she had created, e.g. location based, with whom she felt comfortable sharing information.

By disseminating cross-ideological information and opinions to other citizens via the online public spheres available through social media, people were purposefully trying to expose others to new information as well as interpretations that were counter to their personal viewpoints, which is a major component of depolarization. Informants were attempting to help people understand and accept the varying beliefs of others by exposing them to news articles and opinions from media and lay citizens.

For example, one informant (p10), a writer and Native American political activist living in Idaho, described how he used Twitter not only to follow what the news media and public were saying on all sides of the spectrum, but also to retweet those links to disseminate that argument to his followers. He felt that he was trying to "add to people's understanding of issues by exposing them to different interpretations."

Some informants were disseminating information and opinions to try and persuade others to change their views.

One informant (p11) described how he was overly cautious when posting political links or opinions on Facebook. He did not wish to offend anyone, nor did he want his friends and family to, at times, know his true "feelings". However, he wanted to have "some kind of effect and help people understand other perspectives other than their own" and, as such, began using Twitter and blogs to "try and change people's minds."

Respectful and Reasoned Political Engagement with Diverse Audiences

Social media enabled our informants to have access to a public, heterogeneous group of people with whom they could discuss politics on a more frequent basis. Importantly, people reported using social media to seek out diverse audiences with whom they could engage in "rational" and "reasoned" discussions. When one medium did not provide an environment conducive to constructive discussion with people holding different views—when civic agency was restricted—informants adopted and/or switched to other media.

For three informants, social media did not provide a public sphere through which everyone could interact with others. One described how he has tried "every single social media available" and has not yet found a suitable discussion environment. Another informant explained that she does not feel comfortable discussing politics online due to a lack of personal political knowledge (related to political efficacy). Another informant reported purposefully following and having political discussions with other Twitterers who were aligned with his personal political views.

With respect to the public spaces devoted to the discussion of politics, like politician Facebook pages or the public discussions that take place in the comments sections of YouTube and online media like CNN, the majority of our informants described the discussions in these public spaces as being highly polarized and filled with messages of flaming or support [33]. As such, many did not frequent these interaction spaces because they did not facilitate healthy, constructive interaction as there existed a misalignment in people's values.

Despite these negative accounts, eighteen of our informants described having fruitful discussions in the public spheres available through social media. They sought discussants who respected their values and political identities. However, people had varying experiences depending on the tool they used and they made technological choices accordingly.

Six of our informants reported using Facebook for the purpose of political discussion. Due to the personal nature of Facebook, they were more cognizant of their audience and were more sensitive in how they approached the discussion of issues. They also had access to a large population of discussion participants as friends of friends often interacted with one another via newsfeed discussions. As such, people were exposed to other citizens with diverse viewpoints and perspectives, but interacted in a meaningful way. For example, when friends were perceived to be skewing information, our informants felt they could engage and correct them, without offending them. As described by one informant (p17):

"I know they're my friends, but oftentimes we skew facts even if by accident. So if somebody makes a statement, if they're on Facebook, a close friend or an acquaintance, I like to check it. If they're my friends I can say I think that's wrong without upsetting them. They're close to me and don't get offended... it's not like a blog or Tumblr, where people can attack what you say anonymously. There's no anonymity on Facebook, there's an accountability for your words and actions..."

Informants attempted to use other media like Twitter or blogs in conjunction with Facebook but found them to be lacking. Firstly, they felt that Facebook, unlike Twitter, provided interactional context and was more useful as a discussion tool as you could see how a conversation had unfolded by perusing visible comment streams. Secondly, they felt that the Twitter character limit was restrictive and did not facilitate discussion. Lastly, they felt that the anonymity afforded by other media networks like blogs enabled negative interaction like flaming.

However, for others (twelve informants), the presence of family and friends on Facebook led them to use other media. They felt people on Facebook were, as one informant described, "way too emotional." Our informants wanted to avoid upsetting friends and family members, avoid arguments, and ultimately not ruin their relationships. Even when people felt like they were being reasonable in how they approached a discussion on Facebook, their friends and family would still have a negative emotional response. As described by one informant (p5):

"On Facebook I try not to do too much civil discussion and the only reason why I don't do it is because I know way too many people and they get too emotional and take things way too personally.... I've seen really bad stuff happen..."

In order to engage with others, informants began using one or more media to engage in political discussions. Firstly, they described the informality of other networks as improving the overall discursive experience. For example, when people were emotional or engaging in flaming behavior through Twitter, our informants did not take offense, as they did not know many of the other discussion participants personally. They could simply continue searching for or targeting participants who wished to discuss issues rationally. Secondly, four informants adopted other media to interact anonymously. Lastly, informants described how the integration of opinion with facts via the linking to other resources, e.g. news sites and websites, helped in enabling reasoned discussion.

One informant (p21), who was employed at a cannery, described the desire to "connect with people who could change [his] mind." After several "bad experiences" discussing politics through Facebook, he began using a combination of Twitter, Google+, and Reddit. Although he did not knowingly construct informal networks in each respective tool, during our discussion (in checking his networks via his mobile phone) he determined that his networks were mostly informal, but that they had formed that way organically. He used these tools to interact with different audiences who held diverse perspectives, as he wished to find "intelligent people with who [he] could have intelligent discussions."

Another informant (p20), a social worker, found that his Facebook friends were too easily offended when he disagreed with them, and believed the Twitter character limit to be too restrictive. Using Google+, however, he constructed an informal network through which he could engage in meaningful political discussions:

"Google+ is where I take a lot of my debates... and the reason I do that is because I'm not as emotionally attached to a lot of people on that circuit. If they feel offended they can always uncircle me and I don't care. Most of those people end up respecting me and my point of view. I do keep things on a professional level... if I'm disrespectful to someone it's just not good for real discussions...."

The diverse and rational discussions informants were having, in turn, led some people to alter their views on political issues and form what they considered to be more informed perspectives. They were not simply making pre-conceived judgments about other people's political views; rather, they were interested in better understanding why people "held certain perspectives by putting [themselves] in other people's shoes."

As explained by one informant (p13) who changed his views on the RAIL project—a light-rail system that is being constructed on the island of Oahu. During the most recent Mayoral election in 2012, the RAIL project was the most prevalent issue driving political discourse amongst Oahu's residents:

"On Facebook people are free to post and express their likes and dislikes on certain issues and they're all coming from different places and affected in different ways. So many people... are approaching certain issues and I try to understand why certain issues affect them. This can often lead me to re-think my perspectives... for example, with RAIL, I have some friends who were completely against it. I couldn't understand that perspective, but after talking to my friends on Facebook, I was able to really get a feel for why they didn't want it to happen and how it would impact their lives... and frankly, now I agree with them."

Another informant (p9), after feeling limited in her ability to interact with others through Facebook, Twitter, and online news sites, found a neutral blogging site through which she interacted in reasoned discussions that altered her perspectives on political issues. She described how the rational discussions she held with others helped her understand how certain issues like "having the right to choose" actually impacted others and helped her change her perspectives accordingly:

"Yes, because when people disagree on the blog I frequent, as they often do, they tend to argue in a respectful fashion. Not by calling names. And, they tend to argue by bringing up facts... to make their points. It's a reasoned discussion, I like reasoned discussions. And so a... a political discussion online can sometimes change my views. I can see what I thought about such and such is wrong...."

Contrary to the polarization perspective, our informants were actively seeking discussants with diverse perspectives through which they could better establish common ground and understand opposing viewpoints. The conversations people were having even led some people to change their views.

DISCUSSION

We used Habermas' theory of the public sphere, along with Dahlgren's [11] subsequent elaborations, to provide an analytical frame through which we could interpret our empirical data. We examined the political interactions that emerge across diverse social media in both political and non-political spheres. We used qualitative bottom-up methods to understand how users were appropriating multiple social media to engage in political deliberation.

We found that the ways in which people used social media was an interaction between the characteristics and goals of the user and the affordances of the social media tools. The way in which each respective individual appropriated and/or perceived a tool mediated their interactions in the public sphere. Our data suggests that these politically involved and technology savvy people have learned to shape various online social tools to meet their information gathering, posting and participation needs. The affordances of the social media at hand resulted in uniquely structured public spheres with different qualities. We found that the audiences present within a social network could dictate a user's ability to consume and disseminate information, and engage in discussions—and this caused multi-mediation in the context of political deliberation. People made fluid technology choices based on the audiences within their networks, being concerned with how they were perceived by different audiences, and with how their audiences were influenced by their online political activities.

We return to Papacharissi's [29] hypothesis about the public sphere in the age of social media, where she re-conceptualizes the public sphere as being more akin to "private spheres"—or online spaces that provide people with the autonomy that is most associated with physical private spaces, but with the potential audience of a public act. Our results show that the audience plays an instrumental role in dictating how people interact in the public sphere.

There exists a duality between the private and the public—one where agency can be structured by the public and the public can be structured by the individual. For example, people's ability to disseminate and access diverse information can be dictated by their perceptions of the audience, where the audience is relative to the medium. People can also aim to alter public opinion through the dissemination of information and opinions, or through discussion, thus acting as change agents. However, as we found in our study, the public quality of the private sphere was instrumental in shaping people's interactions. The perceived audience and the potential negative ramifications of their interactions led to multi-mediation, and the various media all varied in relation to how "private" or "public" they were.

Facebook, for example, has at least two distinct types of spaces with differing qualities that can be accessed by any one individual. Firstly, there is the unique private sphere that is constructed by each individual user, composed of an individual's (usually) real-world friend network. When members of the network post political links and opinions, or initiate political discussions, these become points of interaction where people can, in turn, engage others if they so choose. However, with Facebook, much of the discussion may or may not be political. This makes the use of Facebook for political deliberation challenging since users must scroll through their entire newsfeed to seek out political information and discussions. Furthermore, the degree to which differing views are exchanged is also dependent on the network, as the more heterogeneous an individual's network the more likely diverse political exchanges will result. Secondly, there are the group-based public spheres that are open to the public, where people can interact and exchange information, as well as discuss political issues. These public spheres have been the major foci of recent studies of the deliberation that is taking place on Facebook. The unique public spheres and group-based public spheres are connected (posts to groups are usually seen in individual's news feeds), but the behavior encouraged in both situations is potentially very different.

Twitter and Google+ are more "public" than Facebook since people can follow any number of users with public profiles in a non-reciprocal relationship. Interview informants, in understanding the differences between Facebook and more impersonal networks like Twitter, purposefully constructed their networks to obtain political information and be able to engage in meaningful discussions with others. The adoption and use of other media served as a way in which people could work around the challenges of using Facebook as a tool for political deliberation. It also demonstrated the different levels of malleability in these social media tools. Whereas people were unable to effectively shape their Facebook networks for deliberative purposes because their networks were personal their newsfeeds were multidimensional, they were able to mold Twitter and Google+ into a political information acquisition and discussion tool.

Towards Depolarization

Many studies, in looking at the deliberative activities that emerge online, have suggested that the Internet is leading towards *polarization* [e.g. 40]. In contrast, building on previous work [e.g. 27], through our examination of the full spectrum of public spheres (both political and non-political) available through multiple media, we found that people's broader online interactions were *depolarized* in nature.

Papacharissi [29] suggests that the combination of networked activities provides the basis of a participatory culture that may have democratizing consequences. We found that people were participating in these private/public spaces. Contrary to the polarization perspective, our informants were purposefully seeking diverse information and perspectives, disseminating diverse information and perspectives, and engaging with diverse audiences. They accomplished this through the appropriation of multiple media. Some of our informants even reported altering their own political views as a result of the exposure to diverse perspectives and their ability to engage in rational conversations with people holding alternative viewpoints.

Implications for Research

Most scholarly work in this space has focused on a single medium. This may explain why many public sphere scholars share the view that the Internet serves as a polarized and polarizing "echo chamber" in which people only seek political information that is aligned with their beliefs, or discuss political issues and candidates with citizens who are also in support of those issues and candidates [e.g. 2, 16, 40, 43]. In our study, we looked at people's interactions across social media tools and found that people were actively seeking diversity.

In building on Papacharissi's [29] work, we found that people's interactions across multiple public spheres did have a democratizing value. We believe it is important that researchers continue to investigate how individuals appropriate multiple media and interact with multiple audiences across social media.

Implications for Design

Our results clearly demonstrated that our informants were actively seeking an environment through which they could accomplish their personal deliberation goals. Our informants were able to assemble a suitable deliberation environment to accomplish their own personal goals by combining multiple tools with varying affordances. However, this may be beyond the average user's capabilities. Based on our findings, we now elaborate on critical features for the design of new political public spheres.

The ability to view, understand, and select the audience: Our informants' experiences with social media were relative to the tool and their perceptions of the audience present within any given medium. Deliberative environments must provide users with the ability to understand their audience, as well as to select the audience they wish to target, much like how Google+ provides its users with the ability to place their connections into self-determined circles.

The ability to filter information: Our informants described a process whereby they constructed robust information environments using Twitter and Google+. This was counter to the unstructured way in which Facebook displays information to its users. A new deliberation system must afford its users the ability to filter information based on a variety of factors like ideology and sentiment, both for viewing and disseminating information.

The ability to aggregate: Our informants were actively seeking information and opinions from a variety of sources in both public and private contexts. Future deliberation systems must allow users to aggregate and filter whatever they wish, such as information, sources and contacts.

The ability to judge the impact of participation: Our informants were disseminating information with the intention of informing others in the various social media tools at their disposal. They were also engaging in discussions with diverse audiences. These participants cared very much about the impact of their interactions, however, they were unable to easily assess the impact of these interactions. Future tools must allow users to judge the impact of their participation, perhaps providing information, such as who read what a user posted, how many people cared, and what type of impact the activities had.

The ability to adjust identity: Some of our informants expressed how they experienced limitations in their ability to participate through social media as a result of identity management. Future tools should allow users to adjust their identity from being anonymous to completely known, as both served varying purposes in people's online interactions.

Fusion of features: The features above would be best served in an integrated environment which was easy to navigate and understand and in which actions taken in one area (examining impact, for example) had influences in other areas (presentation of self, for example). Hacking multiple tools together, while allowing users to take advantage of multiple affordances, has the limitations of not coordinating actions and states in one tool to actions and states in another.

Limitations

Nearly all of our informants were proactive social media users with some interest in politics. Thus, we cannot generalize our results to people who do not share these characteristics. However, interview informants came from diverse educational and professional backgrounds. They were also diverse with respect to age, gender and political orientation. In an attempt to limit the issues associated with our sampling methodology, we found informants through multiple seeds, which could help to diversify our sample. However, our goal was not to generalize to the entire population. We wished to investigate whether or not social media could be used to directly support political interactions in the public sphere and found that a range of social media was being used as a platform for deliberative democracy. By taking a more ethnographic approach, we provided an introspective view into how individuals interacted across the sprawling public sphere.

Concluding Remarks

Social Media are malleable and users of these technologies can shape them to suit their needs and interests. People are now discovering how to manipulate and integrate multiple social media platforms in order to create the information, dissemination, and discussion environments they desire. As time passes and people's understandings of these technologies evolve (along with the technologies themselves), an even greater number of people will have learned to mold social media to better suit their needs. Thus, it will become increasingly important for us, as a research community, to continue to study users of social media as closely as possible. In contrast to the echo chamber view of social media that is widely shared by public-sphere scholars [e.g. 40], our findings provide a counter-narrative—not only can social media support people's deliberative interactions, but people's interactions through diverse social media may also be depolarized.

ACKNOWLEDGEMENTS

This research was funded by NSF award No. IIS-1064852. Any opinions, findings and conclusions or recommendations expressed in this material are those of the authors and do not necessarily reflect the views of the National Science Foundation. We are grateful to Yong Ming Kow and Yunan Chen for early feedback on the ideas presented in this work.

REFERENCES

1. Adamic, L., and Glance, N. (2005). The political blogosphere and the 2004 U.S. election: Divided they blog. *Proc. of the 3rd ACM International Workshop on Link Discovery*, 36-43.
2. Agre, P. (2002). Real-time politics: The internet and the political process. *The Information Society*, 18, 5, 311-331.
3. Bakshy, E., Rosenn, I., Marlow, C., and Adamic, L. (2012). The role of social networks in information diffusion. *WWW'12 Proc. of the 21st International Conference on the World Wide Web,* 519-528.
4. Biernacki, P. (1981). Snowball sampling: Problems and techniques of chain referral sampling, *Soc. Methods and Research,* 10, 2, 141-163.
5. Bodker, S., and Andersen, P. (2005). Complex Mediation. *Human-Computer Interaction*, 20, 4, 353-402.
6. Boyd, D., and Ellison, N. (2007). Social Network Sites: Definition, History, and Scholarship. *Journal of Computer-Mediated Communication*, 13, 1, 210-230.
7. Chadwick, A. (2009). Web 2.0: New Challenges for the Study of E-Democracy in an Era of Informational Exuberance. *I/S: Journal of Law and Policy for the Information Society*, 5, 1, 9-41.
8. Chambers, S. (2003). Deliberative Democratic Theory, *Annual Review of Political Science*, 6, 307-326.
9. Conover, M., Ratkiewicz, J., Fancisco, M., Goncalves, B., Flammini, A., and Menczer, F. (2011). Political polarization on twitter. *5th International Conference on Weblogs and Social Media.*
10. Dahlgren, P. (2005). The Internet, public spheres, and political communication: Dispersion and deliberation. *Political Communication*, 22, 2, 147-162.
11. Dahlgren, P. (2009). *Media and political engagement: Citizens, communication, and democracy*. University Press, Cambridge, MA.
12. Ellison, N., Steinfield, C., and Lampe, C. (2007). The benefits of Facebook "friends:" Social capital and college students' use of online social network sites. *Journal of Computer-Mediated Communication*, 12, 4, 1143-1168.
13. Farrell, H., and Drezner, D.W. (2008). The power and politics of blogs. *Public Choice*, 134, 15- 30.
14. Foot, K.A., and Schneider, S.M. (2006). *Web campaigning*, MIT Press, Cambridge, MA.
15. Gentzkow, S. (2011). Ideological Segregation Online and Offline. *Quarterly Journal of Economics*, 126, 4, 1799-1839.

16. Gilbert, E., Bergstrom, T., and Karahalios, K. (2009). Blogs are echo chambers: Blogs are echo chambers. *Proc. of the 42nd Hawaii International Conference on System Sciences*, 1-10.

17. Golbeck, J., and Hansen, D. (2011). Computing political preference among twitter followers. *Proc. of the 2011 annual conference on Human factors in computing systems*, 1105-1108.

18. Habermas, J. (1984). *The theory of communicative action: Reason and the rationalization of society*. Heneimann, London.

19. Habermas, J. (1991). *The structural transformation of the public sphere: An inquiry into a category of bourgeois society*. MIT Press, Cambridge, MA.

20. Habermas, J. (1996). *Between facts and norms: Contributions to a discourse theory of law and democracy*. MIT Press, Cambridge, MA.

21. Horrigan, J., Garrett, K., and Resnick, P. (2004). The internet and democratic debate. *Pew Internet and American Life Project*.

22. Lampe, C., Ellison, N., and Steinfield, C. (2006). A face (book) in the crowd: Social searching vs. social browsing. *Proc. of the ACM Conference on Computer Supported Cooperative Work*, 167-170.

23. Madden, M., and K. Zickuhr, K. (2011). 65% of Online Adults Use Social Networking Sites. *Pew Internet and American Life Project*.

24. Milliken, M., Gibson, K., and O'Donnell, S. (2008). User-generated video and the online public sphere: Will YouTube facilitate digital freedom of expression in Atlantic Canada?. *American Communication Journal*, 10, 3.

25. Milliken, M., and O'Donnell, S. (2008). User-generated online video: The next public sphere?, *IEEE International Symp. on Technology and Society*, 1-3.

26. Morgan, J.S., Lampe, C., and Shafiq, M.Z. (2013). Is News Sharing on Twitter Ideoligically Based?. *CSCW'13*.

27. Munson, S., and Resnick, P. (2010). Presenting diverse political opinions: how and how much, *Proc. of the 28th international conference on Human factors in computing systems*, 1457-1466.

28. Munson, S., and Resnick, P. (2011). The prevalence of political discourse in non-political blogs, *Fifth International AAAI Conference on Weblogs and Social Media*.

29. Papacharissi, Z. (2010). *A private sphere: Democracy in a digital age*. Polity Press, Malden, MA.

30. Papacharissi, Z. (2012). The virtual sphere: The internet as a public sphere. *New Media and Society*, 4, 1, 9-27.

31. Poor, N. (2005). Mechanisms of an online public sphere: The website Slashdot. *Journal of Computer-Mediated Communication*, 10, 2.

32. Raine, L., and Smith, A. (2012). Politics on social networking sites. *Pew Internet and American Life Project*.

33. Robertson, S.P., Douglas, S., Maruyama, M., & Semaan, B. (2013). Political discourse on social networking sites: Sentiment, in-group/out-group orientation and rationality. *Information Polity 18(2)*, 107-126.

34. Shamma, D., Kennedy, L., and Churchill, E.F. (2009): Tweet the debates: understanding community annotation of uncollected sources. *Proc. of the first SIGMM workshop on Social media*, 3-10.

35. Shirky, C. (2011): The Political Power of Social Media - Technology, the Public Sphere Sphere, and Political Change, Foreign Aff. 28

36. Sleeper, M., Balebako, R., Das, S., McConahy, A., Wiese, J., Cranor, L. (2013). The Post that Wasn't: Exploring Self-Censorship on Facebook. *Proc. of the ACM Conference on CSCW'13*.

37. Strauss, A. L. and Corbin, J. M. (1998). *Basics of Qualitative Research: Techniques and Procedures for Developing Grounded Theory*. Sage, CA.

38. Stromer-Galley, J. (2003). Diversity of political conversation on the Internet: Users' perspectives. *Journal of Computer-Mediated Communication*, 8, 3.

39. Stroud, N. J. (2007). Media effects, selective exposure, and Fahrenheit 9/11. *Political Communication*, 24, 4, 415–432.

40. Sunstein, C.R. (2007). *Republic.com 2.0*. Princeton University Press, MA.

41. Tremayne, M. (2006): *Blogging, citizenship, and the future of media*. Routledge, New York.

42. Vitak, J., Zube, P., Smock, A., Caleb, T., Carr, C.T., Ellison, N., and Lampe, C. (2011). It's Complicated: Facebook Users' Political Participation in the 2008 Election. *Cyberpsychology, Behavior and Social Networking*, 14, 3, 107-114.

43. Wallsten, K. (2011). Many sources, one message: Political blog links to online videos during the 2008 campaign. *Journal of Political Marketing*, 10, 1-2, 88-114.

44. Williams, B. and Gulati, G. (2008). The political impact of Facebook: Evidence from the 2006 midterm elections and 2008 nomination contest. *Politics and Technology Review*, 1, 11- 21.

Hybrid Media Consumption: How Tweeting During a Televised Political Debate Influences the Vote Decision

Misa Maruyama[1], Scott P. Robertson[2], Sara Douglas[1], Bryan Semaan[2], Heather Faucett[1]
[1]Communication and Information Sciences Program, [2]Information and Computer Sciences Department
University of Hawai'i at Mānoa
Honolulu, HI 96822 USA
{misattm, scott.robertson, sarad, bsemaan, ha8}@hawaii.edu

ABSTRACT
An increasing number of people are using microblogs to broadcast their thoughts in real time as they watch televised political events. Microblogging social network sites (SNSs) such as Twitter generate a parallel stream of information and opinion. It is presumed that the additional content enhances the viewing experience, but our experiment explores the validity of this assumption. We studied how tweeting, or passively observing Twitter during a debate, influenced affect, recall and vote decision. For most measures, participants' average feeling and recall toward the candidates did not depend on Twitter activity, but Twitter activity did matter for vote choice. People who actively tweeted changed their voting choice to reflect the majority sentiment on Twitter. Results are discussed in terms of the possibility that active tweeting leads to greater engagement but that it may also make people more susceptible to social influence.

Author Keywords
Social networking; social media; e-participation; e-citizenship; microblogging; digital democracy

ACM Classification Keywords
K.4.3 [Computers and Society]: Organizational Impacts – Computer-Supported cooperative work

INTRODUCTION
Social networking sites (SNSs), like Facebook and Twitter, have become important tools in the realm of political information seeking, deliberation and decision making. A recent survey by the Pew Internet and American Life project [24] found that 25% of respondents said they used SNSs to discuss or debate political issues with others. Thirty percent of respondents said that their friends post occasionally about politics, and 25% said that they have become more involved politically as the result of information in their social networking feeds.

The study of the use of social media to obtain and discuss political information and candidates has become an active research topic in the HCI and CSCW community. Several types of social media have been studied like political blogs [1, 9, 38, 40], discussion forums [23], online videos [18, 19], and pure SNSs like Facebook and Twitter [14, 25, 26, 27]. Twitter, a popular microblogging SNS, has more recently received particular attention by the research community in the context of political discourse. Tumasjan and colleagues [39] found that sentiment and political topic distribution on Twitter reflect the same patterns as "real-world" sentiment and topic. Designers have begun to discuss how sentiment and content on Twitter might be visualized during live events, like debates, to enhance the experience [7]. In this paper, we wish to understand the cognitive and affective experiences of using Twitter during a live political event from the perspective of the individual.

CSCW'14, February 15–19, 2014, Baltimore, Maryland, USA.

http://dx.doi.org/10.1145/2531602.2531719

Media hybridity
In mass media research, watching television has traditionally been viewed as a solitary and passive activity [30]. However, people are now appropriating interactive media during television broadcasts to create a hybrid media environment. The rise of the Internet has allowed more people to become "networked" viewers who capitalize on the web's interactivity and connectivity to augment their television viewing experience. For example, according to a recent Pew Internet and American Life project survey, about 20% of cellphone owners who use the Internet, e-mail or apps have also used their phone to see what other people are saying online about a TV program they are watching [35]. The same percentage used their phone to post their own comments online [35]. Watching a televised event while connecting with others to talk about the event blurs the line between the one-to-many broadcast audience and the many-to-many networked audience [16].

Twitter use during political debates
Twitter is a form of lightweight chat that allows users to send short messages in real time to people subscribed to their streams. Twitter messages—or "tweets"—can only be 140 characters or less, and can be sent or retrieved using a variety of technologies like laptops and mobile phones.

One main feature of Twitter is the use of the '@' symbol, followed by a user name, i.e. @username, within the text of a message. The use of the '@' symbol is also referred to as an @reply or an @mention, where the message is directed to a specific user or talking about a user. Another major feature of Twitter is the use of the '#' symbol—hashtag—followed by a keyword like #PresidentialDebate. When people compose a tweet that includes a hashtag, the message text is available to the public (barring privacy settings) and will be available to anyone who is searching for any given hashtag and keyword combination. The tweet feeds for hashtag searches are updated while tweets are being posted by Twitter users.

Because Twitter allows people to broadcast their thoughts in real time, people have used it to interact with others during televised political events. This makes watching a debate a social experience and generates a parallel stream of information and opinion that augments the debating candidates' words. Media and campaigns often encourage this activity by suggesting hashtags and mentions that microblogging participants can use. Several studies have examined the role of microblogging during political debates [17, 32, 33, 34]. Mascaro and Goggins [17], for example, found that communities coalesced around hashtags, where tweeters could interact with political officials and journalists. Shamma et al. [32] studied the use of Twitter during President Obama's inauguration and found that tweet activity declined during critical moments, as people were more preoccupied with witnessing the event on television than tweeting about it.

Much of the research on social influence on microblogging platforms has used Social Network Analysis (SNA) to study massive Twitter data sets [2, 4, 11, 13, 21, 29]. Cha, Haddadi, Benevenuto and Gummadi [4] found that the number of retweets and mentions reflect a different kind of influence than the number of followers. Huberman, Romero, and Wu [11] also found that interactional measures may provide a more accurate reflection of a social network than bond-based ties (follower-followee relationships). As further support for these findings, a study by Romero, Galuba, Asur and Huberman [28] found that influence depends not only on the size of an audience, but also on how active or passive the audience members are. As a way to predict influence, Anger and Kittl [2] proposed a quantitative method that not only included the number of followers, but also the frequency of retweets and mentions.

While much of the research on social influence and Twitter has analyzed large data sets, experiments have the potential to show the complex way in which people are influenced on the individual level. Zhu, Huberman and Luon [42] conducted a series of online experiments to gauge social influence in which they asked participants to choose between a pair of images with and without knowledge of others' opinions. They found that social influence caused users to switch their choice, although the effect was nuanced: social influence was stronger for delayed decisions and in situations where users faced a moderate, instead of a large, number of opposing opinions.

In a field experiment, we examined the influence of using Twitter during a political debate on users' affect, cognition and vote choice. This is the first of this type of study, as far as we are aware. The power of an experiment is two-fold. One, through random assignment, we eliminate self-selection bias. Second, we attempt to control the information available during the debate by asking participants to view the debate on a particular channel and, for those who are viewing Twitter, to view a particular hashtag feed. We maintained external validity by asking participants to use Twitter while viewing the debate in their natural environments.

While our exploratory study was not guided by hypotheses, we held a general belief that using Twitter while watching a debate would influence voters' affect, cognition and vote decision. We compared people who could tweet to those who viewed content passively in order to understand how engagement might influence the way users feel, think and vote. Our research questions were:

RQ1: Does exposure to Twitter influence feelings toward political candidates and is this different for people who actively tweet versus those who passively monitor Twitter?

RQ2: Does exposure to Twitter influence what is learned about political candidates and is this different for people who actively tweet versus those who passively monitor Twitter?

RQ3: Does exposure to Twitter influence vote choice and is this different for people who actively tweet versus those who passively monitor Twitter?

METHOD

Participants

Fifty-one Twitter users, 29 women and 22 men, participated in the study. They were recruited through multiple methods and sites. These included our laboratory's Twitter feed, recruitment fliers and in-class recruitment on the University of Hawai`i at Mānoa campus, in-person recruitment at local community meetings for the general public, and an e-mail newsletter announcement distributed via a local online newspaper. Participants were included only if they were in Hawaii, familiar with Twitter (held a Twitter account and had posted at least one tweet), and had agreed to watch a candidate debate on a specific date. Participants were compensated with a $20 gift card for participating on the night of the debate and an additional $10 gift card for participating in a follow-up online questionnaire two weeks later.

The participants represented a diversity of age categories. Eleven participants were 18 to 20 years old, 19 were 21 to 29 years old, 11 were 30 to 39 years old, 6 were 40 to 49 years old, and 4 were 50 or older. Ninety-two percent had completed at least some college, and 46% had completed at least some graduate school. Twenty-three people, or nearly half of our respondents, reported being Independent or Non-Partisan. Twenty-three participants identified as Democrats and four identified as Republican. The average participant's political interest was moderately high. The means, minimums and maximums for political interest and Twitter use are shown in Table 1.

Most of the participants were daily users of Twitter. About 80 percent looked at Twitter at least once a day, and about half of the participants posted a tweet daily. To get a sense of participants' political activity on Twitter, we asked them to rate how frequently they looked at Twitter to learn about politics. Interestingly, a majority of participants never or rarely went to Twitter for political information, yet 60 percent said they stumbled upon political tweets on a daily basis even when they were not looking for them.

Frequency	Mean	Min	Max
Look at Twitter (1=Never)	4.08	1	5
Tweet (1=Never)	3.49	1	5
Political Interest (1=Very low)	3.48	1	5
Stumble upon political tweets (1=Never)	3.62	1	5
Go to Twitter to learn about politics (1=Never)	2.62	1	5
Tweet about politics (1=Never)	2.02	1	5

Table 1: Participant demographics on 1-5 scales.

Setting

We conducted the study during the November 2012 U.S. election. Rather than expose participants to an election they were unfamiliar with, we wanted to present them with an election they may care about. In some of our previous laboratory studies on social media and political deliberation, we exposed participants to content related to an election in a different part of the United States. But the participants shared in post-experiment interviews that the material was not relevant to them, saying for example:

"... I was just not really caring because we previously said it's not in Hawaii. So, it's just like if it doesn't apply to me, I shouldn't, I don't really care."

To ameliorate this issue, our field experiment approach raised external validity by asking participants to learn about real candidates they would be eligible to vote for – with the hope that it would increase engagement with the study material.

We selected the election to replace Hawaii's U.S. Senator Daniel Akaka, who was retiring after serving 22 years in the Senate. Two locally well-known politicians were vying for his seat: sitting U.S. Congresswoman Mazie Hirono (Democratic party candidate), who also served two terms as Hawaii's lieutenant governor, and former two-term Hawaii Governor Linda Lingle (Republican party candidate). We chose this race due to its prominence in local politics as well as its visibility on the national stage. The October 16, 2012, debate was the second of five debates between Hirono and Lingle. It took place three weeks prior to the November 6 general election and lasted one hour. A local news station and a local online newspaper hosted the event.

Design

Three independent groups were formed based on their interaction with Twitter:

- Tweeters: Tweeters watched the debate and tweeted whenever and whatever they pleased. In this condition, we asked participants to log in to their personal Twitter accounts and start by searching #kitvdebate. We asked them to actively tweet during the debate using the hashtag #kitvdebate.
- Twitter Observers: Twitter observers watched the debate and monitored the Twitter stream, but did not tweet. In this condition, we asked participants to log in to their personal Twitter accounts and start by searching #kitvdebate. We asked them to monitor Twitter during the debate but refrain from tweeting.
- No Twitter (Control): Participants in this condition watched the debate and did not look at Twitter.

Measures of affect, knowledge, memory, and vote choice (described below) were taken at three different times relative to the debate: pre-debate, immediately after the debate, and two weeks after the debate.

Thus the design for most analyses was a 3x3 mixed design with independent groups defined by their level of interaction with Twitter and repeated measures defined by the times at which measurements were taken.

At all three times (pre-debate, immediately following the debate, and two weeks after the debate), dependent measures were taken on knowledge, affect, and voting preferences. Recall was taken at only the second and third times (as there would have been nothing to recall prior to the debate). Dependent measures were as follows:

• *Knowledge of the race.* Participants were asked to "Please indicate your general knowledge level of the 2012 U.S. Senate election in Hawaii" and given the response choices of 1=No knowledge to 5=Very high knowledge.

• *Knowledge of the candidate.* Participants were asked to "Please indicate your knowledge about each candidate." Next to the candidate names, the following response choices were provided: 1= "No knowledge" to 5= "Very high knowledge."

• ***Feeling thermometer.*** Subjects were asked to rate the candidates on a "feeling thermometer" with the response choices of 1="Cold" to 7="Warm." Feeling thermometers are commonly used in research on attitudes toward political candidates [41].

• ***Liking the candidate.*** Subjects were asked to "Please indicate how much you like/dislike this candidate" using the response scale of 1="Dislike very much" to 5="Like very much." This item was used as a means of comparison against the feeling thermometer indicator, which also assessed how much respondents liked a candidate.

• *Likelihood of voting for candidate.* Subjects were asked to "Please indicate how likely it is that you would vote for this candidate" using the response scale of 1="Definitely would not," to 5="Definitely would."

• *Feeling toward the candidate.* Participants were asked to rate the candidates on five affective terms: "angry," "hopeful," "afraid," "proud," and "anxious". The first four items on the checklist were used in the American National Election Studies, and "anxious" was added per Marcus, Neuman and MacKuen [15]. The checklist questions were in the form "When you think about <candidate name>, how <affect term> does she make you feel?" The response scale ranged from 1="Not <affect term> at all," to 5="Extremely <affect term>."

• *Vote.* Participants were asked, "If the 2012 U.S. Senate election were held today, whom would you vote for?" using the responses 1="Mazie Hirono" and 2="Linda Lingle."

• *Recall.* The dependent measures for recall were asked as the following two free response items:

- *Debate recall.* Participants were asked to "Please write down as many things as you can remember from the debate. Recall from memory without using any reminders (i.e. open tabs, other windows) or asking anyone who might be with you."

- *Twitter recall.* In addition to the debate recall, participants who looked at Twitter were also asked to "Please write down as many things as you can remember from Twitter during the debate. Recall from memory without using any reminders (i.e. open tabs, other windows) or asking anyone who might be with you."

For the recall measures, the free response entry field for each question was 20 lines long and 100 characters wide. We asked participants not to worry about spelling, punctuation or complete sentences and recommended they spend about 10 minutes on each free recall response.

• *Tweets.* All of the public tweets that included the #kitvdebate hashtag during the debate were collected using the streaming Twitter API. We also used the streaming API to collect all of the tweets posted by the participants during the debate. We conducted a sentiment analysis of the tweets about each candidate to code for positive, negative or neutral sentiment. We identified tweets that mentioned the candidates by first querying the candidates' names, including possible misspellings and wildcards to capture non-exact matches (i.e., possessives and hashtags). The tweets were filtered into three groups: tweets that mentioned only Hirono, tweets that mentioned only Lingle and tweets that mentioned both candidates. If the tweet mentioned only one candidate, it was coded as having positive, negative or neutral sentiment about the candidate. If a tweet mentioned both candidates, two codes were assigned, including one for each candidate. We also coded the participants' tweets to determine whether they declared a winner of the debate.

Procedure

Surveymonkey.com was used for the online consent form and all questionnaires. One hour before the debate, participants were e-mailed a link to directions and the pre-exposure questionnaire. After completing the pre-exposure questionnaire, the participants were randomly assigned to one of the three Twitter conditions (without being told about the other conditions) and asked to prepare to watch the debate. All participants were asked to view the debate either on a televised broadcast on a specific local news channel or as a live stream on the station's website. Immediately after the debate, participants were e-mailed a link to an online post-exposure questionnaire, which they were required to complete within one hour. Two weeks after the debate, participants were again e-mailed a request to complete a follow-up online questionnaire. While it is possible that new information in the subsequent two weeks influenced the dependent measures, we concluded that if a major event disrupted the election, any influence would likely be similar across all of the groups.

We asked participants in the Tweet and Twitter Observer groups to start by searching #kitvdebate on Twitter because the hashtag had been popular during a previous political debate that had aired on the same station. We intentionally exposed the Tweet and Twitter Observer groups to the same Twitter content to keep the conditions consistent while manipulating only their level of engagement with Twitter.

Our intent was to insert our participants into the naturally occurring dialogue on Twitter. Use of the widely distributed #kitvdebate hashtag exposed the participants to enough voices to ensure inconspicuousness. Use of this hashtag also increased the study's external validity, exposing participants to the full diversity of voices – candidates' campaigns, news sources, advocacy groups and citizens – available to all Twitter users. In addition, because participants' perception of their audience influences their communicative acts [16], it was important that they knew the audience was real, broad, and consisted of other Twitter users watching the debate (including those outside of our study).

RESULTS

Rating Scales

Rating scale data was analyzed using a 3x3 mixed design Analysis of Variance, with the exception of the recall data which was analyzed using a 3x2 mixed-design Analysis of Variance. Missing data was replaced by the mean of the relevant scale across all participants, regardless of condition. No more than four values were replaced for any scale.

Since we used six rating scale dependent measures in the same 3x3 design (knowledge of the race, knowledge of the candidate, feeling thermometer, liking, and likelihood of voting), we applied the Bonferroni correction for multiple significance tests when considering this data. With this correction, experimentwise significance at $p<.05$ will require $p<.008$ (.05/6). This correction was applied to all ANOVAs discussed below.

The descriptive statistics for the rating scales suggest the data were fairly normally distributed. Skewness ranged from -.895 to 1.83, and kurtosis ranged from -1.30 to 3.12, which are within normal limits. The standard deviation ranged from .85 to 1.85, which is normal given a 5-point or 7-point scale.

Over time, subjects grew more angry about Hirono, $F(2,96)=17.545$, $p<.001$ (means = 1.61, 2.44, and 2.12 for pre-exposure, immediate post-exposure, and two-week post exposure, respectively) and more afraid regarding Hirono, $F(2,96)=7.275$, $p=.001$ (means = 1.65, 2.12, and 1.80 for pre-exposure, immediate post-exposure, and two-week post exposure, respectively), and more anxious, $F(2,96)=5.543$, $p<.01$ (means = 1.81, 2.28, and 2.04 for pre-exposure, immediate post-exposure, and two-week post exposure, respectively).

Other rating scale measures were not significant.

	Democrat	Republican
Tweet		
Before	11	4
Immediate	7	8
Two Weeks	8	7
Observe Twitter		
Before	6	8
Immediate	5	9
Two Weeks	5	9
No Twitter		
Before	11	7
Immediate	11	7
Two Weeks	13	5

Table 2. Frequencies of participants across the three groups reporting their vote for the Democrat or Republican before, immediately after, and two weeks after the debate.

Vote choice

The vote choice dependent measure was a dichotomous category choice (Hirono or Lingle), thus the data was analyzed in terms of frequencies of participants who chose one or the other candidate and tested using the chi-square statistic.

Table 2 shows the raw frequencies of subjects in all three Twitter groups who reported that they would vote for the Democrat (Hirono) or the Republican (Lingle) before, immediately after, and two weeks after the debate (four subjects were removed from this analysis for missing data).

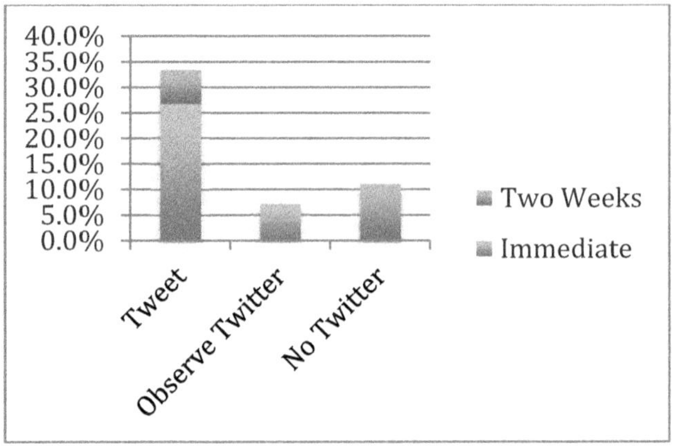

Figure 1: Percentage of participants in the three Twitter groups who changed their vote immediately after and two weeks after the debate.

Figure 1 expresses this data as the percentage of participants in the three Twitter groups who changed their vote (in either direction) immediately after the debate and two weeks later. The Tweet group had far more changes than the other groups, especially immediately but also after a delay. A chi-square test on the change percentages shows a significant contingency between the Twitter group factor and the time measure, $\chi2(2)=27.9$, $p<.0001$. In other words, active Tweeters were the most likely to change their position.

Figure 2 expresses the data as the percentage of Republican votes in each Twitter group at each time period. In Figure 2 we note a strong movement in the active Tweet group toward the Republican candidate immediately after the debate, which was still present two weeks later.

Even though the groups started out in different places (the Twitter Observers had more Republicans to begin with), there was room to see a similar change in the Twitter Observer group.

A chi-square test shows a marginally significant contingency between the Twitter group factor and the time

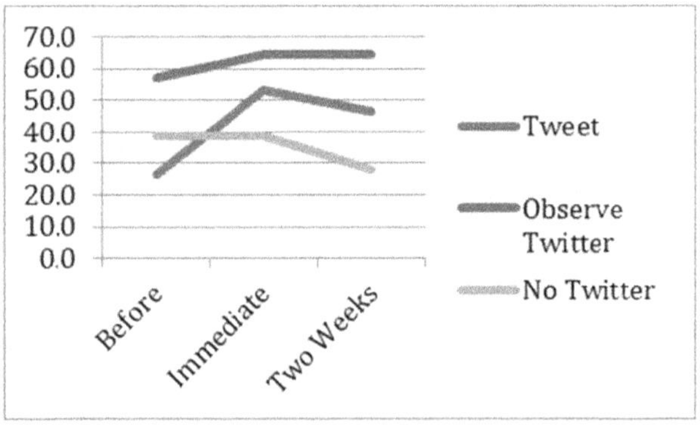

Figure 2. Percentage of subjects in the three Twitter groups reporting that they would vote for the Republican before, immediately after, and two weeks after the debate.

measure for the Republican percentage data, $\chi^2(4)=8.35$, $p<.08$. In other words, active Tweeters were the most likely to change their position toward the Republican candidate immediately, and this change was persistent. We examine reasons for this when we treat the content of the tweets in a subsequent section.

Recall

We analyzed the recall data using a method similar to grounded theory [37], with the goal of identifying what type of information was recalled and whether the types varied across conditions. We define recall as it has been defined in other studies [12]: all ideas presented in the free recall response, including opinions, personal stories and inaccurate memories. Each participant's recall was split into idea units, which were often clauses that contained a subject and predicate. However, sometimes they were as short as a noun or as long as a phrase (if parts of the phrase failed to make sense when standing alone).

A subset of the recall data was independently coded by two authors – not for final coding decisions but to identify situations where the coding scheme did not fit. One additional code was identified through this process and one was eliminated, and through iterative cycles of redefining the codes and reducing under axial coding, we collaboratively identified a set of 13 codes.

The coders independently coded one third of the recall of the debate using Atlas.ti. Inter-rater reliability between the two coders was substantial ($\kappa=.70$). When the coders disagreed on coding a recall item, they discussed the discrepancy to come to an agreement. The first author coded the remaining two-thirds of the recall data.

For brevity, we discuss only the seven codes that were used 15 times or more. These included:

• Candidate Tactics: comments about a candidate's political ploys to influence the meaning of an event, issue or their opponent's identity.

• Political Views: comments about a candidate's political behavior, opinions or platform issues.

• Public speaking: comments about a candidate's verbal and non-verbal communications skills.

• Character: judgments of candidate's integrity, personality.

• Outside References: discussion of events that occurred outside of the debate itself including personal stories, current events and discussions that occurred on Twitter.

• Final Impression: sweeping judgment about a candidate that summarizes a participant's opinion on the candidate

• Candidate Competence: judgments about a candidate's experience, knowledge or understanding of a political topic, or ability to serve.

The mean numbers of recall instances for each code category across all participants are shown in Figure 3. Participants most frequently recalled ideas about Candidate Tactics, Political Views and Public Speaking and Character.

We analyzed the recall data using a 3x2 mixed-design Analyses of Variance. The two independent variables included group and time.

There was a main effect of time for Candidate Tactics, $F(1,45)=5.542$, $p<.05$ (means = 3.77 and 2.50 for immediate post-exposure and two-week post exposure, respectively), and Character, $F(1,45)=5.597$, $p<.05$ (means = 1.00 and .542 for immediate post-exposure and two-week post exposure, respectively). Both decreased from the initial recall to the follow-up recall.

The candidate competence recall showed a main effect of group, $F(2,45)=3.20$, $p<.05$ (means = .16, .67, and .12 for Tweet, Twitter Observer and No Twitter groups, respectively). In other words, Twitter Observers recalled more items in this category than the Tweeters and the No Twitter group. We found no significant difference between the groups for the other recall categories.

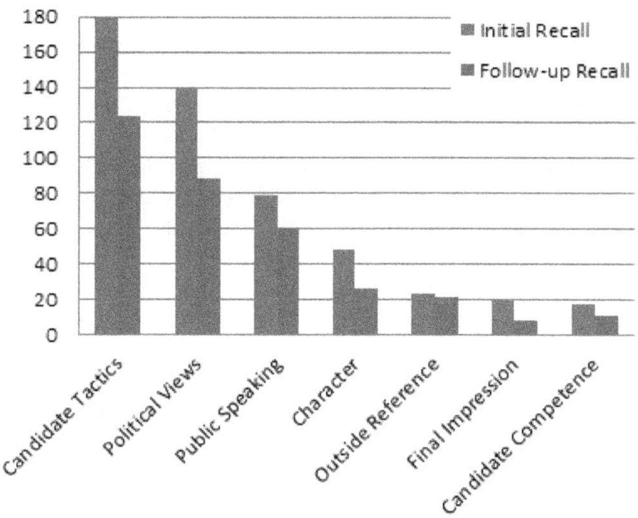

Figure 3: Recall Counts by Code Type

Tweet analysis

We manually coded #kitvdebate tweets that explicitly mentioned the candidates during the debate. We collected 407 tweets that were posted using the #kitvdebate hashtag during the hour-long debate. Of them, 303 mentioned at least one candidate's name, including 102 tweets that mentioned both candidates. The average number of tweets posted by general Twitter users who used the #kitvdebate hashtag was 5.9 tweets. In comparison, Tweeters in our study posted an average of 9.5 tweets, almost double the number posted by all users who included the hashtag.

The analysis showed that tweets about Lingle were mostly favorable and tweets about Hirono were mostly critical. Tweets that mentioned Lingle were 73 percent positive, 16 percent negative and 11 percent neutral. Tweets that mentioned Hirono were 9 percent positive, 87 percent negative and 4 percent neutral. The percentages include tweets that mentioned one of the candidates or both of the candidates. More than a third of the tweets that mentioned both candidates were positive about Lingle and negative about Hirono.

We also conducted an analysis of tweets posted by participants in the Tweet group to determine what they were tweeting during the debate. Our intention was to analyze not only what they saw (tweets posted using the #kitvdebate hashtag) but also what they said (participant tweets). While presenting a complete analysis is beyond the scope of this paper, we were interested in the extent to which participants were vocalizing their support for the candidates.

We found that three of the four "vote switchers" in the Tweet condition posted a tweet declaring that Lingle won the debate. For example, one vote switcher used a well-known local Pidgin English phrase to say that Lingle was winning the debate: "Linda is small kine killing it #kitvdebate." At about 43 minutes into the debate, another vote switcher in the Tweet group modified a retweet saying, "Me too. RT @username: i am a democrat and am 100% siding with Lingle #whatsithis #kitvdebate #hisen". In the last two minutes of the debate, the third vote switcher wrote: "Hirono needs to get to the point with concise responses! I think Lingle nailed it. #kitvdebate." The fourth vote switcher in the Tweet condition did not declare a debate winner and was the only participant who changed her vote back to Hirono two weeks after the debate. In other words, only the vote switchers who declared a debate winner on Twitter stuck with their new vote decision after two weeks. The three other Tweeters who posted a comment about Lingle winning the debate had voted for her prior to the debate and stuck with their vote two weeks later.

DISCUSSION

Our first research question was: Does exposure to Twitter influence feelings toward political candidates and is this different for people who actively Tweet versus those who passively monitor Twitter? We found no effects of Twitter exposure on our rating scales. All participants experienced a surge in negative feelings toward Hirono and positive feelings toward Lingle immediately after the debate, which eased with time but did not quite return to pre-debate levels. We therefore found no evidence to answer “yes” to this research question.

The second research question was: Does exposure to Twitter influence what is learned about political candidates and is this different for people who actively Tweet versus those who passively monitor Twitter? We found only a main effect of Twitter group for the number of Candidate Competence recall items. Mondak and Huckfeldt [20] found that cues about candidate competence influence voting decision even when people receive clear signals about a candidate’s political party and ideology, which was the case in the debate study. However, recall about candidate competence comprised a small fraction of the total number of recall items, so it may not have wielded influence on feeling toward the candidates or vote decision.

Our most interesting finding is related to our third research question: Does exposure to Twitter influence vote choice and is this different for people who actively Tweet versus those who passively monitor Twitter? We found that participants in the Tweet group were significantly more likely to change their vote decision immediately after the debate and to stick with their new vote decision two weeks later. By contrast, the Twitter Observer and No Twitter groups were less swayed by the debate. Their votes remained mostly unchanged after the debate and after the two-week delay. Thus, we can answer that active Tweeting seems to have more of an influence on vote choice than just exposure to Twitter, which in turn is not much different than no exposure to Twitter.

We propose two possible explanations for the observed vote change in the Tweet group: The first explanation is that there existed increased engagement through the cognitive act of creating the messages–allowing for new viewpoints to form [8]. Eveland [8] notes that the act of participating in discussion presents the opportunity to process the information in new ways as it is re-synthesized to produce conversation with others. The reformulation and cognitive elaboration necessary for conversing can then lead to changes in attitude beyond that of those with solitary motives such as to privately view media [8, 31]. It may be that engagement matters beyond observation. Those who engaged in discussion may have processed the information more elaborately or in new ways compared to the other groups because they were expecting to engage in discussion with others.

The second explanation is related to social influence, or, in this case, the majority sentiment on Twitter [5]. The #kitvdebate tweets were predominantly pro-Lingle (tweets that mentioned Lingle were 73 percent positive) and anti-Hirono (tweets that mentioned Hirono were 87 percent negative). To better understand how prevalent group conformity was amongst people in the Twitter conditions (Tweeters and Twitter Observers), the lead author coded the Twitter recall data for mentions of a debate winner. We found that 16 of the 26 respondents who completed the initial recall mentioned a Twitter favorite in the debate. They told the same story: “most” or “many” people on Twitter praised Lingle or criticized Hirono. There was a similar consensus in the follow-up recall. This suggests that participants were cognizant of the majority opinion on Twitter. Research suggests that the greater the size of the majority, the more likely the minority will be to conform [3].

Cialdini and Goldstein [5] describe how social influence, or peer pressure, can lead people to change their beliefs or behavior to reflect the group majority. Conformity tends to take two forms: informational and normative [5]. Informational conformity refers to privately changing your beliefs to reflect the opinions of credible others. Normative conformity means changing behavior to fit in to the crowd, even when this change is not accompanied by a private change in opinion [36].

If the Tweeters switched their opinion to reflect the opinions of people who they deemed to be credible, then this would be an example of informational conformity. On the other hand, tweeting about the popular candidate in order to attain social rewards would demonstrate normative conformity. There was some evidence of social pressure in the #kitvdebate tweet stream, which suggests the possibility of normative conformity. In cases where people showed positive sentiment towards Hirono, their posts were met with criticism (a reflection of group majority sentiment). For example, one person in the minority who tweeted "Hirono is schooling Lingle" met backlash: "Hirono isn't schooling anyone." When the Hirono supporter later wrote, "It's a wrap, Hirono's more genuine, logical and people-oriented. Lingle's all tacticsdirty politics," someone else replied "R U on CRACK?"

Interestingly, three of the four vote switchers declared on Twitter that Lingle was the debate winner. The vote switchers might have been expressing what they believe to be accurate information based on the opinions of knowledgeable others (informational conformity) or they may have been conforming to group norms even though it may not have been attached to a private change in opinion (normative conformity) [36]. The two types of conformity are frequently intertwined [6] and often work in tangent to maintain one's self-concept [5].

For instance, the Tweeters may have declared Lingle as the debate winner to gain social acceptance at first (public compliance) but later changed their vote decision (private acceptance) to maintain a consistent self-concept. Twitter Observers could not commit to a new opinion publicly. They did not have the opportunity to conform to the group norm publicly and did need to modify their vote decision to keep their self-concept intact. We speculate that communicating their pro-Lingle sentiment may have furthered the group bond for the Tweeters and made them more likely to switch their vote to reflect the sentiment of the Twitter majority.

Regardless of why engagement may have influenced the vote decision, it seems that being able to participate can lead to real change whereas merely observing may not. While social media has been criticized for having a polarizing effect [1], our study suggests that this is not always true. People's vote decisions can be swayed, meaning confirmation bias does not always lead people to interpret information in a way that supports pre-existing beliefs [22]. While our study suggests that the majority may be able to sway the opinion of the minority, the reverse is not necessarily true. No one in the Tweet or Twitter Observer groups switched their vote from the Republican favorite on Twitter to the Democratic candidate.

Implications for Theory

Most of the research that has focused on microblogging during live political events has analyzed data on a macro scale [7, 29, 32, 33]. Few studies have studied the cognitive and affective effects of participation during political events on the microbloggers themselves. Although we did not find evidence that engaging on Twitter had any influence on what people knew or how they felt about the candidates, our study did suggest that Twitter engagement mattered when it came to vote choice. This indicates that the relationship between participation and action may be different from the relationship between participation and affect and intention.

We found an interesting pattern in which vote switchers frequently declared a debate winner – a form of public commitment that may have been related to their decision-making process. We suggest future studies include post-experiment interviews to further examine the potential relationship between expressing a belief publicly and the decision-making process.

Our study design allowed us to explore the private beliefs and feelings behind public communication on social media. While big data collection, SNA, and automated content analysis are effective in studying the nature of interaction on social media (behavior), experimental studies can show *how* the interaction influences the thoughts and feelings of users (cognition and affect). Moreover, while research methods such as SNA can study the content created by contributors, they cannot tell the stories of the countless people who do not post. Our study explores the experience of silent social media users by including the Twitter Observer group. Future work should investigate microblogging in different political contexts, including debates in which the political sentiment on Twitter is more even-handed, as well as in national debates.

Implications for Practice

Our study suggests that having the power to tweet about a political event may influence the tweeter's vote decision in ways that reading tweets may not.

We advanced two possible explanations for this: active participation heightened cognitive processing of the debate or it made the minority more susceptible to the influence of the majority opinion. These are not mutually exclusive. If the capacity to tweet led to more elaborate memories (which we did not find in this study), then tweeting could be viewed as a means to developing a more thoughtful electorate willing to listen to the political opposition. On the other hand, listening to the majority may increase cognitive processing of the debate, especially if the majority opinion is different from one's own opinion. But this may not always be good for democracy. If active participation increases group conformity, then tweeting could be viewed as culprit in increased homogenization of political thought. It would also imply that at times decisions can be based on social rewards rather than accurate information, which threatens rational discourse in the public sphere [10]. We cannot determine which explanation is true based on our data. The stakes for democracy are high, which is why we believe more research must be conducted on how social media participation influences the way people think, act and vote.

LIMITATIONS

Our participants were more highly educated, more politically interested, more liberal and had more Twitter experience than the average U.S. citizen; thus, any generalizations are limited to this demographic. However, our study was designed to examine how the use of Twitter influenced a politically interested and technologically experienced group of Twitter users.

Also, importantly, we have several limitations related to our experimental design that should be addressed in future work. Firstly, in our study, we randomly assigned participants to one of the three Twitter conditions. Despite using random assignment, the groups were different prior to the debate on at least one dimension that we cared about: the ratio of people who voted for the Democrat (Mazie Hirono) was higher in the Tweet and the No Twitter groups than in the Twitter Observer group. This may be an indication that our groups were different in a systematic way, which would mean that group differences rather than the treatment may have influenced the results. We attribute the randomization problem to our relatively small sample size. We feel it would be beneficial in future studies to use a larger sample size, which would likely yield groups that were more similar prior to the debate, or to use stratified randomization to control and balance the influence of covariates. Other potential covariates that we did not measure or account for include participants' propensity to change their minds and their susceptibility to social influence. To address these issues, future studies should use existing, or develop new, measures for how willing people are to change their minds or be influenced by others.

Secondly, this was an 'in situ' study that looked at how users behave and feel in their natural tweeting environment, increasing ecological validity. However, as is the nature of this type of approach, the evidence of internal validity is harder to judge since we did not control participants' behavior. We only controlled what we *invited* participants to do. For example, we do not know whether the participants watched and discussed the debate with others physically present with them, nor whether they viewed social media content beyond the assigned hashtag feed. Thus, it is possible that people beyond the #kitvdebate hashtag stream influenced feelings, knowledge and votes. We recommend that future field experiments monitor participants' online and offline behavior more carefully. Future studies may also be conducted in a controlled laboratory setting, where participant behavior can be manipulated, albeit at the expense of ecological validity.

Thirdly, the design of the study allowed Twitter Observers to view tweets posted by the Tweeters. Therefore, it is possible that the Twitter Observers were influenced by both their treatment and the treatment of the Tweet group. To control for this, interaction between groups can be prevented by artificially constructing simulations of identical but *separate* Twitter feeds for each group to view. Because the feeds would be experimental sandboxes, they would not be live nor would they be plugged into real world discourse. Again, ecological validity may decrease with this more controlled approach.

Lastly, our participants' political leanings may have contributed to the way in which our experiment unfolded. Twenty-three participants reported being Independent or Non-Partisan, 23 identified as Democrats and 4 identified as Republican. Because almost half of our respondents identified as Independent or Non-Partisan, our participants may have been more open to changing their vote decisions.

CONCLUSION

An increasing number of people are using social media to learn about and discuss politics, including microbloggers who provide live commentary about televised political debates. The result is a hybrid media environment in which anyone with an Internet connection can watch the conversation unfold or join the discussion. Our study suggests that people who intend to actively post may experience the debate differently than people who do not.

In this experiment, we found that users who could contribute to the conversation on Twitter were more likely to switch their vote to reflect the majority. Additionally, it so happened that vote switching seemed to be related to a public declaration on Twitter of a debate victor. When people post, it is assumed that they have the capacity to influence others. But this study suggests that social media contributors may also have the power to influence themselves.

ACKNOWLEDGMENTS

This material is based upon work supported by the National Science Foundation under Grant No. IIS-1064852. Any opinions, findings and conclusions or recommendations expressed in this material are those of the authors and do not necessarily reflect the views of the National Science Foundation.

REFERENCES

1. Adamic, L., & Glance, N. (2005). The political blogosphere and the 2004 U.S. election: Divided they blog. *Proc. of the International Workshop on Link Discovery*.
2. Anger, I., & Kittl, C. (2011). Measuring influence on Twitter. In *I-KNOW*, 31.

3. Asch, S.E. (1956). Studies of independence and conformity: I. A minority of one against a unanimous majority. *Psychological Monographs*, *70*(9).

4. Cha, M., Haddadi, H., Benevenuto, F., & Gummadi, K. (2010). Measuring user influence in Twitter: The million follower fallacy. *Proc. of the Int'l AAAI Conference on Weblogs and Social Media.*

5. Cialdini, R.B., & Goldstein, N.J., (2004). Social Influence: Compliance and Conformity. *Annual Review of Psychology, 55*, 591-621.

6. David, B., & Turner, J. C. (2001). Majority and minority influence: A single process self-categorization analysis. In C. De Dreu; N. De Vries (Eds.), *Group consensus and minority influence: Implications for innovation* (pp. 91-121). Malden: Blackwell Publishing.

7. Diakopoulos, N. A., & Shamma, D. A. (2010). Characterizing Debate Performance via Aggregated Twitter Sentiment. *Proc. of CHI '10*. New York, NY:ACM.

8. Eveland, W. P. (2004). The effect of political discussion in producing informed citizens: The roles of information, motivation, and elaboration. *Political Communication, 21*(2), 177-193.

9. Farrell, H., & Drezner, D.W. (2008). The power and politics of blogs. *Public Choice*, 134, 15- 30.

10. Habermas, J. (1989). *The structural transformation of the public sphere*. Cambridge: MIT Press.

11. Huberman, B., Romero, D. M., and Wu, F. (2009). Social networks that matter: Twitter under the microscope. *First Monday,* 14. 1-5. http://firstmonday.org/ojs/index.php/fm/article/view/2317/2063

12. Hyman, I.E. (1994). Conversational remembering: Story recall with a peer versus for an experimenter. *Applied Cognitive Psychology*, 8, 49-66.

13. Kivran-Swaine, F., & Naaman, M. (2011). Network properties and social sharing of emotions in social awareness streams. *Proc. of the conference on Computer supported cooperative work*, 379-382. ACM.

14. Lampe, C., Ellison, N., & Steinfield, C. (2006). A face (book) in the crowd: Social searching vs. social browsing. *Proc. of the conference on Computer Supported Cooperative Work.*

15. Marcus, G.E., W.R. Neuman, & M. MacKuen. (2000) *Affective Intelligence and Political Judgment.* Chicago: University of Chicago Press.

16. Marwick, A., & boyd, d. (2011). I Tweet Honestly, I Tweet Passionately: Twitter Users, Context Collapse, and the Imagined Audience. *New Media & Society*, 1-20.

17. Mascaro, C., & Goggins, S.P. (2012). Twitter as Virtual Town Square: Citizen Engagement During a Nationally Televised Republican Primary Debate. APSA 2012 Annual Meeting Paper.

18. Milliken, M., & O'Donnell, S. (2008). User-generated online video: The next public sphere? *IEEE Int'l Symposium on Technology and Society*, 1-3.

19. Milliken, M., Gibson, K., & O'Donnell, S. (2008). User-generated video and the online public sphere: Will YouTube facilitate digital freedom of expression in Atlantic Canada? *American Communication Journal*, 10, 3.

20. Mondak, J.J., & Huckfeldt, R. (2006). The accessibility and utility of candidate character in electoral decision making. *Electoral Studies, 25*(1), 20-34.

21. Naaman, M., Boase, J., & Lai, C. H. (2010). Is it really about me?: message content in social awareness streams. *Proc. of the conference on Computer supported cooperative work.*

22. Nickerson, R. S.(1998) Confirmation bias: A ubiquitous phenomenon in many guises. *Review of General Psychology, 2*(2), 175-220.

23. Poor, N. (2005). Mechanisms of an online public sphere: The website Slashdot. *Journal of Computer-Mediated Communication*, 10, 2.

24. Raine, L., & Smith, A. (2012). Politics on social networking sites. Pew Internet and American Life Project.

25. Robertson, S.P., Douglas, S., Maruyama, M., & Chen, L. (2012). Political dialog evolution in a social network, In *Proc. of the International Digital Government Research Conference.* New York: ACM, 40-48.

26. Robertson, S.P., Douglas, S., Maruyama, M., & Semaan, B. (2013). Political discourse on social networking sites: Sentiment, in-group/out-group orientation and rationality. *Information Polity 18(2)*, 107-126.

27. Robertson, S.P., Vatrapu, R.K., & Medina, R. (2009). The social life of social networks: Facebook linkage patterns in the 2008 U.S. presidential election, *Proc. of the International Digital Government Research Conference.* New York: ACM, 6-15.

28. Romero, D.M., Galuba, W., Asur, S., and Huberman, B.A. (2011). Influence and Passivity in Social Media. *Proc. of the European Conference on Machine Learning and Knowledge Discovery in Databases.*

29. Romero, D.M., Meeder, B., and Kleinberg, J. (2011). Differences in the Mechanics of Information Diffusion Across Topics: Idioms, Political Hashtags, and Complex Contagion on Twitter. *Proc. of the International World Wide Web Conference.*

30. Ruggiero, T. (2000) Uses and Gratifications Theory in the 21st Century. *Mass Communication and Society, 3*(1), 3-37.

31. Scheufele, D. A. (2002). Examining differential gains from mass media and their implications for participatory behavior. *Communication Research*, *29*(1), 46-65.

32. Shamma, D. A., Kennedy, L., & Churchill, E. (2010a). Tweetgeist: Can the twitter timeline reveal the structure of broadcast events. *CSCW Horizons*.

33. Shamma, D. A., Kennedy, L., & Churchill, E. F. (2009). Tweet the debates: understanding community annotation of uncollected sources. *Proc. of the SIGMM Workshop on Social Media.*

34. Shamma, D. A., Kennedy, L., & Churchill, E. F. (2010b). Conversational Shadows: Describing Live Media Events Using Short Messages. *Proc. of ICWSM.*

35. Smith, A., & Boyles, J. (2012). The rise of the 'connected viewer.' *Pew Internet and American Life Project.*

36. Stangor, C. (2004). *Social groups in action and interaction*. Psychology Press.

37. Strauss, A. L. & Corbin, J. M. (1998). *Basics of Qualitative Research: Techniques and Procedures for Developing Grounded Theory*. California: Sage.

38. Tremayne, M. (2006). *Blogging, citizenship, and the future of media*. Routledge, New York.

39. Tumasjan, A., Sprenger, T., Sandner, P., & Welpe, I. (2010) Predicting Elections with Twitter: What 140 Characters Reveal about Political Sentiment. *Proc. of International AAAI Conference on Weblogs and Social Media,* 178-185.

40. Vatrapu, R., S.P. Robertson, and W. Dissanayake. (2008). Are Political Weblogs Public Spheres or Partisan Spheres? *International Reports on Socio-Informatics, 5*(1), 7-26.

41. Weisberg, H.F., and J.G. Rusk. (1970). Dimensions of Candidate Evaluation. *American Political Science Review, 64*, 1167-1185.

42. Zhu, H., Huberman, B.A., Luon, Y. (2012). To switch or not to switch: Understanding influence in online choices. *Proc. of CHI 2012*, 2257-2266.

Voyant: Generating Structured Feedback on Visual Designs Using a Crowd of Non-Experts

Anbang Xu, Shih-Wen Huang, Brian P. Bailey
Department of Computer Science
University of Illinois
Urbana, IL 61801
{xu26, shuang51, bpbailey}@ illinois.edu

ABSTRACT

Feedback on designs is critical for helping users iterate toward effective solutions. This paper presents Voyant, a novel system giving users access to a non-expert crowd to receive perception-oriented feedback on their designs from a selected audience. Based on a formative study, the system generates the elements seen in a design, the order in which elements are noticed, impressions formed when the design is first viewed, and interpretation of the design relative to guidelines in the domain and the user's stated goals. An evaluation of the system was conducted with users and their designs. Users reported the feedback about impressions and interpretation of their goals was most helpful, though the other feedback types were also valued. Users found the coordinated views in Voyant useful for analyzing relations between the crowd's perception of a design and the visual elements within it. The cost of generating the feedback was considered a reasonable tradeoff for not having to organize critiques or interrupt peers.

Author Keywords

Feedback; crowdsourcing; creativity; critique; design.

ACM Classification Keywords

H.5.3 [Information Interface and Presentation]: Group and Organization Interfaces – Collaborative computing.

INTRODUCTION

Feedback is a critical aspect of the creative design process [14, 18]. One key benefit of feedback is that it reveals gaps between what the user intends and what others perceive in a design [12]. For example, Figure 1 shows a poster that a user experienced in design intended to be perceived as Shakespeare, but was surprised to learn of an unintended interpretation (see word cloud, Figure 1). Gaps between intentions and interpretations are not uncommon in design and, if not addressed, can have adverse consequences [40]. Knowing where the gaps exist is therefore critical for helping users iterate toward more effective solutions [9].

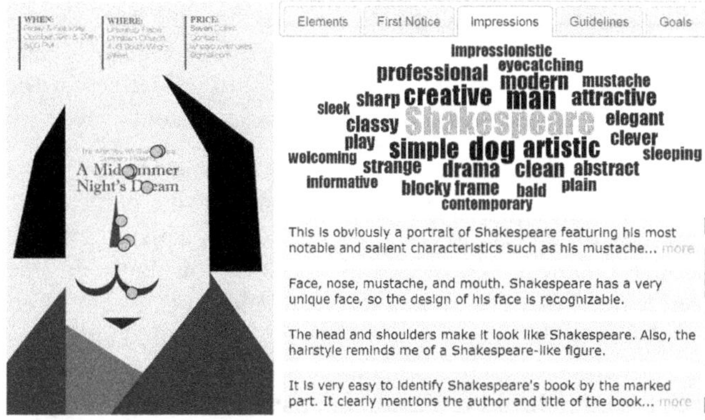

Figure 1. The feedback generated by Voyant on a poster. The interface is showing a word cloud representing the impressions formed when the crowd first viewed the design. Selecting an impression (in orange) shows the corresponding explanations and visual markers associating specific regions of the design.

Feedback also helps remove creative blocks [24], inform design choices [7], and gain insight into the design [31].

A user currently has several options for receiving feedback on designs. One option is organizing a critique [12], where the comprehensive feedback fosters insight into the design problem, solution approach, and strategies utilized. Though organizing a critique is warranted at key checkpoints (e.g. as scheduled by clients or instructors), it can be burdensome otherwise. Also, users without a background in design may not have the desire or peer network to organize a critique.

A second option is to informally ask peers for feedback, which incurs minimal overhead and can yield quick results. However, peer feedback can have an overly positive bias [31]. The user may also feel uncomfortable showing her design to others due to the fear of criticism [6] or may be concerned about interrupting their work [16]. A third option is to submit a design to an online community (e.g. Core77) where diverse feedback is possible. Unfortunately, studies report that little feedback is generated and the quality does not typically exceed judgments such as "I like it" [33, 37].

An emerging option for receiving feedback on designs is harnessing the wisdom of crowds. For example, researchers have recently enabled users to pose design alternatives to a crowd to collect their preferences [8]. The advantage is that crowd workers offer a potentially diverse audience, but the drawback is that the workers do not typically have expertise in design. To enable crowds to provide additional feedback on designs (beyond preferences), it is critical to know what types of feedback users would desire from non-experts and explore how that feedback could be generated by a system and effectively aggregated and presented to users.

In this paper we present *Voyant*, a novel system giving users access to a non-expert crowd to receive structured feedback on the perceptions of their designs from a selected audience. The term *non-expert crowd* is used to refer to a crowd without expertise in design. Voyant generates five types of feedback: a list of elements seen in the design, the order in which the elements are noticed, the impressions formed when the design is first viewed (see Figure 1), and the interpretation of the design relative to guidelines in the domain and the user's stated communicative goals.

For each feedback type, Voyant provides coordinated views that consist of a visual overview of the crowd's perceptions and visual markers overlaid on the design. This interactive model enables analysis of the association between the perceptions of a design and the visual elements within it. To use Voyant, the user imports a design image and configures the crowd demographics. Once generated, the feedback can be utilized to help iterate toward an effective solution.

Any user creating visual designs can use Voyant to assess how non-experts perceive the designs. The audience of our system therefore includes novice and expert designers and non-designers who are creating posters, logos, illustrations, or Web pages for courses, research, or personal interests. We use the term *user* to refer to this broad audience.

Compared to other options for receiving feedback, Voyant does not require scheduling or use of social capital. It reduces the fear of criticism since the user and crowd workers are unlikely to be able to identify each other [26]. It eliminates concern about interrupting other's work by employing paid workers and produces feedback beyond simple judgments by structuring crowd workflows.

The contributions of this paper are:

- Results of a formative study identifying several types of feedback on a design that are desired from non-experts. Our results reveal specific types of feedback (e.g. on the user's goals) that are desired but not directly provided by prior work [8] or existing systems [43-45].
- The design and implementation of a system (Voyant) for generating the desired feedback on designs from a crowd of non-experts. A novel feature is that the user interface of the system provides coordinated views to help users analyze associations between the crowd's perception of a design and the visual elements within it.
- Results of an evaluation demonstrating the utility of the feedback generated by a crowd-based system with users and their designs. The results also demonstrate the utility of the coordinated views and interactions in Voyant.

RELATED WORK

We discuss how our work is original relative to prior efforts that use crowdsourcing in design and existing methods for receiving design feedback. We also describe the creative need for receiving feedback during the design process.

Crowdsourcing in Design

Design is a complex task and researchers have investigated many directions for how a non-expert crowd can aid design. For example, Dow et al. studied how crowd technologies can aid each phase of the design process such as collecting preferences on variations of a design (AB testing) [8]. In the CvC design method, the crowd works with the designer to form a team as part of an open design competition [25]. The designer can leverage these team members to collect their preferences on proposed design solutions. Yu and Nickerson showed how crowds and genetic algorithms can be combined to generate concept sketches [38]. Others have utilized crowds for rating ideas in innovation competitions [36] and testing interfaces based on task performance [21].

Our research is original relative to this prior work because it generates *structured feedback* on designs. For example, our approach generates the crowd's impressions when viewing a design and interpretation of the design according to the user's goals. This feedback extends prior work which solicited only individual preferences (e.g. "I like this one"). The feedback we provide is important since preferences are regarded as the least helpful aspect of design feedback [13].

Crowd-based usability Web sites can also be used to collect feedback on designs [43-45]. For example, when using Fivesecondtest [44], a user can pose free-form questions to the crowd about a design and the site returns a word cloud from the responses. In comparison, our system is original because it provides coordinated views for analyzing the association between the crowd's perception of a design and the visual elements within it. Our system also generates specific feedback (e.g. on the user's goals) not directly provided by these sites. Though the question format of the sites could be used to approximate the questions targeted by our system, the user would need to conceptualize and phrase the questions in a way that yields desired and consistent responses. Finally, we report results of the first study testing the utility of a crowd-based feedback system.

Methods for Receiving Design Feedback

There are at least two approaches for computationally generating feedback on designs. One approach, software critics, is to encode and apply domain-specific knowledge in the form of rules to generate feedback on designs [15]. The limitation of this approach is that it cannot consider the unique goals of the user or nuances of the design problem [29]. In contrast, our approach overcomes this limitation because it is based on the coordination of *human input*. A second approach is to build computational models to predict aesthetics and affect [39], complexity and colorfulness [27], or perceptual groupings [28] using the visual features of a design. Our work generates a broader range of feedback such as feedback on the user's communicative goals and established guidelines in the visual domain. Also, because the feedback is synthesized from human input, it can include explanations and inspiration for improvement.

Besides software tools, a user can use social approaches to receive feedback on designs such as organizing critiques, informally asking peers, and participating in online design communities. Critique is the traditional venue for receiving feedback in the creative design domains [12, 14]. However, the critique imposes the burden of organizing discussions, which are typically needed only at scheduled checkpoints. Users without a background in design may also not have the peer network or desire to organize a critique. A user can ask peers for feedback but may be uncomfortable due to the fear of criticism [6] or concerned about interrupting their work [16]. A design can also be posted to an online community (e.g. Core77 [41] or Dribbble [42]) to receive feedback. Studies of these types of communities, however, report that little feedback is generated and the quality does not typically exceed statements such as "I like it" [33, 37].

In contrast to these social approaches, the feedback in our system can be generated on-demand by any user performing visual design work. It reduces the fear of criticism since the user and crowd workers are unlikely to identify each other and tracing a design to the user should be hard, especially if anonymized, thereby offering anonymity [26]. It removes concern about interrupting other's work because it uses paid workers and it uses structured workflows to generate feedback that surpasses simplistic statements.

The Creative Need for Design Feedback

From a creative cognition perspective, feedback can foster insight or unblock creativity because the feedback serves as retrieval cues that activate new memory items and thought production [24]. This, in turn, can spark new understanding of a design, new solution approaches, or new perspectives on the design problem. For instance, prior work has shown that exposure to external visual stimuli aids brainstorming groups in producing more diverse ideas [24, 32]. Dow et al. showed that designers who receive feedback during iterative design produce higher quality outcomes than those who do not [9] and sharing multiple designs with others, due in part to increased communication, improves design exploration and outcomes [7]. Our system strives to allow these benefits to be realized by enabling users to receive feedback as often as desired during the design process.

FORMATIVE STUDY

A critical challenge for generating design feedback via crowdsourcing is to identify what type of feedback is desirable to the user, yet can be generated by non-experts. To address this challenge, we conducted interviews with twelve participants (six female). Eight were experienced graphic designers (experience ranged from 1 to 8 years; median was 3.5) while the other four occasionally create visual designs (e.g. data graphics, posters for conferences, or personal Web sites) as part of their work or interests but had no formal training in design. Inclusion of these two user categories was intended to tap diverse perspectives on what type of feedback is desired during the design process. Interviews lasted about one hour and were conducted face-to-face in the user's workspace. Participants received $15.

Characterizing Design Feedback
Could you describe a recent or ongoing design project for which you received feedback? How did this feedback influence the design or your approach to the design?
How often do you receive feedback for a design project? How would you characterize effective and ineffective feedback?
Types of Feedback Desired
What type of feedback is most desirable during your process?
How do you usually receive that feedback (informal discussion, formal critique, online community)? What do you see as the key strengths and weaknesses of these methods?
Desirability of Feedback from Non-Experts
Imagine you could interact with a crowd of non-experts during the design process. What questions would you want to ask the crowd? What type of feedback would you want to receive?

Table 1. The main topics and a sample of questions asked within each topic for the semi-structured interviews.

The interviews were semi-structured. The participant was first asked to describe a recent or ongoing design project that served as an initial warm-up and offered context for the discussion. Twelve prepared questions were asked probing the importance of feedback in the design process, what methods are used to receive feedback and from whom, what makes feedback effective, and what type of feedback might be desired from a non-expert crowd (posed as an audience without design knowledge). Additional questions pursued interesting points raised by the participant. Table 1 shows the topics covered and a sample of questions in each one. Following qualitative analysis methods [30], the interview data was coded using a bottom-up approach. The data was segmented into logical units and a first pass was made to assign categories to the units. Subsequent passes were then performed to organize the categories into broader themes.

We had three main findings from the interviews. First, all of the participants emphasized the importance of receiving feedback during the design process. Echoing prior work [4, 29, 31], participants reported that feedback helps them better understand what is (not) being communicated in the design, inform design choices, and remove creative blocks. One participant stated: *"When I get feedback, I start thinking about things in a different way, or I start realizing something that I was overlooking because I spent so much time on the project ... It helps me come to a final thing."* [P1]

Second, we found that participants may struggle to receive the feedback desired using existing methods. For example, similar to results reported in [31], participants reported that feedback received from peers is often overly optimistic and lacks clear direction for improvement: *"They [peers] know what went into it and how hard I worked. Maybe they don't like my project but they don't want to hurt my feelings. So those will be sugar-coated"* [P2]. Participants who leveraged online communities such as Dribbble complained the feedback received was too little and lacked depth (echoing findings in [33, 37]). As one participant stated: *"I post my work and I will get feedback occasionally. But it's usually very shallow and very positive. 'that looks nice or good work'. It is not very often that you get very true feedback on this site. It's also a follower-based community. So I have like 50 followers and some people have thousands. So they get a lot of feedback. Since I have so few, I don't get a lot of feedback."* [P3]. Feedback from others knowledgeable about design was deemed useful but not typically available outside of scheduled critiques or studio work, or if one's peer network does not include designers. *"There is no easy way to access feedback... I don't have many friends who are designers. For graphic design stuff, I haven't received extensive feedback... I usually just pick my favorite layout and color"* [P4]. Requesting feedback is therefore considered a limited resource that must be used judiciously.

Finally, all of the participants expressed that feedback from a non-expert crowd would be useful for comparing the perceptions of the crowd to their own expectations. For example, P5 stated *"We are trained designers to see certain things in certain ways. But if I can get non-trained people to understand my concept. Really see it. That means I did something really well ... There are a lot of people that have designed artifacts that can be only understood by designers. And that's a problem. Because the general public should be able to grasp your concept and understand it."* P3 made a similar argument: *"I'd like to get feedback from people outside of the design world. Because it's so easy to get caught inside the design bubble. A lot of times, if you are surrounded by designers, you only design for designers."*

From the responses, we also identified four types of design feedback that would be desirable from non-experts. One type of feedback relates to assessing the visual hierarchy of a design: *"What is the first thing people see in a design?"* [P1]; *"Does it stand out? What do they first read? What do they first see? What do they think they are gonna see?"* [P6]. A second type of feedback mentioned is capturing first impressions when the design is viewed: *"What are people's initial impressions of it?"* [P4]; *"What's your reaction to this or what does this make you think of? ... So I can see if that's the reaction that I want them to perceive"* [P7]. A third type of feedback is whether the crowd understands the communicative goals of the design: *"Does my design convey the right message to the audience?"* [P8]; *"Here is my goal.... How is this coming across to you?"* [P9]; *"How well do my concepts read?"* [P10].

A fourth type of feedback tacitly mentioned is assessing a design relative to design guidelines, e.g. contrast, proximity, and alignment [34]. This feedback was inferred from many responses expressing the need for technical insights about a design and clear direction for how to improve it: *"I want highly technical feedback and constructive feedback...what's wrong and how to fix it?"* [P11]; *"Do the colors clash or complement each other? Are there any distractions?"* [P4].

Based on findings from the interviews and prior work [35, 37], we designed and implemented a novel Web application called *Voyant* that generates design feedback desired from non-experts. For the non-expert crowd, the system currently uses paid workers from an online labor market. The system accepts a visual design as input, decomposes the feedback generation process into sub-tasks suitable for non-experts, aggregates the results, and presents them to the user.

Figure 2. The interface for configuring the feedback generation process. From this interface, Alice uploads her poster image, configures the desired audience (M/F, USA, 18-35) and selects which feedback is desired. For example, after selecting Goals, Alice enters her communicative goals for the poster.

USER EXPERIENCE OF VOYANT

To demonstrate the utility of our system, we first describe the design feedback that can be generated, interactions for exploring the feedback, and how the feedback benefits the user. Consider a real scenario adopted from our evaluation. Alice, a novice designer, is designing a poster for a dessert station as part of a design project (Figure 2). The goal of the design is to attract attention and create excitement about trying the new service in a restaurant. Alice wants to assess how the poster is perceived by her intended audience and how these perceptions align with her expectations. Figures 2, 3, and 4 illustrate our system in context of this scenario.

To initiate feedback on a design, the user navigates to the main page of our Web application (currently restricted to our institution). From the page, the user uploads a visual design (e.g. poster, logo, or Web page) as an image, selects the feedback desired, and configures any related parameters. Five types of feedback can be selected or configured:

- *Elements* are the individual elements that are visible or otherwise perceived ("seen") in the design including colors, shapes, objects, and activities.
- *First Notice* refers to the visual order in which elements are first noticed in the design.
- *Impressions* are the perceptions formed in one's mind upon first viewing the design.
- *Goals* refer to how well the design is perceived to meet its communicative goals. If selected the user is prompted to briefly state each of her goals for the design.

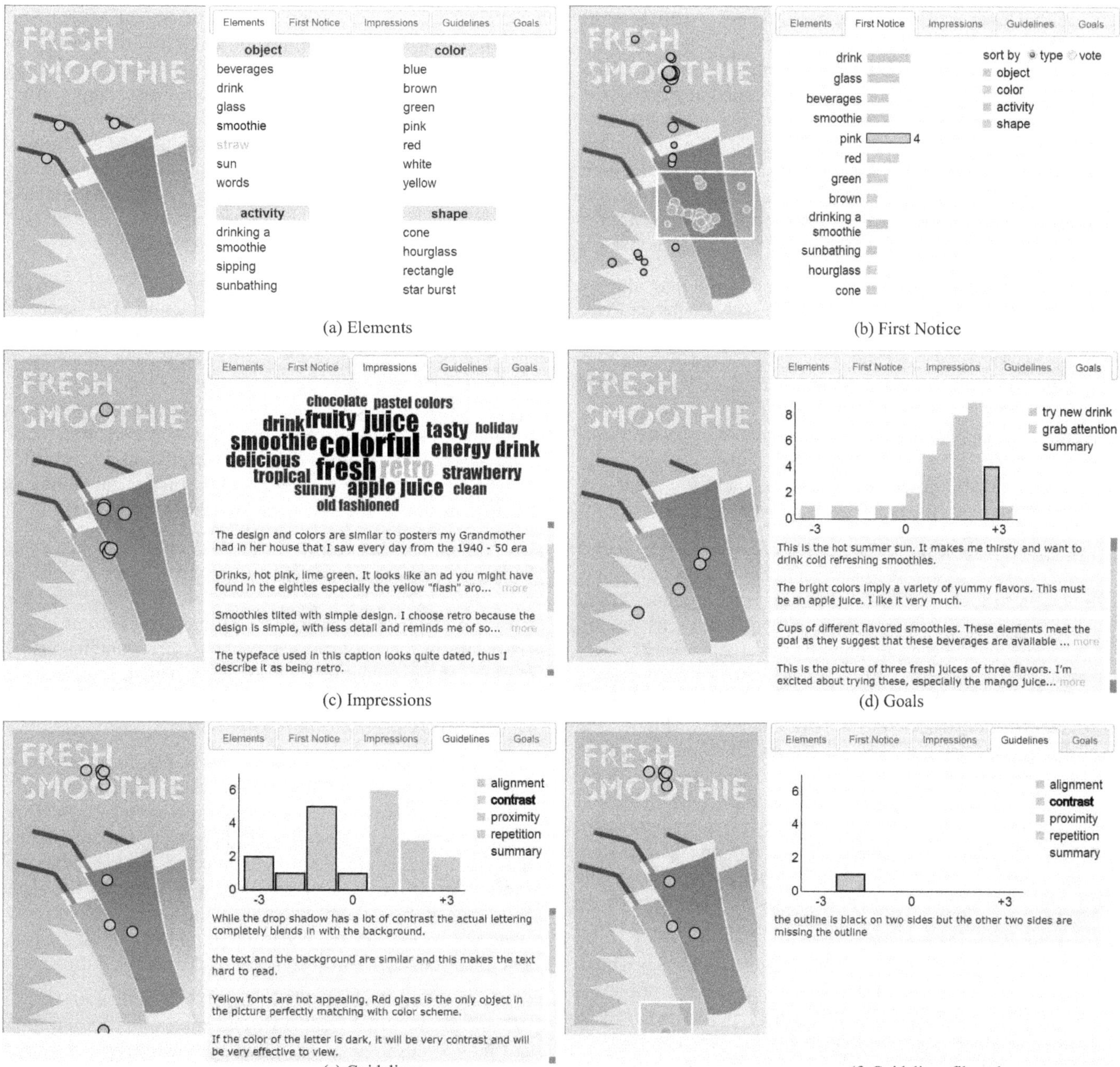

(a) Elements (b) First Notice (c) Impressions (d) Goals (e) Guidelines (f) Guidelines filtered

Figure 3. The user interface offers coordinated views for each type of feedback generated on Alice's poster. In (a), she reviews the list of elements seen by the crowd. In (b), she views which elements and corresponding regions of the design are first noticed and creates a filter to determine which elements relate to the center markers. In (c), a word cloud represents the impressions and their frequency that the crowd had upon first viewing the design. In (d), a set of interactive charts show the distributions of the crowd ratings for each communicative goal. (e) A similar set of charts shows the distributions of the ratings for each design guideline. In (e), the user selects the non-positive ratings to inspect the corresponding explanations and visual markers. In (f), the user further explores the feedback by selecting a subset of the visual markers (bottom center), which filters the ratings shown in the chart and the explanations.

- *Guidelines* refer to how well the design is perceived to meet known guidelines in the domain. Our set includes proximity, alignment, repetition, and contrast [34].

In early prototypes, the *Elements* were produced as part of the workflow for generating *First Notice*. However, user testing revealed that knowing the set of elements seen in the design was useful on its own and was therefore extracted into its own type of feedback. The user may also configure the geography, gender, and age of the audience.

Once the feedback is configured, the system instantiates the crowd workflows, decomposes the complex process of feedback generation into micro-tasks, and submits them to an online labor market (Mechanical Turk). Analogous to [33], the tasks are designed such that they can be performed by crowd workers with little or no design knowledge. The individual task outcomes are then aggregated and presented to the user. Each type of feedback typically requires a few hours to generate and costs a few US dollars. To ensure that the crowd workers match the audience specified by the user, prospective workers first complete a demographic survey and only those workers whose responses match the user's specification are allowed to progress to the feedback tasks.

For each feedback type, Voyant provides coordinated views that consist of a visual overview of the crowd's perceptions (e.g. in the form of a list, word cloud, or bar chart) and visual markers overlaid on the design (see Figure 3). Though coordinated views is an established visualization technique for exploratory analysis [1], we apply this technique to enable analysis of the association between the perceptions of a design and the visual elements within it. Once generated, the feedback is presented as a tabbed interface where each tab contains one type of feedback.

For *Elements*, the user receives a list of the elements "seen" by the crowd. To help the user parse the elements, they are grouped into four categories including object, color, shape, and activity, which were derived from [14]. The set of categories could be easily modified in future work. Each element can be selected to view the regions of the design associated with it. Marked regions appear as visual markers (circles) overlaid on the design. For example, in Figure 3a, selecting the element "straw" shows the corresponding visual markers placed by the workers. The benefit is the user can compare what was "seen" to what was expected. For example, in Figure 3a, some crowd workers perceived the yellow background shape in the bottom right as the "sun." The user can assess whether this perception aligns with her expectation and, if not, can use this discrepancy to seed the next iteration on the design.

The second tab *First Notice* shows the visual order in which the elements are seen. The list can be ordered globally based on the number of workers who reported seeing the element first or ordered separately in each category. Assessing the visual hierarchy is an important aspect of visual design [22]. For example, from the feedback shown in Figure 3b, the user learns that the glass with the red-colored content is the element most frequently seen first as indicated by the concentration of visual markers and the corresponding elements "red," "pink," "drink," "glass," and "beverage." Interestingly, "fresh smoothie" attracts far less attention despite its prominent size and location.

The *Impressions* tab shows a word cloud of the crowd's first impressions of the design (Figure 3c). A word cloud is used as it offers a compact representation and efficiently communicates the more and less frequent impressions. The word size is proportional to the number of workers who shared the impression. If the user selects a word, the system shows the visual markers on the design corresponding to that impression. Conversely, the user can select an individual or group of markers on the design image to view the corresponding impressions in the word cloud and read the explanations offered by the workers. For example, from Figure 3c, one of the most common perceptions was "retro" which was associated with the title and the red and brown drink glasses in the poster. Though not shown in the figure, the user could also explore the markers placed on these elements to identify other words associated, e.g., the glasses were associated with "colorful", "fresh", and "juice".

The two remaining tabs for *Guidelines* and *Goals* provide similar forms of feedback and interaction. For each of these, Voyant presents an interactive bar chart summarizing the ratings from the crowd. The ratings were made on a seven-point scale from strongly disagree (-3) to strongly agree (+3) with whether the design met the given guideline or goal. Also, each worker could place a marker to indicate the region of the design associated with the rating and enter rationale. The user can select subsets of the guidelines or goals to inspect and compare the results (Figure 3d-f).

In addition, the user can select a subset of the bars in a chart to inspect only those markers and explanations associated with the selected ratings. For example, in Figure 3e, the user selects all the non-positive ratings for *contrast* in the chart and is then able to review the corresponding visual markers and explanations. Likewise, as shown in Figure 3f, the user can select a set of visual markers on the design to view the corresponding ratings and explanations.

From the ratings of the goals shown in Figure 3d, the user can have increased confidence that the goals are being reasonably communicated given the positive ratings. But, from the ratings of *Guidelines* in Figure 3e, the user learns that the design could use improved contrast. Inspecting the explanations reveals that many crowd workers felt the color and style of the "fresh smoothie" text did not adequately stand out relative to the background and other colors. This and other feedback can seed additional design iterations.

CROWD WORKFLOWS FOR FEEDBACK GENERATION

Voyant decomposes feedback generation into a description and interpretation phase, inspired by how critique is taught in design education [14]. In each phase, the tasks focus worker attention on specific aspects of a design rather than soliciting holistic evaluations to improve outcomes [33].

Description

The purpose of the first phase is to enumerate what can be "seen" in a design such as objects, colors, shapes, and activities. The inclusion of this step was motivated by how novices are taught to critique visual designs by first describing what elements are seen [14]. Once identified, one can consider how the elements relate to each other, the goals of the designer, or guidelines in the domain.

To generate elements for a design, micro-tasks are created and submitted to the online labor market. The worker task screen shows the design and prompts the worker to enter at

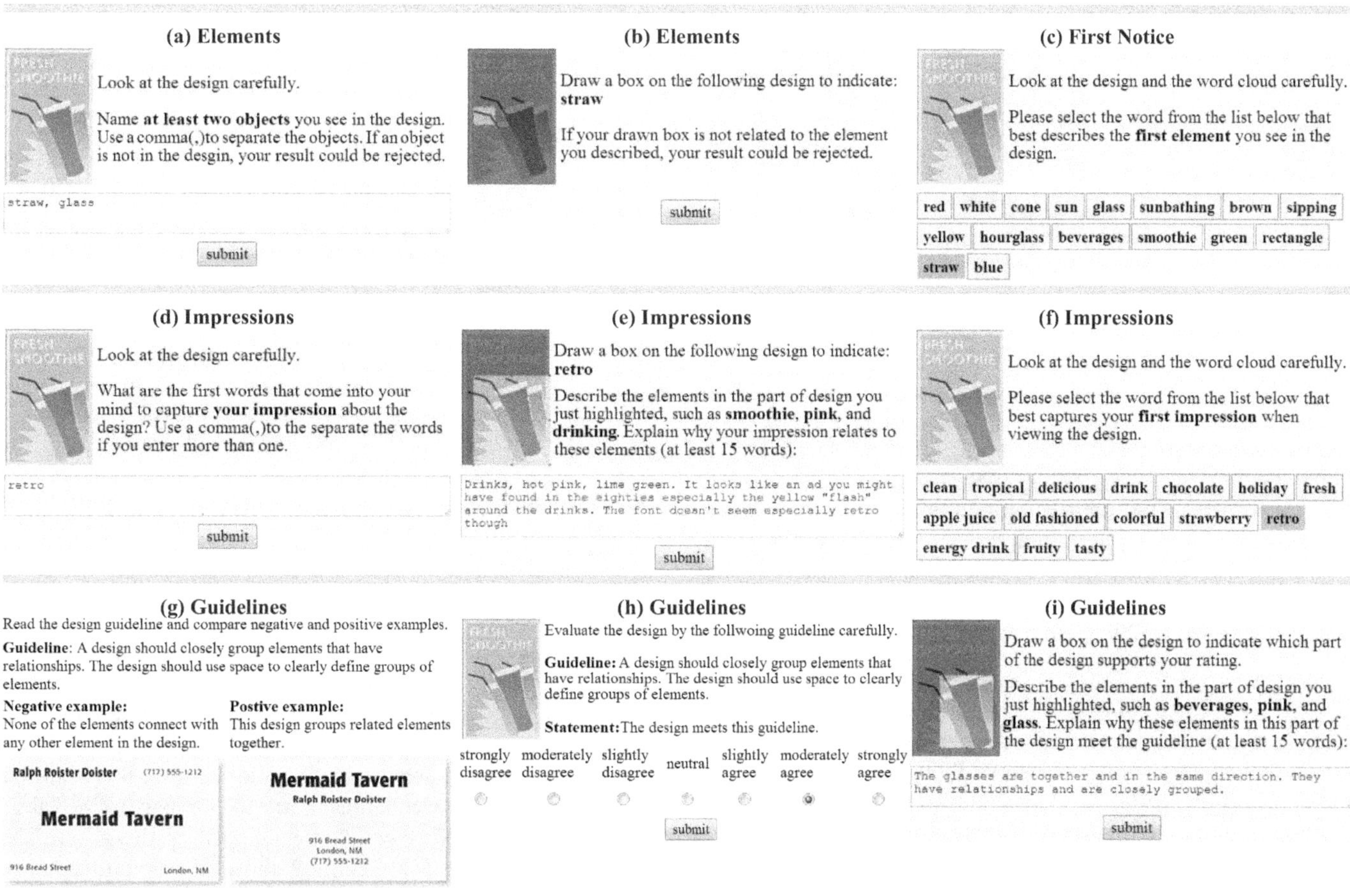

Figure 4. The workflows and related task screens for generating design feedback in Voyant. For *Elements*, (a) the worker enters at least two elements seen or perceived in the design and then (b) sizes and locates a rectangle to locate each element. For *First Notice*, (c) a worker selects which element is first noticed in the design. For *Impressions*, (d) a worker enters the first word(s) that come to mind after viewing the design. For each impression entered, (e) the worker locates the most related area of the design and enters rationale. In (f), additional workers vote on the collected impressions and enter rationale. For *Guidelines*, (g) the worker learns about the guideline, (h) rates the design on the guideline, and (i) locates the area of the design that best supports the rating and enters rationale. The workflow for *Goals* is the same as that for *Guidelines*.

least two elements seen in the design relating to a given category (color, object, shape, or activity). See Figure 4a. The category prompts provide a means for focusing worker attention on the task. After a worker lists two or more elements, s/he is asked to mark regions of the design corresponding to each element listed, if applicable (Figure 4b). The markers provide an efficient mapping from what is described to what is seen. Five tasks are created for each category by default. However, if elements collected for a category are all unique, additional tasks are created for that category until a new element repeats an earlier one (a proxy for saturation). The repeated element is removed and the final set is piped into the second phase - interpretation.

Interpretation

In the second phase, the design is interpreted relative to the visual hierarchy, first impressions, design guidelines, and any communicative goals entered by the end user.

First Notice Workflow

The workflow for *First Notice* creates task screens showing the design and all the elements listed during Description. The ordering of the elements on the screen is randomized to avoid bias (Figure 4c). The worker is prompted to select which element s/he notices first in the design. The worker is then instructed to mark on the design (by placing and sizing a rectangle) where the selected element is located. From experimentation, the number of workers currently recruited is twice the number of elements listed, up to a limit of thirty. The number of times each element is selected is returned and presented to the user (Figure 3b, right panel) along with the corresponding visual markers (Figure 3b, left panel).

Impressions Workflow

The *Impressions* workflow generates task screens showing the design and prompts the worker to enter one or more words that come to mind when first viewing it (Figure 4d). For each word entered, the same worker is prompted to mark the design (place and size a rectangle) to indicate the

Figure 5. The designs collected for the evaluation included Web designs, a magazine cover, and an illustration. P18, P19, and P20's designs were shown in Figures 1, 2, and 6 respectively.

region related to the impression and enter rationale (Figure 4e). As an aid, the system inserts up to three elements from the *Description* phase whose markers are nearest to the one just entered. This workflow ends once twenty tasks have been completed or thirty unique impressions are collected.

From the impression words collected, the system extracts the unique words and their frequency. Additional workers are then recruited to view the design, select which words from the existing set best captures their impression (Figure 4f), and enter rationale. This latter step is performed to further elicit the frequency of impressions from the crowd.

Guidelines Workflow

For the *Guidelines* workflow, a series of tasks are generated where workers rate how well the design adheres to the set of guidelines available in the system. A worker rates his or her perception of how well the design adheres to a guideline on a 7-point scale (Figure 4h). The worker is then prompted to mark a region on the design and describe how the content in that region relates to the rating (Figure 4i). This task is repeated several times per guideline, and then repeated for all guidelines selected by the user during the configuration phase. Because workers are not assumed to have knowledge of visual design, the first part of each task screen explains the guideline to be rated in lay language and shows both a positive and negative example (Figure 4g).

Communicative Goals Workflow

The workflow for *Goals* is similar to *Guidelines*. A series of tasks are created for each goal entered by the user during the configuration phase. A worker views the design and one of the goals and rates how well the design is perceived to meet the goal. As with Guidelines, the worker then marks a region on the design that best relates to the rating and enters rationale. This task is repeated several times per goal.

Workflow	Number of Workers	$US
Elements	20 (5 for each element type)	1.0
First Notice	30	1.5
Impressions	50 (20 for listing; 30 for voting)	2.5
Guidelines	80 (20 for each guideline)	4.0
Goals	40 (e.g. 2 goals; 20 for each goal)	2.0

Table 2. The typical number of workers recruited and cost for each workflow in the current implementation.

Question	Avg (SD)
Q1. The feedback would help me improve my design	5.8 (1.3)
Q2. The "Impressions" feedback was helpful.	6.0 (1.2)
Q3. The "Goals" feedback was helpful.	5.4 (1.2)
Q4. The "First Notice" feedback was helpful.	5.1 (1.0)
Q5. The "Elements" feedback was helpful	4.5 (0.9)
Q6. The "Guidelines" feedback was helpful.	4.1 (1.6)
Q7. The user interface was easy to learn and use	5.2 (1.6)
Q8. The overview for each feedback type was helpful	6.2 (0.7)
Q9. It was easy to inspect details of the feedback	5.5 (1.1)
Q10. The use of the visual markers was helpful	5.4 (1.4)
Q11. I would request feedback more often with Voyant	5.1 (1.1)

Table 3. Participant ratings for the different types of feedback generated and the overall system.

IMPLEMENTATION

Voyant was built as a Web application and can be accessed from most popular Web browsers. The functionality described in this paper has been fully implemented. The user interface was built using JavaScript, JQuery, and D3.js. The micro-tasks generated by the application are submitted to Amazon.com's Mechanical Turk, a popular online labor market. Only workers with >= 95% task approval rate are considered for our tasks. Table 2 shows the default number of workers and total payment made for each feedback type. These values were determined through experimentation and could be easily adjusted or made configurable by the user.

EVALUATION

The purpose of the evaluation was to gauge the helpfulness of the different types of feedback generated by our system, assess the usability of the visual feedback representations and interactions in the interface, and understand how the use of the system may be integrated into the design process.

Eight users (P13-20) were recruited for the study (4 female) and none had prior knowledge of our system. Four of the participants were practicing graphic designers (2-5 years of experience) who worked on print, Web, and interaction design. The other four created visual designs for personal use such as Web pages and illustrations as part of course or research projects. They had no training in visual design.

We collected one in-progress or recently completed visual design from each participant for which feedback was desired. Figure 5 shows the designs collected. For example, P14 was designing a magazine cover and wanted to visually communicate it is about a film festival. P17 was designing a Web site showing positive social work in the community and wanted to convey a warm, inviting feeling. Relevant information such as the goals and intended audience was collected for each design. Our system was then configured and used to generate the full set of feedback on each design. The time to generate the feedback on each design ranged

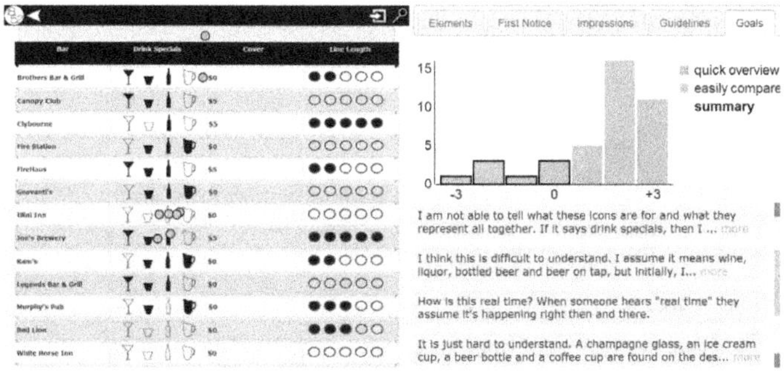

Figure 6. Part of the feedback (Goals) generated by Voyant for a Web design collected from P20. The participant explored the non-positive ratings and learned that the icons were not being perceived the way he intended and needed refinement.

from 22 to 70 hours with a median of 40 hours. The cost ranged from \$10.70 to \$13, with a median of \$11. Interviews were then scheduled with the participants. An interview lasted one hour and remuneration was \$15.

The interview consisted of a warm-up (15 minutes), system walkthrough (30 minutes), and post discussion / survey (15 minutes). In the warm-up, the participant described the feedback previously received on the design, where it came from, and how useful it was. For the walkthrough, we first introduced the system and then the participant used it to explore each feedback type at their own pace while thinking aloud. We prompted discussion about the helpfulness of the feedback, usability of the interface, and how the system can be used in practice. Afterward, the participant completed a survey. It contained eleven questions stated in a neutral manner regarding the helpfulness of the system and each type of feedback. Responses were given using a 7-point Likert-scale ranging from strongly disagree (1) to strongly agree (7). Table 3 summarizes the questions and responses.

Helpfulness of the Feedback Overall

Participants reported that the feedback generated by our system was helpful overall and would help them improve their designs (Q1, μ=5.8). For example, participants stated:

> *"There is some misunderstanding of my poster [see Figure 1]. Many people said that the portrait is not clear enough to show the Shakespeare's figure. They think it's a dog. That's the most important part I learn from the feedback. I will make new sketches based on the feedback."* [P18]

> *"It is useful to see the number of people that have certain issues. I keep getting people's misunderstanding of the icons of the drink specials* [see Figure 6]. *I definitely get right away that was a major issue because there are so many people that talked about it"* [P20]

> *"This is very useful feedback and something that I couldn't get in any other way."* [P17]

Specifically, the feedback helped users identify problems with their designs. For example, one of P15's design goals was to create a rendering of a teapot in Chinese style. However, she learned from the *Goals* feedback that this goal was not well supported. After exploring the visual markers and explanations linked to the lower ratings for this goal, she gained a better understanding of the problem. To address it, she stated she would add tea cups beside the teapot to reinforce the perception of a teapot rather than a coffeepot and add a dragon pattern to communicate Chinese style. Likewise, P20 discovered from *First Notice* that *"not a lot attention is given to the main navigation bar at the top... We need to do something to highlight this area more."* Due to the low ratings and the corresponding explanations about contrast in *Guidelines*, P16 said that he would now increase the contrast between the foreground and background colors.

A second way the feedback was helpful is that it allowed participants to gain insight into their designs. For example, in the poster created by P19 (see Figure 3d), her color selections were intended only to make the poster "colorful." But from the feedback, she discovered that people were associating different flavors with her color selections (e.g. mango or apple to the yellow-orange smoothie) and that she could manipulate the color to cause people to literally 'taste' her design.

A third way the feedback helped is that it allowed participants to consider their designs from different perspectives, especially when the feedback contained conflicting viewpoints. For example, P13 said *"Some of these positive things are contrasting what negative people said. I find myself comparing "+3" to "-3" if they are talking about the same thing... I can see why it worked for one person and see why it didn't work for another person. So it's easy for me to find a compromise between these two."*

Finally, participants felt the feedback was a useful complement to prior feedback received on their designs:

> *"I think the quality of the feedback is really good. Because many parts of the feedback are actually the same as the feedback I got from my professors and my classmates."* [P15]

> *"It is really interesting to get people's feedback, especially if it's coming from non-designers. I'm so used to focusing so much on type. The most surprising thing is that people [non-designers] don't care much about the type as they care about the imagery."* [P14]

> *"I got a lot more critical feedback. That's very hard to get from peers."* [P16]

Helpfulness of the Different Types of Feedback

The *Impressions* feedback was reported as the most helpful among the five types of feedback generated (Q2, μ=6.0). From the perspectives of the participants:

> *"I like this word map [Impressions] and I think this word map is incredibly helpful... Because I can think about what I was trying to achieve with this design and reflect it to the words people are using when describing this. Then I can see if I really did well enough by portraying something in my design."* [P13]

> *"Impressions were the most useful because they brought up more unexpected details.... I'm looking for unusual words or data. I can see the less common terms associated with the design."* [P19]

Participants also agreed that the *Goals* (Q3, μ=5.4) and *First Notice* (Q4, μ=5.1) feedback was helpful:

> *"Goals is helpful for verifying the level achievement of goals that are actionable by the audience. Goals sort of remind me of AB testing if I had multiple iterations of the design and compared the feedback on the goals."* [P17]

> *"What you see first is important. This [First Notice] will give me information on how to make things more attractive and memorable in short time frame."* [P19]

There was moderate agreement the *Elements* feedback was helpful (Q5, μ=4.5). P15 felt the feedback was "*a good check*" on whether design elements are interpreted correctly. He reasoned that *"At a basic level, those things [Elements] are very important to understand. Like if someone says that object looks like an elephant, and it's not supposed to. That's something that could be really helpful to know."* [P15]. Other participants felt the feedback may be too low-level.

The Guidelines feedback received lower ratings, though the average was still on the positive side of neutral (Q6, μ=4.1). Positive reactions included: *"This is useful, especially for me. I'm bad at following common design principles"* [P20]; *"because I'm not a professional designer. I might forget about color, positioning, or grouping elements. If they mentioned these, it's useful for me to keep these in mind."* [P17].

In terms of less positive reactions, some participants had strong pre-conceptions and "*don't necessarily trust non-experts to give technical feedback*" [P18]. However, after reviewing the *Guidelines* feedback on their designs, they became less skeptical: *"I like this comment. This line is not parallel to that line. It doesn't satisfy the alignment design guideline. That's a good point."* [P18]. Finally, two participants commented that some explanations about the given ratings were "*arbitrary*" or "*not related*" and they had to expend effort to filter these irrelevant explanations.

Feedback Representations and Interactions

The coordinated views provided by Voyant enable exploration of the feedback from the perspective of either the overview representation or the markers on the design. Participants reported that this interactive coupling was helpful for analyzing the association between the crowd's perception of a design and the elements within it (Q7-Q10, μ>=5.2). For example, when exploring *Impressions*, we observed participants selecting specific words to identify the locations on the design associated with them and selecting a subset of the markers to identify the associated impressions. This was supported by several statements:

> *"I wasn't expecting the word cloud to be so helpful. Because in general when I see a word cloud I usually just assume people put words together randomly. There is no data behind it. But being able to click on each word and find individual things they cite, like the actual areas in the photo [markers] they think, enforces that. That's really valuable."* [P13]

> *"The most useful part of the interface is that I can check specific parts of the design [using visual filters]. For example, I want to see if my title in the poster works well. So I just draw a box to select this part and look at the ratings and the comments."* [P18]

> *"It is the most efficient way to quickly highlight like that [draw visual filter on the design]. Oh, that part I was concerned about that. Let's see what people thought about that part. It can help me find comments about the areas I am most interested or concerned about. I think that's probably the best feature."* [P14]

In addition, several participants suggested that more ways to explore the feedback would be desirable. For example, some wanted to interactively explore the feedback based on the demographics of the crowd (e.g. age and gender). This may help reveal potential patterns in the responses, aid interpretation, and lead to further insights into the design.

Potential Use in Practice

We shared with participants the costs and response times needed to generate feedback on their designs and discussed how this might affect the use of the system in practice. The participants did not view this as a major limitation, rather they viewed it as a fair tradeoff for not having to organize a face-to-face critique or interrupt others to receive feedback:

> *"No efforts from my side at all. Because I don't need to use my social capital to do this [request feedback]. I have to call my friends at [company] and ask how my website works. They work at [company] and they are busy. But here it's just 10 dollars"* [P17]

> *"I can get feedback at any time I want. For example, I did this project at 10 or 11PM at night. I'm really excited about this. I will upload it to the tool to get feedback. But it's very inappropriate to request feedback from my professor and classmates at that time. Also, when I do freelance projects, I don't have chance to show my designs to them. This tool allows me to work by myself."* [P15]

Participants reported they would use a system like Voyant to receive feedback more often in the design process (Q11, μ=5.1). Participants felt the system would be particularly useful after they had begun iterating on a selected design:

> *"I could see myself using it in the mid to the late phase of the project. Say I have a concrete idea for the way I'm gonna approach the project. From there, after I have done a few iterations on something I was fond of. Then I may send the first or second draft down and get some feedback."* [P14]

> *"When I was doing this, I was maybe about half way through the project. I think that's a pretty good time to take data like this and look at it."* [P16]

Some participants also wanted to use the system to generate and compare feedback on different versions of a design. For example, P13 stated *"I could see this being incredibly useful for having multiple concepts at first. Before this, I did a quite few different sketches and concepts. I could see using the impressions on these would be really useful.... I would do three different versions of this site layout and then compare the impressions."* This and other extensions are described next in Discussion.

DISCUSSION AND FUTURE WORK

Our system helps users identify and understand problems with their designs, but it is up to the users to determine how to best modify the designs to address those problems. The fact that the feedback generated by our system can surface problems with a design is itself a significant outcome, e.g., as iterating on a design requires knowing what problems to address [9]. The user can also inspect the overviews, visual markers, and explanations to not only identify problems but also understand why they occurred. The feasibility of using crowds to brainstorm solutions to the problems identified could be explored in future work. It would also be interesting to observe how Voyant is utilized throughout a design cycle and how the generated feedback prompts iterations on a design. Such a study could reveal how the feedback benefits different design phases and types of designs, and users with different levels of design expertise.

Participants in our study appreciated exploring the feedback through the visual markers placed on their designs. Each marker was placed by a crowd worker to associate an element of the design with her perception during a task. Placing a marker was typically straightforward, but became problematic when the element could not be easily localized, e.g., background color, white space, or relations between multiple elements. System designers could improve this aspect by offering the worker different types of markers, e.g., different shapes, free-form annotation, and selectable areas or groups defined by image segmentation techniques.

The *Guidelines* feedback received ratings lower than the other types. One cause could be that the worker tasks for *Guidelines* were more complex than the others. For instance, when rating a design relative to a guideline, a worker had to comprehend the guideline, review the examples, and apply it to the design. Outcome quality may therefore have been more variable on these tasks. To improve quality, additional scaffolding for workers such as apprenticeship or showing worked examples for the tasks could be explored. For the other feedback, only minimal quality control was performed and participants in our evaluation did notice that some comments were irrelevant, which cast doubt on the corresponding input. Voyant and similar systems should therefore consider adopting additional quality controls such as use of self-assessment [10], find-fix-verify [3], validation questions [19], or task designs [20] to improve feedback. Similarly, future work should explore how to optimize the workflows in terms of the workers, costs, and time required.

Our current system generates feedback on one design at a time. However, if desired, a user could generate feedback on multiple variations of a design or competing concepts. The feedback could be used to conduct deeper comparison between the designs and complement simple AB tests (e.g. as offered in [2, 8]). A related extension is to visualize the feedback history for the evolution of a design. For example, the feedback could be shown and made accessible through an interactive, visual timeline [11]. The system also could allow users to bookmark informative views of the feedback as a way to help guide and explain later design choices [17].

Five types of feedback are generated in Voyant, but other types may also be beneficial. For example, the system could enable dialog between the user and the crowd, e.g., by allowing questions to be posed for each other about the design. Other feedback such as the analysis of a design relative to precedents or contemporary trends [5] would also be useful, but cannot yet be generated. To the degree that a crowdsourcing or other computational approach could generate these types of feedback is an open question.

Our system recruits a crowd of workers from an online labor market, but other crowds such as the employees of a large organization, members of an online community, or students in a large design course could also be used. In the latter case, the perception-oriented feedback generated by our system could complement other forms of peer critique already integrated into the course [23]. A related future study would be to compare the feedback generated by crowds with different levels of design knowledge.

Voyant targets the visual design domain. This domain was selected because it is challenging and more people are performing visual design work due to the increased demand for visual communication skills and the wide availability of graphic design software. But, the concept of receiving structured feedback from non-experts may be applicable to other domains. For example, in architecture, a system like Voyant could enable architects to receive impressions of the form of a building or interpretation of its design goals.

CONCLUSION

Crowdsourcing offers an emerging opportunity for users to receive rapid feedback on their designs. Our work has made three contributions in this direction. First, we contributed results from interviews identifying several types of feedback on a visual design that are desired from non-experts. A second contribution was the design and implementation of a system that generates the desired feedback on designs from a crowd of non-experts. A novel aspect of the system is that it provides coordinated views to help users analyze associations between the crowd's perceptions of a design and the elements within it. Finally, we contributed the results of an evaluation demonstrating the utility of the feedback generated by a crowd-based system for users and their own designs. Users reported that the impressions of the design and the interpretations of their goals were the most helpful, though the other feedback types provided were also valued. Users also appreciated the coordinated views and the interactions for exploring and understanding the feedback generated. Voyant exemplifies how crowdsourcing can be harnessed to enable new forms of computational tools that support design activity.

REFERENCES

1. Baldonado, M.Q.W., Woodruff, A., & Kuchinsky, A., Guidelines for Using Multiple Views in Information Visualization. In *AVI*, (2000), 110-119.

2. Bernstein, M.S., Brandt, J., Miller, R.C., & Karger, D.R., Crowds in Two Seconds: Enabling Realtime Crowd-Powered Interfaces. In *UIST*, (2011), 33-42.
3. Bernstein, M.S., Little, G., Miller, R.C., Hartmann, B., Ackerman, M.S., Karger, D.R., Crowell, D., et al., Soylent: A Word Processor with a Crowd Inside. In *UIST*, (2010), 313-322.
4. Cross, N. Designerly Ways of Knowing. *Design Studies*, *3*, 5, (1982), 221-227.
5. Dannels, D.P. and Martin, K.N. Critiquing Critiques: A Genre Analysis of Feedback Across Novice to Expert Design Studios. *Journal of Business and Technical Communication*, *22*, 2, (2008), 135-159.
6. Diehl, M. and Stroebe, W. Productivity Loss in Brainstorming Groups: Towards the Solution of a Riddle. *Journal of Personality and Social Psychology*, *53*, 3, (1987), 497-509.
7. Dow, S.P., Fortuna, J., Schwartz, D., Altringer, B., & Klemmer, S., Prototyping Dynamics: Sharing Multiple Designs Improves Exploration, Group Rapport, and Results. In *CHI*, (2011), 2807-2816.
8. Dow, S.P., Gerber, E., & Wong, A., A Preliminary Study of Using Crowds in the Classroom. In *CHI*, (2013), 227-236.
9. Dow, S.P., Heddleston, K., & Klemmer, S.R., The Efficacy of Prototyping Under Time Constraints. In *Creativity & Cognition*, (2009), 165-174.
10. Dow, S.P., Kulkarni, A., Klemmer, S., & Hartmann, B., Shepherding the Crowd Yields Better Work. In *CSCW*, (2012), 1013-1022.
11. Dunne, C., Riche, N.H., Lee, B., Metoyer, R.A., & Robertson, G.G., GraphTrail: Analyzing Large Multivariate, Heterogeneous Networks while Supporting Exploration History. In *CHI*, (2012), 1663-1672.
12. Elkins, J. *Art Critiques: A Guide*. New Academia Publishing, Washington DC, 2012.
13. Feldman, E.B. The Teacher as Model Critic. *Journal of Aesthetic Education*, *7*, 1, (1973), 50-57.
14. Feldman, E.B. *Varieties of Visual Experience: Art as Image and Idea*. Prentice-Hall, Englewood Cliffs, N.J., 1981.
15. Fischer, G., Nakakoji, K., Ostwald, J., Stahl, G., & Sumner, T., Embedding Computer-Based Critics in the Contexts of Design. In *CHI*, (1993), 157-164.
16. Fogarty, J., Hudson, S.E., Atkeson, C.G., Avrahami, D., Forlizzi, J., Kiesler, S., Lee, J.C., et al. Predicting Human Interruptibility with Sensors. *TOCHI*, *12*, 1, (2005), 119-146.
17. Heer, J., Viégas, F.B., & Wattenberg, M., Voyagers and Voyeurs: Supporting Asynchronous Collaborative Information Visualization. In *CHI*, (2007), 1029-1038.
18. Hundhausen, C.D., Fairbrother, D., & Petre, M. An Empirical Study of the "Prototype Walkthrough": A Studio-Based Activity for HCI Education. *TOCHI*, *19*, 4, (2012), 1-36.
19. Kittur, A., Chi, E.H., & Suh, B., Crowdsourcing User Studies With Mechanical Turk. In *CHI*, (2008), 453-456.
20. Kittur, A., Nickerson, J.V., Bernstein, M.S., Gerber, E.M., Shaw, A., Zimmerman, J., Lease, M., et al., The Future of Crowd Work. In *CSCW*, (2013), 1301-1318.
21. Komarov, S., Reinecke, K., & Gajos, K.Z., Crowdsourcing Performance Evaluations of User Interfaces. In *CHI*, (2013), 207-216.
22. Kress, G.R. and Leeuwen, T.v. *Reading Images: the Grammar of Visual Design*. Routledge, 1996.
23. Kulkarni, C. and Klemmer, S. Learning Design Wisdom by Augmenting Physical Studio Critique With Online Self-Assessment, Stanford University technical report, 2012.
24. Nijstad, B.A. and Stroebe, W. How the Group Affects the Mind: A Cognitive Model of Idea Generation in Groups. *Personality and Social Psychology Review*, *10*, 3, (2006), 186-213.
25. Park, C.H., Son, K., Lee, J.H., & Bae, S.-H., Crowd vs. Crowd: Large-Scale Cooperative Design through Open Team Competition. In *CSCW*, (2013), 1275-1284.
26. Paulus, P. and Yang, H.-C. Idea Generation in Groups: A Basis for Creativity in Organizations. *Organizational Behavior and Human Decision Processes*, *82*, 1, (2000), 76-87.
27. Reinecke, K., Yeh, T., Miratrix, L., Mardiko, R., Zhao, Y., Liu, J., & Gajos, K.Z., Predicting Users' First Impressions of Website Aesthetics With a Quantification of Perceived Visual Complexity and Colorfulness. In *CHI*, (2013), 2049-2058.
28. Rosenholtz, R., Twarog, N.R., Schinkel-Bielefeld, N., & Wattenberg, M., An Intuitive Model of Perceptual Grouping for HCI Design. In *CHI*, (2009), 1331-1340.
29. Schön, D.A. Designing as Reflective Conversation with the Materials of a Design Situation. *Knowledge-Based Systems*, *5*, 1, (1992), 3-14.
30. Strauss, A.L. *Qualitative Analysis for Social Scientists*. Cambridge University Press, 1987.
31. Tohidi, M., Buxton, W., Baecker, R., & Sellen, A., Getting the Right Design and the Design Right. In *CHI*, (2006), 1243-1252.
32. Wang, H.C., Fussell, S.R., & Cosley, D., From Diversity to Creativity: Stimulating Group Brainstorming with Cultural Differences and Conversationally-Retrieved Pictures. In *CSCW*, (2011), 265-274.
33. Willett, W., Heer, J., & Agrawala, M., Strategies for Crowdsourcing Social Data Analysis. In *CHI*, (2012), 227-236.
34. Williams, R. *The Non-designer's Design Book*. Peachpit Press, 2008.
35. Xu, A. and Bailey, B.P., A Crowdsourcing Model for Receiving Design Critique. In *CHI Extended Abstracts*, (2011), 1183-1188.
36. Xu, A. and Bailey, B.P., A Reference-Based Scoring Model for Increasing the Findability of Promising Ideas in Innovation Pipelines. In *CSCW*, (2012), 1183-1186.
37. Xu, A. and Bailey, B.P., What Do You Think? A Case Study of Benefit, Expectation, and Interaction in a Large Online Critique Community. In *CSCW*, (2012), 295-304.
38. Yu, L. and Nickerson, J.V., Cooks or Cobblers? Crowd Creativity through Combination. In *CHI*, (2011), 1393-1402.
39. Zheng, X.S., Chakraborty, I., Lin, J.J., & Rauschenberger, R., Correlating Low-level Image Statistics with Users' Rapid Aesthetic and Affective Judgments of Web Pages. In *CHI*, (2009), 1-10.
40. Does This JC Penney Tea Kettle Look Like Hitler?, NBC's Today.com, http://www.today.com/news/does-j-c-penney-tea-kettle-look-hitler-6C10100642, Retrieved on May 28 2013.
41. Core77. http://www.core77.com.
42. Dribbble. http://dribbble.com.
43. Feedbackarmy. http://www.feedbackarmy.com.
44. Fivesecondtest. http://fivesecondtest.com.
45. Usabilla. http://www.usabilla.com.

Reviewing versus Doing: Learning and Performance in Crowd Assessment

Haiyi Zhu, Steven P Dow, Robert E Kraut, Aniket Kittur
Human Computer Interaction Institute
Carnegie Mellon University
{haiyiz, spdow, robert.kraut, nkittur}@cs.cmu.edu

ABSTRACT

In modern crowdsourcing markets, requesters face the challenge of training and managing large transient workforces. Requesters can hire peer workers to review others' work, but the value may be marginal, especially if the reviewers lack requisite knowledge. Our research explores if and how workers learn and improve their performance in a task domain by serving as peer reviewers. Further, we investigate whether peer reviewing may be more effective in teams where the reviewers can reach consensus through discussion. An online between-subjects experiment compares the tradeoffs of reviewing versus producing work using three different organization strategies: working individually, working as an interactive team, and aggregating individuals into nominal groups. The results show that workers who review others' work perform better on subsequent tasks than workers who just produce. We also find that interactive reviewer teams outperform individual reviewers on all quality measures. However, aggregating individual reviewers into nominal groups produces better quality assessments than interactive teams, except in task domains where discussion helps overcome individual misconceptions.

Author Keywords

Crowdsourcing, Review, Assessment, Learning.

ACM Classification Keywords

H.5.3 [Information Interfaces and Presentation]: Group and Organization Interfaces – Collaborative computing, Computer-supported cooperative work, Web-based interaction; K.4.3 [Computers and Society]: Organizational Impacts – Computer supported collaborative work.

INTRODUCTION

Crowdsourcing has become a powerful paradigm for accomplishing work at a scale and speed previously impossible. Most online crowdsourcing markets currently have a flat organizational structure where requesters post tasks for workers and then decide retrospectively which workers to pay. Recent crowdsourcing research suggests that peer review strategies can help requesters achieve better results because it provides training for the workers receiving assessment [5, 8]. However, peer review strategies incur real costs for requesters, and thus may be marginally valuable, especially if reviewers lack domain knowledge.

Theory from organization science (e.g., [36]) and learning science (e.g., [20]) would suggest that reviewing others' work can offer an opportunity to make a meaningful impact, induce a sense of responsibility, and improve motivation to master a task domain. This paper explores ancillary benefits—such as learning and performance increases—that peer reviewing can provide to the *reviewers*, not just to workers.

Further, while peer review strategies may provide numerous potential benefits, there is relatively little evidence about how to structure it effectively for crowds. An individual reviewer might not have the complete set of skills needed to be an effective reviewer, especially for subjective or generative tasks where gold standards do not apply. Small teams can help overcome individual limitations by bringing together varying perspectives, knowledge, and expertise [18]. However, interactive teams can endure coordination costs [18,32] and are subject to group polarization [9]. *Nominal groups* aggregate independent actions of individuals and provide a cost-equivalent alternative to interactive teams. Prior research shows that nominal groups can overcome production loss and groupthink, especially during generative brainstorming tasks [10, 23, 32]. Thus, this research also investigates whether peer review quality improves by supporting interactive team versus nominal group reviews and whether team size has an effect.

To understand the tradeoffs on learning and performance for peer review versus production work and for individual versus team strategies, we conducted a between-subjects experiment with workers (N=680) from Amazon's Mechanical Turk [12] across five common task domains. In a three-stage procedure (see Figure 1), participants first completed a single production task (pre-task). Then, we randomly assigned participants to a condition where they either completed a review task or a production task, either individually or in teams (main-task). Finally, participants received an email message inviting them to perform more production tasks (post-task). To measure learning, we compared partic-

CSCW '14, February 15–19, 2014, Baltimore, Maryland, USA.

ACM 978-1-4503-2540-0/14/02...$15.00.
http://dx.doi.org/10.1145/2531602.2531718

ipants' performance across conditions on the pre- and post-task production work. To measure performance on peer review tasks, we calculated the consistency among reviewers, internal coherence, agreement with judges, subjective ratings of the review's helpfulness to production workers, and the review correctness for a mathematics problem.

The study showed that participants who performed peer review tasks had a greater increase in performance between the pre- and post-task than those who only performed production tasks. This indicates that participating in review tasks improves learning in a task domain.

Comparing the different methods for organizing reviewers, we found that interactive reviewer teams outperformed individuals on most quality measures. Moreover, nominal groups outperformed interactive reviewer teams, except when judging the correctness of a mathematics problem. These performance differences were not affected by the size of the team. Also, the organizational structure (individual vs. team vs. nominal) did not affect the performance difference between the pre and post task.

THEORY AND HYPOTHESES

Crowdsourcing researchers and practitioners have recently become interested in incorporating management, feedback and assessment mechanisms in micro-task market places. For example, Mobileworks introduced management strategies to micro-task markets [16]. However, there remains a need for a rigorous scientific foundation for understanding the effectiveness of feedback and assessment mechanisms in crowd work. In the following section, we build on relevant theory to predict the effects of participating in review tasks and the effectiveness of different ways of organizing reviewers in crowd work.

Learning by Reviewing

Reviewing, which is the action of providing information regarding one's task performance (sometimes referred to as providing feedback or assessment), has been investigated in depth in organization and learning science due to its important role in management and education, respectively. Research on organizational behavior shows numerous motivational and performance-oriented benefits of encouraging peers to participate in managerial activities such as evaluating performance and providing feedback, variously termed as self-leadership [21], distributed leadership [1], empowered leadership [29], and shared leadership [26, 37, 39]. Exercising managerial influence such as evaluating others can improve workers' performance by giving them an opportunity to express their voice and make a more meaningful impact [26]. This benefit is consistent with Ryan and Deci's self-determination theory, which argues that people gravitate towards work that allows them to feel competent and autonomous [27].

In the learning sciences, we see a parallel line of research about learning by mentoring [4, 20]. Mentoring also involves providing assessment and instructions to others. Chase and her colleagues demonstrated the so-called "protégé effect" where students made greater effort and learned more when they mentored others [4]. Mentoring others invokes a sense of responsibility that motivates learning, and protects students' egos when confronted with failure [4]. Providing students with opportunities to mentor others can also help them learn by developing meta-cognitive knowledge and skills, that is, students "learn how to learn" [3, 34].

There has been some recent research on peer feedback and reviewing in crowd work. Horton [8] investigated the effects of peer feedback on feedback providers' productivity, finding that evaluating high-output work raised the feedback provider's subsequent productivity compared to evaluating low-output work. Our work similarly focuses on the role of feedback providers, but explicitly compares feedback providers and production workers and additionally looks at learning outcomes. Dow et al. [5] investigated the effects of "self-assessment" (a hybrid of assessing and producing) on learning, showing that self-assessment helps workers improve their task performance over time. However, unlike our study this feedback was self-provided and furthermore did not disentangle assessment from production work. Therefore, our first hypothesis is as follows.

> *H1. Participating in review tasks enhances performance in the task domain.*

Strategies for Organizing Peer Reviewers

While promoting workers to reviewer roles can help them become better workers, they need a considerable set of skills to be an effective reviewer [36]. Reviewers need technical skills (i.e., knowledge about methods, processes, procedures and techniques for conducting a specialized activity) and communication skills (i.e., ability to communicate the judgment clearly and effectively). A single worker might not have the complete skill set to effectively perform review tasks. In contrast, a group of workers acting together are more likely to collectively have the skills needed to effectively review other workers' work [17].

Assuming that groups outperform individuals, requesters still need effective methods to organize people from different backgrounds and perspectives to accomplish a common task. Two alternative methods are plausible: interactive groups and nominal groups [10, 18, 23, 25]. In interactive groups, people interact and communicate with each other while working, while in nominal groups people work individually and their efforts are combined algorithmically, as an average or sum.

Interactive teams might perform worse than nominal teams in a review task because social influence occurring in active discussions might cause the group judgment to move away from the "truth" and towards each other's initial biased positions. The phenomenon is referred to "group polarization" in literature [9]. For example, Schkade et al. reported a study of over 500 mock juries composed of over 3000 jury eligible citizens. They found that deliberation produces a "severity shift" in which the jury's dollar verdict is systematically higher than that of the median of its jurors' pre-deliberation individual judgment [28]. In addition to avoiding unhealthy social influence, nominal teams also avoid other factors that inhibit productivity, such as 1) production blocking preventing members from simultaneously contributing during discussions [30]; 2) free riders do not contribute [10]; 3) time and effort diverted from production to coordinate and resolve conflicts [32]; and 4) "bad apples" who discourage others [6].

Furthermore, although the resources increase with number or people in a group, coordination and other process losses also increase [23]. Therefore, we predict that the performance gap between nominal and interactive teams will increase with group size. To summarize, we hypothesize that:

H2a. Interactive reviewer teams perform better than individual reviewers.

H2b. Nominal reviewer teams will perform better than interactive reviewer teams.

H2c. The performance gap between nominal and interactive teams will increase with team size.

METHOD

Experiment Design

We designed a three-stage experiment: pre-task, main experimental task, and post-task. In the main task, we examined two types of work (production vs. review) and five ways of grouping people (individually vs. four different-sized teams), giving us ten independent conditions (see Figure 1 for details). Half of the participants were in "producer" conditions where they completed five jobs: a writing task, a brainstorming task, a moral judgment task, a mathematics problem, and a summary task. The other half of participants were in "reviewer" conditions where they were required to assess others' work on those same five tasks. For both types of tasks, participants either worked individu-

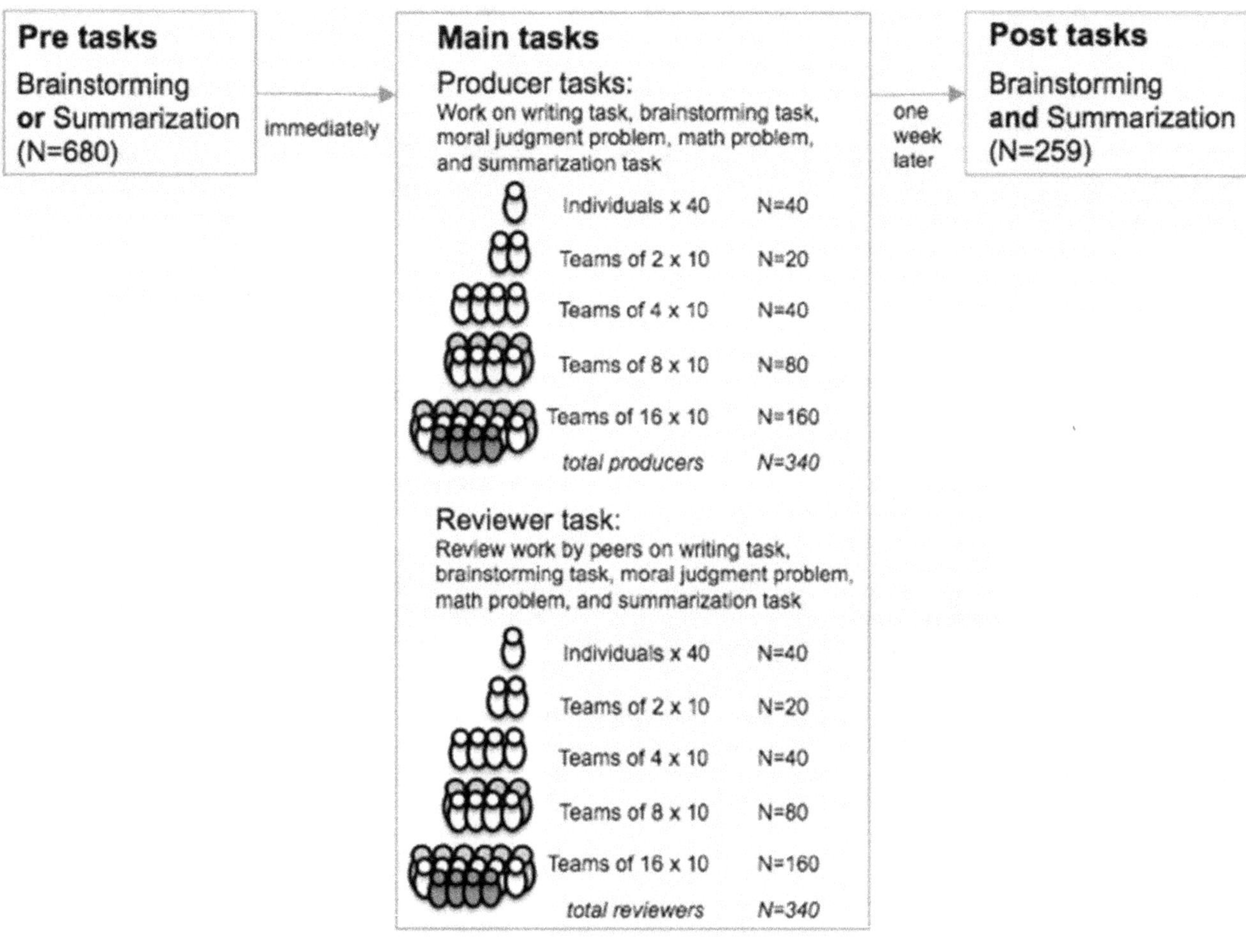

Figure 1: We conducted a three-stage between-subjects experiment with workers from Amazon's Mechanical Turk. To measure learning, we compared participants' performance across conditions on the pre- and post-tasks. *Note that we designed post-task as a separate task to ensure that the baseline study (pre-task plus main task) was not too time-consuming, and thus limit the number of study dropouts. For the same reason, participants were only required to complete one task (either brainstorming or summarization) in the pre-task. Our analysis compared the participants' pre- and post-task difference for only the participants who completed all the three stages.*

ally or in interactive teams with an exponentially increasing number of workers—two, four, eight or sixteen. In the pre-task, half the participants completed a summary task, and the other half completed a brainstorming task. Then participants were randomly assigned to an experimental condition. After the workers finished the main experimental task, we sent emails to invite participants to complete a post-task, which included both a brainstorming task and a summary task.

Production Tasks

We designed tasks for the "producer" conditions according to McGrath [22]'s taxonomy of group tasks, which cover a variety of different skills and group processes.

- *Writing task.* Participants were asked to write a consumer review for a product from the following list: MP3 player, Mobile phone, Digital camera, Headphones, Game console, Computer, and Laptop. Dow et al. previously used this experiment task to study feedback for crowd workers [5].
- *Brainstorming task.* Participants were asked to generate ten ideas for alternative uses for a brick or a pencil [35]. The more creative, the better.
- *Moral judgment.* Participants were asked to judge a moral dilemma [35]. In this case, a college teaching assistant accepted a bribe from a star basketball player to change his exam grade. The workers were required to make decisions that satisfy the conflicting interests between the basketball team (who wanted to retain the player) and the course instructor (who wanted to punish the cheating behavior).
- *Mathematics problem.* Participants were asked to solve a mathematics problem: "A bag contains two red balls, three blue balls and five green balls. Balls are drawn at random. How many balls do you need to draw so that at least two of them are of the same color?"
- *Summarization.* Participants were asked to summarize a paragraph of text in two or three sentences.

Review Tasks

For the review task, participants were asked to assess five production tasks (one of each type). Participants first made Yes/No judgments about the quality of different dimensions of a worker's answer. For example, to assess the summarization task, participants judged whether the summary was accurate or not. Details of the review tasks are shown below. Then participants decided whether they wanted to approve the worker's work and whether the worker deserved a bonus. Finally, participants provided rationale to justify their decisions and qualitative feedback to help the worker improve.

- *Review the writing task.* Participants made seven Yes/No judgments on whether the product review 1) was an original product review; 2) contained sufficient information about the product; 3) was useful; 4) contained personal stories and anecdotes; 5) listed both good and bad aspects of the product; 6) assessed the product's value given its price; and 7) contained any spelling or grammar mistakes.
- *Review the brainstorming task.* Participants judged whether the worker 1) came up with ten different ideas; 2) described the ideas clearly; 3) came up with high quality ideas; 4) came up with creative ideas; and 5) made any spelling or grammar mistakes.
- *Review the moral judgment task.* Participants judged whether 1) the worker's decision took into account the interest of the basketball team who wanted to retain the player; 2) the worker's decision took into account the interest of the course instructor who wanted to punish the cheating behavior; 3) the worker provided good reasons for the decisions; 4) the worker demonstrated good communication skills; and 5) the worker made any spelling or grammar mistakes.
- *Review the mathematics problem.* Participants judged whether the worker 1) gave the correct answer; 2) provided a clear explanation; and 3) made any spelling or grammar mistakes.
- *Review the summary task.* Participants judged whether the worker 1) provided a summary of no more than three sentences; 2) provided a concise summary; 3) provided an accurate summary; 4) included all the key points; and 5) did not have any spelling or grammar mistakes.

Participants

We recruited 680 participants from Amazon Mechanical Turk (MTurk) [12, 24]. To ensure quality, we restricted recruitment to workers with a 90% HIT acceptance rate.

Experiment Procedure

After accepting the MTurk task, participants completed the pre-task. Then we gave participants a link that randomly directed them to an Etherpad that corresponded with one of the ten conditions. When workers finished performing their main tasks on the pad, they went back to MTurk to get paid. Each worker received $1.50 by finishing the pre-task and main experiment. After submitting the main task, workers received a post-task invitation email. Workers received $1 for completing the post-task.

Study Instrument

To perform their work (and to facilitate communication in the interactive team condition) participants used Etherpad-lite, an open-source collaborative editor (see Figure 2). The editor highlights each user's input using a unique color. Users on the same pad can see others' changes in real-time. Users communicate with each other using the chat functionality on the right side. Note that the editor enables participants who arrive asynchronously to collaborate with others: they had access to the entire chat history and the existing output (as a way of interacting with previous workers); and they could leave comments on the pad or on the chat history (to interact with the future workers). We di-

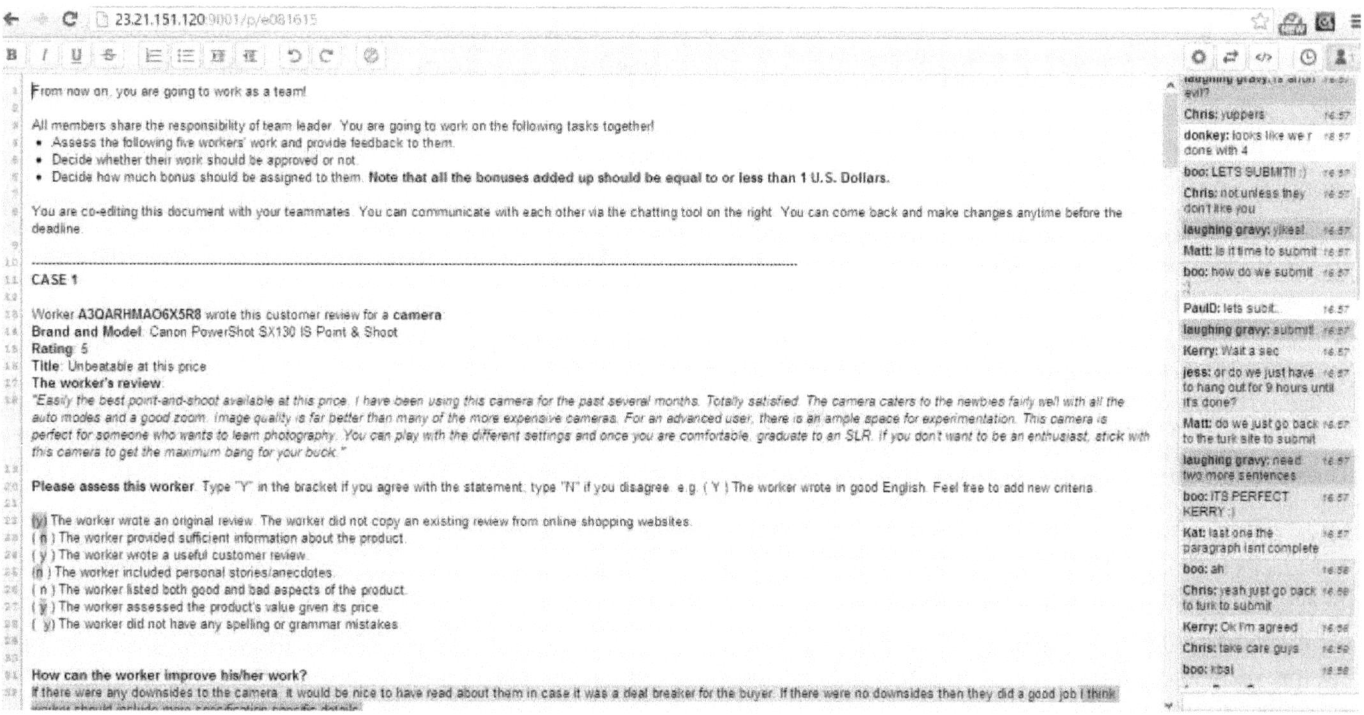

Figure 2. Participants used an Etherpad to perform production work and to perform review task (assessing other workers).

rected participants that were part of the same interactive team to the same pad where they worked together, although sometimes members of a team arrive asynchronously within around half an hour. In contrast, participants in the individual condition worked alone on a single pad.

Measures

To examine the effects of participating in review tasks on reviewers' learning, we compared their performance on the pre-task and post-task. Independent judges blind to condition rated participants' performance on both tasks. For the brainstorming task, judges rated the novelty of the ideas on a scale of 1-5. For the summary task, judges rated the accuracy and conciseness (on a scale of 1-5) of the summary. The change in score from pre-task to post-task indicates the learning gain.

To examine the effectiveness of different review strategies, we calculated five measures about the quality of the assessment task..

- *Consistency among reviewers.* We used intra-class correlation (ICC) to measure how consistently each reviewer or team's assessment agreed with other assessment of the same case. In our experiment ICC is a descriptive statistic that measures how much judgments of the case resemble each other.
- *Internal coherence.* As a measure of the judgment coherence, we calculated the degree to which reviewers' or teams' overall evaluation of a task correlated with their evaluation of more detailed evaluations of the task. For example, were their overall evaluation of a summary predicted by their evaluations of its accuracy and conciseness. We ran a prediction model using the reviewer or reviewer team's Yes/No judgments to predict the same reviewer or reviewer team's decisions on task approval and bonus assignment. Our assumption is that a high coefficient of determination (R-square) indicates that one can predict the final judgment according to its component judgments. The higher the R-square value, the more coherent the assessment.
- *Agreement with judges.* To evaluate the accuracy of participant assessments, we compared them to judgments made by independent assessors — two PhD students not part of our research team. The judges reviewed the tasks together and created an assessment for each. During the main task, reviewers or reviewer teams made a set of assessments, including the Yes/No judgments and the decisions of task approval and bonus assignment. For each reviewer or reviewer team, we transformed their assessment to a vector. For example, one reviewer made the following assessment about a mathematics problem: 1) the worker solved the problem correctly; 2) the worker explained the solution clearly; 3) the work contained some grammar errors; 4) the worker's work should be approved; and 5) the worker does not deserve a bonus. The vector for this reviewer's assessment is (1,1,0,1,0). Then we calculated the distance between the assessments of participants and the independent judges. The shorter the distance, the more the reviewer (team) agreed with

the judges. We calculated the "agreement with the judge" as the reverse distance.

- *Subjective ratings of helpfulness.* Reviewers provided a rationale for their decision about task approval and bonus assignment, and qualitative feedback to help workers to improve their work. To judge the quality of the assessment rationale and qualitative feedback, we recruited a new set of independent Mechanical Turk workers blind to condition to rate the convincingness of the rationale and the usefulness of the feedback on five-point Likert scales.
- *Correctness of judging mathematics problem.* We measured whether the reviewers or reviewer teams made the right judgment about the correctness of the mathematics problem.

Data Preparation

Of the 680 participants recruited for the experiment, half were placed in reviewer conditions and the other half in producer conditions. There were 40 individuals and 40 interactive teams each condition (see Table 1).

Table 1 shows the participation numbers per condition for the pre/main task and post-task. We found no significant difference on the number of people returning for the post-task between reviewer conditions and producer conditions ($\chi^2(1) = 1.40, p=0.24$).

To assess the quality of reviews for different conditions, we include all the reviews from teams and individuals in the analysis and treated incomplete items as missing data. The individual completion rate is higher for reviewers in individual conditions. The dropout rate (i.e., percentage of people did not submit the task) of individual reviewer is 17.5%, while the dropout rate of participants in interactive team review condition is 38% ($\chi^2(1) = 6.47, p=0.01$). However, in terms of the completion of review task as a team (i.e., completing all the assessment items), individual reviewer is 83.3% while review teams are 92%.($\chi^2(1) = 51.9, p<0.01$).

		# of Teams	# of participants (pre/ main task)	# of participants (post-task)	Return rate
Reviewer	Individual	NA	40	16	40%
	Team size 2	10	20	9	45%
	Team size 4	10	40	13	33%
	Team size 8	10	80	30	38%
	Team size 16	10	160	54	34%
Producer	Individual	NA	40	11	28%
	Team size 2	10	20	6	30%
	Team size 4	10	40	12	30%
	Team size 8	10	80	38	48%
	Team size 16	10	160	70	44%

Table 1. Participation numbers per condition for the main task and post-task

Construction of Nominal Teams

To understand if teams should be organized by simply pooling individual efforts, we formed nominal teams by combining the decisions of the individual workers. Specifically, to construct a nominal team of N workers, we randomly selected N individual workers who reviewed the same case and combined their individual outputs as the nominal team output. For Yes/No judgments, we selected the majority opinion as the team judgment. If there was a tie, we randomly selected Yes or No as the output. For qualitative outputs such as rationale for the decisions and feedback, we concatenated the individual output to form the team output. We constructed 10 nominal teams for each team size (2, 4, 8, and 16). Note that nominal teams reuse the data from individual conditions. Therefore, we will not directly compare these two conditions in the analysis since they are interdependent. Our analyses only draw comparison between interactive teams and *either* individuals or nominal teams.

RESULTS

Effect of Reviewing on Task Performance

We found that workers who participated in reviewing had higher learning gain (comparing pre- vs. post-task results) than those who did production work, which supports our hypothesis 1.

Reviewers Learned More

We measured learning gains by comparing participants' task performance on a pre- and post-tasks. For independent variables, we created three dummy variables indicating whether it is pre-task or post task, whether the participant was in the reviewer conditions or in the producers' conditions, and whether the participant worked individually or in groups. We only included participants who finished both pre-task and post-task in the analysis.

	DV: novelty of the ideas in the brainstorming task		
	Model 1	Model 2	Model 3
	Coef. (S.E.)	Coef. (S.E.)	Coef. (S.E.)
Pre-Post (0- pre; 1 -post)	0.13 (0.04)**	-0.07 (0.06)	0.01 (0.18)
Producer–Reviewer (0-producer; 1-reviewer)	-0.02 (0.04)	0.09 (0.05)	0.10 (0.20)
Pre-Post X Producer-Reviewer	NA	0.11 (0.05)*	0.27 (0.17)
Individual-Team (0-individual, 1-team)	NA	NA	0.07 (0.15)
Pre-post X Individual-Team	NA	NA	0.16 (0.14)
Producer-Reviewer XIndividual-Team	NA	NA	-0.03 (0.15)
Pre-post X Producer-Reviewer X Individual-Team	NA	NA	0.15 (0.15)

Table 2. Linear regression models examining the learning gains. All participants improved from pre to post task (p<.01); Reviewers improved more than producers (*p<.05).**

Model 1 in Table 2 shows that participants' brainstorming performance improved significantly from the pre- to post-test (b=.13, p<.05). Model 2, which includes the interaction between "Pre-Post" and "Producer-Reviewer", shows that only participants in the reviewer conditions improved. Performance of those in the producer conditions declined slightly (b= -.07, p> .10), while those in reviewer condition significantly improved (b=.11, p<.05). There was no significant difference between group conditions and individual conditions in brainstorming task (Model 3, Table 2).

There is a significant improvement in performance ratings between pre- and post- versions of the summary task (for accuracy: b=.27, se=.07, p<.01; for conciseness: b=.13, se=.06, p<.05), but the increase is not significantly greater for reviewers than producers (for the interaction of accuracy, b=.15, se=14, p=.31; for the interaction of conciseness, b=.02, se=13, p=.88). We also found no effect of team size on summary task performance.

Effect of Organizational Structures on Review Quality

We found interactive reviewer teams outperformed individual reviewers on all quality measures. Nominal groups outperformed interactive teams on all measures except the correctness of the mathematics problem. However, the gap between nominal teams and interactive teams does not increase as the team becomes larger.

Teams Showed More Consistency

The intra-class correlation among individual reviewers is 0.33; the intra-class correlation among interactive reviewer teams is 0.45; and the intra-class correlation among nominal reviewer teams is 0.61. We used Fisher r-to-z transformation and found that the difference between individual reviewers and interactive reviewer teams is marginally significant (z=1.4, p =0.08) and the difference between interactive teams and nominal teams is significant (z = 2.23, p<0.05).

Nominal Team Assessments Were More Coherent

As described previously, to calculate internal coherence we ran a prediction model using the Yes/No judgments to predict the decisions on task approval and bonus assignment on different assessment tasks. Therefore, the higher the R-square value, the more likely the assessment is coherent. The average R-square of nominal teams is 0.66; and interactive teams is 0.6, and the individual condition is 0.56. (see Table 3). We applied Fisher r-to-z transformation on R (the root square of R square) and found that the difference between individual team and interactive team is not significant (z =0.69, p = 0.25); and the difference between interactive team and nominal team is marginal significant (z = 1.35, p=0.09).

Team Assessments Aligned with Judge Assessments

To evaluate the accuracy of participant assessments, we compared them to those of independent judges. Model 1 in Table 4 shows the interactive reviewer team's assessment agrees with the independent judges more than the individual reviewers (b=.05, p<.05); and the nominal reviewer team's

	R-square		
Tasks	**Individual reviewers**	**Interactive reviewer teams**	**Nominal reviewer teams**
Writing	0.36	0.45	0.67
Brainstorming	0.76	0.78	0.73
Moral judgment	0.60	0.80	0.90
Mathematics	0.57	0.80	0.43
Summary	0.49	0.17	0.57
Average	0.56	0.6	0.66

Table 3. Internal coherence of the assessment. Nominal teams were more internally coherent.

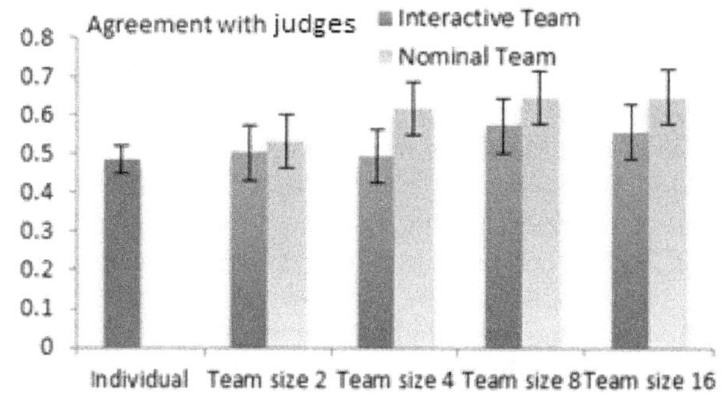

Figure 5. Agreement with judges

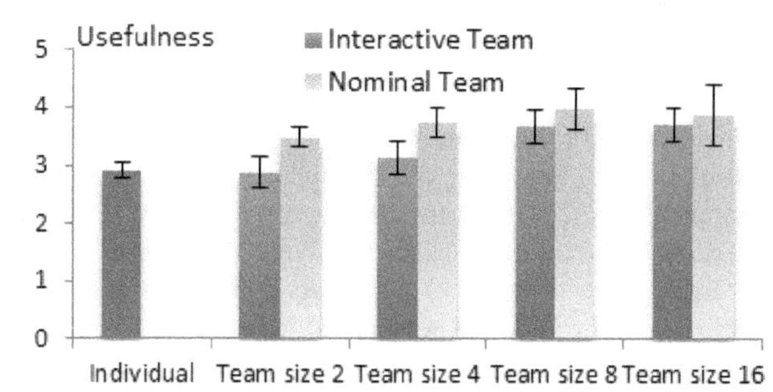

Figure 6. Turkers' rating: perceived usefulness of the feedback

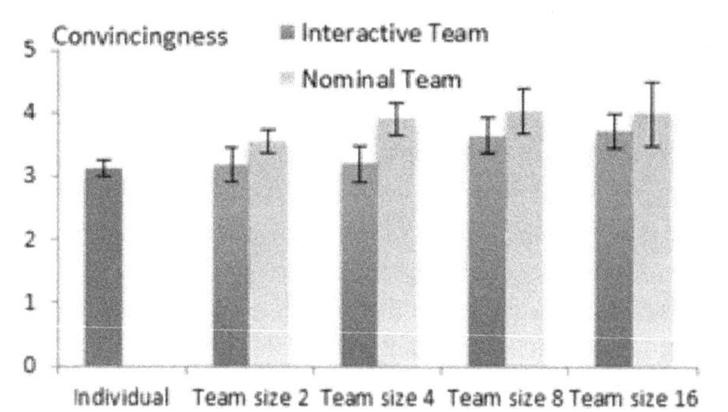

Figure 7. Turkers' rating: perceived convincingness of the rationale.

judgment is even closer than interactive teams (b=.08, p<.01). From Model 1 of Table 5, we found that the assessment of larger groups is not significantly closer to the independent judges (b= .025, p>.10) compared to smaller groups. There is no significant interaction between team size the team type (interactive team versus nominal team). We can see the trend graphically in Figure 5.

Teams Provided More Useful Feedback

Results show that nominal teams provide higher quality rationale and more useful feedback than interactive reviewer teams (see Figure 6 and 7, and Table 4 for p-values). Moreover, interactive reviewer teams significantly outperform individuals. Compared to the individual reviewers, the interactive reviewer teams score 0.45 points higher for perceived usefulness (b=.45; p<.01 in the Model 2 of Table 4) and 0.31 points higher for perceived convincingness (b=.31; p<.05 in the Model 3 of Table 4) on a five-point Likert scale; nominal teams score another 0.29 points higher for perceived usefulness than interactive teams (b=.29; p<.01 in the Model 2 of Table 4) and 0.30 points higher for perceived convincingness (b=.30; p<.01 in the Model 3 of Table 4). Furthermore, ratings of larger groups are higher than ratings of smaller groups. For perceived usefulness, the coefficient of the logarithm of team size is 0.30, p<.01; for perceived convincingness, the coefficient is 0.21, p<.01 See Model 2 and Model 3 in Table 5).

However, the interaction between team size and team type is not significant, indicating that the gap between nominal teams and interactive teams did not increase as team size grows.

Interactive Teams Exert Coordination Effort

Consistent with our hypotheses, interactive reviewer teams exhibited "production loss". Compared to nominal groups, interactive groups had to devote time to interaction and coordination with other team members. For example, in one Etherpad (see Figure 8), "4kwood" expressed different opinions about how to coordinate the work with the rest of the participants. 4kwood wanted the team to work on the task simultaneously, while the other team members wanted to divide the task first and then review the task together at the end. Feeling ignored, 4kwood quit the task and later sent the following message to the research team:

> *"I just returned a task I was working on. A few of the other workers were somewhat offensive and were more concerned about how much they did rather than working as a team. The task became a race to some participants with quite a bit of sarcasm added in as well."*

Interactive Teams Judged Mathematics Problem Best

One exception to the trend thus far was that interactive reviewer teams outperformed nominal teams on judging the correctness of the mathematics problem. Specifically, 31% of individual reviewers correctly judged the mathematics problem; 58% of the interactive reviewer teams judged the math problem correctly; and 47% of the nominal teams judged the math problem correctly. The relationship be-

	Model 1 DV: Agreement with judges Coef. (S.E.)	Model 2 DV: Perceived usefulness Coef. (S.E.)	Model 3 DV: Perceived convincingness Coef. (S.E.)
Interactive-Individual (1-interactive; 0- individual)	0.05* (0.03)	0.45 ** (0.10)	0.31** (0.10)
Nominal-Interactive (1-nominal; 0-interactive)	0.08** (0.03)	0.29 ** (0.10)	0.30** (0.10)

Table 4. Linear regression models examining the agreement with judges, perceived usefulness and perceived convincingness for individual reviewers, interactive reviewer teams and nominal reviewer teams.*p<.05; **p<.01

	Model 1 DV: Agreement with judges Coef. (S.E.)	Model 2 DV: Perceived usefulness Coef. (S.E.)	Model 3 DV: Perceived convincingness Coef. (S.E.)
Nominal-Interactive (1-nominal; 0-interactive)	0.04 (0.08)	0.85** (0.28)	0.47 (0.28)
Logarithm of team size to base two	0.025 (0.015)	0.30** (0.06)	0.21** (0.04)
Nominal-Interactive X team size	00.01 (0.02)	-0.12 (0.09)	-0.001 (0.09)

Table 5. Linear regression models examining the agreement with judges, perceived usefulness and perceived convincingness for different types of teams and different team size.*p<.05; **p<.01

4kwood: *We're all working as a team right? How about slowing down to let everyone do it together.*
P1: *4kwood, do you have anything you're currently working on? Sorry if we're leaving you in the dust! If you don't have anything at the moment we can figure out what would be best for you to work on.*
P2: *We were saying earlier that we could each do them individually and then check them to make sure we agree with the answers. If anyone has a problem we can discuss and decide and go over them all together at the end to decide who gets bonuses.*
P2: *So if you're not working on anything individually feel free to go over and make sure you agree with everything that was written, and add anything you feel could be missing.*
4kwood: *Not leaving me in the dust, I'm just trying to take my time and read everyones input.*
P1: *Thanks, we need a proof-reader. :)*
P2: *Take as much time as you need. feel free to discuss if you need to*

Figure 8. Conversations demonstrating the production

tween the correctness and type of review structure is significant, chi-square with two degrees of freedom is 6.26, $p<.05$.

One reason for this could be that the probability problem was a "truth supported" task [22]. In such tasks, group members may differ in their ability to solve a problem, but can recognize a good solution once a group member had solved it. Since fewer than half of the individual reviewers judged the mathematics problem correctly, the nominal group's structured algorithm to pool the individual results does not effectively select the correct judgment. In other words, individuals in the nominal groups never see their group members' answers, so they never have the opportunity to get struck by the insight. One benefit of interactive teams is that individuals who know the correct answer can influence the whole team through discussions [17]. Specifically, participants who understood the mathematics problem could convince teammates and influence the final judgment, even when they are in the minority. For example, one participant (Martha) successfully convinced other members in the team and led the team to reach the correct judgment on the mathematics problem (see Figure 9).

Anna: *you guys ok with case 4 (math problem) so far? i'm not a math person.*
Martha: *On case 4 you don't need the minimum for there to be a possibility of 2 balls of the same color.*
Martha: *you need to definitely have 2 balls of the same color.*
Martha: *so because there are 3 colors you need 4 balls to be sure that there are two of the same color.*
Lucy: *I agree it is wrong. I'm not good at this sort of math.*

Figure 9. Conversations on mathematics problem.

DISCUSSION

In this paper, we explored the beneficial effects of reviewing others' work on learning and performance. We found that workers who participated in review tasks had higher learning gains than workers who only did production tasks.

We also examined how to organize people into teams and found that interactive reviewer teams outperformed individual reviewers on most quality measures including consistency among reviewers, agreement with judges, subjective ratings of the assessments' helpfulness to workers, and correctness of judging mathematics problems. Moreover, nominal reviewer teams performed even better than interactive teams on all the measures except the correctness of mathematics problem. Qualitative evidence indicates that interactive teams exerted extra coordination efforts. Also, some discussions resulted in unhealthy social influence causing people to move away from the "truth" and towards each other's initial biased positions. With exception of the math problem where discussion may have helped to overcome individual misconceptions, the observations of coordination costs and social biasing may explain why the assessments produced by interactive teams were less consistent, were less coherent, and had lower agreement with independent judges.

Our results showed that the performance gaps between nominal teams and interactive teams were not larger as team size increased. It is possible that the factors inhibiting the effectiveness of interactive teams might have some ceiling effects.

Design Implications

The results demonstrate that providing opportunities to review others can improve workers' learning. In addition, outsourcing the review task should also have a downstream benefit for the production workers who receive the assessment, as shown in previous work [5]. Although we did not explicitly measure the downstream benefit, a separate set of Turkers judged whether the reviewers provided helpful feedback in their assessments. The average score of larger nominal teams (>2) is around 4 in a 5 point scale. Therefore, we have reasons to believe that assessment and feedback generated by peer reviewers should help the production workers improve skills and task performance. In theory, we claim that outsourcing review tasks can facilitate the learning of both reviewers (who assess others' work) and production workers (who receive assessment), and thus benefit the employers to accomplish higher quality work in the long run.

The study also provides guidelines for how employers might structure the review task. For subjective tasks, we suggest employers first allow reviewers to do the assessment task individually and then systematically aggregate their assessment (a nominal team approach). For more objective tasks in which correct answers can "win" through rational discussion (like the Mathematics problem in our study), employers should consider providing communication channels for reviewers so that they can identify the correct judgment through discussion.

Limitations and Future Work

We measured learning gain by comparing workers' pre- to post performance on only two tasks (i.e., brainstorming and summary), and in a specific way (comparing the novelty of the ideas and the accuracy and conciseness of the summaries from pre-task to post-task). It is possible that by reviewing others, workers may have been learning in ways that did not show up on our tests. For example, workers might have improved their task performance on other types of tasks, they might have learned review techniques such as how to provide useful feedback, or they might have learned communication and coordination strategies by working with others. One direction of future work is to further explore what else workers could learn from reviewing others.

Factors such as coordination and free-riding cause production loss and undermine the performance of interactive teams. However, working in interactive teams might have other benefits. For example, Sutton and Hargadon studied a product design firm and found that interactive brainstorming sessions can support organizational memory of design solutions, help members recognize skill variety among team, and build shared ownership of ideas [31]. In our experiment, we also observed that workers appreciate the experience of working together with others. In future work, we plan to measure whether working in interactive teams improves non-quality outcomes such as work satisfaction and loyalty.

We constructed nominal teams using a simple linear algorithm (majority algorithm). Small group research shows that the majority algorithm is better than a single judge (where a single person aggregates all the team members' opinions and makes the final judgment) [1] and other more stringent algorithms (e.g., two-thirds majorities or unanimity) [11]. Our results showed that nominal teams using the majority algorithm did perform best on most quality measures except on judging mathematics problems. It is possible that we can improve nominal teams' performance on these types of tasks by improving the combining algorithm. For example, we can ask each member to assign a confidence parameter for their own judgment and set this parameter as weight when combining members' judgments.

CONCLUSION

Our paper demonstrates that providing workers opportunities to review other workers' work will enhance their understanding of the task domain, and eventually help them become better workers. We investigated the effectiveness of three different strategies for organizing workers to accomplish review tasks: assigning individual reviewers, organizing interactive reviewer teams, and aggregating individual reviewers into nominal teams. Our results provide practical guidelines for employers and crowdsourcing system designers to better structure and train the workforce to accomplish high-quality work.

ACKNOWLEDGMENTS

This work was supported by NSF grants IIS-1149797, IIS-1217559, OCI-0943148, IIS-0968484, IIS-1111124, IIS-1208382, IIS-1217096, Bosch, Google, and Microsoft.

REFERENCES

1. Ariely D, Au WT, Bender RH, Budescu DV, Dietz CB, et al. 2000. The effects of averaging subjective probability estimates between and within judges. J. Exp. Psychol.: Applied 6:130–47.
2. Barry, D.(1991) Managing the bossless team: Lessons in distributed leadership. Organizational Dynamics, 20, 31-47.
3. Brown, A., Bransford, J., Ferrara, R.,& Campione, J.(1983). Learning, remembering, and understanding. In J.H. Flavell & E.M. Markman (Eds.), Handbook of child psychology: Vol.3. Cognitive development (4th ed., pp.77-166). New York: Wiley.
4. Chase C.C., Chin, D.B., Oppezzo, M.A., and Schwartz, D.L. (2009) Teachable Agents and the Protégé Effect: Increasing the Effort Towards Learning. Journal of Science Education and Technology. Volume 18, Number 4 (2009), 334-352.
5. Dow, S.P., Kulkarni, A., Klemmer, S.R., and Hartmann, B.(2012) Shepherding the Crowd Yields Better Work. ACM Conference on Computer Supported Cooperative Work, 2012.
6. Felps, W., Mitchell, T., and Byington, E. How, When, and Why Bad Apples Spoil the Barrel: Negative Group Members and Dysfunctional Groups. Research in Organizational Behavior 27, (2006), 175-222.
7. Guilford, J. P. (1967). The nature of human intelligence. New York, NY: McGraw Hill.
8. Horton, J. J. (2010). Employer expectations, peer effects and productivity: Evidence from a series of field experiments. arXiv preprint arXiv:1008.2437.
9. Isenberg, D. J. (1986). Group polarization: A critical review and meta-analysis. Journal of Personality and Social Psychology, 50(6), 1141.
10. Janis, I.L. Groupthink: Psychological Studies of Policy Decisions and Fiascoes. Wadsworth Publishing, 1982.
11. Kerr, N. L., Tindale, R.S. (2004) Group performance and decision making. Annu. Rev. Psychol. 2004. 55:623–55.
12. Kittur, A., Chi, E.H., and Suh, B. (2008) Crowdsourcing user studies with Mechanical Turk. In Proceedings of the twenty-sixth annual SIGCHI conference on Human factors in computing systems (CHI '08). ACM, New York, NY, USA, 453-456.
13. Kittur, A. and Kraut, R.E. 2008. Harnessing the wisdom of crowds in wikipedia: quality through coordination. In Proceedings of the 2008 ACM conference on Computer supported cooperative work (CSCW '08)
14. Kittur, A., Smus, B., Khamkar, S., and Kraut, R.E. (2011) CrowdForge: crowdsourcing complex work. In Proceedings of the 24th annual ACM symposium on User interface software and technology (UIST '11). ACM, New York, NY, USA, 43-52.
15. Kraut, R. E. & Resnick, P. (2012). Building successful online communities: Evidence-based social design. Cambridge, MA: MIT Press.
16. Kulkarni, A., Gutheim, P., Narula, P., Rolnitzky, D., Parikh, T., & Hartmann, B. (2012). MobileWorks: Designing for Quality in a Managed Crowdsourcing Architecture. IEEE Internet Computing, 16(5), 28-35.
17. Laughlin PR, McGlynn RP. (1986). Collective induction: mutual group and individual influence by exchange of hypotheses and evidence. J. Exp. Soc. Psychol. 22:567–589.
18. Levine, J.M., Moreland, R.L. (1990) Progress in small group research. Annual Review of Psychology, Vol 41, 1990, 585-634.
19. Mannix, E., and Neale, M.A. (2005) What Differences Make a Difference? The Promise and Reality of Diverse Teams in Organizations. Psychological Science in the Public Interest , Vol. 6, No. 2 (Oct., 2005), pp. 31-55.
20. Matsuda, N., Cohen, W. W., Koedinger, K. R., Keiser, V., Raizada, R., Yarzebinski, E., et al. (2012). Studying the Effect of Tutor Learning using a Teachable Agent that asks the Student Tutor for Explanations. In Digital Game and Intelligent Toy Enhanced Learning (DIGITEL), 2012 IEEE Fourth International Conference on (pp. 25-32). IEEE.
21. Manz, C.C., & Sims, H.P., Jr(1993) Business without bosses. New York: Wiley.

22. McGrath, J.E. (1984) Groups: interaction and performance. Prentice Hall, Inc., Englewood Cliffs. N.J.

23. Mullen, B., Johnson C., and Salas E.(1991) "Productivity loss in brainstorming groups: A meta-analytic integration." Basic and Applied Psychology, 12: 2-23.

24. Paolacci, G., Chandler, J., Ipeirotis, P.G. (2010) Running experiments on Amazon Mechanical Turk. Judgment and Decision Making, Vol 5(5), Aug 2010, 411-419.

25. Paulus, P.B., Dzindolet, M.T., Poletes, G., and Camacho, L.M. (1993) "Perceptions of performance in group brainstorming: The illusion of group productivity." Personality and Social Psychology Bulletin, 19: 78-89.

26. Pearce, C.L., and Conger,J. A. (2003) Shared leadership: Reframing the hows and whys of leadership, Sage, Thousand Oaks.

27. Ryan, R. M.; Deci, E L. (2000) Self-determination theory and the facilitation of intrinsic motivation, social development, and well-being. American Psychologist, Vol 55(1), Jan 2000, 68-78.

28. Schkade, D., Sunstein, C. R., & Kahneman, D. (2000). Deliberating about dollars: The severity shift. Columbia Law Review, 1139-1175.

29. Srivastava A., Bartol, K.M., and Locke, E.A.(2006) Empowering Leadership in Management Teams: Effects on Knowledge Sharing, Efficacy, and Performance. The Academy of Management Journal , Vol. 49, No. 6 (Dec., 2006), pp. 1239-1251.

30. Stroebe, W. and Diehl, M. Why Groups are less Effective than their Members: On Productivity Losses in Idea-generating Groups. European Review of Social Psychology 5, (1994), 271.

31. Sutton, R. and Hargadon, A. Brainstorming groups in context: effectiveness in a product design firm. Administrative Science Quarterly, (1996).

32. Van De Ven, A. H., and Delbecq A.L. (1971) Nominal versus Interacting Group Processes for Committee Decision-Making Effectiveness. The Academy of Management Journal, Vol. 14, No. 2 (Jun., 1971), pp. 203-212.

33. Van De Ven, A. H., and Delbecq A.L. (1974) The Effectiveness of Nominal, Delphi, and Interacting Group Decision Making Processes. The Academy of Management Journal, Vol. 17, No. 4 (Dec., 1974), pp. 605-621.

34. White, B.Y. and Frederiksen, J.R. (1998) Inquiry, Modeling, and Metacognition: Making Science Accessible to All Students. Cognition and Instruction, Vol. 16, No. 1 (1998), pp. 3-118.

35. Woolley, A.W., Chabris, C.F., Pentland, A., Hashmi, N., Malone, T.W. (2010) Evidence for a Collective Intelligence Factor in the Performance of Human Groups. Science 29 October 2010: Vol. 330 no. 6004 pp. 686-688

36. Yukl, G. A. (1998). Leadership in organizations (4th ed.). Upper Saddle River, N.J.: Prentice Hall.

37. Zhu, H., Kraut, R.E., & Kittur, A., (2012) Effectiveness of Shared Leadership in Online Communities. CSCW'2012.

38. Zhu, H., Kraut, R., & Kittur, A. (2012, February). Organizing without formal organization: group identification, goal setting and social modeling in directing online production. In Proceedings of the ACM 2012 conference on Computer Supported Cooperative Work (pp. 935-944). ACM.

39. Zhu, H., Kraut, R.E., Wang, Y.C., & Kittur, A. (2011) Identifying Shared Leadership in Wikipedia. In CHI'2011: Proceedings of the 2011 annual conference on Human factors in computing systems. New York: ACM Press.

AskSheet: Efficient Human Computation for Decision Making with Spreadsheets

Alexander J. Quinn[1,2], **Benjamin B. Bederson**[1,2,3]
University of Maryland, College Park
Human-Computer Interaction Lab[1] :: Computer Science[2] :: Institute for Advanced Computer Studies[3]
College Park, Maryland 20740
{aq, bederson}@cs.umd.edu

ABSTRACT
The wealth of resources online has empowered individuals and businesses with an unprecedented volume of information to aid in decision making processes. However, finding the many details needed for a non-trivial decision can be very labor-intensive. We present AskSheet, a general system that leverages human computation to acquire the inputs to an arbitrary decision spreadsheet provided by the user. The key innovation is the ability to prioritize the inputs by analyzing the user's spreadsheet formulas to calculate value of information for each of the blanks. By directing workers to find the details that impact the end result most, it results in a conclusive decision without gathering all of the inputs.

Author keywords
Human computation; crowdsourcing; value of information

ACM Classification Keywords
H.5.m. Information interfaces and presentation (e.g., HCI): Miscellaneous.

INTRODUCTION
The explosive growth in availability of information online has opened a bounty of resources for people making plans and strategic decisions. They can now turn to web pages and online databases for questions requiring objective information. Subjective questions can often be answered by a post on a social network or discussion forum, or even a direct email or chat message to a trusted colleague.

The challenge comes when trying to leverage these mediums for more complex problems that require more thorough analysis. While it may be easy to find an answer to a specific question, a solution to the overarching problem may be more elusive. Consider the following questions:

Where should I buy groceries this week to save money?
Where/when can I vacation to balance cost vs. preference?
What graduate programs should I apply to?

CSCW'14, February 15 - 19 2014, Baltimore, MD, USA
Copyright 2014 ACM 978-1-4503-2540-0/14/02…$15.00.
http://dx.doi.org/10.1145/2531602.2531728

Each person will have a unique set of factors upon which they will base their decision. Of course, there can never be a database with up-to-date details on *every* possible aspect of such decisions. Details may be locale- or time-sensitive.

When the outcome is worth some effort, a tactic used by many decision-makers is to create a spreadsheet with tables containing the relevant dimensions of the decision problem. If the user is fluent with the use of spreadsheet formulas—as many in the business world are—and already has a clear idea *how* she wants to decide (i.e., if she had all information available), then she can even add formulas to display the decision result. At that point, it is only a matter of gathering the details to fill in the blank cells in the spreadsheet.

In reality, time to gather the information is limited, so we compromise. If the value of the outcome does not justify such an effort, we often accept a suboptimal decision based on partial information or take the first option that meets some baseline standard. This behavior by individual decision-makers, termed "satisficing" by Simon [23], results from the inherent tradeoff between the cost of deciding and the benefit of a well-reasoned decision that utilizes as much information as possible. *This project aims to help people do better.*

The rapid development of online task markets, such as Amazon Mechanical Turk, has opened new options. Now, one can easily hire web workers to gather information, paying a small reward for a small amount of work.

A commonly overlooked limitation of most such systems is that they assume every question is mandatory. Requests are sent and then the requester waits until all results have been received. In contrast, individual information foraging tends to follow a dynamic workflow [17]. Especially with decision-making, users seek out the information that will have the greatest impact on the final result, constantly adjusting the strategy based on the information seen so far.

AskSheet is a research prototype we built to demonstrate a new method of coordinating workers to support decision making tasks. To reduce human effort wasted gathering unnecessary information, it leverages a model of the decision provided by the user in the form of a spreadsheet. By efficiently offloading the information task, a decision-maker may be able to avert the all too common tendency to compromise, potentially leading to a more optimal decision.

To use AskSheet, the user (someone with a decision to make) starts with an ordinary spreadsheet with formulas that will calculate the end result. Then, in cells where information is needed, the user enters a special `=ASK(...)` formula to indicate to the server that some information is needed in that cell. The parameters specify such details as the type and range of values that are expected. AskSheet analyzes the formulas and manages the sending of requests. To reduce human effort, it calculates the *value of information* [13,21] of each `=ASK(...)` formula and eliminates those that cannot affect the final result. With this analysis, it aggressively prioritizes the inputs to minimize unnecessary requests.

The key contribution of this paper is a fully operational system for efficiently coordinating crowd workers to gather the input data for spreadsheet decision models.

Although our efforts so far have targeted workflows with Mechanical Turk, our longer-term goals for AskSheet extend to other types of group decision workflows, such as screening job applicants. That vision is reflected in the design of the system, and will be discussed later in the paper.

NEED FOR RESEARCH

AskSheet can be viewed as efficient human computation driven by a declarative notation based on spreadsheets. We examine the related work as such.

Efficient human computation

Human computation is a paradigm for computation that delegates to humans parts of the problem that computers cannot solve adequately [18,25]. Often, it starts with the assumption that you have a set of questions for which you would like to receive answers. Many such systems aim to reduce the number of tasks that workers are asked to perform by adjusting the number of judgments per question [10,22], the number of iterations on incremental improvement jobs [6,8,15,22], the strategy for decomposing tasks into subtasks [2,3], or by delegating some tasks to machines [19].

AskSheet is different in that it optimizes the number of *questions*—akin to telling the user, "No, actually you don't need these ones." A user shopping for a house might ask for several facts about each of many homes for sale, but if AskSheet can determine that some will not affect the user's final choice, those questions will be culled, and not asked. This notion of "efficiency" has been relatively unexplored.

AskSheet is built on the premise that human time is more precious and plentiful than CPU time, and thus any opportunity to use machine cycles to reduce human burden is a positive value proposition. Active learning [24], a machine learning technique, does this to some extent, but its focus is on efficient training of predictive models, as opposed to solving a single, monolithic problem, such as a decision.

Declarative crowdsourcing

Several recent projects have demonstrated a new, declarative approach to describing human computation processes in SQL [7,16]. We see such work (and our own) as exploring a big idea in crowdsourcing: By firmly separating the computational logic from the details of posting tasks and managing responses, the workflow can be optimized using computational methods that are independent of those details.

Spreadsheets

The system with the perhaps most resemblance to AskSheet is SmartSheet, a commercial web-based platform for many kinds of collaboration, including crowdsourcing via Mechanical Turk [9]. Using the site, a user creates a spreadsheet-like document with the row and column headers, and then issues a request for workers to fill in columns with needed data. However, once the process has begun, it has no automatic mechanism to stop once enough information has been gathered to solve the user's overarching problem.

Although not related to crowdsourcing or collaboration, the implementation of AskSheet has parallels with an early spreadsheet system by Lewis that operated on uncertain values, represented as inequality constraints [14]. They were propagated throughout the spreadsheet with formulas. As we will explain, AskSheet treats every cell as a random variable, which is similarly propagated through the formulas.

ASKSHEET

We describe the use of AskSheet with a simplified illustration. Later, we will show how the system supports applications with more realistic requirements.

Example: Grocery stores

Andrew operates a catering business that needs to buy a substantial amount of food each week—typically about 50 items totaling about $1,000. Depending on the week, any of the 5 grocery stores nearby might have some of the items on sale. All of the grocery stores make their weekly flyers available online in PDF format, but there is no API or central database of current grocery prices. Any such database would have to contain prices for every locality, and update them weekly as prices change. Therefore, Andrew will hire web workers to search through the flyers for sale prices on the items so he can get the best deal possible at a single store.

Starting with a blank spreadsheet, he enters the needed ingredients, the names of the stores, and some formulas. (For compactness, we use only 9 items and 3 stores.)

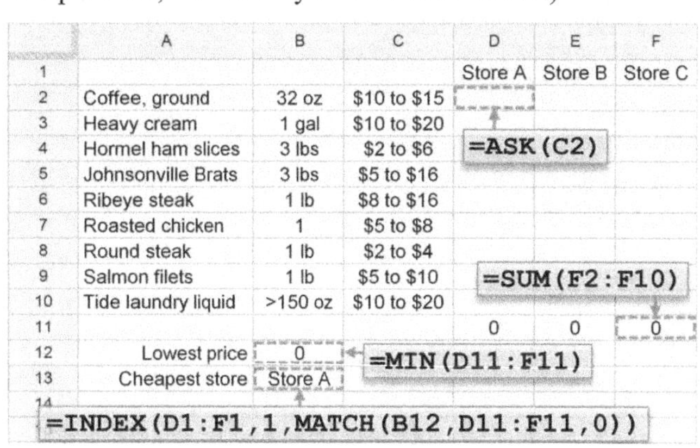

Cells D11, E11, and F11 calculate the sums of the prices at each stores. Cell B12 calculates the minimum of those totals.

Cell B13 selects the name of the store with the lowest total. Note that `=SUM(...)`, `=MIN(...)`, `=INDEX(...)`, and `=MATCH(...)` are standard functions found in most spreadsheet applications; they are not specific to AskSheet.

In cells D2:F10 (columns D through F, rows 2 through 10), he will enter `=ASK(...)` formulas. `=ASK(...)` formulas *are* specific to AskSheet, and indicate requests for information.

The formula in D2, equivalent to `=ASK("$10 to $15")`, means that Andrew expects the 32 ounces of ground coffee to cost between $10 and $15. (More details of the `=ASK(...)` function parameters are given in Figure 2.)

Note that if the price ranges he supplied were too wide, the prioritization might be less effective. The system might request the other value unnecessarily. On the other hand, if the ranges were too narrow, it might stop too soon.

Next, he enters some instructions for the workers and other details the system needs in order to post the tasks and manage the quality of the results. The "Prioritization" slider controls how many inputs to include in each batch.

Recipients

AMT | $ 9.00 per hour (target hourly rate) | Sandbox

Role setup: Shopping

Title: Search for grocery prices — Recipients: AMT

Instructions: Go to the web site of each grocery store, find their current weekly for the zip code 82190, and look for the items listed.

Prioritization: *One at a time* … *All together—no prioritization*

Effort: 1 min, 5 min, 10 min, 15 min, 20 min, 30 min, ___ min

Quality: Trust one response, ___-worker vote, ___-worker average

Inputs: Assume all are answerable, Enforce bounds

Next »

Based on the contents and structure of the spreadsheet, AskSheet generates a form for entering data. If *Enforce bounds* was selected in the setup, then AskSheet will require that workers enter only values in the specified bounds. This may enhance data quality in some cases (e.g., 5-star rating must be between 1 and 5) but would not be appropriate for values like prices where values outside the bounds may be possible, or even desirable (e.g., lower price than expected).

Search for grocery prices
Requester: You Reward: $1.50 HITs Available: 7 Duration: 40 minutes
Qualifications Required: None

Instructions
Go to the web site of each grocery store, find their current weekly for the zip code 82190, and look for the items listed.

		Store A
Heavy cream	1 gal	$
Johnsonville Brats	3 lbs	$
Ribeye steak	1 lb	$
Tide laundry liquid	>150 oz	$

AskSheet posts the tasks and manages the entire process. Andrew can monitor the progress from a dashboard. The braced expressions show the possible range of output values for each cell. The shaded colors indicate the relative priorities of the cells. Obtaining the dark green cells first would provide the greatest opportunity to eliminate other cells. The system will request those inputs first, in order to reduce the overall human effort—and hence, Andrew's cost.

			Store A	Store B	Store C
Coffee, ground	32 oz	$10 to $15	{10…15}	{10…15}	{10…15}
Heavy cream	1 gal	$10 to $20	{10…20}	{10…20}	{10…20}
Hormel ham slices	3 lbs	$2 to $6	{2…6}	{2…6}	{2…6}
Johnsonville Brats	3 lbs	$5 to $16	{5…16}	{5…16}	{5…16}
Ribeye steak	1 lb	$8 to $16	{8…16}	{8…16}	{8…16}
Roasted chicken	1	$5 to $8	{5…8}	{5…8}	{5…8}
Round steak	1 lb	$2 to $4	{2…4}	{2…4}	{2…4}
Salmon filets	1 lb	$5 to $10	{5…10}	{5…10}	{5…10}
Tide laundry liquid	>150 oz	$10 to $20	{10…20}	{10…20}	{10…20}
			{57…115	{57…115	{57…115
Lowest price	{57…115}				
Cheapest store	{3 values}				

As results are received, AskSheet recalculates the priorities based on the new information, and posts new tasks, as needed. When enough data has been entered to calculate a conclusive answer, it displays the result of that formula.

			Store A	Store B	Store C
Coffee, ground	32 oz	$10 to $15	not needed	12	10
Heavy cream	1 gal	$10 to $20	20	not needed	10
Hormel ham slices	3 lbs	$2 to $6	not needed	4	not needed
Johnsonville Brats	3 lbs	$5 to $16	5	not needed	5
Ribeye steak	1 lb	$8 to $16	16	12	10
Roasted chicken	1	$5 to $8	not needed	7	not needed
Round steak	1 lb	$2 to $4	not needed	3	not needed
Salmon filets	1 lb	$5 to $10	not needed	8	5
Tide laundry liquid	>150 oz	$10 to $20	20	not needed	10
			{85…104}	{71…102}	{59…68}
Lowest price	{59…68}				
Cheapest store	Store C				

In this fictional illustration, 16 of the 27 inputs have been entered. The range of possible totals for each of the stores has been constrained just enough that a winner can be conclusively determined. The worst case (upper bound) of Store C ($68) would still be better than the best case (lower bound) of either Store B ($71) or Store A ($85).

A primary benefit of using AskSheet is that it does not need to fulfill all of the requests. It is able to obtain a conclusive result that satisfies the user's spreadsheet model, with only partial information. This is similar to what individuals do when they have seen enough information to make a decision, even without seeing every detail of every alternative. For Andrew, this means lower cost and/or faster turnaround.

It should be emphasized that AskSheet does not depend on this particular decision model. The user starts with a blank spreadsheet and creates a model based on their needs. The example models in this paper are not part of AskSheet itself.

Usability

Like most current research in human computation, our primary focus is on new ways to coordinate the crowd to accomplish work. The interface we use to control AskSheet may someday be adapted for use by general users, but its usability is not an intended contribution of this work. Although many users are fluent with the use of spreadsheet formulas, many more are not. In the future, we plan to refine the user experience of creating models, starting the requests, and viewing progress. To support users who are not experts in spreadsheets, we plan to build simpler interfaces for common models, effectively hiding the spreadsheet details.

AskSheet is however designed to streamline the activities of workers. To that end, it balances the goal of gathering inputs in the most efficient order with the reality that workers can be more efficient if they can gather several inputs from each web search conducted.

IMPLEMENTATION

AskSheet is implemented as a web application coded in Python. The user creates the model in Google Spreadsheets and imports it into AskSheet, which extracts the formulas.

To illustrate how the prioritization algorithms work, we will refer to this very trivial model.

	A	B	C
1	=ASK("1 to 5")	=ASK("1 to 10")	=IF(A1 < B1, "true", "false")

The first step is to parse each formula into an abstract syntax tree (AST). These trees are joined wherever there is a cell reference, resulting in the structure in a structure like this.

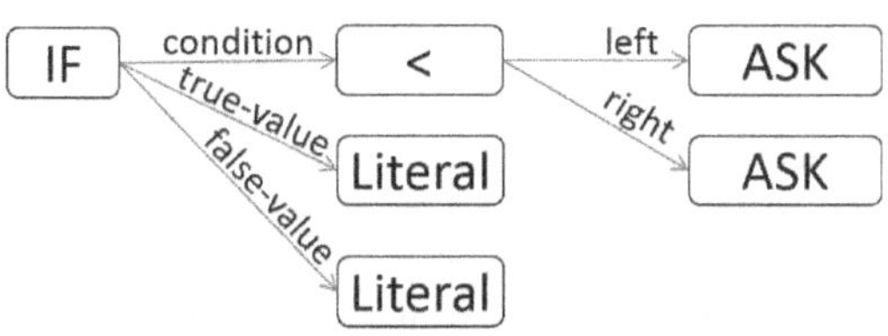

By analyzing the dependence relationships between cells, the planner can infer which cells the user is likely to care about (e.g., the `=INDEX(...)` function in cell B10 of the grocery shopping example). We call these the *roots* of the resulting graph because they depend on other cells, but other cells do not depend on them. The root of this trivial model is C1.

The goal is to find an ordering of the requests that will minimize the expected cost of evaluating the model—finding a conclusive result for all root cells. We think of the *cost of an ordering* as the expected sum of the costs from all requests that would be fulfilled (i.e., not eliminated) if they were gathered in that order. We define the *resulting expected model cost* of fulfilling a particular request as the expected cost of evaluating the entire model, if that request were fulfilled next. This cost should be regarded as a heuristic.

(In this section, we refer to `=ASK(...)` functions as *requests* or *r* since *i* (inputs) would be confusing as a variable name.)

An advantage of using spreadsheets for this work is that the order of evaluation for most operations is effectively arbitrary. Often, evaluating operands in one order can yield a higher probability of eliminating one of the others by short-circuit evaluation or some form of lazy evaluation. This is the fundamental advantage that AskSheet exploits.

When evaluating the comparison in the `=IF(...)` function, we could evaluate A1 and B1 in either order: (A1, B1) or (B1, A1). To prioritize, AskSheet considers the range of possible values for A1 and B1, from the `=ASK(...)` formulas. In our current implementation, every possible value is treated as equally probable, i.e., discrete uniform distribution.

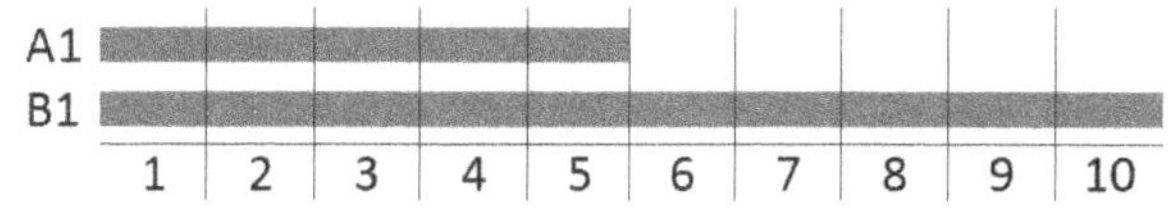

Suppose we choose the latter and evaluate B1 first. If the request in B1 receives any of the values 6, 7, 8, 9, or 10, then the comparison A1 < B1 must be true, no matter which value A1 receives. Also, if B1 is 1, then A1 < B1 must be false. Therefore, we would only need A1 if B1 turns out to be 2, 3, 4, or 5. In other words, Pr(need A1 | have B1) = 0.4.

On the other hand, if we evaluate A1 first, no matter what the value, we will need B1. Thus, Pr(need B1 | have A1) = 1.0.

Based on the above, we can say that the resulting expected model cost of fulfilling A1 first is 2.0 because if A1 is fulfilled next, we will definitely need both B1 (cost=1) and A1 (cost=1) with probability 1.0. The resulting expected model cost of fulfilling B1 is 1.4 because we will need A1 with probability 0.4 and we will need B1 will probability 1.0.

More generally, for any model M we will calculate the expected resulting model cost of fulfilling each request that the root cells depend on. Sorting by that will give us our final ordering. The resulting expected model cost is calculated as:

$$\mathrm{E}\big(\mathrm{C}(M)\big) = \sum_{r \in reqs} \mathrm{C}(r)\Pr(M \text{ needs } r)$$

... where C(r) is the cost specified in the `ASK(...)` function parameters, *reqs* is the set of all requests in the model, C(M) is the cost of evaluating the model, and Pr(M needs r) is the probability that evaluating every root in the model will require fulfilling request r. That can in turn be expressed as the probability that any root node will need request r.

$$\Pr(M \text{ needs } r) = P\left(\bigvee_{n \in roots} n \text{ needs } r\right)$$

The probability that a particular node n needs a request r is calculated recursively:

- If n is a request and $n = r$, then P(n needs r) = 1. (Every request node needs itself.)
- If n is a request and $n \neq r$, then P(n needs r) = 0. (A request node never needs any other nodes.)
- For any other node type, the probability is:

$$\Pr(n \text{ needs } r) = \Pr\left(\bigvee_{op \in Ops_n} op \text{ needs } r \;\wedge\; n \text{ needs } op\right)$$

... where Ops_n is the set of operands (i.e., child nodes) to n.

For simple arithmetic operations, P(n needs op)=1 for all of the operands, since you cannot calculate an arithmetic operation without all of its operands (except for the case of multiplication by zero). For example, to calculate $a + b$, you need both a and b, regardless of the bounds or distributions.

AskSheet prioritizes the requests by the conditional expected model cost E(C(M | r next)), conditioned on acquiring each request r next. It is equivalent to the this utility function:

$$\mathrm{U}(r) = \mathrm{E}(\mathrm{C}(M)) - \mathrm{E}(\mathrm{C}(M) \mid r \text{ next})$$

In essence, this is the expected overall savings if we acquired r next, versus choosing parameters randomly at every step.

Note that the cost is based on marginal probabilities over all possible values of other inputs in the model. The calculations assume parameters are evaluated in random order by default. (For `=IF(...)`, the condition is always evaluated first since it would not make sense to evaluate the value parameters first.)

For operations that can potentially be optimized to eliminate requests—including the comparison operators, `=MIN(...)`, `=MAX(...)`, `=IF(...)`, and many others—calculating the probability that the node needs each operand generally entails calculating the output distribution (probability mass function) of the node—every possible output value and its probability relative to the decision inputs (random variables).

Operations

The current system supports a small but important subset of core spreadsheet formulas: `=IF(...)`, `=MAX(...)`, `=MIN(...)`, `=SUM(...)`, `=AND(...)`, `=OR(...)`, `=NOT(...)`, `=INDEX(...)`, `=MATCH(...)`, and operators (+, -, /, *, =, <, <=, !=, >=, >). Efficient algorithms for calculating the output distribution and need probabilities are specific to each these. Below, we show how these are calculated for one example.

Example: =MAX(...)

The output distribution for `=MAX(...)` is the joint distribution of possible values the formula could take, for all possible values of its parameters.

Since `=MAX(...)` is synonymous with the kth order statistic for a discrete random variable with k possible values, we can use the probability mass function for discrete order statistics:

$$\Pr(\max = k) = \Pr(\max \le k) - \Pr(\max < k)$$

$$= \Pr\left(\bigwedge_{op \in Ops_n} op \le k\right) - \Pr\left(\bigwedge_{op \in Ops_n} op < k\right)$$

The need probability Pr(max needs op) for each operand of `=MAX(...)` is calculated on the premise that an operand is needed only when there was some chance that it could be greater than the maximum. In other words, for each possible max value k in the output distribution calculated above, we temporarily assume that was the max value, and then set the cost for that case as the sum of expected costs for every operand op for which $\Pr(op > k) > 0$. With that, we calculate an expected value over every possible value of k.

Scope

AskSheet offers a unified process for efficient application of crowdsourcing to a wide range of decision making tasks. It is especially suited to decisions that entail gathering a lot of details and then selecting a subset of them, typically based on the relation to the rest. This includes the examples above and, more generally, any problem that can be modeled using operations such as minimum, maximum, if/else, conditionals, and so forth. Since expected bounds of the inputs are specified by the user a priori, such operations can often be precisely computed with only partial information.

AskSheet is not intended for needle-in-a-haystack search problems (e.g., find Mayor X's salary). Also excluded are problems where a large set of information is gathered and all of it is to be used (e.g., find salaries of all mayors in the US).

LIMITATIONS OF CURRENT IMPLEMENTATION

The calculations described above have enabled us to test the core concept embodied by AskSheet. Below, we summarize some known limitations and outline some potential solutions.

Performance

In our current implementation, models with `=MAX(...)` and `=MIN(...)` formulas are currently practical only in modest sizes (i.e., up to around 30-40 parameters). This affects weighted sums models, a common type of decision model.

There is no closed form expression for the running time, since it depends on specifics of the model, such as how closely spaced the weights are. For a weighted sums model with a alternatives each having b attributes with c levels per attribute, and all weights being the same, running time is $O(a^2b^2c)$. The theoretical worst case, $O(a^2b^2c^2)$, could only occur if the weights were spaced in an extremely unlikely pattern. These were determined by analyzing the code.

The algorithm can compute prioritization in polynomial time because instead of considering every possible permutation, it simply ranks requests by the expected cost savings that would result if each one were fulfilled next. That can be calculated in polynomial time for a given request, and so calculating it for every request is also polynomial.

To understand this practically, we measured the time to prioritize inputs in several WSM models. All weights were set equal to 1 (the best case) and we assumed 5 levels for every attribute. This represents a decision where all attributes are scored from 1 to 5 and are equally important. As a spreadsheet, it would occupy $a \times b$ cells, plus the labels.

These were run on a desktop computer with an Intel model i7-3770K 3.50 GHz CPU and 32 GB RAM using the Python 2.7 interpreter. The results are shown in Figure 1.

This time is important because when a worker submits a form, the prioritization must be recalculated in real-time, before the answers are accepted. AskSheet only posts a small number of tasks (HITs) at a given time, to avoid collecting responses that will not be needed. To make this possible, as a worker submits a form, it recalculates the prioritization and, if more inputs from that role (HIT Type) are still needed, it posts another task—all before accepting the worker's data.

number of alternatives	number of attributes: 5	10	15	20	25
10	0.1	0.5	1.1	2.0	2.9
20	0.6	2.2	4.7	8.2	12.0
30	1.5	5.3	11.8	20.9	30.9
40	2.9	10.6	23.4	42.8	61.9
50	5.0	18.3	41.6	73.8	108.8

Figure 1. Time (secs.) to prioritize a benchmark model based on the sum of 5-star ratings for each alternative.

```
=ASK(inputSpec[, itemLabels[, attrLabels[, roleName[, recipientSpec]]]])
```

	inputSpec	itemLabels	attrLabels	roleName	recipientSpec
Description:	Specifies the type and format of the expected input	Label(s), typically identifying the alternative	Label(s), typically identifying the attribute	Name for this task type	Who to direct the task to
Examples:	"1 to 10" "$3 to $6" "score: big > small" G1:G20	"Subaru Outback" "Galaxy S3" A13 A13:B13	"miles per gallon" "screen size G1 G1:G2	"check fuel specs" "check basic specs"	"AMT" "xxxxx@gmail.com"
Default:	(no default)	row heading	column heading	""	"AMT"
Note:	Cell arrays specify a drop-down control. "score" is for *text scoring (*discussed later in this paper).	For worker efficiency, inputs with the same item label into the same task, when possible.	Attribute labels must also appear in the same task with the input, but do not affect batching.	Inputs with the same role will share the same instructions and task setup.	In the future, this will be used to send tasks to internal collaborators by email, etc.

Figure 2. =ASK(...) formula parameters are at the core of the strategy for partitioning inputs into efficient tasks.

To reduce the recalculation time, we could keep the state from the last calculation, and then update the output distributions and need probabilities incrementally. Recalculation time is most important since it affects the delay that workers experience when submitting the form.

To improve the initial calculation time, we are aware of several untapped opportunities for optimizing the code. Using dynamic programming, we previously improved performance of calculations for the =SUM(...) operation. We believe a similar approach could be used for other operations.

For some operations, we have not found computationally feasible algorithms for calculating output distributions and need probabilities. These include =RANK(...) and =LARGE(...) (pick n^{th} largest value). To support those, and also increase the number of parameters that can be supported with the current set of operations, we are exploring options for approximating the probabilities by random sampling. This is complicated by the large number of parameters.

Finally, since AskSheet is implemented in pure Python, these times could be improved by a constant—but substantial—factor by porting critical modules to C and splitting the calculations acrosss multiple CPU cores. The algorithms are extremely parellelizable because they compute the probabilities for a large number of scenarios.

Dependence between formulas

The algorithms that calculate output distribution and need probabilities use only local information (i.e., at the level of a particular function or operator), so they cannot detect dependence between cells. For example, in this simple model, AskSheet *should* detect that A1 and B1 refer to the same quantity, and thus elimincate A1, i.e., Pr(need A1)=0.0.

	A	B	C
1	=ASK("1 to 10")	=A1*1	=IF(A1=B1, "same", "different")

The problem is that when analyzing the condition in C1, it has no knowledge of the relationshiop between A1 and B1. Although it calculates that both A1 and A2 have the same distribution (discrete uniform, 1 to 10), it cannot detect the dependence between the two, and so it fails to eliminate A1.

In our experience, the most common area where this issue is apparent is with comparison operators, as well as spreadsheet functions that depend on comparisons internally, such as table lookups. For example, in the grocery shopping example above, the system will continue to calculate the entire total cost for a store, even though the actual number is not needed to determine which store is the winner.

These issues do not arise with tree-structured models (i.e., each cell referenced by at most one formula). They only arise in DAG-structured models, because the local information used by the probability calculations does not provide information on these relationships.

A potential solution we intend to explore is to simplify the formulas algebraically before calculating need probabilities for comparison operators. Software libraries exist for performing such algebraic manipulation [11]. When algebraic simplification determines two nodes to be the same quantity, then the output distribution of the equality operator will be Pr(node=True)=1.0. This could be applied to functions that inherently involve comparison operations (e.g., table lookups), following a strategy similar to symbolic evaluation, a technique used in software testing [5].

These solutions might not fully eliminate the issue of dependence, which affects any calculation of conjunctions (A ∧ B) or disjunctions (A ∨ B). However, it would reduce the effect on the prioritizations.

BATCHING INPUTS FOR WORKER EFFICIENCY

Up to now, we have assumed that that inputs are acquired one at a time. To make the task more efficient for workers, AskSheet can batch inputs that involve the same type of activity (e.g. searching for fuel economy specifications) and, where possible, the same source information (e.g., pages about a single car model). The user sets the batch size.

In addition, the parameters to =ASK(...) allow it to split the job into multiple roles (HIT Types) which are run in parallel. (See Figure 2.) The example below illustrates how the job of gathering information to find an acceptable pediatrician is split into four separate roles which run in parallel.

Field trial #1: Find a pediatrician

Alan needs to find a pediatrician for his daughter. He values information from doctor rating sites but does not trust one site alone. Recognizing that these sources alone would not be sufficient to find the *best* pediatrician, he will be satisfied to find one that matches his basic requirements:

- Average rating at RateMDs.com is at least 4 stars.
- Average rating at HealthGrades.com is least 80% positive.
- The doctor accepts Alan's insurance, CareFirst.
- Driving to the office takes no more than 20 minutes.

We tested this scenario using the model in Figure 3. The root formula in F53 simply evaluates whether *any* of the doctors conforms. Recall that Alan will be satisfied with any doctor who meets his minimum criteria. Thus, AskSheet's task is ostensibly just to determine whether any doctor satisfies the criteria. Once any doctor has been confirmed to fit the criteria, the value of F53 will be TRUE, and no more inputs are needed. Columns B, C, D, and E each becomes a separate role (HIT Type) which runs in parallel.

Note that the current implementation of AskSheet requires the user to fill in the row labels in the model. For this example, we found a list of pediatricians online. In the future, we plan to extend AskSheet so that workers can gather the row labels and extend the spreadsheet.

We received a conclusive answer in 47 minutes. With the prioritization, AskSheet required only 36 of the 200 inputs. The total cost was \$5.67 with one judgment per input. We paid \$0.63 per task. The 6 workers spent a combined total of 58 minutes, for an average hourly rate of \$5.89 per hour.

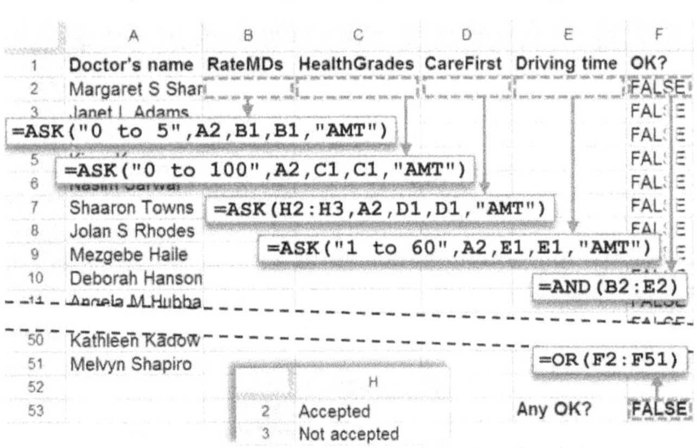

Figure 3. Model for field trial #1 (pediatrician)

Had all of the 200 inputs been fulfilled (i.e., the approach used by tools such as SmartSheet) the total cost would have been \$31.50. The optimizations saved \$25.83 (82%).

OPTIMALITY

Full optimality would be achieved only if a few simplifying assumptions were satisfied. They are listed below. To the extent these are violated, optimality may be diminished.

- *Input values are presumed to be uniformly distributed and mutually independent.* This affects the calculated output distributions, which are used to calculate need probabilities. For =MAX(...), AskSheet effectively prioritizes inputs for the top contenders in order to rapidly differentiate which is the maximum. This assumption may lead to inaccurate selection of the top contenders.
- *Bounds given in =ASK(...) formulas are presumed accurate.* If there are actual values outside the bounds (e.g., lower price than anticipated), it may stop too soon.
- *Each cell is referenced by at most one node.* This is the problem of dependence between formulas described above. It can lead to gathering more inputs than necessary.
- *At each step, only one input is acquired from one worker.* The batching mechanism described above violates this. However, making tasks more efficient for workers may reduce overall cost and completion time. The user controls this tradeoff via the =ASK(...) parameters and the setup.

Single-step assumption

AskSheet considers only the effects of the next input acquired, and greedily acquires whichever maximizes overall expected cost savings. In many value of information applications, this can diminish optimality, especially for those that optimize cost and another utility function [13,21].

Within the above assumptions, the single-step assumption does not affect AskSheet. We will explain with this example.

	A	B	C
1	=ASK("0 to 1")	=ASK("0 to 100")	=AND(A1=0, B1=0)
2	=ASK("0 to 1")	=ASK("0 to 100")	=AND(A2=0, B2=0)
3	=ASK("0 to 1")	=ASK("0 to 100")	=AND(A3=0, B3=0)
4			=OR(C1:C3)

If either A1, A2, or A3 were chosen first, then the expected model cost would be 3.88. However, choosing B1, B2, or B3 first would reduce that to 3.61, for a utility of 0.27. Below, the dashboard is annotated with all of the utilities.

	A	B	C
1	{0...1} U=0.000	{0...100} U=0.27	{false...true}
2	{0...1} U=0.000	{0...100} U=0.27	{false...true}
3	{0...1} U=0.000	{0...100} U=0.27	{false...true}
4			{false...true}

Although the *pair* of (A1, B1)—or (A2, B2) or (A3, B3)—could eliminate the other four cells, AskSheet does not know this. Nevertheless, optimality is not affected, as we will see.

Suppose we enter 0 in cell B1. Then, A1 gets the highest utility since it could eliminate the remaining cells. Taking

A1 next, the expected model cost would be 2.28, versus 3.01 if B2 or B3 were chosen next, or 3.22 if A2 or A3 were next.

	A	B	C
1	{0...1} U=0.93	0	{false...true}
2	{0...1} U=0.00	{0...100} U=0.21	{false...true}
3	{0...1} U=0.00	{0...100} U=0.21	{false...true}
4			{false...true}

The result is the same as if the pair had been selected together. More generally, because utility is based on marginal probabilities over all other values, there is no extra value to selecting pairs (or *n*-tuples) together, as long as the input with single highest utility is acquired at each step.

In practice, it is often more efficient to gather a few related inputs at once. This *can* affect optimality, although the user can control that tradeoff in the setup panel. If the user had set batch size to 2, B1 and B2 would have been acquired first.

QUANTIFYING UNSTRUCTURED INPUTS

Up to this point, we have discussed only models where all inputs are either numbers or discrete choices. AskSheet handles unstructured, non-numeric inputs using a method we call *text scoring*. It leverages the "score" input type mentioned in the =ASK(...) parameters (Figure 2).

Field trial #2: Car shopping

The use of text scoring is illustrated by the following scenario. Jay is shopping for a new car and has these criteria:

- Hatchback with 4-wheel-drive
- Good fuel efficiency
- Wheel base about 100 inches (similar to Jay's former car)
- Abundance of modern safety features
- Seats 5 adults comfortably (for long car trips)

As before, Jay creates a spreadsheet model. The last two criteria are difficult to quantify. Although they are somewhat subjective, Jay will write his criteria and ask workers to simply specify how well each car model fits what he wants.

Workers are given two car models to research at a time. For safety features, they are asked to write a textual description of how spacious they think the inside of the car would be, as it would relate to traveling with 5 adults. They are instructed to look for photographs of the interior or other metrics that

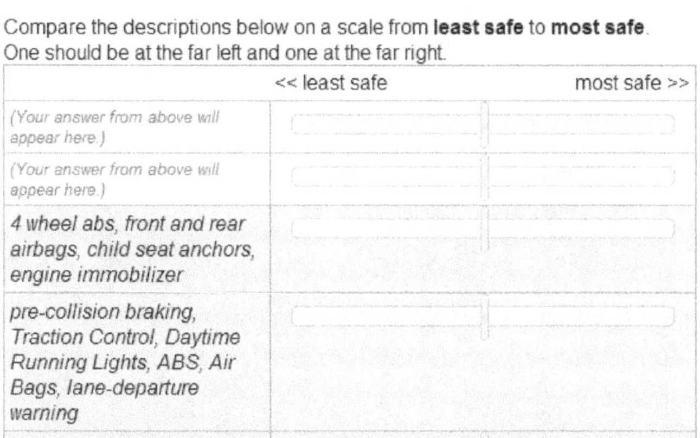

Figure 4. Text scoring interface

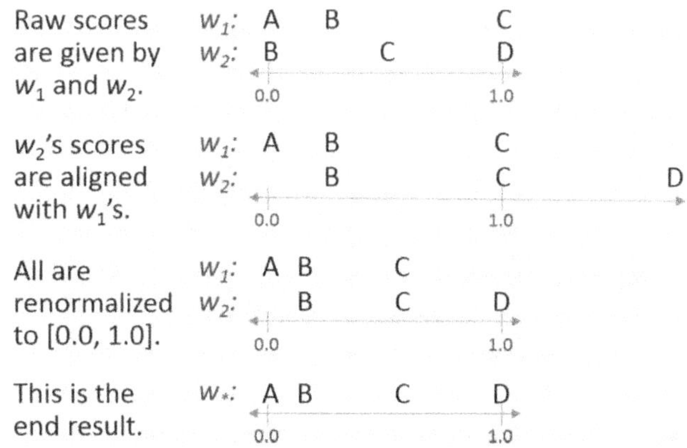

Figure 5. In this minimal example, text scores from two workers who each scored three items are aligned.

would help. The first worker is asked to compare the two models based on which seems to be most spacious. A similar course was used to compare by safety features (Figure 4).

To enable a global view across tasks and/or workers, AskSheet asks subsequent workers to compare the features on the car model they have researched together with the text descriptions entered in up to four prior tasks. Figure 4 shows this comparison with two prior values.

Each subsequent worker who does the task adds some new descriptions and is shown some prior descriptions for reference. To reconcile all of the scores, AskSheet scales and translates all of the scores for a particular field onto a common coordinate system (i.e., offset and scale). This is analagous to if all of the scores were in different unknown units, and there were just a few measurements of the same quantity with which to convert the units of one to another.

Two common scores would be sufficient if the information were perfect. A challenge is that workers may disagree on the relative score of items, and the values on the slider may not be precise, in the absence of more reference points. Therefore, we collect up to four comparative scores with each task in order to accumulate redundant information and use the method of least squares to solve for the set of scale factors and offsets that gives the best fit (Figure 5).

When we ran the model to choose between 20 current model cars, the results for the text scoring agreed with our own assessment of the cars (e.g., Volkswagon CC = 0.14, Volvo C30 = 0.83). Although this method is not designed to be statistically rigorous, in the context of a model with various kinds of information, it allows us to add these unstructured inputs. In this case, because these items were mixed with numeric and choice answers, only 8 of the 20 cars were compared for safety features and spaciousness.

We received a conclusive answer (Subaru Outback) in 54 minutes. With the prioritization, AskSheet required only 48 of the 120 inputs. The total cost was $16.05 with one judgment per input. We paid $0.75 per task. The 8 workers spent a combined total of 57 minutes, for an average hourly rate of $9.40 per hour.

Had all of the 120 inputs been fulfilled the total cost would have been \$33.75. The optimizations saved \$24.75 (73%).

This strategy was adopted to allow a richer set of models, but is not intended to be primary basis of a model. A more thorough study of text scoring is needed to fully understand its ability to reconcile scores from different contributors.

Prioritizing without known bounds

Another challenge is that there is no way to specify bounds a priori for such unstructured quantities. To solve this, at each step, after reconciling the scores received so far, AskSheet estimates how much of the total space has been seen so far.

This is accomplished using maximum spacing estimation (MSE) [20], a method of estimating properties of a distribution based on a limited sample. The MSE formula for uniform distributions gives us an estimate of the global maximum and minimum (e.g., Relative to cars seen so far, what is the most spacious car on the consumer market?).

$$max_{estimate} = \frac{n \cdot max_{samples} - min_{samples}}{n-1}$$

$$min_{estimate} = \frac{n \cdot min_{samples} - max_{samples}}{n-1}$$

Although this relies on our presumption of uniform distribution, which is very unlikely to be accurate for these fields, the effect is what we need: The bounds narrow as more inputs are received. From that, we calculate a scale factor and offset that are applied to all scores in a given field.

$$scalefactor = \frac{1.0}{max_{estimate} - min_{estimate}}$$

$$offset = -min_{estimate} \cdot scalefactor$$

That pushes all values toward the middle of the space from 0.0 to 1.0. The prioritization assumes a minimum and maximum of 0.0 and 1.0, respectively, so this effectively causes the prioritization to assume greater and/or lesser values may still exist. As more values are received, this margin is decreased gradually.

This approach while straightforward, is necessary to enable a richer set of models using a variety of types of data. It is not necessary to discover the absolute maximum or minimum for any one attribute. Eventually, with enough data, one decision alternative in the decision will prevail.

Field trial #3: Smartphone shopping

Another example we have used throughout the project development is comparison shopping. Using a spreadsheet, a user can model their exact personal preferences, and include details that might not be important to all shoppers. The simplest way to model this is with a weighted sums model, which depends on the `=MAX(...)` and `=SUM(...)` formulas. Web workers can be employed to search the web for details about the alternatives.

We created a model to compare seven leading smartphones by the following criteria:

- Weight=1: screen size, material, appearance, CPU cores
- Weight=2: physical shutter button, camera megapixels
- Weight=4: battery talk time, storage potential, RAM

For appearance, workers were asked to look at a photo of the phone and compare based on the scale of "solid" to "cheap-looking". As in the example of car shopping, we separated this unstructured input into a separate role. Because it had a relatively low weight, it was prioritized low and only used to distinguish between the three top contenders: HTC One, Samsung Galaxy S3, and Samsung Galaxy S4. Since this was a more time-intensive task for workers (and we paid a higher rate), this demonstrates how prioritizing inputs can save worker effort. The result is shown in Figure 6.

We received a conclusive answer (Samsung Galaxy S4) in 1 hour 31 minutes. With the prioritization, AskSheet required only 43 of the 63 inputs. The total cost was \$16.05 with one judgment per input. We paid between \$1.05 and \$1.50 per task. The 9 workers spent a combined total of 1 hour 31 minutes for an average rate of \$10.52 per hour.

Had all of the 63 inputs been fulfilled the total cost would have been \$23.45. The optimizations saved \$7.40 (32%).

QUALITY CONTROL

AskSheet includes a few mechanisms for controlling quality. First, in the setup screen, the user can request multiple judgments. The judgments can be aggregated by averaging (for subjective ratings) or voting (for objective information).

	Weights	Nexus 4	Samsung Galaxy S3	Samsung Galaxy S4	Sony Xperia T7	Kyocera Rise	HTC One	iPhone 5
Camera quality	2	8	8	13	12	3	3	8
Battery, talk time	4	12	12	12	5	9	12	8
Screen size	1	not needed	3	4	not needed	not needed	3	not needed
Max storage	4	0	4	4	2	2	4	4
Material	1	not needed	2	4	not needed	not needed	4	not needed
Appearance	1	not needed	0.37	0.26	not needed	not needed	0.74	not needed
CPU, # of cores	1	not needed	4	4	not needed	not needed	4	not needed
RAM	4	4	2	4	0	0	4	2
Shutter button	2	not needed	4	4	not needed	not needed	0	not needed
Score		{68.3⋯93.3}	96.63	111.19	{34.4⋯59.4}	{45.6⋯70.6}	96.34	{60.3⋯85.3}
Best model		Best score						
Samsung Galaxy S4		111.19						

Figure 6. AskSheet's dashboard shows how 20 of the 63 inputs in this smartphone shopping model were eliminated. Note that many of the values shown are the values associated with labels in a drop-down selection control specified in the model.

AskSheet optimizes this, as well, requesting judgments incrementally. For example, if the user requests five judgments and the first three agree, it will not request any more. In fact, it only requests one at a time because there is always a chance that the input might be eliminated by the optimizations. This approach was inspired by Get Another Label [22], although it is far simpler than that system.

In addition to multiple judgments, AskSheet uses the input specification to validate the format and range of the inputs. In the setup screen, the user may specify that blanks not be allowed (i.e., all inputs required) and/or that ranges must be enforced (or not). With these options, the form does not allow submission until the inputs conform.

DISCUSSION

The models we used for these field trials allowed us to demonstrate AskSheet in the context of familiar personal decision problems within the technical boundaries of our current implementation. However, these examples do not capture the full expressive power of this framework.

In creating those models, we were confined by the limitations of our current implementation. We had to limit `=SUM(...)`, `=MIN(...)`, and `=MAX(...)` functions to around 30-40 parameters each. Moreover, the system does not yet support functions related to relative ordering, such as `=RANK(...)`, `=PERCENTILE(...)`, `=MEDIAN(...)`, `=LARGE(...)`, and `=SMALL(...)`. If it did, far richer models would be supported.

Spreadsheets are used in business contexts to model a wide range of decision problems [12]. In fact, the language of spreadsheets formulas can be considered first-order functional programming [1] and, as such, can be used to solve problems as permutations, combinations, and even the Towers of Hanoi problem [4]. The most fundamental requirement imposed by AskSheet—ignoring computational boundaries—is that the decision answer(s) be expressed as a formula(s) somewhere in the spreadsheet. However, some types of problems are more amenable than others.

From our experiences so far, we have learned that the method works best where the decision-maker knows in advance what aspects are important and something about the choices. In addition, there is a trade-off between the time the decision-maker must spend specifying the model and the instructions versus the time that is saved by delegating the work to others.

As we mentioned in the introduction, our vision for AskSheet extends beyond Mechanical Turk to internal organizational decisions that require inputs that are not readily on hand. Besides gathering facts from the web, this could include trusted judgments, such as evaluating materials submitted by applicants to a job or academic program. Spreadsheets have the advantage of creating a record of the decision rationale.

Instead of working through Mechanical Turk, internal users would enter inputs via a private web site. Since they would already be familiar with the context, we expect the burden of writing instructions would be less. However, since the "cost" of asking different people is rarely equal—in terms of hourly rate, social capital, etc.—the decision coordinator who creates the model would need an interface for specifying the relative cost of asking each collaborator. For example, asking the boss could be considered equivalent to asking an administrator five times. If the same model contained tasks for Mechanical Turk *and* internal collaborators, then it would need to relate social capital to monetary cost, as well.

MORE POTENTIAL APPLICATIONS

In this section we outline two use cases that illustrate our vision for the future, and how they can be modeled.

Example: Vacation

Vicky wants to take a vacation sometime in March for a few days. She has three destinations in mind, with a preference for Puerto Rico. Cost is important, too.

She makes a table of the travel dates that are compatible with her work schedule, and her preference (1 to 10) for each. She does the same for the candidate destinations.

Date	Preference
3/1/2013	4
3/2/2013	5
3/3/2013	5

Destination	Preference
Puerto Rico	10
Florida	5
Lake Michigan	5

Elsewhere, she enters weights that describe what aspects are important to here. Finally, she uses formulas to make a table of every combination of destination, departure date, and duration along with a calculated score for each combination.

Itineraries						
To location	*Depart*	*# of Days*	*Return*	*Fare*	Hotel	Score
Puerto Rico	3/1/2013	4	3/5/2013	970	480	48
Puerto Rico	3/1/2013	5	3/6/2013	530	600	72
Puerto Rico	3/1/2013	6	3/7/2013	710	720	27

At the top, a result formula displays the best option of all.

BEST CHOICE			
Destination	Depart	Duration	Return
Florida	3/22/2013	4	3/26/2013

The large number of combinations makes this infeasible with our current implementation. With a future version, Vicky could direct workers to check various travel web sites to find the best airfares, hotels, and other features for each location, date and duration. If the hotels at a destination are expensive, it would skip checking airfares for any of her listed dates.

Example: Reviewing conference paper submissions

The XYZ conference has a very simple review process. It initially assigns three reviewers per paper. For those that are borderline, it adds more until a consensus forms.

This could be modelled as accepting any paper where the median of five scores is at least 4.0 out of 5.0. If the first three are more (or less) than 4.0, then no more are needed.

	A	B	C	D	E	F	G	H
1	Title	R1	R2	R3	R4	R5	Median	Accept
2	Linear Potentials Airy Wave	3	2	3	2	3	3	no
3	Restricted Isometries and G	3	3	1	4	2	3	no
4	Dirichlet mean identities anc	4	4					YES
5	Asymptotic Traffic Flow in a							
6	Finite Bounds for Neighborh	2	1	2	2	1	2	no

=MEDIAN(B2:F2)

=IF(G2 >= 4, "YES", "no")

They could have structured the process in other ways. For example, to target a 25% acceptance rate, it could accept every paper in the top 25 percentile, as this model illustrates:

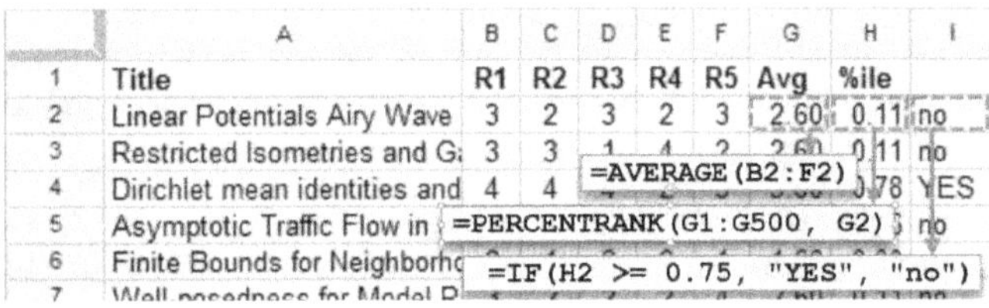

To accept a specific number of papers (e.g., to fit the number of rooms), the `RANK(...)` function could be used as follows:

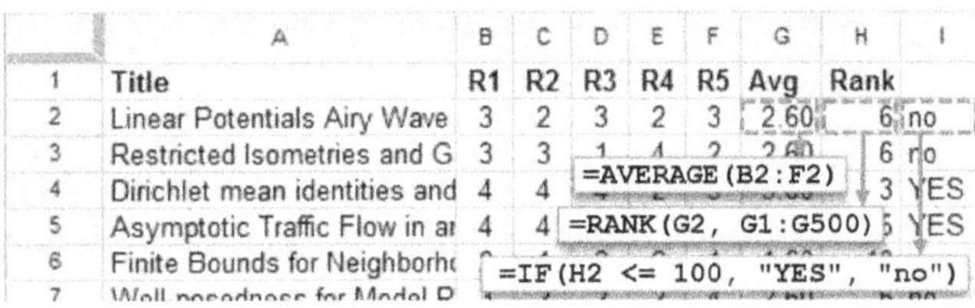

In each case, once there was enough information to be sure the process was complete, it would stop requesting reviews.

Note that since the submissions are confidential, reviewers would of course be trusted experts, not web workers. Also, the scores would be entered on a private, controlled web site.

CONCLUSION

We have presented AskSheet, a system that leverages the structure of a decision spreadsheet to coordinate an efficient human workflow to solve the user's overarching decision problem without necessarily gathering all of the inputs.

The current implementation is fully operational with a basic set of spreadsheet operations. The three field studies all generated decisions in under 1.5 hours for between about \$6 and \$16 using Amazon Mechanical Turk. This shows what we believe to be a financially and temporally viable process.

Extending this to larger, more complex decision models will require solving many technical hurdles. Adding support for spreadsheet functions related to ranking and relative ordering will enable new model types important for decision-making.

The potential benefits extend well beyond saving money or time. The ability to offload a complex task such as gathering information for a decision would give users new flexibility for delegating work. Also, a user who might otherwise choose to satisfice—accept a subpar option to avoid the tedium of researching others—would gain a viable alternative. Ultimately, we see this as an opportunity to effectively connect such users with the people who can help.

ACKNOWLEDGMENTS

We gratefully acknowledge the advice of Nicholas Chen, Chang Hu, Lise Getoor, Piotr Mardziel, Atif Memon, Jay Pujara, Ben Shneiderman, Keith Walker, Tom Yeh, and Ben Zou, as well as thoughtful feedback from the reviewers.

REFERENCES

1. Abraham, R., Burnett, M., & Erwig, M.. 2009. Spreadsheet Programming. *Wiley Encyclopedia of Comp Sci and Eng.*
2. Bernstein, M. S., Brandt, J., Miller, R. C., & Karger, D. R. 2011. Crowds in two seconds: Enabling realtime crowd-powered interfaces. *UIST '10.*
3. Bernstein, M.S., Little, G., Miller, R.C., et al. 2010. Soylent: a word processor with a crowd inside. *UIST '10.*
4. Casimir, R. J. 1992. Real programmers don't use spreadsheets. *ACM Sigplan Notices, 27*, 6, 10-16.
5. Cheatham, Jr, T.E., Holloway, G.H. & Townley, J.A. 1979. Symbolic evaluation and the analysis of programs. *TOSE.*
6. Dai, P., Mausam, & Weld, D. S. 2010. Decision-theoretic control of crowd-sourced workflows. *AAAI '10.*
7. Franklin, M., Kossmann, D., Kraska, T., Ramesh, S., & Xin, R. 2011. CrowdDB: answering queries with crowdsourcing. *SIGMOD '11.*
8. Franklin, M. J., Trushkowsky, B., Sarkar, P., & Kraska, T. 2013. Crowdsourced enumeration queries. *ICDE '13.*
9. Frei, B. 2009. Paid crowdsourcing: Current state & progress toward mainstream business use. Smartsheet.com.
10. Ipeirotis, P.G., Provost, F., & Wang, J. 2010. Quality management on Amazon Mechanical Turk. *HCOMP '10.*
11. Joyner, D., Čertík, O., Meurer, A., & Granger, B.E.. 2012. Open source computer algebra systems: SymPy. *ACM Communications in Computer Algebra,* 45, 3/4, 225-234.
12. Kirkwood, C.W. 1997. *Strategic Decision Making: Multiobjective Decision Anal. w/ Spreadsheets.* Duxbury.
13. Koller, D. & Friedman, N. 2009. *Probabilistic graphical models: principles and techniques.* MIT Press. 1121-1125.
14. Lewis, C. 1985. Extending the spreadsheet interface to handle approximate quantities and relationships. *ACM SIGCHI Bulletin,* 55-59.
15. Little, G., Chilton, L.B., Goldman, M., & Miller, R. C. 2010. Exploring iterative and parallel human computation processes. *HCOMP '10.*
16. Marcus, A., Wu, E., Karger, D.R., Madden, S.R., & Miller, R.C. 2011. Crowdsourced databases: query processing with people. *CIDR '11.*
17. Pirolli, P. & Card, S.K. 1999. Information foraging. *Psychological Review,* 106, 4, 643-675.
18. Quinn, A.J. & Bederson, B.B. 2011. Human computation: a survey and taxonomy of a growing field. *CHI '11.*
19. Quinn, A.J., Bederson, B.B., Yeh, T., & Lin, J. 2010. CrowdFlow: integrating machine learning with Mechanical Turk for speed-cost-quality flexibility. Technical Report HCIL-2010-09, University of Maryland.
20. Ranneby, B. 1984. The maximum spacing method. An estimation method related to the maximum likelihood method". *Scandinavian J. of Statistics*, 11, 2, 93–112.
21. Shachter, R.D, & Peot, M.A. 1992. Decision Making Using Probabilistic Inference Methods. *UAI '92.*
22. Sheng, V., Provost, F., & Ipeirotis, P.. 2008. Get Another Label? Improving Data Quality and Data Mining using multiple noisy labelers. *KDD '08.*
23. Simon, H.A. 1972. Theories of bounded rationality. *Decision and organization 1*, 161-176.
24. Tong, S. & Koller, D. 2002. Support vector machine active learning with applications to text classification. *JMLR.*
25. von Ahn, L. 2005. *Human Computation.* Doctoral Thesis.

Cancer Navigation: Opportunities and Challenges for Facilitating the Breast Cancer Journey

Maia Jacobs, James Clawson, Elizabeth D. Mynatt
College of Computing
Georgia Institute of Technology
Atlanta, GA 30332 USA
mjacobs30@gatech.edu, {jamer, mynatt}@cc.gatech.edu

ABSTRACT
Cancer navigation programs help patients overcome emotional, financial, and logistical challenges not typically addressed by the medical system. In this paper, we provide a detailed description of a rural cancer navigation organization, specifically detailing the roles collaboration and technology play in supporting navigation work. Examining navigation from a CSCW perspective, we see that navigation is a collaborative care system requiring coordination with patients, providers, and other navigators. Our study reveals a number of design opportunities for supporting navigation in the areas of resource monitoring, knowledge transfer, case management, long term navigation, and development of best practices. Supporting cancer navigation will be a critical step towards improving the healthcare experience for cancer patients.

Author Keywords
Cancer; Healthcare; Navigation; Implications for design;

ACM Classification Keywords
H.5.3 **[Group and Organization Interfaces]**: Computer-supported cooperative work

INTRODUCTION
When a person is diagnosed with cancer they must traverse a complex medical network as they obtain treatment, requiring coordination with numerous healthcare providers. Adapting to this new system and schedule often causes patients to face many emotional, financial, and logistical obstacles not addressed through the medical system. To help patients overcome these challenges, government, community, and healthcare organizations have joined forces over the past two decades to develop independent cancer navigation programs. Cancer navigators provide one-on-one support for patients from the time they are diagnosed with cancer until they complete their treatment [10]. Navigators attempt to ensure that nothing impedes a person's ability to obtain medical treatment by helping patients receive an often customized set of resources including counseling, social security benefits, medical insurance, gas money, answers to medical questions and many other crucial resources.

A young and developing practice, cancer navigation operates outside of the conventional healthcare system and yet provides an invaluable service to those diagnosed with cancer. Few studies explore how cancer navigators operate on a daily basis or how they collaborate with patients, physicians, and other cancer navigators. In this paper, we present a detailed case study of how a rural navigation organization collaborates with key stakeholders in an attempt to bridge gaps in the healthcare system and improve the quality of care for cancer patients. While we studied the communication and work practices of the entire organization, we focused on breast cancer navigation as the disease's high incidence and survival rates necessitate a high degree of sustained care management [1].

In this paper we describe the coordination and communication practices of a rural cancer navigation organization, identify the role that technology plays in supporting navigation work, and uncover opportunities where CSCW support could improve cancer navigation. We describe the various roles and responsibilities present in a cancer navigation organization and map these tasks to common phases of the breast cancer journey [12]. We classify our findings into five key categories: resource monitoring, knowledge transfer, case management, long term navigation, and the development of best practices. For each category we review cancer navigators' current strategies, identify challenges, and offer design opportunities. Through our work we offer new insight into how socio-technical systems may support cancer navigation.

Our work makes the following two main contributions to CSCW:

1. We introduce cancer navigation as a collaborative care network, and describe current navigation practices with a focus on communication and coordination techniques and technology usage.
2. We identify opportunities to support cancer navigation through future technological innovation and CSCW

CSCW'14, February 15 - 19 2014, Baltimore, MD, USA

http://dx.doi.org/10.1145/2531602.2531645

research, thus expanding the design opportunities for collaborative health technologies.

Many of the lessons learned from our case study can be applied to other cancer navigation programs or to programs with non-traditional health professionals who play similar roles. As researchers continue to try to understand and improve cooperation within the hospital and healthcare settings, we must consider ways of extending this cooperation to professionals who do not fall within the traditional hospital setting or role, but with whom coordination is imperative for supporting patients. As new technologies, such as personal health records and electronic medical records, are introduced to health systems, an increasing amount of healthcare will occur outside of the hospital walls, making coordination increasingly complex and essential.

HISTORY OF CANCER NAVIGATION

Researchers over the past several decades have documented a severe disparity in healthcare delivery in the United States. People at lower socio-economic levels face higher cancer incidence and lower survival rates [8, 30].

In 1990, Dr. Harold Freeman developed cancer navigation (also called patient navigation) to address this healthcare gap. At that time, only 38% of operable breast cancer patients in Harlem survived for five years, and 25% of the breast cancer patients that came to the hospital were inoperable due to the cancer being too advanced [9]. The goal of the initial program developed by Freeman was to improve the survival rate of patients diagnosed with breast cancer by using trained community health workers to help patients receive the care they need. These health workers helped patients identify and overcome barriers that hindered their ability to successfully interact with the healthcare system. Over a six-year period, this program correlated to a substantial improvement in 5-year survival rates for breast cancer patients—increasing the rates from 39% to 70% [5].

The goals of cancer navigation programs have since progressed. Navigation originally focused only on providing patients with access to cancer screenings and medical treatment but now includes a growing focus on patient experience and improving perceived quality of life. As a result, cancer navigation organizations have increased their ability to provide services related to psychosocial support and quality of life outcomes [24].

While all cancer navigation organizations work to eliminate barriers faced by cancer patients, there is currently no standardized approach to providing this care across the various cancer navigation organizations nationwide. Cancer navigation remains highly localized, which has the benefit of enabling the organizations to provide the cultural sensitivity and understanding necessary to meet the unique needs of their neighborhoods and patients [17].

RELATED WORK

Medical Care Coordination

Many aspects make hospitals and healthcare centers complex adaptive systems. The intricacy of these sociotechnical systems makes studying their cooperation and coordination methods interesting and important for enhancing medical practices. Previous research has examined many aspects of these systems. For example, research exploring healthcare coordination helped explain how health professionals collaboratively search for information [23] and how staff members communicate in emergency departments [14]. Researchers in this area have also studied how patients interact with information in clinical settings [29]. Further, research has shown how technologies can enhance various medical processes. For example, previous studies deployed and evaluated technology for operating suites in order to enhance surgery coordination [3]. This segment of healthcare research shows how enhanced coordination can improve medical practices. However, past research has primarily focused on examining healthcare systems comprised of patients, physicians, nurses, and pharmacists. In contrast to previous work, our work highlights the need for research that examines healthcare professionals who exist outside of the traditional areas of study, such as cancer navigators, since these professionals will become important stakeholders of future healthcare coordination technologies.

Breast Cancer Patient Challenges

Many researchers have specifically examined the struggles encountered by breast cancer patients. This work helps to explain the importance of breast cancer navigators and the services they offer.

From the time of diagnosis, patients often face dramatic changes in their physical and emotional well-being [27]. Patients must manage physical side effects that result from their treatment including fatigue, nausea, and pain [11, 16]. In addition to these side effects, emotional distress, fear, and feelings of loneliness impact patients' quality of life [6, 25]. Managing information about their disease and treatment can also prove complicated for patients especially when working with multiple healthcare providers [13].

The challenges triggered by a breast cancer diagnosis are typically compounded when patients are ethnic minorities or of a low socioeconomic status. Issues such as lack of insurance, lack of transportation, and language barriers are prevalent within these groups [2].

Cancer Navigation Research

Limited work has been done to study cancer navigation. Most studies focus on providing a general definition and overview of navigation duties, as cancer navigation remains a new and evolving field for researchers [18]. Recent research looked at practices for developing lay navigation programs that recruit volunteers and cancer survivors as cancer navigators for newly diagnosed patients [4, 15, 28]. Understanding the cost effectiveness of cancer navigation programs is another area of interest that presents many challenges [21], as well as gauging patient satisfaction with navigation programs [7].

While all of this work helps to explore cancer navigation practices, there remain gaps in the research. To date we are not aware of any investigation into the work practices of any specific cancer navigation organizations in order to gain a deep understanding of its inner workings. Due to the highly localized nature of cancer navigation, concentrated case studies will help clarify the nuances of navigation work, while providing greater insight into the common strategies, challenges, and opportunities for support across navigation organizations.

Further, we are unaware of any research that has examined a cancer navigation organization as a socio-technical system. In order for HCI research to support navigation, we must gain a clearer insight into the interfaces and technological interactions that impact current navigation strategies. Our research expands on the existing knowledge of cancer navigation by providing a focused study that begins to address these specified research gaps.

METHODS

In the investigation of cancer navigation, our goal was to understand the day-to-day routines of navigators and to explore the use of technology to support the navigation process. We worked with a nonprofit organization that provides navigation and counseling services to patients with any form of cancer. We focus specifically on breast cancer navigation for the purposes of our investigation.

Over a six-month period we conducted 7 semi-structured interviews and 1 focus group session with the employees of a rural cancer navigation organization. Our investigation focused on understanding navigation responsibilities, the navigators' primary challenges, and their technology usage. We transcribed the interviews and focus group for later data analysis. To analyze the data we structured the data using two approaches. For the first approach we organized the data along the established cancer journey framework. Once we understood navigation practices as they relate to a general cancer treatment timeline we focused on constructing a framework around future design opportunities. To surface the themes in our data we used an iterative inductive analysis to cluster segments from the transcripts and develop theme concepts. Members of the research team then verified each of the themes and reviewed the transcriptions for theme validation.

Throughout the course of this project we have also collected data from breast cancer survivors and oncologists working with the cancer navigators. While the analysis of this data is ongoing, we were able to reflect on the interviews from patients and healthcare providers to assess the completeness of our portrayal of the practices of cancer navigators. Namely, we do not have additional data that points to unexplored areas in cancer navigation.

FINDINGS

We conducted our investigation of breast cancer navigation practices in Rome, GA, a rural city with a population of approximately 96,000. The city is supported by three distinct cancer clinics: Harbin Clinic, Floyd Medical Center, and Redmond Regional Medical Center. The navigation program under investigation was developed in 2008 as a non-profit organization to serve patients from all three of the local cancer clinics. In 2012, the organization navigated 901 cancer patients, 37% of whom were breast cancer patients.

Organization Structure

The navigation organization we investigated employs seven individuals: an executive director, an office manager, a social worker, two nurse navigators (referred to as N1 and N2) and two service navigators (referred to as S1 and S2). In the following sections we discuss the responsibilities of these navigators as they relate to the typical steps patients encounter as they progress through their cancer care.

Nurse Navigators

Due to their medical background, nurse navigators primarily work on educating patients about their disease and answering medical questions. Both of the nurse navigators in our organization were registered nurses prior to joining the cancer navigation organization.

Service Navigators

Service navigators focus their expertise on understanding the resources available to patients, identifying patients' needs, and helping patients apply for resources for which they are eligible. Prior to joining the navigation organization in Rome, the service navigators in our organization both had careers in social work.

Mapping Navigation to the Breast Cancer Journey

Understanding the steps a breast cancer patient must go through can be difficult as there are many different types of breast cancer, each with different treatment options available to a patient. Hayes et al. found that commonalities exist across individual cancer journeys, which can be described in five major phases: screening and diagnosis, initial information seeking, acute care and treatment, no evidence of disease, and chronic disease and disease management [12]. In order to demonstrate the role of navigation throughout the breast cancer journey, we will explain how the navigation process changes through these phases (table 1 summarizes the responsibilities of the navigators at each phase). Though we do our best to categorize the process, cancer navigation is a flexible and dynamic activity that is tailored to each patient's individual needs and cancer journeys.

Screening and Diagnosis

The first phase of Hayes et al.'s cancer journey is Screening and Diagnosis. In breast cancer, the first step after an abnormal breast cancer screening result is often surgery. The goal of surgery is to remove as much of the cancer

Phase	Role	Responsibility
Screening and Diagnosis	Nurse Navigator	Meet with patients Introduce patients to navigation Answer medical questions Provide emotional and educational support
Initial Information Seeking	Nurse Navigator	Refer patients to service navigators Follow up with patients as needed to address medical/health questions
	Service Navigator	Meet with patients for initial needs assessment Help patients apply for necessary resources Provide emotional support
Acute Care and Treatment	Nurse Navigator	Provide support at health centers during treatment Answer medical questions that come up during treatment
	Service Navigator	Continue work from previous phase Refer patients to social worker for counseling if needed
No Evidence of Disease/Chronic Disease Management	Nurse Navigator	Follow up with patients as needed
	Service Navigator	Follow up with patients as needed

Table 1: Breakdown of Navigation Responsibilities by Breast Cancer Phase

from the body as possible and to prevent the cancer from returning. Navigators attempt to make first contact with the patient at this point in the cancer journey.

The responsibility of making first contact with patients falls on the nurse navigators. Nurse navigators will meet with the newly diagnosed patients during their first meeting with the general surgeon. In this meeting the navigators focus on providing emotional and educational support. Nurse navigator N1 described the meeting as follows:

There's a lot of different focuses. [Answering] questions is one, to just reassure them that I'm there to support them, I become their shadow. That's what I tell them, 'I'm your shadow through all this. And just know I'm here to do whatever you need me to do.' I can look up records; I can tell you what the doctor said. For instance, the patient gets home and everybody in the room forgot what was said, I can actually go online and read what the doctor said word for word. And then it's to reassure them that we have services that are here and readily available to them whenever they're ready and comfortable with coming here or talking to one of the [service navigators].

Initial Information Seeking

After completing surgery, breast cancer patients will often go through additional treatment including chemotherapy, radiation, or a combination of the two. According to the cancer navigators, there is often a three to four week gap between surgery and treatment. During this time a shift occurs where patients will meet less frequently with nurse navigators and more frequently with service navigators. Referrals usually trigger this shift, in which the nurse navigator provides the office manager with the name and contact information of patients requiring service navigation. The service navigators can then contact the patient to set up future meetings at the cancer navigation office. Similar transfers of patients between nurse and service navigators based on phase and needs is seen throughout the cancer journey, particularly when beginning the initial information seeking phase and the acute care and treatment phase.

With service navigators acting as the primary navigators in the initial information seeking phase, S1 described this time as the most important point for them to meet with patients:

A perfect patient, they know what's going to happen but they haven't started treatment yet. So by the time they start to get those resources, about a couple weeks in, it kind of gets them over the hump.

The service navigators utilize numerous resources to provide aid to eligible patients. Based on a patient's needs, these navigators help patients apply for and receive social security benefits, gas cards and other transportation assistance, assistance with rent, food stamps, cell phones to communicate with their providers, dental assistance, as well as Medicaid and other medical insurance benefits. If service navigators are able to meet with patients prior to the commencement of their chemotherapy or radiation, they are better able to help patients access these resources by the time treatment begins. This timeliness can be particularly important for patients whose ability to access treatment relies solely on accessing these resources. Radiation, for instance, usually requires patients to go to the health center every day for several weeks. For many patients, daily transportation to the health center would not be possible without gas cards or other travel assistance.

To determine which resources a patient requires, the first one-on-one meeting between a patient and service navigator focuses primarily on assessing needs, while also providing an opportunity for relationship building. The service navigators have developed their own resource checklist which they complete as they talk to the patient. This checklist includes all of the resources navigators know they have available as well as a rating scale that helps the navigators predict how much time they will need to spend to obtain the necessary resources for the patients. Both of the service navigators indicated relying heavily on these documents. S2 specifically stated:

[The checklist] gives us a guide and ensures that we are going to gauge everything that we know to gauge.

Another aspect of the one-on-one meeting is evaluating a patient's social support and mental well-being. If needed, service navigators will refer patients to the social worker who works in the navigation organization, or they will provide patients with information about local support groups. All of the navigators discussed the importance of providing counseling for their patients. N2 discussed previous incidents that led to this understanding:

Some people have a lot of support, others have no one. That's been shocking. I thought that everybody had somebody in their life, a friend. And sometimes people get embarrassed and they'll say 'I have lots of friends, I don't need you'. And then when I go to the hospital after their surgery there's nobody there. And they'll say 'I lied to you.'

After completing the needs assessment, service navigators will work directly with patients to help them acquire their needed resources. The ultimate goal is to get the resources to the patients by the start of treatment so that no barriers impede the patient's ability to access the treatment they need. Securing aid for the patients in advance of their treatment allows the patients to focus on their health and not worry about whether or not they will actually be able to receive treatment. During the process of obtaining resources, navigators will put some of the responsibility on the patient, as described by S1:

Almost all of the time, we'll start the process but we want to make them finish it. You know like we'll say 'make this call, we're going to talk to them, we're going to tell them your story, but then we're going to hand you the phone'. Just to give them that autonomy and just to give them that responsibility as well. To make sure we're not just doing it for them. It also just gives them that empowerment, I think, because you know they have a problem that's bigger than they are, and then if we give them the tools to do it, they've fought that problem. And so to me it's just a good way to give them back some control.

Acute Care and Treatment

As patients begin their post-surgery medical treatment, the emphasis returns to the nurse navigators. During treatment, nurse navigators often meet patients at the health centers where their treatment takes place to provide an added level of emotional support. In addition, nurse navigators continue to provide education to patients by answering medical questions as they arise throughout the treatment. As patients begin to experience various side effects, this support becomes particularly significant. N2 described the importance of being available to answer these medical questions for patients' emotional stability:

Chemo nurses are really busy... If someone's panicked you don't want to be called back at the end of the day, and you don't want to go to the emergency room. A lot of things that people freak out about is a common side effect. So we try to nip that and that way they are at peace.

Also throughout this phase, service navigators will continue to help a patient apply for available resources if the applications could not be completed prior to treatment. The role of the service navigator then begins to shift towards providing the level of emotional support desired by the patient. Patients may indicate this desire by visiting the cancer navigation office or calling their service navigator. At this point, maintaining continuous communication with navigators is the responsibility of the patient. However, if a navigator determined in the needs assessment that a patient required counseling from the social worker, the social worker will organize counseling sessions during this phase, although the time period will change based on individual needs.

No Evidence of Disease/Chronic Disease Management

As patients move forward in their breast cancer journey, their relationship with the navigation organization can vary. Some patients will stay in close contact and come in to the navigation office frequently while others do not. All charts and files created by the navigators are saved if needed for later reference. As patients go through treatment, the service and nurse navigators will often follow up with them to ensure their care is continuing as expected. N1 detailed how she follows up with patients:

When I get a free day, what I try to do with those is just sit down and call and say 'hey, just wanted to see how you're doing, how's your treatment going' and just follow up. And it may take me several days to do that, just pulling a handful of charts at a time, but I try to follow up with them as much as I can.

DESIGN OPPORTUNITIES

In examining cancer navigators' daily workloads, we found that the majority of their responsibilities revolve around five central themes: resource monitoring, knowledge transfer, case management, long term navigation, and development of best practices. For each of these themes we discuss the strategies developed by the navigators to handle the workload, current challenges, and design implications that may help direct future research in the cancer navigation space.

Resource Monitoring

Current Strategies

Resource tracking is an important and continuous task for the service navigators. Financial institutions such as foundations continuously open and close due to the availability of funds. This fluctuation causes navigators to constantly search for new resources. To find resources and track their availability over time, navigators use basic search engines. Both service navigators mentioned using

Google frequently to look up possible resources for patients. S1 discussed with us how communication between navigators helps promote efficient searching and reduces the potential for overlapping efforts:

We communicate really well together, like, if I go and I get somebody's rent paid I immediately tell [the other service navigator]. Or if she gets somebody's power bill paid then I know about it. So then that way we know, 1) that it worked and 2) just to be careful with it. You know, because we don't want to drain them. And so it's really, there's not an official way of doing it, we just kind of talk it out and tell each other.

Challenges

One of the biggest challenges facing navigators is the decline of money and resources available to patients. As N2 described:

The resources started drying up as the economy, so we didn't have as much to offer.

The distribution of limited resources is an obstacle that navigators address up front through the needs assessment. They work to ensure they do not over-utilize limited resources so that high needs patients are able to access the resources. As S1 discusses, ensuring the availability of resources for those who really need them is not only important for the patients, but for the organization's reputation as well:

We really like to keep our resources kind of close to the chest because we don't want other people to take advantage of them. And then we can kind of do an internal process of screening. You know, like if we know a certain association will pay rent, we don't want to refer everybody that comes through that says 'oh, I need my rent paid'. We don't want to refer them because we know those funds will go out and then they'll stop seeing us as a viable referring agency. So we kind of do our own little screening process

Resources also tend to be limited to patients beginning treatment. Patients who do not inform navigators of their needs early in the process often do not receive needed aid. This lack of flexibility in the aid distribution process inhibits navigators' abilities to assist high needs patients who are at later points in the cancer journey. S1 opened up about recently trying to deal with this issue.

That patient I was telling you that came in yesterday, his last radiation treatment is today, and they came in yesterday. And I know they were struggling. They're a $700 a month income with seven people in the house. And it was hard because it's like I could have gotten you at least $100, but now we're going to have to see if we can even get that.

Design Implications

An intrinsic conflict exists when it comes to collaboration across cancer navigation organizations. Sharing strategies, resources, and services may be key to developing a collective practice that currently does not exist in cancer navigation. Such a collective practice could help in growing existing organizations, providing a larger variety of services to patients in any particular community, and help in building new navigation organizations in communities that do not yet have them.

The decline of available resources, and the risk of depleting available resources further, hinders the development of such a collective practice. If navigators were to share their resources with organizations across the nation they risk not being able to provide for their own patients should the resource become exhausted.

This conflict indicates a direct need for CSCW researchers to explore ways in which cooperation can be promoted amongst navigation organizations that enhance the collective navigation practice and best supports the needs of individual patients and communities. For example, tools which allow navigators across organizations to share search strategies or rank resource providers may prove beneficial. Technologies such as these will allow navigators to find resources more efficiently without the fear of losing specific resources.

Knowledge Transfer

Current Strategies

Throughout any given day, cancer navigators are continuously interacting with providers, patients and with each other. Communication with providers in the community we investigated is particularly crucial for the nurse navigators, who rely on the doctor's schedules to determine when new patients are being diagnosed. Some technological solutions begin to support this collaboration. Nurse navigators in our rural community received access to doctors' calendars and patients' electronic medical records and have included reviewing these sources as part of their daily routine. While the nurse navigators no longer need to wait for clinical nurses to fax individual schedules, N1 did share that sorting through all of the calendars does take a significant amount of time:

Per week I print 14 schedules of the different doctors and their PA's. And what I do is I go through them usually, there's me and there is one other nurse. And what I usually do is go through and each day or the day before I mark for the next day... it may take a good hour to really sit down and look through the system.

In addition to providers, communication between navigators proves important for the organization's success. We already discussed how internal communication helps in sharing resources. Open communication and collaboration also assists navigators in managing the unpredictable nature of their work and their patients. N1 described a recent example:

Yesterday [the other nurse navigators] was out of the office at 4 o'clock, got a call one of her patients was in the hospital in a panic mode, needed somebody here now. So I just dropped everything. I went there and I stayed with him until she got there. So those are things we try to do, we're good about helping each other with those kind of things.

Open communication also helps the cancer navigators provide emotional support to one another. The service navigators discussed how they would usually talk with one another after meeting with a patient, and hold an informal debrief.

Maintaining open communications between navigators also leads to positive effects on the patients, by providing an environment unlike other healthcare facilities. N2 and S2, respectively, shared their perception of this effect:

We're almost like a family. And when they come here, it's not a clinical environment, and if they're having a problem with a doctor or they're uncomfortable about something, this is a safe place and confidential.

There's no task list. We know each other's schedules and we know what's going on in each other's days. I think people that are used to being in an office, it sounds like we are just running amuck. But we're not; we know what we're all doing. And the patients really appreciate it because they'll say 'it feels like I just became part of your family'. They say, 'I have my support system now'.

By using open and casual communication between navigators, the organization has also provided a system that promotes trust and communication with their patients.

Challenges

The nature of cancer navigation provides navigators with the continuous challenge of remaining flexible while distributing their time to as many patients as possible. This challenge affects both nurse and service navigators, who all discussed the unpredictability of every patient meeting they hold. N2 specifically discussed the high degree of variability in regards to meeting times:

You don't ever know how a patient is going to handle something. You might speak with them 10-15 minutes or you could be caught up for 2 hours.

Between organizing appointments around doctors' schedules and continuously holding meetings with irregular time intervals, communicating with stakeholders takes the majority of a navigator's day.

Design Implications

Future work should look at supporting cancer navigators' use of open and continuous communication with providers, patients, and other navigators as this communication greatly benefits the organization. Access to electronic medical records has already helped to alleviate some of the time constraints placed on nurse navigators. Hospitals and healthcare centers continue to implement technology that allows for greater interoperability, providing an increased level of communication between providers and other stakeholders. Cancer navigators should also be considered a primary stakeholder for future implementations. Elevating their role could be a critical step in allowing cancer navigators to spend more time with patients, and thus allowing them to reach a broader group of patients who could benefit from the navigation services. Tools that focus on awareness and allow a navigator to see when the other navigators are available may also help when unpredictable events occur. Ultimately, tools ought to promote flexibility and easier collaboration.

Case Management

Current Strategies

Over the course of a year, each navigator works with hundreds of patients, each with different needs. During cancer navigation, a paper file is created for each patient. This file includes a needs assessment form, navigators' notes, and resource application forms, and is shared across the organization should a patient work with multiple navigators. These files are never thrown away; one navigator even discussed having a specific location for files of deceased patients. While managing caseloads of this magnitude can be complicated, each navigator developed their own personalized method for organizing patient files. S1 described how she places files in certain locations based on her perceptions of the patient:

I have my files that I put everybody in, but then, if I know they're going to be calling me I just kind of keep them, put them in a different spot, just so I can grab their chart when they call.

While service navigators must manage a large number of files, they work entirely from the cancer navigation office building. Nurse navigators developed more complicated strategies to deal with the added mobility required in their job as they meet patients in surgery, chemotherapy, and radiation appointments. Any information or patient files a nurse navigator will need is organized by meeting date so that she can take a day's worth of files with her as she moves between healthcare centers. N1 described her personal strategy:

What I do is I just carry them for the day. The day's worth of files. I pick them up in the mornings because sometimes the doctors go in for an appointment and they may be so far behind and if you don't take your charts what's going to happen is you can't get back to the office to get them.

Although each navigator's case management strategy was different based on where they stored files and when they moved files, each focused on the usage of paper files that included patients' needs assessments, personal notes on the patient, and copies of resource applications that had been submitted.

Challenges

Large workloads place a great deal of pressure on memory and mental capacity. One of the service navigators mentioned struggling to remember patients' names when she runs into them unexpectedly. Further, N1 discussed the challenge of having such a high ratio of cancer patients in the community to available navigators:

There's just so many cancers with two nurses there's no way we can cover them all.

The office space required to store the files for all of the cancer navigation patients presents an additional challenge. Navigators store their files in several locations around the office including desks, drawers, and file cabinets.

Design Implications

Future research ought to examine ways to alleviate the cognitive load placed on cancer navigators working with a large number of patients. Over the course of a month navigators typically manage hundreds of patients.

Improved scheduling systems may help navigators remain adaptable for their patients. For example, scheduling tools that consider the amount of time a navigator spent with each patient in previous meetings could help navigators develop more accurate schedules.

Opportunities for technical implementations to help with file storage, thus saving office space may be particularly important for larger navigation organizations. Reminder based systems may also be useful in following up and tracking information for patients once they begin to meet with navigators less frequently. This shift usually happens once patients progress in their treatment and receive the resources for which they are eligible.

Technological implementations that educate communities about the navigation organization and their services may also help the limited number of navigators reach a higher percentage of cancer patients.

While a large variety of tools may be useful in case management, caution must be taken when introducing new technologies into cancer navigation organizations that support patients of low socioeconomic status. Technological implementations designed to support navigation work must take the physical environment under consideration. Many of the high-needs patients do not have access to technology. Since patients meet the service navigators at the cancer navigation center, obvious technological implementations may cause a disconnect between the navigation environment and the environments patients' are accustomed to.

Preserving the casual atmosphere when navigators meet with patients may be important for maintaining relationships between navigators and their patients. The executive director of the organization described what a drastic effect a building's atmosphere can have on patients:

[We] had a gentleman who was a high needs patient. He was just really resistant to treatment and [S1] talked to him for a few minutes and realized his only pair of shoes was a pair of sneakers with the toes out of them, and so he was embarrassed to go to the fancy cancer center without decent shoes.

This description illustrates one situation in which the environment itself directly impacted a patient's willingness to receive treatment. In order to prevent similar issues from occurring in the navigation center, technologies and changes made to cancer navigation facilities must consider impacts on the patients who work directly with the navigators and the environment navigators promote.

Long-Term Navigation

Current Strategies

When mapping cancer navigators' responsibilities to the breast cancer journey, one can see that the work and services are heavily weighted towards the beginning of the journey. Many of the navigators mentioned that they try to follow up with patients when they get some free time to see how they are doing during or after treatment. However, large caseloads and high demands on their time limit navigators' ability to follow up with all of the patients, as mentioned by S2:

Once I actually give them everything they need, I'll keep [his or her file] next to me for a while then I get rid of it, I have to because our drawer is constantly filling up.

Challenges

The large number of new patients that continue to need navigation support impedes on navigators' ability to work with patients after treatment. According to one of the nurse navigators, as many as eight new consults may occur in a single day. This continuous influx of patients keeps the cancer navigators focused on patients in the beginning of their journey, so that they may help the new patients eliminate any barriers to beginning treatment.

Design Implications

There is a growing need to provide ubiquitous care in chronic cancer management. Research shows that cancer survivors face physical and emotional challenges after completing treatment [6, 31]. For example, Rosedale found that "Survival loneliness," which includes feelings of loneliness caused by an increased awareness of mortality and changed sense of identity, affected survivors even 18 years after treatment [25]. In this study Rosedale also found that discussing their feelings of loneliness led survivors to feel relieved. This finding indicates that emotional support from navigators may help tackle survivorship challenges. Moving cancer navigation from a reactive to a more proactive system could greatly benefit their patients, especially the cancer survivors post-treatment. However, the current time constraints, as discussed above, greatly hamper on the ability for cancer navigation to move in this direction.

One way to assist cancer navigators in providing more long term support is to provide systems that allow navigators to be proactive and structure their follow ups with patients in more efficient ways. Technology in the area of home or continuous monitoring could provide this necessary aid. Projects such as Digital Family Portrait have demonstrated the utility of providing awareness to caregivers while retaining privacy and autonomy for the individual [26]. Similar projects could prove useful as a way for navigators to monitor the well-being of patients they no longer see regularly. This information could be particularly important in allowing navigators to use their time efficiently by being better able to assess from a distance the needs of these patients and gain a sense of which patients they should prioritize.

Development of Best Practices

Current Strategies

The development of best practices for cancer navigation falls outside the scope of the navigators' daily work. However, the advancement and expansion of cancer navigation requires the creation of these practices.

Challenges

One of the biggest challenges in developing a set of best practices for cancer navigation programs is that many of the characteristics that promote the success of individual organizations inhibit the creation of standards. One such characteristic is that the backgrounds of the individual navigators help to define the expertise of their organization. The impact of individual backgrounds on the practice of navigation became apparent when discussing how the service navigators provide social security benefits for their patients. One of the service navigators originally worked for several years in the social security department, and brought to the navigation organization the knowledge of how to efficiently complete social security applications and help patients quickly receive their social security benefits. S1 expressed to us the significance of gaining that knowledge in the organization:

So now I know how to go online and look for the diagnosis that we know we are going be covered. And then we print their policy and we highlight it to show them that we know they [the social security department] have 20 days to get this decision... the patient goes, and within 30 minutes they are in and out of social security... And it's all [S2]. If it wasn't for her, I had never heard of it and I've been in healthcare for 8 years and I had never heard of that. And so that's something that she's taught us.

By leveraging individuals' backgrounds and expertise, this cancer navigation group is able to provide a broad range of services to their patients. However, since each navigation organization is comprised of people with various backgrounds, and no standard training program exists to capture this knowledge, there is currently no way for each organization to follow an encompassing and standardized set of best practices.

The high level of localization also makes developing best practices difficult. As previously mentioned, focusing on local impact has allowed the organization to develop processes that work best for the employees, patients, and local health clinics. The nurse navigators' strategy of accessing the doctors' schedules from the health clinics in order to attend all new consults is one example of a localized strategy. However, this process may not work in larger communities with more than three health clinics or in smaller, rural communities that do not have a nearby hospital. Thus, both the significant role of employees' backgrounds and the high localization of cancer navigation organizations hinder the development of national best practices for cancer navigation programs.

Design Implications

Scaling cancer navigation programs will require substantial work in the development of standard practices. We identified two key components absent from the current navigation structure that inhibit navigation growth: sharing of processes and standardized training.

As we discussed, the cancer navigators in this case study worked for years to establish processes and strategies that allow them to work efficiently and systematically. While organizations such as the one we investigated develop their own effective processes, such as the needs assessment process, no tools currently exist which allow separate organizations to share these practices with each other. Thus, each organization must develop their own practices despite the overlap of goals and tasks. Supporting the sharing of business processes can help encourage collaboration and enable the development of future cancer navigation organizations

Another property not yet developed is a standard training model. Navigators did discuss learning new processes and resources by working at the organization. However, currently no standard training exists to use across multiple cancer navigation organizations. Thus the skills and materials that navigators learn remain highly localized, as do the organizations themselves.

Developing a social network for navigators may provide an initial technique for the creation standard practices. Through an online community navigators could share processes, experiences, and stories with one another. This tool may also promote a sense of community across multiple navigation organizations, fostering greater collaboration.

Summary

Each of the themes described in this section help to identify areas for future cancer navigation support and expand the design opportunities for collaborative health technology. Table 2 provides a summary of the findings presented in each theme. All of these areas point to the need for technical support for the scaling of navigation practices. The reliance on informal communication means that current navigation organizations are limited to small teams that are vulnerable to serious disruption if a navigator unexpectedly

Theme	Current Strategy	Challenge	Design Idea
Resource Monitoring	-Online Google searches -Communication with other navigators within the organization	-Limited available resources -Resources are usually only available for patient beginning treatment	-Tool that allows navigators across multiple organizations to share search strategies and rank resource providers
Knowledge Transfer	-Print multiple doctors' schedules to access meeting times -Open communication with other navigators to deal with unexpected events	-Printing individual schedules is time consuming -Navigators must remain flexible as meetings with patients are unpredictable	-Awareness tool that shows which navigators are available during an unexpected event
Case Management	-Shared paper file created for each patient -Try to call patients during down time	-Work with over a hundred patients in a month -Files require office space for storage	-Scheduling tool that considers the amount of time a navigator spent with each patient in previous meetings to develop more accurate schedules
Long-Term Navigation	-Navigation services focus heavily on the beginning of one's cancer journey	-Continuous influx of patients keep navigators focused on new diagnoses	-Home or continuous monitoring systems that allow navigators to check on former patients
Development of Best Practices	-No current strategy, falls outside scope of navigators' daily work	-Many of the characteristics that promote the success of individual organizations inhibit the creation of standards	-Social network systems that begin to foster greater collaboration and sense of community across navigation organizations

Table 2: Summary of Design Opportunities

leaves the group. These limitations also restrict the number the patients who may benefit from the personalized navigation services.

DISCUSSION

Through a detailed analysis of navigation practices in a rural community, we provide researchers with an introduction to navigation processes. Despite over twenty years of existence, only a small fraction of cancer patients are introduced to navigation services. In order for cancer navigation to experience the growth necessary to provide greater impact in cancer care, new tools and technologies will be needed. In the past, information systems that did not account for the high level of collaboration and flexibility in healthcare have failed [20]. As these are common CSCW concepts, researchers in this field are uniquely positioned to develop the tools necessary to support complex navigation work. Further, the ability for future CSCW research to assist in expanding cancer navigation, thus allowing more patients to benefit from their services, will be vital in developing an improved standard of patient-centric cancer care.

Current research investigating healthcare coordination primarily focuses on supporting doctors, nurses, and patients. As demonstrated with cancer navigators, when designing technologies for health systems, researchers must begin to consider healthcare professionals who work closely with patients and their information, but exist outside of the traditional patient-provider context. Our analysis of cancer navigation begins to provide insight into new technological strategies for healthcare. We discuss two specific technologies that have the potential to support current navigation practices: collaborative information retrieval (CIR) systems and personal health records (PHRs).

Supporting collaboration across navigation organizations will be particularly important for enhancing navigation practices. Improving collaboration support will facilitate the development and maintenance of standard practices, afford the communication of a set of best practices between organizations, as well as potentially assist with regional and national resource management. One tool that successfully engaged collaboration in healthcare is the CIR system, which allowed users to share online search results with one another [22]. By developing this type of technology for navigation, cancer navigators from multiple organizations could share available patient resources with each other. This technology fits very well into current resource management practices as navigators primarily use online searches to find resources. By growing the pool of available resources for all navigators, the need to preserve resources may decrease. We also believe this technology could be vital in promoting communication across navigation organizations. Opening this communication will be a critical first step in sharing navigation processes and best practices on a national level.

In additional to CIR systems, PHRs have the potential to play a vital role in enhancing communication between navigators and patients, as well as between navigators and providers. Examining the themes knowledge transfer, case management, and long-term navigation reveals a need for better social connectivity. Regarding knowledge transfer, we discuss how nurse navigators need a more efficient way of monitoring schedules, so that they ensure that they are present for specific patient-doctor meetings. Within case management and long-term navigation we discussed the need for tools to reduce the cognitive load placed on navigators due to high workloads while also helping navigators remain in contact with patients after treatment. PHRs may provide a solution for all of these areas of interest. Many PHR technologies allow patients to designate a network of people who may access their health information. An easy to use PHR tool could allow navigators to see patients' medical appointments and health status both during and after treatment. Over time, PHRs may provide a new way for navigators to monitor and support patients when they are unable to meet face to face. Ultimately leveraging PHRs may further the broader goal of empowering patients in their own care by centering the care network on the patient and enabling the patient to activate that network when new needs arise. PHRs have already proved to be an interesting technology for CSCW researchers exploring healthcare cooperation [19]. Studying the impact of PHR usage by patients on healthcare facilitators, such as cancer navigators, remains an unexplored area. Investigating the use of CIR and PHR technologies provide potential areas for researchers to investigate in order to enhance navigation practices nationally.

CONCLUSION

In this paper, we provide a detailed description of a rural cancer navigation organization, specifically investigating the roles collaboration and technology play in supporting their work. Examining navigation from a CSCW perspective, we see that navigation is a collaborative care system requiring coordination with patients, providers, and other navigators. Our study reveals a number of design opportunities for supporting navigation in the areas of resource monitoring, knowledge transfer, case management, long term navigation, and development of best practices. Two goals drive the presentation of these opportunities to the CSCW community. First, we wish to introduce researchers to a profession that could greatly benefit from further CSCW research. Second, through navigation we expand the design space for collaborative health system technologies.

Each of the design opportunities present challenges that could be considered in future work. Producing more case studies of cancer navigation organizations is necessary to increase our understanding of navigation trends at a national level and to reveal the impact of localization on these organizations. Investigating a wider range of cancer navigation programs could also assist in developing a more cohesive national cancer navigation program.

Cancer navigators are proving to be valuable supporters of patient-centered research. We are particularly interested in working with cancer navigators in the design and implementation of a PHR-based technology deployment and examining the impact of patient-centric technology on the patient-navigator relationship. Supporting cancer navigation will be a critical next step in improving the healthcare experience for cancer patients.

Cancer navigators provide patients with emotional, financial, and logistical support not available anywhere else in cancer care. As such, cancer navigators are uniquely positioned to have a dramatic positive impact on cancer patients' healthcare experiences. By supporting navigation organizations and aiding in their expansion, our goal is to assist them in their quest to provide the millions of people combating cancer each year with the opportunity to benefit from this critical assistance.

ACKNOWLEDGMENTS

This publication is made possible by the Georgia Department of Community Health (DCH) through a contract managed by Georgia Tech Research Corporation. DCH is not responsible for any misuse of copyright infringement with respect to publication.

REFERENCES

1. American Cancer Society, "Breast Cancer Facts & Figures 2011-2012" (2011). [Online]. Available: http://www.cancer.org/acs/groups/content/@epidemiologysurveilance/documents/document/acspc-030975.pdf. [Accessed 22 May 2013].

2. Ashing-Giwa, K. T., Padilla, G., Tejero, J., Kraemer, J., Wright, K., Coscarelli, A., Clayton, S., et al. Understanding the breast cancer experience of women: a qualitative study of African American, Asian American, Latina and Caucasian cancer survivors. *Psycho-oncology*, *13*, 6 (2004), 408–28.

3. Bardram, J. E., Thomas R. H. Peri-operative coordination and communication systems: A case of CSCW in medical informatics. In *Proc. Of the CSCW 2010 workshop on CSCW Research in Healthcare: Past, Present and Future*, ACM Press (2010).

4. Braun, K. L., Allison, A., Tsark, J. U. Using Community-Based Research Methods to Design Cancer Patient Navigation Training. *Prog Community Health Partnersh, 2*, 4 (2010), 329–340.

5. Calhoun, E., Whitley, E. M., Esparza, A., Ness, E., Greene, A., Garcia, R., & Valverde, P. A national patient navigator training program. *Health promotion practice*, *11*, 2 (2010), 205–15.

6. Cappiello, M., Cunningham, R. S., Knobf, M. T., & Erdos, D. Breast cancer survivors: information and support after treatment. *Clinical nursing research*, *16*, 4 (2007), 278–93.

7. Donelan, K., Mailhot, J. R., Dutwin, D., Barnicle, K., Oo, S. A., Hobrecker, K., Percac-Lima, S., et al. Patient perspectives of clinical care and patient navigation in follow-up of abnormal mammography. *Journal of general internal medicine*, *26*, 2, (2011), 116–22.

8. Freeman, H. P. Race, poverty, and cancer. *Journal of the National Cancer Institute*, *83*, 8 (1991), 526–7.

9. Freeman, H. P. The impact of Clinical Trial Protocols on Patient Care Systems in a Large City Hospital. *Cancer* supplement, *72*, 9 (1993), 2834–2838.

10. Freund, K.M., Battaglia, T., Calhoun, E., Dudley, D.J., Fiscella, K., Paskett, E., Raich, P.C., et al. National Cancer Institute Patient Navigation Research Program: methods, protocol, and measures. *Cancer*, *113*, 12 (2008), 3391–9.

11. Gill, K. M., Mishel, M., Belyea, M., Germino, B., Germino, L.S., Porter, L., LaNey, I.C., Stewart, J. Triggers of uncertainty about recurrence and long-term treatment side effects in older African American and Caucasian breast cancer survivors. *Oncology nursing forum, 31,* 3 (2004), 633-9.

12. Hayes, G.R., Abowd, G.D., Davis, J.S., Blount, M.L., Ebling, M., Mynatt, E.D. Opportunities for Pervasive Computing in Chronic Cancer Care. In *Proc. of Pervasive* (2008). 262-279

13. Klasnja, P., Hartzler, A. C., Unruh, K. T., & Pratt, W. Blowing in the wind: unanchored patient information work during cancer care. In *Proc. CHI 2010,* ACM Press (2010).

14. Lee, Soyoung, et al. Loosely formed patient care teams: communication challenges and technology design. In *Proc. Computer Supported Cooperative Work 2012*, ACM Press (2012).

15. Lorhan, S., Cleghorn, L., Fitch, M., Pang, K., McAndrew, A., Applin-Poole, J., Ledwell, E., et al. Moving the Agenda Forward for Cancer Patient Navigation: Understanding Volunteer and Peer Navigation Approaches. *Journal of cancer education : the official journal of the American Association for Cancer Education*. (2012).

16. "Managing Chemotherapy Side Effects," Breastcancer.org (2013). [Online]. Available: http://www.breastcancer.org/treatment/chemotherapy/side_effects. [Accessed 20 May 2013].

17. Nguyen, T.-U. N., & Kagawa-Singer, M. Overcoming barriers to cancer care through health navigation programs. *Seminars in oncology nursing*, *24*, 4 (2008), 270–8.

18. Pedersen, A., & Hack, T. F. Pilots of oncology healthcare: a concept analysis of the patient navigator role. *Oncology nursing forum*, *37*, 1 (2010), 55–60.

19. Piras, E. M., Zanutto A. Prescriptions, x-rays and grocery lists. Designing a Personal Health Record to support (the invisible work of) health information management in the household. In *Proc. Computer Supported Cooperative Work 2010*, ACM Press (2010).

20. Pratt, W., Reddy, M. C., McDonald, D. W., Tarczy-Hornoch, P., Gennari, J. H. Incorporating ideas from computer-supported cooperative work. *Journal of biomedical informatics*, *37*, 2, (2004) 128–37.

21. Ramsey, S., Whitley, E., Mears, V. W., McKoy, J. M., Everhart, R. M., Caswell, R. J., Fiscella, K., et al. Evaluating the cost-effectiveness of cancer patient navigation programs: conceptual and practical issues. *Cancer, 115*, 23, (2009), 5394-403.

22. Reddy, M. C., Jansen, B. J. A model for understanding collaborative information behavior in context: A study of two healthcare teams. *Information Processing & Management, 44*, 1 (2008), 256-73.

23. Reddy, M. C., Spence, P. R. Collaborative information seeking: A field study of a multidisciplinary patient care team. *Information Processing & Management*, *44*, 1 (2008), 242–255.

24. Robinson-white, S., Conroy, B., & Slavish, K. H. Patient Navigation in Breast Cancer, *Cancer Nursing*, *33*, 2 (2010), 127–140.

25. Rosedale, M. Survivor loneliness of women following breast cancer. *Oncology nursing forum*, *36*, 2 (2009), 175–83.

26. Rowan, J., Mynatt, E.D. Digital family portrait field trial: support for aging in place. In *Proc. CHI 2005*, ACM Press (2005).

27. Salonen, P., Kellokumpu-Lehtinen, P.-L., Tarkka, M.-T., Koivisto, A.-M., & Kaunonen, M. Changes in quality of life in patients with breast cancer. *Journal of clinical nursing*, *20*, 1-2 (2011), 255–66.

28. Steinberg, M. L., Fremont, A., Khan, D. C., Huang, D., Knapp, H., Karaman, D., Forge, N., et al. Lay patient navigator program implementation for equal access to cancer care and clinical trials: essential steps and initial challenges. *Cancer*, *107,* 11 (2006), 2669–77.

29. Unruh, K. T., et al. Transforming clinic environments into information workspaces for patients. In *Proc. CHI 2010,* ACM Press (2010).

30. Wells, B. L., & Horm, J. W. Race and Socioeconomic Factors. *American Journal of Public Health, 82*, 10 (1992), 1383–1385.

31. Zebrack, B. J. Cancer survivor identity and quality of life. *Cancer Practice*, *8*, 5 (2000), 238–243.

Craving, Creating, and Constructing Comfort: Insights and Opportunities for Technology in Hospice

Robert Douglas Ferguson[1], Michael Massimi[2], Emily Crist[1], and Karyn Moffatt[1]

[1] School of Information Studies, McGill University
3661 Peel Street, Montreal, QC, H3A 1X1

[2] Microsoft Research Cambridge
21 Station Road, Cambridge, CB1 2FB, UK

robert.douglas.ferguson@mail.mcgill.ca, mmassimi@microsoft.com,
emily.crist@mail.mcgill.ca, karyn.moffatt@mcgill.ca

ABSTRACT

Hospice is a medical setting for patients with terminal illnesses where active treatment is withdrawn in favor of providing comfort and dignity at the end of life. Providing comfort extends beyond managing physical pain to include social, emotional, spiritual, and environmental aspects of care. We studied technology's role in achieving these multifaceted dimensions of comfort through interviews with 16 family members of past hospice patients. Comfort was an ongoing pursuit, requiring the involvement of diverse stakeholders; communication technologies were selectively chosen in service of this achievement. We provide opportunities and recommendations for technologies in hospice, including the need for varying degrees of richness and symmetry, and for support for life-affirming acts. To our knowledge, this constitutes the first study, in the CSCW and HCI literatures, of communication technology use during the final days of a person's life, with implications both for hospice and for the end of life more broadly.

Author Keywords

Comfort; hospice, palliative, and end of life care; computer-mediated communication; family communication.

ACM Classification Keywords

H.5.m [Information Interfaces and Presentation (e.g. HCI)]: Miscellaneous.

INTRODUCTION

Entrance into hospice care marks withdrawal of active medical intervention aimed at curing fatal conditions, to instead provide "a dignified, comfortable death for the terminally-ill and to care for the patient and family together" [38]. Admission into end of life care—an umbrella term encompassing hospice residences, palliative care facilities, and agencies that provide home-based care services for terminal patients—can be an exceptionally stressful time for family and friends, who seek to provide for the physical, emotional, and social well-being of a dying loved one, in addition to tending to their own needs.

CSCW'14, February 15 - 19 2014, Baltimore, MD, USA
Copyright 2014 ACM 978-1-4503-2540-0/14/02...$15.00.
http://dx.doi.org/10.1145/2531602.2531631

Numerous studies have associated access to strong social support as an important component of quality of life for hospice care patients [16, 17, 42–44], and individuals with higher levels of social support have been found to cope better with pain [39]. Communication-centered therapeutic interventions have also been effective in later reducing grief symptoms for family members [21]. Together, this body of evidence points to the importance of communication and social support as components of high-quality end of life care.

Despite these benefits, opportunities for communication and social support may be limited. Patients will likely experience varying levels of lucidity and alertness across and within days. Family members may have competing responsibilities or geographical constraints that limit the frequency and timing of face-to-face visits. Institutions often have visiting hour limits that can further impede and complicate the task of scheduling and coordinating care. Moreover, while some patients will experience too little interaction and may feel lonely and isolated, others will experience too much and may become overwhelmed with the frequency and duration of visits. Such patients may want to limit visits from their extended social network, enabling them to focus their energy on their closest friends and family. In these cases, they may elect one or two caregivers to act as a spokesperson to their larger network. While this reduces exertion on the part of the patient, this can be an arduous task for caregivers as they are likely already overburdened with other caregiving responsibilities.

In this paper, we present findings from interviews with 16 individuals about their past experiences caring for a close family member or friend in hospice. In describing their interactions with dying relations, participants revealed the provision of comfort as a chief concern and motivating force that extended well beyond simply ensuring that their loved one was free from pain. Rather, comfort was a multi-dimensional state under constant renegotiation. In pursuing comfort, participants spoke of creating home-like spaces and of constructing life-affirming experiences such as the reliving of past memories and the sharing of small talk or a meal. Comfort was also multi-directional: participants described not only their own efforts to comfort patients, but—in describing patients' actions—revealed how the patients themselves acted to comfort caregivers. Lastly, they spoke of the need to comfort and support each other.

Views surrounding technology and its adoption were complex. While face-to-face interaction was prized, technology was seen to provide unique benefits. Mobile phones gave patients autonomy over their social interactions, letting them choose who they wished to contact and when. Low-richness technologies such as texting enabled one participant to filter out the realities of her mother's condition and to momentarily experience pre-diagnosis-like interactions. Email and social networking sites also enabled family and friends efficient means of coordinating care and sharing information. Yet, technology also caused problems. Differing views on its ideal use led to privacy violations, and conflicts surrounding how and when information should be shared. From these findings, we suggest opportunities for design that reflect the unique constraints of the hospice setting, and that are sensitive to the value participants placed on the provision of comfort.

BACKGROUND

To set the stage for our investigation, we first briefly review the current state of research in our field concerning the end of life as a domain of inquiry. Noting that this is the first study in the literature to examine technology use during the final days of a person's life, we present an introduction to the provenance and values of hospice care. This sketch then leads us to review efforts in the nursing and medical fields on introducing technology into the hospice setting. While promising, these explorations (a) focus on introducing existing technologies rather than designing new ones, and (b) seek to improve existing methods of care rather than considering new possibilities.

HCI, CSCW, and the End of Life

The end of life has been a relatively recent, but fruitful, domain for exploring technology use and design in the HCI and CSCW communities. Key themes in this domain include materiality, identity, temporality, and ethics [25]. Massimi and Charise proposed the need for a humanistic design approach to the end of life that they termed thanatosensitive design [24]. Since then, work in the end of life has focused on a few key issues. The first is materiality and how objects and data would be potentially passed down, destroyed, or otherwise handled following a death [15, 32]. Bespoke technology heirlooms have been proposed as a way to address these issues [31]. A second strand of research has focused more on remembrance at the cultural and national levels, with efforts to create digitally-enhanced memorials of genocide [27], made possible by multi-lifespan information systems that permit the safeguarding of data [11]. A final strand has focused on social support and computer-mediated communication regarding the end of life, and highlighted issues concerning "continuing bonds" [22]—the idea that after a death the relationship is not necessarily severed, but continued in a new form [13] and that social media sites may present a space for enacting this relationship [4, 13]. Other work has investigated the features of websites that are helpful for bereavement support groups [23]. It is in this vein of social support that our work most closely fits, but our unique contribution here is that we focus on social support and the achievement of comfort *during the process of dying*, rather than following a death. This is a space that has yet to be directly explored in the HCI and CSCW literatures.

Modern Hospice and End of Life Care

While caring for the dying has been practiced for many centuries and in many contexts, the modern hospice movement can be traced to the 1960s, when Dame Cicely Saunders advocated for medical professionals to view their patients as human beings with multiple needs, rather than simply as sites for treating disease. She referred to this broadened emphasis as "total pain" [6]. From the earliest days, hospice care has placed a primary focus on the concept of comfort; in fact, aspects of hospice care are sometimes referred to as "comfort care" or "palliative care" [26]. This term refers to ongoing, concerted efforts made by a care team to provide for the patient by withdrawing active treatment and instead focusing efforts on maintaining and improving the patient's quality of life [48].

From a traditional medical perspective, comfort is often synonymous with pain reduction and management [6]. In other words, comfort is the absence of physical pain associated with the disease or side effects from its treatment. In this conceptualization, comfort is then a patient state that is achieved through the administration of drugs or application of pain relief devices. Alertness is a secondary, but often present, concern. Both drugs and disease progression may result in drowsiness, sluggishness, and communication problems. Through this lens, achieving comfort is achieving the highest level of alertness possible while alleviating pain with analgesics and narcotics [33].

Hospice advocates have challenged this framing. In hospice care, patients may be encouraged to manage their pain through alternative forms of therapy such as massage or meditation [46]. In addition to an expanded set of treatments for physical pain, the hospice model of care sees patients as people who have needs for emotional and spiritual comfort as well. Emotional support may include suggestions for contacting and communicating with friends and family, or the provision of a therapist or counselor [34]. It may involve occupational therapies such as art or music therapy [8]. A patient's spiritual comfort is another important aspect of their humanity; at the end of life, patients may struggle to find solace and peace with respect to their mortality. Clergy are often present in hospices to tend to patients' spiritual needs.

While most scholarly work focuses on the comfort of the patient, there is a growing literature that addresses the comfort of medical professionals in this setting. Nurses and doctors who deal with death on a regular basis may be negatively impacted by their exposure to the accompanying existential and emotional pain, often called "compassion fatigue" [40]. Medical professionals must not only grieve their own loss of the patient, but must confront the grief of the family and friends who may be present.

Hospice settings are also unique in their provision of support for friends and family of the patient. Many hospices will offer bereavement support groups and assist families in making arrangements after the individual passes away [10]. This is to say little of the ongoing work of managing visitors and providing updates to the family. This support, however, is generally provided informally (e.g., through bedside conversations between staff and visitors). At the same time it is worth noting that hospice has not been proven to reduce subsequent grief reactions [18]. While the loss of a loved one is clearly an important personal event and there is considerable advocacy for supporting family through this transition, the psychology, psychiatry, and medical literatures generally fail to find experimental results that indicate bereavement and its attendant grief cause long-term medically-detectable changes [3, 7].

Technology Use in Hospice Settings

Like other medical settings, stakeholders in hospice care include the patient, his/her family and friends, and the medical care team, staff, community liaisons (e.g., social workers, clergy), and professional caregivers. Each of these has different communication goals and preferences.

For the patient, communication may be impeded by health conditions or treatments that impair vocal, auditory, and motor function. Communication is of course important for sharing care preferences, but it is equally important for acts of spiritual and emotional expression. For example, terminally ill patients may create blogs to share their thoughts regarding their conditions and how they would like to die [41]. In a hospice or palliative care setting, assistive communication technologies may be used to overcome these barriers [37], but more commonly, family members are charged with making health decisions [36].

The shortened lifespan of hospice residents and hurdles to learning new technology near end of life present challenges for researchers when designing and validating technologies for hospice residents [47]. Although many online support communities exist, some evidence suggests they may be used mostly for informal emotional support and the sharing of personal experiences, rather than for formal information seeking [5].

Some patients elect to receive palliative care at home, rather than in a hospice facility. Caring for the patient usually falls to family members, although paid caregivers can sometimes be afforded. Health researchers and social workers have proposed telephone-based interventions that target family members in order to reduce stress and depression by helping caregivers develop coping skills [19].

In home-based hospice settings, telephones, videophones, and telemetric devices can be used to communicate with medical staff regarding the ongoing care of the patient [20]. A number of studies in this space have investigated the barriers to adoption and efficacy of videophones in telehospice [33]. Others have explored the feasibility of operating home-based hospice systems and provide design recommendations for web-based hospice interventions [45]. The use of Skype as a means for geographically-distributed visitors to converse with dying patients has also been explored, with promising results [1].

With the exception of telemetric devices, communication technologies in hospice are usually off-the-shelf devices such as telephones or videophones. Though telephones and videophones provide quality synchronous communication, they offer comparatively limited asynchronous capabilities. Given the sensitivity and gravity of the issues discussed in hospice settings, and the large proportion of time that communicants may be inaccessible, technologies that target asynchronous communication may particularly improve communication for stakeholders in the hospice setting. In all of this, the achievement of comfort remains an unstated goal in the design and application of technology.

METHOD

As noted above, hospice care means providing for the whole person and their family, extending beyond pain management. With this as our starting point, we undertook an empirical interview study to more closely examine what it is that technology might provide in pursuit of a multi-dimensional concept of care consistent with hospice values.

Participants

Over a period of 10 months (May 2012 to Feb 2013), we interviewed adult family members and friends of recently deceased individuals (n=16[1]), asking them to describe their most recent hospice experience. Participants were recruited through advertisements distributed via partnerships with hospices across Canada, posted within the university, and advertised on several hospice and cancer-centric social networks on the web. Interviews were recorded either in person or over the phone. Participants received $10 in compensation for their time.

Participants were between 21 and 69 years of age (mean=40, median=34). The overwhelming majority was female (14/16), which is not surprising in light of previous studies documenting how females generally assume primary responsibilities of informal caregiving [29]. Participants in our sample generally had a higher than average education, with 81% (13) having an undergraduate university degree or higher. One participant described her information and computer technology (ICT) use as "moderate", while the rest reported "heavy" use.

Participants described hospice experiences taking place in Canada (10), the United States (5), and Pakistan (1). Their

[1] Two additional participants were interviewed, but due to equipment failure their interviews were unrecorded, and thus, are not reported here.

experiences involved 14 unique hospice patients, as in two cases we interviewed 2 different family members about the same hospice patient. All interviews took place within ten years of the patient's death. The majority (12) took place within five years, and of these 9 occurred within two years and 6 within one year. The average reported age of former hospice patients (at death) was 66 years (median = 62) of which 11 were female and 3 were male. Most of the hospice patients described in our interviews died following a cancer diagnosis (14/16); one died due to kidney problems associated with old age, and the other died from complications resulting from COPD (chronic obstructive pulmonary disease). Hospice care ranged from 2 weeks to 6 months. The reported level of ICT use during hospice care also varied across interviews with 29% (4) reporting "none", 43% (6) reporting "light use", 14% (2) reporting "moderate use", and 21% (3) reporting "heavy use". Our sample covered a variety of hospice scenarios including home-based care, residential facilities that emulate the home setting, and full institutional settings within hospitals.

Design

We chose a semi-structured approach to data collection to ensure a baseline level of consistency in the themes discussed, while also allowing participants the freedom to diverge into unanticipated topics. In addition to collecting demographic information on both the respondent and the deceased hospice patient, the interviews covered 3 main themes: (1) expectations for hospice, (2) communication during hospice, and (3) the potential role of technology. Each interview took approximately 1 hour to complete.

Data Analysis

Each interview was transcribed and later coded by two graduate student research assistants. Analysis consisted of two passes: the first to create an initial set of inductively generated codes and the second to categorize these codes into unified themes. Data was analyzed section-by-section, question-by-question, across interviews. The initial phase of coding was completed independently by each research assistant who, upon completion, worked collaboratively to develop consensus across the codes and to cluster them into overarching themes inspired by grounded theory [14].

RESULTS

In this section, we first describe our findings, organizing them into two main themes: (1) how our participants interacted and communicated with hospice patients, and (2) how caregivers coordinated and interacted with other members of the patient's social network. The provision of comfort repeatedly presented itself as a driving motivation, appearing in the way hospice settings, conversation topics, and offerings (particularly of food) were chosen. Comfort was also valued in interactions within the larger social network, with participants often noting how interpersonal strains resulted in its absence.

An additional underlying theme was the uncertainty of the hospice experience. Participants expressed having few preconceptions of hospice care. Though many participants recalled prior experiences from childhood, these early encounters did not inform their adult experiences. As a result, participants felt they had under-anticipated the extent of the demands they would encounter, as exemplified here:

Honestly, I never thought of it. You are in high school and then university and you don't even think of something like that. For my mom, it was very sudden and for my aunt, as I said she had it [cancer] 7 years before when I [was] really young; it didn't even click that it would be something I would have to deal with. –P06

Accordingly, communication and coordination activities tended to be a reactionary response to admission. In settings where treatment and palliative care were co-located in the same institution, that distinction was even more blurred and difficult to anticipate for caregivers. The uncharted nature of hospice influenced nearly all their activities and the way they approached decision-making throughout hospice care.

Connecting with Patients: Constantly Seeking Comfort

Creating and maintaining comfort was a primary value that emerged from participants' descriptions of their hospice experiences, and extended beyond ensuring freedom from pain. Participants worked to maintain continuity between life before, during, and after hospice, and to ease difficulties they encountered in the transition from living to dying.

Recreating Normalcy inside the Hospice

Participants involved in selecting a hospice locale for their loved one sought settings that emulated home. Home-based and home-like settings helped alleviate anxiety regarding the potential for isolation:

The fact that my grandmother had her own TV in her own room [was] especially important to my mom [and] to my grandmother. Like that was something that they were really glad that my grandmother had, a TV in her room. And I think it was because it reduced a sense of isolation or socialized-relation; that it replicated what she had back home, and she would, you know, watch previous programs and the news and whatnot. –P02

Here, access to a TV and personal space, in the form of a room, was seen as extending the stability of home life into the uncertain and ambiguous context of hospice care. The consumption of media was seen as providing hospice patients with a window to the outside world, and to a source of comfort and normalcy that carried over from home life.

This desire to create a sense of normalcy extended beyond the selection of home-like spaces to using activities and visits to (re)create feelings of normal. Families in our sample described using conversation to affirm the life of their loved ones by talking about the past and about other family members. As P15 describes below, many conversations were mundane or ordinary, but these helped to extend day-to-day family life into the hospice setting:

I remember her explaining to me about gardening a lot. TV shows a bit. Francophone TV shows. We would talk about school. What plans I had for the future. –P15

Participants also described how the sharing of meals acted as a focal point for bringing families together and enabled them to be present and have meaningful interactions with their loved ones while in the hospice setting:

It was just like he was at home. Right? Up until the day before he died, he'd come out, and we'd cook him dinner, he'd sit at the dining room table. The Saturday that he died, we had a family barbecue. We had 18 people in the backyard [of the hospice] and we had a barbecue for my dad. –P17

Favorite foods were also offered as a means of providing comfort. For example, P07 would call before her visits to see if her mom wanted *"any treats or sweets or anything like that."* The sharing of food was seen as a life-affirming way of maintaining quality of life, and thus great effort was expended to satisfy wants and to get participants to eat:

Whatever [she] wanted to eat we'd try to get her. She was, you know, she had a hankering all of a sudden for eggs; so whatever she wanted, we would do to keep her eating. –P05

Putting Affairs in Order

While the above actions sought to create comfort in the here and now, other actions were undertaken to plan for future comfort. Although most participants indicated that their loved ones had made funeral arrangements prior to their admission into hospice, almost all described having further conversations near the end of life. These discussions provided loved ones with an understanding of how the deceased wished to be remembered and honored. They were also a way for patients to comfort and reduce the burden on caregivers:

She really did talk about the end of her life quite a bit. She was someone who wanted to make sure every single thing was in order. I can't remember anyone having more things in order than her. Very conscious of who received what, making sure everything was very, very fair, right until the last item and penny. It was important for her to actually hand people the jewelry or the items of hers that she wanted them to have. –P05

Participants described their loved one's anxieties surrounding the handling of their estate and their fears that incomplete arrangements would be burdensome after they passed. The decision to give away one's possessions or sell one's house were emotional moments and part of the hospice patients' acknowledgement of dying.

Regulating Information and Emotion

An additional way comfort was sought was through the withholding of information. Some participants expressed feeling the need to control the flow of information to the person in their care and to change their communication style in order to support their loved one by maintaining an air of optimism and hope. Caregivers acknowledged their own need for support during these times in order to deal with the emotional and physical impacts of caregiving:

Usually we would get very bad news so we'd try not to cry in front of [her]. That was a big part of trying to stay strong for her and at times that felt almost impossible. And at a certain point, I remember we broke down in front of her and she said "oh my God, what did they tell you?" because it was impossible to keep it in anymore. So it was just trying to calm her down, um, talk positively to her, lie to her, we did a lot of lying just to give her hope and tell her that there's still hope, that they're still doing this or there is still that option, and after this, we'd just try to joke around and talk about our everyday lives and distract her and just try to like, try to have just a little bit of the past experiences we had? And I would maybe help her eat, or force her to eat. Yeah that's pretty much how they would go. –P14

In this case, we see several ways that comfort was created. As the participant notes, she regulated her own emotional reaction to negative news to protect her loved one from worrying. She lied and distracted her with jokes and food to maintain an air of optimism. Regulating information and emotion in this way can be seen as an effort to comfort not only her loved one but also herself.

Saying Goodbye

Almost all participants expressed either the experience of—or an expectation for—meaningful conversations at the end. However, while some were able to share intimacy and emotions that they might not otherwise share in day-to-day life, others were not able to have these kinds of conversations. Positive experiences were often associated with the emotional impact of thinking of the future and the importance of loved ones sharing their hopes and dreams for after they pass:

He'd talk about his life and children; [Participant starts crying] that he was taking care of us even if he wasn't there and he would talk about my baby [crying again] because at this point, well at this point, I think dad and I really knew he wasn't going to see her. –P01

Dissatisfaction, on the other hand, was often associated with superficiality and inauthenticity, and feelings that interactions were too mundane or ordinary:

Watching the TV with your grandmother who is dying, when you really feel like you're supposed to be having, like, these profound conversations that have some kind of significant meaning, seemed far too pedestrian, far too mundane, and far too insignificant. –P02

In some cases, external supports could help to guide interaction and help broaden discussion. One participant who did report positive interactions described the role of a simple book in prompting discussions about her mother's past that they may have not otherwise thought to discuss, but that were in fact incredibly meaningful:

What the book does is, it invokes memories, for instance for my mom, it invoked memories of her childhood, her relationship with her parents. Um, special things that happened. It was an absolutely wonderful event, shall I say, of discovery for all of us. –P07

Communication Barriers

Though communication played an important role in creating comfort, communication barriers often impeded its achievement. Changes in energy levels and cognition at the end of life represented a significant communication and coordination challenge for loved ones visiting hospice patients. The impact of pain medications and the effects of declining health also had significant effects on the ability of hospice patients to participate in social interactions. Cognitive impairment due to medications made it difficult for hospice patients to carry conversations, to use devices such as the telephone, and to remember recent or past events:

It was just a chemical cocktail so that also made it difficult to focus and really understand sometimes what was going on around her and it made her extremely sensitive so even if we wanted to suggest an activity to make her feel distracted she would take it the wrong way. Her personality changed. –P14

Respondents also described the ways in which physical changes affected the personality of their loved ones. These physical and cognitive changes were difficult for caregivers because they dramatically changed the quality of interactions they had with their loved ones. They described needing to adjust expectations and communication styles. Conversation also became increasingly one-sided and difficult as contact with the world outside of the hospice setting became increasingly foreign to the patient:

The catching up also was really kind of painful as well because it was always one-sided. I had so much going on and so much to share, and my grandmother wanted to hear about it but you can't have a natural "give and take" in a conversation because the last thing she wants to talk about is what's going on in her life, which can be frustrating. –P02

Participants perceived the lack of conversation topics, in conjunction with decreasing mental alertness, as responsible for awkward interactions with their loved one. While these barriers emerged, sometimes conversations were less important than simply being together:

I didn't really have anything to say I just came over and sat next to her and she was like, "What are you doing?" and I'm like, "I don't know, I just thought I would come over and say hi" and she started tearing up and I started tearing up. You know, we didn't have a big conversation, she just said that she was so glad I was there and I said I was glad I was there and we kind of just sat there, and held hands for 5 or 10 minutes, and kind of went on doing what we were doing. You know, those kinds of things you don't do when everybody's fine. And you know I was glad, I wish we had done more of that. –P08

Role of Technology in Hospice Care

Not surprisingly, when asked about ICT use, participants expressed a strong preference for face-to-face contact. For example P10—though acknowledging a supplemental role for technology—emphatically declared, "*I would never want a last interaction with someone to be via some sort of text interface.*" Despite this emphasis on face-to-face interaction, participants also spoke positively about technology. The telephone was the most frequently used ICT by caregivers and hospice patients and preferred for its ease of access:

The cordless phone was a wonder. Like that was an awesome technology for her because she didn't have to get out of bed. And wireless things were like things that seemed to be really remarkable. I remember at some point in her home they got a wireless fireplace control. So that she could like turn it on or off, up or down from the bed. –P02

For this hospice patient, wireless devices enhanced her quality of life and afforded her a level of independence. With access to a cordless phone, she could seek out social interactions autonomously, and alert caregivers when needs were not being met. A fireplace remote control enabled her to independently control her environment.

Contrary to the general emphasis on face-to-face contact, participants sometimes sought less rich communication mediums. Because phones, like face-to-face interaction, carry the emotional tenor of a message, low-richness asynchronous mechanisms such as text messaging were sometimes chosen to maintain emotional distance and filter the realities of the end of life:

A lot of the conversations we had in the clinical setting was her speculating about the cause of her illness and it was really strange because there was a negativity to it... it never felt like I was talking to my mother, but then the text messages she would send me really did. There was a sweetness about them, they weren't ever really about her illness. They were about her and I. So they were kind of an equalizing, leveling, grounding gesture. –P04

In this case, mediation of communication provided a separation of context from message that allowed the participant to connect more directly with her mother and imagine the relationship in a more comforting way.

Almost no one in our sample reported the use of webcams or video chat. While participants spoke positively about the possibility of integrating web cameras into future hospice experiences, they had concerns about their unfamiliarity:

I mean by that point, my sister certainly could have grabbed a laptop with a webcam on it and stuck it in front of her, right? But on her own, the fact that she wasn't already comfortable and familiar with it would just have made it this weird new thing... –P08

Additional concerns surrounded the current symmetry of video chat, and whether it was appropriate to project a video feed of the hospice environment. Some participants expressed concerns about the visual impact of hospice on younger viewers or those who were unfamiliar or unprepared for the physical changes that accompany end of life such as changing skin color and severe weight loss:

If you were willing to take children to visit grandma in the hospital, then I guess, a FaceTime conversation would be fine. But if you didn't want the children to see grandma hooked up to an IV or on some kind of breathing machine, then you wouldn't want them to see it online either. –P07

These quotes point to the need for sensitivity to the reality of the hospice setting and the difficulty of introducing new technologies at the end of life. Relationships are unlikely to be symmetrical; designs that encourage heterogeneous ways of sharing could be valuable for respecting this asymmetry.

Coordinating Care: Comforting Each Other

The admission of a loved one into hospice was extremely disruptive to the day-to-day routines of caregivers. In this section, we shift our focus from how caregivers interacted with the hospice patients to how they interacted with each other and with extended family members. Some participants described dissatisfaction with the division of labor, particularly when they were unexpectedly and unilaterally charged with the majority of caregiving responsibilities. Many felt other potential family caregivers abandoned them, citing their own schedules and responsibilities:

Yeah it was really hard balancing commitments to school and [the] timeline I was on as well. Trying to provide support for her and be there for her because it was an intensely uncomfortable position she was in and she was alone in the city. Like my sister also lives in [the same city] but [I felt like] she was really unavailable because of her work schedule and [that she experienced difficulty] acknowledg[ing] that [our mother] had a life threatening cancer. So I felt a lot of responsibility to care for her also because her partner, my dad, just wasn't really supportive either so it was really difficult. –P04

As has been documented elsewhere [29], participants experienced stress from their multiple responsibilities as caregivers, family members, and employees. They also experienced pressure to perform these roles authentically and completely, and feared how others would judge their performance of the caregiving role:

Well obviously in real life, I found it was much more difficult. I didn't know it was going to be so, I mean of course you always assume that it's going to be sad but it was just an extreme amount of anxiety, insomnia, like just the physical toll that is takes on you; that was unexpected to me. And also, for everyone else life goes on. It's not like the world stops... and it's funny because while I was at the hospital with her, I felt nothing, I felt complete numbness. –P14

Primary caregivers were not always alone in wanting better coordination support. Some secondary caregivers described wanting to provide support but experiencing difficulty in doing so effectively:

It was really about helping [the primary caregiver]. I'm trying to think, it was very challenging. Challenging in that sense because there were times perhaps when she needed help and for whatever reason we weren't there, or couldn't be there, or you know, those were challenges. That was probably the biggest challenge of the whole thing, because it was hard, it was hard for her. I mean it wasn't <u>hard</u> for her. She did a great job, don't get me wrong. It was an emotional... it was a really emotional, straining journey for her. So in that respect, um, I have to say, that was a challenge. Because you wanted to be there to help as much as you could and you couldn't always be there to help. –P05

Communication and Coordination Technology

A desire for better ways of coordinating support also emerged when we asked participants to imagine how technology could have helped. Here, participants described the emotional drain of having to independently call large numbers of individuals and envisioned some sort of management system that would allow caregivers to automate the transmission of repeated information. Emotionally sensitive and time-critical messages were described by interview participants as requiring personalization, thoughtfulness, and the ability to respond to the emotional needs of the receiver. At the same time, the requirement to personalize and respond to the emotional impact of messages added an additional level of challenge that participants saw as amenable to technological support:

It was very difficult to make all those phone calls. If there is a way of having something that is in-between a mass email and individual phone calls for a million people, I don't know what that would look like but something that balances the competing needs of not making it seem like a mass-message impersonal thing but also saving the emotional sanity of the family member because with each new person you tell, they're shocked and they're upset and you're going through it every time with each person. –P08

Participants did make use of email and social networking sites such as Facebook to aid in these tasks, but with mixed success. Email was valued for its ability to transmit documents across distance, communicate across time zones, and accommodate thorough updates and accounts:

Email for me, that's tops. For [the patient] she preferred the telephone I think because she worked online, so it's, you know... For everybody else, I can't really speak, I think probably email was the preferred because a lot of these are distant, you know, they're busy. –P12

Email is for thorough communication, like our emails are very long, like this happened and that happened and then, you know. Oh and we'd scan and send reports. –P06

Technology was also used as an emotional buffer and a means of easing communication when relations were tense:

I don't think [my half-brother is] totally comfortable with me, so texting just kind of made it easier... Well I mean he didn't say much, but I think talking to him would have made it a lot harder for him even to say whatever he had to say. I also didn't want him to hear me on the phone, because I was a bit of a wreck... And if he didn't want to answer, he could just ignore it or leave it for a little bit. And I wasn't necessarily interrupting anything... –P16

Although asynchronous text-based communications were used extensively, some participants expressed concern about overreliance on them. The lag time between sending and receiving messages made these mediums less useful for time sensitive content. They were considered too cold and impersonal for the emotional, sensitive nature of some messages (i.e., the passing of the hospice patient).

Differences in their adoption among concerned parties also limited their usefulness; not everyone who needed to be reached could be reached in the same way. For example, generational differences were pronounced when it came to the use of social networking sites like Facebook. In some cases, the ability to reach a large number of people with relative ease infringed on the agency of the hospice patient and his ability to control the flow of information:

My brother posted on Facebook that my dad was ill and all these people started coming out of the woodwork to visit my dad. People that my dad really didn't want to see. –P17

In other cases, the posting of private information within Facebook's relatively public and general-purpose space caused discomfort for extended family members who received upsetting news at an unexpected place and time:

When my father-in-law passed, all my nephews and nieces on that side of my family, there's a ton of them, and everybody's on Facebook and one of them actually said, "Rest in peace, Grandpa." All of them hadn't been told yet and it created a horrible, horrible family fight. –P07

This is not to say that all social networking experiences were negative. In some cases, they were successfully harnessed to support feelings of connectedness:

Like a year ago I set up like a Facebook group for our family, and this is us putting status updates, and then letting us comment on each other/them. It's increased the amount of communication my family has 10 fold. This Facebook group with my family has recreated intimacy... it's a space I have where I actually can perform the role of [a] "brother", "son", "brother-in-law", "uncle", effectively. And I can only imagine that had my grandmother had access to this, or had she been participating in this, that [it] would have had a different kind of impact... –P02

DISCUSSION: REVISITING COMFORT

As our results suggest, participants were continually in pursuit of comfort in the hospice setting, but this notion of comfort is far more than merely the reduction of pain for the patient. While the hospice setting highlights the pursuit of multiple types of comfort, we must bear in mind that comfort is something that we are always in pursuit of in all social situations. In almost all everyday encounters, we seek to avoid conflicts and pain; the hospice setting provides a unique, instructive lens onto these issues. With this in mind, we remark on how comfort might be more productively unpacked and reconsidered in the context of designing interactive systems.

First, comfort is multidimensional and continually produced. While we often talk about "giving comfort" to others as if it is a commodity that can exchange hands, our work suggests that comfort is better understood as a state that is actively produced and pursued by all involved in the hospice setting. It is not a thing, but a repeated set of actions. Comforting acts are undertaken again and again—medication is given, a meal is shared, a favorite TV show is watched, a mother consoles a crying daughter with gentle words, a hand is held—but none of these actions alone are equivalent to the lived experience of comfort. There are endless forms of such compassionate or pain-reducing acts that one may perform, and they are contributors to comfort, but it is the concerted and continual undertaking of these actions that gives rise to a larger, more effable sense of comfort in the hospice environment. It is in this spirit that we must consider technologies for hospice care, where the technologies allow new or varied actions to take place, but bearing in mind that these technology-mediated actions must be subsumed into a more holistic and sustained effort in order to be eventually recognized as comfort.

Second, the achievement of comfort involves multiple, and non-obvious, stakeholders. Returning to the phrase "giving comfort," we often think of the dying patient as the recipient of this gift and the healthy as benefactors. Our work suggests that patients are much more active and vital to the production of comfort than traditional medical models might suggest. For example, the patient may selectively hide potentially damaging information, or lie about the severity of pain, to make the young and healthy feel less uncomfortable. Family members may be complicit in this act; we may have a child talk to their grandparent on the phone to spare them the pallor and frailty that a face-to-face visit would reveal. While first steps to improve a sense of comfort in hospice might involve technologies that are designed for caregivers to provide for their dying loved ones, it may also be helpful to consider technologies for use by the patient that could enable them to more fully comfort those around them. Further to this point, comfort is something that is sought after by an extended network of family and friends. Family members might comfort one another, or a caregiver might try to comfort herself. While providing comfort to the patient will always be a central concern of stakeholders in this setting, some technologies for producing comfort in hospice may actually have little to do with the patient, but instead focus on the experiences of friends and family.

Finally, achieving comfort is not a process that is limited to the people in the hospice room at a given time; people work to produce comfort in the future, and to produce comfort in places beyond the hospice. Patients would often speak about post-mortem arrangements, ensuring their estates were cleanly divided, that funeral costs were covered, and so on. In this sense these patients are attempting to temper future financial or emotional pain for their loved ones. Because a death is painful but unavoidable, patients exerted control and asserted their personhood by exercising their abilities to minimize avoidable pain. This was not simply on the part of the patient, however. Family members remarked on how some of the most uncomfortable conversations—those ridden with conflict, or those that touched on mortality and death—were the ones that ultimately produced the greatest comfort down the road. Thus, there is no simple path to comfort. Actions causing ephemeral discomfort may be undertaken at one point in time, to create more durable forms of comfort later on. This again ties back to the multi-dimensional nature of comfort: some forms may be mutually exclusive, and not all discomfort can or should be avoided. As we also saw, participants sought to provide comfort to those who were not physically present in addition to those who were. Family members who had demanding work schedules and children were seen to be important stakeholders, but because their commitments or maturity did not permit them to be present, the process of creating comfort had to extend out to them and meet them on their own terms wherever possible. Comfort, therefore, is not simply a property of objects or an environment (e.g., as in a comfortable bed, or a comfortable temperature). Rather, *comfort is a mutually, continually produced state that arises out of a wide variety of actions performed by multiple stakeholders over a long period of time and despite distance*. The upshot of this argument suggests that technology can play a vital role in the production of comfort in hospice, given its unique capabilities to connect human actors across time and space.

OPPORTUNITIES FOR DESIGN

Building on this discussion, we now provide more grounded and succinct design recommendations that are derived from our findings. We anticipate that these recommendations would be helpful not only for designers targeting hospice environments, but additionally for those designing for end of life circumstances more generally.

Information seeking and communication: Because participants felt that admittance into hospice occurred suddenly, they had little idea of what to expect. Participants expressed the desire for better education regarding the dying process in general and administrative procedures governing their loved one's admission into hospice: a role they attributed to the professionals responsible for their loved one's prior treatment and hospice organizations that received their loved ones after the cessation of treatment. Thus, it is unlikely that prospective caregivers would seek out ICTs designed for end-of-life settings independently and preemptively.

Hospice is not the time to introduce new interaction paradigms: Hospice patients typically experience a reduction in their cognitive and physical abilities that would impede the learning and use of unfamiliar technologies. Moreover, learning a new technology is unlikely to be a top priority for hospice patients. This is not to say that new technologies cannot be designed for this setting or that they cannot be innovative; however, the success of a technological intervention will likely hinge on its ability to leverage familiar metaphors and known technologies to control new interactions.

For inspiration in this regard, we can turn to existing design work, such as that done by Blythe et al. [2] to support ludic engagement in residential care settings. In this work designs were introduced to encourage engagement and interaction among residents and across generations, but none of these designs required computer literacy on the part of older users. Similarly, the Photostroller [12] demonstrates how technology can be designed to spark engagement and interaction with a computational system with minimal demands on the user. As a final example, Petrelli et al. [35] used an old fashioned radio as an interaction paradigm for browsing sonic mementos from family vacations. One could imagine adopting a similar metaphor to enable hospice patients to access relevant audio streams, such a pre-recorded messages from loved ones.

Designs could also strive to take advantage of the blurred line between treatment and hospice care to introduce technologies as early as possible, thereby enabling them to leverage earlier learning while slowly adapting to the evolving needs of the patient.

Life-affirming technologies can help provide emotional support: Novel ICTs designed for end-of-life care settings need to be life affirming while at the same time guiding caregivers through the dying process of a loved one. By life affirming, we refer to technologies that focus on the patient's capabilities and opportunities for continued interaction. For example, designing technologies that allow people to achieve their own sense of comfort (thinking here of the cordless phone or fireplace remote control) may be particularly effective. Leveraging existing modes of producing comfort, such as shared meals, conversations, TV/radio shows, favorite activities, and connections to home may also be fruitful. Support for sharing provides a rich space for design to explore, and as our participants revealed, the items shared are often of less significance than the simple act of sharing itself. Technologies along these lines can also look at supporting emotional needs. Our participants described experiences that went beyond conversation to feelings of just being together, and technologies could enable these experiences for those who cannot do so face-to-face.

Returning to the family radio example above, one could imagine linking homes such that a hospice patient could enjoy the sound of familiar routines (e.g., the start of the coffee maker, the running of the shower, the morning news over breakfast), while family members receive a reassuring soundscape of activity from the hospice. Privacy concerns would of course need to be addressed, but techniques such as audio distortion could be employed to provide a sense of connection without revealing unnecessary detail. CSCW research on long-distance couples has revealed openness to this sort of sharing within intimate relationships [30].

Supporting conversation: Designers might consider conversation in two ways: the ability to have one, and the topics that might be discussed. Because alertness and cognizance decline over time, technologies should accommodate changing levels of activity on the part of the patient. Similarly, asymmetry in media richness and availability is a resource for design; hiding the sensual aspects of being in hospice might allow family members to re-experience their loved one as they once were, or allow children who are deigned too young to visit, an opportunity to talk to their loved one. Technologies that help support or guide individuals through interaction (thinking here of the book of questions used by P07) could be potentially helpful for encouraging conversations of the type that family members expect. Alternatively, technologies could focus on bringing in aspects of the outside world to spur conversation or could capture and maintain elements of each visit upon which subsequent visitors could build.

In this vein, we may also consider technologies to connect larger conversation groups. Rather than envisioning video calling as a one-to-one connection between the hospice patient and a remote loved-one, it may be fruitful to explore it as a means for bringing a larger group of remote and co-located visitors together in the hospice room. Used in this way, the patient him or herself need not be capable of managing the technology, and the technology could support communication by reducing (1) the pressure on each individual visitor to sustain conversation topics, (2) the pressure on the patient to participate in conversation when s/he may only have the energy to listen, and (3) the awkwardness of one-sided conversation by offering a more dynamic multi-way interaction.

Coordination support: Technologies should be employed selectively and delicately in spreading news and coordinating care. For example, email was valuable for its asynchrony and ability to target specific people. Social networking sites offer many features that could be helpful, but existing ones might not be the right setting for the types of conversations that hospice entails. In particular, conflict seemed to arise from the sharing of sensitive and private end-of-life information on public and blithe forums such as Facebook. Dedicated systems do exist. For example CaringBridge provides a suite of tools for sharing information, coordinating care, and connecting with others, but no one in our sample used (or seemed to have any awareness of) such tools. This suggests an interesting tension: whereas individuals are unlikely to appropriate new technologies during the disruptive transition to hospice care, end-of-life interactions seem to require a dedicated private space.

Coordination of care has been explored in related domains. For example, Consolvo et al. [9] developed CareNet an ambient display to help the members of an elder's care network coordinate day-to-day care. This display enabled individuals to quickly assess the elder's condition and to monitor events (such as medications, meals, activities, mood, falls, and calendar) to determine whether or not assistance was needed. Similarly, the Digital Family Portraits project sought to enable individuals to remotely monitor the status of an elderly individual [28]. Future research could examine the ability of such systems to meet the needs of individuals in hospice care.

LIMITATIONS

There are a number of limitations to this study that should be noted. Firstly, our participants provided retrospective accounts based on past experiences; in some cases these experiences were quite distant (up to 10 years). Recruiting individuals willing to revisit this period of their life proved difficult, requiring us to be flexible in our inclusion criteria; however, the span of our sample does mean that some details may have been forgotten or modified over time. Encouragingly, caring for a dying loved one appeared particularly salient for our participants; only seldom did a participant indicate forgetting a detail. Secondly, our participants tended to have somewhat above average education levels. This can be at least partially attributed to our recruiting process (which relied heavily on snowball sampling, and also included postings on a university campus). Thus, our results may not fully capture the range of experiences that exist in the population at large. Thirdly, of our 16 interviewees, 10 reported little or no technology use in the hospice. While this is a true representation of our participants' experiences, it may be interesting to contrast our findings with a more technologically-oriented sample. Finally, our interviews captured almost exclusively the point of view of primary caregivers. We felt this was a good starting place for the research; however, additional perspectives are needed to build a holistic picture of the technology use in this setting. Future work could enhance our understanding with accounts from hospice workers, and terminally ill individuals themselves, as well as with more detailed accounts from secondary and tertiary caregivers.

CONCLUSION

We have discussed here the ways in which family members of patients in hospice care view their activities in the hospice setting, and found that the pursuit of comfort was a consistent theme. In achieving comfort, participants remarked on the barriers that they faced, such as difficulty coordinating visits, declining levels of participation on the part of the patient, and the emotional challenges associated with the dying process. While technology was seen as somewhat alien to this process, participants described evocative scenarios where selectively-chosen ICTs allowed them to provide and coordinate support, and reflect on relationships with their loved ones. Our findings suggest that technologies that are designed for hospice should support conversation, coordination, remembrance, and life-affirming activities. At the same time, the hospice is a challenging setting to introduce new technologies, and focusing on well-established interaction paradigms may be effective in early system designs. Our future work will entail a series of design sketches that address some of these needs, with long-term work to include a potential deployment and evaluation of our designs. This work highlights the opportunities for technology to aid families in their pursuit of comfort before, during, and after their encounters with the hospice setting.

ACKNOWLEDGMENTS

We thank all our participants who graciously shared their stories and experiences with us, as well as our community partners who helped with recruitment: Hill House Hospice, CanadianVirtualHospice.ca, CancerConnection.ca, and Better Living Health and Community Services. This work was supported by grants from the Natural Science and Engineering Research Council of Canada (NSERC), and the Graphics, Animation, and New Media Network of Centres of Excellence (GRAND-NCE).

REFERENCES

1. Battley, J., Balding, L., Gilligan, O., O'Connell, C., & O'Brien, T. (2012). From Cork to Budapest by Skype: Living and dying. *BMJ Support. Palliat. Care*, 2, 168–169.
2. Blythe, M. et al. (2010). Age and experience: Ludic engagement in a residential care setting. In *Proc. DIS 2010*. 161–170.
3. Bonanno, G. (2004). Loss, trauma, and human resilience: Have we underestimated the human capacity to thrive after extremely aversive events? *Am. Psychol.*, 59(1), 20–28.
4. Brubaker, J. R., & Hayes, G. R. (2011). We will never forget you [online]: An empirical investigation of post-mortem MySpace comments. In *Proc. CSCW 2011*, 123–132.
5. Buis, L. R. (2008). Emotional and informational support messages in an online hospice support community. *Comput. Inform. Nurs.*, 26(6), 358–367.
6. Clark, D. (2000) Total pain: The work of Cicely Saunders and the hospice movement. *American Pain Society Bulletin*, 10 (4), 13–15. ISSN 1057-1590.
7. Clayton, P. (1979). The sequelae and nonsequelae of conjugal bereavement. *Am. J. Psych.*, 136(12), 1530–1534.
8. Clements-Cortés, A. (2004). The use of music in facilitating emotional expression in the terminally ill. *Am. J. Hosp. Palliat. Me.*, 21(4), 255-260.
9. Consolvo, S., Roessler, P., & Shelton, B. E. (2004). The CareNet display: Lessons learned from an in home evaluation of an ambient display. In *Proc. UBICOMP 2004*, 1–17.
10. Demmer, C. (2003). A national survey of hospice bereavement services. *OMEGA-J. Death Dying*, 47(4), 327–341.
11. Friedman, B., & Nathan, L. P. (2010). Multi-lifespan information system design: A research initiative for the HCI community. In *Proc. CHI 2010*, 2243–2246.
12. Gaver, W. et al. (2011). The Photostroller: Supporting diverse care home residents in engaging with the world. In Proc. CHI 2011, 1757–1766 .
13. Getty, E., Cobb, J., Gabeler, M., Nelson, C., Weng, E., & Hancock, J. (2011). I said your name in an empty room: Grieving and continuing bonds on Facebook. In *Proc. CHI 2011*, 997–1000.
14. Glaser, B. G., & Strauss, A. L. (1967). *The discovery of grounded theory: Strategies for qualitative research.* Chicago: Aldine Pub. Co.
15. Gulotta, R., Odom, W., Forlizzi, J., & Faste, H. (2013). Digital artifacts as legacy: Exploring the lifespan and value of digital data. In *Proc. CHI 2013*, 1813–1822.
16. Heyland, D. K. et al. (2006). What matters most in end of life care: perceptions of seriously ill patients and their family members. *Can. Med. Assoc. J.*, 174(5), 627–633.
17. Houck, K., Avis, N. E., Gallant, J. M., Fuller, A. F., & Goodman, A. (1999). Quality of Life in Advanced Ovarian Cancer: Identifying Specific Concerns. *J. Palliat. Med.* 2(4), 397–402.
18. Kane, R. L., Klein, S., Berstein, L., & Rothenberg, R. (1986). The role of hospice in reducing the impact of bereavement. *J. Chron. Dis.*, 39(9), 735–742.
19. Kilbourn, K. M., Costenaro, A., Madore, S., DeRoche, K., Anderson, D., Keech, T., & Kutner, J. S. (2011). Feasibility of a telephone-based counseling program for informal caregivers of hospice patients. *J Palliat. Med.*, 14(11), 1200–1205.
20. Kinsella, A. (2013). About telehospice care. National Care Planning Council. Retrieved 28 May 2013 from: http://www.longtermcarelink.net/eldercare/telehospice.htm.
21. Kissane, D. W., McKenzie, M., Bloch, S., Moskowitz, C., McKenzie, D. P., & O'Neill, I. (2006). Family Focused Grief Therapy: A Randomized, Controlled Trial in Palliative Care and Bereavement. *Am J Psychiatry*, 163(7), 1208–1218.

22. Klass, D., Silverman, P. R., & Nickman, S. L. (1996). *Continuing bonds: New understandings of grief.* Washington, DC: Taylor & Francis.

23. Massimi, M. (2013). Exploring remembrance and social support behavior in an online bereavement support group. In *Proc. CSCW 2013*, 1169-1180.

24. Massimi, M., & Charise, A. (2009). Dying, death, and mortality: Towards thanatosensitivity in HCI. In *Ext. Abs. CHI 2009*, 2459–2468.

25. Massimi, M., Odom, W., Banks, R., & Kirk, D. (2011). Matters of life and death: Locating the end of life in lifespan-oriented HCI research. In *Proc. CHI 2011*, 987–996.

26. McCann, R., Hall, W., & Groth-Juncker, A. (1994). Comfort care for terminally ill patients: the appropriate use of nutrition and hydration. *J. Am. Med. Assoc.,* 272(16), 1263-1266.

27. Merritt, S., Durrant, A., Reeves, S., & Kirk, D. (2012). In dialogue: Methodological insights on doing HCI research in Rwanda. In *Proc. CHI 2012*, 661–676.

28. Mynatt, E. D., Rowan, J., Craighill, S., & Jacobs, A. (2001). Digital family portraits: Supporting peace of mind for extended family members. In *Proc. CHI 2001*, 333–340.

29. Navaie-Waliser, M., Spriggs, A., Feldman, P. H. (2002). Informal Caregiving: Differential experiences by gender. *Med. Care*, 40(12), 1249–1259.

30. Neustaedter, C. & Greenberg, S. (2012). Intimacy in long-distance relationships over video chat. In *Proc. CHI 2012*, 753–762.

31. Odom, W., Banks, R., Kirk, D., Harper, R., Lindley, S., & Sellen, A. (2012). Technology heirlooms? Considerations for passing down and inheriting digital materials. In *Proc. CHI 2012*, 337–346.

32. Odom, W., Harper, R., Sellen, A., Kirk, D., & Banks, R. (2010). Passing on & putting to rest: Understanding bereavement in the context of interactive technologies. In *Proc. CHI 2010*, 1831–1840.

33. Oliver, D. P., Demiris, G., Wittenberg-Lyles, E., Washington, K., Day, T., & Novak, K. (2012). A Systematic review of the evidence base for telehospice. *Telemed. J. E. Health*, 18(1), 38–47.

34. Oliver, D. P., Wittenberg-Lyles, E., Washington, K. T., & Sehrawat, S. (2009). Social work role in hospice pain management: A national survey. *J. Soc. Work End Life Palliat. Care*, 5(1-2), 61–74.

35. Petrelli, D., Villar, N., Kalnikaite, V., Dib, L., & Whittaker. S. (2010). FM radio: Family interplay with sonic mementos. In *Proc. CHI 2010*, 2371–2380.

36. Prendergast, T. J., Puntillo, K. A. (2002). Withdrawal of life support: intensive caring at the end of life. *J. Am. Med. Assoc.,* 288(21), 2732–2740.

37. Radtke, J. V., Baumann, B. M., Garrett, K. L., & Happ, M. B. (2011). Listening to the voiceless patient: Case reports in assisted communication in the intensive care unit. *J. Palliat. Med.*, 14(6), 791–795.

38. Rhymes, J. (1990). Hospice care in America. *J. Am. Med. Assoc.*, 264(3), 369–72.

39. Rosenfeld, B., Breitbart, W., McDonald, M. V., Passik, S. D., Thaler, H., & Portenoy, R. K. (1996). Pain in ambulatory AIDS patients. II: Impact of pain on psychological functioning and quality of life. *Pain,* 68(2-3), 323–328.

40. Showalter, S. E. (2010). Compassion fatigue: What is it? Why does it matter? Recognizing the symptoms, acknowledging the impact, developing the tools to prevent compassion fatigue, and strengthen the professional already suffering from the effects. *Am. J. Hosp. Palliat. Care*, 27(4), 239–242.

41. Sofka, C., Cupit, I. N., & Gilbert, K. R. (2012). *Dying, Death, and Grief in an Online Universe: For Counselors and Educators*. New York, NY: Springer.

42. Steinhauser, K. E., Christakis, N. A., Clipp, E. C., McNeilly, M., McIntyre, L., & Tulsky, J. A. (2000). Factors Considered Important at the End of Life by Patients, Family, Physicians, and Other Care Providers. *J. Am. Med. Assoc.,* 284(19), 2476–2482.

43. Stewart, A. L., Teno, J., Patrick, D. L., & Lynn, J. (1999). The Concept of Quality of Life of Dying Persons in the Context of Health Care. *J. Pain Symptom Manage.,* 17(2), 93–108.

44. Tang, W., Aaronson, L. S., & Forbes, S. A. (2004). Quality of Life in Hospice Patients with Terminal Illness. *West. J. Nurs. Res.,* 26(1), 113–128.

45. Washington, K. T., Demiris, G., Parker Oliver, D., & Day, M. (2007). Home Internet use among hospice service recipients: Recommendations for web-based interventions. J. Med. Syst., 31(5), 385–389.

46. Wilkie, D. J. et al. (2000). Effects of massage on pain intensity, analgesics and quality of life in patients with cancer pain: A pilot study of a randomized clinical trial conducted within hospice care delivery. *Hosp. J.*, 15(3), 31–53.

47. Willis, L., Demiris, G., & Oliver, D. (2007). Internet Use by Hospice Families and Providers: A Review. *J Med Syst*, 31(2), 97–101.

48. World Health Organization. (2013). WHO definition of palliative care. Retrieved 28 May 2013 from http://www.who.int/cancer/palliative/definition/en/

Life Transitions and Online Health Communities: Reflecting on Adoption, Use, and Disengagement

Michael Massimi[1], Jackie Bender[2], Holly O. Witteman[3], Osman Hassan Ahmed[4]

[1] Microsoft Research
Cambridge, UK
mmassimi@microsoft.com

[2] University Health Network
Toronto, Ontario, Canada
Jackie.bender@rmp.uhn.on.ca

[3]Université Laval
Laval, Quebec, Canada
Holly.Witteman@fmed.ulaval.ca

[4]University of Otago
Dunedin, New Zealand
osman.ahmed@otago.ac.nz

ABSTRACT

Online health communities are places where people can come together in order to exchange social support at a particular point in an individual's life. There are, however, relatively few accounts that look across multiple communities across the lifespan. In this paper, we reflect on four case studies of research on different online health communities in order to identify patterns in how individuals selectively adopt, use, and disengage from these communities throughout their lives. We argue that users leaving communities is not necessarily a failing of the site's design or purpose; rather, it is a logical reaction to changing life circumstances. In characterizing this pattern, we contribute a set of implications for design and management that bear consideration by online community designers, developers, moderators, and end users. Ultimately this may lead to a smoother transition from community to community and ensure that social support needs are being met more consistently in response to changing life circumstances.

Author Keywords

Online communities; social support; health; transitions; lifespan.

ACM Classification Keywords

H.5.3 (Computer-supported cooperative work).

INTRODUCTION

The growth of the internet has resulted in opportunities for organizations and individuals to create specialized websites that address specific concerns. One of the domains that has benefited most from this practice is that of online health-related communities, where users facing health or life conditions can find support. Whether communication in these communities is performed in email lists, forums, social networking sites, or some other technology, they provide a constantly available source of information and support throughout the lifespan as people and their conditions change.

CSCW'14, February 15 - 19 2014, Baltimore, MD, USA

ACM 978-1-4503-2540-0/14/02...$15.00.
http://dx.doi.org/10.1145/2531602.2531622

In this paper, we "zoom out" from use of a single online community to look more broadly at how users joined, used, and left communities of different types and at different points in their lives. By adopting this more multi-community perspective, we speak to the shifting life circumstances that result in some communities being more helpful at certain times than others. Recasting online community use in this broader context allows us to notice more nuanced patterns of behavior that are not as evident, even in longitudinal studies of a single community.

To provide such a perspective, we reflect on case studies of research with four unique online communities addressing different health events from different parts of the lifespan: young adult sports concussion, pregnancy and birth choices, breast cancer, and finally bereavement. We first provide a background on social support and online health communities, noting that most work focuses on a single community or type of community, and that even longitudinal studies rarely look across different stages of life. We then describe our four case studies in more detail and summarize their major findings. Instead of providing rich details about each individual community, we foreground the interdisciplinary discussion that arose from comparing our methods, types of communities, and research aims. Our comparisons among the four communities highlighted issues of community adoption, use, and disengagement, which we illustrate with examples drawn from the cases. We contribute a set of considerations for community managers, developers, and designers.

BACKGROUND

Social Support

Social support has been conceptualized and measured in a variety of different ways. It is often used in a broad sense to refer to any means by which social relationships might promote health and well-being [7]. Cohen, Gottlieb and Underwood conceive of social support in terms of the functional provisions of relationships such as emotional, instrumental and informational resources, and the health benefits accrued from participation in one or more social groups [7]. In this sense, the term "social support" encompasses the social resources that are perceived to be available or are actually received from others and the influence that integration in a social group can have on cognition, emotion, behavior and biological responses that are beneficial to health and well-being. While the exact mechanisms by which social relationships affect health remains unclear, nearly 30 years of research has consistently demonstrated that they have a powerful effect on physical and mental health, and may extend survival [3].

Some researchers have suggested that online support communities offer a form of support that cannot be achieved face-to-face [6]. Frequently reported advantages include the anonymity of the medium and the resulting lack of stigmatization, followed by its availability, diversity of experience, similarity of experience and greater information and resources. Disadvantages include the inability to engage in cues that we normally rely upon in face-to-face settings, including a lack of non-verbal cues which can lead to misunderstandings, flaming or negative comments, deception and slower feedback [42]. Despite these disadvantages, shifting life circumstances can precipitate a turn to online communities for supplemental support.

Online Health Communities

Recent years have seen the launch of many health-specific social networks [31]. Such communities can serve to either support or suppress health-promoting behaviours [2, 9], though they have been noted as having largely positive effects [12]. This is possibly because they offer a means for people to learn more about the day-to-day aspects of living with a disease, managing a health condition or treatment side effects, and other lived experience aspects of health [9].

Within an online health community, people adopt many roles. Maloney-Krichmar & Preece [22] identified examples of classic group membership roles enacted within a longstanding online health community as a means of documenting the social processes and norms within the community. These included task roles (e.g. 'information giver – provides data and facts,' 'opinion seeker – asks for opinions, values & feelings'), socio-emotional roles (e.g. 'harmonizer – mediates conflicts among group members'), and individualistic roles (e.g. 'recognition-seeker – self-aggrandizing').

Researchers have previously focused on user loyalty to an online community, and reasons for leaving. Brandtzaeg and Heim identified 9 reasons people left communities, including a lack of interesting people, poor usability, and poor content [5]. Sandaunet reports that reasons for withdrawal from an online community for breast cancer patients might be due in part to the challenge of "fitting in" [30]. Examples include: a need to avoid painful details about cancer, not being "ill enough" to participate, the challenge of establishing a legitimate position in the group, the organization of everyday life, and illness phases that did not motivate participation. These concerns are mediated by a need to present an appropriate image to a given group (e.g., Facebook vs. a specific health community) [24].

In much of the work in online health communities, the focus has been on creating communities and keeping them active. Although some work has examined obtaining the right "fit" with an online community, it still remains an underexplored

Life event	*Study design*	*Number and type of communities*	*Sample size and method of collection data*	*Moderators*
Sports concussion [1]	1-Arm pre-post feasibility study of a Facebook group intervention	1 (Facebook group)	Questionnaire (n=11) (concussion symptoms)	Health professionals
Birth (pregnancy options) [39]	Cross-sectional content analysis of threads and survey of members in birth online communities	4 (existing websites, 2 very large with>20k members, 1 moderate with 5-10k members, and 1 small with <2k members)	Web-based questionnaire with closed- and open-ended questions (n=744), content analysis (n=60 threads)	Largely volunteers, (some paid staff at larger sites), not health professionals
Breast cancer [4]	Cross-sectional survey and in-depth qualitative interviews with breast cancer survivors who were members of a national support agency	Unrestricted and variable. From a list of 20 websites, users reported using a median of 4 (IQR 4.2)	In-person and web-based questionnaire (n=73), In-person and telephone interviews (n=12)	Largely volunteers (some paid staff at larger sites); one also offered forums moderated by health professionals
Bereavement [21]	Longitudinal prototype deployment study	1 (custom website, prototype)	Interviews, system logs, questionnaires (social support, grief) (n=19)	Trained volunteers from a local support group

Table 1. Characteristics of the communities and studies under consideration. More information about each study can be found in the references listed in the first column.

space [35]. What is even less understood is how life circumstances are affecting patterns of use and adoption, and especially how these change over time [27].

Research into online health communities has generally selected a particular website or type of community for in-depth examination, and reported on findings about usage of that website. For example, Maloney-Krichmar & Preece provide an in-depth analysis of a community for people with knee injuries [22]. Huh and Ackerman focus on a lifelong condition – diabetes – and how it is discussed in a particular online diabetes support community [14]. Newman et al. move closer towards our goals in their study of people's perceptions of Facebook as a place for sharing health information, especially as they highlight how and why people choose to use social networking sites for health concerns [24]. Though they did not study a health community, Lampe et al. move closer to the current study in their longitudinal investigation of a website called Everythings2.com where they found that initial reasons for using the website were different from the ones that kept them there, such as for entertainment or information-sharing purposes – echoing some of the findings of our work [18]. What we notice is that single communities are often studied in depth, and that when multiple communities are studied, it is around a single theme (e.g., diabetes).

CASE STUDIES

Because our research goal was to take a more longitudinal, lifespan-oriented perspective, we saw a need to put multiple, diverse online health communities in conversation with one another. In order to ground our discussion of how users could move from community to community throughout the lifespan, we present brief descriptions of four case studies that stem from our own research and different disciplinary perspectives. Each author of this paper studied a different community in detail, and the cases presented here are summaries of their work. It should be noted that each author was highly familiar with one of the communities; two of the authors designed and deployed the communities under consideration (sports concussion, bereavement). Table 1 provides more information about the topic and format of the case studies.

We do not suggest that a single user might use all four communities in their lives, but we believe that the communities in these case studies are a sufficiently diverse sampling of the types of available communities that people engage with when dealing with changing life circumstances. Comparing and contrasting among four different cases permits us some explanatory power, and as Yin points out, a case study method is appropriate for examining questions of *how* [43] – in this case, we are interested in how people adopt, use, and leave online communities at different stages of life. Adopting a case study approach further allows us to draw upon four rich, but diverse, data sets in our findings.

We begin with a system for young persons dealing with sports concussion. We then turn to early adulthood by examining an online community for pregnant women. Following this we examine a community primarily used by middle-aged women facing breast cancer, before concluding with a case study that examined people of all ages who were dealing with grief in an online bereavement support group.

Sports Concussion

Concussion in sport has been suggested as a major public health issue [39], and is the focus of much current attention in the mainstream media [10]. Although awareness and recognition of sports concussion is rising [34], inconsistencies in the knowledge and understanding of this condition are still being reported at a community level [38]. The use of social networking sites to facilitate the knowledge transfer process and for support have been suggested as a potential strategy to assist individuals recovering from a sports concussion [28], but to date few studies have appraised their use in this manner.

To evaluate the potential for Facebook to assist the management of sports concussion, an interactive concussion management intervention was created using a multi-stage, needs-focused development process. This intervention was a Facebook group which was moderated by experienced healthcare professionals. To test the feasibility of this intervention, a preliminary small-scale pilot study was conducted and the success of this community was measured using a mixed methods approach. User satisfaction with the intervention was the primary outcome measure. Objective measurements of symptoms were also made before and after the trial, using elements of the Sports Concussion Assessment Tool 2, which is the widely-accepted best-practice method of assessing an injured athlete with a suspected concussion [15].

The research team actively recruited participants who had sustained a concussion playing sport at a recreational (non-elite) level, and were aged between 18 and 28 years old. People may have joined the community out of interest as it was a novel approach to healthcare, or because their concussion symptoms were not being adequately managed by existing means (i.e., by consultation with their doctor and by finding information independently either online or in written format). The posts in this community were broadly categorized into groups; "Asking a question" and "Commenting on a link" were the two most common uses of this community by participants, with "Sharing a story/link" and "Sharing updates on progress/recovery" being used to a lesser degree. Only one person left the group before the community ended, with that individual stating that they left the group as they were symptom-free and therefore felt that they did not need to be a part of the community.

The presence of users in this community was only ever intended to be for the duration of the 3-month trial or until their symptoms resolved (whichever came first). Although the community was created for a finite period it was hoped that the concussion education and management principles shared in the group would stay with the users long beyond this, and that it would be of assistance to them should they or anyone they know sustain a concussion in the future. It was expected that positive experiences of being in the group might also prompt users of this community to seek our similar communities in the future for other health-related needs.

Birth Choices

The Internet is a major source of information for pregnant women [17, 19]. In addition to seeking information, they also seek community with other parents and hopeful parents. Women who are pregnant, trying to become pregnant [21], or raising young children may seek out online communities as a substitute for, or supplement to, social interaction in their physical communities [8, 20].

This case study examined women's use of online pregnancy and parenting communities to explore the effects that participating in such communities might have on women's and their families' opinions and choices of birth place (e.g., home, hospital or birth center) and birth attendant (e.g., obstetrician, family physician, midwife, or unassisted birth.) A cross-sectional analysis approach was used to identify 480 relevant threads in four communities, 60 of which were randomly selected for in-depth, interdisciplinary qualitative analysis. Members of these online communities (n=744) were concurrently surveyed, recruiting respondents through postings in these communities and related sites.

Members of these communities were, for the most part, women who were, wanted to become, or had been pregnant. Community members who responded to the survey indicated that their purposes for participating in online pregnancy and parenting communities included getting information from others (97%), emotional support (87%), providing information to others (83%), friendship (65%) and entertainment (62%). The analysis of patterns across communities revealed that different communities espoused different values, and this affected the content and character of information and support provided. For example, some communities' members saw home birth as a valid, safe choice, at least under certain circumstances, whereas members from other communities saw it as a much riskier choice. Survey respondents who made choices more outside the norm (e.g., home birth, unassisted birth) more frequently reported that participating in the communities helped shape their opinions surrounding birth and parenting choices (Chi-squared $(5) = 53.31$, $p < .001$). Observations of community participation suggest that most members participate during periods of greatest need for information or support, typically during and immediately after their pregnancy, but others continue to engage with other community members to discuss parenting and other issues, splinter off into new communities, and may even form offline friendships with other members who may reside in the same geographical area. Those who leave may do so because of pregnancy loss, lack of fit with the group, or a lack of continued interest, especially after they have had their babies.

In the long term, most community members will associate these communities with the intensity of pregnancy and parenting. Their relationships with community members grow from shared experiences of that time. As their children grow and they exit their childbearing years, their interests and attention naturally shift to other topics.

Breast Cancer

Several studies have demonstrated that online communities provide breast cancer survivors with important benefits. These include: reassurance and hope for the future [31, 32, 37]; reduced feelings of isolation and uncertainty [29, 32, 36, 37]; and validation of concerns not dealt with by health professionals [31]. In addition, they enable breast cancer survivors to become better informed [13, 31, 37], better able to cope [29] and prepared for their interactions with health professionals [13, 36]. Little is known about the extent to which breast cancer survivors use online communities, or the conditions that influence use.

This case study examined the use of online communities by breast cancer survivors who are facilitators of face-to-face support groups (c.f., [25]). A cross-sectional survey was used to identify the extent of, and reasons for, online community use. Qualitative interviews with a purposive sample of the survey respondents were used to explore the conditions under which they used online communities. The sample for the survey was drawn from the 2008 and 2009 contact list of the attendees of a Canadian support group facilitator-training program. Participants recruited for the qualitative interview study were survey respondents who had used an online community and agreed to participate in a follow-up interview. In total, 73 of the 100 individuals surveyed returned a completed questionnaire, and 12 survey respondents participated in a follow-up interview.

In this study, respondents used online communities primarily for information and less so for emotional support. Of the 73 participants surveyed, 23 reported having used an online community (31.5%). The top reasons survey respondents reported for using online breast cancer communities were to find information about breast cancer and its treatment (91.3%) and to learn how to manage symptoms and side effects (69.6%). Less than 50% reported joining online communities to obtain emotional support (47.8%). Those who used online communities as a health resource did so intensely (e.g., on a daily basis) when their needs were greatest, which was predominantly during treatment for cancer (73.9%). According to interview participants, online communities played a distinct and supplemental role in comparison to traditional sources of supportive care. Many explained that were dissatisfied with the quality of information provided to them by their physicians, and considered face-to-face groups to be reserved for "emotional stuff". The main factors that motivated use of online communities post-treatment were the experience of a new or worsening symptom, the need for subsequent treatment, or to support other community members.

Most interview participants discovered online communities inadvertently while searching for information to address a particular unmet need. Some learned about online communities through an unsolicited recommendation from a family member, fellow breast cancer survivor, or support group member; only one person was referred to an online community by a health professional. Different online communities were not seen as being equivalent. Several interview participants described testing out a number of online communities before they found one that suited them. Not receiving a timely or supportive response caused some women to leave an online community in search of another. In addition, they appreciated the ability to "come and go" from online communities without incurring social consequences or feeling obligated to reciprocate support. Nearly all women described reaching a point at which they wanted to move beyond cancer and distance themselves from their online community.

As the effects of cancer and its treatment dissipate and individuals begin their transition to life beyond cancer, cancer survivors will have less need for online communities that focus on cancer. Some individuals may continue to participate in online cancer communities in order to support other cancer patients and survivors. Helping others has been reported by other researchers to be one of the primary reasons for staying involved in online cancer support groups [40].

Bereavement and Grief

Throughout their lives, people are inevitably faced with the loss of a loved one. Friends and family – those who have been around the longest – can be helpful in these circumstances. At the same time, the bereaved may not wish to burden these contacts with their own feelings of grief for fear of complicating or straining their relationships [26]. Turning to community-based support groups is one way of handling the situation, and provides the bereaved with an opportunity to talk to a set of compassionate peers.

This case study reports on findings from a 3-year long research project that investigated how the bereaved adopt and perceive sources of online support. The investigation included surveys, interviews, focus groups, and fieldwork with a community-based non-profit organization, ultimately producing a website that permits bereaved individuals to conduct online peer-support groups in a closed forum. The design of the website was based on the best practices established by the community organization, and was deployed in a 10-week exploratory study that collected feedback about design features through interviews and system logs.

Outcomes revealed that participants saw an online support group as a way to complement their existing forms of support. In other words, there were unmet support needs and an online group presented a low enough barrier to entry that participants felt it would be worthwhile to try. Surprisingly, not all participants joining the group did so because they needed support. Some participants reported joining the online support group in order to provide the benefit of their experience coping with their own grief, and sought to comfort others by making themselves available to those with fresher losses.

Once participants actually joined the group, their use was largely dependent on timing in two forms: how much time had passed since they endured the loss, and the timing of delivery of messages in the system. Individuals who had more recent losses tended to log in more frequently than those who had experienced a more distant loss. At the same time, some participants who had already dealt with their loss found that participation in the group could serve to dredge up unwanted emotions. This impacted the amount that people logged in and responded to messages in the support group, with up to an entire day passing between exchanges in the chat system. This lack of a rapid response resulted in situations where participants were sharing intimate and urgent thoughts without a timely acknowledgment of their feelings.

Ultimately participants left the group setting for these two reasons of timing. Those who were closer to their losses moved to more active groups and forms of support, and those who were further along simply stopped logging in as frequently because of the emotional burden it placed on them. A group of participants ultimately chose to take their conversation offline, and decided to hold an in-person weekly meeting instead. Participants often remarked on how helpful it would be in the future to have the option of an online support group available to them, but ideally with more activity.

THEMES AND DISCUSSION

Having described the research and sites in which our discussion is based, we now turn to some of the patterns of adoption, use, and disengagement that were borne out of comparison between these case studies. We arrived at these trends through iterative discussion, secondary review and comparative analysis of our data sets and collaborative writing among the researchers specializing in each of the four case studies, and refer back to these to provide specific examples of the trends we observe. Regular discussions occurred approximately once per month over the course of 8 months; meetings occurred in person, via teleconference, and as part of a panel at a health conference. These discussions were guided by a set of common questions jointly developed and individually answered in written form by each of the authors, and consolidated in an online collaborative document for comparative analysis. Discussion questions included:

- What are the characteristics of the group?
- What are their motivations to use online communities?
- How does this group use online communities?
- What were the effects of participation?
- Who is recognized as an authoritative source of information?
- What is the group's perspective on the nature of the technology?
- What is the group's perspective on what constitutes a successful online community?

Themes emerged from the collaborative writing, and were critiqued in light of the discussion and questions originating from the panel discussion at the health conference.

As the case studies illustrate, each community employed a different set of data collection and analysis procedures – some studies were more quantitative, others more qualitative (Table 1). Some focused on social support, while others were more on providing health information. These differences make direct comparisons difficult, but our goal in this section is to report back on an ongoing interdisciplinary discussion among the authors that draws out themes from our range of experiences.

Our goal in identifying these trends is not to provide an exhaustive list of behaviors, but rather to argue that contextualizing user behavior in a larger trajectory of use can identify overlooked considerations for developers, designers, and community managers. Further we would note that the four sites are drawn from a constellation of potential communities that could be drawn into this argument. Our aim is thus not to generalize behavior across communities, but rather illustrate how changing circumstances are brought to bear on the ways we seek out support online.

Adoption

Across our research studies, there were a number of trends concerning how, and why, users adopted particular communities. Adoption is of particular concern in a health context because participation in a community may create significant benefits for the individual and the health system, and health authorities may create online communities to provide support for their patients.

Self-selection

Observational studies concerning the efficacy of online support networks for health conditions suggest that they may have a beneficial effect [3]. As a result, professionals and policymakers may be eager to commission, encourage, and even "prescribe" these communities to patients. However, some communities may feel too formal or informal, reflect values the patient does not share, or provide information of differing degrees of applicability to a specific subset of the life condition (e.g., finding others who experienced a similar loss or medical information that may or may not apply to one's individual condition). These findings have implications for the design of effectiveness studies, as study participants may have to self-select online communities in order to obtain benefit. Efforts that seek to use health communities as a way to provide care must offer multiple formats and options for the presentation of information. Correspondingly, there is an emerging need for systems that help users find a community that is the best fit for them. More research is also needed on the potential benefits and harms of online communities that promote controversial views on health (e.g., those that encourage eating disorders).

Unmet needs and professional authority

In all four cases, online communities were places where unmet needs could be satisfied, such as obtaining support not available from health care professionals, sharing and validating experiences, and finding practical answers and actionable results. However, the ways in which the communities fit into an authoritative idea of care differed. In the case of the sports concussion community, family doctors and physical therapists working with sports teams referred their clients to participate in the study, and thus, the community was integrated into care. On the other hand, some participants in the breast cancer community felt that their health care professionals did not regard online communities favorably, perhaps because information shared on these sites did not come from a medical authority. Even further along the spectrum, members of some birth communities were actively opposed to professional authorities in the domain of maternity care. Indeed, some of these communities specifically supported choices outside the statistical norm such as midwife-attended home birth or unassisted birth. Online communities are only one source of information and support among many pre-existing professional and personal sources, and depending on how well or poorly the sources align, this can cause tensions in how communities are adopted.

Reasons other than emotional support

When conceptualizing online communities we often imagine a user that is in search of actionable results that are specific to a condition or challenge that the individual is facing. It is well-established that users turn to these sites in order to share their experiences, and to learn more about how to reconcile their condition with their individual circumstances. By looking beyond in-community usage, we see reasons for adoption that are not motivated by the desire for support.

One common reason for joining was for the opportunity to "give back" to an organization or group of individuals as described in the breast cancer and bereavement case study. For example, some participants in the bereavement support group reported joining not because they needed help dealing with their grief, but because they had benefited from support groups in the past and saw it as fitting to repay their debt by listening and offering support. This often fits into larger goals concerning charity and awareness (e.g., contributing to the breast cancer patient community, helping other pregnant women to avoid a negative birth experience). The point in time when an individual joins a community is therefore an opportunity for an ongoing relationship with peers and broader social goals, such as advocacy or fundraising.

Another reason for joining was to develop a better understanding of the condition more generally, without necessarily seeking emotional support. Participants in all four types of communities reported that they were interested in obtaining scientific (and non-scientific) information about their condition, and worked to develop an expertise on the topic through both study and personal experience. Even if the kinds of information were not applicable to their specific condition, the goal of joining was to develop expertise around a more general phenomenon. For these users, the goal was not to seek support, but to observe how supportive behavior was carried out in an online setting and to make personal assessments about its viability as a format for conversation. For these kinds of users, articles and more formal resources concerning the phenomenon in question may be helpful additions to conversation. Indeed, in the case of both the bereavement and sports concussion groups, the people who strove to attain an expert understanding had multiple encounters with their conditions (i.e., multiple concussions or multiple losses). This was also the case in birth communities, where women's previous experiences with pregnancy and birth influenced decision making in subsequent pregnancies.

Use

There are several ways one might use an online health community: to answer a question, to converse, or simply as a way to socialize or pass time. In our work at different stages of the life course, what we have observed is that use of online communities is marked by transience.

We often think of a successful community as one where members are continually participating. This kind of success makes sense for many types of online communities (e.g,, a fantasy football league or an online gaming site). However, this same kind of focus on growing and consistent engagement finds itself out of place in certain health contexts. In the same way that one does not wish to spend one's entire life in a hospital, one does not necessarily want to be part of an online health community forever. In our case studies, health communities were characterized by temporary and intermittent use driven by changing life events. This is especially pronounced in communities for people dealing with "long-term" conditions, such as breast cancer and grief.

Surprise of sticking around

When participants talked about their health event, they often spoke of their perception that the event and its repercussions would be temporary. They imagined that they would eventually move on and find a new normal. Years later, a small number of participants expressed surprise that they were actually still participating in online communities related to their health event. Several participants who signed up for the bereavement support group had experienced their loss over 5 years ago, and one woman in the breast cancer community noted:

"Well actually I'm kind of in a place right now that I didn't anticipate after only five years. I'm realizing how my concerns, my focus is turning and I'm finding that I'm starting to pull away. I'm not quite ready yet to leave the [mailing] list because of the information... but um I didn't anticipate being here at this five year junction. But I'm finding that maybe it's a natural progression for most people."

Motivations for sticking around vary. It may be because sharing expertise is important, or because friendships spring up between users. Whatever the reason, online health communities include people whose use is not in response to a current event, but one that occurred in the more distant past.

At the same time, even the most seasoned participants felt that eventually they would leave, but at an ill-defined point in the future. If people are using online support communities years beyond the incident that brought them there, this raises important issues concerning community management and system design. Specifically, systems should be designed to allow users to grow over time and fill shifting roles – from "newbie" to expert. Moreover as people settle into a community, social functions unrelated to the health event (e.g., so-called "off-topic" discussions) may become more important to the vitality of the community.

This also raises questions concerning the health of individuals who participate in a community for a lengthy period of time. While these websites can be helpful for coping with the health event, they may encourage dependence. Relying on a community for too long may signal an inability to adjust, but it may be difficult to say when discontinuing participation is warranted. This concern warrants further research.

Recurrence

For those that do stop using a community, the constant availability of online health communities makes it easy for them to rejoin. Participants reported becoming active again and seeking support each time they lost a loved one, became pregnant, or their cancer diagnosis changed or a new symptom emerged. Each time a user returns to a community, their circumstances differ. For example, a woman who is having her second child may be seeking answers to a different set of questions than when she had her first. In the case of breast cancer, participants would return to the community upon receiving new information about their treatment or diagnosis; for example, if the disease had progressed further.

Returning to a community following time away is a different experience from joining a community for the first time. Participants who had a negative condition they sought to bounce back from may be hesitant and view their return as a step backwards in terms of recovery. They may expect to find familiar people and conversations, but these kinds of supports may no longer exist, or exist in an altered form. Reintegration may be difficult; their motivations may set them apart from others who are at different points in their lives.

Disengagement

Support found in a community can help people through intense and/or difficult periods in their lives. Over time, the amount of perceived support may decline as questions are answered, and individuals develop their own mechanisms for adjusting to their new circumstances. Moving on from a community should not be seen as a failure of the community; on the contrary, leaving a community can be the result of the community's ability to help them adjust, or events entirely external to their engagement with the community. For example, in the sports concussion study, participants whose symptoms had resolved found little use in continued interaction with the health professionals on the site. Similarly, after giving birth, users of pregnancy-focused communities sometimes tapered off their usage because pregnancy and birth options were simply no longer the foremost issue. In addition to moving on due to the development of adaptive coping strategies, we note several mechanisms that participants used to facilitate this process, and discuss what happens offline when people discontinue their use of these communities.

Changing types and levels of need

Among the more obvious reasons for leaving a community was because an individual found the information they were seeking. Patients seeking specific answers to their health questions were often able to obtain the information they needed. A participant in the breast cancer study explained:

"I was bragging to my doctor about that website...I was telling him 'you have no idea the support systems that women have' ... any question I had was answered, any fear I had was reassured, and I didn't have to seek out as much help."

In contrast, meeting the needs of those seeking emotional support could take more time as interpersonal relationships are established, developed, and ultimately used as a resource for coping. In any case, these types of transactions – interpersonal or emotional – satisfied a need.

This provides a neat endpoint for an articulation of the community's role in providing support to an individual, but a person's needs continue to evolve independently of the community. Patient support needs do not come in the form of individual transactions at a single point in time, but rather needs emerge unevenly and across long periods of time. Mundane forces independent of the health condition, such as attending a social function, can cause new issues to emerge or old issues to dissipate suddenly. For example, a bereaved mother who lost one of her children recounted how she felt she had finally learned to cope until she was at a party where a stranger asked "How many children do you have?" This triggered a return to a support group and brought with it a new set of questions that needed new answers. Correspondingly, in the sports concussion study, the disappearance of symptoms prompted users to quit the community suddenly. This characterization of needs as shifting and unpredictable may help designers and managers to shape interaction flows and organize resources in the community.

Transitioning to face-to-face

Online support communities often act as match-making services that allow people to find others in a similar situation. At the same time, individuals may find an affinity for other users based on their personalities, location, or other factors. In these cases, users may choose to move their interactions to other modalities. In the bereavement study, members of the bereaved parents group set up a time for them to meet at one of the participants' homes and get to know one another in real life. Some members of pregnancy communities similarly moved their conversations to face-to-face.

In the breast cancer case study, all of the individuals surveyed chose to lead a face-to-face support group post-treatment, while only 39% of users of online communities chose to provide support to the members of their online community. In other words, moderating a face-to-face support group was more attractive to participants than moderating an online group. Similarly, in the bereavement support community, moderators reported that moderating online was less fulfilling than experiences leading face-to-face groups. This would suggest that perhaps the rewards of moderating are better felt or appreciated when face-to-face (e.g., being able to see that you've helped someone). The higher quality exchanges made available in face-to-face contact may be a contributor to individuals leaving the online community.

Overexposure

Online support communities necessarily contain a great deal of personal, emotionally-laden material. Engaging with this material on a regular basis can be difficult in a number of ways. For new members, reading through all of this information can be overwhelming. A tension exists: on the one hand, a user is more likely to find what they are looking for in a large community, but at the same time, the plethora of information can suggest that their problem is endlessly complex, unknowable, and capable of overwhelming them.

Beyond the sheer amount of information available, the emotional content of others' stories can be difficult to break away from. As one reads, one inextricably relates to the suffering, confusion, excitement or despair of others in the community. Over time these emotions comingle with one's own emotions, sharpening the intensity of the emotions that one experiences, as a member of the young adults bereavement group described:

"It was very hard for me emotionally and way harder than I thought it would be after hearing everyone's story. I felt like... pretty upset about it truthfully. It was hard for me to come back...hearing all the sad stories again was really hard for me to take because I'm in a different place now... people using it seem to be getting a lot out of it but for me I'm just a bit heartbroken."

What is less well understood, and contributes to disengagement with health communities, is how exposure to negative experiences and information affects adaptive coping processes. This is especially concerning given the pervasiveness of mobile technology that permits people to connect to these communities anytime, and anyplace. The burden of managing exposure is shifted onto the individual, who may not always be able to monitor their own responses.

Communities that comingle participants who are at different stages in reaction to their health event also face a tension. On one hand, more experienced members can offer their expertise and support to people who are closer to the event. On the other, the stories that these community "veterans" share can sometimes lead participants to ask themselves if they will also be "stuck" dealing with the event years from now. In the breast cancer study, reading stories of women who were worse off influenced some participants to withdraw from the online community to avoid anxiety provoking details of cancer.

IMPLICATIONS FOR DESIGN AND MANAGEMENT

In raising these issues in our discussion, we have drawn together some of the commonalities present across our four case studies. We now distill these discussion points into a set of implications for community designers and managers.

Communities grow and shrink – and that's okay.

The case studies and discussion have outlined the ways that people adopt and disengage from a given online health community. In presenting how and why people join and leave, we wish to show that turnover and/or reduction in community membership is always happening due to users' changing life circumstances. Overexposure, for example, is the result of too much use and may result in worse outcomes. We raise this issue to add some nuance to ongoing discussions of how to encourage contribution to online health communities, which often suggest that metrics like popularity and community size are the most important factors for perceived utility (e.g., [16]).

For community managers, this has several implications. First, because communities often rely on a critical mass of individuals in order for users to find meaningful support exchanges, it is important to find ways to keep the community active. This is a well-established concern, however. The second, less obvious implication is that users' departure should be expected and perhaps even facilitated. There are opportunities to make an individual's transition away from the community more graceful and supportive by supporting "ramp down" behavior and by facilitating engagement with a different online community if needed (e.g., transitioning from curative to palliative treatment in the case of breast cancer survivors, or transitioning from pregnancy to parenting). Better support of transitions into and away from the community may lead to better health outcomes in the long-term, and as a byproduct, yield insight into existing users.

Technically speaking, these transitions could take many forms. For example, rather than labeling users who have benefited from the community in the past as "inactive," it might be more useful to denote them as role models or "survivors" depending on the health condition. Alternatively, if users change to a different board, being able to set up a "forwarding address" could be useful. Other systems might allow users to participate in multiple communities simultaneously; for example, a system that aggregates content across communities (similar to an RSS reader) could be useful for helping individuals synthesize and selectively interact with supportive content tailored to their situation.

Help people find the right community more easily.

With the proliferation and diversification of online communities comes a problem of scale. While some users may seek out the oldest, largest, or most well-known community, most people have needs that may be best met through lesser-known communities, or through a combination of multiple communities. Developing more sophisticated means for matching users with the set of communities that could meet their needs at a given point in time is a challenge that remains to be solved, and one that requires attention to presentation of self and the anticipated benefit of participation [24, 35]. Expertise in recommendation systems could be leveraged to help users identify the communities that meet their needs, but could prove challenging because users may have trouble articulating their needs, and because aggregating all communities – who may consider each other as competitors – into a maintainable database would be difficult.

Support reintegration.

Community designers and managers should take note of the needs of individuals who are returning to a community after a period of time away. As we saw in the case studies, people who returned to a community were facing a different set of circumstances from those that they initially arrived at the community with. Helping people to reintegrate could be accomplished technically. For example, providing services to summarize and draw attention to important conversations that occurred would be a helpful tool for returning users. Returning users might also be flagged as returning in the user interface for moderators (e.g., highlighting their username) to pay special attention to their requests for support.

A community's success can be measured in many ways.

The success of a community can be measured in terms of the number of users, how often they log in, the number of discussion topics available or active, and so on. A community's success may also be measured by how well the information or services offered meet the needs of users, and if their expectations regarding the availability and quality of support are met. Did they get a suitable answer to their question? Did they learn a new coping strategy? Measures of how users learn and develop adaptive mechanisms that replace the need for support from an online community are needed.

At the same time, our work suggests that leaving isn't always a failing of the community or its design, but rather a natural part of the community's lifecycle. There are less obvious measures of success related to how well communities support transitions. For example, measures of how well a site supports more experienced users in assisting those seeking information may indicate the richness of the expertise in a community. Designers might consider how to ease this transition from support recipient into support provider (e.g., incorporating ways to train users to become better moderators).

Another measure related to transitions is how well a community connects people in relationships outside the community. Are email lists established? Do people connect on Facebook as well? Do they meet face-to-face? An online community's success may be measured by considering how well it leads to richer, more stable, and more intimate relationships among members. It remains a challenge to both system designers and community managers how to operationalize these measurements, but collecting and tracking this data could demonstrate that an outwardly small, inactive community may still be providing benefit to those who find it.

CONCLUSION

In this paper we have drawn on our experiences with four case studies of online health communities that address different periods in an individual's life. Based on discussion among the authors, we have found thematic elements that cut across cases and identify issues dealing with community adoption, use, and disengagement. As we have shown, online health communities are places that patients strategically and purposefully use to meet their needs in a shifting, ongoing trajectory of health. We suggest that designers and community managers should take note of this by paying better attention to how people transition from community to community. Growth and active participation are not the only measures of success; indeed, the greatest successes of a community, such as the development of coping mechanisms and stronger off-band support channels, may actually result in a reduction in usage. Providing more support for finding, returning to, and transitioning among multiple communities may meet patient needs more fully.

ACKNOWLEDGMENTS

We would like to thank our participants for their time and insight in each of these studies. Thanks also to John Sullivan, Tony Schneiders, and Paul McCrory.

REFERENCES

1. Ahmed, O. H., Sullivan, S. J., Schneiders, A. G., & Mccrory, P. (2010). iSupport: do social networking sites have a role to play in concussion awareness? *Disability & Rehabilitation, 32*(22), 1877-1883.
2. Ancker, J.S. et al., Peer-to-peer communication, cancer prevention, and the internet. *J. Health Comm.*, vol. 14, suppl 1, 2009, 38–46.
3. Berkman, L., Glass, T., Brissette, I. & Seeman, T. From social integration to health: Durkheim in the new millennium. *Soc. Sci. & Med.,* 51, 6, 2000, 843-857.
4. Bender, J. L., Hohenadel, J., Wong, J., Katz, J., Ferris, L. E., Shobbrook, C. et al. (2008). What patients with cancer want to know about pain: a qualitative study. *Journal of Pain and Symptom Management*, *35*(2), 177-187.
5. Brandtzæg, P. & Heim, J. User loyalty and online communities: why members of online communities are not faithful. *Proc. ITETAIN*, 11, 2008.
6. Broom, A. Virtually he@lthy: the impact of internet use on disease experience and the doctor-patient relationship. Qualitative Health Research, 15, 3, 2005, 325-345.
7. Cohen, S., Underwood, L. & Gottlieb, B. Social support measurement and intervention: A guide for health and social scientists. *Oxford University Press* (2000).
8. Drentea, P. & Moren-Cross, J. Social capital and social support on the web: the case of an internet mother site. *Soc. Health & Ill*, 27, 7, 2005, 920–943.
9. Eysenbach, G., et al. Health related virtual communities and electronic support groups: systematic review of the effects of online peer to peer interactions. *Brit Med J*, 328, 2004, 1166.
10. Gladwell, M. How different are dogfighting and football? *The New Yorker*, http://www.newyorker.com/reporting/2009/10/19/091019fa_fact_gladwell, 2009.
11. Hartzler, A & Pratt, W. Managing the personal side of health: How patient expertise differs from the expertise of clinicians. *J. Med. Internet Research*, 13, 3, 2011, 1–18.
12. Hong, Y., Peña-Purcell, N. & Ory, M. Outcomes of online support and resources for cancer survivors: A systematic literature review. *Pat. Ed. And Couns*, 2011, 1–9.
13. Hoybye, M., Johansen, C., & Tjornhoj-Thomsen, T. Online interaction: Effects of storytelling in an internet breast cancer support group. *Psycho-Oncol*, 14, 2005, 211-220.
14. Huh, J. & Ackerman, M. Collaborative help in chronic disease management: supporting individualized problems. *Proc CSCW 2012*, 853-862.
15. Jinguji et al., T. Sport concussion assessment tool – 2: Baseline values for high school athletes. *Brit. J. Sports Med*, 26, 2012, 365-370.
16. Kim, H. and Sundar, S.S. Using interface cues in online health community boards to change impressions and encourage user contribution. *Proc. CHI 2011*, 599-608.
17. Lagan, M., Sinclair, M., & Kernohan, W.G. Internet use in pregnancy informs women's decision making: A web-based survey. *Birth,* 37, 2, 2010, 106–115.
18. Lampe, C., Walsh, R. Velasquez, A., & Ozkaya, E. Motivations to participate in online communities. *Proc. CHI 2010*, 1927-1936.
19. Larsson, M. A descriptive study of the use of the Internet by women seeking pregnancy-related information. *Midwifery*, 25, 1, 2009, 14–20.
20. Ley, B. Vive les roses!: The architecture of commitment in an online pregnancy and mothering group. *J. Computer-Mediated Communication*, 12, 4, 2007, 1388–1408.
21. Malik, S. & Coulson, N. Coping with infertility online: An examination of self-help mechanisms in an online infertility support group. *Pat. Ed. and Couns.*, 2010, 1–4.
22. Maloney-Krichmar, D. & Preece, J. A multilevel analysis of sociability, usability, and community dynamics in an online health community. *TOCHI*, 12, 2, ACM Press (2005), 1–32.
23. Massimi, M. (2013, February). Exploring remembrance and social support behavior in an online bereavement support group. In *Proc. CSCW 2013* (pp. 1169-1180). ACM.
24. Newman, M., Lauterbach, D., Munson, S.A., Resnick, P., and Morris, M. E. "It's not that I don't have problems, I'm just not putting them on Facebook": Challenges and opportunities in using online social networks for health. *Proc. CSCW 2011*, 341-350.
25. Owen, J., Bantum, E. & Golant, M. Benefits and challenges experienced by professional facilitators of

online support groups for cancer survivors. *Psycho-Oncol,* 18, 2, 2009, 144-55.

26. Picton, B., et al. Bereavement support groups: Timing of participation and reasons for joining. *Omega,* 43, 3, 2001, 247-258.

27. Preece, J. Online communities: Designing usability and supporting socialbility. *John Wiley & Sons, Inc*. (2000).

28. Provvidenza, C., et al. From consensus to action: knowledge transfer, education and influencing policy on sports concussion. *Brit. J. Sports Med.*, 2013.

29. Rogers, S. & Chen, Q. Internet community group participation: Psychosocial benefits for women with breast cancer. *J Comput-Mediat Comm,* 10, 1, 2005.

30. Sandaunet, A. A space for suffering? Communicating breast cancer in an online self-help context. *Qual Health Res.*, 18, 12, 2008, 1631-1641.

31. Sharf, B. Communicating breast cancer on-line: support and empowerment on the Internet. *Women Health*, 26, 1997, 65-84.

32. Shaw, B., et al., Experiences of women with breast cancer: exchanging support over the CHESS network. *J Health Comm*, 5, 2000, 135-59.

33. Swan, M. Emerging patient-driven health care models: An examination of health social networks, consumer personalized medicine and quantified self-tracking. *Int. J. Env. Res and Public Health*, 6, 2, 2009, 492-52.

34. Tator, C. Sport concussion education and prevention. *J. Clinical Sport Psychology*, 6, 2012, 293-301.

35. Turner, J.W., Grube, J. A., & Meyers, J. Developing an optimal match within online communities: An exploration of CMC support communities and traditional support. *J. Communication 51*, 2 (2001), 231-251.

36. van Uden-Kraan, C. et al. Empowering processes and outcomes of participation in online support groups for patients with breast cancer, arthritis, or fibromyalgia. *Qual Health Res*, 18, 3, 2008, 405-17, 2008.

37. Vilhauer, R. A qualitative study of the experiences of women with metastatic breast cancer. *Pall. Support Care*, 6, 2008, 249-58.

38. Weber, M. & Edwards, M. Sport concussion knowledge in the UK general public. *Arch. Clin. Neuropsych.*, 27, 3, 2012, 355-61.

39. Wiebe, D., Comstock, R. & Nance, M. Concussion research: A public health priority. *Injury Prevention*, 17, 1, 2011, 69-70.

40. Winefield, H. Support provision and emotional work in an Internet support group for cancer patients. *Pat Ed & Couns*, 62, 2006, 193-7.

41. Witteman et al. Apomediation and women's choices of birth place and attendants.*Proc. Medicine 2.0*, (2009).

42. Wright, K. Social support within an on-line cancer community. *J. App. Comm.*, 30, 3, 2002, 195-209.

43. Yin, R. K. *Case study research.* Sage (2009).

City, Self, Network: Transnational Migrants and Online Identity Work

Jessa Lingel
Microsoft Research
1 Memorial Dr.
Cambridge, MA 02142 USA
jlingel@microsoft.com

Mor Naaman
Cornell Tech
111 8th Ave.
New York, NY 10011 USA
mor.naaman@cornell.edu

danah boyd
Microsoft Research
1 Memorial Dr.
Cambridge, MA 01242 USA
dmb@microsoft.com

ABSTRACT
We use qualitative interviews with 26 transnational migrants in New York City to analyze socio-technical practices related to online identity work. We focus specifically on the use of Facebook, where benefits included keeping in touch with friends and family abroad and documenting everyday urban life. At the same time, many participants also reported experiences of fatigue, socio-cultural tensions and concerns about maintaining a sense of personal privacy. These experiences highlight how transnational practices complicate context collapse, where the geographic dispersal of participants' personal networks renders visible conflicts of "flattened" online networks. Our findings also suggest a kind of technology-enabled code-switching, where transnational migrants leverage social media to perform identities that alternate between communities, nationalities and geographies. This analysis informs HCI research on transnationalism and technological practices, and helps expose the complexities of online identity work in terms of shifting social and spatial contexts.

Author Keywords
Identity work; social media; transnationalism; urban informatics

ACM Classification Keywords
H.1.2. User/Machine Systems, Human Factors.

INTRODUCTION
Transnational migration is a process that involves a range of technologically-mediated practices of information and communication, including research to prepare for living in a new place [2], services to maintain existing social ties and form new ones [3, 24, 37], and tools for navigating a new environment [10]. In this paper, we report on interviews with 26 transnational migrants in New York City, conducted with the goals of understanding how social network sites (SNSs) are used in everyday life, and the socio-cultural tensions that emerge around managing relationships with a social network that spans multiple languages and geographic locales. Throughout our analysis, we use the term "transnational migrant" as a more inclusive alternative to "immigrant," referring people that might otherwise not be associated with the term immigrants, such as exchange students, tourists and temporary workers.

CSCW'14, February 15–19, 2014, Baltimore, Maryland, USA.

http://dx.doi.org/10.1145/2531602.2531l693

Our investigation contributes to a growing body of scholarship addressing transnationalism and information and communication technologies (ICTs) by exploring the role of technology in maintaining social ties. For example, researchers have analysed uses of technology to maintain ties to their communities of origin, such as Castro and Gonzalez's [11] work on the ways in which even very basic ICTs (such as an online guest book) can provide a sense of connection to one's family and local community. Wang and Brown [37] examined the range of ICTs used by families in a remote village in Mexico to keep in touch with family members who had migrated to the U.S. Taking more of an interventionist approach, Weibert and Wulf [38] examined the ways in which a computer-supported collaboration projects enabled cross-cultural interaction between Turkish immigrants and native Germans in Bonn. In these investigations, technology plays a deeply important role in different moments of transnational life, facilitating social connectivity through the production, consumption and circulation of information about everyday life.

Our work addresses two gaps in this body of scholarship, the first being methodological, the second conceptual. First, there is a tendency across literature on transnationalism to focus on a single nationality or ethnicity. In contrast, we gather accounts of 26 transnational migrants from 20 different countries. This allows us to identify practices that emerge across varied experiences of transnationalism. Second, much of the literature on human computer interaction (HCI) and transnationalism constructs ICTs as tools of collapsing geographic boundaries and facilitating communication, without addressing ways in which these same tools of connectivity can generate socio-cultural complications to the point of rupturing or threatening social ties [e.g. 3, 11, 24, 37]. We instead take a holistic approach to transnational experience, gathering narratives that discuss both the benefits and drawbacks of ICT use. Our qualitative approach highlights the importance of looking not just at dominant uses and narratives surrounding technology (e.g. Facebook and connectivity) but also at some of the counter-intuitive, less immediately evident practices and experiences surrounding transnational use of ICTs.

Our analysis bridges research on urban transnationalism and investigations of identity work. Identity work provides a focal point for investigations of the role of technology in shaping the construction of the self, where a number of technological practices are deployed in everyday tasks related to identity. SNSs offer their users highly useful tools of maintaining and building ties in ways that can build social capital [15], where the different choices that users make regarding their online profiles are read as indicators of taste and identity [25]. Transnational migration in particular creates a context in which issues related to identity work are rendered quite clearly, as evidenced by tensions related to managing relationships with a culturally diverse personal network.

We begin by introducing the concepts of *identity work*, *context collapse* and *code switching* as useful frameworks for unpacking the objectives as well as the drawbacks of technological connectivity. We then analyze the use of SNSs (specifically Facebook) among transnational migrants, addressing both positive outcomes (e.g. keeping in touch with friends and family abroad) and drawbacks (e.g. the fatigue of feeling obligated to disclose personal information) of SNS use in the context of everyday life. We conclude with a discussion of how these findings help inform our understanding of identity work and ICTs in a transnational context.

CONCEPTUAL FRAMEWORKS: IDENTITY WORK, CONTEXT COLLAPSE AND CODE-SWITCHING

This paper focuses on technological practices of urban newcomers as tied to identity work, or how "individuals shape and reshape who they are through language, behavior, appearance, and affiliation" [34]. Our conceptualization of identity is a constructionist one, where people make sense of themselves and others by following (or not following) social norms and scripts [19]. This sociological approach to understanding identity provides a framework for how different socio-technical practices are read within a wider socio-cultural context of conventional behavior. This approach is particularly appropriate to a study of transnational migration, which requires navigating different expectations of comportment and social interaction [22].

Within HCI research, scholars have investigated the role of technology in identity work, such as Ames' work on technological practices related to iPhones among university students [1]. In Ames' analysis, access to technology alone is an insufficient signifier of identity – the social consequences of using or not using technology, and the contexts in which those technologies are deployed are far more indicative of identity work as manifest through technology. In the context of designing SNS, Farnham and Churchill [18] argued that people's lives are faceted, meaning that "people maintain social boundaries and show different facets or sites of their character according to the demands of the current social situation" (p. 359). As such, the design of online platforms interpersonal communication should reflect the faceted nature of human identity. In these studies (see also, [12, 15, 25]), identity work becomes a means of gauging the efficacy of various technologies in ways that account for the social (as well as purely functional) objectives.

For scholars interested in issues of online identity work, the notion of *context collapse* offers a useful means of analyzing sources of tension in curating online identity. Context collapses result from a multi-faceted social network being flattened into a single audience, such that users find it difficult to curate content intended for or legible to only part of their personal networks [7] - See also [8, 20, 21, 27, 39]. Offline, people have the option to modify behavior based on their immediate social surroundings or to encode messages and gestures for a select few [18]. On sites like Facebook, such practices are far more challenging, potentially generating tension and fatigue.

The construct of code-switching originated in linguistics to describe the transition between languages in a single conversation among bilingual speakers [30]. From this fairly narrow construction of code-switching as conducted between speakers fluent in two languages, the concept has been expanded to refer to altering between forms of vernacular or between professional identities (e.g. [14]). We use a fairly expansive conceptualization of code-switching, referring both to linguistic shifts and more nuanced alterations in cultural markers of identity, including behavioural norms and social customs.

METHODOLOGY

This project takes a qualitative approach to identifying and analyzing information practices of transnational migrants in the New York City metropolitan area. Interviews were conducted between December of 2011 and September of 2012. Participants were recruited through two methods: 18 were recruited from English as a Second Language (ESL) programs in and around New York City. A second group of eight participants were recruited through word-of-mouth via our personal networks, and consisted mostly of current or former graduate students from countries outside the United States. Participants were screened based on the length of time that they had lived in New York, where we limited the interview pool to those who had arrived within the last two years. In total, the 26 participants hailed from 20 different countries and ranged in age from 22 to 60. For details on participants, see Table 1.

Interviews lasted between 45 and 90 minutes and were audio recorded. Interview questions focused on resources for tasks like finding an apartment and locating ESL classes. Participants were also asked about technologies for keeping in touch with people abroad and the role of SNSs in everyday urban life. Transcripts were coded using NVIVO software. In terms of data analysis, we used an emic/etic coding strategy [29], which involves creating a series of high-level "etic" codes corresponding to themes identified prior to coding: urban space, changing relationships to space over time, personal networks and technological practices. We then nested "emic" subcategories underneath that emerged in participants' own terms. In addition, we used an open coding method [36] to identify emergent themes and concepts, many of which were then brought into the emic/etic hierarchy. A number of themes grew out of this process, including information practices used to become familiar with city space, relationships to the city in terms of navigational as well as ethnicity-based landmarks, and technology and identity work. In this paper, we present findings related to this third area.

It's important to note that although we analyze experiences of transnational migrants, many of our findings are likely also applicable to people who migrate domestically, or even from one part of the city to another. At the same time, our data does not allow us to make claims about the extent to which participant experiences are representative of transnational migrants generally. As a whole, we take an interpretive approach in analyzing narratives of transnational migrants with whom we spoke; rather than using qualitative data as a means of addressing hypotheses, we use participant accounts to draw out themes for discussion of SNS use as it relates to identity work, as manifested in practices of keeping in touch with one's personal network and documenting everyday life.

RESULTS

In this section, we analyze references to identity work in an online context, focusing on Facebook, which was by far the most popular SNS among participants in this study. Online identity work can take place in numerous environments – e.g., video chats, search engine use, online shopping and social media. We focus on SNSs because they were nearly universal among people we interviewed and because analyses of transnational use of SNSs are still not well documented [10]. Among the 26 transnational migrants interviewed in this study, Facebook was by far the most popular SNS, referenced by 24 participants. Other references to SNSs (with the number of participants who referenced each in parentheses) included Twitter (8), LinkedIn (6), foursquare (6) and Weibo (1). Perhaps unsurprisingly, the two oldest participants in this study,

Participant Details

Name	Age	Nationality	Residence in NYC	Profession
Alice	26	Australia	18 months	Barista
Amelie	27	France	2 weeks	Unemployed
Araceli	29	Mexico	7 months	Hostess
Cecille	33	Cameroon	2 years	Teacher
Ishmael	42	Togo	6 months	Unemployed
Julio	60	Dominican Republic	9 months	Unemployed
Jorge	29	Spain	6 months	IT worker
Juan	37	Uruguay	3 months	Factory worker
Kiki	32	Japan	1 year	Nanny
Lalo	35	Chile	4 months	Auto mechanic
Laura	34	Brazil	1 year	Unemployed
Luka	29	Georgia	2 years	NGO
Miao	36	China	1 month	Student
Midori	38	Japan	3 months	Research fellow
Nalan	32	Turkey	2 years	IT worker
Noely	32	Venezuela	1 year	PR person
Raul	22	Honduras	18 months	Student
Rob	28	Puerto Rico	1 year	Delivery person
Carla	26	Philippines	2 years	Student
Dinan	25	India	18 months	IT worker
Gia	32	Indonesia	2 years	Journalist
Jacinta	33	Mexico	2 years	NGO
Javier	26	Brazil	18 months	Student
Lu	28	Mexico	1 year	NGO
Sue	29	Korea	2 years	Student
Wen	26	China	1 year	Student

Table 1. Participant details include age at time of interview, country of origin and the length of time in New York. Julio declined to provide his age, but we estimate him to be about 60. "NGO" denotes participants who worked at a non-government organization. As discussed in the methods section, participants were recruited in two groups – first through ESL classes, and second through word-of-mouth and snowball sampling among transnational graduate students. Gray shading denotes the latter group.

Julio (60, Dominican Republic) and Ishmael (42, Togo) did not use Facebook, or any other SNS.

From its origins in 2004 as an online community for university students, Facebook has grown into the most popular SNS in the world, with over one billion users, and approximately 81% of monthly active Facebook users live outside of the U.S. and Canada [17], indicating the global reach of the site. This is also in contrast to platforms with users bases concentrated in only a few geographic regions (e.g., Weibo in China or Orkut in Brazil and India). Depending on individual configurations of privacy settings, users can see each other's photos, links and messages, and geographic location check-ins. These operational functions have important consequences for norms of disclosure and expectations of privacy, as demonstrated by the choices that participants made in when and how to use Facebook as part of the process of managing their own experiences of newness. In contrast to HCI research that focuses on a single face to social media operations (for example, looking only at photo sharing or location functions), we take a holistic approach in our analysis of Facebook, integrating discussion of messaging, posting, uploading photos and using locative functions. In other words, we sought to understand how different components of Facebook are deployed in the larger socio-technical assemblage of everyday life and online connectivity.

Online identity work: An analysis of Facebook

Benefits of using Facebook included maintaining relationships with friends and family abroad, and providing a platform for garnering prestige, as well as documenting everyday life. At the same time, participants also described drawbacks of SNS use: issues of language and audience; privacy concerns; and the exhaustion of feeling obligated to maintain an online persona.

Facebook and Connectivity

In looking at social media use among people we interviewed, Facebook was used by participants to document everyday life and maintain social ties, both in New York and abroad. This is in keeping with arguments that devoting time to online interaction displays a commitment to the maintenance of social ties [5, 20], and to previous work on transnational use of ICTs [3, 11, 24, 37]. Nalan's (32, Turkey) description of using Facebook is typical of this type of SNS use:

> [Facebook] is very useful, definitely. I keep in touch with my friends, a lot of friends, family, my ex co-workers. It is good, you can see pictures of what's going on in their life, it's good, good. I like Facebook ... I like using technology, especially [because] my family is in Turkey, I'm here, but we don't feel so far away from each other. We can see each other online.

Nalan had lived in New York for about two years and although she visited her native Turkey about once a year, she had no plans to return permanently, and her family had never visited the U.S. Thus SNSs provided a vital means of communicating with family and friends abroad. Although she uses language that emphasizes visual interaction, Nalan is not referring here to videoconferencing tools like Skype or Google Hangouts. Rather, she refers to the sense of connectivity that takes place through online interaction. This use of Facebook confirms much of the literature on use of SNSs (transnational or otherwise) to maintain a sense of intimacy and connectivity with people in one's personal network, irrespective of distance [5, 20]. For Nalan and others in this study, Facebook provides an important means of articulating a social network of her friends and family, and signaling a commitment to interpersonal connectivity across space.

SNSs and Signals of Prestige

Participants also used Facebook as part of a particular kind of identity work intended to impress one's friends and family by documenting visits to well-known places or consumption of particularly famous, location-specific goods. Demonstrating how this process works via use of Facebook's locative functionality, Alice (26, Australia) stated that she mainly used Facebook check-in to "show off" to her friends in Australia: "I was in a bar [I'd seen] from [the TV show] *Sex in the City*. So I had to check in on Facebook. I knew my friends in Adelaide would die." Similarly, Araceli (29, Mexico) referenced using Facebook check in to document visiting "the favorite tapas place [of] Lady Gaga." In both cases, Facebook becomes a means of documenting everyday life, but participants were also motivated by the ability to use Facebook updates as a kind of impression management, gaining status among their connections abroad for having access to iconic foreign locations. These technological practices are fairly complex accounts of signals that traverse space (New York and abroad), media (indirect encounters with celebrity translated into gaining status among one's friends), and technology (showcasing offline spaces to one's online connections).

Even outside of references to celebrities, we noted frequent references to everyday uses of Facebook's check-in functionality as a means of showing off. Sue (29, Korea) noted that she rarely checked in on Facebook in New Jersey, where she was a graduate student, however, "in [New York City] all the time I turn it on, the location function, so that I can just keep track of the location ... I can check in somewhere cool in Facebook or Foursquare. Just try to show off I'm in the city now, something like that." Araceli described similar uses, stating that she used check-in on Facebook on

> happy days, like when ... I was visiting many places with my friends [from Mexico] a few weeks ago. I post because all the time they told me like, please post us in this place, la la la, they didn't have service, phone service, so all the time [they] told me, please post us in this place. So yeah, I use [check-in] sometimes. Or when I want to remember some place, like some good restaurant. I like to do that.

In both Sue's and Araceli's descriptions, the use of locative media accomplishes a number of tasks – it helps them find locations in the city and documents those locations for future reference. Sue and Araceli also noted that Facebook's check-in function allows them to transmit the experience of visiting a location to friends in a way that shows off, garnering prestige. In Araceli's case, there was an external pressure from her friends to check in and tag photos on their behalf as a way of accruing their own markers of status, or what might be called identity work by proxy. Araceli's friends push the efforts of gaining social status onto her own Facebook updates, where online connectivity can produce a shared labor of identity work.

Another facet of collaborative identity work as tied to locative SNS functions took shape via friend-based recommendations. For example, Carla (26, Philippines) noted "I can see recommendations [from my friends] to find places, [so it's] kind of tailored to what you like, I see suggestions based on where my friends are going, which I like." Although Carla had lived in New York for over a year, she still felt that her knowledge of the city was limited to the neighborhoods immediately surrounding her school and where she lived, and Carla commented that seeing updates about where her friends had checked in served as both a motivational and vetting mechanism to visiting new places. As a kind of follow-up function, Javier (26, Brazil) commented on the sense of satisfaction and pride that surfaced when he could post on someone's page that he had been to a location where one of his friends had checked in, effectively demonstrating his familiarity with different bars, clubs and restaurants. This kind of interactive communication is at once spatial and social, and underscores the extent to which identity and information work on Facebook is highly networked, in that identity work isn't solely a matter of what an individual user shares, it is also comprised of the content posted by those in one's personal network, where comments, posts and tags that link users also shape how identity is performed online.

Transnational Facebook Fatigue

Interestingly, some participants expressed discomfort with SNSs precisely because of the possibility of using them to impress one's friends. At the time of our interview, Amelie (27, France) was just two weeks into a three-month stay in New York, during which time she was focused on improving her English. Amelie mentioned that although she had been a Facebook user prior to moving, she rarely updated her page in New York, partly because she wanted to resist a construction of everyday urban life as overly conventional or touristy: "I don't want to post like typical sentences, 'I'm in New York and I do this.' So I don't know, I prefer to send email and maybe I use [Facebook to] send some the message. [I] send message more than like publish something, post something [on Facebook]." For Amelie, the communication functions of Facebook were useful, but the locative functions were more problematic. Voicing similar concerns, Lu (28, Mexico) described a transition in her use of Facebook check-in over time, moving from excitement at checking in to a sense of unease:

> Lu: When I was in a cool place, or when I was with a big group of friends, you know, then I wanted to show it to other people. But now I think it's weird.
>
> Interviewer: Weird?
>
> Lu: I don't know. It's weird … because I don't want to be that person who checks in somewhere because I want people to know I'm living in New York.

Here Lu suggests a kind of backlash to signaling that can be interpreted as posturing or patronizing. Facebook users with transnational connections may want to use functions like Facebook check in largely for personal reasons, like documenting where they've eaten in a given neighborhood, but these actions may still have social consequences in producing unwanted connotations, such as showing off and generating "typical" rather than personalized identities.

Code-switching on Facebook

For 25 of the 26 people interviewed in this project, English was not their native language. Thus one important component of transnational use of SNSs centers on multi-lingualism. Participants explained that decisions about posting on Facebook in one language versus another indicate the intended audience of a given online update or comment. As Araceli (29, Mexico) indicated, "If I want to say something that I think is involved with my friends in New York, I write in English, because I have friends from … many places. Or if I wanna say something just for my friends in Mexico, I will post in Spanish." Bilingualism enables transnational migrants to direct (albeit somewhat loosely) their content to various parts of their personal networks, and they assume that people will take language as an indication of whether or not the message is intended for them.

Bilingual posting can be marked as code-switching, but because of the visibility of this switch, it also becomes a coping mechanism for negotiating collapsed contexts, in keeping with Marwick and boyd's [27] findings on SNS steganography, which refers to practices of hiding things in plain sight. Looking specifically at teenagers, Marwick and boyd found that adolescent Facebook users relied on inside jokes, slang and pop culture references to post content that only some of their connections could parse. Yet, at times, teens would also post encoded language that was explicitly meant to exclude by making it very clear to readers who could not understand the message that they were not part of the intended audience.

Bilingualism and code-switching enable SNS users to draw linguistic boundaries around their social media content, signaling information intended for a specific subset of their social networks. This kind of code-switching takes place not in a single conversation, but in a larger conceptualization of communication as a social awareness stream [31], where a constant feed of information is intended to keep one's connections abreast of activities and events. Unlike teens who are actively obscuring their encoded messages, the transnational migrants we interviewed were actively trying to signal their intended audience through the use of language.

Participants were typically highly tuned to how their networks would respond to content that they couldn't understand. Laura (34, Brazil) described how some of these tensions unfolded on her Facebook page:

> I started to publish, not *all* news that I publish, but *sometimes* I publish in Portuguese and in English. But all photos, all pictures that I publish, I publish with both languages. Because I know that my new friends that don't speak Portuguese want to know what I put in the pictures … I'm trying always to do this. I think, like, [it

> shows I] respect new friends. But sometimes it's only to publish news, some phrase or expression, I forget and I publish in Portuguese. But sometimes I publish in English and my father, my mother, my sister complain, "Oh, we couldn't understand, you need to write in Portuguese!"

In the context of language choices and SNS, Laura's account demonstrates the extent to which language is an indication of audience, such that her family's voicing objections to the language used in Facebook content is moreover an objection to being excluded from information about everyday life because the information being remitted lacks translation.

As a counterpart to earlier comments that signaling location via SNS can be read as posturing, there was an additional complication of feeling that adopting non-native language was presumptuous or haughty. As Jacinta (33, Mexico) explained, "I have some judgment issues with people that use English in Mexico. I don't like it, because it's like snotty, a little bit. I'm like, 'Oh, come on. Oh yeah, we know you're in New York, I see that too.'" Where Facebook check-in was sometimes used to generate status among one's followers in terms of place, here Jacinta reads a similar kind of identity work linked to language in a derogatory sense. Part of the SNS fatigue described earlier can be tied to efforts of code-switching and the continuous shifts between languages as well as normative social scripts. Code-switching allowed participants some leeway in directing social media signals to certain segments of one's personal network, but it also opened up complications of managing a multi-lingual audience that may react negatively to messages perceived as exclusionary or as posturing.

Facebook and breaking ties.

Other modes of using Facebook emerged from interviews that diverged dramatically from participants' typical use of SNSs to keep in touch with friends and family. Although mentioned less often, participants also discussed transnational migration as responsible for radically altering previous Facebook practices. Overall, research on SNSs – and, transnational practices in particular – has been more focused on adoption and tie maintenance than departure and defriending [4, 32]. The following examples are useful precisely because they are atypical, and allow for a counter narrative challenging highly prevalent assumptions about SNSs (and transnational use of ICTs in particular – see [10]) as always, only or predominantly connective.

As a somewhat extreme example of altering SNS practices post-migration, Rob (28) moved from Puerto Rico to New York and promptly deleted the majority of his friends from his Facebook account. As Rob explained: "When I came to New York, I erased most of the people, most of my friends. Because I just wanted to change. I like changes. I wanted to change the past." Rob had been in the city for about a year at the time of our interview, during which time he had held down a string of delivery jobs. Although he had no intention of returning to Puerto Rico permanently, Rob was also not tied to the idea of staying in New York, expressing an interest in moving "somewhere warm, somewhere that's green, with less hipsters."

On the whole, Rob's approach to living in New York seemed rooted in accruing as diverse a social network as possible, which partly explains his willingness to delete his Puerto Rican friends from his Facebook network. This is a marked difference from the typical use of Facebook, at least among participants in this study. Rather than using Facebook to maintain ties, Rob used Facebook as a means of severing them. Rob went on to explain, "I wanted to start over again. I didn't know nobody in New York, so I just deleted people. And eventually, friends grow." Here, Rob describes Facebook as a platform for performing a particular kind of identity work, where removing people from his online social network symbolized his physical removal from Puerto Rico. This can also be constructed as a pre-emptive move to avoid context collapse, effectively homogenizing his Facebook audience, at least in terms of geography.

Jacinta (33, Mexico) echoed Rob's practices in a less drastic way, reducing her engagement with Facebook and Twitter rather than deleting connections altogether. After moving to New York for graduate school, Jacinta found a job with a non-government organization (NGO) and had plans to return to Mexico, although not for another five or six years. Jacinta specifically linked her SNS fatigue to the burden of keeping her personal network in Mexico informed of her life in New York:

> And I don't post anything because it overwhelms me now. I have this visceral reaction to my persona online, that I just quit ... I felt that I was living in Mexico too much, because I was too much monitoring what was going on in there, and I felt pressured to let people know what was going in on my New York life. Like I had to let them know that I was having a great life or something ... So I decided I was not going to tell them anything. And I can see that this is not very well taken from the other side, it is probably a form of selfishness. But for now, it's sort of an unchosen choice. I'm just doing it that way. I wish for some day to be able to find a grey area, you know, when I can serenely do Facebook and Twitter but for now I just feel it's too much maintenance, putting too much out there, like maintaining relationships with people, especially on Twitter, and I feel too exposed ... Too much exposure, I don't want to feel so exposed.

This account highlights tensions that emerge from transnational migration and are borne out online, specifically in terms of identity work via SNSs. Jacinta's desire for a "serene" post-migration engagement with SNSs speaks to a disconnect between the level of engagement desired by Jacinta's contacts and her own need for control and privacy. Thus Jacinta is no longer willing to document information about her everyday life because it requires "too much maintenance, putting too much out there" and "too much exposure." Jacinta's description points to the cost of online identity work as a burden of time and energy, particularly because of the operational limitations at work: SNSs encourage sharing without necessarily providing a way to keep in touch without self-disclosure, which results in the feeling of removing oneself from the present location and, instead, being pulled back into one's country (or at least, personal network) of origin.

DISCUSSION: EVERYDAY URBAN LIFE AND CONTEXT COLLAPSE.

The most popular SNS among participants in this study, Facebook operates on a number of levels in facilitating online identity work. Although this identity work is extremely helpful in connecting with friends and family abroad, using Facebook also generates moments of interpersonal and intercultural tension, as when code-switching between languages generates texts that include and exclude within a social network. Practices of rejecting, restarting or heavily reducing use of Facebook did not surface universally among participants, but are nevertheless useful in understanding drawbacks of SNS use. These experiences provide a useful counter-balance to HCI research on transnationalism that over-emphasizes or over-simplifies the use of ICTs among transnational migrants as linear, unproblematic and primarily about maintaining and forging ties rather than manipulating or breaking them. In the remainder of this article, we offer discussion of key themes from our findings and point to some areas for future work.

Context Collapse Transnational Audiences

For transnational migrants, experiences of context collapse can track along distinctly geographic lines, where SNS users are confronted with posting content to friends, family, and acquaintances spread across the globe. Context collapse hinges on homogenizing diverse audiences, where the heterogeneity of relationships managed through social media has been linked to anxiety or paralysis in terms of what, how and to whom one discloses personal information [39]. But for transnational migrants in this study, the problem was not hesitation at what to post because the audience being imagined was too difficult to conceptualize [7], but rather was imagined quite precisely, both spatially (in terms of whether people lived nearby or abroad) as well as temporally (before or after migration). Thus context collapse is not necessarily best conceived as an individual overwhelmed by an audience so heterogeneous as to be anonymous. Rather, experiences of transnational migrants inform a notion of context collapse that is much more linked to exhaustion of tailoring messages to known and discrete but different audiences. Feelings of exhaustion and fatigue are by no means limited to transnational migrants, and research on leaving or abstaining from SNSs is beginning to address motivations for reducing time spent on Facebook or leaving altogether [4, 32].

Findings from this study also have implications for rethinking code-switching in the context of online identity work. Many transnational migrants we interviewed were deeply familiar with modes of code-switching and we regularly witnessed participants engaging in different forms of this practice, from deploying slang to changes in body language, depending on who else was in the room or engaged in conversation. In the context of advertising, Luna and Peracchio [26] examined the reception of ads that contained both English and Spanish, noting that code-switched slogans activate emotional associations related to the specific language and culture being used. In other words, code-switching takes place on a level that is not only linguistic, but also emotional and social. The emotion and affect at work in code-switching is in fact central to understanding how transnational migrants leverage bilingualism in order to signal an enduring commitment to friends and family abroad. But as in the case of advertising, this affective labor requires substantive knowledge about one's personal network, and specifically their SNS reading practices. This finding underscores the above point about the extent to which context collapse for transnational migrants is experienced not necessarily in vague or paralyzing ways, but far more acutely in terms of personal networks divided geographically. Future work could focus on the reception rather than production of code-switching content. Participants commented on the reactions of their online networks to code-switching, but how are these messages understood and circulated by people whose friends and family have migrated abroad? To what extent is code-switching interpreted as an enduring commitment to one's place of origin?

Bilingualism enabled participants some leeway in guiding content of their online identity work to certain portions of their personal networks. Yet it's worth noting that with a broad definition for code switching, the experiences of transnational migrants have implications for other SNS users. Additional research on online identity work is needed to understand whether different levels of technological use are effective in managing context collapse – for example, using different platforms (e.g. Tumblr versus Facebook) to reach different members of one's personal network, having different accounts within the same network, or using group functionality (like Google+'s circles).

Impression Management of Self and City

Context collapse is frequently constructed as a conflict experienced individually or a crisis of selfhood [21]. For participants in this study, concerns of authentic documentation of everyday life were partly tied to the self and partly tied to place. For example, references to reducing SNS use underscore tensions of producing selfhood both in New York and abroad. New York has its own identity, however, and participants' references to concerns of "showing off" tie context collapse not only to impression management of the self, but of the city. In the socio-technical practices we identified above, experiences of online identity work among transnational migrants in New York highlight the inter-relatedness of self, place and technologies at work in online connectivity. As locative media like Facebook check-in and Foursquare continue to gain popularity, issues of performing personal as well as spatial identity will become increasingly important to understand and untangle.

It's likely that New York's extensive presence in mainstream media heightens the extent to which participants' connections are interested in their experiences of living in the city. Having consumed imagery of New York through film, music and news media, Facebook content of transnational newcomers becomes an additional source of information about New York. Yet even if the stakes of prestige are perhaps higher in New York than places with less visibility in popular media, similar dynamics of using locative functionality to gain status are also likely for other cities. Future work could explore conspicuous consumption in the specific context of using SNS to document purchases and entertainment in a way intended to gain status among one's personal network.

As a whole, our qualitative analysis of transnational newcomers to New York City has discussed the relationships between technology and identity work, demonstrating the extent to which everyday life is technologically messy [13], with complications of language, privacy and socio-cultural differences. Taking a holistic approach to technological practices used by transnational migrants to produce and manage flows of information about everyday life throughout their personal networks, we have sought to consider how these practices provide insight into experiences of transnationalism, as well as more general experiences of online identity work.

ACKNOWLEDGEMENTS

The authors are grateful to Christina Dunbar-Hester, Ingrid Erickson, Heewon Kim, Ben Merriman and the anonymous reviewers for comments on this paper.

REFERENCES

1. Ames, M. Managing mobile multi-tasking: The culture of iphones on Stanford campus. In *Proc. CSCW 2013*, ACM Press, (2013).
2. Amit, K. and Riss, I. The role of social networks in the immigration decision-making process: The case of North American immigration to Israel. *Immigrants & Minorities 25,* 3 (2007), 290-313.
3. Bacigalupe, G. and Cámara, M. Transnational families and social technologies: Reassessing immigration psychology. *Journal of Ethnic and Migration Studies 38* 9 (2012), 1425-1438.
4. Baumer, E. P. S., Adams, P., Khovanskaya, V. D., Liao, T. C., Smith, M. E., Schwanda Sosik, V. and Williams, K. Limiting, leaving, and (re)lapsing: An exploration of Facebook non-use practices and experiences. In *Proc. CHI 2013*, ACM Press (2013).
5. Baym, N. K. *Personal connections in the digital age.* Polity Press, Cambridge, UK, 2010.
6. Bernstein, M. S., Bakshy, E., Burke, M. and Karrer, B. Quantifying the Invisible Audience in Social Networks. In *Proc. CHI 2013,* ACM Press (2013).
7. boyd, d. Taken out of context: American teen sociality in networked publics. PhD Dissertation, UC Berkeley, 2008.
8. boyd, d. and Marwick, A. Social privacy in networked publics: Teens' attitudes, practices, and strategies. Paper presented at the *Oxford Internet Institute Decade in Internet Time Symposium* (2011).
9. Burrell, J. *Invisible users: Youth in the Internet cafes of urban Ghana.* MIT Press, Cambridge, MA, USA, 2012.
10. Caidi, N., Allard, D. and Quirke, L. Information practices of immigrants. *Annual Review of Information Science and Technology* (2010), 493-530
11. Castro, L. A. and Gonzaelz, V. M. Hometown websites: Continuous maintenance of cross-border connections. In *Proc. C&T '09*, ACM Press (2009), 145-154.
12. Donath, J. Signals in social supernets. *Journal of Computer-Mediated Communication 13,* 1 (2008), 231-251.
13. Dourish, P. and Bell, G. *Divining a Digital Future: Mess and Mythology in Ubiquitous Computing.* MIT Press, Cambridge, MA, USA, 2011.
14. Downey, G. L. and Lucena, J. C. Knowledge and professional identity in engineering: code-switching and the metrics of progress. *History and Technology 20,* 4 (2004), 393-420.
15. Ellison, N. B., Steinfield, C. and Lampe, C. The benefits of Facebook "friends:" Social capital and college students' use of online social network sites. *Journal of Computer-Mediated Communication 12,* 4 (2007), 1143–1168.
16. Ellison, N. B., Vitak, J. Steinfeld, C., Gray, R. and Lampe, C. Negotiating privacy concerns and social capital needs in a social media environment. In S. Strepte and L. Reinecke (eds.), *Privacy Online.* 2011. 19-32.
17. Facebook Newsroom. Key facts. http://newsroom.fb.com/Key-Facts
18. Farnham, S. D. and Churchill, E. F. Faceted identity, faceted lives: Social and technical issues with being

yourself online. In *Proc. CSCW 2011*, ACM Press (2011), 359 – 368.

19. Goffman, E. *The presentation of self in everyday life*. Penguin, Harmondsworth, UK, 1971

20. Harper, R. *Texture: Human expression in the age of communications overload*. MIT Press, Cambridge, MA, USA, 2010.

21. Hogan, B. The presentation of self in the age of social media: Distinguishing performances and exhibitions online. *Bulletin of Science, Technology & Society 30,* 6 (2010), 377-386.

22. Kasinitz, P., Mollenkopf, J. H. and Waters, M. C. *Becoming New Yorkers: Ethnographies of the new second generation*. 2003. New York, NY: Russell Sage.

23. Kivran-Swaine, F., Govindan, P. and Naaman, M. The impact of network structure on breaking ties in online social networks: Unfollowing on Twitter. In Proc. CHI '11. ACM Press (2011), 1101-1104.

24. Komito, L. and Bates, J. Migrants' information practices and use of social media in Ireland: Networks and community. In *Proc. iConference 2011*, ACM Press (2011), 289-295.

25. Liu, H. Social network profiles as taste performances. *Journal of Computer-Mediated Communication 13*, 1 (2007).

26. Luna, D. and Peracchio, L. A. Advertising to bilingual consumers. The impact of code-switching on persuasion. *Journal of Consumer Research* 31, 4 (2007), 760-765.

27. Marwick, A. and boyd, d. I tweet honestly, I tweet passionately: Twitter users, context collapse, and the imagined audience. *New Media and Society 13,* 1 (2010), 113-133.

28. Mehra, B. and Papajohn, D. "Glocal" patterns of communication-information convergences in Internet use: Cross cultural behaviour of international teaching assistants in a culturally alien information environment. *International Information & Library Review 39,* 1 (2007), 12-30.

29. Miles, M. B. and Huberman, A. M. *Qualitative data analysis: An expanded sourcebook*. SAGE, Thousand Oaks, CA, USA, 2007.

30. Milroy, L. and Muysken, P. *One speaker, two languages: Cross-disciplinary perspectives on code-switching*. Cambridge University Press, Cambridge, UK, 1995.

31. Naaman, M., Boase, J. and Lai, C. Is it really about me? Message content in social awareness streams. In *Proc. CHI 2009,* ACM Press (2009), 189-192.

32. O'Hara, K., Kindberg, T., Glaney, M., Baptista, L., Sukumaran, B., Kahana, G. and Rowbotham, J. Social Practices in location-based collecting. In *Proc. CHI, 2007*, ACM Press (2007), 1225-1234.

33. Portwood-Stacer, L. Media refusal and conspicuous non-consumption: The performative and political dimensions of Facebook abstention. *New Media & Society* (In press).

34. Quirke, L. C. Public libraries serving newcomers to Canada: A comparison of the Toronto and Windsor public libraries. Unpublished master's thesis, Ryerson University, Toronto, 2006.

35. Shapiro, E. *Gender circuits: Bodies and identities in a technological age.* Routledge, New York, NY, USA, 2010.

36. Strauss, A. L. and Corbin, J. M. *Basics of Qualitative Research: Grounded Theory Procedures and Techniques*. SAGE, Thousand Oaks, CA, USA, 1990.

37. Wang, T. and Brown, B. Ethnography of the telephone: Changing uses of communication technology in village life. In *Proc. Mobile HCI 2011*, ACM Press (2011).

38. Weibert, A. and Wulf, V. "All of a sudden we had this dialogue": Intercultural clubs' contribution to sustainable integration. In *Proc. ICIC 2010,* ACM Press (2010).

39. Wesch, M. Youtube and you: Experiences of self-awareness in the context collapse of the recording webcam. *Explorations in Media Ecology 8,* 2 (2009), 19-34.

Twitter ain't Without Frontiers: Economic, Social, and Cultural Boundaries in International Communication

Ruth Garcia-Gavilanes
Universitat Pompeu Fabra
Barcelona
ruth.garcia@upf.edu

Yelena Mejova
Yahoo Labs
Barcelona
ymejova@yahoo-inc.com

Daniele Quercia
Yahoo Labs
Barcelona
dquercia@acm.org

ABSTRACT

With the advent of Twitter and other lightweight social-networking services, one might think that it is easier than ever to maintain geographically dispersed, weaker social ties. By contrast, in this study we show that the international Twitter communication landscape is not only still largely predetermined by physical distance, but that it also depends on countries' social, economic, and cultural attributes. We describe a study of an international Twitter mention network of 13 million users across over 100 countries. We show that the *Gravity Model*, which hypothesizes that the flow between two areas is proportional to their masses (which we approximate using internet penetration) and inversely proportional to the distance between them, is correlated ($r = 0.68$) with the international communication flow. Using this model, along with other social, economic, and cultural variables, we predict the communication volume at *Adjusted* R^2 of 0.80, with trade, language and racial intolerance especially impacting communication. We discuss the implications of these barriers to communication in the contexts of collaborative work, software design, and recommendation systems.

Author Keywords

Communication; Social Media; Culture

ACM Classification Keywords

J.4 Social and Behavioral Sciences: Sociology

INTRODUCTION

The rise of the Internet and social networks have lead some researchers to hypothesize that "distance is dead" [6] or is not longer important to make social contacts. At the very conception of online networking pundits predicted the loosening of the "grip of geography" [7], foreseeing the strengthening of the bonds between people with the same interest in different parts of the world, and globalization of both the workforce and the scope of governmental considerations. Nevertheless, empirical studies have shown that distance still matters in online communication, including email [32, 25] and instant messages [23], with these new modes of communication reinforcing the strong ties we make in person. However, recently other factors were shown to mediate the effect of distance, including language, air travel frequency [34], and culture [32]. For instance, countries sharing cultural features have a higher affinity in international email exchanges, and can be effectively clustered into "civilizations", as suggested by Samuel Huntington in "The Clash of Civilizations" [16].

Finding whether Internet users are trapped in socio-economic or cultural "bubbles", despite the supposed freedom and multi-cultural nature of the web, is a first step to identifying the blind spots in our communication. Specifically, cultural dimensions have long been studied by sociologists. One way to measure cultural values, as they relate to personal behavior, is using Hofstede's culture indexes [14]. Available for many countries around the world, they characterize authority relations, the relationship between individual and society, gender roles, and social and environmental uncertainties. We bring these into the realm of social media analysis by relating the international communication flows in Twitter to the extent to which countries share these cultural characteristics and various other country-specific attributes.

Recent wide adoption of Twitter has fostered a global network of relatively weak ties based on user interests. As defined by Granovetter [13], the strength of a tie is "a combination of the amount of time, the emotional intensity, the intimacy (mutual confiding), and the reciprocal services which characterize the tie". Since Twitter messages are short (140 characters), and are broadcast publicly, easy to both read and to ignore, Twitter provides a perfect platform for the establishment of weak ties. Also, the connections need not be reciprocal, and users are free to 'follow' (subscribe to) any other user with a public profile in order to see the posts, or status updates, of that user in their timeline. Furthermore, users are free to contact others (being their followers or not) by simply mentioning their users names. The value of such characteristics make Twitter a useful tool for exploring communication in online social media, going beyond the strong ties of personal e-mails or Facebook. Indeed, we find major differences between the importance of economic and cultural factors in Twitter communication as compared to e-mail, as described in [32].

Here, we explore how various factors (distance, social, economic, and cultural dimensions) shape the cross-country communication through the lightweight social networking services. Specifically, we address two questions: (1) To what extent does distance determine the informal communication

CSCW'14, February 15–19, 2014, Baltimore, Maryland, USA.
Copyright © 2014 ACM 978-1-4503-2540-0/14/02$15.00.
http://dx.doi.org/10.1145/2531602.2531725

of users from different nations? and (2) To what extent do social, economic and cultural factors mediate/impede this communication? To tackle these questions, we study user mentions among 13 million geolocated users during a 10 week period from March to May 2011. Using this data, covering 111 countries, along with country-specific statistics gathered from outside sources (CIA, World Banks and World Values Survey), we make two main contributions:

- We employ the *gravity model* [20], which uses node population and physical distance, to construct a baseline communication network, and test to which extent it estimates cross-country Twitter communication. We use the Haversine distance between two countries and two population proxies: country population and the Internet penetration, with the latter showing moderate correlation with the number of mentions and retweets of 5,932 pairs of countries ($r = 0.68$ for unique mentions, and $r = 0.66$ for unique retweets).
- We build a regression model that uses economic, social and cultural country attributes, along with the gravity model to predict communication volume between pairs of countries. We find that the complete model performs well with $Adjusted\ R^2 = 0.80$, illustrating the importance of social economic and cultural variables in bilateral online communication.

We conclude by discussing the design implications of these findings in the realms of collaborative work, software design, and recommendation systems.

RELATED WORK

The emergence of Internet social platforms has enabled, fostered, and recorded social networks of an unprecedented scale. Containing social connections, virtual communities, and the content they produce and share, these platforms enable researchers to study social phenomena, extending the reach of conventional sociological studies [19].

A number of studies have used confidential communication to examine the social connections between individuals across the world. A well known study by Leskovec & Horvitz [23] uses the private messages to build a "planetary scale" social network of 180 million nodes, and examines social phenomena, such as Milgram's "6 degrees of separation" [36] (finding that, indeed, the users of the service had an average path length of 6.6).

Specialized communication has also been considered. A community of travelers on CouchSurfing.com was studied by Lauterbach *et al.* [21], who attempted to predict the trust the users display toward one another. They show that, among more personal variables (such as whether the users have met in person), whether users are from the same country affects the chances of one user vouching for another. Olson *et al.* [27] carried out empirical studies of remote work, both in the field and in the laboratory, concluding that distance impacts the quality of end result, regardless of the technology used. More recently, Takhteyev [33] discussed examples of successful collaboration over long distances by looking at how several cultural and geographic constrains were negotiated in the face of increasingly "global" knowledge and technology.

Across social media, geographical distance has been shown to play a major role in human connections. Scellato *et al.* [29] show that, among the users in Brightkite, Foursquare, and Gowalla communities, 40% of links are made in a radius of under 100km. Similar results were found of a 2,852-user sample of the Twitter network in 2009 by Takhteyev *et al.* [34] with 35% of links being under 100km but they also find that other variables, such as the commonalities in language and the extent of air travel to be more predictive of Twitter communication than physical distance. They speculate that air travel may stand as "a proxy for other kinds of pre-existing connections between places, which in turn influence formation of electronic ties". Inspired by this, we examine social, economic, and cultural factors in international Twitter communication. However, a marked difference between these previous studies and one described here is the network construction process. Instead of using follower or followee edges (subscriptions), which do not necessarily imply active communication or attention [38] with 25% of Twitter users never tweeting at all [2], we use geolocated user mentions in nearly 3 billion posts.

Though first, we use the *Gravity Model* to capture the effect of distance. Inspired by Newtonian physics, it models the importance of physical distance in communication between two populated nodes, using a proportion of the population sizes of the two nodes to the distance between them [20]. For example, it has been applied to modeling road and airline networks [1, 17], phone calls [20], and flows of passengers in a London metro system [31].

We also build on the seminal work by Hofstede [14] to measure cultural differences. In 1980, he conducted a survey of IBM employees from 55 different countries, examining a wide range of cultural values. Specifically, we use six cultural indexes: the power-distance index (PDI), individualism-collectivism (IDV), masculinity-femininity (MAS), uncertainty avoidance (UAI), indulgence-restraint (IVR), and the long term orientation index (LTO). Hofstede's cultural dimensions have also been used to study differences in social media usage, for example previous work has found that culture of a country is associated with the way people use Twitter [10].

Although popular in cross-cultural sociology and psychology literature, these measures have largely not been used in internet-mediated communication studies. A notable exception is an email communication study by State *et al.* [32] who examine the extent to which inter-national communication flows according to the civilization, as defined by Samuel Huntington in *The Clash of Civilizations* [16]. By including geographic, economic and cultural factors in their regression model (including the first four of Hofstede's cultural indexes), they show that the membership in the same Huntington civilization to nearly double the pairwise communication density, increasing it by factor of 1.941. However, since the notion of civilization encompasses both geographic and religious attributes of the countries, we find it unsuitable in our aim of separating geography from culture.

# of geolocated users	13,139,763
# of tweets (with mentions)	2,924,398,138
# of mentions	534,868,476
# of unique mentions	258,534,246
# of countries with $> 1K$ users	111
# of country pairs with complete predictors	481

Table 1: Summary of the dataset. We identified the geolocation of more than 13M users but considered only the countries with more than 1K users, which represents more than 90% of our sample users. In total, we obtained 481 country-pairs with no missing attribute values for regression analysis.

In summary, to the best of our knowledge, we present a previously unattempted study of international Twitter communication which combines cultural information with geographic, economic, and social features, using a variety of outside sources from the CIA and World Bank. Unlike e-mail, Twitter mention graph goes beyond strong ties of interpersonal communication, potentially breaking down barriers of distance and culture. Also, unlike the previous studies on Twitter which use subscriptions instead of tweet content [28, 34], this study focuses on the active conversation and attention beyond the user's immediate follower/followee network. Finally, we use the gravity model and a variety of other predictors to build a communication model based solely on data independent of the particulars of Twitter dataset.

DATASET

We model communication across countries in Twitter by observing mentions and retweets by users in one country involving users from another. Similar to [32], we say that a communication is established from country a to b when a message is posted by a user from a mentioning a user from b. A "mention" consists of any Twitter username preceded by the *at* symbol (@). So, for example, if user @Maria located in Spain creates a post "@BarackObama is the president of the United States," we know two things: a) BarackObama received a notification in his account (although unlikely to answer) and b) a communication was made from Spain to USA. The interpretation of this phenomena consists of both conversation and attention, in that, mentions and retweets may be used in a conversation between users, but may also signify an awareness of another user (as with BarackObama and the notification he received in the previous example). Thus, in this paper, when we refer to the number of mentions or retweets as "communication", we do so loosely.

The data was collected as follows. We first randomly selected 55K users who tweeted at least once on March 2011 and obtained their profile information. From this information, we selected users with out-degree and in-degree in the range of $[100, 1000]$ and crawled their corresponding followee network (for a user u, it is all users who u is following). This choice was made in order not to exceed the limit of the API calls. It also has the added benefit of filtering away less legitimate (e.g., spam) users, since, according to [22], the majority of spam users tend to have out-degree and in-degree outside the range of $[100, 1000]$. Also [35] show that 89% of users following spam accounts have fewer than 10 followers. So,

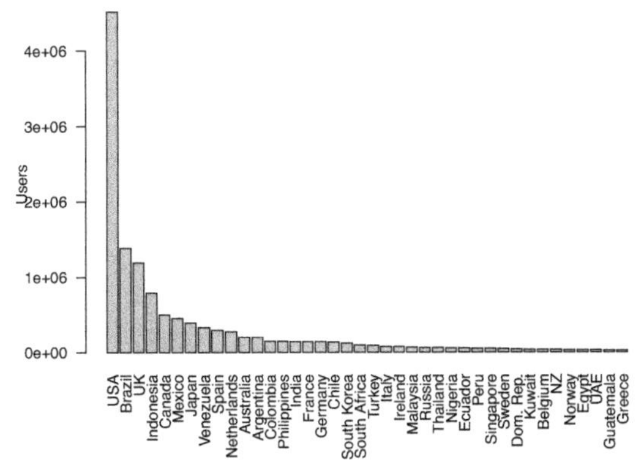

Figure 1: Number of users per the country in the sample (showing top 40 countries).

while we can not guarantee that all users in our dataset are not spammers, previous studies indicate that our sample will indeed have a higher probability of containing legitimate users.

We then proceeded to collect all of the tweets posted by the original 55K users as well as their followees during 10 weeks starting from the second half of Mach 2011. We also collect all tweets containing a mention of any user of our sample (i.e., identified by @username) and the user profile of who posted these tweets.

We continue by finding the geolocation of each user via the location field entered in their profiles. Often these locations are either strings specified by the users themselves or GPS coordinates coming from their mobile devices. We then map these locations into $(long, lat)$ points (using Yahoo! PlaceMaker[1] for user-specified strings), resulting in 13 million geo-located users.

To alleviate any bias due to the selection of seed users and obtain representative samples, we only consider the countries with more than 1,000 users in our sample.

Figure 1 shows sample sizes, with the typical skew across the countries with USA having by far the largest share of Twitter users, followed by Brazil, United Kingdom, and Indonesia. Seven out of the top 10 countries in our sample overlap with the top 10 countries by site traffic in 2011[2] and we also find a *Pearson correlation* of 0.72 to the corresponding logarithm of the number of internet users in 2011 reported by the US's Central Intelligence Agency[3] (CIA). The discrepancy can be attributed to our sampling method which favors users who are mentioned, thus promoting Mexico, Venezuela, and Netherlands in our ranking, excluding Germany, India, and Australia which appear in the traffic ranking.

Table 1 shows statistics about the final dataset, including the number of geolocated users and their tweets, and mentions

[1] `http://www.programmableweb.com/api/yahoo-placemaker`
[2] `http://www.marketinggum.com/twitter-statistics-2011-updated-stats/`
[3] `https://www.cia.gov/library/publications/the-world-factbook/rankorder/2153rank.html`

	Sample Size	γ	Internet Penet.	γ	Country Population	γ
Mentions	0.915	0.83	0.670	0.42	0.489	0.84
Unique mentions	0.919	0.83	0.679	0.43	0.501	0.84
Retweets	0.911	0.88	0.676	0.49	0.505	0.92
Unique retweets	0.904	0.87	0.663	0.48	0.492	0.91

Table 2: Pearson correlation between observed Twitter interactions and gravity model estimations using three different population masses ($N = 5392$ country pairs) and adjusted distance exponent (γ)

found in those tweets. We count "unique" mentions per user, summing the number of unique accounts mentioned by each. On average, for each user-user conversation, there is one duplication, since it is common to mention a specific user more than once (same holds true for unique retweets).

With the geolocation information, we can now analyze the communication across countries. We do this by mapping the country of the mentioned users to the countries of those who posted the tweets, obtaining a country to country graph. Since we are interested in measuring the flow of information between countries and not the direction of it, we obtain an undirected graph of the inter-country communication by adding the bilateral number of mentions and retweets between a pair of countries. Furthermore, we discard self-loop edges since we are interested in communication across countries, not within. This resulted in $5,392$ country-country pairs.

Finally, to tackle our hypotheses and objectives, we obtain geographic, social, economic, and cultural features of these countries. We collect the number of direct flights between each of the countries[4], as well as the spoken languages in each country, as reported by the CIA. Additional social, economic and cultural indicators came from the WorldBank API for R[5]. Each of the variables is explained in the *Social, Economic & Cultural Predictors* section. Since data was missing for some of the countries, we excluded the records with no values. This gave us a total of 481 pairs with complete information for each predictor variable in our model.

GRAVITY MODEL

Definition

In its simplest formulation, the Gravity Model posits that the gravitational interaction between two places is proportional to their mass and inversely proportional to the distance between [41] and it takes the form of:

$$I_{1,2} = k\frac{p_1^{\alpha} * p_2^{\beta}}{d_{1,2}^{\gamma}} \quad (1)$$

where $I_{1,2}$ is the volume of interaction between communities 1 and 2, k is a constant, p_1 and p_2 refer to the "population

[4] `http://openflights.org/data.html`

[5] `http://www.r-chart.com/2010/06/world-bank-api-r-package-available.html`

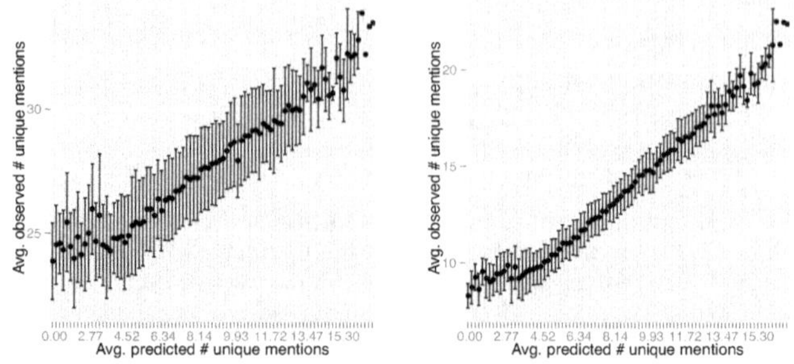

(a) Internet Penetration (b) Sample Size

Figure 2: Unique mentions versus gravity model using (a) internet penetration and (b) sample size, with standard deviations of unique mentions. The country pairs are first binned by estimated flow, then we plot the mean estimated flow in each bin vs. the mean observed flow of the edges in each bin. The error bars show the standard deviation of the observed flows in each bin.

mass" (that is, community size) of communities 1 and 2, and $d_{1,2}$ refers to the distance between these communities. The exponents α, β, γ and the scaling factor k are adjustable parameters chosen to fit the data modeled. The pure gravity model is retained if the population exponents (α and β) are 1 and the distance exponent (γ) is 2; but the formula allows the exponents to be adjusted to finely tune the data being modeled.

It has been previously shown that the gravitational model is applicable to various phenomena such as telecommunication, email and transportation flow between countries, cities and within cities [30]. Since the gravity model can be used to account for any interaction or flow from one place to another, we apply it to estimate the volume of Twitter traffic between two countries and adjust the γ exponent to better fit our data.

We employ several alternative proxies for the "population mass" in the gravity model: (i) sample size, (ii) internet penetration and (iii) country population; and as proxy for distance, we use the Haversine distance[6] (distance between two points on a sphere). We examine the correlation with Twitter bilateral interactions, measured as a) the number of mentions, b) unique mentions, c) retweets, and d) unique retweets. For the case of re-tweets (cases *c* and *d*), we counted only the original authors of a tweet ignoring all other mentions.

Table 2 shows the Pearson correlation between Twitter interactions and gravity model estimations using three different estimates for the population mass, along with the best values of γ for each. Sample size produces the strongest correlation with all four measures, at $r = 0.919$ with unique mentions, with no significant difference in communication flow across countries between re-tweets and mentions. In the following regression experiments, to make sure the dependent variable is not related to the predictors, instead of using sample size we use Internet penetration as a proxy for population.

In Figure 2, we show the distribution of observed unique mentions vs. estimated mentions flows, using (a) internet penetra-

[6] `https://github.com/linkedin/datafu`

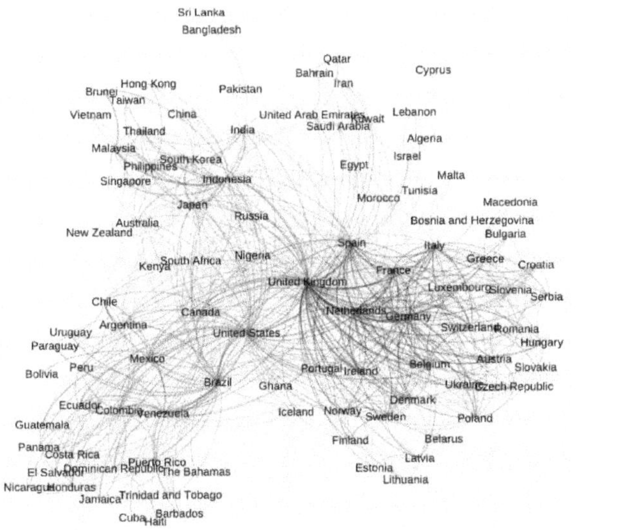

(a) Gravity Model

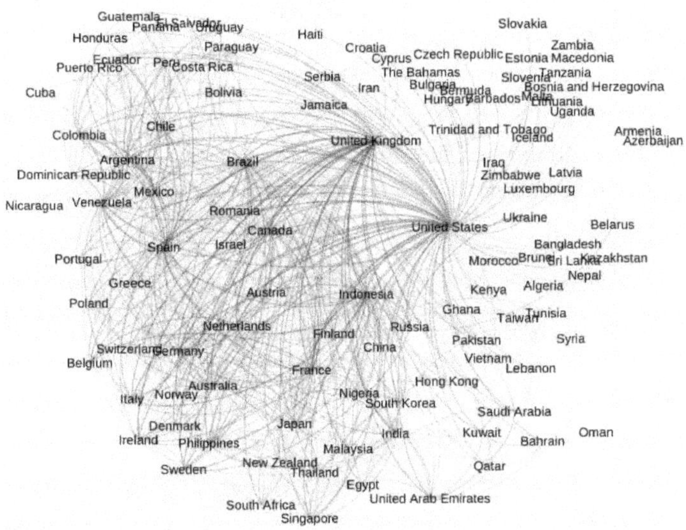

(b) Unique Mentions

Figure 3: Cross-country communication network, 1000 most prominent edges, color-coded by continent.

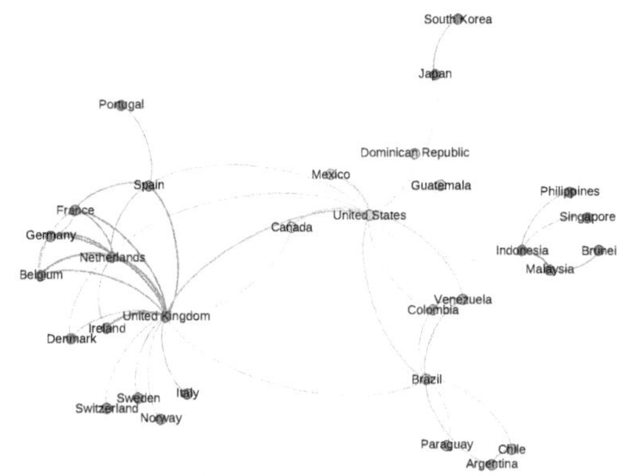

(a) Gravity Model

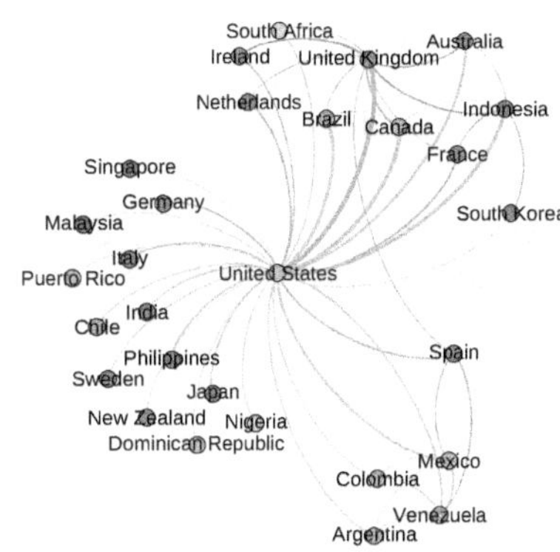

(b) Unique Mentions

Figure 4: Cross-country communication network, 50 most prominent edges, color-coded by continent.

tion and (b) sample size as proxies for population. We see that both versions of gravity model provide estimates which correlate well with observed Twitter interactions. Sample size provides the best estimation, but the standard deviation tends to increase as communication increases.

Finally, we visualize the mention networks induced by these two measures by selecting the top 1000 strongest edges (Figure 3) and top 50 edges (Figure 4). The nodes are positioned using force-directed algorithm using log-transformed edge weights, and colored according to the continent on which they reside. The countries in gravity model network are largely clustered according to their geography, with most populated countries (Brazil, US, UK) connecting them at the center. The network built using unique mentions also has UK and US as central hubs, however the geographical differences between the countries are less pronounced. Now, Spain is much closer to Mexico and its South American peers in language. In larger mentions network, countries with a smaller Twitter use are also pushed out into their own group in the upper right, including countries from Africa, Eastern Europe, and Middle East. Although the major players remain the same (partially because we are using our sample size in the gravity model), the geographic separations are less pronounced in the Twitter-induced network. Next, we examine the extent to which international communication is explained using features other than physical distance.

SOCIAL, ECONOMIC & CULTURAL PREDICTORS

The high correlation of retweets and mentions with the gravity model testifies to the importance of distance. Nevertheless, the standard deviation of the observations seen in Figure

2 show that there are other factors to take into account when studying cross country communication. We observe an acute tendency to overestimate communication flows. This is especially the case for European countries which are very close together and have a large number of people online, including Germany, The Netherlands, Poland, and United Kingdom. Same is true for China and Japan. Similarly, communication between countries which are far apart, such as United States and United Kingdom, and United States and Australia, is underestimated. This behavior suggests that the model does not take into account important information, such as culture and other international connections. We now proceed to study 16 variables that we hypothesize will impact communication. These variables are classified into social, economic and cultural.

Economic Indicators

Does difference in income divide people? Despite the fact that the so called "liberation technologies" have and continue to alter information propagation across countries during crises, the boundaries separating high- from low- income countries affect the daily real world interactions between people, and therefore affect interactions online [24]. In fact, where income differences are bigger, social distances are bigger and social stratification more important [40]. We use predictors (in American dollars) that account for economy described as follows.

Income: We take the GDP per capita for each pair of countries and multiply them. A high product stands for the combination of two wealthy nations.

Similarly, the trade relationships between countries has been shown to be affected by ease of communication [5]. For this reason, we assume the trade between two countries should also be taken as a predictors of communication and we do so under three perspectives (metrics obtained from the World Bank)[7] :

Export importance: We propose a metric that measures the importance of the exports between two countries with regard to the overall exportations of both countries – we add their pair-wise exports and normalize by the total sum of all their exports.

Trade intensity index: The value of trade between two countries on the basis of their importance in the world trade. This metric is defined as the share of one country's exports going to a partner divided by the share of world exports going to the partner. To obtain one value per country pair, we multiply their corresponding trade intensity index.

Trade market share of total exports: It measures how much of the world import demand is covered by the country's exports. Similarly, to obtain a single value per country pair, we multiply the share of total exports for each country.

Social Indicators

We present four social variables expected to affect information flow related to migration and air travel.

[7] `http://wits.worldbank.org/`

	Distribution	Max
Unique Mentions		58,214,512
Gravity Model		2,731,487
Economic Variables		
Income		802,604.5
Exports		0.35
Trade Intensity		395.8
Trade Market Share		92.6
Social Variables		
Routes		6.68
Emigration		0.83
Migration		0.05
Migration Rate		39.9
Cultural Variables		
Language		1
Intolerance		86
Power Distance		82
Individualism		84
Masculinity		90
Uncertainty avoidance		104
Long Term Orientation		88
Indulgence vs. Restrain		97

Table 3: Statistics of regression variables: unique mentions (dependent variable) and 17 independent variables, collected for 5392 country pairs. The distributions begin at zero and end at the adjacent maximum. Language and income group are categorical variables converted to numeric factors. There are 481 pairs having values for all the predictive variables.

The term "transnational migrants" refers to the extent to which immigrants keep cross-border ties when sharing political or religious ideas as well as maintaining cross-border activities of travel, remittance flow and telephone communication with their home-country. These interlocking networks across national boundaries are even more evident with people from border-free travel zones where individuals can work and live in a different country and travel regularly to their home-countries without major bureaucratic barriers.

We propose four migration metrics :

Net migration rate: the difference between the number of persons entering and leaving a country during the year (per 1000 persons). A positive value indicates an excess in immigration and a negative number an excess in emigration. We calculate the absolute difference between these values for each country.

Emigration: obtained by summing the number of emigrants from one country to the other divided by the total number of emigrants for both countries. *Migration*: obtained by summing the number of emigrants from one country to the other divided by the total.

Direct flights: The availability of direct fights has been proven to mediate distance when measuring social interactions [34]. Besides simplifying the process of travel of immigrants to their home-country, it fosters interactions between tourists, visitors and business partners. We consider the number of direct flights between a pair of countries and hypothesize that

Cultural Indicators

One of the most prominent efforts to measure cultural differences is Hofstede's series of surveys [15] administered to the residents of over 70 countries. In his original experiment he administered opinion surveys to IBM employees in over 50 countries. In the following decades his research was expanded to other populations and countries. Using factor analysis, Hofstede identified six main cultural dimensions: 1) Power distance (*PDI*) the level of acceptance of unequal distribution of power, 2) Individualism (*IDV*) the degree to which individuals are integrated into groups, 3) Masculinity (*MAS*) the distribution of emotional roles between the genders, 4) Uncertainty avoidance index (*UAI*) a society's tolerance for uncertainty and ambiguity, 5) Long term orientation (*LTO*), importance to tradition and the future and 6) Indulgence vs. restraint (*IVR*), describes hedonistic behaviors. We take the absolute value of the difference between the cultural indexes of a pair of countries to measure the cultural differences between their inhabitants.

To this, we have also added *Racial intolerance* as one more dimension that can strongly affect communication between people from different countries. Researches have shown that there is a causal relationship between well-being, economic freedom and tolerance [3]. Using the "World Values Survey", racial intolerance was measured in more than 80 countries by asking participants what kinds of people they would not want as neighbors answered and calculating the percentage of those who answered "people of a different race" option. We calculate intolerance as the maximum percentage reported by the survey between a pair of countries: the highest intolerance will determine the level of communication with people from the other country.

Finally, we add *Language* to this category because it defines a culture, through the people who speak it and what it allows speakers to say. Many immigrants and tourists choose to travel to places where they can communicate, as we tend to establish social ties with people who can speak the same language. The CIA provides a rank ordering of spoken languages per country. We set the binary variable *language* to 0 if there is no common language between two countries and to 1 if there is.

REGRESSION

To verify the predictability power of the gravity model, as well as the economic, social and cultural variables (summarized in Table 3), we run a regression analysis, and build a model to predict the normalized volume of mentions between the countries. To avoid an excess of variables versus data points, we only consider the pairs with no missing values (resulting in 481 pairs). Finally, to account for the violations of normality exhibited by the distributions in Table 3, every variable is log transformed and then standardized.

We define communication strength as the communication volume between two countries, as measured by the number of unique user mentions between users of two countries. We choose this measure as it encompasses both conversations and unsolicited mentions of users. We normalize the raw unique mention volume between countries to a scale of $\{0, 1\}$ in order to represent the communication flow strength of a pair of countries in comparison to the the rest. The transformation was made by:

$$s_{i,j} = \frac{m_{i,j} - min_m}{max_m - min_m} \tag{2}$$

where $s_{i,j}$ is a normalized mention volume, $m_{i,j}$ is the number of unique mentions from i to j and vise versa, and min_m and max_m are the minimum and the maximum observed unique mentions between any pair of countries in the dataset.

We use multiple linear regression to predict our dependent variable. Consequently, we model communication strength as a linear combination of the predictive variables and the gravity model:

$$cs_{i,j} = \alpha + \beta_1 G_{i,j} + \beta_2 R_{i,j} + \beta_3 D_{i,j} + \epsilon_{i,j} \tag{3}$$

where $cs_{i,j}$ is the communication strength between the i-th and j-th country, $G_{i,j}$ is the gravitational model variable, $R_{i,j}$ is the vector of remaining predictive variables (classified into social, economic and cultural), $D_{i,j}$ represents the pairwise interactions between all the predictors, and $\epsilon_{i,j}$ is the error term.

Multicollinearity. Before applying the model, we check for multicollinearity among the model's variables. We employ Variance Inflation Factors (VIF), which measure the extent to which errors of the estimated coefficients are inflated by the existence of correlation among the predictor variables in the model [37]. We detected two groups of variables for which VIF was high (above 4): one dealing with trade: Trade Intensity at 7.3 and Trade Market Share at 12.3, and with migration: Migration at 50.2 and Emigration at 48.6. One way of eliminating multicollinearity is to remove one of the violating predictors. Thus, we exclude Trade Intensity and Emigration from the analysis, with the resulting model showing VIFs of under 4.

RESULTS

When predicting the normalized communication volume, the complete model fits the data very well, with an *Adjusted* $R^2 = 0.80$ at $p < 0.001$ and a standard error of 0.087. This error interval is of less significance for countries with communication close to 1. Note that if we use sample size as a proxy for population, the full model achieves *Adjusted* $R^2 = 0.95$, suggesting over-fitting. As mentioned in *Gravity Model* section, we instead use Internet population in order to remove the effects of our sampling method. As part of a regression routine, we have looked for normality of residuals in a QQplot and observed that they follow approximately a

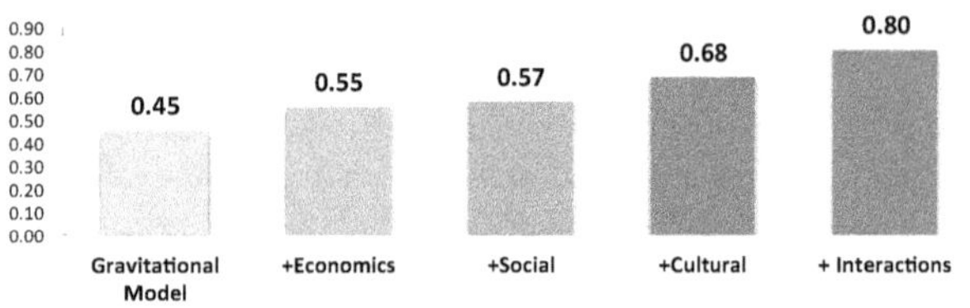

Figure 5: Adjusted R^2 as new dimensions are added to the model. Modeling interactions between dimensions results in substantial performance boost.

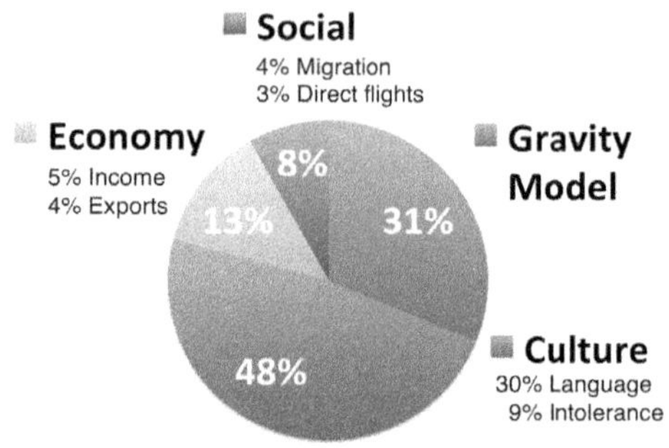

Figure 6: The predictive power of the four dimensions with three most important variables. A dimension's weight is computed by summing the absolute values of the coefficients belonging to it.

normal distribution except for the top and bottom of the line. These outliers are understandable in this situation and therefore should not be considered as evidence for instability of the model [11].

Figure 5 summarizes the model's performance for communication volume broken down by four predictor groups. There are notable gains when adding economic and cultural predictors to the model, but it is the interaction term that is responsible for boosting the performance to *Adjusted* $R^2 = 0.80$.

Figure 6 visualizes the predictive power of the four dimensions as part of communication volume. For this figure, we have not included interactions in order to analyze each dimension individually (recall that we have controlled for the multicollinearity). The weight of a dimension is calculated by summing the coefficients of the variables belonging to it as in [12]. As described in more detail later, cultural factors (most prominently language) and the gravity model play the largest role (also, Figure 5 shows that indeed cultural features are more important in boosting the results).

Next, we add interaction factors to our model. Table 4 presents the coefficients of the top 12 predictive variables ordered by a) beta coefficient and b) *t-value*. Trade, cultural dimension of Masculinity vs. Femininity (MAS), and gravity model and its combinations show the highest significant coefficients. Gravity model alone, as well as in combination with the economic variable of trade, exports, and cultural variable of language is high on the coefficient ranking. However, by the magnitude of the coefficient (at 0.165) Trade Market Share proves to be an even better predictor. Among the cultural variables, we see MAS to have the highest coefficient, followed by intolerance with a negative coefficient at -0.054. Language in combination with the gravity model proves to be a more significant predictor than language alone.

If we consider the *t-values*, which signify a variable's importance in the presence of other variables (the left column of Table 4), we find three significant combinations of cultural attributes. The most significant is the interaction between intolerance and the cultural dimension of Long-Term Orientation (LTO) (*t-value* $= 3.66$) and intolerance and Uncertainty Avoidance (UAI) (*t-value* $= 2.83$). The dimensions of LTO and UAI are linked to tradition, nationalism, and the fear of the unknown [14]. For example, studies show that in Japan (ranking high in LTO and UAI), studies show that people avoid communication with non-Japanese for fear of failing to understand and interact with strangers from different cultures which reflects the way of how strangers are treated [8]. UAI and LTO combined with the intolerance variable, although not explicitly studied by Hofstede, shows that they are indeed related. Also, language, in combination with Masculinity vs Femininity (MAS) (*t-value* $= 2.57$) is more significant than language alone, suggesting its importance in the cultural domain.

The most prominent economic factor is trade market share of total exports – the share of the world's import that is covered by the two countries' exports – with a coefficient of 0.165 – eclipses the direct measure of income groups (at -0.03 not included in the top 12 predictive features), showing trade to be a better indicator of communication than per-capita GDP. Trade agreements are organized over various historic events and through geo-political considerations, thus it is interesting to see them play such an important role in determining everyday online communication. A connection between political climate and communication would be an enticing potential future direction of this research.

Finally, the importance of language (here, considered a cultural feature) is mitigated when we add the interactions, with trade and gravity model playing a more important role than language. This is interesting if we refer to recent studies on cooperative work in software [33] where it was found that English is almost always the working language of such communities, even if their mother tongue is not English and hence reducing the importance of common language other than English.

Figure 7 compares the model's prediction to communication volume. The figure shows a higher accuracy at high communication volumes with worse performance as the communication decreases. In the next section we discuss these results and look at some of the most difficult to predict cases. Finally we look at practical significance of the findings and its limitations.

DISCUSSION

Is distance dead? We show that no, it is still predictive of international communication in Twitter, but cultural and socioeconomic factors, especially that of language, also play an important role. Linguistic and physical separation has been

Variable	β	t-value	p-value	Variable	β	t-value	p-value
Trade Market Share	0.165	3.90	***	Gravity Model	0.072	7.17	***
Exports	-0.151	-1.48		Gravity Model x Trade Market Share	-0.067	-4.67	***
Exports x Language	-0.110	-1.45		Trade Market Share	0.165	3.90	***
MAS	-0.102	-2.76	**	Gravity Model x Language	0.060	3.70	***
Gravity Model x Exports	0.098	2.73	**	Intolerance x LTO	0.022	3.66	***
Gravity Model	0.072	7.17	***	Migration x PDI	0.041	3.24	**
Language	-0.070	-1.70	.	Trade Market Share x Exports	0.016	2.95	**
Gravity Model x Trade Market Share	-0.067	-4.67	***	Gravity Model x MAS	0.031	2.93	**
PDI	0.061	1.63		Intolerance x UAI	0.023	2.83	**
Gravity Model x Language	0.060	3.70	***	MAS	-0.102	-2.76	**
Intolerance	-0.054	-2.11	*	Gravity Model x Exports	0.098	2.73	**
Income group x Migration Rate	-0.051	-2.41	*	Language x MAS	0.042	2.57	*

Table 4: The top 12 predictive variables in the final model (including interaction factors) ordered by beta coefficients (columns 1-4) and *t-value* (columns 6-9). The gravity model was calculated by using internet penetration as a proxy for population. Significance: *** $p < 0.0001$, ** $p < 0.001$, * $p < 0.01$, . $p < 0.05$.

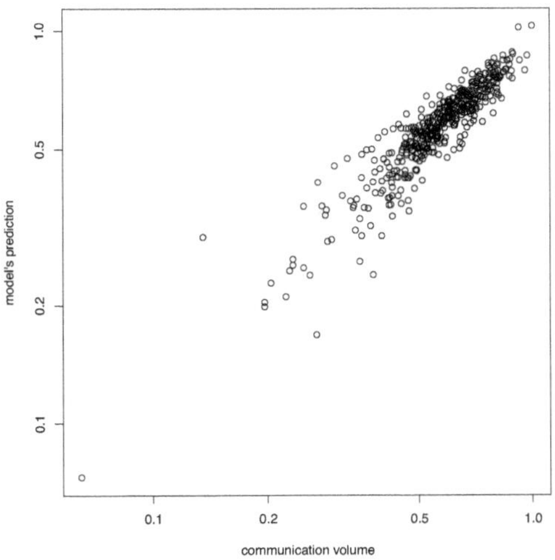

Figure 7: Observed unique mention volume versus the model's predictions.

considered a major obstacle in international communication and collaboration. In 2000 Olson *et al.* [27] argued that distance impacts the effectiveness of collaborative work, with language, trust and cultural differences endanger the quality of project results, despite technological enablement of international communication. However, we show that the language barrier is strongest in combination with cultural factors dealing with intolerance and the fear of the unfamiliar. Finding a common culture, thus, may present a way of overcoming language barriers. For instance, a recent study by Takhteyev *et al.* [33] describes successful international collaborative projects in Open Source software development. This takes place, authors argue, when contributors follow an agreed "common" culture and communicate mostly in English. For example, *Lua*, a programming language developed in Brazil and used in the development of several well-known projects such as *World of Warcraft* and *Angry Birds*, was adapted by the global collaborative circles, such that the manuals were in English rather than in Portuguese, fostering widespread international partnerships. To improve collaboration in a culturally-diverse setting, Kittur *et al.* [18] propose several strategies, including observing behavior of other workers, electing leaders, and passing knowledge to others. Figure 4 (b) shows that many of the strongest ties lie between countries with different native language, such as United States and Japan, Indonesia and South Korea, Spain and United Kingdom, which, although geographically remote, may be connected by common cultural attributes. Thus, our findings show that finding a common culture could be an important barrier which software designers, in particular those who mean to enable international conversation and collaboration, must overcome.

Similarly, State *et al.* [32], find the concept of *civilization* – countries that share the same religion and continent – having a strong positive effect on the private email exchanges. If one ranks the significant coefficients of their model, one finds Colonial Link and Hungtington's Civilization as the top and third most important predictors, respectively. Language, physical distance, and population size also appear at the top (as second, fourth, and fifth in the ranking). For Twitter communication, we show that even though people can subscribe to the majority of users without authorization or reciprocity (unlike the definition of links in [32]), active interactions (through mentions) are still aligned along culture and physical distance.

Practical Implications

Our findings have several implications for the design of social media software. First, we find language and culture to be substantial barriers to Twitter communication. It is noted by Nardi *et al.* [26] that people have to adjust to the technology from other cultures. For instance, Japanese have adapted their writing style to the horizontal typewriter-style word processors, and spelling of words in languages having letters not included in the standard English keyboard has been adjusted accordingly. In the communication network shown in Figure 4, the strongest links are with the United States – the country in which Twitter originates – and the culture of which would drive the design of the software. However, Twitter is already making an effort to diversify its service to embrace non-English languages by providing support for a variety of character sets and automatic translation[8].

One of the major cultural factors we found impacting communication is intolerance, implying that the users of countries associated with higher intolerance would be less likely to communicate with other nations. As discussed by Borning & Muller [4], designers must not assume that some cultural views and values, including those on gender, age, and speech, are universally held [9]. Some of these values could be learned by gathering user behavior data using built-in tools and interaction logs, combined with the cultural attributes extrapolated from user location information and other personalized data, providing potentially better culture-aware services.

However, using a user's cultural preferences, we may want to instead enrich her experience and broaden the reach of information. Including economic, cultural, and social factors, we plan to enhance the recommendations presented to the user. In particular, we'll consider the task of finding people that will most likely re-tweet posts and reach larger audiences [39] not only locally, but internationally.

Limitations

Although we attempt to reduce the effect of multicollinearity in our model and exclude some of the variables, it is impossible to find a complete, and yet altogether independent set of real-world variables. Further, a different selection of country-specific variables would likely somewhat change the observed results. For example, the importance of trade market share may imply that certain economic and trade policies may also be important, as well as official social policies and visa requirements between countries. Also, due to unavailability of some of the predictive variables, the data set for regression was quite limited compared to original data. The missing values are a source of potential selection bias. This happens because the data extracted from the World Bank and CIA does not distinguish between countries that do not report their trade statistics and country pairs with no bilateral trade (resulting in zero values). A more complete dataset would expand the scope and accuracy of such analysis.

Even though Twitter may not be a representative sample of the world's population, our study shows barriers even among the relatively more well-off, technically savvy communities. As a new kind of light-weight, public communication, it is a platform which encourages weak ties between its users. More longitudinal studies are needed to determine whether the development and change of these barriers can be detected in other, more personal or established, means of communication like e-mail and texting.

Finally, we have not considered in our regression inputs that capture how automative or repressive a countries's regime is, nor the imposition of internet censorship[9].

[8]http://gigaom.com/2013/07/03/twitter-enables-translation-on-tweets-from-high-profile-users-amid-egyptian-turmoil/

[9]Twitter was banned in Iran and China before 2011

CONCLUSION

Will distance, economic and social constrains impact communication online forever? Or will eventually ubiquitous internet access, new social platforms and globalization open the door for unrestricted communication between countries despite their economic and social differences? The awareness of these boundaries is prerequisite in our understanding of the kinds of information residents of these countries are likely to consume, and of the constraints on the world-wide information propagation.

In this paper we study online communication and attention as measured in Twitter mentions – a platform which provides an easy way for its users to maintain "weak social ties". We find that, similarly to more personal communication, these weak ties are best predicted using both distance, as well as cultural and socio-economic factors.

We are continuing this line of investigation. In this study, we have unveiled the dynamics of flow between countries, but have not considered directionality and the focus of international attention. Of particular interest would be a deeper study of the language used among residents of different countries as well as the topics discussed in their interactions. By tracking these topics over time, we could detect major shifts in public attention and opinion, especially around crises or other major events.

We are also looking to invert the focus of this research, and attempt to predict socio-economic factors of populated areas, such as city districts, via their online communication. For this, we will attempt to increase the international coverage of our data by including sites like Weibo (an equivalent of Twitter and China) in our dataset.

ACKNOWLEDGMENTS

This research is partially supported by European Community's Seventh Framework Programme FP7/2007-2013 under the ARCOMEM and Social Sensor projects, by the Spanish Centre for the Development of Industrial Technology under the CENIT program, project CEN-20101037 "Social Media", and by Grant TIN2009-14560-C03-01 of the Ministry of Science and Innovation of Spain.

REFERENCES

1. Barrat, A., Barthelemy, M., Pastor-Satorras, R., and Vespignani, A. The architecture of complex weighted networks. *Proceedings of the National Academy of Sciences of the United States of America 101*, 11 (2004), 3747–3752.
2. Beevolve. An exhaustive study of twitter users across the world. http://www.beevolve.com/twitter-statistics/, January 2012.
3. Berggren, N., and Nilsson, T. Does economic freedom foster tolerance? Working Paper Series 918, Research Institute of Industrial Economics, 2012.
4. Borning, A., and Muller, M. Next steps for value sensitive design. In *Proceedings of ACM annual conference on Human Factors in Computing Systems*, (2012), 1125–1134.

5. Hutchinson, W. K. Does ease of communication increase trade? commonality of language and bilateral trade. *Vanderbilt University Department of Economics Working Papers 0217*, June 2002.

6. Brun, J.-F., Carrère, C., Guillaumont, P., and De Melo, J. Has distance died? evidence from a panel gravity model. *The World Bank Economic Review 19*, 1 (2005), 99–120.

7. Cairncross, F. The death of distance: How the communications revolution is changing our lives. Harvard Business Press, 2001.

8. Duronto, P. M., and Nakayama, S. Japanese communication. avoidance, anxiety, and uncertainty during initial encounters. *Journal of East Asian Affairs* (2005), 22–49.

9. Ess, C., and Sudweeks, F. On the edge: Cultural barriers and catalysts to it diffusion among remote and marginalized communities. *New Media & Society 3*, 3 (2001), 259–269.

10. Garcìa-Gavilanes, R., Quercia, D. and Jaimes, A. Cultural Dimensions in Twitter: Time, Individualism and Power. In *Proceedings of the The 7th International AAAI Conference on WebLogs and Social Media* (ICWSM) (2013).

11. Gelman, A., and Hill, J. Data Analysis Using Regression and Multilevel/Hierarchical Models, 1 ed. Cambridge University Press, Dec. 2006.

12. Gilbert, E., and Karahalios, K. Predicting tie strength with social media. In *Proceedings of the SIGCHI Conference on Human Factors in Computing Systems* (CHI) (2009)

13. Granovetter, M. S. The strength of weak ties. *American journal of sociology* (1973), 1360–1380.

14. Hofstede, G. Culture's consequences: International differences in work-related values, vol. 5. *Sage Publications, Incorporated, 1980.*

15. Hofstede, G., Hofstede, G. J., and Minkov, M. Cultures and Organizations: Software Of The Mind. *McGraw-Hill USA, 2010.*

16. Huntington, S. P. The clash of civilizations? *Foreign affairs* (1993), 22–49.

17. Jung, W.-S., Wang, F., and Stanley, H. E. Gravity Model in the Korean Highway. *EPL (Europhysics Letters) 81*, 4 (2008).

18. Kittur, A., Nickerson, J. V., Bernstein, M., Gerber, E., Shaw, A., Zimmerman, J., Lease, M., and Horton, J. The future of crowd work. In *ACM Proceedings of the 2013 conference on Computer supported cooperative work*(CSCW) (2013), 1301–1318.

19. Kleinberg, J. The convergence of social and technological networks. *Communications of the ACM 51*, 11 (2008), 66–72.

20. Krings, G., Calabrese, F., Ratti, C., and Blondel, V. D. Urban gravity: a model for inter-city telecommunication flows. *Journal of Statistical Mechanics: Theory and Experiment* (2009).

21. Lauterbach, D., Truong, H., Shah, T., and Adamic, L. Surfing a web of trust: Reputation and reciprocity on couchsurfing. com. In *the 12th IEEE International Conference on Computational Science and Engineering.* (CSE) (2009).

22. Lee, K., Eoff, B., and Caverlee, J. Seven months with the devils: A long-term study of content polluters on twitter. In *Proceedings of the 5th International AAAI Conference on Weblogs and Social Media* (ICWSM) (2011).

23. Leskovec, J., and Horvitz, E. Planetary-scale views on a large instant-messaging network. In *Proceedings of the ACM 17th international conference on World Wide Web*, (2008).

24. Meier, J. P. Do "Liberation Technologies" Change the Balance of Power Between Repressive States and Civil Society? PhD thesis, The Fletcher School of Law and Diplomacy, 2011.

25. Mok, D., Wellman, B., and Carrasco, J. Does distance matter in the age of the internet? *Urban Studies 47*, 13 (2010), 2747–2783.

26. Nardi, B. A., Vatrapu, R. K., and Clemmensen, T. Comparative informatics. *Interactions 18*, 2 (2011), 28–33.

27. Olson, G. M., and Olson, J. S. Distance matters. *Human-Computer Interaction* (2000), 139–179.

28. Scellato, S., Mascolo, C., Musolesi, M., and Latora, V. Distance matters: geo-social metrics for online social networks. In *the Proceedings of the 3rd Conference on Online Social Networks* (2010).

29. Scellato, S., Noulas, A., Lambiotte, R., and Mascolo, C. Socio-spatial properties of online location-based social networks. In *Proceedings of the 5th International AAAI Conference on Weblogs and Social Media* (2011).

30. Smith, C., Quercia, D., and Capra, L. Anti-gravity underground? In *the 2nd Workshop on Pervasive Urban Applications* (PURBA) (2012).

31. Smith, C., Quercia, D., and Capra, L. Finger on the pulse: identifying deprivation using transit flow analysis. In *Proceedings of the ACM 16th Conference on Computer Supported Cooperative Work* (2013).

32. State, B., Park, P., Weber, I., Mejova, Y., and Macy, M. The mesh of civilizations and international email flows. Tech. Rep. No. arXiv: 1303.0045, 2013.

33. Takhteyev, Y. Coding Places: Software Practice in a South American City. The MIT Press, 2012.

34. Takhteyev, Y., Gruzd, A., and Wellman, B. Geography of twitter networks. *Social Networks 34*, 1 (2012), 73–81.

35. Thomas, K., Grier, C., Song, D., and Paxson, V. Suspended accounts in retrospect: an analysis of twitter spam. In *Proceedings of the 2011 ACM SIGCOMM conference on Internet measurement conference* (2011).

36. Travers, J., and Milgram, S. An experimental study of the small world problem. *Sociometry* (1969), 425–443.

37. University, T. P. S. Stat 501 - regression methods, 2013.

38. Venkataraman, M., Subbalakshmi, K. P., and Chandramouli, R. Measuring and quantifying the silent majority on the internet. In *the 35th IEEE Sarnoff Symposium* (SARNOFF) (2012).

39. Wang, B., Wang, C., Bu, J., Chen, C., Zhang, W. V., Cai, D., and He, X. Whom to mention: expand the diffusion of tweets by @ recommendation on micro-blogging systems. In *Proceedings of the 22nd ACM International Conference on World Wide Web* (2013).

40. Wilkinson, R., and Pickett, K. The Spirit Level: Why Equality is Better for Everyone. *Penguin Books*, 2010.

41. Zipf, G. K. The p 1 p 2/d hypothesis: on the intercity movement of persons. *American sociological review 11*, 6 (1946).

Inferring the Origin Locations of Tweets with Quantitative Confidence

Reid Priedhorsky,* Aron Culotta,† Sara Y. Del Valle*

*Los Alamos National Laboratory
Los Alamos, NM
{reidpr,sdelvall}@lanl.gov

†Illinois Institute of Technology
Chicago, IL
aculotta@iit.edu

ABSTRACT

Social Internet content plays an increasingly critical role in many domains, including public health, disaster management, and politics. However, its utility is limited by missing geographic information; for example, fewer than 1.6% of Twitter messages (*tweets*) contain a geotag. We propose a scalable, content-based approach to estimate the location of tweets using a novel yet simple variant of gaussian mixture models. Further, because real-world applications depend on quantified uncertainty for such estimates, we propose novel metrics of accuracy, precision, and calibration, and we evaluate our approach accordingly. Experiments on 13 million global, comprehensively multi-lingual tweets show that our approach yields reliable, well-calibrated results competitive with previous computationally intensive methods. We also show that a relatively small number of training data are required for good estimates (roughly 30,000 tweets) and models are quite time-invariant (effective on tweets many weeks newer than the training set). Finally, we show that toponyms and languages with small geographic footprint provide the most useful location signals.

INTRODUCTION

Applications in public health [9], politics [29], disaster management [21], and other domains are increasingly turning to social Internet data to inform policy and intervention strategies. However, the value of these data is limited because the geographic origin of content is frequently unknown. Thus, there is growing interest in the task of *location inference*: given an item, estimate its geographic *true origin*.

We propose an inference method based on gaussian mixture models (GMMs) [22]. Our models are trained on geotagged tweets, i.e., messages with user profile and geographic true origin points.[1] For each unique n-gram, we fit a two-dimensional GMM to model its geographic distribution. To infer the origin of a new tweet, we combine previously trained GMMs for the n-grams it contains, using weights inferred from data; Figure 1 shows an example estimate. This approach is simple, scalable, and competitive with more complex approaches.

[1] Our implementation is open source: http://github.com/reidpr/quac

ACM 978-1-4503-2540-0/14/02. LA-UR 13-23557.
http://dx.doi.org/10.1145/2531602.2531607

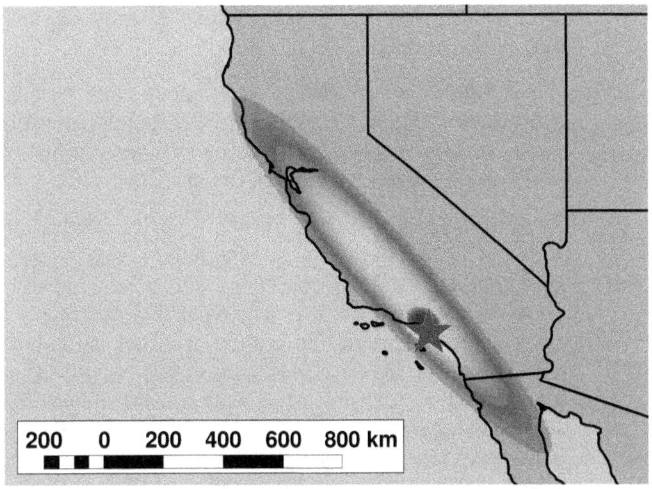

text:	Americans are optimistic about the economy & like what Obama is doing. What is he doing? Campaigning and playing golf? Ignorance is bliss
language:	en
location:	Los Angeles, CA
time zone:	pacifictimeuscanada

Figure 1. A tweet originating near Los Angeles, CA. We show the true origin (a blue star) and a heat map illustrating the density function that makes up our method's estimate. This estimate, whose accuracy was at the 80th percentile, was driven by two main factors. The unigram *ca* from the location field, visible as the large density oval along the California coast, contributed about 12% of the estimate, while *angeles ca*, the much denser region around Los Angeles, contributed 87%. The contribution of four other n-grams (*angeles*, *los angeles*, *obama*, and *los*) was negligible.

Location estimates using any method contain uncertainty, and it is important for downstream applications to quantify this uncertainty. While previous work considers only point estimates, we argue that a more useful form consists of a density estimate (of a probability distribution) covering the entire globe, and that estimates should be assessed on three independent dimensions of accuracy, precision, and calibration. We propose new metrics for doing so.

To validate our approach, we performed experiments on twelve months of tweets from across the globe, in the context of answering four research questions:

RQ1. **Improved approach.** How can the origin locations of social Internet messages be estimated accurately, precisely, and with quantitative uncertainty? Our novel, simple, and scalable GMM-based approach produces well-calibrated estimates with a global mean accuracy error of roughly 1,800 km and precision of 900,000 square kilometers (or better); this is competitive with more complex approaches on the metrics available in prior work.

RQ2. **Training size.** How many training data are required? We find that approximately 30,000 tweets (i.e., roughly 0.01% of total daily Twitter activity) are sufficient for high-quality models, and that performance can be further improved with more training data at a cost of increased time and memory. We also find that models are improved by including rare n-grams, even those occurring just 3 times.

RQ3. **Time dependence.** What is the effect of a temporal gap between training and testing data? We find that our models are nearly independent of time, performing just 6% worse with a gap of 4 months (vs. no gap).

RQ4. **Location signal sources.** Which types of content provide the most valuable location signals? Our results suggest that the user location string and time zone fields provide the strongest signals, tweet text and user language are weaker but important to offer an estimate for all test tweets, and user description has essentially no location value. Our results also suggest that mentioning toponyms (i.e., names of places), especially at the city scale, provides a strong signal, as does using languages with a small geographic footprint.

The remainder of our paper is organized as follows. We first survey related work, then propose desirable properties of a location inference method and metrics which measure those properties. We then describe our experimental framework and detail our mixture model approach. Finally, we discuss our experimental results and their implications. Appendices with implementation details follow the body of the paper.

RELATED WORK

Over the past few years, the problem of inferring the origin locations of social Internet content has become an increasingly active research area. Below, we summarize the four primary lines of work and contrast them with this paper.

Geocoding

Perhaps the simplest approach to location inference is *geocoding*: looking up the user profile's free-text location field in a *gazetteer* (list of toponyms), and if a match is found, inferring that the message originated from the matching place. Researchers have used commercial geocoding services such as Yahoo! Geocoder [32], U.S. Geological Survey data [26], and Wikipedia [16] to do this. This technique can be extended to the message text itself by first using a *geoparser* named-entity recognizer to extract toponyms [13].

Schulz et al. [30] recently reported accurate results using a scheme which combines multiple geocoding sources, including Internet queries. Crucial to its performance was the discovery that an additional 26% of tweets can be matched to precise coordinates using text parsing and by following links to location-based services (FourSquare, Flickr, etc.), an approach that can be incorporated into competing methods as well. Another 8% of tweets – likely the most difficult ones, as they contain the most subtle location evidence – could not be estimated and are not included in accuracy results.

In addition to one or more accurate, comprehensive gazetteers, these approaches require careful text cleaning before geocoding is attempted, as grossly erroneous false matches are common [16], and they tend to favor precision over recall (because only toponyms are used as evidence). Finally, under one view, our approach essentially infers a probabilistic gazetteer that weights toponyms (and pseudo-toponyms) according to the location information they actually carry.

Statistical classifiers

These approaches build a statistical mapping of text to discrete pre-defined regions such as cities and countries (i.e., treating "origin location" as membership in one of these classes rather than a geographic point); thus, any token can be used to inform location inference.

We categorize this work by the type of classifier and by place granularity. For example, Cheng et al. apply a variant of naïve Bayes to classify messages by city [6], Hecht et al. use a similar classifier at the state and country level [16], and Kinsella et al. use language models to classify messages by neighborhood, city, state, zip code, and country [19]. Mahmud et al. classify users by city with higher accuracy than Cheng et al. by combining a hierarchical classifier with many heuristics and gazetteers [20]. Other work instead classifies messages into arbitrary regions of fixed [25, 34] or dynamic size [28]. All of these require aggressively smoothing estimates for regions with few observations [6]

Recently, Chang et al. [5] classified tweet text by city using GMMs. While more related to the present paper because of the underlying statistical technique, this work is still fundamentally a classification approach, and it does not attempt the probabilistic evaluation that we advocate. Additionally, the algorithm resorts to heuristic feature selection to handle noisy n-grams; instead, we offer two learning algorithms to set n-gram weights which are both theoretically grounded and empirically crucial for accuracy.

Fundamentally, these approaches can only classify messages into regions specified before training; in contrast, our GMM approach can be used both for direct location inference as well as classification, even if regions are post-specified.

Geographic topic models

These techniques endow traditional topic models [2] with location awareness [33]. Eisenstein et al. developed a *cascading topic model* that produces region-specific topics and used these topics to infer the locations of Twitter users [10]; follow-on work uses *sparse additive models* to combine region-specific, user-specific, and non-informative topics more efficiently [11, 17].

Topic modeling does not require explicit pre-specified regions. However, regions are inferred as a preprocessing step: Eisenstein et al. with a Dirichlet Process mixture [10] and Hong et al. with K-means clustering [17]. The latter also suggests that more regions increases inference accuracy.

While these approaches result in accurate models, the bulk of modeling and computational complexity arises from the need to produce geographically coherent topics. Also, while topic models can be parallelized with considerable effort, doing so often requires approximations, and their global state limits the potential speedup. In contrast, our approach focusing solely on geolocation is simpler and more scalable.

Finally, the efforts cited restrict messages to either the United States or the English language, and they report simply the mean and median distance between the true and predicted location, omitting any precision or uncertainty assessment. While these limitations are not fundamental to topic modeling, the novel evaluation and analysis we provide offer new insights into the strengths and weaknesses of this family of algorithms.

Social network information

Recent work suggests that using social link information (e.g., followers or friends) can aid in location inference [4, 8]. We view these approaches as complementary to our own; accordingly, we do not explore them more deeply at present.

Contrasting our approach

We offer the following principal distinctions compared to prior work: (a) location estimates are multi-modal probability distributions, rather than points or regions, and are rigorously evaluated as such, (b) because we deal with geographic coordinates directly, there is no need to pre-specify regions of interest; (c) no gazetteers or other supplementary data are required, and (d) we evaluate on a dataset that is more comprehensive temporally (one year of data), geographically (global), and linguistically (all languages except Chinese, Thai, Lao, Cambodian, and Burmese).

EXPERIMENT DESIGN

In this section, we present three properties of a good location estimate, metrics and experiments to measure them, and new algorithms motivated by them.

What makes a good location estimate?

An estimate of the origin location of a message should be able to answer two closely related but different questions:

Q1. What is the *true origin* of the message? That is, at which geographic point was the person who created the message located when he or she did so?

Q2. Was the true origin within a specified geographical region? For example, did a given message originate from Washington State?

It is inescapable that all estimates are uncertain. We argue that they should be quantitatively treated as such and offer probabilistic answers to these questions. That is, we argue that a location estimate should be a *geographic density estimate*: a function which estimates the probability of every point on the globe being the true origin. Considered through this lens, a high-quality estimate has the following properties:

- It is *accurate*: the density of the estimate is skewed strongly towards the true origin (i.e., the estimate rates points near the true origin as more probable than points far from it). Then, Q1 can be answered effectively because the most dense regions of the distribution are near the true origin, and Q2 can be answered effectively because if the true origin is within the specified region, then much of the distribution's density will be as well.
- It is *precise*: the most dense regions of the estimate are compact. Then, Q1 can be answered effectively because fewer candidate locations are offered, and Q2 can be answered effectively because the distribution's density is focused within few distinct regions.
- It is *well calibrated*: the probabilities it claims are close to the true probabilities. Then, both questions can be answered effectively regardless of the estimate's accuracy and precision, because its uncertainty is quantified. For example, the two estimates "the true origin is within New York City with 90% confidence" and "the true origin is within North America with 90% confidence" are both useful even though the latter is much less accurate and precise.

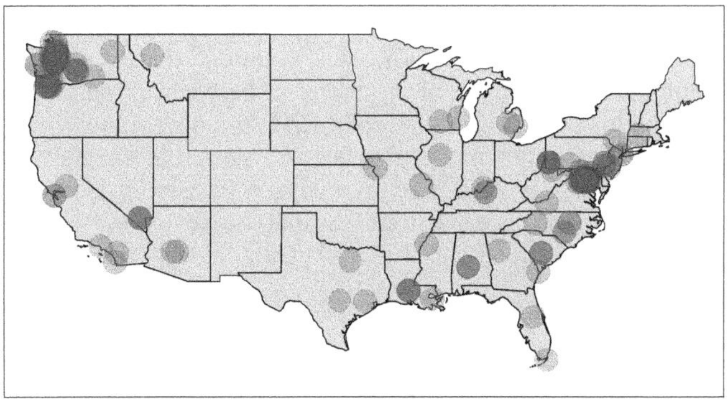

Figure 2. True origins of tweets having the unigram *washington* in the location field of the user's profile.

Our goal, then, is to discover an *estimator* which produces estimates that optimize the above properties.

Metrics

We now map these properties to operationalizable metrics. This section presents our metrics and their intuitive reasoning; rigorous mathematical implementations are in the appendices.

Accuracy

Our core metric to evaluate the accuracy of an estimate is *comprehensive accuracy error* (CAE): the expected distance between the true origin and a point randomly selected from the estimate's density function, or in other words, the mean distance between the true origin and every point on the globe, weighted by the estimate's density value.[2] The goal here is to offer a notion of the distance from the true origin to the density estimate as a whole.

This contrasts with a common prior metric that we refer to as *simple accuracy error* (SAE): the distance from the best single-point estimate to the true origin. Figure 2 illustrates this contrast. The tight clusters around both Washington, D.C.

[2] A similar metric, called Expected Distance Error, has been proposed by Cho et al. for a different task of user tracking [7].

and Washington State suggest that any estimate based on the unigram *washington* is inherently bimodal; that is, no single point at either cluster or anywhere in between is a good estimated location. More generally, SAE is a poor match for the continuous, multi-modal density estimates that we argue are more useful for downstream analysis, because good single-point distillations are often unavailable. However, we report both metrics in order to make comparisons with prior work.

The units of CAE (and SAE) are kilometers. For a given estimator (i.e., a specific algorithm which produces location estimates), we report *mean comprehensive accuracy error* (MCAE), which is simply the mean of each estimate's CAE. CAE ≥ 0, and an ideal estimator has MCAE $= 0$.

Precision

In order to evaluate precision, we extend the notion of one-dimensional prediction intervals [3, 12] to two dimensions. An estimate's *prediction region* is the minimal, perhaps non-contiguous geographic region which contains the true origin with some specified probability (the region's *coverage*).

Accordingly, the metric we propose for precision is simply the area of this region: *prediction region area* (PRA) parameterized by the coverage, e.g., PRA_{50} is the area of the minimal region which contains the true origin with 50% probability.

Units are square kilometers. For a given estimator, we report *mean prediction region area* (MPRA), i.e., the mean of each estimate's PRA. PRA ≥ 0; an ideal estimator has MPRA $= 0$.

Calibration

Calibration is tested by measuring the difference between an estimate's claimed probability that a particular point is the true origin and its actual probability.

We accomplish this by building upon prediction regions. That is, given a set of estimates, we compute a prediction region at a given coverage for each estimate and measure the fraction of true origins that fall within the regions. The result should be close to the specified coverage. For example, for prediction regions at coverage 0.5, the fraction of true origins that actually fall within the prediction region should be close to 0.5.

We refer to this fraction as *observed coverage* (OC) at a given expected coverage; for example, OC_{50} is the observed coverage for an expected coverage of 0.5. (This measure is common in the statistical literature for one-dimensional problems [3].) Calibration can vary among different expected coverage levels (because fitted density distributions may not exactly match actual true origin densities), so multiple coverage levels should be reported (in this paper, OC_{50} and OC_{90}).

Note that OC is defined at the estimator level, not for single messages. OC is unitless, and $0 \leq OC \leq 1$. An ideal estimator has observed coverage equal to expected coverage, an overconfident estimator has observed less than expected, and an underconfident one greater.

Experiment implementation

In this section, we explain the basic structure of our experiments: data source, preprocessing and tokenization, and test procedures.

Data

We used the Twitter Streaming API to collect an approximately continuous 1% sample of all global tweets from January 25, 2012 to January 23, 2013. Between 0.8% and 1.6% of these, depending on timeframe, contained a geotag (i.e., specific geographic coordinates marking the true origin of the tweet, derived from GPS or other automated means), yielding a total of approximately 13 million geotagged tweets.[3]

We tokenized the message text (*tx*), user description (*ds*), and user location (*lo*) fields, which are free-text, into bigrams by splitting on Unicode character category and script boundaries and then further subdividing bigrams appearing to be Japanese using the TinySegmenter algorithm [15].[4] This covers all languages except a few that have low usage on Twitter: Thai, Lao, Cambodian, and Burmese (which do not separate words with a delimiter) as well as Chinese (which is difficult to distinguish from Japanese). For example, the string "Can't wait for 私の" becomes the set of bigrams *can, t, wait, for,* 私, の, *can t, t wait, wait for, for* 私, and 私 の. (Details of our algorithm are presented in the appendices.)

For the language (*ln*) and time zone (*tz*) fields, which are selected from a set of options, we form n-grams by simply removing whitespace and punctuation and converting to lowercase. For example, "Eastern Time (US & Canada)" becomes simply *easterntimeuscanada*.

Experiments

Each experiment is implemented using a Python script on tweets selected with a regular schedule. For example, we might train a model on all tweets from May 1 and test on a random sample of tweets from May 2, then train on May 7 and test on May 8, etc. This schedule has four parameters:

- **Training duration.** The length of time from which to select training tweets. We used all selected tweets for training, except only the first tweet from a given user is retained, to avoid over-weighting frequent tweeters.
- **Test duration.** The length of time from which to select test tweets. In all experiments, we tested on a random sample of 2,000 tweets selected from one day. We excluded users with a tweet in the training set from testing, in order to avoid tainting the test set.
- **Gap.** The length of time between the end of training data and the beginning of test data.
- **Stride.** The length of time from the beginning of one training set to the beginning of the next. This was fixed at 6 days unless otherwise noted.

For example, an experiment with training size of one day, no gap, and stride of 6 days would schedule 61 tests across our 12 months of data and yield results which were the mean of the 58

[3] As in prior work [10, 17, 28], we ignore the sampling bias introduced by considering only geotagged tweets. A preliminary analysis suggests this bias is limited. In a random sample of 11,694,033 geotagged and 17,175,563 non-geotagged tweets from 2012, we find a correlation of 0.85 between the unigram frequency vectors for each set; when retweets are removed, the correlation is 0.93.

[4] More complex tokenization methods yielded no notable effect.

tests with sufficient data (i.e., 3 tests were not attempted due to missing data). The advantage of this approach is that test data always chronologically follow training data, minimizing temporal biases and better reflecting real-world use.

We built families of related experiments (as described below) and report results on these families.

OUR APPROACH: GEOGRAPHIC GMMS

Here, we present our location inference approach. We first motivate and summarize it, then detail the specific algorithms we tested. (Mathematical implementations are in the appendices.)

Motivation

Examining the geographic distribution of n-grams can suggest appropriate inference models. For example, recall Figure 2 above; the two clusters, along with scattered locations elsewhere, suggest that a multi-modal distribution consisting of two-dimensional gaussians may be a reasonable fit.

Based on this intuition and coupled with the desiderata above, we propose an estimator using one of the mature density estimation techniques: *gaussian mixture models* (GMMs). These models are precisely the weighted sum of multiple gaussian (normal) distributions and have natural probabilistic interpretations. Further, they have previously been applied to human mobility patterns [7, 14].

Our algorithm is summarized as follows:

1. For each n-gram that appears more than a threshold number of times in the training data, fit a GMM to the true origin points of the tweets in the training set that contain that n-gram. This n-gram/GMM mapping forms the trained location model.

2. To locate a test tweet, collect the GMMs from the location models which correspond to n-grams in the test tweet. The weighted sum of these GMMs — itself a GMM — is the geographic density function which forms the estimate of the test tweet's location.

It is clear that some n-grams will carry more location information than others. For example, n-gram density for the word *the* should have high variance and be dispersed across all English-speaking regions; on the other hand, density for *washington* should be concentrated in places named after that president.[5] That is, n-grams with much location information should be assigned high weight, and those with little information low weight — but not zero, so that messages with only low-information n-grams will have a quantifiably poor estimate rather than none at all. Accordingly, we propose three methods to set the GMM weights.

Weighting by quality properties

One approach is to simply assign higher weight to GMMs which have a crisper signal or fit the data better. We tested 15 *quality properties* which measure this in different ways.

We tried weighting each GMM by the inverse of (1) the number of fitted points, (2) the spatial variance of these points, and (3) the number of components in the mixture. We also tried metrics based on the covariance matrices of the gaussian components: the inverse of (4) the sum of all elements, and (5) the sum of the products of the elements in each matrix. Finally, we tried normalizing: by both the number of fitted points (properties 6–9) and the number of components (10–13). Of these, property 5, which we call *GMM-Qpr-Covar-Sum-Prod*, performed the best, so we carry it forward for discussion.

Additionally, we tried two metrics designed specifically to test goodness of fit: (14) Akaike information criterion [1] and (15) Bayesian information criterion [31], transformed into weights by subtracting from the maximum observed value. Of this pair, property 14, which we call *GMM-Qpr-AIC*, performed best, so we carry it forward.

Weighting by error

Another approach is to weight each n-gram by its error among the training set. Specifically, for each n-gram in the learned model, we compute the error of its GMM (CAE or SAE) against each of the points to which it was fitted. We then raise this error to a power (in order to increase the dominance of relatively good n-grams over relatively poor ones) and use the inverse of this value as the n-gram's weight (i.e., larger errors yield smaller weights).

We refer to these algorithms as (for example) *GMM-Err-SAE4*, which uses the SAE error metric and an exponent of 4. We tried exponent values from 0.5 to 10 as well as both CAE and SAE; because the latter was faster and gave comparable results, we report only SAE.

Weighting by optimization

The above approaches are advantaged by varying degrees of speed and simplicity. However, it seems plausibly better to learn optimized weights from the data themselves. Our basic approach is to assign each n-gram a set of features with their own weights, let each n-gram's weight be a linear combination of the feature weights, and use gradient descent to find feature weights such that the total error across all n-grams is minimized (i.e., total geo-location accuracy is maximized).

For optimization, we tried three types of n-gram features:

1. The quality properties noted above (*Attr*).

2. Identity features. That is, the first n-gram had Feature 1 and no others, the second n-gram had Feature 2 and no others, and so on (*ID*).

3. Both types of features (*Both*).

Finally, we further classify these algorithms by whether we fit a mixture for each n-gram (*GMM*) or a single gaussian (*Gaussian*). For example, *GMM-Opt-ID* uses GMMs and weights optimized using ID features only.

Baseline weighting algorithms

As two final baselines, we considered *GMM-All-Tweets*, which fits a single GMM to all tweets in the training set and returns

[5] Indeed, Eisenstein et al. attribute the poor performance of several of their baselines to this tendency of uninformative words to dilute the predictive power of informative words [10].

that GMM for all locate operations, and *GMM-One*, which weights all n-gram mixtures equally.

RESULTS

We present in this section our experimental results and discussion, framed in the context of our four research questions. (In addition to the experiments described in detail above, we tried several variants that had limited useful impact. These results are summarized in the appendices.)

RQ1: Improved approach

Here we evaluate the performance of our algorithms, first with a comparison between each other and then against prior work (which is less detailed due to available metrics).

Performance of our algorithms

We tested each of our algorithms with one day of training data and no gap, all fields except user description, and minimum n-gram instances set to 3 (detailed reasoning for these choices is given below in further experiments). With a stride of 6 days, this yielded 58 tests on each algorithm, with 3 tests not attempted due to gaps in the data. Table 1 summarizes our results, making clear the importance of choosing n-gram weights well.

Considering accuracy (MCAE), *GMM-Err-SAE10* is 10% better than the best optimization-based algorithm (*GMM-Opt-ID*) and 26% better than the best property-based algorithm (*GMM-Qpr-Covar-Sum-Prod*); the baselines *GMM-One* and *GMM-All-Tweets* performed poorly. These results suggest that a weighting scheme directly related to performance, rather than the simpler quality properties, is important — even including quality properties in optimization (*-Opt-Attr* and *-Opt-Both*) yields poor results. Another highlight is the poor performance of *Gaussian-Opt-ID* vs. *GMM-Opt-ID*. Recall that the former uses a single Gaussian for each n-gram; as such, it cannot fit the multi-modal nature of these data well.

Turning to precision ($MPRA_{50}$), the advantage of *GMM-Err-SAE10* is further highlighted; it is 50% better than *GMM-Opt-ID* and 38% better than *GMM-Qpr-Covar-Sum-Prod* (note that the relative order of these two algorithms has reversed).

However, calibration complicates the picture. While *GMM-Err-SAE10* is somewhat overconfident at coverage level 0.5 (OC_{50} = 0.453 instead of the desired 0.5), *GMM-Err-SAE4* is calibrated very well at this level (OC_{50} = 0.497) and has better calibration at coverage 0.9 (OC_{90} = 0.775 instead of 0.724). *GMM-Opt-ID* has still better calibration at this level (OC_{90} = 0.864), though worse at coverage 0.5 (OC_{50} = 0.584), and interestingly it is overconfident at one level and underconfident at the other. A final observation is that some algorithms with poor accuracy are quite well calibrated at the 0.9 coverage level (*Gaussian-Opt-ID*) or both levels (*GMM-All-Tweets*). In short, our calibration results imply that algorithms should be evaluated at multiple coverage levels, and in particular gaussians may not be quite the right distribution to fit.

These performance results, which are notably inconsistent between the three metrics, highlight the value of carefully considering and tuning all three of accuracy, precision, and calibration. For the remainder of this paper, we will focus on

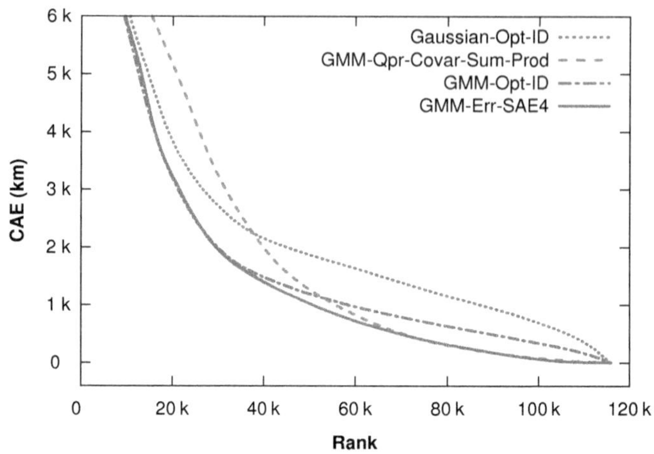

Figure 3. Accuracy of each estimate using selected algorithms, in descending order of CAE.

GMM-Err-SAE4, with its simplicity, superior calibration, time efficiency, and second-best accuracy and precision.

Is CAE necessary?

A plausible hypothesis is that the more complex CAE metric is not needed, and algorithm accuracy can be sufficiently well judged with the simpler and faster SAE. However, *Gaussian-Opt-ID* offers evidence that this is not the case: while it is only 4% worse than *GMM-Err-SAE4* on MSAE, the relative difference is nearly 6 times greater in MCAE.

Several other algorithms are more consistent between the two metrics, so SAE may be appropriate in some cases, but caution should be used, particularly when comparing different types of algorithms.

Distribution of error

Figure 3 plots the CAE of each estimate from four key algorithms. These curves are classic long-tail distributions (as are similar ones for PRA_{50} omitted for brevity); that is, a relatively small number of difficult tweets comprise the bulk of the error. Accordingly, summarizing our results by median instead of mean may be of some value: for example, the median CAE of *GMM-Err-SAE4* is 778 km, and its median PRA_{50} is 83,000 km^2 (roughly the size of Kansas or Austria). However, we have elected to focus on reporting means in order to not conceal poor performance on difficult tweets.

It is plausible that different algorithms may perform poorly on different types of test tweets, though we have not explored this; the implication is that selecting different strategies based on properties of the tweet being located may be of value.

Compared to prior work with the Eisenstein data set

Table 2 compares *GMM-Opt-ID* and *GMM-Err-SAE* to five competing approaches using data from Eisenstein et al. [10], using mean and median SAE (as these were the only metrics reported).

These data and our own have important differences. First, they are limited to tweets from the United States — thus, we expect lower error here than in our data, which contain tweets from across the globe. Second, these data were created for

Algorithm	MCAE	MSAE	$MPRA_{50}$	OC_{50}	OC_{90}	RT
GMM-Err-SAE10	1735 ± 81	1510 ± 76	824 ± 75.8	0.453 ± 0.012	0.724 ± 0.013	10.6
GMM-Err-SAE4	1826 ± 82	1565 ± 78	934 ± 69.9	0.497 ± 0.012	0.775 ± 0.013	10.6
GMM-Opt-ID	1934 ± 77	1578 ± 67	1661 ± 171.0	0.584 ± 0.017	0.864 ± 0.011	29.8
GMM-Err-SAE2	2173 ± 82	1801 ± 76	1192 ± 92.5	0.567 ± 0.012	0.848 ± 0.011	11.0
GMM-Qpr-Covar-Sum-Prod	2338 ± 123	2084 ± 115	1337 ± 123.1	0.485 ± 0.013	0.736 ± 0.013	9.1
Gaussian-Opt-ID	2445 ± 81	1635 ± 69	6751 ± 377.5	0.731 ± 0.015	0.902 ± 0.011	30.2
GMM-Opt-Both	4780 ± 506	4122 ± 469	4207 ± 811.2	0.796 ± 0.078	0.943 ± 0.052	23.4
GMM-Opt-Attr	4803 ± 564	4146 ± 505	4142 ± 811.4	0.801 ± 0.079	0.947 ± 0.053	22.4
GMM-One	5147 ± 221	4439 ± 251	4235 ± 443.9	0.852 ± 0.013	0.982 ± 0.003	10.0
GMM-Qpr-AIC	5154 ± 226	4454 ± 252	4249 ± 474.9	0.851 ± 0.013	0.982 ± 0.003	10.0
GMM-All-Tweets	7871 ± 156	7072 ± 210	5243 ± 882.7	0.480 ± 0.020	0.900 ± 0.012	15.5

Table 1. Performance of key algorithms; we report the mean and standard deviation of each metric across each experiment's tests. MCAE and MSAE are in kilometers, $MPRA_{50}$ is in thousands of km^2, and OC_β is unitless. RT is the mean run time, in minutes, of one train-test cycle using 8 threads on 6100-series Opteron processors running at 1.9 GHz.

Algorithm	SAE Mean	SAE Median	OC_{50}	n-grams
Hong et al. [17]		373		
Eisenstein et al. [11]	845	501		
GMM-Opt-ID	**870**	**534**	**0.50**	**19**
Roller et al. [28]	897	432		
Eisenstein et al. [10]	900	494		
GMM-Err-SAE6	**946**	**588**	**0.50**	**153**
GMM-Err-SAE16	**954**	**493**	**0.36**	**37**
Wing et al. [34]	967	479		
GMM-Err-SAE4	**985**	**684**	**0.55**	**182**

Table 2. Our algorithms compared with previous work, using the dataset from Eisenstein et al. [10]. The *n-grams* column reports the mean number of n-grams used to locate each test tweet.

user location inference, not message location (that is, they are designed for methods which assume users tend to stay near the same location, whereas our model makes no such assumption and thus may be more appropriate when locating messages from unknown users). To adapt them to our message-based algorithms, we concatenate all tweets from each user, treating them as a single message, as in [17]. Finally, the Eisenstein data contain only unigrams from the text field (as we will show, including information from other fields can notably improve results); for comparison, we do the same. This yields 7,580 training and 1,895 test messages (i.e., roughly 380,000 tweets versus 13 million in our data set).

Judged by mean SAE, *GMM-Opt-ID* surpasses all other approaches except for Eisenstein et al. [11]. Interestingly, the algorithm ranking varies depending on whether mean or median SAE is used — e.g., *GMM-Err-SAE16* has lower median SAE than [11] but a higher mean SAE. This trade-off between mean and median SAE also appears in other work – for example, Eisenstein et al. report the best mean SAE but have much higher median SAE [11]. Also, Hong et al. report the best median SAE but do not report mean at all [17].

Examining the results for *GMM-Err-SAE* sheds light on this discrepancy. We see that as the exponent increases from 4 to 16, the median SAE decreases from 684 km to 493 km. How-

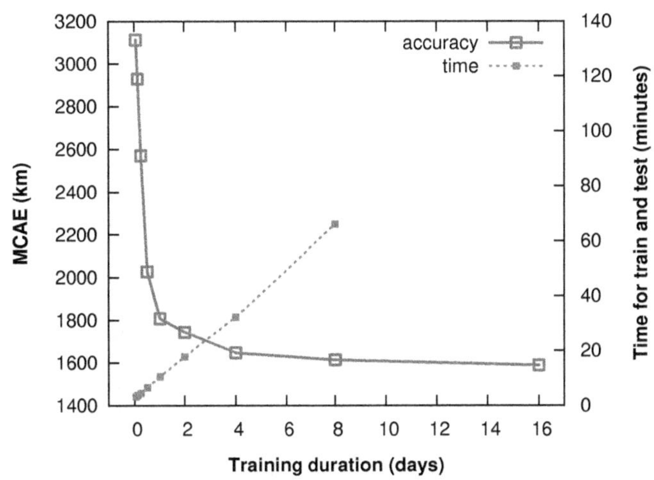

Figure 4. Accuracy of *GMM-Err-SAE4* with different amounts of training data, along with the mean time to train and test one model. Each day contains roughly 32,000 training tweets. (The 16-day test was run in a nonstandard configuration and its timing is therefore omitted.)

ever, calibration suffers rather dramatically: *GMM-Err-SAE16* has a quite overconfident $OC_{50} = 0.36$. This is explained in part by its use of fewer n-grams per message (182 for an exponent of 4 versus 37 for exponent 16).

Moreover, to our knowledge, no prior work reports either precision or calibration metrics, making a complete comparison impossible. For example, the better mean SAE of Eisenstein et al. [11] may coincide with worse precision or calibration. These metrics are not unique to our GMM method, and we argue that they are critical to understanding techniques in this space, as the trade-off above demonstrates.

Finally, we speculate that a modest decrease in accuracy may not outweigh the simplicity and scalability of our approach. Specifically in contrast to topic modeling approaches, our learning phase can be trivially parallelized by n-gram.

RQ2: Training size

We evaluated the accuracy of *GMM-Err-SAE4* on different training durations, no gap, all fields except user description,

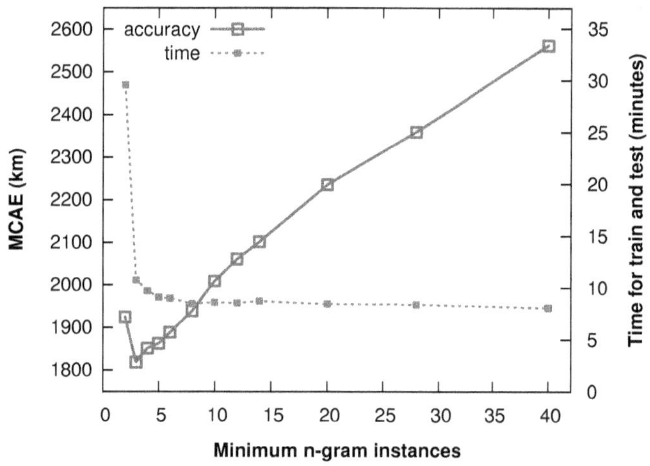

Figure 5. Accuracy and run time of *GMM-Err-SAE4* vs. inclusion thresholds for the number of times an n-gram appears in training data.

and minimum instances of 3. We used a stride of 13 days for performance reasons.

Figure 4 shows our results. The knee of the curve is 1 day of training (i.e., about 30,000 tweets), with error rapidly plateauing and training time increasing as more data are added; accordingly, we use 1 training day in our other experiments.[6]

We also evaluated accuracy when varying minimum instances (the frequency threshold for retaining n-grams), with training days fixed at 1; Figure 5 shows the results. Notably, including n-grams which appear only 3 times in the training set improves accuracy at modest time cost (and thus we use this value in our other experiments). This might be explained in part by the well-known long-tail distribution of word frequencies; that is, while the informativeness of each individual n-gram may be low, the fact that low-frequency words occur in so many tweets can impact overall accuracy. This finding supports Wing & Baldridge's suggestion [34] that Eisenstein et al. [10] pruned too aggressively by setting this threshold to 40.

RQ3: Time dependence

We evaluated the accuracy of *GMM-Err-SAE4* on different temporal gaps between training and testing, holding fixed training duration of 1 day and minimum n-gram instances of 3. Figure 6 summarizes our results. Location inference is surprisingly time-invariant: while error rises linearly with gap duration, it does so slowly – there is only about 6% additional error with a four-month gap. We speculate that this is simply because location-informative n-grams which are time-dependent (e.g., those related to a traveling music festival) are relatively rare.

RQ4: Location signal source

We wanted to understand which types of content provide useful location information under our algorithm. For example, Figure 1 on the first page illustrates a successful estimate by *GMM-Err-SAE4*. Recall that this was based almost entirely on the n-grams *angeles ca* and *ca*, both from the location field. Table 6 in the appendices provides a further snapshot of the algorithm's output. These hint that, consistent with other methods (e.g., [16]), toponyms provide the most important signals; below, we explore this hypothesis in more detail.

[6]We also observed deteriorating calibration beyond 1 day; this may explain some of the accuracy improvement and should be explored.

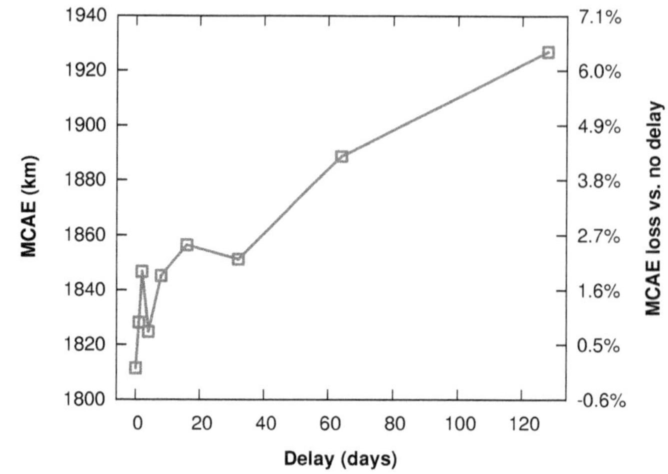

Figure 6. Accuracy of GMM-Err-SAE4 with increasing delay between training and testing.

Field	Alone MCAE	Alone success	Improvement MCAE	Improvement success
user location	2125	65.8%	1255	1.7%
user time zone	2945	76.1%	910	3.0%
tweet text	3855	95.7%	610	7.3%
user description	4482	79.7%	221	3.3%
user language	6143	100.0%	-103	8.5%

Table 3. Value of each field. *Alone* shows the accuracy and success rate of estimation using that field alone, while *Improvement* shows the mean improvement when adding a field to each combination of other fields (in both cases, positive indicates improvement). For example, adding user location to some combination of the other four fields will, on average, decrease MCAE by 1,255 km and increase the success rate by 1.7 percentage points.

Which fields provide the most value?

One framing of this research question is structural. To measure this, we evaluated *GMM-Err-SAE4* on each combination of the five tweet fields, holding fixed training duration at 1 day, gap at zero, and minimum instances at 3. This requires an additional metric: *success rate* is the fraction of test tweets for which the model can estimate a location (i.e., at least one n-gram in the test tweet is present in the trained model).

Table 3 summarizes our results, while Table 4 enumerates each combination. User location and time zone are the most accurate fields, with tweet text and language important for success rate. For example, comparing the first and third rows of Table 4, we see that adding text and language fields to a model that considers only location and timezone fields improves MCAE only slightly (39 km) but improves success rate considerably (by 12.3% to 100.0%). We speculate that while tweet text is a noisier source of evidence than time zone (due to the greater diversity of locations associated with each

Rank	Fields					MCAE	success
1	lo	tz	tx		ln	1823	100.0%
2	lo	tz	tx	ds	ln	1826	100.0%
3	lo	tz				1862	87.7%
4	lo	tz	tx			1878	99.2%
5	lo	tz	tx	ds		1908	99.6%
6	lo	tz		ds		2013	94.1%
7	lo	tz		ds	ln	2121	100.0%
8	lo					2125	65.8%
9	lo		tx	ds	ln	2176	100.0%
10	lo	tz			ln	2207	100.0%
11	lo		tx	ds		2274	99.2%
12	lo		tx		ln	2310	100.0%
13	lo		tx			2383	98.0%
14		tz	tx	ds	ln	2492	100.0%
15	lo			ds		2585	88.3%
16		tz	tx	ds		2594	99.4%
17		tz	tx		ln	2617	100.0%
18		tz	tx			2691	98.7%
19	lo			ds	ln	2759	100.0%
20		tz				2945	76.1%
21		tz		ds		2991	91.8%
22		tz		ds	ln	3039	100.0%
23	lo				ln	3253	100.0%
24			tx	ds	ln	3267	100.0%
25			tx	ds		3426	98.8%
26		tz			ln	3496	100.0%
27			tx		ln	3685	100.0%
28			tx			3855	95.7%
29				ds		4482	79.7%
30				ds	ln	4484	100.0%
31					ln	6143	100.0%

Table 4. Accuracy of including different fields. We list each combination of fields, ordered by increasing MCAE.

n-gram), our algorithm is able to combine these sources to increase both accuracy and success rate.

It is also interesting to compare the variant considering only the location field (row 8 of Table 4) with previous work that heuristically matches strings from the location field to gazetteers. Hecht et al. found that 66% of user profiles contain some type of geographic information in their location field [16], which is comparable to the 67% success rate of our model using only location field.

Surprisingly, user description adds no value at all; we speculate that it tends to be redundant with user location.

Which types of n-grams provide the most value?

We also approached this question by content analysis. To do so, from an arbitrarily chosen test of the 58 successful *GMM-Err-SAE4* tests, we selected a "good" set of the 400 (or 20%) lowest-CAE tweets, and a "bad" set of the 400 highest-CAE tweets. We further randomly subdivided these sets into 100 training tweets (yielding 162 good n-grams and 457 bad ones) and 300 testing tweets (364 good n-grams and 1,306 bad ones, of which we randomly selected 364).

Two raters independently created categories by examining n-grams from the location and tweet text fields in the training sets. These were merged by discussion into a unified hierarchy. The same raters then independently categorized n-grams from the two fields into this hierarchy, using Wikipedia to confirm potential toponyms and Google Translate for non-English n-grams. Disagreements were again resolved by discussion.[7]

Our results are presented in Table 5. Indeed, toponyms offer the strongest signal; fully 83% of the n-gram weight in well-located tweets is due to toponyms, including 49% from city names. In contrast, n-grams used for poorly-located tweets tended to be non-toponyms (57%). Notably, languages with geographically compact user bases, such as Dutch, also provided strong signals even for non-toponyms.

These results and those in the previous section offer a key insight into gazetteer-based approaches [13, 16, 26, 30, 32], which favor accuracy over success rate by considering only toponyms. However, our experiments show that both accuracy and success rate are improved by adding non-toponyms, the latter to nearly 100%; for example, compare rows 1 and 8 of Table 4. Further, Table 5 shows that 17% of location signal in well-located tweets is not from toponyms.

IMPLICATIONS

We propose new judgement criteria for location estimates and specific metrics to compute them. We also propose a simple, scalable method for location inference that is competitive with more complex ones, and we validate this approach using our new criteria on a dataset of tweets that is comprehensive temporally, geographically, and linguistically.

This has implications for both location inference research as well as applications which depend on such inference. In particular, our metrics can help these and related inference domains better balance the trade-off between precision and recall and to reason properly in the presence of uncertainty.

Our results also have implications for privacy. In particular, they suggest that social Internet users wishing to maximize their location privacy should (a) mention toponyms only at state- or country-scale, or perhaps not at all, (b) not use languages with a small geographic footprint, and, for maximal privacy, (c) mention decoy locations. However, if widely adopted, these measures will reduce the utility of Twitter and other social systems for public-good uses such as disease surveillance and response. Our recommendation is that system designers should provide guidance enabling their users to thoughtfully balance these issues.

Future directions include exploring non-gaussian and non-parametric density estimators and improved weighting algorithms (e.g., perhaps those optimizing multiple metrics), as well as ways to combine our approach with others, in order to take advantage of a broader set of location clues. We also plan to incorporate priors such as population density and to compare with human location assessments.

[7] We did a similar analysis of the language and time zone fields, using their well-defined vocabularies instead of human judgement. However, this did not yield significant results, so we omit it for brevity.

Category		Good	Bad	Examples
location		*** **0.83**	**0.19**	
	city	*** 0.49	0.09	edinburgh, roma, leicester, houston tx
	country	** 0.10	0.03	singapore, the netherlands, nederland, janeiro brasil
	generic	0.01	0.02	de mar, puerta de, beach, rd singapore
	state	*** 0.14	0.02	maryland, houston tx, puebla, connecticut
	other lo	*** 0.09	0.02	essex, south yorkshire, yorkshire, gloucestershire
not-location		**0.07**	**0.57** ***	
	dutch word	*** 0.02	0.00	zien, bij de, uur, vrij
	english word	0.01	0.37 ***	st new, i, pages, check my
	letter	0.01	0.04	µ, w, α, s
	slang	0.00	0.08 ***	bitch, lad, ass, cuz
	spanish word	0.00	0.07 ***	mucha, niña, los, suerte
	swedish word	0.00	0.02	rätt, jävla, på, kul
	turkish word	0.02	0.00	kar, restoran, biraz, daha
	untranslated	0.02	0.00	cewe, gading, ung, suria
technical		** **0.03**	**0.02**	
	foursquare	*** 0.03	0.00	paulo http, istanbul http, miami http, brasília http
	url	0.00	0.02	co, http, http t, co h
other		**0.03**	**0.04**	

Table 5. Content analysis of n-grams in the location and text fields. For each category, we show the fraction of total weight in all location estimates from n-grams of that category; e.g., 49% of all estimate weight in the good estimates was from n-grams with category *city* (weights do not add up to 100% because time zone and language fields are not included). Weights that are significantly greater in good estimates than bad (or vice versa) are indicated with a significance code (○ = 0.1, * = 0.05, ** = 0.01, * = 0.001) determined using a Mann-Whitney U test with Bonferroni correction, the null hypothesis being that the mean weight assigned to a category over all n-grams in the *good* set is equal to the mean weight for the same category in the *bad* set. Categories with less than 1.5% weight in both classes are rolled up into *other*. We also show the top-weighted examples in each category.**

ACKNOWLEDGMENTS

Susan M. Mniszewski, Geoffrey Fairchild, and other members of our research team provided advice and support. We thank our anonymous reviewers for key guidance and the Twitter users whose content we studied. This work is supported by NIH/NIGMS/MIDAS, grant U01-GM097658-01. Computation was completed using Darwin, a cluster operated by CCS-7 at LANL and funded by the Accelerated Strategic Computing Program; we thank Ryan Braithwaite for his technical assistance. Maps were drawn using Quantum GIS;[8] base map geodata is from Natural Earth.[9] LANL is operated by Los Alamos National Security, LLC for the Department of Energy under contract DE-AC52-06NA25396.

APPENDIX: MATHEMATICAL IMPLEMENTATIONS

Metrics

This section details the mathematical implementation of the metrics presented above. To do so, we use the following vocabulary. Let m be a message represented by a binary feature vector of n-grams (i.e., sequences of up to n adjacent tokens; we use $n = 2$) $m = \{w_1 \dots w_V\}$, $w_j \in \{0, 1\}$. $w_j = 1$ means that n-gram w_j appears in message m, and V is the total size of the vocabulary. Let $y \in \mathbb{R}^2$ represent a geographic point (for example, latitude and longitude) somewhere on the surface of the Earth. We represent the true origin of a message as y^*; given a new message m, our goal is to construct a geographic density estimate $f(y|m)$, a function which estimates the probability of each point y being the true origin of m.

[8]http://qgis.org

[9]http://naturalearthdata.com

These implementations are valid for any density estimate f, not just gaussian mixture models. Specific types of estimates may require further detail; for GMMs, this is noted below.

CAE depends further on the geodesic distance $d(y, y^*)$ between the true origin y^* and some other point y. It can be expressed as:

$$\text{CAE} = \text{E}_f[d(y, y^*)] = \int_y d(y, y^*) f(y|m)\,\text{d}y \qquad (1)$$

As computing this integral is intractable in general, we approximate it using a simple Monte Carlo procedure. First, we generate a random sample of n points from the density f, $S = \{y_1 \dots y_n\}$ ($n = 1000$ in our experiments).[10] Using this sample, we compute CAE as follows:

$$\text{CAE} \approx \frac{1}{|S|} \sum_{y \in S} d(y, y^*) \qquad (2)$$

Note that in this implementation, the weighting has become implicit: points that are more likely according to f are simply more likely to appear in S. Thus, if f is a good estimate, most of the samples in S will be near the true origin.

To implement PRA, let $R_{f,\beta}$ be a prediction region such that the probability of y^* falling within the geographic region R is its coverage β. Then, PRA_β is simply the area of R:

[10]The implementations of our metrics depend on being able to efficiently (a) sample a point from f and (b) evaluate the probability of any point.

%ile	Tweet text	Location	TZ	L	N-grams	CAE	PRA$_{50}$
100	I'm at Court Avenue Restaurant and Brewing Company (CABCO) (309 Court Avenue, Des Moines) w/ 3 others http://t.co/LW8cKUG3	Urbandale, IA	central	en	0.50 tx moines 0.50 tx des moines	4	34
90	Eyebrow threading time with *@mention* :)	Cardiff , Wales		en	0.73 lo cardiff 0.27 lo wales	17	379
80	Americans are optimistic about the economy & like what Obama is doing. What is he doing? Campaigning and playing golf? Ignorance is bliss	Los Angeles, CA	pacific	en	0.87 lo angeles ca 0.12 lo ca	115	835
70	Extreme Close Up..	Rancagua, Chile	quito	es	1.00 lo chile	272	1,517
60	Reaksinya bakal sama ga yaa? Pengen tau.. http://t.co/8ABEPmKQ	ÜT: -2.9873722,104.7218631	pacific	en	0.97 tx pengen	451	2,974
50	Follow *@mention* exhibition date announced soon #Fabulous	London		en	1.00 lo london	688	967
40	You cannot you on ANY news station and NOT see NEWT being ripped apart.		quito	en	0.99 tx newt	1,008	634,421
30	*@mention* kkkkkk besta		santiago	en	0.91 tx kkkkkk 0.08 tz santiago	1,496	511,405
20	*@mention* eu entrei no site é em dólar, se for real eu compro uma pra vc ir de novo Pra Disney agora.	Belem-PA	brasilia	pt	0.89 tx de novo 0.07 lo pa	2,645	263,576
10	Þegar ég get ekki sofið #hunangsmjolk http://t.co/zx43NoZD			en	0.81 tx get 0.05 ln en 0.02 tx t 0.02 tx zx 0.02 tx co 0.02 tx t co	5,505	2,185,354
0	*@mention* cyber creeping ya mean! I'm in New Zealand not OZ you mad *expletive* haha it's deadly anyways won't b home anytime soon :P			en	1.00 tx *expletive*	18,578	17,827

Table 6. Example output of *GMM-Err-SAE4* for an arbitrarily selected test. *TZ* is the time zone field (with *-timeuscanada* omitted), while *L* is the language code. N-grams which collectively form 95% of the estimate weight are listed. *CAE* is in kilometers, while PRA$_{50}$ is in square kilometers.

$$\mathrm{PRA}_\beta = \int_{R_{f,\beta}} \mathrm{d}y \tag{3}$$

As above, we can use a sample of points S from f to construct an approximate version of R:

1. Sort S in descending order of likelihood $f(y_i|m)$. Let S_β be the set containing the top $|S|\beta$ sample points.
2. Divide S_β into approximately convex clusters.
3. For each cluster of points, compute its convex hull, producing a geo-polygon.
4. The union of these hulls is approximately $R_{f,\beta}$, and the area of this set of polygons is approximately PRA_β.[11]

Finally, recall that OC_β for a given estimator and a set of test messages is the fraction of tests where y^* was within the prediction region $R_{f,\beta}$. That is, for a set $(y_1^*, y_2^*, ... y_n^*)$ of n true message origins:

$$\mathrm{OC}_\beta = \frac{1}{n}\sum_{i=1}^{n} \mathbb{1}[y_i^* \in R_{f,\beta}^i] \tag{4}$$

We do not explicitly test whether $y^* \in R$, because doing so propagates any errors in approximating R. Instead, we count how many samples in S have likelihood less than $f(y^*|m)$; if this fraction is greater than β, then y^* is (probably) in R. Specifically:

$$r(y^*) = \frac{1}{|S|}\sum_{y \in S} \mathbb{1}[f(y) < f(y^*)] \tag{5}$$

$$\mathrm{OC}_\beta \approx \frac{1}{n}\sum_{i=1}^{n} \mathbb{1}[r(y_i^*) > \beta] \tag{6}$$

Gaussian mixture models

As introduced in section "Our Approach", we construct our location model by training on geographic data consisting of a set D of n (message, true origin) pairs extracted from our database of geotagged tweets; i.e., $D = \{(m_i, y_i^*)\}_{i=1}^n$. For each n-gram w_j, we fit a gaussian mixture model $g(y|w_j)$ based on examples in D. Then, to estimate the origin location of a new message m, we combine the mixture models for all n-grams in m into a new density $f(y|m)$. These steps are detailed below.

[11] Because the polygons lie on an ellipsoidal Earth, not a plane, we must compute the *geodesic area* rather than a planar area. This is accomplished by projecting the polygons to the Mollweide equal-area projection and computing the planar area under that projection.

We estimate g for each (sufficiently frequent) n-gram w_j in D as follows. First, we gather the set of true origins of all messages containing w_j, and then we fit a gaussian mixture model of r components to represent the density of these points:

$$g(y|w_j) = \sum_{k=1}^{r} \pi_k^j \, N(y|\mu_k^j, S_k^j) \tag{7}$$

where $\pi^j = \{\pi_1^j \dots \pi_r^j\}$ is a vector of mixture weights and N is the normal density function with mean μ_k^j and covariance S_k^j. We refer to $g(y|w_j)$ as an *n-gram density*.

We fit π and S independently for each n-gram using the expectation maximization algorithm, as implemented in the Python package scikit-learn [27].

Choosing the number of components r is a well-studied problem. While Dirichlet process mixtures [24] are a common solution, they can scale poorly. For simplicity, we instead investigated a number of heuristic approaches from the literature [23]; in our case, $r = \min(m, \log(n)/2)$ worked well, where n is the number of points to be clustered, and m is a parameter. We use this heuristic with $m = 20$ in all experiments.

Next, to estimate the origin of a new message m, we gather the available densities g for each n-gram in m (i.e., some n-grams may appear in m but not in sufficient quantity in D). We combine these n-gram densities into a mixture of GMMs:

$$f(y|m) = \sum_{w_j \in m} \delta_j g(y|w_j) = \sum_{w_j \in m} \delta_j \sum_{k=1}^{r} \pi_k^j \, N(y|\mu_k^j, S_k^j) \tag{8}$$

where $\delta = \{\delta_1 \dots \delta_V\}$ are the *n-gram mixture weights* associated with each n-gram density g. We refer to $f(y|m)$ as a *message density*.

A mixture of GMMs can be implemented as a single GMM by multiplying δ_j by π_k^j for all j, k and renormalizing so that the mixture weights sum to 1. Thus, Equation 8 can be rewritten:

$$f(y|m) = \sum_{w_j \in m} \sum_{k=1}^{r} \tau_k^j \, N(y|\mu_k^j, S_k^j) \tag{9}$$

where $\tau_k^j = \delta_j \pi_k^j / \sum_{j,k} \delta_j \pi_k^j$.

We can now compute all four metrics. CAE and OC_β require no additional treatment. To compute SAE, we distill $f(y|m)$ into a single point estimate by the weighted average of its component means: $\hat{y} = \sum_{w_j \in m} \sum_{k=1}^{r} \tau_k^j \mu_k^j$. Computing PRA_β requires dividing S_β into convex clusters; we do so by assigning each point in S to its most probable gaussian in f.

The next two sections describe methods to set the n-gram mixture weights δ_j.

Setting δ_j weights by inverse error

Mathematically, the inverse error approach introduced above can be framed as a non-iterative optimization problem. Specifically, we set δ by fitting a multinomial distribution to the observed error distribution. Let $e_{ij} \in \mathbb{R}_{\geq 0}$ be the error incurred by n-gram density $g(y|w_j)$ for message m_i; in our implementation, we use SAE as e_{ij} for performance reasons (results with CAE are comparable). Let e_j be the average error of n-gram w_j: $e_j = \frac{1}{N_j} \sum_{i=1}^{N_j} e_{ij}$, where N_j is the number of messages containing w_j. We introduce a model parameter α, which places a non-linear (exponential) penalty on error terms e_j. The problem is to minimize the negative log likelihood, with constraints that ensure δ is a probability distribution:

$$\delta^* \leftarrow \operatorname*{argmin}_{\delta} - \log \prod_j \delta_j^{\frac{1}{e_j^\alpha}} \tag{10}$$

$$\text{s.t.} \sum_j \delta_j = 1 \text{ and } \delta_j \geq 0 \; \forall j \tag{11}$$

This objective can be minimized analytically. While the inequality constraints in Equation 11 will be satisfied implicitly, we express the equality constraints using a Lagrangian:

$$L(\delta, \lambda) = -\log \prod_j \delta_j^{\frac{1}{e_j^\alpha}} + \lambda \left(\sum_j \delta_j - 1 \right) \tag{12}$$

$$= -\sum_j \frac{1}{e_j^\alpha} \log \delta_j + \lambda \left(\sum_j \delta_j - 1 \right) \tag{13}$$

Taking the partial derivative with respect to δ_k and setting to 0 results in:

$$\frac{\partial L}{\partial \delta_k} = -\frac{1}{e_k^\alpha \delta_k} + \lambda = 0 \; \forall k \tag{14}$$

$$= -\frac{1}{e_k^\alpha} + \lambda \delta_k = 0 \; \forall k \tag{15}$$

$$\frac{\partial L}{\partial \delta} = -\sum_k \frac{1}{e_k^\alpha} + \lambda \sum_k \delta_k = 0 \tag{16}$$

The equality constraint lets us substitute $\sum_k \delta_k = 1$ in Equation 16. Solving for λ yields:

$$\lambda = \sum_k \frac{1}{e_k^\alpha} \tag{17}$$

Plugging this into 14 and solving for δ_k results in:

$$\delta_k = \frac{\frac{1}{e_k^\alpha}}{\sum_k \frac{1}{e_k^\alpha}} \tag{18}$$

This brings us full circle to the intuitive result above: that the weight of an n-gram is proportional to its average error.[12]

Setting δ_j weights by optimization

This section details the data-driven optimization algorithm introduced above. We tag each n-gram density function with a feature vector. This vector contains the ID of the n-gram density function, the quality properties, or both of these. For

[12] Our implementation first assigns $\delta_k = \frac{1}{e_k^\alpha}$, then normalizes the weights per-message as in Equation 9.

example, the feature vector for the n-gram *dallas* might be $\{\text{id} = 1234, \text{variance} = 0.56, \text{BIC} = 0.01, ...\}$. We denote the feature vector for n-gram w_j as $\phi(w_j)$, with elements $\phi_k(w_j) \in \phi(w_j)$.

This feature vector is paired with a corresponding real-valued parameter vector $\theta = \{\theta_1, \ldots, \theta_p\}$ setting the weight of each feature. The vectors θ and ϕ are passed through the logistic function to ensure the final weights δ are in the interval [0,1]:

$$\delta_j^\theta = \frac{1}{1 + e^{-\sum_{k=1}^{p} \phi_k(w_j)\theta_k}} \tag{19}$$

The goal of this approach is to assign values to θ such that properties that are predictive of low-error n-grams have high weight (equivalently, so that these n-grams have large δ_j^θ). This is accomplished by minimizing an error function (built atop the same SAE-based e_{ij} as the previous method):

$$\theta^* \leftarrow \underset{\theta}{\operatorname{argmin}} \sum_{i=1}^{|D|} \frac{\sum_{w_j \in m_i} e_{ij}\delta_j^\theta}{\sum_{w_j \in m_i} \delta_j^\theta} \tag{20}$$

After optimizing θ, we assign $\delta^* = \delta^{\theta^*}$. The numerator in Equation 20 computes the sum of mixture weights for each n-gram density weighted by its error; the denominator sums mixture weights to ensure that the objective function is not trivially minimized by setting δ_j^θ to 0 for all j. Thus, to minimize Equation 20, n-gram densities with large errors must be assigned small mixture weights.

Before minimizing, we first augment the error function in Equation 20 with a regularization term:

$$\Phi(D, \theta) = \sum_{i=1}^{|D|} \frac{\sum_{w_j \in m_i} e_{ij}\delta_j^\theta}{\sum_{w_j \in m_i} \delta_j^\theta} + \frac{\lambda}{2}||\theta||^2 \tag{21}$$

The extra term is an ℓ_2-regularizer to encourage small values of θ to reduce overfitting; we set $\lambda = 1$ in our experiments.[13]

We minimize Equation 21 using gradient descent. For brevity, let $n_{ij} = \sum_{w_j \in m_i} e_{ij}\delta_j^\theta$ and $d_{ij} = \sum_{w_j \in m_i} \delta_j^\theta$ be the numerator and denominator terms from Equation 21. Then, the gradient of Equation 21 with respect to θ_k is

$$\frac{\partial \Phi}{\partial \theta_k} = \sum_{i=1}^{|D|} \sum_{w_j \in m_i} \frac{-\phi_k(w_j)\delta_j^\theta(1 - \delta_j^\theta)(e_{ij}d_{ij} - n_{ij})}{d_{ij}^2} + \lambda\theta_k \tag{22}$$

We set Equation 22 to 0 and solve for θ using L-BFGS as implemented in the SciPy Python package [18]. (Note that by decomposing the objective function by n-grams, we need only compute the error metrics e_{ij} once prior to optimization.) Once θ is set, we then find δ according to Equation 19 and use these values to find the message density in Equation 8.

APPENDIX: TOKENIZATION ALGORITHM

This section details our algorithm to convert a text string into a sequence of n-grams, used to tokenize the message text, user description, and user location fields into bigrams (i.e., $n = 2$).

[13] λ could be tuned on validation data; this should be explored.

1. Split the string into candidate tokens, each consisting of a sequence of characters with the same Unicode category and script. Candidates not of the *letter* category are discarded, and letters are converted to lower-case. For example, the string "Can't wait for 私の" becomes five candidate tokens: *can*, *t*, *wait*, *for*, and 私の.
2. Candidates in certain scripts are discarded either because they do not separate words with a delimiter (Thai, Lao, Khmer, and Myanmar, all of which have very low usage on Twitter) or may not really be letters (Common, Inherited). Such scripts pose tokenization difficulties which we leave for future work.
3. Candidates in the scripts Han, Hiragana, and Katakana are assumed to be Japanese and are further subdivided using the TinySegmenter algorithm [15]. (We ignore the possibility that text in these scripts might be Chinese, because that language has very low usage on Twitter.) This step would split 私の into 私 and の.
4. Create n-grams from adjacent tokens. Thus, the final tokenization of the example for $n = 2$ would be: *can*, *t*, *wait*, *for*, 私, の, *can t*, *t wait*, *wait for*, *for* 私, and 私 の.

APPENDIX: RESULTS OF PILOT EXPERIMENTS

This section describes briefly three directions we explored but did not pursue in detail because they seemed to be of limited potential value.

- **Unifying fields.** Ignoring field boundaries slightly reduced accuracy, so we maintain these boundaries (i.e., the same n-gram appearing in different fields is treated as multiple, separate n-grams).
- **Head trim.** We tried sorting n-grams by frequency and removing various fractions of the most frequent n-grams. In some cases, this yielded a slightly better MCAE but also slightly reduced the success rate; therefore, we retain common n-grams.
- **Map projection.** We tried plate carrée (i.e., WGS84 longitude and latitude used as planar X and Y coordinates), Miller, and Mollweide projections. We found no consistent difference with our error- and optimization-based algorithms, though some others displayed variation in MPRA. Because this did not affect our results, we used plate carrée for all experiments, but future work should explore exactly when and why map projection matters.

REFERENCES

1. H. Akaike. A new look at the statistical model identification. *Automatic Control*, 19(6):716–723, 1974. 10.1109/TAC.1974.1100705.
2. D. M. Blei and others. Latent Dirichlet allocation. *Machine Learning Research*, 3:993–1022, 2003. http://dl.acm.org/citation.cfm?id=944937.
3. L. D. Brown et al. Confidence intervals for a binomial proportion and asymptotic expansions. *Annals of Statistics*, 30(1), 2002. 10.1214/aos/1015362189.

4. S. Chandra et al. Estimating Twitter user location using social interactions – A content based approach. In *Proc. Privacy, Security, Risk and Trust (PASSAT)*, 2011. 10.1109/PASSAT/SocialCom.2011.120.

5. H. Chang et al. @Phillies tweeting from Philly? Predicting Twitter user locations with spatial word usage. In *Proc. Advances in Social Networks Analysis and Mining (ASONAM)*, 2012. 10.1109/ASONAM.2012.29.

6. Z. Cheng et al. You are where you tweet: A content-based approach to geo-locating Twitter users. In *Proc. Information and Knowledge Management (CIKM)*, 2010. 10.1145/1871437.1871535.

7. E. Cho et al. Friendship and mobility: User movement in location-based social networks. In *Proc. Knowledge Discovery and Data Mining (KDD)*, 2011. 10.1145/2020408.2020579.

8. C. A. Davis Jr. et al. Inferring the location of Twitter messages based on user relationships. *Transactions in GIS*, 15(6), 2011. 10.1111/j.1467-9671.2011.01297.x.

9. M. Dredze. How social media will change public health. *Intelligent Systems*, 27(4):81–84, 2012. 10.1109/MIS.2012.76.

10. J. Eisenstein et al. A latent variable model for geographic lexical variation. In *Proc. Empirical Methods in Natural Language Processing*, 2010. http://dl.acm.org/citation.cfm?id=1870782.

11. J. Eisenstein et al. Sparse additive generative models of text. In *Proc. Machine Learning (ICML)*, 2011. http://www.icml-2011.org/papers/534_icmlpaper.pdf.

12. S. Geisser. *Predictive Inference: An Introduction*. Chapman and Hall, 1993.

13. J. Gelernter and N. Mushegian. Geo-parsing messages from microtext. *Transactions in GIS*, 15(6):753–773, 2011. 10.1111/j.1467-9671.2011.01294.x.

14. M. C. González et al. Understanding individual human mobility patterns. *Nature*, 453(7196):779–782, 2008. 10.1038/nature06958.

15. M. Hagiwara. TinySegmenter in Python. http://lilyx.net/tinysegmenter-in-python/.

16. B. Hecht et al. Tweets from Justin Bieber's heart: The dynamics of the location field in user profiles. In *Proc. CHI*, 2011. 10.1145/1978942.1978976.

17. L. Hong et al. Discovering geographical topics in the Twitter stream. In *Proc. WWW*, 2012. 10.1145/2187836.2187940.

18. E. Jones et al. SciPy: Open source scientific tools for Python, 2001. http://www.scipy.org.

19. S. Kinsella et al. "I'm eating a sandwich in Glasgow": Modeling locations with Tweets. In *Proc. Workshop on Search and Mining User-Generated Content (SMUC)*, 2011. 10.1145/2065023.2065039.

20. J. Mahmud et al. Where is this Tweet from? Inferring home locations of Twitter users. In *Proc. ICWSM*, 2012. http://www.aaai.org/ocs/index.php/ICWSM/ICWSM12/paper/viewFile/4605/5045.

21. S. McClendon and A. C. Robinson. Leveraging geospatially-oriented social media communications in disaster response. In *Proc. Information Systems for Crisis Response and Management (ISCRAM)*, 2012. http://iscramlive.org/ISCRAM2012/proceedings/136.pdf.

22. G. McLachlan and D. Peel. *Finite Mixture Models*. Wiley & Sons, 2005. 10.1002/0471721182.

23. G. W. Milligan and M. C. Cooper. An examination of procedures for determining the number of clusters in a data set. *Psychometrika*, 50(2):159–179, 1985. 10.1007/BF02294245.

24. R. M. Neal. Markov chain sampling methods for Dirichlet process mixture models. *Computational and Graphical Statistics*, 9(2), 2000. 10.2307/1390653.

25. N. O'Hare and V. Murdock. Modeling locations with social media. *Information Retrieval*, 16(1):1–33, 2012. 10.1007/s10791-012-9195-y.

26. S. Paradesi. Geotagging tweets using their content. In *Proc. Florida Artificial Intelligence Research Society*, 2011. http://www.aaai.org/ocs/index.php/FLAIRS/FLAIRS11/paper/viewFile/2617/3058.

27. F. Pedregosa et al. Scikit-learn: Machine learning in Python. *Machine Learning Research*, 12:2825–2830, 2011. http://dl.acm.org/citation.cfm?id=2078195.

28. S. Roller et al. Supervised text-based geolocation using language models on an adaptive grid. In *Proc. Empirical Methods in Natural Language Processing and Computational Natural Language Learning (EMNLP-CoNLL)*, 2012. http://dl.acm.org/citation.cfm?id=2391120.

29. N. Savage. Twitter as medium and message. *CACM*, 54(3):18–20, 2011. 10.1145/1897852.1897860.

30. A. Schulz et al. A multi-indicator approach for geolocalization of tweets. In *Proc. ICWSM*, 2013.

31. G. Schwarz. Estimating the dimension of a model. *Annals of Statistics*, 6(2):461–464, 1978. 10.1214/aos/1176344136.

32. G. Valkanas and D. Gunopulos. Location extraction from social networks with commodity software and online data. In *Proc. Data Mining Workshops (ICDMW)*, 2012. 10.1109/ICDMW.2012.128.

33. C. Wang et al. Mining geographic knowledge using location aware topic model. In *Proc. Workshop on Geographical Information Retrieval (GIR)*, 2007. 10.1145/1316948.1316967.

34. B. Wing and J. Baldridge. Simple supervised document geolocation with geodesic grids. In *Proc. Association for Computational Linguistics (ACL)*, 2011. https://www.aclweb.org/anthology-new/P/P11/P11-1096.pdf.

Exploring the Social-technological Gap in Telesurgery: Collaboration within Distributed OR Teams

Pieter Duysburgh
iMinds-SMIT-VUB
Pleinlaan 2,
1050 Brussels, Belgium
pieter.duysburgh@vub.ac.be

Shirley Elprama
iMinds-SMIT-VUB
Pleinlaan 2,
1050 Brussels, Belgium
shirley.elprama@vub.ac.be

An Jacobs
iMinds-SMIT-VUB
Pleinlaan 2,
1050 Brussels, Belgium
an.jacobs@vub.ac.be

ABSTRACT
While its technical feasibility has been illustrated over a decade ago, today, robot-assisted telesurgery is not a part of everyday surgical practice. The thresholds for adoption of telesurgery are mostly seen as technical, legal and financial challenges. However, the aim of this paper is to understand collaboration within distributed OR teams, which seems to be under examined in research on telesurgery. By means of a proxy-technology assessment and a series of interviews, collaborative challenges for telesurgery have been identified. These include the unfamiliarity of the remote surgeon with the practices of the local operating room team and the patient. In addition, verbal and non-verbal communication have to be mediated in a telesurgery setting, making it difficult for the remote surgeon to have an overview and stay in control during surgery. With this research, we illustrate how trust issues in distributed teams manifest in OR teams in a telesurgery setting.

Author Keywords
Telesurgery; distributed teams; robot-assisted surgery; robot-assisted telesurgery; team work; surgical teams.

ACM Classification Keywords
H.5.3. **[Group and Organization Interfaces]**: Computer-supported cooperative work; I.2.9. **[Robotics]**: Manipulators; J.3. **[Life and medical sciences]**: Health.

INTRODUCTION
Today, telesurgery is no longer a hot topic. The technical feasibility of telesurgery has been shown in 2001 by Dr Marescaux [15] by operating on a patient in Strasbourg (France) from New York (U.S.). However, since then, telesurgery has not become a part of common surgical practice, and the few publications dedicated to telesurgery in recent years still regard it as a future practice (e.g. [8]). The main issues for adoption of telesurgery practices are considered to be cost efficacy, technical challenges (especially video latency), training, patient outcomes, and the legal and regulatory framework [14].

CSCW '14, February 15–19, 2014, Baltimore, Maryland, USA.
Copyright 2014 ACM 978-1-4503-2540-0/14/02...$15.00.
http://dx.doi.org/10.1145/2531602.2531717

Telesurgery can be understood as a type of robot-assisted surgery where the surgeon (while manipulating a robot with a controller) is not in the same operating room as the rest of the operating room team (OR team) members and the patient (see Figure 1). When using a surgical robot, the surgeon is outside the sterile area, and operates on the patient from a controller, manipulating one or more robot arms that are connected to surgical tools, and inserted in the patient through 'trocars' (small tubes) that are fitted in body ports [11]. Here, a surgical robot is "*a powered, computer-controlled manipulator with artificial sensing that can be programmed to move and position tools to carry out a wide range of surgical tasks.*" [5:71].

In robot-assisted surgery, the surgeon operates from a controller and does not stand next to the patient. As such, all forms of robot-assisted surgery can be understood as a kind of '*remote*' surgery when compared to open surgery or minimally invasive surgery: using surgical robots increases the distance between the surgeon and the rest of the OR team and the patient (see Figure 1).

However, in telesurgery, the distance between the surgeon and the patient is further increased since the surgeon is not located in the same room as the rest of the operating team and the patient. In other words: the OR team is no longer collocated but distributed. As a result, not only the actions of the surgeon on the patient are mediated through technology but all communication between the surgeon and the OR team is mediated.

While all telesurgery is 'robot-assisted', we will not repeat this explicitly throughout the paper. We will use the term 'robot-assisted surgery' when talking about collocated OR teams and both the surgeon(s) and the rest of the OR team find themselves in the same room. When we use the term 'telesurgery', this will always imply that a surgical robot is used and the OR team is distributed.

Advantages of robot-assisted surgery
The importance of robotics in surgical practice has substantially increased and have found their way into everyday surgical practice [4]. Theoretically, a surgical

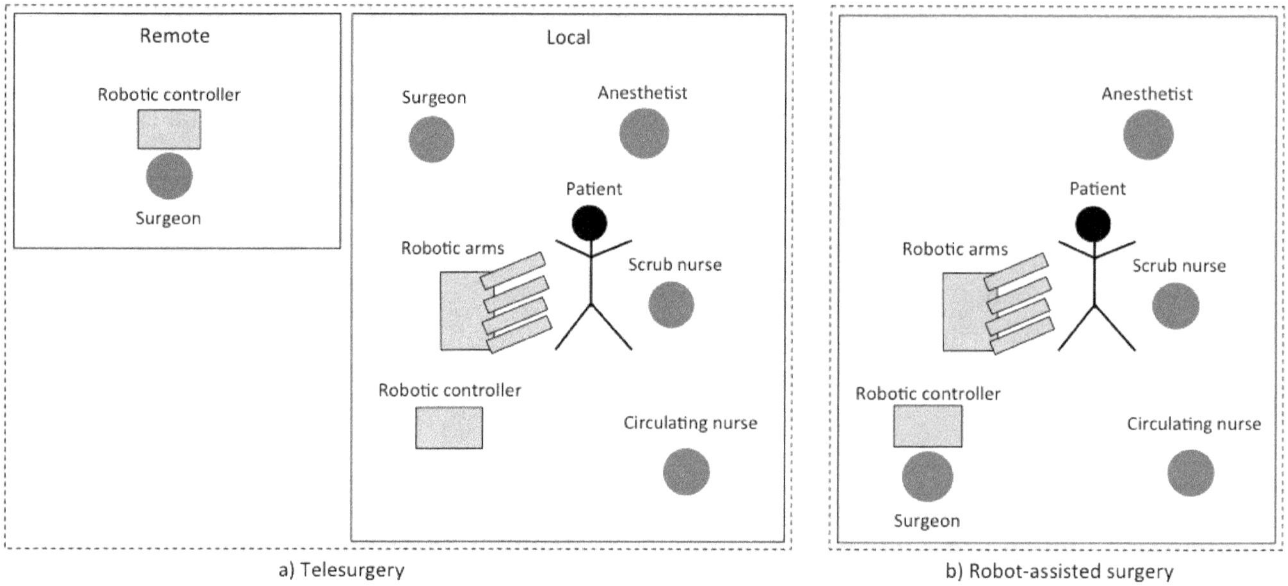

Figure 1: Operating room (a) during telesurgery with distributed teams; (b) during robot-assisted surgery with collocated teams.

robot allows a surgeon to work with more precision than in minimally invasive surgery. The surgeon has a 3D visualization of the body of the patient, and can make use of six to seven degrees of freedom of manipulation and scaled movements (micromotion). However, the acquisition of a surgical robot still is a substantial economical investment for a hospital, and it remains controversial if and to what extent the surgical robots offers medical advantages compared to minimally invasive surgery (e.g. [4, 22]). Still, surgical robots are increasingly being used for procedures in a wide range of medical fields (such as abdominal surgery, pediatric surgery, gynecology, urology, cardiothoracic surgery, and otorhinolaryngology [11]). Especially in Belgium, many hospitals have acquired surgical robots to position themselves as technological front-runners: this country has considerably more surgical robots available than its neighboring countries [4].

With surgical robots becoming more and more commonplace, the question what issues are at play for adoption of telesurgery becomes pertinent. In theory, telesurgery has potentially some clear advantages: the technology can bring the expertise of a surgeon to hospitals in rural areas or extreme locations, such as underwater stations or even space stations [9]. Other application domains are remote areas, warzones, rare interventions or interventions that require a high specialized or skilled surgeon, etc. [8]. However, we have not found any publications detailing to what extent, if at all, telesurgery is being practiced today. Also, none of the surgeons involved in this research were aware of such telesurgery procedures taking place. This paper will look at what issues might be at play with regard to supporting the collaborative practices within OR teams.

The highly collaborative nature of OR teams

An OR team in its basic form consists of a surgeon, an anesthetist, a scrub nurse and a circulating nurse. In some cases, an assisting surgeon and one or more additional nurses are also present in the OR. The role of the circular nurse can be taken up by several people during a single operation. In general, medical personal tends to walk in and out the operating room during interventions. As such, an operation room should not be regarded as a closed environment.

In telesurgery this basic OR team is typically extended with an additional surgeon, who is located at a remote location (see Figure 1). Having a remote surgeon does not change the composition of the local OR team: a second surgeon still needs to be present with the patient, for the start-up of the intervention (e.g. placement of surgical ports) and the end of the operation, or in case the surgery needs to be reverted to open surgery (which may be necessary when complications occur during the intervention). As such, a distributed OR team will usually be larger than a collocated OR team. The local surgeon could at times assist the remote surgeon, or could operate on the patient as well from the local controller. Since both scenarios are possible, we did not decide upon a specific task for the local surgeon while the remote surgeon is operating.

An OR team can be considered as a highly hierarchical and strictly organized collaborative group of medical professionals. The roles in an OR team are strictly defined and often, the members of the OR team have been working together for many years. In any type of surgical intervention, the surgeon is always 'leading' the operation. During robot-assisted surgery, the surgeon is most of the time sitting behind the controller, away from both the rest of the OR team and the patient. The surgeon is required to do complex actions, operating the three or four arms of the surgical robot simultaneously, while being less able to communicate with the rest of the OR team in a non-verbal manner, since the OR team cannot see the surgeon during the operation. As such, in robot-assisted surgery, the complexity of the tasks of the surgeon seems to have increased compared to minimally invasive surgery, which already caused more pressure on the surgeon to perform [2].

Hence, surgical robots pose a challenge for collaboration in the operating room. This might be problematic, since several authors have pointed out the importance of good collaboration in surgery [21, 22, 25]. It is clear that errors resulting from miscommunication can result in grave consequences for patients and all others involved. As such, it is our opinion that collaborative practices should be a focal point in research on robot-assisted surgery and telesurgery. We should also investigate how the introduction of additional technology in the operating room and the increased working distance between the OR team members will influence collaboration. We think that a good understanding of the collaborative challenges related to telesurgery will provide additional insights into why the technology has not (yet) been adopted and how the technology might be improved.

Closing the socio-technical gap in telesurgery

This collaborative element in the OR team has been under examined in publications on telesurgery. The barriers for telesurgery are usually seen as technological, financial, legal, or safety issues. For instance, quite some research effort goes to minimal degradation of the picture, minimal latency, high data quality and a robust communication system [5]. Another focal point is the lack of tactile feedback for the surgeon when using surgical robots, which omits an important source of information for surgeons during the operation [20]. The costs (of the robotic systems, telecommunication, training and research and development) are another important threshold. Finally, having a surgeon working on a patient remotely increases the complexity of the legal framework considerably (e.g., national differences in privacy legislation or surgical accountability in case of a medical error) [5].

While these issues are certainly pertinent, we feel that the issue of collaboration also deserves specific attention. Telesurgery requires a geographically distributed OR team, which may result in new collaborative practices. Studies have shown that technical advances can imply new forms of collaborations in OR teams, since technology may change the tasks and responsibilities [15, 23]. Understanding these changes is crucial to avoid medical errors due to miscommunication.

As such, this paper wishes to explore what Ackerman [1] has described as 'the social-technical gap' to understand how this might impede the adoption of telesurgery. The social-technical gap is "*the great divide between what we know we must support socially and what we can support technically*" [1:180]. According to Ackerman, what is a central intellectual challenge in CSCW is precisely exploring, understanding and ameliorating this social-technical gap. Even though this gap will most probably not go away, it can perhaps be approached better and taken into account.

When applied to telesurgery, we need to understand how the staff in the operation room interacts and communicates, and how these patterns of collaboration occur in telesurgery settings, and where they are problematic. Typically, a process of *mutual shaping* occurs between a technology and users: the users adjust themselves to a new ecology and product, and adjust their working practices to the new conditions [23]. As such, it is to be expected that the new technology in the operating room, and different setup of the people and tools will cause changes in the workflow and how information is accessed in the OR [27]. But a distributed OR team will also adjust itself to this surgical setup and appropriates the technological tools. However, a social-technical gap will remain, and a close examination and good understanding of it, can either steer future developments in telesurgery, or help explaining why telesurgery remains a rare practice.

METHOD

This research consisted of two phases. A first step was an exploratory phase, where a series of interviews and unstructured observations were held to get a better understanding of surgical practices. These observations slowly developed into more structured observations to find specific answers to our research goals. Secondly, a series of interviews were organized with surgeons and scrub nurses to legitimize, adjust and nuance the results of the analysis of the structured observations. As such, this paper elaborates on the results described in prior work [6], but the additional research allowed us to identify central themes in the initial results. Also, this research presents additional insights and more nuanced understandings.

As stipulated in the preceding paper [6], we wanted to verify the findings of this first research phase further with some additional data collection. We called this second phase 'further verification' since we agree with Morse et al. [16] that reliability but also validation cannot simply be limited to a kind of post hoc evaluation. Verification strategies are to be used and kept in mind throughout the whole research process. However, after the first research phase, we found that additional interviews were required, both with some of the medical personal that had participated in the research already, as with some new people. To the medical personnel involved before, we wanted to present the abstractions we had made of their activities and those of others. To interviewees we had not talked to before, we wanted to present the full research, and ask for their opinions. As such, by collecting more data, we wished to continue following the principles of qualitative research, by being self-corrective and working iteratively rather than linearly.

In what follows, we will describe both phases in more detail.

Phase 1: Identifying the barriers

To the best of our knowledge, and according to the surgeons we have encountered during the research, telesurgery interventions have been executed rarely, and mainly for research purposes. We have not found any examples or figures about telesurgery taking place. As a result, we were unable to observe telesurgery.

Consequently, it was decided that robot-assisted surgeries where both the master-side (the controller) and the slave-side (the robotic arms) of the robot are located in the same room would be studied (see Figure 1). By observing how a collocated OR team interacted with and around the robot, we wanted to identify those interactions that potentially could be problematic in a distributed OR team when the main operating surgeon would be in another location.

Such an analysis can be described as a proxy technology assessment (or 'PTA') [13]. Proxy technology assessment is a research method where the users are given a 'future' experience by making use of technology that already exists. PTA has been defined as "*a method for emulating everyday life practices with future technologies and applications by confronting selected user groups with existing similar tools and applications*"[13]. As such, the technology used in the research has some strong similarities with the technology under development, but also misses some key features. In our case, it could be argued that 'local' robot-assisted surgery can be understood as the best proxy available for telesurgery. Key differences between the two technologies are the location of the main operating surgeon and any additional, currently unspecified technical features that would be required to make telesurgery a common practice.

By choosing this method, 'product use' (the surgical robot) is central in our analysis and we regard it as a starting point to understand collaboration in the OR team. We decided to concentrate mainly on the (collaborative) user experience and we do not depart from a general understanding of how OR teams collaborate. While this focus on the product use might be considered as a weakness, we think this approach is useful for understanding how collaboration evolves as a result of using surgical robots. As Olson and Olson [20] have pointed out: if technology is useful, then the constrains of that technology are going to change the way how people will collaborate. Practices will evolve that will fit the tools in the flow of collaborative activity. Therefore, we decided to focus on the use of the product, rather than researching OR team collaboration in general.

In the first phase, we collected data by observing 7 interviews and observing 14 surgical procedures in various hospitals in Belgium.

Interviews

As previously explained, a series of interviews was done at the start of the research project, in order to gain a general understanding of surgical practices and the working procedures. With these interviews, the researchers (who do not have a medical background), wanted to increase their understanding of the general practices and procedures of an OR team involved in minimally invasive surgery and robot-assisted surgery. The researchers interviewed two surgeons, two assistants, one scrub nurse, one bio technician and IT support for the operating room across three different hospitals in Belgium. Both types of surgery were looked at, in order to establish how robot-assisted surgery and minimally invasive surgery are different.

Observation

Next, 14 surgical procedures (9 robot-assisted surgeries and 5 minimally invasive procedures) were examined in four different hospitals in Belgium. Here too, both minimally invasive procedures and robot-assisted surgeries were observed, in order to gain a better understanding how the introduction of the surgical robot in the operating room changed the collaborative practices of the OR team, and as such, be able to understand how telesurgery might further change collaborative practices.

The researchers have observed minimally invasive procedures done by surgeons specialized in gastrointestinal surgery or general surgery. The robot-assisted surgeries (executed with the Da Vinci Surgical System from Intuitive Surgical) were urological interventions and included procedures such as robot-assisted radical prostatectomy and robot-assisted partial nephrectomy.

These observations were done in a structured manner. Based on Forlizzi's product ecology framework [7] an observation scheme was worked out. The framework identified the several components that define product use, in order to describe and investigate how people relate to products and how their relationships change over time. Hence, the scheme included themes such as personnel in the operating theater, the atmosphere in the OR, the interactions amongst the personnel, and other topics. The researchers stopped observing when they reached a point of data saturation and no new information could be observed. During the observations, notes were made and pictures were taken. Also, maps of the OR were drafted, including the positioning and movement of the material and personnel in the operating room. This resulted in one observation report per observed intervention.

Analysis

The analysis of the reports was done using NVIVO software. There were two iterations of coding. In the first iterations, all the actions and interactions between the staff in the operating room were coded. This included any type of communication (questions, agreeing, commenting, instructing, requesting...). These codes were then visualized: the interactions between the members of the OR team were mapped per member of the OR team. This gave the research team a schematized representation of the interactions in the team, allowing for a more direct and visual understanding of the types of interactions and their frequency. These visual representations served as a first point of discussion in identifying potential thresholds for collaboration in a distributed OR team.

Based on this discussion, we returned to the data and the coded interactions were screened in more detail and recoded. During the coding, we now departed from the discussion based on the visual representations of the interactions. Next, they used this to focus on the identification of interactions that are currently challenging, and on the identification of interactions that may become problematic in a telesurgery setting.

This analysis resulted in a first report and paper [6], describing 13 barriers that might impede collaboration in a distributed OR team.

Phase 2: Further verification of the barriers

As detailed before, an additional phase of data gathering was organized after the first part of this research. Not only did the researchers want to validate the findings of the first research phase further, in addition, they wished to move more towards theory building and make a further abstraction of our findings in the first phase.

Participants

For these interviews, the researchers decided to recruit surgeons and scrub nurses. They chose not to include the other OR personnel, since the first phase of the research made clear that it is precisely the relationship between the surgeon and the scrub nurse that is of utmost importance in surgical interventions, and it is this relationship that would change substantially in a telesurgery setting. Most of our initial findings pointed towards barriers related to the collaboration between scrub nurses and surgeons. Therefore, we decided to restrict our additional interviews to this profile. We contacted two surgeons that had already participated in the research (their surgeries were observed) and several others who had experience with robot-assisted surgery, using the Da Vinci robot. Eleven surgeons (working in Belgium) were asked to participate. In the end, 5 of those 14 surgeons agreed to collaborate with the researchers. All 5 surgeons were male, their mean age was 47.2 years (range 40 – 54). On average, they had 21.5 years of experience in general surgery and 7.2 years of experience in robot-assisted surgery. Their specializations included urology, gynecology and digestive surgery. We also contacted 5 scrub nurses, of which 3 agreed to participate in an interview, who worked at two different hospitals. Two scrub nurses were female and one was male; their mean age was 49.3 years (range 45 – 54). All nurses were specialized in assisting at urologic surgeries. Two nurses had no prior experience in being a scrub nurse, while one nurse had 27 years of experience as a scrub nurse. On average, the nurses had 6.5 years experience assisting during robot-assisted surgery (range 1 – 12.5 years).

Interview

During the interviews, the researchers wanted to go over all barriers identified in the previous research, and discuss these with the interviewees. Therefore, the surgeons were sent the report beforehand and were asked to read it in preparation of the interview. The report was not sent to the scrub nurses, because the researchers were concerned that the use of (academic) English in the report would discourage the nurses from participating (English was not the mother tongue of the nurses). In addition, a summary of the results was made, that could be used during the interviews to give them a quick insight in the preliminary results. This summary proved to be useful for the interviews with both the scrub nurses and the surgeons, since not all surgeons had read the report beforehand.

The surgeons that were interviewed had very busy time schedules and several interviews were numerously interrupted by colleagues (the interviews were held during working hours). Hence, it was not possible to discuss all barriers in detail with each interviewee. Also, some participants simply did not want to discuss each barrier separately and gave a more generic feedback on the analysis, while others focused on certain elements in the report or summary they found particularly interesting relevant or, in contrast, did not agree with at all. Nevertheless, despite the fact that the semi-structured setup of the interviews could not always be entirely executed as planned, the researchers felt that these interviews were insightful and substantially enriched the original analysis.

Each interview consisted of three parts. The first set of questions was about personal information such as age, experience with surgery and experience with robot-assisted surgery. Furthermore, we asked the participants about their views on telesurgery. Finally, we presented them with the several challenges to telesurgery and we asked them to which extent they viewed them as legitimate. Each surgeon and scrub nurse was interviewed individually and the interviews lasted on average for 33 minutes (range 15 min - 1 hour).

Analysis

The researchers had originally planned to code the interviews using a structured codebook based on the barriers that were identified in the research. However, since the interviews had to be done in a less structured way than planned beforehand, the analysis of the resulting data also required another approach.

The researchers chose to analyze the data using the affinity diagramming method [3]. For this purpose, the researchers went through the transcribed interviews and identified all potentially relevant and interesting feedback. These were listed per interviewee. Then, the researchers reorganized and categorized these according to similarity of contents. Next, a second categorization was done; now also including the barriers identified in the original report. This final categorization regrouped some of the original barriers into central themes. As such, we made further abstraction of our original findings and decided to describe some of the barriers on a more general level.

In this process, we kept in mind that our participants did not necessary need to judge the analysis to be correct. As clarified by e.g. [16], a simplistic interpretation of the reactions of the interviewees on the first results could in fact be a thread to validity rather than guaranteeing it. Since our data was synthesized, decontextualized and abstracted from individual participants and situations, it might well be possible that our interviewees might not recognize themselves in their data. This is especially true for those participants we had seen and talked to before (which can be understood as a form of 'member check') but also for the interviewees that were new to the research. For instance, a surgeon operating in a commercial hospital might be reluctant to confirm certain barriers specific to robot-surgery given the high investments required by the hospital management for surgical robots, and the strategically importance of the robots in the hospital in attracting certain patients. Research pointing out difficulties with surgical robots (whether or not in a telesurgery setting) might ultimately jeopardize the income stream of the hospital in general and the position of the surgeon specifically. Therefore, during the analysis and interpretation of the results, the background of the interviewees was taken into account, and they remained identifiable in all stages of the data analysis, enabling us to contextualize their answers by relating them to their personal and professional interests, and their working environment.

This research phase allowed the researchers to add more details and nuances to barriers that already described. While none of the results of the original paper were necessarily seen as erroneous, they felt that these additional insights added sufficient information to the original paper for another publication.

RESULTS

When presented with the possible challenges towards conducting telesurgery [6] most interviewees found the results interesting and they recognized their everyday work practices conducting robot-assisted surgery as the researchers described them in the paper. Some challenges for telesurgery were considered trivial by several interviewees (such as planning or language barriers), and most regarded these as easy to overcome. However, at the same time they emphasized that working from a distance is far from ideal, can be stressful and might never be as efficient as working together in the same operating room.

Some interviewees were somewhat surprised by the focus on team collaboration. When contacted beforehand, they were inclined to think of technical or legal barriers with regard to telesurgery. Nonetheless, they acknowledged the 'social' challenges as identified in the previous paper. Also, one of the surgeons explained that although these identified challenges are appropriate, they are not necessary specific to robot-assisted surgery.

A. Remote surgeon as a new member of the local surgical team

A first challenge follows from the hypothesis that in a telesurgery setting a remote surgeon will sometimes have to work together with an OR team that might be unfamiliar with his or her working methods. This is challenging since we observed very close working relationships amongst the OR team, especially between the surgeon and the scrub nurse. Getting familiar with each other's professional preferences results in additional communication flows.

Close working relationship

During the observations and exploratory interviews, we noticed a very tight working relationship between surgeons and their surgical team in minimally invasive surgery and in robot-assisted surgery. Some surgeons compared the relationship they have with the OR team with their marriage. For instance, one surgeon noted *"with some staff members, you have been [working] longer together than with your wife"*. This close working relationship could also clearly be observed in the operating room during interventions: the team members continuously anticipated each other's actions and communicated non-verbally. The whole OR team knows the procedure and the next steps that need to be taken in the intervention.

For instance, we frequently noticed how the scrub nurse anticipates the surgeon's actions and already had the tools ready, before the surgeon requested or needed it. One scrub nurse said: *"I always know what they are going to think."* In an interview, a surgeon confirms this by saying: *"It would be exhausting [to have a new team composition each day]. You would have to ask [for instruments], while now we are used to each other, the nurse knows what we are doing, [she] gives the default instruments and has prepared the things that you need. You just have to reach out with your hand without [verbally] asking for it. And this will be difficult if you would have a new team or changing teams"*.

OR team members do of course change over time, and personnel does leave a team or joins a new team. But (scrub) nurses usually stay longer than assisting surgeons: they are in training and after that will change teams and hospitals. As such, surgeons often invest more time and effort in building up a good professional relationship with scrub nurses than with their assistants.

Professional preferences and increased operating time

Working with a new OR team can have considerable impact on the surgical intervention. Besides having to communicate more when new team members are introduced, the operating time will also increase. A surgeon estimated that the operation time of a surgical intervention increases with more or less 30 minutes when a new nurse or assistant is added to the team.

This has to do with the professional preferences of the surgeon. Even though procedures are roughly the same, there are still some degrees of freedom for each surgeon. All surgeons have their own way of approaching a medical problem, and while the aims of similar surgical interventions are the same, the way to attain that goal can differ amongst surgeons. For instance, one of the surgeons explained the importance of using tools that he is familiar with. In general, he reported to be extremely dependent on his instruments. The choice for the tools he is using now is the result of years of testing to find out which tools work well and which do not. Having to use tools he is not used to, can be an extra element of stress, on top of working with nurses he is not familiar with. A scrub nurse confirms this: *"All surgeons have their preferences. [...] They appreciate it if take these into account."* Therefore, it is for instance very important to communicate the remote surgeons' preferences for specific instruments to the local team so they can prepare the right tools.

Implications for telesurgery

Keeping the above in mind, a surgeon in a telesurgery setting faces several challenges. Having to work with an OR team the surgeon is not familiar is, means the new team members need to get to know each other. Part of this has to do with the professional preferences of the surgeon involved, the way in which the surgeon approaches the medical problem, and the preferred tools and working methods. The combination of these elements makes a telesurgical intervention considerably more challenging for a surgeon. Initially, this will lead to a higher need for communication, both before and during surgery, which results in a higher likelihood of misunderstandings and longer surgeries.

B. Trust between remote surgeon and local surgical team

In a telesurgery setting, a remote surgeon will have to collaborate very closely since a local surgeon will always be needed for the startup and the end of the operation, and has to be stand-by in case the operation needs to be converted to open surgery. However, we learned that collaboration between surgeons is relatively rare. Depending on each other for the placement the trocars, relying on each other's capacities, and trusting other surgeons for referring patients to them might be challenging.

Working with fellow surgeons

Telesurgery forces surgeons to collaborate closely before, during and after surgery. Especially during surgery, usually only one surgeon is present. If another person with surgical training is present, this person is usually the surgeon's assistant. This is important with regard to the hierarchy in the operating room: the operating surgeon is the person in charge, and the rest of the personnel in the operating room mainly follows the surgeon's activities.

When surgeons do collaborate during surgery, this is mostly across medical disciplines, namely, when two types of interventions are done during one operation. Here, surgeons often collaborate smoothly since the surgeons have different expertise and have to rely on each other.

It can be expected that, when both surgeons have similar knowledge, their diverging ideas might be a cause for conflict. Unless when know each other thoroughly and trust each other's judgment. A scrub remembers an operation where two surgeons operated together: *"This went relatively smooth. They talked and discussed a lot, but the operation went well. I have to add that these surgeons have been working together for many years. Together, they started doing robot-assisted surgery at this hospital."*

Relying on the skills of the other surgeon

For certain phases of a telesurgery procedure, a surgeon will have to rely fully on the actions of another surgeon. This is most manifest in when the local surgeon will have to make the incisions to place the trocars in the body of the patient, through which the robot arms would enter the body of the patient. To a large extent, the placement of the trocars at the beginning of the surgery determines the success of a surgery. This requires a high degree of trust and several surgeons confirmed that they definitely prefer to place these trocars themselves, or by an assistant they have trained themselves.

A surgeon detailed that such a trust relationship is something that needs to grow over time. A scrub nurse thought it would be essential for the surgeons to have met and preferably worked in real life before. All interviewees agreed that the surgeon working remotely should be able to have great confidence in the skills of the local operating team. Especially since in case of a medical error, having two surgeons in charge will complicate the question of who is to be held responsible.

Trusting referrals

In this regard, it is important to mention that it is unusual as well for surgeons to operate on patients referred to them by other surgeons. While one of the surgeons commented that he regularly operates on patients he has never seen before and that he can fully rely on the medical record of the patient, the other surgeons never did so. All surgeons had a reserved attitude towards operating on patients from other doctors when reflecting on telesurgery.

For instance, one of the surgeons said he was sometimes "*suspicious*" when other surgeons referred one of their patients to him. He figured that if these surgeons could operate on the patient themselves, there would be no reason to refer the patient to him. The surgical intervention probably would be highly complicated and thus very stressful for the surgeon.

Implications for telesurgery

In the context of telesurgery, the complexity caused by having to work with another surgeon might add considerable stress to the working conditions of a surgeon. The remote surgeon needs to work together with a colleague with similar skills, and has to put a lot of trust in the operating team he or she might not have met before. In addition, they have to execute a surgical intervention that is more likely to be more complicated (since this patient was referred) on a patient they might only know through the medical records. These working conditions make telesurgery a less appealing way of working for the surgeons involved.

C. Keeping overview of OR during procedure

We wonder how in a telesurgery setting, the remote surgeon will be able to have a good overview of all activities and events occurring the OR. We saw that during minimally invasive surgery or open surgery, surgeons are usually aware of all activities going on in the OR. The introduction of the surgical robot, however, has changed this to some extent. One surgeon described the situation as follows: *"When doing open surgery or laparoscopy, you can see the monitors of the anesthetist, you can see who is entering and leaving the OR. (...) You can tell if there is a problem or a discussion is going on. You have a good overview of what is going on. But when sitting at the console, you're unable to see things like that, you cannot even see the patient.*"

Stepping away from the controller

We observed during multiple robot-assisted surgeries that the surgeon frequently steps away from the console to see what was going in the operating room. During one surgery, a surgeon was not aware that an assistant was struggling to attach a new instrument to a robotic arm. After a while, the surgeon left the controller, and walked up to the patient, to then notice that the assistant was having some problems. After walking back to the console, the surgeon asked repeatedly if he could continue operating while the assistant was actually still working on the problem. Similarly, sometimes the robotic arms get entwined and the scrub nurse needs to stop the surgeon from operating further until she has repositioned the robotic arms.

Also, for the OR team it is difficult to see what a surgeon, hidden behind the controller, is doing. He or she can be texting or making phone calls, keeping the rest of the OR team unaware and confused about a seemingly inexplicable stop of activities from the surgeon.

Shortcomings of the setup

Tools are available for both the surgeon and the rest of the OR team to create more contextual awareness: the robot has a communication system installed that allows the surgeon and the rest of the OR team to talk with each other. But what is being said often is incomprehensible due to the noise. One surgeon commented that he often turned off the sound coming from the OR inside his console: "*When I sit behind the console (...) and someone passes the microphone (...) you hear noise, buzzing, and humming through the [speakers]. (...) It drives me crazy. So I shut down the volume (....) so [the surgical team] should speak loud [enough so I can hear it]*".

This example, and the example of the surgeon stepping away from the controller and walking through the operating room may illustrate that the surgeon has a lack of overview and develops coping strategies to compensate for the shortcomings of the setup.

Implications for telesurgery

The problems the surgeons encounter during robotic surgery to keep overview of activities and events, will most likely only increase in telesurgery. The surgeon will not have the opportunity to step away from the console and walk to the patient to see what is going on. If camera views from the operating room are available, he might at most be able to switch views and no longer look through the endoscope. Equally, the others in the OR team will have even more difficulty to know what the surgeon is doing when not operating. The surgeon will have to rely even more on the local OR team when troubles occur with tools or robotic arms. Even though surgeons cannot approach the patient too closely during robotic surgery (since they are not scrubbed in), they are still able to evaluate the situation from a certain distance. The OR team will not be able to rely on the current coping strategies currently used and additional displays and communication tools will have to be provided in order to give both the remote surgeon and the local OR team a better understanding and overview of the activities of all people involved in the intervention.

D. Mediated communication

As we have argued, the introduction of the surgical robot in the operating room has physically moved the surgeon further away from the patient compared to open or minimally invasive surgery. When conducting telesurgery, the remote surgeon will be even further removed from the surgical team and the patient. This distance will most likely increase the difficulty of communication between the surgeon and surgical team, and the surgeon and the patient.

(In)formal communication in the OR

From the observations and the interviews, we learned that besides work-related communication, there is also a lot of informal communication taking place in the operating room. A surgeon says: "*We talk about everything, not only about work [related topics], also about what people did during the weekend...*" As mentioned in the previous section, the surgical robot hampers the surgeon from having an overview of what is going on in the operating room. Similarly, the robot also hinders informal or work related communication and nonverbal communication between the whole surgical team including the surgeon.

Being able to talk about private life during work, also during surgery, was considered to be important for enjoying work. A scrub nurse mentions: *"You like to know what someone did over the weekend. It's important for the team spirit."*

Patient contact

In addition to informal communication during surgery, a surgeon usually frequently talks to the patient both before and after surgery. With the exception of one surgeon we interviewed, all surgeons always encountered their patients and discussed the intervention at hand with them. Most surgeons wish to keep it as such. Patients frequently want a specific surgeon to operate on them. Often, surgeons and patients have a personal relationship.

One surgeon was explicitly worried about surgeons not meeting their patients outside of surgery. According to him, there have been indications that these patients suffer more frequently from complications after surgery. He explained this by the fact that the surgeon is probably unable in these situations to follow up the medical condition of these patients as carefully as is required.

Implications for telesurgery

In telesurgery, all communications between the remote surgeon and the local OR team will be mediated. As becomes clear of the situations described above, this inevitably changes the nature of the interactions. Current teleconferencing systems are becoming more advanced and increasingly give their users a sense of 'presence'. The communication tools should ideally allow the members of the OR team to enjoy each other's company and allow surgeons to communicate with their patients.

E. Incremental changes in effort

To conclude, we discuss two challenges that most surgeons did not see as problematic, but in the end could be a hassle for surgeons and their team or for patients. These have to do with the planning of the operation and the differences in language. In isolation, these challenges might have a minimal impact, but in combination with the previous issues, their impact might be substantial.

Planning

Telesurgery would require planning and coordination between the schedules of two hospitals. Some surgeons considered this to be a minor detail, however, planning might complicate regular activities in hospitals. As one scrub nurse explains: *"Hospitals all work in their own way, and operations do not take place every day. Different hospitals often have different operating days, so you need to take that into account."*

A surgeon added how telesurgery might affect the planning of the hospital where the remote surgeon resides. Patients from the local hospital might have to be on the waiting list longer, because their surgeon first needs to perform some surgeries on patients in other hospitals through telesurgery. This surgeon therefore would not consider telesurgery, as there is already insufficient operation in the hospital he works now.

Language differences

A similar issue is the language difference. For instance in Europe, when doing remote surgery, chances increase that the personnel in the operating room might speak another language. One of the surgeons considered language differences as an extra complication, but expected it to be overcome easily. Another surgeon, however, did not seem to be worried about language issues, since he reported to speak multiple (European) languages and gave as an example that even in the Middle East they speak English in the operating room.

However, a scrub nurse mentioned a lot of communication problems when working with a Dutch surgeon. While his mother tongue is Dutch and hers Flemish (which is a regional variation of Dutch), there were a lot of misunderstandings during the operation. The Dutch surgeon used other names for some of the instruments than she did, and she mentioned frequently *"having to guess"* what instrument he meant.

Implications for telesurgery

Planning might be relatively easy to organize, but hospitals are often organized in different ways, and it may imply that the patients of the remote surgeons will have to wait longer in order to be treated. Similarly, all medical personnel in the operating room might have sufficient knowledge of a language all are familiar with to some extent. However, language differences in addition to unfamiliarity between the surgeon and the OR team, might be a hurdle for successful telesurgery. Keeping in mind that in telesurgery the amount of communication between the members of the OR will probably increase substantially and members of the OR team will often speak different languages, this can further increase the likelihood that misunderstandings will occur.

DISCUSSION AND CONCLUSION

As we have argued, most research on telesurgery is focused on technical, financial and legal barriers, and in our opinion, the collaborative side of telesurgery has been under examined in the research on telesurgery. In this paper, we aimed to explore the socio-technical gap in telesurgery by asking ourselves how the introduction of a surgical robot and a geographical distribution of an OR team might change collaboration between OR teams. As a result of this exercise, we have identified challenges for collaboration between the remote surgeon and the local surgical team during telesurgery. These challenges were discussed with several surgeons and scrub nurses familiar with robotic surgery, and the analysis of these interviews served as a basis to restructure, nuance and correct the original barriers that were identified before [6]. In comparison, the central themes in this paper are formulated on a more general level. Some additional insights were gained in the second research phase. For instance, we highlighted the conflicts that might potentially arise from two surgeons working together, we further explored the relationship between the scrub nurse and the surgeon, and considerable attention was given to the trust issue in OR teams.

This study has a number of limitations. The small sample size is a limitation of any type ethnographical work. As HCI researchers familiar with dealing with recruitment of participants, we found it particularly difficult to find surgeons willing to participate in interviews. The surgeons that agreed to participate were usually under high time pressure and could not go through our results in as much detail as we hoped for. However, we believe these surgeons with different backgrounds still allowed us to present different views on the challenges in telesurgery. Another shortcoming is that we were not able to observe any real telesurgery, which might have given us even more insight in how OR teams collaborate when geographically distributed. Our approach to use robotic surgery as a proxy-technology has its merits, but it is also a pragmatic solution to the fact that we could not give our participants the actual experience of telesurgery.

Since our main interest was to understand how future collaborative experiences of distributed OR teams might differ from current experiences of collocated teams using surgical robots, we decided to concentrate mainly on the (collaborative) user experience and did not depart from a general understanding of how OR teams collaborate. However, as a result of this choice, we are reluctant to state that our research has resulted in what Ackerman [1] has called 'social requirements' of OR teams. But we did identify some challenges for telesurgery that may serve as input for developers and designers working on surgical robots to improve their systems for telesurgery purposes; or will need to be taken into account by the OR team when the technology is implemented in the hospital. The main challenges as described in the results section are:

- making the remote surgeon and the local OR team familiar with each other's working practices and procedures;
- creating trust between the remote surgeon and the local OR team;
- allowing the surgeon to keep control over the operation and allowing all OR team members to keep an overview of the activities of all personnel involved in the intervention;
- allow for supportive mediated communication between both the remote surgeon and the rest of the OR team and the remote surgeon and the patient; and
- finding ways to decrease the complexity created by combined planning and language differences.

Trust is a reoccuring issue in many of these challenges: being able to trust a member of the OR team was an important element brought up by many of the surgeons and scrub nurses at several occasions. This is not really surprising, since trust has been identified as the main component of functional virtual teams [10]. The key components of trust have been understood as 'risk' and 'reliance' (or 'interdependence') [19], or the fact that group members of teams could experience negative outcomes and that the fate of a member of the OR team can be determined by other members of the group. This helps understanding why trust is of such high importance in a telesurgery setting: the members of the OR team heavily have to rely on each other and the risks are high when their reliance on this other person would be unjustified.

In their list of characteristics of collaboration over distance that will be largely resistant to technological support, Olson and Olson mentioned 'trust' [18]. They wonder if the same level of trust can ever be achieved through for instance video chat. However, more recent research seems to show that this is indeed a possibility: Wilson et al [28] have used Walther's Social Information Processing theory [26] for an empirical study in which they demonstrated that initial levels of trust are indeed higher in collocated teams than in distributed teams, but that there is an interaction effect of time, which neutralizes the effect of communication media. The Social Information Processing theory states that people strive for human relationships in any mode of interaction. But since computer-mediated communication affects the rate of information change (there are e.g. no or less nonverbal cues) it takes longer for trust to develop in distributed teams.

This type of research seems to illustrate that it is possible for distributed OR teams to grow a trusted relationship amongst the members. However, it also seems to illustrate that the distributed OR team also needs to have a certain fixed form, since it takes time to grow a trusted relationship, and probably more time than in collocated teams. Thus, most of the measures that will be required to create trust will be non-technological. Perhaps structural collaborations with a limited team of surgeons will be required, perhaps it is better for the remote surgeon and the rest of the OR team to occasionally have a face-to-face meeting, or OR team members will see it necessary to have an easier understanding of the reputation and skills of the other members of the OR team. Also, Hinds et al [12] have illustrated how informal communication (they call it 'spontaneous communication') helps to create a shared identity and context in distributed teams, which helps to reduce the amount of conflicts (both interpersonal and task-related). As they clarify, conflicts typically result from distrust, and they hypothesize that spontaneous communication also results in more trust. How growing a trusted relationship amongst OR team members should be operationalized, and the implications this will have for the telesurgery setup and the distributed OR team, will have to be the focus of future research.

Increasing trust in the team, can involve more communication amongst the team members for collaboration. Ultimately it will be the OR team that decides whether telesurgery brings added value for them to make the additional efforts in order to grow a trusted relationship within a distributed team. Perhaps other forms of remote interactions that require less trust (are less risky and allow the surgeons to rely less on each other) are more likely to become part of surgical practices in the near future. Future research might for instance focus on telementoring (a remote surgeon guides a procedure where the operating surgeon has limited experience with), teleproctoring (remote assessments of skills surgeons performing live surgeries), teleconsultation (a surgeon remote assessing a patient), telestration (a remote surgeon guiding an operating surgeon using live annotations on the video stream coming from the robot) and others [8].

ACKNOWLEDGMENTS

We would like to thank the surgeons and hospital staff for allowing us in their operating rooms to observe. Also, we are thankful to the hospital staff that was willing to be interviewed.

The Telesurgery project is co-funded by iMinds, a research institute founded by the Flemish Government, with projectsupport of IWT. Companies and organizations involved in the project are Barco Healthcare Division and CandIT-Media BVBA.

REFERENCES

1. Ackerman, M.S. The intellectual challenge of CSCW: The gap between social requirements and technical feasibility. *Human-computer interaction 15*, 2 (2000), 179–203.
2. Arora, S., Hull, L., Sevdalis, N., et al. Factors compromising safety in surgery: stressful events in the operating room. *The American Journal of Surgery 199*, 1 (2010), 60–65.
3. Beyer, H. and Holtzblatt, K. *Contextual Design: Defining Customer-Centered Systems*. Elsevier, 1997.
4. Camberlin, Cecile, Senn, Arnaud, Leys, Mark, and De Laet, Chris. *Robotgeassisteerde chirurgie: health technology assessment Health Technology Assessment (HTA).* Federaal Kenniscentrum voor de Gezondheidszorg (KCE), Brussel, 2009.
5. Doarn, C.R. and Moses, G.R. Overcoming Barriers to Wider Adoption of Mobile Robotic Surgery: Engineering, Clinical and Business Challenges. In J. Rosen, B. Hannaford and R. Satava, eds., *Surgical Robotics - Systems, Applications, and Visions.* 2011, 69–102.
6. Elprama, S.A., Kilpi, K., Duysburgh, P., Jacobs, A., Vermeulen, L., and Jan, van L. Identifying barriers in telesurgery by studying current team practices in robot-assisted surgery. *7th International Conference on Pervasive Computing Technologies for Healthcare (Pervasive Health 2013), 5-8 May 2013*, (2013).
7. Forlizzi, J. The product ecology: Understanding social product use and supporting design culture. *Human-Computer Interaction Institute*, (2007), 35.
8. Gambadauro, P. and Torrejón, R. The "tele" factor in surgery today and tomorrow: implications for surgical training and education. *Surgery Today 43*, 2 (2012), 115–122.
9. Haidegger, T., Sándor, J., and Benyó, Z. Surgery in space: the future of robotic telesurgery. *Surgical Endoscopy 25*, 3 (2011), 681–690.
10. Handy, C. Trust and the Virtual Organization. *Harvard Business Review 73*, 3 (1995), 40–50.
11. Herron, D.M. and Marohn, M. A consensus document on robotic surgery. *Surgical Endoscopy 22*, 2 (2008), 313–325.
12. Hinds, P.J. and Mortensen, M. Understanding Conflict in Geographically Distributed Teams: The Moderating Effects of Shared Identity, Shared Context, and Spontaneous Communication. *Organization Science 16*, 3 (2005), 290–307.
13. Pierson, J., Jacobs, A., Dreessen, K., Van den Broeck, I, Lievens, B., and Van den Broeck, W. Walking the interface: uncovering practices through proxy technology assessment. *EPIC 2006 proceedings*, American Anthropological Association.
14. Lendvay, T.S., Hannaford, B., and Satava, R.M. Future of robotic surgery. *Cancer journal (Sudbury, Mass.) 19*, 2 (2013), 109–119.
15. Marescaux, J., Leroy, J., Rubino, F., et al. Transcontinental Robot-Assisted Remote Telesurgery: Feasibility and Potential Applications. *Annals of Surgery 235*, 4 (2002), 487–492.
16. Morse, J.M., Barrett, M., Mayan, M., Olson, K., and Spiers, J. Verification Strategies for Establishing Reliability and Validity in Qualitative Research. *International Journal of Qualitative Methods 1*, 2 (2008), 13–22.
17. Nio, D., Bemelman, W.A., Busch, O.R.C., Vrouenraets, B.C., and Gouma, D.J. Robot-assisted laparoscopic cholecystectomy versus conventional

laparoscopic cholecystectomy: a comparative study. *Surgical endoscopy 18*, 3 (2004), 379–382.

18. Olson, G. and Olson, J. Distance Matters. *Human-Computer Interaction 15*, 2 (2000), 139–178.
19. Rousseau, D.M., Sitkin, S.B., Burt, R.S., and Camerer, C. NOT SO DIFFERENT AFTER ALL: A CROSS-DISCIPLINE VIEW OF TRUST. *Academy of Management Review 23*, 3 (1998), 393–404.
20. Satava, R.M. Future Directions in Robotic Surgery. *Surgical Robotics: Systems Applications and Visions*, (2010), 1.
21. Saunders, S. *Why good communication skills are important for theatre nurses.* 2004.
22. Sexton, J.B., Makary, M.A., Tersigni, A.R., et al. Teamwork in the operating room: frontline perspectives among hospitals and operating room personnel. *Anesthesiology 105*, 5 (2006), 877–884.
23. Silverstone, R., Haddon, L., In Silverstone, R., and Mansell, R. Design and the domestication of ICTs: technical change and everyday life. *Communicating by Design: The Politics of Information and Communication Technologies. Oxford: Oxford University Press. p44–74*, (1996).
24. Tinelli, A., Malvasi, A., Gustapane, S., et al. Robotic assisted surgery in gynecology: current insights and future perspectives. *Recent patents on biotechnology 5*, 1 (2011), 12–24.
25. Undre, S., Healey, A.N., Darzi, A., and Vincent, C.A. Observational assessment of surgical teamwork: a feasibility study. *World journal of surgery 30*, 10 (2006), 1774–1783.
26. Walther, J.B. Interpersonal Effects in Computer-Mediated Interaction: A Relational Perspective. *Communication Research 19*, 1 (1992), 52–90.
27. Webster, J.L. and Cao, C.G.L. Lowering communication barriers in operating room technology. *Human Factors: The Journal of the Human Factors and Ergonomics Society 48*, 4 (2006), 747–758.
28. Wilson, J.M., Straus, S.G., and McEvily, B. All in due time: The development of trust in computer-mediated and face-to-face teams. *Organizational Behavior and Human Decision Processes 99*, 1 (2006), 16–33.

How Beliefs about the Presence of Machine Translation Impact Multilingual Collaborations

Ge Gao[1], Bin Xu[2], Dan Cosley[2], Susan R. Fussell[1,2]
[1]Department of Communication
[2]Department of Information Science
Cornell University
Ithaca NY 14850 USA
[gg365, bx55, drc44, sfussell] @cornell.edu

ABSTRACT

Traditional communication tools tend to make their presence known, e.g., "when my collaborators and I are using IM to discuss our work, how could we *not* realize the actual presence of IM?" In the case of machine translation (MT) mediated collaborations, however, the absence or presence of MT is not obvious. English sentences with poor grammar can result from both a partner's lack of fluency and errors in the MT process. We hypothesize that partners' attributions about the source of the errors affects their collaboration experience. To test this hypothesis, we conducted a laboratory experiment in which monolingual native English speaking participants collaborated with bilingual native-Mandarin speakers on a map navigation task. Participants were randomly assigned into a 2 (beliefs about MT: absence vs. presence) by 2 (actual mediation of MT: absence vs. presence) experiment design. Beliefs about presence of MT significantly impacted the collaboration experience, opening new opportunities for both research and design around MT-mediated collaborations.

Author Keywords

Machine translation; collaboration; multilingual communication

ACM Classification Keywords

H.5.3 Group and Organization Interface: Computer-supported cooperative work

General Terms

Experimentation; Human Factors

INTRODUCTION

With the emergence of distributed organizations and virtual work, people increasingly interact with others who speak different native languages. Such multilingual collaboration is becoming increasingly common and important in distributed work, and a variety of communication tools have been developed to help people overcome language barriers and establish collaboration [e.g.,17,26,31].

Figure 1. The use of machine translation (MT) during multilingual collaborations may not be obvious, leading to confusion about where to attribute errors in communication.

In recent years, machine translation (MT) technology has made it possible for people with different language backgrounds to interact via their own native languages [e.g.,17]. The adoption of MT creates new opportunities as well as challenges for multilingual collaboration. In particular, unlike most CMC tools whose presence is obvious in use, when collaborators communicate via MT, they may or may not realize that MT is operating in the background. Figure 1 illustrates the issue: an English speaking person who receives a message in English from a native Mandarin speaking partner may assume either that the partner has typed this message in English or that he/she has typed the message in Chinese and it was subsequently translated via MT.

This leads to a potential design opportunity for overcoming problems around multilingual collaboration that arise in part because of language disfluency, such as establishing trust and relationships between native and non-native speakers of a shared language [6,14]. If some of the attribution for disfluency in conversation can be shifted to

CSCW'14, February 15–19, 2014, Baltimore, Maryland, USA.

ACM 978-1-4503-2540-0/14/02...$15.00.
http://dx.doi.org/10.1145/2531602.2531702

	Actual MT is *absent*	**Actual** MT is *present*
Believe MT is *absent*	Receive English messages that were directly typed by the partner in their second language.	Receiving English messages that were translated from Chinese via MT, **but** believe the messages were directly typed by the partner in their second language.
Believe MT is *present*	Receive English messages that were directly typed by the partner in their second language, **but** believe the messages were translated from Chinese via MT.	Receive English messages that were translated from Chinese via MT.

Table 1. The 2 × 2 experiment design for native English speakers.

the technology, people's opinions of their conversation partners might improve. On the other hand, if the quality of MT is poorer than what a bilingual speaker could achieve without MT, then the additional disfluency might harm the collaboration.

This tricky situation creates a new space for examining the role of beliefs about MT during multilingual collaboration and their effects on people's experience.

The remainder of this paper presents a laboratory study that explores how beliefs about MT impact collaboration experience in multilingual settings. In the experiment, monolingual English speaking participants performed a collaborative task with a native Mandarin speaking partner who spoke English as a second language. We manipulated both participants' beliefs about the use of MT (absence vs. presence) as well as the actual mediation of MT (absence vs. presence), creating the four collaboration conditions shown in Table 1. Participants assessed five aspects of their collaboration experience: reasons for miscommunications, message clarity, impressions of their partners, quality of the collaboration, and willingness to collaborate in the future.

Our data show significant influences of people's beliefs about the presence or absence of MT on the collaboration experience. Some of these influences were qualified by the actual presence of MT. while others were independent of its actual presence. Insights from this study provide better understanding of MT-mediated collaboration in multilingual settings and suggest ideas for the development of MT-based collaboration tools.

RELATED WORK AND HYPOTHESES

We first describe prior work on MT in CMC and collaborative work settings. We then address how beliefs about MT, which we define as a communicator's belief that the messages received from a partner have been translated via machine translation rather than typed directly, might affect attributions of error. Finally, we describe how such beliefs might shape both current and subsequent collaboration experience and set hypotheses for the study.

Machine Translation as a Communication Tool

Machine translation is a new but fast-developing communication tool. Different from most communication tools such as IM and email, which pass messages more-or-less unchanged, MT takes a more active role in the communication, processing messages via computational translation before sending them. Adding translation capabilities to a communication channel is a promising idea for facilitating multilingual collaborations [e.g., 17].

However, several studies show that MT negatively influences multilingual collaboration. Yamashita and colleagues [28, 29, 30], for example, have shown how the use of MT, as opposed to a shared second language, created confusion about the meaning of referring expressions between multilingual speakers. Wang et al. [27] examined multilingual brainstorming conversations and found that both native and non-native English speakers viewed MT-mediated messages as less comprehensible than English messages. From these studies, it is clear that message understanding plays a fundamental role in multilingual collaboration. When messages with bad translation quality are generated by MT, it hinders the success of communication and collaboration [12].

Machine Translation and Attribution

The studies above show that issues of translation quality affect the usability of MT and the quality of collaboration experience. Theories of attribution [16, 20] paint a more complex picture of how MT might affect collaboration by changing people's beliefs about both the partner and the communication technologies used. Previous studies have shown the importance of attribution, especially the attribution of problems and failures, in shaping both current and subsequent collaboration experience [4].

Much attribution research makes a fundamental distinction between *dispositional attributions* (e.g., attributing problems to a partner's personality or lack of interest) and *situational attributions* (e.g., attributing problems to technological constraints or task difficulty) [e.g., 11, 13, 14, 22, 23]. In general, negative dispositional attributions lead to worse perceptions of partners and collaborations [1,13]. Thus, one plausible strategy for improving people's collaboration experience is to encourage attribution of problems toward the situation rather than toward the partner. For example, cues available during the collaboration, such as the absence or presence of video, can trigger different attributions for communication and performance problems [e.g., 9].

In the current study, we hypothesize that by making the (supposed) presence of MT salient, participants will reassess where communication problems come from. When people believe the collaboration is mediated by MT, they will expect that all the messages they get are processed beforehand by MT, regardless of the actual mediation of MT. In such a case, MT has some agency in the communication and we expect people to attribute some of the responsibility for the collaboration experience to the technology rather than to their partner. This leads to the following pair of hypotheses:

H1a. People will attribute collaboration problems less often to dispositional factors (e.g., the partner's intelligence) when they believe the conversation is mediated by MT rather than conducted in a common language.

H1b. People will attribute collaboration problems more often to situational factors (e.g., quality of the translated message) when they think the conversation is mediated by MT rather than conducted in a common language.

Machine Translation and Collaboration

These attributions based on beliefs about the presence or absence of MT may in turn change people's collaboration experience. Attributing collaboration problems to a partner rather than to situational factors can lead to more negative impressions of that partner [e.g., 1, 13]. This in turn may lead to more negative opinions of the current collaboration and less motivation for future collaboration. On the other hand, attributing collaboration problems to situational factors may lead to more positive impressions of the partner as well as the collaboration. Based on these arguments, we hypothesized that beliefs about MT would influence social experience in the current collaboration and willingness to collaborate in the future:

H2a. People will judge messages from their partners to be higher in clarity when they believe MT is in use.

H2b. People will judge the collaboration to be higher in quality when they believe MT is in use.

H3a. People will be more positive about their partners when they believe MT is in use.

H3b. People will be more willing to collaborate with the same partner in the future when they believe MT is in use.

The above hypotheses pertain to people's beliefs about whether or not their collaboration is mediated by machine translation, and all posit that these beliefs will have effects independent of whether the collaboration is actually mediated by MT or not. As we know of no prior work that has examined interactions between beliefs about MT and the actual presence of MT, we pose the following research question:

RQ. What interactions exist between beliefs about and the actual use of MT for each of our dependent measures?

METHOD

Overview

We conducted a laboratory experiment to examine the effect of beliefs about MT on attributions and collaboration experience. We used the HCRC map navigation task developed by Anderson and colleagues [2], which has been used in previous studies to examine computer-mediated communication and collaboration [e.g., 9, 10].

We paired monolingual native English speaking participants with a Chinese/English bilingual native Mandarin speaking partner using an asymmetric design similar to that used by Wang and colleagues [27]. English speaking participants always typed and received messages in English. We manipulated their beliefs about whether the English messages they received were typed by the partner directly or translated from Chinese via MT. Mandarin speaking participants typed in either English or Mandarin depending on whether MT was actually used to support the collaboration or not. Their beliefs about the presence or absence of MT could therefore not be manipulated. Participants answered a post-task survey after finishing the collaboration task on each map, and answered a post-experiment survey after finishing the whole experiment.

Participants

The study involved a total of 64 participants recruited from a U.S. university. Half (N = 32) were native English speaking undergraduate students (23 female), with a mean age of 20.6 years (SD = 2.12). All had lived in the U.S. for more than 10 years. They reported having some previous experience using MT (M = 3.28, SD = 1.47 on a 7-point scale ranging from 1 = never to 7 = very often).

The other half of the participants (N = 32) were bilingual native-Mandarin speakers (19 female). Their mean age was 26.8 years (SD = 5.67). All spoke English as a second language and on average reported moderate English fluency (M = 4.38, SD = 1.09 on a 7-point scale ranging from 1 = not fluent at all to 7 = very fluent) and some experience using MT (M = 4.09, SD = 2.13).

Because beliefs in the presence or absence of machine translation during the interaction could only be manipulated for the English speakers, we restrict our analysis in this paper to the 32 English speakers.

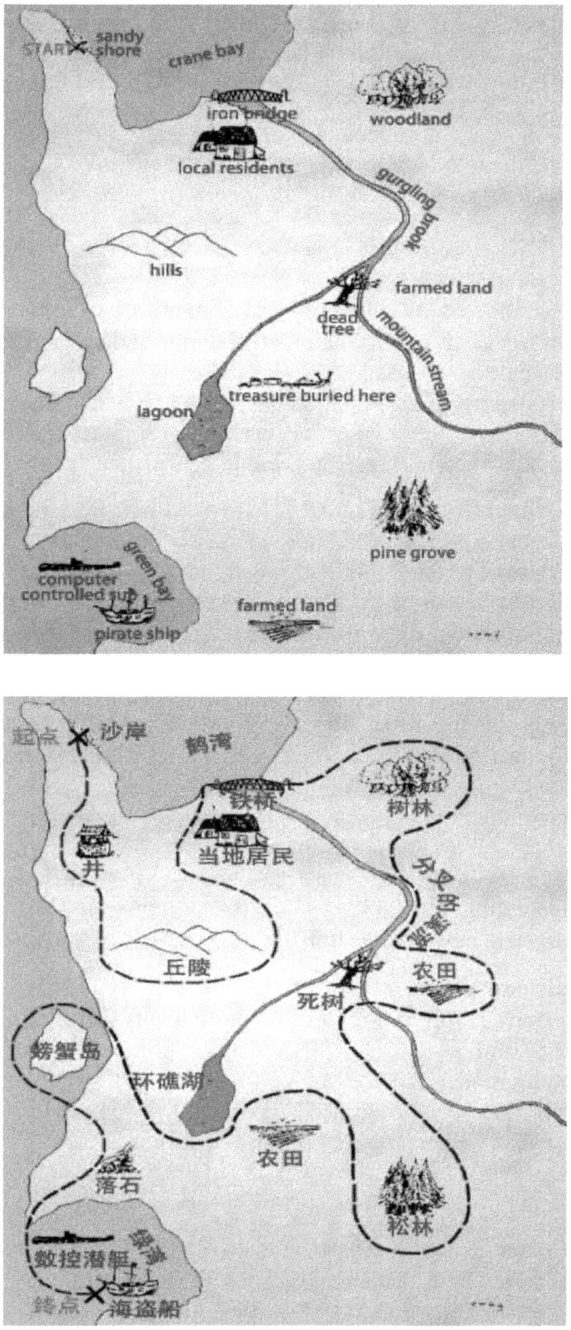

Figure 2. One set of maps used in the navigation task (the top one for the English follower, the bottom one for the Chinese instructor).

Materials

We used two HCRC map navigation tasks of equivalent difficulty [2]. One participant (the instructor) is given a map that shows a prescribed route around a series of landmarks, while a second participant (the follower) is given a map with the landmarks but not the route. The instructor and follower work together to help the follower learn the prescribed route. Figure 2 shows the two versions of one of the HCRC maps used in the study. To further complicate to the task, each pair of HCRC maps has some differences in the depicted landmarks, e.g., a bridge present in one map might be missing in the other. We manually translated the labels on each map into Mandarin Chinese for use in the MT-mediated communication condition.

Software and Equipment

We developed an online chat tool that displayed the map during the task and provided machine translation when appropriate for a participant's condition. Figure 3 shows the two parts of the tool interface: the IM window and the map window.

IM window. On the left side of the interface was an instant messaging window where participants typed messages and saw their partner's messages. For the MT-mediation condition, participants typed in their native language and received messages translated from their partners' language to their own native language using Google Translate. Translations were automatic and no preview or pre-editing of the translated message were afforded by the IM tool. For the MT-absence condition, this module was not available, and all communication was typed in English.

Map window. On the right side of the interface was the given map. Instructors saw the map with both landmarks and the route; followers started with a map that had only landmarks. Followers could use the cursor to draw and/or correct the route they created under the instructor's guidance. For both the followers and the instructors, only the landmarks and route (if any) shown on their own maps could be seen.

Equipment. All participants were seated at Mac Pro laptops with 13.3 inch monitors in a separate room from their partners. They wore headphones during the study so as not to be distracted by outside noise.

Procedure

Participants were assigned to pairs consisting of one native English speaker and one native Chinese speaker and seated in two separate rooms in the lab. All pairs completed the two map navigation tasks using text-based IM (no video or audio was permitted). Pairs were randomly assigned to one of two actual communication medium conditions: MT-mediation (in which actual MT was present) or English as a common language (in which actual MT was absent).

As noted earlier, the manipulation of beliefs about the presence or absence of MT mediation was done only for the native English speakers in each dyad. Half of the English speakers were told that they would be working with a native Mandarin speaking partner using MT (that is, participants believed MT was present). The other half of the English speakers were told that they would be working with a native Mandarin speaking partner using English as a common language (that is, participants believed MT was absent).

Participants then completed two HCRC tasks. During the first task, participants were randomly assigned as either an instructor or a follower and one of the two sets of maps. Participants had 15 minutes to complete the task, after which they answered a post-task survey to assess the perceived clarity of their partner's messages, the quality of the collaboration, and attributions they made for miscommunications during the task. Then, participants switched roles with their partner and completed the second 15-minute task on the other set of maps and answered an identical post-task survey. The order of maps and roles were fully counterbalanced using a Latin Square design.

After completing both tasks, each participant rated his/her impression of the partner and willingness to collaborate with the same partner in the future based on the overall collaboration experience. We then debriefed participants.

Measures

Participants answered a post-task survey after each map task and a post-experiment survey given at the end of the experiment. All measures reflected the communication and collaboration experience of each participant at the individual level.

Post-Task Survey

Clarity of partner's messages. Participants assessed the perceived clarity of their partner's messages using a single item, "I felt my partner always expressed his/her idea clearly". Responses were on a 7-point scale (1 = strongly disagree, 7 = strongly agree).

Quality of collaborations. Participants' evaluation of the quality of their collaboration with their partner was measured using four 7-point Likert scales (e.g., "Generally, I'm satisfied with our collaboration on this task."). The questions formed a reliable scale (Cronbach's α = .92) and were averaged to create a measure of quality of collaboration.

Attribution for miscommunications. Participants' attributions for miscommunication during the collaboration were measured using 18 7-point Likert scales. Factor analysis indicated the presence of five attribution factors (Table 2). Items under each factor were averaged to create a measure for each of the attribution factors, including message quality (Cronbach's α = .91), the partner (Cronbach's α = .62), shared information within pairs (Cronbach's α = .67), oneself (Cronbach's α = .68), and the task (Cronbach's α = .61).

The Post-Experiment Survey

Manipulation checks. Beliefs about the presence or absence of MT were assessed by four single-choice questions. These questions asked which language (English vs. Mandarin) was used to write and receive messages on their partners' side and their own side.

Impression of the partner. Participants' impressions of their partners were measured using ten 7-point Likert scales (e.g., "My partner is extraverted and enthusiastic."). Scores

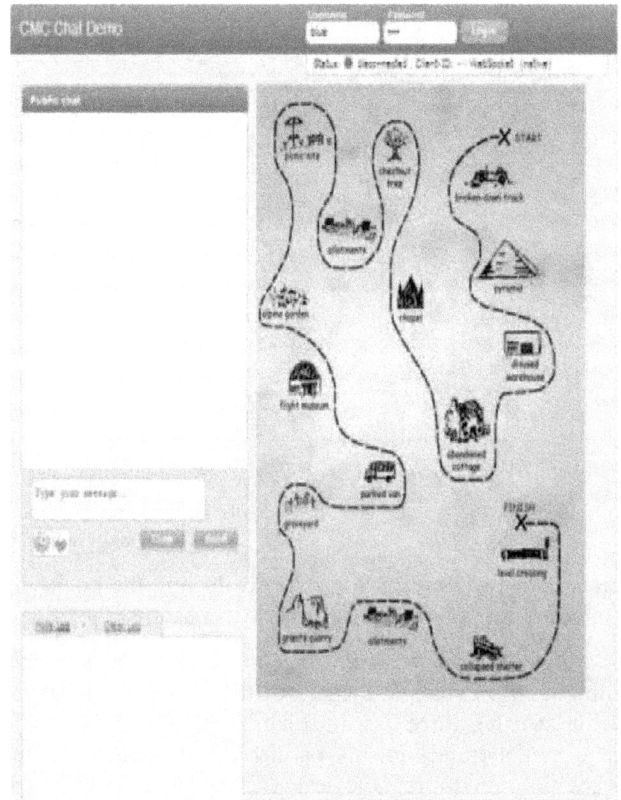

Figure 3. The interface of the chat tool as seen by the instructor.

	I	II	III	IV	V
Problematic sentence structure	.90				
Inaccurate expression	.90				
Inconsistent wording	.90				
Using of MT/English	.81				
Partner's understanding of maps		.75			
Partner's effort		.78			
Partner's intelligence		.58			
Audio cues absence			.79		
Familiarity between partners			.70		
Visual cues absence			.66		
Common background knowledge			.50		
Own intelligence				.78	
Own understanding on maps				.66	
Own effort				.54	
Route complicity					.72
Landmarks					.65
Time limitation					.65
Differences between the maps					.58

Table 2. Attribution for miscommunications, with factor loadings.

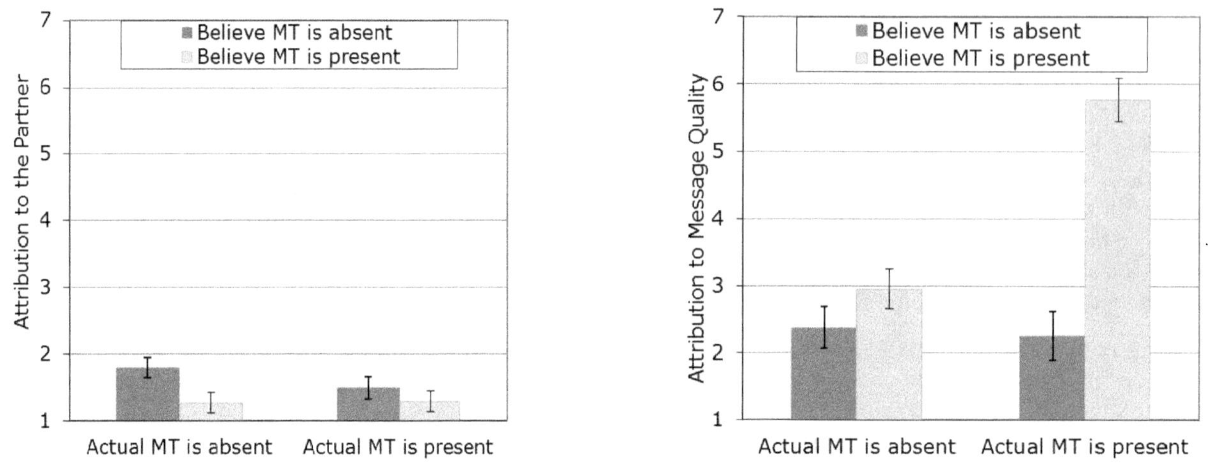

Figure 4. Mean attribution to the partner (left) and message quality (right) ratings by condition. Error bars represent standard errors of the mean.

were averaged to create a measure reflecting the positivity of their impressions of their partner (Cronbach's α = .78).

Willingness to collaborate in the future. Participants' willingness to collaborate again with the same partner was measured using three 7-point Likert scales (e.g., "I would like to collaborate with my partner in other tasks."). The questions formed a reliable scale (Cronbach's α = .87) and were averaged to create a measure of willingness to collaborate again in the future.

RESULTS

To test our hypotheses, we conducted 2 (beliefs about the MT: absence vs. presence) × 2 (actual mediation of MT: absence vs. presence) Mixed Model ANOVAs that took into account the fact that each participant provided two sets of measures, one after each map. As noted earlier, we look only at the data provided by the native English speaking participants, for whom beliefs about the presence or absence of MT could be manipulated. The demographic backgrounds (e.g., age and gender) and previous MT experience of each participant were set as control variables in all the ANOVA models.

Manipulation Checks

The manipulation checks indicated that all manipulations were successful. Regardless of the actual absence or presence of MT, 100% of English speaking participants who were told MT was absent thought their Chinese partners wrote and received messages in English and 100% of those who were told MT was present thought their Chinese partners wrote and received messages in Chinese.

The manipulation check of the actual absence/presence of MT was done by checking the chat tool settings and language using in each conversation. We found that 100% of participants and their partners in the actual presence of MT conditions generated messages in their native languages and used MT to mediate their communication, and 100% of participants and their partners in the actual absence of MT conditions used English as a common language to communicate during the experiment.

Attribution for Miscommunications

To test H1a and H1b, we examined participants' attributions for miscommunications by running Mixed Model ANOVAs of the form outlined above.

For each participant, there was a significant effect of the attribution type regardless of which experiment condition the participant belonged to ($F[4, 25] = 71.81$, $p < .0001$). Generally, participants attributed miscommunications more to situational factors such as message quality ($M = 3.35$, $SE = 0.23$) and the task ($M = 4.09$, $SE = 0.15$), and less to dispositional factors such as the partner ($M = 1.47$, $SE = 0.08$) and oneself ($M = 1.77$, $SE = 0.11$).

There was also an interaction between the actual presence of MT and the beliefs about the presence of MT on attribution ($F[4, 25] = 5.11$, $p < .001$). To get a clearer understanding of this result, we examined each of the five attribution factors separately. No difference was found for the attributions to oneself ($F[1, 28] = 0.05$, $p = .83$), the task ($F[1, 27.45] = 2.60$, $p = .12$), or shared information within pairs ($F[1, 28] = 0.51$, $p = .48$). However, attributions to the partner and message quality both varied with the experiment conditions.

Consistent with H1a, attribution of miscommunication to the partner (left side of Figure 4) was significantly lower when participants believed that MT was present than when they believed MT was absent ($M = 1.28$, $SE = 0.11$ vs. $M = 1.64$, $SE = 0.11$; $F[1, 28.15] = 4.69$, $p = .04$). There was no main effect of the actual presence of MT ($F[1, 28.15] = 1.52$, $p = .23$), nor an interaction between the actual and believed presence of MT ($F[1, 28.15] = 0.53$, $p = .47$).

H1b, about belief in the presence of MT leading to increased attribution of miscommunication to situational factors, was partially supported. Attributions to message quality (right side of Figure 4) were significantly higher for

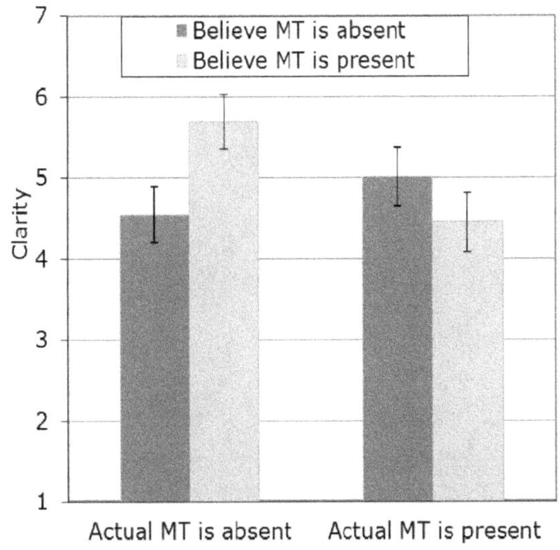

Figure 5. Mean clarity ratings by condition. Error bars represent standard errors of the mean.

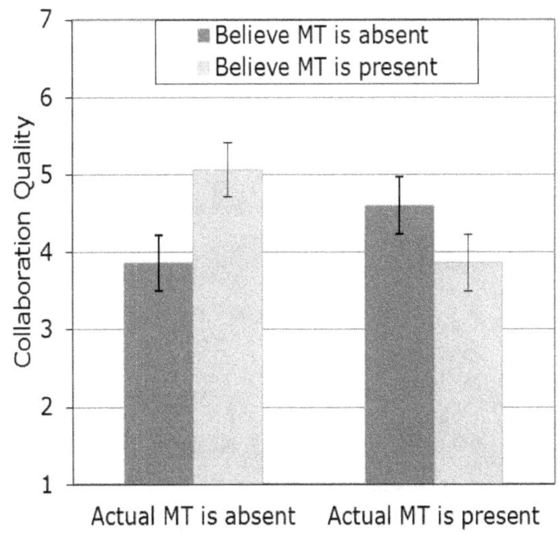

Figure 6. Mean collaboration quality ratings by condition. Error bars represent standard errors of the mean.

both the actual mediation of MT ($F [1, 28] = 17.35$, $p < .001$) and the belief that MT was present ($F [1, 28] = 48.45$, $p < .001$) when looking at main effects. There was also a significant interaction between the actual presence of MT and the belief that MT was present ($F [1, 28] = 23.53$, $p < < .001$). In particular, the combination of MT being present and participants believing it was present led to much higher attributions of miscommunication to message quality (M = 5.77, SE = 0.32) than in other conditions.

Thus, overall, we found that beliefs about the use of MT did affect attributions, as predicted by H1a and H1b. Participants who believed that MT was present were less likely to attribute miscommunications to dispositional factors such as their partner and more likely to attribute them to situational factors such as quality of the translated message. Attributions of miscommunication to dispositional factors were especially pronounced when the actual use of MT corresponded to people's beliefs about its use.

Collaboration Experience during the Task

H2a and H2b predicted that the perceived clarity of partner's messages and collaboration quality during the task would vary depending on whether people believed MT was being used. This prediction was partially supported by participants' responses on the post-task surveys.

For H2a, about perceived clarity (Figure 5), there is a significant interaction between actual and believed use of MT ($F [1, 28] = 8.91$, $p = .01$), though neither the main effect of actual mediation nor the belief that MT was used was significant ($F [1, 28] = 2.06$, $p = .16$; $F [1, 28] = 0.99$, $p = .33$). Here, the *presence* of MT had no strong interaction with beliefs (M = 4.45, SE = 0.36 vs. M = 5.01, SE = 0.34). Instead, the *absence* of MT mattered: participants perceived higher clarity when they believed MT was in use (M = 5.69, SE = 0.36 vs. M = 4.54, SE = 0.34).[1]

For H2b, about perceived collaboration quality (Figure 6), we saw a similar pattern to H2a, with a significant interaction effect ($F [1, 28] = 7.25$, $p = .01$) but no main effect of either the actual or believed presence of MT ($F [1, 28] = 0.41$, $p = .53$; $F [1, 28] = 0.36$, $p = .55$). As with perceived clarity, belief about MT use made no difference when it was actually present (M = 3.86, SE = 0.37 vs. M = 4.60, SE = 0.35). When actual MT was absent, however, participants perceived higher collaboration quality when they believed MT was in use versus when they did not (M = 5.06, SE = 0.37 vs. M = 3.86, SE = 0.36).

Thus overall, beliefs about the use of MT also affected people's collaboration experience during the task. Here, the dominant result is that people who believe that their partner is using MT rate both the clarity of communication and the quality of the collaboration higher—but only when there partner is actually using English as a second language, rather than MT.

Collaboration Preference beyond the Task

H3a and H3b predicted that people's overall impression of partners and willingness to collaborate with them in the future would also vary with beliefs about whether MT was

[1] The clarity question, "I felt my partner always expressed his/her idea clearly", did not specify whether the message to be rated was the original Chinese message or the MT translation. Thus, those who believed MT was absent based their ratings on the English messages, but those who believed MT was present may have rated either the original or the "translated" message. However, since only the interaction between actual MT and beliefs is significant, this indeterminacy does not affect the pattern of results.

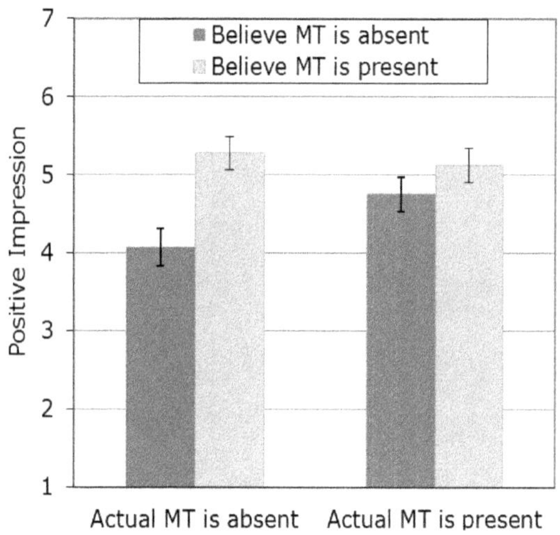

Figure 7. Mean impression of the partner ratings by condition. Error bars represent standard errors of the mean).

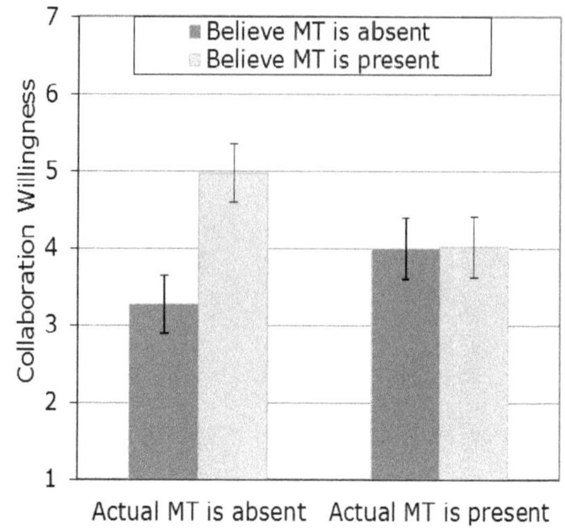

Figure 8. Mean willingness to collaborate in the future by condition. Error bars represent standard errors of the mean.

in use. This prediction was fully supported by participants' responses on the post-experiment surveys.

Consistent with H3a, people's impressions of their partner (Figure 7) were significantly higher when they believed that MT was in use, regardless of the actual presence of MT (M = 5.21, SE = 0.15 vs. M = 4.42, SE = 0.16; F [1, 23] = 13.56, p = .001). Neither the main effect of actual mediation of MT nor the interaction were significant (F [1, 23] = 1.20, p = .29; F [1, 23] = 3.54, p = .07).

We also examined H3b, participants' willingness to The main effect of believing MT was in use led participants to give higher future collaboration ratings (F [1, 25] = 5.16, p = .03) and there was a significant interaction between believed and actual use of MT. As with the ratings of collaboration experience on individual tasks (H2a and H2b), the main effect was driven by what happened when MT was absent. Here, participants who believed MT was in use had higher ratings than those who did not (M = 4.97, SE = 0.40 vs. M = 3.27, SE = 0.38; F [1, 11] = 13.79, p = .003). There were no differences based on belief when MT was actually in use (M = 4.02, SE = 0.40 vs. M = 4.00, SE = 0.38; F [1, 11] = 0.05, p = .83), and no main effect of the actual mediation of MT (F [1, 25] = 0.07, p = .80).

Once again, we see that believing MT is in use has positive effects on both participants' impression of their partner and their willingness to collaborate with them in the future. The effect is stronger when MT is not actually being used.

DISCUSSION

Our results shed new light on the possible effects of MT on collaboration experiences. Previous studies have looked at the impact of MT on collaborations from the perspective of message understanding. Instead, we explore how knowing, or believing, that MT systems are in use might affect how people make attributions about the causes of miscommunication, in turn affecting their perceptions of the partner and of the collaboration experience.

The broadest and most consistent finding is that message receivers who believe their partner's communication is mediated by MT have better communication experiences than those who don't. Belief that MT is in use leads people to make fewer dispositional attributions for miscommunication to their partner, more positive overall ratings of their partner, and a greater willingness to engage in future collaborations.

These beliefs interact with the actual use of MT in interesting ways. In particular, for attributions to situational rather than dispositional factors, the effect of believing that MT is in use is overall enhanced when MT is actually being used. For ratings of communication and partner quality, however, the opposite obtains: on balance this belief primarily affects ratings when MT is *not* being used.

We believe these interaction effects are driven by how the actual quality of messages received matches people's expectations. We suspect that people who believed that MT was in use expected to see lower quality messages on average. When MT was actually in use and people saw the obvious errors that MT sometimes generates, their beliefs about the quality of the technology were confirmed and they blamed situational factors rather than their partner. But the kinds of errors that second language speakers make when generating non-native text are perhaps both less glaring than MT errors and more familiar to native English speakers who have interacted with second language speakers. Thus, incoming non-MT messages were easier than expected to cope with for people who believed MT was being used—leading to better perceptions of their communication and their partner.

Multilingual CMC tools as socio-technical systems

One way to directly address this suspicion would be to marry our analysis of attributions with measures of message quality. Measuring the quality of translated text is non-trivial and typically requires a human gold standard (although using Mechanical Turk to judge translation quality has some promise [5]). The closest measure we have in our study is people's ratings of their partner's message clarity, which was not significantly different whether MT was present or not. On the other hand, Wang et al. [27] found that MT significantly affected perceptions of message comprehensibility.

We think this difference arises because of the nature of the task. HCRC tasks such as those used in the current study are designed to require grounding and repair work by deliberately including mismatches between landmarks on the maps. The confusion induced by these mismatches, along with the relatively constrained domain of the conversation, may have washed out differences in language clarity. In the brainstorming tasks used by Wang et al., the domain is less constrained and the need to build on others' ideas is more central to the task, leading to lower ratings of clarity [27]. Also in that study, participants knew nothing about their partner's background or the use of machine translation; running a version of that study that made clear to participants that MT would be interesting for deepening our understanding of the interplay between beliefs about and actual use of translation.

These results highlight the socio-technical nature of using MT to support collaboration. Most work so far on MT has compared it to second language use and implicated differences in comprehensibility as a problem, but quality is only part of the story. Social and psychological processes, task characteristics, and translation quality all interact to affect how using MT will affect people's experiences and outcomes.

Designing for and with MT

Interface design also can affect those experiences. We suggest several strategies that leverage these results to help people collaborate more effectively via MT by making the fact of MT's use more salient, by helping people improve the quality of messages they generate, and by more directly encouraging attribution of problems to the system rather than to collaborators. We discuss each in turn.

Making MT salient. In our experiment we used explicit instructions to prime people's beliefs that MT was present. However, interface design elements could do this work as well and have been shown in a number of cases to improve both collaboration outcomes and processes. For instance, recent CSCW work demonstrates that priming beliefs about community goals by showing desirable example content in the interface can increase the quality [24], structuring [21], and descriptiveness [18] of content people contribute to a group, Likewise, even small interventions to make group activity [7] and communication [8] more salient can increase attachment to groups, while subtle cues about desirable collaborative behaviors can increase their frequency [3].

A simple way to increase the salience of translation would be to link to the original source text for translated text, or put an icon or the original text itself alongside the translation. The original text might not be useful in and of itself for a monolingual speaker, but it would raise awareness of the translation process in play. The interface might also provide explicit translation controls for senders, to make them aware that they (and, in turn, their partners) might be using translation. Or, if automatic translation is desired, the interface could allow receivers to specify their preferred language and tell other people in the conversation that all text will be automatically translated to partners' preferred languages. This might be especially valuable in groups with more than two native languages.

Increasing message quality. For many of our measures, the strongest effects came when people believed MT was in use, but it was not. And, although our measure of idea clarity did not reveal significant differences, prior work [27, 29] suggests that a main factor is that text generated by second language speakers is on average more readable than machine translations. Thus, systems should strive to help people generate the highest quality messages possible.

Rather than MT being an all or nothing proposition, systems might support seamless transitions between MT and second language use. The idea of auto-translation would also be useful here. People could choose to write in any language and the system could translate only as needed. The interface should also make users aware that they can choose to communicate in either language and that it's probably best to use whichever language is likely to lead to the best translation for their partners.

Another idea would be for the system to help senders generate higher-quality translations. Seeing translated messages, as suggested earlier for making translation more salient, would have useful side effects. People would both know when a particular translation was confusing and learn which kinds of language constructs an MT system tended to struggle with. The system could also allow notify senders when a message is likely to be mistranslated, and allow them to either edit the translation directly, simplify the message so that it's easier for MT to work with, or switch to a different language. The cognitive costs and the delays imposed by such a system might make it impractical, but it is an idea worth exploring.

Increasing perceived agency. Finally, we suspect that part of the effect around increased dispositional attributions comes from people seeing the system as an active agent in the communication channel. Thus, emphasizing not just the salience of MT but also its agency might increase the power of the effect[2]. Borrowing ideas from Nass and colleagues [e.g., 19] around anthropomorphic agents, multilingual collaboration tools that include MT might literally include a "Translation Agent". The agent might present with human-like characteristics such as apologizing for errors or looking confused when translation engines report uncertainty in translation quality or parses of translated text show large deviations from normal grammar. More generally, they could exhibit behaviors that encourage users to attribute errors in communication to the tool rather to than the partner. Finally, following Adar, Tan, and Teevan's defense of benevolent deception in HCI [1], they might even lie a little about how much effect the translation has on quality.

Potential costs. Such deception, and the general goal of encouraging people to attribute problems to the system rather than their partners, does sometimes pose tradeoffs. In situations where multilingual teams are assigned and MT must be part of the collaboration, we see only benefit in reducing friction by putting the blame on the system rather than on teammates.

The picture is more complicated when people have more freedom in choosing partners. One argument in favor of using the aforementioned strategies is that non-native language speakers often face an uphill battle in establishing trust [14] and relationships [6] with native speakers in organizations with a common language. These strategies are one way to help second language speakers move past surface aspects of language disfluency to be judged on deeper merits. However, because MT and second language use do in fact impose communication costs, this may impact their partners or the long-term success of collaboration. Further, because the effects are stronger when MT is not actually in use, this may come at the expense of less fluent or mono-lingual collaborators who must make greater use of MT. These issues will need to be explored as MT tools, and designs that leverage them, become more commonly used for cross-language collaboration.

Limitations

There were several limitations to this study. First, the current study examined how MT influences collaboration only at the individual level. The measurements used here all addressed individuals' experience during the collaboration, without attention to group-level evaluations. Both are important, and future work should examine the relationship between the beliefs about and mediation of MT and collaboration from both individual and group levels. Furthermore, we examined beliefs about MT in a group of people who were relatively unfamiliar with it, and we asked them to perform only two tasks. It would be interesting to see if beliefs had as strong of an effect among a group of heavy MT users, or over a longer time period.

Also, beliefs about presence of MT were only examined from the perspective of monolingual English speakers receiving messages. This was largely a practical consideration that arose because we recruited participants from a U.S. university. Finding monolingual non-English speaking participants is nearly impossible in this setting, and finding enough bilingual native English speakers of Chinese (or pairs of speakers who are bilingual in each other's native language in any language except perhaps Spanish) would also have been a monumental task.

This does leave open the question of how strongly the effect would appear for bilingual receivers, who might better understand the foibles of both manual and machine translation between the languages. The effect may also be less pronounced for language pairs where MT on average works better (such as Chinese-Japanese or translations between many European languages). Finally, we don't know how the effect of beliefs or choices about MT might influence message senders' perception of receivers.

CONCLUSION

Our study both answers and raises questions about the ways that people's beliefs about the use of MT affect multilingual collaboration, and we hope that both the answered and raised questions contribute to our understanding of MT.

At least for message receivers, if they believe that MT is in use, they attribute miscommunication problems to technological constraints (e.g., quality of the translated message) much more than to their partner (e.g., the partner's intelligence). They also give higher ratings of the communication experience and of the partner, particularly when MT is not actually in use, and we suspect this because messages likely seem more natural and/or of higher quality when MT is not used, and thus the level of fluency exceeds their expectations.

Our findings have a number of potential design applications around making the presence and agency of MT in multilingual collaboration systems more salient in order to encourage people to attribute errors to the system rather than to their partners. They also suggest that supporting seamless use of both MT and second language proficiency is likely to increase collaboration quality, especially if bilingual speakers are coached to use tools in ways that maximize translation quality.

From a research perspective, our open questions about monolingual versus bilingual speakers, senders versus receivers, and easy versus hard language pairs provide a set of directions to explore. Finally, our results suggest that the quality of messages and the causes of imperfect messages, along with people's understanding of those causes, all work together to shape individuals' collaboration experience together; none alone can tell the whole story. Research that addresses each chapter of the story will lead to better

[2] Interestingly, there is some debate in both the literary community and the professional translation community about how salient the human translator of texts should be as an active agent in the communication [25].

understanding of and systems for using MT to support multilingual collaboration.

ACKNOWLEDGMENTS

This research was funded in part by National Science Foundation grant #1025425. The material is also based in part on work supported by the National Science Foundation, while Susan Fussell was working at the Foundation. Any opinion, findings, and conclusions or recommendations expressed in this material are those of the authors and do not necessarily reflect the views of the National Science Foundation. We thank Leslie Setlock, Monica Chen, Jean-Carlos Polanco, Christopher Chung and Huaishu Peng for their assistance and the anonymous reviewers for their valuable comments.

REFERENCES

1. Adar, E., Tan, D.S., & Teevan, J. Benevolent Deception in Human Computer Interaction. In *Proc. of CHI 2013*, 1863–1872.
2. Anderson, A., Bader, M., Bard, E., Boyle, E., Doherty, G. M., Garrod, S., Isard, S., Kowtko, J., McAllister, J., Miller, J., Sotillo, C., Thompson, H. S. & Weinert, R. (1991). The HCRC Map Task Corpus. *Language and Speech*, *34*, 351–366.
3. Balaam, M., Fitzpatrick, G., Good, J., & Harris, E. (2011, May). Enhancing interactional synchrony with an ambient display. In *Proceedings of the SIGCHI Conference on Human Factors in Computing Systems* (pp. 867–876). ACM.
4. Bazarova, N.N. & Hancock, J.T. (2011). Attributions after a group failure: Do they matter? *Communication Research*, *40*, 1–24.
5. Callison-Burch, C. (2009, August). Fast, cheap, and creative: evaluating translation quality using Amazon's Mechanical Turk. In *Proceedings of the 2009 Conference on Empirical Methods in Natural Language Processing: Volume 1-Volume 1* (pp. 286–295). Association for Computational Linguistics.
6. Chevrier, S. (2003). Cross-cultural management in multinational project groups. *Journal of World Business*, *38*, 141–149.
7. Dabbish, L., Farzan, R., Kraut, R., & Postmes, T. (2012, February). Fresh faces in the crowd: turnover, identity, and commitment in online groups. In*Proceedings of the ACM 2012 conference on Computer Supported Cooperative Work* (pp. 245–248). ACM.
8. Dabbish, L., Kraut, R., & Patton, J. (2012, May). Communication and commitment in an online game team. In *Proceedings of the 2012 ACM annual conference on Human Factors in Computing Systems* (pp. 879–888). ACM.
9. Diamant, E.I., Fussell, S.R. & Lo, F.I. (2008). Where Did We Turn Wrong? Unpacking the Effects of Culture and Technology on Attributions of Team Performance. In *Proc. of CSCW 2008*, ACM Press, 383–391.
10. Doherty-Sneddon, G., Anderson, A.H., O'Malley, C., Langton, S., Garrod, S., & Bruce, V. (1997). Face-to-face and video mediated communication: A comparison of dialogue structure and task performance. *Journal of Experimental Psychology*, *3*, 105–125.
11. Dweck, C. (1999). Self theories: Their role in motivation, personality and development. Philadelphia, PA: Psychology Press.
12. Gao, G., Wang, H.C., Cosley, D., & Fussell, S.R. (2013). Same translation but different experience: The effects of highlighting on machine-translated conversations. In *Proc. of CHI 2013*, 449–458.
13. Hancock, J.T. & Dunham, P.J. (2001). Impression formation in computer-mediated communication revisited: An analysis of the breadth and intensity of impressions. *Communication Research*, *28*, 325–347.
14. Henderson, J. K. (2005). Language diversity in international management teams. *International Studies of Management and Organization*, *35*, 66–82.
15. Hinds, P. (1999). The cognitive and interpersonal costs of video. *Media Psychology*, 1, 283–312.
16. Kelley, H.H. (1967). Attribution theory in social psychology. *Nebraska Symposium on Motivation.* University of Nebraska Press.
17. Lim, J. & Yang, Y.P. (2008). Exploring computer-based multilingual negotiation support for English-Chinese dyads: Can we negotiate in our native languages? *Behaviour and Information Technology*, *27*, 139–151.
18. Malu, M., Jethi, N., & Cosley, D. (2012, February). Encouraging personal storytelling by example. In *Proceedings of the 2012 iConference* (pp. 611–612). ACM.
19. Nass, C. & Lee, K.M. (2000). Does computer-generated speech manifest personality? An experimental test of similarity-attraction. *Proceedings of CHI 2000* (pp. 329–336). NY: ACM Press.
20. Nisbett, R.E. & Eugene, B. Attribution and the psychology of prediction. *Journal of Personality and Social Psychology*, *35*, 932–950.
21. Solomon, J. & Wash, R. (2012, February). Bootstrapping wikis: developing critical mass in a fledgling community by seeding content. In *Proceedings of the ACM 2012 conference on Computer Supported Cooperative Work* (pp. 261–264). ACM.
22. Storck, J. & Sproull, L. (1995). Through a glass darkly: What do people learn in videoconferences? *Human Communication Research*, *22*, 197–219.
23. Straus, S.G. & McGrath, J.E. (1994). Does the medium really matter? The interaction of task type and

technology on group performance and member reactions. *Journal of Applied Psychology*, *79*, 87–97.

24. Sukumaran, A., Vezich, S., McHugh, M., & Nass, C. (2011, May). Normative influences on thoughtful online participation. In *PART 5 of Proceedings of the 2011 annual conference on Human factors in computing systems* (pp. 3401–3410). ACM.
25. Tymoczko, M. (2007). Enlarging Translation, Empower Translators. Manchester: St. Jerome Press.
26. Wang, H.C., Cosley, D., & Fussell, S.R. (2010). Idea expander: supporting group brainstorming with conversationally triggered visual thinking stimuli. In *Proc. of CSCW 2010*, 103–106.
27. Wang, H.C., Fussell, S.R., & Cosley, D. (2013). Machine translation vs. common language: Effects on idea exchange in cross-lingual groups. In *Proc. of CSCW 2013*, 935–944.
28. Yamashita, N. & Ishida, T. (2006). Automatic prediction of misconceptions in multilingual computer-mediated communication. In *Proc. of IUI 2006*, 62–69.
29. Yamashita, N. & Ishida, T. (2006). Effects of machine translation on collaborative work. In *Proc. CSCW 2006*, 515–523.
30. Yamashita, N., Inaba, R., Kuzuoka, H., & Ishida, T. (2009). Difficulties in establishing common ground in multiparty groups using machine translation. In *Proc. of CHI 2009*, 679–688.
31. Yamashita, N., Kuzuoka, K., Hirata, K., Aoyagi, S., & Shirai, Y. (2011). Supporting fluid tabletop collaboration across distances. In *Proc. of CHI 2011*, ACM Press, 2827–2836

Sounds of Silence: Exploring Contributions to Conversations, Non-Responses and the Impact of Mediating Technologies in *Triple Space*

Joon-Suk Lee
Virginia State University
Dept. of Computer Science,
P.O. Box 9068, Petersburg, VA 23806
jlee@vsu.edu

Deborah Tatar
Virginia Tech
Dept. of Computer Science, MC 0106
2202 Kraft Dr., Blacksburg, VA 24060
tatar@vt.edu

ABSTRACT
We investigate collocated triads as they play a collaborative, problem-solving game using distributed technology on laptops. We examine how different triads attain and maintain mutual understanding in *triple-space*—when working on a hard problem, with communicating technologies and face-to-face interaction. We present qualitative and quantitative evidence that demonstrates the descriptive adequacy of a model of triadic interaction in triple space. We use that model to argue that the notion of *good-enoughness* is not a group attribute, but rather tied to each dyadic pair. This intellectual framework allows us to examine how *non-response* operates within these triple-space interactions when interaction is supported by different media. The results related to non-response raise the possibility that different media may result in subtle influence on the balance of participant goals.

Author Keywords: Triple Space; Triple Factor Space; Grounding; Common Ground; Contributions to Conversations; Non-Responses; Mediating Technologies; Mediated Interaction; Form Factor; Team Sudoku.

ACM Classification Keywords: H.5.m. [Information interfaces and presentation (e.g., HCI)]: Miscellaneous

INTRODUCTION
How do collocated people come to understand each other in carrying out joint activities? Do groups of three do this any differently from groups of two? Does the use of small screen technologies influence ways that collocated people come to understand each other in group settings? This research asks these questions and discusses how Clark and Schaefer's *Contributions to Conversations* model [14] of common ground applies to collocated triads.

CSCW'14, February 15 – 19, 2014, Baltimore, MD, USA.

http://dx.doi.org/10.1145/2531602.2531655

We investigate collocated triads as they play a collaborative, problem-solving game using distributed technologies. Lee, Tatar and Harrison [21] have previously described this increasingly prevalent situation, shown in Figure 1, as representing a "triple space," in which participants are managing not only the cognitive and social functions described by Barron [3], but also the challenge of making sense of the changes to the shared medium caused by the other players. In our case, the participants were all working on the same Sudoku puzzle while sitting in the same room but interacting with the game either on a large shared paper or on their own computers, which are updated in real time. This situation is not unlike, for example, working in a room with Google Docs.

The increasing use of visually segregated small screen technologies such as smartphones, tablets, and laptops among collocated people creates an interactional quandary in which interactors are (1) required to allocate and manage their attentions in carrying out perceptible social interactions within cotemporal/cospacial settings, while at the same time (2) managing concealed cognitively-engrossing digital interactions through transtemporal/transspatial digital media, and (3) also expected to operate across these two heterogeneous interactional channels, the social and the digital. *Triple Space* signifies how we manage our everyday activities within and through these complex, multi-layered, disparate, yet concurrently existing interactional channels.

In investigating triple space interactions and comparing different mediating technology conditions, we examine (1) how triads attain and maintain mutual understandings of the current activities differently from dyads, and (2) if and how the choices of the technological medium impact the grounding process among the triads. In particular, by extending Clark *Contributions to Conversations* model [13,14] we can examine how non-responses can located and interpreted in triads in triple space.

INTERACTIONAL DIFFICULTIES IN TRIPLE SPACE
The belief that people are experts in managing group activities with technology implies that the requirements are simple extrapolations of the already learned techniques. To the con-

trary, many tasks involve much more than simple extrapolations.

For instance, Barron [3] describes how upper elementary school students solving math problems *learn* to manage a dual factor space: social and cognitive. In a dual factor space, people need to manage their internal production of 'computational thinking,' and their social skills in managing group processes. Dual space tasks may ask a group to perform tasks otherwise conceived of as individual. Barron points out that joint problem-solving in dual space requires each participant to both make his/her own thinking visible to the group, and to recognize other participant's thinking. She shows that not all groups know how to work together in dual space, and suggests that communication skills should be taught explicitly [3].

In our research, we look at an even more complex yet increasingly pervasive situation: a *triple space.*

This situation we create experimentally embodies a constellation of three increasingly important situational dilemmas that often co-exist: (1) they must behave in a way that defines the "current purposes" when several different possible goals are palpable—they may satisfice (in Simon's terms [26]) between a focus, for example, on the game and a good interaction with the other players; (2) they must choose mechanisms of engagement with others, that is, people may choose to direct attention to the others through action in the game or through engagement in social space; (3) they must take action in a situation which affects other people but in which the goodness of the action may very difficult to infer or may not be known for a considerable lag. Often coordination research within HCI is concerned with whether one player can see what another player is seeing (as in [27]). The assumption is that seeing the action is sufficient to infer that action's meaning. But in these dual or triple factor spaces, there are two points of failure: the players may not perceive changes in state, or they may not understand the meaning of changes in state.

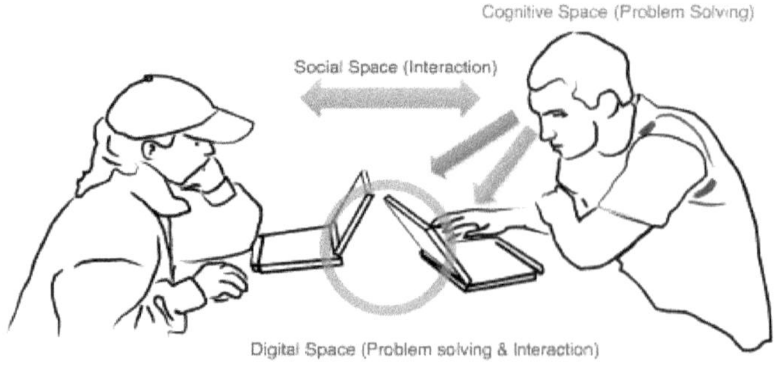

Figure 1: Attention and Task Management in Triple Space

COMMON GROUND

Clark, long ago, arguing that language is a form of joint activity, studied collocated coordinative interaction [9]. He and colleagues (c.f., [10,13,14,15]) examined how people build and maintain mutual understanding in carrying out joint actions in the moment of the interaction. Clark and Schaefer, in particular, argued that people in conversation speak both to advance content specification and to regulate the course of the interaction. To attain such kinds of mutual understandings, conversants collaboratively create units of conversation called *contributions.* Through contributions, interlocutors in conversation collectively try to establish the mutual belief that *everyone* has a *good enough understanding* of what is being discussed at the moment for their *current purposes* [9,10,13,15]. The term *common ground* refers to what the participants need to know for mutual understanding. *Grounding* is the process of attaining and maintaining mutual understanding among interlocutors.

Clark's theory has influenced quite a number of important works not just in CSCW, but in many other fields as well. For instance, much previous research comparing video mediated communications (VMC) with face-to-face interactions has asked how different mediating technologies impact the grounding process in group discourse (e.g., [1,2,24,28]). Some reported that communication technologies often create difficulties in turn-taking among the geographically distributed, technology-mediated groups, resulting in a decrease in the number of turns and an increase in the length of turns compared to face-to-face interactions [24,28]. Such research typically reasons that the grounding process takes longer in computer-mediated settings and therefore people using computers end up talking more. However, other research either found no such result [1] or found contradictory result [2].

Noticing that technology-mediated communications among distributed groups can impair grounding processes, researchers also have proposed various enhancements. Cornelius and Boos [17] reported that common ground is difficult to achieve in text-based computer-mediated communication in general, but mutual understanding as well as satisfaction with the group process can be improved by proper training. Beer et al. [6] suggested that group decision support systems can effectively support grounding processes by explicitly mandating users to verify and explicate their understandings.

Clark's theory has also been applied, tested and extended for groups beyond dyads by different researchers. For example, Anderson and colleagues (c.f. [1,2]) examined how Clark's *common ground* model would apply to three-party interactions as compared to two-party interactions in both face-to-face and technology-mediated settings. They reported information distribution among the group members affected the grounding process and that triadic interactions required more work in the grounding process as compared to dyadic interactions. Birnholtz et al. [7] raised questions about possible ambiguities in Clark's notions of *good enoughness* and *current purposes*. For instance, Clark's theory leaves open the question of how that understanding may be distributed between two or more legitimate participants. Does one's acceptance stand in for the other's? Is this true even when there are substantial questions of attention, as there are in the presence of a difficult problem and visual competition from the screen?

In this paper, we pursue questions that Birnholtz et al. [7] raised and build on the work of Anderson and colleagues (c.f. [1,2]). That is, we ask questions Clark's theory does not fully answer and try to see how Clark's model would apply to groups beyond dyads. Yet, our work is unique in that we try to see how the use of technologies impact the grounding process in triple space instead of comparing technology-mediated, distributed interactions to non-mediated collocated interactions. In addition, unlike many of the previous studies that looked only at effects that the grounding process has on group activities on a macro level, we base our discussions on interactional level analyses.

CONTRIBUTIONS TO CONVERSATIONS

Clark and Schaefer [13,14] argued that people in conversation speak to make contributions to the social process they are engaged in. They saw that contributions to conversations are achieved through content specification and grounding. Through speaking and listening, interlocutors in conversation collectively try to establish the mutual belief that everyone has good enough understandings of what is being discussed at the moment and presumably of the group processes in which they are engaged for their current purposes [10,13,15]. In order to accomplish such kinds of mutual understandings, conversants collaboratively create units of conversation called contributions. Contributions are "stretches of speech and the grounding of the contents" (p. 37, [13]). Building on [25], Clark delineates a two-part process in which a presentation phase is thought to occur prior to an acceptance phase. The acceptance phase is where we expect to see evidence both of interactional trouble and of what constitutes an adequate and acceptable repair [13].

However, the model of contributions does not clearly explicate how it can describe interactions among groups of people larger than two. In this paper, therefore, we consider how the model can be extended to analyze triadic interaction data, and how modifying it can be used to identify ambiguous and potentially problematic places in the interaction.

Extending the Model of Contributions. First, the model of contributions states that the process of making contributions consists minimally of three parts in the case of dyadic interactions (p. 22, [13]):

(a) A presents *u* for B to consider.

(b) B accepts *u*.

(c) A accepts that B accepts *u*.

We can project an extension of this model to accommodate triadic interactions (A, B and C). In theory, the process for triads consists minimally of five parts:

(a) A presents *u* for B and C to consider

(b) B accepts *u*.

(c) C accepts *u*.

(d) A accepts that B accepts *u*.

(e) A accepts that C accepts *u*.

A more complex, fully-crossed model would project that B and C also had to accept one another's contributions. The current work investigates the descriptive power and adequacy of these proposed extensions.

Failure to Signal Repairs. The extension of this model is important because it can provide evidence about how to conceptualize triadic interaction in triple-space. In a dyad, current purposes can easily be seen as a unitary outcome, because they are the product of a focused negotiation between two people. (Participants may have private goals, but until these goals receive some behavioral expression they are not thought to be part of the joint action. If new goals are expressed, they are thought to be worked out through the grounding process.) But when more than two people are involved, the question arises of whether there is, at any given time, a single unitary notion of joint action, or several, separate dyadic notions. Furthermore, Lee, Tatar and Harrison [21] reported cases in which groups successfully solved a complex puzzle problem together without making any contributions to conversations. In a dyad, this is not problematic because, by Clark's model, any action is seen as constituting a response to an immediate or distally prior action by the self or a known other. The triadic situation is intrinsically more complex.

Exploration of this is important because it opens up the possibility of failure to signal the need for repair in more complex groups that does not exist in simpler ones. For example, in such tasks as telephone directory inquiries, if a customer and an operator fail to engage in the activities that signify the achievement of mutual understanding, it clearly signals the need for a repair of the main task—getting necessary information. On the other hand, in Sudoku (and in many other triple space tasks), the absence of activities that signify mutual understanding does not decisively indicate communication failure. It may be considered enough if two of the three people are thought to have conducted a successful communication. Furthermore, because there may be ambiguity about who is the recipient of any particular communication, a non-response may be taken by a speaker or actor as an affirmation of understanding by the listener or viewer who is assumed to be paying attention. In both cases, there may be an expectation gap.

The Meaning of Continued Attention. Clark's model of contribution mandates positive evidence of understanding. Clark and Schaefer [14] list five different types of positive evidence: *continued attention*, *initiation of the relevant next contribution*, *acknowledgement*, *demonstration* and *display*. Most of this list is unproblematic when applied to more complex situations. However, continued attention---when a participant does not show changes in his/her "attentive demeanor or eye contact" (p. 267, [14])---is not only the weakest form of evidence in dyadic interaction, but constitutes a quite problematic source of information in triple space interaction, or indeed, any visual focus on a surface or object not seen by others. When a participant does not display any observable behavioral changes from attention to a private screen, either the listener is maintaining focus or absorbed in something else, and either the speaker is correctly able to infer the listener's state or not. Furthermore, the speaker's inference may or may not be significant for any given contribution. However, in triple-space interaction, we cannot *assume* as analysts that continued attention constitutes evidence of positive understanding.

THE STUDY

The analysis in this paper is based on data from a study we conducted last year [20]. The original study investigated how differences in form factor impacted people's emotions and communicative behaviors.

The study asked participants to play Sudoku games collectively on one of three different mediating technologies (on a shared paper, tablets and laptops) and experimentally compared the three conditions. Our findings showed that people in both the laptop and tablet conditions talked less than people in the paper-control condition, but only people in the laptop condition experienced a significant decrease in positive emotion [20].

This current paper uses the same data set to investigate new questions: whether grounding processes in triple space among triads require more sophisticated theoretical frameworks than previously employed and whether such frameworks lead us to suggestive observations. We report on the new findings not yet been discussed in our previous report.

Procedures

The study was designed as a two-phase, between-subject experiment. During the initial sign-up process, participants were directed to an online survey site and asked to fill out questionnaires about demographics, prior experiences with Sudoku as well as five personality self-report inventories (Big Five [19], Circumplex Scales of Interpersonal Values [22], Circumplex Scales of Interpersonal Efficacy [23], Beck Anxiety Inventory [4] and Beck Depression Inventory [5]). Only the participants who filled out the online questionnaires were allowed to sign-up for phase 2. When participants reported that they did not have prior Sudoku experience, they were directed to a web site that had both descriptions of the Sudoku rules and sample Sudoku games.

In phase 2, participants were brought into a small room and seated in close proximity to one another. They were introduced to one another when they came into the room. After the informed consent process, participants were asked to fill out a pre-game questionnaire (Q1) including questions about their experiences with the game and with the other players, and also the 20-item Positive and Negative Affect Schedule (PANAS) [29] that measures how people are feeling in the moment. After filling out Q1, researchers briefly went over the Sudoku rules (in all conditions) and conducted a software walkthrough (in laptop condition and tablet condition) in order to familiarize participants with the Team Sudoku tool features. The groups were then asked to work together on two Sudoku puzzles, in an order counterbalanced across groups. The groups were given 20 minutes to work on each game. After each game, participants filled out post-game questionnaires (Q2 and Q3), including retaking the PANAS. In Q3, we also asked them to rate how much they were satisfied with the group and the way it worked together on a scale of 1 (not at all) to 7 (very much). There was also a short discussion at the end of the study. Video and audio recordings of all the game sessions were collected as well as computer logs and screen shot movies of the games.

In each game, participants were asked to play Sudoku puzzles either on a 25 x 30.5 inch sheet (base-line, Paper Condition) or on one of two different form-configurations (tablet condition and laptop condition) of tablet PCs. In paper condition (PC), researchers prepared the Sudoku game board manually prior to the study and asked participants to solve the puzzles on that. In both computer conditions, groups were asked to collaboratively solve puzzles on specially designed multiplayer Sudoku software, Team Sudoku.

We made an explicit decision to use a type of computer that has a twist-and-swivel display so that we could configure the same computer both as a laptop and as a tablet. For laptop condition (LC), mice were connected to the systems as the primary input devices, while for tablet condition (TC), stylus pens were provided as the primary input devices. Keyboard input mechanisms were disabled in the systems to maintain compatibility between the laptop condition and the tablet condition in which keyboards are hidden under the laid-down screens, inaccessible to the users.

Clearly, there are many differences between the paper and the computer conditions that are consequences of the types of sharing that they enable. However, the differences between LC and TC include only the configuration and the input device.

Team Sudoku

Team Sudoku is a multi-user, parallel-distributed form of the Sudoku game. Sudoku presents the player with a 9x9 board with digits between 1 and 9 in some cells. The goal of Sudoku is to fill the board so that each of the nine columns, nine rows and nine distinct 3x3 blocks contain exactly one instance of each digit from 1 to 9. Games are differentiated from one another by the number and location of starting digits. In the computerized form, each distinct game initially contains digits that cannot be written over or changed except by starting a new game, and that are a different color (black) from those that are in play (green).

Team Sudoku provides users three distinct features for manipulating the board. A pen tool enables users to insert entries on the board, and a pencil tool allows users to tentatively mark possibilities (note-entries). Users can delete any entries on the game board with an eraser tool. Each user can also highlight a row, a column, a 3x3 block, or a cell at a time using a personalized, color-coded highlighter tool.

Team Sudoku enables multiple players to interact with the game on their own computers, which are updated in real time. That is, when one player fills in a number, erases a number, or uses a highlighter, the results are immediately shared on all players' screens.

Participants

Players were recruited from the Psychology Participant pool at our university, and received extra credit for participation. A total of 138 (75 female, 63 male) college students enrolled in the study, in 24 groups of two and 30 groups of three. Participants' age ranged from 18 to 41 (M = 19 SD = 2.28). Almost all the participants had prior experience with Sudoku. 15 reported initially that they did not know the Sudoku rules, but researchers confirmed that these 15 people were at least fully familiar with the Sudoku rules when they came in for the on-site experiment. Overall, participants reported playing Sudoku quite often (mode = 6, M = 5.35, SD = 1.51) on a scale of 1 (rarely) to 7 (several times a day). If only two participants appeared at the agreed time, the game was run with them, resulting in 24 groups of two. However, our interest was in triadic behavior and only the triads have been analyzed.

There were no groups in which all three participants knew each other prior to the experiment. Six pairs out of 90 participants knew each other before coming to the study. Triads with pairs that knew one another were relatively well spread out among the three conditions: 1 in PC, 3 in LC, and 2 in TC. These groups were excluded from the statistical analysis to ensure that there would exist no interfering effect between the acquaintance status and the groups' behaviors. However, the way these groups solved the interactional challenge of working together was considered fodder for qualitative description.

After the initial analysis of non-responses, a smaller subset of 5 groups per condition was randomly selected for further, more detailed analysis of kinds of non-responses.

METHODS

Four video cameras recorded each session. With one camera facing each participant and one capturing the entire group, we were able to ensure that each player's facial expressions as well as bodily gestures were captured in the video recordings.

The 20-minute video recordings of the first Sudoku game for triads were transcribed using a slightly modified version of Chafe's prosodic transcription system [8]. Transcripts were arranged into intonation and conversational turn units. Descriptions of non-verbal gestures as well as critical changes on the Sudoku board were also added to the transcripts. The final transcripts were reviewed for accuracy several times with the log files and screen-captured videos.

In order to identify non-response places, we first applied the five-part extended *Contributions to Conversations* model to our data and coded each conversational turn for *Pr* (*Presentation*) and *Ac* (*Acceptance*). Researchers went through the transcripts and video recordings in three iterations. During the initial iteration, researchers marked non-response places based solely on verbal evidence. For example, if participant A highlighted a cell and said, "I think a 3 goes here," and no other participants showed any verbal evidence of understanding such as "OK" or "yeah," we marked participant A's turn as having no response from B and C. In the second iteration, researchers revisited all the non-response places and looked for evidence of any gestural responses. For instance, if participant B nodded back when A said, "I think a 3 goes here," we re-marked A's turn as having a response from B, but not from C. During the third iteration, we revisited all the non-response places again, and checked for evidence of understanding within the digital space. So if we saw that participant C inserted a 3 into the cell to which A was referring immediately after A said, "I think a 3 goes here," we re-marked the turn as having responses from both B and C. This initial coding enabled us to pick out dangling presentation turns, that is, all the *Pr* turns that have either no matching *Ac* or just one matching *Ac*.

After marking the non-response places, we randomly selected 5 groups per condition (15 in total) for further analysis. Non-response places were used to develop a coding scheme. Researchers went through the transcripts multiple times, and conducted open and axial coding [16]. The coding scheme consisted of 8 codes under 3 main categories. The three main categories are '*talking-to-oneself*,' '*interrupted-and-delayed contributions*,' and '*absent response*.'

Following practices common in discourse analysis, the analysis of these data was conducted primarily by the first author, with help from research assistants. In this kind of enterprise, validity is thought to devolve from the highly trained focus to detail and the emergent properties of the coding system.

Different Kinds of Non-Responses

Thinking-to-Oneself

The first noticeable kind of non-response was '*talking-to-oneself*.' This category includes the three sub-categories: *Thinking-out-loud, Talking-to-Things,* and *Self-Answering*. *Thinking-out-loud* represents situations in which a speaker murmurs, making the utterances almost incomprehensible to others. Oftentimes participants seemed to narrate (or mark off) possibilities for entries as in "two three four... can't be 3... can't be 2 ((speaker mutters))." In such cases, the utterances did not usually get responses back from the other two players. *Talking-to-Things* refers to incidences in which a participant seems to talk to inanimate objects such as computers. *Self-Answering* codes occasions in which a participant utters a question, and subsequently self-answers it before anyone else has a chance to respond. For instance, in Excerpt 1, Aden first presents a contribution (*c1*) by asking the group if it would be possible to put an eight in a cell to which he is pointing. Both Beck and Cam accept *c1* by saying "m=hm=" and "yeah." Aden then goes on to make the next relevant contribution (*c2*), showing that Aden has accepted that both Beck and Cam understood *c1*. At this point, the group attains a mutual belief that everyone understood the content, *c1*. Yet in presenting the second contribution (*c2*), Aden self-answers his own contribution by saying "nope ok," depriving others of a chance to reply. It is possible for Beck or Cam to still reply to what Aden has said, but in this case, no one responds to Aden. Therefore we code the case as a *self-answering* (*talking-to-oneself*) kind of *non-response*.

line01- Aden: can't be six seven -- Pr (c1)
line02- but it can be eight?
line03- Beck: m=hm= -- Ac
line04- Cam: yeah -- Ac
line05- Aden: and -- Ac, Pr (c2)
line06- what about nine? ((asking a question))
line07- nope ((self answering the question))
line08- ok

Excerpt 1: Non-Response – Self-Answering (paper condition)

Interrupted-and-Delayed-Contributions

In conversations involving more than two people, not all *Presentations* are intended to be understood by all the others [11]. Pairs sometimes create communicative sub-channels within three person groups. One person can also be involved in more than one communicative sub-channel. Moreover different participants can concomitantly present multiple *Presentations,* creating possible interactional conflicts. The *Interrupted-and-Delayed-Contributions* category represents incidences of such conflicts. For instance, in Excerpt 2, Aden presents a contribution (*c1*), but Cam, immediately following Aden, presents another contribution (*c2*) in an assertive manner, masking out *c1*. The group picks up *c2* instead of *c1,* and continues to talk about the content presented in *c2*. Since *c2* and *c1* are not closely related topics, we do not see *c2* as *the relevant next contribution* [14] of *c1*, and do not consider it as accepting *c1*. We see such cases as having two different conflicting contributions. In this case, *c1* gets interrupted by *c2*. Sometimes participants who initiate interrupted contributions, try to re-present the contributions at a later time as Aden re-presents *c1* in line14 ~ line15. When initially interrupted contributions get re-presented at later times, we code that instance as "*delayed-contribution,*" if not, we code it as "*interrupted-contribution.*"

line01- Aden: should we keep it like that and move on to like the next ones and then like= -- Pr (c1)
line02- Cam: wait -- Pr (c2)
line03- you can put three in this one
line04- [this is the only place that three fits]
line05- Beck: yeah it's the only [one that=] -- Ac, Pr
line06- yeah
line07- so put three there
line08- Aden: ok -- Ac, Pr
line09- go head
line10- well hauh is that because that's the only one in that order?
line11- ...
line12- ((the group continues to talk about putting in a 3))
line13- ...
line14- Aden: should we just n like move onto the next -- Pr (c1')

Excerpt 2: Non-Response – Delayed Contributions (paper condition)

Absent Response

As we mentioned, our participants from time to time engaged in dyadic interactions, creating communicative sub-channels within three person groups. For instance, Kim can pose a question directed only to James by saying, "James, why did you put that 4 there?" In this case, Kim creates a sub-channel between herself and the addressee, James. Even though the third player, Linda can still barge in and respond to what Kim says, it is not imperative for Linda to do so. It is also relatively safe to assume that Kim does not expect Linda to respond. In this case, Linda's not responding to Kim's presentation should not be seen as absence of what is expected. Therefore, when a *presentation* is directed specifically to one of two listeners, we only check for an acceptance from the addressee. We do not code the absence of an acceptance from the third player as non-response.

After coding non-response places for '*talking-to-oneself*' and '*interrupted-and-delayed- contributions*,' we were still left with a number of non-response places that did not belong to either category. For reasons that we could not tell, on many occasions, participants still remained non-responsive to other people's utterances. That is, we could not find any positive evidence that showed the listeners (people other than the one presenting the contribution) understood what had been uttered by the presenter (person who presents the contribution). We code these cases as *absent response type1 and absent response type2*: *absent response type 1* represents cases in which a presenter fails to get a response back from one listener; *absent response type 2* represents cases in which a presenter fails to get any response back from both listeners.

RESULTS

Results of the qualitative analysis integrate discussion of observations, as explication of their significance, in evaluating the adequacy and power of the proposed model of interaction in triple space. We argue that dyadic relationships can be set up within the triads and that the notion of *good-enoughness* can be tied to these dyadic pairs. We note that single examples are important in this kind of research because they can reveal the underlying structures that obtain and to define what constitutes an explanation of behavior. For example, in studying phone answering behavior, a person might conclude based on statistics alone that people answer the phone by saying "hello." However, if sometimes people answer the phone by saying "Joe's pizza", this is not a statistical aberration, but information that tells us that an account of phone answering requires a more complex conceptual framework. Numerical (quantitative) analysis is then used to further explore the conjecture that dyadic relationships are important in triadic interaction, to tie the location of non-response to global changes in affect, and to show indications that non-responses may differ by technological condition.

line01- Carol: Well one has to be either in that center block
line02- or to the left with that
line03- ..[because=]
line04- Abel: [Yeah]
line05- cause one two four five that are missing for it
line06- and then if *((points to his screen with a finger))*
line07- you go to the very bottom.
line08- it can't be two four five so=,
line09- I think it might be one for that.
line10- Carol: OK
line11- Abel: Like right=
line12- [oh no]
line13- Carol: [Oh yeah]
line14- I see what you saying right there
line15- ...like that? *((puts blue 1 at cell9,5))*
line16- Abel: Yeah
line17- Carol: OK

Excerpt 3: Two Players Co-constructing a Contribution (laptop condition)

Discourse Findings

In this section, we use examples from our study to discuss how the *expanded Contributions to Conversations* model to explain and highlight issues in triadic interaction. We find evidence of dyadic orientation, of the ability to maintain co-existing dyadic orientations and of the importance in understanding these dyads to understanding the *good-enoughness* of the interaction.

Dyadic Orientation within the Triad

The notion of *Contributions to Conversations* is based on evidence in dyadic conversations in which both conversants have evidence that helps them establish *good enough* understandings for their *current purposes*. This model is powerful. The data from our study show multiple occasions in which contributions to conversations as well as contributions to the joint activity are co-constructed by the group members. For example, Excerpt 3 illustrates a segment of conversation in which group members conjointly build multi-layered and overlapping contributions. In this conversation, Carol poses a stretch of speech intended to specify her contribution, raising a possibility that 1 can go into either one of two possible locations on the board. In response to Carol's specification, Abel replies "Yeah" and elaborates on the reasoning behind Carol's proposal. The fact that Abel says "Yeah" and that Abel is able to elaborate her reasoning acts as evidence for Carol that Abel understands Carol's content well enough.

While showing that he understands what Carol is saying, Abel also adds a new content, a confinement of the previously stated possibilities, which narrows the possible locations where 1 can be placed. In that sense, line01 to line03 form a presentation phase while line04 to line09 act as both an acceptance phase and a new presentation phase. Carol replies to Abel by saying "OK" which in turn acts as evidence that Carol understands what Abel is saying. This shows the processes of the grounding in conversation as well as how co-constructions of contributions can be overlapped. In addition, these different sub-contributions are nested and imbedded in the overarching conversation segment. Excerpt 3 is a prototypical example that shows how contributions are created and maintained interactionally by the participants [15].

However, this account simply ignores the third player, Bob, who does not say anything in this portion of the conversation. When we use the five-part *extended Contributions to Conversations* model to describe this segment of conversation, it becomes apparent that we are missing a response from Bob. Far from needing a fully-crossed model in which Abel and Bob assert that they have understood one another, the interaction does not even motivate positive evidence of understanding between Carol and Bob. Neither Carol nor Abel appear to have evidence that Bob understood the contents that posed in the presentation phases. This suggests that establishing plausible beliefs that the contents of their conversation are understood depends on it being understood by a single other. Dyadic sense-making may be seen to suffice even in the triad.

Another possible explanation that leads to the same conclusion would be to conceptualize the interactions between Carol and Abel as a side sequence [18] and Bob as an overhearer [12]. Since speakers do not monitor overhearers' actions, Bob's acceptance would not be expected. However, the facts that Carol and Abel do not designate a specific addressee when making presentations, and also that Bob constantly makes contributions to the game board even when he is not engaged in group conversation make such an explanation less plausible.

It is true that there may be evidence of understanding that we cannot perceive. Bob's non-response may be perceived by other participants as positive evidence of understanding in the form of *continued attention*. Alternatively, Bob may be thought to have given an *unarticulated consent* that he understood the contents well enough. However, it is difficult to understand how mutual knowledge is in fact ensured in these cases. Occam's Razor suggests that, if Bob does not in fact follow the interaction, he has reduced understanding of the situation. This recalls Barron's finding that students do not automatically know how to work together in teams and her suggestion that teamwork be taught [3].

```
Ann: but that means this
   that means this one has to be a three
Cain: it's gonna be like one of these two
   so it's like
   okay
Ann: and that means that has to be the three
   cause that's the only available three spot
Ben: true that
Ann: so Cain
   write a three there
   that actually looks like a three
Cain: oh yeah
   uhm I don't get your logic but I trust you
```

Excerpt 4: Different Degrees of Good Enough Understanding (paper condition)

Two Concomitant Dyadic Orientations

Birnholtz et al. [7] point out ambiguities in Clark's notions of *good enoughness* and *current purposes* by arguing that participants in the Clark and Wilkes-Gibbs' experiment do not need to have complete understanding of the shapes in order to complete the task [15]. They propose that the use of lightweight text chat can provide sufficient awareness for the task at hand in a large distributed group without necessarily ensuring everyone has a complete understanding of the current situation.

However, they do not analyze how conversations proceed in this case. We show that concomitant dyadic orientation can exist in the triad, with different criteria for understanding.

In Excerpt 4, Ann tries to explain the logic behind a move she is about to make. As Ann describes her logic, Ben responds by saying "true that," indicating he has understood what Ann was saying. Ben's saying "true that" is sufficient evidence for Ann to think Ben understood what she was saying. Both Ann and Ben at this point have sufficient evidence to believe that they have good enough understandings of the current situation.

On the other hand, Cain explicitly states that he does not understand what Ann was saying when he says "uhm I don't get your logic." However, he subsequently says "but I trust you," which shows that for Cain, *not understanding* Ann's logic is good enough for whatever purposes he has for the current activity he is engaged in at the moment. (The purposes could be presumably playing Team Sudoku, but there could also be multiple other goals.) Moreover, Ann also knows that Cain did not understand what she has been saying. But, for Ann, knowing that Cain would trust her logic even though Cain does not understand what she has been saying is also good enough for carrying out the current activity from her perspective.

These examples show that even *not understanding* can be a good enough understanding in some cases. Ben and Cain have different perceptions of what constitutes a good enough understanding, even though they are conjointly experiencing the same group conversation and activity. This fact hints to us that the notion of "*good enougness*" is not bound to the whole group, but rather it is a unique attribute of each dyadic pair. What is good enough for Ann and Cain is different from what is good enough for Ann and Ben.

The Current Purpose

Why is *not understanding* good enough for Cain while it might not be for Ben? The notion of "*good enough understandings*" is defined by Clark and his colleagues as relating to *current purposes* [9,10,13,15]. However, Clark and his colleagues did not fully explore what they meant by current purposes and how the different purposes manifest themselves in the grounding processes. In this section we will examine how different purposes might play roles in defining what would constitute good enough understandings at the moment.

In investigating groups playing puzzle games in triple space, Lee, Tatar and Harrison [21] reported that a relatively significant number of groups remained silent during the gaming sessions, while other groups talked quite a lot. In the current study, we also observed varying levels of contributions to conversations among the groups and individuals: some talked quite a lot; some remained silent. Why, then, would some groups remain silent playing a collaborative puzzle game? Even though we asked the groups to play Sudoku collectively, we can conjecture that individuals' purposes for playing the game might vary. Some might just want to sit in the experiment, spend time, and get their extra credit. Some might want to enjoy playing the game without necessarily expecting to finish the puzzle. Some might be quite eager to finish the puzzle in time. So different individuals can have different purposes for their joint activities.

In addition, individuals can also have concurrent multiple purposes for the joint activity. They might wish to maintain good relationships and do the puzzle.

If people have concurrent multiple current purposes, how would these multiple purposes play roles in shaping their behavior?

line01- Adam: I'm ah=na
line02- Eden's gonna be the first small number
line03- you can you can put be the big number
line04- you can put what number you think the first one is
line05- I'm gonna be the second little number
line06- Bob: no
line07- ..you can't just guess right
line08- I mean it's better if you have like
line09- what are the possible choices than just guessing
line10- ...
line11- *((Bob tries to explain why Adam's plan would not*
line12- *work & Adam says Bob's strategy is confusing.))*
line13- ...
line14- Adam: so we're we're basically doing
line15- three possibilities in each each box but then we can
line16- keep keep moving and it won't be as so so hectic
line17- with four or five answers
line18- Bob: I mean we can all like try different grids
line19- at the same time, like how about
line20- I do this one *((points to one 3x3 box))*
line21- and you do this one *((points to another 3x3 box))*
line22- I mean you do like *((points to yet another 3x3 box))*

Excerpt 5: Shifts in Current Purposes (laptop condition)

Group89 (see Excerpt 5) consists of Adam, Bob and Eden. After playing the 1st game for a while, Adam becomes confused by all the notes Bob has been entering on the board and suggests that everyone should only place one number in the cell by assigning big numbers to one player, the first small note to the second player, the second small note to the third player (line01 to line05). However, the proposed strategy is nonsensical since there is no way in the software of assigning a note in a particular order to a player. Anyone who enters a note into a cell first becomes the owner of the first note. Bob tries to explain the difficulty, but Adam does not see the problem. Upon meeting with misunderstanding, Bob stops trying to explain the difficulty and instead suggests another alternative to simplify the display. He asks the group to divide the board into sections so that each player could work on their own section (line18 to line22).

It is clear at this point that solving the puzzle successfully is not Bob's only purpose at the moment. From the point of view of an outside observer, Bob has a better grasp of the game play situation than Adam. Throughout the game Bob tries to explain how guesswork is not a good strategy for solving the puzzle. He also tries to explain the problem of Adam's plan. But, in the end, Bob compromises his initial strategy of using notes to capture the possible numbers that could go into a cell because Adam does not understand it. If solving the puzzle correctly and maximizing the potential achievement in the game were the only purposes, Bob would not have compromised his initial strategy for a less effective one. From these facts, we can safely infer that Bob's current purpose for the activity at the moment is not to solve the puzzle successfully, but more likely to continue playing the group game without conflicting with other players.

However, neither can we say Bob's current purposes excluded the attempt to try to solve the puzzle correctly. In fact, Bob tried to explain the pitfalls in Adam's strategy for a while and that shows at least at some point during the game, Bob's purpose was to solve the puzzle correctly.

How and why do the shifts in the current purposes occur during the joint activity? The most probable explanation might be that different coexisting current purposes have different levels of tolerance for the efforts required to achieve the goal. It is possible that the efforts required to show Adam the problem in his plan exceeded Bob's effort tolerance threshold for "solving the puzzle correctly." Presumably, Bob's current purpose shifted at this point to "playing the group game without conflicting with other players" which requires much less effort.

We see that multiple current purposes can coexist, each having different levels of effort tolerance thresholds. These concurrently existing purposes sometimes work together to shape people's behaviors as we saw in the case of a player playing Sudoku while talking about non-game related topics. At other times, current purposes shift to new ones when the effort required to realize the existing purpose exceed an individual's tolerance level.

NUMERICAL FINDINGS

Contributions to Conversations: Extended to Triads in Triple-Space

Based on our qualitative discussions, we have suggested that conversants in *triple space do not* usually seek or get positive evidence of understanding from *all* the other participants. In fact, the quantitative result confirmed our conjecture. The data shows that 8.70% of *Presentations* had no matching *Acceptances* from both players, and 43.69% of *Presentations* did not have a matching *Acceptance* from one player. That means, in some cases, people still can conduct joint activities without fully establishing the mutual belief that everyone has understood the contents of conversations.

Groups are Happier When They Have Low Rates of Non-Responses

Interestingly enough, the group's average of differences in individual members' positive emotional states (ΔPA) were negatively correlated with the ratio of non-responses per total conversational turns per group. That is, groups tended to feel happier when they had a lower non-response rate. This relationship is illustrated in Figure 2 ($r^2 = 0.41$, $p < .01$).

Non-Response: Mediating Technology Does Matter

To explore whether and how media might affect the way non-responses were manifested in group interactions, we examined kinds of non-responses in the 15 groups that had been coded for kinds of non-responses.

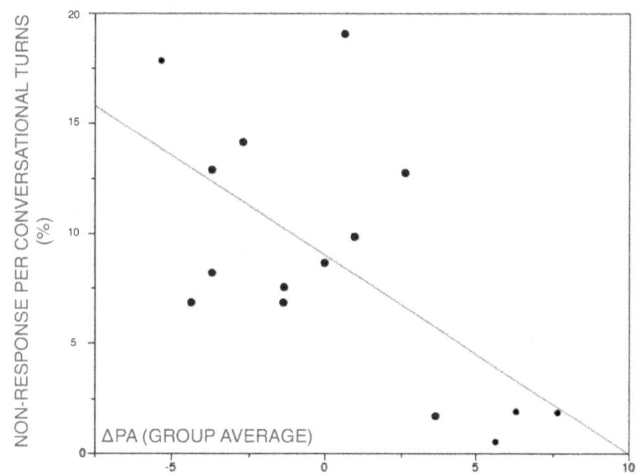

Figure 2: Non-Response per Total Conversational Turns by Changes in Positive Affect (All Condition)

Since we were interested in looking at the ratio of the number of certain types of non-response over the total number of non-responses, the data for the groups that had a very small total number of non-responses did not really enable meaningful interpretation. For example, interpreting a group that had just 1 non-response (whatever kind of non-response it was) during the entire gaming session as having 100% tendency to have that particular type of non-response could indeed be a misleading interpretation.

Six out of 15 groups had more than 10 non-responses. This time, 47% of non-responses were coded as "talking to oneself" in the computer conditions while in the paper condition, 21% of non-response behaviors were coded as "talking to oneself." Figure 3 visualizes the differences between two different media (computer vs. paper) for "talking to oneself" and absent non-responses.

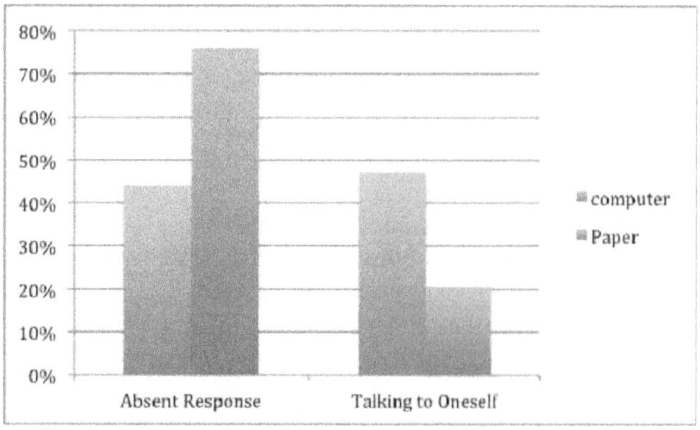

Figure 3. The ratio of "talking to oneself" and "absent responses type 2" by computer and paper conditions based on groups that had more than 10 non-responses

These small numbers do not admit of inferential statistics. However, we find these trends noteworthy. They suggest that participants who used personalized devices tended to talk more to themselves than people who shared a paper. It is the computing technology that nudges us to encapsulate ourselves in a very private personal space around the digital artifacts. By going into these private spaces, we might feel more detached from social interactions and find it easier to talk to ourselves. We plan to conduct an extended study with a larger sample size in the future.

In addition, close examination of two groups (Group 44 and Group 45) in paper condition revealed that *Presentations* coded as '*absent response type 2*' were typically accompanied by presenters' making modifications on the physically shared game board. Group 44 had 17 '*absent response type 2*' non-responses, and in 15 out of these 17 incidences, the speakers either used hand gestures to point to the shared game board or the groups maintained joint focus on the area the speakers were referring to. Group 45 had 32 '*absent response type 2*' non-responses, and in 29 out of 32 cases, the speakers used hand gestures to point to the shared game board. The speakers in the two computer conditions (Group 8 and Group 4) never used the highlighter tool to indicate their referents.

Having a physically shared space, and acting on the shared medium might have given the presenters a certain sense of assurance that other people had seen and heard what had been acted and uttered by the presenter. So in a sense, people in paper condition might have felt it was easier to actually use *continued attention* as evidence of understanding. Even though we did not consider *continued attention* as positive evidence in our analysis, people in paper condition might have utilized *continued attention* in their conversations. Moreover, in the same line of argument, we might presume that the use of digital technologies among collocated groups creates difficulties for the participants to use *continued attention* in their interactions.

CONCLUSION

Increasing use of small screen technologies is creating opportunities to engage in highly coordinative activities for multiple users with multiple screens in collocated settings. *A situation of seeing the other but not being able to see what captures his/her attention is endemic.* Indeed, such situations will only increase as wearable computing devices become more and more ubiquitous. With devices such as Google Glass, we cannot even guarantee that *what the other person sees is what I see* even among the people within the same physical space. It will become enormously difficult to tell if a person is looking at me or looking at the personalized display projected onto his/her glasses. This has the potential to create many unexpected interactional problems such as difficulties for grounding processes.

In this work, we examined how the *Contributions to Conversations* model applies to collocated triads playing a collaborative, problem-solving game on computers in *triple space*.

We propose a descriptive model of triadic interactions in triple space interactions that bring our focus to the importance of dyads, we find that *good-enoughness* is necessarily a group attribute, but may be tied to dyadic pairs. We also discussed and showed how groups and individuals can have multiple coexisting current purposes. We believe that our extension to Clark and Schaefer's *Contributions to Conversations* model is a small but important step forward in the understanding of collocated, coordinative interactions among triads and, possibly, groups with more than three people.

The context of this model allows us to examine and detect kinds of non-responses. In addition, we have also examined how *non-response* affects group processes in increasingly pervasive "triple space" situations. Our data show that not all non-responses are the same. They also raise the possibility that different mediating technologies afford different types of non-responses. This kind of result is important for design in proportion to the meaning of the behaviors for the participants. An East African proverb says "One lie undoes a 1000 truths," signifying that once a lie has been detected, a relationship is forever changed. When we define a situation as, for example, permitting people to talk to themselves, it may similarly change the meaning of the entire interaction.

In the current study, we mainly compared a paper condition to two computer conditions. Many questions on how mediating technologies affect grounding processes and how different kinds of non-response manifest themselves in *triple space* tasks still remain to be answered. We think comparing technologies with different screen sizes (tabletops, desktops, laptops, tablets and mobile phones) will help us further investigate different coordinative issues related to *silence* in grounding processes.

ACKNOWLEDGMENTS

This work was supported by NSF Grant. IIS-1018607 HCC-Small.

REFERENCES

1. Anderson, A. H. (2006). Achieving understanding in face-to-face and video-mediated multiparty interactions. *Discourse processes*, *41*(3), 251-287.
2. Anderson, A. H., Mullin, J., Katsavaras, E., Brundell, P., McEwan, R., Grattan, E., & O'Malley, C. (1999). Multi-mediating multiparty interactions. *Human Computer Interaction (INTERACT99)*, 313-320.
3. Barron, B. (2003). When smart groups fail. *The journal of the learning sciences*,*12*(3), 307-359.
4. Beck, A.T. & Steer, R. A. (1997). Beck Anxiety Inventory.
5. Beck, A. T., Ward, C. H., Mendelson, M., Mock, J., & Erbaugh, J. (1961). An inventory for measuring depression. *Archives of general psychiatry*, *4*(6), 561.
6. Beers, P. J., Boshuizen, H. P., Kirschner, P. A., & Gijselaers, W. H. (2006). Common ground, complex problems and decision making. *Group Decision and Negotiation*, *15*(6), 529-556.
7. Birnholtz, J. P., Finholt, T. A., Horn, D. B., & Bae, S. J. (2005, April). Grounding needs: achieving common ground via lightweight chat in large, distributed, ad-hoc groups. In *Proceedings of the SIGCHI conference on Human factors in computing systems* (pp. 21-30). ACM.
8. Chafe, W. (1993). Prosodic and functional units of language. *Talking data: Transcription and coding in discourse research*, 33-43.
9. Clark, H. H. (1996). *Using language* (Vol. 4). Cambridge: Cambridge University Press.
10. Clark, H. H., & Brennan, S. E. (1991). Grounding in communication. *Perspectives on socially shared cognition*, *13*(1991), 127-149.
11. Clark, H. H., & Carlson, T. B. (1982). Hearers and speech acts. *Language*, 332-373.
12. Clark, H. H., & Krych, M. A. (2004). Speaking while monitoring addressees for understanding. *Journal of Memory and Language*, *50*(1), 62-81.
13. Clark, H. H., & Schaefer, E. F. (1987). Collaborating on contributions to conversations. *Language and cognitive processes*, *2*(1), 19-41.
14. Clark, H. H., & Schaefer, E. F. (1989). Contributing to discourse. *Cognitive science*, *13*(2), 259-294.
15. Clark, H. H., & Wilkes-Gibbs, D. (1986). Referring as a collaborative process.*Cognition*, *22*(1), 1-39.
16. Corbin, J., & Strauss, A. (2007). *Basics of qualitative research: Techniques and procedures for developing grounded theory*. Sage Publications, Incorporated.
17. Cornelius, C., & Boos, M. (2003). Enhancing mutual understanding in synchronous computer-mediated communication by training trade-offs in judgmental tasks. *Communication Research*, *30*(2), 147-177.
18. Jefferson, G. (1972). Side sequences. *Studies in social interaction*, *294*, 338.
19. John, O. P. (1990). The "Big Five" factor taxonomy: Dimensions of personality in the natural language and in questionnaires. In L. Pervin (Ed.), Handbook of personality: Theory and research (pp. 66-100). Guilford Press.
20. Lee, J.S., Tatar, D. (2013, February). Form factor matters. In *Proceedings of the 2013 conference on Computer supported cooperative work* (pp. 1481-1486). ACM.
21. Lee, J. S., Tatar, D., & Harrison, S. (2012, February). Micro-coordination: because we did not already learn everything we need to know about working with others in kindergarten. In *Proceedings of the ACM 2012 conference on Computer Supported Cooperative Work* (pp. 1135-1144). ACM.
22. Locke, K. D. (2000). Circumplex scales of interpersonal values: Reliability, validity, and applicability to interper-

sonal problems and personality disorders. *Journal of Personality Assessment*, *75*(2), 249-267.

23. Locke, K. D., & Sadler, P. (2007). Self-efficacy, values, and complementarity in dyadic interactions: Integrating interpersonal and social-cognitive theory. *Personality and Social Psychology Bulletin*, *33*(1), 94-109.

24. O'Conaill, B., Whittaker, S., & Wilbur, S. (1993). Conversations over video conferences: An evaluation of the spoken aspects of video-mediated communication. *Human-computer interaction*, *8*(4), 389-428.

25. Schegloff, E. A., Jefferson, G., & Sacks, H. (1977). The preference for self-correction in the organization of repair in conversation. *Language*, 361-382.

26. Simon, H. A. (1996). *The sciences of the artificial*. MIT press.

27. Tatar, D. G., Foster, G., & Bobrow, D. G. (1991). Design for conversation: lessons from Cognoter. *International Journal of Man-Machine Studies*, *34*(2), 185-209.

28. van der Kleij, R., Schraagen, J. M., Werkhoven, P., & De Dreu, C. K. (2009). How conversations change over time in face-to-face and video-mediated communication. *Small Group Research*, *40*(4), 355-381

29. Watson, D., Clark, L. A. & Tellegen, A., (1988). Development and validation of brief measures of positive and negative affect: The PANAS scales. *Journal of personality and social psychology*, *54*(6), 1063-1070.

Next Generation Humanitarian Computing

Patrick Meier
Director of Social Innovation
Qatar Computing Research Institute (QCRI)
http://irevolution.net/

ABSTRACT
Humanitarian organizations are completely unprepared to deal with the rise of Big (Crisis) Data--the massive overflow of user-generated content posted on social media during disasters. To be sure, humanitarian organizations have no expertise in advanced computing. At the same time, the overflow of information during disasters can be as paralyzing to humanitarian response as the absence of information. This talk will highlight how the computing community can make a significant difference in humanitarian response. To demonstrate this, the talk will explain how we are experimenting with human and machine computing to make sense of—and verify—Big Crisis Data. For example, we can automatically extract crisis information from Twitter by combining microtasking with machine learning. This would enable UN information management officers to create their own classifiers on the fly. In terms of verification, we can draw on techniques from time-critical crowdsourcing to rapidly collect and triangulate evidence during disasters. This would allow emergency managers to quickly debunk rumors in the immediate aftermath of a crisis. In conclusion, the talk will outline how we can actively bridge the gap between humanitarian and computing communities.

Author Keywords
Big data, citizen journalism, crisis informatics, crowdsourcing, digital activism, twitter

ACM Classification Keywords
K.4.3 Computers and Society: Organizational Impacts: Computer-supported collaborative work.

BIO
Patrick Meier (PhD) is an internationally recognized thought leader on the application of new technologies for humanitarian response. He presently serves as Director of Social Innovation at the Qatar Foundation's Computing Research Institute (QCRI) where he and his team use Advanced Computing to develop Next Generation Humanitarian Technologies. Patrick is also a UNICEF Humanitarian Innovations Fellow, a Rockefeller Foundation and PopTech Fellow, and a Fellow at Harvard University where he previously co-directed the Harvard Humanitarian Initiative's Program on Crisis Mapping. His influential blog iRevolution has received well over 1 million hits and been cited by the New York Times, UK Guardian, Slate, Wired, Scientific American and New Scientist, amongst others. Patrick tweets at @patrickmeier.

CSCW'14, February 15–19, 2014, Baltimore, MD, USA.
ACM 978-1-4503-2540-0/14/02.
http://dx.doi.org/10.1145/2531602.2556856

Author Index

www.ingramcontent.com/pod-product-compliance
Lightning Source LLC
LaVergne TN
LVHW080104011026
849160LV00013B/1028